ISBN 978-1-331-89168-0
PIBN 10250520

English
Français
Deutsche
Italiano
Español
Português

www.forgottenbooks.com

Mythology Photography **Fiction**
Fishing Christianity **Art** Cooking
Essays Buddhism Freemasonry
Medicine **Biology** Music **Ancient
Egypt** Evolution Carpentry Physics
Dance Geology **Mathematics** Fitness
Shakespeare **Folklore** Yoga Marketing
Confidence Immortality Biographies
Poetry **Psychology** Witchcraft
Electronics Chemistry History **Law**
Accounting **Philosophy** Anthropology
Alchemy Drama Quantum Mechanics
Atheism Sexual Health **Ancient History**
Entrepreneurship Languages Sport
Paleontology Needlework Islam
Metaphysics Investment Archaeology
Parenting Statistics Criminology
Motivational

COLLINS'
ETYMOLOGICAL
DICTIONARY

CONTAINING ROOTS AND DERIVATIONS AND
EMBRACING THE MOST RECENT WORDS

ILLUSTRATED

LONDON AND GLASGOW
COLLINS' CLEAR-TYPE PRESS

Manufactured in Great Britain

PREFACE

THE ETYMOLOGICAL DICTIONARY of the English Language has been compiled with a double purpose in view. The vast circulation attained by the cheaper forms of literature, together with the greatly increased range of criticism in periodicals and newspapers, has brought into use a considerable number of new words—some of them technical and scientific terms—which require explanation. The incorporation of many such words and phrases in the Etymological Dictionary brings the book fully abreast of modern requirements, thus making it a boon to the general reader. In addition, its comprehensiveness, conciseness, clarity, and accuracy render it eminently suitable for the schoolroom.

The ORTHOGRAPHY is that usually accepted by lexicographers; but where authorities differ about the spelling or pronunciation of words, both forms are given.

The PRONUNCIATION of all words is indicated by a system of Phonetics, the correct sound being exhibited by re-spelling each word in phonetic form, the syllabification, marked vowel sounds, and proper accentuation being distinctly shown.

With the exception of *g*, the consonants employed in the phonetic spelling retain their name sounds, and the vowels, unless marked, retain their short sounds; H represents the guttural *h* heard in 'loch.' The digraph *aw* represents the sound of *a* heard in 'fall'; *ou* the sound of *ow* heard in 'now'; *oo*, unmarked, the sound heard in 'book'; *ōō* the sound heard in 'moon.' The surd (*sharp, unvoiced*) sound of *th* is indicated by common letters, as in 'thin,' the sonant (*flat, voiced*) sound by small capitals, as in 'THen.' The following key to the long and peculiar vowel sounds,

Fāte, fär, ạdo; mē, hẹr; mīne; nōte; tūne; mōōn.

being repeated at the foot of each page, should prove of much service.

The two Appendixes of ABBREVIATIONS and FOREIGN WORDS AND PHRASES give additional value to the book.

The careful attention paid to the ETYMOLOGY will result, it is hoped, in its being really instructive, and not merely formal. The most recent work in philological research has been consulted, and, as in the 'Home' Dictionary, the steps by which a word has reached its present form have been noted more precisely than is usual in such compilations.

List of Abbreviations

a. . . adjective
abl. . . ablative
acc. . . accusative
ad. . . adverb
aux. . . auxiliary
cf. . . *confer* (compare)
comp. . . comparative
conj. . . conjunction
contr. . . contraction
dim. . . diminutive
e.g. . . *exempli gratia* (for example)
fem. . . feminine

i.e. . . *id est* (that is)
imp. . . imperative
intens. . . intensive
inter. . . interjection
masc. . . masculine
n. . . noun
neg. . . negative
neut. . . neuter
orig. . . originally
p. or *part.* . particle
pass. . . passive
pl. . . plural
pp. . . past participle

ppr. . . present participle
pref. . . prefix
prep. . . preposition
pret. . . preterite
pron. . . pronoun
sing. . . singular
suff. . . suffix
superl. . . superlative
syn. . . synonym
v. . . verb
v.i. . . verb intransitive
v.t. . . verb transitive

A. . . Arabic
A.F. . . Anglo-French
Afr. . . African
Amer. . . American
Anat. . . Anatomy
Astr. . . Astronomy
Astrol. . . Astrology
Austr. . . Australian
Biol. . . Biology
Bot. . . Botany
Braz. . . Brazilian
Bret. . . Breton
C. . . Centigrade
cap. . . capital
Carib. . . Caribbean
Celt. . . Celtic
ch. . . chapter
Chin. . . Chinese
cog. . . cognate
corr. . . corruption
D. . . Dutch
Dan. . . Danish
E. . . East; English
Egypt . . Egyptian
E. Ind. . . East Indian
esp. . . especially
Ethn. . . Ethnology
Etym. . . Etymology
F. . . French
Fahr. . . Fahrenheit
fr. . . from
ft. . . feet
G. . . Greek
Gael. . . Gaelic
Geol. . . Geology
Geom. . . Geometry

Ger. . . German
Goth. . . Gothic
Gram. . . Grammar
H. . . Hebrew
Her. . . Heraldry
Hind. . . Hindustani
Hung. . . Hungarian
Icel. . . Icelandic
Imit. . . Imitative
Ind. . . Indian
Ir. . . Irish
It. . . Italian
L. . . Latin
l. . . line
m. . . miles
Mal. . . Malayan
Math. . . Mathematics
M.D. . . Middle Dutch
M.E. . . Middle English
Med. . . Medicine
Mex. . . Mexican
M. H. Ger. . Middle High German
mt. . . mountain
Mus. . . Music
Myth. . . Mythology
N. . . North
Nat. Hist. . Natural History
Naut. . . Nautical affairs
Norw. . . Norwegian
O.E. . . Old English
O.F. . . Old French
O. H. Ger. . Old High German
O. L. Ger. . Old Low German

orig. . . originally
Per. . . Persian
perh. . . perhaps
pert. . . pertaining
Peruv. . . Peruvian
Pg. . . Portuguese
Phil. . . Philology
Pol. . . Polish
prov. . . provincial
riv. . . river
rt. . . root.
R. . . Roman; River
Rhet. . . Rhetoric
Russ. . . Russian
Scand. . . Scandinavian
Scot. . . Scotland; Scottish
Sculp. . . Sculpture
Singh. . . Singhalese
Skr. . . Sanskrit
Slav. . . Slavonic
S. Afr. D. . South African Dutch
Sp. . . Spanish
sq. . . square
Surg. . . Surgery
Sw. . . Swedish
Syr. . . Syriac
Teut. . . Teutonic
tn. . . town
Turk. . . Turkish
U.S. . . United States
W. . . Welsh; West
Zool. . . Zoology

COLLINS'
ETYMOLOGICAL DICTIONARY

A, called the indefinite article, used before words beginning with the sound of a consonant; any, one. A1 in Lloyd's register denotes a ship of the first class; hence first-rate, excellent.

AARONIC (ā-ron'ik) *a.* pertaining to Aaron, or the Levitical priesthood. [H.]

AARONITE (ā'run-īt) *n.* a descendant of Aaron; a Jew.

AARON'S ROD (ā'runz-rod) *n.* in *Architecture,* a rod with a serpent coiled round it.

ABACK (a-bak') *ad.* backwards; by surprise. [O.E. *on bæc,* on the back.]

ABACUS (ab'a-cus) *n.* the upper part of a column; *pl.* **ABACI.** [L. *abacus,* fr. G. *abax,* a reckoning board.]

ABADDON (a-bad'un) *n.* the destroying angel. [H., fr. *abad,* to be lost.]

ABAFT (a-baft') *ad.* towards the stern. [O.E. *a,* on, and *bæftan,* after. See AFT.]

ABANDON (a-ban'dun) *v.t.* to forsake wholly; to renounce. [F. *abandonner,* to give up, fr. L. *ad* and Low L. *bandum,* a proclamation.]

ABANDONED (a-ban'dund) *a.* given up entirely; very wicked.

ABANDONMENT (a-ban'dun-ment) *n.* entire desertion; a final giving up.

ABASE (a-bās') *v.t.* to bring low; to humble. [L. *ad* and Low L. *bassare,* lower.]

ABASEMENT (a-bās'ment) *n.* the state of being brought low.

ABASH (a-bash') *v.t.* to make ashamed; to confuse. [O.F. *es* = L. *ex* and (part.) *baissant,* expressing astonishment, fr. inter. *bah.*]

ABASING (a-bās'ing) *a.* very humbling.

ABATABLE (a-bā'ta-bl) *a.* that may be abated.

ABATE (a-bāt') *v.t.* to lessen; to diminish in price. [L. *ab* and *batere,* to strike.]

ABATEMENT (a-bāt'ment) *n.* decrease; the sum taken away.

ABATER (a-bāt'er) *n.* one who lessens or takes down the price.

ABBA (ab'a) *n.* father. [H. *ab,* father.]

ABBACY (ab'a-si) *n.* the condition or privileges of an abbot. [an abbot.

ABBE (ab'i) *n.* a title without office or rights;

ABBESS (ab'es) *n.* governess of a nunnery.

ABBOT (ab'ut) *n.* head of a society of monks.

ABBEY (ab'i) *n.* a monastery or convent; *pl.* **ABBEYS** [O.F. *abaie;* but see ABBA.]

ABBREVIATE (a-brē'vi-āt) *v.t.* to shorten. [L. *ad* and *brevis,* short.]

ABBREVIATION (a-brē-vi-ā'shun) *n.* act of shortening; contraction.

ABBREVIATOR (a-brē'vi-ā-tur) *n.* one who abridges or abbreviates.

ABBREVIATURE (a-brē'vi-ā-tūr) *n.* a letter or character used in abridging.

ABDICATE (ab'di-kāt) *v.t.* to abandon an office. [L. *ab,* off or from, and *dicare,* to proclaim.] [resigning a trust.

ABDICATION (ab-di-kā'shun) *n.* the act of

ABDOMEN (ab-dō'men) *n.* the lower part of the belly. [L.]

ABDOMINAL (ab-dom'i-nal) *a.* pertaining to the abdomen. (*Ichth.*) A group of fishes with the barbed fins under the abdomen, as the salmon.

Abdominal Fish.

ABDUCE (ab-dūs') *v.t.* to draw away. [L. *ab,* from, and *ducere,* to lead.]

ABDUCTION (ab-duk'shun) *n.* act of carrying away. [See ABDUCE.]

ABEAM (a-bēm') *ad.* at right angles with the keel. [O.E. *a,* on, and BEAM.]

ABED (a-bed') *ad.* in bed; on the bed. [O.E. *a,* on, and BED.]

ABERRANCE (ab-er'ans) *n.* deviation; error. [L. *ab,* from, and *errare,* to wander.]

ABERRANT (ab-er'ant) *a.* wandering from.

ABERRATION (ab-er-ā'shun) *n.* act of deviating from the line or course; mental derangement.

ABET (a-bet') *v.t.* [*pp.* ABETTED] to encourage; to help. [O.F. *abeter,* to incite, fr. Icel. *beita,* to bait.]

ABETTOR (a-bet'ur) *n.* one who abets.

ABEYANCE (a-bā'ans) *n.* a state of suspense. [F., fr. *à* and *bayer,* fr. L. *ad,* to, and *badare,* to gape.]

ABHOR (ab-hor') *v.t.* to dislike or hate bitterly. [L. *abhorrere,* to shrink from.]

ABHORRENCE (ab-hor'ens) *n.* extreme hatred; detestation.

ABHORRENT (ab-hor'ent) *a.* inconsistent with; detesting.

ABHORRENTLY (ab-hor'ent-li) *ad.* with abhorrence.

ABIDE (a-bīd') *v.i.* [*pret.* and *pp.* ABODE] to stay or dwell in a place; to wait for. [O.E. *abidan,* to remain in a place.]

ABIDING (a-bīd'ing) *a.* lasting.

ABIGAIL (ab'i-gāl) *n.* a lady's maid. [See 1 Samuel xxv. 23, 24.]

ABILITY (a-bil'li-ti) *n.* power; means; skill; *pl.* mental powers. [O.F. *ablété,* fr. L. *habilitas,* possession, fr. *habere,* to hold.]

ABJECT (ab'jekt) *a.* mean; worthless. [L. *abjectus,* thrown away.]

ABJECTION (ab-jek'shun) *n.* meanness of spirit or condition; baseness.

ABJECTNESS (ab'jekt-nes) *n.* state of being low, mean, or base. Also ABJECTEDNESS.

ABJURATION (ab-jōō-rā'shun) *n.* act of abjuring; recantation. [L. *ab,* away, and *jurare,* to swear.]

ABJURE (ab-jōōr') *v.t.* to renounce upon oath; to retract.

ABLATIVE (ab'la-tiv) *a.* one of the cases of Latin substantives. [L. *ablativus,* fr. *ab,* from, and *latus,* taken.]

ABLAZE (a-blāz') *ad.* in a blaze; on fire. [O.E. *a,* on, and *blæse,* flame.]

ABLE (ā'bl) *a.* having power; capable. [L. *habilis,* active.] [of body.

ABLE-BODIED (ā'bl-bod-id) *a.* having strength

ABLUTION (ab-lōō'shun) *n.* the act of washing. [L. *ablutus,* washed away.]

ABLY (ā'bli) *ad.* with ability.

ABNEGATE (ab'ne-gāt) *v.t.* to renounce; repudiate. [L. *ab,* away, and *negare,* to deny.]

ABNEGATION (ab-ne-gā'shun) *n.* self-denial.

ABNORMAL (ab-nor'mal) *a.* against rule. [L. *ab,* away, and *norma,* a rule.]

ABOARD (a-bōrd') *ad.* on a ship or boat. [O.E. *a,* on, and *bord,* the side of a ship.]

ABODE (a-bōd') *n.* place of residence; dwelling-place; continuance; stay. [See ABIDE.]

ABOLISH (a-bol'ish) *v.t.* to do away with; to make void. [L. *abolere,* to destroy.]

ABOLITION (ab-ō-lish'un) *n.* the act of abolishing.

ABOLITIONIST (ab-ō-lish'un-ist) *n.* one who seeks to abolish.

ABOMINABLE (a-bom'i-na-bl) a. detestable. [L. ab, away, and omen, omen.]

ABOMINABLY (a-bom'i-na-bli) ad. in an excessively bad degree; detestably.

ABOMINATE (a-bom'i-nat) v.t. to hate utterly; to abhor.

ABOMINATION (a-bom-i-na'shun) n. extreme hatred; object of hatred.

ABORIGINAL (ab-ō-rij'i-nal) a. first, or primitive. [L. ab, from, and F. origine, from L. origo, the beginning.]

ABORIGINES (ab-ō-rij'i-nēz) n.pl. first inhabitants of a country. [L.]

ABORTION (a-bor'shun) n. a miscarriage. [L. ab, from, and orire, to rise.]

ABORTIVE (a-bor'tiv) a. unsuccessful; untimely; premature.

ABORTIVELY (a-bor'tiv-li) ad. immaturely; without success.

ABORTIVENESS (a-bor'tiv-nes) n. state of being abortive; unproductiveness.

ABOUND (a-bound') v.i. to be in plenty. O.F. abonder, to overflow, fr. L. ab, from, and unda, a wave.]

ABOUT (a-bout') prep. round; near to; concerning; —ad. around; the longest way; every way. [O.E. a, on, and butan (= be, and utan, out).]

ABOVE (a-buv') prep. higher; more than;— ad. in a higher place. [O.E. a, on, and bufan (= be, and ufan, high).]

ABRADE (ab-rād') v.t. to rub off; to scrape away. [L. ab, from, and radere, to scrape.]

ABRASION (ab-rā'zhun) n. a rubbing off.

ABREAST (a-brest') ad. side by side; in a line. [O.E. a, on, and breost, breast.]

ABREPTION (ab-rep'shun) n. act of snatching and carrying away. [L. ab, away, and rapio, I seize.]

ABRIDGE (a-brij') v.t. to contract; to cut short; to deprive of. [O.F. abregier, fr. L. abbreviare, to shorten.]

ABRIDGMENT (a-brij'ment) n. a work abridged; a summary.

ABROAD (a-brawd') ad. out; out of doors. [O.E. a, on, and brad, broad.]

ABROGATE (ab'rō-gāt) v.t. to repeal; to annul. [L. abrogatus, repealed, fr. abrogare.]

ABROGATION (ab-rō-gā'shun) n. act of repealing.

ABRUPT (a-brupt') a. broken; craggy;— sudden; blunt. [L. abruptus, fr. abrumpere, to break off.]

ABRUPTION (ab-rup'shun) n. violent separation of bodies.

ABRUPTLY (a-brupt'li) ad. hastily; suddenly; rudely.

ABRUPTNESS (a-brupt'nes) n. an abrupt manner; suddenness.

ABSCESS (ab'ses) n. a tumour filled with purulent matter. [L. abscessus, going away.]

ABSCIND (ab-sind') v.t. to cut off; to pare off. [L. ab, off, and scindo, I cut.]

ABSCOND (ab-skond') v.i. to hide oneself. [L. abs, away, and condere, to hide.]

ABSCONDER (ab-skond'er) n. one who absconds or hides himself.

ABSENCE (ab'sens) n. state of being absent.

ABSENT (ab-sent') v.t. to keep away;— (ab'sent). a. not present; inattentive. [L. (acc. part.) absentem, being away, fr. abesse, to be away.] [himself.

ABSENTEE (ab-sen-tē') n. one who absents

ABSENTEEISM (ab-sen-tē'izm) n. the practice of a landlord living away from his estate.

ABSOLUTE (ab'sō-lūt) a. not limited; unconditional; arbitrary. [L. absolutus, free.]

ABSOLUTELY (ab'sō-lūt-li) ad. positively; arbitrarily.

ABSOLUTENESS (ab'sō-lūt-nes) n. completeness; arbitrary power.

ABSOLUTION (ab-sō'lū'shun) n. act of absolving; forgiveness. [L. ab, away, and solvere, to loosen.]

ABSOLUTISM (ab'sō-lūt-izm) n. principles of absolute government.

ABSOLVATORY (ab-zol'va-tur-i) a. having power to absolve; containing pardon or release.

ABSOLVE (ab-zolv') v.t. to free from; to pardon. [L. ab, away, and solvere, loosen.]

ABSONANT (ab'so-nant) a. contrary to reason; absurd. [L. ab, from, and sonare, to sound.]

ABSORB (ab-sorb') v.t. [pp. absorbed] to suck up; to imbibe. [L. ab, from, and sorbere, to suck.] [imbibed.

ABSORBABLE (ab-sor'ba-bl) a. that may be

ABSORBENT (ab-sor'bent) n. a substance that sucks up;—a. sucking up; imbibing. Also ABSORBING.

ABSORPTION (ab-sorp'shun) n. act of sucking up.

ABSORPTIVE (ab-sorp'tiv) a. having power to absorb.

ABSTAIN (ab-stān') v.i. to keep or refrain from; to forbear. [L. abs, from, and tenere, to hold.]

ABSTAINER (ab-stān'er) n. one who abstains from intoxicating liquors.

ABSTEMIOUS (ab-stē'mi-us) a. temperate in diet. [L. abs, from, and temetum, wine.]

ABSTEMIOUSLY (ab-stē'mi-us-li) ad. temperately.

ABSTEMIOUSNESS (ab-stē'mi-us-nes) n. a sparing use of food, etc.

ABSTENTION (ab-sten'shun) n. act of holding back, or refraining from.

AESTERGE (ab-sterj') v.t. to cleanse by wiping; to purify. [L. abstergere, to wipe away.]

ABSTERGENT (ab-ster'jent) a. having a cleansing quality.

ABSTINENCE (ab'sti-nens) n. voluntary refraining from food or drink.

ABSTINENT (ab'sti-nent) a. practising abstinence; fasting.

ABSTRACT (ab'strakt) a. separate; existing in the mind only;—n. an abridgment or epitome;—(ab-strakt') v.t. to draw from; to separate; to remove. [L. abstractus, withdrawn.]

ABSTRACTED (ab-strak'ted) a. purloined;— absent in mind.

ABSTRACTION (ab-strak'shun) n. a drawing from; absence of mind.

ABSTRACTLY (ab'strakt-li) ad. by itself.

ABSTRUSE (ab-strōōs') a. difficult to be understood; obscure. [L. abstrusus, concealed.]

ABSTRUSELY (ab-strōōs'li) ad. obscurely.

ABSURD (ab-surd') a. contrary to reason; ridiculous. [L. absurdus, inharmonious, fr. ab, from, and surdus, deaf.]

ABSURDITY (ab-sur'di-ti) n. the quality of being absurd; any foolish act or speech.

ABUNDANCE (a-bun'dans) n. great plenty. [L. abundare to overflow, fr. ab, from, and unda, a wave.]

ABUNDANT (a-bun'dant) a. very plentiful.

ABUSABLE (a-būz'a-bl) a. that may be abused.

ABUSE (a-būs') n. ill-use, treatment, or employment of; rude, reproachful language; the violation of a female;—(a-būz') v.t. to make a wrong use of; treat ill; vilify. [L. abusus, misusing, fr. ab, from, and uti, to use.]

ABUSIVE (a-bū'siv) a. marked by abuse.

ABUT (a-but') v.i. to border upon. [O.F. abouter, to thrust forwards.]

ABUTMENT (a-but'ment) n. that which borders upon; the solid part of a bridge next the land. [less.]

ABYSMAL (a-biz'mal) a. bottomless; fathom-

ABYSS (a-bis') n. a bottomless gulf or depth. [L. abyssus, fr. G. abyssos, bottomless.]

ACACIA (a-kā'sha) n. a genus of thorny, tropical shrubs, with pinnate leaves. [G. akē, a point.]

ACADEMIC (ak-a-dem'ik) a. pertaining to an academy. Also ACADEMICAL.

ACADEMICIAN (ak-ad-e-mish'an) n. a member of an academy.

ACADEMY (a-kad'e-mi) *n.* a school of arts and sciences; a school holding a place intermediate between the common school and college. [G. *Akademia,* the name of the garden near Athens, in which Plato's teaching was given.]

ACANTHA (a-kan'tha) *n.* the prickle of a plant; the spine or prickly fin ot a fish. [G. *ake,* a thorn, and *anthos,* a flower.]

ACANTHOUS (a-kan'thus) *n.* armed with prickles; spiny. Also **ACANTHACEOUS.**

ACANTHUS (a-kan'thus) *n.* a herbaceous prickly plant; an ornament resembling its foliage in the capitals of the Corinthian and Composite orders.

ACARUS (ak'a-rus) *n.* a small spider-like insect, sometimes parasitic; mite. [G. *akares,* very small.]

ACATALEPSY (a-kata-lep'si) *n.* ignorance of the nature and cause of disease. [G. *akatalepsia,* fr. *a,* not, *kata,* completely, and *lepsis,* a seizing.]

ACATALEPTIC (a-kat-a-lep'tik) *a.* incomprehensible.

ACCEDE (ak-sēd') *v.i.* to assent; to quicken. [L. *ad,* to, and *cedere,* to go.]

ACCEDING (ak-sē'ding) *a.* agreeing to; granting.

ACCELERATE (ak-sel'e-rāt) *v.t.* to hasten motion; to quicken. [L. *acceleratus,* quickened, fr. *ad,* to, and *celer,* swift.]

ACCELERATION (ak-sel-e-rā'shun) *n.* act of hastening. [ing the speed.

ACCELERATIVE (ak-sel-e-rā'tiv) *a.* increasing the speed.

ACCENT (ak-sent') *v.t.* to express or note the accent;—(ak'sent) *n.* modulation of voice; a mark to direct the modulation. [L. (acc.) *accentum,* a tone, fr. *ad,* to, and *cantus,* a song.]

ACCENTUATE (ak-sen'tū-āt) *v.t.* to lay stress on the accent; to emphasise.

ACCENTUAL (ak-sen'tū-al) *a.* relating to accent.

ACCEPT (ak-sept') *v.t.* to receive; to admit; to subscribe, and become liable for. [F., fr. L. *acceptus,* received.]

ACCEPTABLE (ak-sep'ta-bl) *a.* likely to be accepted; agreeable.

ACCEPTABILITY (ak-sep-ta-bil'i-ti) *n.* the quality of being acceptable.

ACCEPTABLY (ak-sep-ta'bli) *ad.* agreeably.

ACCEPTANCE (ak-sep'tans) *n.* reception with approbation; a bill accepted.

ACCEPTATION (ak-sep-tā'shun) *n.* acceptance; the commonly received meaning of a word.

ACCEPTED (ak-sep'ted) *a.* kindly received.

ACCEPTER (ak-sep'tçr) *n.* one who accepts.

ACCESS (ak'ses) *n.* approach; increase. [L. *ad,* to, and *cedere,* to go.]

ACCESSARY, ACCESSORY (ak-ses'u-ri) *a.* acceding to; contributing to;—*n.* one who helps to commit a crime, or has guilty knowledge of its commission either before or after the event.

ACCESSIBILITY (ak-ses-i-bil'i-ti) *n.* quality of being easily got at.

ACCESSIBLE (ak-ses'i-bl) *a.* that may be approached. [accessible.

ACCESSIBLY (ak-ses'i-bli) *ad.* so as to be

ACCESSION (ak-sesh'un) *n.* act of coming to; addition.

ACCESSIONAL (ak-sesh'un-al) *a.* additional.

ACCESSORIAL (ak-ses-sō'ri-al) *a.* pertaining to an accessory.

ACCIDENCE (ak'si-dens) *n.* a book of rudiments. [L. *accidere,* to happen.]

ACCIDENT (ak'si-dent) *n.* that which happens unforeseen or undesigned mishap; casualty; —in *Logic* a non-essential.

ACCIDENTAL (ak-si-dent'al) *a.* happening by chance; fortuitous.

ACCIDENTALLY (ak-si-dent'al-i) *ad.* by accident.

ACCLAIM (a-klām') *n.* a shout of joy or welcome. [L. *ad,* to, and *clamare,* to call aloud.] [applause.

ACCLAMATION (ak-la-mā'shun) *n.* a shout of

ACCLAMATORY (a-klam-a'tur-i) *a.* expressing joy or applause.

ACCLIMATE (a-kli'māt) *v.t.* to inure to a climate. Also **ACCLIMATISE.** [G. *klima,* fr. *klinein,* slope.]

ACCLIMATION (ak-li-mā'shun) *n.* process or state of being acclimated. Also **ACCLIMATISATION.**

ACCLIVITY (a-kliv'i-ti) *n.* steepness inclining upward; ascent. [L. (acc.) *acclivitatem,* an upward slope.]

ACCOLADE (ak-ō-lād') *n.* a tap with a sword on the shoulder in conferring knighthood. [L. *ad,* to, and *collum,* the neck.]

ACCOMMODATE (a-kom'ō-dāt) *v.t.* to supply with conveniences; suit; adjust. [L. *accommodatus,* fitted.]

ACCOMMODATING (a-kom'ō-dāt-ing) *a.* disposed to oblige; kind.

ACCOMMODATION (a-kom-ō-dā'shun) *n.* adaptation; adjustment;—provision of necessaries;—loan of money;—*pl.* conveniences; lodgings.

ACCOMPANIMENT (a-kum'pa-ni-ment) *n.* that which accompanies, or is added as ornament.

ACCOMPANIST (a-kum'pa-nist) *n.* the performer in music who takes the accompanying part.

ACCOMPANY (a-kum'pa-ni) *v.t.* to go or be with. [L. *ad,* to, *con,* with, and *panis,* bread —(*ad,* and Late L. (acc) *companiem,* a sharer of bread.)]

ACCOMPLICE (a-kom'plis) *n.* an associate in crime. [L. *ad,* to, and (acc.) *complicem,* interwoven.]

ACCOMPLISH (a-kom'plish) *v.t.* to finish entirely; bring to pass. [O.F. *complisant,* completing, fr. L. *ad,* to, and *complere,* to fill.]

ACCOMPLISHED (a-kom'plisht) *pp.* or *a.* finished; completed; refined.

ACCOMPLISHMENT (a-kum'plish-ment) *n.* fulfilment; attainment; an acquirement which adds grace.

ACCORD (a-kord') *n.* agreement; concurrence; harmony;—*v.t.* to grant or concede;—*v.i.* to agree or harmonise with. [F. *accorder,* to agree, fr. L. *ad,* to, and *cor, cordis,* the heart.]

ACCORDANCE (a-kor'dans) *n.* agreement; harmony. [consequently.

ACCORDINGLY (a-kor'ding-li) *ad.* agreeably;

ACCORDION (a-kor'di-un) *n.* a modern small-keyed instrument with metallic reeds. [Fr. It. See **ACCORD.**]

ACCOST (a-kost') *v.t.* to speak first to; address. [O.F. *acoster,* fr. L. *ad,* to, and *costa,* rib, side.] [familiar.

ACCOSTABLE (a-kos't-a-bl) *a.* easy of access;

ACCOUNT (a-kount') *n.* computation or reckoning; register or statement of money transactions; recital or narrative; reason or motive; importance; estimation; value; behalf; sake;—*v.t.* to reckon or judge;— *v.i.* to answer for. [O.F. *acconter,* fr. L. *ad,* to, and *computare,* to reckon.]

ACCOUNTABILITY (a-koun-ta-bil'i-ti) *n.* liability to give account.

ACCOUNTABLE (a-koun'ta-bl) *a.* subject to account; liable.

ACCOUNTANT (a-koun'tant) *n.* one employed, or skilful, in keeping accounts.

ACCOUTRE (a-kōō'ter) *v.t.* to equip; furnish. [F. *accoutrer,* to dress, array.]

ACCOUTREMENTS (a-kōō'tre-ments) *n.* equipage; trappings.

ACCREDIT (a-kred'it) *v.t.* to give credit, authority, or honour to. [F. *accréditer,* fr. L. *ad,* to, and *creditus,* believed.]

ACCREDITED (a-kred'i-ted) *a.* sent with credentials to a foreign state.

ACCRESCENT (a-kres'ent) *a.* growing or adding to; increasing. [L. *ad,* to, and *crescere,* to grow.]

ACCRETION (a-krē'shun) *n.* the act of growing; increase. [L, *crescere,* grow.]

ACCRETIVE (a-krē'tiv) *a.* increasing by growth or addition.

ACCRUE (a-krōò') *v.i.* to arise; be added. [O.F. *accreu,* grown, fr. L. *ad,* to, and *crescere,* to grow.]

ACCUMULATE (a-kū'mū-lāt) *v.t.* or *i.* to heap together; increase. [L. *accumulatus,* heaped up, fr. *ad,* to, and *cumulus,* a heap.]

ACCUMULATION (a-kū-mū-lā'shun) *n.* the act of accumulating; a heap.

ACCUMULATIVE (a-kū'mū-lā-tiv) *a.* that accumulates.

ACCUMULATOR (a-kū'mū-lā-tur) *n.* one who, or that which, accumulates.

ACCURACY (ak'ū-rā-si) *n.* exactness; closeness. [L. *ad,* to, and *curatus,* cared for, fr. *cura,* care.]

ACCURATE (ak'ū-rāt) *a.* done with care; without error; correct; precise; just.

ACCURATELY (ak'ū-rāt-li) *ad.* exactly; nicely.

ACCURATENESS (ak'ū-rāt-nes) *n.* exactness; correctness; accuracy.

ACCURSED (a-kur'sed, a-kurst') *a.* cursed; execrable. [O.E. *cursian,* curse.] [surable.

ACCUSABLE (a kū'za-bl) *a.* blamable; censurable.

ACCUSATION (ak-ū-zā'shun) *n.* act of accusing; charge of a crime.

ACCUSATIVE (a-kū'za-tiv) *a.* accusing; denoting a case in grammar.

ACCUSATORY (a-kū'za-tur-i) *a.* containing or pertaining to an accusation.

ACCUSE (a-kūz') *v.t.* to charge with a crime; blame; impeach. [L. *ad,* to, and *causa,* a law suit.] [accusation.

ACCUSER (a-kū'zer) *n.* one who brings **ACCUSTOM** (a-kus-tum) *v.t.* to make familiar. [O.F. *acostumer,* fr. O.F. *costume,* fr. L. (acc.) *consuetudinem,* habit.]

ACE (ās) *n.* a unit on cards or dice. [L. *as,* unity or pound.]

ACENTRIC (a-sen'trik) *a.* not having a centre; not centred. [L. *a,* not or away, and *centrum,* fr. G. *kentron,* a prick.]

ACEPHALOUS (a-sef'a-lus) *a.* without a head. [G. *a,* not, and *kephale,* head.]

ACERBITY (a-ser'bi-ti) *n.* bitterness of taste or of spirit. [F., fr. L. (acc.) *acerbitatem,* sourness.]

ACERIC (a-ser'ik) *a.* pertaining to, or got from, the maple. [L. *acer,* a maple-tree.]

ACETIFY (a-sēt'i-fī) *v.t.* or *i.* to turn acid. [L. *acetum,* vinegar.]

ACETIMETRY (as-i-tim'et-ri) *n.* act 'of ascertaining the strength of acids. [L. *acetum,* vinegar, and G. *metron,* a measure.]

ACETOUS (as'-et-ōs, -tus, or a-sē'tus) *a.* having the quality of vinegar; sour. Also **ACETIC**.

ACETYLENE (a-set'i-lēn) *n.* a colourless inflammable gas, C_2H_2.

ACHE (āk) *v.t.* to be in pain;—a continued pain. [O.E. *acan,* to suffer pain.]

ACHIEVABLE (a-chē'va-bl) *a.* that may be performed.

ACHIEVE (a-chēv') *v.t.* to do; perform; obtain. [O.F. *à chef,* to a head, fr. L. *ad,* to, and *caput,* the head.]

ACHIEVEMENT (a-chēv'ment) *n.* a performance; an action.

ACHING (āk'ing) *n.* continued pain.

ACHROMATIC (ak-rō-mat'ik) *a.* destitute of colour. [G. *a,* not, and *chroma,* colour.]

ACICULAR (a-sik'ū-lar) *a.* shaped and sharp as a needle. Also **ACICULATE**. [L. *acicula,* a little needle.]

ACID (as'id) *a.* sour, like vinegar;—*n.* a substance by which salts are formed. [L. *acidus,* sour.]

ACIDIFY (a-sid'i-fī) *v.t.* to convert into acid. [L. *acidus,* sour, and *facere,* to make.]

ACIDITY (a-sid'i-ti) *n.* sourness; sharpness.

ACIDULATE (a-sid'ū-lāt) *v.t.* to tinge with acids.

ACIDULOUS (a-sid'ū-lus) *a.* slightly sour.

ACKNOWLEDGE (ak-nol'ej) *v.t.* to own; confess. [O.E. *on,* in, and *cnawan,* know.]

ACKNOWLEDGMENT (ak-nol'ej-ment) *n.* the owning of a thing; thanks.

ACME (ak'mē) *n.* the highest point; crisis of a thing. [G. *akme,* top.]

ACOLYTE (ak'ō-līt) *n.* a ministering servant or attendant. [G. *akolouthos,* a follower.]

ACONITE (ak'ō-nīt) *n.* wolf's-bane; a poisonous root. [G. *akoniton.*]

ACONTINE (a-kon'i-tin) *n.* an anodyne obtained from aconite, used in neuralgia.

ACORN (ā'korn) *n.* the seed or fruit of the oak, being an oval nut growing in a rough cup. [O.E. *æcern,* fruit, fr. *æcer,* field.]

ACOUSTIC (a-kous'tik) *a.* pertaining to hearing. [G. *akoustikos,* relating to sound.]

Acorn.

ACOUSTICS (a-kous'tiks) *n.pl.* the theory of sounds.

ACQUAINT (a-kwānt') *v.t.* to inform; make familiar with. [O.F. *acointer,* fr. Low L. *accoquitare,* to make known.]

ACQUAINTANCE (a-kwān'tans) *n.* knowledge; one well known.

ACQUAINTED (a-kwān'ted) *a.* informed; known one to the other.

ACQUIESCE (ak-wē-es') *v.i.* to assent to; be satisfied with. [L. *ad,* to, and *quiescere,* to rest.] [compliance.

ACQUIESCENCE (ak-wē-es'ens) *n.* consent; **ACQUIESCENT** (ak-wē-es'ent) *a.* disposed to submit.

ACQUIRABLE (a-kwīr'a-bl) *a.* that may be acquired.

ACQUIRE (a-kwīr') *v.t.* to gain something; to attain to. [L. *acquirere,* to obtain.]

ACQUIREMENT (a-kwīr'ment) *n.* that which is acquired; gain.

ACQUISITION (ak-wi-zish'un) *n.* the act of gaining; the thing acquired. [L. *acquisitus,* obtained.]

ACQUISITIVENESS (a-kwiz'i-tiv-nes) *n.* desire of possession.

ACQUIT (a-kwit') *v.t.* to discharge; to clear from; absolve. [O.F. *acquiter,* to settle a claim.]

ACQUITTAL (a-kwit'al) *n.* formal release from a charge.

ACQUITTANCE (a-kwit'ans) *n.* receipt in full for debt.

ACRE (ā'ker) *n.* a piece of land containing 160 square rods. [O.E. *æcer,* a field.]

ACREAGE (ā'ker-āj) *n.* number of acres in a given field or estate.

ACRID (ak'rid) *a.* hot and biting to the taste; pungent. [L. *acer, acris,* sharp.]

ACRIDITY (a-krid'i-ti) *n.* sharp bitterness; pungency. Also **ACRIDNESS**.

ACRIMONIOUS (ak-ri-mō'ni-us) *a.* full of acrimony; bitter.

ACRIMONY (ak'ri-mun-i) *n.* sharpness; bitterness of feeling or language. [L. *acrimonia,* sharpness of language or temper.]

ACROBAT (ak'ro-bat) *n.* one who practises high-vaulting, rope-dancing, etc. [G. *akrobatos,* tiptoeing.]

ACROPOLIS (a-krop'o-lis) *n.* a citadel. [G. *akros,* on high, and *polis,* a city.]

ACROSPIRE (ak'rō-spīr) *n.* a sprout at the end of a seed. [G. *akros,* summit or end, and *speira,* that which is twisted round.]

ACROSTIC (a-kros'tik) *n.* a poem whose initial letters form a name. [G. *akros,* the extreme, and *stichos,* a verse.]

ACT (akt) v.t. to perform; move;—v.i. to imitate; conduct or behave;—n. a deed; division of a play. [L. actus, done, fr. agere, to do.]

ACTING (ak'ting) n. performing duty; doing temporary duty; performing dramatically.

ACTINIC (ak-tin'ik) a. denoting the chemical power of the rays of the sun. [G. aktis, stem, aktin, ray.]

ACTINISM (ak'tin-izm) n. the chemical action of the sun's rays distinct from light and heat as in photography.

ACTION (ak'shun) n. deed; battle; suit at law; gesticulation;—pl. behaviour; deeds.

ACTIONABLE (ak'shun-a-bl) a. liable to an action at law.

ACTIVE (ak'tiv) a. denoting action; quick motion or advance.

ACTIVELY (ak'tiv-li) ad. in an active, nimble manner.

ACTIVITY (ak-tiv'i-ti) n. quality of being active; nimbleness. [player.

ACTOR (akt'ur) n. a man that acts; a stage-

ACTRESS (ak'tres) n. a female who acts.

ACTUAL (ak'tū-al) a. real; certain.

ACTUALLY (ak'tu-al-i) ad. really; in fact.

ACTUARY (ak'tu-a-ri) n. a registrar or clerk. [L. actuarius, a clerk.]

ACTUATE (ak'tu-āt) v.t. to put in action; excite. [See ACT.]

ACULEATE (a-kū'le-āt) a. having a point or sting; prickly. [L. aculeatus, aculeus, a little needle.]

ACUMEN (a-kū'men) n. quickness of intellect; acuteness. [L. acuere, to sharpen.

ACUPRESSURE (ak-ū-presh'ūr) n. in Surgery, stopping hemorrhage by compressing the arteries with needles or wire. [L. acus, a needle, and pressus, pressed.]

ACUPUNCTURE (ak-ū-pungk'tūr) n. pricking the bodily tissues with a needle to introduce anodynes, etc. [L. acus, a needle, and punctus, pricked.]

ACUTE (a-kūt') a. sharp; ingenious; penetrating; keen.—(Geom.) An angle less than 90°, or less than a right angle. [L. acutus, sharp, fr. acuere, to sharpen.]

ACUTENESS (a-kūt'nes) n. sharpness; quickness of intellect.

Acute Angle.

ADAGE (ad'āj) n. a proverb; maxim; an old saying. [L. adagium, an old saying, fr. aio, I say.]

ADAGIO (a-da'je-ō) n. in Music, a mark of slow time. [It.]

ADAMANT (ad'a-mant) n. a very hard stone; a diamond. [G. adamantos, fr. a, not, and damao, I tame.]

ADAMANTINE (ad-a-mant'in) a. extremely hard; hard as adamant.

ADAM'S-APPLE (ad'amz-ap'pl) n. a species of citron; the prominent part of the throat.

ADAPT (a-dapt') v.t. to fit one thing to another; suit. [L. ad, to, and aptus, fit.]

ADAPTABILITY (a-dap-ta-bil'i-ti) n. the quality of adaptation.

ADAPTABLE (a-dap'ta-bl) a. that may be adapted.

ADAPTED (a-dap'ted) a. suited or fitted.

ADD (ad) v.t. to join or put to; augment or enlarge. [L. addere.]

ADDER (ad'er) n. a venomous serpent. [O.E. nœdre, a snake. An adder is mistaken use for a nadder.]

ADDICTED (a-dik'ted) pp. given up; devoted. [L. addictus, assigned.]

ADDICTEDNESS (a-dik'ted-nes) n. state of being addicted. [voting.

ADDICTION (a-dik'shun) n. the act of de-

ADDITION (a-dish'un) n. an adding to.

ADDITIONAL (a-dish'un-al) a. that is added.

ADDITIVE (ad'i-tiv) a. that may be added.

ADDLE (ad'l) v.t. to make corrupt;—a. barren; empty. [O.E. adela, mud.]

ADDLED (ad'ld) a. morbid; corrupt;—barren.

ADDRESS (a-dres') v.t. to speak or apply to; prepare for; direct to; make love;—n. a speaking to; application; skill; direction of a letter. [F. adresser.]

ADDRESSEE (a-dres'ē) n. the person addressed.

ADDRESSES (a-dres'es) n.pl. courtship; attentions of a lover.

ADDUCE (a-dūs') v.t. to bring forward; allege. [L. ad, to, and ducere, to lead.]

ADDUCTION (a-duk'shun) n. the act of bringing forward. [L. ad, to, and (part.) ductus, led.]

ADEMPTION (a-demp'shun) n. in Law, the revocation of a grant. [L. ad, to, and eme, I buy.]

ADENIFORM (a-den'i-form) a. shaped like a gland. [G. aden, a gland, and L. forma, shape.]

ADENOLOGY (ad-en-ol'o-ji) n. the doctrine of the glands, their nature and uses. [G. aden, a gland, and logos, a discourse.]

ADENOTOMY (ad-en-ot'ō-mi) n. incision of a gland. [G. aden, a gland, and tome, a cutting.]

ADEPT (a-dept') n. a person skilled in any art;—a. skilful. [L. (part.) adeptus, having attained.]

ADEQUATE (ad'e-kwāt) a. fully sufficient; equal to. [L. adequatus, made equal.]

ADHERE (ad-hēr') v.i. to stick close; remain fixed or firm. [L. ad, to, and hœrere, hasum, to stick.]

ADHERENCE (ad-hēr'ens) n. the quality or state of adhering; steady attachment.

ADHERENT (ad-hēr'ent) a. united with or to; sticking to;—n. a follower; a partisan.

ADHERER (ad-hēr'er) n. one who adheres to his leader or party.

ADHESION (ad-hē'zhun) n. the act or state of sticking to.

ADHESIVE (ad-hē'siv) a. sticking to; tenacious.

ADHESIVELY (ad-hē'siv-li) ad. with adhesion.

ADHESIVENESS (ad-hē'siv-nes) n. quality of sticking; tenacity.

ADIEU (a-dū') inter. farewell;—n. act of taking leave. [F. à Dieu, to God.]

ADIPOCERE (ad'i-pō-sēr) n. a substance like spermaceti. [L. adeps, soft fat, and cera, wax.]

ADIPOSE (ad'i-pōz) a. consisting of, or containing, fat; fatty. Also **ADIPOUS**. [L. adiposus, fr. adeps, fat.]

ADIT (ad'it) n. a horizontal entrance into a pit. [L. aditus, entrance.]

ADJACENCY (a-jā'sen-si) n. state of lying close to. [L. ad, to, and jacentem, lying.]

ADJACENT (a-jā'sent) a. lying close to.

ADJECTIVE (ad'jek-tiv) n. a word added to a noun to express some quality or circumstance. [L. adjectivus, fr. adjectus, put near.]

ADJECTIVELY (ad'jek-tiv-li) ad. in the manner of an adjective.

ADJOIN (a-join') v.t. or i. to join or be contiguous to. [F. adjoindre, fr. L. adjungere, to join.]

ADJOINING (a-join'ing) a. joining; adjacent; near.

ADJOURN (a-jurn') v.t. to put off to another time; postpone; defer. [O.F. ajorner, Late L. adjurnare to name a day.]

ADJOURNMENT (a-jurn'ment) n. the act of adjourning; delay; intermission.

ADJUDGE (a-juj') v.t. to sentence; to decide judicially. [O.F. ajouger, fr. L. ad, to, and judicare, to judge.]

ADJUDGMENT (a-juj'ment) n. judicial sentence.

ADJUDICATE (a-jōō'de-kāt) v.t. to determine by law.

ADJUDICATION (a-jŏŏ-de-kā'shun) n. judicial trial or sentence.

ADJUDICATOR (a-jŏŏ'de-kā-tur) n. one who determines a cause.

ADJUNCT (ad'jungkt) n. something joined to another;—a. added to or united with. [L. ad, to, and junctus, joined.]

ADJURATION (ad-jŏŏ-rā'shun) n. act of charging solemnly; form of oath.

ADJURE (ad-jŏŏr') v.t. to charge on oath; enjoin earnestly. [L. ad, to, and jurare, to swear.]

ADJURING (ad-jŏŏr'ing) a. charging or urging solemnly.

ADJUST (a-just') v.t. to make exact or conformable; set right. [F. adjuster, fr. O.F. ajouster, fr. Low L. adjustare, to place side by side.]

ADJUSTABLE (a-jus'ta-bl) a. capable of being adjusted.

ADJUSTER (a-jus'ter) n. one who puts right; that which regulates.

ADJUSTIVE (a-jus'tiv) a. serving or tending to put right.

ADJUSTMENT (a-just'ment) n. a setting in order; regulation; settlement.

ADJUTANCY (ad'jŏŏ-tan-si) n. office of an adjutant.

ADJUTANT (ad'jŏŏ-tant) n. a military officer who assists the major. [L. (acc. part.) adjutantem, assisting.]

ADJUTOR (ad-jŏŏ'ter) n. a helper. [L. ad, to, and juvare, to help.]

ADJUVANT (ad'jŏŏ-vant) a. helping; assisting.

ADMENSURATION (ad-men-sū-rā'shun) n. act of measuring. [L. ad, to, and mensura, a measure.]

ADMINISTER (ad-min'is-ter) v.t. to manage or conduct; supply or dispense; tender, as an oath; settle, as an estate;—v.i. to add something to; contribute. [L. ad, to, and ministrare, to serve.]

ADMINISTRATION (ad-min-is-trā'shun) n. the act of administering; executive part of government.

ADMINISTRATIVE (ad-min'is-trāt-iv) a. that which administers.

ADMINISTRATOR (ad-min-is-trāt'ur) n. a man that manages an intestate estate.

ADMINISTRATORSHIP (ad-min-is-trā'tur-ship) n. the office of an administrator.

ADMINISTRATRIX (ad-min-is-trā'triks) n. a woman that administers.

ADMIRABLE (ad'mi-ra-bl) a. worthy of admiration; excellent. [L. ad, to, and mirari, to wonder.]

ADMIRABLY (ad'mi-ra-bli) ad. wonderfully.

ADMIRAL (ad'mi-ral) n. principal officer of a fleet or navy. [F. amiral, fr. A. amir, a chief.]

ADMIRALSHIP (ad'mi-ral-ship) n. office of admiral.

ADMIRALTY (ad'mi-ral-ti) n. the board or court for administering naval affairs; the official buildings thereof.

ADMIRATION (ad-mi-rā'shun) n. astonishment; wonder; esteem.

ADMIRE (ad-mir') v.t. to regard with wonder; esteem or prize highly;—v.i. to wonder at; marvel. [L. ad, to, and mirari, wonder.]

ADMIRER (ad-mir'er) n. one that admires; a lover.

ADMIRINGLY (ad-mir'ing-li) ad. with admiration; in the manner of an admirer.

ADMISSIBILITY (ad-mis-i-bil'i-ti) n. the quality of being admissible.

ADMISSIBLE (ad-mis'i-bl) a. that may be admitted. [L. admissum, sent, fr. ad, to, and mittere, send.]

ADMISSION (ad-mish'un) n. the act of entering; permission to enter; concession in argument; acknowledgment.

ADMIT (ad-mit') v.t. to allow; let in; receive as true. [L. ad, to, and mittere, send.]

ADMITTANCE (ad-mit'ans) n. act or power of entering; entrance.

ADMITTED (ad-mit'ed) a. granted; allowed.

ADMIX (ad-miks') v.t. to mingle. [L. ad, to, and mixtum, mixed.]

ADMIXTURE (ad-miks'tūr) n. the act of mixing; state of being mingled; the compound made by mixing.

ADMONISH (ad-mon'ish) v.t. to warn; reprove gently; advise. [L. admoneo, I. warn.]

ADMONISHER (ad-mon'ish-er) n. one who admonishes or reproves.

ADMONISHMENT (ad-mon'ish-ment) n. counsel; warning.

ADMONITION (ad-mŏn-ish'un) n. gentle reproof; counsel. [monishes.

ADMONITOR (ad-mon'i-tur) n. one who admonishes; warning.

ADMONITORY (ad-mon'i-tu-ri) a. that admonishes; warning.

ADNASCENT (ad-nas'cnt) a. growing on something else. [L. (acc.) adnascentem, fr. nasci, to grow.]

ADNATE (ad'nāt) a. growing or attached to by its whole length. [L. ad. to, and natus, born.]

ADO (a-dŏŏ') n. trouble; difficulty; bustle; stir. [M.E. at = to and DO.]

ADOBE (a-dō'bā) n. a sun-dried brick. [Sp. adobar, to plaster.]

ADOLESCENCE (ad-ō-les'ens) n. state of growing; youth. [L. (acc. part.) adolescentem, growing up.]

ADOLESCENT (ad-ō-les'ent) a. growing; advancing to manhood.

ADOPT (a-dopt') v.t. to take the child of another and treat it as one's own; choose or select. [L. adoptare, fr. ad, to, and optare, to choose.]

ADOPTION (a-dop'shun) n. the act of adopting.

ADOPTIVE (a-dop'tiv) a. fitted for adopting.

ADORABILITY (a-dŏr-a-bil'i-ti) n. the quality of being adorable. Also ADORABLENESS.

ADORABLE (a-dŏr'a-bl) a. worthy of adoration; divine.

ADORATION (ad-ō-rā'shun) n. divine worship; homage.

ADORE (a-dōr') v.t. to worship; love intensely. [L. adorare, to worship, fr. ad, to, and orare, to pray, fr. os, oris, mouth.]

ADORER (a-dōr'er) n. one who adores; a lover.

ADORINGLY (a-dōr'ing-li) ad. with adoration or love.

ADORN (a-dorn') v.t. to deck; embellish. [L. ad, to, and ornare, to decorate.]

ADORNMENT (a-dorn'ment) n. embellishment.

ADRIFT (a-drift') a. or ad. floating at random. [O.E. a, on, and DRIFT, fr. drifan, to drive.]

ADROIT (a-droit') a. skilful; expert; dexterous; ingenious. [F. à droit, to the right.]

ADROITLY (a-droit'li) ad. ingeniously.

ADROITNESS (a-droit'nes) n. dexterity.

ADULATION (ad-ū-lā'shun) n. excessive flattery. [L. adulare, to fawn upon.]

ADULATORY ad'ū-lā-tō-ri) a. flattering to excess.

ADULT (a-dult') n. a person grown up;—a. grown to maturity. [L. adultus, grown up, fr. adolescere, to grow up.]

ADULTERATE (a-dul'ter-āt) v.t. to debase or corrupt by mixture;—a. debased. [L. adulteratus, corrupted.]

ADULTERATED (a-dul'ter-āt-ed) a. debased; mixed; corrupted.

ADULTERATION (a-dul-te-rā'shun) n. the act of adulterating.

ADULTERER (a-dul'ter-er) n. a man guilty of adultery. [L. adulterium.]

ADULTERESS (a-dul'ter-es) n. a woman guilty of adultery.

ADULTEROUS (a-dul'ter-us) a. guilty of adultery; spurious.

ADULTERY (a-dul'ter-i) n. a violation of the marriage bed.

ADULTNESS (a-dult'nes) *n.* the state of being adult. [See **ADULT**.]

ADUMBRANT (ad-um'brant) *a.* giving a faint shadow.

ADUMBRATE (ad-um'brāt) *v.t.* to shadow out faintly. [L. *adumbratus*, shadowed forth, fr. *ad, to,* and *umbra,* a shade.]

ADUMBRATION (ad-um-brā'shun) *n.* a shadow or faint resemblance.

ADVANCE (ad-vans') *n.* a going forward; promotion; payment beforehand; —*v.t.* to bring forward or higher; raise; promote; pay beforehand; —*v.i.* to improve; rise in rank. [F. *avancer,* fr. *avant,* before, fr. L. *ab,* away, and *ante,* before.]

ADVANCED (ad-vanst') *pp.* or *a.* moved forward; improved; old.

ADVANCEMENT (ad-vans'ment) *n.* act of moving forward; promotion.

ADVANTAGE (ad-van'tāj) *n.* favourable circumstances; superiority; gain; —*v.i.* to benefit; promote. [F. *avantage,* fr. *avant,* before.]

ADVANTAGEOUS (ad-van-tā'jus) *a.* profitable; useful.

ADVANTAGEOUSLY (ad-van-tā'jus-li) *ad.* profitably; conveniently.

ADVENT (ad'vent) *n.* a coming; the season of four weeks before Christmas. [L. *adventus,* fr. *advenire,* to come to.]

ADVENTITIOUS (ad-ven-tish'us) *a.* added; not essentially inherent.

ADVENTURE (ad-ven'tūr) *n.* an extraordinary event; an enterprise; —*v.t.* to try the chance; risk. [L. *adventurus,* about to happen.]

ADVENTURER (ad-ven'tūr-er) *n.* one that risks.

ADVENTUROUS (ad-ven'tūr-us) *a.* daring; bold; enterprising.

ADVERB (ad'verb) *n.* a word which modifies a verb. [L. *ad, to,* and *verbum,* a word.]

ADVERBIAL (ad-ver'bi-al) *a.* relating to, or like an adverb.

ADVERBIALLY (ad-ver'bi-al-i) *ad.* in the manner of an adverb.

ADVERSARY (ad'ver-sar-i) *n.* an opponent; enemy. [L. *adversus,* turned to, fr. *advertere,* to turn to.]

ADVERSE (ad'vers) *a.* contrary to one's desires; calamitous.

ADVERSELY (ad'vers-li) *ad.* with opposition; unfortunately.

ADVERSITY (ad-ver'si-ti) *n.* misfortune; affliction; calamity.

ADVERT (ad-vert') *v.i.* to turn the mind; to notice; refer; allude.

ADVERTENCE (ad-ver'tens) *n.* attention to; heed.

ADVERTENT (ad-ver'tent) *a.* attentive.

ADVERTISE (ad'ver-tiz) *v.t.* to inform; give public notice. [F. *avertissant,* fr. L. *advertere,* to turn to.]

ADVERTISEMENT (ad-ver'tiz-ment) *n.* a public notice. [vertises.

ADVERTISER (ad-ver-ti'zer) *n.* one who advertises.

ADVERTISING (ad-ver-ti'zing) *a.* furnishing or having advertisements.

ADVICE (ad-vis') *n.* opinion or suggestion given; counsel; deliberate consideration; information; notice; —*pl.* commercial letters detailing shipments, drafts, and the like. [O.F. *aviser,* fr. *avis,* fr. L. *ad, to,* and *visum,* seen.]

ADVICE-BOAT (ad-vis'bōt) *n.* a swift vessel to carry despatches.

ADVISABLE (ad-vi'za-bl) *a.* fit to be done.

ADVISABLY (ad-vi'za-bli) *ad.* with advice; prudently.

ADVISE (ad-viz') *v.t.* to give advice; inform of; —*v.i.* to consider.

ADVISEDLY (ad-vi'zed-li) *ad.* with deliberation or advice.

ADVISER (ad-vi'zer) *n.* one who gives advice.

ADVISORY (ad-vi'zur-i) *a.* having power to advise; giving advice.

ADVOCACY (ad'vō-ka-si) *n.* act of pleading; intercession.

ADVOCATE (ad'vō-kāt) *n.* one who pleads for another; —*v.t.* to plead in favour of; support. [L. *advocatus,* one called upon, fr. *ad, to,* and *vocare,* call.]

ADVOCATION (ad-vō-kā'shun) *n.* a pleading for; a plea.

ADVOWEE (ad-vou-ē') *n.* he that has the right of presenting a priest to a benefice. [O.F. *avouson,* patronage, Low L. *advocatus,* a patron.]

ADVOWSON (ad-vou'zn) *n.* the right of presenting a priest to a benefice. [See **ADVOWEE**.]

ADYNAMIC (a-di-nam'ik) *a.* destitute of strength; weak. [See **ADYNAMY**.]

ADYNAMY (a-din'a-mi) *n.* loss of the vital powers; weakness. [G. *a,* not, and *dunamis,* power.]

ADZ or **ADZE** (adz) *n.* a carpenter's tool for chipping, its edge being at right angles to the handle. [O.E. *adesa.*]

AERATE (ā-e-rāt') *v.t.* to combine with carbonic acid; supply with air. [G. *aer,* air.]

Adze.

AERATED (ā-e-rāt-ed) *a.* denoting alkaline beverages impregnated with carbonic acid.

AERATION (ā-e-rā'shun) *n.* exposing to the action of the air. [high.

AERIAL (ā-ē'ri-al) *a.* belonging to the air;

AERIE (ē'ri, ā'ri) *n.* the nest of a bird of prey. [Late L. *area,* the nest of a bird of prey.]

AERIFICATION (ā-e-ri-fi-kā'shun) *n.* act of aerifying.

AERIFY (ā'e-ri-fi) *v.t.* to combine or fill with air. [G. *aer,* air, and L. *facio,* 1 make.]

AERODROME (ā'e-rō-drōm) *n.* an enclosure within which aeroplanes make ascents and descents. [G. *aer,* air, and *dromos,* a course.]

AEROLITE (ā'e-rō-lit) *n.* a meteoric stone.

AEROLOGY (ā-e-rol'ō-ji) *n.* the science of the air and its phenomena. [G. *aer,* air, and *logos,* a discourse.]

AEROMETRY (ā-e-rōm'e-tri) *n.* science of ascertaining the mean bulk of gases. [G. *aer,* air, and *metron,* a measure.]

AERONAUT (ā'e-rō-nawt) *n.* an aerial navigator. [G. *aer,* air, and *nautes,* a sailor.]

AERONAUTIC (ā-e-rō-naw'tik) *a.* pertaining to aerial sailing.

AERONAUTICS (ā-e-rō-naw'tiks) *n.pl.* the art of sailing in the air.

AEROPLANE (ā'e-rō-plān) *n.* a flying machine heavier than air, and supported by one or more plane surfaces. [G. *aer,* air, and L. *planus,* level.]

AEROSCOPY (ā-e-ros'kō-pi) *n.* the observation of the variations of the atmosphere. [G. *aer,* air, and *skopein,* see.]

AEROSTATIC (ā-e-rō-stat'ik) *a.* suspending in air. [G. *aer,* air, and *statos,* standing.]

ÆRUGINOUS (ē-rōō'ji-nus) *a.* pertaining to or containing copper rust. [L. *aerugo,* rust of copper, fr. *aes, aeris,* copper.]

ÆSTHETIC. See ESTHETIC.

AFACE (a-fās') *ad.* in face or front of. [L. *facies,* the face.]

AFAR (a-fär') *ad.* at a great distance. [E. = *on, far.*]

AFFABILITY (af-a-bil'i-ti) *n.* readiness to converse; civility. [L. *affabilis,* ready to speak, fr. *ad, to,* and *fore,* speak.]

AFFABLE (af'a-bl) *a.* easy of manners or conversation.

AFFABLY (af'a-bli) *ad.* in an affable manner; courteously.

AFFAIR (a-fār') *n.* a business matter. [O.F. *afaire,* F. *affaire,* fr. *à* and *faire,* to do, fr. L. *ad, to,* and *facere,* to do.]

AFFECT (a-fekt') *v.t.* to act upon; influence; touch; aim at; make a show of. [L. *affectare*, to apply oneself to.]

AFFECTATION (a-fek-tā'shun) *n.* false show; artificial pretence or manners.

AFFECTED (a-fek'ted) *a.* disposed; distressed; assumed.

AFFECTEDLY (a-fek'ted-li) *ad.* in an affected manner.

AFFECTING (a-fek'ting) *a.* capable of being moved; moving the feelings; pathetic.

AFFECTINGLY (a-fek'ting-li) *ad.* so as to excite emotion.

AFFECTION (a-fek'shun) *n.* love; fondness.

AFFECTIONATE (a-fek'shun-āt) *a.* fond; tender.

AFFECTIONATELY (a-fek'shun-āt-li) *ad.* lovingly; tenderly.

AFFECTIVE (a-fek'tiv) *a.* that affects or excites emotion.

AFFERENT (af'e-rent) *a.* bringing to, or inwards. [L. *ad*, to, and *ferre*, carry.]

AFFIANCE (a-fī'ans) *n.* a marriage contract; confidence; trust;—*v.t.* to give confidence; betroth. [O.F. *afiance*, fr. L. *ad*, to, and *fides*, faith.]

AFFIANCER (a-fī'an-ser) *n.* one who affiances.

AFFIANT (a-fī'ant) *n.* one who makes an affidavit.

AFFIDAVIT (af-i-dā'vit) *n.* a written declaration upon oath. [Late L. *affidavit*, he has pledged his word.]

AFFILIATE (a-fil'i-āt) *v.t.* to adopt as a son; receive into fellowship; ally. [L. *ad*, to, and *filius*, a son.]

AFFILIATION (a-fil-i-ā'shun) *n.* adoption; association.

AFFINITY (a-fin'i-ti) *n.* relation by marriage; connection; resemblance in structure; chemical attraction. [L. *affinis*, neighbouring.]

AFFIRM (a-ferm') *v.t.* to declare positively; aver; to ratify; establish. [O.F. *afermer*, fr. L. *ad*, to, and *firmus*, strong.]

AFFIRMABLE (a-ferm'a-bl) *a.* that may be affirmed. [ratification.

AFFIRMANCE (a-ferm'mans) *n.* confirmation;

AFFIRMATION (a-fer-mā'shun) *n.* a solemn declaration.

AFFIRMATIVE (a-ferm'ma-tiv) *a.* that affirms; —*n.* a word expressing assent; the side which affirms or maintains; opposed to negative.

AFFIRMATIVELY (a-ferm'ma-tiv-li) *ad.* positively; on the *ay* side.

AFFIRMER (a-ferm'mer) *n.* one who affirms or declares.

AFFIX (af'iks) *n.* a syllable or letter joined to the end of a word;—(af-iks') *v.t.* to attach to; fasten to the end. [L. *affixus*, fixed, fr. *ad*, to, and *figere*, to fix.]

AFFLICT (a-flikt') *v.t.* to give pain. [L. *afflictum*, fr. *ad*, to, and *fligere*, to dash to the ground.]

AFFLICTED (a-flik'ted) *a.* troubled; suffering distress.

AFFLICTING (a-flik'ting) *a.* grievous.

AFFLICTION (a-flik'shun) *n.* the state of being afflicted.

AFFLICTIVE (a-flik'tiv) *a.* distressing.

AFFLUENCE (af'loo-ens) *n.* wealth; riches. [L. *ad*, to, and *fluere*, to flow.]

AFFLUENT (af'loo-ent) *a.* wealthy; rich; plentiful;—*n.* a tributary.

AFFLUENTLY (af'loo-ent-li) *ad.* in abundance.

AFFLUX (af'luks) *n.* the act of flowing to. [L. *affluxum*. See AFFLUENCE.]

AFFORD (a-ford') *v.t.* to yield; be able to sell, exchange, or expend; supply. [O.E. *geforthian*, to further.]

AFFOREST (a-for'est) *v.t.* to convert land into forest. [Low L. *afforestare*, fr. *ad*, to, and *foresta*, fr. *foris*, out-of-doors.]

AFFORESTATION (a-for-es-tā'shun) *n.* act of turning land into forest.

AFFRAY (a-frā') *n.* a quarrel with violence; tumult. [O.F. *effraier*, fr. L. *ex*, out, and O. H. Ger. *fridu*, peace.]

AFFRIGHT (a-frit') *v.t.* to frighten; terrify;— *n.* sudden terror. [O.E. *afyrhtan*, to terrify.]

AFFRONT (a-frunt') *n.* open disrespect or illtreatment;—*v.t.* to insult; offend. [O.F. *afronter*, to oppose face to face, fr. L. *ad*, to and *frons*, *frontis*, the forehead.]

AFFRONTIVE (a-frun'tiv) *a.* giving offence; contumelious; abusive. Also **AFFRONTING.**

AFLOAT (a-flōt') *ad.* or *a.* swimming; in a floating state. [O.E. *flotian*, to float.]

AFOOT (a-foot') *ad.* on foot; in action or being planned for action. [O.E. *fot*, foot.]

AFORE (a-for') *ad.* or *prep.* in front. [O.E. *on foran*.]

AFORESAID (a-for'sed) *a.* named before. [See AFORE and SAY.]

AFORETIME (a-for'tim) *ad.* in time past. [See AFORE and TIME.]

AFRAID (a-frād') *a.* struck with fear; fearful; timid. [See AFFRAY.]

AFRESH (a-fresh') *ad.* anew; again. [See FRESH.]

AFT (aft) *ad.* or *a.* astern or toward the stern. [O.E. *æftan*, behind.]

AFTER (af'ter) *prep.* later in time; behind; —*a.* more aft; later;—*ad.* later in time. [O.E. *æfter*, farther away.]

AFTERMATH (af'ter-math) *n.* second crop of grass. [O.E. *after*, and *mæth*, a mowing.]

AFTERMOST (af'ter-mōst) *a.* nearest the stern. [O.E. *æftemest* (a double superlative). Note that *most* here is not the adverb *most*, and that the *r* has been obtruded.]

AFTERNOON (af'-ter-nóón') *n.* the time from noon to evening. [See AFTER and NOON.]

AFTERWARD (af'ter-ward) *ad.* in time subsequent. Also **AFTERWARDS.** [O.E. *æfterweard*.]

AGAIN (a-gen', a-gān') *ad.* once more. [O.E. *ongegn*, fr. *on*, and *gegn*, direct or straight.]

AGAINST (a-genst', a-gānst') *prep.* in opposition to; in provision for.

AGAMIC (a-gam'ik) *a.* not having visible organs of reproduction, as certain plants. [G. *a*, not, and *gamos*, marriage.]

AGAPE (a-gāp') *ad.* with staring eagerness; with surprise. [E. on gape.]

AGATE (ag'āt) *n.* a kind of quartz. [O.F., fr. G. *achates*, so called because found near the River *Achates* in Sicily.]

AGE (āj) *n.* any period of time; decline of life; maturity; a generation; a century. [O.F. *edage* or *dage*, fr. Late L. *ætaticum*, fr. *cetas*, *œtatis*, age.]

AGED (ā'jed) *a.* advanced in age.

AGENCY (ā'jensi) *n.* quality or state of action; business performed by an agent.

AGENDA (a-jen'da) *n.pl.* things to be done; business of the meeting; notebook of such.

AGENT (ā'jent) *n.* a deputy; any active cause or power. [L. (acc.) *agentem*, doing, fr. *agere*, to do.]

AGGLOMERATE (a-glom'e-rāt) *v.t.* to gather into a ball or mass. [L. *agglomaratus*, made into a ball.]

AGGLOMERATION (a-glom-e-rā'shun) *n.* act of gathering into a ball.

AGGLUTINATE (a-gloo'ti-nāt) *v.t.* to cause to adhere. [L. *agglutinatus*, glued together, fr. *ad*, to, and *gluten*, glue.]

AGGLUTINATION (a-gloo'ti-nā'shun) *n.* act of uniting, as by glue.

AGGLUTINATIVE (a-gloo'ti-nā-tiv) *a.* that tends to unite.

AGGRANDISE (ag'gran-diz) *v.t.* to make great; exalt. [O.F. *aggrandisant*, making greater, fr. L. *ad*, to, and *grandire*, to make great.]

AGGRANDISEMENT (a-gran'diz-ment, ag'ran-diz-ment) *n.* the act of aggrandising.
AGGRANDISER (a-gran-di'zer) *n.* one who aggrandises.
AGGRAVATE (ag'ra-vāt) *v.t.* to make worse; exaggerate. [L. *aggravatus*, increased in weight, fr. *ad*, to, and *gravis*, heavy.]
AGGRAVATION (ag-ra-vā'shun) *n.* the act of making worse.
AGGREGATE (ag're-gāt) *v.t.* to collect;—*a.* formed of parts collected;—*n.* the whole. [L. *aggregatus*, gathered into a body, fr. *ad*, to, and *grex*, *gregis*, a flock.]
AGGREGATION (ag-re-gā'shun) *n.* the act of collecting into a mass.
AGGRESS (a-gres') *v.t.* to encroach upon with violence. [L. (acc.) *aggressionem*, fr. *aggressus*, having attacked, fr. *ad*, to, and *gradi*, to step upon.]
AGGRESSION (a-gresh'un) *n.* the first act of hostility or injury. [attack.
AGGRESSIVE (a-gres'iv) *a.* making the first
AGGRESSIVENESS (a-gres'iv-nes) *n.* the quality of being aggressive.
AGGRESSOR (a-gres'ur) *n.* one who begins to attack or injure.
AGGRIEVANCE (a-grē'vans) *n.* injury; wrong. [O.F. *agrever*, to overwhelm, fr. L. *aggravare*, to increase in weight.]
AGGRIEVE (a-grēv') *v.t.* to give pain or sorrow to; afflict; oppress; vex.
AGGRIEVED (a-grēvd') *a.* pained; afflicted.
AGHAST (a-gast') *a.* amazed; terrified. [M. E. *agasted*, terrified.]
AGILE (aj'il) *a.* quick of motion; nimble; active. [L. *agilis*, nimble.]
AGILITY (a-jil'i-ti) *n.* activity; quickness.
AGIO (ā'ji-o, aj'i-ō, ā'ji-ō) *n.* the difference in value between metallic and paper money; premium or discount. [It. *agio*, ease.]
AGITABLE (aj'i-ta-bl) *a.* that may be agitated.
AGITATE (aj'i-tāt) to disturb; to discuss. [L. *agitare*, frequentative of *agere*, to put into motion.]
AGITATION (aj-i-tā'shun) *n.* disturbance; discussion.
AGITATOR (aj'i-tā-tur) *n.* a disturber.
AGLET (ag'let) *n.* a tag; a point at the end of a fringe. [F. *aiguillette*, dim. of *aiguille*, fr. Late L. *acutulam* (acc.) for *acum*, a needle.]
AGNAIL (ag'nāl) *n.* a disease of the nails; a whitlow. [O.E. *ang*, tight, and *naegl*, nail.]
AGNATE (ag'nāt) *a.* related or akin by the father's side. [L. *agnatus*, a relative.]
AGNATION (ag-nā'shun) *n.* relation by the father's side. [See AGNATE.]
AGNOSTIC (ag-nos'tik) *n.* one who holds that we can know nothing of God or of the supernatural. [G. *a*, not, and *gnostikos*, good at knowing.]
AGNOSTICISM (ag-nos'ti-sizm) *n.* system or principles of the Agnostics.
AGO (a-gō') *ad.* in time past. [O.E. *agan*, past.]
AGOING (a-gō'ing) *ppr.* in motion. [See **GO**.]
AGONIC (a-gon'ik) *a.* not forming an angle. [G. *a*, not, and *gonia*, angle.]
AGONISE (ag'ō-niz) *v.i.* or *t.* to writhe with pain; put in severe pain. [G. *agon*, contest.]
AGONISING (ag'ō-niz-ing) *a.* suffering severe pain. [See **AGONISE**.]
AGONISM (ag'ō-nizm) *n.* contention for a prize. [See **AGONISE**.]
AGONISTIC (ag-ō-nist'ik) *a.* relating to athletic combats. [See **AGONISE**.]
AGONY (ag'ō-ni) *n.* excessive pain; anguish. [See **AGONISE**.]
AGOUTI (a-gōō'tē) *n.* a rodent mammal of the West Indies.
AGRARIAN (a-grā'ri-an) *a.* relating to fields or grounds. [L. *agrarius*, fr. *ager*, a field.]
AGRARIANISM (a-grā'ri-an-izm) *n.* an equal division of land or property.

AGREE (a-grē') *v.i.* [*pp.* **AGREED**] to be of one mind; come to terms; resemble; suit. [O.F. *agréer*, to receive kindly, fr. L. *ad*, to, and *gratus*, pleasing.]
AGREEABLE (a-grē'a-bl) *a.* pleasing to the mind or senses; suitable; in conformity with.
AGREEABLENESS (a-grē'a-bl-nes) *n.* the quality of being pleased or suitable.
AGREEABLY (a-grē'a-bli) *ad.* pleasingly.
AGREED (a-grēd') *pp.* settled by consent; determined.
AGREEMENT (a-grē'ment) *n.* state of agreeing; harmony; bargain.
AGRICULTURAL (ag-ri-kul'tūr-al) *a.* relating to agriculture.
AGRICULTURE (ag'ri-kul-tūr) *n.* the art of cultivating the ground. [L. *agri*, of a field, and *culturam* (acc.) culture, fr. *colo*, I till.]
AGRICULTURIST (ag-ri-kul'tūr-ist) *n.* a farmer.
AGROUND (a-ground') *ad.* on the ground. [O.E. *on grund*.]
AGUE (ā'gū) *n.* chilly fit. [O.F. *ague*, fr. *acuta* (*febris*), acute fever.]
AGUISH (ā'gū-ish) *a.* shivering; causing ague. [See AGUE.] [with cold.
AGUISHNESS (ā'gū-ish-nes) *n.* a shivering as
AHEAD (a-hed') *ad.* further on; forward; in advance. [E.]
AID (ād) *v.t.* to help; succour;—*n.* help; support. [F. *aider*, fr. L. *adjutare*, fr. *ad*, to, and *juvare*, help.]
AIGRETTE (ā'gret) *n.* a tuft of feathers. Also **EGRETTE**. [F.]
AIL (āl) *v.t.* to affect with uneasiness. [M.E. *eilen*, fr. O.E. *eglan*, to pain.]
AILMENT (āl'ment) *n.* illness; disease.
AIM (ām) *n.* endeavour; design; direction; —*v.i.* to take sight;—*v.t.* to direct a weapon. [O.F. *aesmer*, fr. L. *adæstimare*, to estimate.]
AIMLESS (ām'les) *a.* without aim.
AIR (ār) *n.* the fluid we breathe; a tune; affected manner or gesture;—*pl.* **AIRS**, disdainful mien;—*v.t.* to give or take air; dry by air and warmth. [G. *aer*, air.]
AIR-CELLS (ār'selz) *n.pl.* cells containing air. [G. *aer*, air, and L. *cellum*, a small room.]
AIR-CUSHION (ār-koosh'un) *n.* an air-tight cushion which can be inflated. [G. *aer*, air, and O.F. *coissin*, fr. L. *coxa*, a hip.]
AIRED (ārd) *pp.* ventilated; warmed.
AIR-GUN (ār'gun) *n.* a gun discharged by air. [G. *aer*, air, and M.E. *gonne*, fr. Welsh = a bowl.]
AIR-HOLE (ār'hōl) *n.* an opening to admit air. [G. *aer*, air, and O.E. *hol*, a hollow place.]
AIRILY (ār'i-li) *ad.* gaily; merrily.
AIRINESS (ār'i-nes) *n.* openness to the air; gaiety.
AIRING (ār'ing) *n.* an excursion to enjoy the air; exposure to the air.
AIRLESS (ār'les) *a.* void of air; close.
AIR-PUMP (ār'pump) *n.* a pump or machine, variously constructed, for exhausting the air from a vessel. [G. *aer*, air, and F. *pompe*, fr. Ger. *Pumpe*.]
AIR-SHIP (ār'ship) *n.* a navigable balloon. [G. *aer*, air, and **SHIP**.]
AIRY (ār'i) *a.* open to the air; gay; unsubstantial.
AISLE (il) *n.* a walk in a church; wing of a choir. [F. *aile*, fr. L. *ala*, a wing.]

Air-Pump.

AJAR (a-jär') *ad.* partly open, as a door. [O.E. *on cyrr*, fr. O.E. *cierran*, to turn.]
AKIMBO (a-kim'bō) *ad.* with a crook; bent. [M.E. *in kenebow*, into a crook-bend.]
AKIN (a-kin') *a.* related; allied by blood. [E. =of kin.]

ALABASTER (al'a-bas-ter) *n.* a variety of gypsum or sulphate of lime. [G. *alabastros*, fr. *Alabastron*, a town in Egypt.]

ALACK (a-lak') *ex.* expressive of sorrow. [E.]

ALACRITY (a-lak'ri-ti) *n.* cheerful willingness; liveliness. [L. (acc.) *alacritatem*, fr. *clacer*, brisk.]

ALARM (a-lärm') *n.* a notice of danger;— *v.t.* to give notice of danger; disturb. [F. *clarme*, It. *ali' arme*, to arms, fr. Late L. *ad* (*illas*) *armas*, to (those) arms.]

ALARM-CLOCK (a-lärm'klok) *n.* a clock to give alarm. [ALARM and O.F. *cloke*, *cloche*, fr. Low L. (acc.) *clocam*, a bell, fr. Celt.]

ALARMING (a-lär'ming) *ppr.* or *a.* exciting apprehension. [alarm.

ALARMIST (a-lär'mist) *n.* one who excites

ALB (alb) *n.* a vestment of white linen. [Low L. *alba*, fr. L. *albus*, white.]

ALBACORE (al'ba-kōr) *n.* a fish of the mackerel kind. [A. *al*, the, and *bukr*, camel.]

ALBATROSS (al'ba-tros) *n.* a large sea-gull in the Southern Ocean. [Formerly *algatross*, fr. Pg. *alcatraz*, a cormorant.]

ALBESCENT (al-bes'ent) *a.* becoming white. [L. *albescens*, fr. *albescere*, to grow white.]

ALBIGENSES (al-bi-jen'sēs) *n.pl.* a sect which separated from the church of Rome in the twelfth century. [*Albi*, a town in Provence.]

ALBINO (al-bi'nō) *n.* a person with exceptionally fair hair and skin and pink eyes. [Sp. *albino*, whitish, fr. L. *albus*, white.]

ALBION (al'bi-on) *n.* England. [Gael. *alp*, height.]

ALBUM (al'bum) *n.* a white table; a blank book. [L. *albus*, white.]

ALBUMEN (al-bū'men) *n.* a viscous constituent of animal and vegetable solids and fluids, found nearly pure in the white of an egg. [L. *albus*, white.]

ALBURNUM (al-bur'num) *n.* the white soft part of wood; sap-wood. [L. *albus*, white.]

ALCHEMIST (al'ke-mist) *n.* one who practises alchemy. [A. *al*, the, and *kimia*, fr. Late G. *chemeia*, chemistry.]

ALCHEMY (al'ke-mi) *n.* occult chemistry; the art of changing base metals into gold. [See **ALCHEMIST**.]

ALCOHOL (al'kō-hol) *n.* pure spirit. [A. *al*, the, and *kohʼl*, powdered antimony.]

ALCOHOLIC (al-kō-hol'ik) *a.* pertaining to alcohol.

ALCOHOLISE (al'kō-hol-iz) *v.t.* to convert into spirit; rectify spirit.

ALCORAN (al-kō-rän') *n.* the book of Mohammedan faith. [A. *al*, the, and *koran*, book.]

ALCOVE (al'kōv) *n.* a recess. [F. *alcove*, fr. Sp. *alcoba*, fr. A.]

ALDER (awl'der) *n.* a tree of several varieties. [O.E. *aler*.]

ALDERMAN (awl'der-man) *n.* a city magistrate;—*pl.* **ALDERMEN**. [O.E. *ealdorman*, chief man.]

ALDINE (awl'din) *a.* denoting books printed by Aldus at Venice in the 16th century; denoting editions in the same form.

ALE (āl) *n.* a fermented malt liquor. [O.E. *calu*.]

ALEAK (a-lēk') *ad.* in a leaking state. [O.E. *a*, on, and Scand. *leak*.]

ALEE (a-lē') *ad.* on the side opposite to the wind. [E.]

ALERT (a-lert') *a.* denoting watchful activity or readiness; lively. [It. *alla*, on the, and *erta*, erect, fr. *erto*, fr. L. *erectus*, erect.]

ALERTNESS (a-lert'nes) *n.* briskness; sprightliness; activity. [See **ALERT**.]

ALEXANDRINE (al-egz-an'drin) *n.* a verse of twelve syllables. [G.]

ALGEBRA (al'je-bra) *n.* a method of computation in which signs stand for arithmetical operations, and letters for numbers and quantities. [A.]

ALGEBRAIC (al-je-brä'ik) *a.* pertaining to or performed by algebra.

ALGEBRAIST (al-je-brä'ist) *n.* one who is skilled in algebra.

ALGERINE (al-je-rēn') *a.* belonging to Algiers.

ALIAS (ā'li-as) *n.* a second writ;—*ad.* otherwise. [L. (ad.) fr. *alius*, another.]

ALIBI (al'i-bi) *n.* elsewhere; in another place. [L. (ad.) elsewhere.]

ALIEN (āl'yen) *a.* estranged from; adverse to;—*n.* a stranger; foreigner. [L. *alienus*, a stranger.]

ALIENABLE (āl'yen-a-bl) *a.* that may be transferred or sold.

ALIENATE (āl'yen-āt) *v.t.* to transfer to another; estrange.

ALIENATION (āl-yen-ā'shun) *n.* a making over; estrangement.

ALIENATOR (āl-yen-ā'tur) *n.* one that transfers. [is sold.

ALICNEE (āl-yen-ē') *n.* one to whom a thing

ALIGHT (a-līt') *v.i.* to fall upon; get off. [M.E. *alihten*, to unload or alight.]

ALIGNMENT (a-lin'ment) *n.* the fixing of a line; the line established. [F. *à ligne*, into line, fr. L. *ad*, to, and *lineam* (acc.) line.]

ALIKE (a-lik') *ad.* in the same manner. [O.E. *onlic*, like.]

ALIMENT (al'i-ment) *n.* that which feeds; nourishment. [L. *alimentum*, fr. *alere*, to nourish.]

ALIMENTAL (al-i-men'tal) *a.* pertaining to food.

ALIMENTATION (al-i-men-tā'shun) *n.* act of nourishing; state of being nourished.

ALIMONY (al'i-mun-i) *n.* allowance to a wife pending or after separation. [L. *alimonia*.]

ALIQUOT (al'i-kwot) *a.* that divides without remainder. [L. *alius*, another, and *quot*, how many.]

ALIVE (a-liv') *a.* not dead; active. [O.E. *a*, on, and *lif*, life.]

ALKALESCENT (al-ka-les'ent) *a.* tending to an alkali. [See **ALKALI**.]

ALKALI (al'ka-li) *n.* a substance which neutralises acids; *pl.* **ALKALIES**. [A. *al*, the, and *qaliy*, ashes.]

ALKALINE (al'ka-lin) *a.* having the qualities of alkali.

ALKALOID (al'ka-loid) *n.* a vegetable substance having the properties of alkali;—*a.* resembling alkali.

ALL (awl) *a.* every one;—*n.* everything;—*ad.* wholly; entirely. [O.E. *eal*.]

ALLAH (al'a) *n.* the one God of Mohammedans. [A. *al-ilah*, he that is worthy of adoration.]

ALLAY (a-lā') *v.t.* to repress or bring down; calm; assuage. [M.E. *aleyen*, fr. O.E. *alecgan*, to lay down.]

ALLEGATION (al-e-gā'shun) *n.* affirmation; plea; excuse.

ALLEGE (a-lej') *v.t.* to declare; plead in excuse. [L. *ad*, to, and *legare*, to send or tell.]

ALLEGIANCE (a-lē'jans) *n.* the duty of a subject to his government; loyalty. [L. *ad*, to, and O.F. *lige*, free.]

ALLEGORIC (al-e-gor'ik) *a.* in the manner of allegory; figurative.

ALLEGORISE (al'e-go-riz) *v.t.* to form an allegory;—*v.i.* to use an allegory.

ALLEGORY (al'e-go-ri) *n.* a figurative speech; a parable. [G. *allegoria*, fr. *allegorein*, to speak in parables.]

ALLEGRO (al-lā'grō) *n.* sprightly movement in music. [It., fr. L. (acc.) *alacrem*, brisk.]

ALLELUIA (al-e-lōō'ya) *n.* give praise to Jehovah. [H. *halelu*, praise ye, and *Jah*, Jehovah.]

ALLEVIATE (a-lē'vi-āt) *v.t.* to make light; ease; lessen. [L. *ad*, to, and *leviatus*, lightened.]

ALLEVIATION (a-lē-vi-ā'shun) *n.* act of relieving, or making light.

ALLEY (al'i) *n.* a narrow walk or passage;— *pl.* **ALLEYS.** [O.F. *alee* (F. *allée*), a passage, fr. *aller*, to go.]

ALL-HALLOW (awl-hal'lō) *n.* the first of November, dedicated to all the saints; All-Saints' Day. [O.E. *eal*, all, and *halig*, holy.]

ALLIANCE (a-lī'ans) *n.* union by treaty or marriage. [O.F. *alier*, fr. L. *alligare*, to bind.]

ALLIED (a-līd') *pp.* connected by marriage, etc.; related.

ALLIGATE (al'i-gāt) *v.t.* to tie together. [See **ALLIANCE.**] [metic.

ALLIGATION (al-i-gā'shun) *n.* a rule of arith-

ALLIGATOR (al-i-gā'tur) *n.* the crocodile. [Sp. *el lagarto*, fr. L. *lacerta*, a lizard.]

ALLITERATION (a-lit-e-rā'shun) *n.* the beginning of two or more successive words with the same letter. [L. *ad*, to, and *literaius*, lettered.]

ALLITERATIVE (a-lit-e-rā'tiv) *a.* pertaining to alliteration.

ALLOCATE (al'o-kāt) *v.t.* to place; distribute; give every one his share. [L. *ad*, to, and *locatus*, placed.]

ALLOCATION (al-o-kā'shun) *n.* act of assigning or allotting; allowance.

ALLODIAL (a-lō'di-al) *a.* not held of a superior; freehold. [Late L. *allodium*, a freehold estate.]

ALLOPATHY (al-op'a-thi) *n.* the ordinary medical treatment of disease, as opposed to **HOMEOPATHY.** [G. *allos*, other, and *pathos*, suffering.]

ALLOT (a-lot') *v.t.* [*pp.* **ALLOTTED**] to give by lot; distribute. [L. *ad*, to, and O.E. *hlot*, share.]

ALLOTMENT (a-lot'ment) *n.* act of allotting; share allotted. [is assigned.

ALLOTTEE (a-lot'ē) *n.* one to whom a share

ALLOW (a-lou') *v.t.* to permit; grant; make abatement. [O.F. *alouer*, to hire out, fr. L. *ad*, to, and *locare*, to place.]

ALLOWABLE (a-lou'a-bl) *a.* that may be allowed. [fulness.

ALLOWABLENESS (a-lou'a-bl-nes) *n.* law-

ALLOWABLY (a-lou'a-bli) *ad.* in an allowable manner; admissibly.

ALLOWANCE (a-lou'ans) *n.* act of allowing; sanction; abatement;—*v.t.* to put upon allowance.

ALLOY (a-loi') *v.t.* to debase by mixing;— *n.* a baser metal mixed with a finer. [O.F. *aleyer*, to combine, fr. L. *ad*, to, and *ligare*, to bind.]

ALLSPICE (awl'spīs) *n.* the berry of the pimenta. [*All* and *spice*, fr. O.F. *espice*, fr. L. *species*, kind.]

ALLUDE (a-lōōd') *v.i.* to refer to; insinuate. [L. *ad*, to, and *ludere*, to play.]

ALLURE (a-lūr') *v.t.* to tempt by the offer of good; entice; decoy. [O.F. *loirre* = F. *leurre*, a decoy.]

ALLUREMENT (a-lūr'ment) *n.* that which entices or allures.

ALLURING (a-lūr'ing) *a.* engaging; having power to allure.

ALLUSION (a-lū'zhun) *n.* indirect reference. [L. *alludere*, fr. *ad*, to, and *ludere*, *lusum*, to play.] [ive.

ALLUSORY (a-lū'so-ri) *a.* insinuating; suggest-

ALLUSIVE (a-lū'siv) *a.* hinting at.

ALLUVIAL (a-lū'vi-al) *a.* deposited by water. [L. *alluvium*, fr. *ad*, to, and *luere* = *lavare*, to wash.]

ALLUVIUM (a-lū'vi-um) *n.* earth deposited by water;—*pl.* **ALLUVIA.**

ALLY (a-lī') *v.t.* [*pp.* **ALLIED**] to unite by treaty or marriage;—(a'lī) *n.* a friend; confederate. [O.F. *alier* to bind.]

ALMANAC (awl'ma-nak) *n.* a calendar of months, weeks, days, etc. [Etym. doubtful, perh. fr. Sp. through A.]

ALMIGHTINESS (awl-mī'ti-nes) *n.* infinite power. [O.E. *ealmihtig*, all-powerful, and *ness*, state of being.]

ALMIGHTY (awl-mī'ti) *a.* all-powerful;—*n.* the omnipotent God.

ALMOND (ä'mund) *n.* the fruit of the almond-tree. [M.E. *almaund*, O.F. *almandre*, fr. G. *amugdalon*, almond.]

ALMONER (al'mun-er) *n.* a distributor of alms for another. [O.E. *ælmœsse*, Low L. *alimosina*, fr. G. *eleemosune*, pity.]

ALMONRY (al'mun-ri) *n.* place for distributing alms.

ALMOST (awl'mōst) *ad.* nearly; wellnigh; for the most part. [E.]

ALMS (ämz) *n. sing.* and *pl.* a gift to the poor.

ALMS-HOUSE (ämz'hous) *n.* a house for the poor who subsist on charity.

ALOE (al'ō) *n.* a tree of several species;— *pl.* **ALOES.** [G. *aloe*, bitter.]

ALONE (a-lōn') *a.* single; solitary;—*ad.* separately. [E. = *all* and *one*.]

ALONG (a-long') *ad.* onward;—*prep.* throughout; by the side of; lengthwise. [E. *and*, against, and *lang*, long.]

ALOOF (a-lōōf') *ad.* at a distance; apart. [M.E. *a*, on, and *lof*, a paddle.]

ALOUD (a-loud') *ad.* loudly. [O.E. *a*, on, and *hlud*, loud.]

ALP (alp) *n.* a high snow-capped mountain; —*pl.* **ALPS**, the mountain ranges of Switzerland, etc. [Celt., akin to L. *albus*, white.]

ALPACA (al-pak'a) *n.* an animal of Peru, having long, fine, woolly hair; a species of the llama; a thin kind of cloth made of the wool of the alpaca, mixed with silk or cotton. [Sp., fr. A. *al*, the, and Peruv. *paco*, the name of the animal.]

ALPENSTOCK (al'pen-stok) *n.* a long stout staff, pointed with iron, used in climbing the Alps. [Ger. *Alpen*, of the Alps, and *Stock*, a stick.] [alphabet. [G.]

ALPHA (al'fa) *n.* the first letter of the Greek

ALPHABET (al'fa-bet) *n.* the letters of a language arranged in order;—*v.t.* to arrange in the order of an alphabet. [G. *alpha*, *beta*, the first two Greek letters.]

ALPHABETIC (al-fa-bet'ik) *a.* in the order of an alphabet. Also **ALPHABETICAL.**

ALPINE (al'pin) *a.* pertaining to the Alps; very high.

ALREADY (awl-red'i) *ad.* before this time; now. [O.E. *eal*, all, and *raede*, ready.]

ALTAR (awl'tar) *n.* a place for offerings; communion table. [L. *altare*, a high place, fr. *altus*, high.]

ALTAR-PIECE (awl'tar-pēs) *n.* a painting above the altar.

ALTER (awl'ter) *v.t.* to make some change in; —*v.i.* to change. [Late L. *alterare*, to alter, fr. L. *alter*, another.]

ALTERABLE (awl'ter-a-bl) *a.* that may be changed; that may vary.

ALTERABLY (awl'ter-a-bli) *ad.* so that it can be changed.

ALTERANT (awl'ter-ant) *a.* producing a change;—*n.* an alternative.

ALTERATION (awl-ter-a-shun) *n.* act of altering; change.

ALTERATIVE (awl'ter-a-tiv) *a.* causing alteration;—*n.* a medicine that gradually produces a change in the habit or constitution.

ALTERCATE (al'ter-kāt) *v.i.* to contend in words. [L. *altercatus*, having disputed, fr. *alter*, another.]

ALTERCATION (al-ter-kā'shun) *n.* an angry dispute; controversy.

ALTERNATE (al'ter-nāt) *a.* being by turns; —*v.t.* to perform by turns;—*v.i.* to happen or to act by turns. [L. *alternatus*, done by turns, fr. *alter*, another.]

ALTERNATELY (al'ter-nāt-li) *ad.* by turns.

ALTERNATION (al-ter-nā'shun) *n.* reciprocal succession.

ALTERNATIVE (al-ter'na-tiv) *n.* choice of two things;—*a.* offering a choice.

ALTERNATIVELY (al-ter'na-tiv-li) *ad.* reciprocally.

ALTHOUGH (awl-THŌ') *conj.* grant; allow; notwithstanding; however. [O.E. *eal*, all, and *theah*, though.]

ALTIMETER (al-tim'e-ter) *n.* an instrument for measuring altitudes. [L. *altus*, high, and G. *metron*, a measure.]

ALTIMETRY (al-tim'e-tri) *n.* art of measuring heights.

ALTITUDE (al'ti-tūd) *n.* the height of a place; elevation. [L. *altitudo*, fr. *altus*, high.]

ALTO (al'tō) *ad.* high;—*n.* the counter tenor. [L. *altus*, high.]

ALTOGETHER (awl-tóó-geTH'er) *ad.* wholly; without exception. [O.E. *eal*, all, and *togædere*, together.]

ALTRUISM (al'tróó-izn) *n.* care or devotion to others; opposed to selfishness. [Ital. *altrui*, another.]

ALUM (al'um) *n.* a mineral salt. [L. *alumen*.]

ALUMINIUM (al-ū-min'i-um) *n.* the metallic base of alumina; a light metal resembling silver. [See ALUM.] [See ALUM.]

ALUMINOUS (al-ū'mi-nus) *a.* containing alum.

ALUMNUS (a-lum'nus) *n.* a pupil;—*n.pl.* **ALUMNI** (a-lum'ni). [L., fr. *alere*, to nurse.]

ALVEARY (al've-ar-i) *n.* a bee-hive; the hollow of the ear. [L. *alviarium*, a bee-hive, fr. *alveus*, a hollow vessel.]

ALVEOLAR (al-vē'o-lar) *a.* pertaining to or resembling the sockets of the teeth. [E.]

ALWAYS (awl'wāz) *ad.* for ever; perpetually.

AM (am) the first person singular, present indicative of the verb *to be.* [E.]

AMAIN (a-mān') *ad.* with all force. [O.E. *a*, on, and *mœgen*, strength.]

AMALGAM (a-mal'gam) *n.* a mixture of quicksilver with another metal. [Late L. *amalgama*, fr. G. *malassein*, to soften.]

AMALGAMATE (a-mal'ga-māt) *v.t.* to mix metals with quicksilver; to join, as companies.

AMALGAMATION (a-mal-ga-mā'shun) *n.* the act of amalgamating.

AMANUENSIS (a-man-ū-en'sis) *n.* a writer of what another dictates;—*pl.* **AMANUENSES**. [L. *a manu*, by hand.]

AMARANTH (am'a-ranth) *n.* a flower that never fades. [G. *amarantos*, unfading.]

AMASS (a-mas') *v.t.* to collect into a heap; accumulate. [L. *ad*, to, and F. *masse*, fr. L., fr. G. *massein*, to knead.]

AMASSMENT (a-mas'ment) *n.* a heap; a collection.

AMATEUR (am-a-tūr') *n.* one who studies or practises any of the fine arts—not being a professional. [F., fr. L. *amator*, a lover.]

AMATIVENESS (am'a-tiv nes) *n.* propensity to love. [See AMATEUR.]

AMATORY (am-'a-tur-i) *a.* relating to or induced by love. [See AMATEUR.]

AMAZE (a-māz') *v.t.* to confound;—*n.* a mingled feeling of surprise and wonder. [O.E. *amasian*, to cause to wonder.]

AMAZEMENT (a-māz'ment) *n.* astonishment; confusion.

AMAZING (a-mā'zing) *a.* wonderful.

AMAZON (am'a-zun) *n.* a warlike woman; a virago. [G.]

AMBASSADOR (am-bas'a-dur) *n.* the representative of one sovereign at the court of another. [It. *ambasciadore*.]

AMBER (am'ber) *n.* a yellow semi-transparent fossil resin. [A.]

AMBERGRIS (am'ber-grēs) *n.* a fragrant drug. [F. *amber gris*, gray amber.]

AMBIDEXTER (am-bi-deks'ter) *n.* one who uses both hands with equal dexterity. [L. *ambo*, both, and *dexter*, the right hand.]

AMBIDEXTERITY (am-bi-deks-ter'i-ti) *n.* the power of using both hands with equal ease.

AMBIDEXTROUS (am-bi-deks'trus) *a.* using either hand.

AMBIENT (am'bi-ent) *a.* encompassing. [L. (acc.) *ambientem*, going round.]

AMBIGUITY (am-bi-gū'i-ti) *n.* doubtfulness of meaning. [L. *ambiguus*, fr. *ambi*, around, and *agere*, to drive.]

AMBIGUOUS (am-big'ū-us) *a.* of uncertain meaning; doubtful.

AMBIGUOUSLY (am-big'ū-us-li) *ad.* equivocally; doubtfully.

AMBITION (am-bish'un) *n.* eager desire of fame or power. [L. (acc.) *ambitionem*, a going round.]

AMBITIOUS (am-bish'us) *a.* desiring to excel; aspiring.

AMBLE (am'bl) *v.i.* to move with an amble; —*n.* peculiar pace of a horse, in which the two legs on the same side move together. [F. *ambler*, to go leisurely, fr. L. *ambulare*.]

AMBLER (am'bler) *n.* a horse which ambles or paces.

AMBROSIA (am-brō'zhi-a) *n.* the imaginary food of the gods; a plant. [G. fr. *ambrotos*, immortal.]

AMBROSIAL (am-brō'zhi-al) *a.* having the qualities of ambrosia.

AMBULANCE (am'bū-lans) *n.* a kind of movable hospital; a carriage for the sick and wounded. [L. (acc.) *ambulantem*, moving about.]

AMBULATION (am-bū-lā'shun) *n.* the act of walking about.

AMBUSCADE (am'bus-kād) *n.* a place of surprise. [Sp., fr. Late L. *amboscatus*, set in a bush.]

AMBUSH (am'bóósh) *n.* the place or act of lying in wait. [See AMBUSCADE.]

AMBUSHED (am'bóóshd) *a.* concealed; lying in wait.

AMBUSHMENT (am'bóósh-ment) *n.* a lying in wait; an ambush.

AMELIORATE (a-mēl'yur-āt) *v.t.* to make better;—*v.i.* to grow better; mend. [F. *améliorer*, fr. L. *ad*, to, and Late L. *meliorare*, to improve.]

AMELIORATION (a-mēl-yur-ā'shun) *n.* making or becoming better.

AMEN (ā-men', also ä'men) *n.* or *inter.* so be it; verily. [H.]

AMENABILITY (a-mē-na-bil'-i-ti) *n.* state of being amenable. [F. *amener*, to lead near, fr. L. *ad*, to, and Late L. *minare*, to drive.]

AMENABLE (a-mē'na-bl) *a.* liable to give account; responsible.

AMEND (a-mend') *v.t.* to make better; alter and improve;—*v.i.* to grow or become better. [F. *amender*, fr. L. *emendare*, to free from errors.]

AMENDABLE (a-men'da-bl) *a.* that may be amended.

AMENDMENT (a-mend'ment) *n.* a change for the better; improvement; proposed alteration of a motion or bill; correction in a writ or process.

AMENDS (a-mendz') *n.pl.* a recompense; compensation.

AMENITY (a-men'i-ti) *n.* pleasantness; agreeableness of situation. [L. (acc.) *amoenitatem*, pleasantness.]

AMERCE (a-mers') *v.t.* to punish with a fine. [O.F., fr. L. *ad*, to, and (acc.) *mercedem*, wages.]

AMERCEMENT (a-mers'ment) *n.* arbitrary fine.

AMERCER (a-mers'er) *n.* one who amerces or sets a fine.

AMERICANISE (a-mer'i-kan-īz) *v.t.* to render American. [Fr. *America*, fr. *Amerigo Vespucci.*]

Fāte, fär, ado; mē, her; mine; nōte; tūne; móón.

AMERICANISM (ɑ-mer'i-kan-izm) *n.* an American idiom.

AMETHYST (am'e-thist) *n.* a precious stone of a violet-blue colour. [G. *amethustos*, not drunken. The stone was supposed to prevent intoxication.]

AMETHYSTINE (am-e-this'tin) *a.* of or like amethyst.

AMIABILITY (ā-mi-ɑ-bil'i-ti) *n.* sweetness of disposition.

AMIABLE (ā'mi-ɑ-bl) *a.* worthy of love. [F. *aimable*, fr. L. *amicabilis*, friendly, :r. *amicus*.]

AMIABLENESS (ā'mi-ɑ-bl-nes) *n.* the quality of being amiable. Also **AMIABILITY**.

AMIABLY (ā'mi-ɑ-bli) *ad.* in an amiable manner.

AMICABLE (am'i-kɑ-bl) *a.* peaceable; friendly; kind. [L. *amicus*, a friend.]

AMID (ɑ-mid') *prep.* in the middle; among. [M.E. *amiddes*, for *amidde* = O.E. *on middan*, in the middle.]

AMISS (ɑ-mis') *a.* or *ad.* improperly. [O.E. *a*, on, and *missan*, to fail.]

AMITY (am'i-ti) *n.* friendship; agreement; goodwill. [O.F. *amiste* (3 syll.) fr. Late L. (acc.) *amicitatem*, friendship.]

AMMONIA (ɑ-mō'ni-ɑ) *n.* a volatile alkali. [Fr. *Jupiter Ammon*.]

AMMONIAC (ɑ-mō'ni-ak) *a.* pertaining to ammonia; *n.* a gum resin extracted from a Persian plant.

AMMUNITION (am-ū-nish'un) *n.* military stores. [O.F. *l'ammunition*, fr. *la munition*.]

AMNESTY (am'nes-ti) *n.* an act of general pardon. [F., fr. G. *amnestis*, a forgetting, fr. *a*, not, and *mnestos*, remembered.]

AMŒBA (ɑ-mē'bɑ) *n.* the simplest form of animal life; a mass of protoplasm, feeding and moving at every point. [L., fr. G. *amoibe*, change.]

AMONG (ɑ-mung') *prep.* mingled with. Also **AMONGST**. [O.E. *onmang*, M.E. *amonge*.]

AMOROUS (am'ur-us) *a.* inclined to love; passionate. [L. *amo*, I love.]

AMOROUSNESS (am'ur-us-nes) *n.* fondness; doting love.

AMORPHOUS (ɑ-mor'fus) *a.* having no determinate form. [G. *a*, not, and *morphe*, shape.]

AMORTISATION (ɑ-mor-ti-zā'shun) *n.* act of redeeming by a sinking fund. [F. *à*, to, and *mort*, death.]

AMORTISE (ɑ-mor'tiz) *v.t.* to alienate in mortmain; convey as lands or funds to a corporation.

AMOUNT (ɑ-mount') *v.i.* to rise to or reach by adding the whole items; — *n.* the sum total; effect; result. [O.F. *amonter*, fr. L. *ad*, to, and (acc.) *montem*, a mountain.]

AMOUR (a-mòòr') *n.* a love intrigue; gallantry. [L. *amor*, love.]

AMPHIBIAN (am-fib'i-an) *n.* an animal that lives on land or in water. [G. *amphi*, on both sides, and *bios*, life.]

AMPHIBIOUS (am-fib'i-us) *a.* living in two different elements.

AMPHIBOLOGY (am-fi-bol'o-ji) *n.* discourse of doubtful meaning. [G. *amphi*, on both sides, and *ballein*, to throw.]

AMPHITHEATRE (am-fi-thē'a-ter) *n.* an edifice of a round or oval form. [G. *amphi*, on both sides, and *theatron*, a theatre.]

AMPLE (am'pl) *a.* large; extended; liberal; diffusive; wide. [F., fr. L. *amplus*, of full dimensions.]

AMPLIFICATION (am-pli-fi-kā'shun) *n.* enlargement; diffuse discourse.

AMPLIFIER (am'pli-fi-er) *n.* one who enlarges.

AMPLIFY (am'pli-fi) *v.t.* to enlarge; treat copiously; — *v.i.* to exaggerate; dilate. [F. *amplifier*, fr. L. *amplificare*, to augment.]

AMPLITUDE (am'pli-tūd) *n.* largeness; extent; capacity. [L. (acc.) *amplitudinem*, largeness.]

AMPLY (am'pli) *ad.* largely; liberally.

AMPUTATE (am'pū-tāt) *v.t.* to cut off a limb. [L. *amputatus*, excised, fr. *amb*, around, and *putare*, to prune.]

AMPUTATION (am-pū-tā'shun) *n.* the act of cutting off a limb.

AMUCK (a-muk') *ad.* in a wild, mad way; against every one or everything in the way. [Malay *amok*, madness.]

AMULET (am'ū-let) *n.* a charm worn to prevent evil. [F. *amuleite*, fr. L. *amuletum*.]

AMUSE (ɑ-mūz') *v.t.* to entertain agreeably; delude; divert. [F. *amuser*.]

AMUSEMENT (ɑ-mūz'ment) *n.* that which amuses.

AMUSER (ɑ-mūz'er) *n.* one who amuses.

AMUSING (ɑ-mūz'ing) *a.* affording amusement.

AN (an) *a.* one; denoting an individual. [O. E. *an*, one.]

ANABAPTIST (an-a-bap'tist) *n.* one who holds that infant baptism is not valid. [G. *ana*, anew, and *baptizein*, to dip in water.]

ANACHRONISM (an-ak'run-izm) *n.* an error in the account of events in time past. [G. *ana*, backwards, and *chronos*, time.]

ANACONDA (an-ɑ-kon'dɑ) *n.* a large serpent in the East. [Perh. Cingalese.]

ANACREONTIC (a-nak-rēon'tik) *a.* pertaining to Anacreon, a Greek poet; — *n.* an amatory poem.

ANÆSTHETIC (an-es-thet'ik) *n.* a substance, as chloroform, that produces sleep or insensibility; — *a.* producing insensibility. [G. *a*, *an*, not, and *aisthesis*, feeling.]

ANAGRAM (an'ɑ-gram) *n.* transposition of the letters of a word or sentence. [G. *ana*, again, and *graphein*, to write.]

ANALOGICAL (an-ɑ-loj'i-kɑl) *a.* according to analogy.

ANALOGOUS (ɑ-nal'o-gus) *a.* having resemblance.

ANALOGY (ɑ-nal'o-ji) *n.* likeness; proportion. [G. *ana*, again or anew, and *logos*, a discourse.]

ANALYSABLE (an-ɑ-līz'ɑ-bl) *a.* susceptible of analysis.

ANALYSE (an'ɑ-līz) *v.t.* to resolve into first principles. [G. *analusis*, decomposition.]

ANALYSER (an'ɑ-līz-er) *n.* one that analyses.

ANALYSIS (ɑ-nal'i-sis) *n.* separation of a body, or of a subject, into its parts; — *pl.* **ANALYSES**.

ANALYST (an'ɑ-list) *n.* one who analyses.

ANALYTIC (an-ɑ-lit'ik) *a.* pertaining to analysis; resolving into parts.

ANAPEST (an'ɑ-pest) *n.* a poetic foot of three syllables, two short and one long. [G. *anapaistos*, reversed.]

ANARCHIC (a-när'kik) *a.* being without government.

ANARCHISM (an'ɑr-kizm) *n.* state of being without rule or law.

ANARCHIST (an'ɑr-kist) *n.* one who promotes lawlessness and disorder.

ANARCHY (an'ɑr-ki) *n.* want of government; lawlessness; disorder. [G. *a*, *an*, not, and *arche*, government.]

ANATHEMA (ɑ-nath'ē-mɑ) *n.* an ecclesiastical curse. [G. *anatithemi*, I lay up an offering.]

ANATHEMATISE (a-nath'ē-mɑ-tīz) *v.t.* to denounce or excommunicate. [See **ANATHEMA**.]

ANATOMICAL (an-ɑ-tom'i-kɑl) *a.* belonging to anatomy.

ANATOMIST (ɑ-nat'ō-mist) *n.* one skilled in anatomy.

ANATOMY (ɑ-nat'ō-mi) *n.* art of dissection; a skeleton. [G. *anatomia*, fr. *anatemnein*, to cut up.]

ANCESTOR (an'ses-tur) *n.* one from whom we descend. [O.F. *ancestre,* fr. L. *antecessor,* a foregoer.]

ANCESTRAL (an-ses'tral) *a.* claimed from ancestors.

ANCESTRY (an-ses-tri) *n.* a line of ancestors; lineage.

ANCHOR (ang'kur) *n.* an iron instrument for holding ships at rest in water;—*v.i.* to cast an anchor;—*v.t.* to place at anchor. [L. *anchora,* fr. G. *angkura.*]

Anchor.

ANCHORAGE (ang'kur-āj) *n.* ground for anchoring.

ANCHORITE (ang'kur-īt) *n.* a hermit; a recluse. [F. *anachorète,* fr. G. *anachoretes,* one who retires.]

ANCHOVY (an-chō'vi) *n.* a small sea-fish, used in seasoning. [Sp.]

ANCIENT (ān'shent) *a.* of former times; not modern; old. [F. *ancien,* fr. Late L, *antianus,* old, fr. *ante,* before.]

ANCIENTLY (ān'shent-li) *ad.* in old times.

ANCIENTS (ān-shents) *n.pl.* men of past ages.

ANCILLARY (an-sil'ar-i) *a.* subservient or subordinate. [L. *ancilla,* a maid-servant.]

AND (and) *conj.* a word joining sentences. [E.]

ANDANTE (an-dan'tā) *n.* in *Music,* a word directing to slow movement. [It.]

ANDIRON (and'ī-ern) *n.* a utensil to hold wood for burning. [M.E. *anderne,* fr. O.F. *andier.*]

ANDROGYNAL (an-drog'i-nal) *a.* having both sexes. [G. *aner, andros,* man, and *gune,* woman.]

ANDROIDES (an-droid'ēz) *n.* a machine in the human form; automaton. [G. *aner, andros,* man.]

ANEAR (a-nēr') *ad.* near; nearly. [O.E. *a, on,* and *neah,* near.]

ANECDOTE (an'ek-dōt) *n.* a short story. [G. *anekdotos,* not given out, fr. *an,* not, *ek,* out, and *dotos,* given.]

ANELE (a-nēl') *v.t.* to give extreme unction to. [O.E. *an,* on, and *ele,* oil]

ANEMOMETER (a-nem-om'e-ter) *n.* an instrument to measure the velocity of the wind. [G. *anemos,* wind, and *metron,* a measure.]

ANEMONE (a-nem'ō-nē) *n.* the wind flower. [G. *anemos,* wind.]

ANENT (a-nent') *prep.* concerning; about. [O.E. *an* and *efen,* even; M.E. *onefent.*]

ANEURISM (an'ū-rizm) *n.* a disease of the arteries. [G. *ana,* up, and *eurunein,* to widen.]

ANEURISMAL (an-ū-ris'mal) *a.* pertaining to aneurism.

ANEW (a-nū') *ad.* afresh; newly. [M.E. of new.]

ANGEL (ān'jel) *n.* a divine messenger; a spirit; a beautiful person. [G. *angelos,* a messenger.]

ANGELIC (an-jel'ik) *a.* belonging to or resembling angels.

ANGELOLOGY (ān-jel'ol-ō-ji) *n.* the doctrine of angelic being. [G. *angelos,* a messenger, and *logos,* a discourse.]

ANGER (ang'ger) *n.* a passion excited by injury; —*v.t.* to provoke; enrage. [Ieel. *angr.*]

ANGINA (an-ji'na) *n.* inflammation of the throat. [L.]

ANGLE (ang'gl) *n.* a point where two lines meet; a corner;—*v.i.* to fish with a rod and hook. [L. *angulus,* a corner; O.E. *angel,* a hook.]

ANGLER (ang'gler) *n.* one who angles for fishes.

ANGLICAN (ang'gli-kan) *a.* English. [L. fr. *Angli,* Angles.]

ANGLICANISM (ang-gli-kan-izm) *n.* attachment to English institutions; the principles of the English Church.

ANGLICISE (ang'gli-sīz) *v.t.* to render into English.

ANGLICISM (ang'gli-sizm) *n.* an English idiom.

ANGLING (ang'gling) *n.* act of fishing.

ANGLO-SAXON (ang'glō-saks-un) *n.* an early Teutonic settler in England;—*a.* denoting the earliest form of the language; Old English.

ANGORA-WOOL (ang-gō'ra-wool) *n.* the long silky hair of the Angora goat.

ANGRILY (ang'gri-li) *ad.* with anger. [See ANGER.]

ANGRY (ang'gri) *a.* moved with anger. [See ANGER.]

ANGUINEAL (an-gwin'e-al) *a.* pertaining to a snake. [L. *anguis, anguinis,* a snake.]

ANGUISH (ang'gwish) *n.* excessive pain. [O.F. *anguisse,* fr. L. *angustia,* straitness, fr. *angere,* to choke.]

ANGULAR (ang'gū-lar) *a.* having an angle or corner; pointed; sharp and stiff. [L. *anguius,* a corner.]

ANGULARITY (ang-gū-lar'i-ti) *n.* the quality of being angular.

ANGULATED (ang'gū-lāt-ed) *a.* formed with angles.

ANILE (an'il) *a.* aged; imbecile. [L. *anus* an old woman.]

ANILINE (an'i-lin) *n.* a dyeing stuff obtained from benzole.

ANILITY (a-nil'i-ti) *n.* old age of a woman; dotage. [See ANILE.]

ANIMADVERSION (an-i-mad-ver'shun) *n.* remarks by way of criticism or reproof. [L. *animadversus,* criticised.]

ANIMADVERT (an-i-mad-vert') *v.i.* to turn the mind to; remark upon.

ANIMAL (an'i-mal) *n.* a living corporeal being, endowed with sensation and voluntary motion;—*a.* pertaining to animals. [L. *animal,* fr *anima,* breath.]

ANIMALCULAR (an-i-mal'kū-lar) *a.* relating to animalcules. [L. *animalculum,* a little animal.]

ANIMALISE (an'i-mal-īz) *v.t.* to give animal life to.

ANIMALISM (an'i-mal-izm) *n.* animal nature; brutishness.

ANIMALITY (an-i-mal'i-ti) *n.* the state of animal existence.

ANIMATE (an'i-māt) *v.t.* to give life to. [L. *anima,* the soul or breath.]

ANIMATING (an'i-māt-ing) *a.* enlivening; giving life to.

ANIMATION (an-i-mā'shun) *n.* quality of being animated; life; spirit.

ANIMATOR (an'i-mā-ter) *n.* one who gives life.

ANIMOSITY (an-i-mos'i-ti) *n.* extreme hatred; malevolence. [L. (acc.) *animositatem,* fr. *animosus,* full of spirit.]

ANIMUS (an'i-mus) *n.* a hostile spirit or prejudice against. [L. = spirit.]

ANISE (an'is) *n.* a plant bearing aromatic seeds. [F., fr. G. *anison.*]

ANKLE (ang'kl) *n.* the joint between the foot and the leg. [O.E. *ancleow.*]

ANKLET (ang'klet) *n.* an ornament or a support for the ankle.

ANNA (an'a) *n.* an Indian coin of the value of three halfpence sterling. [Hind.]

ANNALIST (an'al-ist) *n.* a writer of annals. [F., fr. (*pl.*) *annales,* yearly records, fr. L. *annus,* a year.]

ANNALS (an'alz) *n.pl.* histories related in order of time.

ANNEAL (a-nēl') *v.t.* to temper glass or metals by heat. [O.E. *an,* on, and *ælan,* to kindle.]

ANNEX (a-neks') *v.t.* to join at the end. [L. *annexus,* bound to, fr. *ad,* to, and *nectere,* to tie.]

ANNEXATION (a-neks-ā'shun) *n.* conjunction; addition; union.

ANNEXE (a-neks') *n.* an addition to a building. [F.]

ANNIHILATE (a-ni'hil-āt) *v.t.* to reduce to nothing; destroy the specific form of a thing. [L. *annihilatus*, fr. *ad*, to, and *nihil*, nothing.]

ANNIHILATION (a-ni-hil-ā'shun) *n.* act of annihilating or reducing to nothing.

ANNIHILATOR (a-ni'hi-lā-tẹr) *n.* one who annihilates; a fire-extinguisher.

ANNIVERSARY (an-i-ver'sa-ri) *a.* returning with the year;—*n.* the annual day on which an event is celebrated. [L. *anniversarius*, returning every year; fr. *annus*, a year, and *versus*, turned.]

ANNOTATE (an-ō-tāt) *v.t.* to make comments upon. [L. *annotatus*, fr. *ad*, to, and *nota*, a mark.]

ANNOTATION (an-ō-tā'shun) *n.* an explanatory note.

ANNOTATOR (an'ō-tā-tẹr) *n.* a writer of notes; a commentator.

ANNOUNCE (a-nouns') *v.t.* to give notice of; proclaim. [F. *annoncer*; fr. L. *ad*, to, and *nuntiare*, to report, fr. *nuntius*, a messenger.]

ANNOUNCEMENT (a-nouns'ment) *n.* a declaration or advertisement.

ANNOY (a-noi') *v.t.* to disturb or trouble repeatedly; vex; tease; molest. [O.F. *anoi*, vexation, fr. L. *in odio*, in hatred.]

ANNOYANCE (a-noy'ans) *n.* that which annoys or molests.

ANNUAL (an'ū-al) *a.* coming yearly;—*n.* a plant that lives but one year; a yearly publication. [L. *annualis*, yearly, fr. *annus*, a year.]

ANNUALLY (an'ū-al-li) *ad.* year by year.

ANNUITANT (a-nū'it-ant) *n.* a person who has an annuity.

ANNUITY (a-nū'i-ti) *n.* a yearly allowance. [L. (acc.) *annuitatem.*]

ANNUL (a-nul') *v.t.* [*pp.* **ANNULLED**] to make void; abolish. [L. *annulare*, to bring to nothing; fr. *ad*, to, and *nullus*, nothing; fr. *ne*, not, and *ullus*, anything.]

ANNULAR (an'ū-lar) *a.* having the form of a ring; round. [L. *annulus*, a little ring.]

ANNULATION (an-ū-lā'shun) *n.* a circular, ring-like formation.

ANNULMENT (a-nul'ment) *n.* the act of annulling. [L. *annulare*, to bring to nothing.]

ANNUNCIATE (a-nun'si-āt) *v.t.* to bring tidings; announce.

ANNUNCIATION (a-nun-si-ā'shun) *n.* act of announcing; thing announced.

ANODE (an'ōd) *n.* the positive pole or electrode of a galvanic battery. [G. *ana*, up, and *hodos*, way.]

ANODIC (a-nod'ik) *a.* proceeding upwards; ascending.

ANODYNE (an'ō-dīn) *n.* medicine to assuage pain and dispose to sleep;—*a.* mitigating pain. [L. *anodynus*, fr. G. *a*, not, and *odune*, pain.]

ANOINT (a-noint') *v.t.* to rub with oil; consecrate. [O.F. *part. enoint*, anointed, fr. *enoindre*, fr. L. *in*, in, and *ungere*, to smear.]

ANOINTED (a-noint'ed) *n.* the Messiah.

ANOINTING (a-noint'ing) *n.* an unction; a consecration.

ANOINTMENT (a-noint'ment) *n.* act of anointing.

ANOMALISM (a-nom'a-lizm) *n.* a deviation from rule; anomaly. [G. *anomalia*, exception, fr. *a*, not, and *homalos*, regular.]

ANOMALOUS (a-nom'a-lus) *a.* deviating from rule or analogy.

ANOMALY (a-nom'a-li) *n.* that which deviates from rule; any irregularity.

ANON (a-non') *ad.* soon; quickly. [O.E. *on*, in, and *an*, one.]

ANONYMOUS (a-non'i-mus) *a.* wanting a name; nameless.

ANSERINE (an-se'rin) *a.* belonging to the goose family. [L. *anser*, a goose.]

ANSWER (an'sẹr) *v.i.* to speak in reply; succeed;—*v.t.* to reply to; comply with; suit;—*n.* a reply; return. [O.E. *and*, against, and *swerian*, to speak.]

ANSWERABLE (an'sẹr-a-bl) *a.* accountable; suitable.

ANSWERER (an'sẹr-ẹr) *n.* one who answers.

ANT (ant) *n.* a small insect. [O.E. *æmete.*]

ANTAGONISE (an-tag'ō-nīz) *v.i.* to act in opposition. [G. *antagonistes*, fr. *anti*, against, and *agonizomai*, struggle.]

ANTAGONISM (an-tag'ō-nizm) *n.* opposition of action.

ANTAGONIST (an-tag'ō-nist) *n.* an opponent; —*a.* counteracting; opposing.

ANTAGONISTIC (an-tag-ō-nis'tik) *a.* opposing.

ANTARCTIC (ant-ärk'tik) *a.* opposite to the arctic. [G. *anti*, opposite, and F. *arctique*, fr. L. (acc.) *arcticum*, northern fr. G. *arktikos*, near the constellation of *arktos*, the Bear.]

ANT-BEAR (ant'bār) *n.* an American animal that feeds on ants. [O.E. *æmette*, and *bera*, a bear.]

ANTE (ante), in compound words signifies *before*. [L.]

ANTEACT (an'te-akt) *n.* a preceding act. [L. *ante*, before, and *actus*, done.]

ANTECEDE (an-tē-sēd') *v.i.* to precede; to go before in time, etc. [L. (acc.) *antecedentem*, going before, fr. *ante*, before, and *cedere*, to go.]

ANTECEDENCE (an-tē-sēd'ens) *n.* the act of preceding in time.

ANTECEDENT (an-tē-sē'dent) *n.* that which goes before;—*a.* going before in time; preceding; previous.

ANTECESSOR (an-tē-ses'ẹr) *n.* one who precedes; previous possessor. [L. *ante*, before, and *cessum*, *cedere*, to go.]

ANTECHAMBER (an'tē-chām-bẹr) *n.* a room leading to another. [L. *ante*, before, and F. *chambre*, fr. O.F. *cambre*, fr. L. (acc.) *cameram*, a room.]

ANTEDATE (an'tē-dāt) *v.t.* to date before the true time;—*n.* a prior date. [L. *ante*, before, and *data*, given, fr. *dare*, to give.]

ANTEDILUVIAN (an-tē-di-lōō'vi-an) *a.* being before the flood in Noah's days;—*n.* one who lived before the flood. [L. *ante*, and *diluvium*, the flood.]

ANTELOPE (an'tē-lōp) *n.* a genus of animals between the goat and the deer. [Late L. *antelopus.*]

ANTEMERIDIAN (an-tē-mē-rid'i-an) *a.* being before noon. [L. *ante*, before and (acc.) *meridiem*, midday.]

ANTEMUNDANE (an-tē-mun'dān) *a.* being before the creation. [L. *ante*, before, and *mundus*, the world.]

ANTENNÆ (an-ten'ē) *n.pl.* the feelers of insects. [L. *antenna*, a sailyard.]

ANTENNAL (an-ten'al) *a.* belonging to antennæ.

ANTENUPTIAL (an-tē-nup'shal) *a.* being before marriage. [L. *ante*, before, and F., fr. L. (acc.) *nuptialem*, fr. *nuptiæ*, nuptials.]

ANTEPASCHAL (an-tē-pas'kal) *a.* before Easter. [L. *ante*, before, and *pascha*, fr. H.]

ANTEPENULT (an-tē-pē-nult') *n.* the last syllable but two of a word. [L. *ante*, before, and *penultimus*, all but the last.]

ANTEPENULTIMATE (an-tē-pē-nul'ti-māt) *a.* of the last syllable but two.

ANTEPOSITION (an-tē-po-zish'un) *n.* placing a word before another. [L. *ante*, before, and *positum*, placed.]

ANTERIOR (an-tē'ri-ẹr) *a.* going before in time or place; prior; previous. [L. fr. *ante*, before.]

ANTERIORITY (an-tē-ri-or'i-ti) *n.* the state of being before in time or place.

ANTEROOM (an'ṭē-rôom) *n.* a room leading to the principal apartment. [L. *ante*, before, and O.E. *rum*, a room.]

ANTHEM (an'them) *n.* a hymn sung in parts and set to words from Scripture. [O.E. *antefn*, fr. G. *antiphona*, a sung response.]

ANTHER (an'thẹr) *n.* in *Botany*, the tip of the stamen. [G. *antheros*, in flower.]

ANTHOLOGY (an-thol'ō-ji) *n.* a collection of flowers, or of poems. [G. *anthologia*, fr. *anthos*, a flower, and *legein*, to gather.]

ANTHRACITE (an'thra-sīt) *n.* a sort of hard coal. [G., fr. stem *anthrak-*, of *anthrax*, coal.]

ANTHRACITIC (an-thra-sit'ik) *a.* pertaining to anthracite.

ANTHRAX (an'thraks) *n.* a carbuncle; an ulcer. [G. *anthrax*, coal.]

ANTHROPOID (an'thrō-poid) *a.* resembling the human form. [G. *anthropos*, a man, and *eidos*, form.]

ANTHROPOLOGY (an-thrō-pol'o-ji) *n.* the natural history of the human species. [G. *anthropos*, man, and *logos*, discourse.]

ANTHROPOMORPHISM (an-thrō-po-mor'fizm) *n.* the ascription to God of a human form, passions, and affections. [G. *anthropos*, man, and *morphe*, form.]

ANTHROPOPHAGI (an-thrō-pof'-aji) *n.pl.* cannibals. [G. *anthropo-phagoi*, fr. *anthropos*, man, and *phagein*, to eat.]

ANTHROPOPHAGY (an-thrō-pof'a-ji) *n.* the feeding on human flesh.

ANTIBILIOUS (an-ti-bil'yus) *a.* counteractive of bilious complaints. [G. *anti*, against, and L. *biliosus*, pertaining to bile.]

ANTIC (an'tik) *a.* odd; fanciful;—*n.* a merryandrew. [It., fr. L. *antiquus*, ancient.]

ANTICHRIST (an'ti-krist) *n.* one who opposes Christ. [G. *anti*, against, and *Christ*.]

ANTICHRISTIAN (an-ti-krist'yạn) *n.* an opposer of Christ or Christianity;—*a.* opposing Christianity.

ANTICIPATE (an-tis'i-pāt) *v.t.* to take before; foretaste; foresee. [taste.]

ANTICIPATION (an-tis-i-pā'shun) *n.* fore-

ANTICLIMAX (an-ti-klī'maks) *n.* a falling off or sinking; bathos. [G. *anti*, opposite to, and *klimax*, a ladder.]

ANTICLINAL (an-ti-klī'nạl) *a.* dipping or sloping in opposite directions. [G. *anti*, against, and *klinein*, to lean.]

ANTIDOTAL (an-ti-dōt'ạl) *a.* efficacious against. [F., fr. L. *antidotum*, a remedy; fr. G. *anti*, against, and *doton*, given, fr. *dulomi*.]

ANTIDOTE (an'ti-dōt) *n.* a remedy to counteract evil of any kind.

ANTIFEBRILE (an-ti-feb'ril, an-ti-fē'bril) *a.* good against fever. [G. *anti*, against, and F. *febrile*, fr. L. *febrilis*, fr. *febris*, fever.]

ANTIMONARCHICAL (an-ti-mō-när'ki-kạl) *a.* opposed to monarchy. [G. *anti*, against, *monos*, alone, and *archein*, to rule.]

ANTIMONIAL ((an-ti-mō'ni-ạl) *a.* pertaining to, or composed of, antimony;—*n.* a preparation of antimony. [Low L. *antimonium*, antimony.]

ANTIMONY (an'ti-mun-i) *n.* a metallic ore.

ANTINOMIAN (an-ti-nō'mi-ạn) *n.* one who holds good works to be not necessary to salvation. [G. *anti*, against, and *nomos*, law.]

ANTINOMY (an'tin-ō-mi) *n.* contradiction between two laws.

ANTIPAPAL (an-ti-pā'pạl) *a.* opposing popery. [G. *anti*, against, and L. *papalis*, fr. *papa*, a father or bishop.]

ANTIPATHETIC (an-ti-pa-thet'ik) *a.* having a natural contrariety or aversion to. [G. *anti*, against, and F. *pathétique*, fr. L., fr. G. *pathetikos*, suffering.]

ANTIPATHIC (an-ti-path'ik) *a.* having opposite affections; adverse. [G. *anti*, against and *pathos*, feeling.]

ANTIPATHY (an-tip'a-thi) *n.* natural aversion.

ANTIPESTILENTIAL (an-ti-pes-ti-len'shạl) *a.* counteracting infection. [G. *anti*, against, and F. *peste*, fr. L. (acc.) *pestem*, a fatal epidemic.]

ANTIPHONAL (an-tif'ō-nạl) *a.* relating to alternate singing;—*n.* a book of antiphons or anthems. [See **ANTHEM**.]

ANTIPHONY (an-tif'ō-ni) *n.* alternate singing. [Doublet of **ANTHEM**, which see.]

ANTIPHRASIS (an-tif'ra-sis) *n.* the use of words in a sense opposite to the true one. [G. *anti*, against, and *phrasis*, speech.]

ANTIPODAL (an-tip'ō-dạl) *a.* pertaining to the antipodes. [G. *anti*, against, and *pous*, *podos*, a foot.]

ANTIPODES (an-tip'ō-dēz) *n.pl.* those who live on the opposite side of the globe; the region on the opposite side of the globe from one's own. [See **ANTIPODAL**.]

ANTIPOPE (an'ti-pōp) *n.* one who usurps the popedom. [G. *anti*, against, and L. *papa*, father or bishop.]

ANTIQUARIAN (an-ti-kwā'ri-ạn) *a.* pertaining to antiquity. [L. *antiquus*, old.]

ANTIQUARIANISM (an-ti-kwā'ri-ạn-izm) *n.* study or law of antiquities.

ANTIQUARY (an'ti-kwā-ri) *n.* one versed in antiquities.

ANTIQUATED (an'ti-kwā-ted) *pp.* or *a.* grown out of fashion.

ANTIQUE (an-tēk') *a.* ancient; old;—*n.* a remnant of antiquity.

ANTIQUITY (an-tik'wi-ti) *n.* old times; a relic of old times.

ANTISCORBUTIC (an-ti-skor-bū'tik) *a.* good against the scurvy. [G. *anti*, against, and Late L. *scorbutus*, scurvy.]

ANTISCRIPTURAL (an-ti-skrip'tūr-ạl) *a.* opposed to the doctrines or authority of the Bible. [G. *anti*, against, and L. *scriptura*, fr. *scribere*, to write.]

ANTISEPTIC (an-ti-sep'tik) *a.* counteracting putrefaction. [G. *anti*, against, and *septikos*, putrefying, fr. *septein* to rot.]

ANTITHESIS (an-tith'e-sis) *n.* opposition of words; contrast:—*pl.* **ANTITHESES**. [G. *anti*, against, and *tithenai*, place.]

ANTITHETIC (an-ti-thet'ik) *a.* placed in contrast. [See **ANTITHESIS**.]

ANTITYPE (an'ti-tīp) *n.* that which is prefigured by the type. [G. *anti*, against, and F., fr. L., *typus*, fr. G. *tupos*, a blow, fr. *tuptein*, to strike.]

ANTLER (ant'lẹr) *n.* a branch of a stag's horn. [O.F., fr. Late L. (acc.) *antocularem*, before the eyes: fr. *ante*, and *oculus*, eye.]

ANTLERED (ant'lẹrd) *a.* furnished with antlers.

ANVIL (an'vil) *n.* an iron block, usually with a steel face, on which metals are hammered. [O.E. *anfilte*, M.E. *anvelt*.]

ANXIETY (ang-zī'e-ti) *n.* trouble of mind; solicitude; concern. [L. *anxius*, fr. *angere*, to cause pain.]

ANXIOUS (angk'shus) *c.* greatly solicitous.

Anvil.

ANXIOUSLY (angk'shus-li) *a.* with solicitude.

ANY (en'i) *a.* one, indefinitely; every; whoever. [O.E. *œnig*, fr. *an*, one.]

AORTA (ā-or'ta) *n.* the great artery. [L., fr. G. *aorte*, the 'rising' vein.]

APACE (a-pās') *ad.* quickly; hastily; fast. [O.E. *a*, on, and F. *pas*, fr. L. (acc.) *passum*, stretched, fr. *pandere*.]

APART (a-pärt') *ad.* separately; aside. [F. *à part*, fr. L. *ad partem*, to one side.]

APARTMENT (a-pärt'ment) *n.* a room.

APATHETIC (ap-a-thet'ik) *a.* without feeling; insensible. [G. *a*, not, and *pathetikos*, suffering.]

APATHY (ap'ạ-thi) *n.* want of feeling. [G. *apatheia*, fr. *a*, not, and *pathos*, feeling.]

APE (ấp) *n.* a kind of monkey; a mimic or imitator;—*v.t.* to imitate as an ape; mimic. [O.E. *apa.*]

APERIENT (ạ-pē'ri-ent) *a.* gently purgative; —*n.* a purgative. [L. (acc.) *aperientem,* opening.]

APERTURE (ap'ẹr-tūr) *n.* an opening. [L. (acc.) *aperturam,* fr. *apertus,* open.]

APEX (ā'peks) *n.* the summit or top of a thing;—*pl.* **APICES.** [L. *apex,* the peak of the Flamen's cap.]

APHASIA (ạ-fā'zi-ạ) *n.* loss of power of speech. [G. *a*, not, and *phasis*, speech.]

APHELION (ạ-fē'li-un) *n.* the part of a planet's orbit most distant from the sun. [G. *apo,* far from, and *helios,* the sun.]

APHIDIAN (ạ-fid'i-ạn) *n.* pertaining to the aphides. [Perhaps G. *apheideis,* unsparing.]

APHIS (ā'fis) *n.* the plant-louse or vine fretter; —*pl.* **APHIDES.** [See **APHIDIAN.**]

APHLOGISTIC (af-lō-jis'tik) *a.* burning without flame. [G. *a*, not, and *phlogiston,* flame.]

APHONIA (ạ-fō'ni-ạ) *n.* loss of voice or speech. [G. *a*, not, and *phone*, voice.]

APHORISM (af'ur-izm) *n.* a detached precept in a few words; maxim. [G. *aphorizein,* to ma off, fr. *apo,* far from, and *horos,* limit.]rk

APHORISTIC (af-ur-is'tik) *a.* having the form of an aphorism. [See **APHORISM.**]

APIARY (ā'pi-ạr-i) *n.* a place for bees. [L. *apiarium,* fr. *apis,* a bee.]

APIECE (ạ-pēs') *ad.* to each one's share; for each; each by itself. [O.E, *a*, on, and O.F. *piece,* F. *pièce,* fr. Celt. through Low L.]

APIS (ā'pis) *n.* the sacred bull of the Egyptians; a species of insect; the bee.]

APISH (ā'pish) *a.* like an ape. [See **APE.**]

APLOMB (ạ-plom') *n.* self-possession; assurance; self-confidence. [F., fr. L. *ad,* to, and *plumbum,* lead.]

APOCALYPSE (ạ-pok'ạ-lips) *n.* the Book of Revelation. [G. *apokalupsis,* a revelation; fr. *apo,* far off, and *kalupiein,* to cover.]

APOCALYPTIC (ạ-pok-ạ-lip'tik) *a.* containing revelation; mysterious.

APOCOPE (ạ-pok'ōpē) *n.* the omission of the last syllable or letter of a word. [G. *apo,* far off, and *koptein,* to cut.]

APOCRYPHA (ạ-pok'ri-fạ) *n.* books of doubtful authority. [G. *apokrupha,* fr. *apo,* far off, and *kruptein,* to hide.]

APOCRYPHAL (ạ-pok'ri-fạl) *a.* not canonical; doubtful.

APOGEE (ap'ō-jē) *n.* the point in the moon's orbit most distant from the earth. [G. *apo,* far off, and *ge,* the earth.]

APOLLINARIS WATER (ạ-pol'i-nā-ris-waw'tẹr) *n.* a kind of acidulated soda water.

APOLOGETIC (ạ-pol-ō-jet'ik) *a.* said by way of defence or excuse. Also **APOLOGETICAL.** [G. *apologia,* a defence.]

APOLOGETICS (ạ-pol-ō-jet'iks) *n.pl.* the branch of theology which treats of the external and internal evidences of the truth of the Bible.

APOLOGISE (ạ-pol'ō-jīz) *v.i.* to plead or make excuse for.

APOLOGIST (ạ-pol'ō-jist) *n.* one who makes an apology.

APOLOGUE (ap'ō-log) *n.* a moral fable. [F., fr. G. *apologos,* a fable.]

APOLOGY (ạ-pol'ō-ji) *n.* an excuse; an expression of regret; a make-shift.

APOPLECTIC (ap-ō-plek'tik) *a.* belonging to apoplexy.

APOPLEXY (ap'ō-plek-si) *n.* a sudden deprivation of sense and motion. [G. *apoplexia,* fr. *apo,* far off, and *plessein,* to strike.]

APOSTACY (ạ-pos'tạ-si) *n.* a departure from professed principles. [F., fr. Late G. *apostasia,* a revolt.]

APOSTATE (ạ-pos'tāt) *n.* one that forsakes his principles of religion;—*a.* falling from faith.

APOSTATISE (ạ-pos'tạ-tīz) *v.i.* to abandon one's faith or party.

APOSTLE (ạ-pos'l) *n.* a messenger to preach the Gospel. [O.E. *apostol,* fr. G. *apostolos,* one sent out, fr. *apo,* far off, and *stellein,* to send.]

APOSTLESHIP (ạ-pos'l-ship) *n.* the office of an apostle.

APOSTOLIC (ap-os-tol'ik) *a.* relating to or like an apostle.

APOSTOLICALLY (ap-os-tol'i-kạl-i) *ad.* in the manner of an apostle.

APOSTROPHE (ạ-pos'trō-fē) *n.* in *Rhetoric,* a turning from real auditors to an imaginary one; a mark (') indicating the possessive case, or the omission of one or more letters of a word. [G. *apostrophe,* a turning away, fr. *apo,* far off, and *strephein,* to twist.]

APOTHECARY (ạ-poth'e-kạr-i) *n.* a compounder of medicines. [L. *apothecarius,* a store-keeper, fr. G. *apotheke,* store-house, fr. *apo,* far off, and *tithemi,* I place.]

APOTHEGM (ap'ō-them) *n.* a short instructive saying; a maxim. [G. *apophthegma,* fr. *apo,* far off, and *phthengesthai,* utter.]

APOTHEOSIS (ap-ō-thē'ō-sis) *n.* act of placing among the gods. [G. *apo,* far off, and *theos,* god.]

APOTHEOSISE (ap-ō-thē'ō-siz, ạ-poth-ē-ō'sīz) *v.t.* to deify.

APPAL (ạ-pawl') *v.t.* to smite with terror; dismay; terrify. [O.F. *appalir,* to make pale, fr. L. *ad,* to, and (acc.) *pallidum,* pale.]

APPALLING (ạ-pawl'ing) *a.* adapted to depress or terrify.

APPARATUS (ap-ạ-rā'tus) *n.* instruments, utensils, and the like, provided for scientific operations or experiments;—*pl.* **APPARATUS** or **APPARATUSES.** [L. *ad,* to, and *parare,* to prepare.]

APPAREL (ạ-par'el) *n.* clothing; raiment; equipment;—*v.t.* to dress; clothe; deck. [O.F. *apareiller,* to dress, fr. *à* and *pareil.*]

APPARENT (ạ-par'ent) *a.* visible to the eye; seeming; obvious; evident. [L. *apparere,* to appear.]

APPARENTLY (ạ-par'ent-li) *ad.* in appearance.

APPARITION (ap-ạ-rish'un) *n.* appearance; ghost.

APPEAL (ạ-pēl') *n.* removal of a cause to a higher court;—*v.t.* or *i.* to remove from a lower to a higher court; refer or have recourse to. [O.F. *apeler,* to call, fr. L. *appellare.*]

APPEALABLE (ạ-pēl'ạ-bl) *a.* that may be appealed.

APPEAR (ạ-pēr') *v.i.* to be in sight; seem or be evident. [L. *apparere,* to appear.]

APPEARANCE (ạ-pēr'ạns) *n.* a coming in sight; things seen; probability; show.

APPEASABLE (ạ-pēz'ạ-bl) *a.* that may be appeased. [O.F. *apeser,* to bring to peace, fr. L. (acc.) *pacem,* peace.]

APPEASE (ạ-pēz') *v.t.* to quiet; pacify.

APPEASEMENT (ạ-pēz'ment) *n.* act of appeasing.

APPELLANT (ạ-pel'ạnt) *n.* one who appeals. [See **APPEAL.**]

APPELLATE (ạ-pel'āt) *a.* relating to appeals.

APPELLATION (ap-e-lā'shun) *n.* name by which a person or thing is called.

APPELLATIVE (ạ-pel'ạ-tiv) *a.* common to many; general;—*n.* a common as distinguished from a proper name.

APPELLATORY (ạ-pel'ạ-tur-i) *a.* containing an appeal.

APPELLEE (ap-e-lē') *n.* the defendant in appeal.

APPELLOR (ạ-pel'ur) *n.* the plaintiff in appeal.

APPEND (ạ-pend') v.t. to hang or attach to; subjoin or annex. [L. ad, to, and pendere, to hang.]

APPENDAGE (ạ-pen'dåj) n. something added or annexed.

APPENDANT (ạ-pen'dạnt) n. an adjunct or concomitant;—a. hanging to.

APPENDICITIS (ạ-pen-di-si'tis) n. inflammation of the vermiform appendix of the cæcum.

APPENDIX (a-pen'diks) n. something annexed or added;—pl. APPENDIXES or APPENDICES.

APPERTAIN (ap-ẹr-tān') v.i. to belong to; relate. [L. ad, to, and O.F. partenir, fr. L. per, thoroughly, and tenere, to hold.]

APPETENCY (ap'e-ten-si) n. natural desire or craving for; inherent inclination or propensity. Also APPETENCE. [L. (acc.) appetentem, fr. ad, to, and petere, to seek.]

APPETIBLE (a'pet-i-bl) a. desirable; tempting. [Through F., fr. L. (acc.) appetilum, fr. ad, to, and petere, to seek.]

APPETITE (ap'e-tit) n. desire or relish for food; liking for; inclination.

APPLAUD (ạ-plawd') v.t. to praise by clapping of hands; commend. [L. applaudere, fr. ad, to, and plaudere, to clap hands.]

APPLAUSE (ạ-plawz') n. approbation loudly expressed.

APPLE (ap'l) n. a fruit; pupil of the eye. [O.E. æppel, M.E. appel.]

APPLIANCE (ạ-pli'ạns) n. act of applying; thing applied; means or instrument. [O.F. aplier, fr. L. applicare, to join to.]

APPLICABILITY (ạp-li-kạ-bil'i-ti) n. the quality of being applicable.

APPLICABLE (ap'li-kạ-bl) a. that may be applied.

APPLICANT (ap'li-kạnt) n. one who applies.

APPLICATION (ap-li-kā'shun) n. act of applying; persevering industry.

APPLY (ạ-pli') v.t. to lay on or put to; use or employ; address;—v.i. to suit; refer to; make application. [O.F. aplier, fr. L. applicare, to join to.]

APPOGGIATURA (ạ-poj-ạ-tŏŏ'rạ) n. a small note in music between other notes. [It., fr. appogiare, to lean upon.]

APPOINT (ạ-point') v.t. to settle; provide with; equip; name and commission to an office. [O.F. apointer, fr. Late L. appunctare, to settle.]

APPOINTMENT (ạ-point'ment) n. an order; decree; equipment; designation to office.

APPORTION (ạ-pŏr'shun) v.t. to divide out. [O.F., fr. L. ad, to, and F., fr. L. portio, a part.]

APPORTIONMENT (ạ-pŏr'shun-ment) n. a dividing into shares or portions.

APPOSITE (ap'ŏ-zit) a. proper; suitable. [L. appositus, placed near.]

APPOSITELY (ap'ŏ-sit-li) ad. properly; suitably; fitly.

APPOSITION (ap-ŏ-zish'un) n. the putting of two nouns in the same case.

APPRAISAL (ạ-prā'zạl) n. a valuation by authority.

APPRAISE (ạ-prāz') v.t. to set a price on. [M.E. apraisen, fr. O.F. à, and preis, praise.]

APPRAISEMENT (ạ-prāz'ment) n. act of appraising; valuation.

APPRAISER (ạ-prā'zẹr) n. a person appointed to appraise.

APPRECIABLE (ạ-prē'shi-ạ-bl) a. that may be estimated.

APPRECIATE (ạ-prē'shi-āt) v.t. to value;—v.i. to rise in value. [L. apprecialus, priced, fr. ad, to, and pretium, price.]

APPRECIATION (ạ-prē-shi-ā'shun) n. act of valuing; a just estimate; rising in value.

APPRECIATIVE (ạ-prē'shi-ạ-tiv) a. capable of or showing appreciation.

APPREHEND (ap-rē-hend') v.t. to seize; arrest; understand; think of with fear;—v.i. to be of opinion; believe. [L., fr. ad, to, and prehendere, to grasp.]

APPREHENSION (ap-rē-hen'shun) n. conception of ideas; fear; seizure.

APPREHENSIVE (ap-rē-hen'siv) n. quick to comprehend; fearful.

APPREHENSIVELY (ap-rē-hen'siv-li) ad. fearfully; suspiciously.

APPRENTICE (ạ-pren'tis) n. one bound to a trade or art;—v.t. to bind as an apprentice. [O.F., fr. L. apprehendere, to grasp at.]

APPRENTICESHIP (ạ-pren'tis-ship) n. the time an apprentice serves.

APPRISE (ạ-priz') v.t. to give notice to; inform. [F., apprendre, pp. appris, fr. L. apprehendere, to grasp at.]

APPROACH (ạ-prŏch') v.t. to draw near; approximate;—n. act of drawing near; access; path or avenue. [O.F., fr. L. ad, to, and propius, nearer.]

APPROACHABLE (ạ-prŏ'chạ-bl) a. that may be approached.

APPROACHLESS (ạ-prŏch'les) a. that cannot be approached.

APPROBATE (ap'rŏ-bāt) v.t. to approve officially; license. [L. ad, to, and probare, to prove.]

APPROBATION (ap-rŏ-bā'shun) n. the act of approving; approval; commendation.

APPROBATIVE (ap'rŏ-bā-tiv) a. implying approbation.

APPROBATORY (ap'rŏ-bā-tur-ı) a. containing approbation; approving.

APPROPRIABLE (ạ-prŏ'pri-ạ-bl) a. that may be appropriated.

APPROPRIATE (ạ-prŏ'pri-āt) v.t. to set apart for a purpose, or for oneself; assign;—a. belonging to peculiarly; most suitable. [L. appropriatus, made one's own; fr. ad, to, and proprius, one's own.]

APPROPRIATED (ạ-prŏ'pri-āt-ed) pp. or a. assigned to a particular use.

APPROPRIATELY (ạ-prŏ'pri-āt-li) ad. properly.

APPROPRIATENESS (ạ-prŏ'pri-āt-nes) n. peculiar fitness.

APPROPRIATION (ạ-prŏ-pri-ā'shun) n. application to a particular use; sequestering of a benefice.

APPROPRIATOR (ạ-prŏ'pri-ā-tẹr) n. one who holds an appropriated benefice.

APPROVABLE (ạ-prŏŏ'vạ-bl) a. worthy of approbation.

APPROVAL (ạ-prŏŏv'ạl) n. approbation.

APPROVE (ạ-prŏŏv') v.t. or i. to like or allow of; justify; commend; sanction. [O.F. approver, fr. L. approbare, fr. ad to, and probare, to prove.]

APPROVEMENT (ạ-prŏŏv'ment) n. act of approving; confession of felony with revelation of one's accomplices; turning 'King's' evidence; improvement of common lands by enclosing and tilling them.

APPROVER (ạ-prŏŏ'vẹr) n. one who confesses, and betrays his accomplices.

APPROXIMATE (ạ-prok'si-māt) v.t. or i. to bring or draw near;—a. near to; nearly correct. [L. approximatus, brought near; fr. ad, to, and proximus, very near.]

APPROXIMATELY (ạ-prok'si-māt-li) ad. nearly; closely.

APPROXIMATION (ạ-prok-si-mā'shun) n. approach.

APPURTENANCE (ạ-pur'te-nạns) n. that which belongs to something else. [O.F. apartenance, a belonging.]

APPURTENANT (ạ-pur'te-nạnt) a. belonging to by right.

APRICOT (ā'pri-kot) n. a stone fruit. [F. abricot, fr. Pg. albricoque, fr. A.]

APRIL (ā'pril) n. fourth month of the year. [L. Aprilis, fr. aperire, to open.]

APRON (ā'prun) *n.* a part of dress worn in front. [O.F. *naperon*, a large cloth, fr. *nappa*, a cloth, fr. L. (acc.) *mappam*. Formerly *napron*.]

APROPOS (ap-rō-pō') *ad.* to the purpose; by the way. [F. *à propos*.]

APSE (aps) *n.* a domed or vaulted recess at the east end of the choir or chancel. [L. *apsis*, fr. G. *hapsis*, an arch.]

APT (apt) *a.* liable to; fit; ready; qualified. [L. *aptus*, fit.]

APTERAL (ap'te-rạl) *a.* having columns only in front. [G. *a*, not, and *pteron*, a wing.]

APTEROUS (ap'te-rus) *a.* destitute of wings. [See APTERAL.]

APTERYX (ap'te-riks) *n.* a bird of New Zealand, almost wingless and with no tail.

APTITUDE (ap'ti-tūd) *n.* fitness; adaptation; tendency. [See APT.]

APTLY (apt'li) *ad.* properly; fitly.

APTNESS (apt'nes) *n.* fitness; readiness; tendency.

AQUARIUM (a-kwā'ri-um) *n.* a tank or pond for water plants and fishes; a public collection of such. [L. *aqua*, water.]

AQUATIC (ạ-kwat'ik) *a.* living in water. [L. *aqua*, water.]

AQUATINTA (ak-wạ-tin'ta) *n.* a method of etching on copper;—*v.i.* to etch in aquatint. [L. *aqua*, water, and *tinctum*, coloured.]

AQUEDUCT (ak'wē-dukt) *n.* a conductor, conduit, or artificial channel for conveying water. [L. *aqua*, water, and *ductus*, led.]

AQUEOUS (ā'kwē-us) *a.* watery.

AQUIFORM (ak'wi-form) *a.* in the form of water. [L. *aqua*, water, and *forma*, shape or form.]

AQUILINE (ak'wi-lin, līn) *a.* like an eagle or its beak. [L. *aquila*, an eagle.]

ARAB (ar'ạb) *n.* a native of Arabia; an Arabian horse;—*a.* Arabian.

ARABESQUE (ar'ạ-besk) *a.* in the manner of Arabian architecture. [F., fr. It. *Arabesco*, Arabian-like.]

ARABIC (ar'ạ-bik) *n.* the language of Arabians.

ARABLE (ar'ạ-bl) *a.* fit for ploughing. [F., fr. L. *arabilis*, fr. L. *arare*, to plough.]

ARACHNOID (ạ-rak'noid) *a.* resembling a spider's web; pertaining to the *arachnida*, or spiders. [G. *arachne*, spider.]

ARBITER (ar'bi-tẹr) *n.* an umpire. [L. *arbiter*, a judge.]

ARBITRAMENT (ar-bit'rạ-ment) *n.* will; award of arbitrators.

ARBITRARY (ar'bi-trạ-ri) *a.* dictated by will; despotic. [L. *arbitrarius*, belonging to an umpire.]

ARBITRATE (ar-bi-trāt) *v.i.* or *t.* to hear and judge as an arbitrator. [L. *arbitratus*, judged.]

ARBITRATION (ar-bi-trā'shun) *n.* a hearing before arbitrators.

ARBITRATOR (ar'bi-trā-tẹr) *n.* an umpire.

ARBOREOUS (ar-bō'rē-us) *a.* belonging to trees.

ARBORESCENCE (ar-bur-es'ens) *n.* resembling the growth of a tree.

ARBORESCENT (ar-bur-es'ent) *a.* growing like a tree.

ARBORETUM (ar-bur-ē'tum) *n.* a place in which trees and shrubs are cultivated. [L. *arbor*, a tree.]

ARBORICULTURE (ar-bor-e-kul'tūr) *n.* the art of growing trees and shrubs. [L. *arbor*, a tree, and *colo*, I cultivate.]

ARBOUR (ar'bur) *n.* a shady bower. [L. *arbor*, a tree.]

ARC (ark) *n.* part of a circle or curve. [O.F., fr. L. (acc.) *arcum*, a bow.]

ARCADE (ar-kād') *n.* a walk arched over. [F., fr. It. *arcata*, arched, fr. L. *arcus*, a bow.]

ARCADIAN (ar-kā'di-ạn) *a.* pertaining to Arcadia in the peloponnesus; pastoral;—*n.* an ideal rustic.

ARCH (arch) *a.* chief; waggish;—*n.* a part of a circle;—*v.t.* or *i.* to form an arch. [O.E. *arce*, through L., fr. G. *archi*, fr. *archein*, to rule.]

ARCHÆOLOGY (ar-kē-ol'o-ji) *n.* the science of antiquities. [G. *archaios*, ancient, and *logos*, a discourse.]

ARCHAIC (ar-kā'ik) *a.* ancient; antiquated; obsolete.

ARCHAISM (ar-kā'izm) *n.* an obsolete style, idiom, or word. [G. *archaismos*, fr. *archaizein*, to use an ancient phrase.]

Arch.

ARCHANGEL (ark-ān'jel) *n.* a chief angel. [It., fr. G. (pref.) *archi*, chief, and *angelos*, messenger.]

ARCHBISHOP (arch-bish'up) *n.* a chief bishop. [It., fr. G. (pref.) *archi*, chief, and O.E. *bisceop*, fr. L. *episcopus*, fr. G. *episcopos*, an overseer.]

ARCHBISHOPRIC (arch-bish'up-rik) *n.* diocese or office of an archbishop.

ARCHDEACON (arch-dē'kn) *n.* a bishop's deputy. [G. *archi*, chief, and O.E. *diacon*, fr. L., fr. G. *diakonos*, a servant.]

ARCHDUCHESS (arch-duch'es) *n.* a princess of the house of Austria. [See ARCHDUKE.]

ARCHDUKE (arch-dūk') *n.* a grand-duke; a son of the Emperor of Austria. [G. *archi*, chief, and L. *dux*, a leader.]

ARCHED (archt) *a.* in form of an arch. [O.F. *arc*, fr. L. *arcus*, a bow.]

ARCHELOGY (ar-kel'ō-ji) *n.* the science of first principles. [G. *arche*, beginning, and *logos*, a discourse.]

ARCHER (arch'ẹr) *n.* one who shoots with a bow. [L. *arcus*, a bow.]

ARCHERY (arch'ẹr-i) *n.* art of shooting with a bow.

ARCHETYPAL (ar'ke-ti-pạl) *a.* belonging to the original.

ARCHETYPE (ar'ke-tīp) *n.* an original; a pattern. [G. *archetupon*, pattern.]

ARCHIDIACONAL (ar'ki-di-ak-uh-ạl) *a.* pertaining to an archdeacon. [G. *archi*, chief, and O.E. *diacon*, fr. G. *diakonos*.]

ARCHIEPISCOPAL (ar-ki-ē-pis'kō-pạl) *a.* belonging to an archbishop.

ARCHIPELAGO (ar-ki-pel'ạ-gō) *n.* a chief sea with many isles. [G. *archi*, chief, and *pelagos*, sea.]

ARCHITECT (ar-ki'tekt) *n.* a chief builder, a contriver. [F. *architecte*, fr. L. (acc.) *architectum*, a master builder; fr. G. *archi*, chief, and *tekton*, worker.]

ARCHITECTIVE (ar-ki-tek'tiv) *a.* belonging to architecture.

ARCHITECTURAL (ar-ki-tek'tūr-ạl) *a.* pertaining to building.

ARCHITECTURE (ar-ki-tek'tūr) *n.* the science of building.

ARCHITRAVE (ar'ki-trāv) *n.* a moulding round a door or window. [G. *archi*, chief, and O.F. *traf*, fr. L. *trabs*, a beam.]

ARCHIVES (ar'kivz) *n.pl.* records, or places where they are kept. [F., fr. L. *archivum*, archives, fr. G. *archeion*, a magistrate's residence, fr. *arche*, magistracy.]

ARCHWAY (arch'wā) *n.* a passage under an arch.

ARCTIC (ark'tik) *a.* lying far north. [F. *arctique*, fr. L. (acc.) *arcticum*, northern, fr. G. *arktikos*, near the constellation *arktos*, the Bear.]

ARDENCY (ar'den-si) *n.* eagerness; zeal.

ARDENT (ar'dent) *a.* hot; zealous. [L. (acc.) *ardentem*, fiery, fr. *ardere*, to burn.]

ARDOUR (ar'dur) *n.* warmth; affection. [O.F. *ardor* = F. *ardeur*, fr. L. (acc.) *ardorem*, heat.]

ARDUOUS (ár'dū-us) *a.* hard to climb; laborious. [L. *arduus*, steep.]

AREA (ā'rē-ạ) *n.* an open surface; superficial contents. [L.]

AREFACTION (ar-ē-fak'shun) *n.* the act of drying; dryness. [L. *arefacere*, to make dry, fr. *arere*, to be dry and *facere*, to make.]

ARENA (ạ-rē'nạ) *n.* an open space of ground; any place of public exertion. [L. =sand.]

ARENACEOUS (ar-ē-nā'shus) *a.* consisting of sand.

AREOMETRY (ár-ē-om'e-tri) *n.* art of measuring the specific gravity of liquids. [G. *araios*, thin, and *metron*, measure.]

AREOPAGUS (ar-ē-op'ạ-gus) *n.* the highest tribunal of ancient Athens; Mars' Hill. [G. *areios*, belonging to Ares (Mars).

ARGAL, ARGOL (ár'gal, ár'gol) *n.* crude tartar. [M.E. *argoil*. Etym. doubtful.]

ARGAND (ár'gand) *a.* applied to a wick or a burner that is hollow and circular, increasing the current of air and the brightness of the flame. [Fr. *Aimé Argand.*]

ARGENT (ár'jent) *a.* silvery; white. [F., fr. L. *argentum*, silver.]

ARGENTINE (ár'jent-in) *a.* like silver;—*n.* white metal coated with silver.

ARGIL (ár'jil) *n.* pure clay. [F. *argile*, fr. L. (acc.) *argillam*, white clay, fr. G. *argillos*. fr. *argos*, white.]

ARGIVE (ár'jiv) *a.* used for the Greeks in general. [L., fr. G. *argeia*, belonging to Argos.]

ARGOSY (ár'go-si) *n.* a merchant ship with a rich cargo. [Fr. *Ragusa*, a port in Dalmatia. The word was formerly written *Ragusy, Aragusy.*]

ARGUE (ár'gū) *v.i.* or *t.* to debate or discuss; prove or persuade by reasoning. [M.E. *arguen*, fr. O.F. *arguer*, fr. L. *argutare*, fr. L. (part.) *argutus*, made clear, fr. *arguere*.]

ARGUER (ár-gū'er) *n.* a reasoner.

ARGUMENT (ár-gū'ment) *n.* reason alleged to induce belief; debate.

ARGUMENTATION (ár-gu-men-tā'shun) *n.* act or process of reasoning.

ARGUMENTATIVE (ár-gū-men'tạ-tiv) *a.* consisting of, or addicted to, argument.

ARGUS (ár'gus) *n.* one who watches closely. [G. *argos*, bright.]

ARGUTE (ár-gūt') *a.* subtle; ingenious. [L. *argutus*, made clear by argument.]

ARIAN (ā'ri-ạn) *n.* one who denies the divinity of Christ. [Fr. *Arius* of Alexandria.]

ARIANISM (ā'ri-ạn-izm) *n.* the doctrine of the Arians.

ARID (ar'id) *a.* dry; parched. [L. *aridus*, dry, fr. *arere*, to be dry.]

ARIDITY (ạ-rid'-i-ti) *n.* dryness; absence of moisture.

ARIES (ā'ri-ez) *n.* the ram; one of the twelve signs of the zodiac. [L.]

ARIGHT (ạ-rit') *ad.* rightly. [O.E. *a*, on, and *riht*, right.]

ARISE (ạ-riz') *v.i.* [*pret.* AROSE; *pp.* ARISEN] to rise; mount upward. [O.E. *arisan*, fr. *a*, on, and *risan*, to rise.]

ARISTARCH (ar'is-tárk) *n.* a severe critic. [Fr. *Aristarchus* of Alexandria.]

ARISTOCRACY (ar-is-tok'rạ-si) *n.* government by nobles; nobility. [G. *aristos*, best, and *cratos*, power.]

ARISTOCRAT (ạ-ris'tō-krat) *n.* one who favours aristocracy.

ARISTOCRATIC (ar-is-tō-krat'ik) *a.* partaking of aristocracy.

ARITHMETIC (ạ-rith'met-ik) *n.* the science of numbers. [G. *arithmetika*, fr. *arithmos*, number.]

ARITHMETICAL (ar-ith-met'i-kạl) *a.* according to arithmetic.

ARITHMETICIAN (a-rith-met-ish'ạn) *n.* one skilled in arithmetic.

ARK (árk) *n.* a lumber vessel; chest. [O.E. *arc*, box, fr. L. *arca*, a chest.]

ARLES (ár'lz) *n.* earnest money. [M.E. *erles*, fr. O.F. *erres*, F. *arrhes*, fr. L. *arrha*.]

ARM (árm) *n.* a limb of the body; an inlet of water;—*v.t.* or *i.* to furnish with, or take up, arms. [O.E.]

ARMADA (ár-mā'dạ) *n.* a large fleet of armed ships. [Sp., fr. L. fem. part. *armata*, armed.]

ARMADILLO (ár-mạ-dil'ō) *n.* a small quadruped of South America, armed with a hard bony shell. [Sp. dim. of *armado*, armed.]

ARMAMENT (ár'mạ-ment) *n.* a force equipped for war. [L. *armamenta*, fr. *arma*, arms.]

ARMATURE (ár'mạ-tūr) *n.* armour ; defence. [L. *arma*, arms.]

ARM-CHAIR (árm'chār) *n.* a chair with arms to support the elbows. [ARM and F. *chaire*, fr. L., fr. G. *kathedra*, seat.]

ARMFUL (árm'fool) *n.* as much as the arms can hold.

ARMIGEROUS (ár-mi'jer-us) *a.* bearing arms. [L. *arma*, arms, and *gero*, I bear.]

ARMILLA (ár-mil'ạ) *n.* a bracelet; an iron ring or hoop. [L.]

ARMILLARY (ár'mi-lạ-ri) *a.* consisting of rings like a bracelet.

ARMILLARY SPHERE, an instrument consisting of several brass rings, all circles of the same sphere, designed to represent the positions of the chief circles of the celestial sphere.

Armillary Sphere.

ARMINIAN (ár-min'i-ạn) *n.* one who denies predestination, and holds to universal redemption. [Fr. *Arminius*, a Dutch divine.]

ARMINIANISM (ár-min'i-ạn-izm) *n.* the tenets of the Arminians.

ARMISTICE (ár'mis-tis) *n.* a temporary cessation of fighting. [F., fr. Low L. *armistitium*, fr. L. *arma*, arms, and *sistere*, to stand.]

ARMLET (árm'let) *n.* a bracelet or ornament for the arm.

ARMORIAL (ár-mō'r-iạl) *a.* belonging to arms.

ARMOUR (ár'mur) *n.* defensive arms. [O.F. *armeüre*, fr. L. (acc.) *armaturam*, fr. *armatus*, armed, fr. *armare*, to arm.]

ARMOURER (ár'mur-er) *n.* a person that makes or sells arms.

ARMOURY (ár'mur-i) *n.* a repository of arms.

ARMPIT (árm'pit) *n.* the hollow under the shoulder.

ARMS (ármz) *n.pl.* weapons; ensigns armorial.

ARMY (ár'mi) *n.* a large body of armed men; great number. [O.F. *armée*, fr. fem. part. *armata* armed.]

AROMA (ạ-rō'mạ) *n.* the fragrant quality of plants or other substances. [G.]

AROMATIC (ar-ō-mat'ik) *a.* spicy; fragrant.

AROMATICS (ar-ō-mat'iks) *n.pl.* fragrant spices or perfumes.

AROMATISE (ạ-rō'mạ-tiz) *v.t.* to impregnate with sweet odours.

AROSE (ạ-rōz') *pret.* of ARISE.

AROUND (ạ-round') *prep.* and *ad.* in a circle; on every side. [O.E. *a*, on, and O.F. *roõnd* =F. *rond*; fr. L. *rotundus*, fr. *rota*, a wheel.]

AROUSE (ạ-rouz') *v.t.* to awaken suddenly; stir up; excite. [O.E. *a*, on, and Dan. *ruse*, rush.]

AROW (ạ-rō) *ad.* in a row; successively. O.E. *a*, on, and *raw*, line.]

ARQUEBUSE (ár'ke-bus) *n.* a hand gun. [F. *arquebuse*, fr. *harkibuse*, a form of Dutch *haakbus*.]

ARRACK (ár'ak) *n.* spirit made from the cocoa-nut, rice, or sugar-cane. [A. *araq*, juice.]

ARRAIGN (a-rān') v.t. to call to answer in court. [M.E. arainen, fr. O.F. areisnier, to cite, fr. Low L. arrationare, fr. L. ad, to, and (acc.) rationem, reason]

ARRAIGNMENT (a-rān'ment) n. act of arraigning, accusation.

ARRANGE (a-rānj') v.t. to set in order. [O.F. arengier, fr.à = L.ad, to, and rengier, to rank.]

ARRANGEMENT (a-rānj'ment) n. act of putting in order; adjustment.

ARRANT (ar'ant) a. infamous; bad. [= errant, fr. O.F. errer, fr. L. errare, to stray.]

ARRANTLY (ar'ant-li) ad. notoriously; infamously.

ARRAS (ar'as) n. hangings of tapestry. [Fr. place name Arras.]

ARRAY (a-rā') n. order of men for battle; a body of jurors; arrangement or dress for show;—v.t. to put in order; deck; summon a jury. [O.F. arrai = F. arroi, trappings; fr. L. ad, to, and O.E. geræde, preparation.]

ARREARS (a-rērz') n.pl. that which remains unpaid. [M.E. arere, fr. O.F. ariere = F. arrière; fr. L. ad, to, and retro, back.]

ARREST (a-rest') v.t. to seize by warrant; detain;—n. a seizure by legal warrant; stay of judgment after verdict. [O.F. arrester, to stop, fr. L. ad, to, and restare, to stand still.]

ARRESTATION (ar-es-tā'shun) n. act of arresting.

ARRESTMENT (a-rest'ment) n. seizure and detention of a criminal; seizure of wages, etc., in payment of debt.

ARRIVAL (a-rī'val) n. act of coming.

ARRIVE (a-rīv') v.i. to come to a place; reach. [O.F. ariver, fr. Low L. adripare, fr. ad, to, and (acc.), ripam, the shore.]

ARROGANCE (ar'ō-gans) n. insolence of bearing; haughtiness. [L. arrogatus, claimed, fr. ad, to, and rogare, to ask.]

ARROGANT (ar'ō-gant) a. haughty; proud; insolent.

ARROGANTLY (ar'ō-gant-li) ad. very proudly; haughtily.

ARROGATE (ar'ō-gāt) v.t. to claim unjustly; assume.

ARROGATION (ar-ō-gā'shun) n. act of assuming unjustly or proudly.

ARRONDISSEMENT (a-rong'dēs-mong) n. a district or division of a county in France. [F. arrondir, to make round; fr. L. ad, to, and rotundus, round.]

ARROW (ar'ō) n. a weapon for a bow. [O.E. arwe, M.E. arewe.]

ARROW-HEADED (a-rō-hed'ed) a. shaped like an arrow; said of alphabetical characters which compose the inscriptions found on the monuments at Babylon, Nineveh, etc. Also called **CUNEIFORM**. [O.E. arwe, arrow, and heafod, head.]

ARROWROOT (ar'ō-rōōt) n. a farinaceous substance obtained from the maranta and other roots. It is highly nutritive. [O.E. arwe, arrow, and wrotan, fr. wrot, a snout.]

ARROWY (ar'ō-i) a. shaped or moving like an arrow.

ARSENAL (ár'se-nal) n. a magazine of military stores. [Sp., fr. A.]

ARSENIATE (ár-sē'ni-āt) n. a salt formed by combining arsenic acid with a base.

ARSENIC (ár-sen'ik) n. a mineral poison. [G. fr. arsen, male.]

ARSENICAL (ár-sen'i-kal) a. pertaining to arsenic.

ARSON (ar'sun) n. the malicious burning of a house. [O.F., fr. L. arsus, burnt, fr. L. ardere, to burn.]

ART (árt) second person sing. pr. indic. of the verb BE. [E.]

ART (árt) n. practical skill; dexterity; cunning. [L. (acc.) artem, art.]

ARTERIAL (ár-tē'ri-al) a. belonging to an artery.

ARTERIALISE (ár-tē'ri-al-iz) v.t. to communicate the qualities of arterial blood.

ARTERY (ár'tē-ri) n. a vessel conveying blood from the heart. [L. arteria, the wind-pipe.]

ARTESIAN (ár-tē'zhan) a. denoting wells made by boring for water to a bed lower than the source or fountain. [F. Artésien, belonging to Artois.]

ARTFUL (árt'fool) a. skilful; cunning.

ARTFULLY (árt'fool-i) ad. cunningly; dexterously.

ARTFULNESS (árt'fool-nes) n. quality of being artful; sly, cunning.

ARTHRITIC (ár-thrit'ik) a. pertaining to the joints. [L. arthriticus.]

ARTHRITIS (ár-thrī'tis) n. the gout.

ARTICHOKE (ár'ti-chōk) n. a garden vegetable. [O. It. articiocco.]

ARTICLE (ár'ti-kl) n. a distinct part or particular; item; a substance or commodity; a point of faith; a writing in a periodical; a part of speech;—v.t. to draw up in particulars; bind by agreement;—v.i. to stipulate. [L. articulus, a little joint.]

ARTICULAR (ár-tik'ū-lar) a. belonging to articles or joints.

ARTICULATE (ár-tik'ū-lāt) a. having joints; —v.t. and i. to joint; to pronounce words distinctly. [L. articulatus, jointed.]

ARTICULATION (ár-tik-ū-lā'shun) n. connection by joints; distinct utterance.

ARTIFICE (ár'ti-fis) n. artful contrivance; device; finesse; fraud. [L. artificium, a trade, fr. L. ars, art, and facere, to make]

ARTIFICER (ár-tif'i-ser) n. a skilful worker in some art.

ARTIFICIAL (ár-ti-fish'al) a. made by art; not natural.

ARTIFICIALITY (ár-ti-fish-i-al'i-ti) n. quality of being artificial. Also **ARTIFICIALNESS**.

ARTIFICIALLY (ár-ti-fish'al-i) ad. by art.

ARTILLERIST (ár-til'e-rist) n. one skilled in gunnery.

ARTILLERY (ár-til'e-ri) n. weapons for war; ordnance; troops who manage cannons. [F. artillerie, fr. O.F. artiller, to equip.]

ARTISAN (ár'ti-zan) n. a mechanic. [F. fr. It. artigiano, fr. L. artitus, skilled in the arts.]

ARTIST (ár'tist) n. the professor of an art. [F. artiste.]

ARTISTE (ár-tēst') n. one skilled in any art. [F.]

ARTISTIC (ár-tis'tik) a. conforming to art; pertaining to an artist.

ARTISTICALLY (ár-tis'tik-al-li) ad. in the manner of an artist.

ARTLESS (árt-les) a. without art; simple.

ARTLESSNESS (árt'les-nes) n. want of art.

ARYAN (ár'i-an) n. an Indo-European;—a. belonging to the race of Hindus and Persians in the East; Celts, Greeks, Romans, Teutons, and Slavs, in the West; and to their languages. [Fr. Aria, the Latin form of the ancient name of E. Persia.]

AS (az) ad. even; in like manner;—conj. since;—pron. that. [M.E. as, als, alse.]

ASAFŒTIDA (as-a-fet'i-da) n. a fetid gumlike resin. [Per. asa, name of a gum, and L. fœtidus, stinking.]

ASBESTOS (as-bes'tos) n. a mineral which is fibrous and incombustible. [G. a, not, and sbestos, to be quenched, fr. sbennumi, quench.]

ASCEND (a-send') v.t. or i. to move upwards; rise. [L. ascendere, fr. ad, to, and scandere, to climb.]

ASCENDANT (a-sen'dant) a. superior;—n. superior influence; height.

ASCENDENCY (a-sen'den-si) n. superior influence; authority.

ASCENSION (a-sen'shun) n. the act of ascending.

ASCENT (a-sent') n. an eminence; rise; acclivity.

ASCERTAIN (as-er-tān') v.t. to make certain; establish. [O.F. acertainer, fr. L. ad, to, and certus, fr. cernere, to decide.]

ASCERTAINABLE (as-er-tā'na-bl) a. to be certainly known.

ASCERTAINMENT (as-er-tān'ment) n. a gaining of certainty.

ASCETIC (a-set'ik) n. a devout recluse; a hermit;—a. austere; severe. [G. asketes, one who exercises the body, fr. askein, to work.]

ASCETICISM (a-set'i-sizm) n. the practice of ascetics.

ASCRIBABLE (as-krī'ba-bl) a. that may be attributed.

ASCRIBE (as-krīb') v.t. to attribute; impute. [L. adscribere, fr. ad, to, and scribere, to write.]

ASCRIPTION (as-krip'shun) n. the act of ascribing; the thing ascribed.

ASEPTIC (a-sep'tik) a. not liable to putrefaction. [G. a, not, and septikos, putrefying.]

ASH (ash) n. a well-known tree. [O.E. œsce, M.E. asch.]

ASHAMED (a-shāmd') a. covered with shame. [O.E. a, much, and scamu, modesty.]

ASHAMEDLY (a-shām'ed-li) ad. bashfully.

ASHEN (ash'en) a. made of ash wood.

ASHES (ash'ez) n.pl. the remains of what is burnt; figuratively, a dead body. [O.E. œsce, M.E. asche.]

ASHLAR (ash'lar) n. freestones as they come from the quarry; hewn stones used in facing. [O.F. aiseler, fr. aiselle, fr. L. axilla, a little board, fr. axis, a board.]

ASHORE (a-shōr) ad. at or on shore. [O.E. a, on, and score, shore.]

ASHY (ash'i) a. ash-coloured; like ashes.

ASIATIC (ā-shi-at'ik) a. pertaining to Asia.

ASIDE (a-sīd') ad. on one side;—n. something done aside. [O.E. a, on, and SIDE. Cf. Ger. seite.]

ASININE (as'-nīn) a. pertaining to an ass; stupid [L. asinus, ass-like.]

ASK (ásk) v.t. or i. to make request; question; invite; demand. [O.E. askian, M.E. asken].

ASKANCE (a-skans') ad. towards one corner of the eye; sideways. [Etym. unknown.]

ASKEW (a-skū') ad. obliquely; awry; out of the regular way. [Scand. on the skew, awry.]

ASLANT (a-slant') ad. obliquely; on one side. [Scand.]

ASLEEP (a-slēp') Ud. in a sleeping state [O.E. a, on, and slœpan, to sleep.]

ASP (asp) n. a poisonous serpent. [G. aspis.]

ASPARAGUS (as-par'a-gus) n. a garden plant. [L., fr. G. asparagos.]

ASPECT (as'pekt) n. look; air; appearance. [L. aspectus, appearance, fr. aspectus, seen, fr. ad, to, and specere, to look.]

ASPEN (as'pen) n. a tree; the poplar. [O.E. œspe.]

ASPERITY (as-per'i-ti) n. roughness; harshness; moroseness.

ASPERSE (as-pers') v.t. to attack with slander; defame. [L. aspersus, bespattered, fr. L. ad, to, and spergere, to sprinkle.]

ASPERSER (as-pers'er) n. one who vilifies.

ASPERSION (as-per'shun) n. a sprinkling; calumny; slander.

ASPHALT (as'falt) n. a bituminous substance. [G. asphaltos.]

ASPHALTIC (as-falt'ik) a. bituminous.

ASPHYXIA (as-fik'si-a) n. a fainting; suspended animation. [G. a, not, and sphuxis, pulse.]

ASPIC (as'pik) n. the asp. [See ASP.]

ASPIRANT (as-pīr'ant) n. one who aspires;—a. ambitious.

ASPIRATION (as-pi-rā'shun) n. a breathing after; an ardent wish; an aspirated sound.

ASPIRATE (as'pi-rāt) n. a letter which is aspirated;—v.t. to pronounce with full breath. [L. ad, to, and spirare, to breathe.]

ASPIRATORY (as-pīr'a-tur-i) a. pertaining to breathing; inhaling air freely.

ASPIRE (as-pīr') v.i. to desire eagerly. [L. ad, to, and spirare, to breathe.]

ASPIRER (as-pīr'er) n. one who aspires.

ASPIRING (as-pīr'ing) a. aiming at something great.

ASQUINT (a-skwint') ad. and a. obliquely. [E.]

ASS (as) n. an animal of burden; a stupid fellow. [O.E. assa, fr. older Teut. esol; L. asinus, G. anos.]

ASSAIL (a-sāl') v.t. to assault; attack. [O.F. asaillir, fr. L. ad, to, and salire, to leap.]

ASSAILABLE (a-sāl'a-bl) a. that may be attacked or invaded.

ASSAILANT (a-sāl'ant) n. one who attacks.

ASSAILER (a-sāl'er) n. one who assails.

ASSASSIN (a-sas'in) n. one who kills by secret assault. [A., fr. hashish, an intoxicant.]

ASSASSINATE (a-sas'i-nāt) v.t. to murder by secret assault.

ASSASSINATION (a-sas-i-nā'shun) n. the act of assassinating.

ASSAULT (a-sawlt') n. violent attack; storm of a fort;—v.t. to attack with violence; storm. [L. ad, to, and saltus, a leap, fr. salire, to leap.]

ASSAULTER (a-sawl'ter) n. one who attacks violently.

ASSAY (a-sā') v.t. or i. to try; prove, as metals;—n. a trial; first effort. [O.F. essayer, to try. Doublet of ESSAY.]

ASSAYER (a-sā'er) n. one who tries metals.

ASSAYING (a-sā'ing) n. act or art of testing metals and alloys.

ASSEMBLAGE (a-sem'blāj) n. a collection of individuals. [F. assembler, fr. Late L. assimulare, to gather; fr. ad, to, and simul, together.]

ASSEMBLE (a-sem'bl) v.t. or i. to bring together; meet. [F. assembler, gather.]

ASSEMBLY (a-sem'bli) n. a company assembled; a legislature.

ASSENT (a-sent') v.i. to agree to as true or admissible;—n. the act of agreeing. [O.F. assentire, fr. L. ad, to, and sentire, to think.]

ASSENTER (a-sen'ter) n. one who assents.

ASSERT (a-sert) v.t. to affirm; maintain; claim. [L. assertus, declared free, fr. asserere, to declare positively.]

ASSERTION (a-ser'shun) n. act of asserting; declaration. [asserts.

ASSERTOR (a-ser'ter) n. one who affirms or ASSESS (a-ses') v.t. to fix the value of, for taxation; rate. [F., fr. L., fr. assessor, assistant; fr. assessus, seated near; fr. assidere, to sit.]

ASSESSABLE (a-ses'a-bl) a. that may be assessed.

ASSESSMENT (a-ses'ment) n. act of assessing; the sum assessed.

ASSESSOR (a-ses'er) n. one appointed to apportion taxes. [L.]

ASSETS (a'sets) n.pl. effects of a deceased or insolvent person. [O.F. asez (a-sets'), enough, fr. L. ad, to, and satis, enough.]

ASSEVERATE (a-sev'er-āt) v.t. to affirm solemnly. [L. asseveratus, firmly asserted, fr. ad, to, and severus, firm.]

ASSIDUITY (as-i-dū'i-ti) n. closeness of application; diligence. [L. assiduus, constantly near, fr. assidere. See ASSESS.]

ASSIDUOUS (a-sid'ū-us) a. constant in application; diligent.

ASSIDUOUSLY (a-sid'ū-us-li) ad. diligently; attentively.

ASSIGN (a-sīn') v.t. to mark out; appropriate; make over. [F. assigner, fr. L. assignare to allot; fr. ad, to, and signum, a sign.]

ASSIGNABLE (a-sī'na-bl) a. that may be transferred.

ASSIGNATION (as-ig-nā'shun) n. appointment to meet.

ASSIGNEE (as-ĭ-nē') *n.* one to whom something is assigned.

ASSIGNER (as-ī'nẽr) *n.* one who makes a transfer to another. Also **ASSIGNOR.**

ASSIGNMENT (a-sĭn'ment) *n.* a transfer of title or interest.

ASSIMILATE (a-sĭm'ĭ-lāt) *v.t.* or *i.* to make or become like. [L. *assimilatus,* likened.]

ASSIMILATION (as-sim-ĭ-lā'shun) *n.* the act of making similar. [L. (acc.) *assimilationem,* the act of assimilation.]

ASSIMILATIVE (a-sim'ĭ-lā-tiv) *a.* having power to assimilate.

ASSIST (a-sist') *v.t.* to help; succour; relieve; aid. [L. *assistere,* to stand by, fr. *ad,* to, and *sistere,* to stand.]

ASSISTANCE (a-sis'tans) *n.* help; aid; relief; succour.

ASSISTANT (a-sis'tant) *n.* one who assists;— *a.* helping. [F. (part.) *assistant,* helping.]

ASSISTER (a-sis'tẽr) *n.* one who assists.

ASSIZE (a-sīz') *n.* a court of justice;—*v.t.* to fix measures or rates by authority. [M.E. *assise,* fr. O.F. *assise,* a bench of justices; fr. L. *ad,* to, and *sidere,* to sit.]

ASSIZER (a-sī'zẽr) *n.* one who fixes weights and measures.

ASSOCIABLE (a-sō'shi-a-bl) *a.* that may be associated.

ASSOCIATE (a-sō'shi-āt) *v.t.* or *i.* to join in company; unite with;—*a.* joined in interest; —*n.* a companion; partner; partaker. [L. *associatus,* united, fr. *associare;* fr. *ad,* to, and *socius,* a companion.]

ASSOCIATION (a-sō-shi-ā'shun) *n.* act of joining persons or things; a society bound by mutual interest or to promote a common object.

ASSOCIATIONAL (a-sō-shi-ā'shun-al) *a.* pertaining to an association.

ASSOCIATIVE (a-sō'shi-a-tiv) *a.* capable of, or tending to, association.

ASSORT (a-sort') *v.t.* to arrange or distribute in classes. [O.F. *assorter,* fr. L. *ad,* to, and (acc.) *sortem,* lot.]

ASSORTMENT (a-sort'ment) *n.* a quantity selected or arranged.

ASSUAGE (a-swāj') *v.t.* to bring down or reduce, as pain; pacify; allay. [O.F. *asuager,* to pacify, fr. L. *ad,* to, and *suavis,* gentle.]

ASSUAGEMENT (a-swāj'ment) *n.* mitigation.

ASSUETUDE (as'wē-tūd) *n.* custom; habitual use. [L. *assuetus,* customary.]

ASSUME (a-sūm') *v.t.* to take; undertake; take for granted;—*v.i.* to be arrogant; claim unduly. [L. *ad,* to, and *sumere,* to take.]

ASSUMER (a-sūm'ẽr) *n.* an assuming or arrogant person.

ASSUMING (a-sūm'ing) *a.* arrogant; haughty; —*n.* presumption.

ASSUMPTION (a-sum'shun) *n.* act of assuming; supposition; postulate; taking up to heaven. [L. *assumptus,* taken to oneself.]

ASSURABLE (a-shōōr'a-bl) *a.* that may be assured.

ASSURANCE (a-shōōr'ans) *n.* certain expectation; confidence; want of modesty; security.

ASSURE (a-shōōr') *v.t.* to make sure or certain; give confidence; declare solemnly; insure. [O.F. *aseürer,* fr. L. *ad,* to, and *securus,* safe.]

ASSURED (a-shōōred') *a.* certain; confident.

ASSUREDLY (a-shōōr'ed-li) *ad.* certainly.

ASSUREDNESS (a-shōōr'ed-nes) *n.* certainty; full confidence.

ASSURER (a-shōōr'ẽr) *n.* one that assures.

ASSURINGLY (a-shōōr'ing-li) *ad.* in a way to give assurance or confidence.

ASTER (as'tẽr) *n.* a plant with radiated compound flowers. [G. *aster,* a star.]

ASTERISK (as'tẽ-risk) *n.* the mark (*) in printing. [G. *aster,* a star.]

ASTERISM (as'tẽ-rizm) *n.* a constellation of fixed stars; an asterisk.

ASTERN (a-stẽrn') *ad.* in the hinder part of a ship. [E.]

ASTEROID (as'tẽ-roid) *n.* a name of certain small planets. [G. *aster,* a star, and *eidos,* form.]

ASTHMA (ast'ma) *n.* shortness of breath. [G. *asthma,* panting.]

ASTHMATIC (ast-mat'ik) *a.* troubled with asthma.

ASTONISH (as-ton'ish) *v.t.* to amaze; surprise; confound. [O.F. *estoner,* fr. L. *extonare,* to thunder out.]

ASTONISHING (as-ton'ish-ing) *a.* wonderful.

ASTONISHMENT (as-ton'ish-ment) *n.* emotion created by a sudden or extraordinary event; amazement; wonder; surprise.

ASTOUND (as-tound') *v.t.* to strike with fear and wonder. [See ASTONISH.]

ASTRADDLE (a-strad'l) *ad.* with the legs across; astride. [E.]

ASTRAL (as'tral) *a.* belonging to the stars. [L. *astralis,* fr. *astrum,* fr. G. *astron,* a star.]

ASTRAY (a-strā') *ad.* and *a.* out of the right way. [E.]

ASTRIDE (a-strīd') *ad.* across; with legs apart.

ASTRINGENCY (as-trin'jen-si) *n.* the power of contracting. [L. (acc.) *astringentem,* fr. *ad,* to, and *stringere,* to bind.]

ASTRINGENT (as-trin'jent) *a.* binding;—*n.* a medicine which binds.

ASTROLOGER (as-trol'ō-jẽr) *n.* one who foretells events by the stars. [G. *astrologia,* fr. *astron,* star, and *logos,* discourse.]

ASTROLOGICAL (as-trō-loj'ik-al) *a.* relating to astrology.

ASTROLOGY (as-trol'o-ji) *n.* the art of predicting events by the aspects of the stars.

ASTRONOMER (as-tron'ō-mẽr) *n.* one skilled in astronomy.

ASTRONOMICAL (as-trō-nom'i-kal) *a.* belonging to astronomy.

ASTRONOMY (as-tron'ō-mi) *n.* the science of the heavenly bodies. [G. *astron,* star and *nomos,* law.]

ASTUTE (as-tūt') *a.* shrewd; sagacious; discerning. [L. (acc.) *astutum,* crafty, fr. *astus,* guile.]

ASTUTELY (as-tūt'li) *a.* shrewdly; sharply.

ASTUTENESS (as-tūt'nes) *n.* shrewdness; cunning.

ASUNDER (a-sun'dẽr) *ad.* apart. [O.E. *a,* on, and *sundor,* apart, fr. *syndrian,* to separate.]

ASYLUM (a-sī'lum) *n.* a refuge; sanctuary; a charitable institution. [L., fr. G. *asulon.*]

ATE (āt) *pret.* of EAT.

ATHEISM (ā'the-izm) *n.* disbelief in the existence of a God. [G. *a,* not, and *theos,* god.]

ATHEIST (ā'thē-ist) *n.* one who denies the existence of a God.

ATHEISTICAL (ā-thē-is-ti'kal) *a.* denying a God; impious.

ATHIRST (a-thẽrst') *a.* thirsty; having a keen desire for. [O.E. *a,* very, and *thyrstan,* to thirst.]

ATHLETE (ath'lēt) *n.* a contender for victory in feats of strength. [L., fr. G. *athletes,* a contestant for a prize, *Athlon.*]

ATHLETIC (ath-let'ik) *a.* belonging to trials of strength; strong; vigorous.

ATHWART (a-thwawrt') *ad.* and *prep.* across. [E.]

ATLANTIC (at-lan'tik) *n.* the ocean between Europe and America. [Fr. Mount *Atlas.*]

ATLAS (at'las) *n.* a collection of maps. [G. *atlas.* See ATLANTIC.]

ATMOSPHERE (at'mos-fẽr) *n.* the air that surrounds the earth. [G. *atmos,* air, and *sphaira,* a sphere.]

ATMOSPHERIC (at'mos-fẽr'ik) *a.* belonging to the atmosphere.

ATOLL (at'ol) *n.* a coral island, or a ring of coral surrounding a lagoon. [A Malayan word.]

ATOM (at'um.) *n.* a minute particle. [G. *atomos*, fr. *a*, not, and *tomos*, section, fr. *temnein*, to cut.]

ATOMISE (at'um-īz) *v.t.* to reduce to atoms.

ATOMIC (ạ-tom'ik) *a.* relating to atoms.

ATOMISM (at'um-izm) *n.* the doctrine of atoms.

ATONE (ạ-tōn') *v.i.* to expiate; make satisfaction for;—*v.t.* to reconcile. [E. =*at one.*]

ATONEMENT (ạ-tōn'ment) *n.* satisfaction; expiation for sin.

ATROCIOUS (ạ-trō'shus) *a.* wicked in a high degree; enormous. [L. *atrox, atrocis*, fierce.]

ATROCIOUSLY (ạ-trō'shus-li) *ad.* outrageously.

ATROCITY (ạ-tros'i-ti) *n.* horrible wickedness; any cruel act.

ATROPHY (at'rō-fi) *n.* a wasting away. [G. *atrophia*, fr. *a*, not, and *trophe*, nourishment.]

ATTACH (ạ-tach') *v.t.* to tie or fasten to; connect; take by legal authority; gain over; win;—*v.i.* to be joined or bound up with; belong to. [O.F. *attacher*, fr. L. *ad*, to, and *tache*, a nail.]

ATTACHABLE (ạ-tach'ạ-bl) *a.* that may be taken by attachment.

ATTACHMENT (ạ-tach'ment) *n.* the taking of a person by legal process in a civil suit; affection; fidelity; that which attaches.

ATTACK (ạ-tak') *v.t.* to assault;—*v.i* to make an attack;—*n.* an assault; onset; seizure by disease. [F. *attaquer*, fr. It. *attaccare*.]

ATTAIN (ạ-tān') *v.i.* to reach by efforts; arrive at;—*v.t.* to achieve or gain. [O.F. part. *ateignant*, reaching, fr. *ateindre*; fr. L. *attingere*, fr. *ad*, to, and *tangere*, to touch.]

ATTAINABLE (ạ-tā'nạ-bl) *a.* that may be attained.

ATTAINABLENESS (ạ-tā'nạ-bl-nes) *n.* the state of being attainable.

ATTAINDER (ạ-tān'der) *n.* the act of attainting in law. [O.F. infin. *ateindre*. See ATTAIN.]

ATTAINMENT (ạ-tān'ment) *n.* act of attaining; thing attained. [See ATTAIN.]

ATTAINT (ạ-tānt') *v.t.* to corrupt; find guilty of treason;—*n.* a stain; spot. [M.E. *ateynt*, O.F. *ateint*, convicted.]

ATTAR (at'ạr) *n.* a perfume made from flowers, specifically in Turkey from the cabbage rose. [A.]

ATTEMPT (ạ-temt') *n.* a trial; effort;—*v.t.* to try; endeavour; essay. [O.F. *attempter*, fr. L. *ad*, to, and *tentare*, to handle, fr. *tendere*, to stretch.]

ATTEND (ạ-tend') *v.t.* to accompany; wait on; be present at;—*v.i.* to regard with attention; heed; listen. [L. *ad*, towards, and *tendere*, to stretch.] [waiting.

ATTENDANCE (ạ-ten'dạns) *n.* the act of

ATTENDANT (ạ-ten'dạnt) *a.* accompanying; —*n.* one that attends or accompanies.

ATTENT (ạ-tent') *a.* attentive; listening. [L. *attentus*, stretched towards.]

ATTENTION (ạ-ten'shun) *n.* act of attending or heeding; civility. [See ATTENT.]

ATTENTIVE (ạ-ten'tiv) *a.* heedful; regardful.

ATTENTIVELY (ạ-ten'tiv-li) *ad.* carefully.

ATTENUANT (ạl-ten'ū-ạnt) *a.* making less viscid; thinning;—*n.* a medicine to thin the blood.

ATTENUATE (at-ten'ū-āt) *v.t.* to thin. [L. part. *attenuatus*, made thin; fr. *ad*, to, and *tenuis*, thin.]

ATTENUATION (ạ-ten-ū-ā'shun) *n.* a making thin or slender.

ATTEST (ạ-test') *v.t.* to bear witness. [L. *attestari*, to witness to, fr. *ad*, to, and *testis*, a witness.]

ATTESTATION (at-es-tā'shun) *n.* official testimony.

ATTIC (at'ik) *a.* pertaining to Attica; pure, classical;—*n.* the upper story. [So called because its construction suggested *attic* architecture. G. *Attikos*, Athenian.]

ATTIRE (ạ-tir') *v.t.* to dress;—*n.* clothes; apparel. [O.F. *atirer*, to arrange, fr. *à* = L. *ad*, to, and *tire*, row.]

ATTITUDE (at'i-tūd) *n.* posture of a person; position of things. [F., fr. It., r. L. (acc.) *attitudinem*. See APTITUDE.]

ATTORNEY (ạ-ter'ni) *n.* he who acts for another;—*pl.* ATTORNEYS.

ATTORNMENT (at-tern'ment) *n.* act of a feudal vassal in transferring his service to the new lord or purchaser of the estate.

ATTRACT (ạ-trakt') *v.t.* to draw to; allure; —*v.i.* to be attractive. [L. *attractus*, drawn, fr. *ad*, to, and *trahere*, to draw.]

ATTRACTABILITY (ạ-trak-tạ-bil'i-ti) *n.* quality of being attractable, or being subject to the laws of attraction.

ATTRACTABLE (ạ-trak'tạ-bl) *a.* that may be attracted.

ATTRACTING (ạ-trak'ting) *a.* adapted to allure.

ATTRACTION (ạ-trak'shun) *n.* act or power of attracting; allurement.

ATTRACTIVE (ạ-trak'tiv) *a.* alluring; inviting;—*n.* what draws.

ATTRACTIVENESS (ạ-trak'tiv-nes) *n.* the quality which draws.

ATTRIBUTABLE (ạ-trib'ū-tạ-bl) *a.* that may be ascribed.

ATTRIBUTE (at'ri-būt) *n.* quality, disposition, or characteristic ascribed to a person; a symbol of office;—(ạ-trib'ūt) *v.t.* to ascribe; impute. [L. *attributus*, associated to, fr. *ad*, to, and *tribuere*, to bestow.]

ATTRIBUTION (at-ri-bū'shun) *n.* the act of attributing.

ATTRIBUTIVE (ạ-trib'ū-tiv) *a.* relating to an attribute;—*n.* a word which denotes quality.

ATTRITE (ạ-trit') *a.* worn by rubbing. [L. *ad*, to, and It. *trito*, fr. L. *tritus*, fr. *terere*, to rub.]

ATTRITION (ạ-trish'un) *n.* the act of wearing or rubbing down.

ATTUNE (ạ-tūn') *v.t.* to put in tune. [L. *ad*, towards, and O.E. *tun*, fr. L. *tonus*, fr. G. *tonos*, tone.]

ATYPIC (ạ-tip'ik) *a.* having no type; irregular. [G. *a*, not, and F., fr. L. *typus*, fr. G. *tupos*, fr. *tuptein*, to strike.]

AUBURN (aw'burn) *a.* reddish brown. [O.F. *alborne*, fr. Low L. *alburnus*, blond.]

AUCTION (awk'shun) *n.* a public sale to the highest bidder. [L. (acc.) *auctionem*, increase, fr. *auctus*, increased, fr. *augere*, to increase.]

AUCTIONEER (awk'shun-ēr) *n.* manager of an auction;—*v.t.* or *i.* to sell by auction.

AUDACIOUS (aw-dā'shus) *a.* bold; impudent. [F. *audacieux*, fr. L. stem, *audaci-*, of *audax*, daring.]

AUDACIOUSLY (aw-dā'shus-li) *ad.* impudently.

AUDACITY (aw-das'i-ti) *n.* boldness; daring spirit.

AUDIBLE (aw'di-bl) *a.* that may be heard. [L., fr. *audire*, to hear.]

AUDIBLY (aw'di-bli) *ad.* in a manner to be heard.

AUDIENCE (aw'di-ens) *n.* a hearing; assembly of hearers.

AUDIPHONE (aw'di-fōn) *n.* an instrument to improve the hearing. [L. *audire*, to hear, and G. *phone*, sound.]

AUDIT (aw'dit) *n.* an examination of accounts under authority;—*v.t.* to adjust accounts by persons authorised. [L. *auditus*, hearing.]

AUDITIVE (aw'di-tiv) *a.* having the power of hearing.

AUDITOR (aw'di-ter) *n.* a hearer; an examiner of accounts.

AUDITORY (aw'di-tur-i) *n.* an assembly of hearers;—*a.* that has the power of hearing.

AUGEAN (aw-jē'an) *a.* denoting nuisances or abuses difficult to get rid of; arduous and toilsome. [Fr. *Augeas*, king of Elis.]

AUGER (aw'ger) *n.* a carpenter's tool to bore holes, chiefly in wood; also, an instrument for perforating soils or rocks. [*an auger,* for *a nauger,* fr. O.E. *navu,* nave, and *gar,* a dart.]

Auger.

AUGHT (awt) *n.* anything. [O.E. =*a whit.*]
AUGMENT (awg-ment') *v.t.* to increase;—*v.i.* to grow larger;—(awg'ment) *n.* an increase or state of increase; a prefix to a word. [L. *augmentare,* fr. *augere,* to increase.]
AUGMENTABLE (awg-men'ta-bl) *a.* capable of being increased.
AUGMENTATION (awg-men-tā'shun) *n.* the act of increasing; thing added.
AUGMENTATIVE (awg-men'ta-tiv) *a.* having the quality of augmenting.
AUGMENTER (awg-men'ter) *n.* one who increases.
AUGUR (aw'gur) *n.* a diviner by the flight of birds;—*v.t.* or *i.* to predict by signs or omens. [L., connected with *avis,* a bird.]
AUGURAL (aw'gū-ral) *a.* relating to augurs or augury.
AUGURY (aw'gū-ri) *n.* a prediction by omens; prognostication.
AUGUST (aw'gust) *n.* eighth month of the year. [L. fr. *Augustus* Cæsar.]
AUGUST (aw-gust') *a.* impressing reverence or awe; imposing; majestic. [L., fr. *augere,* to increase.]
AUGUSTAN (aw-gus'tan) *a.* marked by refined literary activity.
AUK (awk) *n.* an aquatic bird of several species. [Icel. *alka.*]
AULIC (aw'lik) *a.* pertaining to a royal court. [L. *aula,* fr. G. *aule,* a hall.]
AUNT (ant) *n.* a father or mother's sister. [O.F. *ante,* fr. L. (acc.) *amitam,* paternal aunt.]
AURAL (aw'ral) *a.* relating to the ear; pertaining to the air. [L. *auris,* the ear.]
AURATED (aw'rāt-ed) *a.* resembling or containing gold. [L. *aurum,* gold.]
AUREOLA (aw-rē'ō-la) *n.* a circle of rays. [L. *aureolus,* dim. of *aureus,* golden.]
AURICLE (aw'ri-kl) *n.* the external ear.
AURICULAR (aw-rik'ū-lar) *a.* pertaining to the ear or hearing; confided to the ear; obtained by hearing. [L. *auriculus,* dim. of *auris,* ear.]
AURICULATE (aw-rik'ū-lāt) *a.* shaped like an ear.
AURIFEROUS (aw-rif'e-rus) *a.* producing gold. [L. *aurum,* gold, and *-ferus,* bearing, fr. *fero,* to bear.]
AURIFORM (aw'ri-form) *a.* shaped like an ear. [L. *auris,* an ear, and *forma,* shape.]
AURIST (aw'rist) *n.* one skilled in disorders of the ear.
AURORA (aw-rō'ra) *n.* the dawning light. [L., fr. *Aurora,* the goddess of dawn.]
AURORA BOREALIS (aw-rō'ra-bō-rē-ā'lis) *n.* the northern lights. [L. *Aurora,* the goddess of dawn, and *borealis,* northern, fr. *Boreas,* the north wind.]
AUSPICE (aws'pis) *n.* omen; influence;—*pl.* **AUSPICES.** [L. fr. *auspex* =*avispex,* fr. *avis,* a bird, and root *spic,* of *specere,* look.]
AUSPICIOUS (aw-spish'us) *a.* having omens of success; propitious. [ously.]
AUSPICIOUSLY (aw-spish'us-li) *ad.* prosper-
AUSTERE (aws-tēr') *a.* severe; rigid. [G. *austeros,* sour.]
AUSTERELY (aws-tēr'li) *ad.* severely.
AUSTERITY (aws-ter'i-ti) *n.* severity; harsh discipline; rigour.
AUSTRAL (aws'tral) *a.* southern. [L. *australis,* fr. *auster,* the south wind.]
AUTHENTIC (aw-then'tik) *a.* genuine; of approved origin or authority. [L., fr. G. *authentikos,* warranted, fr. *authentes,* one who acts for himself.]

AUTHENTICALLY (aw-then'ti-kal-i) *ad.* with genuine proof or evidence.
AUTHENTICATE (aw-then'ti-kāt) *v.t.* to establish by proof.
AUTHENTICATION (aw-then-ti-kā'shun) *n.* the establishing by proof.
AUTHENTICITY (aw-then-tis'i-ti) *n.* genuineness; reality.
AUTHOR (aw'ther) *n.* he that produces anything; a writer. [L. *auctor,* fr. *augere,* to increase.]
AUTHORESS (aw'thur-es) *n.* a female author.
AUTHORISATION (aw-thur-i-zā'shun) *n.* establishment by authority.
AUTHORISE (aw'thur-iz) *v.t.* to give authority; establish by authority; make legal.
AUTHORITATIVE (aw-thor'i-tā-tiv) *a.* having or exercising authority; peremptory; dictatorial.
AUTHORITATIVELY (aw-thor'i-tā-tiv-li) *ad.* in an authoritative manner.
AUTHORITY (aw-thor'i-ti) *n.* legal power; warrant; rule. [L. *auctoritatem,* acc. of *auctoritas,* fr. *auctor,* fr. *augere,* to increase.]
AUTHORSHIP (aw-thur'ship) *n.* the state of being an author.
AUTOBIOGRAPHER (aw-tō-bī-og'ra-fer) *n.* one who relates his own history. [G. *auto,* for *autos,* self, *bios,* life, and *graphein,* to write.]
AUTOBIOGRAPHICAL (aw-tō-bī-ō-graf'i-kal) *a.* relating to autobiography.
AUTOBIOGRAPHY (aw-tō-bī-og'ra-fi) *n.* the writing of one's own life.
AUTOCAR (aw'tō-kar) *n.* a road vehicle, carrying its own motive power. [G. *autos,* self, and **CAR.**]
AUTOCRACY (aw-tok'ra-si) *n.* supreme independent power. [F. *autocratie,* fr. G. *autos,* self, and *kratein,* to rule.]
AUTOCRAT (aw'tō-krat) *n.* an absolute sovereign. [to autocracy.]
AUTOCRATIC (aw'tō-krat'ik) *a.* pertaining
AUTO DA FE (aw'tō-dä-fā) *n.* the punishment of a heretic by burning; also, the sentence then read.;—*pl.* **AUTOS DA FE.** [Pg., a judgment of faith.]
AUTOGRAPH (aw'tō-graf) *n.* a person's own handwriting. [G. *autos,* self, and *graphein,* to write.]
AUTOGRAPHIC (aw-tō-graf'ik) *a.* consisting in one's own handwriting.
AUTOMATIC (aw-tō-mat'ik) *a.* having independent motion; self-acting. [G. *autos,* self, and stem *mat-,* to move.]
AUTOMATICALLY (aw-tō-mat'i-ka-li) *ad.* independently; without other power than itself.
AUTOMATISM (aw-tom'a-tizm) *n.* automatic action; power of self-motion.
AUTOMATON (aw-tom'a-ton) *n.* a machine moved by invisible springs;—*pl.* **AUTOMATA.** [G. *automatos,* self-acting.]
AUTOMATOUS (aw-tom'a-tus) *a.* having power of self-motion.
AUTOMOBILE aw-tō-mo'bil) *a.* self-moving; —*n.* a motor-car. [G. *autos,* self, and L. *mobilis,* that may be moved.]
AUTONOMY (aw-ton'ō-mi) *n.* the power or right of self-government. [G. *autos,* self, and *nomos,* law.]
AUTUMN (aw'tum) *n.* the third season of the year. [L. *auctumnus,* the season of increase, fr. *auctus,* fr. *augere,* to increase.]
AUTUMNAL (aw-tum'nal) *a.* of or belonging to autumn.
AUXILIARIES (awg-zil'ya-riz) *n.pl.* troops assisting another nation.
AUXILIARY (awg-zil'ya-ri) *a.* helping; assisting;—*n.* a helper. [L. *auxiliarius,* helping.]
AVAIL (a-vāl') *v.t.* or *i.* to be of use or value; profit; assist; benefit;—*n.* advantage, profit. [O.F. *à,* and *valoir,* to be of value; fr. L. *ad,* to, and *valere,* to be strong.]

AVAILABILITY (ạ-vā-lạ-bil′i-ti) *n.* quality of being available.

AVAILABLE (ạ-vā′lạ-bl) *a.* able to be used to advantage.

AVAILABLY (ạ-vā′lạ-bli) *ad.* so that it may be used to advantage.

AVAILS (a-vālz′) *n.pl.* proceeds of property sold.

AVALANCHE (av′ạ-lansh) *n.* a large body of ice or snow sliding down a mountain. [F., fr. O.F. *à val*, into the valley; fr. L. *ad*, to, and (acc.) *vallem*, the valley.]

AVARICE (av′ạ-ris) *n.* excessive love of gain. [F., fr. L. (acc.) *avaritiam*, greediness.]

AVARICIOUS (av-ạ-rish′us) *a.* greedy of wealth.

AVAST (ạ-vast′) *inter.* cease; hold; stop. [D. *houd vast*, hold fast.]

AVATAR (av′ạ-tår) *n.* the visible appearance of a deity on earth. [Sanskrit.]

AVAUNT (ạ-vawnt′) *inter.* get away; begone. [F., for *en avant* forward.]

AVE-MARY (ā′vē-mā′ri) *n.* a prayer to the Virgin Mary. [L. *imper.* = *hail*, and *Maria*, Mary.]

AVENAGE (av-e′nǎj) *n.* amount of grain paid to a landlord in lieu of rent. [L. *avena*, oats.]

AVENGE (ạ-venj′) *v.t.* to take just satisfaction; punish. [O.F. *avengier*, fr. L. *ad*, to, and *vindicare*, to vindicate.]

AVENGEFUL (ạ-venj′fōōl) *a.* revengeful.

AVENGER (ạ-ven′jer) *n.* one who avenges.

AVENUE (av′e-nū) *n.* an entrance; way; side street. [F. (part.) *avenu*.]

AVER (ạ-ver′) *v.t.* to declare positively. [F., fr. Low L. *averare*, to affirm, fr. *ad*, to, and *verus*, true.]

AVERAGE (av′e-rāj) *n.* a mean proportion; medium; — *a.* relating to a mean; — *v.t.* or *i.* to reduce to a mean. [Fr. F. *avarie*, loss from sea-damaged freight, hence the proportion borne by each owner; connected with O.F. *aver* = F. *avoir*, possessions, fr. L. *habere*, to have.]

AVERMENT (ạ-ver′ment) *n.* positive assertion.

AVERSE (ạ-vers′) *a.* disinclined; unwilling; reluctant. [L. part. *aversus*, turned away.]

AVERSION (ạ-ver′shun) *n.* hatred; dislike; the cause of aversion.

AVERT (ạ-vert′) *v.t.* to turn away, from, off, or aside. [L. *avertere*, to turn away, fr. *ab*, away, and *vertere*, to turn.]

AVIARY (ā′vi-ạ-ri) *n.* a place for keeping birds. [L. *aviarium*, fr. *avis*, a bird.]

AVIATION (ā-vi-ā′shun) *n.* the art of air navigation. [L. *avis*, a bird.]

AVIATOR (ā-vi-ā′ter) *n.* one who devotes himself to the art of aviation.

AVIDIOUS (ạ-vid′i-us) *a.* greedy; eager. [L. *avidus*, greedy.]

AVIDITY (ạ-vid′i-ti) *n.* greediness; eagerness; intense desire. [L. *aviditas*, greed.]

AVOCATION (av-ō-kā′shun) *n.* business that calls away; occupation. [L. *ad*, to, and *vocare*, to call.]

AVOCATIVE (ạ-vok′ạ-tiv) *a.* calling off; dissuasive.

AVOID (ạ-void′) *v.t.* or *i.* to keep at a distance from; shun; make or become void. [O.F. *cs* = L. *ex*, and *vuide*, *voide*, empty, fr. L. *viduus*, deprived.]

AVOIDABLE (ạ-voi′dạ-bl) *a.* that may be avoided.

AVOIDANCE (ạ-voi′dạns) *n.* the act of avoiding or shunning.

AVOIDLESS (ạ-void′les) *a.* inevitable.

AVOIRDUPOIS (av-ur-dū-polz′) *n.* a weight of sixteen ounces to the pound. [F. *avoir de pois*, to have (goods) of weight, fr. L. *habere*, to have, and *pensum*, weighed.]

AVOUCH (ạ-vouch′) *v.t.* to affirm; declare; maintain. [O.F. *avochier*, fr. L. *ad*, to, and *vocare*, to call.]

AVOUCHABLE (ạ-vouch′ạ-bl) *a.* that may be avouched.

AVOUCHER (ạ-vouch′er) *n.* one who avouches.

AVOUCHMENT (ạ-vouch′ment) *n.* act of avouching.

AVOW (ạ-vow′) *v.t.* to declare en : own and justify. [F. *avouer*, fr. Lọwdvọcare, fr. L. *ad*, to, and *vocare*, to call.]

AVOWABLE (ạ-vou′ạ-bl) *a.* capable of being justified.

AVOWAL (ạ-vou′ạl) *n.* a frank declaration.

AVOWANT (ạ-vou′ạnt) *n.* the defendant who avows and justifies an action of distress of goods.

AVOWEDLY (ạ-vou′ed-li) *ad.* in an open manner.

AVOWER (ạ-vou′er) *n.* one who avows.

AVOWRY (ạ-vou′ri) *n.* act of justifying a distress of goods by avowing that the distrainer took them in his own right.

AVULSION (ạ-vul′shun) *n.* act of tearing and pulling away. [L. *avellere*, *avulsum*, to tear away.]

AVUNCULAR (ạ-vung′kū-lạr) *c.* of or through an uncle. [L. *avunculus*, maternal uncle.]

AWAIT (ạ-wāt′) *v.t.* to wait for. [O.F. *a* = L. *ad*, to, and *awaiter*, fr. *waite*, a watchman, fr. O. H. Ger. *Wahta*, a watchman.]

AWAKE (ạ-wāk′) *a.* not sleeping; — *v.t.* or *i.* [*pret.* AWAKED or AWOKE] to rouse from sleep; cease to sleep. [O.E. *a-wœcncn*.]

AWAKEN (ạ-wā′kn) *v.t.* or *i.* to awake.

AWAKENING (ạ-wā′kn-ing) *n.* a rousing from sleep.

AWARD (a-wawrd′) *v.t.* to adjudge; — *n.* a judgment; a sentence. [O.F., fr. *es* = L. *ex*, and O. Ger. *warten*, to inspect.]

AWARE (ạ-wār′) *a.* foreseeing; watchful; apprised. [O.E. *gewœr*, conscious.]

AWAY (ạ-wā′) *ad.* at a distance; absent. [O.E. *a*, on, and *weg*, way.]

AWE (aw) *n.* reverential fear; — *v.t.* to strike with fear or reverence. [Scand.]

AWEARY (ạ-wē′ri) *a.* weary; tired. [O.E. *a*, on, and *werig*, tired.]

AWFUL (aw′fool) *a.* striking awe.

AWFULNESS (aw′fool-nes) *n.* the quality of striking with awe.

AWHILE (ạ-hwil′) *ad.* for some time. [O.E. *a*, on, and *hwil*, pause.]

AWKWARD (awk′wạrd) *a.* clumsy; unhandy; inelegant. [M.E. *auk*, wrong.]

AWKWARDNESS (awk′wạrd-nes) *n.* ungracefulness; clumsiness.

AWL (awl) *n.* a tool for piercing holes. [O.E. *awel*.]

AWNING (aw′ning) *n.* a covering from the sun or weather.

AWRY (ạ-ri′) *a.* or *ad.* obliquely; unevenly; aside; crooked; perverse. [O.E. *a*, on, and *wrigian*, to twist.]

AXE (aks) *n.* a cutting tool. [O.E. *œx.*]

AXIAL (ak′si-ạl) *a.* pertaining to an axis. [See **AXIS**.]

AXIOM (ak′si-um) *n.* a self-evident proposition or truth. [G. *axioma*, fr. *axioein*, to think worthy.]

AXIOMATIC (ak-si-ō-mat′ik) *a.* of the nature of an axiom.

AXIS (ak′sis) *n.* the line on which a thing revolves; — *pl.* AXES. [L. = an axle.]

AXLE (ak′sl) *n.* a shaft on which carriage wheels turn. [O.E. *eaxl*, connected with *axis*.]

AZALEA (ạ-zā′le-ạ) *n.* a shrub with richly-coloured flowers. [G.]

AZIMUTH (az′i-muth) *n.* an arc of the horizon between the meridian of a place and a vertical circle passing through the sun, moon, or stars. [A.]

AZOIC (ạ-zō′ik) *a.* destitute of organic life. [G. *a*, not, and *zoe*, life.]

AZURE (azh′ūr, ā′zhūr) *a.* blue; sky-coloured; *n.* a light blue; the sky.

Fāte, får, çdo; mē, her; mine; nōte; tūne; mŏŏn.

B

BAA (bà) *v.i.* to cry like a sheep;—*n.* the bleat of a sheep. [Imitative word.]
BABBLE (bab'l) *v.i.* to talk idly;—*n.* senseless prattle. [Imitative word.]
BABBLER (bab'ler) *n.* an idle talker.
BABBLING (bab'ling) *n.* foolish talk. Also **BABBLEMENT** .
BABE (bāb) *n.* an infant; a girl's doll. [M.E. *bab*, perh. fr. **BABBLE**.]
BABEL (bā'bel) *n.* confusion of sounds; disorder; tumult. [H. See Gen. xi.]
BABOON (ba-bòòn') *n.* a large monkey. [F. *babouin*, fr. *babine*, hanging lip in certain animals.]
BABY (bā'bi) *n.* an infant; a girl's doll. [See **BABE**.]
BABY-FARMING (bā-bi-farm'ing) *n.* the trade of rearing infants away from their parents, often insufficiently. [**BABY**, and O.E. *feorm*, M.E. *ferme*, goods or entertainment, fr. L. *firma*, a fixed payment.]
BABYISH (bā'bi-ish) *a.* like a babe; childish.
BACCHANALIAN (bak-a-nā'li-an) *a.* revelling in intemperance. [L. *Bacchus*, the god of revelry.]
BACHELOR (bach'e-ler) *n.* an unmarried man; one who takes his first degree in any profession. [O.F. *bacheler*, fr. Low L. *baccalarius*, a small farmer.]
BACHELOR'S BUTTONS (bach'e-lurz-but'ns) *n.pl.* a species of ranunculus.
BACHELORSHIP (bach'e-lur-ship) *n.* state of being a bachelor.
BACK (bak) *n.* the hinder part in man and the upper part in beasts; the rear;—*ad.* backward;—*v.t.* to mount a horse; support. [O.E. *bæc*.]
BACKBITE (bak'bīt) *v.t.* to slander an absent person.
BACKBITER (bak'bī-ter) *n.* one who slanders the absent. [tion.
BACKBITING (bak'bī-ting) *n.* secret detrac-
BACKBONE (bak'bōn) *n.* the bone of the back.
BACKDOOR (bak'dōr) *n.* a door behind a house. [O.E. *bæc*, and *duru*. Cf. Ger. *Thor*, a door.]
BACKGROUND (bak'ground) *n.* ground behind; a place of obscurity or shade.
BACKING (bak'ing) *n.* putting or going back; mounting; endorsing; supporting.
BACKSHEESH (bak'shesh) *n.* a gift or gratuity; drink money. [A.] [tise.
BACKSLIDE (bak'slid) *v.i.* to fall off; aposta-
BACKSLIDER (bak-slī'der) *n.* an apostate.
BACKSLIDING (bak-slī'ding) *n.* a falling back or away.
BACKSTAIRS (bak'stārs) *n.* private stairs in the back of a house;—*a.* indirect; underhand. [O.E. *bæc*, back, and *stæger*, a stair, fr. *stigan*, to climb.]
BACKWARD (bak'werd) *a.* unwilling; slow.
BACKWARDLY (bak'werd-li) *ad.* unwillingly.
BACKWARDNESS (bak'werd-nes) *n.* a want of will; dullness.
BACKWOODSMAN (bak-woodz'man) *n.* an inhabitant of the western frontier.
BACON (bā'kun) *n.* hog's flesh cured with salt and dried. [O.F., fr. Low L. (acc.) *baconem*, fr. Teut.]
BAD (bad) *a.* ill; wicked; hurtful. [M.E. *badde*, fr. O.E. *bœdling*, a womanish fellow.]
BADE (bad) past tense of **BID**.
BADGE (baj) *n.* a mark of distinction;—*v.t.* to mark with a badge. [M.E. *bage*, fr. Low L. *bagia*, fr. Low L. *baga* = F. *bague*, ring, fr. L. *bacca*, a berry or chain link.]
BADGER (baj'er) *n.* a quadruped;—*v.t.* to tease; to worry. [Fr. **BADGE**, which ,see.]
BADINAGE (bad-i-nāj') *n.* playful discourse. [F., fr. *badin*, frivolous.]

BADLY (bad'li) *ad.* in a bad manner; poorly.
BADNESS (bad'nes) *n.* the state of being bad, evil, or wicked.
BAFFLE (baf'l) *v.t.* to elude or defeat by artifice; frustrate. [Fr. Scot. *baffull*, abuse, fr. Scand.]
BAG (bag) *n.* a sack; pouch; purse;—*v.t.* to put into a bag;—*v.i.* to swell like a bag. [M.E. *bagge*, connected with **BULGE**.]
BAGATELLE (bag-a-tel') *n.* a thing of no importance; a kind of game. [F., fr. It.]
BAGGAGE (bag'āj) *n.* utensils of an army; clothing; lumber.
BAGGING (bag'ing) *n.* cloth for bags.
BAGNIO (ban'yō) *n.* a bathing-house; enclosure for slaves. [It. *bagno*, fr. L. *balneum*, a bath.]
BAGPIPE (bag'pip) *n.* a musical wind instrument. [**BAG**, and O.E. *pipe*.]
BAH (bà) *inter.* an exclamation of contempt or disgust.
BAIL (bāl) *n.* a surety for another's appearance; the security given;—*v.t.* to give security; set free on security; lave out water. [O.F. *bailler*, to keep secure, fr. L. *bajulare*, to bear a burden, fr. *bajulus*, a porter.]
BAILABLE (bā'la-bl) *a.* that may be bailed.
BAILBOND (bāl'hond) *n.* a bond given by a prisoner and his surety.
BAILER (bā'ler) *n.* one who delivers goods in trust.
BAILIE (bā'li) *n.* a Scotch magistrate. [O.F. *bailli*, a land-steward.]
BAILIFF (bā'lif) *n.* an executive officer; an under-steward. [O.F. *baillif*, a justice, fr. *bailler*. See **BAIL**.]
BAILMENT (bāl'ment) *n.* delivery of goods on trust.
BAIT (bāt) *v.t.* or *i.* to put on a hook so as to catch fish; provoke or harass; give or take food on a journey;—*n.* anything to allure; enticement; food; provender. [Icel. *beita*, to cause to bite.]
BAITING (bā'ting) *n.* food or refreshment on a journey.
BAIZE (bāz) *n.* a coarse woollen stuff. [O.F. *baies*, pl. of *baie*, at first a red brown cloth. See **BAY**.]
BAKE (bāk) *v.t.* or *i.* to heat or harden by heat. [O.E. *bacan*, M.E. *baken*.]
BAKEHOUSE (bāk'hous) *n.* a place for baking bread, cakes, etc.
BAKER (bā'ker) *n.* a person whose trade is to bake.
BAKERY (bā'ker-i) *n.* trade of a baker; a bakehouse.
BAKING (bā'king) *n.* drying by heat; quantity baked at once.
BAKSHISH (bak'shesh) *n.* a gratuity. [See **BACKSHEESH**.]
BALANCE (bal'ans) *n.* a pair of scales; the difference of accounts;—*v.t.* to make equal;—*v.i.* to hesitate. [F., fr. L. (acc.) *bilancem*, having two scales, fr. *bi*=*bis*, twice, and *lanx*,a platter.]

Letter Balance.

BALCONIED (bal'kō-nid) *a.* having balconies.
BALCONY (bal'kō-ni) *n.* a frame or gallery before a window. [It. *balcone*, originally a stage, fr. O. H. Ger. *Balcho*, a scaffold or beam.]
BALD (bawld) *a.* without hair; naked; mean; unadorned. [Celt.]
BALDERDASH (bal'der-dash) *n.* a jumble of words. [Scand.]
BALDLY (bawld'li) *ad.* meanly; inelegantly

BALDNESS (bawld'nes) *n.* want of hair; bareness or inelegance of style.

BALE (bāl) *n.* a pack of goods;—*v.t.* to put into or make up into bales. [F. *bale* = *balle*. See BALL.]

BALEFUL (bāl'fool) *a.* sorrowful; sad.

BALIZE (ba-lēz') *n.* a seamark.

BALK (bawk) *n.* a great rafter; a hindrance or disappointment;—*v.t.* to disappoint; to frustrate.

BALL (bawl) *n.* any round body; a bullet; an entertainment of dancing;—*v.i.* to form into a ball. [F. *balle*, fr. M. H. Ger. *Balle*.]

BALLAD (bal'ad) *n.* a little song. [F. *ballade*, a popular song.]

BALLAST (bal'ast) *n.* weight to steady a ship;—*v.t.* to load with ballast. [D.]

BALLOON (ba-lōōn') *n.* a bag or hollow vessel, made of silk or other light material, to be filled with gas. [F. *ballon*, fr. *balle*. See BALL.]

BALLOONIST (ba-lōō'nist) *n.* one who ascends in a balloon.

BALLOT (bal'ut) *n.* a ball or ticket used in voting;—*v.i.* to vote by ballot. [F. *ballotte*, a little ball, fr. *balle*. See BALL.]

BALLOTING (bal'ut-ing) *n.* the act of voting by ballot.

BALM (bám) *n.* an odoriferous plant; an ointment. [O.F. *bausme*, fr. L. *balsamum*. Doublet of BALSAM.]

BALMILY (bá'mi-li) *ad.* soothingly; fragrantly.

BALMY (bá'mi) *a.* sweet; fragrant.

BALSAM (bawl'sam) *n.* an aromatic substance flowing from trees; a species of plant. [See BALM.]

BALSAMIC (bawl-sam'ik, bal-sam'ik) *a.* healing; soft.

BALUSTER (bal'us-ter) *n.* a rail; a small pillar or column. [F. *balustre*, fr. L. *balaustium*, G. *balaustion*, the flower of the pomegranate, which it usually resembled in form.]

BALUSTRADE (bal'us-trād) *n.* a row of balusters or rails.

BAMBOO (bam-bōō') *n.* a plant of India. [Malay.]

BAMBOOZLE (bam-bōō'zl) *v.t.* to deceive.

BAN (ban) *n.* a public notice; interdict; curse;—*v.t.* to curse; execrate. [O.E. *gebann*, proclamation. Cf. O. Ger. *Bann*, a proclamation.]

BANAL (ban'al) *a.* commonplace; trite; stale. [F. = for public use, fr. *ban*. See BAN.]

BANANA (ba-ná'na) *n.* a plantain tree, and its fruit. [Sp.]

BANCO (bang'kō) *n.* a bench; a sitting of all the judges. [It. See BANK.]

BAND (band) *n.* anything that binds; a company;—*v.t.* to unite together. [O.E. *bindan*, to bind. Also F. *bande*, fr. Ger. *Bande*, a gang.]

BANDAGE (ban'dāj) *n.* a fillet.

BANDANA (ban-dan'a) *n.* a kind of silk handkerchief. [Hind.]

BANDBOX (band'boks) *n.* a light box for bands, ribbons, etc.

BANDEAU (ban-dō') *n.* headband or fillet. [F.]

BANDICOOT (ban'di-kōōt) *n.* a marsupial animal of Australia; a large rat in India. [Telegu.]

BANDIT (ban'dit) *n.* an outlaw; a robber; —*pl.* BANDITS, BANDITTI [It. (part.) *bandito*, fr. *bandire*, fr. Low L. *bandire*, to proclaim, fr. Ger. See BAN.]

BANDOG (ban'dog) *n.* a fierce dog.

BANDY (ban'di) *n.* a club for striking a ball; —*v.t.* or *i.* to beat about. [F. *bander*, to bend a bow.]

BANDYLEG (ban'di-leg) *n.* a crooked leg.

BANE (bān) *n.* poison; mischief; ruin. [O.E. *bana*, a murderer, fr. Scand.]

BANEFUL (bān'fool) *a.* poisonous; hurtful; destructive.

BANG (bang) *v.t.* to beat; thump;—*n.* a blow; thump. [Scand.]

BANGLE (bang'gl) *n.* an ornamental ring for the wrists or ankles; the hoop of a mast or spar. [Hind.]

BANISH (ban'ish) *v.t.* to exile from one's country. [O.F. *banisant*, banishing, fr. *banir*, fr. Low L. *bannire*, to proclaim as an outlaw, fr. Ger. See BAN.]

BANISHMENT (ban'ish-ment) *n.* expulsion from one's own country.

BANJO (ban'jō) *n.* a musical instrument with six strings, played on with the fingers. [Corr. fr. F., fr. L. (acc.) *panduram*, fr. G. = a three-stringed instrument invented by Pan.]

BANK (bangk) *n.* a ridge of earth; side of a stream; place where money is deposited; —*v.t.* to raise a bank. [O.F. *banc*, a bench or table; fr. M. H. Ger. *Banc*.]

BANKABLE (bangk'a-bl) *a.* that may be received by a bank.

BANK-BOOK (bangk'book) *n.* a small book for private bank accounts.

BANKER (bang'ker) *n.* one who deals in money or discount notes.

BANKING (bang'king) *n.* the business of a banker;—*a.* pertaining to a bank.

BANKRUPT (bangk'rupt) *n.* one who cannot pay his debts;—*a.* insolvent;—*v.t.* to render unable to pay debts. [F. *banqueroute*, fr. It. *banca rotta*, broken counter.]

BANKRUPTCY (bangk'rupt-si) *n.* state of a bankrupt; failing in trade.

BANK-STOCK (bangk'stok) *n.* shares in a banking capital.

BANNER (ban'er) *n.* a military standard. [O.F. *baniere*, fr. Low L. *banderia*, fr. Ger. *Band*.]

BANNERET (ban'er-et) *n.* a higher kind of knight created on the field of battle; a small banner.

BANNOCK (ban'uk) *n.* a cake of oatmeal. [Gael.]

BANNS (banz) *n.pl.* proclamation of marriage. [See BAN.]

BANQUET (bang'kwet) *n.* a grand entertainment; a feast;—*v.t.* to give a feast. [F. dim. of *banque*. See BANK.]

BANQUETING (bang'kwet-ing) *ppr.* feasting; —*n.* act of feasting.

BANSHEE (ban'shē) *n.* an Irish fairy attached to the family of a house. [Irish Celt.]

BANTAM (ban'tam) *n.* or *a.* a small species of domestic fowl. [Fr. *Bantam* in Java.]

BANTER (ban'ter) *v.t.* to rally; ridicule;— *n.* raillery; joke.

BANTLING (bant'ling) *n.* an infant. [BAND, which see, and E. dim. *ling*.]

BANYAN (ban'yan) *n.* an Indian tree of the fig family. [Pg. *banian*, perh. through A.]

BAOBAB (bā'ō-bab) *n.* the African calabash tree, which grows to an enormous girth. [Afr.]

BAPTISE (bap-tīz') *v.t.* to administer baptism by sprinkling or immersion. [O.F. fr. Late L. *baptizare*, fr. G. *baptizein*, fr. *baptein*, to dip.]

BAPTISM (bap'tizm) *n.* the application of water to the body; one of the Christian sacraments. [G. *baptizma*, a dipping.]

BAPTISMAL (bap-tiz'mal) *a.* pertaining to baptism.

BAPTIST (bap'tist) *n.* one who holds to baptism by immersion.

BAPTISTERY (bap-tis'ter-i) *n.* a place for baptising.

BAPTISTIC (bap-tis'tik) *a.* pertaining to baptism.

BAR (bár) *n.* a bolt; stop; enclosure in an inn or court-room; division in music; bank of sand in a river; body of lawyers;—*v.t.* to fasten; shut out; hinder. [O.F. *barre*, fr. Celt.]

BARB (bárb) *n.* anything like a beard; the backward point in a hook; a horse or pigeon from Barbary. [F. *barbe*, fr. L. (acc.) *barbam*, a beard.]

BARBARIAN (bár-bā'ri-an) *n.* a savage; a man uncivilised;—*a.* savage; rude; cruel. [L. *barbaria*, a foreign land, fr. G. *barbaros*, foreign.]

BARBARIC (bár-bar'ik) *a.* foreign; rude.

BARBARISE (bár-ba-ríz) *v.t.* to reduce to barbarism.

BARBARISM (bár'ba-rizm) *n.* savageness; incorrect form of speech.

BARBARITY (bár-bar'i-ti) *n.* a savage state; cruelty.

BARBAROUS (bár'ba-rus) *a.* rude; cruel; uncivilised.

BARBED (bárbd) *a.* bearded; armed.

BARBER (bár'ber) *n.* one whose business is to shave beards.

BARBERRY (bár'ber-i) *n.* a thorny shrub, and its small red acid fruit. [L. *barbaris*.]

BARBETTE (bár-bet') *n.* a terrace inside the parapet on which guns can be mounted so as to fire over the top of it instead of through an embrasure. [F.]

BARCAROLE (bár'ka-rōl) *n.* boat song of the Venetian gondoliers. [It. *barcaruolo*, a boatman, or *barca*, a boat.]

BARD (á d) *n.* a Celtic minstrel; a poet. [Celt. lb r

BARDIC (bár'dik) *a.* pertaining to bards.

BARE (bár) *a.* naked; plain; poor;—*v.t.* to make naked. [O.E. *bœr*, bare.]

BAREFACED (bár'fást) *a.* shameless; impudent.

BAREFOOT (bár'foot) *a.* without shoes or stockings.

BAREGE (ba-rāzh') *n.* a thin fabric of worsted and silk. [Fr. *Beréges*, in the Pyrenees.]

BARENESS (bár'nes) *n.* nakedness; leanness; poverty.

BARGAIN (bar'gin) *n.* agreement; the thing bought or sold;—*v.t.* to make a contract. [O.F. *bargaigner*, fr. L. *barcaniare*, to buy and sell, fr. L. *barca*, a trading-ship.]

BARGE (bárj) *n.* a large row-boat. [F. *barge*, fr. L. (acc.) *barcam*, a trading vessel.]

BARITONE (bar'i-tōn) *n.* a voice partaking of the common bass and tenor. [G. *taros*, heavy, and *tonos*, tone.]

BARK (bárk) *n.* rind of a tree;—*v.t.* to make the noise of dogs; strip trees. [O.E. *beorcan*, M.E. *barken*, to bark. Also Scand. =the covering of a tree.]

BARKING (bár'king) *n.* clamour of a dog.

BARLEY (bár-li) *n.* grain of which malt is made. [O.E. *bœrlic*, fr. *bere*, barley, and *lic*, like.]

BARLEYCORN (bár'li-korn) *n.* a grain of barley; third part of an inch. [O.E. *bœrlic*, and *corn*, conn. with L. *granum*, grain.]

BARLEYMEAL (bár'li-mēl) *n.* barley ground into meal or flour. [O.E. *bœrlic*, and *melu*, meal. Cf. Ger. *mahlen*, to grind.]

BARM (bárm) *n.* yeast. [O.E. *beorma* conn. with Ger. *Barme*.]

BARMAID (bár'mād) *n.* female who attends the bar of a tavern or public-house. [O.F. BAR, which see, and O.E. *moegden*, a virgin.]

BARMECIDE (bár'me-sīd) *a.* unreal; imaginary; mock. [Fr. Barmecide in the *Arabian Nights*.]

BARMY (bár'mi) *a.* containing barm.

BARN (bárn) *n.* a house for hay and other farm produce. [O.E. *bern*, fr. *bere*, barley, and *ern*, room.]

BARNACLE (bár'na-kl) *n.* a shell-fish. [O.F. *bernaque*, perh. fr. L. *perna*, a kind of shell-fish.]

BARNACLES (bár'na-klz) *n.* irons on horses' noses.

BAROMETER (ba-rom'e-ter) *n.* an instrument to measure the weight of the atmosphere, and hence the actual and probable changes of weather, or height of any ascent. [G. *baros*, weight, and *metron*, a measure.]

Barometer.

BAROMETRICAL (bar-ō-met'ri-kal) *a.* relating to a barometer.

BARON (bar'un) *n.* rank of nobility next to a viscount. [F., fr. Low L. (acc.) *baronem*, fr. O. H. Ger. *Bar*, a freeman.]

BARONAGE (bar'un-āj) *n.* body of barons.

BARONESS (bar'un-es) *n.* a baron's lady.

BARONET (bar'un-et) *n.* the title next to a baron.

BARONETCY (bar'un-et'si) *n.* the rank, state, or title of a baronet.

BARONIAL (ba-rō'ni-al) *a.* belonging to a barony.

BARONY (bar'un-i) *n.* lordship or fee of a baron.

BAROSCOPE (bar'o-skōp) *n.* a sort of barometer. [G. *baros*, weight, and *skopein*, to see.]

BAROUCHE (ba-rōōsh') *n.* a four-wheeled open carriage. [Ger. *Barutsche*, fr. It. *biroccio*, a two-wheeled carriage; fr. L. *bi=bis*, twice, and *rota*, a wheel.]

BARQUE (bárk) *n.* a ship with three masts; the mizzen-mast rigged as a schooner without yards; any small vessel. [F. *barque*, fr. L. (acc.) *barcam*, a trading-vessel.]

BARRACK (bar'ak) *n.* a building for soldiers. [Fr. F. *baraque*, fr. Celt.]

BARRATOR (bar'a-ter) *n.* one who excites law-suits. [O.F. *barateor*, fr. *barat*, deceit.]

BARRATROUS (bar'a-trus) *a.* fraudulent.

BARREL (bar'el) *n.* a cask; a cylinder;—*v.t.* to put in a barrel. [F. *baril*, fr. Celt.]

BARRELLED (bar'eld) *pp.* put in a barrel; —*a.* having a barrel or tube.

BARREN (bar'en) *a.* not prolific; unfruitful; dull;—*n.* an unfertile tract of land. [O.F.]

BARRENNESS (bar'en-nes) *n.* unfruitfulness.

BARRICADE (bar'i-kād) *n.* a hastily-made fortification; a bar;—*v.t.* to fasten; fortify. [F., fr. Sp. *barricada*, originally an obstruction made of barrels of earth.]

BARRIER (bar'i-er) *n.* a limit; defence; obstruction; boundary. [O.F. *barrière*, fr. *barre*. See BAR.]

BARRING (bár'ing) *prep.* excepting.

BARRISTER (bar'is-ter) *n.* a lawyer qualified to plead in the superior courts. [Late L., made fr. BAR.]

BARROW (bar'ō) *n.* a hand carriage; a mound. [O.E. *beran*, to bear, M.E. *barrowe*; also, O.E. *beorg*, a mound, M.E. *bergh*. Cf. Ger. *Berg*.]

BAR-SHOT (bár-shot) *n.* two balls joined by a bar, used in naval combat. [BAR, which see, and O.E. *sceotan*, to shoot.]

BARTER (bár'ter) *v.t.* to traffic by exchanging articles;—*n.* traffic by exchange. [O.F. *barat*, deceit.]

BARTERER (bár'ter-er) *n.* one who traffics by exchange.

BARTIZAN (bár'ti-zan) *n.* a small overhanging turret. [Introduced by Sir Walter Scott; a corr. of *brattising*.]

BASAL (bā'sal) *a.* constituting the base. [See BASE.]

BASALT (ba-sawlt') *n.* a grayish mineral. [L. *basaltus*, black basalt.]

BASALTIC (ba-sawl'tik) *a.* pertaining to basalt.

BASE (bās) *n.* foundation; pedestal; lowest part in music;—*a.* low in value, rank, spirit, etc.; mean; vile;—*v.t.* to found, set, or lay. [F. *cas* (fem. *basse*), fr. Low L. (acc.) *bassum*, low.]

BASE-BORN (bās'born) *a.* illegitimate.
BASELESS (bās'les) *a.* without support.
BASEMENT (bās'ment) *n.* the ground floor.
BASENESS (bās'nes) *n.* meanness; vileness; deepness of sound.
BASHAW (bȧ-shaw') *n.* a pasha; a proud, imperious man. [Turk.]
BASHFUL (bash'fool) *a.* wanting confidence; modest; shy. [=*abashful.* See ABASH.]
BASHFULNESS (bash'fool-nes) *n.* extreme modesty; rustic shame.
BASIC (bās'ik) *a.* relating to a base.
BASIL (baz'il) *n.* the skin of a sheep tanned; an aromatic culinary herb. [O.F. *basile,* fr. L. *basilica,* fr. G. *basilikon,* pertaining to a king.]
BASILICON (bȧ-sil'i-kun) *n.* a kind of salve. [G., lit. sovereign.]
BASILISK (bas'i-lisk) *n.* a cockatrice; a kind of cannon. [G. *basiliskos,* royal, fr. *basileus,* king.]
BASIN (bā'sn) *n.* a small vessel; a dock; a pond. [O.F. *bacin,* fr. Celt.]
BASIS (bā'sis) *n.* foundation; support;— *pl.* BASES. [See BASE.]
BASK (bask) *v.i.* to lie in warmth. [Scand.]
BASKET (bas'ket) *n.* a domestic vessel made of twigs, etc., interwoven;—*v.t.* to put in a basket. [Etym. uncertain.]
BAS-RELIEF (bás-re-lēf') *n.* sculpture in which the figures do not stand far out from the surface. [See BASE and RELIEF.]
BASS (bás) *n.* a fish; a species of tree; matting made from its bark. [O.E. *bœrs,* M.E. *barse, bace.*]
BASS (bās) *n.* in *Music,* the base.
BASSET (bas'set) *n.* a game at ca,ds; the surface edge of strata;—*a.* inclining upwards as strata. [F. *bas,* low.]
BASSINET (bas'i-net) *n.* a cradle of wickerwork with a hood. [F. dim. of *bassin,* basin.]
BASSOON (bȧ-sòòn') *a.* a reed wind instrument of bass compass. [F. *basson,* fr. It. *bassone,* aug. of *basso,* var=F. *basse.*]
BASTARD (bas'tȧrd) *n.* a spurious child. [O.F. *bastard,* fr. O.F. *bât,* or *bast,* a pack saddle.]
BASTARDISE (bas'tȧr-diz) *v.t.* to declare illegitimate.
BASTARDY (bas'tȧr-di) *n.* state of being a bastard.
BASTE (bāst) *v.t.* to beat; sew lightly; drip butter. [Scand. Also O.F. *baster,* to stitch loosely, fr. It. *basta,* a long stitch.]
BASTILLE (bas-tēl') *n.* the state prison formerly at Paris; a fortified castle. [O.F. *bastille,* a building, fr. O.F. *bastir,* to build.]
BASTINADO (bas-ti-nā'dō) *v.t.* to beat with a cudgel;—*n.* a cudgelling. [Sp. *bastonada,* F. *bastonnade,* fr. *bâion.* See BATON.]
BASTING (bās'ting) *n.* a beating; a moistening with fat.
BASTION (bast'yun) *n.* a mass of earth standing out from a rampart. [F., fr. O.F. *bastillon,* a little fort.]
BAT (bat) *n.* a flat club; a piece of brick; a sheet of cotton for quilting; a mammal, like a mouse, with large extensive wings. [Celt. Also M.E. *bakke,* a bat, fr. Scand.]
BATCH (bach) *n.* quantity of bread baked at one time; number produced or despatched. [M.E. *bacche,* a baking. See BAKE.]
BATE (bāt) *v.t.* and *i.* [See ABATE.]
BATEAU (ba-tō') *n.* a long light boat. [F., fr. O.F. *batel,* a boat.]
BATH (bá) *n.* place to bathe in. [O.E. *bœth.*] th
BATHBRICK (báth'brik) *n.* a brick or calcareous earth for polishing metals.
BATH-BUN (báth'bun) *n.* a sweet currant bun, first made at Bath.
BATH-CHAIR (báth'chȧr) *n.* a wheeled chair for invalids.

BATHE (bāTH) *v.t.* to wash in a bath; soften by washing;—*n.* act of bathing especially in the sea. [O.E. *bathian,* to wash.]
BATHING (bāTH'ing) *n.* the act of using a bath.
BATHOS (bā'thos) *n.* descent in poetry. [G. *bathos,* depth.]
BATING (bā'ting) *prep.* excepting.
BATON (bat'un) *n.* a staff; a club. [F. *bâton,* fr. O.F. *baston,* fr. L. (acc.) *bastonem,* a stick.]
BATTALION (bȧ-tal'yun) *n.* a division of an army. [F. *bataillon,* fr. *bataille.*]
BATTEN (bat'n) *v.t.* or *i.* to make fat;—*n.* a narrow piece of board. [A form of BATON.]
BATTER (bat'er) *v.t.* to beat down;—*n.* a mixture of flour, water, eggs, etc. [F. *battre,* fr. L. *batere,* fr. *batuere,* to beat. Also O.F. *bature,* a beating up.]
BATTERING-RAM (bat'er-ing-ram) *n.* an engine for beating down walls.
BATTERY (bat'er-i) *n.* a raised work for cannons; line of cannon. [F. *baterie,* beating, fr. *battre,* to beat.]
BATTING (bat'ing) *n.* cotton or wool in sheets for quilting.
BATTLE (bat'l) *n.* a combat; engagement; a fight;—*v.i.* to contend in fight. [M.E. *bataile,* fr. O.F. *bataille,* fr. Low L. (acc.) *bataliam,* a fight; fr. *batere,* for *batuere,* to beat.]
BATTLE-ARRAY (bat'l-ȧ-rā) *n.* order of battle. [BATTLE and ARRAY, which see.]
BATTLE-AXE (bat'l-aks) *n.* a weapon anciently used in battle.
BATTLEDORE (bat'l-dōr) *n.* an instrument to strike shuttlecocks. [Corr. of Sp. *batidor,* beater.]
BATTLEMENT (bat'l-ment) *n.* a wall with embrasures. [M.E. *batilment,* fr. O.F. *bastiller,* to fortify.]
BATTUE (ba'tòò) *n.* driving the game towards the sportsmen; the game so driven. [F., fr. adj. *battu,* trodden, fr. *battre,* to beat.]
BAUBLE (baw'bl) *n.* a gew-gaw; a trifle. [O.F. *baub-el,* a toy, fr. It., fr. Low L. *babulus,* a simpleton.]
BAWDINESS (baw'di-nes) *n.* obscenity. [O. F. *baud,* gay, fr. O.H. Ger. *bald,* BOLD, which see.]
BAWL (bawl) *v.i.* or *t.* to speak loud; proclaim, as a crier;—*n.* a long, loud cry. [Scand.]
BAY (bā) (1) *v.i.* to bark as a dog;—(2) *a.* brown, inclining to chestnut;—(3) *n.* an arm of the sea; an enclosure in a barn; (4) a species of laurel tree;—*pl.* garlands or marks of distinction. [(1) O.F. *abbaier,* fr. L. *ad,* and *baudari,* to bark gently; (2) O.F. *bai,* fr. L. *badius,* chestnut-coloured; (3) F. *baie,* fr. *bayer,* to be open, fr. Low L. *badere,* to gape; (4) F. *baie,* a berry, fr. L. (acc.) *bacam,* a berry.]
BAYONET (bā'ō-net) *n.* a dagger fixed to a musket;—*v.t.* to stab. [F. *baïonnette,* fr. *Bayonne.*]
BAYOU (bā'òò) *n.* outlet of a lake, etc. [F.]
BAY-RUM (bā'rum) *n.* a spirit obtained by distilling leaves of the bay-tree.
BAY-SALT (bā'sawlt) *n.* salt formed by evaporation. [BAY, which see, and L. (acc.) *saltem,* salt.]
BAZAAR (bȧ-zȧr') *n.* a market-place for sale of goods. [Per.]
BE (bē) *v.i.* and *aux.* [*pret.* WAS] to exist.
BEACH (bēch) *n.* a sandy shore; strand. [Etym. uncertain.]
BEACHED (bēcht) *a.* drawn or driven on the beach.
BEACHY (bē'chi) *a.* having beaches.
BEACON (bē'kn, bē'kun) *n.* a light to direct seamen; light-house. [O.E. *beacen.*]
BEAD (bēd) *n.* a little globule strung on thread, used for necklaces. [O.E. *bed,* M.E. *bede,* prayer, fr. O.E. *beddan,* to pray.]

BEADLE (bē'dl) *n.* a crier; a messenger. [O.F. *bedel, bedeau,* fr. Teut; conn. with O.E. *beodan,* to bid.]

BEADROLL (bēd'rōl) *n.* a list of persons to be prayed for.

BEADSMAN (bēdz'man) *n.* one who prays for others; a monk.

BEAGLE (bē'gl) *n.* a hunting dog. [Etym. unknown.]

BEAK (bēk) *n.* the bill of a bird; anything like a beak. [F. *bec,* fr. Celt.]

BEAKED (bēkt) *a.* having a beak.

BEAKER (bē'ker) *n.* a drinking-cup. [Scand.]

BEAK-IRON (bēk'i-ern) *n.* a pointed tool used by blacksmiths.

BEAM (bēm) *n.* a main timber; part of a balance; ray of light;—*v.i.* or *t.* to emit rays. [O.E. *beam,* a tree; conn. with Ger. *Baum.*]

BEAMING (bēm'ing) *ppr.* or *a.* emitting rays or beams.

BEAMLESS (bēm'les) *a.* emitting no rays of light.

BEAMY (bē'mi) *a.* shining; radiant.

BEAN (bēn) *n.* the name of many kinds of pulse. [O.E. *bean;* conn. with Ger. *Bohne.*]

BEAR (bār) *v.t.* [*pret.* BORE; *pp.* BORN] to bring forth, as young;—*v.t.* [*pret.* BORE; *pp.* BORNE] to carry; endure; sustain;— *v.i.* to press upon; tend or be situated; be fruitful;—*n.* a wild animal; a stock-jobber interested in depressing stocks. [O.E. *beran,* to support. Also O.E. *bera,* a bear.]

BEARABLE (bār'a-bl) *a.* that may be borne.

BEARD (bērd) *n.* hair on the chin;—*v.t.* to pull by the beard; oppose to the face. [O.E. *beard.*]

BEARDED (hēr'ded) *a.* having a beard.

BEARDIE (bēr'di) *n.* a lively little song-bird; a small fish like the carp.

BEARDLESS (bērd'les) *a.* without a beard.

BEARER (bār'er) *n.* a carrier of anything.

BEAR-GARDEN (bār'gär-den) *n.* a noisy, turbulent assembly. [BEAR, and O.F. *gardin* = F. *jardin,* fr. Teut.]

BEARING (bār'ing) *n.* deportment.

BEARISH (bār'ish) *a.* like a bear.

BEAR'S-GREASE (bārz'grēz) *n.* fat of bears; pomatum. [E. BEAR, and O.F. *gresse,* fatness, fr. *gros,* fat, fr. L. *crassus,* fat.]

BEAST (bēst) *n.* an irrational animal. [O.F. *beste* = F. *bête,* fr. L. (acc.) *bestiam.*]

BEASTLINESS (bēst'li-nes) *n.* brutality; filthiness.

BEASTLY (bēst'li) *a.* like a beast.

BEAT (bēt) *v.t.* [*pret.* BEAT; *pp.* BEAT, BEATEN] to strike with repeated blows; outdo; conquer;—*v.i.* to throb, as a pulse; —*n.* a short recurring stroke; throb; a round or course; rise or fall of the hand in marking time. [O.E. *beatan.*]

BEATIFIC (bē-a-tif'ik) *a.* making happy. [F. *béatifier,* fr. L. *beatificare,* fr. *beata* (fem.), happy, and *facere,* to make.]

BEATIFICATION (bē-at-i-fi-kā'shun) *n.* admission to heavenly honours.

BEATIFY (bē-at'i-fi) *v.t.* to make happy.

BEATING (bē'ting) *n.* act of striking.

BEATITUDE (bē-at'i-tūd) *n.* blessedness; perfect felicity.

BEAU (bō) *n.* a man of dress; a lover.—*pl*: **BEAUX.** [F., formed from *bel,* handsome.]

BEAU IDEAL (bō-i-dē'al) *n.* a model of beauty or excellence in the mind.

BEAUISH (bō'ish) *a.* gay; foppish; gallant.

BEAU-MONDE (bō-mongd') *n.* the fashionable world. [F. *beau,* fine, and *monde,* world.]

BEAUTEOUS (bū'tē-us) *a.* handsome; pleasing; elegant.

BEAUTIFIER (bū'ti-fi-er) *n.* that which makes beautiful.

BEAUTIFUL (bū'ti-fool) *a.* elegant in form.

BEAUTIFY (bū'ti-fi) *v.t.* to make beautiful; adorn; embellish.

BEAUTILESS (bū'ti-les) *a.* without beauty.

BEAUTY (bū'ti) *n.* whatever pleases the eye. [F. *beauté,* fr. O.F. *beltet,* fr. Low L. (acc.) *bellitatem,* fr. *bellus,* fair.]

BEAUTY-SPOT (bū'ti-spot) *n.* a spot to heighten beauty; foil.

BEAVER (bē'ver) *n.* an animal and his fur; a hat;—*a.* made of beaver fur. [O.E. *befer,* M.E. *bever.*]

BECALM (bē-kām') *v.t.* to quiet. [E. pref. *be-,* and CALM.]

BECAME (bē-kām') *pret.* of BECOME.

BECAUSE (bē-kawz') *conj.* for the reason that. [O.E. *bi,* by, and CAUSE.]

BECK (bek) (1) *n.* a sign with the hand or head; —*v.i.* to make a sign. [O.E. *becnan, beacnian,* M.E. *becnen,* to make a sign.] (2) *n.* a brook. [Scand.]

BECKON (bek'n) *v.i.* or *t.* to make a sign to another. [See BECK.]

BECLOUD (bē-kloud') *v.t.* to obscure.

BECOME (bē-kum') *v.t.* [*pret.* BECAME; *pp.* BECOME] to fit or befit;—*v.i.* to be made. [O.E. *becuman.*]

BECOMING (bē-kum'ing) *a.* suitable; fit; graceful.

BED (bed) *n.* place in which anything rests; sleeping place; bottom of a stream;—*v.t.* or *i.* to place in bed; plant and cover; go to bed. [O.E. *bed.*]

BEDASH (bē-dash') *v.t.* to wet by spattering.

BEDAUB (bē-dawb') *v.t.* to besmear. [See DAUB.]

BEDAZZLE (bē-daz'l) *v.t.* to confound the sight. [E. pref. *be-,* and DAZZLE.]

BED-CHAIR (bed'chār) *n.* a chair with a movable back for the sick.

BED-CHAMBER (bed'chām'ber) *n.* a chamber for a bed.

BED-CLOTHES (bed'klothz) *n.* sheets, blankets, etc.

BEDDING (bed'ing) *n.* materials for a bed.

BEDECK (bē-dek') *v.t.* to deck; trim. [E. pref. *be-,* and DECK.]

BEDEL (bē'dl) *n.* a beadle in universities. [See BEADLE.]

BEDEVIL (bē-dev'l) *v.t.* to throw into confusion; destroy.

BEDEW (bē-dū') *v.t.* to moisten gently. [E. pref. *be-,* and DEW.]

BEDFELLOW (bed'fel-ō) *n.* one lying in the same bed.

BEDIM (bē-dim') *v.t.* to make dim. [E. pref. *be-,* and DIM.]

BEDIZEN (bē-di'zn) *v.t.* to dress out gaudily. [E. pref. *be-* and *dise* = Low Ger. *Diesse,* the bunch of flax on a distaff.]

BEDLAM (bed'lam) *n.* a madhouse. [Corr. fr. *Hospital of S. Mary of Bethlehem.*]

BEDLAMITE (bed'lam-īt) *n.* a madman.

BED-QUILT (bed'kwilt) *n.* a quilted covering for a bed.

BEDRAGGLE (bē-drag'l) *v.t.* to soil. [E. pref. *be-,* and DRAGGLE, freq. of drag.]

BEDRENCH (bē-drensh') *v.t.* to soak completely. [E. pref. *be-,* and DRENCH.]

BEDRIDDEN (bed'rid-n) *a.* confined to bed. [M.E. *bedreden,* bed-riders; O.E. *bedrida,* fr. O.E. *rida,* a horseman.]

BEDROOM (bed'room) *n.* an apartment for a bed.

BEDROP (bē-drop') *v.t.* to sprinkle over. [E. pref. *be-,* and DROP.]

BEDSTEAD (bed'sted) *n.* a frame for a bed.

BEDTICK (bed'tik) *n.* a piece of strong cloth to hold the feathers or other materials of a bed. [E. BED, and G. *theke,* a case.]

BEDTIME (bed'tim) *n.* the hour of going to rest.

BEDYE (bē-di') *v.t.* to dye; stain. [E. pref. *be-,* and O.E. *deagan,* M.E. *deyen,* to give a new colour to.]

BEE (bē) *n.* an insect which produces honey and wax. [O.E. *beo.*]

BEE-BREAD (bē'bred) *n.* the pollen of flowers.

BEECH (bēch) *n.* the name of a tree. [O.E. *bece.*]

BEECHEN (bē'chen) *a.* belonging to or made of beech.

BEEF (bēf) *n.* the flesh of an ox or cow. [O. F. *boef*, fr. L. (acc.) *bovem*, an ox.]

BEEF-EATER (bēf'ē-tẽr) *n.* a gross person; a yeoman of the guard. [Corr. fr. F. *buffetier*, keeper of the buffet or sideboard.]

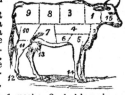

BEEFSTEAK (bēf' stāk) *n.* a slice of beef broiled or for broiling.

BEEFTEA (bēf'tē) *n.* soup made by boiling beef without other ingredient.

1, neck; 2, shaking-piece; 3, chine; 4, ribs; 5, clod; 6, brisket; 7, flank; 8, loin, sirloin; 9, rump; 10, round; 11, leg; 12, foot; 13, udder; 14, shin; 15, cheek.

BEE-HIVE (bē'hīv) *n.* a box or case or other hollow vessel for holding bees.

BEELZEBUB (bē-el'zē-bub) *n.* the prince of demons. [H. *Baal*, lord.]

BEEN (bin, bēn) *pp.* of BE.

BEER (bēr) *n.* a liquor made of malt and hops. [O.E. *beor*, conn. with Ger. *bier*.]

BEERY (bēr'i) *a.* affected by beer; muddled; stained with beer.

BEESWAX (bēz'waks) *n.* the wax collected by bees. [BEE and WAX, which see.]

BEET (bēt) *n.* a garden vegetable. [O.E. *bete*, fr. L. *beta*.]

BEETLE (bē'tl) *n.* a mallet; insect;—*v.i.* to jut out; hang over. [O.E. *bitel*, *bytel*, a biter, fr. *bitan*, to bite.] [hanging.

BEETLING (bēt'ling) *a.* prominent; over-

BEETROOT (bēt'rōōt) *n.* a vegetable used for the table and for making sugar.

BEEVES (bēvz) *n.pl.* cattle. [See BEEF.]

BEFALL (bē-fawl') *v.t.* [*pret.* BEFELL; *pp.* BEFALLEN] to happen to. [O.E. *befeallen*, to happen.]

BEFIT (bē-fit') *v.t.* to become; suit.

BEFITTING (bē-fit'ing) *a.* suiting; becoming.

BEFOOL (bē-fōōl') *v.t.* to make a fool of; delude; lead astray. [E. pref. *be-*, and FOOL.]

BEFOG (bē-fog') *v.i.* to mystify; confuse. [E. pref. *be-*, and FOG.]

BEFORE (bē-fōr') *prep.* in front of; prior to; in presence of;—*ad.* previously to. [O.E. *bī-*, *be-foran*; fr. *bi* = by, and FORE.]

BEFOREHAND (bē-fōr'hand) *ad.* previously; —*a.* well provided.

BEFORETIME (bē-fōr'tīm) *ad.* of old time.

BEFOUL (bē-foul') *v.t.* to make foul. [E. pref. *be-*.]

BEFRIEND (bē-frend') *v.t.* to favour. [E. pref. *be-*, and FRIEND.]

BEFRINGE (bē-frinj') *v.t.* to adorn with fringes [E. pref. *be-*, and FRINGE.]

BEG (beg) *v.t.* to ask earnestly;—*v.i.* to live on alms. [Etym. unknown; perhaps fr. a religious brotherhood of lay beggars of the Netherlands, the *Beghards*.]

BEGET (bē-get') *v.t.* [*pret.* BEGAT; *pp.* BEGOT, BEGOTTEN] to generate or produce. [O.E. *begitan*, acquire. See GET.]

BEGETTER (bē-get'ẽr) *n.* one who begets.

BEGGAR (beg'ẳr) *n.* one who begs, or one who lives by begging;—*v.t.* to bring to want.

BEGGARLINESS (beg'ẳr-li-nes) *n.* the state of being beggarly; meanness.

BEGGARLY (beg'ẳr-li) *a.* very poor; mean; —*ad.* meanly.

BEGGARY (beg'ẳr-i) *n.* indigence.

BEGGING (beg'ing) *ppr.* asking alms;—*n.* practice of asking alms.

BEGIN (bē-gin') *v.t.* [*pret.* BEGAN; *pp.* BEGUN] to take rise; enter upon something new; do the first act. [O.E. *beginnan*.]

BEGINNER (bē-gin'ẽr) *n.* one who begins.

BEGINNING (bē-gin'ing) *n.* the first part of time; first cause; commencement.

BEGIRD (bē-gerd') *v.t.* [*pret.* BEGIRDED; *pp.* BEGIRT] to surround. [E. pref. *be-*, and GIRD.]

BEGONE (bē-gon') *inter.* go away! depart! [E. pref. *be-*, and GONE.]

BEGREASE (bē-grēz') *v.t.* to daub with grease. [E. pref. *be-*, and GREASE.]

BEGRIME (bē-grīm') *v.t.* to soil deeply with dirt. [E. pref. *be-*, and GRIME.]

BEGRUDGE (bē-gruj') *v.t.* to envy the possession of. [E. pref. *be-*, and GRUDGE.]

BEGUILE (bē-gīl') *v.t.* to impose upon; deceive; amuse. [E. pref. *be-*, and GUILE.]

BEGUILEMENT (bē-gīl'ment) *n.* act of beguiling.

BEGUM (bē'gum) *n.* in India, a lady of high rank. [Hind.]

BEGUN (bē-gun') *pp.* of BEGIN.

BEHALF (bē-hâf') *n.* favour; cause. [O.E. *be healfe*, by the side; M.E. *behalve*.]

BEHAVE (bē-hāv') *v.t.* or *i.* to carry; act; demean; conduct oneself. [Formed from *be-*, and HAVE.]

BEHAVIOUR (bē-hāv'yur) *n.* course of life; conduct; deportment.

BEHEAD (bē-hed') *v.t.* to cut off the head.

BEHELD (bē-held') *pret.* of BEHOLD.

BEHEMOTH (bē'hē-moth) *n.* a large beast [Egypt.]

BEHEST (bē-hest') *n.* a command. [O.E. *behœs*, fr. *hœs*, fr. *hatan*, to call.]

BEHIND (bē-hīnd') *prep.* or *ad.* at the back; after; inferior to. [E. pref. *be-*, and HIND.]

BEHINDHAND (bē-hīnd'hand) *ad.* in arrears.

BEHOLD (bē-hōld') *v.t.* [*pret.* and *pp.* BEHELD] to see;—*inter.* lo! see! [O.E. *behealdan*, to fix with the eyes.]

BEHOLDEN (bē-hōl'dn) *a.* indebted.

BEHOLDER (bē-hōl'dẽr) *n.* a spectator.

BEHOOF (bē-hōōf') *n.* profit; advantage. [O.E. *behof*, advantage.]

BEHOOVABLE (bē-hōōv'ẳ-bl) *a.* useful; fit.

BEHOOVE (bē-hōōv') *v.t.* to be necessary, fit, or proper to. [O.E. *behovian*, to be necessary for.]

BEING (bē'ing) *v.i.* and *aux.* [*ppr.* of BE] existing;—*n.* existence; anything that exists.

BEIRAM (bā'ram) *n.* a Mohammedan festival corresponding to Easter. Also BAIRAM. [Per.]

BELABOUR (bē-lā'bur) *v.t.* to thump; beat soundly. [E. pref. *be-*, and LABOUR.]

BELATED (bē-lā'ted) *a.* detained till late, or too late. [E. pref. *be-*, and LATE.]

BELAUD (bē-lawd') *v.t.* to praise highly. [E. pref. *be-*, and LAUD.]

BELAY (bē-lā') *v.t.* to lie in wait for; block up; fasten. [O.E. *belecgan*. See LAY.]

BELCH (belsh) *v.t.* or *i.* to eject wind from the stomach;—*n.* the act of belching. [O.E. *bealcan*.]

BELEAGUER (bē-lē'gẽr) *v.t.* to besiege. [D. *belegeren*, to besiege.]

BEL-ESPRIT (bel-es-prē') *n.* a man of wit. [F.]

BELFRY (bel'fri) *n.* a place where bells are rung. [M.E. *berfray*, fr. O.F. *berfroi*, a watch-tower; fr. M. H. Ger. *Berfrit*, place of security fr. *bercen* (= Ger. *bergen*), and *frit* (= Ger. *Friede*), peace.]

BELIAL (bēl'yạl) *n.* Satan; the devil. [H.]

BELIE (bē-lī') *v.t.* to speak falsely of. [E. pref. *be-*, and LIE.]

BELIEF (bē-lēf') *n.* credit given to evidence; the thing believed. [M.E. *beleven*, to hold dear, fr. O.E. *leof*, dear.]

BELIEVABLE (bĕ-lē'va-bl) *a.* that may be believed.

BELIEVE (bĕ-lēv') *v.t.* or *i.* to be persuaded of as true; confide in; think or suppose. [See **BELIEF**.]

BELIEVER (bĕ-lē'ver) *n.* one who believes.

BELIEVING (bĕ-lē'ving) *a.* having faith or belief.

BELIEVINGLY (bĕ-lē'ving-li) *ad.* with belief or confiding trust.

BELIKE (bĕ-lik') *ad.* perhaps; probably. [E. pref. *be-*, and **LIKE**.]

BELL (bel) *n.* a hollow vessel made of a composition of metals used for making sounds; —*v.i.* to grow like a bell. [O.E. *belle*, imit. Cf. *bellan*, to bellow.]

BELLADONNA (bel-a-don'a) *n.* deadly nightshade. [It. Cf. pop. F. *belle dame* =fair lady.]

BELLE (bel) *n.* a handsome lady. [F. fem. *belle*, fair, fr. O.F. *bel*, fr. L. *bellus*, handsome.]

BELLFOUNDER (bel-foun'der) *n.* one who casts or founds bells. [**BELL** and **FOUNDER**.]

BELLICOSE (bel'i-kōz) *a.* inclined to war; contentious. [L. *bellicosus*, fr. *bellum*, war.]

BELLIED (bel'id) *a.* swelled out in the middle. [See **BELLY**.]

BELLIGERENT (bel-lij'e-rent) *a.* carrying on war;—*n.* a nation at war. [L. (acc.) *belligerantem*, waging war.]

BELLMAN (bel'man) *n.* one who rings a bell; a public or town crier.

BELL-METAL (bel'met-al) *n.* a composition of copper, tin, zinc, and antimony.

BELLOW (bel'ō) *v.i.* to roar like a bull;—*n.* a loud outcry; a roar. [See **BELL**.]

BELLOWING (bel'ō-ing) *n.* a loud roaring.

BELLOWS (bel'ōz, bel'us) *n.* a machine to blow with. [See **BELLY**.]

BELL-PULL (bel'pool) *n.* a cord to ring a bell.

BELL-RINGER (bel'ring-er) *n.* one who rings a bell.

BELL-WETHER (bel'weTH-er) *n.* a sheep which carries a bell. [**BELL**, and O.E. *wither*, a castrated ram.]

BELLWORT (bel'wurt) *n.* a herbaceous plant with bell-shaped flowers. [**BELL**, and O.E. *wyrt*, a plant.]

BELLY (bel'i) *n.* the part of the body containing the bowels;—*v.i.* to bulge; project. [M.E. *belu*, O.E. *bœlig*, a bag.]

BELLY-BAND (bel'i-band) *n.* a girth for a horse.

BELONG (bĕ-long') *v.i.* to be the property of; appertain to. [E. pref. *be-*, intens., and *langian*, to stretch.]

BELONGINGS (bĕ-long'ingz) *n.pl.* qualities; possessions.

BELOVED (bĕ-luv'ed) *a.* dear; much loved; —(bĕ-luvd') *pp.* greatly loved. [E. pref. *be-*, intens., and **LOVE**.]

BELOW (bĕ-lō') *prep.* and *ad.* under in time or place; inferior. [O.E. *be* =by, and **LOW**.]

BELT (belt) *n.* a girdle; sash; band. [O.E.]

BELTANE (bel'tān) *n.* an ancient festival held on the first day of May (Scot.) [Possibly conn. with *Baal*, but etym. doubtful.]

BELTED (bel'ted) *a.* wearing a belt; worn in the belt.

BEMIRE (bĕ-mir') *v.t.* to sink or drag in the mire. [E. pref. *be-*, and **MIRE**.]

BEMOAN (bĕ-mōn') *v.t.* to lament; bewail. [E. pref. *be-*, and **MOAN**.]

BEMUDDLE (bĕ-mud'l) *v.t.* to confuse; stupefy. [E. pref. *be-*, and **MUDDLE**.]

BEN (ben) *n.* a mountain. [Gael. *beann*.]

BENCH (bensh) *n.* a long seat; a judge's seat; body of judges. [M.E. *benche*, fr. O.E. *benc*.]

BENCHER (ben'sher) *n.* a senior in the English inns of court.

BEND (bend) *v.t.* and *i.* [*pret.* and *pp.* **BENDED**, **BENT**] to crook; bow; submit;—*n.* a curve or flexure. [O.E. *bendan*, to fasten a string to; fr. *bend*, a fastening, fr. *binnan*, to bind.]

BENEATH (bĕ-nēth') *prep.* and *ad.* under; below. [O.E. *beneothan*, pref. *be* =by.]

BENEDICT (ben'ĕ-dikt) *n.* a newly married man. [Fr. Benedick, in Shakespeare's *Much Ado About Nothing*.]

BENEDICTION (ben-e-dik'shun) *n.* blessing; invocation of happiness; thanks. [F., fr. L. (acc.) *benedictionem*, fr. *benedictus*, blessed.]

BENEFACTION (ben-e-fak'shun) *n.* charitable gift. [L. (acc.) *benefactionem*, fr. *bene*, well, and *facere*, do.]

BENEFACTOR (ben-e-fak'ter) *n.* he who confers a benefit.

BENEFACTRESS (ben-e-fak'tres) *n.* she who confers a benefit.

BENEFICE (ben'e-fis) *n.* a church living. [F. *bénéfice*, fr. L. *beneficium*.]

BENEFICED (ben'e-fist) *a.* possessed of a benefice.

BENEFICENCE (be-nef'i-sens) *n.* active goodness; bounty.

BENEFICENT (be-nef'i-sent) *a.* conferring benefits, helpful.

BENEFICENTLY (be-nef'i-sent-li) *ad.* charitably; generously.

BENEFICIAL (ben-e-fish'al) *a.* useful; advantageous.

BENEFICIALLY (ben-e-fish'al-i) *ad.* advantageously; usefully.

BENEFICIARY (ben-e-fish'i-a-ri) *n.* one who holds a benefice; one benefited by another.

BENEFIT (ben'e-fit) *n.* advantage; profit; favour conferred;—*v.t.* to do good. [O.F. *bienfet* =F. *bienfait*, fr. L. *benefactum*. See **BENEFACTION**.]

BENEVOLENCE (be-nev'ō-lens) *n.* disposition to do good; goodwill. [L. (acc.) *benevolentem*, well-wishing, fr. *bene*, well, and *volens*, wishing.]

BENEVOLENT (be-nev'ō-lent) *a.* having goodwill; kind; affectionate.

BENIGN (bĕ-nin') *a.* gracious; kind. [O.F. *benigne*, fr. L. *benignus*, kind.]

BENIGNANT (be-nig'nant) *a.* kind; gracious; favourable.

BENIGNITY (be-nig'ni-ti) *n.* graciousness.

BENIGNLY (be-nin'li) *ad.* favourably; graciously.

BENISON (ben'i-zn) *n.* a blessing. [Doublet of **BENEDICTION**, which see.]

BENT (bent) [*pret.* and *pp.* of **BEND**] *n.* (1) a curve; tendency; (2) stiff grass. [(1) See **BEND**; (2) O.E. *beonet*, stiff grass.]

BENUMB (bĕ-num') *v.t.* to deprive of feeling. [E. pref. *be-*, intens., and **NUMB**.]

BENZINE (ben'zēn) *n.* a distilled liquid used to remove grease spots.

BENZOIN (ben'zō-in, ben'zoin) *n.* a resinous juice. [F. *benjoine*, fr. A.]

BEQUEATH (bĕ-kwēTH') *v.t.* to give by will. [O.E. *becwethan*, to declare.]

BEQUEST (bĕ-kwest') *n.* a legacy left by will. [O.E. *be*, by, and *cwithe*, saying. Confused with **QUEST**.]

BEREAVE (bĕ-rēv') *v.t.* [*pret.* and *pp.* **BEREAVED**, **BEREFT**] to deprive of; take away from. [O.E. *be-*, intens. pref., and *reafian*, to spoil.]

BEREAVEMENT (bĕ-rēv'ment) *n.* deprivation.

BEREFT (bĕ-reft') *pret.* and *pp.* of **BEREAVE**.

BERI-BERI (ber-i'-ber'i) *n.* a dropsical disease common in Africa. [African.]

BERRY (ber'i) *n.* any small fruit with naked seeds. [M.E. *berie*, fr. O.E. *berie*.]

BERTH (berth) *n.* a ship's station at anchor; a room or sleeping place. [Doublet of **BIRTH**, which see.]

BERYL (ber'il) *n.* a greenish mineral or gem. [O.F., fr. L. *beryllus*, fr. G. *berullos*.]

BESEECH (bĕ-sēch') *v.t.* [*pret.* and *pp.* **BESOUGHT**] to entreat; pray; beg. [M.E. *besechen*, =O.E. pref. intens. *be-*, and **SEEK**.]

BESEEM (be-sēm') v.t. to become; befit. [Eng. pref. be-, and SEEM.]
BESEEMING (bē-sē'ming) a. becoming;—n. comeliness.
BESEEMLY (bē-sēm'li) a. fit; decent.
BESET (be-set') v.t. [pret. and pp. BESET] to enclose on all sides. [O.E. be-, by, and SET.]
BESETTING (bē-set'ing) a. habitually attending or harassing.
BESHREW (bē-shrōō') v.t. to wish a curse to. [See SHREW.]
BESIDE (bē-sīd') prep. at the side. [O.E. be-, by, and sidan, of side.]
BESIDES (bē-sīdz') ad. over and above.
BESIEGE (bē-sēj') v.t. to lay siege to.
BESIEGER (bē-sē'jer) n. one who besieges.
BESMEAR (bē-smēr') v.t. to daub; soil; smear over [Eng. pref. be-, and SMEAR.]
BESMOKE (bē-smōk') v.t. to foul with smoke; dry with smoke. [Eng. pref. be-, and SMOKE.]
BESOM (bē'zum) n. a brush of twigs. [M.E. besum, fr O.E. besma.]
BESOT (bē-sot') v.t. to make sottish. [See SOT.]
BESOTTED (bē-sot'ed) a. stupefied with liquor; stupid.
BESOUGHT (bē-sawt') pret. and pp. of BESEECH.
BESPANGLE (bē-spang'gl) v.t. to adorn with spangles. [Eng. pref. be-, and SPANGLE.]
BESPATTER (bē-spat'er) v.t. to spatter over with water and dirt. [Eng. pref. be-, and SPATTER.]
BESPEAK (bē-spēk') v.t. [pret. BESPOKE; pp. BESPOKEN] to speak for beforehand.
BESPREAD (bē-spred') v.t. to spread over.
BESPRINKLE (bē-spring'kl) v.t. to scatter over.
BESSEMER (bes'e-mer) a. denoting the process of converting cast-iron into steel. [Fr. Sir H. Bessemer.]
BEST (best) a. superlative, most good. [O.E. betst=betest, fr. bet. [See BETTER.]
BESTEAD (bē-sted') pp. placed; disposed; circumstanced.
BESTIAL (bes'ti-al) a. belonging to a beast; filthy. [F., fr. L. bestialis, fr. bestia a beast.]
BESTIR (bē-ster') v.t. to move quickly.
BESTOW (bē-stō') v.t. to give; confer. [O.E. be, and stow, a place.]
BESTOWER (bē-stō'er) n. one who bestows.
BESTOWMENT (bē-stō'ment) n. act of conferring; the thing given; donation.
BESTREW (bē-strō', bē-strōō') v.t. to scatter over; sprinkle.
BESTRIDE (bē-strīd') v.t. [pret. BESTRID; pp. BESTRID, BESTRIDDEN] to place one leg over, so that a leg shall be on each side.
BESTUD (bē-stud') v.t. to adorn with studs or bosses.
BET (bet) n. a wager; stake;—v.t. [pp. BET or BETTED] to lay a wager. [See ABET.]
BETAKE (bē-tāk') v.t. [pret. BETOOK; pp. BETAKEN] to have recourse to.
BETHINK (bē-think') v.t. and i. [pret. BETHOUGHT] to reflect; recollect; consider.
BETIDE (bē-tīd') v.t. or i. to befall.
BETIMES (bē-tīmz') ad. in good time; seasonably.
BETOKEN (bē-tō'kn) v.t. to signify.
BETOOK (bē-took') pret. of BETAKE.
BETRAY (bē-trā') v.t. to disclose treacherously; to entrap. [E. pref. be-, and O.F. trair, fr. L. tradere, give up.]
BETRAYAL (bē-trā'al) n. breach of trust.
BETRAYER (bē-trā'er) n. one who betrays; a traitor.
BETROTH (bē-trōth', be-troth') v.t. to pledge marriage to. [E. pref. be-, and TROTH, TRUTH.]

BETROTHMENT (bē-trōth'ment, be-troth'ment) n. contract of marriage.
BETTER (bet'er) a. comparative of GOOD, more good;—v.t. to make better; improve. [O.E. betera.]
BETTERMENT (bet'er-ment) n. improvement.
BETTERS (bet'erz) n.pl. superiors.
BETTING (bet'ing) ppr. laying a wager;—n. act of laying a wager. [See ABET.]
BETTOR (bet'er) n. one who bets.
BETWEEN (bē-twēn') prep. in the middle. [O.E. betweonum, fr. be, by, and (dat. pl.) tweonum, twain.]
BEVEL (bev'el) n. a kind of rule used by masons, pointed at one end; a slant or inclination; —a. slanting; denoting any angle other than 45° or 90°;—v.t. [pp. BEVELLED] to cut to a bevel angle. [F. biveau, a carpenter's rule; of unknown etymology.]
BEVEL-WHEELS (bev'el-hwēlz) n. wheels working in different places, having their teeth cut at right angles. [BEVEL and WHEEL.]
BEVERAGE (bev'e-rāj) n. liquor; drink. [O.F. bevrage, fr. bevre, beivre, to drink; fr. L. bibere, drink.]
BEVY (bev'i) n. a flock of birds; brood. [Prob. fr. O.F. buvee, drink, a drinking party.]
BEWAIL (bē-wāl') v.t. to lament; grieve for. [E. pref. be-, and WAIL.]
BEWAILABLE (bē-wā'la-bl) a. that may be lamented.
BEWAILER (bē-wā'ler) n. one who laments.
BEWAILINGLY (bē-wā'ling-li) ad. in a bewailing manner.
BEWARE (bē-wār') v.i. to be cautious. [O.E. be, and wær, cautious.]
BEWILDER (bē-wil'der) v.t. to puzzle; lose in pathless places. [E. pref. be-, and M.E. wilderne, a desert.]
BEWILDERING (bē-wil'der-ing) ppr. or a involving in perplexity.
BEWILDERMENT (bē-wil'der-ment) n. state of being bewildered.
BEWITCH (bē-wich') v.t. to charm; fascinate; enchant. [See WITCH.]
BEWITCHERY (bē-wich'er-i) n. power of charming; fascination. Also BEWITCHMENT.
BEWITCHING (bē-wich'ing) a. having power to charm; fascinating.
BEWITCHINGLY (bē-wich'ing-li) ad. with power to charm and influence.
BEY (bā) n. a Turkish governor. [Turk.]
BEYOND (bē-yond') prep. on the farther side; —ad. at a distance. [O.E. be=by, and geond, across.]
BIAS (bī'as) n. weight on one side; partiality; propensity;—v.t. to incline to some side. [F. biais, an oblique line; fr. L. (acc.) bifacem looking two ways, fr. bi, and facies.]
BIASED (bī'ast) pp. or a. inclined to one side.
BIB (bib) n. a cloth under the chin; a fish of the cod family. [L. bibere, to drink.]
BIBBER (bib'er) n. a drinker; tippler.
BIBLE (bī'bl) n. the book that contains the sacred Scriptures. [L. biblia, n. G. (plu.) biblia, booklets, fr. biblos, book.]
BIBLICAL (bib'li-kal) a. relating to the Bible.
BIBLIOGRAPHIC (bib-li-ō-graf'ik) a. pertaining to a description of books.
BIBLIOGRAPHY (bib-li-og'ra-fi) n. a history or account of books. [BIBLE, and graphein, write.]
BIBLIOMANIAC (bib-li-ō-mā'ni-ak) n. one who has a rage for books. [BIBLE, and MANIA.]

BIBLIST (bĭ-blĭst, bĭb'lĭst) *n.* one conversant with the Bible. Also **BIBLICIST**.
BIBULOUS (bĭb'ū-lus) *a.* apt to imbibe.
BICARBONATE (bī-kär'bo-nāt) *n.* a carbonate containing two equivalents of carbon to one of a base.
BICENTENARY(bī-sen'te-nȧ-ri, bī-sen-te'nȧ-ri) *n.* two hundred years. [L. *bis*, twice, and *centum*, a hundred.]
BICEPHALOUS (bī-sef'ȧ-lus) *a.* having two heads. [L. *bi*, double, and G. *kephale*, a head.]
BICEPS (bī'seps) *n.* a muscle having two heads;—*a.* two-headed. [L. *bi*, double, and *caput*, the head.]
BICKER (bik'ẽr) *v.i.* to contend petulantly about trifles. [Perh. Celtic.]
BICKERING (bik'ẽr-ing) *n.* contention.
BICYCLE (bī'si-kl) *n.* a two-wheeled veloci-pede. [L. *bi*, double, and *kuklos*, a circle.]

Bicycle.

BID (bid) *v.t.* [*pret.* **BID, BADE**; *pp.* **BID, BIDDEN**] to offer; command;—*n.* an offer of price. [O.E. *beodan*, to command.]
BIDDABLE (bid'ȧ-bl) *a.* inclined to obey or do what is required.
BIDDEN (bid'n) *pp.* of **BID**.
BIDDER (bid'ẽr) *n.* one that offers.
BIDDING (bid'ing) *n.* an invitation; command; offer at an auction.
BIDE (bīd) *v.t.* or *i.* to dwell. [O.E. *bīdan*. See **ABIDE**.]
BIENNIAL (bī-en'i-ȧl) *a.* happening every two years. [L. *biennium*, a space of two years; fr. *bi*, twice, and *annus*, a year.]
BIER (bēr) *n.* a carriage to bear the dead. [O.E. *bær*, fr. *beran*, to bear.]
BIFLOROUS (bī-flō'rus) *a.* having two flowers. [L. *bi*, double, and (acc.) *florem*, a flower.]
BIFORM (bī'form) *a.* having two forms. [L. *bi*, double, and *forma*, form.]
BIFURCATE (bī-fur'kāt) *a.* having two branches. [Low L. (part.) *bifurcatus*, forked. See **FORK**.]
BIFURCATION (bī-fur-kā'shun) *n.* a forking into two branches.
BIG (big) *a.* large; swelled; pregnant. [Perh. Scand.]
BIGAMIST (big'ȧ-mist) *n.* one who has two wives or husbands.
BIGAMOUS (big'ȧ-mus) *a.* involving bigamy.
BIGAMY (big'ȧ-mi) *n.* the crime of having two wives or husbands at once. [Late L. (acc.) *bigamiam*, hybrid; fr. L. pref. *bi-*, and G. *gamos*, marriage.]
BIGHT (bīt) *n.* a small bay; the coil of a rope. [O.E. *byht*, fr. *bugan*, to bend.]
BIGNESS (big'nes) *n.* size; bulk.
BIGOT (big'ut) *n.* one unreasonably devoted to a party or creed. [F., of unknown origin.]
BIGOTED (big'ut-ed) *a.* unduly devoted.
BIGOTRY (big'ut-ri) *n.* great prejudice.
BIJOU (bē-zhōō') *n.* a jewel. [F., of uncertain origin.]
BIJOUTRY (bē-zhōō'tri) *n.* jewellery; trinkets.
BILBO (bil'bō) *n.* rapier; sword. [Fr. *Bilbao*, in Spain.]
BILBOES (bil'bōz) *n.pl.* stocks for the feet.
BILE (bīl) *n.* a liquor secreted in the liver. [F., fr. L. *bilis*.]

BILGE (bilj) *n.* the protuberant part of a cask; the broadest part of a ship's bottom;—*v.i.* to leak from fracture. [See **BULGE**.]
BILGE-WATER (bilj'waw-tẽr) *n.* water lying in the bilge.
BILIARY (bil'yȧ-ri) *a.* belonging to the bile.
BILINGUOUS (bī-ling'gwus) *a.* speaking two languages. Also **BILINGUAL**. [L. *bi-*, double, and *lingua*, the tongue.]
BILIOUS (bil'yus) *a.* pertaining to bile. [L. *biliosus*.]
BILL (bil) *n.* beak of a bird; an account; a note; draft of a law;—*v.i.* to caress; fondle. [O.E. *bile*: also Low L. *billa*=*bulla*, a schedule. See **BULL**.]
BILLED (bild) *a.* furnished with a bill.
BILLET (bil'et) *n.* a small note or letter; a stick of wood;—*v.t.* to quarter soldiers. [F., dim. fr. Low L. *billa*, a block of wood or a ball.]
BILLIARDS (bil'yȧrdz) *n.pl.* a game played on a table with balls and cues. [F. *billard*, fr. *bille*, fr. Low L. (acc.) *billam*, a ball.]
BILLINGSGATE (bil'ingz-gāt) *n.* foul, abusive language. [Fr. *Billingsgate*, a London fish-market.]
BILLION (bil'yun) *n.* a million of millions. [Coined fr. L. *bi*, double, and **MILLION**.]
BILLOW (bil'ō) *n.* a large wave of the sea;—*v.i.* to swell or roll like a wave. [Scand., conn. with **BULGE**.]
BILLOWY (bil'ō-i) *a.* swelling like a wave.
BIMENSAL (bī-men'sȧl) *a.* occurring once in two months. Also **BIMESTRIAL**. [L. *bis*, twice, and (acc.) *mensem*, a month.]
BIMETALLISM (bī-met'al-izm) *n.* the employment of two metals in the currency of a country. [L. *bi*, double, and **METAL**.]
BIMONTHLY (bī-munth'li) *a.* every two months. [L. pref. *bi-*.]
BIN (bin) *n.* a receptacle for corn, coal, etc.; a partition in a cellar for wine bottles;—*v.t.* to store in a bin. [O.E. *binn*, crib.]
BINARY (bī'nȧ-ri) *a.* composed of two. [L. *binarius*, fr. *bini*, two at a time.]
BIND (bīnd) *v.t.* or *i.* [*pret.* and *pp.* **BOUND**] to tie; confine; gird; restrain; oblige by kindness; confirm; form a border round; make costive. [O.E. *bindan*, to bind, conn. with Ger. *binden*.]
BINDER (bīn'dẽr) *n.* one who binds books.
BINDERY (bīn'dẽr-i) *n.* place for binding books.
BINDING (bīn'ding) *ppr.* confining;—*n.* a bandage; cover of a book.
BINNACLE (bin'ȧ-kl) *n.* the compass-box of a ship, with a light to show it at night. [Formerly *bittacle*, fr. Pg., fr. L. *habitaculum*, a little dwelling-place.]
BINOCLE (bin'o-kl) *n.* a telescope with two tubes. [F., fr. L. *binus*, double, and *oculus*, an eye.]
BINOCULAR (bī-nok'ū-lȧr) *a.* having two eyes.
BINOMIAL (bī-nō'mi-ȧl) *a.* having two names. [L. pref. *bi-*, double, and *nomen*, a name.]
BINOMINAL (bī-nom'i-nȧl) *a.* having two terms, connected by the sign *plus* + or *minus* —. [See **BINOMIAL**.]
BIOGRAPHER (bī-og'rȧ-fẽr) *n.* writer of biography. [See **BIOGRAPHY**.]
BIOGRAPHIC (bī-ō-graf'ik) *n.* pertaining to the history of a person's life.
BIOGRAPHY (bī-og'rȧ-fi) *n.* a history of one's life and character. [G. *bios*, life, and *graphein*, write.]
BIOLOGY (bī-ol'ō-ji) *n.* the science of life. [G. *bios*, life, and *logos*, discourse.]
BIOSCOPE (bī'o-scōp) *n.* See **KINEMATO-GRAPH**. [G. *Bios* life, and *scopein*, view.]
BIPAROUS (bip'ȧr-us) *a.* bringing forth two at a birth. [L. *bis*, two at a time, and *parere*, bring forth.]
BIPARTITE (bī-pär'tīt) *a.* that may be divided into w parts. [L. *bipartitus*, divided into two.] o

BIPARTITION (bī-pär-tish'un) *n.* division into two parts.

BIPED (bī'ped) *n.* an animal having only two feet. [L. stem *biped-*, of *bipes*, an animal with two feet.]

BIPLANE (bī-plān) *n.* an aeroplane supported by two plane surfaces. L. *bi*, double, and *planus*, level.]

BIRCH (berch) *n.* the name of a tree. [O.E. *beorc* (cf. Ger. *Birke*, and Scot. *birk*); M.E. *birche*.]

BIRD (berd) *n.* the name of the feathered race. [M.E.; O.E. *brid*.]

BIRD-EYED (berd'īd) *a.* quick-sighted.

BIRD-LIME (berd'līm) *n.* a glutinous substance to catch birds.

BIRD'S-EYE (berdz'ī) *a.* seen as if by a flying bird above;—*n.* a kind of tobacco.

BIRETTA (bi-ret'a) *n.* a square cap worn by Roman Catholic clergymen. [It. *berretta*.]

BIRTH (berth) *n.* the act of coming into life. [M.E. *birthe*, perh. fr. Scand.]

BIRTHDAY (berth'dā) *n.* anniversary of one's birth.

BIRTHPLACE (berth'plās) *n.* the place where one was born.

BIRTHRIGHT (berth'rīt) *n.* the rights to which one was born.

BISCUIT (bis'kit) *n.* hard bread in the form of small cakes; a kind of unglazed earthenware. [F., fr. *bis* = L. *bis*, twice, and (part.) *cuit*, fr. L. (acc. part.) *coctum*, cooked, fr. *coquere*, cook.]

BISECT (bī-sekt') *v.t.* to divide into two equal parts. [L. *bi*, twice, and *sectus*, cut.]

BISECTION (bī-sek'shun) *n.* a division into two equal parts.

BISHOP (bish'up) *n.* the head of a diocese. [O.E. *bisceop*; but see ARCHBISHOP.]

BISHOPDOM (bish'up-dum) *n.* jurisdiction of a bishop.

BISHOPRIC (bish'up-rik) *n.* a diocese.

BISMUTH (bis'muth) *n.* a brittle, yellow metal used in the arts and in medicine. [Ger.]

BISON (bis'un, bī'sun) *n.* a wild ox or species of buffalo. [L. *bison*, fr. Teut.]

BISSEXTILE (bi-seks'til) *n.* leap year. [L., fr. *bis-sextus* (dies), the 24th Feb., the 6th day before the Calends or 1st Mar., which was counted twice in leap years.]

BISULPHATE (bī-sul'fāt) *n.* a double sulphate. [L. *bi*, double. See SULPHUR.]

BIT (bit) *n.* the iron of a bridle; a morsel; a boring tool;—*v.t.* to put the bit in the mouth. [See BITE.]

BITCH (bich) *n.* a she-dog. [O.E. *bicce*, fr 'Scand.]

BITE (bit) *v.t.* [*pret.* BIT; *pp.* BITTEN] to seize or crush with the teeth; cheat;—*n.* act of biting; a wound made by the teeth; a mouthful; a trick or cheat. [O.E. *bitan*; cf. Ger. *bessen*.]

BITER (bī'tẹr) *n.* one that bites.

BITING (bī'ting) *a.* that bites; sharp; severe; sarcastic.

BITINGLY (bī'ting-li) *ad.* in a sharp, sarcastic manner.

BITTEN (bit'n) *pp.* wounded with the teeth.

BITTER (bit'ẹr) *a.* sharp; severe; afflictive. [O.E. *biter*, fr. *bitan*, bite.]

BITTERISH (bit'ẹr-ish) *a.* somewhat bitter.

BITTERN (bit'ẹrn) *n.* a bird of the heron family. [M.E. *bitoure*, fr. F. *butor*, fr. Low L. Cf. L. *bubare*, to cry like the bittern.]

BITTERNESS (bit'ẹr-nes) *n.* a bitter taste; extreme hatred. [See BITTER.]

BITTERS (bit'ẹrz) *n.pl.* a bitter drink.

BITUMEN (bi-tū'men, bit'ū-men) *n.* a strong-smelling inflammable substance. [L.]

BITUMINOUS (bi-tū'mi-nus) *a.* containing bitumen.

BIVAVLE (bī'valv) *n.* that which has two valves;—*a.* having two valves. [L. *bi-* double, and VALVE.]

BIVOUAC (biv'ŏŏ-ak, biv'wak) *v.i.* to watch or be on guard; encamp in the open air;—*n.* encampment without tents—said of the whole army in the field. [F., fr. Ger. *bei* by, and *Wacht*, watch.]

BLACK (blak) *a.* destitute of light; dark; cloudy; dismal;—*n.* an African; darkest colour;—*v.t.* to make black. [O.E. *blæc*. M.E. *blak*, black.]

BLACKAMOOR (blak'a-mŏŏr) *n.* a negro.

BLACK-ART (blak'ärt) *n.* magic.

BLACKBALL (blak'bawl) *n.* a composition for blacking shoes;—*v.t.* to reject by black ballots.

BLACK-BEER (blak'bēr) *n.* a black, syrupy beer; Dantzic beer.

BLACKBERRY (blak'bẹr-i) *n.* the fruit of the bramble.

BLACKBIRD (blak'berd) *n.* a song-bird of the thrush family.

BLACKBOARD (blak'bōrd) *n.* a board used for writing on with chalk.

BLACK-CAP (blak'kap) *n.* a small song-bird; mock nightingale.

BLACKCOCK (blak'kok) *n.* the heathcock or black grouse. [*fem.*

BLACKEN (blak'n) *v.t.* to make black; de-

BLACKGUARD (blag'ärd) *n.* a person of foul language.

BLACKISH (blak'ish) *a.* somewhat black.

BLACKLEAD (blak'led) *n.* plumbago; graphite.

BLACKLEG (blak'leg) *n.* a notorious gambler and cheat; a term applied by strikers to workmen who do the labour against the conditions of which the strike is taking place.

BLACKLETTER (blak'let-ẹr) *n.* the old English letter or character.

BLACK-LIST (blak'list) *n.* a printed list of insolvents, bankrupts, etc.

BLACKMAIL (blak'māl) *n.* a tribute paid for protection from robbery and pillage; extortion by threats of exposure, etc.

BLACKNESS (blak'nes) *n.* black colour; enormous wickedness.

BLACK-SHEEP (blak'shēp) *n.* a person of bad character.

BLACKSMITH (blak'smith) *n.* a smith that works in iron.

BLACKTHORN (blak'thorn) *n.* the sloe tree.

BLADDER (blad'ẹr) *n.* a vessel containing some liquid in the body; a blister; a pustule; a bag inflated with air. [O.E. *blædre*, blister, from *blawen*, to blow.]

BLADE (blād) *n.* a spire of grass; the cutting part of an instrument; flat part of an oar. [O.E. *blæd*, a leaf. Cf. Ger. *Blatt*.]

BLADE-BONE (blād'bōn) *n.* the scapula or upper bone of the shoulder.

BLADED (blā'ded) *a.* having a blade.

BLAIN (blān) *n.* a blister; blotch. [O.E. *blegen*, a boil; conn. with BLOW.]

BLAMABLE (blā'ma-bl) *a.* deserving blame; culpable; censurable.

BLAMABLY (blā'ma-bli) *ad.* culpably; faultily.

BLAME (blām) *v.t.* to censure; charge with a fault;—*n.* expression of disapprobation; imputation of a fault. [O.F. *blasmer* = F. *blâmer*, fr. L. *blasphemare*, to reproach.]

BLAMEFUL (blām'fool) *a.* faulty; censurable.

BLAMELESS (blām'les) *a.* without blame; guiltless.

BLAMEWORTHY (blām'wur-THi) *a.* deserving blame; censurable.

BLANCH (blänsh) *v.t.* or *i.* to whiten; evade; shift. [F. *blanchir*, bleach. Doublet of BLANK.]

BLANC-MANGE (bla-mawngzh') *n.* a preparation of isinglass, milk, sugar, etc., boiled. [F. *blanc-manger*, fr. *manger*, to eat.]

Fäte, fàr, ạdo; mē, hẹr; mīne; nōte; tūne; mŏŏn.

BLAND (bland) *a.* courteous; mild; gentle. [L. *blandus*, smooth.]
BLANDISH (blan'dish) *v.t.* to smooth; wheedle; caress. [O.F. *blandisant*, flattering, fr. *blandir*, fr. L. *blandiri*, to caress.]
BLANDISHMENT (blan'dish-ment) *n.* soothing speech.
BLANDNESS (bland'nes) *n.* state of being bland; mildness.
BLANK blangk) *a.* white; pale; unwritten; without rhyme; empty; straightforward; *—n.* void space; disappointment. [See BLANCH.]
BLANK-CARTRIDGE (blangk-kår'trij) *n.* cartridge of powder only.
BLANKET (blang'ket) *n.* a woollen covering for a bed. [O.F. *blanchet*, dim. of *blanc*. See BLANK.]
BLANKLY (blangk'li) *ad.* in a blank manner.
BLANK-VERSE (blangk'vers) *n.* unrhymed verse; the heroic verse of five feet.
BLARE (blâr) *v.i.* to roar; bellow;*—a.* loud sound; roar. [M.E. *blaren*, also *blasen*, fr. O.E. *blœsan*, to blow.]
BLARNEY (blår'ni) *n.* smooth, deceitful talk; flattery. [Fr. *Blarney*-stone in Castle Blarney, near Cork, reputed to give any one that kisses it the faculty of wheedling.]
BLASPHEME (blas-fēm') *v.t.* to speak with irreverence of God. [L., fr. G. *blasphemein*, to speak ill of, fr. *blapsis*, hurt, and *pheme*, speech.] [reviles God.
BLASPHEMER (blas-fē'mer) *n.* a person who blasphemy. [blasphemous way.
BLASPHEMOUS (blas'fe-mus) *a.* containing
BLASPHEMOUSLY (blas'fe-mus-li) *ad.* in a
BLASPHEMY (blas'fe-mi) *n.* language uttered impiously against God.
BLAST (blast) *n.* a gust of wind; sound made by blowing; blight; explosion of powder; *—v.t.* to cause to wither; split with powder; injure. [O.E. *blœst*, fr. *blœsan*, to blow. See BLOW.]
BLASTING (blas'ting) *n.* a blast; explosion.
BLATANT (blā'tant) *n.* bellowing; noisy. [Etym. unknown.]
BLATTER (blat'ter) *v.i.* to patter; talk idly. [L. *blaterare*, to prate.]
BLAZE (blāz) *v.t.* to cut a mark on a tree;— *v.i.* to flame; diffuse a report;*—n.* a flame; a stream of light. [M.E. *blase*, fr. O.E. *blœse*, flame.]
BLAZING (blā'zing) *a.* emitting flame; making conspicuous.
BLAZON (blā'zn) *v.t.* to display with ostentation;*—n.* the art of heraldry. [F. *blason*, a shield.]
BLAZONRY (blā'zn-ri) *n.* the art of describing coats of arms.
BLEACH (blēch) *v.t.* or *i.* to whiten. [O.E. *blœcan*, fr. *blœc*, shining.]
BLEAK (blēk) *a.* open; exposed; cold; cheerless; dreary. [O.E. *blœc*, *blåc*, pale.]
BLEAKLY (blēk'li) *ad.* coldly.
BLEAKNESS (blēk'nes) *a.* exposedness to the wind; coldness.
BLEAR (blēr) *a.* dim with watery rheum;— *v.t.* to make the eyes watery. [Scand., conn. with BLUR.]
BLEAR-EYED (blēr'īd) *a.* having eyes dim with rheum.
BLEAT (blēt) *v.i.* to cry like a sheep;*—n.* the cry of a sheep. [O.E. *blœtan*.]
BLEB (bleb) *n.* a little tumour or blister; a bubble. [Perhaps conn. with BULB.]
BLEED (blēd) *v.t.* or *i.* [*pret.* and *pp.* BLED] to let blood. [O.E. *bledan*, fr. *blod*.]
BLEEDING (blē'ding) *n.* letting of blood with the lancet; discharge of blood.
BLEMISH (blem'ish) *v.t.* to disfigure; mark with deformity; hurt;*—n.* a deformity; disgrace; taint. [O.F. *blemisant*, bruising, discolouring; fr. *bleme* = F. *blême*, livid, fr. Scand.]

BLENCH (blensh) *v.i.* to shrink or start back; flinch. [O.E. *blencan*, make blink, deceive; confused with BLINK.]
BLEND (blend) *v.t.* to confound in a mass; mingle together. [M.E. *blenden*, fr. O.E. *blandan*, to mix.]
BLESS (bles) *v.t.* to wish happiness to; praise; consecrate. [O.E. *bletsian*, to bless; conn. with *blod*, blood.]
BLESSED (bles'ed, blest) *a.* happy; holy.
BLESSEDNESS (bles'ed-nes) *n.* happiness; heavenly joy.
BLESSING (bles'ing) *n.* divine favour; benediction.
BLEST (blest) *a.* blessed; made happy or holy.
BLEW (blū) *pret.* of BLOW.
BLIGHT (blīt) *n.* a disease; mildew;*—v.t.* to affect with blight; blast; frustrate. [Etym. uncertain.]
BLIND (blīnd) *a.* destitute of sight; dark; obscure;*—v.t.* to prevent from seeing;*—n.* anything that intercepts the sight. [O.E. *blind*, blind.]
BLIND-FIRE (blīnd'fīr) *n.* fuel in a grate ready for kindling.
BLINDFOLD (blīnd'fōld) *a.* having the eyes covered;*—v.t.* to cover the eyes.
BLINDLY (blīnd'li) *ad.* without examination or judgment.
BLINDNESS (blīnd'nes) *n.* a want of sight; ignorance.
BLINDSIDE (blīnd'sīd) *n.* the side most assailable; a foible.
BLINDWORM (blīnd'wurm) *n.* a small reptile; slow-worm.
BLINK (blingk) *v.i.* to wink; glimmer;*—v.t.* to evade;*—n.* a glance; glimpse; a glimmer. [M.E. *blenken*, to shine; conn. with O.E. *blisan*, to glitter.]
BLINKERS (bling'kerz) *n.pl.* broad pieces of leather shading a horse's eye sideways.
BLISS (blis) *n.* the highest happiness; blessedness. [O.E. *blids*, *bliths*, blitheness.]
BLISSFUL (blis'fool) *a.* very happy; blessed.
BLISSFULNESS (blis'fool-nes) *n.* exalted happiness; felicity.
BLISTER (blis'ter) *n.* a thin bladder on the skin; a plaster;*—v.t.* to raise blisters:— *v.i.* to rise in blisters. [M.E., conn. with O.E. *blœsan*, to blow.]
BLISTERY (blis'ter-i) *a.* full of blisters.
BLITHE (blīth) *a.* gay; airy; joyous. [O.E. *blithe*, joyous.]
BLITHEFUL (blīth'fool) *a.* gay; jocund.
BLITHELY (blīth'li) *ad.* joyfully.
BLITHESOME (blīth'sum) *a.* gay; joyous; merry.
BLIZZARD (bliz'ard) *n.* a violent snowstorm with intense cold. [Onomatopœic word.]
BLOAT (blōt) *v.t.* to cause to swell;*—v.i.* to puff up. [Scand. = soft, effeminate.]
BLOATED (blō'ted) *a.* puffed; swelled.
BLOATER (blō'ter) *n.* a herring dried in smoke.
BLOB (blob) *n.* anything small and globular, as a dewdrop; a careful brush impression in colouring. [Form of BLEB.]
BLOCK (blok) *n.* a piece of wood in which a pulley runs; a heavy piece of timber, or massive body; an obstruction;*—v.t.* to shut up or stop; shape roughly. [Celt. Doublet of PLUG.]
BLOCKADE (blo-kād') *n.* a close siege;*—v.t.* to surround with a force; shut up.
BLOCKHEAD (blok'hed) *n.* a person of dull intellect.
BLOCKHOUSE (blok'hous) *n.* a wooden fortress.
BLOCKISH (blok'ish) *a.* deficient in understanding; stupid.
BLONDE (blond) *n.* a lady with fair complexion, light hair and eyes;*—a.* fair complexioned. [F.]

BLOOD (blud) *n.* the red fluid which circulates in animals; kindred; race; life;—*v.t.* to stain with or let blood. [O.E. *blod,* conn. with *blowan,* to flourish.]

BLOOD-BOUGHT (blud'bawt) *a.* got at the price of blood.

BLOOD-GUILTINESS (blud'gil-ti-nes) *n.* guilt of shedding blood unlawfully. [BLOOD, and O.E. *gylt,* crime.]

BLOOD-HEAT (blud'hēt) *n.* heat of the same degree as the blood.

BLOOD-HORSE (blud'hors) *n.* a horse of the purest breed, for racing.

BLOODHOUND (blud'hound) *n.* a ferocious kind of dog employed to track fugitive slaves. [BLOOD, and O.E. *hund,* dog.]

BLOODILY (blud'i-li) *ad.* cruelly.

BLOODLESS (blud'les) *a.* without blood.

BLOODSHED (blud'shed) *n.* slaughter.

BLOODSHOT (blud'shot) *a.* red and inflamed.

BLOODSTONE (blud'stōn) *n.* a green stone spotted with jasper.

BLOOD-SUCKER (blud'suk-ẹr) *n.* a leech; a cruel man. [BLOOD, and O.E. *sucan,* to suck.]

BLOODTHIRSTY (blud'thẹrs-ti) *a.* eager for blood. [BLOOD, and O.E. *thyrst.*]

BLOOD-VESSEL (blud'ves-el) *n.* an artery or vein. [BLOOD, and O.F. *vaissel,* a VESSEL, which see.]

BLOODY (blud'i) *a.* stained with blood.

BLOOM (blōōm) *n.* blossom; the flush on the cheek; square iron bar;—*v.i.* to yield blossoms. [Scand. Cf. Ger. *Blume,* flower.]

BLOOMING (blōō'ming) *a.* thriving with youth, health, and beauty.

BLOOMY (blōō'mi) *a.* full of bloom; flowery.

BLOSSOM (blos'um) *n.* the flower of plants; —*v.i.* to put forth blossoms. [M.E. *blosme,* fr. O.E. *blostma,* fr. *blowan,* to bloom.]

BLOT (blot) *v.t.* [*pp.* BLOTTED] to stain; spot with ink; efface;—*n.* spot; disgrace. [Scand.]

BLOTCH (bloch) *n.* an inflamed spot on the skin. [Perh. fr. BLOT.]

BLOTTER (blot'ẹr) *n.* one who blots; a blotting book; a waste book.

BLOTTING (blot'ing) *n.* drying of blots; un-sized paper used to dry up wet ink.

BLOUSE (blouz) *n.* a light loose outer garment. [F.]

BLOW (blō) *n.* a stroke; calamity; egg of a fly;—*v.i.* or *t.* [*pret.* BLEW; *pp.* BLOWN] to make a current of air; pant; breathe; blossom; deposit eggs in. [M.E. *blowe.* Cf. Ger. *bläuen,* strike. Also O.E. *bleowan.* Cf. Ger. *blühen.*]

BLOWER (blō'ẹr) *n.* a plate of iron to increase a current of air.

BLOW-HOLE (blō'hōl) *n.* the nostril of a whale; an air-hole.

BLOW-PIPE (blō'pīp) *n.* a tube by which a current of air is forced through flame upon any substance.

BLOWY (blō'i) *a.* windy; breezy.

BLUBBER (blub'ẹr) *n.* the fat of whales;—*v.i.* to weep so as to swell the cheeks. [E., conn. with BLOB.]

BLUCHER (blōō'chẹr) *n.* a kind of half boot. [Fr. Von *Blucher.*]

BLUDGEON (bluj'un) *n.* a short, thick club. [Celt.]

BLUE (blōō) *a.* of a blue colour;—*n.* one of the primary colours;—*v.t.* to dye or stain blue. [M.E. *blew, bleu;* fr. O.F. *bloe, bleu,* fr. Ger.]

BLUEBELL (blōō'bel) *n.* a plant with blue, bell-shaped flowers.

BLUEBERRY (blōō'bẹr-i) *n.* a plant and its fruit; whortleberry.

BLUE-BOOK (blōō'book) *n.* a publication issued by Parliament.

BLUENESS (blōō'nes) *n.* the quality of being blue.

BLUE-RIBBON (blōō'rib-un) *n.* the badge of the Order of the Garter; any object of ambitious rivalry.

BLUES (blōōz) *n.pl.* lowness of spirits.

BLUE-STOCKING (blōō-stok'ing) *n.* a literary lady.

BLUFF (bluf) *a.* swelled; blustering; steep; frank; hearty;—*n.* a steep bank overhanging the sea or a river. [Perh. D.]

BLUISH (blōō'ish) *a.* blue in a small degree.

BLUNDER (blun'dẹr) *v.i.* to mistake grossly; —*n.* gross mistake; error. [M.E. *blondren* to puzzle over; fr. Scand.]

BLUNDERBUSS (blun'dẹr-bus) *n.* a short gun with large bore. [Corrupt. fr. D. *donderbus,* thunder-tube.]

BLUNDERER (blun'dẹr-ẹr) *n.* one who commits blunders.

BLUNDERING (blun'dẹr-ing) *a.* mistaking grossly; stumbling.

BLUNT (blunt) *a.* dull on the edge or point; rude; abrupt;—*v.t.* to dull; depress. [Scand., conn. with BLUNDER.]

BLUNTLY (blunt'li) *ad.* in a blunt manner.

BLUNTNESS (blunt'nes) *n.* a want of edge or point; plainness; abruptness.

BLUR (blur) *n.* a blot; spot; stain;—*v.t.* to obscure without quite effacing. [Form of BLEAR.]

BLURT (blurt) *v.t.* to utter inadvertently or suddenly. [Onomatopœic word.]

BLUSH (blush) *v.i.* to redden in the face;— *n.* a red colour caused by shame or confusion. [O.E. *blyscan,* shine.]

BLUSHING (blush'ing) *n.* act of turning red; —*a.* reddish; modest.

BLUSHINGLY (blush'ing-li) *ad.* with blushes.

BLUSTER (blus'tẹr) *v.i.* to roar; bully; —*n.* a roar; tumult; boast; swagger. [Scand., conn. with BLAST.]

BLUSTERING (blus'tẹr-ing) *n.* tumult; noise.

BLUSTERINGLY (blus'tẹr-ing-li) *ad.* in a blustering manner.

BLUSTEROUS (blus'tẹr-us) *a.* noisy; tumultuous. Also **BLUSTROUS.**

BOA (bō'a) *n.* a genus of large serpents; a long round piece of fur, resembling a serpent, worn round the neck by ladies. [L.]

Boa.

BOAR (bōr) *n.* a male swine. [O.E. *bar* the male swine.]

BOARD (bōrd) *n.* a piece of timber sawn thin and broad; a table; food; a council;— *v.t.* or *i.* to lay with boards; enter a ship by force; give or receive diet. [O.E. *bord,* board, ship's side.]

BOARDER (bōrd'ẹr) *n.* one who pays for food taken at another's table; one who enters a ship by force.

BOARD-WAGES (bōrd'wā-jes) *n.pl.* allowance to servants to keep themselves.

BOARISH (bōr'ish) *a.* swinish; brutal.

BOAST (bōst) *v.i.* or *t.* to talk ostentatiously; glory in;—*n.* a vaunting speech. [Prob. E.]

BOASTER (bōs'tẹr) *n.* one who boasts.

BOASTFUL (bōst'fool) *a.* vain; haughty.

BOASTFULLY (bōst'fool-i) *ad.* in a boastful manner.

BOASTING (bōs'ting) *n.* act of boasting.

BOASTINGLY (bōs'ting-li) *ad.* in a boasting, ostentatious manner.

BOAT (bōt) *n.* a small open vessel;—*v.t.* to convey in a boat;—*v.i.* to go in a boat. [O.E. *bat,* fr. Celt. Cf. F. *bateau.*]

BOAT-HOOK (bōt'hook) *n.* a pole with an iron point and hook to push or pull a boat. [BOAT, and O.E. *hoc*, hook.]

BOATING (bō'ting) *n.* act or practice of rowing in a boat. [boat.

BOATMAN (bōt'man) *n.* one who manages a boat.

BOATSWAIN (bō'sn, bōt'swān) *n.* an officer in a ship who has charge of the boats and rigging. [See SWAIN.]

BOB (bob) *n.* something that plays loosely; a blow; a short wig;—*v.t.* to move with a jerk; beat;—*v.i.* to play backward and forward; play loosely. [Etym. uncertain.]

BOBTAIL (bob'tāl) *n.* a tail cut short; the rabble.

BODE (bōd) *v.t.* or *i.* to presage; foreshow. [O.E. *bodian*, to announce; fr. *bod*, a message. Conn. with BID.]

BODEFUL (bōd'fool) *n.* ominous of evil.

BODICE (bod'is) *n.* a close-fitting garment for the body, worn by women.

BODIED (bod'id) *a.* having a body.

BODILESS (bod'i-les) *a.* without a body.

BODILY (bod'i-li) *a.* relating to the body.

BODING (bō'ding) *n.* an omen.

BODKIN (bod'kin) *n.* an instrument to bore holes; a dagger. [Perh. Celt.]

BODY (bod'i) *n.* the whole trunk of an animal; person; main part; mass; system. [E.]

BODYGUARD (bod'i-gärd) *n.* a guard of a person. [BODY, and O.F. *garder*, guard; O.E. *weardian*. See WARD.]

BOER (bŏŏr) *n.* a Dutch farmer at the Cape. [D. Cf. BOOR, Ger. *Bauer*.]

BOG (bog) *n.* a fen o morass. [Celt.]

BOGGLE (bog'l) *v.i.* to hesitate from fear of difficulties. [Fr. BOGLE.]

BOGGLER (bog'ler) *n.* one that hesitates.

BOGGY (bog'i) *a.* marshy; swampy.

BOGIE (bō'gi) *n.* a truck running on four wheels to take sharp curves. [Etym. unknown.]

BOGLE (bō'gl) *n.* a spectre or imaginary object of terror. [Celt., fr. BUG.]

BOG-TROTTER (bog'tro'ter) *n.* one who lives among bogs; an Irishman.

BOGUS (bō'gus) *a.* counterfeit; spurious. [Amer. coinage.]

BOHEA (bō-hē') *n.* a coarse kind of black tea. [Fr. Chinese.]

BOHEMIAN (bō-hē'mi-an) *n.* an artist or literary man, who lives a free, unconventional life. [Fr. *Bohemia*.]

BOIL (boil) *n.* a sore swelling;—*v.i.* to bubble through heat;—*v.t.* to cause to boil. [O.F. *boillir*, fr. L. *bullire*, fr. *bulla*, a bubble.]

BOILER (boi'ler) *n.* a vessel for boiling.

BOILERY (boi'ler-i) *n.* a place for boiling.

BOISTEROUS (hois'ter-us) *a.* violent; noisy. [E., of uncertain etym.]

BOISTEROUSLY (bois'ter-us-li) *ad.* in a boisterous manner.

BOISTEROUSNESS (hois'ter-us-nes) *n.* turbulence; disorderly noise.

BOLD (bōld) *a.* having or requiring courage; brave; valiant; prominent. [O.E. *beald*, *bald*, daring.]

BOLD-FACED (hōld'fāst) *a.* impudent.

BOLDLY (bōld'li) *ad.* in a bold manner.

BOLDNESS (bōld'nes) *n.* courage; confidence; impudence. [cylindrical body.

BOLE (bōl) *n.* the body or stem of a tree; any

BOLL (bōl) *n.* a pod; a seed-vessel;—*v.i.* to form into a round pod. [Form of BOWL.]

BOLSTER (bōl'ster) *n.* a long pillow;—*v.t.* to pad; support. [E., conn. with BULGE.]

BOLSTERING (bōl'ster-ing) *n.* a prop or support.

BOLT (bōlt) *n.* bar of a door; an arrow; lightning; a piece of canvas of 38 yards; —*v.t.* to fasten; sift;—*v.i.* to leave suddenly. [E.; also fr. O.F. *bulter* = *bureter*, sift, fr. *bure*, canvas, fr. Low L. (acc.) *burram*, coarse red cloth, fr. L. *burrus*, red.]

BOLTER (bōl'ter) *n.* a sieve to separate flour from bran. [See BOLT.]

BOLTING-CLOTH (bōl'ting-kloth) *n.* a linen or hair cloth used for sifting.

BOLUS (bō'lus) *n.* a large pill. [L., fr. G. *bolos*, a clod.]

BOMB (bom) *n.* an iron shell to be filled with powder and discharged from a mortar.

BOMBARD (bum'bärd) *n.* a short cannon. [F. *bombe*, fr. L., fr. G. *bombos*, a hollow sound, BOOM.]

BOMBARD (bum-bärd', bom-bärd') *v.t.* to attack with bombs. [F. *bombarde*, a cannon.]

BOMBARDIER (bum-bar-dēr', bom-bar-dēr') *n.* one who serves a mortar.

BOMBARDMENT (bum'bärd-ment, bom-bärd'ment) *n.* an attack with bombs.

BOMBAST (bum'bast, bom'bast) *n.* high-sounding language;—*a.* consisting of swelling words. [It., fr. Low L. *bombax*, fr. G. *bombux*, cotton wadding.]

BOMBASTIC (bum-bas'tik, bom-bas'tik) *a.* inflated; extravagant.

BOMBAZINE (bum-ba-zēn', bom-ba-zēn') *n.* a slight twilled stuff. [F. *bombasin*, fr. Low L. (acc.) *bombacinum*, of cotton. See BOMBAST.]

BOND (bond) *n.* anything that binds;—*v.t.* to secure by bond;—*a.* in a servile state; captive. [M.E. *bond*, or *band*; see BAND.]

BONDAGE (bon'dāj) *n.* slavery; captivity; imprisonment.

BONDING (bon'ding) *n.* storing goods under the custom house till the duties are paid.

BONDMAID (bond'mād) *n.* a woman slave.

BONDMAN (bond'man) *n.* a man slave.

BONDSERVANT (bond'ser-vant) *n.* a slave. [BOND, and L. *servus*, a slave.]

BONDSMAN (bondz'man) *n.* one bound as surety for another.

BONDWOMAN (bond'woom-an) *n.* a woman slave.

BONE (bōn) *n.* the firm, hard substance which forms the framework of an animal. [O.E. *ban*. Cf. Ger. *Bein*.]

BONELESS (bōn'les) *a.* wanting bones.

BONE-SETTER (bōn'set-er) *n.* a man that sets broken bones.

BONFIRE (bon'fir) *n.* a triumphal fire. [BONE and FIRE.]

BONNET (bon'et) *n.* a covering for the head. [F., of unknown etym.]

BONNY (bon'i) *a.* handsome; merry. [Scot., fr. F. *bonne* (fem.), fr. *bon*.]

BONUS (bō'nus) *n.* a premium, as on a loan or other privilege. [L. *bonus*, good.]

BONY (bō'ni) *a.* full of bones; strong.

BOOBY (bŏŏ'bi) *n.* a dunce; a bird. [Sp. *bobo*. Cf. F. *baube*, fr. L. *balbus*, stammering.]

BOOK (book) *n.* a volume;—*v.t.* to enter in a book. [O.E. *boc*, beech, and then book.]

BOOK-ACCOUNT (book'a-kount) *n.* account of debit and credit on some branch of trade —distinguished from *personal* account.

BOOKBINDER (book'bin-der) *n.* one who binds books.

BOOKCASE (book'kās) *n.* a case for books. [BOOK, and O.F. *casse*, fr. L. (acc.) *capsam*, from *capere*, take.]

BOOKING (book'ing) *n.* registry in a book; entering in a ledger.

BOOKING-OFFICE (book'ing-of-fis) *n.* place where passengers and parcels are booked.

BOOK-KEEPER (book'kē-per) *n.* a keeper of accounts.

BOOK-KEEPING (book'kē-ping) *n.* the keeping of accounts.

BOOK-MAKING (book'mā-king) *n.* art of compiling books; systematic betting on horse races.

BOOKMAN (book'man) *n.* a learned or scholarly man.

BOOK-MUSLIN (book'mus-lin) *n.* a fine kind of muslin. [BOOK, and O.F. *mosolin*, fr. It., fr. *Mosul*, in Asiatic Turkey.]

BOOKSELLER (book'sel-ẹr) *n.* a retailer of books.

BOOKWORM (book'wurm) *n.* a close student. [BOOK, and O.E. *wyrm*, a worm.]

BOOM (bŏŏm̃) *n.* a spar to extend the bottom of a sail; a bar across a river; a deep sound;—*v.i.* to rush; roar. [D. = a tree. Cf. BEAM, Ger. *Baum*. Also M.E. *bommen*, to make a hollow sound.]

BOOMERANG (bŏŏ'me-rang) *n.* a missile of hard wood, so constructed as to return to the thrower. [Australian.]

BOOMING (bŏŏ'ming) *ppr.* or *a.* rushing with violence; roaring like waves.

BOON (bŏŏn) *a.* gay; merry; kind;—*n.* a gift; present; favour. [Fr. F. *bon*, gay; also Scand. Cf. O.E. *ben*, a blessing.]

BOOR (bŏŏr) *n.* a clown; countryman. [D. *Boer*.]

BOORISH (bŏŏr'ish) *a.* clownish; rustic.

BOOT (bŏŏt) *v.t.* to profit; put on boots;— *n.* profit; a covering for the feet. [O.E. *bot*, profit. Conn. with BATTEN, BETTER. Also O.F. *boute* (= F. *botte*), fr. Low L. (acc.) *bottam*, a sort of barrel.]

BOOTEE (bŏŏ-tē') *n.* a short boot; a kind of muslin.

BOOTH (bŏŏth) *n.* a temporary shelter of slight construction. [Scand.]

BOOTIED (bŏŏ'tid) *a.* laden with plunder. [See BOOT.]

BOOTJACK (bŏŏt'jak) *n.* a stock for pulling off boots.

BOOTLESS (bŏŏt'les) *a.* unprofitable; useless.

BOOTS (bŏŏts) *n.* a servant in an hotel.

BOOT-TREE (bŏŏt'trē) *n.* a wooden mould or block to shape a boot.

BOOTY (bŏŏ'ti) *n.* pillage; plunder; spoil.

BORACIC (bō-ras'ik) *a.* pertaining to borax.

BORAGE (bur'āj) *n.* a plant, the flowers of which were infused as a cordial. [Low L. *borago*.]

BORAX (bō'raks) *n.* a compound of boracic acid and soda, used as a styptic. [Low L., fr. Per. *burah*.]

BORDER (bor'dẹr) *n.* an edge; boundary;— *v.t.* or *i.* to adorn with a border; make a border. [F. *bordure*, fr. D.]

BORDERER (bor'dẹr-ẹr) *n.* one who dwells near a border.

BORE (bōr) *v.t.* to make a hole with an auger; weary;—*n.* a hole made by boring; a tiresome person. [O.E. *borian*. Cf. Ger. *bohren*.]

BOREAL (bō'rē-ạl) *a.* northern.

BOREAS (bō'rē-as) *n.* the north wind. [L. *Boreas*, the north wind.]

BORER (bōr'ẹr) *n.* a piercing tool; a seaworm.

BORN (born) *pp.* brought forth.

BORNE (bôrn) *pp.* of BEAR, carried.

BOROUGH (bur'ō) *n.* a corporation town. [O.E. *burh* or *burg*, a fort or city, fr. *beorgan*, to protect. Cf. Ger. *Burg*.]

BORROW (bor'ō) *v.t.* to obtain the use of for a time. [M.E. *borwen*, fr. O.E. *borgian*, fr. *borh*, pledge.]

BORROWER (bor'ō-ẹr) *n.* one who borrows.

BORT (bort) *n.* fragments of diamonds, ground and used in polishing. [F.]

BOSH (bosh) *n.* nonsense; idle talk; used also as an *interjection*. [Turk.]

BOSOM (bŏŏ'zum) *n.* the breast; heart;—*v.t.* to conceal. [O.E. *bosme*.]

BOSS (bos) *n.* a stud; knob. [F. *bosse*, a hump, a swelling.]

BOSSED (bost) *a.* ornamented with bosses.

BOSSY (bos'i) *a.* containing bosses.

BOTANIC (bō-tan'ik) *a.* relating to plants.

BOTANISE (bot'ạ-nīz) *v.i.* to study plants.

BOTANIST (bot'ạ-nist) *n.* a person skilled in plants.

BOTANY (bot'ạ-ni) *n.* that branch of natural history that treats of plants. [F., fr. G. *botanikos*, relating to plants, fr. *botane*, herb.]

BOTCH (boch) *n.* swelling; work ill-finished; —*v.t.* to mend clumsily. [O.F. *bose* = F. *bosse*. Doublet of BOSS. Also D. *botsen*, strike.]

BOTFLY (bot'flī) *n.* the gadfly. [Etym. unknown; conn. with BITE improbable.]

BOTH (bŏth) *a.* two taken together. [Scand. Cf. Ger. *beide*, O.E. *ba*, L. *am-bo*, G. *am-pho*.]

BOTHER (boTH'ẹr) *v.t.* to perplex. [Celt.]

BOTHERATION (boTH-e-rā'shun) *n.* trouble; worry.

BOTHERSOME (boTH'ẹr-sum) *a.* causing trouble.

BOTTLE (bot'l) *n.* a narrow-mouthed vessel for liquor;—*v.t.* to put into bottles. [O.F. *bouteille*, fr. O.F. *boute*, barrel. See BOOT.]

BOTTLE-GLASS (bot'l-glás) *n.* a coarse green glass.

BOTTLE-HOLDER (bot'l-hōl-dẹr) *n.* one who aids a boxer in a prize fight.

BOTTLE-NOSE (bot'l-nōs) *n.* a kind of whale.

BOTTLER (bot'lẹr) *n.* one who bottles liquors.

BOTTOM (bot'um) *n.* the lowest part; the ground under water; a valley; dregs;—*v.t.* to found or build upon. [O.E. *botm*. Cf. Ger. *Boden*.]

BOTTOMLESS (bot'um-les) *a.* without a bottom.

BOTTOMRY (bot'um-ri) *n.* the act of borrowing money on a ship.

BOUDOIR (bŏŏ'dwár) *n.* a small private apartment. [F., fr. *bouder*, to be ill-humoured.]

BOUGH (bou) *n.* a branch. [O.E. *boᵹ, boh*.]

BOUGHT (bawt) *pret.* and *pp.* of BUY, purchased.

BOUGIE (bŏŏ'zhi) *n.* a wax candle; a surgical instrument. [F. = candle, fr. *Bugia*, in Algeria.]

BOUILLI (bŏŏl'yĕ, bŏŏ'i-yi) *n.* boiled meat. [F., fr. O.F. *boillir*.]

BOULDER (bōl'dẹr) *n.* a roundish mass of rock. [Scand.]

BOULEVARD (bŏŏ'le-várd, bŏŏl'várd, bŏŏl'-vár) *n.* a rampart; a street or promenade planted with trees. [F. for Ger. *Bollwerk*. See BULWARK.]

BOUNCE (bouns) *v.i.* to leap; spring;—*n.* a leap; sudden noise; a boast. [D. *bonzen*, to strike.]

BOUNCER (boun'sẹr) *n.* a boaster; a liar.

BOUNCING (houn'sing) *a.* stout; plump and strong; boasting.

BOUND (bound) *v.t.* or *i.* to limit; restrain; spring;—*a.* destined; going to. [O.F. *boune, bodne*, fr. Celt. Also Scand. = prepared.]

BOUNDARY (boun'dạ-ri) *n.* a limit; mark; barrier.

BOUNDEN (boun'den) *a.* required; necessary, as our *bounden* duty.

BOUNDLESS (bound'les) *a.* unlimited.

BOUNTEOUS (boun'te-us) *a.* liberal; kind. [See BOUNTY.]

BOUNTIFUL (boun'ti-fool) *a.* liberal; generous. [See BOUNTY.]

BOUNTIFULLY (boun'ti-fool-i) *ad.* generously.

BOUNTIFULNESS (boun'ti-fool-nes) *n.* generosity.

BOUNTY (boun'ti) *n.* liberality in giving; a premium. [F. *bonté*, goodness, fr. L. (acc.) *bonitatem*.]

BOUQUET (bŏŏ-kā', bŏŏ'kā) *n.* a bunch of flowers. [O.F. *boscage*, fr. Low L. (acc.) *boscum*, a thicket.]

BOURGEOIS (bur-jois') *n.* a kind of printing type. [F.]

BOURN (bôrn, bŏŏrn) *n.* a bound; limit. [F. *borne*, O.F. *bonne*. See BOUND.]

BOURSE (bóórs) *n.* a French Exchange. [See PURSE]

BOUT (bout) *n.* a turn; trial; essay. [Doublet of BIGHT, which see.]

BOVINE (bō'vīn) *a.* relating to cattle. [L. *bovinus*, fr. stem *bov-* of *bos*, an ox.]

BOW (bou) *v.t.* and *i.* to bend down;—*n.* an act of reverence or respect; the rounded part of a ship's side forward.

BOW (bō) *n.* an instrument to shoot arrows; anything curved; a fiddlestick. [M.E. *bowen*, *bogen*, fr. O.E. *bugan*, to bend. Also O.E. *boga*, bow.]

BOWELS (bou'elz) *n.pl.* the intestines. [O.F. *boel*, fr. L. *botellum*, a small sausage.]

BOWER (bou'er) *n.* an arbour; an anchor at the bow. [O.E. *bur*, a dwelling.]

BOWERY (bou'er-i) *a.* full of bowers; shady.

BOWING (bō'ing) *n.* art of using the bow on the strings;—(bou'ing) inclination.

BOWL (bōl) *n.* a deep vessel. [O.E. *bolla*.]

BOWLER (bō'ler) *n.* one who plays at bowls; one who pitches the ball in cricket. [O.F. *boule*, fr. L. (acc.) *bullam*.]

BOWLINE (bō'lin) *n.* a rope to hold a sail to the wind.

BOWLING-GREEN (bō'ling-grēn) *n.* a green for bowlers.

BOWMAN (bō'man) *n.* an archer;—(bou'man) foremost rower.

BOWSPRIT (bō'sprit) *n.* a spar projecting from a ship's head. [D. *boegspriet*.]

BOWSTRING (bō'string) *n.* a string for a bow; a Turkish punishment. [BOW, and O.E. *strenge*, a cord, fr. *strang*, strong.]

BOW-WINDOW (bō'win-dō) *n.* a projecting window.

BOX (boks) *n.* a tree; a wooden case; blow on the ear;—*v.t.* or *i.* to put in a box; strike. [O.E. *box*, box-tree, fr. L. *buxus*, fr. G. *puksos*.]

BOXEN (bok'sn) *a.* made of box.

BOXER (bok'ser) *n.* one who fights with the fists.

BOY (boi) *n.* a male child; lad. [M.E. *boi*, fr. Teut.]

BOYCOTT (boi'kot) *v.t.* to seclude from intercourse or dealings with. [Fr. Captain *Boycott*.]

BOYHOOD (boi'hood) *n.* state of being a boy.

BOYISH (boi'ish) *a.* like a boy; trifling.

BOYISHNESS (boi'ish-nes) *n.* the manners of a boy.

BRACE (brās) *n.* that which holds; a strap; a pair;—*v.t.* to bind; tie; tighten. [O.F. *brace* =F. *bras*, arm, fr. L. (pl.), *brachia*, arms.]

BRACELET (brās'let) *n.* an ornament for the wrist. [F. dim. See BRACE.]

BRACHIAL (brak'i-al, brā'ki-al) *a.* belonging to the arm. [L. *brachia*, arms.]

BRACING (brā'sing) *a.* giving strength or tone.

BRACKEN (brak'en) *n.* a species of fern. [Scand. Cf. BRAKE.]

BRACKET (brak'et) *v.t* to put within or connect by brackets; *n.* a small support of wood;—*pl.* = hooks, thus [ ]. for enclosing words. [F. *bragu-ette*, fr. L. *braccae*, breeches.]

BRACKISH (brak'ish) *a.* saltish; salt. [D. *brak*, briny.]

BRACT (brakt) *n.* a small leaf on the stalk of a flower. [L. *bractea*, a thin plate.]

BRAD (brad) *n.* a slender nail without a head. [Scand.]

BRAG (brag) *v.i.* to boast; swagger; puff; —*n.* a boast; a game at cards. [Celt.]

BRAGGADOCIO (brag-a-dō'chi-ō) *n.* a vain boaster. [*Braggadochio*, a boaster in Spenser's *Faerie Queene*.]

BRAGGART (brag'art) *n.* a boaster; a vain fellow.

BRAHMIN (brā'min) *n.* a Hindu priest. [Hind. *Brahma*, the Creator.]

BRAHMINICAL (brä-min'i-kal) *a.* pertaining to the Brahmins.

BRAID (brād) *v.t.* to weave three or more strands to form one;—*n.* a textile band formed by plaiting silk, cotton, and wool. [M.E. *breiden*, fr. O.E. *bregdan*, *bredan*.]

BRAIDING (brā'ding) *n.* act of plaiting; a collection of braids.

BRAIN (brān) *n.* a soft substance within the skull; the understanding; the fancy;—*v.t.* to dash out the brains of. [O.E. *brœgen*.]

BRAINLESS (brān'les) *a.* destitute of thought.

BRAINPAN (brān'pan) *n.* the skull.

BRAIN-SICK (brān'sik) *a.* disordered in intellect; crazy.

BRAIRD (brārd) *n.* the first springing up of the corn. [O.E. *brerd*.]

BRAKE (brāk) old *pret.* of BREAK;—*n.* an instrument for dressing flax; a piece of mechanism for retarding motion by friction. [Teut.]

BRAKE (brāk) *n.* a fern; a thicket. [O.E. *bracce*.]

BRAKEMAN (brāk'man) *n.* one who manages the brake on railroads.

BRAKY (brā'ki) *a.* full of brakes.

BRAMAH-PRESS (brā'ma-pres) *n.* the hydraulic press. [Fr. Joseph *Bramah*, its inventor.]

BRAMBLE (bram'bl) *n.* a prickly shrub. [O.E. *brembel*.]

BRAMBLING (bram'bling) *n.* the mountain finch.

BRAMBLY (bram'bli) *a.* full of brambles.

BRAN (bran) *n.* the outer coats of grain separated from the flour. [O.F. fr. Celt.]

BRANCH (bransh) *n.* a limb; a bough;—*v.t.* or *i.* to divide into branches. [F. *branche*, fr. Low L. *branca*, a paw.]

BRANCHING (bran'shing) *a.* a shooting out from.

BRANCHLET (bransh'let) *n.* a little branch. [Dim. of BRANCH, which see.]

BRANCHY (bran'shi) *a.* full of branches.

BRAND (brand) *v.t.* to burn with a hot iron; stigmatise;—*n.* a burnt piece of wood; an iron to burn the figure of letters; the mark burnt; a stigma. [O.E. *brand*, a burning, or a sword, fr. *beornan*, to burn.]

BRANDER (bran'der) *n.* one who brands; a gridiron.

BRAND-GOOSE (brand'gōōs) *n.* a kind of wild goose.

BRANDISH (bran'dish) *v.t.* to wave; flourish. [F. (part.) *brandissant*, waving, fr. O.F. *brand*, sword, fr. Scand. Cf. BRAND.]

BRAND-NEW (brand'nū) *a.* quite new.

BRANDY (bran'di) *n.* a spirit distilled from wine, cider, or fruit. [D. *brandewijn*, fr. *branden*, burn. See BRAND.]

BRASIER (brā'zher) *n.* one who works in brass; a pan for holding coals. [See BRASS.]

BRASS (bras) *n.* a yellow metal composed of copper and zinc; impudence. [O.E. *brœs*.]

BRASSY (bras'i) *a.* made of brass.

BRAT (brat) *n.* a contemptuous name for a child. [O.E. *bratt*, a pinafore, fr. Celt.]

BRAVADO (bra-vä'do, bra-vä'dō) *n.* an arrogant threat; boasting fellow. [Sp.]

BRAVE (brāv) *a.* fearless of danger; valiant; bold;—*v.t.* to encounter with firmness; defy. [F., of uncertain etym.]

BRAVELY (brāv'li) *ad.* gallantly; generously.

BRAVERY (brā'ver-i) *n.* courage; heroism.

BRAVO (brā'vō) *n.* a daring villain. [It.]

BRAVO (brā-vō') *inter.* well done! [It.]

BRAWL (brawl) *v.i.* to make a great noise; quarrel noisily;—*n.* a quarrel; squabble. [F., fr. Scand.]

BRAWLER (braw'ler) *n.* a wrangler; a noisy fellow.

BRAWN (brawn) *n.* a boar's flesh; a muscular part of the body; strength. [O.F. *braon*, flesh for roasting, fr. Teut. Cf. Ger. *braten*, to roast.]

BRAWNY (braw'ni) *a.* having large, strong muscles.

BRAY (brā) *v.t.* to beat in a mortar;—*v.i.* to make a harsh noise;—*n.* the cry of an ass. [O.F. *breier*. Also O.F. *braire*, fr. Celt.]

BRAYING (brā'ing) *n.* the cry of an ass.

BRAZE (brāz) *v.t.* to cover with brass; solder. [See BRASS.]

BRAZEN (brā'zn) *a.* made of brass; bold;—*v.i.* to be impudent.

BRAZENNESS (brā'zn-nes) *n.* a brazen quality.

BRAZIL-NUT (brạ-zil'nut) *n.* the fruit of the Brazil palm.

BRAZIL-WOOD (brạ-zil'wood) *n.* a heavy red wood used for dyeing.

BREACH (brēch) *n.* a gạp; quarrel. [F. *brèche*, fr. Ger. *brechen*, to break.]

BREAD (bred) *n.* food made of flour; support of life. [O.E. *bread*, a bit of bread. Cf. Ger. *Brot*.]

BREADSTUFF (bred'stuf) *n.* that of which bread is made.

BREADTH (bredth) *n.* width. [M.E. *brede*, fr. O.E. *brædu*. See BROAD.]

BREAK (brāk) *v.t.* and *i.* [*pret.* BROKE; *pp.* BROKE, BROKEN] to part by force; tame; become a bankrupt; dawn, as the day; remove from office;—*n.* an opening; failure. [M.E. *breken*, fr. O.E. *brecan*, to break. Cf. Ger. *brechan*.]

BREAKAGE (brā'kāj) *n.* act of breaking; an allowance for things broken.

BREAK-DOWN (brāk'down) *n.* overthrow; collapse; a lively dance at the end.

BREAKER (brā'ker) *n.* one that breaks; a rock on which waves break; the waves so broken; a small water-cask.

BREAKFAST (brek'fạst) *n.* the first meal of the day;—*v.i.* to eat breakfast. [BREAK, and O.E. *fæstnien*, to fast, fr. *fæst*, firm.]

BREAKING-IN (brā'king-in) *n.* training of a horse; irruption, as of water.

BREAK-UP (brāk'up) *n.* disruption; separation.

BREAKWATER (brāk'waw-ter) *n.* a mole to break the force of the waves.

BREAST (brest) *n.* part of the body;—*v.t.* to meet in front. [O.E. *breost*.]

BREAST-PLATE (brest'plāt) *n.* armour for the breast.

BREAST-WHEEL (brest'hwēl) *n.* a water-wheel that receives the water about the middle.

BREAST-WORK (brest'wurk) *n.* a low parapet for defence.

BREATH (breth) *n.* life; air respired. [M.E. *breth*; O.E. *brǣth*.]

BREATHE (brēTH) *v.i.* to respire; live; utter softly.

BREATHING (brē'TH-ing) *n.* respiration.

Breast-wheel.

BREATHLESS (breth'les) *a.* out of breath; exhausted; dead.

BREECH (brēch) *n.* the lower part of the body behind; the part of a cannon behind the closed end of the bore;—*v.t.* to put into breeches. [O.E. *brac*. Cf. D. *brock*.]

BREECH-LOADER (brēch'lō'der) *n.* a fire-arm that receives its load at the breach instead of at the muzzle.

BREED (brēd) *v.t.* and *i.* [*pret.* and *pp.* BRED] to generate; hatch; bring up;—*n.* off-spring; progeny. [O.E. *bredan*, to cherish, fr. *brod*.]

BREEDING (brē'ding) *n.* a bringing up; education; manners.

BREEZE (brēz) *n.* a gentle wind. [F. *brise*.]

BREEZY (brē'zi) *a.* airy; windy.

BRENT (brent) *n.* (=brindled) the brandgoose; —*a.* burnt; high; steep. [Cf. BRAND. Also O.E. *brant*, steep.]

BRETHREN (breTH'ren) *n.pl.* of BROTHER.

BREVET (brev'et) *n.* a commission which entitles an officer to rank above his pay. [F. =certificate, fr. *bref*, short letter (O.F. *brief*.) See BRIEF.]

BREVIARY (brēv'yạ-ri) *n.* the prayer-book of the Roman Catholic Church. [F., fr. L. *breviarium*, an abridgment.]

BREVIER (bre-vēr') *n.* a small printing letter. [Conn. with BREVIARY, for printing which this type was first used.]

BREVITY (brev'i-ti) *n.* shortness; conciseness.

BREW (brōō) *v.i.* to make beer;—*v.t.* to mingle; contrive. [O.E. *breowan*. Cf. Ger. *brauen*.]

BREWAGE (brōō'āj) *n.* drink brewed.

BREWER (brōō'er) *n.* one who brews.

BREWERY (brōō'er-i) *n.* a house for brewing.

BRIBABLE (brī'bạ-bl) *a.* that may or can be bribed.

BRIBE (brīb) *n.* gift to corrupt the conduct; —*v.t.* to corrupt by gifts. [O.F. =bread as alms.]

BRIBER (brī'ber) *n.* one that bribes.

BRIBERY (brī'ber-i) *n.* the giving or receiving bribes.

BRIC-A-BRAC (brik'ạ-brak) *n.* old china and other articles of curiosity. [F.]

BRICK (brik) *n.* a square mass of burnt clay; —*v.t.* to lay with bricks;—*a.* built of brick. [F. *brique*, fr. D., fr. *breken*, break.]

BRICKBAT (brik'bat) *n.* a broken brick.

BRICK-FIELD (brik'fēld) *n.* field or yard where bricks are made.

BRICK-KILN (brik'kil) *n.* a kiln for burning bricks. [BRICK, and O. E. *cyln*, fr. L. *culina*, a kitchen.]

BRICKLAYER (brik'lā-er) *n.* a brick-mason.

BRICKMAKER (brik'mā-ker) *n.* one who makes bricks.

BRICKWORK (brik'wurk) *n.* place where bricks are made; laying of bricks; a building made of bricks.

BRIDAL (brī'dạl) *a.* belonging to marriage;— *n.* a wedding. [BRIDE, and O.E. *ealu*, ALE.]

BRIDE (brīd) *n.* a woman about to be or newly married. [O.E. *bryd*. Cf. Ger. *Braut*.]

BRIDEGROOM (brīd'grōōm) *n.* a man newly married or about to be married. [BRIDE, and O.E. *guma*, a man.]

BRIDEMAID (brīd'mād) *n.* a woman who attends the bride. Also BRIDESMAID.

BRIDGE (brij) *n.* a building on which to pass over water; a support;—*v.t.* to form a bridge over. [M.E. *brigge, brugge*, fr. O.E. *brycg*.]

BRIDLE (brī'dl) *n.* an instrument to restrain a horse;—*v.t.* to put on a bridle; restrain. [O.E. *bridel*.]

BRIDLE-HAND (brī'dl-hand) *n.* the left hand.

BRIEF (brēf) *a.* short; concise;—*n.* an epitome or short writing. [F. *brief, bref*, fr. L. (acc.) *brevem*, short.]

BRIEFLESS (brēf'les) *a.* without a brief.

BRIEFLY (brēf'li) *ad.* in few words.

BRIEFNESS (brēf'nes) *n.* shortness; concise-ness.

BRIER (brī'er) *n.* a prickly shrub. [O.E. *brer*.]

BRIERY (brī'er-i) *a.* full of briers; rough.

BRIG (brig) *n.* a vessel with two masts square-rigged like a ship's main-mast and fore-mast. [Short form of BRIGANTINE, which see.]

BRIGADE (bri-gād') *n.* troops under a brigadier;—*v.t.* to form into brigades. [F. =a troop, fr. It., fr. Low L. *briga*, a quarrel. Cf. F. *brigue*, intrigue.]

BRIGADIER (brig-a-dẽr') *n.* an officer commanding a brigade.

BRIGAND (brig'and) *n.* one of a band of robbers. [F. =a robber, fr. It., fr. Low L. *briga*, an intrigue.]

BRIGANDAGE (brig'an-dáj) *n.* highway robbery.

BRIGANTINE (brig'an-tin) *n.* a light two-masted vessel without a deck. [F. *brigantin*, a piratical vessel, fr. It. See **BRIGAND.**]

BRIGHT (brit) *a.* shining; clear; promising. [O.E. *beorht.*]

BRIGHTEN (bri'tn) *v.t.* or *i.* to make or become bright.

BRIGHTNESS (brit'nes) *n.* lustre; splendour; acuteness.

BRILLIANCE (bril'yans) *n.* sparkling lustre.

BRILLIANT (bril'yant) *a.* shining;—*n.* a diamond cut into angles. [F. *brillant*, fr. O.F. *bril*, lustre, lustrous, fr. L. (acc.) *beryllum*. See **BERYL.**]

BRILLIANTLY (bril'yant-li) *a.* lustrously; splendidly.

BRIM (brim) *n.* the edge; side; bank. [E.]

BRIMFUL (brim'fool) *a.* full to the brim.

BRIMLESS (brim'les) *a.* having no brim.

BRIMMING (brim'ing) *a.* full to the brim.

BRIMSTONE (brim'stōn) *n.* a mineral sulphur. [M.E. *brenstoon* =burning stone, fr. *brennen*, to burn.]

BRINDED (brin'ded) *a.* streaked; spotted. Also **BRINDLED.** [Scand.]

BRINE (brin) *n.* water impregnated with salt; the ocean. [O.E. *bryne*, flame, heat, brine.]

BRINE-PAN (brin'pan) *n.* a pit to hold salt water for evaporation. [**BRINE**, and O.E. *panne*, a shallow vessel.]

BRING (bring) *v.t.* [*pret.* and *pp.* **BROUGHT**] to convey or carry to; fetch from. [O.E. *bringan.* Cf. Ger. *bringen.*]

BRINISH (bri'nish) *a.* somewhat salt; saltish.

BRINK (bringk) *n.* the edge; border. [Scand.]

BRINY (bri'ni) *a.* consisting of brine.

BRISK (brisk) *a.* quick; full of life. [Celt.]

BRISKET (bris'ket) *n.* part of the breast. [O.F.]

BRISKNESS (brisk'nes) *n.* activeness.

BRISTLE (bris'l) *n.* a part of swine's hair;—*v.i.* to raise the bristles. [M.E. *bristle*, *birstle*, fr. O.E. *byrst.*]

BRISTLY (bris'li) *ad.* set thick with bristles.

BRITANNIA-METAL (bri-tan'va-met'al) *n.* a metallic compound consisting chiefly of block-tin.

BRITANNIC (bri-tan'ik) *a.* British.

BRITISH (brit'ish) *a.* pertaining to Britain.

BRITON (brit'un) *n.* a native of Britain.

BRITTLE (brit'l) *a.* apt to break. [O.E. *breotan*, to break.]

BRITTLENESS (brit'l-nes) *n.* aptness to break; fragility.

BROACH (brōch) *n.* a spit;—*v.t.* to tap; utter. [F. *brocher*, to pierce, fr. *broche*, a spit.]

BROACHER (brō'cher) *n.* one who broaches; a spit.

BROAD (brawd) *a.* extended from side to side; wide; comprehensive. [O.E. *brad.*]

BROAD-ARROW (brawd'ar-ō) *n.* the mark on Government implements, etc.

BROAD-AXE (brawd'aks) *n.* an axe for hewing timber.

BROADCAST (brawd'kast) *n.* a scattering of seed with the hand;—*a.* widely spread; diffused;—*ad.* largely; widely.

BROADCLOTH (brawd'kloth) *n.* a woollen cloth. [**BROAD**, and O.E. *clath.* Cf. Ger. *Kleid*, garment.]

BROADEN (braw'dn) *v.t.* or *i.* to make or grow broad.

BROADLY (brawd'li) *a.* widely; openly.

BROADNESS (brawd'nes) *n.* breadth; coarseness.

BROADSIDE (brawd'sid) *n.* a discharge of all the guns on one side of a ship.

BROADSWORD (brawd'sōrd) *n.* a sword with a broad blade and a cutting edge.

BROCADE (brō-kād') *n.* silk stuff variegated with gold and silver. [Sp., fr. part. *brocado*, embroidered, fr. *broca*ᵣ =F. *brocher.*]

BROCADED (brō-kā'ded) *a.* worked, or dressed, in brocade.

BROCCOLI (brok'ō-li) *n.* a kind of cauliflower. [It. pl. dim. fr. *brocco*, a skewer.]

BROCHURE (brō-shōōr') *n.* a pamphlet. [F., fr. *brocher*, to stitch.]

BROCKET (brok'et) *n.* a red deer two years old.

BROGAN (brō'gan) *n.* a thick shoe.

BROGUE (brōg) *n.* a coarse, light shoe; a peculiar dialect or pronunciation. [Celt.]

BROIDER (broi'der) *v.t.* to adorn with figures in needlework. [See **EMBROIDER.**]

BROIDERY (broi'der-i) *n.* ornamental needle-work.

BROIL (broil) *n.* a tumult; quarrel;—*v.t.* or *i.* to dress over coals; to be in a heat. [F. *brouiller*, confuse; of uncertain etym.]

BROILER (broi'ler) *n.* one who broils.

BROKEN (brō'kn) *pp.* or *a.* of **BREAK.**

BROKENLY (brō'kn-li) *ad.* in a broken, interrupted manner.

BROKENNESS (brō'kn-nes) *n.* a state of being broken.

BROKER (brō'ker) *n.* an agent who transacts business on commission. [M.E. *brocour*; of uncertain etym.]

BROKERAGE (brō'ker-āj) *n.* business of a broker; commission of a broker.

BROMIDE (brō'mid, brō'mid) *n.* a compound of bromic acid with a base.

BROMINE (brō'min, brō'min) *n.* one of the elementary substances. [G. *bromos*, stench.]

BRONCHIAL (brong'ki-al) *a.* relating to the throat. [G. *bronchia*, the bronchial tubes.]

BRONCHITIS (brong-ki'tis) *n.* a throat affection.

BRONZE (bronz) *n.* a compound of copper and tin. [F., fr. It. *bronzo*; conn. with **BROWN.**]

BROOCH (brōch) *n.* a jewel. [F. *broche*, a spit, fr. Low L. (acc.) *broccam*, a pin, fr. L. *broccus*, pointed.]

BROOD (brōōd) *n.* an offspring; hatch;—*v.t.* and *i.* to sit, as on eggs; cover chickens. [O.E. *brod.*]

BROODING (brōō'ding) *a.* sitting, as a hen; thinking deeply.

BROOD-MARE (brōōd'mãr) *n.* a mare kept for breeding.

BROOK (brook) *n.* a natural stream less than a river;—*v.t.* to bear; endure; submit to. [O.E. *broc.* Also O.E. *brucan*, to use or enjoy.]

BROOKLET (brook'let) *n.* a small brook.

BROOM (brōōm) *n.* a shrub; a besom to sweep with. [O.E. *brom.*]

BROOMSTICK (brōōm'stik) *n.* the staff or handle of a broom. [**BROOM**, and O.E. *sticca*, a rod.]

BROOMY (brōō'mi) *a.* full of broom.

BROTH (broth) *n.* liquor in which flesh has been boiled. [O.E., fr. (part.) *trowen*, brewed.]

BROTHEL (broth'el) *n.* a house of ill-fame. [O.E. (part.) *brothen*, undone, fr. *breothan.*]

BROTHER (bruTH'er) *n.* a male born of the same parents; an associate. [O.E. *brothor*, conn. with L. *frater.*]

BROTHERHOOD (bruTH'er-hood) *n.* state of being a brother; fraternity.

BROTHERLY (bruTH'er-li) *a.* like brothers.

BROUGHAM (brōōm, brōō'am) *n.* a one-horse close carriage. [Fr. Lord *Brougham*, d. 1868.]

BROUGHT (brawt) *pret.* and *pp.* of **BRING.**

BROW (brou) *n.* the forehead; the edge. [O.E. *bru*, *breau*, eyebrow.]

BROWBEAT (brou'bēt) *v.t.* to beat down.

BROWBEATING (brou'bē-ting) *n.* act of depressing by stern looks or words.

BROWN (broun) *a.* dusky; inclining to red; —*n.* name of a reddish colour;—*v.t.* to make brown. [O.E. *brun*; conn. with BURN.]

BROWNIE (brou'ni) *n.* a kind of supposed good-natured spirit. [Dim. of BROWN.]

BROWNISH (brou'nish) *a.* inclined to brown.

BROWN-STUDY(broun'stud-i) *n.*deep thought-fulness; reverie.

BROWSE (brouz) *v.t.* or *i.* to feed on the shoots of shrubs. [O.F. *brouster*, to crop, fr. *broust*, a shoot, fr. Ger.]

BROWSE (brous) *n.* the twigs of shrubs.

BRUIN (broo'in) *n.* name of a bear. [D. = brown.]

BRUISE (brooz) *v.t.* to hurt with blows;—*n.* a contusion. [O.E. *brysan*, break; confused with O.F. *bruser* = F. *briser*, to break.]

BRUIT (broot) *n.* report; rumour;—*v.t.* to report.

BRUNETTE (broo-net') *n.* a woman of a dark complexion. [F.]

BRUNT (brunt) *n.* shock; attack; onset. [E., conn. with BURN.]

BRUSH (brush) *n.* a hairy instrument; brisk attack; thicket;—*v.t.* to rub or sweep with a brush;—also *intrans.* [O.F. *brosse*, brush-wood, fr. Low L. (acc.) *brusciam*, fr. Teut.]

BRUSHWOOD (brush'wood) *n.* underwood.

BRUSHY (brush'i) *a.* like a brush; shaggy.

BRUSQUE (brusk, broosk) *a.* rude; abrupt in manner. [F.]

BRUTAL (broo'tal) *a.* savage; cruel. [See BRUTE.]

BRUTALISE (broo'tal-iz) *v.t.* to make brutal; —*v.i.* to become brutal.

BRUTALITY (broo-tal'i-ti) *n.* savageness.

BRUTE (broot) *n.* an irrational animal;—*a.* senseless; savage. [F. *brut*, fr. L. (acc.) *brutum*, irrational.]

BRUTIFY (broo'ti-fi) *v.t.* to make brutish or unfeeling.

BRUTISH (broo'tish) *a.* bestial; savage.

BRUTISM (broo'tizm) *n.* extreme stupidity.

BUBBLE (bub'l) *n.* a small bladder of water; a false show; empty project;—*v.i.* and *t.* to rise in bubbles. [Onomatopœic word.]

BUCCANEER (buk-a-ner') *n.* a piratical adventurer. [F. *boucanier*, fr. Carib. *boucan*, a grill.]

BUCK (buk) *n.* male of rabbits, deer, etc; a dandy;—*v.t.* to steep clothes in lye. [M.E. *bukke*, fr. O.E. *bucca*, he-goat. Cf. Ger. *Bock*.]

BUCKET (buk'et) *n.* a vessel to draw or carry water in. [O.E. *buc*, a pitcher+suff. -*et*.]

BUCKISH (buk'ish) *a.* pertaining to a gay fellow; foppish.

BUCKLE (buk'l) *n.* an instrument for fasten-ing straps;—*v.t.* to fasten with a buckle; apply;—*v.i.* to join in battle. [M.E. *bokel*, fr. O.F. *bocle* = F. *boucle*, a ring, fr. L. (acc.) *bucculam*, a mouth, fr. *bucca*.]

BUCKLER (buk'ler) *n.* a shield.

BUCKRAM (buk'ram) *n.* a coarse linen cloth stiffened with glue;—*a.* stiff; formal. [O.F. *boucaran*, goat's skin, fr. *bouc*, he-goat, fr. Teut.]

BUCKSKIN (buk'skin) *n.* the leather from a buck.

BUCKTHORN (buk'thorn) *n.* a shrub used in dyeing.

BUCKWHEAT (buk'hwet) *n.* a plant; an edible grain.

BUCOLIC (bu-kol'ik) *a.* relating to shepherds; pastoral;—*n.* a pastoral poem. [L., fr. G. *boukolos*, cow-herd.]

BUD (bud) *n.* first shoot of a plant;—*v.i.* to put forth buds. [Prob. E.]

BUDDHISM (bood'dizm) *n.* the religion of Asia and the Indian islands, founded by Buddha. [Skr. *buddha*, wise.]

BUDGE (buj) *v.i.* to stir; go; move. [F. *bouger*, to move, fr. It. *bulicare*, to boil, fr. L. *bullire*.]

BUDGET (buj'et) *n.* a bag; a pouch; the annual financial statement made by the Chancellor of the Exchequer. [F. *bouge* (*bougette*), fr. L. (acc.) *bulgam*, bag fr. Celt.]

BUDLET (bud'let) *n.* a little bud or shoot.

BUFF (buf) *n.* a leather dressed with oil. [F. *buffle*, buffalo, fr. L. *bubulus*, an antelope.]

BUFF (buf) *a.* made of buff leather; light yellow;—*n.* a leather prepared from the skin of the buffalo and other animals, dressed in oil.

BUFFALO (buf'a-lo) *n.* a kind of wild ox;— *pl.* BUFFALOES. [Sp., fr. L. *bubulus*, an antelope. See BUFF.]

BUFFER (buf'er) *n.* an apparatus with strong springs to deaden concussion, as at the ends of a railway carri-age. [M.E. *buffen*, to strike.]

BUFFET (buf'et) *v.t.* to box; beat; strike with the fist; —*n.* a blow with the fist. [Dim. of O.F. *buffe*. Cf. Ger. *buffen*.]

Buffer.

BUFFETED (buf'et-ed) *pp.* struck; beaten.

BUFFO (buf'o) *n.* a comic singer in Italian opera. [It. *buffo*, fr. *buffare*, to jest.]

BUFFOON (bu-foon') *n.* an arch fellow. [See BUFFO.]

BUFFOONERY (bu-foon'er-i) *n.* low jests.

BUG (bug) *n.* a generic term for various insects. [Celt.]

BUGBEAR (bug'bar) *n.* a frightful object. [BUG, fr. Celt. =spectre, and BEAR.]

BUGGY (bug'i) (1) *a.* full of or having bugs;— (2) *n.* a light carriage. [(1) See BUG. (2) Etym. unknown.]

BUGLE (bu'gl) *n.* a military instrument of music; a hunting-horn; a glass bead. [O.F., fr. L. *buculus*, a young ox; shortened from bugle-horn. Also fr. M. H. Ger. *Bouc, Boug*, ring.]

BUHL (bool) *n.* metallic figures inlaid in dark wood, etc. [Fr. *Boule*, a French cabinet-maker.]

BUHRSTONE (bur'ston) *n.* a species of quartz, used for millstones. [Perh. conn. with BURR.]

BUILD (bild) *v.t.* and *i.* [*pret.* and *pp.* BUILT] to raise a structure; construct. [O.E. *byldan*, fr. *bold*, house. Cf. Ger. *bilden*.]

BUILDER (bil'der) *n.* one who builds.

BUILDING (bil'ding) *n.* an edifice.

BUILT (bilt) *pret.* and *pp.* of BUILD.

BULB (bulb) *n.* a round root. [F. *bulbe*, fr. L. (acc.) *bulbum*, fr. G. *bolbos*, onion.]

BULBOUS (bul'bus) *a.* having round roots or heads.

BULGE (bulj) *v.i.* to swell in the middle. [F., fr. Celt. Cf. O.E. (part.) *bolgen*, swollen with rage.]

BULGING (bulj'ing) *a.* swelling; protuberant.

BULK (bulk) *n.* size; substance in general; main mass or body. [Scand.]

BULKHEAD (bulk'hed) *n.* a partition in a ship.

BULKINESS (bul'ki-nes) *n.* largeness of size.

BULKY (bul'ki) *a.* of great size.

BULL (bool) (1) *n.* an animal; (2) the pope's edict; (3) a blunder. [(1) M.E. *bole*; conn. with BELLOW. (2) L. *bulla*, a boss or seal. (3) Et m. uncertain, perh. fr. O.F. *boul*, cheat.ly

BULLDOG (bool'dog) *n.* a variety of dog of great courage and ferocity.

BULLET (bool'et) *n.* a ball for a gun. [F. *boulet*, bullet; dim. of *boule*, ball.]

BULLETIN (bool'e-tin) *n.* official report. [F., fr. It.]

BULL-FIGHT (bool'fit) *n.* a fight with a bull.

BULLFINCH (bool-finsh) *n.* a singing bird.

BULL-FROG (bool'frog) *n.* a large species of frog.

BULLION (bool'yun) *n.* uncoined silver or gold. [Etym. uncertain.]

BULLIRAG (bool'i-rag) *n.* to abuse; badger. Also **BULLYRAG.** [Etym. uncertain.]

BULLOCK (bool'uk) *n.* a young bull. [O.E. *bulluca,* a little bull.]

BULL'S-EYE (boolz'i) *n.* a small window or lantern of rounded or projecting glass; the centre of a target.

BULL-TERRIER (bool'ter-i-er) *n.* a cross between a bull-dog and a terrier.

BULL-TROUT (bool'trout) *n.* a large species of trout.

BULLY (bool'i) *n.* a quarrelsome fellow;—*v.t.* to threaten with noisy menaces. [Etym. uncertain.]

BULRUSH (bool'rush) *n.* a rush growing in water.

BULWARK (bool'wark) *n.* a fortification;— also *v.t.* [Cf. Ger. *Bollwerk.* See **BOULEVARD.**]

BUMP (bump) *n.* a swelling; a blow;—*v.t.* or *i.* to make a loud noise. [Onomatopoeic.]

BUMPER (bum'per) *n.* a glass filled to the brim.

BUMPKIN (bump'kin) *n.* an awkward person; a clown. [E. *bumkin,* a thick log, fr. D.]

BUMPTIOUS (bump'shus) *a.* self-important; forward.

BUN (bun) *n.* a small cake, or sweet bread. [O.F. = a swelling, fr. Scand.]

BUNCH (bunsh) *n.* a cluster; a hard lump;— *v.i.* to grow in knobs. [Scand.]

BUNCHY (bun'shi) *a.* full of bunches.

BUNDLE (bun'dl) *n.* a number of things bound together;—*v.t.* to tie together. [Dim. fr. O.E. *bund,* bundle, fr. part. *bunden.*]

BUNG (bung) *n.* a stopper for a barrel;—*v.t.* to stop with a bung. [Etym. uncertain.]

BUNGALOW (bung'ga-lō) *n.* a country house in India. [Hind. *bangla,* fr. *Banga,* Bengalese.]

BUNGHOLE (bung'hōl) *n.* the hole of a cask. [Perh. Scand.]

BUNGLE (bung'gl) *n.* a gross blunder;—*v.i.* to do clumsily. [Perh. Sw. *bangla,* work to no purpose. The etym. is obscure.]

BUNGLER (bung'gler) *n.* a clumsy workman.

BUNGLING (bung'gling) *a.* very clumsy.

BUNION (bun'yun) *n.* an excrescence on the toe. [Fr. the Scand. root of **BUN.**]

BUNK (bungk) *n.* a case of boards for a bed. [Scand.]

BUNKER (bung'ker) *n.* a bin or receptacle; a kind of chest.

BUNTING (bun'ting) *n.* a thin cloth; a small bird. [Etym. unknown.]

BUOY (boi) *n.* a piece of wood or cork floating on the water for a direction, or to bear a cable;—*v.t.* or *i.* to keep afloat; sustain. [D. *boei,* fr. F., fr. L. (pl.) *boiae,* collar.]

BUOYANCY (boi'an-si) *n.* the quality of floating; specific lightness; vivacity of spirit.

BUOYANT (boi'ant) *a.* floating; light.

BUOYANTLY (boi'ant-li) *ad.* in a light, floating manner.

BUR (bur) *n.* the prickly head of a plant. [Scand.]

BURDEN (bur'dn) *n.* that which is borne;— *v.t.* to load; oppress. [O.E. *byrthen,* fr. part. *boren,* borne.]

BURDENSOME (bur'dn-sum) *a.* grievous to be borne; heavy; oppressive.

BURDENSOMELY (bur'dn-sum-li) *ad.* in a burdensome manner.

BURDENSOMENESS (bur'dn-sum-nes) *n.* heaviness; oppressiveness.

BUREAU (bū-rō', bū'rō) *n.* a chest of drawers for holding papers or clothes; an office or department of government. [F., originally a coarse, woollen cloth, fr. O.F. *burel,* fr. L. *burrus,* red-brown.]

BUREAUCRACY (bū-rō'kra-si) *n.* government by departments under the control of a chief. [Hybrid, imitated fr. **ARISTOCRACY.**]

BURG (burg) *n.* a borough; burgh. [O.E. See **BOROUGH.**]

BURGAGE (bur'gāj) *n.* a tenure of lands or houses in a burgh.

BURGESS (bur'ges) *n.* a freeman of a city [O.F. *burgeis.* Doublet of **BOURGEOIS.**]

BURGHAL (bur'gal) *a.* pertaining to a borough.

BURGHER (bur'ger) *n.* a freeman of a borough.

BURGLAR (burg'lar) *n.* one who breaks into a house by night. [O.F. *borg,* a borough, and *leres,* fr. L. *latro,* robber.]

BURGLARIOUS (burg'lā-ri-us) *a.* consisting in burglary.

BURGLARY (burg'la-ri) *n.* the crime of housebreaking by night, with intent to steal.

BURGOMASTER (bur'gō-mas-ter) *n.* a magistrate. [O.E. *burh,* and D. *meister,* fr. F. See **MASTER.**]

BURGUNDY (bur'gun-di) *n.* wine made in Burgundy. [Fr. *Burgundy* in France.]

BURGUNDY-PITCH (bur'gun-di-pich) *n.* a resin obtained from spruce and other pines.

BURIAL (ber'i-al) *n.* the act of burying; a funeral. [O.E. *byrgels,* tomb. See **BURY.**]

BURIED (ber'rid) *pp.* or *a.* covered with earth; concealed.

BURIN (bū'rin) *n.* a graving tool. [F., fr. It. *burino,* conn. with **BORE.**]

BURKE (burk) *v.t.* to murder and sell the body for dissection; smother; shelve. [Fr. *Burke,* an Irish murderer who sold the corpses of his victims for dissection, 1829.]

BURL (burl) *v.t.* to pick knots, etc., from cloth in fulling. [See **BURLY.**]

BURLESQUE (bur-lesk') *a.* tending to excite laughter;—*n.* a ludicrous representation;— *v.t.* to make ludicrous; turn to ridicule. [F., fr. It. *burla,* waggery, fr. L. (pl.) *burræ,* nonsense.]

BURLINESS (bur'li-nes) *n.* state of being burly.

BURLY (bur'li) *a.* large and strong; lusty; coarse; loud. [M.E. *burliche,* of uncertain etym.]

BURN (burn) *v.t.* or *i.* [*pret.* and *pp.* **BURNED, BURNT**] to consume by fire; scorch; be inflamed; be on fire;—*n.* a hurt caused by fire. [O.E. *byrnan,* and *beornan,* to burn.]

BURNER (bur'ner) *n.* one who sets on fire; appendage to a lamp.

BURNING (bur'ning) *n.* combustion; heat;— *a.* flaming; vehement.

BURNISH (bur'nish) *v.t.* to polish; brighten; —*n.* a gloss; brightness. [O.F. (part.) *burnissant,* polishing, fr. *burnir,* fr. Teut.]

BURNISHER (bur'nish-er) *n.* a person that burnishes; a tool for polishing.

BURNT (burnt) *pret.* and *pp.* of **BURN.**

BURR (bur) *n.* a rough, prickly covering of some seeds; the lobe of the ear; a kind of chisel; a guttural pronunciation of the letter *r.* [E., conn. with **BUR**]

BURROW (bur'ō) *n.* a lodge in the earth for rabbits, etc ;—*v.i.* to lodge in the earth; work a way under. [A form of **BOROUGH,** which see.]

BURSAR (bur'sar) *n.* the treasurer of a college; a charity student. [Late L. *bursarius,* a purse-bearer, fr. L. *bursa,* a purse.]

BURSARY (bur'sar-i) *n.* a treasury.

BURST (burst) *v.i.* [*pret.* and *pp.* **BURST**] to break or fly open; rush forth;—*v.t.* to rend or force with violence;—*n.* a sudden outbreak; spasmodic effort. [O.E. *berstan.*]

BURTHEN (bur'THen). See **BURDEN.**

BURY (ber'i) *v.t.* to inter in a grave; conceal. [M.E. *burien,* fr. O.E. *byrigan.*]

BURYING (ber'i-ing) *ppr.* depositing in the grave;—*n.* interment; burial.

BUS (bus) *n.* an omnibus. [Abbrev. of **OMNIBUS.**]

BUSH (boosh) *n.* a shrub; a bough; a tavern sign; the tail of a fox; the backwoods of Australia;—*v.i.* to grow thick. [M.E. *busch, busk,* fr. Teut.]

BUSHEL (boosh'el) *n.* a dry measure of eight gallons, or four pecks. [O.F. *boissel,* a little box, fr. *boiste,* fr. L. *burum.*]

BUSHELAGE (boosh'el-āj) *n.* duty levied by the bushel.

BUSHRANGER (boosh'rān-jer) *n.* a convict who escapes to and lives in the woods of Australia.

BUSHY (boosh'i) *a.* full of bushes; thick.

BUSIED (biz'ed) *a.* fully occupied or employed.

BUSILY (biz'i-li) *ad.* with constant occupation.

BUSINESS (biz'nes) *n.* employment; occupation.

BUSK (busk) (1) *n.* a piece of steel or whalebone worn in corsets;—(2) *v.t.* to dress. [(1) F. *buse,* perh. conn. with **BUST.** (2) Scand.]

BUSKIN (busk'in) *n.* a half-boot. [Etym. uncertain.]

BUSKINED (bus'kind) *a.* wearing buskins.

BUSKY (bus'ki) *a.* woody; overgrown with shrubs.

BUSS (bus) *n.* a kiss;—*v.t.* to kiss. [M.E. *bass,* fr. O. Ger. *bussen,* to kiss, fr. L. *basium,* a kiss; conn. with F. *baiser.*]

BUST (bust) *n.* a statue of the head and shoulders. [F.. fr. It. *busto,* fr. Late L. *bustum,* the trunk.]

BUSTARD (bus'tard) *n.* a kind of wild turkey. [Formerly also *bistard,* fr. O.F., fr. L. (*a)vis tarda,* the slow bird.]

BUSTLE (bus'l) *v.i.* to be busy; *n.* a tumult; hurry; commotion. [Scand.]

BUSTLER (bus'ler) *n.* a stirring person.

BUSY (biz'i) *a.* employed with earnestness; officious; *v.t.* to employ. [O.E. *bysig.*]

Bust.

BUSYBODY (biz'i-bod-i) *n.* a meddling, officious person.

BUT (but) *prep.* except; unless;—*con.* more; further;—*n.* end; limit; bound;—*v.t.* to be bounded; touch with the end. Used for **ABUT.** [O.E. *butan,* fr. *be,* by, and *utan,* outside.]

BUTCHER (booch'er) *n.* one who kills animals to sell;—*v.t.* to slay inhumanly. [O.F. *bochier,* one who kills goats. See **BUSH.**]

BUTCHER-BIRD (booch'er-berd) *n.* a species of perching bird; the shrike.

BUTCHERLY (booch'er-li) *a.* cruel; bloody.

BUTCHER'S-BROOM (booch'er's-brōōm) *n.* a kind of stiff, spiny-leaved shrubs, used as brooms by butchers.

BUTCHERY (booch'er-i) *n.* the slaughter of cattle for market; cruel murder.

BUTLER (but'ler) *n.* a servant who has the care of liquors. [M.E. *boteler,* fr. *botel,* **BOTTLE.**]

BUTLERAGE (but'ler-āj) *n.* the duty paid on imported wines.

BUTLERSHIP (but'ler-ship) *n.* the office of a butler.

BUTLERY (but'ler-i) *n.* a butler's pantry.

BUTT (but) (1) *n.* a mark to shoot at; one who is ridiculed; (2) a cask capable of

containing 126 gallons of wine;—(3) *v.t.* to strike with the head. [(1) fr. Teut. (2) O.F. *boute,* cask, fr. Low L. (acc.) *buttam.* (3) O.F. *boter,* fr. Teut.]

BUTT-END (but'end) *n.* the thicker end of a thing.

BUTTER (but'er) *n.* an oily substance from cream;—*v.t.* to spread with butter. [O.E. *butere,* L. *butyrum,* fr. G. *bouturon.*]

BUTTERCUP (but'er-kup) *n.* a plant with bright yellow flowers; ranunculus.

BUTTERFLY (but'er-fli) *n.* a genus of insects; an inconstant person.

BUTTERINE (but'er-in) *n.* a compound of animal fat and milk used as butter. Now called **MARGARINE.**

BUTTERMILK (but'er-milk) *n.* the milk which remains after the butter is separated.

BUTTER-NUT (but'er-nut) *n.* the nut of a South American tree.

BUTTER-PRINT (but'er-print) *n.* a stamp for butter.

BUTTERTOOTH (but'er-tōōth) *n.* a broad fore-tooth.

BUTTERY (but'er-i) *n.* a room where provisions are kept.

BUTTOCK (but'uk) *n.* upper part of the thigh. [Dim. of **BUTT.**]

BUTTON (but'n) *n.* a knob for fastening;—*v.t.* to fasten with buttons. [F. *bouton,* a knob, fr. *bouter,* thrust.]

BUTTONHOLE (but'n-hōl) *n.* a hole for a button; *v.t.* to stop a person and hold him in conversation against his will.

BUTTON-WOOD (but'n-wōōd) *n.* the plane-tree of America.

BUTTRESS (but'res) *n.* a projecting support to the exterior of a wall or building; prop; —*v.t.* to support by external means. [O.F. (pl.) *bouterez,* prop, fr. *bouter,* **BUTT.**]

BUTTS (buts) *n.pl.* targets for rifle shooting or archery; pieces of stout sole leather.

BUTYRINE (bū'ti-rin) *n.* oily matter in butter. [See **BUTTER.**]

BUXOM (buk'sum) *a.* lively; brisk. [M.E. *buk-sum, boxom,* fr. O.E. *bugan,* bend; affix *-some.*]

BUXOMLY (buk'sum-li) *ad.* briskly.

BUXOMNESS (buk'sum-nes) *n.* plumpness; liveliness; jollity.

BUY (bi) *v.t.* [*pret.* and *pp.* **BOUGHT**] to purchase; bribe; redeem. [O.E. *bycgan.*]

BUYER (bi'er) *n.* a purchaser.

BUZZ (buz) *n.* a humming sound;—*v.i.* to make a low sound; whisper. [Onomat.]

BUZZARD (buz'ard) *n.* a species of hawk. [F. *busard,* fr. *busc,* fr. Late L., fr. L. *butes,* a sparrow-hawk.]

BUZZING (buz'ing) *n.* a low humming noise or talk.

BY (bi) *prep.* near; in presence. [O.E. *bi, big.* Cf. Ger. *bei.*]

BY-AND-BY (bi'and-bi) *ad.* presently; soon.

BY-ELECTION (bi-ē-lek'shun) *n.* an election between general elections to fill a vacancy in Parliament.

BY-END (bi'end) *n.* private interest.

BY-GONE (bi'gōn) *a.* past; gone by.

BY-LAW (bi'law) *n.* a subordinate law made for a town by a corporation, etc.

BYPATH (bi'path) *n.* a private path.

BYSSINE (his'in) *a.* made of silk. [L., fr. G. *byssos,* fine flax.]

BYSTANDER (bi-stan'der) *n.* a looker-on.

BYWORD (bi'wurd) *n.* a common saying; a proverb.

BYZANTIAN (bi-zan'shan) *a.* pertaining to Byzantium or Constantinople.

BYZANTINE (bi-zan'tin) *a.* Byzantian;—*n.* a bezant.

C

CAB (kab ((1) n. a Hebrew measure of three pints; (2) a one-horse hackney carriage. [(1) **H.** (2) Shortened form of CABRIOLET.]

CABAL (ka-bal') n. a small party united for a secret purpose or intrigue;—v.i. to plot. [H.]

CABALISTIC (kab-a-lis'tik) a. pertaining to the mysteries of tradition; occult. [H.]

CABBAGE (kab'āj) v.i. to steal pieces in cutting cloths;—n. a garden plant. [M.E. cabache, fr. F. caboche, a big head.]

CABBAGE-ROSE (kab'āj-rōz) n. a large compact rose.

CABBAGE-TREE (kab'āj-trē) n. a kind of palm-tree.

CABIN (kab'in) n. part of a ship; hut;—v.i. to live in a cabin;—v.t. to confine in a cabin. [F. cabine, fr. cabane, a hut, fr. Celt.]

CABINET (kab'in-et) n. a set of drawers; closet; executive of a state. [Dim. of CABIN.]

CABINETMAKER (kab'in-et-māk-ęr) n. a maker of wooden furniture.

CABLE (kā'bl) n. a strong rope or chain to hold a vessel at anchor; the covering of a telegraphic wire under water. [O.F., fr. Late L. (acc.) capulam, fr. L. capere, to hold.]

CABLEGRAM (kā'bl-gram) n. a message by oceanic telegraph cable. [CABLE, and G. graphein, to write.]

CABMAN (kab'man) n. the driver of a cab.

CABRIOLET (kab-ri-ō-lā') n. a covered carriage with two or four wheels, drawn by one horse. The short form of this word is CAB. [F. =cab, fr. cabriole, O.F. capriole.]

CACAO (ka-kā'o) n. the chocolate tree. [Mex.]

CACKLE (kak'l) v.i. to make the noise of a hen;—n. the noise of a hen or goose. [M.E. cakelen; con. with D. kakelen.]

CACTUS (kak'tus) n. a tropical plant with prickly leaves. [G.]

CADAVEROUS (ka-dav'e-rus) a. like a dead body. [L., fr. cadaver, a corpse, fr. cadere, to fall.]

CADDIE (kad'i) n. a person who attends a golfer. See CADET.

CADDIS (kad'is) n. a grub or worm; lint for dressing wounds. [Etym. unknown.]

CADDY (kad'i) n. a small box for tea. [Malay kati, weight.]

CADENCE (kā'dens) n. a fall or modulation of the voice;—v.t. to regulate by musical measure. [F. fr. L. (part. stem) cadent-, falling.]

CADET (ka-det') n. a younger or the youngest son; a volunteer serving for a commission; a military pupil. [F., fr. O.F. capdet, fr. dim. fr. L. caput, the head.]

CAFÉ (ka'fā) n. a coffee-house; restaurant. [F.]

CAFFEINE (ka-fē'in) n. a bitter crystallisable substance obtained from coffee. [F. caféine.]

CAGE (kāj) n. a box to confine birds;—v.t. to shut up in a cage. [F., fr. L. cavea, a hollow place.]

CAIRN (kārn) n. a round or conical heap of stones. [Celt.]

CAISSON (kā'sun) n. an ammunition chest; a kind of floating dock. [F.]

CAITIFF (kā'tif) n. a base fellow; a villain;—a. base; servile. [O.F., fr. L. (acc.) captivum. Doublet of CAPTIVE.]

CAJOLE (ka-jōl') v.t. to deceive by flattery; wheedle. [F., of uncertain etym.]

CAJOLER (ka-jōl'ęr) n. one who flatters.

CAJOLERY (ka-jōl'ęr-i) n. flattery.

CAKE (kāk) n. a small mass of bread, etc.; —v.i. to form into a hard mass. [Scand.]

CALABASH (kal'a-bash) n. a large gourd. [Fr. Pers.]

CALAMITOUS (ka-lam'i-tus) a. distressing.

CALAMITY (ka-lam'it-i) n. a condition producing great distress; disaster. [F., fr. L. (acc.) calamitatem.]

CALCAREOUS (kal-kā'rē-us) a. having the properties of lime. [L. calcarius, fr. stem calc-, of calx, lime.]

CALCINATION (kal-si-nā'shun) n. the operation of calcining.

CALCINE (kal-sin') v.t. to reduce to a powder by heat. [F. calciner, to calcify.]

CALCULATE (kal'kū-lāt) v.t. to compute; reckon;—v.i. to make a computation. [L. part. calculatus, reckoned, fr. L. calculus, a pebble.]

CALCULATION (kal-kū-lā'shun) a. computation.

CALCULATOR (kal'kū-lā-tęr) n. one who computes.

CALCULUS (kal'kū-lus) n. stone in the bladder; a method of computation;—pl. CALCULI [L. =a counter; dim. fr. calx, stone, lime.]

CALDRON (kawl'drun) n. a large kettle. [M.E. cauderon, fr. O.F. chauderon, fr. L. caldarium, a hot bath.]

CALENDAR (kal'en-dar) n. an almanac. [L. calendarium, an account book, fr. Calendae, the calends, when interest was payable.]

CALENDER (kal'en-dęr) v.t. to give gloss to cloth or paper;—n. a hot press.

CALENDS (kal'endz) n.pl. first day of each month, among the Romans.

CALF (kāf) (1) n. the young of a cow; the thick part of the leg; (2) a kind of leather; —pl. CALVES. [(1) O.E. cealf. (2) Scand.]

CALIBRE (kal'i-bęr) n. the bore of fire-arms; mental capacity. [F., fr. A.]

CALICO (kal'i-kō)n. a stuff made of cotton; —pl. CALICOES. [F. calicot, fr. Calicut.]

CALIPERS (kal'i-pęrz) n.pl. compasses with curved legs for measuring the diameters of round bodies. [Corr. of CALIBRE.]

CALISTHENICS, CALLISTHENICS (kal-is-then'iks) n.pl. exercises to promote bodily strength and graceful movement. [G. kallisthenes, fr. kali=kalos, fair, and sthenos, strength.]

CALK (kawk) v.t. arm with sharp points;—n. a sharp point on a shoe.

CALL (kawl) v.t. or i. to cry aloud; make a short visit; name; summon;—n. summons; demand; short visit; cry of a bird. [O.E. ceallian.]

CALLIGRAPHIC (kal-e-graf'ik) a. pertaining to fine writing. [G., fr. kali =kalos, fair, and graphein, to write.]

CALLING (kawl'ing) n. employment.

CALLOUS (kal'us) a. hard; indurated; unfeeling. [L. callosus, fr. callum, thick skin.]

CALLOUSLY (kal'us-li) ad. in a cold, unfeeling manner.

CALLOUSNESS (kal'us-nes) n. hardness; insensibility.

CALLOW (kal'ō) a. unfledged; naked. [O.E. calu, bald.]

CALM (kām) a. still; quiet; undisturbed;—n. serenity; quiet;—v.t. to make quiet; soothe;—v.i. to become quiet. [Late L. (acc.) cauman, the heat of the day.]

CALMNESS (kām'nes) n. serenity; stillness.

CALOMEL (kal'ō-mel) n. a preparation of mercury. [G. kalos, fair, and melos, black.]

CALORIC (ka-lōr'ik) n. the principle or element of heat. [F., fr. L. calor, heat.]

CALORIFIC (kal-ō-rif'ik) a. producing heat. [L. calor, heat, and facere, to make.]

CALORIMETER (kal-ō-rim'e-tęr) n. an apparatus for measuring heat. [L. calor, heat, and metron, a measure.]

CALUMNIATE (ka-lum'ni-āt) v.t. to accuse falsely. [L. part. columniatus.]

CALUMNIATION (ka-lum-ni-ā'shun) n. slander.

CALUMNIATOR (ka-lum'ni-ā-tur) n. a false accuser; a slanderer.

CALUMNIOUS (ka-lum'ni-us) a. defamatory.

CALUMNY (kal'um-ni) n. malicious accusation; slander. [F., fr. L. (acc.) columniam.]

CALVARY (kal'va-ri) n. a place of skulls. [= Golgotha place of skulls: L. calveria, a skull, fr. calvus, bald.]

CALVE (kāv) v.i. to give birth to a calf. [O.E. cealfian.]

CALVINISM (kal'vin-izm) n. the doctrines of **CALVINIST** (kal'vin-ist) n. one who adheres to Calvinism. [Calvin.

CAM (kam) n. the projection on a wheel or axle to produce reciprocating motion. [D.]

CAMBER (kam'ber) n. a slight arching or convexity upwards ;—v.i. to arch or bend upwards. [F., fr. L. camerare, to vault.]

CAMBRIC (kām'brik) n. a fine linen or cotton. [Fr. Kamerijk, Cambray.]

CAMEL (kam'el) n. an animal of Arabia. [F. fr. L. (acc.) camelum, fr. H.]

CAMELLIA (ka-mēl'ya) n. an evergreen shrub with beautiful white flowers. [Fr. Kamel, a Jesuit traveller.]

CAMEO (kam'ē-ō) n. a precious stone sculptured in relief;—pl. **CAMEOS**. [It., of unknown etym.]

CAMERA (kam'er-a) n. an apparatus used in taking pictures by photography; an arched roof or ceiling. [Doublet of **CHAMBER**, which see.]

CAMP (kamp) n. a place where troops pitch their tents; the collection of tents; the troops in it;—v.i. to pitch tents; lodge. [F., fr. L. (acc.) campum, a field.]

CAMPAIGN (kam-pān') n. the time an army keeps the field. [F. campagne, fr. L. (acc.) campaniam, open country.]

CAMPAIGNER (kam-pā'ner) n. an old experienced soldier.

CAMPHOR (kam'fur) n. a solid white gum. [F. camphre.]

CAMPHORATED (kam'fur-āt-ed) a. impregnated with camphor.

CAMPHORIC (kam-for'ik) a. pertaining to camphor.

CAMWHEEL (kam'hwēl) n. a wheel moving eccentrically. [D., and **WHEEL**.]

CAN (kan) (1) v.i. [pret. **COULD**] to be able; —(2) n. a cup or vessel for liquors. [(1) O.E. (pres. indic.) can, fr. cunnan, know. (2) O.E. canne.]

CANAL (ka-nal') n. a watercourse; a pipe. [F., fr. L. canalis.]

CANARD (ka-nárd') n. an idle rumour or report. [F.]

CANARY (ka-nā'ri) n. a kind of wine; a species of singing-bird. [Fr. Canary Islands.]

CANCEL (kan'sel) v.t. to blot out; efface; obliterate. [L. cancellare, to cancel by scoring, fr. L. cancelli (pl.), a lattice.]

CANCELLATED (kan'se-lā-ted) a. marked by cross lines.

CANCELLATION (kan-se-lā'shun) n. a defacing.

CANCER (kan'ser) n. a sign in the zodiac; a virulent ulcer. [L. = a crab.]

CANCEROUS (kan'se-rus) a. consisting of, or relating to, a cancer.

CANCRIFORM (kang'kri-form) a. having the form of a crab.

CANDELABRUM (kan-dē-lā'brum) n. a candle-stick with branches;—pl. **CANDELABRA**. [L., fr. candela, a candle.]

CANDID (kan'did) a. frank; ingenuous. [F. candide, fr. L. candidus, white, fair.]

CANDIDATE (kan'di-dāt) n. one who sues or is proposed for an office. [L. candidatus, white-robed; white being worn by those seeking office.]

CANDIDATURE (kan'di-dā-tūr) n. state or position of being a candidate.

CANDIDLY (kan'did-li) ad. fairly; frankly.

CANDLE (kan'dl) n. a light made of tallow or wax. [O.E. candel, fr. L. candela.]

CANDLEMAS (kan'dl-mas) n. a feast of the Church of Rome on 2nd February. [**CANDLE** and **MASS**.]

CANDOUR (kan'dur) n. fairness; frankness. [L. candere, to shine.]

CANDY (kan'di) v.t. or i. to conserve with sugar;—n. a sweetmeat. [F., fr. A.]

CANE (kān) n. a reed; the sugar-plant; a walking stick;—v.t. to beat with a cane. [F. canne, fr. L., fr. G. kanna, reed.]

CANE-BRAKE (kān'brāk) n. a thicket of canes. [See **BRACKEN**.]

CANHOOK (kan'hook) n. an instrument to sling a cask by its ends.

CANINE (ka-nīn') a. having the properties of a dog. [L. canis, a dog.]

CANISTER (kan'is-ter) n. a small tin box. [Fr. G. kanastron, pannier, fr. kanna, reed.]

CANKER (kang'ker) n. a disease in animals and plants;—v.i. to become corrupt;—v.t. to corrode; infect. [F., fr. L. cancer, a crab.]

CANKERED (kang'kerd) pp. or a. corroded; ill-natured; crabbed.

CANKEROUS (kang'ker-us) a. corroding like a canker.

CANKER-WORM (kang'ker-wurm) n. a worm that destroys plants and fruit.

CANNABINE (kan'a-bin) n. a narcotic derived from hemp. [Fr. plant name Cannabis Indica.]

CANNIBAL (kan'i-bal) n. a man-eater. [Sp. Caribal, a Carib.]

CANNIBALISM (kan'i-bal-izm) n. the eating of human flesh by man.

CANNON (kan'un) n. a great gun for throwing balls or other instruments of destruction by the force of gunpowder. [F. canon, gun-barrel, cannon, fr. canne. See **CANE**.]

CANNONADE (kan-un-ād') n. the firing of cannon with ball;—v.t. to attack with cannon.

CANNONEER (kan-un-ēr') n. one who manages a cannon.

CANNON-SHOT (kan'un-shot) n. a cannon ball.

CANNOT (kan'not) can and not [not properly connected].

CANOE (ka-nòò') n. a boat made of the trunk of a tree, or of bark and skins. [Sp., fr. Ind.]

CANON (kan'un) n. a church law or rule; the genuine books of the Bible; a prebendary of a cathedral. [G. kanon, rule.]

CANONICAL (ka-non'i-kal) a. according to canons; ecclesiastical.

Canoe.

CANONIST (kan'un-ist) n. one versed in canon law.

CANOPY (kan'ō-pi) n. a covering over the head, throne, or bed;—v.t. to cover with a canopy. [F. canopé, fr. L., fr. G. konopeion, a net over a bed.]

CANT (kant) (1) v.t. to incline or place on the edge; tilt over;—(2) v.i. to speak with affected solemnity;—n. inclination from the level; a toss or jerk; affected speech; jargon of a sect. [(1) Dutch. (2) L. cantare, fr. (part.) cantus, sung.]

CANTANKEROUS (kan-tang'ke-rus) a. ill-tempered; cross; quarrelsome. [Etym. unknown.]

CANTATA (kan-tā'ta) n. a poem set to music. [It.]

CANTEEN (kan-tēn') n. a tin vessel for liquors; the sutler's shop in a garrison. [F., fr. It. cantina, a cellar.]

CANTER (kan'ter) v.i. to move in a moderate gallop;—n. a moderate gallop. [Fr. Canter-bury-gallop, the easy pace of pilgrims riding to Canterbury.]

CANTERBURY (kan'ter-ber-i) *n.* a stand with divisions for holding music books.

CANTHARIDES (kan-thar'i-dēz) *n.* Spanish blister-flies. [L. *cantharis*, a beetle. pl. *cantharides*.]

CANTICLE (kan'ti-kl) *n.* a song. CANTICLES, the Song of Solomon. [L. *canticulum*, a little song.]

CANTILEVER, CANTALIVER (kan'ti-lēv-er, kan'ta-liv-er.) *n.* a bracket for supporting a cornice or balcony. The cantilever principle is employed in bridge-building to support very heavy weights. [D. *kant*, an angle, and F. *lever*, to raise.]

CANTING (kant'ing) *a.* speaking with a whine.

CANTO (kan'tō) *n.* a division of a poem;—*pl.* CANTOS. [It., fr. L. (acc.) *cantum*, a song.]

CANTON (kan'ton) *n.* a division of a country; —*v.t.* to divide into districts. [O.F. *canton*, fr. It. *cantone*, a district.]

CANTONMENT (kan'tun-ment) *n.* a district occupied by soldiers.

CANVAS (kan'vas) *n.* a coarse cloth for sails, etc.; sails in general. [O.F. *canevas*, fr. Late L. *canabacius*, hempen, fr. L. *cannabis*, hemp.]

CANVASS (kan'vas) *v.t.* or *i.* to examine; solicit votes;—*n.* seeking to obtain votes, etc. [See CANVAS.]

CANVASSER (kan'vas-er) *n.* one who solicits votes or orders.

CAOUTCHOUC (kōō'chook) *n.* india-rubber or gum elastic. [F., fr. S. Amer.]

CAP (kap) *n.* a cover for the head; top;— *v.t.* to cover the head or top; excel. [Low L. *cappa*, a cape.]

CAPABILITY (kā-pa-bil'i-ti) *n.* capacity; qualification.

CAPABLE (kā'pa-bl) *a.* having capacity or ability; competent. [L. *capabilis*, fr. *capere*, to take.]

CAPABLY (kā'pa-bli) *ad.* with capability.

CAPACIOUS (ka-pā'shus) *a.* wide; large. [L. stem *capaci-*, of *capax*, able to hold much.]

CAPACIOUSNESS (ka-pā'shus-nes) *n.* power of holding or receiving.

CAPACITY (ka-pas'i-ti) *n.* the power of receiving and containing.

CAPARISON (ka-par'i-sun) *n.* trappings for a horse;—*v.t.* to dress pompously. [F., fr. Sp., fr. Low L. *cappa*, a cape.]

CAPE (kāp) (1) *n.* a headland; neck-piece of a coat; (2) a loose covering for the shoulders. [(1) F. *cap*, fr. It., fr. L. *caput*, the head. (2) Low L. *cappa*, a cape.]

CAPER (kā'per) (1) *n.* bud of the caper-bush; (2) a leap;—*v.i.* to skip; leap. [(1) F., fr. G. *kapparis*, fr. A. (2) Short form of It. *capriole*. See CABRIOLET.]

CAPILLARY (kap'i-lar-i, kap-ll'ar-i) *a.* resembling a hair;—*n.* a small tube, or fine, hair-like fibre. [L. *capillaris*, hair-like.]

CAPITAL (kap'i-tal) *n.* principal sum; stock; large letter; chief city; upper part of a column; —*a.* relating to the head; principal. [L., fr. stem *capit-*, of *caput*, the head.]

CAPITALISE (kap'i-tal-īz) *v.t.* to convert into capital; estimate the present value of deferred payments or rents.

Capital.

CAPITALIST (kap'i-tal-ist) *n.* one who employs or has capital.

CAPITATION (kap-i-tā'shun) *n.* numeration by heads; a poll-tax. [L. (acc.) *capitationem*, a poll-tax.]

CAPITULATE (ka-pit'ū-lāt) *v.i.* to surrender on conditions. [L. *capitulatus*, agreed, of terms.]

CAPITULATION (ka-pit-ū-lā'shun) *n.* a surrender on terms.

CAPITULATOR (ka-pit'ū-lā-ter) *n.* one who capitulates.

CAPRICE (ka-prēs') *n.* sudden or unreasonable change of mind or humour. [F., fr. It., fr. L. (acc.) *caprum*, a goat.]

CAPRICIOUS (ka-prish'us) *a.* whimsical; fanciful.

CAPRICORN (kap'ri-korn) *n.* one of the signs in the zodiac. [L., fr. *caper*, a goat, and *cornu*, a horn.]

CAPSIZE (kap-sīz') *v.t.* to overturn. [Etym. unknown.]

CAPSTAN (kap'stan) *n.* a machine to raise great weights, principally used in ships for raising an anchor. [F. *capestan*, fr. Low L., fr. L. *capistrum*, a halter, fr. *capere*.]

CAPSULAR (kap'sū-lar) *a.* hollow, like a chest. [L. *capsula*; dim. fr. *capsa*, a case.]

CAPSULE (kap'sūl) *n.* the seed-vessel of a plant; a small dish; a metal cover placed over the mouth of a corked bottle; a gelatinous envelope containing some nauseous medicine.]

CAPTAIN (kap'tān, kap'tin) *n.* a commander in the army or navy. [O.F. *capitaine*, fr. Late L. *capitanus*, a chief of soldiers, fr. *caput*, the head.]

CAPTAINCY (kap'tin-si) *n.* the rank or commission of a captain. Also CAPTAINSHIP.

CAPTIOUS (kap'shus) *a.* apt to cavil; fault-finding; censorious. [F., fr. L. *captiosus*, cavilling, fr. L. *captio*, a fallacy, fr. *capere*, to take.]

CAPTIOUSNESS (kap'shus-nes) *n.* disposition to cavil.

CAPTIVATE (kap'ti-vāt) *v.t.* to take prisoner; please exceedingly; fascinate.

CAPTIVATING (kap'ti-vāt-ing) *a.* charming.

CAPTIVE (kap'tiv) *n.* one taken in war;—*a.* made prisoner. [F. *captif*, fr. L. *captivus*, fr. *capere*, to take. Doublet of CAITIFF.]

CAPTIVITY (kap-tiv'i-ti) *n.* subjection; bondage. [or prisoner.

CAPTOR (kap'ter) *n.* one who takes a prize

CAPTURE (kap'tūr) *n.* seizure of a prize;— *v.t.* to take or seize by force or fraud.

CAR (kär) *n.* a light vehicle; a railway or tramway carriage. [F., fr. Celt.]

CARAFE (ka-räf') *n.* a glass water-bottle for the table or toilet. [F., fr. A.]

CARAMEL (kar'a-mel) *n.* burnt sugar used for colouring spirits. [F.]

CARAT (kar'at) *n.* a weight of four grains. [F., fr. A., fr. G. *keration*, a seed, very light weight.

CARAVAN (kar-a-van') *n.* a body of travelling pilgrims or traders; a large, close carriage. [Per.]

CARAVANSARY (kar-a-van'sar-i) *n.* a house for travellers in Asia. [Per.]

CARAWAY (kar'a-wā) *n.* an aromatic plant. [Sp., fr. A.]

CARBINE (kär'bīn) *n.* a short light gun borne by horsemen. [F., of uncertain etym.]

CARBINEER (kar-bi-nēr') *n.* a man who carries a carbine.

CARBOLIC (kär-bol'ik) *n.* a disinfecting fluid obtained from coal tar. [L. *carbo*, coal.]

CARBON (kär'bon) *n.* pure charcoal. [L. *carbo*, coal.]

CARBONIC (kär-bon'ik) *a.* pertaining to carbon.

CARBOY (kär'boi) *n.* a globular bottle protected by basket work. [Per.]

CARBUNCLE (kär'bung-kl) *n.* an inflammatory tumour; a red gem. [L. *carbunculus*, a little coal, fr. L. *carbo*.]

CARBURETTED (kär'bū-ret-ed) *a.* combined with carbon. [L. *carbo*, coal.]

CARBURETTER (kar'bu-ret-er) *n.* that part of a petrol engine in which the petrol vapour is carbonised prior to ignition.

CARCASS (kär'kas) *n.* a dead body; framework or main parts. [F., fr. It. *carcassa*, a shell.]

CARD (kård) (1) *n.* a written note; a paper containing an address; (2) a large comb for wool; a printed paper;—*v.t.* to comb wool. [(1) F. *carte.* Doublet of **CHART.** (2) F. *carde,* fr. L. (acc.) *cardum* = *carduum,* a thistle.]

CARDIAC (kår'di-ak) *a.* pertaining to the heart;—*n.* a stimulating medicine; a cordial. [L., fr. G. *kardiakos,* pertaining to the heart.]

CARDINAL (kår'di-nal) *a.* principal; chief; —*n.* a dignitary of the Roman Catholic Church. [L., fr. stem *cardin-,* fr. *cardo,* a hinge.]

CARD-TABLE (kård'tā-bl) *n.* a small table with one leaf.

CARE (kār) *n.* uneasiness of mind; caution; management;—*v.i.* to be anxious; heed. [O.E. *caru.*]

CAREEN (ka-rēn') *v.t.* or *i.* to heave or incline on one side. [L. *carina,* a keel.]

CAREER (ka-rēr') *n.* a course; race; time or mode of action;—*v.i.* to go or move on rapidly. [F. *carrière,* orig. a chariot course.]

CAREFUL (kār'fool) *a.* anxious; watchful; saving.

CAREFULNESS (kār'fool-nes) *n.* great care; caution.

CARELESS (kār'les) *a.* heedless; having no care.

CARELESSLY (kār'les-li) *ad.* without care.

CARELESSNESS (kār'les-nes) *n.* negligence.

CARESS (ka-res') *v.t.* to embrace; fondle;— *n.* act of endearment. [F. *caresse,* fr. It., fr. L. *carus,* dear.]

CARET (kā'ret) *n.* this mark (∧), denoting omission. [L. = is wanting, fr. *carere.*]

CAREWORN (kār'worn) *a.* worn or vexed with care.

CARGO (kår'gō) *n.* a ship's freight. [Sp., fr. Low L. *carricare,* to load, fr. *carrus,* a car.]

CARIBOU (kar'i-boo) *n.* the American reindeer. [Canadian F.]

CARICATURE (kar-i-ka-tūr') *n.* a description exaggerated to deformity;—*v.t.* to represent ludicrously. [It., fr. *caricare,* load.]

CARILLON (kar'i-lun) *n.* a chime of small bells; a tune or air to be played thereon. [F.]

CARL (kårl) *n.* a rough, elderly man; a kind of hemp; a heap of wool. Also **CARLE.** [Scand; conn. with **CHURL.**]

CARMAN (kår'man) *n.* one who drives a car.

CARMINE (kår'min) *n.* a bright red powder or pigment. [Sp., fr. Low L. *carmesinus,* fr. A. See **CRIMSON.**]

CARNAGE (kår'nāj) *n.* destruction of lives; slaugh . [F., fr. L. stem *carn-,* of *caro,* flesh.] ter

CARNAL (kår'nal) *a.* fleshly; sensual. [See **CARNAGE.**]

CARNALIST (kår'nal-ist) *n.* one given to lust.

CARNALITY (kår-nal'i-ti) *n.* fleshly desires.

CARNALLY (kår'nal-i) *ad.* according to the flesh.

CARNATION (kår-nā'shun) *n.* flesh colour; a beautiful flower. [F., fr. L. (acc.) *carnationem,* fleshiness.]

CARNELIAN (kår-nē'li-an) *n.* a precious stone. [L. *carnis,* of flesh.]

CARNIVAL (kår'ni-val) *n.* a festival during twelve days before Lent. [F. *carnaval,* fr. It., fr. Low L. *carnevale,* the taking away of flesh, fr. L. (acc.) *carnem,* flesh, and *levare,* remove.]

CARNIVORA (kår-niv'ō-ra) *n.pl.* animals which feed on flesh.

CARNIVOROUS (kår-niv'ō-rus) *a.* feeding on flesh.

CAROL (kar'ul) *n.* a song of joy;—*v.i.* to warble. [O.F. *carole,* a dance song; of uncertain etym.]

CAROTID (ka-rot'id) *a.* a term applied to two principal arteries. [G. *karos,* stupor, caused, it was thought, by a stoppage of the flow of blood.]

CAROUSAL (ka-rouz'al) *n.* a drunken revel.

CAROUSE (ka-rouz') *v.i.* to drink freely and jovially;—*n.* a drinking bout. [O.F. *carous,* fr. Ger. *gar-aus* (drink) right out.]

CARP (kårp) (1) *n.* a pond fish;—(2) *v.i.* to find fault; cavil. [(1) O.F. *carpe,* fr. Teut. (2) Scand.]

CARPENTER (kår'pen-ter) *n.* a worker in timber for building houses or ships. [O.F. *carpentier,* fr. L. (acc.) *carpentarium,* a carriage-maker, fr. *carpentum,* a car.]

CARPET (kår'pet) *n.* a covering for a floor;— *v.t.* [*pp.* or *a.* **CARPETED**] to cover with a carpet. [O.F. *carpite,* fr. Late L. (acc.) *carpitam,* cloth made from shred, fr. L. *carpere,* pluck.]

CARPETING (kår'pet-ing) *n.* carpets in general.

CARPING (kår'ping) *a.* captious; censorious; —*n.* cavil; censure. [See **CARP** (2).]

CARRIAGE (kar'ij) *n.* a vehicle; conveyance; behaviour. [See **CARRY.**]

CARRIER (kar'i-er) *n.* one who carries; a species of pigeon.

CARRION (kar'i-un) *n.* putrid flesh. [M.E. and O.F. *caroigne,* fr Late L. (acc.) *caroniam,* carcass, L. *caro,* flesh.]

CARROT (kar'ut) *n.* a reddish or yellowish edible root. [F. *carotte,* fr. L. (acc.) *carrotam,* fr. G.]

CARRY (kar'i) *v.t.* to bear; behave. [O.F. *carier,* fr. Late L. *carricare,* to load, fr. L. *carrus.* See **CAR.**]

CART (kårt) *n.* a carriage with two wheels for heavy loads;—*v.t.* to convey in a cart. [Scand. or E.]

CARTAGE (kår'tāj) *n.* act of carting; the price paid for carting.

CARTER (kår'ter) *n.* one who drives a cart.

CARTILAGE (kår-ti-låj) *n.* gristle. [F., fr. L. (acc.) *cartilaginem,* gristle, fr. *cartilago.*]

CARTILAGINOUS (kår-ti-laj'i-nus) *a.* gristly; of or like cartilage.

CARTOGRAPHY (kår-tog'ra-fi) *n.* the art of preparing charts or maps. [O.F. *charte,* fr. L. (acc.) *chartam, cartam,* a paper, fr. G. *charte.*]

CARTOON (kår-tòòn') *n.* a design for fresco or tapestry; any large sketch or illustration. [F. *carton,* fr. It., fr. L. *charta, carta,* paper.]

CARTRIDGE (kår'trij) *n.* a paper case for powder and ball. [= *cartidge,* fr. F. *cartouche.*]

CARTRIDGE-BOX (kår'trij-boks) *n.* a box for cartridges.

CARTULARY (kår'tu-lar-i) *n.* a register-book of a monastery; place for storing records. [Late L. *chartula,* a document, dim. of *charta.*]

CARTWRIGHT (kårt'rit) *n.* a maker or mender of carts.

CARVE (kårv) *v.t.* to cut wood, stone, or meat. [O.E. *ceorfan.*]

CARVER (kår'ver) *n.* one who carves; a sculptor; a large knife.

CASCADE (kas'kåd) *n.* a waterfall. [F., fr. It., fr. L. *casare,* totter, fr. *cadere,* fall.]

CASE (kås) (1) *a.* a covering; box; state; variation of nouns;—(2) *v.t.* to put in a case. [(1) O.F. *casse,* fr. L. (acc.) *capsam,* fr. *capere,* to take. (2) M.E. *cas,* fr. F. *cas.*]

CASE-HARDEN (kås'hard-en) *v.t.* to make hard on the outside.

CASEIN (kā'sē-in) *n.* the curd or coagulable part of milk of which cheese is made. [F., fr. L. *caseus,* cheese.]

CASE-KNIFE (kås'nif) *n.* a table-knife.

CASEMATE (kås'måt) *n.* a vault or covered archwork. [F., fr. It.]

CASEMENT (kås'ment) *n.* a part of a window.

CASEOUS (kā'sē-us) *a.* resembling cheese.

CASH (kash) *n.* money; coin;—*v.t.* to convert into money. [= orig. a money **CASE** (1).]

CASH-BOOK (kash'böòk) *n.* a book in which accounts of money are kept.

CASHIER (kash-ēr') *n.* one who has the charge of money ;—*v.t.* to dismiss from office. [D., fr. F. *casser*, annul, dismiss, fr. L. *cassare*, **fr.** *cassus*, empty.]

CASHMERE (kash'mēr) *n.* a rich kind of shawl; a fine woollen stuff. [Fr. *Cashmere* in India.]

CASK (kask) *n.* a small barrel. [Sp. *casco*, shell, cask, fr. L.]

CASKET (kas'ket) *n.* a small case for jewels.

CASQUE (kask) *n.* a helmet. [Doublet of **CASK.**]

CASSATION (ka-sā'shun) *n.* the chief court of appeal in France. [F., fr. *casser*.]

CASSOCK (kas'uk) *n.* a close frockcoat for clergymen. [F., fr. It.]

CASSOWARY (kas'ŏ-wạ-ri) *n.* a very large bird, allied to the ostrich. [Malay.]

CAST (kast) *v.t.* [*prep.* and *pp.* **CAST**] to throw; fling; found or form; calculate ;—*n.* a throw; motion; turn; appearance. [Scand.]

CASTANET (kas'tạ-net) *n.* a rattling instrument used in dancing. [F. (pl.) *castagnettes*, fr. Sp. *castañeta*, fr. L. *castanea*, a chestnut-tree.]

CASTAWAY (kast'ạ-wā) *n.* one abandoned to destruction ;—*a.* rejected; useless.

CASTE (kast) *n.* an exclusive class or rank in society. [Pg. *casta*, fr. L. *castus*, pure.]

CASTELLATED (kas'te-lāt-ed) *a.* turreted, like a castle.

CASTER (kas'tẹr) *n.* a thrower; a small wheel on a swivel on which furniture is rolled; a phial stand.

CASTERS (kas'tẹrz) *n.pl.* a stand for bottles; little wheels.

CASTIGATE (kas'ti-gāt) *v.t.* to chastise. [L. *castigatus*, chastened, fr. *castus*, pure.]

CASTIGATION (kas-ti-gā'shun) *n.* correction.

CASTING (kas'ting) *n.* act of casting; anything shaped in a mould.

CASTING-VOTE (kas'ting-vōt) *n.* a vote that decides when the others are equally divided.

CAST-IRON (kast'i-urn) *n.* iron melted and run into moulds.

CASTLE (kas'l) *n.* a fortified house; a piece in chess. [O.E. *castel*, fr. L. *castellum*, dim. for *castrum*, a fort.]

CASTLED (kas'ld) *a.* furnished with castles.

CASTOR (kas'tẹr) *n.* a beaver; a substance secreted in the groin of the beaver; a hat made of its fur. [L., fr. G. *kastor*.]

CASTRATE (kas'trāt) *v.i.* to emasculate or geld; make imperfect. [L. (part.) *castratus*, cut, fr. *castrare*.]

CASUAL (kazh'ū-ạl) *a.* happening without design; accidental; occasional. [L., fr. *casus*; see **CASE** (2).]

CASUALTY (kazh'ū-ạl-ti) *n.* an accident, resulting in injury or loss of life.

CASUIST (kazh'ū-ist) *n.* a resolver of doubtful cases of right and wrong. [F. *casuiste*; see **CASE** (2).]

CASUISTIC (kazh-ū-is'tik) *a.* relating to cases of conscience.

CASUISTRY (kazh'ū-is'tri) *n.* the skill or practice of a casuist.

CATAFALQUE (kat'ạ-falk) *n.* a temporary structure in imitation of a tomb. [It.; of unknown origin.]

CAT (kat) *n.* a domestic animal; a strong tackle; a double tripod; a lash of nine cords. [O.E. *cat.*]

CATACOMB (kat'ạ-kōm) *n.* a cave for the dead. [G. *kata*, downward, and *kumbos*, cavity.]

CATACOUSTICS (kat-ạ-kous'tiks) *n.pl.* science of echoes or reflected sounds.

CATALEPSY (kat'ạ-lep-si) *n.* sudden suppression of sensation and volition. [G. *kata*, outright, and *lepsis*, seizure.]

CATALOGUE (kat'ạ-log) *n.* a list; register of names ;—*v.t.* to make a list of. [G., fr. *kata*, throughout, and *legein*, speak.]

CATAMOUNT (kat'ạ-mount) *n.* a wild cat. [Formed fr. *cat o' mountain*.]

CATAPLASM (kat'ạ-plazm) *n.* a poultice. [G., fr. *kata-plassein*, plaster over.]

CATAPULT (kat'ạ-pult) *n.* a military engine for throwing stones, etc. [G. *katapeltes*, fr. *kata*, against, and *pallein*, to launch.]

CATARACT (kat'ạ-rakt) *n.* a large waterfall; disorder in the eye. [G. *katarhaktes*, fr. *kata*, down, and *rhegnumi*, break.]

CATARRH kạ-tạr') *n.* a defluction from the nose. [L. *catarrhus*, fr. G. *katarrhous*, a flowing down, fr. *rheein*, flow.]

Catapult.

CATASTROPHE (kạ-tas'trō-fē) *n.* a final event; calamity; disaster. [G. = an overturning, fr. G. *kata*, down, and *strephein*, turn.]

CATCALL (kat'kawl) *n.* a squeaking instrument.

CATCH (kach) *v.t.* [*prep.* and *pp.* **CAUGHT**] to seize; take in a net or by sympathy, contagion, etc.; come upon; overtake ;—*v.i.* to keep hold; grasp at ;—*n.* act of seizing; sudden advantage; play upon words; a kind of glee. [O.F. Doublet of **CHASE.**]

CATCHER (kach'ẹr) *n.* one who catches.

CATCHING (kach'ing) *a.* infectious; apt to catch. [publication.

CATCHPENNY (kach'pen-i) *n.* a worthless

CATECHETICAL (kat-ē-ket'i-kạl) *a.* consisting of question and answer. [G. *katechizein*, to instruct.]

CATECHISE (kat'ē-kīz) *v.t.* to instruct; interrogate by questions and answers.

CATECHISER (kat'ē-kīz-ẹr) *n.* one who catechises. [tions and answers.

CATECHISM (kat'ē-kizm) *n.* a book of ques-

CATECHUMEN (kat-ē-kū'men) *n.* one being taught the rudiments of Christianity. [L., fr. G. part. *katechoumenos*, instructed orally, fr. *katechein*, fr. *kata*, down, and *echein*, to sound.]

CATEGORICAL (kat-ē-gor'i-kạl) *a.* absolute; positive. [G. *kategorikos*, pertaining to a category.]

CATEGORY (kat'ē-gor-i) *n.* a class or order of ideas; a rule or condition. [G., fr. *kata*, down, and *agoreuein*, to assert.]

CATENA (ka-tē'na) *n.* a chain; series; bond of union. [L.]

CATENARY (kat'e-nạr-i) *a.* relating to or like a chain. [L. *catenarius*, pertaining to a chain.]

CATER (kā'tẹr) *v.i.* to provide food. [M.E. *catour*, caterer, fr. O.F. *acat*, through Low L. *accipere*, receive, buy.]

CATERER (kā'tẹr-ẹr) *n.* one who provides food.

CATERPILLAR (kat'ẹr-pil-ạr) *n.* the larva or worm state of insects. [Corr. of O.F. *chatepelose*, lit. hairy cat.]

CATERWAUL (kat'ẹr-wawl) *v.i.* to cry as a cat. [**CAT**, and *waul*, which is probably onomatopœic.]

CATGUT (kat'gut) *n.* intestines dried and twisted for violin and other musical instrument strings.

CATHARTIC (kạ-thär'tik) *a.* purgative ;—*n.* a purge. [G., fr. *katharos*, pure.]

CATHEDRAL (kạ-thē'dral) *n.* the principal church in a diocese. [L. *cathedralis (ecclesia)*, (church) with the bishop's throne; fr. G. *kath-, kata*, down, and *hedra*, a seat.]

CATHOLIC (kath'u-lik) *a.* universal; liberal; pertaining to all Christians ;—*n.* an adherent of the Roman Church. [L., fr. G. *katholikos*, general, **fr.** G. *kata*, according to, and *holos*, whole.]

Fāte, fár, ạdo; mē, hẹr; mīne; nōte; tūne; mŏŏn.

CATHOLICISM (ka-thol'i-sizm) *n.* adherence to the Roman Catholic Church.

CATHOLICITY (kath-o-lis'i-ti) *n.* liberality in religion; breadth of thought, feeling, etc.

CAT'S-PAW (kats'paw) *n.* the dupe or tool of another; a light breeze of wind.

CATTLE (kat'l) *n.pl.* beasts of pasture. [O.F. *catel*. Doublet of CHATTELS.]

CAUCUS (kaw'kus) *n.* a party meeting to arrange future political action. [Etym. unknown.]

CAUDAL (kaw'dal) *a.* pertaining to the tail. [L. *cauda*, a tail.]

CAUDLE (kaw'dl) *n.* a warm drink for sick persons. [O.F. *chaudel*, fr. *chald*, hot, fr. L. (acc.) *calidum*.]

CAUGHT (kawt) *pret.* and *pp.* of CATCH.

CAULIFLOWER (kaw'li-flou-er) *n.* a species of cabbage. [M.E. *col*, fr. O.F., fr. L. *caulis*, cabbage.]

CAULK (kawk) *v.t.* to stop seams of a ship. [O.F. *cauquer* to press, fr. L. *calx*, a heel.]

CAUSAL (kaw'zal) *a.* implying causes. [See CAUSE.]

CAUSALITY (kaw-zal'i-ti) *n.* the agency of a cause.

CAUSATION (kaw-za'shun) *n.* the act of causing or producing.

CAUSE (kawz) *n.* that which produces an effect; a suit in law;—*v t.* to make to exist; bring about. [F., fr. L. *causa*, a cause or lawsuit.]

CAUSELESS (kawz'les) *a.* without cause; original. [or reason.]

CAUSELESSLY (kawz'les-li) *ad.* without cause

CAUSEWAY (kawz'wā) *n.* a raised way or path paved with stones. Sometimes written **CAUSEY** (kawz'e). [O.F. *caucie* = F. *chaussée*, fr. Late L. *calciata* (*via*), trodden (way), fr. stem *calc-*, of *calx*, a heel.]

CAUSTIC (kaws'tik) *a.* corroding; severe; cutting;—*n.* a burning application. [G., fr. *kaustos*, burned, fr. *kaiein*.]

CAUSTICITY (kaws-tis'i-ti) *n.* the quality of burning.

CAUTERISE (kaw'ter-īz) *v.t.* to burn or sear with a hot iron, etc.

CAUTERY (kaw'ter-i) *n.* a searing with a hot iron or caustic medicines. [G. *kauterion*, branding-iron.]

CAUTION (kaw'shun) *n.* prudence; care;—*v.t.* to advise against. [F., fr. L. (acc.) *cautionem* = *cavitinum*, fr. *cavere*, beware.]

CAUTIONARY (kaw'shun-a-ri) *a.* containing caution.

CAUTIONER (kaw'shun-er) *n.* cne who becomes security for another.

CAUTIOUS (kaw'shus) *a.* watchful against danger; wary.

CAUTIOUSLY (kaw'shus-li) *ad.* prudently.

CAUTIOUSNESS (kaw'shus-nes) *n.* prudence.

CAVALCADE (kav'al-kād) *n.* a procession on horseback. [F., fr. It. *cavaliere*, horseman.]

CAVALIER (kav-a-lēr') *n.* a horseman;—*a.* brave; haughty; disdainful. [F., fr. It. *cavaliere*, fr. L. (acc.) *caballarium*, fr. L. *caballus*. Doublet of CHEVALIER.]

CAVALRY (kav'al-ri) *n.* mounted troops. [O.F., fr. It. *cavalleria*. Doublet of CHIVALRY.]

CAVE (kāv) *n.* a den; a hollow place in the earth;—*v.i.* to fall in;—*v.t.* to scoop out. [O.F., fr. Low L. (acc.) *cavam*, a cave, fr. *cavus*, hollow.]

CAVERN (kav'ern) *n.* a large cave. [F., fr. L. *caverna*, fr. *cavus*, hollow.]

CAVERNOUS (kav'er-nus) *a.* hollow; full of cavities.

CAVIARE (kav-i-är') *n.* the roes of certain fish salted. [F., fr. Turk.]

CAVIL (kav'il) *v.i.* to raise false or trifling objections; carp;—*n.* a captious or specious argument. [L. *cavillori*, fr. *cavilla*, a quibble.]

CAVILLING (kav'il-ing) *n.* disputation; groundless objection.

CAVITY (kav'i-ti) *n.* a hollow place.

CAW (kaw) *v.i.* to cry as a rook, crow, or raven. [Onomatopœic word.]

CAYENNE (kā-en') *n.* a pungent pepper. [Fr. *Cayenne*, America.]

CAYMAN (kā'man) *n.* an alligator in America. [Sp. *caiman*. probably fr. Carib.]

CEASE (sēs) *v.i.* to stop; leave off. [F. *cesser*, fr. L. *cessare*.]

CEASELESS (sēs'les) *a.* never ceasing.

CEASELESSLY (sēs'les-li) *ad.* without intermission; continually.

CEDAR (sē'dar) *n.* an evergreen tree. [F. *cedre*, fr. L. (acc.) *cedrum*, fr. G. *kedros*.]

CEDE (sēd) *v.t.* to yield; give up. [L. *cedere*.]

CEDILLA (sē-dil'a) *n.* a mark under *c*, thus (¸). [Sp., fr. It. *zediglia*, fr. G. *zeta*, z.]

CEIL (sēl) *v.t.* to cover or line; roof. [M.E. *ceelen*, to ceil, fr. F. *ciel*, fr. L. *cœlum*, the sky.]

CEILING (sē'ling) *n.* covering of the inner roof.

CELEBRANT (sel'e-brant) *n.* the officiating priest or minister. [L. (part.) *celebratus* honoured, fr. *celeber*, frequented.]

CELEBRATE (sel'e-brāt) *v.t.* to praise; extol; observe; commemorate.

CELEBRATION (sel-e-brā'shun) *n.* an honouring with praise or solemnities.

CELEBRITY (se-leb'ri-ti) *n.* fame; distinction; a person of distinction or fame. [L. (acc.) *celebritatem*, fame.]

CELERITY (se-ler'i-ti) *n.* swiftness; speed. [F., fr. L. (acc.) *celeritatem*, swiftness, fr. *celer*, swift.]

CELERY (sel'er-i) *n.* a plant cultivated for the table. [F. *céleri*, fr. L., through Prov. It., fr. G. *selinon*, parsley.]

CELESTIAL (se-lest'yal) *a.* heavenly;—*n.* an inhabitant of heaven. [L. *cœlestis*, fr. *cœlum*, heaven.]

CELIBACY (sel'i-ba-si) *n.* single life; unmarried state. [L., fr. stem *cœlib-*, cf *cœlebs*, unmarried.]

CELIBATE (sel'i-bāt) *n.* an unmarried person.

CELL (sel) *n.* a small room; any small cavity or hollow place. [L. *cella*, a small room.]

CELLAR (sel'ar) *n.* a room under a house. [O.F. *celer*, fr. L. *cellarium*, a pantry.]

CELLARAGE (sel'ar-āj) *n.* cellars in general; space for cellars.

CELLARER (sel'ar-er) *n.* the monk who had charge of the cellars.

CELLARET (sel'ar-et) *n.* an ornamental case in a room for holding liquor bottles.

CELLULAR (sel'ū-lar) *a.* consisting of cells or small vesicles.

CELLULOSE (sel'lu-lōs) *a.* containing cells;—*n.* the substance of vegetable cells.

CELTIC (sel'tik) *a.* pertaining to the primitive inhabitants of Western Europe. [L. (pl.) *Celtae*, fr. Celt.]

CEMENT (sē-ment', sem'ent) *n.* an adhesive substance which unites bodies;—*v.t.* to join closely;—*v.i.* to unite; cohere. [O.F. *ciment*, fr. L. *cœmentum*, stone-chippings.]

CEMENTATION (sem-en-tā'shun) *n.* the act of uniting by cement.

CEMETERY (sem'ē-ter-i) *n.* a place where the dead are buried. [Late L. *cœmetarium*, a sleeping place, fr. G. *koimao*, I lull to sleep.]

CENSER (sen'ser) *n.* an incense-pan. [O.F. *censier* = *encensier*, see INCENSE.]

CENSOR (sen'ser) *n.* a Roman magistrate; one who examines manuscripts for the press; a severe critic. [L. = critic, fr. *censere*, to estimate.]

CENSORIAL (sen-sō'ri-al) *a.* belonging to a censor.

CENSORIOUS (sen-sō'ri-us) *a.* severe; prone to find fault.

CENSORIOUSLY (sen-sō'ri-us-li) *ad.* in a censorious manner.

CENSORIOUSNESS (sen-sō'ri-us-nes) *n.* act or habit of finding fault.

CENSORSHIP (sen'sur-ship) *n.* office, or term of office, of a censor.

CENSURABLE (sen'shŭr-a-bl) *a.* deserving of censure.

CENSURE (sen'shŭr) *n.* blame;—*v.t.* to blame; reprove; reprimand. [F., fr. L. (acc.) *censuram*, opinion.]

CENSUS (sen'sus) *n.* an official enumeration of inhabitants. [L. =a rating.]

CENT (sent) *n.* a hundred; a copper coin of the United States, being the hundredth part of a dollar, or one halfpenny sterling. [L. *centum*.]

CENTAUR (sen'tawr) *n.* a fabulous monster, half man, half horse. [L., fr. G. *kentauros*.]

CENTENARY (sen'ten-a-ri) *a.* pertaining to a hundred;—*n.* commemoration after a hundred years. [L. *centeni*, a hundred at a time, fr. *centum*.]

CENTERING (sen'ter-ing) *n.* the framework of any vaulted structure.

CENTESIMAL (sen-tes'i-mal) *n.* the hundredth part. [L., fr. *centesimus*, hundredth.]

CENTIGRADE (sen'ti-grād) *a.* divided into a hundred degrees. [F., fr. L. pref. *centi-*, for *centum*, and GRADE.]

CENTIME (sen'tēm) *n.* the hundredth part of a franc.

CENTIPEDE (sen'ti-pēd) *n.* an insect with many legs. [L. *centum*, a hundred, and stem *ped-*, of *pes*, a foot.]

CENTRAL (sen'tral) *a.* relating to the centre; near the centre.

CENTRALISATION (sen-tral-i-zā'shun) *n.* act of centralising.

CENTRALISE (sen'tral-īz) *n.* to make central; draw to a centre.

CENTRE (sen'ter) *n.* the middle point;—*v.t.* or *i.* to place or meet on the middle point. [F., fr. L. *centrum*, fr. G. *kentron*, prick, fr. *kentein*, to goad.]

CENTRE-BIT (sen'ter-bit) *n.* an instrument for boring holes in wood.

CENTRIFUGAL (sen-trif'ū-gal) *a.* tending from the centre. [L. *centrum*, the centre, and *fugere*, to flee.]

CENTRIPETAL (sen-trip'e-tal) *a.* tending to the centre. [L. *centrum*, the centre, and *petere*, to move toward.]

CENTURIAL (sen-tūr'i-al) *a.* pertaining to a century.

CENTURION (sen-tūr'i-un) *n.* a Roman officer over a hundred men. [L. (acc.) *centurionem*.]

CENTURY (sen'tū-ri) *n.* a hundred years. [L. *centuria*.]

CEREAL (sē'rē-al) *a.* pertaining to grain;—*n.* an edible grain. [L., fr. *Ceres*, the goddess of agriculture.]

CEREMENT (sēr'ment) *n.* cloth dipped in wax, used in embalming. Also **CERE-CLOTH**.

CEREMONIAL (ser-e-mō'ni-al) *a.* relating to rites;—*n.* outward form.

CEREMONIOUS (ser-ē-mō'ni-us) *a.* formal; exact.

CEREMONY (ser'ē-mō-ni) *n.* outward rite. [F. *cérémonie*, fr. L. (acc.) *cærimoniam*, a rite.]

CERIFEROUS (sē-rif'er-us) *a.* producing wax. [L. *cera*, wax, and *fero*, I bear or carry.]

CERISE (sē-rēz') *a.* cherry-coloured. [F. = cherry.]

CEROGRAPHY (sē-rog'ra-fi) *n.* the art of engraving on wax. [L. *cera*, wax, and G. *graphein*, to write.]

CERTAIN (ser'tin) *a.* sure; regular. [F., fr. L. *certus*, fr. *cernere*, decide.]

CERTAINTY (ser'tin-ti) *n.* full assurance.

CERTIFICATE (ser-tif'i-kāt) *n.* a testimony in writing. [F. *certificat*, fr. L. *certificare*, fr. *certus*, decided, and *facere*, to make.]

CERTIFY (ser'ti-fī) *v.t.* to give certain notice; testify in writing. [doubt.]

CERTITUDE (ser'ti-tūd) *n.* freedom from

CERULIAN (se-rōō'le-an) *a.* sky-coloured; blue. [L. *cæruleus*, fr. *cœlum*, the sky.]

CERVICAL (ser'vi-kal) *a.* relating to the neck. [L. *cervix, cervicis*, the neck.]

CESSATION (se-sā'shun) *n.* stopping or ending; discontinuance. [F., fr. L. (acc.) *cessationem*.]

CESSION (sesh'un) *n.* a giving up; surrender.

CESSPOOL (ses'pōōl) *n.* a reservoir to receive drainage, etc. (Perhaps short for *se-cess pool*. See **SECEDE**.]

CESURAL (sē-zūr'al) *a.* relating to a cesura. [L. *cædere, cæsum*, to cut off.]

CETACEAN (sē-tā'shan) *n.* an animal of the whale family. [L. *cetus*, G. *ketos*, any large sea-animal.]

CETACEOUS (sē-tā'shus) *a.* of the whale kind.

CHAFE (chāf) *v.t.* and *i.* to fret; wear by friction;—*n.* irritation. [M.E. *chaufen*, warm, fr. O.F. *chauffer*.]

CHAFF (chaf) (1) *n.* the husks of grain; cut straw; worthless matter;—(2) *v.t.* to banter. [(1) O. E. *ceaf*. (2) Form of CHAFE =irritation.]

CHAFFER (chaf'er) *v.t.* or *i.* to bargain.

CHAFFERER (chaf'er-er) *n.* one who treats about buying.

CHAFING-DISH (chā'fing-dish) *n.* a dish for holding hot coals, etc.

CHAGRIN (sha-grēn') *n.* ill-humour; vexation; —*v.t.* to vex; mortify. [F., of unknown etym.]

CHAIN (chān) *n.* a line of links;—*v.t.* to fasten with a chain; enslave. [F. *chaine*, fr. L. (acc.) *catenam*.]

CHAIR (chār) *n.* a movable seat; an official seat;—*v.t.* to carry in triumph. [F. *chaire*, fr. L., fr. G. *kathedra*.]

CHAIRMAN chār'man) *n.* a presiding officer.

CHAISE (shāz) *n.* a two-wheeled carriage. [F., a form of *chaire*.]

CHALET (sha-lā') *n.* a Swiss cottage. [F.]

CHALICE (chal'is) *n.* a communion cup. [O.F. *calice*, fr. L. (acc.) *calicem*, a cup, fr. G. *kulix*.]

CHALK (chawk) *n.* a white calcareous earth; —*v.t.* to mark with chalk. [O.E. *cealc*, fr. L. stem *calc-*, of *calx*, lime.]

CHALLENGE (chal'enj) *v.t.* to claim; call to fight; object to;—*n.* a summons to a contest; exception to a juror. [O.F. *chalenge*, accusation, claim; fr. L. (acc.) *calumniam*.]

CHALLENGER (chal'enj-er) *n.* one who challenges.

CHALYBEATE (ka-lib'ē-āt) *a.* impregnated with iron. [Fr. G. stem *chalyb-*, of *chalyps*, steel, fr. the *Chalybes*, who made it first.]

CHAMBER (chām'ber) *n.* a room; an office; hall of justice or legislation; a legislative or corporate body; a hollow or cavity;—*v.i.* to reside in; be wanton. [F. *chambre*, fr. O.F. *cambre*, fr. L. (acc.) *cameram*.]

CHAMBERLAIN (chām'ber-lān) *n.* an overseer of the chambers; city treasurer. [O.F. *chambrelene*, fr. O. Ger.; suff. fr. Ger. *ling* =E. *ling*.]

CHAMBER-MAID (chām'ber-mād) *n.* a female who has charge of bed-chambers.

CHAMELEON (ka-mēl'yun) *n.* a species of lizard whose colour changes. [L., fr. G. *chamaileon*, a dwarf lion, fr. *chamai*, on the ground, and *leon*.]

CHAMOIS (sham'waw) *n.* a kind of a goat; a soft leather made from its skin. [F., fr. O. Ger. *gamz* =Ger. *gemse*.]

CHAMP (champ) *v.t.* or *i.* to chew; bite. [Imitative.]

CHAMPAGNE (sham-pān') *n.* a brisk, sparkling wine. [Fr. *Champagne*, France.]

CHAMPION (cham'pi-un) *n.* a combatant for another, or for a cause. [O.F., fr. L. (acc.) *campionem*, a combatant, fr. *campus*, a field.]

CHAMPIONSHIP (cham'pi-un-ship) *n.* the rank of being first in any trial of strength or skill.

Fāte, fär, ado; mē, her; mīne; nōte; tūne; mōōn.

CHANCE (chans) *n.* an unforeseen occurrence, accident; opportunity;—*v.i.* to happen;—*v.t.* to risk. [O.F. *cheance,* fr. Late L. (acc.) *cadentiam.* Doublet of **CADENCE.**]

CHANCEL (chan'sel) *n.* part of a church where the altar stands. [O.F., fr. L. (pl.) *cancelli,* a screen, dim. of (pl.) *cancri,* lattices.]

CHANCELLOR (chan'sel-ęr) *n.* president of a court, university, or jury, etc. [F. *chancelier,* fr. Late L. (acc.) *cancellarium,* fr. the screen before the judgment seat, *cancelli.*]

CHANCELLORSHIP (chan'sel-ęr-ship) *n.* office of a chancellor.

CHANCERY (chan'sęr-i) *n.* a court of equity. [M.E. *chancelrie,* fr. O.F. *chancellerie.*]

CHANDELIER (shan-dē-lēr') *n.* a frame with branches for candle or gas lights. [F., fr. Late L. (acc.) *candelarium,* a candle-holder, fr. L. *candela.*]

CHANDLER (chand'lęr) *n.* one who deals in candles; a general dealer. [F. *chandelier,* here, candle-merchant.]

CHANGE (chānj) *v.t.* or *i.* to alter; exchange; —*n.* alteration; small money. [F., fr. Late L. *cambiare* (= *cambire*) to barter.]

CHANGEABLE (chānj'ja-bl) *a.* subject to change; fickle.

CHANGEFUL (chānj'fool) *a.* full of change.

CHANGELESS (chānj'les) *a.* constant.

CHANGELING (chānj'ling) *n.* a child substituted in place of another; one apt to change.

CHANNEL (chan'el) *n.* course for a stream; a furrow; strait;—*v.t.* to cut into channels; groove. [O.F., fr. L. (acc.) *canalem.* Doublet of **CANAL.**]

CHANT (chant) *v.t.* or *i.* to sing;—*n.* a song or singing. [F. *chanter,* fr. L. *cantare,* sing. fr. *canere.*]   [the tenor in the bagpipes.

CHANTER (chan'tęr) *n.* a singer in a cathedral;

CHANTICLEER (chan'ti-klēr) *n.* the male of domestic fowls. [M.E. *chaunticleer,* clear-singing.]   [intoning the church service.

CHANTING (chant'ing) *n.* art or practice of

CHAOS (kā'os) *n.* confused mass; confusion. [G. = empty space.]   [confused.

CHAOTIC (kā-ot'ik) *a.* resembling chaos;

CHAP (chap) (1) *v.t.* or *i.* to open; crack;—*n.* a cleft or chink; (2) the jaw; (3) a young fellow. [(1) E. (2) Usually pl., perh. Scand. (3) Short for **CHAPMAN.** O.E. *ceapman.* See **CHEAP.**]

CHAPBOOK (chap'book) *n.* a short tract or pamphlet hawked by pedlars.

CHAPEL (chap'el) *n.* a place of worship. [O.F. *chapele,* fr. Late L. (acc.) *cappellam,* orig. fr. a building holding the *cappa,* cape of S. Martin.]

CHAPERON (shap'e-rōn) *v.t.* to attend on a lady;—*n.* a matron who introduces a young lady to public assemblies. [F. (orig. = a man,ie) dim. fr. *chape,* **CAPE.**]

CHAPFALLEN (chap'fawln) *a.* dejected; dispirited.

CHAPLAIN (chap'lin) *n.* a clergyman of the army or navy, etc. [F. *chapelain,* fr. Late L. (acc.) *cappellanum.*]

CHAPLAINCY (chap'lin-si) *n.* the office of a chaplain.

CHAPLET (chap'let) *n.* a garland or wreath. [O.F., dim. fr. *chapel,* head-gear, fr. *chape.*]

CHAPMAN (chap'man) *n.* a small merchant; hawker; pedlar.

CHAPTER (chap'tęr) *n.* a division of a book; an organised branch of some society. [F. *chapitre,* fr. L. *capitulum,* a chapter, a synod (where a ' chapter ' was read), dim. fr. *caput,* the head.]

CHAR (chär) (1) *v.t.* to reduce to charcoal; hew or work, as stone;—(2) *v.i.* to work by the day;—*n.* a day's work; a job. [(1) Etym. unknown. (2) Orig. a turn, fr. O.E. *cierran,* turn.]

CHARACTER (kar'ak-tęr) *n.* a distinctive sign or letter; the peculiar qualities of a person or thing; estimate or certificate of such; a peculiar person;—*v.t.* to engrave; portray. [G. = a branding.]

CHARACTERISE (kar'ak-tęr-īz) *v.t.* to describe by peculiar qualities.

CHARACTERISTIC (kar-ak-tęr-is'tik) *a.* constituting character;—*n.* that which marks the character.

CHARACTERISTICALLY (kar-ak-tęr-is'ti-kal-i) *ad.* in a manner to reveal individual qualities.

CHARADE (sha-rād', sha-rād') *n.* a kind of riddle. [F.]

CHARCOAL (chär-kōl) *n.* a kind of coal artificially prepared from wood.

CHARGE (chärj) *v.t.* to enjoin; load; accuse; make an onset;—*n.* care; expense. [F., fr. Late L. *carricare* to load.]

CHARGEABLE (chär'ja-bl) *a.* that may be charged.

CHARGER (chär'jęr) *n.* a large dish; a war-horse.

CHARILY (chār-i-li) *ad.* warily; frugally. [O.E. *cearig,* full of **CARE.**]

CHARIOT (char'i-ot) *n.* a carriage of pleasure or state. [F., fr. *char.* See **CAR.**]

CHARIOTEER (char-i-o-tēr') *n.* driver of a chariot.

CHARITABLE (char'i-ta-bl) *a.* liberal; kind. [O.F. *charitet,* fr. L. (acc.) *caritatem,* affection, fr. *carus,* dear.]

CHARITY (char'i-ti) *n.* love; a charitable institution; liberality; alms; benevolence.

CHARLATAN (shär'la-tan) *n.* a quack. [F., fr. It. *ciarlatano,* a chatterer.)

CHARM (chärm) *n.* magic power; attractive power;—*v.t.* to fascinate; subdue; to delight or please greatly. [F. *charme,* fr. L. *carmen,* a song.]

CHARMER (chär'męr) *n.* one who enchants.

CHARMING (chär'ming) *a.* delightful.

CHARNEL-HOUSE (chär'nel-hous) *n.* a place for bones of the dead. [O.F., *charnel,* fr. L. *caro, carnis,* flesh.]

CHARRED (chärd) *a.* reduced to charcoal; slightly burned.

CHART (chärt) *n.* a delineation of coasts, etc.; map. [O.F. *charte,* fr. L. (acc.) *chartam,* a paper, fr. G. *charte.*)

CHARTER (chär'tęr) *n.* a patent; grant;—*v.t.* to let or hire, as vessels.

CHARTER-PARTY (chär'tęr-pär-ti) *n.* an agreement between the owner of a vessel and him who hires or freights it.

CHARTISM (chär'tizm) *n.* principles of the Chartists.

CHARY (chār'i) *a.* careful; cautious.

CHARTIST (chär'tist) *n.* an English ultra-radical reformer.

CHASE (chās) (1) *v.t.* to hunt; pursue;—*n.* pursuit; (2) *v.t.* engrave; emboss; cut into the form of a screw;—(3) *n.* a printer's frame. [(1) F. *chasser,* fr. a late form of L. *captare,* to try to catch. (2) = enchase, fr. F. *enchásser,* to place in a *chásse,* **CASE.** (3) fr. L. *capsa,* a box. Doublet of **CASE.**]

CHASM (kazm) *n.* a cleft; gap; opening. [G. *chaskein,* to gape.]

CHASSIS (sha'sē) *n.* the frame and engine of an automobile without the carriage body. [F.]

CHASTE (chāst) *a.* undefiled; pure. [O.F., fr. L. (acc.) *castum,* pure.]

CHASTELY (chāst'li) *ad.* purely; modestly.

CHASTEN (chā'sn) *v.t.* to punish; correct in order to reclaim. [Fr. **CHASTE,** fr. L. (acc.) *castum,* pure.]

CHASTENESS (chāst'nes) *n.* state or quality of being chaste.

CHASTENING (chā'sn-ing) *n.* correction.

CHASTISE (chas-tīz') *v.t.* to correct. [Fr. **CHASTE.**]

CHASTITY (chas'ti-ti) *n.* purity of body or speech.

CHAT (chat) *v.i.* to talk familiarly;—*n.* idle or familiar talk. [Imit.]

CHATEAU (shả-tō') *n.* a castle or country seat. [F. *château*, fr. O.F. *chastel*. Doublet of **CASTLE**.]

CHATELAINE (shat-e-lăn) *n.* a chain worn by ladies with keys and other domestic articles attached. [F., fr. O.F. *chastelaine*.]

CHATTEL (chat'l) *n.* any movable property. [O.F. *chatel*, property, fr. F. *capitale*. Doublet of **CAPITAL**, **CATTLE**.]

CHATTER (chat'ẹr) *v.i.* to talk idly;—*n.* a prating; noise of birds. [Onomatopœic word.]

CHATTERER (chat'ẹr-ẹr) *n.* one that chatters.

CHAUFFEUR (shōf'fẹr) *n.* a motor-car attendant. [F.]

CHEAP (chēp) *a.* of low price; common. [M.E. *chep*, *cheep*, fr. O.E. *ceap*, a bargain.]

CHEAPEN (chē'pn) *v.t.* to ask the price; lessen the price.

CHEAPENER (chē'pn-ẹr) *n.* one who cheapens.

CHEAPLY (chēp'li) *ad.* at a low price or cost.

CHEAPNESS (chēp'nes) *n.* lowness of price.

CHEAT (chēt) *n.* a trick; a deceiver;—*v.t.* to defraud; impose on. [Short for **ESCHEAT**.]

CHEATERY (chē'tẹr-i) *n.* fraud; deception; habit of cheating.

CHECK (chek) *v.t.* to curb or restrain; mark, as in a list;—*n.* restraint. [O.F. *eschek*, chess term = ' watch the king '; fr. Per. *shāh*, king.]

CHECKER (chek'ẹr) *v.t.* to diversify. Also written **CHEQUER**. [O.F. *eschequier*, chess-board.]

CHECKERS (chek'ẹrz) *n.pl.* a game on a checkered board.

CHECKMATE (chek'māt) *n.* a movement in chess that ends the game;—*v.t.* to defeat; baffle. [A. *shah-mat* = king is dead.]

CHEDDAR (ched'ạr, ched'ẹr) *n.* a rich kind of cheese made in Somersetshire. [Fr. *Cheddar*, in Somerset.]

CHEEK (chēk) *n.* the side of the face. [M.E. *cheke*, *cheoke*, fr. O.E. *ceace*.]

CHEER (chēr) *n.* mirth; a shout of joy;—*v.t.* to salute with joy; enliven. [O.F. *cherc*, face, fr. Late L. (acc.) *caram*.]

CHEERFUL (chēr'fool)*a.*lively; gay; sprightly.

CHEERFULNESS (chēr'fool-nes) *n.* gaiety.

CHEERLESS (chēr'les) *a.* comfortless.

CHEESE (chēz) *n.* the curd of milk coagulated and pressed. [O.E. *cese*, *cyse*, fr. L. *caseus*.]

CHEESEMONGER (chēz'mung-ẹr) *n.* one who deals in or sells cheese. [**CHEESE**, and O.E. *mangere*, merchant, fr. L. *mango*, a dealer.]

CHEMICAL (kem'i-kạl) *a.* pertaining to chemistry. [A. *kimia*, fr. Late G. *chemei*, chemistry.]

CHEMISE (she-mēz') *n.* an under-garment of a female. [F., fr. Late L. (acc.) *camisiam*, a shirt.]

CHEMIST (kem'ist) *n.* one versed in chemistry.

CHEMISTRY (kem'ist-ri) *n.* the science which shows the nature and properties of element-ary substances.

CHEQUE (chek) *n.* an order for money. [Form of **CHECK**.]

CHERISH (cher'ish) *v.t.* to treat with tender-ness; nourish; foster. [F. part. *chérissant*, cherishing, fr. *cher*, fr. L. *carus*, dear.]

CHERRY (chẹr'i) *n.* a small stone fruit;—*a.* red; like a cherry. [O.F. *cheris* = F. *cérise*, through L., fr. G. *kerasos*, perhaps fr. *Kerasos*.]

CHERUB (cher'ub) *n.* a celestial spirit. [H.]

CHERUBIC (che-rōō'bik) *a.* angelic.

CHERUBIM (chẹr'ōō-bim) *n.* Hebrew plural of **CHERUB**.

CHESS (ches) *n.* an ingenious game played on a chequered board. [Fr. O.F. (pl.) *esches*, fr. *eschec*. See **CHECK**.]

CHEST (chest) *n.* a large box; the thorax. [O.E. *cist*, fr. L. *cistả*, fr. G. *kiste*.]

CHESTNUT (ches'nut) *n.* a kind of tree; its fruit or nut; well-worn or stale joke (*slang*);—*a.* of the colour of the chestnut; reddish-brown. [=*chesten-nut*, fr. O.F. *chastaigne*, fr. L. (acc.) *castaneam*, a chestnut-tree, fr. G. *kastanon*.]

CHEVALIER (shev-a-lẹr') *n.* a knight; horse-man. [Doublet of **CAVALIER**.]

CHEW (chōō) *v.t.* to grind with the teeth. [M.E. *chewen*, fr. O.E. *ceowan*.]

CHICK (chik) *n.* the young of fowls; a child. Also **CHICKEN** ([O.E. *cicen*.]

CHICKWEED (chik'wēd) *n.* a low creeping weed which birds are fond of.

CHIDE (chīd) *v.t.* [*pret.* **CHID**; *pp.* **CHID**, **CHIDDEN**] to scold; reprove. [O.E. *cidan*.]

CHIEF (chēf) *a.* highest in office; principal;—*n.* a leader; the head of a clan. [O.F. *chef*, chief, head, fr. L. *caput*, the head.]

CHIEFLY (chēf'li) *ad.* principally; especially.

CHIEFTAIN (chēf'tin) *n.* a captain or leader. [O.F. *chevetaine*, doublet of **CAPTAIN**.]

CHIEFTAINSHIP (chēf'tin-ship) *n.* office of a chieftain.

CHILBLAIN (chil'blān) *n.* a swelling or sore caused by cold. [**CHILL** and **BLAIN**.]

CHILD (chīld) *n.* a son or daughter. [O.E. *cild*, child.]

CHILDBED (chīld'bed) *n.* the state of travail or childbirth.

CHILDBIRTH (chīld'berth) *n.* travail; labour.

CHILDHOOD (chīld'hood) *n.* state of being a child.

CHILDISH (chil'dish) *a.* like a child; simple; trifling.

CHILDISHLY (chil'dish-li) *ad.* in a childish manner.

CHILDISHNESS (chil'dish-nes) *n.* triflingness; simpleness; puerility.

CHILDLESS (chīld'les) *a.* having no child.

CHILDLIKE (chīld'lik) *a.* like or becoming a child; dutiful.

CHILDREN (chil'dren) *n.pl.* of **CHILD**. [Fr. *childer* =O.E. (pl.) *cildru*.]

CHILL (chil) *a.* cold; inducing a shivering;—*n.* moderate cold;—*v.t.* to make cold; dis-courage; *v.i.* to cool suddenly. [O.E. *cele*, *ciele*, coldness.]

CHILLINESS (chil'i-nes) *n.* coldness.

CHILLINGLY (chil'ing-li) *ad.* in a cold, dis-couraging manner.

CHILLY (chil'i) *a.* somewhat cold.

CHIME (chīm) (1) *n.* a set of bells arranged to ring in a tune; the sound thus produced; *v.t.* or *i.* to strike or sound in harmony;—(2) edge of a cask. [(1) =M.E. *chimbe*, orig. **CYMBAL**. (2) O.E. *cim*. Cf. Ger. *Kimme*, edge.]

CHIMERA (ki-mē'rạ) *n.* a vain, idle fancy. [G. *chimaira*, orig. =she-goat.]

CHIMERICAL (ki-mer'i-kạl) *a.* imaginary; fanciful.

CHIMNEY (chim'ni) *n.* a flue or passage for smoke;—*pl.* **CHIMNEYS**. [F. *cheminée*, fireplace, through L., fr. G. *kaminos*, oven.]

CHIMPANZEE (chim-pan'zē) *n.* a large African ape. [W. Afr.]

CHIN (chin) *n.* lower end of the face. [O.E. *cin*.]

CHINA (chī'nạ) *n.* fine earthenware.

CHINE (chīn) *n.* the backbone of an animal; a part of it cut for cooking; the edge or rim of a cask;—*v.t.* to cut through the backbone. [O.F. *eschine* =F. *échine*, spine, fr. Teut.]

CHINK (chingk) *n.* a narrow opening; cleft;—*v.i.* to split or crack. [M.E. *chine*, cleft, fr. O.E. *cinu*.]

CHINK (chingk) *v.t.* to rattle or jingle, as small coin;—*v.i.* to sound by concussion;—*n.* the ring or clink of coin. [Onomatopœic word.]

CHINTZ (chintz) *n.* cotton cloth printed with colours. [Hind. *chint*; orig. pl.]

CHIP (chip) *n.* a piece cut off; a fragment;— *v.t.* to cut into small pieces. [Conn. with *chop.*]

CHIPPER (chip'er) *a.* active; lively; cheerful.

CHIROGRAPHER (ki-rog'ra-fer) *n.* a writer. [G., fr. *cheiro-*, for *cheir.* hand, and *graphein*, write.]

CHIROGRAPHY (ki-rog'ra-fi) *n.* handwriting; penmanship.

CHIROPODIST (ki-rop'o-dist) *n.* one who extracts corns from feet. [G. *cheiro-*, for *cheir*, hand, and stem *pod-*, of *pous*, foot.]

CHIRP (cherp) *v.i.* to make the noise of small birds. [Imit.]

CHIRPING (cher'ping) *n.* the cheerful noise of birds.

CHISEL (chiz'el) *n.* a tool of iron or steel to pare with, used in carpentry, etc.;—*v.t.* to cut with a chisel; cut close in a bargain; cheat. [O.F., fr. Late L. (acc.) *cisellum*, scissors, fr. L. part. *cisus* = *cœsus*, cut, fr. *cœdere*.]

CHISELLED (chiz'eld) *a.* cut with a chisel; clean-cut; statuesque.

CHIT (chit) *n.* a shoot; small child. [O.E. *cith*, a shoot.]

CHIVALROUS (shiv'al-rus) *a.* pertaining to chivalry; gallant.

CHIVALROUSLY (shiv'al-rus-li) *ad.* boldly; gallantly.

CHIVALRY (shiv'al-ri) *n.* body of knights; knight errantry; valour. [F. *chevalerie*, fr. *cheval*, horse. Doublet of **CAVALRY**.]

CHLORAL (klō'ral) *n.* a narcotic compound of chlorine and alcohol. [G. *chloros*, pale green, and *al*-cohol.]

CHLORATE (klō'rāt) *n.* a compound of chloric acid with a salifiable base. [G. *chloros*, pale green.]

CHLORIDE (klō'rīd) *n.* a compound of chlorine with another element.

CHLORINE (klō'rīn) *n.* a gaseous substance obtained from common salt, used in bleaching and disinfecting. [G. *chloros*, pale green.]

CHLORODINE (klō'rō-dīn) *n.* a medicine possessing anodyne and other remedial properties. [G. *chloros*, pale green, and *odune*, pain.]

CHLOROFORM (klō'rō-form) *n.* a volatile liquid used to produce temporary insensibility. [Fr. *chlor*(ine) and *form*(yl).]

CHOCK (chok) *n.* a kind of wedge. [Form of CHOKE.]

CHOCK-FULL (chok'fool) *a.* quite full.

CHOCOLATE (chok'ō-lāt) *n.* a paste made from cacao and sugar. [Mex. Sp.]

CHOICE (chois) *n.* act of choosing; the thing chosen; the best part;—*a.* select; precious. [M.E. *chois*, fr. O.F. *chois* = F. *choix*, fr. Teut.]

CHOICELY (chois'li) *ad.* with care in choosing.

CHOICENESS (chois'nes) *n.* nicety; excellence.

CHOIR (kwir) *n.* part of a church; the chancel; a body of singers. [O.F. *choeur*, fr. L. (acc.) *chorum*. Doublet of **CHORUS**.]

CHOKE (chōk) *v.t.* to stop the breath; stifle; suppress;—*v.i.* to have the windpipe stopped; swell with rage. [E.]

CHOKE-DAMP (chōk'damp) *n.* suffocating vapour in pits or wells.

CHOLER (ko'ler) *n.* bile; anger. [O.F. *colere*. Doublet of **CHOLERA**.]

CHOLERA (kol'e-ra) *n.* bilious vomiting and purging. [See **CHOLER**. L., fr. G. *chole*, bile.]

CHOLERIC (kol'e-rik) *a.* passionate; irascible.

CHOOSE (chōōz) *v.t.* [pret. **CHOSE**; pp. **CHOSEN, CHOSE**] to make choice of; prefer; elect. [O.E. *ceosan*.]

CHOP (chop) *v.t.* or *i.* to cut; mince; shift; —*n.* a small piece of meat. [See **CHAP**.]

CHOP-HOUSE (chop'hous) *n.* a dining-house.

CHOPPER (chop'er) *n.* a butcher's cleaver.

CHOPPING (chop'ing) *a.* large; plump.

CHOPS (chops) *n.pl.* the jaws.

CHOPSTICKS (chop'stiks) *n. pl.* two pieces of wood, ivory, etc., with which the Chinese eat.

CHORAL (kō'ral) *a.* belonging to a choir.

CHORD (kord) *n.* string of a musical instrument; concord; a line in geometry uniting the extremities of the arc of a circle. [Fr. L., fr. G. *chorde*, a string.]

CHORISTER (kor'is-ter) *n.* a member of a choir; a chorist.

CHORUS (kō'rus) *n.* a company of singers; part of music in which all join. [L., fr. G. *choros*. Doublet of **CHOIR**.]

CHOUGH (chuf) *n.* a bird of the crow family; jackdaw. [E.]

CHOUSE (chous) *v.t.* to cheat; trick;—*n.* a trick or imposition; a dupe or tool. [Perh. fr. a Turkish *chiaus*, or interpreter, who perpetrated a swindle in London, 1609.]

CHRISM (krizm) *n.* consecrated oil. [G. *chriein*, to anoint.]

CHRIST (krist) *n.* the Anointed; the Messiah. [L., fr. G. *christos*, anointed, fr. *chriein*, to anoint.]

CHRISTEN (kris'n) *v.t.* to baptise and name.

CHRISTENDOM (kris'n-dum) *n.* territory of Christians.

CHRISTENING (kris'n-ing, kris'ning) *n.* baptism.

CHRISTIAN (krist'yan) *n.* a disciple of Christ; a believer; an adherent of Christ's church; a baptised person;—*a.* pertaining to Christ or to Christianity.

CHRISTIANITY (kris-ti-an'i-ti) *n.* the religion taught by Christ.

CHRISTMAS (kris'mas) *n.* the feast of Christ's nativity. [See **MASS**.]

CHRISTMAS-BOX (kris'mas-boks) *n.* a box for Christmas presents; a Christmas gift.

CHROMATE (krō'māt) *n.* a salt of chromic acid. [G. *chroma*, colour.]

CHROMATIC (krō-mat'ik) *a.* relating to colours and musical semitones. [G., fr. stem *chromat-*, fr. *chroma*, colour.]

CHROMATICS (krō-mat'iks) *n.pl.* the science of colours.

CHROME (krōm) *n.* a metal from which coloured preparations are made. [G. *chroma*, colour.]

CHROMOGRAPH (krō'mō-graf) *n.* a coloured print. [G. *chroma*, colour, and *graphein*, write.]

CHROMO-LITHOGRAPHY (krō-mō-li-thog'ra-fi) *n.* printing with colours off stone. [G. *chroma*, colour, *lithos*, stone, and *graphein* write.]

CHROMO-TYPOGRAPHY (krō-mō-ti-pog'ra-fi) *n.* printing with types in different colours. [G. *chroma*, colour, and F., fr. L. *typus*, fr. G. *tupos*, fr. *tuptein*, to strike; and G. *graphein*, to write.]

CHRONIC (kron'ik) *a.* relating to time; periodical; long-continued. [G. *chronikos*, fr. *chronos*, time.]

CHRONICLE (kron'i-kl) *n.* a register of events; —*v.t.* to record in history. [O.F. *cronique*, through Late L., fr. G. (neut. pl.) *chronika*, annals.]

CHRONOLOGIST (krō-nol'ō-jist) *n.* one who studies or explains chronology. [G. *chronos*, time, and *logos*, discourse.]

CHRONOLOGY (krō-nol'ō-ji) *n.* the science of computing dates; a register of events and dates.

CHRONOMETER (krō-nom'e-ter) *n.* a very exact timepiece. [G. *chronos*, time, and *metron*, measure.]

CHRYSALIS (kris'a-lis) *n.* the form of a butterfly before it reaches the winged state. [G. *chrusallis*, fr. *chrusos*, gold.]

CHRYSANTHEMUM (kris-an'thē-mum) *n.* a genus of composite plants, flowering in winter. [G. *chrusos*, gold, and *anthemon*, flower.]

CHRYSOLITE (kris'ō-līt) *n.* a greenish stone with a golden tinge. [L., fr. G. *chrusos*, gold, and *lithos*, stone.]

CHUB (chub) *n.* a river-fish allied to the carp. [E.]

CHUBBY (chub'i) *a.* plump; short and thick; fat and florid in the cheeks.

CHUCK (chuk) (1) *v.t.* or *i.* to make a noise as a hen; (2) touch under the chin; throw or toss quickly;—*n.* the call of a hen; a touch under the chin; an appendage to a lathe. [(1) Imit. (2) F. *choquer*, to jolt.]

CHUCKLE (chuk'l) *v.t.* or *i.* to laugh inwardly; call as a hen.

CHUFF (chuf) *n.* a clownish person. [M.E. *chuffe*, *choffe*; conn. with Scot. *coof*, akin to Icel. *kueif*.]

CHUFFY (chuf'i) *a.* blunt; surly.

CHUM (chum) *n.* a chamber-fellow in a college, etc.;—*v.i.* to live and mess with another; fraternise. [Etym. unknown.]

CHURCH (church) *n.* a place of worship; a body of Christians;—*v.t.* to perform the giving of thanks in church. [M.E. *chirche*, fr. O.E. *circe*, fr. G. (neut.) *kuriakon*, belonging to the Lord, *Kurios*.]

CHURCHMAN (church'man) *n.* an Episcopalian; a clergyman.

CHURCHWARDEN (church'wawr-den) *n.* an officer of the church; a long clay pipe.

CHURCHYARD (church'yard) *n.* a graveyard near a church.

CHURL (churl) *n.* a countryman; rustic; an ill-bred fellow; a niggard. [O.E. *ceorl*, man. Cf. Ger. *Kerl*.]

CHURLISH (chur'lish) *a.* surly; rude.

CHURLISHLY (chur'lish-li) *ad.* rudely; roughly.

CHURLISHNESS (chur'lish-nes) *n.* rudeness of manners; moroseness.

CHURN (churn) *n.* a vessel in which cream is agitated;—*v.t.* to agitate cream for making butter. [O.E. *cyrin*.]

CHURNING (chur'ning) *n.* the making of butter by means of a churn; the quantity made at one time.

CHUTNEE (chut'ne) *n.* an Indian condiment. [Hind.]

CHYLE (kīl) *n.* a milky fluid formed in the stomach by digesting. [F., fr. G. *chulos*, juice, fr. G. *cheein*, to pour.]

CHYME (kīm) *n.* the pulpy matter formed by digested food in the stomach. [G. *chumos*, juice, fr. *cheein*, to pour.]

CICATRICE (sik'a-tris) *n.* scar; mark. [F., fr. L. (acc.) *cicatricem*, fr. *cicatrix*.]

CICATRISATION (sik-a-tri-zā'shun) *n.* the process of healing a wound.

CICATRISE (sik'a-triz) *v.t.* or *i.* to heal a wound by forming a skin over it.

CICERONE (che-chā-rō'nā, sis-e-rō'ne) *n.* one who points out objects of interest in a place to strangers, and is eloquent, like Cicero, in describing them; a guide. [It., fr. L. (acc.) *Ciceronem*, fr. *Cicero*.]

CIDER (sī'der) *n.* a liquor made from the juice of apples. [O.F. *cisdre*, for *cisre*, fr. L., fr. G. *sikera*, strong drink, fr. H.]

CIGAR (si-gár') *n.* a roll of tobacco for smoking. [Sp.]

CIGARETTE (sig-a-ret') *n.* a roll of cut tobacco in paper for smoking.

CILIA (sil'i-a) *n.pl.* the eyelashes; long hairs on plants. [L. *cilium*, pl. *cilia*, eyelashes.]

CIMMERIAN (si-mē'ri-an) *a.* dark. [Fr. the *Cimmerii*, who are said to have dwelt in darkness.]

CINCHONA (sin-kō'na) *n.* Peruvian bark, or a bark tree. [Sp., fr. the Countess of *Chinchon*, who was cured by it in 1638.]

CINCTURE (singk'tūr) *n.* a belt; a girdle. [L. *cinctura*, fr. part. *cinctus*, girt.]

CINDERS (sin'derz) *n.pl.* coal or other matter charred by fire. [O.E. *sinder*, slag.]

CINEMATOGRAPH (sin-e-mat'ō-graph) *n.* See **KINEMATOGRAPH.**

CINNAMON (sin'a-mun) *n.* the inner bark of a species of laurel. [Fr. H.]

CINQUE (singk) *n.* the number five; *used in games.* [F. *cinq*, fr. L. *quinque*.]

CIPHER (sī'fer) *n.* the figure (0); initial letters of a name inwoven; a secret writing; —*v.i.* to use figures. [O.F. *cifre* = F. *chiffre*, figure, fr. A.]

CIPHERING (sī'fer-ing) *n.* act of performing sums in arithmetic.

CIRCLE (ser'kl) *n.* a round figure; a ring; a sphere; surrounding company;—*v.t.* to move round;—*v.i.* to move in a round or compass. [O.E. *circul*, fr. L. *circulus*, dim. fr. **CIRCUS.**]

CIRCUIT (ser'kit) *n.* that which encircles; space enclosed; periodical visitation by judges; district visited. [F., fr. L. (acc.) *circuitum*, a going round, fr. L. (part.) *circuitus*, gone round, fr. *circum*, round, and *ire*, to go.]

CIRCUITOUS (ser-kū'i-tus) *a.* round about.

CIRCULAR (ser-kū'lar) *a.* round; like a circle; ending in itself;—*n.* an intimation addressed to a number of persons.

CIRCULATE (ser'kū-lāt) *v.i.* to move round; —*v.t.* to cause to pass round. [L. (part.) *circulatus*, fr. *circulari*, come round.]

CIRCULATION (ser-kū-lā'shun) *n.* a passing round; currency.

CIRCUMAMBIENT (ser-kum-am'bi-ent) *a.* surrounding. [L. *circum*, round, and *ambire*, to go round.]

CIRCUMCISE (ser'kum-sīz) *v.t.* to deprive of the foreskin. [L. *circum*, round, and *cisum*, cut, fr. *cædere*.]

CIRCUMCISION (ser-kum-sizh'un) *n.* act of circumcising.

CIRCUMFERENCE (ser-kum'fer-ens) *n.* the line that bounds a circle. [L. *circum*, round, and (part. stem.) *ferentc-*, fr. *ferre*, to carry.]

CIRCUMFERENTIAL (ser-kum-fer-en'shal) *a.* pertaining to the circumference.

CIRCUMFERENTOR (ser-kum-fer-en'ter) *n.* a surveyor's instrument for measuring angles.

CIRCUMFLECT (ser'kum-flekt) *v.t.* to bend round; mark with a circumflex. [L. *circum*, round, and (part.) *flexus*, bent, fr. *flectere*.]

CIRCUMFLEX (ser'kum-fleks) *n.* an accent marked thus (ʌ).

CIRCUMFUSE (ser-kum-fūz') *v.t.* to pour round. [L. *circum*, round and (part.) *fusus*, poured, fr. *fundere*.]

CIRCUMGYRATE (ser-kum-jī'rāt) *v.t.* to roll or turn round; whirl. [L. *circum*, round, and *gyrare*, turn.]

CIRCUMJACENT (ser-kum-jā'sent) *a.* lying around. [L. *circum*, round, and (part. stem.) *jacent-*, lying, fr. *jacere*.]

CIRCUMLOCUTION (ser-kum-lō-kū'shun) *n.* the use of indirect expression. [L. *circum*, round, and *loqui*, *loculus*, to speak.]

CIRCUMLOCUTORY (ser-kum-lok'ū-tur-i) *a.* consisting in roundabout words.

CIRCUMNAVIGABLE (ser-kum-nav'i-ga-bl) *a.* that may be sailed round. [L. *circum*, round, and **NAVIGATE.**]

CIRCUMNAVIGATE (ser-kum-nav'i-gāt) *v.t.* to sail round. [L. *circum*, round, and **NAVIGATE.**]

CIRCUMNAVIGATION (ser-kum-nav-i-gā'shun) *n.* a sailing round.

CIRCUMNAVIGATOR (ser-kum-nav'i-gā-ter) *n.* one who has sailed round the globe.

CIRCUMPOLAR (ser-kum-pō'lar) *a.* about one of the poles of the earth. [L. *circum*, round, and **POLAR.**]

CIRCUMROTARY (ser-kum-rō'ta-ri) *a.* revolving round. [L. *circum*, round, and *rota*, a wheel.]

CIRCUMSCRIBABLE (ser-kum-scrī'ba-bl) *a.* that may be circumscribed.

CIRCUMSCRIBE (sęr-kum-scrīb') *v.t.* to enclose; limit. [L. *circum*, round, and *scribere*, to write.]

CIRCUMSCRIPTION (sęr-kum-skrip'shun) *n.* limitation; bound; confinement.

CIRCUMSPECT (sęr'kum-spekt) *a.* guarded; prudent. [L. *circum*, round, and *specere*, *spectum*, to look.]

CIRCUMSPECTION (sęr-kum-spek'shun) *n.* caution.

CIRCUMSPECTIVE (sęr-kum-spek'tiv) *a.* cautious; wary; careful of consequences.

CIRCUMSPECTLY (sęr'kum-spekt-li) *ad.* watchfully; warily.

CIRCUMSTANCE (sęr'kum-stans) *n.* something pertaining to a fact, but not essential thereto; event; incident. [F. *circonstance*, fr. L. (part. stem) *circumstant-*, standing round, fr. *stare*.]

CIRCUMSTANCES (sęr'kum-stan-ses) *n.pl.* state as to property.

CIRCUMSTANTIAL (sęr-kum-stan'shąl) *a.* particular; minute; abounding with circumstances.

CIRCUMVENT (sęr-kum-vent') *v.t.* to get round or outwit; delude. [L. (part.) *circumventus*, encompassed, fr. *venire*.]

CIRCUMVENTION (sęr-kum-ven'shun) *n.* deception; imposture.

CIRCUMVOLUTION (sęr-kum-vō-lū'shun) *n.* a rolling round. [L. *circum*, round, and *volvere*, *volutum*, to roll.]

CIRCUS (sęr'kus) *n.* an enclosed place for games or feats of horsemanship. [L.]

CIRRO-STRATUS (sir-ō-strā'tus) *n.* a long, dense cloud, fringed or fleecy in the margin. [L. *cirrus*, curly-haired, and *stratus*, paved.]

CISTERN (sis'tern) *n.* a large vessel for water, etc.; reservoir. [F., fr. L. (acc.) *cisternam*, fr. *cista*, CHEST.]

CITABLE (sī'tą-bl) *a.* that may be cited.

CITADEL (sit'ą-del) *n.* a fortress in a city. [It., dim. fr. *citta*, CITY.]

CITATION (sī-tā'shun) *n.* a summons; quotation.

CITE (sīt) *v.t.* to summon; quote. [F. *citer*, fr. L. *citare*, fr. *ciere*, to rouse.]

CITHERN (sith'ern) *n.* a kind of guitar. Also **CITHARA**. [L., fr. G. *kithara*, lyre.]

CITIZEN (sit'i-zn) *n.* an inhabitant of a city; a freeman. [L. *civis*.]

CITIZENSHIP (sit'i-zn-ship) *n.* the freedom of a city.

CITRIC (sit'rik) *a.* belonging to lemons.

CITRON (sit'run) *n.* a species of lemon. [F., fr. L. *citrus*, fr. G.]

CITY (sit'i) *n.* an incorporated town. [O.F. *cite* =F. *cité*, fr. L. (acc.) *civitatem*, a state, fr. *civis*. Doublet of CITADEL.]

CIVET (siv'et) *n.* a small carnivorous animal; perfume obtained from it. [Fr. A.]

CIVIC (siv'ik) *a.* relating to civil life. [L. *civicus*.]

CIVICS (siv'iks) *n.* that branch of science which concerns itself with the training and duties of citizens.

CIVIL (siv'il) *a.* pertaining to society. [L. *civilis*.]

CIVILIAN (si-vil'yąn) *n.* one versed in civil law; one in a civil capacity. [L. *civilis*.]

CIVILISATION (siv-il-iz-ā'shun) *n.* act or result of civilising.

CIVILISE (siv'il-iz) *v.t.* to reclaim from barbarism.

CIVILISED (siv'il-izd) *a.* polished; polite.

CIVILITY (si'vil'i-ti) *n.* politeness.

CIVILLY (siv'i-li) *ad.* courteously; politely.

CLAD (klad) *pp.* of CLOTHE.

CLAIM (klām) *v.t.* to demand;—*n.* demand as of right; thing claimed. [O.F. *clamer*, *claimer*, fr. L. *clamare*, to cry out.]

CLAIMABLE (klā'mą-bl) *a.* that may be demanded.

CLAIMANT (klā'mąnt) *n.* one who demands.

CLAIRVOYANCE (klār-voi'ąns) *n.* discernment of things through mesmeric influence. [F.]

CLAM (klam) (1) *n.* a bivalvular shell-fish; (2) *v.t.* to clog with viscous matter. [(1) O.E. *clam*, fetter; (2) O.E. *clœman*, anoint.]

CLAMANT (klam'ąnt, klā'mąnt) *a.* crying earnestly. [L. (acc.) *clamantem*. [See CLAIM.]

CLAMBER (klam'bęr) *v.i.* to climb with difficulty. [Perhaps Scand.]

CLAMMINESS (klam'i-nes) *n.* stickiness. [O.E. *clœman*, to anoint.]

CLAMMY (klam'i) *a.* viscous; sticky.

CLAMOROUS (klam'ur-us) *a.* noisy with the tongue; loud. [noise or words.

CLAMOROUSLY (klam'ur-us-li) *ad.* with loud

CLAMOUR (klam'ur) *n.* loud outcry; uproar; —*v.i.* to shout loudly; demand importunately. [L. *clamor*.]

CLAMP (klamp) *n.* an iron fastening;—*v.t.* to strengthen by a clamp. [D.]

CLAMP (klamp) *n.* a heavy footstep or tread; —*v.i.* to tread heavily. [Imit.]

CLAN (klan) *n.* a family; tribe; sect. [Celt.]

CLANDESTINE (klan-des'tin) *a.* concealed. [L. *clandestinus*, secretly.]

CLANDESTINELY (klan-des'tin-li) *ad.* secretly.

CLANG (klang) *v.i.* to make a shrill sound;— *n.* a shrill sound. [L. *clangere*. Imit.]

CLANGOUR (klang'gur) *n.* a loud, harsh sound.

CLANK (klangk) *n.* a sharp, shrill sound;— *v.t.* to make a noise, as of a chain. [Imit.]

CLAP (klap) *v.t.* to strike quickly; put in place; shut hastily; applaud with the hands;—*v.i.* to come together with noise; move briskly;—*n.* a loud noise or explosion; a stroke or blow. [E.]

CLAPPER (klap'ęr) *n.* one who claps; the tongue of a bell; the clack of a mill. [E.]

CLARET (klar'et) *n.* a French wine. [F. *clairet*, fr. *clair*. See CLEAR.]

CLARIFICATION (klar-i-fi-kā'shun) *n.* act of making clear or fining. [O.F. *clarifier*, fr. L. *clarificare*, fr. L. *clarus*, clear, and *facere*, to make.]

CLARIFIER (klar'i-fī-ęr) *n.* he who clarifies; a vessel in which liquor is clarified.

CLARIFY (klar'i-fī) *v.t.* to make clear. [L. *clarus*, clear, and *facere*, to make.]

CLARION (klar'i-un) *n.* a kind of trumpet, of a shrill, clear tone. [O.F. =F. *clairon*, fr. Late L. *clarionem*, fr. L. *clarus*.]

CLARIONET (klar'i-o-net) *n.* a musical wind instrument of the reed kind, the leading instrument in a military band. [See CLARION.]

CLARY (klā'ri) *n.* a plant of the sage family. [Low L. *sclarea*.]

CLASH (klash) *v.t.* or *i.* to strike noisily;—*n.* noisy collision. [Imit.]

CLASHING (klash'ing) *a.* contrary; opposing; —*n.* opposition; conflict.

CLASP (klasp) *n.* a hook; a close embrace;— *v.t.* to embrace; hold fast; enclose. [M.E. *clapse*, conn. with CLIP, to embrace.]

CLASPER (klas'pęr) *n.* tendril.

CLASP-KNIFE (klasp'nif) *n.* a knife whose blade folds into the handle.

CLASS (klas) *n.* a rank; an order;—*v.t.* to arrange in a class or classes. [F., fr. L. (acc.) *classem*]

CLASSIC (klas'ik) *n.* an author of rank;—*a.* pertaining to authors of high order. [L. *classicus*, of the first CLASS.]

CLASSIFICATION (klas-i-fi-kā'shun) *n.* act of arranging in classes.

CLASSIFY (klas'i-fī) *v.t.* to arrange; put in its proper class. [F. *classifier*; *-fier* =L. *ficare* =*facere*, to make.]

CLATTER (klat'ęr) *n.* a rattling noise;—*v.i.* to make noises; rattle; talk fast and idly. [Fr. CLACK.]

CLATTERING (klat'ẽr-ing) *n.* a clatter; confusion of sounds.

CLAUSE (klawz) *n.* part of a sentence, contract, bill, etc. [F. *clause*, fr. L. (acc. part), *clausum*, shut, fr. *claudere*.]

CLAVICLE (klav'i-kl) *n.* the collar-bone. [F., fr. L. dim., fr. L. *clavis*, a key.]

CLAVIER (klav'i-er, kla-vēr') *n.* the keyboard of an organ or piano. [See **CLAVICLE**.]

CLAW (klaw) *n.* a hooked nail; grasp;—*v.t.* to tear with claws; clutch. [M.E. *clau*, fr. O.E. *clawu*. Cf. Ger. *Klaue*.]

CLAY (klā) *n.* a plastic earth; earth in general; the body; a corpse;—*v.t.* to purify with clay. [M.E. *clev*, fr. O.E. *clæg*.]

CLAYMORE (klā'mōr) *n.* a large two-edged broadsword. [Celt. = great sword.]

CLEAN (klēn) *a.* free from dirt; pure;—*v.t.* to free from dirt;—*ad.* fully; entirely. [O.E. *clæne*. Cf. Ger. *klein*, small.]

CLEANLINESS (klen'li-nes) *n.* neatness; purity.

CLEANSE (klenz) *v.t.* to purify.

CLEANSER (klen'zẽr) *n.* that which purifies.

CLEAR (klēr) *a.* free from mixture; pure; indisputable;—*v.t.* or *i.* to free from impurities; acquit;—*ad.* completely. [O.F. *cler*, *clair*, fr. L. (acc.) *clarum*, clear.]

CLEARANCE (klēr'ans) *n.* act of removing; free space or profit; permit to sell.

CLEARER (klēr'ẽr) *n.* that which clears.

CLEARING (klēr'ing) *n.* a justification; a tract of land cleared of wood.

CLEARLY (klēr'li) *ad.* plainly; evidently; brightly. [perspicuity.

CLEARNESS (klēr'nes) *n.* plainness; fairness;

CLEAT (klēt) *n.* a piece of wood in joinery nailed on to strengthen or fasten; a piece of wood with two projecting ends, round which ropes are belayed. [E.]

CLEAVE (klēv) *v.i.* [*pret.* **CLEAVED**; *pp.* **CLEFT**, **CLOVEN**, **CLEAVED**] to stick; adhere;—*v.t.* to split. [O.E. *cleofan*. Cf. Ger. *klieben*.]

CLEAVER (klē'vẽr) *n.* a butcher's axe.

CLEAVABLE (klē'va-bl) *a.* capable of being cleaved.

CLEAVAGE (klē'vij) *n.* act of cleaving; quality of splitting or dividing naturally.

CLEF (klef) *n.* a character in music to determine position and pitch of scale. [F., fr. L. (acc.) *clavem*, a key.]

CLEFT (kleft) *pp.* or *a.* split; divided;—*n.* an opening made by splitting; fissure; crack. [Scand., conn. with **CLEAVE**.]

CLEG (kleg) *n.* the horse-fly. [Icel. *kleggi*.]

CLEMENCY (klem'en-si) *n.* a disposition to treat with lenity; mildness; tenderness. [F., fr. L. (acc.) *clementiam*, leniency.]

CLEMENTLY (klem'ent-li) *ad.* in a clement manner.

CLERGY (klẽr'ji) *n.* the ministers of the gospel. [F. *clergé*, fr. Late L. *clericatum*, priestly office.]

CLERGYMAN (klẽr'ji-man) *n.* a minister of the gospel.

CLERICAL (kler'i-kal) *a.* pertaining to the clergy, or to a writer or transcriber. [O.E. *clerc*, a priest, fr. Late L. *clericus*.]

CLERK (klārk, klerk) *n.* a writer for another. [See **CLERICAL**.]

CLEVER (klev'ẽr) *a.* quick-witted; dexterous; skilful; neatly done.

CLEVERLY (klev'ẽr-li) *ad.* skilfully; ably; fitly.

CLEVERNESS (klev'ẽr-nes) *n.* skill. [Etym. doubtful.

CLEW (klōō) *n.* a ball of thread; anything serving to discover or solve; the corner of a sail;—*v.t.* to truss up to the yard, as a sail. [O.E. *cliwen*, *cleowe*.]

CLIENT (klī'ent) *n.* the employer of an attorney; a dependant of a patron. [L. (acc.) *clientem* = orig. a listener, fr. *cliens* = (part.) *cluens*, hearing, fr. *cluere*.]

CLIENTELE (klī'en-tēl) *n.* clients or customers collectively. [F., fr. L. *clientela*.]

CLIENTSHIP (klī'ent-ship) *n.* state or condition of a client.

CLIFF (klif) *n.* a steep rock; a precipice. [O.E. *clif*.]

CLIMACTERIC (klī-mak'te-rik, klī-mak-ter'ik) *n.* a critical period of human life. [F., fr. G. *klimakter*, gradation, fr. stem *klimak-*, of **CLIMAX**.]

CLIMATE (klī'māt) *n.* condition of a country in respect of temperature, atmospheric changes, etc. [F., fr. L., fr. G. stem *klimat-*, of *klima*. Doublet of **CLIME**.]

CLIMATIC (klī-mat'ik) *a.* relating to climate.

CLIMATOLOGY (klī-ma-tol'ō-ji) *n.* the science of climates. [**CLIMATE**, and G. *logos*, discourse.]

CLIMAX (klī'maks) *n.* gradation; ascent; the highest point; acme. [G. = ladder, fr. *klinein*, to slope.]

CLIMB (klīm) *v.t.* or *i.* to mount by the hands and feet. [O.E. *climban*; conn. with **CLAMBER**.]

CLIME (klīm) *n.* a climate. [See **CLIMATE**.]

CLINCH (klinsh) *v.t.* to gripe; hold fast;—*n.* fast hold; part of a cable. [Form of *klink*, to hit smartly. Cf. Ger. *klinken*, to rivet a bolt.]

CLINCHER (klin'shẽr) *n.* a clamp or iron fastening; a decisive argument.

CLING (kling) *v.i.* [*pret.* and *pp.* **CLUNG**] to adhere; hang upon. [O.E. *clingan*, to shrivel up, become matted.]

CLINIC, CLINIQUE (klin'ik) *a.* pertaining to a sick-bed;—*n.* a patient confined to bed. [F., fr. L. (acc.) *clinicum*, a patient kept in bed; fr. G. *kline*, bed.]

CLINKER (klingk'ẽr) *n.* vitreous matter. or slag which collects in furnaces. [D.]

CLINKSTONE (klingk'stōn) *n.* an igneous felspathic rock.

CLIP (klip) *v.t.* to cut short; curtail. [Scand.]

CLIPPER (klip'ẽr) *n.* one who clips; a sharp, fast-sailing vessel. [See **CLIP**.]

CLOAK (klōk) *v.t.* to cover with a cloak; conceal;—*n.* a loose outer garment; a disguise or pretext. [O.F. *cloke*, bell, bell-cape. See **CLOCK**.]

CLOCK (klok) *n.* a timepiece. [O.F. *cloke*, *cloche*, fr. Low L. (acc.) *clocam*, a bell, fr. Celt. Cf. Ger. *Glocke*.]

CLOCK-MAKER (klok-mā'kẽr) *n.* one who makes clocks.

CLOCKWORK (klok'wurk) *n.* well-adjusted machinery.

CLOD (klod) *n.* a lump of earth;—*v.i.* to harden into a lump;—*v.t.* to pelt with clods. [O.E., fr. **CLOT**.]

CLOG (klog) *v.t.* to hinder in motion;—*n.* obstruction; a shoe with a wooden sole. [E.]

CLOGGY (klog'i) *a.* apt to clog; thick.

CLOISTER (klois'tẽr) *n.* a nunnery or monastery; arcade or piazza;—*v.t.* to immure in a cloister. [O.F. *cloistre* = F. *cloitre*, fr. L. *claustrum*, an enclosure. [See **CLAUSE**.]

CLOISTERED (klois'tẽrd) *a.* provided with cloisters; living in a cloister.

CLOISTRAL (klois'tral) *a.* pertaining to a cloister.

Cloister.

CLOSE (klōz) *v.t.* or *i.* to shut; finish;—*n.* conclusion; end. [F. (pr. ind.) *clos*, fr. L. *claudere*, to shut in, fr. *closer*, to shut in, fr. L. *claudere*, to bring together.]

CLOSE (klōs) *n.* a small enclosed field; passage off a street;—*a.* shut fast; private. [F. (part.) *clos,* shut in, fr. *clore.*]

CLOSELY (klōs'li) *ad.* in a close manner; very near.

CLOSENESS (klōs'nes) *n.* compactness; want of air; penuriousness.

CLOSET (kloz'et) *n.* a small private apartment;—*v.t.* to shut up in privacy. [O.F. *closet,* dim. of *clos.* See CLOSE.]

CLOSING (klō'zing) *n.* end; conclusion;—*a.* that concludes.

CLOSURE (klōz'ūr) *n.* a closing; enclosure; summary ending of a debate in Parliament. [See CLOSE.]

CLOT (klot) *n.* a concretion; coagulation;—*v.t. i.* to form clots. [E. =clod. Cf. Ger. *Klotz.*]

CLOTH (kloth) *n.* any material formed by weaving. [O.E. *clath.* Cf. Ger. *Kleide.*]

CLOTHE (klōтн) *v.t.* [*pret.* and *pp.* CLAD, CLOTHED] to furnish with garments; (dress.

CLOTHES (klōтнz, klōz) *n.pl.* dress; garments.

CLOTHIER (klōтн'yer) *n.* one who makes or sells woollen cloth or clothing.

CLOTHING (klō'тнing) *n.* garments.

CLOUD (kloud) *n.* collection of vapours; anything that obscures; a veil; a multitude;—*v.t.* to darken with clouds; obscure. [O.E. *clud.*]

CLOUDINESS (klou'di-nes) *n.* state of being cloudy.

CLOUDLESS (kloud'les) *a.* free from clouds.

CLOUDLESSLY (kloud'les-li) *ad.* in a cloudless manner.

CLOUDLET (kloud'let) *n.* a little cloud.

CLOUDY (klou'di) *n.* covered with clouds; obscure.

CLOUT (klout) *n.* a patch; cloth for any mean use; a blow;—*v.t.* to patch; join clumsily; beat. [O.E. *clut.*]

CLOVE (klōv) *n.* an Indian spice. [M.E. *clow,* fr. F. *clou,* nail, clove (fr. the shape), fr. L. (acc.) *clavum.*]

CLOVEN (klō'vn) *pp.* or *a.* of CLEAVE, cleft; split.

CLOVEN-FOOTED (klō'vn-foot'ed) *a.* having the hoof in two parts.

CLOVER (klō'ver) *n.* a genus of plants; grass. [M.E. *claver,* fr. O.E. *clafre.*]

CLOWN (kloun) *n.* a rustic; buffoon. [Scand.]

CLOWNISH (klou'nish) *a.* coarse; rustic.

CLOWNISHLY (klou'nish-li) *ad.* in a clownish manner.

CLOWNISHNESS (klou'nish-nes) *n.* rusticity; awkwardness.

CLUB (klub) *n.* a heavy stick; one of a suit at cards; an association for social, literary, political, or other purposes;—*v.t.* or *i.* to join in common expense. [Scand.]

CLUBBABLE (klub'a-bl) *a.* disposed to club life; sociable.

CLUB-FOOTED (klub'foot-ed) *a.* crooked in the feet.

CLUB-LAW (klub'law) *n.* violence in place of law.

CLUCK (kluk) *v.i.* to call as a hen;—*n.* the call of a hen; a kind of articulation. [Imit.]

CLUE (klōō) *n.* a ball of thread; lower corner of a sail; a direction or guide. [See CLEW.]

CLUMP (k um) *n.* a cluster of trees. [Perh. Scand.] p

CLUMSY (klum'zi) *a.* awkward. [Scand.]

CLUSTER (klus'ter) *n.* a bunch; group; swarm;—*v.t.* or *i.* to unite in a bunch. [E., conn. with CLOT.]

CLUTCH (kluch) *n.* a gripe; grasp; claw;—*pl.* talons; claws; hands;—*v.t.* to hold fast; gripe. [M.E. *clucchen,* fr. O.E. *clyccean.*]

CLUTTER (klut'er) *n.* a noise; confusion;—*v.t.* to crowd together in disorder;—*v.i.* to make a noise or bustle. [Form of CLATTER.]

CLYSTER (klis'ter) *n.* an injection. [L., fr., G. =syringe.]

COACH (kōch) *n.* a large, close, four-wheeled carriage for pleasure or travelling;—*v.t.* to convey in a coach;—*v.i.* to ride by coach. [F. *coche,* perhaps fr. *Kocs* (kotsh).]

COACHFUL (kōch'fool) *n.* as many as the coach will hold.

COACHMAN (kōch'man) *n.* one who drives a coach. [driving.

COACHMANSHIP (kōch'man-ship) *n.* skill in

COACTION (kō-ak'shun) *n.* compulsion; force. [L. *cogere, coactum,* to compel.]

COADJUTANT (kō-a-jōō'tant) *a.* assisting.

COADJUTOR (kō-a-jōō'ter) *n.* an assistant. [L. *co=con*=with, and *adjutor,* a helper.]

COADJUTORSHIP (kō-a-jōō'tur-ship) *n.* joint assistance.

COADJUTRIX (kō-a-jōō'triks) *n.* a female assistant.

COAGULABLE (kō-ag'ū-la-bl) *a.* that may coagulate.

COAGULATE (kō-ag'ū-lāt) *v.t.* or *i.* to curdle. [L. *coagulatus,* curdled, fr. *coagulatum,* rennet, fr. *cogere,* to gather together.]

COAGULATION (kō-ag-ū-lā'shun) *n.* the process of curdling.

COAGULUM (kō-ag'ū-lum) *n.* a coagulated mass, as curd; rennet. [See COAGULATE.]

COAL (kōl) *n.* wood charred; a fossil used for fuel;—*v.t.* to burn to charcoal; supply with coal;—*v.i.* to take in coal. [O.E. *col.*]

COALESCE (kō-a-les') *v.i.* to grow together; unite. [L. *co=cum*=together, and *alescere,* to grow up.]

COALESCENCE (kō-a-les'ens) *n.* the act of uniting; union.

COALING (kō'ling) *ppr., n.* act of supplying coals or receiving them.

COALITION (kō-a-lish'un) *n.* union of persons, particles, or states.

COAL-MEASURE (kōl'me-zhūr) *n.* a bed or stratum of coal.

COAL-SCUTTLE (kōl'skut-l) *n.* a parlour utensil for holding coal.

COAL-TAR (kōl'tár) *n.* a pitchy substance condensed in the distillation of gas from coal.

COARSE (kōrs) *a.* gross; rude; rough. [E., fr. *in course.*]

COARSEN (kōr'sn) *v.t.* to make coarse.

COARSENESS (kōrs'nes) *n.* grossness; rudeness.

COAST (kōst) *n.* land next the sea;—*v.t.* or *i.* to sail along the shore. [O.F. *coste* =F. *côte,* fr. L. (acc.) *costam,* a rib, side.]

COASTER (kōs'ter) *n.* a person or vessel that sails near a coast.

COASTING (kōs'ting) *n.* a sailing near land.

COAT (kōt) *n.* a man's upper garment; a covering; a layer;—*v.t.* to cover; spread over. [O.F. *cote* =F. *cotte,* perh. fr. Teut.]

COATING (kō'ting) *n.* cloth for coats; act of covering.

COAX (kōks) *v.t.* to wheedle; persuade by flattery. [Etym. unknown.]

COAXER (kōk'ser) *n.* one who entices.

COAXINGLY (kōk'sing-li) *ad.* in a wheedling manner.

COB (kob) *n.* spike of maize; a stout, strong pony or horse. [E.]

COBALT (kō'bawlt) *n.* a mineral. [Ger.]

COBBLE (kob'l) (1) *n.* a roundish stone;—(2) *v.t.* to mend coarsely or clumsily. [(1) E. (2) Etym. unknown.]

COBBLER (kob'ler) *n.* a mender of shoes. [Etym. unknown.]

COBLE (kob'l) *n.* a small fishing boat. [Celt.]

COBWEB (kob'web) *n.* a spider's web;—*a.* thin; flimsy. [M.E. *coppe,* spider, short for O.E. *attor-coppa,* fr. *attor,* poison, and *cop,* head.]

COCA (kō'ka) *n.* the dried leaf of a Peruvian plant. [Native S. Amer. name.]

Fāte, fár, ạdo; mē, hẹr; mīne; nōte; tūne; mōòn.

COCAGNE, COCKAIGNE (kō-kān') *n.* a name applied to London or cockneydom; lotus-land. [F., of uncertain etym.]

COCAINE (kō-kān', kō'kā-in) *n.* a drug made from coca leaves, used as 'an anæsthetic in minor surgical operations. [See COCA.]

COCHINEAL (koch'i-nēl) *n.* an insect used to dye scarlet. [F., fr. L. *coccinus*, scarlet, fr. *coccum*, a berry, (for which the insect was taken) fr. G.]

COCK (kok) (1) *v.t.* to set erect;—*n.* the male of birds; a vane; a tap; lock of a firearm; (2) a pile of hay. [(1) O.E. *cocc*, imit.; (2) Scand.]

COCKADE (kō-kād') *n.* a knot of ribbon worn on the hat. [See COCK (1).]

COCKATOO (kok-ȧ-tōō') *n.* a kind of tufted parrot. [Malay.]

COCKATRICE (kok'ȧ-tris) *n.* a serpent. [O.F., fr. Late L. (acc.) *cocatricem* = the treader, fr. stem *calc*-, of *calx*, the heel.]

COCKBOAT (kok'bōt) *n.* a small boat. [Etym. uncertain.]

COCKLE (kok'l) (1) *n.* a weed; (2) a shell-fish;—*v.t.* to wrinkle. [(1) E.; (2) F. *coquille*, fr. G. *kongche* shell, through L.]

COCKNEY (kok'ni) *n.* a native of London;— *pl.* COCKNEYS. [F., of uncertain etym. See COCAGNE.]

COCKNEYISM (kok'ni-izm) *n.* manners of a Cockney.

COCKPIT (kok'pit) *n.* an area where cocks fight; a room in a ship under a gun-deck.

COCKROACH (kok'rōch) *n.* a troublesome insect; a kind of beetle.

COCKSCOMB (koks'kōm) *n.* a comb of a cock; a plant.

COCKSWAIN (kok'swān, kok'sn) *n.* an officer who has the care of a boat and boat's crew. [Fr. COCK (boat) and SWAIN.]

COCOA (kō'kō) *n.* the chocolate-tree, and a decoction of the nut or the paste. [Corr. fr. cacao.]

COCOA-NUT (kō'kō-nut) *n.* the nut of a kind of palm-tree. [Sp. and Pg. *coco*, bug-bear.]

COCOON (kō-kōōn') *n.* a ball spun by the silk-worm. [F., fr. O.F. *coque*, shell, fr. L. (acc.) *concham*.]

COD (kod) *n.* a sea-fish; a husk or envelope; a bag; a pillow. [O.E. *codd*, a small bag.]

CODDLE (kod'l) *v.t.* to parboil; nurse; fondle.

CODE (kōd) *n.* a system or digest of laws. [F., fr. L. (acc.) *codicem*, a manuscript.]

CODGER (koj'ẽr) *n.* a clownish fellow. [Etym. uncertain.]

CODICIL (kod'i-sil) *n.* supplement to a will. [L. *codicillus*, a short writing.]

CODIFICATION (kō-di-fi-kā'shun) *n.* act of reducing laws to a system.

CODIFY (kō'di-fi) *v.t.* to reduce to a code. [See CODE.]

CODLING (kod'ling) *n.* a young cod-fish; a cooking apple. [Etym. uncertain.]

COEFFICIENT (kō-e-fish'ent) *a.* co-operating; —*n.* that which co-operates. [L. *co = cum*, and EFFICIENT.]

COEQUAL (kō-ē'kwal) *a.* equal with another. [L. *co = cum*, and EQUAL.]

COERCE (kō-ẽrs') *v.t.* to restrain by force; compel; constrain. [L. *coercere*, fr. *co = cum*, and *arcere*, to confine.]

COERCION (kō-ẽr'shun) *n.* compulsory force; legal restraint.

COERCIVE (kō-ẽr'siv) *a.* restraining by force.

CO-ESSENTIAL (kō-e-sen'shal) *a.* partaking of the same essence. [L. *co = cum*, and ESSENTIAL.]

CO-ETERNAL (kō-ē-tẽr'nal) *a.* equally eternal. [L. *co = cum*, and ETERNAL.]

COEVAL (kō-ē'val) *a.* of the same age;—*n.* one of the same age. [L. *co = cum*, and *ævum*, an age.]

CO-EXIST (kō-eg-zist') *v.i.* to exist together. [L. *co = cum*, and EXISTENCE.]

CO-EXISTENCE (kō-eg-zis'tens) *n.* existence at the same time. [L. *co = cum*, and EXISTENCE.]

CO-EXTEND (kō-eks-tend') *v.t.* or *t.* to extend to the same limit. [L. *co = cum*, and EXTEND.]

CO-EXTENSIVE (kō-eks-ten'siv) *a.* equally extensive.

COFFEE (kof'ē) *n.* the berry of the coffee-tree; the 'liquor made from it. [A., through Turkl]

COFFEE-POT (kof'ē-pot) *n.* a pot for coffee.

COFFER (kof'ẽr) *n.* a chest; a treasure. [O.F. *cofre*, *cofin* = F. *coffre*. Doublet of COFFIN.]

COFFERED (kof'ẽrd) *a.* furnished with coffers.

COFFIN (kof'in) *n.* a chest for a dead human body;—*v.t.* to put in a coffin. [O.F. *cofin*, a box, fr. L. (acc.) *cophinum*, Fr. G. *kophinos*, basket.]

COG (kog) *n.* the tooth of a wheel;—*v.t.* to cheat or deceive; load, as dice;—*v.i.* to wheedle. [Scand.]

COGENCY (kō'jen-si) *n.* power; urgency; strength.

COGENT (kō'jent) *a.* having great force; forcible; convincing. [L. (acc. part.) *cogentem*, compelling, fr. *cogere*, fr. *co = cum*, together, and *agere*, drive.]

COGITATE (koj'i-tāt) *v.i.* to think; meditate. [L. *cogitare*, to think.]

COGITATION (koj-i-tā'shun) *n.* deep thought. [L. part. *cogitatus*, well-considered, fr. *cogitare*, think.]

COGITATIVE (koj'i-tā-tiv) *a.* able to think. [L. part. *cogitatus*, well-considered, fr. *cogitare*, think.]

COGNAC (kōn'yak) *n.* the best brandy. [F., fr. name of town *Cognac*.]

COGNATE (kog'nāt) *a.* born together; allied by blood. [L. *co = cum*, together, and *gnatus*, old form of *natus*, born.]

COGNISANCE (kog'ni-zans, kon'i-zans) *n.* knowledge; judicial notice; jurisdiction; a badge or crest. [Conformed to L.; O.F. *connoissance*.]

COGNISANT (kog'ni-zant, kon'i-zant) *a.* having knowledge of. [Conformed to L.; O.F. *connoissance*.]

COGNITION (kog-nish'un) *n.* knowledge. [F., fr. L. (acc.) *cognitionem*.]

COGNOMEN (kog-nō'men) *n.* family name; surname. [L.]

COHABIT (kō-hab'it) *v.i.* to live together as man and wife. [L. *co = cum*, and *habitare*, to dwell.]

COHABITATION (kō-hab-i-tā'shun) *n.* a living together.

CO-HEIR (kō-ār') *n.* a joint heir. [L. *co = cum*, and HEIR.]

CO-HEIRESS (kō-ār'es) *n.* a joint heiress. [See CO-HEIR.]

COHERE (kō-hēr') *v.i.* to stick together; be well connected or consistent. [L. *co = cum*, and *hærere*, to stick.]

COHERER (kō-hēr-ẽr) *n.* part of the apparatus used in wireless telegraphy.

COHERENCE (kō-hēr'ens) *n.* union of parts.

COHERENT (kō-hēr'ent) *a.* consistent; connected. [L. (acc. part.) *cohærentem*, cleaving.]

COHESION (kō-hē'zhun) *n.* state of union; union.

COHESIVE (kō-hē'siv) *a.* sticking; adhesive. [L. *cohæsus*, held together.]

COHESIVENESS (kō-hē'siv-nes) *n.* quality of sticking together.

COHORT (kō'hort) *n.* a body of soldiers. [F., fr. L. (acc.) *cohortem*. Doublet of COURT.]

COIF (koif) *n.* a head-dress;—*v.t.* to cover with a coif. [F. *coiffe*, fr. Low L. (acc.) *coffam*, a kind of helmet, fr. O. Ger. *Chuppha*, cap.]

COIFFURE (koif'ūr) *n.* a head-dress. [F., see COIF.]

COIGNE (koin) *n.* a corner; a corner-stone; a wedge. [Form of COIN.]

COIL (koil) v.t. to wind into a ring;—n. circular form of a rope or serpent. [O.F. coillir = F. cueillir, gather, fr. L. colligere.]

COIN (koin) n. money stamped;—v.t. to stamp metal; mint; invent; forge. [O.F., fr. L. (acc.) cuneum, wedge.]

COINAGE (koi'nāj) n. act of coining; money. [See COIN.]

COINCIDE (kō-in-sīd') v.i. to agree; concur. [L. co = cum, and incidere. See INCIDENT.]

COINCIDENCE (kō-in'si-dens) n. agreement.

COINCIDENT (kō-in'si-dent) a. occurring or agreeing together.

COINER (koi'nẹr) n. a maker of money.

CO-INHERITANCE (kō-in-hẹr'i-tạns) n. joint inheritance. [L. co = cum, and INHERITANCE.]

CO-INHERITOR (kō-in-hẹr'i-tẹr) n. a joint heir; co-heir.

COIR (koir) n. the fibre of the cocoa-nut; rope made from it. [Tamil.]

COKE (kōk) n. mineral coal charred. [Etym. unknown.]

COLATION (kō-lā'shun) n. act of straining; filtration. [L. colum, a strainer.]

COLD (kōld) a. not warm; reserved;—n. sensation produced by want of heat; disorder caused by cold. [O.E. ceald; cf. Ger. kalt.]

COLDLY (kōld'li) ad. without warmth; with reserve. [unconcern.

COLDNESS (kōld'nes) n. want of heat; reserve;

COLEWORT (kōl'wurt) n. a young cabbage. [M.E. col, caul, fr. O.E. caul, fr. L. caulis, a stalk, and O.E. wyrt, plant. Cf. KAIL.]

COLIC (kol'ik) n. a pain in the bowels. [F., fr. L., fr. G. kolikos, pert. to the large intestine, kolon.]

COLLABORATOR (ko-lab'ō-rā-tẹr) n. an associate in literary labour. [Fr. F. collaborateur.]

COLLAPSE (ko-laps') v.i. to fall together;—n. a falling together; sudden prostration or failure. [L. (part.) collapsus, fallen in, fr. col = cum, and LAPSE.]

COLLAPSED (ko-lapst') a. fallen together; closed.

COLLAR (kol'ạr) n. something worn around the neck;—v.t. to put on a collar; seize by the collar. [M.E. coler, fr. O.F., fr. L. collare, a neck-band, fr. collum, the neck.]

COLLATABLE (ko-lā'tạ-bl) a. capable of being collated.

COLLATE (ko-lāt') v.t. to compare; gather and place in order; present to a benefice. [L. (part.) collatus, collected, fr. conferre.]

COLLATERAL (ko-lat'e-rạl) a. being side by side; indirect. [L. col = cum, and stem later-, of latus, side.]

COLLATION (ko-lā'shun) n. a repast; gift; act of comparing.

COLLATOR (ko-lā'tẹr) n. one who collates.

COLLEAGUE (kol'ēg) n. an associate in office. [F. collègue, fr. L. (acc.) collegam, a partner.]

COLLECT (1) (ku-lekt') v.t. or i. to gather; assemble; infer; (2) (kol'ekt) n. a short prayer. [(1) L. (part.) collectus, fr. col = cum, and legere, to gather] [(2) L. collecta, a meeting for prayer].

COLLECTED (ku-lek'ted) a. gathered; cool; not disturbed.

COLLECTION (ku-lek'shun) n. act of collecting; that which is collected.

COLLECTIVE (ku-lek'tiv) a. formed by gathering; inferring. [L. collectivus.

COLLECTIVELY (ku-lek'tiv-li) ad. in a body. [L. collectivus.

COLLECTOR (ku-lek'tẹr) n. a gatherer; a receiver of taxes.

COLLECTORSHIP (ku-lek'tur-ship) n. the office of a collector.

COLLEGE (kol'ej) n. an assembly; a seminary of learning. [O.F., fr. L. collegium, a society, fr. collega, COLLEAGUE.]

COLLEGIAN (ko-lē'ji-ạn) n. a member of a college.

COLLEGIATE (ko-lē'ji-āt) a. pertaining to a college.

COLLET (kol'et) n. the ring in which a stone is set. [F., dim. fr. L. collum, the neck.]

COLLIDE (ko-līd') v.i. to dash together. [L., col = cum, and lœdere, to strike.]

COLLIE (kol'i) n. a shepherd's dog. [Etym. uncert.]

COLLIER (kol'yẹr) n. a digger of or dealer in coals; a coal-ship. [M.E. colier.]

COLLIERY (kol'yẹr-i) n. a coal-mine.

COLLISION (ku-lizh'un) n. a striking together. [Fr. L. (part.) collisus, dashed together.]

COLLOCATE (kol'ō-kāt) v.t. to set in order. [L. col = cum, and LOCATE.]

COLLOCATION (kol-ō-kā'shun) n. a placing together; arrangement.

COLLOCUTION (kol-ō-kū'shun) n. conversation; conference. [L. col = cum, and loqui, to speak.] [a dialogue.

COLLOCUTOR (ko-lok'ū-tẹr) n. a speaker in

COLLODION (ko-lō'di-un) n. a solution of gun cotton in ether. [Fr. G. kollodes, glue-like, fr. kolla, glue, and eidos, appearance.]

COLLOP (kol'up) n. a cut or slice. [Etym. unknown.]

COLLOQUIAL (ko-lō'kwi-ạl) a. pertaining to conversation. [L. colloquium, fr. col = cum, and loqui, speak.]

COLLOQUIALISM (ko-lō'kwi-ạl-izm) n. an expression used only in conversation.

COLLOQUY (kol'ō-kwi) n. a mutual conversation between two.

COLLUSION (ko-lū'zhun) n. a secret agreement to deceive. [L. col = cum, and (part.) lusus, played, fr. ludere.]

COLLUSIVE (ko-lū'siv) a. fraudently concerted.

COLOGNE (kō-lōn') n. a compound of alcohol and aromatic oils used in the toilet. [Fr. town, Cologne.]

COLON (kō'lun) (1) n. the point (:); (2) the largest of the intestines. [(1) G. kolon. a limb. (2) G. See COLIC.]

COLONEL (kẹr'nel) n. the commander of a regiment. [F., fr. It. colonello, fr. L. columna, a column.]

COLONIAL (ko-lō'ni-ạl) a. belonging to a colony or colonies.

COLONIALISM (ko-lō'ni-ạl-izm) n. colonial peculiarity.

COLONISATION (kol-ō-ni-zā'shun) n. the settling of a colony.

COLONISE (kol'ō-nīz) v.t. to plant or settle with inhabitants.

COLONIST (kol'ō-nist) n. an inhabitant of a colony.

COLONNADE (kol-o-nād') n. a row or range of columns. [F., fr. It. colonna, fr. L. columna, a column.]

COLONY (kol'ō-ni) n. a body of people who remove and settle in a distant country, continuing subject to the parent state; the country colonised. [L. colonia, fr. colonus, a farmer, fr. colere, to cultivate.]

COLOSSAL (kō-los'ạl) a. huge in size; gigantic.

COLOSSUS (ko-los'us) n. a statue of gigantic size;—pl. COLOSSI. [L., fr. G.]

COLOUR (kul'ur) n. a property of light; paint; tint; hue; false show;—v.t. to dye; stain; —v.i. to blush. [O.F. colour, = F. couleur, fr. L. (acc.) colorem.]

COLOURABLE (kul'ur-ạ-bl) a. designed to cover and deceive; plausible.

COLOURABLY (kul'ur-ạ-bli) ad. speciously; plausibly.

COLOURATION (kul-ur-ā'shun) n. art of colouring; state of being coloured. [See COLOUR.]

COLOUR-BLIND (kul'ur-blīnd) a. having an imperfect sense of colour.

COLOURING (kul'ur-ing) n. act of dyeing; specious appearance.

COLOURIST (kul'ur-ist) *n.* one who excels in colouring.

COLOURLESS (kul'ur-les) *a.* without colour.

COLOURS (kul'urz) *n.pl.* a banner; flag; ensign.

COLOUR-SERGEANT (kul'ur-sár-jent) *n.* the chief sergeant of a company. [COLOUR and SERGEANT, which see.]

COLPORTEUR (kol'pôr-ter) *n.* one who travels for the sale of religious books, tracts, etc. [F., fr. *colporter*, to carry on the neck, fr. L. *collum*, neck, and PORTER.]

COLT (kōlt) *n.* a young horse. [E.]

COLTER (kōl'ter) *n.* the fore-iron of a plough. Also written COULTER. [O.E. *culter*, fr. L.]

COLUMBINE (kol'um-bin) *n.* a genus of plants; the heroine of a pantomime. [L. *columbinus*, dove-like, fr. *columba*.]

COLUMN (kol'um) *n.* a cylindrical pillar; row of lines in a book; a body of troops. [L. *columna*, fr. *columen*, a prop.]

COLUMNAR (ku-lum'nar) *a.* like a column.

COLURES (ko-lûrz') *n.pl.* two great circles intersecting the solstitial or equinoctial points. [G. *kolouros*, cut short (by horizon), fr. *kolos*, docked, and *oura*, tail.]

COMA (kō'ma) (1) *n.* hairiness of a comet; (2) lethargy; disposition to sleep. [(1) L., fr. G. *kome*, hair of the head. (2) G. *koma*.]

COMATOSE (kō'ma-tōs) *a.* drowsy.

COMB (kōm) *n.* an instrument for cleaning hair; crest of a cock; substance in which bees lodge honey;—*v.t.* to dress with a comb. [O.E. *camb*.]

COMBAT (kom'bat, kum'bat) *n.* a battle; fight; duel;—*v.t.* or *i.* to fight; oppose. [F.]

COMBATANT (kom'ba-tant) *n.* a champion.

COMBATIVE (kom'ba-tiv) *a.* disposed to combat.

COMBATIVENESS (kom'ba-tiv-nes) *n.* disposition to fight.

COMBINATION (kom-bi-nā'shun) *n.* union or association; coalition; conjunction.

COMBINE (kum-bin') *v.t.* or *i.* to join; agree. [L. *combinare*, fr. *com* = *cum*, and *bini*, two by two.]

COMBUSTIBILITY (kum-bus-ti-bil'i-ti) *n.* capacity of burning or being burnt. [See COMBUSTION.]

COMBUSTIBLE (kum-bus'ti-bl) *a.* capable of burning; apt to burn.

COMBUSTION (kum-bust'yun) *n.* a burning. [L. (acc.) *combustionem*, fr. part. *combustus*, burned, fr. *com* = *cum*, and *urere*, burn.]

COME (kum) *v.i.* [*pret.* CAME; *pp.* COME] to move forward; draw near; arrive at; happen. [O.E. *cuman*.]

COMEDIAN (ko-mēd'yan) *n.* an actor or writer of comedies.

COMEDY (kom'e-di) *n.* a humorous dramatic piece. [F. *comédie*, fr. L. (acc.) *comœdiam*, fr. G. *komos*, revel, and *aeidein*, sing.]

COMELINESS (kum'li-nes) *n.* grace; beauty.

COMELY (kum'li) *a.* handsome; graceful; becoming. [O.E. *cyme*, fair.]

COMESTIBLE (ko-mes'ti-bl) *a.* eatable;—*n.pl.* eatables. [L. *com* = *cum*, and *edere*, to eat.]

COMET (kom'et) *n.* a heavenly body with a train of luminous matter. [G. = long-haired star, fr. *kome*, hair.]

COMFIT (kom'fit) *n.* a dry sweetmeat. [F. *confit*, fr. O.F. *confire*, make up, fr. L. *conficere*. See CONFECTION.]

COMFORT (kum'furt) *v.t.* to cheer under affliction or depression;—*n.* relief from pain; consolation. [O.F. *conforter*, fr. L. *confortare*, strengthen much, fr. L. *con* = *cum*, and *fortis*, strong.]

COMFORTABLE (kum'fur-ta-bl) *a.* enjoying or giving comfort. [See COMFORT.]

COMFORTABLY (kum'fur-ta-bli) *ad.* with ease and comfort.

COMFORTER (kum'fur-ter) *n.* one who comforts; the Holy Spirit; a woollen neck-wrap or scarf.

COMFORTLESS (kum'furt-les) *a.* without comfort.

COMIC (kom'ik) *a.* relating to comedy; droll. [L., fr. G. *komikos*, relating to a *komos*. See COMEDY.]

COMICAL (kom'i-kal) *a.* diverting; droll.

COMING (kum'ing) *a.* future;—*n.* approach.

COMITIAL (kō-mish'i-al) *a.* relating to public assemblies. [L. *comitia*, electoral assemblies.]

COMITY (kom'i-ti) *n.* courtesy of intercourse; civility. [L. (acc.) *comitatem*, fr. *comis*, kind.]

COMMA (kom'a) *n.* the point (,) noting a short pause in reading. [G. = clause, fr. *koptein*, to cut.]

COMMAND (ko-mánd') *v.t.* to order; direct; govern;—*n.* an order; injunction. [F. *commander*, fr. L. *commendare*. Doublet of COMMEND.]

COMMANDANT (kom-an-dánt') *n.* a commanding officer. [F.]

COMMANDER (ku-mán'der) *n.* one who directs.

COMMANDING (ko-mán'ding) *a.* controlling by influence or dignity; imperious.

COMMANDINGLY (ko-mán'ding-li) *ad.* in an authoritative manner.

COMMANDMENT (ko-mánd'ment) *n.* command; a precept of the moral law.

COMMEMORABLE (ko-mem'or-a-bl) *a.* worthy to be remembered.

COMMEMORATE (ko-mem'o-rāt) *v.t.* to celebrate. [L. part. *commemoratus*, kept in mind, fr. *com* = *cum*, and *memorare*, recount.]

COMMEMORATION (ko-mem-o-rā'shun) *n.* solemn celebration.

COMMEMORATIVE (ko-mem'o-ra-tiv) *a.* preserving the memory of.

COMMENCE (ku-mens') *v.t.* to begin; originate; —*v.i.* to take rise. [O.F. *comencer*, fr. L. *com-* = *cum*, and *initiare*, to begin.]

COMMENCEMENT (ku-mens'ment) *n.* beginning; the thing begun.

COMMEND (ku-mend') *v.t.* to praise. [L. *commendare*, entrust, fr. *com* = *cum*, and *mandare*, order.]

COMMENDABLE (ku-men'da-bl) *a.* worthy of praise; laudable.

COMMENDABLY (ku-men'da-bli) *ad.* in a praiseworthy manner.

COMMENDATARY (ku-men'da-tar-i) *n.* one who holds a benefice in trust;—*a.* holding *in commendam*.

COMMENDATORY (ku-men'da-tur-i) *a.* tending to commend.

COMMENSAL (ko-men'sal) *a.* living together; eating at the same table. [L. *com* = *cum* and *mensa*, table.]

COMMENSURABILITY (ku-men'sū-ra-bil-i-ti) *a.* capacity of having a common measure.

COMMENSURABLE (ku-men'sū-ra-bl) *a.* having a common measure.

COMMENSURATE (ku-men'sū-rāt) *a.* of equal measure; proportioned to. [L. *com* = *cum*, and *mensura*, a MEASURE.]

COMMENSURATELY (ku-men'sū-rāt'li) *ad.* correspondingly; adequately.

COMMENT (ku-ment', kom'ent) *v.i.* to explain;—*n.* note or remark for explanation. [F., fr. L. *comment-are* (= -*ari*), think over, fr. (part.) *commentus*, devised, fr. *com* = *cum*, and stem of *mens*, mind.]

COMMENTARY (kom'en-tar-i) *n.* comment; exposition; a book of comments.

COMMENTATION (kom-en-tā'shun) *n.* act of commenting; annotation.

COMMENTATOR (kom'en-tā-ter) *n.* one who writes a commentary; expositor.

COMMERCE (kom'ers) *n.* interchange of commodities; trade; traffic; intercourse; a game at cards. [F., fr. L. *commercium*, fr. *com*, together, and *merx*, *mercis*, merchandise.]

Fāte, fär, ado; mē, her; mine; nōte; tūne; mōon.

COMMERCIAL (ku-mer'shal) *a.* relating to trade.

COMMINATION (kom-i-nā'shun) *n.* a threat; denunciation of punishment. [L. *com,* intensive word, and *minari,* threaten.]

COMMINATORY (ko-min'a-tur-i) *a.* threatening.

COMMINGLE (ko-ming'gl) *v.t.* to mix together. [L. *com,* and MINGLE.]

COMMISERABLE (ku-miz'e-ra-bl) *a.* deserving of pity.

COMMISERATE (ku-miz'e-rāt) *v.t.* to pity. [L. *commiseratus,* having pitied, fr. *com = cum,* and *miser,* wretched.]

COMMISERATION (ku-miz-e-rā'shun) *n.* compassion; pity.

COMMISERATOR (ku-miz'e-rā-ter) *n.* one who pities.

COMMISSARIAT (kom-i-sā'ri-at) *n.* the department which supplies provisions, etc., for the army; the body of officers in it.

COMMISSARY (kom'i-sar-i) *n.* a commissioner.

COMMISSION (ku-mish'un) *n.* a trust; compensation for transacting business;—*v.t.* to give a commission to; authorise; empower. [L. (acc.) *commissionem,* fr. *committere,* COMMIT.]

COMMISSIONAIRE (ku-mish'un-ār) *n.* a light porter or messenger.

COMMISSIONER (ku-mish'un-er) *n.* one empowered to act.

COMMIT (ku-mit') *v.t.* to entrust; imprison; pledge; perpetrate. [L. *committere,* fr. *com = cum,* and *mittere,* send.]

COMMITMENT (ku-mit'ment) *n.* act of committing.

COMMITTAL (ku-mit'al) *n.* a pledge, actual or implied.

COMMITTEE (ku-mit'ē) *n.* persons specially appointed to manage any business.

COMMIXTION (ko-mikst'yun) *n.* a blending. [See MIX.]

COMMODIOUS (ku-mō'di-us) *a.* affording ease and convenience. [O.F. *commodieux =* F. *commode,* fr. Late L. *commodiosus,* useful, fr. *commodus,* fit.]

COMMODIOUSNESS (ku-mō'di-us-nes) *n.* convenience; fitness.

COMMODITY (ku-mod'i-ti) *n.* anything convenient or useful; an article of traffic. [F., fr. L. (acc.) *commoditatem.*]

COMMODORE (kom'o-dōr) *n.* the commander of a squadron. [Formerly also *commandore,* fr. D. = COMMANDER.]

COMMON (kom'un) *a.* public; usual; vulgar; mean;—*n.* an open public ground;—*v.i.* to board together. [F. *commun,* fr. L. (acc.) *communem,* originally *serving together,* fr. *com = cum,* and *munis,* ready to serve.]

COMMONALTY (kom'un-al-ti) *n.* the common people.

COMMONER (kom'un-er) *n.* one not noble; a member of the House of Commons.

COMMONITION (kom-ō-nish'un) *n.* warning; instruction. [L. *com = cum,* and *moneo,* warn.]

COMMONLY (kom'un-li) *ad.* usually; frequently; ordinarily.

COMMONPLACE (kom'un-plās) *n.* a general idea; a trite remark; a note;—*a.* ordinary; hackneyed.

COMMONS (kom'unz) *n.pl.* common people; lower House of Parliament; common land; food at a common table.

COMMON-SENSE (kom'un-sens) *n.* sound practical judgment;—*a.* marked by plain good sense.

COMMONWEAL (kom'un-wēl) *n.* public welfare.

COMMONWEALTH (kom'un-welth) *n.* a state; body politic.

COMMOTION (ku-mō'shun) *n.* disturbance. [L. *com = cum,* and *moveo, motum,* move.]

COMMUNE (kom'ūn) *n.* a territorial district in France. [F., fr. *commun,* common.]

COMMUNE (ko-mūn') *v.i.* to converse together familiarly; confer. [O.F. *communer,* fr. *commun,* common.]

COMMUNICABLE (ku-mū'ni-ka-bl) *a.* that may be communicated.

COMMUNICANT (ku-mū'ni-kant) *n.* a partaker of the Lord's Supper.

COMMUNICATE (ku-mū'ni-kāt) *v.t.* or *i.* to impart; give information; partake of the Lord's Supper; have intercourse with. [L. *communicatus,* imparted, fr. *communis,* common.]

COMMUNICATION (ku-mū-ni-kā'shun) *n.* act of imparting intercourse by letter, etc.; passage from place to place; intelligence; news.

COMMUNICATIVE (ku-mū'ni-kā-tiv) *a.* ready to impart.

COMMUNION (ku-mūn'yun) *n.* intercourse; fellowship; a taking of the Lord's Supper; a body of Christians. [L. (acc.) *communionem,* fr. *communis,* common.]

COMMUNISM (kom'ū-nizm) *n.* community of property among all the people; socialism. [See COMMUNE.]

COMMUNIST (kom'ū-nist) *n.* an adherent of communism.

COMMUNISTIC (kom-ū-nis'tik) *a.* relating to communism.

COMMUNITY (ku-mū'ni-ti) *n.* common possession; the body politic; the public. [L. (acc.) *communitatem.*]

COMMUTABILITY (ku-mū-ta-bil'i-ti) *n.* capacity of being interchanged. [See COMMUTE.]

COMMUTABLE (ku-mū'ta-bl) *a.* that may be exchanged.

COMMUTATION (kom-ū-tā'shun) *n.* exchange; alteration; substitution of a less for a greater.

COMMUTATIVE (ku-mū'ta-tiv) *a.* relating to exchange.

COMMUTE (ku-mūt') *v.t.* to exchange one thing for another. [L., fr. *com = cum,* and *mutare,* change.]

COMPACT (kum-pakt') *a.* firm; dense; close; brief;—*v.t.* to press together; consolidate; unite firmly. [L. *com = cum,* and *pactus,* fixed, fr. *pangere,* fix.]

COMPACT (kom'pakt) *n.* an agreement uniting parties; league. [L. *com = cum,* and PACT.]

COMPACTED (kum-pak'ted) *a.* pressed close; firmly united.

COMPACTEDLY (kum-pak'ted-li) *ad.* closely; compendiously.

COMPACTEDNESS (kum-pak'ted-nes) *n.* closeness of parts; density.

COMPACTNESS (kum-pakt'nes) *n.* closeness; density; firmness.

COMPANION (kum-pan'yun) *n.* an associate. [F. *compagnon,* fr. Low L. *companium* fr. L. *com = cum,* and (acc.) *panem,* bread.]

COMPANIONABLE (kum-pan'yun-a-bl) *a.* sociable; agreeable.

COMPANIONABLY (kum-pan'yun-a-bli) *ad.* in a companionable manner.

COMPANIONSHIP (kum-pan'yun-ship) *n.* fellowship; association.

COMPANY (kum'pa-ni) *n.* persons assembled or acting together;—*v.i.* to associate with. [M.E. *companye,* fr. F. *compagnie.* See COMPANION.]

COMPARABLE (kom'par-a-bl) *a.* that may be compared; worthy of equal regard.

COMPARABLY (kom'par-a-bli) *ad.* in a manner deserving equal regard.

COMPARATIVE (kum-par'a-tiv) *a.* estimated by comparison.

COMPARATIVELY (kum-par'a-tiv-li) *ad.* by comparison.

COMPARE (kum-pãr´) v.t. to examine together; liken; inflect;—v.i. to be like. [F., fr. L. comparare, fr. com = cum, and par, equal.]

COMPARISON (kum-par´-i-sun) n. act of comparing; comparative estimate; simile.

COMPARTMENT (kum-pãrt´ment) n. a division or separate part. [F. compartiment.]

COMPASS (kum´pas) v.t. to surround; obtain; —n. a circle; spa e; limit; extent; c a magnetised needle used in steering ships. [F. conpas, fr. Late L. (acc.) compassum, circumference, fr. L. com = cum, and passus. PACE.]

Compass.

COMPASSES (kum´pas-ez) n.pl. an instrument with two legs for describing circles, etc. [See COMPASS.]

COMPASSION (kum-pash´un) n. sorrow for another's suffering; commiseration; pity. [F., fr. L. (acc.) compassionem, fellow-feeling, fr. com = cum, and PASSION.]

COMPASSIONATE (kum-pash´un-ãt) a. inclined to pity; merciful;—v.t. to pity.

Compasses.

COMPATIBILITY (kom-pat-i-bil´i-ti) n. quality of suiting or agreeing; suitableness.

COMPATIBLE (kum-pat´i-bl) a. consistent with; suitable to; congruous. [L. com = cum, and pati, bear, suffer.]

COMPATRIOT (kom-pã´tri-ut) n. one of the same country. [L. com = cum, and PATRIOT.]

COMPEER (kom-pēr´) n. an equal; colleague; companion. [L. com = cum, and PEER.]

COMPEL (kum-pel´) v.t. to drive by force; constrain; oblige. [L. com = cum, and pellere, drive.]

COMPEND (kum´pend) n. abridgment; summary; epitome. Also COMPENDIUM. [L., originally a hanging together. See DEPEND.]

COMPENDIOUS (kom-pen´di-us) a. short; concise; brief.

COMPENSABLE (kom-pens´a-bl) a. that may be compensated.

COMPENSATE (kom´pen-sãt) v.t. to make up for; recompense; requite;—v.i. to make amends. [L. compensatus, weighed against something, fr. com = cum, and part. pensus, weighed.]

COMPENSATION (kom-pen-sã´shun) n. amends; recompense. [amends.

COMPENSATIVE (kom-pen´sa-tiv) a. making

COMPETE (kum-pēt´) v.i. to strive for a like end; rival. [L., fr. com = cum, and petere, seek.]

COMPETENCE (kom´pe-tens) n. sufficiency; legal capacity or right. Also COMPETENCY. [See COMPETENT.]

COMPETENT (kom´pe-tent) a. adequate to some end or duty; having legal capacity; sufficient; qualified. [O.F. (part.), fr. L. (acc. part.) competentem, corresponding.]

COMPETENTLY (kom´pe-tent-li) ad. sufficiently; fitly.

COMPETITION (kom-pe-tish´un) n. rivalry.

COMPETITIVE (kum-pet´i-tiv) a. pertaining to competition.

COMPETITOR (kum-pet´i-ter) n. a rival.

COMPILATION (kom-pi-lã´shun) n. a selection from authors.

COMPILE (kum-pīl´) v.t. to put together or collect from books or documents. [F. compiler, fr. L. com = cum, and pilare, rob.]

COMPLEMENT (kom-pil´ment) n. act of compiling.

COMPILER (kum-pī´ler) n. one who compiles.

COMPLACENCE (kum-plã´sens) n. pleasure; satisfaction of mind; civility. Also COMPLACENCY.

COMPLACENT (kum-plã´sent) a. showing satisfaction; gracious; mild; pleasing; civil. [L. (part. stem) complacent-, pleasing.]

COMPLACENTLY (kum-plã´sent-li) ad. with satisfaction.

COMPLAIN (kum-plãn´) v.i. to murmur; lament; make a charge; be ill. [O.F. (part.) complaignant, lamenting, fr. complaindre fr. com = L. cum, and L. plangere, bewail.]

COMPLAINANT (kum-plã´nant) n. one who complains; a prosecutor.

COMPLAINING (kum-plã´ning) n. expression of grief or injury.

COMPLAINT (kum-plãnt´) n. a murmuring; accusation; illness.

COMPLAISANCE (kom´plã-zans) n. civility. [F., fr. complaire, fr. L. com = cum, and placere, PLEASE.

COMPLAISANT (kom´plã-zant) a. polite, courteous; affable.

COMPLAISANTLY (kom´plã-zant-li) ad. in an obliging, affable manner.

COMPLEMENT (kom´ple-ment) n. the full number or quantity; that which supplies a deficiency. [L., fr. complere, fill up, fr. com = cum, and plere, fill.]

COMPLEMENTARY (kom-ple-men´ta-ri) a. serving to complete.

COMPLETE (kum-plēt´) a. finished; perfect. [L. (part.) completus, filled up. See COMPLEMENT, COMPLY.]

COMPLETELY (kum-plēt´li) ad. perfectly.

COMPLETENESS (kum-plēt´nes) n. state of being complete.

COMPLETION (kum-plē´shun) n. act of finishing; perfect state.

COMPLEX (kom´pleks) a. of many parts; intricate. [L. com = cum, and (part.) plexus, twined, fr. plectere.]

COMPLEXION (kum-plek´shun) n. the colour of the face; general aspect or appearance; texture. [F., fr. L. (acc.) complexionem, bodily constitution.]

COMPLEXITY (kum-plek´si-ti) n. a complex state; intricacy.

COMPLEXLY (kom-pleks´li) ad. intricately.

COMPLIANCE (kum-plī´ans) n. a yielding; submission; consent. [See COMPLY.]

COMPLIANT (kum-plī´ant) a. yielding; bending; obliging. [See COMPLY.]

COMPLICATE (kom´pli-kãt) v.t. to make intricate; entangle; involve;—a. involved. [L. (part.) complicatus, folded together, fr. com = cum, and plicare.]

COMPLICATED (kom´pli-kãt-ed) a. intricate.

COMPLICATION (kom-pli-kã´shun) n. a mixture of many things.

COMPLIMENT (kom´pli-ment) n. act or expression of civility; a present;—v.t. to bestow praise upon; congratulate;—v.i. to use compliments. [F., fr. L. complere, fill up, through It.]

COMPLIMENTARY (kom-pli-men´ta-ri) a. expressive of praise.

COMPLOT (kom´plot) n. a joint plot; conspiracy. [F.]

COMPLY (kum-plī´) v.i. to yield to; consent. [L. complere, fill up, through It.]

COMPONENT (kum-pō´nent) a. constituent; —n. an elementary part; ingredient. [L. (part. stem) component-, putting together, fr. com-ponere.]

COMPORT (kum-pōrt´) v.t. or i. to agree; suit. [F., fr. L. com = cum, and portare, carry.]

COMPORTABLE (kum-pōr´ta-bl) a. consistent.

COMPORTMENT (kum-pōrt´ment) n. behaviour; demeanour. [See COMPORT.]

COMPOSE (kum-pōz´) v.t. to allay; write as an author. [F. composer, fr. com = L. cum, and poser, POSE.]

COMPOSED (kum-pōzd') *a.* calm; tranquil.

COMPOSEDLY (kum-pō'zed-li) *ad.* calmly.

COMPOSER (kom-pō'zer) *n.* one who calms; an author.

COMPOSITE (kom'poz-it) *a.* made up of parts or elements pertaining to a certain order of architecture;—*n.* a compound; composition.

COMPOSITION (kom-pō-zish'un) *n.* a mixture; writing.

COMPOSITOR (kum-poz'i-ter) *n.* one who sets types.

COMPOST (kom'post) *n.* a mixture for manure. [O.F., fr. L. (neut. part.) *composit-um.* Doublet of **COMPOSITE**.]

COMPOSURE (kum-pō'zhūr) *n.* a composed state of mind; calmness.

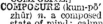

Composite Order.

COMPOTE (kom'pōt) *n.* stewed or preserved fruit. [F., see **COMPOST**.]

COMPOUND (kom'pound) (1) *a.* formed of two or more ingredients;—*n.* a mixture; (2) *n.* an enclosure about a house. [(1) M.E. *componen,* fr. L. *componere,* through O.F. (2) Malay.]

COMPOUND (kum-pound') *v.t.* to mix in one mass; adjust; settle.

COMPOUNDER (kum-poun'der) *n.* one who compounds.

COMPREHEND (kom-prē-hend') *v.t.* to contain; include; understand. [L., fr. *com* =*cum,* and *prehendere,* take. Doublet of **COMPRISE**.]

COMPREHENSIBLE (kom-prē-hen'si-bl) *a.* that can be understood. [See **COMPREHEND**.]

COMPREHENSION (kom-prē-hen'shun) *n.* act of comprehending; capacity.

COMPREHENSIVE (kom-prē-hen'siv) *a.* embracing much; capacious; extensive.

COMPREHENSIVENESS(kom-prē-hen'siv-nes) *n.* quality of including much.

COMPRESS (kum'-pres) *v.t.* to press together; condense. [L., fr. part. *compressus,* pressed together, fr. *com* =*cum,* and **PRESS**.]

COMPRESS (kom'pres) *n.* a soft bandage used by surgeons.

COMPRESSIBILITY (kum-pres-i-bil'i-ti) *n.* quality of being compressible.

COMPRESSIBLE (kum-pres'i-bl) *a.* that may be compressed. [pressing together.

COMPRESSION (kum-presh'un) *n.* act of

COMPRISE (kum-priz') *v.t.* to contain; include. [O.F. (part.) *compris,* included, fr. *comprendre,* fr. L. *com-prehendere.* Doublet of **COMPREHEND**, which see.]

COMPROMISE (kon_'rō-mīz) *n.* settlement of differences by mutual concession;—*v.t.* to settle by mutual agreement; pledge or hazard, as the honour of another. [L. *com,* and *promittere.* See **PROMISE**.]

COMPULSION (kum-pul'shun) *n.* act of compelling; constraint; coercion. [L. (part). *compulsus,* driven together, fr. *compellere.*]

COMPULSIVE (kum-pul'siv) *a.* compelling; forcing.

COMPULSORILY (kum-pul'sur-i-li) *ad.* in a compulsory manner.

COMPULSORY (kum-pul'sur-i) *a.* compelling; using or constrained by force.

COMPUNCTION (kum-pungk'shun) *n.* reproach of conscience; remorse. [O.F., fr. Late L., fr. L. (part.) *compunctus,* conscience-stricken, fr. *com* =*cum,* and *pungere,* to prick.]

COMPUTABLE (kum-pū'ta-bl) *a.* capable of being computed. [ing.

COMPUTATION (kom-pū-tā'shun) *n.* reckon-

COMPUTE (kum-pūt') *v.t.* to calculate; reckon. [L. *com* =*cum,* and *putare,* reckon.]

COMPUTER (kum-pū'ter) *n.* one who computes or reckons.

COMRADE (kom'rād, kum'rād) *n.*an associate; mate; companion. [F. *camerade* fr. L. *camera,* chamber, through Sp.]

CON (kon) *v.t.* to know; read carefully; learn; direct how to steer. [O.E. *cunnian,* investigate; conn. with *cunnan,* know.]

CONCATENATE (kon-kat'e-nāt) *v.t.* to link together; unite in a series. [L. *con* =*cum,* and *catena,* a chain.]

CONCATENATION (kon-kat-e-nā'shun) *n.* a series of links or things united.

CONCAVE (kon'kāv) *a.* hollow;—*n.* a hollow; arch or vault;—*v.t.* to make hollow. [F., fr. L. *con* =*cum,* and **CAVE**.]

CONCAVELY (kon-kāv'li) *ad.* so as to be concave.

CONCAVITY (kon-kav'i-ti) *n.* the inner surface of, or the space contained in, a hollow body; hollowness.

CONCAVO-CONCAVE (kon-kā'vō-kon'kāv) *a.* concave on both sides. [See **CONCAVE**.]

CONCEAL (kun-sēl') *v.t.* to keep secret; hide; disguise; secrete. [O.F. *conceler,* fr. L., fr. *con* =*cum,* and *celare,* hide.]

CONCEALMENT (kun-sēl'ment) *n.* act of keeping secret; suppression of the truth; state of being hid; hiding-place.

CONCEDE (kun-sēd') *v.t.* to give up; surrender; grant;—*v.i.* to admit as true; allow. [L. *concedere,* give way.]

CONCEDED (kun-sēd'ed) *a.* yielded.

CONCEIT (kun-sēt') *n.* self-importance; vanity; a pleasant or an affected idea or expression. [Fr. **CONCEIVE**, on the anal. of *deceit*.]

CONCEITED (kun-sē'ted) *a.* having a high opinion of oneself; vain.

CONCEITEDLY (kun-sē'ted-li) *ad.* with vain opinion.

CONCEIVABLE (kun-sē'va-bl) *a.* that may be conceived.

CONCEIVABLY (kun-sē'va-bli) *ad.* in such a manner as to be imagined or understood.

CONCEIVE (kun-sēv') *v.t.* to form in the mind; imagine;—*v.i.* become with child. [O.F. *concever* =F. *concevoir,* fr. L. *concipere,* fr. *con* =*cum,* and *capere,* take.]

CONCEIVING (kun-sēv'ing) *n.* conception.

CONCENT (kun'sent) *n.* concert of voices; harmony. [L. *consentire,* fr. *con* =*cum,* and *sentire,* feel or think.]

CONCENTRATE (kon-sen'trāt) *v.t.* to bring to a $com mon$ centre or to a closer union;—*v.i.* to meet in one centre. [L. *con* =*cum,* and **CENTRE**.]

CONCENTRATION (kon-sen-trā'shun) *n.* act of drawing to a centre; condensation.

CONCENTRATIVE (kon-sen'tra-tiv) *a.* tending to concentrate.

CONCENTRE (kon-sen'ter) *v.i.* to come to or meet in a centre or point. [See **CONCENTRATE**.]

CONCENTRIC (kon-sen'trik) *a.* having a common centre. [See **CONCENTRATE**.]

CONCENTRICITY (kon-sen-tris'i-ti) *n.* state of being concentric.

CONCEPT (kon'sept) *n.* an abstract idea or conception. [L. *conceptus,* fr. *concipere.* See **CONCEIVE**.]

CONCEPTIBILITY (kun-sep-ti-bil'i-ti) *n.* quality of being conceivable.

CONCEPTIBLE (kun-sep'ti-bl) *a.* capable of being conceived.

CONCEPTION (kun-sep'shun) *n.* act of conceiving; idea.

CONCEPTIONAL (kun-sep'shun-al) *a.* having the nature of a conception.

CONCEPTIVE (kun-sep'tiv) *a.* capable of conceiving.

CONCEPTUAL (kun-sep'tū-al) *a.* pertaining to conception.

CONCEPTUALISM (kun-sep′tū-al-izm) *n.* a theory intermediate between realism and nominalism.

CONCERN (kun-sern′) *v.t.* to affect; interest; belong to;—*n.* an affair; anxiety; solicitude. [F., fr. L. *concernere*, mingle (later) concern, fr. *con* = *cum*, and *cernere*, sift.]

CONCERNING (kun-ser′ning) *prp.* pertaining to.

CONCERNMENT (kun-sern′ment) *n.* business; interest; importance; anxiety.

CONCERT (kun-sert′) *v.t.* to contrive together; plan. [F. *concerter*, fr. L. *concertare*, fr. *con* = *cum*, and *certare*, strive, through It.]

CONCERT (kon′sert) *n.* agreement; a musical entertainment.

CONCERTINA (kon-ser-tē′na) *n.* a musical instrument on the accordion principle. [See **CONCERT**.]

CONCERTO (kon-chär′tō) *n.* a composition for a solo instrument with orchestral accompaniments. [See **CONCERT**.]

CONCESSION (kun-sesh′un) *n.* act of yielding; the thing conceded. [See **CONCEDE**.]

CONCESSIVE (kun-ses′iv) *a.* implying concession.

CONCH (kongk) *n.* a marine shell. [L. *concha*, fr. G. *kongke*, fr. Skr. *cankha*, shell.]

CONCHOIDAL (kong-koi′dal) *a.* resembling a marine shell. [See **CONCH**.]

CONCILIATE (kun-sil′i-āt) *v.t.* to gain by favour; reconcile; propitiate. [L. (part.) *conciliatus*, brought together, fr. *concilium*.]

CONCILIATING (kun-sil′i-āt-ing) *a.* gaining favour; winning; engaging.

CONCILIATION (kun-sil-i-ā′shun) *n.* act of reconciling.

CONCILIATOR (kun-sil′i-ā-ter) *n.* one who conciliates.

CONCILIATORY (kun-sil′i-ā-tur-i) *a.* tending to reconcile.

CONCISE (kun-sīs′) *a.* brief; short. [L. (part.) *concisus*, cut up, fr. *con* = *cum*, and *cædere*.]

CONCISELY (kun-sīs′li) *ad.* in a few words; tersely.

CONCISENESS (kun-sīs′nes) *n.* brevity in speaking or writing.

CONCISION (kun-sizh′un) *n.* a cutting off; a division; a sect.

CONCLAVE (kon′klāv) *n.* an assembly of cardinals; a close assembly. [F., fr. L. *conclave*, a locked place, fr. *con* = *cum*, and *clavis*, key.]

CONCLUDE (kun-klōōd′) *v.t.* to bring to an end; close; settle;—*v.i.* to come to an end; infer; determine. [L. *con* = *cum*, and *claudere*, shut.]

CONCLUDING (kun-klōō′ding) *a.* ending; closing; final.

CONCLUSION (kun-klōō′zhun) *n.* end; inference; determination. [See **CONCLUDE**.]

CONCLUSIVE (kun-klōō′siv) *a.* decisive.

CONCLUSIVELY (kun-klōō′siv-li) *ad.* decisively.

CONCLUSIVENESS (kun-klōō′siv-nes) *n.* quality of being conclusive.

CONCOCT (kun-kokt′) *v.t.* to solve by digestion; compound or make up; devise; mature. [L. (part.) *concoctus*, cooked, fr. *con* = *cum*, and *coquere*, cook.]

CONCOCTION (kun-kok′shun) *n.* digestion; ripening; devising.

CONCOCTIVE (kun-kok′tiv) *a.* tending to digest or mature.

CONCOMITANCE (kun-kom′i-tans) *n.* a being together.

CONCOMITANT (kun-kom′i-tant) *a.* accompanying; conjoined with;—*n.* he or that which accompanies. [L. *con* = *cum*, and (part. stem) *comitant*-, accompanying, fr. stem *comit*-, of *comes*, companion.]

CONCORD (kong′kord) *n.* agreement; union; harmony. [F. *concorde*, fr. L. (acc.) *concordiam*, fr. stem *cord*-, of *cor*, heart.]

CONCORDANCE (kon-kor′dans) *n.* an index to the leading words of a book.

CONCORDANT (kon-kor′dant) *a.* agreeing; suitable; harmonious.

CONCORDANTLY (kon-kor′dant-li) *ad.* correspondently; harmoniously.

CONCOURSE (kong′kōrs) *n.* an assembly. [F. *concours*, fr. L. (acc.) *concursum*, fr. *currere*, run.]

CONCRETE (kon′krēt) *n.* a mass of lime, sand, gravel, and cement;—*a.* formed by massing several things into one body; not abstract; —*v.t.* or *i.* to unite in a mass. [L. (part.) *concretus*, grown together, fr. *crescere*, grow.]

CONCRETION (kon-krē′shun) *n.* act of concreting. [See **CONCRETE**.]

CONCRETIONAL (kon-krē′shun-al) *a.* pertaining to or formed by concretion. Also **CONCRETIONARY**.

CONCRETIVE (kon-krē′tiv) *a.* causing to concrete.

CONCUBINAGE (kun-kū′bi-nāj) *n.* living together as man and wife without being married; state of a concubine.

CONCUBINE (kong′kū-bīn) *n.* a woman in keeping; a mistress. [F., fr. L., fr. *concubare*, fr. *cumbere*, lie.]

CONCUR (kun-kur′) *v.i.* or *t.* to agree; tend to one point; unite in opinion; assent. [L. *con* = *cum*, and *currere*, run.]

CONCURRENCE (kun-kur′ens) *n.* union of minds; joint action; assent. [See **CONCUR**.]

CONCURRENT (kun-kur′ent) *a.* acting together. [See **CONCUR**.]

CONCURRENTLY (kun-kur′ent-li) *ad.* in concert.

CONCUSSION (kun-kush′un) *n.* a shaking; a sudden jar. [F., fr. L. (acc.) *concussionem*, a shaking, fr. (part.) *cussus*, shaken, fr. *-cutio* = *-quatio*.]

CONCUSSIVE (kun-kus′iv) *a.* able to shake.

CONDEMN (kun-dem′) *v.t.* to pronounce to be wrong, guilty, or unfit; sentence; doom. [L. *condemnare*, fr. *damnare*, condemn.]

CONDEMNABLE (kun-dem′na-bl) *a.* deserving condemnation.

CONDEMNATION (kon-dem-nā′shun) *n.* act of condemning; sentence.

CONDEMNATORY (kun-dem′na-tur-i) *a.* implying condemnation.

CONDENSABLE (kun-den′sa-bl) *a.* that may be condensed.

CONDENSATE (kun-den′sāt) *v.t.* to make dense; —*a.* made dense.

CONDENSATION (kon-den-sā′shun) *n.* act of condensing.

CONDENSE (kun-dens′) *v.t.* or *i.* to reduce into smaller compass. [F., fr. L., fr. *con-densus*, very thick, fr. *densus*, DENSE.]

CONDENSER (kun-den′ser) *n.* he or that which condenses.

CONDESCEND (kon-dē-send′) *v.i.* to waive a privilege of rank; stoop; deign. [F., fr. Late L. *condescendare* (= descend with), fr. **DESCEND**.]

CONDESCENDENCE (kon-dē-sen′dens) *n.* condescension.

CONDESCENDING (kon-dē-sen′ding) *a.* yielding to inferiors; obliging.

CONDESCENSION (kon-dē-sen′shun) *n.* act of condescending. [See **CONDESCEND**.]

CONDIGN (kun-dīn′) *a.* deserved; suitable; merited. [O.F., fr. L. (acc.) *con-dignum*, very worthy.]

CONDIGNLY (kun-dīn′li) *ad.* fitly; suitably.

CONDIMENT (kon′di-ment) *n.* a seasoning. [L., fr. *condire*, preserve.]

CONDITION (kun-dish′un) *n.* state; position; quality; term of agreement;—*v.t.* or *i.* to make terms; stipulate. [F., fr. L. (acc. part.) *conditionem*, a setting up, situation, fr. *conditus*, founded, fr. *condere*.]

CONDITIONAL (kun-dish′un-al) *a.* implying terms.

CONDITIONALLY (kun-dish'un-al-i) *ad.* with certain limitations; on certain terms.

CONDITIONED (kun-dish'und) *a.* stipulated; having terms, qualities, etc.

CONDOLE (kun-dōl') *v.t.* to grieve with others. [L., fr. *con* = *cum* and *dolere*, grieve.]

CONDOLEMENT (kun-dōl'ment) *n.* sorrow with others. [another.

CONDOLENCE (kun-dō'lens) *n.* grief for

CONDONATION (kon-dō-nā'shun) *n.* act of pardoning.

CONDONE (kun-dōn') *v.t.* to pardon; overlook. [L. *condonare*, remit, fr. *donare*.]

CONDOR (kon'dor) *n.* a large vulture found in South America. [Sp., fr. Peruv.]

CONDUCE (kon-dūs') *v.i.* to tend to. [L. *conducere*, lead together.]

CONDUCIBLE (kun-dū'si-bl) *a.* promotive.

CONDUCIVE (kun-dū'siv) *a.* tending to.

CONDUCIVENESS (kun-dū'siv-nes) *n.* tendency to promote.

CONDUCT (kon'dukt) *n.* behaviour; guidance. [L. *conductum*, led together.]

CONDUCTIBLE (kun-duk'ti-bl) *a.* that may be conducted. [See **CONDUCE**.]

CONDUCTIVITY (kun-duk-tiv'i-ti) *n.* the power of transmitting heat or other forces. [See **CONDUCE**.]

CONDUCTOR (kun-duk'ter) *n.* a leader; director; manager; a substance that transmits heat, sound, or electricity. [See **CONDUCE**.]

CONDUIT (kon'dit) *n.* a water-pipe; a canal. [O.F. *conduit*, fr. Late L. (acc.) *conductum*, an escort, tube, fr. (part.) *conductus*, led together, fr. **CONDUCE**.]

CONE (kōn) *n.* a solid body tapering to a point from a circular base. [O.F., fr. L., fr. G. *konos*.]

CONFABULATE (kon-fab'ū-lāt) *v.i.* to talk together; chat. [L. (part.) *confabulatus*, having conversed, fr. *fabulari*, talk.]

CONFABULATION (kon-fab-ū-lā'shun) *n.* familiar talk.

CONFECTION (kun-fek'shun) *n.* a sweetmeat. [L. (part.) *confectus*, prepared, fr. *conficere*. See **COMFIT**.]

CONFECTIONER (kun-fek'shun-er) *n.* one who makes or sells sweetmeats, etc.

CONFECTIONERY (kun-fek'shun-er-i) *n.* a place where sweetmeats are made or sold; sweetmeats in general.

CONFEDERACY (kun-fed'er-a-si) *n.* a mutual contract or league; the men or states bound by league.

CONFEDERATE (kun-fed'er-āt) *a.* united in a common cause;—*v.t.* to unite in alliance. [L. *con* = *cum*, and *fœdus*, league.]

CONFEDERATION (kun-fed-er-ā'shun) *n.* a league or alliance; parties to a league.

CONFEDERATIVE (kon-fed'er-āt-iv) *a.* constituting a federal compact.

CONFER (kun-fer') *v.t.* to grant; award; contribute;—*v.i.* to talk or consult together. [L. *con*, and *ferre*, carry.]

CONFERENCE (kon'fer-ens) *n.* formal meeting for consultation, discussion, etc.

CONFERRABLE (kun-fer'a-bl) *a.* that may be conferred.

CONFESS (kun-fes') *v.t.* or *i.* to own; avow; admit; hear or make confession. [O.F. *confesser*, fr. L. (part.) *confessus*, having confessed, fr. *cum*, wholly, and *fateri*, to admit.]

CONFESSEDLY (kun-fes'ed-li) *ad.* avowedly.

CONFESSION (kun-fesh'un) *n.* acknowledgment; act of confessing to a person.

CONFESSIONAL (kun-fesh'un-al) *n.* a place where confession is made.

CONFESSOR (kun-fes'er) *n.* one who confesses or hears confession.

CONFIDANT (kon-fi-dant') *n.* a male bosom friend.

CONFIDANTE (kon-fi-dant') *n.* a female bosom friend.

CONFIDE (kun-fīd') *v.t.* or *i.* to trust fully; entrust to; rely on. [L. *cum*, fully, wholly, and *fidere*, trust.]

CONFIDENCE (kon'fi-dens) *n.* firm belief; trust; self-reliance; boldness.

CONFIDENT (kon'fi-dent) *a.* having full belief or assurance.

CONFIDENTIAL (kon-fi-den'shal) *a.* given in confidence; trustworthy.

CONFIDENTLY (kon'fi-dent-li) *ad.* without doubt; assuredly.

CONFIDING (kon-fīd'ing) *n.* trustful; trusting; credulous. [fiding manner.

CONFIDINGLY (kon-fīd'ing-li) *ad.* in a confiding manner.

CONFIDINGNESS (kon-fīd'ing-nes) *n.* trustfulness; a disposition to trust.

CONFIGURATION (kon-fig-ū-rā'shun) *n.* external form; aspect of planets. [F., fr. L. (acc.) *configurationem*.]

CONFINABLE (kon-fī'na-bl) *a.* that may be confined or limited.

CONFINE (kon'fīn) *n.* a limit; border;— (kon-fīn') *v.t.* to shut up. [O.F. *confin*, fr. L. (acc.) *confinem*, bounding with, fr. *con* = *cum*, and *finis*, a boundary.]

CONFINED (kon-fīnd') *a.* limited; shut up; close and narrow; constipated; in child-bed.

CONFINEMENT (kon-fīn'ment) *n.* restraint.

CONFINER (kon-fī'ner) *n.* a borderer; neighbour.

CONFIRM (kon-ferm') *v.t.* to make certain; admit to Christian communion. [O.F. *confermer*, fr. L. *confirmare*, fr. *con* = *cum*, wholly, and **FIRM**.]

CONFIRMABLE (kon-fer'ma-bl) *a.* that may be confirmed.

CONFIRMATION (kon-fer-mā'shun) *n.* act of establishing; admitting to Christian communion.

CONFIRMATIVE (kun-fer'ma-tiv) *a.* serving to confirm; corroborating.

CONFIRMATORY (kun-fer'ma-tur-i) *a.* adapted to confirm. [firms.

CONFIRMER (kun-fer'er) *n.* one who confirms.

CONFIRMINGLY (kun-fer'ming-li) *ad.* in a manner to confirm.

CONFISCATE (kon-fis'kāt) *v.t.* to forfeit to the public treasury; seize on as forfeited. [L. (part.) *confiscatus*, laid up in coffer, fr. *con* = *cum*, and *fiscus*, a basket.]

CONFISCATION (kon-fis-kā'shun) *a.* the act of forfeiting or confiscating.

CONFISCATOR (kon'fis-kā-ter) *n.* one who confiscates to the public use.

CONFLAGRATION (kon-fla-grā'shun) *n.* a great fire. [L. *conflagrare*, fr. *con* = *cum*, and *flagrare*, burn.]

CONFLICT (kon'flikt) *n.* a contest; struggle;— (kon-flikt') *v.t.* to strive; contend. [L. *conflictus*, struck together, fr. *con* = *cum*, and *fligere*, strike.] [opposing.

CONFLICTING (kon-flikt'ing) *a.* contradictory;

CONFLICTIVE (kon-flik'tiv) *a.* tending to conflict. Also **CONFLICTORY**.

CONFLUENCE (kon'floo-ens) *n.* a flowing together; a concourse. [L. *confluere*, fr. *con* = *cum*, and *fluere*, flow.]

CONFLUENT (kon'floo-ent) *a.* running together. [See **CONFLUENCE**.]

CONFLUX (kon'fluks) *n.* a junction of currents; a gathering; crowd. [L. (part.) *confluxus*, fr. *confluere*.]

CONFORM (kon-form') *v.t.* to make like;— *v.i.* to comply with. [F., fr. L. *conformare*, **FORM**.]

CONFORMABLE (kon-form'ma-bl) *a.* suitable; compliant.

CONFORMABLY (kon-for'ma-bli) *ad.* suitably.

CONFORMATION (kon-for-mā'shun) *n.* disposition of parts; structure.

CONFORMIST (kon-for'mist) *n.* one who complies with established rules.

CONFORMITY (kon-for'mi-ti) *n.* compliance; with; consistency; likeness.

Fāte, fär, ado; mē, her; mine; nōte; tūne; mōōn.

CONFOUND (kun-found') v.t. to mix; perplex; confuse; destroy. [F. *confondre*, fr. L. *confundere*, to pour together. Doublet of CONFUSE.]

CONFOUNDED (kun-foun'ded) pp. or a. mingled; confused; astonished; enormous; detestable.

CONFOUNDEDLY (kun-foun'ded-li) ad. excessively; abominably.

CONFRATERNITY (kon-frạ-tẹr'ni-ti) n. a brotherhood, usually a religious one. [L. *con = cum*, and *frater*, brother.]

CONFRONT (kun-frunt') v.t. to stand face to face; oppose. [F. *confronter*, fr. Late L., fr. *con = cum*, together, and FRONT.]

CONFUSE (kun-fūz') v.t. to confound; abash. [L. *confusus*, poured together. Doublet of CONFOUND.] [fused manner.

CONFUSEDLY (kun-fū'zed-li) ad. in a confused or distinct manner.

CONFUSEDNESS (kun-fū'zed-nes) n. want of order or distinctness.

CONFUSION (kun-fū'zhun) n. disorder; tumult; indistinctness; shame; ruin.

CONFUTABLE (kun-fū'tạ-bl) a. that may be disproved.

CONFUTATION (kon-fū-tā'shun) n. act of disproving; refutation.

CONFUTE (kun-fūt') v.t. to disprove; prove to be wrong. [F., fr. L. *confutare*, to cool hot liquid by adding cold. See FUTILE.]

CONGEAL (kun-jēl') v.t. or i. to freeze; stiffen. [F. *congeler*, make to freeze, fr. L. *con = cum*, and *gelu*, frost.]

CONGEALABLE (kun-jēl'ạ-bl) a. that may be congealed.

CONGEALMENT (kun-jēl'ment) n. mass formed by congelation.

CONGELATION (kon-je-lā'shun) n. the process of congealing. [See CONGEAL.]

CONGENERIC (kon-je-ner'ik) a. of the same kind. [L. *con = cum*, and *genus*, *generis*, kind.]

CONGENEROUS (kon-jen'e-rus) a. of the same kind or nature; belonging to the same genus. [See CONGENERIC.]

CONGENIAL (kun-jēn'yạl) a. of kindred nature or disposition. [L. *con*, and *genialis*, genial.]

CONGENIALITY (kun-jē-ni-al'i-ti) n. natural affinity; suitableness.

CONGENITAL (kun-jen'i-tạl) a. of the same birth. [L. *con = cum*, and *genitus*, born.]

CONGER (kong'gẹr) n. the sea-eel. [L., fr. G. *gongros*.]

CONGERIES (kun-jē'ri-ēz) n. a mass of small bodies. [L.]

CONGEST (kun-jest') v.t. to heap up; collect in a mass. [L. (part.) *congestus*, carried together, fr. *con = cum*, and *gerere*, carry.]

CONGESTIBLE (kun-jes'ti-bl) a. that may be congested.

CONGESTION (kun-jest'yun) n. a diseased accumulation of blood in any part.

CONGESTIVE (kun-jes'tiv) a. indicating an accumulation of blood or humours.

CONGLOMERATE (kun-glom'e-rāt) v.t. to gather into a round mass;—a. gathered as a ball. [L. pref. *cum*. Cf. AGGLOMERATE.]

CONGLOMERATION (kun-glom-e-rā'shun) n. a gathering into a mass; collection.

CONGLUTINANT (kun-glöö'ti-nạnt) a. gluing; uniting; healing.

CONGLUTINATE (kun-glöö'ti-nāt) v.t. to glue together. [L. *con = cum*. See AGGLUTINATE.]

CONGLUTINATION (kun-glöö-ti-nā'shun) n. a gluing together.

CONGLUTINATIVE (kun-glöö'ti-nā-tiv) a. tending to cause union.

CONGRATULATE (kun-grat'ū-lāt) v.t. to profess joy to. [L. (part.) *congratulatus*, fr. *con = cum*, wholly, and *gratulari*, congratulate, fr. *gratus*, pleasing.]

CONGRATULATION (kun-grat-ū-lā'shun) n. an expression of joy.

CONGRATULATOR (kun-grat'ū-lā-tẹr) n. one who offers congratulation.

CONGRATULATORY (kun-grat'ū-lạ-tur-i) a. expressing joy.

CONGREGATE (kong'gre-gāt) v.t. or i. to gather together; assemble. [L. *don = cum*. See AGGREGATE.]

CONGREGATION (kong-gre-gā'shun) n. a religious assembly.

CONGREGATIONAL (kong-gre-gā'shun-ạl) a. relating to a congregation; independent.

CONGREGATIONALISM (kong-gre-gā'shun-ạl-izm) n. a form of church government in which each church or congregation regulates itself; independency.

CONGREGATIONALIST (kong-gre-gā'shun-ạl-ist) n. an adherent to the congregational mode of government.

CONGRESS (kong'gres) n. the legislature of the United States; a meeting. [L., fr. (part.) *congressus*, having met, fr. *congredi*, fr. *con = cum*, and *gradi*, walk.]

CONGRESSIONAL (kong-gresh'un-ạl) a. pertaining to congress.

CONGRESSIVE (kong-gres'iv) a. meeting.

CONGRUENCE (kong'groo-ens) n. agreement; consistency.

CONGRUENT (kong'groo-ent) a. agreeing; suitable. [L. *congruus*, of uncertain etym.]

CONGRUITY (kon-gröö'i-ti) n. consistency. [See CONGRUENT.]

CONGRUOUS (kong'groo-us) a. agreeable to. [See CONGRUENT.]

CONIC (kon'ik) a. like a cone; pertaining to cones. Also CONICAL.

CONICALLY (kon'i-kạl-i) ad. in the form of a cone.

CONICS (kon'iks) n.pl. the science which treats of the properties of the cone.

CONIFEROUS (kō-nif'e-rus) a. bearing cones, as the pine. [CONE, and L. *ferre*, carry.]

CONIFORM (kō'ni-form) a. in the form of a cone. [CONE, and L. *forma*, shape.]

CONJECTURAL (kun-jek'tūr-ạl) a. depending on conjecture.

CONJECTURE (kun-jek'tūr) n. a supposition or opinion without proof; surmise;—v.t. to guess; forecast. [F., fr. L. (acc.) *conjecturam*, a casting together, fr. *con = cum*, and (part.) *-jectus = jactus*, thrown, fr. *jacere*.]

CONJECTURABLE (kun-jek'tūr-ạ-bl) a. that may be guessed.

CONJOIN (kun-join') v.t. to connect; unite; —v.i. to join or league together. [L. *con = cum*, and JOIN.]

CONJOINT (kun-joint') a. united; connected; mutual. [efforts.

CONJOINTLY (kun-joint'li) ad. with united

CONJUGAL (kon'joo-gạl) a. relating to marriage. [F., fr. L. (acc.) *conjugem*, spouse, fr. *conjux*. See CONJUGATE.]

CONJUGATE (kon'joo-gāt) v.t. to inflect, as verbs; unite. [L., fr. (part.) *conjugatus*, yoked together, fr. *con = cum*, and *jugum*, yoke.]

CONJUGATION (kon-joo-gā'shun) n. the form of inflecting verbs.

CONJUNCT (kun-jungkt') a. joint; concurrent. [L. (part.) *conjunctus*, conjoined, fr. *con = cum*, and *jungere*, JCIN.]

CONJUNCTION (kun-jungk'shun) n. a meeting; a connecting word. [unite.

CONJUNCTIVE (kun-jungk'tiv) a. serving to unite.

CONJUNCTURE (kun-jungk'tūr) n. a critical time; union.

CONJURATION (kon-joo-rā'shun) n. an earnest prayer or entreaty; a magic spell. [F., fr. L. (acc.) *conjurationem*, fr. *conjuratus*, bound by oath.]

CONJURE (kun'jer) (1) v.t. or i. to practise charms; play tricks;—(kun-jöör') (2) v.t. to call on by a sacred name; implore earnestly. [(1) Fr. CONJURE, (kun-jöör'). (2) Fr. F., fr. L., fr. *con = cum*, and *jurare*, swear.]

CONJURER (kun'jer-er) *n.* an enchanter.

CONNECT (ku-nekt') *v.t.* to link together; unite. [L., fr. *con* =*cum*, and *nectere*, bind.]

CONNECTEDLY (ku-nek'ted-li) *ad.* by connection.

CONNECTION (ku-nek'shun) *n.* act of joining; a relation by blood or marriage.

CONNECTIVE (ku-nek'tiv) *a.* that serves to connect;—*n.* a word that connects sentences.

CONNEXION. See CONNECTION.

CONNEXIONAL (ku-nek'shun-al) *a.* having connexion or connection.

CONNIVANCE (ku-ni'vans) *n.* the act of winking at a fault; voluntary blindness to an act.

CONNIVE (ku-niv') *v.i.* to wink at. [F., fr. L. *connivere*.]

CONNIVENT (ku-ni'vent) *a.* converging.

CONNIVER (ku-niv'er) *n.* one who connives.

CONNOISSEUR (kon-i-ser') *n.* a critical judge of the fine arts. [F. (now *connaisseur*), fr. (part.) *connoissant*, knowing. See COGNISANT.]

CONNOISSEURSHIP (kon-i-ser'ship) *n.* skill or taste of a connoisseur.

CONNOTATIVE (ko-nō'ta-tiv) *a.* implying; signifying.

CONNOTE (ko-nōt') *v.t.* to include in the meaning. [L., fr. *con* =*cum*, and NOTE.]

CONNUBIAL (ku-nū'bi-al) *a.* pertaining to marriage. [L., fr. *connubium*, wedlock.]

CONOID (kō'noid) *n.* anything that has a figure like a cone. [See CONE.]

CONOIDAL (kō-noi'dal) *a.* nearly conical.

CONQUER (kong'ker) *v.t.* to gain by force; overcome; surmount; —*v.i.* to be victorious. [O.F., fr. Late L., fr. L. *cum*, and *quærere*, seek.]   Conoid.

CONQUERABLE (kong'ker-a-bl) *a.* that may be subdued.

CONQUERINGLY (kong'ker-ing-li) *ad.* in a victorious manner.

CONQUEROR (kong'ker-er) *n.* one who subdues or conquers.

CONQUEST (kong'kwest) *n.* act of conquering; thing conquered.

CONSANGUINEOUS (kon-sang-gwin'ē-us) *a.* of the same blood.

CONSANGUINITY (kon-sang-gwin'i-ti) *n.* relation by blood. [L., fr. *cum*, and stem *sanguin-*, of *sanguis*, blood.]

CONSCIENCE (kon'shens) *n.* internal or self-knowledge; moral judgment; sense of duty. [F., fr. L. (acc.) *conscientiam*, consciousness, fr. *cum*, and SCIENCE.]

CONSCIENTIOUS (kon-shi-en'shus) *a.* regulated by conscience.

CONSCIENTIOUSLY (kon-shi-en'shus-li) *ad.* according to conscience.

CONSCIENTIOUSNESS (kon-shi-en'shus-nes) *n.* a scrupulous regard to conscience.

CONSCIONABLE (kon'shun-a-bl) *a.* reasonable. [See CONSCIENCE.]

CONSCIOUS (kon'shus) *a.* inwardly persuaded; having or done with the knowledge of. [See CONSCIENCE.]

CONSCIOUSLY (kon'shus-li) *ad.* with inward persuasion.

CONSCIOUSNESS (kon'shus-nes) *n.* perception of what passes in the mind.

CONSCRIPT (kon'skript) *n.* an enrolled militiaman;—*a.* written. [L. (part.) *conscriptus*, fr. *cum*, and SCRIPT.]

CONSCRIPTION (kun-skrip'shun) *n.* act of enrolling or registering.

CONSECRATE (kon'se-krāt) *v.t.* to set apart for a sacred use or office. [L. (part.) *consecratus*, hallowed, fr. *cum*, and *sacrare*.]

CONSECRATION (kon-se-krā'shun) *n.* the act of dedicating to sacred uses.

CONSECRATOR (kon'se-krā-ter) *n.* one who consecrates.

CONSECUTIVE (kun-sek'ū-tiv) *a.* following in order. [L. *consecutus*, having followed after, fr. *cum*, and *sequi*.]

CONSECUTIVELY (kun-sek'ū-tiv-li) *ad.* in succession.

CONSENT (kun-sent') *n.* agreement to something proposed;—*v.i.* to accord in mind; comply; yield. [F. *consentir*, fr. L. *cum*, and *sentire*, feel.]

CONSENTANEOUS (kon-sen-tā'nē-us) *a.* accordant. [See CONSENT.]

CONSENTIENT (kun-sen'shi-ent) *a.* agreeing in opinion. [See CONSENT.]

CONSEQUENCE (kon'se-kwens) *n.* that which follows; effect; inference; importance. [L. (part. stem) *consequent-*, following. See CONSECUTIVE.]

CONSEQUENT (kon'se-kwent) *a.* following.

CONSEQUENTIAL (kon-se-kwen'shal) *a.* conceited; important.

CONSEQUENTIALLY (kon-se-kwen'shal-i) *ad.* by consequence; pompously.

CONSEQUENTLY (kon'se-kwent-li) *ad.* by consequence.

CONSERVATION (kon-ser-vī'shun) *n.* preservation from loss or injury.

CONSERVATISM (kun-ser'va-tizm) *n.* the principles of the Conservative party.

CONSERVATIVE (kun-ser'va-tiv) *a.* tending to or desiring to preserve;—*n.* one opposed to political changes; a Tory.

CONSERVATOIRE (kon-ser-va-twor') *n.* a public school for music and the fine arts. [F.]

CONSERVATOR (kun-ser'va-ter) *n.* a preserver.

CONSERVATORY (kun-ser'va-tur-i) *a.* tending to preserve;—*n.* a greenhouse for exotic plants.

CONSERVE (kon'serv) *n.* a sweetmeat;—(kun-serv') *v.t.* to keep whole or sound; candy or pickle, as fruit. [L., fr. *cum*, and SERVE.]

CONSIDER (kun-sid'er) *v.t.* or *i.* to think upon with care; deliberate; take into account. [O.F., fr. L. *considerare*, originally gaze at the stars, fr. *con* =*cum*, and stem *sider-*, of *sidus*, star.]

CONSIDERABLE (kun-sid'er-a-bl) *a.* worthy of regard; moderately large.

CONSIDERABLY (kun-sid'er-a-bli) *ad.* in a considerable degree.

CONSIDERATE (kun-sid'er-āt) *a.* given to reflection; thoughtful; prudent.

CONSIDERATELY (kun-sid'er-āt-li) *ad.* with serious thought.

CONSIDERATENESS (kun-sid'er-āt-nes) *n.* quality of being considerate.

CONSIDERATION (kun-sid-er-ā'shun) *n.* serious thought; prudence; importance; motive or reason; equivalent.

CONSIDERING (kun-sid'er-ing) *prp.* regarding; having regard to.

CONSIDERINGLY (kun-sid'er-ing-li) *ad.* with thought or deliberation.

CONSIGN (kun-sin') *v.t.* to transfer to another; entrust; send to an agent. [F., fr. L. *consignare*, to attest.]

CONSIGNEE (kon-si-nē') *n.* one to whom a thing is consigned.

CONSIGNER (kun-si'ner) *n.* one who commits to another in trust or for sale.

CONSIGNMENT (kun-sin'ment) *n.* act of consigning; goods consigned.

CONSIMILITUDE (kon-si-mil'i-tūd) *n.* resemblance. [L. *con* =*cum*, and *similis*, like.]

CONSIST (kun-sist') *v.i.* to be made up of; be fixed; agree. [L. *con* =*cum*, and *sisto*, stand.]

CONSISTENCE (kun-sis'tens) *n.* fixed state.

CONSISTENT (kun-sis'tent) *a.* agreeing; firm; solid.

CONSISTENTLY (kun-sis'tent-li) *ad.* without contradiction.

Fāte, fär, ado; mē, her; mine; nōte; tūne; mōōn.

CONSISTORIAL (kon-sis-tō'ri-al) a. relating to a consistory. [See CONSIST.]

CONSISTORY (kon'sis-tur-i) n. a spiritual court; an assembly or council. [See CONSIST.]

CONSOCIATION (kun-sō-shi-ā'shun) n. a meeting of the clergy and delegates. [L. con = cum, and sociare, to associate, fr. socius, a companion.]

CONSOLABLE (kun-sōl'a-bl) a. admitting comfort.

CONSOLATION (kon-sō-lā'shun) a. alleviation of misery or distress; comfort; cause of comfort.

CONSOLATORY (kon-sol'a-tur-i) a. tending to the alleviation of misery.

CONSOLE (kun-sōl') v.t. to comfort; cheer under sorrow. [L. con, intensive, and solari, comfort.]

CONSOLE (kon'sōl) n. a bracket or projecting ornament to support a cornice, bust, or vase. [F. console; perhaps conn. with CONSOLIDATE.]

CONSOLIDANT (kun-sol'i-dant) a. uniting and healing wounds;—n. a medicine that unites wounded flesh.

CONSOLIDATE (kun-sol'i-dāt) v.t. or i. to make or grow solid. [L. consolidare, fr. solidus, firm.]

CONSOLIDATION (kun-sol-i-dā'shun) n. act of making hard or firm.

CONSOLIDATIVE (kun-sol'i-dā-tiv) a. tending to consolidate; healing.

CONSOLS (kon'solz) n.pl. certain funds in the British stock market bearing two-and-a-half per cent. interest. [Short for Consolidated Annuities.]

CONSONANCE (kon'sō-nans) n. agreement of sounds; concord.

CONSONANT (kon'sō-nant) a. agreeable; consistent;—n. a letter which cannot be sounded by itself. [F., fr. L. (acc.) consonantem, fr. cum, and SONANT.]

CONSONANTLY (kon'sō-nant-li) ad. consistently; agreeably.

CONSONOUS (kon'sō-nus) a. agreeing in sound. [See CONSONANT.]

CONSORT (kon'sort) n. a husband or wife; companion; partner;—(kun-sort') v.i. to associate. [F., fr. L. (acc.) consortem, partner, fr. cum, and stem sort-, of sors, lot.]

CONSPICUOUS (kun-spik'ū-us) a. obvious to the sight; eminent; prominent. [L. conspicuus, fr. cum, perfectly, and specere, see.]

CONSPICUOUSLY (kun-spik'ū-us-li) ad. evidently; eminently.

CONSPICUOUSNESS (kun-spik'ū-us-nes) n. openness to view; clearness.

CONSPIRACY (kun-spir'a-si) n. a plot.

CONSPIRATION (kun-spir-ā'shun) n. concurrence of things to the same end.

CONSPIRATOR (kun-spir'a-ter) n. a plotter of evil.

CONSPIRE (kun-spir') v.i. to unite for an evil purpose. [L. con, together, and spiro, breathe.]

CONSPIRER (kun-spir'er) n. a plotter.

CONSTABLE (kun'sta-bl) n. an officer of the peace. [O.F. conestable = F. connétable, fr. L. comes stabuli, Count of the stable.]

CONSTABLESHIP (kun'sta-bl-ship) n. office of a constable.

CONSTABULARY (kun-stab'ū-lar-i) n. pertaining to constables;—n. the body of constables.

CONSTANCY (kon'stan-si) n. firmness of mind; stability. [See CONSTANT.]

CONSTANT (kon'stant) a. firm; unchanging; faithful in affection;—n. a fixed law or quantity. [F., fr. L. (acc.) constantem, standing together, fr. cum, and stare, stand.]

CONSTANTLY (kon'stant-li) ad. invariably; firmly.

CONSTELLATION (kon-ste-lā'shun) n. a cluster of fixed stars. [F., fr. L., fr. cum, and stellatus, starred, fr. stella, star.]

CONSTERNATION (kon-ster-nā'shun) n. terror that confounds. [F., fr. L., fr. (part.) consternatus, frightened, fr. con, and sternere, strew.]

CONSTIPATE (kon'sti-pāt) v.t. to compress; shut up; make costive. [L. (part.) constipatus, fr. cum, and stipare, pack. Doublet of COSTIVE.] [ness.

CONSTIPATION (kon-sti-pā'shun) n. costive-

CONSTITUENCY (kon-stit'ū-en-si) n. the whole body of electors.

CONSTITUENT (kun-stit'ū-ent) a. serving to form or compose; elementary;—n. an essential part; an elector.

CONSTITUTE (kon'sti-tūt) v.t. to set up; establish; compose; elect. [L. (part.) constitutus, set together, fr. con = cum, and -stituere = statuere. See STATUE.]

CONSTITUTION (kon-sti-tū'shun) n. frame of body, mind, or government.

CONSTITUTIONAL (kon-sti-tū'shun-al) a. consistent with the constitution;—n. a walk for the sake of health.

CONSTITUTIONALISM (kon-sti-tū'shun-al-ism) n. adherence to the constitution; conservatism.

CONSTITUTIONALIST (kon-sti-tū-shun'al-ist) n. an adherent to a constitution.

CONSTITUTIONALITY (kon-sti-tū-shun-al'i-ti) n. consistency with the constitution.

CONSTITUTIONALLY (kon-sti-tū'shun-al-i) ad. in consistency with the constitution.

CONSTITUTIVE (kon'sti-tū-tiv) a. that which composes, enacts, or establishes.

CONSTRAIN (kun-strān') v.t. to urge with force; compel; hold back; confine. [O.F. constraindre = F. contraindre, fr. L. constringere, fr. cum, and stringere, STRAIN.]

CONSTRAINABLE (kun-strā'na-bl) a. that may be constrained.

CONSTRAINT (kun-strānt') n. compulsion; confinement.

CONSTRICT (kun-strikt') v.t. to bind; cramp. [L. (part.) constrictus, drawn together, fr. constringere, CONSTRAIN.]

CONSTRICTION (kun-strik'shun) n. contraction; compression.

CONSTRICTOR (kun-strik'ter) n. a muscle which draws together; a kind of serpent.

CONSTRINGENT (kun-strin'jent) a. binding. [See CONSTRAIN.]

CONSTRUCT (kun-strukt') v.t. to build; compose; devise. [L. (part.) constructus, built, fr. construere. Doublet of CONSTRUE.]

CONSTRUCTION (kun-struk'shun) n. act of forming; an edifice; structure; act of construing; meaning.

CONSTRUCTIONIST (kun-struk'shun-ist) n. one who construes a public instrument.

CONSTRUCTIVE (kun-struk'tiv) a. by construction; deduced.

CONSTRUCTIVELY (kun-struk'tiv-li) ad. by inference or interpretation.

CONSTRUCTIVENESS (kun-strukt'iv-nes) n. the faculty which constructs.

CONSTRUE (kon'strōō) v.t. to explain; arrange the words of a sentence so that the meaning may be obvious. [L. construere, fr. cum, and struere, pile up. Doublet of CONSTRUCT.]

CONSUBSTANTIATE (kon-sub-stan'shi-āt) v.t. to unite in one substance or nature. [L. con = cum, and SUBSTANCE.]

CONSUBSTANTIAL (kon-sub-stan'shal) a. having the same substance. [See CONSUBSTANTIATE.]

CONSUBSTANTIALITY (kon-sub-stan-shi-al'i-ti) n. participation in the same substance or nature.

CONSUBSTANTIATION (kon-sub-stan-shi-ā'shun) n. union of the body of Christ with the sacramental elements.

Fāte, fär, ado; mē, her; mine; nōte; tūne; mōōn.

CONSUL (kon'sul) *n.* the chief magistrate in ancient Rome; an officer appointed by government to reside in foreign ports to superintend the commerce of his own country. [L.]

CONSULAGE (kon'sul-aj) *n.* duty or tax levied for the support of a consul. [See CONSUL.]

CONSULAR (kon'sū-lar) *a.* pertaining to a consul. [See CONSUL.]

CONSULATE (kon'sū-lāt) *n.* the office, or jurisdiction, or residence of a consul; his term of office.

CONSULSHIP (kon'sul-ship) *n.* the office of a consul.

CONSULT (kun-sult') *v.t.* or *i.* to ask advice of; take counsel together; consider. [F., fr. L., fr. (part.) *consultus*, consulted, fr. *consulere*, of uncertain etym.]

CONSULTATION (kon-sul-tā'shun) *n.* act of consulting; a meeting of physicians or lawyers to consult.

CONSULTER (kun-sul'ter) *n.* one who consults.

CONSULTIVE (kun-sul'tiv) *a.* deliberate; done advisedly.

CONSUMABLE (kun-sū'ma-bl) *a.* that may be consumed.

CONSUME (kun-sūm') *v.t.* or *i.* to waste; spend. [L., fr. *con* = *cum*, altogether, and *sumere*, take.]

CONSUMER (kun-sū'mer) *n.* one who consumes.

CONSUMMATE (kon'sūm-āt) *v.t.* to complete; perfect; — (kun-sum'āt) *a.* accomplished; complete. [L (part.) *consummatus*, originally added together, fr. *cum*, and *summare*, fr. *summa*, SUM.]

CONSUMMATION (kon-sum-ā'shun) *n.* completion; termination.

CONSUMPTION (kun-sum'shun) *n.* a wasting disease of the lungs; use; expenditure. [See CONSUME.]

CONSUMPTIVE (kun-sum'tiv) *a.* inclined to consumption.

CONSUMPTIVENESS (kun-sum'tiv-nes) *n.* tendency to consumption.

CONTACT (kon'takt) *n.* touch; close union. [L. (part.) *contactus*, fr. *contingere*. See CONTINGENT.]

CONTAGION (kun-tā'jun) *n.* communication of disease by contact; infection; noxious influence. [F fr. L. (acc.) *contagionem*, a touching, fr. *con* = *cum*, and *tangere*, touch.]

CONTAGIOUS (kun-tā'jus) *a.* having the quality of infecting.

CONTAIN (kun-tān') *v.t.* to hold; comprise. [O.F., fr. L. *continere*, hold together, fr. *cum*, and *tenere*.]

CONTAINABLE (kun-tā'na-bl) *a.* that may be contained.

CONTAMINATE (kun-tam'i-nāt) *v.t.* to defile; corrupt; — *a.* tainted; defiled. [L., fr. stem *contamin-*, of *contamen* (= *contagmen*), CONTAGION.]

CONTAMINATION (kun-tam-i-nā'shun) *n.* pollution.

CONTEMN (kun-tem') *v.t.* to despise; scorn; reject. [F., fr. L. *contemnere*, despise, fr. *con* = *cum*, thoroughly, and *temnere*, place low value upon.]

CONTEMPER (kun-tem'per) *v.t.* to temper; reduce by mixture. [L. *contemperare*, blend together.]

CONTEMPERATION (kun-tem-pe-rā'shun) *n.* proportionate mixture.

CONTEMPLATE (kun-tem'plāt) *v.t.* or *i.* to meditate; consider; design; intend. [L. *contemplatus*, having observed, fr. *con* = *cum*, and *templum*, temple.]

CONTEMPLATION (kon-tem-plā'shun) *n.* serious and continued thought.

CONTEMPLATIVE (kun-tem'pla-tiv) *a.* given to thought.

CONTEMPLATIVELY (kun-tem'pla-tiv-li) *ad.* thoughtfully; studiously.

CONTEMPLATIVENESS (kun-tem'pla-tiv-nes) *n.* disposition to be thoughtful.

CONTEMPLATOR (kon'tem-plā-ter) *n.* one engaged in deep thought.

CONTEMPORANEOUS (kun-tem-pō-rā'nē-us) *a.* living or being at the same time.

CONTEMPORARY (kon-tem'pō-ra-ri) *a.* living, acting, or happening at the same time. [L. *con* = *cum*, and TEMPORARY.]

CONTEMPT (kun-temt') *n.* act of despising; disdain; disgrace; disobedience of the rules of a court. [See CONTEMN.]

CONTEMPTIBLE (kun-tem'ti-bl) *a.* mean.

CONTEMPTIBLY (kun-tem'ti-bli) *ad.* meanly; despicably.

CONTEMPTUOUS (kun-tem'tū-us) *a.* scornful.

CONTEMPTUOUSLY (kun-tem'tū-us-li) *ad.* in a scornful manner.

CONTEND (kun-tend') *v.i.* to fight with or against; strive for; dispute. [L. *contendere*, strain after, fr. *con* = *cum*, and TEND.]

CONTENDER (kun-ten'der) *n.* a combatant.

CONTENDING (kun-ten'ding) *a.* striving for; opposing; rival.

CONTENT (kon'tent) *n.* that which is contained; extent; area; — *pl.* an index of heads in a book. [L. (part.) *contentus*, contained.]

CONTENT (kun-tent') *a.* satisfied; quiet; — *n.* satisfaction of mind; — *v.t.* to satisfy; please. [F., fr. L. (part.) *contentus*, contained, fr. *continere*. See CONTAIN.]

CONTENTED (kun-ten'ted) *a.* satisfied; pleased.

CONTENTEDNESS (kun-ten'ted-nes) *n.* state of being content.

CONTENTION (kun-ten'shun) *n.* strife; debate. [See CONTEND.]

CONTENTIOUS (kun-ten'shus) *a.* given to strife; quarrelsome.

CONTENTIOUSLY (kun-ten'shus-li) *ad.* in a quarrelsome manner.

CONTENTIOUSNESS (kun-ten'shus-nes) *n.* disposition to contend or debate.

CONTENTMENT (kun-tent'ment) *n.* satisfaction of mind; gratification.

CONTERMINABLE (kon-ter'mi-na-bl) *a.* capable of the same bounds. [L. *conterminus*, neighbouring, fr. *con* = *cum*, and *terminus*, a boundary.]

CONTERMINATE (kon-ter'mi-nāt) *a.* having the same bounds.

CONTERMINOUS (kon-ter'mi-nus) *a.* bordering upon; contiguous.

CONTEST (kon'test) *n.* strife in arms; fight; strife in argument; dispute; — (kun-test') *v.t.* to strive to gain or to hold; controvert; resist; — *v.i.* to contend; dispute. [F. *contester*, fr. L. *contestari*, to cite to a lawsuit fr. *con* = *cum*, and *testis*, a witness.]

CONTESTABLE (kun-tes'ta-bl) *a.* that may be contested.

CONTEXT (kon'tekst) *n.* order of discourse; the parts that precede and follow a sentence. [L. (part.) *contextus*, knit together, fr. *con* = *cum*, and *texere*, weave.]

CONTIGUITY (kon-ti-gū'i-ti) *n.* contact; nearness in situation or place. [L. *contiguus*, fr. *con* = *cum*, and *tangere*, touch.]

CONTIGUOUS (kun-tig'ū-us) *a.* joining at the surface or border.

CONTIGUOUSLY (kun-tig'ū-us-li) *ad.* in close junction.

CONTIGUOUSNESS (kun-tig'ū-us-nes) *n.* close union or nearness.

CONTINENCE (kon'ti-nens) *n.* forbearance of sensual indulgence. [See CONTINENT.]

CONTINENT (kon'ti-nent) *a.* containing; self-restraining; chaste; temperate; — *n.* a great division of the earth; the mainland of Europe. [F., fr. L. (acc.) *continentem*, containing.]

CONTINENTAL (kon-ti-nen'tal) *a.* pertaining to a continent.

CONTINENTLY (kon'ti-nent-li) *ad.* temperately.

CONTINGENCY (kun-tin'jen-si) n. casual event; accident; possibility of happening. [See **CONTINGENT**.]

CONTINGENT (kun-tin'jent) a. accidental; dependent upon;—n. chance; proportion of troops furnished by a contracting power. [L. (part. stem) *contingent-*, touching, happening, fr. *con* = *cum*, and *tingere* = *tangere*. [See **TANGENT**.]

CONTINGENTLY (kun-tin'jent-li) ad. by chance.

CONTINUABLE (kun-tin'ū-a-bl) a. that may be continued.

CONTINUAL (kun-tin'ū-al) a. uninterrupted.

CONTINUALLY (kun-tin'ū-al-i) ad. without intermission.

CONTINUANCE (kun-tin'ū-ans) n. duration; permanence; stay; continuation.

CONTINUATION (kun-tin-ū-ā'shun) n. constant succession; extension; prolongation. [L. (part.) *continuatus*, made all in one.]

CONTINUATOR (kun-tin'ū-ā-ter) n. one who continues.

CONTINUE (kun-tin'ū) v.i. to remain; stay; —v.t. to protect; persevere in. [F. *continuer*, fr. L. *continuare*.]

CONTINUER (kun-tin'ū-er) n. one who continues.

CONTINUINGLY (kon-tin'ū-ing-li) ad. without interruption.

CONTINUITY (kon-ti-nū'i-ti) n. uninterrupted connection. [L. (acc.) *continuitatem*.]

CONTINUOUS (kun-tin'ū-us) a. closely united as it were into one. [L. *continuus*, fr. *continere*, hold together.]

CONTINUOUSLY (kun-tin'ū-us-li) ad. in continuation.

CONTINUOUSNESS (kun-tin'ū-us-nes) n. quality of being continuous.

CONTORT (kun-tort') v.t. to twist; writhe. [L. (part.) *contortus*, twisted, fr. *con* = *cum* and *torquere*, twist.]

CONTORTION (kun-tor'shun) n. a twisting; a wry motion; partial dislocation.

CONTORTIONIST (kun-tor'shun-ist) n. one who practises contortions.

CONTOUR (kon-tóór') n. the general outline of a figure. [F., fr. It., fr. L. *con* = *cum*, and *tornare*, **TURN**.]

CONTRA (kon'tra) a Latin preposition signifying *against*.

CONTRABAND (kon'tra-band) a. prohibited; —n. illegal trade. [Fr. It., fr. L. *contra*, against, and Late L. *bannum*, **BAN**.]

CONTRABANDIST (kon'tra-ban-dist) n. a smuggler. [See **CONTRABAND**.]

CONTRACT (kon'trakt) n. an agreement or bargain; a betrothment; a formal writing or deed of agreement. [F., fr. L. (acc.) *contractum*, an agreement.]

CONTRACT (kun-trakt') v.t. to draw together or nearer; incur; shorten;—v.i. to shrink; bargain. [L. (part.) *contractus*, drawn together, fr. *con* = *cum*, and **TRACT**.]

CONTRACTED (kun-trak'ted) a. narrow; selfish.

CONTRACTEDNESS (kun-trak'ted-nes)n.state of being contracted; narrowness.

CONTRACTIBILITY (kun-trak-ti-bil'i-ti) n. quality of suffering contraction.

CONTRACTIBLE (kun-trak'ti-bl) a. that may contract.

CONTRACTILE (kun-trak'til) a. capable of contracting.

CONTRACTILITY (kon-trak-til'i-ti) n. the quality of contracting or shrinking.

CONTRACTION (kun-trak'shun) n. a shrinking; a shortening. [L. (acc.) *contractionem*.]

CONTRACTOR (kun-trak'ter) n. one who contracts.

CONTRA-DANCE (kon'tra-dans) n. a dance with partners opposite, commonly termed **COUNTRY-DANCE**. [L. *contra*, against, fr. F. *contre-danse*, imit. fr. E. *Country Dance*.]

CONTRADICT (kon-tra-dikt') v.t. to oppose verbally; gainsay; deny. [L. (part.) *contradictus*, spoken against, fr. *contra*, and *dicere*.]

CONTRADICTION (kon-tra-dik'shun) n. a denying.

CONTRADICTIOUS (kon-tra-dik'shus) a. inclined to contradict.

CONTRADICTORILY (kon-tra-dik'tur-i-li) ad. in a contradictory manner.

CONTRADICTORINESS (kon-tra-dik'tur-i-nes) n. disposition to contradict.

CONTRADICTORY (kon-tra-dik'tur-i) a. inconsistent; disagreeing.

CONTRADISTINCT (kon-tra-dis-tingkt') a. distinguished by opposite qualities.

CONTRADISTINCTION (kon-tra-dis-tingk'-shun) n. distinction by opposites.

CONTRADISTINGUISH (kon-tra-dis-ting'-gwish) v.t. to distinguish by opposites. [L. *contra*, against, and **DISTINGUISH**.]

CONTRALTO (kun-tral'tō) n. the counter-tenor. [It., fr. L. *contra*, against, and **ALTO**.]

CONTRARIES (kon'tra-riz) n.pl. things of opposite qualities. [See **CONTRARY**.]

CONTRARIETY (kon-tra-rī'et-i) n. opposition; inconsistency.

CONTRARIOUS (kon-trā'ri-us) a. opposed to. [See **CONTRARY**.]

CONTRARIWISE (kon'tra-ri-wīz) ad. on the contrary; oppositely.

CONTRARY (kon'tra-ri) a. in direct opposition. [L. *contrarius*, fr. *contra*, against.]

CONTRAST (kon'trast) n. opposition in things; —(kun-trast') v.t. or i. to place or stand in opposition. [F. *contraster*, fr. L. *contra*, in opposition to, and *stare*, stand.]

CONTRAVENE (kon-tra-vēn') v.t. to oppose; obstruct; transgress. [L. *contra*, in opposition to, and *venire*, come.]

CONTRAVENTION (kon-tra-ven'shun) n. opposition; violation.

CONTRAVERSION (kon-tra-ver'shun) n a turning to the opposite side. [L. *contra*, in opposition to, and *vertere*, turn.]

CONTRETEMPS (kong-tr-tong') n. an unexpected accident. [F.]

CONTRIBUTABLE (kun-trib'ū-ta-bl) a. that may be contributed.

CONTRIBUTARY (kun-trib'ū-ta-ri) a. adding something to; auxiliary.

CONTRIBUTE (kun-trib'ūt) v.t. to give for a common purpose; pay a share;—v.i. to bear a part in; aid. [L. *con* = *cum*, and *tribuere*, grant, impart.]

CONTRIBUTION (kon-tri-bū'shun) n. act of contributing; sum given. [L. (acc.) *contributionem*.]

CONTRIBUTIVE (kun-trib'ū-tiv) a. tending to promote.

CONTRIBUTOR (kun-trib'ū-ter) n. one who contributes.

CONTRIBUTORY (kun-trib'ū-tur-i) a. advancing the same end.

CONTRITE (kon'trīt) a. worn with sorrow; penitent. [F. *contrit*, fr. L. *contritus*, worn out, fr. *con* = *cum*, and *terere*, rub.]

CONTRITELY (kon-trīt'li) ad. ; a contrite manner.

CONTRITENESS (kon-trīt'nes) n. state of being contrite. [sin.

CONTRITION (kun-trish'un) n. deep sorrow for **CONTRIVABLE** (kun-trī va-bl) a. that may be contrived.

CONTRIVANCE (kun-trī-vans) n. scheme; thing contrived.

CONTRIVE (kun-trīv') v.t. to invent; project. [M.E. *controven*, fr. O.F. *controver*, find out. See **TROVER**.]

CONTRIVER (kun-trī'ver) n. an inventor.

CONTROL (kun-trōl') n. power to govern:— v.t. to restrain; govern. [Fr. O.F. *controrole* = F. *contrôle*, double register, fr. L. *contra*, against, and **ROLL**.]

CONTROLLABLE (kun-trō'lạ-bl) *a.* subject to control.

CONTROLLER (kun-trō'lẹr) *n.* one who controls; an officer who checks other officers by a counter register of accounts.

CONTROLLERSHIP (kun-trō'lẹr-ship) *n.* the office of controller.

CONTROVERSIAL (kon-trō-vẹr'shạl) *a.* relating to controversy. [See CONTROVERT.]

CONTROVERSIALIST (kon-trō-vẹr'shạl-ist) *n.* one engaged in controversy.

CONTROVERSIALLY (kon-trō-vẹr'shạl-i) *ad.* in a controversial manner.

CONTROVERSY (kon'trō-vẹr-si) *n.* a discussion or dis u a on in writing; the matter disputed; t ti

CONTROVERT (kon'trō-vert) *v.t.* to dispute; deny; refute. [L. *contro* = *contra*, against, and *vertere*, turn.]

CONTROVERTIBLE (kon-trō-vẹr'ti-bl) *a.* that may be controverted.

CONTROVERTIBLY (kon-trō-vẹr'ti-bli) *ad.* in a controvertible manner.

CONTROVERTIST (kon-trō-vẹr'tist) *n.* a disputant.

CONTUMACIOUS (kon-tū-mā'shus) *a.* obstinate.

CONTUMACIOUSLY (kon-tū-mā'shus-li) *ad.* with obstinacy.

CONTUMACIOUSNESS (kon-tū-mā'shus-nes) *n.* stubbornness; obstinacy.

CONTUMACY (kon'tū-mạ-si) *n.* unyielding resistance to rightful authority; obstinacy. [F., fr. L. (acc.) *contumaciem*, fr. stem *contumaci-*. of *contumax*, stubborn; conn. with *tumere*, swell.]

CONTUMELIOUS (kon-tū-mē'li-us) *a.* reproachful; abusive; insolent. [See CONTUMELY.]

CONTUMELIOUSLY (kon-tū-mē'li-us-li) *ad.* reproachfully; insolently.

CONTUMELY (kon'tū-me-li) *n.* contemptuous language; reproach. [L. *contumelia*. Cf. CONTUMACY.]

CONTUSE (kon-tūz') *v.t.* to bruise or injure by beating. [L. *contusus*, bruised, fr. *con* = *cum*, thoroughly, and *tundere*, bruise.]

CONTUSION (kun-tū'zhun) *n.* a bruise in the flesh.

CONUNDRUM (kō-nun'drum) *n.* a riddle turning on a point of resemblance between things very unlike. [Etym. doubtful.]

CONVALESCE (kon-vạ-les') *v.i.* to recover health. [L. *convalescere*, fr. *con* = *cum*, thoroughly, and *valere*, be strong.]

CONVALESCENCE (kon-vạ-les'ens) *n.* recovery from sickness.

CONVALESCENT (kon-vạ-les'ent) *a.* recovering health.

CONVECTION (kun-vek'shun) *n.* act or process of transmission, esp. of heat, by means of currents in liquids or gases. [L. (part.) *convectus*, carried together, fr. *con* = *cum*, and *vehere*, carry.]

CONVENABLE (kun-vē'nạ-bl) *a.* that may be convened. [See CONVENE.]

CONVENE (kun-vēn') *v.t.* to call together; — *v.i.* to assemble. [F. *convenir*, fr. L. *con* = *cum*, and *venire*, come.]

CONVENIENCE (kun-vēn'yens) *n.* accommodation; fitness; commodiousness.

CONVENIENT (kon'vēn'yent) *a.* fit; suitable.

CONVENIENTLY (kon-vēn'yent-li) *ad.* suitably.

CONVENT (kon'vent) *n.* a religious house. [L. *conventus*, assembly, fr. *convenire*, CONVENE.]

CONVENTICLE (kun-ven'ti-kl) *n.* a dissenter's meeting-house; an assembly for worship. [L. *conventiculum*, small assembly, fr. CONVENT.]

CONVENTION (kun-ven'shun) *n.* an assembly; a compact; temporary treaty. [L. (acc.) *conventionem*, meeting, agreement, fr. CONVENT.]

CONVENTIONAL (kun-ven'shun-ạl) *a.* agreed on; customary.

CONVENTIONALISE (kun-ven'shun-ạl-īz) *v.t.* to form or represent according to conventional work.

CONVENTIONALISM (kun-ven'shun-ạl-izm) *n.* that which is received by tacit agreement and common usage.

CONVENTIONALITY (kun-ven-shun-al'i-ti) *n.* anything established by the customary usage of so..e.y.

CONVENTIONALLY (kun-ven'shun-ạl-i) *ad.* in a conventional manner.

CONVENTUAL (kun-ven'tū-ạl) *a.* belonging to a convent; — *n.* a monk; a nun.

CONVERGE (kun-vẹrj') *v.i.* to tend toward one point. [L. *con* = *cum*, and VERGE.]

CONVERGENCE (kun-vẹr'jens) *n.* tendency to one point.

CONVERGENT (kun-vẹr'jent) *a.* tending to a point.

CONVERSABLE (kun-vẹr'sạ-bl) *a.* inclined to converse; affable; sociable.

CONVERSABLY (kun-vẹr'sạ-bli) *ad.* in a conversable manner.

CONVERSANT (kon'vẹr-sạnt) *a.* familiar with.

CONVERSATION (kon-vẹr-sa'shun) *n.* familiar discourse.

CONVERSATIONAL (kon-vẹr-sā'shun-ạl) *a.* pertaining to conversation.

CONVERSAZIONE (kon-vẹr-sat-si-ō'nā) *n.* assembly for conversation, chiefly on literature. *pl.* CONVERSAZIONI. [It.]

CONVERSE (kun-vẹrs') *v.i.* to discourse; talk familiarly. [F., fr. L. *conversari*, associate with, fr. (part.) *conversus*, turned towards. See CONVERT.]

CONVERSELY (kun-vẹrs'li) *ad.* by change of order.

CONVERSIBLE (kun-vẹr'si-bl) *a.* that may be made converse.

CONVERSION (kun-vẹr'shun) *n.* act of turning or changing; alteration.

CONVERT (kon'vẹrt) *n.* one who has changed his opinions or religion; — (kun-vẹrt') *v.t.* to change to another form or state. [L. *convertere*, turn round, alter, fr. *con* = *cum*, entirely, and *vertere*, turn.]

CONVERTER (kun-vẹr'tẹr) *n.* one who converts.

CONVERTIBILITY (kun-vẹr-ti-bil'i-ti) *n.* capability of being converted.

CONVERTIBLE (kun-vẹr'ti-bl) *a.* that may be interchanged.

CONVEX (kon'veks) *a.* roundish on the outside. [L. *convexus*, arched, fr. *con* = *cum*, together, and *vehere*, carry.]

CONVEXED (kon'vekst) *a.* made convex.

CONVEXITY (kon-vek'si-ti) *n.* spherical form on the outside.

CONVEXLY (kon'veks-li) *ad.* in a convex form.

CONVEXO-CONCAVE (kon-vek'sō-kon-kāv) *a.* convex on one side, concave on the other. [Fr. CONVEX and CONCAVE.]

CONVEXO-PLANE (kon-vek'so-plān) *a.* convex on one side, plane on the other. [CONVEX, and L. *planus*, level.]

CONVEY (kun-vā') *v.t.* to carry; transmit; make over to; impart; steal. [O.F. *convener* = F. *convoyer*. Doublet of CONVOY.]

CONVEYABLE (kun-vā'ạ-bl) *a.* that may be conveyed. [See CONVEY.]

CONVEYANCE (kun-vā'ạns) *n.* act of conveying; that which conveys.

CONVEYANCER (kun-vā'ạn-sẹr) *n.* one who draws deeds, etc.

CONVEYANCING (kun-vā'ạn-sing) *n.* the business of a conveyancer.

CONVEYER (kun-vā'ẹr) *n.* one who conveys or carries.

CONVICT (kon'vikt) *n.* a person found guilty of crime; (kun-vikt') *v.t.* to prove to be guilty; find guilty; convince.

CONVICTION (kun-vik'shun) *n.* a proving guilty; state of being convinced. [L. *convictus*, overcome, fr. *convincere*, CONVINCE.]

CONVICTIVE (kun-vik'tiv) *a.* adapted to convict.

CONVINCE (kun-vins') *v.t.* to satisfy by evidence; persuade; refute. [L. *convincere*, fr. *con* = *cum*, thoroughly, and *vincere*, conquer.]

CONVINCEMENT (kun-vins'ment) *n.* satisfaction by proof.

CONVINCIBLE (kun-vin'si-bl) *a.* capable of being convinced.

CONVINCINGLY (kun-vin'sing-li) *ad.* in a manner to persuade or satisfy.

CONVIVIAL (kun-viv'i-al) *a.* festive; jovial; social. [L. *convivium*, banquet, fr. L. *con* = *cum*, thoroughly, and *vivere*, live.]

CONVIVIALITY (kun-viv-i-al'i-ti) *n.* a festive disposition; mirth and jollity at a feast.

CONVOCATE (kon'vō-kāt) *v.t.* to call together. [F. *convoquer*, fr. L. *convocare*, fr. *con* = *cum*, and *vocare*, call.]

CONVOCATION (kon-vō-kā'shun) *n.* act of convoking; an assembly of the clergy, or heads of a university.

CONVOKE (kun-vōk') *v.t.* to call together by summons; convene.

CONVOLUTION (kon-vō-lū'shun) *n.* the act of rolling together. [L. (part.) *convolulus*, fr. *con* = *cum*, and *volvere*, roll.]

CONVOLVE (kun-volv') *v.t.* to roll together.

CONVOLVULUS (kun-vol'vū-lus) *n.* a genus of plants; bindweed. [L.]

CONVOY (kun-voi') *v.t.* to accompany for defence;—(kon'voi) *n.* attendance for protection; a protecting force; the ships protected. [F. *convoyer*, fr. *con* = *cum*, and *voie*, a way, fr. L. (acc.) *viam*. Doublet of CONVEY.]

CONVULSE (kun-vuls') *v.t.* to affect by violent motion. [L. (part.) *convulsus*, rent, fr. *con* = *cum* thoroughly, and *vellere*, to pluck.]

CONVULSION (kun-vul'shun) *n.* a violent spasm; any irregular commotion.

CONVULSIONARY (kun-vul'shun-a-ri) *a.* relating to convulsions. Also CONVULSIONAL.

CONVULSIVE (kun-vul'siv) *a.* producing convulsion.

CONVULSIVELY (kun-vul'siv-li) *ad.* in a convulsive manner.

CONY (kō'ni) *n.* a rabbit. Also CONEY. [M.E. *coni*, fr. O.F. *conil*, fr. L. (acc.) *cuniculum*, little.]

COO (kōō) *v.i.* to make a noise as a dove. [Imit.]

COOK (kook) *n.* one who dresses victuals;—*v.t.* to prepare food for the table. [O.E. *coc*, fr. L. *coquus*, a cook.]

COOKERY (kook'e-ri) *n.* act of dressing victuals. [See COOK.]

COOL (kōōl) *a.* somewhat cold; lacking warmth; calm; deliberate; indifferent;—*v.t.* to make moderately cold;—*v.i.* to grow cool. [O.E. *col*. Cf. Ger. *kühl*.]

COOLER (kōō'ler) *n.* a vessel for cooling; that which cools.

COOLIE (kōō'li) *n.* an East India carrier. [Perh. Tamil.]

COOLISH (kōō'lish) *a.* somewhat cool.

COOLLY (kōōl'li) *ad.* without heat.

COOLNESS (kōōl'nes) *n.* moderate cold.

COOMB (kōōm) *n.* a dry measure of four bushels. [O.E. *cumb*.]

COOMBE (kōōm) *n.* a valley between hills. Also COMBE. [O.E. *cumb*.]

COOP (kōōp) *n.* a cage for fowls, etc.; a barrel;—*v.t.* to cage; shut up. [O.E. *cype*, jar, fr. L. *cupa*, tub. See CUP.]

COOPER (kōō'per) *n.* a maker of casks;—*v.t.* to mend or repair. [See COOP.]

COOPERAGE (kōō'per-āj) *n.* a cooper's workshop; price for cooper's work.

CO-OPERANT (kō-op'e-rant) *a.* co-operating.

CO-OPERATE (kō-op'e-rāt) *v.i.* to work together. [L. *co* = *cum*, and OPERATE.]

CO-OPERATION (kō-op-e-rā'shun) *n.* joint labour.

CO-OPERATIVE (kō-op'e-rā-tiv) *a.* promoting the same end.

CO-OPERATOR (kō-op'e-rā-ter) *n.* one who co-operates with others.

CO-ORDINATE (kō-or'di-nāt) *a.* holding the same rank or degree;—*v.t.* to make equal. [L. *co* = *cum*, and ORDINATE.]

CO-ORDINATELY (kō-or'di-nāt-li) *ad.* with equal rank.

CO-ORDINATENESS (kō-or'di-nāt-nes) *n.* state of being co-ordinate.

CO-ORDINATES (kō-or'din-āts) *n.pl.* a system of lines or angles drawn about a point to determine the place or magnitude of others.

CO-ORDINATION (kō-or'di-nā'shun) *n.* arranging in ranks; state of being arranged.

COOT (kōōt) *n.* a small black wading bird. [E. of uncertain etym.]

COPAL (kō'pal) *n.* a Mexican gum, used in varnishing. [Sp., fr. Mex.]

COPARTNER (kō-pärt'ner) *n.* a joint partner. [L. *co* = *cum*, and PARTNER.]

COPARTNERSHIP (kō-pärt'ner-ship) *n.* joint concern in business.

COPARTNERY (kō-pärt'ner-i) *n.* copartnership; the parties in a joint business.

COPE (kōp) *n.* a priest's cloak; a hood; archwork;—*v.t.* or *i.* to contend; strive; oppose with success. [*n.* Form of CAPE. *v.t.* or *i.* O.F. *couper*, strike, cut, fr. *coup*, *colp*, fr. L. (acc.) *colaphum*, a blow with the fist.]

COPESTONE (kōp'stōn) *n.* head or top stone.

COPIER (kop'i-er) *n.* one who transcribes or imitates.

COPING (kō'ping) *n.* the top or cover of a wall.

COPIOUS (kō'pi-us) *a.* plentiful; abundant; rich in supplies; diffuse. [L. *copiosus*, fr. *copia*, abundance.]

COPIOUSLY (kō'pi-us-li) *ad.* abundantly; amply. [See COPIOUS.]

COPIOUSNESS (kō'pi-us-nes) *n.* full supply. [See COPIOUS.]

COPPER (kop'er) *n.* a metal; a large boiler;—*v.t.* to cover with sheets of iron. [O.E. *copor*, fr. L. *cuprum*, for *Cyprium aes*, Cyprian brass, fr. G. *kupros*, Cyprus.]

COPPERAS (kop'e-ras) *n.* sulphate of iron; green vitriol. [O.F. *coperose*, perhaps fr. L. *cupri rosa*, copper-flower.]

COPPERISH (kop'er-ish) *a.* containing or resembling copper. [See COPPER.]

COPPERPLATE (kop'er-plāt) *n.* a plate of copper engraved, or its impression. [See COPPER.]

COPPERSMITH (kop'er-smith) *n.* one who makes copper utensils. [See COPPER.]

COPPERY (kop'er-i) *a.* containing copper. [See COPPER.]

COPPICE (kop'is) *n.* a wood of small growth cut down from time to time. [O.F. *copeiz* wood often cut, fr. *coper*, fr. G. *kolaphos* blow. See COPE and COPSE.]

COPPIN (kop'in) *n.* the cone of thread formed on the spindle in spinning. [O.F. *cop*, *copp*.]

COPRA (kop'ra) *n.* the dried kernel of the cocoa-nut. [Malay.]

CO-PRESBYTER (kō-pres'bi-ter) *n.* member of the same presbytery. [co- = *con* = L. *cum*, and G. *presbuteros*, an elder, orig. (compar.) older, fr. *presbus*, old.]

COPSE (kops) *n.* a wood of small growth. [See COPPICE.]

COPULA (kop'ū-la) *n.* a bond or tie; the word that unites the subject and predicate of a proposition. [L. = band. See COUPLE.]

COPULATION (kop-ū-lā'shun) *n.* act of embracing in pairs. [See COPULA.]

COPULATIVE (kop'ū-lā-tiv) *a.* that unites;—*n.* a conjunction. [See COPULA.]

COPULATORY (kop'ū-la-tur-i) *a.* pertaining to copulation; serving to connect. [See COPULA.]

COPY (kop'i) *n.* a manuscript; pattern; imitation;—*v.t.* to transcribe; imitate;—*v.i.* to follow an example. [O.F. *copie*, orig. =plenty, fr. L. (acc.) *copiam*.]

COPY-BOOK (kop'i-book) *n.* a book for practising writing. [See COPY.]

COPYHOLD (kop'i-hōld) *n.* a tenure in England by copy of record. [See COPY.]

COPYIST (kop'i-ist) *n.* one who copies. [See COPY.]

COPYRIGHT (kop'i-rit) *n.* the sole right to publish a book. [See COPY.]

COQUET (kō-ket') *v.t.* to attempt to excite admiration from vanity ;—*v.i.* to trifle in love. [F. *coqueter*.]

COQUETRY (kō-ket'ri) *n.* trifling in love. [See COQUET.]

COQUETTE (kō-ket') *n.* a vain, trifling woman; a flirt; a jilt. [See COQUET.]

COQUETTISH (kō-ket'ish) *a.* befitting a coquette. [See COQUET.]

COQUETTISHLY (kō-ket'ish-li) *ad.* in a coquettish manner. [See COQUET.]

CORACLE (kor'ạ-kl) *n.* a boat made of wickerwork and covered with leather. [Celt.]

CORAL (kor'ạl) *n.* a genus of animals and their shells, growing in the sea ;—*a.* made of coral. [O.F. =F. *corail*, fr. L., fr. G. *korallion*.]

CORB (korb) *n.* a basket. [L. *corbis*, a basket.]

CORBAN (kor'bạn) *n.* an alms-basket. [H.]

CORBEL (kor'bel) *n.* a projection on the wall to support statues; the vase of the Corinthian column. [O.F. =F. *corbeau*, fr. Low L. dim. *corbellus*, fr. *corvus*, a raven.]

CORD (kord) *n.* a small rope or thick string; a measure of 128 cubic feet;—*v.t.* to bind with a cord. [F. *corde*, fr. Late L. (acc.) *cordam* =L. *chordam*. Doublet of CHORD.]

CORDAGE (kor'dāj) *n.* ropes of a ship. [See CORD.]

CORDATE (kor'dāt) *a.* heart-shaped. [F., fr. L. stem *cord*-, of *cor, cordis*, heart.]

CORDIAL (kord'yal) *n.* an exhilarating liquor; anything that cheers;—*a.* hearty; sincere; warm. [L., fr. stem *cord*-, of *cor, cordis*, heart.] [warm affection. [See CORDIAL.]

CORDIALITY (kor-di-al'i-ti) *n.* sincerity;

CORDIALLY (kord'yal-i) *ad.* with sincere affection. [See CORDIAL.]

CORDIFORM (kor'di-form) *a.* heart-shaped. [L. stem *cord*-, of *cor, cordis*, heart, and *forma*, shape.]

CORDITE (kor'dit) *n.* a smokeless explosive. [*cord*, from the appearance of the grains.]

CORDON (kor'dun) *n.* a line of military posts or troops; a ribbon as a badge of honour. [F.]

CORDOVAN (kor'dō-vạn) *n.* Spanish leather. [Fr. *Cordova*, in Spain.]

CORDUROY (kor-du-roi') *n.* thick cotton stuff, corded or ribbed. [F. =king's CORD.]

CORE (kōr) *n.* the heart or inner part. [Etym. doubtful; perhaps fr. L. *cor*, heart.]

CO-REGENT (kō-rē'jent) *n.* a joint ruler. [L. *co*- =*con* =*cum*, and REGENT.]

CO-RESPONDENT (kō-rē-spon'dent) *n.* a joint respondent. [*co*- =*con* =L. *cum*, and RESPONDENT.]

CORF (korf) *n.* a basket used in mines. [See CORB.]

CORIANDER (kor-i-an'der) *n.* an aromatic plant and its seed. [F., fr. L. *coriandrum*, fr. G. *koriannon*.]

CO-RIVAL (kō-ri'vạl) *n.* a fellow-competitor. [*co*- =*con* =L. *cum*, and RIVAL.]

CO-RIVALRY (kō'ri-vạl-ri) *n.* joint rivalry. [See CO-RIVAL.]

CORK (kork) *n.* a tree or its bark; a stopper; —*v.t.* to stop with a cork. [L. (acc.) *corticem*, bark, fr. *cortex*, through Sp.]

CORKED (korkt) *a.* stopped with a cork; tasting of the cork. [See CORK.]

CORKSCREW (kork'skroo) *n.* a screw to draw corks from bottles. [See CORK and SCREW.]

CORKY (kor'ki) *a.* like cork. [See CORK.]

CORMORANT (kōr'mō-rạnt) *n.* a voracious bird; a glutton. [F. *cormoran*, fr. L. *corvus marinus*, sea-crow.]

CORN (korn) *n.* (1) grain; maize; (2) a hard tumour;—*v.t.* to preserve with salt. [(1) O.E., conn. with L. *granum*, GRAIN. (2) O.F. =F. *cor*, fr. L. *cornu*, horn.]

CORNCRAKE (korn'krāk) *n.* the landrail.

CORNEA (kor'nē-ạ) *n.* the horny membrane in the fore part of the eye. [L. fem., fr. *corneus* horny.]

CORNELIAN (kor-nēl'yạn) *n.* a precious stone; a kind of cherry-tree. [Formerly *cornaline*, fr. F., fr. L. *cornu*, horn.]

CORNEOUS (kor'nē-us) *a.* horny; like horn; hard. [L. See CORNEA.]

CORNER (kor'nẹr) *n.* an angle; a secret place. [O.F. *corniere*, fr. Late L., fr. L. *cornu*, horn.]

CORNER-STONE (kor'nẹr-stōn) *n.* the principal stone. [See CORNER.]

CORNET (kor'net) *n.* a musical instrument; a cavalry officer. [F., dim. of *corne*, horn, fr. Late L. (acc.) *cornam* =L. *cornu*, horn.]

CORNETCY (kor'net-si) *n.* office of a cornet. [See CORNET.]

CORNICE (kor'nis) *n.* the top of a wall or column; a moulding. [F., fr. It. of uncertain etym.]

CORNUCOPIA (kor-nū-kō'pi-ạ) *n.* the horn of plenty, from which fruits and flowers are represented as proceeding. [L. *cornu*, horn, and (gen.) *copiae*, of plenty.]

CORNUTED (kor-nū'ted) *a.* having horns. [L. *cornu*, horn.]

CORNWALLITE (korn' wal-īt) *n.* a mineral found in Cornwall It consists of a hydrous arseniate of copper, combined with phosphoric acid. [Fr. placename *Cornwall*.]

Cornucopia.

CORNY (kor'ni) *a.* hard; like horn; producing grain; tasting of malt. [See CORN.]

COROLLA (kō-rol'ạ) *n.* the inner covering of a flower. [Dim. of L. *corona*, CROWN.]

COROLLARY (kor'ul-lạ-ri) *n.* an inference or deduction from a truth or proposition. [L. *corollarium*, fr. *corolla*, fr. *corona*, crown.]

CORONAL (kor'ō-nạl) *n.* a crown; garland; the frontal bone;—*a.* pertaining to the top of the head. [L. *corona*, crown.]

CORONATED (kor'ō-nā-ted) *a.* surmounted with crown-like eminences. [See CORONAL.]

CORONATION (kor-ō-nā'shun) *n.* act of crowning. [See CORONAL.]

CORONER (kor'ō-nẹr) *n.* an officer who inquires into the cause of any sudden death. [See CORONAL.]

CORONET (kor'ō-net) *n.* an inferior crown worn by the nobility; an ornamental headdress. [See CORONAL.]

CORPORAL (kor'pō-rạl) *n.* a non-commissioned officer;—*a.* pertaining to the body. [O.F., fr. Late L. *corporalis*, fr. stem *corpor*- of *corpus*, body.]

CORPORALITY (kor-pō-ral'i-ti) *n.* state of being embodied. [See CORPORAL.]

CORPORALLY (kor'pō-rạl-i) *ad.* bodily. [See CORPORAL.]

CORPORATE (kor'pō-rāt) *a.* united in a community. [L. (part.) *corporatus*, embodied.]

CORPORATELY (kor'pō-rāt'li) *ad.* in a corporate capacity. [See CORPORATE.]

CORPORATION (kor-pō-rā'shun) *n.* a society acting as an individual. [See CORPORATE.]

CORPORATOR (kor'pō-rā-tẹr) *n.* a member of a corporation. [See CORPORATE.]

CORPOREAL (kor-pō'rē-ạl) *a.* having a body; not spiritual. [See CORPORATE.]

CORPOREALLY (kor-pō′rē-ạl-i) *ad.* in a bodily form or manner. [See CORPORATE.]

CORPOREITY (kor-pō-rē′i-ti) *n.* bodily substance. [See CORPORATE.]

CORPS (kōr) *n.* a body of troops. [F., fr. L. *corpus*, body.]

CORPSE (korps) *n.* dead body of a human being. [F., fr. L. *corpus*, body. Cf. CORSE.]

CORPULENCE (kor′pū-lens) *n.* fleshiness. [F., fr. L. *corpulentia*, fatness, fr. *corpulentus*, fr. CORPUS.]

CORPULENT (kor′pū-lent) *a.* very fleshy; bulky. [See CORPULENCE.]

CORPULENTLY (kor′pu-lent-li) *ad.* in a corpulent manner. [See CORPULENCE.]

CORPUS (kor′pus) *n.* a body. [L.]

CORPUSCLE (kor′pus-l) *n.* an atom; a particle. [See CORPUS.]

CORRADIATE (kō-rā′di-āt) *v.t.* to concentrate, as rays.

CORRAL (ko-rál′) *n.* an enclosure for cattle or for defence. [Sp. =a yard, ' run,' fr. L. *currere*. Cf. KRAAL.]

CORRECT (ku-rekt′) *v.t.* to punish; make right;—*a.* exact; accurate. [L. (part.) *correctus*, put right, fr. *corrigere*, fr. *cor-* = *cum*, thoroughly, and *regere*, rule.]

CORRECTION (ku-rek′shun) *n.* act of correcting. [See CORRECT.]

CORRECTIONAL (ku-rek′shun-ạl) *a.* intended to correct. [See CORRECT.]

CORRECTIVE (ku-rek′tiv) *a.* tending to correct;—*n.* that which corrects. [See CORRECT.]

CORRECTLY (ku-rekt′li) *ad.* exactly; justly. [See CORRECT.]

CORRECTNESS (ku-rekt′nes) *n.* accuracy. [See CORRECT.]

CORRECTOR (ku-rek′ter) *n.* one who corrects. [See CORRECT.]

CORREGIDOR (ko-rej′i-dor) *n.* the chief magistrate of a Spanish town.

CORRELATE (kor′e-lāt) *v.i.* to be mutually related, as father and son. [L. *co-* = *cum*, and RELATE.]

CORRELATIVE (ko-rel′ạ-tiv) *a.* having mutual relation. [See CORRELATE.]

CORRELATIVELY (ko-rel′ạ-tiv-li) *ad.* in a correlative relation. [See CORRELATE.]

CORRESPOND (kor-e-spond′) *v.i.* to suit; agree; write to. [L. *cor-* = *con* = *cum*, with, and RESPOND.]

CORRESPONDENCE (kor-e-spon′dens) *n.* agreement; interchange of letters. [See CORRESPOND.]

CORRESPONDENT (kor-e-spon′dent) *a.* suitable; congruous;—*n.* one who has intercourse by letters. [See CORRESPOND.]

CORRIDOR (kor′i-dor) *n.* a gallery or open passage in a building. [F., fr. It., fr. L. *currere*, run.]

CORRIE (kor′i) *n.* a steep hollow in a hill. [Gael.]

CORRIGENDA (kor-i-jen′dạ) *n.pl.* corrections to be made in a book. [L. gerund pl. of *corrigere*, CORRECT.] [CORRECT.]

CORRIGENT (kor′i-jent) *a.* correcting. [See

CORRIGIBLE (kor′i-ji-bl) *a.* that may be corrected. [See CORRECT.]

CORROBORANT (ko-rob′ō-rạnt) *a.* strengthening. [See CORROBORATE.]

CORROBORATE (ko-rob′ō-rāt) *v.t.* to confirm; strengthen. [L. (part.) *corroboratus*, strengthened, fr. L. *cor-* = *cum* and stem *robor-*, of *robur*, strength.]

CORROBORATION (ko-rob-ō-rā′shun) *n.* act of confirming. [See CORROBORATE.]

CORROBORATIVE (ko-rob′ō-rā′tiv) *a.* tending to strengthen. [See CORROBORATE.]

CORRODE (ku-rōd′) *v.t.* to eat away or consume by degrees. [L. *cor-* = *cum*, thoroughly, and *rodere*, gnaw.]

CORRODENT (ku-rō′dent) *a.* having the power of corroding. [See CORRODE.]

CORRODIBLE (ku-rō′di-bl) *a.* that may be corroded. [See CORRODE.]

CORROSION (ku-rō′zhun) *n.* act of eating away. [L. (part.) *corrosus*, gnawed away.]

CORROSIVE (ku-rō′siv) *a.* eating away gradually. [See CORRODE.]

CORROSIVELY (ku-rō′siv-li) *ad.* in a corrosive manner. [See CORRODE.]

CORROSIVENESS (ku-rō′siv-nes) *n.* quality of corroding; acrimony. [See CORRODE.]

CORRUGATE (kor′ū-gāt) *v.t.* to wrinkle; contract. [L. (part.) *corrugatus*, wrinkled, fr. *cor-* = *cum*, and *rugare*, fr. *ruga*, wrinkle.]

CORRUGATION (kor-ū-gā′shun) *n.* contraction into wrinkles. [See CORRUGATE.]

CORRUGATOR (kor′ū-gā-ter) *n.* a muscle which contracts the skin. [See CORRUGATE.]

CORRUPT (ku-rupt′) *v.t.* to make putrid; defile; deprave; bribe;—*v.i.* to become putrid; —*a.* decayed; debauched. [L. (part.) *corruptus*, spoiled, fr. *cor-* = *cum*, wholly, and *rumpere*, break.]

CORRUPTER (ku-rup′ter) *n.* he or that which corrupts. [See CORRUPT.]

CORRUPTIBILITY (ku-rup-ti-bil′i-ti) *n.* capacity of being corrupted. [See CORRUPT.]

CORRUPTIBLE (ku-rup′ti-bl) *a.* capable of being corrupted. [See CORRUPT.]

CORRUPTION (ku-rup′shun) *n.* putrescence; depravity of morals. [See CORRUPT.]

CORRUPTIVE (ku-rup′tiv) *a.* tending to corrupt. [See CORRUPT.]

CORRUPTLY (ku-rupt′li) *ad.* with depravity. [See CORRUPT.]

CORRUPTNESS (ku-rupt′nes) *n.* depravity. [See CORRUPT.]

CORSAIR (kor′sār) *n.* a pirate; the vessel of a pirate [F. *corsaire*, fr. It. *corsa*, COURSE.]

CORSE (kors) *n.* a corpse. [O.F. *cors* = F. *corps*, body, fr. L. *corpus*.]

CORSELET (kors′let) *n.* light armour for the breast. [F. dim. suffs. *-el*, *-et*.]

CORSET (kor′set) *n.* a bodice for ladies. [F., dim. suff. *-et*.]

CORTEGE (kor′tāzh) *n.* a train of attendants.

CORTES (kor′tes) *n.pl.* the national assemblies of Spain and Portugal. [Sp. and Pg.]

CORTEX (kor′teks) *n.* the bark of a tree; a covering. [L.]

CORTICAL (kor′ti-kạl) *a.* belonging to bark. [See CORTEX.]

CORTILE (kor-tē′lē, kor′ti-lā) *n.* a court in the interior of a building. [It.]

CORUSCANT (ko-rus′kạnt) *a.* flashing; glittering. [See CORUSCATE.]

CORUSCATE (kor′us-kāt) *v.i.* to sparkle; glitter. [L. *coruscare*, to vibrate, glitter.]

CORUSCATION (kor-us-kā′shun) *n.* a sudden flash of light. [See CORUSCATE.]

CORVETTE (kor-vet′) *n.* a sloop of war. [F. fr. Sp., fr. L. *corbita*, a slow ship of burden, fr. *corbis*, basket.]

COSEY (kō′zi) *a.* snug; comfortable; chatty. Also COSY. [Scot., of unknown etym.]

COSILY (kōz′i-li) *ad.* snugly; comfortably. [See COSEY.]

COSINE (kō′sin) *n.* the sign of the complement of an arc or angle.

COSMETIC (koz-met′ik) *a.* promoting beauty; —*n.* a wash for improving beauty. [G., fr. *kosme-ein*, adorn, fr. *kosmos*, order.]

COSMICAL (koz′mi-kạl) *a.* rising or setting with the sun. Also COSMIC. [G. *kosmos*.]

COSMOGONY (koz-mog′ō-ni) *n.* science of the formation of the world. [G. *kosmos*, order, and *-gonia*, creation, fr. *gignesthai*, become.]

COSMOGRAPHER (koz-mog′rạ-fer) *n.* a describer of the world. [G. *kosmos*, order, and *graphein*, write.]

COSMOGRAPHIC (koz-mo-graf′ik) *a.* relating to the description of the world. [See COSMOGRAPHER.]

COSMOGRAPHY (koz-mog'ra-fi) *n.* a description of the world. [See COSMOGRAPHER.]

COSMOLOGY (koz-mol'ŏ-ji) *n.* science of the world or universe. [G. *kosmos*, order, and *logos*, discourse.]

COSMOPOLITAN (koz-mō-pol'i-tan) *a.* common to all the world; universal. [See COSMOPOLITISM.]

COSMOPOLITE (koz-mop'ŏ-lit) *n.* a citizen of the world. [See COSMOPOLITISM.]

COSMOPOLITISM (koz-mop'ŏ-li-tizm) *n.* citizenship of the world. [Also COSMOPOLITANISM. [G. *kosmos*, order, and *polites*. citizen, fr. *polis*, city.]

COSMORAMA (koz-mō-rá'ma) *n.* an optical exhibition of views of the world. [G. *kosmos*, order, and *korama*, spectacle.]

COSMOS (koz'mos) *n.* the whole world; a system of order and law in creation. [G.]

COSSET (kos'et) *v.t.* to pet; fondle. [Etym. doubtful.]

COST (kost) *n.* price paid; charge;—*v.i.* [*pret.* and *pp.* COST] to be had at the price of. [O.F. *coster* = F. *couter*, fr. L. *constare*, stand together.]

COSTAL (kos'tal) *a.* pertaining to the ribs. [L. *costa*, a rib.]

COSTARD (kos'tard) *n.* a kind of apple; the head. [Perh. = ribbed apple, fr. O.F., fr. L. *costa*, a rib.]

COSTERMONGER (kos'ter-mung-ger) *n.* a hawker of fruit and vegetables. [= *costard monger*. See COSTARD.]

COSTIVE (kos'tiv) *a.* bound in the bowels. [O.F. *costevé* = F. *constipé*. Doublet of CONSTIPATED.]

COSTIVENESS (kos'tiv-nes) *n.* state of being costive; constipation. [See COSTIVE.]

COSTLINESS (kost'li-nes) *n.* expensiveness. [See COST.]

COSTLY (kost'li) *a.* expensive; dear. [See COST.]

COSTUME (kos'tūm) *n.* style or mode of dress. [F., fr. It. *costume*. Doublet of CUSTOM.]

COSTUMIER (kos-tū'mi-er) *n.* a dealer in fancy dresses. [F.]

COT (kot) *n.* (1) a hut; a small bed;—(2) a small dwelling; a cottage;—(3) a small boat. [(1) Hind. *khat*. (2) O.E. *cot*. (3) Ir.]

CO-TANGENT (kō-tan'jent) *n.* the tangent of the complement of an arc or angle.

COTE (kōt) *n.* a pen; a sheep-fold. [O.E. *cote*. See COT.]

COTEMPORANEOUS (kō-tem-pō-rā'nē-us) *a.* being at the same time with another. [See COTEMPORARY.]

COTEMPORARY (kō-tem'pō-ra-ri) *n.* one who lives in the same age.

Co-tangent.

COTERIE (kō'te-ri) *n.* a fashionable association. [F., fr. root of COT.]

COTILLION (kō-til'yun) *n.* a brisk, lively dance and tune. [F., fr. *cotte*, a coat, fr. Low L. *cotta*, a tunic. See COAT.]

COTTAGE (kot'āj) *n.* a small house; a hut. [O.E. *cot*, a small house.]

COTTAGER (kot'a-jer) *n.* one living in a cottage. Also COTTAR. [See COTTAGE.]

COTTON (kot'n) *n.* vegetable wool; cloth made from it;—*a.* consisting of cotton;—*v.i.* to rise with a nap; associate with. [F. *coton*, fr. Sp., fr. A.]

COUCH (kouch) *v.i.* to lie or squat down; stoop, as in fear;—*v.t.* to hide; express; remove a cataract from the eye;—*n.* a seat; a bed. [O.F. *colcher* = F. *coucher*, fr. L. *collocare*, place with, fr. *col*—*cum*, and *locus*, place. Doublet of COLLOCATE.]

COUCHANT (kouch'ant) *a.* lying down with the head erect. [F.]

COUGAR (kōō'gär) *n.* a carnivorous animal of the cat family. [Fr. native S. Amer. name, through F.]

COUGH (kof) *n.* effort of the lungs to throw off phlegm;—*v.i.* to try to throw off phlegm. [E. Cf. Ger. *keuchen*, gasp.]

COULD (kood) *pret.* of CAN. [M.E. *coude*, fr. O.E. *cutha*.] [*culter*, fr. L.]

COULTER (kōl'ter) *n.* a ploughshare. [O.E.

COUNCIL (koun'sil) *n.* an assembly for consultation. [F. *concile*, fr. L. *concilium*, fr. *cum*, and *calare*, summon.]

COUNCILLOR (koun'sil-er) *n.* a member of a council. [See COUNCIL.]

COUNSEL (koun'sel) *n.* advice; an advocate;—*v.t.* to give advice; design; purpose. [O.F. *conseil*, fr. L. *consilium*, fr. *consulere*, CONSULT.]

COUNSELLOR (koun'sel-er) *n.* one who gives advice; a lawyer. [See COUNSEL.]

COUNT (kount) (1) *v.t.* or *i.* to reckon; number; esteem; be counted; rely on;—*n.* act of numbering; number; an item of a charge; —(2) *n.* foreign title. [(1) O.F. *conter* = F. *compter*, fr. L. *computare*, reckon. Doublet of COMPUTE. (2) F. *comte*, fr. L. (acc.) *comitem*, fr. *comes*.]

COUNTENANCE (koun'te-nans) *n.* the face; air; look; support;—*v.t.* to support; patronise. [O.F., fr. Late L. (acc.) *continentiam*, demeanour.]

COUNTER (koun'ter) (1) *n.* one who counts; a piece of metal used in counting; a shop table;—(2) *n.* an arched space in the stern of a ship;—*a.* contrary; opposite. [(1) See COUNT. (2) F. *contre*, fr. L. *contra*, opposite.]

COUNTERACT (koun-ter-akt') *v.t.* to act in opposition to. [See COUNTER and ACT.]

COUNTERACTION (koun-ter-ak'shun) *n.* contrary action; hindrance. [See COUNTERACT.]

COUNTERACTIVE (koun-ter-ak'tiv) *a.* tending to counteract;—*n.* that which counteracts. [See COUNTERACT.]

COUNTER - ATTRACTION (koun-ter-a-trak'shun) *n.* opposite attraction or allurement. [See COUNTERACT.]

COUNTERBALANCE (koun-ter-bal'ans) *v.t.* to weigh against;—*n.* an opposite equivalent force. [See COUNTER and BALANCE.]

COUNTERCHANGE (koun'ter-chānj) *v.t.* to cause to change places;—*n.* exchange; reciprocation. [See COUNTER and CHANGE.]

COUNTERCHECK (koun'ter-chek) *n.* anything that hinders or stops; a rebuke. [See COUNTER and CHECK.]

COUNTERFEIT (koun'ter-fit) *v.t.* to copy; imitate; forge;—*a.* fabricated in imitation; forged;—*n.* a forged imitation; an impostor. [O.F. (part.) *contrefait*, imitated, fr. *contre*, and *faire*, fr. L. *contra*, against, and *facere*, make or do.]

COUNTERFEITER (koun'ter-fit-er) *n.* a forger. [See COUNTERFEIT.]

COUNTERFOIL (koun'ter-foil) *n.* the corresponding part of a cheque or tally. [See COUNTER and FOIL.]

COUNTERMAND (koun'ter-mand) *n.* a contrary order. [F. *contremander*, fr. L. *contra*, against, and *mandare*, command.]

COUNTERMAND (koun-ter-mand') *v.t.* to revoke a command.

COUNTERMARCH (koun'ter-märch) *n.* a change of the wings or face of a battalion; —*v.i.* to march back. [See COUNTER and MARCH.]

COUNTERMARK (koun'ter-mark) *n.* an after mark on goods or coin. [See COUNTER and MARK.]

COUNTERMINE (koun'ter-min) *n.* a gallery excavated to frustrate the use of another; —(koun-ter-min') *v.t.* to defeat secretly. [See COUNTER and MINE.]

COUNTERMOTION (koun'tẹr-mō-shun) *n.* an opposite motion. [See COUNTER and MOTION.]

COUNTERPANE (koun'tẹr-pān) *n.* the cover of a bed. [Corr. fr. a F. corr. of L. *culcita puncta*, stitched QUILT.]

COUNTERPART (koun'tẹr-pàrt) *n.* correspondent part. [See COUNTER and PART.]

COUNTERPLOT (koun'tẹr-plot) *n.* a plot against a plot. [See COUNTER and PLOT.]

COUNTERPOINT (koun'tẹr-point) *n.* musical notation or composition; a bed-cover. [Fr. L. *punctum contra punctum*, note against note.]

COUNTERPOISE (koun'tẹr-poiz) *n.* equal weight in opposition;—*v.t.* to balance. [See COUNTER and POISE.]

COUNTER-REVOLUTION (koun-tẹr-rev-u-lū'shun) *n.* a change to a former state. [See COUNTER and REVOLUTION.]

COUNTERSIGN (koun-tẹr-sīn') *v.t.* to sign as secretary or subordinate official;—(koun'tẹr-sīn) *n.* a military watchword. [See COUNTER and SIGN.]

COUNTER-TENOR (koun-tẹr-ten'or) *n.* part between the treble and the tenor; contralto. [See COUNTER and TENOR.]

COUNTERVAIL (koun-tẹr-vāl') *v.t.* to act against equally. [F. See COUNTER and AVAIL.]

COUNTERWORK (koun-tẹr-wurk') *v.t.* to work in opposition. [See COUNTER and WORK.]

COUNTESS (koun'tes) *n.* the lady of an earl or count. [See COUNT (2).]

COUNTING-HOUSE (koun'ting-hous) *n.* an apartment for the keeping of accounts. [See COUNT (1).]

COUNTLESS (kount'les) *a.* numberless; innumerable. [See COUNT (1).]

COUNTRY (kun'tri) *n.* land around a city; a kingdom or state; native place;—*a.* rural; rustic; rude. [O.F. *contrée*, fr. Low L. *contrada* (country), facing, formed fr. *contra*, against.]

COUNTRYMAN (kun'tri-man) *n.* one of the same country; a rustic. [See COUNTRY.]

COUNTRY-SEAT (kun'tri-sēt) *n.* a country residence of a city gentleman. [See COUNTRY.]

COUNTY (koun'ti) *n.* a shire; a district. [O.F. *counte* (2 syll.) = F. *comte*, fr. Late L. (acc.) *comitatum*.]

COUPLE (kup'l) *n.* two; a pair; a brace;—*v.t.* or *i.* to join together; unite. [F., fr. L. (acc.) *copulam*, fr. *co-* = *cum*, and *apere*, join. Doublet of COPULA.]

COUPLET (kup'let) *n.* two verses; a pair. [See COUPLE.]

COUPLING (kup'ling) *n.* that which couples or connects. [See COUPLE.]

COUPON (kōō'pong) *n.* an interest certificate attached to transferable bonds. [F., fr. *couper*, cut.]

COURAGE (kur'āj) *n.* boldness to encounter danger; bravery; daring. [O.F. *corage*, fr. *cor* = F. *cœur*, heart, fr. L. *cor*.]

COURAGEOUS (ku-rā'jus) *a.* brave; bold; daring. [See COURAGE.]

COURAGEOUSLY (ku-rā'jus-li) *ad.* bravely. [See COURAGE.]

COURIER (kōō'ri-ẹr) *n.* a messenger sent in haste; a travelling servant. [F. *courrier*, fr. L. *currere*, run.]

COURSE (kōrs) *n.* a passing or running; career; progress; a race; ground run over; series or range; a service of part of a dinner; —*v.t.* or *i.* to chase; hunt;—*pl.* the lower sails of a ship. [F., fr. L. (acc.) *cursum*, a course, fr. *currere*, run.]

COURSER (kōr'sẹr) *n.* a swift horse. [See COURSE.]

COURSING (kōrz'ing) *n.* hunting. [See COURSE.]

COURT (kōrt) *n.* residence or retinue of a prince; a legal tribunal; the judges; polite attention; a yard or area;—*v.t.* to woo; solicit;—*v.i.* to act the courtier or lover. [O.F. *cort*, fr. L. (acc.) *cortem*, for *cohortem*, enclosure.]

COURTEOUS (kurt'yus) *a.* polite; civil; complaisant. [M.E. *corteis*, fr. O.F.]

COURTEOUSLY (kurt'yus-li) *ad.* politely. [See COURTESY (kur'te-si).]

COURTESY (kur'te-si) *n.* politeness; civility. [O.F. *cortesie*.]

COURTIER (kōrt'yẹr) *n.* one who frequents court; one who solicits favours. [See COURT.]

COURTLIKE (kōrt'līk) *a.* well-bred. [See COURT.]

COURTLINESS (kōrt'li-nes) *n.* complaisance with dignity. [See COURT.]

COURTLING (kōrt'ling) *n.* a retainer to a court. [See COURT.]

COURTLY (kōrt'li) *a.* politely; elegant. [See COURT.]

COURT-MARTIAL (kōrt-mär'shạl) *n.* a court to try crimes in military or naval affairs. [See COURT and MARTIAL.]

COURT-PLASTER (kōrt'plàs-tẹr) *n.* sticking-piaster on silk. [See COURT and PLASTER.]

COURTSHIP (kōrt'ship) *n.* solicitation in marriage. [See COURT.]

COURTYARD (kōrt'yárd) *n.* an enclosure or area round a house. [See COURT and YARD.]

COUSIN (kuz'n) *n.* the child of an uncle or aunt. [F., fr. Late L. *cosinus*, fr. L. *consobrinus*, fr. *con-* = *cum*, and *sobrinus* = *sororinus*, of a sister, *soror*.]

COUSIN-GERMAN (kuz'n-jẹr-man) *n.* a first cousin.

COVE (kōv) *n.* a small creek or bay; a concave moulding or vault;—*v.t.* to arch over. [O.E. *cofa*, chamber. Cf. Ger. *Kobin*, cabin.]

COVENANT (kuv'e-nạnt) *n.* a mutual agreement; the writing containing it;—*v.t.* or *i.* to bind, grant, or promise by agreement. [O.F. fr. (part.) *co-venant* (= *con*) agreeing. See CONVENE.]

COVENANTEE (kuv-en-ạnt-ē') *n.* one to whom a covenant is made. [See COVENANT.]

COVENANTER (kuv'e-nạn-tẹr) *n.* one who makes a covenant. [See COVENANT.]

COVER (kuv'ẹr) *v.t.* to spread over; clothe; conceal; incubate; be sufficient for;—*n.* shelter; pretence. [O.F. *covrir*, *courrir*, fr. L. *co-operire*, fr. *cum-*, quite, and *operire*, hide.]

COVERING (kuv'ẹr-ing) *n.* anything spread over. [See COVER.]

COVERLET (kuv'ẹr-let) *n.* an upper bedcover. [O.F. *covrir*, and *lit*, bed, fr. L. (acc.) *lectum*.]

COVERT (kuv'ẹrt) *a.* hid; secret;—*n.* a shelter; defence. [O.F. (part.) *covert*, covered.]

COVERTLY (kuv'ẹrt-li) *ad.* secretly; closely. [See COVERT.]

COVERTNESS (kuv'ẹrt-nes) *n.* secrecy; privacy. [See COVERT.]

COVERTURE (kuv'ẹr-tūr) *n.* the state of a married woman (legal). [See COVER.]

COVET (kuv'et) *v.t.* to desire unlawfully or earnestly. [O.F., fr. L. (acc.) *cupiditatem*, desire, fr. *cupidus*, greedy.]

COVETABLE (kuv'e-tạ-bl) *a.* that may be coveted. [See COVET.]

COVETER (kuv'e-tẹr) *n.* one who covets. [See COVET.]

COVETINGLY (kuv'e-ting-li) *ad.* with eager desire to possess. [See COVET.]

COVETOUS (kuv'e-tus) *a.* avaricious; greedy for gain. [See COVET.]

COVETOUSLY (kuv'e-tus-li) *ad.* eagerly; avariciously. [See COVET.]

COVETOUSNESS (kuv'e-tus-nes) *n.* an eager desire of gain. [See COVET.]

COVEY (kuv'i) n. a brood of birds;—pl. COVEYS. [O.F. covée, brood, orig. part. = hatched, fr. cover, fr. L. cubare, lie down.]

COVIN (kuv'in) n. deceitful agreement; collusion. [O.F. fr. co venir. See COVENANT.]

COW (kou) (1) n. female of the bull;—(2) v.t. to depress with fear; dishearten. f.(1) O.E. cu. Cf. Ger. Kuh. (2) Scand.]

COWARD (kou'ard) n. one wanting courage; a poltroon;—a. timid; base. [F. couard, fr. O.F. coe, tail, fr. L. (acc.) caudam, tail.]

COWARDICE (kou'ar-dis) n. want of courage; timidity. [See COWARD.]

COWARDLY (kou'ard-li) a. meanly timid;— ad. with mean timidity. [See COWARD.]

COW-CATCHER (kou'kach-er) n. an iron frame in front of locomotives to throw off obstructions from the rails. [See COW and CATCH.]

COWER (kou'er) v.i. to sink or waver through fear. [Scand. Cf Ger. kauern.]

COW-HEEL (kou'hēl) n. the feet of an ox or cow boiled into gelatine. [See COW and HEEL.]

COWHERD (kou'herd) n. one who tends cattle. [See COW and HERD.]

COWHIDE (kou'hid) n. the hide of a cow;— v.t. to beat with a cowhide. [See COW and HIDE.]

COWL (koul) n. a monk's hood. [O.E. cugle, fr. (Eccl.) L. cuculla, a hood.]

COWRY (kou'ri) n. a small shell used as money in India and Africa. [Hind.]

COWSLIP (kou'slip) n. a wild flower of the primrose family. [O.E. cu-slyppe, a piece of dung.]

COXCOMB (koks'kōm) n. a red notched ribbon worn by jesters; a showy fool; a fop; a plant bearing red flowers. [Fr. the cock's comb of red cloth on a jester's cap.]

COXCOMBRY (koks'kom-ri) n. the manners of a coxcomb. [See COXCOMB.]

COY (koi) a. shrinking from familiarity; reserved; shy; bashful. [O.F. coi, fr. Low L. (acc.) quietum, fr. L. quietum. Doublet of QUIET.]

COYISH (koi'ish) a. somewhat coy. [See COY.]

COYLY (koi'li) ad. with reserve; shyly. [See COY.]

COYNESS (koi'nes) n. unwillingness to be familiar; bashfulness; affected modesty. [See COY.]

COZEN (kuz'n) v.t. to cheat; deceive. [F. cousiner, to play the COUSIN in order to sponge upon people.]

COZENAGE (kuz'n-āj) n. fraud in bargaining. [See COZEN.]

COZENER (kuz'n-er) n. a cheater. [See COZEN.]

CRAB (krab) n. a well-known shell-fish; a sign of the zodiac;—a. sour; rough; austere. [O.E. crabba. Cf. Ger. Krabbe.]

CRAB-APPLE (krab'ap-pl) n. a small sour apple. [Perhaps Scand.]

CRABBED (krab'ed) a. peevish; difficult. [See CRAB.]

CRABBEDLY (krab'ed-li) ad. in a crabbed manner. [See CRAB.]

CRABBEDNESS (krab'ed-nes) n. peevishness. [See CRAB.]

CRACK (krak) n. a sudden noise; a fissure; —v.t. or i. to break into chinks; split; disorder; make a quick, sharp sound; talk freely;—a. first-rate. [O.E. cracian. Cf. Ger. krachen.]

CRACK-BRAINED (krak'brānd) a. crazed. [See CRACK.]

CRACKER (krak'er) n. a firework; a hard biscuit. [See CRACK.]

CRACKLE (krak'l) v.i. to make sharp noises. [See CRACK.]

CRACKLING (krak'ling) n. the noise of something that crackles; the rind of roast pork. [See CRACK.]

CRACKNEL (krak'nel) n. a hard, brittle biscuit or cake. [Corr. fr. F. craquelin, fr. D. = crackling.]

CRADLE (krā-dl) n. a machine for rocking children, and one for cutting grain;—v.t. to lay or rock in a cradle; cut and lay with a cradle. [O.E. cradol.]

CRAFT (kräft) n. manual art; trade; cunning; small vessels. [O.E. craft. Cf. Ger. Kraft, force.]

CRAFTILY (kräf'ti-li) ad. with cunning. [See CRAFT.]

CRAFTINESS (kräf'ti-nes) n. artfulness; dexterity; wiliness. [See CRAFT.]

CRAFTSMAN (kräfts'man) n. a mechanic. [See CRAFT.]

CRAFTY (kräf'ti) a. cunning; artful. [See CRAFT.]

CRAG (krag) n. a rough, steep rock. [Celt.]

CRAGGED (krag'ed) a. rugged with broken rocks. Also CRAGGY. [See CRAG.]

CRAGGINESS (krag'i-nes) n. fullness of crags. [See CRAG.]

CRAKE (krāk) n. a bird of the rail family; corncrake;—v.i. to cry like the bird. [Imit.]

CRAM (kram) v.t. or i. to press close; fill full; stuff; prepare or qualify for an examination. [O.E. crammian.]

CRAMBO (kram'bō) n. a word rhyming with another; a game of rhymes. [Perhaps fr. crambe repetita (said of stale speeches), cabbage served up again.]

CRAMP (kramp) n. a spasm;—v.t. to confine; hinder. [O.F. crampe, fr. Teut.]

CRAMPFISH (kramp'fish) n. the torpedo. [See CRAMP.]

CRAMPONS (kramp'ons) n.pl. hooked pieces of iron for raising stones, logs, etc. [See CRAMP.]

CRAN (kran) n. a measure of herrings, holding about 750 fish. [Prob. Gael.]

CRANAGE (krā'nāj) n. liberty to use a crane; price paid for its use.

CRANBERRY (kran'ber-i) n. a berry growing in swamps. [Etym. uncertain.]

CRANE (krān) n. a migratory fowl; a machine for raising, lowering, and moving heavy weights; a pipe for drawing liquor out of a cask. [O.E. cran.]

CRANESBILL (krānz'bil) n. the geranium—a plant of several species. [See CRANE.]

CRANIAL (krā'ni-al) a. relating to the skull. [See CRANIUM.]

CRANIOLOGY (krā-ni-ol'ō-ji) n. the science of, or a treatise on, the cranium. [G. kranion, skull and logos, a discourse.]

CRANIUM (krā'ni-um) n. the skull. [Late L. fr. G. kranion, skull; conn. with kara, head.]

CRANK (krangk) n. the end of an axis bent, used as a handle for communicating circular motion;—a. bold; easily overset. [E.]

CRANNIED (kran'id) a. full of chinks. [See CRANNY.]

CRANNY (kran'i) n. crevice; narrow opening; hole. [F. cran, notch, of uncert. etym.]

CRAPE (krāp) n. a loosely-woven stuff used in mourning. [F. crêpe, fr. O.F. crespe, lit crisped, fr. L. crispus. Doublet of CRISP]

Crank.

CRASH (krash) v.i. to make a noise, as of things falling;—n. a loud noise, as of things falling and breaking. [Imit.]

CRASHING (krash'ing) n. a mingled sound of things breaking. [See CRASH.]

CRASIS (krā'sis) n. the healthy constitution of the blood; a contraction. [G.]

CRASS (kras) a. thick; coarse; dull; obtuse. [L. crassus, through O.F. cras.]

CRASSAMENT (kras'ạ-ment) *n.* the red thick part of the blood. [See CRASIS.]
CRATE (krāt) *n.* a wicker pannier for earthenware. etc. [L. *crates*, wickerwork.]
CRATER (krā'tẹr) *n.* the mouth or aperture of a volcano. [G. = a large mixing-bowl.]
CRAUNCH (krȧnsh) *v.t.* to crush with the teeth; chew. [Imit.]
CRAVAT (krạ-vat') *n.* a neckcloth. [F. *cravate*, a tie worn by *Cravates*, or *Croatians*.]
CRAVE (krāv) *v.t.* to ask earnestly; long for. [O.E. *crafian*.]
CRAVING (krā'ving) *a.* greatly longing for;— *n.* urgent longing for. [See CRAVE.]
CRAW (kraw) *n.* the crop of birds. [E.]
CRAWFISH (kraw'fish) *n.* a small kind of lobster found in rivers. Also CRAYFISH. [Corr. fr. M.E. *crevisse*, fr. O.F. = F. *écrevisse*, fr. O. Ger. *Crebiz*, crab.]
CRAWL (krawl) *v.i.* to creep; move as a worm. [Scand.]
CRAYON (krā'un) *n.* a pencil of coloured chalk; a drawing made with crayons;— *v.t.* to sketch. [F., fr. *craie*, chalk.]
CRAZE (krāz) *v.t.* to impair the intellect. [Scand.]
CRAZILY (krā'zi-li) *n.* in a crazy manner. [See CRAZE.]
CRAZINESS (krā'zi-nes) *n.* state of being deranged; weakness. [See CRAZE.]
CRAZY (krā'zi) *a.* broken; deranged. [See CRAZE.]
CREAK (krēk) *v.i.* to make a grating sound. [Imit.]
CREAKING (krēk'ing) *n.* a harsh, continuing noise. [See CREAK.]
CREAM (krēm) *n.* the oily part of milk;— *v.t.* or *i.* to gather cream; skim; froth. [O.F. = *crème*, fr. Late L. *chrisma*, holy oil, fr. G.]
CREAM-CHEESE (krēm'chēz) *n.* cheese made of cream. [See CREAM and CHEESE.]
CREAMY (krē'mi) *a.* full of cream; rich. [See CREAM.]
CREASE (krēs) *n.* a mark left by folding;— *v.t.* to mark by folding. [Form of (*creast* =) CREST.]
CREATE (krē-āt') *v.t.* to bring into existence; form anew; bring forth; cause. [L. (part.) *creatus*, created, fr. *creare*.]
CREATION (krē-ā'shun) *n.* the act of creating; the universe; any new form or production. [See CREATE.]
CREATIVE (krē-ā'tiv) *a.* having power to create. [See CREATE.]
CREATOR (krē-ā'tẹr) *n.* one who gives existence; a maker; God. [See CREATE.]
CREATURE (krē'tūr) *n.* a being or thing created. [O.F., fr. L. (acc.) *creaturam*.]
CREDENCE (krē'dens) *n.* belief. [O.F., fr. L. (acc.) *credentiam*, fr. *credere*, trust.]
CREDENTIAL (krē-den'shal) *a.* giving a title to credit. [See CREDENCE.]
CREDENTIALS (krē-den'shalz) *n pl.* documents certifying that one is entitled to confidence, or has a valid commission. [See CREDENCE.]
CREDIBILITY (kred-i-bil'i-ti) *n.* just claim to belief. [See CREDENCE.]
CREDIBLE (kred'i-bl) *a.* worthy of credit. [See CREDENCE.]
CREDIBLY (kred'i-bli) *ad.* in a credible manner. [See CREDENCE.]
CREDIT (kred'it) *a.* belief; trust; influence; esteem;— *v.t.* to believe; trust; confide in. [L. (part.) *creditus*, believed, fr. *credere*.]
CREDITABLE (kred'i-tạ-bl) *a.* reputable. [See CREDIT.]
CREDITABLY (kred'i-tạ-bli) *ad.* reputably; without disgrace. [See CREDIT.]
CREDITOR (kred'i-tẹr) *n.* one to whom a debt is due. [See CREDIT.]
CREDO (krē'do) *n.* a creed; a musical setting of a creed. [L. *credo*, I believe (beginning of the Apostles' Creed in Latin).]

CREDULITY (kre-dū'li-ti) *n.* easiness of belief; readiness to believe. [See CREDULOUS.]
CREDULOUS (kred'ū-lus) *a.* apt to believe; easily imposed on. [L. *credulus*.]
CREDULOUSNESS (kred'ū-lus-nes) *n.* credulity. [See CREDULOUS.]
CREED (krēd) *n.* belief; summary of the articles of the Christian religion. [O.E. *creda*, fr. CREDO.]
CREEK (krēk) *n.* a small inlet or bay [Perh. Scand.]
CREEKY (krē'ki) *a.* containing creeks. [See CREEK.]
CREEL (krēl) *n.* an osier basket. [Etym. unknown.]
CREEP (krēp) *v.i.* [*pret.* CREPT, CREEPED] to move as a worm; move slowly. [O.E. *creopan*.]
CREEPER (krē'pẹr) *n.* a creeping plant; a small bird. [See CREEP.]
CREEPINGLY (krē'ping-li) *ad.* by creeping. [See CREEP.]
CREMATION (krē-mā'shun) *n.* burning the dead body. [L. (part.) *crematus*, burned, fr. *cremare*.]
CREMONA (krē-mō'-nạ) *n.* a superior kind of violin. [Fr. place name *Cremona*, in Italy.]
CRENATED (krē'nā-ted) *a.* notched; indented. [L. *crena*, a notch.]
CREOLE (krē'ōl) *n.* a native of the West Indies and Spanish America, descended from European parents. [F., fr. Sp.]
CREOSOTE (krē'ō-sōt) *n.* an oily liquid having the quality of preserving flesh from corruption. [G. *kreo-*, fr. *kreas*, flesh, and *soter*, preserver.]
CREPITATE (krep'i-tāt) *v.i.* to crackle. [L. *crepitare*, fr. *crepare*, to crack.]
CREPITATION (krep-i-tā'shun) *n.* crackling sounds. [See CREPITATE.]
CREPON (krep'on) *n.* a fabric of silk, wool, or wool and silk mixed, resembling CRAPE. [F.]
CREPT (krept) *pret.* of CREEP.
CRESCENDO (kre-shen'dō) *ad.* with increasing volume of sound. [It. = growing stronger.]
CRESCENT (kres'ent) *a.* increasing; growing; — *n.* the increasing moon; Turkish standard. [L. stem *crescent-*, increasing, fr. *crescere*, grow.]
CRESCENTED (kres'ent-ed) *a.* having, or draped like, a crescent. [See CRESCENT.]
CRESS (kres) *n.* a plant used as a salad. [O.E. *cressae*, *cerse*.]
CREST (krest) *n.* the comb of a cock; a tuft of hair or feathers; the foamy top of a wave; summit of a hill. [O.F. *creste*, = F. *crête*, fr. L. (acc.) *cristam*.]
CRESTED (kres'ted) *a.* wearing a crest. [See CREST.]
CRESTFALLEN (krest'fawl-n) *a.* dejected; cowed. [See CREST and FALL.]
CRETACEOUS (krē-tā'shus) *a.* of the nature of chalk. [L. *creta*, chalk.]
CRETIN (krē'tin) *n.* an idiot of the Alpine valleys. [F.]
CRETINISM (krē'tin-izm) *n.* a kind of idiocy attended with deformity, notably with goitre. [See CRETIN.]
CRETONNE (krē-ton') *n.* a stout cotton cloth, patterned on one side. [F.]
CREVICE, CREVASSE (krev'is, kre-vas') *n.* a small crack. [F. fr. *crever*, burst, fr. L. *crepare*, crack.]
CREW (krōō) *n.* (1) a ship's company;— (2) *pret.* of CROW. [(1) F. *crue*, increase. See ACCRUE. (2) See CROW.]
CREWEL (krōō'el) *n.* a ball of yarn; two-threaded worsted. [Etym. unknown.]
CRIB (krib) *n.* a manger; stall; bin; box; bedstead; hut;— *v.t.* to shut in; pilfer. [E.]
CRIBBAGE (krib'āi) *n.* a game at cards. [See CRIB, the *crib* being cards laid aside.]

CRIBBLE (krib'l) n. a corn sieve. [L. cribellum, dim. of cribrum, sieve.]

CRICK (krik) n. a spasmodic affection or cramp. [E.]

CRICKET (krik'et) n. (1) a small insect;—(2) a game. [(1) O.F. criquer, chirp, fr. Teut.; (2) F., fr. D. kricke, a CRUTCH.]

CRICKETER (krik'et-er) n. one who plays at cricket. [See CRICKET (2).]

CRIED (krid) pret. and pp. of CRY.

CRIER (kri'er) n. one who cries. [See CRY.]

CRIME (krim) n. a violation of law; offence; sin. [F., fr. L. crimen, a charge.]

CRIMINAL (krim'i-nal) a. guilty of a crime;— n. a person guilty of a crime. [L., fr. stem crimin-, of criminis, of a charge.]

CRIMINALITY (krim-i-nal'i-ti) n. the quality of being criminal. [See CRIMINAL.]

CRIMINALLY (krim'i-nal-i) ad. with guilt.

CRIMINATE (krim'i-nāt) v.t. to charge with crime. [L. (part) criminatus, having accused, fr. criminari.]

CRIMINATION (krim-i-nā'shun) n. accusation. [See CRIMINATE.]

CRIMINATORY (krim'i-nā-tur-i) a. accusing. [See CRIMINATE.]

CRIMINOUS (krim'i-nus) a. implying great crime; heinous. [See CRIMINAL.]

CRIMP (krimp) a. that crumbles easily; brittle;—v.t. to catch; pinch; curl; decoy. [E.]

CRIMPAGE (krim'pāj) n. act of crimping. [See CRIMP.]

CRIMPLE (krim'pl) v.t. to lay in plaits. [See CRIMP.]

CRIMSON (krim'zn) n. a deep red colour; a. coloured as crimson;—v.t. to tinge with red; —v.i. to blush. [M.E. cremosin, fr. O.F. cramoisin, fr. Low L. cramesinus, fr. A. Doublet of CARMINE.]

CRINGE (krinj) n. a low bow; servility;—v.i. to bow with servility; flatter meanly. [O.E. crincan, cringan, to fall in battle.]

CRINKLE (kringk'l) v.i. to bend in turns or flexures;—n. one of several folds. [Conn. with CRINGE.]

CRINOLINE (krin'ō-lin) n. a hooped petticoat. [F. = orig. hair-cloth, fr. crin, fr. L. (acc.) crinem, and lin, LINEN.]

CRINOSE (kri'nōs) a. hairy. [L. crinis, hair.]

CRIPPLE (krip'l) n. a lame person;—v.t. to make lame. [O.E. creopan, creep. Cf. Ger. Krüppel.]

CRISIS (kri'sis) n. a critical time or turn;— pl. CRISES. [L., fr. G., fr. krinein, judge. See CRITIC.]

CRISP (krisp) v.t. to curl; make brittle;—a. curled; frizzled; short and brittle; brisk. [L. crispus. Doublet of CRAPE.]

CRISPLY (krisp'li) ad. with crispness. [See CRISP.]

CRISPNESS (krisp'nes) n. state of being crisp, curled, or brittle. [See CRISP.]

CRISPY (kris'pi) a. brittle; short; curled; friable. [See CRISP.]

CRISTATE (kris'tāt) a. crested; tufted. [L. crista, a crest.]

CRITERION (kri-tē'ri-un) n. a standard of judging;—pl. CRITERIA. [G., see CRITIC.]

CRITIC (krit'ik) n. one skilled in judging literary or artistic work. [L., fr. G. kritikos, discerning, fr. krites, judge, fr. krinein, judge.]

CRITICAL (krit'i-kal) a. relating to criticism; nice; indicating a crisis. [See CRITIC.]

CRITICALLY (krit'i-kal-i) ad. in the manner of a critic; exactly. [See CRITIC.]

CRITICALNESS (krit'i-kal-nes) n. exactness; niceness; accuracy. [See CRITIC.]

CRITICISE (krit'i-siz) v.t. or i. to examine and judge; act as a critic. [See CRITIC.]

CRITICISM (krit'i-sizm) n. the art or act of judging well; a critical judgment expressed in writing. [See CRITIC.]

CRITIQUE (kri-tēk') n. a critical examination or article. [F., fr. L. (acc.) criticum.]

CROAK (krōk) n. cry of a frog;—v.i. to utter a rough sound like a frog. [Imit.]

CROAKER (krō'ker) n. a grumbler. [See CROAK.]

CROCK (krok) n. a pot; black matter on pots, kettles, etc.;—v.t. to blacken. [O.E. croc. Cf. Ger. Krug. Perhaps fr. Celt.]

CROCKERY (krok'e-ri) n. all kinds of coarse earthenware. [See CROCK.]

CROCODILE (krok'ō-dil) n. an amphibious animal of the lizard kind. [F., fr. L., fr. G. krokodeilos, lizard.]

CROCUS (krō'kus) n. an early spring flower; saffron. [L. crocus, fr. G. krokos.]

CROFT (kroft) n. a little home-field. [E.]

CROFTER (krof'ter) n. one who rents a small farm. [See CROFT.]

CROMLECH (krom'lek) n. a circle of standing stones. [W.]

CRONE (krōn) n. an old woman. [Etym. uncertain.]

CRONY (krō'ni) n. an old and familiar friend. [Etym. unknown.]

CROOK (krook) n. a bend; a shepherd's staff; —v.t. or i. to bend. [Scand.]

CROOKED (krook'ed) pp. or a. [pp. pronounced krookt, and a. krook'ed] bent; curving. [See CROOK.]

CROOKEDNESS (krook'ed-nes) n. state of being crooked; perverseness. [See CROOK.]

CROON (kroōn) n. a low moaning; a simple melody. [Imit.]

CROP (krop) n. the harvest; the stomach of a bird;—v.t. to cut off; reap. [E. = orig. a bunch.]

CROQUET (krō'kā) n. an outdoor game for ladies and gentlemen, played with balls and mallets. [F., dim of croc, hook.]

CROQUETTE (krō-ket') n. a forcemeat ball fried. [F.]

CROSIER (krō'zher) n. a bishop's pastoral staff. [M.E. croce, fr. O.F. = F. crosse, fr. Low L. (acc.) crociam, fr. O.F. croc, a hook.]

CROSLET (kros'let) n. a small cross. [See CROSS.]

CROSS (kros) n. a straight body crossing another; a gibbet; adversity;—a. athwart; peevish;—v.t. to lay athwart; cancel; obstruct. [L. (acc.) crucem, of crux, through Celt.]

CROSSBAR (kros'bär) n. a transverse bar, or one lying in a cross direction. [See CROSS and BAR.]

CROSS-BEARER (kros-bär'er) n. in the Roman Catholic Church, the chaplain of an archbishop, who bears a cross before him. [See CROSS and BEAR.]

CROSS-BILL (kros'bil) n. a defendant's bill in chancery; a kind of bird. [See CROSS and BILL.]

CROSSBOW (kros'bō) n. a bow placed crosswise on a stock for shooting arrows. [See CROSS and BOW.]

CROSS-BUN (kros'bun) n. a cake marked with a cross, eaten at Easter. [See CROSS and BUN.]

CROSS-EXAMINATION (kros-eg-zam-i-nā'shun) n. a close questioning of a witness by the opposing counsel. [See CROSS and EXAMINE.]

CROSS-EXAMINE (kros-eg-zam'in) v.t. to examine by the opposite party. [See CROSS and EXAMINE.]

CROSS-GRAINED (kros'grānd) a. with the fibres irregular; perverse; untractable. [See CROSS and GRAINED.]

CROSSING (kros'ing) ppr. passing over;—n. place of passing; thwarting. [See CROSS.]

CROSSLY (kros'li) ad. athwart; adversely; peevishly. [See CROSS.]

CROSSNESS (kros'nes) n. peevishness. [See CROSS.]

CROSS-PURPOSE (kros'pur-pos) *n.* a contrary purpose; an enigma. [See CROSS and PURPOSE.]

CROSS-QUESTION (kros'kwest-yun) *v.t.* to cross-examine. [See CROSS and QUESTION.]

CROSS-ROAD (kros'rōd) *n.* a way or road that crosses another. [See CROSS and ROAD.]

CROSSWISE (kros'wiz) *ad.* in the form of a cross. [See CROSS and wise = O.E. *wise*, way, fr. *wis*, wise.]

CROTCHED (krocht) *a.* forked. [Etym. unknown.]

CROTCHET (kroch'et) *n.* a note of half a minim; a whim. [F. *crochet*, a hook, now *croche*.]

CROTCHETY (kroch'et-i) *a.* whimsical; fanciful. [See CROTCHET.]

CROTON-OIL (krō'tun-oil) *n.* a violent purgative obtained from the seeds of a genus of tropical plants. [G. *kroton*, a mite resembling the seed of the plant.]

CROUCH (krouch) *v.i.* to stoop low; cringe. [O.F. *croche*, *croc*, crook.]

CROUP (krōōp) *n.* (1) a disease in the throat; (2) buttocks of a horse; rump of a fowl. [(1) Imit. F. fr. Scand.]

CROUPIER (krōō'pi-er, krōō'pēr) *n.* vice-chairman at a public dinner-party. [F.]

CROW (krō) *n.* a black fowl; the cock's voice; *v.t.* [*pret.* CROWED] to utter the cry of a cock; — *v.i.* to boast; exult. [O.E. *crawan*.]

CROWBAR (krō'bär) *n.* (bar with a beak), a heavy iron bar bent at one end, and used as a lever.

CROWD (kroud) *n.* a number of persons or things without order; throng; — *v.t.* to press close; urge; — *v.i.* to press together in a crowd. [O.E. *crudan*, to gather together.]

CROWN (kroun) *n.* the top of the head; a royal ornament; a garland; — *v.t.* to invest with a crown; dignify; complete. [O.F. *corone* = F. *couronne*, fr. L. (acc.) *coronam*, a wreath or garland.]

CROWN-GLASS (kroun'glas) *n.* a fine glass for windows. [See CROWN and GLASS.]

CROWNING (kroun'ing) *n.* act of crowning; the finish. [See CROWN.]

CROWN-PRINCE (kroun'prins) *n.* the prince who succeeds to the throne. [See CROWN and PRINCE.]

CRUCIAL (krōōsh'yal) *a.* transverse; intersecting; searching; testing. [F., fr. stem *cruci-*, of *crux*, cross.]

CRUCIBLE (krōō'si-bl) *n.* a chemical vessel. [Late L., perhaps fr. stem *cruci-*, CROSS.]

CRUCIFIER (krōō'si-fi-er) *n.* one who crucifies. [L. stem *cruci-*, of *crux*, CROSS, and *figere*, fix.]

CRUCIFIX (krōō'si-fiks) *n.* a cross, or representation of a cross, with the figure of Christ crucified. [L. (part.) *crucifixus*, crucified.]

CRUCIFIXION (krōō-si-fik'shun) *n.* a nailing to a cross. [See CRUCIFIX.]

CRUCIFORM (krōō'si-form) *a.* in the form of a cross. [L. stem *cruci-*, of *crux*, CROSS, and *forma*, shape.]

CRUCIFY (krōō'si-fi) *v.t.* to fasten and put to death on a cross; mortify. [L. *crucificare*, for *crucifigere*, to fix to a cross.]

CRUDE (krōōd) *a.* in a raw or rough state; unfinished; unripe. [L. *crudus*, raw.]

CRUDELY (krōōd'li) *ad.* with rawness.

CRUDENESS (krōōd'nes) *n.* rawness; roughness; immatureness. [See CRUDE.]

CRUDITY (krōō'di-ti) *n.* undigested matter; immaturity. [See CRUDE.]

CRUEL (krōō'el) *a.* inhuman; void of pity. [O.F. *cruel*, fr. L. (acc.) *crudelem*, cruel.]

CRUELLY (krōō'el-i) *ad.* in a barbarous manner; inhumanly. [See CRUEL.]

CRUELTY (krōō'el-ti) *n.* quality of being cruel; a cruel act; inhuman treatment. [See CRUEL.]

CRUET (krōō'et) *n.* a vial for sauces. [O.F. *cruie*, pitcher, fr. Teut. Cf. CROCK, Ger. *Krug*.]

CRUISE (krōōz) *v.i.* to rove back and forth on the sea; — *n.* a cruising voyage. [D. *kruisen*, CROSS (the sea), fr. *Kruis*, fr. L. (acc.) *crucem*, CROSS.]

CRUISER (krōō'zer) *n.* a person or vessel that cruises. [See CRUISE.]

CRUMB (krum) *n.* a fragment or piece, as of bread; — *v.t.* to break into crumbs. [O.E. *cruma*. Cf. Ger. *Krume*.]

CRUMB-CLOTH (krum'kloth) *n.* a cloth laid under the table to keep the carpet clean from crumbs. [See CRUMB and CLOTH.]

CRUMBLE (krum'bl) *v.t.* to break into small pieces; — *v.i.* to fall to decay. [See CRUMB.]

CRUMMY (krum'i) *a.* full of crumbs. [See CRUMB.]

CRUMP (krump) *a.* crooked. [O.E. *crump*, fr. *crumb*, crooked, conn. with CRAMP, CRIMP.]

CRUMPET (krum'pet) *n.* a soft cake or muffin. [See CRUMP.]

CRUMPLE (krum'pl) *v.t.* to draw into wrinkles. [See CRUMP.]

CRURAL (krōō'ral) *a.* pertaining to the leg. [L., fr. stem *cruri-*, of *crus*, leg.]

CRUSADE (krōō'sād) *n.* a military expedition to recover the Holy Land. [F. *croisade*, fr. Late L. (fem. part.) *cruci-ata*, marked with a CROSS.]

CRUSADER (krōō-sā'der) *n.* one employed in a crusade. [See CRUSADE.]

CRUSE (krōōz) *n.* a small cup or vial. [Icel. *krus*, a pot.]

CRUSH (krush) *v.t.* to bruise or break by pressure; subdue; ruin; — *n.* a violent collision and bruising; pressure by a crowd. [O.F., fr. Teut.]

CRUST (krust) *n.* a hard covering; — *v.t.* or *i.* to cover with a hard case. [O.F. *crouste* = F. *croûte*, fr. L. (acc.) *crustam*, rind.]

CRUSTACEOUS (krus-tā'shus) *a.* of the nature of a crust or shell. Also **CRUSTACEAN.** [See CRUST.]

CRUSTATED (krus-tā-ted) *a.* covered with a crust. [See CRUST.]

CRUSTILY (krus'ti-li) *ad.* peevishly; testily. [See CRUST.]

CRUSTINESS (krus'ti-nes) *n.* shortness and sharpness of temper or manner. [See CRUST.]

CRUSTY (krus'ti) *a.* like crust; snappish. [See CRUST.]

CRUTCH (kruch) *n.* a staff for cripples; — *v.t.* to support on crutches. [M.E. *crucche*, fr. O.E. *crycc*. Cf. CRICKET.]

CRY (kri) *v.t.* or *i.* to call; weep; proclaim; — *n.* a bawling; outcry; yell; a weeping. [F. *crier*, fr. L. *quiritare*, lament.]

CRYPT (kript) *n.* a cell or chapel under a church. [L., fr. G. *krupte*, vault, fr. *kruptein*, hide.]

CRYPTIC (krip'tik) *a.* hidden; secret. [See CRYPT.]

CRYPTOGAMY (krip-tog'a-mi) *n.* concealed fructification, as of ferns, mosses, etc. [G. *kruptos*, hidden, and *gamos*, marriage.]

CRYPTOGRAPHY (krip-tog'ra-fi) *n.* art of writing in secret characters. [G. *kruptos*, hidden, and *graphein*, write.]

CRYSTAL (kris'tal) *n.* a regular solid transparent body; a fine kind of glass; — *a.* made of or like crystal; clear. [O.F. *cristal*, fr. L. *crystallum*, fr. G. *krustallos*, ice, fr. *kruos*, cold.]

CRYSTALLINE (kris'ta-lin) *a.* consisting of crystal; resembling crystal. [See CRYSTAL.]

CRYSTALLISATION (kris-ta-li-zā'shun) *n.* the process of forming crystals. [See CRYSTAL.]

Fāte, fär, ado; mē, her; mīne; nōte; tūne; mōōn.

CRYSTALLISE (kris'ta-liz) v.t. or i. to form into crystals. [See CRYSTAL.]

CRYSTALLOGRAPHY (kris-ta-log'ra-fi) n. the science of crystallisation. [CRYSTAL, and G. graphein, write.]

CUB (kub) n. the young of many beasts, as the bear or fox. [Etym. unknown.]

CUBATION (kū-bā'shun) n. act of lying down; reclining. [L. cubo, lie down.]

CUBATURE (cū'ba-tūr) n. the finding the exact cubic contents of a body. [See CUBE.]

CUBE (kūb) n. a regular solid body with six equal sides; the third power of a root. [F., fr. L. (acc.) cubum, fr. G. kubos, a die.]

CUBIC (kū'bik) a. having the form of a cube. [L., fr. G. kubikos.]

CUBICLE (kū'bi-kl) n. a small bed-room. [L. cubiculum, fr. cubare, lie down.]

Cube.

CUBICULAR (kū-bik'ū-lar) a. belonging to a chamber.

CUBIFORM (kū'bi-form) a. in form of a cube. [L. (gen.) cubi, of a cube, and forma, shape.]

CUBIT (kū'bit) n. the fore-arm; measure of a man's arm from the elbow to the tip of the middle finger, 18 inches. [L. cubitum, elbow.]

CUCKOO (koo'kŏŏ) n. a well-known bird, deriving its name from its note. [Imit.]

CUCULATED (kū'ku-lā-ted) n. covered with or resembling a hood or cowl. [L. cucullatus, fr. cucullus, hood.]

CUCUMBER (kū'kum-ber) n. a garden plant; its fruit. [L. (acc.) cucum-berem.]

CUD (kud) n. a portion of food or of tobacco chewed. [O.E. cwidu, cudu.]

CUDDY (kud'i) n. a ship's cabin. [Etym. uncert.]

CUDGEL (kud'jel) n. a thick heavy stick; v.t. to beat with a stick. [M.E. kuggel, fr. O.E. cycgel.]

CUE (kū) n. the end or tail of a thing; a straight rod; a hint or intimation; the last words of an actor's speech. [F. queue, fr. L. cauda, tail.]

CUFF (kuf) n. (1) a blow; v.t. to strike with the fist; (2) n. part of a sleeve. [(1) Scand. (2) Etym. uncert.]

CUIRASS (kwi-ras') n. a breastplate. [O.F. cuirace = F. cuirasse, fr. cuir, leather, fr. L. corium.]

CUIRASSIER (kwi-ra-sēr') n. a soldier wearing a cuirass. [F.]

CUISINE (kwi-zēn') n. the kitchen; style of cooking. [F. =kitchen.]

CULDEE (kul-dē') n. a Celtic order of monks in the 6th century. [Celt.]

CUL-DE-SAC (kool'de-sak) n. a street open at one end only. [F. =sack-bottom.]

CULINARY (kū'lin-ar-i) a. belonging to the kitchen. [L. culina, a kitchen.]

CULL (kul) v.t. to select from others. [O.F. cuillir = F. cueillir, fr. L. colligere, COLLECT.]

CULLENDER (kul'en-der) n. a strainer. [L. (part. stem) colant-, straining, fr. colum, strainer.]

CULLION (kul'yun) n. a mean fellow; a bulbous root. [F. couillon, coward, fr. L. coleus, a leather bag.]

CULLY (kul'i) n. the dupe of a woman; —v.t. to impose on. [See CULLION.]

CULMINATE (kul'mi-nāt) v.i. to be on the meridian; to reach the highest point. [Fr. L. stem culmin-, of culmen, top.]

CULMINATION (kul-mi-nā'shun) n. most elevated position. [See CULMINATE.]

CULPABILITY (kul-pa-bil'i-ti) n. blamableness; faultiness; guilt. [See CULPABLE.]

CULPABLE (kul'pa-bl) a. faulty; blamable. [O.F., fr. L. culpabilis, fr. culpa, blame.]

CULPABLY (kul'pa-bli) ad. with blame. [See CULPABLE.]

CULPRIT (kul'prit) n. one arraigned for a crime; a criminal. [In legal phraseology made up of O.E. cul- = culpable, and prit = prest = F prêt, ready.]

CULT (kult) n. veneration for some person or thing; a system of religious belief. [L. cultus, worship, fr. (part.) cultus, cultivated, fr. colere.]

CULTIVABLE (kul'ti-va-bl) a. that may be tilled. [See CULTIVATE.]

CULTIVATE (kul'ti-vāt) v.i. to till; dress; foster; refine. [Late L. (part.) cultivatus, tilled, fr. (part.) cultus, tilled, fr. colo.]

CULTIVATED (kul'ti-vāt-ed) vp. or a. improved or raised by culture. [See CULTIVATE.]

CULTIVATION (kul-ti-vā'shun) n. improvement by tillage or by study. [See CULTIVATE.]

CULTIVATOR (kul'ti-vā-ter) n. one who tills; a kind of harrow. [See CULTIVATE.]

CULTURE (kul'tūr) n. act of cultivating; instruction; training; enlightenment; refinement; —v.t. to cultivate. [See CULT.]

CULTURED (kul'tūrd) a. well educated; refined. [See CULT.]

CULVERT (kul'vert) n. an arched drain. [F., fr. couler, flow, fr. L. colare, strain.]

CULVERTAIL (kul'ver-tāl) n. dove-tail. [O.E. culfre, dove.]

CUMBER (kum'ber) v.t. to clog; burden. [F. combrer, fr. Late L. cumbruo, a heap.]

CUMBERLESS (kum'ber-les) n. free from care or trouble. [See CUMBER.]

CUMBERSOME (kum'ber-sum) a. burdensome. [See CUMBER.]

CUMBERSOMENESS (kum'ber-sum-nes) n. the quality of being cumbersome. [See CUMBER.]

CUMBRANCE (kum'brans) n. burden; clog. [See CUMBER.]

CUMBROUS (kum'brus) a. troublesome; oppressive. [See CUMBER.]

CUMBROUSLY (kum'brus-li) ad. in a cumbrous manner. [See CUMBER.]

CUMMERBUND (kum'er-bund) n. a broad sash worn as a waistband. [Per. kamarband, a loin-cloth.]

CUMULATE (kūm'ū-lāt) v.t. to heap together. [L. (part.) cumulatus, heaped up, fr. CUMULUS.]

CUMULATION (kūm-ū-lā'shun) n. act of heaping together; a heap. [See CUMULATE.]

CUMULATIVE (kūm'ū-lā-tiv) a. augmenting by addition. [See CUMULATE.]

CUMULUS (kūm'ū-lus) n. a cloud in convex masses piled up one upon another. [L.]

CUNEAL (kū'nē-al) a. shaped like a wedge. [L. (gen.) cunei, of cuneus, a wedge.]

CUNEIFORM (kū-nē'i-form) a. denoting the wedge-shaped characters or inscriptions found in Nineveh, etc. [L. (gen.) cunei, of cuneus, a wedge, and FORM.]

CUNNING (kun'ing) a. artful; crafty; —n. art; skill; craft; artifice. [O.E. cunnan, to know.]

CUNNINGLY (kun'ing-li) ad. with art. [See CUNNING.]

CUP (kup) n. a drinking vessel; —v.t. to procure a discharge of blood by scarifying and applying a cupping glass. [O.E., fr. L. cupa, a tub, a drinking cup. Cf. F. coupe.]

CUPBOARD (kub'urd) n. a case or enclosure with shelves for cups, plates, etc. [See CUP and BOARD.]

CUPEL (kū'pel) n. a little cup used in refining. [See CUP.]

CUPELLATION (kū-pe-lā'shun) n. the process of refining metals. [See CUP.]

CUPID (kū'pid) n. the god of love. [L.]

CUPIDITY (kū-pid'i-ti) *n.* inordinate desire, particularly of wealth. [F. *cupidité*, fr. L. (acc.) *cupidi-tatem*, fr. *cupidus*, covetous.]

CUPOLA (kū'pō-la) *n.* a dome; an arched roof;—*pl.* CUPOLAS. [It., fr. L. dim. *cupula*, fr. *cupa*, cask. See CUP.]

CUPREOUS (kū'prē-us) *a.* of or like copper. [L. *cuprum*, copper.]

CUR (kur) *n.* a dog; a snappish fellow. [E.]

CURABLE (kūr'a-bl) *a.* that may be cured. [O.F., fr. L. (acc.) *curam*, care. See CARE.]

CURAÇOA (kŏŏ-ra-so') *n.* a cordial flavoured with orange peel and spices. [F., *Curaçao*, West Indies.]

CURACY (kū'ra-si) *n.* office of a curate. [See CURATE.]

CURATE (kū'rāt) *n.* a clergyman who assists the rector or vicar of a parish. [Late L. *curatus*, fr. L. *cura*, CARE.]

CURATIVE (kū'ra-tiv) *a.* tending to cure. [See CURE.]

CURATOR (kū-rā'ter) *n.* a guardian; a superintendent. [See CARE.]

CURB (kurb) *v.t.* to bend; restrain or check; bridle;—*n.* part of a bridle; box round a well; restraint. [F. *courber*, fr. L. *curvus*, bent.]

CURB-STONE (kurb'stŏn) *n.* the stone on the outer edge of a pavement. [See CURB.]

CURD (kurd) *n.* coagulated milk. [Celt.]

CURDLE (kur'dl) *v.t.* or *i.* to coagulate; congeal; thicken.

CURE (kūr) *n.* remedy; a healing;—*v.t.* to restore to health; salt and dry. [O.F., fr. L. (acc.) *curam*, care.]

CURELESS (kūr'les) *a.* incurable. [See CURE.]

CURER (kūr'er) *n.* one who preserves meats. [See CURE.]

CURFEW (kur'fū) *n.* an evening bell. [O.F. *covrefeu* = F. *couvre-feu*, fr. *couvrir*, COVER, and *feu*, fr. L. (acc.) *focum*, hearth.]

CURIOSITY (kū-ri-os'i-ti) *n.* great inquisitiveness; a rarity. [See CURIOUS.]

CURIOUS (kū'ri-us) *a.* inquisitive; nice; singular; rare. [O.F. *curios* = F. *curieux*, fr. L. *curiosus*, fr. *cura*, care.]

CURIOUSLY (kū'ri-us-li) *ad.* inquisitively; neatly; artfully. [See CURIOUS.]

CURIOUSNESS (kū'ri-us-nes) *n.* state or quality of being curious. [See CURIOUS.]

CURL (kurl) *n.* a ringlet of hair;—*v.t.* or *i.* to form or bend into ringlets. [M.E. *crul*. Cf. Ger. *Krolle*.]

CURLINESS (kur'li-nes) *n.* state of being curly. [See CURL.]

CURLING (kur'ling) *n.* a game played like bowling, but with stones upon the ice. [See CURL.]

CURLY (kur'li) *a.* having curls. [See CURL.]

CURMUDGEON (kur-muj'un) *n.* a miser; a churl. [Formerly also *cornmudgin*, as if fr. E. CORN, and O.F. *mucier*, hide.]

CURMUDGEONLY (kur-muj'un-li) *a.* churlish; avaricious. [See CURMUDGEON.]

CURRANT (kur'ant) *n.* a shrub and its fruit; a dried grape. [Fr. F. *Corinthe*, Corinth.]

CURRENCY (kur'en-si) *n.* circulation; paper passing for money. [See CURRENT.]

CURRENT (kur'ent) *a.* circulating; common; now passing;—*n.* a stream; course. [L. (part. stem) *current-*, running. fr. *currere*.]

CURRENTLY (kur'ent-li) *ad.* with general reception; commonly. [See CURRENT.]

CURRENTNESS (kur'ent-nes) *n.* circulation; fluency. [See CURRENT.]

CURRICLE (kur'i-kl) *n.* a chaise of two wheels for two horses. [Doublet of CURRICULUM.]

CURRICULUM (ku-rik'ū-lum) *n.* a racecourse; a prescribed course of study. [L. *currere*, run.]

CURRIER (kur'i-er) *n.* a dresser of tanned leather. [See CURRY (2).]

CURRISH (kur'ish) *a.* like a cross dog; snappish. [See CUR.]

CURRY (kur'i) *n.* (1) a highly-spiced seasoning powder; a stew mixed with it;—*v.t.* to season with curry;—(2) rub and clean. [(1) Tamil. (2) O.F. = F. *corroyer*, fr. *couroi*, gear; fr. L. *con* = *cum*, and *roi*, order. See ARRAY.]

CURRYCOMB (kur'i-kŏm) *n.* a comb to clean horses. [See CURRY (2).]

CURSE (kurs) *v.t.* to wish evil to;—*n.* a wish of evil; execration. [O.E. *cursian*, fr. *curs*, curse.]

CURSED (kurst) *pp.* execrated. [See CURSE.]

CURSED (kurs'ed) *a.* deserving a curse; vexatious; hateful. [See CURSE.]

CURSEDLY (kur'sed-li) *ad.* miserably; shamefully. [See CURSE.]

CURSING (kurs'ing) *n.* execration; swearing. [See CURSE.]

CURSIVE (kur'siv) *a.* flowing; running. [Late L. *cursivus*, fr. L. (part.) *cursus*, run, fr. *currere*.]

CURSORILY (kur'sur-i-li) *ad.* in a cursory manner; hastily. [See CURSORY.]

CURSORY (kur'sur-i) *a.* hasty; superficial. [L., fr. stem *cursori-*, of *cursor*, runner.]

CURT (kurt) *a.* short; brief; concise. [L. *curtus*, short.]

CURTAIL (kur-tāl') *v.t.* to cut short; abridge; cut off. [See CURT. Through O.F. *courtault*; old spelling was *curtal*.]

CURTAILMENT (kur-tāl'ment) *n.* abridgment.

CURTAIN (kur'tin) *n.* a hanging cloth for a bed or window;—*v.t.* to enclose or furnish with a curtain. [O.F. *cortine*, fr. Low L. (acc.) *cortinam*, dim. of *cohortem*, COURT.]

CURTLY (kurt'li) *ad.* shortly; concisely.

CURTSY, CURTSEY (kurt'si) *n.* a salutation made by slightly bending the knees and bowing;—*v.i.* to make a curtsy. [See COURTESY.] [See CURTSEY.]

CURVATION (kur-vā'shun) *n.* act of bending.

CURVATURE (kur'va-tūr) *n.* a curve. [See CURVE.]

CURVE (kurv) *a.* bending; inflected;—*n.* anything bent;—*v.t.* to inflect; to bend [L. *curvus*.]

CURVILINEAR (kur-vi-lin'ē-ar) *a.* having a curved line. [L. *curvus*, a curve, and *linea*, a line.]

Curve.

CURVITY (kur'vi-ti) *n.* a bent state. [See CURVE.]

CUSHAT (kush'at) *n.* the ring-dove. [O.E. *cusceote*, fr. *cwic*, active, and *sceotan*, shoot.]

CUSHION (koosh'un) *n.* a pillow for a seat;—*v.t.* to furnish with cushions. [O.F., fr. L. *coxa*, a hip.]

CUSP (kusp) *n.* the point of the new moon; a projecting point. [L. *cuspis*, a point.]

CUSPIDAL (kus'pi-dal) *a.* ending in a point. [See CUSP.]

CUSTARD (kus'tard) *n.* a composition of milk, eggs and sugar. [M.E. *crustade*, fr. O.F. *croustade*, pie, fr. It., fr. L. *crustatus*, made with CRUST.]

CUSTARD-APPLE (kus'tard-ap-pl) *n.* a West Indian fruit with a yellow soft pulp. [See CUSTARD.]

CUSTODIAN (kus-tō'di-an) *n.* one who has the care of a public building. [See CUSTODY.]

CUSTODY (kus'tu-di) *n.* a keeping or guarding; imprisonment. [L. *custodia*, fr. stem *custodi-*, of *custos*, guardian.]

CUSTOM (kus'tum) *n.* habitual practice; established usage; business support. [O.F. *costume*, fr. Low L., corr. of L. (acc.) *consuetudinem*.] Doublet of COSTUME.]

CUSTOMARILY (kus'tum-ar-i-li) *ad.* habitually. [See CUSTOM.]

CUSTOMARY (kus'tum-ar-i) *a.* conformable to custom. [See CUSTOM.]

CUSTOMER (kus'tum-er) *n.* an accustomed buyer at a shop. [See CUSTOM.]

CUSTOM-HOUSE (kus'tum-hous) *n.* the house where duties are paid. [See CUSTOM.]

CUSTOMS (kus'tumz) *n.pl.* duties on goods imported or exported. [See CUSTOM.]

CUT (kut) *v.t.* or *i.* [*pret.* and *pp.* CUT] to carve; hew; chop;—*n.* a cleft or gash; a slice. [Perh. Celt.]

CUTE (kūt) *a.* sharp; clever. [Short for ACUTE.]

CUTICLE (kū'ti-kl) *n.* the outermost skin of the body. [L. *cutis*, the skin.]

CUTLASS (kut'las) *n.* a broad, curving sword. [F. *coutelas*, fr. O.F. *coutel*, knife, fr. L. (acc.) *cultellum*, dim. fr. *coulter*, CUTLER.]

CUTLER (kut'ler) *n.* a maker of knives and edged tools. [O.F. *cotelier*, fr. Late L. (acc.) *cultellarium*. See CUTLASS.]

CUTLERY (kut'ler-i) *n.* the articles made by cutlers. [See CUTLER.]

CUTLET (kut'let) *n.* a small piece of meat off the ribs for cooking. [F. *côtelette*, dim. of *côte*, rib, fr. L. (acc.) *costam*.]

CUTTER (kut'er) *n.* a swift sailing vessel, with one mast and a straight running bowsprit. [W. *cwtan*, to make short.]

CUTTING (kut'ing) *a.* severe; pungent:—*n.* a piece cut off. [See CUT.]

CUTTINGLY (kut'ing-li) *ad.* pungently; severely. [See CUT.]

CUTTLE-FISH (kut'l-fish) *n.* a mollusc, which ejects a black fluid when pursued. [O.E. *cudele*. Cf. Ger. *Kuttelfisch*.]

CUT-WATER (kut'waw-ter) *n.* the fore part of a ship's prow. [See CUT.]

CYCLE (sī'kl) *n.* a circle; round of time; short form of bicycle. [G. *kuklos*, circle.]

CYCLIC (sī'klik) *a.* pertaining to a cycle. [See CYCLE.]

CYCLOID (sī'kloid) *n.* a geometrical curve. [G. *kuklos*, circle, and *eidos*, form.]

CYCLOIDAL (sī-kloi'dal) *a.* pertaining to a cycloid. [See CYCLOID.]

CYCLOMETRY (sī-klom'e-tri) *n.* art of measuring cycles. [G. *kuklos*, circle, and *metron*, measure.]

Cycloid.

CYCLONE (sī'klōn) *n.* a violent rotatory wind. [G. *kukloein*, whirl round.]

CYCLOPEAN (sī-klō-pē'an) *a.* pertaining to the Cyclops; vast; gigantic. [See CYCLOPS.]

CYCLOPEDIA (sī-klō-pē'di-a) *n.* a body or circle of sciences. [G. *kuklos*, circle, and *paideia*, learning.]

CYCLOPS (sī'klops) *n. sing.* and *pl.* in *fabulous history*, a class of giants. [G.]

CYCLORAMA (sī-klō-rä'ma) *n.* an exhibition or series of moving views. [G. *kuklos*, circle, and *horama*, view.]

CYCLOSTYLE (sī'klō-stīl) *n.* a kind of copying press. [G. *kuklos*, circle, and STYLE.]

CYGNET (sig'net) *n.* a young swan. [Dim. fr. O.F. *cigne* = F. *cygne*, swan, through L., fr. G. *kuknos*.]

CYGNUS (sig'nus) *n.* the swan. [See CYGNET.]

CYLINDER (sil'in-der) *n.* a roller-like body whose ends are equal and parallel circles. [F., fr. L., fr. G. *kulindros*, fr. *kuliein*, to make to roll.]

CYLINDRICAL (sil-in'dri-kal) *a.* of the nature of a cylinder. [See CYLINDER.]

CYNIC (sin'ik) *n.* a morose man. [G. *kunikos*, dog-like.]

CYNICAL (sin'i-kal) *a.* surly; snarling; satirical. [See CYNIC.]

CYNICALLY (sin'i-kal-i) *ad.* in a sneering, morose manner. [See CYNIC.]

CYNICISM (sin'i-sizm) *n.* a morose contempt of the pleasures and acts of life.

CYNOSURE (sin'o-shōor, sī'no-shōor) *n.* the star nearest the north pole; that which attracts. [G. (gen.) *kunos*, of the dog, and *oura*, tail.]

CYPRESS (sī'pres) *n.* a hard-wood evergreen tree; an emblem of mourning. [O.F. *cypres* = F. *cyprès*, fr. L., fr. G. *kuparissos*.]

CYST (sist) *n.* a bar in animal bodies enclosing matter. [L., fr. G. *kustis*, bladder.]

CYSTIC (sis'tik) *a.* contained in a bag. [See CYST.]

CYSTITIS (sis-tī'tis) *n.* inflammation of the bladder. [See CYST.]

CYSTOSE (sist'ōz) *a.* containing cysts. [See CYST.]

CZAR, TZAR (zär) *n.* the emperor of Russia. [Russ., fr. L. *Cæsar*.]

CZARINA (za-rē'na) *n.* the empress of Russia. [See CZAR.]

CZAREVITCH (zär'e-vich) *n.* the eldest son of the Czar. [See CZAR.]

D

DAB (dab) *v.t.* to hit gently with something moist;—*n.* a gentle blow; a soft lump; an expert; a small flat fish. [M.E. *dabben*, strike. Cf. Ger. *Tappe*, paw.]

DABBLE (dab'l) *v.i.* to play in water; meddle with; trifle;—*v.t.* to wet with dabs; sprinkle or splash. [Freq. of DAB.]

DABBLER (dab'ler) *n.* one who dabbles. [See DABBLE.]

DABSTER (dab'ster) *n.* one who is expert. [See DAB.]

DA CAPO (dä-kä'pō) *n.* musical direction to repeat a piece from the beginning. [It.]

DACE (dās) *n.* a small river-fish. [O.F. *dars*. See DART.]

DAD, DADDY (dad, dad'i) *n.* a child's term for father. [E.]

DADO (dä'dō) *n.* the square part of a pedestal; the moulding round the lower part of the walls of a room. [It.]

DAFFODIL (daf'ō-dil) *n.* a plant with yellow flowers. [For M.E. *affodille*, fr. F. *affrodille*, fr. L. (acc.) *aspodelum*, fr. G. *asphodelos*.]

DAGGER (dag'er) *n.* a short sword. [F. *dague*, of unknown etym.]

DAGGLE (dag'l) *v.i.* to trail in the dirt. [Scand.]

DAGON (dä'gon) *n.* a god, half man, half fish. [Heb. *dag*, a fish.]

DAGUERREOTYPE (dag-er'ō-tīp) *n.* a picture taken by means of light thrown on a surface covered with the iodide of silver. [Formed fr. *Daguerre*, the discoverer.]

DAHLIA (dāl'ya) *n.* a plant that bears a large beautiful compound flower of every variety of colour. [Fr. *Dahl*, a Swedish botanist.]

DAILY (dā'li) *a.* being every day;—*ad.* every day; day by day.

DAINTILY (dān'ti-li) *ad.* nicely; deliciously.

DAINTY (dān'ti) *a.* nice; fastidious;—*n.* a nice bit; delicacy. [O.F. *daintie*, worth, fr. L. (acc.) *dignitatem*. Doublet of DIGNITY.]

DAIRY (dā'ri) *n.* the place where milk is set and butter and cheese made. [Scand.]

DAIS (dā'is) *n.* a platform or high table at the upper end of the dining-hall. [O.F. *deis*, fr. Low L. (acc.) *discum*, table, fr. G. *diskos*, a quoit.]

DAISY (dā'zi) *n.* a common plant of several varieties. [O.E. *dœges-eáye,* day's eye, sun.]

DAKOIT (da-koit') *n.* one of a gang of robbers or river pirates. [Hind.]

DALE (dāl) *n.* a space between hills; a vale. [O.E. *dœl.* Doublet of **DELL.**]

DALLIANCE (dal'i-ans) *n.* act of fondness; mutual embrace; trifling delay. [See **DALLY.**]

DALLY (dal'i) *v.i.* to delay; trifle with; fondle. [M.E. *dalien,* fr. root of **DULL.**]

DALTONISM (dal'tun-izm) *n.* colour-blindness. [Fr. John *Dalton,* chemist, who had this defect.]

DAM (dam) *n.* (1) a mother of brutes:—(2) a bank to confine water;—*v.t.* to confine or shut in water by dams. [(1) F., form of **DAME.** (2) [E.]

DAMAGE (dam'āj) *n.* injury; hurt;—*v.t.* to injure; hurt. [O.F., through Late L., fr. L. *damnum,* loss.]

DAMAGEABLE (dam'āj-a-bl) *a.* liable to receive damage. [See **DAMAGE.**]

DAMASK (dam'ask) *n.* a silk woven with flowers;—*v.t.* to weave flowered work on stuffs. [Fr. *Damascus.*]

DAMASKED (dam'askt) *pp.* or *a.* woven into flowers. [See **DAMASK.**]

DAMASKEEN (dam-as-kēn') *v.t.* to fill incisions in iron or steel with gold or silver wire. [F. *damosquiner.*]

DAME (dām) *n.* a lady; a woman. [F., fr. L. (acc.) *dominam.*]

DAMN (dam) *v.t.* to condemn. [F. *damner,* fr. L. *damnare,* **CONDEMN,** fr. *damnum,* loss.]

DAMNABLE (dam'na-bl) *a.* deserving damnation; odious. [See **DAMN.**]

DAMNABLY (dam'na-bli) *ad.* so as to incur damnation. [See **DAMN.**]

DAMNATORY (dam'na-tur-i) *a.* tending to condemn. [See **DAMN.**]

DAMP (damp) *n.* moist air; fog;—*a.* moist; humid; watery;—*v.t.* to wet; dispirit. [E. Cf. Ger. *Dampf,* vapour.]

DAMPEN (dam'pn) *v.t.* or *i.* to make or become moist. [See **DAMP.**]

DAMPER (dam'per) *n.* a valve to stop air; that which damps. [See **DAMP.**]

DAMPISH (dam'pish) *a.* moist; humid. [See **DAMP.**]

DAMPNESS (damp'nes) *n.* humidity. [See **DAMP.**]

DAMPS (damps) *n.pl.* noxious exhalations. [See **DAMP.**]

DAMSEL (dam'zel) *n.* a young maiden. [O.F. *dameisele,* fr. Late L. (acc.) *domicellam,* fr *domina.*]

DAMSON (dam'zn) *n.* a small black plum. [Short for *Damascene.*]

DANCE (dans) *v.i.* to leap; move to music with varied motions of the feet;—*v.t.* to dandle;—*n.* a leaping and stepping to the sound of music. [O.F. *danser,* fr. O. H. Ger. *danson,* drag along.]

DANCER (dan'ser) *n.* one who dances. [See **DANCE.**]

DANDELION (dan-de-li'un) *n.* the plant lion's tooth or taraxacum. [F. *dent de lion.*]

DANDLE (dan'dl) *v.t.* to shake on the knee; fondle. [E. Cf. Ger. *tändeln,* fr. *Tand.*]

DANDY (dan'di) *n.* a fop; a coxcomb. [Etym. uncertain.]

DANDYISM (dan'di-izm) *n.* the peculiarities of a dandy. [See **DANDY.**]

DANGER (dān'jer) *n.* exposure to risk. [O.F. *dangier,* absolute power, through Late L.; fr. L. *dominus,* master.]

DANGEROUS (dān'jer-us) *a.* full of danger. [See **DANGER.**]

DANGEROUSLY (dān'jer-us-li) *ad.* with danger or hazard. [See **DANGER.**]

DANGLE (dang'gl) *v.i.* to hang loose;—*v.t.* to swing. [Scand.]

DANK (dangk) *a.* moist; humid; damp. [Scand.]

DANSEUSE (dong-sez') *n.* a female professional dancer. [F. See **DANCE.**]

DAPPER (dap'er) *a.* little; active. [D. = brave.]

DAPPLED (dap'ld) *a.* variegated with spots. [Scand.]

DARE (dār) *v.i.* (1) [*pret.* **DURST**] to have courage; venture;—*v.t.* (2) to challenge; defy. [(1) O.E. *dearr* (I) dare. (2) M.E. *daren,* to be in fear, to frighten.]

DARING (dār'ing) *a.* having great courage; fearless; intrepid. [See **DARE.**]

DARINGLY (dār'ing-li) *ad.* boldly. [See **DARE.**]

DARK (därk) *a.* wanting light; obscure;—*n.* darkness; gloom. [M.E. *derk,* fr. O.E. *deorc.*]

DARKEN (där'kn) *v.t.* to make dark;—*v.i.* to grow dark. [See **DARK.**]

DARKISH (där'kish) *a.* rather dark; dusky. [See **DARK.**]

DARKLY (därk'li) *ad.* obscurely; blindly. [See **DARK.**]

DARKNESS (därk'nes) *n.* want of light; infernal gloom. [See **DARK.**]

DARLING (där'ling) *a.* dearly beloved;—*n.* one much loved. [M.E. *derling,* fr. O.E. *deorling,* fr. **DEAR.**]

DARN (därn) *v.t.* to mend holes in clothes. [Perh. Celt.]

DART (därt) *n.* a pointed missile weapon;—*v.t.* or *i.* to thrust; fly as a dart. [O.F. *dart,* fr. Teut. Cf. O.E. *daroth.* See **DACE.**]

DASH (dash) *v.t.* or *i.* to throw or break hastily; strike against; blot out;—*n.* a slight infusion; this mark (—); a blow; flourish; parade. [Scand.]

DASH-BOARD (dash'bōrd) *n.* a board on the front of a vehicle to keep off water, mud, etc. [See **DASH.**]

DASHING (dash'ing) *a.* impetuous; spirited; showy. [See **DASH.**]

DASTARD (das'tard) *n.* one who meanly shrinks from danger; coward; poltroon. [Scand.]

DATA (dā'ta) *n.pl.* propositions given and admitted. [See **DATE.**]

DATE (dāt) *n.* (1) the time of an event;—*v.t.* to note the time of;—*v.i.* to count or begin from;—(2) *n.* the fruit of the palm-tree. [(1) Fr. L. *datum,* fr. (neut. pl. part.) *data,* given, fr. *dare.* (2) O.F. *date* = F. *datte,* fr. L. (acc.) *dactulus.*]

DATELESS (dāt'les) *a.* having no date. [See **DATE.**]

DATIVE (dā'tiv) *a.* or *n.* one of the six Latin cases. [L. *dativus,* pertaining to giving, fr. *dare.*]

DAUB (dawb) *v.t.* to smear with mortar; paint coarsely. [O.F. *dauber,* fr. L. *de-albere,* white-wash, fr. L. *de,* and *albus.*]

DAUBER (daw'ber) *n.* one that daubs. [See **DAUB.**]

DAUBERY (dawb'er-i) *n.* coarse painting. [See **DAUB.**]

DAUBY (daw'bi) *a.* sticky; ropy; glutinous. [See **DAUB.**]

DAUGHTER (daw'ter) *n.* a female child. [M.E. *doghter,* fr. O.E. *dohtor.*]

DAUGHTERLY (daw'ter-li) *ad.* becoming a daughter. [See **DAUGHTER.**]

DAUNT (dänt, also dawnt) *v.t.* to check by fear of danger; intimidate; dishearten. [O.F., fr. L. *domitare,* fr. *domare,* tame.]

DAUNTLESS (dänt'les) *a.* fearless; intrepid. [See **DAUNT.**]

DAUPHIN (daw'fin, dō-fang') *n.* eldest son of the king of France. [F.]

DAVITS (dā'vits) *n.pl.* iron projections over a ship's side, with tackling to hoist up a boat. [F., of uncertain origin.]

DAWN (dawn) *v.i.* to begin to grow light;—*n.* break of day; beginning; first rise. [M.E. *dawen*, fr. O.E. *dagian*, fr. *dæg*, day.]

DAY (dā) *n.* the time from sunrise to sunset; the twenty-four hours. [O.E. *dæg*. Cf. Ger. *Tag*.]

DAY-BOOK (dā'bóók) *n.* a daily journal of accounts. [See DAY.]

DAYBREAK (dā'brāk) *n.* the first appearance of day. [See DAY.]

DAYDREAM (dā'drēm) *n.* an idle fancy. [See DAY and DREAM.]

DAYLIGHT (dā'līt) *n.* the light of the sun. [See DAY.]

DAY-SPRING (dā'spring) *n.* the dawn. [See DAY.]

DAY-STAR (dā'stár) *n.* the morning star. [See DAY.]

DAYTIME (dā'tīm) *n.* time between sunrise and sunset. [See DAY.]

DAZE (dāz) *v.t.* to confuse; stupefy. [Scand.]

DAZZLE (daz'l) *v.t.* to overpower with light or splendour. [Scand.]

DAZZLINGLY (daz'ling-li) *ad.* in a dazzling manner. [See DAZE.]

DEACON (dē'kn) *n.* a church official. [O.E. *diacon*, fr. L., fr. G. *diakonos*, a servant.]

DEACONESS (dē'kn-es) *n.* a female deacon. [See DEACON.]

DEACONSHIP (dē'kn-ship) *n.* the office of a deacon; deaconry. [See DEACON.]

DEAD (ded) *a.* destitute of life;—*n.* stillness; gloom; silence;—*ad.* wholly; completely. [O.E. *dead*.]

DEADEN (ded'n) *v.t.* to weaken; make lifeless. [See DEAD.]

DEADLINESS (ded'li-nes) *n.* the quality of being deadly. [See DEAD.]

DEADLY (ded'li) *a.* mortal; destructive. [See DEAD.]

DEAD-MARCH (ded'march) *n.* solemn music played at a funeral procession. [See DEAD and MARCH.]

DEADNESS (ded'nes) *n.* want of life. [See DEAD.]

DEAD-RECKONING (ded'rek-un-ing) *n.* calculation of a ship's position by the log merely. [*Dead*, intensive, and RECKON.]

DEAD-SHOT (ded'shot) *n.* a sure marksman. [*Dead*, intensive, and SHOT.]

DEAF (def) *a.* wanting the sense of hearing. [O.E. *deaf*.]

DEAFEN (def'n) *v.t.* to make deaf; render a floor impervious to sound by filling in mortar, etc. [See DEAF.]

DEAF-MUTE (def'mūt) *n.* one who is both deaf and dumb. [See DEAF and DUMB.]

DEAFNESS (def'nes) *n.* want of hearing; refusing to hear. [See DEAF.]

DEAL (dēl) *n.* a part; quantity; boards, etc.; distribution;—*v.t.* [*pret.* DEALT] to distribute;—*v.i.* to transact business; behave; distribute cards. [O.E. *dœlan*.]

DEALER (dē'ler) *n.* a trader. [See DEAL.]

DEALING (dē'ling) *n.* manner of acting; behaviour; intercourse in trade. [See DEAL.]

DEAN (dēn) *n.* the second dignitary of a diocese; the head of a college or faculty. [O.F. *deien* = F. *doyen*, fr. L. *decanus*, chief of ten, fr. *decem*.]

DEANERY (dē'ner-i) *n.* office or residence of a dean. [See DEAN.]

DEAR (dēr) *c.* costly; of high value; beloved; —*n.* a person beloved. [M.E. *dere*, fr. O.E. *deore*. Cf. Ger. *thauer*.]

DEARLY (dēr'li) *ad.* at high price. [See DEAR.]

DEARNESS (dēr'nes) *n.* a high price. [See DEAR.]

DEARTH (derth) *n.* great scarcity.

DEATH (deth) *n.* the extinction of life. [M.E. *deeth*, fr. O.E. *death* (2 syll.).]

DEATH-BED (deth'bed) *n.* bed of a dying person; last illness. [See DEATH.]

DEATH-BLOW (deth'blō) *n.* blow extinguishing life or hope. [See DEATH.]

DEATHLESS (deth'les) *a.* immortal. [See DEATH.]

DEATHLIKE (deth'līk) *a.* resembling death. [See DEATH.]

DEATH-RATE (deth'rāt) *n.* proportion of deaths in a given time and area. [See DEATH and RATE.]

DEATH'S-HEAD (dethz'hed) *n.* a figure of a human skull; a kind of moth. [See DEATH.]

DEATH-WARRANT (deth'wor-ant) *n.* a warrant for an execution. [See DEATH and WARRANT.]

DEATH-WATCH (deth'woch) *n.* a small kind of beetle. [See DEATH.]

DEBAR (de-bár') *v.t.* to hinder from entering or enjoying. [F., fr. *dé* = L. *dis*, and BAR.]

DEBARK (de-bárk') *v.t.* or *i.* to disembark. [F. *débarquer*, fr. *dé* = *dis*, and BARQUE.]

DEBARKATION (de-bár-kā'shun) *n.* act of disembarking. [See DISEMBARK.]

DEBASE (de-bās') *v.t.* to degrade; adulterate; vitiate. [Fr. *dé* = L. *dis*, and BASE.]

DEBASEMENT (de-bās'ment) *n.* degradation. [See DEBASE.]

DEBASING (de-bās'ing) *a.* tending to lower or degrade. [See DEBASE.]

DEBATABLE (de-bā'ta-bl) *a.* disputable. [See DEBATE.]

DEBATE (de-bāt') *v.t.* or *i.* to dispute; discuss;—*n.* public discussion. [O.F. *debatre*, fr. *dé* = L. *dis*, and *battre*, to fight.]

DEBATER (de-bā'ter) *n.* one who debates. [See DEBATE.]

DEBATINGLY (de-bāt'ing-li) *ad.* in the manner of debate. [See DEBATE.]

DEBAUCH (de-bawch') *n.* unrestrained indulgence of the appetites;—*v.t.* to corrupt; seduce. [O.F. *desbaucher*, seduce, fr. *des* = L. *dis*, apart, and *bauche*, place of work.]

DEBAUCHEE (deb-ō-shē') *n.* a drunkard; a rake. [See DEBAUCH.]

DEBAUCHERY (de-baw'cher-i) *n.* seduction from duty, etc.; habitual intemperance or lewdness. [See DEBAUCH.]

DEBENTURE (de-ben'tūr) *n.* a writing acknowledging a debt; a certificate entitling to a drawback. [L. (pres. ind.) *debentur*, they are owing, fr. *debere*. Acknowledgments began *debentur mihi*.]

DEBILITATE (de-bil'i-tāt) *v.t.* to weaken. [L. (part.) *debilitatus*, weakened, fr. *debilis*.]

DEBILITY (de-bil'i-ti) *n.* feebleness. [See DEBILITATE.]

DEBIT (deb'it) *n.* the debtor side of an account book;—*v.t.* to charge with debt. [L. *debitum*. See DEBT.]

DEBRIS (de-brē') *n.* ruins; fragments of rocks. [F. *briser*, to break.]

DEBT (det) *n.* what is due. [O.F. *dette*, fr. Low L. (acc.) *debitam*, fr. L. (part.) *debitus*, owed, fr. L. *debere*, to owe.]

DEBTEE (det'ē) *n.* a creditor. [See DEBT.]

DEBTLESS (det'les) *a.* free from debt. [See DEBT.]

DEBTOR (det'er) *n.* one who owes. [O.F. *deteur*, fr. L. (acc.) *debitorem*.]

DEBUT (dā-bōō') *n.* a first appearance. [F.]

DEBUTANT (dā-bōō-tang') *n.* one who makes his first public appearance;—*fem.* DEBUTANTE (dā-bōō-tant') [F.]

DECADE (dek'ād) *n.* the number of ten. [F., fr. L., fr. G. stem, *dekad-*, of *dekas*, a ten, fr. *deka*, ten.]

DECADENCE (de-kā'dens) *n.* a state of decay. [F., fr. L. *de*, down, and CADENCE.]

DECAGON (dek'a-gon) *n.* a figure of ten sides and ten angles. [G. *deka*, ten, and *gon-ia*, corner, angle.]

DECAHEDRON (dek-a-hē'drun) *n.* a solid figure having ten sides. [Fr. G. *deka*, ten, and *hedra*, seat, face.]

DECALOGUE (dek'a-log) *n.* the ten commandments. [F. *décalogue*, fr. L., fr. G. *dekalogos*, fr. *deka*, ten, and *logos*, saying.]

DECAMP (de-kamp') *v.i.* to depart from a camp; march off. [F., fr. *de* = L. *dis*, and CAMP.]

DECAMPMENT (de-kamp'ment) *n.* act of marching off. [See DECAMP.]

DECANT (de-kant') *v.t.* to pour off or out. [F., fr. L. *de*, out of, and *canthus*, neck of a bottle, fr. G.]

DECANTATION (dē-kan-tā'shun) *n.* act of decanting. [See DECANT.]

DECANTER (de-kan'tẹr) *n.* a glass vessel. [See DECANT.]

DECAPITATE (de-kap'i-tāt) *v.t.* to behead. [L. (part.) *decapitatus*, beheaded, fr. *de*, and stem *capit-*, of *caput*, head.]

DECAPITATION (de-kap-i-tā'shun) *n.* act of beheading. [See DECAPITATE.]

DECAY (de-kā') *n.* a falling off; decline;—*v.i.* to decline; wither. [O.F. *decair* = F. *décheoir*, fail, through Low L., fr. L. *de*, and *cadere*.]

DECEASE (de-sēs') *n.* departure from life; death;—*v.i.* to depart from life. [O.F. *deces* = F. *décès*, fr. L. (acc.) *decessum*, departure, fr. L., fr. *de*, and *cedere*, withdraw.]

DECEASED (de-sēst') *a.* departed from life; dead. [See DECEASE.]

DECEIT (de-sēt') *n.* device intended to deceive; artifice; fraud. [O.F. (part.) = deceived.]

DECEITFUL (de-sēt'fool) *a.* full of guile. [See DECEIT.]

DECEITFULLY (de-sēt'fool-i) *ad.* in a deceitful manner; fraudulently. [See DECEIT.]

DECEIVABLE (de-sē'va-bl) *a.* liable to be deceived. [See DECEIVE.]

DECEIVE (de-sēv') *v.t.* to mislead the mind; impose on; disappoint. [O.F. *deceveiz* = F. *décevoiz*, fr. L. *decipere*, fr. *de*, and *capere*, take.]

DECEIVER (de-sē'vẹr) *n.* one that deceives or misleads. [See DECEIVE.]

DECEMBER (de-sem'bẹr) *n.* the twelfth or last month of the year. [L.]

DECENCY (dē'sen-si) *n.* fitness; propriety; modesty. [See DECENT.]

DECENNIAL (dē-sen'i-al) *a.* continuing ten years. [L.]

DECENT (dē'sent) *a.* suitable or becoming; seemly; m des; moderate; sufficient. [O.F., fr. L. (acct.part.) *decentem*, becoming, fr. *decere*.] [See DECENT.]

DECENTLY (dē'sent-li) *ad.* fitly; properly.

DECENTRALISATION (dē-sen-tral-i-zā'shun) *n.* transferring administrative power from the metropolis to provincial or local authorities. [L. *de*, away, and CENTRE.]

DECEPTION (de-sep'shun) *n.* act of deceiving; cheat; fraud. [O.F., fr. L. (acc.) *deceptionem*, fr. (part.) *deceptus*, deceived, fr. *decipere*, DECEIVE.]

DECEPTIVE (de-sep'tiv) *a.* tending to deceive; deceitful; false. [See DECEIVE.]

DECIDE (de-sīd') *v.t.* or *i.* to determine; finish; give judgment. [F. *décider*, fr. L. *decidere*, cut off, settle, fr. *de* and *caedere*.]

DECIDED (de-sī'ded) *a.* clear; resolute. [See DECIDE.]

DECIDEDLY (de-sī'ded-li) *ad.* with determination; fixedly. [See DECIDE.]

DECIDUOUS (de-sid'ū-us) *a.* falling off after a time. [L. *decidu-us*, fr. *decidere*, fall off, fr. *de* and *cadere*.]

DECIMAL (des'i-mal) *a.* tenth;—*n.* a tenth. [O.F., fr. L. *decima*, a tenth part, fr. L. *decimus*.]

DECIMALISE (des'i-mal-īz) *v.t.* to reduce to decimals. [See DECIMAL.]

DECIMALISM (des'i-mal-izm) *n.* the system of weights, measures, and currency, in which the standard unit is multiplied or divided by ten. [See DECIMAL.]

DECIMATE (des'i-māt) *v.t.* to take one in every ten. [L. (part.) *decimatus*, decimated, fr. *decimare*.]

DECIMATION (des-i-mā'shun) *n.* the taking of every tenth. [See DECIMATE.]

DECIPHER (de-sī'fẹr) *v.t.* to explain ciphers; unravel. [F. (pref.) *dé* = L. *dis*.]

DECIPHERABLE (de-sī'fẹr-a-bl) *a.* that may be deciphered. [See DECIPHER.]

DECIPHERER (de-sī'fẹr-ẹr) *n.* one who deciphers or unravels. [See DECIPHER.]

DECISION (de-sizh'un) *n.* act of settling; conclusion; final judgment; decree; firmness of purpose; resolution. [See DECIDE.]

DECISIVE (de-sī'siv) *a.* that determines. [See DECIDE.] [See DECIDE.]

DECISIVELY (de-sī'siv-li) *ad.* conclusively.

DECISIVENESS (de-sī'siv-nes) *n.* quality of deciding or of being decided. [See DECIDE.]

DECISORY (de-sī'sor-i) *a.* able to decide. [See DECIDE.]

DECK (dek) *v.t.* to dress; adorn; set off or embellish;—*n.* the floor of a ship. [D., conn. with THATCH; Ger. *decken*, to cover.]

DECKING (dek'ing) *n.* act of adorning; that which adorns. [See DECK.]

DECLAIM (de-klām') *v.i.* to speak an oration; harangue. [For *declame*, fr. L., fr. *de*, and *clamare*, cry.]

DECLAIMER (de-klā'mẹr) *n.* one who declaims. [See DECLAIM.]

DECLAMATION (dek-la-mā'shun) *n.* a harangue; a passionate rhetorical speech. [See DECLAIM.]

DECLAMATORY (de-klam'a-tur-i) *a.* in the style of declamation. [See DECLAIM.]

DECLARANT (de-klā'rant) *n.* one who declares. [See DECLARE.]

DECLARATION (dek-la-rā'shun) *n.* affirmation. [See DECLARE.]

DECLARATIVE (de-klar'a-tiv) *a.* that declares; explanatory. [See DECLARE.]

DECLARATORY (de-klar'a-tur-i) *a.* affirmative; clearly expressive. [See DECLARE.]

DECLARE (de-klār') *v.t.* or *i.* to make known; affirm; assert; decide in favour of. [F. *déclarer*, fr. L. *declarare*, manifest, fr. *de*, fully, and *clarus*, clear.]

DECLENSION (de-klen'shun) *n.* tendency to fail; refusal; variation of nouns. [O.F. *declinaison*, fr. L. (acc.) *declinationem*.]

DECLINABLE (de-kli'na-bl) *a.* that may be grammatically varied. [See DECLINE.]

DECLINAL (de-kli'nal) *a.* sloping downwards. [See DECLINE.]

DECLINATE (dek'li-nāt) *a.* bending or bent downwards. [See DECLINE.]

DECLINATION (dek-li-nā'shun) *n.* act of bending; deviation; decay; distance from the equator; declension of a noun. [See DECLINE.]

DECLINATORY (de-klin'a-tur-i) *a.* intimating refusal. [See DECLINE.]

DECLINATURE (de-klin'a-tūr) *n.* act of refusing or rejecting. [See DECLINE.]

DECLINE (de-klīn') *v.i.* to fall; decay;—*v.t.* to shun; refuse;—*n.* decay; diminution. [O.F. *decliner*, fr. L. *declinare*.]

DECLIVITOUS (de-kliv'i-tus) *a.* sloping; not precipitous. [See DECLIVITY.]

DECLIVITY (de-kliv'i-ti) *n.* inclination downward; a sloping surface. [F., fr. L., fr. *declivis*, sloping down, fr. *de* and *clivus*.]

DECOCT (de-kokt') *v.t.* to boil; seethe; digest; invigorate. [L. (part.) *decoctus*, boiled down, fr. *de*, and *coquere*, cook.]

DECOCTION (de-kok'shun) *n.* preparation made by boiling; the extract obtained. [See DECOCT.]

DECOCTIVE (de-kok'tiv) *a.* that may be easily decocted.

DECOLLATE (dē-kol'āt) *v.t.* to behead. [L. (part.) *decollatus*, beheaded, fr. *de*, and *collum*, neck.]

Fāte, fär, ado; mē, hẹr; mīne; nōte; tūne; moón.

DECOLORATION (dē-kul-ur-ā'shun) *n.* removal or absence of colour. [F. (pref.) *dé* = L. *dis*, and COLOUR.]

DECOMPOSABLE (dē-kum-pō'zạ-bl) *a.* that may be decomposed. [See DECOMPOSE.]

DECOMPOSE (dē-kum-pōz') *v.t.* to resolve into original elements. [F. (pref.) *dé* =*dis*, and COMPOSE.]

DECOMPOSITION (dē-kom-pō-zish'un) *n.* resolution or separation into parts. [See DECOMPOSE.]

DECOMPOUND (dē-kom-pound') *v.t.* to compound a second time. [L. (pref.) *de*, and COMPOUND.]

DECORATE (dek'u-rāt) *v.t.* to adorn; embellish. [L. (part.) *decoratus*, adorned, fr. stem, *decor-*, of *decus*, ornament.]

DECORATION (dek-u-rā'shun) *n.* ornamentation; ornament; a badge. [See DECORATE.]

DECORATIVE (dek'-u-rā-tiv) *a.* fitted to adorn. [See DECORATE.]

DECOROUS (de-kō'rus) *a.* becoming; behaving with decorum. [L. *decorus*, seemly, fr. *decor*, seemliness.]

DECOROUSLY (de-kō'rus-li) *ad.* decently; becomingly. [See DECOROUS.]

DECORUM (de-kō'rum) *n.* propriety of speech and behaviour. [L. neut.]

DECOY (de-koi') *v.t.* to allure into a snare or net;—*n.* anything used to ensnare or lead into danger. [Fr. D.=cage, fr. L. (acc.) *caveam*. L. (pref.) *de*.]

DECOY-DUCK (de-koi'duk) *n.* a bird used to draw wild fowls towards the sportsman. [See DECOY.]

DECREASE (de-krēs') *v.t.* to make less;—*v.i.* to grow less;—*n.* a becoming less; decay. [O.F. *descreis*, *descrois*, a decrease, fr. *discroistre*, fr. L. *dis*, and *crescere*, increase.]

DECREE (de-krē') *v.t.* to determine; order;—*n.* an edict; order. [O.F. *decret*, fr. L. (neut. part.) *decretum*, decreed, fr. L. *decernere*.]

DECREPIT (de-krep'-it) *a.* infirm; wasted. [L. *de* =*down* and *crepitare*, creak.]

DECREPITATE (de-krep'i-tāt) *v.t.* to roast in heat with crackling;—*v.i.* to crackle in the fire.

DECREPITATION (de-krep-i-tā'shun) *n.* the act of roasting with a crackling noise. [See DECREPITATE.]

DECREPITUDE (de-krep'i-tūd) *n.* broken state of the body by age. [See DECREPIT.]

DECRESCENDO (dā-kre-shen'dō) *ad.* with gradual lessening of the sound. [L. *de* = down, and *crescere*, grow.]

DECRESCENT (de-kres'ent) *a.* decreasing. [L. (acc. part.) *dicrescentem*. See DECREASE.]

DECRETAL (de-krē'tạl) *a.* containing a decree; —*n.* a decree of the pope; a book of edicts. [See DECREE.]

DECRETIVE (de-krē'tiv) *a.* having the force of a decree. [See DECREE.]

DECRETORY (de-krē'tur-i, dek're-tur-i) *a.* established by decree. [See DECREE.]

DECRETORILY (de-krē'tur-i-li, dek're-tur-i-li) *ad.* definitively. [See DECREE.]

DECRY (de-krī') *v.t.* to cry down; censure; disparage. [F. (pref.) *des* =L. *dis*.]

DECUMBENT (de-kum'bent) *a.* lying down; prostrate; bending down. [L. (part. stem), *decumbent-*, fr. *de*, down, and *cumbere*, lie.]

DECUMBENTLY (de-kum'bent-li) *ad.* in a decumbent posture. [See DECUMBENT.]

DECURRENT (de-kur'ent) *a.* running or extending down. [L. *de*, down, and *curro*, run.]

DECURRENTLY (de-kur'ent-li) *ad.* in a decurrent manner. [See DECURRENT.]

DECURSIVE (de-kur'siv) *a.* running down; decurrent. [See DECURRENT.]

DECUSSATE (de-kus'āt) *v.t.* to intersect at acute angles. [L. (part.) *decussatus*, marked with an X, fr. *decussis*, ten =*as*, piece, stamped with X, fr. *decem*, and stem *assi-*, of *as*.]

DECUSSATION (dē-kus-ā'shun) *n.* a crossing at unequal angles. [See DECUSSATE.]

DEDICATE (ded'i-kāt) *v.t.* to consecrate; devote to. [L. (part.) *dedicatus*, devoted, fr. *de*, and *dicare*, declare.]

DEDICATION (ded-i-kā'shun) *n.* consecration; inscription of a book to a friend or patron. [See DEDICATE.]

DEDICATOR (ded'i-kā-ter) *n.* one who dedicates. [See DEDICATE.]

DEDICATORY (ded'i-kā-tur-i) *a.* comprising a dedication. [See DEDICATE.]

DEDUCE (de-dūs') *v.t.* to draw as an inference. [L. *deducere*, bring down, fr. *de* and *ducere*.]

DEDUCIBLE (de-dū'si-bl) *a.* that may be inferred or deduced. [See DEDUCE.]

DEDUCT (de-dukt') *v.t.* to subtract. [L. (part.) *deductus*, brought down.]

DEDUCTION (de-duk'shun) *n.* inference; conclusion; abatement; subtraction. [L. (acc.) *deductionem*.]

DEDUCTIVE (de-duk'tiv) *a.* that may be deduced. [See DEDUCE.]

DEDUCTIVELY (de-duk'tiv-li) *ad.* by fair reasoning; by inference. [See DEDUCE.]

DEED (dēd) *n.* an action; exploit; a writing to convey property;—*v.t.* to transfer by deed. [O.E. *dǽd*, DO. Cf. Ger. *That*.]

DEEM (dēm) *v.t.* to think; judge;—*v.i.* to suppose. [O.E. *dēman*, judge, conn. with DOOM.]

DEEP (dēp) *a.* far to the bottom; profound; artful; intricate;—*n.* the sea; an abyss. [O.E. *dēop*. Cf. Ger. *tief*.]

DEEPEN (dē'pn) *v.t.* to make more deep or dark;—*v.i.* to grow more deep. [See DEEP.]

DEEPLY (dēp'li) *ad.* to a great depth; profoundly; gravely. [See DEEP.]

DEER (dēr) *n.* an animal hunted for venison. [O.E. *dēor*. Cf. Ger. *Thier*.]

DEER-STALKING (dēr-stawk'ing) *n.* shooting the red deer or stag by approaching them warily or stealthily. [See DEER and STALK.]

DEFACE (de-fās') *v.t.* to disfigure; erase. [O.F., fr. *des* =L. *dis*, and FACE.]

DEFACEMENT (de-fās'ment) *n.* injury to the surface; erasure. [See DEFACE.]

DEFALCATE (de-fal'kāt) *v.t.* to lop off. [Late L. (part.) *defalcatus*, cut away, fr. L. *de*, and stem *falc-*, of *falx*, sickle.]

DEFALCATION (dē-fal-kā'shun) *n.* that which is cut off; diminution; a fraudulent deficit; embezzlement. [See DEFALCATE.]

DEFALCATOR (def'al-kā-ter) *n.* one who embezzles money entrusted to his care. [See DEFALCATE.]

DEFAMATION (def-a-mā'shun) *n.* slander; calumny. [See DEFAME.]

DEFAMATORY (de-fam'ạ-tur-i) *a.* slanderous; calumnious. [See DEFAME.]

DEFAME (de-fām') *v.t.* to slander. [O.F. *diffamer*, fr. L. *diffamare*, fr. *dis*, and FAME.] [See DEFAME.]

DEFAMER (de-fā'mer) *n.* one that slanders.

DEFAMING (de-fā'ming) *n.* defamation; slander. [See DEFAME.]

DEFAULT (de-fawlt') *n.* omission; nonappearance in court;—*v.t.* to call in court, and record for not appearing. [O.F. *defaute*, fr. *defaillir*, fail, fr. L. *de*, and FAIL.]

DEFAULTER (de-fawl'ter) *n.* one in default; a peculator.

DEFEASANCE (de-fē'zans) *n.* the act of annulling. [Fr. O.F. (part.) *defeisant*, undoing, fr. *defaire*, fr. L. *dis*, and *facere*, make.]

DEFEASIBLE (de-fēz'i-bl) *a.* that may be annulled. [See DEFEASANCE.]

DEFEASIBLENESS (de-fēz'i-bl-nes) *n.* the quality of being made void or annulled. [See **DEFEASANCE**.]

DEFEAT (de-fēt') *v.t.* to rout; frustrate; overthrow;—*n.* overthrow; discomfiture; frustration. [O.F. (part.) *defait*.]

DEFECT (de-fekt') *n.* want or deficiency; fault; blemish. [L. *defectus*, a failure, fr. *deficere*, fail.]

DEFECTION (de-fek'shun) *n.* a falling away; revolt; apostacy. [See **DEFECT**.]

DEFECTIVE (de-fek'tiv) *a.* full of defects; imperfect; incomplete. [See **DEFECT**.]

DEFECTIVELY (de-fek'tiv-li) *ad.* with defect. [See **DEFECT**.]

DEFENCE (de-fens') *n.* anything that defends; protection; vindication; answer to a charge. [O.F. *defense*, fr. L. fr. (acc. part.) *defensum*, defended, fr. **DEFEND**.]

DEFENCELESS (de-fens'les) *a.* wanting defence; unprotected. [See **DEFENCE**.]

DEFENCELESSLY (de-fens'les-li) *ad.* without defence. [See **DEFENCE**.]

DEFENCELESSNESS (de-fens'les-nes) *n.* state of being without protection or vindication. [See **DEFENCE**.]

DEFEND (de-fend') *v.t.* or *i.* to guard from injury; protect; resist or contest, as a legal claim;—*v.i.* to enter a defence or legal plea. [O.F., fr. L. *defendere*.]

DEFENDABLE (de-fen'da-bl) *a.* that may be defended. [See **DEFEND**.]

DEFENDANT (de-fen'dant) *a.* making defence; —*n.* a defender; the person accused or sued in law. [See **DEFEND**.]

DEFENDER (de-fen'der) *n.* one who guards. [See **DEFEND**.]

DEFENSIBLE (de-fen'si-bl) *a.* capable of being defended. [See **DEFENCE**.]

DEFENSIVE (de-fen'siv) *a.* that defends. [See **DEFEND**.]

DEFER (de-fer') (1) *v.t.* to put off; delay;— (2) *v.i.* to yield to the opinions or wishes of another. [(1) O.F. *differer*, fr. L. *dis*, apart, and *ferre*, bear. (2) O.F., fr. L. fr. *deferre*, bring before one, fr. *de*, and *ferre*, carry.]

DEFERENCE (def'er-ens) *n.* respect to another. [See **DEFER**.]

DEFERENTIAL (def-e-ren'shal) *a.* expressing deference. [See **DEFER**.]

DEFERENTIALLY (def-e-ren'shal-i) *ad.* with deference. [See **DEFER**.]

DEFIANCE (de-fi'ans) *n.* a challenge to fight; contempt of danger. [O.F., fr. L. (acc.) *diffidentiam*, want of faith.]

DEFIANT (de-fi'ant) *a.* bidding defiance. [See **DEFY**.]

DEFIANTLY (de-fi'ant-li) *ad.* with defiance. [See **DEFY**.]

DEFICIENCY (de-fish'en-si) *n.* defect; want; imperfection. [See **DEFICIENT**.]

DEFICIENT (de-fish'ent) *a.* wanting; imperfect. [L. (part. stem) *de-ficienti-*, failing. [See **DEFECT**.]

DEFICIENTLY (de-fish'ent-li) *ad.* in a defective manner. [See **DEFICIENT**.]

DEFICIT (def'i-sit) *n.* deficiency of revenue compared with expenditure. [L. (pres. ind.) =it fails fr. *de-ficere*, fail.]

DEFILE (de-fil') *n.* a narrow passage, as between hills;—*v.t.* to make foul or impure; corrupt; violate;—*v.i.* to go off file by file. [F., fr. *dé*=L. *dis*, and **FILE**. Also L. *de*, and O.E. *fylan*, to pollute; conn. with **FOUL**.]

DEFILEMENT (de-fil'ment) *n.* pollution. [See **DEFILE**.]

DEFINABLE (de-fi'na-bl) *a.* that may be defined. [See **DEFINE**.]

DEFINE (de-fin') *v.t.* to limit; explain. [O.F., fr. L. *definere*.]

DEFINITE (def'i-nit) *a.* having fixed limits; precise; exact. [See **DEFINE**.]

DEFINITELY (def'i-nit-li) *ad.* with certain limitation. [See **DEFINE**.]

DEFINITENESS (def'i-nit-nes) *n.* certainty of extent or of signification. [See **DEFINE**.]

DEFINITION (def-i-nish'un) *n.* explanation in words. [L. (acc.) *definitionem*.]

DEFINITIVE (de-fin'i-tiv) *a.* limiting; determining; positive; final;—*n.* an adjective limiting the signification of a noun. [See **DEFINE**.]

DEFINITIVELY (de-fin'i-tiv-li) *ad.* positively. [See **DEFINE**.]

DEFINITUDE (de-fin'i-tūd) *n.* exactness; precision. [See **DEFINE**.]

DEFLAGRATE (def'la-grāt) *v.t.* to burn; consume;—*v.i.* to burn rapidly. [L., fr. *de* and *flagrare*, burn.]

DEFLAGRATION (def-la-grā'shun) *n.* a rapid and sparkling combustion. [See **DEFLAGRATE**.]

DEFLAGRATOR (def'la-grā-ter) *n.* a galvanic instrument for producing combustion. [See **DEFLAGRATE**.]

DEFLECT (de-flekt') *v.i.* or *t.* to turn aside; bend; deviate. [L., fr. *de*, down, and *flectere*, bend.]

DEFLECTION (de-flek'shun) *n.* a turning; deviation. [See **DEFLECT**.]

DEFLORATION (dē-flō-rā'shun) *n.* act of deflouring. [O.F. *defleurer*, fr. *de*, off, and **FLOWER**.]

DEFOLIATION (dē-fō-li-ā'shun) *n.* the fall of the leaf; time of shedding leaves. [Low L., fr. L. *de*, down and *folvum*, leaf.]

DEFORCE (de-fōrs') *v.t.* to keep out of possession by force. [O.F. *deforcer*, fr. *de*=L. *dis*, and **FORCE**.]

DEFORCEMENT (de-fōrs'ment) *n.* dispossession by force; resistance to the execution of a legal writ or warrant. [See **DEFORCE**.]

DEFORM (de-form') *v.t.* to mar the form; disfigure. [L. *deformis*, uncouth, fr. *de* and **FORM**.]

DEFORMED (de-formd') *a.* disfigured; misshapen; ugly. [See **DEFORM**.]

DEFORMITY (de-for'mi-ti) *n.* an unnatural shape; anything that destroys symmetry or beauty. [See **DEFORM**.]

DEFRAUD (de-frawd') *v.t.* to deprive of right by fraud; withhold wrongfully. [O.F., fr. *defraudare*, fr. *de* and **FRAUD**.]

DEFRAY (de-frā') *v.t.* to bear or pay the expenses of. [O.F. *desfrayer*, *des*=L. *dis*, and *frai*=F. (pl.) *frais*, expense.]

DEFRAYMENT (de-frā'ment) *n.* payment of charges. [See **DEFRAY**.]

DEFUNCT (de-funkt') *a.* deceased; dead. [L (part.) *defunctus*, having discharged (all), fr. *de*, fully, and *fungi*, discharge.]

DEFY (de-fi') *v.t.* to dare; challenge; set at naught. [O.F. *desfier*, fr. Late L. *diffidare*, renounce faith, fr. L. *dis*, and *fidus*, faithful.]

DEGENERACY (de-jen'er-a-si) *n.* decline in good qualities; decay of ancestral virtue. [See **DEGENERATE**.]

DEGENERATE (de-jen'er-āt) *a.* having declined in natural or moral worth;—*v.i.* to decline in physical or moral qualities; grow worse than one's ancestors. [L. *degener* (part.) *de-generatus* made unlike one's race, fr. *de* and stem *gener-*, of *genus*, race.]

DEGENERATENESS (de-jen'er-āt-nes) *n.* a degenerate state. [See **DEGENERATE**.]

DEGENERATION (de-jen-er-ā'shun) *n.* a growing worse. [See **DEGENERATE**.]

DEGENERATIVE (de-jen'er-ā-tiv) *a.* tending to degenerate. [See **DEGENERATE**.]

DEGLUTINATE (dē-glōo'ti-nāt) *v.t.* to unglue. [L., fr. *de*, and stem *glutin-*, of *gluten*, glue.]

DEGLUTITION (deg-lōo-tish'un) *n.* act or power of swallowing. [L., fr. *de*, and *glutire*, to swallow.]

DEGRADATION (deg-ra-dā'shun) *n.* a depriving of rank; disgrace; deposition; reduction. [See **DEGRADE**.]

DEGRADE (de-grād') *v.t.* to deprive of rank or title; lessen. [F., fr. Late L. *degradare*, fr. *de* and **GRADE**.]

DEGRADED (de-grā'ded) *pp.* or *a.* reduced in rank; lowered. [See **DEGRADE**.]

DEGREE (de-grē') *n.* a grade or step; position; extent; rank; a mark of distinction; the 360th part of a circle; sixty geographical miles. [O.F. *degre* = F. *degré*, fr. L. *de*, down, and *gradus*, step.]

DEIFICATION (dē-i-fi-kā'shun) *n.* the act of enrolling among deities. [See **DEITY**.]

DEIFORM (dē'i-torm) *a.* of a godlike form. [L. *dei-*, for *deus*, God, and **FORM**.]

DEIFY (dē'i-fi) *v.t.* to exalt to the rank of deity. [O.F. *deifier*, fr. Late L. *deificare*, fr. L. *dei*, for *deus*, god, and *facere*, make.]

DEIGN (dān) *v.i.* to condescend;—*v.t.* to grant. [F. *daigner*, fr. *dignare*, think worthy, fr. L. *dignus*, worthy.]

DEISM (dē'izm) *n.* belief in a God apart from revelation; natural religion. [F. *déisme*, fr. L. *deus*, god.]

DEIST (dē'ist) *n.* one who denies a revelation from God. [See **DEISM**.]

DEISTICAL (dē-is'ti-kạl) *a.* pertaining to deism. [See **DEISM**.]

DEITY (dē'i-ti) *n.* Godhead; God. [O.F., fr. L. (acc.) *deitatem*, the Godhead; L. *deus.* God.]

DEJECT (de-jekt') *v.t.* to dispirit; discourage. [L. (part.) *dejectus*, cast down, fr. *de*, and *jacere*, throw.]

DEJECTED (de-jek'ted) *a.* cast down. [See **DEJECT**.]

DEJECTION (de-jek'shun) *n.* lowness of spirits; depression; evacuation. [See **DEJECT**.]

DEJECTORY (de-jek'tur-i) *a.* promoting evacuation. [See **DEJECT**.]

DEJEUNER (dā-zhẹ-na') *n.* breakfast; a fashionable luncheon. [F.]

DELAINE (de-lān') *n.* a thin muslin for ladies' dresses. [F. = of wool.]

DELAY (de-lā') *v.t.* to put off; detain;—*n.* hindrance; detention; a stay or stop. [O.F. *delayer*, through Low L., fr. L. (part.) *dilatus*, deferred, fr. *differe* **DEFER**.]

DELECTABLE (de-lek'ta-bl) *a.* delightful. [F., fr. L. *delectabilis*, fr.*delectare*, **DELIGHT**.]

DELEGATE (del'e-gāt) *v.t.* to send away;— *n.* a deputy. [L. (part.) *delegatus*, sent as **LEGATE**, fr. *de* and *legare*.]

DELEGATION (del-e-gā'shun) *n.* a sending away; persons delegated; commission. [See **DELEGATE**.]

DELETE (de-lēt') *v.t.* to erase; efface. [L. (part.) *deletus*, destroyed, fr. *delere*.]

DELETERIOUS (del-e-tē'ri-us) *a.* destructive; highly injurious. [Fr. Late L., fr. G. *deleterios*, fr. *dele-omai*, I harm.]

DELETION (dẹ-lē'shun) *n.* act of blotting out; erasure. [See **DELETE**.]

DELF (delf) *n.* earthenware glazed. [*Delf*(*t*), in Holland.]

DELIBERATE (de-lib'e-rāt) *v.t.* or *i.* to weigh in the mind; hesitate;—*a.* circumspect. [L. (part.) *deliberatus*, well weighed, fr. *de*, fully, and *librare*, fr. *libra*, balance.]

DELIBERATELY (de-lib'e-rāt-li) *ad.* slowly. [See **DELIBERATE**.]

DELIBERATION (de-lib-e-rā'shun) *n.* act of weighing in the mind; mature reflection; mutual discussion; prudence. [See **DELIBERATE**.]

DELIBERATIVE (de-lib'e-rā-tiv) *a.* proceeding from or acting by deliberation. [See **DELIBERATE**.]

DELICACY (del'i-kạ-si) *n.* refinement of sensibility or taste; fineness; softness; anything that pleases the appetite. [L. *de*, and *lacere*, entice.]

DELICATE (del'i-kāt) *a.* nice; pleasing to the taste; tender; refined. [L. *delicatus*, conn with **DELICIOUS**.]

DELICATELY (del'i-kāt-li) *ad.* with nicety; daintily. [See **DELICATE**.]

DELICATENESS (del'i-kāt-nes) *n.* state of being delicate; effeminacy. [See **DELICATE**.]

DELICIOUS (de-lish'us) *a.* sweet to the palate or other sense. [O.F., fr. L. *deliciosus*, fr. *delicia*, delight.]

DELICIOUSLY (de-lish'us-li) *ad.* in a delicious manner. [See **DELICIOUS**.]

DELICIOUSNESS (de-lish'us-nes) *n.* quality of being highly pleasing to the taste or mind. [See **DELICIOUS**.]

DELIGHT (de-līt') *n.* great joy or pleasure;— *v.t.* or *i.* to give pleasure to; take pleasure in. [For *delite*; fr. O.F. *deliter*, fr. L. *delectare*, fr. *delicere*, entice.]

DELIGHTED (de-lī'ted) *a.* greatly pleased. [See **DELIGHT**.]

DELIGHTEDLY (de-lī'ted-li) *ad.* with delight. [See **DELIGHT**.]

DELIGHTFUL (de-līt'fool) *a.* very pleasant. [See **DELIGHT**.]

DELIGHTFULLY (de-līt'fool-i) *ad.* charmingly. [See **DELIGHT**.]

DELIGHTLESS (de-līt'les) *a.* affording no pleasure. [See **DELIGHT**.]

DELIGHTSOME (de-līt'sum) *a.* pleasing; enjoyable. [See **DELIGHT**.]

DELINEATE (de-lin'ē-āt) *v.t.* to draw the outline; portray; describe. [L. (part.) *delineatus*, outlined, fr. *de*, and *lineare*, **LINE**.]

DELINEATION (de-lin-ē-ā'shun) *n.* act of drawing the outline of a thing; a verbal description. [L. (acc.) *delineationem*.]

DELINEATOR (de-lin'ē-ā-tẹr) *n.* one who delineates. [See **DELINEATE**.]

DELINQUENCY (de-lin'kwen-si) *n.* failure or neglect of duty; fault; crime. [See **DELINQUENT**.]

DELINQUENT (de-lin'kwent) *a.* failing in duty;—*n.* one who fails to do his duty; transgressor; criminal. [L. (part. stem) *delinquent-*, failing, fr. *de*, and *linquere*, leave.]

DELIQUESCE (del-i-kwes') *v.i.* to melt by absorbing moisture from the air. [L. *deliquescere*, to become fluid, fr. *de*, and *liquere*, to be fluid.]

DELIQUESCENCE (del-i-kwes'ens) *n.* a becoming liquid, or liquid in the air. [See **DELIQUESCE**.]

DELIQUESCENT (del-i-kwes'ent) *a.* liquefying in the air. [See **DELIQUESCE**.]

DELIRIOUS (dē-lir'i-us) *a.* in a state of delirium. [See **DELIRIUM**.]

DELIRIUM (de-lir'i-um) *n.* derangement of the brain; any strong excitement. [L., fr. *delirus*, crazy, lit. 'out of the furrow,' fr. *de*, from, and *lira*.]

DELIVER (de-liv'ẹr) *v.t.* to free; release; utter. [F. *délivrer*, fr. L. *de*, and *liberare*, set free, *liber*.]

DELIVERANCE (de-liv'ẹr-ans) *n.* act of freeing; rescue; a legal judgment; acquittal. [See **DELIVER**.]

DELIVERER (de-liv'ẹr-ẹr) *n.* one who delivers. [See **DELIVER**.]

DELIVERY (de-liv'ẹr-i) *n.* transfer; rescue; manner of speaking; child-birth. [See **DELIVER**.]

DELL (del) *n.* a little valley. [Doublet of **DALE**.]

DELTA (del'tạ) *n.* an alluvial deposit at the mouth of a river. [G.]

DELTOID (del'toid) *a.* triangular. [Fr. G. *eid-os*, form. See **DELTA**.]

DELUDABLE (de-lū'dạ-bl) *a.* that may be deceived. [See **DELUDE**.]

DELUDE (de-lūd') *v.t.* to deceive; mislead by false representation. [L. *deludere*, mock, *de*, and *ludere*, play.]

DELUGE (del'ūj) *n.* a general inundation;— *v.t.* to overflow; drown; overwhelm. [O.F. *deluge*, fr. L. *diluvium*, a washing away, fr. *di* = *dis*, and *luere*, wash.]

DELUSION (de-lu'zhŭn) *n.* act of deluding [L. (acc.) *delusionem*, fr. (part.) *delusus*, mocked.]

DELUSIVE (de-lū'siv) *a.* tending to deceive; a false impression. [See **DELUSION.**]

DELUSIVELY (de-lū'siv-li) *ad.* in a delusive manner. [See **DELUSION.**]

DELUSORY (de-lū'sur-i) *a.* apt to delude; deceptive. [See **DELUSION.**]

DELVE (delv) *v.t.* or *i.* to dig or open with a spade. [O.E. *delfan.*]

DEMAGOGUE (dem'a-gog) *n.* a ringleader of the rabble. [F., fr. G. *demagogos*, fr. *demos*, people, and *agogos*, fr. *ageo*, lead.]

DEMAND (de-mand') *v.t.* to claim; require; question;—*n.* a claim by right. [F., fr. L. *demandare*, to entrust (later, *demand*). fr. *de*, and *mandare*, commit.]

DEMANDABLE (de-man'da-bl) *a.* that may be demanded. [See **DEMAND.**]

DEMANDANT (de-man'dant) *n.* the plaintiff. [F. (part.) *démandant*, suing.]

DEMARKATION (dē-mär-kā'shun) *n.* division of territory; boundary. Often written **DEMARCATION.** [F., *de* = L. *de*, and *marquer*, **MARK.**]

DEMEAN (de-mēn') *v.t.* to behave; conduct; lessen; debase. [O.F., fr. *dé*, and *mener*, lead.

DEMEANOUR (de-mē'nur) *n.* manner of behaving; deportment. [See **DEMEAN.**]

DEMENT (de-ment') *v.t.* to make mad; infatuate. [L. *dementare*, to drive out of one's wits, fr. *de*, from, and stem *ment-*, of *mens*, mind.]

DEMENTED (de-men'ted) *a.* imbecile in mind; infatuated. See **DEMENT.**]

DEMERIT (dē-mer'it) *n.* ill desert; fault. [O.F. *demerite*, **MERIT**, fault; fr. L. *de*, fully, and *merere*.]

DEMESNE (de-mēn') *n.* a manor-house, and the land attached to it;—*pl.* estates in land. [O.F. form of **DOMAIN.**]

DEMI (dem'i) *a.* prefix, signifying *half.* [F., fr. L. *dimidium* ha f, fr. *di* =*dis*, and *medius*, mid.]

DEMIGOD (dem'i-god) *n.* a deified hero. [See **DEMI** and **GOD.**]

DEMISE (de-mīz') *n.* death; a lease;—*v.t.* to convey by lease; bequeath by will. [O.F. (part.) *demis*, sent away, fr. *demettre*, fr. L. *dimittere*, **DISMISS.**]

DEMOBILISE (dē-mob'i-līz) *v.t.* to disband, as troops. [F. pref *de* =L. *dis*, and **MOBILISE.**]

DEMOCRACY (de-mok'ra-si) *n.* government by the people. [F., fr. G. *dem -kratia*, fr. *demos*, the people, and *kratein*, rule.]

DEMOCRAT (dem'ō-krat) *n.* an adherent to democracy. [See **DEMOCRACY.**]

DEMOCRATIC (dem-ō-krat'ik) *a.* relating to a popular government. [See **DEMOCRACY.**]

DEMOLISH (de-mol'ish) *v.t.* to destroy. [O.F. (part.) *demolissant*, demolishing, fr. *demolir*, fr. L. *demolire*, fr. *de*, and *moles*, heap.]

DEMOLITION (de-mō-lish'un) *n.* act of overthrowing buildings. [See **DEMOLISH.**]

DEMON (dē'mon) *n.* an evil spirit. [L., fr. G. *daimon*.]

DEMONIAC (de-mō'ni-ak) *a.* belonging to or influenced by demons;—*n.* one possessed by an evil spirit. [L., fr. G. *daimoniakos*.]

DEMONISM (dē'mun-izm) *n.* belief in demons or inferior gods. [See **DEMON.**]

DEMONOLOGY (dē-mun-ol'ō-ji) *n.* a treatise on evil spirits. [Fr. G. *logia*, science fr. *legein*. See also **DEMON.**]

DEMONSTRABLE (de-mon'stra-bl) *a.* that may be fully proved. [See **DEMONSTRATE.**]

DEMONSTRABLY (de-mon'stra-bli) *ad.* in a manner to prove beyond doubt [See **DEMONSTRATE.**]

DEMONSTRATE (dem'un-strāt, de-mon'strat) *v.t.* to point out; exhibit; prove fully [L. (part.) *demonstratus*, fully shown, fr. *de* and *monstrare*.]

DEMONSTRATION (dem-un-strā'shun) *n.* proof to a certainty. [L. (acc.) *demonstrationem*.]

DEMONSTRATIVE (de-mon'stra-tiv) *a.* conclusive. [See **DEMONSTRATE.**]

DEMONSTRATOR (dem'un-strā-ter) *n.* one who demonstrates. [See **DEMONSTRATE.**]

DEMORALISATION (dē-mor-al-i-zā'shun) *n.* destruction of morals. [See **DEMORALISE.**]

DEMORALISE (dē-mor'al-īz) *v.t.* to render corrupt. [F., fr. *de* = L. *dis*, and *moral*, **MORAL.**]

DEMULCENT (dē-mul'sent) *a.* softening;—*n.* a medicine that soothes irritation [L. (part. stem), *de-mulcent-*, stroking down.]

DEMUR (de-mur') *v.i.* to hesitate; scruple;—*n.* hesitation. [O.F. *demourer* =F. *demeurer*. stay, fr. L. *de*, fully, and *morari*, fr. *mora*, delay.]

DEMURE (de-mūr') *a.* affectedly modest. [O.F. *de murs* =of (good) manners, fr. L. *de* and *mores*.]

DEMURELY (de-mūr'li) *ad.* with reserve. [See **DEMURE.**]

DEMURRAGE (dē-mur'āj) *n.* expense for the delay of a ship. [See **DEMUR.**]

DEMURRER (dē-mur'er) *n.* one who demurs; a pause in law. [See **DEMUR.**]

DEMY (de-mī') *n.* a paper 22½ by 17½ inches in size. [See **DEMI.**]

DEN (den) *n.* a cave; lodge of a beast. [O.E. *denn.*]

DENATIONALISE (dē-nash'un-al-īz) *v.t.* to divest of national character or rights. [See **NATION.**]

DENATURALISE (dē-nat'ūr-al-īz) *v.t.* to make unnatural; deprive of civil rights. [See **NATURE.**]

DENDRIFORM (den'dri-form) *a.* having the figure of a tree. [G. *dendron*, tree, and **FORM.**]

DENIABLE (de-nī'a-bl) *a.* that may be denied. [See **DENY.**]

DENIAL (de-nī'al) *n.* refusal; contradiction. [See **DENY.**]

DENIZATION (den-i-zā'shun) *n.* act of making a citizen. [See **DENIZEN.**]

DENIZEN (den'i-zn) *n.* one made a citizen. [O.F. *deinzein*, fr. *deinz* =F. *dans*, within, fr. L. *de intus*, from within.]

DENOMINATE (de-nom'i-nāt) *v.t.* to give a name to; call. [L. (part.) *denominatus*, named, fr. *de*, fully, and **NOMINATE.**]

DENOMINATION (de-nom-i-nā'shun) *n.* a name; a title; a religious body or sect. [See **DENOMINATE.**]

DENOMINATIONAL (de-nom-i-nā'shun-al) *a.* relating to a religious body or sect. [See **DENOMINATE.**]

DENOMINATIVE (de-nom'i-nā-tiv) *a.* conferring a name or appellation. [See **DE-NOMINATE.**]

DENOMINATOR (de-nom'i-nā-ter) *n.* the lower number in vulgar fractions. [See **DENOMINATE.**]

DENOTATION (dē-nō-tā'shun) *n.* the act of denoting. [See **DENOTE.**]

DENOTE (de-nōt') *v.t.* to indicate; signify. [F. *dénoter*, fr. L. *de*, and *notare*, mark, fr. *nota*, sign.]

DENOUEMENT (dā-nóō'mong) *n.* the winding up of a plot; the issue or result. [F.]

DENOUNCE (de-nouns') *v.t.* to accuse or censure publicly; threaten. [O.F. *dénoncer*, fr. L. *de* and *nuntiare*.]

DENOUNCEMENT (de-nouns'ment) *n.* act of proclaiming a threat. [See **DENOUNCE.**]

DENSE (dens) *a.* crowded; having its parts closely pressed together; compact. [L. *densus.*]

DENSITY (den'si-ti) *n.* compactness; closeness of parts. [L. (acc.) *densitatem.*]

DENT (dent) *n.* a small hollow; indentation;—*v.t.* to make a dent. [Form of **DINT.**]

DENTAL (den'tal) *a.* pertaining to the teeth. [Fr. L. stem *dent-*, of *dens*, a tooth.]

DENTATE (den'tāt) *a.* toothed; notched. [L. (part.) *dentatus*, toothed.]

DENTED (den'ted) *a.* impressed with little hollows. [See **DENT**.]

DENTIFORM (den'ti-form) *a.* formed as tooth. [L. stem *dent-*, of *dens*, a tooth, and **FORM**.]

DENTIFRICE (den'ti-fris) *n.* something to cleanse the teeth. [F., fr. L. *dentifricium*, fr. stem *dent-*, and *fricare*, rub.]

DENTIST (den'tist) *n.* an operator on the teeth. [L. stem *dent-*, of *dens*, a tooth.]

DENTISTRY (den'tis-tri) *n.* the business of a dentist. [See **DENTIST**.]

DENTITION (den-tish'un) *n.* the cutting of teeth; the system of teeth peculiar to an animal. [L., fr. (part.) *dentitus*, cut (of teeth.)]

DENTOID (den'toid) *a.* tooth-shaped. [Fr. L. stem *dent-*, of *dens*, a tooth, and G. *eidos*, form.]

DENUDE (de-nūd') *v.t.* to lay bare. [L., fr. *de*, and *nudus*, **NUDE**.]

DENUNCIATION (de-nun-shi-ā'shun) *n.* declaration of a threat. [See **DENOUNCE**.]

DENUNCIATOR (de-nun'shi-ā-ter) *n.* one who threatens. [See **DENOUNCE**.]

DENUNCIATORY (de-nun'shi-a-tur-i) *a.* containing a threat. [See **DENOUNCE**.]

DENY (de-nī') *v.t.* to disown; refuse; withhold. [M.E. *denien*, fr. O.F. *denier*, fr. *denegare*, to deny utterly, fr. L. *de* and *negare*.]

DEOBSTRUENT (dē-ob'strōō-ent) *a.* removing obstruction. [L. *de*, away, and *obstruere*, obstruct.]

DEODORISATION (dē-ō-dur-i-zā'shun) *n.* act of removing noxious effluvia. [See **DEODORISE**.]

DEODORISE (dē-ō'dur-īz) *v.t.* to take away foul air or smell. [L. *de*, and **ODOUR**.]

DEODORISER (dē-ō'-dur-īz-er) *n.* chemical substance used in deodorising. [See **DEODORISE**.]

DEOXIDATE (dē-ok'si-dāt) *v.t.* to reduce from the state of an oxide. [L. *de*, and **OXIDE**.]

DEOXIDATION (dē-ok-si-dā'shun) *n.* abstraction of oxygen. Also **DEOXIDISATION**. [L. *de*, and **OXIDE**.]

DEOXIDISE (dē-ok'si-dīz) *v.t.* to deprive of oxygen. [L. *de*, and **OXIDE**.]

DEPART (de-pärt') *v.i.* to go away; forsake; die. [O.F. *despartir*, fr. *des* = L. *dis*, away from, and *partire*, **PART**.]

DEPARTMENT (de-pärt'ment) *n.* a separate office or division. [See **DEPART**.]

DEPARTMENTAL (de-pärt-men'tal) *a.* pertaining to a department. [See **DEPART**.]

DEPARTURE (de-pär'tūr) *n.* a going away; decease. [See **DEPART**.]

DEPEND (de-pend') *v.i.* to hang from; rely on; be in suspense. [F., fr. L. *dependere*, hang from, fr. *de* and *pendere*.]

DEPENDABLE (de-pen'da-bl) *a.* that may be relied on. [See **DEPEND**.]

DEPENDENCE (de-pen'dens) *n.* reliance; trust. [See **DEPEND**.]

DEPENDENT (de-pen'dent) *a.* relying on;— *n.* one subordinate to another. Also written **DEPENDANT**. [L. (part. stem) *dependent-*, hanging down.]

DEPENDENTLY (de-pen'dent-li) *ad.* in a subordinate manner. Also written **DEPENDANTLY**. [See **DEPEND**.]

DEPICT (de-pikt') *v.t.* to paint; portray; represent in words. [L. (part.) *depictus*, fully portrayed, fr. *de*, and *pingere*, paint.]

DEPILATORY (de-pil'a-tur-i) *a.* taking off the hair; — *n.* a cosmetic for removing hair. [Fr. L. (part.) *de-pilatus*, deprived of hair, fr. *de* and *pilus*.]

DEPLETE (de-plēt') *v.t.* to reduce or draw off the strength, as by venesection. [L. (part.) *dent'etus*, emptied, fr. *de* =un, and *plere*, fill.]

DEPLETION (de-plē'shun) *n.* blood-letting. [See **DEPLETE**.]

DEPLETIVE (de-plē'tiv) *a.* tending to reduce blood or habit. [See **DEPLETE**.]

DEPLETORY (de-plē'tur-i) *a.* fitted to reduce fullness of body. [See **DEPLETE**.]

DEPLORABLE (de-plō'ra-bl) *a.* lamentable; pitiable; grievous. [See **DEPLORE**.]

DEPLORABLENESS (de-plō'ra-bl-nes) *n.* the state of being deplorable. [See **DEPLORE**.]

DEPLORABLY (de-plō'ra-bli) *ad.* lamentably; miserably. [See **DEPLORE**.]

DEPLORE (de-plōr') *v.t.* to lament. [L. fr. *de*, much, and *plorare*, weep.]

DEPLOY (de-ploi') *v.t.* to display in a long line; —*v.i.* to extend in line. [F. *déployer*, unfold, fr. L. *displicare*. Doublet of **DISPLAY**. L. *dis*, and *plicare*, fold.]

DEPOLARISE (dē-pō'la-rīz) *v.t.* to deprive of polarity. [L. *de*, and *polaris*, of a pole.]

DEPONE (de-pōn') *v.t.* or *i.* to testify upon oath; lay down. [L., fr. *de*, down, and *ponere*, lay.]

DEPONENT (de-pō'nent) *a.* laying down;— *n.* one who gives testimony on oath. [F., fr. L. (acc. part.) *deponentem*, witnessing.]

DEPOPULATE (de-pop'ū-lāt) *v.t.* to dispeople. [L. (part.) *depopulatus*, laid waste, fr. *de*, and **POPULATE**.]

DEPOPULATION (de-pop-ū-lā'shun) *n.* act of dispeopling; laying waste. [See **DEPOPULATE**.]

DEPORT (de-pōrt') *v.t.* to behave; carry; demean. [O.F., fr. L., fr. *de*, down, and *portare*, carry.]

DEPORTATION (dē-pōr-tā'shun) *n.* a carrying away; exile. [See **DEPORT**.]

DEPORTMENT (dē-pōrt'ment) *n.* manner of acting. [O.F. *deportement*. See **DEPORT**.]

DEPOSABLE (de-pō'za-bl) *a.* that may be deprived of office. [See **DEPOSE**.]

DEPOSAL (de-pō'zal) *n.* act of deposing. [See **DEPOSE**.]

DEPOSE (de-pōz') *v.t.* to dethrone:—*v.i.* to testify under oath. [O.F. *deposer*, fr. *de* = L. *de*, away, and **POSE**.]

DEPOSIT (de-poz'it) (1) *v.t.* to lodge in any place; lay aside;— (2) *n.* that which is laid down or aside; anything entrusted. [(1) O.F., fr. Late L. *depositare*, lay down. (2) L. *depositum*. Doublet of **DEPOT**.]

DEPOSITARY (de-poz'i-ta-ri) *n.* one with whom something is left in trust. [See **DEPOSIT**.]

DEPOSITION (de-pō-zish'un) *n.* act of dethroning or degrading; an affidavit. [F., fr. L. (acc.) *depositionem*.]

DEPOSITOR (de-poz'i-ter) *n.* one who deposits. [See **DEPOSIT**.]

DEPOSITORY (de-poz'i-tur-i) *n.* a place for depositing. [See **DEPOSIT**.]

DEPOT (dep'ō, dē-pō') *n.* place of deposit; railroad station. [O.F. *deposit* = F. *dépôt*, fr. L. (neut. part.) *depositum*, thing laid down, fr. *deponere*, **DEPONE**.]

DEPRAVATION (dep-ra-vā'shun) *n.* act of making worse. [See **DEPRAVE**.]

DEPRAVE (de-prāv') *v.t.* to corrupt; vitiate. [O.F., fr. L. *depravare*, pervert, fr. *de*, quite, and *pravus*, vicious.]

DEPRAVED (de-prāvd') *a.* wicked; vile. [See **DEPRAVE**.]

DEPRAVITY (de-prav'i-ti) *n.* corruption of morals. [See **DEPRAVE**.]

DEPRECATE (dep're-kāt) *v.t.* to pray deliverance from; plead against; regret deeply. [L. (part.) *deprecatus*, having prayed against, fr. *de-*, and *precari*, **PRAY**.]

DEPRECATINGLY (dep're-kā-ting-li) *ad.* with deprecation. [See **DEPRECATE**.]

DEPRECATION (dep-re-kā'shun) *n.* act of deprecating. [See **DEPRECATE**.]

DEPRECATORY (dep're-kā-tur-i) *a.* serving to deprecate; humbly entreating. [See **DEPRECATE**.]

DEPRECIATE (de-prē'shi-āt) v.i. to decline in value; v.t. to undervalue. [L. (part.) *depretiatus*, depreciated, fr. *de*, down, and *pretium*, PRICE.]

DEPRECIATION (de-prē-shi-ā'shun) n. act of depreciating. [See DEPRECIATE.]

DEPRECIATORY (de-prē'shi-ā-tur-i) a. tending to depreciate; undervaluing. [See DEPRECIATE.]

DEPREDATE (dep're-dāt) v.t. to plunder; despoil; lay waste. [L. (part.) *deprædatus*, having plundered, fr. *de*, much, and *prædare*, PREY.]

DEPREDATION (dep-re-dā'shun) n. a robbing; pillaging. [See DEPREDATE.]

DEPREDATORY (dep're-dā-tur-i) a. plundering. [See DEPREDATE.]

DEPRESS (de-pres') v.t. to sink; humble; lower or let down. [L. (part.) *depressus*, pressed down, fr. *de*, and PRESS.]

DEPRESSION (de-presh'un) n. dejection; low state. [L. (acc.) *depressionem*, a hollow. See DEPRESS.]

DEPRESSIVE (de-pres'iv) a. tending to depress. [See DEPRESS.]

DEPRESSOR (de-pres'er) n. one who or that which presses down. [See DEPRESS.]

DEPRIVABLE (de-pri'va-bl) a. that may be deprived. [See DEPRIVE.]

DEPRIVATION (dep-ri-vā'shun) n. act of depriving; loss; bereavement. [See DEPRIVE.]

DEPRIVE (de-priv') v.t. to take from; dispossess; depose; bereave. [O.F., fr. Late L. *deprivare*, reduce in rank, fr. L. *de*, entirely, and *privare*, deprive.]

DEPTH (depth) n. deepness; profundity. [See DEEP.]

DEPUTATION (dep-ū-tā'shun) n. the persons deputed. [See DEPUTE.]

DEPUTE (de-pūt') v.t. to send by appointment. [F. *députer*, fr. L. *deputare*, to cut off (esp. for an end), fr. *de*, and *putare*, cut.]

DEPUTED (de-pū'ted) a. authorised; sent. [See DEPUTE.]

DEPUTY (dep'ū-ti) n. one appointed to act for another. [F. *député* = (part.) deputed.]

DERANGE (de-rānj') v.t. to put out of order; confuse. [O.F. *desranger* = F. *déranger*, fr. *des* = L. *dis*, and RANGE.]

DERANGED (de-rānjd') a. disordered in mind. [See DERANGE.]

DERANGEMENT (de-rānj'ment) n. state of disorder; insanity. [See DERANGE.]

DERELICT (der'e-likt) n. thing abandoned;— a. abandoned. [L. (part.) *derelictus*, forsaken, fr. *de*, and RELICT.]

DERELICTION (der-e-lik'shun) n. act of forsaking; state of being forsaken. [L. (acc.) *derelictionem*, desertion.]

DERIDE (de-rid') v.t. to laugh at in scorn; mock. [L., fr. *de*. intens., and *ridere*, laugh at.]

DERIDER (de-ri'der) n. mocker; scoffer. [See DERIDE.] [See DERIDE.]

DERIDINGLY (de-ri'ding-li) ad. in derision.

DERISION (de-rizh'un) n. a laughing at in contempt. [L. (acc.) *derisionem*, fr. (part.) *derisus*, mocked.]

DERISIVE (de-ri'siv) a. mocking; ridiculing. [L. (part.) *derisus*, mocked.]

DERISIVELY (de-ri'siv-li) ad. with mockery or contempt. [See DERISIVE.]

DERISIVENESS (de-ri'siv-nes) n. quality of being derisive. [See DERISIVE.]

DERISORY (de-ri'sur-i) a. mocking; ridiculing. [See DERISIVE.]

DERIVABLE (de-ri'va-bl) a. that may be derived. [See DERIVE.]

DERIVABLY (de-ri'va-bli) ad. by derivation. [See DERIVE.]

DERIVATION (der-i-vā'shun) n. deduction from a source. [F., fr. L. (acc.) *derivationem*, deviation, etymology, fr. (part.) *derivatus*, diverted.]

DERIVATIVE (de-riv'a-tiv) a. derived;— n. word derived. [See DERIVE.]

DERIVATIVELY (de-riv'a-tiv-li) ad. in a derivative manner. [See DERIVE.]

DERIVE (de-riv') v.t. to draw, receive, or infer from; trace to its source;—v.i. to proceed from. [O.F. *deriver*, to drain, deviate, fr. L. *derivare*, fr. *de*, and *rivus*, stream, brook.]

DERMA (der'ma) n. the true skin. [G.]

DERMAL (der'mal) a. pertaining to skin. Also, DERMIC. [See DERMA.]

DERMATOLOGY (der-ma-tol'o-ji) n. science of the skin. [G. stem *dermat-*, skin, and *logos*, discourse.]

DEROGATE (der'ō-gāt) v.t. or i. to take from. [L. (part.) *derogatus*, repeated, withdrawn, fr. *de*, and *rogare*, ask.]

DEROGATION (der-ō-gā'shun) n. a detracting. [See DEROGATE.]

DEROGATORILY (de-rog'a-tur-i-li) ad. in a detracting manner. [See DEROGATE.]

DEROGATORY (de-rog'a-tur-i) a. detracting from; disparaging. [L., fr. *derogator*, detractor.]

DERRICK (der'ik) n. a kind of crane for raising heavy weights. [Fr. D. name *Derrick*, borne by a London hangman, 17th century.]

DERVIS (der'vis) n. a Mohammedan monk. Also DERVISH. [Per. = poor.]

DESCANT (des-kant') v.i. to sing; comment at large;—(des'kant) n. song in parts; a discourse; comment. [O.F. *descanter* = F. *déchanter*, to change one's tone, fr. *des* = L. *dis*, apart, and CHANT.]

DESCEND (de-send') v.t. or i. to go or come down. [O.F., fr. L. *descendere*, orig. to climb down, *de*, and *scandere*. See SCAN.]

DESCENDANT (de-sen'dant) n. offspring of an ancestor. [O.F. (part.) = descending.]

DESCENDENT (de-sen'dent) a. falling. [See DESCEND.]

DESCENSION (de-sen'shun) n. act of descending; degradation; declension. [See DESCEND.]

DESCENT (de-sent') n. progress downward; declivity; derivation; issue. [F. *descente*.]

DESCRIBABLE (de-skri'ba-bl) a. that may be described. [See DESCRIBE.]

DESCRIBE (de-skrib') v.t. to represent by lines, words, or other signs. [L., fr. *de*, completely, and *scribere*, write. Doublet of DESCRY.]

DESCRIBER (de-skri'ber) n. one who describes. [See DESCRIBE.]

DESCRIER (de-skri'er) n. one who descries. [See DESCRY.]

DESCRIPTION (de-skrip'shun) n. act of describing. [L. (acc.) *descriptionem*, fr. (part.) *descriptus*, delineated.]

DESCRIPTIVE (de-skrip'tiv) a. that describes. [See DESCRIBE.]

DESCRY (de-skri') v.t. to discover. [O.F. *descrire* -*scrire*, describe, fr. L. *describere*. Doublet of DESCRIBE.]

DESECRATE (des'e-krāt) v.t. to pervert from a sacred purpose. [By confusion, fr. L. (part.) *desecratus*, consecrated, fr. *de*, w., and *sacrare*, to make SACRED.]

DESECRATION (des-e-krā'shun) n. a diverting from a sacred purpose. [See DESECRATE.]

DESERT (de-zert') (1) n. merit; reward;— (2) v.t. to abandon;—v.i. to run away. [(1) O.F. (part.) *desert*. (2) L. (part.) *desertus*, abandoned, fr. *de*, neg. *de*, and *serere*, join.]

DESERT (dez'ert) a. solitary;—n. a wilderness; a sandy plain; a solitude. [L. *desertum*, a waste.]

DESERTER (de-zer'ter) n. one who forsakes his colours, etc. [See DESERT.]

DESERTION (de-zer'shun) n. act of abandoning. [See DESERT.]

DESERTLESS (de-zėrt'les) *a.* without claim to favour or reward. [See DESERT.]

DESERVE (de-zėrv') *v.t.* or *i.* to earn by service; merit; be worthy of. [O.F., fr. L. *de*, fully and *servire*, SERVE.]

DESERVED (de-zėrvd') *a.* merited. [See DESERVE.]

DESERVEDLY (de-zėr'ved-li) *ad.* according to desert; justly. [See DESERVE.]

DESHABILLE (des-a-bil') *n.* an undress. [F., fr. O.F. *des* = L. *dis*-, un-, and *habiller*, dress.]

DESICCATE (de-sik'āt) *v.t.* to dry up;—*v.i.* to become dry. [L. (part.) *desiccatus*, dried up, fr. *de*, wholly, and *siccare*.]

DESICCATION (des-i-kā'shun) *n.* process of making dry. [See DESICCATE.]

DESICCATIVE (de-sik'a-tiv) *a.* tending to dry. [See DESICCATE.]

DESIDERATE (de-sid'e-rāt) *v.t.* to desire earnestly; miss greatly. [L. (part.) *desideratus*, wanted, regretted, fr. DESIRE.]

DESIDERATIVE (de-sid'e-rā-tiv) *a.* having or expressing desire:—*n.* an object of desire. [See DESIDERATE.]

DESIDERATUM (de-sid-e-rā'tum) *n.* a thing desired;—*pl.* DESIDERATA. [L. (neut. part.)]

DESIGN (de-zīn') *v.t.* (1) to propose; plan; draw or sketch;—*n.* a purpose; intention; —(2) a sketch or plan. [(1) O.F. = F. *désiner*, indicate, fr. L. *de*, down, and *signare*, to mark. (2) F. (doublet) *dessiner*.]

DESIGNATE (des'ig-nāt) *v.t.* to point out. [L. (part.) *designatus*, marked out.]

DESIGNATION (des-ig-nā'shun) *n.* act of pointing or marking out. [L. (acc.) *designationem*.]

DESIGNEDLY (de-zī'ned-li) *ad.* by design; purposely. [See DESIGN.]

DESIGNER (de-zī'nėr) *n.* a contriver; a drawer. [See DESIGN.]

DESIGNING (de-zī'ning) *a.* artful;—*n.* the art of drawing patterns. [See DESIGN.]

DESIRABLE (de-zī'ra-bl) *a.* that may be wished for; pleasing. [See DESIRE.]

DESIRABLENESS (de-zī'ra-bl-nes) *ad.* quality of being desirable. [See DESIRE.]

DESIRABLY (de-zī'ra-bli) *ad.* in a desirable manner. [See DESIRE.]

DESIRE (de-zir') *n.* a wish to obtain;—*v.t.* to wish for; ask. [F., fr. L. *desiderare*, of uncertain etym.]

DESIROUS (de-zī'rus) *a.* full of desire; longing after. [See DESIRE.]

DESIST (de-sist') *v.i.* to cease; stop. [L., fr. *de*, away, and *sistere*, stand, fr. *stare*.]

DESISTANCE (de-sis'tans) *n.* act of desisting; cessation. [See DESIST.]

DESK (desk) *n.* an inclined table; a pulpit. [Late L. *desca*, fr. L. *discus*, DISK, later, table, whence DAIS.]

DESOLATE (des'u-lāt) *v.t.* to lay waste;—*a.* laid waste; solitary; comfortless. [L. (part.) *desolatus*, forsaken, fr. *de*, completely, and *solare*, to make alone.]

DESOLATION (des-u-lā'shun) *n.* act of laying waste; destruction; a desolate place or state. [L. (acc.) *desolationem*, loneliness.]

DESPAIR (de-spār') *n.* utter loss of hope;—*v.i.* to abandon hope. [O.F., fr. L. *desperare*, fr. *de*, and orig. stem, *sper*-, of *spes*, hope.]

DESPATCH (des-pach') *n.* speedy performance; a government message;—*v.t.* to send away; execute hastily. Sometimes written DISPATCH. [Through Sp., fr. L. *dis*-, away, un-, and (part.) *pactus*, fastened.]

DESPERADO (des-pėr-ā'dō) *n.* a desperate man; a madman. [Sp., fr. L. (part.) *desperatus*.]

DESPERATE (des'pėr-āt) *a.* without hope; violent; furious. [L. (part.) *desperatus*. See DESPAIR.]

DESPERATELY (des'pėr-āt-li) *ad.* in a desperate manner. [See DESPERATE.]

DESPERATION (des-pėr-ā'shun) *a.* hopelessness. [See DESPERATE.]

DESPICABLE (des'pi-ka-bl) *a.* contemptible; base; mean. [L. *despicabilis*, fr. DESPISE.]

DESPICABLY (des'pi-ka-bli) meanly. [See DESPICABLE.]

DESPICABLENESS (des'pi-ka-bl-nes) *n.* extreme meanness; vileness. [See DESPICABLE.]

DESPISE (de-spīz') *v.t.* to contemn; scorn; disdain. [Fr. O.F. (part.) *despisant*, despising, fr. *despire*, fr. L. *despicere*, fr. *de*, down, and *spicere*, look.]

DESPITE (de-spīt') *n.* malice; defiance. [O.F. *despit* = F. *dépit*, SPITE, fr. DESPISE.]

DESPITEFUL (de-spīt'fool) *a.* full of hate. [See DESPITE.]

DESPOIL (de-spoil') *v.t.* to spoil; rob. [O.F. fr. *de* = L. *de*, intens., and SPOIL.]

DESPOILER (de-spoil'ėr) *n.* a plunderer. [See DESPOIL.]

DESPOND (de-spond') *v.i.* to lose hope. [L. = give up, lose heart, fr. *de*, and *spondere*, promise.]

DESPONDENCY (de-spon'den-si) *n.* loss of hope; dejection of spirit. [See DESPOND.]

DESPONDENT (de-spon'dent) *a.* despairing. [L. (acc. part. stem) *despondent*, despairing.]

DESPONDING (de-spon'ding) *a.* yielding to discouragement. [See DESPOND.]

DESPONDINGLY (de-spon'ding-li) *ad.* in a despondent manner. [See DESPOND.]

DESPOT (des'pot) *n.* an absolute prince; a tyrant. [O.F., *despot*, fr. Late L. (acc.) *despotum*, fr. G. *despotes*, master, lord.]

DESPOTIC (des-pot'ik) *a.* absolute in power; tyrannical; arbitrary. [See DESPOT.]

DESPOTISM (des'pu-tizm) *n.* absolute power. [See DESPOT.]

DESQUAMATE (des'kwa-māt, de-skwā'māt) *v.i.* to peel off in scales. [L. (part.) *desquamatus*, scaled off, fr. *d.*, and *squama*, scale.]

DESQUAMATION (des-kwa-mā'shun) *n.* to come off in scales; to peel off. [See DESQUAMATE.]

DESQUAMATORY (des-kwam'a-tur-i) *a.* marked by desquamation. [See DESQUAMATE.]

DESSERT (de-zėrt') *n.* the last course of a dinner; fruit, etc. [O.F., fr. *desservir*, clear the table, fr. *des* = L. *dis*, and SERVE.]

DESTINATION (des-ti-nā'shun) *n.* ultimate purpose or object; use or place. [Fr. L. (part.) *destinatus*, ordained.]

DESTINE (des'tin) *v.t.* to appoint to a certain use or state; fix unalterably. [O.F., fr. L. *destinare*, fr. *de*, and root of *stare*, stand.]

DESTINY (des'ti-ni) *n.* state or condition predetermined; fate. [See DESTINE.]

DESTITUTE (des'ti-tūt) *a.* in want of; needy. [L. (part.) *destitutus*, abandoned, fr. *de*, from, and *stituere*, for *statuere*, set, fr. *stare*, stand.]

DESTITUTION (des-ti-tū'shun) *n.* utter want. [See DESTITUTE.]

DESTROY (de-stroi') *v.t.* to demolish; ruin. [O.F. *destruire* = F. *détruire*, fr. L., fr. *destruere*, unbuild, fr. *de*-, un-, and *struere*.]

DESTROYER (de-stroi'ėr) *n.* one who ruins. [See DESTROY.]

DESTRUCTIBILITY (de-struk-ti-bil'i-ti) *n.* liability to be destroyed. [See DESTRUCTION.]

DESTRUCTIBLE (de-struk'ti-bl) *a.* liable to destruction. [See DESTRUCTION.]

DESTRUCTION (de-struk'shun) *n.* ruin; eternal death. [Fr. L. (acc.) *destructionem*, fr. (part.) *destructus*, destroyed.]

DESTRUCTIVE (de-struk'tiv) *a.* ruinous. [See DESTRUCTION.]

DESTRUCTIVELY (de-struk'tiv-li) *ad.* ruinously; mischievously. [See DESTRUCTIVE.]

DESTRUCTIVENESS (de-struk'tiv-nes) *n.* propensity to destroy. [See **DESTRUCTIVE**.]

DESUETUDE (des'we-tūd) *n.* disuse. [Fr. L. *desuetudo*, fr. (part.) *desuetus*, disused, fr. *de*, and *suescere*, to be wont.]

DESULTORY (des'ul-tur-i) *a.* without method; unconnected. [L. *desultorius*, pertaining to a *desultor*, circus-rider, fr. *de*, down, and (part.) *sultus*, for *saltus*, fr. *salire*, leap.]

DETACH (de-tach') *v.t.* to send off a party; separate; disunite. [F. (pref.) *dé* = L. *dis*, apart. See **ATTACH**.]

DETACHED (de-tacht') *a.* separate. [See **DETACH**.]

DETACHMENT (de-tach'ment) *n.* a party sent from the main army, etc. [See **DETACH**.]

DETAIL (dē'tāl de-tāl') *n.* a minute account or item;—*v.t.* de-tāl' to narrate; enumerate; particularise. [Fr. F. = cut up in pieces, fr. *dé* = L. *de*, and *tailler*, cut. See **TAILOR**.]

DETAIN (de-tān') *v.t.* to withhold; restrain from departure; keep in custody. [O.F., fr. L., fr. *de*, away, and *tenere*, hold.]

DETAINER (de-tā'nẹr) *n.* one that detains. [See **DETAIN**.]

DETAINMENT (de-tān'ment) *n.* detention. [See **DETAIN**.]

DETECT (de-tekt') *v.t.* to bring to light; find out; expose. [L. (part.) *detectus*, lit. uncovered, fr. L. *detegere*, fr. *de*, priv., and *tegere*, cover.]

DETECTABLE (de-tek'ta-bl) *a.* that may be detected. [See **DETECT**.]

DETECTION (de-tek'shun) *n.* discovery. [L. (acc.) *detectionem*.]

DETECTIVE (de-tek'tiv) *n.* a policeman in plain clothes;—*a.* employed in detecting. [See **DETECT**.]

DETENTION (de-ten'shun) *n.* the act of detaining. [L. (acc.) *detentionem*, fr. (part.) *detentus*, detained.]

DETER (de-tẹr') *v.t.* to prevent; hinder. [L., fr. *de*, and *terrere*, frighten, **TERRIFY**.]

DETERIORATE (de-tē'ri-u-rāt) *v.t.* or *i.* to impair; become worse. [L. (part.) *deterioratus*, made worse, fr. *deterior*, lower.]

DETERIORATION (de-tē-ri-u-rā'shun) *n.* act of becoming worse. [See **DETERIORATE**.]

DETERMINABLE (de-tẹr'mi-na-bl) *a.* that may be decided. [See **DETERMINE**.]

DETERMINATE (de-tẹr'mi-nāt) *a.* limited; definite; conclusive. [L. (part.) *determinatus*, limited.]

DETERMINATELY (de-tẹr'mi-nāt-li) *ad.* decisively; with fixed resolve. [See **DETERMINATE**.]

DETERMINATION (de-tẹr-mi-nā'shun) *n.* resolution taken; end; decision. [See **DETERMINATE**.]

DETERMINE (de-tẹr'min) *v.t.* to limit; define;—*v.i.* to decide; resolve. [F., fr. L. *determinare*, to limit, fr. *de*, and **TERMINUS**.]

DETERMINED (de-tẹr'mind) *a.* resolute. [See **DETERMINE**.]

DETERMINEDLY (de-tẹr'mind-li) *ad.* resolutely. [See **DETERMINE**.]

DETERRENT (de-tẹr'ent) *n.* that which hinders or prevents. [L. (part. stem) *deterrent-*, frightening off.]

DETEST (de-test') *v.t.* to hate extremely; abhor. [F., fr. L. *detestari*, lit. to invoke a god, in cursing, fr. *de*, and *testari*, **TESTIFY**.]

DETESTABLE (de-tes'ta-bl) *a.* very hateful. [See **DETEST**.]

DETESTATION (dē-tes-tā'shun) *n.* abhorrence. [See **DETEST**.]

DETHRONE (de-thrōn') *v.t.* to divest of royalty; depose. [L. (pref.) *de*, down, and **THRONE**.]

DETHRONEMENT (de-thrōn'ment) *n.* the act of dethroning. [See **DETHRONE**.]

DETONATE (det'u-nāt) *v.t.* to cause to explode; —*v.i.* to burn with explosions. [L. (part.) *detonatus*, fr. *de*, and *tonare*, thunder.]

DETONATION (det-u-nā'shun) *n.* explosion. [See **DETONATE**.]

DETOUR (de-tōōr') *n.* a winding; a circuitous route. [F., fr. *dé* = L. *dis*, apart, and *tour*, a **TURN**.]

DETRACT (de-trakt') *v.t.* or *i.* to lessen; disparage; defame; take away. [L. (part.) *detractus*, deducted, fr. *de*, and *trahere*, draw.]

DETRACTION (de-trak'shun) *n.* defamation. [L. (acc.) *detractionem*.]

DETRACTOR (de-trak'tẹr) *n.* one who detracts. [L.]

DETRACTORY (de-trak'tur-i) *a.* defamatory. [See **DETRACTOR**.]

DETRIMENT (det'ri-ment) *n.* loss; damage. [L. *detrimentum*, loss, fr. (part.) *detritus*, rubbed away, fr. *de* and *terere*.]

DETRIMENTAL (det-ri-men'tal) *a.* causing loss; injurious. [See **DETRIMENT**.]

DETRITUS (de-trī'tus) *n.* fragments or particles of rock or soil carried down and deposited by floods or rivers. [See **DETRIMENT**.]

DETRUNCATE (de-trung'kāt) *v.t.* to lop off; shorten by cutting. [L. (part.) *detruncatus*, lopped off, fr. *de* and *truncare*, fr. *truncus*. See **TRUNK**.]

DEUCE (dūs) *n.* a card or die with two spots; the devil. [O.F. *deus* = F. *deux*, fr. L. (acc.) *duos*.]

DEVASTATE (dev'as-tāt) *v.t.* to lay waste; ravage. [L. (part.) *devastatus*, laid waste, fr. *de* and *vastare*, fr. *vastus*, waste.]

DEVASTATION (dev-as-tā'shun) *n.* a laying waste; havoc. [See **DEVASTATE**.]

DEVELOP (de-vel'up) *v.t.* to disengage; lay open to view;—*v.i.* to grow or come to view gradually. [O.F. *desveloper*, fr. *des* = L. *dis*, and root of E. **WRAP** (M.E. *ulappen*).]

DEVELOPMENT (de-vel'up-ment) *n.* an unfolding; disclosure. [See **DEVELOP**.]

DEVIATE (dē'vi-āt) *v.i.* to wander; go astray. [L. (part.) *deviatus*, fr. *de*, and *via*, way.]

DEVIATION (dē-vi-ā'shun) *n.* a departure from rule; an error. [See **DEVIATE**.]

DEVICE (de-vīs') *n.* scheme; contrivance; an emblem or motto. [O.F. *devise*, fr. L., fr. Low L. (acc.) *devisam*, a DIVISION, plan.]

DEVIL (dev'il) *n.* the evil one. [O.E. *deofol*, fr. L., fr. G. *diabolos*. See **DIABOLICAL**.]

DEVILISH (dev'il-ish) *a.* diabolical; excessively bad or wicked. [See **DEVIL**.]

DEVILRY (dev'il-ri) *n.* diabolical or mischievous conduct. [See **DEVIL**.]

DEVIOUS (dē'vi-us) *a.* going astray. [L. *devious*.]

DEVISABLE (dē-vī'za-bl) *a.* that may be devised or contrived; that may be bequeathed. [See **DEVISE**.]

DEVISE (de-vīz') *v.t.* to contrive; bequeath; —*n.* a will. [O.F. *deviser*.]

DEVISER (de-vī'zẹr) *n.* one who contrives. [See **DEVISE**.]

DEVITALISE (dē-vī'tal-īz) *v.t.* to deprive of living power. [L. *de* = *dis*, and **VITAL**.]

DEVOID (de-void') *a.* not possessing; void; empty; destitute. [= *devoided*, fr. O.F. *de* = L. *dis*.]

DEVOIR (dev-wawr') *n.* duty; act of civility. [F., fr. L. *debere*, owe.]

DEVOLUTION (de-vō-lū'shun) *n.* act of devolving; transference. [L. (part.) *devolutus*, lit. rolled down.]

DEVOLVE (de-volv') *v.t.* or *i.* to roll down; fall by succession. [L., fr. *de*, and *volvere*, roll.]

DEVOTE (de-vōt') *v.t.* to dedicate; appropriate by vow. [L. (part.) *devotus*, vowed, fr. *de*, and *vovere*. See **DEVOUT**.]

DEVOTED (de-vō'ted) *a.* dedicated; strongly attached; zealous. [See **DEVOTE**.]

DEVOTEDNESS (de-vō'ted-nes) *n.* attachment to a cause, principle, or party; state of being devoted. [See **DEVOTE**.]

DEVOTEE (dev-u-tē') *n.* one devoted; a bigot. [See **DEVOTE**.]

DEVOTION (de-vō'shun) *n.* consecration; piety; prayer; ardent attachment to a cause or person. [L. (acc.) *devotionem*.]

DEVOTIONAL (de-vō'shun-al) *a.* pertaining to devotion. [See **DEVOTION**.]

DEVOUR (de-vour') *v.t.* to eat up ravenously; consume or destroy rapidly. [O.F. (*ie*) *devoure*, (1) devour, fr. L., fr. *de*, quite, and *vorare*, swallow up.]

DEVOUT (de-vout') *a.* pious; religious. [O.F. *devot*, fr. L. (acc. part.) *devotum*. See **DEVOTE**.]

DEVOUTLY (de-vout'li) *ad.* piously. [See **DEVOUT**.]

DEVOUTNESS (de-vout'nes) *n.* quality or state of being devout. [See **DEVOUT**.]

DEW (dū) *n.* moisture on the earth deposited at night;—*v.t.* to wet, as with dew. [O.E. *deaw*. Cf. Ger. *Thau*.]

DEWLAP (dū'lap) *n.* the flesh under an ox's throat. [Fr. DEW, and O.E. *lappa*, sew. See DEW.]

DEWY (dū'i) *a.* moist with dew. [See DEW.]

DEXTER (deks'ter) *a.* right, as opposed to *left*. [L. *dexter*, the right hand.

DEXTERITY (deks-ter'i-ti) *n.* activity and expertness; adroitness; skill. [L. (acc.) *dexteritatem*.]

DEXTEROUS (deks'ter-us) *a.* expert in manual acts; adroit; handy; skilful.

DEXTEROUSLY (deks'ter-us-li) *ad.* with skill. [See **DEXTEROUS**.]

DIABETES (dī-a-bē'tez) *n.* excessive discharge of urine. [G.]

DIABOLICAL (dī-a-bol'i-kal) *a.* devilish. [L., fr. G. *diabolicos*, fr. *diabolos*, DEVIL.]

DIABOLICALLY (dī-a-bol'i-kal-i) *ad.* in a diabolical manner. [See **DIABOLICAL**.]

DIACONATE (dī-ak'u-nāt) *n.* office of a deacon; deaconship. [Fr. L. *diaconus*, DEACON.]

DIADEM (dī'a-dem) *n.* a crown. [L., fr. G. *diadema*, fr. *dia*, across, and *deein*, bind.]

DIÆRESIS (dī-ē're-sis) *n.* a mark (¨) placed over one of two vowels to note that they are pronounced separately. [L., fr. G. =separation, fr. *di* =*dia*, apart, and *hairein*, take.]

DIAGNOSIS (dī-ag-nō'sis) *n.* the science or art of distinguishing one disease from another by means of its symptoms. [G., fr. *dia*, and *gignoskein*, know.]

DIAGNOSTIC (dī-ag-nos'tik) *a.* symptomatic; —*n.* the symptoms of a disease;—*pl.* **DIAGNOSTICS**, the study of symptoms. [See **DIAGNOSIS**.]

DIAGONAL (dī-ag'u-nal) *n.* a right line drawn from angle to angle. [L., fr. G. *diagonios*, *dia*, through, and *gonia*, angle.]

DIAGONALLY (dī-ag'u-nal-i) *ad.* in a diagonal direction. [See **DIAGONAL**.]

DIAGRAM (dī'a-gram) *n.* a figure or drawing made to illustrate a statement, or facilitate a demonstration. [L., fr. G. *diagramma*, fr. *diagraphein*, mark out by lines.]

DIAL (dī'al) *n.* a plate to show the hour by the sun's shadow; any face or plate with a movable index or pointer. [Fr. Late L. *dialis*, pertaining to the day. L. *dies*.]

DIALECT (dī'a-lekt) *n.* language; peculiar or local form of speech. [F., fr. L. *dialectus*, a manner of speaking, fr. G., fr. *dialeg-omai*, converse, fr. *dia*, and *legein*, speak.]

DIALECTICAL (dī-a-lek'ti-kal) *a.* pertaining to dialect. [See **DIALECT**.]

DIALECTICIAN (dī-a-lek-tish'an) *n.* one skilled in formal reasoning. [See **DIALECT**.]

DIALECTICS (dī-a-lek'tiks) *n.pl.* the science of reasoning; the forms and rules of argument. [Fr. G. *dialektike*, technically, art of disputation.]

DIALOGUE (dī'a-log) *n.* discourse between two or more. [F., fr. L., fr. *dialogos*, conversation. See **DIALECT**.]

DIALYSIS (dī-al'i-sis) *n.* separation; exhaustion; diæresis. [G., fr. *dialuein*, part asunder, dissolve.]

DIAMETER (dī-am'e-ter) *n.* a right line passing through the centre of a circle. [F., fr. G. *dia*, across, and METER.]

DIAMETRICAL (dī-a-met'ri-kal) *a.* describing a diameter; direct. [See **DIAMETER**.]

DIAMETRICALLY (dī-a-met'ri-kal-i) *ad.* directly. [See **DIAMETER**.]

Diameter.

DIAMOND (dī'a-mund) *n.* the hardest and costliest of gems; a rhomboidal figure; the smallest printing type;—*a.* made of or set with diamonds. [Fr. O.F. *diamant*, for G. *adamas*, ADAMANT.]

DIANA (dī-an'a) *n.* the virgin goddess of the moon, of hunting, and of health. [L.]

DIAPASON (dī-a-pā'zun) *n.* the whole compass of the tones of an instrument; an organ stop. [G. fr. *dia*, throughout, and (gen.) *pason*, all (the notes).]

DIAPER (dī'a-per) *n.* figured linen. [O.F. *dia(s)pre*, through Late L., fr. Late G. *diaspros*, white throughout.]

DIAPHRAGM (dī'a-fram) *n.* the midriff. [G. *diaphragma*, partition; conn. with *diaphragnunai*, to fence.]

DIARRHŒA (dī-a-rē'a) *n.* morbidly frequent evacuation of the intestines. [G., fr. *dia*, through, and *rhein*, flow.]

DIARY (dī'a-ri) *n.* a register of daily events or transactions;—*a.* lasting for a day. [L. *diarium*, fr. *dies*, day.]

DIATHERMAL (dī-a-ther'mal) *a.* permeable by ea. [G. *dia*, through, *thermos*, and heath] t

DIATONIC (dī-a-ton'ik) *a.* ascending or descending, as in sound. [Fr. G. *diatonos*, extended, fr. *dia*, and *teinein*, stretch.]

DIATRIBE (dī'a-trib) *n.* a continued discourse or disputation; an invective. [F., fr. L. *diatriba*, a place for disputations, fr. G. *diatribein*, to spend time in (discussing), fr. *dia*, through, and *tribein*, rub.]

DIBBLE (dib'l) *n.* a tool for planting;—*v.t.* to make holes in the earth for seed;—*v.i.* to dip, in angling. [Conn. with DAB, DIP.]

DICE (dīs) *n.pl.* of **DIE**. [M.E. *dees*, fr. O.F. *dez*.]

DICE-BOX (dīs'boks) *n.* a box for dice. [See DICE.]

DICKEY (dik'i) *n.* a seat behind a carriage; a linen front worn over the shirt. [Etym. uncertain.]

DICTATE (dik'tāt) *v.t.* to tell another what to do, say, or write; prescribe or direct authoritatively;—*n.* an order, rule, or direction. [L. (part.) *dictatus*, said repeatedly, *dictare*, fr. *dicere*.]

DICTATION (dik-tā'shun) *n.* act of dictating; a school exercise. [See **DICTATE**.]

DICTATOR (dik-tā'ter) *n.* one temporarily invested with absolute power.

DICTATORIAL (dik-ta-tō'ri-al) *a.* unlimited in power; imperious. [See **DICTATOR**.]

DICTATORSHIP (dik-tā'tur-ship) *n.* office of a dictator. [See **DICTATOR**.]

DICTION (dik'shun) *n.* manner of expression; choice of words; style. [F., fr. L. (acc. *dictionem*, fr. (part.) *dictus*, said, fr. *dicere*, say.]

DICTIONARY (dik'shun-ar-i) *n.* a book in which words are explained. [Late L. *diction-arium*.]

DICTUM (dik'tum) *n.* an authoritative word or assertion;—*pl.* DICTA. [L. =thing said.]

DID (did) *pret.* of DO. [O.E. *dyde*.]

DIDACTIC (di-dak'tik) *a.* intended to instruct. [G., fr. *didaskein* =(*didak*) teach.]

DIDACTICS (di-dak'tiks) *n.pl.* the science or art of teaching. [See **DIDACTIC**.]

DIE (di) *v.i.* to lose life; expire. [M.E. *deven*, fr. Scand.]

DIE (di) *n.* a small cube;—*pl.* **DICE**; a stamp; —*pl.* **DIES**. [O.F. *det* = F. *dé*, fr. Late L. (part.) *datum*, cast, fr. *dare*.]

DIET (di'et) *n.* food; an assembly of princes or estates;—*v.t.* to supply with food;—*v.i.* to eat by medical rule. [O.F., fr. L., fr. G. *diaita*, manner of living.]

DIETETIC (di-e-tet'ik) *a.* pertaining to diet. [See DIET.]

DIETETICS (di-e-tet'iks) *n.pl.* the science that relates to food. [See DIET.]

DIFFER (dif'er) *v.i.* to be unlike; be at variance. [L. *differre*, carry away, fr. *dis*, and *ferre*.]

DIFFERENCE (dif'e-rens) *n.* disagreement; disparity; contention; point in dispute; remainder after subtraction. [L. *differentia*.]

DIFFERENT (dif'e-rent) *a.* not the same. [L. (part. stem) *different-*, differing.]

DIFFERENTIAL (dif-e-ren'shal) *a.* creating a difference; special; pertaining to the science of fluxions. [See DIFFERENCE.]

DIFFERENTIATE (dif'e-ren'shi-āt) *v.t.* to mark the difference of; discriminate between. [See DIFFERENCE.]

DIFFERENTLY (dif'e-rent-li) *ad.* variously. [See DIFFERENT.]

DIFFICULT (dif'i-kult) *a.* hard to be done; hard to please. [See DIFFICULTY.]

DIFFICULTY (dif'i-kult-i) *n.* hardness to be done; obstacle; perplexity; objection. [O.F., fr. L. (acc.) *difficultatem*, fr. *difficilis*, difficult, fr. *dis-*, and FACILE.]

DIFFIDENCE (dif'i-dens) *n.* want of confidence; embarrassment; timidity; distrust. [See DIFFIDENT.]

DIFFIDENT (dif'i-dent) *a.* distrustful; bashful. [L. (part. stem) *diffident-*, distrusting, fr. *dis-*, and *fidere*.]

DIFFIDENTLY (dif'i-dent-li) *ad.* with distrust; modestly. [See DIFFIDENT.]

DIFFUSE (di-fūz') *v.t.* to pour out; spread abroad; (di-fūs') *a.* copious; widely spread. [L. (part.) *diffusus*, spread, fr. *dis-*, and *fundere*, pour.]

DIFFUSELY (di-fūs'li) *ad.* widely; copiously. [See DIFFUSE.]

DIFFUSIBLE (di-fū'zi-bl) *a.* that may be diffused. [See DIFFUSE.]

DIFFUSION (di-fū'zhun) *n.* a spreading; expansion; extension. [See DIFFUSE.]

DIFFUSIVE (di-fū'siv) *a.* that spreads widely; extending; circulating. [See DIFFUSE.]

DIG (dig) *v.t.* or *i.* [*pret.* and *pp.* **DIGGED**, **DUG**] to turn up with a spade. [O.F. *diguer*, fr. *digue*, DIKE, fr. D.] [DIGEST.]

DIGEST (di'jest) *n.* a collection of laws. [See

DIGEST (di-jest') *v.t.* to dissolve in the stomach; arrange or distribute; bear with patience; soften by heat. [L. (part.) *digestus*, separated, fr. *di* = *dis*, and *gerere*, carry.]

DIGESTIBLE (di-jes'ti-bl) *a.* capable of being digested. [See DIGEST.]

DIGESTION (di-jest'yun) *n.* the process of digesting. [L. (acc.) *digestionem*.]

DIGESTIVE (di-jes'tiv) *a.* causing digestion. [See DIGEST.]

DIGIT (dij'it) *n.* a finger; three-fourths of an inch; the 12th of the diameter of the sun or moon; any number under ten. [L. *digitus*, finger.]

DIGITAL (dij'i-tal) *a.* relating to a digit. [See DIGIT.]

DIGNIFIED (dig'ni-fīd) *a.* marked with honour; lofty; stately. [See DIGNIFY.]

DIGNIFY (dig'ni-fi) *v.t.* to invest with honour; exalt. [O.F. *dignifier*, fr. Late L., fr. L. *digni* = *dignus*, and *ficare* = *facere*, make.]

DIGNITARY (dig'ni-tar-i) *n.* one that possesses exalted rank, especially ecclesiastical rank. [See DIGNITY.]

DIGNITY (dig'ni-ti) *n.* elevation of rank, mind, character, or mien; nobleness; high office; preferment. [F., fr. L. (acc.) *dignitatem*, fr. *dignus*, worth.]

DIGRESS (di-gres') *v.i.* to turn from the main subject. [L. (part.) *digressus*, gone aside, fr. *di* = *dis*, and *gredi* = *gradi*, go. See GRADE.]

DIGRESSION (di-gresh'un) *n.* a turning aside from the theme of discourse; deviation from the right path. [L. (acc.) *digressionem*.]

DIGRESSIVE (di-gres'iv) *a.* tending to digress. See DIGRESS.]

DIKE (dik) *n.* a ditch; a mound of earth;— *v.t.* to surround with a bank or dike. [O.E. *dic*. Cf. Ger. *Teich*, DIG.]

DILAPIDATE (di-lap'i-dāt) *v.t.* or *i.* to pull down; squander; go to ruin. [L. (part.) *dilapidatus*, pulled down (of stones), fr. *di* = *dis*, and stem, *lapid-*, of *lapis*, stone.]

DILAPIDATED (di-lap'i-dā-ted) *a.* gone to ruin. [See DILAPIDATE.]

DILAPIDATION (di-lap-i-dā'shun) *n.* state of decay or ruin; wasting of church property. [See DILAPIDATE.]

DILATABLE (di-lā'ta-bl) *a.* capable of extension. [See DILATE.]

DILATATION (dil-a-tā'shun) *n.* act of dilating. [See DILATE.]

DILATE (di-lāt') *v.t.* or *i.* to expand, extend, or enlarge in all directions; speak diffusely. [F., fr. L. *dilatare*, make broad, fr. *di* = *dis*, and *latus*, broad.]

DILATORILY (dil'a-tur-i-li) *ad.* tardily. [See DILATORY.]

DILATORY (dil'a-tur-i) *a.* tardy; off-putting; procrastinating. [L. *dilator*, *differe*, delay.]

DILEMMA (di-lem'a) *n.* a perplexing state; an argument with two alternatives, both conclusive against an opponent. [G., fr. *di*, twice, double, and *lemma*, an assumption.]

DILETTANTE (dil-e-tan'te) *n.pl.* **DILETTANTI** (dil-e-tan'tē) an admirer of the fine arts; a would-be critic. [It., fr. L. *delectare*, to DELIGHT.]

DILIGENCE (dil'i-jens) *n.* steady application to business. [F., fr. L. (acc.) *diligentiam*.]

DILIGENT (dil'i-jent) *a.* constant in application to business. [O.F. fr. L. (acc.) *diligentem* orig. (part.) loving, choosing, fr. *di* = *dis*, and *legere*.]

DILIGENTLY (dil'i-jent-li) *ad.* with steady application. [See DILIGENT.]

DILUENT (dil'ū-ent) *a.* making thin, as liquor. [L. (part. stem) *diluent-*, washing away.]

DILUTE (di-lūt') *v.t.* to make more thin;— *a.* thin; dilated. [L. (part.) *dilutus*, melted away, fr. *di* = *dis-*, and *luere*, *diluere*.]

DILUTION (di-lū'shun) *n.* act of diluting; a weak liquid. [See DILUTE.]

DILUVIAL (di-lū'vi-al) *a.* relating to a flood. [See DILUVIUM.]

DILUVIUM (di-lū'vi-um) *n.* a deposit of earth, etc., caused by a flood. [L., fr. *diluere*. See DILUTE.] [cloud; obscure. [E.]

DIM (dim) *a.* not clear; obscure;—*v.t.* to

DIME (dim) *n.* a silver coin, the tenth of a dollar = fivepence sterling. [F. *dime*, tithe, fr. O.F. *disme*, fr. L. (acc.) *decimam*. See DECIMAL.]

DIMENSION (di-men'shun) *n.* bulk; size; extent of body. [O.F., fr. L. (acc.) *dimensionem*, fr. *di* = *dis*, and (part.) *mensus*. See MENSURATION.]

DIMINISH (di-min'ish) *v.t.* or *i.* to make or become less; take from; reduce. [L. pref. *di* = *dis-*, and O F. *menusser*, fr. Low L. = to make minute.]

DIMINUTION (dim-i-nū'shun) *n.* a making or growing smaller. [L. (acc.) *diminutionem*.]

DIMINUTIVE (di-min'ū-tiv) *a.* very small in size or value;—*n.* a derivative word expressing littleness, as *manikin* from *man*. [See DIMINISH.]

DIMINUTIVELY (di-min'ū-tiv-li) *ad.* in a diminutive manner. [See DIMINISH.]

DIMITY (dim'i-ti) *n.* a kind of stout, white cotton cloth, ribbed or figured. [It., fr. Late L., fr. G. *dimitos*, double thread.]

DIMLY (dim'li) *ad.* obscurely. [See DIM.]

DIMMISH (dim'ish) *a.* somewhat dim. [See DIM.]

DIMNESS (dim'nes) *n.* dullness. [See DIM.]

DIMPLE (dim'pl) *n.* a little hollow in the cheek;—*v.i.* to form dimples. [Probably conn. with DIP.]

DIN (din) *v.t.* to stun with noise;—*n.* a loud continued sound. [E., fr. O.E. *dynnan*, to resound.]

DINE (din) *v.i.* to eat a dinner;—*v.t.* to give a dinner to. [F. *diner*, fr. O.F. *disner*, through Low L. forms, fr. L. *dis-*, and *jejunare*, fast. Cf. *Déjeuner*.]

DINGHY (ding'gi) *n.* a small kind of ship's boat. [Native Bengal name.]

DINGINESS (din'ji-nes) *n.* a dusky hue. [See DINGY.]

DINGLE (ding'gl) *n.* a hollow between hills; a dale. [E., conn. with DIMPLE.]

DINGO (ding'gō) *n.* the native dog of Australia. [Native Australian name.]

DINGY (din'ji) *a.* dusky; soiled; foul. [E. conn. with DUNG.]

DINNER (din'ẹr) *n.* the chief meal of the day. [F. *diner*, dinner.]

DINT (dint) *n.* a blow; mark of a blow; force; power;—*v.t.* to mark by a blow. [M.E. *dint*, DENT, *dunt*, fr. O.E.]

DIOCESAN (di-os'e-sạn) *a.* pertaining to a diocese;—*n.* a bishop. [See DIOCESE.]

DIOCESE (di'ō-sẹs) *n.* the jurisdiction of a bishop. [F., fr. L. (acc.) *diœcesem*, parish, fr. G. *dioikesis*, administration, fr. *dia-*, throughout, and *oikein*, keep house. See ECONOMY.]

DIORAMA (di-ō-rà'mạ) *n.* an ingenious optical contrivance. [Fr. G. *di* = *dia*, through, and *horama*, sight, fr. *horaein*, see.]

DIORAMIC (di-ō-ram'ik) *a.* pertaining to diorama. [See DIORAMA.]

DIP (dip) *v.t.* to plunge;—*v.i.* to bathe; sink; enter or look into; incline;—*n.* immersion; inclination; a small candle. [O.E. *dippan*.]

DIPHTHERIA (dif-thē'ri-ạ) *n.* a dangerous epidemic disease of the throat and air passages. [Fr. G. *diphthera*, leather.]

DIPHTHONG (dif'thong) *n.* a union of two vowels in one sound or syllable. [L., fr. G., fr. *di* = *dis-*, double, and *phthongos*, sound.]

DIPHTHONGAL (dif-thong'gal) *a.* consisting of a diphthong. [See DIPHTHONG.]

DIPLOMA (di-plō'mạ) *n.* a document conferring some privilege or honour. [G. = licence (folded), fr. *diploos*, double-folded.]

DIPLOMACY (di-plō'mạ-si) *n.* the art and the forms of international negotiation; political skill and dexterity. [See DIPLOMATIST.]

DIPLOMATIC (dip-lu-mat'ik) *a.* pertaining to diplomacy. [See DIPLOMATIST.]

DIPLOMATIST (di-plō'mạ-tist) *n.* one skilled in diplomacy. [Fr. G. stem, *diplomat-*, of DIPLOMA.]

DIPSOMANIA (dip-so-mā'ni-ạ) *n.* a morbid craving for alcoholic drinks. [Fr. G. *dipsa*, thirst. See MANIA.]

DIRE (dir) *a.* dreadful; highly calamitous. [L. *dirus*.]

DIRECT (di-rekt') *a.* straight; leading to; in line; straightforward; express;—*v.t.* to guide; prescribe; order; superscribe. [L. (part.) *directus*, directed, fr. *di* = *dis-*, and *rigere* for *regere*, rule.]

DIRECTION (di-rek'shun) *n.* act of directing; line, course, or end of motion; address on a letter; board of directors. [See DIRECT.]

DIRECTIVE (di-rek'tiv) *a.* giving direction. [See DIRECT.]

DIRECTLY (di-rekt'li) *ad.* immediately. [See DIRECT.]

DIRECTNESS (di-rekt'nes) *n.* straightness; tendency to a point. [See DIRECT.]

DIRECTOR (di-rek'tẹr) *n.* one who directs; a superintendent. [See DIRECT.]

DIRECTORATE (di-rek'tu-rāt) *n.* body of directors; office of director. Also DIRECTORSHIP. [See DIRECT.]

DIRECTORY (di-rek'tur-i) *n.* a book of directions; a guide-book;—*a.* tending to direct. [L. *directorius*, guiding.]

DIREFUL (dir'fool) *a.* dreadful; horrible.

DIREFULNESS (dir'fool-nes) *n.* calamitousness; dreadfulness. [See DIRE.]

DIRENESS (dir'nes) *n.* dismalness; horror.

DIRGE (derj) *n.* a funeral song. [Corr. fr. L. (imp.) *dirige*, direct (beginning the Office for the Dead). See DIRECT.]

DIRIGIBLE (di'ri-gi-bl) *a.* that may be guided or steered;—*n.* a balloon that may be steered. [See DIRECT.]

DIRK (derk) *n.* a kind of dagger. [Etym. uncertain.]

DIRT (dert) *n.* any foul or filthy substance;—*v.t.* to make dirty. [Scand.]

DIRTILY (der'ti-li) *ad.* filthily; meanly.

Dirk.

DIRTY (der'ti) *a.* foul or filthy; defiled; shabby; mean;—*v.t.* to soil with dirt; sully. [See DIRT.]

DISABILITY (dis-ạ-bil'i-ti) *n.* want of power or qualifications. [L. *dis*. See ABLE.]

DISABLE (dis-ā'bl) *v.t.* to deprive of power; disqualify. [See DISABILITY.]

DISABLEMENT (dis-ā'bl-ment) *n.* loss or want of strength; legal hindrance. [See DISABILITY.]

DISABUSE (dis-ạ-būz') *v.t.* to undeceive. [L. *dis*. See ABUSE.]

DISACCOMMODATION (dis-ạ-kom-u-dā'shun) *n.* state of being unsuited or unprepared. [L. *dis*. See ACCOMMODATION.]

DISADVANTAGE (dis-ạd-van'tāj) *n.* loss of advantage; unfavourable state. [L. *dis*. See ADVANTAGE.]

DISADVANTAGEOUS (dis-ad-vạn-tā'jus) *a.* unfavourable to success; inconvenient; prejudicial. [See DISADVANTAGE.]

DISADVANTAGEOUSLY (dis-ad-van-tā'jus-li) *ad.* with disadvantage. [See DISADVANTAGE.]

DISAFFECT (dis-ạ-fekt') *v.t.* to make less friendly or loyal. [L. *dis*. See AFFECT.]

DISAFFECTED (dis-ạ-fek'ted) *a.* not disposed to good or affection. [See DISAFFECT.]

DISAFFECTION (dis-ạ-fek'shun) *n.* want of affection; dislike; disloyalty. [See DISAFFECT.]

DISAFFIRM (dis-ạ-ferm') *v.t.* to deny. [L. *dis*. See AFFIRM.]

DISAFFIRMANCE (dis-ạ-fer'mạns) *n.* denial; negation; legal annulment. [L. *dis*. See AFFIRM.]

DISAGGREGATE (dis-ag're-gāt) *v.t.* to separate a mass into its component parts. [L. *dis*. See AGGREGATE.]

DISAGREE (dis-ạ-grē') *v.i.* to differ in opinion; be unsuitable; dissent. [L. *dis*. See AGREE.]

DISAGREEABLE (dis-ạ-grē'ạ-bl) *a.* unpleasant to the mind or senses. [See DISAGREE.]

DISAGREEABLY (dis-ạ-grē'ạ-bli) *ad.* unpleasantly. [See DISAGREE.]

DISAGREEMENT (dis-ạ-grē'ment) *n.* difference; unsuitableness; dissension; dispute. [L. *dis*. See AGREE.]

DISALLOW (dis-ạ-lou') *v.t.* to deny; refuse permission. [L. *dis*. See ALLOW.]

DISALLOWABLE (dis-a-lou'a-bl) *a.* not allowable. [L. *dis.* See ALLOW.]

DISALLOWANCE (dis-a-lou'ans) *n.* disapprobation; prohibition. [L. *dis.* See ALLOW.]

DISANNUL (dis-a-nul') *v.t.* to annul completely. [L. *dis.*, intens. See ANNUL.]

DISAPPEAR (dis-a-pēr') *v.i.* to vanish from sight. [L. *dis.* See APPEAR.]

DISAPPEARANCE (dis-a-pēr'ans) *n.* an end of appearance; removal from sight. [L. *dis.* See APPEAR.]

DISAPPOINT (dis-a-point') *v.t.* to defeat of expectation. [O.F. *desapointer*, fr. *des =* L. *dis,* away, and *apointer,* to appoint. See APPOINT.]

DISAPPOINTMENT (dis-a-point'ment) *n.* defeat of hopes or expectation. [See DISAPPOINT.]

DISAPPROBATION (dis-ap-ru-bā'shun) *n.* a disapproving; censure; displeasure; dislike. [L. *dis.* See APPROBATE.]

DISAPPROVAL (dis-a-prōo'val) *n.* disapprobation; dislike. [L. *dis.* See APPROVE.]

DISAPPROVE (dis-a-prōov') *v.t.* to censure or condemn; disallow; reject. [L. *dis.* See APPROVE.]

DISAPPROVINGLY (dis-a-prōo'ving-li) *ad.* by disapprobation. [L. *dis.* See APPROVE.]

DISARM (dis-ärm') *v.t.* to deprive of arms. [L. *dis.* See ARM.]

DISARRANGE (dis-a-rānj') *v.t.* to put out of order. [L. *dis.* See ARRANGE.]

DISARRANGEMENT (dis-a-rānj'ment) *n.* act disturbing order. [See DISARRANGE.]

DISARRAY (dis-a-rā') *v.t.* to undress; throw into disorder;—*n.* want of order; disorder; undress. [O.F. *desarroi, des =* L. *dis,* away, *arroi,* see ARRAY.]

DISASTER (di-zas'tẽr) *n.* unfortunate event; mishap; calamity. [O.F. *desastre, des =* L. *dis,* with evil sense, *astre =* L. *astrum,* a star, destiny.]

DISASTROUS (di-zas'trus) *a.* unlucky; calamitous. [See DISASTER.]

DISASTROUSLY (di-zas'trus-li) *ad.* with loss, suffering, etc. [See DISASTER.]

DISAVOW (dis-a-vou') *v.t.* to disown; deny knowledge or approval of. [O.F. *desavouer, des =* L. *dis,* away, *avouer,* to avow.]

DISAVOWAL (dis-a-vou'al) *n.* act of disowning; repudiation; disclaimer. [See DISAVOW.]

DISBAND (dis-band') *v.t.* or *i.* to dismiss from military service. [O.F. *desbander, des =* L. *dis,* neg., *bander.*]

DISBELIEF (dis-be-lēf') *n.* refusal of belief. [L. *dis.* See BELIEF.]

DISBELIEVE (dis-be-lēv') *v.t.* to discredit. [L. *dis.* See BELIEVE.]

DISBELIEVER (dis-be-lē'vẽr) *n.* an unbeliever; sceptic. [L. *dis.* See BELIEVE.]

DISBURDEN (dis-bur'dn) *v.t.* to ease of a burden; relieve;—*v.i.* to unload or discharge. [L. *dis.* See BURDEN.]

DISBURSE (dis-burs') *v.t.* to expend; pay out; spend. [O.F. *desbourser, fr. des =* L. *dis,* and BOURSE.]

DISBURSEMENT (dis-burs'ment) *n.* act of disbursing; sum spent. [See DISBURSE.]

DISBURSER (dis-bur'sẽr) *n.* one who pays out or disburses money. [See DISBURSE.]

DISBURTHEN (dis-bur'THen) *v.t.* or *i.* to disburden. [See DISBURDEN.]

DISC (disk) *n.* any flat circular surface; face of the sun or a planet. Also DISK. [L. *discus,* disc (used in quoiting), fr. G. Doublet of DAIS, DESK, DISH.]

DISCARD (dis-kärd') *v.t.* to throw away or cast off; discharge; dismiss. [L. *dis.* See CARD.]

DISCERN (di-sẽrn') *v.t.* to distinguish clearly; apprehend; discriminate; judge. [L., fr. *dis,* and *cernere,* separate.]

DISCERNIBLE (di-zẽr'ni-bl) *a.* that may be seen. [See DISCERN.]

DISCERNIBLY (di-zẽr'ni-bli) *ad.* in a manner to be discerned. [See DISCERN.]

DISCERNING (di-zẽr'ning) *a.* quick in perception; acute; penetrating. [See DISCERN.]

DISCERNINGLY (di-zẽr'ning-li) *ad.* with clear perception or understanding. [See DISCERN.]

DISCERNMENT (di-zẽrn'ment) *n.* act of seeing; penetration; discrimination. [See DISCERN.]

DISCHARGE (dis-chärj') *v.t.* to free from; unload; let fly or fire; pay; receipt; dismiss; perform;—*v i.* to emit matter;—*n.* unloading; acquittance; dismissal; performance; matter emitted. [L. *dis.* See CHARGE.]

DISCIPLE (di-sī'pl) *n.* a learner; a scholar or follower of another;—*v t.* to train; make followers of. [F., fr. L. (acc.) *discipulum,* learned, fr. *discere,* learn.]

DISCIPLESHIP (di-sī'pl-ship) *n.* state of a disciple. [See DISCIPLE.]

DISCIPLINABLE (dis'i-plin-a-bl) *a.* capable of instruction. [See DISCIPLINE.]

DISCIPLINARIAN (dis-i-pli-nā'ri-an) *n.* one who keeps good discipline. [See DISCIPLINE.]

DISCIPLINARY (dis'i-plin-ar-i) *a.* intended for discipline. [See DISCIPLINE.]

DISCIPLINE (dis'i-plin) *n.* education and government; penal infliction; correction; —*v.t.* to instruct and govern; regulate; chastise. [F., fr. L. (acc.) *disciplinam,* learning, fr. DISCIPLE.]

DISCLAIM (dis-klām') *v.i.* to disown; disavow; reject. [L. *dis.* See CLAIM.]

DISCLAIMER (dis-klā'mẽr) *n.* one who disclaims; renunciation; disavowal. [L. *dis.* See CLAIM.]

DISCLOSE (dis-klōz') *v.t.* to uncover; reveal. [L. *dis.* See CLOSE.]

DISCLOSER (dis-klō'zẽr) *n.* one who discloses or reveals. [L. *dis.* See CLOSE.]

DISCLOSURE (dis-klō'zhŭr) *n.* a revealing; that which is disclosed. [L. *dis.* See CLOSE.]

DISCOLOUR (dis-kul'ur) *v.t.* to stain or change the colour. [L. *dis.* See COLOUR.]

DISCOLOURATION (dis-kul-u-rā'shun) *n.* change of colour. [See DISCOLOUR.]

DISCOLOURED (dis-kul'erd) *a.* changed in colour. [See DISCOLOUR.]

DISCOMFIT (dis-kum'fit) *v.t.* to cause to flee; rout; defeat. [O.F. (part.) *disconfit,* undone.]

DISCOMFITURE (dis-kum'fi-tŭr) *n.* defeat. [See DISCOMFIT.]

DISCOMFORT (dis-kum'furt) *n.* uneasiness; disquiet;—*v.t.* to disturb peace. [L. *dis,* See COMFORT.]

DISCOMMODE (dis-ku-mōd') *v.t.* to incommode. [L. *dis.* See COMMODIOUS.]

DISCOMMODIOUS (dis-ku-mō'di-us) *a.* inconvenient. [L. *dis.* See COMMODIOUS.]

DISCOMMODITY (dis-ku-mod'i-ti) *n.* inconvenience; trouble. [L. *dis.* See COMMODITY.]

DISCOMPOSE (dis-kum-pōz') *v.t.* to disarrange; unsettle; disturb the temper. [L. *dis.* See COMPOSE.]

DISCOMPOSURE (dis-kum-pō'zhŭr) *n.* disorder; disturbance. [See DISCOMPOSE.]

DISCONCERT (dis-kun-sẽrt') *v.t.* to disturb; unsettle the mind. [L. *dis.* See CONCERT.]

DISCONNECT (dis-ku-nekt') *v.t.* to disunite. [L. *dis.* See CONNECT.]

DISCONNECTION (dis-ku-nek'shun) *n.* separation; want of union. [See DISCONNECT.]

DISCONSOLATE (dis-kon'su-lāt) *a.* void of comfort; hopeless; deeply dejected. [L. *dis.* See CONSOLE.]

DISCONSOLATELY (dis-kon'su-lāt-li) *ad.* in a disconsolate manner. [See DISCONSOLATE.]

DISCONTENT (dis-kun-tent') *n.* uneasiness. [L. *dis.* See CONTENT.]

DISCONTENTED (dis-kun-ten'ted) *a.* dissatisfied. [See DISCONTENT.]

DISCONTENTEDLY (dis-kun-ten'ted-li) ad. in a discontented manner or mood. [See DIS-CONTENT.]

DISCONTINUANCE (dis-kun-tin'ū-ans) n. a ceasing. [See DISCONTINUE.]

DISCONTINUE (dis-kun-tin'ū) v.t. or i. to leave off; cease. [L. dis. See CONTINUE.]

DISCONTINUITY (dis-kun-tin-ū'i-ti) n. separation of parts. [See DISCONTINUE.]

DISCORD (dis'kord) n. disagreement; contrariety; variance; strife; union of inharmonious notes. [O.F., fr. descorder, to clash, fr. L., fr. dis. and stem, cord-, of cor. heart.]

DISCORDANCE (dis-kor'dans) n. disagreement; inconsistency. [See DISCORD.]

DISCORDANT (dis-kor'dant) a. inconsistent; not harmonious. [See DISCORD.]

DISCOUNT (dis'kount) n. deduction of a sum; allowance;—(dis-kount') v.t. or i. to allow discount; lend and deduct interest at the time. [L. dis. See COUNT.]

DISCOUNTABLE (dis-koun'ta-bl) a. that may be discounted. [See DISCOUNT.]

DISCOUNTENANCE (dis-koun'te-nans) v.t. to discourage;—n. disfavour. [L. dis. See COUNTENANCE.]

DISCOUNTER (dis-koun'ter) n. one who advances money on bills, etc., less the interest. [See DISCOUNT.]

DISCOURAGE (dis-kur'ij) v.t. to dishearten; depress. [L. dis. See COURAGE.]

DISCOURAGEMENT (dis-kur'ij-ment) n. that which abates courage. [See DISCOURAGE.]

DISCOURAGING (dis-kur'ij-ing) a. depressing the courage; unfavourable. [See DIS-COURAGE.]

DISCOURAGINGLY (dis-kur'ij-ing-li) ad. in a manner to discourage. [See DISCOURAGE.]

DISCOURSE (dis-kōrs') n. a treatise; a sermon;—v.t. to utter;—v.i. to converse; treat of formally; reason. [O.F. discours, fr. L. (acc. discursum.]

DISCOURSER (dis-kōr'ser) n. a speaker; writer of a treatise. [See DISCOURSE.]

DISCOURSIVE (dis-kōr'siv) a. argumentative; conversational; conversable. [See DIS-COURSE.]

DISCOURTEOUS (dis-kur'tyus) a. uncivil; rude. [L. dis. See COURTEOUS.]

DISCOURTEOUSLY (dis-kur'tyus-li) ad. in a discourteous manner. [See DISCOUR-TEOUS.]

DISCOURTESY (dis-kur'te-si) n. incivility; ill manners. [L. dis. See COURTESY.]

DISCOVER (dis-kuv'er) v.t. to find out; disclose. [O.F. descouvrir = F. découvrir, fr. dis and COVER.]

DISCOVERABLE (dis-kuv'er-a-bl) a. that may be discovered. [See DISCOVER.]

DISCOVERER (dis-kuv'er-er) n. one who discovers. [See DISCOVER.]

DISCOVERY (dis-kuv'er-i) n. a finding; disclosure. [See DISCOVER.]

DISCREDIT (dis-kred'it) n. want of credit or of repute;—v.t. to disbelieve; distrust disgrace. [L. dis. See CREDIT.]

DISCREDITABLE (dis-kred'i-ta-bl) a. injurious to reputation. [See DISCREDIT.]

DISCREDITABLY (dis-kred'i-ta-bli) ad. in a disreputable manner. [See DISCREDIT.]

DISCREET (dis-krēt') a. prudent; cautious; wary; judicious. [O.F. discret, fr. L. (acc. part.) discretum, separated, fr. DISCERN. L. discretus, pp. of discernere.]

DISCREETLY (dis-krēt'li) ad. prudently. [See DISCREET.]

DISCREETNESS (dis-krēt'nes) n. discretion. [See DISCREET.]

DISCREPANCY (dis'krep-an-si, dis'kre-pan-si) n. difference; disagreement. [Fr. L. (part. stem) discrepant-, sounding differently, fr. dis, and crepare, creak.]

DISCREPANT (dis'krep'ant, dis'kre-pant) a. different; disagreeing; contrary. [See DISCREPANCY.]

DISCRETION (dis-kresh'un) n. prudence; sound judgment; freedom of choice or action. [See DISCREET.]

DISCRETIONALLY (dis-kresh'un-al-i) ad. according to one's judgment or option. [See DISCREET.]

DISCRETIONARY (dis-kresh'un-ar-i) a. to be governed by judgment only. [See DIS-CREET.]

DISCRETIVE (dis-krē'tiv) a. noting separation or opposition. [Fr. L. discretus. See DIS-CREET.]

DISCRIMINATE (dis-krim'i-nāt) v.t. to distinguish; select from;—v.i. to make a distinction. [L. (part.) discriminatus, separated, fr. dis, and root of DISCERN, CRIME.]

DISCRIMINATING (dis-krim'i-nā-ting) a. that discriminates. [See DISCRIMINATE.]

DISCRIMINATION (dis-krim-i-nā'shun) n. act of distinguishing. [See DISCRIMINATE.]

DISCRIMINATIVE (dis-krim'i-nā-tiv) a. serving to distinguish. [See DISCRIMINATE.]

DISCRIMINATIVELY (dis-krim'i-nā-tiv-li) ad. with due observance of distinction. [See DISCRIMINATE.]

DISCRIMINATOR (dis-krim'i-nā-ter) n. one who notes and makes a distinction. [See DISCRIMINATE.]

DISCRIMINATORY (dis-krim'i-nā-tur-i) a. distinguishing; characteristic. [See DIS-CRIMINATE.]

DISCURSION (dis-kur'shun) n. a running about; desultory talk; act of reasoning. [See DISCURSUS.]

DISCURSIVE (dis-kur'siv) a. argumentative; rational; desultory; digressive. [See DIS-CURSUS.]

DISCURSIVELY (dis-kur'siv-li) ad. in a discursive manner. [See DISCURSUS.]

DISCURSUS (dis-kur'sus) n. a reasoned argument. [L. = a running about, fr. dis-, and cursus, a COURSE.]

DISCUSS (dis-kus') v.t. to break up; disperse; examine and sift by mutual reasoning; partake of, as viands. [L. (part.) discussus, shaken apart, fr. dis-, and quatere, shake.]

DISCUSSION (dis-kush'un) n. dispersion; reciprocal reasoning or debate; disquisition. [See DISCUSS.]

DISDAIN (dis-dān') n. haughty contempt; —v.t. to scorn; despise; deem worthless. [O.F. desdegnier = F. dédaigner, fr. dis- and DEIGN.]

DISDAINFUL (dis-dān'fool) a. scornful; haughty; contemptuous. [See DISDAIN.]

DISDAINFULLY (dis-dān'fool-i) ad. with scorn. [See DISDAIN.]

DISDAINFULNESS (dis-dān'fool-nes) n. contemptuousness; scornfulness. [See DIS-DAIN.]

DISDAINING (dis-dān'ing) n. haughty scorn; contempt. [See DISDAIN.]

DISEASE (di-zēz') n. derangement; disorder; malady;—v.t. to affect with sickness. [O.F. desaise, fr. dis-, and EASE.]

DISEMBARK (dis-em-bárk') v.t. or i. to put or go on shore. [L. dis. See EMBARK.]

DISEMBARKATION (dis-em-bár-kā'shun) n. a landing or going ashore. [See DISEM-BARK.]

DISEMBARRASS (dis-em-bar'as) v.t. to free from embarrassment. [L. dis. See EM-BARRASS.]

DISEMBODIED (dis-em-bod'id) pp. or a. divested of body. [L. dis. See EMBODY.]

DISEMBODY (dis-em-bod'i) v.t. to divest of a body; disband, as military forces. [L. dis. See EMBODY.]

DISEMBOWEL (dis-em-bou'el) v.t. to take out the bowels of. [L. dis. See BOWELS.]

DISENCHANT (dis-en-chant') v.t. to free from enchantment. [L. dis. See ENCHANT.]

DISENCUMBER (dis-en-kum'ber) v.t. to free from obstruction. [L. dis. See ENCUMBER.]

DISENCUMBRANCE (dis-en-kum'brans) *n.* deliverance from burden or trouble; release from debt. [L. *dis.* See ENCUMBER.]

DISENFRANCHISE (dis-en-fran'chiz) *v.t.* to deprive of privileges or rights. [L. *dis.* See ENFRANCHISE.]

DISENGAGE (dis-en-gāj') *v.t.* to free from an engagement or a tie; release; withdraw. [L. *dis.* See ENGAGE.]

DISENGAGED (dis-en-gājd') *a.* vacant; at leisure. [See DISENGAGE.]

DISENGAGEMENT (dis-en-gāj'ment) *n.* release from engagement; leisure. [See DISENGAGE.]

DISENNOBLE (dis-e-nō'bl) *v.t.* to deprive of title or dignity; degrade. [L. *dis.* See NOBLE.]

DISENROLL (dis-en-rōl') *v.t.* to erase from a roll or list. [L. *dis.* See ENROL.]

DISENTANGLE (dis-en-tang'gl) *v.t.* to unravel; disengage; set free from difficulties. [L. *dis.* See TANGLE.]

DISENTHRAL (dis-en-thrawl') *v.t.* to free from thraldom; to emancipate. [L. *dis.* See ENTHRAL.]

DISENTHRONE (dis-en-thrōn') *v.t.* to dethrone. [L. *dis.* See THRONE.]

DISESTABLISH (dis-es-tab'lish) *v.t.* to remove from an established state; unsettle. [L. *dis.* See ESTABLISH.]

DISESTABLISHMENT (dis-es-tab'lish-ment) *n.* withdrawal from a church of its position and privileges as established by the State. [L. *dis.* See ESTABLISH.]

DISESTEEM (dis-es-tēm') *n.* want of esteem; —*v.t.* to dislike. [L. *dis.* See ESTEEM.]

DISFAVOUR (dis-fā'vur) *n.* unpropitious regard;—*v.t.* to discountenance. [L. *dis.* See FAVOUR.]

DISFIGURATION (dis-fig-u-rā'shun) *n.* act of disfiguring. [L. *dis.* See FIGURE.]

DISFIGURE (dis-fig'ur) *v.t.* to injure the form of; deface. [L. *dis.* See FIGURE.]

DISFIGUREMENT (dis-fig'ur-ment) *n.* a defacement. [L. *dis.* See FIGURE.]

DISFRANCHISE (dis-fran'chiz) *v.t.* to deprive of citizenship. [L. *dis.* See FRANCHISE.]

DISFRANCHISEMENT (dis-fran'chiz-ment) *n.* a deprivation of privileges. [L. *dis.* See FRANCHISE.]

DISGARNISH (dis-gär'nish) *v.t.* to strip of ornaments. [O.F. *garnir*, furnish.]

DISGORGE (dis-gorj') *v.t.* to vomit; discharge; give up. [O.F. *desgorger*, fr. *des* = L. *dis-*, and GORGE.]

DISGRACE (dis-grās') *n.* state of shame; disfavour; dishonour;—*v.t.* to deprive of favour; bring shame upon; dishonour. [O.F., through It. *disgrazia*, fr. L. *dis-*, and *gratia*, grace.]

DISGRACEFUL (dis-grās'fool) *a.* shameful. [See DISGRACE.]

DISGRACEFULLY (dis-grās'fool-i) *ad.* shamefully; ignominiously. [See DISGRACE.]

DISGUISE (dis-giz') *n.* a dress to conceal; false appearance;—*v.t.* to conceal by unusual dress; counterfeit; dissemble. [O.F. *desguiser*, fr. *des* = L. *dis-*, and GUISE.]

DISGUISED (dis-gizd') *a.* concealed by an assumed habit; intoxicated. [See DISGUISE.]

DISGUST (dis-gust') *n.* distaste; dislike; aversion;—*v.t.* to give dislike. [O.F. *desgouster*, fr. L. *dis-*, and *gustare*, taste.]

DISGUSTING (dis-gus'ting) *a.* provoking dislike. [See DISGUST.]

DISH (dish) *n.* a vessel to serve food;—*v.t.* to put in dishes. [M.E. *disch*, fr. O.E. *disc*, fr. L. *discus*. Doublet of DAIS, DESK, DISC.]

DISHEARTEN (dis-här'tn) *v.t.* to discourage; depress. [L. *dis.* See HEART.]

DISHEVEL (di-shev'el) *v.t.* to spread the hair disorderly. [O.F. *descheveler*, fr. L. *dis-*, and *chevel* = F. *cheveu*, fr. L. (acc.) *capillum*, hair.]

DISHONEST (dis-on'est) *a.* void of honesty; marked by fraud. [L. *dis.* See HONEST.]

DISHONESTLY (dis-on'est-li) *ad.* knavishly. [See DISHONEST.]

DISHONESTY (dis-on'est-i) *n.* want of honesty or integrity; fraud; any fraudulent act. [See DISHONEST.]

DISHONOUR (dis-on'ur) *n.* whatever injures the reputation; disgrace;—*v.t.* to bring shame on; refuse payment of. [L. *dis.* See HONOUR.]

DISHONOURABLE (dis-on'ur-a-bl) *a.* reproachful; disgraceful; base. [See DISHONOUR.]

DISHONOURABLY (dis-on'ur-a-bli) *ad.* in a dishonourable manner. [See DISHONOUR.]

DISILLUSION (dis-i-lōō'zhun) *n.* dispelling of a deception or false idea. [L. *dis.* See ILLUSION.]

DISINCLINATION (dis-in-kli-nā'shun) *n.* slight dislike or aversion; unwillingness. [See DISINCLINE.]

DISINCLINE (dis-in-klīn') *v.t.* to produce dislike; make unwilling. [L. *dis.* See INCLINE.]

DISINFECT (dis-in-fekt') *v.t.* to purify from infection. [L. *dis.* See INFECT.]

DISINFECTANT (dis-in-fek'tant) *n.* any agent used in disinfecting. [See DISINFECT.]

DISINFECTION (dis-in-fek'shun) *n.* a purifying from infection. [See DISINFECT.]

DISINGENUOUS (dis-in-jen'ū-us) *a.* wanting in frankness and honesty; insincere; crafty. [L. *dis.* See INGENUOUS.]

DISINGENUOUSLY (dis-in-jen'ū-us-li) *ad.* not openly or candidly; artfully. [See DISINGENUOUS.]

DISINHERIT (dis-in-her'it) *v.t.* to cut off from inheriting. [L. *dis.* See INHERIT.]

DISINTEGRATE (dis-in'te-grāt) *v.t.* to separate into parts. [L. *dis.* See INTEGER.]

DISINTEGRATION (dis-in-te-grā'shun) *n.* a separation of integral parts. [See DISINTEGRATE.]

DISINTER (dis-in-ter') *v.t.* to take out of a grave; revive. [L. *dis.* See INTER.]

DISINTERESTED (dis-in'ter-es-ted) *a.* free from self-interest. [L. *dis.* See INTERETS.]

DISINTERESTEDNESS (dis-in'ter-es-ted-nes) *n.* freedom from self-interest. [See DISINTERESTED.]

DISINTERMENT (dis-in-ter'ment) *n.* act of taking out of a grave. [See DISINTER.]

DISJOIN (dis-join') *v.t.* to separate; disunite; —*v.i.* to be separated; part. [L. *dis.* See JOIN.]

DISJOINT (dis-joint') *v.t.* to separate joints; dislocate. [L. *dis.* See JOINT.]

DISJOINTED (dis-join'ted) *a.* unconnected; out of joint; inconsistent. [See DISJOINT.]

DISJUNCT (dis-jungkt') *a.* separate. [L. (part.) *disjunctus*, disjoined, fr. *dis-*, and JOIN.]

DISJUNCTION (dis-jungk'shun) *n.* disunion. [See DISJUNCT.]

DISJUNCTIVE (dis-jungk'tiv) *a.* that disjoins; —*n.* a word or proposition that disjoins. [See DISJUNCT.]

DISK [See DISC.]

DISLIKE (dis-līk') *n.* absence of affection; aversion;—*v.t.* to disapprove; have no taste for. [L. *dis.* See LIKE.]

DISLOCATE (dis'lō-kāt) *v.t.* to displace; put out of joint;—*a.* out of joint. [Late L. *dislocatus*, displaced.]

DISLOCATED (dis'lō-kā-ted) *pp.* or *a.* put out of joint; displaced. [See DISLOCATE.]

DISLOCATION (dis-lō-kā'shun) *n.* a displacing; a joint or bone put out. [See DISLOCATE.]

DISLODGE (dis-loj') *v.t.* to drive from a place of rest or a station. [L. *dis.* See LODGE.]

DISLODGMENT (dis-loj'ment) *n.* displacement; removal. [L. *dis.* See LODGE.]

DISLOYAL (dis-loi'al) *a.* not true to allegiance; unfaithful. [L. *dis.* See LOYAL.]

DISLOYALLY (dis-loi'al-i) *ad.* in a disloyal manner. [See DISLOYAL.]

DISLOYALTY (dis-loi'al-ti) *n.* want of fidelity; treacherousness. [See DISLOYAL.]

DISMAL (diz'mal) *a.* dark; gloomy; sorrowful; dreadful. [O.F., fr. (pl.) *dismal,* bad days, fr. L. *dies mali.*]

DISMALLY (diz'mal-i) *ad.* in a dismal manner. [See DISMAL.]

DISMANTLE (dis-man'tl) *v.t.* to strip of dress, furniture, or outworks. [O.F. *desmanteller,* fr. L. *dis-,* and MANTEL.]

DISMAST (dis-mast') *v.t.* to deprive of masts. [L. *dis.* See MAST.]

DISMAY (dis-mā') *v.t.* to discourage;—*n.* loss of courage; state of fear or alarm. [O.F.—orig. to fail in strength, fr. L. *dis-,* and O. H. Ger. *magan.* Cf. Ger. *mögen,* MAY.]

DISMEMBER (dis-mem'bẹr) *v.t.* to separate member from member. [L. *dis.* See MEMBER.]

DISMEMBERMENT (dis-mem'bẹr-ment) *n.* separation; division. [See DISMEMBER.]

DISMISS (dis-mis') *v.t.* to send away; discharge; despatch; reject. [Fr. L. *dis-,* and (part.) *missus,* sent, fr. *mittere.*]

DISMISSAL (dis-mis'al) *n.* discharge; dismission. [See DISMISS.]

DISMISSION (dis-mish'un) *n.* a sending away. [See DISMISS.]

DISMISSIVE (dis-mis'iv) *a.* giving leave to go. [See DISMISS.]

DISMOUNT (dis-mount') *v.i.* to alight from a horse, etc.;—*v.t.* to unhorse; bring down or remove; shatter. [L. *dis.* See MOUNT.]

DISOBEDIENCE (dis-ō-bēd'yens) *n.* neglect or refusal to obey. [See DISOBEY.]

DISOBEDIENT (dis-ō-bē'di-ent) *a.* refusing to obey. [See DISOBEY.]

DISOBEY (dis-ō-bā') *v.t.* to refuse or neglect to obey; break the commands of. [L. *dis.* See OBEY.]

DISOBLIGE (dis-ō-blīj') *v.t.* to offend by unkindness or incivility. [L. *dis.* See OBLIGE.]

DISOBLIGING (dis-ō-blī'jing) *a.* not gratifying; unkind. [See DISOBLIGE.]

DISOBLIGINGLY (dis-ō-blī'jing-li) *ad.* in a disobliging manner. [See DISOBLIGE.]

DISOBLIGINGNESS (dis-ō-blī'jing-nes) *n.* indisposition to oblige. [See DISOBLIGE.]

DISORDER (dis-or'dẹr) *n.* confusion; disease; —*v.t.* to throw into confusion; make sick. [L. *dis.* See ORDER.]

DISORDERED (dis-or'dẹrd) *pp.* put out of order;—*a.* indisposed. [See DISORDER.]

DISORDERLINESS (dis-or'dẹr-li-nes) *n.* state of being disorderly. [See DISORDER.]

DISORDERLY (dis-or'dẹr-li) *a.* confused; irregular; lawless; vicious. [See DISORDER.]

DISORGANISATION (dis-or-ga-ni-zā'shun) *n.* subversion of order or system. [See DISORGANISE.]

DISORGANISE (dis-or'ga-nīz) *v.t.* to derange an organised body. [L. *dis.* See ORGAN.]

DISORGANISER (dis-or'ga-ni-zẹr) *n.* one who disorganises. [See DISORGANISE.]

DISOWN (dis-ōn') *v.t.* to disavow; renounce. [L. *dis.* See OWN.]

DISPARAGE (dis-par'ij) *v.t.* to match unequally; detract from. [O.F. *desparager,* fr. L. *dis-,* and *parage,* rank, fr. Late L. *paraticum,* equality. See PEER (1).]

DISPARAGEMENT (dis-par'ij-ment) *n.* injurious comparison with something else; detraction. [See DISPARAGE.]

DISPARAGINGLY (dis-par'ij-ing-li) *ad.* in a manner to depreciate. [See DISPARAGE.]

DISPARATE (dis'pa-rāt) *a.* unequal; unlike. [L. *dis-, paratus,* fr. *parare,* make equal.]

DISPARITY (dis-par'i-ti) *n.* inequality in form, character, years, etc. [See DISPARATE.]

DISPART (dis-pärt') *v.t.* or *i.* to part; divide. [L. *dis.* See PART.]

DISPASSION (dis-pash'un) *n.* freedom from passion. [L. *dis.* See PASSION.]

DISPASSIONATE (dis-pash'un-āt) *a.* cool; calm; impartial. [See DISPASSION.]

DISPASSIONATELY (dis-pash'un-āt-li) *ad.* without passion; impartially. [See DISPASSION.]

DISPASSIONED (dis-pash'und) *a.* free from passion. [See DISPASSION.]

DISPATCH [See DESpATCH.]

DISPEACE (dis-pēs') *n.* want of peace or quiet; dissension. [L. *dis.* See PEACE.]

DISPEL (dis-pel') *v.t.* to drive away; scatter; dissipate;—*v.i.* to be dispersed. [L., fr. *dis-,* apart, and *pellere,* drive.]

DISPENSABLE (dis-pen'sa-bl) *a.* that may be dispensed. [See DISPENSE.]

DISPENSARY (dis-pen'sa-ri) *n.* a place for dispensing medicines. [See DISPENSE.]

DISPENSATION (dis-pen-sā'shun) *n.* distribution; exemption from a law; system of divine truths and rites. [See DISPENSE.]

DISPENSATORY (dis-pen'sa-tur-i) *a.* having power of granting dispensation;—*n.* a book for compounding medicines. [See DISPENSE.]

DISPENSE (dis-pens') *v.t.* to deal out in portions; distribute; administer;—*v.i.* to do without; excuse from. [O.F. *dispenser,* fr. L. *dispensare,* weigh out, fr. *dis-,* and *pendere.*]

DISPENSER (dis-pen'sẹr) *n.* one who dispenses. [See DISPENSE.]

DISPEOPLE (dis-pē'pl) *v.t.* to depopulate. [L. *dis.* See PEOPLE.]

DISPERSE (dis-pẹrs') *v.t.* to scatter; spread abroad;—*v.i.* to go in different directions; vanish. [O.F., fr. L. *di=dis-,* and (part.) *-spersus,* for *sparsus,* scattered, fr. *spargere.*]

DISPERSER (dis-pẹr'sẹr) *n.* one who disperses. [See DISPERSE.]

DISPERSION (dis-pẹr'shun) *n.* act of scattering, or state of being scattered. [See DISPERSE.]

DISPERSIVE (dis-pẹr'siv) *a.* tending to disperse. [See DISPERSE.]

DISPIRIT (dis-pir'it) *v.t.* to discourage. [L. *di=dis.* See SPIRIT.]

DISPLACE (dis-plās') *v.t.* to put out of place. [L. *dis.* See PLACE.]

DISPLACEMENT (dis-plās'ment) *n.* the act of displacing. [L. *dis.* See PLACE.]

DISPLANT (dis-plant') *v.t.* to move a plant; remove from its right place. [L. *dis.* See PLANT.]

DISPLAY (dis-plā') *v.t.* to spread wide; open; exhibit;—*v.i.* to make a show;—*n.* exhibition; ostentatious show; parade. [O.F. *desplayer*=F. *déployer,* unfold, fr. L., fr. *dis-,* and *plicare.* Doublet of DEPLOY.]

DISPLEASE (dis-plēz') *v.t.* to give offence to; —*v.i.* to disgust. [L. *dis.* See PLEASE.]

DISPLEASING (dis-plē'zing) *a.* offensive. [L. *dis.* See PLEASE.]

DISPLEASURE (dis-plezh'ur) *n.* slight anger; irritation; cause of offence. [L. *dis.* See PLEASE.]

DISPORT (dis-pōrt') *n.* play; sport; pastime; —*v.t.* or *i.* to sport; play; wanton. [O.F. *(se) desporter,* to divert (oneself) from work, fr. L. *dis-,* and *portare,* carry.]

DISPOSABLE (dis-pō'za-bl) *a.* capable of being disposed. [See DISPOSE.]

DISPOSAL (dis-pō'zal) *n.* power of bestowing; management. [See DISPOSE.]

DISPOSE (dis-pōz') *v.t.* to place; incline; adapt or fit. [O.F. *disposer,* arrange, fr. L. *dis-,* and *poser,* to POSE.]

DISPOSER (dis-pō'zẹr) *n.* one who disposes. [See DISPOSE.]

DISPOSITION (dis-pō-zish'un) *n.* order; distribution; temper; deed of gift. [See DISPOSE.]

DISPOSSESS (dis-pu-zes') *v.t.* to put out of possession. [L. *dis.* See **POSSESS.**]
DISPOSSESSION (dis-pu-zesh'un) *n.* act of dispossessing. [L. *dis.* See **POSSESS.**]
DISPRAISE (dis-prāz') *n.* censure; blame; dishonour;—*v.t.* to blame. [L. *dis.* See **PRAISE.**]
DISPRAISINGLY (dis-prā'zing-li) *ad.* with some degree of blame. [See **DISPRAISE.**]
DISPROOF (dis-prŏŏf') *n.* refutation. [L. *dis* and **PROOF.**]
DISPROPORTION (dis-prō-pōr'shun) *n.* want of proportion or symmetry;—*v.t.* to make unsuitable. [L. *dis.* See **PROPORTION.**]
DISPROPORTIONABLE(dis-prō-pōr'shun-a-bl) *a.* unsuitable; inadequate. [See **DISPROPORTION.**]
DISPROPORTIONAL (dis-prō-pōr'shun-al) *a.* unequal; without proportion. [See **DISPROPORTION.**]
DISPROPORTIONATE (dis-prō-pōr'shun-āt) *a.* not proportioned; unsymmetrical; inadequate. [See **DISPROPORTION.**]
DISPROVABLE (dis-prŏŏv'a-bl) *a.* capable of being disproved. [See **DISPROVE.**]
DISPROVE (dis-prŏŏv') *v.t.* to show to be false; confute. [L. *dis.* See **PROVE.**]
DISPUTABLE (dis'pū-ta-bl) *a.* that may be disputed. [See **DISPUTE.**]
DISPUTANT (dis'pū-tant) *n.* one who disputes. [See **DISPUTE.**]
DISPUTATION (dis-pū-tā'shun) *n.* act of disputing; contest in argument. [See **DISPUTE.**]
DISPUTATIOUS (dis-pū-tā'shus) *a.* given to dispute. [See **DISPUTE.**]
DISPUTE (dis-pūt') *v.t.* or *i.* to debate; call in question;—*n.* contest in words. [L. *dis-,* and *putare* think.]
DISPUTER (dis-pū'ter) *n.* one who disputes. [See **DISPUTE.**]
DISQUALIFICATION (dis-kwol-i-fi-kā'shun) *n.* that which disqualifies. [See **DISQUALIFY.**]
DISQUALIFY (dis-kwol'i-fī) *v.t.* to make unfit; disable. [L. *dis.* See **QUALIFY.**]
DISQUIET (dis-kwī'et) *v.t.* to make uneasy; vex; fret;—*n.* restlessness; uneasiness. [L. *dis.* See **QUIET.**]
DISQUIETING (dis-kwī'et-ing) *a.* tending to disturb the mind. [See **DISQUIET.**]
DISQUIETUDE (dis-kwī'e-tūd) *n.* uneasiness. [See **DISQUIET.**]
DISQUISITION (dis-kwi-zish'un) *n.* a formal discourse concerning important points; inquiry. [L. (acc.) *disquisitionem,* fr. (part.) *disquisitus,* investigated, fr. *dis-,* and *quærere,* seek.]
DISREGARD (dis-rē-gârd') *n.* slight; neglect;—*v.t.* to slight; pay no heed to. [L. *dis.* See **REGARD.**]
DISREGARDFUL (dis-re-gârd'fool) *a.*negligent. [L. *dis.* See **REGARD.**]
DISRELISH (dis-rel'ish) *n.* distaste; dislike;—*v.t.* to dislike the taste of. [L. *dis.* See **RELISH.**]
DISREPAIR (dis-re-pār') *n.* state of being out of repair. [L. *dis.* See **REPAIR.**]
DISREPUTABLE (dis-rep'ū-ta-bl) *a.* not creditable; disgraceful. [See **DISREPUTE.**]
DISREPUTABLY (dis-rep'ū-ta-bli) *a.* in a disreputable manner. [See **DISREPUTE.**]
DISREPUTE (dis-rē-pūt') *n.* want of reputation or esteem. [L. *dis.* See **REPUTE.**]
DISRESPECT (dis-re-spekt') *n.*want of respect; incivility. [L. *dis.* See **RESPECT.**]
DISRESPECTFUL (dis-re-spekt'fool) *a.* uncivil; rude. [See **DISRESPECT.**]
DISRESPECTFULLY (dis-re-spekt'fool-i) *ad.* with incivility; irreverently. [See **DISRESPECT.**]
DISROBE (dis-rōb') *v.t.* to undress. [L. *dis-,* and F. *robe,* garment.]
DISROOT (dis-rŏŏt') *v.t.* to tear up by the roots; loosen. [L. *dis.* See **ROOT.**]

DISRUPT (dis-rupt') *v.t.* to break asunder; rend. [L. *disruptus,* pp. of *disrumpere,* break asunder.]
DISRUPTION (dis-rup'shun) *n.* act of breaking asunder; breach. [tion.
DISRUPTIVE (dis-rup'tiv) *a.* causing disruption.
DISRUPTURE (dis-rup'tūr) *v.t.* to rend; tear asunder;—*n.* disruption.
DISSATISFACTION (dis-sat-is-fak'shun) *n.* discontent; dislike; displeasure. [See **DISSATISFY.**]
DISSATISFACTORY (dis-sat-is-fak'tur-i) *a.* causing dissatisfaction; displeasing.
DISSATISFIED (dis-sat'is-fid) *a.* discontented; not pleased.
DISSATISFY (dis-sat'-is-fī) *v.t.* to displease. [L. *dis,* apart, and **SATISFY.**]
DISSECT (di-sekt') *v.t.* to divide and examine minutely. [L. *dis,* and *secare,* cut.]
DISSECTION (di-sek'shun) *n.* the act of dissecting; anatomy. [See **DISSECT.**]
DISSECTOR (di-sek'ter) *n.* an anatomist.
DISSEMBLANCE (di-sem'blans) *n.* want of resemblance; dissembling.
DISSEMBLE (di-sem'bl) *v.t.* or *i.* to conceal real views; disguise; pretend. [O.F., fr. L. *dis,* and *similis,* like.]
DISSEMBLER (di-sem'bler) *n.* a hypocrite.
DISSEMINATE (di-sem'i-nāt) *v.t.* to spread in various directions. [L. *dis,* and *seminare,* sow, fr. *semen,* seed.]
DISSEMINATION (di-sem-i-nā'shun) *n.* act of spreading, as seed.
DISSEMINATIVE (di-sem'i-nā-tiv) *a.* tending to spread or propagate.
DISSEMINATOR (di-sem'i-nā-ter) *n.* one who propagates.
DISSENSION (di-sen'shun) *n.* disagreement; discord; strife. [L. See **DISSENT.**]
DISSENT (di-sent') *v.t.* to disagree in opinion; differ;—*n.* disagreement; separation from the Established Church. [L. *dis,* and *sentire,* feel, think, judge.]
DISSENTER (di-sen'ter) *n.* one who dissents; one who withdraws from the State Church; Nonconformist.
DISSENTIENT (di-sen'shent) *a.* disagreeing; declaring dissent;—*n.* one who declares his dissent.
DISSENTING (di-sen'ting) *a.* disagreeing; separating from the State Church; belonging to a body of dissenters.
DISSERTATION (dis-er-tā'shun) *n.* a discourse; an essay. [L. *dissertare,* discuss.]
DISSERVE (di-serv') *v.t.* to injure. [L. *dis.* See **SERVE.**]
DISSERVICEABLE (dis-ser'vis-a-bl) *a.* hurtful; not useful. [juriously.
DISSERVICEABLY (dis-ser'vis-a-bli) *ad.* injuriously.
DISSEVER (dis-sev'er) *v.t.* to part in two. [L. *dis.* See **SEVER.**]
DISSEVERANCE (di-sev'er-ans) *n.* the act of separating.
DISSIDENCE (dis'i-dens) *n.* disagreement.
DISSIDENT (dis'i-dent) *n.* a dissenter. [L. *dis,* and *sedere,* sit.]
DISSIMILAR (di-sim'i-lar) *a.* unlike. [L. *dis,* and **SIMILAR.**]
DISSIMILARITY (di-sim-i-lar'i-ti) *n.* unlikeness; want of resemblance.
DISSIMILITUDE (di-sim-il'i-tūd) *n.* want of resemblance; unlikeness; a comparison by contrast. [See **DISSIMILAR.**]
DISSIMULATE (di-sim'ū-lāt) *v.t.* to dissemble; feign.
DISSIMULATION (di-sim-ū-lā'shun) *n.* feigning; false pretension; hypocrisy.
DISSIPATE (dis'i-pāt) *v.t.* to drive asunder; scatter. [L. *dissipare,* throw asunder.]
DISSIPATED (dis'i-pā-ted) *a.* loose in manners; given to pleasure.
DISSIPATION (dis-i-pā'shun) *n.* dispersion; diversion or distraction; a dissolute course of life; squandering; debauchery.

DISSOCIABLE (di-sō'sha-bl) *a.* not well associated; ill-matched.

DISSOCIATE (di-sō'shi-āt) *v.t.* to disunite. [L. (part.) *dissociatus*, separated, fr. *socius*, ally.]

DISSOCIATION (di-sō-shi-ā'shun) *n.* separation; disunion.

DISSOLUBILITY (dis-o-lū-bil'i-ti) *n.* capacity of being converted into fluid by heat or moisture.

DISSOLUBLE (dis'u-lū-bl, di-sol'ū-bl) *a.* capable of being diss d. [L. *dissolubilis*, fr. DISSOLVE.] olve

DISSOLUTE (dis'u-lūt) *a.* loose in morals. [L. (part.) *dissolutus*, DISSOLVED.]

DISSOLUTELY (dis'u-lūt-li) *ad.* in a loose or wanton manner.

DISSOLUTENESS (dis'u-lūt-nes) *n.* looseness of behaviour.

DISSOLUTION (dis-u-lū'shun) *n.* act of dissolving; death.

DISSOLVABLE (di-sol'va-bl) *a.* that may be dissolved.

DISSOLVE (di-solv') *v.t.* or *i.* to melt; separate; liquefy. [L. *dissolvere*, fr. *dis*, and *solvere*, to loose, free.]

DISSOLVENT (di-sol'vent) *n.* that which dissolves;—*a.* having power to melt.

DISSONANCE (dis'u-nans) *n.* discord.

DISSONANT (dis'u-nant) *a.* discordant; harsh to the ear. [F., fr. L. (acc. part.) *dissonantem*, disagreeing in SOUND, fr. *sonus*.]

DISSUADE (di-swād') *v.t.* to advise or exhort against. [F., fr. L. *dis*, and *suadere*, to persuade.]

DISSUASION (di-swā'zhun) *n.* act of dissuading. [See DISSUADE.]

DISSUASIVE (di-swā'siv) *a.* tending to dissuade;—*n.* argument employed to deter.

DISSUASIVELY (di-swā'siv-li) *ad.* in a way to dissuade.

DISSUASORY (di-swā'sor-i) *a.* serving to dissuade;—*n.* a dissuasive argument.

DISSYLLABIC (dis-i-lab'ik) *a.* consisting of two syllables only.

DISSYLLABLE (di-sil'a-bl) *n.* a word of two syllables. [Pref. G. *di*, double, and *sullabe*, that which is held together.]

DISTAFF (dis'taf) *n.* a staff from which flax is drawn in spinning. [O.E. *distæf*; fr. be-*dizen*, and STAFF.]

DISTAIN (dis-tān') *v.t.* to stain; blot. [O.F. (part.) *desteignant*, discolouring, fr. *des* = *dis*, and *teindre*, fr. L. *tingere*, TINGE.]

DISTANCE (dis'tans) *n.* space in length between bodies; remoteness; reserve; coldness;—*v.t.* to leave behind, as in a race. [O.F., fr. L. (acc.) *distantiam*.]

DISTANCED (dis'tanst) *a.* left far behind; cast out of the race.

DISTANT (dis'tant) *a.* remote in time or place, connection, etc.; separate; far; indistinct; cool; haughty. [O.F., fr. L. (acc. part.) *distantem*, standing apart, fr. *stare*.]

Distaff.

DISTASTE (dis-tāst') *n.* disrelish; disgust;—*v.t.* to dislike; loathe. [L. *dis*. See TASTE.]

DISTASTEFUL (dis-tāst'fool) *a.* offensive; unpleasant to the taste.

DISTASTEFULLY (dis-tāst'fool-i) *ad.* in a displeasing manner.

DISTEMPER (dis-tem'per) (1) *n.* morbid state of the body; disease;—*v.t.* to affect with disease; disturb;—(2) *n.* a kind of painting in opaque colours mixed with size;—*v.t.* to mix opaque colours. [(1) L. *dis*, and *temperare*, moderate. (2) O.F., fr. *des* = *dis*, and *temprer* = F. *tremper*, steep, fr. L. *temperare*, TEMPER.]

DISTEND (dis-tend') *v.t.* or *i.* to stretch in any direction; spread apart; swell. [L. *distendere*, fr. TEND.]

DISTENSIBILITY (dis-ten-si-bil'i-ti) *n.* capacity for being distended.

DISTENSIBLE (dis-ten'si-bl) *a.* that may be distended.

DISTENSION (dis-ten'shun) *n.* a stretching.

DISTICH (dis'tik) *n.* a couplet, or two poetic lines. [L. *distichus*, fr. G. *di* = *dis*, twofold, and *stichos*, row.]

DISTIL (dis-til') *v.t.* or *i.* to drop gently; extract spirit; rectify; use a still. [F., fr. L. *destillare*, to drip down, fr. *de* and *stillare*.]

DISTILLABLE (dis-til'a-bl) *a.* fit for distillation.

DISTILLATION (dis-ti-lā'shun) *n.* the act of distilling.

DISTILLER (dis-til'er) *n.* one who distils.

DISTILLERY (dis-til'er-i) *n.* a place for distilling.

DISTINCT (dis-tingkt') *a.* separate; different; clear, not confused. [L. (part.) *distinctus*, DISTINGUISHED.]

DISTINCTION (dis-tingk'shun) *n.* difference; separation; eminence; mark of honour. [F., fr. L. *distinctionem*.]

DISTINCTIVE (dis-tingk'tiv) *a.* marking distinction or difference.

DISTINCTLY (dis-tingkt'li) *ad.* in a distinct manner.

DISTINCTNESS (dis-tingkt'nes) *n.* clearness; precision.

DISTINGUISH (dis-ting'gwish) *v.t.* or *i.* to note the difference; discriminate; honour. [L. *distinguere*, *distinctum*, fr. *di* = *dis*, and root of *stigma*, mark.]

DISTINGUISHABLE (dis-ting'gwish-a-bl) *a.* capable of being distinguished.

DISTINGUISHABLY (dis-ting'gwish-a-bli) *ad.* in a manner to be distinguished.

DISTINGUISHED (dis-ting'gwisht) *a.* eminent; celebrated.

DISTINGUISHINGLY (dis-ting'gwish-ing-li) *ad.* with some marks of preference.

DISTORT (dis-tort') *v.t.* to twist; writhe. [L. (part.) *distortus*, twisted aside, fr. *torquere*.]

DISTORTION (dis-tor'shun) *n.* the act of distorting.

DISTORTIVE (dis-tor'tiv) *a.* causing distortion.

DISTRACT (dis-trakt') *v.t.* to draw different ways; perplex; confuse; disorder the reason. [L. (part.) *distracius*, drawn aside, fr. *trahere*.]

DISTRACTED (dis-trak'ted) *a.* deranged.

DISTRACTEDLY (dis-trak'ted-li) *ad.* wildly; madly.

DISTRACTION (dis-trak'shun) *n.* confusion; state of disordered reason.

DISTRACTIVE (dis-trak'tiv) *a.* causing perplexity.

DISTRAIN (dis-trān') *v.t.* to seize goods for debt. [O.F. *destraindre*, harass, fr. L. *distringere*. See DISTRESS.]

DISTRAINABLE (dis-trā'na-bl) *a.* liable to be seized for debt.

DISTRAINER (dis-trā'ner) *n.* he who seizes goods for debt.

DISTRAINT (dis-trānt') *n.* a seizure for debt.

DISTRESS (dis-tres') *n.* act of distraining; thing seized; extreme pain;—*v.t.* to pain; afflict. [O.F., through Low L., fr. L. (part.) *districtus*, pulled asunder, fr. *stringere*, draw tight.]

DISTRESSFUL (dis-tres'fool) *a.* giving anguish; full of distress.

DISTRESSFULLY (dis-tres'fool-i) *ad.* in a painful or calamitous manner.

DISTRESSING (dis-tres'ing) *a.* afflicting.

DISTRIBUTE (dis-trib'ūt) *v.t.* to divide among a number. [L. (part.) *distributus*, allotted, fr. *tribuere*, assign. See TRIBUTE.]

DISTRIBUTER (dis-trib'ū-ter) *n.* one who distributes.

DISTRIBUTION (dis-tri-bū'shun) *n.* act of distributing.

DISTRIBUTIVE (dis-trib'ū-tiv) *a.* that distributes.

DISTRIBUTIVELY (dis-trib'ū-tiv-li) *ad.* by distribution; singly.

DISTRICT (dis'trikt) *n.* a circuit; region;—*v.t.* to divide into circuits. [O.F., fr. Late L. (acc.) *districtum*, domain, fr. L. *distringere*, occupy. Cf. **DISTRAIN**.]

DISTRUST (dis-trust') *v.t.* to suspect; doubt; disbelieve;—*n.* want of confidence. [L. *dis*. See **TRUST**.]

DISTRUSTFUL (dis-trust'fool) *a.* suspicious.

DISTRUSTFULLY (dis-trust'fool-i) *ad.* with doubt or suspicion. Also **DISTRUSTINGLY**.

DISTURB (dis-turb') *v.t.* to perplex; disquiet; agitate. [L. *disturbare*, fr. *turbare*, disorder, fr. *turba*, mob.]

DISTURBANCE (dis-tûr'bans) *n.* agitation; excitement of feeling.

DISTURBER (dis-tur'ber) *n.* one who causes disturbance.

DISUNION (dis-ūn'yun) *n.* want of union. [L. *dis*. See **UNION**.]

DISUNITE (dis-ū-nit') *v.t.* to separate. [L. *dis*. See **UNITE**.]

DISUNITY (dis-ū'ni-ti) *n.* a state of separation; want of unity.

DISUSAGE (dis-ū'zāj) *n.* cessation of use. [L. *dis*. See **USAGE**.]

DISUSE (dis-ūz') *v.t.* to cease to make use of; —(dis-ūs') *n.* cessation of use.

DISUSED (dis-ūzd') *a.* no longer used; obsolete.

DITCH (dich) *n.* a trench in the earth;—*v.t.* or *i.* to trench. [M.E. *diche*. Doublet of **DIKE**.]

DITTY (dit'i) *n.* a poem to be sung. [O.F. *dité*, fr. L. (neut. part.) *dictatum*, **DICTATED**.]

DIURETIC (di-ū-ret'ik) *a.* promoting urine. [L., fr. G. *diouretikos*, fr. *dia*, through, and *ouron*, urine.]

DIURNAL (di-ur'nal) *a.* constituting a day; daily;—*n.* a day-book. [L., fr. *diurnus*, fr. *dies*, day.]

DIURNALLY (di-ur'nal-i) *ad.* daily; every day.

DIUTURNAL (di-ū-tur'nal) *a.* being of long continuance.

DIUTURNITY (di-ū-tur'ni-ti) *n.* length of time.

DIVAGATION (di-va-gā'-shun) *n.* a wandering or deviation. [L. *divagari*, wander.]

DIVARICATE (di-var'i-kāt) *v.i.* to divide into two. [L. (part.) *divaricatus*, spread apart, fr. *di* =*dis*, and *varicare*, to straddle.]

DIVARICATION (di-var-i-kā'shun) *n.* a separation into two branches.

DIVE (div) *v.i.* to plunge under water; go deep. [O.E. *dyfan*, conn. with **DIP**.]

DIVER (di'ver) *n.* one who dives; a water-fowl.

DIVERGE (di-verj') *v.i.* to tend various ways from one point; turn aside;—*v*ary. [Pref. L. *di* =*dis*, and *vergere*, incline.]

DIVERGENCE (di-ver'-jens) *n.* receding from; going aside.

DIVERGINGLY (di-ver'-jing-li) *ad.* in a diverging manner.

DIVERS (di'verz) *a.* several; sundry. [O.F., fr. L. *diversus*, lit. separated, fr. **DIVERT**.]

DIVERSE (di'vers, de-vers') *a.* varied; different; various. [Form of **DIVERS**.]

Diver.

DIVERSELY (di'vers-li) *ad.* in different ways or directions; variously.

DIVERSIFICATION (di-ver-si-fi-kā'shun) *n.* the act of making various.

DIVERSIFY (di-ver'si-fi) *v.t.* to make different from another. [F. *diversifier*, fr. **DIVERS**, and L. *ficare* =*facere*, make.]

DIVERSION (di-ver'shun) *n.* a turning aside; anything that diverts; amusement; feigned attack. [See **DIVERT**.]

DIVERSITY (di-ver'si-ti) *n.* difference; unlikeness; variety.

DIVERT (di-vert') *v.t.* to turn aside; amuse; please; draw away. [O.F. *divertir*, fr. L., fr. *di* =*dis*, and *vertere*, turn.]

DIVERTING (di-ver'ting) *a.* pleasing.

DIVERTISSEMENT (di-ver'tiz-ment) *n.* a short ballet or piece between the acts of a drama. Also **DIVERTISEMENT**. [F.]

DIVEST (di-vest') *v.t.* to strip off clothes; deprive. [O.F. *devester*, fr. L. *devestire*, fr. *de*, from, and *vestire*, clothe. See **VEST**.]

DIVESTURE (di-ves'tûr) *n.* the act of putting off. Also **DIVESTITURE**.

DIVIDABLE (di-vid'a-bl) *a.* that may be divided.

DIVIDE (di-vid') *v.i.* to part or separate a whole; keep apart; distribute; share;—*v.t.* to open; cleave; vote. [L. *dividere*.]

DIVIDEND (div'i-dend) *n.* number to be divided; share divided. [L. (gerund.) *dividendus*, to be divided.]

DIVIDER (di-vi'der) *n.* he or that which divides:—*pl.* compasses.

DIVINATION (div-i-nā'shun) *n.* a foretelling.

DIVINE (di-vin') (1) *a.* pertaining to God;—*n.* a minister of the gospel;—(2) *v.t.* or *i.* to foretell. [(1) L. *divinus*; conn. with *deus*. (2) L. *divinare*.]

DIVINELY (di-vin'li) *ad.* in a godlike manner.

DIVING-BELL (di'ving-bel) *n.* a hollow vessel, bell-shaped and air-tight except at the bottom, which is open, in which a person may descend in deep water.

DIVINING-ROD (di-vi'ning-rod) *n.* a forked hazel wand used by pretending discoverers of minerals, etc., under ground.

DIVINITY (di-vin'i-ti) *n.* divine nature; Deity; theology. [L. (acc.) *divinitatem*.]

DIVISIBILITY (di-viz-i-bil'i-ti) *n.* quality of being divisible.

DIVISIBLE (di-viz'i-bl) *a.* that may be divided.

DIVISION (di-vizh'un) *n.* act of dividing; partition; separation; portion of an army or fleet; a rule in arithmetic. [L. (acc.) *divisionem*, fr. (part.) *divisus*, **DIVIDED**.]

DIVISIONAL (di-vizh'un-al) *a.* relating to division.

DIVISOR (di-vi'zur) *n.* a number that divides another. [L.]

DIVORCE (di-vôrs') *n.* dissolution of marriage; —*v.t.* to separate a husband and wife; disunite. [O.F., fr. L. *divortium*· fr. *di* =*dis*, and *vortere*, for *vertere*, turn.]

DIVORCEE (di-vôrs'ē) *n.* a person divorced. [See **DIVORCE**.]

DIVORCEMENT (di-vôrs'ment) *n.* legal dissolution of marriage.

DIVULGE (di-vulj') *v.t.* to publish; disclose or make known. [F. *divulger*, fr. L. *divulgare*, fr. *di* =*dis*, and *vulgus*, the many.]

DIVULGER (di-vul'jer) *n.* he that reveals.

DIVULSION (di-vul'shun) *n.* the act of plucking apart. [L. fr. (part.) *divulsus*, turn apart, fr. *di* =*dis*, and *vellere*.]

DIVULSIVE (di-vul'siv) *a.* tending to pull asunder; rending.

DIZZINESS (diz'i-nes) *n.* giddiness; vertigo. [See **DIZZY**.]

DIZZY (diz'i) *a.* affected with vertigo; giddy. [O.E. *dysig*, foolish.]

DO (dōō) *v.t.* [*pret.* **DID**; *pp.* **DONE**] to perform; execute; practise; finish; cook completely; deceive or hoax;—*v.i.* to behave; fare in health; succeed; suit or avail. [M.E. *doon*, fr. O.E. *don*. Cf. Ger. *thun*.]

DOCILE (dō'sil, dos'il) *a.* ready to be taught.
[F., fr. L. (acc.) *docilem*, fr. *docere*, teach.]
DOCILITY (dō-sil'i-ti) *n.* teachableness.
DOCK (dok) *n.* a place for ships; a box in
court where the accused stands;—*v.t.* to
put a ship in dock. [D. Cf. Ger. *Docke.*]
DOCK (dok) (1) *n.* a common weed; stump of
a beast's tail; case or cover;—(2) *v.t.* to
cut off; shorten; deduct from. [(1) O.E.
docce. (2) Probably E.]
DOCKAGE (dok'āj) *n.* pay for using a dock.
DOCKET (dok'et) *n.* a label tied to goods; a
register of cases in court;—*v.t.* to mark with
titles. [Conn. with DOCK (2).]
DOCKYARD (dok'yärd) *n.* a yard for naval
stores.
DOCTOR (dok'tur) *n.* a title in divinity, law,
etc.; a physician;—*v.t.* to treat medically;
adulterate or falsify. [L. =teacher, fr.
docere, teach.]
DOCTORATE (dok'tu-rāt) *n.* the degree of a
doctor.
DOCTORING (dok'tur-ing) *n.* adulteration of
liquors; falsification of accounts.
DOCTRINAIRE (dok'tri-nār) *n.* a political
theorist. [F., fr. *doctrine*.]
DOCTRINAL (dok'tri-nal) *a.* consisting in or
containing doctrine;—*n.* something that is
part of doctrine.
DOCTRINE (dok'trin) *n.* what is taught; a
gospel truth; tenet. [F., fr. L. (acc.)
doctrinam, teaching, fr. DOCTOR.]
DOCUMENT (dok'ū-ment) *n.* written instruction; proof;—*v.t.* to furnish with documents.
[F., fr. L. *documentum*, lesson, proof, fr.
docere, teach.]
DOCUMENTARY (dok-ū-men'ta-ri) *a.* consist-
ing in written evidence.
DODGE (doj) *v.t.* or *i.* to start suddenly aside;
evade. [Etym. unknown.]
DODO (dō'dō) *n.* a large, clumsy bird, now
extinct. [Pg. *doudo*, silly.]
DOE (dō) *n.* a female deer. [O.E. *da*.]
DOER (dōō'ẹr) *n.* one who performs.
DOES (duz) third person singular of DO,
indicative mood, present tense.
DOESKIN (dō'skin) *n.* skin of the doe; a
twilled woollen cloth.
DOFF (dof) *v.t.* to put off; strip. [Short fr.
DO OFF.]
DOG (dog) *n.* a domestic animal;—*v.t.* to follow
continually. [M.E. *dogge*, fr. O.E. *docga*.]
DOG-CART (dog'kärt) *n.* a two or four wheel
one-horse open machine for sportsmen.
DOG-DAYS (dog'dāz) *n.pl.* the days when the
dog-star rises and sets with the sun, from
the end of July to the beginning of Septem-
ber. [*Dog* here =Sirius the dog-star.]
DOGE (dōj) *n.* the chief magistrate in Venice,
etc. [It. Doublet of DUKE.]
DOGFISH (dog'fish) *n.* a fish of the shark
family.
DOGGED (dog'ed) *a.* sullen; morose.
DOGGEDLY (dog'ed-li) *ad.* sullenly; morosely.
DOGGEDNESS (dog'ed-nes) *n.* obstinacy;
sullenness.
DOGGER (dog'ẹr) *n.* a two-masted fishing
vessel. [D.]
DOGGEREL (dog'ẹr-el) *n.* a kind of irregular
measure in poetry. Also written DOGGREL.
[E.]
DOGGISH (dog'ish) *a.* snappish.
DOGGISHNESS (dog'ish-nes) quality of being
snappish or churlish.
DOGMA (dog'ma) *n.* point of belief, doctrine,
considered as finally established. [G., fr.
doke-ein, think.]
DOGMATIC (dog-mat'ik) *a.* positive; authori-
tative; dictatorial. Also DOGMATICAL.
[G., fr. stem *dogmat-*, of DOGMA.]
DOGMATICALLY (dog-mat'i-kal-i) *ad.* posi-
tively; arrogantly.
DOGMATICS (dog-mat'iks) *n.pl.* doctrinal
theology.

DOGMATISE (dog'ma-tiz) *v.i.* to assert positively without proof.
DOGMATISM (dog'ma-tizm) *n.* positiveness in
opinion; arrogant assertion.
DOGMATIST (dog'ma-tist) *n.* one who is a
confident asserter.
DOILY (doi'li) *n.* a small napkin. [After the
first maker.]
DOIT (doit) *n.* a small piece of money; a
trifle. [D.]
DOLCE (dol'chā) *ad.* softly; sweetly. [It.]
DOLE (dōl) (1) *n.* a thing dealt out; alms;
—(2) pain; grief;—*v.t.* to deal out; distribute.
[(1) Doublet of DEAL. (2) O.F. *doel* =F.
deuil, fr. L., fr. *dolere*, grieve.]
DOLEFUL (dōl'fool) *a.* expressing or causing
grief; sorrowful; melancholy. [See DOLE
(2).]
DOLEFULLY (dōl'fool-i) *ad.* sadly; dismally.
DOLEFULNESS (dōl-fool-nes) *n.* dismal state.
DOLESOME (dōl'sum) *a.* gloomy. [See
DOLE (2).]
DOLL (dol) *n.* a puppet for a girl. [Fr. *Dolly*,
for Dorothy.]
DOLLAR (dol'ar) *n.* a silver coin of the
United States, worth 100 cents, or about
4s. 2d. sterling. [Corr. fr. Ger. *Thaler*.]
DOLMAN (dol'man) *n.* a lady's mantle. [F.,
fr. Turk.]
DOLMEN (dol'men) *n.* a stone table; cromlech.
[F., fr. Celt.]
DOLORIFIC (do-lu-rif'ik) *a.* causing sorrow.
[See DOLOUR.]
DOLOROUS (dol'u-rus) *a.* sorrowful.
DOLOUR (dō'lur) *n.* pain; distress. [O.F.,
fr. L. (acc.) *dolorem*, fr. L. *dolere*, grieve.]
DOLPHIN (dol'fin) *n.* a cetaceous fish. [O.F.
daulphin =F. *dauphin*, fr. Low L., fr. L.
(acc.) *delphinum*, fr. G.]
DOLT (dōlt) *n.* a stupid fellow. [M.E. *dult*
=dulled, fr. DULL.]
DOLTISH (dōl'tish) *a.* stupid; blockish.
DOMAIN (do-mān') *n.* extent of territory or
sway; estate. [F. *domaine*, fr. Late L.
domanium, for L. *dominium*, DOMINION.
Doublet of DEMESNE.]
DOME (dōm) *n.* an arched roof or cupola.
[F. *dôme*, fr. Late L. (acc.) *domain*, house
(of God), fr. *domus*.]
DOMESTIC (do-mes'tik) *a.* belonging to home;
—*n.* a house servant. [F. *domestique*, fr. L.
(acc.) *domesticum*, pertaining to the home,
domus.]
DOMESTICATE (do-mes'ti-kāt) *v.t.* to make
domestic or tame.
DOMICILE (dom'i-sil) *n.* a permanent dwelling;
—*v.t.* to establish a fixed residence. [O.F.,
fr. L. *domicilium*.]
DOMICILIARY (dom-i-sil'i-ar-i) *a.* pertaining
to an abode.
DOMINANCE (dom'i-nans) *n.* ascendancy;
authority.
DOMINANT (dom'i-nant) *a.* ruling; prevailing;—*n.* the fifth tone of the musical scale.
[L. (part. stem) *dominant-*, bearing sway, fr.
dominari, fr. *dominus*.]
DOMINATE (dom'i-nāt) *v.t.* to govern; prevail over.
DOMINATION (dom-i-nā'shun) *n.* rule;
tyranny. [See DOMINANT.]
DOMINEER (dom-i-nēr') *v.i.* to rule with
insolence. [See DOMINANT. Through D.]
DOMINICAL (do-min'i-kal) *a.* denoting the
Lord's Day. [L. *dominus*, lord.]
DOMINICANS (do-min'i-kanz) *n.pl.* an order
of monks. [Fr. St. Dominic.]
DOMINION (do-min'yun) *n.* sovereign authority; territory or subjects governed. [O.F.,
fr. Late L. (acc.) *dominionem*, fr. L. *dominium*,
sway, fr. *dominus*.]
DOMINO (dom'i-nō) *n.* a hood or cloak;—*pl.*
(dom'i-nōz) name of a game played with
dotted pieces of wood. [F., fr. *dominus* =
churchman.]

DON (don) (1) *n.* a Spanish title; a leading man in a college; an important personage;—(2) *v.t.* to put on; invest with. [(1) Sp., fr. **L.** (acc.) *dominum*. (2) Short, fr. **DO ON.**]

DONATION (do-nā'shun) *n.* a gift; present. [**F.,** fr. **L.** (acc.) *donationem*, fr. (part.) *donatio*, gifted, fr. *donum*, gift.]

DONATIVE (don'a-tiv) *n.* a gift; a largess. [See **DONATION.**]

DONKEY (dong'ki) *n.* an ass;—*pl.* **DONKEYS.** [Dim. fr. **DUN**, in allusion to its colour.]

DONKEY-ENGINE (dong'ki-en'jin) *n.* a small assistant engine fed from the main boilers.

DONNA (don'a) *n.* a lady. **PRIMA DONNA**, the leading female singer in an opera troupe. [It., doublet of **DAME, DUENNA.**]

DONOR (dō'ner) *n.* one who gives. [See **DONATION.**]

DOOM (dōōm) *v.t.* to sentence; destine;—*n.* sentence given; fate; ruin. [O.E. *dom*, conn. with *deman*, **DEEM.**]

DOOMSDAY (dōōmz'dā) *n.* the day of judgment. [O.E. *domes*, of judgment.]

DOOR (dōr) *n.* the entrance of a house or room. [O.E. *dor.* Cf. Ger. *Thor.*]

DORIC (dor'ik) *a.* noting an order of architecture. [Fr. *Doris* in ancient Greece.]

DORKING (dor'king) *n.* a domestic fowl. [Fr. *Dorking*, in Surrey.]

DORMANCY (dor'man-si) *n.* quiescence.

DORMANT (dor'mant) *a.* sleeping; in a sleeping posture; not used or claimed.

Doric Order.

[F. (part.) *dormant*, sleeping, fr. *dormir*, fr. **L.** *dormire*, sleep.]

DORMER (dor'mer) *n.* a window in the sloping roof of a house. [Lit. a bedroom, *dormer*, window.]

DORMITORY (dor'mi-tur-i) *n.* a place to sleep in. [L. *dormitorium.*]

DORMOUSE (dor'mous) *n.* a small rodent animal. [Prov. E. *dorm*, sleep.]

DORSAL (dor'sal) *a.* relating to the back. [L. *dorsum*, the back.]

DORY (dō'ri) *n.* a spiky-finned fish of delicate flavour. [F. *dorée*, orig. (fem. part.) gilded.]

DOSE (dōs) *n.* as much medicine as is taken at one time;—*v.t.* to give in doses; physic. [G. *dosis*, fr. *didonai*, give.]

DOST (dust) the second person of **DO.**

DOT (dot) *n.* a point used in writing and printing;—*v.t.* to mark with dots. [D.]

DOTAGE (dō'tāj) *n.* imbecility of mind; excessive fondness.

DOTAL (dō'tal) *a.* pertaining to dower. [L. *dotalis*, fr. *dos*, dowry.]

DOTARD (dō'tard) *n.* one whose mind is impaired by age.

DOTATION (dō-tā'shun) *n.* an endowment. [L. *dotare*, endow, fr. *dos* (dower).]

DOTE (dōt) *v.i.* to be silly through age; be excessively in love. [D. *doten.*]

DOTINGLY (dō'ting-li) *ad.* with silly fondness.

DOTTED (dot'ed) *pp.* marked with dots.

DOUBLE (dub'l) *a.* two-fold;—*v.t.* to make two-fold; pass round a headland;—*v.i.* to grow twice as much; turn or wind in running; —*n.* twice the quantity. [F., fr. **L.** *duplex*, fr. *duo*, two, and *plus.*]

DOUBLE-DEALING (dub'l-dēl'ing) *n.* dealing with duplicity.

DOUBLE-ENTENDRE (dōō'bl-ang-tong'dr) *n.* an expression with a double meaning. [F.]

DOUBLE-ENTRY (dub'l-en'tri) *n.* a mode of book-keeping in which every transaction is entered to the debit of one account and to the credit of another.

DOUBLENESS (dub'l-nes) *n.* duplicity.

DOUBLET (dub'let) *n.* a pair; a waistcoat; —*pl.* the same number on both dice, etc. [Dim. of **DOUBLE.**]

DOUBLING (dub'ling) *n.* act of making double; a fold; artifice; sailing round.

DOUBLOON (dub-lōōn') *n.* a Spanish coin of about twenty-one shillings. [Sp. *doblon.*]

DOUBLY (dub'li) *ad.* with twice the quantity.

DOUBT (dout) *v.i.* to hesitate;—*v.t.* to distrust;—*n.* hesitation; distrust. [L. *dubitare*, fr. *dubius*, doubtful, moving in two (*duo*) directions.]

DOUBTER (dout'er) *n.* one who doubts.

DOUBTFUL (dout'fool) *a.* uncertain; ambiguous; suspicious.

DOUBTFULLY (dout'fool-i) *ad.* with doubt.

DOUBTFULNESS (dout'fool-nes) *n.* uncertainty of mind, meaning, or issue.

DOUBTLESS (dout'les) *ad.* without doubt; unquestionably.

DOUCEUR (dōō-ser') *n.* a gift; bribe. [F.]

DOUCHE (dōōsh) *n.* a jet of water thrown on some part of the body. [F.]

DOUGH (dō) *n.* unbaked paste. [O.E. (stem) *dag-*, of *dah.* Cf. Ger. *Teig.*]

DOUGHTY (dou'ti) *a.* brave; valiant; able; strong. [O.E. *dohtig*, or *dyh-*, tr. *dugan*, be able.]

DOUGHY (dō'i) *a.* like dough.

DOUSE (dous) *v.t.* or *i.* to plunge overhead into water; lower hastily; extinguish. [Etym. doubtful.]

DOVE (duv) *n.* a domestic pigeon. [O.E. *dofa.* Cf. Ger. *Taube.*]

DOVECOTE (duv'kot) *n.* a place for pigeons.

DOVELIKE (duv'lik) *a.* gentle; innocent.

DOVETAIL (duv'tāl) *n.* a joint in form of a dove's tail spread;—*v.t.* to join by dovetail.

DOWAGER (dou'a-jer) *n.* a widow with a jointure. [O.F., fr. *douage.* See **ENDOW.**]

DOWDY (dou'di) *n.* an awkward, ill-dressed woman. [Etym. unknown.]

DOWDYISH (dou'di-ish) *a.* like a dowdy. [See **DOWDY.**]

DOWER (dou'er) *n.* the portion of a married woman or widow. [F. *douaire*, fr. Late **L.** *dotarium*, fr. **L.** *dotare*, endow.]

DOWERED (dou'erd) *a.* portioned.

DOWERLESS (dou'er-les) *a.* having no portion or fortune.

DOWN (doun) *prep.* along a descent;—(1) *ad.* below the horizon; on the ground; in a low state;—(2) *n.* bank of sand; (3) soft feathers or tender hair. [(1) Short fr. *adown.* (2) O.E. *dun*, fr. Celt. (3) Scand.]

DOWNCAST (doun'kast) *a.* bent downwards; dejected;—*n.* a shaft for sending air down a mine.

DOWNFALL (doun'fawl) *n.* a sudden descent of, or from.

DOWNHILL (doun'hil) *n.* declivity; slope of a hill;—*a.* descending.

DOWNRIGHT (doun'rit) *a.* open; plain;—*ad.* plainly; frankly.

DOWNSITTING (doun'sit-ing) *n.* a sitting down; rest; repose.

DOWNWARD (doun'ward) *a.* descending;— *ad.* to a lower place or state. Also **DOWN-WARDS.** [See **DOWN** (1).]

DOWNY (dou'ni) *a.* like down; soft. [See **DOWN** (3).]

DOWRY (dou'ri) See **DOWER.**

DOXOLOGY (doks-ol'ō-ji) *n.* a hymn or form of giving praise to God. [L., fr. G., fr. *doxa*, opinion, glory, and *legein*, speak.]

DOZE (dōz) *v.i.* to slumber;—*n.* imperfect sleep. [Scand.]

DOZEN (duz'n) *a.* or *n.* twelve things. [O.F. *dosaine* = F. *douzaine*, fr. *doz*, twelve, fr. **L.** *duodecim.*]

DOZINESS (dō'zi-nes) *n.* drowsiness. [See **DOZE.**]

DOZY (dō'zi) *a.* drowsy; sleepy.

DRAB (drab) n. (1) a sluttish woman;—(2) a thick gray woollen cloth;—a. of a dun colour. [(1) E. (2) F. drap, cloth. See DRAPE.]

DRACHM (dram) n. the eighth part of an ounce, apothecaries' weight. Also DRAM. [O.F. drame, fr. L., fr. Drachma.]

DRACHMA (drak'ma) n. a Greek silver coin, in value ninepence three-farthings. [G.]

DRAFF (draf) n. dregs; lees; refuse. [E.]

DRAFFY (draf'i) a. dreggy; waste; worthless.

DRAFT (draft) n. order for money; a sketch; a detachment;—v.t. to draw; select. [Form of DRAUGHT.]

DRAFTSMAN (drafts'man) n. one who draws designs or plans; also written DRAUGHTS-MAN.

DRAG (drag) v.t. to pull with force;—n. a net; a harrow; a skid. [Scand., conn. with DRAW.]

DRAGGLE (drag'l) v.t. or i. to make or become wet and dirty by drawing. [See DRAG.]

DRAGNET (drag'net) n. a net to be drawn.

DRAGOMAN (drag'-man) n. an interpreter. [Sp., fr. A.]   o

DRAGON (drag'un) n. a winged serpent. [F., fr. L. (acc.) draconem, fr. G. drakon.]

DRAGONET (drag'un-et) n. a little dragon; a fish of the goby family. [See DRAGON.]

DRAGON-FLY (drag'un-fil) n. a large stinging fly. [a dragon.

DRAGONISH (drag'un-ish) a. in the form of

DRAGOON (dra-gōōn') n. a horse soldier;—v.t. to persecute; compel by force. [F. dragon (orig. a standard).]

DRAIN (drān) n. a channel for water;—v.t. or i. to draw off gradually; exhaust. [O.E. drehnian.]

DRAINABLE (drā'na-bl) a.that can be drained.

DRAINAGE (drā'nij) n. a drawing off; system of drains.

DRAINER (drā'ner) n. a kitchen utensil; he or that which drains or exhausts.

DRAKE (drāk) n. a male duck. [Perh. short fr. a form conn. with Ger. Enterich, fr. Ente, duck.]

DRAM (dram) n. a glass of spirits; one-sixteenth of an ounce, avoirdupois.

DRAMA (drä'ma) n. a theatrical entertainment; a play; a series of interesting events in life. [G. =lit. act. fr. draein, do.]

DRAMATIC (dra-mat'ik) a. pertaining to the drama. [G. (stem) dramat-, of DRAMA.]

DRAMATISE (dram-a-tīz) v.t. to compose in the form of a play.

DRAMATIST (dram'a-tist) n. a dramatic author or writer of plays.

DRANK (drangk) pret. and pp. of DRINK.

DRAPE (drāp) v.t. to cover with drapery. [F. draper, fr. drap, cloth, fr. Late L.]

DRAPER (drā'per) n. one who deals in cloths.

DRAPERIED (drā'per-id) a. hung with drapery.

DRAPERY (drā'per-i) n. cloth; woollen or linen stuffs; hangings of any kind; the dress of human figures; occupation of a draper.

DRASTIC (dras'tik) a. powerful; active;—n. a quick, effective purgative. [G., fr. draein, do. See DRAMA.]

DRAUGHT (draft) n. act of drawing; quantity drunk at once; a current of air; sketch or outline; money order; depth to which a ship sinks in water. [Fr. DRAW.]

DRAUGHT-HORSE (draft'hors) n. a horse for drawing.

DRAUGHTS (drafts) n.pl. a game played by two persons on a chequered board.

DRAW (draw) v.t. or i. [pret. DREW; pp. DRAWN] to pull along or up; inhale; attract; extract; allure; unsheathe; delineate; lengthen; deduce or infer;—v.i. to pull; act as a weight; suck, as a blister; shrink or contract; approach; practise drawing; write a cheque or bill on. [O.E. dragan. Cf. Ger. tragen.]

DRAWBACK (draw'bak) n. duty refunded on goods; any loss of advantage; hindrance of enjoyment.

DRAWBRIDGE (draw'brij) n. a bridge to be drawn up or aside.

DRAWER (draw'er) n. one who draws a bill; a sliding box;—pl. an under-garment for the lower parts of the body.

DRAWING (draw'ing) n. the act of pulling, sketching, etc.; a picture drawn; allocation of prizes and blanks at a lottery; pl. money drawn for sales in a shop.

DRAWING-ROOM (draw'ing-rōōm) n. a room for receiving company.

DRAWL (drawl) v.t. or i. to lengthen in speaking;—n. a slow, monotonous utterance. [Fr. DRAW.]

DRAWN (drawn) pp. of DRAW.

DRAW-WELL (draw'wel) n. a deep well from which water is drawn by ropes and buckets.

DRAY (drā) n. a low, strong cart on wheels, used for heavy burdens. [O.E. drœge, fr. DRAW.]

DRAYAGE (drā'aj) n. charge for the use of a dray. [See DRAY.]

DRAYHORSE (drā'hors) n. a horse used in a dray. [dray.

DRAYMAN (drā'man) n. a man that drives a

DREAD (dred) n. great and continuing fear; terror;—v.t. or i. to fear, or be in great fear; —a. awful; terrible. [Fr. O.E. on-drœdan, to fear.]

DREADFUL (dred'fool) a. inspiring dread or awe; frightful; terrible.

DREADFULLY (dred'fool-i) ad. terribly.

DREADFULNESS (dred'fool-nes) n. frightfulness; fearfulness.

DREADLESS (dred'les) a. fearless; bold.

DREADNOUGHT (dred'nawt) n. a thick cloth with a long pile; an overcoat made of it; name given to a class of warships.

DREAM (drēm) n. thoughts in sleep; an idle fancy; reverie;—v.t. or i. [pret. and pp. DREAMED, DREAMT] to think in sleep; fancy. [E. Cf. Ger. Traum.]

DREAMER (drē'mer) n. one who dreams.

DREAMLESS (drēm'les) a. free from dreams.

DREAMT (dremt) pret. and pp. of DREAM.

DREAMY (drē'mi) a. full of dreams; visionary; fanciful.

DREAR (drēr) a. dismal; gloomy; cheerless. [O.E. dreorig, orig. bloody. Cf. Ger. trauria.]

DREARILY (drēr'i-li) ad. gloomily; dismally.

DREARINESS (drēr'i-nes) n. gloominess.

DREARY (drēr'i) a. sorrowful; dismal; gloomy; cold and uninteresting.

DREDGE (drej) n. an oyster-net;—v.t. to sprinkle flour on; gather with a dredge. [E., conn. with DRAW.]

DREDGER (drej'er) n. a man who fishes with a dredge; a dredging machine.

DREDGING-BOX (drej'ing-boks) n. a box for sprinkling with flour.

DREDGING-MACHINE (drej'ing-ma-shēn) n. an apparatus for taking up mud from the bottom of harbours, etc.

DREGS (dregs) n.pl. lees; refuse. [Scand.]

DRENCH (drensh) v.t. to wet thoroughly;— n. a dose for a beast. [O.E. drencan, give to drink, fr. drincan. Cf. Ger. tränken.]

DRESS (dres) v.t. [pret. and pp. DRESSED, DREST] to clothe; deck; cook; cover a wound; adjust; trim;—n. clothes worn; a lady's gown; style of attire. [O.F. dresser, through Late L., fr. L. (part.) directus, directed.]

DRESSER (dres'er) n. one who dresses; a kitchen sideboard.

DRESSING-CASE (dres'ing-kās) n. a box fitted with toilet requisites.

DRESSING-GOWN (dres'ing-goun) n. a light gown used while a person is dressing.

DRESSING-ROOM (dres'ing-rōōm) n. a room for dressing in.

DRESSMAKER (dres'mā-kẹr) *n.* one who makes ladies' dresses.

DRESSY (dres'i) *a.* showy in dress.

DRIBBLE (drib'l) *v.i.* to fall in drops; slaver; to keep the ball moving by giving slight kicks, in football. [Fr. **DRIP**.]

DRIBBLET (drib'let) *n.* small quantity; a petty sum. [See **DRIBBLE**.]

DRIFT (drift) *n.* a pile of snow or sand; direction; object; meaning;—*r.t.* or *i.* to float or be driven along; form in heaps. [O.E. *drifan*. **DRIVE**.]

DRIFTY (drif'ti) *a.* forming drifts.

DRILL (dril) *n.* a tool for boring holes; a furrow;—*v.t.* to bore; train soldiers by exercise. [E.]

DRILLING (dril'ing) *n.* a coarse cotton cloth used for trousers. [E.]

DRINK (dringk) *v.t.* or *i.* [*pret.* **DRANK**; *pp.* **DRUNK**] to swallow liquor; take in; absorb; be intemperate;—*n.* a draught; intoxicating liquor. [O.E. *drincan.* Cf. Ger. *trinken.*]

DRINKABLE (dring'ka-bl) *a.* that may be drunk.

DRINKER (dring'kẹr) *n.* one who drinks; a tippler.

DRINKING (dringk'ing) *n.* act of swallowing liquors.

DRIP (drip) *v.t.* or *i.* to fall in drops;—*n.* falling in drops; that which falls; the edge of a roof. [M.E. *druppen,* fr. O.E. *dryppan.* Cf. Ger. *triefen.*]

DRIPPING-PAN (drip'ing-pan) *n.* a pan for fat of roast meat.

DRIPPING (drip'ing) *n.* fat falling from roasting meat.

DRIVE (driv) *v.t.* or *i.* [*pret.* **DROVE**; *pp.* **DRIVEN**] to urge; compel; rush on; guide or go in a carriage;—*n.* a carriage excursion; carriage road. [O.E. *drifan.* Cf. Ger. *treiben.*]

DRIVEL (driv'l) *v.i.* to slaver;—*n.* slaver; spittle. [E.; conn. with **DRIBBLE**.]

DRIVELLER (driv'l-ẹr) *n.* a simpleton.

DRIVELLING (driv'l-ing) *n.* a silly speech.

DRIVEN (driv'n) *pp.* of **DRIVE**.

DRIVER (dri'vẹr) *n.* one who drives.

DRIZZLE (driz'l) *v.i.* to fall in small drops. [Fr. M.E. *dresen,* fr. O.E. *dreosan,* fall.]

DRIZZLY (driz'li) *a.* shedding small drops.

DROLL (drōl) *a.* comical; odd;—*n.* a jester; a farce;—*v.i.* to jest. [F. *drôle,* fr. D.]

DROLLERY (drō'le-ri) *n.* buffoonery; funny sayings or antics.

DROLLISH (drōl'ish) *a.* somewhat droll.

DROMEDARY (drum'e-dar-i) *n.* a camel with one hump. [F. *dromedaire,* through Late L., fr. G. stem *dromad-,* of *dromas,* a runner, fr. *dromein,* run.]

DRONE (drōn) *n.* the male bee; a sluggard; —*v.i.* to live idly; hum. [O.E. *dran.*]

DRONISH (drō'nish) *a.* like a drone; lazy; idle.

DRONISHLY (drō'nish-li) *ad.* lazily; idly; sluggishly.

DRONISHNESS (drō'nish-nes) *n.* quality of being dronish.

DROOP (drōōp) *v.i.* to pine; languish; be dispirited. [Scand.; conn. with **DROP**.]

DROOPING (drōōp'ing) *a.* hanging down; languishing.

DROOPINGLY (drōōp'ing-li) *ad.* in a languishing manner.

DROP (drop) (1) *n.* a globule of moisture; a small quantity; an ear-ring; part of a gallows;—(2) *v.i.* to fall in drops;—*v.t.* to let fall. [(1) O.E. *dropa.* (2) O.E. *dropian.*]

DROPLET (drop'let) *n.* a little drop.

DROPPINGS (drop'ingz) *n.pl.* that which falls in drops.

DROPS (drops) *n.pl.* medicine in a liquid form; the dose measured by so many drops.

DROPSICAL (drop'si-kal) *a.* diseased with dropsy.

DROPSY (drop'si) *n.* a collection of water in the body. [Short for *ydropsy,* *hydropsy.*]

DROSKY (dros'ki) *n.* a low, light, four-wheeled carriage. [Russ. *droshki.*]

DROSS (dros) *n.* the scum of metals; worthless matter. [O.E. *dros.*]

DROSSY (dros'i) *a.* full of dross.

DROUGHT (drout) *n.* dry weather; dryness; thirst. [O.E. *drugath,* fr. *drugian,* to be **DRY**.]

DROUGHTY (drou'ti) *a.* dry; wanting rain.

DROUTH (drouth) *n.* want of rain; dryness; thirstiness. [See **DROUGHT**.]

DROUTHY (drou'thi) *a.* dry; thirsty. [See **DROUGHT**.]

DROVE (drōv) *pret.* of **DRIVE**;—*n.* a number of animals driven.

DROVER (drō'vẹr) *n.* one who drives cattle.

DROWN (droun) *v.t.* to suffocate in water; overflow. [Scand.]

DROWSE (drouz) *v.i.* to grow heavy with sleep. [O.E. *drusian.*]

DROWSINESS (drou'zi-nes) *n.* sleepiness.

DROWSY (drou'zi) *a.* sleepy; heavy.

DRUB (drub) *n.* a thump; a blow;—*v.t.* to beat heartily. [Etym. uncertain.]

DRUBBING (drub'ing) *n.* a beating.

DRUDGE (druj) *v.i.* to labour in mean offices toil;—*n.* a slave to work. [E.]

DRUDGERY (druj'ẹr-i) *n.* hard labour; toil.

DRUG (drug) *n.* any substance used in medicine; —*v.t.* to administer drugs. [M.E. *drogue,* *drugve,* fr. O.F. *drogue* (of unknown etym).]

DRUGGET (drug'et) *n.* a coarse woollen cloth. [O.F. *droguet,* dim. fr. *drogue,* **DRUG**, trash.]

DRUGGIST (drug'ist) *n.* one who deals in drugs.

DRUID (drōō'id) *n.* an ancient Celtic priest. [Celt.]

DRUIDESS (drōō'id-es) *n.* a female Druid.

DRUIDICAL (drōō-id'i-kal) *a.* pertaining to the Druids.

DRUIDISM (drōō'id-izm) *n.* religion of the Druids.

DRUM (drum) *n.* a military instrument; part of the ear; a cylinder; evening assembly; —*v.i.* to beat a drum. [Probably Imit.]

DRUMMER (drum'ẹr) *n.* one who beats a drum.

DRUM-STICK (drum'stik) *n.* a stick for beating drums.

DRUNK (drungk) *a.* intoxicated. [O.E. *druncen.*]

DRUNKARD (drung'kard) *n.* one addicted to excess in drinking alcoholic liquors. [F. suff. = *ard.* See **DRUNK**.]

DRUNKEN (drung'kn) *a.* intoxicated.

DRUNKENNESS (drung'kn-nes) *n.* intoxication; inebriation.

DRUPE (drōōp) *n.* a fruit without valves, as the plum. [L. *drupa,* G. *druppa,* an overripe olive; *drupepes,* ripened on the tree, fr. *drus,* a tree, and *peptein,* to cook. Cf. *drupetes-,* fr. *drus,* and *piptein,* to fall.]

DRY (dri) *a.* having no moisture; thirsty; sarcastic;—*v.t.* or *i.* to free from moisture. [O.E. *dryge.* See **DROUGHT**.]

DRYLY (dri'li) *ad.* coldly; sarcastically.

DRYNESS (dri'nes) *n.* thirst; drought.

DRY-ROT (dri'rot) *n.* a decay of timber.

DRYSALTER (dri'sawl-tẹr) *n.* a dealer in drugs, dyestuffs, and chemicals. [See **DRY** and **SALT**.]

DRY-SHOD (dri'shod) *a.* having the feet dry.

DUAL (dū'al) *a.* expressing the number two. [L. *dualis,* fr. *duo,* two.]

DUALISM (dū'al-izm) *n.* two-fold state or division; a theory that there are two opposite principles in nature and in the constitution of man.

DUALIST (dū'al-ist) *n.* a believer in dualism.

DUALISTIC (dū'al-is'tik) *a.* pertaining to duality or dualism.

DUALITY (dū-al'i-ti) *n.* state of being two.

DUB (dub) *v.t.* to confer a title. [O.E. *dubban.*]

DUBIETY (dū-bi'e-ti) *n.* doubtfulness.

DUBIOUS (dū'bi-us) *a.* of uncertain issue; not clear or plain; doubtful. [L. *dubiosus*, fr. *dubium*, doubt; conn. with *duo*, two.]

DUBIOUSLY (dū'bi-us-li) *ad.* doubtfully.

DUBIOUSNESS (dū'bi-us-nes) *n.* hesitation; uncertainty.

DUBITABLE (dū'bi-ta-bl) *a.* that may be doubted.

DUBITATION (dū-bi-tā'shun) *n.* the act of doubting; doubt.

DUCAL (dū'kal) *a.* pertaining to a duke. [F., fr. *duc*, DUKE.]

DUCAT (duk'at) *n.* a foreign coin, struck in the dominions of a duke. [O.F., fr. It.]

DUCHESS (duch'es) *n.* the wife of a duke. [O.F. *duchesse*, fr. L. *dux*, DUKE.]

DUCHY (duch'i) *n.* the territory of a duke. [F. *duché*, fr. Late L. (acc.) *ducatum*.]

DUCK (duk) *n.* (1) a species of canvas;—(2) a water-fowl;—*v.t.* or *i.* to plunge in water; dip; dive; stoop or nod. [(1) D. *doeck*, linen. (2) O.E. *duce*, duck, fr. *ducan*, dive.]

DUCKING (duk'ing) *n.* immersion of the head in water.

DUCKLING (duk'ling) *n.* a young duck.

DUCKWEED (duk'wēd) *n.* a plant growing in shallow waters.

DUCT (dukt) *n.* a tube; a canal; a passage. [L. *ductilis*, fr. (part.) *ductus*, led.]

DUCTILE (duk'til) *a.* easily led; flexible. [L. *ductilis*, fr. (part.) *ductus*, led.]

DUCTILITY (duk-til'i-ti) *n.* the quality of being easily extended.

DUE (dū) *a.* owed; owing to; proper;—*n.* a debt; right; claim;—*ad.* directly. [O.F. (part.) *deu*=F. *dû*, owed, fr. *devoir*, fr. L. *debere*. Doublet of DEBT.]

DUEL (dū'el) *n.* a fight between two. [It., fr. L. *duellum*, old form of *bellum*, fr. *duo*, two.]

DUELLIST (dū'el-ist) *n.* a frequent fighter in duels.

DUELLO (dū-el'ō) *n.* the art or the rules of duelling. [See DUEL.]

DUENNA (dū-en'a) *n.* an elderly lady in charge of a younger. [Sp. Doublet of DONNA.]

DUET (dū-et') *n.* a song or piece in two parts. [It., fr. L. *duo*, two.]

DUG (dug) (1) *n.* the pap or nipple of a beast; —(2) *v. pret.* and *pp.* of DIG. [(1) Scand.]

DUKE (dūk) *n.* one of the highest order of nobility; a sovereign prince. [O.F. *duc*, fr. L. (acc.) *ducem*, leader, fr. *dux*. Doublet of DOGE.]

DUKEDOM (dūk'dum) *n.* estate of a duke.

DUKELING (dūk'ling) *n.* a petty or mock duke.

DULCET (dul'set) *a.* sweet; harmonious; melodious. [Fr. O.F. *dols*=F. *doux*, fr. L. *dulcis*, sweet.]

DULCIFICATION (dul-si-fi-kā'shun) *n.* the act of sweetening.

DULCIFY (dul'si-fi) *v.t.* to sweeten. [F. *dulcifier*, fr. L. *ficare*=*facere*, make.]

DULCIMER (dul'si-mer) *n.* a musical instrument of wire strings played on with sticks. [O.F., corr. fr. Sp. *dulce-mele*, lit. sweet MELODY.]

DULL (dul) *a.* stupid; slow; blunt; cloudy; dim; sad;—*v.t.* to blunt; stupefy;—*v.i.* to become blunt. [O.E. *dol.* Cf. Ger. *toll*, mad.]

DULLARD (dul'ard) *n.* a stupid person.

DULLY (dul'i) *ad.* stupidly; sadly.

DULLNESS (dul'nes) *n.* state of being dull; bluntness; slowness; dimness; stupidity.

DULY (dū'li) *ad.* fitly; properly; regularly. [See DUE.]

DUMB (dum) *a.* mute; incapable of speech. [E. Cf. Ger. *dumm*, stupid.]

DUMB-BELLS (dum'belz) *n.* weights used for exercise.

DUMBLY (dum'li) *ad.* without using words.

DUMBNESS (dum'nes) *n.* inability to speak; muteness.

DUMB-SHOW (dum'shō) *n.* gestures without words.

DUMFOUND (dum-found') *v.t.* to strike dumb; confuse greatly. Also DUMFOUNDER.

DUMMY (dum'i) *n.* a dumb person; a sham package in a shop; the fourth or exposed hand when only three persons play at whist. [Fr. DUMB.]

DUMPLING (dump'ling) *n.* a mass of boiled dough or paste, with or without fruit. [Dim. of *dump*, in DUMPY.]

DUMPS (dumps) *n.pl.* a moping state. [Prob. related to Old D. *domp*, mist; or Ger. *dumpf*, gloomy.]

DUMPY (dum'pi) *a.* short and thick. [From a provincial form *dump*, a clumsy piece.]

DUN (dun) (1) *a.* of a dark colour; gloomy; —*n.* (2) a dark colour;—(3) a clamorous creditor;—(4) *v.t.* to urge for a debt. [(1) and (2) O.E. *dun*, most probably Celt.; W. *dwn*, dusky; Gael. *donn*. (3) and (4) allied to DIN (Scand.).]

DUNCE (duns) *n.* a blockhead. [Originally a follower of Duns Scotus, a churchman opposed to the Renaissance.]

DUNDERHEAD (dun'der-hed) *n.* a dunce. [Perh. for THUNDER.]

DUNE (dūn) *n.* a low hill of sand on the sea-coast. [D.] [manure. [E.]

DUNG (dung) *n.* excrement of animals;

DUNGEON (dun'jun) *n.* a close prison. [O.F. *donjon*, tower, fr. Late L. (acc.) *domnionem*, lit. DOMINION.

DUNGHILL (dung'hil) *n.* a heap of dung or manure;—*a.* of low origin; base; mean. [E.]

DUODECIMAL (dū-ō-des'i-mal) *a.* proceeding by twelves. [L., fr. *duodecim*, DOZEN.]

DUODECIMO (dū-ō-des'i-mō) *n. pl.* DUODECIMOS a book having twelve leaves to a sheet. [L. (abl.)=twelfth, fr. *duodecim*.]

DUODENUM (dū-o-dē'num) *n.* the first of the small intestines. [L., fr. its length, twelve fingers'-breadth.]

DUPE (dūp) *n.* one easily deceived;—*v.t.* to impose on. [F.=the hoopoe. Cf. GULL, PIGEON.]

DUPLICATE (dū'pli-kāt) *v.t.* to double;— *n.* an exact copy;—*a.* double; twofold. [L. (part.) *duplicatus*, doubled.]

DUPLICATION (dū-pli-kā'shun) *n.* act of doubling.

DUPLICATURE (dū'pli-kā-tūr) *n.* a fold.

DUPLICITY (dū-plis'i-ti) *n.* doubleness of heart or speech; deceit. [F. *duplicité*, fr. L. (acc.) *duplicitatem*.]

DURABILITY (dū-ra-bil'i-ti) *n.* power of lasting without perishing.

DURABLE (dū'ra-bl) *a.* able to last or endure; permanent; hardy. [F., fr. L. (acc.) *durabilem*, fr. *durare*, last.]

DURABLENESS (dū'ra-bl-nes) *n.* power of lasting; continuance.

DURABLY (dū'ra-bli) *ad.* in a lasting manner.

DURANCE (dū'rans) *n.* continuance; imprisonment. [O.F., fr. *durer*, last, fr. L. *durare*.]

DURATION (dū-rā'shun) *n.* continuance in time; time during which anything exists. [See DURANCE.]

DURBAR (dur'bär) *n.* an audience chamber; a state council or levee. [Per.]

DURING (dū'ring) *ppr.* continuing. [Orig. part. of *dure*, fr. F. See DURANCE.]

DURST (durst) *pret.* of DARE. [O.E. *dorste*.]

DUSK (dusk) *a.* slightly dark;—*n.* a tending to darkness. [Scand.]

DUSKILY (dus'ki-li) *ad.* darkly; cloudily.

DUSKINESS (dus'ki-nes) *n.* moderate blackness or darkness.

DUSKY (dus'ki) *a.* partially dark; dark coloured; gloomy.

DUST (dust) *n.* particles of dry earth; a low condition;—*v.t.* to brush dust from. [O.E. *dust*. Cf. Ger. *Dunst*.]

Fāte, fär, ado; mē, her; mine; nōte; tūne; mōon.

DUSTER (dus'ter) *n.* a cloth or brush for removing dust.
DUSTY (dus'ti) *a.* covered with dust.
DUTEOUS (dū'te-us) *a.* fulfilling duty. [See DUTY.]
DUTEOUSLY (dū'te-us-li) *ad.* in a duteous manner.
DUTIABLE (dū'ti-ạ-bl) *a.* subject to duties.
DUTIFUL (dū'ti-fool) *a.* obedient to parents; respectful.
DUTIFULLY (dū'ti-fool-i) *ad.* obediently; respectfully.
DUTIFULNESS (dū-ti-fool'nes) *n.* obedience.
DUTY (dū'ti) *n.* what one is bound to perform; military service; obedience; tax or customs. [Fr. DUE.]
DWARF (dwawrf) *n.* a person or plant below the common size;—*v.t.* to hinder from growing;—*a.* below the natural size. [O.E. *dweorg.* Cf. D. *Dwerg,* Ger. *Zwerg.*]
DWARFISH (dwawr'fish) *a.* below the usual size; little; low.
DWELL (dwel) *v.i.* [*pret.* DWELLED, DWELT] to live in a place; reside; hang on; continue. [O.E. *dwellan,* tarry.]
DWELLER (dwel'er) *n.* an inhabitant.
DWELLING (dwel'ing) *n.* place of residence; house; abode.
DWELT (dwelt) *pret.* and *pp.* of DWELL.
DWINDLE (dwin'dl) *v.i.* to become less; diminish; grow feeble; degenerate. [Fr. O.E. *dwinan,* pine.]

DWINE (dwin) *v.t.* to waste away; decline.
DYE (dī) *v.t.* to colour; stain;—*n.* colouring liquor; tinge. [M.E. *deyen,* fr. O.E. *deagan.*]
DYEING (dī'ing) *vpr.* staining;—*n.* art of colouring cloths. [See DYE.]
DYER (dī'er) *n.* one whose trade is to colour cloths, etc.
DYING (dī'ing) *ppr.* expiring. [See DIE.]
DYNAMICS (di-nam'iks) *n.* that branch of mechanics which treats of bodies in motion. [G., fr. *dunamis,* power, fr. *dunamai,* I am strong.]
DYNAMITARD (dī'nạ-mi-tárd) *n.* one who uses dynamite with criminal intent.
DYNAMITE (dī'nạ-mīt, din'ạ-mīt) *n.* a highly explosive compound of nitro-glycerine and a siliceous earth. [See DYNAMICS.]
DYNASTY (din'ạs-ti) *n.* a race of kings of the same family; sovereignty. [F., fr. Late L. *dynastia,* dominion, fr. G., fr. *dunastes,* lord, fr. *dunamai,* I am strong.]
DYSENTERIC (dis-en-ter'ik) *a.* pertaining to dysentery. [See DYSENTERY.]
DYSENTERY (dis'en-ter-i) *n.* a bloody flux. [G., fr. (pref.) *dus-,* badly, and (pl.) *entera,* entrails, fr. *en* = IN.]
DYSPEPSIA (dis-pep'si-ạ) *n.* indigestion or difficulty of digestion. [G., fr. (pref.) *dus-,* badly, and *peptein,* digest.]
DYSPEPTIC (dis-pep'tik) *a.* afflicted with indigestion or pertaining to it.

E

EACH (ēch) *a.* and *pron.* denoting every one separately. [M.E. *eche, elch,* fr. O.E. *œlc.*]
EAGER (ē'ger) *a.* keenly desirous; ardent; impetuous; sharp. [O.F. *egre* = F. *aigre,* fr. L. (acc.) *acrem,* fr. *acer,* sharp. See VINEGAR.]
EAGERLY (ē'ger-li) *ad.* with ardent desire; keenly. [See EAGER.]
EAGERNESS (ē'ger-nes) *n.* ardent desire; fervour; keenness. [See EAGER.]
EAGLE (ē'gl) *n.* a bird of prey. [O.F. *aigle,* fr. L. (acc.) *aquilam.*]
EAGLESS (ē'gles) *n.* a female eagle. [See EAGLE.]
EAGLET (ē'glet) *n.* a young eagle. [See EAGLE.]
EAR (ēr) *n.* the organ of hearing; a spike of corn;—*v.i.* to shoot into ears. [(1) O.E. *eare.* Cf. Ger. *Ohr,* L. *auris.* (2) O.E. *ear.* Cf. Ger. *Ahre.*]
EARACHE (ēr'āk) *n.* pain in the ear. [See EAR and ACHE.]
EARING (ēr'ing) *n.* ploughing of land. [O.E. *erian.* Cf. L. *arare,* G. *aroein.*]
EARL (erl) *n.* a title of nobility. [O.E. *eorl.*]
EARLDOM (erl'dum) *n.* dominion or dignity of an earl. [See EARL.]
EARLESS (ēr'les) *a.* without ears. [See EAR.]
EARLINESS (er'li-nes) *n.* advance in time. [See EARLY.]
EARLY (er'li) *a.* being in good time or season; —*ad.* soon; in good time. [O.E., fr. *œr.* early, and *-lic, -ly,* like.]
EARN (ern) *v.t.* to gain by labour. [O.E. *earnian.*]
EARNEST (er'nest) (1) *a.* strongly desirous; determined;—(?) *n.* money advanced. [(1) O.E. *eornest,* zeal. Cf. Ger. *ernst.* (2) Etym. unknown.]
EARNESTLY (er'nest-li) *ad.* eagerly.
EARNESTNESS (er'nest-nes) *n.* fixed desire; seriousness.
EARNINGS (er'ningz) *n.pl.* the rewards of services. [See EARN.]
EAR-RING (ēr'ring) *n.* jewel for the ear.

EARTH (erth) *n.* the globe we inhabit; the world; land; country; soil of all kinds;—*v.t.* to cover with mould;—*v.i.* to burrow. [O.E. *eorthe,* Cf. Ger. *Erde.*]
EARTHEN (er'thn) *a.* made of earth or clay.
EARTHENWARE (er'thn-wār) *n.* domestic vessels made of clay; crockery.
EARTHLING (erth'ling) *n.* an inhabitant of the earth; a mortal.
EARTHLY (erth'li) *ad.* pertaining to earth.
EARTHQUAKE (erth'kwāk) *n.* a shaking or trembling of the earth.
EARTHWARD (erth'ward) *ad.* towards the earth.
EARTHWORK (erth'wurk) *n.* a fortification of earth; any cutting or embankment of earth.
EARTHY (er'thi) *a.* consisting of earth.
EAR-TRUMPET (ēr'trum-pet) *n.* a tube to aid the ear in hearing.
EAR-WITNESS (ēr'wit-nes) *n.* one who attests what he has heard.
EASE (ēz) *n.* freedom from pain; rest; facility;—*v.t.* to relieve from pain; assuage; slacken; move or shift. [O.F. *aise,* of unknown etym.]
EASEFUL (ēz'fool) *a.* quiet.
EASEL (ē'zl) *n.* a frame on which pictures are placed while being painted. [Ger. *Esel,* ass, easel.]
EASELESS (ēz'les) *a.* wanting ease.
EASEMENT (ēz'ment) *n.* that which gives ease or relief.
EASILY (ē'zi-li) *ad.* with ease; gently.
EAST (ēst) *n.* the quarter where the sun rises; —*a.* toward the rising sun. [O.E. (adv.) *east.* Cf. Ger. *ost.* Conn. with G. *eos,* dawn.]
EASTER (ēs'ter) *n.* the feast of Christ's resurrection. [O.E. *Eastre,* orig. the goddess of the spring.]
EASTERLY (ēs'ter-li) *a.* pertaining to the east; —*ad.* toward the east.
EASTERN (ēs'tern) *a.* being in or from the east; Oriental.
EASTWARD (ēst'ward) *ad.* toward the east.
EASY (ē'zi) *a.* free from pain; not difficult; comfortable; compliant.

EASY-CHAIR (ē′zi-chār) *n.* a large, soft-padded arm-chair.

EAT (ēt) *v.t.* [*pret.* ATE; *pp.* EAT, EATEN] to take food; corrode;—*v.i.* to take food. [O.E. *etan.* Cf. Ger. *essen,* L. *edere.*]

EATABLE (ē′ta-bl) *a.* fit to be eaten;—*n.* anything that may be eaten.

EAU DE COLOGNE (ō-de-kō-lōn′) *n.* a perfumed spirit for the toilet. [F.]

EAU DE VIE (ō-de-vē′) *n.* water of life; brandy. [F.]

EAVES (ēvz) *n.pl.* lower edges of a roof. [M.E. (sing.) *evese,* fr. O.E. *efis,* hedge.]

EAVESDROP (ēvz′drop) *n.* water that drops from the eaves;—*v.i.* to stand outside listening. [See EAVES.]

EAVESDROPPER (ēvz′drop-ẹr) *n.* an insidious listener.

EBB (eb) *v.i.* to flow back; decay; decline;—*n.* a recess of the tide; decline. [O.E. *ebba.*]

EBB-TIDE (eb′tīd) *n.* the retiring tide.

EBON (eb′un) *a.* like ebony. [See EBONY.]

EBONY (eb′un-i) *n.* a species of hard, heavy wood. [Formerly *ebone,* fr. F., fr. L. *ebenus,* fr. H. =stone.]

EBRIETY (ē-brī′e-ti) *n.* drunkenness. [F., fr. L. fr. *ebrius,* drunk.]

EBULLIENCE (ē-bul′yens) *n.* a boiling over; overflow.

EBULLIENT (ē-bul′yent) *a.* boiling over. [L. (part. stem) *ebullient-,* boiling up, fr. *e =ex,* out, and *bullire,* BOIL.]

EBULLITION (ē-bu-lish′un) *n.* act of boiling; outburst of feeling.

ECCENTRIC (ek-sen′trik) *n.* a wheel or disc having its axis out from the centre;—*a.* irregular; anomalous. [F. *excentrique,* fr. Late L. (acc.) *eccentricum,* from the centre, fr. G. *ek,* and CENTRE.]

ECCENTRICALLY (ek-sen′tri-kạl-i) *ad.* with eccentricity.

ECCENTRICITY (ek-sen-tris′i-ti) *n.* deviation from a centre; irregularity.

ECCLESIASTES (e-klē-zi-as′tes) *n.* a canonical book of the Old Testament. [L., fr. G., fr. *ek-klesia,* an assembly, church, fr. *ek,* out, and *kletos,* called, fr. *kalein.*]

ECCLESIASTIC (e-klē-zi-as′tik) *n.* a clergyman.

ECCLESIASTICAL (e-klē-zi-as′ti-kạl) *a.* pertaining to the church or clergy.

ECCLESIASTICUS (e-klē-zi-as-ti-kus) *n.* a book of the Apocrypha.

ECHINUS (ē-ke′nus) *n.* a hedgehog; the sea-urchin; a form of moulding. [L., fr. G. *echinos,* hedgehog.]

ECHO (ek′ō) *n.* a sound reflected or reverberated;—*v.t.* or *i.* to reverberate or resound. [G.]

ECLAT (e-klä′) *n.* striking effect; applause; renown. [F.]

ECLECTIC (ek-lek′tik) *a.* selecting;—*n.* one who chooses his opinions from different thinkers. [G., fr. *eklegein,* fr. *ek,* out, and *legein,* choose.]

ECLECTICISM (ek-lek′ti-sizm) *n.* the practice of selecting from different systems.

ECLIPSE (e-klips′) *n.* the obscuration of a heavenly body by some other body; — *v.t.* to darken; throw in the shade; surpass. [O.F., fr. L., fr. G. *ek-leipsis,* failure, fr. *ek,* out, and *leipein,* leave.]

Eclipse.

ECLIPTIC (e-klip′tik) *n.* the apparent path of the sun. [L. *ec-lipticus.*]

ECONOMICAL (ē-ku-nom′i-kạl) *a.* saving; frugal.

ECONOMICALLY (ē-ku-nom′i-kạl-i) *ad.* with economy.

ECONOMICS (ē-ku-nom′iks) *n.* political economy.

ECONOMISE (ē-kon′u-mīz) *v.t.* or *i.* to use with economy.

ECONOMIST (ē-kon′u-mist) *n.* one who is frugal.

ECONOMY (ē-kon′u-mi) *n.* frugal use of money; arrangement or disposition; regular operation. [F., fr. L. *œconomia,* household management, fr. G., fr. *oikonomos,* steward, fr. *oikos,* house, and *nomos,* law.]

ECSTASY (ek′sta-si) *n.* excessive joy; rapture; enthusiasm. [G. *ekstasis,* lit. trance, fr. *ek,* out of, and *stasis,* standing.]

ECSTATIC (ek-stat′ik) *a.* entrancing. [See ECSTASY.]

ECUMENICAL (ek-ū-men′i-kạl) *a.* general; universal. [L., fr. G., fr. (part.) *oikoumene (ge)* inhabited (earth), fr. *oikos,* house.]

EDACIOUS (ē-dā′shus) *a.* greedy.

EDACIOUSLY (ē-dā′shus-li) *ad.* greedily.

EDACITY (ē-das′i-ti) *n.* greediness. [L. stem, *edaci-,* of *edax,* gluttonous., fr. *edere,* eat.]

EDDY (ed′i) *n.* circular motion of water or air; —*v.i.* to move round and round. [O.E. pref. *ed-,* back.]

EDEN (ē′den) *n.* paradise; any delightful region or residence. [H.]

EDGE (ej) *n.* sharp side; brink; border; sharpness; keenness;—*v.t.* to sharpen; fringe; urge on;—*v.i.* to move sideways. [M.E. *egge,* fr. O.E. *ecg.* Cf. Ger. *Ecke.*]

EDGED (ejd) *a.* sharp.

EDGELESS (ej′les) *a.* without an edge.

EDGE-TOOL (ej′tōōl) *n.* a cutting instrument.

EDGEWISE (ej′wiz) *ad.* with the edge forward.

EDGING (ej′ing) *n.* a narrow lace; a border.

EDIBLE (ed′i-bl) *a.* fit to be eaten. [L. *edere,* eat.]

EDICT (ē′dikt) *n.* a law promulgated; a decree. [L. (part.) *edictus,* proclaimed, fr. *e, ex,* out, and *dicere,* say.]

EDIFICATION (ed-i-fi-kā′shun) *n.* a building up; instruction.

EDIFICE (ed′i-fis) *n.* a large structure. [L. *œdificare,* build.]

EDIFY (ed′i-fi) *v.t.* to build up, or instruct; improve. [F. *édifier,* build, fr. L., fr. stem *œdi-,* of *œdes,* house, and *-ficare =facere,* make.]

EDIT (ed′it) *v.t.* to prepare for publication. [L. (part.) *editus,* given out, fr. *e, ex,* and *dare,* give.]

EDITION (ē-dish′un) *n.* publication of a literary work; the whole number of copies issued at one publication. [F., fr. L. (acc.) *editionem.*]

EDITOR (ed′i-tẹr) *n.* one who prepares for publication. [L.]

EDITORIAL (ed-i-tō′ri-ạl) *a.* pertaining to an editor;—*n.* a leading article in a newspaper.

EDITORIALLY (ed-i-tō′ri-ạl-i) *ad.* in the character or manner of an editor.

EDITORSHIP (ed′it-ẹr-ship) *n.* the business of an editor.

EDUCATE (ed′ū-kāt) *v.t.* to bring up; train; teach. [L. *educatus,* brought up, fr. *e, ex,* and *ducere,* lead.]

EDUCATION (ed-ū-kā′shun) *n.* bringing up and out the powers of body and mind; instruction; training.

EDUCATIONAL (ed-ū-kā′shun-ạl) *a.* pertaining to education.

EDUCATIONIST (ed-ū-kā′shun-ist) *n.* one versed in or promoting education.

EDUCATOR (ed′ū-kā-tẹr) *n.* he or that which educates.

EDUCE (ē-dūs′) *v.t.* to draw out; elicit; extract. [L. *educere,* fr. *e, ex,* and *ducere,* lead.]

EDUCIBLE (ē-dū′si-bl) *a.* that may be adduced.

EDUCTION (ē-duk′shun) *n.* the act of drawing out.

EEL (ēl) *n.* a genus of creeping fish. [M.E. *el,* fr. O.E. *œl.* Cf. Ger. *Aal.*]

EFFABLE (ef′a-bl) *a.* that may be uttered. [F., fr. L. *effari,* fr. *e, ex,* and *fari,* speak.]

EFFACE (e-fās') *vt.*. to blot or rub out; wear away; remove. [F. *effacer*, fr. *ef-* = L. *ex*, and FACE.]

EFFACEABLE (e-fā'sa-bl) *a.* that may be effaced.

EFFACEMENT (e-fās'ment) *n.* act of effacing.

EFFECT (e-fekt') *n.* that which is produced by an agent or cause *n.pl.* goods;—*v.t.* to bring to pass; accomplish. [L. (part.) *effectus*, worked out; fr. *e*, *ex*, and *-ficere* = *facere*, do.]

EFFECTIBLE (e-fek'ti-bl) *a.* that may be effected.

EFFECTION (e-fek'shun) *n.* creation or production.

EFFECTIVE (e-fek'tiv) *a.* able for service; operative; powerful.

EFFECTIVELY (e-fek'tiv-li) *ad.* with effect.

EFFECTUAL (e-fek'tū-al) *a.* producing effect.

EFFECTUALLY (e-fek'tū-al-i) *ad.* thoroughly; completely.

EFFECTUATE (e-fek'tū-āt) *v.t.* to bring to pass.

EFFEMINACY (e-fem'i-na-si) *n.* womanish delicacy. [See EFFEMINATE.]

EFFEMINATE (e-fem'i-nat) *a.* womanish; weak; voluptuous;—*v.t.* (e-fem'i-nāt) to unman; weaken. [L. (part.) *effeminatus*, made womanish, fr. *ef* = *ex*, and *femina*, a woman.]

EFFEMINATELY (e-fem'i-nat-li) *ad.* weakly; softly.

EFFEMINATENESS (e-fem'i-nat-nes) *n.* unmanly weakness or delicateness.

EFFENDI (e-fen'di) *n.* a title of distinction in Turkey. [Turk., fr. Mod. G. *authentes* (av-then-tes), ruler.]

EFFERVESCE (ef-er-ves') *v.t.* to escape, as air or gas, from a liquid with a bubbling and hissing sound. [L., fr. *ef* = *ex*, and *fervescere*, begin to boil, fr. *fervere*, boil.]

EFFERVESCENCE (ef-er-ves'ens) *n.* commotion; bubbling.

EFFERVESCENT (ef-er-ves'ent) *a.* gently boiling or bubbling.

EFFERVESCIBLE (ef-er-ves'i-bl) *a.* capable of effervescence.

EFFETE (e-fēt') *a.* barren; exhausted; worn out. [L. *effetus*, weak from bearing young, fr. *ef* = *ex*, and FETUS.]

EFFICACIOUS (ef-i-kā'shus) *a.* productive of effects. [L., fr. stem *efficac-*, of *efficax*, effectual, fr. *efficere*, EFFECT.]

EFFICACIOUSLY (ef-i-kā'shus-li) *ad.* with the desired effect.

EFFICACY (ef'i-ka-si) *n.* power to produce a given effect.

EFFICIENCY (e-fish'en-si) *n.* power of producing effect.

EFFICIENT (e-fish'ent) *a.* that produces effect; competent;—*n.* an active cause. [L. (part. stem) *efficient-*, effecting.]

EFFICIENTLY (e-fish'ent-li) *ad.* with effect.

EFFIGY (ef'i-ji) *n.* an image of a person; impression of the head on a coin. [F. *effigie*, fr. L. (acc.) *effigiem*, fr. *ef* = *ex*, and stem of *fingere*, to FIGURE.]

EFFLORESCE (ef-lo-res') *v.i.* to form a mealy powder on the surface. [L., fr. *ef* = *ex*, and *florescere*, blossom.]

EFFLORESCENCE (ef-lo-res'ens) *n.* production of flowers; time of flowering; an eruption.

EFFLORESCENT (ef-lo-res'ent) *a.* shooting out like flowers.

EFFLUENCE (ef'lōō-ens) *n.* a flowing out.

EFFLUENT (ef'lōō-ent) *a.* flowing from. [L. (part. stem) fr. *ef* = *ex*, out, and *fluere*, flow.]

EFFLUVIAL (e-flōō'vi-al) *a.* pertaining to effluvia. [See EFFLUVIUM.]

EFFLUVIUM (e-flōō'vi-um) *n.* exhalation from putrefying substances;—*pl.* EFFLUVIA. [L., fr. *effluere*, flow out.]

EFFLUX (ef'luks) *n.* a flowing out. [See EFFLUVIUM.]

EFFLUXION (e-fluk'shun) *n.* a flowing out. [See EFFLUVIUM.]

EFFORT (ef'ert) *n.* exertion of strength. [F. fr. Late L., fr. L. *ex*, and *fortis*. See FORCE.]

EFFORTLESS (ef'ert-les) *a.* making no effort.

EFFRONTERY (e-frun'ter-i) *n.* impudence. [O.F., fr. *effronté*, impudent, fr. L. *ef* = *ex*, and FRONT.]

EFFULGENCE (e-ful'jens) *n.* a flood of light.

EFFULGENT (e-ful'jent) *a.* shining brightly; luminous. [L. (part. stem) *effulgent-*, flashing out, fr. *ef* = *ex*, and *fulgere*, shine.]

EFFULGENTLY (e-ful'jent-li) *ad.* in a splendid manner.

EFFUSE (e-fūz') *v.t.* to pour out. [L. *effusus*, poured out, fr. *ef* = *ex*, and *fundere*, pour.]

EFFUSION (e-fū'zhun) *n.* a pouring out; that which is poured out.

EFFUSIVE (e-fū'siv) *a.* pouring out largely; gushing.

EFFUSIVELY (e-fū'siv-li) *ad.* in an effusive manner.

EFFUSIVENESS (e-fū'siv-nes) *n.* quality of pouring out copiously.

EGG (eg) *n.* (1) a body formed in the females of birds, from which their young is produced;—(2) *v.t.* to urge on; instigate. [(1) E. Cf. Ger. *Ei* and O.E. *aeg.* (2) Scand., conn. with EDGE.]

EGLANTINE (eg'lan-tīn) *n.* the sweet brier. [O.F., fr. a derivative of L. *acus*, needle.]

EGOISM (eg'ō-izm) *n.* excessive love of self. [L. *ego*, I.]

EGOIST (eg'ō-ist) *n.* a philosopher who thinks everything uncertain but personal existence. [See EGOISM.]

EGOTISE (eg'u-tīz) *v.i.* to talk or write much of oneself. [See EGOISM.]

EGOTISM (eg'u-tizm) *n.* self-commendation; vanity. [See EGOISM.]

EGOTIST (eg'u-tist) *n.* one always talking of himself. [See EGOISM.]

EGOTISTIC (eg-u-tis'tik) *a.* addicted to egotism; conceited; full of self.

EGREGIOUS (e-grē'jus) *a.* remarkable; extraordinary. [L. *e-gregius*, fr. *e*, *ex*, and stem *greg-*, of *grex*, herd.]

EGREGIOUSLY (e-grē'jus-li) *ad.* enormously.

EGRESS (ē'gres) *n.* act of going out; power or right to depart. [L., fr. part. *egressus*, gone out, fr. *e*, *ex*, and *gradi*, go forth.]

EGRESSION (ē-gresh'un) *n.* the act of going out.

EGRET (ē'gret) *n.* the lesser white heron. [F. *aigrette*, fr. O. Ger.]

EGRETTE (ē-gret') *n.* an ornament of feathers, ribbons, etc. [See EGRET.]

EGYPTOLOGY (e-jip-tol'ō-ji) *n.* science of Egyptian antiquities. [*Egypt.*, and G. *logos*, discourse.]

EIDER (ī'der) *n.* a species of duck. [Scand.]

EIDER-DOWN (ī'der-doun) *n.* soft feathers of the eider duck. [Scand., and DOWN.]

EIGHT (āt) *n.* or *a.* twice four. [O.E. *eahta.* Cf. Ger. *acht*, L. *octo*, G. *okto*.]

EIGHTEEN (ā'tēn) *n.* or *a.* twice nine. [EIGHT, and O.E. *tien*, ten.]

EIGHTEENTH (ā'tēnth) *a.* denoting one of eighteen.

EIGHT-FOLD (āt'fōld) *a.* eight times. [EIGHT and FOLD = times. fr. O.E. *fealdan*.]

EIGHTH (ātth) *a.* denoting one of eight;—*n.* the interval of an octave. [See EIGHT.]

EIGHTHLY (ātth'li) *ad.* in the eighth place.

EITHER (ē'THer, ī'THer) *a.* or *pron.* one or the other; one of two; each. [O.E. *aegther.*]

EJACULATE (ē-jak'ū-lāt) *v.t.* to throw out; utter suddenly and briefly. [L. (part.) *ejaculatus*, fr. *e*, *ex*, out, and *jaculum* dart.[

EJACULATION (ē-jak-ū-lā'shun) *n.* a short prayer or utterance.

EJACULATORY (ē-jak'ū-lā-tur-i) *a.* suddenly darted out.

EJECT (e-jekt') *v.t.* to cast out; dismiss; expel. [L. (part.) *ejectus*, fr. *e*, *ex*, and *jacere*, hurl.]

EJECTION (ê-jek'shun) *n.* a casting out.

EJECTMENT (ê-jekt'ment) *n.* expulsion; dispossession; an action for the recovery of possession of lands or tenements.

EKE (ēk) *v.t.* to increase; lengthen;—*ad.* also; moreover. [O.E. *ecan*.]

ELABORATE (e-lab'u-rąt) *v.t.* to produce with labour;—*a.* finished with exactness. [L. (part.) *elaboratus*, worked out, fr. *e*, *ex*, out, and LABOUR.]

ELABORATED (e-lab'u-rā-ted) *pp.* or *a.* produced with labour or study.

ELABORATELY (e-lab'u-rąt-li) *ad.* with great care, study, etc.

ELABORATION (e-lab-u-rā'shun) *n.* a producing with labour; a natural process of growth in living organisms.

ELAND (ē'land) *n.* a species of antelope. [D.]

ELAPSE (e-laps') *v.i.* to pass away. [L. (part.) *elapsus*, having slipped away, fr. *e*, *ex*, and LAPSE.]

ELASTIC (e-las'tik) *a.* having elasticity. [G., fr. *ela-ein* = *elaunein*, drive, push.]

ELASTICITY (e-las-tis'i-ti) *n.* the property by which bodies recover a former state after being bent or compressed.

ELATE (e-lāt') *a.* flushed with success;—*v.t.* to puff up. [L. (part.) *elatus*, lifted up, fr. *e*, *ex*, and (part.) *latus*, borne.]

ELATEDLY (e-lāt'ed-li) *ad.* with pride or triumph.   [pride.

ELATION (e-lā'shun) *n.* self-esteem; vanity;

ELBOW (el'bō) *n.* the bend of the arm;—*v.t.* or *i.* to push with the elbow. [O.E. *elboga*. See ELL and BOW.]

ELBOW-ROOM (el'bō-rōom) *n.* space for moving or acting.

ELDER (el'dęr) (1) *a.* having lived longer;—*n.* an older person; an ecclesiastical officer; (2) a tree. [(1) O.E. *aeldra*. (2) M.E. *eiler*, fr. O.E. *ellacru*.]

ELDERLY (el'dęr-li) *a.* somewhat old.

ELDERSHIP (el'dęr-ship) *n.* seniority; office of an elder; body of elders.

ELDEST (el'dest) *a.* oldest; most aged. [O.E. *aeldesta*, oldest.]

ELECT (e-lekt') *v.i.* to choose for office; prefer; —*a.* chosen;—*n.* one chosen. [L. (part.) *electus*, chosen out, fr. *e*, *ex*, and *-ligere* = *legere*, choose.]

ELECTION (el-ek'shun) *n.* power of choosing; choice; preference.

ELECTIONEER (e-lek-shu-nēr') *v.t.* to make interest for office. [See ELECT.]

ELECTIONEERING (e-lek-shu-nēr'ing) *n.* use of efforts to gain an office.

ELECTIVE (e-lek'tiv) *a.* relating to or regulated by choice.

ELECTOR (e-lek'tęr) *n.* one who elects or has the right of voting.

ELECTORAL (e-lek'tu-rąl) *a.* belonging to an elector or elections.

ELECTRIC (e-lek'trik) *n.* a substance that exhibits electricity by friction; a non-conductor. [G. *elektron*, amber, through L. *electrum*.]

ELECTRICAL (e-lek'tri-kąl) *a.* pertaining to electricity.   [tricity.

ELECTRICALLY (e-lek'tri-kąl-i) *ad.* by elec-

ELECTRICIAN (e-lek-trish'ąn) *n.* one versed in electricity.

ELECTRICITY (e-lek-tris'i-ti) *n.* a subtle, mysterious power in nature, evoked by friction or other disturbance of molecular conditions, and producing light, heat, attraction, repulsion, etc.; the science of these phenomena.

ELECTRIFIABLE (e-lek'tri-fi-ą-bl) *a.* capable of becoming electric.

ELECTRIFY (e-lek'tri-fi) *v.t.* to communicate electricity to.

ELECTRISE (e-lek'triz) *v.t.* to electrify.

ELECTRODE (e-lek'trōd) *n.* either pole of the electric current.

ELECTRO-DYNAMICS (e-lek-trō-di-nam'iks) *n.* the science of electricity as a motive power. [ELECTRICITY, and G. *dunamos*, force.]

ELECTROMETER (e-lek-trom'e-tęr) *n.* an instrument for measuring the quantity or intensity of electricity, or its quality; or an instrument for discharging it from a jar. [ELECTRICITY, and G. *metron*, measure.]

ELECTROPLATE (e-lek'trō-plāt) *v.t.* to plate or cover with a coating of metal by electricity. [ELECTRICITY and PLATE.]

ELECTROTYPE (e-lek'trō-tip) *n.* a facsimile taken in metal deposited by an electrochemical process. [ELECTRICITY and TYPE.]

ELECTRUM (e-lek'trum) *n.* amber; also an alloy of gold and silver. [L.]

ELECTUARY (e-lek'tū-ąr-i) *n.* a medicine. [O.F. *electuaire*, of uncertain etym.]

ELEEMOSYNARY (el-ē-mos'i-na-ri) *n.* given in or living on charity. [L., fr. G. *eleemosune*, pity.]

ELEGANCE (el'e-gąns) *n.* state or quality of being elegant.

ELEGANT (el'e-gąnt) *a.* pleasing to the eye or taste; graceful; neat; shapely; polished; refined. [F., fr. L. (acc.) *elegantem*, fastidious, fr. *e*, *ex*, and root of *legere*, choose.]

ELEGANTLY (el'e-gąnt-li) *ad.* with pleasing propriety; gracefully.

ELEGIAC (el-e-ji'ak) *a.* used in elegy. [L. *elegiacus*, fr. G.]

ELEGIST (el'e-jist) *n.* a writer of elegies.

ELEGY (el'e-ji) *n.* a mournful or plaintive poem. [L. *elegia*, fr. G. *elegos*, lament.]

ELEMENT (el'e-ment) *n.* a first principle; a constituent part; ingredient; proper sphere. [L. *elementum*, of uncertain etym.]

ELEMENTAL (el-e-men'tąl) *a.* pertaining to first principles.

ELEMENTARY (el-e-men'ta-ri) *a.* primary.

ELEPHANT (el'e-fąnt) *n.* the largest quadruped. [L. *elephantus*, fr. G. *elephas*.]

ELEPHANTINE (el-e-fan'tin) *a.* huge; bulky.

ELEVATE (el'e-vāt) *v.t.* to raise to a higher place; elate; cheer; excite. [L. (part.) *elevatus*, lifted up, fr. *e*, *ex*, and *levare*, fr. *levis*, light.]

ELEVATION (el-e-vā'shun) *n.* act of raising; a high station.

ELEVATOR (el'e-vā-tęr) *n.* a muscle or machine that lifts up.

ELEVEN (e-lev'n) *n.* or *a.* one more than ten. [O.E. *endleofon*. Cf. Goth. *ainlif*.]

ELEVENTH (e-lev'nth) *n.* the next in order to the tenth. [See ELEVEN.]

ELF (elf) *n.* a diminutive fairy, supposed to inhabit desolate places and to delight in mischief; *pl.* ELVES. [O.E. *aelf*.]

ELFIN (el'fin) *n.* a little fairy or urchin. [See ELF.]

ELFISH (el'fish) *a.* mischievous; tricky.

ELICIT (e-lis'it) *v.t.* to draw out; deduce; extort. [L. (part.) *elicitus*, fr. *e*, *ex*, out, and *licere*, bring to light.]

ELIDE (e'lid) *v.t.* to cut off; suppress. [L. *e*, *ex*, out, and *laedere*, strike.]

ELIGIBILITY (el-i-ji-bil'i-ti) *n.* fitness to be chosen to office.

ELIGIBLE (el'i-ji-bl) *a.* capable of being elected; desirable. [F., fr. L. *eligibilis*, fr. *eligere*, ELECT.]

ELIGIBLY (el'i-ji-bli) *ad.* in a way to be worthy of choice.

ELIMINATE (e-lim'i-nāt) *v.t.* to leave out of consideration; throw off. [L. (part.) *eliminatus*, turned out of doors, fr. *e*, *ex*, and stem *limin-*, of *limen*, threshold.]

ELIMINATION (e-lim-i-nā'shun) *n.* the act of setting aside or throwing out.

ELISION (e-lizh'un) *n.* the cutting off of a vowel or syllable.
ELITE (ā-lēt') *n.* the select or best in society. [F.]
ELIXIR (e-lik'ser) *n.* a compound tincture; any invigorating cordial. [A.]
ELK (elk) *n.* a species of stag. [Scand.]
ELL (el) *n.* a yard and a quarter. [O.E. *eln,* orig. arm. Cf. Ger. *Elle.*]
ELLIPSE (e-lips') *n.* an oval figure; path which the planets describe round the sun. [For EL-LIPSIS, which see.]
ELLIPSIS (e-lip'sis) *n.* in *Grammar,* the omission of a word or phrase. [L., fr. G. *el-leipsis,* defect, fr. *en,* in (behind), and *leipein,* leave.]

Ellipse.

ELLIPTICAL (e-lip'ti-kąl) *a.* oval; having a part omitted.
ELLIPTICITY (el-ip-tis'i-ti) *n.* deviation from the form of a circle.
ELM (elm) *n.* a forest tree, valued for its timber. [E. Cf. L. *ulmus.*]
ELOCUTION (el-u-kū'shun) *n.* pronunciation or delivery of words. [L. *e, ex,* out, and LOCUTION.]
ELOCUTIONARY (el-u-kū'shun-ąr-i) *a.* pertaining to elocution.
ELOCUTIONIST (el-u-kū'shun-ist) *n.* one versed in elocution.
ELOHIM (ē-lō'him) *n.* one of the names of God. [H.]
ELOHISTIC (el-ō-his'tik) *a.* denoting passages in the Pentateuch in which Elohim is used and not Jehovah. [H.]
ELONGATE (ē-long'gāt) *v.t.* to draw out in length. [L. *e, ex,* out, and LONG.]
ELONGATION (ē-long-gā'shun) *n.* a lengthening; distance.
ELOPE (e-lōp') *v.i.* to run away without permission. [Etym. uncertain.]
ELOPEMENT (e-lōp'ment) *n.* a departure clandestinely.
ELOQUENCE (el'ō-kwens) *n.* beauty, power, and appropriateness of oral or written discourse.
ELOQUENT (el'ō-kwent) *a.* speaking with eloquence or persuasive power. [F., fr. L. (acc. part.) *eloquentem,* speaking out, fr. *e, ex,* and *loqui.*]
ELOQUENTLY (el'ō-kwent-li) *ad.* in an eloquent manner.
ELSE (els) *a.* and *pron.* other; one or something besides;—*conj.* otherwise; if it were not so. [O.E. *elles.*]
ELSEWHERE (els'hwār) *ad.* in some other place.
ELUCIDATE (e-lū'si-dāt) *v.t.* to make clear; bring out the meaning of. [L. *e, ex,* and LUCID.]
ELUCIDATION (e-lū-si-dā'shun) *n.* act of throwing light on an obscure topic; exposition.
ELUCIDATIVE (e-lū'si-dā-tiv) *a.* making plain or clear.
ELUCIDATOR (e-lū'si-dā-ter) *n.* one who explains.
ELUDE (e-lūd') *v.t.* to escape by stratagem; remain undiscovered. [L., fr. *e, ex,* and *ludere,* play.]
ELUSION (ē-lū'zhun) *n.* escape; evasion. [See ELUDE.]
ELUSIVE (e-lū'siv) *a.* practising elusion.
ELUSORY (e-lū'su-ri) *a.* tending to elude.
ELVISH (el'vish) *a.* elfish; mischievous. [See ELF.]
ELYSIAN (e-lizh'ąn) *a.* very delightful.
ELYSIUM (e-lizh'i-um) *n.* a place of unmixed happiness. [L., fr. G.]
EMACIATE (e-mā'shi-āt) *v.i.* to lose flesh;—*v.t.* to reduce to leanness;—*a.* wasted; thin. [L. (part.) *emaciatus,* made thin, fr. *e, ex,* and *macies,* leanness.]

EMACIATION (e-mā-shi-ā'shun) *n.* act of becoming lean.
EMANANT (em'ą-nąnt) *a.* issuing from.
EMANATE (em'ą-nāt) *v.i.* to flow from. [L. (part.) *emanatus,* fr. *e, ex,* out, and *manare,* flow.]
EMANATION (em-ą-nā'shun) *n.* act of flowing from; that which proceeds from.
EMANATIVE (em'ą-nāt-iv) *a.* issuing; flowing forth.
EMANCIPATE (e-man'si-pāt) *v.t.* to free from servitude. [L. (part.) *emancipatus,* declared free, fr. *e, ex,* out, and *mancipare,* formally to transfer, fr. *manus,* hand, and *capere,* take.]
EMANCIPATION (e-man-si-pā'shun) *n.* act of emancipating; liberation; release; freedom.
EMANCIPATOR (ē-man'si-pā-ter) *n.* one who frees from slavery. [L.]
EMASCULATE (e-mas'kū-lāt) *v.t.* to deprive of manly vigour or spirit; render effeminate. [L. *e, ex,* out, and *masculus,* MASCULINE.]
EMBALM (em-bäm') *v.t.* to preserve from decay with aromatics; cherish or perpetuate. [F. *embaumer.*]
EMBANK (em-bangk') *v.t.* to enclose or defend with mounds or ditches. [F. (pref.) *em* =L. *in,* and BANK.]
EMBANKMENT (em-bangk'ment) *n.* a mound or bank.
EMBARGO em-bär'gō) *n.* prohibition of vessels from sailing; any restraint. [Sp., conn. with BAR.]
EMBARK (em-bärk') *v.t.* or *i.* to enter on board; engage in. [F. *embarquer,* fr. Late L. *imbarcare,* fr. *in,* and BARK.]
EMBARKATION (em-bär-kā'shun) *n.* act of putting or going on board.
EMBARRASS (em-bar'ąs) *v.t.* to perplex. [F. *embarrasser,* lit. keep back, fr. Sp., conn. with BAR.]
EMBARRASSING (em-bar'ąs-ing) *a.* tending to perplex or abash.
EMBARRASSMENT (em-bar'as-ment) *n.* perplexity; pecuniary distress.
EMBASSY (em'bą-si) *n.* the charge or commission of an ambassador; the dwelling or suite of an ambassador. [F. *ambassee.* See AMBASSADOR.]
EMBELLISH (em-bel'ish) *v.t.* to make beautiful by adornment. [F. *embellissant,* beautifying, fr. O.F. (pref.) *em-,* and *bel,* fair.]
EMBELLISHMENT (em-bel'ish-ment) *n.* act of adorning; decoration.
EMBER-DAYS (em'ber-dāz) *n.pl.* certain days appointed for fasting—three in each quarter. [O.E. *ymbryne,* a circuit, fr. *ymb,* round, and *rinnan,* run.]
EMBERS (em'berz) *n.pl.* hot cinders. [M.E. *emeres.*]
EMBEZZLE (em-bez'l) *v.t.* to appropriate by breach of trust. [O.F., of uncertain etym.]
EMBEZZLEMENT (em-bez'l-ment) *n.* unlawful appropriation of what is entrusted to one's care.
EMBEZZLER (em-bez'ler) *n.* one who embezzles.
EMBLAZON (em-blā'zn) *v.t.* to adorn with figures of heraldry; deck in glaring colours. [F. *em,* and *blazon,* shield.]
EMBLAZONRY (em-blā'zn-ri) *n.* display of figures on shields.
EMBLEM (em'blem) *n.* a picture or representation imaging forth a truth; a type. [F., fr. L., fr. G. *emblema,* work in relief, fr. *en,* on, and *ballein,* throw.]
EMBLEMATICAL (em-ble-mat'i-kąl) *a.* comprising an emblem.
EMBLEMATICALLY (em-ble-mat'i-kąl-i) *ad.* by or with an emblem.
EMBODY (em-bod'i) *v.t.* or *i.* to form into a body, as troops; give form or expression to. [*Em,* in, and BODY.]
EMBOGUE (em-bōg') *v.i.* to discharge itself, as a river. [Sp., fr. L. *in,* and *bucca,* mouth.]

EMBOLDEN (em-bōl'dn) v.t. to give courage to. [See BOLD.]

EMBOLISM (em'bu-lizm) n. the obstruction of a blood-vessel by a clot of fibrin; insertion of days or periods in a calendar; intercalation. [L., fr. G. embolismos, insertion, fr. en, in, and ballein, throw.]

EMBOLUS (em'bu-lus) n. a clot of fibrine obstructing a blood-vessel and causing embolism; a piston or driver. [See EMBOLISM.]

EMBOSS (em-bos') v.t. to adorn with protuberances. [See BOSS.]

EMBOSSMENT (em-bos'ment) n. raised work.

EMBOUCHURE (äng-bōō-shōōr') n. mouth of a river, cannon, etc.; mouth-hole of a flute, etc. [F., fr. bouche, mouth, fr. L. (acc.) buccam.]

EMBOWER (em-bou'er) v.t. to place in a bower. [See BOWER.]

EMBRACE (em-brās') v.t. to clasp in the arms; cherish; surround; include; accept eagerly; —n. clasp with the arms. [F. embrasser, fr. bras, arm. See BRACE.]

EMBRASURE (em-brā'zhur) n. an opening through which cannon are pointed. [F., of uncertain etym.]

EMBROCATE (em'bru-kāt) v.t. to moisten and rub a diseased part. [O.F., fr. Late L. (part.) embrocatus, fomented, fr. G. embroche, fomentation.]

Embrasure.

EMBROCATION (em-bro-kā'shun) n. a moistening and rubbing with cloth, etc., a diseased part.

EMBROIDER (em-broi'der) v.t. to border with figured needlework. [O.F. embroder, fr. em, and broder, prob. Celt.]

EMBROIDERY (em-broi'der-i) n. variegated needlework.

EMBROIL (em-broil') v.t. to disturb; confuse. [F. embrouiller, confuse, fr. BROIL.]

EMBROILMENT (em-broil'ment) n. a state of contention or confusion; disturbance.

EMBRYO (em'bri-ō) n. the rudiments of an animal or plant;—a. denoting anything in its first rudiments. [Formerly embryon, fr. F., fr. G. embruon.]

EMBRYOLOGY (em-bri-ol'ō-ji) n. the science of the development of embryos. [Fr. G. logia, science, fr. legein. See EMBRYO.]

EMENDABLE (e-men'da-bl) a. that may be amended.

EMENDATION (ē-men-dā'shun) n. correction.

EMENDATOR (ē-men-dā'ter) n. one who corrects or improves.

EMENDATORY (ē-men'da-tur-i) a. amending.

EMERALD (em'e-rald) n. a precious stone of a green colour; a small printing type. [M.E. esmeraude, fr. O.F., corr. fr. L. smaragdus, fr. G. smaragdos.]

EMERGE (e-merj') v.i. to rise out of a fluid; come into view. [L. emergere, fr. e, ex, and mergere, plunge. See MERGE.]

EMERGENCY (e-mer'jen-si) n. a rising out from; a sudden event; pressing necessity.

EMERGENT (e-mer'jent) a. rising out of; urgent; pressing.

EMERITUS (ē-mer'i-tus) n. one who has honourably retired from office. [L. =a veteran, fr. e, out, and merere, MERIT.]

EMERODS (em-er-ods) n. the piles. Also written HEMORRHOIDS. [G. haima, and rhein, flow.]

EMERSION (ē-mer'shun) n. a rising out of. [Fr. L. (part.) emersus, raised.]

EMERY (em'e-ri) n. a mineral used in polishing. [Fr. emcril, fr. O.F. esmeril, through It., fr. G. smeris.]

EMETIC (e-met'ik) a. producing vomiting; —n. a medicine producing vomits. [G., fr. eme-ein, vomit.]

EMIGRANT (em'i-grant) a. removing from one country or state to another for residence; —n. one who emigrates. [See EMIGRATE.]

EMIGRATE (em'i-grāt) v.i. to remove from one country or state to another for residence. [L., fr. e, ex, and MIGRATE.]

EMIGRATION (em-i-grā'shun) n. act of emigrating to another country.

EMINENCE (em'i-nens) n. a rising; distinction; title of cardinals.

EMINENT (em'i-nent) a. exalted in rank or public estimation; distinguished; conspicuous; celebrated. [L. (part. stem) eminent-, standing out. fr. eminere.]

EMINENTLY (em'i-nent-li) ad. conspicuously; in a high degree.

EMIR (e-mēr') n. an Arabian chief; a title of honour in Turkey. [A. amir.]

EMISSARY (em'i-sar-i) n. a secret agent;— a. exploring. [L., fr. (part.) emissus, sent out.]

EMISSION (e-mish'un) n. act of sending out; circulation; issue.

EMISSIVE (e-mis'iv) a. sending out. [L., fr. e, ex, and mittere, send.]

EMIT (e-mit') v.t. to send out. [L. fr. e, ex, and mittere, send.]

EMMET (em'et) n. an ant; pismire. [M.E., fr. O.E. Doublet of ANT.]

EMOLLIATE (e-mol'i-āt) v.t. to soften.

EMOLLIENT (e-mol'i-ent) a. softening. [O.F., fr. L. (acc. part.) emollientem, softening, fr. e, ex, and mollire.]

EMOLUMENT (e-mol'ū-ment) n. profit; gain. [L. =orig. exertion, fr. e, ex, outright, and moliri, toil.]

EMOTION (e-mō'shun) n. excitement of the feelings; agitation of mind. [L. e, ex, much, and movere, to move.]

EMOTIONAL (e-mō'shun-al) a. exciting or excited by the feelings.

EMOTIONALISM (e-mō'shun-al-izm) n. tendency to excitement.

EMPALE (em-pāl') v.t. to enclose with pickets; fix on a stake. [F. empaler, fr. L. in, and palus, a stake.]

EMPALEMENT (em-pāl'ment) n. a fortifying with stakes; an impaling.

EMPANEL (em-pan'el) v.t. to form or enrol a jury. [L. in, and PANEL. Also IMPANEL.]

EMPEROR (em'per-er) n. the sovereign of an empire. [O.F. empereor (4 syll.), fr. L. (acc.) imperatorem, fr. imperare, command.]

EMPHASIS (em'fa-sis) n. force impressed by pronunciation;—pl. EMPHASES. [L., fr. G. =force, fr. en, in, and phainein, show.]

EMPHASISE (em'fa-sīz) v.t. to utter with a particular stress of voice.

EMPHATIC (em-fat'ik) a. forcible; strong; uttered with emphasis.

EMPHATICALLY (em-fat'i-kal-i) ad. with emphasis; forcibly; decidedly.

EMPIRE (em'pir) n. dominions of an emperor; supreme control. [F., fr. L. imperium.]

EMPIRIC (em-pir'ik) n. a quack. [L., fr. G. empeirikos, fr. en, in, and peira, trial.]

EMPIRICAL (em-pir'i-kal) a. used and applied without science.

EMPIRICALLY (em-pir'i-kal-i) ad. by experiment.

EMPIRICISM (em-pir'i-sizm) n. quackery.

EMPLOY (em-ploi') v.t. to use; exercise; engage; hire;—n. business; occupation; service of another. [F. employer, fr. L. implicare. Doublet of IMPLY, IMPLICATE.]

EMPLOYEE (em-ploi-ē') n. one who is employed. [F., fr. (part.) employé, employed.]

EMPLOYER (em-ploi'er) n. one who employs.

EMPLOYMENT (em-ploi'ment) n. business; office; avocation.

EMPORIUM (em-pō'ri-um) n. a place of merchandise; a mart. [L., fr. G., fr. emporos, trader, traveller, fr. en, in, and poros, way.]

EMPOWER (em-pou'er) *v.t.* to authorise.
EMPRESS (em'pres) *n.* a woman invested with imperial dignity. [See **EMPEROR**.]
EMPRISE (em-prīz') *n.* undertaking; adventure. [O.F. (fem. part.) = undertaken, fr. *em* = L. *in*, and *prise*, a taking, fr. L. *prehendere*, take.]
EMPTINESS (emp'ti-nes) *n.* vanity; vacuity.
EMPTY (emp'ti) *a.* void; unfurnished;—*v.t.* or *i.* to exhaust. [O.E. *æmtig*, leisurely, fr. *æmta*.]
EMPYREAL (em-pir'ē-al) *a.* formed of pure fire or light.
EMPYREAN (em-pi-rē'an) *n.* the highest and purest heaven. [L., fr. G. *empuros*, lit. in fire, fiery, fr. *en*, and *pur*.]
EMU (ē'mū) *n.* a large running bird of Australia. [Port.]
EMULATE (em'ū-lāt) *v.t.* to vie with; strive to equal. [L. (part.) *æmulatus*, having vied.]
EMULATION (em-ū-lā'shun) *n.* rivalry.
EMULATIVE (em'ū-lāt-iv) *a.* inclined to contend for superiority.
EMULATOR (em'ū-lā-ter) *n.* a competitor.
EMULOUS (em'ū-lus) *a.* rivalling. [L. *æmulus*.]
EMULOUSLY (em'ū-lus-li) *ad.* with desire to equal or excel another.
EMULSION (ē-mul'shun) *n.* a softening medicine. [Fr. L. (part.) *emulsus*, milked out, fr. *e*, *ex*, and *mulgere*.]
EMULSIVE (ē-mul'siv) *a.* mollifying.
EN (en) a prefix, usually signifies *in* or *on*. [O.F. and F., fr. L. *in*.]
ENABLE (en-ā'bl) *v.t.* to make able.
ENABLEMENT (en-ā'bl-ment) *n.* the act of enabling; ability.
ENACT (en-akt') *v.t.* to establish by law; perform.
ENACTIVE (en-ak'tiv) *a.* having power to establish, as law.
ENACTMENT (en-akt'ment) *n.* the passing of a bill into a law; a law or act; playing of a part or character.
ENACTOR (en-ak'ter) *n.* one who enacts or acts. [See **ENACT**.]
ENAMEL (en-nam'el) *n.* a substance imperfectly vitrified; substance on teeth;—*v.t.* to cover with enamel. [O.F. *enamailer*, fr. *amaile*. *esmail* = F. *émail*, enamel, fr. Teut.]
ENAMELLER (en-nam'el-er) *n.* one who enamels.
ENAMELLING (e-nam'el-ing) *n.* the art of laying on enamel.
ENAMOUR (e-nam'ur) *v.t.* to inflame with love; make fond. [F., fr. *en amour*, in love.]
ENCAMP (en-kamp') *v.t.* or *i.* to pitch tents.
ENCAMPMENT (en-kamp'ment) *n.* act of pitching tents; a camp.
ENCAUSTIC (en-kaws'tik) *a.* or *n.* painting in heated or burnt wax. [L., fr. G., fr. *en*, in, and **CAUSTIC**.]
ENCEINTE (áng-sangt') *n.* ground enclosed within a wall or rampart;—*a.* pregnant. [F.]
ENCEPHALIC (en-se-fal'ik) *a.* pertaining to the head or brain. [G. *en*, in, and *kephale*, head.]
ENCEPHALITIS (en-sef-al-ī'tis) *n.* inflammation of the brain.
ENCHANT (en-chánt') *v.t.* to charm. [F. *enchanter*, fr. L. *incantare*, to sing an **INCANTATION**.]
ENCHANTER (en-chán'ter) *n.* a magician.
ENCHANTINGLY (en-chán'ting-li) *ad.* with the power of enchantment.
ENCHANTMENT (en-chánt'ment) *n.* fascination; irresistible influence.
ENCHANTRESS (en-chán'tres) *n.* a sorceress.
ENCHASE (en-chās') *v.t.* to adorn by embossed work. [F. *enchâsser*, to place in a *châsse*, **CASE**.]
ENCIRCLE (en-ser'kl) *v.t.* to enclose by a circle; embrace; surround.

ENCLITIC (en-klit'ik) *a.* that inclines or leans upon;—*n.* a particle suffixed to another word. [G. *egklitikos* (*eng*-), fr. *en*, in, on, and *klinein*, lean.]
ENCLOISTER (en-klois'ter) *v.t.* to shut up in a cloister.
ENCLOSE (en-klōz') *v.t.* to inclose.
ENCLOSURE (en-klōz'ūr) *n.* inclosure.
ENCLOUDED (en-kloud'ed) *a.* covered with clouds.
ENCOMIAST (en-kō'mi-ast) *n.* one who praises another. [G. *eukomiastes*.]
ENCOMIUM (en-kō'mi-um) *n.* panegyric; formal and high praise. [Fr. G. *egkomion*, a song of revelry, praise, fr. *en*, and *komos*, revel.]
ENCOMPASS (en-kum'pas) *v.t.* to go round; encircle; surround; enclose.
ENCORE (ang-kōr') *n.* a call for a repetition of some performance;—*v.t.* to call for repetition. [F.]
ENCOUNTER (en-koun'ter) *n.* a sudden meeting; combat; engagement;—*v.t.* to meet face to face; meet suddenly. [O.F. *encontrer*, fr. *contre*, against, fr. L. *contra*.]
ENCOURAGE (en-kur'ij) *v.t.* to give courage to; animate. [F. *encourager*.]
ENCOURAGEMENT (en-kur'ij-ment) *n.* incitement; hope.
ENCOURAGING (en-kur'ij-ing) *a.* favouring.
ENCOURAGINGLY (en-kur'ij-ing-li) *ad.* so as to give hope of success.
ENCROACH (en-krōch') *v.i.* to intrude on another's rights; infringe. [O.F. *encrochier*, seize, lit. hook, fr. *croc*, a hook.]
ENCROACHMENT (en-krōch'ment) *n.* unlawful intrusion; inroad.
ENCUMBER (en-kum'ber) *v.t.* to impede action by a load or burden. [O.F. *encombrer*.]
ENCUMBERINGLY (en-kum'ber-ing-li) *ad.* in a way to burden or impede.
ENCUMBRANCE (en-kum'brans) *n.* a load; clog; burden on an estate.
ENCYCLICAL (en-sik'lik-al) *a.* sent to many persons or places. [Fr. G. *enkuklios*, circular fr. *en*, and *kuklos*, circle.]
ENCYCLOPEDIA (en-si-klō-pē'di-a) *n.* a work that embodies the whole circle of sciences. Also written **ENCYCLOPÆDIA**. [Fr. G. for *en(g)kuklios*, **ENCYCLICAL**, circular, and *paideia*, instruction, fr. stem *paid*-, of *pais*, boy.]
END (end) *n.* extreme point; ultimate object; close; death;—*v.t.* or *i.* to finish; close. [O.E. *ende*. Cf. Ger. *Ende*.]
ENDANGER (en-dān'jer) *v.t.* to bring into peril.
ENDANGERMENT (en-dān'jer-ment) *n.* peril; hazard.
ENDEAR (en-dēr') *v.t.* to render dear.
ENDEARMENT (en-dēr'ment) *n.* that which excites tender affection; state of being fondly loved.
ENDEAVOUR (en-dev'ur) *n.* effort; attempt; —*v.i.* to exert oneself; labour; try;—*v.t.* to strive after; attempt. [M.E. *devoir*, duty, fr. F.]
ENDEMIC (en-dem'ik) *a.* peculiar to a people or a district;—*n.* a disease in a particular place or season. [Fr. G. *endemos* popular, fr. *en*, in, and *demos*, a people.]
ENDING (end'ing) *n.* termination.
ENDIVE (en'div) *n.* a garden vegetable. [F., fr. L.]
ENDLESS (end'les) *a.* having no end.
ENDLESSLY (end'les-li) *ad.* without end.
ENDOGENOUS (en-doj'en-us) *a.* increasing by internal growth, as the palm, etc. [Fr. G. *endon*, within, and root *gen*-, of *gignesthai*, be born, *genes*, born.]
ENDORSE [See **INDORSE**.]
ENDOW (en-dou') *v.t.* to furnish with dower, funds, or other gift. [Norman F. *endouer*, fr. L. *dotare*, fr. *dos*, marriage portion.]

ENDOWMENT (en-dou'ment) *n.* act of settling a fund; property or revenue; talent; gift.

ENDURABLE (en-dūr'a-bl) *a.* that can be borne.

ENDURANCE (en-dūr'ans) *n.* continuance; suffering; patience.

ENDURE (en-dūr') *v.i.* to continue;—*v.t.* to bear or undergo. [O.F. *endurer*, fr. L. *indurare*, fr. *durus*, hard.]

ENEMA (e-nē'ma) *n.* an injection of fluid into the bowels by the rectum. [G. *enieni*, send in.]

ENEMY (en'e-mi) *n.* a foe; adversary. [L. *inimicus*, fr. *in*, negative, and *amicus*, friend.]

ENERGETIC (en-er-jet'ik) *a.* operating with vigour; active; effective; vigorous.

ENERGETICS (en-er-jet'iks) *n.* the science of physical and mechanical forces. [See **ENERGY**.]

ENERGISE (en'er-jīz) *v.i.* to act with energy; —*v.t.* to employ with energy.

ENERGY (en'er-ji) *n.* internal strength; force of expression; vigour; spirit; resolution. [G. *en*, in, and *ergon*, work.]

ENERVATE (ē-ner'vāt) *v.t.* to deprive of nerve. [L. *enervare*, weaken, fr. *e*, out, and *nervus*, nerve.]

ENERVATION (en-er-vā'shun) *n.* act of weakening.

ENFEEBLE (en-fē'bl) *v.t.* to weaken.

ENFEEBLEMENT (en-fē'bl-ment) *n.* a weakening; enervation.

ENFILADE (en-fi-lād') *n.* a straight line;— *v.t.* to rake with shot through the whole length of a line or work. [F. *en*, and *fil*, a thread.]

ENFORCE (en-fōrs') *v.t.* to put in execution. [O.F., fr. L. *in*, and **FORCE**.]

ENFORCEMENT (en-fōrs'ment) *n.* act of enforcing; compulsion.

ENFORCER (en-fōr'ser) *n.* one who carries into effect.

ENFORCIBLE (en-fōr'si-bl) *a.* capable of being enforced.

ENFOREST (en-for'est) *v.t.* to turn land into forest.

ENFRANCHISE (en-fran'shiz) *v.t.* to set free; admit to civil and political privileges. [F. *en* and *franc*, free.]

ENFRANCHISEMENT (en-fran'shiz-ment) *n.* act of setting free; admission to civil and political rights.

ENGAGE (en-gāj') *v.t.* to encounter; bind by contract. [F. *engager*, fr. *en*, and *gage*, pledge.]

ENGAGED (en-gājd') *a.* promised; attached; occupied.

ENGAGEMENT (en-gāj'ment) *n.* a battle; obligation; promise; occupation.

ENGAGING (en-gā'jing) *a.* attractive; winning.

ENGAGINGLY (en-gā'jing-li) *ad.* in a way to win or attract; pleasingly.

ENGENDER (en-jen'der) *v.t.* to beget; produce. [F. *engendrer*, fr. L. *in*, and *generare*, produce, beget.]

ENGINE (en'jin) *n.* an instrument of action; machine. [L. *ingenium*, skill, invention.]

ENGINEER (en-ji-nēr') *n.* one skilled in mathematics and mechanics, and who superintends works for military or civil objects.

ENGINEERING (en-ji-nēr'ing) *n.* the art of an engineer.

ENGIRD (en-gerd') *v.t.* [*pret.* and *pp.* **ENGIRDED, ENGIRT**] to encompass; encircle. [See **GIRD**.]

ENGLISH (ing'glish) *a.* pertaining to England; —*n.* the people or language of England. [O.E. *Englisc*, fr. *Engle*, the Angles.]

ENGORGE (en-gorj') *v.t.* or *i.* to swallow greedily; devour.

ENGORGED (en-gorjd') *a.* too full of blood; congested.

ENGORGEMENT (en-gorj'ment) *n.* act of devouring; congestion.

ENGRAIN (en-grān') *v.t.* to dye in grain; dye deep. [Orig. to dye, *i.e.* with cochineal berries.]

ENGRAVE (en-grāv') *v.t.* [*pret.* **ENGRAVED**; *pp.* **ENGRAVEN**] to cut with a chisel or graver; impress deeply. [F. *en* = L. *in*, and **GRAVE**.]

ENGRAVER (en-grā'ver) *n.* one who engraves.

ENGRAVING (en-grā'ving) *n.* the art of engraving; that which is engraved.

ENGROSS (en-grōs') *v.t.* to seize or buy the whole; write in a large hand. [Fr. F. *en grosse*, in a large hand.]

ENGROSSER (en-grō'ser) *n.* a monopoliser; one who writes a fair hand.

ENGROSSING (en-grōs'ing) *n.* copying deeds or documents; monopolising.

ENGROSSMENT (en-grōs'ment) *n.* act of engrossing; exorbitant acquisition.

ENGULF (en-gulf') *v.t.* to throw or absorb, as in a gulf.

ENHANCE (en-hans') *v.t.* to heighten in price; aggravate;—*v.i.* to grow larger; swell. [O.F. *enhauncer*, *-haucer*, fr. Late L. *inaltiare*, fr. L. *altus*, high.]

ENHANCEMENT (en-hans'ment) *n.* act of increasing; state of being increased.

ENIGMA (e-nig'ma) *n.* an obscure question; riddle; anything unaccountable. [L., fr. G. *ainigma*.]

ENIGMATICAL (e-nig-mat'i-kal) *a.* containing a riddle; obscure.

ENIGMATIST (e-nig'ma-tist) *n.* a dealer in enigmas or riddles.

ENJOIN (en-join') *v.t.* to command; order; forbid judicially. [F. *enjoindre*, fr. L. *injungere*, ordain, lit. join into.]

ENJOINER (en-join'er) *n.* one who enjoins.

ENJOINMENT (en-join'ment) *n.* direction; command.

ENJOY (en-joi') *v.t.* to feel, perceive, possess, or use with pleasure. [O.F., fr. *en*, and *joie*, joy.]

ENJOYMENT (en-joi'ment) *n.* possession with pleasure; fruition.

ENKINDLE (en-kin'dl) *v.t.* to set on fire; excite;—*v.i.* to take fire.

ENLARGE (en-lärj') *v.t.* or *i.* to swell; increase; amplify.

ENLARGEMENT (en-lärj'ment) *n.* increase of bulk; release.

ENLIGHTEN (en-li'tn) *v.t.* to illuminate; instruct.

ENLIGHTENER (en-li'tn-er) *n.* one who illuminates or instructs.

ENLIGHTENMENT (en-li'tn-ment) *n.* act of enlightening; state of being enlightened.

ENLIST (en-list') *v.t.* or *i.* to enter a name on a list; enroll. [*ing*.

ENLISTMENT (en-list'ment) *n.* act of enlist-

ENLIVEN (en-li'vn) *v.t.* to animate; cheer.

ENLIVENER (en-li'vn-er) *n.* one who animates.

ENMESH (en-mesh') *v.t.* to entangle; entrap.

ENMITY (en'mi-ti) *n.* ill-will; hatred; hostility. [O.F. *enemite*, *enemis-tié* (*-tya*), fr. L. *in-*, negative, and **AMITY**.]

ENNOBLE (e-nō'bl) *v.t.* to make noble. [See **NOBLE**.]

ENNOBLEMENT (e-nō'bl-ment) *n.* act of ennobling; dignity.

ENNUI (ä'nü-e) *n.* lassitude; languor; dullness of spirit. [O.F. = *anui*. See **ANNOY**.]

ENORMITY (e-nor'mi-ti) *n.* atrociousness. [See **ENORMOUS**.]

ENORMOUS (e-nor'mus) *a.* beyond all natural or ordinary limits; immense; excessive. [Formerly *enorm*, fr. O.F., fr. L. (*ace.*) *enormem*, fr. *e*, *ex*, and *norma*, a rule. See **NORM**.]

ENORMOUSLY (e-nor'mus-li) *ad.* beyond measure; atrociously.

ENOUGH (e-nuf') *a.* sufficient;—*n.* sufficiency; —*ad.* sufficiently. [M.E. *enogh,* fr. O.E. *genog.* Cf. Ger. *genug.*]

ENRAGE (en-rāj') *v.t.* to irritate; provoke to fury.

ENRAPTURE (en-rap'tūr) *v.t.* to throw into rapture.

ENRAVISH (en-rav'ish) *v.t.* to throw into ecstasy.

ENRAVISHINGLY (en-rav'ish-ing-li) *ad.* so as to produce extreme delight.

ENRAVISHMENT (en-rav'ish-ment) *n.* rapture.

ENREGISTER (en-rej'is-ter) *v.t.* to enrol; record.

ENRICH (en-rich') *v.t.* to make rich.

ENRICHMENT (en-rich'ment) *n.* the state of being enriched; decoration.

ENRIDGE (en-rij') *v.t.* to form into ridges.

ENROBE (en-rōb') *v.t.* to attire.

ENROLL (en-rōl') *v.t.* to register.

ENROLMENT (en-rōl'ment) *n.* a registering.

ENSAMPLE (en-sâm'pl) *n.* an example. [O.F. *es-sample.* See SAMPLE.]

ENSCONCE (en-skons') *v.t.* to shelter; hide safely.

ENSEMBLE (âng-sâm'bl) *n.* all parts taken together. [F.]

ENSHIELD (en-shēld') *v.t.* to shield.

ENSHRINE (en-shrīn') *v.t.* to enclose in a chest; lay up choicely; cherish.

ENSHROUD (en-shroud') *v.t.* to cover, as with a shroud.

ENSIGN (en'sīn) *n.* an officer that carries a standard; a flag. [F. *enseigne,* fr. Late L. (pl.) *insignia,* standards. See SIGN, INSIGNIA.]

ENSIGNCY (en'sīn-si) *n.* rank or commission of an ensign. [See ENSIGN.]

ENSILAGE (en'si-lij) *n.* a mode of preserving fodder in pits. [F., through Sp., fr. L. *in,* and *sirus,* a pit for grain, fr. G.]

Ensign.

ENSLAVE (en-slāv') *v.t.* to deprive of liberty; subject.

ENSLAVEMENT (en-slāv'ment) *n.* state of servitude; slavery.

ENSNARE (en-snār') *v.t.* to catch in a snare; to entangle.

ENSUE (en-sū') *v.t.* to pursue; follow;—*v.i.* to come after, as an event or consequence; succeed. [O.F. *ensuir* = F. *ensuivre,* fr. Late L. *insequere.* fr. L. *insequi,* follow.]

ENSUING (en-sū'ing) *ppr.* next following.

ENTABLATURE (en-tab'la-tūr) *n.* part of a column over the capital. [O.F., fr. *en,* and L. *tabula,* board.]

ENTAIL (en-tāl') *n.* an estate entailed;—*v.t.* to settle an estate so as to descend to a particular heir. [Fr. *en,* and F. *tailler,* cut. See RETAIL, TAILOR.]

ENTAILMENT (en-tāl'ment) *n.* act of limiting an estate to a particular heir.

ENTANGLE (en-tang'gl) *v.t.* to make intricate; perplex; involve. [*cacy.*

ENTANGLEMENT (en-tang'gl-ment) *n.* intri-

ENTER (en'ter) *v.t.* to go or come into; penetrate; insert; enroll; record; begin; attain; take possession;—*v.i.* to go or come in; engage in; form a part of. [F. *entrer,* fr. L. *intrare,* to go into, fr. *in,* and root of *trans,* across. Cf. PENETRATE.]

ENTERIC (en-ter'ik) *a.* relating to the intestines. [G., fr. *enteron,* intestine, fr. *entos,* within.]

ENTERITIS (en-te-rī'tis) *n.* inflammation of the intestines. [See ENTERIC.]

ENTERPRISE (en'ter-priz) *n.* an undertaking; a bold attempt. [O.F., fr. (part.) *entrepris,* undertaken, fr. *entre,* among, and *prendere,* L. *inter,* and *prehendere.* See PRIZE.]

ENTERPRISING (en'ter-prī-zing) *a.* bold or resolute to undertake.

ENTERTAIN (en-ter-tān') *v.t.* to treat with hospitality; amuse; cherish; maintain;— *v.i.* to receive guests. [O.F. *entretenir,* maintain, fr. L. *inter,* among, and *tenere,* hold.]

ENTERTAINING (en-ter-tā'ning) *a.* amusing.

ENTERTAINMENT (en-ter-tān'ment) *n.* amusement; hospitality.

ENTHRAL (en-thrawl') *v.t.* to enslave. [O.E. *thræl,* slave, fr. *thrægian,* run.]

ENTHRONE (en-thrōn') *v.t.* to place on a throne.

ENTHRONEMENT (en-thrōn'ment) *n.* act of enthroning.

ENTHRONISATION (en-thrō-ni-zā'shun) *n.* placing of a bishop in his cathedral throne or stall.

ENTHUSIASM (en-thū'zi-azm) *n.* ardent zeal in respect to some object or pursuit; heat of imagination. [G., fr. *enthousiazein,* to be inspired, fr. *entheos,* lit. having a god within, fr. *en* and *theos.*]

ENTHUSIAST (en-thū'zi-ast) *n.* one intensely earnest for a cause or object. [G. *enthousiastes.*]

ENTHUSIASTIC (en-thū-zi-as'tik) *a.* full of enthusiasm.

ENTHUSIASTICALLY (en-thū-zi-as'ti-kal-i) *ad.* with enthusiasm.

ENTICE (en-tīs') *v.t.* to incite to evil; allure. [O.F. *ticier,* excite, fr. L. *in,* and root of *titio,* firebrand.]

ENTICEMENT (en-tīs'ment) *n.* the act or means of alluring.

ENTICER (en-tī'ser) *n.* one who entices.

ENTICINGLY (en-tī'sing-li) *ad.* in a winning or attractive manner; charmingly. [See ENTICE.]

ENTIRE (en-tīr') *a.* forming an unbroken whole; complete; full; pure. [O.F. *entier,* fr. L. (acc.) *integrum.* Doublet of INTEGER.]

ENTIRELY (en-tīr'li) *ad.* wholly; fully.

ENTIRENESS (en-tīr'nes) *n.* fullness; completeness. [whole.

ENTIRETY (en-tīr'ti) *n.* completeness; the

ENTITLE (en-tī'tl) *v.t.* to give a right to.

ENTITY (en'ti-ti) *n.* real existence. [Fr. L. stem *enti-,* of *ens,* a being, fr. *esse,* to be.]

ENTOMB (en-tōòm') *v.t.* to deposit in a tomb.

ENTOMBMENT (en-tōòm'ment) *n.* burial.

ENTOMOLOGICAL (en-tu-mu-loj'i-kal) *a.* pertaining to the science of insects. [See ENTOMOLOGY.]

ENTOMOLOGIST (en-tu-mol'ō-jist) *n.* one versed in entomology.

ENTOMOLOGY (en-tu-mol'ō-ji) *n.* description of insects. [Fr. G. *entomon,* insect = orig. (neut. adj.) cut into, fr. *en,* and *temnein,* to cut, and *logia,* science.]

ENTRAILS (en'trālz) *n.pl.* the bowels; intestines. [O.F. *entraille,* fr. Late L. (neut. pl.) *intralia,* fr. *inter,* within.]

ENTRAIN (en-trān') *v.t.* to despatch by rail, as troops.

ENTRANCE (en'trans) *n.* a going or coming in. [See ENTER.]

ENTRANCE (en-trans') *v.t.* to put into a trance or into ecstasy. [See TRANCE.]

ENTRANT (en'trant) *n.* one who begins a study, profession, or career.

ENTRAP (en-trap') *v.t.* to catch in a trap.

ENTREAT (en-trēt') *v.t.* or *i.* to supplicate; importune; use or manage. [O.F. *entraitre,* to treat with; pref. *en.*]

ENTREATINGLY (en-trē'ting-li) *ad.* in an importunate manner.

ENTREATY (en-trē'ti) *n.* urgent prayer or petition.

ENTREE (âng-trā') *n.* freedom of access; a course of dishes; one of the course. [F.]

ENTRUST (en-trust') *v.t.* to give in trust; to commit, as to the fidelity of another. Also INTRUST.

ENTRY (en'tri) *n.* entrance; passage; committing to writing; item written; taking possession. [F. *entrée.*]

ENTWINE (en-twīn') *v.t.* to twine or wreathe round.

ENUMERATE (e-nū'mer-āt) *v.t.* to number; detail; account. [L. (part.) *enumeratus*, counted out, fr. *e*, *ex*, and *numerare*, NUMBER.]

ENUMERATION (e-nū-mer-ā'shun) *n.* act of numbering; detailed account; a summing up.

ENUMERATIVE (e-nū'mer-āt-iv) *a.* reckoning up.

ENUNCIATE (ē-nun'shi-āt) *v.t.* to declare; utter; pronounce. [L. (part.) *enunciatus*, fully reported, fr. *e*, *ex*, and *nuntiare*.]

ENUNCIATION (ē-nun-shi-ā'shun) *n.* utterance of words.

ENVELOP (en-vel'up) *v.t.* to cover on all sides by wrapping or folding; hide. [O.F. *enveloper*, fr. *en*, and Teut. root of WRAP. M.E. *wlappen*.]

ENVELOPE (en'vel-ōp) *n.* a wrapper; a cover for a letter.

ENVELOPMENT (en-vel'up-ment) *n.* a wrapping.

ENVENOM (en-ven'um) *v.t.* to poison.

ENVIABLE (en'vi-a-bl) *a.* that may excite envy; desirable.

ENVIABLY (en'vi-a-bli) *ad.* so as to excite envy.

ENVIOUS (en'vi-us) *a.* feeling envy.

ENVIOUSLY (en'vi-us-li) *ad.* with envy.

ENVIRON (en-vī'run) *v.t.* to surround. [F., fr. *en* = L. *in*, and *virer*, VEER.]

ENVIRONMENT (en-vī'run-ment) *n.* act of surrounding.

ENVIRONS (en-vī'ronz) *n.pl.* places that lie around a town.

ENVOY (en'voi) *n.* a public minister to a foreign court; a postscript. [O.F. *envoy* = F. *envoi*, a sending, fr. *en voie*, upon the way, fr. L. *in viam*. See CONVOY.]

ENVY (en'vi) *v.t.* to grieve at another's good; grudge; — *n.* pain excited by another's prosperity. [O.F. *envie*, L. (acc.) *invidiam*. See INVIDIOUS.]

ENWRAP (en-rap') *v.t.* to wrap up; envelop.

EOCENE (ē'ō-sēn) *a.* early; first of the tertiary formations. [Imit. *Epicene*, etc., fr. G. *eos*, dawn, and *kainos*, recent.]

EOLIAN (ē-ō'li-an) *a.* pertaining to Æolus, or the winds.

EON, ÆON (ē'on) *n.* an age or era; an eternal virtue, a i u e, or perfection. [G. *aion*, an age.] ttr b t

EPACT (ē'pakt) *n.* the excess of the solar month beyond the lunar. [G. *epaktos*, added, fr. *epi*, unto, and *agein*, bring.]

EPAULEMENT (ē-pawl'ment) *n.* a sidework, in fortification. [F. *épauler*, to protect, fr. *épaule*, shoulder.]

EPAULET, EPAULETTE (ep'awl-et) *n.* a shoulder-knot worn by naval and military officers to denote rank. [F. dim., fr. *épaule*, fr. L. (acc.) *spatulam*.]

EPERGNE (e-pern') *n.* an ornamental stand for flowers, etc., in the centre of the dining-table. [F.]

EPHEMERA (e-fem'er-a) *n.* an insect that lives one day only. [G. = (neut. pl.) lasting but a day, fr. *eph* = *epi*, for, and *hemera*, day.]

EPHEMERAL (e-fem'er-al) *a.* lasting one day. [See EPHEMERA.]

EPIC (ep'ik) *a.* containing heroic narration; — *n.* an epic poem. [G. *epikos*, fr. *epos*, word.]

EPICENE (ep'e-sēn) *a.* common to both sexes. [L. *epi-cœnus*, fr. G., fr. *epi*, among, and *koinos*, common.]

EPICURE (ep'i-kūr) *n.* a luxurious and dainty eater. [L., fr. G. *Epicouros*.]

EPICUREAN (ep-i-kū-rē'an) *a.* luxurious; sensual; — *n.* an epicure.

EPICURISM (ep'i-kūr-izm) *n.* devotion to luxurious living.

EPIDEMIC (ep-i-dem'ik) *n.* a prevailing disease. [Fr. L. *epidemus*, fr. G., fr. *epi*, among, and *demos*, the people.]

EPIDEMICAL (ep-i-dem'i-kal) *a.* common; generally prevailing.

EPIDERMIS (ep-i-der'mis) *n.* the cuticle or scarf skin. [G., fr. *epi*, upon, and *derma*, skin.]

EPIGASTRIC (ep-i-gas'trik) *a.* relating to the upper part of the stomach. [G. *epi*, and *gaster*, belly.]

EPIGLOTTIS (ep-i-glot'is) *n.* a cartilage that prevents food entering the windpipe. [G., fr. *epi*, upon, and GLOTTIS.]

EPIGRAM (ep'i-gram) *n.* a short poem with point. [F., fr. L. *epigramma*, short poem, fr. G. *epigramma*, inscription. See EPIGRAPH.]

EPIGRAMMATIC (ep-i-gra-mat'ik) *a.* concise and pointed; poignant.

EPIGRAMMATIST (ep-i-gram'a-tist) *n.* one who writes epigrams.

EPIGRAPH (ep'i-graf) *n.* an inscription on a building, book, etc. [G. *epi*, round, and *graphein*, write. Cf. EPIGRAM.]

EPILEPSY (ep'i-lep-si) *n.* the falling sickness. [O.F., fr. L., fr. G. *epilepsia*, attack, fr. *epi*, on, and stem *leps-*, of *lambanein*, seize.]

EPILEPTIC (ep-i-lep'tik) *a.* diseased with epilepsy.

EPILOGICAL (ep-i-loj'i-kal) *a.* pertaining to the conclusion of a speech.

EPILOGUE (ep'i-log) *n.* a concluding speech. [F. *épilogue*, fr. L., fr. G. *epilogos*, fr. *epi*, to, and *logos*, speech.]

EPIPHANY (ē-pif'a-ni) *n.* a festival held the 12th day after Christmas. [O.F., fr. L., fr. G. *epiphania*, fr. *epi*, to, and *phainein*, show.]

EPISCOPACY (e-pis'kō-pa-si) *n.* government of the church by bishops.

EPISCOPAL (e-pis'kō-pal) *a.* governed by or vested in bishops. [L. *episcopalis*, fr. G. *episkopos*, overseer, BISHOP.]

EPISCOPALIAN (e-pis-kō-pā'li-an) *n.* one of the Episcopal church.

EPISCOPALIANISM (e-pis-kō-pā'li-an-izm) *n.* system or practice of episcopacy.

EPISCOPALLY (e-pis'kō-pal-i) *a.* by authority of a bishop.

EPISCOPATE (e-pis'kō-pāt) *n.* a bishopric.

EPISODE (ep'i-sōd) *n.* a separate story, event, or action. [G., fr. *epi*, upon, and *eisodios*, coming in, fr. *eis*, into, and *hodos*, way.]

EPISODICAL (ep-i-sōd'i-kal) *a.* pertaining to an episode.

EPISTLE (ē-pis'l) *n.* a letter. [O.F. *epistle* = F. *epître*, fr. L. (acc.) *epistolam*.]

EPISTOLARY (e-pis'tu-lar-i) *a.* contained in letters.

EPITAPH (ep'i-taf) *n.* a monumental inscription. [F. *épitaphe*, fr. L., fr. G. *epi*, upon, and *taphos*, tomb.]

EPITHET (ep'i-thet) *n.* a title or name. [G., fr. *epi*, to, besides, and *thetos*, placed.]

EPITOME (e-pit'ō-me) *n.* an abridgment; brief summary. [G., fr. *epi*, and *temnein*, cut.]

EPITOMISE (e-pit'ō-mīz) *v.t.* to abridge.

EPITOMISER (e-pit'ō-mi-zer) *n.* one who abridges. Also EPITOMIST.

EPOCH (ē'pok, ep'ok) *n.* a remarkable period of time. [G. *epoche*, stop, check, fr. *ep* = *epi*, to, upon, and *echein*, to hold.]

EPODE (ep'ōd) *n.* the third or last part of an ode. [G., fr. *ep* = *epi*, after, and *ode*, an ode.]

EPSOM SALT (ep'sum sawlt) *n.* a purgative; sulphate of magnesia. [Fr. *Epsom*, in Surrey England.]

EQUABILITY (ē-kwa-bil'i-ti) *n.* uniformity of mind or temper.

EQUABLE (ē-kwa-, ek'wa-bl) *a.* equal and uniform; not variable. [L. *æquabilis* fr. *æquare*, to EQUAL.]

EQUABLY (ē′kwạ-, ek′wạ-bli) *ad.* with uniformity.

EQUAL (ē′kwạl) *a.* like in any quality; fit; adequate; even; just; fair;—*n.* one of the same age, rank, or merit;—*v.t.* or *i.* to make equal. [L. *æqualis*, fr. *æquus*, equal.]

EQUALISATION (ē-kwạl-i-zā′shun) *n.* state of equality.

EQUALISE (ē′kwạl-īz) *v.t.* to make equal.

EQUALITY (ē′kwol′i-ti) *n.* state or quality of being equal. [L. (acc.) *æqualitatem*.]

EQUALLY (ē′kwạl-i) *ad.* in the same degree.

EQUANIMITY (ē-kwạ-nim′i-ti) *n.* evenness of mind. [L., fr. *æquanimis*, of even mind, fr. *æquus*, equal, and *animus*, the mind.]

EQUATION (ē-kwā′shun) *n.* a proposition stating the equality of two quantities.

EQUATOR (ē-kwā′tẹr) *n.* a great circle dividing the earth into northern and southern hemispheres.

EQUATORIAL (ē-kwạ-tō′ri-ạl) *a.* pertaining to the equator;—*n.* an astronomical instrumen .

EQUATORIALLY (ē-kwạ-tō′ri-ạl-i) *ad.* in a line with the equator.

EQUERRY (ek′we-ri, ē-kwer′i) *n.* one who has the care of horses. [Orig. stable, fr. F. *écurie*, fr. Late L. (acc.) *scuriam*, fr. Teut. Cf. Ger. *Scheuer*.]

EQUESTRIAN (ē-kwes′tri-ạn) *a.* pertaining to horses or horsemanship. [Fr. L. (stem) *equestri-*, of *equester*, fr. *eques*, horseman, fr. *equus*, horse.]

EQUIANGULAR (ē-kwi-ang′gū-lạr) *a.* of equal angles. [L. pref. *æqui-*, fro *æquus*, EQUAL.]

EQUIDISTANCE (ē-kwi-dis′tạns) *n.* equal distance or remoteness.

EQUIDISTANT (ē-kwi-dis′tạnt) *a.* being at the same distance. [L. *æquus*, and *distare*, stand apart.]

EQUILATERAL (ē-kwi-lat′e-rạl) *a.* having the sides equal, as an equilateral triangle. [L. *æquus*, and *latus*, side.]

EQUILIBRATE (ē-kwi-lī′brāt) *v.t.* to balance equally. [See EQUILIBRIUM.]

EQUILIBRATION (ē-kwi-li-brā′shun) *n.* equipoise. [See EQUILIBRIUM.]   Equilateral Triangle.

EQUILIBRIUM (ē-kwi-lib′ri-um) *n.* equipoise. [L. *æquilibris*, balanced, fr. *libra*, balance.]

EQUINOCTIAL (ē-kwi-nok′shạl) *n.* the great circle which the sun describes when the days and nights are equal;—*a.* pertaining to the equinox. [See EQUINOX.]

EQUINOX (ē′kwi-noks) *n.* the time when the days and nights are of equal length. [F., fr. L. *æquinoctium*, fr. *æquus*, and stem, *nocti-*, of *nox*, night.]

EQUIP (e-kwip′) *v.t.* to furnish or prepare for service; fit out; accoutre. [O.F. *equiper*, *eskipper*, fr. Scand.; conn. with SKIPPER.]

EQUIPAGE (ek′wi-pij) *n.* furniture; a carriage and attendants; retinue.

EQUIPMENT (e-kwip′ment) *n.* act of equipping; any apparatus furnished.

EQUIPOISE (ē′kwi-poiz) *n.* equality of weight or force.   [of power or force.

EQUIPOLLENCE (ē-kwi-pol′ens) *n.* equality

EQUIPOLLENT (ē-kwi-pol′ent) *a.* having equal force. [L., fr. (part. stem) *pollent-*, being able, fr. *pollere*.]

EQUIPONDERANCE (ē-kwi-pon′dẹr-ạns) *n.* equality of weight.

EQUIPONDERANT (ē-kwi-pon′dẹr-ạnt) *a.* of the same weight. [L., fr. (part. stem) *ponderant-*, weighing.]

EQUITABLE (ek′wi-tạ-bl) *a.* giving or disposed to give each his due; impartial; fair; upright.

EQUITABLY (ek′wi-tạ-bli) *ad.* impartially.

EQUITATION (ek-wi-tā′shun) *n.* act of riding on horseback.

EQUITY (ek′wi-ti) *n.* justice; impartiality. [F. *équité*, fr. L. (acc.) *æquitatem*, fr. *æquus*.]

EQUIVALENCE (e-kwiv′ạ-lens) *n.* equality of worth.

EQUIVALENT (e-kwiv′ạ-lent) *a.* equal in worth, force, value, meaning, etc.;—*n.* that which is equal in value, worth, etc. [L. (acc. part.) *æquivalentem*, equalling in power, fr. *valere*, be worth.]

EQUIVOCAL (e-kwiv′ō-kạl) *a.* ambiguous. [L. *æquivocis*, fr. stem, *voc-* of *vox*, voice.]

EQUIVOCALLY (e-kwiv′ō-kạl-i) *ad.* doubtfully.

EQUIVOCATE (e-kwiv′ō-kāt) *v.t.* to use words of double meaning.

EQUIVOCATION (e-kwiv-ō-kā′shun) *n.* ambiguity of speech.

EQUIVOCATOR (e-kwiv′ō-kā-tẹr) *n.* one who equivocates.

EQUIVOCATORY (e-kwiv′ō-kā-tur-i) *a.* of an evasive or quibbling character.

EQUIVOKE (ō′kwi-vōk) *n.* an ambiguous term; quibble. [See EQUIVOCAL.]

ERA (ē′rạ) *n.* a point or period of time from which to compute; an epoch. [L. *æra*, a basis for calculation = orig. (pl.) counters, fr. *æs*, brass.]   [eradicated.

ERADICABLE (e-rad′i-kạ-bl) *a.* that may be

ERADICATE (e-rad′i-kāt) *v.t.* to extirpate. [L. (part.) *eradicatus*, rooted out, fr. *e*, *ex*, and stem *radic-*, of RADIX.]

ERADICATION (e-rad-i-kā′shun) *n.* act of rooting out.

ERASABLE (e-rās′ạ-bl) *a.* that may be erased.

ERASE (e-rās′) *v.t.* to blot out; efface; rub or scrape out. [L. (part.) *erasus*, fr. *e*, *ex*, and *radere*.]

ERASEMENT (e-rās′ment) *n.* obliteration.

ERASER (e-rā′zẹr) *n.* one who or that which erases.

ERASION (ē-rā′zhun) *n.* act of erasing.

ERASURE (e-rā′zhūr) *n.* act of rubbing or scratching; part or word that has been erased.

ERE (ār) *ad.* before; sooner than;—*prep.* before. [O.E. *ær*. Cf. Ger. *eher*.]

EREBUS (er′e-bus) *n.* darkness; the region of the dead. [L., fr. G.]

ERECT (e-rekt′) *a.* upright; perpendicular; bold;—*v.t.* to set upright; build. [L. (part.) *erectus*, set upright, fr. *e*, *ex*, and *rigere* = *regere*, set straight.]

ERECTION (e-rek′shun) *n.* a setting upright; act of building; a building of any kind.

ERECTLY (e-rekt′li) *ad.* in an erect posture.

ERELONG (ār′long) *ad.* before long; soon. [See ERE and LONG.]

EREMITE (er′e-mīt) *n.* a hermit. [Late L. *eremita*, fr. G. *eremites*, dweller in a desert, *erimia*. Doublet of HERMIT.]

ERGO (er′gō) *ad.* therefore; consequently. [L.]

ERGOT (er′gut) *n.* a protuberance on a horse's leg; an excrescence on rye and other grasses. [F.]

ERIN (er′in) *n.* Ireland. [Celt.]

ERMINE (er′min) *n.* a species of animal or its fur. [O.F. *ermine* = F. *hermine*, weasel, fr. Teu.]

EROSION (e-rō′zhun) *n.* act or state of eating or being eaten away. [L. (part.) *erosus*.]

EROSIVE (e-rō′siv) *a.* corrosive.

EROTIC (e-rot′ik) *a.* pertaining to love; amatory. [G., fr. stem *erot-*, of *eros*, love.]

ERR (er) *v.i.* [pret. ERRED] to wander from the right way; to mistake. [O.F. *errer*, fr. L. *errare*, to stray.]

ERRAND (er′and) *n.* a message. [O.E. *ærende*.]

ERRANT (er′ant) *a.* wandering; roving. [F., fr. L. Doublet of ARRANT.]

ERRANTRY (er′ant-ri) *n.* an errant state.

ERRATIC (e-rat′ik) *a.* wandering.

ERRATICALLY (e-rat′ik-ạl-i) *ad.* without rule; irregularly.

ERRATUM (e-ra'tum) *n.* error or mistake in printing or writing;—*pl.* **ERRATA.** [L.]

ERRONEOUS (e-rŏ'ne-us) *a.* containing error; mistaking; misleading. [L. *erroneus.*]

ERRONEOUSLY (e-rŏ'ne-us-li) *ad.* by mistake.

ERROR (er'ur) *n.* a mistake; blunder; sin. [L.]

ERRORIST (er'ur-ist) *n.* one who errs or teaches error.

ERSE (ers) *n.* the language of the Celts of Irish origin in Scotland. [Corr. for IRISH.]

ERST (erst) *ad.* at first; long ago. [O.E. *œrest,* fr. *œr,* ERE.]

ERUBESCENT (er-ū-bes'ent) *a.* red; blushing. [L., fr. *erubescere,* redden, fr. *e,* and *rubere,* be red. See RUBRIC.]

ERUCTATION (ē-ruk-tā'shun) *n.* a belching. [L. (part.) *eructatus,* belched out, fr. *e, ex,* and *ructare.*]

ERUDITE (er'oo-dīt) *a.* learned. [L. (part.) *eruditus,* polished, fr. *e, ex,* and *rudis,* rough. See RUDE.]

ERUDITION (er-oo-dish'un) *n.* knowledge gained by study of books; scholarship.

ERUPT (e-rupt') *v.t.* to throw out; emit. [L. (part.) *eruptus,* fr. *e, ex,* and *rumpere.*]

ERUPTION (e-rup'shun) *n.* a breaking forth; pustules on the skin.

ERUPTIVE (e-rup'tiv) *a.* bursting out; having eruption.

ERYSIPELAS (er-i-sip'e-las) *n.* St Anthony's fire; the rose. [L., fr. G., fr. *eruthros,* red, and *pella,* skin.]

ESCALADE (es-ka-lād') *n.* a scaling of walls; —*v.t.* to mount by ladders. [F. through Sp., fr. L. *scala,* ladder. See SCALE.]

ESCAPE (es-kāp') *v.t.* to avoid; shun by flight; —*v.i.* to become free;—*n.* act of avoiding; flight; a getting free. [O.F. *escaper* = F. *échapper,* fr. L. *ex,* and *cappa,* cloak, CAPE (1).

ESCAPEMENT (es-kāp'ment) *n.* that part of a timepiece which regulates its movements.

ESCHALOT (esh'a-lot) *n.* a species of small onion. [O.F. *eschalotte.* See SHALLOT.]

ESCHATOLOGY (es-ka-tol'ō-ji) *n.* the doctrine of the last or final things. [G. *eschatos,* last, and *-logia,* science.]

ESCHEAT (es-chēt') *n.* a falling of lands to the lord of the manor or the State for want of heirs;—*v.i.* to revert, as land, to the crown, etc. [O.F. *eschete,* rent, fr. *eschcoir* = F. *échoir,* fall due, fr. L. *e, ex,* and *cadere.*]

Escapement.

ESCHEW (es-chōo') *v.t.* to shun or avoid. [O.F. *eschever,* fr. Teut. Cf. Ger. *scheuen.*]

ESCORT (es-kort') *v.t.* to attend and guard;— (es'kort) *n.* a guard. [F. *escorte,* fr. It. *scorta,* guide, fr. L. *ex,* and *corrigere,* CORRECT.]

ESCRITOIRE (es-kri-twor') *n.* a box with conveniences for writing. [O.F. *escriptoire,* fr. L. See SCRIPT.]

ESCULAPIAN (es-kū-lā'pi-an) *a.* pertaining to the healing art. [Fr. *Æsculapius,* god of medicine.]

ESCULENT (es'kū-lent) *a.* good for food. [L. *esculentus,* fr. *esca* = *edsca,* food, fr. *edere.*]

ESCUTCHEON (es-kuch'un) *n.* a shield or coat of arms. [O.F. *escuchon,* fr. Late L., fr. L. *scutum,* shield.]

ESOPHAGUS (ē-sof'a-gus) *n.* the gullet. [G.]

ESOTERIC (es-ō-ter'ik) *a.* secret. [G., fr. *esoteros,* inner, fr. *eso,* within.]

ESOTERICS (es-ō-ter'iks) *n.pl.* secret or mysterious doctrines.

ESPALIER (es-pal'yer) *n.* a frame or trellis for fruit trees. [O.F., fr. It. *spalliera,* support for the shoulder, *spalla,* fr. SPATULA.]

ESPARTO (es-pär'tō) *n.* a strong grass used in paper-making. [Sp.]

ESPECIAL (es-pesh'al) *a.* principal; chief; particular. [O.F. *especial,* SPECIAL, fr. L., fr. *species,* kind.]

ESPECIALLY (es-pesh'al-i) *ad.* chiefly.

ESPIAL (es-pi'al) *n.* act of espying. [See ESPY.]

ESPIONAGE (es'pi-u-nij) *n.* practice of employing spies; secret watching. [Fr. *espionnage,* fr. *espion,* a spy.]

ESPLANADE (es-pla-nād') *n.* an open space before a fortification; any clear space used for public walks or drives. [F., fr. L. *ex,* and *planus,* flat.]

ESPOUSAL (es-pouz'al) *a.* relating to espousals; —*n.* act of espousing or betrothal; adoption;—*n.pl.* a contracting of marriage. [F. *épusailles,* fr. L. *sponsalis,* belonging to betrothal.]

ESPOUSE (es-pouz') *v.t.* to betroth; marry; embrace. [F. *épouser,* fr. L. *sponsare,* to betroth, fr. *spondere,* promise.]

ESPY (es-pi') *v.t.* to see at a distance; descry; discover;—*v.i.* to watch; spy. [O.F. *espier,* fr. Teut. Cf. Ger. *spahen,* SPY.]

ESQUIRE (es-kwir') *n.* a title of dignity next to a knight; a title of courtesy. [O.F. *escuyer,* SQUIRE, fr. *escu* = F. *écu,* fr. L. *scutum.*]

ESSAY (es-sā') *v.t.* to attempt;—(es'ā) *n.* a trial; short treatise. [O.F. *essai,* fr. L. *exanium,* a weighing, fr. *ex,* and *agere,* move. Doublet of ASSAY.]

ESSAYIST (es'ā-ist) *n.* a writer of essays.

ESSENCE (es'ens) *n.* the nature of a thing; perfume; scent;—*v.t.* to perfume. [F., fr. L. (acc.) *essentiam,* fr. *esse,* be.]

ESSENTIAL (e-sen'shal) *a.* necessary to existence; rectified;—*n.* something necessary; chief point.

ESSENTIALITY (e-sen-shi-al'i-ti) *n.* the quality of being real or necessary. [in effect.

ESSENTIALLY (e-sen'shi-al-i) *ad.* necessarily;

ESTABLISH (es-tab'lish) *v.t.* to settle firmly; ordain; found; confirm. [O.F. (part.) *etablissant,* establishing, fr. L. *stabilire,* to make STABLE.]

ESTABLISHMENT (es-tab'lish-ment) *n.* settlement; confirmation; place of residence or business; style of living; the State Church.

ESTATE (es-tāt') *n.* condition; property, especially landed property. [O.F. *estat* = F. *état.* Doublet of STATE.]

ESTEEM (es-tēm') *v.t.* to value; regard; think;—*n.* high value in opinion. [O.F. *estimer,* fr. L. *œstimare,* to value, ESTIMATE.]

ESTHETIC (es-thet'-ik) *a.* relating to the beautiful in nature or art. [G. *aisthetikos,* perceptive.]

ESTIMABLE (es'ti-ma-bl) *a.* worthy of esteem; valuable.

ESTIMABLY (es'ti-ma-bli) *ad.* in a manner to deserve regard or esteem.

ESTIMATE (es'ti-māt) *v.t.* to set a value on;— *n.* calculation; value set. [L. (part.) *œstimatus,* valued, fr. *œstimare.*]

ESTIMATION (es-ti-mā'shun) *n.* a valuing; esteem; honour; opinion.

ESTIVATION (es-ti-vā'shun) *n.* act of passing the summer; the disposition of the petals within the flower bud. [L. *œstivalis* fr. *œstas,* summer.]

ESTRANGE (es-trānj') *v.t.* to keep at a distance; withdraw; divert; alienate. [O.F., fr. *estrange,* STRANGE.]

ESTREAT (es-trēt') *n.* a true copy of a writing or record. [O.F. (fem. part.) *estraite,* fr. L. (acc. part. fem.) *extractam.* Doublet of EXTRACT.]

ESTUARY (es'tū-a-ri) *n.* an arm of the sea. [L. *œstuarium,* fr. *œstuare,* surge, fr. *œstus,* heat, tide.]

ETCH (ech) *v.t.* to engrave by drawing lines through wax and corroding them with nitric acid. [G. *ätzen,* lit. make to eat, fr. *essen.*]

ETCHING (ech'ing) *n.* impression from an etched plate.

ETERNAL (ē-tẹr'nạl) *a.* having no beginning or end;—*n.* an appellation of God. [O.F. *eternel*, fr. L. *æternus* (= *æviternus*), fr. *ævum*, age.]

ETERNALLY (ē-tẹr'nạl-i) *ad.* perpetually.

ETERNISE (ē-tẹr'nīz) *v.t.* to immortalise; make endless. [See ETERNAL.]

ETERNITY (ē-tẹr'ni-ti) *n.* duration without beginning or end; state or time after death.

ETESIAN (ē-tē'zi-ạn) *a.* denoting certain periodical winds. [G. *etesios*, annual, fr. *etos*, year.]

ETHER (ē'thẹr) *n.* the subtle fluid supposed to fill space; a volatile fluid. [L., fr. G. *aither*, upper air.]

ETHEREAL (ē-thē'rē-ạl) *a.* consisting of ether; heavenly. [See ETHER.]

ETHEREALISE (ē-thē'rē-ạl-īz) *v.t.* to convert into ether; make spiritual.

ETHEREALLY (ē-thē'rē-ạl-i) *ad.* in a heavenly manner.

ETHERISATION (ē-thẹr-i-zā'shun) *n.* administration of ether; state of being under the influence of ether. [influence of ether.

ETHERISE (ē'thẹr-īz) *v.t.* to subject to the

ETHICAL (eth'i-kạl) *a.* relating to morals. [L., fr. G. *ethikos*, moral, fr. *ethos*, morals.]

ETHICALLY (eth'i-kạl-i) *ad.* according to ethics.

ETHICS (eth'iks) *n.* the science of moral principles and duties.

ETHNIC (eth'nik) *a.* concerning nations or races; pertaining to the heathen. [L., fr. G. *ethnikos*, pertaining to a nation, *ethnos*.]

ETHNOLOGY (eth-nol'ō-ji) *n.* science of the varieties of the human race. [See ETHNIC.]

ETIQUETTE (et-i-ket') *n.* forms of ceremony. [F. = a label, fr. Ger. *stecken*, stick.]

ETYMOLOGICAL (et-i-mu-loj'i-kạl) *a.* relating to etymology. [in etymology.

ETYMOLOGIST (et-i-mol'ō-jist) *n.* one versed

ETYMOLOGY (et-i-mol'ō-ji) *n.* derivation of words from their originals. [G. *etumos*, true, and *-logia*, science, *legein*.]

EUCALYPTUS (ū-kạ-lip'tus) *n.* a gigantic evergreen tree of Australia; the gum-tree, yielding a medicinal oil. [G. *eu*, well, and *kalup-tos*, hidden, (as the stamens are).]

EUCHARIST (ū'kạ-rist) *n.* the Lord's Supper. [L., fr. G. *eucharicta*, fr. *eu*, and *charizomai*, thank.]

EUCHARISTIC (ū-kạ-ris'tik) *a.* pertaining to the eucharist.

EUDIOMETER (ū-di-om'et-ẹr) *n.* an instrument employed in estimating the proportions of any gaseous mixture. [G. *eudios*, fine, and *metron*, measure.]

EUGENICS (ū-jen'iks) *n.* the doctrine of evolution in the human race through improved conditions in the relations of the sexes. [G. *eu*, well, and *gignesthai*, to be produced.]

EULOGISE (ū'lō-jīz) *v.t.* to praise by eulogy; commend.

EULOGIUM (ū-lō'ji-um) *n.* commendation; praise. [L., fr. G. *eulogia*, fr. *eu*, well, and *legein*, speak.]

EULOGY (ū'lō-ji) *n.* marked or studied praise; encomium; pane-Eudiometer. gyric.

EUNUCH (ū'nuk) *n.* a defective man. [G.] fr *eune*, couch, and *echein*, have, keep.]

EUPHEMISM (ū'fe-mizm) *n.* a delicate word or expression used for one that is offensive. [G., fr. *eu*, well, and *phemi*, speak.]

EUPHONIC (ū-fon'ik) *a.* having a sound agreeable to the ear. [See EUPHONY.]

EUPHONY (ū'fu-ni) *n.* an agreeably sounding enunciation. [G., fr. *euphonos*, sweet-voiced, fr. *eu*, well, and *phone*, sound.]

EUPHUISM (ū'fū-izm) *n.* fastidious delicacy in the choice of words. [Fr. *Euphues* (G. = well-shaped), the book by John Lyly, which influenced the courtiers of Elizabeth.]

EURASIAN (ū-rā'shạn) *n.* one born of a European and an Asiatic parent. [From a combination of Europe and Asia.]

EUROCLYDON (ū-rok'li-don) *n.* a tempestuous easterly wind. [G., fr. *euros*, the east wind, *klydon*, a wave, *klyzein*, to dash over.]

EUROPEAN (ū-ru-pē'ạn) *a.* pertaining to Europe;—*n.* a native of Europe.

EURUS (ū'rus) *n.* the south-east wind. [L., fr. G. *euros*, the east wind.]

EUTHANASIA (ū-thạ-nā'si-ạ) *n.* easy death. [G. *euthanasia*, fr. *eu*, well, and *thanatos*, death.]

EVACUANT (ē-vak'ū-ạnt) *n.* a medicine that evacuates;—*a.* emptying; purgative. [See EVACUATE.]

EVACUATE (ē-vak'ū-āt) *v.t.* to make empty; quit. [L. (part.) *evacuatus*, emptied, fr. *e*, *ex*, and *vacuus*, empty.]

EVACUATION (ē-vak-ū-ā'shun) *n.* act of ejecting; withdrawing from; discharge.

EVACUATOR (ē-vak-ū-ā'tẹr) *n.* one who evacuates or makes void.

EVADE (ē-vād') *v.t.* to avoid; elude; slip away. [L., fr. *e*, *ex*, and *vadere*, go.]

EVANESCENCE (ev-ạ-nes'ens) *n.* a gradual vanishing. [L. *e*, *ex*, and *vanescere*, vanish, fr. *vanus*.]

EVANESCENT (ev-ạ-nes'ent) *a.* vanishing; fleeting; passing away.

EVANGEL (e-van'jel) *n.* good news; glad tidings; the Gospel. [L., fr. G. *eua(n)ggelion* good tidings, fr. *eu*, well, and *a(n)ggelos*, messenger, ANGEL.]

EVANGELICAL (ē-van-jel'i-kạl) *a.* according to or contained in the Gospel.

EVANGELISE (e-van'jel-īz) *v.t.* to instruct in the Gospel of Christ.

EVANGELISM (e-van'jel-izm) *n.* promulgation of the Gospel.

EVANGELIST (e-van'jel-ist) *n.* one of the four writers of the Gospel; preacher; missionary.

EVAPORATE (e-vap'ō-rāt) *v.i.* to pass off in vapour; waste insensibly. [L. (part.) *evaporatus*, fr. *e*, *ex*, and *vaporare*, to steam, fr. VAPOUR.]

EVAPORATION (e-vap-ō-rā'shun) *n.* conversion of a fluid into vapour.

EVASION (e-vā'zhun) *n.* artifice; equivocation. [L. (part.) *evasus*, evaded.]

EVASIVE (e-vā'siv) *a.* using evasion.

EVASIVELY (e-vā'siv-li) *ad.* by means of evasion.

EVASIVENESS (e-vā'siv-nes) *n.* the quality or state of being evasive.

EVE (ēv) *n.* evening. [Short for EVEN.]

EVEN (ē'vn) *a.* level; smooth;—*v.t.* to make level or smooth;—*ad.* likewise; in like manner; indeed; still. [O.E. *efen*. Cf. Ger. *eben*.] [partial.

EVEN-HANDED (ē'vn-han-ded) *a.* fair; im-

EVENING (ēv'ning) *n.* the close of the day. [O.E. *æfnung*.]

EVENNESS (ē'vn-nes) *n.* the state of being even. [See EVEN.]

EVENT (e-vent') *n.* that which happens; incident; issue; result. [L. *eventus*, fr. *e*, *ex*, and *venire*, come.]

EVENTFUL (e-vent'fool) *a.* full of incidents.

EVENTIDE (ē'vn-tīd) *n.* time of evening.

EVENTUAL (e-vent'ū-ạl) *a.* consequential; final. [See EVENT.]

EVENTUALITY (e-ven-tū-ạl'i-ti) *n.* a contingent occurrence; a happening.

EVENTUALLY (e-vent'ū-ạl-i) *a.* in the end; finally.

EVENTUATE (e-ven'tū-āt) *v.i.* to come to pass or to an end. [See EVENT.]

EVER (ev'ẹr) *ad.* at any time; always. [O.E. *æfre*.]

EVERGREEN (ev'er-grēn) *n.* a plant or shrub always green.

EVERLASTING (ev-er-lås'ting) *a.* continuing without end; eternal. [nally.

EVERLASTINGLY (ev-er-lås'ting-li) *ad.* eter-

EVERMORE (ev'er-mōr) *ad.* eternally.

EVERSION (e-ver'shun) *n.* turning outwards; overthrow. [See EVERT.]

EVERSIVE (e-ver'siv) *a.* tending to overthrow. [See EVERT.]

EVERT (e-vert') *v.t.* to overthrow; turn outwards. [L. *evertere*, overturn.]

EVERY (ev'ri) *a.* each one of a whole. [M.E. *everich*, fr. O.E. *œfre*, ever, and *œlc*, each.]

EVERYDAY (ev'ri-dā) *a.* common; usual.

EVERYTHING (ev'ri-thing) *pron.* all things; all.

EVERYWHERE (ev'ri-hwār) *ad.* in every place.

EVICT (e-vikt') *v.t.* to dispossess by judicial process. [L. (part.) *evictus*, expelled. fr. *e*, *ex*, and *vincere*, conquer.]

EVICTION (e-vik'shun) *n.* dispossession.

EVIDENCE (ev'i-dens) *n.* that which proves or shows facts; testimony; witness;—*v.t.* to show; prove.

EVIDENT (ev'i-dent) *a.* clear; plain. [O.F., fr. L. (acc.) *evidentum*, visible. fr. *e*, *ex*, clearly, and *videre*, see.]

EVIDENTIAL (ev-i-den'shal) *a.* affording evidence.

EVIDENTLY (ev'i-dent-li) *ad.* clearly.

EVIL (ē'vil) *a.* ill; wicked;—*n.* calamity; wickedness;—*ad.* injuriously. [M.E. *evel*, fr. O.E. *yfel*.]

EVIL-DOER (ē-vil-dōō'er) *n.* one who commits sin or crime habitually.

EVIL-EYE (ē'vil-i) *n.* a supposed power of injuring by a hostile look.

EVIL-SPEAKING (ē'vil-spē'king) *n.* slander; censoriousness.

EVINCE (e-vins') *v.t.* to prove; show in a clear manner. [L. *evincere*, prevail, prove outright, fr. *e*, *ex*, and *vincere*, conquer.]

EVINCIBLE (e-vins'i-bl) *a.* capable of proof. [See EVINCE.] [See EVINCE.]

EVINCIVE (e-vin'siv) *a.* tending to prove.

EVISCERATE (ē-vis'e-rāt) *v.t.* to take out the bowels. [L. (part.) *evisceratus*, gutted, fr. *e*, *ex*, and *riscera*, bowels.]

EVISCERATION (ē-vis-e-rā'shun) *n.* act of disembowelling.

EVOCATION (ev-ō-kā'shun) *n.* a calling forth. [Fr. L. (part.) *evocatus*, called forth.]

EVOKE (e-vōk') *v.t.* to call forth. [F. *evoquer*, fr. L. *e*, *ex*, and *vocare*, call.]

EVOLUTION (ev-ol-ū'shun) *n.* act of unfolding; development; extraction of roots; movement ' of troops or war-ships; the scientific theory according to which the higher forms of life have gradually developed from simple and rudimentary forms. [L. (part.) *evolutus*, unrolled.]

EVOLUTIONARY (ev-ol-ū'shun-ar-i) *a.* pertaining to evolution.

EVOLUTIONIST (ev-ol-ū'shun-ist) *n.* one skilled in military movements; a believer in the evolutionary theory.

EVOLVE (ē-volv')* *v.t.* to unfold; expand; emit;—*v.i.* to come out. [L., fr. *e*, *ex*, out, and *volvere*, roll.]

EVULSION (ē-vul'shun) *n.* act of plucking or tearing out. [L. (part.) *evulsus*, plucked out, fr. *e*, *ex*, and *vellere*.]

EWE (ū) *n.* a female sheep. [O.E. *eowu*. Cf. L. *ovis*, G. *ois*.]

EWER (ū'er) *n.* a large pitcher with a wide spout, used for carrying water. [O.F., fr. L. *aquarium*, a watering-place, fr. *aqua*.]

EX (eks) a prefix, signifies *out of* or *from*.

EXACERBATE (eg-zas'er-bāt) *v.t.* to irritate. [L. (part.) *exacerbatus*, irritated, fr. *ex*, and *acerbus*, bitter.]

EXACERBATION (eg-zas-er-bā'shun) *n.* increased violence of a disease.

EXACT (eg-zakt') *a.* closely correct or regular; punctual; accurate; precise;—*v.t.* to demand; require; extort. [L. (part.) *exactus*, lit. weighed out, fr. *exigere*, fr. *ex*, and *agere*, drive.]

EXACTION (eg-zak'shun) *n.* act of extorting.

EXACTLY (eg-zakt'li) *ad.* accurately; nicely.

EXACTNESS (eg-zakt'nes) *n.* accuracy; nicety.

EXAGGERATE (eg-zaj'e-rāt) *v.t.* to heighten in representation. [L. (part.) *exaggeratus*, heaped up, fr. *ex*, fully, and *agger*, heap.]

EXAGGERATION (eg-zaj-e-rā'shun) *n.* a representation beyond the truth.

EXALT (eg-zawlt') *v.t.* to lift high; elevate; elate; extol; refine. [F. *exalter*, fr. L. *ex*, out of, and *altus*, high.]

EXALTATION (eg-zawl-tā'shun) *n.* a raising; elevation; refinement or rectification.

EXALTED (eg-zawl'ted) *a.* elevated; lofty; extolled; elated.

EXALTEDNESS (eg-zawl'ted-nes) *n.* the state of being exalted.

EXAMINATION (eg-zam-i-nā'shun) *n.* inquiry. [L. (part.) *examinatus*, examined.]

EXAMINE (eg-zam'in) *v.t.* to inspect; search into; question. [F., fr. L. *examinare*, fr. stem *examin-*, of *examen = exagmen*, the tongue of a balance. See EXACT.]

EXAMINER (eg-zam'i-ner) *n.* one who examines.

EXAMPLE (eg-zàm'pl) *n.* a pattern; instance. [O.F. = F. *exemple*, fr. L. *exemplum*, a sample, fr. *eximeri*, to take out. See EXEMPT.]

EXASPERATE (eg-zas'pe-rāt) *v.t.* to make very angry; enrage. [L. (part.) *exasperatus*, provoked, fr. *ex*, and *asper*, rough.]

EXASPERATION (eg-zas-pe-rā'shun) *n.* irritation.

EXCAVATE (eks'ka-vāt) *v.t.* to make hollow. [L. (part.) *excavatus*, hollowed out, fr. *ex*, and *cavus*.]

EXCAVATION (eks-ka-vā'shun) *n.* a making hollow; a cavity or hollow made by cutting or digging.

EXCEED (ek-sēd') *v.t.* or *i.* to surpass; excel. [O.F. *exceder*, fr. L. *ex*, beyond, and *cedere*, go.]

EXCEEDING (ek-sēd'ing) *ppr.* going beyond; —*a.* very great.

EXCEEDINGLY (ek-sēd'ing-li) *ad.* to a great degree; very much.

EXCEL (ek-sel') *v.t.* or *i.* to surpass. [O.F., fr. L. *excellare*, fr. *ex*, out, up, and root of *celsus*, lofty.]

EXCELLENCE (ek'se-lens) *n.* superior goodness or worth. [See EXCEL.]

EXCELLENCY (ek'se-len-si) *n.* a title of honour.

EXCELLENT (ek'se-lent) *a.* having great value; eminent. [O.F., fr. L. (acc. part.) *excellentem*, surpassing.]

EXCELLENTLY (ek'se-lent-li) *ad.* in an excellent degree.

EXCEPT (ek-sept') *v.t.* to take out:—*pp.* or *prep.* not including;—*conj.* unless. [F., fr. L. *exceptare*, fr. (part.) *exceptus*, taken out, fr. *ex*, and *cipere*, fr. *capere*, take.]

EXCEPTING (ek-sep'ting) *ppr.* taking or leaving out. [tion.

EXCEPTION (ek-sep'shun) *n.* exclusion; objec-

EXCEPTIONABLE (ek-sep'shun-a-bl) *a.* liable to objection.

EXCEPTIONAL (ek-sep'shun-al) *a.* forming an exception; peculiar.

EXCESS (ek-ses') *n.* more than enough; intemperance. [O.F. *exces* = F. *excès*, fr. L. (acc.) *excessum*, a going out. See EXCEED.]

EXCESSIVE (ek-ses'iv) *a.* exceeding just limits; extreme.

EXCESSIVELY (ek-ses'iv-li) *ad.* exceedingly.

EXCHANGE (eks-chānj') *v.t.* to give one thing for another;—*n.* act of bartering; balance of money; place where merchants meet. [O.F. *eschangier*, fr. *es = L. ex*, and *changier*, to CHANGE.]

EXCHANGEABLE (eks-chānj'ą-bl) *a.* that may be exchanged.

EXCHEQUER (eks-chek'ẽr) *n.* a court in England that tries questions of the king's revenue; the public treasury. [O.F. *eschequier*, chess-board, chequered cloth, fr. *eschec*, CHESS.]

EXCISABLE (ek-sī'zą-bl) *a.* subject to excise.

EXCISE (ek-sīz') *n.* a duty on goods;—*v.t.* to lay a duty on goods. [O.F. *acceis*, tax, fr. Late L. *accensus*, tax, fr. L. *ad*, to, and *census*, tax.]

EXCISEMAN (ek-sīz'man) *n.* one who inspects excised goods.

EXCISION (ek-sizh'un) *n.* cutting off; extirpation; a cutting out or cutting off any part of the body. [L. (part.) *excisus*, cut off, fr. *ex*, out, and -*cidere*, for *cædere*, cut.]

EXCITABILITY (ek-si-tą-bil'i-ti) *n.* capacity of being easily excited.

EXCITABLE (ek-sī'tą-bl) *a.* that can be roused into action.

EXCITATION (ek-si-tā'shun) *n.* act of rousing.

EXCITE (ek-sīt') *v.t.* to stir; rouse. [F., fr. L. *excitare*, fr. *ex*, and *ciere*, call.]

EXCITED (ek-sī'ted) *a.* inflamed.

EXCITEMENT (ek-sīt'ment) *n.* act of rousing.

EXCITING (ek-sī'ting) *ppr.* or *a.* producing excitement.

EXCLAIM (eks-klām') *v.i.* to cry out. [F. *exclamer*, fr. L. *ex*, and *clamare*, cry out.]

EXCLAMATION (eks-klą-mā'shun) *n.* a loud outcry; the mark (!) noting some emotion.

EXCLAMATORY (eks-klam'ą-tur-i) *a.* using exclamation.

EXCLUDE (eks-klūd') *v.t.* to shut out; debar. [L., fr. *ex*, and -*cludere*, for *claudere*, shut.]

EXCLUSION (eks-klōō'zhun) *n.* rejection. [L. (part.) *exclusus*, shut out.]

EXCLUSIONIST (eks-klōō'zhun-ist) *n.* one who would debar another from a privilege.

EXCLUSIVE (eks-klōō'siv) *c.* shutting out; not including.

EXCLUSIVELY (eks-klōō'siv-li) *ad.* to the exclusion of others.

EXCLUSIVENESS (eks-klōō'siv-nes) *n.* state of being exclusive.

EXCLUSORY (eks-klōō'sur-i) *a.* serving or able to exclude.

EXCOGITATE (eks-koj'i-tāt) *v.t.* to think out; discover or invent by thinking. [L. pref. *ex*-, thoroughly, and *cogitare*, think.]

EXCOGITATION (eks-koj-i-tā'shun) *n.* act of thinking or scheming out.

EXCOMMUNICATE (eks-ku-mū'ni-kāt) *v.t.* to exclude from communion. [L. (part.) *excommunicatus*, shut out from (communion).]

EXCOMMUNICATION (eks-ku-mū-ni-kā'shun) *n.* act of excluding from the ordinances of the church.

EXCORIATE (eks-kō'ri-āt) *v.t.* to flay; strip off skin. [L., fr. *ex*, and *corium*, skin.]

EXCORIATION (eks-kō-ri-ā'shun) *n.* act of stripping off skin.

EXCREMENT (eks'kre-ment) *n.* matter discharged from the body. [L. *excrementum*, fr. (part.) *excretus*. See EXCRETE.]

EXCREMENTAL (eks-kre-men'tąl) *a.* pertaining to excrement.

EXCREMENTITIOUS (eks-kre-men-tish'us) *a.* pertaining to or containing excrement.

EXCRESCENCE (eks-kres'ens) *n.* preternatural growth or protuberance. [F., fr. L. *excrescentia*, outgrowth, fr. *ex*, and *crescere*.]

EXCRESCENT (eks-kres'ent) *a.* growing out.

EXCRETE (eks-krēt') *v.t.* to discharge through the pores. [L. (part.) *excretus*, sifted, fr. *ex*, and *cernere*.]

EXCRETION (eks-krē'shun) *n.* throwing out matter from the animal system; that which is thrown out; excrement.

EXCRETIVE (eks-krē'tiv, eks'krē-tiv) *a.* tending to excrete.

EXCRETORY (eks-krē'tur-i, eks'krē-tur-i) *n.* a little duct for secreting a fluid.

EXCRUCIATE (eks-krōō'shi-āt) *v.t.* to torture. [L. (part.) *excruciatus*, tortured, fr. *ex*, and *cruciare*, slay on a cross, fr. stem *cruci-*, of *crux*, CROSS.]

EXCRUCIATING (eks-krōō'shi-ā-ting) *a.* distressing; very painful.

EXCRUCIATINGLY (eks-krōō'shi-ā-ting-li) *ad.* with extreme pain or severity.

EXCRUCIATION (eks-krōō-shi-ā'shun) *n.* torture; extreme vexation.

EXCULPABLE (eks-kul'pą-bl) *a.* that may be cleared of blame.

EXCULPATE (eks-kul'pāt) *v.t.* to clear from a charge of fault or crime. [Fr. L. *ex*, and *culpa*, fault.]

EXCULPATION (eks-kul-pā'shun) *n.* act of clearing from blame.

EXCULPATORY (eks-kul'pą-tur-i) *a.* clearing from blame.

EXCURSION (eks-kur'shun) *n.* a trip for health or pleasure; expedition; digression. [L. (acc.) *excursionem*, a running out, fr. *excursus*.]

EXCURSIONIST (eks-kur'shun-ist) *n.* one who goes on an excursion.

EXCURSIVE (eks-kur'siv) *a.* wandering. [See EXCURSION.]

EXCURSIVELY (eks-kur'siv-li) *ad.* in a desultory or random manner.

EXCURSIVENESS (eks-kur'siv-nes) *n.* disposition to wander or digress.

EXCUSABLE (eks-kū'zą-bl) *a.* that may be excused. [See EXCUSE.]

EXCUSABLY (eks-kū'zą-bli) *ad.* in a way to be excused.

EXCUSE (eks-kūz') *v.t.* to free from blame or obligation; ask or give pardon for;— (eks-kūs') *n.* apology; that which excuses. [F., fr. L. *excusare*, release from a charge, fr. *ex*, and *causa*.]

EXECRABLE (ek'se-krą-bl) *a.* detestable.

EXECRABLY (ek'se-krą-bli) *ad.* abominably.

EXECRATE (ek'se-krāt) *v.t.* to curse. [L. (part.) *ex(s)ecratus*, having cursed, fr. *ex*, greatly, and *sacrare*, consecrate, devote, fr. *sacer*, holy.]

EXECRATION (ek-se-krā'shun) *n.* imprecation of evil.

EXECUTE (ek'se-kūt) *v.t.* to carry into effect; put to death by law; complete; perform. [F. *exécuter*, fr. L. (part.) *ex(s)ecutus*, having followed up, fr. *ex*, and *sequi*, follow.]

EXECUTION (ek-se-kū'shun) *n.* act of executing; performance; achievement; capital punishment; style of performance in music, painting, and other works of art.

EXECUTIONER (ek-se-kū'shun-ẽr) *n.* one who puts to death by law.

EXECUTIVE (eg-zek'ū-tiv) *a.* carrying into effect;—*n.* the person or power that executes the law.

EXECUTOR (eg-zek'ū-tẽr) *n.* one who administers the will of a testator. [See EXECUTE.]

EXECUTORSHIP (eg-zek'ū-tur-ship) *n.* office of executor.

EXECUTORY (eg-zek'ū-tur-i) *a.* performing official duties.

EXECUTRIX (eg-zek'ū-triks) *n.* a female executor. [L.]

EXEGESIS (ek-se-jē'sis) *n.* science of interpretation. [G., fr. *ex*, and *hegeomai*, guide.]

EXEGETICAL (ek-se-jet'i-kąl) *a.* explanatory. [See EXEGESIS.]

EXEMPLAR (eg-zem'plär) *n.* copy; pattern. [L., fr. *exemplum*.]

EXEMPLARILY (eg'zem-plą-ri-li) *ad.* by way of example.

EXEMPLARY (eg'zem-plą-ri) *a.* worthy of imitation; commendable. [L. *exemplaris*.]

EXEMPLIFICATION (eg-zem-pli-fi-kā'shun) *n.* illustration by example; a copy. [See EXEMPLIFY.]

EXEMPLIFIER (eg-zem'pli-fi-er) *n.* one who exemplifies.

EXEMPLIFY (eg-zem'pli-fi) *v.t.* to illustrate by example. [Suff. *fy.* fr. F. *-fier*, fr. L. *-ficare*, =*facere*, make. See EXEMPLAR.]

EXEMPT (eg-zemt') *a.* free;—*v.t.* to free from; —*n.* one who is not subject. [L. (part.) *exemptus*, taken out, fr. *ex*, and *emere*, take.]

EXEMPTION (eg-zem'shun) *n.* freedom; immunity.

EXERCISE (ek'ser-siz) *n.* use; practice; lesson; task;—*v.t.* to train by use; practise; occupy; give authority to;—*v.i.* to use action or exertion. [F. *exercice*, fr. L. *exercitium*, fr. (part.) *exercitus*, exercised, lit. shut out, (to work), fr. *ex*, out, and *arcere*, enclose.]

EXERT (eg-zert') *v.t.* to put forth; put in action; strain. [L. (part.) *exertus*, of *exerere*, fr. *ex*, and *serere*, bind together.]

EXERTION (eg-zer'shun) *n.* act of exerting; effort.

EXFOLIATE (eks-fō'li-āt) *v.i.* to scale off. [L. (part.) *exfoliatus*, of *exfoliare*, to strip of leaves, fr. *ex*, and *folium*, leaf.]

EXFOLIATION (eks-fō-li-ā'shun) *n.* act of scaling off.

EXHALABLE (eks-hā'la-bl) *a.* that may be exhaled. [See EXHALE.]

EXHALANT (ekz-hā'lant) *a.* sending forth vapours or odours. [See EXHALE.]

EXHALATION (eks-ha-lā'shun) *n.* evaporation; vapour. [See EXHALE.]

EXHALE (ekz-hāl') *v.t.* to emit, as vapour; evaporate;—*v.i.* to rise or be given off, as vapour. [L. *ex*, and *halare*, breathe.]

EXHALEMENT (eks-hāl'ment) *n.* matter exhaled; vapour.

EXHAUST (eg-zawst') *v.t.* to drain to emptiness; expend entirely; weary. [L. (part.) *exhaustus*, fr. *ex*, and *haurire*, to draw.]

EXHAUSTIBLE (eg-zaws'ti-bl) *a.* that may be exhausted.

EXHAUSTION (eg-zaws'tyun) *n.* act of exhausting; state of being emptied or wearied.

EXHAUSTIVE (eg-zaws'tiv) *a.* serving to exhaust. [exhausted.]

EXHAUSTLESS (eg-zawst'les) *a.* not to be

EXHIBIT (eg-zib'it) *v.t.* to display; present officially; administer;—*n.* anything exhibited. [L. (part.) *exhibitus*, fr. *ex*, and *habere*, to have, hold.]

EXHIBITION (ek-si-bish'un) *n.* a setting forth; public show; a bursary.

EXHIBITIONER (ek-si-bish'un-er) *n.* one who has a bursary or pension at a university.

EXHIBITORY (eg-zib'i-tur-i) *a.* showing.

EXHILARATE (eg-zil'a-rāt) *v.t.* to make cheerful. [L. (part.) *exhilaratus*, greatly gladdened, fr. *ex*, and *hilaris*, blithe. See HILARIOUS.]

EXHILARATING (eg-zil'a-rā'ting) *a.* enlivening; gladdening.

EXHILARATINGLY (eg-zil'a-rā-ting-li) *ad.* in an exhilarating manner.

EXHILARATION (eg-zil-a-rā'shun) *n.* act of exhilarating.

EXHORT (eg-zort') *v.t.* to advise or warn; incite to good;—*v.i.* to give good advice. [L., fr. *ex*, greatly, and *hortari*, urge.]

EXHORTATION (ek-sor-tā'shun) *n.* a persuasive discourse. [L. fr. (part.) *exhortatus*, having exhorted.]

EXHORTATORY (eg-zor'ta-tur-i) *a.* tending to exhort. Also EXHORTATIVE. [See EXHORTATION.]

EXHUMATION (eks-hū-mā'shun) *n.* a digging from the grave. [See EXHUME.]

EXHUME (eks-hūm') *v.t.* to disinter. [F., fr. Late L. *exhumare*, fr. L. *ex*, and *humus*, ground.]

EXIGENCY (ek'si-jen-si) *n.* urgent demand; pressing necessity; a case of distress. [See EXIGENT.]

EXIGENT (ek'si-jent) *a.* pressing. [L. (part. stem) *exigent-*, exacting, fr. *ex*, and *agere*, drive.]

EXIGIBLE (ek'si-ji-bl) *a.* that may be exacted.

EXILE (ek'sil) *n.* banishment; a person banished;—*v.t.* to banish. [O.F. *exil*, fr. L. *ex(s)ilium*, conn. with *solium*, SOIL.]

EXIST (eg-zist') *v.t.* to be; live; occur; endure. [L. *ex(s)istere*, stand out, fr. *ex*, and *sistere*, cause to stand, fr. *stare*.]

EXISTENCE (eg-zis'tens) *n.* being; life.

EXISTENT (eg-zis'tent) *a.* having being.

EXISTING (eg-zis'ting) *ppr.* or *a.* having being or life.

EXIT (eks'it) *n.* a going out; departure; way out; death. [L. =he goes out.]

EXODUS (ek'sō-dus) *n.* departure from a place; the second book in the Bible. [L., fr. G. *exodos*, a going out, fr. *ex*, and *hodos*, a journey.]

EXOGEN (ek'sō-jen) *n.* a plant that grows by new layers to the outside of the stem. [G. *exo*, outside, and root *gen*, of *gignomai*, I am born.]

EXOGENOUS (ek-soj'e-nus) *a.* growing by additions to the outside.

EXONERATE (eg-zon'e-rāt) *v.t.* to unload; free from a charge. [L. (part.) *exoneratus*, disburdened, fr. *ex*, and *onerare*.]

EXONERATION (eg-zon-e-rā'shun) *n.* act of exonerating.

EXORABLE (eg'zō-ra-bl) *a.* that may be moved by entreaty. [L., fr. *ex*, out, and *orare*, pray, beseech.]

EXORBITANCE (eg-zor'bi-tans) *n.* extravagance; enormity.

EXORBITANT (eg-zor'bi-tant) *a.* excessive. [L. (part. stem) *exorbitant-*, leaving the track, fr. *ex*, and *orbita*, ORBIT, fr. *orbis*, circle.]

EXORBITANTLY (eg-zor'bi-tant-li) *ad.* excessively; enormously.

EXORCISE (ek'sor-siz) *v t.* to expel, as evil spirits by conjuration. [Fr. G. *ex*, and *horkizein*, bind by an oath, fr. *horkos*, through Late L.]

EXORCISM (ek'sor-sizm) *n.* act of exorcising.

EXORCIST (ek'sor-sist) *n.* one who casts out evil spirits. [See EXORCISE.]

EXORDIAL (eg-zor'di-al) *a.* pertaining to the beginning. [See EXORDIUM.]

EXORDIUM (eg-zor'di-um) *n.* introduction; preface, or preamble. [L., fr. *ex*, and *ordiri*, begin.]

EXOTIC (eg-zot'ik) *a.* foreign;—*n.* anything of foreign origin. [L., fr. G. *exotikos*, fr. *exo*, outside.]

EXPAND (ek-spand') *v.t.* or *i.* to open; spread; dilate. [L., fr. *ex*, and *pandere*, spread out.]

EXPANSE (ek-spans') *n.* wide extent of space or body. [L. (part.) *expansus*, spread out.]

EXPANSIBILITY (ek-span-si-bil'i-ti) *n.* capacity of being expanded.

EXPANSIBLE (eks-pan'si-bl) *a.* capable of being expanded.

EXPANSIBLY (eks-pan'si-bli) *ad.* in an expansible manner.

EXPANSION (ek-span'shun) *n.* act of expanding; extent.

EXPANSIVE (ek-span'siv) *a.* capable of expanding or of being expanded.

EXPANSIVELY (eks-pan'siv-li) *ad.* by expansion.

EXPANSIVENESS (eks-pan'siv-nes) *n.* quality of being expansive.

EXPATIATE (eks-pā'shi-āt) *v.i.* to rove; wander; enlarge upon. [L. (part.) *ex(s)-patiatus*, having wandered, fr. *ex*, and *spatiari*, walk abroad, fr. *spatium*, SPACE.]

EXPATIATION (eks-pā-shi-ā'shun) *n.* enlarging in discourse or writing.

EXPATRIATE (eks-pā'tri-āt) *v.t.* to banish from one's country. [Late L., fr. *ex*, and *patria*, fatherland, fr. *pater*.]

EXPATRIATION (eks-pā-tri-ā'shun) *n.* banishment; voluntary emigration.

EXPECT (eks-pekt') *v.t.* to look for or anticipate. [L., fr. *ex*, and *spectare*, look.]

EXPECTANCY (eks-pek'tan-si) *n.* a state of waiting.

EXPECTANT (eks-pek'tant) *n.* waiting; looking for; —*n.* one who is expecting.

EXPECTATION (eks-pek-tā'shun) *n.* act or state of looking for; hope or prospect of future good. [L. (part.) *expectatus*, expected]

EXPECTORANT (eks-pek'tō-rant) *n.* a medicine that promotes discharges from the lungs. [See EXPECTORATE.]

EXPECTORATE (eks-pek'tu-rāt) *v.i.* to discharge from the lungs. [L., fr. *ex*, and stem *pector-*, of *pectus*, breast.]

EXPECTORATION (eks-pek-tu-rā'shun) *n.* act of discharging from the lungs.

EXPECTORATIVE (eks-pek'tu-rat-iv) *a.* serving to promote expectoration; —*n.* a medicine for the purpose. [See EXPECTORATE.]

EXPEDIENCE (eks-pē'di-ens) *n.* suitableness; self-interest; time serving.

EXPEDIENCY (eks-pē'di-en-si) *n.* fitness; propriety.

EXPEDIENT (eks-pē'di-ent) *a.* fit; proper; —*n.* means to an end; shift; device. [L. (part. stem) *expedient-*, fr. *expedire*. See EXPEDITE.] [with advantage.

EXPEDIENTLY (eks-pē'di-ent-li) *ad.* fitly;

EXPEDITE (eks'pe-dīt) *v.t.* to hasten forward; render easy; accelerate. [L. (part.) *expeditus*, made ready, lit. of a foot, fr. *ex*, and stem *ped-*, of *pes*, foot.]

EXPEDITION (eks-pe-dish'un) *n.* haste; despatch; a voyage; an enterprise.

EXPEDITIONARY (eks-pe-dish'un-a-ri) *a.* belonging to or forming an expedition.

EXPEDITIOUS (eks-pe-dish'us) *a.* done with despatch; speedy; prompt. [See EXPEDITE.]

EXPEDITIOUSLY (eks-pe-dish'us-li) *ad.* with expedition or despatch.

EXPEL (eks-pel') *v.t.* to drive or force out; banish. [L., fr. *ex*, and *pellere*, drive.]

EXPEND (eks-pend') *v.t.* to spend for an object; lay out; consume; waste. [L. *expendere*, lit. weigh out, fr. *ex*, and *pendere*.]

EXPENDITURE (eks-pen'di-tūr) *n.* act of spending; sum expended. [Fr. Late L. (part.) *expenditus* = *espensus*.]

EXPENSE (eks-pens') *n.* cost; charge. [O.F., fr. L. (acc.) *expensam* (*pecuniam*), (money) disbursed.]

EXPENSIVE (eks-pen'siv) *a.* costly; dear.

EXPENSIVELY (eks-pen'siv-li) *ad.* with great expense.

EXPENSIVENESS (eks-pen'siv-nes) *n.* habit of spending much money; extravagance.

EXPERIENCE (eks-pē'ri-ens) *n.* trial or series of trials; —*v.t.* to try; know by practice. [O.F., fr. L. *experientia*, fr. (part. stem) *experiri*, trying thoroughly, fr. *experiri*.]

EXPERIMENT (eks-per'i-ment) *n.* trial; essay; —*v.i.* to make trial. [L. *experimentum*.]

EXPERIMENTAL (eks-per-i-men'tal) *a.* founded on trial or experience.

EXPERIMENTALIST (eks-per-i-men'tal-ist) *n.* one who makes experiments.

EXPERIMENTALLY (eks-per-i-men'tal-i) *ad.* by experiment; by personal trial.

EXPERIMENTER (eks-per-i-men'tėr) *n.* one who makes experiments.

EXPERT (eks-pert') *a.* skilful; dexterous; — (eks'pert) *n.* a specialist; a scientific or professional witness. [L. (part.) *expertus*, having tested. See EXPERIENCE.]

EXPERTLY (eks-pert'li) *ad.* with skill.

EXPERTNESS (eks-pert'nes) *n.* readiness; dexterity; practical skill.

EXPIATE (eks'pi-āt) *v.t.* to atone for, as a crime. [L. (part.) *expiatus*, atoned for, fr. *ex*, fully, and *piare*, fr. *pius*, PIOUS.]

EXPIATION (eks-pi-ā'shun) *n.* atonement; satisfaction.

EXPIATORY (eks'pi-ā-tur-i) *a.* that makes expiation.

EXPIRATION (eks-pi-rā'shun) *n.* act of breathing out; end.

EXPIRATORY (eks-pīr'ā-tur-i) *a.* pertaining to the emission of breath.

EXPIRE (eks-pīr') *v.t.* [*pret.* EXPIRED] to breathe out; —*v.i.* to terminate; die. [O.F. *expirer*, fr. L. *ex*, and *spirare*, breathe.]

EXPIRING (eks-pī'ring) *a.* dying; pertaining to or uttered at death.

EXPLAIN (eks-plān') *v.t.* to make plain; expound; elucidate; —*v.i.* to give explanations. [O.F., fr. L. *ex*, quite, and *planare*, to level.]

EXPLAINABLE (eks-plā'na-bl) *a.* that may be explained.

EXPLANATION (eks-pla-nā'shun) *n.* act of making plain.

EXPLANATORY (eks-plan'a-tur-i) *a.* serving to explain.

EXPLETIVE (eks'ple-tiv) *n.* a word inserted to fill a space; an oath. [L. (part.) *expletus*, filled out, fr. *ex*, and *plere*.]

EXPLETORY (eks'ple-tur-i) *a.* serving to fill up. [See EXPLETIVE.]

EXPLICABLE (eks'pli-ka-bl) *a.* that can be explained.

EXPLICATE (eks'pli-kāt) *v.t.* to unfold; explain; show. [L. (part.) *explicatus*, unfolded, fr. *ex*, and *plicare*.]

EXPLICATION (eks-pli-kā'shun) *n.* an explanation.

EXPLICATIVE (eks'pli-kā-tiv) *a.* tending to explain.

EXPLICIT (eks-plis'it) *a.* clear; plain; express; not obscure. [L. (part.) *explicitus*, = *ex-plicatus*.]

EXPLICITLY (eks-plis'it-li) *ad.* plainly; expressly.

EXPLICITNESS (eks-plis'it-nes) *n.* plainness of language.

EXPLODE (eks-plōd') *v.i.* to burst with noise; —*v.t.* to drive into disrepute. [L. *explodere*, lit. to hoot off (the stage), fr. *ex*, and *plaudere*, clap (the hands).]

EXPLOIT (eks-ploit') *n.* a heroic deed; —*v.t.* to work up and utilise, for one's own ends. [O.F. *esploit*, fr. L. *explicitum*, thing finished. See EXPLICIT.]

EXPLOITATION (eks-ploi-tā'shun) *n.* successful application of industry and skill to any object. [See EXPLOIT.]

EXPLORATION (eks-plō-rā'shun) *n.* act of exploring.

EXPLORATORY (eks-plor'a-tur-i) *a.* serving to search out; examining.

EXPLORE (eks-plōr') *v.t.* to search through; examine thoroughly. [F. *explorer*, fr. L. *explorare*, orig. to cry out. See DEPLORE.]

EXPLORING (eks-plōr'ing) *ppr.* or *a.* searching; examining.

EXPLOSION (eks-plō'zhun) *n.* a sudden bursting with noise. [L. (part.) *explosus*, driven away.]

EXPLOSIVE (eks-plō'siv) *a.* liable to or causing explosion.

EXPLOSIVELY (eks-plō'siv-li) *ad.* in an explosive manner.

EXPONENT (eks-pō'nent) *n.* one who or that which sets forth; an algebraic letter or number. [L. (part. stem) *exponent-*, setting out, fr. *ex*, and *ponere*, place.]

EXPORT (eks-pōrt') *v.t.* to transport from one country to another; —(eks'pōrt) *n.* a commodity sent abroad. [L., fr. *ex*, and *portare*, carry.]

EXPORTABLE (eks-pōr'ta-bl) *a.* that can be exported.

EXPORTATION (eks-pōr-tā'shun) *n.* the carrying of goods out of a country.

EXPORTER (eks-pōr'tėr) *n.* one who exports.

Fāte, fär, ado; mē, her; mine; nōte; tūne; mōŏn.

EXPOSE (eks-pōz') *v.t.* to lay open or bare; put in danger. [O.F., fr. *ex*—L. *ex*, and *poser*, place, POSE.]

EXPOSE (eks-pō-zā') *n.* a formal statement of a case; exposure of something wrong. [F.]

EXPOSED (eks-pōzd') *a.* laid out for sale; open to attack.

EXPOSITION (eks-pu-zish'un) *n.* explanation; exhibition.

EXPOSITOR (eks-pōz'i-tẹr) *n.* an interpreter; expounder.   [exegetical.

EXPOSITORY (eks-poz'i-tur-i) *a.* explaining.

EXPOSTULATE (eks-pos'tū-lāt) *v.i.* to remonstrate earnestly with. [L. (part.) *expostulatus*, demanded, fr. *ex*, and *postulare*.]

EXPOSTULATION (eks-pos-tū-lā'shun) *n.* reasoning with.

EXPOSTULATORY (eks-pos'tū-lā-tur-i) *a.* containing expostulation.

EXPOSURE (eks-pō'zhŭr) *n.* act of exposing or state of being exposed.

EXPOUND (eks-pound') *v.t.* to explain. [O.F. *espondre*, fr. L. *exponere*. See EXPONENT.]

EXPOUNDER (eks-poun'dẹr) *n.* one who interprets or explains. [See EXPOUND.]

EXPRESS (eks-pres') *v.t.* to press out; utter in language; represent; exhibit; declare; designate;—*a.* plain; explicit;—*n.* a special messenger or message; fast conveyance. [O.F. *expresser*, fr. L. *ex*, out, and *pressare*, freq. of *premere* (part. *pressus*), to press. See PRESS.]

EXPRESSED (eks-prest') *pp.* or *a.* despatched by express; uttered; squeezed out.

EXPRESSIBLE (eks-pres'i-bl) *a.* that may be uttered.

EXPRESSION (eks-presh'un) *n.* a pressing out; utterance or representation; feature; look; phrase; diction; musical tone or feeling.

EXPRESSIVE (eks-pres'iv) *a.* adapted to express.

EXPRESSIVELY (eks-pres'iv-li) *ad.* with force.

EXPRESSLY (eks-pres'li) *ad.* in direct terms; plainly.

EXPUGN (eks-pūn') *v.t.* to take by assault.

EXPUGNABLE (eks-pug'nạ-bl, eks-pū'nạ-bl) *a.* that may be conquered. [L. *ex*, out, and *pugna*, fight.]

EXPULSION (eks-pul'shun) *n.* act of expelling. [O.F., fr. L. (part.) *expulsus*, driven out, fr. EXPEL.]

EXPULSIVE (eks-pul'siv) *a.* having power to expel.

EXPUNGE (eks-punj') *v.t.* to blot out. [L. *expungere*, prick out, to remove, fr. *ex*, and *pungere*, prick.]

EXPURGATE (eks-pur'gāt, eks'pur-gāt) *v.t.* to cleanse; purify; expunge. [L. (part.) *expurgatus*, thoroughly purged, fr. *ex*, and *purgare*, PURGE.]

EXPURGATION (eks-pur-gā'shun) *n.* act of purifying.

EXPURGATORY (eks-pur'gạ-tur-i) *a.* purifying. [See EXPURGATE.]

EXQUISITE (eks'kwi-zit) *a.* very fine; excellent; keenly felt;—*n.* a fop or dandy. [L. (part.) *exquisitus*, sought out, fr. *ex*, and *quærere*, seek.]

EXQUISITELY (eks'kwi-sit-li) *ad.* nicely.

EXQUISITENESS (eks'kwi-zit-nes) *n.* nicety; keenness; perfection.

EXTANT (eks'tạnt) *a.* now in being. [L. (part.-stem) *extant-*, outstanding, fr. *ex*, and *stare*.]

EXTEMPORANEOUS (eks-tem-pu-rā'ne-us) *a.* uttered without previous study. [See EXTEMPORE.]

EXTEMPORARY (eks-tem'pu-rā-ri) *a.* performed without previous preparation. [See EXTEMPORE.]

EXTEMPORE (eks-tem'pu-re) *ad.* without previous study. [L. *ex tempore*, at the time.]

EXTEMPORISE (eks-tem'pu-rīz) *v.i.* to utter without study. [See EXTEMPORE.]

EXTEND (eks-tend') *v.t.* or *i.* to stretch out; spread; prolong. [L., fr. *ex*, and *tendere*, to stretch, TEND.]

EXTENSIBILITY (eks-ten-si-bil'i-ti) *n.* quality of being extensible.

EXTENSIBLE (eks-ten'si-bl) *a.* that can be extended. [See EXTEND.]

EXTENSION (eks-ten'shun) *n.* act of extending; enlargement. [F., fr. L. (acc.) *extensionem*, fr. (part.) *extensus*, extended.]

EXTENSIVE (eks-ten'siv) *a.* large; of great extent. [See EXTENSION.]   [largely.

EXTENSIVELY (eks-ten'siv-li) *ad.* widely;

EXTENSIVENESS (eks-ten'siv-nes) *n.* extent; largeness; wideness. [See EXTENSION.]

EXTENSOR (eks-ten'sẹr) *n.* a muscle that serves to extend or straighten. [See EXTENSION.]

EXTENT (eks-tent') *n.* space; compass. [See EXTENSION.]

EXTENUATE (eks-ten'ū-āt) *v.t.* to palliate; lessen; draw out; make thin. [L. (part.) *extenuatus*, thinned, fr. *ex*, and *tenuare*, make thin, *tenuis*.]

EXTENUATION (eks-ten-ū-ā'shun) *n.* act of extenuating; palliation.

EXTENUATOR (eks-ten'ū-ā-tẹr) *n.* one who extenuates.

EXTERIOR (eks-tē'ri-ẹr) *a.* outward; foreign; —*n.* the outside; surface. [L. (comp.) fr. *exterus*, external, fr. *ex*.]

EXTERMINATE (eks-tẹr'mi-nāt) *v.t.* to root out. [L. (part.) *exterminatus*, banished, fr. *ex*, and *terminus*, boundary.]

EXTERMINATION (eks-tẹr-mi-nā'shun) *n.* destruction.

EXTERMINATOR (eks-tẹr'mi-nā-tẹr) *n.* one who exterminates.

EXTERN (eks-tẹrn') *a.* not inherent; outward; visible;—*n.* a pupil who lives outside the seminary. [See EXTERNAL.]

EXTERNAL (eks-tẹr'nạl) *a.* outward. [L. *externus*, fr. *exterus*, external. See EXTERIOR.]

EXTERNALLY (eks-tẹr'nạl-i) *ad.* outwardly.

EXTERNALS (eks-tẹr'nạlz) *n.pl.* outward rites; exterior form.

EXTINCT (eks-tingkt') *a.* extinguished; no longer in force; dead. [L. (part.) *extinctus*, extinguished. See EXTINGUISH.]

EXTINCTION (eks-tingk'shun) *n.* destruction; suppression. [See EXTINCT.]

EXTINGUISH (eks-ting'gwish) *v.t.* to put out; quench; destroy. [L., fr. *ex*, thoroughly, and *stinguere*, quench.]

EXTINGUISHABLE (eks-ting'gwish-ạ-bl) *a.* that may be quenched or put out.

EXTINGUISHER (ex-ting'gwish-ẹr) *n.* a utensil to put on a candle to extinguish it.

EXTINGUISHMENT (eks-ting'gwish-ment) *n.* a putting out or quenching; abolition.

EXTIRPABLE (eks-tẹr'pạ-bl) *a.* that may be rooted or cut out.

EXTIRPATE (eks-tẹr'pāt, eks'tẹr-pāt) *v.t.* to root or cut out; destroy totally. [L. (part.) *extirpatus*, rooted out, fr. *ex*, and *stirps*, the stem (with root).]

EXTIRPATION (eks-tẹr-pā'shun) *n.* the act of rooting out.

EXTOL (eks-tōl') *v.t.* to praise greatly; magnify; eulogise; glorify. [L., fr. *ex*, and *tollere*, lift.]

EXTORT (eks-tort') *v.t.* to wrest or gain by force; exact;—*v.i.* to practise extortion. [L. (part.) *extortus*, wrung out, fr. *ex*, and *torquere*.]

EXTORTION (eks-tor'shun) *n.* unlawful exaction.   [sive.

EXTORTIONATE (eks-tor'shun-āt) *a.* oppres-

EXTORTIONER (eks-tor'shun-ẹr) *n.* one who practises extortion.

EXTRA (eks'trạ) *prefix*, signifying without or beyond;—*n.* an additional item in an estimate of expenses. [L. = beyond.]

Fāte, fär, ado; mē, hẹr; mïne; nōte; tūne; mōŏn.

EXTRACT (eks-trakt') *v.t.* to draw out; take out; select;—(eks'trakt) *n.* a substance drawn from another; a passage from a book. [L. (part.) *extractus*, drawn out, fr. *ex*, and *trahere*, draw.]

EXTRACTION (eks-trak'shun) *n.* a drawing out; lineage; finding the root of a number.

EXTRACTIVE (eks-trak'tiv) *a.* that may be extracted.

EXTRACTOR (eks-trak'ter) *n.* he or that which extracts.

EXTRADITE (eks-tra-dīt') *v.t.* to deliver up, as by one nation to another. [See EXTRADITION.]

EXTRADITION (eks-tra-dish'un) *n.* delivery on the part of one government to another of an accused person. [Fr. L. *ex*, and (acc.) *traditionem*, a giving up. See TRADITION.]

EXTRADOS (eks-trā'dos) *n.* the exterior curve of an arch. [F., fr. L *extra*, and *dorsum*, back.]

EXTRANEOUS (eks-trā'ne-us) *a.* foreign; not intrinsic. [L. *extraneus*, fr. EXTRA. Doublet of STRANGE.]

EXTRANEOUSLY (eks-trā'ne-us-li) *ad.* in an extraneous manner.

EXTRAORDINARILY (eks-tra-or'di-na-ri-li, eks-tror'di-na-ri-li) *ad.* in an uncommon degree.

EXTRAORDINARY (eks-tra-or'di-na-ri, eks-tror'di-na-ri) *a.* uncommon; remarkable; special. [L. *extraordinarius*.]

EXTRAVAGANCE (eks-trav'a-gans) *n.* lavish expense; excess.

EXTRAVAGANT (eks-trav'a-gant) *a.* exceeding due bounds; lavish in expenses; irregular; profuse. [F., fr. L. *extra*, and (acc. part.) *vagantem*, wandering, fr. *vagari*.]

EXTRAVAGANTLY (eks-trav'a-gant-li) *ad.* in an extravagant manner.

EXTRAVASATE (eks-trav'a-sāt) *v.t.* to let out of the proper vessels, as blood. [Fr. L. *extra*, and *vas*, vessel.]

EXTREME (eks-trēm') *a.* outermost; utmost; greatest;—*n.* utmost limit; extremity. [O.F. = F. *extrême*, fr. L. (superl.) *extremus*, fr. *exterus*. See EXTERIOR.]

EXTREMELY (eks-trēm'li) *ad.* in the utmost degree; intensely.

EXTREMITY (eks-trem'i-ti) *n.* utmost point or degree; end; necessity.

EXTRICABLE (eks'tri-ka-bl) *a.* that may be extricated.

EXTRICATE (eks'tri-kāt) *v.t.* to disentangle; set free. [L. (part.) *extricatus*, disentangled, fr. *extricare*, fr. *tricæ*, hindrances.]

EXTRICATION (eks-tri-kā'shun) *n.* act of disentangling.

EXTRINSIC (eks-trin'sik) *a.* outward; external; unessential. [O.F. = F. *extrinsèque*, fr. L. *extrinsecus*, from, on the outside, fr. *exter*, outward, and *secus*, beside.]

EXTRINSICALLY (eks-trin'si-kal-i) *ad.* from without; externally.

EXTRUDE (eks-trŏŏd') *v.t.* to thrust out; expel. [L., fr. *ex* and *trudere*, to thrust]

EXTRUSION (eks-trŏŏ'zhun) *n.* act of thrusting out. [L. (part.) *extrusus*, thrust out.]

EXUBERANCE (ek-sū'be-rans) *n.* over abundance; luxuriance.

EXUBERANT (ek-sū'be-rant) *a.* over abundant; superfluous. [L. (part. ster.) *exuberant-*, abounding, fr. *ex*, and *uberare*, to be fertile, fr. *uber*, rich.]

EXUBERANTLY (ek-sū'be-rant-li) *ad.* abundantly; very copiously.

EXUDATION (ek-sū-dā'shun) *n.* the act of sweating out.

EXUDE (ek-sūd') *v.t.* to discharge through the pores;—*v.i.* to flow; issue forth. [L., fr. *ex*, and *sudare*, to sweat.]

EXULT (eg-zult') *v.i.* to rejoice greatly. [L. *ex(s)ultare*, fr. *ex-silire*, leap forth, fr. *ex*, and *salire*.]

EXULTATION (eg-zul-tā'shun) *n.* great joy or rapturous delight.

EYAS (ī'as) *n.* a young hawk. [An *eyas* for a *nyas*, fr. F. *niais*, orig. unfledged, fr. L. *nidus*, nest, through Late L.]

EYE (ī) *n.* the organ of sight;—*v.t.* to watch; observe. [M.E. *eye*, *eighe*, fr. O.E. *eage*. Cf. Ger. *Auge*.]

EYEBALL (ī'bawl) *n.* the ball of the eye.

EYEBOLT (ī'bōlt) *n.* a bar of iron with an eye at one end for hooking tackle to.

EYEBROW (ī'brou) *n.* hairy arch over the eyes.

EYELASH (ī'lash) *n.* hair on the eyelid.

EYELESS (ī'les) *n.* having no eyes; blind.

EYELET-HOLE (ī'let-hōl) *n.* a hole for lace or cord. [O.F. *œillet*, dim. of *œil*, eye.]

EYELID (ī'lid) *n.* movable cover of the eyeball.

EYESALVE (ī'sav) *n.* ointment for the eye.

EYE-SERVANT (ī'ser-vant) *n.* a servant that requires watching.

EYE-SERVICE (ī'ser-vis) *n.* service done under the employer's eye.

EYESIGHT (ī'sīt) *n.* sight of the eye; power of seeing.

EYESORE (ī'sōr) *n.* something offensive to the sight.

EYETOOTH (ī'tŏŏth) *n.* an upper tooth next the grinders.

EYE-WATER (ī'waw-ter) *n.* lotion for sore eyes.

EYEWITNESS (ī'wit-nes) *n.* one who saw what he testifies.

EYRE (ār) *n.* a circuit of judges. [O.F. *eire*, journey, fr. L. *iter*.]

EYRY (ī'ri) *n.* a place where birds of prey build and hatch; a brood of such birds. [See AERIE.]

F

FABIAN (fā'bi-an) *a.* delaying; dilatory;—*n.* a member of a group of Socialists bearing this name. [Fr. *Fabius Maximus*, called *Cunctator* the delayer, who wore out Hannibal by cautious tactics.]

FABLE (fā'bl) *n.* a fiction enforcing a useful truth; plot of a poem; falsehood;—*v.t.* or *i.* to feign; invent; lie. [F., fr. L. *fabula*, fr. *fari*, speak.]

FABLED (fā'bld) *a.* told in fables.

FABRIC (fab'rik) *n.* a building; a manufactured article, as cloth. [F. *fabrique*, fr. L. (acc.) *fabricam*, workshop, fr. stem *fabri-*, of *faber*, artisan. Doublet of FORGE.]

FABRICATE (fab'ri-kāt) *v.t.* to form by art and labour; build; manufacture; devise falsely. [See FABRIC.]

FABRICATION (fab-ri-kā'shun) *n.* act of framing, constructing, or devising; that which is fabricated.

FABRICATOR (fab'ri-kā-ter) *n.* one who constructs.

FABULIST (fab'ū-list) *n.* one who writes or invents fables.

FABULOUS (fab'ū-lus) *a.* feigned; invented; unreal; false.

FABULOUSLY (fab'ū-lus-li) *ad.* in a feigned or false manner.

FACADE (fa-säd') *n.* a front elevation of a building. [Fr., Fr. It. = face.]

FACE (fās) *n.* the visage; front;—*v.t.* to meet in front. [F., fr. L. *facies*.]

FACET (fas'et) *n.* a little face. [See FACE.]

FACETIOUS (fa-sē'shus) *a.* humorous; witty. [L., fr. *facetus*, witty.]

FACETIOUSLY (fa-sē'shus-li) *ad.* with humour.

FACETIOUSNESS (fa-sē'shus-nes) *n.* jocoseness; pleasant jesting.

FACIAL (fā'shal) *a.* pertaining to the face. [See FACE.]

FACILE (fas'il) *a.* easy to be done; yielding; pliant; ready; dexterous. [F., fr. L. (acc.) *facilem*, easily done, fr. *facere*.]

FACILITATE (fa-sil'i-tāt) *v.t.* to make easy. [See FACILE.]

FACILITY (fa-sil'i-ti) *n.* ease; easiness;—*pl.* means to render easy. [Doublet of FACULTY.]

FACING (fā'sing) *n.* a covering in front for ornament or defence;—*pl.* movements in drilling troops;—*a.* fronting.

FACSIMILE (fak-sim'i-le) *n.* exact likeness. [L. =do-a-like-thing.]

FACT (fakt) *n.* an act; deed; reality; circumstance. [L. *factum*, orig. (neut. part.) thing done, fr. *facere*, Doublet of FEAT.]

FACTION (fak'shun) *n.* a political party; dissension. [F., fr. L. (acc.) *factionem*, lit. a doing. See FACT.]

FACTIONIST (fak'shun-ist) *n.* one who promotes faction.

FACTIOUS (fak'shus) *a.* given to faction. [See FACTION.]

FACTIOUSLY (fak'shus-li) *ad.* in a factious manner.

FACTITIOUS (fak-tish'us) *a.* made by art; artificial. [L. *factitius*, fr. *facere*, make.]

FACTITIOUSLY (fak-tish'us-li) *ad.* in an unnatural manner.

FACTOR (fak'ter) *n.* an agent in trade; anything which contributes to a result or forms a product. [L. =doer.]

FACTORAGE (fak'tur-ij) *n.* commission allowed to a factor.

FACTORY (fak'tur-i) *n.* house of a factor; a manufactory; body of factors.

FACTOTUM (fak-tō'tum) *n.* a servant employed in all sorts of work. [L. =do-everything.]

FACULTY (fak'ul-ti) *n.* power of the mind; ability; officers of a college; members of the learned professions. [F. *faculté*, fr. L. (acc.) *facultatem*, fr. *facilis*. Doublet of FACILITY.]

FAD (fad) *n.* a favourite notion or theory; crotchet; hobby. [Etym. uncertain.]

FADE (fād) *v.i.* to wither or decay; lose colour, freshness, or distinctness. [O.F. *fader*, fr. *fade*, insipid, flat, fr. L. (acc.) *vapidum*, VAPID.]

FADING (fā'ding) *a.* subject to decay.

FAG-END (fag'end) *n.* untwisted end of a rope; refuse or meaner part of anything.

FAGGOT (fag'ut) *n.* a bundle of twigs;—*v.t.* to bind in a bundle. Also FAGOT. [F. *fagot*, perh. fr. a dim. fr. L. *fagus*, beech-tree.]

FAGGOT-VOTE (fag'ut-vōt) *n.* a fictitious vote created by parcelling an estate into as many lots as will supply separate voters.

FAIL (fāl) *v.i.* to become deficient or weak; come short of; decay; cease; miss; become insolvent;—*v.t.* to neglect or omit; disappoint;—*n.* deficiency; want. [F. *faillir*, fr. L. *fallere*, deceive.]

FAILURE (fāl'ur) *n.* deficiency; omission; decay; want of success; bankruptcy.

FAIN (fān) *a.* glad;—*ad.* gladly. [O.E. *fægen*, glad.]

FAINT (fānt) *a.* weak; languid; indistinct; feeble;—*v.i.* to swoon; sink with fatigue. [O.F. (part.) *feint*, fr. *feindre*, FEIGN.]

FAINTING (fān'ting) *n.* a swoon.

FAINTISH (fān'tish) *a.* slightly faint.

FAINTLY (fānt'li) *ad.* feebly; weakly.

FAINTNESS (fānt'nes) *n.* loss of strength, colour, or respiration; feebleness; indistinctness.

FAIR (fār) (1) *a.* free from blemish, perversion, etc; frank; moderate;—*ad.* openly; frankly; civilly;—(2) *n.* a stated market. THE FAIR, the female sex. [(1) O.E. *fæger*. (2) O.F. *feire* =F. *foire*, fr. L. (acc.) *feriam*, holiday.]

FAIRLY (fār'li) *ad.* openly; honestly.

FAIRNESS (fār'nes) *n.* just conduct; honesty; distinctness; clearness of skin.

FAIR-PLAY (fār-plā') *n.* equitable conduct or treatment.

FAIRY (fā'ri) *n.* a fabled spirit;—*a.* belonging to the fairies. [O.F. *faerie*, enchantment, fr. *fae*, fairy.]

FAITH (fāth) *n.* trust; confidence; belief; fidelity; truth or religious system believed. [M.E. *feith*, fr. O.F. *fei(d)* =F. *foi*, fr. L. (acc.) *fidem*, fr. *fides*.]

FAITHFUL (fāth'fool) *a.* firm to the truth; loyal; honest; true.

FAITHFULLY (fāth'fool-i) *ad.* honestly.

FAITHFULNESS (fāth'fool-nes) *n.* firm adherence to truth or trust.

FAITHLESS (fāth'les) *a.* without faith; unbelieving; treacherous; disloyal; false.

FAITHLESSNESS (fāth'les-nes) *n.* want of faith; treachery.

FAKE (fāk) *v.t.* to cheat, or deceive. [D. *facken*, to catch.]

FAKIR (fā-kēr') *n.* a mendicant priest in India. [A. =a poor man.]

FALCATE (fal'kāt) *a.* bent like a sickle; crescent. Also FALCATED. [L. *falcatus*, bent, fr. stem *falc-*, of *falx*, sickle.]

FALCHION (fawl'shun) *n.* a short crooked sword. [O.F. *fauchon*, through it., fr. L. *falx*. See FALCATE.]

FALCON (faw'kn, fal'kun) *n.* a hawk trained for sport. [O.F. *fauc-, faulcon*, fr. L. (acc.) *falconem*, named from its **FALCATED** tail.]

Falchion.

FALCONER (faw'kn-er) *n.* one who trains or sports with hawks.

FALCONRY (faw'kn-ri) *n.* the art of training hawks; hawking.

FALL (fawl) *v.i.* [*p.* FELL; *pp.* FALLEN] to drop down; decline; sink; be killed; disembogue; happen; come upon; assail; be transferred; be uttered;—*n.* descent; declivity; cascade; declension; diminution in value; lady's veil; end of a tackle; musical cadence. [O.E. *feallan*. Cf. Ger. *fallen*.]

FALLACIOUS (fa-lā'shus) *a.* producing mistake; deceitful.

FALLACY (fal'a-si) *n.* a deceptive argument; sophism. [O.F., fr. L. (acc.) *fallaciam*, fr. stem *fallac-*, of *fallax*, deceitful.]

FALLIBILITY (fal-i-bil'i-ti) *n.* liableness to err.

FALLIBLE (fal'i-bl) *a.* liable to err or be deceived. [L., fr. *fallere*, deceive.]

FALLIBLY (fal'i-bli) *ad.* in a fallible manner.

FALLOW (fal'ō) *a.* pale red or yellow; ploughed but not sown;—*n.* land left untilled;—*v.t.* to plough and harrow without sowing. [O.E. *fealu*.]

FALLOW-DEER (fal'ō-dēr) *n.* a species of deer, smaller than the stag, domesticated in English parks.

FALSE (fawls) *a.* not true; counterfeit; not faithful; hypocritical. [O.F. *fals*, fr. L. (acc.) *falsum*, fr. *fallere*, deceive.]

FALSEHOOD (fawls'hood) *n.* want of truth or veracity; untruth; lie. [See FALSE. E. suff. *-hood*, denoting state.]

FALSELY (fawls'li) *ad.* untruly; treacherously.

FALSENESS (fawls'nes) *n.* want of truth or integrity.

FALSETTO (fawl-set'ō) *n.* tones higher in compass than those of the natural voice. [It., dim. fr. *falso*, FALSE.]

FALSIFICATION (fawls-i-fi-kā'shun) *n.* act of misstating or misrepresenting.

FALSIFIER (fawls-i-fi'ẹr) *n.* a liar.

FALSIFY (fawls'i-fī) *v.t.* to represent falsely; prove to be untrue or erroneous;—*v.i.* to tell lies. [See FALSE. -fy = F. *fier* = L. -*ficare*, for *facere*, make.]

FALSITY (fawls'i-ti) *n.* quality of being false; a false assertion.

FALTER (fawl'tẹr) *v.i.* to hesitate in speech; waver. [Etym. uncertain.]

FALTERING (fawl'tẹr-ing) *a.* hesitating.

FAME (fām) *n.* reputation; renown. [F., fr. L. (acc.) *famam.*]

FAMED (fāmd) *a.* celebrated.

FAMILIAR (fạ-mil'yạr) *a.* intimate; well-known; knowing intimately; common;— *n.* an intimate acquaintance; a demon. [L. *familiaris*, pertaining to the FAMILY.]

FAMILIARISE (fạ-mil'yạ-rīz) *v.t.* to accustom; make easy by practice or study.

FAMILIARITY (fạ-mil-i-ar'i-ti) *n.* intimate acquaintance; ease in intercourse.

FAMILIARLY (fạ-mil'yạr-li) *ad.* without constraint or formality; commonly.

FAMILY (fam'i-li) *n.* household; lineage; class. [L. *familia*, fr. *famulus*, servant.]

FAMINE (fam'in) *n.* a general scarcity of food; dearth. [F., fr. L. *fames*, hunger, through Late L.]

FAMISH (fam'ish) *v.i.* to die of hunger;—*v.t.* to starve. [See FAMINE.]

FAMOUS (fā'mus) *a.* renowned; noted. [L. *famosus.*] [L. *famosus.*]

FAMOUSLY (fā'mus-li) *ad.* with great renown.

FAN (fan) *n.* an instrument to blow and cool the face, and one to winnow grain;—*v.t.* to blow with a fan; winnow; stimulate; excite. [O.E. *fann*, fr. L. *vannus*, fan.]

FANATIC (fạ-nat'ik) *n.* an enthusiast; a bigot. [F. *fanatique*, fr. L. (acc.) *fanaticum*, inspired, fr. *fanum*, FANE.]

Fan.

FANATICAL (fạ-nat'i-kạl) *a.* wild and enthusiastic in opinions.

FANATICALLY (fạ-nat'i-kạl-i) *ad.* in an enthusiastic or bigoted manner.

FANATICISM (fạ-nat'i-sizm) *n.* extravagant notions; religious frenzy.

FANCIED (fan'sid) *a.* imaginary; liked.

FANCIER (fan'si-ẹr) *n.* one who has special liking for, or keeps for sale, birds, dogs, etc.

FANCIFUL (fan'si-fool) *a.* dictated by fancy; whimsical; strange.

FANCY (fan'si) *n.* notion; groundless opinion; preference; taste;—*v.t.* or *i.* to imagine; —*a.* pleasing the fancy; fine. [Contr. fr. FANTASY.]

FANE (fān) *n.* a temple; a church. [L. *fanum*, probably fr. *fari*, speak.]

FANFARE (fan'fār) *n.* a flourish of trumpets. [F.; imit.]

FANFARONADE (fan'fạr-o-nād) *n.* a vain boasting; ostentation.

FANG (fang) *n.* tusk of an animal; claw; talon. [O.E. = lit. a catching, fr. (part.) *gefangen*, seized, fr. *fōn*. Cf. Ger. *Fang.*]

FANGLESS (fang'les) *a.* having no fangs.

FANNER (fan'ẹr) *n.* one who fans; a ventilator;—*pl.* an implement to separate grain from chaff.

FANTASIA (fan-tä'zi-ạ) *n.* a fanciful piece of music. [It.]

FANTASTIC (fan-tas'tik) *a.* fanciful; whimsical. [See FANTASY.]

FANTASTICALLY (fan-tas'ti-kạl-i) *ad.* in a fantastic manner.

FANTASY (fan'tạ-si) *n.* a fancy; conceit. [M.E. *fantasye*, fr. O.F. = F. *fantaisie*, fr. Late L. *phantasia*, imagining, imagination, fr. G., fr. *phantazo*, I display.]

FAR (fär) *a.* distant; remote;—*ad.* at or to a great distance; very much. [O.E. *feor.*]

FARCE (färs) *n.* a ludicrous play;—*v.t.* to stuff. [F. *farce*, stuffing, a farce, fr. *farcir*, to stuff.]

FARCICAL (fär'si-kạl) *a.* belonging to a farce. [See FARCE.]

FARE (fār) *v.i.* to be in any state, good or bad; —*n.* price of passage; the person conveyed; food. [O.E. *faran*, go.]

FAREWELL (ā -wel') *n.* wish of welfare; act of taking leave;—*a.* parting; valedictory. FARE and WELL.

FAR-FETCHED (fär'fecht) *a.* brought from afar; forced; elaborately strained.

FARINA (fa-rī'nạ, fa-rē'nạ) *n.* pollen of flowers; the flour of grain, starch, etc. [L. meal, flour, fr. *far*, a sort of grain.]

FARINACEOUS (fär-in-ā'shi-us) *a.* consisting of meal or flour; mealy. [See FARINA.]

FARM (färm) *n.* land occupied by a tenant;— *v.t.* or *i.* to lease or rent for a price; cultivate land. [M.E. *ferme*, fr. O.E. *feorm*, goods, entertainment, fr. L. *firma*, a fixed payment, rent, lease.]

FARMER (fär'mẹr) *n.* one who cultivates a farm.

FARMING (fär'ming) *n.* the business of tilling land.

FARRAGO (far-rā-'gō) *n.* a medley. [L. *farrago*, mixed food for cattle, fr. *far* (gen. *farris*), a kind of grain.]

FARRIER (far'i-ẹr) *n.* one who cures the diseases of horses; a smith who shoes horses. [O.F. *ferrier*, fr. L. *ferrum*, iron.]

FARRIERY (far'i-ẹr-i) *n.* the business of a farrier.

FARROW (far'rō) *n.* a litter of pigs;—*v.t.* or *i.* to bring forth, as pigs;—*a.* not producing a calf in the year. [O.E. *fearh*, pig.]

FARTHER (fär'THẹr) *a.* being at a greater distance. [See FURTHER.]

FARTHEST (fär'THest) *a.* or *ad.* at or to the greatest distance. [See FAR.]

FARTHING (fär'THing) *n.* the fourth of a penny. [O.E. *feortha*, fourth, and dim. -*ing.*]

FARTHINGALE (fär'THing-gāl) *n.* a hoop for a petticoat. [O.F. *verdugalle*, fr. Sp. *verdugado*, a hoop, fr. *verdugo*, a rod, fr. L. *viridis*, green.]

FASCINATE (fas'i-nāt) *v.t.* to charm; captivate. [L. (part.) *fascinatus*, fr. *fascinare*, to enchant.]

FASCINATION (fas-i-nā'shun) *n.* the power of charming.

FASHION (fash'un) *n.* form; custom; mode; —*v.t.* to form; mould. [O.F. *fachon*, make, shape, fr. L. (acc.) *factionem*, of *factio*, a making. Doublet of FACTION.]

FASHIONABLE (fash'un-ạ-bl) *a.* according to the prevailing mode; stylish.

FASHIONABLY (fash'un-ạ-bli) *ad.* in a fashionable manner.

FASHIONER (fash'un-ẹr) *n.* one who fashions.

FASHIONLESS (fash'un-les) *a.* out of the prevailing fashion.

FAST (fäst) (1) *v.i.* to abstain from food;— *n.* abstinence from food; a time for fasting; —(2) *a.* close; firm; faithful; permanent; rapid; swift; dissipated;—*ad.* firmly; rapidly. [(1) O.E. *fœsten*, to fast, fr. *fœst*, firm, strict. (2) O.E. *fœst*, firm.]

FAST-DAY (fäst'dā) *n.* a day set apart for fasting and prayer.

FASTEN (fäs'n) *v.t.* to make firm; hold together. [O.E. *fœstnian*, fr. *fœst*, fixed.]

FASTENING (fäs'ning) *ppr.* making firm;—*n.* that which confines or makes fast. [See FASTEN.]

FASTER (fäs'tẹr) (1) *n.* one who fasts;—(2) *ad.* more quickly.

FASTIDIOUS (fas-tid'i-us) *a.* difficult to please; squeamish. [L. *fastidiosus*, fr. *fastus*, pride, and *taedium*, loathing.]

FASTIDIOUSLY (fas-tid´i-us-li) *a.* with squeamishness.

FASTIDIOUSNESS (fas-tid´i-us-nes) *n.* excessive delicacy of taste, appetite, etc.

FASTING (fas´ting) *n.* abstinence from food; religious mortification. [See FAST (1).]

FASTNESS (fäst´nes) *n.* state of being fast; a strong fort. [See FAST (2).]

FAT (fat) *n.* oily part of animal bodies;—*a.* plump; gross; greasy;—*v.t.* or *i.* to make or grow fat. [O.E. *fæt*.]

FATAL (fä´tål) *a.* deadly; destructive; necessary. [L. *fatalis*, fr. *fari*, speak.]

FATALISM (fä´tål-izm) *n.* the doctrine of fate or inevitable necessity.

FATALIST (fä´tål-ist) *n.* one who holds to fatalism.

FATALITY (fa-tal´i-ti) *n.* invincible necessity; mortality.

FATALLY (fä´tål-i) *ad.* mortally; necessarily.

FATE (fät) *n.* inevitable necessity; destiny; doom; death. [L. *fatum*, a prediction, fr. *fari*, speak.]

FATED (fä´ted) *a.* decreed by fate.

FATES (fäts) *n.pl.* the destinies supposed to preside over men.

FATHER (fä´THer) *n.* a male parent; ancestor; dignitary or authority in the Church; first person of the Trinity;—*v.t.* to adopt as one's own. [M.E. *fader*, O.E. *fæder*, L. *pater*, G. *pater*, fr. root *pa*, to feed.]

FATHERHOOD (fä´THer-hood) *n.* state of being a father; character or conduct of a father. [See FATHER. E. suff. -*hood*, denoting state.]

FATHERLAND (fä´THer-land) *n.* the land of one's fathers.

FATHERLESS (fä´THer-les) *a.* having no father.

FATHERLINESS (fä´THer-li-nes) *n.* tenderness of a father.

FATHERLY (fä´THer-li) *a.* like a father.

FATHOM (faTH´um) *n.* six feet; depth;—*v.t.* to try the depth of; penetrate. [O.E. *fœthum*, the space reached by the extended arms, a grasp.]

FATHOMABLE (faTH´um-a-bl) *a.* that may be fathomed.

FATHOMLESS (faTH´um-les) *a.* bottomless.

FATIGUE (fa-tēg´) *n.* great weariness; toil; —*v.t.* to weary to excess; tire. [O.F., fr. *fatiguer*, to weary, fr. L. *fatigare*, to weary.]

FATLING (fat´ling) *n.* a fat animal. [See FAT.]

FATNESS (fat´nes) *n.* fleshiness; fertility.

FATTEN (fat´n) *v.t.* to make fat.

FATTY (fat´i) *a.* consisting of fat; greasy.

FATUITY (fa-tū´i-ti) *n.* weakness of mind. [See FATUOUS.]

FATUOUS (fat´ū-us) *a.* foolish; weak; silly. [L. *fatuus*, foolish.]

FAUCES (faw´sēz) *n.pl.* back part of the mouth. [L.]

FAUCET (faw´set) *n.* a pipe for drawing liquors. [O.F. *fausset*, fr. *fausser*, falsify.]

FAUGH (faw) *inter.* an expression of dislike or contempt. [Imit.]

FAULT (fawlt) *n.* a defect; offence. [O.F. *faute*, fr. L. *fallita* (Folk L.), a defect, fem. of new part. *fallitus*, fr. *fallere*, deceive.]

FAULTILY (fawl´ti-li) *ad.* imperfectly; blamably.

FAULTINESS (fawl´ti-nes) *n.* state of being defective or erroneous.

FAULTLESS (fawlt´les) *a.* free from fault.

FAULTLESSNESS (fawlt´les-nes) *n.* freedom from fault or defect.

FAULTY (fawl´ti) *a.* guilty of a fault; defective.

FAUN (fawn) *n.* a rural deity. [L. *faunus*, fr. *favere*, to favour.]

FAUNA (faw´na) *n.* the entire group of animals belonging to a country. [See FAUN.]

FAUNIST (faw´nist) *n.* a naturalist. [See FAUN.]

FAVONIAN (fa-vō´ni-an) *a.* gentle; favourable. [L. *favonius*, the western breeze.]

FAVOUR (fä´vur) *n.* kind regard; a gift; kind act; letter; advantage; partiality; —*v.t.* to regard with kindness; support; render easy; resemble in feature. [O.F., fr. L. (acc.) *favorem*, of *favor*, favour, fr. *favere*, to favour.]

FAVOURABLE (fä´vur-a-bl) *a.* propitious to success; kind; conducive to. [See FAVOUR.]

FAVOURABLY (fä´vur-a-bli) *ad.* with favour or affection.

FAVOURER (fä´vur-er) *n.* one who favours.

FAVOURITE (fä´vur-it) *n.* a particular friend; —*a.* preferred.

FAVOURITISM (fä´vur-i-tizm) *n.* undue disposition to favour; partiality.

FAWN (fawn) (1) *n.* a young deer;—(2) *v.i.* to flatter servilely. [(1) F. *faon*, fr. L. *fœtus*, offspring. (2) M.E. *faunen*, fr. Scand.]

FAWNER (faw´ner) *n.* a flatterer.

FAWNINGLY (faw´ning-li) *ad.* with servile adulation.

FAY (fä) *n.* a fairy; an elf. [O.F. *fae*, F. *fée*, fr. L. *fata*, a fate, goddess of destiny.]

FEALTY (fē´al-ti) *n.* fidelity; loyalty; faithfulness. [O.F. *fealte*, fidelity, fr. L. (acc.) *fidelitatem*, of L. *fidelitas*, fr. *fidelis*, faithful.]

FEAR (fēr) *n.* apprehension of evil;—*v.t.* or *i.* to apprehend evil; be afraid. [O.E. *fœr*, fear, danger.]

FEARFUL (fēr´fool) *a.* afraid; timorous; terrible.

FEARFULLY (fēr´fool-i) *a.* timorously; frightfully.

FEARFULNESS (fēr´fool-nes) *n.* fear; alarm.

FEARLESS (fēr´les) *a.* free from fear; undaunted.

FEARLESSLY (fēr´les-li) *ad.* without fear.

FEARLESSNESS (fēr´les-nes) *n.* freedom from fear; courage.

FEASIBILITY (fē-zi-bil´i-ti) *n.* practicability. [See FEASIBLE.]

FEASIBLE (fē´zi-bl) *a.* that can be performed. [F. *faisible*, that can be done, fr. *faisant*, part. of *faire*, make, fr. L. *facere*, make, do.]

FEAST (fēst) *n.* a sumptuous entertainment; a festival;—*v.i.* to eat sumptuously;—*v.t.* to entertain sumptuously. [O.F. *feste*, F. *fête*, fr. L. *festum*, a holiday, fr. *festus*, solemn.]

FEAT (fēt) *n.* an extraordinary action; exploit. [F. *fait*, fr. L. *factum*, a deed, fr. *facere*, do, make.]

FEATHER (feTH´er) *n.* a plume; that which forms the covering of birds;—*v.t.* to cover with plumage; adorn. [O.E. *fether*.]

FEATHERLESS (feTH´er-les) *a.* destitute of feathers.

FEATHERY (feTH´e-ri) *a.* covered with or resembling feathers.

FEATURE (fē´tūr) *n.* form of the face; lineament; distinguishing part of anything. [O.F. *faiture*, fashion, fr. L. *factura*, fut. part. of *facere*, make.]

FEATURELESS (fē´tūr-les) *a.* having no distinct features.

FEBRILE (fē´bril, feb´ril) *a.* pertaining of fever. [F. *fébrile*, fr. L. *febrilis*, fr. *febris*, fever.]

FEBRUARY (feb´rŏŏ-a-ri) *n.* the second month of the year. [L. *Februarius*, fr. *Februa*, the Roman festival of purification, fr *februare*, to purify.]

FECES (fē´sez) *n.pl.* excrement. Also written **FÆCES**. [Pl. of L. *fœx*, *fœcis*, grounds, dregs.]

FECKLESS (fek´les) *a.* feeble and wanting spirit. [Scot. Also *fectless*, short for *effectless*.]

FECUND (fek´und, fē-kund´) *a.* fruitful. [L. *fecundus*, fruitful.]

FECUNDATE (fē-kun´dät, fek´un-dät) *v.t.* to make prolific.

FECUNDATION (fek-un-dā'shun) *n.* act of making fruitful.

FECUNDITY (fē-kun'di-ti) *n.* fruitfulness.

FED (fed) *pret.* and *pp.* of **FEED**. [See **FEED**.]

FEDERAL (fed'e-ral) *a.* pertaining to a league or contract. [F. *fédéral*, fr. L. stem, *fœder-*, of *fœdus*, league.]

FEDERALISE (fed'e-ral-īz) *v.t.* to unite in compact, as different states.

FEDERALISM (fed'e-ral-izm) *n.* the principles of federalists.

FEDERALIST (fed'e-ral-ist) *n.* an advocate of union; a supporter of the authority of the Federal Government, in opposition to the Confederates who supported that of the separate States.

FEDERATE (fed'e-rāt) *a.* leagued. [L. *fœderatus*, fr. *fœdus*.]

FEDERATION (fed-e-rā'shun) *n.* act of uniting in a league. [See **FEDERATE**.]

FEDERATIVE (fed'e-rā-tiv) *a.* joining in league.

FEE (fē) *n.* a reward; recompense; possession in land by right or tenure; fief;—*v.t.* to retain by a fee. [O.E. *feoh*, cattle, whence M.E. *fee*, cattle, property.]

FEEBLE (fē'bl) *a.* wanting in strength or activity; infirm; imbecile; languid; faint. [O.F. *foible*, fr. L. *flebilis*, wretched, fr. *flere*, weep.]

FEEBLENESS (fē'bl-nes) *n.* infirmity.

FEEBLY (fē'bli) *ad.* weakly; faintly.

FEED (fēd) *v.t.* or *i.* [*pret.* and *pp.* **FED**] to supply with food; eat; supply;—*n.* food; provender; pasture. [O.E. *fedan*, to feed.]

FEEDER (fē'der) *n.* one that feeds; any medium of supply.

FEEDING (fē'ding) *n.* pasture.

FEEL (fēl) *v.t.* or *i.* [*pret.* and *pp.* **FELT**] to perceive by the touch; be affected;—*n.* sense of feeling; sensation given or received by touching. [O.E. *felan*.]

FEELER (fē'ler) *n.* one who feels; something thrown out to ascertain the views of others; —*pl.* organs of touch in insects.

FEELING (fē'ling) *n.* touch; sensibility.

FEELINGLY (fē'ling-li) *ad.* tenderly.

FEE-SIMPLE (fē-sim'pl) *n.* an estate held by one in his own right.

FEET (fēt) *n. pl.* of **FOOT**.

FEE-TAIL (fē'tāl) *n.* an estate limited to a man and particular heirs of his body.

FEIGN (fān) *v.t.* to imagine; pretend; dissemble. [F. *feindre*, to feign, fr. L. *fingere*, to form.]

FEINT (fānt) *n.* a false show; a mock attack; pass in fencing. [F. *feint*, past part. of *feindre*.]

FELICITATE (fe-lis'i-tāt) *v.t.* to make happy; congratulate.

FELICITATION (fe-lis-i-tā'shun) *n.* kind wish.

FELICITOUS (fe-lis'i-tus) *a.* happy; well expressed; appropriate.

FELICITOUSLY (fe-lis'i-tus-li) *ad.* happily.

FELICITY (fe-lis'i-ti) *n.* happiness; prosperity; a happy art or skill. [O.F. *félicité*, fr. L. (acc.) *felicitatem*, fr. stem *felici-*, of *felix*, happy.]

FELINE (fē'līn) *a.* pertaining to cats. [F. *felinus*, belonging to cats, fr. *felis*, cat.]

FELL (fel) (1) *a.* fierce; savage; cruel;—(2) *v.t.* to knock or cut down;—(3) *v.i.* past tense of the verb **FALL**;—(4) *n.* skin or hide of a beast. [(1) O.E. *fel*, cruel. (2) O.E. *fellan*, *fyllan*, to cut down, causative form of *feallan*, to fall. (3) See **FALL**. (4) O.E. *fel*, skin, allied to L. *pellis*, skin.]

FELLAH (fel'a) *n.; pl.* **FELLAHS, FELLAHIN** (fel'az, fel'a-hēn) a peasant, or cultivator of the soil, among the Egyptians, Syrians, etc. [A., tiller of the soil.]

FELLOW (fel'ō) *n.* an associate or equal;— *v.t.* to match. [M.E. *felawe*, fr. Scand.]

FELLOWSHIP (fel'ō-ship) *n.* society; companionship; station in a college or university.

FELON (fel'un) *n.* one guilty of felony; a painful tumour;—*a.* malicious; depraved. [F. *felon*, fr. Late L. (acc.) *felonem*, of *fel.* traitor.]

FELONIOUS (fē-lō'ni-us) *a.* containing felony; villainous. [manner.

FELONIOUSLY (fē-lō'ni-us-li) *ad.* in a felonious manner.

FELONY (fel'un-i) *n.* a heinous crime. [See **FELON**.]

FELSPAR (fel'spár) *n.* a crystalline mineral constituent of granite and other volcanic rocks. Also **FELDSPAR**. [G. *feldspath*, fr. *feld*, field, and *spath*, spar.]

FELT (felt) *pret.* and *pp.* of **FEEL**;—*n.* cloth or stuff of wool. [(1) See **FEEL**. (2) O.E. *felt*.]

FELUCCA (fe-luk'a) *n.* a Mediterranean boat with lateen sails. [It. *feluca*, fr. A. *fulk*, a ship.]

FEMALE (fē'māl) *n.* the sex that bears young; —*a.* feminine. [F. *femelle*, fr. L. *femella*, dim. of *femina*, woman.]

FEMININE (fem'i-nin) *a.* pertaining to females of the human race; tender; cheminate. [O.F. *feminin*, fr. L. *femininus*, fr. L. *femina*, woman.]

FEMORAL (fem'u-ral) *a.* belonging to the thigh. [See **FEMUR**.]

FEMUR (fē'mur) *n.* the thigh bone. [L. *femur*, *femoris*, the thigh.] [marsh.]

FEN (fen) *n.* a marsh; a bog. [O.E. *fenn*.

FENCE (fens) *n.* a wall or other structure to enclose land; fencing; skill in fencing or argument; a receiver of stolen goods;— *v.t.* to enclose with a fence;—*v.i.* to practise fencing. [Abbrev. of **DEFENCE**.]

FENCELESS (fens'les) *a.* destitute of a fence. [See **FENCE**.]

FENCIBLES (fen'si-blz) *n.pl.* soldiers enlisted for home service only.

FENCING (fen'sing) *n.* materials for fencing; art of defence by the small sword. [See **FENCE**.]

FEND (fend) *v.t.* or *i.* to keep or ward off; shut out;—*v.i.* to resist. [Abbrev. of **DEFEND**.]

FENDER (fen'der) *n.* a metal utensil before a fireplace to confine the ashes, etc.; something to protect the sides of a ship from injury by collision.

FENIANISM (fē'ni-an-izm) *n.* a secret organisation to overthrow British rule in Ireland. [Ir. *Fianna Eirionn*, the champions of Erin—the name applied, in traditions, to those that formed the militia of the ancient kings of Ireland.]

FENNEL (fen'el) *n.* an aromatic plant with yellow flowers. [O.E. *finol*, fr. L. *feniculum*, fennel, double dim. of *fenum*, hay.]

FEOFF (fef) *v.t.* to invest with the fee of land. [O.F. *feoffer*, fr. **FIEF**.]

FEOFFMENT (fef'ment) *n.* grant of a fee of land; conveyance by actual delivery or legal deed; the deed itself.

FERMENT (fer'ment) *n.* any substance which produces fermentation; commotion; agitation. [L. *fermentum*, short for *fervimentum*, leaven, fr. *fervere*, to boil.]

FERMENT (fer-ment') *v.t.* to cause fermentation; excite by internal motion;—*v.i.* to undergo fermentation.

FERMENTABLE (fer-men'ta-bl) *a.* susceptible of fermentation.

FERMENTATION (fer-men-tā'shun) *n.* a gaseous change in an organic substance by decomposition, heat, etc.; fermenting; high activity or excitement.

FERMENTATIVE (fer-men'ta-tiv) *a.* causing fermentation.

FERN (fern) *n.* a genus of plants which have their fructification on the back of the fronds or leaves. [O.E. *fearn*.]

FERNERY (fer'ne-ri) *n.* a place where ferns are cultivated.

FEROCIOUS (fe-rō'shus) *a.* savage; fierce. [See **FEROCITY**.]

FEROCIOUSLY (fe-rō'shus-li) *ad.* with savage cruelty; fiercely. [fierceness.

FEROCIOUSNESS (fe-rō'shus-nes) *n.* savage

FEROCITY (fe-ros'i-ti) *n.* savage fierceness; cruelty. [O.F. *ferocité*, fr. L. (acc.) *ferocitatem*, fierceness, fr. *feroci-*, stem of *ferox*, fierce.]

FERREOUS (fer'e-us) *a.* made of or pertaining to iron. [L. *ferreus*, made of iron, fr. *ferrum*, iron.]

FERRET (fer'et) (1) *v.t.* to drive or hunt out from a lurking place; search out and discover;—*n.* an animal of the weasel kind;—(2) narrow tape. [(1) O.F. *furet*, *ferret*, fr. L. *fur*, thief. (2) Corr. of It. *fioretto*, little flower, fr. L. *flos*, *floris*, flower.]

FERRUGINOUS (fe-rōō'ji-nus) *a.* partaking of or containing iron. [L. *ferrugineus*, *ferrugineum*, iron-rust, fr. *ferrum*, iron.]

FERRULE (fer'ōōl, fer'il) *n.* a ring round the end of a stick to strengthen it. [Corr. (through L. t. *ferrum*.) fr. O.F. *virole*, fr. L. *viriola*, a little bracelet.]

FERRY (fer'i) *n.* a place for passing a river or lake; a boat;—*v.t.* to convey over water in a boat. [O.E. *ferian*, carry; conn. with **FARE**.]

FERRYMAN (fer'i-man) *n.* one who attends a ferry.

FERTILE (fer'til, fer'til) *a.* fruitful; producing much. [F., fr. L. *fertilis*, fr. *ferre*, bear.]

FERTILISE (fer'ti-liz) *v.t.* to make fruitful or productive; enrich, as soil.

FERTILITY (fer-til'i-ti) *n.* productiveness; fruitfulness; abundance of resources. [See **FERTILE**.]

FERULE (fer'ōōl, fer'il) *n.* a rod to punish children at school;—*v.t.* to punish with the rod or cane. [L. *ferula*, a rod.]

FERVENCY (fer'ven-si) *n.* heat; extreme eagerness; zeal. Also **FERVENTNESS**.

FERVENT (fer'vent) *a.* warm; ardent. [L. (part. stem) *fervent-*, boiling, fr. *fervere*.]

FERVENTLY (fer'vent-li) *ad.* with fervour. [See **FERVENT**.]

FERVID (fer'vid) *a.* warm; vehement. [L. *fervidus*.]

FERVIDLY (fer'vid-li) *ad.* with glowing warmth; very hotly.

FERVOUR (fer'vur) *n.* heat; warmth of mind; ardour; zeal.

FESTAL (fes'tal) *a.* relating to a feast. [Fr. L. *festum*, a holiday. **FEAST**, **FÊTE**.]

FESTER (fes'ter) *v.i.* to suppurate; grow virulent; rankle;—*v.t.* to cherish;—*n.* a small purulent tumour. [O.F. *festre*, fistle, fr. **FISTULA**.]

FESTIVAL (fes'ti-val) *a.* pertaining to a feast; —*n.* a feast; a day of civil or religious joy.

FESTIVE (fes'tiv) *a.* pertaining to or becoming a feast; joyous; gay. [L. *festivus*, festive, fr. *festum*, a feast.]

FESTIVITY (fes-tiv'i-ti) *n.* social joy or mirth. [See **FESTIVE**.]

FESTOON (fes-tōōn') *n.* a chain of flowers and foliage, or folds of drapery, suspended from two points in flowing curves;—*v.t.* to hang or decorate with ornamental curves. [F. *feston*, fr. Late L. *festo*, a garland, fr. L. *festum*.]

Festoon.

FETCH (fech) *v.t.* to go and bring; derive; obtain; arrive at;—*n.* a stratagem or trick; ghost. [O.E. *feccan*, bring.]

FETE (fāt) *n.* a festival; holiday celebration; —*v.t.* to feast. [F., fr. L. *festum*.]

FETICH or **FETISH** (fē'tish) *n.* any false object of worship. [Pg. =artificial, fr. L. *facere*, make.]

FETID (fē'tid) *a.* offensive in smell; stinking. [L. *foetidus*, fr. *foetere*, have an ill smell.]

FETLOCK (fet'lok) *n.* hair behind the pastern joints of a horse. [Fr. **FEET**, or **FOOT**, and **LOCK**.]

FETTER (fet'er) *n.* a chain for the feet;—*v.t.* to chain; shackle; bind. [O.E. *fetor*, fr. *fet*, feet, fr. *fot*, foot.]

FETTERLESS (fet'er-les) *a.* free from fetters• unrestrained.

FETUS (fē'tus) *n.* an animal in the womb;— *pl.* **FETUSES**. [L. *fetus*, a bringing forth.]

FEU (fū) *n.* a fief; land held on payment of rent;—*v.t.* to grant or let in feu. [Scot. a form of **FEUD** (2).]

FEUD (fūd) (1) *n.* quarrel; broil;—(2) *n.* a feudal tenure. [O.E. *foehth*, hostility, fr. *fah*, hostile. (2) Late L. *feudum*, a fief.]

FEUDAL (fū'dal) *a.* held of a lord or superior by tenure.

FEUDALISM (fū'dal-izm) *n.* the system of feudal tenures.

FEVER (fē'ver) *n.* a disease marked by heat, thirst, and accelerated pulse. [O.E. *fefor*, fr. L. *febris*.]

FEVERISH (fē'ver-ish) *a.* affected with slight fever.

FEW (fū) *a.* small in number. [O.E. *feawe*.]

FEWNESS (fū'nes) *n.* smallness of number.

FEZ (fez) *n.* a cap without a brim, and with a tassel at the crown, worn by Turks. [Fr. *Fez*, a town in Morocco.]

FIASCO (fē-ás'kō) *n.* a signal failure. [It.]

FIAT (fi'at) *n.* a decree; an order. [L. =let it be done.]

FIB (fib) *n.* a story; falsehood;—*v.i.* to tell what is false. [An abbreviation of **FABLE**.]

FIBRE (fi'ber) *n.* a slender thread of an animal or plant. [F., fr. L. *fibra*, a thread.]

FIBRIL (fi'bril) *n.* a small fibre.

FIBRINE (fi'brin) *n.* an organic compound found in animals and vegetables. [See **FIBRE**.]

FIBROUS (fi'brus) *a.* consisting of fibres.

FICHU (fi-shōō') *n.* a light silk or lace cape worn by ladies. [F., fr. *ficher*, to pin up.]

FICKLE (fik'l) *a.* changeable in mind. [O.E. *ficol*, fr. *fic*, fraud.]

FICKLENESS (fik'l-nes) *n.* inconstancy.

FICTION (fik'shun) *n.* an invented story; novel; romance; a falsehood. [L. *fictio*, -*ionis*, fr. *fingere*.]

FICTIONIST (fik'shun-ist) *n.* a writer of novels.

FICTITIOUS (fik-tish'us) *a.* feigned; counterfeit.

FICTITIOUSLY (fik-tish'us-li) *ad.* falsely.

FIDDLE (fid'l) *n.* a stringed instrument of music; a violin;—*v.i.* to play on a violin. [O.E. *fithele*, a fiddle; conn. with Late L. *vidula*, violin.]

FIDDLER (fid'ler) *n.* one who plays on a fiddle. [See **FIDDLE**.]

FIDELITY (fi-del'i-ti) *n.* faithfulness; loyalty; honesty. [L. *fidelitas*, fr. *fides*, faith, fr. *fidere*, to trust.]

FIDGET (fij'et) *v.i.* to move by fits and starts; —*n.* uneasy motion of the body. [Dim. of *fidge*, fr. *fike*, move up and down, fr. Scand.]

FIDGETY (fij'et-i) *a.* restless; uneasy. [See **FIDGET**.]

FIDUCIAL (fi-dū'shal) *a.* confident; held in trust. [L. *fiducia*.]

FIE (fi) *ex.* denoting dislike. [Scand.]

FIEF (fēf) *n.* a fee; feud. [F., fr. Late L. *feudum*.]

FIELD (fēld) *n.* a piece of enclosed land; a battle-ground; compass; extent. [O.E. *feld*.]

FIELD-BED (fēld'bed) *n.* a bed for the field.

FIELD-BOOK (fēld'book) *n.* a book used in surveying.

FIELDFARE (fēld'fār) *n.* a bird of the thrush family.

FIELD-MARSHAL (fēld'mär-shạl) *n.* a military officer of the highest rank.

FIELD-OFFICER (fēld'of-i-sẹr) *n.* a major, lieutenant-colonel, or colonel.

FIELD-PIECE (fēld'pēs) *n.* a small cannon.

FIEND (fēnd) *n.* an implacable enemy; the devil. [O.E. *feond*, fr. *feon*, to hate.]

FIENDISH (fēn'dish) *a.* malicious; diabolical.

FIENDISHLY (fēn'dish-li) *ad.* in a fiendish manner.

FIERCE (fērs) *a.* violent; eager in attack; furious. [O.F. *fers*, bold, fr. L. *ferus*, wild.]

FIERCENESS (fērs'nes) *n.* violence; rage.

FIERINESS (fir'i-nes) *n.* great warmth. [See **FIERY**.]

FIERY (fir'i) *a.* consisting of fire; hot; irritable; fierce.

FIFE (fīf) *n.* a small musical pipe;—*v.i.* to play on a fife. [F. *fifre*, fr. L. *pipare*, to chirp.]

FIFER (fī'fẹr) *n.* one who plays the fife.

FIFTEEN (fif-tēn') *a.* and *n.* five and ten. [O.E. *fiftyne*, fr. *fif*, five, and *tyn*, ten.]

FIFTEENTH (fif-tēnth') *a.* noting fifteen

FIFTH (fifth) *a.* noting five;—*n.* an interval of three tones and a semitone. [O.E. *fifta*.]

FIFTIETH (fif'ti-eth) *a.* noting the number fifty. [O.E. *fifteogotha*.]

FIFTY (fif'ti) *n.* or *a.* sum of five tens added. [O.E. *fiftig*.] [L. *ficus*.]

FIG (fig) *n.* a tree and its fruit. [F. *figue*, fr.

FIGHT (fīt) *v.i.* [*pret.* and *pp.* **FOUGHT**] to contend in battle;—*v.t.* to war against;— *n.* a battle; a combat. [O.E. *feohtan*.]

FIGHTER (fī'tẹr) *n.* one who fights.

FIGMENT (fig'ment) *n.* invention; fiction. [L. *figmentum*, fr. *fingere*, feign.]

FIGURATIVE (fig'ū-ra-tiv) *a.* representing by figure; typical; abounding in figures of speech; florid.

FIGURATIVELY (fig'ū-ra-tiv-li) *ad.* by figure or metaphor.

FIGURE (fig'ur) *n.* a character for a number; a type; shape; image;—*v.t.* or *i.* to form into any shape; make figures; represent; imagine. [L. *figura*, fr. *fingere*, to form.]

FILAMENT (fil'ạ-ment) *n.* a slender thread; a fibre. [F., fr. L. *filum*, thread.]

FILATORY (fil'ạ-tur-i) *n.* a machine for spinning threads. [See **FILAMENT**.]

FILATURE (fil'ạ-tūr) *n.* the reeling of silk from cocoons; the reel itself; silk factory.

FILBERT (fil'bẹrt) *n.* a nut of the hazel kind. [Fr. St. *Philibert*.]

FILCH (filsh) *v.t.* to steal; pilfer. [Prob. for *filk*, fr. M.E. *felen*, conceal.]

FILCHER (fil'shẹr) *n.* a petty thief.

FILCHINGLY (fil'shing-li) *ad.* in a thievish manner.

FILE (fīl) (1) *n.* a tool for smoothing iron;— *v.t.* to smooth with a file;—(2) *n.* a series; a wire on which papers are strung; a line of soldiers;—*v.t.* place in order, as papers; —*v.i.* to march in file. [(1) O.E. *feol*. (2) F., fr. L. *filum*, thread.]

FILIAL (fil'yạl) *a.* pertaining to or becoming a child. [L. *filius*, son, *filia*, daughter.]

FILIALLY (fil'yạl-i) *ad.* in a filial manner.

FILIATION (fil-i-ā'shun) *n.* the relation of a child to a parent.

FILIBUSTER (fil'i-bus-tẹr) *n.* a lawless military adventurer; a buccaneer. [Sp. *filibustero*, fr. D. = freebooter.]

FILIGREE (fil'i-grē) *n.* ornamental work in fine gold or silver wire. [It. and Sp. *filigrana*, fr. L. *filum*, thread, and *granum*, a grain.] [by a file.

FILINGS (fī'lingz) *n.pl.* particles rubbed off

FILL (fil) *v.t.* or *i.* to make or become full; occupy; expand;—*n.* as much as fills or satisfies. [O.E. *fyllan*, fr. *ful*, full.]

FILLER (fil'ẹr) *n.* a tube or funnel for filling bottles, casks, etc.

FILLET (fil'et) *n.* a head-band; fleshy part of the thigh; meat rolled together and tied round;—*v.t.* to bind with a fillet. [F. *filet*, dim. of *fil*, thread, fr. L. *filum*.]

FILLIBEG (fil'i-beg) *n.* a kilt or short dress worn in the Highlands of Scotland. [Gael. =small kilt.]

FILLING (fil'ing) *n.* that which fills up.

FILLIP (fil'ip) *v.t.* to strike with the nail of the finger; to incite; spur on;—*n.* a stroke with the finger. [Another form of **FLIP**.]

FILLY (fil'i) *n.* a young mare. [Dim. of **FOAL**.]

FILM (film) *n.* a thin skin or pellicle on the eye. [O.E. *film*, fr. *fell*, a skin.]

FILTER (fil'tẹr) *n.* a liquor-strainer;—*v.t.* to purify by passing through a strainer;—*v.i.* to pass through. [F. *filtre*, fr. Late L. *filtrum*, felt.]

FILTH (filth) *n.* foul or dirty matter. [O.E. *fuldh*, fr. *ful*, foul.]

FILTHILY (filth'i-li) *ad.* dirtily.

FILTHINESS (filth'i-nes) *n.* dirtiness.

FILTHY (filth'i) *a.* abounding in filth; foul; dirty; obscene; impure.

FILTRATE (fil'trāt) *v.t.* or *i.* to filter; percolate. [Late L. *filtrare*, to filter.]

FILTRATION (fil-trā'shun) *n.* the act of filtering.

FIN (fin) *n.* a membrane in a fish serving to balance and propel it in the water. [O.E. *finn*, allied to L. *pinna*, fin.]

FINABLE (fī'nạ-bl) *a.* liable to a fine.

FINAL (fī'nạl) *a.* ending; conclusive. [L. *finalis*, fr. *finis*, end.]

FINALE (fē-nä'lā) *n.* last piece in music; termination. [It.]

FINALITY (fī-nal'i-ti) *n.* final state or arrangement; doctrine of final causes.

FINALLY (fī'nạl-i) *ad.* in conclusion.

FINANCE (fi-nans') *n.* the science of raising and investing money;—*pl.* funds; public revenue; private income. [Late L. *finare*, pay a fine fr. *finis*, end.]

FINANCIAL (fi-nan'shạl) *a.* pertaining to finance. [financial matters.

FINANCIER (fi-nan'sẹr) *n.* one skilled in

FINCH (finsh) *n.* a small singing bird. [O.E. *finc*, finch.]

FIND (fīnd) *v.t.* [*pret.* and *pp.* **FOUND**] to discover; gain; supply;—*v.i.* to give a verdict; —*n.* thing found; discovery [O.E. *findan*.]

FINDING (fīn'ding) *n.* verdict of a jury.

FINE (fīn) (1) *a.* thin; delicate; keen; sharp; nice; handsome; showy;—(2) *n.* penalty; forfeiture;—*v.t.* to inflict a penalty; to purify; refine. [(1) F. *fin*, fr. L. *finitus*, fr. *finire*, to finish. (2) Low L. *finis*, a fine or payment, fr. L. *finis*, end.]

FINE-DRAW (fīn'draw) *v.t.* to sew up neatly; reenter.

FINELY (fīn'li) *ad.* gaily; dexterously.

FINENESS (fīn'nes) *n.* slenderness; showiness; purity; sharpness; delicacy.

FINER (fī'nẹr) *n.* one who purifies metals.

FINERY (fī'nẹr-i) *n.* fine dress, jewels, trinkets, etc.; splendour.

FINESPUN (fīn'spun) *a.* drawn out minutely; too elaborate.

FINESSE (fi-nes') *n.* art; artifice; stratagem; —*v.i.* to use stratagem. [F.]

FINGER (fing'gẹr) *n.* an extremity of the hand; —*v.t.* to handle; touch; pilfer. [O.E. *finger*.]

FINGERING (fing'gẹr-ing) *n.* act or manner of touching with the fingers.

FINICAL (fin'i-kạl) *a.* nice in trifles; fastidious; foppish. [Fr. **FINE**.]

FINICALLY (fin'i-kạl-i) *ad.* with great nicety.

FINIS (fī'nis) *n.* the end; conclusion. [L.]

FINISH (fin'ish) *v.t.* to bring to an end; perfect;—*v.i.* to come to an end;—*n.* the last touch to a work; polish. [F. (pres. part.) *finissant*, fr. *finir*, fr. L. *finire*, fr. *finis*, end.]

FINISHER (tin'ish-er) *n.* one who completes.

FINITE (fi'nit) *a.* bounded; limited. [L. (past part.) *finitus*, fr. *finire*.]

FINITELY (fi'nit-li) *ad.* within limits.

FINNY (fin'i) *a.* furnished with fins; pertaining to fins or to fish.

FIORD (fyord) *n.* a long narrow firth bounded by high rocks. [Scand. *fiord*.]

FIR (fer) *n.* a resinous cone-bearing tree or its wood. [O.E. *furh*.]

FIRE (fir) *n.* heat and light; anything burning; passion;—*v.t.* to set on fire; discharge; —*v.i.* to take fire. [O.E. *fyr*, allied to G. *pur*.]

FIREARMS (fir'armz) *n.pl.* guns, pistols, etc.

FIRE-BASKET (fir'bas-ket) *n.* a small portable grate.

FIREBRAND (fir'brand) *n.* a piece of wood on fire; incendiary; mischief-maker.

FIRE-BRIGADE (fir'bri-gād) *n.* a body of men for extinguishing fires.

FIREDAMP (fir'damp) *n.* a highly explosive gas generated in coal mines.

FIRE-ENGINE (fir'en-jin) *n.* an engine to extinguish fires.

FIRE-ESCAPE (fir'es-kāp) *n.* a machine for escaping from a building on fire.

FIRE-IRONS (fir'i-crnz) *n.pl.* tongs, poker, and shovel.

FIRELOCK (fir'lok) *n.* a musket.

FIREMAN (fir'man) *n.* a man who extinguishes fires or tends engine fires.

FIRE-OFFICE (fir'of-is) *n.* office for insuring against loss by fire.

FIRE-PLUG (fir'plug) *n.* a plug for drawing water at fires.

FIRE-POLICY (fir'pol-i-si) *n.* policy of insurance against loss by fire.

FIREPROOF (fir'proof) *a.* incombustible.

FIRE-SHIP (fir'ship) *n.* a ship to set an enemy's vessels on fire.

FIRESIDE (fir'sid) *n.* the family hearth; home.

FIREWORKS (fir'wurks) *n.pl.* preparations of powder for exploding in the air.

FIRING (firing) *n.* act of discharging firearms; fuel.

FIRKIN (fer'kin) *n.* a vessel of eight or nine gallons; small cask. [O.D. *vier*, four, and suff. *-kin*.]

FIRLOT (fer'lot) *n.* the fourth part of a boll. [O.D. *vier*, four, and E. *lot*, part.]

FIRM (ferm) (1) *a.* strong; compact; fixed; steady; secure;—(2) *n.* a partnership. [(1) L. *firmus*. (2) It. *firma*, signature, fr. L. *firmus*.]

FIRMAMENT (fer'ma-ment) *n.* the region of the air; the sky. [L. *firmamentum*, fr. *firmus*.]

FIRMAMENTAL (fer-ma-men'tal) *a.* belonging to the firmament.

FIRMAN (fer'man, fer-mán') *n.* a Turkish permit or decree. [Per.]

FIRMLY (ferm'li) *ad.* strongly; steadily; with fixedness.

FIRMNESS (ferm'nes) *n.* compactness; solidity; constancy. [See FIRM (1).]

FIRST (ferst) *a.* earliest; chief;—*ad.* in the first place, time, etc. [O.E. *fyrst*, superl. of FORE.]

FIRST-BORN (ferst'born) *n.* the eldest child.

FIRST-FRUITS (ferst'froots) *n.pl.* first produce or results.

FIRSTLING (ferst'ling) *n.* offspring of cattle first produced.

FIRTH, FRITH (ferth, frith) *n.* the opening of a river into the sea.

FISCAL (fis'kal) *a.* pertaining to a treasury; —*n.* revenue; a treasurer. [Short for *Procurator-fiscal*, fr. O.F., fr. L. *fiscus*, a purse.]

FISH (fish) *n.* an animal living in water;— *v.t.* to search, as for fish;—*v.i.* to try to catch fish. [O.E. *fisc*, a fish.]

FISHED (fisht) *a.* strengthened with pieces of wood, as a mast.

FISHERY (fish'er-i) *n.* the business or place of fishing.

FISH-HOOK (fish'hook) *n.* a hook for catching fish.

FISHING (fish'ing) *n.* the practice of catching fish.

FISH-MARKET (fish'mar-ket) *n.* a market for fish.

FISHMONGER (fish'mung-ger) *n.* a dealer in fish.

FISH-POND (fish'pond) *n.* a pond for fish.

FISH-SLICE (fish'slis) *n.* broad knife for dividing fish at table.

FISH-SPEAR (fish'spēr) *n.* a harpoon; leister.

FISHY (fish'i) *a.* consisting of fish; like a fish; seedy; equivocal.

FISSURE (fish'ūr) *n.* a cleft; a narrow chasm. [F., fr. L. *fissura*, fr. part. *fissus*, fr. *findere*, to cleave.]

FIST (fist) *n.* the hand clenched;—*v.t.* to beat with the fist. [O.E. *fyst*.]

FISTICUFFS (fis'ti-kufs) *n.pl.* blows with the fist.

FISTULA (fis'tū-la) *n.* a deep, callous ulcer; a pipe or reed. [L.]

FISTULOUS (fis'tū-lus) *a.* hollow like a pipe.

FIT (fit) (1) *n.* a sudden attack, impulse, or whim;—(2) *a.* suitable; convenient;—*v.t.* to suit; adapt; equip; qualify;—*v.i.* to be suitable; become. [(1) O.E. *fitt*, a struggle. (2) Etym. doubtful.]

FITFUL (fit'fool) *a.* varied by fits.

FITLY (fit'li) *ad.* suitably; conveniently.

FITNESS (fit'nes) *n.* state of being fit.

FIVE (fiv) *n.* the sum of four and one; a symbol representing this number, as 5 or V.;—*a.* one more than four. [O.E. *fif*.]

FIVEFOLD (fiv'fōld) *a.* taken five times.

FIX (fiks) *v.t.* to set firmly; fasten; make permanent;—*v.i.* to become firm; settle; —*n.* a difficult position; predicament. [L. (part.) *fixus*, fr. *figere*, to fix.]

FIXABLE (fik'sa-bl) *a.* that may be fixed.

FIXEDLY (fik'sed-li) *ad.* firmly; steadfastly.

FIXEDNESS (fik'sed-nes) *n.* state of being fast.

FIXITY (fik'si-ti) *n.* coherence; fixedness.

FIXTURE (fiks'tūr) *n.* fixed state; anything permanently attached, as to a house, business, etc.

FIZZ (fiz) *v.i.* to make a hissing sound. [Imit.]

FLABBILY (flab'i-li) *ad.* in a flabby manner.

FLABBINESS (flab'i-nes) *n.* a flabby state. [Fr. FLAP.]

FLABBY (flab'i) *a.* soft; yielding; loose; easily shaken.

FLACCID (flak'sid) *a.* weak and limber. [L., fr. *flaccus*, flabby.]

FLACCIDITY (flak-sid'i-ti) *n.* laxness; want of tension.

FLACCIDLY (flak'sid-li) *ad.* in a flaccid manner.

FLAG (flag) (1) *v.i.* to become weak; droop; —(2) *v.t.* to lay with flags or flat stones;— *n.* a flat stone used for paving;—(3) an ensign or colours. [(1) Etym. doubtful. (2) Scand.; a form of FLAKE. (3) D. or Scand.]

FLAGELLATE (flaj'e-lāt) *v.t.* to scourge. [L. (past part.) *flagellatus*, fr. *flagellare*, to scourge, fr. *flagellum*, a little whip.]

FLAGELLATION (flaj-e-lā'shun) *n.* a whipping.

FLAGEOLET (flaj'e-let) *n.* a kind of flute. [F.]

FLAGITIOUS (fla-jish'us) *a.* extremely wicked. [L. *flagitium*, a disgraceful act, fr. *flagrare*, to burn.]

FLAGITIOUSLY (fla-jish'us-li) *ad.* atrociously; grossly.

FLAGITIOUSNESS (fla-jish'us-nes) *n.* extreme wickedness; villainy.

FLAGON (flag'un) *n.* a vessel with a narrow mouth. [F.]

FLAGRANCY (flā'gran-si) *n.* burning heat; enormity.

FLAGRANT (flā´grant) *a.* burning; glowing; glaring; notorious; enormous. [L. (part. stem) *flagrant-*, fr. *flagrare*, to burn.]

FLAGRANTLY (flā´grant-li) *ad.* notoriously.

FLAG-SHIP (flag´ship) *n.* the ship which bears the commander of a squadron.

FLAG-STAFF (flag´staf) *n.* a staff to support a flag.

FLAG-STONE (flag´stōn) *n.* a flat stone for a pavement.

FLAIL (flāl) *n.* an instrument for thrashing grain. [L. *flagellum*, a whip.]

FLAKE (flāk) *n.* a flock of snow; a stratum; a scaffold;—*v.i.* to form into flakes;—*v.i.* to break into laminæ. [Scand.]

FLAKY (flā´ki) *a.* consisting of flakes. [See FLAKE.]

FLAMBEAU (flam´bō) *n.* a lighted torch. [F. *flambe*, fr. L. *flamma*, flame.]

FLAME (flām) *n.* light emitted from fire; blaze; ardour;—*v.i.* to burn with a blaze; shine as fire;—*v.t.* to excite. [L. *flamma*.]

FLAMING (flā´ming) *a.* burning with a blaze; bright; violent.

FLAMINGO (fla-ming´gō) *n.* a bird remarkable for its long neck and legs and bent bill. [Sp. *flamenco*, fr. L. *flamma*, flame, from its red colour.]

FLAMMABILITY (flam-a-bil´i-ti) *n.* Flambeau. aptness to take fire.

FLANGE (flanj) *n.* a projecting edge or rim on a wheel to keep it on the rails. [O.F. *flanche*, F. *flanc*, side; conn. with FLANK.]

FLANK (flangk) *n.* side of the body or of an army or fleet;—*v.t.* to attack or turn the flank; border;—*v.i.* to be posted on the side of. [M.E. *flanc*, fr. F. *flanc*, side.]

FLANKER (flang´ker) *n.* a lateral fortification; a skirmisher;—*v.t.* or *i.* to attack or defend sideways.

FLANNEL (flan´el) *n.* a soft woollen cloth. [W., fr. *gwlan*, wool, Prov. E. *flannen*, F. *flanelle*.]

FLANNELETTE (flan-el-et´) *n.* a cotton material having the appearance of wool.

FLAP (flap) *n.* anything that hangs broad and loose; the motion of it, or a stroke with it;—*v.t.* to move as wings;—*v.i.* to make a motion as with wings. [M.E. *flappen*, to beat; Imit.]

FLAPPER (flap´er) *n.* he or that which flaps.

FLARE (flār) *v.i.* to burn or shine with an unsteady light. [Scand.=to blaze.]

FLARING (flār´ing) *a.* making a display.

FLASH (flash) *n.* a sudden burst of light;—*v.t.* or *i.* to send out or burst suddenly, as light. [Scand.; M.E. *flaschen*, to dash; conn. with FLARE.]

FLASHILY (flash´i-li) *ad.* with empty show.

FLASHY (flash´i) *a.* dazzling; showy.

FLASK (flask) *n.* a bottle; a powder-horn. [O.E. *flasce*, fr. Late L. *flasca*, fr. L. *vasculum*, a flask.]

FLAT (flat) *a.* level; insipid; positive; in *Music*, depressed;—*n.* a level piece of land; a shoal; mark of depression in music; a simpleton; floor of a house;—*v.t.* to make flat;—*v.i.* to become flat. [Scand.]

FLATLY (flat´li) *ad.* horizontally; peremptorily.

FLATNESS (flat´nes) *n.* evenness; vapidness.

FLATTEN (flat´n) *v.t.* or *i.* to make or grow flat.

FLATTER (flat´er) *v.t.* to praise falsely. [O.F. *flater*, smooth, fr. *flatter*, to flatter.]

FLATTERER (flat´er-er) *n.* one that flatters.

FLATTERING (flat´er-ing) *a.* exciting hopes; favourable.

FLATTERY (flat´er-i) *n.* false praise.

FLATTISH (flat´ish) *a.* rather flat.

FLATULENCE (flat´ū-lens) *n.* wind in the stomach.

FLATULENT (flat´ū-lent) *a.* windy; puffy. [Late L. *flatulentus*, fr. L. (part.) *flatus*, fr. *flare*, to blow.]

FLATULENTLY (flat´ū-lent-li) *ad.* windily; emptily.

FLATUS (flā´tus) *n.* a puff of air; a breath; flatulence.

FLAUNT (flänt) *v.t.* or *i.* to display ostentatiously; flourish or toss;—*n.* boast; brag; gibe. [Etym. doubtful, prob. Imit.]

FLAUNTING (flän´ting) *a.* making a display for show; gaudy.

FLAUNTINGLY (flän´ting-li) *ad.* in a flaunting manner.

FLAUTIST (flaw´tist) *n.* a player on the flute [It. *flauto*, flute; of uncertain origin.]

FLAVOUR (flā´vur) *n.* a peculiar taste or smell; relish;—*v.t.* to give a pleasant taste or smell to. [O.F. *fleiur*, *flaur*, smell; perh. influenced by form f SAVOUR.]

FLAVOURLESS (flā´vur-les) *a.* without flavour; tasteless.

FLAW (flaw) *n.* a break; defect; sudden gust;—*v.t.* to break; injure. [Scand.]

FLAWLESS (flaw´les) *a.* free from crack or defect.

FLAX (flaks) *n.* plant of which linen is made. [O.E. *fleax*.]

FLAXEN (flak´sn) *a.* made of or like flax; fair and flowing. Also FLAXY.

FLAY (flā) *v.t.* to strip off the skin. [O.E. *flean*.]

FLEA (flē) *n.* an insect. [M.E. *flee*, pl. *fleen*, fr. O.E. *fleah*.]

FLEAM (flēm) *n.* an instrument for opening veins. [F., fr. Late L. *fletoma*, a lancet, fr. G. *phlebotomon*, a lancet, fr. *phlebo-*, stem of *phleps*, a vein, and *temnein*, to cut.]

FLECK (flek) *n.* a spot; streak; speckle;—*v.t.* to flecker. [Scand.]

FLECKER (flek´er) *v.t.* to spot; streak or stripe.

FLECTION (flek´shun) *n.* act of bending. [L., better form *flexion*, fr. (acc.) *flexionem*, a bending, fr. (part.) *flexus*, fr. *flectere*.]

FLED (fled) *pret.* and *pp.* of FLEE.

FLEDGE (flej) *v.t.* to furnish with wings or feathers. [M.E. *flegge*, ready to fly, fr. O.E. *flycge*, in compound *unflycge*, unfeathered.]

FLEDGELING (flej´ling) *n.* a young bird just fledged.

FLEE (flē) *v.i.* [*pret.* and *pp.* FLED] to run with rapidity; run away;—*v.t.* to shun or avoid. [O.E. *fleon*.]

FLEECE (flēs) *n.* coat of wool from a sheep; —*v.t.* to deprive of a fleece; strip by severe exactions; furnish with a fleece. [O.E. *fleos*. Cf. Ger. *Fliess*.]

FLEECY (flē´si) *a.* covered with wool; woolly.

FLEET (flēt) (1) *a.* swift in motion; nimble; light;—*v.i.* to fly swiftly; to flit;—(2) *n.* a number of ships in company; a navy. [(1) Scand. Cf. O.E. *fleotig*, swift. (2) O.E. *fleot*, a ship, fr. *fleotan*, to float.]

FLEETING (flē´ting) *a.* not durable; passing swiftly.

FLEETNESS (flēt´nes) *n.* swiftness; speed.

FLESH (flesh) *n.* the softer solids of animals; animal nature; human family;—*v.t.* to feed with flesh; satiate; initiate. [O.E. *flaesc*. Cf. Ger. *Fleisch*.]

FLESH-BRUSH (flesh´brush) *n.* a brush to excite action of the skin.

FLESH-COLOUR (flesh´kul-ur) *n.* the colour of the flesh.

FLESHER (flesh´er) *n.* a butcher; fleshmonger. [Scot. See FLESH.]

FLESHINESS (flesh´i-nes) *n.* corpulence.

FLESHLY (flesh´li) *a.* carnal; corporeal.

FLESHMONGER (flesh´mung-ger) *n.* a dealer in animal food; flesher.

FLESHY (flesh´i) *a.* pertaining to the flesh; full of flesh; plump; pulpy.

FLETCH (flech) *v.t.* to feather an arrow. [F. *flèche*, an arrow.]

FLEW (flōō) *pret.* of FLY, which see.

FLEX (fleks) *v.t.* to bend. [L. (part.) *flexus*, bent, fr. *flectere*, to bend.]

FLEXIBILITY (flek-si-bil'i-ti) *n.* pliability; pliancy. Also FLEXIBLENESS.

FLEXIBLE (flek'si-bl) *a.* capable of being bent; pliant; tractable; manageable.

FLEXIBLY (flek'si-bli) *ad.* in a flexible manner.

FLEXION (flek'shun) *n.* act of bending; a fold; a turn.

FLEXOR (flek'sur) *n.* a muscle which contracts the joints in stooping.

FLEXUOUS (flek'sū-us) *a.* bending; winding.

FLEXURE (flek'sūr) *n.* a bending or winding.

FLICK (flik) *v.t.* to strike lightly, as with a whip; to flip;—*n.* a light, smart stroke. FLACK, to flutter. [E., imit. Cf. FLIP.]

FLICKER (flik'ẽr) *v.i.* to flutter; flap the wings; waver; twinkle;—*n.* a wavering gleam. [Frequent. of FLICK.]

FLICKERING (flik'ẽr-ing) *a.* wavering;—*n.* a fluttering.

FLIER (flī'ẽr) *n.* one that flies or flees. [See FLY.]

FLIGHT (flīt) *n.* act of flying; flock of birds. [O.E. *flyht*, fr. *fleogan*, to fly.]

FLIGHTINESS (flī'ti-nes) *n.* capricious feeling. [See FLIGHT.]

FLIGHTY (flī'ti) *a.* fleety; changeful; volatile; giddy.

FLIMSY (flim'zi) *a.* thin; slight; weak. [Mod. E.; first recorded use 1702. Prob. Imit.]

FLINCH (flinsh) *v.i.* to draw back; shrink from; irresolution. [O.E. *flenchr*, to turn aside; of unknown origin.]

FLING (fling) *v.t.* [*pret.* and *pp.* FLUNG] to cast from the hand; hurl; shed; scatter; throw down;—*v.i.* to kick; toss about; rush away;—*n.* a throw or cast; gibe; a kind of dance; sneer. [Scand.]

FLINT (flint) *n.* a hard stone. [O.E.; perhaps cognate with G. *plinthos*, a brick.]

FLINTY (flin'ti) *a.* made of flint; hard.

FLIP (flip) *v.t.* to flick; to toss with the fingers; to twitch; to fillip;—*n.* a flick; a snap. [E., init. Cf. FLAP.]

FLIP (flip) *n.* a drink made of beer, spirit, and sugar. [Probably fr. FLIP, to beat.]

FLIPPANCY (flip'an-si) *n.* volubility of tongue. [See FLIPPANT.]

FLIPPANT (flip'ant) *a.* rapid in speech; talkative, forward; pert. [Scand., M.E. (part.) *flippand*, prattling.]

FLIPPANTLY (flip'ant-li) *ad.* in a flippant manner.

FLIRT (flẽrt) *v.t.* to throw with a jerk;—*v.i.* to coquet;—*n.* a jerk; a volatile girl. [E., Imit. Cf. FLIP (1), FLAP.]

FLIRTATION (flẽr-tā'shun) *n.* desire of attracting notice; coquetry.

FLIT (flit) *v.i.* to flutter; dart along; remove. [Scand.] [*flicce*.]

FLITCH (flich) *n.* a side of pork cured. [O.E.

FLITTING (flit'ing) *a.* variable; flying;—*n.* a fluttering.

FLOAT (flōt) *n.* something that swims; a raft;—*v.t.* or *i.* to swim on the surface. [O.E. *flotian*.]

FLOATAGE (flō'tij) *n.* anything that floats.

FLOATING (flō'ting) *a.* spreading plaster on walls. [See FLOAT.]

FLOCCULENCE (flok'ū-lens) *n.* adhesion in small locks. [See FLOCK.]

FLOCCULENT (flok'ū-lent) *a* adhering in small locks. [See FLOCK.]

FLOCK (flok) (1) *n.* a collection of small animals,—*v.i.* to gather in a crowd; assemble; a lock of wool. [(1) O.F. *flocc*, a company. (2) L. *floccus*, lock of hair.]

FLOCK-BED (flok'bed) *n.* a bed filled with locks of wool.

FLOCK-PAPER (flok'pā-pẽr) *n.* a wall-paper with raised figures of cloth or flock.

FLOCKY (flok'i) *a.* full of flocks or woolly locks.

FLOE (flō) *n.* a mass of floating ice. [Scand. *flage*, in *üs-flage*, lit. an ice-flake, ice floe.]

FLOG (flog) *v.t.* to whip; lash; punish by whipping. [Etym. doubtful.]

FLOGGING (flog'ing) *n.* act of one who flogs; a whipping for punishment.

FLOOD (flud) *n.* a great body of moving water; inundation; deluge; flowing in of the tide; overflow; superabundance;—*v.t.* to overflow; inundate. [O.E. *flod*, fr. *flowan*, to flow.]

FLOODGATE (flud'gāt) *n.* a gate to stop or let out water.

FLOODMARK (flud'märk) *n.* the point to which the tide rises.

FLOOR (flōr) *n.* the bottom of a room; a story; platform;—*v.t.* to lay with a floor; strike or put down; overthrow. [O.E. *flor*.]

FLOORING (flōr'ing) *n.* laying a floor; materials for floors.

FLOP (flop) *v.t.* or *i.* to strike or clap; let down suddenly; plump down. [Variant of FLAP.]

FLORA (flō'ra) *n.* the goddess of flowers; the plants of a given country or period; a list or description of such. [L. *Flora*, the goddess of flowers, fr. *flor-*, stem of *flos*, a flower.]

FLORAL (flō'ral) *a.* pertaining to flowers. [See FLORA.]

FLORESCENCE (flo-res'ens) *n.* the season of flowering in plants. [L. :part. stem) *florescent-*, of *florescens*, fr. *florescere*, fr. *flos*, a flower.]

FLORICULTURE (flo'ri-kul-tūr) *n.* cultivation of flowering plants. [L. *flori-*, stem of *flos*, a flower, and CULTURE.]

FLORID (flor'id) *a.* flowery; bright with colour; highly embellished; ornate. [L. *floridus*, abounding with flowers, rosy, fr. *flori-*, stem of *flos*, a flower.]

FLORIDNESS (flor'id-nes) *n.* freshness of colour; embellishment. Also FLORIDITY.

FLORIN (flor'in) *n.* a coin of different values —British value, 2s. [F., fr. It. *florino*, a coin of Florence which bore a lily, fr. L. (acc.) *florem*, of *flos*, a flower.]

FLORIST (flor'ist) *n.* one who cultivates flowers. [See FLORA.]

FLOSS (flos) *n.* a downy substance on the husks of certain plants; ravelled silk filaments. [O.F. *flocher*, to form into flocks or tufts; F. *floc*.]

FLOTAGE (flō'tij) *n.* something that floats. [See FLOAT.]

FLOTILLA (flō-til'a) *n.* a fleet of small vessels. [Sp. = a little fleet, dim. of *flota*, a fleet.]

FLOUNCE (flouns) (1) *v.t.* to adorn with flounces;—*n.* a plaited border on a dress; —(2) *v.i.* to struggle violently;—*n.* a sudden jerk or dash. [(1) M.E. *frounce*, a plait, fr. O.F. *froncer*, to fold. (2) E. Cf. Sw. *flunsa*, to plunge.]

FLOUNDER (floun'dẽr) (1) *v.i.* to flounce; struggle violently;—(2) *n.* a small flat fish. [(1) E., etym. doubtful. (2) F., fr. Scand.; A.F. *floundre*.]

FLOUR (flour) *n.* finely ground meal of wheat or other substance;—*v.t.* to grind and bolt; sprinkle with flour. [F. *fleur*, short for *fleur de farine*, flour of wheat.]

FLOURISH (flur'ish) *v.t.* or *i.* to thrive; embellish; brandish;—*n.* a fanciful stroke of the pen or graver; showy display; embellishment. [O.F. *floriso-* (part. stem) of *florir*, to flourish, fr. L. *florere*, to blossom, fr. *flos*, a flower.]

FLOURISHINGLY (flur'ish-ing-li) *ad.* in a thriving or prosperous manner.

FLOUT (flout) *v.t.* to treat with contempt;—*v.i.* to sneer at;—*n.* contemptuous mock or sneer. [Scand. = to play the flute, to jeer.]

FLOW (flō) *v.t.* and *i.* to move as a liquid; rise as the tide; hang loose and waving;—*n.* a stream; current. [O.E. *flowan.*]

FLOWER (flou'er) *n.* the blossom of a plant; the prime or best of anything;—*v.i.* to blossom forth;—*v.t.* to embellish with figures. [O.F. *flour*, F. *fleur*, fr. L. (acc.) *florem*, of *flos*, a flower.]

FLOWERINESS (flou'er-i-nes) *n.* state of being flowery.

FLOWERY (flou'er-i) *a.* full of flowers; highly ornamented.

FLOWING (flō'ing) *a.* liquid; fluent.

FLOWN (flōn) *pp.* of FLY.

FLUCTUATE (fluk'tū-āt) *v.i.* to waver; rise and fall. [L. *fluctuare*, pp. *fluctuatus*, fr. *fluere*, to flow.]

FLUCTUATION (fluk-tū-ā'shun) *n.* unsteadiness.

FLUE (flōō) *n.* a passage for smoke. [Etym. uncert.; probably M.E. *fluen*, to flow.]

FLUENCY (flōō'en-si) *n.* facility of utterance.

FLUENT (flōō'ent) *a.* liquid; flowing; smooth; ready in the use of words; voluble. [L. (part. stem) *fluent-*, of *fluens*, flowing, fr. *fluere*, to flow.]

FLUENTLY (flōō'ent-li) *ad.* with flow of utterance; volubly.

FLUID (flōō'id) *a.* having parts which easily move, as water; liquid;—*n.* a liquid substance. [O.F., fr. L. *fluidus*, fr. *fluere*, to flow.]

FLUIDITY (flōō-id'i-ti) *n.* the quality of being fluid.

FLUKE (flōōk) (1) *n.* the part of an anchor which fastens in the ground; (2) a small flat fish. [(1) E., etym. doubtful. (2) O.E. *floc*, a plaice.]

FLUME (flōōm) *n.* a channel for water. [L. *flumen*, a river, fr. *fluere*, flow.]

FLUMMERY (flum'er-i) *n.* a kind of jelly; empty talk or compliment. [W. =sour oatmeal boiled and jellied.]

FLUNG (flung) *pret.* and *pp.* of FLING.

FLUNKEY (flung'ki) *n.* a livery servant; lackey; a mean-spirited fellow. [F. *flanquer*, to run along by the side of, fr. F. *flanc*, side.]

FLUNKEYISM (flung'ki-izm) *n.* qualities of a flunkey; mean servility.

FLUOR-SPAR (flōō'or-spär) *n.* a beautiful mineral. [L. *fluor*, lit. a flowing, fr. *fluere*, to flow.]

FLURRY (flur'i) *n.* a hasty blast; sudden commotion;—*v.t.* to agitate. [imit., fr. *flurr*, to whirr. Cf. FLUTTER.]

FLUSH (flush) (1) *a.* fresh; full of vigour;—*v.i.* to redden suddenly;—*v.t.* to cause to blush;—*n.* a flow of blood to the face;—(2) *v.t.* to cleanse by a run of water;—(3) *v.t.* to start;—(4) *a.* level; even. [(1) E., prob. fr. Scand. (2) Imit. Cf. FLUSH, to fly up quickly. Perhaps conn. with F. *flux*, fr. L. *fluere*, flow. (3) Conn. with FLUSTER. (4) Etym. doubtful.]

FLUSTER (flus'ter) *v.t.* to confuse;—*v.i.* to be agitated. [Scand.]

FLUTE (flōōt) *n.* a musical pipe;—*v.i.* to play on a flute;—*v.t.* to furrow or channel. [O.F. *flaute*, F. *flûte*, of uncert. origin; perhaps fr. L. (part.) *flatus*, fr. *flare*, to blow.]

FLUTING (flōō'ting) *n.* fluted work. [See FLUTE.]

FLUTIST (flōō'tist) *n.* a performer on the flute.

FLUTTER (flut'er) *v.i.* to move or flap the wings rapidly; *v.t.* to agitate; hurry the mind;—*n.* rapid motion; hurry; confusion. [O.E. *flotorian*, to float about, fr. *flot*, the sea.]

FLUVIAL (flōō'vi-al) *a.* belonging or pertaining to rivers. [L. *fluvius.*]

FLUX (fluks) *n.* a flowing; looseness;—*v.t.* to melt or fuse. [O.F. fr. L. (acc.) *fluxum*, of *fluxus*, a flowing, fr. *fluere*, to flow.]

FLUXIBILITY (fluks-i-bil'i-ti) *n.* capacity of being fused.

FLUXIBLE (fluks'i-bl) *a.* capable of being melted.

FLY (flī) *v.i.* [*pret.* FLEW; *pp.* FLOWN] to move with the wings; move rapidly; float; flutter;—*v.t.* to quit; shun;—*n.* a winged insect; a light carriage. [O.E. *fleogan.*]

FLYBLOW (flī'blō) *n.* the egg of a fly. [See FLY. [E. *blots*, eggs of maggots.]

FLYBLOWN (flī'blōn) *a.* tainted; impure.

FLY-FISHING (flī'fish-ing) *n.* angling for fish with flies.

FLY-LEAF (flī'lēf) *n.* a blank leaf at the beginning or end of a book.

FLY-WHEEL (flī'hwēl) *n.* a large wheel for equalising the motive power of a machine.

FOAL (fōl) *n.* the young of a mare; she-ass, etc.;—*v.t.* or *i.* to bring forth a colt or filly. [O.E. *fola.*]

FOAM (fōm) *v.i.* to froth; be in a rage;—*n.* froth; rage. [O.E. *fam.*]

FOAMY (fō'mi) *a.* covered with froth; frothy.

FOB (fob) *n.* a small watch-pocket;—*v.t.* to trick; defraud. [Ger.]

FOCAL (fō'kal) *a.* belonging to a focus.

FOCALISE (fō'kal-īz) *v.t.* to bring to a focus.

FOCUS (fō'kus) *n.* the point in which rays of light meet when reflected or refracted; meeting point;—*pl.* FOCUSES, FOCI. [L. =a hearth.]

FODDER (fod'er) *n.* food for cattle;—*v.t.* to feed as cattle. [O.E. *fodor*, food.]

FOE (fō) *n.* an enemy; an adversary; an ill-wisher. [O.E. *fah*, hostile.]

FOG (fog) *n.* a thick vapour from the earth or water. [Etym. unknown; M.E. *fogge* = coarse grass.]

FOGGINESS (fog'i-nes) *n.* state of being foggy.

FOGGY (fog'i) *a.* dark with a fog; filled with fog; misty; obscure.

FOGY (fō'gi) *n.* an old-fashioned fellow; one behind the times. Also FOGEY. [Etym. unknown.]

FOIBLE (foi'bi) *n.* a moral weakness or failing; a weak point. [O.F.; F. *faible*, weak, feeble.]

FOIL (foil) (1) *v.t.* to frustrate; blunt; dull; —*n.* a defeat; a blunt sword;—(2) a thin leaf of metal. [(1) and (2) F. *fouler*, trample on. (3) F., fr. L. *folium*, a leaf.]

FOILABLE (foil'a-bl) *a.* that may be foiled.

FOILER (foi'ler) *n.* one who frustrates another.

FOIST (foist) *v.t.* to insert wrongfully or secretly; interpolate. [D. =to take in the hand.]

FOLD (fōld) (1) *n.* a doubling; a plait;—*v.t.* or *i.* to double over; wrap; embrace; be closed;—(2) a pen for sheep. [(1) O.E. *fealdan*, to wrap, to fold. (2) O.E. *fald.*]

FOLDER (fōl'der) *n.* an instrument to fold paper.

FOLIACEOUS (fō-li-ā'shus) *a.* leafy or with scales. [L. *foliaceus.*]

FOLIAGE (fō'li-ij) *n.* leaves of trees. [F., fr. L. (pl.) *folia*, of *folium*, a leaf.]

FOLIATE (fō'li-āt) *v.t.* to beat into a thin plate.

FOLIATION (fō-li-ā'shun) *n.* the beating into plates.

FOLIATURE (fō'li-ā-tūr) *n.* leafage; state of being beaten into a foil.

FOLIO (fō'li-ō) *n.* a book of two leaves to a sheet; a page;—*pl.* FOLIOS. [L., fr. the phrase, *in folio*, abl. of *folium*, a leaf.]

FOLK (fōk) *n.* people in general;—*pl.* FOLKS. [O.E. *folc.*]

FOLLICLE (fol'i-kl) *n.* a univalvular pericarp; a little bag; gland. [F. *follicule*, little bag, fr. L. *folliculus*, double dim. of *follis*, a bag.]

FOLLOW (fol'ō) *v.t.* or *i.* to go or come after; pursue; copy; practise; succeed; result from. [O.E. *folgian.*]

FOLLOWER (fol'ō-er) *n.* one who follows; a disciple.

FOLLOWING (fol'ō-ing) a. being the next after; subsequent;—n. business; occupation; body of followers.

FOLLY (fol'i) n. absurd action; criminal weakness. [O.F. folie, fr. fol, foolish.]

FOMENT (fō-ment') v.t. to supply warm lotions; encourage or abet. [L. fomentum, fr. fovere, to warm.]

FOMENTATION (fō-men-tā'shun) n. a bathing with warm lotions.

FOND (fond) a. foolish; silly; loving. [M.E. (part.) fond, or fonn-ed, of fonnen, to act as a fool, fr. fon, a fool.]

FONDLE (fon'dl) v.t. or i. to dote on; caress.

FONDLING (fond'ling) n. one fondled or caressed much.

FONDLY (fond'li) ad. lovingly.

FONDNESS (fond'nes) n. affection; love; liking; inclination; relish.

FONT (font) n. a baptismal basin. [(1) O.E. font, fr. L. (acc.) fontem, of fons, a fount.

FOOD (food) n. that which supplies nutriment, provisions; aliment. [O.E. foda, fr. root pa, to nourish.]

FOOL (fool) n. one destitute of reason;—v.t. to impose on; spend foolishly;—v.i. to act like a fool; trifle. [O.F. fol, fr. L. (acc.) follem, of follis, a wind-bag; pl. folles, puffed cheeks; Late L. follis, a fool.]

Font.

FOOLERY (fool'e-ri) n. acts of folly.

FOOLHARDINESS (fool'hár-di-nes) n. courage without sense; mad rashness. Also FOOL-HARDIHOOD.

FOOLHARDY (fool'hàr-di) a. madly rash or adventurous.

FOOLISH (fool'ish) a. silly; indiscreet. [See FOOL.]

FOOLISHLY (fool'ish-li) ad. weakly; absurdly.

FOOLISHNESS (fool'ish-nes) n. want of understanding.

FOOLSCAP (foolz'kap) n. a paper 17 by 14 inches in size. [Fr. watermark, fool's cap and bells, used by old paper-makers.]

FOOT (foot) n. that on which a thing stands; the bottom of the leg; 12 inches; measure in poetry; infantry;—pl. FEET;—v.i. to dance; walk;—v.t. to tread; sum up; put a foot on. [O.E. fot, pl. fet. Cf. Ger. Fuss, L. pes, G. pous.]

FOOTBALL (foot'bawl) n. a leathern ball to be kicked in sport; the game itself.

FOOTBOY (foot'boi) n. a boy in livery.

FOOTFALL (foot'fawl) n. a footstep.

FOOTING (foot'ing) n. ground for the foot; support; position; measured step or dance; addition of figures; sum total of such.

FOOTMAN (foot'man) n. a man-servant.

FOOTNOTE (foot'nōt) n. a note of reference at the foot of the page.

FOOTPATH (foot'path) n. a way for foot passengers.

FOOTPRINT (foot'print) n. impression of the foot.

FOOTRULE (foot'rool) n. a measure 12 inches long.

FOOTSTEP (foot'step) n. mark of a foot; track; way.

FOP (fop) n. a vain, trifling man; a coxcomb. [E.]

FOPPERY (fop'er-i) n. foolish vanity in dress or manners.

FOPPISH (fop'ish) a. vain; gaudy; foolish.

FOR (for) prep. or con. because of. [O.E.]

FORAGE (for'ij) n. food for horses or cattle; provisions;—v.i. to go in search of provisions. [O.F. fourage, F. feurre, fodder, fr. Late L. fodrum, fodder.]

FORAMEN (fo-rā'men) n. a small hole or opening. [L., fr. forare, to bore.]

FORASMUCH (for'az-much) ad. or con. since; seeing. [E.]

FORAY (for'ā) n. a pillaging excursion. [Scot., a form of FORAGE.]

FORBADE (for-bad') pret. of FORBID. [See FORBID.]

FORBEAR (for-bār') v.t. or i. [pret. FORBORE; pp. FORBORNE] to cease; abstain; delay. [Pref. for-, away, and BEAR.]

FORBEARANCE (for-bār'ans) n. long-suffering.

FORBID (for-bid') v.i. [pret. FORBID; pp. FORBIDDEN] to prohibit. [Pref. for-, away, and BID.]

FORBIDDING (for-bid'ing) a. repulsive.

FORCE (fōrs) n. strength; active power; efficacy; armament;—v.t. to compel; urge; ravage; strain; ripen artificially. [O.F., fr. Late L. fortia, strength, fr. fortis, strong.]

FORCEMEAT (fōrs'mēt) n. spiced meat chopped fine. [F. farce, stuffing, fr. farcir, fr. L. farcire, so stuff.]

FORCEPS (for'seps) n. a pair of pincers for delicate operations. [L. for formiceps, fr. formus, hot, and capere, to hold; orig. used for holding hot iron.]

FORCIBLE (fōr'si-bl) a. manifesting force; violent; having force; cogent; binding.

FORCIBLY (fōr'si-bli) ad. powerfully; impressively.

FORD (fōrd) n. a shallow place where water is passed on foot;—v.t. to pass by wading. [O.E. ford, fr. faran, to go.]

FORDABLE (fōr'da-bl) a. passable on foot.

FORE (fōr) a. coming or going first;—ad. before; in the fore part. [O.E.]

FOREARM (fōr-àrm') v.t. to arm beforehand.

FOREBODE (fōr-bōd') v.t. to prognosticate; predict, especially evil. [See FORE and O.E. bodian, to warn.]

FOREBODING (fōr-bō'ding) n. prognostication.

FORECAST (fōr-kàst') v.t. or i. to plan beforehand; foresight.

FORECASTLE (fōk'sel) n. the forepart of a ship.

FORECLOSE (fōr-klōz') v.t. to shut up; preclude; cut off from right of redemption. [O.F. forclos, fr. for-, fr. L. foris, outside, and O.F. clorre, to shut, fr. L. claudere.]

FORECLOSURE (fōr-klō'zhūr) n. act of precluding.

FOREFATHER (fōr'fà-THer) n. an ancestor.

FOREFEND (fōr'fend) v.t. to avert; prohibit; secure. [Pref. for-, away, and fend, abbrev. of DEFEND.]

FOREFINGER (fōr'fing-ger) n. the finger next the thumb.

FOREFRONT (fōr'frunt) n. the foremost part or place.

FOREGO (fōr-gō') v.t. [pp. FOREGONE] (1) to forbear to possess; renounce;—(2) go before; precede. [(1) Better FORGO; fr. O.E. forgan, to pass over, fr. pref. for- and GO.]

FOREGOING (fōr'gō-ing) a. preceding.

FOREGONE (fōr-gon') a. formed beforehand; relinquished.

FOREGROUND (fōr'ground) n. the front part of a picture.

FOREHAMMER (fōr'ham-er) n. the sledge hammer.

FOREHANDED (fōr'han-ded) a. early; timely; easy in property.

FOREHEAD (for'hed) n. upper part of the face.

FOREIGN (for'en) a. belonging to another country; not to the purpose; alien; remote; exotic. [O.F. forain, alien, fr. Late L. forancus, fr. foras, out-of-doors.]

FOREIGNER (for'en-er) n. an alien; one from another country.

FOREIGNNESS (for'en-nes) n. remoteness; want of relation.

FOREJUDGE (fōr-juj') *v.t.* to judge beforehand.

FOREKNOW (fōr-nō') *v.t.* to know before.

FOREKNOWLEDGE (fōr-nol'ej) *n.* knowledge of future events.

FORELAND (fōr'land) *n.* a promontory or cape.

FORELOCK (fōr'lok) *n.* a lock of hair on the forehead.

FOREMAN (fōr'man) *n.* the chief man of a jury or in a shop.

FOREMAST (fōr'mast) *n.* the forward mast of a vessel.

FOREMOST (fōr'most) *a.* first in time, place, rank, etc. [Double superl., fr. O.E. *formest*, a by-form of *fyrmest*, fr. *forma*, first.]

FORENOON (fōr' nōōn) *n.* first half of the day.

FORENSIC (fō-ren'sik) *a.* relating to courts of law. [Fr. L. *forensis* belonging to the *forum*, fr. *forum*, market-place.]

FOREORDAIN (fōr-or-dān') *v.t.* to ordain beforehand.

FOREORDINATION (fōr-or-di-nā'shun) *n.* previous ordination or appointment.

FOREPART (fōr'part) *n.* the part before.

FORERANK (fōr'rangk) *n.* the first or front rank.

FORERUN (fōr-run') *v.t.* to precede.

FORERUNNER (fōr'run-er) *n.* one sent before; a precursor.

FORESAIL (fōr'sāl) *n.* a sail extended on the yard of the foremast.

FORESEE (fōr-sē') *v.t.* [*pp.* **FORESEEN**] to see beforehand.

FORESHORE (fōr'shōr) *n.* the sloping part of the shore between high and low water mark.

FORESHORTEN (fōr-short'n) *v.t.* to paint figures as they appear when viewed obliquely.

FORESHOW (fōr-shō') *v.t.* [*pp.* **FORESHOWN**] to indicate beforehand.

FORESIGHT (fōr'sit) *n.* a seeing beforehand; penetration; prudent care. [See FORESEE.]

FOREST (for'est) *n.* an extensive wood. [O.F., fr. Late L. *forestis*, open space of hunting-ground, fr. *foris*, out-of-doors.]

FORESTALL (fōr-stawl') *v.t.* to buy goods before they reach the market.

FORESTER (for'es-ter) *n.* one who guards or lives in a forest. [See FOREST.]

FORESTRY (for'es-tri) art of cultivating forests.

FORETASTE (fōr'tāst) *n.* anticipation;—*v.t.* to anticipate.

FORETELL (fōr-tel') *v.t.* or *i.* [*pret.* and *pp.* FORETOLD] to predict; prophesy.

FORETHOUGHT (fōr'thawt) *n.* previous thought; provident care.

FORETOKEN (fōr-tō'kn) *v.t.* to foreshow;—*n.* a previous sign; prognostic.

FORETOLD (fōr-tōld') *a.* told or uttered before. [See FORETELL.]

FORETOP (fōr'top) *n.* hair on the forehead; platform at the head of the foremast.

FOREVER (for-ev'er) *ad.* through endless ages; to eternity.

FOREWARN (fōr-wawrn') *v.t.* to admonish beforehand.

FOREWARNING (fōr-wawr'ning) *n.* previous admonition.

FORFEIT (for'fit) *v.t.* to lose by an offence;—*a.* liable to seizure;—*n.* what is lost by an offence. [O.F. *forfait*, fr. L. *foris*, out of doors, and *facere*, make.]

FORFEITABLE (for'fi-ta-bl) *a.* subject to forfeiture.

FORFEITURE (for'fi-tūr) *n.* act of forfeiting; thing forfeited.

FORGAVE (for-gāv') *pret.* of FORGIVE. [See FORGIVE.]

FORGE (fōrj) *n.* a place where iron is beaten into form;—*v.t.* to form by hammering; counterfeit. [F., fr. L. *faber*, smith.]

FORGER (fōr'jer) *n.* one who forges.

FORGERY (fōr'jer-i) *n.* act of counterfeiting or falsifying.

FORGET (for-get') *v.t.* [*pret.* FORGOT; *pp.* FORGOT, FORGOTTEN] to lose the remembrance of; overlook; neglect. [O.E. *forgitan*, fr. *for*, away, and *gitan*, to get.]

FORGETFUL (for-get'fool) *a.* apt to forget.

FORGETFULNESS (for-get'fool-nes) *n.* aptness to forget; neglect.

FORGET-ME-NOT (for-get'me-not) *n.* a small blue flower—emblem of friendship.

FORGETTER (for-get'er) *n.* one who forgets.

FORGING (for'jing) *n.* beating into shape; counterfeiting; any work of hammered iron or steel.

FORGIVE (for-giv') *v.t.* [*pret.* FORGAVE; *pp.* FORGIVEN] to pardon; remit. [O.E. *for*, away, and *giefan*, give.]

FORGIVENESS (for-giv'nes) *n.* pardon. [See FORGIVE.]

FORK (fork) *v.t.* or *i.* to shoot into branches; divide;—*n.* an instrument with prongs. [O.E. *forca*, fr. L. *furca*.]

FORKED (forkt) *a.* divided into branches or prongs.

FORKY (for'ki) *a.* divided into shoots. [See FORK.]

FORLORN (for-lorn') *a.* forsaken and wretched; helpless. [O.E. (part.) *forloren*, cf *forleosan*, to lose. Cf. Ger. (part.) *verloren*, of *verlieren*.]

FORM (form) *n.* shape; manner; model; order; show; a long bench;—*v.t.* to model; plan; make;—*v.i.* to take position, as troops. [O.F. *forme*, fr. L. *forma*, shape.]

FORMAL (for'mal) *a.* according to form; essential; methodical; conventional; external.

FORMALISM (for'mal-izm) *n.* quality of being formal.

FORMALIST (for'mal-ist) *n.* an observer of forms.

FORMALITY (for-mal'i-ti) *n.* observance of form or ceremony.

FORMALLY (for'mal-i) *ad.* according to forms.

FORMATION (for-mā'shun) *n.* act of forming, production; structure; arrangement.

FORMATIVE (form'a-tiv) *a.* that forms; tending to form;—*n.* a word formed agreeably to some analogy.

FORMER (for'mer) (1) *n.* one who makes;— (2) *a.* first of two; preceding; previous. [(1) See FORM. (2) Double compar. formed by adding *er* to base of (superl.) *forma*, first.]

FORMERLY (for'mer-li) *ad.* in time past.

FORMIDABLE (for'mi-da-bl) *a.* adapted to excite fear; tremendous. [L. *formidabilis*, fr. *formido*, fear.]

FORMIDABLY (for'mi-da-bli) *ad.* in a manner to excite fear.

FORMLESS (form'les) *a.* having no regular form.

FORMULA (for'mū-la) *n.* prescribed form;— *pl.* FORMULÆ. [L., dim. of *forma*, form.]

FORMULARY (for'mū-la-ri) *n.* a book of stated forms;—*a.* stated. [See FORMULA.]

FORMULATE (for'mū-lāt) *v.t.* to reduce to a formula; express in definite terms. Also FORMULARISE. [See FORMULA.]

FORNICATE (for'ni-kāt) *v.i.* to commit lewdness. [L. *fornicatus*, fr. stem *fornic-*, cf *fornix*, vault.]

FORNICATION (for-ni-kā'shun) *n.* incontinence of unmarried persons.

FORNICATOR (for'ni-kā-ter) *n.* one guilty of fornication.

FORSAKE (for-sāk') *v.t.* [*pret.* FORSOOK; *pp.* FORSAKEN] to quit entirely; abandon; relinquish; renounce. [O.E., fr. *for*, and *sacan*, to contend, strive.]

FORSAKEN (for-sā'kn) *a.* abandoned.

FORSOOTH (for-sŏŏth') *ad.* in truth; verily. [O.E. *for sothe,* for truth.]

FORSWEAR (for-swär') *v.t.* or *i.* [*pret.* FOR-SWORE; *pp.* FORSWORN] to denounce or deny upon oath; swear falsely. [O.E. *for,* and *swerian,* to swear.]

FORT (fŏrt) *n.* a fortress; castle. [L. *fortis,* strong.]

FORTE (for'tă) *ad.* in *Music,* a direction to play or sing with force. [It.]

FORTE (fŏrt) *n.* that in which one excels. [It. *forte,* fr. L. *fortis.*]

FORTH (fŏrth) *ad.* forward; abroad. [O.E., fr. *fore,* before.]

FORTHCOMING (fŏrth'kum-ing) *a.* ready to appear.

FORTHWITH (fŏrth-wiᴛʜ') *ad.* immediately. [See **FORTH** and **WITH.**]

FORTIETH (for'ti-eth) *a.* the tenth taken four times. [O.E. *fcower-tigetha.*]

FORTIFICATION (for-ti-fi-ka'shun) *n.* military architecture; a work for defence. [See **FORTIFY.**]

FORTIFY (for'ti-fi) *v.t.* to erect works for defence; confirm. [L. *fortis,* strong, and *facere,* to make.]

FORTITUDE (for'ti-tŭd) *n.* firmness of mind to endure; resolution; endurance. [L. *fortitudo,* courage, fr. *fortis.*]

FORTNIGHT (fort'nit) *n.* the space of two weeks. [Contr. of *fourteen nights.*]

FORTNIGHTLY (fort'nit-li) *ad.* once a fortnight.

FORTRESS (fŏr'tres) *n.* a fortified place. [O.F. *forteresse,* L. *fortis,* strong.]

FORTUITOUS (for-tū'i-tus) *a.* accidental. [L. *fortuitus,* casual, fr. stem *fort-,* of *fors,* chance.]

FORTUITOUSLY (for-tū'i-tus-li) *ad.* accidentally; by chance.

FORTUNATE (for'tū-năt) *a.* lucky; successful.

FORTUNATELY (for'tū-năt-li) *ad.* successfully.

FORTUNE (for'tūn) *n.* the good or ill that befalls man; luck; riches;—*v.i.* to happen; befall. [F., fr. L. *fortuna,* fr. *fors, fortis,* chance, fr. *ferre,* to bear.]

FORTY (for'ti) *a.* or *n.* four tens added. [O.E. *feower,* and *tig,* ten.]

FORUM (fō'rum) *n.* a public place in Rome; court of justice; tribunal. [L.]

FORWARD (for'ward) *a.* being before; prompt; bold;—*v.t.* to advance; promote;—*ad.* in front; onward. [O.E., fr. *fore,* before, and *weard,* towards.]

FORWARDLY (for'ward-li) *ad.* hastily; eagerly.

FORWARDNESS (for'ward-nes) *n.* eagerness; boldness; precocity.

FOSSE (fos) *n.* a ditch; a moat. [F., fr. L. *fossa,* ditch, fr. (part.) *fossus,* of *fodere,* to dig.]

FOSSIL (fos'il) *a.* dug from the earth;—*n.* a substance dug from the earth. [F. *fossile,* fr. L. *fossilis,* fr. *fodere,* to dig.]

FOSSILIFEROUS (fos-i-lif'e-rus) *a.* containing fossil or organic remains. [See **FOSSIL.**]

FOSSILISE (fos'il-iz) *v.t.* or *i.* to change into a fossil or petrefaction.

FOSSILIST (fos'il-ist) *n.* one versed in fossils. [See **FOSSIL.**]

FOSTER (fos'ter) *v.t.* to nurse; feed; cherish. [O.E. *fostrian,* to nourish, fr. *fostor,* food.]

FOSTER-BROTHER (fos'ter-bruᴛʜ'er) *n.* a brother by nursing, not by birth.

FOSTER-CHILD (fos'ter-child) *n.* a child nursed by another than its parent.

FOSTER-SISTER (fos'ter-sis'ter) *n.* a sister by nursing, not by birth.

FOSTER-SON (fos'ter-sun) *n.* one fed and educated like a son.

FOUGHT (fawt) *pret.* and *pp.* of **FIGHT.** [See **FIGHT.**]

FOUL (fo̤ul) *a.* turbid; impure; entangled; unfair;—*v.t.* or *i.* to make filthy; come into collision. [O.E. *ful.*]

FOULLY (foul'i) *ad.* filthily.

FOULNESS (foul'nes) *n.* filthiness.

FOUND (found) (1) *pret.* and *pp.* of **FIND;**—(2) *v.t.* to lay a basis; establish; endow; (3) cast vessels of metal. [(1) See **FIND.** (2) F. *fonder,* fr. L. *fundare,* fr. *fundus,* the bottom. (3) F. *fondre,* fr. L. *fundere,* to pour.]

FOUNDATION (fo̤un-dā'shun) *n.* bottom support; establishment; endowed institution.

FOUNDER (foun'der) (1) *n.* one who founds, originates, or endows;—(2) *n.* a caster of wares;—(3) *v.t.* to fill and sink; to make lame. [(1) See **FOUND** (2). (2) See **FOUND** (3). (3) L. *fundus,* bottom.]

FOUNDRY (foun'dri) *n.* a place for casting metals. [See **FOUND** (3).]

FOUNDLING (found'ling) *n.* a deserted or exposed child. [See **FIND.**]

FOUNTAIN (foun'tan) *n.* a spring; source; artificial jet; head of a river; first cause. [F. *fontaine,* fr. L. stem *font-,* of *fons,* fr. *fundere,* to pour.]

FOUR (fŏr) *n.* or *a.* two and two added. [O.E. *feower.*]

FOURFOLD (fŏr'fōld) *a.* or *n.* four times as much.

FOUR-FOOTED (fŏr'fo̤ot-ed) *a.* having four feet.

FOURSCORE (fŏr'skŏr) *a.* eighty.

FOURSQUARE (fŏr'skwär) *a.* having four equal sides.

FOURTEEN (fŏr'tēn) *n.* or *a.* four and ten.

FOURTEENTH (fŏr'tēnth) *n.* one of fourteen parts or persons. [O.E. *feower* and *tien.*]

FOURTH (fŏrth) *n.* one of four parts or persons;—*ad.* the ordinal of four. [O.F. *feortha.*]

FOURTHLY (fŏrth'li) *a.* in the fourth place.

FOWL (foul) *n.* a winged animal; a bird. [O.E. *fugel.* Cf. Ger. *Vogel.*]

FOWLER (fou'ler) *n.* a sportsman who catches birds.

FOWLING-PIECE (fou'ling-pēs) *n.* a gun for shooting birds.

FOX (foks) *n.* an animal remarkable for cunning; a cunning fellow. [O.E. Cf. Ger. *Fuchs.*]

FOXCHASE (foks'chās) *n.* a fox hunt.

FOXGLOVE (foks'gluv) *n.* digitalis; a narcotic plant. [O.E. *foxes-glofa.*]

FOXHOUND (foks'hound) *n.* a hound for chasing foxes.

FOXTAIL (foks'tāl) *n.* the tail of a fox; a species of grass.

FOXY (fok'si) *a.* wily as a fox.

FRACAS (fra-kä') *n.* a noisy quarrel. [F., fr. *fracasser,* to break, fr. It. *fracassare,* to make an uproar.]

FRACTION (frak'shun) *n.* a broken part; part of an integer. [O.F. *fraccion,* fr. L. (acc.) *fractionem,* fr. (part.) *fractus,* of *frangere,* to break.]

Foxglove.

FRACTIONAL (frak'shun-al) *a.* consisting in fractions.

FRACTIOUS (frak'shus) *a.* apt to quarrel; cross; fretful. [See **FRACTION.**]

FRACTIOUSLY (frak'shus-li) *ad.* snappishly; fretfully.

FRACTIOUSNESS (frak'shus-nes) *n.* a cross or fretful temper.

FRACTURE (frak'tūr) *n.* a breach of a solid; —*v.t.* to break or crack, as a bone. [L. *fractura.*]

FRACTURED (frak'tūrd) *a.* broken; cracked.

FRAGILE (fraj'il) *a.* easily broken; brittle; weak. [F., fr. L. *fragilis,* fr. *frangere,* to break.]

FRAGILITY (fra-jil'i-ti) *n.* brittleness; frailty; weakness. [See **FRAGILE**.]

FRAGMENT (frag'ment) *n.* a piece broken off; a small portion. [L. *fragmentum*, fr. *frangere*, to break.]

FRAGMENTARY (frag'men-ta-ri) *a.* composed of fragments.

FRAGRANCE (frā'grans) *n.* sweetness of smell.

FRAGRANT (frā'grant) *a.* sweet-smelling. [F., fr. L. (part. stem) *fragrant-*, of *fragrare*, to smell.]

FRAGRANTLY (frā'grant-li) *ad.* with a pleasant smell.

FRAIL (frāl) *a.* weak; liable to error; of easy virtue. [O.F. *fraile*, fr. L. *fragilis*.]

FRAILNESS (frāl'nes) *n.* state of being frail; weakness.

FRAILTY (frāl'ti) *n.* weakness; infirmity; foible.

FRAME (frām) *v.t.* to fit to something else; form;—*n.* fabric; order; form; structure; temperament; timbers of an edifice. [O.E. *fremman*, to make.]

FRAMEWORK (frām'wurk) *n.* outline or skeleton of a fabric; structure.

FRANC (trangk) *n.* a French coin, value tenpence sterling. [F., fr. the legend on the first coin. *Francorum rex*.]

FRANCHISE (fran'chiz) *n.* a privilege; immunity;—*v.t.* to make free. [F., fr. *franc*, *franche*, free.]

FRANCHISEMENT (fran'chiz-ment) *n.* release from burden or restriction.

FRANCISCAN (fran-sis'kan) *n.* one of an order of monks; gray friar. [L. *Franciscus*, Francis.]

FRANGIBILITY (fran-ji-bil'i-ti) *n.* state of being frangible.

FRANGIBLE (fran'ji-bl) *a.* liable to break. [L., fr. *frangere*, break.]

FRANGIPANI (fran-ji-pa'ni) *n.* a kind of perfume from the West Indies. [F., fr. a personal name.]

FRANK (frangk) *a.* free in uttering sentiments; without disguise; candid; liberal; generous;—*n.* a free letter;—*v.t.* to exempt from postage. [F. *franc*, free, fr. O. H. Ger. *Franko*, one of the tribe called *Franks*, a free man.]

FRANKINCENSE (frangk'in-sens) *n.* a resinous aromatic substance. [O.F. *franc encens*, pure incense.]

FRANKLY (frangk'li) *ad.* freely; openly.

FRANKNESS (frangk'nes) *n.* ingenuousness; openness.

FRANTIC (fran'tik) *a.* distracted; raving; furious; wild and noisy. [O.F. *frenetique*, mad, fr. *freneticus*, fr. G. *phrenetikos*, fr. *phren*, the mind.]

FRANTICNESS (fran'tik-nes) *n.* excitement of fury or passion. [See **FRANTIC**.]

FRATERNAL (fra-ter'nal) *a.* brotherly. [F., fr. Late L. *fraternalis*, fr. *frater*, a brother, fr. G. *phrater*, a clansman.]

FRATERNALLY (fra-ter'nal-i) *ad.* in a brotherly manner.

FRATERNISE (frat'er-niz) *v.i.* to associate as brothers.

FRATERNITY (fra-ter'ni-ti) *n.* a brotherhood. [L. *fraternitas*.]

FRATRICIDAL (frat'ri-si-dal) *a.* pertaining to fratricide.

FRATRICIDE (frat'ri-sid) *n.* murder, or the murderer, of a brother. [L. (stem) *fratr-*, of *frater*, a brother, and *cædere*, to kill.]

FRAUD (frawd) *n.* any act or course to deceive and injure another. [O.F., fr. L. (stem) *fraud-*, of *fraus*, fraud.]

FRAUDFULLY (frawd'fool-i) *ad.* in a manner to deceive and gain the advantage of another.

FRAUDULENCE (fraw'dū-lens) *n.* deceitfulness; trickery. Also **FRAUDULENCY**. [See **FRAUD**.]

FRAUDULENT (fraw'dū-lent) *a.* using fraud; designing; obtained by fraud; dishonest.

FRAUDULENTLY (fraw'dū-lent-li) *ad.* by fraud. [See **FRAUD**.]

FRAUGHT (frawt) *a.* loaded; full. [Scand.]

FRAY (frā) (1) *n.* a quarrel; a riot;—(2) *n.* a fret or chafe in cloth;—*v.t.* or *i.* to wear away by rubbing. [(1) Contr. of **AFFRAY**. (2) O.F. *frayer*, fr. L. *fricare*, to rub.]

FREAK (frēk) *n.* a whim; caprice. [O.E. *frec*, bold, rash.]

FREAKISH (frē'kish) *a.* whimsical; odd.

FRECKLE (frek'l) *n.* a spot on the skin. [Dim. of *freak*, to spot.]

FRECKLED (frek'ld) *a.* full of freckles.

FRECKLY (frek'li) *a.* marked with spots.

FREE (frē) *a.* being at liberty; open; liberal; rude;—*v.t.* to deliver from restraint; clear; absolve. [O.E. *freo*. Cf. Ger. *frei*.]

FREEBOOTER (frē'bōō-ter) *n.* a robber. [D.]

FREEBORN (frē'born) *a.* born free.

FREEDMAN (frēd'man) *n.* a man freed from slavery.

FREEDOM (frē'dum) *n.* exemption from control; liberty; ease or facility; franchise; undue familiarity.

FREEHOLD (frē'hōld) *n.* land held by free tenure.

FREEHOLDER (frē'hōl-der) *n.* the owner of a freehold.

FREELY (frē'll) *ad.* at liberty; willingly; liberally.

FREEMAN (frē'man) *n.* one who enjoys liberty, or is entitled to the privileges of citizenship.

FREEMASON (frē-mā'sun) *n.* a member of a secret friendly society.

FREE-PORT (frē'pōrt) *n.* a port where goods may enter free from duties.

FREE-SCHOOL (frē'skōōl) *n.* a school open to all.

FREESTONE (frē'stōn) *n.* any stone composed of sand or grit.

FREETHINKER (frē'thing-ker) *n.* one who disbelieves revelation.

FREE-TRADE (frē'trād) *n.* interchange of commodities between nations without protective duties.

FREE-WILL (frē-wil') *n.* power of acting at pleasure;—*a.* voluntary.

FREEZE (frēz) *v.t.* or *i.* [*pret.* **FROZE**; *pp.* **FROZEN**] to congeal; die by cold. [O.E. *freosan*.]

FREIGHT (frāt) *n.* lading of a ship; hire of a ship; charge for carrying goods;—*v.t.* to load, as a vessel. [A late form of **FRAUGHT**.]

FREIGHTAGE (frāt'ij) *n.* charge for transporting goods; cargo.

FRENCH (frensh) *a.* belonging to France;—*n.* the language or people of France.

FRENZY (fren'zi) *n.* distraction of mind. [Through F. and L., fr. G. *phrenitis*, inflammation of the brain, fr. *phren*, the mind.]

FREQUENCY (frē'kwen-si) *n.* a common occurrence; repetition.

FREQUENT (frē'kwent) *a.* happening often; common. [L. (stem)fr. *frequent-*, of *frequens*.]

FREQUENT (frē-kwent') *v.t.* to visit often.

FREQUENTATIVE (frē-kwen'ta-tiv) *a.* denoting frequent repetition.

FREQUENTER (frē-kwen'ter) *n.* one who visits a place often.

FREQUENTLY (frē'kwent-li) *ad.* often.

FRESCO (fres'kō) *n.* coolness; a kind of painting on fresh plaster. [It. =fresh.]

FRESH (fresh) *a.* cool; new; brisk; healthy in look; not salt or stale. [O.E. *fresci*. Cf. Ger. *freisch*.]

FRESHEN (fresh'n) *v.t.* to make fresh; revive.

FRESHET (fresh'et) *n.* a flood in rivers.

FRESHLY (fresh'li) *ad.* briskly; recently; newly; coolly.

FRESHMAN (fresh'man) *n*. one of the younger class in college.

FRESHNESS (fresh'nes) *n*. state of being fresh; coolness.

FRET (1) (fret) *v.t.* or *i*. to wear away by rubbing; corrode; agitate; irritate; be peevish;—*n*. agitation of liquor; irritation of mind. [O.E. *fretan*, to gnaw, fr. *etan*, to eat.]

FRET (2) (fret) *n*. ornamental work, consisting of perforations;—*v.t.* to ornament with frets. [O.F. *frete*, trellis-work, fr. Late L. *ferrata*, grating of a window.]

FRETFUL (fret'fool) *a*. disposed to fret; peevish; cross. [See FRET (1).]

FRETFULLY (fret'fool-i) *ad*. in a peevish manner; angrily. [See FRET (1).]

FRETFULNESS (fret'fool-nes) *n*. peevishness. [See FRET (1).]

FRETWORK (fret'wurk) *n*. raised work. [See FRET (2).]

FRIABILITY (fri-a-bil'i-ti) *n*. the quality of being easily reduced to powder.

FRIABLE (fri'a-bl) *a*. easily crumbled. [L. *friabilis*, fr. *friare*, to break into pieces.]

FRIAR (fri'ar) *n*. a begging monk. [O.F. *frere*, fr. L. *frater*, brother.]

FRIARY (fri'ar-i) *n*. a monastery.

FRIBBLE (frib'l) *a*. frivolous; trifling; silly; —*n*. a trifling fellow;—*v.i.* to trifle; totter. [imit.]

FRICANDEAU (frek-ȧn-dō') *n*. dish of veal larded and stewed. [F.]

FRICASSEE (frik-a-sē') *n*. dish of stewed or fried chickens, rabbits, etc.;—*v.t.* to dress in fricassee. [F.]

FRICTION (frik'shun) *n*. a rubbing; attrition. [F., fr. L. (acc.) *frictionem*, fr. (part.) *frictus*, of *fricare*, to rub.]

FRICTIONAL (frik'shun-al) *a*. relating to or caused by friction.

FRICTIONLESS (frik'shun-les) *a*. having no friction.

FRIDAY (fri'dā) *n*. the sixth day of the week. [O.E. *Frigedaeg*, fr. *Frigu*, the wife of the god Odin, and *daeg*, day.]

FRIEND (frend) *n*. a person attached to another by affection; a Quaker. [O.E. *freond*, fr. *freon*, to love.]

FRIENDLESS (frend'les) *a*. without friends.

FRIENDLINESS (frend'li-nes) *n*. kind disposition; goodwill.

FRIENDLY (frend'li) *a*. kind; favourable.

FRIENDSHIP (frend'ship) *n*. intimacy based on mutual esteem.

FRIEZE (frēz) *n*. a coarse woollen cloth, with a nap; part of an entablature of a column. [F. *frise*.]

FRIGATE (frig'at) *n*. a ship of war of the 18th and early part of the 19th century, carrying from 30 to 60 guns. [F. *frégate*, fr. It.; etym. uncert.]

FRIGHT (frit) *n*. sudden violent fear; ugly or ill-dressed person;—*v.t.* to frighten. [O.E. *fyrhtu*. Cf. Ger. *Furcht*, fear.]

.Frigate.

FRIGHTEN (fri'tn) *v.t.* to affect with fear; terrify; scare.

FRIGHTFUL (frit'fool) *a*. adapted to excite fear; shocking; dreadful.

FRIGHTFULLY (frit'fool-i) *ad*. dreadfully; shockingly.

FRIGHTFULNESS (frit'fool-nes) *n*. the quality of impressing terror. [See FRIGHT.]

FRIGID (frij'id) *a*. cold; dull; insensible. [L. *frigidus*, fr. *frigere*, to be cold, fr. *frigus*, cold.]

FRIGIDITY (fri-jid'i-ti) *n*. coldness; dullness.

FRIGIDLY (frij'id-ii) *ad*. coldly; unfeelingly.

FRILL (fril) *n*. an edging or ruffle:—*v.i.* to shiver with cold;—*v.t.* to decorate with frills or ruffles. [O.F. *friller*, to shiver.]

FRINGE (frinj) *n*. a kind of trimming;—*v.t.* to adorn with fringe. [O.F. *frenge*, fr. L. *fimbria*, threads.]

FRINGELESS (frinj'les) *a*. having no fringe.

FRINGY (frin'ji) *a*. adorned with fringes.

FRIPPERY (frip'er-i) *n*. cast-off things; trifles; trumpery;—*a*. trifling; useless. [F., fr. *friper*, to wear.]

FRISK (frisk) *v.i.* to leap; dance; skip;— *n*. a caper; frolic. [O.F. *frisque*, fr. Scand.]

FRISKET (fris'ket) *n*. a frame to confine sheets of paper in printing. [F. *frisquette*.]

FRISKINESS (fris'ki-nes) *n*. liveliness; airiness; gaiety.

FRISKY (fris'ki) *a*. lively; frolicsome.

FRITH. See FIRTH. [Scand. *fiord*.]

FRITTER (frit'er) *n*. a kind of pancake:— *v.t.* to break into fragments. **TO FRITTER AWAY**, to diminish gradually. [O.F. *friture*, fr. L. (part.) *frictus*, of *frigere*, to fry.]

FRIVOLITY (fri-vol'i-ti) *n*. trifling acts or habits. [See FRIVOLOUS.]

FRIVOLOUS (friv'u-lus) *a*. silly; trifling. [F. *frivole*, fr. L. *frivolus*.]

FRIVOLOUSLY (friv'u-lus-li) *ad*. in a trifling manner.

FRIVOLOUSNESS (friv'u-lus-nes) *n*. quality of being frivolous.

FRIZZ (friz) *v.t.* to curl or crisp;—*n*. anything curled. [O.F. *friser*, to curl.]

FRIZZLE (friz'l) *v.t.* to crisp in short curls; a lock of hair curled. [Dim. of FRIZZ.]

FRO (frō) *ad*. from; back. [Short for FROM.]

FROCK (frok) *n*. an outer garment. [O.F. *froc*, a monk's frock, fr. Late L. *froceus*, fr. L. *floccus*, flock of wool; or fr. Teut.]

FROCKCOAT (frok'kōt) *n*. a body-coat with broad skirts, shorter than a surtout.

FROG (frog) *n*. an amphibious animal; a tag or tassel for a coat or robe. [O.E. *frogga*.]

FROGGED (frogd) *a*. ornamented with tassels or braid.

FROGGING (frog'ing) *n*. a kind of braiding on a coat.

FROLIC (frol'ik) *a*. gay; full of pranks; playful;—*n*. a wild prank; merriment;—*v.t.* to be merry; gambol. [D. Cf. Ger. *fröhlich*, joyful.]y

FROLICKING (frol'ik-ing) *ppr*. or *a*. playing pranks; frolicsome.

FROLICSOME (frol'ik-sum) *a*. full of gaiety; sportive.

FROM (from) *prep*. away; out of; by reason of. [O.E.]

FROND (frond) *n*. the leaf peculiar to plants and ferns. [L. stem *frond-*, of *frons*, a leaf.]

FRONDESCENCE (fron-des'ens) *n*. the time of the year when a plant puts forth its leaves. [L. *frondescere*.]

FRONT (frunt) *n*. the fore part;—*v.t.* to stand before; stand or oppose face to face. [L. stem *front-*, of *frons*, the forehead.]

FRONTAGE (frun'tij) *n*. the front part of an edifice or lot.

FRONTAL (frun'tal) *a*. belonging to the forehead or front;—*n*. a pediment over a small door or window.

FRONTED (frun'ted) *a*. formed with a front.

FRONTIER (frun'tēr) *n*. the utmost verge of a country;—*a*. bordering. [F. *frontier*, fr. L. *frons*.]

FRONTISPIECE (fron'tis-pēs) *n*. a picture facing the first page of a book. [L. *frontispicium*, fr. stem *fronti-*, of *frons*, front, and *specere*, to look at.]

FRONTLET (frunt'let) *n*. a band worn on the forehead. [Dim. of FRONT.]

FROST (frost) *n*. the effect of cold producing ice;—*v.t.* to cover with something like frost, as cake. [O.E. *frost*, fr. *freosan*, freeze.]

FROSTBITTEN (frost'bit-n) *a*. nipped or withered by frost.

FROSTILY (fros'ti-li) *ad*. with frost; coldly; ungraciously.

·Fāte. fār. ade: mē. her: mīne: nōte: tūne: mōon.

FROSTINESS (fros'ti-nes) *n.* state of being frosty. [See **FROST**.]

FROST-WORK (frost'wurk) *n.* work resembling hoar-frost. Also **FROSTING**.

FROSTY (fros'ti) *a.* like frost; freezing.

FROTH (froth) *n.* foam; unsubstantial matter; showy but empty speech. [Scand.]

FROTHINESS (froth'i-nes) *n.* state of being frothy.

FROTHY (froth'i) *a.* full of foam; empty.

FROWARD (frō'ward) *a.* perversely disobedient; peevish; wayward; cross. [O.E. *fra,* away, and affix *-ward*.]

FROWARDLY (frō'ward-li) *ad.* in a forward manner.

FROWARDNESS (frō'ward-nes) *n.* perverseness; peevishness.

FROWN (froun) *n.* a look of displeasure;— *v.i.* to express displeasure by contracting the brow; scowl. [F. *se refrogner,* knit the brow.]

FROWNINGLY (frou'ning-li) *ad.* with a frown.

FROZE (frōz) *pret.* of **FREEZE**. [See **FREEZE**.]

FROZEN (frō'zn) *pp.* of **FREEZE**.

FRUCTESCENCE (fruk-tes'ens) *n.* the time when fruit ripens. [L. *fructescere,* to bear fruit.]

FRUCTIFEROUS (fruk-tif'e-rus) *a.* producing fruit. [See **FRUCTIFY**.]

FRUCTIFY (fruk'ti-fī) *v.t.* to make fruitful; fertilise;—*v.i.* to produce fruit. [L. *fructus,* fruit, and *facere,* make.]

FRUGAL (frōō'gal) *a.* saving of expenses. [L. *frugalis,* fr. stem *frug-,* of *frux,* fruit.]

FRUGALITY (frōō'gal-i-ti)*n.* prudent economy; thrift.

FRUGALLY (frōō'gal-i) *ad.* with economy.

FRUGIFEROUS (frōō-jif'e-rus) *a.* producing fruit. [L. stem *frugi-,* of *frux,* fruit, and *ferre,* to bear.]

FRUIT (frōōt) *n.* produce of the earth, of trees, or animals; effect or consequence;—*v.i.* to produce fruit. [O.F. *fruit, fruict,* fr. L. (part.) *fructus,* of *frui,* to enjoy.]

FRUITAGE (frōō'tij) *n.* fruit in general.[1]

FRUITERER (frōō'ter-er) *n.* one who deals in fruit.

FRUITFUL (frōōt'fool) *a.* producing fruit; fertile; prolific.

FRUITFULNESS (frōōt'fool-nes) *n.* productiveness.

FRUITION (frōō-ish'un) *n.* realised possession or use of something striven or hoped for; enjoyment. [F., fr. *frui,* to enjoy, to use.]

FRUITLESS (frōōt'les) *a.* destitute of fruit.

FRUITLESSLY (frōōt'les-li) *ad.* unprofitably.

FRUITLESSNESS (frōōt'les-nes) *n.* quality of being fruitless or unprofitable.

FRUITY (frōō'ti) *a.* having the flavour of fruit.

FRUMENTACEOUS (frōō-men-tā'shus) *a.* made of or resembling grain. [L. *frumentum,* corn.]

FRUMP (frump) *n.* a cross, formal old woman; a dowdy person. [Etym. doubtful.]

FRUMPISH (frum'pish) *a.* old-fashioned; ill-tempered.

FRUSTRATE (frus'trāt) *v.t.* to disappoint; defeat; nullify;—*a.* ineffectual; null and void. [L. (part.) *frustratus,* of *frustari,* to deceive, fr. *frustra,* in vain.]

FRUSTRATION (frus-trā'shun) *n.* disappointment; defeat.

FRUTESCENT (frōō-tes'ent) *a.* becoming shrubby. [L. *frutex,* shrub.]

FRY (frī) *v.t.* to cook in a frying-pan;—*v.i.* to be heated;—*n.* a crowd of small fish. [F. *frire,* fr. L. *frigere,* to roast.]

FRYING-PAN (frī'ing-pan) *n.* a kitchen utensil.

FUCHSIA (fū'sha) *n.* a beautiful flowering plant of many species. [Leonhard *Fuchs* (1501-66), Ger. botanist.]

FUDGE (fudj) *int.* a word expressing contempt.

FUEL (fū'el) *n.* any substance that feeds fire. [O.F. *fouaille,* fr. L. *focus,* fireplace.]

FUGACITY (fū-gas'i-ti) *n.* volatility; instability. [L. stem *fugaci-,* of *fugax,* apt to flee, fr. *fugere,* flee.]

FUGITIVE (fū'ji-tiv) *a.* flying; wandering;— *n.* a runaway; a deserter. [F., fr. L. *fugitivus,* fr. *fugere,* to flee.]

FUGLEMAN (fū'gl-man) *n.* one who stands in front of soldiers at drill to show them the movements. [Ger. *Flügel-mann,* the leader of a file, fr. *Flügel,* wing.]

FUGUE (fūg) *n.* a chase of parts in music. [F., fr. L. *fuga,* flight.]

FULCRUM (ful'krum) *n.* the prop on which a lever rests;—*pl.* **FULCRA** or **FULCRUMS**. [L., fr. *fulcire,* to prop.]

FULFIL (fool-fil') *v.t.* to perform what was promised; complete.

FULFILMENT (fool-fil'ment) *n.* performance.

Fulcrum.

FULGENCY (ful'jen-si) *n.* brightness.

FULGENT (ful'jent) *a.* shining. [L. (part. stem) *fulgent-,* of *fulgere,* to shine.]

FULL (fool) (1) *a.* having all it can contain; complete; ample;—*n.* complete measure; —*ad.* fully; quite;—(2) *v.t.* to thicken and scour cloth in a mill. [(1) O.E. Cf. Ger. *voll.* (2) O.F. *fuler,* fr. Late L. *fullare,* fr. L. *fullo,* a cloth-fuller.]

FULLAGE (fool'ij) *n.* price paid for fulling cloth. [See **FULL** (2).]

FULL-BLOWN (fool'blōn) *a.* fully expanded.

FULLER (fool'er) *n.* one who fulls cloth. [See **FULL** (2).]

FULLER'S-EARTH (fool'erz-erth) *n.* a soft friable clay which absorbs grease or oil. [See **FULL** (2).]

FULLERY (fool'er-i) *n.* a place or works for fulling cloth. [See **FULL** (2).]

FULLY (fool'i) *ad.* to the full; entirely.

FULMINATE (ful'mi-nāt) *v.t.* or *i.* to thunder; explode; utter denunciation;—*n.* an explosive compound. [L. (part.) *fulminatus,* of *fulminare,* for *fulmen,* for *fulgimen,* fr. *fulgere,* to shine.]

FULMINATION (ful-mi-nā'shun) *n.* denunciation of censure; chemical explosion.

FULLNESS (fool'nes) *n.* repletion; plenty.

FULSOME (fool'sum) *a.* gross; disgusting; nauseous. [See **FULL** (1) and **SOME**.]

FULSOMENESS (fool'sum-nes) *n.* offensive grossness.

FULVID (ful'vid) *a.* yellow; tawny. Also **FULVOUS**. [L. *fulvus,* deep yellow, fr. *fulgere,* to shine.]

FUMBLE (fum'bl) *v.i.* to attempt awkwardly; grope about. [D.]

FUMBLER (fum'bler) *n.* an awkward person. [D.]

FUME (fūm) *n.* smoke; vapour; rage;—*v.i.* to smoke; rage. [L. *fumus,* smoke.]

FUMIGATE (fū'mi-gāt) *v.t.* to smoke; purify; perfume. [L. *fumus,* smoke, and *agere* to drive.]

FUMIGATION (fū-mi-gā'shun) *n.* diffusion of smoke or vapours.

FUMY (fū'mi) *a.* producing fumes.

FUN (fun) *n.* sport; merriment. [Probably Ir. *fonn,* delight.]

FUNAMBULATORY (fū-nam'bū-la-tur-i) *a.* performing on the tight rope; narrow, like the rope.

FUNAMBULIST (fū-nam'bū-list) *n.* a rope-dancer. [L. *funis,* rope, and *ambulare,* to walk.]

FUNCTION (fungk'shun) *n.* office; employment; organic action or power. [L. (acc.) *functionem,* fr. (part.) *functus,* of *fungi,* to perform.]

FUNCTIONAL (fungk'shun-al) *a.* pertaining to some office.

FUNCTIONALLY (fungk'shun-al-i) *ad.* by means of functions.

FUNCTIONARY (fungk'shun-a-ri) *n.* one who holds an office or trust.

FUND (fund) *n.* a stock; capital; ample store;—*pl.* public securities;—*v.t.* to invest in funds. [F. *fond*, fr. L. *fundus*, the bottom.]

FUNDAMENT (fun'da-ment) *n.* the seat. [L. *fundamentum*, fr. *fundus*, the bottom.]

FUNDAMENTAL (fun-da-men'tal) *a.* pertaining to the foundation; essential.

FUNDAMENTALLY (fun-da-men'tal-i) *ad.* primarily; essentially.

FUNDHOLDER (fund'hōl-der) *n.* one who has property in the public funds.

FUNERAL (fū'ne-ral) *n.* a burial;—*a.* used at the interment of the dead. [O.F., fr. Late L. *funeralis* fr. L. *funus-eris* a funeral procession.]

FUNEREAL (fū-nē're-al) *a.* suiting a funeral.

FUNEREALLY (fū-nē're-al-i) *ad.* mournfully; dismally.

FUNGOID (fung'goid) *a.* resembling a mushroom. [See FUNGUS.]

FUNGOUS (fung'gus) *a.* like a mushroom; spongy. [See FUNGUS.]

FUNGUS (fung'gus) *n.* a mushroom; proud flesh. [L. a mushroom, fr. G. *sphonggos*, a sponge.]

FUNNEL (fun'el) *n.* passage for smoke; a tunnel for pouring liquors in bottles. [L. *infundi-bulum*, fr. *infundere*, pour in.]

FUNNY (fun'i) *a.* droll; comical.

FUR (fur) *n.* fine, soft hair; skins;—*v.t.* to line with fur. [O.F. *fourre*, a sheath.]

FURBISH (fur'bish) *v.t.* to polish; burnish. [O.F. *fourbiss*, *fourbir*, fr. O. H. Ger.]

FURCATE (fur'kāt) *a.* forked. [L., fr. *furca*, fork.]

FURIOUS (fū'ri-us) *a.* rushing violently; transported with passion; vehement; boisterous; frenzied. [O.F. *furieux*, L. *furiosus*, fr. *furia*, rage.]

FURIOUSLY (fū'ri-us-li) *ad.* with great vehemence; madly.

FURL (furl) *v.t.* to fold and fasten to a yard, etc. [O.F. *fardel*, a bundle.]

FURLONG (fur'long) *n.* the eighth of a mile. [O.E. *furh*, furrow, and *lang*, long.]

FURLOUGH (fur'lō) *n.* temporary leave of absence;—*v.t.* to furnish with a furlough. [D. Cf. Ger. *Verlaub*.]

FURNACE (fur'nes) *n.* a place for melting metals, or for heating water; enclosed fireplace; place of trial. [O.F. *fornais*, fr. L. *fornus*, an oven.]

FURNISH (fur'nish) *v.t.* to supply; provide; equip. [F. *fournir*, fr. O. H. Ger.]

FURNISHER (fur'nish-er) *n.* one who supplies.

FURNITURE (fur'ni-tūr) *n.* whatever is put into a house for use or ornament; materials for work. [F. *fourniture*, fr. *fournir*, to furnish.]

FURRIER (fur'i-er) *n.* a dealer in furs. [See FUR.]

FURRIERY (fur'i-er-i) *n.* furs in general; trade in furs.

FURROW (fur'ō) *n.* a trench made by a plough; a wrinkle;—*v.t.* to cut in furrows; wrinkle. [O.E. *furh*.]

FURROWY (fur'ō-i) *a.* full of ridges or channels; furrowed.

FURRY (fur'i) *a.* covered with fur. [See FUR.]

FURTHER (fur'THer) (1) *a.* more distant; additional;—*ad.* to a greater distance;— (2) *v.t.* to assist; promote; advance. [(1) O.E.; comp. of FORE or *furth*. (2) O.E. *furthran*.]

FURTHERANCE (fur'THer-ans) *n.* act of helping forward; advancement. [See FURTHER (2).]

FURTHERER (fur'THer-er) *n.* a promoter. [See FURTHER (2).]

FURTHERMORE (fur'THer-mōr) *ad.* moreover. [See FURTHER (1).]

FURTHERMOST (fur'THer-mōst) *a.* most remote. [See FURTHER (1).]

FURTHEST (fur'THest) *a.* most distant in time or space;—*ad.* at the greatest distance. [Superl. of FORE.]

FURTIVE (fur'tiv) *a.* gotten by stealth; secret. [L. *furtivus*, fr. *fur*, thief.]

FURTIVELY (fur'tiv-li) *ad.* by stealth.

FURY (fū'ri) *n.* violent rushing; angry passion; rage; a raging woman. [F. *furie*, fr. L. *furia*, fr. *furere* to rage.]

FURZE (furz) *n.* a thorny evergreen shrub with yellow flowers. [O.E. *fyrs*.]

FUSE (fūz) (1) *v.t.* to liquefy by beat;—*v.i.* to be melted;—(2) *n.* a tube filled with combustibles, used in blasting, etc. [(1) L. (part.) *fusus*, of *fundere*, to pour, melt. (2) It. *fuso*, fr. L. *fusus*, a spindle.]

FUSEE (fū-zē') (1) *n.* a firelock; a fuse; a match used by smokers;—(2) *n.* the wheel of a watch or clock, round which the chain is wound, to equalise the power of the mainspring. [(1) F., fr. L. *focus*, fireplace. (2) O.F. *fusée*, a spindleful, fr. L. *fusus*, spindle.]

Fusee.

FUSIBILITY (fū-zi-bil'i-ti) *n.* the quality of being fusible. [See FUSE (1).]

FUSIBLE (fū'zi-bl) *a.* that may be melted. [See FUSE (1).]

FUSIL (fū'zil) *n.* a light musket. [O.F. *fuisil*, firelock, fr. L. *focus*, fireplace.]

FUSILIER (fū-zi-lēr') *n.* a soldier armed with a fusil. [See FUSIL.]

FUSILLADE (fū-zi-lād') *n.* a simultaneous discharge of fire-arms.

FUSION (fū'zhun) *n.* the operation of converting a solid into a liquid by heat; melting by heat; state of being melted; union. [See FUSE (1).]

FUSS (fus) *n.* a tumult; a bustle;—*v.i.* to make ado about trifles. [O.E. *fus*, ready].

FUSSILY (fus'i-li) *ad.* in a fussy manner.

FUSSINESS (fus'i-nes) *n.* heedless hurry or bustle.

FUSSY (fus'i) *a.* bustling in small matters.

FUST (fust) *n.* the shaft of a column; a musty smell;—*v.i.* to grow mouldy; smell ill.

FUSTED (fus'ted) *a.* mouldy; ill-smelling.

FUSTIAN (fust'yan) *n.* a cotton stuff; bombast;—*a.* made of fustian; bombastic. [O.F. *fustaigne*, fr. Late L., fr. A. *Fostat*, near Cairo, where the cloth was first made.]

FUSTIC (fus'tik) *n.* a West India wood used for dyeing. [F. fr. L. *fustis*, stick.]

FUSTINESS (fus'ti-nes) *n.* mouldiness; rankness. [*fuste*, cask.]

FUSTY (fus'ti) *a.* mouldy; ill-smelling. [O.F. *fusty* (fū-til) *a.* trifling; worthless; ineffectual. [F., fr. L. *futilis*, fr. *fundere*, pour.]

FUTILE (fū'til) *a.* trifling; worthless; ineffectual. [F., fr. L. *futilis*, fr. *fundere*, pour.]

FUTILITY (fū-til'i-ti) *n.* worthlessness.

FUTURE (fū'tūr) *a.* that is to come or be hereafter;—*n.* time to come. [L. *futurus*, future part. of *esse*, to be.]

FUTURISM (fū'tūr-ism) *n.* a modern school of art, thought and ideals.

FUTURITY (fū-tūr'i-ti) *n.* time to come.

FUZZ (fuz) *v.i.* to fly off in small particles;—*n.* fine volatile particles. [Etym. doubtful.]

FY (fī) *ex.* expressing dislike, blame, or disgust. [Same as FIE.]

G

GAB (gab) (1) *n.* the mouth;—(2) idle talk; —*v.i.* to prate; talk idly. [(1) Scot. (2) Fr. Icel. *gabba.*]

GABBLE (gab'l) *v.i.* to talk fast or without meaning;—*n.* rapid, inarticulate utterances. [Freq. of **GAB.**]

GABION (gā'bi-un) *n.* a wicker-basket filled with earth, used in hasty defences. [F., fr. L. *cavea,* cage.]

GABLE (gā'bl) *n.* triangular part of the end of a house, etc. [M. H. Ger. *Gabele,* fork.]

GAD (gad) (1) *n.* a wedge; a punch;—(2) *v.i.* to ramble or rove. [(1) O.E. (2) Scand.]

GADFLY (gad'flī) *n.* a fly that stings cattle, and deposits its eggs in their skin. [Fr. O.E. *gad,* a goad.]

Gabion.

GAELIC (gā'lik) *a.* belonging to the Celtic inhabitants of Scotland;—*n.* their language. [Gael. *Gaid-healach.*]

GAFF (gaf) *n.* a light spear; a small boom. [F. *gafe,* iron hook.]

GAFFER (gaf'er) *n.* an old man; foreman or overseer. [Contr. for grandfather.]

GAG (gag) *v.t.* to stop the mouth;—*n.* something to stop the mouth. [Imit.]

GAGE (gāj) (1) *n.* a pledge or pawn; standard 'measure;—(2) a kind of plum;—(3) *v.t.* to pledge; measure, as a cask. [(1) and (3) O.F. *gauge,* fr. Teut. (2) From Sir William Gage.]

GAIETY (gā'e-ti) *n.* merriment. [See **GAY.**]

GAILY (gā'li) *ad.* finely; merrily. [See **GAY.**]

GAIN (gān) *n.* profit; advantage;—*v.t.* to obtain; reach;—*v.i.* to advance. [O.F., fr. Teut.]

GAINABLE (gān'a-bl) *a.* that may be obtained or reached.

GAINFUL (gān'fool) *a.* producing profit; lucrative.

GAININGS (gā'ningz) *n.pl.* the acquisitions of labour.

GAINLESS (gān'les) *a.* unprofitable; useless; without gain.

GAINSAY (gān'sā) *v.t.* [*pret.* and *pp.* **GAINSAID**] to deny; oppose; contradict. [O.E. *gegn,* against, and **SAY.**]

GAINSAYER (gān'sā-er) *n.* one who denies; an opposer.

GAIT (gāt) *n.* manner of walking. [Variant of **GATE.**]

GAITER (gā'ter) *n.* a covering of cloth for the leg, fitting down upon the shoe. [F. *guêtre.*]

GALA (gā'la) *n.* show; festivity. [F.]

GALANTINE (gal'an-tin) *n.* a dish of veal or poultry, without bone, served cold with jelly. [O.F., fr. Late L. *galatina,* for *gelatina,* jelly.]

GALAXY (gal'ak-si) *n.* the milky way; a splendid assemblage. [Through F. and L., fr. G. *galaxias,* fr. *gala,* milk.]

GALE (gāl) *n.* a strong wind. [Scand.]

GALIOT (gal'i-ut) *n.* a little brig. [F.]

GALL (gawl) (1) *n.* bile; rancour;—(2) an excrescence on the oak;—(3) *v.t.* to hurt the skin; fret; vex. [(1) O.E. *gealla.* (2) F., fr. L. *galla,* an oak-apple. (3) O.E. *callus,* hard, thick skin.]

GALLANT (ga-lant') *n.* a lover; an attendant; —*v.t.* to wait on a lady;—*a.* civil; attentive to ladies. [F. *galant.*]

GALLANT (gal'ant) *a.* high-spirited; noble; brave; courageous; showy; splendid.

GALLANTLY (gal'ant-li) *ad.* bravely; in the manner of a wooer.

GALLANTRY (gal'ant-ri) *n.* bravery; nobleness; civility to ladies.

GALLEON (gal'e-un) *n.* a large Spanish ship. [Sp. *galeon.*]

GALLERY (gal'er-i) *n.* a covered walk; corridor; upper floor of a church or theatre; collection of paintings, etc. [O.F. *galerie.*]

GALLEY (gal'i) *n.* a low, flat-built vessel; a frame which receives the types from a composing-stick; kitchen of a ship;—*pl.* **GALLEYS.** [O.F. *galie.*]

GALLEY-SLAVE (gal'i-slāv) *n.* one condemned to work at the oar in a galley.

GALLIC (gal'ik) *a.* French. [L. *Gallia,* Gaul.]

GALLICISM (gal'i-sizm) *n.* a French idiom. [See **GALLIC.**]

GALLINACEOUS (gal-i-nā'shus) *a.* designating fowls of the barn-door or pheasant kind. [L. *gallina,* hen.]

GALLIPOT (gal'i-pot) *n.* a pot painted and glazed, used by apothecaries. [D.]

GALL-NUT (gawl'nut) *n.* an excrescence on a species of oak used in dyeing, etc. [See **GALL** (2) and **NUT.**]

GALLON (gal'un) *n.* a measure of four quarts. [O.F.] [Sp. *galon.*]

GALLOON (ga-lōōn') *n.* narrow close lace.

GALLOP (gal'up) *v.i.* to move by leaps, as a horse;—*n.* swift leaping movement. [O.F. *galoper.*]

GALLOPADE (gal-u-pād') *n.* a curveting gallop; a sprightly dance; the music to it;—*v.i.* to perform the dance. [F.]

GALLOWS (gal'ōz) *n.* a frame for the execution of criminals; braces for trousers. [O.E. *galga.*]

GALOCHE (ga-losh') *n.* an over-shoe. [F.]

GALVANIC (gal-van'ik) *a.* pertaining to galvanism.

GALVANISE (gal'va-nīz) *v.t.* to affect by galvanism; electro-plate; restore to activity.

GALVANISM (gal'va-nizm) *n.* a species of electricity. [Fr. *Galvani,* of Bologna, the discoverer, 1737-1798.]

GALVANOMETER (gal-va-nom'e-ter) *n.* an instrument for measuring electric currents. [Fr. G. *metron,* **METRE.** See **GALVANISM.**]

GAMBIT (gam'bit) *n.* an opening move in chess-playing. [F.]

GAMBIER (gam'bir) *n.* a brown substance from Singapore, used in tanning and dyeing. Also **GAMBIER.**

GAMBLE (gam'bl) *v.i.* to play for money. [O.E. *gamen,* to game.]

GAMBLER (gam'bler) *n.* one that gambles.

GAMBLING (gam'bling) *n.* the practice of gambling for money.

GAMBOGE (gam-bōj') *n.* a gum-resin, used as a pigment and cathartic. [Fr. Cambodia, in Asia, whence brought about 1600.]

GAMBOL (gam'bol) *n.* a skipping and leaping; —*v.i.* to leap and skip. [O.F., fr. Late L. *gamba,* leg.]

GAMBREL (gam'brel) *n.* the hind leg of a horse. [O.F. *gambe,* leg.]

GAMBROON (gam-brōōn') *n.* a twilled linen cloth for linings. [Prob. Gambroon, in Persia.]

GAME (gām) *n.* play; scheme; animals hunted;—*v.i.* to play for money; sport;—*a.* brave; plucky. [O.E. *gamen,* to play.]

GAMECOCK (gām'kok) *n.* a cock bred for fighting.

GAMESOME (gām'sum) *a.* gay; sportive.

GAMESTER (gām'ster) *n.* one addicted to gaming.

GAMMON (gam'un) (1) *n.* thigh of a hog smoked;—*v.t.* to pickle and smoke;—(2) *v.t.* impose upon. [(1) O.F. *gambon,* big leg. (2) O.E. *gamen,* game.]

GAMUT (gam'ut) *n.* a scale of notes in music. [G. *gamma*, the third letter of the Greek alphabet, and *ut*, the name of a musical note.]

GANDER (gan'der) *n.* the male of the goose kind. [O.E. *gandra*, for *ganra*. Cf. Ger. *Gans*, a goose.]

GANG (gang) *n.* a crew; a band.

GANGLION (gang'gli-un) *n.* a tumour in the tendinous parts. [G. *ganglion*, a swelling.]

GANGLIONIC (gang-gli-on'ik) *a.* pertaining to a ganglion. Also **GANGLIAC.**

GANGRENE (gang'grēn) *n.* mortification of flesh. [F., fr. L. *gangrœna*, fr. G. *grainein*, gnaw.]

GANGRENOUS (gang'gre-nus) *a.* mortified.

GANGWAY (gang'wā) *n.* a narrow passage of any kind. [O.E. *gangweg*.]

GANTLET (gánt'let) *n.* a kind of military or naval punishment. [Scand.]

GAOL (jāl) *n.* a jail. [O.F.]

GAP (gap) *n.* an opening; cleft; interstice; hiatus; flaw. [Scand. = mouth.]

GAPE (gāp) *v.i.* to open the mouth wide; yawn; stare;—*n.* act of gaping; width of the opened mouth. [Scand.]

GARAGE (gar'azh) *n.* a depot for storing and repairing motor cars. [F. *gare*, railway station, and suffix, *-age*.]

GARB (gárb) *n.* clothes; dress; appearance. [O.F. *garbe*, dress.]

GARBAGE (gár'bij) *n.* offals of animals; refuse matter. [M.E.; etym. uncertain.]

GARBLE (gár'bl) *v.t.* to pick out or sift; select or suppress for a purpose. [A.]

GARDEN (gár'dn) *n.* a place for the cultivation of plants, fruits, flowers, etc.;—*v.i.* to cultivate a garden. [O.F. *gardin* = F. *jardin*, fr. Teut.]

GARDENER (gár'dn-er) *n.* one who tills a garden.

GARDENING (gár'dn-ing) *n.* horticulture.

GARGARISE (gár'ga-riz) *v.t.* to gargle.

GARGLE (gár'gl) *v.t.* to wash the throat;—*n.* a liquid for washing the throat. [O.F. *gargouille*, throat.]

GARGOYLE (gár'goil) *n.* a projecting waterspout in ancient buildings, carved grotesquely. [O.F. *gargouille*, fr. L. *gurgulio*, throat.]

GARISH (gár'ish) *a.* gaudy; dazzling; flighty. [O.F. *garer*, watch.]

GARISHLY (gár'ish-li) *ad.* showily; in a flighty manner.

GARLAND (gár'land) *n.* a wreath of flowers; principal thing; choice collection. [O.F. *garlande*, prob. fr. Teut.]

GARLIC (gár'lic) *n.* a bulbous plant of the onion tribe. [O.E. *garleac*, fr. *gar*, a spear, and *leac*, leak.]

GARMENT (gár'ment) *n.* an article of clothing. [O.F. *garniment*, fr. *garnir*, to furnish.]

GARNER (gár'ner) *n.* a store-house for grain; —*v.t.* to store; hoard. [O.F. *gernier* = F. *grenier*, fr. L. *granarium*, a granary, fr. *granum*, grain.]

GARNET (gár'net) *n.* a precious stone of a red colour; a kind of tackle in ships. [O.F. *grenat*, fr. Late L. *granatum*, pomegranate.]

GARNISH (gár'nish) *v.t.* to adorn; ornament or set off with something; furnish; warn; give notice;—*n.* decoration. Also **GARNISHMENT.** [O.F. *garnir*, furnish.]

GARNITURE (gár'ni-tūr) *n.* furniture; ornament.

GARRET (gar'et) *n.* a room directly under the roof. [O.F. *garite*, a place of refuge.]

GARRETEER (gar-e'tēr) *n.* one who lives in a garret.

GARRISON (gar'i-sn) *n.* a body of troops in a fort;—*v.t.* to place soldiers in a garrison. [O.F., fr. *garnir*, furnish.]

GARROTE (ga-rot') *n.* strangling by a collar screwed tight round the neck; a mode of capital punishment in Spain;—*v.t.* to choke and rob. [Sp.]

GARRULITY (gar-ūl'i-ti) *n.* talkativeness.

GARRULOUS (gar'ū-lus) *a.* disposed to talk much; talkative; loquacious. [L., fr. *garrire*, chatter.]

GARTER (gár'ter) *n.* a band to hold up a stocking; the highest order of knighthood in England; the badge of it; its herald; —*v.t.* to fasten with a garter. [O.F. *gartier*, garter = F. *jarretière*, fr. O.F. *garet*, the ham of the leg.]

GAS (gas) *n.* an aeriform elastic fluid;—*pl.* **GASES.** [A word invented by Van Helmont, Dutch chemist, 1577-1644. Cf. Ger. *Geist*, spirit.]

GASALIER (gas-a-lēr') *n.* a metal frame hanging from the ceiling with branches for gas-burners. [See **GAS.**]

GASEOUS (gā'shus) *a.* in the form of gas.

GAS-FITTER (gas'fit-ter) *n.* workman who fits up the apparatus for gas burning.

GASH (gash) *v.t.* to cut deep;—*n.* a deep and long cut. [O.F. *garser*, scarify.]

GASKET (gas'ket) *n.* a flat plaited cord used in furling or tying sails to the yard. [F. *garcette*.]

GASKINS (gas'kinz) *n.pl.* wide, open hose.

GAS-LIGHT (gas'līt) *n.* light produced by gas.

GAS-METER (gas'mēt-er) *n.* an instrument for measuring the consumpt of gas. [See **GAS.** G. *metron*, **METRE.**]

GASOMETER (gas-om'e-ter) *n.* a reservoir for collecting gas. [See **GAS.** G. *metron*, **METRE.**]

GASP (gasp) *v.t.* or *i.* to open the mouth to catch breath; pant; long for;—*n.* effort to catch breath. [Scand.]

GASTRIC (gas'trik) *a.* belonging to the stomach. [G. *gaster*, *gastros*, belly, stomach.]

GASTRONOMER (gas-tron'u-mer) *n.* one who likes good living.

GASTRONOMIC (gas-trō-nom'ik) *a.* pertaining to gastronomy.

GASTRONOMY (gas-tron'u-mi) *n.* art or science of good eating. [G. *gaster*, belly, and *nomos*, law.]

GATE (gāt) *n.* a large door; a way or passage; —*v.t.* to supply with a gate. [O.E. *geat*, a passage-way in a wall.]

GATEWAY (gāt'wā) *n.* a way through a gate.

GATHER (gath'er) *v.t.* or *i.* to collect; plait; infer;—*n.* a plait or fold. [O.E. *gaderian*, fr. *gador*, together, fr. *gead*, company.]

GATHERER (gath'er-er) *n.* one who gathers.

GATHERING (gath'er-ing) *n.* an assembly of people; charitable collection; suppurating tumour.

GAUD (gawd) *n.* ornament; trinket. [L. *gaudium*, joy, fr. *gaudere*, to rejoice.]

GAUDILY (gaw'di-li) *ad.* with much show; ostentatiously.

GAUDY (gaw'di) *a.* showy; ostentatiously fine.

GAUFFER (gaw'fer) *v.t.* to plait; crimp; flute. Also **GOFFER.** [O.F. *gauffrer*.]

GAUGE (gāj) *v.t.* to measure the contents of a cask;—*n.* a measure; a rod for measuring. [O.F. *gauger*.]

GAUGER (gā'jer) *n.* one who gauges. [See **GAUGE.**]

GAUNT (gánt) *a.* lean; thin. [Scand.]

GAUNTLET (gánt'let) *n.* an iron glove. [F. *gantelet*, double dim. of *gant*, glove, fr. Scand.]

GAUZE (gawz) *n.* a thin silk or linen. [O.F. *gaze*.]

GAUZY (gaw'zi) *a.* like gauze; very thin.

GAVE (gāv) *pret.* of **GIVE.**

GAVOT (ga-vot') *n.* a lively dance after the minuet. Also **GAVOTTE.** [F., fr. a dance of the Gavotes, a people of the Upper Alps.]

GAWK (gawk) *n.* a cuckoo; a fool. [O.E. *geac*.]

GAWKY (gaw'ki) *a.* foolish; awkward.

GAY (gā) *a.* cheerful; merry; jovial; fine; showy. [O.F. *gai*.]

GAZE (gāz) *v.i.* to look intently;—*n.* a fixed or eager look. [Scand.]

GAZEFUL (gāz'fool) *a.* looking with fixed attention.

GAZELLE (ga-zel') *n.* a species of antelope. [F., fr. A. =a wild goat.]

GAZETTE (ga-zet') *n.* a newspaper;—*v.i.* to insert or publish officially. [It. *gazzetta*, a small coin, through F.]

GAZETTEER (gaz-e-tēr') *n.* a book of topographical descriptions; a writer for a gazette.

GAZOGENE (gaz'u-jēn) *n.* an apparatus for making aerated waters. [E. *gas*, and G. root *gen*, fr. *gignesthai*, to become.]

GEAN (gēn) *n.* the wild cherry tree or its fruit. [O.F. *guigne*.]

GEAR (gēr) *n.* apparatus; harness;—*v.t.* to put on gear. [O.E.]

GEE (jē) *v.i.* to turn to the offside of the driver; move faster—used in the imperative. [Etym. doubtful.]

GEESE (gēs) *n.pl.* of GOOSE.

GELATINE (jel'ə-tin) *n.* an animal tissue, soluble in boiling water, and cooling down into a jelly. [F., fr. It. *gelatina*, jelly, fr. L. *gelare*.]

GELATINOUS (je-lat'i-nus) *a.* of the nature of gelatine.

GELD (geld) *v.t.* to deprive of an essential part. [Scand.]

GELID (jel'id) *a.* cold, or very cold. [L. *gelidus*, fr. *gelu*, frost.]

GEM (jem) *n.* a bud; a jewel; a precious stone;—*v.t.* to adorn with jewels;—*v.i.* to bud. [O.E. *gim*, fr. L. *gemma*, a bud.]

GEMINATION (jem-i-nā'shun) *n.* a doubling.

GEMINI (jem'i-nī) *n.pl.* the Twins, Castor and Pollux; third sign of the zodiac. [L., twins, pl. of *geminus*, twin-born.]

GEMMATION (je-mā'shun) *n.* form of budding in plants.

GEMMY (jem'i) *a.* resembling gems.

GENAPPE (je-nap') *n.* a smooth worsted yarn used for making fringes. [*Genappe*, in Belgium.]

GENDER (jen'dẹr) *n.* sex, male or female. [F. *genre*, fr. L. *genus*, *generis*, kind.]

Gemini.

GENEALOGICAL (jen-e-a-loj'i-kạl) *a.* pertaining to genealogy.

GENEALOGIST (jen-ē-al'o-jist) *n.* one skilled in genealogy or descents.

GENEALOGY (jen-e-al'ō-ji) *n.* history of descents; lineage; pedigree. [F., fr. L., fr. G. *genealogia*, fr. *genea*, birth, and *logos*, discourse, fr. *legein*, to speak of.]

GENERA (jen'e-rạ) *n.pl.* of GENUS.

GENERAL (jen'e-rạl) *a.* common; public; usual; lax or vague; abstract;—*n.* the whole; main part; chief of an order of monks; officer commanding whole or part of an army. [F., fr. L. *generalis*, fr. *genus*.]

GENERALISATION (jen-e-rạl-i-zā'shun) *n.* the act of generalising.

GENERALISE (jen'e-rạl-īz) *v.t.* to arrange under general heads.

GENERALISSIMO (jen-e-rạ-lis'i-mō) *n.* commander in chief. [It.]

GENERALITY (jen-e-rạl'i-ti) *n.* state of being general; the greatest part.

GENERALLY (jen'e-rạl-i) *ad.* commonly.

GENERALSHIP (jen'e-rạl-ship) *n.* the skill or conduct of a general.

GENERATE (jen'e-rāt) *v.t.* to beget; produce; originate. [L. (part.) *generatus*, of *generare*, fr. *genus*, a kind.]

GENERATION (jen-e-rā'shun) *n.* a race; family; an age.

GENERATIVE (jen'e-rā-tiv) *a.* able to produce.

GENERATOR (jen'e-rā-tẹr) *n.* one who produces or begets.

GENERIC (je-ner'ik) *a.* comprehending a genus. [See GENUS.]

GENERICALLY (je-ner'i-kạl-i) *ad.* with regard to genus.

GENEROSITY (jen-e-ros'i-ti) *n.* liberality of soul; nobleness; munificence.

GENEROUS (jen'e-rus) *a.* liberal; free; noble; bountiful. [L. *generosus*, of noble birth, fr. *genus*, birth.]

GENEROUSLY (jen'e-rus-li) *ad.* with liberality; magnanimously.

GENESIS (jen'e-sis) *n.* the first book of Scripture; origin or explanation of anything. [L., fr. G., fr. *gignesthai*, to be produced.]

GENEVA (je-nē'vạ) *n.* a spirit distilled from grain, and flavoured with juniper berries. [F., *genièvre*, fr. L. *juniperus*, juniper.]

GENIAL (jē'nyạl) *a.* contributing to production; enlivening; natural. [L. *genialis*, fr. *genius*, the spirit of social enjoyment.]

GENIALITY (jē-ni-al'i-ti) *n.* sympathetic cheerfulness.

GENIALLY (jē'nyạl-i) *ad.* naturally; with cheerful kindness.

GENICULATION (je-nik-ū-lā'shun) *n.* kneeling at worship; state of having knots or joints like the knee. [L. *geniculare*, fr. *geniculum*, dim. of *genu*, knee.)

GENIE (jē'ni-ē) *n.*, *pl.* GENII, spirits; demons. [A. *corr.* fr. *jinnee*, through confusion with *genius*.]

GENISTA (je-nis'tạ) *n.* a leguminous shrub with yellow flowers. [L. =Sp. broom.]

GENITAL (jen'i-tạl) *a.* pertaining to generation. [L. *genitalis*, fr. (part.) *genitus*, of *gignere*, to beget.]

GENITIVE (jen'i-tiv) *a.* *gram.* the case denoting the class or kind to which a thing belongs. [L. *genitivus*, fr. *gignere*, to beget.]

GENIUS (jē'nyus) *n.* a good or evil spirit;—*vi.* GENII. [L., fr. *gignere*, to beget.]

GENIUS (jē'nyus) *n.* nature; disposition; a man of great mental powers;—*pl.* GENIUSES. [L., tr. *gignere*, to beget.]

GENTEEL (jen-tēl') *n.* polished in manners; polite. [F. *gentil*, fr. L. *gentilis*, fr. *gens*, race.]

GENTEELLY (jen-tēl'li) *ad.* with polite manners.

GENTEELNESS (jen'tēl-nes) *n.* elegance; politeness; good breeding.

GENTILE (jen'til) *n.* any one not a Jew; a heathen;—*a.* pertaining to heathen. [L. *gentilis*, belonging to the same *gens*, clan, or nation.] [*gentilitas*.]

GENTILITY (jen-til'i-ti) *n.* politeness. [L.

GENTLE (jen'tl) *a.* of mild feelings; not rough or coarse; not wild; tame; mild; meek. [F., fr. L. *gentilis*, fr. *gens*, clan.]

GENTLEFOLK (jen'tl-fōk) *n.pl.* people of good family and breeding.

GENTLEMAN (jen'tl-man) *n.* a man of good breeding and education.

GENTLEMANLIKE (jen'tl-man-līk) *a.* becoming a gentleman; polite.

GENTLENESS (jen'tl-nes) *n.* sweetness of disposition; tenderness; mild treatment.

GENTLY (jen'tli) *ad.* softly; with care.

GENTRY (jen'tri) *n.* people of good position; the wealthy and well-born. [O.F.]

GENUFLECTION (jen-ū-flek'shun) *n.* act of bending the knee. [L. *genu*, knee, and *flectere*, bend.]

GENUINE (jen'ū-in) *a.* free from adulteration; natural; real. [L. *genuinus*, fr. *gignere*, beget.]

GENUINELY (jen'ū-in-li) *ad.* really; truly.

GENUINENESS (jen'ū-in-nes) *n.* a genuine quality; purity.

GENUS (jē'nus) *n.* a class embracing many species;—*pl.* **GENERA.** [L. *genus, generis,* birth.]

GEOGRAPHER (je-og'ra-fer) *n.* one skilled in geography. [See **GEOGRAPHY.**]

GEOGRAPHICAL (jē-u-graf'i-kal) *a.* relating to geography.

GEOGRAPHY (jĕ-og'ra-fi) *n.* description of the earth's surface, etc. [F., fr. L., fr. G. *geographia,* fr. *ge,* and *graphein,* to write.]

GEOLOGICAL (jē-u-loj'i-kal) *a.* pertaining to geology. [geology.

GEOLOGIST (jē-ol'ō-jist) *n.* one versed in

GEOLOGY (jē-ol'ō-ji) *n.* the science of the structure and mineral constituents of the earth, and the changes in its form and contents. [F. *géologie,* fr. G. *ge,* and *logos,* discourse.]

GEOMETRICAL (jē-u-met'ri-kal) *a.* pertaining to geometry.

GEOMETRICALLY (jē-u-met'ri-kal-i) *ad.* according to geometry.

GEOMETRICIAN (jē-om-e-trish'an) *n.* one skilled in geometry.

GEOMETRY (jē-om'e-tri) *n.* the science of magnitude; mensuration of lines, angles, surfaces, or solids. [F. *géométrie,* fr. L., fr. G. *geometria,* fr. *ge,* and *metron,* measure.]

GEONOMY (jē-on'u-mi) *n.* the science of the physical conditions of the earth. [G. *ge,* earth, *nomos,* law.]

GEORGE (jorj) *n.* an ornament worn by Knights of the Garter having the figure of St George on horseback; a brown loaf.

GEORGIAN (jor'ji-an) *a.* pertaining to the reign of the four English Georges.

GEORGIC (jor'jik) *a.* relating to agriculture; —*n.* a rural poem. [L. *georgicus,* fr. G. *georgikos,* fr. *georgia,* agriculture, fr. *ge,* and *ergon,* work.]

GERANIUM (je-rā'ni-um) *n.* a greenhouse flower. [L., fr. G. *geranos,* a crane.]

GERM (jerm) *n.* a seed-bud of a plant; first principle. [F. *germe,* fr. L. *germen,* bud.]

GERMAN (jer'man) *a.* belonging to Germany; —*n.* a native or inhabitant of Germany; the German language. [L. *Germani.*]

GERMAN (jer'man) *a.* related by blood. [O.F. *germain,* fr. L. *germanus,* near akin.]

GERMANE (jer-mān') *a.* entirely appropriate; relevant.

GERMINAL (jer'mi-nal) *a.* pertaining to the germ or seed-bud. [L. *germen,* a bud.]

GERMINATE (jer'mi-nāt) *v.i.* to bud; sprout.

GERUND (jer'und) *n.* a verbal noun. [L. *gerundium,* fr. *gerere,* to bear.]

GESTATION (jes-tā'shun) *n.* act of carrying young in the womb. [L. (acc.) *gestationem,* fr. *gestare,* carry, fr. *gerere,* bear.]

GESTICULATE (jes-tik'ū-lāt) *v.i.* to use gestures. [L. (part.) *gesticulatus,* of *gesticulari,* fr. *gesticulus,* dim. of *gestus,* gesture, fr. *gerere,* to carry.]

GESTICULATION (jes-tik-ū-lā'shun) *n.* act of making gestures.

GESTURE (jes'tūr) *n.* movement of the body or hand expressive of feeling. [Late L. *gestura,* fr. L. *gestus,* fr. *gerere,* to bear.]

GET (get) *v.t.* [*pret.* GOT; *pp.* GOT, GOTTEN] to gain; obtain; win; learn;—*v.i.* to arrive at; become. [O.E. *gitan.*]

GEWGAW (gū'gaw) *n.* a showy trifle. [O.E. reduplication of *gifan,* to give; prov. E. **GIFF-GAFF.**]

GEYSER (gī'zer) *n.* a fountain which spouts boiling water. [Icel. *geysa,* to gush.]

GHASTLINESS (gast'li-nes) *n.* a death-like look; paleness.

GHASTLY (gast'li) *a.* pale; death-like. [O.E. *gæstlic,* terrible.]

GHAUT (gawt) *n.* a mountain pass; a landing-place or staircase. [Hind.]

GHERKIN (ger'kin) *n.* a pickled cucumber. [D. *agurkje.*]

GHOST (gōst) *n.* a spirit; an apparition. [O.E. *gast.* Cf. Ger. *Geist.*]

GHOSTLY (gōst'li) *a.* like a ghost; pale; spiritual.

GIANT (jī'ant) *n.* a man of extraordinary stature;—*a.* like a giant; unusually large. [O.F. *geant* = F. *géant,* fr. L., fr. G. *stem gigant-,* of *gigas,* a giant.]

GIANTESS (jī'an-tes) *n.* a female giant.

GIANTLIKE (jī'ant-līk) *a.* like a giant; gigantic; huge.

GIBBER (gib'er) *v.i.* to speak rapidly and inarticulately. [Conn. with **GABBLE.**]

GIBBERISH (gib'er-ish) *n.* rapid, inarticulate speech.

GIBBET (jib'et) *n.* a gallows;—*v.t.* to hang, or expose, as on a gibbet. [O.F. *gibet,* stick.]

GIBBON (gib'un) *n.* a species of ape noted for the length of its arms. [F.]

GIBBOSITY (gi-bos'i-ti) *n.* protuberance; convexity; roundness.

GIBBOUS (gib'us, gib'ōs) *a.* convex; swelling; protuberant. [L. *gibbosus* = *gibberosus,* fr. *gibber,* a hump.]

GIBE (jib) *v.t.* or i. to rail at sneeringly;—*n.* a sneer; taunt; scoff. [Scand.]

GIBLETS (jib'lets) *n.pl.* the heart, liver, gizzard, etc., of a fowl. [O.F. *gibelet,* of uncertain origin.]

GIDDILY (gid'i-li) *ad.* unsteadily; heedlessly.

GIDDINESS (gid'i-nes) *n.* a swimming of the head; unsteadiness; levity.

GIDDY (gid'i) *a.* reeling; dizzy; inconstant; thoughtless. [O.E. *giddian,* to sing, fr. *gid,* song.]

GIFF-GAFF (gif'-gaf) *n.* mutual giving and taking; mutual obligation. [O.E. *gifen,* give.]

GIFT (gift) *n.* anything given; an offering; faculty; power. [O.E. *gifan,* =to give.]

GIFTED (gif'ted) *a.* endowed with a faculty.

GIG (gig) *n.* a thing that whirls; a light chaise; a long, light boat. [M.E. *gigge,* a whirling thing. Cf. **WHIRLIGIG.**]

GIGANTIC (ji-gan'tik) *a.* like a giant; mighty. [L. (acc.) *gigantem,* of *gigas,* a giant.]

GIGGLE (gig'l) *n.* a laugh with short catches of breath;—*v.i.* to laugh; titter. [Imit.]

GIGOT (jig'ut) *n.* a leg of mutton; a hipjoint. [F., fr. O.E. *gigue,* leg.]

GILD (gild) *v.t.* [*pret.* and *pp.* GILDED, GILT] to overlay with gold; illuminate. [O.E. *gyldan.*]

GILDER (gil'der) *n.* one who overlays with gold leaf or gold dust.

GILDING (gil'ding) *n.* art of overlaying with gold; a superficial coating.

GILL (jil) *n.* the fourth of a pint; a plant. [O.F. *gelle.*] [Scand.]

GILL (gil) *n.* organ of respiration in fishes.

GILLIE (gil'i) *n.* an outdoor male servant. [Gael. =a lad.]

GILLYFLOWER (jil'i-flow'er) *n.* a plant that flowers about July, of a clove-like odour. [O.F. *giroflée,* fr. G. *karuophullon,* clove-tree, fr. *karuon,* a nut, and *phullon,* leaf.]

GILT (gilt) *a.* overlaid with gold. [See **GILD.**]

GIMBALS (gim'balz) *n.pl.* two brass rings used in suspending the mariner's compass. [F., fr. L. *gemelli,* twins.]

GIMCRACK (jim'krak) *n.* a trivial mechanism or device; a toy. [Prov. E., fr. *jim,* neat, and *crack,* a lively lad.]

GIMLET (gim'let) *n.* a small borer. [O.F. *gimbelet,* fr. Teut.]

GIMP (gimp) *n.* silk twist or lace; edging. [F. *guimpe,* fr. Teut.]

GIN (jin) (1) *n.* a distilled spirit, flavoured with juniper berries;—(2) *n.* a machine for raising heavy weights, etc., or driving piles; a machine for separating the seeds from cotton; a snare; a trap;—*v.t.* to clear cotton of its seed by a machine. [(1) Contr. and corr. of **GENEVA.** (2) Contr. of **ENGINE.**]

GINGER (jin'jer) *n.* a plant and its hot and spicy root. [M.E. *gingivere.* fr. O.F. *gengibre,* fr. L. *zingiber,* fr. G.]

GINGERBREAD (jin'jer-bred) *n.* a sweet-cake flavoured with ginger.

GINGERLY (jin'jer-li) *ad.* cautiously.

GINGHAM (ging'am) *n.* a kind of striped cotton cloth. [F. *guingan,* corr. fr. *Guingamp,* in Brittany.]

GIPSY (jip'si) *n.* one of a nomadic Indian tribe; their language; a tricky young woman;—*pl.* GIPSIES. [Corr. fr. *Egyptian.*]

GIRAFFE (ji-raf') *n.* the camelopard, the tallest of animals. [F., fr. A.]

GIRD (gerd) *v.t.* [*pret.* and *pp.* GIRDED, GIRT] to bind; tie round; surround; enclose;—*v.i.* to sneer at; jibe. [O.E. *gyrdan.*]

GIRDER (ger'der) *n.* the chief timber in a floor.

GIRDLE (ger'dl) *n.* a band round the waist; —*v.t.* to bind; cut a ring round a tree. [O.E. *gyrdel,* fr. *gyrdan,* to bind.]

GIRL (gerl) *n.* a female child; a young woman. [Perhaps fr. Old Low Ger. *Gör,* child.]

GIRLHOOD (gerl'hood) *n.* the state of a girl.

GIRLISH (ger'lish) *a.* like a girl; giddy.

GIRLISHNESS (ger'lish-nes) *n.* girlish manners or disposition; youthful levity.

GIRT (gert) *v.t.* to gird; surround.

GIRTH (gerth) *n.* a strap for a saddle; a circular bandage; measure round the waist.

GIST (jist) *n.* the main point or pith of a matter. [F. *gésir,* lie.]

GIVE (giv) *v.t.* or *i.* [*pret.* GAVE; *pp.* GIVEN] to bestow; yield; grant; utter; produce; allow;—*v.i.* to grow soft; recede; yield to pressure. [O.E. *giefan.* Cf. Ger. *geben.*]

GIVER (giv'er) *n.* one who gives.

GIVING (giv'ing) *n.* the act of bestowing gratuitously.

GIZZARD (giz'ard) *n.* the muscular stomach of a fowl. [O.F. *gezier,* fr. L. *gigeria,* the cooked entrails of poultry.]

GLACIAL (glā'shal) *a.* pertaining to ice or its action; frozen. [See GLACIER.]

GLACIATE (glā'shi-āt) *v.t.* to become ice.

GLACIATION (glā-shi-ā'shun) *n.* act of freezing; process of being covered over with glaciers.

GLACIER (glā'sher) *n.* a field or mass of ice continuing in valleys on high mountains. [F., fr. *glace,* fr. L. *glacies,* ice.]

GLACIS (glā'sis) *n.* a sloping bank. [O.F. *glacer,* fr. *glace,* ice.]

GLAD (glad) *a.* affected with pleasure; happy; bright; giving pleasure;—*v.t.* to make glad. [O.E. *glæd.*]

GLADDEN (glad'n) *v.t.* to make glad.

GLADE (glād) *n.* an opening through a wood or ice. [Scand.]

GLADIATOR (glad'i-ā-ter) *n.* a sword-player. [L. =a swordsman, fr. *gladius,* a sword.]

GLADIATORIAL (glad-i-a-tō'ri-al) *a.* pertaining to combats or prize fights.

GLADLY (glad'li) *ad.* with pleasure; joyfully; cheerfully.

GLADNESS (glad'nes) *n.* joy; pleasure.

GLADSOME (glad'sum) *a.* pleased; gay; causing joy.

GLADSOMENESS (glad'sum-nes) *n.* moderate joy.

GLAIR (glār) *n.* the white of an egg; any viscous transparent substance;—*v.t.* to varnish with glair. [O.F. *glaire,* fr. Late L. *clara ovi,* white of egg, fr. L. *clarus,* clear.]

GLAIRY (glār'i) *a.* resembling glair.

GLANCE (glāns) *n.* a sudden shoot of light; a cast of the sight;—*v.t.* or *i.* to dart; fly off; twinkle; allude to. [Fr. Teut.]

GLAND (gland) *n.* a soft fleshy organ in animals and plants. [F. *glande,* fr. L. stem *gland-,* of *glans,* acorn.]

GLANDERS (glan'derz) *n.pl.* a disease of horses.

GLANDIFORM (glan'di-form) *a.* resembling a gland or nut.

GLANDULAR (glan'dū-lar) *a.* consisting of glands. Also GLANDULOUS.

GLANDULATION (glan-dū-lā'shun) *n.* structure of glands or secreting vessels in plants.

GLANDULE (glan'dūl) *n.* a small gland.

GLARE (glār) *n.* a bright, dazzling light; a fixed, piercing look;—*v.t.* or *i.* to emit or shine out, as light; flare; stare. [Cf. O.E. *glær,* amber.]

GLARING (glār'ing) *a.* shining brightly; open and bold; notorious.

GLARINGLY (glār'ing-li) *ad.* in a barefaced or notorious manner.

GLASS (glās) *n.* a transparent substance; mirror; telescope; barometer; drinking vessel;—*a.* made of glass; vitreous;—*v.t.* to case in glass; glaze; reflect. [O.E. *glæs.*]

GLASSINESS (glās'i-nes) *n.* smoothness, like glass.

GLASSY (glās'i) *a.* made of or like glass.

GLAUBER'S-SALT (glaw'berz-sawlt) *n.* sulphate of soda—a strong cathartic. [Fr. *Glauber,* a German chemist of 17th century.]

GLAVE (glāv) *n.* a kind of short, curved sword; falchion. Also GLAIVE. [O.F. *glaive,* fr. L. *gladius,* a sword.]

GLAZE (glāz) *v.t.* to furnish with glass; cover with a vitreous substance. [M.E. *glasen,* fr. O.E. *glæs,* glass.]

GLAZIER (glā'zher) *n.* one who sets window glass; dealer in glass.

GLAZING (glā'zing) *n.* the vitreous substance on potter's ware; art of setting glass.

GLEAM (glēm) *n.* a faint shoot of light;—*v.i.* to shine with flashes of light; glimmer. [O.E. *glæm.*]

GLEAMY (glē'mi) *a.* darting light; flashing.

GLEAN (glēn) *v.t.* or *i.* to gather after the reaper, or what is thinly scattered; cull; select;—*n.* act of gleaning; that which is gleaned. [O.F. *glener,* glean = F. *glaner,* fr. Teut.]

GLEANER (glē'ner) *n.* one who gathers.

GLEANING (glē'ning) *n.* act of gathering the remains.

GLEBE (glēb) *n.* turf; soil; church land. [F., fr. L. *gleba,* a clod, soil.]

GLEE (glē) *n.* joy; merriment; a song in parts. [O.E. *gleo,* mirth.]

GLEEFUL (glē'fool) *a.* merry; laughing; gay. Also GLEESOME. [See GLEE.]

GLEN (glen) *n.* a narrow valley; dale. [Gael. *gleann.*]

GLIB (glib) *a.* smooth; slippery. [D.]

GLIBLY (glib'li) *ad.* smoothly; volubly.

GLIBNESS (glib'nes) *n.* smoothness; volubility of tongue.

GLIDE (glīd) *v.i.* to flow gently;—*n.* the act of passing smoothly. [O.E. *glidan,* to slide. Cf. Ger. *gleiten.*]

GLIDINGLY (glī'ding-li) *ad.* smoothly.

GLIMMER (glim'er) *v.i.* to shoot scattered rays; shine faintly or unsteadily. [M.E. *glimeren,* fr. Scand.]

GLIMMERING (glim'er-ing) *a.* a faint view.

GLIMPSE (glimps) *n.* a slight view; faint tinge; inkling. [M.E. *glimsen,* shine faintly; variant of GLIMMER.]

GLISTEN (glis'n) *v.t.* to sparkle with light. [M.E. *glisien,* fr. O.E. *glisnian.*]

GLISTER (glis'ter) *v.i.* to shine; be bright.

GLITTER (glit'er) *v.i.* to shine brightly;—*n.* sparkling light; brilliancy; showy lustre. [M.E. *gliteren.*]

GLOAMING (glō'ming) *n.* twilight; dusk. [O.E. *glomung,* akin to GLOOM.]

GLOAT (glōt) *v.i.* to look with eagerness, desire, or malice. [Scand.]

GLOBATE (glō'bāt) *a.* round; spherical.

GLOBE (glōb) *n.* a round body; a sphere; the earth. [L. *globus,* ball.]

GLOBOSE (glō-bōs') *a.* round; globular.

GLOBOSITY (glō-bos'i-ti) *n.* roundness; sphericity.

GLOBULAR (glob'ū-lar) *a.* spherical.

GLOBULE (glob'ūl) *n.* a small, round mass or particle; corpuscle in the blood; small pill. [L. dim. of *globus*.]

GLOBULOUS (glob'ū-lus) *a.* round; globular.

GLOMERATE (glom'e-rāt) *v.t.* to gather into a ball. [L. (part.) *glomeratus*, of *glomerare*, fr. stem *glomer-*, of *glomus*, a clew of yarn.]

GLOMERATION (glom-e-rā'shun) *n.* the act of forming into a ball; a spherical body.

GLOOM (glōōm) *n.* darkness; obscurity; heaviness of mind; sad, hopeless state;—*v.i.* to be dark or cloudy; be dejected or sullen. [O.E. *glom*.]

GLOOMILY (glōō'mi-li) *ad.* darkly; obscurely; sullenly.

GLOOMY (glōō'mi) *a.* dark; melancholy.

GLORIFICATION (glō-ri-fi-kā'shun) *n.* act of making glorious.

GLORIFY (glō'ri-fī) *v.t.* to make glorious; extol; exalt. [L. *gloria*, and *facere*, make.]

GLORIOUS (glō'ri-us) *a.* splendid; renowned.

GLORIOUSLY (glō'ri-us-li) *ad.* illustriously. [See GLORY.]

GLORY (glō'ri) *n.* brightness; splendour; honour; renown;—*v.i.* to exult; boast. [O.F. *glorie*, fr. L. *gloria*.]

GLOSS (glos) (1) *n.* brightness, from a smooth surface; polish; a specious appearance; —*v.t.* to make smooth and shining; to render plausible;—(2) *n.* an explanatory note upon some word or passage in a text, written on the margin or between the lines;—*v.t.* to explain by a note. [(1) Scand. (2) L. *glossa*, a word to be explained, fr. G. *glossa*, tongue.]

GLOSSARIAL (glo-sā'ri-al) *a.* containing explanations. [See GLOSS (2).]

GLOSSARY (glos'a-ri) *n.* a vocabulary for explaining obsolete or peculiar words.

GLOSSINESS (glos'i-nes) *n.* the lustre of a surface; polish. [See GLOSS (1).]

GLOSSOLOGIST (glo-sol'ō-jist) *n.* one who defines technical terms.

GLOSSOLOGY (glo-sol'ō-ji) *n.* definition of terms; comparative science of language. [G. *glossa*, tongue, and *logos*, discourse.]

GLOSSY (glos'i) *a.* smooth and shining; bright. [See GLOSS (1).]

GLOTTAL (glot'al) *a.* pertaining to the glottis.

GLOTTIS (glot'is) *n.* the opening of the windpipe. [G. *glotta*, *glossa*, the tongue.]

GLOVE (gluv) *n.* a cover for the hand;—*v.t.* to cover with a glove. [O.E. *glof*.]

GLOVER (gluv'er) *n.* one who makes or sells gloves.

GLOW (glō) *v.i.* to shine with intense heat; be flushed; rage with passion;—*n.* white heat; brightness of colour; intense earnestness; vehemence. [O.E. *glowan*.]

GLOWING (glō'ing) *a.* white with heat; ardent; vehement.

GLOW-WORM (glō'wurm) *n.* a female insect of the beetle tribe, which emits a greenish light in the dark.

GLOZE (glōz) *v.i.* to talk smoothly; to smooth over;—*n.* specious show. [M.E. *glosen*.]

GLOZING (glō'zing) *n.* specious representation or comment.

GLUE (glōō) *n.* a tenacious gelatinous substance;—*v.t.* to cement with glue; unite. [O.F. *glu*, fr. Late L. *glus*, *glutis*, glue, fr. *gluere*, to draw together.]

GLUEY (glōō'i) *a.* glutinous.

GLUM (glum) *a.* sullen; moody; silent. Also **GLUMPY.** [M.E. *glommen*, to frown.]

GLUMNESS (glum'nes) *n.* sullenness; moroseness. Also **GLUMPINESS.**

GLUT (glut) *v.t.* to swallow greedily; cloy; supply in excess;—*n.* that which is swallowed; over supply; anything to block a passage. [L. *glutire*, to swallow.]

GLUTEN (glōō'ten) *n.* a viscid substance in grain which gives adhesiveness to dough or paste. [L. *gluten*, fr. stem *glut-*, of *glus*, glue.]

GLUTINATE (glōō'ti-nāt) *v.t.* to unite with glue. [L. (part.) *glutinatus*, of *glutinare*, to cement.]

GLUTINOUS (glōō'ti-nus) *a.* viscous; viscid.

GLUTTON (glut'n) *n.* a voracious eater; a carnivorous quadruped. [O.F. *gloton*, fr. L. *gluttire*, devour.]

GLUTTONISE (glut'n-īz) *v.i.* to eat voraciously; gormandise.

GLUTTONOUS (glut'n-us) *a.* given to excessive eating.

GLUTTONOUSLY (glut'n-us-li) *ad.* in a voracious manner; excessively.

GLUTTONY (glut'n-i) *n.* excess in eating.

GLYCERINE (glis'e-rin) *n.* a sweet viscid liquid obtained from fat, oils, etc. [G. *glukeros*, fr. *glukus*, sweet.]

GLYPTIC (glip'tik) *a.* pertaining to engraving figures on gems; figured. [G. *gluphein*, to carve.]

GNARL (närl) (1) *v.i.* to growl; snarl;—(2) *n.* a knot in timber. Also **GNARL.** [(1) Imit. (2) Teut.]

GNARLED (närld) *a.* full of knots.

GNASH (nash) *v.t.* or *i.* to strike the teeth together in pain or anger. [M.E. *gnasten*.]

GNASHING (nash'ing) *n.* striking together or grinding of the teeth in pain or rage.

GNAT (nat) *n.* a small insect that bites. [O.E. *gnæt*.]

GNAW (naw) *v.t.* or *i.* to bite or prick with the teeth; bite in pain or rage; corrode. [O.E. *gnagan*.]

GNEISS (nīs) *n.* a primary stratified rock. [Ger.]

GNOME (nōm) *n.* an imaginary being supposed to inhabit the inner parts of the earth, and to be the guardian of mines, quarries. [G. *gnome*, an opinion, fr. *gnonai*, *gignoskein*, to know.]

GNOMIC (nō'mik) *a.* dealing in axioms. [See GNOME.]

GNOMON (nō'mon) *n.* the style or pin of a dial. [G. *gnomon*, interpreter, fr. *gnonai*, know.]

GNOMONICS (nō-mon'iks) *n.pl.* art of dialing.

GNOSTICS (nos'tiks) *n.pl.* persons who held all beings to be emanations from the Deity. [G. *gnostikos*, good at knowing, fr. *gignoskein*, to know.]

GO (gō) *v.i.* [*pret.* WENT; *pp.* GONE] to move; depart; circulate; extend; avail; happen; fare:—*n.* the fashion; mode. [O.E. *gan*, fr. *gangan*, go. Cf. Ger. *gehen*.]

GOAD (gōd) *n.* a pointed stick to drive oxen; —*v.t.* to prick with a goad; urge. [O.E. *gad*.]

GOAL (gōl) *n.* a starting-post; mark; end; final purpose. [F. *gaule*, pole.]

GOAT (gōt) *n.* a ruminating animal, seemingly between a deer and a sheep. [O.E. *gat*.]

GOATHERD (gōt'herd) *n.* one who tends goats.

GOATISH (gō'tish) *a.* like a goat; rank in smell.

GOATSKIN (gōt'skin) *n.* dressed leather from the skin of a goat.

GOBBLE (gob'l) *v.t.* to swallow hastily;—*v.i.* to make a noise as a turkey. [O.F. *gober*, to devour.]

GOBLET (gob'let) *n.* a drinking vessel. [O.F. *gobelet*.]

GOBLIN (gob'lin) *n.* an evil spirit. [O.F. *gobelin*, fr. Late L., fr. G. *kobalos*, a mischievous spirit.]

GOD (god) *n.* the Supreme Being. [O.E. Cf. Ger. *Gott*.]

GODDAUGHTER (god'daw-ter) *n.* a girl for whom one becomes sponsor at baptism.

GODDESS (god'es) *n.* a female deity. [See GOD.]

GODFATHER (god'fȧ-ᴛʜẹr) *n.* a male sponsor, at baptism. [See **GOD** and **FATHER.**]

GODHEAD (god'hed) *n.* divine nature.

GODLESS (god'les) *a.* ungodly; wicked.

GODLIKE (god'līk) *a.* resembling God.

GODLINESS (god'li-nes) *n.* real piety; a religious life.

GODLY (god'li) *a.* pious; religious.

GODMOTHER (god'muᴛʜ-ẹr) *n.* a female sponsor at baptism.

GODSEND (god'send) *n.* an unexpected gift or acquisition.

GODSON (god'sun) *n.* a boy for whom one becomes sponsor at baptism.

GOGGLE (gog'l) *v i.* to roll the eyes;—*a.* full, round, and staring;—*n.* a roll or stare of the eye. [Gael. *gog,* a nod.]

GOGGLES (gog'lz) *n.pl.* glasses to protect the eyes.

GOING (gō'ing) *n.* moving or walking; procedure; behaviour; course of life.

GOITRE (goi'tẹr) *n.* bronchocele; swelled neck. [F., fr. L. *guttur,* throat.]

GOLD (gōld) *a.* a precious metal; money; a bright yellow colour; centre of the target;—*a.* made of gold; golden. [O.E.]

GOLD-BEATER (gōld'bēt-ẹr) *n.* one who beats gold into thin leaves

GOLDEN (gōl'dn) *a.* made of gold; like gold; yellow; precious; auspicious.

GOLDFINCH (gōld'finsh) *n.* a small singing bird.

GOLDFISH (gōld'fish) *n.* a small gold-coloured fish.

GOLDLEAF (gōld'lēf) *n.* gold beaten into a thin leaf.

GOLDSMITH (gōld'smith) *n.* a worker in gold.

GOLDY-LOCKS (gōl-di-loks) *n.* a plant with tufts of yellow flowers.

GOLF (golf) *n.* a game played with a small ball and a club bent at the lower end. [D.]

GONDOLA (gon'du-lạ) *n.* a pleasure-boat used in Venice. [It.]

GONDOLIER (gon-du-lēr') *n.* one who rows a gondola.

GONE (gon) *pp.* of **GO,** departed.

GONG (gong) *n.* a kind of metal drum. [Malay.]

GONIOMETER (gō-ni-om'e-tẹr) *n.* an instrument for measuring angles. [G. *gonia,* angle, and *metron,* measure.]

Gondola.

GOOD (good) *a.* valid; sound; suitable; virtuous; benevolent; beneficial;—*n.* that which affords happiness; advantage. [O.E. *god.* Cf. Ger. *gut.*]

GOOD-BREEDING (good-brēd'ing) *n.* polite education and manners.

GOOD-BYE (good-bī') *n.* or *inter.* farewell. [Contr. fr. 'God be with you.']

GOODLINESS (good'li-nes) *n.* beauty; grace.

GOODLY (good'li) *a.* beautiful; comely.

GOODNESS (good'nes) *n.* excellence.

GOODS (goodz) *n.pl.* movables; chattels; wares; merchandise.

GOOSE (goos) *n.* a fowl; a tailor's utensil;—*pl.* **GEESE.** [O.E. *gos.* Cf. Ger. *Gans.*]

GORDIAN-KNOT (gord'yạn-not) *n.* an inextricable difficulty. [Fr. *Gordius.*]

GORE (gōr) (1) *n.* clotted blood;—triangular piece of cloth or land;—(2) *v.t.* to wound with the horns; cut in a triangular form. [(1) O.E. *gor,* blood, dirt. (2) O.E. *gar,* spear with triangular blade.]

GORGE (gorj) *n.* the throat;—*v.t.* to swallow with greediness; satiate;—*v.i.* to feed greedily. [O.F. fr. L. *gurges,* whirlpool.]

GORGEOUS (gor'jus) *a.* very fine or showy. [O.F. *gorgias,* beautiful, fr. *gorge,* the throat.]

GORGEOUSLY (gor'jus-li) *ad.* splendidly.

GORGON (gor'gun) *n.* a fabulous monster of terrific aspect, with snakes intertwined in place of hair, and by her look turning the beholders into stone. [L., fr. G. *gorgo,* fr. *gorgos,* grim.]

GORILLA (go-ril'ạ) *n.* the largest of the ape species, is found in Western Africa, and when full grown is from 5 to 7 feet in height. [Afr.]

GORMAND (gor'mạnd) *n.* a glutton. [F. *gourmand.*]

GORMANDISE (gor'mạn-dīz) *v.i.* to eat greedily.

GORMANDISER (gor'mạn-dī-zẹr) *n.* a voracious eater.

GORSE (gors) *n.* a thick prickly shrub. [O.E. *gorst,* furze.]

GORY (gō'ri) *a.* stained with gore.

GOSLING (gos'ling) *n.* a young goose. [O.E. *gos,* and double dim. *-l-ing.*]

GOSPEL (gos'pel) *n.* good news or tidings; the Christian revelation; one or all of the four Scriptural narratives of the life of Christ; the whole system of Christian doctrine. [O.E. *god-spell,* fr. *god,* good, and *spell,* story.]

GOSSAMER (gos'ạ-mẹr) *n.* the down of plants floating in the air. [M.E. *gossomer,* fr. **GOOSE** and **SUMMER.**]

GOSSIP (gos'ip) *n.* one that tattles; mere talk; idle rumour;—*v.i.* to go about talking or telling stories about one's neighbours. [M.E. *gossib,* fr. *god,* God, and *sib,* related.]

GOSSIPING (gos'ip-ing) *a.* prating or tattling.

GOSSIPY (gos'ip-i) *a.* full of gossip. [See **GOSSIP.**]

GOSSOON (go-soon') *n.* a boy; a young messenger. [F. *garçon,* boy.]

GOT (got) *pret.* of **GET.**

GOTH (goth) *n.* a barbarian. [L. *Gothi.*]

GOTHIC (goth'ik) *a.* pertaining to the Goths; noting a style of architecture with sharp pointed arches.

GOTHICISM (goth'i-sizm) *n.* a Gothic idiom; barbarism.

GOUDA (gou'dạ) *n.* a kind of cheese, first made in Holland. [Fr. *Gouda,* in Holland.]

GOUGE (gouj) *n.* a chisel with a round edge; —*v.t.* to cut with a gouge; scoop out. [O.F., fr. Late L. *guvia,* chisel.]

GOURD (goord, gōrd) *n.* a plant and its fruit. [O.F. *gourde,* fr. L. *cucurbita.*]

GOURMAND (goor'mạnd) *n.* a ravenous eater; epicure. [F.]

GOURMET (goor'mā, goor'met) *n.* a judge of good living; connoisseur in wines and meats. [F.]

GOUT (gout) *n.* a painful disease of the great and small joints. [O.F. *goutte,* fr. L. *gutta,* drop.]

GOUT (goo) *n.* taste; relish. [F., fr. L. *gustus,* taste.]

GOUTY (gou'ti) *a.* diseased with or pertaining to gout.

GOVERN (guv'ẹrn) *v.t.* or *i.* to rule; control; exercise authority. [O.F. *governer,* fr. L. *gubernare,* to steer a ship.]

GOVERNABLE (guv'ẹr-nạ-bl) *a.* subject to rule; obedient; controllable.

GOVERNANCE (guv'ẹr-nạns) *n.* direction; management; deportment.

GOVERNESS (guv'ẹr-nes) *n.* a female who governs or instructs.

GOVERNMENT (guv'ẹrn-ment) *n.* control; executive power; an empire or state.

GOVERNMENTAL (guv-ẹrn-men'tạl) *a.* pertaining to government.

GOVERNOR (guv'er-nur) *n.* chief magistrate; a regulator.

GOWAN (gou'an) *n.* the daisy. [Scot.]

GOWN (goun) *n.* a woman's garment; a long loose robe worn by professional men, etc. [M.E. *goune*, fr. W. *gwn*, gown.]

GRAB (grab) *v.t.* to seize; clutch. [Sc.]

GRACE (grās) *n.* favour; mercy; divine influence; ease of manner; embellishment; a short prayer at meals; —*v.t.* to adorn; dignify; favour. [F., fr. L. *gratia*, favour, fr. *gratus*, agreeable.]

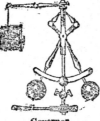
Governor.

GRACEFUL (grās'fool) *a.* beautiful with dignity; elegant.

GRACELESS (grās'les) *a.* destitute of grace.

GRACES (grās'ez) *n.pl.* elegant manners; a game with hoop and sticks; three Greek goddesses who attended on Venus and the Muses.

GRACIOUS (grā'shus) *a.* kind; favourable; condescending; pleasing; virtuous. [L. *gratiosus*, fr. *gratia*, favour, fr. *gratus*, agreeable.]

GRACIOUSLY (grā'shus-li) *ad.* kindly.

GRADATION (gra-dā'shun) *n.* orderly arrangement or progress; a step or degree in a series.

GRADATIONAL (gra-dā'shun-al) *a.* proceeding step by step.

GRADE (grād) *n.* degree; rank;—*v.t.* to reduce to a regular slope. [F., fr. L. *gradus*, fr. *gradi*, to step.]

GRADIENT (grād'yent) *n.* moving by steps;—*n.* degree of ascent or descent on a railroad. [L. (part. stem) *gradient-*, of *gradi*.]

GRADUAL (grad'ū-al) *a.* proceeding by degrees; step by step; slow.

GRADUALLY (grad'ū-al-i) *ad.* by degrees.

GRADUATE (grad'ū-āt) *v.i.* to receive an academical degree;—*v.t.* to mark with degrees;—*n.* one who has received a degree.

GRADUATION (grad-ū-ā'shun) *n.* regular progression; act of marking with degrees.

GRADUATOR (grad'ū-ā-ter) *n.* an instrument for dividing into small regular spaces or intervals.

GRAFT (gráft) *n.* a scion inserted in a stock; —*v.t.* to insert a shoot or scion into another tree. [O.F. *grafe*, fr. L. *graphium*, a style for writing with, fr. G. *graphein*, write.]

GRAIL (grāl) *n.* in mediæval legend, the Holy Cup used by Christ at the Last Supper. [Fr. O.F. *graal* or *greal*, a flat dish; Late L. *gradale*, a flat dish, app. a corr. of *cratella*, a dim. of *crater*, a bowl.]

GRAIN (grān) *n.* corn; a small seed; a minute particle; a small weight; disposition; texture;—*v.t.* to granulate; paint like grains of wood. [F., fr. L. *granum*, seed.]

GRAIP (grāp) *n.* a spade with forks or prongs. [Variant of GROPE.]

GRALLATORIAL (gral-a-tōr'i-al) *a.* pertaining to the wading birds. [L. *grallator*, *grallæ*, stilts, contr. of *gradulæ*, dim. of *gradus*, a step.]

GRAMINIVOROUS (gram-i-niv'u-rus) *a.* feeding on grass. [L. *stem*, *gramin-*, of *gramen*, grass, and *vorare*, to eat greedily.]

GRAMMAR (gram'ar) *n.* a system of rules for speaking and writing a language; an elementary text-book or catechism. [O.F. *gramaire*, fr. G. *gramma*, writing, fr. *graphein* write.]

GRAMMARIAN (gra-mā'ri-an) *n.* one versed in grammar.

GRAMMATICAL (gra-mat'i-kal) *a.* according to the rules of grammar.

GRAMMATICISE (gra-mat'i-sīz) *v.t.* to render grammatical.

GRAMOPHONE (gram-u-fōn) *n.* an instrument for recording and reproducing sounds. [G. *gramma*, a letter, and *phone*, sound.]

GRANARY (gran'a-ri) *n.* a store-house for grain. [L. *granaria*, fr. *granum*, grain.]

GRAND (grand) *a.* very great; magnificent. [F., fr. L. *grandis*. great.]

GRANDAM (gran'dam) *n.* grandmother.

GRANDEE (gran-dē') *n.* a man of high rank. [Sp.]

GRANDEUR (gran'dūr) *n.* magnificence; vastness; loftiness; splendour. [F.]

GRANDILOQUENCE (gran-dil'u-kwens) *n.* lofty speaking. [L. *grandis*, grand, and *loqui*, speak.]

GRANDIOSE (gran'di-ōs) *a.* grand and impressive—in a real or affected style.

GRAND-JURY (grand-jōōr'i) *n.* a preliminary jury to decide as to whether the person accused should be put on trial.

GRANDSIRE (grand'sir) *n.* a grandfather.

GRANDSON (grand'sun) *n.* the son of a son or daughter.

GRANGE (grānj) *n.* a farm with the buildings, etc. [O.F. =a barn, fr. L. *granum*, grain.]

GRANITE (gran'it) *n.* a stone composed of quartz, feldspar, and mica. [It. *granito*, grained, fr. *granum*, grain.]

GRANITIC (gra-nit'ik) *a.* pertaining to granite.

GRANIVOROUS (gra-niv'u-rus) *a.* subsisting on grain. [L. *granum*, grain, and *vorare*, eat greedily.]

GRANT (gránt) *v.t.* to bestow; yield;—*n.* a thing granted. [O.F. *graanter*, to promise, as fr. Late L. *credentare*, fr. *credere*, to believe.]

GRANTEE (grán-tē') *n.* one to whom a grant is made.

GRANTER (grán'ter) *n.* one who makes a grant.

GRANTOR (grán'ter) *n.* one who makes a conveyance in law.

GRANULAR (gran'ū-lar) *a.* consisting of grains.

GRANULATE (gran'ū-lāt) *v.t.* or *i.* to form into grains.

GRANULATION (gran-ū-lā'shun) *n.* act of forming into grains.

GRANULE (gran'ūl) *n* a particle. [L. *granulum*, dim. of *granum*, grain.]

GRANULOUS (gran'ū-lus) *a.* full of grains.

GRAPE (gráp) *n.* the fruit of the vine. [O.F. *grappe*, bunch of grapes.]

GRAPERY (grā'per-i) *n.* place where grapes are cultivated.

GRAPE-SHOT (gráp'shot) *n.* a cluster of small shot in a bag.

GRAPH (graf) *n.* a representation by means of lines of the variation of some phenomenon according to stated conditions;—*v.t.* to show the variation of some phenomenon by means of lines. [G. *graphein*, write.]

GRAPHIC (graf'ik) *a.* well delineated or described. [G. *graphe*, a writing, fr. *graphein*, write.]

GRAPHICALLY (graf'i-kal-i) *ad.* in a graphic manner.

GRAPNEL (grap'nel) *n.* a small anchor. [O.F. *grappin*, fr. *grappe*, a hook, with dim. suff. *-el*.]

GRAPPLE (grap'l) *v.t.* to lay fast hold of;—*v.i.* to contend closely;—*n.* a seizing; a hook. [O.F. *grappil*, fr. *grappe*, a hook.]

GRASP (grásp) *v.t.* to seize and hold;—*n.* gripe of the hands. [M.E. *graspen*=*grapsen*.]

GRASPING (grás'ping) *a.* greedy; avaricious.

GRASPINGLY (grás'ping-li) *ad.* in a grasping manner.

GRASS (grás) *n.* herbage;—*v.t.* or *i.* to grow over with grass. [O.E. *gœrs*, *grœs*.]

GRASS-CLOTH (grás'kloth) *n.* a beautiful light fabric made in the East Indies from the fibres of plants.

GRASS-GREEN (gràs'grēn) *a.* dark green;—*n.* the colour of grass.

GRASSHOPPER (gràs'hop-er) *n.* a jumping insect of the locust family.

GRASSINESS (gràs'i-nes) *n.* the state of abounding with grass.

GRASSY (gràs'i) *a.* covered with grass.

GRATE (grāt) (1) *v.t.* or *i.* to rub hard; fret; vex;—(2) *n.* frame of iron bars for holding coals used as fuel. [(1) O.F. *grater*, scrape. (2) Late L. *grata*, fr. L. *crates*, a hurdle.]

GRATEFUL (grāt'fool) *a.* having a sense of favours; affording pleasure; thankful; agreeable; welcome. [L. *gratus*.]

GRATEFULLY (grāt'fool-i) *ad.* with gratitude.

GRATER (grā'ter) *n.* an instrument for grating. [See **GRATE** (1).]

GRATIFICATION (grat-i-fi-kā'shun) *n.* pleasure enjoyed; satisfaction.

GRATIFY (grat'i-fi) *v.t.* to indulge; please; humour. [L. *gratus*, pleasing, thankful, and *facere*, make.]

GRATING (grā'ting) (1) *a.* fretting; harsh;—(2) *n.* a partition of bars or lattice-work. [(1) See **GRATE** (1). (2) See **GRATE** (2).]

GRATINGLY (grā'ting-li) *ad.* harshly; offensively. [See **GRATE** (1).]

GRATIS (grā'tis) *ad.* for nothing. [L. contr. of *gratiis*, ablative pl. of *gratia*, favour.]

GRATITUDE (grat'i-tūd) *n.* thankfulness or gratefulness for benefits. [L. *gratus*, pleasing.]

GRATUITOUS (gra-tū'i-tus) *a.* free; voluntary; asserted without proof. [reward.]

GRATUITOUSLY (gra-tū'i-tus-li) *ad.* without

GRATUITY (gra-tū'i-ti) *n.* a free gift; reward for service. [F., fr. Late L. (acc.) *gratuitatem*, fr. *gratus*, pleasing.]

GRATULATE (grat'ū-lāt) *v.t.* to express joy at another's prosperity. [L. (part.) *gratulatus*, of *gratulare*, fr. *gratus*, pleasing.]

GRATULATION (grat-ū-lā'shun) *n.* expression of joy. [ing joy.

GRATULATORY (grat'ū-lā-tur-i) *a.* express-

GRAVAMEN (gra-vā'men) *n.* burden; substantial part of a complaint or charge. [L., fr. *gravis*, heavy.]

GRAVE (grāv) (1) *n.* a place of burial; tomb; sepulchre;—*v.t.* to carve or cut; to engrave; to practise engraving;—(2) *a.* weighty; important; (*Mus.*) slow; low in tone; deep; —(3) *v.t.* to clean a ship's bottom by burning or scraping off seaweeds, barnacles, etc., and covering it over with pitch. [(1) O.E., fr. *grafan*, dig. Cf. Ger. *graben*. (2) F., fr. L. *gravis*, heavy. (3) Scand.]

GRAVEDIGGER (grāv'dig-er) *n.* one who digs graves; sexton. Also **GRAVEMAKER**.

GRAVEL (grav'el) *n.* pebbles; concretions in the kidneys;—*v.t.* to cover with gravel; puzzle. [O.F. *gravele*, sand = F. *gravier*, fr. Celt.]

GRAVELLY (grav'el-i) *a.* full of gravel.

GRAVELY (grāv'li) *ad.* seriously.

GRAVENESS (grāv'nes) *n.* seriousness.

GRAVER (grā'ver) *n.* a tool to engrave with.

GRAVESTONE (grāv'stōn) *n.* a stone set up as a memorial of the dead.

GRAVEYARD (grāv'yàrd) *n.* a burial place.

GRAVING-DOCK (grā'ving-dok) *n.* a dry dock in which ships' bottoms are graved.

GRAVITATE (grav'i-tāt) *v.i.* to tend towards the centre. [to the centre.

GRAVITATION (grav-i-tā'shun) *n.* tendency

GRAVITY (grav'i-ti) *n.* seriousness; force which draws toward the centre of attraction. [F. *gravité*, fr. L. (acc.) *gravitatem*, fr. *gravis*, heavy.]

GRAVY (grā'vi) *n.* juice that comes from flesh in cooking; sauce or soup made from it. [Prob. fr. **GREAVES**.]

GRAY (grā) *a.* hoary; white with a mixture of black. [O.E. *grœg.* Cf. Ger. *grau.*]

GRAYBEARD (grā'bērd) *n.* an old man; an earthen jar for holding liquor.

GRAYISH (grā'ish) *a.* somewhat gray.

GRAYLING (grā'ling) *n.* a small fish of the salmon family.

GRAYNESS (grā'nes) *n.* the state of being gray.

GRAZE (grāz) (1) *v.t.* to eat grass;—(2) rub slightly. [(1) O.E., fr. **GRASS**. (2) Etym. doubtful.]

GRAZIER (grā'zher) *n.* one who feeds cattle.

GREASE (grēs) *n.* animal fat;—*v.t.* to smear with grease. [O.F. *gresse*, fatness, fr. *gras*, fat, fr. L. *crassus*, gross.]

GREASINESS (grē'zi-nes) *n.* state of being greasy.

GREASY (grē'zi) *a.* fat; oily.

GREAT (grāt) *a.* large; chief; pregnant. [O.E.]

GREATLY (grāt'li) *ad.* in a great degree.

GREATNESS (grāt'nes) *n.* quality of being great.

GREAVES (grēvz) *n.pl.* armour for the legs. [O.F., fr. *greve*, shin-bone.]

GRECIAN (grē'shan) *a.* pertaining to Greece. [F. *Grec*, fr. L. *Grœcus*, Greek, fr. G. *Graikos*]

GRECISM (grē'sizm) *n.* an idiom of the Greek language.

GREED (grēd) *n.* eager desire; covetousness. [O.E. *grœdig*, hungry.]

GREEDILY (grē'di-li) *ad.* ravenously.

GREEDINESS (grē'di-nes) *n.* ravenousness; ardent desire.

GREEK (grēk) *n.* a native of Greece; language of Greece;—*a.* belonging to Greece. [See **GRECIAN**.]

GREEK-FIRE (grēk'fīr) *n.* a combustible which burns under water, said to consist of asphalt, sulphur, and nitre.

GREEN (grēn) *a.* of the colour of growing plants; fresh; raw; not dry; not ripe; —*n.* a green colour; a grassy plot;—*v.t.* to make green. [O.E. *grene*, allied to *grow*. Cf. Ger. *grun*.]

GREEN-CROP (grēn'krop) *n.* growing crop; crop of grass, turnips, etc. [plum.

GREENGAGE (grēn'gaj) *n.* a choice kind of

GREENHORN (grēn'horn) *n.* a raw youth.

GREENHOUSE (grēn'hous) *n.* a house to keep plants.

GREENING (grē'ning) *n.* a kind of apple which is green in colour when ripe.

GREENISH (grē'nish) *a.* somewhat green.

GREENNESS (grēn'nes) *n.* green colour; unripeness; inexperience.

GREEN-ROOM (grēn'rŏŏm) *n.* the retiring-room of actors in a theatre.

GREENS (grēnz) *n.pl.* the leaves of kale, spinach, etc., boiled for the table.

GREENSWARD (grēn'swawrd) *n.* a close green turf.

GREET (grēt) *v.t.* to salute; congratulate. [O.E. *gretan*, to go to meet.]

GREGARIOUS (gre-gā'ri-us) *a.* keeping in flocks. [L. *gregarius*, fr. (acc.) *gregem*, of *grex*, flock.]

GRENADE (gre-nād') *n.* a ball filled with gunpowder. [F., fr. Sp. *granada*, fr. L. *granatus*, full of seeds, fr. *granum*, grain.]

GRENADIER (gren-a-dēr') *n.* originally, a soldier who threw grenades; then, a member of the first company of every battalion of foot; now, one of a regiment of guards attached to the court.]

GREY (grā). [See **GRAY**.]

GREYHOUND (grā'hound) *n.* a tall, fleet dog used to hunt hares. [M.E. *greihund*, fr. Scand.]

GRIDDLE (grid'l) *n.* a broad, shallow pan, or circular plate of metal, for baking cakes. [O.F. *gredil*, fr. Late L. *craticulum*, dim. of L. *cratis*, a grate.]

GRIDIRON (grid'ī-ern) *n.* a frame of iron bars for broiling flesh or fish. [M.E. *gredire*, a griddle.]

GRIEF (grēf) *n.* a painful sense of loss. [F., fr. L. *gravis*, heavy.] [grief.

GRIEVANCE (grē'vans) *n.* that which causes

GRIEVE (grēv) *v.i.* to mourn;—*v.t.* to wound acutely. [O.F. *grever*, fr. L. *gravare*, fr. *gravis*, heavy.]

GRIEVOUS (grē'vus) *a.* giving pain; afflictive; burdensome.

GRIEVOUSLY (grē'vus-li) *ad.* painfully.

GRIFFIN (grif'in) *n.* a fabled animal, part lion and part eagle. [F. *griffon*, fr. L., fr. G. *grupos*, hook-nosed.]

GRILL (gril) *v.t.* to broil. [F. *griller*, fr. *gril*, a gridiron, fr. L. *craticula*, a small gridiron, fr. *cratis*, a grate.]

GRILSE (grils) *n.* a young salmon. [Scand. = gray salmon.]

GRIM (grim) *a.* fierce; hideous. [O.E.]

GRIMACE (gri-mās') *n.* a wry mouth. [F.]

GRIMALKIN (gri-mál'kin) *n.* an old cat. [Fr. **GRAY**, and *malkin*, a hare, a dim. of *Moll* = Mary.]

GRIME (grim) *v.t.* to sully deeply;—*n.* dirt deeply ingrained. [Scand.]

GRIMLY (grim'li) *ad.* in a surly manner.

GRIMNESS (grim'nes) *n.* sternness of visage.

GRIN (grin) *v.i.* to show the teeth;—*n.* a showing of the teeth; a forced smile. [O.E. *grennian*.]

GRIND (grind) *v.t.* or *i.* to reduce to powder; rub together; sharpen; prepare or work for examination; oppress;—*n.* hard study. [O.E. *grindan*.]

GRINDER (grin'der) *n.* one who grinds; a double or molar tooth.

GRINDSTONE (grind'stōn) *n.* a flat circular stone to grind edged tools on.

GRIP (grip) *n.* a seizing; a grasping; tenacious power or hold;—*v.t.* or *i.* to clutch; hold fast; bite.

GRIPE (grip) *v.t.* to seize; clutch; give pain to the bowels;—*n.* a squeeze; a grasp; oppression. [O.E. *gripan*.]

GRIPING (grī'ping) *a.* grasping; greedy;—*n.* pain in the bowels.

GRIS (grē, gris) *n.* a kind of gray fur. [F.]

GRISETTE (gri-zet') *n.* a young workwoman in France. [F. = a gray gown.]

GRISLY (griz'li) *a.* horrible; frightful. [O.E. *gristic*, fr. *grisan*, to shudder.]

GRIST (grist) *n.* corn ground, or for grinding, at one time; supply; provision. [O.E. = a grinding.]

GRISTLE (gris'l) *n.* a cartilage. [O.E., fr. **GRIST**.]

GRISTLY (gris'li) *ad.* like gristle.

GRIT (grit) *n.* coarse part of meal; sand; gravel; a hard sandstone; spirit; pluck. [O.E. *greot*, bran, dust.]

GRITTINESS (grit'i-nes) *n.* the quality of being gritty.

GRITTY (grit'i) *a.* full of grit; spirited; resolute.

GRIZZLE (griz'l) *n.* a gray colour. [M.E. *grisel*, fr. F. *gris*, gray.]

GROAN (grōn) *v.i.* to breathe with a deep noise;—*n.* a deep, mournful sound. [O.E. *granian*.]

GROANING (grō'ning) *n.* act of uttering groans; lamentation.

GROAT (grōt) *n.* fourpence sterling. [O. L. Ger. *Grote*, a coin of Bremen.]

GROATS (grōts) *n.pl.* oats coarsely ground. [O.E. *gratan*.]

GROCER (grō'ser) *n.* a dealer in sugar, tea, liquors, spices, etc. [Formerly written *grosser*, one that sells by the *gross*, or wholesale.]

GROCERY (grō'ser-i) *n.* goods of grocers; a grocer's store.

GROG (grog) *n.* spirit and water. [Fr. 'Old *Grog*,' the nickname of Admiral Vernon, who introduced it about 1745; he wore *grogram* breeches.]

GROGRAM (grog'ram) *n.* a stuff made of silk and hair. [O.F. *grosgrain* of a coarse texture.]

GROIN (groin) *n.* the part between the belly and the thigh; angular curve made by the crossing of two arches. [Scand.]

GROOM (grōom) *n.* one who tends horses; a newly-married man;—*v.t.* to tend or curry, as a horse. [Prob. fr. O.E. *guma* (in bride*groom*), a man.]

GROOMSMAN (grōomz'man) *n.* one who attends a bridegroom at his marriage.

GROOVE (grōov) *n.* a furrow; a long hollow cut by a tool;—*v.t.* to cut a furrow or channel. [D., a channel. Cf. E. **GRAVE**.]

GROPE (grōp) *v.i.* to feel in the dark;—*v.t.* to search by feeling. [O.E. *grapian*, seize, allied to **GRIPE**.]

GROSS (grōs) *a.* thick; bulky; corpulent; indelicate; coarse; plain; dull; entire; —*n.* the whole bulk; twelve dozen. [O.F. *gros*, fr. L. *grossus*, thick.]

GROSSLY (grōs'li) *ad.* thickly; coarsely; palpably.

GROSSNESS (grōs'nes) *n.* thickness; coarseness; enormity.

GROTESQUE (grō-tesk') *a.* wildly formed; odd. [F., fr. It. *grotta*.]

GROTTO (grot'ō) *n.* a cavern; an ornamental cave. [It. *grotta*, fr. L. *crypta*, fr. G. *kruptein*, to hide.]

GROUND (ground) *n.* surface of the earth; land; floor; place of action; foundation; basis; primary colour;—*pl.* sediment;—*v.t.* to lay or fix firmly; instruct in first principles;—*v.i.* to strike the bottom and become fixed. [O.E. *grund*.]

GROUNDLESS (ground'les) *a.* void of foundation.

GROUND-PLOT (ground'plot) *n.* the site of a building.

GROUND-RENT (ground'rent) *n.* rent for building ground.

GROUNDSEL (ground'sel) *n.* a common annual weed. [O.E. *grund* and *swelgan*, to swallow.]

GROUND-SWELL (ground'swel) *n.* a broad deep swell of the sea after the gale has ceased.

GROUND-WORK (ground'wurk) *n.* foundation; first principle.

GROUP (grōop) *n.* cluster; crowd; throng; assemblage;—*v.t.* to form a cluster; arrange in order. [F. *groupe*, cluster.]

GROUSE (grous) *n.* one of a family of game birds, red or black; moor-fowl; blackcock; —*v.i.* to shoot grouse. [Prob. fr. O.F. *griesche*, gray.]

GROUT (grout) *n.* coarse meal; lees; a thin kind of mortar;—*v.t.* to fill up with grout, as spaces between stones. [O.E. *grut*.]

GROVE (grōv) *n.* a small shady wood or group of trees. [O.E. *graf*, grove.]

GROVEL (grov'l) *v.t.* to creep on the earth. [M.E. adv. *grovelling*, flat on the ground, fr. Scand.]

GROVELLING (grov'l-ing) *a.* mean.

GROW (grō) *v.t.* or *i.* [*pret.* **GREW**; *pp.* **GROWN**] to vegetate; increase; raise; extend; become. [O.E. *growan*. Conn. with **GREEN**.]

GROWL (groul) *v.t.* or *i.* to grumble; snarl; —*n.* murmur of a cross dog. [D.]

GROWLER (grou'ler) *n.* a snarling cur; a grumbler.

GROWTH (grōth) *n.* increase of size; progress; vegetation; product.

GRUB (grub) *n.* a small destructive worm; that which is grubbed up; victuals;—*v.t.* or *i.* to dig in; eradicate. [M.E. *grobben*, allied to **GRAVE**, engrave.]

GRUBBER (grub'er) *n.* a tool for eradicating weeds, roots, etc.

GRUDGE (gruj) *v.t.* or *i.* to envy the enjoyment of another; give or take unwillingly; —*n.* secret envy or enmity; old cause of quarrel. [M.E. *grochen*, fr. O.F. *groucer*, grumble.]

Fāte, fär, ado; mē, her; mine; nōte; tūne; mōōn.

GRUDGINGLY (gruj'ing-li) *ad.* unwillingly.
GRUEL (gróo'el) *n.* food of meal boiled in water. [O.F., fr. Late L. *gruium*, meal.]
GRUFF (gruf) *a.* stern; surly; glum. [D.]
GRUFFLY (gruf'li) *ad.* with surliness.
GRUMBLE (grum'bl) *v.i.* to murmur with discontent; growl. [O.D. *grommelen*, to keep on muttering.]
GRUMBLER (grum'bler) *n.* one who mutters or complains.
GRUMBLING (grum'bling) *n.* a murmuring.
GRUMPY (grum'pi) *a.* gruff; surly.
GRUNT (grunt) *v.i.* to utter a sound like a hog;—*n.* the sound of a hog. [Imit., O.E. *grunian*, allied to L. *grunnire*.]
GRUNTER (grun'ter) *n.* a pig; a fish of the gurnard kind.
GUANO (gwä'nō) *n.* a valuable manure, consisting of sea-fowl dung, brought from the coasts of South America and Africa. [Sp. *guano* or *huano*, fr. Peruv.]
GUARANTEE (gar-an-tē') *v.t.* to warrant;— *n.* a surety for performance. [O.F. (part.) *garantie*, of *garantir*, to warrant.]
GUARANTEED (gar-an-tēd') *pp.* warranted; vouched for.
GUARD (gård) *n.* a watch; defence; sentinel; conductor; watch chain; posture in fencing; —*v.t.* or *i.* to protect; defend; bind; watch;—*n.pl.* troops attached to the person of a prince. [O F. *garder*, guard; O.E. *weardian*. See WARD.]
GUARDED (går'ded) *a.* cautious; reserved.
GUARDIAN (går'dyan) *n.* one who has the care of another;—*a.* protecting.
GUARDIANSHIP (går'dyan-ship) *n.* the office of a guardian.
GUARDSMAN (gårdz'man) *n.* a soldier of the guards.
GUAVA (gwå'va) *n.* a tropical tree and its fruit. [Sp.]
GUDGEON (guj'un) (1) *n.* a fish;—(2) pin on which a wheel turns. [(1) O.F. *goujon*, fr. L. (acc.) *gobionem*, fr. G. *kobios*. (2) O.F. *goujon*, pin of a pulley.]
GUERDON (ger'dun) *n.* a reward; a recompense;—*v.t.* to reward. [O.F., corr. fr. Teut.]
GUERRILLA (ger-ril'a) *n.* an irregular warfare by independent bands of peasants; a member of the band. [Sp., fr. *guerra*, war; F. *guerre*, fr. Teut.]
GUESS (ges) *v.t.* to conjecture;—*n.* a conjecture. [M.E. *gessen*, fr. Scand.]
GUEST (gest) *n.* a visitor who is received and entertained with hospitality. [O.E. *gest*, *cerst*. Cf. Ger. *Gast*.]
GUFFAW (gu-faw') *n.* a loud laugh. [Imit.]
GUIDANCE (gi'dans) *n.* direction; care.
GUIDE (gid) *v.t.* to lead; direct;—*n.* one who shows the way; a regulator. [F. *guider*, allied to O.E. *witan*, to know.]
GUIDELESS (gid'les) *a.* having no guide.
GUIDE-POST (gid'pōst) *n.* a post to direct the way.
GUILD (gild) *n.* a corporation or fraternity of merchants, tradesmen, or craftsmen. [O.E. *gild*, money, fr. *gildan*, to pay.]
GUILDHALL (gild'hawl) *n.* the hall of a corporation; town-hall.
GUILE (gil) *n.* cunning; craft; deceit. [O.F. —deceit. Cf. O.E. *wil*.]
GUILEFUL (gil'fool) *a.* deceitful; crafty.
GUILELESS (gil'les) *a.* free from guile; artless.
GUILLOTINE (gil-o-tēn') *n.* a machine for beheading. [F., fr. *Guillotin* (1738-1814) the inventor.]
GUILT (gilt) *n.* criminality; sin. [O.E. *gylt*, crime (orig. fine for an offence), fr. *gildan* to pay.]
GUILTINESS (gil'ti-nes) *n.* criminality.
GUILTLESS (gilt'les) *a.* without guilt.
GUILTY (gil'ti) *a.* criminal; wicked.

GUINEA (gin'e) *n.* a gold coin formerly current in Great Britain, value 21s. sterling. [Fr. *Guinea*, in W. Africa.]
GUINEA-FOWL (gin'e-foul) *n.* a dark gray fowl with white spots.
GUIPURE (gē-pōor') *n.* an imitation of old lace. [F.]
GUISE (giz) *n.* manner; garb. [O.F. Cf. Ger. *weise*, away.]
GUISER (gi'zer) *n.* a Christmas masker or mummer. Also GUISARD. [See GUISE.]
GUITAR (gi-tär') *n.* a stringed instrument of music. [F. *guitare*, fr. L. *cithara*, fr. G. *kithara*, a lyre or lute.]
GULF (gulf) *n.* an arm of the sea extending into land; an abyss. [F. *golfe*, Late G. *kolphos*, fr. G. *kolpos*, the bosom.]
GULL (gul) *v.t.* to cheat; defraud;—*n.* a web-footed sea-fowl. [Celt.]
GULLET (gul'et) *n.* the passage for food; the throat. [O.F. *goulet*, fr. L. *gula*, throat.]
GULLIBILITY (gul-i-bil'i-ti) *n.* great credulity.
GULLIBLE (gul'i-bl) *a.* easily imposed on.
GULLY (gul'i) *n.* a channel worn by water;— *v.t.* to wear by water into a channel. [O.F. *goulet*. Cf. GULLET.]
GULP (gulp) *v.t.* to swallow eagerly;—*n.* a swallow. [D. = a great draught.]
GUM (gum) (1) *n.* the fleshy substance that encloses the teeth;—(2) mucilage of vegetables hardened. [(1) O.E. *gome*, jaws. (2) O.F. *gomme*, fr. L. *gummi*, fr. G. *kommi*.]
GUMBOIL (gum'boil) *n.* a boil on the gum.
GUMMY (gum'i) *a.* consisting of gum.
GUMPTION (gun'shun) *n.* capacity; shrewdness; address; the act of preparing colours. [Prob. O.E. *gyman*, observe.]
GUN (gun) *n.* a cannon, musket, etc. [M.E. *gonne*, fr. Welsh = a bowl.]
GUNNER (gun'er) *n.* one who works a gun.
GUNNERY (gun'er-i) *n.* the art and science of firing guns.
GUNPOWDER (gun'pow-der) *n.* a composition of saltpetre, sulphur, and charcoal mixed, dried, and granulated.
GUNSHOT (gun'shot) *n.* the reach or range of a shot. [firearms.
GUNSMITH (gun'smith) *n.* a maker of small
GUNSTOCK (gun'stok) *n.* the stock or wood in which the barrel of a gun is fixed.
GUNWALE (gun'l) *n.* upper part of a ship's side.
GURGLE (gur'gl) *v.i.* to flow with noise, as water from a bottle;—*n.* the sound of air forced through a liquid. [Through It., fr. L. *gurges*.]
GURNARD (gur'nard) *n.* a sea-fish of several species. Also GURNET. [O.F. *gronguard*, fr. *grogner*, to grunt, fr. L. *grunnire*, to grunt.]
GUSH (gush) *v.i.* to rush out as a fluid;—*n.* a sudden flow. [D.]
GUSSET (gus'et) *n.* a small piece of cloth inserted in a garment to enlarge or strengthen the part. [F. *gousset*, armpit.]
GUST (gust) (1) *n.* a sudden blast of wind; violent burst of temper;—(2) taste; relish; critical perception. [(1) Scand. = a blast. (2) L. *gustus*, taste.]
GUSTATORY (gus'ta-tur-i) *a.* relating to taste. [See GUST (2).]
GUSTO (gus'tō) *n.* relish; taste. [It.]
GUSTY (gus'ti) *a.* subject to blasts of wind; stormy.
GUT (gut) *n.* the intestinal canal; a narrow channel; fiddle-string;—*v.t.* to eviscerate; destroy or remove the contents of. [O.E. *gut*, *geotan*, to pour. Cf. Ger. *Gosse*, a drain.]

Guitar.

GUTTA-PERCHA (gut'ą-pẽr'chą) *n.* a substance exuding from certain trees in Asia, and used variously. [Malay.]

GUTTER (gut'ẽr) *n.* a passage for water;— *v.t.* to hollow;—*v.i.* to be hollowed; run in drops. [O.F. *goutiere*, fr. L. *gutta*, a drop.]

GUTTURAL (gut'u-rąl) *a.* belonging to the throat. [F., fr. L. *guttur*, throat.]

GUY (gi) *n.* a rope to keep a body steady in hoisting. [O.F. *guie*, a guide.]

GUZZLE (guz'l) *v.t.* or *i.* to swallow much or frequently. [O.F. *desgouziller*, to swallow down, fr. *gosier*, the throat.]

GUZZLER (guz'lẽr) *n.* an immoderate eater or drinker.

GYMNASIUM (jim-nā'zi-um) *n.* a place of exercise; school for the higher branches of literature or science. [L., fr. G. *gumnasion*, fr. *gumnos*, naked.]

GYMNASTIC (jim-nas'tik) *a.* pertaining to athletic exercises for health.

GYMNASTICS (jim-nas'tiks) *n.pl.* the art of performing athletic exercises.

GYNECOCRACY (jin-e-kok'rą-si) *n.* female ascendancy or government. Also written **GYNOCRACY.** [G. *gune*, *gunaikos*, woman, and *kratein*, to rule.]

GYPSUM (jip'sum) *n.* plaster of Paris. [L., fr. G. *gupsos*, chalk.]

GYRATE (ji'rāt) *v.i.* to revolve round a central point; to move spirally. [L. (part.) *gyratus*, of *gyrare*, to move in a circle.]

GYRATION (ji-rā'shun) *n.* a circular motion.

GYRATORY (ji'rą-tur-i) *a.* moving in a circle. [See **GYRATE.**]

GYROSCOPE (ji'ro-skōp) *n.* a rotating wheel mounted in a ring or rings for illustrating the dynamics of rotation. [G. *guros*, circle, and *skopein*, view.]

GYVE (jiv) *n.* a fetter or shackle for the legs; —*v.t.* to shackle; fetter. [M.E., fr. A.F. *gives*.]

H

HA (hä) *ex.* denoting surprise or other emotion; when repeated, laughter. Also **HAH**, *v.i.* to express surprise. [imit.]

HABEAS CORPUS (hä'be-as kor'pus) *n.* a writ ordering a jailer to produce the body of a prisoner in court. [L., thou must produce the body.]

HABERDASHER (hab'ẽr-dash-ẽr) *n.* a dealer in drapery stuffs, as silks, muslin, lace, etc., or in small wares, as ribbons, tapes, etc. [O.F. *hapertas*, of uncertain etym.]

HABERDASHERY (hab'ẽr-dash-ẽr-i) *n.* drapery wares in general.

HABERGEON (ha-bẽr'jun) *n.* mailed armour to defend the neck and breast. [F. *haubergeon*, dim. of O.F. *hauberc*.]

HABILIMENT (hą-bil'i-ment) *n.* dress; clothing. [F., fr. *habiller*, to dress, fr. L. *habilis*, ready, fr. *habere*, to have.]

HABIT (hab'it) *n.* temperament of body or mind; aptitude gained by practice; custom; manner; dress; a long-skirted garment worn by ladies on horseback;—*v.t.* to clothe; array. [O.F., fr. L. *habitus*, attire, fr. *habere*, to have.]

HABITABLE (hab'i-tą-bl) *a.* that can be inhabited. [L. *habitabilis*, fr. *habitare*, to dwell, fr. *habere*, to have.]

HABITANCY (hab'i-tąn-si) *n.* legal residence.

HABITATION (hab-i-tā'shun) *n.* a place of abode.

HABITUAL (hą-bit'ū-ąl) *a.* acquired by habit; customary; usual. [customarily.]

HABITUALLY (hą-bit'ū-ąl-i) *ad.* by habit;

HABITUATE (hą-bit'ū-āt) *v.t.* to accustom to a practice or usage;—*a.* formed by habit or frequent use.

HABITUDE (hab'i-tūd) *n.* customary practice; habit; state.

HABITUE (hą-bit'ū-ā) *n.* one who frequents a place, especially a place of amusement.

HACK (hak) (1) *v.t.* to cut awkwardly; notch; —*v.i.* to cough; hawk;—*n.* a notch; a cut; —(2) *n.* a horse let out for hire; a literary drudge;—*a.* hired; worn out;—(3) *n.* a rack for feeding cattle; a frame for drying cheese or fish. [(1) O.E. *haccian*. (2) Contr. for **HACKNEY.** (3) Fr. **HATCH.**]

HACKING (hak'ing) *a.* short and interrupted, as a cough.

HACKLE (hak'l) *v.t.* to comb, as flax or hemp; question severely; heckle;—*n.* a comb for dressing flax; a fly for angling. [D.]

HACKNEY (hak'ni) *n.* a horse or coach for hire;—*a.* let for hire; common;—*v.t.* to use much; make common. [O.F. *haquenee*, a pacing horse.]

HACKNEY-COACH (hak'ni-kōch) *n.* a coach for hire.

HACKNEYED (hak'nid) *a.* used much.

HAD (had) *pret.* and *pp.* of **HAVE.**

HADDOCK (had'uk) *n.* a small sea-fish of the cod kind. [M.E.]

HADES (hā'dēz) *n.* the abode of the dead; state of departed souls. [G., the unseen, fr. *a*, not, and *idein*, to see.]

HAFT (häft) *n.* a handle; hilt;—*v.t.* to set in a haft. [O.E. *hæft*. Cf. Ger. *Heft*.]

HAG (hag) *n.* an ugly old woman; a witch. [Fr. O.E. *hægtesse*, a witch. Cf. Ger. *Hexe*.]

HAGGARD (hag'ard) *a.* lean and wasted; ghastly; wild or untamed;—*n.* a species of hawk. [O.F. *hagard*.]

HAGGIS (hag'is) *n.* a sheep's pluck chopped up with suet, oatmeal, onions, etc., and boiled in its maw. [Per. fr. *hag*, to chop.]

HAGGLE (hag'l) *v.t.* to mangle in cutting; —*v.i.* be difficult in making a bargain. [Freq. of *hag*, chop.]

HAGGLER (hag'lẽr) *n.* one who mangles.

HAGIOGRAPHER (hā'ji-og'rą-fẽr, hag-i-og'rą-fẽr) *n.* a writer of sacred books. [G., fr. *hagios*, holy, and *graphein*, to write.]

HAGIOGRAPHY (hā-ji-og'rą-fi, hag-i-og'rą-fi) *n.* sacred writings; the last of the three Jewish divisions of the Old Testament.

HAGIOLOGY (hā-ji-ol'ō-ji, hag-i-ol'ō-ji) *n.* the history of the lives or legends of the saints. [G. *hagios*, and *logos*, a discourse.]

HAIL (hāl) (1) *n.* frozen rain; *v.i.* to fall in frozen drops; (2) *v.t.* to call after; salute; *inter.* or *n.* wish of health. [(1) O.E. *hagol*. Cf. Ger. *Hagel.* (2) Scand. =health.]

HAILSHOT (hāl'shot) *n.* small shot scattered like hail.

HAILSTONE (hāl'stōn) *n.* a single pellet of hail; frozen rain-drop.

HAILSTORM (hāl'storm) *n.* a heavy, tempestuous fall of hail.

HAIR (hār) *n.* a small animal filament; the mass of such which covers the head or body; anything very small and fine. [O.E. *hær.* Cf. Ger. *Haar*.]

HAIRBREADTH (hār'bredth) *n.* a very small distance.

HAIRCLOTH (hār'kloth) *n.* cloth made of hair.

HAIRDRESSER (hār'dres-ẽr) *n.* one who cuts or dresses hair.

HAIRINESS (hār'i-nes) *n.* state of being hairy.

HAIRLESS (hār'les) *a.* destitute of hair; bald.

HAIR-SPLITTING (hār'split-ing) *a.* or *n.* making fine distinctions in reasoning.

HAIR-STROKE (hār'strōk) *n.* a fine stroke in writing or drawing.

HAIR-TRIGGER (här'trig-ẹr) *n.* a trigger for discharging a firearm with a very fine spring.
HAIRY (här'i) *a.* full of hair; made of hair.
HAKE (ā) *n.* a sea-fish of the cod family. [Scand.] k
HALBERD (hal'bẹrd) *n.* an ancient military weapon, partly axe, partly dagger or spear. [O.F. *halebarde*, fr. Teut.]
HALBERDIER (hal-bẹr-dēr') *n.* one armed with a halberd.
HALCYON (hal'si-un) *a.* calm; quiet. [L., ḻ, fr. G. *alkyon*, wrongly derived fr. *hals*, sea. and *kyein*, to breed.]
HALE (hāl) (1) *a.* healthy; sound of body;— (2) *v.t.* to haul; drag. [(1) M.E. *hal*. (2) Variant of HAUL.]
HALF (häf) *n.* one of two equal parts;—*pl.* HALVES. [O.E. *healf*. Cf. Ger. *halb*.]
HALF-BLOOD (häf'blud) *n.* a relation by one parent. [Hindu and a European.
HALF-CASTE (häf'kast) *n.* one born of a
HALF-LENGTH (häf'length) *a.* presenting the upper part of the body.
HALF-MEASURE (häf'mezh-ŭr) *n.* a feeble or inadequate plan of operation.
HALF-PAY (häf'pā) *n.* reduced pay.
HALIBUT (hal'i-but) *n.* a large, flat fish. [M.E. *hali*, holy, and *butte*, flounder, that fish being much eaten on fast-days.]
HALL (hawl) *n.* entrance of a house; a public room; college. [O.E. *heal*, fr. *helan*, to cover.]
HALLELUJAH (hal-e-lōō'yạ) *n.* praise ye the Lord. Also written HALLELUIAH. [H. = praise ye, and *Jah*, Jehovah.]
HALLOW (hal'ō) *v.t.* to consecrate. [O.E. *halig*, holy.]
HALLUCINATION (ha-lōō-si-nā'shun) *n.* a delusion of the imagination. [L. (acc.) *hallucinationem*, fr. *hallucinari*, to wander in mind.]
HALLO (hạ'lō) *v.i.* to call or cry out loudly. Also written HOLLO. [F. *holà*, fr. *ho*, and *là*, there.]
HALO (hā'lō) *n.* a luminous circle round the sun; a bright ring;—*pl.* HALOS. [L., fr. G. *halos*, threshing-floor, and also the disc of the sun or moon.]
HALT (hawlt) *v.t.* or *i.* to limp; stop;—*a.* lame, crippled;—*n.* a stop; a limping; hesitation in speech. [O.E. *healtian*, to limp.]
HALTER (hawl'tẹr) *n.* a rope to tie a horse; a hangman's rope;—*v.t.* to put a halter on. [O.E. *hælftre*.]
HALVE (häv) *v.t.* to divide into equal parts.
HALYARD (hal'yård) *n.* a rope to raise or lower yards or sails. [Fr. HALE (2) or HAUL, and YARD.]
HAM (ham) *n.* the thigh of a beast, especially a hog, salted and dried; the hind part of the knee. [O.E. *hamm*.] [D.]
HAMES (hāmz) *n.pl.* a kind of collar for horses,
HAMLET (ham'let) *n.* a small village. [O.F. *hamel*, and dim. *-let*. Cf. Ger. *Heim*; O.E. *ham*, a dwelling.]
HAMMER (ham'ẹr) *n.* an instrument for driving nails;—*v.t.* to drive with a hammer; forge; form with labour. [O.E. *hamor*.]
HAMMOCK (ham'uk) *n.* a hanging bed used in ships. [Sp. *hamaca* of W. Indian origin.)]
HAMPER (ham'pẹr) (1) *n.* a covered basket; — (2) a fetter;—*v.t.* to shackle; embarrass. [(1) Fr. *hanaper*, fr. O.F. *hanap*, a drinking-cup. (2) O.E. *hamelian*, to maim.]
HAMSTRING (ham'string)*n.* one of the tendons of the ham;—*v.t.* to lame by cutting the tendon of the ham.
HAND (hand) *n.* the palm with the fingers; pointer of a clock or watch; a workman; performance; skill; side; direction; manner of writing;—*v.t.* to give; deliver; lead; trim or furl. [O.E.]
HANDBILL (hand'bil) *n.* a pruning hook; a loose printed sheet for circulation.

HANDBOOK (hand'book) *n.* a guide-book.
HANDCUFF (hand'kuf) *n.* a manacle to confine the hands;—*v.t.* to fetter with handcuffs.
HANDFUL (hand'fool) *n.* as much as the hand can hold.
HAND-GALLOP (hand'gal-up) *n.* a gentle gallop.
HAND-GLASS (hand'glås) *n.* a small g ass frame placed over plants to foster them.
HANDICAP (han'di-kap) *n.* a race run with additional weights or allowances to the competitors.
HANDICRAFT (han'di-kräft) *n.* manual occupation. [ously.
HANDILY (han'd-li) *ad.* skilfully; dexter-
HANDINESS (han'di-nes) *n.* ease in performance.
HANDIWORK (han'di-wurk) *n.* work done by skill of hand; any work or product.
HANDKERCHIEF (hang'kẹr-chif) *n.* a cloth used for the face or neck.
HANDLE (han'dl) *v.t.* to touch; manage; treat of;—*n.* the part by which the thing is held. [O.E., fr. HAND.]
HAND-LOOM (hand'lōōm) *n.* a loom worked by the hand.
HANDMAID (hand'mād) *n.* a waiting-maid.
HAND-MILL (hand'mil) *n.* a mill for grinding coffee, pepper, etc., worked by the hand.
HANDSEL (hand'sel, han'sel) *n.* earnest;— *v.t.* to use or do for the first time. [O.E. *handselen*.]
HANDSOME (han'sum) *a.* well-formed, beautiful; generous. [O.E., fr. HAND and suff. *-sum*.] [liberally.
HANDSOMELY (han'sum-li) *ad.* gracefully;
HANDY (han'di) *a.* ready; dexterous.
HANG (hang) *v.t.* or *i.* (*pret.* HANGED, HUNG) to suspend; put to death on a gallows; display; swing free; lean on; linger. [O.E. *hangian*.]
HANGAR (hang'ẹr) *n.* a shed in which aeroplanes are kept. [F.]
HANGER (hang'ẹr) *n.* a broadsword; that by which anything hangs.
HANGER-ON (hang'ẹr-on) *n.* a servile dependant.
HANK (hangk) *n.* a skein of thread. [Scand. =a hasp.]
HANKER (hang'kẹr) *v.i.* to long for. [Freq. of HANG.]
HANKERING (hang'kẹr-ing) *n.* an eager craving.
HANSOM (han'sum) *n.* a two-wheeled cab, with the driver's seat behind. [Fr. *Hansom* the inventor, 1803-1882.]
HAP (hap) *n.* that which comes unexpectedly; chance; fortune; lot;—*v.i.* to happen; befall. [Scand. =good luck.]
HAPHAZARD (hap-haz'ạrd) *n.* a chance; accident.
HAPLESS (hap'les) *a.* unhappy; unfortunate.
HAPLY (hap'li) *ad.* perhaps; by chance.
HAPPEN (hap'n) *v.i.* to come to pass.
HAPPILY (hap'i-li) *ad.* luckily; fortunately.
HAPPINESS (hap'i-nes) *n.* state of enjoyment.
HAPPY (hap'i) *a.* in a state of felicity; fortunate; ready; easy; favourable. [Fr. HAP.]
HARANGUE (hạ-rang') *n.* a popular pompous speech; declamation;—*v.t.* or *i.* to make such a speech. [O.F., fr. O. H. Ger. =a ring of auditors.]
HARASS (har'ạs) *v.t.* to fatigue; vex; annoy; torment. [F. *harasser*.] [or vex.
HARASSING (har'ạs-ing) *a.* tending to annoy
HARBINGER (här'bin-jẹr) *n.* a forerunner. [M.E. *herbergeour*. See HARBOUR.]
HARBOUR (här'bur) *n.* a haven for ships;— *v.t.* to lodge; shelter; entertain. [M.E., *herberwe*, fr. O.E. *here*, an army and *beorgan* to protect. Cf. Ger. *Herberge*.]
HARBOURAGE (här'bur-ij) *n.* a place of shelter; entertainment.

HARBOUR-DUES (här'bur-düz) *n.pl.* charges for accommodation in a harbour.

HARD (härd) *ad.* close; near; diligently;—*a.* not easily penetrated; difficult to understand, do, or bear; unjust; unfeeling; close; stiff. [O.E. *heard*. Cf. Ger. *hart*.]

HARDEN (här'dn) *v.t.* or *i.* to make or grow hard.

HARD-HEARTED (härd'bär-ted) *a.* unfeeling.

HARDIHOOD (här'di-hood) *n.* boldness.

HARDILY (här'di-li) *ad.* boldly; stoutly.

HARDINESS (här'di-nes) *n.* firm intrepidity; assurance.

HARDLY (härd'li) *ad.* not easily; scarcely; harshly. [hard.

HARDNESS (härd'nes) *n.* the quality of being hard.

HARDSHIP (härd'ship) *n.* severe toil; burden of any kind.

HARDWARE (härd'wär) *n.* wares made of iron, etc.

HARDY (här'di) *a.* strong; stout; bold. [O.F. *hardi*.]

HARE (här) *n.* a small, timid animal. [O.E. *hara*. Cf. Ger. *Hase*.]

HAREBELL (här'bel) *n.* a plant with bell-shaped blue flowers; bluebell.

HARE-BRAINED (här'bränd) *a.* wild; giddy.

HAREHOUND (här'hound) *n.* a dog for hunting hares. [hare's.

HARELIP (här'lip) *n.* a divided lip like a

HAREM (hä'rem, hä'rem) *n.* in an Eastern house the apartments reserved for females; the inmates. [A. =sacred.]

HARICOT (har'i-kō) *n.* the French kidney bean; a stew of meat and vegetables. [F.]

HARK (härk) *v.i.* to hear; listen;—*inter.* hear. [Fr. HEARKEN.]

HARLEQUIN (här'le-kwin) *n.* a buffoon. [F., perhaps of Teut. origin.]

HARLOT (här'lut) *n.* a lewd woman. [O.F. *arlot*, a base fellow.]

HARLOTRY (här'lut-ri) *n.* trade or practice of prostitution.

HARM (härm) *n.* injury; hurt;—*v.t.* to injure; hurt. [O.E. *hearm*.]

HARMFUL (härm'fool) *a.* hurtful; injurious.

HARMLESS (härm'les) *a.* innocent; not hurtful; unhurt.

HARMLESSLY (härm'les-li) *ad.* without inflicting or receiving injury.

HARMONICAL (här-mon'i-kạl) *a.* relating to harmony; musical.

HARMONIOUS (här-mō'ni-us) *a.* agreeing together; musical.

HARMONIOUSLY (här-mō'ni-us-li) *a.* with harmony.

HARMONISE (här'mu-niz) *v.t.* or *i.* to make harmonious; agree; adjust; reconcile.

HARMONIST (här'mu-nist) *n.* a composer of music; one who shows the harmony of parallel passages, as in the four gospels.

HARMONIUM (här-mō'ni-um) *n.* a musical wind instrument resembling a small organ.

HARMONY (här'mu-ni) *n.* concord of sound; agreement. [F., fr. L., fr. G. *harmonia*, fr. *harmos*, fitting, fr. *arein*, to fit.]

HARNESS (här'nes) *n.* furniture for a horse, etc.;—*v.t.* to put on harness. [O.F. *harneis*, armour.]

HARP (härp) *n.* instrument of music;—*v.i.* to play on a harp; dwell on. [O.E. *hearpe*. Cf. Ger. *Harfe*.]

HARPER (här'per) *n.* one who plays on a harp.

HARPOON (här-pōōn') *n.* a barbed spear;—*v.t.* to strike with a harpoon. [F. *harpon*, fr. *harpe*, a clamp, fr. L. *harpa*, fr. G. *harpe*, a sickle.]

HARPOONER (här-pōō'ner) *n.* one who throws the harpoon.

Harp.

HARPSICHORD (härp'si-kord) *n.* a stringed instrument of music. [F. *harpe-chorde*.]

HARPY (här'pi) *n.* a fabulous animal; an extortioner. [O.F. *harpie*, fr. L. *harpyia*, fr. G. (pl.) *harpyiai*, snatches, fr. G. *harpazein* to snatch.]

HARQUEBUSE (här'kwe-bus) *n.* a kind of hand-gun supported on a rest. [See ARQUE-BUSE.]

HARRIER (har'i-er) *n.* a hound for hunting hares; a kind of hawk. [Fr. HARE.]

HARROW (har'ō) *n.* an instrument to break or smooth land;—*v.t.* to break with a harrow; harass. [O.E. *hearge*.]

HARROWING (har'ō-ing) *a.* heartrending; distressful.

HARRY (har'i) *v.t.* or *i.* to plunder; pillage; ravage. [O.E. *hergian*, ravage, fr. *here*, army.]

HARSH (härsh) *a.* rough to the touch, taste, ear, or feelings. [M.E. *harsk*, fr. Scand.]

HARSHLY (härsh'li) *ad.* roughly; gratingly; rudely.

HARSHNESS (härsh-nes) *n.* roughness; severity.

HART (härt) *n.* a stag or male deer. [O.E. *heort*, literally the horned animal. Cf. Ger. *Hirsch*.]

HARTBEEST (härt'bēst) *n.* a large African antelope. Also **HARTEBEEST**. [D.]

HARTSHORN (härts'horn) *n.* horn of harts; sal-ammonia.

HART'S-TONGUE (härts'tung) *n.* a common British fern.

HARUM-SCARUM (här'um-skär'um) *a.* wild; flighty; rash. [Fr. HARE, fr. its unreasoning haste and fright, and SCARE, terrify.]

HARVEST (här'vest) *n.* the season for gathering ripe grain; the crop gathered; effects; —*v.t.* to gather a crop when ripe. [O.E. *hærfest*. Cf. Ger. *Herbst*.]

HASH (hash) *v.t.* to mince; chop;—*n.* minced meat; mess; bungled state. [F. *hacher*, fr. *hache*, hatchet.]

HASP (hasp) *n.* a clasp for a staple. [O.E. *hæpse*. Cf. Ger. *Haspe*.]

HASSOCK (has'uk) *n.* a mat to kneel on. [O.E. *hassuc*, tuft of coarse grass.]

HAST (hast) second person of HAVE.

HASTE (hāst) *n.* celerity of motion or action; hurry; speed; despatch;—*v.t.* or *i.* to make speed; hurry. [O.F. *haste* =F. *hâte*, fr. Teut. Cf. Ger. *Hast*.]

HASTILY (hās'ti-li) *ad.* with haste.

HASTY (hās'ti) *a.* quick in action; passionate; rash; forward. [*hœt*.

HAT (hat) *n.* a covering for the head. [O.E.

HATCH (hach) (1) *v.t.* to produce young from eggs; contrive;—*n.* a brood;—(2) an opening in a deck or a floor; lid or cover of such opening. [(1) Etym. unknown. (2) O.E. *hœc*, hurdle.]

HATCHES (hach'ez) *n.pl.* the opening in a ship's deck. [See HATCH (2).]

HATCHET (hach'et) *n.* a small axe. [F. *hachette*, dim. of *hache*, an axe.]

HATCHWAY (hach'wä) *n.* an opening in a ship's deck. [See HATCH (2).]

HATE (hāt) *v.t.* to dislike greatly;—*n.* great dislike; enmity. [O.E. *hete*, fr. *hatian*. Cf. Ger. *Hass*.]

HATEFUL (hāt'fool) *a.* exciting great dislike.

HATEFULNESS (hāt'fool-nes) *n.* quality of exciting dislike or aversion.

HATRED (hā'tred) *n.* ill-will; hate.

HATTER (hat'er) *n.* a maker or seller of hats.

HAUBERK (haw'berk) *n.* a coat or shirt formed of interwoven steel rings. [O.F. *hauberc*, fr. O. H. Ger. *Hals*, neck, and *beorgan*, protect.]

HAUGH (häh) *n.* a piece of low-lying, flat ground near a river. [Scot., fr. O.E. *healh*.]

HAUGHTILY (haw'ti-li) *ad.* with pride and contempt.

HAUGHTINESS (haw'ti-nes) *n.* supercilious pride.

Fāte, fär, ạdo; mē, her; mīne; nōte; tūne; mōōn.

HAUGHTY (haw'ti) *a.* proud and overbearing. [O.F. *hautain*, fr. *haut*, high, fr. L. *altus*, high.]

HAUL (haul) *v.t.* to draw with force;—*n.* a pull; draught. [Same as HALE (2).]

HAULAGE (haw'lij) *n.* act of hauling; charge for hauling. [See HAUL.]

HAULM (hawm) *n.* stalk of grain of any kind; straw. [O.E. *healm.*]

HAUNCH (hänsh) *n.* the thigh. [O.F. *hanche*, fr. O. H. Ger.]

HAUNT (hänt) *v.t.* or *i.* to frequent;—*n.* a place of frequent resort. [O.F. *hanter.*]

HAVE (hav) *v.t.* [*pret.* and *pp.* HAD] to hold; possess; obtain; receive; procure; beget; produce; contain; be under constraint or obligation. [O.E. *habban*. Cf. Ger. *haben.*]

HAVEN (hā'vn) *n.* a harbour. [O.E. *hæfent*; Ger. *Hafen.*]

HAVERSACK (hav'er-sak) *n.* strong cloth bag, in which a soldier carries his rations. [F. *havresac*, fr. Ger. *Habersack*, oatsack, fr. *Haber*, *Hafer*, oats.]

HAVOC (hav'uk) *n.* waste; destruction;— *v.t.* to lay waste. [O.F. *havot*, plunder.]

HAWK (hawk) (1) *v.t.* or *i.* to force up phlegm; —(2) cry goods;—(3) *n.* a bird of prey. [(1) Imit. (2) O. L. Ger. (3) O.E. *hafoc.*]

HAWKER (haw'ker) *n.* one who hawks. [See HAWK (2).]

HAWK-EYED (hawk'id) *a.* having acute sight.

HAWSER (haw'zer) *n.* a small cable; a large rope. [Scand. *hals*, neck.]

HAY (hā) *n.* grass dried for fodder;—*v.t.* to dry grass for preservation. [O.E. *hig.* Cf. Ger. *Heu.*]

HAYLOFT (hā'loft) *n.* a scaffold for hay.

HAYMAKER (hā'mā-ker) *n.* one who cuts and dries grass for hay.

HAZARD (haz'ard) *n.* risk of loss or evil; danger;—*v.t.* or *i.* to expose to chance; run a risk. [F. *hasard*, fr. A. through Sp.]

HAZARDOUS (haz'ar-dus) *a.* that exposes to danger; perilous; uncertain.

HAZE (hāz) *n.* a thin mist or fog. [Etym. unknown.]

HAZEL (hā'zl) *n.* a shrub bearing nuts;—*a.* like a hazel-nut; brown. [O.E. *hæsel.* Cf. Ger. *Hasel.*]

HAZINESS (hā'zi-nes) *n.* state of being hazy. [See HAZE.]

HAZY (hā'zi) *a.* foggy; misty; obscure. [See HAZE.]

HE (hē) *pron.* of the third person, masculine gender, referring to some man or male. [O.E.]

HEAD (hed) *n.* upper part of the body; the chief; front; source; brain; topic; point; strength; resistance;—*v.t.* or *i.* to lead; top. [O.E. *heafod.* Cf. Ger. *Haupt.*]

HEADACHE (hed'āk) *n.* pain in the head.

HEAD-DRESS (hed'dres) *n.* covering worn on the head.

HEADER (hed'er) *n.* one who heads pins or nails; a leap into the water head foremost.

HEADINESS (hed'i-nes) *n.* rashness; intoxicating quality in liquors.

HEADING (hed'ing) *n.* timber for heads of casks; lines at the head; title. [See HEAD.]

HEADLAND (hed'land) *n.* a promontory.

HEADLONG (hed'long) *a.* rash; precipitate; —*ad.* precipitately.

HEADMOST (hed'most) *a.* most advanced; first in the line.

HEADPIECE (hed'pēs) *n.* a helmet; the head as the seat of the understanding.

HEADQUARTERS (hed'kwawr-terz) *n.pl.* quarters of a chief commander.

HEADSTALL (hed'stawl) *n.* part of a bridle.

HEADSTONE (hed'stōn) *n.* corner stone of a building; stone at the head of a grave.

HEADSTRONG (hed'strong) *a.* obstinate.

HEADWAY (hed'wā) *n.* progress of an advancing ship.

HEAD-WIND (hed'wind) *n.* wind blowing against the ship's head.

HEADY (hed'i) *a.* hasty; rash; wilful; intoxicating.

HEAL (hēl) *v.t.* to cure;—*v.i.* to become well. [O.E. *hælan*, fr. *hal*, whole. Cf. Ger. *heil.* See HAIL, HALE, WHOLE.]

HEALTH (helth) *n.* freedom from sickness; sound state of body and mind. [O.E. *hælth*, fr. *hal*, whole.]

HEALTHFUL (helth'fool) *a.* free from disease; wholesome.

HEALTHINESS (hel'thi-nes) *n.* state of being in health.

HEALTHY (hel'thi) *a.* free from disease.

HEAP (hēp) *n.* a pile; accumulation;—*v.t.* to pile; amass; accumulate. [O.E.]

HEAR (hēr) *v.t.* to perceive by the ear;—*v.i.* to be told. [O.E. *hyran.* Cf. Ger. *hören.*]

HEARER (hēr'er) *n.* one who hears.

HEARING (hēr'ing) *n.* the sense of perceiving sounds; audience.

HEARKEN (bār'kn) *v.i.* to listen; lend the ear; attend to; grant. [O.E. *hyrcnian*, fr. *hyran*, hear.]

HEARSAY (hēr'sā) *n.* report; rumour; common talk.

HEARSE (hers) *n.* a carriage to bear the dead. [O.F. *herce*, fr. L. *hirpex*, harrow.]

HEART (härt) *n.* the organ of the blood's motion; inner part; seat of love; spirit. [O.E. *heorte.* Cf. Ger. *Herz.*]

HEARTACHE (härt'āk) *n.* deep sorrow.

HEARTBURN (härt'burn) *n.* an acrid sensation in the stomach.

HEARTBURNING (härt'bur-ning) *n.* secret discontent or enmity.

HEARTFELT (härt'felt) *a.* sincere; deep.

HEARTH (härth) *n.* place on which fire is made. [O.E. *heorth.* Cf. Ger. HERD.]

HEARTILY (här'ti-li) *ad.* from the heart; sincerely.

HEARTINESS (här'ti-nes) *n.* sincerity.

HEARTLESS (härt'les) *a.* spiritless; void of affection.

HEARTLESSNESS (härt'les-nes) *n.* want of affection.

HEARTY (här'ti) *a.* healthy; sincere.

HEAT (hēt) *n.* great warmth; glow;—*v.t.* to make hot;—*v.i.* to grow hot. [O.E. *hætu*, fr. *hat*, hot.]

HEATER (hē'ter) *n.* a lump of hot iron, enclosed in an iron box, for smoothing clothes.

HEATH (hēth) *n.* a shrub; a place overgrown with shrubs. [O.E. *hæth.* Cf. Ger. *Heide.*]

HEATHEN (hē'THn) *n.* a pagan; gentile; one who is ignorant of the true God;—*a.* Gentile; pagan. [O.E. *hæthen*, lit. a heath-dweller. Cf. PAGAN.]

HEATHENISH (hē'THn-ish) *a.* like heathen; rude; idolatrous.

HEATHENISM (hē'THn-izm) *n.* paganism.

HEATHER (heTH'er) *n.* heath. [See HEATH.]

HEATHY (hē'thi) *a.* full of heath. Also **HEATHERY.** [See HEATH.]

HEATING (hē'ting) *a.* imparting heat.

HEAVE (hēv) *v.t.* [*pret.* and *pp.* HEAVED, HOVE.] to lift; cause to swell; pant; cast;—*v.i.* to rise and fall; swell; pant; retch;—*n.* throw; upward motion; swell. [O.E. *hebban.* Cf. Ger. *heben.*]

HEAVEN (hev'n) *n.* the region of the air; expanse of the sky; place of the blessed. [O.E. *heofon*, orig. ceiling; conn. with HEAVE.]

HEAVENLY (hev'n-li) *a.* pertaining to heaven. [See HEAVEN.]

HEAVENWARD (hev'n-ward) *ad.* toward heaven.

HEAVER (hē'ver) *n.* one who heaves.

HEAVINESS (hev'i-nes) *n.* weight; depression.

HEAVY (hev'i) *a.* weighty; grievous; dull; burdensome; stiff; dense; copious; gloomy; expensive. [O.E. *hefig*, fr. HEAVE.]

HEBE (hē'bē) *n.* the goddess of youth. [Myth.]

HEBETUDE (heb'e-tūd) *n.* bluntness; dullness. [L.]

HEBRAIC (hē-brā'ik) *a.* pertaining to the Hebrews. [See **HEBREW**.]

HEBRAICALLY (hē-brā'i-kal-i) *ad.* in the manner of the Hebrews; from right to left. [See **HEBREW**.]

HEBRAIST (hē'brā-ist) *n.* one versed in Hebrew. [See **HEBREW**.]

HEBREW (hē'brōō) *n.* a Jew; language of the Jews. [F. *hébreu*, fr. L., fr. G. *hebraios*, fr. H. =those across Euphrates.]

HECATOMB (hek'a-tom, hek'a-tōōm) *n.* a sacrifice of a hundred oxen. [G., fr. *hekaton*, 100, and *bous*, ox.]

HECTIC (hek'tik) *n.* a kind of fever attending consumption;—*a.* feverish; consumptive. [G. *hektikos*, orig. habitual, fr. *hexis*, habit, fr. *hexo*, I shall have.]

HECTOR (hek'ter) *n.* a bully;—*v.t.* or *i.* to threaten; bully; bluster. [Fr. G. *Hector*, the Trojan hero.]

HEDGE (hej) *n.* a thicket of shrubs;—*v.t.* to make a hedge; fence; obstruct;—*v.i.* to skulk; bet on both sides. [O.E. *heog.* Cf. Ger. *Hecke.*]

HEDGE-BILL (hej'bil) *n.* a cutting hook for dressing hedges.

HEDGEHOG (hej'hog) *n.* a small insectivorous quadruped covered with prickly spines.

HEED (hēd) *v.t.* to mind; observe;—*n.* care; attention; notice. [O.E. *hedan.*]

HEEDFUL (hēd'fool) *a.* attentive; watchful.

HEEDFULLY (hēd'fool-i) *ad.* attentively; cautiously.

HEEDFULNESS (hēd'fool-nes) *n.* attention; wary caution.

HEEDLESS (hēd'les) *a.* careless; inattentive; negligent.

HEEDLESSLY (hēd'les-li) *ad.* negligently.

HEEDLESSNESS (hēd'les-nes) *n.* carelessness.

HEEL (hēl) (1) *n.* the hind part of a foot;— *v.t.* to add a heel.— (2) *v.i.* to lean. [(1) O.E. *hela.* (2) O.E. *hyldan.*]

HEFT (heft) *n.* a handle; an effort to lift; a heave.

HEGIRA (he-jīr'a) *n.* the Mohammedan epoch, reckoned from the flight of Mohammed from Mecca, July 16, 622. [A. =flight.]

HEIFER (hef'er) *n.* a young cow. [O.E. *heahfore.*]

HEIGH-HO (hī'hō) *ex.* denoting languor, etc. [Imit.]

HEIGHT (hīt) *n.* distance from a point below; an elevated place; summit; utmost degree. [For *highth*, fr. O.E. *heahthu*, fr. **HIGH**.]

HEIGHTEN (hī'tn) *v.t.* to raise higher; advance.

HEINOUS (hā'nus) *a.* characterised by great wickedness; atrocious; flagrant. [O.F., fr. *haine*, hate, fr. *hair*, fr. Teut.]

HEINOUSLY (hā'nus-li) *ad.* hatefully.

HEIR (ār) *n.* he who inherits the property of another;—*v.t.* to inherit. [O.F., fr. L. (acc.) *herem*, for *heredem.* See **HEREDITY**.]

HEIR-APPARENT (ār-a-pār'ent) *n.* one having full right to the succession.

HEIRESS (ār'es) *n.* a female heir.

HEIRLESS (ār'les) *a.* without heirs.

HEIRLOOM (ār'lōōm) *n.* any movable property which descends to the heir. [Fr. **HEIR** and **LOOM** =a belonging.]

HEIRSHIP (ār'ship) *n.* state of an heir.

HELD (held) *pret.* and *pp.* of **HOLD**.

HELIOGRAPH (hē'li-u-graf) *n.* an apparatus for telegraphing by the sun's rays. [Fr. G. *helios*, the sun, and *graphein*, write.]

HELIOLATRY (hē-li-ol'a-tri) *n.* worship of the sun. [G. *helios*, the sun, and *latreia*, worship.]

HELL (hel) *n.* the place of the devil and the damned. [O.E. *hel*, orig. that which hides.]

HELM (helm) (1) *n.* the instrument by which a ship is steered;— (2) *n.* a helmet. [(1) O.E. *helma.* (2) O.E. *helm.*]

HELMET (hel'met) *n.* armour for the head. [Dim. of **HELM** (2).]

HELMSMAN (helmz'man) *n.* man at the helm; steersman. [See **HELM** (1) and **MAN**.]

HELOT (hē'lot, hel'ut) *n.* a Spartan slave. [L., fr. G. *Heilos*, pl. *Heilotes*.]

HELP (help) *v.t.* to aid; assist; prevent;— *v i.* to lend aid; contribute;—*n.* aid; support; relief. [O.E. *helpan.* Cf. Ger. *helfen.*]

HELPER (hel'per) *n.* one who assists.

HELPFUL (help'fool) *a.* affording aid.

HELPLESS (help'les) *a.* destitute of help or of relief; irremediable.

HELPLESSLY (help'les-li) *ad.* without help; without effort.

HELPLESSNESS (help'les-nes) *n.* want of help or support.

HELPMATE (help'māt) *n.* companion or helper. Also written **HELPMEET**.

HELTER-SKELTER (hel'ter-skel'ter) *ad.* in hurried confusion. [Imit.]

HEM (hem) *n.* border of a garment; sort of half cough;—*v.t.* to form a border; shut in;—*v.i.* to cough; hesitate. [E., conn. with *ham* in place names.]

HEMISPHERE (hem'i-sfēr) *n.* the half of a sphere. [G. *hemi-*, half.]

HEMISPHERICAL (hem-i-sfer'i-kal) *a.* containing half a sphere.

HEMLOCK (hem'lok) *n.* a poisonous plant. [O.E. *hymlice.*]

HEMORRHAGE (hem'u-rij) *n.* a flowing of blood from a rupture. [F., fr. L., fr. G., fr. *haima*, and *rhegnunai*, burst.]

HEMP (hemp) *n.* a plant whose fibres are used for cloth and cordage. [O.E. *hænep.*]

HEMPEN (hem'pn) *a.* made of hemp.

HEN (hen) *n.* the female of birds. [O.E. *henn*, fr. *hana*, cock. Cf. Ger. *Henne*, fr. *Hahn*.]

HENBANE (hen'bān) *n.* a poisonous plant, sometimes used for opium.

HENCE (hens) *ad.* from this place, time, cause, or source. [M.E. *hennes*, fr. O.E. *heonan*; adv. suff. *-s*.]

HENCEFORTH (hens'fōrth) *ad.* from this time.

HENCEFORWARD (hens-for'ward) *ad.* from this time forward.

HENCHMAN (hensh'man) *n.* an attendant; a page. [For *hengestman*, fr. O.E. *hengest*, horse.]

HENCOOP (hen'kōōp) *n.* a large cage for poultry.

HENPECKED (hen'pekt) *a.* ruled over by a wife.

HEPATIC (he-pat'ik) *a.* belonging to the liver. [G.]

HEPTAGON (hep'ta-gun) *n.* a figure of seven sides and angles. [G. *hepta*, seven, and *gonia*, angle.]

HEPTAGONAL (hep-tag'u-nal) *a.* having seven sides.

HEPTARCHY (hep'tar-ki) *n.* government by seven rulers. [Fr. G. *hepta*, seven, and *archia*, fr. *archein*, rule.]

HER (her) *a.* belonging to a female;—*pron. obj.* of *she.* [O.E. *hire* (gen. dat.) *heo*, she.]

Heptagon

HERALD (her'ald) *n.* an officer who regulates coats of arms; a forerunner;—*v.t.* to proclaim; usher in. [O.F. *heralt*, fr. O. H. Ger. *Hari*, army, and *walt-an*, **WIELD**.]

HERALDIC (he-ral'dik) *a.* pertaining to heraldry.

HERALDRY (her'ald-ri) *n.* the art or office of a herald.

HERB (herb) *n.* a plant with a succulent stalk. [F. *herbe*, fr. L. (acc.) *herbam*.]

HERBACEOUS (her-bā'shus) *a.* belonging to herbs. [See **HERB**.]

HERBAGE (her'bij) *n.* herbs collectively; grass; pasture.

HERBAL (her'bal) *n.* a book on plants; collection of plants dried;—*a.* pertaining to herbs.

HERBALIST (her'bal-ist) *n.* one skilled in herbs.

HERBARY (her'ba-ri) *n.* a garden of herbs.

HERBIFEROUS (her-bif'e-rus) *a.* bearing herbs. [HERB and L. *fero,* carry.]

HERBORISE (her'bu-riz) *v.i.* to search 'for plants; botanise; to take a plant-like form, as minerals. [See HERB.]

HERCULEAN (her-kū'le-an) *a.* very strong, great, or difficult. [Fr. G. *Hercules.*]

HERD (herd) *n.* a collection; drove;—*v.t.* or *i.* to associate; tend cattle. [O.E. *heord.* Cf. Ger. *Heirde.*]

HERDSMAN (herdz'man) *n.* one who tends herds; an owner of cattle.

HERE (hēr) *ad.* in this place or state. [O.E. *her.* Cf. Ger. *hier.*]

HEREABOUTS (hēr'a-bouts) *ad.* about or near this place.

HEREAFTER (hēr-áf'ter) *ad.* in time after the present.

HEREAT (hēr-at') *ad.* at this; on this account.

HEREBY (hēr-bi') *ad.* by this.

HEREDITARILY (he-red'i-ta-ri-li) *ad.* by inheritance.

HEREDITARY (he-red'i-ta-ri) *a.* descending by inheritance.

HEREDITY (he-red'i-ti) *n.* transmission of qualities from ancestors to their offspring. [L. (acc.) *hereditatem,* fr. stem *heredi-,* of *heres,* HEIR.]

HEREIN (hēr-in') *ad.* in this.

HEREOF (hēr-ov') *ad.* of this; from this.

HEREON (hēr-on') *ad.* upon this.

HERESIARCH (he-rē'zi-ärk) *n.* a chief in heresy. [G., fr. *-archos,* leader, fr. *archein,* rule. See HERESY.]

HERESY (her'e-si) *n.* error in doctrines; any unsound opinion. [O.F., fr. L. *hæresis,* choice, heresy, fr. G., fr. *hair-ein,* take.]

HERETIC (her'e-tik) *n.* one who errs in religious faith. [G. *haireticos,* able to choose.]

HERETICAL (he-ret'i-kal) *a.* containing heresy.

HERETICALLY (he-ret'i-kal-i) *ad.* in a heretical manner.

HERETOFORE (hēr-tu-fōr') *ad.* formerly.

HEREUNTO (hēr-un-tôô') *ad.* to this.

HEREWITH (hēr-with') *ad.* with this.

HERITABLE (her'i-ta-bl) *a.* that may be inherited. [Fr. F. *hériter,* fr. L. *hereditare,* fall HEIR to.]

HERITAGE (her'i-tij) *n.* inheritance. [See HERITABLE.]

HERITOR (her'i-ter) *n.* a landlord in a parish.

HERMENEUTICS (her-me-nū'tiks) *n.pl.* art or science of interpretation. [G., fr. *hermeneutes,* interpreter; conn. with *Hermes.*]

HERMETIC (her-met'ik) *a.* perfectly close. [Fr. *Hermes,* patron of alchemists, who called their science 'Hermetic science.']

HERMETICALLY (her-met'i-kal-i) *ad.* closely.

HERMIT (her'mit) *n.* one who lives in solitude. [F. *hermite,* fr. Late L. (acc.) *heremitam.* Doublet of EREMITE.]

HERMITAGE (her'mi-tij) *n.* a hermit's dwelling.

HERNIA (her'ni-a) *n.* a rupture or protusion of any internal organ. [L.]

HERO (hē'rō) *n.* a brave man;—*pl.* HEROES. [O.F. *heroe* (3 syll.), fr. L. (acc.) *heroem,* fr. G. *heros.*]

HEROIC (he-rō'ik) *a.* becoming a hero.

HEROICALLY (he-rō'i-kal-i) *ad.* intrepidly.

HEROINE (her'ō-in) *n.* a female hero.

HEROISM (her'ō-izm) *n.* distinguished bravery; gallantry.

HERON (her'un) *n.* a large water-fowl. [O.F. *hairon* =F. *héron,* fr. O. Ger. *heiger.* See EGRET.]

HERO-WORSHIP (hē'rō-wur-ship) *n.* inordinate admiration of a great man.

HERPES (her'pēz) *n.* a disease of the skin. [L., fr. G.]

HERPETIC (her-pet'ik) *a.* relating to herpes. [See HERPES.]

HERRING (her'ing) *n.* a small sea-fish. [O.E. *hæring.* Cf. Ger. *Häring.*]

HERRINGBONE (her'ing-bōn) *a.* denoting a kind of cross stitch in worsted work, and of ashlar in masonry.

HERSELF (her-self') *pron.* the female in person; used emphatically or reflexively.

HESITANCY (hez'i-tan-si) *n.* uncertainty; doubt. [See HESITATE.]

HESITATE (hez'i-tāt) *v.i.* to pause in deciding or acting; be in doubt or suspense; stammer. [L. (part.) *hæsitatus,* fr. *hæsitare,* stick fast, fr. (part.) *hæsus,* stuck, fr. *hærere.* See ADHERE.]

HESITATION (hez-i-tā'shun) *n.* a pausing; a stammering in speech.

HESPER (hes'per) *n.* the evening star. Also **HESPERUS.** [L., fr. G. *Hesperos.*]

HETERODOX (het'e-ru-doks) *a.* contrary to Scripture doctrine; heretical. [Fr. G. *heteros,* other, and *doxa,* opinion.]

HETERODOXY (het'e-ru-dok-si) *n.* heresy.

HEW (hū) *v.t.* [*pret.* HEWED; *pp.* HEWED, HEWN] to cut off chips and pieces; chop. [O.E. *heawan.* Cf. Ger. *hauen.*]

HEXAGON (hek'sa-gun) *n.* a figure with six sides and angles. [G. *hex,* six, and *gonia,* angle.]

HEXAGONAL (hek-sag'u-nal) *a.* having six sides and angles.

HEXAHEDRON (hek-sa-hē'drun) *n.* a body of six equal sides; a cube. [G. *hex,* six, and *hedra,* base.]

Hexagon.

HEXAMETER (hek-sam'e-ter) *n.* a verse of six metrical feet. [L., fr. G. *hex,* six, and *metron,* a measure.]

HIATUS (hi-ā'tus) *n.* a chasm; gap. [L. (part.) *hiatus,* fr. *hiare,* to gape.]

HIBERNAL (hi-ber'nal) *a.* pertaining to winter. [Fr. *hibernus,* wintry, fr. *hiems,* winter.]

HIBERNATE (hi-ber'nāt) *v.i.* to pass the winter in a torpid state. [L. (part.) *hibernatus,* fr. *hibernare,* fr. *hibernus,* wintry.]

HIBERNATION (hi-ber-nā'shun) *n.* wintering in torpor or close quarters.

HIBERNIAN (hi-ber'ni-an) *n.* a native of Ireland;—*a.* belonging to Ireland. [L.]

HICCOUGH, HICCUP (hik'up) *n.* a spasmodic affection of the stomach;—*v.i.* to have a hiccough. Also written HICKUP. [Imit. Cf. Ger. *Hickup.*]

HICKORY (hik'u-ri) *n.* a walnut-tree. [Amer. Indian.]

HIDALGO (hi-dal'gō) *n.* a man of noble birth. [Sp.]

HIDDEN (hid'n) *a.* not seen or known. [See HIDE (1).]

HIDE (hid) (1) *v.t.* or *i.* [*pret.* HID; *pp.* HID, HIDDEN] to conceal; cover; keep close; —(2) *n.* the skin of a beast;—(3) *n.* an old measure of land. [(1) O.E. *hydan,* to hide. (2) O.E. *hyd,* the cover. Cf. Ger. *Haut;* L. *cutis.* (3) *higid.*]

HIDEBOUND (hid'bound) *a.* having the skin too tight.

HIDEOUS (hid'e-us) *a.* shocking to the eye or ear; very ugly; discordant. [O.F. *hidos,* *hidus,* hideous.]

HIE (hi) *v.i.* to go in haste; repair to. [O.E. *higian,* make haste.]

HIERARCH (hi'e-rärk) *n.* the chief of a sacred order. [G., fr. *hieros,* sacred, and *archos,* leader, fr. *archein.*]

HIERARCHICAL (hi-e-rär'ki-kal) *a.* pertaining to church government.

HIERARCHY (hi'e-rär-ki) *n.* dominion in sacred things; order of celestial beings.

HIEROGLYPHIC (hī'e-ru-glif'ik) n. a mystical symbol in ancient writings;—a. expressive of meaning by symbols. [L., fr. G., fr. hieros, and glyphein, to carve.]

HIEROGRAPHIC (hī-e-ru-graf'ik) a. Pertaining to sacred writings.

HIEROGRAPHY (hi-e-rog'ra-fi) n. sacred writing. [G. hieros and graphein.]

HIEROPHANT (hī'e-ru-fant) n. a chief priest. [G. hierophantes, fr. hieros, sacred, phain- -ein, to show.]

HIGGLE (hig'l) v.i. to carry provisions about for sale; dispute and be hard in bargaining. [Variant of HAGGLE.]

HIGGLEDY-PIGGLEDY (hig'l-di-pig'l-di) ad. in utter confusion. [See HIGGLE.]

HIGGLER (hig'ler) n. one who higgles.

HIGH (hī) a. elevated; lofty; eminent; loud; severe; difficult; costly; intense; sharp; remote; vivid; tainted; sacred;—ad. aloft; eminently; profoundly;—n. an elevated place. [O.E. heah. Cf. Ger. hoch.]

HIGH-BORN (hī'born) a. being of noble extraction.

HIGH-FLIER (hī'flī-er) n. one of extravagant opinions.

HIGH-FLOWN (hī'flōn) a. elevated; turgid; extravagant.

HIGH-HANDED (hī'han-ded) a. overbearing; arbitrary.

HIGHLAND (hī'land) n. a mountainous country. [taineer.

HIGHLANDER (hī'lan-der) n. a Scotch moun-

HIGHLY (hī'li) ad. in a great degree.

HIGHNESS (hī'nes) n. altitude; a title of honour.

HIGH-PRESSURE (hī'presh-ūr) n. pressure exceeding that of atmosphere.

HIGH-PRIEST (hī'prēst) n. the chief priest.

HIGH-ROAD (hī'rōd) n. a public road; high-way.

HIGH-SEAS (hī'sēz) n.pl. the open ocean.

HIGH-SEASONED (hī'sē-znd) a. made rich and piquant with spices, etc.

HIGH-SPIRITED (hī'spir-i-ted) a. full of natural spirit; daring; irritable.

HIGH-WATER (hī'waw-ter) n. highest state of the tide.

HIGHWAY (hī'wā) n. a public road.

HIGHWAYMAN (hī'wā-man) n. a robber on the road.

HIGH-WROUGHT (hī'rawt) a. neatly finished.

HILARIOUS (hi-lā'ri-us) a. mirthful; jovial; jolly. [O.F., fr. L., fr. G. hilaros, cheerful.]

HILARITY (hi-lar'i-ti) n. mirth; gaiety. [See HILARIOUS.]

HILL (hil) n. an elevation of land;—v.t. to draw earth around. [O.E. hyll.]

HILLOCK (hil'uk) n. a small eminence. [Dim. of HILL.]

HILL-SIDE (hil'sid) n. the sloping face of a hill. [See HILL and SIDE.]

HILLY (hil'i) a. abounding with hills.

HILT (hilt) n. the handle of a sword, etc. [O.E.]

HIM (him) objective case of HE. [O.E.]

HIMSELF (him-self') pron. the emphatic form of HE.

HIND (hind) (1) a. backward; back;—(2) n. a she-stag;—(3) n. a rustic. [(1) O.E. hindan, back, hinder, backwards. (2) O.E. (3) O.E. hina, genitive pl. of hiwan, domestics.]

HINDER (hin'der) a. on the rear. [See HIND (1).]

HINDER (hin'der) v.t. to impede progress; keep back; interrupt; check; retard;— v.i. to raise obstacles. [O.E. hindrian. Cf. Ger. hindern.]

HINDERANCE (hin'der-ans) n. act of hinder-ing; that which hinders; obstruction; obstacle. Also HINDRANCE.

HINDERMOST (hin'der-mōst) a. behind all others. Also written HINDMOST.

HINDU (hin'dōō, hin-dōō') n. a native of Hindostan. [Skr.=Indies.]

HINDUSTANEE (hin-dōō-stā'ni) n. the language of the Hindus. [See HINDU.]

HINGE (hinj) n. the joint on which a door turns; that on which anything depends; —v.t. or i. to hang, turn, or depend upon. [M.E. heng, fr. hengen, to hang.]

HINT (hint) v.t. to suggest;—v.i. to allude to; —n. slight allusion. [Fr. O.E. hentan, to seize.]

HIP (hip) (1) n. joint of the thigh;—(2) n. fruit of the brier or wild dog-rose. [(1) O.E. hype. (2) O.E. heope.]

HIPPODROME (hip'u-drōm) n. a circus for horse-races, etc. [G. hippos, horse, and dromos, a course.]

HIPPOPOTAMUS (hip-u-pot's-mus) n. the river-horse. [G., fr. hippos, horse, and potamos, river.]

HIRE (hīr) v.t. to engage for pay; bribe;— n. wages; reward. [O.E. hyran, to hire, fr. hyr, wages. Cf. Ger. Heuer.]

HIRELING (hīr'ling) n. a mercenary;—a. serving for wages.

HIS (hiz) pron. possessive of HE. [O.E.]

HISS (his) v.t. or i. to make a sibilant sound; condemn by hissing;—n. a sibilant noise; expression of disapprobation. [Imit.]

HISSING (his'ing) n. noise of a hiss; expres-sion of dislike or condemnation; object of scorn.

HIST (hist) inter. hush; be silent. [Imit.]

HISTOLOGY (his-tol'ō-ji) n. the science that treats of the minute structure of the tissues of plants, animals, etc. [G., fr. histos, tissue, and logos, discourse.]

HISTORIAN (his-tō'ri-an) n. a writer or com-piler of history.

HISTORICAL (his-tor'i-kal) a. pertaining to history; containing history.

HISTORIOGRAPHER (his-tō-ri-og'ra-fer) n. a writer of history.

HISTORIOGRAPHY (his-tō-ri-og'ra-fi) n. the writing of history. [HISTORY, and G. graphein, write.]

HISTORY (his'tu-ri) n. a continuous narrative of past events; narration; description. [L., fr. G. historia, a learning by inquiry, fr. histor, knowing.]

HISTRIONIC (his-tri-on'ik) a. pertaining to the theatre. [L. histrionicus, fr. histrio, actor.]

HIT (hit) v.t. or i. [pret. and pp. HIT] to strike, reach, or touch a given point; suit; succeed; —n. a stroke or blow; lucky chance; happy thought or expression. [Scand.=to meet with.]

HITCH (hich) v.t. to hook; catch;—v.i. to move by jerks; be caught;—n. a catch or hook; sudden halt; defect or break; knot or noose in a rope; jerk. [M.E.]

HITCHING (hich'ing) n. fastening in a harness; bent knot; coil.

HITHER (hiTH'er) ad. to this place;—a. nearest to the speaker. [O.E. hider.]

HITHERMOST (hiTH'er-mōst) a. nearest this way.

HITHERTO (hiTH'er-tōō) ad. to this time.

HITHERWARD (hiTH'er-ward) ad. this way. [See HITHER; WARD for TOWARD.]

HITTER (hit'er) n. one who hits.

HIVE (hīv) n. a box for bees; a swarm of bees;—v.t. or i. to collect into a hive; lay up in store; dwell in company. [O.E. hyf.]

HOAR (hōr) a. gray with age; white. [O.E. har.]

HOARD (hōrd) v.t. to collect; amass;—n. a store laid up; a treasure. [O.E. hord.]

HOAR-FROST (hōr'frost) n. dew frozen.

HOARINESS (hōr'i-nes) n. state of being hoary.

HOARSE (hōrs) a. having the voice rough. [O.E. has.]

HOARSELY (hōrs'li) ad. with a hoarse voice.

HOARSENESS (hōrs'nes) n. state of being hoarse.

HOARY (hōr'i) *a.* gray; white.

HOAX (hōks) *n.* deception for sport;—*v.t.* to deceive; impose on. [Corr. fr. HOCUS.]

HOB (hob) (1) *n.* the nave of a wheel; side of a grate;—(2) *n.* a clown; a fairy. [(1) Cf. HUB. (2) Corr. fr. Rob*in*, Rob*ert*.]

HOBBLE (hob'l) *v.i.* to walk lamely;—*v.t.* to tie the legs together; clog;—*n.* a halting walk. [Freq. of HOP.]

HOBBLEDEHOY (hob'l-de-hoi) *n.* a lad between man and boy. [Etym. unknown.]

HOBBY (hob'i) *n.* a strong nag; a kind of hawk; a favourite plan or pursuit; a child's horse. [M.E. *hobin*, a nag.]

HOBGOBLIN (hob-gob'lin) *n.* apparition. [See HOB (2).]

HOBNAIL (hob'nāl) *n.* a thick-headed nail; a clown.

HOB-NOB (hob'nob) *v.i.* to drink familiarly. [O.E. *habban*, to have, and *nabban*, not to have.]

HOCK (hok) (1) *n.* the joint between the knee and fetlock;—(2) *n.* a Rhenish wine. [(1) O.E. *hoh*, heel. Cf. HOUGH. (2) Fr. *Hockheim*, in Germany.]

HOCKEY (hok'i) *n.* a game played with a ball and hooked club. [Perhaps fr. O.F. *hoquet*, a crook.]

HOCUS-POCUS (hō'kus-pō'kus) *n.* a juggler, or juggler's trick. [Corr. fr. L. *Hoc est corpus*, this is the body.]

HOD (hod) *n.* a bricklayer's tray for mortar. [Cf. F. *hotte*, basket.]

HODGE-PODGE (hoj'poj) *n.* a mixed mass. Also written HOTCH-POTCH. [F. *hocher*, to shake, and *pot*, pot.]

HOE (hō) *n.* a garden tool for weeds, etc.;—*v.t.* to cut with a hoe. [O.F. *houe*.]

HOG (hog) *n.* a swine; a sheep of a year old; a gluttonous fellow. [M.E. *hogge*, hog, a gelded hog, a young sheep, perhaps fr. *hag*, to cut.]

HOGGISH (hog'ish) *a.* filthy; greedy.

HOGSHEAD (hogz'hed) *n.* a measure of 63 gallons.

HOGSKIN (hog'skin) *n.* leather tanned from the skin of swine.

HOG'S-LARD (hogz'lärd) *n.* the fat of swine used as an ointment.

HOIDEN, HOYDEN (hoi'dn) *n.* a bold girl; a romp. [O.D. = a gipsy.]

HOIST (hoist) *v.t.* to raise; lift;—*n.* act of raising up; a machine for raising or lowering persons or goods; height of a sail. [M.E. *hoise*.]

HOITY-TOITY (hoi'ti-toi'ti) *ex.* noting surprise or disapprobation.

HOLD (hōld) (1) *v.t.* [*pret.* and *pp.* HELD] to stop; restrain; grasp; receive; keep;—*v.i.* to endure; refrain;—*n.* catch; support; custody;—(2) *n.* interior of a ship. [(1) O.E. *healdan*. (2) D. = a hole.]

HOLDER (hōld'er) *n.* one who or that which holds; tenant; clip; clasp.

HOLDFAST (hōld'fast) *n.* an iron hook.

HOLDING (hōld'ing) *n.* tenure; influence; farm held of a superior.

HOLE (hōl) *n.* a hollow place; a perforation; cell;—*v.t.* or *i.* to perforate; drive or go into a hole. [O.E. *hol*.]

HOLIDAY (hol'i-dā) *n.* a festival day. [E. = holy day.]

HOLINESS (hō'li-nes) *n.* perfect rectitude; moral purity; sanctity; title of the Pope. [See HOLY.]

HOLLAND (hol'and) *n.* a fine kind of linen. [From *Holland*.]

HOLLANDS (hol'andz) *n.* gin made in Holland. [See HOLLAND.]

HOLLOW (hol'ō) *a.* empty; deceitful; low; deep;—*n.* a low place; a hole;—*v.t.* to make hollow. [O.E. *holh*, a hollow place, fr. *hol*, hole.]

HOLLOWNESS (hol'ō-nes) *n.* state of being hollow; insincerity.

HOLLY (hol'i) *n.* an evergreen tree. [O.E. *holegn*.]

HOLLYHOCK (hol'i-hok) *n.* a tall garden plant bearing flowers of various colours. [HOLY, and O.E. *hoc*, mallows.]

HOLM (hōm) (1) *n.* evergreen oak;—(2) *n.* low, flat, rich land. [(1) M.E. *holin*, holly. (2) O.E. *holm*.]

HOLOGRAPH (hol'u-graf) *n.* a deed or testament written wholly by the grantor's or testator's own hand. [G., fr. *holos*, whole, and *graphein*, to write.]

HOLOGRAPHIC (hol-u-graf'ik) *a.* written wholly by the author or testator.

HOLOMETER (ho-lom'e-ter) *n.* an instrument for taking all kinds of measurements. [G. *holos*, whole, and *metron*, a measure.]

HOLSTER (hōl'ster) *n.* a horseman's case for pistols. [D.]

HOLY (hō'li) *a.* perfectly pure; consecrated; pious; godly; sacred. [O.E. *halig*, healthy, perfect, fr. *hal*, sound. Cf. HEAL, HAIL, HALE, WHOLE.]

HOMAGE (hom'ij) *n.* reverence; worship; respect. [O.F., fr. Late L. *homaticum*, fr. L. *homo*, a man.]

HOME (hōm) *n.* one's dwelling-house; one's country; a charitable institution;—*a.* domestic; close; severe; poignant;—*ad.* to the point. [O.E. *ham*. Cf. Ger. *Heim*.]

HOME-BRED (hōm'bred) *a.* native; domestic; plain.

HOME-FELT (hōm'felt) *a.* felt inwardly.

HOMELESS (hōm'les) *a.* without a home.

HOMELINESS (hōm'li-nes) *n.* plainness.

HOMELY (hōm'li) *a.* plain; coarse.

HOME-MADE (hōm'mād) *a.* made at home.

HOMEOPATHIC (hō-me-u-path'ik) *a.* pertaining to homeopathy.

HOMEOPATHY (hō-me-op'a-thi) *n.* a theory founded on the principle that a medicine which will cause will also cure a disease. [G., fr. *homoios*, like, and *pathos*, feeling.]

HOMERIC (hō-mer'ik) *a.* relating to Homer, the Greek poet.

HOME-RULE (hōm'rool) *n.* claim in Ireland for a separate parliament for local and internal affairs.

HOMESICK (hōm'sik) *a.* longing after home.

HOMESPUN (hōm'spun) *a.* made in the family.

HOMESTEAD (hōm'sted) *n.* place of the mansion.

HOMEWARD (hōm'ward) *ad.* toward home.

HOMICIDAL (hom'i-si-dal) *a.* pertaining to homicide; murderous.

HOMICIDE (hom'i-sid) *n.* the killing of one man by another; a manslayer. [F., fr. L. *homo*, man, and *caedere*, kill.]

HOMILIST (hom'i-list) *n.* one who preaches homilies or sermons. [See HOMILY.]

HOMILY (hom'i-li) *n.* a familiar religious discourse. [G. *homilia*, an assembly, a sermon; fr. *homos*, same, and *ile*, crowd.]

HOMOGENEITY (ho-mu-je-ne'i-ti) *n.* participation of the same principles or nature; similitude in kind. [See HOMOGENEOUS.]

HOMOGENEOUS (ho-mu-je'ne-us) *a.* of the same kind. [G., fr. *homos*, same, and *genos*, kind, fr. *genein*, beget.]

HOMOLOGATE (ho-mol'u-gāt) *v.t.* to confirm by assent; approve; confirm. [See HOMOLOGOUS.]

HOMOLOGOUS (ho-mol'u-gus) *a.* corresponding in position, structure, etc. [G., fr. *homos*, same, and *logos*, speech.]

HOMOLOGUES (hō'mō-lōgz) *n.* corresponding parts or organs, as the arm of a man, the foreleg of a horse, and the wing of a bird.

HOMOLOGY (hō-mol'u-ji) *n.* affinity in structure, but not in form or use.

Fāte, fär, ado; nē her; mine; nōte; tūne; moon.

HONE (hōn) *n.* a whetstone for sharpening;— *v.t.* to sharpen on a hone. [O.E. *han*, a stone.]

HONEST (on'est) *a.* upright in dealing; just; sincere; decent; chaste; honourable. [F., fr. L. *honestus*, honourable, fr. *honor*.]

HONESTLY (on'est-li) *ad.* uprightly; sincerely.

HONESTY (on'es-ti) *n.* integrity; uprightness; candour; plain dealing.

HONEY (hun'i) *n.* sweet juice collected by bees from flowers. [O.E. *hunig*. Cf. Ger. *Höniy.*]

HONEYBAG (hun'i-bag) *n.* stomach of the honey-bee.

HONEYCOMB (hun'i-kōm) *n.* cells of wax for holding honey.

HONEYCOMBED (hun'i-kōmd) *a.* perforated; full of flaws or holes.

HONEYED (hun'id) *a.* covered with honey; sweet.

HONEYMOON (hun'i-mōon) *n.* first month after marriage.

HONORARIUM (on-u-rā'ri-um) *n.* a voluntary or extra fee tendered to a professional man. [L. *honorarium (donum)*, honorary (gift).]

HONORARY (on'ur-ar-i) *a.* conferring honour. [L. *honorarius*, honorary, fr. *honor*.]

HONOUR (on'ur) *n.* esteem paid to worth; reputation; a title;—*v.i.* to esteem; exalt; accept and pay. [F., fr. L. *honor*.]

HONOURABLE (on'ur-a-bl) *a.* actuated by noble motives; illustrious; a title of distinction.

HOOD (hood) *n.* a covering for the head. [O.E. *hod*, hat. Cf. Ger. *Hut*.]

HOODWINK (hood'wingk) *v.t.* to blind; cover; impose on.

HOOF (hōof) *n.* the horny part of a beast's foot. [O.E. *hof*. Cf. Ger. *Huf*.]

HOOFED (hōoft) *a.* furnished with hoofs.

HOOK (hook) *n.* a bent piece of iron;—*v.t.* to fix on a hook; catch with a hook; steal; —*v.i.* to be curved; bend. [O.E. *hoc*, hook. Cf. Ger. *Haken*, a personal name.]

Hood.

HOOLIGAN (hool'i-gan) *n.* one of a band of young street roughs.

HOOLIGANISM (hool'i-ga-nizm) *n.* the disorderly or criminal practices of hooligans.

HOOP (hōop) *n.* a band of wood or iron for a cask;—*v.t.* to fasten with hoops;—*v.i.* to cry out; whoop. [O.E. *hop*.]

HOOPING-COUGH (hōo'ping-kof) *n.* a convulsive cough; chin-coughs. Also **WHOOPING-COUGH**. [F. *houper*.]

HOOPOE (hōo'poo) *n.* a bird with a large crest. [L. *up-upa*, fr. G. *epops*, so called from its cry.]

HOP (hop) (1) *v.i.* to leap on one leg;—*n.* a leap on one leg;—(2) *n.* a bitter plant used in brewing;—*v.i.* to gather hops. [(1) O.E. *hoppian*, to dance. Cf. Ger. *hupfen*. (2) D.]

HOPE (hōp) *n.* desire of good joined with expectation;—*v.t.* or *i.* to desire with expectation. [O.E. *hopa*.]

HOPEFUL (hōp'fool) *a.* full of hope.

HOPEFULLY (hōp'fool'i) *ad.* with hope.

HOPELESS (hōp'les) *a.* destitute of hope; desponding; desperate.

HOPELESSLY (hōp'les-li) *ad.* without hope.

HOPELESSNESS (hōp'les-nes) *n.* destitution of hope; despair.

HOPPER (hop'er) *n.* one who hops; a funnel or trough by which grain passes into a mill; a steam barge for removing the mud raised by a dredging machine.

HORDE (hōrd) *n.* a migratory tribe. [F., fr. Turk.]

HOREHOUND (hōr'hound) *n.* a bitter medicinal plant. [O.E. *har*, hoar, white, and *hune*, hoarhound.]

HORIZON (ho-rī'zun) *n.* the apparent line or circle between the earth and the sky. [F., fr. L., fr. G. *horizein*, to bound, fr. *horos*, a limit.]

HORIZONTAL (hor-i-zon'tal) *a.* parallel to the horizon; level.

HORIZONTALLY (hor-i-zon'tal-i) *ad.* in a horizontal direction.

HORN (horn) *n.* a hard-pointed substance on an animal's head; wind instrument; drinking cup; powder flask; symbol of strength. [O.E. Cf. L. *cornu*, G. *keras*.]

HORNED (hornd) *a.* furnished with horns.

HORNLESS (horn'les) *a.* having no horns.

HORNPIPE (horn'pip) *n.* a tune; dance.

HORNY (hor'ni) *a.* made of or like horn.

HOROGRAPHY (ho-rog'ra-fi) *n.* art of constructing dials; an account of the hours. [G. *hora*, an hour, *graphein*, to describe.]

HOROLOGE (hor'u-lōj) *n.* a clock; any instrument that tells the hours. [O.F., fr. L., fr. G., fr. *hora*, an hour, and *legein*, tell.]

HOROLOGY (hor-ol'ō-ji) *n.* art of measuring time.

HOROSCOPE (hor'u-skōp) *n.* aspect of planets at the hour of birth. [F., fr. L., fr. G. *hora*, and *skopein*, to observe.]

HORRIBLE (hor'i-bl) *a.* tending to excite horror; frightful; awful. [See **HORROR**.]

HORRIBLY (hor'i-bli) *ad.* frightfully.

HORRID (hor'id) *a.* dreadful; hideous. [See **HORROR**.]

HORRIDLY (hor'id-li) *ad.* shockingly.

HORRIFIC (ho-rif'ik) *a.* causing horror. [See **HORROR**.]

HORRIFY (hor'i-fi) *v.t.* to strike with horror. [See **HORROR**.]

HORROR (hor'ur) *n.* a shuddering with fear; terror. [L. *horror*, fr. *horrere*, to bristle.]

HORSE (hors) *n.* a quadruped; cavalry; a wooden frame; a foot rope;—*v.t.* to mount; sit astride; carry on the back; provide with a horse. [O.E. Cf. Ger. *Ross*.]

HORSEBACK (hors'bak) *n.* back of a horse.

HORSE-BREAKER (hors'brā-ker) *n.* tamer of horses.

HORSE-CHESTNUT (hors'ches-nut) *n.* a flowering tree.

HORSEHAIR (hors'hār) *n.* the hair of horses.

HORSE-LEECH (hors'lēch) *n.* a large leech that bites horses.

HORSE-LITTER (hors'lit-er) *n.* a carriage on poles borne between horses.

HORSEMAN (hors'man) *n.* one skilled in riding.

HORSEMANSHIP (hors'man-ship) *n.* art of riding and training horses.

HORSEPLAY (hors'plā) *n.* rough, rude play.

HORSE-POWER (hors'pou-er) *n.* power of a horse or its equivalent; power which will raise 33,000 pounds avoirdupois one foot per minute—used to express the power of a steam-engine. [horse.

HORSESHOE (hors'shōo) *n.* a shoe for a horse.

HORSEWHIP (hors'hwip) *n.* a whip for driving horses;—*v.t.* to lash.

HORTATION (hor-tā'shun) *n.* act of advising. [L., fr. *hortari*, to incite.]

HORTATIVE (hor'ta-tiv) *a.* giving advice;— *n.* an encouraging advice or precept. [See **HORTATION**.]

HORTATORY (hor'ta-tur-i) *a.* giving advice or encouragement; inciting. [See **HORTATION**.]

HORTICULTURAL (hor-ti-kul'tūr-al) *a.* pertaining to horticulture.

HORTICULTURE (hor'ti-kul-tūr) *n.* culture of a garden. [L., fr. *hortus*, garden, and *cultura*, culture, fr. *colere*, to cultivate.]

HORTICULTURIST (hor-ti-kul'tūr-ist) *n.* one skilled in gardening.

HOSANNA (hŏ-zan'ạ) *n.* praise to God. [H. =Save now, I pray.]

HOSE (hōz) *n.* stockings; coverings for the legs; a leathern tube;—*pl.* HOSE. [O.E. *hosa*, pl. *hosan*. Cf. Ger. *Hose.*]

HOSIER (hŏ'zhẹr) *n.* one who deals in stockings and underclothing. [See HOSE.]

HOSIERY (hŏ'zhẹr-i) *n.* hose in general.

HOSPITABLE (hos'pi-tạ-bl) *a.* kind to strangers or guests; generous; liberal. [L., fr. *hospes*, guest.]

HOSPITABLY (hos'pi-tạ-bli) *ad.* in a hospitable manner.

HOSPITAL (hos'pi-tạl) *n.* a building for the sick, aged, or insane. [O.F., fr. Late L. *hospitale*, fr. L. *hospes*, guest.]

HOSPITALITY (hos-pi-tal'i-ti) *n.* entertainment of strangers and guests. [See HOSPITAL.]

HOSPITALLER (hos'pi-tạl-ẹr) *n.* one of a religious brotherhood for the care of the sick; a knight of St John.

HOSPODAR (hos-pu-dår') *n.* a prince or governor. [Slav.]

HOST (hōst) (1) *n.* one who entertains others; —(2) *n.* an army;—(3) *n.* sacrifice of the mass. [(1) O.F. *hoste*, fr. L. stem *hospit-*, of *hospes*. (2) O.F., fr. L. *hostis*, enemy. (3) L. *hostia*, sacrifice, victim.]

HOSTAGE (hos'tij) *n.* a person given as a pledge for the performance of certain conditions. [O.F. =F. *ôtage*, fr. L. stem *obsid-*, of *obses*, hostage.]

HOSTEL (hos'tel) *n.* an old term for an inn or lodging; now HOTEL. [O.F. *hostel.*]

HOSTESS (hōs'tes) *n.* a female host; a landlady.

HOSTILE (hos'til) *a.* warlike; adverse; unfriendly. [L. *hostilis*, fr. *hostis*, enemy.]

HOSTILITY (hos-til'i-ti) *n.* enmity; active opposition;—*pl.* acts of warfare. [See HOSTILE.]

HOSTLER (os'lẹr) *n.* one who has the care of horses. [See HOSTEL.]

HOT (hot) *a.* having heat; eager; fiery. [O.E. *hat.* Cf. Ger. *heiss.*]

HOTBED (hot'bed) *n.* a garden-bed covered with glass.

HOT-BLAST (hot'blast) *n.* a current of heated air blown into a furnace to increase the heat.

HOT-BLOODED (hot'blud-ed) *a.* high-spirited; irritable.

HOTEL (hŏ-tel') *n.* an inn for travellers. [F., fr. O.F. *hostel.*]

HOT-HEADED (hot'bed-ed) *a.* passionate; [violent; rash.

HOTHOUSE (hot'hous) *n.* a house kept warm to shelter plants.

HOTLY (hot'li) *ad.* violently; keenly.

HOTNESS (hot'nes) *n.* violence; vehemence; fury.

HOT-PRESSED (hot'prest) *a.* pressed while heat is applied.

HOTSPUR (hot'spur) *n.* a violent, rash man; a kind of early pea.

HOTTENTOT (hot'n-tot) *n.* a native of South Africa. [D. To the first settlers the language sounded like a repetition of *hot-en* and *tot.*]

HOUDAH (hou'dạ) *n.* a seat fixed on an elephant's back. [Hind.]

HOUGH, HOH (hok) *n.* the ham;—*v.t.* to hamstring. [O.E. *hoh*, heel.]

HOUND (hound) *n.* a dog for hunting:—*v.t.* to set on; hunt; incite. [O.E. *hund*, dog.]

HOUR (our) *n.* twenty-fourth part of a day; particular time. [O.F. *hore* =F. *heure*, fr. L. *hora*, hour.]

HOUR-GLASS (our'glạs) *n.* a glass to measure time by the running of sand from one glass to another.

HOUR-HAND (our'hand) *n.* the hand of a clock or watch that points to the hour.

HOURI (hou'ri, hou'ri) *n.* a nymph of the Mohammedan paradise. [Perhaps fr. A. = having fine black eyes.]

HOURLY (our'li) *a.* done every hour; frequent;—*ad.* every hour.

HOUSE (hous) *n.* a place of abode; a family; branch of the legislature; a quorum. [O.E. *hus.* Cf. Ger. *Haus.*]

HOUSEBOAT (hous'bōt) *n.* a covered boat.

HOUSEBREAKER (hous'brā-kẹr) *n.* one who breaks into a house feloniously.

HOUSEBREAKING (hous'brā-king) *n.* the act of breaking into a house.

HOUSECRAFT (hous'kråft) *n.* the science and art of housekeeping.

HOUSEHOLD (hous'hōld) *n.* a family living together;—*a.* domestic; belonging to the family. [occupies a house.

HOUSEHOLDER (hous'hōl-dẹr) *n.* one who

HOUSEKEEPER (hous'kē-pẹr) *n.* one who keeps a house; a superior female servant.

HOUSELESS (hous'les) *a.* destitute of a house.

HOUSEMAID (hous'mād) *n.* a female servant.

HOUSEWIFE (hous'wif, huz'if) *n.* mistress of a family; female economist; a little case holding sewing materials.

HOUSEWIFERY (hous'wif-ri, huz'if-ri) *n.* female domestic economy. [houses.

HOUSEWRIGHT (hous'rit) *n.* builder of

HOUSING (hou'zing) (1) *n.* a saddle-cloth; —(2) *n.* sheltering. [(1) O.F. *housse*, mantle. (2) See HOUSE.]

HOVEL (hov'el) *n.* a shed; a small, mean dwelling. [Dim. of O.E. *hof*, a dwelling.]

HOVER (hov'ẹr) *v.i.* to flap the wings; hang fluttering; move about and near. [Etym. doubtful.]

HOW (hou) *ad.* in what manner. [O.E. *hu.*]

HOWBEIT (hou-bē'it) *ad.* nevertheless.

HOWEVER (hou-ev'ẹr) *ad.* nevertheless.

HOWITZER (hou'it-sẹr) *n.* a kind of mortar or cannon. [Ger. *Haubitze*, fr. Bohemian.]

HOWL (houl) *v.i.* to cry as a dog or wolf;— *n.* the cry of a dog or wolf. [Imit. Cf. L. *ululare*, to howl, fr. *ulula*, an owl. Cf. Ger. *heulen.*]

HOWLET (hou'let) *n.* a bird of the owl kind.

HOWSOEVER (hou-sō-ev'ẹr) *ad.* in whatever manner; notwithstanding.

HOY (hoi) (1) *n.* a small coasting vessel;— (2) *ex.* ho! stop! [(1) D. (2) Imit.]

HUB (hub) *n.* the nave of a wheel. [A variant of HOB.]

HUBBLE-BUBBLE (hub'l-bub'l) *n.* a tobacco pipe in which the smoke is drawn through water. [Redupl. from BUBBLE.]

HUBBUB (hub'ub) *n.* uproar; tumult. [Imit.]

HUCKABACK (huk'a-bak) *n.* a kind of linen with raised figures, used for tablecloths and towels. [Low Ger.]

HUCKSTER (huk'stẹr) *n.* a retailer of small articles; hawker. [Orig. fem. of HAWKER.]

HUDDLE (hud'l) *v.t.* or *i.* to crowd together; —*n.* a crowd without order; confusion. [M.E. *hodren.* Cf. HIDE.]

HUDIBRASTIC (hū-di-bras'tik) *a.* pertaining to Hudibras or to doggerel poetry.

HUE (hū) *n.* colour; dye; a clamour. [O.E. *hiw.*]

HUFF (huf) *n.* a swell of anger;—*v.t.* or *i.* to swell up; take offence; bluster. [Imit.]

HUFFINESS (huf'i-nes) *n.* petulance; sulky; ill humour.

HUFFISH (huf'ish) *a.* insolent; arrogant.

HUFFY (huf'i) *a.* swelled; petulant.

HUG (hug) *v.t.* to embrace closely or fondly; take pride in; sail close to;—*n.* a close embrace; clasp or gripe. [Scand.]

HUGE (hūj) *a.* bulky; vast. [O.F. *ahuge*, vast.]

HUGENESS (hūj'nes) *n.* enormous bulk; vastness.

HUGGER-MUGGER (hug'gẹr-mug'gẹr) *n.* secrecy; slovenly confusion;—*a.* sly; confused; slovenly. [Fr. HUG.]

HUGUENOT (hū'ge-not, hū'ge-nō) *n.* a Protestant in France, formerly. [M. H. Ger. *Hug*, Hugh; F. *Hugon.*]

HULK (hulk) *n.* the body of an old ship. [Late L. *hulka*, fr. G. *helkein*, to draw.]

HULL (hul) *n.* the outer covering of a nut; frame of a ship;—*v.t.* to strip; husk; hit or pierce the hull. [O.E. *hulu*, covering.]

HUM (hum) *v.t.* or *i.* to sing low;—*n.* a buzzing sound. [Imit. Cf. Ger. *hummen*.]

HUMAN (hū'man) *a.* belonging to mankind; not divine. [F., fr. L. *humanus*, fr. *homo*, a man.]

HUMANE (hū-mān') *a.* benevolent; kind. [See HUMAN.]

HUMANELY (hū-mān'li) *ad.* with kindness.

HUMANISE (hū'man-iz) *v.t.* to render humane.

HUMANIST (hū'man-ist) *n.* student of human nature, or of the humanities.

HUMANITARIAN (hū-man-i-tā'ri-an) *n.* one who holds that Christ was merely a man.

HUMANITIES (hū-man'i-tiz) *n.pl.* polite literature; study of the classics, poetry, etc.

HUMANITY (hū-man'i-ti) *n.* the nature of man; kind disposition.

HUMANKIND (hū'man-kind) *n.* the human race. [of men.

HUMANLY (hū'man-li) *ad.* after the manner

HUMBLE (hum'bl) *a.* low in feelings or condition; lowly; modest; unassuming; meek; —*v.t.* to make humble; bring low; abase. [F., fr. L. *humilis*, low, fr. *humus*, the earth.]

HUMBLE-BEE (num'bl-bē) *n.* a large black hairy bee with orange bands. [Freq. of HUM.]

HUMBLY (hum'bli) *ad.* without pride.

HUMBUG (hum'bug) *n.* an imposition;—*v.t.* to impose upon. [Fr. HUM, delude, and BUG, a dreadful object.]

HUMDRUM (hum'drum) *a.* commonplace; dull; monotonous;—*n.* a droning tone; a stupid fellow. [Prob. fr. HUM and DRUM.]

HUMID (hū'mid) *a.* moist; damp. [F., fr. L. *humidus*, fr. *humere*, to be moist.]

HUMIDITY (hū-mid'i-ti) *n.* moisture; dampness. Also HUMIDNESS.

HUMILIATE (hū-mil'i-āt) *v.t.* to humble; depress; abase. [L. (part.) *humiliatus*, fr. L. *humiliare*.]

HUMILIATION (hū-mil-i-ā'shun) *n.* act of humbling; state of being abased.

HUMILITY (hū-mil'i-ti) *n.* lowliness of mind; modesty. [See HUMILIATE.]

HUMMING (hum'ing) *n.* noise of bees or flies.

HUMMING-BIRD (hum'ing-berd) *n.* a tropical bird with brilliant plumage.

HUMORAL (hū'mur-al, ū'mur-al) *a.* pertaining to the humours. [See HUMOUR.]

HUMORIST (hū'mur-ist, ū'mur-ist) *n.* a playful or fanciful writer; a wag. [See HUMOUR.]

HUMOROUS (hū'mur-us, ū'mur-us) *a.* jocular; pleasant; playful.

HUMOROUSLY (hū'mur-us-li, ū'mur-us-li) *ad.* with pleasantry.

HUMORSOME (hū'mur-sum, ū'mur-sum) *a.* peevish; odd.

HUMOUR (hū'mur, ū'mur) *n.* moisture; any animal fluid; a rash; temper; caprice; mood; petulance; pleasantry; wit;—*v.t.* to gratify; indulge by compliance. [O.F. *humor*=F. *humeur*, fr. L. *humere*, be moist.]

HUMP (hump) *n.* a swelling, as of flesh; protuberance. [Perhaps nasalised form of HEAP.]

HUMPBACK (hump'bak) *n.* a crooked back; one having such; a kind of whale.

HUNCH (hunsh) *n.* a protuberance;—*v.t.* to push with the elbow; crook the back. [Prov. E. *hunk*, a lump.]

HUNCHBACK (hunsh'bak) *n.* one having a hunch or hump on his back.

HUNCHBACKED (hunsh'bakt) *a.* deformed in the back.

HUNDRED (hun'dred) *a.* ten times ten;—*n.* the sum of ten times ten. [O.E., fr. *hund*, a hundred, with superfluous *red*, *ræd*, a reckoning.]

HUNDREDFOLD (hun'dred-fōld) *n.* a hundred times as much.

HUNDREDTH (hun'dredth) *a.* the ordinal of a hundred;—*n.* one of a hundred parts.

HUNDREDWEIGHT (hun'dred-wāt) *n.* a weight of 112 pounds avoirdupois—written CWT.

HUNGER (hung'ger) *n.* a desire or craving for food;—*v.i.* to crave food; long for;—*v.t.* to famish. [O.E. *hungor*.]

HUNGRY (hung'gri) *a.* feeling pain from want of food. [See HUNGER.]

HUNT (hunt) *v.t.* to chase, as game; search for; pursue;—*v.i.* to follow the chase;—*n.* chase of game; pursuit; pack of hounds; body of huntsmen. [O.E. *huntian*. Cf. O.E. *hentan*, to seize.]

HUNTER (hun'ter) *n.* one who hunts; a hunting horse or dog; a kind of watch.

HUNTRESS (hunt'res) *n.* a female hunter.

HUNTSMAN (hunts'man) *n.* a man who hunts.

HURDLE (hur'dl) *n.* a texture of twigs; a crate; a sledge; movable fence. [O.E. *hyrdel*. Cf. Ger. *Hürde*.]

HURL (hurl) *v.t.* to throw with violence; utter forcibly; wheel;—*v.i.* to be driven or move with noise; play at ball;—*n.* cast; throw; drive; tumult. [M.E. *hurlen*. Imit.]

HURLING (hur'ling) *n.* throwing with force; a game of throwing a ball.

HURLY-BURLY (hur'li-bur'li) *n.* tumult; bustle. [O.F. *hurler*, fr. L. *ululare*, to yell, and *burly* (a rhyming addition).]

HURRA (hu-rä') *ex,* of joy, triumph, or applause. Also written HURRAH. [Ger.]

HURRICANE (hur'i-kān) *n.* a storm with extreme violence and sudden changes of the wind. [Sp. *huracan* (fr. Caribbean).]

HURRICANE-DECK (hur'i-kān-dek) *n.* the uppermost deck in steamboats.

HURRY (hur'i) *v.t.* to hasten;—*v.i.* to move hastily;—*n.* great haste. [M.E. *horien.* Imit.]

HURT (hurt) *n.* harm; mischief; wound or bruise; injury; damage;—*v.t.* to injure; wound; harm. [O.F. *hurter*=F. *heurter*, to run against.] [chievous; harmful.

HURTFUL (hurt'fool) *a.* injurious; mis-

HURTFULNESS (hurt'fool-nes) *a.* quality of doing harm.

HURTLE (hur'tl) *v.t.* or *i.* to push or whirl forcibly; clash; jostle. [Freq. of HURT.]

HUSBAND (huz'band) *n.* a married man;—*v.t.* to manage frugally. [*Husbonda*, fr. Icel. *hus*, house, and *buandi*, inhabiting, fr. *bua*, dwell.]

HUSBANDMAN (huz'band-man) *n.* a farmer.

HUSBANDRY (huz'band-ri) *n.* tillage; domestic economy; thrift.

HUSH (hush) *a.* still; silent;—*v.t.* to silence; quiet. [Imit. Cf. HISS, HIST, WHISHT.]

HUSH-MONEY (hush'mun-i) *n.* a bribe to induce secrecy.

HUSK (husk) *n.* the covering of certain fruits; —*v.t.* to strip the husks from. [Dim. fr. O.E. *hus*, house, M.E. *huske*. Cf. Ger. *Hülse*.]

HUSKILY (hus'ki-li) *ad.* dryly; roughly.

HUSKINESS (hus'ki-nes) *n.* dryness; harshness.

HUSKY (hus'ki) *a.* abounding with husks; harsh; rough in sound.

HUSSAR (hoo-zär') *n.* a light-armed horse-soldier. [Slav.=a gooseherd.]

HUSSY (huz'i) *n.* a pert, frolicsome girl.

HUSTINGS (hus'tingz) *n.pl.* a temporary stage for speakers. [O.E. =a council, fr. Scand.]

HUSTLE (hus'l) *v.t.* or *i.* to shake or push together; handle roughly; jostle. [D.]

HUT (hut) *n.* a small mean house; a wooden tent;—*v.t.* or *i.* to lodge or be lodged in huts, as troops. [F. *hutte*.]

HUTCH (huch) *n.* a corn-chest; a rabbit-box. [F. *huche*, a chest, fr. Late L. *hutica*, a box.]

HUZZA (hoo-zä') *n.* a shout of joy;—*v.i.* to shout in joy. [Ger.]

HYACINTH (hi'a-sinth) *n.* a flowering bulbous plant; its flower; a gem; jacinth. [L. *hyacinthus*, fr. G. *huakinthos*. Doublet of **JACINTH.**]

HYACINTHINE (hi-a-sin'thin) *a.* resembling hyacinth; dark auburn or brown.

HYALINE (hi'a-lin) *a.* like glass. [L. *hyalinus*, fr. G. *hualos*, glass.]

HYBRID (hi'brid) *a.* of different species; mongrel;—*n.* an animal or plant produced from two different species; a word compounded of different languages. [F., fr. L. *hibrida*, a mongrel.]

HYDRA (hi'dra) *n.* a monster with many heads. [L., fr. G. *hudra*, fr. *hudor*, water.]

HYDRANT (hi'drant) *n.* a machine for raising water; a fire-plug. [G. *hudor*, water.]

HYDRAULIC (hi-draw'lik) *a.* relating to hydraulics. [F., fr. G., fr. *hudor*, water, and *aulos*, a pipe.]

HYDRAULICS (hi-draw'liks) *n.pl.* the science which treats of fluids in motion.

HYDRODYNAMICS (hi-dru-di-nam'iks) *n.* the science of the motive power or pressure of fluids. [G. *hudor*, water, and **DYNAMICS.**]

HYDROGEN (hi'dru-jen) *n.* a gas which is one of the elements of water. [G. *hudor*, and the stem *gen-*, of *gignomai*, to produce.]

HYDROGENOUS (hi-droj'e-nus) *a.* pertaining to hydrogen. [makes sea-charts.]

HYDROGRAPHER (hi-drog'ra-fer) *n.* one who

HYDROGRAPHIC (hi-dru-graf'ik) *a.* relating to hydrography.

HYDROGRAPHY (hi-drog'ra-fi) *n.* description and representation by charts of seas, rivers, etc. [G. *hudor*, and *graphein*, to write.]

HYDROLOGY (hi-drol'ō-ji) *n.* science of water. [Fr. *hudor*, and *logos*, a discourse.]

HYDROMETER (hi-drom'e-ter) *n.* an instrument for determining the specific gravities, and thence the strength of liquids. [G. *hudor*, and *metron*, measure.]

HYDROPATHIC (hi-dru-path'ik) *a.* pertaining to hydropathy.

HYDROPATHY (hi-drop'a-thi) *n.* the water cure. [G. *hudor*, and *pathos*, suffering, fr. *pathein*, to suffer.]

HYDROPHOBIA (hi-dru-fō'bi-a) *n.* dread of water; canine madness. [G. *hudor*, and *phobos*, fear.]

HYDROPHOBIC (hi-dru-fō'bik) *a.* pertaining to canine madness.

HYDROPLANE (hi'dru-plān) *n.* an aeroplane which can be made to float on the surface of water. [G. *hudor*, water, and L. *planus*, level.]

HYDROSCOPE (hi'dru-skōp) *n.* an instrument to measure the moisture in air or gases. Also **HYGROSCOPE.** [G. *hudor*, water, and *skopein*, to view.]

HYDROSTATIC (hi-dru-stat'ik) *a.* relating to hydrostatics. [G. *hudor*, and *statikos*, causing to stand, fr. *histanai*, to stand.]

HYDROSTATICS (hi-dru-stat'iks) *n.* the science which treats of the properties of fluids at rest. [water.]

HYDROUS (hi'drus) *a.* watery. [G. *hudor*,

HYEMAL (hi'e-mal) *a.* pertaining to winter. [L. *hiems*, winter.]

HYENA (hi-ē'na) *n.* a savage carnivorous quadruped of the dog family. [L., fr. G. *huaina*, fr. *hus*, a sow.]

HYGIENE (hi'ji-ēn) *n.* science of, or medical treatment for, the preservation of health. [Fr. G. *hugies*, healthy.]

HYGROMETER (hi-grom'e-ter) *n.* an instrument for measuring the degree of moisture in the atmosphere, or its relative humidity. [G. *hugros*, moist, and *metron*, measure.]

HYMEN (hi'men) *n.* the god of marriage. [L., fr. G.]

HYMENEAL (hi-me-nē'al) *a.* pertaining to marriage;—*n.* a marriage song. [See **HYMEN.**]

HYMN (him) *n.* a song of praise;—*v.t.* to praise in songs. [L., fr. G. *humnos*, a festive song.]

HYMNIC (him'nik) *a.* relating to hymns. [See **HYMN.**]

HYMNOLOGIST (him-nol'ō-jist) *n.* a writer of hymns. [hymns.

HYMNOLOGY (him-nol'ō-ji) *n.* a collection of

HYPERBOLA (hi-per'bu-la) *n.* one of the conic sections. [G. *huper*, beyond, and *ballein*, to throw.]

HYPERBOLE (hi-per'bu-lē) *n.* a rhetorical figure; exaggeration. [Doublet of **HYPERBOLA.**]

HYPERBOLICAL (hi-per-bol'i-kal) *a.* exaggerating or exceeding the truth.

HYPERBOLISE (hi-per'bu-liz) *v.t.* or *i.* to represent or speak with exaggeration.

HYPERBOLISM (hi-per'bu-lizm) *n.* use of, or a, hyperbolical expression. Hyperbola.

HYPERBOREAN (hi-per-bō're-an) *a.* northern; —*n.* an inhabitant of the extreme north. [G., fr. *huper*, beyond, and *Boreas*, the north wind.]

HYPERCRITIC (hi-per-krit'ik) *n.* a critic exact beyond reason. [G. *huper*, over, and *kritikos*, critical.]

HYPERCRITICAL (hi-per-krit'i-kal) *a.* critical beyond use or reason.

HYPHEN (hi'fen) *n.* the mark (-) between syllables and compound words. [G., fr. *hupo*, under, and *hen*, one.]

HYPNOTIC (hip-not'ik) *a.* causing sleep; soporific. [G. *hupnos*, sleep; coined in 1843.]

HYPNOTISM (hip'nu-tizm) *n.* a kind of mesmeric sleep.

HYPOCHONDRIA (hip-u-kon'dri-a) *n.* gloomy depression of spirits. [L., fr. G., fr. *hupo*, under, and *chondros*, a cartilage.]

HYPOCHONDRIAC (hip-u-kon'dri-ak) *n.* one affected with low spirits.

HYPOCHONDRIACAL (hip-u-kon'dri-a-kal) *a.* melancholy; dejected.

HYPOCRISY (hi-pok'ri-si) *n.* dissimulation; deceitful appearance. [G. *hupokrisis*, acting a part, fr. *hupo*, and *krinein*, to decide.]

HYPOCRITE (hip'u-krit) *n.* a dissembler; false pretender. [See **HYPOCRISY.**]

HYPOCRITICAL (hip-u-krit'i-kal) *a.* insincere; dissembling.

HYPODERMIC (hi-pu-der'mik) *a.* pertaining to parts underlying the skin;—*n.* a medicine introduced under the skin. [G., fr. *hupo*, and *derma*, skin.]

HYPOTENUSE (hi-pot'e-nūs) *n.* longest side of a right-angled triangle. Also written **HYPOTHENUSE.** [F., fr. G. *hupotenousa*, (gramme) (a line) stretching under, fr. *hupo*, under, and *teinein*, to stretch.]

HYPOTHEC (hi-poth'ek) *n.* legal security for debt, which a landlord or creditor has over crops, effects, goods, etc. [F., fr. L. *hupotheca*, fr. G. *hupotheke*, pledge.]

HYPOTHECATE (hi-poth'e-kāt) *v.t.* to pledge for the security of a creditor. [See **HYPOTHEC.**]

HYPOTHECATION (hi-poth-e-kā'shun) *n.* act of pledging as security.

HYPOTHESIS (hi-poth'e-sis) *n.* supposition; proposition assumed. [G. *hupothenai*, to place under.]

HYPOTHETICAL (hi-pu-thot'i-kal) *a.* supposed. **HYPOTHETICALLY** (hi-pu-thet'i-kal-i) *ad.* upon supposition.

HYSON (hi'sun) *n.* a fine kind of green tea. [Chinese, F., fr. L. *hyssopum*, fr. G. *hussopos*.]

HYSSOP (his'up) *n.* an aromatic plant. [Fr. H.]

HYSTERICAL (his-ter'i-kal) *a.* pertaining to hysteria; affected with fits of a certain kind.

HYSTERICS (his-ter'iks) *n.* a nervous affection peculiar to women. Also written **HYSTERIA.** [G. *hustera*, womb.]

I

I (i) *pron.* used by a speaker or writer when mentioning his individual self. [O.E. Cf. Ger. *ich*, L. *ego*, G. *ego*.]

IAMBIC (i-am'bik) *a.* pertaining to the Iambus. [L., fr. G. *iambikos*, fr. *iambos*, an iambic foot, iambic verse, fr. *iaptein*, to assail, this metre being first used in satire.]

IAMBUS (i-am'bus) *n.* a poetic foot of a long and a short syllable. [See **IAMBIC**.]

IBEX (i'beks) *n.* an animal of the goat kind. [L.]

IBIDEM (i-bi'dem) *ad.* in the same place. Usually printed **IBID**. [L.]

IBIS (i'bis) *n.* a wading bird resembling the stork. [L., fr. G.]

ICARIAN (i-kā'ri-an) *a.* soaring in flight; too adventurous. [Fr. *Icarus*, who fell into the sea on his flight from Crete, his wings of wax having melted by the sun's heat.]

ICE (is) *n.* water congealed to hardness; concreted sugar;—*v.t.* to cover with ice or concreted sugar. [O.E. *is.* Cf. Ger. *Eis*.]

ICEBERG (is'berg) *n.* a floating mountain of ice. [r m **ICE** and Scand. *berg*, a mountain.] F o

ICE-BOUND (is'bound) *a.* totally surrounded with ice.

ICE-CREAM (is'krēm) *n.* cream flavoured and frozen.

ICE-HOUSE (is'hous) *n.* a place for keeping ice.

ICICLE (i'si-kl) *n.* a pendant mass of ice. [O.E. *isgicel*, fr. *isesgicel* = an icicle of ices.]

ICILY (i'si-li) *ad.* in a cold manner; frigidly.

ICON (i'kon) *n.* an image or representation. [L., fr. G.]

ICONOCLASM (i-kon'u-klazm) *n.* the act of breaking images.

ICONOCLAST (i-kon'u-klast) *n.* a breaker of images. [G. *eikon*, image, and *klastes*, breaker.]

ICONOCLASTIC (i-kon-u-klas'tik) *a.* breaking idols or images.

ICONOGRAPHY (i-ko-nog'ra-fi) *n.* description of ancient statues. [G. *eikon*, and *graphein*, describe.]

ICTERIC (ik-ter'ik) *a.* affected with jaundice; —*n.* a remedy for jaundice. [G. *ikteros*.]

ICTUS (ik'tus) *n.* stress of voice on an accented syllable. [L. =a blow.]

ICY (i'si) *a.* abounding with ice; cold.

IDEA (i-dē'a) *n.* mental image; conception; thought; notion. [L., fr. G., fr. *idein*, see.]

IDEAL (i-dē'al) *a.* existing in idea or in fancy; visionary; imaginary;—*n.* the conception of a thing in its most perfect state.

IDEALISM (i-dē'a-lizm) *n.* the doctrine of ideal existence.

IDEALITY (i-dē-al'i-ti) *n.* capacity for imaginary thought.

IDEALLY (i-dē'al-i) *ad.* in imagination.

IDENTICAL (i-den'ti-kal) *a.* the same. [L. *idem*, the same.]

IDENTICALLY (i-den'ti-kal-i) *ad.* in the same way or form; exactly.

IDENTIFY (i-den'ti-fi) *v.t.* or *i.* to prove to be the same; recognise; combine with. [F. *identifier*, fr. L. *idem*, same, and *facere*, make.]

IDENTITY (i-den'ti-ti) *n.* sameness.

IDES (idz) *n.* the 15th day of March, May, July, and October, and the 13th of the other months. [F., fr. L. *Idus*.]

IDIOCY (id'i-u-si) *n.* defect of understanding; imbecility. [See **IDIOT**.]

IDIOM (id'i-um) *n.* an expression peculiar to a language. [L., fr. G. *idioma*, peculiarity, fr. *idios*, one's own.]

IDIOMATIC (id-i-u-mat'ik) *a.* peculiar to a language.

IDIOSYNCRASY (id-i-u-sin'kra-si) *n.* a peculiarity of constitution, mind, or character. [G. *idios*, peculiar, and *sunkrasis*, a mixing together, fr. *sun*, together, and *krasis* a mixing.]

IDIOT (id'i-ut) *n.* a natural fool. [F., fr. L., fr. G. *idiotes*, a private person, then an ignorant, or foolish person, fr. *idios*, one's own.]

IDIOTIC (id-i-ot'ik) *a.* like an idiot.

IDIOTISM (id'i-ot-izm) *n.* an idiom; idiocy. [G. *idiotismos*.]

IDLE (i'dl) *a.* empty; vain; unoccupied; lazy; useless; trifling; vacant;—*v.t.* or *i.* to spend or waste in inaction. [O.E. Cf. Ger. *eitel*.]

IDLENESS (i'dl-nes) *n.* indolence.

IDLER (id'ler) *n.* a lazy person.

IDLY (id'li) *ad.* sluggishly; vainly.

IDOL (i'dul) *n.* an image worshipped. [O.F., fr. L. *idolum*, fr. G. *eidolon*, fr. *eidos*, what is seen, fr. *idein*, to see.]

IDOLATOR (i-dol'a-ter) *n.* a worshipper of idols. [Fr. **IDOL**, and G. *latreuein*, to worship.]

IDOLATRESS (i-dol'a-tres) *n.* a female idolator.

IDOLATROUS (i-dol'a-trus) *a.* given to idolatry.

IDOLATROUSLY (i-dol'a-trus-li) *ad.* in an idolatrous manner.

IDOLATRY (i-dol'a-tri) *n.* the worship of idols; excessive attachment.

IDOLISE (i-dul'īz) *v.t.* to love to excess or adoration.

IDYL (i'dil) *n.* a short pastoral poem. Also **IDYLL**. [L., fr. G. *idullion*, fr. *eidos*, image.]

IDYLLIC (i-dil'ik) *a.* belonging to idyls; pastoral.

IF (if) *conj.* in case that; granting or supposing that. [O.E. *gif*.]

IGNEOUS (ig'ne-us) *a.* consisting of fire. [L. *igneus*, fr. *ignis*, fire.]

IGNIS-FATUUS (ig-nis-fat'ū-us) *n.* a kind of meteor in the night; a delusion. [L. *ignis*, fire, and *fatuus*, foolish.]

IGNITE (ig-nīt) *v.t.* or *i.* to kindle. [L. (part.) *ignitus*, fr. *ignire*, to set on fire, fr. *ignis*, fire.]

IGNITIBLE (ig-ni'ti-bl) *a.* capable of being ignited.

IGNITION (ig-nish'un) *n.* the act of taking fire.

IGNOBLE (ig-nō'bl) *a.* of low birth; mean. [F., fr. L. *ignobilis*, fr. *in*, not, and (*g*)*nobilis*, noble.]

IGNOBLY (ig-nō'bli) *ad.* meanly; basely.

IGNOMINIOUS (ig-nu-min'i-us) *a.* very shameful; dishonourable.

IGNOMINIOUSLY (ig-nu-min'i-us-li) *ad.* meanly; disgracefully.

IGNOMINY (ig'nu-min-i) *n.* disgrace; infamy. [F., fr. L. *ignominia*, fr. *in*, not and (*g*)*nomen*, name.]

IGNORAMUS (ig-nu-rā'mus) *n.* an ignorant person. [L. =we are ignorant, fr. *ignorare*.]

IGNORANCE (ig'nu-rans) *n.* want of knowledge.

IGNORANT (ig'nu-rant) *a.* wanting knowledge. [F., fr. L. (part. stem) *ignorant-* fr. *ignorare*.]

IGNORANTLY (ig'nu-rant-li) *ad.* without knowledge.

IGNORE (ig-nōr') *v.t.* to leave out of account; disregard; throw out or reject. [L. *ignorare*, not to know, fr. *in*, not, and (*g*)*noscere*, know.]

IL (il) *pref.* for *in*, not, before adjectives, etc., as *il-legal*, *il-legible*, *il-licit*, *il-logical*; *in*, into, or upon, before verbs, etc. Also *im*, *ir*; as *im-pend*, *im-pede*, *im-pale*, *ir-rigate*. [L.]

ILIAC (il'i-ak) *a.* pertaining to the lower bowels. [F., fr. L., fr. *ilia*, groin, flank, small intestines.]

ILL (il) *a.* bad; evil; unfortunate; sick; diseased; improper; incorrect; cross;—*n.* evil; wickedness; misfortune;—*ad.* not well; not rightly; with difficulty. [Scand.; the root occurs in O.E. *yfel*, evil.]

ILLATION (i-lā'shun) *n.* an inference. [F., fr. L. (acc.) *illationem*, fr. part. *illatus*, fr. *inferre*, fr. *in*, into, and *ferre*, to bear.]

ILLATIVE (il-ā'tiv) *a.* that may be inferred. [See ILLATION.]

ILL-BRED (il'bred) *a.* impolite.

ILL-BREEDING (il-brē'ding) *n.* incivility; rudeness.

ILLEGAL (i-lē'gal) *a.* contrary to law. [L. *in*, and *legalis*, fr. stem *leg-* of *lex*, law.]

ILLEGALISE (i-lē'gal-iz) *v.t.* to render unlawful.

ILLEGALITY (il-e-gal'i-ti) *n.* unlawfulness.

ILLEGALLY (i-lē'gal-i) *ad.* unlawfully.

ILLEGIBLE (i-lej'i-bl) *a.* that cannot be read. [L. *in*, and *legibilis*, legible, fr. *legere*, to read.]

ILLEGIBLY (i-lej'i-bli) *ad.* so that it cannot be read.

ILLEGITIMACY (il-e-jit'i-ma-si) *n.* bastardy.

ILLEGITIMATE (il-e-jit'i-mat) *a.* born out of wedlock; not authorised or inferred; illogical. [L. *in*, and *legitimus*.]

ILL-FAVOURED (il-fā'verd) *a.* ugly; deformed.

ILLIBERAL (i-lib'e-ral) *a.* not generous; mean; not candid. [L. *in*, and *liberalis*.]

ILLIBERALITY (i-lib-e-ral'i-ti) *n.* narrowness of mind; parsimony.

ILLIBERALLY (i-lib'e-ral-i) *ad.* ungenerously; uncharitably; parsimoniously.

ILLICIT (i-lis'it) *a.* not allowed; unlicensed; unlawful. [L. *in*, and *licitus*, allowed.]

ILLICITLY (i-lis'it-li) *ad.* unlawfully; lawlessly.

ILLIMITABLE (i-lim'i-ta-bl) *a.* that cannot be bounded or limited. [L. *in*, and LIMITABLE. See LIMIT.]

ILLITERATE (i-lit'e-rat) *a.* unlearned; wanting culture or grace. [L. *in*, and *literatus*, learned.]

ILLITERATENESS (i-lit'e-rat-nes) *n.* want of learning.

ILL-JUDGED (il'jujd) *a.* badly devised; likely to fail; injudicious.

ILL-NATURE (il-nā'tūr) *n.* habitual badness of temper.

ILL-NATURED (il-nā'tūrd) *a.* cross; peevish.

ILLNESS (il'nes) *n.* indisposition; sickness; wickedness.

ILLOGICAL (i-loj'i-kal) *a.* not according to logic.

ILL-STARRED (il'stärd) *a.* fated to be unfortunate.

ILLUDE (i-lūd') *v.t.* to mock or deceive. [O.F., fr. L. *in*, upon, and *ludere*, play.]

ILLUME (i-lūm') *v.t.* to make bright; enlighten; adorn. Also ILLUMINE. [See ILLUMINATE.]

ILL-TEMPERED (il-tem'perd) *a.* cross; peevish; fretful.

ILLUMINATE (i-lū'mi-nāt) *v.t.* to enlighten; illustrate. [L. (part.) *illuminatus*, fr. *illuminare*, fr. *in*, and *luminare*, to cast light, fr. *lumen* = *lucimen*, light, fr. *lucere*, to shine.]

ILLUMINATION (i-lū-mi-nā'shun) *n.* act of enlightening; display of light for festive occasions.

ILLUSION (i-lū'zhun) *n.* false show; error. [L. (part.) *illusus*, fr. *illudere*.]

ILLUSIONIST (i-lū'zhun-ist) *n.* one given to illusion.

ILLUSIVE (i-lū'siv) *a.* deceiving by false show.

ILLUSTRATE (i-lus'trāt, il'us-trāt) *v.t.* to explain; make clear; elucidate. [L. (part.) *illustratus*, fr. *illustrare*, to light up, fr. *illustris*, bright.]

ILLUSTRATION (il-us-trā'shun) *n.* explanation.

ILLUSTRATIVE (i-lus'tra-tiv) *a.* tending to explain.

ILLUSTRIOUS (i-lus'tri-us) *a.* shining; brilliant; conferring honour; renowned; distinguished.

ILLUSTRIOUSLY (i-lus'tri-us-li) *ad.* in an illustrious manner.

ILL-WILL (il-wil') *n.* unkind or hostile feeling.

IMAGE (im'ij) *n.* a likeness; statue; idol; idea;—*v.t.* to form a likeness in idea. [L. *imago*.]

IMAGERY (im'ij-er-i) *n.* lively description; figures of speech.

IMAGINABLE (i-maj'i-na-bl) *a.* possible to be conceived.

IMAGINABLY (i-maj'i-na-bli) *ad.* in an imaginable manner.

IMAGINARY (i-maj'i-na-ri) *a.* existing only in imagination; unreal; fanciful.

IMAGINATION (i-maj-i-nā'shun) *n.* faculty of forming mental images; conception; idea.

IMAGINATIVE (i-maj'i-nā-tiv) *a.* gifted with or pertaining to imagination.

IMAGINATIVENESS (i-maj'i-nā-tiv-nes) *n.* high degree of fancy or invention.

IMAGINE (i-maj'in) *v.t.* or *i.* to think; conceive; contrive; devise. [O.F. *imaginer*, fr. L. *imaginare*, fr. *imago*.]

IMBECILE (im'be-sēl) *a.* weak in mind or body;—*n.* a weak or impotent man. [O.F., fr. L. *imbecillis*, weak.]

IMBECILITY (im-be-sil'i-ti) *n.* weakness of body or mind.

IMBED (im-bed') *v.t.* to sink or cover, as in a bed. [Fr. pref. *im* = in, and BED.]

IMBIBE (im-bib') *v.t.* to drink in; receive and retain. [L. *in*, in, and *bibere*, to drink.]

IMBITTER (im-bit'er) *v.t.* to make bitter or more severe; exasperate. Also EMBITTER.

IMBOSOM (im-bōō'zum) *v.t.* to embrace or hold in the bosom. Also written EMBOSOM.

IMBRICATED (im'bri-kā-ted) *a.* laid one under another, as tiles. [L. (part.) *imbricatus*, fr. *imbricare*, fr. *imbrex*, a gutter, fr. *imber*, a shower.]

IMBRICATION (im-bri-kā'shun) *n.* overlapping of the edges; a concave indenture.

IMBROWN (im-broun') *v.t.* to make brown.

IMBRUE (im-brōō') *v.t.* to steep; wet. [O.F. *embruer*, fr. *bevre* = F. *boire*, fr. L. *bibere*, to drink.]

IMBUE (im-bū') *v.t.* to tincture deeply; instruct with; instil. [O.F. *imbuer*, fr. L. *imbuere*, fr. *in*, and *bibere*, to drink.]

IMITABLE (im'i-ta-bl) *a.* that may be imitated.

IMITATE (im'i-tāt) *v.t.* to follow a pattern or example; copy; counterfeit. [L. (part.) *imitatus*, fr. *imitari*.]

IMITATION (im-i-tā'shun) *n.* act of imitating; a copy; forged resemblance.

IMITATIVE (im'i-tā-tiv) *a.* tending to or aiming at likeness.

IMITATOR (im'i-tā-ter) *n.* one who imitates.

IMMACULATE (i-mak'ū-lat) *a.* without blemish; morally spotless. [L. (part.) *immaculatus*, fr. *in*, and *macula*, a spot.]

IMMANENCY (im-a'nen-si) *n.* internal dwelling.

IMMANENT (im'a-nent) *a.* inherent; having permanent existence. [L. (part. stem) *immanent-*, fr. L. *immanere*, remain near, fr. *in*, and *manere*, to remain.]

IMMANUEL (i-man'ū-el) *n.* God with us— an appellation of the Saviour. [H.]

IMMATERIAL (im-a-tē'ri-al) *a.* not consisting of matter; unimportant. [Fr. *in*, and MATERIAL.]

IMMATERIALISM (im-ȧ-tō'ri-ȧl-izm) *n.* doctrine of spiritual existence.

IMMATERIALITY (im-ȧ-tē-ri-al'i-ti) *n.* quality of being distinct from matter.

IMMATERIALLY (im-ȧ-tē'ri-ȧl-i) *ad.* to an unimportant degree; without matter.

IMMATURE (im-ȧ-tūr') *a.* unripe; unseasonable. [L. *in*, and **MATURE**.]

IMMATURITY (im-ȧ-tūr'i-ti) *n.* unripeness; incompleteness. Also **IMMATURENESS**.

IMMEASURABLE (i-mezh'ūr-ȧ-bl) *a.* that cannot be measured. [L. *in*, and **MEASURABLE**.]

IMMEASURABLY (i-mezh'ūr-ȧ-bli) *ad.* beyond all measure.

IMMEDIATE (i-mē'di-ȧt) *a.* without a medium; instant; direct; near at hand. [Late L. *immediatus*, fr. L. *in*, and *medius*, middle.]

IMMEDIATELY (i-mē'di-ȧt-li) *ad.* closely; directly; instantly.

IMMEMORIAL (im-ē-mō'ri-ȧl) *a.* beyond memory, record, or tradition; out of mind. [L. *in*, and **MEMORIAL**.]

IMMEMORIALLY (im-ē-mō'ri-ȧl-i) *ad.* from a past time beyond memory.

IMMENSE (i-mens') *a.* vast in extent; without known limit; huge; enormous. [F., fr. L. *immensus*, fr. *in*, and (part.) *mensus*, fr. *metiri*, to measure.]

IMMENSELY (i-mens'li) *ad.* vastly.

IMMENSITY (i-men'si-ti) *n.* unlimited extension; vastness.

IMMERGE (i-merj') *v.t.* to immerse. [L. *in*, in, and *mergere*, to plunge.]

IMMERSE (i-mers') *v.t.* to put into a fluid; engage deeply. [L. (part.) *mersus*, fr. *mergere*.]

IMMERSION (i-mer'shun) *n.* the act of immersing, or state of being immersed.

IMMIGRANT (im'i-grant) *n.* one who immigrates. [See **IMMIGRATE**.]

IMMIGRATE (im'i-grāt) *v.i.* to remove into a country for residence. [L. (part.) *immigratus*, fr. *in*, in, and *migrare*, to migrate.]

IMMIGRATION (im-i-grā'shun) *n.* removal into a country.

IMMINENCE (im'i-nens) *n.* impending evil or danger.

IMMINENT (im'i-nent) *a.* impending; threatening. [L. (part. stem) *imminent-*, fr. *imminere*, project.]

IMMINENTLY (im'i-nent-li) *a.* in a threatening manner.

IMMOBILE (im-mōb'il) *a.* not mobile; fixed. [L. *in*, and *mobilis*, movable, fr. *movere*, move.]

IMMOBILITY (im-ō-bil'i-ti) *n.* resistance to motion; immovableness.

IMMODERATE (i-mod'e-rȧt) *a.* excessive; exorbitant; intemperate. [From *in*, and **MODERATE**.]

IMMODERATELY (i-mod'e-rȧt-li) *ad.* in an excessive degree.

IMMODEST (i-mod'est) *a.* indecent; indelicate. [L. *in*, and **MODEST**.]

IMMODESTLY (i-mod'est-li) *ad.* without reserve.

IMMODESTY (i-mod'es-ti) *n.* want of modesty.

IMMOLATE (im'ō-lāt) *v.t.* to sacrifice. [L. (part.) *immolatus*, fr. *immolare*, to sprinkle a victim with sacrificial meal, fr. *mola*, meal.]

IMMOLATION (im-ō-lā'shun) *n.* act of sacrificing; a sacrifice.

IMMOLATOR (im'ō-lā-ter) *n.* one who offers in sacrifice.

IMMORAL (i-mor'ȧl) *a.* evil; wicked. [L. *in*, and **MORAL**.]

IMMORALITY (im-u-ral'i-ti) *n.* any act that is contrary to the divine law.

IMMORALLY (i-mor'ȧl-i) *ad.* viciously.

IMMORTAL (i-mor'tȧl) *a.* never-dying; everlasting; imperishable. [L. *in*, and **MORTAL**.]

IMMORTALISE (i-mor'tȧl-iz) *v.t.* to make immortal.

IMMORTALITY (im-or-tal'i-ti) *n.* immortal existence.

IMMORTALLY (i-mor'tȧl-i) *ad.* with exemption from death.

IMMOVABILITY (i-mōō-vȧ-bil'i-ti) *n.* quality of being immovable; steadfastness. Also **IMMOVABLENESS**.

IMMOVABLE (i-mōō'vȧ-bl) *a.* that cannot be moved. [L. *in*, and **MOVABLE**.]

IMMOVABLY (i-mōō'vȧ-bli) *ad.* firmly; unchangeably.

IMMUNE (i-mūn') *a.* exempt; free.

IMMUNITY (i-mū'ni-ti) *n.* exemption from duty, tax, office, or the like; preservation from. [F., fr. L. *in*, and *munis*, serving.]

IMMURE (i-mūr') *v.t.* to enclose within walls. [F., fr. L. *in*, and *murus*, wall.]

IMMUTABILITY (i-mū-tȧ-bil'i-ti) *n.* unchangeableness.

IMMUTABLE (i-mū'tȧ-bl) *a.* that cannot be changed; invariable. [O.F., fr. L. *in*, and **MUTABLE**.]

IMMUTABLY (i-mū'tȧ-bli) *ad.* unchangeably.

IMP (imp) *n.* offspring; a little devil; mischievous child;—*v.t.* to graft; extend or strengthen by addition. [O.E. *impe*, fr. Late L. *impotus*, a graft.]

IMPACT (im-pakt') *v.t.* to drive close;—(im'pakt) *n.* a forcible touch; stroke or shock of two bodies in collision. [L. (part.) *impactus*, fr. O.F., fr. L. *impingere*, strike.]

IMPAIR (im-pār') *v.t.* to make worse; injure; weaken;—*v.i.* to grow worse; decrease. [O.F. *empeirer*, fr. L. *in*, and *pejor*, worse.]

IMPALE (im-pāl') *v.t.* to fix on a stake. [F. *empaler*, fr. L. *in*, and *palus*, a stake.]

IMPALEMENT (im-pāl'ment) *n.* act of impaling.

IMPALPABILITY (im-pal-pȧ-bil'i-ti) *n.* quality of not being palpable or perceptible by the touch.

IMPALPABLE (im-pal'pȧ-bl) *a.* that cannot be felt or apprehended. [L. *in*, and **PALPABLE**.]

IMPALPABLY (im-pal'pȧ-bli) *ad.* in a way not readily felt or perceived.

IMPARITY (im-par'i-ti) *n.* inequality. [L. *in*, and *par*, equal.]

IMPART (im-pärt') *v.t.* to grant; bestow on another; disclose. [O.F. *empartir*, fr. L. *impartire*, fr. *in*, and *pars*, part.]

IMPARTIAL (im-pär'shal) *a.* free from bias; unprejudice; equitable. [Fr. L. *in*, and **PARTIAL**.]

IMPARTIALITY (im-pär-shi-al'i-ti) *n.* freedom from bias; equitableness.

IMPARTIALLY (im-pär'shal-i) *ad.* without bias or prejudice.

IMPASSABLE (im-pas'ȧ-bl) *a.* that cannot be passed; impervious. [L. *in*, and *passus*, step.]

IMPASSABLY (im-pas'ȧ-bli) *ad.* so as to prevent passage.

IMPASSIBILITY (im-pas-i-bil'i-ti) *n.* exemption from suffering or pain.

IMPASSIBLE (im-pas'i-bl) *a.* incapable of passion or pain. [F., fr. L. *in*, and (part.) *passus*, fr. *pati*, to suffer.]

IMPASSION (im-pash'un) *v.t.* to affect with passion. [L. *in*, and (acc.) *passionem*, fr. *passus*, fr. *pati*, to suffer.]

IMPASSIONATE (im-pash'un-āt) *v.t.* to affect powerfully; *a.* powerfully affected; without passion or feeling.

IMPASSIONED (im-pash'und) *a.* expressive of strong feeling or emotion.

IMPASSIVE (im-pas'iv) *a.* not susceptible of pain; not exhibiting feeling. [L. *in*, and **PASSIVE**.]

IMPASSIVELY (im-pas'iv-li) *ad.* without sensibility to pain.

IMPASSIVENESS (im-pas'iv-nes) *n.* insensibility. Also **IMPASSIVITY**.

IMPATIENCE (im-pā'shens) *n.* uneasiness under suffering, delay, etc.; restlessness. [L. *in*, and *patiens*, suffering.]

IMPATIENT (im-pā'shent) *a.* not able to endure or to wait; fretful; restless; eager for. [See IMPATIENCE.]

IMPATIENTLY (im-pā'shent-li) *ad.* with uneasiness or eagerness.

IMPEACH (im-pēch') *v.t.* to charge with crime, especially to charge a high official; call in question; disparage. [O.F. *empescher* = F. *empêcher*, to hinder, fr. Late L. *impedicare*, to entangle, or fr. L. (part.) *impactus*, fr. *impingere*, strike against.]

IMPEACHABLE (im-pē'cha-bl) *a.* liable to impeachment.

IMPEACHMENT (im-pēch'ment) *n.* accusation of a public officer; discredit or disparagement of one's rectitude, motives, etc.

IMPEARL (im-perl') *v.t.* to adorn with pearls.

IMPECCABILITY (im-pek-a-bil'i-ti) *n.* the quality of not being liable to sin. [L. *in*, and PECCABLE.]

IMPECCABLE (im-pek'a-bl) *a.* not liable to sin. [L. *in*, and PECCABLE.]

IMPECCANCY (im-pek'an-si) *n.* freedom from sin or failure; impeccability.

IMPECCANT (im-pek'ant) *a.* sinless. [See IMPECCABLE.]

IMPECUNIOUS (im-pe-kū'ni-us) *a.* not having money; poor. [L. *in*, and *pecunia*, money.]

IMPEDE (im-pēd') *v.t.* to hinder; obstruct. [L. *impedire*, to entangle the feet, fr. *in*, and stem *ped-*, of *pes*, a foot.]

IMPEDIMENT (im-ped'i-ment) *n.* obstruction; hindrance in speech. [See IMPEDE.]

IMPEL (im-pel') *v.t.* to urge forward. [L. *impellere*, to drive.]

IMPEND (im-pend') *v.i.* to hang over. [L. *in*, and *pendere*, hang.]

IMPENDING (im-pen'ding) *a.* hanging over; imminent.

IMPENETRABILITY (im-pen-e-tra-bil'i-ti) *n.* quality of not being penetrable.

IMPENETRABLE (im-pen'e-tra-bl) *a.* that cannot be penetrated. [L. *im* = *in*, not.]

IMPENETRABLY (im-pen'e-tra-bli) *ad.* so as not to be penetrated.

IMPENITENCE (im-pen'i-tens) *n.* obduracy; hardness of heart.

IMPENITENT (im-pen'i-tent) *a.* not repenting of sin. [L. *in*, and PENITENT.]

IMPENITENTLY (im-pen'i-tent-li) *ad.* without repentance.

IMPERATIVE (im-per'a-tiv) *a.* expressive of command;—*n.* mood of a verb which orders, exhorts, etc. [L. *imperativus*, fr. *imperare*, to command, fr. *in*, and *parare*, to prepare.]

IMPERATIVELY (im-per'a-tiv-li) *ad.* with command.

IMPERCEPTIBLE (im-per-sep'ti-bl) *a.* not to be perceived. [L. *in*, and PERCEPTIBLE.]

IMPERCEPTIBLENESS (im-per-sep'ti-bl-nes) *n.* quality of not being perceptible.

IMPERCEPTIBLY (im-per-sep'ti-bli) *ad.* so as not to be perceived.

IMPERFECT (im-per'fekt) *a.* not perfect; defective; weak; frail;—*n.* a past tense. [L. *in*, and PERFECT.]

IMPERFECTION (im-per-fek'shun) *n.* defect; want; blemish.

IMPERFECTLY (im-per'fekt-li) *ad.* not fully.

IMPERIAL (im-pē'ri-al) *a.* belonging to an empire or an emperor; noting a standard measure or a large size of paper;—*n.* a case for luggage on the top of a coach; a tuft of hair on a man's lower lip. [L. *imperialis*, fr. *imperium*, command, empire.]

IMPERIALISM (im-pē'ri-al-izm) *n.* the spirit of empire or arbitrary power.

IMPERIALIST (im-pē'ri-al-ist) *n.* an advocate of imperial government.

IMPERIL (im-per'il) *v.t.* to bring into danger. [Fr. *in*, and PERIL.]

IMPERIOUS (im-pē'ri-us) *a.* commanding; haughty; dictatorial; urgent. [L. *imperiosus*, full of command, fr. *imperium*.]

IMPERIOUSLY (im-pē'ri-us-li) *ad.* insolently.

IMPERIOUSNESS (im-pē'ri-us-nes) *n.* dictatorial manner; arrogance.

IMPERISHABLE (im-per'i-sha-bl) *a.* not liable to perish. [L. *in*, and PERISHABLE.]

IMPERISHABLENESS (im-per'i-sha-bl-nes) *n.* indestructibility.

IMPERMEABILITY (im-per-me-a-bil'i-ti) *n.* quality of not being permeable.

IMPERMEABLE (im-per'me-a-bl) *a.* that cannot be passed through. [L. *in*, and PERMEABLE.]

IMPERSONAL (im-per'sun-al) *a.* not personal; individual; noting verbs used only in the third person with *it* for a nominative. [L. *in*, and PERSONAL.]

IMPERSONALITY (im-per-su-nal'i-ti) *n.* want of individuality; anonymous character.

IMPERSONALLY (im-per'sun-al-i) *ad.* without a personal nominative.

IMPERSONATE (im-per'sun-āt) *v.t.* to personify; act. [L. *in*, and PERSONATE.]

IMPERTINENCE (im-per'ti-nens) *n.* rudeness.

IMPERTINENT (im-per'ti-nent) *a.* irrelevant; meddling; intrusive; rude. [L. *in*, and PERTINENT.]

IMPERTINENTLY (im-per'ti-nent-li) *ad.* officiously; rudely.

IMPERTURBABILITY (im-per-tur-ba-bil'i-ti) *n.* coolness of mind and temper; self-possession.

IMPERTURBABLE (im-per-tur'ba-bl) *a.* not to be disturbed. [L., fr. *in*, and *perturbare*, to disturb.]

IMPERVIOUS (im-per'vi-us) *a.* not to be penetrated. [L. *in*, and PERVIOUS.]

IMPERVIOUSLY (im-per'vi-us-li) *ad.* impenetrably; without entrance or passage.

IMPETUOSITY (im-pet-ū-os'i-ti) *n.* violence; vehemence.

IMPETUOUS (im-pet'ū-us) *a.* rushing with violence; rapid; hasty; vehement; passionate. [L. *impetuosus*.]

IMPETUOUSLY (im-pet'ū-us-li) *ad.* furiously.

IMPETUS (im'pe-tus) *n.* force of motion; strong tendency or inclination. [L., fr. *impetere*, rush upon, fr. *in*, and *petere*, seek.]

IMPIETY (im-pī'e-ti) *n.* ungodliness. [See IMPIOUS.]

IMPINGE (im-pinj') *v.t.* to dash against; touch upon; infringe. [L. *impingere*, fix, strike.]

IMPIOUS (im'pi-us) *a.* irreverent towards God; profane; scoffing. [L. *in*, and PIOUS.]

IMPIOUSLY (im'pi-us-li) *ad.* with irreverence; profanely.

IMPLACABILITY (im-pla-ka-bil'i-ti) *n.* quality or state of being implacable.

IMPLACABLE (im-plak'a-bl) *a.* not to be appeased; inexorable; stubborn. [L. *in*, and *placabile*, placable.]

IMPLACABLY (im-plak'a-bli) *ad.* with unappeasable enmity.

IMPLANT (im-plant') *v.t.* to insert; fix. [L. *in*, and PLANT.]

IMPLANTATION (im-plan-tā'shun) *n.* act of implanting.

IMPLEMENT (im'ple-ment) *n.* a tool or instrument; utensil;—*v.t.* to fulfil a contract or engagement. [L. *implementum*, fr. *implere*, to fill up.]

IMPLETION (im-plē'shun) *n.* act of filling; state of being full.

IMPLICATE (im'pli-kāt) *v.t.* to involve; connect with. [L. (part.) *implicatus*, fr. *in*, and *plicare*, to fold.]

IMPLICATION (im-pli-kā'shun) *n.* act of involving; entanglement; inference.

IMPLICATIVE (im'pli-kā-tiv, im-plik'a-tiv) *a.* having implication.

IMPLICIT (im-plis'it) *a.* tacitly implied; unreserved; relying entirely. [L. *implicitus.*]

IMPLICITLY (im-plis'it-li) *ad.* by inference; unreservedly.

IMPLIEDLY (im-pli'ed-li) *ad.* by implication. [See **IMPLY.**]

IMPLORE (im-plōr') *v.t.* to call upon in supplication; beseech. [L. *implorare,* to cry aloud.]

IMPLORER (im-plōr'er) *n.* one who implores.

IMPLORINGLY (im-plōr'ing-li) *ad.* with earnest entreaty.

IMPLY (im-pli') *v.t.* to contain by inference; signify; mean. [O.F., fr. L. *implicare,* to implicate.]

IMPOLICY (im-pol'i-si) *n.* inexpedience. [L. *in,* and **POLICY.**]

IMPOLITE (im-pō-lit') *a.* not having politeness; uncivil; rude. [L. *in,* and **POLITE.**]

IMPOLITELY (im-pō-lit'li) *ad.* uncivilly.

IMPOLITENESS (im-pō-lit'nes) *n.* want of manners; incivility.

IMPOLITIC (im-pol'i-tik) *a.* not politic; inexpedient; imprudent. [L. *in,* and **POLITIC.**]

IMPONDERABLE (im-pon'der-a-bl) *a.* that cannot be weighed. [L. *in,* and stem *ponder*—of *pondus,* weight.]

IMPORT (im-pōrt') *v.t.* to bring from another country or port; imply; signify;—(im'pōrt) *n.* thing imported; signification; moment. [F., fr. L. *in,* and *portare,* carry.]

IMPORTABLE (im-pōr'ta-bl) *a.* that may be imported.

IMPORTANCE (im-pōr'tans) *n.* weight; consequence.

IMPORTANT (im-pōr'tant) *a.* weighty; momentous.

IMPORTANTLY (im-pōr'tant-li) *ad.* with importance.

IMPORTATION (im-pōr-tā'shun) *n.* act of importing; commodities imported.

IMPORTER (im-pōr'ter) *n.* one who brings goods from abroad.

IMPORTUNATE (im-por'tū-nāt) *a.* earnest in request or demand; exacting; overpressing. [See **IMPORTUNE.**]

IMPORTUNATELY (im-por'tū-nat-li) *ad.* with urgent solicitation.

IMPORTUNE (im-por-tūn', im-por'tūn) *v.t.* to solicit earnestly and frequently; dun; —*a.* unseasonable. [F., fr. L. *importunus,* fr. *in,* and *portus,* harbour.]

IMPORTUNITY (im-por-tū'ni-ti) *n.* urgent and repeated request.

IMPOSABLE (im-pō'za-bl) *a.* that may be laid on. [See **IMPOSE.**]

IMPOSE (im-pōz') *v.t.* to put or lay on; enjoin or command; pass off; palm. [F. *imposer,* to lay upon, fr. L. *in,* and *ponere,* to place.]

IMPOSING (im-pō'zing) *a.* impressive; commanding.

IMPOSINGLY (im-pō'zing-li) *ad.* as if by authority.

IMPOSITION (im-pu-zish'un) *n.* act of laying on; deception.

IMPOSSIBILITY (im-pos-i-bil'i-ti) *n.* that which cannot be.

IMPOSSIBLE (im-pos'i-bl) *a.* that cannot be, or be done. [L. *in,* and **POSSIBLE.**]

IMPOST (im'pōst) *n.* a tax or duty, especially upon imports; the part of a pillar or pier on which the weight of the arch rests. [O.F. = F. *impôt,* fr. L. *imponere,* to lay on.]

IMPOSTOR (im-pos'ter) *n.* a deceiver. [L. *imponere,* impose upon.]

IMPOSTURE (im-pos'tūr) *n.* imposition.

IMPOTENCE (im'pu-tens) *n.* weakness; imbecility.

IMPOTENT (im'pu-tent) *a.* weak; wanting competent power. [L. *in,* and **POTENT.**]

IMPOTENTLY (im'pu-tent-li) *ad.* weakly.

IMPOUND (im-pound') *v.t.* to confine in a pound or enclosure. [L. *in,* and **POUND.**]

IMPOUNDAGE (im-poun'dij) *n.* act of impounding, as cattle.

IMPOUNDER (im-poun'der) *n.* one who impounds.

IMPOVERISH (im-pov'er-ish) *v.t.* to make poor; exhaust fertility. [O.F., fr. L. *in,* and *pauper,* poor.]

IMPOVERISHER (im-pov'er-ish-er) *n.* one who makes poor; that which impairs fertility.

IMPOVERISHMENT (im-pov'er-ish-ment) *n.* reduction to poverty; exhaustion.

IMPRACTICABILITY (im-prak-ti-ka-bil'i-ti) *n.* state or quality of being not practicable.

IMPRACTICABLE (im-prak'ti-ka-bl) *a.* that cannot be done; impossible; stubborn. [L. *in,* and **PRACTICABLE.**]

IMPRACTICABLY (im-prak'ti-ka-bli) *ad.* in an impracticable manner.

IMPRACTICAL (im-prak'ti-kal) *a.* not practical; visionary. [See **IMPRACTICABLE.**]

IMPRECATE (im'pre-kāt) *v.t.* to invoke a curse on any one. [L. (part.) *imprecatus,* fr. *in,* and *precari,* pray.]

IMPRECATION (im-pre-kā'shun) *n.* prayer for evil; curse; execration.

IMPRECATORY (im'pre-kā-tur-i) *a.* containing a curse; maledictory. [See **IMPRECATE.**]

IMPREGNABLE (im-preg'na-bl) *a.* that cannot be taken; invincible. [F. *imprenable,* fr. L. *in,* and *prenere, prehendere,* take.]

IMPREGNABILITY (im-preg-na-bil'i-ti) *n.* state of being invincible or unattainable.

IMPREGNABLY (im-preg'na-bli) *ad.* in a manner to defy force.

IMPREGNATE (im-preg'nāt) *v.t.* to make pregnant; infuse; imbue. [L. (part.) *impregnatus,* fr. *impregnare.*]

IMPREGNATION (im-preg-nā'shun) *n.* the act of impregnating.

IMPRESS (im-pres') *v.t.* to stamp; print; force into service as seamen; fix in the mind; inculcate;—(im'pres) *n.* mark; stamp; likeness; device. [L. *in,* and (part.) *pressus,* fr. *premere,* to press.]

IMPRESSIBILITY (im-pres-i-bil'i-ti) *n.* susceptibility of impressions.

IMPRESSIBLE (im-pres'i-bl) *a.* that may receive impression.

IMPRESSIBLY (im-pres'i-bli) *ad.* in a manner to leave an impression.

IMPRESSION (im-presh'un) *n.* stamp; edition; influence; effect; faint notion.

IMPRESSIVE (im-pres'iv) *a.* producing effect; earnest; solemn; susceptible.

IMPRESSIVELY (im-pres'iv-li) *ad.* so as to make impression.

IMPRESSMENT (im-pres'ment) *n.* the act of forcing men into service.

IMPRESSURE (im-presh'ūr) *n.* mark by pressure.

IMPRIMATUR (im-pri-mā'tur) *n.* a licence to print and publish; a mark of approval. [L. =let it be printed.]

IMPRIMIS (im-pri'mis) *ad.* in the first place. [L. *in,* and *primus,* first.]

IMPRINT (im-print') *v.t.* to mark by pressure; to fix deep;—(im'print) *n.* the publisher's name, with date and place of publication. [L. *in,* and **PRINT.**]

IMPRISON (im-priz'n) *v.t.* to put in a prison; confine. [L. *in,* and **PRISON.**]

IMPRISONMENT (im-priz'n-ment) *n.* confinement.

IMPROBABILITY (im-prob-a-bil'i-ti) *n.* unlikelihood.

IMPROBABLE (im-prob'a-bl) *a.* not likely. [L. *in,* and **PROBABLE.**]

IMPROBABLY (im-prob'a-bli) *ad.* in a manner not likely.

IMPROBITY (im-prob'i-ti) *n.* dishonesty. [L. *improbitas,* fr. *in,* and *probitas,* probity.]

Fāte, fär, ado; mē, her; mine; nōte; tūne; mōōn.

IMPROMPTU (im-promp'tŭ) *a.* or *ad.* without previous study; off-hand. [L., in readiness, fr. *promptus*, ready. Cf. **PROMPT**.]

IMPROPER (im-prŏp'ẽr) *a.* not proper. [L. *in*, and **PROPER**.]

IMPROPERLY (im-prop'ẽr-li) *ad.* unsuitably; not fitly.

IMPROPRIETY (im-prŏ-prī'e-ti) *n.* unsuitableness to time, place, or character; any unbecoming act.

IMPROVABLE (im-prŏŏv'va-bl) *a.* that may be improved.

IMPROVABLENESS (im-prŏŏv'va-bl-nes) susceptibility of improvement. Also **IMPROVABILITY**.

IMPROVE (im-prŏŏv') *v.t.* to make better; use to advantage;—*v.i.* to grow better. [O.F. *aproer, approuer*, to benefit, fr. *a* = L. *ad*, and *prou*, profit. Variant of **APPROVE**.]

IMPROVEMENT (im-prŏŏv'ment) *n.* progress from one condition to a better; instruction;—*pl.* valuable additions.

IMPROVIDENCE (im-prov'i-dens) *n.* want of foresight.

IMPROVIDENT (im-prov'i-dent) *a.* not making provision for the future. [L. *in*, and **PROVIDENT**.]

IMPROVIDENTLY (im-prov'i-dent-li) *ad.* without forethought.

IMPROVISATION (im-prov-i-sā'shun) *n.* art of composing extemporaneously.

IMPROVISE (im-prŏ-viz') *v.i.* to compose extemporaneously. [L. *in*, and *provisus*, foreseen, fr. *videre*, to see.]

IMPROVISO (im-prŏ-vi'zŏ) *ad.* offhand. [It.]

IMPRUDENCE (im-prŏŏ'dens) *n.* want of prudence; rashness; a rash act.

IMPRUDENT (im-prŏŏ'dent) *a.* wanting prudence; inconsiderate; injudicious. [L. *in*, and **PRUDENT**.] [creetly.

IMPRUDENTLY (im-prŏŏ'dent-li) *ad.* indis-

IMPUDENCE (im'pū-dens) *n.* shameless effrontery.

IMPUDENT (im'pū-dent) *a.* wanting modesty; shamelessly bold. [L. *impudens*, fr. *in*, and *pudere*, to be ashamed.]

IMPUDENTLY (im'pū-dent-li) *ad.* with shameless effrontery.

IMPUGN (im-pūn') *v.t.* to call in question; contradict. [L. *in*, and *pugnare*, fight.]

IMPUGNABLE (im-pū'na-bl) *a.* that may be called in question.

IMPUGNER (im-pū'nẽr) *n.* one who impugns.

IMPULSE (im'puls) *n.* force communicated; influence; motive; instigation. [L. (part.) *impulsus*, fr. *impellere*, to urge on.]

IMPULSION (im-pul'shun) *n.* act of impelling.

IMPULSIVE (im-pul'siv) *a.* communicating force; acting from impulse.

IMPULSIVELY (im-pul'siv-li) *ad.* with sudden energy.

IMPULSIVENESS (im-pul'siv-nes) *n.* quality of acting or being moved to act hastily.

IMPUNITY (im-pū'ni-ti) *n.* exemption from punishment. [L. *impunitas*, impunity, fr. *in*, and *pœna*, punishment.]

IMPURE (im-pūr') *a.* not pure; mixed; unclean; unholy; unchaste. [L. *in*, and **PURE**.]

IMPURITY (im-pū'ri-ti) *n.* foulness; anything impure in thought, act, or word.

IMPUTABLE (im-pū'ta-bl) *a.* that may be imputed.

IMPUTATION (im-pū-tā'shun) *n.* act of imputing; charge; attribution.

IMPUTATIVE (im-pū'ta-tiv) *a.* that may be imputed.

IMPUTE (im-pūt') *v.t.* to charge upon; attribute. [L. *in*, and *putare*, reckon, think.]

IMPUTER (im-pū'tẽr) *n.* one who imputes.

IN (in) (1) *prep.* within; on behalf of; on account of; by; through; because;—*ad.* inside; closely;—(2) L. *pref.* meaning *not* before adjectives and adverbs, and *in* or *into* before verbs. [(1) O.E. (2) L.]

INABILITY (in-a-bil'i-ti) *n.* want of power, means, skill, etc. [L. *in*, and **ABILITY**.]

INACCESSIBILITY (in-ak-ses-i-bil'i-ti) *n.* the quality of being beyond reach.

INACCESSIBLE (in-ak-ses'i-bl) *a.* that cannot be reached. [L. *in*, and **ACCESSIBLE**.]

INACCURACY (in-ak'ū-ra-si) *n.* want of accuracy; a mistake.

INACCURATE (in-ak'ū-rat) *a.* not exact or correct; erroneous. [L. *in*, and **ACCURATE**.]

INACCURATELY (in-ak'ū-rat-li) *ad.* not correctly; erroneously.

INACTION (in-ak'shun) *n.* want of action; state of rest; idleness.

INACTIVE (in-ak'tiv) *a.* not active; inert; indolent; idle. [L. *in*, and **ACTIVE**.]

INACTIVELY (in-ak'tiv-li) *ad.* without effort or employment.

INACTIVITY (in-ak-tiv'i-ti) *n.* want of activity; idleness.

INADEQUACY (in-ad'e-kwa-si) *n.* insufficiency.

INADEQUATE (in-ad'e-kwat) *a.* not equal to the purpose; insufficient; defective. [L. *in*, and **ADEQUATE**.]

INADEQUATELY (in-ad'e-kwat-li) *ad.* not fully or sufficiently.

INADEQUATENESS (in-ad'e-kwat-nes) *n.* insufficiency; inequality.

INADHESION (in-ad-hē'zhun) *n.* want of adhesion. [L. *in*, and **ADHESION**.]

INADHESIVE (in-ad-hē'siv) *a.* not adhering.

INADMISSIBILITY (in-ad-mis-i-bil'i-ti) *n.* quality of being inadmissible.

INADMISSIBLE (in-ad-mis'i-bl) *a.* not proper to be admitted or allowed. [L. *in*, and **ADMISSIBLE**.]

INADVERTENCE (in-ad-vẽr'tens) *n.* negligence; oversight. Also **INADVERTENCY**.

INADVERTENT (in-ad-vẽr'tent) *a.* heedless; inattentive; absent in mind. [L. *in*, and **ADVERTENT**.]

INADVERTENTLY (in-ad-vẽr'tent-li) *ad.* with negligence.

INALIENABLE (in-āl'yen-a-bl) *a.* that cannot be alienated or transferred. [L. *in*, and **ALIEN**.]

INALIENABLY (in-āl'yen-a-bli) *ad.* in a way to prevent transference.

INANE (in-ān') *a.* void; empty; wanting sense;—*n.* empty space. [L. *inanis*.]

INANIMATE (in-an'i-mat) *a.* void of life. [L. *in*, and **ANIMATE**.]

INANIMATION (in-an-i-mā'shun) *n.* want of spirit; lifelessness.

INANITION (in-a-nish'un) *n.* want of fullness; emptiness; exhaustion from want of food.

INANITY (in-an'i-ti) *n.* emptiness; vanity.

INAPPEASABLE (in-a-pē'za-bl) *a.* not to be appeased. [L. *in*, and **APPEASE**.]

INAPPLICABILITY (in-ap-li-ka-bil'i-ti) *n.* quality of not being applicable.

INAPPLICABLE (in-ap'li-ka-bl) *a.* that may not be applied; unfit. [L. *in*, and **APPLICABLE**.]

INAPPLICATION (in-ap-li-kā'shun) *n.* want of application; indolence.

INAPPRECIABLE (in-a-prē'shi-a-bl) *a.* not to be estimated. [L. *in*, and **APPRECIATE**.]

INAPPREHENSIVE (in-ap-re-hen'siv) *a.* not apprehensive; regardless. [L. *in*, and **APPREHEND**.]

INAPPROPRIATE (in-a-prŏ'pri-at) *a.* unsuitable. [L. *in*, and **APPROPRIATE**.]

INAPT (in-apt') *a.* not apt; unsuited; unfit. [L. *in*, and **APT**.]

INAPTITUDE (in-ap'ti-tūd) *n.* unfitness.

INARCH (in-ärch') *v.t.* to graft by joining a scion to a stock without separating it from its parent tree. [L. *in*, and **ARCH**.]

INARTICULATE (in-är-tik'ū-lat) *a.* not uttered with articulation; not jointed. [L. *in*, and **ARTICULATE**.]

INARTICULATELY (in-är-tik'ū-lat-li) *ad.* not with distinct syllables.

INARTICULATION (in-ár-tik-ū-lā'shun) n. indistinctness of utterance.

INARTIFICIAL (in-ár-ti-fish'ạl) a. not done by art; artless; simple. [L. in, and ARTIFICIAL.]

INASMUCH (in-az-much') ad. since; seeing that; this being the fact. [IN, AS, MUCH.]

INATTENTION (in-ạ-ten'shun) n. neglect.

INATTENTIVE (in-ạ-ten'tiv) a. heedless. [L. in, and ATTENTION.] [lessly.

INATTENTIVELY (in-ạ-ten'tiv-li) ad. care-

INAUDIBLE (in-aw'di-bl) a. that cannot be heard; making no sound. [L. in, and AUDIBLE.]

INAUDIBLY (in-aw'di-bli) ad. so as not to be heard.

INAUGURAL (in-aw'gū-rạl) a. relating to installation.

INAUGURATE (in-aw'gū-rāt) v.t. institute formally; exhibit; invest with office. [L. (part.) inauguratus, fr. in, and augurare, to augur.]

INAUGURATION (in-aw-gū-rā'shun) n. act of inducting into office with appropriate ceremonies.

INAUSPICIOUS (in-aw-spish'us) a. unfortunate; unfavourable. [L. in, and AUSPICIOUS.]

INAUSPICIOUSLY (in-aw-spish'us-li) ad. with ill omens.

INAUSPICIOUSNESS (in-aw-spish'us-nes) n. unluckiness; unfavourableness.

INBEING (in'bē-ing) n. inherent existence. [Fr. in, and BEING.]

INBORN (in'born) a. implanted by nature. [Fr. in, and BORN.]

INBREATHE (in-brēᴛʜ') v.t. to infuse by breathing. [Fr. in, and BREATHE.]

INBRED (in'bred) a. bred within; natural. [Fr. in, and BREED.]

INCA (ing'kạ) n. the native prince of ancient Peru. [Sp. inca, fr. Peruv. inca.]

INCALCULABLE (in-kal'kū-lạ-bl) a. that cannot be calculated. [L. in, and CALCULATE.]

INCALCULABLY (in-kal'kū-lạ-bli) ad. beyond reckoning; inconceivably.

INCANDESCENCE (in-kan-des'ens) n. a white heat.

INCANDESCENT (in-kan-des'ent) a. glowing with heat. [L. (part. stem), fr. incandescere, to become warm, fr. candere, to glow.]

INCANTATION (in-kan-tā'shun) n. magical charm; enchantment. [L. (acc.) incantationem, fr. incantare, to chant.]

INCAPABILITY (in-kā-pạ-bil'i-ti) n. incapacity; want of qualifications.

INCAPABLE (in-kā'pạ-bl) a. wanting power; disqualified. [L. in, and CAPABLE.]

INCAPABLY (in-kā'pạ-bli) ad. in an incapable manner.

INCAPACIOUS (in-kạ-pā'shus) a. not capacious.

INCAPACITATE (in-kạ-pas'i-tāt) v.t. to deprive of power. [L. in, and CAPACITATE, fr. CAPACITY.]

INCAPACITY (in-kạ-pas'i-ti) n. want of capacity; inability; incompetency.

INCARCERATE (in-kár'se-rāt) v.t. to imprison. [L. in, and carcer, prison.]

INCARCERATION (in-kár-se-rā'shun) n. imprisonment.

INCARNADINE (in-kár'nạ-dīn) a. flesh-coloured;—v.t. to dye red or flesh colour. [F.]

INCARNATE (in-kár'nạt) a. clothed in flesh. [L. (part.) incarnatus, fr. in, and caro, carnis, flesh.]

INCARNATION (in-kár-nā'shun) n. act of clothing with flesh; assumption of a human body; striking exemplification.

INCARNATIVE (in-kár'nạ-tiv) a. generating flesh.

INCASE (in-kās') v.t. to enclose in a case. [L. in, and CASE.]

INCASEMENT (in-kās'ment) n. act of enclosing; any enclosing substance.

INCAUTIOUS (in-kaw'shus) a. unwary. [L. in, and CAUTIOUS.]

INCAUTIOUSLY (in-kaw'shus-li) ad. without caution; heedlessly.

INCAUTIOUSNESS (in-kaw'shus-nes) n. heedlessness.

INCENDIARISM (in-sen'dyạ-rizm) n. crime of house-burning. [L. incendere, to set on fire.]

INCENDIARY (in-sen'dyạ-ri) n. one who maliciously burns a house or foments strife;—a. inflammatory; seditious. [L. incendiarius, fr. incendium, fr. incendere.]

INCENSE (in'sens) n. perfume exhaled by fire;—v.t. to perfume with incense or odours.

INCENSE (in-sens') v.t. to kindle; inflame with anger; enrage. [L. (part.) incensus, fr. incendere, to kindle.]

INCENTIVE (in-sen'tiv) a. inciting; encouraging;—n. that which encourages; motive or spur. [L. incentivus, striking up a tune, fr. incinere, to sing, fr. in, and canere, to sing.]

INCEPTION (in-sep'shun) n. a beginning. [L. (acc.) inceptionem, fr. (part.) inceptus, fr. incipere, to begin.]

INCEPTIVE (in-sep'tiv) a. beginning.

INCEPTIVELY (in-sep'tiv-li) ad. in an inceptive manner.

INCERTITUDE (in-ser'ti-tūd) n. uncertainty. [L. in, and CERTITUDE.]

INCESSANCY (in-ses'ạn-si) n. unintermitted continuance.

INCESSANT (in-ses'ạnt) a. unceasing. [L. (part. stem) incessant-, fr. in, and cessare, cease.]

INCESSANTLY (in-ses'ạnt-li) ad. without intermission.

INCEST (in'sest) n. cohabitation of persons within the prohibited degrees of kindred. [F., fr. L. in, and castus, chaste.]

INCESTUOUS (in-ses'tū-us) a. consisting in or guilty of incest.

INCESTUOUSLY (in-ses'tū-us-li) ad. in an incestuous manner.

INCESTUOUSNESS (in-ses'tū-us-nes) n. state or quality of being incestuous.

INCH (insh) (1) n. the twelfth part of a foot;—(2) n.a small island. [(1) O.E. ynce. from L. uncia, twelfth part of anything. Cf. OUNCE. (2) Gael. innis.]

INCHOATE (in'kō-āt) a. begun. [L. (part.) inchoatus, fr. inchoare, to begin.]

INCIDENCE (in'si-dens) n. the direction in which a body, ray of light, etc., falls on any surface.

Incidence.
ABF, angle of incidence; CBF, angle of reflection.

INCIDENT (in'si-dent) a. falling on;—n. that which happens; event; fact; circumstance. [F., fr. L. (part stem) incident-, fr. incidere, to fall, fr. in, on, and cadere, to fall.]

INCIDENTAL (in-si-den'tạl) a. accidental.

INCIDENTALLY (in-si-den'tal-i) ad. by accident.

INCINERATE (in-sin'e-rāt) v.t. to burn to ashes. [L. (part.) incineratus, fr. in, and cinis, cineris, ashes.]

INCIPIENCY (in-sip'i-en-si) n. beginning.

INCIPIENT (in-sip'i-ent) a. commencing. [L. (part. stem) incipient-, fr. incipere, to begin.]

INCIPIENTLY (in-sip'i-ent-li) ad. at first.

INCISE (in-siz') v.t. to cut in; to carve; to engrave. [L. (part.) incisus, fr. incidere, to cut.]

INCISION (in-sizh'un) n. a cut; gash; a wound.

INCISIVE (in-sī'siv) a. cutting; sharp; biting; trenchant.

INCISOR (in-si'ser) *n.* a cutter; a fore-tooth.
INCISORY (in-si'su-ri) *a.* having the quality of cutting.
INCISURE (in-sizh'ūr) *n.* a cut.
INCITANT (in'si-tant) *n.* that which incites to action.
INCITATION (in-si-tā'shun) *n.* act of inciting; that which incites.
INCITE (in-sit') *v.t.* to move or rouse to action. [L. *incitare*, to rouse, fr. *citare*, fr. *ciere*, to put in motion.]
INCITEMENT (in-sit'ment) *n.* that which moves the mind; motive; inciting cause.
INCIVILITY (in-si-vil'i-ti) *n.* want of civility; disrespect; rudeness. [L. *in*, and CIVIL.]
INCLEMENCY (in-klem'en-si) *n.* severity.
INCLEMENT (in-klem'ent) *a.* severe, as applied to weather; rough; boisterous; stormy; cold. [L. *in*, and CLEMENCY.]
INCLINABLE (in-kli'na-bl) *a.* leaning or tending to.
INCLINATION (in-kli-nā'shun) *n.* a leaning; tendency; disposition.
INCLINE (in-klin') *v.t.* or *i.* to lean; bend; dispose; feel disposed;—(in'klin) an ascent or descent; a grade; a slope. [L. *inclinare*, to bend down, fr. *in*, towards, and *clinare*, to lean.]
INCLOSE (in-klōz') *v.t.* to surround; put in a case or envelope. [F. *enclos*, fr. L. *in*, and *claudere*, to shut.]
INCLOSER (in-klō'zer) *n.* one or that which encloses.
INCLOSURE (in-klō'zhūr) *n.* act of enclosing; place or thing enclosed; fence.
INCLUDE (in-klōōd') *v.t.* to comprehend; comprise. [L. (part.) *inclusus*, fr. *includere*, to shut in.]
INCLUSION (in-klōō'zhun) *n.* act of including.
INCLUSIVE (in-klōō'siv) *a.* comprehending; enclosing.
INCLUSIVELY (in-klōō'siv-li) *ad.* so as to include.
INCOGNISABLE (in-kog'ni-za-bl, in-kon'i-za-bl) *a.* that cannot be recognised, known, or distinguished. [See INCOGNITO.]
INCOGNITO (in-kog'ni-tō) *a.* or *ad.* in disguise; in private. [It., fr. L. *incognitus*, unknown, fr. *in*, and *cognitus*, known, fr. *cognoscere*, to know.]
INCOHERENCE (in-kō-hēr'ens) *n.* want of connection.
INCOHERENT (in-kō-hēr'ent) *a.* not connected. [L. *in*, and COHERENT.]
INCOHERENTLY (in-kō-hēr'ent-li) *ad.* without coherence.
INCOMBUSTIBILITY (in-kum-bus-ti-bil'i-ti) *n.* quality of being incombustible.
INCOMBUSTIBLE (in-kum-bus'ti-bl) *a.* that will not burn. [L. *in*, and COMBUSTIBLE.]
INCOME (in'kum) *n.* rent; revenue; profits, interest, etc. [L. *in*, and COME.]
INCOMMENSURABLE (in-ku-men'sū-ra-bl) *a.* having no common standard of comparison. [L. *in*, *con*, with, and *mensura*, measure.]
INCOMMENSURATE (in-ku-men'sū-rat) *a.* not of equal extent.
INCOMMODE (in-ku-mōd') *v.t.* to give inconvenience to. [L. *in*, and *commodus*, convenient.]
INCOMMODIOUS (in-ku-mō'di-us) *a.* inconvenient; unsuitable.
INCOMMUNICABLE (in-ku-mū'ni-ka-bl) *a.* not transferable; unspeakable.
INCOMMUNICATIVE (in-ku-mū'ni-kā-tiv) *a.* not free or disposed to impart. [L. *in*, and COMMUNICATE.]
INCOMPARABLE (in-kom'pa-ra-bl) *a.* that admits no comparison; matchless. [L. *in*, and COMPARE.]
INCOMPARABLY (in-kom'pa-ra-bli) *ad.* beyond comparison.
INCOMPATIBILITY (in-kum-pat-i-bil'i-ti) *n.* inconsistency; inherent difference.

INCOMPATIBLE (in-kum-pat'i-bl) *a.* inconsistent; incongruous. [L. *in*, and COMPATIBLE.]
INCOMPETENCE (in-kom'pe-tens) *n.* inability; want of means or of legal power; incapability. [L. *in*, and COMPETENT.]
INCOMPETENT (in-kom'pe-tent) *a.* not competent; improper; unfit.
INCOMPETENTLY (in-kom'pe-tent-li) *ad.* inadequately; unsuitably.
INCOMPLETE (in-kum-plēt') *a.* not finished. [L. *in*, and COMPLETE.]
INCOMPLETELY (in-kum-plēt'li) *ad.* imperfectly; partially.
INCOMPLETENESS (in-kum-plēt'nes) *n.* unfinished state.
INCOMPREHENSIBLE (in-kom-pre-hen'si-bl) *a.* that cannot be understood. [L. *in*, and COMPREHENSIBLE.]
INCOMPREHENSIVE (in-kom-pre-hen'siv) *a.* not extensive; limited.
INCOMPRESSIBILITY (in-kum-pres-i-bil'i-ti) *n.* the quality of being able to resist compression.
INCOMPRESSIBLE (in-kum-pres'i-bl) *a.* that cannot be reduced into a smaller compass. [L. *in*, and COMPRESS.]
INCOMPUTABLE (in-kum-pū'ta-bl) *a.* that cannot be reckoned; incalculable. [L. *in*, and COMPUTE.]
INCONCEIVABLE (in-kun-sē'va-bl) *a.* that cannot be conceived. [L. *in*, and CONCEIVE.]
INCONCLUSIVE (in-kun-klōō'siv) *a.* not determining a question. [L. *in*, and CONCLUSIVE.]
INCONGRUENT (in-kong'grōō-ent) *a.* inconsistent.
INCONGRUITY (in-kung-grōō'i-ti) *n.* unsuitableness.
INCONGRUOUS (in-kong'grōō-us) *a.* not consistent; unfit; inappropriate. [L. *in*, and CONGRUOUS.]
INCONSEQUENT (in-kon'se-kwent) *a.* not following the premises; illogical. [L. *in*, and CONSEQUENT.]
INCONSIDERABLE (in-kun-sid'er-a-bl) *a.* of small amount or importance; trifling. [L. *in*, and CONSIDER.]
INCONSIDERATE (in-kun-sid'er-at) *a.* thoughtless; careless. [L. *in*, and CONSIDERATE.]
INCONSIDERATELY (in-kun-sid'er-at-li) *ad.* heedlessly; without thought.
INCONSIDERATION (in-kun-sid-e-rā'shun) *n.* want of consideration.
INCONSISTENCY (in-kun-sis'ten-si) *n.* want of agreement; incongruity.
INCONSISTENT (in-kun-sis'tent) *a.* incongruous; unsuitable. [L. *in*, and CONSISTENT.]
INCONSISTENTLY (in-kun-sis'tent-li) *ad.* incongruously.
INCONSOLABLE (in-kun-sō'la-bl) *a.* not admitting comfort. [L. *in*, and CONSOLE.]
INCONSOLABLY (in-kon-sō'la-bli) *ad.* so as not to admit comfort.
INCONSPICUOUS (in-kun-spik'ū-us) *a.* not conspicuous. [L. *in*, and CONSPICUOUS.]
INCONSTANCY (in-kon'stan-si) *n.* changeableness in temper or affection.
INCONSTANT (in-kon'stant) *a.* subject to change of opinion or purpose; not uniform; variable; fickle. [L. *in*, and CONSTANT.]
INCONSTANTLY (in-kon'stant-li) *ad.* not steadily; variably.
INCONTESTABLE (in-kun-tes'ta-bl) *a.* that cannot be disputed. [L. *in*, and CONTEST.]
INCONTESTABLY (in-kun-tes'ta-bli) *ad.* beyond dispute.
INCONTINENCE (in-kon'ti-nens) *n.* want of restraint; unchastity.
INCONTINENT (in-kon'ti-nent) *a.* not restraining the passions or the natural discharges. [L. *in*, and CONTINENT.]

Fāte, fär, ado; mē, her; mīne; nōte; tūne; mōŏn.

INCONTINENTLY (in-kon'ti-nent-li) *ad.* without due restraint; immediately.

INCONTROVERTIBLE (in-kon-tru-vėr'ti-bl) *a.* that cannot be disputed. [L. *in*, and CONTROVERT.]

INCONTROVERTIBLY (in-kon-tru-vėr'ti-bli) *ad.* beyond dispute.

INCONVENIENCE (in-kun-vēn'yens) *n.* want of convenience; anything unsuitable or annoying;—*v.t.* to put out of one's way; hinder or trouble.

INCONVENIENT (in-kun-vēn'yent) *a.* unsuitable; unfit; giving trouble or annoyance. [L. *in*, and CONVENIENT.]

INCORPORATE (in-kor'po-rāt) *v.t.* or *i.* to form into a body; unite;—*a.* immaterial; mixed; associated. [L. *in*, and CORPORATE.]

INCORPORATION (in-kor-pō-rā'shun) *n.* act of incorporating; embodiment; the body or association formed.

INCORPOREAL (in-kor-pō'rē-al) *a.* not consisting of matter; not material. [L. *in*, and CORPOREAL.]

INCORRECT (in-ku-rekt') *a.* inaccurate; containing faults. [L. *in*, and CORRECT.]

INCORRECTLY (in-ku-rekt'li) *ad.* inaccurately.

INCORRECTNESS (in-ku-rekt'nes) *n.* want of accuracy.

INCORRIGIBLE (in-kor'i-ji-bl) *a.* that cannot be corrected. [L. *in* and *corrigere*, CORRECT.]

INCORRIGIBLY (in-kor'i-ji-bli) *ad.* beyond hope of amendment.

INCORRUPT (in-ku-rupt') *a.* free from corruption; honest; pure. [L. *in*, and CORRUPT.]

INCORRUPTIBILITY (in-ku-rup-ti-bil'i-ti) *n.* the quality of being incorruptible.

INCORRUPTIBLE (in-ku-rup'ti-bl) *a.* that cannot be corrupted.

INCORRUPTION (in-ku-rup'shun) *n.* exemption from decay.

INCORRUPTNESS (in-ku-rupt'nes) *n.* purity; integrity.

INCRASSATE (in-kras'āt) *v.t.* to make thick. [L. *in*, and *crassare*, make thick.]

INCRASSATION (in-kra-sā'shun) *n.* act of making thick; state of being thickened.

INCREASE (in-krēs') *v.i.* to grow;—*v.t.* to cause to grow; advance; extend. [M.E., fr. O.F., fr. L. *in*, and *crescere*, grow.]

INCREASE (in'krēs) *n.* augmentation; produce.

INCREASINGLY (in-krē'sing-li) *ad.* in a growing manner or degree.

INCREDIBILITY (in-kred-i-bil'i-ti) *n.* quality of being incredible.

INCREDIBLE (in-kred'i-bl) *a.* that cannot be believed. [L. *in*, and CREDIBLE.]

INCREDIBLY (in-kred'i-bli) *ad.* so as not to deserve belief.

INCREDULITY (in-kre-dū'li-ti) *n.* indisposition to believe.

INCREDULOUS (in-kred'ū-lus) *a.* not believing. [L. *in*, and CREDULOUS.]

INCREMENT (in'kre-ment) *n.* increase. [L. *incrementum*. Cf. INCREASE.]

INCRIMINATE (in-krim'i-nāt) *v.t.* to charge with a crime or fault. [L. *in*, and CRIME.]

INCRIMINATORY (in-krim'i-nā-tu-ri) *a.* charging with crime.

INCRUST (in-krust') *v.t.* to cover with a crust or hard coat. [L. *in*, and CRUST.]

INCRUSTATION (in-krus-tā'shun) *n.* act of encrusting; a hard coat.

INCUBATE (in'kū-bāt) *v.i.* to sit on, as eggs. [L. (part.) *incubatus*, fr. *in*, and *cubare*, lie down.]

INCUBATION (in-kū-bā'shun) *n.* act of sitting on eggs.

INCUBATOR (in'kū-bā-tėr) *n.* an apparatus for hatching eggs.

INCUBUS (in'kū-bus) *n.* the nightmare. [L. *incubare*.]

INCULCATE (in-kul'kāt) *v.t.* to enforce or urge. [L. (part.) *inculcatus*, fr. *in*, and *calcare*, tread, fr. *calx*, heel.]

INCULCATION (in-kul-kā'shun) *n.* act of inculcating.

INCULPABLE (in-kul'pa-bl) *a.* not blamable; without fault.

INCULPATE (in-kul'pāt) *v.t.* to censure. [L. (part.) *inculpatus*, fr. *in*, and *culpa*, fault.]

INCUMBENCY (in-kum'ben-si) *n.* the possession of an office.

INCUMBENT (in-kum'bent) *n.* one who has a benefice or an office;—*a.* imposed as a duty; lying upon. [L. (part. stem) *incumbent-*, fr. *incumbere*, to lie down, fr. *in*, and *cumbere*, lie down.]

INCUR (in-kur') *v.t.* to become liable to. [L. *in*, and *currere*, run.]

INCURABLE (in-kūr'a-bl) *a.* that cannot be cured. [L. *in*, and CURE.]

INCURABLY (in-kūr'a-bli) *ad.* so as to be incurable.

INCURIOUS (in-kū'ri-us) *a.* not having curiosity. [L. *in*, and CURIOUS.]

INCURSION (in-kur'shun) *n.* an inroad; invasion. [See INCUR.]

INCURSIVE (in-kur'siv) *a.* making attack; aggressive.

INCURVATE (in-kur'vāt) *v.t.* to make crooked; —*a.* bent or curved inward or upward.

INCURVE (in-kurv') *v.t.* to bend. [L. *in*, and CURVE.]

INDEBTED (in-det'ed) *a.* being in debt. [L. *in*, and DEBT.]

INDEBTEDNESS (in-det'ed-nes) *n.* state of being in debt.

INDECENCY (in-dē'sen-si) *n.* that which is unbecoming in manner or language; immodesty.

INDECENT (in-dē'sent) *a.* offensive to delicacy. [L. *in*, and DECENT.]

INDECENTLY (in-dē'sent-li) *ad.* so as to offend delicacy.

INDECIPHERABLE (in-de-sī'fėr-a-bl) *a.* that cannot be deciphered. [L. *in*, and DECIPHER.]

INDECISION (in-de-sizh'un) *n.* want of decision.

INDECISIVE (in-de-sī'siv) *a.* not decisive. [L. *in*, and DECISIVE.]

INDECLINABLE (in-de-klī'na-bl) *a.* not varied in termination. [L. *in*, and DECLINE.]

INDECOROUS (in-de-kō'rus, in-dek'u-rus) *a.* violating good manners; unbecoming; indecent. [L. *in*, and DECOROUS.]

INDECORUM (in-de-kō'rum) *n.* impropriety of conduct.

INDEED (in-dēd') *ad.* in fact; in truth.

INDEFATIGABLE (in-de-fat'i-ga-bl) *a.* not yielding to fatigue; unremitting. [F., fr. L. *in*, *de*, and *fatigare*, to tire.]

INDEFATIGABLY (in-de-fat'i-ga-bli) *ad.* without weariness.

INDEFEASIBILITY (in-de-fē-zi-bil'i-ti) *n.* quality of being indefeasible.

INDEFEASIBLE (in-de-fē'zi-bl) *a.* that cannot be defeated. [O.F. *defaire*, to undo, fr. *faire*, L. *facere*, make.]

INDEFENSIBLE (in-de-fen'si-bl) *a.* that cannot be defended. [L. *in*, and DEFEND.]

INDEFINABLE (in-de-fī'na-bl) *a.* that cannot be defined. [L. *in*, and DEFINE.]

INDEFINITE (in-def'i-nit) *a.* not precise; unlimited; uncertain. [L. *in*, and DEFINITE.]

INDEFINITELY (in-def'i-nit-li) *ad.* without limitation.

INDEFINITENESS (in-def'i-nit-nes) *n.* quality of being indefinite.

INDELIBLE (in-del'i-bl) *a.* that cannot be blotted out. [L. *in*, and *delere*, destroy, blot out.]

INDELIBLY (in-del'i-bli) *ad.* so as not to be effaced.

INDELICACY (in-del'i-kạ-si) *n.* want of delicacy.

INDELICATE (in-del'i-kăt) *a.* offensive to purity. [L. *in*, and DELICATE.]

INDELICATELY (in-del'i-kăt-li) *ad.* indecently.

INDEMNIFICATION (in-dem-ni-fi-kă'shun) *n.* act of indemnifying; that which indemnifies.

INDEMNIFY (in-dem'ni-fi) *v.t.* to secure against loss; make good. [L. *in*, and *damnum*, damage, loss, and *facere*, to make.]

INDEMNITY (in-dem'ni-ti) *n.* security against loss or penalty; compensation.

INDENT (in-dent') *v.t.* to notch; bind to service;—*n.* a notch in the margin. [Late L. *indentare*, fr. *in*, and stem *dent-*, of *dens*, tooth.]

INDENTATION (in-den-tā'shun) *n.* a cut; notch.

INDENTURE (in-den'tūr) *n.* a written contract or agreement;—*v.t.* to bind by contract.

INDEPENDENCE (in-de-pen'dens) *n.* exemption from control.

Indented.

INDEPENDENT (in-de-pen'dent) *a.* not relying on others; not subject to control;—*n.* a congregationalist. [L. *in*, and DEPENDENT.]

INDEPENDENTLY (in-de-pen'dent-li) *ad.* without dependence.

INDESCRIBABLE (in-des-kri'bạ-bl) *a.* that cannot be described. [L. *in*, and DESCRIBE.]

INDESCRIPTIVE (in-di-skrip'tiv) *a.* not containing description. [L. *in*, and DESCRIPTION.]

INDESTRUCTIBLE (in-de-struk'ti-bl) *a.* that cannot be destroyed. [L. *in*, and DESTRUCTIVE.]

INDETERMINABLE (in-de-tẹr'mi-nạ-bl) *a.* that cannot be determined. [L. *in*, and DETERMINE.]

INDETERMINATE (in-de-tẹr'mi-năt) *a.* indefinite; not fixed; uncertain.

INDETERMINATELY (in-de-tẹr'mi-năt-li) *ad.* without certainty.

INDETERMINATION (in-de-tẹr-mi-nā'shun) *n.* wavering or unsettled state of mind.

INDEX (in'deks) *n.* something that points; table of contents;—*pl.* INDEXES or INDICES. [L., fr. *indicare*, to show.]

INDEXER (in'dek-sẹr) *n.* maker of an index.

INDIA (in'di-ạ) *n.* a country in Asia, so named from the River Indus. [L., fr. Hind., fr. Skr. = river.]

INDIAMAN (in'di-ạ-mạn) *n.* a large ship in the India trade. [See INDIA.]

INDIAN (in'di-ạn) *a.* pertaining to the Indies;—*n.* a native of the Indies. [See INDIA.]

INDIAN CORN (in'di-ạn korn) *n.* a species of maize, native of America. [Fr. INDIA and CORN.]

INDIAN INK (in'di-ạn ingk) *n.* a water colour made of lamp black and animal glue. [Fr. INDIA and INK.]

INDIA-PAPER (in'di-ạ-pā'pẹr) *n.* a fine paper used for first proofs of engravings. [Fr. INDIA and PAPER.]

INDIA-RUBBER (in'di-ạ-rub'ẹr) *n.* caoutchouc. used for rubbing out pencil-marks, etc. [Fr. INDIA and RUB.]

INDICANT (in'di-kạnt) *a.* showing.

INDICATE (in'di-kăt) *v.t.* to show; point to. [L. (part.) *indicatus*, fr. *in*, and *dicare*, to proclaim.]

INDICATION (in-di-kā'shun) *n.* anything indicative; token.

INDICATIVE (in-dik'a-tiv) *a.* pointing out; —*n.* the positive mood of a verb.

INDICATOR (in'di-kă-tẹr) *n.* he or that which shows.

INDICATORY (in'di-kă-tu-ri) *a.* serving to point out.

INDICT (in-dit') *v.t.* to charge and summon for ria. [L. *indictare*, fr. *in*, and *dicere*, say.]

INDICTABLE (in-di'tạ-bl) *a.* subject to indictment.

INDICTION (in-dik'shun) *n.* declaration; a cycle of fifteen years.

INDICTIVE (in-dik'tiv) *a.* proclaimed.

INDICTMENT (in-dit'ment) *n.* accusation by a grand jury; any formal charge.

INDIFFERENCE (in-dif'e-rens) *n.* impartiality; unconcernedness.

INDIFFERENT (in-dif'e-rent) *a.* impartial; not good; middling; neutral; unconcerned. [L. *in*, and DIFFERENT.]

INDIFFERENTLY (in-dif'e-rent-li) *ad.* tolerably.

INDIGENCE (in'di-jens) *n.* state of destitution; poverty; want; need.

INDIGENOUS (in-dij'e-nus) *a.* native to a country. [L. *in*, and *gignere*, to produce.]

INDIGENT (in'di-jent) *a.* needy; poor. [L. (part. stem) *indigent-*, fr. *indigere*, stand in need of, fr. *in*, and *egere*, need.]

INDIGESTIBLE (in-di-jes'ti-bl) *a.* that cannot be digested. [L. *in*, and DIGESTIBLE.]

INDIGESTION (in-di-jest'yun) *n.* want of digestive powers.

INDIGNANT (in-dig'nạnt) *a.* affected with anger; feeling wrath and scorn. [L., fr. *in*, not, and *dignari*, to deem worthy.]

INDIGNATION (in-dig-nā'shun) *n.* anger with contempt.

INDIGNITY (in-dig'ni-ti) *n.* insult; contemptuous conduct.

INDIGO (in'di-gō) *n.* an Indian plant used in dyeing blue. [L. *indicum*, indigo, fr. *Indicus*, Indian.]

INDIMINISHABLE (in'di-min-ish-ạ-bl) *a.* that cannot be lessened or reduced. [L. *in*, and DIMINISH.]

INDIRECT (in-di-rekt') *a.* not direct; circuitous; inferential; unfair. [L. *in*, and DIRECT.]

INDIRECTION (in-di-rek'shun) *n.* oblique course or means.

INDIRECTLY (in-di-rekt'li) *ad.* not directly.

INDIRECTNESS (in-di-rekt'nes) *n.* obliquity.

INDISCERNIBLE (in-di-zẹr'ni-bl) *a.* that is not visible. [L. *in*, and DISCERN.]

INDISCERNIBLY (in-di-zẹr'ni-bli) *ad.* so as not to be seen or discovered.

INDISCREET (in-dis-krēt') *a.* injudicious; wanting discretion. [L. *in*, and DISCREET.]

INDISCREETLY (in-dis-krēt'li) *ad.* without prudence.

INDISCRETION (in-dis-kresh'un) *n.* imprudence; an imprudent act.

INDISCRIMINATE (in-dis-krim'i-năt) *a.* not making a distinction. [L. *in*, and DISCRIMINATE.]

INDISCRIMINATELY (in-dis-krim'i-năt-li) *ad.* without distinction.

INDISCRIMINATION (in-dis-krim-i-nā'shun) *n.* want of distinction.

INDISPENSABLE (in-dis-pen'sạ-bl) *a.* not to be dispensed with; necessary. [L. *in*, and DISPENSE.]

INDISPENSABLENESS (in-dis-pen'sạ-bl-nes) *n.* state of being absolutely necessary.

INDISPENSABLY (in-dis-pen'sạ-bli) *ad.* necessarily.

INDISPOSE (in-dis-pōz') *v.t.* to render unfit or unfavourable; disqualify; disorder. [L. *in*, and DISPOSE.]

INDISPOSED (in-dis-pōzd') *a.* not inclined; slightly unwell.

INDISPUTABLE (in-dis'pū-tạ-bl) *a.* that cannot be controverted. [L. *in*, and DISPUTE.]

INDISPUTABLY (in-dis'pū-tạ-bli) *ad.* without question.

INDISSOLUBLE (in-dis'o-lū-bl) a. not capable of being melted; binding. [L. *in*, and **DISSOLUBLE**.]

INDISSOLUBLY (in-dis'o-lū-bli) ad. so as not to be separated.

INDISSOLVABLE (in-di-zol'va-bl) a. that cannot be dissolved. [L. *in*, and **DISSOLVE**.]

INDISTINCT (in-dis-tingkt') a. confused; obscure; faint. [L. *in*, and **DISTINCT**.]

INDISTINCTION (in-dis-tingk'shun) n. confusion; equality in rank or condition.

INDISTINCTLY (in-dis-tingkt'li) ad. not clearly; obscurely.

INDISTINCTNESS (in-dis-tingkt'nes) n. want of distinctness or clearness.

INDISTINGUISHABLE (in-dis-ting'gwish-a-bl) a. that cannot be distinguished. [L. *in*, and **DISTINGUISH**.]

INDITE (in-dīt') v.t. to compose in writing; dictate. [O.F. *enditer*. Cf. **INDICT**.]

INDITER (in-dī'ter) n. one who indites.

INDITEMENT (in-dīt'ment) n. act of inditing.

INDIVIDUAL (in-di-vid'ū-al) a. single; numerically one;—n. a single person or thing. [L. *individuus*, fr. *in*, and *dividuus*, divisible, fr. *dividere*, to divide.]

INDIVIDUALISE (in-di-vid'ū-al-īz) v.t. to single out and distinguish one from others. Also **INDIVIDUATE**.

INDIVIDUALISM (in-di-vid'ū-al-izm) n. exclusive regard to one's personal interest.

INDIVIDUALITY (in-di-vid-ū-al'i-ti) n. separate existence; distinctive character.

INDIVIDUALLY (in-di-vid'ū-al-i) ad. by itself; separately.

INDIVISIBILITY (in-di-viz-i-bil'i-ti) n. property of being indivisible.

INDIVISIBLE (in-di-viz'i-bl) a. that cannot be divided. [L. *in*, and **DIVISIBLE**.]

INDIVISIBLY (in-di-viz'i-bli) ad. so as not to be capable of division.

INDOCILE (in-dō'sil) a. not teachable. [L. *in*, and **DOCILE**.]

INDOLENCE (in'du-lens) n. habitual idleness. [L. *in*, and (part. stem) *dolent-*, fr. *dolere*, feel pain.] [lazy.

INDOLENT (in'du-lent) a. habitually idle or

INDOLENTLY (in'du-lent-li) ad. listlessly.

INDOMITABLE (in'dom-i-ta-bl) a. that cannot be subdued; untamable. [L., fr. *in*, and *domitare*, to tame.]

INDOOR (in'dōr) a. being within the house; domestic. [Fr. O.E. *in*, and **DOOR**.]

INDORSE (in-dors') v.t. to write on the back of a paper; assign by indorsement. [L. *in*, and *dorsum*, the back.]

INDORSEE (in-dor-sē') n. one to whom a note is indorsed.

INDORSEMENT (in-dors'ment) n. a writing on the back of a note.

INDORSER (in-dor'ser) n. one who indorses a note or bill.

INDUBIOUS (in-dū'bi-us) a. not doubtful; not doubting. [L. *in*, and **DUBIOUS**.]

INDUBITABLE (in-dū'bi-ta-bl) a. admitting no doubt.

INDUBITABLY (in-dū'bi-ta-bli) ad. certainly.

INDUCE (in-dūs') v.t. to lead by persuasion; actuate; cause; produce. [L. *inducere*, to lead in, fr. *in*, and *ducere*, to lead.]

INDUCEMENT (in-dūs'ment) n. anything which induces.

INDUCIBLE (in-dū'si-bl) a. that may be induced.

INDUCT (in-dukt') v.t. to put in possession of a benefice or office; instal. [L. (part.) *inductus*, fr. *inducere*, to lead in. Cf. **INDUCE**.]

INDUCTILE (in-duk'til) a. not capable of being drawn. [L. *in*, and **DUCTILE**.]

INDUCTILITY (in-duk-til'i-ti) n. incapacity of being extended by drawing.

INDUCTION (in-duk'shun) n. introduction; inference or conclusion. [See **INDUCT**.]

INDUCTIVE (in-duk'tiv) a. leading to inference; drawing conclusions. [See **INDUCT**.]

INDUCTIVELY (in-duk'tiv-li) ad. by induction or inference. [See **INDUCT**.]

INDUCTOR (in-duk'ter) n. one who introduces to office, etc.

INDUE (in-dū') v.t. to invest; clothe.

INDULGE (in-dulj') v.t. or i. to gratify; humour; permit; enjoy. [L. *indulgere*, to be kind to, fr. *in*, and (perhaps) *dulcis*, sweet.]

INDULGENCE (in-dul'jens) n. forbearance of restraint; favour; liberty; fond kindness.

INDULGENT (in-dul'jent) a. yielding to wishes.

INDULGENTLY (in-dul'jent-li) ad. with indulgence.

INDURATE (in'dū-rāt) v.t. or i. to harden; grow hard;—a. hard-hearted; callous. [L. (part.) *induratus*, fr. *in*, and *durare*, harden, fr. *durus*, hard.]

INDURATION (in-dū-rā'shun) n. act of hardening.

INDUSTRIAL (in-dus'tri-al) a. consisting in industry.

INDUSTRIOUS (in-dus'tri-us) a. habitually diligent; assiduous; laborious.

INDUSTRIOUSLY (in-dus'tri-us-li) ad. diligently.

INDUSTRY (in'dus tri) n. constant diligence; assiduity. [F., fr. L. *industria*.]

INDWELL (in'dwel) v.t. or i. to abide in; occupy. [E. *in*, within, and **DWELL**.]

INDWELLER (in'dwel-er) n. one who lives in a place; inhabitant.

INDWELLING (in'dwel-ing) a. abiding in the heart;—n. residence within.

INEBRIANT (in-ē'bri-ant) a. intoxicating;—n. anything that intoxicates.

INEBRIATE (in-ē'bri-āt) v.t to make drunk; —n. an habitual drunkard. [L. (part.) *inebriatus*, fr. *in*, and *ebrius*, drunk.]

INEBRIATION (in-ē-bri-ā'shun) n. drunkenness; intoxication. Also **INEBRIETY**.

INEDITED (in-ed'i-ted) a. not edited. [L. *in*, and **EDIT**.]

INEFFABLE (in-ef'a-bl) a. not to be expressed; unspeakable. [L. *in*, not, and *effabilis*, effable.

INEFFABLY (in-ef'a-bli) ad. inexpressibly.

INEFFACEABLE (in-e-fā'sa-bl) a. that cannot be effaced. [L. *in*, and **EFFACE**.]

INEFFECTIVE (in-e-fek'tiv) a. producing no effect; useless. [L. *in*, and **EFFECTIVE**.]

INEFFECTUAL (in-e-fek'tū-al) a. not producing effect. [L. *in*, and **EFFECTUAL**.]

INEFFECTUALLY (in-e-fek'tū-al-i) ad. without effect.

INEFFICACIOUS (in-ef-i-kā'shus) a. not producing effect.

INEFFICACY (in-ef'i-ka-si) n. want of power to produce the desired effect. [L. *in*, and *efficax*, fr. *er*. out, and *facere*, make.]

INEFFICIENCY (in-e-fish'en-si) n. want of power to produce the effect.

INEFFICIENT (in-e-fish'ent) a. not efficient; not active. [L. *in*, and **EFFICIENT**.]

INEFFICIENTLY (in-e-fish'ent-li) ad. without effect.

INELASTIC (in-e-lás'tik) a. not elastic. [L. *in*, and **ELASTIC**.]

INELASTICITY (in-e-lás-tis'i-ti) n. want of elastic power.

INELEGANCE (in-el'e-gans) n. want of elegance.

INELEGANT (in-el'e-gant) a. wanting elegance. [L. *in*, and **ELEGANT**.]

INELEGANTLY (in-el'e-gant-li) ad. without elegance.

INELIGIBILITY (in-el-i-ji-bil'i-ti) n. incapacity of being elected to office.

INELIGIBLE (in-el'i-ji-bl) a. not capable of being elected; inexpedient. [L. *in*, and **ELIGIBLE**.]

INEPT (in-ept') a. unfit; useless. [F., fr. L. *in*, and *aptus*, ap.]

INEPTITUDE (in-ep'ti-tūd) n. unfitness; foolishness.

INEPTLY (in-ept'li) ad. unfitly; unsuitably.

INEQUALITY (in-ē-kwol'i-ti) n. want of equality. [L. *in*, and EQUALITY.]

INEQUITABLE (in-ek'wi-ta-bl) a. not equitable. [L. *in*, and EQUITABLE.]

INERADICABLE (in-e-rad'i-ka bl) a. that cannot be rooted out. [L. *in*, and ERADICABLE.]

INERRABLE (in-er'a-bl) a. that cannot err; infallible. [L. *in*, and *errare*, wander.]

INERT (in-ert') a. sluggish; inactive; slothful. [F., fr. L. stem *inert-*, fr. *in*, and *ars*, art.]

INERTIA (in-er'shia) n. inactivity; sluggishness.

INERTLY (in-ert'li) ad. sluggishly.

INERTNESS (in-ert'nes) n. quality of being inert.

INESTIMABLE (in-es'ti-ma-bl) a. that is above price; invaluable. [L. *in*, and ESTIMABLE.]

INESTIMABLY (in-es'ti-ma-bli) ad. so as not to be estimated.

INEVITABLE (in-ev'i-ta-bl) a. that cannot be avoided. [F., fr. L. *in*, and *evitare*, avoid.]

INEVITABLY (in-ev'i ta-bli) ad. unavoidably.

INEXACT (in-eg-zakt') a. not exact; incorrect. [L. *in*, and EXACT.]

INEXACTNESS (in-eg-zakt'nes) n. want of exactness.

INEXCUSABLE (in-eks-kū'za-bl) a. that cannot be excused or justified. [L. *in*, and EXCUSE.]

INEXCUSABLENESS (in-eks-kū'za-bl-nes) n. quality of not being excusable.

INEXCUSABLY (in-eks-kū'za-bli) ad. so as not to be excusable.

INEXHAUSTED (in-eg-zaws'ted) a. not emptied.

INEXHAUSTIBLE (in-eg-zaws'ti-bl) a. that cannot be exhausted. [L. *in*, and EXHAUST.]

INEXHAUSTIVE (in-eg-zaws'tiv) a. not to be exhausted or spent.

INEXORABLE (in-ek'su-ra-bl) a. not to be moved by entreaty; inflexible; unyielding; relentless. [L. *in*, not, *ex*, from, and *orare*, entreat.]

INEXORABLY (in-ek'su-ra-bli) ad. so as not to be moved by entreaty.

INEXPEDIENCY (in-eks-pē'di-en-si) n. want of fitness.

INEXPEDIENT (in-eks-pē'di-ent) a. not suitable. [L. *in*, and EXPEDIENT.]

INEXPERIENCE (in-eks-pē'ri-ens) n. want of experience. [L. *in*, and EXPERIENCE.]

INEXPERIENCED (in-eks-pē'ri-enst) a. not having experience; unskilled.

INEXPERT (in-eks-pert') a. unskilful. [L. *in*, and EXPERT.]

INEXPIABLE (in-eks'pi-a-bl) a. admitting no atonement. [L. *in*, and EXPIATE.]

INEXPLICABLE (in-eks'pli-ka-bl) a. that cannot be explained. [L. *in*, and EXPLICABLE.]

INEXPLICABLY (in-eks'pli-ka-bli) ad. so as not to be explained.

INEXPLICIT (in-eks-plis'it) a. not clear or precise. [L. *in*, and EXPLICIT.]

INEXPRESSIBLE (in-eks-pres'i-bl) a. unutterable. [L. *in*, and EXPRESS.]

INEXPRESSIBLY (in-eks-pres'i-bli) ad. in an unutterable manner.

INEXPRESSIVE (in-eks-pres'iv) a. not expressive.

IN EXTENSO (in eks-ten'sō) ad. at full length. [L.]

INEXTINGUISHABLE (in-eks-ting'gwish-a-bl) a. that cannot be extinguished. [L. *in*, and EXTINGUISH.]

INEXTRICABLE (in-eks'tri-ka-bl) a. not to be disentangled. [L. *in*, and EXTRICABLE.]

INEXTRICABLY (in-eks'tri-ka-bli) ad. so as not to be extricable.

INFALLIBILITY (in-fal-i-bil'i-ti) n. the quality of being incapable of error. [L. *in*, and FALLIBLE.]

INFALLIBLE (in-fal'i-bl) a. incapable of error or mistake.

INFALLIBLY (in-fal'i-bli) ad. certainly.

INFAMOUS (in'fa-mus) a. notoriously bad; detestable.

INFAMOUSLY (in'fa-mus-li) ad. most vilely.

INFAMY (in'fa-mi) n. public disgrace. [F., fr. L. *in*, and *fama*, report.]

INFANCY (in'fan-si) n. the first part of life; the beginning.

INFANT (in'fant) n. a young child;—a. pertaining to infants. [L. *infans*, fr. *in*, not, and *fari*, speak.]

INFANTA (in-fan'ta) n. in Spain and Portugal, a princess of the blood royal. [Sp.]

INFANTICIDE (in-fan'ti-sīd) n. the murder or murderer of an infant. [L. *infans*, and *cædere*, to kill.]

INFANTILE (in'fan-tīl) a. pertaining to infants. Also INFANTINE.

INFANTRY (in'fan-tri) n. foot-soldiers. [It. *infanteria*, foot-soldiers, fr. *infante*, an infant.]

INFATUATE (in-fat'ū-āt) v.t. to affect with folly. [L. (part.) *infatuatus*, fr. *in*, and *fatuus*, foolish.]

INFATUATION (in-fat-ū-ā'shun) n. deprivation of reason.

INFECT (in-fekt') v.t. to taint with disease; corrupt; contaminate. [L. (part.) *infectus*, fr. *inficere*, *in*, into, and *facere*, make.]

INFECTION (in-fek'shun) n. propagation of disease by contact; a prevailing disease; that which taints or corrupts.

INFECTIOUS (in-fek'shus) a. that may communicate disease.

INFECTIOUSLY (in-fek'shus-li) ad. by infection.

INFECTIOUSNESS (in-fek'shus-nes) n. quality of being infectious.

INFELICITOUS (in-fe-lis'i-tus) a. not felicitous; unhappy.

INFELICITY (in-fe-lis'i-ti) n. unhappiness. [L. *in*, not, and (acc.) *felicitatem*, fr. *felicitas*, fr. *felix*, happy.]

INFER (in-fer') v.t. to deduce as a fact or consequence. [L. *inferre*, fr. *in*, and *ferre*, to bring.]

INFERABLE (in-fer'a-bl) a. that may be inferred.

INFERENCE (in'fer-ens) n. deduction from premises.

INFERENTIAL (in-fe-ren'shal) a. deducible by inferences.

INFERENTIALLY (in-fe-ren'shal-i) ad. by way of inference.

INFERIOR (in-fē'ri-er) a. lower in age, place, or value;—n. one who is lower in age or place. [L. comp. of *inferus*, low.]

INFERIORITY (in-fē-ri-or'i-ti) n. a lower state.

INFERNAL (in-fer'nal) a. pertaining to hell; —n. a inhabitant of hell. [F., fr. L. *infernus*, fr. *inferus*, lower.]

INFERTILE (in-fer'til) a. unfruitful. [Fr. *in*, and FERTILE.]

INFERTILITY (in-fer-til'i-ti) n. unfruitfulness; barrenness.

INFEST (in-fest') v.t. to disturb; annoy. [L. *infestus*, hostile.]

INFESTATION (in-fes-tā'shun) n. molestation.

INFESTER (in-fes'ter) n. one who or that which infests.

INFESTERED (in-fes'terd) a. rankling; inveterate.

INFIDEL (in'fi-del) n. not believing the Scriptures; unbelieving;—n. one who denies the Scriptures and Christianity; an unbeliever. [F., fr. L. *infidelis*, fr. *in*, and *fidelis*, faithful, fr. *fides*, faith.]

INFIDELITY (in-fi-del′i-ti) *n.* disbelief of Christianity; atheism; breach of trust; unfaithfulness in married persons.

INFILTRATE (in-fil′trāt) *v.t.* to enter by the pores. [From *in* and **FILTER.**]

INFILTRATION (in-fil-trā′shun) *n.* act of entering the pores.

INFINITE (in′fi-nit) *a.* unlimited in time, space, power, excellence, etc.; indefinitely great or extensive. [L. *in*, and **FINITE.**]

INFINITELY (in-fi-nit′li) *ad.* without limit or end.

INFINITENESS (in′fi-nit-nes) *n.* boundless extent.

INFINITESIMAL (in-fi-ni-tes′i-mal) *a.* infinitely small.

INFINITIVE (in-fin′i-tiv) *a.* without limitation of person or number.

INFINITUDE (in-fin′i-tūd) *n.* infinity.

INFINITY (in-fin′i-ti) *n.* unlimited extent or number.

INFIRM (in-ferm′) *a.* weak; sickly; irresolute; unstable. [L., fr. *in*, and *firmus*, strong.]

INFIRMARY (in-fer′ma-ri) *n.* a place to lodge and nurse the sick.

INFIRMITY (in-fer′mi-ti) *n.* weakness; failing; defect; imbecility.

INFIRMLY (in-ferm′li) *ad.* in a weak manner or degree.

INFIX (in-fiks′) *v.t.* to fix deep; implant. [L. *in*, and (part.) *fixus*, fr. *figere*, to fix.]

INFLAME (in-flām′) *v.t.* to set on fire; provoke; excite. [O.F., fr. L. *inflammare*, fr. *in*, into, and *flamma*, a flame.]

INFLAMMABILITY (in-flam-a-bil′i-ti) *n.* susceptibility of taking fire.

INFLAMMABLE (in-flam′a-bl) *a.* easily set on fire.

INFLAMMATION (in-fla-mā′shun) *n.* a setting on fire; a redness and swelling.

INFLAMMATORY (in-flam′a-tu-ri) *a.* showing inflammation; tending to excite.

INFLATE (in-flāt′) *v.t.* to swell; puff up. [L. (part.) *inflatus*, fr. *inflare*, blow in, fr. *in*, and *flare*, to blow.]

INFLATE (in-flāt′) *a.* distended; bombastic. Also **INFLATED.**

INFLATION (in-flā′shun) *n.* a swelling with wind or vanity.

INFLATUS (in-flā′tus) *n.* breathing into; inspiration.

INFLECT (in-flekt′) *v.t.* to bend; decline; conjugate; modulate. [L., fr. *in*, and *flectere*, to bend.]

INFLECTION (in-flek′shun) *n.* act of bending; variation of ending in words; modulation of voice.

INFLECTIONAL (in-flek′shun-al) *a.* pertaining to inflection.

INFLECTIVE (in-flek′tiv) *a.* able to bend.

INFLEX (in-fleks′) *v.t.* to bend; make crooked.

INFLEXIBILITY (in-flek-si-bil′i-ti) *n.* unyielding stiffness; obstinacy.

INFLEXIBLE (in-flek′si-bl) *a.* that cannot be bent; unyielding; firm in purpose. [F., fr. L. *in*, and **FLEXIBLE.**]

INFLEXIBLY (in-flek′si-bli) *ad.* with firmness.

INFLICT (in-flikt′) *v.t.* to lay or bring on. [L. *in*, and (part.) *flictus*, fr. *fligere*, strike.]

INFLICTION (in-flik′shun) *n.* the act of inflicting; punishment.

INFLICTIVE (in-flik′tiv) *a.* tending to inflict.

INFLORESCENCE (in-flo-res′ens) *n.* mode of flowering. [F., fr. L. (part.) *inflorescens*, fr. *inflorescere*, to begin to blossom.]

INFLOW (in-flō′) *v.i.* to flow in;—*n.* act of flowing into; that which flows in. [L. *in*, and **FLOW.**]

INFLUENCE (in′floo-ens) *n.* moving or directing power;—*v.t.* to move by moral power; persuade; act upon. [L. *influentia*, fr. *in*, and *fluere*, to flow.]

INFLUENCER (in′floo-ens-er) *n.* one who or that which influences.

INFLUENTIAL (in-floo-en′shal) *a.* exerting influence or power.

INFLUENTIALLY (in-floo-en′shal-i) *ad.* so as to influence or direct.

INFLUENZA (in-floo-en′za) *n.* an epidemic catarrh. [It.; variant of **INFLUENCE.**]

INFLUX (in′fluks) *n.* act of flowing in; importation in abundance. [L. (part.) *influxus* fr. *influere*, to flow in.] [mission.

INFLUXION (in-fluk′shun) *n.* infusion; intro-

INFOLD (in-fōld′) *v.t.* to inwrap; enclose; embrace. [L. *in*, and **FOLD.**]

INFORM (in-form′) *v.t.* to give shape to; animate; acquaint with; apprise; instruct; —*a.* without form; shapeless. [O.F., fr. *in*, and *formare*, to form.]

INFORMAL (in-for′mal) *a.* wanting form; irregular.

INFORMALITY (in-for-mal′i-ti) *n.* want of usual forms.

INFORMALLY (in-for′mal-i) *ad.* without the usual forms.

INFORMANT (in-for′mant) *n.* one who tells.

INFORMATION (in-for-mā′shun) *n.* notice given; intelligence; knowledge.

INFORMER (in-for′mer) *n.* one who prefers accusations against others.

INFRACTION (in-frak′shun) *n.* breach; violation. [L. *in*, and (part.) *fractus*, fr. *frangere*, to break.]

INFRANGIBLE (in-fran′ji-bl) *a.* that cannot be broken. [L., fr. *in*, and *frangere*, to break.] [ness; rarity.

INFREQUENCY (in-frē′kwen-si) *n.* uncommon-

INFREQUENT (in-frē′kwent) *a.* not usual; rare. [L. *in*, and **FREQUENT.**]

INFRINGE (in-frinj′) *v.t.* to break, as contracts; violate. [L. *infringere*, fr. *in*, and *frangere*, break.]

INFRINGEMENT (in-frinj′ment) *n.* violation.

INFURIATE (in-fū′ri-āt) *v.t.* to enrage:— (in-fū′ri-at) *a.* like a fury. [L. *in*, and (part.) *furiatus*, fr. *furiare*, to enrage, fr. *furia* fury.]

INFUSE (in-fūz′) *v.t.* to pour in; steep in liquor; inspire. [L. *in*, and (part.) *fusus*, fr. *fundere*, to pour.]

INFUSIBILITY (in-fū-zi-bil′i-ti) *n.* capacity of being poured in; incapability of fusion.

INFUSIBLE (in-fū′-zi-bl) *a.* that may be infused; that cannot be made liquid.

INFUSION (in-fū′zhun) *n.* act of pouring in; liquor made by infusion.

INGATHERING (in-gaᴛʜ′er-ing) *n.* collecting and securing the harvest. [L. *in*, and **GATHER.**]

INGENIOUS (in-jēn′yus) *a.* possessed of genius; inventive; curious in contrivance. [L. *ingeniosus*, fr. *ingenium*, natural capacity; fr. *in*, and root *gen-*, of *gignere*, to beget.]

INGENIOUSLY (in-jēn′yus-li) *ad.* with ingenuity.

INGENIOUSNESS (in-jēn′yus-nes) *n.* ingenuity.

INGENUITY (in-je-nū′i-ti) *n.* ready invention; clever or curious skill in contriving, adapting, etc.

INGENUOUS (in-jen′ū-us) *a.* free from reserve or dissimulation; frank; artless; noble; honourable. [L. *ingenuus*, of good birth.]

INGENUOUSLY (in-jen′ū-us-li) *ad.* openly; frankly.

INGENUOUSNESS (in-jen′ū-us-nes) *n.* openness of heart; frankness; fairness.

INGESTION (in-jest′yun) *n.* act of throwing into. [L. (part.) *ingestus*, fr. *in*, and *gerere*.]

INGLE (ing′gl) *n.* a fire, or fireplace. [Gael.]

INGLORIOUS (in-glō′ri-us) *a.* bringing no glory; disgraceful. [L. *in*, and **GLORIOUS.**]

INGLORIOUSLY (in-glō′ri-us-li) *ad.* without glory.

INGOING (in′gō-ing) *a.* entering in or upon. [Fr. *in*, and **GOING.**]

INGOT (ing′gut) *n.* a bar or wedge of metal. [O.E. *in*, in, and *geotan*, to pour.]

INGRAFT (in-gráft′) *v.t.* to insert a scion in a stock. Also written **INGRAFF**. [Fr. **IN**, and **GRAFT**.]

INGRAFTMENT (in-gráft′-ment) *n.* act of ingrafting.

INGRAIN (in-grān′) *v.t.* to dye in the raw state; fix deeply; imbue. [Fr. **IN**, and **GRAIN**.]

INGRATE (in′grāt) *n.* an ungrateful person. [L. *in*, and *gratus*, pleasing.]

INGRATIATE (in-grā′shi-āt) *v.t.* to get oneself into favour. [L. *in*, into, and *gratia*, favour.]

INGRATITUDE (in-grat′i-tūd) *n.* want of a sense of favours.

INGREDIENT (in-grēd′yent) *n.* a component part. [L. (part. stem) *ingredient*-, fr. *ingredi*, to enter.]

INGRESS (in′gres) *n.* entrance. [L. *in*, and (part.) *gressus*, fr. *gradi*, to go.]

INGRESSION (in-gresh′un) *n.* act of entering.

INGUINAL (ing′gwi-nal) *a.* pertaining to the groin. [L. *inguen*, *inguinis*, the groin.]

INGURGITATE (in-gur′ji-tāt) *v.t.* to swallow greedily; drink largely. [L. (part.) *ingurgitatus*, fr. *ingurgitare*, fr. *in*, into, and *gurges*, gulf.]

INHABIT (in-hab′it) *v.t.* to occupy; live in; —*v.i.* to dwell or abide. [F., fr. L. *in*, and *habitare*, dwell.]

INHABITABLE (in-hab′i-ta-bl) *a.* that may be inhabited.

INHABITANCY (in-hab′it-an-si) *n.* legal residence. Also **INHABITANCE**.

INHABITANT (in-hab′i-tant) *n.* a dweller. Also **INHABITER**.

INHABITATION (in-hab-i-tā′shun) *n.* act of residence.

INHALATION (in-hā-lā′shun) *n.* act of drawing in with the breath.

INHALE (in-hāl′) *v.t.* to draw into the lungs. [L., fr. *in*, and *halare*, breathe.]

INHALER (in-hā′ler) *n.* a machine for inhaling vapour.

INHARMONIOUS (in-hár-mō′ni-us) *a.* unmusical; discordant. [L. *in*, and **HARMONIOUS**.]

INHERE (in-hēr′) *v.i.* to be fixed in. [L. *in*, and *hærere*, to stick.]

INHERENCE (in-hēr′ens) *n.* existence in something else.

INHERENT (in-hēr′ent) *a.* existing in something; innate.

INHERENTLY (in-hēr′ent-li) *ad.* by inheritance.

INHERIT (in-her′it) *v.t.* or *i.* to receive or possess by nature of birth. [O.F. *enhériter*, fr. Late L. *hereditare*, to inherit, fr. L. *in*, and *heres*, heir.]

INHERITABLE (in-her′i-ta-bl) *a.* that may be inherited.

INHERITANCE (in-her′i-tans) *n.* a hereditary estate; any valuable possession or blessing.

INHERITOR (in-her′i-ter) *n.* a man who inherits.

INHERITRIX (in-her′i-triks) *n.* a female who inherits.

INHESION (in-hē′zhun) *n.* state of inhering.

INHIBIT (in-hib′it) *v.t.* to restrain; forbid; interdict. [L. *inhibere*, fr. *in*, and *habere*, to have.]

INHIBITION (in-hi-bish′un) *n.* act of prohibiting; restraint; writ of interdict.

INHIBITORY (in-hib′i-tu-ri) *a.* prohibiting or interdicting.

INHOSPITABLE (in-hos′pi-ta-bl) *a.* not disposed to entertain strangers; affording no shelter or means of subsistence. [L. *in*, and **HOSPITABLE**.]

INHOSPITABLY (in-hos′pi-ta-bli) *ad.* unkindly to strangers.

INHOSPITALITY (in-hos-pi-tal′i-ti) *n.* want of hospitality.

INHUMAN (in-hū′man) *a.* barbarous; cruel. [L. *in*, and **HUMAN**.]

INHUMANITY (in-hū-man′i-ti) *n.* want of human feeling; any cold or cruel deed.

INHUMANLY (in-hū′man-li) *ad.* barbarously.

INIMICAL (i-nim′i-kal) *a.* unfriendly; adverse; hurtful. [L. *inimicalis*, fr. *inimicus*. fr. *in*, and *amicus*, friendly.]

INIMICALLY (i-nim′i-kal-i) *ad.* in an unfriendly manner.

INIMITABILITY (in-im-i-ta-bil′i-ti) *n.* quality of being inimitable.

INIMITABLE (in-im′i-ta-bl) *a.* that cannot be imitated. [L. *in*, and **IMITATE**.]

INIMITABLY (in-im′i-ta-bli) *ad.* beyond imitation.

INIQUITY (i-nik′wi-ti) *n.* injustice; crime; depravity. [F., fr. L. (acc.) *iniquitatem*, fr. *iniquus*, unjust, fr. *in*, and *æquus*, equal.]

INITIAL (i-nish′al) *a.* placed at the beginning; commencing;—*n.* the first letter of a word. [L. *initialis*, fr. *initium*, beginning, fr. *inire*, to go in.]

INITIATE (i-nish′i-āt) *v.t.* to instruct in rudiments; introduce.

INITIATION (i-nish-i-ā′shun) *n.* instruction in first principles.

INITIATIVE (i-nish′i-ā-tiv) *n.* serving to initiate;—*n.* first step or essay; right to lead or originate.

INITIATORY (i-nish′i-ā-tu-ri) *a.* introductory; serving to initiate.

INJECT (in-jekt′) *v.t.* to throw in. [L. (part.) *injectus*, fr. *injicere*, fr. *in*, and *jacere*, to throw.]

INJECTION (in-jek′shun) *n.* act of throwing in; a clyster.

INJUDICIAL (in-jōō-dish′al) *a.* not in the forms of law. [L. *in*, and **JUDICIAL**.]

INJUDICIOUS (in-jōō-dish′us) *a.* not wise. [L. *in*, and **JUDICIOUS**.]

INJUDICIOUSLY (in-jōō-dish′us-li) *ad.* without judgment.

INJUDICIOUSNESS (in-jōō-dish′us-nes) *n.* want of judgment; indiscretion.

INJUNCTION (in-jungk′shun) *n.* command; order; a legal writ or process. [L. *in*, and (part.) *junctus*, fr. *jungere*, to join.]

INJURE (in′jōōr) *v.t.* to hurt; damage. [F. *injurier*, fr. L. *injuria*, fr. *in*, and *jus*, *juris*, law.]

INJURIOUS (in-jōō′ri-us) *a.* hurtful.

INJURIOUSLY (in-jōō′ri-us-li) *ad.* hurtfully.

INJURIOUSNESS (in-jōō′ri-us-nes) *n.* quality of being injurious.

INJURY (in′joo-ri) *n.* hurt; detriment; damage; wrong.

INJUSTICE (in-jus′tis) *n.* any violation of what is right and due to others. [L. *in*, and **JUSTICE**.]

INK (ingk) *n.* a liquor used in writing and printing;—*v.t.* to mark with ink. [O.F. *enque* = F. *encre*, fr. Late L. *encaustum*, the purple-red ink used by the later Roman emperors, fr. G. *eykauston*, ink, fr. *eykaiein*, to burn in.]

INKHORN (ingk′horn) *n.* a vessel for holding ink. [See **INK** and **HORN**.]

INKINESS (ing′ki-nes) *n.* state of being inky.

INKLING (ingk′ling) *n.* a hint; desire. [Etym. doubtful.]

INKSTAND (ingk′stand) *n.* a vessel for holding ink. [See **INK** and **STAND**.]

INKY (ing′ki) *a.* made of or resembling ink.

INLAND (in′land) *a.* remote from the sea;—*n.* the interior of a country. [L. *in*, and **LAND**.]

INLANDER (in′lan-der) *n.* one who lives in the interior.

INLAY (in-lā′) *v.t.* to diversify with other substances;—(in′lā) *n.* pieces of wood, ivory, etc., inlaid. [See **IN** and **LAY**.]

INLAYER (in-lā′er) *n.* one who inlays.

INLET (in′let) *n.* passage; means of entrance; a small bay, creek, or channel. [See **IN** and **LET**.]

INLY (in′li) *ad.* internally; secretly;—*a.* inward; secret. [Fr. **IN**.]

INMATE (in'māt) *n.* one who lives in the same house. [Fr. **IN** and **MATE.**]

INMOST (in'mōst) *a.* deepest within. [L. *in.*]

INN (in) *n.* a house of entertainment for travellers. [O.E.]

INNATE (in'nāt, in-nāt') *a.* inborn; natural. [L. *in,* and (part.) *natus,* fr. *nasci,* to be born.]

INNATELY (in'nāt-li) *ad.* naturally.

INNATENESS (in'nāt-nes) *n.* the quality of being innate.

INNER (in'ẹr) *a.* interior; farther inward. [L. *in.*]

INNERMOST (in'ẹr-mōst) *a.* deepest or farthest within. [INNER and MOST.]

INNING (in'ing) *n.* ingathering of corn;—*pt.* the turn for using the bat in cricket; lands recovered from the sea. [O.E. *inn.* in, within.]

INNOCENCE (in'u-sens) *n.* freedom from guilt; harmlessness.

INNOCENT (in'u-sent) *a.* free from guilt; pure; harmless;—*n.* an imbecile. [F., fr. L. *in,* and (part. stem) *nocent-,* fr. *nocere,* to harm.]

INNOCENTLY (in'u-sent-li) *ad.* harmlessly.

INNOCUOUS (i-nok'ū-us) *a.* harmless. [L. *innocuus,* fr. *in,* not, and *nocere,* to hurt.]

INNOCUOUSLY (i-nok'ū-us-li) *ad.* without injurious effects.

INNOMINATE (i-nom'i-nąt) *a.* having no name. [L. (part.) *innominatus,* fr. *in,* not, and *nomen,* a name.]

INNOVATE (in'u-vāt) *v.t.* or *i.* to introduce novelties or changes. [L. (part.) *innovatus,* fr. *in,* and *novus,* new.]

INNOVATION (in-u-vā'shun) *n.* introduction of novelties; any change in custom, etc.

INNOVATOR (in'u-vā-tẹr) *n.* one who innovates.

INNOXIOUS (i-nok'shus) *a.* harmless; innocent. [Fr. *in,* and **NOXIOUS.**]

INNOXIOUSLY (i-nok'shus-li) *ad.* harmlessly.

INNUENDO (in-ū-en'dō) *n.* a distant hint; indirect insinuation. [L, fr. *innuere,* fr. *in,* and *nuere,* to nod.]

INNUENT (in'ū-ent) *a.* conveying a hint; significant.

INNUMERABILITY (i-nū-me-rą-bil'i-ti) *n.* state of being innumerable.

INNUMERABLE (i-nū'me-rą-bl) *a.* that cannot be numbered. [L. *in,* and **NUMBER.**]

INNUMERABLY (i-nū'me-rą-bli) *ad.* beyond number.

INNUTRITION (in-ū-trish'un) *n.* want of nourishment. [L. *in,* and **NUTRITION.**]

INNUTRITIOUS (in-ū-trish'us) *a.* not nourishing.

INOBSERVANCE (in-ub-zẹr'vąns) *n.* disregard; negligence. [L. *in,* and **OBSERVANCE.**]

INOBTRUSIVE (in-ob-trōō'siv) *a.* not obtrusive. [L. *in,* and **OBTRUSION.**]

INOCULATE (in-ok'ū-lāt) *v.t.* to insert a scion in a stock; communicate disease by inserting infectious matter; imbue with;—*v i.* to practise vaccination. [L. (part.) *inoculatus,* fr. *inoculare,* fr. *in,* and *oculus,* an eye.]

INOCULATION (in-ok-ū-lā'shun) *n.* act of inoculating.

INOCULATOR (in-ok'ū-lā-tor) *n.* one who inoculates.

INODOROUS (in-ō'du-rus) *a.* destitute of smell. [L. *in,* and **ODOUR.**]

INOFFENSIVE (in-u-fen'siv) *a.* giving no offence. [L. *in,* and **OFFENSIVE.**]

INOFFENSIVELY (in-u-fen'siv-li) *ad.* harmlessly; without offence.

INOPERATIVE (in-op'e-rą-tiv) *a.* inactive. [L. *in,* and **OPERATE.**]

INOPPORTUNE (in-op'ur-tūn) *a.* not seasonable. [L. *in,* and **OPPORTUNE.**]

INOPPORTUNELY (in-op'ur-tūn-li) *ad.* unseasonably.

INORDINACY (in-or'di-ną-si) *n.* want of moderation.

INORDINATE (in-or'di-nąt) *a.* immoderate. [L. *in,* and **ORDINATE.**]

INORDINATELY (in-or'di-nąt-li) *ad.* immoderately; excessively.

INORGANIC (in-or-gan'ik) *a.* void of organs. [L. *in,* and **ORGANIC.**]

INQUEST (in'kwest) *n.* judicial inquiry. [O.F., fr. L. (part.) *inquisitus,* fr. *inquirere* = to inquire.]

INQUIETUDE (in-kwī'e-tūd) *n.* a restless state of mind; uneasiness. [L. *in,* and **QUIETUDE.**]

INQUIRE (in-kwīr') *v.t.* or *i.* to ask questions; seek or search for; investigate. [L. *inquirere,* fr. *in,* in, and *quærere,* to seek.]

INQUIRER (in-kwīr'ẹr) *n.* one who inquires.

INQUIRINGLY (in-kwīr'ing-li) *ad.* by way of inquiry.

INQUIRY (in-kwīr'i) *n.* act of inquiring; a question; examination; research.

INQUISITION (in-kwi-zish'un) *n.* judicial inquiry; a popish tribunal for sifting out of heresy. [L. (acc.) *inquisitionem,* a searching for, fr. *inquirere.*]

INQUISITIONAL (in-kwi-zish'un-ąl) *a.* pertaining to inquiry.

INQUISITIVE (in-kwiz'i-tiv) *a.* given to inquiry; curious.

INQUISITIVELY (in-kwiz'i-tiv-li) *ad.* with curiosity.

INQUISITIVENESS (in-kwiz'i-tiv-nes) *n.* busy curiosity.

INQUISITOR (in-kwiz'i-tẹr) *n.* a member of the Inquisition.

INQUISITORIAL (in-kwiz-i-tō'ri-ąl) *a.* pertaining to inquisition.

INROAD (in'rōd) *n.* sudden invasion.

INSALUBRIOUS (in-są-lū'bri-us) *a.* unhealthy. [L. *in,* and **SALUBRIOUS.**]

INSALUBRITY (in-są-lū'bri-ti) *n.* unwholesomeness.

INSALUTARY (in-sal'ū-tą-ri) *a.* unfavourable to health. [L. *in,* and **SALUTARY.**]

INSANE (in-sān') *a.* unsound in mind. [L. *in,* and *sanus,* sound.]

INSANELY (in-sān'li) *ad.* madly; foolishly.

INSANITY (in-san'i-ti) *n.* derangement of intellect.

INSATIABLE (in-sā'shą-bl) *a.* that cannot be satisfied. [L., fr. *in,* and *satiare,* satiate.]

INSATIABLENESS (in-sā'shą-bl-nes) *n.* insatiable greediness. Also **INSATIABILITY.**

INSATIABLY (in-sā'shą-bli) *ad.* with greediness not to be satisfied.

INSATIATE (in-sā'shi-āt) *a.* not to be satisfied.

INSATIETY (in-są-tī'i-ti) *n.* insatiableness.

INSCRIBABLE (in-skrī'bą-bl) *a.* that may be inscribed.

INSCRIBE (in-skrīb') *v.t.* to write on; address; dedicate. [L. *in,* and *scribere,* to write.]

INSCRIBER (in-skrī'bẹr) *n.* one who inscribes.

INSCRIPTION (in-skrip'shun) *n.* that which is written on something; title; address.

INSCRIPTIVE (in-skrip'tiv) *a.* of the nature of an inscription.

INSCRUTABILITY (in-skrōō-tą-bil'i-ti) *n.* the quality of being inscrutable.

INSCRUTABLE (in-skrōō'tą-bl) *a.* unsearchable; undiscoverable. [F., fr. L. *inscrutabilis,* fr. *in,* and *scrutari,* to search.]

INSCRUTABLY (in-skrōō'tą-bli) *ad.* beyond finding out.

INSEAM (in-sēm') *v.t.* to impress or mark with a seam. [IN and **SEAM.**]

INSECT (in'sekt) *n.* a small animal, as a grasshopper. [F., fr. L. (part.) *insectus,* fr. *insecare,* fr. *in,* and *secare,* to cut.]

INSECTILE (in-sek'til) *a.* having the nature of insects.

INSECTION (in-sek'shun) *n.* a cutting in; incision.

INSECTIVOROUS (in-sek-tiv'u-rus) *a.* feeding on insects.

INSECURE (in-se-kūr') *a.* unsafe; not confident of safety. [L. *in*, and SECURE.]
INSECURELY (in-se-kūr'li) *ad.* unsafely; with hazard.
INSECURITY (in-se-kū'ri-ti) *n.* want of safety.
INSENSATE (in-sen'sạt) *a.* senseless; stupid. [L. *insensatus*, fr. *in*, and *sensatus*, fr. *sensus*, feeling.]
INSENSIBILITY (in-sen-si-bil'i-ti) *n.* want of emotion or affection.
INSENSIBLE (in-sen'si-bl) *a.* destitute of feeling; imperceptible. [L. *in*, and SENSIBLE.]
INSENSIBLY (in-sen'si-bli) *ad.* imperceptibly; gradually.
INSENTIENT (in-sen'shi-ent) *a.* not having perception or sensibility. [L. *in*, and SENTIENT.]
INSEPARABLE (in-sep'ạ-rạ-bl) *a.* that cannot be disjoined. [L. *in*, and *separare*, to separate.]
INSEPARABLENESS (in-sep'ạ-rạ-bl-nes) *n.* quality of being inseparable.
INSEPARABLY (in-sep'ạ-rạ-bli) *ad.* with indissoluble union.
INSERT (in-sẹrt') *v.t.* to set in or among; introduce. [L., fr. *in*, and (part.) *sertus*, fr. *serere*, to join.]
INSERTION (in-sẹr'shun) *n.* act of inserting; thing inserted.
INSESSORES (in-se-sō'rēz) *n.pl.* an order of birds whose feet are formed for perching. [L. *in*, and (part.) *sessus*, fr. *sedere*, to sit.]
INSHEATHE (in-shēтн') *v.t.* to cover with a sheath. [L. *in*, and SHEATHE.]
INSHORE (in'shōr) *ad.* by or along the shore. [L. *in*, and SHORE.]
INSIDE (in'sid) *n.* the inner part or place.
INSIDIOUS (in-sid'i-us) *a.* lying in wait; designing; artful. [L. *insidiosus*, fr. *insidiœ*, an ambush, fr. *insidere*, fr. *in*, and *sedere*, to set.]
INSIDIOUSLY (in-sid'i-us-li) *ad.* deceitfully.
INSIGHT (in'sit) *n.* sight of the interior; clear perception; full knowledge. [L. *in*, and SIGHT.]
INSIGNIA (in-sig'ni-ạ) *n.pl.* badges of distinction. [L., fr. *in*, and *signum*, a sign.]
INSIGNIFICANCE (in-sig-nif'i-kạns) *n.* want of meaning; unimportance
INSIGNIFICANT (in-sig-nif'i-kạnt) *a.* void of meaning; without weight of character; small; trivial. [L. *in*, and SIGNIFICANT.]
INSINCERE (in-sin-sēr') *a.* hypocritical; false. [L. *in*, and SINCERE.]
INSINCERELY (in-sin-sēr'li) *ad.* hypocritically.
INSINCERITY (in-sin-sẹr'i-ti) *n.* deceitfulness.
INSINUATE (in-sin'ū-āt) *v.t.* or *i.* to introduce gently; instil; hint; wind or work into. [L. (part.) *insinuatus*, fr. *in*, and *sinus*, bosom.]
INSINUATION (in-sin-ū-ā'shun) *n.* act of insinuating; a hint.
INSINUATOR (in-sin'ū-ā-tor) *n.* one who insinuates.
INSIPID (in-sip'id) *a.* void of taste; vapid. [L., *in*, and *sapidus*, savoury, fr. *sapere*, to taste.]
INSIPIDITY (in-si-pid'i-ti) *n.* want of taste; want of life and spirit.
INSIPIDLY (in-sip'id-li) *ad.* without taste.
INSIPIENCE (in-sip'i-ens) *n.* want of wisdom.
INSIST (in-sist') *v.i.* to persist in urging; dwell on in discourse. [L., fr. *in*, and *sistere*, stand, fr. *stare*.]
INSNARE (in-snār') *v.t.* to entangle. [L. *in*, and SNARE.]
INSOBRIETY (in-sō-bri'i-ti) *n.* intemperance. [L. *in*, and SOBRIETY.]
INSOLATE (in'su-lāt) *v.t.* to expose to the sun's rays. [L. (part.) *insolatus*, fr. *insolare*, fr. *in*, and *sol*, the sun.]
INSOLENCE (in'su-lens) *n.* overbearing pride; any rude, offensive speech or act.

INSOLENT (in'su-lent) *a.* haughty and contemptuous; insulting; abusive. [L. *in*, and *solere*, to be accustomed.]
INSOLENTLY (in'su-lent-li) *ad.* haughtily.
INSOLIDITY (in-su-lid'i-ti) *n.* want of solidity. [L. *in*, and SOLID.]
INSOLUBILITY (in-sol-ū-bil'i-ti) *n.* the quality of being insoluble.
INSOLUBLE (in-sol'ū-bl) *a.* that cannot be dissolved in a fluid. [L. *in*, and SOLUBLE.]
INSOLVABLE (in-sol'vạ-bl) *a.* that cannot be solved or explained. [L. *in*, and SOLVE.]
INSOLVENCY (in-sol'ven-si) *n.* inability to pay debts.
INSOLVENT (in-sol'vent) *a.* unable to pay debts;—*n.* a bankrupt. [L. *in*, and SOLVENT.]
INSOMNIA (in-som'ni-ạ) *n.* sleeplessness. [L., fr. *in*, and *somnus*, sleep.]
INSOMUCH (in-sō-much') *ad.* so that. [Fr. IN, SO, MUCH.]
INSOUCIANT (in-söö'si-ạnt, áng-söö'syáng') *a.* unconcerned; careless. [F. *in*, and *souciant*, fr. *souci*, care.]
INSPECT (in-spekt') *v.t.* to examine; superintend. [L. *in*, and (part.) *spectus* fr. *srecere*, to look.]
INSPECTION (in-spek'shun) *n.* examination; view.
INSPECTOR (in-spek'tẹr) *n.* an examiner; a superintendent.
INSPECTORSHIP (in-spek'tur-ship) *n.* office or district of an inspector. Also INSPECTORATE.
INSPIRABLE (in-spir'ạ-bl) *a.* that may be inspired.
INSPIRATION (in-spi-rā'shun) *n.* act of drawing in the breath; divine infusion into the mind.
INSPIRE (in-spir') *v.i.* to draw in breath;—*v.t.* to breathe into; infuse; animate supernaturally. [L., fr. *in*, and *spirare*, breathe.]
INSPIRIT (in-spir'it) *v.t.* to animate. [L. *in*, and SPIRIT.]
INSPISSATE (in-spis'āt) *v.t.* to thicken, as liquids. [L. *in*, and *spissare*, to thicken, fr. *spissus*, thick.]
INSPISSATION (in-spi-sā'shun) *n.* the act of thickening.
INSTABILITY (in-stạ-bil'i-ti) *n.* inconstancy.
INSTABLE (in-stā'bl) *a.* inconstant; unsteady. [L. *in*, and STABLE.]
INSTALL (in-stawl') *v.t.* to invest with office. [F., fr. Late L. *installare*, fr. *in*, and *stallum*, seat.]
INSTALLATION (in-staw-lā'shun) *n.* the giving possession of an office.
INSTALMENT (in-stawl'ment) *n.* act of installing; payment of part.
INSTANCE (in'stạns) *n.* solicitation; example; a case occurring;—*v.t.* or *i.* to produce an example.
INSTANT (in'stạnt) *n.* a moment;—*a.* present; urgent. [L. (part. stem) *instant-*, fr. *instare*, *in*, and *stare*, to stand.]
INSTANTANEOUS (in-stan-tā'ne-us) *a.* done in an instant.
INSTANTANEOUSLY (in-stan-tā'ne-us-li) *ad.* in an instant.
INSTANTER (in-stan'tẹr) *ad.* instantly. [L.]
INSTANTLY (in'stạnt-li) *ad.* immediately.
INSTATE (in-stāt') *v.t.* to place in a condition. [L. *in*, and STATE.]
INSTEAD (in-sted') *ad.* in place of. [O.E. *on stede*, in the place.]
INSTEP (in'step) *n.* the upper part of the foot. [Perhaps fr. E. *on*=*in*, and STOOP.]
INSTIGATE (in'sti-gāt) *v.t.* to urge on; incite. [L. (part.) *instigatus*, fr. *instigare*, incite.]
INSTIGATION (in-sti-gā'shun) *n.* incitement to a crime.
INSTIGATOR (in'sti-gā-tẹr) *n.* one who incites.

INSTIL (in-stil') v.t. to pour into by drops; infuse by degrees, as truth into the mind. [L., fr. *instillare*, fr. *in*, and *stillare*, to drop.]

INSTILLATION (in-sti-lā'shun) n. act of instilling; thing instilled. Also **INSTIL-MENT.**

INSTINCT (in'stingkt) n. natural impulse; unreasoning or involuntary desire or aversion;—a. urged from within; animated with. [L. *instinctus*, fr. *instinguere*, to incite.]

INSTINCTIVE (in-stingk'tiv) a. prompted by instinct.

INSTINCTIVELY (in-stingk'tiv-li) ad. by instinct.

INSTITUTE (in'sti-tūt) v.t. to establish; commence; ordain;—n. established law; a literary or scientific body;—pl. a book of elements or principles. [L. (part.) *institutus* fr. *instituere*, fr. *in*, and *statuere*, to cause to stand.]

INSTITUTION (in-sti-tū'shun) n. act of establishing; system established.

INSTITUTIONAL (in-sti-tū'shun-al) a. instituted by authority; elementary. Also **INSTITUTIONARY.**

INSTRUCT (in-strukt') v.t. to teach; direct. [L. (part.) *instructus*, fr. *instruere*, fr. *in*, and *struere*, to pile up.]

INSTRUCTION (in-struk'shun) n. act of teaching; information; direction; order.

INSTRUCTIVE (in-struk'tiv) a. affording instruction.

INSTRUCTIVENESS (in-struk'tiv-nes) n. quality of furnishing instruction.

INSTRUCTOR (in-struk'ter) n. one who teaches.

INSTRUCTRESS (in-struk'tres) n. a female teacher.

INSTRUMENT (in'stroo-ment) n. a tool; machine; a writing; an agent. [F., fr. L. *instrumentum*, fr. *instruere*. Cf. INSTRUCT.]

INSTRUMENTAL (in-stroo-men'tal) a. conducive to some end.

INSTRUMENTALIST (in-stroo-men'tal-ist) n. one who plays a musical instrument.

INSTRUMENTALITY (in-stroo-men-tal'i-ti) n. subordinate agency; means or influence.

INSUBJECTION (in-sub-jek'shun) n. state of disobedience. [L. *in*, and SUBJECTION.]

INSUBORDINATE (in-sub-or'di-nat) a. not submissive; unruly. [L. *in*, and SUBORDINATE.]

INSUBORDINATION (in-sub-or-di-nā'shun) n. disobedience to superior authority.

INSUBSTANTIAL (in-sub-stan'shal) a. not real; is na . [L. *in*, and SUBSTANTIAL.]v o ry

INSUFFERABLE (in-suf'er-a-bl) a. not to be borne. [L. *in*, and SUFFERABLE.]

INSUFFICIENCY (in-su-fish'en-si) n. want of sufficiency.

INSUFFICIENT (in-su-fish'ent) a. inadequate. [L. *in*, and SUFFICIENT.]

INSULAR (in'sū-lar) a. belonging to an island; surrounded by water. [F., fr. L. *insularis*, fr. *insula*, island.]

INSULARITY (in-sū-lar'i-ti) n. state of being insular; narrowness of view.

INSULATE (in'sū-lāt) v.t. to set detached; make an isle.

INSULATION (in-sū-lā'shun) n. act of insulating; state of being insulated.

INSULT (in'sult) n. sudden attack; gross abuse in word or action. [L. *insultare*, leap upon.]

INSULT (in-sult') v.t. to treat with abuse or insolence.

INSULTING (in-sul'ting) a. containing gross abuse.

INSULTINGLY (in-sul'ting-li) ad. with insolent triumph.

INSUPERABLE (in-sū'pe-ra-bl) a. that cannot be overcome. [L. *insuperabilis*, fr. *in*, and *superare*, overcome, fr. *super*, above.]

INSUPERABLY (in-sū'pe-ra-bli) ad. so as not to be surmounted.

INSUPPORTABLE (in-su-pōr'ta-bl) a. that cannot be endured. [L. *in*, and SUPPORT-ABLE.]

INSUPPORTABLY (in-su-pōr'ta-bli) ad. beyond endurance.

INSUPPRESSIBLE (in-su-pres'i-bl) a. not to be suppressed. [L. *in*, and SUPPRESSIBLE]

INSURABLE (in-shōōr'a-bl) a. that may be insured.

INSURANCE (in-shōōr'ans) n. act of insuring against loss; premium paid.

INSURE (in-shōōr') v.t. to make sure; contract for indemnity for loss of life or property; —v.i. to undertake insurances; underwrite. [O.F. *enseurer*, fr. L. *in*, and *securus*, secure.]

INSURER (in-shōōr'er) n. one who insures.

INSURGENT (in-sur'jent) n. exciting sedition; —n. one who rises against lawful authority. [L. (part. stem) *insurgent*-, fr. *insurgere*, fr. *in*, and *surgere*, to rise.]

INSURMOUNTABLE (in-sur-moun'ta-bl) a. not to be overcome; insuperable. [L. *in*, and SURMOUNTABLE.]

INSURMOUNTABLY (in-sur-moun'ta-bli) ad. insuperably.

INSURRECTION (in-su-rek'shun) n. rising in opposition to lawful authority; rebellion. [L. (acc.) *insurrectionem*, fr. *insurgere*.]

INSURRECTIONARY (in-su-rek'shun-a-ri) a. relating to insurrection.

INSUSCEPTIBILITY (in-su-sep-ti-bil'i-ti) n. want of capacity to feel.

INSUSCEPTIBLE (in-su-sep'ti-bl) a. not capable of feeling or admitting. Also **INSUSCEPTIVE.** [L. *in*, and SUSCEPTIBLE.]

INTACT (in-takt') a. untouched; unhurt; entire. [L. (part.) *intactus*, fr. *in*, and *tangere*, to touch.]

INTAGLIO (in-tal'yō) n. a precious stone with a head engraved on it. [It. *in*, into, and *tagliare*, to cut (rods), fr. L. *talea* a twig.]

INTANGIBILITY (in-tan-ji-bil'i-ti) n. quality of being intangible.

INTANGIBLE (in-tan'ji-bl) a. that cannot be handled or dealt with. [Fr. L. *in*, and *tangere*, to touch.]

INTEGER (in'te-jer) n. a whole number. [L., fr. *in*, and *tangere*, to touch.]

INTEGRAL (in'te-gral) n. an entire thing;— a. whole; entire.

INTEGRANT (in'te-grant) a. necessary to constitute a thing.

INTEGRATE (in'te-grāt) v.t. to form one whole; renew; give the sum total.

INTEGRATION (in-te-grā'shun) n. formation of a whole; completion.

INTEGRITY (in-teg'ri-ti) n. wholeness; uprightness; purity.

INTELLECT (in'te-lekt) n. thinking or reasoning faculty; understanding. [L. (part.) *intellectus*, fr. *intelligere*, to understand, fr. *inter*, and *legere*, to choose.]

INTELLECTION (in-te-lek'shun) n. simple apprehension of ideas.

INTELLECTIVE (in-te-lek'tiv) a. pertaining to the intellect.

INTELLECTUAL (in-te-lek'tū-al) a. pertaining to the understanding; mental; rational.

INTELLECTUALITY (in-te-lek-tū-al'i-ti) n. mental power.

INTELLECTUALLY (in-te-lek'tū-al-i) ad. by means of the understanding.

INTELLIGENCE (in-tel'i-jens) n. understanding; information; news; an intelligent being.

INTELLIGENT (in-tel'i-jent) a. knowing; instructed; skilful. [L. (part. stem) *intelligent*-, fr. *intelligere*.]

INTELLIGENTIAL (in-tel-i-jen'shal) a. consisting of mind.

INTELLIGIBLE (in-tel'i-ji-bl) a. that may be comprehended.

INTELLIGIBLY (in-tel'i-ji-bli) ad. so as to be understood.

INTEMPERANCE (in-tem'per-ans) n. excess; drunkenness.

INTEMPERATE (in-tem'per-at) a. excessive; addicted to the use of spirituous liquors; passionate. [L. in, and TEMPERATE.]

INTEND (in-tend') v.t. or i. to purpose. [O.F. entendre, fr. L. intendere, to stretch, fr. in, and tendere.]

INTENDANCY (in-ten'dan-si) n. office or district of an attendant.

INTENDANT (in-ten'dant) n. an overseer.

INTENDEDLY (in-ten'ded-li) ad. purposely.

INTENSE (in-tens') a. tightly drawn or stretched; extreme in degree; severe; keen. [L. (part.) intensus, fr. intendere, to stretch.]

INTENSELY (in-tens'li) ad. to a high degree.

INTENSENESS (in-tens'nes) n. intensity.

INTENSIFY (in-ten'si-fi) v.t. or i. to make or become more intense. [See INTENSE; fv, fr. L. faire, to make.]

INTENSION (in-ten'shun) n. act of straining.

INTENSITY (in-ten'si-ti) n. extreme degree of active power, feeling, application, etc.

INTENSIVE (in-ten'siv) a. giving force.

INTENT (in-tent') a. using close application; —n. purpose; aim. [Fr. INTEND.]

INTENTION (in-ten'shun) n. design; purpose.

INTENTIONAL (in-ten'shun-al) a. designed.

INTENTIONALLY (in-ten'shun-al-i) ad. purposely.

INTENTLY (in-tent'li) ad. with close attention.

INTENTNESS (in-tent'nes) n. close application.

INTER (in-ter') v.t. to bury. [L. in, and terra, the earth.]

INTERACT (in'ter-akt) n. performance between acts. [L. inter, between, and ACT.]

INTERCALARY (in-ter'ka-la-ri) a. inserted; added.

INTERCALATE (in-ter'ka-lat) v.t. to insert a day. [L. (part.) intercalatus, fr. intercalare, fr. inter, and calare, to call.]

INTERCEDE (in-ter-sed') v.i. to interpose; plead for another. [L. intercedere, fr. inter, and cedere, to go.]

INTERCEDENT (in-ter-sed'ent) a. mediating.

INTERCEDING (in-ter-sed'ing) n. mediation.

INTERCEPT (in-ter-sept') v.t. to seize on its passage; obstruct; cut off; cut short. [L. (part.) interceptus, fr. intercipere, fr. inter, and capere, to take.]

INTERCEPTION (in-ter-sep'shun) n. act of intercepting. [obstruct.

INTERCEPTIVE (in-ter-sep'tiv) a. tending to

INTERCESSION (in-ter-sesh'en) n. mediation. [See INTERCEDE.]

INTERCESSOR (in-ter-ses'ur) n. a mediator.

INTERCESSORY (in-ter-ses'u-ri) a. containing intercession. Also INTERCESSIONAL.

INTERCHAIN (in-ter-chan') v.t. to link together. [L. inter, between, and CHAIN.]

INTERCHANGE (in-ter-chanj') v.t. to change by giving and receiving;—(in'ter-chanj) n. mutual exchange; barter. [L. inter, and CHANGE.]

INTERCHANGEABLE (in-ter-chan'ja-bl) a. that may be given and taken mutually.

INTERCHANGEABLY (in-ter-chan'ja-bli) ad. with mutual exchange.

INTERCOLONIAL (in-ter-ku-lo'ni-al) a. between colonies. [L. inter, and COLONIAL.]

INTERCOMMUNICATE (in-ter-ku-mu'ni-kat) v.i. to hold mutual communication. [L. inter, and COMMUNICATE.]

INTERCOMMUNICATION (in-ter-ku-mu-ni-ka'shun) n. reciprocal intercourse.

INTERCOMMUNION (in-ter-ku-mun'yun) n. mutual communion.

INTERCOURSE (in'ter-kors) n. mutual dealings; connection. [O.F. entrecours, fr. L. intercursus, a running between, fr. inter, and currere, to run.]

INTERDICT (in-ter-dikt') v.t. to forbid;—(in'ter-dikt) n. a prohibition. [L. (part.) interdictus, fr. interdicere, fr. inter, and dicere, to say.]

INTERDICTION (in-ter-dik'shun) n. act of prohibiting. [to prohibit.

INTERDICTORY (in-ter-dik'tu-ri) a. serving

INTEREST (in'ter-est) v.t. to concern or relate to; affect;—n. concern; share; premium for the use of money. [O.F. interesse, to concern, fr. L. interest, it concerns.]

INTERESTED (in'ter-es-ted) a. having an interest or share in; personally affected.

INTERESTING (in'ter-es-ting) a. exciting interest; pleasing.

INTERFERE (in-ter-fer') v.i. to interpose; act reciprocally; clash. [O.F., fr. L. inter, and ferire, strike.]

INTERFERENCE (in-ter-fer'ens) n. interposition; intermeddling.

INTERFUSED (in-ter-fuzd') a. fused together. [L. inter, and (part.) fusus, fr. fundere, to pour.]

INTERIM (in'ter-im) n. the mean time. [L., fr. inter, between.]

INTERIOR (in-te'ri-ur) n. internal; being within;—n. the inward part. [L. comp. of interus, inward; internal; inner.]

INTERJACENT (in-ter-ja'sent) a. lying between. [L. (part. stem) interjacent-, fr. interjacere, to lie between.]

INTERJECT (in-ter-jekt') v.t. to throw in between; insert. [L. (part.) interjectus, fr. inter, and jacere, throw.]

INTERJECTION (in-ter-jek'shun) n. a word of exclamation.

INTERLACE (in-ter-las') v.t. to intermix; insert. [L. inter, and LACE.]

INTERLARD (in-ter-lard') v.t. to intermix. [L. inter, and LARD.]

INTERLEAVE (in-ter-lev') v.t. to insert leaves. [L. inter, and LEAF.]

INTERLINE (in-ter-lin') v.t. to write between lines. [L. inter, and LINE.]

INTERLINEAR (in-ter-lin'e-ar) a. written between lines.

INTERLINEATION (in-ter-lin-e-a'shun) n. a writing between lines.

INTERLOCK (in-ter-lok') v.t. or i. to unite, flow, or communicate with each other. [L. inter, and LOCK.]

INTERLOCUTOR (in-ter-lok'u-ter) n. one who speaks in dialogue. In Law, an intermediate act or decree before final judgment. [F., fr. L. (acc.) interlocutionem, fr. interloqui, to speak between.]

INTERLOCUTORY (in-ter-lok'u-tur-i) a. consisting of dialogue.

INTERLOPE (in-ter-lop') v.t. to come between and forestall; interfere. [L. inter, and D. loopen, to run.]

INTERLOPER (in'ter-lo-per) n. an intruder.

INTERLUDE (in'ter-lud) n. entertainment between the acts of a play. [L. inter, and ludus, a play, fr. ludere, to play.]

INTERMARRIAGE (in-ter-mar'ij) n. the act of connecting families or races by a marriage between two of their members.

INTERMARRY (in-ter-mar'i) v.i. to become related by marriages among their members, as families and clans. [L. inter, and MARRY.]

INTERMEDDLE (in-ter-med'l) v.i. to meddle in the affairs of others. [L. inter, and MEDDLE.] [officious person.

INTERMEDDLER (in-ter-med'ler) n. an

INTERMEDIATE (in-ter-me'di-at) a. lying between. [L. inter, and medius, middle.]

INTERMEDIATION (in-ter-me-di-a'shun) n. agency between; intervention.

INTERMEDIATELY (in-ter-me'di-at-li) ad. by way of intervention.

INTERMEDIUM (in-ter-me'di-um) n. an intervening agent or space.

INTERMENT (in-ter′ment) *n.* a burying. [See **INTER.**]

INTERMEZZO (in-ter-met′zō, in-ter-med′zō) *n.* an interlude; a light dramatic entertainment between the acts of a tragedy, grand opera, etc. [It., fr. L. *intermedius*, that is between.]

INTERMINABLE (in-ter′mi-nə-bl) *a.* admitting of no end; boundless; endless. [L. *in*, and *terminare*, fr. *terminus*, boundary.]

INTERMINGLE (in-ter-ming′gl) *v.t.* to mingle together. [L. *inter*, and **MINGLE.**]

INTERMISSION (in-ter-mish′un) *n.* cessation for a time.

INTERMISSIVE (in-ter-mis′iv) *a.* coming at times.

INTERMIT (in-ter-mit′) *v.t.* or *i.* to cease for a time; suspend. [L. *inter*, and *mittere*, to send.]

INTERMITTENT (in-ter-mit′ent) *a.* ceasing at intervals;—*n.* a disease that intermits.

INTERMIX (in-ter-miks′) *v.t.* or *i.* to mix together; intermingle. [L. *inter*, and **MIX.**]

INTERMIXTURE (in-ter-miks′tūr) *n.* a mixture.

INTERN (in-tern′) *v.t.* to confine in a neutral country. [F., fr. L. *internus*, internal.]

INTERNAL (in-ter′nəl) *a.* inward; interior; domestic.

INTERNALLY (in-ter′nəl-i) *ad.* inwardly.

INTERNATIONAL (in-ter-nash′un-əl) *a.* existing between nations.

INTERNECINE (in-ter-nē′sin) *a.* mutually destructive. [L., fr. *internecare*, fr. *inter*, and *necare*, to kill.]

INTERNUNCIO (in-ter-nun′shi-ō) *n.* a pope's representative. [L. *internuncius*, messenger.]

INTERPELLATION (in-ter-pe-lā′shun) *n.* interposition; a question put to government during a debate. [L. *interpellare*, to disturb by speaking, fr. L. *inter*, and *pellere*, to drive.]

INTERPOLATE (in-ter′pu-lāt) *v.t.* to insert, as spurious matter in writing. [L. (part.) *interpolatus*, fr. *interpolare*, fr. *inter*, and *polire*, to polish.]

INTERPOLATION (in-ter-pu-lā′shun) *n.* the act of inserting spurious words in a writing.

INTERPOSAL (in-ter-pō′zəl) *n.* act of interposing.

INTERPOSE(in-ter-pōz′)*v.t.* to step in between; mediate;—*v.t.* to place between. [F., fr. L. *inter*, and F. *poser*, to place. Cf. **POSE.**]

INTERPOSITION (in-ter-pu-zish′un) *n.* being or coming between; anything interposed.

INTERPRET (in-ter′pret) *v.i.* to explain the meaning of; translate; decipher. [F., fr. L. *interpres*, interpreter.]

INTERPRETABLE (in-ter′pre-tə-bl) *a.* capable of interpretation.

INTERPRETATION (in-ter-pre-tā′shun) *n.* act of interpreting; exposition given; translation; power of explaining.

INTERPRETER (in-ter′pre-ter) *n.* one who expounds; translator.

INTERREGNUM (in-ter-reg′num) *n.* the time a throne is vacant between the death of a king and the accession of his successor. [L. *inter*, and *regnum*, rule.]

INTERROGATE (in-ter′u-gāt) *v.t.* to examine by question;—*v.i.* to ask questions. [L.(part.) *interrogatus*, fr. *inter*, and *rogare*, to ask.]

INTERROGATION (in-ter-u-gā′shun) *n.* act of questioning; a question put; the point (?) denoting a question.

INTERROGATIVE (in-te-rog′ə-tiv) *a.* denoting a question.

INTERROGATOR (in-ter′u-gā-ter) *n.* one who asks questions.

INTERROGATORY (in-te-rog′ə-tu-ri) *n.* a question;—*a.* containing a question.

INTERRUPT (in-te-rupt′) *v.t.* to break into or between; divide. [L. *interruptus*, fr. *inter*, and (part.) *ruptus*, fr. *rumpere*, to break.]

INTERRUPTION (in-te-rup′shun) *n.* interposition; stop; hinderance.

INTERSECT (in-ter-sekt′) *v.t.* to divide; cross; —*v.i.* to meet and cross. [L. (part.) *intersectus*, fr. *intersecare*, fr. *inter*, and *secare*, to cut.]

INTERSECTION (in-ter-sek′shun) *n.* act of crossing; point where two lines cut each other.

INTERSPACE (in′ter-spās) *n.* an intervening space. [L. *inter*, and **SPACE.**]

INTERSPERSE (in-ter-spers′) *v.t.* to scatter among. [L. (part.) *interspersus*, fr. *interspergere*, fr. *inter*, and *spargere*, to scatter.]

INTERSPERSION (in-ter-sper′shun) *n.* act of scattering.

INTERSPINOUS (in-ter-spī′nus) *a.* between the processes of the spine. Also **INTERSPINAL.** [L. *inter*, and **SPINE.**]

INTERSTELLAR (in-ter-stel′ər) *a.* being among the stars. [L. *inter*, and **STELLAR.**]

INTERSTICE (in-ter′stis) *n.* a space between things. [F., fr. L. *inter*, and *sistere*, stand.]

INTERTIE (in′ter-ti) *n.* a short timber framed between two upright posts to support them. [L. *inter*, and **TIE.**]

INTERTROPICAL (in-ter-trop′i-kəl) *a.* between or within the tropics. [L. *inter*, and **TROPICAL.**]

INTERTWINE (in-ter-twin′) *v.t.* or *i.* to unite by twining. [L. *inter*, and **TWINE.**]

INTERVAL (in′ter-vəl) *n.* a space between; time between events. [F., fr. L. *intervallum*, fr. *inter*, and *vallum*, wall.]

INTERVENE (in-ter-vēn′) *v.i.* to come between. [F., fr. L. *inter*, and *venire*, come.]

INTERVENTION (in-ter-yen′shun) *n.* interposition.

INTERVIEW (in′ter-vū) *n.* a formal meeting; conference;—*v.t.* to visit a public character, and report what he says. [O.F. *entrevue*, fr. *entre*, and *voir*, to see.]

INTERWEAVE (in-ter-wēv′) *v.t.* to weave one into another. [L. *inter*, and **WEAVE.**]

INTESTABLE (in-tes′tə-bl) *a.* not qualified to make a will.

INTESTATE (in-tes′tət) *a.* dying without a will;—*n.* one who dies without leaving a will. [L. *intestatus*, fr. *in*, and *testari*, to make a will.]

INTESTINAL (in-tes′ti-nəl) *a.* pertaining to the bowels.

INTESTINE (in-tes′tin) *a.* internal; domestic. [the bowels. [F., fr. L. *intestinus*, fr. *intus*, within.]

INTESTINES (in-tes′tinz) *n.pl.* the bowels.

INTHRAL. See **ENTHRAL.**

INTIMACY (in′ti-mə-si) *n.* close familiarity; friendship.

INTIMATE (in′ti-mət) *v.t.* to hint; suggest; point out;—*a.* inmost; near;—*n.* a familiar associate or friend. [L. (part.) *intimatus*, fr. *intimare*, fr. *intimus*, innermost, fr. *intus*, within.]

INTIMATELY (in′ti-mət-li) *ad.* closely; familiarly; thoroughly.

INTIMATION (in-ti-mā′shun) *n.* a hint; suggestion; notice; announcement.

INTIMIDATE (in-tim′i-dāt) *v.t.* to make timid; dishearten; deter. [L. *in*, and *timidus*, fearful.]

INTIMIDATION (in-tim-i-dā′shun) *n.* the act of intimidating.

INTITULED (in-tit′ūld) *a.* entitled; distinguished by a title or heading. [L. *in*, and **TITLE.**]

INTO (in′too) *prep.* denoting entrance or transition from one place or state to another. [Fr. **IN** and **TO.**]

INTOLERABLE (in-tol′e-rə-bl) *a.* not to be borne or endured. [L. *in*, and **TOLERABLE.**]

INTOLERABLY (in-tol′e-rə-bli) *ad.* beyond endurance.

INTOLERANCE (in-tol′e-rəns) *n.* want of toleration.

INTOLERANT (in-tol'e-rant) *a.* unable to bear; not suffering difference of opinion.

INTOLERANTLY (in-tol'e-rant-li) *ad.* in an intolerant manner.

INTOLERATION (in-tol-e-rā'shun) *n.* refusal to give liberty to others in their opinions, worship, etc.

INTONATION (in-tō-nā'shun) *n.* manner of utterance; modulation.

INTONE (in-tōn') *v.t.* or *i.* to chant; read in a singing style. [L. (part.) *intonatus*, fr. *intonare*, fr. *in*, and *tonus*, tone.]

INTOXICATE (in-tok'si-kāt) *v.t.* to inebriate; excite greatly. [Late L. (part.) *intoxicatus*, fr. L. *in*, and *toxicum*, fr. G. *toxikon*, a poison in which arrows were dipped, fr. *toxon*, an arrow.]

INTOXICATION (in-tok-si-kā'shun) *n.* state of drunkenness.

INTRACTABLE (in-trak'ta-bl) *a.* unmanageable; obstinate; unruly. [L. *in*, and TRACTABLE.]

INTRACTABLY (in-trak'ta-bli) *ad.* in an ungovernable manner.

INTRANSITIVE (in-tran'si-tiv) *a.* expressing an action or state that does not pass to an object. [L. *in*, and TRANSITIVE.]

INTRENCH (in-trensh') *v.t.* or *i.* to dig or fortify with a trench; encroach. Also **ENTRENCH**.

INTRENCHMENT (in-trensh'ment) *n.* a ditch and parapet for defence; encroachment.

INTREPID (in-trep'id) *a.* fearless; bold. [L, fr. *in*, and *trepidus*, alarmed.]

INTREPIDITY (in-tre-pid'i-ti) *n.* undaunted bravery.

INTRICACY (in'tri-ka-si) *n.* entanglement; perplexed state; obscurity.

INTRICATE (in'tri-kāt) *a.* entangled or involved; complex; complicated. [L. *intricatus*, fr. *in*, and *tricæ*, hindrances.]

INTRICATELY (in'tri-kāt-li) *ad.* with entanglement.

INTRIGUE (in-trēg') *n.* stratagem; amour; —*v.i.* to carry on secret designs. [F. *intriguer*, fr. L. *intricare*, to make difficulties.]

INTRINSIC (in-trin'sik) *a.* internal; inherent; essential; real. [F., fr. L. *intrinsecus*, fr. L. *intra*, within, and *secus*, following.]

INTRINSICALLY (in-trin'si-kal-i) *ad.* internally; in its real nature.

INTRODUCE (in-tru-dūs') *v.t.* to bring in; preface; make known to; present; bring into practice. [L. *intro*, within, and *ducere*, to lead.]

INTRODUCTION (in-tru-duk'shun) *n.* act of introducing; a preface.

INTRODUCTORILY (in-tru-duk'tu-ri-li) *ad.* by way of introduction.

INTRODUCTORY (in-trō-duk'tu-ri) *a.* serving to introduce.

INTROMISSION (in-trō-mish'un) *n.* act of sending in; dealing with.

INTROMIT (in'tru-mit) *v.t.* to send in; admit; —*v.i.* to deal with or manage the property of another. [L., fr. *intro*, within, and *mittere*, to send.]

INTROSPECTION (in-tru-spek'shun) *n.* view of the inside; self-inspection. [L., fr. *intro*, within, and *specere*, to look.]

INTROVERT (in-tru-vert') *v.t.* to turn inward. [L. *intro*, within, and *vertere* (part. *versus*), to turn.]

INTRUDE (in-trōōd') *v.t.* to thrust or force in; —*v.i.* to enter uninvited or unwelcome. [L., fr. *in*, and *trudere* (part. *trusus*,) thrust.]

INTRUSION (in-trōō'zhun) *n.* entrance without right.

INTRUSIVE (in-trōō'siv) *a.* apt to intrude.

INTRUSIVELY (in-trōō'siv-li) *ad.* forwardly.

INTRUSIVENESS (in-trōō'siv-nes) *n.* forward or impertinent spirit.

INTRUST (in-trust') *v.t.* to commit to the care of. [L. *in*, and TRUST.]

INTUITION (in-tū-ish'un) *n.* immediate perception; a direct conception or notion. [L., fr. *in*, and (part.) *tuitus*, fr. *tueri*, to look.]

INTUITIVE (in-tū'i-tiv) *a.* perceived by the mind immediately.

INTUITIVELY (in-tū'i-tiv-li) *ad.* by immediate perception.

INTWIST (in-twist') *v.t.* to twist together. [L. *in*, and TWIST.]

INUNDATE (in-un'dāt, in'un-dāt) *v.t.* to overflow; deluge. [L. (part.) *inundatus*, fr. *in*, and *undare*, rise in waves, fr. *unda*, a wave.]

INUNDATION (in-un-dā'shun) *n.* an overflow of water.

INURE (in-ūr') *v.t.* or *i.* to accustom; harden by use. [E. *in*, and *ure*, use, practice, fr. O.F. *eure*, *ovre*, work.]

INUREMENT (in-ūr'ment) *n.* practice; habit.

INURN (in-urn') *v.t.* to put in an urn. [L. *in*, and URN.]

INUTILITY (in-ū-til'i-ti) *n.* uselessness. [L. *in*, and UTILITY.]

INVADE (in-vād') *v.t.* to enter in a hostile manner; attack. [F., fr. L. *in*, and *vadere*, go.]

INVADER (in-vā'der) *n.* one who invades.

INVALID (in-val'id) *a.* weak; null; void; infirm; feeble; — (in'val-id, in-va-lēd') *n.* one disabled or sick. [L., fr. *in*, and *valere*, be strong.]

INVALIDATE (in-val'i-dāt) *v.t.* to make void; weaken.

INVALIDITY (in-va-lid'i-ti) *n.* weakness; want of legal force.

INVALUABLE (in-val'ū-a-bl) *a.* beyond valuation; priceless. [L. *in*, and VALUABLE.]

INVARIABLE (in-vā'ri-a-bl) *a.* unchangeable. [L. *in*, and VARIABLE.]

INVARIABLENESS (in-vā'ri-a-bl-nes) *n.* unchangeableness.

INVARIABLY (in-vā'ri-a-bli) *ad.* without change; uniformly.

INVASION (in-vā'shun) *n.* hostile entrance; infringement.

INVASIVE (in-vā'siv) *a.* entering with hostile purpose; aggressive.

INVECTIVE (in-vek'tiv) *n.* a severe utterance of censure; sarcasm; satire. [L. (part.) *invectus*, fr. *invehere*, to bring against.]

INVEIGH (in-vā') *v.i.* to rail against; reproach.

INVEIGHER (in-vā'er) *n.* one who inveighs. [O.F. *enveoglir*, to blind, F. *aveugle*, blind, fr. L. *ab*, from, and *oculus*, eye.]

INVEIGLE (in-vē'gl) *v.t.* to entice; wheedle; seduce. [meant; enticing.

INVEIGLEMENT (in-vē'gl-ment) *n.* an enticement.

INVEIGLER (in-vē'gler) *n.* one who seduces; a deceiver.

INVENT (in-vent') *v.t.* to devise something not known before; frame by imagination; contrive; fabricate. [L. (part.) *inventus*, fr. *invenire*, fr. *in*, and *venire*, to come.]

INVENTION (in-ven'shun) *n.* act of finding out; that which is invented.

INVENTIVE (in-ven'tiv) *a.* quick in contrivance; ready with expedients.

INVENTIVELY (in-ven'tiv-li) *ad.* by the power of invention.

INVENTIVENESS (in-ven'tiv-nes) *n.* the faculty of inventing.

INVENTOR (in-ven'ter) *n.* one who finds out or contrives.

INVENTORY (in'ven-tu-ri) *n.* list of articles; —*v.t.* to make a list. [F. *inventaire*, fr. L. *inventarium*, a list of things found.]

INVERSE (in-vers') *a.* inverted; contrary.

INVERSELY (in-vers'li) *ad.* in a contrary order or manner.

INVERSION (in-ver'shun) *n.* change of order, time, or place.

INVERT (in-vert') *v.t.* to turn upside down; reverse. [L. *in*, and *vertere*, to turn.]

INVERTED (in-ver'ted) *a.* reversed.

INVERTEDLY (in-ver'ted-li) *ad.* in an inverted order.

Fāte, fär, ado; mē, her; mine; nōte; tūne; mōōn.

INVEST (in-vest') v.t. to clothe; endow; place in office; lay siege to; lay out money;—v.i. to make an investment. [L. investire, fr. in, and vestire, to clothe.]

INVESTIGATE (in-ves'ti-gāt) v.t. to search into; examine with care. [L. (part.) investigatus, fr. in, and vestigare, to track. Cf. **VESTIGE**.]

INVESTIGATION (in-ves-ti-gā'shun) n. a searching for truth; examination.

INVESTIGATOR (in-ves'ti-gā-ter) n. one who searches or examines with care.

INVESTITURE (in-ves'ti-tūr) n. act of giving possession.

INVESTMENT (in-vest'ment) n. act of investing; blockade; laying out of money; money invested.

INVESTOR (in-ves'ter) n. one who invests.

INVETERACY (in-vet'e-ra-si) n. long continuance; obstinacy confirmed by time.

INVETERATE (in-vet'e-rat) a. firmly established; habitual; obstinate. [L. (part.) inveteratus, fr. inveterare, to grow old, fr. in, and vetus, old.]

INVIDIOUS (in-vid'i-us) a. likely to excite envy or ill will. [L. invidiosus, fr. invidia, envy.]

INVIDIOUSLY (in-vid'i-us-li) ad. enviously.

INVIGORATE (in-vig'u-rāt) v.t. to strengthen. [L., fr. in, and vigor, force.]

INVIGORATION (in-vig-u-rā'shun) n. act of invigorating.

INVINCIBLE (in-vin'si-bl) a. not to be conquered; insuperable; insurmountable. [L. in, and vincere, conquer.]

INVINCIBLY (in-vin'si-bli) ad. unconquerably.

INVIOLABILITY (in-vī-u-la-bil'i-ti) n. quality of being inviolable. Also **INVIOLABLENESS**.

INVIOLABLE (in-vī'u-la-bl) a. that cannot or ought not to be broken.

INVIOLABLY (in-vī'u-la-bli) ad. without breach or failure.

INVIOLATE (in-vī'u-lat) a. not broken, injured, or profaned. [L., fr. in, and violare, to violate.]

INVISIBILITY (in-viz-i-bil'i-ti) n. the state of being invisible.

INVISIBLE (in-viz'i-bl) a. that cannot be seen. [L. in, and **VISIBLE**.]

INVISIBLY (in-viz'i-bli) ad. so as not to be seen.

INVITATION (in-vi-tā'shun) n. act of inviting; request to attend.

INVITE (in-vīt') v.t. to request the company of; allure; attract;—v.i. to ask to anything pleasing. [F., fr. L. invitare.]

INVITINGLY (in-vi'ting-li) ad. so as to invite or allure.

INVOCATE (in'vō-kāt) v.t. to invoke in prayer; supplicate. [L., fr. in, and vocare, to call, fr. vox, vocis, voice. See **INVOKE**.]

INVOCATION (in-vō-kā'shun) n. act of invoking, judicial order.

INVOICE (in'vois) n. a bill of goods with the prices annexed;—v.t. to make a list of, with the prices. [F. envois, pl. of envoi, a sending, fr. O.F. en voie, on the way.]

INVOKE (in-vōk') v.t. to address in prayer; implore. [See **INVOCATE**.]

INVOLUNTARILY (in-vol'un-ta-ri-li) ad. without consent of the will.

INVOLUNTARY (in-vol'un-ta-ri) a. not done willingly; unwillingly; not affecting the will; independent. [L. in, and **VOLUNTARY**.]

INVOLUTE (in'vu-lūt) a. rolled inward;—n. a kind of curve. [See **INVOLVE**.]

INVOLUTION (in-vu-lū'shun) n. action of involving.

INVOLVE (in-volv') v.t. to envelop; infold; comprise; complicate; bring into debt or difficulty. [L. involvere, fr. in, and volvere, (part. volutus), to roll.]

INVULNERABILITY (in-vul-ne-ra-bil'i-ti) n. quality or state of being invulnerable.

INVULNERABLE (in-vul'ne-ra-bl) a. that cannot be wounded. [L. in, and **VULNERABLE**.]

INVULNERABLY (in-vul'ne-ra-bli) ad. so as to be secure from injury, etc.

INWARD (in'ward) a. being within;—ad. within; internal; in the heart or soul. [O.E. inneweard.]

INWARDLY (in'ward-li) ad. in the inner part; internally.

INWARDS (in'wardz) n.pl. intestines.

INWEAVE (in-wēv') v.t. [pret. **INWOVE**; pp. **INWOVE, INWOVEN**] to weave together. [L. in, and **WEAVE**.]

INWROUGHT (in-rawt') a. worked in or among other things. [L. in, and **WROUGHT**.]

IODIDE (i'u-dīd) n. non-acid compound of iodine with other substance. [See **IODINE**.]

IODINE (i'u-dīn) n. an elementary body obtained from the ashes of seaweeds. [G. ioeides, violet-like, fr. ion, violet, and eidos, form.]

IONIC (i-on'ik) a. pertaining to Ionia; denoting the second of the Greek architectural orders.

IOTA (i-ō'ta) n. a tittle; a jot. [G; the smallest letter of Greek alphabet = E. i.]

I.O.U. (i'ō-ū) n. a written acknowledgment of a loan. [I owe you.]

IPECACUANHA (ip-e-kak-ū-á'na) n. an emetic obtained from the root of a South American plant. [Brazilian.]

IRASCIBILITY (i-ras-i-bil'i-ti) n. quality of being easily provoked.

Ionic.

IRASCIBLE (i-ras'i-bl) a. irritable; easily provoked to anger. [F., fr. L. irascibilis, fr. irasci, be angry, fr. ira, anger.]

IRE (īr) n. anger; wrath. [L. ira.]

IREFUL (īr'fool) a. angry; wroth; furious with anger.

IRIS (i'ris) n. the rainbow; the coloured circle round the pupil of the eye; a flower. [L., fr. G. iris, rainbow.]

IRISH (i'rish) a. pertaining to Ireland;—n. the people of Ireland; the language of the Irish.

IRISH-STEW (i'rish-stū) n. a hash of meat and potatoes.

IRK (erk) v.t. to weary; to give pain to; to distress (used impersonally.). [M.E. irken, fr. Scand.]

IRKSOME (erk'sum) a. tedious; tiresome.

IRKSOMELY (erk'sum-li) ad. tediously; vexatiously.

IRKSOMENESS (erk'sum-nes) n. tediousness.

IRON (i'ern) n. the most useful metal; an instrument or utensil made of iron;—a. made of or like iron; hard; stern;—pl. fetters; handcuffs;—v.t. to smooth with a hot iron; arm with iron plates; fetter. [O. E. iren. Cf. Ger. Eisen.]

IRONCLAD (i'ern klad) a. covered with iron or steel plates;—n. a vessel thus armed. [See **IRON** and **CLAD**.]

IRONFOUNDER (i'ern-found-er) n. one who makes iron castings. [See **IRON** and **FOUNDER**.]

IRONICAL (i-ron'i-kal) a. spoken in irony. [See **IRONY**.]

IRONICALLY (i-ron'i-kal-i) ad. by way, or by the use, of irony.

IRONMASTER (i'ern-mas-ter) n. a manufacturer of iron. [See **IRON** and **MASTER**.]

IRONMONGER (i'ern-mung-ger) n. dealer in iron wares. [See **IRON** and **MONGER**.]

IRONY (i'ru-ni) n. speech intended to convey a contrary signification; sarcasm. [F., fr. L. ironia, fr. G. eironeia, fr. eiron, a dissembler, fr. eirein, to talk.]

IRRADIANCE (i-rā'di-ans) *n.* beams of light; splendour. [L. *in*, and *radiare*, to radiate.]
IRRADIATE (i-rā'di-āt) *v.t.* or *i.* to emit rays; illuminate. [L. *in*, and *radiare*, to radiate.]
IRRADIATION (i-rā-di-ā'shun) *n.* emission of rays.
IRRATIONAL (i-rash'un-al) *a.* void of reason. [L. *in*, and RATIONAL.]
IRRATIONALLY (i-rash'un-al-i) *ad.* absurdly; without reason.
IRRECLAIMABLE (ir-e-klā'ma-bl) *a.* that cannot be reclaimed. [L. *in*, and RECLAIMABLE.]
IRRECONCILABLE (i-rek-un-si'la-bl) *a.* that cannot be reconciled. [L. *in*, and RECONCILABLE.]
IRRECOVERABLE (ir-e-kuv'er-a-bl) *a.* that cannot be recovered. [L. *in*, and RECOVERABLE.]
IRREDEEMABLE (ir-e-dē'ma-bl) *a.* that cannot be redeemed. [L. *in*, and REDEEMABLE.]
IRREDEEMABLY (ir-e-dē'ma-bli) *ad.* beyond redemption or calling back.
IRREDUCIBLE (ir-e-dū'si-bl) *a.* that cannot be reduced. [L. *in*, and REDUCIBLE.]
IRREFRAGABLE (i-ref'ra-ga-bl) *a.* that cannot be refuted. [F., fr. L. *in*, and *frangere*, to break.]
IRREFUTABLE (ir-e-fū'ta-bl, i-ref'ū-ta-bl) *a.* that cannot be refuted. [L. *in*, and REFUTABLE.]
IRREGULAR (i-reg'ū-lar) *a.* not according to rule; immethodical;—*n.* a soldier not in the ordinary army service. [L. *in*, and REGULAR.] [from rule.]
IRREGULARITY (i-reg-ū-lar'i-ti) *n.* deviation
IRREGULARLY (i-reg'ū-lar-li) *ad.* without method, rule, or order.
IRRELEVANCY (i-rel'e-van-si) *n.* state of being irrelevant.
IRRELEVANT (i-rel'e-vant) *a.* not bearing on the matter in hand. [L. *in*, and RELEVANT.]
IRRELIGION (ir-ē-lij'un) *n.* want of religion; impiety. [L. *in*, and RELIGION.]
IRRELIGIOUS (ir-e-lij'us) *a.* ungodly; impious; profane.
IRREMEDIABLE (ir-e-mēd'ya-bl) *a.* that cannot be remedied. [L. *in*, and REMEDIABLE.]
IRREMEDIABLY (ir-e-mēd'ya-bli) *ad.* beyond remedy or correction.
IRREPARABLE (i-rep'a-ra-bl) *a.* that cannot be recovered or regained. [L. *in*, and REPARABLE.]
IRREPARABLY (i-rep'a-ra-bli) *ad.* beyond cure or recovery.
IRREPREHENSIBLE (i-rep-re-ben'si-bl) *a.* not to be blamed. [L. *in*, and REPREHENSIBLE.]
IRREPRESSIBLE (ir-e-pres'i-bl) *a.* that cannot be repressed. [L. *in*, and REPRESSIBLE.]
IRREPRESSIBLY (ir-e-pres'i-bli) *ad.* in a way to preclude repression.
IRREPROACHABLE (ir-e-prō'cha-bl) *a.* that cannot be reproached. [L. *in*, and REPROACHABLE.]
IRREPROACHABLY (ir-e-prō'cha-bli) *ad.* so as not to deserve reproach.
IRREPROVABLE (ir-e-prōó'va-bl) *a.* that cannot be justly reproved. [L. *in*, and REPROVABLE.]
IRRESISTIBLE (ir-e-zis'ti-bl) *a.* that cannot be resisted with success. [L. *in*, and RESISTIBLE.]
IRRESISTIBLY (ir-e-zis'tl-bli) *ad.* so as not to be resisted.
IRRESOLUTE (i-rez'u-lūt) *a.* not firm in purpose; wanting decision; hesitating. [L. *in*, and RESOLUTE.]
IRRESOLUTELY (i-rez'u-lūt-li) *ad.* without firmness or decision.
IRRESOLUTION (i-rez-u-lū'shun) *n.* want of firmness of mind; indecision. Also **IRRESOLUTENESS.**

IRRESPECTIVE (ir-e-spek'tiv) *a.* not regarding circumstances or conditions. [L. *in*, and RESPECTIVE.]
IRRESPECTIVELY (ir-e-spek'tiv-li) *ad.* without regard to.
IRRESPONSIBLE (ir-e-spon'si-bl) *a.* not responsible. [L. *in*, and RESPONSIBLE.]
IRRETRIEVABLE (ir-e-trē'va-bl) *a.* irrecoverable. [L. *in*, and RETRIEVABLE.]
IRRETRIEVABLY (ir-e-trē'va-bli) *ad.* irrecoverably.
IRREVERENCE (i-rev'e-rens) *n.* want of reverence or veneration.
IRREVERENT (i-rev'e-rent) *a.* wanting in reverence. [L. *in*, and REVERENT.]
IRREVERENTLY (i-rev'e-rent-li) *ad.* in an irreverent manner.
IRREVERSIBLE (ir-e-ver'si-bl) *a.* that cannot be reversed. [L. *in*, and REVERSIBLE.]
IRREVERSIBLY (ir-e-ver'si-bli) *ad.* beyond reversal or repeal.
IRREVOCABLE (i-rev'u-ka-bl) *a.* that cannot be recalled. [L. *in*, and REVOCABLE.]
IRREVOCABLY (i-rev'u-ka-bli) *ad.* so as not to admit of recall.
IRRIGATE (ir'i-gāt) *v.t.* to water, or wet. [L. (part.) *irrigatus*, fr. *in*, and *rigare*, to wet.]
IRRIGATION (ir-i-gā'shun) *n.* act of watering.
IRRITABILITY (ir-i-ta-bil'i-ti) *n.* capacity of being irritated.
IRRITABLE (ir'i-ta-bl) *a.* easily provoked.
IRRITABLY (ir'i-ta-bli) *ad.* in an irritable manner.
IRRITANT (ir'i-tant) *n.* that which excites or irritates.
IRRITATE (ir'i-tāt) *v.t.* to excite heat or redness in the skin; excite anger in; provoke. [L. (part.) *irritatus*, fr. *irritare*, fr. *irrire*, to snarl.]
IRRITATION (ir-i-tā'shun) *n.* act of exciting; —*a.* morbid sensation in the skin or nerves; provocation to anger.
IRRITATIVE (ir'i-tā-tiv) *a.* serving to excite action or irritation.
IRRITATORY (ir'i-iā-tu-ri) *a.* producing irritation; exciting.
IRRUPTION (i-rup'shun) *n.* sudden invasion; a violent inroad. [L. (acc.) *irruptionem*, fr. (part.) *irrumpus*, fr. *irrumpere*, to break in.]
IRRUPTIVE (i-rup'tiv) *a.* rushing in or upon.
IS (iz) third person singular of the verb TO BE. [O.E.]
ISLAM (iz'lam) *n.* the Mohammedan religion; the people who profess it. [A.=obedience to God.]
ISLAND (i'land) *n.* land surrounded by water. [M.E. *iland*, fr. O.E. *igland*, fr. *ig*, island (as in Sel*sea*, Alder*ney*), and LAND.]
ISLANDER (i'lan-der) *n.* inhabitant of an island.
ISLE (il) *n.* an island. [O.F. *isle*=F. *île*, fr. L. *insula*, island.]
ISLET (i'let) *n.* a little island.
ISOBAR (i'gu-bar) *n.* a line on a map connecting places with the same mean barometric pressure. [G. *isos*, equal, and *baros*, weight.]
ISOLATE (i-su-lāt) *v.i.* to place in a detached situation. [It. *isolare*, fr. *isola*, fr. L. *insula*, island.]
ISOLATION (i-su-lā'shun) *n.* state of being alone.
ISRAELITE (iz'rā-el-īt) *n.* a descendant of Israel; a Jew.
ISSUABLE (ish'ū-a-bl) *a.* that may be issued.
ISSUE (ish'ū) *n.* offspring; final result; a small ulcer kept open;—*v.i.* to come or send out; result;—*v.t.* to put in circulation. [O.F., fr. L. *exire*, go out, fr. *ex*, out, and *ire*, to go.]
ISTHMUS (ist'mus, is'mus) *n.* a neck of land connecting larger portions of land. [L., fr. G. *isthmos*, a passage.]
IT (it) *pron.* that thing. [O.E. *hit*, neut. of *he*.]

ITALIAN (i-tal′yạn) *a.* pertaining to Italy;—*n.* a native of Italy; language of Italy.
ITALIC (i-tal′ik) *a.* relating to Italy or to its letters. [letters.
ITALICISE (i-tal′i-sīz) *v.t.* to print in italic
ITALICS (i-tal′iks) *n.pl. letters inclining as these.*
ITCH (ich) *n.* a cutaneous disease;—*v.i.* to have irritation in the skin; to long for. [O.E. *giccan*, to itch. Cf. Ger. *jucken*; Scot. *youk*.]
ITCHY (ich′i) *a.* affected with itch.
ITEM (ī′tem) *n.* a separate particular:—*ad.* also *v.t.* to make a note of. [L.]
ITERATE (it′e-rāt) *v.t.* to repeat. [L. (part.) *iteratus*, fr. *iterare*, fr. *iterum*, again. See ITINERATE.]
ITERATION (it-e-rā′shun) *n.* act of repeating.
ITINERANCY (I-tin′e-rạn-si) *n.* passing from place to place.

ITINERANT (I-tin′e-rạnt) *n.* one who travels from place to place;—*a.* wandering; unsettled. [L. (part. stem) *itinerant-*, fr. *itinerans*, fr. stem *itiner-*, of *iter*, a journey.]
ITINERARY (I-tin′e-rạ-ri) *n.* a book of travels; —*a.* travelling; done on a journey. [See ITINERATE.]
ITINERATE (i-tin′e-rāt) *v.i.* to travel. [L. *itinerare*, make a journey.]
ITSELF (it-self′) *pron.* the neuter reciprocal pronoun applied to things. [See IT and SELF.]
IVIED (ī′vid) *a.* covered with ivy.
IVORY (ī′vu-ri) *n.* the tusk of an elephant;—*a.* made of ivory. [O.F. *ivurie* = F. *ivoire*, fr. L. *ebur*, *eboris*, ivory.]
IVY (ī′vi) *n.* a parasitic creeping or climbing plant. [O.E. *ifig*.]

J

JABBER (jab′ẹr) *v.i.* to talk rapidly and indistinctly;—*n.* rapid talk. [Fr. root of GABBLE.] [and indistinctly.
JABBERER (jab′ẹr-ẹr) *n.* one who talks fast
JACK (jak) *n.* a saucy fellow; a playing card; a sailor; a young pike; a leathern bottle; a contrivance for turning a spit or raising heavy weights; a bowler's tee; a flag. [F. *Jacques*, James, the most common name in France, used for John, the most common name in England.]
JACKAL (jak′awl) *n.* a carnivorous animal allied to the wolf. [Per.]
JACKANAPES (jak′a-nāps) *n.* a monkey; an ape. [Fr. *Jack o′ apes*, a man that exhibited performing monkeys.]
JACKASS (jak′as) *n.* the male of the ass; a blockhead. [*Jack*, the male, and ASS.]
JACKBOOTS (jak′bōōts) *n.pl.* very large boots. [Fr. JACK and BOOTS.]
JACKDAW (jak′daw) *n.* a bird of the crow family. [Fr. JACK and *daw*.]
JACKET (jak′et) *n.* a short coat. [O.F. *jaquette*, a sleeveless jacket, a dim. of O.F. *jaque*, a coat of mail.]
JACK-KNIFE (jak′nif) *n.* a large pocket-knife. [Fr. JACK and KNIFE.]
JACOBIN (jak′u-bin) *n.* an opponent of constitutional government. [F., fr. L. *Jacobus*, James.]
JACOBINICAL (jak-u-bin′i-kạl) *a.* pertaining to secret clubs against government.
JACOBINISM (jak′u-bin-izm) *n.* revolutionary doctrines.
JACOBITE (jak′u-bīt) *a.* pertaining to the adherents of James II. of England and the Stuarts. [L. *Jacobus*, James.]
JADE (jād) *n.* a tired horse; a worthless woman;—*v.t.* or *i.* to exhaust by labour; tire; become weary. [Scand.]
JAG (jag) *n.* a notch;—*v.t.* to notch; indent. [Etym. unknown.]
JAGUAR (jag-wär′) *n.* a carnivorous animal allied to the leopard. [Brazilian.]
JAIL (jāl) *n.* a prison. [O.F. *gaole* = F. *geôle*, fr. Late L. *gabiola*, a cage, dim. of *gabia*, a cage, corr. fr. *cavea*, a cage, fr. L. *cavus*, hollow.]
JAILER (jā′lẹr) *n.* one who keeps a jail.
JALAP (jal′ạp) *n.* a plant or drug used as a cathartic. [So called from *Jalapa* or *Xalapa*, in Mexico.]
JAM (jam) *n.* a conserve of fruits;—*v.t.* to squeeze closely; wedge in. [Cf. CHAMP.]
JAMB (jam) *n.* side piece of a chimney. [F. *jambe*, leg.]
JANGLE (jang′gl) *v.t.* or *i.* to wrangle; quarrel; —*n.* discordant sound; contention. [Imit., fr. O.F. *jangler*.]

JANGLER (jang′glẹr) *n.* a wrangler.
JANITOR (jan′i-tẹr) *n.* a doorkeeper. [L., fr. *janua*, a door.]
JANIZARY (jan′i-zạ-ri) *n.* a Turkish soldier of the guards. [F. *Janissaire*, fr. Turk., new soldier.]
JANUARY (jan′ū-ạ-ri) *n.* the first month of the year. [L. *Januarius*, fr. *Janus*, a Roman deity, to whom this month was sacred.]
JAPAN (jạ-pan′) *n.* varnish or varnished work;—*v.t.* to varnish; black and gloss. [Fr. *Japan*.]
JAPHETIC (ja-fet′ik) *a.* pertaining to Japheth.
JAR (jär) (1) *v.t.* to cause to shake;—*v.i.* to strike together slightly; interfere;—*n.* a shaking; a clash;—(2) a stone or glass vessel. [(1) Imit. (2) O.F. *jare*, fr. A., fr. Per. =water-vessel.]
JARGON (jär′gun) *n.* confused talk. [F.]
JASMINE (jas′min) *n.* a climbing plant with white fragrant flowers. Also JESSAMINE. [F., fr. A., fr. Per.]
JASPER (jas′pẹr) *n.* an opaque variety of quartz. [F. *jaspe*, fr. L. and G. *iaspis*, fr. A.]
JAUNDICE (jän′dis) *n.* a disease in which the body becomes yellow. [F. *jaunisse*, fr. *jaune*, yellow, fr. L. *galbinus*, fr. *galbus*, yellow.]
JAUNDICED (jän′dist) *a.* affected with jaundice; prejudiced.
JAUNT (jänt) *v.i.* to make an excursion;—*n.* an excursion. [Etym. doubtful.]
JAUNTILY (jän′ti-li) *ad.* airily; briskly. Also written JANTILY.
JAUNTY (jän′ti) *a.* airy; showy. Also written JANTY. [F. *gentil*, fr. G. *gentilis*.]
JAUNTINESS (jän′ti-nes) *n.* airiness; sprightliness; briskness.
JAVELIN (jav′e-lin) *n.* a kind of spear. [F.]
JAW (jaw) *n.* the bone in which the teeth are fixed;—*v.t.* to scold. [Old form CHAW, fr. root of CHEW.]
JAY (jā) *n.* a chattering bird with beautiful plumage. [O.F. *jay*, a jay.]
JEALOUS (jel′us) *a.* suspicious. [O.F. *jalous*, = F. *jaloux*, fr. L. *zelus*, emulation, fr. G. *zelos*.]
JEALOUSLY (jel′us-li) *ad.* with jealousy.
JEALOUSY (jel′us-i) *n.* suspicion; fear of losing some good which another may obtain.
JEAN (jān) *n.* a cotton cloth twilled. [It. *Genova*, Geneva.]
JEER (jēr) *v.i.* to scoff; deride;—*n.* a scoffing jest; taunt. [M.D. =jest.]
JEERINGLY (jēr′ing-li) *ad.* with scorn; in mockery.
JEHOVAH (Je-hō′vạ) *n.* the Hebrew name of God. [H.]

JEJUNE (je-jōōn') *a.* empty; wanting interest. [L. *jejunus*, hungry.]
JEJUNENESS (je-jōōn'nes) *n.* barrenness.
JELLY (jel'i) *n.* any gelatinous substance; inspissated juice of fruit. [F. *gelée*, fr. L. *gelare*, to freeze.]
JEMMY (jim'i) *n.* a small crowbar used by burglars. [Fr. *James*.]
JENNET (jen'et) *n.* a small Spanish horse. [O F. *genette*, fr. Sp. *ginette*, fr. A.]
JENNY (jen'i) *n.* a machine for spinning cotton. [Corr. fr. GIN, contr. of ENGINE.]
JEOPARD (jep'ard) *v.t.* to put in danger; risk; peril; endanger. [F. *jeu parti*, a divided game, fr. Late L. *jocus partitus*, fr. *jocus*, a game, and *partiri*, to divide.]
JEOPARDOUS (jep'ar-dus) *a.* hazardous.
JEOPARDY (jep'ar-di) *n.* danger; peril.
JERK (jerk) *v.t.* or *i.* to throw or pull with sudden motion;—*n.* a sudden thrust, or twitch, or spring. [Scot. *yerk*, to strike. Cf. *yard*, a rod.]
JERKIN (jer'kin) *n.* a jacket or short coat. [D.]
JERSEY (jer'zi) *n.* a very fine wool; a woollen shirt. [Fr. the island *Jersey*.]
JESS (jes) *n.* a short strap or ribbon used in falconry. [O.F. *ject*, fr. L. *jactare*, fr. L. *jacere*, to throw.]
JEST (jest) *v.i.* to make sport;—*n.* a joke. [M.E. *geste*, a tale, a deed, fr. O.F., fr. L. *gesta*, fr. *gerere*, to do.]
JESTER (jes'ter) *n.* one who jests; a buffoon.
JESTING (jes'ting) *n.* talk to excite laughter.
JESUIT (jez'ū-it) *n.* one of a religious order; a crafty person. [*Jesus*.]
JESUITICAL (jez-ū-it'i-kạl) *a.* designing; cunning.
JESUITICALLY (jez-ū-it'i-kạl-i) *a.* craftily; cunningly. [the Jesuit.
JESUITISM (jez'ū-it-izm) *n.* the principles of
JET (jet) (1) *n.* a very black fossil;—(2) a spout of water; a gas branch with one opening;—*v.i.* to shoot forward. [(1) O.F. *jaet*, fr. G. *gagates*, fr. *Gagas*, a town in Asia Minor. (2) O.F. *jetter*, fr. L. *jactare*, fr. *jacere*, to throw.]
JETTY (jet'i) (1) *a.* made of jet: black;—(2) *n.* a small pier. [(1) See JET (1). (2) O.F. *jetée*, thrown out. Cf. JET (2).]
JEW (jōō) *n.* a Hebrew or Israelite. [O.F. *Juis*, fr. L. *Judœus*, Jew, fr. G. *Ioudaios*, fr. H. = *Judah*.]
JEWEL (jōō'el) *n.* a precious stone;—*v.t.* to fit or dress with jewels. [O.F. *jouel* = F. *joyau*, fr. L. *gaudium*, joy, or fr. *jocus*, play.]
JEWELLER (jōō'el-er) *n.* one who deals in jewels.
JEWELLERY (jōō'el-ri) *n.* jewels in general; the art or trade of a jeweller.
JEWISH (jōō'ish) *a.* pertaining to the Jews.
JIB (jib) *n.* foremost sail of a ship. [Scand.]
JIBE (jib) *v.t.* or *i.* to shift from one side to the other. [Scand.]
JIG (jig) *n.* a light dance; a dance tune. [O.F. *gige, gigue*, a fiddle, a dance.]
JILT (jilt) *n.* a woman who trifles with her lover;—*v.t.* or *i.* to encourage and then reject; coquet. [Contr. of *jillet*, dim. of *Jill*.]
JINGLE (jing'gl) *v.i.* to cause to sound with a sharp noise;—*v.i.* to clink; tinkle;—*n.* a sharp, clinking sound; a little rattle. [Imit.]
JINGLING (jing'gling) *n.* a sharp, rattling sound, as of bells.
JINGO (jing'gō) *n.* an oath; an advocate of a warlike policy;—*pl.* JINGOES. [Etym. doubtful. Political sense due to the use made of the words of a music-hall song in a *Daily News* leader.]
JINRIKISHA (jin-rik'i-sha) *n.* a small two-wheeled carriage drawn by one or more men. [Jap.]
JOB (job) *n.* a piece of work;—*v.t.* or *i.* to do small work; deal in stocks; hire or let out for hire. [O.F. *gob*, a mouthful. Cf. GOBBLE.]

JOBBER (job'er) *n.* a dealer in stocks; one who works by the job.
JOCKEY (jok'i) *n.* one who rides horses in a race; horse-dealer;—*pl.* JOCKEYS;—*v.t.* to jostle in riding; overreach; cheat. [Dim. of *Jock*, JACK.]
JOCOSE (jō-kōs') *a.* given to jesting. [L. *jocosus*, fr. *jocus*, joke.]
JOCOSELY (jō-kōs'li) *ad.* in jest; merrily.
JOCULAR (jok'ū-lạr) *a.* jocose; merry. [L. *jocularis*, fr. *jocus*, joke.]
JOCULARITY (jok-ū-lar'i-ti) *n.* disposition to jest.
JOCULARLY (jok'ū-lạr-li) *ad.* jocosely; merrily.
JOCUND (jok'und) *a.* merry; gay; lively. [L. *jocundus*, fr. *jocus*, jest.]
JOG (jog) *v.t.* or *i.* to push with the elbow; walk slowly;—*n.* a push with the elbow. [W.]
JOGGLE (jog'l) *v.t.* to shake slightly. [Dim. of JOG.]
JOG-TROT (jog'trot) *n.* a slow, regular pace; *a.* monotonous. [See JOG and TROT.]
JOIN (join) *v.t.* or *i.* to couple; unite; combine; close; adhere; be in contact. [O.F. *joindre*, fr. L. *jungere*.]
JOINER (join'er) *n.* an artisan in woodwork.
JOINERY (join'er-i) *n.* a joiner's art.
JOINT (joint) *n.* union of bones; knot;—*v.t.* to form into joints;—*a.* shared by two or more. [F. *joint*. Cf. JOIN.]
JOINTED (join'ted) *a.* having joints.
JOINTER (join'ter) *n.* a large plane.
JOINTLY (joint'li) *ad.* unitedly.
JOINT-TENANT (joint-ten'ant) *n.* one who holds by joint tenancy. [See JOIN and TENANT.]
JOINTURE (join'tūr) *n.* an estate settled on a wife;—*v.t.* to settle a jointure on. [L. *junctura*, a joining, fr. (part.) *junctus*, fr. *jungere*, to join.]
JOIST (joist) *n.* one of the timbers to which the flooring of a house is fastened. [O.F. *giste*, fr. L. *jacere*, to lie.]
JOKE (jōk) *n.* a jest;—*v.t.* or *i.* to jest; banter. [L. *jocus*.]
JOLLITY (jol'i-ti) *n.* noisy mirth; gaiety; festivity. Also JOLLINESS.
JOLLY (jol'i) *a.* merry; gay; lively; plump; very pleasing. [O.F. *joli*, *joli*, merry, fr. Scand.]
JOLT (jōlt) *v.t.* or *i.* to shake with jerks;—*n.* a sudden shake or shock. [O.E.]
JONQUIL (jon'kwil) *n.* a bulbous plant of the genus Narcissus, allied to the daffodil. [F. *jonquille*, fr. L. *juncus*, a rush.]
JOSS (jos) *n.* a Chinese idol. [Corr. of Pg. *deos*, god.]
JOSTLE (jos'l) *v.t.* or *i.* to push or run against; move as in a crowd. [Freq. of JOUST.]
JOT (jot) *n.* an iota; a tittle;—*v.t.* to write briefly; make a note of. [G. *iota*, the letter *i*.]
JOTTING (jot'ing) *n.* a memorandum.
JOURNAL (jur'nạl) *n.* an account of daily transactions; a diary. [F., fr. L. *diurnalis*, fr. *diurnus*, belonging to the day, fr. *dies*, a day.]
JOURNALISE (jur'nạl-īz) *v.t.* to enter in a journal.
JOURNALIST (jur'nạl-ist) *n.* one who keeps a journal; writer in a newspaper or periodical.
JOURNEY (jur'ni) *n.* travel;—*v.i.* to travel from one place to another;—*pl.* JOURNEYS. [F. *journée*, fr. *jour*, a day, fr. L. *diurnus*.]
JOURNEYMAN (jur'ni-man) *n.* a hired workman.
JOUST (jōōst) *n.* a tournament;—*v.i.* to fight on horseback; tilt. [O.F *jousie*, fr. L. *juxta*, near.]
JOVE (jōv) *n.* Jupiter, the supreme deity of the Romans. [L. *Jupiter, Jovis*.]

JOVIAL (jō'vi-ạl) a. merry; jolly; gay. [L. Jovialis, fr. Jupiter, Jovis.]
JOVIALITY (jō-vi-al'i-ti) n. merriment; festivity. Also JOVIALNESS.]
JOVIALLY (jō'vi-ạl-i) ad. with mirth; gaily.
JOY (joi) n. gladness; happiness; exultation; —v.t. or i. to rejoice. [F. joie, fr. L. gaudium, fr. gaudere, to rejoice.]
JOYFUL (joi'fool) a. full of joy; glad.
JOYFULLY (joi'fool-i) ad. with joy; gladly.
JOYFULNESS (joi'fool-nes) n. great joy.
JOYLESS (joi'les) a. void of joy.
JOYLESSLY (joi'les-li) ad. without joy.
JOYLESSNESS (joi'les-nes) n. state of being joyless.
JOYOUS (joi'us) a. glad; merry; cheerful.
JOYOUSLY (joi'us-li) ad. with joy or gladness.
JOYOUSNESS (joi'us-nes) n. state of being joyous.
JUBILANT (jōō'bi-lạnt) a. uttering songs of triumph. [L. (part. stem) jubilant-, fr. jubilare, to shout for joy.]
JUBILATION (jōō-bi-lā'shun) n. joyfulness; exultation.
JUBILEE (jōō'bi-lē) n. the fiftieth year, in which slaves and lands were released; any season of public rejoicing. [F. jubilé, fr. L. jubilæus, fr. H. =a blast of a trumpet.]
JUDAICAL (jōō-dā'i-kạl) a. pertaining to the Jews.
JUDAISM (jōō'dā-izm) n. the religion of the Jews. [L. Judaicus, fr. H. Juda, Judah.]
JUDGE (juj) n. one authorised to determine causes in court;—v.t. or i. to hear and determine; try; sentence; compare; distinguish; reckon. [F. juger, fr. L. judicare, fr. L. judex, fr. jus, law, and dicere, to speak.]
JUDGESHIP (juj'ship) n. the office of a judge.
JUDGMENT (juj'ment) n. act of judging; faculty which judges; opinion formed; verdict; sentence; discernment; good taste; a special calamity.
JUDICATORY (jōō'di-kā-tu-ri) n. a court of justice:—a. dispensing justice.
JUDICATURE (jōō'di-kā-tūr) n. power of distributing justice.
JUDICIAL (jōō-dish'ạl) a. pertaining to courts; inflicted as a penalty. [L. judicialis, fr. judicium, judgment, fr. judex.]
JUDICIALLY (jōō-dish'ạl-i) ad. in the forms of justice.
JUDICIARY (jōō-dish'ạ-ri) a. pertaining to law courts;—n. the judges collectively. [L. judiciarius.]
JUDICIOUS (jōō-dish'us) a. prudent; acting with judgment.
JUDICIOUSLY (jōō-dish'us-li) ad. wisely.
JUG (jug) (1) n. a vessel for liquids; a pitcher; a ewer;—v.t. to boil or stew, as in a jug;—(2) v.i. to utter a note or call, as the nightingale. [(1) Etym. uncertain (2) Imit.]
JUGGLE (jug'l) v.i. to play tricks; conjure. [O.F., fr. L. joculari, to jest, fr. jocus, a jest.]
JUGGLER (jug'lẹr) n. one who juggles.
JUGGLERY (jug'lẹr-i) n. sleight of hand.
JUGGLING (jug'ling) n. act of playing tricks; imposture.
JUGULAR (jug'ū-lạr) a. belonging to the throat. [L. jugulum, the collar-bone, fr. jungere, to join.]
JUICE (jōōs) n. the sap of vegetables; fluid part of animal substances. [F., fr. L. jus, broth.]
JUICELESS (jōōs'les) a. without juice.
JUICINESS (jōō'si-nes) n. succulence.
JUICY (jōō'si) a. full of juice.
JUJUBE (jōō'jōōb) n. a pulpy fruit; confection of sugar and juice; any fruity lozenge. [F., fr. L. zizyphum, fr. Per.]
JULEP (jōō'lep) n. a liquor or syrup. [F., fr. Sp., fr. A. and Per. =rose-water.]
JULY (jōō-lī') n. seventh month of the year. [Fr. Julius, the surname of Caius Cæsar, who was born in this month.]

JUMBLE (jum'bl) v.t. to mix;—n. a confused mixture; a small cake. [Perh. freq. of JUMP.]
JUMP (jump) v.i. to spring by raising both feet;—v.t. to pass by a leap; skip over;—n. leap; bound; distance leapt; fault in strata. [Fr. Teut. Cf. Sw. gumpa, and M. H. Ger. gumpen, to jump.]
JUMPER (jum'pẹr) n. a cheese mite; a long iron chisel; one who jumps in religious service.
JUNCTION (jungk'shun) n. act of joining; union; place where two lines of railway meet. [L., fr. jungere, to join.]
JUNCTURE (jungk'tūr) n. a joining; point of time. [L. junctura.]
JUNE (jōōn) n. sixth month of the year. [L. Junius.]
JUNGLE (jung'gl) n. land covered with trees, brushwood, etc.; a wooded swamp. [Skr. =desert.]
JUNIOR (jōōn'yur) a. younger in years; lower in position or practice;—n. one who is younger or lower. [L. comp. of juvenis, young.]
JUNIPER (jōō'ni-pẹr) n. an evergreen shrub. [L. juniperus, fr. juvenis, young, and parere, bring forth.]
JUNK (jungk) (1) n. a Chinese ship;—(2) old ropes; hard, salt beef. [(1) Pg. junco, fr. Malay, fr. Chin. =a boat. (2) L. juncus, a rush.]
JUNKET (jung'ket) n. a sweetmeat; a feast; —v.t. or i. to feast. [It. giuncata, fr. L. juncus, a rush.]
JUNO (jōō'nō) n. a heathen goddess; one of the smaller planets. [L.]
JUNTO (jun'tō) n. a cabal; a faction. [Sp. junta.]
JUPITER (jōō'pi-tẹr) n. the supreme deity of the pagan world; the largest of the planets. [L. Jovis pater, heaven-father, fr. G. Zeus pater.]
JURIDICAL (jōō-rid'i-kạl) a. used in courts of justice. [L. juridicus, fr. stem. jur-, of jus, law, and dicere, to speak.]
JURISDICTION (jōō-ris-dik'shun) n. legal authority, or the space over which it extends. [F., fr. L. (acc.) jurisdictionem, fr. jus, law, and dicere, to speak.]
JURISDICTIONAL (jōō-ris-dik'shun-ạl) a. according to legal authority.
JURISPRUDENCE (jōō-ris-prōō'dens) n. the science of law. [F., fr. L., fr. stem, jur-, of jus, law, and prudentia, knowledge of.]
JURISPRUDENT (jōō-ris-prōō'dent) a. understanding law;—n. one versed in law.
JURISPRUDENTIAL (jōō-ris-prōō-den'shạl) a. belonging to jurisprudence.
JURIST (jōō'rist) n. a professor of the civil law; a civilian. [F. juriste, fr. L. jus, juris, law.]
JUROR (jōō'rur) n. one who serves on a jury; a juryman.
JURY (jōō'ri) n. persons empanelled and sworn to deliver truth on evidence in court. [F. juré, sworn, fr. jurer, fr. L. jurare, to swear.]
JURYMAN (jōō'ri-man) n. one who serves on a jury. [See JURY and MAN.]
JURYMAST (jōō'ri-mȧst) n. a temporary mast set up in place of one carried away. [O.F. ajurie, fr. L. adjutare, to aid. See MAST.]
JUST (just) a. lawful; true; upright; exact; righteous; full; fair; equitable;—ad. near at hand or in time; exactly; barely. [F., fr. L. justus, fr. jus, law.]
JUSTICE (jus'tis) n. the giving to every one his due; integrity; impartiality; desert; retribution; a judge; magistrate. [F., fr. L. justitia, fr. justus, just, fr. jus, law.]
JUSTICIARY (jus-tish'i-ạ-ri) n. one who administers justice.

JUSTIFIABLE (jus'ti-fi-ạ-bl) *a.* that can be justified.
JUSTIFIABLY (jus'ti-fi-ạ-bli) *ad.* so as to be justified.
JUSTIFICATION (jus-ti-fi-kā'shun) *n.* act of justifying; vindication.
JUSTIFIER (jus'ti-fi-ẽr) *n.* one who justifies.
JUSTIFICATORY (jus-ti-fi-kā'tu-ri) *a.* defensory; vindicatory.
JUSTIFY (jus'ti-fi) *v.t.* to prove to be just; vindicate; treat as righteous; space out in even lines. [F., fr. L. *justificare*, fr. *justus*, just, and *facere*, to make.]
JUSTLY (just'li) *ad.* equitably; uprightly; accurately.

JUSTNESS (just'nes) *n.* equity; fairness; propriety; exactness.
JUT (jut) *v.i.* to shoot out or project;—*n.* a projection. [A form of JET.]
JUTE (jōōt) *n.* a substance like hemp, from which a coarse kind of cloth is woven. [Bengali.]
JUVENILE (jōō've-nil) *a.* young; youthful. [L. *juvenilis*, fr. *juvenis*, young.]
JUVENILITY (jōō-ve-nil'i-ti) *n.* youthfulness.
JUXTAPOSITION (juks-tạ-pō-zish'un) *n.* placing or being placed near; contiguity. [L. *juxta*, near, and (part.) *positus*, of *ponere*, to place.]

K

KAFIR, KAFFIR (kaf'ẽr) *n.* one of a woolly-haired race inhabiting the eastern part of South Africa; the language of the Kaffirs. [A. =an unbeliever.]
KAIL (kāl) *n.* a kind of cabbage. Also written **KALE.** [O.E. *cawel*, fr. L. *caulis*, stalk.]
KAISER (ki'zẽr, kā'zẽr) *n.* an emperor. [Ger., fr. L. *Cæsar.*]
KALEIDOSCOPE (kạ-li'du-skōp) *n.* an optical instrument which multiplies an object into an endless variety of coloured figures. [G., fr. *kalos*, beautiful, *eidos*, form, and *skopein* to view.]
KAMPTULICON (kamp-tū'li-kun) *n.* a kind of floorcloth. [G., fr. *kamptos*, flexible, and *oulos*, thick.]
KANGAROO (kang-gạ-rōō') *n.* a marsupial quadruped of Australia. [Austr.]
KAOLIN (kā'u-lin) *n.* a fine kind of porcelain clay. [Chin.]
KAW (kaw). See CAW.
KAROO, KARROO (kạ-rōō') *n.* the name given to immense clayey table-lands in South Africa. [Hottentot = hard.]
KEA (kē'ạ) *n.* the sheep-killing parrot of New Zealand. [Ma₀ri.]
KEDGE (kej) *n.* a small anchor;—*v.t.* to warp by means of a kedge. [F.]
KEEL (kēl) *n.* the lower timber of a ship. [O.E. *ceol.* Cf. Ger. *Kiel.*]
KEELHAUL (kēl'hawl) *v.t.* to haul under the keel. [See KEEL and HAUL.]
KEEN (kēn) *a.* eager; sharp; piercing. [O.E. *cene.* Cf. Ger. *kühn*, bold.]
KEENLY (kēn'li) *ad.* sharply; bitterly.
KEEP (kēp) *v.t.* [*pret.* and *pp.* KEPT] to preserve; hold; watch; protect; observe; fulfil; conceal;—*v.i.* to remain in; endure; —*n.* a stronghold; central tower; maintenance; cost of boarding. [O.E. *cepan.*]
KEEPER (kē'pẽr) *n.* one who preserves or guards.
KEEPING (kē'ping) *n.* custody; care.
KEEPSAKE (kēp'sāk) *n.* a token of remembrance. [See KEEP and SAKE.]
KEG (keg) *n.* a small cask. [Icel. =cask.]
KELP (kelp) *n.* the calcined ashes of seaweed. [Etym. unknown.]
KELT (kelt) *n.* a spent or spawned salmon. [Celt.]
KENNEL (ken'el) *n.* a cot for dogs; a pack of hounds; hole; gutter;—*v.t.* or *i.* to lodge in a kennel. [O.F. *chenil*, fr. Late L. *canile*, a house for a dog, fr. L. *canis*, a dog.]
KEPT (kept) *pret.* and *pp.* of KEEP.
KERB (kẽrb). See CURB-STONE.
KERCHIEF (kẽr'chif) *n.* a cloth to cover the head. [Contr. fr. M.E. *couerchef*, fr. O.F. *covrir*, to cover, and *chef*, the head.]
KERNEL (kẽr'nel) *n.* anything enclosed in a husk or shell; grain; seed; central part; gist; core;—*v.i.* to form a kernel. [O.E. *cyrnel*, fr. *corn*, grain, seed, and dim. *-el.* Cf. CORN.]

KEROSENE (kẽr'u-sēn) *n.* a bituminous oil used for lamps. [F., fr. G. *keros*, wax.]
KERSEY (kẽr'zi) *n.* a woollen cloth. [Prob. fr. *Kersey*, in Suffolk.]
KERSEYMERE (kẽr'zi-mēr) *n.* a thin woollen cloth, generally woven from the finest wool. [Corr. fr. *cassimere*, cashmere.]
KESTREL (kes'trel) *n.* a small slender hawk, of a reddish-fawn colour. [O.F. *quercerelle*, fr. L. *querquedula.*]
KETCH (kech) *n.* a vessel having two masts —a main and a mizen. [Etym. doubtful.]
KETCHUP (kech'up) *n.* a sauce. [E. Ind.]
KETTLE (ket'l) *n.* a vessel for boiling. [O.E. *cetel.* Cf. Ger. *Kessel.* Perh. fr. L. *catillus*, a small bowl, dim. of *catinus*, a deep cooking vessel.]
KETTLEDRUM (ket'l-drum) *n.* a drum of metal except the head. [See KETTLE and DRUM.]
KEY (kē) *n.* an instrument to fasten and open locks; middle stone of an arch; a small screw or lever; fundamental tone; solution; a book of answers to exercises. [O.E. *cæg.*]
KEYED (kēd) *a.* furnished with keys.
KEYHOLE (kē'hōl) *n.* hole in a lock or door which receives the key. [See KEY and HOLE.]
KEYSTONE (kē'stōn) *n.* the top stone of an arch. [See KEY and STONE.]
KHAKI (kä'kē) *a.* dust-coloured, or gray;—*n.* a cloth of this colour, used for the uniforms of soldiers on active or foreign service. [E. Ind. =dusty, earthy.]

Keystone.

KHEDIVE (ke-dēv') *n.* the title of the ruler of Egypt, since 1867. [F., fr. Per. =prince.]
KICK (kik) *n.* a blow with the foot;—*v.t.* or *i.* to strike with the foot. [M.E. *kiken*, fr. W.]
KID (kid) (1) *n.* a young goat; leather made of its skin;—(2) a small wooden tub. [(1) Scand. Cf. Ger. *Kitze.* (2) Cf. KIT.]
KIDNAP (kid'nap) *v.t.* to steal; as persons. [E. *Kid*, slang for child, and *nab*, to steal.]
KIDNAPPER (kid'nap-ẽr) *n.* one who steals a human being.
KIDNEY (kid'ni) *n.* that part of the viscera which secretes the urine;—*pl.* KIDNEYS. [M.E. *kidneer*, fr. Scand. Cf. Ger. *Niere*, a kidney.]
KILDERKIN (kil'dẽr-kin) *n.* a small barrel. [O.D. *kindeken*, a small barrel, dim. of *kind*, child.] [fr. Scand.]
KILL (kil) *v.t.* to slay; quell. [M.E. *killen*, **KILN** (kil) *n.* an oven for drying or burning anything. [O.E. *cyln*, fr. L. *culina*, a kitchen.]
KILOGRAMME (kil'u-gram) *n.* a French measure of weight, equal to 2·20462 lb. avoir. [F., fr. G. *chilioi*, 1000, and *gramma*, a weight.]

KILT (kilt) *n.* a Highlander's petticoat. [Scand. = to tuck up.]

KILTED (kil'ted) *a.* tucked up; shortened; dressed in a kilt.

KIN (kin) *n.* kindred; relation. [O.E. *cynn.* Cf. L. *genus,* G. *genos,* birth, race.]

KIND (kind) *a.* noting a humane disposition; benevolent; gracious;—*n.* a genus; race; sort. [O.E. *cynd, gecynd,* nature, fr. *cynn.*]

KINDERGARTEN (kin-der-går'tn) *n.* a school for the training of infants. [Ger. = garden of children.]

KINDLE (kin'dl) *v.t.* to set on fire;—*v.i.* to ignite. [Scand. = a torch.]

KINDLER (kind'ler) *n.* he or that which kindles.

KINDLINESS (kind'li-nes) *n.* affectionate disposition; benevolence.

KINDLY (kind'li) *ad.* with goodwill;—*a.* mild; favourable.

KINDNESS (kind'nes) *n.* sympathising benevolence; goodness; any friendly act.

KINDRED (kin'dred) *n.* people related to each other; relatives;—*a.* allied by birth; congenial; of like nature. [O.E. *cynn,* kin.]

KINE (kin) *n.* old *pl.* of COW. [M.E. *kyen,* double pl., fr. O.E. *cy,* pl. of *cu,* cow. Cf. Scot. *kye.*]

KINEMATOGRAPH (kin-e-mat'u-graf) *n.* an instrument by means of which a series of photographs taken in rapid succession can be projected so as to reproduce to the eye the movements of the original scene. [G. *kinema,* motion, and *graphein,* to write.]

KINETIC (ki-net'ik) *a.* producing motion;—*n.pl.* the science of forces producing motion. [G. *kinetikos,* fr. *kinein,* to move.]

KING (king) *n.* a monarch; a playing card; chief piece in chess. [O.E. *cyning,* fr. *cyn,* tribe, and *-ing,* son of.]

KINGDOM (king'dum) *n.* the territory subject to a king; a region; a scientific division.

KINGLY (king'li) *a.* royal; like a king.

KINSFOLK (kinz'fōk) *n.* relations; kindred. [See KIN and FOLK.]

KINSMAN (kinz'man) *n.* a relation. [See KIN and MAN.]

KIPPER (kip'er) *n.* salmon out of season; salmon, haddock, herring, etc., salted and dried;—*v.t.* to cure or preserve, as salmon. [O.E. *cypera,* a kipper-salmon.]

KIPSKIN (kip'skin) *n.* leather prepared from the skin of young cattle.

KIRK (kerk) *n.* the church, as in Scotland. [O.E. *circe.* Cf. CHURCH.]

KIRTLE (ker'tl) *n.* a short upper garment for women. [O.E. *cyrtel.*]

KISS (kis) *n.* a salute with the lips;—*v.t.* to salute with the lips. [O.E. *cyssan,* to kiss, fr. *coss,* a kiss. Cf. Ger. *küssen.*]

KIT (kit) *n.* a soldier's or sailor's outfit. [O.D. = a beaker, a decanter.]

KITCHEN (kich'en) *n.* a room for cooking. [O.E. *cycene,* fr. L. *coquina,* fr. *coquere,* to cook. Cf. Ger. *Kuche,* F. *cuisine.*]

KITE (kit) *n.* a rapacious bird of the hawk family; a child's paper toy for flying; an accommodation bill. [O.E. *cyta.*]

KITH (kith) *n.* a person or persons well known; kindred. [O.E. *cuth,* fr. *cunnan,* to know.]

KITTEN (kit'n) *n.* the young of a cat. [Dim. of CAT.]

KITTIWAKE (kit'i-wāk) *n.* a gull common on British coasts. [Imit., fr. its cry.]

KLEPTOMANIA (klep-tu-mā'ni-a) *n.* a morbid desire to steal. [G., fr. *kleptein,* to steal, and *mania,* madness.]

KNACK (nak) *n.* a toy; contrivance; dexterity. [Imit. Cf. Ger. *knacken.*]

KNAP (nap) *n.* (1) a protuberance; button;—(2) *v.t.* or *i.* to bite; strike with a sharp sound; snap. [(1) Cf. KNOB. (2) D.]

KNAPSACK (nap'sak) *n.* a soldier's sack. [D., fr. *knappen,* to eat, and *zak,* sack.]

KNAVE (nāv) *n.* a rascal; a playing card. [O.E. *cnafa, cnapa,* a youth. Cf. Ger. *Knabe,* a boy.] [mischievous practices.

KNAVERY (nā'ver-i) *n.* dishonesty; trickery;

KNAVISH (nā'vish) *a.* dishonest.

KNEAD (nēd) *v.t.* to work and mix with the hands. [O.E. *cnedan.* Cf. Ger. *kneten.*]

KNEE (nē) *n.* the joint connecting the two principal parts of the leg; a timber like a bent knee. [O.E. *cneo.* Cf. Ger. *Knie,* L. *genu,* G. *gonu.*]

KNEEL (nēl) *v.i.* to fall on the knees.

KNEEPAN (nē'pan) *n.* the round bone of the knee.

KNELL (nel) *n.* the sound of a bell;—*v.t.* to ring; toll. [O.E. *cnyllan,* to beat with a loud noise.]

KNEW (nū) *pret.* of KNOW.

KNICKERBOCKERS (nik'er-bok'erz) *n.pl.* loose trousers gathered in at the knee. [D.]

KNICK-KNACK (nik'nak) *n.* a trifle or toy. [Reduplication of KNACK.]

KNIFE (nif) *n.* an instrument for cutting;—*pl.* KNIVES. [O.E. *cnif.* Cf. Ger. *Kneif.*]

KNIGHT (nit) *n.* a title of honour; champion; a piece in chess;—*v.t.* to create a knight. [O.E. *cniht.* Ger. *Knecht.*]

KNIGHT-ERRANT (nit-er'ant) *n.* a roving knight. [See KNIGHT and ERRANT.]

KNIGHTHOOD (nit'hōod) *n.* the dignity of a knight; the body of knights. [Fr. KNIGHT and suff. *hood.*]

KNIGHTLY (nit'li) *a.* pertaining to or becoming a knight.

KNIT (nit) *v.t.* [*pret.* and *pp.* KNIT, KNITTED] to unite, as threads with needles; join closely;—*v.i.* to interweave; grow together. [O.E. *cnyttan,* fr. *cnotta,* a knot.]

KNITTING-NEEDLE (nit'ing-nē-dl) *n.* a needle used for knitting. [Fr. KNIT and NEEDLE.]

KNOB (nob) *n.* a knot; a protuberance. [Variant of KNOP.]

KNOBBY (nob'i) *a.* full of knots; hard.

KNOCK (nok) *v.t.* or *i.* to hit; strike; dash;—*n.* a blow; a dashing; a rap. [O.E. *cnucian.* Cf. KNACK.]

KNOCKER (nok'er) *n.* a hammer on a door.

KNOLL (nōl) *n.* a little hill. [O.E. *cnol.*]

KNOP (nop) *n.* a knob; button; round bunch of flowers. [O.E. *cnœp.*]

KNOT (not) *n.* a tie; joint of a plant; bond of union; cluster; group; epaulette; a nautical mile; a porter's pad;—*v.t.* to form knots. [O.E. *cnotta.* Cf. KNIT.]

KNOTTY (not'i) *a.* full of knots; intricate.

KNOUT (nout) *n.* a Russian instrument of punishment. [Russ.]

KNOW (nō) *v.t.* [*pret.* KNEW; *pp.* KNOWN] to understand; perceive; recognise. [O.E. *cnavan.* Cf. L. *noscere, gnoscere,* to know; G. *gignoskein.*] [deliberately.

KNOWINGLY (nō'ing-li) *ad.* with knowledge;

KNOWLEDGE (nol'ej) *n.* clear perception; information; instruction; practical acquaintance. [M.E. *knowlege, knauleche,* fr. KNOW, and O.E. *lac,* play, gift. Cf. *lock,* in WEDLOCK.]

KNUCKLE (nuk'l) *n.* a joint of the fingers, etc.;—*v.i.* to submit to in contest. [M.E. *knokil.* Cf. KNACK, KNOCK.]

KORAN (kō-rän', kō'ran) *n.* the Mohammedan book of faith. [A. = the book.]

KRAAL (krål) *n.* a Hottentot hut or village. [D., fr. Pg. *curral,* fr. L. *currere,* to run.]

KREUTZER (kroit'zer) *n.* an old German coin, equal to 1d.; a modern Austrian coin, value about a farthing. [Ger. *Kreuzer,* fr. *Kreuz,* a cross; so called because once stamped with a cross.]

KYANISE (kī'an-iz) *v.t.* to preserve timber from the dry rot by the use of corrosive sublimate. [Fr. *Kyan,* 1774-1830, inventor of the process.]

KYLOES (kī'lōz) *n.pl.* Highland cattle. [Gael.]

L

LA (lå) *n.* a note in music.
LA (law) *inter.* look ! [O.E. *la.*]
LAAGER (lä'ger) *n.* in South Africa, an encampment. [D., a variant of *leger*, a camp.]
LABEL (lå'bel) *n.* a slip of paper, etc., containing a name or title, tied to anything; —*v.t.* to affix a label. [O.F.]
LABIAL (lå'bi-ạl) *a.* pertaining to the lips; —*n.* a letter uttered by the lips. [F., fr. L. *labium*, lip.]
LABORATORY (lab'ur-ạ-tu-ri, lạ-bor'ạ-tu-ri) *n.* a place for chemical operations. [L. *laboratorium*, fr. *laborare*, to labour, fr. *labor*, work.]
LABORIOUS (lạ-bō'ri-us) *a.* diligent in work; requiring labour.
LABORIOUSLY (lạ-bō'ri-us-li) *ad.* with great toil.
LABOUR (lå'bur) *n.* work; toil; travail;— *v.t.* or *i.* to work; toil. [O.F., fr. L. *labor.*]
LABOURER (lå'bur-ẹr) *n.* a workman.
LABURNUM (lạ-bur'num) *n.* a small tree bearing beautiful clusters of yellow flowers. [L.]
LABYRINTH (lab'i-rinth) *n.* a place full of windings; maze; any perplexing difficulty. [F., fr. L., fr. G. *laburinthos*, maze.]
LABYRINTHIAN (lab-i-rinth'i-ạn) *a.* winding; intricate. Also **LABYRINTHINE.**
LAC (lak) (1) *n.* a resinous substance;— (2) in India, 100,000. [(1) Per. (2) Hind.]
LACE (lås) *n.* work composed of fine threads; a plaited string;—*v.t.* to fasten or trim with lace; lash. [O.F. *las*, fr. L. *laqueus*, a noose.]
LACERATE (las'ẹr-åt) *v.t.* to rend; tear; wound deeply. [L. (part.) *laceratus*, fr. *lacerare*, *lacer*, mangled.]
LACERATION (las-ẹr-å'shun) *n.* act of tearing; a rent.
LACERATIVE (las'ẹr-ạ-tiv) *a.* tending to tear.
LACHRYMOSE (lak'ri-môs) *a.* generating or shedding tears; mournful. [L. *lacryma*, a tear.]
LACING (lå'sing) *n.* fastening with a cord through eyelet holes; the cord itself.
LACK (lak) *v.t.* or *i.* to be in want; be wanting; —*n.* want or need of. [Fr. O. L. Ger.]
LACKADAISICAL (lak-ạ-då'zi-kạl) *a.* affectedly pensive.
LACKADAY (lak-ạ-då') *ex.* alas ! the day. [For *alack-a-day.*]
LACKEY (lak'i) *n.* a footman;—*v.t.* or *i.* to attend; wait upon with servility. [O.F. *laquay* = F. *laquais.*]
LACONIC (lạ-kon'ik) *a.* pertaining to Lacedemonia, Sparta, or to the Lacones, its inhabitants; brief; pithy; concise.
LACONICALLY (lạ-kon'i-kạl-i) *ad.* concisely.
LACONISM (lak'u-nism) *n.* a pithy phrase or expression.
LACQUER (lak'ẹr) *v.t.* to varnish;—*n.* a yellow varnish. [F. *lacre*, fr. Per. = *lac.*]
LACTATION (lak-tå'shun) *n.* suckling or time of suckling. [L. *lacteus*, milky, fr. stem *lact-*, fr. *lac*, milk.]
LAD (lad) *n.* a boy; a young man. [M.E. *ladde*, servant, perh. fr. *led* (part.) of **LEAD.**]
LADDER (lad'ẹr) *n.* a frame with round steps; gradual rise. [O.E. *hlœder.* Cf. Ger. *Leiter.*]
LADE (låd) *v.t.* [*pret.* **LADED**; *pp.* **LADED, LADEN**] to load; throw out with a dipper. [O.E. *hladan*, to load, to draw out water.]
LADING (lå'ding) *n.* load; cargo.
LADLE (lå'dl) *n.* a dipper with a handle. [O.E. *hlœdel*, fr. *hladan* to load, to drain.]
LADY (lå'di) *n.* mistress of a house; wife; a title of respect. [O.E. *hlœfdige*, fr. *hlaf*, a loaf, and *dœge*, a kneader, or, contr. fr. *hlafweardige*, loaf-keeper, and thus fem. of **LORD.**]

LADYSHIP (lå'di-ship) *n.* title of a lady.
LAG (lag) *v.i.* to move slowly; stay behind; loiter;—*a.* tardy; late;—*n.* the last; fagend. [Celt.]
LAGER-BEER (lå'gẹr-bër) *n.* a strong German beer. [Ger. *lager*, a store-house, and *Bier*, beer.]
LAGOON (la-gōōn') *n.* a shallow pond; a lake in a coral island. [It. and Sp. *laguna*, fr. L. *lacuna.*]
LAIC (lå'ik) *n.* a layman;—*a.* belonging to the laity. Also **LAICAL.**
LAIR (lår) *n.* couch of a wild beast. [O.E. *leger*, a bed, fr. *licgan*, to lie down. Cf. Ger. *Lager.*]
LAIRD (lård) *n.* a landowner; lord of a manor. [A form of **LORD.**]
LAITY (lå'i-ti) *n.* the people, as distinct from the clergy. [See **LAY** (4).]
LAKE (låk) (1) *n.* a body of water surrounded by land;— (2) a deep red colour. [(1) A.F. *lac*, fr. L. *lacus.* (2) F. *laque*, fr. Per. See **LAC.**]
LAKELET (låk'let) *n.* a little lake; pond.
LAMA (lå'mạ) *n.* a Buddhist priest in Tibet. [Tibetan = spiritual teacher.]
LAMB (lam) *n.* a young sheep;—*v.t.* or *i.* to bring forth lambs. [O.E. Cf. Ger. *Lamm.*]
LAMBENT (lam'bent) *a.* playing over the surface; flickering. [L. (part. stem) *lambent-*, fr. *lambere*, to lick.]
LAMBKIN (lam'kin) *n.* a young lamb.
LAME (låm) *a.* unsound in limb;—*v.t.* to make lame. [O.E. *lama* lame; Ger. *lahm.*]
LAMELLA (lạ-mel'ạ) *n.* a very thin plate or scale. [L. dim. of *lamina.*]
LAMELLAR (lạ-mel'ạr) *a.* formed in thin plates. [*fectly.*
LAMELY (låm'li) *ad.* like a cripple; imperfectly.
LAMENESS (låm'nes) *n.* the state of a cripple; weakness.
LAMENT (lạ-ment') *v.t.* or *i.* to weep or mourn for; deplore; regret. [F. *lamenter*, fr. L. *lamentare.*]
LAMENTABLE (lam'en-tạ-bl) *a.* deserving or expressing sorrow.
LAMENTABLY (lam'en-tạ-bli) *ad.* pitifully; despicably.
LAMENTATION (lam-en-tå'shun) *n.* expression of sorrow.
LAMISH (låm'ish) *a.* somewhat lame; halting.
LAMMAS (lam'mạs) *n.* the first day of August. [O.E. *hlaf-mœsse*, fr. *hlaf*, loaf, and *mœsse*, feast.]
LAMP (lamp) *n.* a vessel with a wick for light. [F. *lampe*, fr. G. *lampas*, torch, fr. *lampein*, to shine.]
LAMPBLACK (lamp'blak) *n.* a fine soot from the smoke of resinous substances.
LAMPLIGHTER (lamp'li-tẹr) *n.* one who lights street lamps. [Fr. **LAMP** and **LIGHT.**]
LAMPOON (lam-pōōn') *n.* a personal satire; —*v.t.* to abuse with satire. [O.F. *lampon*, orig. a drinking song with refrain *lampons* = let us drink.]
LAMPOONER (lam-pōō'nẹr) *n.* one who lampoons.
LAMPREY (lam'pri) *n.* a fish like an eel. [O.F. *lamproie*, fr. Late L. *lampetra*, fr. *lambere*, to lick, and *petra*, rock.]
LANCE (låns) *n.* a long spear;—*v.t.* to pierce; open with a lancet; throw or dart. [F., fr. L. *lancea*, fr. G. *longche*, a lance.]
LANCER (lån'sẹr) *n.* a light cavalry soldier; *pl.* a kind of dance.
LANCET (lan'set) *n.* a surgical instrument to let blood. [F.]
LAND (land) *n.* ground; country; region; soil; an estate;—*v.t.* to put on shore;— *v.i.* to come on shore. [O.E.]

LANDAU (lan'daw) *n.* a kind of four-wheeled carriage. [Ger. *Landauer*, from Landau.]

LAND-COURT (land'kort) *n.* a court held to arrange fair rents.

LANDING (lan'ding) *n.* a place for going on shore; level part of a staircase between the flights.

LANDLADY (land'lā-di) *n.* a female who has tenants holding from her; the mistress of an inn. [Fr. LAND and LADY.]

LANDLESS (land'les) *a.* having no land.

LANDLOCK (land'lok) *v.t.* to enclose by land.

LANDLORD (land'lord) *n.* the lord of land; master of an inn. [Fr. LAND and LORD.]

LANDLUBBER (land'lub-er) *n.* any one who is not a sailor.

LANDMARK (land'märk) *n.* mark of bounds to land; an elevated object. [Fr. LAND and MARK.]

LAND-OFFICE (land'of-is) *n.* office for the disposal of land. [Fr. LAND and OFFICE.]

LANDSCAPE (land'skāp) *n.* the aspect or a picture of a portion of country. [D. *landschap*.]

LANDSLIP (land'slip) *n.* a portion of land sliding down a mountain. [Fr. LAND and SLIP.]

LANDSMAN (landz'man) *n.* a sailor serving for the first time at sea. [Fr. LAND and MAN.]

LANDWARD (land'ward) *ad.* towards land.

LANE (lān) *n.* a narrow passage or street. [O.E.]

LANGUAGE (lang'gwij) *n.* human speech; style or expression peculiar to a nation or an individual. [F. *langage*, fr. O.F. *langue*, fr. L. *lingua*, tongue.]

LANGUID (lang'gwid) *a.* weak; faint; feeble. [F., fr. L. *languidus*, fr. *languere*, to be weak.]

LANGUIDLY (lang'gwid-li) *ad.* faintly; weakly.

LANGUISH (lang'gwish) *v.t.* to droop; pine away; grow dull. [F. *languir*, fr. L. *languescere*, fr. *languere*, to be faint. Cf. LANGUID.]

LANGUISHINGLY (lang'gwish-ing-li) *ad.* faintly; tenderly.

LANGUOR (lang'gwer) *n.* faintness; lassitude. [L.]

LANK (langk) *a.* thin; slender; loose. [O.E. *hlanc*.]

LANKNESS (langk'nes) *n.* a want of flesh.

LANKY (lang'ki) *a.* tall and slender.

LANOLINE, LANOLIN (lan'u-lin) *n.* an oily substance obtained from wool. [L., fr. *lana*, wool, and *oleum*, oil.]

LANTERN (lan'tern) *n.* a transparent case for a candle or lamp. [F. *lanterne*, L. *lanterna*, fr. G. *lampter*, fr. *lampein*, to give light.]

LANYARDS (lan'yardz) *n.pl.* small ropes. [F. *lanière*.]

LAP (lap) (1) *n.* the loose part of a coat; part between the knees and the body when seated; border; edge;—*v.t.* or *i.* to lay over;—(2) lick. [(1) O.E. *læppa*, a loosely hanging part. (2) O.E. *lapian*.]

LAPDOG (lap'dog) *n.* a small pet dog. [Fr. LAP and DOG.]

LAPFUL (lap'fool) *n.* as much as the lap can hold. [Fr. LAP and FULL.]

LAPIDARY (lap'i-da-ri) *n.* a dealer in precious stones. [L. *lapidarius*, fr. stem *lapid*-, fr. *lapis*, *lapidis*, a stone.]

LAPPET (lap'et) *n.* part of a garment hanging loose. [Dim. of LAP.]

LAPSE (laps) *v.i.* to slip; slide; to deviate from rectitude;—*n.* passing; failing in duty; fault. [L. (part.) *lapsus*, fr. *labi*, to slide.]

LAPSTONE (lap'stōn) *n.* a stone on which shoemakers beat leather.

LAPWING (lap'wing) *n.* a bird of the plover family. [O.E. *hleape-wince*, fr. *hleapan*, to run, and *wince*, one that runs.]

LARBOARD (lär'burd) *n.* left-hand side of a ship. [Etym. doubtful.]

LARCENOUS (lär'se-nus) *a.* of the nature of theft.

LARCENY (lär'se-ni) *n.* theft. [O.F., fr. L. *latrocinium*, fr. *latro*, thief.]

LARCH (lärch) *n.* a coniferous tree having deciduous leaves in whorls or clusters. [L., fr. G. *larix*.]

LARD (lärd) *n.* the fat of swine;—*v.t.* to stuff with pork. [O.F., fr. L. *laridum*, *lardum*.]

LARDER (lär'der) *n.* a place where meat is kept. [F. *lardier*, fr. .. *lardum*.]

LARGE (lärj) *a.* bulky; Lwide; liberal. [F., fr. L. *largus*.]

LARGELY (lärj'li) *ad.* extensively.

LARGENESS (lärj'nes) *n.* great size.

LARGESS (lär'jes) *n.* a gift; present. [F. *largesse*, fr. L. *largiri*, to give freely, fr. *largus*.]

LARK (lärk) (1) *n.* a small song-bird;—(2) a prank or frolic;—*v.i.* to make sport. [(1) M.E. *laverock*, fr. O.E. *lawerce*. Cf. Ger. *Lerche*. (2) O.E. *lac*, play, fr. *lacan*, to play.]

LARVA (lär'va) *n.* an insect in the first stage after leaving the egg;—*pl.* LARVÆ. [L.]

LARYNX (lar'ingks) *n.* the windpipe. [G.]

LASCIVIOUS (la-siv'i-us) *a.* wanton; lewd; lustful. [L. *lascivus*, lustful.]

LASH (lash) *n.* the thong of a whip; a stroke with a whip;—*v.t.* to strike with a lash; tie with a cord; censure severely;—*v.i.* to ply the whip; break out. [M.E. *lasshe*. Cf. Ger. *Lasche*, a flap.]

LASS (las) *n.* a young maiden.

LASSITUDE (las'i-tūd) *n.* languor of body; weariness. [F., fr. L. *lassitudo*, fr. *lassus*, faint.]

LASSO (las'ō) *n.* a rope with a noose;—*pl.* LASSOS. [Sp. *lazo*, fr. L. *laqueus*, a noose.]

LAST (last) (1) *a.* following all the rest; hindmost;—*ad.* the last time; in conclusion;—(2) *n.* a form to shape a shoe;—(3) *n.* a weight of 4000 lb.;—(4) *v.i.* to continue in time. [(1) Contr. fr. LATEST. (2) O.E. *last*, a trace. (3) O.E. *hlæst*, fr. *hladan*, to load. (4) O.E. *læstan*, to continue in a track.]

LASTING (las'ting) *a.* continuing long; permanent; durable. [See LAST (1).]

LASTINGLY (las'ting-li) *ad.* in a lasting manner.

LASTLY (last'li) *ad.* in the last place; finally. [See LAST (1).]

LATCH (lach) *n.* the catch of a door;—*v.t.* to fasten with a latch. [O.E. *læccan*, to catch.]

LATE (lāt) *a.* coming after the time; slow; tardy; recent; near the close; departed;—*ad.* far in the day or night. [O E. *læt*, slow. Cf. Ger. *lass*, weary.]

LATELY (lāt'li) *ad.* not long ago.

LATENCY (lā'ten-si) *n.* state of being concealed. [See LATENT.]

LATENESS (lāt'nes) *n.* state of being late.

LATENT (lā'tent) *a.* hidden; secret. [L. (part. stem) *latent*-, fr. *latere*, to lie hid or concealed.]

LATER (lā'ter) *a.* comp. more late; posterior.

LATERAL (lat'e-ral) *a.* pertaining to, or proceeding from, the side. [L. *lateralis*, fr. stem *later*-, fr. *latus*, a side.]

LATERALLY (lat'e-ral-li) *ad.* by the side; sidewise.

LATH (läth) *n.* a thin strip of wood to support plaster;—*v.t.* to cover with laths. [O.E. *lætt*. Cf. Ger. *Latte*, thin plate.]

LATHE (lāTH) *n.* a turner's machine. [Scand.]

LATHER (laTH'er) *n.* froth of soap and water;—*v.t.* to spread with lather. [O.E. *leathor*.]

LATHING (läth'ing) *n.* covering with laths; the laths used in covering a wall.

LATHY (läth'i) *a.* thin as a lath.

LATIN (lat'in) *a.* pertaining to the Roman language;—*n.* the ancient language of the Romans. [L. *Latinus*, belonging to *Latium*, the district round Rome.]

LATINISE (lat'in-īz) *v.t.* to turn into Latin.
LATINISM (lat'in-ism) *n.* an idiom of the Latin.
LATINITY (la-tin'i-ti) *n.* purity of Latin style.
LATITUDE (lat'i-tūd) *n.* distance from the equator; breadth. [L. (acc.) *latitudinem*, fr. *latus*, broad.]
LATITUDINAL (la-ti-tū'di-nal) *a.* in the direction of latitude.
LATITUDINARIAN (lat-i-tū-di-nā'ri-an) *n.* one who exercises freedom in thinking;—*a.* unrestrained in religious opinion.
LATITUDINOUS (la-ti-tū'di-nus) *a.* of great extent.
LATTEN (lat'en) *n.* iron plate covered with tin; a kind of bronze. [O.F. *laton* = F. *laiton*. Cf. Ger. *Latte*, a lath.]
LATTER (lat'er) *a.* the last of two; more recent; final. [Variant of **LATER**.]
LATTERLY (lat'er-li) *ad.* of late; lately.
LATTICE (lat'is) *n.* network of cross bars;—*v.t.* to form with cross bars. [F. *lattis*, fr. Ger. *Latte*, lath.]
LAUD (lawd) *n.* commendation; praise in worship;—*v.t.* to praise; extol. [L. *laudare*, fr. stem *laud-*, of *laus*, praise.]
LAUDABLE (law'da-bl) *a.* pra eworthy.
LAUDABLY (law'da-bli) *ad.* so as to deserve praise.
LAUDANUM (law'da-num) *n.* opium dissolved in spirit of wine. Sometimes written **LADANUM**. [Variant of *Ladanum*, L., fr. Per. *ladan*.]
LAUDATORY (law'da-tu-ri) *a.* containing praise.
LAUGH (laf) *v.t.* or *i.* to express pleasure, mirth, etc.; smile; chuckle; be gay or happy;—*n.* an expression of mirth peculiar to man. [Imit., O.E. *hlihan*, to laugh.]
LAUGHABLE (laf'a-bl) *a.* that may excite laughter.
LAUGHTER (laf'ter) *n.* convulsive expression of mirth, ridicule, etc.
LAUNCH (lånsh) *v.t.* or *i.* to throw; send forth; slide into water; go forth; expatiate; —*n.* act of launching; the largest boat in a ship. [O.F. *lanchier* = F. *lancer*. Cf. **LANCE**.]
LAUNDRESS (lån'dres) *n.* a washerwoman.
LAUNDRY (lån'dri) *n.* a place where clothes are washed and dressed. [O.F. *lavandier*, fr. L. gerundive of *lavare*, to wash.]
LAUREATE (law're-āt) *a.* invested with a laurel wreath;—*n.* the court poet;—*v.t.* to confer a degree on.
LAUREL (lor'el) *n.* the bay tree. [F. *laurier*, fr. L. *laurus*.]
LAVA (lä'va) *n.* melted matter flowing from a volcano. [It. *lava*, a stream, fr. L. *lavare*, to wash.]
LAVATORY (lav'a-tu-ri) *n.* a place for washing; a lotion for a diseased part. [See **LAVE**.]
LAVE (lāv) *v.t.* or *i.* to wash; bathe. [F. *laver*, L. *lavare*, to wash.]
LAVENDER (lav'en-der) *n.* an aromatic plant; a grayish blue colour. [F. *lavande*, fr. L. *lavare*, to wash.]
LAVER (lā'ver) *n.* a large basin. [L. *lavare*.]
LAVEROCK (lav'er-ok) *n.* the skylark. [M.E. Cf. **LARK**.]
LAVISH (lav'ish) *a.* expending with profusion; prodigal; wasteful;—*v.t.* to expend profusely; squander. [E. **LAVE**, to throw out.]
LAVISHLY (lav'ish-li) *ad.* with wasteful profusion.
LAW (law) *n.* rule of action or motion; statute; decree. [O.E. *lagu*, law, fr. *licgan*, to lie, fr. Scand.]
LAWFUL (law'fool) *a.* conformable to law; legal; rightful.
LAWFULNESS (law'fool-nes) *n.* legality.
LAWGIVER (law'giv-er) *n.* a legislator. [Fr. **LAW** and **GIVE**.]
LAWLESS (law'les) *a.* not restrained by law.

LAWLESSLY (law'les-li) *ad.* without the restraints of law.
LAWN (lawn) (1) *n.* an open space covered with grass;—(2) a fine linen or cambric; a bishop's robe. [(1) M.E. *laund*, fr. O.F. *lande*, a plain;—(2) F., fr. *Laon*, a town near Rheims.]
LAWSUIT (law'sūt) *n.* a process in law. [Fr. **LAW** and **SUE**.]
LAWN-TENNIS (lawn-ten'nis) *n.* a game played with rackets and balls. [Fr. **LAWN** (1) and **TENNIS**.]
LAWYER (law'yer) *n.* one who is versed in or who practises law.
LAWYERLY (law'yer-li) *a.* like a lawyer; legal; formal.
LAX (laks) *a.* loose; vague; slack. [L. *laxus*.]
LAXATIVE (lak'sa-tiv) *a.* having the quality of relieving costiveness.
LAXITY (lak'si-ti) *n.* slackness; looseness; vagueness; dissoluteness; openness of the bowels.
LAXLY (laks'li) *ad.* loosely.
LAY (lā) (1) *v.t.* [*pret.* and *pp.* **LAID**] to place; beat down; spread; calm; wager; produce eggs;—(2) *n.* a song;—(3) *n.* a stratum; a row;—(4) *a.* pertaining to the laity. [(1) O.E. *lecgan*, causative form of *licgan*, to lie. Cf. Ger. *legen*. (2) O.F. *lai*, fr. Celt. (3) Ger. *Lage*. (4) O.F. *lai*, fr. L. *laicus* fr. G. *laikos*, fr. *laos*, the people.]
LAYER (lā'er) *n.* a stratum; bed; a course; a shoot or twig. [M.E. *leir*, lair.]
LAY-FIGURE (lā'fig-ūr) *n.* a wooden figure of the human body; artist's model. [D.]
LAYMAN (lā'man) *n.* one not a clergyman.
LAZAR (lā'zar, laz'ar) *n.* a person with a pestilential disease. [F. *lazare*, fr. *Lazarus*, the beggar in the parable, Luke xvi. 20.]
LAZARETTO (laz-a-ret'tō) *n.* a pest-house for diseased persons. [It.]
LAZILY (lā'zi-li) *ad.* in a slothful manner.
LAZINESS (lā'zi-nes) *n.* habitual inaction; sluggishness.
LAZY (lā'zi) *a.* slothful; sluggish. [O.F. *lasche* = F. *lâche*, fr. L. *laxus*, loose.]
LEAD (led) *n.* a soft metal; a plummet; thin plate of type metal; stick of plumbago;— *v.t.* to cover or fit with lead. [O.E. *lead*.]
LEAD (lēd) *v.t.* or *i.* [*pret.* and *pp.* **LED**] to go before; guide; direct; precede; tend to. [O.E. *lædan*, to lead. Cf. Ger. *leiten*.]
LEADEN (led'n) *a.* consisting of lead.
LEADER (lē'der) *n.* one who leads; chief of a party; principal wheel; editorial article.
LEADERSHIP (lē'der-ship) *n.* office or authority of a leader.
LEAF (lēf) *n.* part of a plant; part of a book; one side of a double door;—*pl.* **LEAVES**;—*v.i.* to put forth leaves. [O.E.]
LEAFAGE (lē'fij) *n.* leaves collectively; season of leafing.
LEAFLESS (lēf'les) *a.* destitute of leaves.
LEAFLET (lēf'let) *n.* a small leaf.
LEAFY (lē'fi) *a.* full of leaves.
LEAGUE (lēg) (1) *n.* a combination or alliance; international compact;—*v.i.* to unite for mutual interest; —(2) *n.* three miles. [(1) F. *ligue*, fr. Late L. *liga*, fr. L. *ligare*, to bind. (2) O.F. *legue*, fr. L. *leuca*, a Gallic mile of 1500 Roman paces, fr. Celt.]
LEAK (lēk) *n.* a crack or hole that permits a fluid to pass; the escape of a fluid;—*v.i.* to let a fluid in or out. [Scand.]
LEAKAGE (lē'kij) *n.* loss, or allowance for loss, by leaking.
LEAKY (lē'ki) *n.* letting or apt to let water out or in.

LEAL (lēl) *a.* loyal; faithful; true-hearted. [O.F. Cf. LOYAL.]

LEAN (lēn) (1) *a.* thin; slender; — *n.* flesh without fat; — (2) *v.i.* to incline; bend. [(1) O.E. *hlǽne*. (2) *hlǽnan*, to make to lean.]

LEANNESS (lēn'nes) *n.* want of flesh.

LEAP (lēp) *v.i.* to spring; bound; — *n.* a jump; bound; skip. [O.E. *hleapan.* Cf. Ger. *laufen*, to run.]

LEAPFROG (lēp'frog) *n.* a boy's game of leaping over one another who stoops down. [Fr. LEAP and FROG.]

LEAP-YEAR (lēp'yēr) *n.* every fourth year, which has one day more than others. [Fr. LEAP and YEAR.]

LEARN (lėrn) *v.t.* or *i.* to gain knowledge or skill; receive information or instruction. [O.E. *leornian.* Cf. Ger. *lernen.*]

LEARNED (lėr'ned) *a.* having learning.

LEARNEDLY (lėr'ned-li) *ad.* with erudition.

LEARNER (lėr'nėr) *n.* one who is acquiring knowledge.

LEARNING (lėr'ning) *n.* knowledge acquired by study, instruction, or experience.

LEASABLE (lē'sa-bl) *a.* that may be leased.

LEASE (lēs) *n.* a letting for hire; the contract or the term for such letting; — *v.t.* to let for use by hire. [F. *laisser*, to leave, fr. L. *laxare*, to loose, fr. *laxus*, loose.]

LEASEHOLD (lēs'hōld) *n.* a tenure held by lease. [Fr. LEASE and HOLD.]

LEASH (lēsh) *n.* a leather thong; a band; a brace-and-a-half. [O.F. *lesse* = F. *laisse*, a thong, fr. L. *laxus*, loose.]

LEAST (lēst) *a.* smallest; — *ad.* in the lowest degree. [O.E. *lǽst*, superl. of LITTLE.]

LEATHER (leᴛн'ėr) *n.* the hide of an animal dressed. [O.E. *lether.* Cf. Ger. *Leder.*]

LEATHERN (leᴛн'ėrn) *a.* made of leather.

LEAVE (lēv) (1) *n.* liberty granted; permission; licence; a formal parting; — (2) *v.t.* [*pret.* and *pp.* LEFT] to quit; suffer to remain; have at death; bequeath; permit; — *v.i.* to depart; desist. [(1) O.E. *leaf.* (2) O.E. *lefan*, to leave a heritage.]

LEAVEN (lev'n) *n.* a mass of sour dough for making other dough light; — *v.t.* to raise and make light; taint; imbue. [F. *levain*, fr. L. *levamen, levare*, to raise, fr. *levis*, light.]

LEAVINGS (lē'vingz) *n.pl.* things left. [See LEAVE (2).]

LECHER (lech'ėr) *n.* a man given to lewdness. [O.F. *lecher*, to lick. Cf. LICK.]

LECHEROUS (lech'ėr-us) *a.* lustful; lascivious.

LECTERN (lek'tėrn) *n.* a bookstand for holding the volumes from which the church service is read. [Corr. for Low L. *lectrinum*, fr. *lectrum*, a pulpit, fr. G. *lektron*, a couch.]

LECTION (lek'shun) *n.* a reading. [L. *legere*, (part.) *lectus*, to read.]

LECTURE (lek'tūr) *n.* a discourse; recital; reproof; — *v.t.* or *i.* to read lectures; reprove. [L. (part.) *lectus*, fr. *legere*, to read.]

LECTURER (lek'tūr-ėr) *n.* a teacher by lectures.

LECTURESHIP (lek'tūr-ship) *n.* office of a lecturer.

LED (led) *pret.* and *pp.* of LEAD.

LEDGE (lej) *n.* a layer; shelf; a ridge; a moulding; prominent part. [Scand.]

LEDGER (lej'ėr) *n.* a chief book of accounts. [Cf. D. *legger*, one that lies down.]

LEE (lē) *n.* side opposite to the wind. [O.E. *hleow.*]

LEECH (lēch) *n.* an aquatic blood-sucking worm; a physician; edge of a sail; — *v.t.* to bleed with leeches. [O.E. *lœce*, one that heals.]

LEEK (lēk) *n.* a garden plant allied to the oni n. [O.E. *leac*, a leek plant. Cf. hem-lock.]

LEER (lēr) *n.* an oblique or arch look; — *v.i.* to look obliquely or archly. [O.E. *hleor*, the cheek, or face.]

LEES (lēz) *n.pl.* dregs; sediment of liquor. [F. *lie.*]

LEE-SHORE (lē'shōr) *n.* the shore toward which the wind blows. [Fr. LEE and SHORE.]

LEE-SIDE (lē'sīd) *n.* side of a vessel opposite to the direction of the wind; sheltered side. [Fr. LEE and SIDE.]

LEET (lēt) *n.* a court of record; a list of candidates for office. [Icel. *leiti*, a share. Cf. LOT.]

LEEWARD (lē'wȧrd, lōō'ȧrd) *ad.* towards the lee.

LEEWAY (lē'wā) *n.* movement towards the lee.

LEFT (left) (1) *pret.* and *pp.* of LEAVE; — (2) *a.* opposite to the right. [(1) See LEAVE. (2) O.E. *left, luft*, weak.]

LEFT-HANDED (left'han-ded) *a.* using the left hand with most dexterity.

LEG (leg) *n.* limb of an animal used to support the body. [Scand.]

LEGACY (leg'a-si) *n.* a bequest by will. [L *legatum*, fr. *legare*, to bequeath.]

LEGAL (lē'gal) *a.* according to law; permitted by law. [F., fr. L. *legalis*, fr. stem *leg-*, fr. *lex*, law.]

LEGALISE (lē'gal-iz) *v.t.* to make lawful; authorise.

LEGALITY (lē-gal'i-ti) *n.* lawfulness; observance of the letter of the law. Also LEGAL-ISM.

LEGALLY (lē'gal-i) *ad.* according to law.

LEGATE (leg'at) *n.* ambassador of the pope; deputy. [F. *légat*, fr. L. *legatus*, fr. *legare*, to send with a commission.]

LEGATEE (leg-a-tē') *n.* one who has a legacy. [See LEGACY.]

LEGATION (le-gā'shun) *n.* an embassy; suit of an ambassador.

LEGATOR (leg-a-tor' le-gā'tėr) *n.* one who bequeaths.

LEGEND (lej'end) *n.* an ancient tale or tradition; any marvellous story; motto or inscription. [L. *legendus*, fr. *legere*, to read.]

LEGENDARY (lej'en-da-ri) *a.* fabulous; romantic.

LEGERDEMAIN (lej-ėr-de-mān') *n.* sleight of hand. [F. *léger*, light, *de*, of, and *main*, hand, fr. L. *manus.*]

LEGER-LINE (lej'ėr-līn) *n.* in *Music*, a line above or under the staff. [O.F. fr. L. *levis*, light.]

LEGIBILITY (lej-i-bil'i-ti) *n.* quality or state of being easily read. Also LEGIBLENESS.

LEGIBLE (lej'i-bl) *a.* that can be read. [L. *legibilis*, fr. *legere*, to read.]

LEGIBLY (lej'i-bli) *ad.* so that it can be read.

LEGION (lē'jun) *n.* a body of soldiers; a great number. [F., fr. L. (acc.) *legionem*, fr. *legere*, to levy.]

LEGIONARY (lē'jun-a-ri) *a.* pertaining to legions.

LEGISLATE (lej'is-lāt) *v.t.* to make laws. [L. stem *leg-*, fr. *lex*, law, and (part.) *latus*, fr. *ferre*.]

LEGISLATION (lej-is-lā'shun) *n.* the act of making laws.

LEGISLATIVE (lej'is-lā-tiv) *a.* passing laws.

LEGISLATOR (lej'is-lā-tėr) *n.* one who makes laws.

LEGISLATURE (lej'is-lā-tūr) *n.* the body that makes laws.

LEGIST (lē'jist) *n.* one skilled in the laws.

LEGITIMACY (le-jit'i-ma-si) *n.* lawfulness of birth; genuineness; logical sequence.

LEGITIMATE (le-jit'i-māt) *a.* lawful; lawfully begotten; fairly deduced; authorised; — *v.t.* to make lawful. [Late L. (part.) *legitimatus*, fr. *legitimare*, fr. *legitimus*, lawful, fr. *lex*, law.]

LEGITIMATELY (le-jit'i-māt-li) *ad.* lawfully.

LEISURE (lezh'ur, lē'zhur) *n.* freedom from occupation; spare time; convenience. [O.F. *leisir*, fr. L. *licere*, to be permitted.]

LEISURELY (lezh'ur-li, lē'zhur-li) *ad.* slowly; —*a.* deliberate.

LEMMA (lem'a) *n.* a previous or assumed proposition. [G. *lemma*, a thing taken, fr. *lambanein*, to take, assume.]

LEMMING (lem'ing) *n.* a burrowing animal of the rat family. [Norw. *lemende, lemming*, fr. *lemja*, to beat.]

LEMON (lem'un) *n.* an acid fruit of the orange sort; the tree that produces lemons. [F. *limon*, fr. Per. *limun*.]

LEMONADE (lem-un-ād') *n.* water, sugar, and lemon-juice rendered effervescent.

LEMUR (lē'mur) *n.* an animal of the monkey kind. [L., a ghost, so nicknamed from its nocturnal habits.]

LEND (lend) *v.t.* [*pret.* and *pp.* LENT] to grant on condition of receiving the thing again or an equivalent. [O.E. *lænan*, fr. *læn*, a loan.]

LENDER (len'der) *n.* one who lends money on interest.

LENGTH (length) *n.* extent from end to end; extension; reach; long duration. [O.E. *length*, fr. *lang*, long.]

LENGTHEN (leng'thn) *v.t.* to make longer; —*v.i.* to grow longer.

LENGTHINESS (leng'thi-nes) *n.* prolixity in speech; undue length.

LENGTHWISE (length'wiz) *ad.* in direction of the length.

LENGTHY (leng'thi) *a.* somewhat long.

LENIENCY (lēn'yen-si) *n.* mildness; clemency.

LENIENT (lēn'yent) *a.* softening; mild. [L. *lenire*, to soften, fr. (part. stem) *lenient-*, fr. *lenis*, gentle.]

LENITIVE (len'i-tiv) *a.* assuasive; easing; softening;—*n.* a mild purgative.

LENITY (len'i-ti) *n.* mildness; mercy.

LENO (lē'no) *n.* a kind of cotton gauze. [It.]

LENS (lenz) *n.* a glass by which rays of light are refracted and objects are magnified and diminished. [L., a lentil, so called from its shape.]

LENT (lent) *pret.* and *pp.* of LEND;—*n.* the time of fasting forty days before Easter. [O.E. *lencten*, spring, lent.]

LENTEN (len'ten) *a.* pertaining to Lent; used in Lent.

LENTIL (len'til) *n.* an annual plant allied to the bean. [O.F. *lentille*, fr. L. *lens, lentis*.]

LEO (lē'ō) *n.* the lion; fifth sign of the zodiac. [L.]

LEONINE (lē'u-nīn) *a.* having the qualities of a lion.

LEOPARD (lep'ard) *n.* a spotted beast of prey. [O.F., fr. L., fr. G. *leon*, lion, and *pardos*, pard.]

LEPER (lep'er) *n.* one infected with leprosy. [F., fr. L., fr. G. *lepra*, leprosy, fr. *lepein*, to peel.]

LEPORINE (lep'u-rin) *a.* pertaining to a hare. [L. *lepus, leporis*, hare.]

LEPROSY (lep'ru-si) *n.* a cutaneous disease.

LEPROUS (lep'rus) *a.* affected with leprosy.

LESION (lē'zhun) *n.* hurting; wound; injury. [F., fr. L. (acc.) *læsionem*, fr. (part.) *læsus*, fr. *lædere*, to hurt.]

LESS (les) *a.* smaller; not so large;—*ad.* in a smaller degree;—*n.* a smaller portion; the younger. [O.E. *læssa, læs*.]

LESSEE (le-sē') *n.* one to whom a lease is made. [O.F. (part.) *lesse*, fr. *lesser*, to let go. Cf. LEASE.]

LESSEN (les'n) *v.t.* or *i.* to make or become less in any sense.

LESSER (les'er) *a.* smaller of two; inferior.

LESSON (les'n) *n.* a portion of a book to be read or learned; a doctrine inculcated. [F. *leçon*, fr. L. (acc.) *lectionem*, a reading, fr. *legere*, to read.]

LESSOR (les-er') *n.* he who grants a lease.

LEST (lest) *con.* for fear that. [O.E.]

LET (let) (1) *v.t.* [*pret.* and *pp.* LET] to permit; lease;—*v.i.* to be leased;— (2) *n.* hinderance; delay. [(1) O.E. *lættan*, to permit. Cf. Ger. *lassen*. (2) O.E. *lettan*, to delay, fr. *læt*, late, slow.]

LETHAL (lē'thal) *a.* mortal; deadly. [L. *lethalis*, mortal, fr. *letum*, death.]

LETHARGIC (le-thär'jik) *a.* sleepy; drowsy.

LETHARGICALLY (le-thär'ji-kal-i) *ad.* in a dull or drowsy manner.

LETHARGY (leth'ar-ji) *n.* morbid drowsiness; dullness. [F., fr. L., fr. G. *lethargia*, forgetfulness, fr. *lethe*, forgetfulness.]

LETHE (lē'thē) *n.* oblivion; death. [G. *letho*, old form of *lanthanein*, to forget.]

LETTER (let'er) *n.* one who leases; an alphabetical character; a written message; a printing type; the literal meaning;—*v.t.* to stamp with letters. [F. *lettre*, fr. L. *litera*, letter.]

LETTERED (let'erd) *a.* learned; docqueted; stamped with name or title.

LETTERPRESS (let'er-pres) *n.* print, from type.

LETTERS (let'erz) *n.pl.* learning; literature.

LETTUCE (let'is) *n.* a garden plant eaten as a salad. [O.F. *laictuce* =F. *laitue*, fr. L. *lactuca*, fr. *lac*, milk.]

LEVANT (le-vant') *n.* the eastern countries along the Mediterranean;—*a.* eastern. [It. *levante*, east wind, eastern country where the sun rises, fr. L. *levare*, to raise.]

LEVANTER (le-van'ter) (1) *n.* a strong east wind in the Levant;— (2) *n.* one who absconds without paying his bets. [(1) See LEVANT. (2) Sp. *levantar*, to move, fr. L. *levare*, to raise.]

LEVEE (lev'ē) *n.* assembly of people on a morning or evening visit to a great personage; a bank of earth. [F., fr. *lever*, to raise.]

LEVEL (lev'el) *a.* even; flat; plain;—*v.t.* to make even;—*n.* a plain; a flat surface; equality. [O.F. *livel*, fr. L. *libella*, a water-level, dim. of *libra*, a balance.]

LEVELLER (lev'el-er) *n.* one who levels.

LEVELLING (lev'el-ing) *n.* act of bringing to a level.

LEVER (lē'ver) *n.* a bar, turning on a prop, for raising weights. [F. *levier*, fr. L. *levare*, to raise.]

LEVERAGE (lē'ver-ij) *n.* mechanical power or purchase of a lever.

LEVERET (lev'er-et) *n.* a young hare. [O.F. *levrault, leveret*, a young hare, fr. L. stem *lepor-*, fr. *lepus*, a hare.]

Lever.

LEVIABLE (lev'i-a-bl) *a.* that may be levied.

LEVIATHAN (le-vī'a-than) *n.* a large sea animal. [H.]

LEVITE (lē'vīt) *n.* one of the tribe of Levi.

LEVITICAL (le-vit'i-kal) *a.* pertaining to the Levites.

LEVITICUS (le-vit'i-kus) *n.* the third book of the Old Testament scriptures.

LEVITY (lev'i-ti) *n.* want of weight; lightness; thoughtlessness; trifling disposition; frivolity. [L. *levitatem*, fr. *levitas*, lightness, fr. *levis*, light.]

LEVY (lev'i) *v.t.* to raise; collect;—*n.* the act of raising money or troops; the amount or number raised. [F. *lever*, fr. L. *levare*, to raise.]

LEWD (lūd) *a.* given to the indulgence of lust; licentious; lascivious. [O.E. *læwede*, belonging to the laity.]

LEWDLY (lūd'li) *ad.* wantonly.

LEWDNESS (lūd'nes) *n.* unlawful indulgence of lust; unchastity.

LEXICAL (lek'si-kạl) *a.* pertaining to a lexicon.

LEXICOGRAPHER (lek-si-kog'rạ-fẹr) *n.* the writer of a dictionary. [G. *lexicon,* dictionary, and *graphein,* to write.]

LEXICOGRAPHICAL (lek-si-kō-graf'i-kạl) *a.* pertaining to lexicography.

LEXICOGRAPHY (lek-si-kog'rạ-fi) *n.* the art of composing dictionaries.

LEXICON (lek'si-kun) *n.* a dictionary. [G. *lexikos,* of, or belonging to, words, fr. *lexis,* a saying, fr. *legein,* to speak.]

LEYDEN-JAR (li'dn-jàr) *n.* a jar used to accumulate electricity, invented in Leyden, Holland.

LIABILITY (li-ạ-bil'i-ti) *n.* a state of being liable; responsibility; tendency.

LIABLE (li'ạ-bl) *a.* bound in law; subject or exposed to; responsible. [F., fr. L. *ligare,* to bind.]

LIAR (li'ạr) *n.* one who utters falsehood. [E. *lie.* [See **LIE** (1).]

LIBATION (li-bā'shun) *n.* an offering of wine. [L. (acc.) *libationem,* fr. *libare,* fr. G. *leibein,* to pour.]

LIBEL (li'bel) *n.* a defamatory writing; a lampoon;—*v.t.* to defame by writing. [L. *libellus,* dim. of *liber,* a book.]

LIBELLER (li'bel-ẹr) *n.* one who libels.

LIBELLOUS (li'bel-us) *a.* defamatory.

LIBERAL (lib'e-rạl) *a.* free in giving; enlarged; candid;—*n.* an advocate of greater freedom in political institutions. [F., fr. L. *liberalis,* befitting a freeman, fr. *liber.* tree.]

LIBERALISE (lib'e-rạl'īz) *v.t.* to free from narrow views.

LIBERALITY (lib-e-ral'i-ti) *n.* generosity; largeness of mind; impartiality.

LIBERALLY (lib'e-rạl-i) *ad.* generously.

LIBERATE (lib'e-rāt) *v.t.* to set free. [L. (part.) *liberatus,* fr. *liberare,* fr. *liber,* free.]

LIBERATION (lib-e-rā'shun) *n.* a setting free.

LIBERATOR (lib'e-rā-ter) *n.* one who liberates or sets free.

LIBERTINE (lib'ẹr-tin) *n.* a dissolute man;— *a.* licentious. [L. *libertinus,* a freedman, fr. *liber,* free.]

LIBERTINISM (lib'ẹr-tin-izm) *n.* licentiousness of doctrine or life.

LIBERTY (lib'ẹr-ti) *n.* freedom; permission; immunity. [F., fr. L. (acc.) *libertatem,* fr. *libertas,* fr. *liber,* free.]

LIBIDINOUS (li-bid'in-us) *a.* lustful; lewd; licentious. [L. *libido, libidinis,* desire, lust.]

LIBRA (li'brạ) *n.* the balance; seventh sign of the zodiac. [L.]

LIBRARIAN (li-brā'ri-ạn) *n.* one who has charge of a library.

LIBRARY (li'brạ-ri) *n.* a collection of books; place for books. [L. *librarium,* fr. *liber,* a book.]

LIBRATE (li'brāt) *v.t.* or *i.* to balance; poise. [L. *librare,* fr. (part.) *libratus,* fr. *libra,* a balance.]

LIBRATION (li-brā'shun) *n.* act of balancing.

LIBRATORY (li'brạ-tu-ri) *a.* moving like a balance.

LIBRETTO (li-bret'ō) *n.* a book of the words of an opera. [It., dim. of *libro,* fr. L. *liber,* book.]

LICE (lis) *pl.* of **LOUSE.**

LICENCE (li'sens) *n.* leave; grant of permission to practice or deal in; the document itself; excess or abuse of freedom;— **LICENSE,** *v.t.* to permit by legal warrant; authorise. [F., fr. L. *licentia,* fr. *licere,* to be permitted.]

LICENTIATE (li-sen'shi-āt) *n.* one who has a licence.

LICENTIOUS (li-sen'shus) *a.* loose in morals; dissolute. [F. *licencieux,* fr. L. *licentia,* fr. *licet.*]

LICENTIOUSLY (li-sen'shus-li) *ad.* dissolutely; loosely.

LICENTIOUSNESS (li-sen'shus-nes) *n.* excessive freedom in principles or practice.

LICH-GATE (lich'gāt) *n.* a churchyard gate, with a porch in which the bier may stand while the introductory part of the burial service is read. [O.E. *lic,* a corpse, and E. *gate.*]

LICK (lik) *v.t.* to pass over with the tongue; lap;—*n.* a stroke; a salt spring. [O.E. *liccian.* Cf. Ger. *lecken.*]

LICKERISH (lik'ẹr-ish) *a.* delicate; dainty; tempting. [Fr. obsolete *lickerous,* lecherous.]

LICTOR (lik'tur) *n.* an officer attending a Roman magistrate, who bore an axe and rods as ensigns of office. [L., fr. *ligare,* to bind.]

LID (lid) *n.* a cover of a vessel or box. [O.E. *hlid.*]

LIE (li) (1) *n.* a false statement uttered to deceive;—*v.i.* to utter falsehood;—(2) *v.i.* [*pret.* **LAY;** *pp.* **LAIN**] to rest horizontally; lean; remain. [(1) O.E. *leogan.* (2) M.E. *lyen,* fr. O.E. *licgan.* Cf. L. *lectus,* bed.]

LIEF (lēf) *ad.* willingly. [O.E. *leof;* Ger. *lieb,* loved.]

LIEGE (lēj) *a.* bound by tenure; sovereign. [O.F. *lige,* free, fr. O. H. Ger.; confused with L. *ligatus,* bound.]

LIEN (li'en, lē'en) *n.* a legal claim. [F. tie, band, fr. L. *ligamen,* fr. *ligare,* to bind.]

LIEU (lū) *n.* stead; place. [F., fr. L. *locus,* place.]

LIEUTENANCY (lef-ten'ạn-si) *n.* office or commission of a lieutenant.

LIEUTENANT (lef-ten'ạnt) *n.* a deputy; an officer next below a captain. [F., fr. *lieu,* place, and (part.) *tenant,* fr. *tenir* to hold.]

LIFE (lif) *n.* vitality; existence; energy; spirit; manner of living. [O.E. *lif.*]

LIFE-BLOOD (lif'blud) *n.* blood necessary to life. [Fr. **LIFE** and **BLOOD.**]

LIFEBOAT (lif'bōt) *n.* a boat rendered buoyant by air-tight chambers, etc. [Fr. **LIFE** and **BOAT.**]

LIFEGUARD (lif'gàrd) *n.* the guard of a king's person. [Fr. **LIFE** and **GUARD.**]

LIFE-INSURANCE (lif'-in-shōōr-ạns) *n.* a contract for payment of a sum of money at a person's death. [Fr. **LIFE** and **INSURANCE.**]

LIFELESS (lif'les) *a.* without life or spirit; dull; dead.

LIFELESSNESS (lif'les-nes) *n.* quality of being without life.

LIFE-PRESERVER (lif'pre-zẹr-vẹr) *n.* apparatus for saving life. [Fr. **LIFE** and **PRESERVE.**]

LIFETIME (lif'tim) *n.* period or whole time in which one lives.

LIFT (lift) *v.t.* to raise; exalt;—*n.* act of lifting; rise; a hoist. [Scand.]

LIGAMENT (lig'ạ-ment) *n.* anything that unites one thing to another; a substance serving to bind one bone to another. [F., a tie, fr. L. *ligamentum,* fr. *ligare,* to bind.]

LIGATURE (lig'ạ-tūr) *n.* a bandage. [See **LIGAMENT.**]

LIGHT (lit) *n.* that by which we see; that which gives or admits light; point of view; knowledge; enlightenment;—*a.* bright; nimble; not heavy;—*v.t.* to illuminate; kindle. [O.E. *leoht.*]

LIGHTEN (li'tn) *v.i.* to flash with light;—*v.t.* to make light; alleviate.

LIGHTER (li'tẹr) *n.* one who lights; a strong barge for loading or unloading ships.

LIGHT-HEADED (lit'hed-ed) *a.* delirious; giddy; thoughtless. [Fr. **LIGHT** and **HEAD.**]

LIGHT-HORSE (lit'hors) *n.* light-armed cavalry. [Fr. **LIGHT** and **HORSE.**]

LIGHTHOUSE (lit'hous) *n.* a house with a light to direct seamen. [Fr. **LIGHT** and **HOUSE.**]

LIGHTLY (līt'li) *ad.* nimbly; with levity; easily.

LIGHT-MINDED (līt'mind-ed) *a.* volatile. [Fr. **LIGHT** and **MIND**.]

LIGHTNESS (līt'nes) *n.* levity; brightness; want of weight.

LIGHTNING (līt'ning) *n.* a flash of electricity. [M.E. *lightnen*, to flash.]

LIGHTNING-ROD (līt'ning-rod) *n.* a metallic rod for diverting the electric current from buildings, etc. [Fr. **LIGHTNING** and **ROD**.]

LIGHTS (līts) *n.pl.* lungs of animals. [Fr. their lightness.]

LIGHTSOME (līt'sum) *a.* lively; cheering.

LIGNIFY (līg'ni-fī) *v.t.* or *i.* to convert into or become wood. [L. *lignum*, and *facere*, to make.]

LIKE (līk) (1) *a.* equal; similar; probable; —*n.* that which resembles;—*ad.* in the same manner;—(2) *v.t.* to approve; relish. [(1) O.E. *lic*, as in *gelic*. Cf. Ger. *gleich*. (2) O.E. *lician*, to please.]

LIKELIHOOD (līk'li-hood) *n.* probability. [See **LIKE** (1).]

LIKELINESS (līk'li-nes) *n.* probability. [See **LIKE** (1).]

LIKELY (līk'li) *a.* probable. [=*like-like*.]

LIKEN (lī'kn) *v.t.* to represent as like; compare. [See **LIKE** (1).]

LIKENESS (līk'nes) *n.* resemblance; portrait; picture. [See **LIKE** (1).]

LIKEWISE (līk'wīz) *ad.* in like manner; moreover; also. [See **LIKE** (1).]

LIKING (lī'king) *n.* inclination; desire. [See **LIKE** (2).]

LILAC (lī'lak) *n.* a flowering shrub. [Sp., fr. A.]

LILIPUTIAN (lil-i-pū'shan) *a.* diminutive; pertaining to the imaginary island of Lilliput.

LILT (lilt) *n.* a lively tune or song;—*v.i.* to play or sing cheerfully. [Norw. *lilla*, to sing. Cf. **LULL**.]

LILY (lil'i) *n.* a bulbous plant; its beautiful fragrant flower. [L. *lilium*, fr. G. *leirion*.]

LIMB (lim) *n.* an extremity of the body; a branch of a tree; edge of a disc or circle; —*v.t.* to dismember. [O.E. *lim*.]

LIMBER (lim'bėr) (1) *a.* easily bent; flexible; pliant;—(2) *n.* front part of a gun carriage. [(1) Fr. **LIMP**. (2) Etym. unknown.]

LIMBERNESS (lim'bėr-nes) *n.* flexibility; pliancy. [See **LIMBER** (1).]

LIMBO (lim'bō) *n.* the borders of hell; a place of restraint. [L. *in limbo*, abl. of *limbus*, border.]

LIME (lim) (1) *n.* a viscous substance; calcareous earth; *v.t.* to smear with lime; to ensnare;—(2) *n.* the linden tree;—(3) *n.* a fruit allied to the lemon. [(1) O.E. *lim*, cement. Cf. **LOAM**. (2) Corr. fr. O.E. *lind*, the linden tree. (3) F., fr. Per. =*citron*.]

LIMEKILN (lim'kil) *n.* a kiln for burning lime. [See **LIME** (1) and **KILN**.]

LIMESTONE (lim'stōn) *n.* a calcareous stone. [Fr. **LIME** (1).]

LIMIT (lim'it) *n.* a bound; border;—*v.t.* to confine within certain bounds. [F., fr. L. stem *limit-*, fr. *limes*, a boundary.]

LIMITABLE (lim'i-ta-bl) *a.* that may be bounded or restrained.

LIMITARY (lim'i-ta-ri) *a.* placed at the boundaries.

LIMITATION (lim-i-tā'shun) *n.* restriction.

LIMITLESS (lim'it-les) *a.* without limit; infinite.

LIMN (lim) *v.t.* to draw or paint. [O.F. *enluminer*, to illuminate, fr. L. *illuminare*, fr. *lumen*, light.]

LIMNER (lim'nėr) *n.* a portrait-painter.

LIMP (limp) (1) *v.i.* to walk lamely;—*n.* limping or halting step;—(2) *a.* wanting stiffness; flexible; weak. [(1) Cf. O.E. *lemphealt*, halting. (2) Etym. uncertain.]

LIMPET (lim'pet) *n.* a shellfish which adheres to bare rocks. [O.E. *lempedu*, a lamprey, fr. L. *lampreda*, lamprey.]

LIMPID (lim'pid) *a.* pure; transparent. [F., fr. L. *limpidus*, clear.]

LIMPIDITY (lim-pid'i-ti) *n.* cleanness; purity. Also **LIMPIDNESS**.

LIMPINGLY (lim'ping-li) *ad.* in a halting manner, as if lame. [See **LIMP** (1).]

LIMY (li'mi) *a.* containing or resembling lime; viscous; sticky. [See **LIME** (1).]

LINDEN (lin'den) *n.* the lime-tree. [O.E. *lind*. Cf. Ger. *Linde*, and **LIME** (2).]

LINE (lin) *n.* a string or cord; an extended mark; a row or rank; a course; business; a verse; the equator; the twelfth of an inch; a short letter or note; lineage; infantry;—*v.t.* to mark out; cover on the inside. [L. *linea*, fr. *linum*, flax.]

LINEAGE (lin'e-ij) *n.* direct descendants; progeny. [F. *lignage*, fr. *ligne*, line, fr. L. *linea*, line.]

LINEAL (lin'e-al) *a.* composed of lines; being in a direct line. [L. *linealis*, fr. *linea*, line.]

LINEALLY (lin'e-al-i) *ad.* in a direct line.

LINEAMENT (lin'e-a-ment) *n.* outline; feature. [F., fr. L. *lineamentum*, a drawing, fr. *lineare*, to draw a line, fr. *linea*.]

LINEAR (lin'e-ar) *a.* like a line; straight; slender. [L. *linearis*, fr. *linea*.]

LINEATION (lin-e-ā'shun) *n.* delineation.

LINEN (lin'en) *a.* made of flax or hemp;—*n.* cloth of flax or hemp. [O.E. *lin*. fr. L. *linum*, flax.]

LINEN-DRAPER (lin'en-drā-pėr) *n.* one who deals in linen. [Fr. **LINEN** and **DRAPER**.]

LINER (li'nėr) *n.* a vessel of a regular line of packets. [See **LINE**.]

LING (ling) *n.* a fish of the cod family. [O.E. *lenge*, length. Cf. *lang*.]

LINGER (ling'gėr) *v.i.* to remain long; delay. [M.E. *lengen*, to tarry, fr. O.E. *lang*, long.]

LINGERER (ling'gėr-ėr) *n.* one who loiters or hesitates.

LINGERING (ling'gėr-ing) *a.* slow; tardy.

LINGERINGLY (ling'gėr-ing-li) *ad.* in a lingering manner.

LINGO (ling'gō) *n.* language; slang. [Corr. fr. L. *lingua*, tongue.]

LINGUAL (ling'gwal) *a.* pertaining to the tongue. [L. *lingua*, tongue.]

LINGUIST (ling'gwist) *n.* one skilled in languages.

LINGUISTIC (ling-gwis'tik) *a.* relating to language;—*n.pl.* the science of languages.

LINIMENT (lin'i-ment) *n.* a soft ointment. [L. *linimentum*, fr. *linire*, to anoint.]

LINK (lingk) (1) *n.* part of a chain or series; a measure; 7'92 inches;—*v.t.* or *i.* to connect by links. (2) a torch. [(1) Scand. (2) D. Cf. **LINSTOCK**.]

LINNET (lin'et) *n.* a small singing bird. [O.F. *linette*, fr. L. *linum*, flax, so called from feeding on flax-seed.]

LINOLEUM (li-nō'le-um) *n.* a kind of floorcloth. [L. *linum*, flax, and *oleum*, oil.]

LINSEED (lin'sēd) *n.* seed of the flax plant. [O.E. *lin*, flax, and **SEED**.]

LINSTOCK (lin'stok) *n.* a cannonier's staff to hold a match. [*Lint*, or *lunt*, fr. D.]

LINT (lint) *n.* soft scrapings of linen. [L. *linteum*, a linen cloth, fr. *linum*, flax.]

LINTEL (lin'tel) *n.* the upper part of a doorframe. [O.F., fr. Low L. *lintellus*, for *limitellus*, dim. of *limes*, a border.]

LION (li'un) *n.* a rapacious quadruped; any person or object of interest. [L. *leo*, (acc.) *leonem*, fr. *leonis*.]

LIONESS (li'un-es) *n.* a female lion.

LION-LIKE (li'un-lik) *a.* bold; fierce.

LIP (lip) *n.* the border of the mouth; edge of anything. [O.E. *lippa*; allied to L. *labium*, lip.]

LIPPED (lipt) *a.* having lips.

LIP-SALVE (lip'salv) *n.* ointment for chapped lips. [Fr. **LIP** and **SALVE**.]

LIQUEFACTION (lik-we-fak'shun) *n.* act of melting. [See **LIQUEFY**.]

LIQUEFIABLE (lik'wĕ-fī-a-bl) *a.* that may be melted.

LIQUEFIER (lik'we-fī-ẽr) *n.* that which dissolves.

LIQUEFY (lik'we-fī) *v.t.* or *i.* to melt; become fluid. [L., fr. *liquere*, to be liquid, and *facere*, to make.]

LIQUEUR (li-kẽr') *n.* a preparation of distilled spirits. [F.]

LIQUID (lik'wid) *a.* fluid; flowing; soft and smooth; —*n.* a fluid substance; a letter, as *l* or *r*. [F., fr. L. *liquidus*, ir. *liquere*, to be fluid.]

LIQUIDATE (lik'wi-dāt) *v.t.* to adjust; pay; wind up. [L. (part.) *liquidatus*, fr. *liquidus*, liquid.] [liquidating.

LIQUIDATION (lik-wi-dā'shun) *n.* act of

LIQUIDATOR (lik'wi-dā-tẽr) *n.* one who liquidates.

LIQUIDITY (lik-wid'i-ti) *n.* the quality of being liquid.

LIQUOR (lik'ur) *n.* a liquid; strong drink; — *v.i.* to drink spirits. [O.E. *licur*, O.F. *liqeur*, fr. L. *liquor*, fr. *liquere*, to be liquid.]

LIQUORICE (lik'u-ris) *n.* a plant, the root of which abounds with a sweet juice; the juice obtained from the root. Also **LICORICE**. [O.F. *liquerice*, fr. L., fr. G. *glukus*, sweet, and *rhiza*, root.]

LISP (lisp) *v.i.* to clip words in pronunciation; —*n.* a defective articulation. [M.E. *lispen*, fr. O.E. *wlisp*, stammering. Cf. Ger. *lispeln*, to lisp.]

LISSOME (lis'um) *a.* supple; nimble; loose and free. Also **LITHESOME**.

LIST (list) (1) *n.* a line enclosing a field for combat; —(2) *n.* the outer edge or selvage of cloth; —(3) *n.* a roll; a catalogue; —*v.t.* to enlist; to sew or border; to enrol for service; —(4) *v.i.* to lean or incline—hence to desire or choose; to lean to one side; — (5) *v.i.* to listen. [(1) O.F. *lisse*. Cf. Late L. *liciœ*, barriers. (2) O.E. *list*, a list of cloth. Cf. Ger. *Leiste*. (3) O. H. Ger. *Lista*. (4) O.E. *lystan*, to desire, fr. *lust*, pleasure. (5) See **LISTEN**.]

LISTEL (lis'tel) *n.* in *Architecture*, a fillet.

LISTEN (lis'n) *v.t.* or *i.* to attend to; hearken; follow advice. [O.E. *hlystan*, fr. *hlyst*, hearing.]

LISTENER (lis'nẽr) *n.* one who listens.

LISTLESS (list'les) *a.* heedless; indifferent. [O.E. *lust*, pleasure.]

LISTLESSLY (list'les-li) *ad.* without attention; heedlessly.

LITANY (lit'a-ni) *n.* a solemn form of public prayer. [O.F. *letanie*, fr. L., fr. G. *litaneia*, a prayer.]

LITERAL (lit'e-ral) *a.* according to the letter or exact meaning; not figurative. [O.F., fr. *literalis*, fr. L. *litera*, a letter.]

LITERALLY (lit'er-al-i) *ad.* with adherence to words.

LITERARY (lit'e-ra-ri) *a* relating to literature. [L. *literarius*, fr. *litera*, a letter.]

LITERATURE (lit'e-ra-tūr) *n.* acquaintance with books; the whole books written in a country or period, or on a given subject. [F., fr. L. *literatura*.]

LITHE (lith) *a.* pliant; flexible; limber. [O.E. *lithe*, *lith*, gentle.]

LITHOGRAPH (lith'u-graf) *v.t.* to trace on stone, and transfer to paper by printing; —*n.* a print from a drawing on stone. [G., fr. *lithos*, stone, and *graphein*, to write.]

LITHOGRAPHIC (lith-u-graf'ik) *a.* pertaining to lithography.

LITHOGRAPHY (li-thog'ra-fi) *n.* the art of tracing letters, etc., on stone, and of transferring them to paper by impression.

LITHOLOGY (li-thol'ō-ji) *n.* the natural history of stones. [G. *lithos*, stone, and *logos*, discourse.]

LITHOTOMY (li-thot'u-mi) *n.* the operation of cutting for stone in the bladder. [G. *lithos*, stone, and *temnein*, to cut.]

LITIGANT (lit'i-gant) *n.* one engaged in a lawsuit; —*a.* contesting in law.

LITIGATE (lit'i-gāt) *v.t.* or *i.* to contest by a lawsuit. [L. (part.) *litigatus*, fr. *litigare*, to dispute.]

LITIGATION (lit-i-gā'shun) *n.* contention in law.

LITIGIOUS (li-tij'us) *a.* inclined to go to law. [L. *litigium*, quarrel.]

LITTER (lit'ẽr) *v.t.* to bring forth; strew with scraps; —*n.* a portable bed; brood of pigs; loose matter strewed about. [O.F. *litiere*, fr. Late L. *lectaria*, fr. L. *lectus*, couch.]

LITTLE (lit'l) *a.* small; paltry; mean; —*n.* a small quantity or extent; —*ad.* not much; in a small degree. [O.E. *lytel*.]

LITTLENESS (lit'l-nes) *n.* smallness; meanness.

LITTORAL (lit'u-ral) *a.* belonging to the seashore; —*n.* a strip of land between high and low water mark. [L stem *litor-*, fr. *litus*, the sea-shore.]

LITURGICAL (li-tur'ji-kal) *a.* pertaining to a liturgy.

LITURGIST (it'ur-jist) *n.* one who favours or is versed in liturgies.

LITURGY (lit'ur-ji) *n.* a formulary of prayers. [O.F. *liturgie* fr. G., fr. *leitos*, public, and *ergon*, work.]

LIVE (liv) (1) *v.t.* or *i.* to exist; subsist; abide; dwell; last; spend; — (2) (liv) *a.* having life; more active. [(1) O.E. *lifian*. Cf. Ger. *leben*. (2) Contr. fr. **ALIVE** = O.E. *on life*, in life.]

LIVELIHOOD (liv-li-hood) *n.* the means of living. [O.E. *lif*, life, and *lad*, a leading, way. Cf. **LODE**.]

LIVELINESS (liv'li-nes) *n.* sprightliness.

LIVELONG (liv'long) *a.* long in passing.

LIVELY (liv'li) *a.* brisk; active; lifelike; vivid; —*ad.* in a brisk manner. [M.E. *lifly*, lifelike.]

LIVER (liv'ẽr) *n.* an organ which secretes bile. [O.E. *lifer*.]

LIVERY (liv'er-i) *n.* a giving of possession; a particular dress; keeping and feeding for h re; a body of freemen in London. [F. *livrée*, fr. *livrer*, fr. L. *liberare*, to give freely.]

LIVES (livz) *n.pl.* of **LIFE**.

LIVESTOCK (liv'stok) *n.* cattle, horses, etc. [See **LIVE** (2).]

LIVID (liv'id) *a.* discoloured by a bruise; lead-coloured. [F., fr. L. *lividus*, bluish, fr. *livere*, to be of a lead colour.]

LIVIDNESS (liv'id-nes) *n.* a livid colour.

LIVING (liv'ing) *n.* subsistence; support; a benefice.

LIZARD (liz'ard) *n.* a scaly reptile. [F., fr. L. *lacerta*, a lizard.]

LLAMA (lä'ma) *n.* a woolly quadruped of South America. [Peruv.]

LLOYDS (loidz) *n.* exchange of underwriters and insurance brokers in London, so called from Edward Lloyd, in whose coffee-house the first meetings were held in the 17th century.

LO (lō) *ex.* look ! see ! behold ! [O E. *la*.]

LOACH (lōch) *n.* a small river fish. [F. *loche*.]

LOAD (lōd) *n.* that which is carried; weight; encumbrance; —*v.t.* to burden; freight; charge. [O.E. *hladan*, to load.]

LOADING (lō'ding) *n.* a cargo; charge.

LOAF (lōf) (1) *n.* a lump or mass of bread or sugar; —*pl.* **LOAVES**; —(2) *v.i.* to spend time in idleness. [(1) O.E. *hlaf*. (2) Ger. *laufer*, fr. *laufen*, to run about.]

LOAFER (lō'fẽr) *n.* a low idler. [See **LOAF** (2).]

LOAM (lōm) *n.* a rich earth; marl. [O.E. *lam*. Cf. **LIME**.]

LOAN (lōn) *n.* act of lending; the thing lent; —*v.t.* to lend. [O.E. *lœn.*]

LOATH (lōth) *ad.* unwilling; reluctant. Also written **LOTH**. [O.E. *lath*, hateful.]

LOATHE (lōth) *v.t.* to hate; be disgusted by.

LOATHSOME (lōth'sum) *a.* exciting disgust.

LOATHSOMENESS (lōth'sum-nes) *n.* quality that excites disgust.

LOBATE (lō'bāt) *a.* having lobes. Also **LOBED**.

LOBBY (lob'i) *n.* an opening before a room; a hall. [Late L. *lobia*, a covered way, fr. M. H. Ger. *Loube*, arbour.]

LOBBY-MEMBER (lob'i-mem'bėr) *n.* one who frequents the lobby of a legislature. [Fr. **LOBBY** and **MEMBER**.]

LOBE (lōb) *n.* part of the lungs; lower part of the ear. [F., fr. L., fr. G. *lobos*, lobe of the ear.]

LOBELIA (lō-bē'li-a) *n.* an ornamental herb and its flower. [*Lobel*, a Flemish botanist.]

LOBSTER (lob'stėr) *n.* a crustaceous fish. [O.E. *loppestre, lopust*, corr. fr. L. *locusta*, lobster.]

LOBULAR (lob'ū-lar) *a.* like a lobule.

LOBULE (lob'ūl) *n.* a small lobe.

LOCAL (lō'kal) *a.* pertaining to a place. [Fr. Late L. *localis*, fr. L. *locus*, place.]

LOCALISE (lō'kal-īz) *v.t.* to place or assign to a definite place.

LOCALISM (lō'kal-izm) *n.* attachment to a place; a local phrase or custom.

LOCALITY (lō-kal'i-ti) *n.* existence in place; situation.

LOCALLY (lō'kal-i) *ad.* with respect to place.

LOCATE (lō'kāt) *v.t.* to place or set.

LOCATION (lō-kā'shun) *n.* the act of placing; position.

LOCH (loH) *n.* a lake; an arm of the sea. [Gael.]

LOCK (lok) (1) *n.* a tuft or tress of hair;—(2) *n.* fastening for a door; part of a gun; works to confine water in a canal;—*v.t.* to fasten with a lock; embrace closely. [(1) O.E. *locc.* (2) O.E. *ioc*, a fastening.]

LOCKAGE (lok'ij) *n.* materials for locks.

LOCKER (lok'ėr) *n.* a drawer or close place fastened by a lock.

LOCKET (lok'et) *n.* a catch; an ornamental case. [F. *loquet*, a door latch, fr. O.F. *loc*, lock.]

LOCKJAW (lok'jaw) *n.* spasmodic contraction of the muscles of the jaw. [See **LOCK** (2) and **JAW**.]

LOCKSMITH (lok'smith) *n.* a maker of locks. [See **LOCK** (2) and **SMITH**.]

LOCK-UP (lok'up) *n.* a place for confining persons for a short time.

LOCOMOTION (lō-ku-mō'shun) *n.* act or power of moving from place to place. [L., fr. *locus*, place, and **MOTION**.]

LOCOMOTIVE (lō-ku-mō'tiv) *a.* producing motion; able to change place;—*n.* a steam engine on wheels.

LOCUS (lō'kus) *n.* a geometrical line, all of whose points satisfy a certain geometrical condition to the exclusion of all other points. [L., a place.]

LOCUST (lō'kust) *n.* a jumping winged insect; name applied to several plants and trees. [L. *locusta*.]

LODE (lōd) *n.* a course or vein containing metallic ore. [O.E. *lad*, course. Cf. *lœdan*, to lead.]

LODESTAR (lōd'stár) *n.* the pole-star; the cynosure. Also written **LOADSTAR**. [Cf. **LODE**.]

LODESTONE (lōd'stōn) *n.* an ore of iron; a native magnet. Also written **LOAD-STONE**. [Cf. **LODE**.]

LODGE (loj) *n.* a small house; a den; an association of masons; their meeting-place; —*v.t.* or *i.* to deposit; settle; rest; dwell; lay or lie flat. [O.F. *loge.*]

LODGER (loj'ėr) *n.* one who lodges.

LODGMENT (loj'ment) *n.* act of lodging; position secured by assailants.

LOFT (loft) *n.* an elevated floor. [M.E. *loft*, air, fr. Scand. =sky, upper room; O.E. *luft.*]

LOFTINESS (loft'i-nes) *n.* altitude; haughtiness; pride.

LOFTY (loft'i) *a.* high; proud; stately.

LOG (log) *n.* a bulky piece of wood; apparatus for measuring a ship's velocity. [Scand.]

LOGARITHM (log'a-rithm) *n.* a mathematical term. [G., fr. *logos*, a word, ratio, and *arithmos*, number.]

LOG-BOOK (log'bŏok) *n.* register of a ship's way. [Fr. **LOG** and **BOOK**.]

LOGIC (loj'ik) *n.* the art of reasoning. [G. *logike* (sc. *techne*, logic, art), fr. *logikos*, reasonable, fr. *legein*, to speak.]

LOGICAL (loj'i-kal) *a.* according to logic.

LOGICALLY (loj'i-kal-i) *ad.* according to the rules of logic.

LOGICIAN (lo-jish'an) *n.* a person versed in logic.

LOG-LINE (log'lin) *n.* a line to measure a ship's way. [Fr. **LOG** and **LINE**.]

LOGWOOD (log'wood) *n.* a wood used in dyeing.

LOIN (loin) *n.* the back of an animal cut for food;—*pl.* the lower part of the back in man. [O.F. *logne*, fr. L. *lumbus*, loin.]

LOITER (loi'tėr) *v.i.* to linger on the way; delay. [D.]

LOITERER (loi'tėr-ėr) *n.* one who loiters.

LOLL (lol) *v.i.* to lie at ease;—*v.t.* to hang out the tongue. [O.D.]

LONE (lōn) *a.* single; solitary. [Contr. of **ALONE**.]

LONELINESS (lōn'li-nes) *n.* solitude; want of company.

LONELY (lōn'li) *a.* solitary; retired.

LONESOME (lōn'sum) *a.* secluded from society; wanting company.

LONESOMELY (lōn'sum-li) *ad.* in a lonesome manner.

LONESOMENESS (lōn'sum-nes) *n.* state of being alone; dismal seclusion.

LONG (long) (1) *a.* extended in space or time; protracted; far-reaching;—*ad.* to a great extent;—(2) *v.i.* to desire earnestly. [(1) O.E. *lang.* (2) O.E. *langian*, to desire.]

LONGER (long'gėr) *a.* more long or extended.

LONGEVITY (lon-jev'i-ti) *n.* length of life. [L., fr. *longus*, long, and *ævus* (*ætas*) age.]

LONG-HEADED (long'hed-ed) *a.* far-seeing; shrewd. [Fr. **LONG** and **HEAD**.]

LONGING (long'ing) *n.* an earnest desire; continual wish. [See **LONG** (2).]

LONGINGLY (long'ing-li) *ad.* with eager desire.

LONGISH (long'gish) *a.* somewhat long. [See **LONG** (1).]

LONGITUDE (lon'ji-tūd) *n.* distance from east to west; length. [F., fr. L. *longitudo*, fr. *longus*, long.]

LONGITUDINAL (lon-ji-tū'di-nal) *a.* being in the direction of the length.

LONGPRIMER (long'pri-mėr) *n.* a printing type between small pica and bourgeois.

LONG-RUN (long'run) *n.* the final issue or result.

LONG-SUFFERING (long'su-fėr-ing) *a.* forbearing; not easily provoked;—*n.* great patience. [See **LONG** (1) and **SUFFER**.]

LONG-WINDED (long-wind'ed) *a.* tedious; prolix.

LONGWISE (long'wiz) *ad.* lengthwise.

LOO (lōō) *n.* a game at cards. [F. *lanturelu, lanturlu.*]

LOOF (lōōf) *n.* after part of a ship's bow. [M.E. *lof*, a large paddle once used to assist the helm. Cf. Scot. *loof*, Ger. *Lofa*, palm of the hand. Cf. **LUFF**.]

LOOK (look) *v.i.* to behold; appear; search for;—*n.* cast of countenance; appearance; view. [O.E. *locian.*]

LOOKING-GLASS (look'ing-glas) *n.* a glass that reflects images. [See **LOOK** and **GLASS.**]

LOOKOUT (look'out) *n.* watching for; place of observation; watchman.

LOOM (1) *n.* a weaver's frame;—(2) *v.t.* to appear above, indistinctly or in the distance. [(1) O.E. *geloma,* a tool. (2) O.F. *lumer,* fr. L. *luminare.*]

LOON (loon) *n.* (1) a simple fellow;—(2) a kind of bird. [(1) M.E. *lown,* fr. O. Low Ger. (2) Scand.]

LOOP (loop) *n.* a noose in a rope or string. [Scand.]

LOOPHOLE (loop'hol) *n.* a hole for a string; means of escape. [O.F. *loup.*]

LOOSE (loos) *v.t.* to untie; release; open; —*a.* unbound; wanton. [O.E. *leas.*]

LOOSELY (loos'li) *ad.* negligently.

LOOSEN (loo'sn) *v.t.* to relax.

LOOSENESS (loos'nes) *n.* freedom; flux.

LOOT (loot) *n.* plunder; booty;—*v.t.* to plunder. [Hind., fr. Skr.]

LOP (lop) *v.t.* to cut short. [D. =to maim.]

LOQUACIOUS (lo-kwa'shus) *a.* addicted to talking. [L. stem *loquaci-,* fr. *loquax,* fr. *loqui,* to speak.]

LOQUACITY (lo-kwas'i-ti) *n.* talkativeness.

LORD (lord) *n.* a master; tyrant; baron; God; the Supreme Ruler;—*v.i.* to domineer; rule despotically. [O.E. *hlaford,* fr. *hlafweard,* the loaf-keeper. Cf. **LOAF.**]

LORDLINESS (lord'li-nes) *n.* haughtiness.

LORDLING (lord'ling) *n.* a petty lord.

LORDLY (lord'li) *a.* proud; haughty.

LORD'S DAY (lordz'da) *n.* Christian Sabbath.

LORDSHIP (lord'ship) *n.* dominion; a title given to a lord.

LORD'S SUPPER (lordz'sup-er) *n.* holy communion. [Fr. **LORD** and **SUPPER.**]

LORE (lor) *n.* learning; instruction. [O.E. *lar.*]

LORGNETTE (lor-nyet') *n.* an opera glass. [F.]

LORICATE (lor'i-kat) *v.t.* to plate over. [L. *lorum,* a thong.]

LORICATION (lor-i-ka'shun) *n.* the act of plating over.

LORN (lorn) *a.* forsaken; lost; lonely. [(Part.) *loren,* fr. *lesen,* to lose. Cf. **LOSE.**]

LOSE (looz) *v.t.* [*pret.* and *pp.* **LOST**] to suffer loss; miss; let slip;—*v.i.* not to win. [O.E. *leosan.*]

LOSS (los) *n.* privation; destruction or ruin; waste. [O.E. *los.*]

LOST (lost) *pret.* and *pp.* of **LOSE.**

LOT (lot) *n.* state; portion; share; parcel; number; chance; a field; —*v.t.* to allot; share; separate; catalogue. [O.E. *hlot,* share.]

LOTION (lo'shun) *n.* a medicinal wash. [F., fr. L. (part.) *lotus,* fr. L. *larare,* to wash.]

LOTTERY (lot'er-i) *n.* a distribution of prizes by chance. [F. *lot,* a lot, prize.]

LOUD (loud) *a.* noisy; high in tone or pitch. [O.E. *hlud.* Cf. Ger. *laut.*]

LOUDLY (loud'li) *ad.* noisily; clamorously.

LOUDNESS (loud'nes) *n.* force of sound.

LOUGH (loH) *n.* a lake. [Celt. *loch.*]

LOUNGE (lounj) *v.i.* to spend time lazily; loiter. [F. *longis,* an idle, stupid fellow.]

LOUNGER (loun'jer) *n.* an idle person.

LOUR (lou'er) *v.i.* to appear dark; threaten. [M.E. *louren,* to frown.]

LOUSE (lous) *n.* an insect;—*pl.* **LICE.** [O.E. *lus,* pl. *lys.*]

LOUSY (lou'zi) *a.* swarming with lice; dirty; low.

LOUT (lout) *n.* an awkward person. [O.E. *lutan,* to bow.]

LOUTISH (lou'tish) *a.* awkward; clownish.

LOVABLE (luv'a-bl) *a.* deserving of love.

LOVE (luv) *v.t.* to regard with affection;—*n.* an affection excited by beauty or whatever is pleasing; courtship; benevolence; person loved; a term of endearment. [O.E. *lufu.* Cf. Ger. *Liebe.*]

LOVE-FEAST (luv'fest) *n.* a religious festival. [See **LOVE** and **FEAST.**]

LOVE-KNOT (luv'not) *n.* a knot emblematical of love. [See **LOVE** and **KNOT.**]

LOVELESS (luv'les) *a.* not attracting love.

LOVE-LETTER (luv'let-er) *n.* a letter of courtship. [See **LOVE** and **LETTER.**]

LOVELINESS (luv'li-nes) *n.* qualities that excite love; gentle beauty.

LOVELY (luv'li) *a.* exciting love; amiable.

LOVER (luv'er) *n.* one who loves.

LOVE-SICK (luv'sik) *a.* languishing through love. [See **LOVE** and **SICK.**]

LOVE-SONG (luv'song) *n.* a song expressing love. [See **LOVE** and **SONG.**]

LOVING (luv'ing) *a.* expressing love or kindness.

LOVINGLY (luv'ing-li) *ad.* with affection.

LOW (lo) (1) *a.* deep; poor; cheap;—*ad.* with a low voice; cheaply;—(2) *v.i.* to bellow as an ox. [(1) Scand.] (2) O.E. *hlowan.*]

LOW-BRED (lo'bred) *a.* bred in low condition; vulgar; rude. [See **LOW** and **BREED.**]

LOWER (lo'er) *v.t.* or *i.* to let down; sink; diminish. [E. *lower,* comp. of *low.*]

LOWERMOST (lo'er-most) *a.* lowest; deepest. [See **LOUR.**]

LOWERY (lou'er-i) *a.* cloudy; threatening rain. [See **LOUR.**]

LOWLAND (lo'land) *n.* land low and flat.

LOWLINESS (lo'li-nes) *n.* humbleness of mind.

LOWLY (lo'li) *a.* humble; meek; mean;—*ad.* humbly; meekly.

LOWNESS (lo'nes) *n.* depression; dejection; meanness.

LOW-WINES (lo'winz) *n.pl.* the first run of the still. [See **LOW** and **WINE.**]

LOYAL (loi'al) *a.* faithful to a prince, to plighted love, or duty. [F., fr. L. *legalis,* fr. *lex, legis,* law.]

LOYALIST (loi'al-ist) *n.* one who is faithful to his sovereign or country.

LOYALLY (loi'al-i) *ad.* with fidelity.

LOYALTY (loi'al-ti) *n.* fidelity.

LOZENGE (loz'enj) *n.* a rhomb; a small cake of sugar. [O.F. *losange,* flattery, prob. fr. O.F. *lauze,* a flat stone.]

LUBBER (lub'er) *n.* a heavy, idle fellow. [W.]

LUBBERLY (lub'er-li) *a.* bulky and lazy; awkward;—*ad.* clumsily; awkwardly.

LUBRICANT (loo'bri-kant) *n.* any oily or greasy substance.

LUBRICATE (loo'bri-kat) *v.t.* to make slippery. [L. (part.) *lubricatus,* fr. *lubricare,* to make slippery.]

LUBRICITY (loo-bris'i-ti) *n.* smoothness; instability; lewdness.

LUBRICOUS (loo'bri-kus) *a.* slippery.

LUCE (loos) *n.* a fresh-water fish; a pike. [O.F. *lus,* fr. G. *lukos,* a wolf, a (ravenous) fish.]

LUCERN (loo-sern') *n.* a plant grown for fodder. [F. *luzerne.*]

LUCID (loo'sid) *a.* clear; transparent; easily understood; intellectually bright. [L. *lucidus,* bright, fr. *lux, lucis,* light.]

LUCIDITY (loo-sid'it-i) *n.* clearness of statement or exposition.

LUCIDNESS (loo'sid-nes) *n.* clearness; transparency.

LUCIFER (loo'si-fer) *n.* the planet Venus; Satan; a combustible match lighted by friction. [L., fr. *lux, lucis,* light, and *ferre,* to bring.]

LUCK (luk) *n.* chance; accident; good fortune. [D.]

LUCKILY (luk′i-li) *ad.* by good chance.

LUCKLESS (luk′les) *a.* unfortunate.

LUCKY (luk′i) *a.* fortunate; successful by chance. [ful.

LUCRATIVE (lōō′kra̤-tiv) *a.* profitable; gain-

LUCRE (lōō′kẹr) *n.* profit; gain. [F., fr. L. *lucrum.*]

LUDICROUS (lōō′di-krus) *a.* exciting laughter; funny; ridiculous. [L. *ludicrus*, fr. *ludus*, sport, fr. *ludere*, to play.]

LUDICROUSLY (lōō′di-krus-li) *ad.* in a ludicrous manner.

LUFF (luf) *n.* the part toward the wind;— *v.i.* to turn the head of a ship toward the wind. [Cf. LOOF.]

LUG (lug) *v.t.* to pull or carry with force or difficulty;—*n.* a load; lobe of the ear; handle of a vessel; a kind of sail. [Scand.]

LUGGAGE (lug′ij) *n.* baggage. [Fr. LUG. and F. suffix.] [sails.

LUGGER (lug′ẹr) *n.* a small vessel with lug

LUGUBRIOUS (lōō-gū′bri-us) *a.* mournful. [L. *lugubris*, fr. *lugere*, to mourn.]

LUKEWARM (lōōk′wawrm) *a.* moderately warm; indifferent. [M.E. *leuk*, *luke*, tepid.]

LUKEWARMNESS (lōōk′wawrm-nes) *n.* want of zeal; indifference.

LULL (lul) *v.t.* or *i.* to soothe; compose; subside;—*n.* a season of calm. [Scand. Imit. fr. repetition of *lu*, *lu*.]

LULLABY (lul′a̤-bi) *n.* a song to quiet infants.

LUMBAGINOUS (lum-baj′i-nus) *a.* pertaining to lumbago.

LUMBAGO (lum-bā′gō) *n.* a rheumatic pain in the small of the back.

LUMBAR (lum′ba̤r) *a.* pertaining to or near the loins. [L. *lumbus*, loin.]

LUMBER (lum′bẹr) *n.* anything useless or cumbersome; rough timber;—*v.t.* to heap carelessly together;—*v.i.* to move heavily. [F. *Lombard*, fr. *Lombard-room*, the room of a Lombard, a banker, or pawnbroker.]

LUMBER-ROOM (lum′bẹr-rōōm) *n.* a place for useless things.

LUMINARY (lōō′mi-na̤-ri) *n.* any body that gives light. [O.F. *luminarie*, fr. L. *lumen*, light.]

LUMINOUS (lōō′mi-nus) *a.* giving light; shining; clear; lucid.

LUMINOUSLY (lōō′mi-nus-li) *ad.* in a clear or vivid manner.

LUMINOUSNESS (lōō′mi-nus-nes) *n.* clearness; perspicuity. Also **LUMINOSITY.**

LUMP (lump) *n.* a shapeless mass;—*v.t.* to throw into a mass; take in the gross. [Scand.]

LUMPISH (lum′pish) *a.* heavy; dull.

LUMPISHLY (lum′pish-li) *ad.* heavily.

LUMPY (lum′pi) *a.* full of lumps.

LUNACY (lōō′na̤-si) *n.* mental derangement; madness in general.

LUNAR (lōō′na̤r) *a.* pertaining to the moon. [L. *lunaris*, fr. *luna*, the moon.]

LUNARIAN (lōō-nā′ri-a̤n) *n.* inhabitant of the moon.

LUNATIC (lōō′na̤-tik) *a.* affected with lunacy; —*n.* a madman. [F., fr. L. *lunaticus*, mad-affected by the moon, fr. L. *luna*, the moon.]

LUNCH (lunsh) *n.* food taken between breakfast and dinner. Also **LUNCHEON.** [Fr. *lunch*, a lump.]

LUNETTE (lōō-net′) *n.* a detached bastion; a kind of lens; a watch glass flattened in the centre. [F., fr. L. *luna*.]

LUNG (lung) *n.* organ of respiration. [O.E. *lunge.*]

LUNGE (lunj) *n.* a sudden push or thrust with a sword. [F. *allonger*, to lengthen, fr. *ad*, to, and *longus*, long.]

LUNT (lunt) *n.* a match-cord to fire a cannon. [D. *lont*, a match. Cf. Ger. *Lunte*.]

LUNULAR (lōō′nū-la̤r) *a.* shaped like a new moon. [L. *lunula*, dim. of *luna*.]

LURCH (lurch) *n.* a sudden roll of a ship; deserted condition;—*v.i.* to roll to one side; lie in wait; lurk. [Variant of LURK.]

LURCHER (lur′cher) *n.* one who lies in wait; a kind of sporting dog.

LURE (lūr) *n.* that which allures;—*v.t.* to entice. [O.E. *loirre*, *loerre* = F. *leurre*.]

LURID (lū′rid) *a.* ghastly pale; gloomy; dismal. [L. *luridus*, pale yellow.]

LURK (lurk) *v.t.* to lie in wait; lie close or out of sight. [Scand.]

LURKING-PLACE (lurk′ing-plās) *n.* a hiding-place.

LUSCIOUS (lush′us) *a.* sweet or rich, so as to cloy. [Old form *lushious*, fr. LUSTY.]

LUST (lust) *n.* carnal appetite;—*v.t.* to desire eagerly or improperly. [O.E. *lust*, pleasure.]

LUSTFUL (lust′fool) *a.* having irregular or evil desires.

LUSTILY (lus′ti-li) *ad.* stoutly; boldly.

LUSTINESS (lus′ti-nes) *n.* bodily strength; robustness. Also **LUSTIHOOD.**

LUSTRAL (lus′tra̤l) *a.* used in purification.

LUSTRATE (lus′trāt) *v.t.* to purify; survey. [L. *lustrare*, to purify. Cf. LUSTRUM.]

LUSTRATION (lus-trā′shun) *n.* purification; a surveying.

LUSTRE (lus′tẹr) *n.* brightness; a kind of lamp. [F., fr. It., fr. Late L. *lustrum*, window, fr. L. *lustrare*, to shine.]

LUSTRING (lus′tring) *n.* a glossy silk. [E. *lustre.*]

LUSTROUS (lus′trus) *a.* bright; luminous; shining.

LUSTRUM (lus′trum) *n.* a period of five years. [L., fr. *luere*, to wash, purify.]

LUSTY (lus′ti) *a.* vigorous; robust; stout; hearty. [O.E. *lust*, pleasure.]

LUTE (lōōt) *n.* (1) instrument of music;—(2) *n.* a composition like clay;—*v.t.* to coat with lute. [(1) O.F. *lut* = F. *luth*, fr. Pg., fr. A. (2) *lutum*, clay, fr. *luere*, to wash.]

LUTESTRING (lōōt′string) *n.* string of a lute.

LUTHERAN (lōō′thẹr-a̤n) *a.* pertaining to Luther.

LUXATE (luk′sāt) *v.t.* to put out of joint; dislocate. [L. *luxare*, to dislocate, dislocated, fr. G. *loxos*, slanting, oblique.]

LUXURIANCE (lug-zhŏŏ′ri-a̤ns) *n.* rank growth; exuberance.

LUXURIANT (lug-zhŏŏ′ri-a̤nt) *a.* exuberant in growth.

LUXURIATE (lug-zhŏŏ′ri-āt) *v.i.* to grow to excess; indulge in; expatiate on.

LUXURIOUS (lug-zhŏŏ′ri-us) *a.* given to luxury; furnished with luxuries; enervating by pleasure.

LUXURIOUSLY (lug-zhŏŏ′ri-us-li) *ad.* voluptuously; exuberantly.

LUXURY (luk′zhu-ri) *n.* excess in eating, dress, or equipage; any expensive habit or article. [O.F. *luxurie*, fr. L. *luxuria*, luxury, fr. L. *luxus*, excess.]

LYCEUM (li-sē′um) *n.* a literary association, or the place where they meet. [L.]

LYE (li) *n.* a solution of alkaline salt. [O.E. *leah.*]

LYING (li′ing) (1) *n.* the vice of falsehood;— (2) *a.* recumbent. [(1) See LIE (1). (2) See LIE (2).]

LYMPH (limf) *n.* a colourless animal fluid. [L. *lympha*, water.]

LYNCH (linsh) *v.t.* to punish, as a criminal without legal trial. [Fr. a Virginian planter, Charles *Lynch* (1736-96).]

LYNX (lingks) *n.* a wild animal of the cat kind, noted for its keen sight. [G.]

LYRE (lir) *n.* instrument of music; a kind of harp much used by the ancients. [F., fr. L. *lyra*, fr. G. *lyra.*]

LYRIC (lir′ik) *a.* pertaining to a lyre; written in stanzas;—*n.* a lyric poem.

LYRIST (li′rist) *n.* one who plays on the harp or lyre; a composer of lyrics.

M

MAB (mab) *n.* queen of the fairies. [W.]

MACADAMISE (ma-kad'am-īz) *v.t.* to form or cover a road with small broken stones. [Fr. *Macadam*, the inventor.]

MACARONI (mak-a-rō'ni) *n.* a finical fellow; a food made of wheaten paste formed into long slender tubes. [It.]

MACAW (ma-kaw') *n.* a showy kind of parrot. [Fr. Braz.]

MACE (mās) *n.* (1) a club; a cue; an ensign of authority;—(2) a spice. [(1) O.F.=F. *masse*, fr. L. (2) F., fr. G. *maker*.]

MACERATE (mas'e-rāt) *v.t.* to make lean. [L. (part.) *maceratus*, steeped, fr. *macerare*.]

MACERATION (mas-e-rā'shun) *n.* the act of making lean or soft.

MACHIAVELIAN (mak-i-a-vē'li-an) *a.* politically cunning; crafty. [Fr. *Machiavelli*, an Italian writer.]

MACHINATE (mak'i-nāt) *v.t.* to plot; contrive. [L. (part.) *machinatus*, having designed.]

MACHINATION (mak-i-nā'shun) *n.* act or art of scheming or plotting; an artful design.

MACHINE (ma-shēn') *n.* an engine; any mechanical contrivance to produce or regulate force; a mere tool. [F., fr. L. (acc.) *machinam*, fr. G. *mechane*, a device, ruse.]

MACHINERY (ma-shē'ne-ri) *n.* works of a machine; machines collectively.

MACHINIST (ma-shē'nist) *n.* constructor of machines.

MACKEREL (mak'e-rel) *n.* a small sea fish spotted with blue. [O.F., of unknown etym.]

MACULATE (mak'ū-lāt) *v.t.* to spot; defile. [L. (part.) *maculatus*, spotted.]

MAD (mad) *a.* insane; enraged; furious. [Short fr. O.E. (part.) *ge-mæd-ed*, maddened.]

MADAM (mad'am) *n.* complimentary address to a woman. [F. *ma*, fr. L. *mea*, my, and **DAME**.]

MADCAP (mad'kap) *n.* a rash, hot-headed person.

MADDEN (mad'n) *v.t.* or *i.* to make or become mad.

MADDER (mad'er) *n.* a plant whose roots yield a rich red dye. [O.E. *mædere*.]

MADE (mād) *pret.* and *pp.* of **MAKE**.

MADEIRA (ma-dē'ra) *n.* a wine made in Madeira; a kind of cake.

MADLY (mad'li) *ad.* furiously; foolishly.

MADMAN (mad'man) *n.* an insane·man.

MADNESS (mad'nes) *n.* state of being mad; extreme folly.

MADONNA (ma-don'a) *n.* the Virgin Mary or her picture. [It. Cf. **MADAM**.]

MADRIGAL (mad'ri-gal) *n.* a short lyric poem or song; the same vocalised and harmonised. [It., fr. *mandra*, flock, fr. L., fr. G.]

MAELSTROM (māl'strom) *n.* a kind of whirlpool. [Dan.]

MAESTRO (ma-es'trō) *n.* a musical composer. [It.]

MAGAZINE (mag-a-zēn') *n.* a storehouse; a periodical publication. [O.F.=F. *magasin*, warehouse, fr. A.]

MAGENTA (ma-jen'ta) *n.* a bright pink red colour. [Fr. the time of its discovery—the year (1859) of the battle of *Magenta*.]

MAGGOT (mag'ut) *n.* a grub; worm; egg of the green fly; whim; caprice. [Celt.]

MAGI (mā'ji) *n.pl.* eastern enchanters or astrologers. [L.]

MAGIC (maj'ik) *n.* a dealing with spirits; enchantment. [L., fr. G. *magikos*.]

MAGIC-LANTERN (maj'ik-lan'tern) *n.* an optical instrument for magnifying small painted figures on the walls of a dark room. [See **MAGIC** and **LANTERN**.]

MAGICAL (maj'i-kal) *a.* produced by magic.

MAGICALLY (maj'i-kal-i) *ad.* by magic.

MAGICIAN (ma-jish'an) *n.* one skilled in magic.

MAGISTERIAL (maj-is-tē'ri-al) *a.* proud; lofty; authoritative. [L. *magisterius*, fr. *magister*, master.]

MAGISTERIALLY (maj-is-tē'ri-al-i) *ad.* arrogantly.

MAGISTRACY (maj'is-tra-si) *n.* the office of a magistrate; the body of magistrates.

MAGISTRATE (maj'is-trāt) *n.* a civil officer with limited judicial and executive powers. [F. *magistrat*, fr. L. (acc.) *magistratum*, fr. *magister*.]

MAGNA CARTA (mag'na kàr'ta) *n.* the great charter of English rights. [L., great charter.]

MAGNANIMITY (mag-na-nim'i-ti) *n.* greatness of mind; generosity.

MAGNANIMOUS (mag-nan'i-mus) *a.* great in mind; generous; noble in thought or deed. [L. fr. *magnus*, great, and *animus*, mind.]

MAGNANIMOUSLY (mag-nan'i-mus-li) *ad.* nobly; bravely.

MAGNATE (mag'nāt) *n.* a person of rank, opulence, and influence. [F. *magnat*, fr. L., fr. *magnus*.]

MAGNESIA (mag-nē'shi-a) *n.* a white powder, aperient and antacid.

MAGNESIUM (mag-nē'shi-um) *n.* the metallic base of magnesia. [L., fr. G.=pert. to *Magnesia*, Asia Minor.]

MAGNET (mag'net) *n.* the lodestone, an ore which attracts iron. [O.F. *magnete*, fr. L. (acc.) *magnetem*, Magnesian (ore).]

MAGNETIC (mag-net'ik) *a.* having the properties of the magnet; attractive.

MAGNETICALLY (mag-net'i-kal-i) *ad.* by magnetism; by attraction.

MAGNETISE (mag'ne-tīz) *v.t.* or *i.* to impart or receive the properties of the magnet.

MAGNETISM (mag'ne-tizm) *n.* properties of the magnet; attraction.

MAGNIFIC (mag-nif'ik) *a.* great; noble. [L. *magnificus*.]

MAGNIFICENCE (mag-nif'i-sens) *n.* grandeur.

MAGNIFICENT (mag-nif'i-sent) *a.* splendid.

MAGNIFICENTLY (mag-nif'i-sent-li) *ad.* splendidly; pompously.

MAGNIFIER (mag'ni-fi-er) *n.* one who magnifies; a glass that enlarges objects to the sight.

MAGNIFY (mag'ni-fī) *v.t.* to make great. [F. *magnifier*, fr. L. *magni-*, for *magnus*, and *-ficare*, for *facere*, make.]

MAGNILOQUENCE (mag-nil'u-kwens) *n.* high-sounding language.

MAGNILOQUENT (mag-nil'u-kwent) *a.* speaking pompously. [Fr. L. (part. stem) *loquent-*, speaking, fr. *loqui*.]

MAGNITUDE (mag'ni-tūd) *n.* greatness of size or importance; largeness; bulk. [L. *magnitudo*.]

MAGNOLIA (mag-nō'li-a) *n.* a beautiful flowering shrub. [Fr. *Magnol*, a French botanist, d. 1715.]

MAGPIE (mag'pi) *n.* a chattering bird. [F. *Magot*, *Margot*, Margaret (also magpie) and *pie*, fr. L. (acc.) *picam*, magpie.]

MAHOGANY (ma-hog'a-ni) *n.* a beautiful hardwood used in making furniture. [S. Amer.]

MAHOMETAN (ma-hom'e-tan) *n.* See **MOHAMMEDAN**.

MAID (mād) *n.* a young unmarried woman. [Short for **MAIDEN**.]

MAIDEN (mād'n) *n.* a young, unmarried woman;—*a.* fresh; pure. [O.E. *mœgden*.]

MAIDENHAIR (mād'n-hār) *n.* a fern with graceful slender stalks.

MAIDENHOOD (mād'n-hood) *n.* state of virginity; freshness; purity Also **MAIDENHEAD.**

MAIDENLIKE (mād'n-līk) *a.* like a maid.

MAIDENLY (mād'n-li) *a.* modest.

MAIL (māl) (1) *n.* a coat of steel;—*v.t.* to arm with mail;—(2) *n.* a bag for conveying letters;—*v.t.* to send by mail; to post. [(1) O.F. *maille*, mail, fr. L. (acc.) *maculam*, mesh, spot. (2) M.E. *male*, fr. O.F. *male* = F. *malle*, a bag, fr. O. H. Ger.]

MAIL-COACH (māl'kōch) *n.* a coach that conveys a mail. [See MAIL (2), and COACH.]

MAIM (mām) *v.t.* to disable a limb;—*n* lameness; injury. [O.F. *mahoyn*, *mehaing*, of uncert. etym.]

MAIN (mān) (1) *a.* chief; principal;—*n.* the gross; the ocean; continent; main pipe; —(2) *n.* strength; force. [(1) O.F., fr. L. *magnus*. (2) O.E. *mœgen*, might.]

MAINLAND (mān'land) *n.* a continent. [See MAIN (1) and LAND.]

MAINLY (mān'li) *ad.* chiefly; principally.

MAINMAST (mān'mast) *n.* the chief or middle mast.

MAINSAIL (mān'sāl) *n.* the principal sail.

MAINSHEET (mān'shēt) *n.* rope that hauls down the mainsail to the leeside of a ship.

MAINSPRING (mān'spring) *n.* moving spring of a watch; chief source or motive of action.

MAINSTAY (mān'stā) *n.* rope extending from the foremast foot to the maintop; chief support.

MAINTAIN (mān-tān') *v.t.* to keep; preserve; support with food; uphold. [F. *maintenir*, fr. L. (abl.) *manu*, by the hand, and *tenere*, hold.]

MAINTAINABLE (mān-tā'na-bl) *a.* that may be maintained

MAINTENANCE (mān'te-nans) *n.* sustenance.

MAINTOP (mān'top) *n.* a platform at the head of the mainmast.

MAIZE (māz) *n.* Indian corn. [Sp. *maiz*, fr. W. Ind.]

MAJESTIC (ma-jes'tik) *a.* stately; grand.

MAJESTICALLY (ma-jes'ti-kal-i) *ad.* with dignity or grandeur.

MAJESTY (maj'es-ti) *n.* dignity; grandeur; a title. [F., fr. L. (acc.) *majestatem*; conn. with MAJOR.]

MAJOLICA (ma-jol'i-ka) *n.* a kind of enamelled pottery. [It., fr. *Majorca*.]

Maintop.

MAJOR (mā'jur) *a.* greater; elder;—*n.* a military officer next above a captain. [L. comp. of *magnus*.]

MAJORITY (ma-jor'i-ti) *n.* the greater number; full age; rank of a major.

MAKE (māk) *v.t.* [*pret.* and *pp.* MADE] to compel; cause to be; create;—*n.* form; structure. [O.E. *macian*. Cf. Ger. *machen*.]

MAKER (mā'ker) *n.* one who forms or creates.

MAKESHIFT (māk'shift) *n.* a temporary expedient.

MALADMINISTRATION (mal-ad-min-is-trā'shun) *n.* bad management of affairs. [Pref. F. *mal*, ill, fr. L. *male*.]

MALADY (mal'a-di) *n.* sickness; disease; bodily ailment. [F., fr. *malade*, corr. fr. L. *male*, badly, and (part.) *habitus*, conditioned, fr. *habere*, have.]

MALAPERT (mal'a-pert) *a.* bold; saucy. [O.F. *mal apert*, fr. L. *male*, ill, and (acc.) *apertum*, open.]

MALARIA (ma-lā'ri-a) *n.* noxious exhalation. [It.]

MALARIOUS (ma-lā'ri-us) *a.* pertaining to malaria.

MALCONTENT (mal'kun-tent) *a.* discontented; —*n.* one who is dissatisfied. Also written **MALECONTENT.** [Pref. F. *mal* (badly).]

MALE (māl) *a.* belonging to the male sex;— *n.* one of the sex that begets young. [O.F. *masle* = F. *mâle*, fr. L. (acc.) *masculum*. See MASCULINE.]

MALEDICTION (mal-e-dik'shun) *n.* evil speaking; cursing; a curse. [Pref. L. *male*, evilly.]

MALEFACTOR (mal-e-fak'tur) *n.* one guilty of a crime; a felon; convict. [Pref. L. *male*.]

MALEVOLENCE (ma-lev'u-lens) *n.* ill will.

MALEVOLENT (ma-lev'u-lent) *a.* ill-disposed. [L. (part. stem) *volent*-, willing, fr. *volo*.]

MALICE (mal'is) *n.* extreme enmity. [F., fr. L. (acc.) *malitiam*, badness, fr. *malus*.]

MALICIOUS (ma-lish'us) *a.* ill-disposed; malignant.

MALICIOUSLY (ma-lish'us-li) *ad.* with evil intention.

MALIGN (ma-līn') *v.t.* to traduce; slander; —*a.* malicious. [O.F. (fem.) *maligne*, fr. L. *malignus* = *mali-genus*, of evil nature, fr. *malus*, bad, and rt. *gen*-, of *gignere*, beget.]

MALIGNANCY (ma-lig'nan-si) *n.* malevolence; virulence.

MALIGNANT (ma-lig'nant) *a.* malicious; dangerous to life. [L. (part. stem) *malignant*-, maligning, fr. *malignari*.]

MALIGNITY (ma-lig'ni-ti) *n.* extreme virulence; deadly evil.

MALINGERER (ma-ling'ger-er) *n.* a person who avoids duty by feigning illness. [F. *mal*, ill, and O.F. *heingre*, lean, fr. Ger. *hager*.]

MALISON (mal'i-zun) *n.* malediction. [O.F., fr. MALEDICTION.]

MALL (mal, mel) (1) *n.* a public walk;—(2) *n.* a kind of hammer. [(1) Orig. a place where *Pall-Mall* was played. (2) See MAUL.]

MALLARD (mal'ard) *n.* a wild drake. [O.F., fr. *male*, *masle*, MALE.]

MALLEABLE (mal'e-a-bl) *a.* that can be extended by beating. [Fr. L. *malleus*, hammer.]

MALLET (mal'et) *n.* a kind of wooden hammer. [F. dim. fr. O.F. *mal*, fr. L. (acc.) *malleum*, hammer.]

MALLOWS (mal'ōz) *n.* an emollient plant. Also written **MALLOW.** [O.E. *malue*, fr. L. *malva*.]

MALMSEY (mām'zi) *n.* a sort of grape; a strong, sweet wine. [Corr. fr. O.F. *malvoisie*, fr. *Malvasia*, in the Morea.]

MALPRACTICE (mal-prak'tis) *n.* evil practice. [Pref. F. *mal*, ill.]

MALT (mawlt) *n.* barley steeped and dried; —*v.t.* or *i.* to make or become malt. [O.E. *mealt*. Cf. O. Ger. *Malz*.]

MALTREAT (mal-trēt') *v.t.* to treat ill. [Pref. F. *mal*, ill.]

MALTREATMENT (mal-trēt'ment) *n.* ill usage; abuse.

MALTSTER (mawlt'ster) *n.* a malt-maker.

MALVERSATION (mal-ver-sā'shun) *n.* fraudulent or corrupt act or conduct in office. [F., fr. L. *male*, ill, and (part.) *versatus*, having engaged in, fr. *versari*.]

MAMMA (ma-mä') *n.* word for mother. Also **MAMA.** [Fr. the infantine *ma*.]

MAMMAL (mam'al) *n.* an animal that suckles its young. [L. *mammalis*, fr. *mamma*, breast.]

MAMMALIA (ma-māl'ya) *n.pl.* animals which suckle their young. [L. (neut. pl.).]

MAMMIFEROUS (ma-mif'e-rus) *a.* nourishing its young by breasts. [L. *mammi*, for *mamma*, and *ferus*, bearing.]

MAMMILLARY (mam'i-la-ri) *a.* belonging to the breasts. Also **MAMMARY.**

MAMMON (mam'un) *n.* riches; wealth; the god or spirit of riches. [G., fr. Syr.]

MAMMOTH (mam'uth) *n.* a huge quadruped now extinct;—*a.* gigantic. [Russ., fr. Tartar.]

MAN (man) *n.* a human being; mankind; an adult male; husband; a piece in playing chess, etc.;—*pl.* **MEN**;—*v.t.* to furnish with men. [O.E. Cf. Ger. *Mann.*]

MANACLE (man'a-kl) *n.* a handcuff;—*v.t.* to shackle the hands. [Fr. F. *manicle*, fr. L. (acc.) *maniculam*, little sleeve, fr. *manus*, hand.]

MANACLES (man'a-klz) *n.pl.* chains for the hands.

MANAGE (man'ij) *v.t.* or *i.* to conduct; transact; husband. [O.F. *manege*, handling, through It., fr. L. *manus.*]

MANAGEABLE (man'ij-a-bl) *a.* governable; easily managed.

MANAGEMENT (man'ij-ment) *n.* conduct or direction of affairs; skilful treatment; managing body.

MANAGER (man'ij-er) *n.* a conductor; director; good economist.

MANATEE (man-a-tē') *n.* an herb-eating fish of the whale family. [Sp., fr. W. Ind.]

MANCHET (man'chet) *n.* a small loaf of fine bread. [Etym. uncert.]

MANDARIN (man-da-rēn') *n.* a Chinese governor. [Pg., fr. Skr.]

MANDATE (man'dāt) *n.* an order; command. [O.F. *mandat*, fr. L. (neut. part.) *mandatum* (a thing) enjoined, from *mandare.*]

MANDATORY (man'da-tur-i) *a.* enjoining.

MANDIBLE (man'di-bl) *n.* the jaw. [L., fr. *mandere*, chew.]

MANDIBULAR (man-dib'ū-lar) *a.* belonging to the jaw.

MANDOLIN (man'du-lin) *n.* a kind of guitar. [F., fr. It.]

MANDRAKE (man'drāk) *n.* a narcotic plant with curious forked roots. [Short fr. (Shak.) *mandragora*, through F. and L., fr. G. *mandragoras.*]

MANDREL (man'drel) *n.* a turner's instrument. [Etym. uncert.]

MANDUCATE (man'dū-kāt) *v.t.* to chew; to eat. [L. (part.) *manducatus*, chewed, fr. *manducare*, fr. *mandere.*]

MANDUCATION (man-dū-kā'shun) *n.* act of chewing.

MANE (mān) *n.* long hair on the neck of a beast. [O.E. *mann.* Cf. Ger. *Mähne.*]

MANEGE (ma-nāzh') *n.* horsemanship; a riding school. [F., see **MANAGE.**]

MANES (mā'nēz) *n.pl.* departed souls. [L.]

MANFUL (man'fool) *a.* bold; brave; having the spirit of a man.

MANFULLY (man'fool-i) *ad.* like a man.

MANGANESE (mang-ga-nēz') *n.* a gray metal, hard and brittle. [O.F. corr. fr. **MAGNESIA.**]

MANGE (mānj) *n.* the itch on cattle. [Fr. **MANGY.**]

MANGER (mān'jer) *n.* an eating-trough for cattle. [O.F. *mangeure*, fr. *manger.* See **MANGY.**]

MANGLE (mang'gl) (1) *v.t.* to cut roughly or coarsely;—*v.t.* (2) smooth linen;—*n.* a calender for smoothing linen. (1) Perh. fr. O.F. *mehainger*, to **MAIM.** (2) D., through Late L., fr. G. *manganon*, a war-engine worked by a winch.]

MANGLER (mang'gler) *n.* one who mangles. [See **MANGLE** (2).]

MANGO (mang'gō) *n.* an East Indian fruit; a pickled musk-melon. [Pg., fr. Malay.]

MANGROVE (man'grōv) *n.* a tropical tree, whose bark is used in tanning. [Fr. Malay native name, and **GROVE.**]

MANGY (mān'ji) *a.* scabby, as a beast. [F. (part.) *mangé*, eaten, fr. *manger*, fr. L. *manducare.*]

MAN-HATER (man'hāt-er) *n.* a misanthrope. [See **MAN** and **HATE.**]

MANHOOD (man'hood) *n.* state of being a man; full age; manly quality.

MANIA (mān'ya) *n.* madness; any excessive desire or propensity. [L., fr. G.]

MANIAC (mā'ni-ak) *a.* raving with madness; —*n.* a madman.

MANIACAL (ma-nī'a-kal) *a.* affected with madness.

MANIFEST (man'i-fest) *a.* clearly visible; apparent; evident;—*v.t.* to show plainly; reveal; declare;—*n.* an invoice of a cargo. [F., fr. L. *manifestus* of uncert. etym.]

MANIFESTATION (man-i-fes-tā'shun) *n.* exhibition; display.

MANIFESTLY (man'i-fest'li) *ad.* evidently.

MANIFESTO (man-i-fes'tō) *n.* a public declaration;—*pl.* **MANIFESTOS.** [It.]

MANIFOLD (man'i-fōld) *a.* many; diverse. [Fr. **MANY** and **FOLD.**]

MANIKIN (man'i-kin) *n.* a little man. [Fr. D.]

MANILLA (ma nil'a) *n.* a kind of cheroot made in *Manila.*

MANIPULAR (ma-nip'ū-lar) *a.* pertaining to a hand.

MANIPULATE (ma-nip'ū-lāt) *v.t.* or *i.* to work with the hands; operate so as to produce a desired result. [Fr. L. *manipulus*, a handful, fr. *mani-*, for *manus*, and rt. of *plere*, fill.]

MANIPULATION (ma-nip-ū-lā'shun) *n.* manual operation; skilful treatment.

MANKIND (man'kind) *n.* the human race.

MANLIKE (man'lik) *a.* becoming a man.

MANLINESS (man'li-nes) *n.* bravery; dignity; qualities of a man.

MANLY (man'li) *a.* pertaining to manhood; becoming a man.

MANNA (man'a) *n.* the juice of a tree, used as a medicine. [G., fr. H.]

MANNER (man'er) *n.* form; mode; air or mien; custom; sort; style; deportment. [O.F. *maniere* = F. *manière*, fr. Late L. (acc.) *maneriam*, kind, fr. L. *manus.*]

MANNERISM (man'er-izm) *n.* peculiarity or sameness of manner or literary style.

MANNERLY (man'er-li) *a.* civil; decent; well-behaved.

MANŒUVRE (ma-nöö'ver, ma-nū'ver) *n.* adroit movement or arrangement;—*v.t.* or *i.* to change the position of ships or troops; manage artfully. [F. = orig. handiwork, fr. L. (abl.) *manu*, by hand and *opera*, work. Doublet of **MANURE.**]

MANOMETER (ma-nom'e-ter) *n.* an instrument for measuring the density of gases. Also **MANOSCOPE.** [Fr. G. *manos*, rare, and **METRE.**]

MANOR (man'ur) *n.* a lord's estate in land. [O.F., fr. *manoir*, dwell, fr. L. *manere.*]

MANORIAL (ma-nō'ri-al) *a.* pertaining to a manor.

MANSE (mans) *n.* dwelling-house attached to a church for the clergyman. [O.F. = a holding, fr. Late L. (acc.) *mansam*, fr. L. (part.) *mansus*, fr. *manere*, stay.]

MANSION (man'shun) *n.* a large dwelling-house. [O.F., fr. L. (acc.) *mansionem*, a staying, quarters.]

MANSLAUGHTER (man'slaw-ter) *n.* the killing of a person in passion, without malice.

MANTEL (man'tl) *n.* the piece of timber or stone over the fireplace. [Form of **MANTLE.**]

MANTELET (man'tel-et) *n.* a small mantle or cloak for women. [F.]

MANTILLA (man-til'a) *n.* a kind of hood or veil; a lady's light cloak of silk. [Sp. dim., fr. L. *mantum*, a Spanish cloak.]

MANTLE (man'tl) *n.* a loose garment or cloak; a cover;—*v.t.* or *i.* to cloak; cover; disguise; rise and spread; be diffused. [O.F. *mantel* = F. *manteau* fr. L. *mantellum*, a cloak.]

MANTUA (man'tū-a) *n.* a woman's gown. [For It. *manto*, as if from *Mantua.*]

MANTUAMAKER (man'tū-ạ-māk-ẽr) *n.* a dressmaker.

MANUAL (man'ū-ạl) *a.* performed by the hand; —*n.* a small book; keyboard of an organ. [L. *manualis,* pert. to the hand, *manus.*]

MANUFACTORY (man-ū-fak'tur-i) *n.* a place where goods are made.

MANUFACTURE (man-ū-fak'tūr) *n.* anything made by the hand;—*v.t.* to form by the hand or by art. [O.F., fr. L. (abl.) *manu,* by hand, and (acc.) *facturam,* a making, fr. (part.) *factus,* made.]

MANUFACTURER (man-ū-fak'tūr-ẽr) *n.* one who manufactures.

MANUMISSION (man-ū-mish'un) *n.* act of freeing slaves.

MANUMIT (man-ū-mit') *v.t.* to release from slavery. [Fr. L. (abl.) *manu,* by hand, and *mittere,* send.]

MANUMOTOR (man'ū-mō-tẽr) *n.* a small wheeled carriage moved by the hand.

MANURE (mạ-nūr') *n.* anything that fertilises land;—*v.t.* to apply fertilising substances to land. [Short. fr. MANŒUVRE =to hand-cultivate.]

MANX (mangks) *a.* denoting the Isle of Man, its people, or its language.

MANUSCRIPT (man'ū-skript) *n.* any writing done by hand;—*a.* written; not printed. [Fr. L. (abl.) *manu,* by hand, and SCRIPT.]

MANY (men'i) *a.* numerous;—*n.* a great number; the people. [O.E. *manig.* Cf. Ger. *manch.*]

MAORI (mou'ri) *n.* a native of New Zealand.

MAP (map) *n.* a delineation on a plane of the surface of the earth or heavens, or a portion thereof; outline; representation;—*v.t.* to draw or describe distinctly. [O.F. = F. *mappemonde,* fr. L. (acc.) *mappam* (*mundi*), a (painted) cloth (of the world).]

MAPLE (mā'pl) *n.* a tree of several species. [O.E. *mœpul* (-*treo*).]

MAPPERY (map'ẽr-i) *n.* the art of designing maps.

MAR (mår) *v.t.* to hurt; impair; disfigure; —*n.* hurt; blemish. [O.E. Cf. *amerran.*]

MARANATHA (mar-ạ-nā'thạ, mar-ạ-nath'ạ) *n.* an anathema; the Lord comes to judge. [Syr.]

MARAUD (mạ-rawd') *v.i.* to rove for plunder. [F., of uncert. etym.]

MARAUDER (mạ-raw'dẽr) *n.* a plunderer.

MARBLE (mår'bl) *n.* a calcareous stone;—*v.t.* to vein like marble;—*a.* made of marble. [O.F. *marbre,* fr. L. (acc.) *marmorem,* for *marmor.*]

MARCH (mårch) (1) *n.* third month of the year;—(2) *n.* regulated movement of troops; procession; step; distance marched over; a piece of music;—*v.t.* to cause to march or go;—*v.i.* to move in military order; —(3) *n.* a frontier of a territory. [(1) *Mars,* the god of war. (2) F. *marcher,* of uncert. etym. (3) O.E. *mearc,* doublet of MARK (1), MARQUE.]

MARCHES (mårch'ez) *n.pl.* borders; confines. [See MARCH (3).]

MARCHIONESS (mår'shun-es) *n.* the wife of a marquis. [See MARQUIS.]

MARCONIGRAM (mar-kō'ni-gram) *n.* a message carried by wireless telegraphy. [Fr. *Marconi,* a person name.]

MARE (mår) *n.* the female of the horse kind. [O.E. *mere,* fr. *mearh,* horse. Cf. Ger. *Mähre.*]

MARGARINE (mår'gạ-rin) *n.* an imitation of butter made from animal fat; butterine. [Made fr. L. *margarita,* pearl, fr. G.]

MARGIN (mår'jin) *n.* an edge; border;—*v.t.* to form a border. [L. stem *margin-,* of *margo,* brim, brink.]

MARGINAL (mår'ji-nạl) *a.* placed in the margin.

MARIGOLD (mar'i-gōld) *n.* a plant with a yellow flower. [Fr. MARY and GOLD.]

MARINE (mạ-rēn') *a.* pertaining to the sea; —*n.* a soldier doing duty in a ship; the navy. [F. *marin,* fr. L. (acc.) *marinum,* pert. to the sea, *mare.*]

MARINER (mar'i-nẽr) *n.* a seaman; a sailor.

MARIOLATRY (mā-ri-ol'ạ-tri) *n.* worship of the Virgin Mary. [Fr. G. *latreia,* worship.]

MARITAL (mar'i-tạl) *a.* pertaining to a husband. [L., fr. *maritus,* a husband, fr. stem *mari-,* of *mas,* MALE.]

MARITIME (mar'i-tim) *a.* pertaining to the sea. [F.]

MARJORAM (mår'jo-rạm) *n.* an aromatic plant used in cookery. [Corr. through O.F. *marjorane,* and Low L., fr. G. *amarakos.*]

MARK (mårk) (1) *n.* a stroke drawn; impression; trace; proof; distinction; rank; object aimed at;—*v.t.* or *i.* to draw a mark upon; write on; note; observe;—(2) *n.* a silver German coin, worth about a shilling. [(1) O.E. *mearc.* Doublet of MARCH (3). Cf. MARQUIS. (2) O.E. *marc,* Ger. *Mark.*]

MARKET (mår'ket) *n.* a place or time of sale; rate of sale; value;—*v.i.* to deal in market. [O.F. = F. *marché,* fr. L. (acc.) *mercatum,* traffic, fr. *mercari.*]

MARKETABLE (mår'ket-ạ-bl) *a.* fit for market.

MARKETING (mår'ket-ing) *n.* articles in market.

MARKSMAN (mårks'man) *n.* a man skilful in shooting. [See MARK (1).]

MARL (mårl) *n.* a rich clayey earth;—*v.t.* to manure with marl. [F., fr. Low L. (acc.) *margillam,* dim. for L. *marga,* fr. Celt.]

MARLINE (mår'lin) *n.* a small line of two strands. [D.; conn. with MOOR.]

MARLINESPIKE (mår'lin-spīk) *n.* an iron tool for separating the strands of a rope.

MARMALADE (mår'mạ-lād) *n.* a preserve or jam of oranges. [F., fr. Pg. =quince, fr. L. *melimelum,* lit. honey-apple, fr. G.]

MARMOT (mår'mot) *n.* a rodent animal, native of the Alps. [F. = mountain-rat, through It., fr. L. stem, *mur-,* of *mus,* mouse, and stem, *mont-,* of *mons,* mountain.]

Marmot.

MAROON (mạ-rōōn') (1) *n.* a free black on the West Indian mountains; — *v.t.* to put on shore on a desolate island;—(2) *n.* a brownish-red. [(1) F. *marron,* fugitive, fr. Sp. *cimarron,* of uncert. etym. (2) F. *marron,* a chestnut, of unknown etym.]

MARQUE (mårk) *n.* letter of marque is a commission to make reprisal on an enemy. [O.F., fr. M. H. Ger. *Marke,* MARCH (1).]

MARQUEE (mår-kē') *n.* a large field tent. [Orig. *marquees* =tent of a *Marquise.*]

MARQUETRY (mår'ket-ri) *n.* inlaid work of shells, etc. [F., fr. *marqueter,* to inlay, MARK out, fr. Ger.]

MARQUIS (mår'kwis) *n.* a title of nobility. [F., fr. Late L., fr. O. H. Ger. *Marcha,* MARK (1), in Great Britain a nobleman ranking next below a duke.]

MARRIAGE (mar'ij) *n.* state or condition of being married; matrimony.

MARRIAGEABLE (mar'ij-ạ-bl) *a.* of a fit age to be married.

MARROW (mar'ō) *n.* a soft substance in bones; essence of a thing. [M.E. *marow,* fr. O.E. *mearh.* Cf. Ger. *Mark.*]

MARROW-BONE (mar'ō-bōn) *n.* a bone containing marrow;—*pl.* the knees.

MARROWFAT (mar'ō-fat) *n.* a large delicious pea.

MARROWY (mar'ō-i) *a.* full of marrow.

MARRY (mar'i) *v.i.* to be joined in wedlock; —*v.t.* to join in wedlock. [F. *marier*, fr. L. *maritare*, to marry, fr. *marita*, wife. See **MARITAL**.]

MARS (mārz) *n.* the god of war; a planet. [L.]

MARSALA (mär-sä'lò) *n.* a light kind of sherry wine. [Fr. *Marsala*, Sicily.]

MARSELLAISE (mär'se-lāz, mär-se-lyāz') *n.* song or hymn of the French revolution. [Sung first by Marseilles volunteers, 1792.]

MARSH (märsh) *n.* low wet ground; morass or fen; —*a.* swampy; boggy. [O.E. *mersc*, fr. *merisc*, full of **MERES**.]

MARSHAL (mär'shạl) *n.* chief military commander; a civil officer; one who directs processions, etc.;—*v.t.* to arrange in due order. [O.F. *mareschal*, groom, fr. O. H. Ger., fr. *Marah*, horse. Cf. **MARE**; and *scalk*, servant. Cf. Ger. *Schalk*.]

MARSHY (mär'shi) *a.* wet; boggy.

MARSUPIAL (mär-sū'pi-ạl) *a.* having a pouch to carry its young, as the kangaroo. [Fr. L. *marsupium*, pouch, fr. G. dim. of *marsupos*, bag.]

MART (märt) *n.* a place of public sale. [Short for **MARKET**.]

MARTELLO (mär-tel'ō) *n.* a small round fort on the coast. [It. =F. *martel*, hammer (for beating alarms), fr. L.]

MARTEN (mär'ten) *n.* a kind of weasel. [F. *martre*, fr. Teut. Cf. O.E. *mearth*.]

MARTIAL (mär'shạl) *a.* warlike; bold. [F., fr. L., fr. *Mars*.]

MARTIN (mär'tin) *n.* a kind of swallow. [F., nicknamed fr. *St Martin*.]

MARTINET (mär'ti-net) *n.* a strict disciplinarian. [Fr. a French officer, *Martinet*, under Louis XIV.]

MARTINGALE (mär'tin-gāl) *n.* a strap to curb a horse; a spar under the bowsprit. [F., of uncert. etym.]

MARTINMAS (mär'tin-mạs) *n.* festival of St Martin, 11th November. [Fr. **MASS** (2).]

MARTYR (mär'ter) *n.* one who is put to death for the truth;—*v.t.* to make a martyr of; torment. [O.E., fr. L., fr. G. *martur*, witness.]

MARTYRDOM (mär'ter-dum) *n.* the death of a martyr.

MARTYROLOGY (mär-ter-ol'ō-ji) *n.* history of martyrs. [G. *logia*, science.]

MARVEL (mär'vel) *v.i.* to wonder;—*n.* anything astonishing. [F. *merveille*, fr. L. (neut. pl.) *mirabilia*, wonderful things, fr. *mirari*, **ADMIRE**.]

MARVELLOUS (mär've-lus) *a.* wonderful.

MARVELLOUSLY (mär've-lus-li) *ad.* in a wonderful manner.

MASCULINE (mas'kū-lin) *a.* male; like a man; not effeminate. [F. *masculin*, fr. L. *masculus*, dim. fr. *mas*. Doublet of **MALE**.]

MASH (mash) *n.* a mixture of things; bran and water for cattle; ground malt steeped in hot water for brewing;—*v.t.* to bruise into a soft mass; crush. [E. Cf. Ger. *meischen*, mix.]

MASHER (mash'er) *n.* a young silly dandy or fop.

MASHING (mash'ing) *n.* a process in brewing; quantity of malt used in brewing.

MASK (mask) *n.* a cover for the face;—*v.t.* to disguise. [Fr. **MASQUE**.]

MASKER (mas'ker) *n.* one who wears a mask; mummer.

MASON (mā'sn) *n.* an artificer in bricks and stone. [O.F. *masson*=F. *maçon*, fr. Low L. (acc.) *macionem*, fr. Teut. Cf. Ger. *Steinmetz*.]

MASONIC (mạ-son'ik) *a.* pertaining to masonry.

MASONRY (mā'sn-ri) *n.* work of a mason; craft of freemasons.

MASQUE (mask) *n.* See **MASK**. [F., short fr. *masquerer*, fr. Sp. *mascara*, a masquerader, fr. A.]

MASQUERADE (mas-ke-rād') *n.* a nocturnal assembly of persons in disguise;—*v.i.* to assemble in masks; go in disguise. [O.F. and F. *muscarade*.]

MASS (mas) (1) *n.* a lump; an assemblage; —*v.t.* to heap together; assemble;—(2) *n.* a Roman Catholic service. [(1) F. *masse*, fr. L., fr G. *massein*, knead. (2) O.E. *mæsse*, fr. Late L. *messa*, *missa*, fr. L. (part.) *missus*, sent, fr. *mittere*, fr. the announcement in church. 'Ite, missa est,'=Go (the congregation) is dismissed.]

MASSACRE (mas'ạ-ker) *n.* promiscuous slaughter;—*v.t.* to kill promiscuously or with cruelty. [F., of uncert. etym.]

MASSETER (mas'e-ter, ma-sē'ter) *n.* a muscle which raises the under jaw. [G., fr. *massaomai*, chew.]

MASSINESS (mas'i-nes) *n.* bulk; ponderousness. [See **MASS** (1).]

MASSIVE (mas'iv) *a.* bulky; heavy; ponderous. Also **MASSY**.

MASSIVENESS (mas'iv-nes) *n.* great bulk and weight.

MAST (mȧst) (1) *n.* the long upright timber of a ship set on the keel for supporting the yards, sails, and rigging;—(2) *n.* nut of the beech, oak, etc. [(1) O.E. *mæst*. (2) O.E. *mæst*.]

MASTER (mȧs'ter) *n.* a ruler; superior; proprietor; teacher; chief;—*v.t.* to conquer. [O.F. *maistre*=F. *maître*, fr. L. (acc.) *magistrum*. Cf. **MAGISTERIAL**.]

MASTERLY (mȧs'ter-li) *a.* becoming a master.

MASTERPIECE (mȧs'ter-pēs) *n.* a chief performance.

MASTERY (mȧs'ter-i) *n.* superiority over; supremacy; attainment of skill or power.

MASTIC (mas'tik) *n.* a resin from a tree. Also written **MASTICH**. [F., fr. L., fr. G. *mastiche*, a sweet gum.]

MASTICATE (mas'ti-kāt) *v.t.* to chew. [L. (part.) *masticatus*, chewed, fr. *masticare* (orig.) to chew (**MASTIC**).]

MASTICATION (mas-ti-kā'shun) *n.* the act of chewing.

MASTIFF (mas'tif) *n.* a large dog. [O.F. *mastin* (confused with *mestif*, mongrel), fr. Teut.]

MAT (mat) *n.* a texture of rushes;—*v.t.* to weave into a mat. [O.E., fr. L. *matta*.]

MATADORE (mat'ạ-dōr) *n.* a bull-fighter; cards at the game of ombre and quadrille. [Sp.]

MATCH (mach) (1) *n.* a contest; an equal marriage;—*v.t.* to pair; suit; marry;—(2) *n.* something to take fire. [(1) M.E. *macche*, fr. O.E. *mæcca*. Cf. **MATE**. (2) O.F. *mesche* =F. *mèche*, fr. L. (acc.) *myxam*, nozzle of a lamp, fr. G. *muxa*.]

MATCHLESS (mach'les) *a.* having no equal. [See **MATCH** (1).]

MATCHLOCK (mach'lok) *n.* a musket fired by a match. [See **MATCH** (2).]

MATE (māt) *n.* a companion; second officer of a vessel. [D.]

MATE (mä'te) *n.* a plant used as a substitute for tea in South America. [Sp.]

MATERIAL (mạ-tē'ri-ạl) *a.* consisting of matter; corporeal; essential; important; —*n.* the substance of which anything is made. [L. *materialis*.]

MATERIALISE (mạ-tē'ri-ạl-īz) *v.t.* to reduce to a state of matter; regard as mere matter.

MATERIALISM (mạ-tē'ri-ạl-izm) *n.* the doctrine of materialists.

MATERIALIST (mạ-tē'ri-ạl-ist) *n.* one who denies the existence of spiritual substances.

MATERIALITY (mạ-tē-ri-al'i-ti) *n.* material existence.

MATERIALLY (mạ-tē'ri-ạl-i) *ad.* in a state of matter; essentially.

MATERNAL (mạ-ter'nạl) *a.* motherly. [Fr. L. *maternus*, pert. to a mother, *mater*.]

MATERNITY (mǝ-tẽr′ni-ti) *n.* state or relation of a mother.

MATH (math) *n.* a mowing. O.E. *mœdh*, fr. *mawan*, **MOW.**

MATHEMATICAL (math′e-mat′i-kǝl) *a.* pertaining to mathematics.

MATHEMATICALLY (math-e-mat′i-kǝl-i) *ad.* by mathematics.

MATHEMATICIAN (math-e-mǝ-tish′ǝn) *n.* one versed in mathematics.

MATHEMATICS (math-e-mat′iks) *n.* the science of quantities, magnitudes, and numbers. [O.F. *mathematique*, fr. L. (acc.) *mathematicam*, fr. G., fr. stem *mathemat-*, of *mathema*, a lesson.]

MATINEE (mat′i-nā) *n.* a morning reception; a morning musical performance. [F.]

MATINS (mat′inz) *n.pl.* morning worship or service. [F., fr. L. (acc.) *matutinum*, in the morning.]

MATRASS (mat′rǎs) *n.* a chemical vessel. [F., of uncert. etym.]

MATRICIDE (mat′ri-sīd) *n.* the murder or murderer of a mother. [F., fr. L., fr. stem *matri-*, of *mater*, and *-cidere* = *cædere*, slay.]

MATRICULATE (mǝ-trik′ū-lāt) *v.t.* to admit to membership, as in a college;—*n.* one entered in a college, etc. [Fr. L. *matricula*, a register, fr. **MATRIX.**]

MATRICULATION (mǝ-trik-ū-lā′shun) *n.* the act of admitting to membership.

MATRIMONIAL (mat-ri-mō′ni ǝl) *a.* pertaining to marriage.

MATRIMONY (mat′ri-mu-ni) *n.* marriage; wedlock. [L. *matrimonium* = orig. maternity, fr. *mater*.]

MATRIX (mā′triks) *n.* the womb; a mould. [L. = womb.]

MATRON (mā′trun) *n.* a married woman, especially an elderly one; female superintendent of an hospital. [L. *matrona*, fr. *mater*.]

MATRONLY (mā′trun-li) *a.* becoming a wife or matron.

MATTER (mat′ẽr) *n.* elementary substance of the earth or of living bodies; things treated of; inducing cause; small amount; affair; concern; pus;—*v.i.* to be of importance; signify; form pus. [O.F. *matiere* = F. *matière*, fr. **MATERIAL.**]

MATTOCK (mat′uk) *n.* a pickaxe. [O.E. *mattuc*.]

MATTRESS (mat′res) *n.* a quilted bed. [O.F., fr. A.]

MATURE (mǝ-tūr′) *a.* ripe; full grown; well digested;—*v.t.* to bring to perfection; prepare for use;—*v.i.* to become payable. [L. *maturus*, ripe, timely.]

Mattock.

MATURELY (mǝ-tūr′li) *ad.* with ripeness.

MATURITY (mǝ-tūr′i-ti) *n.* a mature state; ripeness; full growth; expiry of the time that a bill has to run.

MAUDLIN (mawd′lin) *a.* half-drunk; silly; weakly sentimental. [Fr. O.F. *Maudeleine*, Mary *Magdalen*, painted as weeping.]

MAUL (mawl) *n.* a wooden hammer;—*v.t.* to beat and bruise. [M.E. *mallen*, to beat with a *malle*, fr. F.]

MAUNDER (mawn′dẽr) *v.i.* to mutter; talk incoherently. [Orig. *n.* =beggar, fr. his *maund*, O.E *mand*, basket.]

MAUSOLEUM (maw-sō-lē′um) *n.* a magnificent tomb or monument. [=orig. tomb of *Mausolus*, king of Caria.]

MAUVE (mawv) *n.* a pretty purple or violet colour. [F. =a **MALLOW.**]

MAVIS (mā′vis) *n.* a singing bird; song thrush. [F., fr. Celt.]

MAW (maw) *n.* stomach of a beast. [O.E. *maga*. Cf. Ger. *Magen*.]

MAWKISH (maw′kish) *a.* apt to cause satiety and loathing. [M.E. *mawk*, a maggot, fr. Scand.]

MAXILLARY (mak′si-lar-i) *a.* pertaining to the jawbone. [L., fr. *maxilla*, jawbone.]

MAXIM (mak′sim) *n.* an established principle; adage; proverb. [F., fr. L. *maxima* (*sententiarum*), the greatest (of opinions).]

MAXIMUM (mak′si-mum) *n.* the greatest quantity, number, or degree. [L.]

MAY (mā) (1) *n.* the fifth month of the year; —(2) *v. aux.* [*pret.* **MIGHT**] to be possible; be able; have licence. [(1) F., fr. L. *Maius*. (2) O.E. *mæg*, may, fr. *muyan*, to be able to. Cf. Ger. (*ich*) *mag*.]

MAY-DAY (mā′dā) *n.* the first day of May. [See **MAY** (1).]

MAYOR (mā′ur) *n.* chief magistrate of a corporation. [F. *maire*, fr. L. (acc.) *majorem*, doublet of **MAJOR.**]

MAYORALTY (mā′ur-ǝl-ti) *n.* the office of a mayor.

MAZE (māz) *n.* a labyrinth; confusion of thought;—*v.t.* to bewilder. [Conn. with **AMAZE.**]

MAZURKA (mǝ-zöör′kǝ) *n.* a Polish dance; the music set for it. [Pol.]

MAZY (mā′zi) *a.* intricate; perplexed.

ME (mē) *pron.* objective case of *I*. [O.E. *me*.]

MEAD (mēd) (1) *n.* honey and water fermented and spiced;—(2) *n.* meadow. [(1) O.E. *medu*. (2) O.E. *mæd*; conn. with **MOW, MATH.**]

MEADOW (med′ō) *n.* low or grass land.

MEAGRE (mē′gẽr) *a.* lean; thin; poor. [F. *maigre*, fr. L. (acc.) *macrum*, thin.]

MEAGRELY (mē′gẽr-li) *ad.* poorly; thinly.

MEAGRENESS (mē′gẽr-nes) *n.* leanness; scantiness.

MEAL (mēl) (1) *n.* grain ground to powder; —(2) food taken at one time; act or time of eating. [(1) O.E. *melu*. Cf. Ger. *mahlen*, grind. (2) O.E. *mæl.* Cf. Ger. *Mahl, Mal*, a time.]

MEALY (mē′li) *a.* resembling meal.

MEAN (mēn) (1) *a.* low; base;—(2) *a.* middle; moderate;—*n.* the middle point; rate; degree;—*pl.* medium; instrument; income; —(3) *v.t.* or *i.* to have in view; intend; design; signify. [(1) O.E. (*ge*)*mæne.* Cf. Ger. *gemein*. (2) O.F. *meien* = F. *moyen*, fr. L. (acc.) *medianum*, fr. *medius*, middle. (3) O.E. *mænan*. Cf. Ger. *meinen*.]

MEANDER (mē-an′dẽr) *n.* a winding course; —*v.i.* to run in windings. [L., fr. G. *Maiandros*, a winding river in Asia Minor.]

MEANING (mē′ning) *n.* intention; signification. [See **MEAN** (3).]

MEANINGLESS (mē′ning-les) *a.* wanting meaning. [See **MEAN** (3).]

MEANLY (mēn′li) *ad.* without dignity. [See **MEAN** (1).]

MEANNESS (mēn′nes) *n.* lowness; sordidness; baseness. [See **MEAN** (1).]

MEANT (ment) *pret.* and *pp.* of **MEAN.** [See **MEAN** (3).]

MEANTIME (mēn′tim) *ad.* in the intervening time. [See **MEAN** (2).]

MEASLED (mē′zld) *a.* infected with measles.

MEASLES (mē zlz) *n.* an eruptive disease. [M.E. *maseles*, fr. O.E. *mæsle*, a spot.]

MEASURABLE (mezh′ur-ǝ-bl) *a.* that may be measured.

MEASURE (mezh′ur) *n.* that which measures; extent; time in music; degree; means to an end;—*v.t.* to ascertain extent or quantity of; estimate; adjust; allot;—*v.i.* to have a certain extent. [O.F. *mesure*, fr. L. (acc.) *mensuram*, measure. See **MENSURATION.**]

MEASURELESS (mezh′ur-les) *a.* boundless.

MEASUREMENT (mezh′ur-ment) *n.* act of measuring; dimensions.

MEASURER (mezh'ur-ẹr) *n.* one who measures.

MEAT (mēt) *n.* food in general; flesh for food. [O.E. *mete.*]

MECHANIC (me-kan'ik) *n.* artisan. [L., fr. G. *mechanike,* science of machines. See **MACHINE.**]

MECHANICAL (me-kan'i-kạl) *a.* pertaining to machines; acting by physical power; without thought; unconscious; pertaining to artisans.

MECHANICALLY (me-kan'i-kạl-i) *ad.* by physical force; unconsciously.

MECHANICIAN (mek-ạ-nish'ạn) *n.* one skilled in mechanics.

MECHANICS (me-kan'iks) *n.* the science that treats of the laws of motion and force.

MECHANISM (mek'ạ-nizm) *n.* structure of a machine.

MECHANIST (mek'ạ-nist) *n.* one skilled in machines.

MECHLIN (mek'lin) *n.* a fine kind of lace, made at Mechlin (Malines), in Belgium.

MEDAL (med'ạl) *n.* a coin with a device. [O.F. *medaille,* through late L. forms, fr. L. *metallum,* **METAL.**]

MEDALLIST (med'ạl-ist) *n.* a person skilled in medals.

MEDDLE (med'l) *v.i.* to interpose; interfere officiously. [Fr. O.F. *medler,* for *mesler* = F. *mêler,* to mix, fr. L. *misculare,* fr. *miscere,* mix.]

MEDDLER (med'lẹr) *n.* a busybody.

MEDDLESOME (med'l-sum) *a.* apt to meddle.

MEDIÆVAL (med-i-ē'vạl) *a.* relating to the middle ages. Also **MEDIEVAL.** [Fr. L. *medius,* middle, and *ævum,* age.]

MEDIAL (mēd'yạl) *a.* noting a mean or average. [L. fr. *medius,* middle.]

MEDIATE (mē di-āt) *v.t.* or *i.* to interpose between two parties as a friend of both; arbitrate; intercede; (mē'-di-ạt) *a.* middle. [L. (part.) *mediatus,* halved, fr. *medius.*]

MEDIATELY (mē'di-ạt-li) *ad.* by a secondary cause.

MEDIATION (mē-di-ā'shun) *n.* agency between parties; interposition; intercession.

MEDIATOR (mē'di-ā-tẹr) *n.* an intercessor. (L.)

MEDIATORIAL (mē-di-ạ-tō'rí-ạl) *a.* belonging to a mediator.

MEDIATORSHIP (mē'di-ā-tur-ship) *n.* office of a mediator.

MEDICABLE (med'i-kạ-bl) *a.* capable of being cured.

MEDICAL (med'i-kạl) *a.* pertaining to the art of healing. [Fr. L. *medicus,* physician, fr. *mederi,* to heal.]

MEDICAMENT (med'i-kạ-ment) *n.* a healing application. [L. *medica-mentum.*]

MEDICATE (med'i-kāt) *v.t.* to tincture with medicines; treat with medicine.

MEDICINAL (me-dis'i-nạl) *a.* healing.

MEDICINALLY (me-dis'i-nạl-i) *ad.* by medicine.

MEDICINE (med'i-sin, med'sin) *n.* anything that cures; a remedy. [O.F. *medecine,* fr. L. (acc.) *medicinam.*]

MEDIOCRE (mē-di-ō'kẹr) *a.* of moderate degree. [F., fr. L. (acc.) *mediocrem,* fr. *medius.*]

MEDIOCRITY (mē-di-ok'ri-ti) *n.* middle state; moderate degree.

MEDITATE (med'i-tāt) *v.t.* or *i.* to think; muse; contemplate. [L. (part.) *meditatus,* having pondered, fr. *meditari*]

MEDITATION (med-i-tā'shun) *n.* contemplation; continued thought.

MEDITATIVE (med'i-tā-tiv) *a.* given to contemplation.

MEDIUM (mē'di-um) *a.* middle;—*n.* a means or instrument; middle term;—*pl.* **MEDIA** or **MEDIUMS.** [L. (neut.) =a mean.]

MEDLAR (med'lẹr) *n.* a small tree and its fruit. [O.F. *meslier,* the tree, fr. *mesle,* the fruit, fr. L. (acc.) *mespilum,* fr. G.

MEDLEY (med'li) *n.* a mixture; a miscellany. [O.F. (part.) *medle,* confused, fr. *medler* for *mesler.* See **MEDDLE.**]

MEDOC (me-dok') *n.* a French red wine from *Médoc,* Gironde, France.

MEDULLA (me-dul'ạ) *n.* marrow; pith. [L.]

MEDULLARY (me-dul'ạr-i) *a.* consisting of marrow, or resembling it.

MEED (mēd) *n.* a reward; recompense. [O.E. *med.* Cf. Ger. *Miethe.*]

MEEK (mēk) *a.* mild; soft; gentle. [Scand.]

MEEKLY (mēk'li) *ad.* mildly; softly.

MEEKNESS (mēk'nes) *n.* mildness of temper; gentleness.

MEERSCHAUM (mēr'shawm) *n.* sea-scum; a mineral; a kind of tobacco-pipe. [Ger. =sea-foam.]

MEET (mēt) *v.t.* or *i.* [*pret.* and *pp.* **MET**] to come together; join; receive; satisfy; assemble;—(2) *a.* fit; suitable. [(1) O.E. *metan,* fr. *mot,* **MOOT.** (2) O.E. *gemet,* fit. See **METE.**]

MEETING (mē'ting) *n.* an assembly; an interview. [See **MEET** (1).]

MEETLY (mēt'li) *ad.* fitly; suitably; duly. [See **MEET** (2).]

MELANCHOLY (mel'ạn-kol-i) *a.* dejected;—*n.* dejection of spirits. [F. *mélancolie.*]

MELEE (mā-lā') *n.* a confused fight; scuffle. [F., fr. O.F. *mesle,* **MEDLEY.**]

MELIORATE (mēl'yu-rāt) *v.t.* to make better. [L. (part.) *melioratus,* made better, fr. *melior,* better.]   [ment.

MELIORATION (mēl-yu-rā'shun) *n.* improve-

MELLIFEROUS (me-lif'e-rus) *a.* producing honey. [L. stem *melli-,* of *mel,* honey, and *-ferus,* bearing, fr *ferre.*]

MELLIFLUOUS (me-lif'lŏŏ-us) *a.* sweetly flowing. [Fr. L. *-fluus,* flowing, fr. *fluere.*]

MELLOW (mel'ō) *a.* soft with ripeness;—*v.t.* or *i.* to ripen to softness. [E.; conn. with **MEALY.**]   [ness.

MELLOWNESS (mel'ō-nes) *n.* softness; ripe-

MELODEON (me-lō'de-un) *n.* an organ with metallic reeds. [See **MELODY.**]

MELODIOUS (me-lō'di-us) *a.* sounding sweetly; harmonious.

MELODISE (mel'u-dīz) *v.t.* to make melodious.

MELODY (mel'u-di) *n.* an agreeable succession of sounds; air; tune. [O.F. *melodie,* fr. L. (acc.) *melodiam,* fr. G. *melos,* and *ode,* song. ODE.]

MELON (mel'un) *n.* a plant and its edible fruit. [F., fr. L., fr. G. *melon,* apple.]

MELT (melt) *v.t.* or *i.* to dissolve; soften; dissipate; become mild. [O.E. *meltan.*]

MELTINGLY (mel'ting-li) *ad.* so as to melt.

MEMBER (mem'bẹr) *n.* a limb of the body; one of a society or legislature. [F. *membre,* fr. L. *membrum.*]

MEMBERSHIP (mem'bẹr-ship) *n.* the state of being a member.

MEMBRANE (mem'brān) *n.* a thin animal or vegetable tissue which covers the organs or parts. [L. *membrana,* parchment, lit. the skin of a limb, **MEMBER.**]

MEMENTO (me-men'tō) *n.* that which reminds;—*pl.* **MEMENTOES.** [L. (imper.) = remember, fr. *meminisse.*]

MEMOIR (mem'wor, mem'oir) *n.* a written account of personal recollections or the transactions of a society; short sketch. [O.F. Doublet of **MEMORY.**]

MEMORABILIA (mem-u-rạ-bil'i-ạ) *n.pl.* things to be remembered. [L. (neut. pl.)]

MEMORABLE (mem'u-rạ-bl) *a.* worthy of remembrance. [F., fr. L. *memorabilis.*]

MEMORABLY (mem'u-rạ-bli) *ad.* in a way to be remembered.

MEMORANDUM (mem-u-ran'dum) *n.* a note to help the memory;—*pl.* **MEMORANDA.**

MEMORIAL (me-mō'ri-ạl) *a.* preserving remembrance;—*n.* that which preserves remembrance; statement with petition.

MEMORIALISE (me-mō′ri-al-īz) *v.t.* to present a memorial to.

MEMORIALIST (me-mō′ri-al-ist) *n.* one who presents a memorial.

MEMORISE (mem′u-riz) *v.t.* to cause to be remembered.

MEMORY (mem′u-ri) *n.* the faculty by which ideas are retained in the mind; recollection. [O.F. *memorie* = F. *mémoire*, fr. L. (acc.) *memoriam*, fr. *memor*, mindful.]

MEN (men) *pl.* of MAN.

MENACE (men′as) *v.t.* to threaten;—*n.* a threat. [O.F., fr. L. stem *minac-*, of *minax*, full of threats, *minœ*.]

MENACINGLY (men′as-ing-li) *ad.* in a threatening way.

MENAGE (me-näzh′) *n.* housekeeping; a household; training of horses. [F.]

MENAGERIE (me-naj′e-ri) *n.* a collection of wild or exotic animals. [F., fr. *ménager*, to keep house, through Late L. forms, fr. L. *mansio*, MANSION.]

MEND (mend) *v.t.* or *i.* to repair; correct; improve. [Short. fr. AMEND.]

MENDACIOUS (men-dā′shus) *a.* given to deception; lying; false. [Fr. L. stem *mendac-*, fr. *mendax*, lying.]

MENDACITY (men-das′i-ti) *n.* falsehood.

MENDER (men′dėr) *n.* one who repairs.

MENDICANT (men′di-kant) *n.* a beggar. [L. (part. stem) *mendicant-*, begging, fr. *mendicare*, fr. *mendicus*, beggar.]

MENDICITY (men-dis′i-ti) *n.* state of beggary; life of a beggar.

MENIAL (mēn′yal) *a.* servile; mean;—*n.* an inferior servant; a mean-spirited fellow. [Fr. O.F. *mesnee*, household, MENAGE.]

MENSTRUAL (men′strŏŏ-al) *a.* monthly. [Fr. L. *menstruus*, monthly.]

MENSURABLE (men′shū-ra-bl) *a.* measurable.

MENSURATION (men-shū-rā′shun) *n.* act of measuring. [L. (acc.) *mensurationem*, fr. (part.) *mensuratus*, fr. *mensura*, MEASURE.]

MENTAL (men′tal) *a.* belonging to the mind. [Fr. L. stem *ment-*, of *mens*, mind.]

MENTALLY (men′tal-i) *ad.* in mind.

MENTION (men′shun) *n.* notice; remark;—*v.t.* to notice briefly; name. [F., fr. L. (acc.) *mentionem*, fr. *mens*, mind.]

MENTIONABLE (men′shun-a-bl) *a.* that may be mentioned.

MENTOR (men′tėr) *n.* a wise adviser or monitor. [Fr. G. *Mentor*, tutor of Telemachus.]

MENU (men′ū) *n.* a bill of fare. [F. = small, fr. L. (acc.) *minutum*, MINUTE.]

MERCANTILE (mėr′kan-tīl) *a.* commercial. [F., fr. Late L. (part. stem) *mercant-*, trading, fr. *mercari*.]

MERCATOR'S CHART (mėr-kā′turs chärt) *n.* a map of the earth's surface upon a plane projection. [Fr. *Mercator*, a geographer.]

MERCENARY (mėr′se-nar-i) *a.* that may be hired; greedy of gain; venal;—*n.* a soldier hired for foreign service. [L. *merce(d)narius*, fr. stem *merced-*, of *merces*, wages.]

MERCER (mėr′sėr) *n.* one who deals in silks. [F., *mercier*, trader, fr. Late L. (acc.) *mercerium*, fr. stem *merc-*, of L. *merx*, goods.]

MERCERY (mėr′sėr-i) *n.* the goods of mercers.

MERCHANDISE (mėr′chan-dīz) *n.* goods for sale; trade. [F. *marchandise*.]

MERCHANT (mėr′chant) *n.* an exporter or importer of goods; a trader on a large scale;—*a.* pertaining to trade; trading. [O.F. *marchant*, fr. L. (acc. part.) *mercantem*, trading, fr. *mercari*.]

MERCHANTABLE (mėr′chant-a-bl) *a.* fit for sale.

MERCHANTMAN (mėr′chant-man) *n.* a ship employed in trade.

MERCIFUL (mėr′si-fool) *a.* compassionate; forgiving; tender.   [passion.

MERCIFULLY (mėr′si-fool-i) *ad.* with com-

MERCILESS (mėr′si-les) *a.* hard-hearted; unfeeling; cruel.   [cruelly.

MERCILESSLY (mėr′si-les-li) *ad.* unsparingly;

MERCURIAL (mėr-kū′ri-al) *a.* composed of quicksilver; spirited; active.

MERCURY (mėr′kū-ri) *n.* the name of a Roman divinity; quicksilver; the planet nearest the sun. [L. *Mercurius*, Mercury.]

MERCY (mėr′si) *n.* tenderness toward an offender; pardon; grace; act of kindness; discretion. [O.F. *merci*, fr. Late L. *mercedem*, mercy. See MERCENARY.

MERE (mēr) (1) *a.* pure; unmixed; alone; absolute. (2) (mēr) *n.* a pool or lake. [(1) L. *merus*, undiluted. (2) O.E. *mere*. Cf. Ger. *Meer*, sea. See MERMAID.]

MERELY (mēr′li) *ad.* singly; only.

MERETRICIOUS (mer-e-trish′us) *a.* lewd; gaudy, showy, and deceitful. [L., fr. stem *meretric-*, of *meretrix*, fr. *merere*, to receive hire.]

MERGANSER (mėr-gan′sėr) *n.* a sea duck. [Fr. L. See MERGE.]

MERGE (mėrj) *v.t.* or *i.* to immerse; be lost in. [L. *mergere*.]

MERIDIAN (me-rid′yan) *n.* a great circle which the sun crosses at noon; noon. [L. *meridianus*, fr. *meridies* = *medidies*, midday, fr. *medius*, and *dies*.]

MERIDIONAL (me-rid′yu-nal) *a.* pertaining to the meridian.

MERINO (me-rē′nō) *n.* a variety of sheep or th ir wool; a thin cloth made of the wool. [Sp.]

MERIT (mėr′it) *n.* desert; worth; reward;—*v.t.* to earn by services; deserve. [O.F., fr. L. *meritum*, desert, fr. *merere*.]

MERITED (mėr′i-ted) *a.* deserved; earned.

MERITORIOUS (mėr-i-tō′ri-us) *a.* deserving reward. [L. *meritorius*.]

MERK (mėrk) *n.* an old Scottish silver coin. [See MARK.]

MERLE (mėrl) *n.* a blackbird. [O.F., fr. L. (acc.) *merulam*.]

MERMAID (mėr′mād) *n.* a fabled sea-woman. [E. = MERE (2), and MAID.]

MERRILY (mėr′i-li) *ad.* with mirth.

MERRIMENT (mėr′i-ment) *n.* gaiety with laughter; noisy sport.

MERRY (mėr′i) *a.* gay; jovial; sportive; cheerful. [M.E. *merie*, fr. O.E. *myrge*, *myrige*.]

MESENTERY (mes′en-tėr-i) *n.* a membrane in the intestines. [Fr. G.]

MESH (mesh) *n.* a space between threads in a net;—*v.t.* to catch in a net. [M.E. *maske*, fr. O.E. *max*.]

MESHY (mesh′i) *a.* formed like network.

MESMERIC (mez-mėr′ik) *a.* relating to or by mesmerism.

MESMERISE (mez′mėr-iz) *v.t.* to cause the patient to fall into a trance or sleep, and seem to influence his thoughts and actions.

MESMERISM (mez′mėr-izm) *n.* animal magnetism; magnetic sleep. [Fr. *Mesmer*, a German quack.]   [merises.

MESMERIST (mez′mėr-ist) *n.* one who mesmerises.

MESS (mes) (1) *n.* a dish of food; a company who eat together;—*v.i.* to join in a mess; —(2) *n.* medley; confusion. [(1) O.F. *mes*, fr. L. (neut. part.) *missum*, that which is sent, fr. *mittere*. (2) Corr. fr. *mesh*, for MASH.]

MESSAGE (mes′ij) *n.* notice sent; official communication; errand. [F., fr. Late L. *missaticum*, fr. (part.) *missus*, sent, fr. *mittere*, to send.]

MESSENGER (mes'en-jer) *n.* one who bears a message; a harbinger. [M.E. *messager.*]

MESSIAH (me-sī'ạ) *n.* the anointed; *Christ.* [H. =anointed.]

MESSIANIC (mes-i-an'ik) *a.* relating to the Messiah.

MESSIAHSHIP (me-sī'ạ-ship) *n.* office of the Messiah.

MESSMATE (mes'māt) *n.* one who eats ordinarily at the same table. [See MESS (1).]

MESSUAGE (mes'wij) *n.* a house and adjoining land. [O.F.; form of MENAGE.]

METAL (met'ạl) *n.* a simple, fixed, opaque substance fusible by heat, as iron, etc. [O.F., fr. L., fr. G. *metallon,* a mine, metal.]

METALLIC (me-tal'ik) *a.* partaking of metal.

METALLIFEROUS (met-ạ-lif'e-rus) *a.* producing metals. [Fr. L. *-ferus,* bearing, fr. *ferre.*]

METALLINE (met'ạl-īn) *a.* like metal.

METALLIST (met'ạl-ist) *n.* one skilled in metals.

METALLURGIC (met-ạ-lur'jik) *a.* pertaining to metallurgy.

METALLURGY (met'ạ-lur-ji) *n.* art of separating and refining metals. [O.F., fr. Late L. *metallurgia,* fr. G. *metallourgia,* fr. *metallon,* and *ergon,* work.]

METAMORPHOSE (met-ạ-mor'fōz) *v.t.* to transform or change the shape of.

METAMORPHOSIS (met-ạ-mor'fō-sis) *n.* change of form or structure; transformation. [L., fr. G., fr. *meta,* denoting change, and *morphoein,* to form.]

METAPHOR (met'ạ-fur) *n.* a similitude. [L., fr. G. *metaphora,* transference, fr. *meta,* over, and *pherein,* carry.]

METAPHORICAL (met-ạ-for'i-kạl) *a.* containing a metaphor; figurative.

METAPHORICALLY (met-ạ-for'i-kạl-i) *ad.* by a figure.

METAPHYSICAL (met-ạ-fiz'i-kạl) *a.* according to metaphysics; abstract.

METAPHYSICIAN (met-ạ-fiz-ish'ạn) *n.* one versed in metaphysics.

METAPHYSICS (met-ạ-fiz'iks) *n.* science of the mind. [G. *meta (ta) phusika,* after (the) physics, because the study came after physics in Aristotle's *Organon.*]

METE (mēt) *v.t.* to measure; —*n.* measure; boundary. [O.E. *metan.* Cf. *messen.*]

METEOR (mē'te-ur) *n.* a luminous body passing in the air; any transient wonder. [G. *meteoron,* lit. anything heavenly or atmospheric.]

METEORIC (mē-te-or'ik) *a.* pertaining to or proceeding from meteors.

METEOROLITE (mē'te-ur-u-līt) *n.* a meteoric stone. [Fr. G. *lithos,* stone.]

METEOROLOGICAL (mē-te-ur-u-loj'i-kạl) *a.* pertaining to meteorology.

METEOROLOGY (mē-te-ur-ol'ō-ji) *n.* the science of the atmosphere. [G. *meteoron,* and *-logia,* science, fr. *legein.*]

METER (mē'ter) *n.* an instrument for measuring. [See METE.]

METHINKS (mē-thingks') *v.imp.* it seems to me. [E., fr. O.E. *thyncan,* to seem.]

METHOD (meth'ud) *n.* orderly arrangement; way of doing things; mode; manner. [Fr. F. *méthode,* fr. L. (acc.) *methodum,* lit. an inquiry, fr. G., fr. *meth =meta,* after, and *hodos,* a way.]

METHODICAL (me-thod'i-kạl) *a.* exhibiting method; orderly; formal.

METHODICALLY (me-thod'i-kạl-i) *ad.* in due order.

METHODISE (meth'ud-īz) *v.t.* to reduce to method.

METHODISM (meth'ud-izm) *n.* doctrines and worship of Methodists, founded by Wesley.

METHODIST (meth'ud-ist) *n.* an adherent to Methodism.

METHODISTIC (meth-u-dis'tik) *a.* resembling the Methodists.

METRE (mē'ter) *n.* verse; harmonic measure. [F., fr. L., fr. G. *metron,* measure.]

METRIC (met'rik) *a.* denoting the French system of weights and measures; decimal. [F. *métrique,* fr. L., fr. G. *metrikos.*]

METRICAL (met'ri-kạl) *a.* pertaining to poetic measure.

METRONOME (met'ru-nōm) *n.* an instrument to measure the time of a musical note or bar. [Fr. G. *nomos,* law, division.]

METROPOLIS (me-trop'u-lis) *n.* chief city. [G. =mother-city, fr. *metro-,* for *meter,* mother, and *polis,* city.]

METROPOLITAN (met-ru-pol'i-tạn) *a.* pertaining to the chief city; —*n.* an archbishop.

METTLE (met'l) *n.* substance; stuff; spirit; courage. [Form of METAL.]

METTLESOME (met'l-sum) *a.* spirited.

MEW (mū) (1) *n.* a kind of sea-gull; —(2) *n.* a cage or coop; —*pl.* stables; —*v.t.* to shut up; —*v.i.* to cast the feathers; moult; —(3) *n.* the cry of a cat; —*v.t.* to cry as a cat. [(1) O.E. *mœw.* Cf. Ger. *Möwe.* (2) O.F. *muer,* to moult, fr. L. *mutare.* (3) Imit.]

MEWL (mūl) *v.i.* to cry as a child. [F. *miauler;* imit.]

MEZZO (med'zō) *a.* middle. [It.]

MEZZOTINT (med'zō, mez'o-tint) *n.* an engraving on copper, effected by scraping and burnishing. [It.]

MIASMA (mi-az'mạ) *n.* noxious effluvia. [G., fr. *mici-mein,* to stain.]

MICHAELMAS (mik'el-mạs) *n.* feast of St Michael, 29th September.

MICROBE (mī'krōb) *n.* a minute organism; a bacterium. [G. *mikros,* small, and *bios,* life.]

MICROPHONE (mī'kru-fōn) *n.* an instrument to make faint sounds more audible. [Fr. G. *mikros,* and *phone,* voice.]

MICROSCOPE (mī'kru-skōp) *n.* an optical instrument for magnifying. [G. *mikros,* and *skopein,* to see.]

MICROSCOPIC (mī-kru-skop'ik) *a.* very small. [MID (mid) *a.* middle; intervening. [O.E. *mid, midd.*]

MIDDAY (mid'dā) *n.* noon.

MIDDEN (mid'n) *n.* a heap of dung, ashes, etc. [Scand.]

MIDDLE (mid'l) *a.* equally distant from the ends; intermediate; —*n.* the point equally remote from the extremes. [O.E. *middel,* fr. MID. Cf. Ger. *Mitte.*]

MIDDLING (mid'ling) *a.* of middle rank, quality, size, etc.; moderate.

MIDGE (mij) *n.* a small kind of fly. [M.E. *migge,* O.E. *micg.* Cf. Ger. *Mücke.*]

MIDLAND (mid'lạnd) *a.* being in the interior of a country.

MIDNIGHT (mid'nīt) *n.* twelve o'clock at night; —*a.* very dark.

MIDRIFF (mid'rif) *n.* the diaphragm. [Fr. O.E. *hrif,* the belly.]

MIDSHIPMAN (mid'ship-mạn) *n.* a naval cadet or young officer. [See MID.]

MIDST (midst) *n.* the middle; —*ad.* in the middle. [M.E.]

MIDWAY (mid'wā) *n.* the middle; —*a.* or *ad.* in the middle.

MIDWIFERY (mid'wif-ri) *n.* assistance in child-birth.

MIEN (mēn) *n.* look; air; manner; bearing. [F. *mine,* perh. fr. Celt.]

MIGHT (mīt) (1) *pret.* of MAY; —(2) *n.* power; strength; force. [(1) O.E. *mihte.* (2) O.E. *miht.* Cf. Ger. *Macht* and MIGHT (1).]

MIGHTILY (mī'ti-li) *ad.* powerfully.

MIGHTINESS (mī'ti-nes) *n.* power; a title of dignity.

MIGHTY (mī'ti) *a.* powerful; vigorous; valiant; huge; important; wonderful.

MIGNONETTE (min-yu-net') *n.* a fragrant plant. [F. See MINION.]

MIGRATE (mī'grāt) *v.i.* to remove to a distant country. [L. (part.) *migratus,* fr. *migrare.*]

MIGRATION (mī-grā'shun) *n.* act of migrating.
MIGRATORY (mī'grạ-tur-i) *a.* disposed to migrate.
MILCH (milsh) *a.* giving milk. [Form of **MILK.**]
MILD (mīld) *a.* gentle; calm; soft; moderate; mellow. [E.]
MILDEW (mil'dū) *n.* a fungus growth or coating on leaves, cloth paper, etc.;—*v.t.* or *i.* to taint with mildew. [O.E. *mele, mildeaw*, lit., honey-dew. Cf. L. *mel*.]
MILDLY (mīld'li) *ad.* gently; softly.
MILDNESS (mīld'nes) *n.* quality of being mild; gentleness.
MILE (mīl) *n.* a linear measure of 320 rods, 1760 yards, or 5280 feet. [O.E. *mīl*, fr. L. (pl.) *millia*, a thousand (paces).]
MILEAGE (mīl'ij) *n.* fees for travel by the mile.
MILITANT (mil'i-tạnt) *a.* engaged in warfare; fighting. [L. (part. stem) *militant-*, serving in arms, fr. stem *milit-*, of *miles*.]
MILITARY (mil'i tạr-i) *a.* suiting a soldier;— *n.* soldiers; the army.
MILITATE (mil'i-tāt) *v.i.* to contend against; be inconsistent with.
MILITIA (mi-lish'ạ) *n.* national military force. [L. = warfare, troops.]
MILK (milk) *n.* a white liquor drawn from the female of certain animals, and from plants; —*v.t.* to draw milk. [O.E. *meolc*. Cf. Ger. *Milch*; **MILCH**.]
MILKER (mil'kẹr) *n.* one that milks.
MILKINESS (mil'ki-nes) *n.* qualities like milk; softness.
MILKMAID (milk'mād) *n.* a woman employed in a dairy.
MILKMAN (milk'mạn) *n.* a man that carries milk to market.
MILK-PAIL (milk'pāl) *n.* a vessel for milk.
MILKSOP (milk'sop) *n.* bread steeped in milk; a weak, effeminate person. [Fr. **SOP.**]
MILK-WHITE (milk'whīt) *a.* pure; spotless.
MILKY (mil'ki) *a.* made of or like milk.
MILKYWAY (mil'ki-wā) *n.* a white track in the heavens; galaxy.
MILL (mil) *n.* a machine for grinding; a manufactory;—*v.t.* to grind; stamp coin; full, as cloth. [O.E. *mylen*, fr. Late L. *mulina*, fr. L. *mola*.]
MILL-COG (mil'kog) *n.* cog of a mill-wheel.
MILL-DAM (mil'dam) *n.* a dam to keep water for a mill. Also **MILL-POND.**
MILLED (mild) *a.* grained and stamped as coin; fulled, as cloth.
MILLENARIAN (mil-e-nā'ri-ạn) *n.* one who believes in the millennium.
MILLENARY (mil'e-nạr-i) *a.* consisting of a thousand. [L. *millenarius*.]
MILLENNIAL (mi-len'i-ạl) *a.* pertaining to the millennium.
MILLENNIUM (mi-len'i-um) *n.* the thousand years of Christ's reign on earth. [L., fr. *mille*, a thousand, and *annus*, a year.]
MILLEPORE (mil-e-pōr) *n.* a kind of coral. [L. *mille*, a thousand, and *porus*, passage.]
MILLER (mil'ẹr) *n.* one who attends a mill.
MILLET (mil'et) *n.* a kind of grass yielding an edible grain; the grain itself. [F., dim. fr. *mil*, fr. L. *milium*, millet.]
MILLINER (mil'i-nẹr) *n.* one who makes ladies' caps and hats. [For *Milaner*, trader in Milan wares.]
MILLINERY (mil'i-nẹr-i) *n.* head-dresses.
MILLION (mil'yun) *n.* ten hundred thousand. [F., fr. Late L. (acc.) *millionem*, fr. L. *mille*.]
MILLIONAIRE (mil-yun-ār') *n.* one worth a million of money.
MILLIPEDE (mil'i-ped) *n.* an insect having many feet. [L. *mille*, a thousand, and *pes, pedis*, foot.]
MILL-RACE (mil'rās) *n.* a canal to convey water to a mill-wheel.

MILLSTONE (mil'stōn) *n.* one of two stones used in grinding corn.
MILLWRIGHT (mil'rīt) *n.* a mechanic who makes or repairs mills.
MILT (milt) *n.* the spleen; roe of fishes. [O.E. *milte*.]
MIME (mīm) *n.* a mimic actor. [L., fr. G. *mimos*.]
MIMETIC (mi-met'ik) *a.* apt to imitate; imitative.
MIMIC (mim'ik) *n.* one who imitates;—*v.t.* to imitate for sport; ape. [L., fr. G. *mimikos*.]
MIMICKER (mim'i-kẹr) *n.* one who mimics.
MIMICRY (mim'ik-ri) *n.* ludicrous imitation for sport.
MIMOSA (mi-mō'sạ) *n.* a leguminous plant. [G., fr. **MIME.**]
MINARET (min'ạ-ret) *n.* a small spire. [Sp., fr. A. = lighthouse.]
MINATORY (min'ạ-tur-i) *a.* threatening. [L. *minatorius*, fr. (part.) *minatus*, having **MENACED.**]
MINCE (mins) *v.t.* or *i.* to chop into small pieces; clip; suppress; walk with short steps. [O.E. *minsian*, fr. *min*, small. Cf. F. *mince*, L. *minor*.]
MINCINGLY (mins'ing-li) *ad.* in small parts; affectedly.
MIND (mīnd) *n.* the intelligent power in man; purpose; opinion; inclination; remembrance;—*v.t.* to heed; regard. [O.E. *gemynd*, fr. *munan*, think.]
MINDED (mīn'ded) *a.* disposed; inclined.
MINDFUL (mīnd'fool) *a.* regardful; attentive; observant.
MINE (mīn) (1) *a.* belonging to me;—(2) *n.* a pit where minerals are dug; an excavation;—*v.t.* or *i.* to dig; sap. [(1) O.E., fr. *min*, of me. (2) F., fr. Celt.]
MINER (mī'nẹr) *n.* one who digs mines.
MINERAL (min'e-rạl) *n.* a substance not organic, existing on or in the earth;—*a.* impregnated with mineral substances. [O.F. fr. **MINE** (2).]
MINERALISE (min'e-rạl-īz) *v.t.* or *i.* to combine with a metal in forming an ore; seek minerals.
MINERALOGICAL (min-e-rạ-loj'i-kạl) *a.* pertaining to mineralogy.
MINERALOGIST (min-e-ral'ō-jist) *n.* one versed in minerals.
MINERALOGY (min-e-ral'ō-ji) *n.* the science of minerals. [**MINE** (2), and G. *-logia*, science, fr. *legein*.]
MINERVA (mi-nẹr'vạ) *n.* the goddess of wisdom, war, and liberal arts. [L.]
MINGLE (ming'gl) *v.t.* or *i.* to mix; blend. [O.E. *mengan*.]
MINIATURE (min'i-tūr) *n.* a small likeness;—*a.* on a small scale. [It., fr. (part.) *miniato*, painted (with cinnabar), fr. L. *minium* (much used in illuminating MSS.), paint.]
MINIM (min'im) *n.* a dwarf; a note in music; a small liquid measure; a drop. [O.F. *minime*, fr. L. See **MINIMUM.**]
MINIMISE (min'i-mīz) *v.t.* to reduce to the smallest degree.
MINIMUM (min'i-mum) *n.* the least quantity;—*pl.* **MINIMA.** [L. superl. Cf. **MINOR.**] **Minim.**
MINION (min'yun) *n.* a favourite; a small type. [F. *mignon*, of uncert. etym.]
MINISTER (min'is-tẹr) *n.* an agent; an ambassador; a pastor;—*v.t.* or *i.* to give; communicate; supply; serve. [L.]
MINISTERIAL (min-is-tē'ri-ạl) *a.* pertaining to a minister; acting under authority; sacerdotal.
MINISTRATION (min-is-trā'shun) *n.* office of a minister; service.

Fäte, fär, ạdo; mē, hẹr; mīne; nōte; tūne; mōōn.　　　　H

MINISTRY (min'is-tri) *n.* office; service; ecclesiastical function; ministers of state. [L. *ministerium*.]

MINIVER (min'i-vĕr) *n.* the fur of the Siberian squirrel. [O.F. *menu vair*, fr. MENU, and L. (acc.) *varium*, variegated.]

MINNOW (min'ō) *n.* a small fresh-water fish. [M.E. *menow*, fr. O.E. *myne*.]

MINOR (mī'nẹr) *a.* less; smaller; lower in tone;—*n.* a person under the age of twenty-one. [L. (comp.). Cf. MINIMUM.]

MINORITY (mī-nor'i-ti) *n.* state of being under age; smaller number. [F. *minorité*.]

MINOTAUR (min'u-tawr) *n.* a fabled monster, half man, half bull. [G.]

MINSTER (min'stẹr) *n.* a cathedral. [O.E. *mynster*, fr. L. =MONASTERY.]

MINSTREL (min'strel) *n.* a singer and player on an instrument. [O.F. *menestrel*, fr. Late L. (acc.) *ministralem*, retainer, fr. L. MINISTER.]

MINSTRELSY (min'strel-si) *n.* art or work of a minstrel; a volume of songs; a body of minstrels.

MINT (mint) (1) *n.* the place where money is coined; a place of invention or production; —*v.t.* to coin; invent;—(2) *n.* an aromatic plant. [(1) O.E. *mynet*, fr. L. *moneta*. See MONEY. (2) O.E. *minte*, fr. L. *menta*, fr. G. *mintha*.]

MINTAGE (min'tij) *n.* that which is coined or stamped; duty paid for coining. [See MINT (1).]

MINUEND (min'ū-end) *n.* the number from which another is to be subtracted. [L. (gerund.) *minuendus*, to be lessened, fr. *minuere*.]

MINUET (min'ū-et) *n.* a graceful dance. [O.F. *menuet* (3-syll.), dim. fr. MENU.]

MINUS (mī'nus) *a.* an algebraic term denoting subtraction; less. [L.]

MINUTE (min'it) *n.* (1) the sixtieth part of an hour or degree; short note or sketch;— *v.t.* to set down in short notes or minutes; (2) (mi-nūt') *a.* very small; single; slight; particular; detailed. [(1) See MINUTE (2). (2) Fr., fr. L. *minutus*. Cf. MINOR.]

MINUTE-BOOK (min'it-book) *n.* a book for short notes. [See MINUTE (1).]

MINUTE-GUN (min'it-gun) *n.* a gun fired every minute. [See MINUTE (1).]

MINUTELY (mi-nūt'li) *ad.* to a small point. [See MINUTE (2).]

MINUTENESS (mi-nūt'nes) *n.* smallness.

MINUTIÆ (mi-nū'shi-ē) *n.pl.* less important details; trifling particulars. [L.]

MINX (mingks) *n.* a pert, forward girl. [O. H. Ger. *minni*, love, affection. Conn. with MIGNON, which see.]

MIRACLE (mir'ạ-kl) *n.* an act or event beyond human power. [F., fr. L. *miraculum*, fr. *mirare*, wonder.]

MIRACULOUS (mir-ak'ū-lus) *a.* supernatural; wonderful.

MIRAGE (mi-räzh') *n.* an optical illusion, presenting an image of water in sandy deserts, or elevating objects in the air. [F., fr. *mirer*, to look at. See ADMIRE.]

MIRE (mīr) *n.* soft, wet earth; mud;—*v.t.* to fix in mud. [Scand.]

MIRROR (mir'ur) *n.* a looking-glass; an exemplar;—*v.t.* to reflect. [O.F. *mireor* (3 syll.), fr. *mirer*. See MIRAGE.]

MIRTH (mẹrth) *n.* noisy gaiety; glee; hilarity; merriment. [O.E. *myrgth*, fr. *myrge*, MERRY.]

MIRTHFUL (mẹrth'fool) *a.* merry; gay.

MIRTHFULLY (mẹrth'fool-i) *ad.* with mirth.

MIRTHLESS (mẹrth'les) *a.* having no gaiety.

MIRY (mī'ri) *a.* full of mire.

MISADVENTURE (mis-ad-ven'tūr) *n.* a mischance; misfortune. [O.F. *mesaventure*, fr. *mes* =F. *mé-*, fr. L. *minus*, and ADVENTURE, *mis* denoting bad, and E. *adventure*.]

MISADVISED (mis-ad-vizd') *a.* ill-directed or counselled. [E. pref. *mis-*, badly, wrongly.]

MISALLIANCE (mis-ạ-lī'ạns) *n.* improper association or marriage. [F. *mésalliance*, fr. L. *minus*, and ALLIANCE.]

MISANTHROPE (mis'ạn-thrōp) *n.* a hater of mankind; one disgusted with society and its ways. [G., fr. *misein*, to hate, and *anthropos*, man.]

MISANTHROPIC (mis-ạn-throp'ik) *a.* hating mankind.

MISANTHROPIST (mis-ạn'thrō-pist) *n.* a hater of mankind.

MISANTHROPY (mis-an'thrō-pi) *n.* hatred of mankind. [G. *misanthropia*.]

MISAPPLICATION (mis-ap-li-kā'shun) *n.* wrong application.

MISAPPLY (mis-ạ-plī') *v.t.* to apply wrongly. [O.E. *mis*, denoting wrong, and E. *apply*.]

MISAPPREHEND (mis-ap-rē-hend') *v.t.* to misunderstand. [E. *mis-*, and APPREHEND.]

MISAPPREHENSION (mis-ap-rē-hen'shun) *n.* a mistaken idea; misunderstanding.

MISAPPROPRIATE (mis-ạ-prō'pri-āt) *v.t.* to assign to the wrong person or purpose. [E. *mis-*, and APPROPRIATE.]

MISBECOME (mis-be-kum') *v.t.* to suit ill. [E. *mis-*, and BECOME.]

MISBEGOTTEN (mis-be-got'n) *a.* begotten irregularly. [E. *mis-*, and BEGET.]

MISBEHAVE (mis-be-hāv') *v.i.* to behave improperly. [E. *mis-*, and BEHAVE.]

MISBEHAVIOUR (mis-bē-hāv'yur) *n.* ill conduct.

MISBELIEF (mis-be-lēf') *n.* erroneous belief.

MISBELIEVE (mis-be-lēv') *v.t.* to believe erroneously; doubt or question. [E. *mis-* and BELIEVE.]

MISCALCULATE (mis-kal'kū-lāt) *v.t.* to calculate wrongly. [E. *mis-*, and CALCULATE.]

MISCALL (mis-kawl') *v.t.* to call by a wrong name. [E. *mis-*, and CALL.]

MISCARRIAGE (mis-kar'ij) *n.* failure; abortion.

MISCARRY (mis-kar'i) *v.i.* to fail of success; have an abortion. [E. *mis-*, and CARRY.]

MISCELLANEOUS (mis-e-lā'nē-us) *a.* mixed; consisting of various kinds. [L., fr. *miscere*, mix.]

MISCELLANY (mis'el-ạ-ni, mi-sel'ạ-ni) *n.* a collection of writings; a mixture.

MISCHANCE (mis-chans') *n.* ill luck; mishap. [E. *mis-*, and CHANCE.]

MISCHARGE (mis-chärj') *v.t.* to charge in error;—*n.* an erroneous charge. [E. *mis*, and CHARGE.]

MISCHIEF (mis'chif) *n.* evil, whether intended or not; damage; harm.

MISCHIEVOUS (mis'chi-vus) *a.* making or inclined to make mischief.

MISCHIEVOUSLY (mis'chi-vus-li) *ad.* hurtfully; maliciously.

MISCIBLE (mis'i-bl) *a.* that can be mixed.

MISCITATION (mis-si-tā'shun) *n.* a wrong quotation. [E. *mis*, and CITE.]

MISCOMPUTATION (mis-kom-pū-tā'shun) *n.* false reckoning.

MISCOMPUTE (mis-kom-pūt') *v.t.* to compute wrongly. [E. *mis-*, and COMPUTE.]

MISCONCEIVE (mis-kun-sēv') *v.t.* to have a wrong notion of. [E. *mis-*, and CONCEIVE.]

MISCONCEPTION (mis-kun-sep'shun) *n.* wrong conception.

MISCONDUCT (mis-kon'dukt) *n.* bad behaviour or management;—(mis-kon-dukt') *v.t.* or *i.* to conduct or behave badly. [E. *mis-*, and CONDUCT.]

MISCONJECTURE (mis-kon-jekt'ūr) *n.* a wrong conjecture. [E. *mis-*, and CONJECTURE.]

MISCONSTRUCTION (mis-kun-struk'shun) *n.* wrong interpretation.

MISCONSTRUE (mis-kon'strŏŏ) v.t. to interpret wrongly. [E. mis-, and CONSTRUE.]
MISCOUNT (mis-kount') v.t. or i. to mistake in counting. [O.F. mesconter, fr. mes = F. mé-, fr. L. minus, and COUNT.]
MISCREANT (mis'kre-ant) n. a vile wretch. [O.F. mescreant, fr. mes = F. mé-, fr. L. minus, and (acc.) part. credentem, believing. See CREDENCE.]
MISDATE (mis-dāt') v.t. to date erroneously; —n. a wrong date. [E. mis-, and DATE.]
MISDEAL (mis-dēl') n. a wrong deal in cards;—also v.t. and i. [E. mis-, and DEAL.]
MISDEED (mis-dēd') n. an evil action; wicked deed. [E. mis-, and DEED.]
MISDEEM (mis-dēm') v.t. to judge amiss. [E. mis-, and DEEM.]
MISDEMEAN (mis-dē-mēn') v.i. to behave ill. [E. mis-; O.F. desmener, de, down, mener, lead, fr. Low L. menare, to drive cattle, fr. minare, to threaten.]
MISDEMEANOUR (mis-de-mē'nur) n. ill-behaviour; any petty indictable offence.
MISDIRECT (mis-di-rekt') v.t. to direct to a wrong person or place. [E. mis-, and DIRECT.]
MISDIRECTION (mis-di-rek'shun) n. addressing wrongly; wrong address; error of a judge in charging a jury.
MISDO (mis'dŏŏ) v.t. or i. to do wrong; commit crime. [E. mis-, and DO.]
MISDOER (m·s'dŏŏ-ẹr) n. one who commits a fault or evil deed.
MISDOING (mis-dŏŏ'ing) n. a wrong done.
MISEMPLOY (mis-em-ploi') v.t. to use to a wrong purpose; misuse. [E. mis-, and EMPLOY.]
MISER (mi'zẹr) n. one covetous to excess; a niggard. [L. = wretched.]
MISERABLE (miz'ẹr-a-bl) a. wretched; unhappy; worthless. [O.F., fr. L. (acc.) miserabilem, deplorable.]
MISERABLY (miz'ẹr-a-bli) ad. wretchedly.
MISERLY (mi'zẹr-li) a. very covetous.
MISERY (miz'e-ri) n. wretchedness; distress; calamity. [L. miseria.]
MISESTIMATE (mis-es'tim-āt) v.t. to estimate at a wrong value. [E. mis-, and ESTIMATE.]
MISFORTUNE (m·s-for'tūn) n. ill luck; an evil accident; any harm or loss. [E. mis-, and L. fortuna.]
MISGIVE (mis-giv') v.t. or i. to fill with doubt; fail in confidence. [E. mis-. and G VE.]
MISGIVING (mis-giv'ing) n. a weakening of confidence; distrust.
MISGOTTEN (mis-got'n) a. obtained unjustly. [E. mis-, and GET.]
MISGOVERN (mis-guv'ẹrn) v.t. to govern amiss. [E. mis-, and GOVERN.]
MISGOVERNMENT (mis-guv'ẹrn-ment) n. bad administration.
MISGUIDANCE (mis-gī'dans) n. wrong direction.
MISGUIDE (mis-gīd') v.t. to lead or guide into error. [E. mis-, and GUIDE.]
MISHAP (mis-hap') n. ill chance or accident; misfortune.
MISHNA (mish'na) n. a collection of Jewish interpretations of the Old Testament. [H. shanah, to repeat.]
MISIMPROVE (mis-im-prŏŏv') v.t. to use to no purpose, or to a bad one. [E. mis-, and IMPROVE.]
MISINFORM (mis-in-form') v.t. to give erroneous information. [E. mis-, and INFORM.]
MISINFORMATION (mis-in-for-mā'shun) n. wrong information.
MISINTERPRET (mis-in-tẹr'pret) v.t. to explain erroneously; misconstrue. [E. mis-, and INTERPRET.]
MISINTERPRETATION (mis-in-tẹr-pre-tā'shun) n. interpreting erroneously.
MISJUDGE (mis-juj') v.t. to judge amiss. [E. mis-, and JUDGE.]

MISJUDGMENT (mis-juj'ment) n. a wrong judgment.
MISLAY (mis-lā') v.t. to lay in a wrong place, or place not remembered. [E. mis-, and LAY.]
MISLEAD (mis-lēd') v.t. to lead into error. [E. mis-, and LEAD.]
MISLED (mis-led') pret. of MISLEAD.
MISMANAGE (mis-man'ij) v.t. or i. to manage ill. [E. mis-, and MANAGE.]
MISMANAGEMENT (mis-man'ij-ment) n. bad management.
MISNAME (mis-nām') v.t. to call by a wrong name. [E. mis-, and NAME.]
MISNOMER (mis-nō'mẹr) n. a wrong name. [O.F. mesnommer, to misname, fr. mes-, fr. L. minus, and nommer.]
MISOGAMIST (mi-sog'a-mist) n. a hater of marriage.
MISOGAMY (mi-sog'a-mi) n. hatred of marriage. [Fr. G. misos, hatred, and gamos, marriage.]
MISOGYNIST (mi-sog'i-nist, mi-soj'i-nist) n. a woman hater.
MISOGYNY (mi-sog'i-ni, mi-soj'i-ni) n. hatred of woman. [Fr. G. misos, and gune, woman.]
MISPLACE (mis-plās') v.t. to place wrong. [E. mis-, and PLACE.]
MISPRINT (mis-print') v.t. to print wrong;—n. an error in printing. [E. mis-, and PRINT.]
MISPRISION (mis-prish'un) n. oversight; neglect. [O.F., fr. mes, fr. L. minus, and prise, a seizing.]
MISPRIZE (mis-priz') v.t. to undervalue; slight. [E. mis- and PRIZE, O.F., fr. mes = F. mé-, fr. L. minus, and priser, esteem, fr. pris, PRICE.]
MISPRONOUNCE (mis-pru-nouns') v.t. to pronounce incorrectly. [E. mis-, and PRONOUNCE.]
MISPRONUNCIATION (mis-pru-nun-si-ā'shun) n. improper pronunciation.
MISPROPORTION (mis-pru-pōr'shun) v.t. to distribute without due proportion. [E. mis-, and PROPORTION.]
MISQUOTATION (mis-kwō-tā'shun) n. act of quoting wrongly.
MISQUOTE (mis-kwōt') v.t. to quote incorrectly. [E. mis-, and QUOTE.]
MISRECKON (mis-rek'n) v.t. to compute erroneously. [E. mis-, and RECKON.]
MISRELATE (mis-re-lāt') v.t. to relate erroneously. [E. mis-, and RELATE.]
MISRELATION (mis-re-lā'shun) n. erroneous relation.
MISREPORT (mis-re-pōrt') v.t. to report erroneously;—n. a false report. [E. mis-, and REPORT.]
MISREPRESENT (mis-rep-re-zent') v.t. to represent incorrectly. [E. mis-, and REPRESENT.]
MISREPRESENTATION (mis-rep-re-zen-tā'shun) n. untrue or unfair account.
MISRULE (mis-rŏŏl') n. confusion; unjust domination. [E. mis-, and RULE.]
MISS (mis) (1) n. a young unmarried female; —(2) v.t. to err; not to hit. [(1) Short. fr. MISTRESS. (2) O.E. missan; conn. with E. pref. mis-, badly.]
MISSAL (mis'al) n. the Roman Catholic mass-book. [Late L. missale, a MASS-book.]
MISSHAPE (mis-shāp') v.t. [pp. or a. MIS-SHAPEN] to shape ill. [E. mis-, and SHAPE.]
MISSILE (mis'il) n. a weapon to be thrown.
MISSING (mis'ing) a. lost; absent.
MISSION (mish'un) n. act of sending; persons sent; duty on which one is sent; purpose in life. [O.F., fr. L. (acc.) missionem, a sending. See MISSILE.]
MISSIONARY (mish'un-ar-i) n. one sent to spread religion;—a. pertaining to missions.

MISSIVE (mis'iv) a. sent or that may be sent;—n. a message or letter sent. (Scots. Law) a written contract sent for signature. [F., fr. L. (part.) *missus*, sent, fr. *mittere*.]

MISSPELL (mis-spel') v.t. [pret. and pp. **MISSPELLED MISSPELT**] to spell erroneously. [E. *mis-*, and **SPELL**.]

MISSPEND (mis-spend') v.t. [pret. and pp. **MISSPENT**] to waste or spend ill. [E. *mis-*, and **SPEND**.]

MISSTATE (mis-stāt') v.t. to state inaccurately. [E. *mis-*, and **STATE**.]

MIST (mist) n. rain in very fine drops;—v.i. to rain in fine drops. [O.E. =gloom.]

MISTAKE (mis-tāk') n. unintentional error; —v.t. or i. to understand wrongly; err. [Scand.; pref. =E. *mis-*.]

MISTAKEN (mis-tāk'n) pp. or a, used of things, misunderstood; used of persons, wrong; being in error.

MISTEACH (mis-tēch') v.t. pret. and pp. **MISTAUGHT** to teach wrong. [E. *mis-*, and **TEACH**.]

MISTER (mis'tẽr) n. a title of address, used for master. [Form of **MASTER**.]

MISTERM (mis-tẽrm') v.t. to name erroneously. [E. *mis-*, and **TERM**.]

MISTHINK (mis-thingk') v.t. to think erroneously. [E. *mis-*, and **THINK**.]

MISTHOUGHT (mis-thawt') pp. of **MIS-THINK**.

MISTILY (mis'ti-li) ad. obscurely; vaguely.

MISTIME (mis-tim') v.t. not to time aright. [E. *mis-*, and **TIME**.]

MISTINESS (mis'ti-nes) n. state of being misty; obscurity.

MISTLETOE (mis'l-tō, miz'l-tō) n. a plant that grows on trees. [O.E. *mistel tan*, mistletoe twig. Cf. Ger. *Mistel*.]

MISTOOK (mis-tóók') pret. of **MISTAKE**.

MISTRANSLATE (mis-trans-lāt') v.t. to translate erroneously. [E. *mis-*, and **TRANSLATE**.]

MISTRANSLATION (mis-trans-lā'shun) n. erroneous translation.

MISTRESS (mis'tres) n. a woman who governs; a term of address. [O.F. *maistresse* =F. *maîtresse*, fr. **MASTER**.]

Mistletoe.

MISTRUST (mis-trust') n. want of confidence; suspicion;—v.t. to regard with suspicion; doubt. [E. *mis-*, and **TRUST**.]

MISTRUSTFUL (mis-trust'fool) a. suspicious.

MISTRUSTFULLY (mis-trust'fool-i) ad. with doubt or suspicion.

MISTRUSTLESS (mis-trust'les) a. not apt to suspect.

MISTY (mis'ti) a. raining in very fine drops; cloudy with mist.

MISUNDERSTAND (mis-un-dẽr-stand') v.t. to misconceive; mistake. [E. *mis-*, and **UNDERSTAND**.]

MISUNDERSTANDING (mis-un-dẽr-stan'ding) n. misconception; disagreement.

MISUSAGE (mis-ū'zij) n. bad treatment.

MISUSE (mis-ūz') v.t. to abuse; treat ill. [E. *mis-*, and **USE** (1).]

MISUSE (mis-ūs') n. bad use; abuse. [E. *mis-*, and **USE** (2).]

MITE (mit) (1) n. a minute insect;—(2) n. a very small coin, one-twelfth of a penny; anything very small. [(1) O.E. *mite*. (2) O.D.]

MITIGABLE (mit'i-gə-bl) a. capable of mitigation.

MITIGATE (mit'i-gāt) v.t. to lessen; alleviate. [L. *mitis*, mild. and *agere*, make.]

MITIGATION (mit-i-gā'shun) n. alleviation; relief; abatement.

MITRE (mi'tẽr) n. a bishop's cap. [G. *mitra*, head-band.]

MITTEN (mit'n) n. a cover for the hand. [O.F. *mitaine*.]

MITTIMUS (mit'i-mus) n. a warrant of commitment to prison. [L. = we send.]

MIX (miks) v.t. [pret. and pp. **MIXED** or **MIXT**] to unite and blend promiscuously; —v.i. to mingle; associate. [O.E. *miscian*. Cf. Ger. *mischen*, L. *miscere*, G. *misgein*.]

MIXABLE (mik'sǝ-bl) a. capable of being mixed.

MIXED (mikst) a. not pure; various; confused.

MIXEDLY (mik'sed-li) ad. in a confused manner.

MIXTURE (miks'tūr) n. a mingled mass. [L. *mixtura*, fr. (part.) *mixtus*, mixed, fr. *miscere*.]

MIZENMAST (miz'n-mast) n. the mast nearest the stern. [F. *misaine*, a fore-mast, fr. It. =fr. L. *medius*, middle, orig. a sail of middle size. See **MEZZO**.]

MNEMONIC (nē-mon'ik) a. assisting the memory.

MNEMONICS (nē-mon'iks) n.pl. the art or science of assisting memory. [G., fr. stem *mnemon-*, of *mnemon*, mindful.]

MOAN (mōn) n. a low sound expressing pain or grief;—v.t. or i. to groan; lament. [Fr. O.E. *mænan*.]

MOANFUL (mōn'fool) a. expressing sorrow.

MOAT (mōt) n. a ditch round a castle, etc.; —v.t. to surround with a moat. [O.F. *mote*, a dike, trench, fr. Teut.]

MOB (mob) n. a tumultuous crowd;—v.t. to attack as a crowd. [Short. fr. L. *mobile vulgus*, the fickle, common people. See **MOBILE**.]

MOBILE (mō'bil) a. easily moved or excited. [F., fr. L. (acc.) *mobilem*, *movibil-*, fr. *movere*, move.]

MOBILISE (mob'i-liz) v.t. to call into active service, as troops. [F. *mobiliser*.]

MOBILITY (mō-bil'i-ti) n. activity; fickleness; the populace.

MOCCASIN (mok'ǝ-sin) n. a shoe of soft leather, without a sole; a poisonous water serpent. [N. Amer. Ind. name.]

MOCK (mok) v.t. or i. to deride; mimic; disappoint; jeer;—n. a sneer; ridicule;—a. unreal; assumed. [O.F. *mocquer*, of uncert. etym.]

MOCKER (mok'ẽr) n. scorner; scoffer.

MOCKERY (mok'ẽr-i) n. derision; scorn. [O.F. *mocquerie*.]

MOCKING-BIRD (mok'ing-bẽrd) n. an American singing bird.

MODAL (mō'dǝl) a. relating to mode.

MODE (mōd) n. form; method; fashion; manner of conjugating a verb. [F., fr. L. (acc.) *modum*, measure, manner.]

MODEL (mod'el) n. a structure designed to be imitated; copy; pattern; example; standard;—v.t. to plan; shape;—also v.i. to make a model. [O.F. *modelle* =F. *modèle*, fr. It., dim. fr. *modus*, measure.]

MODERATE (mod'e-rat) a. not extreme; temperate; average;—v.t. to restrain; reduce; qualify;—v.i. to become less violent; preside. [L. (part.) *moderatus*, controlled, fr. *modus*, measure.]

MODERATELY (mod'e-rǝt-li) ad. not excessively; temperately.

MODERATION (mod-e-rā'shun) n. state of being moderate. [L. (acc.) *moderationem*.]

MODERATISM (mod'e-rǝ-tizm) n. moderate spirit or opinions in religion.

MODERATOR (mod'e-rā-tẽr) n. one who presides over a meeting; regulator. [L.]

MODERN (mod'ẽrn) a. of the present time; not ancient; recent. [F., fr. L. *modernus*, pert. to the present **MODE**.]

MODERNISE (mod'ẽr-niz) v.t. to make modern.

MODERNISER (mod'er-ni-zer) *n.* one that renders modern.
MODERNISM (mod'er-nizm) *n.* recent practice, manners, etc.
MODERNS (mod'ernz) *n.pl.* people of modern times.
MODEST (mod'est) *a.* not forward; moderate; chaste. [F., fr. L. *modestus.* MODERATE.]
MODESTLY (mod'est-li) *ad.* with diffidence.
MODESTY (mod'es-ti) *n.* absence of conceit; chastity.
MODICUM (mod'i-kum) *n.* a small portion. [L. (neut.) =moderate.]
MODIFICATION (mod-i-fi-kā'shun) *n.* act of modifying.
MODIFIER (mod'i-fī-er) *n.* he or that which modifies.
MODIFY (mod'i-fī) *v.t.* to change the form; reduce; qualify. [F. *modifier,* fr. L. *modi-,* for *modus,* measure, and *-ficare,* for *facere,* make.]
MODISH (mō'dish) *a.* fashionable.
MODISHLY (mō'dish-li) *ad.* fashionably.
MODISTE (mō-dēst') *n.* a female artiste in dress. [F.]
MODULATE (mod'ū-lāt) *v.t.* to vary sounds; inflect;—*v.i.* to pass from one key to another. [L. (part.) *modulatus,* having measured, fr. *modulus.* dim. fr. *modus,* measure.]
MODULATION (mod-ū-lā'shun) *n.* the act of modulating.
MODULATOR (mod'ū-lā-ter) *n.* that which varies sounds.
MODULE (mod'ūl) *n.* a model or representation. [F., fr. L. (acc.) *modulum,* a small measure.]
MOGUL (mō-gul') *n.* a Mongolian; formerly emperor of the Moguls in Asia.
MOHAIR (mō'hār) *n.* a stuff of goat's hair. [Fr. A.]
MOHAMMEDAN (mō-ham'e-dan) *a.* pertaining to Mohammed;—*n.* a follower of Mohammed. Also MAHOMETAN. [Fr. A.]
MOHR (mōr) *n.* the African antelope.
MOIETY (moi'e-ti) *n.* half; part; share. [F. *moitié,* fr. L. (acc.) *medietatem,* half, fr. *medius,* middle.]
MOIL (moil) *v.t.* or *i.* to work with painful effort; drudge; soil; dirty. [O.F. *moiller* =F. *mouiller* wet, fr. L. *mollis,* soft.]
MOIRE (mwär) *n.* a fine kind of watered silk. [F., fr. E. MOHAIR.]
MOIST (moist) *a.* damp; wet in a small degree. [O.F., of uncert. etym.]
MOISTEN (moi'sn) *v.t.* to make damp; wet slightly.
MOISTNESS (moist'nes) *n.* dampness.
MOISTURE (mois'tūr) *n.* slight wetness; quantity of liquid in the air or other body.
MOLAR (mō'lar) (1) *a.* adapted to grind;—*n.* a grinding or double tooth; (mō'lar) *a.* pertaining to a mass. [(1) L., fr. *mola,* mill. (2) Fr. L. *moles,* great mass.]
MOLASSES (mu-las'ez) *n.* the syrup which drains from sugar; treacle. [Formerly *melasses,* through Pg., fr. L. *mel,* honey.]
MOLE (mōl) (1) *n.* a natural spot on the skin;—(2) a pier; a mound;—(3) a little animal. [(1) O.E. *mal.* (2) F. *môle* fr. L. (acc.) *molem,* mass. See MOLAR (2). (3) M.E. *moldwerp,* lit. earth-thrower, fr. MOULD and WARP. Cf. Ger. *Maulwurf.*]
MOLECULAR (mō-lek'ū-lar) *a.* pertaining to molecules.
MOLECULE (mol'e-kūl) *n.* a very minute particle of matter. [Fr. L. *moles,* mass. See MOLAR (2).]
MOLEHILL (mōl'hil) *n.* a hillock raised by a mole. [See MOLE (3).]
MOLESKIN (mōl'skin) *n.* a strong twilled fustian. [See MOLE (3).]

MOLEST (mu-lest') *v.t.* to render uneasy; annoy. [Fr. L., fr. *molestus,* troublesome, fr. root of *molere,* grind; MOLAR (1).]
MOLESTATION (mol-es-tā'shun) *n.* annoyance.
MOLLIFIABLE (mol'i-fī-a-bl) *a.* that may be softened or assuaged.
MOLLIFIER (mol'i-fī-er) *n.* that which softens.
MOLLIFY (mol'i-fī) *v.t.* to soften; assuage. [F. *mollifier,* fr. L. *mollis,* soft, and *-ficare,* for *facere,* make.]
MOLLUSC (mol'usk) *n.* an animal with a fleshy, inarticulate body, as the snail, oyster, etc. [L. *molliusca,* a soft nut, fr. *mollis,* soft.]
MOLTEN (mōlt'n) *a.* melted, or made of melted metal. [See MELT.]
MOMENT (mō'ment) *n.* a portion of time; importance; weight. [F., fr. L. *momentum* =*movi-,* fr. *morere,* move. Doublet of MOMENTUM.]
MOMENTARILY (mō'men-ta-ri-li) *ad.* every moment.
MOMENTARY (mō'men-ta-ri) *a.* lasting a moment only. [L. *momentarius.*]
MOMENTLY (mō'ment-li) *ad.* in a moment.
MOMENTOUS (mō-men'tus) *a.* important; weighty.
MOMENTUM (mō-men'tum) *n.* force of a moving body;—*pl.* MOMENTA. [L. See MOMENT.]
MONACHISM (mon'a-kizm) *n.* monastic life. [L. *monachus,* monk.]
MONAD (mon'ad) *n.* an atom. [G. stem *monad-,* of *monas,* unity, fr. *monos,* alone.]
MONADIC (mu-nad'ik) *a.* having the nature of a monad.
MONARCH (mon'ark) *n.* a sole supreme ruler; hereditary sovereign; the chief of its kind. [L. *monarcha,* fr. G., fr. *monos,* alone, and *archein,* to rule.]
MONARCHICAL (mu-när'ki-kal) *a.* pertaining to a monarch.
MONARCHIST (mon'ar-kist) *n.* a friend to monarchy.
MONARCHY (mon'ar-ki) *n.* government vested in one man; a kingdom. [L., fr. G. *monarchia.*]
MONASTERY (mon'as-te-ri) *n.* a house of religious retirement; convent; nunnery. [L., fr. G. *monasterion,* fr. G. *monastes,* a recluse, fr. *monazein,* to be alone, *monos.*]
MONASTIC (mu-nas'tik) *a.* pertaining to monks; recluse;—*n.* a monk. [Fr. G. *monastikos.*]
MONASTICISM (mu-nas'ti-sizm) *n.* monastic life.
MONDAY (mun'dā) *n.* second day of the week. [M.E. *mone(n)day,* fr. O.E. (gen.) *monan,* of the MOON, and DAY.]
MONETARY (mun'e-ta-ri) *a.* relating to or consisting of money. [L. *moneta,* money.]
MONEY (mun'i) *n.* coin for current use in trade, or a substitute for it;—*pl.* MONEYS. [O.F. *moneie* =F. *monnaie,* fr. L. (acc.) *monetam.* Doublet of MINT (1).]
MONEY-BROKER (mun'i-brōk-er) *n.* a broker who deals in money.
MONEYED (mun'id) *a.* rich; possessed of money. Also written MONIED.
MONEY-LENDER (mun'i-len-der) *n.* one who advances money on security.
MONEY-MARKET (mun'i-mär-ket) *n.* the exchange; state of the funds, bank, or other shares.
MONGER (mung'ger) *n.* a trader. [O.E. *mangere,* a merchant, fr. L. *mango,* dealer.]
MONGREL (mung'grel) *a.* of a mixed breed;—*n.* an animal of a mixed breed. [=*mong-er-el,* double dim. fr. O.E. *mang* mixture; conn. with MINGLE.]
MONITION (mo-nish'un) *n.* a warning; instruction. [F., fr. L. (acc.) *monitionem,* fr. (part.) *monitus,* warned, fr. *monere.*]

MONITIVE (mon'i-tiv) *a.* conveying warning or instruction.

MONITOR (mon'i-ter) *n.* one who warns; a subordinate instructor; an ironclad ship of war. [L.]

MONITORIAL (mon-i-to'ri-al) *a.* pertaining to a monitor.

MONITORY (mon'i-tu-ri) *a.* giving warning.

MONITRESS (mon-i-tres) *n.* a female monitor.

MONK (mungk) *n.* one who lives in a monastery. [O.E. *munuc*, fr. L. *monachus*, fr. G. *monos*, alone.]

MONKEY (mung'ki) *n.* an animal like the ape; —*pl.* MONKEYS. [Fr. It., fr. *monna* = MADONNA.]

MONKEY-JACKET (mung'ki-jak-et) *n.* a thick, close-fitting woollen jacket.

MONKEY-WRENCH (mung'ki-rensh) *n.* a wrench with a movable jaw.

MONKISH (mung'kish) *a.* like a monk; monastic.

MONKSHOOD (mungks'hood) *n.* a poisonous herb; aconite. [See MONK and HOOD.]

MONODIST (mon'u-dist) *n.* a writer of monodies.

MONODY (mon'u-di) *n.* a mournful song by one person. [G. *monodia*, fr. *monos*, and ODE.]

MONOGAMY (mu-nog'a-mi) *n.* marriage to one wife. [G., fr. *monos*, and *gamos*, marriage.]

MONOGRAM (mon'u-gram) *n.* a cipher composed of letters interwoven. [G., fr. *monos*, and *gramma*, letter.]

MONOGRAPH (mon'u-graf) *n.* an account of a single thing. [Fr. G. *monos*, and *-graphia*, description, fr. *graphein*, write.]

MONOGRAPHIC (mon-u-graf'ik) *a.* pertaining to a monograph.

Monogram.

MONOLITH (mon'u-lith) *n.* a pillar or column of a single stone. [L., fr. G., fr. *monos*, and *lithos*, stone.]

MONOLOGUE (mon'o-log) *n.* a speech by one person. [F., fr. G. *monos*, and *logos*, speech.]

MONOMANIA (mon-u-mā'ni-a) *n.* derangement of the mind on one subject only. [Fr. G. *monos*, alone, and MANIA.]

MONOMANIAC (mon-u-mā'ni-ak) *n.* a person affected by monomania.

MONOPLANE (mon'o-plān) *n.* a flying-machine supported by one plane surface. [G. *monos*, single, and F. *plane*, flat.]

MONOPOLISE (mu-nop'u-līz) *v.t.* to engross the whole. [monopolises.]

MONOPOLIST (mu-nop'u-list) *n.* one who monopolises.

MONOPOLY (mu-nop'u-li) *n.* entire control or appropriation. [L., fr. G. *monopolia*, fr. *monos*, and *polein*, sell.]

MONORAIL (mon'o-rāl) *n.* a one-rail track along which a suspended car travels. [G. *monos*, alone, and RAIL.]

MONOSYLLABIC (mon-u-si-lab'ik) *a.* of one syllable only.

MONOSYLLABLE (mon'u-sil-a-bl) *n.* a word of one syllable. [Fr. G. *monos*.]

MONOTHEISM (mon'u-thē-izm) *n.* the belief in one God only. [Fr. G. *monos*, alone, and *Theos*, God.]

MONOTONE (mon'u-tōn) *n.* a sound or succession of sounds in the same pitch or key. [Fr. G. *monos*.]

MONOTONOUS (mu-not'u-nus) *a.* in the same tone; without variety.

MONOTONOUSLY (mu-not'u-nus-li) *ad.* in an unvarying, wearisome manner.

MONOTONOUSNESS (mu-not'u-nus-nes) *n.* irksomeness; sameness.

MONOTONY (mu-not'u-ni) *n.* uniformity of tone; want of variety.

MONSOON (mon'sōōn) *n.* a periodical wind. [Fr. A.]

MONSTER (mon'ster) *n.* something horrid or unnatural. [F., fr. L. *monstrum*, portent; conn. with *monere*, warn.]

MONSTROSITY (mon-stros'i-ti) *n.* state of being monstrous.

MONSTROUS (mon'strus) *a.* unnatural; shocking; enormous.

MONSTROUSLY (mon'strus-li) *ad.* in a shocking, unnatural manner.

MONTH (munth) *n.* one revolution of the moon; the twelfth part of the year. [O.E. *monath*, fr. MOON. Cf. Ger. *Monat*.]

MONTHLY (munth'li) *a.* happening every month;—*n.* a periodical published once a month;—*ad.* once a month.

MONUMENT (mon-ū-ment) *n.* a memorial; a tomb. [F., fr. L. *monumentum*, fr. *monere*, remind.]

MONUMENTAL (non-ū-men'tal) *a.* preserving memory.

MOOD (mōōd) *n.* temper of mind; humour; variation in inflection of a verb; form of a syllogism; key tone in music. [O.E. *mod*. Cf. Ger. *Muth*. Doublet of MODE.]

MOODINESS (mōō'di-nes) *n.* peevishness.

MOODY (mōō'di) *a.* governed by moods of feeling; ill-humoured. [O.E. *modig*.]

MOON (mōōn) *n.* a satellite of this earth, and revolving round it; a month. [O.E. *mona*. Cf. Ger. *Mond*.]

MOONBEAM (mōōn'bēm) *n.* ray of light from the moon.

MOONLIGHT (mōōn'līt) *n.* light of the moon.

MOOR (mōōr) (1) *n.* a black man;—(2) *n.* a marsh;—(3) *v.t.* to secure a vessel by cables and anchors. [(1) F. *More*, fr. L., fr. G. *Mauros*. (2) O.E. *mor*. (3) D.]

MOORAGE (mōōr'ij) *n.* a place for mooring ships. [See MOOR (3).]

MOORFOWL (mōōr'fowl) *n.* the red grouse. Also MOORCOCK. [See MOOR (2).]

MOORINGS (mōōr'ingz) *n.pl.* anchors, chains, etc., to hold a ship. [See MOOR (3).]

MOORISH (mōōr'ish) *a.* marshy; fenny. [See MOOR (2).]

MOORLAND (mōōr'land) *n.* marshy land;—also *a.* [See MOOR (2).]

MOORY (mōōr'i) *a.* marshy; fenny. [See MOOR (2).]

MOOSE (mōōs) *n.* the largest animal of the deer kind. [An Amer. Ind. name.]

MOOT (mōōt) *v.t.* or *i.* to discuss or debate;—*a.* disputable. [O.E. *motian*, to address a *mot*, meeting.]

MOOT-CASE (mōōt'kās) *n.* a case admitting of discussion or debate. Also MOOT-POINT.

MOP (mop) *n.* a cloth or collection of thrums for cleaning floors, etc.;—*v.t.* to wipe with a mop. [Perhaps a form of MAP.]

MOPE (mōp) *v.i.* to be dull or spiritless;—*n.* a stupid person. [D.]

MOPISH (mō'pish) *a.* dull; spiritless.

MOPPET (mop'et) *n.* a puppet made of cloth. [See MOP.]

MORAL (mor'al) *a.* pertaining to right or wrong in a man's manners, duties, and conduct; virtuous; responsible; probable;—*n.* the precept inculcated by a fable;—*pl.* the doctrine or practice of the duties of life. [F., fr. L. stem, *mor-*, of *mores*, morals.]

MORALE (mo-räl') *n.* the moral condition, especially of a body of men. [F.]

MORALISE (mor'al-īz) *v.t.* to discourse on moral subjects; apply to moral purposes.

MORALIST (mor'a-list) *n.* one who teaches or practises morality.

MORALITY (mu-ral'i-ti) *n.* system or practice of moral duties. [F., fr. L. (acc.) *moralitatem*, character.]

MORALLY (mor'ạl-i) *ad.* in a moral sense or manner; certainly.

MORASS (mo-ras') *n.* a marsh; fen. [D. Cf. **MARSH.**]

MORBID (mor'bid) *a.* not sound or healthy; diseased. [L. *morbidus*, fr. *morbus*, disease.]

MORBIDNESS (mor'bid-nes) *n.* a diseased state.

MORBIFIC (mor-bif'ik) *a.* causing disease.

MORDACIOUS (mor-dā'shus) *a.* biting; sarcastic. [Fr. L. *stem mordaci-*, of *mordax*, snappish.]

MORDACITY (mor-das'ĭ-ti) *n.* the quality of biting.

MORDANT (mor'dạnt) *n.* a substance to fix colours in cloth;—*a.* biting; sarcastic. [F. (part.) =biting, fr. *mordre*, to bite, fr. L. *mordere*.]

MORE (mōr) (1) *a.* greater in quantity or number;—(2) *ad.* to a greater degree. [(1) M.E. *more*, fr. O.E. *mara*, greater. (2) Fr. M.E. *mo*, fr. O.E. *ma*.]

MOREOVER (mōr-ō'vẹr) *ad.* further; besides; in addition to. [See **MORE** (2).]

MORESQUE (mō-resk') *a.* done after the manner of the Moors, as paintings. [F., fr. **MOOR** (1).]

MORIBUND (mor'i-bund) *a.* dying; at the point of death. [L., fr. *mori*, to die.]

MORMON (mor'mun) *n.* one of a religious sect that advocates polygamy, etc. [Fr. the fictitious Book of *Mormon*.]

MORMONISM (mor'mun-izm) *n.* principles of the Mormons.

MORN (morn) *n.* the first part of the day. [M.E. *morwen*, fr. O.E. *morgen*. Cf. Ger. *Morgen*.]

MORNING (mor'ning) *n.* the first part of the day. Also written **MORN.** [M.E. *morwening*, fr. **MORN.**]

MOROCCO (mo-rok'ō) *n.* leather of goat or sheep-skin dressed. [Fr. *Morocco*, where first made.]

MOROSE (mu-rōs') *a.* sour; severe; sullen. [L. *morosus*, self-willed, fr. *stem mor-*, of *mos*, self-will; conn. with **MORAL.**]

MOROSELY (mu-rōs'li) *ad.* sullenly.

MOROSENESS (mu-rōs'nes) *n.* sullenness.

MORPHIA (mor'fi-ạ) *n.* an alkali extracted from opium; a powerful anodyne. [Fr. G. *Morpheus*, the god of sleep and dreams.]

MORRIS (mor'is) *n.* a kind of dance. [Fr. Sp. *Morisco*, Moorish.]

MORROW (mor'ō) *n.* next day after the present. [M.E. *morwe(n)*, fr. O.E. *morgen*. See **MORN.**]

MORSE (mors) *n.* the walrus or sea-horse. [Finnish.]

MORSEL (mor'sel) *n.* a bite; small piece. [O.F. =F. *morceau*; dim. fr. L. *morsus*, a bite, fr. *mordere*.]

MORTAL (mor'tạl) *a.* subject to death; deadly; human;—*n.* a human being. [L. *mortalis*.]

MORTALITY (mor-tal'i-ti) *n.* subjection to death; frequent death; death-rate.

MORTALLY (mor'tạl-i) *ad.* so as to cause death; fatally.

MORTAR (mor'tạr) (1) *n.* cement for building; —(2) a vessel for pounding substances with a pestle; a piece of ordnance for throwing bombs. [(1) F. *mortier*. (2) L. *mortarium*.]

MORTGAGE (mor'gāj) *n.* a pledge of real estate;—*v.t.* to pledge or convey for securing a debt. [O.F. =dead pledge, fr. L. (part.) *mortuus*, dead, and **GAGE.**]

MORTGAGEE (mor-gā-jē') *n.* one to whom a mortgage is given.

MORTGAGER (mor'gāj-ẹr) *n.* one who executes a mortgage.

MORTIFICATION (mor-ti-fi-kā'shun) *n.* dying, or death of a part of the body; subjection by bodily severities; vexation; chagrin.

MORTIFY (mor'ti-fi) *v.t.* or *i.* to destroy or lose vitality; subdue by discipline; humiliate. [F. *mortifier*, fr. L. *mortificare*, destroy, fr. s em *morti-*, of *mors*, death, and *facere*, make.)

MORTIFYING (mor'ti-fi-ing) *a.* tending to humble; humiliating.

MORTISE (mor'tis) *n.* an opening or cut to receive a tenon;—*v.i.* to form with a mortise. [F., of uncert. etym.]

MORTMAIN (mort'mān) *n.* an inalienable estate. [Fr. F. *morte main*, dead hand.]

MORTUARY (mor'tū-ár-i) *n.* a dead-house; —*a.* pertaining to death and burial. [L. *mortuarius*.]

MOSAIC (mō-zā'ik) *n.* work variegated by shells and stones of various colours;—*a.* composed of mosaic; pertaining to Moses. [F. *mosaique*, through It., fr. Late L. *musaicus*, fr. G. *mouseion*, lit. artistic work, fr. **MUSE.**]

MOSELLE (mō-zel') *n.* a light French wine. [F.]

MOSLEM (moz'lem) *n.* a Mohammedan;—*a.* pertaining to the creeds or followers of Mohammed. [A.]

MOSQUE (mosk) *n.* a Mohammedan house of worship. [F., *mosquée*, fr. Sp., fr. A.]

MOSQUITO (mus-kē'tō) *n.* a stinging gnat or fly, common in tropical countries; *pl.* **MOSQUITOES.** [Sp. (dim.), fr. L. *musca*, ṵ fly.]

MOSS (mos) *n.* a small herb; ground covered with moss; a bog;—*v.t.* to cover with moss. [O.E. *mos.* Cf. Ger. *Moos.*]

MOSSY (mos'i) *a.* overgrown with moss.

MOST (mōst) *a.* the greatest number or quantity; greatest;—*ad.* in the greatest degree. [O.E. *maest* =*ma-est.* Cf. Ger. *meist.*]

MOSTLY (mōst'li) *ad.* for the greatest part.

MOTE (mōt) *n.* a very small particle; speck. [O.E. *mot.*] [*mothe.*]

MOTH (moth) *n.* a winged insect. [O.E.

MOTHER (muтн'ẹr) (1) *n.* a female parent; —*a.* natural; native;—*v.i.* to concrete;— *v.t.* to adopt as a child;—(2) *n.* thick dregs in liquids. [(1) M.E. *moder*, fr. O.E. *modor.* Cf. Ger. *Mutter.* (2) orig. *mudder*, fr. D. Cf. Ger. *Moder.*]

MOTHERHOOD (muтн'ẹr-hood) *n.* the state of a mother.

MOTHERLY (muтн'ẹr-li) *a.* like a mother.

MOTHER-WIT (muтн'ẹr-wit) *n.* native wit.

MOTION (mō'shun) *n.* act of changing place; a proposal made. [F., fr. L. (acc.) *motionem*, fr. (part.) *motus*, moved, fr. *movere*.]

MOTIONLESS (mō'shun-les) *a.* quiescent.

MOTIVE (mō'tiv) *a.* causing to move;—*n.* that which incites to volition or action; inducement. [O.F. *motif*, fr. Late L. (acc.) *motivum*, causing **MOTION,** L. *movere*.]

MOTIVITY (mō-tiv'i-ti) *n.* power of motion.

MOTLEY (mot'li) *a.* variegated in colour. [Etym. uncert.]

MOTOR (inō'tẹr) *n.* moving power; a self-propelling carriage;—*v.i.* to drive in a self-propelling carriage. [L. See **MOTION.**]

MOTOR-CAR (mō'tur-kạr) *n.* a carriage for the road, propelled by steam or electricity.

MOTTO (mot'ō) *n.* a sentence prefixed to an essay; an inscription;—*pl.* **MOTTOES.** [It., fr. L. *muttum*, a murmur.]

MOULD (mōld) (1) *n.* fine, soft soil; the earth; —*v.t.* to cover with mould;—(2) *n.* a hollow form for casting; shape;—*v.t.* to cast or shape;—(3) *v.i.* to become mouldy. [(1) O.E. *molde.* (2) F. *molde*, *molle* =F. *moule*, fr. L. (acc.) *modulum.* See **MODULATE.** (3) M.E. *moule*, fr. Scand.]

MOULDER (mōl'dẹr) (1) *v.i.* to decay;—(2) *n.* a castor of metal. [(1) See **MOULD** (1). (2) See **MOULD** (2).]

MOULDY (mōl'di) *a.* covered with mould. [See **MOULD** (3).]

MOULT (mōlt) *v.i.* to shed hair, feathers, horns, etc. [M.E. *mouten*, fr. O.E., fr. L. *mutare*, change.]

MOULTING (mōl'ting) *n.* act of shedding feathers, hair, etc.

MOUND (mound) *n.* a natural or artificial elevation for defence;—*v.t.* to fortify with a mound. [O.E. *mund*, a protection. Cf. Ger. *Vormund*.]

MOUNT (mount) *n.* a hill; mountain; heap; —*v.i.* to rise; soar;—*v.t.* to climb; get or put on horseback, etc.; set; embellish. [F. *mont*, fr. L. (acc.) *montem*, fr. *mons*, MOUNTAIN.]

MOUNTABLE (moun'ta̤-bl) *a.* that may be ascended.

MOUNTAIN (moun'tin) *n.* ground higher than the country around;—*a.* pertaining to mountains. [O.F. = F. *montagne*, through Late L., fr. L. *montanus*, mountainous, fr. MOUNT.]

MOUNTAINEER (moun'ti-nēr) *n.* an inhabitant, or a climber, of mountains.

MOUNTAINOUS (moun'ti-nus) *a.* abounding with mountains.

MOUNTEBANK (moun'te-bangk) *n.* a pretender; quack. [It. *montambanco* = one that mounts a BENCH or BANK.]

MOUNTED (moun'ted) *a.* raised; embellished.

MOUNTING (moun'ting) *n.* an ascent; setting; material or frame in which a thing is set.

MOURN (mōrn) *v.t.* or *i.* to grieve; lament; wear mourning. [O.E. *murnan*.]

MOURNER (mōr'nẹr) *n.* one who laments.

MOURNFUL (mōrn'fool) *a.* sorrowful; lamentable.

MOURNFULLY (mōrn'fool-i) *ad.* with sorrow.

MOURNING (mōr'ning) *n.* act of sorrowing; dress of mourners;—*a.* sorrowing.

MOUSE (mous) *n.* a small rodent quadruped which infests houses and fields;—*v.t.* to watch and catch mice;—*pl.* MICE. [O.E. *mus*, pl. *mys*. Cf. Ger. *Maus*, L. and G. *mus*.]

MOUSER (mou'zẹr) *n.* a cat that catches mice.

MOUSTACHE (mus-tâsh') *n.* See MUSTACHE.

MOUTH (mouth) *n.* the aperture of an animal for eating and speaking; an opening; speech; boasting; grimace. [O.E. *muth*. Cf. Ger. *Mund*.]

MOUTH (mourн) *v.t.* or *i.* to speak or utter with affected emphasis.

MOUTHFUL (mouth'fool) *n.* as much as the mouth holds at once.

MOUTHPIECE (mouth'pēs) *n.* part of an instrument for the mouth; one who speaks for another.

MOVABLE (mōo'va̤-bl) *a.* that can be moved.

MOVABLES (mōo'va̤-blz) *n.pl.* goods, furniture, etc.

MOVE (mōov) *v.t.* or *i.* to put in motion; excite; change place; propose or recommend. [M.E. *moven*, fr. O.F. *movoir*, fr. L. *movere*.]

MOVER (mōo'vẹr) *n.* one that moves.

MOVEMENT (mōov'ment) *n.* the act of moving; change of place; excitement; emotion.

MOVING (mōo'ving) *a.* changing place; pathetic.

MOVINGLY (mōo'ving-li) *ad.* with feeling.

MOW (mō) (1) *n.* a pile of hay in a barn;—*v.t.* to heap up in a barn:—(2) *v.t.* or *i.* [*pret.* MOWED; *pp.* MOWED, MOWN] to cut down with a scythe; cut grass; cut down in great numbers. [(1) O.E. *muga*, heap. (2) O.E. *mawan*. to mow. Cf. Ger. *mähen*.]

MOWER (mō'ẹr) *n.* one who mows.

MOWING (mō'ing) *n.* act of cutting with a scythe.

MUCH (much) *a.* great in quantity, amount, or time;—*n.* a great quantity or burden; a strange thing;—*ad.* in a great degree; by far; often or long; almost. [M.E. *muche*(*l*), *michel*, fr. O.E. *micel*; by-form, *mickle*.]

MUCILAGE (mū'si-lij) *n.* a slimy or viscous solution of gum. [F., fr. L., fr. MUCUS.]

MUCILAGINOUS (mū-si-laj'i-nus) *a.* slimy; ropy.

MUCK (muk) *n.* a mass of moist dung; anything filthy;—*v.t.* to manure with muck. [Scand.]

MUCKWORM (muk'wurm) *n.* a miser.

MUCKY (muk'i) *a.* filthy.

MUCOUS (mū'kus) *a.* slimy; viscous.

MUCUS (mū'kus) *n.* a slimy fluid. [L.]

MUD (mud) *n.* wet earth; slime; mire;—*v.t.* to make foul with mud; bespatter. [E.; conn. with MOTHER (2).]

MUDDILY (mud'i-li) *ad.* in a muddy manner.

MUDDINESS (mud'i-nes) *n.* foul or turbid state.

MUDDLE (mud'l) *v.t.* to make muddy or confused;—*n.* a confused state; mess. [Fr. MUD.]

MUDDY (mud'i) *a.* foul; dirty; turbid;—*v.t.* to make foul.

MUEZZIN (mōo-ed'zin) *n.* a Mohammedan official who calls the hours of prayer. [A.]

MUFF (muf) *n.* a warm fur cover for the hands. [Low Ger. and Dan. *muff*, *muffe*, sleeve.]

MUFFIN (muf'in) *n.* a light cake. [Perhaps fr. MUFF.]

MUFFLE (muf'l) *v.t.* to cover close. [See MUFF.]

MUG (mug) *n.* a cup or vessel to drink from. [Scand.]

MUGGY (mug'i) *a.* damp and close. [Scand.]

MULATTO (mū-lat'ō) *n.* the child of a black and a white person. [Sp., fr. A.]

MULBERRY (mul'her-i) *n.* a tree and its fruit. [M.E. *mool berry*, fr. O.E. *mor*, fr. L. *morus*, a mulberry, and BERRY.]

MULCH (mulsh) *n.* half-rotten straw. Also MULSH. [E. Cf. Ger. *mulsch*, rotten.]

MULCT (mulkt) *n.* pecuniary penalty;—*v.t.* to punish by a fine. [L. *mulcta*.]

MULE (mūl) *n.* an animal or plant of a mongrel kind. [F., fr. L. (acc.) *mulum*.]

MULETEER (mū-le-tēr') *n.* a driver of mules. [F. *muletier*.]   [perverse.

MULISH (mū'lish) *a.* like a mule; stubborn;

MULL (mul) (1) *v.t.* to spice and sweeten wine; —(2) *n.* a headland; promontory (Scot.) [(1) Fr. MULLED. (2) Celt.]

MULLED (muld) *a.* spiced and sweetened, as wine, ale, etc. [Fr. M.E. *molde*, feast-ale, funeral feast.]

MULLER (mul'ẹr) *n.* a stone for grinding colours. [See MULLED.]

MULLET (mul'et) *n.* a small sea-fish which frequents the shores. [F. *mulet*, dim. fr. L. *mullus*.]

MULLIGATAWNY (mul-i-ga-taw'ni) *n.* a soup of white meat and curry powder. [Tamil.]

MULLION (mul'yun) *n.* a bar in a window frame. [L. *mancus*, maimed.]

MULTIFARIOUS (mul-ti-fā'ri-us) *a.* having great variety. [L., fr. *multi-*, for *multus*, many.]

MULTIFARIOUSNESS (mul-ti-fā'ri-us-nes) *a.* manifold diversity.

MULTIFORM (mul'ti-form) *a.* having various forms or shapes. [L. *multi-*, many.]

MULTIFORMITY (mul-ti-for'mi-ti) *n.* diversity of forms.

MULTIPAROUS (mul-tip'a̤-rus) *a.* producing many at a birth. [L. *multus*, many, and *parere*, bear.]

MULTIPLE (mul'ti-pl) *n.* a number exactly divisible by another. [F., fr. Late L. *multiplus*, fr. *multus*, many. Cf. TRIPLE.]

MULTIPLEX (mul'ti-pleks) *a.* many-fold. [L.]

MULTIPLIABLE (mul'ti-pli-a̤-bl) *a.* that may be multiplied.

MULTIPLICAND (mul-ti-pli-kand') *n.* a number to be multiplied. [L. (gerund.) *multiplicandum*.]

MULTIPLICATION (mul-ti-pli-kā′shun) *n.* act of multiplying. [F., fr. L. (acc.) *multiplicationem,* fr. (part.) *multiplicatus,* multiplied.]

MULTIPLICITY (mul-ti-plis′i-ti) *n.* a great number or variety. [L. *multiplex.*]

MULTIPLIER (mul′ti-pli-ẹr) *n.* one that multiplies.

MULTIPLY (mul′ti-pli) *v.t.* to increase in numbers. [F. *multiplier,* fr. L. *multiplicare,* fr. stem *multiplic-,* of MULTIPLEX.]

MULTITUDE (mul′ti-tūd) *n.* a great number; crowd; the populace. [F., tr. L. (acc.) *multitudinem,* fr. *multus.*]

MULTITUDINOUS (mul-ti-tū′di-nus) *a.* consisting of a great number.

MULTURE (mul′tūr) *n.* grinding of grain; quantity ground at one time; charge for grinding. [O.F., fr. L. (acc.) *molituram,* a grinding; fr. *mola.*]

MUM (mum) (1) *a.* silent;—*inter.* be silent; —(2) *n.* a kind of beer. [(1) Imit. Cf. L. and G. *mu.* (2) Fr. *Mumme,* a 15th century brewer, of Brunswick.]

MUMBLE (mum′bl) *v.t.* or *i.* to mutter. [M.E. *momelen,* fr. MUM (1).]

MUMMER (mum′ẹr) *n.* a masker; buffoon. [D.]

MUMMERY (mum′ẹr-i) *n.* sport in masks; foolery.

MUMMY (mum′i) *n.* a dead human body embalmed. [F. *momie,* fr. A.]

MUMP (mump) *v.t.* to munch; to grumble; —*v.i.* to mumble; to grin. [D.; conn. with MUMBLE.]

MUMPISH (mum′pish) *a.* grim; sullen.

MUMPS (mumps) *n.* a disease of the neck; sullenness.

MUNCH (munsh) *v.t.* or *i.* to chew with closed mouth. [E.; imit.]

MUNDANE (mun′dān) *a.* belonging to this world. [L. *mundanus,* fr. *mundus,* world.]

MUNICIPAL (mū-nis′i-pl) *a.* belonging to a city. [L., fr. *municipium,* township, fr. *munia,* duties, and *capere,* take.]

MUNICIPALITY (mū-nis-i-pal′i-ti) *n.* a municipal district.

MUNIFICENCE (mū-nif′i-sens) *n.* liberality. [F., fr. L. (acc.) *munificentiam,* fr. *munus,* gift, and *facere,* make.]

MUNIFICENT (mū-nif′i-sent) *a.* giving generously; very liberal.

MUNIMENT (mū′ni-ment) *n.* fortification; charter; title deed. [L. *munimentum,* fr. *munire,* fortify.]

MUNITION (mū-nish′un) *n.* materials for war. [F., fr. L. (acc.) *munitionem,* fr. (part.) *munitus,* fortified.]

MURAL (mū′rạl) *a.* pertaining to a wall. [L., fr. *murus,* wall.]

MURDER (mur′dẹr) *n.* the act of killing a human being with premeditated malice;—*v.t.* to kill; assassinate; destroy. Also **MURTHER.** [Fr. O.E. *morthor.*]

MURDERER (mur′dẹr-ẹr) *n.* one who is guilty of murder.

MURDEROUS (mur′dẹr-us) *a.* guilty of murder.

MUREX (mū′reks) *n.* a sort of marine shellfish, from which the ancients obtained purple dye. [L. =the murex; a pointed rock.]

MURICATED (mū′ri-kā-ted) *a.* armed with sharp points. [Fr. L. stem *muric-,* of MUREX.]

MURK (murk) *n.* darkness. [Scand.]

MURKY (mur′ki) *a.* dark; gloomy.

MURMUR (mur′mur) *v.i.* to mutter; purl; complain;—*n.* continued complaint; a purling sound. [L.; imit.]

MURMURER (mur′mur-ẹr) *n.* one who murmurs.

MURRAIN (mur′in) *n.* an infectious disease among cattle;—also *a.* affected with murrain. [O.F. *murine,* carcass, fr. L. *mori,* die.]

MUSCATEL (mus′ka-tel) *n.* a rich kind of grape; wine made from it; a raisin; a pear. Also **MUSCADEL** and **MUSCADINE.** [O.F., through It., fr. MUSK.]

MUSCLE (mus′l) *n.* the fleshy fibre in animals. [O.F., fr. L. *musculus.*]

MUSCULAR (mus′kū-lạr) *a.* relating to the muscles; brawny.

MUSCULARITY (mus-kū-lar′i-ti) *n.* state of being muscular.

MUSE (mūz) (1) *n.* a fit of meditation; deep thought;—*v.t.* or *i.* to think deeply; consider; wonder at; be absent in mind;—(2) *n.pl.* the nine goddesses presiding over the arts. [(1) F. *muser,* lit. to sniff about, fr. O.F. *muse,* MUZZLE. (2) F., fr. L., fr. G. *Mousa.*]

MUSEFUL (mūz′fool) *a.* silently thoughtful. [See MUSE (1).]

MUSER (mū′zẹr) *n.* one who muses; daydreamer. [See MUSE (1).]

MUSEUM (mū-zē′um) *n.* a repository or collection of curiosities in nature or art. [L., fr. G. *mouseion,* temple of the MUSES.]

MUSH (mush) *n.* food of maize meal. [Form of MASH.]

MUSHROOM (mush′rŏŏm) *n.* an edible fungus; an upstart;—*a.* from mushrooms; shortlived. [M.E. *muscheron,* fr. O.F. *mousseron,* fr. *mousse,* MOSS.]

MUSIC (mū′zik) *n.* science of harmonical sounds; melody or harmony. [F. *musique,* fr. L., fr. G. *mousike,* fr. MUSE (2).]

MUSICAL (mū′zi-kạl) *a.* melodious.

MUSICALLY (mū′zi-kạl-i) *ad.* in a harmonious manner.

MUSICIAN (mū-zish′ạn) *n.* one skilled in music.

MUSK (musk) *n.* an animal, and a strong-scented substance procured from it;—*v.t.* to perfume with musk. [F., fr. L. *muscus,* fr. G. *moschos.*]

MUSKET (mus′ket) *n.* a species of fire-arms. [F. *mousquet,* fr. It. =orig. a small hawk, fr. L. *musca,* fly.]

MUSKETRY (mus′ket-ri) *n.* muskets in general; practice in discharging muskets.

MUSLIN (muz′lin) *n.* a fine cotton cloth. [O.F. *mosolin,* fr. It., fr. *Mosul,* in Asiatic Turkey.]

MUSLIN-DE-LAINE (muz′lin-de-lān) *n.* a light fabric of cotton and wool. [F. *mousseline de laine.*]

MUSROLE (muz′rōl) *n.* the noseband of a horse's bridle. [F. *muserolle,* fr. O.F. *muse,* MUZZLE.]

MUSSEL (mus′l) *n.* a shell-fish. [See MUSCLE.]

MUSSULMAN (mus′ul-man) *n.* a believer in the Koran;—*pl.* MUSSULMANS. [Pers. fr. A. *moslim,* MOSLEM.]

MUST (must) (1) *v.i.* to be obliged; be morally fit;—(2) *v.t.* to grow mouldy;—*n.* new wine unfermented. [(1) O.E. (past tense). Cf. Ger. *musse.* (2) O.E., fr. L. *mustum.*]

MUSTACHE (mŏŏs-tàsh′) *n.* long hair on the upper lip;—*pl.* MUSTACHES. Also **MOUSTACHE.** [F., fr. It., fr. G. stem *mustak-,* of *mustax,* upper lip.]

MUSTARD (mus′tạrd) *n.* a plant and its seed—used as a condiment when ground, and for blistering. [O.F. *mostarde* =F. *moutarde,* fr. MUST (2), with which it was mixed.]

MUSTER (mus′tẹr) *v.t.* or *i.* to assemble; collect; meet in one place;—*n.* a review of troops; register of forces. [O.F. *mostre,* show =F. *monstre,* MONSTER.]

MUSTINESS (mus′ti-nes) *n.* mouldiness. [See MUST (2).]

MUSTY (mus′ti) *a.* affected with mould; spoiled by damp or age.

MUTABILITY (mū-ta-bil′i-ti) *n.* change of mind; instability.

MUTABLE (mū′ta-bl) *a.* subject or given to change; inconstant; variable. [L. *mutabilis,* fr. *mutare,* change.]

MUTCHKIN (much'kin) *n.* a Scotch liquid measure of four gills. [D.]
MUTE (mūt) *a.* silent; speechless; not sounded;—*n.* one who is silent or dumb; an undertaker's attendant. [L. *mutus.*]
MUTELY (mūt'li) *ad.* silently.
MUTENESS (mūt'nes) *n.* silence; aversion to speech.
MUTILATE (mū'ti-lāt) *v.t.* to cut off a limb, or part. [L. (part.) *mutilatus,* maimed, fr. *mutilus,* maimed.]
MUTILATION (mū-ti-lā'shun) *n.* deprivation of an essential part.
MUTINEER (mū-ti-nēr') *n.* one who joins in a mutiny.
MUTINOUS (mū'ti-nus) *a.* seditious; disorderly.
MUTINY (mū'ti-ni) *n.* an insurrection of soldiers or seamen;—*v.i.* to rise against lawful authority. [O.F. (v.) *mutiner,* fr. *mute,* a rebellion, fr. Low L. (part.) *movitus* =*motus.* See **MOTION**.]
MUTTER (mut'er) *v.t.* or *i.* to speak low or indistinctly; grumble;—*n.* obscure utterance; murmur. [Imit. Cf. L. *muttere.*]
MUTTERER (mut'er-er) *n.* a grumbler.
MUTTERING (mut'er-ing) *n.* a grumbling.
MUTTERINGLY (mut'er-ing-li) *ad.* with low, indistinct articulation.
MUTTON (mut'n) *n.* flesh of sheep. [O.F. = F. *mouton,* fr. Low L. (acc.) *multonem,* sheep.]
MUTTON-CHOP (mut'n-chop) *n.* a rib or slice of mutton for broiling.
MUTUAL (mū'tū-al) *a.* pertaining to both sides; reciprocal; given or received by each party. [L. *mutuus,* fr. *mutare,* change.]
MUTUALITY (mū-tū-al'i-ti) *n.* state of being mutual.
MUTUALLY (mū'tū-al-i) *ad.* reciprocally.
MUZZLE (muz'l) *v.t.* to fasten the mouth of an animal;—*n.* a mouth; a fastening for the mouth. [O.F. *musel* =F. *museau,* fr. *muse,* snout, fr. L. *morsus,* bite. See **MORSEL**.]
MUZZY (muz'i) *a.* tipsy; bewildered. [Conn. with **MUSE** (1).]

MY (mi) *a.* belonging to me. [Short. fr. **MINE**.]
MYOLOGY (mi-ol'ō-ji) *n.* science or description of the muscles. [Fr. G. *mus, muos,* muscle, and *-logia,* science, fr. *legein.*]
MYOPIA (mi-ō'pi-a) *n.* short-sightedness. Also **MYOPY**. [G., fr. *myo,* shut, and *ops,* eye.]
MYRIAD (mir'i-ad) *n.* the number of ten thousand; a large number. [G. stem *muriad-,* fr. *murios,* 10,000, numberless.]
MYRMIDON (mer'mi-don) *n.* a rough soldier; ruffian. [G. = one of a tribe that followed Achilles.]
MYRRH (mer) *n.* an inspissated aromatic gum resin. [F., fr. L., fr. G. *murr(h)a.*]
MYRTLE (mer'tl) *n.* an evergreen shrub. [O.F. dim. fr. *myrte,* fr. L., fr. G. *murtos.*]
MYSELF (mi-self') *pron.* I or me—used emphatically and reflexively.
MYSTERIOUS (mis-tē'ri-us) *a.* full of mystery; obscure; incomprehensible.
MYSTERIOUSLY (mis-tē'ri-us-li) *ad.* obscurely.
MYSTERY (mis'te-ri) *n.* a deep secret; an enigma; a truth known by revelation only; a truth not revealed; trade; calling. [L. *mysterium,* fr. G. *mustes,* one initiated, fr. *muein,* to shut, (lips or eyes).]
MYSTIC (mis'tik) *n.* one who professes to have direct intercourse with God;—*a.* mystical. [L. *mysticus,* pertaining to the rites, fr. G. *mustes.* See **MYSTERY**.]
MYSTICAL (mis'ti-kal) *a.* obscure; involving a secret meaning; emblematical.
MYSTICALLY (mis'ti-kal-i) *ad.* with a secret meaning.
MYSTICISM (mis'ti-sizm) *n.* obscurity of doctrine; the doctrines of mystics.
MYSTIFY (mis'ti-fi) *v.t.* to render obscure or complex. [F. *fier* =L. *ficare* =*facere,* make.]
MYTH (mith) *n.* a fable; moral or religious legend. [L. fr. G. *muthos.*]
MYTHIC (mith'ik) *a.* fabulous.
MYTHOLOGICAL (mith-ō-loj'i-kal) *a.* pertaining to mythology. [in mythology.]
MYTHOLOGIST (mi-thol'ō-jist) *n.* one versed in mythology.
MYTHOLOGY (mi-thol'ō-ji) *n.* a science of or treatise on myths. [G. *muthos,* and *-logia,* science, fr. *legein.*]

N

NAB (nab) *v.t.* to catch; seize. [Scand.]
NABOB (nā'bob) *n.* a prince in India; a very rich man. Also **NAWAB**. [Hind., fr. A.]
NACRE (nā'ker) *n.* mother of pearl. [F., fr. Per.]
NACREOUS (nī'krē-us) *a.* having an iridescent lustre.
NADIR (nā'dir) *n.* point directly opposite the zenith. [F., fr. A.]
NAG (nag) (1) *n.* a small horse;— (2) *v.i.* to find fault constantly; carp at. [(1) D. (2) Scand.; conn. with **GNAW**.]
NAIAD (nī'ad) *n.* a water-nymph;—*pl.* **NAIADES**. [G. stem *naiad-,* of *naias,* fr. *naein,* flow.]
NAIL (nāl) *n.* a claw; a horny substance on the ends of the fingers; an iron pin; a boss; two inches and a quarter;—*v.t.* to fasten or stud with nails. [O.E. *nœgel.* Cf. Ger. *Nagel.*]
NAILER (nā'ler) *n.* a maker of nails.
NAILERY (nā'ler-i) *n.* manufactory for making nails.
NAIVE (nä-ēv') *a.* simple; frank; ingenuous. [F. fem., fr. *naïf,* fr. L. (acc.) *nativum,* doublet of **NATIVE**.]
NAIVETE (nä-ēv'tā) *n.* native simplicity.
NAKED (nā'ked) *a.* having no covering; unprotected; bare; plain or evident; simple. [O.E. *nacod.* Cf. Ger. *nackt.*]
NAKEDLY (nā'ked-li) *ad.* openly; plainly; barely.

NAKEDNESS (nā'ked-nes) *n.* want of covering; bareness.
NAME (nām) *n.* designation; title; reputation; remembrance; appearance; behalf; race or family;—*v.t.* to mention by name; denominate. [O.E. *nama.* Cf. Ger. *Name;* L. *nomen,* **NOUN**.]
NAMELESS (nām'les) *a.* having no name.
NAMELY (nām'li) *ad.* that is to say.
NAMER (nā'mer) *n.* one who names or designates.
NAMESAKE (nām'sāk) *n.* a person of the same name.
NANKEEN (nan-kēn') *n.* a buff-coloured cotton cloth. [After *Nankin,* where first made.]
NAP (nap) (1) *n.* a short sleep;—*v.i.* to sleep a short time;— (2) *n.* a woolly substance on cloth. [(1) O.E. *hnœppian.* (2) Fr. D.]
NAPE (nāp) *n.* the joint of the neck behind. [E.; conn. with **KNOB**.]
NAPERY (nā'per-i) *n.* linen for the household, especially linen for the table. [O.F. *naperie.*]
NAPHTHA (nap'tha, naf'tha) *n.* a bituminous and inflammable liquid which exudes from the earth. [G., fr. A.]
NAPKIN (nap'kin) *n.* a handkerchief; a cloth to wipe the hands. [O.F. *nape,* a cloth, fr. Late L. (acc.) *napam,* for L. *mappam.* See **MAP**; E. dim. suff. *-kin.*]

Fāte, fár, ado; mē, her; mīne; nōte; tūne; mòòn.

NAPLESS (nap'les) *a.* without nap; threadbare. [See NAP (2).]

NARCISSUS (når-sis'us) *n.* a genus of bulbous flowering plants. [L., fr. G., fr. its properties.

NARCOTIC.]

NARCOTIC (når-kot'ik) *a.* inducing sleep. [G. fr. *narkoein*, benumb, fr. *narke*, numbness.]

NARCOTINE (når'kō-tin) *n.* the active principle in opium.

NARD (nård) *n.* an aromatic plant; an ointment. [G., fr. Per.]

NARRATE (nạ-rāt') *v.t.* to tell; relate. [L. (part.) *narratus*, narrated, fr. *gnarus*, knowing.]

NARRATION (nạ-rā'shun) *n.* that which is narrated; rehearsal. [F., fr. L. (acc.) *narrationem*, tale.]

Narcissus.

NARRATIVE (nar'ạ-tiv) *n.* recital of particulars; a story; —*a.* relating particulars.

NARRATOR (nạ-rā'tẹr) *n.* one who narrates.

NARROW (nar'ō) *a.* having little width; close; covetous; —*v.t.* to contract; —*v.i.* to become less broad. [M.E. *narowe*, fr. O.E. *nearu*.]

NARROWING (nar'ō-ing) *n.* the part of a stocking which is narrowed.

NARROWLY (nar'ō-li) *ad.* closely; nearly; hardly.

NARROWNESS (nar'ō-nes) *n.* want of breadth; meanness.

NARROWS (nar'ōz) *n.pl.* a narrow passage.

NASAL (nā'zạl) *a.* pertaining to the nose; —*n.* a sound uttered through the nose. [Late L. *nasalis*, fr. *nasus*, NOSE.]

NASCENT (nas'ent) *a.* beginning to exist. [L. (part. stem) *nascent-*, being born, fr. *nasci*.]

NASTY (nås'ti) *a.* dirty; filthy. [Formerly *nasky*, fr. Scand.]

NATAL (nā'tạl) *a.* relating to nativity. [F., fr. L. (acc.) *natalem*, fr. (part.) *natus*, born, fr. *nasci*, to be born.]

NATANT (nā'tạnt) *a.* floating. [L. (part. stem) *natant-*, swimming, fr. *natare*.]

NATHLESS (nath'les) *ad.* nevertheless. [=not by that less, fr. O.E. *na thy læs*.]

NATION (nā'shun) *n.* a people living under one government; race; great number. [F., fr. L. (acc.) *nationem*, lit. birth. See NATAL.]

NATIONAL (nash'un-ạl) *a.* pertaining to a nation.

NATIONALISE (nash'un-ạl-īz) *v.t.* to make national.

NATIONALITY (nash-un-al'i-ti) *n.* love of one's nation; national character or bias.

NATIONALLY (nash'un-al-i) *ad.* as a whole nation.

NATIVE (nā'tiv) *a.* produced by nature; pertaining to the place of one's birth; original; —*n.* one born in a place or country. [L. *nativus*, natural. See NATAL. Doublet of NAIVE.]

NATIVITY (nạ-tiv'i-ti) *n.* birth; time, place, or manner of birth. [L. (acc.) *nativitatem*.]

NATTY (nat'i) *a.* trim; neat; tidy; spruce. [Cf. NEAT.]

NATURAL (nat'ū-rạl) *a.* pertaining to nature; inborn; normal; not revealed; not artificial; illegitimate; —*n.* an idiot; a fool. [L. *naturalis*.]

NATURALISATION (nat-ū-rạl-i-zā'shun) *n.* admission to native privileges.

NATURALISE (nat'ū-rạl-īz) *v.t.* to confer the rights of citizenship.

NATURALISM (nat'ū-rạl-izm) *n.* mere state of nature; natural religion; denial of supernatural agency.

NATURALIST (nat'ū-rạl-ist) *n.* one versed in natural history.

NATURALLY (nat'ū-rạl-i) *ad.* according to nature.

NATURALNESS (nat'ū-rạl-nes) *n.* state of being produced by nature.

NATURE (nā'tūr) *n.* whatever is made; essential qualities; constitution; regular course; natural affection; sort; kind. [F., fr. L. (acc.) *naturam*. See NATAL.]

NAUGHT (nawt) *n.* nothing. [O.E. *nawhit*, lit. not a WHIT. Doublet of NOT.]

NAUGHTILY (naw'ti-li) *ad.* in a naughty manner.

NAUGHTINESS (naw'ti-nes) *n.* slight wickedness; bad behaviour.

NAUGHTY (naw'ti) *a.* wicked; mischievous; perverse. [=orig. worth NAUGHT.]

NAUSEA (naw'shạ, naw'she-ạ) *n.* sickness at the stomach; loathing. [L., fr. G. *nausia*, sea-sickness, fr. *naus*, ship.]

NAUSEATE (naw'she-āt) *v.t.* or *i.* to affect with disgust; loathe.

NAUSEOUS (naw'shus) *a.* loathsome; disgusting. [L. *nauseosus*.]

NAUTICAL (naw'ti-kạl) *a.* pertaining to seamen or navigation. [Fr. L. *nauticus*, fr. G. *naus*, ship.]

NAVAL (nā'vạl) *a.* belonging to ships. [L., fr. *navis*, ship; conn. with G. *naus*; NAUSEA; NAUTICAL; NAVE.]

NAVE (nāv) (1) *n.* the central piece, or hub, from which the spokes of a wheel radiate; —(2) *n.* the body of a church, from the choir to the entrance. [(1) O.E. *nafu, nabu*. Cf. Ger. *Nabe*. (2) O.F. =F. *nef*, fr. L. (acc.) *navem*, ship; suggested by the long shape.]

NAVEL (nā'vl) *n.* the middle of the abdomen. [O.E. *nafela*; conn. with NAVE.]

NAVIGABLE (nav'i-ga-bl) *a.* passable for ships.

NAVIGATE (nav'i-gāt) *v.t.* or *i.* to pass on water with ships; sail. [L. (part.) *navigatus*, navigated, fr. *navis*, ship, and *-igare* =*agere*, lead.]

NAVIGATION (nav-i-gā'shun) *n.* the act or art of navigating; ships in general.

NAVIGATOR (nav'i-gā-tẹr) *n.* one who directs the course of a ship.

NAVVY (nav'i) *n.* a labourer employed in cutting railways, etc. [Short. fr. NAVIGATOR. Orig. of labourers about canals.]

NAVY (nā'vi) *n.* a fleet of ships. [O.F. *navie*, a ship, fr. L. (acc.) *naviam*, for *nave*. See NAVE.]

NAY (nā) *ad.* no; not only so; but also; —*n.* denial; refusal. [Scand.]

NAZARENE (naz'ạ-rēn) *n.* a term of contempt for Christ and early Christians. [G.]

NAZARITE (naz'ạ-rīt) *n.* a Jew who professed extraordinary purity of life.

NEAP (nēp) *n.* the pole of a cart; —*a.* low, as *neap* tides. [O.E. *nep*.]

NEAP-TIDE (nēp'tīd) *n.* a low tide.

NEAR (nēr) (1) *a.* not distant; close; intimate; dear; covetous; —*v.t.* to approach; —(2) *ad.* within a little. [(1) M.E. *nerre*, fr. O.E. *neah*, fr. *nigher*, fr. (ad.) *near*, NIGH. (2) M.E. *ner*.]

NEARLY (nēr'li) *ad.* at hand; closely; almost; stingily. [See NEAR (1).]

NEARNESS (nēr'nes) *n.* closeness; intimacy; stinginess.

NEAT (nēt) *a.* trim; tidy; clean; pure; finished; refined. [Doublet of NET (2).]

NEAT-CATTLE (nēt'kat-l) *n.pl.* oxen; cows. [O.E. *neat*.]

NEATLY (nēt'li) *ad.* cleanly; nicely.

NEATNESS (nēt'nes) *n.* cleanliness; niceness; purity.

NEB (neb) *n.* a nose; beak of a bird. [O.E. *nebb*, the face; cog. with D. *neb*, beak.]

NEBULA (neb'ū-lạ) *n.* a light gauzy cloud; cluster of stars forming a misty cloud; film in the eye; —*pl.* NEBULÆ. [L. =mist.]

NEBULOUS (neb'ū-lus) *a.* resembling a collection of vapours.

NECESSARIES (nes'e-sẹr-iz) *n.pl.* things needful.

NECESSARILY (nes'e-sẹr-i-li) *ad.* from necessity; inevitably.

NECESSARY (nes'e-sẹr-i) *a.* that must be; inevitable; compulsory. [L., fr. (a.) *necesse*, needful.]

NECESSITARIAN (ne-ses-i-tā'ri-ạn) *n.* one who denies the freedom of the will.

NECESSITATE (ne-ses'i-tāt) *v.t.* to compel.

NECESSITOUS (ne-ses'i-tus) *a.* very needy.

NECESSITOUSLY (ne-ses'i-tus-li) *ad.* by or from necessity.

NECESSITY (ne-ses'i-ti) *n.* that which must be; compulsion; requisite; indigence; overruling fate. [L. (acc.) *necessitatem*.]

NECK (nek) *n.* the part between the head and body; a narrow tract of land. [O.E. *hnecca*. Cf. Ger. *Nacken*.]

NECKCLOTH (nek'kloth) *n.* a cloth for men's necks.

NECKERCHIEF (nek'ẹr-chif) *n.* a cloth for the neck.

NECKLACE (nek'les) *n.* a string of beads, etc., for the neck.

NECROLOGIST (nek-rol'ō-jist) *n.* a recorder of deaths.

NECROLOGY (nek-rol'ō-ji) *n.* a register of the dead or of deaths. [Fr. G. *necros*, corpse, and *-logia*, science, fr. *legein*, speak.]

NECROMANCER (nek'ru-man-sẹr) *n.* a conjurer.

NECROMANCY (nek'ru-man-si) *n.* conjuration. [Fr. G. *nekros*, corpse, and *manteia*, divination.]

NECROPOLIS (nek-rop'u-lis) *n.* a public cemetery. [Fr. G. *nekros*, corpse, and *polis*, a city.]

NECTAR (nek'tạr) *n.* the fabled drink of the gods; any pleasant beverage; honey of flowers. [L., fr. G.]

NECTAREAN (nek-tā're-ạn) *a.* like nectar.

NECTARIAL (nek-tā'ri-ạl) *a.* pertaining to the nectary of a plant.

NECTARINE (nek'tạ-rin) *n.* a fruit of the peach kind.

NECTARY (nek'tạ-ri) *n.* the honey cup of a flower.

NEED (nēd) *n.* occasion for something; want; pressing necessity; poverty;—*v.t.* to want; —*v.i.* to be wanted. [O.E. *nead*. Cf. Ger. *Noth*.]

NEEDFUL (nēd'fool) *a.* necessary; requisite.

NEEDINESS (nē'di-nes) *n.* want; indigence.

NEEDLE (nē'dl) *n.* a pointed instrument for sewing, and for the mariner's compass;— *v.t.* to form into crystals. [O.E. *nœdl*. Cf. Ger. *Nadel*.]

NEEDLESS (nēd'les) *a.* unnecessary.

NEEDLESSLY (nēd'les-li) *ad.* without necessity.

NEEDS (nēdz) *ad.* indispensably.

NEEDY (nē'di) *a.* necessitous; poor.

NE'ER (nàr) *ad.* a contraction of NEVER.

NEFARIOUS (ne-fā'ri-us) *a.* abominably wicked; villainous; impious. [L., fr. *nefas*, wickedness, fr. *ne-*, not, and *fas*, law.]

NEFARIOUSLY (ne-fā'ri-us-li) *ad.* with extreme wickedness.

NEFARIOUSNESS (ne-fā'ri-us-nes) *n.* villainy.

NEGATION (ne-gā'shun) *n.* denial. [O.F., fr. L. (acc.) *negationem*.]

NEGATIVE (neg'ạ-tiv) *a.* implying denial; prohibitory; vetoing;—*n.* a word or proposition that denies;—*v.t.* to prove the contrary; refuse; reject by vote. [L., fr. (part.) *negatus*, denied, fr. *negare*.]

NEGATIVELY (neg'ạ-tiv-li) *ad.* with or by denial.

NEGLECT (neg-lekt') *v.t.* to omit by carelessness; disregard; slight;—*n.* omission to do; inattention; indifference. [L. (part.) *neglectus*, neglected, fr. *neg*, *ne*, not, and *legere*, to gather.]

NEGLECTFUL (neg-lekt'fool) *a.* heedless.

NEGLIGEE (neg'li-zhā) *n.* a loose gown or dress; a long coral necklace. [F. (part.) neglected.]

NEGLIGENCE (neg'li-jens) *n.* habitual omission of that which ought to be done. [F., fr. L. (acc.) *negligentiam*, fr. (acc. part.) *negligentem*, neglecting.]

NEGLIGENT (neg'li-jent) *a.* heedless; inattentive.

NEGLIGENTLY (neg'li-jent-li) *ad.* heedlessly.

NEGOTIABLE (ne-gō'shi-ạ-bl) *a.* that may be negotiated.

NEGOTIATE (ne-gō'shi-āt) *v.t.* or *i.* to transact business; treat with; procure or sell; transfer for value. [L. (part.) *negotiatus*, having trafficked, fr. *negotium*, business, fr. *ne(g)*, *ne*, not, and *otium*, leisure.]

NEGOTIATION (ne-gō-shi-ā'shun) *n.* a treaty of business.

NEGOTIATOR (ne-gō'shi-ā-tẹr) *n.* one who negotiates. [L.]

NEGRESS (nē'gres) *n.* a female of the black African race.

NEGRO (nē'grō) *n.* an African by birth, or a descendant of one. [Sp., fr. L. (acc.) *nigrum*, black.]

NEGUS (nē'gus) *n.* wine, water, sugar, and lemon-juice mixed. [After the inventor, Col. *Negus*.]

NEIGH (nā) *v.i.* to whinny;—*n.* voice of a horse. [O.E. *hnœgan*.]

NEIGHBOUR (nā'bur) *n.* one who lives near; a country or nation near;—*v.t.* or *i.* to adjoin; be or live near to. [O.E. *neahgebur*, fr. NIGH, and *ge-bur*, farmer, BOOR.]

NEIGHBOURHOOD (nā'bur-hood) *n.* state of being near; adjoining district; the people who live in it.

NEIGHBOURING (nā'bur-ing) *a.* near.

NEIGHBOURLY (nā'bur-li) *a.* cultivating familiar intercourse.

NEITHER (nē'THẹr, nī'THẹr) *pron.* not either; —*con.* nor. [Fr. O.E. *ne*, not, and EITHER.]

NEOLITHIC (nē-u-lith'ik) *a.* belonging to the later Stone Age. [Fr. G. *neos*, new, and *lithos*, stone.]

NEOLOGIST (nē-ol'u-jist) *n.* one who holds to neology.

NEOLOGY (nē-ol'ō-ji) *n.* rationalistic views in theology. [Fr. G. *neos*, and *-logia*, science, fr. *legein*.]

NEOPHYTE (nē'u-fīt) *n.* a new convert; a novice. [L., fr. G. *neos*, and *phutos*, grown, fr. *phuein*.]

NEPHEW (nev'ū) *n.* son of a brother or sister. [M.E. *neveu*, fr. F., fr. L. (acc.) *nepotem*. Cf. Ger. *Neffe*.]

NEPHRITIC (nef-rit'ik) *a.* pertaining to the kidneys. [G., fr. *nephros*, kidney.]

NEPOTISM (nē'put-izm, nep'u-tizm) *n.* favouritism to relations. [F., fr. L. stem *nepot-*, of *nepos*, grandson or NEPHEW.]

NEPTUNE (nep'tūn) *n.* the god of the sea; a planet beyond Uranus. [L.]

NEREID (nē'rē-id) *n.* a sea-nymph. [G. = a daughter of *Nereus*.]

NERVE (nerv) *n.* an organ of sensation and motion in animals; firmness; strength;— *v.t.* to give vigour to. [F. *nerf* (ner-f), fr. L. (acc.) *nervum*, sinew.]

NERVELESS (nerv'les) *a.* without strength.

NERVINE (ner'vin) *a.* good for the nerves.

NERVOUS (ner'vus) *a.* strong; robust; forcible; weak in the nerves; shaky. [L. *nervosus*.]

NERVOUSLY (ner'vus-li) *ad.* with strength; with agitation.

NERVOUSNESS (ner'vus-nes) *n.* strength; vigour; weakness of the nerves.

NESS (nes) *n.* promontory; headland. [O.E. *nœss*.]

NEST (nest) *n.* a bed for birds or insects; a number of boxes inserted one into another; —*v.i.* to build or live in a nest. [F.]

NESTLE (nes'l) *v.i.* to lie close; move restlessly. [O.E. *nestlian*.]

NESTLING (nes'ling) *n.* a bird just hatched.

NET (net) (1) *n.* an instrument for catching fish and fowls;—*v.t.* to make network; take with a net;—(2) *a.* pure; clear of all charges and reductions;—*v.t.* to produce in clear profit. [(1) E. Cf. Ger. *Netz*. (2) F.; fem. *nette*; fr. L. (acc.) *nitidum*.]

NETHER (neTH'er) *a.* lower; infernal. [O.E. *neothera*. Cf. Ger. *nieder*.]

NETHERMOST (neTH'er-mōst) *a.* lowest.

NETTING (net'ing) *n.* network. [See NET (1).]

NETTLE (net'l) *n.* a prickly plant;—*v.t.* to sting; vex. [O.E. *netele*. Cf. Ger. *Nessel*.]

NETWORK (net'wurk) *n.* work wrought for or like a net. [See NET (1).]

NEURALGIA (nū-ral'ji-a) *n.* a pain in the nerves. [Fr. G. *neuron*, nerve, and *algos*, pain.]

NEURALGIC (nū-ral'jik) *a.* pertaining to neuralgia.

NEUROLOGY (nū-rol'ō-ji) *n.* a description of the nerves.

NEUTER (nū'ter) *a.* of neither party; of neither gender. [L. = neither, sexless.]

NEUTRAL (nū'tral) *a.* not of either party; indifferent;—*n.* one that takes no part in a contest.

NEUTRALISATION (nū-tral-i-zā'shun) *n.* the act of rendering neutral.

NEUTRALISE (nū'tral-iz) *v.t.* to render neutral.

NEUTRALITY (nū-tral'i-ti) *n.* state of being neutral.

NEVER (nev'er) *ad.* at no time; in no degree. [O.E. *noefre*, fr. *ne*, not, and EVER.]

NEVERTHELESS (nev-er-THe-les') *ad.* notwithstanding. [Cf. NATHLESS.]

NEW (nū) *a.* fresh; recent. [O.E. *neowe*. Cf. Ger. *neu*. L. *novus*. G. *neos*.]

NEWFANGLED (nū-fang'gld) *a.* newly formed; fond of new things. [-fangled, for O.E. *fangel*, ready to seize. See FANG.]

NEWLY (nū'li) *ad.* freshly; lately.

NEWNESS (nū'nes) *n.* freshness; novelty; recent change.

NEWS (nūz) *n.* fresh information. [Orig. pl. = new things.]

NEWSMONGER (nūz'mung-ger) *n.* a dealer in news. [See NEWS and MONGER.]

NEWSPAPER (nūz'pā-per) *n.* a periodical paper to circulate news. [See NEWS and PAPER.]

NEXT (nekst) *a.* nearest in place, time, or rank;—*ad.* at the time or turn nearest. [M.E. *nehest*, *next*, fr. NIGH.]

NEXUS (nek'sus) *n.* connecting link or principle. [L.]

NIB (nib) *n.* point of a pen; end of a beak; —*v.t.* to point; cut off the point. [Form of NEB.]

NIBBLE (nib'l) *n.* a little bite;—*v.t.* or *i.* to bite at; bite slowly; find fault in trifles. [Fr. NIP.]

NIBBLER (nib'ler) *n.* one that nibbles.

NICE (nis) *a.* exact; fine; delicate; fastidious. [O.F. = simple, fr. L. *nescius*.]

NICELY (nis'li) *ad.* accurately; delicately.

NICETY (nis'e-ti) *n.* accuracy; minuteness; delicacy.

NICHE (nich) *n.* a small recess in the side of a wall for a statue. [F., through It., fr. L. *mitulus*, a mussel.]

NICK (nik) *n.* a notch; score; exact point; —*v.t.* to cut in notches. [Fr. Ger.]

Niche.

NICKEL (nik'el) *n.* a grayish-white metal used for alloys. [Ger.]

NICK-NACKS (nik'naks) *n.pl.* small wares; trifles. [See KNICK-KNACK.]

NICKNAME (nik'nām) *n.* a name in sport or contempt;—*v.t.* to name in contempt. [A *neke name*, for an EKE name.]

NICOTINE (nik'u-tin) *n.* a poisonous oil found in tobacco. [Fr. *Nicot*, who first sent tobacco to France. 1560.]

NICTATE (nik'tāt) *v.i.* to wink. [L. *nictare*, *atum*.]

NICTATION (nik-tā'shun) *n.* the act of winking.

NIECE (nēs) *n.* a daughter of a brother or sister. [F. *niece*, fr. Late L. (acc.) *neptiam*, fr. L. *neptis*. See NEPHEW.]

NIGGARD (nig'ard) *n.* a stingy person. [Scand.]

NIGGARDLY (nig'ard-li) *a.* or *ad.* miserly; meanly saving.

NIGGER (nig'er) *n.* a negro. [See NEGRO.]

NIGH (ni) *a.* near; allied closely;—*ad.* nearly; closely;—*prep.* near to. [M.E. *neh*, fr. O.E. *neah*, *neh*. Cf. Ger. (a.) *nahe*.]

NIGHNESS (ni'nes) *n.* nearness.

NIGHT (nit) *n.* time when the sun is beneath the horizon; darkness; adversity; death. [O.E. *niht*, *neaht*. Cf. Ger. *Nacht*.]

NIGHTFALL (nit'fawl) *n.* close of day.

NIGHTINGALE (ni'tin-gāl) *n.* a small bird that sings at night. [Fr. O.E. *galan*, sing. Cf. Ger. *Nachtigall*.]

NIGHTLY (nit'li) *a.* done by night;—*ad.* every night.

NIGHTMARE (nit'mār) *n.* sensation of weight about the breast in sleep. [Fr. O.E. *mara*, incubus. Cf. Ger. *Nachtmahr*.]

NIGHTSHADE (nit'shād) *n.* a family of narcotic or poisonous plants.

NIGHT-WATCH (nit'woch) *n.* guard at night.

NIHILISM (ni'hil-izm) *n.* absolute scepticism; revolutionary communism. [Fr. L. *nihil*, nothing.]

NIMBLE (nim'bl) *a.* brisk; light and quick in motion. [M.E. *nimel*, fr. O.E. *niman*, to catch.]

NIMBLENESS (nim'bl-nes) *n.* briskness.

NIMBLY (nim'bli) *ad.* with agility.

NIMBUS (nim'bus) *n.* a rain cloud; a circle of rays round the head. [L.]

NINCOMPOOP (nin'kum-pōop) *n.* a silly fellow. [Corr. fr. L. *non compos* (*mentis*), not of sound mind.]

NINE (nin) *a.* eight and one added. [O.E. *nigen*. Cf. Ger. *neun*. L. *novem*.]

NINETEEN (nin'tēn) *a.* nine and ten. [Fr. TEN.]

NINETIETH (nin'ti-eth) *a.* ordinal of 90.

NINETY (nin'ti) *a.* nine times ten.

NINNY (nin'i) *a* simpleton. [It. *ninno*, child; imit.]

NINTH (ninth) *n.* the ordinal of nine.

NIP (nip) (1) *v.t.* to pinch or bite off; blast; destroy;—*n.* a pinch; a cutting off;—(2) *n.* small glassful. [(1) E. (2) Scand.]

NIPPERS (nip'erz) *n.pl.* small pincers.

NIPPLE (nip'l) *n.* a teat. [Dim. of NIP (1).]

NIT (nit) *n.* the egg of insects. [E.]

NITRATE (ni'trāt) *n.* a salt formed of nitric acid and a base.

NITRE (ni'ter) *n.* nitrate of potash. [F., fr. L., fr. G. *netron*, fr. H.]

NITRIC (ni'trik) *a.* containing nitre.

NITRIFY (ni'tri-fi) *v.t.* or *i.* to convert into or become nitre. [-fy, fr. F. *fier*, fr. L. *ficare* = *facere*.]

NITROGEN (ni'tru-jen) *n.* an inodorous gas, the chief ingredient in common air. [Fr. G. root *gen-*, of *gignein*, produce.]

NITROUS (ni'trus) *a.* pertaining to nitre. Also NITRY.

NO (nō) (1) *ad.* a word of denial or refusal; —(2) *a.* not any; none. [(1) O.E. *na*. (2) Short. fr. NONE.]

NOB (nob) *n.* the head; a man of rank; a swell. [Short. fr. **NOBLEMAN**.]

NOBILITY (nō-bil'i-ti) *n.* dignity of mind; distinction of family or rank; body of nobles.

NOBLE (nō'bl) *a.* dignified from rank, intellect, or character; stately; lofty; generous; splendid; ingenuous;—*n.* a person of rank; peer. [F., fr. L. (acc.) *nobilem*, orig. noted, fr. root of *noscere*, know.]

NOBLEMAN (nō'bl-man) *n.* a man of rank; a peer. [See N_OB_LE and **MAN**.]

NOBLENESS (nō'bl-nes) *n.* greatness of mind; dignity; worth; splendour.

NOBLESSE (nō-bles') *n.* body of nobles. [F.]

NOBLY (nō'bli) *ad.* with greatness of soul; illustriously; splendidly.

NOBODY (nō'bod-i) *n.* not any person; a person of no importance. [See **NO** (2).]

NOCENT (nō'sent) *a.* hurtful; injurious. [L. *nocere*, to hurt.]

NOCTAMBULATION (nok-tam-bū-lā'shun) *n.* walking in sleep. [L. *nor, noctis*, night, and *ambulare, -atum*, to walk.]

NOCTAMBULIST (nok-tam'bū-list) *n.* one who walks in sleep.

NOCTURN (nok'turn) *n.* a religious song for worship by night; **NOCTURNE,** a picture or a piece of music descriptive of a night scene. [L.]

NOCTURNAL (nok-tur'nal) *a.* nightly.

NOCUOUS (nok'ū-us) *a.* noxious; hurtful. [L.]

NOD (nod) *v.t.* or *i.* to bend the head quickly, or in assent; be drowsy;—*n.* a quick inclination of the head. [E.]

NODATED (nō'dā-ted) *a.* knotted.

NODDLE (nod'l) *n.* the head.

NODDY (nod'i) *n.* a simpleton; a sea-**fowl** easily taken.

NODE (nōd) *n.* point where the orbit of a planet intersects the ecliptic; a knot; a knob. [L. *nodus*. Cf. **KNOT**.]

NODOSE (nō'dōs) *a.* knotty.

NODULAR (nod'ū-lar) *a.* in the form of a knot.

NODULE (nod'ūl) *n.* a small knot or lump. [L. dim. *nodulus*.]

NOGGIN (nog'in) *n.* a wooden cup. [Scand.]

NOISE (noiz) *n.* sound of any kind;—*v.t.* or *i.* to sound; spread by report. [O.F. *noise*, quarrel, noise, of uncert. etym.]

NOISELESS (noiz'les) *a.* making no noise.

NOISELESSLY (noiz'les-li) *ad.* without noise.

NOISILY (noi'zi-li) *ad.* with noise.

NOISOME (noi'sum) *a.* offensive; injurious. [M.E. *noy*.]

NOISY (noi'zi) *a.* clamorous; turbulent.

NOMAD (nom'ad) *n.* one who leads a wandering and pastoral life. [G. stem *nomad-*, of *nomas*, fr. *nomos*, pasture, fr. *nemein*, allot.]

NOMADIC (nō-mad'ik) *a.* pastoral; wandering for pasturage; roving.

NOMENCLATURE (nō'men-klā-tūr) *n.* the names appropriated to any art or science. [L., fr. *nomen*, and *calare*, call.]

NOMINAL (nom'i-nal) *a.* existing in name only; not real. [L. *nominalis*, fr. stem *nomin-*, of *nomen*, name.]

NOMINALLY (nom'i-nal-i) *ad.* in name only.

NOMINATE (nom'i-nāt) *v.t.* to name, designate, or propose for office. [L. (part.) *nominatus*, named.]

NOMINATION (nom-i-nā'shun) *n.* act of nominating; state of being nominated.

NOMINATIVE (nom'i-nā-tiv) *a.* pertaining to a name;—*n.* first case in grammar.

NOMINATOR (nom'i-nā-ter) *n.* one who names or nominates.

NOMINEE (nom-i-nē') *n.* one designated by another.

NONAGE (non'ij) *n.* minority in age. [L. *non*, not, and **AGE**.]

NONCE (nons) *n.* present time or occasion. [*The nonce*, corr. fr. *then once*.]

NONCHALANCE (non'sha-lans) *n.* indifference; coolness.

NONCHALANT (non'sha-lant) *a.* careless; indifferent. [F. (part.), fr. O.F. *non*, and *chaloir*, to be ardent, fr. L. *non*, and *calere*.]

NON-COMMISSIONED (non-ku-mish'und) *a.* noting all petty officers under the rank of lieutenant. [L. *non*, and **COMMISSION**.]

NON-CONDUCTOR (non-kun-duk'ter) *n.* a substance that does not transmit heat or electricity. [L. *non*, and **CONDUCTOR**.]

NONCONFORMIST (non-kun-for'mist) *n.* one who refuses to conform to the established church. [L. *non*, and **CONFORM**.]

NONCONFORMITY (non-kun-for'mi-ti) *n.* want of conformity.

NONDESCRIPT (non'de-skript) *a.* that has not been described. [L. *non*, and (part.) *descriptus*, described.]

NONE (nun) *a.* not any. [M.E. *non*, fr. O.E. *nan*, fr. *ne*, not, and *an*, **ONE**.]

NON-ELECT (non-e-lekt') *n.* one not elected. [L. *non*, and **ELECT**.]

NONENTITY (non-en'ti-ti) *n.* a thing not existing; an insignificant person or thing. [L. *non*, not, and **ENTITY**.]

NONES (nōnz) *n.pl.* in Rome, the 7th of March, May, July, and October, and the 5th of the other months. [(Fem.) *nona*, ninth day (reckoning inclusively). See **NOON**.]

NONESUCH (nun'such) *n.* that which has not its equal.

NON-EXISTENCE (non-eg-zis'tens) *n.* want of existence. [L. *non*, and **EXIST**.]

NON-JUROR (non-jōō'rer) *n.* one who refuses to swear allegiance. [L. *non*, and **JUROR**.]

NON-OBSERVANCE (non-ob-zer'vans) *n.* neglect of observance. [L. *non*, and **OBSERVE**.]

NONPAREIL (non-pa-rel') *n.* a small printing type;—*a.* unequalled; matchless. [F., fr. L. *non*, and Late L. (acc.) *pariculum*, for L. *par*, equal.]

NONPLUS (non'plus) *n.* a puzzle;—*v.t.* to put to a stand; puzzle. [L. = not farther.]

NONSENSE (non'sens) *n.* words without meaning or importance. [L. *non*, and **SENSE**.]

NONSENSICAL (non-sen'si-kal) *a.* unmeaning.

NONSUIT (non'sūt) *n.* the stoppage of a suit at law;—*v.t.* to adjudge that a plaintiff drops his suit. [L. *non*, and **SUIT**.]

NOOK (nook) *n.* a corner; recess. [E.]

NOON (nōōn) *n.* the middle of the day; twelve o'clock. [O.E. *non*, fr. *nona*, ninth (hour), 3 p.m. The church service for this hour was changed to midday.]

NOONDAY (nōōn'dā) *n.* midday; time of noon;—*a.* pertaining to midday.

NOOSE (nōōs) *n.* a running knot;—*v.t.* to catch in a noose. [O.F. *nous*, fr. *nodus*, knot.]

NOR (nor) *con.* a word that denies. [Short for M.E. *nother*, fr. O.E. *nawther*. Doublet of **NEITHER**.]

NORM (norm) *n.* a rule; typical form. [L. *norma*, rule.]

NORMAL (nor'mal) *a.* according to rule; regular;—*n.* perpendicular.

NORMALLY (nor'mal-i) *ad.* in a normal manner.

NORMAL SCHOOL (nor'mal skōōl) *n.* an institution for training teachers. [Fr. **NORMAL** and **SCHOOL**.]

NORMAN (nor'man) *a.* pertaining to Normandy; noting a style of architecture. [O.F. *Normand*, fr. Scand. = Northman.]

Norman Arch.

NORNS (nornz) *n.pl.* the three fates—past, present, and future. [Scand. myth.]

NORSE (nors) a. pertaining to ancient Scandinavia;—n. the language of ancient Scandinavia. [Icel. *Norske*; Norw. *Norsk*.]

NORTH (north) n. the point opposite the south;—a. being in the north. [O.E. Cf. Ger. *Nord*.]

NORTH-EAST (north-ēst') n. the point between the north and east. [See **NORTH** and **EAST**.]

NORTH-EASTERN (north-ēs'tern) a. pertaining to the north-east.

NORTHERLY (nor'THer-li) a. being toward the north; from the north.

NORTHERN (nor'THern) a. being in or toward the north.

NORTHENER (nor'THern-er) n. a native of the north.

NORTHWARD (north'ward) a. being toward the north;—ad. in a northern direction.

NORTH-WEST (north-west') n. the point between the north and west;—a. being in or proceeding from the north-west. [See **NORTH** and **WEST**.]

NORTH-WESTERN (north-wes'tern) a. pertaining to the north-west.

NOSE (nōz) n. prominent part of the face; organ of smell; power of smelling; end of anything;—v.t. to smell; track;—v.i. to snivel. [O.E. *nosu*. Cf. Ger. *Nase*, L. *nasus*.]

NOSEGAY (nōz'gā) n. a bunch of flowers.

NOSOLOGY (nos-ol'ō-ji) n. classification of diseases. [Fr. G. *nosos*, disease, and *-logia*, fr. *legein*, speak.]

NOSTRIL (nos'tril) n. a passage through the nose. [M.E. *nosethirel*, fr. O.E. *nosu*, nose, and *thyrel*, perforation.]

NOSTRUM (nos'trum) n. a medicine, the ingredients of which are not made public. [L. = our own.]

NOT (not) ad. a word that expresses denial. [Short. fr. **NAUGHT**.]

NOTABLE (nō'ta-bl) a. worthy of being known; remarkable; distinguished;—n. a person or thing of note. [F., fr. L. (acc.) *notabilem*, noteworthy, fr. *nota*, **NOTE**.]

NOTABILITY (nō-ta-bil'i-ti) n. quality of being easily known; a remarkable person.

NOTARIAL (nō-tā'ri-al) a. relating to or done by a notary.

NOTARY (nō'ta-ri) n. an officer who attests writings. [L. *notarius*, a secretary, fr. **NOTE**.]

NOTATION (nō-tā'shun) n. the act of noting by marks, figures, or characters. [L., fr. (part.) *notatus*, noted.]

NOTCH (noch) n. a cut or nick;—v.t. to cut a hollow in. [For (an) *otch*, fr. O.F. *oche*.]

NOTE (nōt) (1) n. a visible sign; mark; short remark or letter; character representing a musical sound; the sound itself; acknowledgment of debt; fame; reputation; —(2) v.t. to observe closely; record in writing; furnish with notes. [(1) F., fr. L. *nota*. (2) L. *notare*.]

NOTEBOOK (nōt'book) n. book for notes. [Fr. **NOTE** and **BOOK**.]

NOTED (nō'ted) a. known by reputation or report.

NOTEWORTHY (nōt'wur-THi) ad. deserving observation. [See **NOTE** and **WORTHY**.]

NOTHING (nuth'ing) n. not any thing; of no importance, use, etc.; a trifle; a cipher. [Fr. **NO THING**.]

NOTHINGNESS (nuth'ing-nes) n. non-existence; no value.

NOTICE (nō'tis) n. remark; regard; public intimation;—v.t. to observe; regard; attend to; mention. [F., fr. L. (acc.) *notitiam*, knowledge, fr. (part.) *notus*.]

NOTICEABLE (nō'tis-a-bl) a. worthy of observation.

NOTIFICATION (nō-ti-fi-kā'shun) n. act of giving notice; notice given; paper giving notice.

NOTIFY (nō'ti-fi) v.t. to make known; give notice of. [F. *notifier*, fr. L. (part.) *notus*, known, and *-ficare*=*facere*.]

NOTION (nō'shun) n. conception; opinion; sentiment. [F., fr. L. (acc.) *notionem*. See **NOTICE**.]

NOTIONAL (nō'shun-al) a. existing in idea only; imaginary; ideal; fanciful.

NOTORIETY (nō-tō-rī'e-ti) n. public knowledge or exposure.

NOTORIOUS (nō-tō'ri-us) a. publicly known; known to disadvantage; infamous. [Fr. L. *notoria*, a pointing out, fr. *notare*, to **NOTE**.]

NOTORIOUSLY (nō-tō'ri-us-li) ad. in a notorious manner; openly.

NOTORIOUSNESS (nō-tō'ri-us-nes) n. state of being well known; notoriety.

NOTWITHSTANDING (not-with-stand'ing) ppr. not opposing; nevertheless.

NOUGHT (nawt). See **NAUGHT**.

NOUN (noun) n. name of anything. [O.F. = F. *nom*, fr. L. *nomen*. Cf. **NAME**, G. *onoma*.]

NOURISH (nur'ish) v.t. to support with food; cherish; encourage. [O.F. (part.) *nourissant*, nourishing, fr. *nourir*, fr. L. *nutrire*.]

NOURISHER (nur'ish-er) n. he or that which nourishes.

NOURISHMENT (nur'ish-ment) n. act of nourishing; anything that nourishes.

NOUS (nous) n. intellect; brain power. [G.]

NOVEL (nov'el) a. new; unusual;—n. a fictitious tale. [O.F.=F. *nouveau*, fr. L. (acc.) *novellum*, new, fr. *novus*.]

NOVELETTE (nov-el-et') n. a short novel.

NOVELIST (nov'el-ist) n. a writer of novels; an innovator.

NOVELTY (nov'el-ti) n. newness; anything new or strange. [O.F., fr. L. (acc.) *novellitatem*.]

NOVEMBER (nō-vem'ber) n. eleventh month of the year. [L. *Novembris* (*mensis*), the ninth (month of the Roman year), fr. *novem*, nine.]

NOVICE (nov'is) n. one new in anything; a beginner. [F., fr. L. *novitius*, fr. *novus*.]

NOVITIATE (nō-vish'i-āt) n. state or period of being a novice. [L. *novitius*.]

NOW (now) ad. at this time. [O.E. *nu*. Cf. Ger. *nun*, L. *nunc*.]

NOWADAYS (now'a-dāz) ad. in the present age;—n. the present time. [Fr. **NOW** and **DAY**.]

NOWHERE (nō'hwār) ad. not in any place or state. [See **NO**.]

NOWISE (nō'wiz) ad. in no way or degree. [See **NO**.]

NOXIOUS (nok'shus) a. hurtful; destructive; unwholesome. [L. *noxius*, fr. *noxa* hurt, fr. *nocere*.]

NOZZLE (noz'l) n. a little nose; an extremity with an aperture. [Dim. fr. **NOSE**.]

NUANCE (nōō-ăngs') n. a delicate shade or degree of difference. [F., fr. *nuer*, assort colours, fr. L. *nutare*, change, dye.]

NUBILE (nū'bil) a. marriageable. [L. *nubilis*, fr. *nubere*, to marry.]

NUCLEUS (nū'klē-us) n. a body about which anything is collected; body of a comet;—pl. **NUCLEI** or **NUCLEUSES**. [L., fr. stem, *nuc-*, of *nux*, nut.]

NUDE (nūd) a. bare; naked. [L. *nudus*.]

NUDGE (nuj) v.t. to touch gently with the elbow;—n. a gentle touch or push. [E.]

NUDITY (nū'di-ti) n. nakedness.

NUGATORY (nū'ga-tur-i) a. of no force; trifling; futile. [L. *nugax*, trifles.]

NUGGET (nug'et) n. a lump of metal or ore. [E.]

NUISANCE (nū'sans) n. that which annoys, troubles, or is offensive. [F., fr. (part.) *nuisant*, harming, fr. *nuire*, fr. L. *nocere*.]

NULL (nul) a. void; of no force. [L. *nullus*, fr. *ne*, not, and *ullus*, any.]

Fāte, fár, ado; mē her; mine; nōte; tūne; mōōn.

NULLIFY (nul'i-fi) *v.t.* to make void; deprive of force. [-*fy*, fr. F. -*fier*, fr. L. -*ficare* - *facere*, make.]

NULLITY (nul'i-ti) *n.* want of force.

NUMB (num) *a.* torpid; deprived of sensation or motion;—*v.t.* to deprive of feeling; deaden. [M.E. (part.) *nomen*, seized, fr. O.E. *niman*, take.]

NUMBER (num'bẹr) *n.* a unit; any assemblage of units; measure; a grammatical inflection; part or division of a book; verse; —*v.t.* to count; reckon; enumerate. [F. *nombre*, fr. L. (acc.) *numerum*, fr. *numerus*.]

NUMBERLESS (num'bẹr-les) *a.* more than can be counted.

NUMBERS (num'bẹrz) *n.* fourth book of the Old Testament.

NUMBNESS (num'nes) *n.* state of being numb.

NUMERABLE (nū'mẹr-ȧ-bl) *a.* that may be numbered.

NUMERAL (nū'mẹr-ạl) *a.* relating to or expressing number;—*n.* a letter for a number, as L. for fifty. [L. *numeralis*.]

NUMERARY (nū'mẹr-ạr-i) *a.* belonging to a number.

NUMERATE (nū'mẹr-āt) *v.t.* to count in numbers; mention by number. [L. (part.) *numeratus*, counted, fr. *numerare*.]

NUMERATION (nū-mẹr-ā'shun) *n.* act or art of numbering.

NUMERATOR (nū'mẹr-ā-tur) *n.* one who numbers; a number that shows how many parts are taken. [L.]

NUMERICAL (nū-mẹr'i-kạl) *a.* denoting number. [respect to number.

NUMERICALLY (nū-mẹr'i-kạl-i) *ad.* with

NUMEROUS (nū'mẹr-us) *a.* containing many. [O.F. *numereux*, fr. L. *numerosus*.]

NUMISMATICS (nū-mis-mat'iks) *n.pl.* the science of coins and medals. [L. stem *numismat*-, of *numisma*, piece of money, fr. G., fr. *nomos*, usage.] [NUMBskull.]

NUMSKULL (num'skul) *n.* a blockhead. [For

NUN (nun) *n.* a female secluded in a cloister under religious vows; a kind of pigeon. [O.E., fr. L. *nonna* ~ crig. mother.]

NUNCIO (nun'shi-ō) *n.* an ambassador of the pope. [It., fr. L. *nuntius*, messenger.]

NUNCUPATIVE (nun'kū-pā-tiv) *a.* verbally pronounced; not written. Also NUNCUPATORY, [L. (part.) *nuncupatus*, called by name, fr. *nomen*, and *capere*.]

NUNNERY (nun'ẹr-i) *n.* a house for nuns; convent.

NUNNISHNESS (nun'ish-nes) *n.* habits or manners of nuns.

NUPTIAL (nup'shạl) *a.* pertaining to marriage. [F., fr. L. (acc.) *nuptialem*, fr. *nuptiæ*, nuptials.]

NUPTIALS (nup'shạlz) *n.pl.* marriage.

NURSE (nurs) *n.* one who tends a child or sick person;—*v.t.* to tend in infancy or sickness; bring up; cherish; manage with economy. [Short. fr. M.E. *norice*, fr. O.F. -F. *nourrice*, fr. L. (acc. fem.) *nutriciam*, one that nurses, fr. *nutrire*.]

NURSERY (nur'sẹr-i) *n.* a room for young children; ground for rearing fruit, flowers, etc.

NURSLING (nurs'ling) *n.* an infant.

NURTURE (nur'tūr) *n.* upbringing; training; instruction; nourishment;—*v.t.* to nourish; feed; bring up; educate. [O.F. - F. *nourriture*, fr. L. (acc.) *nutrituram*, fr. *nutrire*.]

NUT (nut) *n.* a fruit consisting of a shell and kernel; a small metal block with a concave screw inside;—*v.i.* to gather nuts. [O.E. *hnutu*. Cf. Ger. *Nuss*.]

NUTATION (nū-tā'shun) *n.* an apparent vibratory motion of the earth's axis. [L., fr. *nutare*, nod.]

NUTCRACKER (nut'krak-ẹr) *n.* an instrument for breaking nuts by pressure. [Fr. NUT and CRACK.]

NUTGALL (nut'gawl) *n.* excrescence of the oak. [Fr. NUT and GALL.]

NUTMEG (nut'meg) *n.* a kind of aromatic nut. [M.E. *note-mugge*, fr. E. NUT, and O.F. *mugue*, MUSK.]

NUTRIMENT (nū'tri-ment) *n.* that which nourishes; aliment; food. [L. *nutrimentum*.]

NUTRIMENTAL (nū-tri-men'tạl) *a.* nourishing.

NUTRITION (nū-trish'un) *n.* act of nourishing; that which nourishes; food. [Fr. L. (part.) *nutritus*, nourished.]

NUTRITIOUS (nū-trish'e-us) *a.* having the quality of nourishing.

NUTRITIVE (nū'tri-tiv) *a.* nutritious.

NUTTING (nut'ing) *n.* gathering nuts.

NUTTY (nut'i) *a.* abounding in nuts; tasting like nuts.

NUX VOMICA (nuks vom'i-kạ) *n.* the fruit of an Indian tree; strychnine. [L.]

NUZZLE (nuz'l) *v.t.* or *i.* to lie snug; poke with the nose; nestle. [Fr. NOSE.]

NYMPH (nimf) *n.* a goddess; a graceful young lady. [F. *nymphe*, fr. L., fr. G. *numphe*.]

NYMPHA (nim'fạ) *n.* the chrysalis of an insect. [L.]

NYMPHEAN (nim-fē'ạn) *a.* pertaining to nymphs.

O

OAF (ōf) *n.* a foolish child; a changeling; a dolt. [Scand.]

OAFISH (ō'fish) *a.* dull; stupid.

OAK (ōk) *n.* a valuable tree. [O.E. *ac*. Cf. Ger. *Eiche*.]

OAKEN (ō'ken) *a.* made of oak.

OAKLING (ōk'ling) *n.* a young oak.

OAKUM (ō'kum) *n.* old rope untwisted. [O.E. *acumba*, tow.]

OAR (ōr) *n.* an instrument to row boats. [M.E. *ore*, fr. O.E. *ar*.]

OARSMAN (ōrz'mạn) *n.* one who rows with the oar. [See OAR and MAN.]

OASIS (ō-ā'sis, ō'ȧ-sis) *n.* a fertile spot in a desert. [L., fr. G., fr. Egypt.]

OAT (ōt) *n.* a plant and its seed. [O.E. *ate*.]

OATCAKE (ōt'kāk) *n.* a cake made of oatmeal. [See OAT and CAKE.]

OATEN (ō'ten) *a.* pertaining to oats.

OATH (ōth) *n.* a solemn affirmation with an appeal to God for its truth. [O.E. *ath*. Cf. Ger. *Eid*.]

OATMEAL (ōt'mēl) *n.* meal made of oats. [See OAT and MEAL.]

OBDURACY (ob'dū-rȧ-si) *n.* hardness of heart.

OBDURATE (ob'dū-rạt) *a.* hardened in heart or feelings; stubborn. [L. (part.) *obduratus*, hardened, fr. *ob*, and *durus*, hard.]

OBDURATELY (ob'dū-rạt-li) *ad.* stubbornly; inflexibly.

OBEDIENCE (ō-bēd'yens) *n.* compliance with a command.

OBEDIENT (ō-bēd'yent) *a.* submissive to authority; dutiful. [O.F., fr. L. (acc. part.) *obedientem*, obeying.]

OBEDIENTLY (ō-bēd'yent-li) *ad.* with submission to commands.

OBEISANCE (ō-bā'sạns) *n.* act of reverence or respect; a bow. [O.F., fr. (part.) *obeissant*, obeying.] [of an obelisk.

OBELISCAL (ob-e-lis'kạl) *a.* being in the form

OBELISK (ob'e-lisk) *n.* a quadrangular pillar or pyramid. [G. *obeliskos*, dim. fr. *obelos*, spit.]

OBESE (ō-bēs') *a.* fat; fleshy. [L., fr. *ob*, intens., and *edere*, eat.]

OBESITY (ō-bēs'i-ti) *n.* fatness; corpulence.

OBEY (ō-bā') *v.t.* to comply with; yield to; do as told. [O.F. *obeir*, fr. L. *obedire*, fr. *ob*, towards, and *audire*, hear.]

OBIT (ō'bit, ob'it) *n.* death; decease. [O.F. fr. L. (acc.) *obitum*, fr. *obire*, meet (death), fr. *ob*, towards, and *ire*, go.]

OBITUARY (ō-bit'ū-ạr-i) *n.* a register of deaths;—*a.* relating to deaths.

OBJECT (ob'jekt) *n.* anything set before the mind or senses; thing sought for; aim; design; end in view. [L. *objectus*, orig. (part.) thrown towards, fr. *ob*, and *-jicere* = *jacere*.]

OBJECT (ob-jekt') *v.t.* or *i.* to oppose by words or reasons; urge against. [F. *objecter*, fr. L. *objectare*.]

OBJECTION (ob-jek'shun) *n.* adverse reason.

OBJECTIONABLE (ob-jek'shun-ạ-bl) *a.* liable to objections. [object. [F. *objectif*.]

OBJECTIVE (ob-jekt'iv) *a.* contained in the

OBJECTOR (ob-jek'tẹr) *n.* one who objects.

OBJURGATE (ob-jur'gāt) *v.t.* to chide; reprove. [L. (part.) *objurgatus*, rebuked, fr. *ob*, and *jurgare*, scold.]

OBJURGATION (ob-jur-gā'shun) *n.* act of chiding; reproof.

OBLATE (ob'lāt) *a.* broad or flattened at the poles. [L. *oblatus*, thrust out (at the equator), fr. *ob*, and *latus* carried, and fr. *tollere*, bear.]

OBLATION (ob-lā'shun) *n.* anything offered in divine worship; sacrifice. [F., fr. L. (acc.) *oblationem*, fr. (part.) *oblatus*, offered.]

OBLIGATE (ob'li-gāt) *v.t.* to bind over by contract or duty. [L. (part.) *obligatus*, tied up, fr. *obligare*, OBLIGE.]

OBLIGATION (ob-li-gā'shun) *n.* the binding force of a vow, law, or duty; a bond.

OBLIGATORY (ob'li-gạ-tur-i) *a.* imposing an obligation; binding.

OBLIGE (ō-blīj') *v.t.* to constrain; bind; gratify. [F. *obliger*, fr. L., fr. *ob*, and *ligare*, bind. See LIGAMENT.]

OBLIGEE (ob-li-jē') *n.* the person obliged, or to whom a bond is given.

OBLIGING (ō-blī'jing) *a.* disposed to do favours; kind; complaisant.

OBLIGINGLY (ō-blī'jing-li) *ad.* civilly.

OBLIQUE (ob-lēk') *a.* deviating from a right line; not parallel; indirect. [F., fr. L. (acc.) *obliquum*.]

OBLIQUELY (ob-lēk'li) *ad.* not directly.

OBLIQUITY (ob-lik'wi-ti) *n.* deviation from a right line, or from moral rectitude. Also OBLIQUENESS.

OBLITERATE (ob-lit'e-rāt) *v.t.* to blot out; efface. [L. (part.) *oblitteratus*, covered, of writing, fr. *ob*, over, and *litera*, LETTER.]

OBLITERATION (ob-lit-e-rā'shun) *n.* act of blotting out; extinction.

OBLIVION (ob-liv'i-un) *n.* forgetting; state of being forgotten; general pardon. [F., fr. L. (acc.) *oblivionem*, fr. *oblivisci*, forget.]

OBLIVIOUS (ob-liv'i-us) *a.* causing forgetfulness; forgetful. [L. *oblivosus*.]

OBLONG (ob'long) *a.* longer than broad;— *n.* a figure longer than it is broad. [F., fr. L., fr. *ob*, over, and *longus*, LONG.]

OBLOQUY (ob'lu-kwi) *n.* censorious language; calumny; abuse. [L. *obloquium*, fr. *ob*, against, and *loqui*, speak.]

OBNOXIOUS (ob-nok'shus) *a.* liable; exposed; offensive; odious. [L. *obnoxius*, exposed to, fr. *ob*, and *noxa*, hurt.]

OBOE (ō'boi) *n.* a musical wind instrument sounded by a reed. [It., fr. F. *hautbois*.]

OBSCENE (ob-sēn') *a.* grossly indelicate and disgusting; lewd; licentious. [L. *obscenus*, of uncert. etym.]

OBSCENITY (ob-sen'i-ti) *n.* impurity in act or word; indecency; lewdness. Also OBSCENENESS.

OBSCURANTISM (ob-skū'rạn-tizm) *n.* system or principles opposed to progress and enlightenment.

OBSCURATION (ob-skū-rā'shun) *n.* the act of darkening; state of being hidden.

OBSCURE (ob-skūr') *a.* dark; gloomy; not easily understood; not much known;— *v.t.* to darken; cloud; dim; tarnish. [F. *obscur*, fr. L. (acc.) *obscurum*, lit. covered over, fr. *ob*, and root of *scutum*, shield.]

OBSCURELY (ob-skūr'li) *ad.* darkly

OBSCURITY (ob-skū'ri-ti) *n.* state of being obscure; darkness; privacy; low condition.

OBSECRATE (ob'se-krāt) *v.t.* to beseech; to entreat. [L. (part.) *obsecratus*, implored, fr. *ob*, and *secrare*. See SACRED.]

OBSECRATION (ob-se-krā'shun) *n.* act of imploring; entreaty.

OBSEQUIES (ob'se-kwiz) *n.pl.* funeral solemnities. [O.F., fr. L. (acc. pl.) *obsequias*.]

OBSEQUIOUS (ob-sē'kwi-us) *a.* submissive or compliant to excess. [Fr. L. *obsequiosus*, fr. *obsequium*, compliance, lit. a following near, fr. *ob*, and *sequi*.]

OBSEQUIOUSLY (ob-sē'kwi-us-li) *ad.* with servile compliance.

OBSEQUIOUSNESS (ob-sē'kwi-us-nes) *n.* mean compliance; servility.

OBSERVABLE (ob-zẹr'vạ-bl) *a.* that may be observed; remarkable.

OBSERVABLY (ob-zẹr'vạ-bli) *ad.* in a manner worthy of note.

OBSERVANCE (ob-zẹr'vạns) *n.* careful notice; attentive performance; a religious rite; rule of practice.

OBSERVANT (ob-zẹr'vạnt) *a.* taking notice; attentive; adhering to in practice.

OBSERVATION (ob-zẹr-vā'shun) *n.* act of seeing; state of being noticeable; remark; due performance; angular measurement of the sun, etc. [F. L. (part.) *observatus*.]

OBSERVATORY (ob-zẹr'vạ-tur-i) *n.* a place for astronomical observations.

OBSERVE (ob-zẹrv') *v.t.* or *i.* to notice; regard attentively; comply with; keep religiously; remark. [O.F. *observer*, fr. L. *ob*, near, and *servare*, keep.]

OBSERVER (ob-zẹr'vẹr) *n.* one who takes notice; one who keeps any custom or rite.

OBSERVINGLY (ob-zẹr'ving-li) *ad.* attentively.

OBSESSION (ob-sesh'un) *n.* act of besieging. [L. pref. *ob*, near, and *sidere*, seat.]

OBSOLESCENT (ob-su-les'ent) *a.* going out of use.

OBSOLETE (ob'su-lēt) *a.* gone out of use; old-fashioned. [L. *obsoletus*, grown old, fr. *obsolescere*, perh. fr. *obs* = *ob*, and root of ADCLESCENT.]

OBSOLETENESS (ob'su-lēt-nes) *n.* state of disuse.

OBSTACLE (ob'stạ-kl) *n.* that which hinders; obstruction. [F., fr. L. *obstaculum*, fr. *ob*, against, and *stare*, stand.]

OBSTETRIC (ob-stet'rik) *a.* pertaining to midwifery. [L., fr. stem. *obstetric-*, of *obstetrix*, midwife, fr. *ob*, at hand, before, and *stare*, stand.]

OBSTETRICS (ob-stet'riks) *n.pl.* science or art of midwifery.

OBSTINACY (ob'sti-nạ-si) *n.* unyielding firmness; stubbornness. Also OBSTINATENESS.

OBSTINATE (ob'sti-nạt) *a.* stubborn; self-willed; not easily subdued. [L. *obstinatus*, resolved, fr. *ob*, against, and root of *stare*. See DESTINE.]

OBSTINATELY (ob'sti-nạt-li) *ad.* stubbornly.

OBSTREPEROUS (ob-strep'e-rus) *a.* clamorous; loud; noisy. [L. *obstreperus*, fr. *ob*, against, and *strepere*, make a noise.]

OBSTREPEROUSLY (ob-strep'e-rus-li) *ad.* with tumultuous noise.

Fāte, fär, ạdo; mē, hẹr; mine; nōte; tūne; moon.

OBSTRUCT (ob-strukt') *v.t.* to hinder; stop; block up. [L. (part.) *oöstructus*, lit. built against, fr. *ob*, and *struere*. See CONSTRUCT.]

OBSTRUCTION (ob-struk'shun) *n.* act of obstructing; stoppage; impediment; obstacle.

OBSTRUCTIONIST (ob-struk'shun-ist) *n.* one who hinders progress in legislation.

OBSTRUCTIVE (ob-struk'tiv) *a.* hindering.

OBSTRUENT (ob'strōō-ent) *a.* blocking up; —*n.* anything that closes a natural passage. [L. (part. stem) *obstruent-*, impeding.]

OBTAIN (ob-tān') *v.t.* to gain; get; hold; continue in use. [F. *obtenir*, fr. L. *obtinere*, fr. *ob*, near, and *tenere*, hold.]

OBTAINABLE (ob-tā'na-bl) *a.* that may be obtained.

OBTEST (ob-test') *v.t.* or *i.* to beseech; protest. [L., fr. *ob*, and *testari*, call as a witness, *testis*.]

OBTESTATION (ob-tes-tā'shun) *n.* supplication; entreaty; solemn protest.

OBTRUDE (ob-trōōd') *v.t.* to thrust into; urge upon against the will;—*v.i.* to enter without invitation. [L., fr. *ob*, against, and *trudere*, thrust.]

OBTRUDER (ob-trōō'der) *n.* one who obtrudes.

OBTRUSION (ob-trōō'zhun) *n.* an entering without invitation; thrusting upon. [Fr. L. (acc.) *obtrusionem*, fr. (part.) *obtrusus*, obtruded.]

OBTRUSIVE (ob-trōō'siv) *a.* apt to obtrude.

OBTRUSIVELY (ob-trōō'siv-li) *ad.* by way of intrusion.

OBTUSE (ob-tūs') *a.* not pointed, acute, or shrill; dull. [F. *obtus*, fr. L. (acc. part.) *obtusum*, blunted, fr. *ob*, against, and *tundere*, beat.]

OBTUSENESS (ob-tūs'nes) *n.* want of sharpness or readiness; dullness; bluntness.

OBTUSION (ob-tū'zhun) *n.* act of blunting.

OBVERSE (ob'vers) (1) *n.* the principal face of a coin;—(ob-vers') (2) *a.* having the base narrower than the top. [L. (part.) *obversus*, turned towards, fr. *ob*, and *vertere*.]

OBVIATE (ob'vi-āt) *v.t.* to meet; prevent; remove. [L. (part.) *obviatus*, fr. *obviare*, meet, withstand, fr. *ob*, against, and *via*, way.]

OBVIOUS (ob'vi-us) *a.* evident; clear. [L. *obvius*, in the way.]

OBVIOUSLY (ob'vi-us-li) *ad.* evidently.

OBVIOUSNESS (ob'vi-us-nes) *n.* state of being evident.

OCCASION (o-kā'zhun) *n.* a cause; occurrence; opportunity; need; requirement;—*v.t.* to cause; produce. [F., fr. L. (acc.) *occasionem*, fr. *ob*, and (part.) *casus*, fr. *cadere*, fall.]

OCCASIONAL (o-kā'zhun-al) *a.* occurring at times.

OCCASIONALLY (o-kā'zhun-al-i) *ad.* upon occasion; at times.

OCCIDENT (ok'si-dent) *n.* the west. [O.F., fr. L. (acc.) *occidentem*, west, orig. (part.) setting, fr. *ob*, down, and *cadere*, fall.]

OCCIDENTAL (ok-si-den'tal) *a.* western.

OCCIPITAL (ok-sip'i-tal) *a.* pertaining to the back part of the head.

OCCIPUT (ok'si-put) *n.* the hinder part of the head. [L., fr. *ob*, against, and *caput*, head.]

OCCULT (o-kult', ok'ult) *a.* secret; hidden. [F. *occulte*, fr. (acc. part.) *occultus*, concealed, fr. *occulere*, fr. *ob*, and root of *celare*, hide.]

OCCULTATION (ok-ul-tā'shun) *n.* act of hiding; temporary concealment.

OCCUPANCY (ok'ū-pan-si) *n.* possession.

OCCUPANT (ok'ū-pant) *n.* one who takes or holds possession. [F.]

OCCUPATION (ok-ū-pā'shun) *n.* act of taking possession; employment; business; tenure.

OCCUPY (ok'ū-pi) *v.t.* to hold; keep; employ; use; fill or cover. [F. *occuper*, fr. L. *occupare*, fr. *ob*, and *capere*, seize.]

OCCUR (o-kur') *v.i.* to come to the mind; happen; appear; be found here and there. [L., fr. *ob*, against, and *currere*, to run.]

OCCURRENCE (o-kur'ens) *n.* any accidental event.

OCEAN (ō'shan) *n.* the largest body of water on the earth. [O.F., fr. L. (acc.) *oceanum*, fr. G. *okeanos*.]

OCEANIC (ō-she-an'ik) *a.* pertaining to the ocean.

OCHLOCRACY (ok-lok'ra-si) *n.* government by the populace. [Fr. G. *ochlos*, mob; imit. fr. ARISTOCRACY.]

OCHRE (ō'ker) *n.* clay used as a pigment. [F. *ocre*, fr. L., fr. G. *ochra*, yellow earth, fr. *ochros*, wan.]

OCHREOUS (ō'krē-us) *a.* of or resembling ochre. Also OCHREY.

OCTAGON (ok'ta-gon) *n.* a figure of eight sides and angles. [Fr. G. *okto*, and *gonia*, angle.]

OCTAGONAL (ok-tag'u-nal) *a.* containing eight angles and sides.

OCTAHEDRON (ok-ta-hē'dron) *n.* a solid figure of eight equal faces. [Fr. G. *hedra*,'seat, base.]

Octagon.

OCTAVE (ok'tāv) *a.* consisting of eight;—*n.* the eighth day after; an interval or sound eight tones higher. [F., fr. L. *octavus*, eighth, fr. *octo*.]

OCTAVO (ok-tā'vō) *a.* having eight leaves to a sheet;—*n.* a book of this size. Written 8vo.

OCTOBER (ok-tō'ber) *n.* tenth month of the year. [L., ancient Rom., the eighth month of the year.]

OCTOGENARIAN (ok-tō-je-nā'ri-an) *n.* a person eighty years of age. [L. *octogenarius*, of eighty, fr. *octogeni*, eighty each.]

OCTOROON (ok'tu-rōōn) *n.* child of a quadroon and a white person. [Imit. after QUADROON; fr. L. *octo*.]

OCULAR (ok'ū-lar) *a.* known by or relating to the eye. [L., fr. *oculus*, eye.]

OCULARLY (ok'ū-lar-li) *a.* by the eye or actual view. [of the eye.

OCULIST (ok'ū-list) *n.* one skilled in diseases

ODD (od) *a.* uneven in number; strange; peculiar; spare. [Scand.]

ODDITY (od'i-ti) *n.* singularity; a singular person.

ODDLY (od'li) *ad.* unevenly; strangely.

ODDNESS (od'nes) *n.* singularity.

ODDS (odz) *n.pl.* inequality; excess; advantage in a wager; scraps.

ODE (ōd) *n.* a short poem; song. [F., fr. L. (acc.) *odam*, fr. G. *ode*, fr. *aeidein*.]

ODIOUS (ō'di-us) *a.* hateful; disgusting; repulsive. [L. *odiosus*.]

ODIOUSLY (ō'di-us-li) *ad.* hatefully.

ODIOUSNESS (ō'di-us-nes) *n.* quality of being hateful or repulsive.

ODIUM (ō'di-um) *n.* quality of provoking dislike or hate; hatred. [L., fr. *odi*, I hate.]

ODORIFEROUS (ō-du-rif'e-rus) *a.* fragrant. [Fr. L. *-ferus*, bearing, fr. *ferre*.]

ODOROUS (ō'dur-us) *a.* sweet of scent. [L. *odorus*.]

ODOUR (ō'dur) *n.* any smell; scent; perfume; estimation. [F. *odeur*, fr. L. (acc.) *odorem*.]

O'ER (ōr) contraction of OVER.

OF (ov) *pret.* from; concerning. [O.E. Cf. Ger. *ab*; L. *ab*.]

OFF (of) *a.* on the farther side; most distant; —*ad.* away from; in the opposite direction; —*prep.* not on;—*inter.* begone! [Form of OF.]

OFFAL (of'al) *n.* refuse; entrails. [Fr. OFF and FALL. Cf. Ger. *Abfall*.]

OFFENCE (o-fens') *n.* any cause of displeasure; wrong; injury; resentment; assault. [O.F., fr. L. (acc.) *offensam*, fr. (part.) *offensus*, offended.]

OFFENCELESS (o-fens'les) *a.* innocent.
OFFEND (o-fend') *v.t.* or *i.* to make angry; affront; transgress; give offence; sin. [L., fr. *ob*, against, and *-fendere*, strike. See **DEFEND.**]
OFFENDER (o-fen'dẹr) *n.* one who offends.
OFFENSIVE (o-fen'siv) *a.* displeasing; injurious; making, or used in, attack;—*n.* act of, or posture in, attacking.
OFFENSIVELY (o-fen'siv-li) *ad.* so as to give displeasure.
OFFER (of'ẹr) *v.t.* or *i.* to present; propose; bid;—*n.* a proposal; price bid. [L., fr. *ob*, near, and *ferre*, bring.]
OFFERING (of'ẹr-ing) *n.* a sacrifice; anything offered.
OFFERTORY (of'ẹr-tur-i) *n.* church service during the collection of alms; the alms collected. [Late L. *offertorium*, place to which offerings were brought.]
OFFICE (of'is) *n.* public employment; function; place of business. [F., fr. L. *officium*, perh. for *opificium*, fr. *opus*, work, and *facere*, do.]
OFFICER (of'i-sẹr) *n.* one who holds an office;—*v.t.* to furnish with officers. [F. *officier*.]
OFFICIAL (o-fish'ạl) *a.* derived from office;—*n.* a subordinate public officer.
OFFICIALLY (o-fish'ạl-i) *ad.* by authority.
OFFICIATE (o-fish'i-āt) *v.i.* to perform an office.
OFFICINAL (o-fis'i-nạl, of-i-si'nạl) *a.* belonging to a shop.
OFFICIOUS (o-fish'us) *a.* doing kind offices; busy; intermeddling. [L. *officiosus*.]
OFFICIOUSLY (o-fish'us-li) *ad.* kindly; forwardly.
OFFICIOUSNESS (o-fish'us-nes) *n.* eagerness to serve.
OFFING (of'ing) *n.* the sea at a distance from shore. [Fr. **OFF.**]
OFFSCOURING (of'skour-ing) *n.* refuse or rejected matter. [See **OFF** and **SCOUR.**]
OFFSET (of'set) *n.* a shoot or sprout; equivalent;—*v.t.* to set one account against another. [See **OFF** and **SET.**]
OFFSPRING (of'spring) *n.* a child or children; issue; production. [See **OFF** and **SPRING.**]
OFT (oft) *ad.* frequently. [M.E. *ofte*, fr. O.E. *oft*.]
OFTEN (of'n) *ad.* frequently. [M.E. *often*.]
OGEE (ō-jē') *n.* a moulding formed like the letter S. [F. *ogive*, fr. Sp., fr. A.]
OGLE (ō'gl) *v.t.* or *i.* to look at fondly with side glances;—*n.* a side glance. [Fr. D. = to eye.]
OGLER (ō'glẹr) *n.* one who ogles.
OGRE (ō'gẹr) *n.* a giant or monster in fairy tales. [F., of uncert. etym.]
Ogee.
OGRESS (ō'gres) *n.* a female ogre.
OH (ō) *ex.* denoting surprise or pain. [F.]
OIL (oil) *n.* an unctuous liquid;—*v.t.* to smear with oil. [O.F. *oile* = F. *huile*, fr. L. *oleum*, fr. G. *elaion*; conn. with **OLIVE.**]
OILCAKE (oil'kāk) *n.* a cake made of compressed flax seed.
OILCLOTH (oil'kloth) *n.* a cloth oiled for floors, etc.
OILINESS (oil'i-nes) *n.* unctuousness.
OILY (oil'i) *a.* like oil; smooth.
OINTMENT (oint'ment) *n.* any soft unctuous matter; unguent. [M.E. *oinement*, fr. O.F., fr. *oigner*, anoint, fr. L. *unguere*.]
OLD (ōld) *a.* having existed a long time; aged; ancient; out of date; decayed. [O.E. *ald*, *eald*. Cf. Ger. *alt*.]
OLDEN (ōl'den) *a.* old; ancient.
OLDISH (ōl'dish) *a.* somewhat old.
OLDNESS (ōld'nes) *n.* state of being old.
OLEASTER (ō-lē-as'tẹr) *n.* wild olive. [L., fr. *olea*, **OLIVE.**]

OLEOGRAPH (ō'lē-ō-graf) *n.* print in oil colours. [Fr. L. *oleo*, **OIL**, and G. *graphein*, write.]
OLFACTORY (ol-fak'tu-ri) *a.* having the sense of smelling. [L. *olfactus*, smelled, fr. (part.) *olere*, smell, and *facere*, cause.]
OLIGARCHY (ol'i-gär-ki) *n.* government in the hands of a few men. [G., fr. *oligos*, few, and *arche*, rule.]
OLIO (ō'li-ō) *n.* a mixture of various pieces; medley. [Sp., fr. L. *olla*, pot.]
OLIVE (ol'iv) *n.* a tree yielding oil; the emblem of peace. [F., fr. L. (acc.) *olivam*, fr. G. *elaia*, olive-tree.]
OLYMPIAD (ō-lim'pi-ad) *n.* the period of four years in Grecian history.
OLYMPIC (ō-lim'pik) *a.* pertaining to Olympia and its games. [G.]
OMBRE (om'bẹr) *n.* a game at cards. [F., fr. Sp. *hombre*, fr. L. *homo*.]
OMEGA (ō-meg'ạ, ō'me-gạ) *n.* the last Greek letter; the last. [G.]
OMELET (om'e-let) *n.* a fritter of eggs, etc. [F., of uncert. orig.]
OMEN (ō'men) *n.* a prognostic; a sign — *v.t.* to augur; predict;—*v.i.* to augur. [L.]
OMINOUS (om'i-nus) *a.* foreboding ill. [L. *ominosus*, fr. stem *omin-*, of *omen*.]
OMISSION (ō-mish'un) *n.* neglect of duty; failure; anything left out or forgotten. [L. (acc.) *omissionem*, fr. (part.) *omissus*, omitted.]
OMIT (ō-mit') *v.t.* to pass by; leave out; neglect. [L., fr. *ob*, and *mittere*.]
OMNIBUS (om'ni-bus) *n.* a large vehicle for conveying passengers. [L.]
OMNIPOTENCE (om-nip'u-tens) *n.* unlimited or infinite power.
OMNIPOTENT (om-nip'u-tent) *a.* having all power;—*n.* the Almighty. [Pref. L. *omnis*, all.]
OMNIPRESENCE (om-ni-prez'ens) *n.* presence in every place. [Pref. L. *omnis*, all.]
OMNIPRESENT (om-ni-prez'ent) *a.* present in every place.
OMNISCIENCE (om-nish'ens) *n.* universal knowledge or wisdom. [Pref. L. *omnis*, all.]
OMNISCIENT (om-nish'ent) *a.* having infinite knowledge.
ON (on) *prep.* upon; at; near;—*ad.* forward; onward; above;—*inter.* go on. [O.E. Cf. Ger. *an*.]
ONCE (wuns) *ad.* one time; at a former time. [O.E. *anes*; ad. suff. *-s*.]
ONE (wun) *a.* single; any. [O.E. *an*. Cf. Ger. *ein*; L. *unus*.]
ONENESS (wun'nes) *n.* singleness; unity.
ONERARY (on'e-rạ-ri) *a.* fitted for or entailing burdens.
ONEROUS (on'e-rus) *a.* burdensome; oppressive. [L. *onerosus*, fr. stem *oner-*, of *onus*, burden.]
ONEROUSLY (on'e-rus-li) *ad.* in an onerous manner.
ONE-SIDED (wun'sid-ed) *a.* limited to one side; partial. [See **ONE** and **SIDE.**]
ONGOING (on'gō-ing) *n.* doings; proceeding.
ONION (un'yun) *n.* a plant with a bulbous root. [L. *unio*.]
ONLOOKER (on'look-ẹr) *n.* a spectator. [See **ON** and **LOOK.**]
ONLY (ōn'li) *a.* single; alone;—*ad.* singly; merely;—*conj.* but. [O.E. *anlic*, fr. **ONE** and **LIKE.**]
ONSET (on'set) *n.* an attack; assault. [Fr. **ON** and **SET.**]
ONSLAUGHT (on'slawt) *n.* violent attack; onset.
ONTOLOGY (on-tol'ō-ji) *n.* the science of being. [G. (part. stem) *ont-*, of *on*, being, and *-logia*, fr. *legein*, speak.]
ONUS (ō'nus) *n.* the burden. [L.]
ONWARD (on'wạrd) *ad.* forward; farther; —*a.* advancing; improving.

ONYX (on'iks) *n.* a gem used for cameos. [L., fr. G. *onux*, finger-nail; fr. the colour.]

OOLITE (ō'a-līt) *n.* a kind of limestone. [Fr. G. *oon*, egg, and *lithos*, stone.]

OOZE (ōōz) *n.* soft mud; —*v.i.* to flow gently. [M.E. *wose*, fr. O.E. *wase*.]

OOZY (ōō'zi) *a.* miry; slimy.

OPACITY (ō-pas'i-ti) *n.* want of transparency.

OPAL (ō'pạl) *n.* a stone of changeable colours. [L. *opalus*.]

OPALESCENT (ō-pạl-es'ent) *a.* reflecting light.

OPALINE (ō'pạl-in) *a.* pertaining to or like opal.

OPAQUE (ō-pāk') *a.* not transparent. Also **OPACOUS**. [F., fr. L. (acc.) *opacum*.]

OPE (ōp) *v.t.* to open.

OPEN (ō'pn) *v.t.* or *i.* to unclose; divide; unfold; begin; —*a.* not shut; free; frank; clear; public. [O.E. Cf. Ger. *offen*.]

OPENING (ō'pning) *n.* an aperture; a breach; beginning; opportunity.

OPENLY (ō'pn-li) *ad.* publicly; plainly; frankly.

OPENNESS (ō'pn-nes) *n.* state or quality of being open.

OPERA (op'e-rạ) *n.* a dramatic composition set to music. [It., fr. L. *opera*, work.]

OPERATE (op'e-rāt) *v.i.* to act; work. [L. (part.) *operatus*, having worked, fr. *operari*, fr. stem *oper-*, of *opus* work.]

OPERATIC (op-e-rat'ik) *a.* pertaining to the opera.

OPERATION (op-e-rā'shun) *n.* action; agency.

OPERATIVE (op'e-rạ-tiv) *a.* acting; having power to act; —*n.* a labouring person. Also **OPERANT**.]

OPERATOR (op'e-rā-tẹr) *n.* one who operates. [L.]

OPHICLEIDE (of'i-klīd) *n.* a large brass wind instrument. [=the old 'serpent' with keys added; fr. G. *ophis*, a serpent, and stem *kleid-*, of *kleis*, key.]

OPHIDIAN (ō-fid'i-ạn) *a.* relating to serpents. [Fr. G. *ophidion*, a little serpent.]

OPHIOLOGY (of-i-ol'ō-ji) *n.* history and description of serpents. [Fr. G. *ophis*, and *-logia*, fr. *legein*.] [eyes.

OPHTHALMIA (of-thal'mi-ạ) *n.* a disease of the

OPHTHALMIC (of-thal'mik) *a.* relating to the eye. [Fr. G. *ophthalmos*.]

OPIATE (ō'pi-āt) *n.* a medicine that contains opium; —*a.* causing sleep. [See **OPIUM**.]

OPINE (ō-pīn') *v.i.* to think; suppose. [F. *opiner*, fr. L. *opinari*.]

OPINION (ō-pin'yun) *n.* the judgment formed by the mind; notion; estimation. [F., fr. L. *opinio*.]

OPINIONATIVE (ō-pin'yun-ā-tiv) *a.* unduly fond of one's own opinion.

OPIUM (ō'pi-um) *n.* the inspissated juice of the poppy. [L., fr. G. *opion*, poppy juice, fr. *opos*, juice.]

OPOSSUM (ō-pos'um) *n.* an American marsupial quadruped. [Amer. Ind.]

OPPONENT (o-pō'nent) *a.* that opposes; —*n.* an opposer. [L. (part. stem) *opponenti-*, opposing, fr. *ob*, against, and *ponere*, place.]

OPPORTUNE (op-ur-tūn') *a.* timely; seasonable. [L. *opportunus*, lit. before the PORT, fr. *ob*, and *portus*.]

OPPORTUNELY (op-ur-tūn'li) *ad.* seasonably.

OPPORTUNITY (op-ur-tū'ni-ti) *n.* fit or favourable time or place. [Fr. L. (acc.) *opportunitatem*.]

OPPOSABLE (o-pō'zạ-bl) *a.* that may be opposed.

OPPOSE (o-pōz') *v.t.* or *i.* to resist; withstand; make objection. [F. *opposer*, fr. *poser* to **POSE** with L. pref. *ob*.]

OPPOSER (o-pō'zẹr) *n.* one who opposes.

OPPOSITE (op'u-zit) *a.* contrary in position; adverse. [F., fr. L. (part.) *oppositus*, opposed, fr. *ob*, and *ponere*, place.]

OPPOSITION (op-u-zish'un) *n.* resistance; contradiction; an opposite party.

OPPOSITIONIST (op-u-zish'un-ist) *n.* one of the opposite party.

OPPRESS (o-pres') *v.t.* to burden; overpower; treat cruelly; lie heavy on. [F. *oppresser*, fr. L. (part.) *oppressus*, oppressed, fr. *ob*, near, and *-primere*, for *premere*, to **PRESS**.]

OPPRESSION (o-presh'un) *n.* act of oppressing.

OPPRESSIVE (o-pres'iv) *a.* burdensome; unjustly severe; exacting.

OPPRESSIVELY (o-pres'iv-li) *ad.* in an oppressive or cruel manner.

OPPRESSIVENESS (o-pres'iv-nes) *n.* quality of being oppressive.

OPPRESSOR (o-pres'ẹr) *n.* one who oppresses; a tyrant. [L.]

OPPROBRIOUS (o-prō'bri-us) *a.* reproachful; abusive.

OPPROBRIOUSLY (o-prō'bri-us-li) *ad.* reproachfully; scurrilously.

OPPROBRIUM (o-prō'bri-um) *n.* contemptuous reproach; infamy. [L., fr. *ob*, over, and *probrum*, disgrace.]

OPPUGN (o-pūn') *v.t.* to oppose; resist. [F. *oppugner*, fr. *ob*, against, and *pugnare*, fight. See **PUGILIST**.]

OPTATIVE (op'tā-tiv, op-tā'tiv) *a.* expressing desire or wish. [L., fr. (part.) *optatus*, wished, fr. *optare*.]

OPTIC (op'tik) *n.* an organ of sight; —*a.* pertaining to sight or to optics. [F. *optique*, fr. G. *optikos*, fr. root of *opsomai*, I shall see.]

OPTICAL (op'ti-kạl) *a.* pertaining to vision or to optics.

OPTICIAN (op-tish'ạn) *n.* a person skilled in optics; dealer in spectacles, etc.

OPTICS (op'tiks) *n.pl.* science of the nature and laws of light and vision.

OPTIMISM (op'ti-mizm) *n.* the doctrine that everything is for the best. [Fr. L. *optimus*, best.]

OPTIMIST (op'ti-mist) *n.* an adherent of optimism.

OPTION (op'shun) *n.* right of choosing; choice. [F., fr. L. (acc.) *optionem*; conn. with **OPTATIVE**.]

OPTIONAL (op'shun-ạl) *a.* left to choice.

OPULENCE (op'ū-lens) *n.* wealth; riches.

OPULENT (op'ū-lent) *a.* very rich; wealthy. [L. *opulentus*, fr. stem of *opes*, riches.]

OPULENTLY (op'ū-lent-li) *a.* richly; affluently.

OPUS (ō'pus) *n.* a work; a musical composition. [L.]

OR (or) *con.* uniting alternatives—as, you may go *or* stay. [Short. fr. M.E. **OTHER**.]

ORACLE (or'ạ-kl) *n.* an opinion deemed infallible; a wise man or sentence. [F., fr. L. *oraculum*, fr. *orare*, speak, pray. See **ORAL**.]

ORACLES (or'ạ-klz) *n.pl.* the revelations of God.

ORACULAR (ō-rak'ū-lạr) *a.* uttering oracles; authoritative.

ORACULARLY (ō-rak'ū-lạr-li) *ad.* authoritatively; positively.

ORAL (ō'rạl) *a.* delivered by the mouth. [Fr. L. stem *or-*, of *os*, mouth.]

ORALLY (ō'rạl-i-) *ad.* by word of mouth.

ORANGE (or'inj) *n.* the pulpy fruit of a tree. [O.F. *orenge*, by association with *or*, gold. fr. It. *arancia*, fr. A. *naranj*.]

ORANGE-BLOSSOM (or'inj-blos'um) *n.* the flower of the orange; a bride's ornament.

ORANGEMAN (or'inj-mạn) *n.* an Irish Protestant. [Fr. William III., Prince of *Orange*.]

ORANGE-PEEL (or'inj-pēl) *n.* the rind of an orange.

ORANGERY (or'inj-ri) *n.* a plantation of orange-trees.

Fāte, fár, ạdo; mē, hẹr; mīne; nōte; tūne; mōon.

ORANG-OUTANG (ŏ-rang'-ŏŏ-tang) *n.* the great ape, having a deformed resemblance to man. [Mal. =man of the woods.]

ORATION (ŏ-rā'shun) *n.* a public speech. [F., fr. L. (acc.) *orationem.*]

ORATOR (or'a-tẹr) *n.* an eloquent speaker; a petitioner. [L.]

ORATORICAL (or-a-tor'i-kạl) *a.* pertaining to an orator or to oratory; rhetorical.

ORATORICALLY (or-a-tor'i-kạl-i) *ad.* in a rhetorical manner.

ORATORIO (or-a-tō'ri-ō) *n.* a sacred drama set in music; a chapel. [It.]

ORATORY (or'a-tu-ri) *n.* art of public speaking; a small private chapel.

ORB (orb) *n.* a round body; a sphere; any rolling body; the eye. [F. *orbe*, fr. L. (acc.) *orbem*, fr. *orbis.*]

ORBED (orbd) *a.* round; circular.

ORBICULAR (or-bik'ū-lạr) *a.* circular; spherical. [L., fr. *orbiculus*, a little disc.]

ORBIT (or'bit) *n.* path of a planet or comet round its centre; cavity of the eye. [L. *orbita.*]

ORCHARD (or'chạrd) *n.* an assemblage or garden of fruit-trees. [O.E. *orceard, ortgeard.* [See WORT and YARD.]

ORCHESTRA (or'kes-tra) *n.* the part of a theatre for the musicians; the musicians. [G., fr. *orchesthai*, to dance.]

ORCHESTRAL (or-kes'trạl) *a.* pertaining to an orchestra.

ORCHIS (or'kis) *n.* a plant with fleshy tubers and fragrant flowers; orchid. [G. *orchis.*]

ORDAIN (or-dān') *v.t.* to put in order; regulate; decree; set apart for office in the church. [M.E. *ordeyne*, fr. O.F. *ordener* = F. *ordonner*, fr. L. *ordinare*, set in ORDER.]

ORDEAL (or'dē-ạl) *n.* trial by fire or water; any severe test or trial. [O.E. *ordel*, judgment; conn. with DEAL.]

ORDER (or'dẹr) *n.* arrangement; method; command; rule; care; class; commission to pay money or supply goods;—*v.t.* or *i.* to arrange; regulate; give command;— *pl.* ordination or office in the church. [F. *ordre*, O.F. *ordine*, fr. L. (acc.) *ordinem*, fr. *ordo.*] [management.

ORDERING (or'dẹr-ing) *n.* arrangement.

ORDERLY (or'dẹr-li) *a.* regular; well regulated; being on duty;—*ad.* methodically; according to rule;—*n.* a private soldier who attends on an officer.

ORDINAL (or'di-nạl) *a.* noting order;—*n.* a book of rites. [L. *ordinalis*, denoting ORDER.]

ORDINANCE (or'di-nạns) *n.* appointment by authority; any established rule; rite. [O.F. fr. (part.) *ordenant*, ordaining.]

ORDINARILY (or'di-nạr-i-li) *ad.* usually.

ORDINARY (or'di-nạr-i) *a.* usual; common; inferior;—*n.* an ecclesiastical judge; an eating-house, or the meal provided at fixed charges.

ORDINATE (or'di-nạt) *a.* regular; methodical; *n.* a line used to fix the position of a point in space. [L. (part.) *ordinatus*, ordained.]

ORDINATION (or-di-nā'shun) *n.* act of ordaining; state of being ordained.

ORDNANCE (ord'nạns) *n.* heavy artillery; cannon. [Form of ORDNANCE.]

ORDURE (or'dūr) *n.* dung; filth. [F., fr. O.F. *ord*, vile, fr. L. (acc.) *horridum*, HORRID.]

ORE (ōr) *n.* any mineral substance from which metal is extracted; the metal itself. [O.E. *ora.*]

ORGAN (or'gạn) *n.* an instrument of action or motion; a wind instrument of music. [F. *organe*, fr. L., fr. G. *organon*, an implement.]

ORGANIC (or-gan'ik) *a.* containing or produced by organs. [L., fr. G. *organikos.*]

ORGANISATION (or-gạn-i-zā'shun) *n.* act of organising.

ORGANISE (or'gạn-iz) *v.t.* to furnish with organs; form in due order.

ORGANISM (or'gạn-izm) *n.* organic structure; any living or active being or agency.

ORGANIST (or'gạn-ist) *n.* one who plays on an organ.

ORGASM (or'gazm) *n.* immoderate excitement or action.

ORGIES (or'jiz) *n.pl.* drunken and disorderly revels. [F. *orgie*, fr. L., fr. G. (pl.) *orgia;* orig. feast of Bacchus.]

ORIEL (ō'ri-el) *n.* a large projecting bay window. [M.E. *oriol*, fr. O.F. fr. Late L. *oriolum*, small room (gilded), fr. *aurum*, gold.]

ORIENT (ō'ri-ent) *a.* rising as the sun; eastern; shining;—*n.* the east. [F., fr. L. (acc.) *orientem*, east, orig. (part.) rising, fr. *oriri*, rise.]

ORIENTAL (ō-i-ren'tạl) *a.* eastern;—*n.* a native of the east.

ORIENTALIST (ō-ri-en'tạl-ist) *n.* one versed in the eastern languages or literature.

Oriel Window.

ORIFICE (or'i-fis) *n.* an opening; aperture. [F., fr. L. *orificium*, fr. *os*, mouth, and *facere*, make.]

ORIFLAMME (or'i-flam) *n.* the ancient royal standard of France. [F., fr. L. *aurum*, gold, and *flamma*, FLAME.]

ORIGIN (or'i-jin) *n.* first beginning; cause; source; derivation. [F. *origine*, fr. L. (acc.) *originem*, fr. *oriri*, rise.]

ORIGINAL (o-rij'i-nạl) *a.* first; primitive;— *n.* origin; first copy.

ORIGINALITY (o-rij-i-nal'i-ti) *n.* quality of being original; power of producing new ideas or expressions of thought.

ORIGINALLY (o-rij'i-nạl-i) *ad.* at first; at the time of formation.

ORIGINATE (o-rij'i-nāt) *v.t.* to bring into existence;—*v.i.* to take rise; begin.

ORIGINATOR (o-rij'i-nā-tẹr) *n.* one who originates.

ORION (ō-ri'un) *n.* a southern constellation. [G., name of a myth. hunter.]

ORISON (or'i-zun) *n.* a prayer. [O.F. =F. *oraison*, fr. L. (acc.) *orationem.*]

ORLOP (or'lop) *n.* the lower deck of a ship. [D.]

ORMOLU (or'mō-lōō) *n.* brass or copper gilt. [Fr. F. =pounded gold.]

ORNAMENT (or'na-ment) *n.* decoration;— *v.t.* to embellish. [M.E. *ornement*, fr. O.F., fr. L. *ornamentum.* See ORNATE.]

ORNAMENTAL (or-na-men'tạl) *a.* tending to adorn or embellish.

ORNAMENTATION (or-na-men-tā'shun) *n.* act or art of ornamenting; decoration.

ORNATE (or'nāt) *a.* adorned; decorated. [L. (part.) *ornatus*, adorned, fr. *ornare.*]

ORNATENESS (or-nāt'nes) *n.* state of being adorned.

ORNITHOLOGIST (or-ni-thol'ō-jist) *n.* one skilled in the science of birds.

ORNITHOLOGY (or-ni-thol'ō-ji) *n.* the science which treats of birds. [Fr. G. stem *ornith-*, of *ornis*, bird, and *-logia*, discourse, fr. *legein.*]

ORPHAN (or'fạn) *n.* a fatherless or motherless child. [Fr. G. *orphanos*, destitute.]

ORPHANAGE (or'fạn-ij) *n.* the state of an orphan; a home for orphans.

ORPHANED (or'fạnd) *a.* bereft of parents.

ORPHEAN (or-fē'ạn) *a.* pertaining to Orpheus.

ORPIMENT (or'pi-ment) *n.* a yellow sulphuret of arsenic used in dyeing. [F., fr. L. *auripigmentum.* See PIGMENT.]

ORRERY (or'.e-ri) *n.* an instrument to show the revolutions of the planets. [The Earl of *Orrery*, for whom one was made in 1715.]

ORRIS (or'is) *n.* a plant with a fragrant root; a kind of gold lace. [Form of IRIS.]

ORT (ort) *n.* a fragment, as of a meal; used mostly in the plural, ORTS (ortz). [O.E. *or. out*, and *etan*, eat.]

ORTHODOX (or'thu-doks) *a.* correct in doctrine. [L. *orthodoxus*, fr. G., fr. *orthos*, right, and *doxa*, opinion.]

ORTHODOXY (or'thu-dok-si) *n.* soundness in opinion and doctrine. Also ORTHODOXNESS.

ORTHOEPIST (or'thō-e-pist) *n.* a person well skilled in pronunciation.

ORTHOEPY (or'thō-e-pi, or-thō'e-pi) *n.* correct pronunciation of words. [G,. fr. *orthos*, right, and *epos*, word.]

ORTHOGRAPHER (or-thog'ra-fer) *n.* one versed in orthography.

ORTHOGRAPHIC (or-thu-graf'ik) *a.* pertaining to orthography.

ORTHOGRAPHICALLY (or-thu-graf'i-kal-i) *ad.* according to rules of spelling.

ORTHOGRAPHY (or-thog'ra-fi) *n.* the spelling or writing of words with the proper letters. [G. *orthos*, right, and *graphein*, write.]

ORTOLAN (or'tu-lan) *n.* a small singing bird of southern Europe, prized as a delicacy for the table. [O.F. *hortolan*, fr. L. (acc.) *hortulanum*, gardener, fr. *hortus*, garden.]

OSCILLATE (os'i-lāt) *v.i.* [*ppr.* or *a.* OSCILLATING] to swing to and fro; vibrate. [L., fr. *oscillum*, a swing.]

OSCILLATION (os-i-lā'shun) *n.* a vibration.

OSCILLATORY (os'i-la-tu-ri) *a.* moving as a pendulum.

OSCULANT (os'kū-lant) *a.* kissing; closely adhering.

OSCULATE (os'kū-lāt) *v.t.* to salute with a kiss; touch. [L., fr. *osculum*, lit. a little mouth, fr. *os*.]

OSIER (ō'zher) *n.* a willow-like plant, with flexible branches, used in basket-making; —*a.* made of, or like, osiers. [F., of uncert. etym.]

OSSEOUS (os'ē-us) *a.* bony; like bone. [L. *osseus*, fr. *os*.]

OSSICLE (os'i-kl) *n.* a small bone.

OSSIFIC (o-sif'ik) *a.* having power to ossify.

OSSIFICATION (os-i-fi-kā'shun) *n.* the process of changing to bone.

OSSIFY (os'i-fi) *v.t.* or *i.* to change to bone. [-*fy*, fr. F. *fier*, fr. L. *-ficare* = *facere*, make.]

OSTENSIBLE (os-ten'si-bl) *a.* apparent; plausible. [Fr. L. [part.) *ostensus*, shown, fr. *ostendere*, fr. *ob*, before, and *tendere*, stretch. [See TEND, TENT.]

OSTENSIBLY (os-ten'si-bli) *n.* in appearance.

OSTENSIVE (os-ten'siv) *a.* tending to show; exhibiting.

OSTENTATION (os-ten-tā'shun) *n.* ambitious display; pompous parade. [F., fr. L. (acc.) *ostentationem*, fr. *ostentare*, parade, fr. *ostendere*.]

OSTENTATIOUS (os-ten-tā'shus) *a.* fond of, or intended for, show or vain display.

OSTENTATIOUSLY (os-ten-tā'shus-li) *ad.* boastfully; vainly.

OSTEOLOGY (os-tē-ol'ō-ji) *n.* description of bones. [Fr. G. *osteon*, bone, and *-logia*, fr. *legein*, to discourse.]

OSTRACISE (os'tra-siz) *v.t.* to banish by the voice of the people. [G. *ostrakizein*, to banish (for ten years) by popular vote, fr. *ostrakon*, voting-tablet. See OYSTER.]

OSTRACISM (os'tra-sizm) *n.* banishment by ostracising. [G. *ostrakismos*.]

OSTRICH (os'trich) *n.* a large bird with very short wings and fine feathers. [O.F. *ostruce*, fr. L. *avis*, bird, and *struthio*, fr. G. *strouthion*, ostrich.]

OTHER (uTH'er) *pron.* and *a.* not the same; different. [O.E. *other*.]

OTHERWISE (uTH'er-wiz) *ad.* in a different manner; by other causes; in other respects.

OTIOSE (ō'shi-ōs) *a.* being at ease; indolent. [L., fr. *otium*, ease.]

OTOLOGY (ō-tol'ō-ji) *n.* science of the ear. [Fr. G. stem *ot-*, of *ous*, ear, and *-logia*, fr. *legein*, discourse.]

OTTER (ot'er) *n.* an amphibious quadruped. [O.E. *otor*. Cf. Ger. *Otter*.]

OTTO (ot'ō) *n.* essential oil of roses. Also written OTTAR, ATTAR. [See ATTAR.]

OTTOMAN (ot'u-man) *n.* a stuffed seat without a back; a native of Turkey;—*a.* relating to Turkey. [F., fr. the sultan *Othman* or *Osman*, founder of Turkish empire.]

OUBLIETTE (òò-bli-et') *n.* an underground dungeon. [F., fr. *oublli*, OBLIVION.]

OUCH (ouch) *n.* the bezel or socket of a ring. [O.F. *nusche*, fr. Ger.]

OUGHT (awt) *v.i.* to be morally necessary; be obliged. [O.E. (pret.) *ahte*, fr. OWE.]

OUNCE (ouns) *n.* 12th of a pound troy, and 16th of a pound avoirdupois; a kind of leopard. [O.F., fr. L. *uncia*. Doublet of INCH.]

OUR (our) *a.* pertaining or belonging to us. [O.E. *ure*.]

OURS (ourz) *pron.* noting what belongs to us.

OURSELVES (our-selvz') *pron. pl.* we; not others.

OUSEL (òò'zl) *n.* a kind of thrush. [O.E. *osle*. Cf. Ger. *Amsel*.]

OUST (oust) *v.t.* to eject with force. [O.F. = F. *ôter*; of uncert. etym.]

OUT (out) *ad.* abroad; not at home; fully; freely; in error; at a loss;—*inter.* away! begone! [O.E. *utan*, *ut*.]

OUTBID (out-bid') *v.t.* to bid more than another. [Fr. OUT and BID.]

OUTBOUND (out'bound) *a.* proceeding to a foreign port.

OUTBREAK (out'brāk) *n.* a breaking forth. [Fr. OUT and BREAK.]

OUTCAST (out'kast) *n.* a person banished. [Fr. OUT and CAST.]

OUTCRY (out'kri) *n.* clamour; loud cry. [Fr. OUT and CRY.]

OUTDO (out-dóó') *v.t.* [*pp.* OUTDONE] to surpass; excel.

OUTDOOR (out'dōr) *ad.* or *a.* abroad; out of the house.

OUTER (out'er) *a.* that is without; exterior. [O.E. (comp.) *uttera*, *utera*. Doublet of UTTER.]

OUTERMOST (out'er-mōst) *a.* farthest from the middle.

OUTFACE (out-fās') *v.t.* to bear down or brave with impudence.

OUTFIT (out'fit) *n.* complete equipment for a voyage, etc.; the articles or expenses necessary for such.

OUTGENERAL (out-jen'e-ral) *v.t.* to exceed in generalship.

OUTGO (out-gō') *v.t.* to surpass.

OUTGOING (out'gō-ing) *n.* act of going out; expenditure.

OUTGROW (out-grō') *v.t.* to surpass in growth.

OUT-HEROD (out-her'ud) *v.t.* to exceed in cruelty or absurdity. [Fr. *Herod*, as type of ferocity.]

OUTHOUSE (out'hous) *n.* an appendage to the mansion.

OUTLAW (out'law) *n.* one excluded from the benefit of the law;—*v.t.* to deprive of the benefit of the law; proscribe. [O.E. *ut laga*.]

OUTLAWRY (out'law-ri) *n.* act of depriving of the benefit or protection of the law.

OUTLAY (out'lā) *n.* expenditure.

OUTLET (out'let) *n.* a passage outward.

OUTLINE (out'lin) *n.* the exterior line of a figure; a sketch.

OUTLIVE (out-liv') *v.t.* to survive.

Fāte, fär, ado; mē, her; mine; nōte; tūne; mòòn.

OUTLOOK (out′look) *n.* vigilant watch; prospect; a watch tower;—(out-look′) *v.t.* to stare down.

OUTLYING (out-ll′ing) *a.* lying out or beyond; on the frontier.

OUTMOST (out′mŏst) *a.* farthest in the extremity.

OUTNUMBER (out-num′bẹr) *v.t.* to exceed in number.

OUTPACE (out-pās′) *v.t.* to leave behind in walking.

OUTPOST (out′pŏst) *n.* a station without a camp, or at a distance.

OUTPOUR (out-pōr′) *v.t.* to pour out.

OUTPOURING (out′pōr-ing) *n.* effusion.

OUTRAGE (out′rāj) *v.t.* or *i.* to treat with violence; injure; abuse;—*n.* injurious violence; wanton abuse. [F., fr. *outre*, beyond, fr. O.F. *oltre*, fr. L. *ultra*.]

OUTRAGEOUS (out-rā′jus) *a.* exceeding propriety, sense, etc.; abusive; furious; exorbitant.

OUTREACH (out-rēch′) *v.t.* to go or extend beyond.

OUTRIDE (out-rid′) *v.t.* to ride faster than.

OUTRIDER (out′ri-der) *n.* an attending servant on horseback.

OUTRIGHT (out′rit) *ad.* immediately; completely. [thing.

OUTRIVAL (out-ri′val) *v.t.* to surpass in anything.

OUTRUN (out-run′) *v.t.* to surpass in running; exceed. [sailing.

OUTSAIL (out-sāl′) *v.t.* to leave behind in

OUTSELL (out-sel′) *v.t.* to exceed in amount of sales, or in the selling price.

OUTSET (out′set) *n.* beginning; opening.

OUTSHINE (out-shin′) *v.t.* to excel in brightness.

OUTSIDE (out′sid) *n.* the outward part; the utmost;—*a.* exterior;—*adv.* and *prep.* on the exterior (of).

OUTSKIRT (out′skẹrt) *n.* border; suburb.

OUTSPREAD (out-spred′) *v.t.* to spread open; diffuse.

OUTSTANDING (out-stan′ding) *a.* not collected; unpaid.

OUTSTRETCH (out-strech′) *v.t.* to extend far; expand.

OUTSTRIP (out-strip′) *v.t.* to outgo; exceed; leave behind.

OUTVOTE (out-vŏt′) *v.t.* to exceed in the number of votes.

OUTWALK (out-wawk′) *v.t.* to leave behind in walking.

OUTWARD (out′wạrd) *a.* external;—*ad.* towards the outside. Also **OUTWARDS**. [O.E., fr. *ute*, *utan* OUT, and suff. -*weard*, expressing direction.]

OUTWARD-BOUND (out′wạrd-bound) *a.* going to a foreign port; going seaward.

OUTWEAR (out-wãr′) *v.t.* to endure or wear longer than.

OUTWEIGH (out-wā′) *v.t.* to exceed in weight or value.

OUTWIT (out-wit′) *v.t.* to overcome by superior ingenuity.

OUTWORK (out-wurk′) *v.t.* to surpass in work or labour.

OUTWORK (out′wurk) *n.* a part of a fortress outside the principal lines of defence.

OVAL (ō′val) *a.* of the form of an egg; oblong; —*n.* a body shaped like an egg. [F., fr. L. *ovum*, egg.]

OVARIOUS (ō-vā′ri-us) *a.* consisting of eggs.

OVARY (ō′va-ri) *n.* place where eggs are formed. [Fr. L. *ovum*, egg.   Oval.

OVATE (ō′vāt) *a.* egg-shaped, as a leaf.

OVATION (ō-vā′shun) *n.* a lesser triumph; any expression of popular applause. [F., fr. L. *ovatio*, a lesser triumph, fr. *ovare*, to triumph, exult.]

OVEN (uv′n) *n.* an arched cavity for baking, heating, drying, etc. [O.E. *ofen*. Cf. Ger. *Ofen*.]

OVER (ō′vẹr) *prep.* across; above; upon; on the surface;—*ad.* from side to side; more than; throughout;—*a.* upper; past. [O.E. *ofer*. Cf. Ger. *über*; L. *super*; G. *huper*.]

OVERACT (ō-vẹr-akt′) *v.t.* to perform to excess.

OVERALLS (ō′vẹr-awlz) *n.* a kind of long, loose trousers.

OVERARCH (ō-vẹr-ȧrch′) *v.t.* to cover with an arch; —*v.i.* to hang over.

OVERAWE (ō-vẹr-aw′) *v.t.* to restrain by awe.

OVERBALANCE (ō-vẹr-bal′ạns) *v.t.* to weigh down; preponderate.

OVERBEAR (ō-vẹr-bãr′) *v.t.* to bear down; overpower; repress.

OVERBEARING (ō-vẹr-bãr′ing) *a.* haughty and dogmatical.

OVERBOARD (ō′vẹr-bōrd) *ad.* out of the ship.

OVERBURDEN (ō-vẹr-bur′dn) *v.t.* to load to excess.

OVERCAST (ō-vẹr-kast) *v.t.* to cloud; darken; rate too high; sew over slightly.

OVERCHARGE (ō-vẹr-chȧrj′) *v.t.* to load or charge to excess.

OVERCHARGE (ō′vẹr-charj) *n.* excessive load or charge.

OVERCOAT (ō′vẹr-kŏt) *n.* a coat worn over the ordinary clothing; topcoat.

OVERCOME (ō-vẹr-kum′) *v.t.* to get the better of; conquer.

OVERDO (ō-vẹr-dŏŏ′) *v.t.* to do too much.

OVERDOSE (ō′vẹr-dŏs) *n.* too great a dose.

OVERDRAW (ō-vẹr-draw′) *v.t.* to draw orders beyond the credit.

OVERDUE (ō′vẹr-dū) *a.* past the time of payment.

OVERFLOW (ō-vẹr-flō′) *v.t.* or *i.* to flow or run over; flood; cover; be more than full.

OVERFLOW (ō′vẹr-flō) *n.* inundation; deluge; superabundance.

OVERFLOWING (ō-vẹr-flō′ing) *a.* flowing over; abundant; copious.

OVERGROW (ō-vẹr-grō′) *v.t.* or *i.* to cover with herbage; *v.i.* grow beyond the natural size.

OVERGROWTH (ō′vẹr-grōth) *n.* exuberant or excessive growth.

OVERHANG (ō′vẹr-hang) *v.t.* or *i.* to hang over; project over.

OVERHAUL (ō-vẹr-hawl′) *v.t.* to turn over and examine; overtake.

OVERHEAD (ō-vẹr-hed′) *ad.* above; aloft.

OVERHEAR (ō-vẹr-hēr′) *v.t.* to hear by accident.

OVERHEAT (ō-vẹr-hēt′) *v.t.* to heat to excess.

OVER-ISSUE (o-vẹr-ish′ū) *n.* issue of notes or bills beyond capital or public wants.

OVERJOY (ō-vẹr-joi′) *v.t.* to transport with delight.

OVERLAND (ō′vẹr-land) *a.* carried by land.

OVERLAY (ō-vẹr-lā′) *v.t.* to spread over; cover; smother.

OVERLEAP (ō-vẹr-lēp′) *v.t.* to leap over.

OVERLIE (ō′vẹr-li) *v.t.* to lie above or upon.

OVERLOAD (ō-vẹr-lŏd′) *v.t.* to load too heavily; fill to excess.

OVERLOOK (ō-vẹr-look′) *v.t.* to inspect; neglect; excuse.

OVERLOOKER (ō′-vẹr-look-ẹr) *n.* a superintendent.

OVERMATCH (ō-vẹr-mach′) *v.t.* to be too powerful for.

OVERMATCH (ō′vẹr-mach) *n.* one superior in power or skill.

OVERMUCH (ō′vẹr-much) *a.* too much.

OVERPASS (ō-vẹr-pas′) *v.t.* to go over; cross; omit.

OVERPAY (ō-vẹr-pā′) *v.t.* to pay too much.

Fāte, fár, ạdo; mē, hẹr; mīne; nōte; tūne; moŏn.

OVERPLUS (ō'vẹr-plus) *n.* more than is wanted; surplus. [Fr. pref. OVER-, and PLUS.]

OVERPOISE (ō'vẹr-poiz) *n.* preponderant weight.

OVERPOWER (ō-vẹr-pou'ẹr) *v.t.* to vanquish by superior force; affect too strongly.

OVERPRODUCTION (ō'vẹr-prō-duk-shun) *n.* supply beyond the demand.

OVERRATE (ō-vẹr-rāt') *v.t.* to rate too high or beyond the truth.

OVERREACH (ō-vẹr-rēch') *v.t.* to extend beyond; get the better of; cheat.

OVERRULE (ō-vẹr-rōōl') *v.t.* to rule over or against; control; supersede.

OVERRULER (ō-vẹr-rōōl'ẹr) *n.* one who over-rules.

OVERRULING (ō-vẹr-rōōl'ing) *a.* exerting superior power.

OVERRUN (ō-vẹr-run') *v.t.* to spread over; outrun; ravage;—*v.i.* to overflow; run over.

OVERSEA (ō'vẹr-sē) *a.* from beyond sea.

OVERSEE (ō-vẹr-sē') *v.t.* to superintend.

OVERSEER (ō-vẹr-sēr') *n.* a supervisor

OVERSET (ō-vẹr-set') *v.t.* or *i.* to overturn; subvert; capsize.

OVERSHADE (ō-vẹr-shād') *v.t.* to cover with shade.

OVERSHADOW (ō-vẹr-shad'ō) *v.t.* to cover with shade.

OVERSHOE (ō'vẹr-shōō) *n.* a waterproof shoe worn over the ordinary shoe.

OVERSHOOT (ō-vẹr-shōōt') to shoot or go beyond the mark.

OVERSHOT (ō'vẹr-shot) *a.* shot over; having the water falling from above, as a wheel.

OVERSIGHT (ō'vẹr-sīt) *n.* watchful care; failing to notice. [long.

OVERSLEEP (ō-vẹr-slēp') *v.t.* to sleep too

OVERSMAN (ō'vẹrz-man) *n.* an umpire.

OVERSPENT (ō-vẹr-spent') *a.* wearied to excess.

OVERSPREAD (ō-vẹr-spred') *v.t.* to cover over.

OVERSTATE (ō-vẹr-stāt') *v.t.* to exaggerate.

OVERSTEP (ō-vẹr-step') *v.t.* to step beyond or over.

OVERSTOCK (ō-vẹr-stok') *v.t.* to fill too full.

OVERSTORY (ō'vẹr-stō-ri) *n.* the upper story.

OVERSTRAIN (ō-vẹr-strān') *v.t.* to strain or stretch too far.

OVERSTREW (ō-vẹr-strōō', ō-vẹr-strō') *v.t.* to spread or scatter over.

OVERT (ō'vẹrt) *a.* open; public. [O.F. (part.) =opened, fr. *ovrir*. See COVERT.]

OVERTAKE (ō-vẹr-tāk') *v.t.* [*pret.* OVER-TOOK; *pp.* OVERTAKEN] to come up with.

OVERTASK (ō-vẹr-task') *v.t.* to impose too much work on.

OVERTHROW (ō-vẹr-thrō') *v.t.* to throw down; upset; defeat utterly.

OVERTHROW (ō'vẹr-thrō) *n.* ruin; defeat.

OVERTLY (ō'vẹrt-li) *ad.* openly; publicly.

OVERTOP (ō-vẹr-top') *v.t.* to rise above; surpass.

OVERTURE (ō'vẹr-tūr) *n.* an opening; proposal; an introductory piece of music.

OVERTURN (ō-vẹr-turn') *v.t.* to throw down; destroy;—(ō'vẹr-turn) *n.* overthrow; to interfere with, as a decision.

OVERVALUE (ō-vẹr-val'ū) *v.t.* to estimate too highly.

OVERWEENING (ō-vẹr-wē'ning) *a.* self-conceited; arrogant.

OVERWEIGH (ō-vẹr-wā') *v.t.* to exceed in weight.

OVERWEIGHT (ō'vẹr-wāt) *n.* preponderance; greater weight.

OVERWHELM (ō-vẹr-hwelm') *v.t.* to spread over and crush; immerse and bear down.

OVERWISE (ō-vẹr-wīz') *a.* wise to affectation.

OVERWORK (ō-vẹr-wurk') *v.t.* [*pp.* OVER-WROUGHT] to cause to labour too much.

OVERWORN (ō'vẹr-worn) *a.* worn out by toil; spoiled by use.

OVERWROUGHT (ō'vẹr rawt) *a.* tired by labour; worked all over.

OVIFORM (ō'vi-form) *a.* egg-shaped. [L. *ovum,* an egg.]

OVIPAROUS (ō-vip'a-rus) *a.* producing eggs. [L., fr. *ovum,* egg, and *parere,* bring forth.]

OVOLO (ō'vu-lō) *n.* a round moulding. [It., fr. L. *ovum,* egg.]

OVULE (ō'vūl) *n.* rudiment of a seed. [L. *ovum.*]

OWE (ō) *v.t.* or *i.* to possess; be indebted to; be obliged for. [M.E. *awen, owen,* fr. O.E. *agan,* possess.]

OWING (ō'ing) *ppr.* or *a.* due; imputable to.

OWL (oul) *n.* a fowl that flies at night. [O.E. *ule.* Cf. Ger. *Eule.*]

OWLET (ou'let) *n.* a little owl.

OWN (ōn) *a.* noting property; belonging to; —*v.t.* to avow; possess. [O.E. (part.) *agen,* possessing, fr. *agan.* See OWE.]

OWNER (ō'nẹr) *n.* the rightful proprietor of anything.

OWNERSHIP (ō'nẹr-ship) *n.* exclusive right of possession.

OX (oks) *n.* a male of the bovine genus;—*pl.* OXEN. [O.E. *oxa; pl. oxan.* Cf. Ger. *Ochse.*]

OXIDE (ok'sīd) *n.* a compound of oxygen and a base. [G. *oxus,* sharp. See OXYGEN.]

OXIDISE (ok'si-diz) *v.t.* to convert into an oxide.

OXYGEN (ok'si-jen) *n.* a gaseous element which supports life and combustion; the respirable part of air. [=acid generator, fr. G., fr. *oxus,* acid, and root *gen-,* of *gignesthai,* be born.]

OYER (ō'yẹr) *n.* a hearing or trial of causes. [A.F., fr. L. *audire,* hear.]

OYSTER (ois'tẹr) *n.* a bivalvular shellfish. [O.F. = F. *huître,* fr. L., fr. G. *ostreon,* fr. *osteon,* shell, bone. Conn. with OSTRA-CISE.]

OZONE (ō'zōn) *n.* oxygen in the atmosphere made more active by electricity. [G., fr. *ozein,* smell.]

P

PABULAR (pab'ū-lẹr) *a.* pertaining to food. [L., conn. with *pasci,* feed; **PASTOR.**]

PACE (pās) *n.* a step; gait; measure of five feet;—*v.t.* or *i.* to measure by steps; walk slowly; amble. [F. *pas,* fr. L. (acc.) *passum,* tr. (part.) *passus* stretched, fr. *pandere.* Cf. **EXPANSION.**]

PACER (pā'sẹr) *n.* a horse that paces.

PACIFIC (pa-sif'ik) *a.* appeasing; peaceful; mild;—*n.* the ocean between Asia and America. [L.]

PACIFICATION (pa-sif-i-kā'shun) *n.* act of making peace. [L.]

PACIFICATORY (pa-sif'i-kā-tu-ri) *a.* tending to peace.

PACIFIER (pas'i-fī-ẹr) *n.* one who appeases. Also **PACIFICATOR.**

PACIFY (pas'i-fī) *v.t.* to appease; soothe. [F. *pacifier,* fr. L. *pacificare,* fr. stem *paci-,* of *pax,* peace, and *facere.*]

PACK (pak) *n.* a bundle; load; bale; set of playing cards; number of hounds, etc.;—*v.t.* or *i.* to press together and fasten; load; send or go in hates; fill beforehand, as a meeting. [Etym. uncert. Cf. Ger. *Pack.*]

PACKAGE (pak'ij) *n.* a bundle; a bale.

PACKER (pak'er) *n.* one who packs goods.
PACKET (pak'et) *n.* a small package; a vessel for dispatches, or for passengers. [F. *paquet*, fr. Teut.]
PACKINGSHEET (pak'ing-shēt) *n.* a kind of coarse cloth; a wet sheet used in the water cure.
PACKMAN (pak'man) *n.* a pedlar.
PACKTHREAD (pak'thred) *n.* strong thread for binding parcels.
PACT (pakt) *n.* a contract; covenant. [L. *pactum*, orig. (neut. part.) *thing* covenanted. fr. *pacisci*, to make PEACE.]
PAD (pad) (1) *n.* an easy-paced horse; a footpad or robber;—*v.i.* to travel slowly; to tread;—(2) *n.* a soft saddle or cushion; package of blotting paper;—*v.t.* to stuff with padding. [(1) = pad-horse; fr. D. *pad*, PATH. (2) Etym. uncert. Cf. POD.]
PADDING (pad'ing) *n.* stuffing with some soft substance; inferior matter inserted to extend an article or book.
PADDLE (pad'l) *v.i.* to play in water;—*n.* a short, broad oar. [Prob. fr. PAD (1).]
PADDOCK (pad'uk) (1) *n.* a small enclosure; —(2) a toad or frog. [(1) Corr. fr. M.E. *parrock*, PARK. (2) Dim. fr. M.E. *padde*, frog, fr. Scand.]
PADLOCK (pad'lo') *n.* a lock for a staple. [Fr. Prov. E. *pad*, pannier. See PEDLAR.]
PÆAN (pē'an) *n.* a song of triumph or joy. [G. *paian*, *Paion*, Apollo.]
PAGAN (pā'gan) *n.* a heathen; *a.* heathenish. [L. *paganus*, lit. PEASANT, the cities having first received Christianity; fr. *pagus*, village. Cf. HEATHEN.]
PAGANISE (pā'gan-īz) *v.t.* to convert to heathenism.
PAGANISM (pā'gan-izm) *n.* heathenism.
PAGE (pāj) (1) *n.* a boy or youth attending persons of rank;—(2) one side of a leaf;—*v.t.* to number the leaves of. [(1) F., of uncert. etym. (2) F., fr. L. (acc.) *paginam*, fr. root of *pangere*, fasten (compose).]
PAGEANT (paj'ent, pā'jent) *n.* a pompous show; public spectacle. [Low L. *pagina*, a stage (fixed up). See PAGE (2).]
PAGEANTRY (paj'ent-ri, pā'jent-ri) *n.* pompous exhibition; show.
PAGODA (pa-gō'da) *n.* an Indian idol, temple, and coin. [Pg., fr. Per.]
PAID (pād) *pret.* and *pp.* of PAY.
PAIL (pāl) *n.* a vessel for water, milk, etc. [O.E. *pægel*.]
PAILFUL (pāl'fool) *n.* as much as a pail holds.
PAIN (pān) *n.* bodily or mental uneasiness or suffering; labour; punishment; penalty; —*v.t.* to distress; afflict. [F. *peine*, fr. L. (acc.) *poenam*, fr. G. See PENALTY.]
PAINFUL (pān'fool) *a.* full of pain; requiring labour.
PAINFULLY (pān'fool-i) *ad.* laboriously.
PAINT (pānt) *v.t.* to cover with colours;—*v.i.* to practise painting;—*n.* a colouring substance. [F. (part.) *peint*, painted, fr. *peindre*, fr. L. *pingere*. See PIGMENT, PICTURE.]
PAINTER (pān'ter) *n.* (1) one who paints;—(2) a rope to fasten a boat. [(1) See PAINT. (2) M.E. *panter*, fr. G. *pantheros*, catching all.]
PAINTING (pān'ting) *n.* art of forming figures in colours; a picture.
PAIR (pār) *n.* two things suited or used together; a couple;—*v.i.* or *i.* to join in couples. [F., fr. *pair*, equal, fr. L. (acc.) *parem*, fr. *par*. See PAR, PEER (1).]
PALACE (pal'ās) *n.* a magnificent house; a royal or episcopal residence. [M.E. *palais*, fr. F., fr. L. *palatium*, orig. palace on the *Palatine* hill.]
PALADIN (pal'a-din) *n.* a knight-errant. [F., fr. It. = lit. of the palace. See PALATINE.]

PALANQUIN (pal-an-kēn') *n.* a covered carriage borne on the shoulders. [Hind., fr. Skr.]
PALATABLE (pal'a-ta-bl) *a.* pleasing to the taste.
PALATAL (pal'a-tal) *a.* pertaining to the palate;—*n.* a letter uttered by the aid of the palate.
PALATE (pal'at) *n.* the roof of the mouth; taste; relish. [O.F. *palat*, fr. L. *palatum*.]
PALATIAL (pa-lā'shal) *a.* pertaining to a palace; magnificent.
PALATINE (pal'a-tin, tin) *n.* one invested with royal privileges;—*a.* possessing royal privileges. [Fr. L. *palatinus*. See PALACE.]
PALAVER (pa-lā'ver) *v.t.* to flatter;—*n.* idle talk; a public conference;—*v.i.* to talk idly. [Pg. *palavra*, fr. L. *parabola*, PARABLE.]
PALE (pāl) (1) *a.* destitute of colour; white of look; wan; faint;—*v.i.* to turn pale;— (2) *n.* a pointed stake; fence; district;— *v.t.* to enclose with pales. [(1) O.F. = F. *pâle*, fr. L. (acc.) *pallidum*, PALLID. (2) F. *pal*, fr. L. *palus*.]
PALENESS (pāl'nes) *n.* state of being pale; defect of colour.
PALETOT (pal'e-tō) *n.* a light, loose overcoat. [F.]
PALETTE (pal'et) *n.* a thin oval board used by painters in mixing their colours. [F., fr. It. = orig. flat blade, fr. L. *pala*, spade.]
PALFREY (pol'fri) *n.* a small saddle horse; a lady's horse. [O.F. *palefrei*, spare horse, fr. Low L. *para* (= G. *para*), beside, and *veredus*, post-horse, fr. Celt.]
PALIMPSEST (pal'imp-sest) *n.* a parchment written upon twice. [G.]

Palette.

PALISADE (pal-i-sād') *n.* a fortification of stakes;—*v.t.* to fortify with pales or posts. [F., fr. L. *palus*, stake.]
PALING (pāl'ing) *n.* pales in general; a fence or enclosure made with pales.
PALISH (pā'lish) *a.* somewhat pale.
PALL (pawl) (1) *n.* cloak; a consecrated garment; a cloth thrown over a coffin at a funeral;—*v.t.* or *i.* to cloak;—(2) *n.* make or become vapid. [(1) O.E. *pæll*, fr. L. *pallium*. (2) Short. fr. APPAL, in same sense.]
PALLET (pal'et) (1) *n.* a mean mattress or couch;— (2) *n.* a tool for shaping or spreading used by potters, gilders, etc. [(1) M.E. *paillet*, fr. F. *paille*, straw, fr. L. (acc.) *paleam*. (2) Form of PALETTE.]
PALLIASSE (pal'-i-as, pal-yas') *n.* an under-bed of straw. [F. *paillasse*.]
PALLIATE (pal'i-āt) *v.t.* to cover; excuse or extenuate; mitigate. [L. *palliatus*, cloaked, fr. *pallium*.]
PALLIATION (pal-i-ā'shun) *n.* extenuation; mitigation.
PALLIATIVE (pal'i-ā-tiv) *n.* that which extenuates;—*a.* mitigating.
PALLID (pal'id) *a.* pale; wan. [L. *pallidus*.]
PALL-MALL (pel-mel') *n.* an old game in which a wooden ball was driven with a mallet through an iron arch. [O.F. *pale-maille*, through It., fr. O.G. *palla*, ball, and L. *malleus*, a mallet.]
PALM (päm) (1) *n.* the inner part of the hand; —*v.t.* to conceal with the hand; to impose by fraud;—(2) *n.* a tropical tree; its leaf or branch; a symbol of victory. [(1) L. *palma*. (2) O.E. *palm*, fr. L. *palma*.]
PALMARY (pal'mar-i) *a.* worthy of the palm or prize.
PALMER (pä'mer) *n.* a pilgrim or crusader.
PALMETTO (pal-met'ō) *n.* a palm tree. [Sp.]

PALMHOUSE (pám'hous) *n.* a glass hot-house for tropical plants.

PALMISTER (pal'mis-tẹr) *n.* a fortune-teller.

PALMISTRY (pal'mis-tri) *n.* art of telling fortunes by the hand. See PALM (1).

PALPABLE (pal'pạ-bl) *a.* that may be felt; obvious; gross. [F., fr. L. *palpabilis,* fr. *palpare,* handle.]

PALPITATE (pal'pi-tāt) *v.t.* to throb or beat, as the heart. [L., fr. *palpitare,* throb.]

PALPITATION (pal-pi-tā'shun) *n.* irregular beating of the heart.

PALSIED (pawl'zid) *a.* paralytic.

PALSY (pawl'zi) *n.* loss of the power of voluntary muscular motion; paralysis;—*v.t.* to strike with palsy; paralyse. [M.E. *parlesy,* fr. F. *paralysie.* Doublet of PARALYSIS.]

PALTER (pawl'tẹr) *v.i.* to trifle; shift; shuffle; equivocate. [Scand.]

PALTRINESS (pawl'tri-nes) *n.* meanness.

PALTRY (pawl'tri) *a.* mean; insignificant; worthless.

PAMPAS (pam'pạs) *n.pl.* vast treeless plains in South America. [Sp., fr. Peruv.]

PAMPER (pam'pẹr) *v.t.* to feed to the full. [Low Ger. *pampen,* cram.]

PAMPHLET (pam'flet) *n.* a literary publication in book form, stitched but not bound. [Etym. uncert.]

PAMPHLETEER (pam-fle-tēr') *n.* one who writes pamphlets.

PAN (pan) *n.* a broad, shallow vessel; part of a gun-lock; hard stratum of earth. [O.E. *panne.* Cf. Ger. *Pfanne.*]

PANACEA (pan-ạ-sē'ạ) *n.* a universal remedy. [G.]

PANCAKE (pan'kāk) *n.* a thin cake of eggs, flour, and milk fried in a pan.

PANCREAS (pan'krē-as) *n.* a soft gland of the body; the sweetbread. [G. =sweetbread.]

PANCREATIC (pan-krē-at'ik) *a.* pertaining to the pancreas.

PANDECT (pan'dekt) *n.* a treatise which contains the whole of any science. [F. *pandectes,* fr. L., fr. G. *pandectes,* comprehensive, fr. *pan-,* and *dechesthai,* receive.]

PANDEMONIUM (pan-dē-mō'ni-um) *n.* the council-hall of evil spirits, any disorderly place or gathering. [L., fr. G., fr. *pan.,* all, and DEMON.]

PANDER (pan'dẹr) *n.* a pimp;—*v.t.* or *i.* to play or minister to the designs or lusts of others. [Fr. *Pandarus,* in the story of *Troilus and Cressida.*]

PANE (pān) *n.* a sheet or plate of glass. [F. *pan,* piece, PANEL, fr. L. (acc.) *pannum.*]

PANEGYRIC (pan-e-jir'ik) *n.* a laudatory speech;—*a.* containing praise. [L., fr. G. *panegurikos* (speech) for a festival, fr. *paneguris,* full assembly, fr. *pan-,* and *agora,* assembly.]

PANEGYRISE (pan'e-ji-riz) *v.t.* to praise highly.

PANEL (pan'el) *n.* square of wainscot; jury roll; a body of doctors serving under the Insurance Act;—*v.t.* to form with panels. [O.F. =F. *panneau,* fr. PANE.]

PANG (pang) *n.* a sudden violent pain; throe. [Perh. conn. with PRONG.]

PANIC (pan'ik) *n.* sudden fright without good cause;—*a.* extreme or sudden. [G. =orig. (fear) excited by *Pan.*]

PANNIER (pan'yẹr) *n.* a basket to be carried on a horse's back. [F. *panier,* bread-basket, fr. L., fr. *panis,* bread.]

PANOPLY (pan'u-pli) *n.* armour covering the whole body. [G. *panoplia,* fr. *pan-,* and *hopla,* arms.]

PANORAMA (pan-u-rä'mạ) *n.* complete view; a picture of several scenes unrolled before the spectators. [G. *pan-,* and *horama,* a view.]

PANORAMIC (pan-u-ram'ik) *a.* pertaining to or like a panorama.

PANSLAVISM (pan-slav'izm) *n.* a movement for union of all the Slavic nations. [G. *pan-,* all.]

PANSY (pan'zi) *n.* the garden violet; heart's ease. [F. *pensée,* a thought, fr. *penser,* to think, fr. L. *pensare,* ponder.]

PANT (pant) *v.i.* to breathe rapidly; gasp; desire ardently;—*n.* quick breath; palpitation. [O.F., of uncert. etym.]

PANTALOON (pan-tạ-lōōn') *n.* a buffoon in pantomimes;—*pl.* tight-fitting trousers. [F. *pantalon,* St *Pantaleone,* patron saint of Venice.]

PANTHEISM (pan'thē-izm) *n.* the doctrine that the universe is God. [G. *pan,* all, and *theos,* god.]

PANTHEIST (pan'thē-ist) *n.* one who believes in pantheism.

PANTHEISTIC (pan-thē-is'tik) *a.* relating to pantheism.

PANTHEON (pan-thē'un, pan'thē-on) *n.* a temple in Rome dedicated to all the deities. [G.]

PANTHER (pan'thẹr) *n.* a spotted carnivorous animal. [L. *panther,* fr. G.]

PANTOGRAPH (pan'tu-graf) *n.* an instrument to copy any drawing. [G. *panto-,* fr. *pan,* all, and *graphein,* to write.]

PANTOGRAPHY (pan-tog'rạ-fi) *n.* general description.

PANTOMIME (pan'tu-mim) *n.* a representation in dumb show; a Christmas theatrical entertainment. [F. fr. L. *pantomimus,* fr. G., fr. *panto* =*pan-* all, and *mimos,* mime.]

PANTOMIMIC (pan-tu-mim'ik) *a.* representing characters and actions by dumb show.

PANTRY (pan'tri) *n.* a store-room for provisions. [O.F. *paneterie,* fr. Late L. *paneta,* maker of bread, fr. L. *panis.*]

PAP (pap) *n.* a nipple; soft food for infants. [E., fr. *pa-pa,* in baby speech.]

PAPA (pạ-pä') *n.* a father; (pạ'pạ) the pope. [Imit. See PAP.]

PAPACY (pā'pạ-si) *n.* office and dignity of the pope.

PAPAL (pā'pạl) *a.* belonging to the pope. [F., fr. L. *papalis,* fr. *papa,* father, bishop. Cf. PAPA.]

PAPALIST (pā'pạl-ist) *n.* one who favours popery.

PAPAVEROUS (pạ-pav'ẹ-rus) *n.* resembling the poppy. [L., fr. *papaver,* poppy.]

PAPER (pā'pẹr) *n.* a substance for writing or printing on; a piece of it; a written or printed article or document; a journal; money, as notes, bills, etc.; hanging for walls;—*a.* made of paper;—*v.t.* to cover with paper. [O.E., fr. PAPYRUS.]

PAPIER-MACHE (pap'yä-mä'shä) *n.* articles made of the pulp of paper japanned, as tea-boards, trays, etc. [F.]

PAPIST (pā'pist) *n.* an adherent to the Roman Catholic religion. [F. *papiste,* fr. *pape,* POPE.]

PAPISTIC (pạ-pis'tik) *a.* pertaining to popery. Also PAPISTICAL.

PAPPY (pap'i) *a.* like pap; succulent.

PAPYRUS (pạ-pi'rus) *n.* an Egyptian plant and the paper made from it. [L., fr. G. *papuros,* an Egyptian rush.]

PAR (pär) *n.* state of equality; equal value or condition. [L. =equal.]

PARABLE (par'ạ-bl) *n.* an allegorical narrative or similitude embodying a truth or doctrine. [G. *parabole,* a comparison, fr. O.F., fr. L. (acc.) *parabolam.* Doublet of PARABOLA.]

PARABOLA (pạ-rab'u-lạ) *n.* a conic section. [L., fr. G. *parabole,* fr. *ballein,* cast.]

PARABOLIC (par-ạ-bol'ik) *a.* expressed by parable or similitude. Also PARABOLI-CAL.

PARACHUTE (par′ạ-shòòt) *n.* an apparatus in the form of an umbrella to break the fall in descending from a balloon. [F., fr. G. *para-*, against, and *chute*, a fall.]

PARACLETE (par′ạ-klēt) *n.* an advocate; the Holy Spirit. [L., fr. G. *parakletos*, called to help, fr. *para-*, and *kalein*, call.]

PARADE (pạ-rād′) *n.* a pompous exhibition; military display; a place for such display; —*v.t.* or *i.* to show off; marshal; march; walk as if for show. [F., fr. Sp. *parada*, a halt. L. *parare*, prepare.]

PARADIGM (par′ạ-dim) *n.* an example; a model. [F. *paradigme*, fr. L., fr. G. *paradeigma*, a model, fr. *para-*, and *deiknunai*, show.]

PARADISE (par′ạ-dīz) *n.* Eden; a place of bliss; heaven. [L. *paradisus*, fr. G. *paradeisos*, park, fr. Per.]

PARADISIACAL (par-ạ-di-sī′ạ-kạl) *a.* pertaining to paradise.

PARADOX (par′ạ-doks) *n.* a tenet seemingly absurd, yet true. [G. *paradoxon*, fr. *para-*, against, and *doxa*, opinion.]

PARADOXICAL (par-ạ-dok′si-kạl) *a.* having the nature of a paradox.

PARAFFIN,PARAFFINE (par′-ạ-fin,par′ạ-fēn) *n.* a white fatty substance, and a clear burning oil, distilled from bituminous coal or wood. [Fr. L. *parum*, little, and *affinis*, akin (with acids and alkalies).]

PARAGON (par′ạ-gon) *n.* a perfect pattern of excellence. [O.F., fr. Sp., of uncert. etym.]

PARAGRAPH (par′ạ-graf) *n.* a reference mark (¶); a short article or remark. [G. *paragraphos*, marginal mark showing new paragraph, fr. *para-*, and *graphein*, write.]

PARALLAX (par′ạ-laks) *n.* apparent change of place in a heavenly body as viewed from different points. [G., fr. *para-*, and *allassein*, to change.]

PARALLEL (par′ạ-lel) *a.* side by side; equally extended and distant; exactly like in

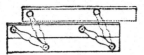

Parallel Ruler.

essential points;—*n.* an extended equidistant line; a comparison made; counterpart; a wide trench; a reference mark (‖); —*v.t.* to compare; equal; correspond to. [F., fr. L., fr. G. *parallelos*, fr. *para*, beside, and (gen.) *allelon*, one another.]

PARALLELISM (par′ạ-lel-izm) *n.* state of being parallel.

PARALLELOGRAM (par-ạ-lel′u-gram) *n.* a right-lined figure of four sides, whose opposite sides are equal and parallel. [Fr. G. *para*, beside, and *gramma*, line.]

PARALOGISM (pạ-ral′u-jizm) *n.* reasoning which is false in logical form. [F., fr. L., fr. G. *paralogismos*, fr. *para*, beside, and *logismos*, fr. *logos*, a discourse.]

PARALYSE (par′ạ-līz) *v.t.* to strike with palsy; destroy or weaken action or energy.

PARALYSIS (pạ-ral′i-sis) *n.* loss of voluntary motion or sensation in any part of the body; palsy. [L., fr. G., fr. *para*, beside, and *luein*, to loosen. Doublet of **PALSY**.]

PARALYTIC (par-ạ-lit′ik) *a.* palsied;—*n.* one affected with palsy.

PARAMATTA (par-ạ-mat′ạ) *n.* a fabric of wool and cotton. [*Paramatta*, Austr.]

PARAMOUNT (par′ạ-mount) *a.* chief; superior to all ers. [F. *par amont*, at the top, fr. L. *per* and **AMOUNT**.]

PARAMOUNTLY (par′ạ-mount-li) *ad.* in a superior manner or degree.

PARAMOUR (par′ạ-mòòr) *n.* a lover; a mistress, in a bad sense. [F. *par amour*, with love, fr. L. *per*, and (acc.) *amorem*.]

PARAPET (par′ạ-pet) *n.* a wall breast-high on a bridge or for defence. [F., fr. It. *parapetto*, a wall breast-high, prepare, guard (**PARRY**), and *pectus*, breast.]

PARAPHERNALIA (par-ạ-fẹr-nā′li-ạ) *n.pl.* apparel and ornaments. [Fr. Late L. *parapherna*, besides, the dowry, fr. G., fr. *pherne*, dowry, fr. *pherein*, bring.]

PARAPHRASE (par′ạ-frāz) *n.* a copious explanation; free translation; Scripture hymn;—*v.t.* or *i.* to translate or interpret freely and fully; write in hymn form. [G. *paraphrasis*, fr. *phrasis*, **PHRASE**, fr. *phrazein*, speak.]

PARAPHRAST (par′ạ-frast) *n.* one who interprets.

PARASITE (par′ạ-sīt) *n.* a hanger-on; a plant growing on another. [F., fr. L. (acc.) *parasitum*, lit. one that eats with another, fr. G., fr. *sitos*, food.]

PARASITIC (par-ạ-sit′ik) *a.* living on others; fawning. Also **PARASITICAL**.

PARASOL (par′ạ-sol) *n.* a small umbrella used by ladies. [F., through It., fr. L. *parare*, guard, **PARRY**, and *sol*, sun.]

PARBOIL (pár′boil) *v.t.* to boil partly. [O.F. *parboillir*, boil thoroughly, fr.L. *per*, through, and *bullire*, **BOIL**.]

PARBUCKLE (pár′buk-l) *n.* a purchase of a single rope used in hoisting spars or casks; —*v.t.* to sling with a rope and hoist. [Prob. L. *par*, equal, and **BUCKLE**.]

PARCEL (pár′sel) *n.* a portion; collection; quantity; small bundle or package;—*v.t.* to divide into portions; make up into parcels;—*ad.* in part. [F. *parcelle*, fr. Late L., dim. fr. *pars*, **PART**.]

PARCEL-BOOK (pár′sel-book) *n.* a book for registering the despatch or delivery of parcels.

PARCEL-POST (pár′sel-pòst) *n.* post for conveyance of small parcels.

PARCELLING (pár′sel-ing) *n.* narrow strips of canvas wound round a rope and tarred.

PARCH (párch) *v.t.* or *i.* to burn the surface; scorch slightly; dry up. [Etym. uncert.]

PARCHMENT (párch′ment) *n.* the skin of a sheep or goat dressed for writing on. [O.F. *parchemin*, fr. L. (acc.) *pergaminam*, lit. (paper) of *Pergamos*, in Asia Minor, fr. G.]

PARD (párd) *n.* the leopard; any spotted beast. [G. *pardos*.]

PARDON (pạr′-dun, pár′dn) *n.* forgiveness; remission of penalty ;—*v.t.* to forgive; excuse. [F., fr. *paraonner*, to forgive, fr. L. *per-donare*, fr. *per*, fully, and *donare*, give.]

PARDONABLE (pár′dun-ạ-bl) *a.* that may be forgiven.

PARDONER (pár′dun-ẹr) *n.* one who forgives.

PARE (pār) *v.t.* to cut off or away little by little. [F., fr. L. *parare*, **PREPARE**.]

PAREGORIC (par-e-gor′ik) *n.* a medicine that mitigates pain. [G., fr. *paregorein*, to address a meeting, fr. *para*, beside, and *agora*, assembly.]

PARENT (pár′ent) *n.* a father or mother; cause; origin. [F. =*relative*, fr. L. (acc.) *parentem*, lit. (part.) *begetting*, fr. *parere*.]

PARENTAGE (pár′en-tij) *n.* birth; extraction.

PARENTAL (pạ-ren′tạl) *a.* pertaining to or becoming parents.

PARENTHESIS (pạ-ren′the-sis) *n.* a sentence, or part of it, included in curved lines, thus ( ). [G., fr. *para*, beside, *en*, in, and *thesis*, a placing.]

PARENTHETICAL (par-en-thet′i-kạl) *a.* pertaining to or included in a parenthesis.

PARENTLESS (pár′ent-les) *a.* deprived of parents.

PARER (pár′ẹr) *n.* an instrument for paring.

PARGET (pár'jet) *n.* gypsum; plaster-stone; —*v.t.* to cover with plaster. [F., fr. L.]

PARHELION (pár-hē'li-on) *n.* a mock sun; —*pl.* **PARHELIA**. [G., fr. *parelior*, beside the sun, fr. *helios*, sun.]

PARIAH (pā'ri-a) *n.* the lowest caste in Hindustan; an outcast. [Tamil.]

PARIAN (pā'ri-an) *n.* a native of Paros; a fine kind of marble; a rich porcelain clay.

PARIETAL (pa-rī'e-tal) *a.* pertaining to or forming a wall. [L., fr. stem *pariet-*, of *paries*, partition wall.]

PARING (pār'ing) *n.* a thin strip cut off.

PARISH (par'ish) *n.* a district or division of town or country under a Christian minister, having the cure of souls therein;—*a.* belonging to a parish. [F. *paroisse*, fr. L. (acc.) *parœciam*, fr .G., fr. *paroikos*, dwelling beside, fr. *oikos*, a dwelling.]

PARISHIONER (pa-rish'un-er) *n.* one belonging to a parish.

PARISIAN (pa-riz'i-an) *n.* an inhabitant of Paris;—*a.* of, or belonging to Paris.

PARITY (par'i-ti) *n.* equality of number, likeness, quantity, etc. [F., fr. L. (acc.) *paritatem*, fr. **PAR**.]

PARK (párk) *n.* a piece of enclosed ground; a place for, or a train of, artillery;—*v.t.* to enclose in a park. [M.E. *parrock*, fr. O.E. *pearruc*. Doublet of **PADDOCK**.]

PARLANCE (pár'lans) *n.* conversation; form of speech; idiom. [F., fr. (part.) *parlant*, speaking, fr. *parler*, fr. Late L. *parabolare*.]

PARLEY (pár'li) *n.* mutual discourse; conference with an enemy;—*v.i.* to speak with, confer or treat with. [F. *parler*. See **PARLANCE**.]

PARLIAMENT (pár'li-ment) *n.* the legislature of Great Britain. [F. *parlement*. See **PARLANCE**.]

PARLIAMENTARY (pár-li-men'ta-ri) *a.* pertaining to, done by, or according to the forms and usages of parliament.

PARLOUR (pár'lur) *n.* the ordinary sitting-room in a family house. [O.F. *parloir*, a room for conversation. See **PARLANCE**.]

PARMESAN (pár-me-zan') *n.* a fine kind of cheese made in Parma, a town in Italy.

PARNASSIAN (pár-nas'yan) *a.* pertaining to Parnassus, a mountain in Greece, sacred to Apollo and the Muses.

PAROCHIAL (pa-rō'ki-al) *a.* belonging to a parish. [Fr. L. *parochia* = *parœcia*. **PARISH**.]

PARODIST (par'u-dist) *n* a writer of parodies.

PARODY (par'u-di) *n.* a composition in which the words and ideas of another are copied and burlesqued;—*v.t.* to imitate and burlesque. [F., fr. G. *parodia*, a song sung beside (imitating) another, fr. *ode*, a song.]

PAROLE (pa-rōl') *n.* word of mouth; a verbal promise; military password;—*a.* oral; verbal. [F., fr. Late L., fr. L. (acc.) *parabolam*. See **PARLANCE**.]

PAROQUET (par'u-ket) *n.* a small parrot. [See **PARRAKEET**.]

PAROXYSM (par'uk-sizm) *n.* a violent fit of pain; any sudden, violent action. [F. *paroxysme*, fr. L., fr. G. *paroxusmos*, fr. *para*, beyond, and *oxunein*, sharpen, fr. *oxus*, sharp.]

PARRAKEET (par'a-kēt) *n.* a small parrot with a long tail. [Sp. *periquito*, dim. of *Perico*, Peter. See **PARROT**.]

PARRICIDE (par'i-sīd) *n.* (1) one who murders his parent;—(2) murder of a parent. [(1) F., fr. L. *parricida*, fr. rt. of **PARENT**, and *cædere*, kill. (2) L. *parricidium*.]

PARROT (par'ut) *n.* a tropical, parti-coloured talking bird. [F. *perrot*, *pierrot*, little *Pierre* or Peter, a nickname.]

PARRY (par'i) *v.t.* to ward off. [F. *parer*, fr. L. *parare*, to **PREPARE**, ward off.]

PARSE (párz) *v.t.* to find or tell the parts of speech and their relations in a sentence. [L. *pars*, a part (of speech).]

PARSEE (pár-sē') *n.* an adherent of the Persian religion living in India; a worshipper of the sun or fire. [Per. = Persian.]

PARSIMONIOUS (pár-si-mō'ni-us) *a.* frugal; sparing; penurious.

PARSIMONY (pár'si-mu-ni) *n.* frugality; niggardliness. [F. *parsimonie*. fr. L. (acc.) *parcimoniam*, fr. *parcus*, frugal.]

PARSLEY (párs'li) *n.* well-known pot herb. [O.F. *peresil*, fr. L., fr. G. *petroselinon*, rock parsley, fr. *petros*, and *selinon*. See **CELERY**.]

PARSNIP (párs'nip) *n.* a plant and edible root. [Corr. fr. O.F. *pasinague*, fr. L. (acc.) *pastinacum*, of uncert. etym.]

PARSON (pár'sn) *n.* the clergyman of a parish. [L. *persona*, **PERSON**, later a personage, curate.]

PARSONAGE (pár'sun-ij) *n.* house of the minister of a parish.

PART (párt) *n.* a portion; share; side;—*v.t.* or *i.* to divide; share; separate. [F., fr. L. (acc.) *partem*, of *pars*.]

PARTAKE (pár-tāk') *v.t.* to have or take part in; share. [Fr. **PART** and **TAKE**.]

PARTAKER (pár-tā'ker) *n.* one who shares.

PARTIAL (pár'shal) *a.* including a part; not general; biased. [Low L. *partialis*, fr. stem *parti-*, of *pars*, **PART**.]

PARTIALITY (pár-shi-al'i-ti) *n.* undue bias.

PARTIALLY (pár'shal-i) *ad.* in part only; with undue bias.

PARTICIPANT (par-tis'i-pant) *a.* sharing; partaking;—*n.* a partaker.

PARTICIPATE (pár-tis'i-pāt) *v.t.* to partake. [L. (part.) *participatus*, made **PARTAKER** of, fr. stem *parti-*, of *pars*, and *-cipare*, for *capere*, take.]

PARTICIPATION (pár-tis-i-pā'shun) *n.* a sharing; distribution.

PARTICIPIAL (pár-ti-sip'i-al) *a.* of the nature of, or formed from, a participle.

PARTICIPLE (pár'ti-si-pl) *n.* a word partaking of the properties of a noun and a verb. [F. *participe*, fr. L. *participium*, lit. a sharing. See **PARTICIPATE**.]

PARTICLE (pár'ti-kl) *n.* a minute portion of matter; an atom. [F. *particule*, fr. L. (acc.) *particulam*, a little **PART**.]

PARTICULAR (pár-tik'ū-lar) *a.* pertaining to a single person or thing; special; exact; nice; peculiar;—*n.* a single part, point, or instance;—*pl.* details. [L. *particularis*, fr. *particula*, **PARTICLE**.]

PARTICULARISE (pár-tik'ū-lar-īz) *v.t.* or *i.* to mention in detail; specify.

PARTICULARITY (pár-tik-ū-lar'i-ti) *n.* something peculiar; minuteness of detail.

PARTICULARLY (pár-tik'ū-lar-li) *ad.* singly; specially.

PARTING (pár'ting) *n.* act of separating or breaking.

PARTISAN (pár'ti-zan) *n.* an adherent to a party;—*a.* adhering to a party. [F., fr. It. *partisano*, partner, fr. L. (part.) *partitus*. See **PARTITION**.]

PARTISANSHIP (pár'ti-zan-ship) *n.* the state of being a partisan.

PARTITION (pár'tish-un) *n.* division; a dividing wall or board; place where separation is made. [F., fr. L. (part.) *partitus*, divided, fr. *partire*, fr. **PART**.]

PARTITIVE (pár'ti-tiv) *a.* distributive; *n.* a word denoting a part.

PARTNER (párt'ner) *n.* associate in business; a sharer; husband or wife. [Corr. fr. O.F. *parcener*, through Late L., fr. L. (acc.) *partitionem*, **PARTITION**. See **PARTISAN**.]

PARTNERSHIP (párt'ner-ship) *n.* union or joint interest in business.

PARTRIDGE (pár'trij) *n.* a well-known bird of game. [M.E. *pertriche*, fr. O.F. *perdrix*, fr. L. (acc.) *perdicem*, of *perdix*, fr. G.]

PARTS (párts) *n.pl.* faculties; talents.

PARTURIENT (pár-tū'ri-ent) *a.* giving birth to young.

PARTURITION (pár-tū-rish'un) *n.* act of giving birth. [L., fr. (part.) *parturitus*, fr. *parturire*, to be in travail, fr. *parere*, produce.]

PARTY (pár'ti) *n.* a select assembly; faction; side; one of two litigants; a detachment of soldiers;—*a.* of or belonging to a party or side. [O.F. *partie*, side, part, fr. *partir*, divide, fr. L. *partire*. See PARTITION.]

PASCHAL (pas'kal) *a.* pertaining to the passover. [L., fr. *pascha*, fr. H.]

PASHA (pᴀ-shaw', pá'shᴀ) *n.* a Turkish official of high rank. [Per. =great SHAH.]

PASQUINADE (pas'kwi-nād) *n.* a satirical writing. [Fr. *Pasquino*, a witty Roman cobbler, on whose statue people afterwards wrote lampoons.]

PASS (pas) *v.t.* or *i.* to go by, over, beyond, etc.; spend; omit; transfer; utter; enact; thrust; die; disappear; elapse; bear inspection;—*n.* a narrow way; licence to pass; a thrust. [F. *passer*, fr. Late L. *passare*, fr. L. *passus*, PACE.]

PASSABLE (pas'ᴀ-bl) *a.* that may be passed; tolerable.

PASSAGE (pas'ij) *n.* act of passing; way; incident; cause or portion of a book; voyage; time or price of voyage.

PASS-BOOK (pas'book) *n.* a book to enter articles bought on credit.

PASSENGER (pas'en-jer) *n.* one that travels in some public conveyance. [M.E. *passager*.]

PASSIBILITY (pas-i-bil'i-ti) *n.* capacity of receiving impressions.

PASSIBLE (pas'i-bl) *a.* susceptible of impressions. [L., fr. (part.) *passus*, having suffered. See PASSION.]

PASSING (pas'ing) *n.* act of going by;—*a.* surpassing;—*ad.* exceedingly.

PASSION (pash'un) *n.* that which is suffered; any strong emotion; extreme desire. [F., fr. L. (acc.) *passionem*, lit. suffering, fr. (part.) *passus*, fr. *pati*, suffer. See PATIENT.]

PASSIONATE (pash'un-ᴀt) *a.* easily excited.

PASSIONATELY (pash'un-ᴀt-li) *ad.* with passion; ardently.

PASSIONLESS (pash'un-les) *a.* not easily excited; calm.

PASSIVE (pas'iv) *a.* suffering; unresisting; receptive. [F. *passif*, fr. L. *passivus*. See PASSION.]

PASSIVELY (pas'iv-li) *ad.* in a submissive manner.

PASSIVENESS (pas'iv-nes) *n.* unresisting submission to external influence.

PASSIVITY (pᴀ-siv'i-ti) *n.* tendency to remain in a given state; inertia.

PASS-KEY (pas'kē) *n.* a key to open several locks; a latchkey.

PASSOVER (pas'ō-ver) *n.* a feast reminding the Jews that God *passed over* them when he slew the first-born in Egypt; the lamb sacrificed.

PASSPORT (pas'pōrt) *n.* a written permission to pass or travel; ready entrance. [F. *passeport*, lit. pass gate. See PORT (1).]

PASSWORD (pas'wurd) *n.* a word to be given before one can pass into a camp, fortification, or certain secret society meetings.

PAST (pást) *a.* gone by; former; ended;—*n.* former time;—*prep.* beyond in time or place; above; out of reach or control;—*ad.* by.

PASTE (pāst) *n.* a cement of flour boiled in water; flour or clay prepared for baking; a fine kind of glass of which artificial jewels are made;—*v.t.* to fasten with paste. [O.F. =F. *pâté*, fr. Late L., fr. G. *paste*.]

PASTEBOARD (pást'bōrd) *n.* a species of thick paper.

PASTERN (pas'tern) *n.* joint of a horse next the foot. [O.F. *pasturon* =F. *pâturon*, the shackle of a horse at PASTURE.]

PASTILLE (pas'tēl) *n.* a coloured crayon; an aromatic roll used in fumigating; a lozenge. Also *Pastel, Pastil*. [F., fr. L. *pastillus*, dim. fr. *pastus*, food, fr. *pascere*, feed.]

PASTIME (pás'tim) *n.* amusement; recreation. [Fr. PASS and TIME.]

PASTOR (pás'tur) *n.* a shepherd; minister of a church. [L. =herdsman, fr. (part.) *pastus*, fed, fr. *pascere*. See PASTURE.]

PASTORAL (pás'tu-rᴀl) *a.* rural; relating to a pastor;—*n.* a poem describing rural life. [L. *pastoralis*.]

PASTORATE (pás'tu-rᴀt) *n.* the office of a pastor.

PASTRY (pás'tri) *n.* pies, tarts, cake, etc.

PASTURABLE (pás'tūr-ᴀ-bl) *a.* fit for pasture.

PASTURAGE (pás'tūr-ij) *n.* lands grazed by cattle; grass for cattle.

PASTURE (pás'tūr) *n.* land for grazing;—*v.t.* or *i.* to graze. [F., fr. L. *pastere, pp. pastus*, fed.]

PASTY (pás'ti) *a.* like paste or dough;—*n.* a pie made of paste. [O.F. *pasté* =F. *pâté*.]

PAT (pat) *a.* fit; exactly suitable;—*n.* a light blow; a small mass;—*v.t.* to tap with the fingers. [Imit.]

PATCH (pach) *n.* a piece of cloth;—*v.t.* to put a patch on [Etym. uncert.]

PATCHWORK (pach'wurk) *n.* bits of cloth sewed together; bungling work.

PATE (pat) *n.* the head; skin of a calf's head. [O.F.]

PATEN (pat'en) *n.* a small plate used for the bread in the eucharist. [L. *patena*, fr. G. *patane*.]

PATENT (pā'tent, pat'ent) *n.* a grant from the crown of a title or of a right in an invention;—*v.t.* to grant or to secure by patent; —*a.* manifest; protected by patent. [F., fr. L. (acc. part.) *patentem*, lying open, fr. *patere*.]

PATENTEE (pā-ten-tē', pat-en-tē') *n.* one to whom a patent is granted. [E. *patenteé*.]

PATERNAL (pᴀ-ter'nᴀl) *a.* fatherly; hereditary. [F. *paternel*, fr. Late L., fr. L. *paternus*, of a father, *pater*.]

PATERNITY (pᴀ-ter'ni-ti) *n.* the relation of a father.

PATERNOSTER (pā'ter-nos-ter,pat'er-nos-ter) *n.* the Lord's Prayer. [Fr. the first words *pater noster*, L. =Our Father.]

PATH (páth) *n.* a way trodden by man or beast; course of life. [O.F. *pœth*. Cf. Ger. *Pfad*.]

PATHETIC (pᴀ-thet'ik) *a.* affecting or moving the feelings. [F. *pathétique*, fr. L., fr. G. *pathetikos*.]

PATHETICALLY (pᴀ-thet'i-kal-i) *ad.* in a way to excite pity, sorrow, etc.

PATHLESS (páth'les) *a.* having no path.

PATHOLOGIC (path-u-loj'ik) *a.* pertaining to pathology.

PATHOLOGIST (pᴀ-thol'ō-jist) *n.* one who treats of pathology.

PATHOLOGY (pᴀ-thol'ō-ji) *n.* the science of diseases. [Fr. G. *pathos*, suffering, and *-logia*, discourse, fr. *legein*.]

PATHOS (pā'thos) *n.* the expression of deep or tender feeling; quality of exciting the same. [G., fr. stem *path-*, of *paschein*, suffer.]

PATHWAY (páth'wā) *n.* a path conducting to any point; course of action.

PATIENCE (pā'shens) *n.* the power of suffering; forbearance; perseverance.

PATIENT (pā'shent) *a.* enduring without murmuring;—*n.* a sick person. [F., fr. L. (acc. part.) *patientem*, suffering, fr. *pati*.]

PATIENTLY (pā'shent-li) *ad.* without discontent; calmly.

PATNESS (pat'nes) n. fitness; appropriateness.

PATOIS (pat-waw') n. a provincial or vulgar idiom. [F.]

PATRIARCH (pā'tri-àrk) n. the head of a family or church. [L., fr. G. *patriarches*, chief, fr. *patria*, clan, and *archein*, rule.]

PATRIARCHAL (pā-tri-àr'kąl) a. pertaining to a patriarch.

PATRICIAN (pą-trish'ąn) n. of noble family; senatorial;—n. a nobleman. [L. *patricius*, fr. *pater, patris*, a father.]

PATRIMONIAL (pat-ri-mō'ni-ąl) a. possessed by inheritance.

PATRIMONY (pat'ri-mu-ni) n. an estate derived by inheritance; church estate or revenue. [L. *patrimonium*, fr. stem *patri-*, of *pater*, father.]

PATRIOT (pā'tri-ut, pat'ri-ut) n. one who loves his country. [O.F. *patriote*, fr. Late L., fr. G. *patriotes*, lit. a compatriot, fr. *patria*, tribe, clan, fr. *pater*, father.]

PATRIOTIC (pāt-ri-ot'ik, pat-ri-ot'ik) a. having love to one's country.

PATRIOTISM (pā'tri-ut-izm, pat'ri-ut-izm) n. love of one's country.

PATRISTIC (pą-tris'tik) a. pertaining to the fathers of the early Christian church. [Fr. L. stem *patri-*, of *pater*, father.]

PATROL (pą-trōl') n. going round, or the persons that go round a camp at night;—v.t. or i. to go the rounds of a camp or district. [O.F., of uncert. etym.]

PATRON (pā'trun) n. one who countenances or protects; one who can present to a church living. [F., fr. L. (aec.) *patronum*, protector, fr. *pater*, father.]

PATRONAGE (pā'trun-ij, pat'run-ij) n. support; protection; advowson.

PATRONESS (pā'trun-es) n. a female patron.

PATRONISE (pā'trun-iz, pat'run-iz) v.t. to act the patron to; support; assume the air of a superior.

PATRONYMIC (pat-ru-nim'ik) n. a name derived from a father or ancestor. [L. *patronymicus*, fr. G., fr. *patronumia*, a name, fr. *pater*, father, and *onoma*.]

PATTEN (pat'en) n. the base of a column; a wooden shoe with an iron ring. [F. *patin*, fr. O.F. *pate*, paw, fr. PAT.]

PATTER (pat'ęr) v.t. or i. to strike and sound, as hail or rain; speak rapidly;—n. glib utterance; slang. [A freq. of PAT.]

PATTERN (pat'ęrn) n. a model for imitation;—v.i. to copy. [F. *patron*, a PATRON; also model.]

PAUCITY (paw'si-ti) n. fewness. [F. *paucité*, fr. L. (acc.) *paucitatem*, fr. *paucus*, few, little.]

PAULINE (paw'lin) a. pertaining to Saint Paul or his epistles.

PAUNCH (pànsh, pawnsh) n. the belly. [O.F. *panche*, fr. L. (acc.) *panticem*, of *pantex*.]

PAUPER (paw'pęr) n. a poor person; one who receives alms. [L. =poor.]

PAUPERISE (paw'pęr-iz) v.t. to reduce to pauperism.

PAUPERISM (paw'pęr-izm) n. state of complete indigence.

PAUSE (pawz) n. a temporary stop; cessation; suspense; a break in writing; a mark for suspending or continuing the voice;—v.i. to make a short stop; hesitate. [F., fr. L. (acc.) *pausam*, fr. G., fr. *pauesthai*, to cease.]

PAVE (pāv) v.t. to lay with stone or brick; prepare. [F. *paver*, fr. Late L. *pavare*, fr. L. *pavire*, beat.]

PAVEMENT (pāv'ment) n. a causeway of stone or brick; the material for such. [F., fr. L. *pavimentum*.]

PAVER (pā'vęr) n. one who lays or repairs pavements. Also **PAVIER, PAVIOR.** [F. *paveur*.]

PAVILION (pą-vil'yun) n. a tent; a building with a dome. [F. *pavillon*, fr. L. (acc.) *papilionem*, fr. *papilio*, butterfly, tent.]

PAW (paw) n. the foot of a beast;—v.t. or i. to scrape with the foot; handle roughly. [C'elt.]

PAWKILY (paw'ki-li) ad. in an arch or sly manner.

PAWKINESS (paw'ki-nes) n. quality of being pawky.

PAWKY (paw'ki) a. artfully insinuating; shrewd. [Scot.]

PAWL (pawl) n. a short bar to check the revolution of a windlass, etc. [O.F. *paul, pal*. See PALE (2).]

PAWN (pawn) n. a pledge deposited;—v.t. to leave as security; give in pledge. [F. *pan*, fr. D. Cf. Ger. *Pfand*.]

PAWNBROKER (pawn'brō-kęr) n. one who lends money on pledge.

PAWNBROKING (pawn'brō-king) n. business of a pawnbroker.

PAY (pā) v.t. or i. [pret. and pp. PAID] to discharge a debt or duty; recompense; punish; coat with tar;—n. compensation; wages. [O.F. *paier* =F. *payer*, fr. L. *pacare*, pacify, fr. stem *pac-*, of *pax*, PEACE.]

PAYABLE (pā'ą-bl) a. that is due.

PAYEE (pā-ē') n. one to whom a note is made payable.

PAYMASTER (pā'màs-tęr) n. an officer who makes payment.

PAYMENT (pā'ment) n. act of paying; money paid.

PEA (pē) n. a plant and its fruit;—pl. PEAS, PEASE. [M.E. (sing.) *pese*, fr. O.E. *pisa*, fr. L. *pisum*.]

PEACE (pēs) n. quiet; freedom from war or disturbance; calm; rest. [O.F. *pais* =F. *paix*, fr. L. (acc.) *pacem*, fr. *pax*, conn. with PACT.]

PEACEABLE (pē'są-bl) a. disposed to peace; quiet.

PEACEABLY (pē'są-bli) ad. quietly.

PEACEFUL (pēs'fool) a. having or making peace; quiet; mild.

PEACEFULLY (pēs'fool-i) ad. quietly.

PEACE-OFFICER (pēs'of-is-ęr) n. a civil officer; constable.

PEACH (pēch) n. a delicious stone-fruit. [F. *pêche*, fr. O.F. *pesche*, fr. L. *persicum* (*malum*), Persian apple.]

PEACOCK (pē'kok) n. a beautiful fowl. [M.E. *pecok*, fr. O.E. *pea, pawa*, fr. L. *pavo*, PEACOCK; and COCK.]

PEAHEN (pē'hen) n. female of the peacock.

PEAK (pēk) n. the top of a hill; a point. [F. *pic*; conn. with PIKE.]

PEAL (pēl) n. a loud sound; a set of bells; changes rung on them;—v.t. or i. to ring or sound. [Short. fr. APPEAL.]

PEAR (pār) n. a tree and its fruit. [O.E. *pera*, fr. L. *pirum*.]

PEARL (pęrl) n. a gem found in the oyster; anything round and clear; a white speck; a small sort of type;—v.t. to adorn with pearls. [F. *perle*, of unknown etym.]

PEARLASH (pęrl'ash) n. refined potash.

PEARLY (pęr'li) a. like pearl.

PEASANT (pez'ant) n. one who lives by rural labour. [O.F. *paisan(t)* =F. *paysan*, fr. *pais*, country, through Late L., fr. *pagus*, village. See PAGAN.]

PEASANTRY (pez'ant-ri) n. rustics.

PEAT (pēt) n. a species of turf used as fuel. [Etym. uncert.]

PEBBLE (peb'l) n. a roundish stone. [E.]

PEBBLY (peb'li) a. full of pebbles.

PECCABILITY (pek-ą-bil'i-ti) n. capacity of sinning.

PECCABLE (pek'ą-bl) a. liable to sin. [Fr. L. *peccare* sin.]

PECCADILLO (pek-a-dil'ō) *n.* a slight fault. [Sp. dim. fr. *pecado,* sin, fr. L. *peccatum.*]

PECCANT (pek'ant) *a.* criminal; faulty. [F., fr. L. (acc. part.) *peccantem,* sinning.]

PECK (pek) *n.* fourth of a bushel;—*v.t.* to strike with the beak or something pointed; pick up with the beak. [Form of **PICK**.]

PECTIN (pek'tin) *n.* the gelatinising principle in some fruits. [G. *pektikos,* congealing, fr. *pegnunai,* to make solid.]

PECTINAL (pek'tin-al) *a.* like a comb. [L. *pecten,* a comb.]

PECTORAL (pek'tu-ral) *a.* belonging to the breast;—*n.* a breastplate; a medicine for the breast. [L., fr. stem *pector-,* of *pectus,* breast.]

PECULATE (pek'ū-lāt) *v.i.* to appropriate public money. [L. (part.) *peculatus,* fr. *peculari,* embezzle; conn. with **PECULIAR**.]

PECULATION (pek-ū-lā'shun) *n.* embezzlement.

PECULATOR (pek'ū-lā-ter) *n.* one who embezzles or steals money.

PECULIAR (pē-kūl'yar) *a.* appropriate; singular; special; odd. [O.F. *peculier,* fr. L., fr. *peculium,* private property; conn. with **PECUNIARY**.]

PECULIARITY (pē-kū-li-ar'i-ti) *n.* anything special or characteristic in an individual.

PECULIARLY (pē-kūl'yar-li) *ad.* particularly; especially.

PECUNIARY (pē-kū'ni-a-ri) *a.* relating to or consisting of money. [L., fr. *pecunia,* money, property, orig. in cattle, fr. *pecus,* cattle.]

PEDAGOGIC (ped-a-goj'ik) *a.* suiting a pedagogue.

PEDAGOGICS (ped-a-goj'iks) *n.pl.* the science of teaching.

PEDAGOGISM (ped'a-gog-izm) *n.* business of a pedagogue.

PEDAGOGUE (ped'a-gog) *n.* a schoolmaster. [O.F., fr. L. (acc.) *pædagogum,* fr. G. *paidagogos,* a slave who took boys to school, fr. stem *paid-,* of *pais,* boy, and *agein,* lead.]

PEDAL (ped'al) *a.* pertaining to the foot;—*n.* the foot keys of an organ. [L. *pedalis,* fr. stem *ped-,* of *pes,* foot.]

PEDANT (ped'ant) *n.* one who makes a vain display of his learning. [O.F., fr. It. *pedante* (=*pedagogante*). See **PEDAGOGUE**.]

PEDANTIC (pe-dan'tik) *a.* displaying pedantry.

PEDANTRY (ped'an-tri) *n.* vain and formal display of learning.

PEDDLE (ped'l) *v.t.* or *i.* to travel and retail goods; hawk. [Formed fr. **PEDLAR**.]

PEDDLING (ped'ling) *a.* trifling.

PEDESTAL (ped'es-tal) *n.* the base of a column, statue, etc. [F. *piedestal,* fr. It., fr. L. stem *ped-,* of *pes,* foot, and Ger. *Stoll.*]

PEDESTRIAN (pe-des'tri-an) *a.* on foot;—*n.* one who walks. [Fr. L. stem *pedestri-,* of *pedester,* fr. stem *ped-,* of *pes.* See **PEDAL**.]

PEDESTRIANISM (pe-des'tri-an-izm) *n.* walking; art or practice of walking for a wager.

PEDICEL (ped'i-sel) *n.* a short stem or foot stalk. [F., fr. L. dim. of stem *ped-,* of *pes,* foot.]

PEDIGREE (ped'i-grē) *n.* genealogy; lineage. [Perh. fr. O.F. *pied de grue,* crane's foot, from a mark used to denote descent.]

PEDIMENT (ped'i-ment) *n.* a triangular ornamental facing over porticoes, windows, etc. [Fr. L. stem *ped-,* of *pes,* foot.]

PEDLAR, PEDLER, PEDDLER (ped'lar) *n.* a travelling trader in small wares. [Perh. fr. *peddar,* fr. prov. E. *ped,* basket.]

Pediment.

PEDOMETER (pe-dom'e-ter) *n.* an instrument to measure the distance traversed in walking. [Fr. L. stem *ped-,* of *pes,* foot, and **METRE**.]

PEDUNCLE (pe-dung'kl) *n.* the stem of the flower or of the fruit of a plant. [Fr. L. stem *ped-,* of *pes,* foot.]

PEEL (pēl) (1) *v.t.* or *i.* to strip off skin or rind; pare; come off, as skin;—*n.* rind; bark;—(2) *n.* a large fire shovel. [(1) F. *peler,* fr. O.F. *pel,* skin, fr. L. (acc.) *pellem,* fr. *pellis.* (2) O.F. *pele,* fr. L. *pala,* a spade.]

PEELER (pē'ler) *n.* (1) one who or that which peels;—(2) a policeman. [(1) See **PEEL** (1). (2) Fr. Sir Robert *Peel.*]

PEEP (pēp) *n.* sly look; first appearance; cry of chickens;—*v.i.* to begin to appear; cry as a chicken. [Imit. Cf. Ger. *piepen,* L. *pipire.* Cf. **PIPE**.]

PEER (pēr) (1) *n.* an equal; a nobleman;—(2) *v.i.* to look narrowly; appear. [1) O.F. *per* =F. *pair,* fr. L. (acc.) *parem,* of **PAR**. (2) O.F. *perer,* fr. L. *parere.* See **APPEAR**.]

PEERAGE (pēr'ij) *n.* rank of a peer; body of peers.

PEERESS (pēr'es) *n.* a peer's lady.

PEERLESS (pēr'les) *a.* without an equal.

PEEVISH (pē'vish) *a.* easily vexed; fretful; hard to please; discontented. [Of uncert. etym.]

PEEVISHNESS (pē'vish-nes) *n.* fretfulness.

PEG (peg) *n.* a small wooden pin;—*v.t.* to fasten with a peg. [E.; conn. with **PEAK**, **PIKE**.]

PEGASUS (peg'a-sus) *n.* a winged horse; a northern star cluster. [L., fr. G.]

PEKOE (pē'kō, pek'ō) *n.* fine kind of black tea. [Chinese = white down.]

PELAGIAN (pe-lā'ji-an) *a.* pertaining to the sea or to Pelagius;—*n.* one who denies the received doctrines of original sin, free grace, and good works.

PELAGIANISM (pe-lā'ji-an-izm) *n.* doctrinal system of Pelagius.

PELARGONIUM (pel-ár-gō'ni-um) *n.* a plant allied to the geranium. [G.]

PELERINE (pel'-e-rin) *n.* a lady's long cape. [Fr. F. *pélerin,* **PILGRIM**.]

PELF (pelf) *n.* money, in a bad sense. [O.F. *pelfre,* spoil. See **PILFER**.]

PELISSE (pe-lēs') *n.* a silk habit for a female. [F., fr. L., fr. *pellis,* skin.]

PELLET (pel'et) *n.* a little ball. [O.F. *pelote,* little ball, fr. L. *pila.*]

PELLICLE (pel'i-kl) *n.* thin external skin; film. [F. *pellicule,* fr. L. dim. fr. *pellis,* a skin.]

PELL-MELL (pel'mel) *ad.* confusedly. [O.F., for *pesle-mesle.* See **MEDLEY**.]

PELLUCID (pe-lū'sid) *a.* clear; transparent; not opaque. [L., fr. *per,* very, and **LUCID**.]

PELT (pelt) (1) *n.* an undressed hide or skin; —(2) *v.t.* to throw at; strike with something thrown. [(1) Short, fr. **PELTRY**. (2) M.E. *pelten, pulten,* fr. L. *pultare,* beat.]

PELTRY (pel'tri) *n.* skins; furs. [F. *pelleterie,* prepared skins, fr. O.F. *pel,* skin.]

PELVIS (pel'vis) *n.* the bony cavity which forms the lower part of the belly. [L. = basin.]

PEN (pen) *n.* an instrument for writing; the quill, as of a goose;—*v.t.* to compose and commit to paper. [L. *penna,* feather.]

PENAL (pē'nal) *a.* exacting, inflicting, or incurring punishment. [F., fr. L. *pœna.* G. See **PAIN**.]

PENALLY (pē'nal-i) *n.* by way of punishment.

PENALTY (pen'al-ti) *n.* punishment attached to the commission of a crime.

PENANCE (pen'ans) *n.* suffering inflicted or self-imposed for sin. [O.F., fr. L. (acc.) *pœnitentiam,* **PENITENT**.]

PENCE (pens) *n.pl.* of **PENNY**.

PENCHANT (päng'shäng) *n.* a strong liking or taste for. [F.]

PENCIL (pen'sil) *n.* a small brush used by painters; an instrument of black lead, for writing. [O.F., *pincel*, small brush, fr. L. dim. for *penis*, tail.]

PENDANT (pen'dant) *n.* an ear-ring; a flag. [F. =orig. (part.) hanging, fr. *pendre*, fr. L. *pendere*.]

PENDENCY (pen'den-si) *n.* suspense; delay of decision.

PENDENT (pen'dent) *a.* hanging; projecting. [L. (part. stem) *pendent-*, hanging, fr. *pendere*.]   [during.

PENDING (pen'ding) *a.* undecided;—*prep.*

PENDULOUS (pen'dū-lus) *a.* swinging. [L. *pendulus*, hanging.]

PENDULUM (pen'dū-lum) *n.* a body suspended and vibrating. [L.]

PENETRABLE (pen'e-tra-bl) *a.* that may be penetrated.

PENETRATE (pen'e-trāt) *v.t.* or *i.* to pierce into; enter; affect deeply; find out. [L. (part.) *penetratus*, pierced into, fr. rt. of *penitus*, within.]

PENETRATING (pen'e-trā-ting) *a.* piercing; quick to understand; acute.

PENETRATION (pen'e-trā'shun) *n.* physical piercing and entering; mental insight or acumen.

PENGUIN (pen'gwin) *n.* a web-footed marine bird. [Etym. unknown.]

PENINSULA (pe-nin'sū-la) *n.* land nearly surrounded by water. [L., fr. *pene*, almost, and *insula*, island.]

PENINSULAR (pe-nin'sū-lar) *a.* in the form of a peninsula.

PENINSULATE (pe-nin'sū-lāt) *v.t.* to form a peninsula.

PENITENCE (pen'i-tens) *n.* sorrow of heart for sin; contrition.

PENITENT (pen'i-tent) *a.* suffering sorrow for sin;—*n.* one sorrowful for sin. [O.F., fr. L. (part. stem) *pœnitent-*, fr. *pœnitere*, to make repent, fr. *pœna*.]

PENITENTIAL (pen-i-ten'shal) *a.* expressing penitence;—*n.* a book of rules for Roman Catholic penitents.

PENITENTIARY (pen-i-ten'sha-ri) *a.* relating to penance;—*n.* a house of correction.

PENKNIFE (pen'nif) *n.* a knife for making or mending pens;—*pl.* PENKNIVES.

PENMAN (pen'man) *n.* one who writes a good hand; an author.

PENMANSHIP (pen'man-ship) *n.* manner of writing; use of the pen.

PENNANT (pen'ant) *n.* a small flag or streamer; a tackle for hoisting. [O.F. *pennon* =F. *penon*, fr. L. *penna*, feather.]

PENNATE (pen'āt) *a.* winged. [L. *penna*, feather.]   [posed.

PENNED (pend) *a.* cooped up; written; com-

PENNILESS (pen'i-les) *a.* having no money.

PENNY (pen'i) *n.* twelfth of a shilling;—*pl.* PENNIES, PENCE. [M.E. *peni*; pl. *penies*, *pens*, fr. O.E. *penig*. Cf. Ger. *Pfennig*.]

PENNYWEIGHT (pen'i-wāt) *n.* a troy weight of 24 grains.

PENNYWISE (pen'i-wiz) *a.* saving small sums at the risk of larger.

PENNYWORTH (pen'i-wurth) *n.* as much as a penny will buy; a good bargain; a small quantity.

PENSION (pen'shun) *n.* a settled yearly allowance for past service;—*v.t.* to grant a pension to. [F., fr. L. (acc.) *pensionem*, payment, fr. (part.) *pensus*, weighed out, of money, fr. *pendere*.]

PENSIONER (pen'shun-er) *n.* one who receives a pension.

PENSIVE (pen'siv) *a.* thoughtful, or expressing thought with sadness. [F. *pensif*, fr. *penser*, think, fr. L. *pensare*, weigh well, ponder. See PANSY, PENSION.]

PENSIVENESS (pen'siv-nes) *n.* melancholy thoughtfulness.

PENTAGON (pen'ta-gon) *n.* a figure of five sides and five angles. [F., fr. L., fr. G., fr. *penta-*, for *pente*, five, and *gonia*, angle.]

PENTAGONAL (pen-tag'u-nal) *a.* having five angles.

PENTAMETER (pen-tam'e-ter) *n.* a poetic verse of five feet. [L., fr. G. *penta metros*, fr. *pente*, five, and *metron*, measure. METRE.]

Pentagon.

PENTATEUCH (pen'ta-tūk) *n.* the first five books of the Old Testament. [G., fr. *pente*, five, and *teuchos*, book.]

PENTECOST (pen'te-kost) *n.* a Jewish festival fifty days after the Passover; a church festival in commemoration of the descent of the Holy Spirit on the apostles. [G. *pentekost*, fiftieth (day after Passover.)]

PENTHOUSE (pent'hous) *n.* a shed standing aslope from the main building. [Corr. fr. *pentice*, fr. O.F. *appentis*, fr. L. *appendicium*, fr. *ad*, and *pendere*, hang.]

PENTROOF (pent'rōōf) *n.* a roof with a slope on one side only. [Fr. F. *pente*, a slope, fr. *pendre*, hang, fr. L. *pendere*.]

PENULT (pē'nult) *n.* the last syllable but one. [L. *penultimus*, all but the last, pref. *pene*, almost.]

PENULTIMATE (pe-nul'ti-māt) *a.* of the last syllable but one.

PENUMBRA (pe-num'bra) *n.* an imperfect or partial shadow; point where light and shade blend. [Fr. L. *pene*, almost, and *umbra*, shade.]

PENURIOUS (pe-nū'ri-us) *a.* excessively saving; miserly.

PENURIOUSLY (pe-nū'ri-us-li) *ad.* with parsimony.

PENURY (pen'ū-ri) *n.* poverty; indigence. [L. *penuria*.]

PEONY (pē'u-ni) *n.* a perennial plant and flower. [L. *pœonia*, lit. (fem. adj.) healing, fr. G. *Paion*, *Paian*, Apollo, who healed the gods. See PÆAN.]

PEOPLE (pē'pl) *n.* persons generally; inhabitants; community;—*v.t.* to stock with inhabitants. [L. *populus*.]

PEPPER (pep'er) *n.* a plant and its seed;—*v.t.* to sprinkle with pepper. [O.E. *pipor*, fr. L., fr. G. *piperi*.]

PEPPER-BOX (pep'er-boks) *n.* box with perforated lid for sprinkling pepper.

PEPPERMINT (pep'er-mint) *n.* an aromatic pungent plant; a liquor distilled from it.

PEPPERY (pep'er-i) *a.* of the nature of pepper; hot and pungent.

PERAMBULATE (per-am'bū-lāt) *v.t.* to walk round or over. [L., fr. *ambulare*, to walk about. See AMBLE.]

PERAMBULATION (per-am-bū-lā'shun) *n.* a passing over.

PERAMBULATOR (per-am'bū-lā-ter) *n.* a wheel to measure distances traversed on roads; a two-wheeled carriage for children drawn by the hand.

PERCEIVABLE (per-sē'va-bl) that may be perceived.

PERCEIVE (per-sēv') *v.t.* to take in from the senses; observe; understand. [O.F. *percever*, fr. L. *percipere*, fr. *per*, perfectly, and *capere*, take.]

PERCENTAGE (per-sen'tij) *n.* allowance, interest, or commission on a hundred. [Fr. *cent*; L. pref. *per*, by.]

PERCEPTIBLE (per-sep'ti-bl) *a.* that can be seen or understood.

PERCEPTIBLY (per-sep'ti-bli) *ad.* so as to be perceived.

PERCEPTION (per-sep'shun) *n.* act or power of perceiving; cognition; discernment. [L. fr. (part.) *perceptus*.]

PERCEPTIVE (per-sep'tiv) *a.* able to perceive.

PERCEPTIVITY (per-sep-tiv'i-ti) *n.* faculty of perceiving.

PERCH (perch) (1) *n.* a fresh-water fish; a pole;—(2) *n.* measure of 16½ feet; a roost;—*v.t.* to place upon:—*v.i.* to settle on; roost. [(1) F., fr. L. (acc.) *percam*, fr. G. *perke*. (2) O.F. *perche*, fr. L. (acc.) *perticam*, pole.]

PERCHANCE (per-châns') *ad.* perhaps.

PERCOLATE (per'kō-lāt) *v.t.* or *i.* to strain through; filter. [L., fr. *per*, through, and *colare*, filter.]

PERCOLATION (per-kō-lā'shun) *n.* a passing through interstices.

PERCUSSION (per-kush'un) *n.* the act or effect of striking; a stroke. [L. (part.) *percussus*, struck, fr. *per*, thoroughly, and *quatere*, shake.]

PERDITION (per-dish'un) *n.* utter loss or ruin. [F., fr. L., fr. (part.) *perditus*, lost, fr. *perdere*.]

PERDU (per-dū') *ad.* lost; in a state of concealment. [F. = (part.) lost, fr. *perdre*, fr. L. *perdere*. See PERDITION.]

PEREGRINATE (per'e-gri-nāt) *v.i.* to travel. [L. (part.) *peregrinatus*, having travelled, fr. *peregrinus*. See PILGRIM.]

PEREGRINATION (per-e-gri-nā'shun) *n.* a travelling; a wandering.

PEREMPTORILY (per'emp-tu-ri-li) *ad.* positively.

PEREMPTORY (per'emp-tu-ri) *a.* authoritative; decisive; forbidding expostulation. [L. *peremptorius*, fr. (part.) *peremptus*, destroyed, fr. *per* thoroughly, and *imere*, for *emere*, take, buy.]

PERENNIAL (pe-ren'i-al) *a.* lasting through the year; perpetual. [Fr. L. *perennis*, fr. *per*, through, and *annus*, year.]

PERFECT (per'fekt) *a.* complete; finished; faultless; pure; certain;—*v.t.* to complete; instruct fully. [L. (part.) *perfectus*, finished, fr. *per*, thoroughly, and *facere*, make.]

PERFECTER (per'fek-ter) *n.* one who makes complete.

PERFECTIBILITY (per-fek-ti-bil'i-ti) *n.* capability of being made perfect.

PERFECTIBLE (per-fek'ti-bl) *a.* that may be perfected. [perfect.

PERFECTION (per-fek'shun) *n.* state of being

PERFECTIVE (per-fek'tiv) *a.* conducive to perfection.

PERFECTLY (per'fekt-li) *ad.* in a perfect manner.

PERFIDIOUS (per-fid'i-us) *a.* false to trust.

PERFIDY (per'fi-di) *n.* violation of faith; treachery. [L. *perfidia*, treachery, fr. *fides*, faith.]

PERFORATE (per'fu-rāt) *v.t.* to bore or pierce through. [L. (part.) *perforatus*, bored through, fr. *per*, and *forare*.]

PERFORATION (per-fu-rā'shun) *n.* act of boring through; a hole bored.

PERFORATOR (pe'-fu-rā-ter) *n.* an instrument for boring.

PERFORCE (per-fōrs') *ad.* by force. [L. pref. *per*, by.]

PERFORM (per-form') *v.t.* or *i.* to do thoroughly; discharge; fulfil; act a part; play upon. [M.E. *parfournen*, fr. O.F., fr. *par* = L. *per*, thoroughly, and *fournir*. FURNISH.]

PERFORMABLE (per-for'ma-bl) *a.* that can be done.

PERFORMANCE (per-for'mans) *n.* act of performing; deed; mode of performing; execution; public representation of skill.

PERFORMER (per-for'mer) *n.* one that performs in public.

PERFUME (per-fūm') *v.t.* to scent.

PERFUME (per'fūm) *n.* a sweet scent. [F. *parfum*, fr. L. *per*, through, and *fumus*, smoke. See FUME.]

PERFUMERY (per-fū'mer-i) *n.* perfumes in general.

PERFUNCTORILY (per-fungk'tu-ri-li) *ad.* in a perfunctory manner.

PERFUNCTORY (per-fungk'tu-ri) *a.* done in a slovenly way; slight and careless. [L., fr. (part.) *perfunctus*, having discharged, fr. *per*, quite, and *fungi*, do. See FUNCTION.]

PERHAPS (per-haps') *ad.* by chance. [Imit. fr. PERCHANCE. See HAP.]

PERI (pē'ri) *n.* a female fairy. [Per. = winged fairy.]

PERICARDIUM (per-i-kar'di-um) *n.* the membrane enclosing the heart. [L., fr. G. *peri*, around, and *kardia*, heart.]

PERICARP (per'i-karp) *n.* the seed-vessel of a plant. [Fr. G. *peri*, around, and *karpos*, fruit.]

PERIGEE (per'i-jē) *n.* that point in the orbit of the moon nearest to the earth. [Fr. G. *peri*, around, and *ge*, earth.]

PERIHELION (per-i-hē'li-on) *n.* the point in a planet's orbit nearest the sun. [Fr. G. *peri*, around, and *helios*, sun.]

PERIL (per'il) *n.* danger; risk; threatened evil;—*v.t.* to expose to danger; risk. [O.F., fr. L. *periculum*.]

PERILOUS (per'i-lus) *a.* full of danger.

PERILOUSLY (per'i-lus-li) *ad.* dangerously; with hazard.

PERIMETER (pe-rim'e-ter) *n.* the outer boundary of a figure. [L., fr. G., fr. *peri*, and *metron*, measure. See METRE.]

PERIOD (pē'ri-ud) *n.* a circuit; time of a revolution; series of years; end; full stop, thus—(.). [O.F. *periode*, fr. L., fr. G. *peri*, and *hodos*, way.]

PERIODICAL (pē-ri-od'i-kal) *a.* returning or happening at regular times;—*n.* a publication issued at stated times.

PERIODICALLY (pē-ri-od'i-kal-i) *ad.* at stated periods.

PERIODICITY (pē'ri-u-dis'i-ti) *n.* state of recurring at stated intervals of time.

PERIPATETIC (per-i-pa-tet'ik) *a.* pertaining to Aristotle or his philosophy;—*n.* one who walks about. [L., fr. G. *peripatetikos*, fr. *peri*, about, and *patein*, walk.]

PERIPHERY (pe-rif'e-ri) *n.* circumference of a circle or curvilinear figure. [G. *peri-phereia*, fr. *peri*, and *pherein*, bear.]

PERIPHRASIS (pe-rif'ra-sis) *n.* a roundabout mode of expression. [L., fr. G., fr. *peri*, and *phrazein*, speak. See PHRASE.]

PERIPHRASTIC (per-i-fras'tik) *a.* expressing or expressed in many words.

PERISH (per'ish) *v.i.* to decay; die; go to ruin. [O.F. (part.) *perissant*, perishing, fr. *perir*, fr. L. *perire*, fr. *per*, altogether, and *ire*, go.]

PERISHABLE (per'ish-a-bl) *a.* liable to decay or destruction; mortal.

PERISTYLE (per'i-stil) *n.* a range of columns round an edifice. [G. pref. *peri*, around, and *stulos*, a column.]

PERIWIG (per'i-wig) *n.* a small wig. [M.E. *perwike*, corr. fr. PERRUQUE.]

PERIWINKLE (per'i-wing-kl) *n.* a small shell-fish. [Fr. O.E. *pervince*, fr. L. *pervinca*, fr. *per*, and *vincere*, bind.]

PERJURE (per'jur) *v.t.* to swear lawfully and testify falsely; forswear. [F. *parjurer*, fr. L. *perjurare*, forswear, fr. *per*, and *jurare*. See JURY.]

PERJURY (per'ju-ri) *n.* the crime of giving false evidence on oath; false swearing.

PERK (perk) *a.* brisk; smart; trim;—*v.i.* to hold up the head affectedly; *v.t.* or *i.* make smart; dress up. [Celt.]

PERKIN (per'kin) *n.* a kind of cider. [Dim. fr. PERRY.]

PERKY (per'ki) *a.* perk.

PERMANENCY (per'ma-nen-si) *n.* continuance in the same place or state; duration. Also **PERMANENCE.**

PERMANENT (per'ma-nent) *a.* durable; lasting; without change. [F., fr. L. (acc. part.) *permanentem*, enduring, fr. *per*, through, and *manere*, REMAIN.]

PERMANENTLY (per'ma-nent-li) *ad.* durably.

PERMEABLE (per'me-a-bl) *a.* that may be passed through.

PERMEATE (per'me-āt) *v.t.* to pass through the interstices or pores. [L. (part.) *permeatus*, fr. *per*, through, and *meare*, pass.]

PERMEATION (per-me-ā'shun) *n.* the act of passing through pores.

PERMISSIBLE (per-mis'i-bl) *a.* that may be allowed.

PERMISSION (per-mish'un) *n.* act of permitting. [F., fr. L., fr. (part.) *permissus*, permitted.]

PERMISSIVE (per-mis'iv) *a.* granting liberty.

PERMIT (per-mit') *v.t.* or *i.* to grant leave or liberty; allow; tolerate;—(per'mit) *n.* a written warrant or licence. [L. *permittere*, lit. let pass through, fr. *per*, and *mittere*, send.]

PERMUTATION (per-mū-tā'shun) *n.* mutual exchange; possible combination of given letters or figures. [L., fr. *per*, throughly, and *mutare*, change.]

PERNICIOUS (per-nish'us) *a.* tending to injure; hurtful; destructive. [F., fr. L. *perniciosus*, destructive, fr. *per*, and stem *neci-*, of *nex*, death by violence.]

PERNICIOUSLY (per-nish'us-li) *ad.* in an injurious manner.

PERNICIOUSNESS (per-nish'us-nes) *n.* the quality of being very injurious or destructive.

PERORATION (per-u-rā'shun) *n.* the closing part of an oration. [L., fr. (part.) *peroratus* completed (of a speech), fr. *per*, thoroughly, and *orare*, speak. See ORATION.]

PERPEND (per-pend') *v.t.* to weigh in the mind. [L. *perpendere*, fr. *per*, intens., and *pendere*, to weigh.]

PERPENDICULAR (per-pen-dik'ū-lar) *a.* upright; crossing at right angles:—*n.* anything at right angles. [F., fr. L. *perpendicularis*, fr. *perpendiculum*, plummet, fr. *per*, through, and *pendere*, weigh.]

PERPENDICULARLY (per-pen-dik'ū-lar-li) *ad.* at right angles.

PERPETRATE (per'pe-trāt) *v.t.* to do or commit, in a bad sense. [L. (part.) *perpetratus* accomplished thoroughly, fr. *per*, and *patrare*, perform.]

PERPETRATION (per-pe-trā'shun) *n.* commission of something wrong.

PERPETRATOR (per'pe-trā-ter) *n.* one who commits a crime.

PERPETUAL (per-pet'ū-al) *a.* never ceasing. [O.F. *perpetuel*, fr. L. (acc.) *perpetuatem*.]

PERPETUALLY (per-pet'ū-al-i) *ad.* unceasingly.

PERPETUATE (per-pet'ū-āt) *v.t.* to make perpetual. [L. *perpetuus*, constant, fr. *per*, through, and rt. of *petere*, seek.]

PERPETUITY (per-pe-tū'i-ti) *n.* endless duration.

PERPLEX (per-pleks') *v.t.* to make intricate; trouble with ambiguity, suspense, etc. [L. (part.) *perplexus*, entangled, fr. *per*, thoroughly, and *plectere*, weave, PLAIT.]

PERPLEXITY (per-plek'si-ti) *n.* state of intricacy; embarrassment.

PERQUISITE (per'kwi-sit) *n.* a fee or allowance beyond the stated wages. [Late L., fr. L. (part.) *perquisitus*, sought after, fr. *per*, and *quaerere*, QUERY.]

PERRY (per'i) *n.* a drink made of pears. [L. *pirum*, a PEAR.]

PERSECUTE (per'se-kūt) *v.t.* to pursue with malignity; harass. [Fr. L. (part.) *persecutus*, pursued, fr. *per*, and *sequi*, follow. See SEQUENCE.]

PERSECUTION (per-se-kū'shun) *n.* act or practice of persecuting; state of being persecuted.

PERSECUTOR (per'se-kū-ter) *n.* one who persecutes.

PERSEVERANCE (per-se-vēr'ans) *n.* act or state of persevering.

PERSEVERE (per-se-vēr') *v.i.* to continue doing or labouring; proceed steadily. [O.F. *perseverer*, fr. L., fr. *per*, thoroughly, and *severus*, earnest, SEVERE.]

PERSEVERINGLY (per-se-vēr'ing-li) *ad.* with perseverance.

PERSIST (per-sist') *v.i.* to persevere steadily and firmly. [L. *per*, through, and *sistere*, STAND, fr. *stare*.]

PERSISTENCE (per-sis'tens) *n.* steady consistence in, or pursuit of; obstinacy; duration. Also PERSISTENCY.

PERSISTIVE (per-sis'tiv) *a.* persevering.

PERSON (per'sun) *n.* a man, woman, or child; bodily form; character represented; a distinction in the Godhead. [F., fr. L. *persona*, an actor's mask, a personage fr. *per*, and *sonare*, sound.]

PERSONABLE (per'sun-a-bl) *a.* having a well-formed body.

PERSONAGE (per'sun-ij) *n.* a person of distinction.

PERSONAL (per'sun-al) *a.* belonging to a person; done or said by, or against a person.

PERSONALITY (per-su-nal'i-ti) *n.* that which constitutes or distinguishes a person; individuality; a remark offensive to a person.

PERSONALLY (per'sun-al-i) *ad.* in person.

PERSONALTY (per'sun-al-ti) *n.* personal estate.

PERSONATE (per'sun-āt) *v.t.* or *i.* to assume the character and act the part of.

PERSONATION (per-sun-ā'shun) *n.* act of representing or acting.

PERSONATOR (per'sun-ā-ter) *n.* one who assumes another's character.

PERSONIFICATION (per-sun-i-fi-kā'shun) *n.* act of personifying.

PERSONIFY (per-son'i-fi) *v.t.* to speak of inanimate things, etc., as though they were persons; represent a character. [See PERSON, *fy.* = F. *fier*. L. *ficare* = *facere*.]

PERSONNEL (per-son-nel') *n.* the body or staff of persons in a public service. [F.]

PERSPECTIVE (per-spek'tiv) *a.* relating to vision;—*n.* art of drawing on a plain surface objects as they appear to the eye; a view; a picture in perspective. [L. (part.) *perspectus*, fr. *per*, and *specere*, look.]

PERSPICACIOUS (per-spi-kā'shus) *a.* quicksighted; discerning. [Fr. L. stem *perspicaci-*, of *perspicax*, keen of sight, fr. *perspicere*. See PERSPECTIVE.]

PERSPICACITY (per-spi-kas'i-ti) *n.* acuteness of discernment or sight. Also PERSPICACIOUSNESS.

PERSPICUITY (per-spi-kū'i-ti) *n.* clearness in statement. Also PERSPICUOUSNESS.

PERSPICUOUS (per-spik'ū-us) *a.* clear; not obscure or ambiguous. [L. *perspicuus*.]

PERSPIRABLE (per-spīr'a-bl) *a.* that may be perspired.

PERSPIRATION (per-spi-rā'shun) *n.* act of perspiring; matter perspired.

PERSPIRATORY (per-spīr'a-tu-ri) *a.* causing or performing perspiration.

PERSPIRE (per-spīr') *v.t.* or *i.* to emit fluid matter through the pores; sweat. [L., fr. *per*, through, and *spirare*, breathe. See SPIRIT.]

PERSUADE (per-swād') *v.t.* to influence successfully by statement of motives, considerations, etc.; convince; induce. [F., fr. L. *per*, outright, and *suadere*, persuade.]

PERSUASIBLE (per-swā'si-bl) *a.* that may be persuaded.

PERSUASIVE (per-swā'siv) *a.* tending or having power to persuade;—*n.* that which persuades; inducement.

PERSUASIVENESS (per-swā'siv-nes) *n.* quality of being persuasive.

PERT (pert) *a.* smart; brisk; saucy. [O.F. *apert.* See **MALAPERT**.]

PERTAIN (per-tān') *v.i.* to belong or have relation to. [O.F. *partenir,* fr. L., fr. *per,* thoroughly, and *tenere,* hold.]

PERTINACIOUS (per-ti-nā'shus) *a.* holding firmly to any opinion or purpose; resolute; obstinate. [F., fr. L. stem *pertinaci-,* of *pertinax,* fr. *per,* and *tenax,* **TENACIOUS**.]

PERTINACIOUSLY (per-ti-nā'shus-li) *ad.* resolutely; obstinately.

PERTINACITY (per-ti-nas'i-ti) *n.* constancy in adhering; obstinacy. Also **PERTINACIOUSNESS**.

PERTINENCE (per'ti-nens) *n.* fitness; suitableness.

PERTINENT (per'ti-nent) *a.* appropriate to the case; apposite. [F., fr. L. (acc. part.) *pertinentem,* pertaining. See **PERTAIN**.]

PERTINENTLY (per'ti-nent-li) *ad.* to the purpose.

PERTLY (pert'li) *ad.* smartly; saucily.

PERTNESS (pert'nes) *n.* forwardness; smartness; sauciness.

PERTURB (per-turb') *v.t.* to disturb; agitate. [O.F. *perturber,* fr. L., fr. *per,* thoroughly, and *turbare* **DISTURB**.]

PERTURBATION (per-tur-bā'shun) *n.* disturbance of the mind or passions; disorder; irregularity in a planet's orbital motion.

PERUKE, PERRUQUE (pe-rōōk', per'ūk, per-ūk') *n.* an artificial cap of hair. [F. *perruque,* fr. It. *pelo,* fr. L. *pilus,* hair.]

PERUSAL (pe-rōō'zal, per-ū'zal) *n.* act of reading.

PERUSE (pe-rōōz', per-ūz') *v.t.* to read with attention. [L. pref. *per,* thoroughly, and *uti, usum,* use.]

PERVADE (per-vād') *v.t.* to pass through; spread through the whole. [L., fr. *per,* and *vadere,* go.]

PERVASION (per-vā'shun) *n.* act of pervading.

PERVASIVE (per-vā'siv) *a.* tending or able to pervade.

PERVERSE (per-vers') *a.* obstinate in the wrong; froward; stubborn. [L. (part.) *perversus,* overturned, fr. *per,* and *vertere,* turn.]

PERVERSENESS (per-vers'nes) *n.* quality of being perverse.

PERVERSION (per-ver'shun) *n.* a diverting from the truth or duty, or from the true sense and meaning.

PERVERSITY (per-ver'si-ti) *n.* cross disposition.

PERVERSIVE (per-ver'siv) *a.* tending to pervert.

PERVERT (per-vert') *v.t.* to turn from the right course, or the true use or meaning. [L. *per,* through, and *vertere,* to turn.]

PERVERT (per'vert) *n.* one who has changed from truth to error.

PERVERTIBLE (per-ver'ti-bl) *a.* that can be perverted.

PERVIOUS (per'vi-us) *a.* that may be penetrated. [L., fr. *per,* and *via,* way.]

PERVIOUSNESS (per'vi-us-nes) *n.* quality of being pervious.

PESSIMIST (pes'i-mist) *n.* one who regards everything in the world as radically bad. [L. *pessimus,* worst.]

PEST (pest) *n.* a deadly epidemic disease; anything destructive or troublesome. [F. *peste,* fr. L. (acc.) *pestem,* of *pestis.*]

PESTER (pes'ter) *v.t.* to harass with little vexations; annoy. [Low L. *pastorium,* a foot-shackle, fr. L. *pascere,* pp. *pastus,* to feed.]

PEST-HOUSE (pest'hous) *n.* an hospital for contagious diseases.

PESTIFEROUS (pes-tif'e-rus) *a.* pestilential. [L. *pestis,* and *ferre,* bear.]

PESTILENCE (pes'ti-lens) *n.* contagious distemper; plague.

PESTILENT (pes'ti-lent) *a.* noxious to health, life, morals, etc.; corrupting; troublesome.

PESTILENTIAL (pes-ti-len'shal) *a.* containing, or tending to, pestilence; destructive.

PESTLE (pes'l) *n.* an instrument for pounding things in a mortar;—*v.t.* to pound with a pestle. [O.F., fr. L. *pistillum,* a small pestle.]

PET (pet) *n.* fit of peevishness; a little animal loved and indulged; a word of endearment; —*v.t.* [*pp.* **PETTED**] to treat as a pet; fondle. [Ir.]

PETAL (pet'al) *n.* a flower-leaf. [G. *petalon,* leaf, fr. rt. of *petannumi,* spread.]

PETALINE (pet'a-lin) *a.* resembling or attached to a petal.

PETALOID (pet'a-loid) *a.* having the form of a petal.

PETALOUS (pet'a-lus) *a.* having petals. Also **PETALED**.

PETARD (pe-tärd') *n.* a *a.* Petals. piece of ordnance for blowing up works. [O.F., fr. *rel,* an explosion, fr. L., fr. *pedere,* break wind.]

PETER-PENCE (pē'ter-pens) *n.* an annual tax of a silver penny paid to the pope.

PETIOLE (pet'i-ōl) *n.* a leaf-stalk. [F., fr. L. *petiolus.*]

PETIT (pet'i) *a.* small; mean. [F.]

PETITION (pe-tish'un) *n.* a formal request; prayer; memorial;—*v.t.* to supplicate. [L. (acc.) *petitionem,* a suit, fr. L. (part.) *petitus,* sought, fr. *petere.*]

PETITIONARY (pe-tish'un-a-ri) *a.* bringing a petition.

PETITIONER (pe-tish'un-er) *n.* one who offers a petition.

PETIT-MAITRE (pet'i-mā'tr) *n.* a dangler about females. [F.]

PETREL (pet'rel) *n.* a long-winged, web-footed ocean bird. [Dim. fr. *Pêtre,* Peter, so called from its appearing, like St Peter, to walk on thhe sea.]

PETRIFACTION (pet-ri-fak'shun) *n.* conversion into stone.

PETRIFACTIVE (pet-ri-fak'tiv) *a.* having power to change into stony matter.

PETRIFY (pet'ri-fī) *v.t.* to convert into stone; —*v.i.* to become stone. [O.F. *petrifier,* fr. L. *petra,* rock, fr. G., and *-ficare = facere,* make.]

PETROL (pet'-rol) an oil derived from petroleum and used in motor-engines. [Fr. F. *pétrole,* L. *petra,* rock, and *oleum,* **OIL**.]

PETROLEUM (pe-trō'le-um) *n.* a bituminous liquid; rock-oil. [Fr. L. *petra,* rock, and *oleum,* **OIL**.]

PETTICOAT (pet'i-kōt) *n.* a woman's undergarment. [Fr. **PETTY** and **COAT**.]

PETTIFOGGER (pet'i-fog-er) *n.* a petty lawyer. [Fr. **PETTY**, and D. *focker,* wholesale merchant.]

PETTIFOGGERY (pet'i-fog-er-i) *n.* mean business of a lawyer.

PETTIFOGGING (pet'i-fog-ing) *a.* doing small law business; mean.

PETTISH (pet'ish) *a.* fretful; peevish.

PETTISHLY (pet'ish-li) *ad.* peevishly.

PETTITOES (pet'i-tōz) *n.pl.* the toes of a pig. [Fr. **PETTY** and **TOE**.]

PETTY (pet'i) *a.* small; trifling. [F. *petit,* of uncert. etym.]

PETULANCE (pet'ū-lans) *n.* peevishness.

Fāte, får, ado; mē, her; mīne; nōte; tūne; mōōn.

PETULANT (pet'ū-lant) *a.* pert with ill humour; freakish; fretful. [L. (stem) *petulant-*, pert, fr. *petere*, seek, attack.]

PETULANTLY (pet'ū-lant-li) *ad.* in a petulant manner.

PEW (pū) *n.* an enclosed seat in a church. [O.F. *pui*, platform, fr. L. *podium*, balcony, fr. G. *podion*, orig. a stool, fr. stem *pod-*, of *pous*, foot.]

PEWIT (pē'wit) *n.* a water fowl; the lapwing. Also written PEWET. [Imit.]

PEWTER (pū'ter) *n.* a compound of tin and lead; vessels made of it. [O.F. *peutre*, of uncert. etym.]

PHAETON (fā'e-tun) *n.* an open four-wheeled carriage. [F., fr. G. *Phaeton*. son of Phœbus, who guided the chariot of the sun.]

PHALANX (fā'langks, fal'angks) *n.* a compact body of soldiers. [G.]

PHANTASM (fan'tazm) *n.* image of an object; a fancied vision; illusion. [L., fr. G. *phantasma*, fr. *phainein*, to show. Doublet of PHANTOM.]

PHANTASMAL (fan-taz'mal) *a.* like a phantom.

PHANTASMAGORIA (fan-taz-ma-gō'ri-a) *n.* a magic lantern representation; group of shadowy figures. [Fr. G. rt. of *agora*, assembly.]

PHANTOM (fan'tum) *n.* an apparition; airy spirit; ghost. [O.F. *fantosme*, fr. L. *phantasma*. Doublet of PHANTASM.]

PHARISAICAL (far-i-sā'i-kal) *a.* like the Pharisees; formal.

PHARISAISM (far'i-sā-izm) *a.* formality in religion; profession of superior sanctity.

PHARISEE (far'i-sē) *n.* a Jew strict in the externals of religion; a self-righteous man. [L. *pharisæus*, fr. G., fr. H. *parash*, to separate.]

PHARMACEUTIC (fár-ma-sū'tik) *a.* pertaining to pharmacy.

PHARMACEUTICS (fár-ma-sū'tiks) *n.* science of preparing medicines.

PHARMACY (fár'ma-si) *n.* art or trade of compounding medicines. [O.F. *farmacie*, fr. L., fr. G. *pharmakeia*, fr. *pharmakon*, drug.]

PHAROS (fā'ros) *n.* a lighthouse. [*Pharos*, off Alexandria, noted for lighthouse.]

PHASE (fāz) *n.* appearance; apparent state at a given time of any variable object. [Late L., fr. G. *phasis*, an appearance.]

PHASIS (fā'sis) *n.* appearance of the moon or planets;—*pl.* PHASES. [G.]

PHEASANT (fez'ant) *n.* a bird with brilliant plumage preserved as game. [O.F. *faisan*, fr. L. *Phasiana* (*avis*), (bird) from the *Phasis*, a Colchian river, fr. G.]

PHENOMENAL (fe-nom'e-nal) *a.* noting that which is unaccountable or unusual.

PHENOMENON (fe-nom'e-non) *n.* an appearance; anything remarkable;—*pl.* PHENOMENA, [L., fr. G. *phainomenon*, orig. (neut. part.) thing shown, fr. *phainein*.]

PHIAL (fī'al) *n.* small glass bottle. [O.F. *phiole*, fr. L., fr. G. *phiale*, a shallow cup.]

PHILANTHROPIC (fil-an-throp'ik) *a.* having goodwill to mankind.

PHILANTHROPIST (fi-lan'thru-pist) *n.* a person of general benevolence.

PHILANTHROPY (fi-lan'thru-pi) *n.* the love of mankind at large. [L., fr. G. *philanthropia*, fr. *philos*, friendly, and *anthropos*, man.]

PHILHARMONIC (fil-hár-mon'ik) *a.* loving harmony; musical. [G.; pref. *philos*, loving.]

PHILIPPIC (fi-lip'ik) *n.* any invective declamation. [L. *Philippicum*, one of the famous orations of Demosthenes against *Philip* of Macedon.]

PHILOLOGICAL (fil-u-loj'i-kal) *a.* pertaining to philology.

PHILOLOGIST (fi-lol'ō-jist) *n.* one versed in philology.

PHILOLOGY (fi-lol'ō-ji) *n.* the science or study of languages in their formation, growth, and relations. [L., fr. G. *philologia*, fr. *philos*, loving, and *logos*, discourse, fr. *legein*, speak.]

PHILOMEL (fil'u-mel) *n.* the nightingale. [Fr. *Philomela*, of Athens, who was changed into a nightingale.]

PHILOPROGENITIVENESS (fil-u-pru-jen'i-tiv-nes) *n.* the love of offspring. [G. pref. *philos*, loving, *pro*, before, and *genitor*, a parent, fr. *gignere*, to beget.]

PHILOSOPHER (fi-los'u-fer) *n.* one skilled in philosophy; rational thinker.

PHILOSOPHICAL (fil-u-sof'i-kal) *a* pertaining or according to philosophy; rational.

PHILOSOPHICALLY (fil-u-sof'i-kal-i) *ad.* according to philosophy; calmly.

PHILOSOPHISE (fi-los'u-fiz) *v.t.* to reason like a philosopher.

PHILOSOPHY (fi-los'u-fi) *n.* general laws or principles of knowledge—material, mental, or moral. [F., fr. L., fr. G. *philosophia*, fr. *philos*, loving, and *sophia*, wisdom.]

PHILTER (fil'ter) *n.* a potion to excite love. [F., fr. L., fr. G. *philtron*, fr. *philos*, loving, dear.]

PHLEBOTOMIST (fle-bot'u-mist) *n.* one who lets blood with a lancet.

PHLEBOTOMY (fle-bot'u-mi) *n.* act or art of opening a vein. [O.F. *phlebotomie*, fr. L., fr. G. *phlebotomia*, fr. *phleps*, vein, and *tomos*, cutting. See TOME.]

PHLEGM (flem) *n.* cold animal fluid. [F., fr. G. *phlegma*, inflammation, fr. *phlegein*, to burn.]

PHLEGMATIC (fleg-mat'ik) *a.* abounding with phlegm; cold; sluggish.

PHONETIC (fō-net'ik) *a.* pertaining to or representing the sound of the voice. [G. *phonetikos*, fr. *phone*, sound.]

PHONETICS (fō-net'iks) *n.* the science of vocal sounds; phonography.

PHONOGRAPH (fō'nu-graf) *n.* an instrument which registers and repeats sound. [Fr. G. *phone*, sound, and *graphein*, to write.]

PHONOGRAPHY (fō-nog'ra-fi) *n.* a representation of sounds, each by its distinctive character; shorthand writing.

PHONOLOGY (fō-nol'ō-ji) *n.* the science of vocal elementary sounds. [Fr. G. *phone*, sound, and *-logia*, fr. *legein*, discourse.]

PHONOTYPE (fō'nu-tip) *n.* a type or character representing a sound. [Fr. G. *phone*, sound and TYPE.]

PHOSPHATE (fos'fāt) *n.* a salt of phosphoric acid.

PHOSPHORESCE (fos-fo-res') *v.i.* to exhibit a phosphoric light.

PHOSPHORESCENCE (fos-fo-res'ens) *n.* a faint light or luminousness.

PHOSPHORESCENT (fos-fo-res'ent) *a.* shining like phosphorus.

PHOSPHORIC (fos-for'ik) *a.* obtained from phosphorus. Also PHOSPHOROUS.

PHOSPHORUS (fos'fo-rus) *n.* a combustible substance exhibiting a faint light in the dark. [L., fr. G. *phosphoros*, light-bringing, fr. *phos*, light, and *pherein*, bring.]

PHOTOGRAPH (fō'tu-graf) *n.* a picture obtained by photography.

PHOTOGRAPHY (fō-tog'ra-fi) *n.* art of producing pictures by the action of sunlight on chemically-prepared surfaces. [Fr. G. stem *phot-*, of *phos*, light, and *graphein*, write.]

PHOTOLOGY (fō-tol'ō-ji) *n.* the science of light. [Fr. G. *phos*, light, and *-logia*, fr. *legein*, discourse.]

PHOTOMETER (fō-tom'e-ter) *n.* an instrument for measuring the intensity of light. [Fr. G. *phos*, light, and *metron*, measure, METRE.]

PHRASE (frāz) *n.* part of a sentence; a pithy word or term; form of speech;—*v.t.* or *i.* to put in words; style; speak drawlingly. [F., fr. L., fr. G. *phrasis*, a speech, fr. *phrazein*, speak.]

Fāte, fár, ado; mē, her; mine; nōte; tūne; mŏŏn.

PHRASEOLOGY (frā-ze-ol'ō-ji) *n.* mode of speech; peculiar diction; a collection of phrases.

PHRENETIC (fre-net'ik) *a.* mad; frantic. [G. *phren,* diaphragm, mind.]

PHRENOLOGY (fre-nol'ō-ji) *n.* science of the mind, or supposed organs of thought. [G. *phren,* the mind, and *-logia,* fr. *legein,* discourse.]

PHTHISICAL (tiz'i-kal) *a.* having or pertaining to pulmonary consumption.

PHTHISIS (thi'sis) *n.* tubercular disease in the lungs; consumption. Also **PHTHISIC**. [L., fr. G., fr. *phthiein,* to waste away, decay.]

PHYLACTERY (fi-lak'te-ri) *n.* a parchment with a passage of Scripture written on it, worn on the forehead and left arm. [L. *phylacterium,* fr. G. *phulassein,* to guard.]

PHYSIC (fiz'ik) *n.* the art of healing; medicine; *—v.t.* to purge; cure with medicine. [L. *physica,* natural philosophy, fr. G. *phusikos,* natural, fr. *phuein,* to produce.]

PHYSICAL (fiz'i-kal) *a.* pertaining to nature; external; bodily.

PHYSICALLY (fiz'i-kal-i) *ad.* according to nature. [physic.

PHYSICIAN (fi-zish'an) *n.* one who practises

PHYSICS (fiz'iks) *n.pl.* science of nature or natural objects.

PHYSIOGNOMIST (fiz-i-og'nu-mist, fiz-i-on'u-mist). *n.* one skilled in physiognomy.

PHYSIOGNOMY (fiz-i-og'nu-mi, fiz-i-on'-u-mi) *n.* the art of discerning the character of the mind from the face. [O.F. *phisonomie,* fr. Late L., fr. G. *phusis,* nature, and *gnomon,* judge.]

PHYSIOGRAPHY (fiz-i-og'ra-fi) *n.* a general introduction to the study of inorganic nature; physical geography (with additional phenomena). [G. *phusis,* and *graphein,* write.]

PHYSIOLOGICAL (fiz-i-u-loj'i-kal) *a.* pertaining to physiology.

PHYSIOLOGIST (fiz-i-ol'ō-jist) *n.* one versed in physiology.

PHYSIOLOGY (fiz-i-ol'ō-ji) *n.* the science of living beings. [L., fr. G. *phusis,* nature, being, and *-logia,* fr. *legein,* discourse.]

PHYSIQUE (fi-zēk') *n.* bodily form or constitution. [F.]

PHYTOLOGY (fi-tol'ō-ji) *n.* doctrine of plants. [G. *phuton,* a plant, and *-logia.*]

PIACULAR (pi-ak'ū-lar) *a.* expiatory. [L., fr. *piaculum,* propitiatory, fr. *piare,* appease.]

PIANIST (pi-an'ist) *n.* a player on the pianoforte.

PIANOFORTE (pi-an'u-for-te) *n.* a musical keyed instrument. [It., fr. L. *planus,* smooth, soft, and *fortis,* strong.]

PIASTRE (pi-as'ter) *n.* a small silver coin of value varying in different countries. [It. *piastra.*] [It.]

PIAZZA (pi-az'a, pē-ad'za) *n.* a covered walk.

PIBROCH (pē'broH) *n.* an air or march played on the bagpipe. [Gael.; conn. with **PIPE**.]

PICA (pi'ka) *n.* a large printing type. [L. = magpie, fr. the contrast made by print and paper.]

PICK (pik) *v.t.* to choose; gather; pierce; open; steal;—*v.i.* to eat or do anything nicely;—*n.* a sharp-pointed tool; choice; right of selection. [Fr. Low L. *pica,* a pike; or Celt.]

PICKAXE (pik'aks) *n.* an axe that has a point. [Corr. fr. M.E. *pikois,* fr. O.F. *picquois,* mattock, fr. *pic,* a **PICK**.]

PICKED (pikt) *a.* selected; choice; pointed.

PICKET (pik'et) *n.* a sharpened stake; a small guard or outpost. [F. *piquet,* a small **PICK**, fr. *pic.*]

PICKLE (pik'l) *n.* a liquid in which food is preserved; brine; vinegar; thing pickled; *—v.t.* to preserve in brine, etc. [Etym. uncert.]

PICKPOCKET (pik'pok-et) *n.* one who picks another's pocket.

PICNIC (pik'nik) *n.* a pleasure party in which each one furnishes refreshment. [Fr. **PICK** =to nibble, and *nic,* for *knick,* a trifle.]

PICTORIAL (pik-tō'ri-al) *a.* pertaining to or illustrated by pictures.

PICTURE (pik'tūr) *n.* a resemblance in colours; any graphic representation or description; *—v.t.* to paint or represent. [L. *pictura,* painting, fr. (part.) *pictus,* painted, fr. *pingere.*]

PICTURESQUE (pik-tu-resk') *a.* beautiful to the eye; graphic; vivid. [Fr. It. *pittoresco.*]

PIE (pi) (1) paste baked with something in it or under it; (2) the magpie. [(1) Fr. **PIE** (2), in the sense of a contrast, or mix-up. (2) O.F., fr. L. (acc.) *picam.* See **PICA**.]

PIEBALD (pi'bawld) *a.* of various colours. [F. *bald* =streaked.]

PIECE (pēs) *n.* a part; a patch; a literary or artistic work; coin; gun; a woman; bit of bread;—*v.t.* or *i.* to enlarge by addition; patch; unite. [O.F. *piece* =F. *pièce,* fr. Celt., through Low L.]

PIECEMEAL (pēs'mēl) *a.* single;—*ad.* in or by parts. [M.E. suff. *-mele,* fr. O.E. *mǣlum,* by parts. See **MEAL** (2).]

PIED (pid) *a.* party-coloured.

PIER (pēr) *n.* support of an arch; a mole projecting into the sea; a wharf. [O.F. *piere* =F. *pierre,* stone, fr. L., fr. G. *petra,* rock.]

PIERAGE (pēr'ij) *n.* toll for using a pier or wharf.

PIER-GLASS (pēr'glas) *n.* a glass between windows.

PIERCE (pērs) *v.t.* or *i.* to thrust or enter into; penetrate; affect deeply. [F. *percer,* fr O.F. *pertuisier,* through Late L. forms, fr. L. (part.) *pertusus,* bored, fr. *per,* through, and *tundere,* beat.]

PIERCER (pēr'ser) *n.* a perforating instrument.

PIERCING (pēr'sing) *a.* keen; sharp.

PIETISM (pi'e-tizm) *n.* strong religious feeling.

PIETY (pi'e-ti) *n.* veneration with love of God; filial duty. [O.F. *pieté,* fr. L. (acc.) *pietatem,* fr. *pius,* **PIOUS**.]

PIG (pig) *n.* the young of swine; mass of metal. [E.]

PIGEON (pij'un) *n.* a dove. [F., fr. L. (acc.) *pipionem,* fr. *pipire,* to **PIPE**.]

PIGEON-HOLE (pij'un-hōl) *n.* a little division in a case for papers.

PIGMENT (pig'ment) *n.* a colour for painting. [L. *pigmentum,* fr. rt. of *pingere,* paint. See **PICTURE**.]

PIGMY (pig'mi) *n.* a dwarf. Also written **PYGMY**. [F. *pygmé,* fr. L., fr. G. *pugme,* measure of 13 inches.]

PIKE (pik) *n.* a lance; a fish. [O.E. *pic,* a point.]

PIKED (pikt) *a.* ending in a point.

PILASTER (pi-las'ter) *n.* a square column. [F., fr. It. *pilastro,* fr. L. *pila,* **PILE** (2).]

PILCHARD (pil'chard) *n.* a fish resembling the herring. [Etym. unknown.]

PILE (pil) (1) *n.* hair; fur; the fibre of wool or cotton; the nap;—(2) *n.* a mass or collection; a heap;—*v.t.* to throw into a pile or heap;—(3) *n.* a beam driven into the earth to support a building, bridge, etc.;—*v.t.* to drive piles into. [(1) L. *pilus,* hair. (2) O.E. *pil,* fr L. *pila,* **PILLAR**. (3) O.E. *pil,* a stake, fr. L. *pilum,* javelin.]

PILES (pilz) *n.pl.* tumour on the verge of the anus. [Fr. L. *pila,* ball.]

PILFER (pil'fer) *v.t.* or *i.* to steal small things or in small quantities. [O.F. *pelfrer;* conn. with **PELF**.]

PILFERER (pil'fer-er) *n.* one guilty of petty theft.

Fāte, fär, ado; mē, her; mine; nōte; tūne; moon.

PILGRIM (pil'grim) *n.* a traveller to holy places; a wanderer. [It. *pellegrino*, fr. L. *peregrinus*.]

PILGRIMAGE (pil'gri-mij) *n.* a journey to a place deemed sacred.

PILL (pil) *n.* a medicine in form of a little ball. [Short. fr. F. *pilule*, fr. L. (acc). *pilulam*, dim. fr. *pila*, ball.]

PILLAGE (pil'ij) *n.* that which is taken by force; plunder;—*v.t.* to plunder; spoil. [F., fr. *piller*, plunder, fr. L. *pilare*.]

PILLAR (pil'ar) *n.* a stone column; anything that supports. [O.F. *piler*, fr. Late L. *pilare*, fr. *pila*, **PILE** (2).]

PILLION (pil'yun) *n.* a cushion for a female to ride on. [Through F. =saddle-cloth, fr. L. *pellis*, skin.]

PILLORY (pil'u-ri) *n.* a frame to confine criminals by the neck and hands;—*v.t.* to put in the pillory; expose to public abuse. [F. *pilori*, of unknown etym.]

PILLOW (pil'ō) *n.* a cushion for the head;—*v.t.* to rest on a pillow. [M.E. *pilwe*, fr. O.E. *pyle*, fr. L. *pulvinus*, cushion.]

PILLOWCASE (pil'ō-kās) *n.* a cloth cover for a pillow.

PILOSE (pī'lōs) *a.* hairy. Also **PILOUS**.

PILOT (pī'lut) *n.* one who steers a ship;—*v.t.* to steer; guide. [O.F. *pilot*, *pedot*, through It., fr. G. *pedon*, oar.]

PILOTAGE (pī'lu-tij) *n.* the pay or office of a pilot.

PIMP (pimp) *n.* a pander;—*v.i.* to pander. [F. *pimper*, dress up; conn. with **PIMPLE**.]

PIMPLE (pim'pl) *n.* a small pointed elevation on the skin. [Etym. doubtful.]

PIN (pin) *n.* a pointed instrument; peg; bolt; thing of no value;—*v.t.* to fasten with a pin. [O.E. *pinn*, fr. L. *pinna*, feather.]

PINAFORE (pin'a-fōr) *n.* a little apron. [Fr. **PIN** and **AFORE**.]

PINCH (pinsh) *v.t.* to squeeze;—*n.* a squeezing or gripe; a difficulty. [F. *pincer*, perh. fr. Teut.]

PINCHBECK (pinsh'bek) *n.* a yellow mixture of copper and zinc. [Fr. the name of a London watchmaker.]

PINCHERS (pinsh'erz) *n.pl.* a tool for drawing nails. Also written **PINCERS**.

PINCUSHION (pin'kŏŏsh-un) *n.* a pad for pins.

PINE (pin) (1) *n.* a forest-tree;—(2) *v.i.* to languish. [(1) O.E. *pin*, fr. L. *pinus*. (2) Fr. O.E. *pin*, **PAIN**, fr. L. *pœna*, punishment.]

PINEAPPLE (pin'ap-l) *n.* a fruit which resembles the cone of pines.

PINION (pin'yun) *n.* wing of a fowl; a small toothed wheel; fetter;—*v.t.* to bind the wings or arms. [O.F. *pignon*, fr. L. *pinna*, feather.]

PINK (pingk) *n.* a fragrant flower; a light red colour; a small eye; the minnow;—*a.* flesh-coloured;—*v.t.* to pierce with small holes; scollop; stab. [M.E. *pinken*, prick; form of **PICK**.]

PIN-MONEY (pin'mun-i) *n.* a wife's pocket-money.

PINNACE (pin'as) *n.* a small vessel; a boat with eight oars. [F. *pinasse*, fr. It., fr. L. *pinus*, **PINE** (1), fr. the material used.]

PINNACLE (pin'a-kl) *n.* turret; summit; highest point. [F., fr. dim., fr. L. *pinna*, a feather, peak.]

PINNATE (pin'āt) *a.* shaped like a feather. [L., fr. *pinna*, feather.]

PINT (pint) *n.* half a quart. [O.F. *pinte*, fr. Late L. (acc.) *pinctam*, lit. a part of a measure marked off, fr. (part.) *pictus*, painted. See **PICTURE**.]

PIONEER (pī-u-nēr') *n.* one who goes before to clear the way. [O.F., fr. *peon*, foot-soldier.]

PIOUS (pī'us) *a.* religious; godly. [Fr. L. *pius*.]

PIP (pip) (1) *n.* a disease in fowls;—(2) *n.* the seed of an apple, orange, etc;—(3) *v.i.* to chirp as a chick. [(1) O.F., fr. Late L. *pipita*, fr. L. *pipuita*, slime, phlegm. (2) Short. fr. **PIPPIN**. (3) Form of **PIPE** (2).]

PIPE (pip) (1) *n.* a wind instrument; the voice; any long, hollow tube; cask;—(2) *v.t.* or *i.* to play on or call with a pipe. [(1) O.E. *pipe*, fr. L. *pipa*. (2) L. *pipare*.]

PIPECLAY (pip'klā) *n.* a kind of white clay.

PIPING (pī'ping) *a.* boiling; feeble; sickly.

PIPKIN (pip'kin) *n.* a small earthen boiler. [Dim. of **PIPE** = wine-measure.]

PIPPIN (pip'in) *n.* a species of apple. [F. *pepin*, seed of fruit, perh. fr. G. *pepon*, melon.]

PIQUANCY (pē'kan-si) *n.* sharpness; severity.

PIQUANT (pē'kant) *a.* stimulating to the taste; sharp; lively; pungent. [F.]

PIQUANTLY (pē'kant-li) *ad.* in a piquant manner.

PIQUE (pēk) *n.* resentment of an offence; wounded pride;—*v.t.* to touch with pride or envy; excite to action. [F.]

PIQUET (pi-ket') *n.* a game at cards. [F.]

PIRACY (pī'ra-si) *n.* robbery on the seas; literary theft.

PIRATE (pī'rat) *n.* one that robs on the seas; —*v.t.* or *i.* to rob on the sea; take without permission. [F., fr. L. *pirata*, fr. G. *pirates*, one who attempts, fr. *peiraein*, attempt.]

PIRATICAL (pi-rat'i-kal) *a.* practising piracy.

PIRATICALLY (pi-rat'i-kal-i) *ad.* in a piratical manner.

PIRN (pern) *n.* a bobbin; reel. [Etym. doubtful.]

PIROGUE (pi-rōg') *n.* a canoe formed of the

Pirogue.

trunk of a tree. [F., fr. W. Ind. native name.]

PIROUETTE (pir-ŏŏ-et') *n.* a rapid whirling on the toes in ballet dancing;—*v.i.* to turn about. [F.]

PISCATORIAL (pis-ka-tō'ri-al) *a.* that relates to fish or fishing. Also **PISCATORY**. [Fr. L. *piscator*, fisher.]

PISTACHIO (pis-tā'shi-ō) *n.* a small Syrian tree; its fragrant edible nut. [Sp., fr. G. *pistakion*, fr. Per.]

PISTIL (pis'til) *n.* the seed-bearing organ of a plant. [L. *pistillum*, a pestle, fr. (part.) *pistus*, pounded, fr. *pinsere*.]

PISTOL (pis'tul) *n.* the smallest of fire-arms; —*v.t.* to shoot with a pistol. [F., fr. It., fr. *Pistola* or *Pistoia*, in Italy, where first made.]

PISTOLE (pis'tul) *n.* a gold coin of Spain, worth about sixteen shillings sterling. [F. *pistolet*, lit. a little **PISTOL**.]

PISTON (pis'tun) *n.* a short cylinder fitted to a hollow one within which it moves. [F. =*pestle*, fr. Late L. *pistare*, pound, fr. L. (part.) *pistus*. See **PISTIL**.]

PIT (pit) *n.* a deep hole; any hollow or indentation; floor of a theatre;—*v.t.* to lay in a pit; mark with pits; set in competition. [O.E. *pyt*, fr. L. *puteus*.]

PITAPAT (pit'a-pat) *n.* a light, quick step;— *ad.* in a fluttering manner. [A reduplication of PAT.]

PITCH (pich) *n.* a substance which exudes from the pine or obtained from boiling down tar;—*v.t.* to smear with pitch. [M.E. *pich*, fr. O.E. *pic*, fr. L.]

PITCH (pich) *n.* point or degree of elevation or depression;—*v.t.* to throw or hurl; fix or set in array; strike the keynote of a tune;—*v.i.* to settle; fall headlong; rise and fall, as a ship. [Form of PICK.]

PITCHER (pich'er) *n.* a vessel with a spout for holding water. [O.F. *picher*, fr. Late L. *picarium*, a goblet.]

PITCHFORK (pich'fork) *n.* a fork to throw sheaves.

PITCHPIPE (pich'pip) *n.* an instrument to give the keynote.

PITEOUS (pit'e-us) *a.* that may excite pity; sorrowful; compassionate; paltry. [M.E. *pitous.*]

PITEOUSLY (pit'e-us-li) *ad.* in a piteous manner.

PITFALL (pit'fawl) *n.* a pit slightly covered, as a trap.

PITH (pith) *n.* the soft substance in plants; strength or force. [O.E. *pitha.*]

PITHILY (pith'i-li) *ad.* with brief energy.

PITHY (pith'i) *a.* consisting of pith; energetic; forcible.

PITIABLE (pit'i-a-bl) *a.* deserving pity; lamentable; wretched.

PITIFUL (pit'i-fool) *a.* compassionate; despicable.

PITIFULLY (pit'i-fool-i) *ad.* in a pitiful manner; contemptibly.

PITILESS (pit'i-les) *a.* void of pity.

PITSAW (pit'saw) *n.* a large saw to be used vertically by two men.

PITTANCE (pit'ans) *n.* a small allowance or portion. [F. *pitance*, allowance of food in a monastery, fr. L. *pietas*, pity.]

PITY (pit'i) *n.* sympathy for another's distresses; compassion;—*v.t.* to have sympathy for. [O.F. *pite* = F. *pitié*, fr. L. (acc.) *pietatem*. Doublet of PIETY.]

PIVOT (piv'ut) *n.* a pin on which anything turns. [F., fr. Low L. *pipa*, a PIPE, through it.]

PLACABILITY (plak-a-bil'i-ti) *n.* quality of being placable. Also **PLACABLENESS.**

PLACABLE (plak'a-bl) *a.* capable of being pacified or appeased. [L. *placabilis*, fr. *placare*, pacify.]

PLACARD (pla-kård', plak'ard) *n.* a printed paper posted in a public place;—*v.t.* to notify publicly. [F., fr. *plaque*.]

PLACE (plås) *n.* a portion of space; rank; office; room; residence; stead; passage in a book;—*v.t.* to put in a particular spot, or condition; settle; invest; ascribe. [F., fr. L. *platea*, a broad way, fr. G., fr. *platus*, flat, broad.]

PLACEMAN (plås'man) *n.* one holding an office under government.

PLACID (plas'id) *a.* pleased; serene; gentle. [L. *placidus*, fr. *placere*, please.]

PLACIDITY (pla-sid'i-ti) *n.* calmness; unruffled state or disposition.

PLACIDLY (plas'id-li) *ad.* calmly; mildly.

PLAGIARISM (plå'ji-a-rizm) *n.* literary theft. [F., fr. L. *plagiarius*, a kidnapper, fr. *plaga*, snare.]

PLAGIARIST (plå'ji-a-rist) *n.* one who purloins the writings of another.

PLAGUE (plåg) *n.* a contagious disease; anything that troubles;—*v.t.* to trouble; vex. [O.F.—F. *plaie*, fr. L. (acc.) *plagam*, blow, stroke, fr. G. *plege*.]

PLAGUY (plå'gi) *a.* vexatious; annoying.

PLAICE (plås) *n.* a flat fish allied to the flounder. [O.F. *plais*, fr. L., fr. G. rt. of *platus*, broad. See PLACE.]

PLAIN (plån) (1) *a.* level; smooth; simple; open; evident; sincere; bare; coarse; not seasoned or ornamented;—*n.* level land; field of battle;—*v.i.* or *i.* to level; —*ad.* distinctly; simply;—(2) *v.t.* or *i.* to lament. [(1) F., fr. L. *planus*. (2) Short. fr. COMPLAIN.]

PLAINLY (plån'li) *ad.* sincerely; bluntly; clearly.

PLAINNESS (plån'nes) *n.* flatness; clearness; want of ornament.

PLAINT (plånt) *n.* a complaint; cry of distress. [O.F. *pleinte*, fr. L. (acc.) *planctam*, lit. (part.) bewailed, fr. *plangere*.]

PLAINTIFF (plån'tif) *n.* he who commences a lawsuit. [F. *plaintif*.]

PLAINTIVE (plån'tiv) *a.* mournful; sad.

PLAIT (plåt) *n.* a fold, as of cloth; braid, as of hair;—*v.t.* to fold; braid; interweave. [O.F. *pleit*, fr. Late L., fr. L. (part.) *plicatus*, folded. See COMPLICATE.]

PLAN (plan) *n.* draught; anything devised; a scheme;—*v.t.* to make a sketch of; scheme; contrive in thought. [F., fr. *plan*, flat, fr. L. (acc.) *planum*. See PLAIN (1).]

PLANCH (plansh) *v.t.* to plank.

PLANE (plån) *n.* a level surface; a joiner's tool;—*v.t.* to smooth with a plane;—*a.* even; level. [F. (fem) *plane*, flat. See PLAN.]

PLANET (plan'et) *n.* a celestial body revolving about another. [O.F. *planete*, fr. L., fr. G. *planetes*, wanderer.]

PLANETARY (plan'e-ta-ri) *a.* pertaining to, or consisting of, planets.

PLANE-TREE (plån'trē) *n.* a tall tree with large broad leaves. [F., fr. L. *platanus*, plane-tree, fr. G., fr. *platus*, broad.]

PLANISPHERE (plan'i-sfēr) *n.* a sphere projected on a plane, as a map.

PLANK (plangk) *n.* a thick, strong board;— *v.t.* to cover with planks. [O.F. *planke* = F. *planche*, fr. L. *planca*.]

PLANT (plånt) *n.* an organic vegetable production; tree; herb; sprout; fixtures; machinery; tools; a fraudulent device;— *v.t.* to set in the earth; settle. [O.E. *plante*, fr. L. *planta*.]

PLANTAIN (plan'tån) *n.* a West Indian tree and its fruit; an astringent herb. [F., fr. L. *plantago*, *plantaginis*.]

PLANTATION (plan-tå'shun) *n.* act of planting; place planted; a colony; a cultivated estate.

PLANTER (plån'ter) *n.* one who plants; one who owns a plantation.

PLANTICLE (plan'ti-kl) *n.* a plant in embryo.

PLANTIGRADE (plan'ti-grād) *a.* walking on the sole of the foot;—*n.* an animal that does so. [Fr. L. *planta*, sole, and *gradi*, walk.]

PLASH (plash) (1) *n.* a puddle of water;— *v.t.* to dabble in water;—(2) cut and interweave branches. [(1) E. (2) Form of PLEACH.]

PLASHY (plash'i) *a.* abounding in puddles; watery.

PLASM (plazm) *n.* a mould; a matrix used in casting. [G.]

PLASMA (plaz'ma) *n.* elementary matter from which organic tissues are developed. [G. See PLASTIC.]

PLASMATIC (plaz-mat'ik) *a.* giving shape.

PLASTER (plas'ter) *n.* a composition of lime, sand, and water; an adhesive salve;—*v.t.* to cover with plaster. [O.E., fr. L., fr. G. *emplastron*, a plaster; conn. with PLASTIC.]

PLASTERER (plas'ter-er) *n.* one who works in plaster.

PLASTERING (plas'ter-ing) *n.* a covering of plaster.

PLASTIC (plas'tik) *a.* giving form; capable of being formed; pertaining to moulding. [L., fr. G. *plastikos*, fr. *plassein*, mould.]

PLASTICITY (plas-tis'i-ti) *n.* the quality of being plastic.

PLAT (plat) (1) *v.t.* to interweave;—(2) *n.* a small level piece of ground. [(1) Form of PLAIT. (2) Form of PLOT (1).]

PLATE (plãt) *n.* a flat sheet of metal; wrought gold or silver articles; a round shallow dish; trencher; an engraved piece of metal; the impression from it;—*v.t.* to coat with metal; beat into thin plates. [O.F., fr. Low L. *platta*, a lamina.]

PLATEAU (pla-tō') *n.* broad, flat, elevated land; an ornamental centre dish. [F.]

PLATEFUL (plãt'fool) *n.* as much as a plate will hold.

PLATEGLASS (plãt'glas) *n.* a fine kind of glass cast in large thick plates.

PLATEMARK (plãt'märk) *n.* legal mark showing the quality of the metal.

PLATEN (plat'en) *n.* the flat part of a printing-press.

PLATFORM (plat'form) *n.* a floor of wood, stone, or earth, raised above the general level; groundwork of a plan; scheme of united policy or action. [F., fr. (fem.) *plate*, flat (see PLATE), and *forme*, FORM.]

PLATINUM (plat'i-num) *n.* a metal. [Through Sp., fr. O.F. *plate* = silver PLATE.]

PLATITUDE (plat'i-tūd) *n.* insipidity; a trite, empty remark. [F., fr. *plat*, flat. See PLATE.]

PLATONIC (pla-ton'ik) *a.* relating to Plato; intellectually refined.

PLATONISM (plā'tu-nizm) *n.* the philosophy of Plato.

PLATOON (pla-tóón') *n.* a small body of soldiers. [Fr. F. See PELLET.]

PLATTER (plat'er) *n.* a broad shallow dish.

PLAUDIT (plaw'dit) *n.* praise bestowed. [L. (imper.) *plaudite*, clap your hands, fr. *plaudere*, praise.]

PLAUSIBILITY (plaw-zi-bil'i-ti) *n.* speciousness; appearance of right.

PLAUSIBLE (plaw'zi-bl) *a.* adapted to satisfy or convince; specious. [L., fr. (part.) *plausus*, praised. See PLAUDIT.]

PLAUSIBLY (plaw'zi-bli) *ad.* with fair show.

PLAY (plā) *v.t.* or *i.* to sport; contend in a game; act; perform upon; put in motion; —*n.* any exercise for amusement or contest for victory; dramatic piece or performance; motion; room for motion. [O.E. *plega*, a game.]

PLAYBILL (plā'bil) *n.* advertisement of a play.

PLAYER (plā'er) *n.* one who plays.

PLAYFELLOW (plā'fel-ō) *n.* a companion in sports.

PLAYFUL (plā'fool) *a.* full of play; sportive.

PLAYFULNESS (plā'fool-nes) *n.* sportiveness.

PLAYHOUSE (plā'hous) *n.* a theatre.

PLAYMATE (plā'māt) *n.* a playfellow.

PLAYTHING (plā'thing) *n.* a toy.

PLEA (plē) *n.* what is alleged in proof or defence of a cause; a lawsuit; excuse; apology. [O.F. *plai*, fr. Late L. *placitum*, decree, fr. L. *placere*, seem good.]

PLEACH (plēch) *v.t.* to intertwine the branches of. [O.F., fr. L. *plectere*, to plait.]

PLEAD (plēd) *v.t.* or *i.* to allege or argue in support of or in defence against; offer in excuse; supplicate earnestly; admit or deny a charge. [O.F. *plaider*, fr. *plaid* = *plai*, PLEA.]

PLEADER (plē'der) *n.* one who pleads.

PLEADING (plē'ding) *a.* urging; imploring; —*n.* act or form of advocating;—*pl.* statements of the opposite counsel.

PLEASANT (plez'ant) *a.* gratifying; delightful; gay. [O.F. (part.) *plaisant* pleasing.]

PLEASANTLY (plez'ant-li) *ad.* in a pleasant manner; gaily.

PLEASANTRY (plez'ant-ri) *n.* cheerfulness; sprightly talk.

PLEASE (plēz) *v.t.* to give pleasure; delight; satisfy;—*v.i.* to choose; like. [O.F. *plaisir* = F. *plaire*, fr. L. *placere*.]

PLEASING (plē'zing) *a.* giving pleasure; agreeable; delightful. Also PLEASURABLE.]

PLEASURE (plezh'ur) *n.* gratification; delight; will; choice; thing done to please;—*v.t.* to please. [F. *plaisir*.]

PLEBEIAN (ple-bē'an) *a.* common; popular; —*n.* one of the common people. [F., fr. L. *plebeius*, pert. to the common people.]

PLEDGE (plej) *n.* security; surety; written promise;—*v.t.* to give as security; pawn. [O.F. *plege*, a surety, fr. Teut.]

PLEDGET (plej'et) *n.* a small tent of lint. [Dim. fr. PLUG.]

PLEIADS (plī'adz) *n.pl.* a cluster of seven stars in Taurus. [G.]

PLENARILY (plē'na-ri-li) *ad.* fully; entirely.

PLENARY (plē'na-ri) *a.* full; complete. [L., fr. *plenus*, full.]

PLENIPOTENCE (ple-nip'u-tens) *n.* fullness of power.

PLENIPOTENT (ple-nip'u-tent) *a.* of full power.

PLENIPOTENTIARY (plen-i-pō-ten'sha-ri) *a.* having full power;—*n.* an envoy invested with the highest powers. [Fr. L. *plenus*, full, and stem *potent*-, POTENT.]

PLENITUDE (plen'i-tūd) *n.* fullness; completeness.

PLENTEOUS (plen'tē-us) *a.* having plenty; fully sufficient; ample.

PLENTEOUSLY (plen'tē-us-li) *ad.* in abundance; copiously.

PLENTIFUL (plen'ti-fool) *a.* yielding plenty; copious; yielding full crops.

PLENTIFULLY (plen'ti-fool-i) *ad.* in great abundance.

PLENTIFULNESS (plen'ti-fool-nes) *n.* abundance.

PLENTY (plen'ti) *n.* full or adequate supply; abundance;—*a.* plentiful. [O.F. *plente*, fr. L. (acc.) *plenitatem*, fullness, fr. *plenus*, full.]

PLEONASM (plē'u-nazm) *n.* redundancy of words. [Fr. G. *pleion*, more.]

PLEONASTIC (plē-u-nas'tik) *a.* redundant.

PLETHORA (pleth'ō-ra) *n.* fullness of blood; repletion. G. =fullness, fr. *plethos*, a crowd.]

PLETHORIC (ple-thor'ik) *a.* having a full habit of body.

PLEURA (plóó'ra) *n.* the membrane that covers the inside of the thorax. [G. = side.]

PLEURISY (plóó'ri-si) *n.* inflammation of the pleura. [F. *pleurésie*, fr. L., fr. G. *pleuritis*.]

PLEURITIC (plóó-rit'ik) *a.* diseased with pleurisy.

PLEXIFORM (plek'si-form) *a.* like network. [Fr. L. *plexus*.]

PLIABILITY (plī-a-bil'i-ti) *n.* the quality of being pliable.

PLIABLE (plī'a-bl) *a.* easily bent; yielding readily. [F., fr. *plier*, PLY, fr. L. *plicare*.]

PLIANCY (plī'an-si) *n.* state of being pliant, morally or physically.

PLIANT (plī'ant) *a.* bending; easily bent; easily influenced or persuaded.

PLIERS (plī'erz) *n.pl.* an instrument to bend small things.

PLIGHT (plīt) *v.t.* to pledge, as the hand, faith, honour;—*n.* pledge; condition. [O.E. *pliht*, danger.]

PLIGHTER (plī'ter) *n.* one that pledges.

PLINTH (plinth) *n.* the square member at the base of a column. [G. *plinthos*, brick.]

PLOD (plod) *v.i.* to travel or work slowly but steadily. [E.]

PLODDER (plod'er) *n.* a dull, slow, laborious person.

PLODDING (plod'ing) *n.* a slow motion or study.

PLOT (plot) (1) *n.* a small piece of level ground; a plantation;—(2) *n.* any complicated plan or scheme;—*v.t.* or *i.* to plan; contrive; conspire. [(1) O.E. (2) Fr. F. *complot.*]

PLOTTER (plot'er) *n.* one who plots or contrives.

PLOTTING (plot'ing) *n.* act of contriving schemes or conspiracies; delineating on paper the lines of a survey.

PLOUGH (plou) *n.* an instrument to turn and break the soil;—*v.t.* to trench and turn up the ground. Also written PLOW. [O.E. *ploh*, plot. Cf. Ger. *Pflug.*]

PLOUGHMAN (plou'man) *n.* one who holds the plough.

PLOUGHSHARE (plou'shar) *n.* the iron blade of a plough. [Fr. PLOUGH, and O.E. *scear*, a share of a plough, a shearing, fr. *sceran*, to cut.]

PLOVER (pluv'er) *n.* a grallatorial bird. [F. *pluvier*, lit. rain-bird, fr. L. *pluvia.*]

PLUCK (pluk) *v.t.* to pull with sudden force; snatch; strip off;—*n.* the heart, liver, and lights of an animal; spirit; courage. [O.E. *pluccian.* Cf. Ger. *pflücken.*]

PLUG (plug) *n.* stopper of a hole in a vessel or cask;—*v.t.* to stop with a plug. [D.]

PLUM (plum) *n.* a garden tree and its fruit. [O.E. *plume*, fr. L. *prunum.* See PRUNE.]

PLUMAGE (plöö'mij) *n.* feathers of a bird. [F., fr. PLUME.]

PLUMB (plum) *n.* a leaden weight on a line; —*a.* perpendicular;—*v.t.* to adjust by a plumb line; sound the depth of. [L. *plumbum*, lead.]

PLUMBER (plum'er) *n.* one who works in lead.

PLUMBERY (plum'er-i) *n.* work done by a plumber.

PLUMBIC (plum'bik) *a.* pertaining to lead.

PLUMB-LINE (plum'lin) *n.* a perpendicular line.

PLUME (plöóm) *n.* a feather; token of honour; pride;—*v.t.* to adjust feathers; pride; value. [F., fr. L. (acc.) *plumam.*]

PLUMIPED (plöó'mi-ped) *n.* a bird that has feathers on its feet. [Fr. L. stem *ped-*, of *pes*, foot.]

PLUMMET (plum'et) *n.* a piece of lead for sounding; plumb-line. [O.F. *plommet*, *plombet.*]

PLUMP (plump) *a.* fat; sleek; full; round; —*v.t.* to fatten; swell;—*v.i.* to fall down; vote for one only;—*ad.* with a sudden fall. [Perh. D.]

PLUMPER (plum'per) *n.* a vote given to one candidate only; a deliberate lie.

PLUMPNESS (plump'nes) *n.* fatness; fullness of skin.

PLUNDER (plun'der) *v.t.* to take by pillage or open force; sack; rifle;—*n.* spoil taken by open force. [Ger., fr. *Plunder*, lumber, baggage.]

PLUNDERER (plun'der-er) *n.* a pillager.

PLUNGE (plunj) *v.t.* or *i.* to thrust or force into; dive; rush into; pitch; heave;— *n.* act of plunging. [F. *plonger*, through Late L., fr. L. *plumbum*, lead.]

PLUNGER (plun'jer) *n.* a diver; a cylinder used as a forcer of pumps; a heavy bettor at races.

PLURAL (plöó'ral) *a.* expressing more than one. [O.F. *plurel* = F. *pluriel*, fr. L. stem *plur-*, of *plus*, more.]

PLURALIST (plöó'ral-ist) *n.* one who holds more than one church benefice or office.

PLURALITY (plöö-ral'i-ti) *n.* state of being plural; two or more; the majority.

PLUSH (plush) *n.* a shaggy cloth. [F. *peluche*, fr. L. *pilus*, hair, through Late L.]

PLUTOCRACY (plöö-tok'ra-si) *n.* government by the rich classes. [Fr. G. *ploutos*, wealth, and *kratein*, rule.]

PLUTONIC THEORY (plöö-ton'ik thē'u-ri) *n.* the theory that the crust of the earth was formed by the action of fire. [L., fr. G. *Ploutonios*, fr. *Plouton*, Pluto, the god of the nether world.]

PLUVIAL (plöó'vi-al) *a.* rainy; wet. [F., fr. L. fr. *pluvia*, rain.]

PLUVIOMETER (plöó-vi-om'e-ter) *n.* an instrument for measuring the rainfall. G. *metron*, measure.

PLY (pli) *v.t.* or *i.* [*pret.* and *pp.* PLIED] to work at closely; urge; come and go between; —*n.* a fold or plait. [F. *plier*, fold, fr. *plicare.*]

PNEUMATIC (nū-mat'ik) *a.* relating to air; moved by air; relating to spiritual essence. [G. *pneumatikos*, fr. *pneuma*, wind, air.]

PNEUMATICS (nū-mat'iks) *n.pl.* the science of the air and other elastic fluids; doctrine of the soul and spiritual being.

PNEUMONIC (nū-mon'ik) *a.* pertaining to the lungs.

PNEUMONITIS (nū-mu-ni'tis) *n.* inflammation of the lungs. Also PNEUMONIA. [G., fr. *pneumon*, lung.]

POACH (pōch) (1) *v.t.* or *i.* to pierce; be swampy;—(2) *v.t.* or *i.* trespass and steal game;—(3) *v.t.* or *i.* dress eggs by breaking them in boiling water. [(1) O.F. (2) Etym. uncert. (3) F., of uncert. etym.]

POACHER (pō'cher) *n.* one who steals game.

POACHY (pō'chi) *a.* soft; wet.

POCK (pok) *n.* a pustule on the skin in smallpox. [O.E. *poc*, a pustule. Cf. Ger. *Pocke.*]

POCKET (pok'et) *n.* a small bag;—*v.t.* to put in the pocket. [F. *pochette*, dim of *poche*, pouch; Icel. *poki*, a bag.]

POCKET-BOOK (pok'et-book) *n.* a book to be carried in the pocket.

POCKY (pok'i) *a.* full of pustules.

POD (pod) *n.* capsule; seed-case;—*v.i.* to grow, as pods. [E.]

POEM (pō'em) *n.* a composition in verse. [L. *poema*, fr. G. *poiema*, lit. work, fr. *poiein*, make.]

POESY (pō'e-si) *n.* art of writing poems; metrical composition. [O.F. fr. L., fr. G. *poiesis.*]

POET (pō'et) *n.* one who writes poetry. [L. *poeta*, fr. G. *poietes*, maker.]

POETASTER (pō'et-as-ter) *n.* a poor or mediocre writer of verse.

POETESS (pō'et-es) *n.* a female poet.

POETICAL (pō-et'i-kal) *a.* written in verse; suitable to poetry.

POETISE (pō'et-iz) *v.i.* to compose verses.

POET-LAUREATE (pō'et-law'rē-at) *n.* the Court poet.

POETRY (pō'et-ri) *n.* any embodiment in rhythmical form of ideal beauty vivified by imagination or fancy, and by strong emotion; metrical composition; verse; collection of poems.

POIGNANCY (poi'nan-si) *n.* sharpness; point.

POIGNANT (poi'nant) *a.* piercing; pungent; very keen or painful. [F. (part.) =stinging, fr. *poindre*, prick, fr. L. *pungere.*]

POIGNANTLY (poi'nant-li) *ad.* with keen point.

POINT (point) *n.* a sharp end; a stop; dot; spot; place; degree; verge; object; end; gist of an argument; railway switch;— *v.t.* or *i.* to sharpen; direct; indicate; punctuate; fill with mortar, as stones in a wall. [O.F. *point*, pride, fr. L. *punctum*, fr. *pungere.*]

POINTED (poin'ted) *a.* having a sharp point; keen; direct.

POINTEDLY (poin'ted-li) *ad.* with point.

POINTER (poin'ter) *n.* an index; a dog.

POINTING (poin'ting) *n* punctuation; directing; filling with mortar.

POINTLACE (point'läs) *n.* a fine kind of lace.

POINTLESS (point'les) *a.* having no point.

POINTSMAN (points'man) *n.* a man who looks after the switches on railways.

POISE (poiz) *n* balance; that which balances; —*v.t.* to load with weight; balance; examine. [O.F *poiser*, fr. *pois*, weight, fr. L., fr. (part.) *pensus*, weighed, fr. *pendere*.]

POISON (poi'zn) *n.* anything deadly or malignant; —*v.t.* to infect with poison. [F., fr. L. (acc) *potionem*, fr. *potare*, to drink. Doublet of POTION.]

POISONOUS (poi'zn-us) *a.* having the qualities of poison.

POKE (pōk) (1) *n.* a pocket; a sack; — (2) *n.* thrust; push; —*v.t.* or *i.* to thrust at; search for; grope. [(1) Scand. (2) E.]

POKER (pō'kẹr) *n* an iron bar for stirring the fire.

POLAR (pō'lạr) *a.* pertaining to the poles.

POLARISATION (pō-lạr-i-zā'shun) *n.* act of polarising light.

POLARISE (pō'lạr-iz) *v.t.* to communicate polarity to.

POLARITY (pō-lar'i-ti) *n.* the property of having, or being influenced by, attractive or repellant points, called poles.

POLARY (pō'lạr-i) *a.* tending to a po.e.

POLE (pōl) (1) *n.* a long piece of wood; a measure of length; — (2) *n.* one of the extremities of the earth's axis; one of the points of attraction or repulsion in magnetic bodies; — (3) *n.* a native of Poland. [(1) O.E. *pal*, fr. L. *palus*, a stake. (2) O.F. *pol*, fr. L., fr. G. *polos*, pivot.]

POLE-AXE (pōl'aks) *n.* hatchet fixed on a long handle.

POLEMIC (po-lem'ik) *n.* a disputant; —*a.* controversial. [G. *polemikos*, pertaining to war, *polemos*.]

POLEMICS (po-lem'iks) *n pl.* history of dogmas and discussions in the Christian Church.

POLE-STAR (pōl'står) *n.* a star vertical to the pole of the earth.

POLICE (pu-lēs') *n.* government of a city; body of civil officers in a town or district. [F., fr. L. (acc.) *politiam*, government, fr. G., fr. *polis*, city.]

POLICED (pu-lēst') *a.* regulated by a system of laws.

POLICEMAN (pu-lēs'man) *n.* one of the ordinary civil force in a town or county.

POLICY (pol'i-si) (1) *n.* art or system of government; prudence; dexterity; —(2) contract of insurance. [(1) F., fr. L. *politia*. Doublet of POLICE. (2) F., fr. G. *polus*, many, and *plux*, *pluxhos*, fold.]

POLISH (pol'ish) *v.t.* or *i.* to make or become smooth and glossy; refine; —*n.* artificial gloss; elegance of manners. [F. (part.) *polissant*, polishing, fr. *polir*, fr. L. *polire*. See POLITE.]

POLISHER (pol'ish-ẹr) *n.* person or thing that polishes.

POLITE (pu-lit') *a.* polished; refined. [L. (part.) *politus*, polished. See POLISH.]

POLITELY (pu-lit'li) *ad.* genteelly; elegantly; with courtesy.

POLITENESS (pu-lit'nes) *n.* good breeding.

POLITIC (pol'i-tik) *a.* well-devised or adapted; judicious; prudent. [G. *politikos*. See POLICE.]

POLITICAL (pu-lit'i-kạl) *a.* relating to public affairs or to politics.

POLITICALLY (pu-lit'i-kạl-i) *ad.* with reference to a state or to politics.

POLITICIAN (pol-i-tish'ạn) *n.* one versed in politics.

POLITICS (pol'i-tiks) *n.pl.* the science of government.

POLITY (pol'i-ti) *n.* form or constitution of civil government.

POLKA (pōl'kạ) *n.* a fashionable dancẹ; the music played for it; a short jacket worn by females. [Pol.]

POLL (pōl) *n.* the head; register of electors; election; place of election; —*v.t.* to lop; clip; register; bring to the voting place; —*v.i.* to vote. [Teut.]

POLLARD (pol'ạrd) *n.* a tree lopped, that it may throw out branches. [Fr. POLL.]

POLLED (pōld) *a.* wanting horns, as black cattle.

POLLEN (pol'en) *n.* the fecundating dust of plants. [L. =fine flour.]

POLL-TAX (pōl'taks) *n.* a tax levied by the poll or head.

POLLUTE (po-lūt') *v.t.* to make foul or unclean; profane; violate. [L. (part.) *pollutus*, defiled, fr. *polluere*.]

POLLUTION (po-lū'shun) *n.* defilement; impurity.

POLO (pō'lō) *n.* a game, like hockey, played on horseback. [E. Ind.]

POLONY (pu-lō'ni) *n.* a kind of meat sausage. [Fr. *Bologna*, where first made.]

POLTROON (pol-trōon') *n.* a coward. [F. = sluggard, fr. It.]

POLTROONERY (pol-trōon'e-ri) *n.* want of spirit or courage.

POLYANTHUS (pol-i-an'thus) *n.* a variety of the primrose, or its flower. [L., fr. G.]

POLYGAMIST (po-lig'ạ-mist) *n.* one who vindicates polygamy.

POLYGAMY (po-lig'ạ-mi) *n.* plurality of wives or husbands at the same time. [Fr. G. *polus*, many, and *gamos*, marriage.]

POLYGLOT (pol'i-glot) *n.* a book or version of the same text in several languages. [Fr. G. *polus*, many, and *glotta*, tongue.]

POLYGON (pol'i-gon) *n.* a figure of many angles and sides. [Fr. G. *polus*, many, and *gonia*, angle.]

POLYGONAL (po-lig'u-nạl) *a.* of many angles.

POLYGRAPH (pol'i-graf) *n.* an instrument to multiply copies of a writing.

POLYGRAPHY (po-lig'rạ-fi) *n.* the art of writing in various ciphers. [Fr. G. *polus*, many, and *graph-ein*, to write.]

Polygon.

POLYHEDRON (pol-i-hē'drun) *n.* a body having many sides. [Fr. G. *polus*, many, and *hedra*, seat, base.]

POLYPUS (pol'i-pus) *n.* an animal with many feet; a tumour. [L.]

POLYSYLLABIC (pol-i-si-lab'ik) *a.* having many syllables.

POLYSYLLABLE (pol-i-sil'ạ-bl) *n.* a word of more syllables than three.

POLYTECHNIC (pol-i-tek'nik) *a.* comprehending many arts. [G. *polus*, many, and *techne*, an art.]

POLYTHEISM (pol'i-thē-izm) *n.* the doctrine of a plurality of gods. [G. *polus*, many, and *theos*, a god.]

POLYTHEIST (pol'i-thē-ist) *n.* one who believes in a plurality of gods.

POLYTHEISTIC (pol'i-thē-is'tik) *a.* pertaining to polytheism.

POMACE (pom'is) *n.* substance of apples crushed. [Fr. L. *pomum*, apple.]

POMANDER (pō-man'dẹr) *n.* a perfumed ball or powder. [O.F. *pomme d'ambre*, lit. apple of AMBER.]

POMATUM (pu-mā'tum) *n.* an unguent for the hair. [F. *pommade*, fr. L. *pomum*, apple, through It.]

POMEGRANATE (pom'gran-ạt) *n.* a tree and its fruit. [F., fr. It., fr. L. *pomum*, fruit, and *granatus*, having many seeds.]

POMMEL (pum'el) *n.* a knob on a saddle bow, or hilt of a sword; —*v.t.* to beat; thump. [O.F. =orig. small apple, fr. L. *pomum*.]

POMOLOGY (po-mol'ō-ji) *n.* the art of raising fruit. [Fr. G. -*logia*, fr. *legein*, discourse.]

POMP (pomp) *n.* procession or show of grandeur or splendour. [F., fr. L., fr. G. *pompe*, procession, fr. *pempein*, send.]

POMPON (pom′pon) *n.* an ornamental tuft on a military cap. [F.]

POMPOSITY (pom-pos′i-ti) *n.* act or state of being pompous.

POMFOUS (pom′pus) *a.* showing grandeur; dignified; ostentatious; boastful.

POMPOUSLY (pom′pus-li) *ad.* with parade or display.

POND (pond) *n.* a body of standing water. [E.; conn. with **POUND** (3).]

PONDER (pon′dẹr) *v.t.* to think upon deliberately; weigh in the mind; consider. [L. *ponderare*, weigh over, fr. stem *ponder-*, of *pondus*, weight.]

PONDEROSITY (pon-dẹr-os′i-ti) *n.* weight; gravity.

PONDEROUS (pon′dẹr-us) *a.* heavy; massy; momentous; forcible.

PONIARD (pon′yård) *n.* a small dagger. [F. *poignard*, fr. *poign*, fist, fr. L. (acc.) *pugnum*.]

PONTIFF (pon′tif) *n.* a high priest; the pope. [F., fr. L. *pontifex*.]

PONTIFICAL (pon-tif′i-kạl) *a.* belonging to a high priest; —*n.* a book of rites and forms; —*pl.* the full dress of a pontiff.

PONTIFICATE (pon-tif′i-kạt) *n.* office of high priest; office or reign of the pope.

PONTOON (pon-tŏŏn′) *n.* a floating bridge or bridge of boats, used by armies in crossing rivers. [F., fr. L. (acc.) *pontonem*, of *ponto*, a boat.]

PONY (pō′ni) *n.* a small horse. [O.F. *poulenet*, little colt, fr. Late L., fr. L. *pullus*, colt.]

POODLE (pŏŏ′dl) *n.* a lap-dog. [Ger.]

POOH (pŏŏ) *ex.* of disdain. [imit.]

POOL (pŏŏl) (1) *n.* a small pond; —(2) *n.* stakes at cards; a kind of game in billiards. [(1) O.E. *pol.* Cf. Ger. *Pfuhl.* (2) F. *poule*, hen, stakes being regarded as eggs to be gained from the hen.]

POOP (pŏŏp) *n.* the stern of a ship; —*v.t.* to strike upon the stern. [F., fr. L. *puppis*.]

POOR (pŏŏr) *a.* lean; indigent; mean; unfertile; trifling; contrite. [O.F. *povre*, fr. L. (acc.) *pauperem.* Doublet of **PAUPER**.]

POORLY (pŏŏr′li) *ad.* without wealth; with poor success; meanly; —*a.* somewhat ill.

POORNESS (pŏŏr′nes) *a.* state of being poor.

POP (pop) *n.* a smart quick sound; —*v.t.* or *i.* to dart suddenly; offer suddenly. [imit.]

POPE (pōp) *n.* the head of the Roman Catholic Church. [O.E. *papa*, fr. L. *papa.* See **PAPAL**.]

POPEDOM (pōp′dom) *n.* the dignity or jurisdiction of the pope.

POPERY (pō′pẹr-i) *n.* the Roman Catholic religion.

POPINJAY (pop′in-jā) *n.* a parrot; a woodpecker; a fop. [F. *papegai*, a parrot.]

POPISH (pō′pish) *a.* relating to the pope or popery.

POPLIN (pop′lin) *n.* a stuff of silk and worsted. [F. *popeline*.]

POPPY (pop′i) *n.* a soporific plant. [O.E. *popæg*, fr. L. *papaver*.]

POPULACE (pop′ū-lạs) *n.* the people. [F. fr. It., fr. *popolo*, **PEOPLE**.]

POPULAR (pop′ū-lạr) *a.* pleasing to the people; prevailing; plain. [L. *popularis*, pertaining to the **PEOPLE**, *populus*.]

POPULARISE (pop′ū-lạr-iz) *n.* to make suitable and familiar to the common mind.

POPULARITY (pop-ū-lạr′i-ti) *n.* public favour.

POPULARLY (pop-ū-lạr-li) *ad.* with general favour.

POPULATE (pop′ū-lāt) *v.t.* to furnish with inhabitants.

POPULATION (pop-ū-lā′shun) *n.* the whole people of a place or country.

POPULOUS (pop′ū-lus) *a.* full of people.

POPULOUSNESS (pop′ū-lus-nes) *n.* the state of being populous.

PORCELAIN (pors′lān) *n.* finest species of earthenware. [F., fr. It. *porcellana*, a delicate shell-fish, shaped like a pig's back, fr. L. *porcus*, pig.]

PORCH (pōrch) *n.* an entrance to a building; a portico. [F., fr. L. *porticus*, gallery. See **PORTICO**.]

PORCUPINE (por′kū-pin) *n.* an animal with a bristly hide and erectile quills. [Through F., fr. L. *porcus*, pig, and *spina*, **SPINE**.]

PORE (pōr) *n.* a passage in the skin; a small hole; —(2) *v.i.* to look steadily. [(1) F., fr. L., fr. G. *poros*, passage. (2) Cp. Sw. *pora*, to work slowly.]

PORK (pōrk) *n.* the flesh of swine. [F. *porc*, fr. L. (acc.) *porcum*, pig.]

POROSITY (pō-ros′i-ti) *n.* the quality of having pores. Also **POROUSNESS**.

POROUS (pō′rus) *a.* having pores.

PORPHYRITIC (por-fi-rit′ik) *a.* resembling porphyry.

PORPHYRY (por′fi-ri) *n.* a fine speckled marble. [L. *porphyrites*, fr. G., fr. *porphura*, the **PURPLE** fish.]

PORPOISE (por′pus) *n.* a sea fish of the whale family. [O.F. *porpeis*, fr. L. *porcus*, hog, *piscis*, fish.]

PORRIDGE (por′ij) *n.* a mixture of meal or flour and water or milk boiled. [Form of **POTTAGE**.]

PORT (pōrt) (1) *n.* a harbour; —(2) *n.* a gate; —(3) *n.* mien; demeanour; —(4) *n.* wine from Oporto; —(5) *n.* the larboard or left side of a ship; —*v.t.* to turn to the left, as the helm. [(1) O.E. *port*, fr. L. *portus.* (2) F., fr. L. *porta.* (3) F., fr. *porter*, carry, fr. L. *portare.* (5) Etym. obscure.]

PORTABLE (pōr′tạ-bl) *a.* that may be carried.

PORTAGE (pōr′tij) *n.* carrying; price of carriage.

PORTAL (pōr′tạl) *n.* a small gate; the framework of a gateway; arch over it.

PORTCULLIS (pōrt-kul′is) *n.* a framework of crossed timbers for obstructing a passage. [F. *porte coulisse*, through Late L., fr. L. *porta*, gate, and *colare*, to glide.]

PORT-DUES (pōrt′dūz) *n.pl.* rates leviable on goods entering or leaving a port.

PORTE (pōrt) *n.* the Ottoman court. [F.]

PORTEND (pōr-tend′) *v.t.* to indicate the future; forebode. [L., fr. *por-*, forth, and *tendere*, to stretch.]

PORTENT (por′-tent) *n.* an omen of ill.

PORTENTOUS (por-ten′tus) *a.* foreshadowing evil; monstrous.

PORTER (pōr′tẹr) *n.* a door-keeper; a carrier; a kind of malt liquor.

PORTERAGE (pōr′tẹr-ij) *n.* money for carriage.

PORTFOLIO (pōrt-fō′li-ō) *n.* a portable case for papers.

PORT-HOLE (pōrt′hōl) *n.* an opening in a ship's side for cannon, or for air, light, etc.

PORTICO (pōr′ti-kō) *n.* a covered space or entrance enclosed by columns; —*pl.* **PORTICOES**. [It., fr. L. *porticus*, fr. *porta*, gate.]

PORTION (pōr′shun) *v.t.* to divide; allot; endow; —*n.* part assigned; share; wife's fortune. [F., fr. L. *portio*.]

PORTLINESS (pōrt′li-nes) *n.* dignity of mien or personal appearance.

PORTLY (pōrt′li) *a.* having an imposing form or carriage of body.

PORTMANTEAU (pōrt-man′tō) *n.* a leathern bag for carrying apparel on a journey. [See **PORT** (3), and **MANTLE**.]

PORTRAIT (pōr′trạt) *n.* a picture or likeness of a person; description in words. [O.F. *pourtrait*, orig. (part.) portrayed.]

PORTRAY (pōr-trā′) *v.t.* to paint the likeness of; describe. [F. *pourtraire*, fr. L. *protrahere*, draw forth.]

PORTRAYAL (por-trā′ạl) *n.* the act or art of portraying.

PORTRAYER (pŏr-trā'ẹr) *n.* one who paints or describes.

POSE (pōz) *n.* attitude; assumed or affected position;—*v.t.* to stand or sit with a view to effect; puzzle by questioning. [F., fr. *poser*, place, fr. Late L. *pausare*, fr. L. *pausa*, PAUSE.]

POSITION (pō-zish'un) *n.* situation; attitude; station; proposition or principle in reasoning; social condition. [F., fr. L., fr. (part.) *positus*, placed, fr. *ponere*.]

POSITIVE (poz'i-tiv) *a.* explicit; direct; actual; real; confident; absolute; decisive. [L. *positivus*, fr. (part.) *positus*, set, fr. *ponere*.]

POSITIVELY (poz'i-tiv-li) *ad.* in a positive manner.

POSITIVISM (poz'i-tiv-izm) *n.* system or doctrine which limits man's knowledge to the positive phenomena in nature, their laws and relations.

POSSESS (pu-zes') *v.t.* to have or hold as one's own; seize; inform. [L. (part.) *possessus*, possessed, fr. *possidere*.]

POSSESSION (pu-zesh'un) *n.* the state of owning; the thing possessed.

POSSESSIVE (pu-zes'iv) *a.* denoting possession.

POSSESSOR (pu-zes'ẹr) *n.* the person who holds or occupies.

POSSET (pos'et) *n.* milk curdled with wine or other liquors. [O.F. *possette*. Cf. W. *posel*, curdled milk, posset.]

POSSIBILITY (pos-i-bil'i-ti) *n.* the power of being or doing.

POSSIBLE (pos'i-bl) *a.* that may be, happen, or be done. [F., fr. L. *possibilis*.]

POSSIBLY (pos'i-bli) *ad.* peradventure; perchance.

POST (pōst) (1) in compounds, signifies *after*; —(2) *n.* a piece of timber; pillar;—(3) place; stage; office; messenger; mail; a sort of writing paper;—*v.t.* to station; put in the post office; transfer to the ledger; —*v.i.* to travel with speed. [(1) L. (2) O.E., fr. L. *postis*. (3) F. *poste*, through It., fr. L. (part.) *positus* set, fr. *ponere*.]

POSTAGE (pōs'tij) *n.* money paid for conveyance of letters.

POSTAL (pōs'tạl) *a.* belonging to the post office.

POST-CHAISE (pōst'shāz) *n.* a travelling carriage.

POST-DATE (pōst-dāt') *v.t.* to date after the true time.

POSTDILUVIAN (pōst-di-lū'vi-ạn) *a.* being after the deluge. [POST, after, and *diluvium*, flood.]

POSTER (pōs'tẹr) *n.* a courier; a large bill or placard.

POSTERIOR (pos-tē'ri-ur) *a.* later in time or order; subsequent. [L. (comp.) fr. *posterus*, after, fr. POST.]

POSTERIORS (pos-tē'ri-urs) *n.pl.* the hinder parts of an animal.

POSTERITY (pos-ter'i-ti) *n.* descendants. [F., fr. L. *posteritas*, fr. *posterus*, after.]

Postern.

POSTERN (pos'tẹrn) *a.* back; private;—*n.* back gate; door under a rampart. [F. = back door, fr. L. *posterus*.]

POSTFIX (pōst'fiks) *n.* a letter or syllable added; an affix.

POSTFIX (pōst-fiks') *v.t.* to annex at the end.

POSTHASTE (pōst-hāst') *ad.* as fast as possible.

POSTHUMOUS (pos'tū-mus) *a.* being after one's decease. [Corr. (through confusion with L. *humus*, ground, grave), L. (superl.) *postumus*, latest (born).]

POSTILION (pōs-til'yun) *n.* one who rides a coach horse. [F., fr. It., fr. *postal* POST.]

POSTMASTER (pōst'mȧs-tẹr) *n.* one who superintends a post office.

POSTMERIDIAN (pōst-me-rid'i-ạn) *a.* being in the afternoon.

POST-OFFICE (pōst'of-is) *n.* a place where mail letters are received and distributed.

POSTPONE (pōst-pōn') *v.t.* to put off; delay. [L., fr. *post*, and *ponere*, put.]

POSTPONEMENT (pōst-pōn'ment) *n.* a putting off; temporary delay.

POSTSCRIPT (pōst'skript) *n.* a part added to a writing. [L., fr. *post*, after, and (neut. part.) *scriptum*, written, fr. *scribere*.]

POSTULATE (pos'tū-lāt) *n.* anything assumed without proof;—*v.t.* to assume without proof; demand. [L. (part.) *postulatus*, demanded, fr. *postulare*, fr. *poscere*, to ask.]

POSTULATION (pos-tū-lā'shun) *n.* an assumption without proof.

POSTURE (pos'tūr) *n.* attitude; position; situation. [F., fr. L. *positura*, placing, fr. (part.) *positus*, set, fr. *ponere*.]

POSY (pō'zi) *n.* a motto on a ring; a nosegay; —*pl.* POSIES. [Form of POESY.]

POT (pot) *n.* a metallic or earthen vessel; a quart; a size of paper (generally written POTT);—*v.t.* to put into or preserve in pots. [O.E. *pott*.]

POTABLE (pō'tạ-bl) *a.* fit for drinking. [L., fr. *potare*, drink.]

POTASH (pot'ash) *n.* an alkaline salt from the ashes of plants. [Fr. POT and ASH.]

POTATION (pō-tā'shun) *n.* a drinking; excessive draught.

POTATO (pō-tā'tō) *n.* an esculent root. [Sp. *patata*, fr. Hayti *batata*, yam.]

POTENCY (pō'ten-si) *n.* power, strength, or efficacy.

POTENT (pō'tent) *a.* having great power, authority, or influence; puissant; powerful; efficient. [L. (part. stem) *potent-*, of *potens*, powerful, fr. *posse*, to be able.]

POTENTATE (pō'ten-tāt) *n.* any one having or exercising great power.

POTENTIAL (pō-ten'shạl) *a.* having possible or latent power; expressing power.

POTENTIALLY (pō-ten'shạl-i) *ad.* in possibility, not in act.

POTENTLY (pō'tent-li) *ad.* powerfully.

POTHER (poṭH'ẹr) *n.* confusion; stir. [Form of POTTER.]

POT-HERB (pot'ẹrb) *n.* any vegetable used in cookery.

POT-HOOK (pot'hook) *n.* a hook on which pots are hung over the fire; a scrawled letter.

POTION (pō'shun) *n.* a draught; a liquid medicine. [F., fr. L. (acc.) *potionem*, fr. *potus*, drunken. Doublet of POISON.]

POT-LUCK (pot'luk) *n.* whatever may be provided for dinner.

POTSHERD (pot'sherd) *n.* a piece of a broken pot. [Fr. O.F. *sceard*, a SHRED.]

POTTAGE (pot'ij) *n.* porridge. [F. *potage*, soup, fr. *pot*, POT, fr. Teut.]

POTTER (pot'ẹr) (1) *n.* one who makes earthen vessels;—(2) *v.i.* to busy about trifles. [(1) See POT. (2) Fr. Prov. E. *put*, to thrust.]

POTTERY (pot'ẹr-i) *n.* the wares of a potter.

POTTLE (pot'l) *n.* a measure of four pints; small fruit basket. [Dim. fr. POT.]

POUCH (pouch) *n.* a small bag;—*v.t.* to pocket. [O.F. *pouche*, fr. D.]

POULT (pōlt) *n.* a young chicken, turkey, etc.; pullet. [F. *poulet*, dim. fr. *poule*, a hen, fr. Late L. *pulla*.]

POULTERER (pōl'tẹr-ẹr) *n.* a dealer in fowls.

POULTICE (pōl'tis) *n.* a soothing application for sores;—*v.t.* to apply a poultice to. [L. *stem pult-*, of *puls, pultis*, thick pap.]

POULTRY (pōl'tri) *n.pl.* domestic fowls. [O.F. *pouletric.*]

POUNCE (pouns) (1) *n.* the claw of a bird;—*v.i.*to fall on and seize;—(2) *n.* a fine powder; *v.t.* to sprinkle with pounce. [(1) Through O.F., fr. L. (part.) *punctus*, pricked, fr. *pungere*. (2) F., fr. L. (acc.) *pumicem*, fr. *pumex*, PUMICE.]

POUND (pound) (1) *n.* a weight of 16 ounces avoirdupois, or 12 of troy; twenty shillings; —(2) *v.t.* to beat;—(3) *n.* an enclosure in which stray cattle are confined;—*v.t.* to confine in a pound. [(1) O.E. *pund*, fr. L. *pondo*, orig. (abl.) by weight. (2) M.E. *ponnen*, fr. O.E. *punian*. (3) O.E. *pund*, enclosure. Doublet of POND.]

POUNDAGE (poun'dij) *n.* a duty or allowance on the pound.

POUR (pōr, pour) *v.t.* to throw out or into in a continuous stream;—*v.i.* to issue; flow. [F. *purer*, to make PURE, fr. L., fr. *purus*.]

POUT (pout) *n.* a sullen look; a fish;—*v.i.* to push out the lips. [Form of POULT.]

POUTING (pou'ting) *n.* childish sullenness.

POVERTY (pov'ęr-ti) *n.* want of means, ideas, words, style, or ornament. [O.F. = F. *pauvreté*, fr. L. (acc.) *pauperitatem*, fr. PAUPER.]

POWDER (pou'dęr) *n.* a fine dust; composition for firing guns;—*v.t.* to sprinkle with powder; reduce to dust; salt. [O.F. *puldre*, *poldre*, fr. L. (acc.) *pulverem*, fr. *pulvis*, dust.]

POWDERED (pou'dęrd) *a.* sprinkled with powder; salted.

POWDER-FLASK (pou'dęr-flask) *n.* a small flask in which sportsmen carry gunpowder.

POWDER-MILL (pou'dęr-mil) *n.* mill in which gunpowder is made.

POWDERY (pou'dęr-i) *a.* resembling powder; friable; dusty.

POWER (pou'ęr) *n.* faculty of doing; force; strength; influence; a state; legal authority; any mechanical agent. [O.F. *poeir* = F. *pouvoir*, fr. L. *potere*, to be able.]

POWERFUL (pou'ęr-fool) *a.* having power; strong; forcible; efficacious.

POWERFULLY (pou'ęr-fool-i) *ad.* with great force.

POWERLESS (pou'ęr-les) *a.* without power; weak; impotent.

POX (poks) *n.* an eruptive disease. [Orig. pl. of POCK.]

PRACTICABILITY (prak-ti-kạ-bil'i-ti) *n.* the quality or state of being practicable.

PRACTICABLE (prak'ti-kạ-bl) *a.* that can be done or traversed; feasible.

PRACTICABLY (prak'ti-kạ-bli) *ad.* in a practicable manner.

PRACTICAL (prak'ti-kạl) *a.* relating to practice.

PRACTICALLY (prak'ti-kạl-i) *ad.* by use.

PRACTICE (prak'tis) *n.* customary use; habit; performance. [Fr. PRACTISE.]

PRACTISE (prak'tis) *v.t.* or *i.* to do frequently or habitually; exercise a profession; perpetrate. [O.F., fr. Late L. *practicare*, fr. L., fr. G. *praktikos*, practical, fr. *prassein*, do.]

PRACTITIONER (prak-tish'un-ęr) *n.* one engaged in a profession.

PRAGMATICAL (prag-mat'i-kạl) *a.* very positive or officious. [L., fr G. *pragmatikos*, skilled in business, fr. *pragma*, a thing done. Conn. with PRACTICE.]

PRAGMATISM (prag'mạ-tism) *n.* that system of philosophy which considers events with relation to their condition, causes, and results.

PRAIRIE (prā'ri) *n.* an extensive tract of land with few trees. [F., through Late L., fr. L. *pratum*, meadow.]

PRAISE (prāz) *n.* commendation; object or ground of praise;—*v.t.* to commend; extol, in words, song, or hymn. [O.F. *preis*, merit, fr. L. *pretium*, price.]

PRANCE (prāns) *v.i.* to spring; leap. [Form of PRANK.]

PRANK (prangk) *v.t.* to adorn;—*n.* a frolic; a trick. [E.]

PRATE (prāt) *v.t.* or *i.* to talk idly; utter without meaning; tattle;—*n.* trifling talk. [E.]

PRATIQUE (prā'-tēk, prat'ēk) *n.* a licence to trade after performing quarantine. [F. = PRACTICE, fr. L. (acc.) *practicam*.]

PRÆTOR (prē'tęr) *n.* a Roman magistrate. [L.]

PRÆTORIUM (prē-to'ri-um) *n.* a Roman judgment hall; general's tent. [L.]

PRATTLE (prat'l) *n.* childish talk. [Fr. PRATE.]

PRATTLER (prat'lęr) *n.* one that prattles.

PRAWN (prawn) *n.* a small crustaceous fish. [Etym. uncert.]

PRAY (prā) *v.t.* or *i.* to ask with earnestness; supplicate; address God. [O.F. *preier*, fr. *precari*, to pray.]

PRAYER (prār) *n.* a petition; entreaty; form of devotion; habit of praying.

PRAYER-BOOK (prār'book) *n.* a book containing forms of prayers.

PRAYERFUL (prār'fool) *a.* given to prayer.

PRAYERFULLY (prār'fool-i) *ad.* with prayer.

PRAYERLESS (prār'les) *a.* habitually neglecting prayer.

PRAYERLESSNESS (prār'les-nes) *n.* habitual neglect of prayer.

PRAYER-MEETING (prār-mēt'ing) *n.* a stated meeting for public prayer.

PREACH (prēch) *v.t.* or *i.* to discourse publicly on a religious subject. [O.F. *prescher* = F. *prêcher*, fr. L. *prædicare*. See PREDICATE.]

PREACHER (prē'chęr) *n.* one who preaches.

PREACHMENT (prēch'ment) *n.* a serious discourse, used ironically.

PREAMBLE (prē'am-bl) *n.* an introductory writing; preface to a statute. [F. *préambule*, L. *præ*, before, *ambulare*, to go.]

PREBEND (preb'end) *n.* a stipend in a cathedral church. [O.F., fr. L. *præbenda*, stipend, fr. *præbere*, furnish, fr. *præ*, before, and *habere*, have.]

PREBENDAL (preb'en-dạl) *a.* belonging to a prebend.

PREBENDARY (preb'en-dạ-ri) *n.* the stipendiary of a cathedral.

PRECARIOUS (prē-kā'ri-us) *a.* held by a doubtful tenure; uncertain. [L. = lit. won only by prayer, fr. *precari*, pray.]

PRECARIOUSLY (prē-kā'ri-us-li) *ad.* uncertainly; dependently.

PRECAUTION (prē-kaw'shun) *n.* previous care; a preventive measure.

PRECAUTIONARY (prē-kaw'shun-ạ-ri) *a.* with a view to prevent evil or secure good.

PRECAUTIOUS (prē-kaw'shus) *a.* taking preventive measures.

PRECEDE (prē-sēd') *v.t.* to go before in time, place, importance, etc. [L. *præ*, and *cedere*, to go.]

PRECEDENCE (prē-sē'dens) *n.* priority of time; superior rank or influence.

PRECEDENT (prē-sē'dent) *a.* going before; anterior; antecedent.

PRECEDENT (pres'e-dent) *n.* something done or said that serves as an example.

PRECEDENTED (pres'e-den-ted) *a.* authorised by example.

PRECEDENTLY (prē-sē'dent-li) *ad.* at a former time.

PRECENTOR (prē-sen'tęr) *n.* leader of the choir or of psalmody in a church. [L., fr. *præ*, and *cantor*, singer.]

PRECEPT (prē'sept) *n.* a commandment; order; rule of action; writ. [L. *præ*, and (part.) *captus*, taken, fr. *capere*.]

PRECEPTIVE (pre-sep'tiv) *a.* giving precepts.
PRECEPTOR (pre-sep'tur) *n.* a teacher.
PRECEPTORY (prē-sep'tu-ri) *n.* a religious college of the Knights Templar.
PRECEPTRESS (prē-sep'tres) *n.* female teacher.
PRECESSION (prē-sesh'un) *n.* a going before. [Fr. L. (part.) *cessus*, fr. *cedere*, go.]
PRECINCT (prē'singt) *n.* an outward limit; territorial district. [Fr. L. (part.) *cinctus*, girdled, fr. *cingere*.]
PRECIOUS (prosh'us) *a.* of great price or value. [O.F. =F. *précieux*, fr. L. *pretiosus*, fr. *pretium*, PRICE.]
PRECIOUSLY (presh'us-li) *ad.* in a costly way; in great esteem.
PRECIOUSNESS (presh'us-nes) *n.* state of being highly valued or esteemed.
PRECIPICE (pres'i-pis) *n.* a steep descent of land or rock. [F. *précipice*, fr. *præceps*, headlong, fr. *præ*, before, and stem *capit-*, of *caput*, head.]
PRECIPIENT (pre-sip'i-ent) *a.* directing.
PRECIPITANCE (pre-sip'i-tans) *n.* great or rash haste.
PRECIPITANT (pre-sip'i-tant) *a.* rushing hastily or headlong.
PRECIPITATE (pre-sip'i-tāt) *v.t.* or *i.* to throw headlong; hasten; cast or fall to the bottom of a vessel;—*a.* very hasty; headlong; rash;—*n.* that which is cast to the bottom; sediment. [L. (part.) *præcipitatus*, cast headlong, fr. stem *præcip-*, of *præceps*, headlong.]
PRECIPITATION (pre-sip-i-tā'shun) *n.* rash haste; headlong hurry.
PRECIPITATELY (pre-sip'i-tāt-li) *ad.* headlong; rashly.
PRECIPITOUS (pre-sip'i-tus) *a.* very steep.
PRECIPITOUSLY (pre-sip'i-tus-li) *ad.* descending rapidly.
PRECIS (prā-sē') *n.* a brief abstract or summary. [F.]
PRECISE (pre-sis') *a.* exact; definite; exessively nice; finical. [O.F. *precis*, fr. L. (part.) *præcisus*, cut off, concise, fr. *præ*, and *cædere*.]
PRECISELY (pre-sis'li) *ad.* exactly; correctly.
PRECISENESS (pre-sis'nes) *n.* exactness.
PRECISIAN (pre-zish'an) *n.* a strict observer of rules or forms. [accuracy.
PRECISION (pre-zizh'un) *n.* exactness;
PRECLUDE (pre-klōōd') *v.t.* to hinder beforehand; prevent from taking place. [L., fr. *præ*, and *claudere*, to shut.]
PRECLUSION (pre-klōō'zhun) *n.* act of preventing; state of being prevented.
PRECLUSIVE (pre-klōō'siv) *a.* precluding; tending to preclude.
PRECOCIOUS (pre-kō'shus) *a.* ripe prematurely. [L. *præcox*, fr. *præ*, before, and *coquere*, cook.]
PRECOCITY (pre-kos'i-ti) *n.* premature growth and ripeness.
PRECOGNITION (prē-kog-nish'un) *n.* previous knowledge or examination.
PRECOGNOSCE (prē-kog-nos') *v.t.* to examine witnesses, and find out the grounds for prosecution. [L. *præ*, before, and *cognoscere*, know.]
PRECONCEIT (prē-kun-sēt') *n.* notion or idea previously formed.
PRECONCEIVE (prē-kun-sēv') *v.t.* to conceive beforehand.
PRECONCEPTION (prē-kun-sep'shun) *n.* previous opinion or idea.
PRECONCERT (prē-kun-sert') *v.t.* to concert beforehand.
PRECONCERTED (prē-kun-sert'ed) *a.* previously planned.
PRECURSOR (prē-kur'ser) *n.* he or that which precedes; harbinger. [L. *præ*, and *currere*.]
PRECURSORY (prē-kur'su-ri) *a.* preceding; preliminary.

PREDACEOUS (pre-dā'shus) *a.* living by plunder. [Fr. L. *præda*, prey.]
PREDAL (prē'dal) *a.* pertaining to prey.
PREDATORY (pred'a-tu-ri) *a.* plundering.
PREDECEASE (prē-de-sēs') *v.i.* to die before another person or date.
PREDECESSOR (prē-de-ses'er) *n.* one who has gone before in place or office.
PREDESTINARIAN (prē-des-ti-nā'ri-an) *n.* one who believes in predestination.
PREDESTINATE (prē-des'ti-nāt) *v.t.* to foreordain.
PREDESTINATION (prē-des-ti-nā'shun) *n.* the unchangeable purpose of God.
PREDETERMINATION (prē-de-ter-mi-nā'shun) *a.* previous determination.
PREDIAL (prē'di-al) *a.* belonging to land. [L., fr. *prædium*, farm.]
PREDICABILITY (pred-i-ka-bil'i-ti) *n.* the quality of being predicable.
PREDICABLE (pred'i-ka-bl) *a.* that may be affirmed of or attributed to.
PREDICAMENT (pre-dik'a-ment) *n.* class or genus; condition; trying situation.
PREDICATE (pred'i-kāt) *n.* what is affirmed or denied;—*v.t.* or *i.* to affirm one thing of another; imply. [L. (part.) *prædicatus*, declared, fr. *præ*, and *dicare*, publish.]
PREDICATION (pred-i-kā'shun) *n.* act of affirming; assertion or denial.
PREDICT (pre-dikt') *v.t.* to foretell; prophesy. [L., fr. *præ*, before, and (part.) *dictus*, told, fr. *dicere*.]
PREDICTED (pre-dik'ted) *a.* told before.
PREDICTION (pre-dik'shun) *n.* act of foretelling; prophecy; warning of evil.
PREDICTIVE (pre-dik'tiv) *a.* foretelling.
PREDICTOR (pre-dik'ter) *n.* one who foretells.
PREDILECTION (prē-di-lek'shun) *n.* a previous liking. [L., fr. *præ*, and (part.) *dilectus*, chosen, fr. *diligere*.]
PREDISPOSE (prē-dis-pōz') *v.t.* to incline or adapt previously.
PREDISPOSITION (prē-dis-pō-zish'un) *n.* previous propensity.
PREDOMINANCE (pre-dom'i-nans) *n.* ascendency; superiority.
PREDOMINANT (pre-dom'i-nant) *a.* prevalent.
PREDOMINATE (pre-dom'i-nāt) *v.t.* or *i.* to rule over; surpass in influence; prevail.
PRE-EMINENCE (prē-em'i-nens) *n.* superiority; priority of place or rank.
PRE-EMINENT (prē-em'i-nent) *a.* surpassing others.
PRE-EMINENTLY (prē-em'i-nent-li) *ad.* in a pre-eminent degree.
PRE-EMPTION (prē-em'shun) *n.* act or right of buying before others. [L. *præ*, and *emere*, buy.
PREEN (prēn) *v.t.* to clean and adjust the feathers, as birds. [Form of PRUNE.]
PRE-ENGAGE (prē-en-gāj') *v.t.* to engage by previous contract or influence.
PRE-ENGAGEMENT (prē-en-gāj'ment) *n.* a prior obligation or attachment.
PRE-EXIST (prē-eg-zist') *v.i.* to exist beforehand. [existence.
PRE-EXISTENCE (prē-eg-zis'tens) *n.* previous
PRE-EXISTENT (prē-eg-zis'tent) *a.* existing in time previous.
PREFACE (pref'as) *n.* an introductory speech or writing;—*v.t.* to introduce by remarks. [O.F., fr. L. *præfatio*, fr. *præ*, and *fari*, speak. See FATE.]
PREFATORY (pref'a-tu-ri) *a.* introductory.
PREFECT (prē'fekt) *n.* a governor or chief officer. [L. *præfectus*, orig. (part.) set before, fr. *præ*, and *facere*.]
PREFECTURE (prē'fek-tūr) *n.* office or jurisdiction of a prefect. Also **PREFECTSHIP**.
PREFER (pre-fer') *v.t.* to esteem above another; offer; choose; advance. [L., fr. *præ*, and *ferre*, bear.]

PREFERABLE (pref'er-a-bl) *a.* worthy of preference.

PREFERABLY (pref'er-a-bli) *ad.* in preference.

PREFERENCE (pref'er-ens) *n.* choice of one thing rather than another; thing preferred.

PREFERENTIAL (pref-e-ren'shal) *a.* having a prior right or claim.

PREFERMENT (pre-fer'ment) *n.* advancement to a higher station or o'fice.

PREFIGURATION (prē-fig-ū-rā'shun) *n.* previous representation.

PREFIGURATIVE (prē-fig'ū-rā-tiv) *a.* showing by previous types.

PREFIGURE (prē-fig'ur) *v.t.* to show by a figure beforehand.

PREFIX (prē-fiks') *v.t.* to place before.

PREFIX (prē'fiks) *n.* a letter or word prefixed.

PREGNANCY (preg'nan-si) *n.* a state of being with young; fertility of thought; fullness of meaning.

PREGNANT (preg'nant) *a.* being with young; productive; suggestive. [F., fr. L. *prægnans*, orig. (part.) being about to bear; conn. with NATAL.]

PREHENSIBLE (prē-ben'si-bl) *a.* that may be seized. [L., fr. (part.) *prehensus*, seized, fr. *prehendere*.]

PREHENSILE (prē-hen'sil) *a.* grasping; adapted to clasp.

PREHISTORIC (prē-his-tor'ik) *a.* relating to times or events before historical writings.

PREJUDGE (prē-juj') *v.t.* to judge before hearing; condemn beforehand.

PREJUDGMENT (prē-juj'ment) *n.* judgment without trial or examination.

PREJUDICATE (prē-jōō'di-kāt) *v.t.* or *i.* to judge or decide without examination.

PREJUDICE (prej'oo-dis) *n.* previous judgment; bent or bias; injury;—*v.t.* to bias unduly; prepossess; injure. [F., fr. L., fr. *præ*, and *judicium*, judgment.]

PREJUDICIAL (prej-oo-dish'al) *a.* likely to injure; hurtful.

PREJUDICIALLY (prej-oo-dish'al-i) *ad.* injuriously.

PRELACY (prel'a-si) *n.* office of a prelate.

PRELATE (prel'at) *n.* an archbishop, bishop, or patriarch. [L. *prælatus*, orig. (part.) set, borne, before.]

PRELATICAL (prē-lat'i-kal) *a.* pertaining to prelates or prelacy.

PRELATIST (prel'a-tist) *n.* one who supports prelacy.

PRELECT (prē-lekt') *v.i.* to read a discourse in public; lecture. [Fr. L. (part.) *lectus*, read. See LECTURE.]

PRELECTION (prē-lek'shun) *n.* a public lecture or discourse.

PRELIBATION (prē-li-bā'shun) *n.* a foretaste.

PRELIMINARY (prē-lim'i-na-ri) *a.* that precedes; introductory; preparatory;—*n.* a first step; introduction. [L., fr. *præ*, and stem *limin-*, of *limen*, threshold.]

PRELUDE (prel'ūd) *n.* in *Music*, something introductory; preface. [Fr. L. *ludere*, play.]

PRELUDE (pre-lūd') *v.t.* or *i.* to preface.

PRELUSIVE (pre-lū'siv) *a.* serving to introduce.

PREMATURE (pre'-, prē'ma-tūr) *a.* ripe too soon; too hasty.

PREMATURELY (pre'-, prē'ma-tūr-li) *ad.* before the proper time.

PREMEDITATE (prē-med'i-tāt) *v.t.* or *i.* to meditate beforehand.

PREMEDITATED (prē-med'i-tāt-ed) *a.* conceived beforehand.

PREMEDITATION (prē-med-i-tā'shun) *n.* previous deliberation or design.

PREMIER (prē'mi-er) *n.* first minister of state;—*a.* first; chief. [F., fr. L. *primarius*, of the first rank, fr. *primus*, first.]

PREMIERSHIP (prē'mi-er-ship) *n.* office of the first minister.

PREMISE (pre-miz') *v.t.* or *i.* to lay down propositions for subsequent reasoning; preface. [Fr. O.F. *premisse*, fr. L., fr. *præ*, and (part.) *missus*, sent, (stated), fr. *mittere*.]

PREMISES (prem'is-ez) *n.pl.* propositions admitted; a building and its adjuncts.

PREMISSES (prem'is-ez), *n.* propositions laid down upon which subsequent reasoning is based. See PREMISE.

PREMIUM (prē'mi-um) *n.* reward; bounty; payment for insurance; rise in value above par. [L.]

PREMONITION (prē-mu-nish'un) *n.* previous notice or warning. [L. *præ*, and *monere*, warn.]

PREMONITORY (prē-mon'i-tur-i) *a.* giving previous notice.

PREMUNITION (prē-mū-nish'un) *n.* an anticipation of objections. [L. *præ*, and *munire*, fortify.]

PREOCCUPANCY (prē-ok'ū-pan-si) *n.* act or right of taking possession before.

PREOCCUPY (prē-ok'ū-pi) *v.t.* to take possession before another.

PREORDAIN (prē-or-dān') *v.t.* to ordain or determine beforehand.

PREORDINATION (prē-or-di-nā'shun) *n.* act of foreordaining.

PREPAID (prē-pād') *a.* paid previously.

PREPARATION (prep-a-rā'shun) *n.* act of making ready; state of being prepared; a medical compound.

PREPARATIVE (pre-par'a-tiv) *n.* adapted to prepare;—*n.* that which prepares.

PREPARATORY (pre-par'a-tur-i) *a.* preparing for; introductory.

PREPARE (pre-pār') *v.t.* or *i.* to make fit or ready; qualify; provide. [L., fr. *præ*, before, and *parare*, make ready.]

PREPAY (prē-pā') *v.t.* to pay in advance, as postage. [advance.

PREPAYMENT (prē-pā'ment) *n.* payment in advance.

PREPENSE (pre-pens') *a.* preconceived. [Fr. F. (part.) *prepensé*, premeditated, fr. L. *præ*, before and *pensare*, weigh.]

PREPONDERANCE (pre-pon'der-ans) *n.* superiority of weight or power.

PREPONDERANT (pre-pon'der-ant) *a.* superior in weight or influence.

PREPONDERATE (pre-pon'der-āt) *v.t.* or *i.* to outweigh. [L., fr. *præ*, and (part.) *ponderatus*, weighed. See PONDER.]

PREPONDERATION (pre-pon-de-rā'shun) *n.* act of outweighing.

PREPOSITION (prep-u-zish'un) *n.* a word put before another to express relation, etc. [L., fr. (part.) *præpositus*, set before, fr. *præ*, before, and *ponere*, place.]

PREPOSITIONAL (prep-u-zish'un-al) *a.* pertaining to a preposition.

PREPOSITIVE (prē-poz'i-tiv) *a.* put before.

PREPOSSESS (prē-pu-zes') *v.t.* to preoccupy; bias.

PREPOSSESSING (prē-pu-zes'ing) *a.* adapted to invite favour.

PREPOSSESSION (prē-pu-zesh'un) *n.* prior impression; a feeling for or against.

PREPOSTEROUS (pre-pos'te-rus) *a.* absurd. [L. =hindside foremost, fr. *præ*, before, and *posterus*, after.]

PREREQUISITE (prē-rek'wi-zit) *a.* previously necessary;—*n.* something previously necessary.

PREROGATIVE (pre-rog'a-tiv) *n.* an exclusive or peculiar privilege. [L., fr. *præ*, and (part.) *rogatus*, asked, fr. *rogare*.]

PRESAGE (pres'ij, prē'sāj) *n.* anything that foretells. [L., fr. *præ*, and *sagire*, perceive acutely.]

PRESAGE (prē-sāj') *v.t.* or *i.* to foretell; forebode.

PRESBYTER (pres'bi-ter) *n.* an elder in the church; pastor; priest. [G. *presbuteros*, an elder, orig. (compar.) older, fr. *presbus*, old.]

PRESBYTERIAN (pres-bi-tē'ri-an) a. pertaining to, or consisting of, presbyters;—n. one that belongs to the Presbyterian church.

PRESBYTERIANISM (pres-bi-tē'ri-an-izm) n. principles and government of Presbyterians.

PRESBYTERY (pres'bi-ter-i) n. a body of pastors and ruling elders.

PRESCIENCE (prē'shi-ens) n. foreknowledge. [O.F., fr. L. præscientia, foreknowledge. See SCIENCE.]

PRESCIENT (prē'shi-ent) a. foreknowing.

PRESCRIBE (pre-skrib') v.t. or i. to direct; lay down as a rule. [L., fr. præ. and scribere, to write.]

PRESCRIPT (prē'skript) n. an official or authoritative direction.

PRESCRIPTION (pre-skrip'shun) n. medical direction of remedies; claim from use or possession.

PRESCRIPTIVE (pre-skrip'tiv) a. acquired by or pleading the right of long use.

PRESENCE (prez'ens) n. state of being here or in view; appearance; person of a prince; persons about him; readiness.

PRESENT (prez'ent) (1) a. being here or at this time; ready at hand;—n. this time; a gift; (2) (pre-zent') v.t. to exhibit to view; point, as a gun; give; appoint; lay before for consideration. (1) O.F., fr. L. præsens, being near. (2) [L. præsentare, to place before, fr. præsens, PRESENT.]

PRESENTABLE (pre-zen'ta-bl) a. that may be presented.

PRESENTATION (prez-en-tā'shun) n. act of presenting; exhibition; appointment.

PRESENTEE (prez-en-tē') n. one presented to a benefice.

PRESENTIMENT (prē-zen'ti-ment) n. previous apprehension.

PRESENTLY (prez'ent-li) ad. shortly; soon.

PRESENTMENT (pre-zent'ment) n. accusation by a grand jury.

PRESERVATION (prez-er-vā'shun) n. act of preserving; safety.

PRESERVATIVE (pre-zer'va-tiv) a. having power to preserve;—n. that which preserves.

PRESERVE (pre-zerv') v.t. to keep safe; defend; season; maintain;—n. fruit preserved. [L., fr. præ, and servare, save.]

PRESERVER (pre-zerv'er) n. he or she that preserves.

PRESIDE (pre-zid') v.i. to exercise superintendence or control. [O.F. presider, fr. L. præ, and sedere, sit.]

PRESIDENCY (prez'i-den-si) n. office, residence, or jurisdiction of a president.

PRESIDENT (prez'i-dent) n. one at the head of a state or society; chairman.

PRESIDENTIAL (prez-i-den'shal) a. pertaining to a president.

PRESIDENTSHIP (prez'i-dent-ship) n. office of a president, or his term of once.

PRESIGNIFY (pre-sig'ni-fi) v.t. to signify beforehand.

PRESS (pres) v.t. or i. to squeeze; urge; drive; distress;—n. a machine for squeezing; a printing machine; printed literature; crowd; stress; a closet. [O.F. presser, fr. L. (part.) pressus, pressed, fr. premere.]

PRESSGANG (pres'gang) n. a crew that impresses men as seamen. [Fr. prest = ready, fr. O.F., fr. L. præstare, to stand forth.]

Press.

PRESSING (pres'ing) a. urgent.

PRESSMAN (pres'man) n. the man who impresses the sheets in printing.

PRESSURE (presh'ur) n. act of pressing; weight; urgency.

PRESUMABLE (pre-zū'ma-bl) a. that may be presumed.

PRESUME (pre-zūm') v.t. or i. to take for granted; suppose; venture without leave. [O.F., fr. L. præ, and sumere, take.]

PRESUMPTION (pre-zum'shun) n. strong probability; supposition; forward conduct.

PRESUMPTIVE (pre-zum'tiv) a. partaking of presumption.

PRESUMPTUOUS (pre-zum'tū-us) a. bold and confident; wilful.

PRESUMPTUOUSLY (pre-zum'tū-us-li) ad. with presumption.

PRESUPPOSAL (prē-sup-pōz'al) n. previous supposition.

PRESUPPOSE (prē-su-pōz') v.t. to suppose as previous; take for granted.

PRESUPPOSITION (prē-sup-u-zish'un) n. previous supposition or surmise.

PRETENCE (pre-tens') n. a simulated claim or assumption; pretext.

PRETEND (pre-tend') v.t. to hold out an appearance; claim; affect;—v.i. to put in a claim to; aspire to. [O.F., fr. L. præ, and tendere, stretch.]

PRETENDEDLY (pre-ten'ded-li) ad. with pretence.

PRETENDER (pre-ten'der) n. one who pretends or lays claim.

PRETENSION (pre-ten'shun) n. claim, true or false; pretence.

PRETENTIOUS (pre-ten'shus) a. making great pretensions.

PRETERIT (pret'er-it) a. past, or perfectly past. [L. præter, beyond, and (part.) -itus, it, ire, go.]

PRETERMISSION (prē-ter-mish'un) n. the act of omitting.

PRETERMIT (prē-ter-mit') v.t. to pass by; omit. [Fr. L. mittere, send.]

PRETERNATURAL (prē-ter-nat'u-ral) a. beyond what is natural.

PRETEXT (pre-tekst', prē'tekst) n. a simulated reason or motive; pretence. [F., fr. L. prætextum, orig. (part.) woven in front, fr. præ, and texere.]

PRETTILY (prit'i-li) ad. neatly; pleasingly.

PRETTY (prit'i) a. neat; graceful; tasteful; affected; mean;—ad. in some degree. [O.E. prættig, crafty, wily.]

PREVAIL (pre-vāl') v.i. to overcome; be in force or use; induce. [O.F. stem prevail-of prevaloir, to prevail, fr. L. præ, and valere, be strong.]

PREVAILING (pre-vā'ling) a. prevalent; most general; current.

PREVALENCE (prev'a-lens) n. predominance.

PREVALENT (prev'a-lent) a. powerful; most generally received.

PREVALENTLY (prev'a-lent-li) ad. powerfully; successfully.

PREVARICATE (pre-var'i-kāt) v.t. to avoid giving a direct answer; equivocate. [L. præ, before, and varicari, straddle, fr. varus, awry.]

PREVARICATION (pre-var-i-kā'shun) n. act of quibbling.

PREVARICATOR (pre-var'i-kā-ter) n. one who quibbles; a shuffler.

PREVENT (pre-vent') v.t. to hinder; obviate; precede. [L., fr. præ, before, and venire, come.]

PREVENTION (pre-ven'shun) n. act of hindering; hindrance; anticipation.

PREVENTIONAL (prē-ven'shun-al) a. tending to prevent.

PREVENTIVE (pre-ven'tiv) a. tending to hinder;—n. that which prevents.

PREVIOUS (prē'vi-us) a. going before in time; prior; former. [L., fr. præ, before, and via, way.]

PREVIOUSLY (prē'vi-us-li) ad. antecedently.

PREVISION (prē-vizh'un) n. foresight.

PREWARN (prē-wawrn') v.t. to give previous notice of.

Fāte, fár, ado; mē, her; mine; nōte; tūne; mōŏn.

PREY (prā) *n.* spoil; booty;—*v.i.* to seize and devour; plunder; weigh heavily. [O.F *preie* = F. *proie*, fr. L. (acc.)* *prœdam*. See PREDATORY.]

PRICE (pris) *n.* equivalent paid for anything; reward; worth. [O.F. *pris*, fr. L. *pretium*. See PRECIOUS.]

PRICELESS (pris'les) *a.* invaluable; having no value.

PRICK (prik) (1) *v.t.* to pierce; spur; raise up;—*v.i.* to become acid; ride forward;— (2) *n.* a spur; a sharp, stinging pain; a point; a mark. [(1) O.E. *prician*. (2) O.E. *prica*.]

PRICKLE (prik'l) *n.* a small, sharp shoot or spine;—*v.t.* to prick. [Dim. fr. PRICK.]

PRICKLINESS (prik'li-nes) *a.* fullness of prickles.

PRICKLY (prik'li) *a.* full of prickles.

PRIDE (prid) *n.* inordinate self-esteem; generous elation of heart; dignity;—*v.t.* to be proud of. [O.E. *pryte*, fr. *prut*, PROUD.]

PRIEST (prēst) *n.* a man in orders; a clergyman. [O.E. *preost*, fr. L. *presbyter*. See PRESBYTER.]

PRIESTCRAFT (prēst'kraft) *n.* priestly policy or fraud.

PRIESTESS (prēs'tes) *n.* a female priest.

PRIESTHOOD (prēst'hood) *n.* the office of a priest. [priest.

PRIESTLINESS (prēst'li-nes) *n.* manners of a

PRIESTLY (prēst'li) *a.* becoming a priest; sacerdotal.

PRIG (prig) *n.* a conceited fellow. [Fr. PRICK = deck out.]

PRIGGISH (prig'ish) *a.* conceited.

PRIM (prim) *a.* formal; concise;—*v.t.* to deck with nicety. [O.F. *prime*, PRIME, slight, delicate, fr. L (acc.) *primum*, first.]

PRIMACY (pri'ma-si) *n.* office or dignity of an archbishop.

PRIMAGE (pri'mij) *n.* a duty or allowance for loading or unloading a ship. [L. *prime*, first.]

PRIMAL (pri'mal) *a.* first; original. [L. *primalis*. See PRIME.]

PRIMARILY (pri'ma-ri-li) *ad.* originally.

PRIMARY (pri'ma-ri) *a.* original; first in time, meaning, or rank.

PRIMATE (pri'mat) *n.* an archbishop. [O.F. *primat*, fr. L. (acc.) *primatem*, fr. *primas*, a chief.]

PRIME (prim) (1) *a.* first; original; chief; early;— (2) *n.* the dawn; spring; the best part; the height;—*v.t.* to put powder in the pan; lay the first colour in painting. [(1) O.F., fr. L. (acc. fem.) *primam*, first. See PRIM. (2) O.F., fr. L. *prima* (*hora*), first (hour).]

PRIMER (prim'er pri'-mer) *n.* a small first book for children.

PRIMEVAL (pri-mē'val) *a.* belonging to the earliest age. [L. *primus*, first, and *œvum*, age.]

PRIMING (pri'ming) *n.* powder in the pan; first colour laid.

PRIMITIAL (pri-mish'al) *a.* being of the first order.

PRIMITIVE (prim'i-tiv) *a.* first; original; ancient;—*n.* an original or root word. [L. *primitivus*, fr. *primus*, for the first time. See PRIME.]

PRIMNESS (prim'nes) *n.* affected niceness of formality.

PRIMOGENITAL (pri-mō-jen'i-tal) *a.* firstborn. [Fr. L., fr. *primo*-, for *primus*, and *genitus*, born, fr. root of *gignere*, beget.]

PRIMOGENITURE (pri-mō-jen'i-tūr) *n.* seniority by birth.

PRIMORDIAL (pri-mor'di-al) *a.* first in order; existing from the beginning. [L. *primus*, first, and *ordere*, begin.]

PRIMROSE (prim'rōz) *n.* an early flowering plant;—*a.* gay; flowery; yellow. [O.F. *primerole*, fr. Late L. (acc.) *primulam*, fr. *primus*.]

PRINCE (prins) *n.* a king's son; a ruler. [F., fr. L. *princeps*, fr. *primus*. first, and *capere*, take.]

PRINCEDOM (prins'dum) *n.* the dignity of a prince; sovereignty.

PRINCELY (prins'li) *a.* royal; grand.

PRINCESS (prin'ses) *n.* the consort of a prince; a king's daughter.

PRINCIPAL (prin'si-pal) *a.* chief; highest in rank, character, or importance;—*n.* a chief person or thing; head; chief party or actor; capital sum at interest; an organ stop. [F., fr. L. *principalis*, fr. stem *princip*-, chief. See PRINCE.]

PRINCIPALITY (prin-si-pal'i-ti) *n.* a prince's domain.

PRINCIPALLY (prin'si-pal-i) *ad.* chiefly; above all.

PRINCIPIA (prin-sip'ia) *n.pl.* first principles. [L.]

PRINCIPLE (prin'si-pl) *n.* fundamental truths; axiom; rule; original element. [Fr. F. *principe*, fr. L. *principium*, beginning. See PRINCIPAL.]

PRINK (pringk) *v.t.* or *i.* to dress for show. [Conn. with PRICK = deck out.]

PRINT (print) *v.t.* to mark by impression;— *v.i.* to use typography; publish;—*n.* a mark made by pressure; engraving; calico. [Short. fr. O.F. *empreintere*, IMPRINT.]

PRINTER (prin'ter) *n.* one who prints.

PRINTING (prin'ting) *n.* the art or practice of a printer.

PRINTSELLER (print'sel-er) *n.* a dealer in engravings.

PRINTWORKS (print'wurks) *n.* manufactory for printing cottons, calicoes, etc.

PRIOR (pri'ur) *a.* former; antecedent;—*n.* the superior of a monastery. [L. =former.]

PRIORESS (pri'ur-es) *n.* the lady superior of a convent.

PRIORITY (pri-or'i-ti) *n.* state of being first in time, rank, etc.

PRIORY (pri'ur-i) *n.* a convent.

PRISE (priz) *v.t.* to raise, as by means of a lever; to force up. [O.F. *prise*, a hold, fr. *prendre*, grasp, fr. L. *prehendere*.]

PRISM (prizm) *n.* a solid whose bases are similar, equal, parallel, plane figures, and whose sides are parallelograms. [Fr. G. *prisma*.]

PRISMATIC (priz-mat'ik) *a.* formed by prisms.

PRISMOID (priz'moid) *n.* a body something like a prism. [G. *eidos*, form.]

PRISON (priz'n) *v.t.* to shut up; confine;—*n.* a jail. [O.F. *prisun*, fr. *prise*. See PRISE.]

PRISONER (priz'ner) *n.* one under arrest.

PRISTINE (pris'tin) *a.* ancient. [L. *pristinus*, fr. *priscus*, of old.]

PRITHEE (priTH'ē) *ad.* I pray thee.

PRIVACY (pri'va-si, priv'a-si) *n.* retirement; secrecy.

PRIVATE (pri'vat) *a.* peculiar to oneself; alone; secret. [L. *privatus*, orig. (part.) deprived, fr. *privus*, single.]

PRIVATEER (pri-va-tēr') *n.* a private ship of war commissioned to take prizes;—*v.i.* to cruise in a privateer.

PRIVATEERSMAN (pri-va-tērs'man) *n.* officer or seaman of a privateer.

PRIVATELY (pri'vat-li) *ad.* clandestinely.

PRIVATION (pri-vā'shun) *n.* act of depriving; state of being deprived; absence; destitution. [See PRIVATE.]

PRIVATIVE (priv'a-tiv) *a.* causing privation; —*n.* a prefix to a word which gives it a negative signification.

PRIVET (priv'et) *n.* a shrub used for hedges. [Etym. uncert.]

PRIVILEGE (priv'i-lij) *v.t.* to invest with peculiar rights;—*n.* peculiar advantage; prerogative; liberty. [L., fr. *privatus*, PRIVATE, and stem *leg*, of *lex*, law.]

PRIVILY (priv'i-li) *ad.* secretly.

PRIVITY (priv'i-ti) *n.* privacy; joint knowledge.

PRIVY (priv'i) *a.* privately knowing and consenting. [O.F. *privé* (prē-vā'), fr. L. *privatus*, PRIVATE.]

PRIZE (priz) (1) *n.* a reward; something taken from an enemy;—(2) *v.t.* to value highly. [(1) O.F. *prise*. See PRISE. (2) F. *priser*, value much.]

PRIZE-MONEY (priz'mun-i) *n.* the whole, or a share of, the value of what has been captured.

PRIZE-RING (priz'ring) *n.* an enclosure for pugilistic fights; boxing.

PROBABILITY (prob-a-bil'i-ti) *n.* appearance of truth; likelihood.

PROBABLE (prob'a-bl) *a.* likely to be, or to be true. [F., fr. L. *probabilis*, that may be proved. See PROVE.]

PROBABLY (prob'a-bli) *ad.* in likelihood.

PROBATE (prō'bat) *n.* proof of a will. [Fr. L. (part.) *probatus*, proved. See PROVE.]

PROBATION (prō-bā'shun) *n.* act of proving or of testing; trial; time of trial. [F., fr. L. (acc.) *probationem*. See PROBATE.]

PROBATIONARY (prō-bā'shun-a-ri) *a.* serving for trial or probation. Also **PROBATIONAL**.

PROBATIONER (prō-bā'shun-er) *n.* one upon trial; a novice.

PROBATIVE (prō'ba-tiv) *a.* serving for proof or trial. Also **PROBATORY**.

PROBE (prōb) *n.* a surgeon's instrument:—*v.t.* to try with a probe; search thoroughly. [Fr. L. *probare*, PROVE, test.]

PROBITY (prob'i-ti) *n.* tried virtue or integrity; honesty. [F., fr. L., fr. *probus*, honest.]

PROBLEM (prob'lem) *n.* a question to be solved; any practical difficulty. [L. *problema*, fr. G., fr. *pro*, forward, and *ballein*, throw.]

PROBLEMATICAL (prob-le-mat'i-kal) *a.* questionable.

PROBOSCIS (pro-bos'is) *n.* the snout or trunk of an elephant, etc. [G., fr. *pro*, before, and *boskein*, feed.]

PROCEDURE (prō-sē'dūr) *n.* act or manner of proceeding; process; conduct.

PROCEED (prō-sēd') *v.i.* to go forward; advance; issue. [O.F. *proceder*, fr. L., fr. *pro*, forward, and *cedere*, go.]

PROCEEDING (prō-sē'ding) *n.* advancing movement; step; measure; transaction.

PROCEEDS (prō'sēdz) *n.* results; sum realised from sale; produce.

PROCESS (prō'ses) *n.* a proceeding method. [F. *procès*, fr. L. *processus*, fr. *procedere*, PROCEED.]

PROCESSION (pru-sesh'un) *n.* act of advancing; a train of persons.

PROCESSIONAL (pru-sesh'un-al) *a.* consisting in procession.

PROCLAIM (prō-klām') *v.t.* to pronounce publicly and solemnly; make widely known. [F. *proclamer*, fr. L., fr. *pro*, before, and *clamare*.]

PROCLAMATION (prok-la-mā'shun) *n.* a public announcement or declaration.

PROCLIVITY (prō-kliv'i-ti) *n.* habitual or natural inclination. Fr. L., fr. *pro-*, and *clivius*, slope.]

PROCRASTINATE (prō-kras'ti-nāt) *v.t.* or *i.* to put off from day to day; be dilatory. [L., fr. *procrastinus*, of to-morrow, fr. *cras*, to-morrow.]

PROCRASTINATION (prō-kras-ti-nā'shun) *n.* delay; dilatoriness.

PROCREATE (prō'kre-āt) *v.t.* to generate. [Fr. L. (part.) *procreatus*, generated, fr. *pro*, and *creare*, CREATE.]

PROCREATION (prō-kre-ā'shun) *n.* production of young.

PROCTOR (prok'ter) *n.* an attorney in ecclesiastical courts; an official in a university. [M.E. *proketour*, PROCURATOR.]

PROCTORIAL (prok-tō'ri-al) *a.* pertaining to a proctor.

PROCURABLE (pru-kūr'a-bl) *a.* obtainable.

PROCURATION (prok-ū-rā'shun) *n.* act of managing another's affairs; document conferring this power. [See PROCURE.]

PROCURATOR (prok'ū-rā-ter) *n.* manager of another's affairs; legal agent or prosecutor.

PROCURE (pru-kūr') *v.t.* to obtain; acquire; bring about. [F. *procurer*, fr. L. *procurare*, fr. *curare*. See CURE.]

PROCUREMENT (pru-kūr'ment) *n.* act of obtaining.

PRODIGAL (prod'i-gal) *a.* lavish; wasteful; —*n.* a spendthrift. [O.F., fr. L., fr. *prodigus*, prodigal.]

PRODIGALITY (prod-i-gal'i-ti) *n.* wasteful expenditure; extravagance; profusion.

PRODIGALLY (prod'i-gal-i) *ad.* lavishly.

PRODIGIOUS (pru-dij'us) *a.* very great; astonishing; enormous.

PRODIGIOUSLY (pru-dij'us-li) *ad.* astonishingly; enormously.

PRODIGY (prod'i-ji) *n.* any surprising thing; a wonder. [F. *prodige*, fr. L. *prodigium*, portent.]

PRODUCE (pru-dūs') *v.t.* to bring forth; yield; exhibit; cause; extend. [L., fr. *pro*, before, in front, and *ducere*, lead.]

PRODUCE (prod'ūs) *n.* that which is produced or yielded; gain.

PRODUCER (pru-dū'ser) *n.* he or that which produces.

PRODUCIBLE (pru-dū'si-bl) *a.* that may be produced.

PRODUCT (prod'ukt) *n.* a thing produced; effect; result; sum. [L. (part.) *productus*, produced.

PRODUCTILE (pru-duk'til) *a.* capable of being extended.

PRODUCTION (pru-duk'shun) *n.* act of producing; fruit; product.

PRODUCTIVE (pru-duk'tiv) *a.* fertile; efficient.

PRODUCTIVELY (pru-duk'tiv-li) *ad.* with fruitful abundance.

PRODUCTIVENESS (pru-duk'tiv-nes) *n.* the quality of producing.

PROEM (prō'em) *n.* a preface; prelude. [F. fr. L. *proœmium*, fr. G. *pro*, and *oimos*, path.]

PROFANATION (prof-a-nā'shun) *n.* a violation of sacred things; desecration.

PROFANE (pru-fān') *a.* impious; unholy; secular; impure; —*v.t.* to put to a wrong use; abuse or debase anything sacred. [F. fr. L., fr. *pro*=outside, and *fanum*, FANE.]

PROFANELY (pru-fān'li) *ad.* irreverently.

PROFANITY (pru-fan'i-ti) *n.* irreverence of sacred things; profane language.

PROFESS (pru-fes') *v.t.* or *i.* to own freely; declare; avow knowledge or skill in. [L. (part.) *professus*, avowed, fr. *fateri*, utter. See CONFESS.]

PROFESSEDLY (pru-fes'ed-li) *ad.* by avowal.

PROFESSION (pru-fesh'un) *n.* open declaration of confession; calling; employment; taking of a religious vow; body of men in the same calling.

PROFESSIONAL (pru-fesh'un-al) *a.* belonging to one's profession;—*n.* an artist, as opposed to an amateur.

PROFESSOR (pru-fes'er) *n.* one who declares his faith; a public and authorised teacher.

PROFESSORSHIP (pru-fes'ur-ship) *n.* office of a professor.

PROFFER (prof'er) *v.t.* to propose for acceptance;—*n.* an offer; attempt. [O.F. *proferer*, fr. L. *proferre* bring forward, fr. *ferre*.]

PROFICIENCY (pru-fish'en-si) *n.* improvement or skill acquired in any art or practice.

PROFICIENT (pru-fish'ent) *a.* well advanced or skilled in anything;—*n.* an adept; expert. [L. (part. stem) *proficient-*, lit. making forward, fr. *pro*, before, and *facere*, make.]

PROFILE (prō'fīl, prō'fēl) *n.* outline; side face;—*v.t.* to draw a side view. [It. *profilo*, lit. line in front, fr. L. *pro*, and *filum*, thread.]

PROFIT (prof'it) *n.* gain; advantage; pecuniary benefit;—*v.t.* or *i.* to gain or receive advantage; benefit; improve. [F., fr. L. (part.) *profectus*, fr. *proficere*, advance. See **PROFICIENT.**]

PROFITABLE (prof'i-tạ-bl) *a.* yielding advantage; lucrative.

PROFITABLY (prof'i-tạ-bli) *ad.* with advantage.

PROFITLESS (prof'it-les) *a.* void of gain or advantage.

PROFLIGACY (prof'li-gạ-si) *n.* a vicious course of life.

PROFLIGATE (prof'li-gạt) *a.* lost to virtue; dissolute; prodigal;—*n.* a vicious man. [L.=abandoned, fr. *pro-*, forward and *fligere*, dash.]

PROFOUND (pro-found') *a.* deep; low; intense; deeply felt; intellectually deep;—*n.* the sea or ocean; an abyss. [F. *profond*, fr. L. (acc) *profundum*, deep, fr. *pro* =downward, and *fundus*, bottom.]

PROFOUNDLY (pro-found'li) *ad.* deeply.

PROFUNDITY (pro-fun'di-ti) *n.* depth of place, of knowledge, etc.

PROFUSE (pro-fūs') *a.* liberal to excess; exuberant; lavish; prodigal. [L. (part.) *profusus*, poured gently, fr. *fundere*, pour.]

PROFUSELY (pro-fūs'li) *ad.* prodigally.

PROFUSION (pro-fū'zhun) *n.* great abundance; extravagance.

PROGENITOR (prō-jen'i-tẹr) *n.* a direct ancestor; forefather.

PROGENY (proj'e-ni) *n.* offspring; race. [O.F. *progenie*, fr. L. (acc.) *progeniem*, offspring, fr. *genus*, kin.]

PROGNOSIS (prog-nō'sis) *n.* the art or act of foretelling the course of a disease by its symptoms. [G., fr. *gignoskein*, know.]

PROGNOSTIC (prog-nos'tik) *a.* foreboding;—*n.* a sign or symptom of disease; medical opinion thereof. [L., fr. G. *prognostikon*, an omen.]

PROGNOSTICATE (prog-nos'ti-kāt) *v.t.* to foreshow.

PROGNOSTICATION (prog-nos-ti-kā'shun) *n.* the act of foretelling.

PROGNOSTICATOR (prog-nos'ti-kā-tẹr) *n.* one who foretells.

PROGRAMME (prō'gram) *n.* an outline of some public performance. [Fr. G. =a public writing, fr. *pro*, before, and *graphein*, write.]

PROGRESS (prō'gres, prog'res) *n.* a course onward; advance; procession; improvement. [F., fr. L. (part) *progressus*, gone forward, fr. *gradi*, walk.]

PROGRESS (prō-gres') *v.i.* to advance.

PROGRESSION (pro-gresh'un) *n.* regular and gradual advance.

PROGRESSIONAL (pro-gresh'un-ạl) *a.* tending to advance.

PROGRESSIONIST (pro-gresh'un-ist) *n.* one who believes in the progress of mankind.

PROGRESSIVE (pro-gres'iv) *a.* going onward; advancing.

PROGRESSIVELY (pro-gres'iv-li) *ad.* by gradual advance.

PROHIBIT (prō-hib'it) *v.t.* to forbid. [L. (part.) *prohibitus*, lit. held in the way, fr. *pro*, in front, and *habere*, have.]

PROHIBITER (prō-hib'i-tẹr) *n.* one who prohibits.

PROHIBITION (prō-hi-bish'un) *n.* act of forbidding.

PROHIBITIVE (prō-hib'i-tiv) *a.* implying prohibition; forbidding. Also **PROHIBITORY.**

PROJECT (proj'ekt) *n.* a plan; scheme;—(pro-jekt') *v.t.* or *i.* to jut or throw out; form a plan. [O.F. =F. *projet*, fr. L. (part.) *projectus*, lit. thrown forward, fr. *jacere*, throw.]

PROJECTILE (pro-jek'til) *a.* impelling forward;—*n.* a body projected by force.

PROJECTION (prō-jek'shun) *n.* act of projecting; plan; delineation.

PROJECTOR (pro-jek'tẹr) *n.* one who plans.

PROJECTURE (pro-jek'tūr) *n.* a jutting out.

PROLAPSUS (prō-lap'sus) *n.* a falling down; protrusion. [L. See **LAPSE.**]

PROLEPTIC (prō-lep'tik) *a.* previous. Also **PROLEPTICAL.** [Fr. G. *lambanein*, take.]

PROLETARIAN (prō-lē-tā'ri-ạn) *n.* one of the poorest labouring class;—*a.* common; vulgar. [F., fr. L. *proletarius*, in ancient Rome a citizen that served the state by the help of his children only, fr. *proles*, offspring.]

PROLETARIAT, PROLETARIATE (prō-le-tā'ri-at, āt) *n.* the lowest labouring class.

PROLIFIC (prō-lif'ik) *a.* fruitful. [F., fr. L. *proles*, offspring, and *-ficus*, making, fr. *jacere.*]

PROLIFICACY (prō-lif'i-kạ-si) *n.* fruitfulness. Also **PROLIFICNESS.**

PROLIX (prō'liks) *a.* long; tedious. [F., fr. L. *prolixus*, extended, fr. *liquere*, flow.]

PROLIXITY (prō-lik'si-ti) *n.* great length; tediousness.

PROLOGUE (prō'log) *n.* introduction to a play. [F., fr. L., fr. G. *prologos*, a speech before, fr. *legein*, to speak.]

PROLONG (pro-long') *v.t.* to lengthen in time or space; continue. [F. *prolonger*, fr. L., fr. *pro-*, and *longus*, LONG.]

PROLONGATION (pro-long-gā'shun) *n.* a lengthening in space or time; delay.

PROMENADE (prom-e-nād', nād') *n.* a walk for pleasure; the place for walking;—*v.i.* to walk up and down. [F., fr. O.F. *promener*, walk, fr. L. *pro-*, and *minare*, drive. See **MENACE.**]

PROMINENCE (prom'i-nens) *a.* state of being prominent.

PROMINENT (prom'i-nent) *a.* standing out; eminent; conspicuous. [L. (part. stem) *prominent-*, projecting; conn. with **PROMENADE.**]

PROMINENTLY (prom'i-nent-li) *ad.* eminently.

PROMISCUOUS (pro-mis'kū-us) *a.* mixed; indiscriminate. [L., fr. *miscere*, to mix. See **MISCELLANY.**]

PROMISCUOUSLY (prō-mis'kū-us-li) *ad.* without distinction.

PROMISE (prom'is) *n.* declaration which binds the one who makes it, expectation;—*v.t.* to engage by declaration; give hopes. [M.E. *promes*, fr. O.F., fr. L. (part.) *promissus*, lit. put forward, fr. *mittere*, send.]

PROMISEE (prom-i-sē') *n.* one to whom a promise is made.

PROMISING (prom'i-sing) *a.* affording ground for hope.

PROMISOR (prom'i-sẹr) *n.* one who promises.

PROMISSORY (prom'i-sụ-ri) *a.* containing a promise.

PROMONTORY (prom'un-tu-ri) *n.* a headland; high cape. [L. *promonturium*, fr. stem *mont-*, of *mons*, MOUNT.]

PROMOTE (pro-mōt') *v.t.* to forward; advance; encourage; raise in rank or office. [L. (part.) *promotus*, lit. moved forward, fr. *movere*. See **MOTION.**]

PROMOTER (pro-mō'tẹr) *n.* an encourager.

PROMOTION (pro-mō'shun) *n.* advancement; furtherance; preferment.

PROMOTIVE (pro-mō'tiv) *a.* tending to advance or aid.

PROMPT (promt) *a.* ready; quick;—*v.t.* to incite to action; dictate; suggest. [F., fr. L. *promptus* =*pro-emptus*, lit. (part.) brought forward, fr. *emere*, bring, buy.]

PROMPTER (promt'ẹr) *n.* one who reminds an actor of the next words.

PROMPTLY (promt'li) *ad.* with readiness.

PROMPTITUDE (prom'ti-tūd) *n.* readiness; alacrity.

PROMULGATE (pro-mul'găt) *v.t.* to make known by open declaration; publish. [L. (part.) *promulgatus*, fr. *promulgare*; of uncert. etym.]

PROMULGATION (pro-mul-gă'shun) *n.* a notice; open publication.

PROMULGATOR (prom'ul-gă-ter) *n.* one who publishes or makes known.

PRONE (prōn) *a.* bending downward; head-long; mentally disposed; inclined. [F., fr. L. *pronus*.]

PRONENESS (prōn'nes) *n.* inclination of mind, temper, etc.

PRONG (prong) *n.* the branch of a fork. [E.]

PRONOMINAL (pro-nom'i-nal) *a.* belonging to a pronoun.

PRONOUN (prō'noun) *n.* a word used for a noun. [Fr. *pro* = for, and NOUN.]

PRONOUNCE (pro-nouns') *v.t.* to speak; utter rhetorically; declare. [F. *prononcer*, fr. L. = tell forth, fr. *nuntiare*, ANNOUNCE.]

PRONOUNCEABLE (pro-noun'sa-bl) *a.* that can be pronounced.

PRONUNCIATION (prō-nun-si-ā'shun) *n.* act or mode of utterance.

PROOF (prŏŏf) *n.* test or trial; demonstration; convincing evidence; an impression taken for correction; early impression of an engraving; a certain strength in alcoholic spirits;—*a.* firm in resisting. [F. *preuve*, a trial, fr. Late L. (acc.) *probam*, L. *probare*, PROVE.]

PROP (prop) *n.* that on which a body rests; support;—*v.t.* to support; uphold. [E.]

PROPAGANDA (prop-a-gan'da) *n.* an institution for disseminating religious tenets or opinions. [L. = things to be propagated.]

PROPAGANDIST (prop-a-gan'dist) *n.* a person who propagates opinions.

PROPAGATE (prop'a-găt) *v.t.* to generate; multiply; spread; extend. [L. (part.) *propagatus*, lit. fastened down, fr. *pangere*, set.]

PROPAGATION (prop-a-gā'shun) *n.* spreading or extending; extension.

PROPAGATOR (prop'a-gā-ter) *n.* one who propagates.

PROPEL (pro-pel') *v.t.* to drive forward. [L. *propellere*, urge forward, fr. *pro*, before, and *pellere*, drive.]

PROPELLER (pro-pel'er) *n.* a screw-wheel in the stern for propelling a steamboat

PROPENSE (pro-pens') *a.* inclined. [L. *propensus*, hanging down, fr. (part.) *pensus*, fr. *pendere*, hang.] Propeller.

PROPENSION, PRO-PENSITY (pro-pen'shun, pro-pen'si-ti) *n.* inclination; bent of mind; tendency.

PROPER (prop'er) *a.* one's own; peculiar; suitable; correct; becoming. [F. *propre*, fr. L. (acc.) *proprium*, one's own.]

PROPERLY (prop'er-li) *ad.* fitly; suitably.

PROPERTY (prop'er-ti) *n.* inherent quality; ownership; an estate. [F., fr. L. *proprietas*. See PROPER.]

PROPHECY (prof'e-si) *n.* prediction. [F., fr. L. *prophetia*, fr. G. *propheteia*.]

PROPHESY (prof'e-si) *v.t.* or *i.* to foretell events; predict; foreshow.

PROPHET (prof'et) *n.* one who foretells future events. [G. *prophetes*, fr. *pro*, before, and *phemi*, I speak.]

PROPHETESS (prof'et-es) *n.* a female that predicts.

PROPHETICAL (pro-fet'i-kal) *a.* unfolding future events.

PROPHYLACTIC (prof-i-lak'tik) *a.* preventing disease;—*n.* a preventive medicine. [G. See PHYLACTERY.]

PROPINQUITY (pro-ping'kwi-ti) *n.* nearness in place, time, or relation. [L., fr. *propinquus*, neighbouring, fr. *prope*, near.]

PROPITIABLE (pro-pish'i-a-bl) *a.* that may be propitiated.

PROPITIATE (pro-pish'i-āt) *v.t.* or *i.* to make favourable; conciliate; atone. [L. (part.) *propitiatus*, made PROPITIOUS.]

PROPITIATION (pro-pish-i-ā'shun) *n.* act of appeasing; atonement.

PROPITIATOR (pro-pish-i-ā-ter) *n.* one who propitiates.

PROPITIATORY (pro-pish'i-a-tu-ri) *a.* adapted to atone;—*n.* the mercy-seat.

PROPITIOUS (pro-pish'us) *a.* highly favourable to success; disposed to be kind or gracious. [L. *propitius*.]

PROPITIOUSLY (pro-pish'us-li) *n.* favourably.

PROPITIOUSNESS (pro-pish'us-nes) *n.* kindly or favourable disposition.

PROPONENT (pro-pō'nent) *n.* one who makes a proposal. [L. See OPPONENT.]

PROPORTION (pro-pōr'shun) *n.* comparative relation; equal share; the rule of three;—*v.t.* to adjust parts to each other. [F., fr. L., fr. *pro* = in relation to, and *portio*, PORTION.]

PROPORTIONABLE (pro-pōr'shun-a-bl) *a.* that may be proportioned.

PROPORTIONATE (pro-pōr'shun-at) *a.* having proportion.

PROPORTIONALLY (pro-pōr'shun-al-i) *ad.* in due proportion.

PROPOSAL (pro-pō'zal) *n.* anything offered for consideration or acceptance.

PROPOSE (pro-pōz') *v.t.* to offer for consideration;—*v.i.* to make an offer of marriage. [F. *proposer*, fr. L. *pro-*, and F. *poser*, set. See E.]

PROPOSITION (prop-u-zish'un) *n.* a thing proposed; offer of terms. [L. fr. (part.) *propositus*, lit. set before, fr. *ponere*, put.]

PROPOSITIONAL (prop-u-zish'un-al) *a.* belonging to or contained in a proposition.

PROPOUND (pro-pound') *v.t.* to offer for consideration; set forth in words. [Formerly *propoune*, fr. L. *proponere*. See PROPOSITION.]

PROPOUNDER (pro-poun'der) *n.* one who proposes or offers.

PROPRIETARY (pro-pri'e-ta-ri) *n.* an owner; body of owners;—*a.* belonging to an owner.

PROPRIETOR (pro-pri'e-ter) *n.* a possessor in his own right; owner. [See PROPERTY.]

PROPRIETY (pro-pri'e-ti) *n.* fitness; justness; decorum. [L. *proprietas*. Doublet of PROPERTY.]

PROPULSION (pro-pul'shun) *n.* act of driving forward. [Fr. L. (part.) *propulsus*, propelled. See PROPEL, PULSE.]

PROROGATION (prō-ru-gā'shun) *n.* act of proroguing parliament.

PROROGUE (pro-rōg') *v.t.* to adjourn and continue the sitting of parliament; protract; delay. [F., fr. L. *prorogare*, lit. ask in public, fr. *rogare*, ask.]

PROSAIC (prō-zā'ik) *a.* consisting in or like prose; commonplace.

PROSAICALLY (prō-zā'i-kal-i) *ad.* in a prosaic or dull manner.

PROSCENIUM (prō-sē'ni-um) *n.* the part of the stage before the drop-scene. [L. See SCENE.]

PROSCRIBE (pro-skrib') *v.t.* to denounce; interdict; prohibit. [L., fr. *pro*, publicly, and *scribere*, write.]

PROSCRIPTION (pro-skrip'shun) *n.* a dooming to death; utter rejection. [L., fr. (part.) *proscriptus*, proscribed.]

PROSCRIPTIVE (pro-skrip'tiv) *a.* serving to proscribe.

PROSE (prōz) *n.* language not in verse;—*a.* not poetical; dull;—*v.i.* to talk or write tediously. [F., fr. L. *prosa* (*oratio*), direct (speech), short. fr. *proversus*, orig. (part.) turned forwards, fr. *vertere*.]

PROSECUTE (pros'e-kūt) *v.t.* or *i.* to follow; continue; pursue by law. [L. (part.) *prosecutus,* having pursued, fr. *sequi,* follow. Doublet of **PURSUE.**]

PROSECUTION (pros-e-kū'shun) *n.* act of prosecuting.

PROSECUTOR (pros'e-kū-tẹr) *n.* one who prosecutes.

PROSELYTE (pros'e-līt) *n.* a new convert;— *v.t.* to convert. [F., fr. L., fr. G. *proselutos,* lit. incomer, fr. *pros,* forward, and *elthein,* come.]

PROSELYTISE (pros'e-li-tīz) *v.t.* to make converts; convert.

PROSELYTISM (pros'e-li-tizm) *n.* zeal to make converts; conversion.

PROSODIST (pros'u-dist) *n.* one skilled in prosody.

PROSODY (pros'u-di) *n.* the part of grammar which treats of syllables, accent, and versification. [G., fr. *pros,* to, and *ode,* song.]

PROSPECT (pros'pekt) *n.* a view; object of view; reason to hope;—*v.t.* to look forward; seek. [L. (part.) *prospectus,* fr. *prospicere,* to look forward, fr. *specere,* to look.]

PROSPECTING (pros-pekt'ing) *n.* searching a district for signs of gold or silver.

PROSPECTION (pro-spek'shun) *n.* looking forward and providing for the future.

PROSPECTIVE (pro-spek'tiv) *a.* looking forward; regarding the future.

PROSPECTUS (pro-spek'tus) *n.* plan of a proposed literary work or public undertaking; syllabus. [L.]

PROSPER (pros'pẹr) *v.i.* to be successful; succeed;—*v.t.* to favour; render successful. [L. *prosper,* fr. *pro-,* according to, and *spes,* hope.]

PROSPERITY (pros-per'i-ti) *n.* good fortune; success.

PROSPEROUS (pros'pẹr-us) *a.* successful.

PROSPEROUSLY (pros'pẹr-us-li) *ad.* successfully; fortunately.

PROSTITUTE (pros'ti-tūt) *v.t.* to debase;— *a.* vicious for hire;—*n.* a female devoted to lewdness. [L., f . *pro-,* and *statuere,* place.]

PROSTITUTION (pros-ti-tū'shun) *n.* act of prostituting.

PROSTRATE (pros'trāt) *a.* lying at length;— *v.t.* to throw down; lay flat; overthrow; reduce; bow in reverence. [L. (part.) *prostratus,* thrown forward, fr. *sternere,* strew. See **STRATUM.**]

PROSTRATION (pros-trā'shun) *n.* act of prostrating; dejection.

PROSTYLE (prō'stīl) *a.* having a range of columns in front. [G. *pro,* before, and *stulos,* column.]

PROSY (prō'zi) *a.* dull and tedious in speech or writing.

PROTEAN (prō-tē'an) *a.* changing shape. [Fr. *Proteus,* a sea-god who had the faculty of assuming different shapes.]

PROTECT (pro-tekt') *v.t.* to cover from danger; defend; shelter. [L. (part.) *protectus,* lit. covered in front, fr. *pro,* before, and *tegere,* to cover.]

PROTECTION (pro-tek'shun) *n.* defence from injury or danger; refuge; guard; passport.

PROTECTIONIST (pro-tek'shun-ist) *n.* one who would favour home industry by taxing foreign.

PROTECTIVE (pro-tek'tiv) *a.* defensive.

PROTECTOR (pro-tek'tẹr) *n.* a defender from injury; guardian. [protects.

PROTECTRESS (pro-tek'tres) *n.* a female who

PROTEGE (pro-tā-zhā') *n.* one protected. [F.]

PROTEST (prō-test') *v.i.* to affirm solemnly; —*v.t.* to declare against; note, as a bill for non-payment. [F., fr. L., fr. *pro-,* publicly, and *testari,* **TESTIFY.**]

PROTEST (prō'test) *n.* a formal declaration.

PROTESTANT (prot'es-tant) *n.* one who protests against popery.

PROTESTANTISM (prot'es-tan-tizm) *n.* the reformed religion.

PROTESTATION (prot-es-tā'shun) *n.* solemn declaration—usually of dissent.

PROTESTER (pro-tes'tẹr) *n.* one who protests.

PROTOCOL (prō'tu-kol) *n.* the first copy of a diplomatic despatch or treaty. [F., fr. Late L. *protocollum,* lit. a fly-leaf bearing author's name, etc., glued on to MS., fr. G. *protos,* first, and *kolla,* glue.]

PROTOMARTYR (prō'tō-mär-tẹr) *n.* the first martyr, Stephen. [G. *protos,* first.]

PROTOTYPE (prō'tu-tīp) *n.* an original model. [G. *protos,* first.]

PROTRACT (pro-trakt') *v.t.* to lengthen in time; prolong; defer. [L. (part.) *protractus* lit. drawn forward, fr. *pro,* forward, and *trahere,* draw.]

PROTRACTION (pro-trak'shun) *n.* act of lengthening out.

PROTRACTIVE (pro-trak'tiv) *a.* delaying.

PROTRACTOR (pro-trak'tẹr) *n.* an instrument for laying down angles.

PROTRUDE (pro-trōōd') *v.t.* or *i.* to thrust or shoot forward or out. [L. *protrudere,* fr. *pro,* forward, and *trudere,* thrust.]

PROTRUSION (pro-trōō'zhun) *n.* act of thrusting out.

PROTRUSIVE (pro-trōō'siv) *a.* impelling outward.

PROTUBERANCE (pro-tū'bẹ-rans) *n.* a prominence; a swelling.

PROTUBERANT (pro-tū'bẹ-rant) *a.* prominent; swelling. [L. (part. stem) *protuberant,* bulging out, fr. *tuber,* swelling.]

PROTUBERATE (pro-tū'bẹ-rāt) *v.i.* to become prominent.

PROUD (proud) *a.* having inordinate self-esteem; arrogant; ostentatious. [O.E. *prud.*]

PROUDFLESH (proud'flesh) *n.* growth of flesh on a wound or sore.

PROUDLY (proud'li) *ad.* haughtily.

PROVABLE (prōō'va-bl) *a.* that may be proved.

PROVE (prōōv) *v.t.* or *i.* to try by experiment, by a standard, or by suffering; demonstrate; deduce; turn out to be. [O.E. *profian,* fr. L. *probare,* test, fr. *probus,* good, proper.]

PROVENDER (prov'en-dẹr) *n.* dry food for cattle and horses. [O.F. *provendre, provende,* fr. Late L. *præbenda,* allowance, stipend. See **PREPEND.**]

PROVERB (prov'ẹrb) *n.* a wise saying; maxim; a byword. [L. *proverbium,* fr. *pro*=publicly, and *verbum,* word.]

PROVERBIAL (pro-vẹr'bi-al) *a.* pertaining to proverb; widely spoken.

PROVERBIALLY (pro-vẹr'bi-al-i) *ad.* commonly; generally.

PROVIDE (pro-vīd') *v.t.* or *i.* to make ready beforehand; prepare; supply. [L. *providere,* to foresee, fr. *videre,* see.]

PROVIDED (pro-vī'ded) *conj.* on the condition or understanding that.

PROVIDENCE (prov'i-dens) *n.* foresight; the care of God over His creatures; God; prudence.

PROVIDENT (prov'i-dent) *a.* preparing beforehand.

PROVIDENTIAL (prov-i-den'shal) *a.* effected by providence.

PROVIDENTIALLY (prov-i-den'shal-i) *ad.* by means of providence.

PROVIDENTLY (prov'i-dent-li) *ad.* with prudent foresight.

PROVINCE (prov'ins) *n.* a conquered country, or one governed by a delegate. [F., fr. L. *provincia*; perh. conn. with *vincere,* conquer.]

PROVINCIAL (pro-vin'shal) *n.* an inhabitant of a province;—*a.* belonging to a province; unpolished; not general.

Fāte, fär, ado; mē, hẹr; mine; nōte; tūne; mōōn.

PROVINCIALISM (pro-vin'shal-izm) *n.* peculiarity of speech in a province.

PROVISION (pru-vizh'un) *n.* something provided; food;—*v.t.* to supply with stores. [F., fr. L. (acc.) *provisionem*, foresight, fr. (part.) *provisus*, foreseen. See **PROVIDE**.]

PROVISIONAL (pru-vizh'un-ạl) *a.* prepared for the occasion; temporary. Also **PROVISIONARY**.

PROVISIONALLY (pru-vizh'un-ạl-i) *ad.* by way of provision.

PROVISO (prō-vī'zo) *n.* conditional stipulation;—*pl.* **PROVISES.** [L. *proviso quod*, it being provided that.]

PROVISORY (prō-vī'zur-i) *a.* conditional; temporary.

PROVOCATION (prov-u-kā'shun) *n.* act of provoking; any offence or cause of anger.

PROVOCATIVE (pru-vō'kạ-tiv) *a.* that excites.

PROVOKE (pru-vōk') *v.t.* to excite to action or to anger; incense; offend; challenge. [F. *provoquer*, fr. L. *provocare*, call forth, fr. *vocare*, call.]

PROVOST (prov'ust) *n.* a chief officer or magistrate. [O.F. *provost*, It. *prevost*, fr. (acc. part.) *præpositum*, one set over, fr. *præ*, and *ponere*, place.]

PROW (prow) *n.* forepart of a ship. [F. *proue*, fr. L. (acc.) *proram*, fr. G., fr. *pro*, before.]

PROWESS (prow'es) *n.* bravery; valour. [O.F., fr. *prou* =F. *preux*, good, of uncert. etym.]

PROWL (prowl) *v.i.* to rove for prey;—*n.* a roving for prey. [M.E. *prollen*, fr. Teut.]

PROXIMATE (prok'si-mạt) *a.* having intimate relation; next; immediate. [L. (part.) *proximatus*, fr. *proximare*, draw near.]

PROXIMATELY (prok'si-mạt-li) *ad.* by immediate relation; immediately.

PROXIMITY (prok-sim'i-ti) *n.* immediate nearness. [F., fr. L., fr. *proximus*, nearest, fr. *prope*, near.]

PROXIMO (prok'si-mō) *n.* the next or the coming month.

PROXY (prok'si) *n.* one deputed to act for another; the writing by which he is deputed. [Short. fr. **PROCURACY.** See **PROCTOR.**]

PRUDE (prōōd) *n.* a woman of affected modesty. [F., conn. with *preux*, **PROWESS.**]

PRUDENCE (prōō'dens) *n.* practical wisdom; caution.

PRUDENT (prōō'dent) *a.* practically wise; cautious; discreet; careful; frugal. [F., fr. L. (acc.) *prudentem* = (*providentem*). **PROVIDENT.**]

PRUDENTIAL (prōō-den'shạl) *a.* proceeding from prudence.

PRUDENTLY (prōō'dent-li) *ad.* discreetly.

PRUDERY (prōō'dẹ-ri) *n.* affected modesty. Also **PRUDISHNESS.**]

PRUDISH (prōō'dish) *a.* affectedly modest; very precise or reserved.

PRUDISHLY (prōō'dish-li) *ad.* in a prudish manner.

PRUNE (prōōn) (1) *n.* a dried plum;—(2) *v.t.* or *i.* to cut off branches; dress; trim. [(1) F., fr. L., fr. G. *proumnon, prounon.* (2) Etym. uncert.]

PRUNELLA (prōō-nel'ạ) *n.* a strong black woollen stuff. [F. *prunelle*, a sloe, dim. fr. *prune*, **PRUNE.**]

PRURIENCE (prōō'ri-ens) *n.* itching desire.

PRURIENT (prōō'ri-ent) *a.* uneasy with desire. [L. (part. stem) *prurient-*, itching, fr. *prurire.*]

PRY (pri) *v.i.* to inspect closely. [O.F. *prier*, to pillage, fr. Late L. *predare*, to plunder, to investigate. See **PREY.**]

PSALM (sám) *n.* a sacred song. [O.E. *sealm*, fr. L., fr. G. *psalmos*, fr. *psallein*, to play on a stringed instrument.]

PSALMIST (sà'mist, sal'mist) *n.* a writer of psalms.

PSALMODIST (sà'mu-dist, sal'mu-dist) *n.* one who sings sacred songs.

PSALMODY (sà'mu-di, sal'mu-di) *n.* the art or practice of singing sacred songs. [G. *ode*, song, ode.]

PSALTER (sawl'tẹr) *n.* the book of psalms. [Form of **PSALTERY.**]

PSALTERY (sawl'tẹr-i) *n.* an instrument of music. [L. *psalterium*, fr. G. *psalterion.* See **PSALM.**]

PSEUDONYM (sū'dō-nim) *n.* a fictitious name. [G. *pseudonumos*, fr. *onoma*, name.]

PSHAW (shaw) *ex.* expressing contempt.

PSYCHOLOGIC (si-kō-loj'ik) *a.* pertaining to the soul or to the science of the same.

PSYCHOLOGIST (si-kol'ō-jist) *n.* one versed in psychology.

PSYCHOLOGY (si-kol'ō-ji) *n.* the doctrine of the soul. [Fr. G. *psuche*, soul, and *-logia*, fr. *legein*, discourse.]

PTARMIGAN (tár'mi-gạn) *n.* a bird of the grouse family. [Celt.]

PUBERTY (pū'bẹr-ti) *n.* ripe age in the sexes. [F. *puberté*, fr. L. (acc.) *pubertatem*, fr. *pubes*, signs of manhood.]

PUBESCENCE (pū-bes'ens) *n.* a state of puberty; the soft, short hairs on plants.

PUBLIC (pub'lik) *a.* pertaining to a community; common; open;—*n.* the body of a people. [F., fr. L. *publicus = poplicos*, fr. *populus*, people.]

PUBLICAN (pub'li-kạn) *n.* an innkeeper; a collector of toll or tribute; licensed dealer in spirituous liquors.

PUBLICATION (pub-li-kā'shun) *n.* the act of publishing; thing published.

PUBLICIST (pub'li-sist) *n.* a writer on current political topics.

PUBLICITY (pub-lis'i-ti) *n.* state of being public.

PUBLICLY (pub'lik-li) *ad.* openly.

PUBLISH (pub'lish) *v.t.* to make known; proclaim; put into circulation. [Fr. F. *publier*, fr. L. *publicare*, make **PUBLIC.**]

PUBLISHER (pub'lish-ẹr) *n.* one who publishes books.

PUCE (pūs) *a.* of a brownish purple colour. [F. =flea-colour, fr. O.F. *pulce*, fr. L. (acc.) *pulicem*, flea.]

PUCK (puk) *n.* a small tricky fairy. [O.E. *puca.*]

PUCKER (puk'ẹr) *v.t.* to gather into small folds;—*n.* a fold; wrinkle. [Scand.]

PUDDING (poo'ding) *n.* a kind of food variously compounded. [E.]

PUDDLE (pud'l) *n.* a small pool of muddy water;—*v.t.* to make muddy; stop up with clay; convert cast iron into wrought. [M.E. *podel*, fr. O.E. *pudd*, ditch.]

PUERILE (pū'ẹr-il) *a.* childish; boyish. [L., fr. *puer*, child, boy.]

PUERILITY (pū-ẹr-il'i-ti) *n.* childishness.

PUERPERAL (pū-ẹr'pẹr-ạl) *a.* pertaining to childbirth. [L. *puerpera*, a lying-in woman, fr. *puer*, child, and *parere*, so bear]

PUFF (puf) *n.* a slight blast of wind;—*v.t* or *i.* to swell with wind; pant; praise vainly. [Imit.]

PUG (pug) *n.* a monkey or little dog. [E.; conn. with **PUCK.**]

PUGILISM (pū'ji-lizm) *n.* a fighting with the fist. [Fr. L. *pugil*, boxer. Cf. *pugnus*, fist.]

PUGILIST (pū'ji-list) *n.* a boxer.

PUGILISTIC (pū-ji-lis'tik) *a.* pertaining to fighting with the fist.

PUGNACIOUS (pug-nā'shus) *a.* inclined to fight; quarrelsome. [L. stem *pugnaci-*, of *pugnax*, fr. *pugnare* to fight.]

PUGNACITY (pug-nas'i-ti) *n.* disposition to fight.

PUG-NOSE (pug'nōz) *n.* a short, thick nose.

PUISNE (pū'ne) *a.* younger; inferior. [Form of **PUNY.**]

PUISSANCE (pū′i-sans) *a.* power; strength.
PUISSANT (pū′i-sant) *a.* powerful. [F., through Late L., fr. L. *posse*, be able.]
PUKE (pūk) *v.i.* to vomit;—*n.* a vomit. [E.]
PULE (pūl) *v.i.* to whine like a child. [Imit.]
PULL (pool) *v.t.* or *i.* to draw; haul; tear; pluck; gather; tug;—*n.* act of pulling; effort; advantage in a contest. [O.E. *pullian.*]
PULLET (pool′et) *n.* a young hen. [F. *poulette*, dim. fr. *poule*, hen, fr. L. *pulla*.]
PULLEY (pool′i) *n.* a small wheel in a block, with a groove for a running cord ; — *pl.* **PULLEYS.** [Perh. fr. F. *poulie*, fr. E. *pull*.]
PULMONARY (pul′mu-na-ri) *a.* affecting the lungs. [L. *pulmonarius*, fr. stem *pulmon-*, of *pulmo*, lung.]
PULP (pulp) *n.* the soft part of fruit;—*v.t.* to deprive of pulp. [F., fr. L. *pulpa*.]

Pulley.

PULPIT (pool′pit) *n.* an elevated station or desk for a preacher. [O.F. *pulpite*, fr. L. *pulpitum*, a stage.]
PULPY (pul′pi) *a.* like pulp; soft.
PULSATE (pul′sāt) *v.i.* to throb or beat. [L. (part.) *pulsatus*, fr. *pulsare*, throb. See **PULSE.**]
PULSATION (pul-sā′shun) *n.* a beating.
PULSATIVE (pul′sa-tiv) *a.* beating like a pulse. Also **PULSATORY.**
PULSE (puls) (1) *n.* a beating of arteries;—(2) *n.* peas, beans, etc. [(1) F. *pouls*, fr. L. (acc.) *pulsum*, beating, fr. *pellere*. (2) L. *puls*, pottage.]
PULVERISABLE (pul-ve-rī′za-bl) *a.* that may be reduced to fine powder.
PULVERISATION (pul-ve-ri-zā′shun) *n.* a reducing to powder.
PULVERISE (pul′ver-iz) *v.t.* to reduce to powder. [F., fr. Late L. *pulverizare*, fr. L. stem *pulver-*, of *pulvis*, dust.]
PUMA (pū′ma) *n.* a carnivorous quadruped of the cat family. [Peruv.]
PUMICE (pū′mis, pum′is) *n.* a porous substance ejected from volcanoes. [O.E. fr. L. stem *pumic-*, of *pumex*.]
PUMP (pump) *n.* an engine for raising water or other fluids;—*v.t.* or *i.* to work a pump. [F. *pompe*, fr. Ger. *Pumpe*; conn. with **PLUMP.**]
PUMPKIN (pump′kin) *n.* a plant and its fruit. [F. *pompon*, fr. G. *pepon*, ripe.]
PUN (pun) *n.* a word or expression with two meanings;—*v.i.* to play upon words. [Fr. O.E. *punian*, to beat.]
PUNCH (punsh) (1) *n.* a tool for making holes; *v.t.* to perforate; (2) a liquor; (3) a buffoon; (4) a blow; *v.t.* to thrust. [Contr. fr. **PUNCHEON.** (2) Skr. =five. (3) Short. fr. *Punchinello*. (4) Prob. fr. **PUNISH.**]
PUNCHEON (pun′shun) *n.* a tool; a cask. [O.F. =F. *poincon*, fr. L. (acc.) *punctionem*, pricking, fr. (part.) *punctus*, pricked. See **PUNCTURE.**]
PUNCTILIO (pungk-til′i-ō, pungk-til′yō) *n.* a nice point in behaviour or ceremony. [Sp. *puntillo*, dim. fr. *punto*, POINT.]
PUNCTILIOUS (pungk-til′i-us) *a.* exact in ceremony or behaviour; very formal.
PUNCTUAL (pungk′tū-al) *a.* exact; strict; nice. [Late L. *punctualis*, fr. L. *punctum*, POINT.]
PUNCTUALITY (pungk-tū-al′i-ti) *n.* scrupulous exactness in time.
PUNCTUALLY (pungk′tū-al-i) *ad.* exactly.
PUNCTUATE (pungk′tū-āt) *v.t.* to mark with written points. [Late L. *punctuatus*, pointed off. See **POINT.**]

PUNCTUATION (pungk-tū-ā′shun) *n.* the act or art of dividing sentences by points.
PUNCTURE (pungk′tūr) *n.* piercing or pricking; a small hole made by a point;—*v.t.* to prick with a pointed instrument. [L. *punctura*, fr. (part.) *punctus*, pricked, fr. *pungere*. See **PUNGENT.**]
PUNDIT (pun′dit) *n.* a learned man. [Hind. *pandit.*]
PUNGENCY (pun′jen-si) *n.* sharpness; keenness; severity.
PUNGENT (pun′jent) *a.* sharp; biting; keen; stinging. [L. (part. stem) *pungent*, pricking, fr. *pungere.*]
PUNIC (pū′nik) *a.* pertaining to Carthage; faithless. [L. *Punicus*, fr. *Pœnus*, Carthaginian.]
PUNINESS (pū′ni-nes) *n.* littleness and weakness.
PUNISH (pun′ish) *v.t.* to inflict pain for an offence; chastise; correct. [F. (part.) *punissant*, punishing, fr. *punir*, fr. L. *punire*, fr. *pœna*, PENALTY.]
PUNISHABLE (pun′ish-a-bl) *a.* worthy to be punished.
PUNISHER (pun′ish-er) *n.* one that punishes.
PUNISHMENT (pun′ish-ment) *n.* any pain, loss, or suffering inflicted for a fault or crime.
PUNITIVE (pū′ni-tiv) *a.* awarding or inflicting punishment. Also **PUNITORY.**
PUNKAH (pung′ka) *n.* a large fan swung from the ceiling of a room to ventilate it. [Hind.]
PUNT (punt) *n.* a flat-bottomed boat;—*v.t.* to propel a boat with a pole. [O.E., fr. L. *ponto*, a punt, FONTOON.]
PUNY (pū′ni) *a.* little and weak. [O.F. *puisné*, lit. born after, fr. L. *post natus.*]
PUPA (pū′pa) *n.* a chrysalis. [L.]
PUPIL (pū′pil) *n.* a scholar; a ward; the apple of the eye. [O.F., fr. L. *pupillus*, *pupilla*, dim. of *pupus*, boy, and *pupa*, girl.]
PUPILAGE (pū′pil-ij) *n.* the state of being a scholar or ward; minority.
PUPILARY (pū′pi-la-ri) *a.* pertaining to a ward or to the pupil of the eye.
PUPPET (pup′et) *n.* a doll; a figure moved by wires in a show; one entirely under the control of another. [O.F. *poupette*, fr. L. *pupa*, girl. See **PUPIL.**]
PUPPY (pup′i) *n.* a young dog; a conceited young fellow. [F. *poupée*, doll, baby; conn. with **PUPPET.**]
PUPPYISM (pup′i-izm) *n.* affectation or conceit in young men.
PURBLIND (pur′blind) *a.* near-sighted. [Fr. **PURE**=whole, and **BLIND.** Cf. **PAR-BOIL.**]
PURBLINDNESS (pur′blind-nes) *n.* dimness of vision.
PURCHASABLE (pur′cha-sa-bl) *a.* that can be bought or acquired.
PURCHASE (pur′chas) *v.t.* to buy; obtain by outlay of money or effort;—*n.* a buying; thing bought; power of a lever. [O.F. *purchacer*, fr. *pur*=F. *pour*, fr. L. *pro*, for, and *chacer*, CHASE.]
PURCHASER (pur′cha-ser) *n.* one who buys.
PURE (pūr) *a.* clear; real; unmixed; unpolluted; mere. [F., fr. L. *purus.*]
PURELY (pūr′li) *ad.* in a pure manner; merely.
PURGATION (pur-gā′shun) *n.* the act of cleansing.
PURGATIVE (pur′ga-tiv) *a.* cleansing;—*n.* a cathartic.
PURGATORIAL (pur-ga-tō′ri-al) *a.* pertaining to purgatory.
PURGATORY (pur′ga-tu-ri) *n.* a place after death, where souls are supposed to be purified from venial sins; any state or time of trial and suffering. [Fr. L. (part.) *purgatus*, purged. See **PURGE.**]

PURGE (purj) *n.* cathartic medicine;—*v.t.* or *i.* to make pure; cleanse; clear; evacuate the bowels. [F. *purger*, fr. L. *purgare*, fr. *purus*, **PURE**, and *agere*, bring.]

PURIFICATION (pū-ri-fi-kā'shun) *n.* act of purifying; a cleansing.

PURIFIER (pū'ri-fi-ẹr) *n.* that which purifies; a refiner.

PURIFY (pū'ri-fi) *v.t.* or *i.* to cleanse; refine; grow pure. [F. *purifier*, fr. L., fr. *purus*, and *ficare* = *facere*, make.]

PURIST (pūr'ist) *n.* one nice in the choice of words.

PURITAN (pū'ri-tẹn) *n.* a dissenter from the Church of England;—*a.* puritanic. [Made fr. **PURITY**.]

PURITANIC (pū-ri-tan'ik) *a.* pertaining to the dissenters and their doctrines; rigid.

PURITANISM (pū'ri-tẹn-izm) *n.* the notions or practice of Puritans.

PURITY (pū'ri-ti) *n.* cleanness; chastity. [F. *pureté*, fr. *pur*, **PURE**.]

PURL (purl) (1) *v.i.* to flow with a gentle noise;—*n.* a gentle murmur of a stream; —(2) a border; lace. (1) E. (2) Also **PEARL**. Form of *purfle*.]

PURLIEU (pur'lū) *n.* a border or environ; district. [Formerly *pourallee*, fr. O.F. *pur* = F. *pour*, fr. L. *pro*, for, and *alee*, going. See **ALLEY**.]

PURLOIN (pur-loin') *v.t.* to steal; pilfer. [O.F. *purloigner*, lit. detain, fr. L. *prolongare*, **PROLONG**.]

PURLOINER (pur-loi'nẹr) *n.* one who steals.

PURPLE (pur'pl) *a.* red tinged with blue;— *n.* a colour composed of red and blue; robe of an emperor or cardinal; cardinalate; —*v.t.* to dye or clothe with purple. [O.F. *purpre*, fr. L., fr. G. *porphura*, the purple-fish.]

PURPORT (pur-pōrt') *n.* that which is meant; tendency;—*v.t.* to mean; signify. [O.F. *purporter*, declare, fr. *pur* = F. *pour*, fr. L. *pro*, for, and *portare*, carry.]

PURPOSE (pur'pus) (1) *n.* object to be accomplished; determined choice; intention; aim;—(2) *v.t.* or *i.* to intend; design; resolve. [(1) O.F.; form of *propos*, fr L. *propositum*. See **PROPOSITION**. (2) O.F. *pourposer*]

PURPOSELESS (pur'pus-les) *a.* without meaning or effect.

PURPOSELY (pur'pus-li) *ad.* on purpose.

PURR (pur) *v.i.* to murmur as a cat;—*n.* a sound made by cats. [imit.]

PURSE (purs) *n.* a small money-bag;—*v.t.* to put in a purse. [O.F. *borse* = F. *bourse*, fr. Late L., fr. G. *bursa*, hide.]

PURSE-PRIDE (purs'prid) *n.* pride of money.

PURSER (pur'sẹr) *n.* paymaster of a ship.

PURSUANCE (pur-sū'ạns) *n.* a following; prosecution; consequence.

PURSUANT (pur-sū'ạnt) *a.* done in consequence; agreeable.

PURSUE (pur-sū') *v.t.* to follow; chase; prosecute. [O.F. *porsuir* = F. *poursuivre*, fr. L. *pro*, forward, and *sequi*, follow.]

PURSUER (pur-sū'ẹr) *n.* one that follows.

PURSUIT (pur-sūt') *n.* act of following; chase; course of business; occupation.

PURSUIVANT (pur'swi-vạnt) *n.* a state messenger. [F. (part.) = pursuing.]

PURSY (pur'si) *a.* fat and short-breathed. [O.F. *poursif* = *poulsif*, fr. *pouls*, **PULSE**.]

PURULENCE (pū'rū-lens) *n.* generation of pus.

PURULENT (pū'rū-lent) *a.* consisting of pus. [F., fr. L. *purulentus*, fr. stem *pur*-, of *pus*, **PUS**.]

PURVEY (pur-vā') *v.t.* or *i.* to provide; procure; cater. [O.F. = *purveier* = F. *pourvoir*, fr. L. *providere*, to **PROVIDE**.]

PURVEYANCE (pur-vā'ạns) *n.* procurement of provisions.

PURVEYOR (pur-vā'ẹr) *n.* one that provides.

PURVIEW (pur'vū) *n.* the body of a statute; scope; extent. [O.F. (part.) *purveu*, provided. See **PURVEY**.]

PUS (pus) *n.* the matter of an ulcer. [L.]

PUSEYISM (pū'zi-izm) *n.* high church doctrines or principles advanced by Dr *Pusey* and other Oxford divines in 1830-47.

PUSEYIST (pū'zi-ist) *n.* a follower of Dr Pusey or of his teaching. Also **PUSEYITE**.

PUSH (poosh) *v.t.* or *i.* to press against with force; urge; impel; make an effort;—*n.* a thrust; pressure or force applied; emergency. [O.F. *pousser*, *poulser*, fr. L. *pulsare*, **PULSATE**.]

PUSILLANIMITY (pū-si-lạ-nim'i-ti) *n.* a weakness of mind; cowardice.

PUSILLANIMOUS (pū-si-lan'i-mus) *a.* destitute of courage; cowardly; dastardly. [L. *pusillus*, very little, and *animus*, spirit.]

PUSS (poos) *n.* a cat; a hare. [imit., from noise made by cat in spitting.]

PUSSY (poos'i) *n.* the diminutive of **PUSS**.

PUSTULATE (pus'tū-lāt) *v.i.* to form into pustules.

PUSTULE (pus'tūl) *n.* a small pimple containing pus. [F., fr. L. *pustula*, a pimple.]

PUSTULOUS (pus'tū-lus) *a.* having pustules.

PUT (poot) *v.t.* [*pret.* and *pp.* **PUT**] to lay in a place; apply; propose; exhibit; express in words. [O.E. *potian*, to push.]

PUTATIVE (pū'tạ-tiv) *a.* supposed; reputed. [F., fr. L., fr. (part.) *putatus*, supposed, fr. *putare*.]

PUT-OFF (poot'of) *n.* a shift or excuse for delay.

PUTREFACTION (pū-tre-fak'shun) *n.* process of rotting.

PUTREFACTIVE (pū-tre-fak'tiv) *a.* making rotten.

PUTREFY (pū'tre-fi) *v.t.* or *i.* to dissolve or rot, as organised matter. [F. *putrifier*, fr. Late L., fr. L. *putris*, **PUTRID**, and *facere*, make.]

PUTRESCENCE (pū-tres'ens) *n.* state of rotting or decomposition.

PUTRESCENT (pū-tres'ent) *n.* dissolving, as organised bodies.

PUTRESCIBLE (pū-tres'i-bl) *a.* liable to become putrid.

PUTRID (pū'trid) *a.* corrupt; rotten. [L. *putridus*, stinking, fr. *putris*, rotten.]

PUTRIDITY (pū-trid'i-ti) *n.* state of being putrid. Also **PUTRIDNESS**.

PUTTOCK (put'uk) *n.* a species of kite. [E., of unknown etym.]

PUTTY (put'i) *n.* a paste of whiting and linseed oil, used by glaziers;—*v.t.* to cement with putty. [F. *potée*, orig. a potful, fr. *pot*, **POT**.]

PUZZLE (puz'l) *n.* perplexity; an ingenious toy;—*v.t.* to perplex, as the mind. [Short. fr. *opposayle* = *opposal*.]

PUZZLER (puz'lẹr) *n.* an awkward question or objection.

PYGMEAN (pig-mē'ạn) *a.* dwarfish. [F. *pygme*, fr. L., fr. G. *pugme*, measure of 13¼ inches.]

PYLON (pi'lon) *n.* a mark set up to guide aeroplanes during a flight over a stated course. [G. *pule*, a gate.]

PYRAMID (pir'ạ-mid) *n.* a solid having a rectilinear base, and its sides triangles having a common vertex. [L. stem *pyramid*-, of *pyramis*, fr. G. *puramis*.]

PYRAMIDICAL (pir-a-mid'i-kal) *a.* having the form of a pyramid. Also **PYRAMIDAL**.

PYRE (pir) *n.* a funeral pile. [L., fr. G. *pura*, funeral pile, fr. *pur*, fire.]

PYRITES (pi-ri'tēz) *n.* a compound of sulphur with a metal. [L., fr. G. *purites*, flint, lit. pertaining to fire, *pur*, fire.]

PYROLATRY (pi-rol'ạ-tri) *n.* worship of fire. [Fr. G. *pur*, fire, and *latreia*, worship.]

PYROLOGY (pī-rol'ō-ji) *n.* science of heat. [G. *pur*, fire, and *logia*, fr. *legein*.]

PYROMANCY (pī'ru-man-si) *n.* divination by fire. [G. *pur*, fire, and *manteia*, divination.]

PYROMETER (pī-rom'e-ter) *n.* an instrument to measure degrees of heat. [Fr. G. *pur*, fire, and *metron*, measure, **METRE**.]

PYROTECHNICS (pī-ru-tek'niks) *n.* the art of making fireworks, as rockets. [G. *pur*, and *technikos*, fr. *techne*, an art.]

PYROTECHNIST (pī-ru-tek'nist) *n.* one skilled in pyrotechny.

PYRRHONISM (pir'u-nizm) *n.* universal scepticism. [*Pyrrho*, Greek philosopher, 360-270 B.C.]

PYTHIAN (pith'i-an) *a.* pertaining to the priestess of Apollo, and also to certain games. [G. *Puthios*.]

PYTHON (pī'thon) *n.* a genus of large serpents. [G.]

PYX (piks) *n.* among *Roman Catholics*, the box in which the consecrated host is kept. Also written PIX. [L., fr. G. *puxis*, a **BOX**, fr. *puxos*, BOX-wood.]

Q

QUACK (kwak) *v.i.* to cry like a duck; boast; —*n.* a pretender to medical skill. [Imit. Cf. Ger. *quaken*.]

QUACKERY (kwak'e-ri) *n.* boastful pretensions to skill in medicine.

QUACKISH (kwak'ish) *a.* like a quack.

QUADRANGLE (kwod'rang-gl) *n.* a figure of four angles [L. *quad-*, fr. rt. of *quatuor*, four, and *angulus*, **ANGLE**.]

QUADRANGULAR (kwod-rang'gū-lar) *a.* having four angles.

QUADRANT (kwod'rant) *n.* a fourth part; an instrument for taking altitudes; 90 degrees. [Fr. L. *quadrans*, a fourth part.]

QUADRANTAL (kwod-ran'tal) *a.* pertaining to a quadrant.

QUADRAT (kwod'rat) *n.* piece of metal to fill a space in printing. [Fr. L. (part.) *quadratus*, squared, fr. root of *quatuor*, four.]

QUADRATE (kwod'rāt) *a.* square; suited;— *v.t.* to square; fit; suit. [L. (part.) *quadratus*, squared. See QUADRAT.]

Quadrant.

QUADRATIC (kwod-rat'ik) *a.* pertaining to a square.

QUADRATURE (kwod'ra-tūr) *n.* a square; the act of squaring.

QUADRILLE (ka-dril', kwo-dril') *n.* game at cards played by four; a dance in sets of four couples; the music for it. [F., through Sp., fr. Late L. *quadrus*, square, fr. L. root of *quatuor*, four.]

QUADRIPARTITE (kwod-ri-pär'tit) *a.* consisting of four parts. [L. pref. *quadri-*, fr. root of *quatuor*, four.]

QUADROON (kwod-röön') *n.* the child of a mulatto and a white man. [Sp. *cuarteron*, fr. L. *quartus*, fourth.]

QUADRUMANOUS (kwod-roo'ma-nus) *a.* having four hands. [L. *quadru-*, four times, and *manus*, a hand.]

QUADRUPED (kwod'roo-ped) *n.* an animal having four feet. [L., fr. *quadru-*, four times, and stem *ped-*, of *pes*, foot.]

QUADRUPLE (kwod'roo-pl) *a.* fourfold. [L. *quadruplus*, fr. *quadru*, four times.]

QUADRUPLICATE (kwod-roo'pli-kāt) *a.* fourfold;—*v.t.* to make fourfold. [L. *quatuor*, and *plicare*, to fold.]

QUADRUPLICATION (kwod-roo-pli-kā'shun) *n.* a making fourfold.

QUAFF (kwaf) *v.t.* or *i.* to drink largely. [Celt.]

QUAGMIRE (kwag'mir) *n.* a bog that shakes under the feet. [=QUAKEMIRE.]

QUAICH (kwāh) *n.* a small drinking cup. Also QUAIGH. [Celt.]

QUAIL (kwāl) (1) *n.* a bird of the partridge kind;—(2) *v.t.* or *i.* to sink or depress; shrink; cower. [(1) O.F. *quaille* =F. *caille*. (2) O.E. *cwelan*, to die.]

QUAINT (kwānt) *a.* neat and ingenious, but peculiar; curious and fanciful. [O.F. *coint*, neat, fr. L. (acc. part.) *cognitum*, known. See COGNITION, ACQUAINT.]

QUAINTLY (kwānt'li) *ad.* in a quaint manner.

QUAINTNESS (kwānt'nes) *n.* a singular ingenuity or neatness in thought or diction.

QUAKE (kwāk) *v.i.* to shake or tremble with cold or fear;—*n.* a shake; shudder. [O.E. *cwacian*.]

QUAKER (kwā'ker) *n.* one of the Society of Friends.

QUAKERESS (kwā'ker-es) *n.* female Quaker.

QUAKERISM (kwā'ker-izm) *n.* system of the Quakers.

QUALIFIABLE (kwol'i-fī-a-bl) *a.* that may be abated or modified.

QUALIFICATION (kwol-i-fi-kā'shun) *n.* legal requisite; endowment; abatement; modification.

QUALIFIER (kwol'i-fī-er) *n.* one who or that which qualifies.

QUALIFY (kwol'i-fī) *v.t.* or *i.* to make fit or capable; limit by modifications; reduce the strength of. [F. *qualifier*, fr. Late L., fr. L. *qualis*, of what kind, and *facere*, make.]

QUALITY (kwol'i-ti) *n.* an attribute; inherent nature or character; rank; person of high station. [F. *qualité*, fr. L. (acc.) *qualitatem*, fr. *qualis*, of what kind.]

QUALM (kwäm) *n.* nausea; scruple of conscience. [O.E. *cwealm*, death.]

QUALMISH (kwä'mish) *a.* affected with sickness at the stomach.

QUANDARY (kwon'da-ri) *n.* a state of difficulty or perplexity. [Corr. fr. HYPOCHONDRIA.]

QUANTITATIVE (kwon'ti-tā-tiv) *a.* relating to or determining the quantity.

QUANTITY (kwon'ti-ti) *n.* a large extent, number, or portion; weight; bulk; measure; amount. [F. *quantité*, fr. L. *quantitatem*, fr. *quantus*, how much.]

QUANTUM (kwon'tum) *n.* a quantity; amount. [L.]

QUARANTINE (kwor'an-tēn) *n.* prohibition of intercourse with the shore. [O.F. =forty days, fr. *quarante*, forty, fr. L. *quadraginta*.]

QUARREL (kwor'el) *n.* an angry dispute between friends; brawl;—*v.t.* to disagree or dispute violently. [O.F., fr. L. *querela*, fr. *queri*, to complain.]

QUARRELSOME (kwor'el-sum) *a.* inclined to quarrel.

QUARRY (kwor'i) (1) *n.* a place where stones are dug;—*v.t.* to dig stones;— (2) *n.* game pursued; the entrails of game given to the dogs. [(1) O.F. *quarriere*, lit. a place where stones were squared, fr. Late L., fr. L. *quadrare*. See QUADRATE. (2) O.F. *cuiree*, intestines of game, wrapped in skin given to hounds; *cuir*, fr. L. *corium*, skin.]

QUARRYMAN (kwor'i-man) *n.* one who works in a quarry. Also QUARRIER.

QUART (kwort) *n.* fourth of a gallon. [F., fr. L. *quarta*, fourth (part of a gallon).]

QUARTAN (kwor'tan) a. designating a fourth; —n. an ague occurring every fourth day. [F., fr. L. quartanus, pertaining to the fourth, fr. quartus.]

QUARTER (kwor'ter) n. a fourth part of anything; 8 bushels; 28 pounds; region or division; afterpart of a ship's side; mercy to a beaten foe;—v.t. to divide into four parts; station soldiers; lodge. [O.F. quartier, fr. L. quartarius, fourth part, fr. quartus.]

QUARTERAGE (kwor'ter-ij) n. a quarterly allowance.

QUARTER-DAY (kwor'ter-dā) n. the day when quarterly rents are paid.

QUARTER-DECK (kwor'ter-dek) n. upper deck between the mainmast and stern.

QUARTERLY (kwor'ter-li) a. happening every three months;—ad. once in the quarter of a year;—n. a work published quarterly.

QUARTERMASTER (kwor'ter-mas'ter) n. an officer who regulates the quarters and provisions of an army.

QUARTERN (kwor'tern) n. the fourth part of a pint or of a peck;—a. weighing four pounds, as a loaf. [O.F. quarteron, fr. L. quartus.]

QUARTERS (kwor'terz) n.pl. lodgings, especially for soldiers.

QUARTETTE (kwor-tet') n. a company of four persons; a musical composition for four parts. Also written **QUARTET**. [F.]

QUARTO (kwor'tō) n. a book in which a sheet is folded into four leaves;—pl. **QUARTOS**. [Fr. L. in quarto, in a fourth part.]

QUARTZ (kworts) n. a mineral of pure silica; rock crystal. [Ger. Quarz.]

QUASH (kwosh) v.t. to crush; subdue; annul. [O.F. quasser = F. casser, fr. L. quassare, to shake.]

QUASI (kwā'sī) ad. as it were. [L.]

QUASSATION (kwas-ā'shun) n. a shaking.

QUASSIA (kwash'i-a) n. a medicinal bark. [Fr. the name of a negro, Quassi, who prescribed this article as a specific.]

QUATERNION (kwa-ter'ni-un) n. a set or file of four. [Fr. L. quaterni, four each, fr. quatuor, four.]

QUAVER (kwā'ver) v.i. to shake the voice; vibrate;—n. a note half the length of a crochet; a rapid vibration. [Cf. **QUAKE**.]

QUAY (kē) n. a mole or wharf. [O.F. = F. quai, fr. Celt.]

QUAYAGE (kē'ij) n. money paid for the use of a quay.

QUEAN (kwēn) n. a worthless woman. [O.E. cwen, woman. See **QUEEN**.]

QUEASY (kwē'zi) a. squeamish; sick. [Scand.]

QUEEN (kwēn) n. the consort of a king; a female sovereign; a playing card; piece in chess;—v.i. to play the queen. [O.E. cwen, a woman; conn. with **QUEAN**.]

QUEER (kwēr) a. odd; strange; singular. [Ger.]

QUEERLY (kwēr'li) ad. oddly.

QUEERNESS (kwēr'nes) n. oddity or singularity.

QUELL (kwel) v.t. to crush; allay; appease. [O.E. cwellan, to kill.]

QUENCH (kwensh) v.t. to extinguish; repress; allay. [O.E. cwencan.]

QUERN (kwern) n. a hand-mill for grinding corn. [O.E. cweorn.]

QUERIST (kwē'rist) n. one who inquires.

QUERULOUS (kwer'ū-lus) a. habitually complaining. Also **QUERIMONIOUS**. [L., fr. queri, complain.]

QUERY (kwē'ri) n. a question; mark of interrogation;—v.t. or i. to inquire into; question; doubt. [L. (imper.) quære ! enquire ! fr. quærere, to seek for.]

QUEST (kwest) n. act of seeking; search; pursuit; desire. [O.F. = F. quête, fr. L. (part.) quæsita (res), (thing) sought, fr. quærere.]

QUESTION (kwest'yun) n. act of asking; inquiry; doubt; subject of discussion;—v.t. or i. to ask questions; examine by questions; doubt. [F., fr. L. (acc.) quæsitionem, a seeking. See **QUEST**.]

QUESTIONABLE (kwest'yun-a-bl) a. doubtful; suspicious.

QUESTIONER (kwest'yun-er) n. one who interrogates.

QUESTIONLESS (kwest'yun-les) ad. without doubt; certainly.

QUIBBLE (kwib'l) n. an evasion of the truth; a cavil; a low play on words;—v.i. to evade the point at issue with quirks; prevaricate. [Conn. with **QUIP**.]

QUIBBLER (kwib'ler) n. one who quibbles.

QUICK (kwik) a. moving or acting with celerity; living; pregnant;—ad. soon; rapidly;—n. a living animal or plant; living flesh; any sensible part. [O.E. cwic, alive.]

QUICKEN (kwik'n) v.t. to make alive; hasten.

QUICKLIME (kwik'līm) n. lime unslacked.

QUICKLY (kwik'li) ad. in a short time; speedily.

QUICKNESS (kwik'nes) n. speed; haste; activity; acuteness; keen sensibility.

QUICKSAND (kwik'sand) n. sand sinking under the feet.

QUICKSET (kwik'set) a. made of living shrubs, as a hedge;—v.t. to plant with shrubs.

QUICKSILVER (kwik'sil-ver) n. mercury; a fluid metal. [O.E. cwic seolfor, living silver.]

QUIDDITY (kwid'i-ti) n. essence or nature of a thing; any trifling question. [L. quidditas, fr. quid? what ?]

QUIDNUNC (kwid'nungk) n. one curious to know everything. [L. = what now ?]

QUIESCENCE (kwi-es'ens) n. rest; silence.

QUIESCENT (kwi-es'ent) a. at rest; silent. [Fr. L. quiescere, rest.]

QUIET (kwi'et) a. free from motion or disturbance; still; calm; silent; reserved;—n. rest; tranquillity;—v.t. to make quiet; calm; allay. [L. quietus.]

QUIETISM (kwi'et-izm) n. mental peace; rest found in a form of religious meditation.

QUIETLY (kwi'et-li) ad. calmly.

QUIETNESS (kwi'et-nes) n. stillness; repose; peace; silence.

QUIETUDE (kwi'et-ūd) n. tranquillity.

QUIETUS (kwi-ē'tus) n. final discharge; repose; death.

QUILL (kwil) n. a large, strong feather; a pen; a piece of reed;—v.t. to weave in ridges; wind on a quill. [Prob. E.]

QUILT (kwilt) n. the cover of a bed;—v.t. to stitch one cloth upon another. [O.F. cuilte, fr. L. (acc.) culcitam, a bed cushion.]

QUINARY (kwi'na-ri) a. consisting of or arranged in fives. [L. quinarius, five by five, quini, five each.]

QUINCE (kwins) n. a tree and its fruit. [M.E. (pl.) quynes, coins, fr. O.F. coin, through L., fr. G. kudonion (melon), (apple) of Cydonia, in Crete.]

QUININE (kwi-nin', kwi-nēn') n. an alkaloid obtained from cinchona. [Peruv.]

QUINQUAGESIMA (kwin-kwa-jes'i-ma) n. Shrove Sunday. [L. quinquagesima, fiftieth.]

QUINQUENNIAL (kwin-kwen'i-al) a. occurring once in five years. [Fr. L. quinque, and annus, year.]

QUINSY (kwin'zi) n. inflammation of the tonsils or throat. [O.F. quinancie, fr. G. kuna(n)gke, fr. kuon, dog, and a(n)gchein, to choke.]

QUINTAIN (kwin'tan) n. a post with a turning crosspiece to be tilted at. [O.F., fr. L. quintanus, fr. quintus, fifth.]

QUINTAL (kwin'tal) n. a hundred pounds. [F., through A., fr. L. centum, a hundred.]

QUINTAN (kwin'tan) n. a fever or ague recurring every fifth day. [See **QUINTAIN**, fr. L. quintus, fifth.]

QUINTESSENCE (kwin-tes'ens) n. the fifth or highest essence; concentrated extract. [L. *quinta essentia*, fifth ESSENCE.]

QUINTETTE, QUINTET (kwin-tet') n. a composition for five voices or instruments. [F., fr. It.]

QUINTUPLE (kwin'tū-pl) a. fivefold;—v.t. to make fivefold. [F.; imit. fr. QUADRUPLE.]

QUIP (kwip) n. a sarcastic taunt; smart retort;—v.t. or i. to taunt; scoff. [Formerly *quippy*, fr. L. *quippe*, ' forsooth.']

QUIRE (kwir) n. 24 sheets of paper. [O.F. *quaier* = F. *cahier*, fr. Late L. *quaternum*, a collection of four sheets.]

QUIRK (kwerk) n. an artful evasion; quibble; shift. [Etym. uncert.]

QUIT (kwit) v.t. to leave; forsake;—a. clear; free; absolved. [F. *quitter*, fr. O.F. *quite*, discharged, from Late form of L. *quietus*, quiet.]

QUIT-CLAIM (kwit'klām) n. release of a claim; deed of release;—v.t. to release by deed.

QUITE (kwit) ad. entirely; wholly. [M.E. *quite*, free, QUIT.]

QUIT-RENT (kwit'rent) n. a rent by which a tenant is discharged from other service.

QUITS (kwits) ad. square; on equal terms.

QUITTANCE (kwit'ans) n. discharge from a debt; repayment.

QUIVER (kwiv'er) (1) n. a case for arrows;— (2) n. a slight, tremulous motion;—v.i. to shake; tremble; shiver. [(1) O.F. *cuivre*, fr. Ger. (2) Fr. O.E. *cwifer*, to be eager.]

QUIXOTIC (kwiks-ot'ik) a. like Don Quixote; romantic.

QUIXOTISM (kwiks'ot-izm) n. romantic and absurd notions.

QUIZ (kwiz) n. a riddle; hoax; an odd fellow; —v.t. to make sport of; banter; spy or peer into. [Etym. unknown.]

QUIZZICAL (kwiz'i-kal) a. comical.

QUOIF (koif) n. a cap or hood; coif. [See COIF.]

QUOIN (koin) n. a corner; a wedge. [F. *coin*. See COIN.]

QUOIT (koit) n. a flat iron ring to be pitched at a mark;—pl. the game itself;—v.t. to play the game. [Etym. unknown.]

QUONDAM (kwon'dam) a. former. [L. = formerly.]

QUORUM (kwō'rum) n. a bench of justices; a number for doing business. [L. = of whom.]

QUOTA (kwō'ta) n. a share or part assigned to each. [L. *quota (pars)*, how great (a part).]

QUOTABLE (kwō'ta-bl) a. that may be quoted.

QUOTATION (kwō-tā'shun) n. a passage cited; naming a price; the price named.

QUOTE (kwōt) v.t. to cite, as the words of another; name, as a price. [O.F. *quoter*, fr. Late L. *quotare*, to number, as chapters, fr. L. *quotus*, how many.]

QUOTH (kwoth) v.i. to say; speak; used only in the phrases *quoth I*, *quoth he*. [O.E. *cwœth*, said, fr. *cwethan*, say.]

QUOTIDIAN (kwō-tid'i-an) a. occurring daily; —n. a fever recurring daily. [L. *quotidianus*, fr. *quotus*, how many, and *dies*, day.]

QUOTIENT (kwō'shent) n. the number resulting from the division of one number by another. [Fr. L. (adv.) *quotiens*, how often, fr. *quot*, how many.]

R

RABBET (rab'et) v.t. to pare down the edge of a board for lapping;—n. a groove in the side of a board. [F., of uncert. etym.]

RABBI (rab'i, rab'ī) n. a Jewish teacher or doctor of the law. Also RABBIN. [H. = my master.]

RABBINICAL (ra-bin'i-kal) a. pertaining to rabbins.

RABBIT (rab'it) n. a small quadruped of the hare tribe. [Fr. Ger.]

RABBIT-WARREN (rab'it-wor-en) n. piece of ground where rabbits burrow and breed.

RABBLE (rab'l) n. a tumultuous crowd; a mob. [D.]

RABID (rab'id) a. furious; mad. [L. *rabidus*.]

RABIDNESS (rab'id-nes) n. madness; intense bitterness.

RABIES (rā'bi-ez, n. canine madness—a disease from which hydrophobia is communicated. [L.]

RACCOON (ra-kōōn') n. an American quadruped valued for its fur. [Amer. Ind.]

RACE (rās) (1) n. a running; trial of speed; a rapid current; progress;—(2) n. a breed; family; a root; flavour. [(1) Scand. (2) F., fr. It. *razza*, of uncert. etym.]

RACEHORSE (rās'hors) n. a horse kept for running.

RACEME (ra'sēm) n. a cluster of flowers or fruit arranged along a stem. [F., fr. L. *racemus*, a cluster.]

RACIAL (rā'shal) a. pertaining to a race or breed.

RACINESS (rā'si-nes) n. the quality of being racy.

RACK (rak) n. an engine of torture; extreme pain; a wooden grate for hay; flying broken clouds;—v.t. to torture; strain. [E.]

RACKET, RAQUET (rak'et) (1) n. a clattering noise;—(2) n. a bat used in tennis. [(1) E.; imit. (2) O.F. *raquette*, through Sp., fr. A.]

RACK-RENT (rak'rent) n. rent raised to the utmost.

RACY (rā'si) a. highly flavoured; spirited; piquant.

RADIAL (rā'di-al) a. pertaining to a ray or radius.

RADIANCE (rā'di-ans) n. sparkling brightness; brilliance.

RADIANT (rā'di-ant) a. emitting rays of light or heat; beaming; sparkling. [L. (part. stem) *radiant-*, shining, fr. *radius*, RAY.]

RADIATE (rā'di-āt) v.t. or i. to emit rays. [L. (part.) *radiatus*, fr. *radiare*, send out rays, fr. *radius*, RAY.]

RADIATION (rā-di-ā'shun) n. emission of rays.

RADIATOR (rā'di-ā-tur) n. a body from which rays of light or heat emanate.

RADICAL (rad'i-kal) a. original; implanted by nature; thorough; ultra liberal;—n. root of a word; a democrat. [Fr. L. stem *radic-*, of *radix*, root.]

RADICALLY (rad'i-kal-i) ad. originally; essentially; completely.

RADICATION (rad-i-kā'shun) n. the process of taking root.

RADICLE (rad'i-kl) n. the part of a seed which becomes a root. [L. *radicula*, dim. of *radix*.]

RADIOGRAPH (rā'di-u-graf) n. a photograph taken by means of Röntgen rays. [L. *radius*, a ray, G. *graphein*, to write.]

RADISH (rad'ish) n. an annual plant; its root, which is eaten as a salad. [F. *radis*, through It., fr. L. *radix*, a root.]

Radius.

RADIUS (rā'di-us) n. the semi-diameter of a circle. [L.]

RADIX (rā'diks) n. a root;—pl. RADICES. [L. = a root.]

RAFFLE (raf′l) *v.t.* or *i.* to dispose of by raffle; engage in a raffle;—*n.* a kind of lottery. [F., fr. Ger. *raffeln*, snatch up.]

RAFT (raft) *n.* a float of timber. [Scand.]

RAFTERS (raf′tẹrz) *n.pl.* roof-timbers of a building. [O.E. *ræfter*, fr. **RAFT**.]

RAG (rag) *n.* a torn piece of cloth; anything rent or worn out. [Scand.]

RAGAMUFFIN (rag′a-muf-in) *n.* a mean fellow. [Etym. doubtful.]

RAGE (rāj) *n.* violent anger; fury; object of desire;—*v.i.* to be furious with anger; act or prevail with violence. [F. *rage*, fr. L. (acc.) *rabiem*. See **RABIES**.]

RAGGED (rag′ed) *a.* torn into tatters; dressed in tatters.

RAGGEDNESS (rag′ed-nes) *n.* state of being dressed in rags; irregularity in rocks; unevenness in rhymes.

RAGING (rā′jing) *a.* furious; violent.

RAGOUT (ra-gōō′) *n.* a highly-seasoned stew of meat and herbs. [F.]

RAGS (ragz) *n.pl.* worn-out garments.

RAID (rād) *n.* a hostile incursion; a foray; —*v.t.* to make a raid upon;—*v.i.* to go upon a raid. [Form of **ROAD**.]

RAIL (rāl) (1) *n.* a bar of wood or iron;—*v.t.* to enclose with rails; to send by rail;—(2) *n.* a wading bird;—(3) *v.i.* to use abusive language. [(1) O.F. *reille*, fr. L. (acc.) *regulam*, bar. See **RULE**. (2) F. *râle*; imit. (3) F. *railler*; of unknown etym.]

RAILING (rā′ling) *n.* insulting language; a series of rails.

RAILLERY (ra′lẹr-i) *n.* banter; jesting language.

RAILWAY (rāl′wā) *n.* a way laid with iron rails on which carriages run.

RAIMENT (rā′ment) *n.* clothing in general; garments. [Short. fr. *arraiment*. See **ARRAY**.]

RAIN (rān) *n.* moisture falling in drops;— *v.t.* or *i.* to pour or fall in drops. [O.E. *regn*. Cf. Ger. *Regen*.]

RAINBOW (rān′bō) *n.* a many-coloured arch formed by the refraction and reflection of the sun's rays.

RAINFALL (rān′fawl) *n.* amount of rain in a given place and period.

RAIN-GAUGE (rān′gāj) *n.* instrument for measuring the rainfall.

RAINY (rā′ni) *a.* attended or abounding with rain.

RAISE (rāz) *v.t.* to lift; set upright; produce; breed; grow; excite; recall from death; levy; swell. [Scand.]

RAISIN (rā′zn) *n.* a dried grape. [O.F., fr. form of L *racemus*, cluster.]

RAJAH (rā′ja) *n.* in *India*, a native prince. [Skr.]

RAKE (rāk) (1) *n.* a gardener's tool;—*v.t.* or *i.* to level or collect with a rake;—(2) *n.* a loose-living man;—(3) *v.i.* to incline from the perpendicular. [(1) O.E *raca*. Cf. Ger. *Rechen*. (2) Scand. (3) Scand.]

RAKISH (rā′kish) *a.* loose; debauched.

RALLY (ral′i) *v.t.* or *i.* to collect and put in order disordered troops; reunite; recover strength; banter;—*n.* act of reuniting troops, or of recovering strength; a good-humoured jest. [F., fr. *re-*, again, and *allier*, to **ALLY**.]

RAM (ram) *n.* a male sheep; a mechanical contrivance;—*v.t.* to drive with violence; force in; cram. [O.E. Cf. Ger. *Ramm*.]

RAMBLE (ram′bl) *n.* a going from place to place; short walk;—*v.i.* to rove about; be desultory or incoherent. [M.E. *ramen*.]

RAMBLER (ram′blẹr) *n.* one who rambles.

RAMBLING (ram′bling) *a.* wandering; desultory;—*n.* irregular excursion.

RAMIFICATION (ram-i-fi-kā′shun) *n.* process of separating into branches; a branch or division.

RAMIFY (ram′i-fi) *v.t.* or *i.* to shoot or separate into branches. [F. *ramifier*, fr. L. *ramus*, a branch, and *-ficare* = *facere*, to make.]

RAMMER (ram′ẹr) *n.* an instrument for driving down; a ramrod.

RAMOSE, RAMOUS (rā-mōs rā′mus) *a.* full of branches. [Fr. L. *ramus*, a branch.]

RAMP (ramp) *v.i.* to climb, as a plant; leap; bound;—*n.* a leap; a spring. [F. *ramper*, fr. Teut.]

RAMPANCY (ram′pan-si) *a.* exuberance of growth.

RAMPANT (ram′pant) *a.* overgrowing bounds or restraint; standing on the hind legs.

RAMPART (ram′part) *n.* a wall or mound round a fortified place. [F., fr. *remparer*, repair, fr. L. *re*, again, *in*, in, and *parare* get ready.]

RAMROD (ram′rod) *n.* a rod used to ram down the charge in a gun.

RANCID (ran′sid) *a.* having a rank smell; musty; sour. [L. *rancidus*.]

RANCIDITY (ran-sid′i-ti) *n.* a strong, sour smell; mustiness. Also **RANCIDNESS**.

RANCOUR (rang′kur) *n.* malignity; inveterate enmity. [O.F. *rancour*, fr. L. (acc.) *rancorem*. Conn. with **RANCID**.]

RANCOROUS (rang′kur-us) *a.* very spiteful or malicious.

RANDOM (ran′dum) *a.* done or uttered by chance;—*n.* a course without direction or method; range. [O.F. strong current, fr. Ger. *Rand*, edge.]

RANG (rang) *pret.* of **RING**.

RANGE (rānj) *v.t.* or *i.* to set in a row or in order; pass over; sail near;—*n.* a row or rank; class; wandering; room for passing; extent or variety; a rung; a long cooking stove. [F. *ranger*, fr. *rang*, a **RANK**.]

RANGER (rān′jẹr) *n.* a rover; a sporting dog; keeper of a park.

RANK (rangk) (1) *a.* strong-scented; high-tasted; luxuriant;—(2) *n.* a line of men; row; degree; dignity;—*v.t.* to place in a line;—*v.i.* to have a degree of dignity. [(1) O.E. *ranc*. (2) O.F. *reng* = F. *rang*, fr. Ger.]

RANKLE (rangk′l) *v.t.* to become inflamed or violent. [See **RANK** (1).]

RANKNESS (rangk′nes) *n.* luxuriance in growth; grossness; a strong musty taste or smell.

RANSACK (ran′sak) *v.t.* to search narrowly; pillage completely. [Scand.]

RANSOM (ran′sum) *n.* release or the price paid to redeem a person or goods from an enemy;—*v.t.* to redeem from captivity by a price. [O.F. *raenson*, fr. L. (acc.) *redemptionem*. Doublet of **REDEMPTION**.]

RANSOMER (ran′sum-ẹr) *n.* one who redeems.

RANSOMLESS (ran′sum-les) *a.* without ransom.

RANT (rant) *n.* extravagant language; empty declamation;—*v.i.* to rave. [D.]

RANTER (ran′tẹr) *n.* a boisterous talker or preacher.

RANUNCULUS (ra-nun′kū-lus) *n.* a flowering plant of several species. [L. = a little frog, a plant, dim. fr. *rana*, a frog.]

RAP (rap) *n.* a quick, smart blow;—*v.t.* or *i.* to strike; seize. [Scand.]

RAPACIOUS (ra-pā′shus) *a.* inclined to plunder; greedy. [L. stem *rapaci-*, of *rapax*, grasping, fr. *rapere*, grasp.]

RAPACIOUSLY (ra-pā′shus-li) *ad.* in a rapacious manner.

RAPACITY (ra-pas′i-ti) *n.* disposition to plunder or make gain.

RAPE (rāp) *n.* a plant of the turnip family; the oil extracted from its seeds;—(2) *n.* violation by force. [(1) L. *rapa*. (2) Corr. fr. O.F. *rapt*, a rape, fr. L., fr. (part.) *raptus*, seized, fr. *rapere*.]

RAPID (rap'id) *a.* very swift; quick in motion or utterance. [F. *rapide*, fr. L. *rapidus*, fr. *rapere*, to snatch.]

RAPIDITY (rạ-pid'i-ti) *n.* swiftness; velocity; haste.

RAPIDLY (rap'id-li) *ad.* swiftly; with quick motion.

RAPIDS (rap'idz) *n.pl.* the part of a river where the bed descends rapidly.

RAPIER (rā'pi-ẹr) *n.* a light sword with a narrow blade used in duels. [F., fr. Sp.]

RAPINE (rap'in) *n.* act of plundering by violence; pillage. [F., fr. L. *rapina*, plundering, fr. *rapere*.]

RAPPEE (ra-pē') *n.* a kind of snuff. [F. *râpé*, lit. (part.) grated, fr. *râper*, RASP.]

RAPT (rapt) *a.* transported in ecstasy. [L. (part.) *raptus*, snatched away, fr. *rapere*.]

RAPTURE (rap'tūr) *n.* extreme joy; ecstasy.

RAPTUROUS (rap'tūr-us) *a.* causing rapture.

RARA-AVIS (rā'ra-ā'vis) *n.* a rare bird; an uncommon person or thing. [L.]

RARE (rār) (1) *a.* not dense; porous; uncommon; scarce; very valuable;—(2) underdone. [F., fr. L. *rarus.*]

RAREFACTION (rā-re-fak'shun) *n.* expansion of bodies.

RAREFY (rā're-fi) *v.t.* or *i.* to make or become thin or less dense. [Fr. L. *rarus*, RARE, and *-ficare = facere*, make.]

RARELY (rār'li) *ad.* seldom; not often.

RARITY (rā'ri-ti, rar'i-ti) *n.* uncommonness; thinness; something valued for its scarceness.

RASCAL (ras'kạl) *n.* a dishonest or worthless fellow; scoundrel. [O.F. *raskaile* = F. *racaille*, the rabble, through Late L., tr. L. (part.) *rasus*, scraped. See RASE.]

RASCALITY (ras-kal'i-ti) *n.* conduct of a rascal; the mob.

RASCALLY (ras'kạl-i) *a.* worthless; vile.

RASE (rāz) *v.t.* to erase; level; raze. [F. *raser*, fr. Late L., fr. L. (part.) *rasus*, scraped, fr. *radere*.]

RASH (rash) (1) *a.* hasty in counsel or action; incautious; headstrong; sudden;—(2) *n.* an eruption on the skin. [(1) E. Cf. Ger *rasch*. (2) O.F. *rasche*, itch, fr. *raser*, scrape, RASE.]

RASHER (rash'ẹr) *n.* a thin slice of bacon. [Fr. RASH = quick, because quickly cooked.]

RASHLY (rash'li) *ad.* hastily; adventurously.

RASHNESS (rash'nes) *n.* inconsiderate haste.

RASP (rasp) *n.* a rough file; a grater; a garden berry and its fruit;—*v.t.* to rub or grate with a rasp. [O.F. *rasper* = F. *râper*, fr. O. Ger. Cf. Ger. *raspeln.*]

RASPBERRY (raz'bẹr-i) *n.* a kind of bramble; a rasp.

RAT (rat) *n.* a small rodent animal infesting houses, ships, etc.; one who deserts his party or fellow workmen;—*v.i.* to desert one's party or associates. [O.E. *ræt.* Cf. Ger. *Ratte.*] [rated.

RATABLE (rā'tạ-bl) *a.* liable to be taxed or

RATCHET (rach'et) *n.* a tooth at the bottom of the fusee of a watch to stop it in winding up. [E.]

RATE (rāt) *n.* proportion; standard; value; price; class of a ship; movement fast or slow; a tax;—*v.t.* or *i.* to estimate; value; place or be placed in a certain class. [F., fr. Low L. *rata*, fr. L. (part.) *rata*, determined, fr. *reor*, I judge.]

Ratchet.

RATEPAYER (rāt'pā-ẹr) *n.* one who is assessed for poor-rates, etc.

RATHER (rȧᴛн'ẹr) *ad.* more willingly; somewhat. [O.E. (compar.) *hrǣthor*, sooner.]

RATIFICATION (rat-i-fi-kā'shun) *n.* the act of sanctioning.

RATIFIER (rat'i-fi-ẹr) *n.* one who sanctions.

RATIFY (rat'i-fi) *v.t.* to approve and sanction. [F. *ratifier*, fr. L. *ratus*, settled, and *-ficare = facere*, make. See RATE.]

RATIO (rā'shi-ō) *n.* proportion; rate. [L.]

RATIOCINATION (rash-i-os-i-nā'shun) *n.* act or process of reasoning. [L. *ratiocinari-*, *atus*, fr. *rato*, reason.]

RATION (rā'shun) *n.* allowance of provisions for a day. [F., fr. L. *ratio*, reckoning. RATIO. Doublet of REASON.]

RATIONAL (rash'un-ạl) *a.* endowed with reason; agreeable to reason. [L. *rationalis*, fr. RATIO.]

RATIONALE (rash-u-nā'le) *n.* detailed explanation of the ground or reasons of a fact, truth, principle, etc.

RATIONALIST (rash'un-ạl-ist) *n.* one who is guided solely by reason in religious opinion.

RATIONALITY (rash-un-al'i-ti) *n.* the power of reasoning; reasonableness.

RATIONALLY (rash'un-ạl-i) *ad.* in a rational manner.

RATLINE (rat'lin) *n.* a small rope traversing the shrouds of a ship. Also RATTLING. [E.; formerly *raddelines*, of uncert. etym.]

RATSBANE (rats'bān) *n.* poison for rats.

RATTAN, RATAN (ra-tan') *n.* a kind of palm; a cane or walking-stick made from it. [Malay.]

RATTING (rat'ing) *n.* act of deserting a party.

RATTLE (rat'l) *v.t.* or *i.* to clatter;—*n.* a succession of sharp sounds; a toy. [E. Cf. Ger. *rasseln.*]

RATTLESNAKE (rat'l-snāk) *n.* a poisonous snake with bones in the tail which rattle.

RATTLING (rat'ling) *n.* succession of sharp sounds. [*raucus.*

RAUCOUS (raw'kus) *a.* hoarse; harsh. [L.

RAVAGE (rav'ij) *v.i.* to lay waste in various ways; sack; pillage; destroy;—*n.* violent destruction; ruin; plunder. [F., fr. *ravir*, fr. term of L. *rapere*, to carry off.]

RAVE (rāv) *v.i.* to be delirious; talk wildly; —*n.* upper timber of a cart. [O.F., fr. L. *rabere*, to be mad.]

RAVEL (rav'el) *v.t.* or *i.* to untwist; entangle; involve; be confused. [O.D. *ravelen.*]

RAVELIN (rav'lin) *n.* a detached work in fortification. [F., fr. It.]

RAVEN (rav'n) (1) *v.t.* or *i.* to prey upon; devour greedily;—*n.* rapine;—(rāv'n) (2) *n.* a kind of crow;—*a.* black. [(1) O.F. *ravine*, fr. L. (acc.) *rapinam*, plunder, RAPINE. (2) O.E. *hræfn.* Cf. Ger. *Rabe.*]

RAVENOUS (rav'e-nus) *a.* voracious; rapacious; greedy.

RAVENOUSLY (rav'e-nus-li) *ad.* with raging hunger.

RAVINE (rạ-vēn') *n.* a long hollow between hills. [See RAVEN (1).]

RAVING (rā'ving) *a.* furious.

RAVINGLY (rā'ving-li) *ad.* in a raving manner.

RAVISH (rav'ish) *v.t.* to carry away by force; transport with delight; violate. [F. (part.) *ravissant*, ravishing. See RAVAGE.]

RAVISHER (rav'ish-ẹr) *n.* one who ravishes.

RAVISHMENT (rav'ish-ment) *n.* act of ravishing; ecstasy.

RAW (raw) *a.* not cooked; crude; unmanufactured; not mixed or prepared; undressed; unfinished; bleak; bare; sore. [O.E. *hreaw.* Cf. Ger. *roh.*]

RAWNESS (raw'nes) *n.* state of being raw.

RAY (rā) *n.* a line of light or heat; intellectual beam; perception; a kind of flat fish; —*v.t.* to send forth; shoot; streak. [O.F. *raye* = F. *raie*, fr. L. (acc.) *radium*, beam, or rod, RADIUS.]

RAYLESS (rā'les) *a.* without a ray.

RAZOR (rā'zẹr) *n.* an instrument for shaving. [F. *rasoir*, fr. *raser*, scrape, RASE.]

RE-, pref. again; over; back. Also red. [L.]

REACH (rēch) v.t. or i. to extend; hand over; arrive at; gain; include;—n. extent; influence; contrivance; straight portion of a stream. [O.E. rœcan.]

REACT (rē-akt') v t. or i. to return an impulse; act one upon the other. [L. pref. re, again, over, back.]

REACTION (rē-ak'shun) n. counter action or mutual action; backward tendency.

REACTIONARY (rē-ak'shun-ar-i) a. having a backward tendency from reform or progress.

REACTIVE (rē-ak'tiv) a. tending to react.

READ (rēd) v.t. or i. to utter aloud written or printed words; peruse; study; learn. [O.E. rœdan, interpret, to read. Cf. Ger. rathen, advise.]

READ (red) pp. perused; versed in books.

READABLE (re'da-bl) a. fit to be read.

READER (rē'der) n. one who reads; a reading book.

READILY (red'i-li) ad. quickly; with facility; promptly; cheerfully.

READINESS (red'i-nes) n. willingness; preparedness; alacrity.

READING (rē'ding) n. perusal; interpretation of a passage; public lecture or recital.

READJUST (rē-a-just') v.t. to adjust again. [L. re, again.]

READMISSION (rē-ad-mish'un) n. second admission.

READMIT (rē-ad-mit') v.t. to admit again. [L. re, again.]

READOPT (rē-a-dopt') v.t. to take up again. [L. re, again.]

READORN (rē-a-dorn') v.t. to deck with fresh ornaments or attractions. [L. re, again.]

READY (red'i) a. prepared; willing; near; easy. [O.E. rœde. Cf. Ger. bereit.]

READY-MADE (red'i-mād) n. made and ready for use.

REAL (rē'al) a. having positive existence; not imaginary; actual. [Late L. realis, belonging to the thing, fr.]

REALISATION (rē-al-i-zā'shun) n. act of realising.

REALISE (rē'al-īz) v.t. or i. to bring into being or act; understand by experience; convert into real property; gain or receive money. [Fr. REAL.]

REALISM (rē'al-izm) n. a philosophical system opposed to nominalism and idealism.

REALISTIC (rē-al-ist'ik) a. representing events or scenes as in real life.

REALITY (rē-al'i-ti) n. certainty.

REALLY (rē'al-i) ad. in fact; truly.

REALM (relm) n. a royal jurisdiction; kingdom. [O.F. realme =F. royaume, through Late L., fr. L. regalis, REGAL.]

REALTY (rē'al-ti) a. immobility of real property.

REAM (rēm) n. a bundle of 20 quires, or 480 sheets, of paper. [O.F. raime, fr. Sp., fr. A.]

REANIMATE (rē-an'i-māt) v.i. to restore to life. [L. re, again.]

REANNEX (rē-a-neks') v.t. to annex again. [L. re, again.]

REANNEXATION (rē-an-ek-sā'shun) n. act of annexing again.

REAP (rēp) v.t. or i. to cut grain with a sickle; gather the crop; receive as a reward for labour, etc. [O.E. repan.]

REAPER (rē'per) n. one who reaps.

REAPPEAR (rē-a-pēr') v.i. to appear again.

REAPPOINT (rē-a-point') v.t. to appoint again.

REAPPOINTMENT (rē-a-point'ment) n. a second or new appointment. [L. re, again.]

REAR (rēr) (1) n. the part behind;—(2) v.t. to raise; bring up; elevate the fore-legs. [(1) O.F. riere, fr. L. retro, behind. See ARREARS. (2) O.E. rœran.]

REARGUARD (rēr'gärd) n. the body that marches in the rear.

REARWARD (rēr'wawrd) n. the rearguard.

REASCEND (rē-a-send') v.i. to ascend again.

REASON (rē'zn) n. the faculty of judging; motive; cause; consideration; just view; moderation; common sense;—v.t. or i. to argue; debate. [O.F. reison =F. raison, fr. L. (acc.) rationem, reckoning. Doublet of RATION.]

REASONABLE (rē'zn-a-bl) a. governed by reason; just; moderate; considerable.

REASONABLENESS (rē'zn-a-bl-nes) n. agreeable to reason.

REASONABLY (rē'zn-a-bli) ad. agreeably to reason; moderately.

REASONER (rē'zn-er) n. one who argues.

REASONING (rē'zn-ing) n. act of drawing conclusions from premisses.

REASSERT (rē-a-sert') v.t. to affirm again.

REASSIGN (rē-a-sīn') v.t. to transfer back.

REASSUME (rē-a-sūm') v.t. to assume again; resume.

REASSURE (rē-a-shōòr') v.t. to assure again.

REAVE (rēv) v.t. [pret. and pp. REFT] to take away by violence. [O.E. reaftan, to rob.]

REBAPTISE (rē-bap-tīz') v.t. to baptise a second time.

REBATE (re-bāt') v.t. to diminish; deduct for prompt payment;—n. a groove on the edge of a board; discount. [F. rebatre, beat back, fr. re-, and battere =L. battuere, to beat.]

REBATEMENT (re-bāt'ment) n. abatement; deduction.

REBEL (reb'el) n. one who opposes lawful authority;—a. acting in revolt. [F. rebelle, Fr. L. (acc.) rebellem, lit. renewing war, fr. re-, and bellum.]

REBEL (re-bel') v.i. to rise in opposition to lawful authority.

REBELLION (re-bel'yun) n. open opposition to government.

REBELLIOUS (re-bel'yus) a. engaged in rebellion.

REBELLIOUSNESS (re-bel'yus-nes) n. spirit of resistance to lawful authority.

REBOUND (re-bound') v.i. to spring back;—n. act of springing back.

REBUFF (re-buf') n. a sudden check; repulse; refusal;—v.t. to repel. [Fr. It.]

REBUILD (rē-bild') v.t. to build anew.

REBUKE (re-būk') v.t. to put down with reproof; chide; check;—n. a direct reproof. [O.F., fr. re-, again, and bouquer, to stop up, fr. L. vucca (cheek), mouth.]

REBUS (rē'bus) n. a kind of riddle. [L. =by things.]

REBUT (re-but') v.t. or i. to oppose by argument; return an answer. [O.F. rebouter, fr. Ger.]

REBUTTER (re-but'er) n. answer of a defendant to a plaintiff's rejoinder; refutation.

RECALCITRATE (re-kal'si-trāt) v.i. to kick against; oppose. [L., fr. re-, and calcitrare, kick, fr. stem calc-, of calx, heel.]

RECALL (re-kawl') v.t. to call back; revoke; remember;—n. revocation.

RECANT (re-kant') v.i. to retract an opinion or declaration. [L. recantare, lit. sing back, fr. cantare, sing. See CANT (2), CHANT.]

RECANTATION (rē-kan-tā'shun) n. act of recanting.

RECAPITULATE (rē-ka-pit'ū-lāt) v.t. or i. to repeat in a summary way. [L., fr. re, and capitulare, fr. capitulum, a small head.]

RECAPITULATION (rē-ka-pit-ū-lā'shun) n. a summary; a recapitulating.

RECAPITULATORY (rē-ka-pit'ū-la-tur-i) a. repeating in a summary way.

RECAPTURE (rē-kap'tūr) n. act of retaking; a prize retaken;—v.t. to retake.

RECAST (re-kast') v.t. [pret. and pp. RE-CAST] to cast or mould a second time.

RECEDE (re-sēd') v.t. or i. to draw back; give back; retire. [L., fr. re, back, and cedere, to go.]

RECEIPT (re-sēt') *n.* reception: a writing that something has been received; a receipe;— *v.t.* to give a writing for something received.

RECEIVABLE (re-sē'va-bl) *a.* that may be received.

RECEIVE (re-sēv') *v.t.* to take what is offered; admit; allow; entertain; contain; take in stolen goods. [O.F. *receivre*, fr. L. *recipere*, lit. take back, fr. *capere*, take.]

RECEIVER (re-sē'ver) *n.* one who receives; a glass vessel used in several chemical processes.

RECENCY (rē'sen-si) *n.* newness; freshness.

RECENSION (re-sen'shun) *n.* revising the text of an old author; the text after revision. [L., fr. (part.) *recensus*, revised, fr. *censere*, value.]

RECENT (rē'sent) *a.* new; late; fresh. [O.F., fr. L. (acc.) *recentem*, lit. beginning again; conn. with G. *kainos*, new.]

RECENTLY (rē'sent-li) *ad.* newly; lately.

RECENTNESS (rē'sent-nes) *n.* freshness; lateness in time or origin.

RECEPTACLE (re-sep'ta-kl) *n.* a place to receive things in.

RECEPTION (re-sep'shun) *n.* act of receiving; admission. [L., fr. (part.) *receptus*, received. See **RECEIVE**.]

RECEPTIVE (re-sep'tiv) *a.* having the quality of receiving.

RECEPTIVITY (rē-sep-tiv'i-ti) *n.* capacity of receiving impressions.

RECESS (re-ses') *n.* a withdrawing; retirement; seclusion; niche in a room; period in which parliament or the law courts do not sit. [L. *recessus*, fr. *recedere*, **RECEDE**.]

RECESSION (re-sesh'un) *n.* act of ceding back.

RECHARGE (rē-chärj') *v.t.* to attack anew.

RECHARTER (rē-chär'ter) *v.t.* to charter again.

RECHEAT (rē-chēt') *n.* a recall to dogs in hunting;—*v.t.* to sound the recheat. [O.F. *recct*.]

RECHERCHE (re-sher'shā) *a.* sought out with care; nice. [F.]

RECHOOSE (rē-chōōz') *v.t.* to choose a second time.

RECIPE (res'i-pē) *n.* medical prescription; any formula for making up compounds of food, drink, etc. [L. (imper.) =**RECEIVE** thou.]

RECIPIENCY (re-sip'i-en-si) *n.* act of receiving.

RECIPIENT (re-sip'i-ent) *n.* one who receives; —*a.* receiving. [L. (part. stem) *recipient-*, receiving. See **RECEIVE**.]

RECIPROCAL (re-sip'ru-kal) *a.* mutual; acting in return. [L. *reciprocus*.]

RECIPROCALLY (re-sip'ru-kal-i) *ad.* so that each affects and is affected by the other.

RECIPROCATE (re-sip'ru-kāt) *v.t.* or *i.* to act by turns; interchange; requite.

RECIPROCATION (re-sip-ru-kā'shun) *n.* a giving and receiving in return.

RECIPROCITY (res-i-pros'i-ti) *n.* reciprocal obligation; action and reaction.

RECITAL (re-sī'tal) *n.* repetition of words of another, or of a writing; rehearsal; account; narration.

RECITATION (res-i-tā'shun) *n.* act of reciting; a public reading.

RECITATIVE (res-i-ta-tēv') *n.* a kind of chant; —*a.* reciting.

RECITE (re-sīt') *v.t.* or *i.* to read aloud; repeat from memory; enumerate; narrate. [O.F. *reciter*, fr. L., fr. *re-*, and *citare*, **CITE**.]

RECITER (re-sī'ter) *n.* one who recites.

RECK (rek) *v.t.* or *i.* to care; mind; heed. [O.E. *recan*, to care for.]

RECKLESS (rek'les) *a.* careless of consequences; heedless.

RECKLESSLY (rek'les-li) *ad.* carelessly.

RECKLESSNESS (rek'les-nes) *n.* heedlessness; carelessness.

RECKON (rek'n) *v.t.* or *i.* to number; compute; esteem. [O.E. *gerecenian*, to explain. Cf. Ger. *rechnen*.]

RECKONER (rek'n-er) *n.* one who reckons; a book of tables to aid in calculations of moneys and weights.

RECKONING (rek'n-ing) *n.* act of counting; settlement of accounts; bill of charges; estimation; calculation of a ship's position.

RECLAIM (re-klām') *v.t.* to recall; reform; restore to use, as land.

RECLAIMABLE (re-klā'ma-bl) *a.* that may be reclaimed.

RECLAIMANT (re-klā'mant) *n.* one who reclaims.

RECLAIMING (re-klā'ming) *a.* recalling; appealing.

RECLAMATION (rek-la-mā'shun) *n.* demand for restoration; recovery.

RECLINATION (rek-li-nā'shun) *n.* act of leaning or reclining.

RECLINE (re-klīn') *v.t.* or *i.* to lean back; rest upon; repose. [L. *reclinare*. See **INCLINE**.]

RECLUSE (re-klōōs') *a.* living in retirement; solitary;—*n.* one who lives in retirement from society. [O.F. (part.) *reclus*, shut up, fr. Late L. *recludere*, fr. *claudere*, shut.]

RECLUSION (re-klōō'zhun) *n.* state of retirement. [*ment*.

RECLUSIVE (re-klōō'siv) *a.* affording retirement.

RECOGNISABLE (rek-ug-nī'za-bl) *a.* that may be acknowledged.

RECOGNISANCE (re-kog'ni-zans) *n.* a legal bond of obligation taken before a magistrate. [O.F., fr. (part.) *recognisant*, knowing again, fr. *recognoistre*, fr. L. *recognoscere*.]

RECOGNISE (rek'ug-nīz) *v.t.* to know again; acknowledge. [Fr. **RECOGNISANCE**.]

RECOGNISOR (re-kog-ni-zer') *n.* one who gives a legal bond of obligation.

RECOGNITION (rek-ug-nish'un) *n.* an acknowledgment; avowal.

RECOGNITOR (re-kog'ni-ter) *n.* one of the jury on an assize.

RECOIL (re-koil') *v.i.* to move or fall back; —*n.* a falling backward; rebound. [O.F., fr. *re-*, back, and *cul*, the part behind, fr. L. (acc.) *culum*.]

RECOILMENT (re-koil'ment) *n.* the act of recoiling.

RECOIN (rē-koin') *v.t.* to coin again.

RECOINAGE (re-koi'nij) *n.* a coining again; new coinage.

RECOLLECT (rek'u-lekt) *v.t.* to recall or bring to memory; collect again.

RECOLLECTION (rek-u-lek'shun) *n.* a recalling; remembrance.

RECOMBINE (rē-kom-bīn') *v.t.* to combine again.

RECOMMENCE (rē-ku-mens') *v.t.* to begin anew.

RECOMMEND (rek-u-mend') *v.t.* to commend; praise.

RECOMMENDATION (rek-u-men-dā'shun) *n.* act of praising; that which commends to favour.

RECOMMENDATORY (rek-u-men'da-tur-i) *a.* that recommends.

RECOMMIT (rē-ku-mit') *v.t.* to commit anew. [L. *re*, again.]

RECOMMITMENT (rē-ku-mit'ment) *n.* a second commitment. Also **RECOMMITTAL**.

RECOMPENSE (rek'um-pens) *v.t.* to give as equivalent for; requite; compensate; remunerate;—*n.* requital; reward. [O.F. *recompenser*, fr. L. *re-*, and *compensare*, **COMPENSATE**.]

RECONCILABLE (rek-un-sī'la-bl) *a.* that may be adjusted or made to agree.

RECONCILE (rek'un-sil) *v.t.* to conciliate anew; make consistent. [O.F., fr. L. *re-*, and *conciliare*, **CONCILIATE**.]

RECONCILIATION (rek-un-sil-i-ā'shun) *n.* renewal of friendship.

RECONDITE (rek'on-dīt) *a.* secret; abstruse; profound. [L. (part.) *reconditus*, hidden away, fr. *re-*, and *condere*, hide.]

RECONDITORY (re-kon'di-tu-ri) *n.* a repository.

RECONNAISSANCE (rē-kon'ā-sạns) *n.* the examination of a tract of country, usually for warlike purposes. [F.]

RECONNOITRE (rek-un-noi'tẹr) *v.t.* to survey. [O.F. *reconoistre*. See RECOGNISANCE.]

RECONQUER (rē-kong'kẹr) *v.t.* to conquer again; recover. [again.

RECONSIDER (rē-kun-sid'ẹr) *v.t.* to consider

RECONSIDERATION (rē-kun-sid-ẹr-ā'shun) *n.* renewed consideration.

RECONSTRUCTION (rē-kun-struk'shun) *n.* rebuilding; forming upon renewed principles.

RECONVEY (rē-kun-vā') *v.t.* to convey back.

RECONVEYANCE (rē-kun-vā'ạns) *n.* a transferring back.

RECORD (re-kord') *v.t.* to register; enrol. [O.F., fr. L. *recordare*, call to mind, fr. *re-*, and stem *cord-*, of *cor*, heart.]

RECORD (rek'ord) *n.* register; authentic memorial.

RECORDER (re-kor'dẹr) *n.* one who records or keeps records.

RECORDERSHIP (re-kor'dẹr-ship) *n.* office of a recorder.

RECOUNT (rē-kount') *v.t.* to relate in detail. [O.F. *reconter*, to relate again, fr. *re*, and *conter*, COUNT.]

RECOUP (re-kööp') *v.t.* or *i.* to recover or make up for; indemnify. [F., fr. *couper*, cut.]

RECOURSE (re-kōrs') *n.* application, as for help; resort. [F. *recours*, fr. L. (acc.) *recursum*, running back, fr. *re*, and *currere*, run.]

RECOVER (re-kuv'ẹr) *v.t.* or *i.* to regain what was lost; revive; retrieve; obtain judgment or damages; regain health. [O.F. *recuvrer*, fr. L. *recuperare*, RECUPERATE.]

RECOVERABLE (re-kuv'ẹr-ạ-bl) *a.* that may be recovered.

RECOVERY (re-kuv'ẹr-i) *n.* act of recovering.

RECREANT (rek're-ạnt) *a.* cowardly; mean and false; apostate;—*n.* a mean-spirited fellow. [O.F., *recreant*, half-hearted, orig. (part.) giving in, fr. *recroire*, believe again, fr. L. *re-*, and *credere*.]

RECREATE (rek're-āt) (1) *v.t.* to refresh after labour; amuse;—(2) (rē-kre-āt') *v.t.* to create or form anew. [L. *re*, again.]

RECREATION (rek-re-ā'shun) (1) *n.* refreshment or diversion after toil; amusement;—(2) (rē-kre-ā'shun) *n.* a forming anew; new creation.

RECREATIVE (rek're-ā-tiv) *a.* tending to refresh after labour.

RECREMENT (rek're-ment) *n.* refuse. [L.]

RECREMENTAL (rek-re-men'tạl) *a.* containing refuse; drossy.

RECRIMINATE (re-krim'i-nāt) *v.t.* or *i.* to return an accusation. [L. *re*, again, and *crimen*, a crime.]

RECRIMINATION (re-krim-i-nā'shun) *n.* accusation retorted.

RECRIMINATIVE (re-krim'i-nā-tiv) *a.* retorting accusation.

RECRUIT (re-krööt') *v.i.* to gain new supplies of anything;—*v.t.* to supply deficiency, as of troops;—*n.* a new soldier. [Corr. fr. F. *recrue*, levy (lit. reformed), fr. *recroître*, fr. L. *re-*, and *crescere*, grow.]

RECTANGLE (rek'tang-gl) *n.* a right-angled parallelogram. [F., fr. L., fr. L. *rectus*, right, and *angulus*, ANGLE.]

RECTANGULAR (rek-tang'gū-lạr) *a.* having right angles.

RECTIFICATION (rek-ti-fi-kā'shun) *n.* act of correcting or refining.

RECTIFY (rek'ti-fi) *v.t.* to correct; refine by distillation. [F. *rectifier*, fr. Late L. *recti-ficare*, fr. *rectus*, right, and *facere*, make.]

Rectangle.

RECTILINEAR (rek-ti-lin'e-ạr) *a.* consisting of right lines. [L., fr. *rectus*, right, and *linea*, line.]

RECTITUDE (rek'ti-tūd) *n.* uprightness; integrity. [F., fr. L. *rectitudo*, uprightness, fr. *rectus*.]

RECTOR (rek'tẹr) *n.* a minister of a parish; ruler or governor. [L.]

RECTORIAL (rek-tō'ri-ạl) *a.* belonging to a rector.

RECTORSHIP (rek'tur-ship) *n.* the rank or office of a rector.

RECTORY (rek'tur-i) *n.* the mansion of a rector; a parish church.

RECTUM (rek'tum) *n.* the third of the large intestines. [L.]

RECUMBENCY (re-kum'ben-si) *n.* a lying down; repose.

RECUMBENT (re-kum'bent) *a.* reclining; reposing; idle. [L. (part. stem) *recumbent-*, reclining, fr. *cumbere*, lie.]

RECUPERATE (re-kū'per-āt) *v.i.* to recover health. [L. Doublet of RECOVER.]

RECUPERATIVE (re-kū'per-ā-tiv) *a.* pertaining to or tending to recovery.

RECUR (re-kur') *v.i.* to resort; return to the mind. [L., fr. *re*, again, and *currere*, to run.]

RECURRENCE (re-kur'ens) *n.* return; resort.

RECURRENT (re-kur'ent) *a.* returning at intervals.

RECUSANCY (rek'ū-zạn-si) *n.* nonconformity.

RECUSANT (rek'ū-zạnt) *a.* refusing to conform;—*n.* one who refuses to conform to the established church. [F. (part.) *récusant*, rejecting, fr. *récuser*, fr. L. *recusare*, oppose a cause, fr. *causa*, CAUSE.]

RED (red) *a.* of a bright colour, like blood; —*n.* a red colour. [O.E. *read*. Cf. Ger. *roth*.]

REDACTION (re-dak'shun) *n.* arranging in systematic order; digest. [L., fr. (part.) *redactus*, brought back, fr. *re-*, *red-*, and *agere*, to put in motion, to drive.]

REDAN (re-dan') *n.* a kind of rampart. [O.F. *redent*, a double notching, fr. L. *re-*, back, and stem *dent-*, of *dens*, tooth.]

RED-DEER (red'dēr) *n.* the common stag.

REDDEN (red'n) *v.t.* or *i.* to make or grow red; blush.

REDDISH (red'ish) *a.* somewhat red.

REDDITION (re-dish'un) *n.* restitution; surrender; rendering. [L., fr. (part.) *redditus*, restored, fr. *reddere*.]

REDEEM (re-dēm') *v.t.* to ransom; atone for; rescue; discharge; recover; spend wisely. [Fr. L. *red-*, back, and *emere*, to buy.]

REDEEMABLE (re-dē'mạ-bl) *a.* that may be redeemed.

REDEEMER (re-dē'mẹr) *n.* one who ransoms; the Saviour.

REDELIVER (rē-de-liv'ẹr) *v.t.* to deliver back or again.

REDEMPTION (re-dem'shun) *n.* act of redeeming; repurchase; ransom.

REDEMPTORY (re-dem'tur-i) *a.* serving to redeem. Also REDEMPTIVE.

RED-HOT (red'hot) *a.* heated to redness.

REDINTEGRATE (re-din'ti-grāt) *v.t.* to renew. [L. *re*, again, and *integrare*, to make whole.]

REDISPOSE (rē-dis-pōz') *v.t.* to dispose or adjust again.

REDNESS (red'nes) *n.* the quality of being red.

REDOLENCE (red'u-lens) *n.* sweetness of scent.

REDOLENT (red'u-lent) *a.* diffusing a sweet scent. [O.F., fr. L. (acc. part.) *redolentem*, emitting a scent, fr. *red-*, again, and *olere*.]

REDOUBLE (rē-dub'l) *v.t.* or *i.* to increase by doubling.

REDOUBT (re-dout') *n.* an outwork in fortifications. [F. *redoute*, fr. L. (part.) *reductus*, drawn back, fr. *ducere*.]

REDOUBTABLE (re-dou'tạ-bl) *a.* formidable.

REDOUND (re-dound') *v.i.* to conduce; contribute. [L. *re*, again, and *undare*, to surge, fr. *unda*, a wave.]

REDRAFT (rē-draft') *v.t.* to draft anew;—*n.* a second copy.

REDRAW (rē-draw') *v.t.* to draw again.

REDRESS (re-dres') *v.t.* to set right; relieve from wrongs, etc.;—*n.* remedy for wrong.

REDRESSIVE (re-dres'iv) *a.* affording redress.

RED-START (red'stàrt) *n.* a small singing bird. [Fr. RED, and *start*, a tail, fr. O.E. *steort.*]

RED-TAPE (red'tàp) *n.* tape used in public offices; official routine or formality.

RED-TAPISM (red-tàp'izm) *n.* adherence to official routine.

REDUCE (re-dūs') *v.t.* to lower; subdue. [L., fr. *re-*, back, and *ducere*, to lead.]

REDUCIBLE (re-dū'si-bl) *a.* that may be reduced.

REDUCTION (re-duk'shun) *n.* act of reducing; the bringing of different denominations to one. [L., fr. (part.) *reductus*, led back.]

REDUCTIVE (re-duk'tiv) *a.* having power to reduce.

REDUNDANCE (re-dun'dans) *n.* superfluous quantity; excess.

REDUNDANT (re-dun'dant) *a.* exceeding what is necessary; superfluous in words or figures. [L. (part. stem) *redundant-*, redounding. See REDOUND.]

REDUNDANTLY (re-dun'dant-li) *ad.* superfluously.

REDUPLICATE (rē-dū'pli-kàt) *v.t.* to double again; repeat often.

REDUPLICATION (rē-dū-pli-kā'shun) *n.* the act of doubling.

RE-ECHO (rē-ek'ō) *v.t.* or *i.* to echo back again;—*n.* echo of an echo.

REED (rēd) *n.* a hollow, jointed stalk; a musical pipe. [O.E. *hreod.*]

REEDED (rē'ded) *a.* covered with reeds; formed with channels or ridges.

REEDY (rē'di) *a.* abounding with reeds; sounding like a reed.

REEF (rēf) *v.t.* or *i.* to take in and roll up part of a sail; reduce sail;—*n.* portion of a sail;—*n.* a chain of rocks near the surface of water. [D.]

REEFER (rē'fer) *n.* one who reefs; a midshipman.

REEFY (rē'fi) *a.* full of reefs.

REEK (rēk) *n.* steam; vapour;—*v.i.* to send forth steam or smoke. [O.E. *rec.* Cf. Ger. *Rauch.*]

REEKY (rē'ki) *a.* soiled with smoke; sending out smoke.

REEL (rēl) (1) *n.* a frame to wind yarn or thread on;—*v.t.* or *i.* to wind; stagger;—(2) *n.* a lively dance. [(1) O.E. *hreol.* (2) Gael.]

RE-ELECT (rē-e-lekt') *v.t.* to elect again.

RE-ELECTION (rē-e-lek'shun) *n.* a second or repeated election.

RE-ELIGIBLE (rē-el'i-ji-bl) *a.* capable of being elected again.

RE-EMBARK (rē-em-bàrk') *v.t.* or *i.* to embark again.

RE-ENACT (rē-en-akt') *v.t.* to act anew.

RE-ENACTMENT (rē-en-akt'ment) *n.* the renewal of a law.

RE-ENGAGE (rē-en-gàj') *v.t.* to engage a second time.

RE-ENTER (rē-en'ter) *v.t.* to enter again.

RE-ENTRANCE (rē-en'trans) *n.* act of entering again.

RE-ESTABLISH (rē-es-tab'lish) *v.t.* to establish again.

RE-ESTABLISHMENT (rē-es-tab'lish-ment) *n.* act of establishing again.

REEVE (rēv) *v.t.* to pass the end of a rope through a block, thimble, etc. [D.]

REEVE (rēv) *n.* a magistrate; head bailiff; a steward. [O.E. *gerefa.*]

RE-EXAMINE (rē-eg-zam'in) *v.t.* to examine again.

RE-EXPORT (rē-eks-pōrt') *v.t.* to export what has been imported.

REFECTION (re-fek'shun) *n.* refreshment; repast. [O.F., fr. L. (acc.) *refectionem*, fr. (part.) *refectus*, re-make, fr. *facere.*]

REFECTIVE (re-fek'tiv) *a.* refreshing.

REFECTORY (rē-fek'tu-ri) *n.* a place for refreshment.

REFER (re-fer') *v.t.* or *i.* to submit to another; assign; direct to; have recourse; allude; respect. [L., fr. *re-*, back, and *ferre*, to bear.]

REFERABLE (re-fer'a-bl) *a.* that may be referred.

REFEREE (ref-e-rē') *n.* one to whom something is referred.

REFERENCE (ref'er-ens) *n.* act of referring; allusion to.

REFERENTIAL (ref-e-ren'shal) *a.* that contains a reference.

REFERRIBLE (re-fer'i-bl) *a.* that may be referred; referable.

REFINE (re-fin') *v.t.* or *i.* to clear from impurities; polish; grow pure; make nice or subtle distinctions. [L. *re*, intens.]

REFINED (re-find') *a.* freed from extraneous matter; purified; polished; polite.

REFINEMENT (re-fin'ment) *n.* act of refining; state of being refined; polish or elegance in manners, etc.

REFINER (re-fi'ner) *n.* he or that which refines.

REFINING (re-fi'ning) *n.* act of purifying; minute subtlety in argument or speech.

REFIT (rē-fit') *v.t.* or *i.* to fit out a second time; repair.

REFLECT (re-flekt') *v.t.* or *i.* to throw back, consider attentively. [L. *reflectere*, lit. to bend back, fr. *flectere.*]

REFLECTING (re-flek'ting) *a.* throwing back, as light; given to thought.

REFLECTION (re-flek'shun) *n.* act of throwing back; attentive consideration; reproach.

REFLECTIVE (re-flek'tiv) *a.* throwing back images.

REFLECTIVELY (re-flek'tiv-li) *ad.* by reflection.

REFLECTOR (re-flek'ter) *n.* one who, or a polished surface that, reflects.

REFLEX (rē'fleks) *a.* directed backwards; bent back;—*n.* reflected light.

REFLEXIVE (re-flek'siv) *a.* that respects something past.

REFLEXIVELY (re-flek'siv-li) *ad.* in a direction backward.

REFLORESCENCE (rē-flō-res'ens) *n.* a blossoming anew.

REFLUENCE (ref'loo-ens) *n.* a flowing back.

REFLUENT (ref'loo-ent) *a.* flowing back; returning.

REFLUX (rē'fluks) *n.* a flowing back of water; ebb.

REFORM (rē-form') *v.t.* or *i.* to form anew; repair; reclaim; amend; become better; improve;—*n.* improvement; correction; any political change for the better. [F. *reformer*, fr. L. *re-*, again, and *formare*, to FORM.]

REFORMATION (ref-ur-mā'shun) *n.* act of reforming; amendment.

REFORMATION (rē-for-mā'shun) *n.* formation anew. [L. (part.) *reformatus*, formed again.]

REFORMATORY (re-for'ma-tur-i) *n.* an institution for juvenile offenders.

REFORMER (re-for'mer) *n.* one who promotes reform.

REFRACT (re-frakt') *v.t.* to break the direct course of. [L. (part.) *refractus*, lit. broken back, fr. *frangere*, break.]

REFRACTION (re-frak'shun) *n.* deviation of a ray from a direct course.

REFRACTIVE (re-frak'tiv) *a.* that has power to refract.

REFRACTORINESS (re-frak'tur-i-nes) *n.* obstinacy.

REFRACTORY (re-frak'tur-i) *a.* perverse; unruly; obstinate.

REFRAIN (re-frān') (1) *v.t.* or *i.* to curb; keep from action; restrain oneself; abstain;— (2) *n.* words repeated at the end of each verse of a song. [(1) O.F., fr. L. *re*, back, and *frenum*, a rein. (2) O.F., fr. L. *re*, again, and *frangere*, to break.]

REFRANGIBILITY (re-fran-ji-bil'i-ti) *n.* capability of being refracted.

REFRANGIBLE (re-fran'ji-bl) *a.* that may be refracted. [L., fr. *re*, again, back, and *frangere*, to break.]

REFRESH (re-fresh') *v.t.* to revive; cool; restore; enliven. [O.F. *refreschir*, fr. *re-*, back, and Ger. *frisch*, FRESH.]

REFRESHING (re-fresh'ing) *a.* reviving; cooling.

REFRESHMENT (re-fresh'ment) *n.* act of refreshing; that which refreshes; food; rest.

REFRIGERANT (re-frij'er-ant) *a.* cooling;— *n.* a cooling medicine or application.

REFRIGERATE (re-frij'er-āt) *v.t.* to cool. [L., fr. *frigerare*, make cool, fr. *frigus*, cold. See FRIGID.]

REFRIGERATION (re-frij-er-ā'shun) *n,* a cooling.

REFRIGERATOR (re-frij'er-ā-ter) *n.* an airtight box for keeping things cool by means o ice.

REFRIGERATORY (re-frij'er-ā-tur-i) *n.* a vessel for cooling; =*a.* cooling.

REFUGE (ref'ūj) *n.* a shelter from danger; stronghold; asylum; resource; expedient. [F., fr. L. *refugium*, escape, fr. *re*, back, and *fugere*, flee.]

REFUGEE (ref-ū-jē') *n.* one who flees for safety to a foreign power.

REFULGENCE (re-ful'jens) *n.* brilliancy; bright radiance.

REFULGENT (re-ful'jent) *a.* casting a bright light; splendid. [L., fr. *re*, and *fulgere*, shine.]

REFUND (re-fund') *v.t.* to pay back; repay; restore. [L., fr. *re*, again, back, and *fundere*, to pour.]

REFUSAL (re-fū'zal) *n.* denial; right of choice; option.

REFUSE (re-fūz') *v.t.* to deny; reject;—*v.i.* not to comply with. [O.F. *refuser*, fr. L., fr. (part.) *fusus*, poured, fr. *fundere*.]

REFUSE (ref'ūs) *n.* waste matter; dregs;— *a.* worthless. [O.F. *refus*.]

REFUSER (re-fū'zer) *n.* one who refuses or rejects.

REFUTABLE (re-fū'ta-bl) *a.* that may be refuted.

REFUTATION (ref-ū-tā'shun) *n.* act of refuting.

REFUTE (re-fūt') *v.t.* to overthrow by argument; prove wrong; disprove. [L., fr. *refutare*; conn. with REFUSE.]

REGAIN (re-gān') *v.t.* to obtain again; recover. [F.]

REGAL (rē'gal) *a.* royal; kingly. [O.F., fr. L. (acc.) *regalem*, fr. stem *reg-*, of *rex*, king.]

REGALE (re-gāl') *v.t.* or *i.* to entertain sumptuously; refresh; delight; feast. [O.F.]

REGALEMENT (re-gāl'ment) *n.* refreshment; entertainment.

REGALIA (re-gā'li-a) *n.pl.* ensigns of royalty, as the crown, sceptre, etc. [L. =royal (insignia).]

REGALITY (re-gal'i-ti) *n.* royalty.

REGALLY (rē'gal-i) *ad.* as befits a sovereign.

REGARD (re-gärd') *v.t.* to observe; heed; keep; respect; esteem; consider;—*n.* attention; respect; esteem; reference. [F. *regarder*, fr. *garder*, observe, GUARD.]

REGARDFUL (re-gärd'fool) *a.* taking notice; heedful; attentive.

REGARDLESS (re-gärd'les) *a.* heedless; careless; indifferent.

REGATTA (re-gat'a) *n.* a race of yachts; any rowing or sailing match. [It.]

REGENCY (rē'jen-si) *n.* government by a regent.

REGENERATE (re-jen'er-āt) *v.t.* to produce anew; renew the moral nature; convert; —*a.* born again; born of the Spirit. [L. *regenerate.*]

REGENERATION (re-jen-er-ā'shun) *n.* the new birth; reproduction.

REGENERATIVE (re-jen'er-āt-iv) *a.* tending to regenerate.

REGENT (rē'jent) *n.* one who governs in the place of a king; a ruler;—*a.* ruling. [O.F., fr. L. (acc. part.) *regentem*, ruling, fr. *regere*.]

REGICIDE (rej'i-sīd) *n.* the killer or killing of a king. [Fr. L. stem *regi-*, of *rex*, king, and *-cida*, fr. *cædere*, slay.]

REGIME (rā-zhēm') *n.* mode of living; form of government. [F.]

REGIMEN (rej'i-men) *n.* orderly government; any beneficial regulation; rule of diet. [L., fr. *regere*, to guide, to rule.]

REGIMENT (rej'i-ment, rej'ment) *n.* a body of troops under a colonel. [F., fr. Late L. *regimentum*, government, fr. *regere*.]

REGIMENTAL (rej-i-men'tal) *a.* belonging to a regiment.

REGIMENTALS (rej-i-men'talz) *n.pl.* the uniform of a regiment.

REGION (rē'jun) *n.* a tract of land; country. [O.F., fr. L. (acc.) *regionem*, fr. *regere*, rule.]

REGISTER (rej'is-ter) *n.* a written record; the book containing it; the keeper of it; an organ stop; musical compass; a sliding plate in a furnace;—*v.t.* to record; enrol. [O.F., fr. Late L. *registrum*, *regestum*, fr. (part.) *regestus*, recorded, fr. *re*, back, and *gerere*, carry.]

REGISTRAR (rej'is-trär) *n.* an officer who keeps public records.

REGISTRATION (rej-is-trā'shun) *n.* act of registering; enrolment.

REGISTRY (rej'is-tri) *n.* a registering place where a register is kept.

REGLET (reg'let) *n.* a flat, narrow moulding; a printer's lead. [F. dim. of *règle*, fr. L. *regula*, a rule.]

REGNANCY (reg'nan-si) *n.* rule; predominance.

REGNANT (reg'nant) *a.* reigning. [L., ppr. of *regnare*, to reign.]

REGRESS (rē'gres) *n.* return; power of returning. [L., fr. (part.) *regressus*, having gone back, fr. *gradi*, go.]

REGRESSION (re-gresh'un) *n.* act of passing back.

REGRESSIVE (re-gres'iv) *a.* passing back.

REGRET (re-gret') *n.* pain of mind at something untoward; sorrow for anything; remorse; repentance;—*v.t.* to feel sorrow for; grieve for; repent. [O.F. *regrater*, of uncert. etym.]

REGULAR (reg'ū-lar) *a.* agreeable to rule; stated; orderly;—*n.* a soldier of the standing army. [L., fr. *regula*, a RULE.]

REGULARITY (reg-ū-lar'i-ti) *n.* certain order; method.

REGULARLY (reg'ū-lar-li) *ad.* statedly; in due order.

REGULATE (reg'ū-lāt) *v.t.* to adjust by rule or method; put in good order. [L. (part.) *regulatus*, directed, fr. *regulare*. See REGULAR.]

REGULATION (reg-ū-lā'shun) *n.* act of adjusting; prescribed rule.

REGULATOR (reg'ū-lā-tur) *n.* he or that which regulates.

REHABILITATE (rē-ha-bil'i-tāt) *v.t.* to restore to a former state, right, etc. [L.]

REHABILITATION (rē-ha-bil-i-tā'shun) *n.* act of reinstating; restoration.

REHEARSAL (re-hers'al) *n.* recital; preparatory repetition.

REHEARSE (re-hers') v.t. to repeat what has been said; narrate; recite before public exhibition. [O.F. reherser, to harrow over again. See HEARSE.]

REIGN (rān) n. royal authority or government; prevalence; controlling influence;—v.i. to rule. [O.F. regne, fr. L. regnum, kingdom, fr. regere, rule.]

REIGNING (rā'ning) a. predominant; prevailing.

REIMBURSE (rē-im-burs') v.t. to repay. [Fr. F. rembourser, fr. re, back, em, in, and bourse, PURSE.]

REIMBURSEMENT (rē-im-burs'ment) n. repayment.

REIMPORT (rē-im-pōrt') v.t. to import back, as export goods.

REIN (rān) n. strap of a bridle; leading string; means of governing or restraining; —v.t. to guide by a bridle; restrain. [O.F. reine, fr. Late L., fr. L. retinere, hold back, fr. tenere, hold.]

REINDEER (rān'dēr) n. an animal of the deer kind. [Scand.]

REINFORCE (rē-in-fōrs')v.t.to strengthen with new force.

REINFORCEMENT (rē-in-fōrs'ment) n. additional supply of troops or ships.

REINS (rānz) n.pl. the kidneys; the inward parts. [O.F. (pl.) renes.]

REINSERT (rē-in-sert') v.t. to insert again.

REINSPECTION (rē-in-spek'shun) n. a second inspection.

Reindeer.

REINSTATE (rē-in-stāt') v.i. to replace in possession or in a former state.

REINSTATEMENT (rē-in-stāt'ment) n. a placing in a former state.

REINSURANCE (rē-in-shōōr'ans) n. insurance of property already insured.

REINSURE (rē-in-shōōr') v.t. to insure a second time.

REINVEST (rē-in-vest') v.t. to invest anew.

REINVESTMENT (rē-in-vest'ment) n. a new investment.

REINVIGORATE (rē-in-vig'ur-āt) v.t. to give new strength to; reanimate.

REISSUE (rē-ish'ū) v.t. to issue a second time; —n. republication.

REITER (rī'ter) n. a mounted trooper. [Ger.]

REITERATE (rē-it'er-āt) v.t. to do or say again and again; repeat frequently. [L. re, and iter, again.]

REITERATION (rē-it-er-ā'shun) n. act of reiterating.

REJECT (re-jekt') v.t. to cast off; discard; refuse. [L. (part.) rejectus, thrown back, fr. jacere, throw.]

REJECTION (re-jek'shun) n. act of rejecting.

REJOICE (re-jois') v.t. or i. to be glad; exult; gladden; cheer. [O.F. (part.) resjoisant, rejoicing, fr. resjoir, fr. L. re-, again, ex, greatly, and gaudere, be glad.]

REJOICING (re-jois'ing) n. expression of joy.

REJOICINGLY (re-jois'ing-li) ad. with joy.

REJOIN (re-join') v.t. or i. to join again.

REJOINDER (re-join'der) n. a reply to an answer.

REJUDGE (rē-juj') v.t. to examine or try again.

REJUVENATE (re-jōō'ven-āt) v.t. to render young again. [L. re, again, and juvenis, young.]

REJUVENESCENCE (rē-jōō-ven-es'ens) n. a being young again. [L. re-, again, and juvenescent.]

REKINDLE (rē-kin'dl) v.t. to kindle again.

RELAPSE (re-laps') v.i. to fall back; return to a former state;—n. a falling back. [L. (part.) relapsus, back-slidden. See LAPSE.]

RELATE (re-lāt') v.t. or i. to tell; narrate; ally; refer. [O.F. relater, fr. Late L., fr. L. (part.) relatus, lit. brought back, fr. referre.]

RELATION (re-lā'shun) n. act of relating; any connection established; kindred.

RELATIONAL (re-lā'shun-al) a. having relation.

RELATIONSHIP (re-lā'shun-ship) n. state of being related.

RELATIVE (rel'a-tiv) a. having relation;—n. one allied by blood; that which relates to something else.

RELATIVELY (rel'a-tiv-li) ad. with relation to something else.

RELAX (re-laks') v.t. or i. to slacken; remit in effort, attention, or severity; make or become feeble. [L., fr. re-, back, again, and laxare, loosen. See LAX.]

RELAXATION (rē-lak-sā'shun) n. a slackening; relief from laborious or painful duties.

RELAXATIVE (re-lak'sa-tiv) a. tending to relax.

RELAY (re-lā') (1) n. a supply of horses at the stages of a journey; anything laid up in store;—(2) v.t. to lay again. [(1) F. relais, lit. a ' rest,' fr. relaissier, to RELAX.]

RELEASE (re-lēs') v.t. to free from restraint, obligation, pain, grief, etc.; discharge; relinquish;—n. setting free; discharge; a quit-claim. [O.F. relessier = relaissier. See RELAY (1).]

RELEGATE (rel'e-gāt) v.t. to despatch; to send into exile; to banish. [L., fr. re, again, back, and legare, to send with a commission. See LEGATE.]

RELEGATION (rel-e-gā'shun) n. exile.

RELENT (re-lent') v.i. to soften in temper; yield to pity. [F. ralentir, slacken, fr. L. re-, ad, and lentus, slow.]

RELENTLESS (re-lent'les) a. unmoved by pity.

RELEVANCY (rel'e-van-si) n. state of being relevant.

RELEVANT (rel'e-vant) a. bearing on the point or purpose; pertinent. [F. (part.) relevant, helping, lit. raising up, fr. relever.]

RELIEVE.]

RELIABILITY (re-lī-a-bil'i-ti) n. state or quality of being reliable.

RELIABLE (re-lī'a-bl) a. that may be relied on or trusted; trustworthy. [Fr. RELY.]

RELIANCE (re-lī'ans) n. trust; dependence.

RELIC (rel'ik) n. remains of a dead body; any memorial of the dead. [F. (pl.) reliques, fr. L. (acc. pl.) reliquias, remains, fr. relinquere, leave behind, fr. linquere, leave.]

RELICT (rel'ikt) n. a woman left a widow. [L. (fem. part.) relicta, left behind.]

RELIEF (re-lēf') n. alleviation of pain or evil; aid; support; relief from a military post; relievo. [O.F. relief.]

RELIEVABLE (re-lē'va-bl) a. that may be relieved.

RELIEVE (re-lē-v) v.t. to ease; help; mitigate; release; redress; set off by contrast. [F. relever, raise up, help, fr. L. relevare, fr. levare, raise, fr. levis, light.]

RELIEVO (re-lē'vō, rel-yā'vō) n. prominence of figures in sculpture or painting.

RELIGION (re-lij'un) n. a system of faith and worship; pious practice. [F., fr. L. (acc.) religionem, conn. with religens, devout.]

RELIGIONISM (re-lij'un-izm) n. practice of or adherence to religion.

RELIGIONIST (re-lij'un-ist) n. one devoted to a religion.

RELIGIOUS (re-lij'us) a. pertaining to religion; sacred; pious; godly; conscientious.

RELIGIOUSLY (re-lij'us-li) ad. piously; sacredly; exactly.

RELINQUISH (re-ling'kwish) *v.t.* to withdraw from; give up; quit. [L. *relinquere*, to leave behind. See RELIC.]
RELINQUISHMENT (re-ling'kwish-ment) *n.* act of forsaking.
RELIQUARY (rel'i-kwor-i) *n.* a small chest or casket for holding relics. [F. *reliquaire*, fr. L. *reliquiæ*, RELICS.]
RELIQUIÆ (re-lik'wi-ē) *n.pl.* fossil remains of plants or animals. [L.]
RELISH (rel'ish) *n.* a pleasing taste; flavour; —*v.t.* to give flavour to; like the taste of; enjoy;—*v.i.* to have a pleasant flavour. [O.F. *reles, relais*, that which is left behind. See RELAY.]
RELISHABLE (rel'ish-a-bl) *a.* that may be relished.
RELUCTANCE (re-luk'tans) *n.* unwillingness.
RELUCTANT (re-luk'tant) *a.* averse to; granted unwillingly. [L., fr *re-* back and *luctari*, struggle, fr *lucta*, a tussle.]
RELUCTANTLY (re-luk'tant-li) *ad.* with unwillingness.
RELY (re-lī') *v.i.* to rest or confide in; depend on. [F. *relier*, bind up, fr. L. *re*, back, and *ligare*, to bind.]
REMADE (re-mād') *pret.* and *pp.* of REMAKE.
REMAIN (re-mān') *v.i.* to stay behind; continue; be left; last [O.F. *remaindre*, fr. L. *remanere*, fr. *re-* behind, and *manere.*]
REMAINDER (re-mān'der) *n.* anything left.
REMAINS (re-mānz') *n.pl.* what is left; relics.
REMAKE (re-māk') *v.t.* to make anew.
REMAND (re-mand') *v.t.* to send back in custody; recommit. [L. *re* back, and *mandare*, to order.]
REMANENT (rem'a-nent) *a.* remaining. See REMAIN.
REMARK (re-märk') *v.t.* or *i.* to take notice of; observe; express in words; animadvert; —*n* notice; observation; casual expression. [F. *remarquer*, fr. *re*, again, and *marquer* to mark.]
REMARKABLE (re-mär'ka-bl) *a.* worthy of note; extraordinary; distinguished.
REMARKABLY (re-mär'ka-bli) *ad.* in a remarkable manner or degree.
REMARRY (re-mar'i) *v.t.* to marry again.
REMEDIABLE (re-mē'di-a-bl) *a.* capable of remedy.
REMEDIAL (re-mē'di-al) *a.* affording remedy.
REMEDILESS (rem'e-di-les) *a.* admitting no cure; without remedy.
REMEDY (rem'e-di) *n.* that which is adapted to cure, or which counteracts an evil;—*v.t.* to cure; remove; repair. [L. *remedium*, fr. *re*, again, and *mederi*, to cure.]
REMEMBER (re-mem'ber) *v.t.* to have or keep in mind; keep sacred; celebrate. [O.F. fr L. *rememorari*, fr. *re*, again, and *memor*, mindful.]
REMEMBRANCE (re-mem'brans) *n.* power of remembering; memory; recollection; memorial.
REMEMBRANCER (re-mem'bran-ser) *n.* a recorder; officer of the exchequer; memento; memorial.
REMIND (re-mīnd') *v.t.* to put in mind; bring to recollection or consideration. [L. *re*, again, and O.E. *gemynd*, fr. *munan*, to think.]
REMINDER (re-mīn'der) *n.* one who or that which reminds.
REMINISCENCE (rem-i-nis'ens) *n.* recollection; any suggestion of the past; narrative of past personal experience.
REMINISCENT (rem-i-nis'ent) *a.* inclined to call to mind. [L., fr. (part. stem) *reminiscent-*. fr. *reminisci*, to call to mind.]
REMISS (re-mis') *a.* slack; negligent. [L. (part.) *remissus*, slackened, lit. sent back. See REMIT.]
REMISSIBLE (re-mis'i-bl) *a.* that may be remitted.

REMISSION (re-mish'un) *n.* pardon; diminution of intensity. [L.]
REMISSLY (re-mis'li) *ad.* negligently; carelessly.
REMISSNESS (re-mis'nes) *n.* negligence.
REMIT (re-mit') *v.t.* or *i.* to send money; forgive; relax; refer; abate. [L., fr. *re-* back, and *mittere*, to send.]
REMITTAL (re-mit'al) *n.* a giving back.
REMITTANCE (re-mit'ans) *n.* act of remitting money in payment; sum transmitted.
REMITTENT (re-mit'ent) *a.* increasing and abating in turn.
REMNANT (rem'nant) *n.* what is left;—*a.* remaining. [O.F (part.) *remnant*, remaining, fr. L., fr. *remanere*, REMAIN.]
REMODEL (re-mod'ell) *v.t.* to model anew.
REMOLTEN (re-mōl'ten) *a.* melted again.
REMONSTRANCE (re-mon'strans) *n.* expostulation; reproof.
REMONSTRANT (re-mon'strant) *n.* one who remonstrates.
REMONSTRATE (re-mon'strāt) *v.i.* to urge reasons against; expostulate. [Late L. (part.) *remonstratus*, opposed by argument, fr. L. *re-* again, back, and *monstrare*, show.]
REMORA (rem'u-ra) *n.* the sucking fish. [L. *remorari*, to delay.]
REMORDENCY (re-mor'den-si) *n.* compunction.
REMORSE (re-mors') *n.* pain or reproach of conscience; compunction. [O.F. *remors* fr. Late L. (acc.) *remorsum* fr. L. *re*, again and (part.) *morsus* bitten, fr. *mordere.*]
REMORSEFUL (re-mors'fool) *a.* full of a sense of guilt.
REMORSELESS (re-mors'les) *a.* unpitying.
REMOTE (re-mōt') *a.* distant in place or time; alien; slight; not primary. [L. (part.) *remotus*, lit. moved back. See REMOVE.]
REMOTELY (re-mōt'li) *ad.* at a distance; in a slight degree.
REMOTENESS (re-mōt'nes) *n.* state of being remote; distance.
REMOULD (re-mōld') *v.t.* to mould or shape anew.
REMOUNT (re-mount') *v.t.* or *i.* to reascend.
REMOVABLE (re-mōō'va-bl) *a.* that may be removed.
REMOVAL (re-mōō'val) *n.* act of moving from a place.
REMOVE (re-mōōv') *v.t.* or *i.* to change place; —*n.* change of place; step. [L., fr. *re*, back, and *movere*, to move.]
REMUNERATE (re-mū'ne-rāt) *v.t.* to recompense for any act. [L., fr. *re-*, again, back, and *munerare*, give a present to, fr. stem *muner-*, of *munus*, present.]
REMUNERATION (re-mū-ne-rā'shun) *n.* reward; recompense.
REMUNERATIVE (re-mū'ne-rā-tiv) *a.* fitted to remunerate; lucrative.
RENAISSANCE (re-nā'sans) *n.* revival of arts and letters in the 15th century; *n.* noting a style in art more florid than the classic of ancient Greece. [F =new birth.]
RENAL (rē'nal) *a.* pertaining to the kidneys. [L. *renes*, the kidneys or REINS.]
RENASCENT (re-nas'ent) *a.* growing again. [L. *re-*, again, and (part. stem) *nascent-*, fr. *nasci*, to be born.]
RENCOUNTER (ren-koun'ter) *n.* a sudden or casual combat; clash;—*v.t.* or *i.* to meet; clash. [F., fr. *rencontrer*, meet, fr. *re-*, again, and *encontrer* ENCOUNTER.]
REND (rend) *v.t.* [*pret.* and *pp.* RENT] to split; tear asunder. [O.E. *rendan*, to cut.]
RENDER (ren'der) *v.t.* or *i.* to return; restore; make up and deliver; translate; perform; plaster roughly; yield. [F. *rendre*, fr. L. *reddere*, fr. *re-*, back. and *dare*, to give.]
RENDERING (ren'der-ing) *n.* act of returning; a version; rough plastering.

RENDEZVOUS (räng'dā-vōō) *n.* a place of meeting; a meeting appointed;—*v.t.* or *i.* to assemble, as troops. [F. =RENDER yourselves !]

RENDITION (ren-dish'un) *n.* a giving back; surrender; translation; performance of a part, song, or the like.

RENEGADE (ren'e-gād) *n.* an apostate; deserter from his party. [Sp. *renegado,* one that denies the faith, fr. L. *re,* again, and *negare,* to deny.]

RENEW (re-nū') *v.t.* or *i.* to make new; restore; begin again; repeat; grant or accept a new money bill; regenerate.

RENEWABLE (rē-nū'a-bl) *a.* that may be renewed.

RENEWAL (re-nū'al) *n.* act of renewing; restoration; regeneration.

RENEWER (re-nū'er) *n.* one who renews.

RENNET (ren'et) (1) *n.* the concreted milk found in the stomach of a calf; (2) a kind of apple. [(1) M.E. *rennen,* RUN, congeal. Cf. Ger. *rinnen* =congeal. (2) F.]

RENOUNCE (re-nouns') *v.t.* to disown; cast off formally. [F. *renoncer,* fr. L., fr. *re-,* again, and *nuntiare,* bring a message, fr. *nuntius,* messenger.]

RENOUNCEMENT (re-nouns'ment) *n.* act of renouncing.

RENOVATE (ren'u-vāt) *v.t.* to renew. [L., fr. *re-,* again, and *novare,* to make NEW.]

RENOVATION (ren-u-vā'shun) *n.* renewal.

RENOWN (re-noun') *n.* fame; celebrity. [O.F. *renoun,* fr. *renomer,* to make famous, fr. L. *re-,* again, and *nomen,* name.]

RENOWNED (re-nound') *a.* famous; celebrated.

RENT (rent) (1) *pret.* of REND, torn asunder; —*n.* a fissure; tear:—(2) *n.* money received or paid for the use of property;—*v.t.* or *i.* to let or occupy by payment of rent; lease. [(2) F. *rente,* fr. Late L. (acc.) *reddilam,* fr. *reddere,* to give back, to pay.]

RENTABLE (ren'ta-bl) *a.* that may be rented.

RENTAL (ren'tal) *n.* annual amount of rents; rent-roll.

RENTER (ren'ter) *n.* tenant or occupier of property let on rent.

RENTER (ren'ter) *v.t.* to sew finely or artfully; fine-draw. [F. *rentraire,* fr. L. *re-,* again, and *trahere,* draw.]

RENT-ROLL (rent'rōl) *n.* a list of rents and tenants.

RENUNCIATION (re-nun-si-ā'shun) *n.* act of disowning; rejection; refusal. [L., fr. *renuntiare,* RENOUNCE.]

REORGANISATION (rē-or-gan-i-zā'shun) *n.* organisation anew.

REORGANISE (rē-or'ga-nīz) *v.t.* to organise anew.

REP (rep) *n.* a dress stuff with a corded surface. [Prob. corr. fr. RIB.]

REPAID (rē-pād') *pret.* of REPAY.

REPAIR (re-pār') (1) *v.t.* to mend; to refit; —*n.* mending; patching; restoration;— (2) *v.i.* to go; to resort. [(1) O.F. *reparer,* fr. L., fr. *re-,* again, and *parare,* to prepare. (2) O.F. *repairer,* fr. L. *repatriare,* to return home again, fr. *patria,* native land.]

REPAIRER (re-pār'er) *n.* one who repairs.

REPARABLE (rep'a-ra-bl) *a.* that may be repaired.

REPARATION (rep-a-rā'shun) *n.* restitution; amends.

REPARATIVE (re-par'a-tiv, rep'a-ra-tiv) *a.* amending defects;—*n.* that which makes amends.

REPARTEE (rep-ar-tē') *n.* a smart reply; witty retort. [O.F., fr. (part.) *reparti,* replied, fr. *repartir,* lit. to re-divide, fr. L., fr. *partire,* fr. stem *part-,* of *pars,* PART.]

REPAST (re-past') *n.* act of taking food; food taken; a meal. [O.F. *repast,* fr. L., fr. *re-,* again, and *pascere,* to eat, feed.]

REPAY (re-pā') *v.t.* to pay back; recompense; requite.

REPAYABLE (re-pā'a-bl) *a.* that is to be repaid.

REPAYMENT (re-pā'ment) *n.* act of repaying; thing repaid.

REPEAL (re-pēl') *v.t.* to revoke by authority; abrogate;—*n.* revoking; annulling. [Fr. O.F. *rapeler,* fr. *re,* back, and *appeler,* APPEAL.]

REPEALABLE (re-pē'la-bl) *a.* that may be repealed.

REPEALER (re-pē'ler) *n.* one who advocates dissolution of the union between Great Britain and Ireland.

REPEAT (re-pēt') *v.t.* or *i.* to do or speak again; recite; quote from memory; strike the hours; recur. [O.F. *repeter,* fr. L., fr. *re-,* again, and *petere,* attack, seek.]

REPEATEDLY (re-pē'ted-li) *ad.* frequently.

REPEATER (re-pē'ter) *n.* one who or that which repeats; a watch that strikes the hours.

REPEL (re-pel') *v.t.* to drive back; resist. [L., fr. *re,* back, and *pellere,* to drive.]

REPELLENCY (re-pel'en-si) *n.* quality that repels.

REPELLENT (re-pel'ent) *a.* tending to repel.

REPENT (re-pent') *v.t.* or *i.* to feel sorrow for something done or left undone; remember with sorrow; change and amend one's ways. [F. *repentir,* fr. L. *re-,* again, back, and *pœnitere,* make PENITENT.]

REPENT (rep'ent) *a.* creeping, as a plant. [L. (part. stem) *repent-,* fr. *repere,* to creep.]

REPENTANCE (re-pen'tans) *n.* sorrow for sins; penitence.

REPENTANT (re-pen'tant) *a.* sorrowful for sin; contrite; sorry for; expressing sorrow; —*n.* a penitent.

REPEOPLE (rē-pē'pl) *v.t.* to supply anew with inhabitants.

REPERCUSSION (rē-per-kush'un) *n.* act of driving back; rebound. [L. *re-,* back, *percutio,* I drive.]

REPERCUSSIVE (rē-per-kus'iv) *a.* beating back.

REPERTORY (rep'er-tu-ri) *n.* place where things are kept; a magazine. [L. *repertorium,* inventory, fr. *repertor,* discoverer, fr. *repertire.*]

REPERUSAL (rē-pe-rū'zal) *n.* a second perusal.

REPETITION (rep-e-tish'un) *n.* act of repeating.

REPINE (re-pīn') *v.i.* to fret oneself; grieve at. See PINE.

REPLACE (re-plās') *v.t.* to put again in its place; substitute.

REPLANT (rē-plant') *v.t.* to plant again.

REPLENISH (re-plen'ish) *v.t.* to fill again; supply. [L. *re-,* again, and *plenere,* to fill.]

REPLETE (re-plēt') *a.* full; completely filled. [L. (part.) *repletus,* filled full, fr. L. *re-,* again, and *plere,* fill.]

REPLETION (re-plē'shun) *n.* superabundant fullness.

REPLETIVE (re-plē'tiv) *a.* replenishing.

REPLEVIABLE (re-plev'i-a-bl) *a.* that may be replevied.

REPLEVIN (re-plev'in) *n.* a writ to recover goods distrained.

REPLEVY (re-plev'i) *v.t.* to set at liberty on security; bail. [L. *re-,* again, and O.F. *plevir,* to be surety.]

REPLICA (rep'li-ka) *n.* a copy of a picture made by the artist of the original. [It.]

REPLICATE (rep'li-kāt) *a.* folded back or down.

REPLICATION (rep-li-kā'shun) *n.* a plaintiff's reply to a defendant's plea. [L. (part.) *replicatus,* lit. folded backwards, fr. *plicare.* See PLY, REPLY.]

REPLIER (re-plī'er) *n.* one who answers.

REPLY (re-plï') v.i. to answer;—n. return in words; response. [O.F. replier, fr. L. replicare, to fold back, fr. plicare.]

REPORT (re-pórt') v.t. or i. to return as an answer; circulate publicly; take notes of and write for the press;—n. a formal or official statement; rumour; repute; explosive sound. [F. reporter, fr. L., fr. re-, back, and portare, to bring.]

REPORTER (re-pōr'ter) n. one who reports.

REPOSAL (re-pō'zal) n. act of reposing.

REPOSE (re-pōz') v.t. to lay at rest; place in trust;—v.i. to rest upon; lie still;—n. rest; sleep. [F. reposer, fr. Late L. repousare, pause, fr. L. re-, again, and pausa, PAUSE.]

REPOSIT (rē-poz'it) v.t. to lodge for safety.

REPOSITORY (rē-poz'i-tu-ri) n. a place where things are stored. [O.F. repositoire, storehouse, fr. L. (part.) repositus stored up, fr. ponere, place.]

REPREHEND (rep-re-hend') v.t. to blame. [L. reprehendere, lit. hold back, check, fr. prehendere, seize.]

REPREHENSIBLE (rep-re-hen'si-bl) a. deserving censure.

REPREHENSIBLY (rep-re-hen'si-bli) ad. in a reprehensible manner.

REPREHENSION (rep-re-hen'shun) n. reproof; blame.

REPREHENSIVE (rep-re-hen'siv) a. containing reproof.

REPRESENT (rep-re-zent') v.t. to show; personate; stand for; act for. [O.F., fr. L. representare.]

REPRESENTATION (rep-re-zen-tā'shun) n. act of representing; thing represented; likeness; exhibition; appearance for another.

REPRESENTATIVE (rep-re-zen'ta-tiv) a. exhibiting likeness;—n. one acting for another.

REPRESENTATIVELY (rep-re-zen'ta-tiv-li) ad. by substitution.

REPRESS (re-pres') v.t. to put down; subdue. [L. re-, back, and pressus, (part.) of premere, to press.]

REPRESSIBLE (re-pres'i-bl) a. that may be repressed. [ing.

REPRESSION (re-presh'un) n. act of repressing.

REPRESSIVE (re-pres'iv) a. tending to repress.

REPRIEVE (re-prēv') v.t. to respite for a time;—n. respite after sentence of death. [O.F. (pres. ind.) repreuve, fr. reprover. Doublet. of REPROVE.]

REPRIMAND (rep'ri-mand) n. reproof for a fault;—v.t. to chide; reprove. [F., fr. L. reprimendum, a thing that ought to be repressed, fr. reprimere, to REPRESS.]

REPRINT (rē-print') v.i. to print again; print a new edition.

REPRINT (rē'print) n. a new impression.

REPRISAL (re-prī'zal) n. seizure by way of retaliation; that which is seized. [O.F. represaille, a seizing on, through lt., fr. L. reprehendere, to lay hold of.]

REPROACH (re-prōch') v.t. to blame or censure severely; upbraid;—n. censure; cause or object of blame or disgrace. [F. reprocher, through Late L., fr. L. re-, again, and proprius, nearer.]

REPROACHABLE (re-prō'cha-bl) a. deserving reproach.

REPROACHFUL (re-prōch'fool) a. opprobrious.

REPROACHFULLY (re-prōch'fool-i) ad. with reproach.

REPROBATE (rep'ru-bat) a. lost to virtue;—n. one abandoned to sin;—(rep'ru-bāt) v.t. to disapprove; reject. [L. (part.) reprobatus, rejected after trial, fr. re-, back, and probare, try.] [condemnation.

REPROBATION (rep-ru-bā'shun) n. rejection.

REPRODUCE (rē-pru-dūs') v.t. to produce anew.

REPRODUCTION (rē-pru-duk'shun) n. a producing anew.

REPRODUCTIVE (rē-pru-duk'tiv) a. producing again.

REPROOF (re-prōōf') n. censure expressed.

REPROVABLE (re-prōō'va-bl) a. worthy of reproof; culpable.

REPROVAL (rē-prōō'val) n. reproof.

REPROVE (re-prōōv') v.t. to censure to the face; rebuke; reprimand. [O.F. reprover, fr. L. reprobare, reject. See REPROBATE, REPRIEVE.]

REPROVER (re-prōō'ver) n. one who reproves or blames.

REPTILE (rep'til) a. creeping; grovelling; —n. a creeping animal. [F., fr. L. reptilis, creeping, fr. (part.) reptus, fr. repere, creep.]

REPTILIAN (rep-til'i-an) a. pertaining to reptiles.

REPUBLIC (re-pub'lik) n. a state governed by representatives elected by the citizens. [F., fr. L. respublica, fr. res, a thing, an affair, and publicus, PUBLIC.]

REPUBLICAN (re-pub'li-kan) a. pertaining to, or consistent with, a republic;—n. one who prefers a republic.

REPUBLICANISE (re-pub'li-kan-īz) v.t. to convert to republican principles.

REPUBLICANISM (re-pub'li-kan-izm) n. system of republican government.

REPUBLICATION (rē-pub-li-kā'shun) n. a new publication; reprint.

REPUBLISH (rē-pub'lish) v.t. to publish anew.

REPUDIATE (re-pū'di-āt) v.t. to disavow; divorce; reject; disclaim. [L., fr. repudiare, cast off, fr. (acc.) repudiam, divorce, fr. rt. of pudor, shame.]

REPUDIATION (rē-pū-di-ā'shun) n. act of disclaiming; divorce.

REPUGNANCE (re-pug'nans) n. unwillingness.

REPUGNANT (re-pug'nant) a. contrary; adverse; distasteful. [F. (part.) repugnant, fighting against, fr. repugner, fr. L., fr. re-, back, again, and pugnare, fight.]

REPUGNANTLY (re-pug'nant-li) ad. in an adverse manner; unwillingly.

REPULSE (rē-puls') n. a check in advancing; refusal;—v.t. to repel; beat off. [L. (part.) repulsus, driven off, fr. repellere, REPEL.]

REPULSELESS (re-puls'les) a. that cannot be repelled.

REPULSION (re-pul'shun) n. the act of driving back.

REPULSIVE (re-pul'siv) a. forbidding; cold; reserved.

REPULSIVENESS (re-pul'siv-nes) n. quality of being forbidding.

REPURCHASE (rē-pur'chās) v.t. to buy back.

REPUTABLE (rep'ū-ta-bl) a. of good repute.

REPUTABLENESS (rep'u-ta-bl-nes) n. quality of being reputable.

REPUTABLY (rep'u-ta-bli) ad. with credit.

REPUTATION (rep-u-tā'shun) n. general estimation; good name; honour derived from public esteem.

REPUTE (re-pūt') v.t. to hold in estimation; think;—n. established opinion; estimate; good character. [O.F. reputer, L. reputare, to count over, to consider, fr. L. re-, again, and putare, to think.]

REPUTED (re-pū'ted) a. reckoned.

REPUTEDLY (re-pū'ted-li) ad. in the general regard.

REQUEST (re-kwest') v.t. to ask earnestly; entreat;—n. petition; prayer; desire; demand. [O.F., fr. L. (part.) requisitus, asked again, fr. re-, again, and quærere, seek.]

REQUICKEN (re-kwik'n) v.i. to revive; reanimate.

REQUIEM (rē-kwi-em') n. a hymn or prayer for the dead. [L. (acc.) =rest.]

REQUIRABLE (re-kwīr'a-bl) a. that may be required.

REQUIRE (re-kwīr') v.t. to make necessary; ask as a right; demand; exact; need. [L. requirere, to REQUEST, fr. re-, again, and quærere.]

REQUIREMENT (re-kwir'ment) *n.* demand; thing required.

REQUISITE (rek'wi-zit) *a.* required; necessary;—*n.* that which is necessary; anything indispensable. [L. (part.) *requisitus*, requested. See REQUEST.]

REQUISITION (rek-wi-zish'un) *n.* act of requiring; demand; a written request; quota of supplies demanded;—*v.t.* to lay a demand for supplies.

REQUITAL (re-kwi'tal) *n.* recompense.

REQUITE (re-kwit') *v.t.* to recompense; pay back in kind. [Fr. L. *re-*, back, and QUIT.]

REREDOS (rēr'dos) *n.* screen behind the altar; ornamental screen. [F.]

REREWARD (rēr'wawrd) *n.* rearguard.

RESCIND (re-sind') *v.t.* to appeal. [F. *rescinder*, fr. L., fr. *re-*, again, and *scindere*, to cut, split.]

RECISSION (re-sizh'un) *n.* act of abrogating.

RESCRIPT (rē'skript) *n.* official answer; edict; decree. [O.F. *rescript*, a written reply, fr. L., fr. *re-*, back, and (part.) *scriptus*, written, fr. *scribere*.]

RESCRIPTIVE (rē-skrip'tiv) *a.* having power to decide and decree.

RESCUE (res'kū) *v.t.* to deliver from danger or confinement;—*n.* deliverance from arrest or danger; forcible release. [O.F. *rescourre*, to rescue, fr. Late L. *rescutere*, to drive away again, fr. L. *re*, *ex*, and *quatere*, to shake.]

RESEARCH (re-serch') *n.* diligent inquiry.

RESEAT (rē-sēt') *v.t.* to seat again.

RESEIZE (rē-sēz') *v.t.* to seize again.

RESEMBLANCE (re-zem'blans) *n.* likeness.

RESEMBLE (re-zem'bl) *v.t.* to be like; liken; compare. [O.F. *resembler*, fr. L., fr. *re-*, again, and *simulare*, to make like. See SIMULATE.]

RESENT (re-zent') *v.t.* to be angry at; take ill. [F., fr. L. *re-*, again, and *sentire*, to feel.]

RESENTFUL (re-zent'fool) *a.* apt to resent.

RESENTMENT (re-zent'ment) *n.* sense of injury or affront; continued anger.

RESERVATION (rez-ėr-vā'shun) *n.* act of reserving; a proviso.

RESERVE (re-zėrv') *v.t.* to keep in store; retain;—*n.* that which is kept back; coldness; concealment; caution. [O.F., fr. L., fr. *re-*, back, and *servare*, to keep.]

RESERVED (re-zėrvd') *pp.* withheld;—*a.* not frank; cautious.

RESERVEDLY (re-zėr'ved-li) *ad.* with reserve; coldly.

RESERVOIR (rez'ėr-vwor) *n.* a large cistern. [F.]

RESET (rē-set') *v.t.* to set again, as a jewel, plant, or printed matter.

RESIDE (re-zid') *v.i.* to dwell habitually. [O.F. *resider*, fr. L., fr. *re*, back, and *sedere*, to sit.]

RESIDENCE (rez'i-dens) *n.* a place of abode.

RESIDENCY (rez'i-den-si) *n.* the official dwelling of a government officer.

RESIDENT (rez'i-dent) *n.* dwelling; living;—*n.* one who dwells in a place.

RESIDUAL (re-zid'ū-al) *a.* left after a part is taken.

RESIDUARY (re-zid'ū-a-ri) *a.* pertaining to or receiving the remainder.

RESIDUE (rez'i-dū) *n.* remainder, or what is left. [O.F., fr. *residuum*.]

RESIDUUM (re-zid'ū-um) *n.* that which remains; residue. [L. (neut.) =remaining, fr. *residere*, lit. sit back.]

RESIGN (re-zin') *v.t.* to give up in a formal manner. [O.F. *resigner*, fr. L., fr. *re*, back, and *signare*, to sign.]

RESIGN (rē-sin') *v.t.* to sign again.

RESIGNATION (rez-ig-nā'shun) *n.* act of resigning; quiet submission.

RESIGNED (re-zind') *a.* submissive to the will of God.

RESIGNEE (re-zi-nē') *n.* party to whom anything is resigned.

RESILE (re-zil') *v.i.* to start back; withdraw from an engagement. [L. *resilire*, leap back, fr. *salire*. See SALIENT.]

RESILIENCE (rē-zil'i-ens) *n.* a recoil.

RESILIENT (rē-zil'i-ent) *a.* leaping back.

RESIN (rez'in) *n.* an inflammable substance from the pine. [F., fr. L. *resina*, fr. G. *retine*, resin.]

RESINOUS (rez'in-us) *a.* containing resin.

RESIST (re-zist') *v.t.* or *i.* to act in opposition to; withstand; oppose. [L., fr. *re*, back, and *sistere*, to stand, fr. *stare*, stand.]

RESISTANCE (re-zis'tans) *n.* act of resisting; opposition.

RESISTANT (rē-zis'tant) *n.* he or that which resists.

RESISTIBILITY (re-zis-ti-bil'i-ti) *n.* the quality of resisting.

RESISTIBLE (re-zis'ti-bl) *a.* that may be resisted.

RESISTLESS (re-zist'les) *a.* that cannot be withstood.

RESOLUBLE (rez'u-lū-bl) *a.* that may be dissolved.

RESOLUTE (rez'u-lūt) *a.* firm to one's purpose. [L. (part.) *resolutus*, fr. *resolvere*, RESOLVE.]

RESOLUTELY (rez'u-lūt-li) *ad.* with steadiness and courage.

RESOLUTION (rez-u-lū'shun) *n.* act of resolving; firmness of purpose; formal declaration.

RESOLVABLE (re-zol'va-bl) *a.* that may be resolved.

RESOLVE (re-zolv') *v.t.* to separate component parts; analyse;—*v.i.* to determine;—*n.* fixed purpose. [L., fr. *re-*, back, again, and *solvere*, to dissolve, to decide.]

RESOLVENT (re-zol'vent) *n.* that which causes solution.

RESONANCE (rez'u-nans) *n.* a reverberation of sound or sounds.

RESONANT (rez'u-nant) *a.* echoing back. [L., fr. *re*, back, and *sonare*, to sound.]

RESORT (re-zort') *v.i.* to have recourse; repair; go;—*n.* concourse of people; place of habitual meeting; recourse. [O.F. *resortir*, lit. go forth again, fr. L., fr. *re*, again, and *sortir*, orig. to appeal, fr. L. *sortire*, to obtain.]

RESOUND (re-zound') *v.t.* or *i.* to sound back; echo. [O.F. *resoner*, fr. L., fr. *re*, again, and *sonare*, SOUND.]

RESOURCE (re-sōrs') *n.* any source of aid or support; expedient;—*pl.* means of any kind; pecuniary means. [O.F. *resource*, fr. *resoudre*, fr. L. *resurgere*, to rise again.]

RESPECT (re-spekt') *v.t.* to regard with esteem; relate to;—*n.* regard to worth; deference; relation; reference. [O.F., fr. L., fr. (part.) *respectus*, fr. *respicere*, to look back at, fr. *specere*.]

RESPECTABILITY (re-spek-ta-bil'i-ti) *n.* the quality of deserving respect.

RESPECTABLE (re-spek'ta-bl) *a.* worthy of respect.

RESPECTABLY (re-spek'ta-bli) *ad.* so as to merit respect.

RESPECTED (re-spek'ted) *a.* held in estimation.

RESPECTER (re-spek'tėr) *n.* one who respects.

RESPECTFUL (re-spekt'fool) *a.* full of respect.

RESPECTFULLY (re-spekt'fool-i) *ad.* with respect.

RESPECTIVE (re-spek'tiv) *a.* having relation to; particular.

RESPECTIVELY (re-spek'tiv-li) *ad.* as relating to each.

RESPIRABLE (re-spir'a-bl) *a.* that may be breathed.

RESPIRATION (res-pi-rā'shun) *n.* act of breathing.

RESPIRATOR (res'pi-rā-tėr) *n.* an instrument of fine wire for covering the mouth to protect weak lungs from cold.

RESPIRATORY (re-spir′ạ-tu-ri, res′pi-rā-tu-ri) *a.* serving for respiration.

RESPIRE (re-spir′) *v.t.* or *i.* to breathe. [F., fr. L., fr. *re,* back, and *spirare,* to breathe.]

RESPITE (res′pit) *n.* delay; interval of rest; suspension of punishment;—*v.t.* to suspend execution; delay. [O.F. *respit,* fr. L. (acc.) *respectum,* **RESPECT.**]

RESPLENDENCY (rẹ-splen′den-si) *n.* brilliant lustre.

RESPLENDENT (re-splen′dent) *a.* bright; splendid; shining. [L., fr. *resplendere,* to glitter, fr. *splendere,* to shine.]

RESPOND (re-spond′) *v.t.* to answer; reply; —*n.* a short anthem. [L., fr. *re,* back, again, and *spondere,* to promise.]

RESPONDENT (re-spon′dent) *n.* an answerer in an action;—*a.* answering.

RESPONSAL (re-spon′sạl) *a.* answering to;— *n.* answer of the people to the priest.

RESPONSE (re-spons′) *n.* an answer; reply. [L. (part.) *responsus,* fr. *respondere,* **RE-SPOND.**]

RESPONSIBILITY (re-spon-si-bil′i-ti) *n.* liability to answer or pay.

RESPONSIBLE (re-spon′si-bl) *a.* liable to account; accountable; answerable.

RESPONSIBLY (re-spon′si-bli) *ad.* in a responsible manner.

RESPONSIONS (re-spon′shuns) *n.* the first examination at Oxford; Little Go.

RESPONSIVE (re-spon′siv) *a.* answering; correspondent.

RESPONSORY (re-spon′su-ri) *a.* containing an answer;—*n.* an answer.

REST (rest) *n.* quiet; peace; sleep; a pause; —*v.i.* to be quiet; sleep; lean on; come to an end;—*v.t.* to place on a support; quiet; —(2) *n.* that which is left; the others; undivided profits in a bank balance. [(1) O.E. Cf. Ger. *Rast,* F. *rester,* fr. L. *restare,* fr. *re,* again, and *stare,* stand.]

RESTAURANT (res′to-rạng) *n.* an eating-house. [F.]

RESTAURATEUR (res-tō′rạ-tẹr) *n.* the keeper of an eating-house.

RESTFUL (rest′fool) *a.* giving rest; being at rest.

RESTITUTION (res-ti-tū′shun) *n.* act of restoring. [L. (part.) *restitutus,* restored, fr. *re,* back, and *statuere,* place.]

RESTIVE (res′tiv) *a.* unwilling to go; obstinate. [O.F. *restif,* stubborn, fr. *rester,* **REST** (1).]

RESTIVENESS (res′tiv-nes) *n.* obstinate reluctance.

RESTLESS (rest′les) *a.* void of rest; unsettled; unquiet.

RESTLESSLY (rest′les-li) *ad.* unquietly.

RESTLESSNESS (rest′les-nes) *n.* uneasiness of body or mind.

RESTORABLE (re-stōr′ạ-bl) *a.* that may be restored.

RESTORATION (res-tu-rā′shun) *n.* renewal; recovery.

RESTORATIVE (re-stōr′ạ-tiv) *a.* that tends to renew;—*n.* that which restores.

RESTORE (re-stōr′) *v.t.* to bring back; give back; revive; recover; resuscitate; re-establish. [O.F. *restorer,* fr. L. *restaurare.*]

RESTRAIN (re-strān′) *v.t.* to check; repress; hold back. [O.F. *restraindre,* fr. L., fr. *re,* back, and *stringere,* to bind.]

RESTRAINABLE (re-strā′nạ-bl) *a.* that may be restrained.

RESTRAINT (re-strānt′) *n.* that which restrains; a hindering; check. [O.F. (fem. part.) *restrainte,* held back.]

RESTRICT (re-strikt′) *v.t.* to limit; restrain; confine.] [L. part. *restrictus* fr. *restringere.*]

RESTRICTION (re-strik′shun) *n.* limitation.

RESTRICTIVE (re-strik′tiv) *a.* restraining.

RESTRINGENCY (re-strin′jen-si) *n.* power of contracting.

RESTRINGENT (re-strin′jent) *a.* astringent.

RESULT (re-zult′) *v.i.* to follow as a consequence; issue in;—*n.* consequence; conclusion; decision. [F., fr. L. *resultare.*]

RESULTANT (re-zul′tạnt) *a.* resulting from combination;—*n.* effect of two or more forces.

RESUMABLE (re-zū′mạ-bl) *a.* that may be resumed.

RESUME (rē-zūm′) *v.t.* to take back or up; begin again. [L., fr. *re,* back, and *sumere,* to take.]

RESUME (rā-zū-mā′) *n.* a summing up; summary. [F.]

RESUMPTION (re-zum′shun) *n.* act of resuming. [L. (part.) *resumptus,* taken again.]

RESURRECTION (rez-u-rek′shun) *n.* revival from the grave; the future state. [O.F., fr. L. (acc.) *resurrectionem,* fr. (part.) *resurrectus,* fr. *re,* again, and *surgere,* rise.]

RESUSCITATE (re-sus′i-tāt) *v.t.* to revive. [L., fr. *re,* again, and *suscitare,* to raise, rouse, fr. *cidere,* **CITE.**]

RESUSCITATION (re-sus-i-tā′shun) *n.* act of resuscitating.

RESUSCITATIVE (re-sus′i-tā-tiv) *a.* reviving.

RETAIL (re-tāl′) *v.t.* to sell in small quantities; report, as news;—(rē′tāl) *n.* small sales. [O.F. *retail,* small piece, fr. *re,* again, and *tailler,* to cut. See **TAILOR.**]

RETAILER (re-tā′lẹr) *n.* one who sells in small quantities.

RETAIN (re-tān′) *v.t.* to keep in possession, or in pay. [F. *retenir,* fr. L. *retinere,* fr. *re,* back, and *tenere,* to hold.]

RETAINABLE (re-tā′nạ-bi) *a.* that may be retained.

RETAINER (re-tā′nẹr) *n.* one who retains; a dependent; a fee to engage counsel.

RETAKE (rē-tāk′) *v.t.* to take again.

RETALIATE (re-tal′i-āt) *v.t.* or *i.* to return like for like; repay. [L., fr. *retaliare,* fr. *re,* back, and stem *tali-,* of *talis,* such.]

RETALIATION (re-tal-i-ā′shun) *n.* return of like for like.

RETALIATIVE (re-tal′i-ā-tiv) *a.* giving like for like. Also **RETALIATORY.**

RETARD (re-tárd′) *v.t.* to keep back; delay; hinder. [F. *retarder,* fr. L., fr. *re,* back, again, and *tardus,* slow, **TARDY.**]

RETCH (rech) *v.i.* to make an effort to vomit. [O.E. *hræcan.*]

RETENTION (re-ten′shun) *n.* act of retaining memory; restraint. [L. (part.) *retentus,* kept back. See **RETAIN.**]

RETENTIVE (re-ten′tiv) *a.* having power to retain; tenacious.

RETENTIVELY (re-ten′tiv-li) *ad.* with a firm hold of memory.

RETENTIVENESS (re-ten′tiv-nes) *n.* power of retaining. [silence.

RETICENCE (ret′i-sens) *n.* concealment by silence.

RETICENT (ret′i-sent) *a.* concealing by silence; close; reserved. [L. (part. stem) *reticent-,* being taciturn, fr. *re,* again, and *tacere,* be silent.]

RETICULAR (re-tik′ū-lạr) *a.* having the form of a net.

RETICULATE (re-tik′ū-lāt) *a.* made of or resembling network.

RETICULATION (re-tik-ū-lā′shun) *n.* network.

RETICULE (ret′i-kūl) *n.* a network bag; lady's bag. [F., fr. L. (acc.) *reticulum,* small net, fr. *rete,* net.]

RETIFORM (rē′ti-form) *a.* having the form of a net. [L. *rete,* a net, and *forma,* form.]

RETINA (ret′i-nạ) *n.* one of the coats of the eye resembling network;—*pl.* **RETINÆ.** [Fr. L. *rete,* a network.]

RETINUE (ret′i-nū) *n.* a train of attendants. [O.F. (part.) *retenu,* retained. See **RETAIN.**]

RETIRE (re-tīr') v.t. or i. to retreat; withdraw. [F., fr. re, back, and tirer, to draw. See TIRADE.]

RETIRED (re-tīrd') a. withdrawn.

RETIREMENT (re-tīr'ment) n. act of living in seclusion.

RETORT (re-tort') v.t. or i. to throw back; return; answer sharply; —n. a sharp and witty reply; a chemical vessel for distillation. [L., fr. F. (part.) retort, twisted back, fr. retordre, fr. L., fr. re, back, and torquere. See TORTURE.]

RETOUCH (re-tuch') v.t. to improve by new touches. Retort.

RETRACE (rē-trās') v.t. to trace back.

RETRACT (re-trakt') v t. or i. to take back; recall; recant. [L. (part.) retractus, drawn back, fr. re, back, and trahere, to draw.]

RETRACTABLE (re-trak'ta-bl) a. that may be recalled.

RETRACTIBLE (re-trak'ti-bl) a. that may be drawn back.

RETRACTILE (re-trak'til) a. capable of being drawn back.

RETRACTION (re-trak'shun) n. recantation.

RETRACTIVE (re-trak'tiv) a. withdrawing.

RETREAT (re-trēt') n. a retiring; place of privacy; shelter; withdrawal of troops; signal to withdraw;—v.t. or i. to draw back; retire. [O.F. retrete, fr. L. (part.) retractus, wi drawn, fr. re, back, and trahere, to draw.]

RETRENCH (re-trensh') v.t. or i. to lessen; curtail; economise. [O.F. retrencher = F. retrancher, fr. L. re, off, and F. trencher, to cut, perh. fr. L. truncare, to cut.]

RETRENCHMENT (re-trensh'ment) n. a cutting off; reduction; inner work of a fort.

RETRIBUTE (rē-trib'ūt) v.t. to pay back.

RETRIBUTION (ret-ri-bū'shun) n. repayment; requital. [L. (acc.) retributionem, fr. retribuere, to give back, fr. re, back, and tribuere, give.]

RETRIBUTIVE (re-trib'ū-tiv) a. rewarding or punishing.

RETRIEVABLE (re-trē'va-bl) a. that may be retrieved.

RETRIEVE (re-trēv') v.t. to recover; regain. [O.F. retreuver = F. retrouver, fr. re, again, and trouver, to find, fr. Late L. tropare, to tromis, a song, fr. G. tropos, fr. trepein, turn.]

RETRIEVEMENT (re-trēv'ment) n. act of retrieving; retrieval.

RETRIEVER (re-trē'ver) n. a kind of dog that picks up game.

RETROACT (rē-trō-akt') n. to act backward or in return. [L. (part.) retroactus, of retroagere, fr. retro, backwards, and agere, to do.]

RETROACTION (rē-trō-ak'shun) n. action in return.

RETROCEDE (rē'trō-sēd) v.t. to grant back; —v.i. to go back; retire. [F., fr. L. retrocedere, fr. retro, backward, and cedere, to go.]

RETROCESSION (rē-trō-sesh'un) n. act of going or of ceding back.

RETROFLEX (rē'trō-fleks) a. bent backward. [L. (part.) retroflexus, bent back, fr. retro, back, and flectere, to bend.]

RETROGRADE (ret'rō-grād, rē'trō-grād) a. going backward;—v.i. to go backward. [L. (part.) retrogradus, going backward, fr. retro, back, and gradi, to go.]

RETROGRESSION (rē-trō-gresh'un) n. a going backward. [L. retrogressus, fr. retrogradi.]

RETROGRESSIVE (rē-trō-gres'iv) a. moving backward.

RETROSPECT (ret'rō-spekt, rē'trō-spekt) n. a view of things past. [L. (part.) retrospectus, of retrospicere, fr. retro, back, and specere, to look.]

RETROSPECTION (ret-rō-spek'shun, rē-trō-spek'shun) n. a looking back.

RETROSPECTIVE (ret-rō-spek'tiv, rē-trō-spek'tiv) a. looking back.

RETROSPECTIVELY (ret-rō-spek'tiv-li, rē-trō-spek'tiv-li) ad. by way of retrospect.

RETROVERT (rē'trō-vert) v.t. to turn back. [L., fr. retro, back, and vertere, to turn.]

RETURN (re-turn') v.i. to come or go back; —v.t. to send back; repay;—n. a going back; restitution; profit of capital or labour; official report;—pl. light tobacco. [F., fr. re, back, and tourner, to turn, fr. L. tornare, to turn.]

RETURNABLE (re-tur'na-bl) a. that may be returned.

REUNION (rē-ūn'yun) n. act of reuniting; a second union. [F., fr. L. (acc.) reunionem, fr. re, back, and (acc.) unionem, of unio, fr. unus, one.]

REUNITE (rē-ū-nīt') v.t. or i. to unite things disjoined; join again after variance. [L., fr. re, back, and (part.) unitus, of unire, to unite, fr. unus, one.]

REVEAL (re-vēl') v.t. to make known; disclose; divulge. [O.F. reveler = F. révéler, fr. L. revelare, fr. re, back, and velum, a veil.]

REVEALABLE (re-vē'la-bl) a. that may be revealed.

REVEALER (re-vē'ler) n. one who reveals.

REVEL (rev'el) v.i. to carouse;—n. a noisy feast. [O.F. reveler = F. rebeller, fr. L. rebellare, to rebel.]

REVEILLE (re-vāl'yā, re-vā'yā) n. the morning beat of drum or sound of bugle. [O.F. reveil, fr. re, again, and esveiller, to awake, fr. L. ex, out, and vigilare, fr. vigil, awake, watchful.]

REVELATION (rev-e-lā'shun) n. act of disclosing; divine communication; the Bible; the Apocalypse.

REVELRY (rev'el-ri) n. a carousing.

REVENGE (re-venj') v.i. to inflict pain or injury for injury received; avenge;—n. act of revenging; injury inflicted; passion for retaliation. [O.F. revenger, revencher = F. revancher, fr. L. re, in return, and vindicare, to lay claim to, fr. (acc.) vim, of vis, power, and dicare, to proclaim, fr. dicere, to say.]

REVENGEFUL (re-venj'fool) a. disposed to revenge; vindictive.

REVENGEFULLY (re-venj'fool-i) ad. vindictively.

REVENGELESS (re-venj'les) a. being without revenge.

REVENGER (re-ven'jer) n. one who revenges.

REVENGINGLY (re-ven'jing-li) ad. by or with revenge.

REVENUE (rev'e-nū) n. income of a state or an individual. [F. (part.) revenu, of revenir, to return.]

REVERBERANT (re-ver'ber-ant) a. resounding.

REVERBERATE (re-ver'ber-āt) v.t. or i. to resound; echo; bound back; reflect. [L. (part.) reverberatus, of reverberare, fr. re, back, and verberare, to beat, fr. verber, a lash.]

REVERBERATION (re-ver-ber-ā'shun) n. act of reverberating.

REVERBERATORY (re-ver'ber-a-tu-ri) a. beating back.

REVERE (re-vēr') v.t. to regard with reverence; venerate. [O.F. reverer = F. révérer, fr. L. revereri, fr. re (intens.) and vereri, to feel awe.]

REVERENCE (rev'er-ens) n. veneration; respectful awe; act of obeisance; title of the clergy;—v.t. to revere.

REVEREND (rev'er-end) a. deserving reverence; venerable; title of the clergy.

REVERENT (rev'er-ent) a. that may be revered.

REVERENTIAL (rev-er-en'shal) a. expressing reverence.

REVERENTLY (rev'ẽr-ent-li) *ad.* in a reverent manner.

REVERIE (rev'ẽr-i) *n.* loose, irregular train of thought. [O.F. *resverie* = F. *rêverie*, fr. *rêver*, to dream.]

REVERSAL (re-vẽr'sạl) *n.* change to the opposite; overthrowing or annulling.

REVERSE (re-vẽrs') *v.t.* to change from one position to the opposite; make void; revoke; subvert;—*n.* back or opposite side; change of fortune;—*a.* turned backward. [L. (part.) *reversus*, of *revertere*, to turn back, fr. *re*, back, and *vertere*, to turn.]

REVERSELESS (re-vẽrs'les) *a.* not to be reversed.

REVERSIBLE (re-vẽrs'i-bl) *a.* that may be reversed.

REVERSION (re-vẽr'shun) *n.* the return of an estate to the grantor or his heirs; future succession.

REVERSIONARY (re-vẽr'shun-ạr-i) *a.* that is to be enjoyed in succession.

REVERSIONER (re-vẽr'shun-ẽr) *n.* one entitled to a reversion.

REVERT (re-vẽrt') *v.t.* or *i.* to turn back; reverse; fall back; return to;—*n.* recurrence. [O.F., fr. L. *re*, again, and *vertere*, to turn.]

REVERTIBLE (re-vẽr'ti-bl) *a.* that may revert.

REVIEW (re-vū') *v.t.* to consider again; revise; inspect;—*n.* careful examination; inspection of troops; a periodical containing essays and critical notices. [F. (part.) *revue*, of *revoir*, to see again, fr. L. *re*, again, and *videre*, to see.]

REVIEWER (re-vū'ẽr) *n.* one who reviews.

REVIGORATE (rē-vig'ur-āt) *v.t.* to add new strength to.

REVILE (re-vil') *v.t.* to treat with abusive language. [O.F. *avilir*, to make vile, fr. *a* = *ad*, to, and *vilis*, cheap.]

REVILER (re-vi'lẽr) *n.* one who reviles.

REVISE (re-viz') *v.t.* to examine with care for correction;—*n.* a second proof-sheet. [F. *reviser*, fr. L. *revisere*, fr. *re*, back, and *visere*, intens. of *videre*, to see.]

REVISER (re-vi'zẽr) *n.* one who revises.

REVISION re-vizh'un) *n.* act of revising or reviewing.

REVISIONAL (re-vizh'un-ạl) *a.* containing revision.

REVISIT (rē-viz'it) *v.t.* to visit again.

REVIVAL (re-vi'vạl) *n.* return to life; a religious awakening.

REVIVALIST (re-vi'vạl-ist) *n.* one who promotes revivals.

REVIVE (re-viv') *v.t.* to restore or bring to life;—*v.i.* to recover life and vigour. [F. *revivre*, fr. L. *re*, again, and *vivere*, to live.]

REVIVIFICATION (rē-viv-i-fi-kā'shun) *n.* act of returning to life.

REVIVIFY (rē-viv'i-fi) *v.t.* to recall to life.

REVIVISCENT (rē-vi-vis'ent) *a.* restoring to life or action.

REVOCABLE (rev'u-kạ-bl) *a.* that may be recalled.

REVOCATION (rev-u-kā'shun) *n.* act of recalling; repeal.

REVOKE (re-vōk') *v.t.* to recall or repeal;—*v.i.* to renounce or not follow suit. [O.F. *revocquer*, fr. L. *revocare*, to recall.]

REVOLT (re-vōlt') *v.t.* or *i.* to turn away; renounce allegiance; shock;—*n.* renunciation of allegiance; rebellion. [O.F. *revolte*. It. *rivolta*; fr. L. (part.) *revolutus*, of *revolvere*, fr. *re*, back, and *volvere*, to turn.]

REVOLUTION (rev-u-lū'shun) *n.* motion round a centre; a radical change in the government of a country.

REVOLUTIONARY (rev-u-lū'shun-ạr-i) *a.* producing great and sudden change.

REVOLUTIONISE rev-u-lū'shun-iz) *v.t.* to effect a radical change in government or principles.

REVOLUTIONIST (rev-u-lū'shun-ist) *n.* one who favours a revolution.

REVOLVE (re-volv') *v.i.* to move round;—*v.t.* to turn in the mind. [F., fr. L. (part.) *revolutus*, of *revolvere*, fr. *re*, back, and *volvere*, to turn.]

REVOLVENCY (re-vol'ven-si) *n.* the act or state of revolving.

REVOLVER (re-vol'vẽr) *n.* a pistol, the barrel of which revolves.

REVULSION (re-vul'shun) *n.* act of drawing or turning back; marked repugnance or hatred. [L. (acc.) *revulsionem*, of *revulsio*, fr. (part.) *revulsus*, of *revellere*, fr. *re*, away, and *vellere*, to tear.]

REVULSIVE (re-vul'siv) *a.* having the power of revulsion.

REWARD (re-wawrd') *v.t.* to recompense; requite;—*n.* compensation; pay. [O.F. *reswarder* = F. *regarder*, fr. *re*, again, and *warder*, *guarder*, to guard, fr. Teut.]

REWARDABLE (re-wawr'dạ-bl) *a.* deserving to be rewarded.

REWARDER (re-wawr'dẽr) *n.* one who recompenses.

REWRITE (rē-rit') *v.t.* to write a second time or again.

REYNARD (rā'nạrd, ren'ạrd) *n.* a fox. [F. *renard*, fr. O.G. *Reinaerd*, *Reginhart*, lit. 'strong in counsel.']

RHABDOMANCY (rab'du-man-si) *n.* divination by rods. [G., fr. *rhabdos*, a rod, and *manteia*, divination.]

RHADAMANTINE (rad-ạ-man'tin) *a.* judicially severe; inflexible. [L. *Rhadamanthus*, a fabled judge of the lower world.]

RHAPSODICAL (rap-sod'i-kạl) *a.* consisting in rhapsody; unconnected.

RHAPSODIST (rap'su-dist) *n.* one who writes or sings rhapsodies.

RHAPSODY (rap'su-di) *n.* an unconnected writing or discourse. [F. *rhapsodie*, fr. L., fr. G. *rhapsodia*, fr. *rhaptein*, to sew, and *ode*, a song.]

RHENISH (ren'ish) *a.* pertaining to the River Rhine.

RHETORIC (ret'u-rik) *n.* the art of speaking with propriety, elegance, and force. [F. *rhétorique*, fr. L., fr. G. *rhetorike* (*techne*), the rhetorical (art), fr. *rhetor*, a speaker, fr. *erein*, to speak.]

RHETORICIAN (ret-u-rish'ạn) *n.* one who teaches rhetoric; a practised or artificial orator.

RHEUM (room) *n.* a thin fluid secreted by the glands. [F. *rhume*, fr. L., fr. G. *rheuma*, fr. *rhein*, to flow.]

RHEUMATIC (roo-mat'ik) *a.* affected with rheumatism. [G. *rheumatikos*.]

RHEUMATISM (roo'ma-tizm) *n.* a painful disease of the joints and muscles.

RHEUMY (roo'mi) *a.* full of rheum.

RHODODENDRON (rō-du-den'dron) *n.* an evergreen shrub having brilliant rose-like flowers. [G. *rhodon*, the rose, and *dendron*, tree.]

RHOMB (rom) *n.* a figure of four equal sides, but unequal angles. [L., fr. G. *rhombos*, fr. *rhombein*, to turn round and round.]

RHOMBIC (rom'bik) *a.* having the figure of a rhomb.

RHOMBOID (rom'boid) *n.* a figure like a rhomb, having only the opposite sides equal. [G. *rhombos*, and *eidos*, shape.]

Rhomb.

RHOMBOIDAL (rom-boi'dạl) *a.* having the form of a rhomboid.

RHUBARB (roo'bärb) *n.* a plant—its stalk is used in cookery, its roots as a cathartic. [O.F. *rheubarbe*, fr. Late L. *rheubarbarum*, fr. G. *rheon barbaron*, fr. *rheon*, the rha-plant, fr. *Rha*, the Volga.]

RHYME (rīm) *v.i.* to accord in sounds;—*v.t.* to turn into rhyme;—*n.* correspondence of sounds at the end of verses. [Properly *rime*, the *hy* being due to the influence of **RHYTHM**. O.E. *rim*, number.]

RHYMER (rī'mẹr) *n.* one who makes rhymes.

RHYTHM (rithm) *n.* flow and proportion of sounds in verse; two verses that rhyme; periodical accent; metre. [G. *rhythmos*, fr. *rhein*, to flow.]

RHYTHMICAL (rith'mi-kạl) *a.* pertaining to rhythm or metre.

RIB (rib) *n.* a bone in the side; a strengthening piece of timber in a ship; a vein; narrow strip;—*v.t.* to furnish with ribs; form with rising lines. [O.E. *ribb*. Cf. Ger. *Rippe*.]

RIBALD (rib'ạld) *n.* a low, vulgar fellow;—*a.* low; base. [O.F. = F. *ribaud*, fr. Teut.]

RIBALDRY (rib'al-dri) *n.* vulgar language.

RIBAND. See **RIBBON**.

RIBBED (ribd) *a.* furnished with ribs.

RIBBON (rib'un) *n.* a fillet of silk;—*v.t.* to adorn with ribbons. [O.F. *riban* = F. *ruban*.]

RICE (rīs) *n.* an esculent grain. [O.F. *ris*, fr. L., fr. G. *oruza*, fr. O. Pers.]

RICH (rich) *a.* opulent; valuable; sumptuous; fertile; bright. [O.E. *rice*, rich. Cf. Ger. *reich*.]

RICHES (rich'es) *n.pl.* wealth. [F. *richesse*, wealth, fr. O. H. Ger. *rihhi*, rich.]

RICHLY (rich'li) *ad.* abundantly.

RICHNESS (rich'nes) *n.* wealth; fertility.

RICK (rik) *n.* a long pile of hay or grain or straw. [O.E. *hreac*.]

RICKETS (rik'ets) *n.pl.* a disease of children. [M.E. *wrikken*, to twist, allied to O.E. *wringan*, to twist.]

RICKETY (rik'e-ti) *a.* affected with rickets.

RICOCHET (rik'u-shā, rik'u-shet) *v.t.* to fire guns so as to cause balls to rebound from one point to another;—*n.* rebound of a ball; skip of a flat stone on water. [F., of uncert. etym.]

RID (rid) *v.t.* [*pret.* and *pp.* **RID**] to free; clear; drive away; disencumber. [O.E. *hreddan*, to snatch away. Cf. Ger. *retten*.]

RIDDANCE (rid'ạns) *n.* a clearing away.

RIDDLE (rid'l) (1) *n.* a grain sifter;—*v.t.* to separate, as grain from the chaff, with a riddle;—(2) *n.* an enigma;—*v.t.* to solve; to speak in riddles. [(1) O.E. *hridder*. (2) O.E. *rædelse*, fr. *rædan*, to guess, to read, fr. *ræd*, counsel. Cf. Ger. *Rat*.]

RIDE (rīd) *v.i.* [*pret.* **RODE**; *pp.* **RID**, **RIDDEN**] to be carried on horseback, or in a vehicle;—*n.* an excursion on horseback. [O.E *ridan*. Cf. Ger. *reiten*.]

RIDER (rī'dẹr) *n.* one who rides; an additional clause to a bill.

RIDGE (rij) *n.* top of the back; a long elevation of land; strip thrown up by the plough;—*v.t.* to form into ridges. [M.E. *rigge*, fr. O.E. *hrycg*, the back. Cf. Ger. *Rücken*, back.]

RIDICULE (rid'i-kūl) *n.* laughter with contempt;—*v.t.* to laugh at, or expose to laughter; mock; deride. [L. *ridiculus*, fr. *ridere*, to laugh.]

RIDICULOUS (ri-dik'ū-lus) *a.* deserving ridicule.

RIDING (rī'ding) *a.* used to or suitable for travel;—*n.* act of one who rides; road; district; one of the three divisions of Yorkshire. [Corr. of Scand. *thriding*, a third.]

RIDING-HABIT (rī'ding-hab-it) *n.* long cloth skirt worn by ladies on horseback.

RIDING-MASTER (rī'ding-mas-tẹr) *n.* instructor in the art of riding.

RIFE (rīf) *a.* prevalent; abundant. [O.E.]

RIFENESS (rīf'nes) *n.* frequency; prevalence.

RIFFRAFF (rif'raf) *n.* sweepings; refuse. [M.E. *rif* and *raf*.]

RIFLE (rī'fl) (1) *n.* a gun with grooved bore; —(2) *v.t.* to rob; plunder. [(1) O.F. *rifler*, to scratch, fr. Dan. *rifle*, a groove. (2) O.F. *rifler*, to spoil, fr. Teut.]

RIFLEMAN (rī'fl-man) *n.* one armed with a rifle.

RIFLER (rī'flẹr) *n.* a robber; a plunderer.

RIFT (rift) *n.* a cleft; a fissure;—*v.t.* to rive; cleave. [Fr. *rive*, to rend.]

RIFTY (rif'ti) *a.* having fissures.

RIG (rig) *v.t.* to fit with rigging; dress; clothe. [Scand.]

RIGGER (rig'ẹr) *n.* one who fits a ship with tackling.

RIGGING (rig'ing) *n.* the ropes of a ship.

RIGHT (rīt) *a.* straight; correct; opposed to left; direct; true; just; proper; containing 90 degrees;—*n.* justice; just claim; property; privilege; side opposed to left; —*ad.* in a straight line; according to rule; —*v.t.* to do justice to;—*v.i.* to take a proper position. [O.E. *riht*. Cf. Ger. *recht*, L. *rectus*.]

RIGHT-ANGLE (rīt'ang-gl) *n.* an angle of 90 degrees.

RIGHTEOUS (rīt'yus) *a.* just; religious; virtuous; merited; equitable. [O.E. *rihtwis*, fr. *riht*, right, and *wis*, wise.]

RIGHTEOUSLY (rīt'yus-li) *ad.* justly; honestly; religiously.

RIGHTEOUSNESS (rīt'yus-nes) *n.* justice; virtue; holiness; equity.

Right-angle.

RIGHTFUL (rīt'fool) *a.* having a right.

RIGHTFULLY (rīt'fool-i) *ad.* according to right.

RIGHTLY (rīt'li) *ad.* properly; justly.

RIGID (rij'id) *a.* difficult to bend; strict; exact; severe. [L. *rigidus*, fr. *rigere*, to be stiff with cold.]

RIGIDITY (ri-jid'i-ti) *n.* strictness; stiffness.

RIGIDLY (rij'id-li) *ad.* exactly; severely.

RIGMAROLE (rig'ma-rōl) *n.* confused or nonsensical talk. [Corr. of *ragmanroll*, a list of many names.]

RIGOUR (rig'ur) *n.* strictness; severity; stiffness; chilliness. [L., fr. *rigere*, to be stiff.]

RIGOROUS (rig'ur-us) *a.* strict; severe.

RIGOROUSLY (rig'ur-us-li) *ad.* strictly.

RILL (ril) *n.* a small brook. [Ger. *Rille*, a channel.]

RIM (rim) *n.* a border; edge;—*v.t.* to put on a rim. [O.E. *rima*.]

RIME (rīm) *n.* hoar-frost; a chink. [O.E. *hrim*.]

RIND (rīnd) *n.* skin, bark, or outer coat. [O.E. *rinde*.]

RING (ring) (1) *n.* a circular thing;—(2) *n.* a metallic sound;—*v.t.* [*pret.* and *pp.* **RUNG**] to cause to sound;—*v.i.* to sound. [(1) O.E. *hring*. (2) O.E. *hringan*.]

RING-BOLT (ring'bōlt) *n.* a ring through the head of a bolt.

RINGLEADER (ring'lēd-ẹr) *n.* the leader of a lawless association.

RINGLET (ring'let) *n.* a curl of hair. [Dim. of **RING**.]

RINSE (rins) *v.t.* to cleanse by agitating in the water. [O.F *rinser* = F. *rincer*, fr. Scand.]

RIOT (rī'ut) *n.* uproar; tumult;—*v.i.* to make an uproar; revel. [O.F. *riote*, brawling; of uncert. etym.]

RIOTER (rī'ut-ẹr) *n.* one who joins in a riot.

RIOTOUS (rī'ut-us) *a.* disposed to riot.

RIOTOUSLY (rī'ut-us-li) *ad.* in a riotous manner.

RIOTOUSNESS (rī'ut-us-nes) *n.* state or quality of being riotous.

RIP (rip) *v.t.* to cut or tear asunder; take out;—*n.* a tear; a rent. [M.E. *ripen*, to search into, fr. Scand. *ripa*, to scratch.]

RIPARIAN (ri-pā'ri-an) *a.* belonging to the bank of a river. [L. *ripa*, a river bank.]

RIPE (rip) *a.* perfect in growth; fit; ready; plump; ruddy. [O.E. *ripe*, conn. with *rip*, harvest. Cf. Ger. *reif*.]

RIPELY (rip'li) *ad.* maturely.

RIPEN (ri'pn) *v.t.* to mature; prepare;—*v.i.* to grow ripe.

RIPENESS (rip'nes) *n.* maturity; perfection

RIPPER (rip'er) *n.* one who rips or cuts up.

RIPPLE (rip'l) (1) *v.t.* or *i.* to fret on the surface; curl;—*n.* a little wave or undulation; (2) *v.t.* to separate the seed from flax. [(1) Variant of *rimple*, fr. O.E. *hrimpan*, to wrinkle. (2 M.E. *ripplen*, fr. *ripple*, a flax comb, fr. O.E. *ripan*, to reap.]

RIPPLING (rip'ling) *n.* noise of water agitated.

RISE (riz) *v.i.* [*pret.* **ROSE**; *pp.* **RISEN**] to get up; spring; grow; increase; amount; adjourn. [O.E. *risan*.]

RISE (riz) *n.* act of rising; ascent; origin.

RISEN (ri'zn) *pp.* ascended.

RISER (ri'zer) *n.* one who rises.

RISIBILITY (riz-i-bil'i-ti) *n.* inclination to laughter.

RISIBLE (riz'i-bl) *a.* exciting laughter. [L. *risibilis*, fr. (part.) *risus*, of *ridere*, to laugh.]

RISING (ri'zing) *n.* act of getting up; insurrection; adjournment; resurrection.

RISK (risk) *n.* hazard; danger; peril;—*v.t.* to expose to danger or loss. [F. *risque*, fr. L. *resecare*, to cut off, fr. *re*, off, and *secare*, to cut.]

RITE (rit) *n.* a ceremonial observance. [L. *ritus*, a custom.]

RITUAL (rit'ū-al) *n.* a book of rites;—*a.* according to rites. [L. *ritualis* fr. *ritus*.]

RITUALISM (rit'ū-al-izm) *n.* system of forms and rites.

RIVAL (ri'val) *n.* one in pursuit of the same object as another; competitor;—*a.* standing in competition;—*v.t.* compete with; try to excel; emulate. [L. *rivales*, two neighbours having the same brook in common, fr. *rivus*, a stream.]

RIVALRY (ri'val-ri) *n.* strife for superiority; competition.

RIVE (riv) *v.t.* [*pret.* **RIVED**; *pp* **RIVEN**] to split. [Scand.]

RIVEN (riv'n) *pp.* of **RIVE**.

RIVER (riv'er) *n.* a large stream. [O.F. *riviere*, fr. Late L. *riparia*, a shore district, fr. *ripa*, a bank; It. *Riviera*, shore, river.]

RIVET (riv'et) *v.t.* to fasten with rivets; clinch;—*n.* a pin clinched. [O.F. *rivet*, fr. Scand.]

RIVULET (riv'ū-let) *n.* a small stream. [L., fr. *rivulus*, dim. *rivus*, · brook.]

ROACH (rōch) *n.* a fresh-water silvery fish. [O.F. *roche*, fr. Teut.]

ROAD (rōd) *n.* a public way for travelling; a place where ships ride at anchor. [O.E. *rad*, p.t. of *ridan*, to ride.]

ROADSTEAD (rōd'sted) *n.* a place where ships can anchor.

ROADSTER (rōd'ster) *n.* a vessel at anchor in the bay; a horse fitted for the road.

ROAM (rōm) *v.i.* to rove; ramble. [M.E. *romen*, influenced by *Rome-rennere*, a pilgrim.]

ROAMER (rō'mer) *n.* one who roams.

ROAN (rōn) *a.* of a dark colour variegated with spots;—*n.* a roan colour; a roan horse; dressed sheep's skin. [O.F. *roan*, fr. F. *rouan*, fr. Late L. *rufanus*, fr. *rufus*, red.]

ROAR (rōr) *v.i.* to make a loud noise; cry aloud; bawl;—*n.* cry of a beast; loud sound; outcry; peal. [O.E. *rarian*. Cf. Ger. *röhren*, to cry as a stag.]

ROARING (rōr'ing) *n.* a loud noise; a disease in breathing among horses.

ROAST (rōst) *v.t.* to cook before a fire;—*n.* that which is roasted. [O.E. *rostian*, fr. O.F. *rostir*, fr. O. H. Ger. *Rost*, a gridiron.]

ROASTER (rōs'ter) *n.* a contrivance for roasting.

ROASTING (rōs'ting) *n.* act of roasting.

ROB (rob) *v.t.* to take property without the owner's consent; plunder; steal. [M.E. *robben*, fr. O.F. *rober*. Cf. Ger. *rauben*.]

ROBBER (rob'er) *n.* one who robs.

ROBBERY (rob'er-i) *n.* a taking of property without consent.

ROBE (rōb) *n.* a long gown;—*v.t.* to invest with a robe. [F., fr. O. H. Ger. *Raup*, booty.]

ROBUST (rō-bust') *a.* strong; healthy. [L. *robustus*, fr. *robur*, an oak, strength.]

ROBUSTNESS (rō-bust'nes) *n.* great and hearty strength.

ROCHET (roch'et) *n.* a linen habit worn by bishops. [O.F., fr. Late L. *roccus*, fr. O. H. Ger. *Roch*, a coat.]

ROCK (rok) (1) *n.* a large mass of stone;— (2) *v.t.* or *i.* to move from side to side. [(1) O.F. *roke*, *rocque*, *roche*. (2) M.E. *rokken*, fr. O.E. *roccian*.]

ROCK-ALUM (rok'al-um) *n.* pure alum.

ROCKER (rok'er) *n.* one or that which rocks.

ROCKET (rok'et) *n.* a projectile firework. [Old It. *rocchetto*.]

ROCKINESS (rok'i-nes) *n.* abundance of rocks.

ROCK-CRYSTAL (rok'kris-tal) *n.* pure crystals of quartz.

ROCKERY (rok'er-i) *n.* pile of small rocks and earth for growing plants.

ROCK-SALT (rok'sawlt) *n.* salt in masses like rock.

ROCKY (rok'i) *a.* full of rocks; hard.

ROD (rod) *n.* a twig; a pole or perch; five-and-a-half yards. [O.E.]

RODE (rōd) *pret.* and *pp.* of **RIDE**.

RODOMONTADE (rod-u-mon-tād') *n.* empty bluster. [Fr. *Rodomonte*, in Ariosto's *Orlando Furioso*.]

ROE (rō) (1) *n.* a female of the hart;— (2) *n.* spawn. [(1) O.E. *rah*. (2) Scand.]

ROEBUCK (rō'buk) *n.* male of the roe.

ROGATION (rō-gā'shun) *n.* supplication; the litany. [L. (acc.) *rogationem*, fr. *rogare*, to ask.]

ROGUE (rōg) *n.* a dishonest person; knave; sly fellow. [O.F. *rogue*, proud; uncert. etym.]

ROGUERY (rō'ger-i) *n.* knavery; dishonest tricks; waggery.

ROGUISH (rō'gish) *a.* knavish; waggish.

ROIL (roil) *v.t.* to make turbid by stirring; excite. [F.]

ROLL (rōl) *v.t.* or *i.* to turn; revolve;—*n.* a thing rolled; a turn; a cylinder of wood, etc.; kind of bread; twist of tobacco; a list of names. [M.E. *rollen*, fr. O.F. *roler* =F. *rouler*, fr. Late L. *rotula*, a little wheel fr. *rota*, a wheel.]

ROLLER (rō'ler) *n.* one who or that which rolls.

ROLLING-PIN (rō'ling-pin) *n.* a round piece of wood.

ROMAN (rō'man) *a.* pertaining to Rome.— *n.* a native of Rome. [L. *Romanus*, fr. *Roma*, Rome.]

ROMANCE (rō-mans') *n.* a tale of exciting adventures; a fiction;—*v.i.* to write or tell marvellous tales. [O.F. *romanz*, a romance, fr. Late L. (ad.) (*loqui*) *romanice* (to speak) in the Latin tongue, fr. L. *Romanicus*, Roman.]

ROMANISM (rō'man-izm) *n.* tenets of the Church of Rome.

ROMANIST (rō'man-ist) *n.* a Roman Catholic.

ROMANTIC (rō-man'tik) *a.* wild; fanciful.

ROMISH (rō'mish) *a.* belonging to Rome.

ROMP (romp) *n.* a rude, noisy girl;—*v.i.* to play rudely or boisterously. [Variant of **RAMP**.]

ROMPISH (rom'pish) *a.* inclined to rough play.

RONDEAU (ron'dō) *n.* a poem or musical composition in three recurring parts. [F., fr. O.F. *rondel*. Also **RONDO**.]
ROOD (rōōd) *n.* the fourth of an acre; a crucifix. [O.E. *rod*, rod, cross.]
ROOF (rōōf) *n.* cover of a building; vault of the mouth;—*v.t.* to cover with a roof. [O.E. *hrof*.]
ROOFLESS (rōōf'les) *a.* having no roof.
ROOK (rook) *v.t.* or *i.* to cheat; rob;—*n.* a bird like a crow; a cheat. [O.E. *hroc*.]
ROOKERY (rook'ęr-i) *n.* a collection of rooks' nests; a pile of dilapidated buildings.
ROOKY (rook'i) *a.* inhabited by rooks.
ROOM (rōōm) *n.* space; extent; an apartment;—*v.t.* to lodge. [O.E. *rum*.]
ROOMILY (rōō'mi-li) *ad.* with plenty of room.
ROOMINESS (rōō'mi-nes) *n.* spaciousness.
ROOMY (rōō'mi) *a.* having ample room; spacious; capacious.
ROOST (rōōst) *n.* a place on which birds or fowls rest;—*v.i.* to rest as a bird. [O.E. *hrost*.]
ROOSTER (rōōst'ęr) *n.* male of domestic fowl.
ROOT (rōōt) (1) *v.t.* or *i.* to plant in earth; take root; implant deeply; sink deep;—*n.* part of a plant in the earth; bottom; cause or occasion; primitive word;—(2) *v.t.* or *i.* to turn up with the snout, as swine —hence, to tear up by the root; to extirpate. [(1) O.E. *wyrt*, fr. Scand. (2) O.E. *wrotan*, fr. *wrot*, a snout.]
ROPE (rōp) *n.* a thick twisted cord;—*v.i.* to draw out in a slender string. [O.E. *rap*.]
ROPEMAKER (rōp'māk-ęr) *n.* a maker of ropes.
ROPE-WALK (rōp'wawk) *n.* a place where ropes are made.
ROPE-YARN (rōp'yárn) *n.* threads to be twisted into ropes.
ROPINESS (rō'pi-nes) *n.* stringiness.
ROPY (rō'pi) *a.* stringy; glutinous.
ROQUELAURE (rō'ke-lōr) *n.* a man's cloak. [F.]
RORQUAL (ror'kwąl)*n.*a genus of large whales. [Scand.]
ROSARY (rō'zą-ri) *n.* a bed of roses; a string of beads.
ROSE (rōz) *n.* a plant and flower of many species. [L. *rosa*, fr. G. *rhodon*.]
ROSEATE (rō'ze-āt) *a.* full of roses; blooming. [L. *roseus*, prepared from roses.]
ROSET (rō'zet') *n.* a red colour used by painters.
ROSETTE (rō-zet') *n.* an ornament made of ribbons. [F. dim. of *rose*, a rose.]
ROSE-WATER (rōz'waw-tęr) *n.* water tinctured with roses by distillation.
ROSIN (roz'in) *n.* turpentine thickened by evaporation. [F. *resine*.]
ROSINESS (rō'zi-nes) *n.* state of being rosy.
ROSINY (rōz'i-ni) *a.* partaking of rosin.
ROSTER (ros'tęr) *n.* a list of persons for duty. [D. *rooster*, a corruption of *register*.]
ROSTRAL (ros'trąl) *a.* resembling or pertaining to a beak.
ROSTRUM (ros'trum) *n.* a beak; a platform for speakers. [L. *rostrum*, a beak, fr. *rodere*, to gnaw.]
ROSY (rō'zi) *a.* like a rose; red as a rose.
ROT (rot) *v.t.* or *i.* to putrefy;—*n.* putrefaction; a distemper in sheep. [O.E. *rotian*.]
ROTARY (rō'tąr-i) *a.* turning like a wheel on an axis.
ROTATE (rō'tāt) *a.* wheel-shaped;—*v.t.* or *i.* to cause to turn; revolve round an axis. [L. *rota*, wheel.]
ROTATION (rō-tā'shun) *n.* a turning, as a wheel; regular succession.
ROTATORY (rō'tą-tu-ri) *a.* turning on an axis; following in succession.
ROTE (rōt) *n.* repetition of words by memory. [O.F. *rote*, track, fr. *rupta*, a road, fr. (part.) *ruptus*, of *rumpere*, to break.]

ROTTEN (rot'n) *a.* putrid; unsound.
ROTTENNESS (rot'n-nes) *n.* a putrid state.
ROTTENSTONE (rot'n-stōn) *n.* a soft stone used to clean and polish metals.
ROTUND (rō-tund') *a.* round; circular. [L. *rotundus*, fr. *rota*, a wheel.]
ROTUNDNESS (rō-tund'nes) *n.* sphericity; roundness.
ROTUNDA (rō-tun'dą) *n.* a building circular within and without. Also **ROTUNDO**. [It., fr. L.]
ROUBLE (rōō'bl) *n.* a silver coin of Russia, equal to 2s. 10d. Also **RUBLE**. [Russ.]
ROUE (rōō'ā) *n.* a dissipated man; a fashionable rake. [F. = one broken on the wheel, part. of *rouer*, fr. L. *rota*, a wheel.]
ROUGE (rōōzh) *n.* a red paint;—*v.t.* to tinge with rouge. [F., fr. L. *rubeus*, red.]
ROUGH (ruf) *a.* having an uneven surface; coarse. [O.E. *ruh*, rough, hairy. Cf. Ger. *rauch, rauh*.]
ROUGH-CAST (ruf'kast) *v.t.* to cover with plaster and gravel;—*n.* a rude model; plaster mixed with gravel.
ROUGH-DRAUGHT (ruf'dráft) *n.* a first drawing, sketch, or copy.
ROUGH-DRAW (ruf'draw) *v.t.* to draw coarsely.
ROUGH-HEW (ruf'hū) *v.t.* to hew roughly; give the first form or shape.
ROUGHLY (ruf'li) *ad.* harshly; rudely.
ROUGHNESS (ruf'nes) *a.* ruggedness.
ROUGH-SHOD (ruf'shod) *a.* having shoes armed with points; caulked.
ROULEAU (rōō-lō') *n.* a little roll of coins in paper. [F., dim. of O.F. *role*, a roll.]
ROULETTE (rōō-let') *n.* a game of chance. [F., dim. of O.F. *roule*, wheel.]
ROUND (round) *a.* spherical; circular;—*n.* a circle; a regular course;—*v.t.* to make round;—*v.i.* to become round;—*ad.* or *prep.* about; near. [O.F. *roōnd* = F. *rond*, fr. L. *rotundus*, fr. *rota*, a wheel.]
ROUNDABOUT (round'ą-bout) *a.* indirect; loose; encompassing.
ROUNDELAY (roun'dē-lā) *n.* a kind of song. [O.F. *rondelet*, fr. *rond*, round.]
ROUNDISH (roun'dish) *a.* somewhat round.
ROUNDLY (round'li) *ad.* openly; boldly.
ROUNDNESS (round'nes) *n.* quality of being round; sphericity.
ROUSE (rouz) *v.t.* to stir; excite; wake from rest. [Scand.]
ROUT (rout) *n.* a defeat; a multitude; fashionable assembly;—*v.t.* to put to flight. [O.F. *route*, a band, fr. Late L. *rupta*, thing broken, fr. (part.) *ruptus*, of *rumpere*, to break.]
ROUTE (rōōt) *n.* a course or way. [F., fr. L. *rupta* (*via*), a broken (way), fr. *rumpere*, to break.]
ROUTINE (rōō-tēn') *n.* regular course. [F.]
ROVE (rōv)*v.t.* to ramble. [Fr. *rover*, a robber.]
ROVER (rō'vęr) *n.* a wanderer; a pirate.
ROW (rou) *n.* a riot. [Scand.]
ROW (rō) (1) *n.* a line of persons or things;— (2) *v.t.* or *i.* to impel with oars; work at the oar;—*n.* sail in a rowing boat. [(1) O.E. *raw*. (2) O.E. *rowan*.]
ROWAN-TREE (rou'ąn-trē) *n.* the mountain ash. [Scand.]
ROWDYISM (rou'di-izm) *n.* rude or riotous conduct.
ROWEL (rou'el) *n.* a little wheel; seton;— *v.t.* to insert a rowel. [O.F. *rouelle*, a little wheel, fr. Late L. *rotella*, dim. of *rota*, a wheel.]
ROWER (rō'ęr) *n.* one who rows.
ROWLOCKS (rul'uks, rō'loks) *n.pl.* two pins between which the oars work.
ROYAL (roi'ąl) *a.* regal; kingly. [F., fr. O.F. *roial*, fr. L. *regalis*. Cf. **REGAL**.]
ROYALIST (roi'ąl-ist) *n.* an adherent to kingly government.

ROYALTY (roi'ạl-ti) *n.* office, state, or character of a king.

RUB (rub) *v.t.* to wipe; clean; scour; erase; —*v.i.* to move along with pressure;—*n.* friction; difficulty; grate; jibe. [M.E. *rubben*, perh. fr. Celt.]

RUBBER (rub'ẹr) *n.* one who rubs; contest of three games.

RUBBISH (rub'ish) *n.* waste matter; ruins of buildings; nonsense. [O.F. *robeux*, pl. of *robel*, dim. of *robe*, trash.]

RUBBLE (rub'l) *n.* small undressed stones used in coarse masonry. [O.F. *robel*, dim. of *robe*, *robbe*, trash.]

RUBIED (rŏŏ'bid) *a.* red as a ruby.

RUBRIC (rŏŏ'brik) *a.* red; placed in red letters;—*n.* directions in a prayer-book. [L. *rubrica*, red earth, fr. *ruber*, red.]

RUBY (rŏŏ'bi) *n.* a gem of a red colour; a small printing type;—*a.* of a red colour;—*v.t.* to make red. [O.F. *rubi*, fr. L. *rubeus*, red, fr. *ruber*, red.]

RUCK (ruk) *v.t.* to wrinkle;—*n.* a wrinkle; a heap. [Scand.] redness.]

RUDD (rud) *n.* a fresh-water fish. [O.E. *rudu*.

RUDDER (rud'ẹr) *n.* the instrument by which a ship is steered. [O.E. *rother*. Cf. Ger. *Ruder*, an oar.]

RUDDINESS (rud'i-nes) *n.* redness.

RUDDOCK (rud'ok) *n.* the redbreast or robin. [O.E.]

RUDDY (rud'i) *a.* of a red colour. [O.E. *rudig*.]

RUDE (rŏŏd) *a.* uncivilised; rough. [F., fr. L. *rudis*, rough.]

RUDELY (rŏŏd'li) *ad.* roughly; harshly.

RUDENESS (rŏŏd'nes) *n.* incivility; coarseness; unskilfulness.

RUDIMENT (rŏŏ'di-ment) *n.* first principle; original; element;—*pl.* first book;—*v.t.* to ground in first principles. [L. *rudimentum*, fr. *rudis*, rude.]

RUDIMENTAL (rŏŏ-di-men'tạl) *a.* pertaining to elements; initial.

RUE (rŏŏ) (1) *n.* a very bitter plant;—(2) *v.t.* to lament; regret. [(1) F., fr. L. *ruta*, fr. G. *rhute.* (2) O.E. *hreowan*, to be sorry for.]

RUEFUL (rŏŏ'fool) *a.* sorrowful.

RUFF (ruf) (1) *n.* a plaited cloth round the neck; applaud by beating the floor or benches;—(2) *v.t.* to trump instead of following suit. [(1) Fr. **RUFFLE.** (2. It.]

RUFFIAN (ruf'i-ạn) *n.* a boisterous, brutal fellow; a cut-throat;—*a.* brutal; savage. [O.F.=F. *rufien*, fr. It. *ruffiano*.]

RUFFIANISM (ruf'i-ạn-izm) *n.* the act or conduct of a ruffian. [violent.

RUFFIANLY (ruf'i-ạn-li) *a.* like a ruffian;

RUFFLE (ruf'l) *v.t.* to wrinkle; vex; disturb; —*v.i.* to grow rough; flutter;—*n.* a plaited article of dress; disturbance; roll of a drum. [imit.]

RUG (rug) *n.* a coarse woollen cloth or coverlet; a mat. [Scand.]

RUGGED (rug'ed) *a.* rough; harsh; shaggy.

RUGGEDLY (rug'ed-li) *ad.* in a rugged manner.

RUGGEDNESS (rug'ed-nes) *n.* roughness; unevenness of surface.

RUGOSE (rŏŏ'gōs) *a.* wrinkled; full of wrinkles. Also **RUGOUS.** [L. *rugosus*, *ruga*, a wrinkle.]

RUIN (rŏŏ'in) *n.* overthrow; destruction; remains of buildings, etc.;—*v.t.* to destroy utterly; impoverish. [F., fr. L. *ruina*, fr. *ruere*, to fall down.]

RUINATE (rŏŏ'i-nāt) *v.t.* to destroy wholly.

RUINATION (rŏŏ-i-nā'shun) *n.* total ruin or destruction.

RUINOUS (rŏŏ'i-nus) *a.* destructive; fatal.

RULE (rŏŏl) *n.* sway; principle; standard; maxim; order; instrument for drawing lines;—*v.t.* or *i.* to govern; settle; decide; mark with lines; range or stand, as prices in the market. [O.F. *reule*=F. *règle*, fr. L. *regula*, fr. *regere*, to govern.]

RULER (rŏŏ'lẹr) *n.* one who rules; a governor; an instrument for drawing lines.

RUM (rum) *n.* a spirituous liquor distilled from molasses. [Contr. fr. *rumbullion* or *rumbowling*, a sailor's name for grog.]

RUMBLE (rum'bl) *v.i.* to make a low continued noise;—*n.* a low, heavy sound; a seat for servants behind a carriage. [Teut.]

RUMBLING (rum'bling) *n.* a low, heavy sound.

RUMINANT (rŏŏ'mi-nạnt) *a.* chewing the cud.

RUMINATE (rŏŏ'mi-nāt) *v.t.* to chew the cud; meditate. [L. (part.) *ruminatus*, of *ruminare*, fr. *rumen*, the gullet.]

RUMINATION (rŏŏ-mi-nā'shun) *n.* act of ruminating; calm reflection.

RUMINATOR (rŏŏ'mi-nā-tẹr) *n.* one who ruminates.

RUMMAGE (rum'ij) *n.* a close search;—*v.t.* to tumble about in searching. [For *roomage*, fr. **ROOM.**]

RUMMER (rum'ẹr) *n.* a large drinking glass. [D. *roemer*, a wine-glass.]

RUMOUR (rŏŏ'mur) *n.* a flying or popular report;—*v.t.* to report; circulate by report. [F., fr. L. *rumor*, a noise.]

RUMP (rump) *n.* end of the backbone; buttocks. [Scand.]

RUMPLE (rum'pl) *v.t.* to wrinkle;—*n.* a wrinkle; a fold. [O.E. *hrimpan*.]

RUMPUS (rum'pus) *n.* a disturbance; noisy confusion.

RUN (run) *v.t.* or *i.* [*pret.* **RAN** or **RUN**; *pp.* **RUN**] to move with rapidity; flow; form in a mould; smuggle; melt; discharge matter; incur;—*n.* course; small stream; range of ground; distance sailed. [O.E. *rinnan.* Cf. Ger *rennen*.]

RUNAGATE (run'ạ-gāt) *n.* a runaway; vagabond. [Corr. of **RENEGADE**; modified by **RUN.**]

RUNAWAY (run'ạ-wā) *n.* a fugitive; a deserter.

RUNDLE (run'dl) *n.* round of a ladder. [Fr. **ROUND.**]

RUNNEL (run'el) *n.* a small brook; rivulet. [O.E. *rynel*, dim. of *ryne*, a stream, fr. *rinnan*, to run.]

RUNNER (run'ẹr) *n.* one that runs; a messenger.

RUNG (rung) *n.* round of a ladder; cudgel. [O.E. *hrung*, a beam.]

RUNLET (run'let) *n.* a small cask. [F,]

RUNT (runt) *n.* a dwarfed animal; stalk or stem of cabbage. [O.E. *hryther*.]

RUPEE (rŏŏ-pē') *n.* an East Indian silver coin, equal to 2s.; if of gold, 29s. [Hind.]

RUPTURE (rup'tūr) *n.* a breach; a burst; hernia;—*v.t.* to break; burst. [F., fr. Late L. *ruptura*, fr. (part.) *ruptus*, of *rumpere*, to break.]

RURAL (rŏŏ'rạl) *a.* belonging to the country. [F., fr. L. *ruralis*, fr. stem *rur-*, of *rus*, the country.]

RUSH (rush) (1) *n.* impetuous onset or flow; —*v.i.* to pass with vehemence; enter into hastily;—(2) *n.* a kind of reed. [(1) M.E. *ruschen.* (2) O.E. *risce*.]

RUSH-LIGHT (rush'lit) *n.* a candle of rushwick.

RUSHY (rush'i) *a.* abounding with rushes.

RUSK (rusk) *n.* a species of cake. [Sp. *rosca de mar*, sea-rusks, a biscuit, fr. *rosca*, a roll of bread.]

RUSSET (rus'et) *a.* of a reddish brown colour; —*n.* rustic dress; an apple of a russet colour. [O.F. *rousset*, fr. L. *russus*, red.]

RUSSIA LEATHER (rush'ạ-leᴛн-ẹr) *n.* a fine soft leather highly prized for bookbinding.

RUST (rust) *n.* crust which forms on metals; —*v.i.* to gather rust;—*v.t.* to make rusty. [O.E. *rust*, rust, redness. Cf. Ger. *Rost*.]

RUSTIC (rus'tik) *a.* rural;—*n.* an inhabitant of the country. [F. *rustique*, fr. L. *rusticus*, fr. *rus*, the country.]

RUSTICATE (rus'ti-kāt) *v.t.* or *i.* to reside in or banish to the country.

RUSTICATION (rus-ti-kā'shun) *n.* residence in, or banishment to, the country.

RUSTICITY (rus-tis'i-ti) *n.* rustic manners; rudeness; simplicity.

RUSTINESS (rus'ti-nes) *n.* state or quality of being rusty.

RUSTLE (rus'l) *v.i.* to make a quick, low sound by rubbing of leaves, silk, etc.;—*n.* such a sound. [Scand.]

RUSTY (rus'ti) *a.* covered with rust.

RUT (rut) *n.* the track of a wheel;—*v.i.* to cut in ruts. [O.F. *route*, fr. Late L. *rupta*, a way, fr. (part.) *ruptus*, of *rumpere*, to break.]

RUTH (rōōth) *n.* mercy; pity; tenderness. [O.E. *hreow*.]

RUTHLESS (rōōth'les) *a.* cruel; pitiless.

RUTHLESSLY (rōōth'les-li) *ad.* without pity.

RUTTY (rut-i) *a.* full of ruts.

RYE (rī) *n.* a kind of grain. [O.E. *ryge*.]

RYOT (rī'ut) *n.* a renter of land in Hindustan. [Hind., fr. A. =a tenant.]

S

SABAOTH (sa-bā'oth) *n.* armies; hosts. [H.]

SABBATARIAN (sab-a-tā'ri-an) *a.* pertaining to the Sabbath;—*n.* a strict observer of the Sabbath.

SABBATH (sab'ath) *n.* the day of religious rest; Sunday. [L. *Sabbatum*, fr. G. *Sabbaton*, fr. H. *Shabbath*, rest.]

SABBATHLESS (sab'ath-les) *a.* without intermission of labour.

SABBATICAL (sa-bat'i-kal) *a.* pertaining to the Sabbath.

SABIAN (sā'bi-an) *n.* a worshipper of the sun, moon, and stars. [H. *tsaba*, a host.]

SABIANISM (sā'bi-an-izm) *n.* worship of the heavenly bodies.

SABLE (sā'bl) *n.* an animal of the weasel kind, valued for its fur;—*a.* dark; black; made of sable. [O.F.]

SABRE (sā'ber) *n.* a sword with a broad blade. [F.]

SABRETACHE (sā'ber-tash) *n.* a leathern case worn by cavalry.

SACCHARINE (sak'a-rin) *a.* having the qualities of sugar. [F. *saccharin*, fr. L. *saccharum*, sugar, fr. G.]

SACERDOTAL (sas-er-dō'tal) *a.* priestly. [L. stem *sacerdot-*, of *sacerdos*, a priest, fr. *sacer*, sacred, and *dare*, to give.]

SACHEM (sā'chem) *n.* an Indian chief.

SACK (sak) (1) *n.* a bag;—(2) *n.* pillage of a town;—*v.t.* to pillage; plunder;—(3) *n.* a sweet wine, sherry; canary. [(1) O.E. *sacc*, fr. L. *saccus*, fr. G. *sakkos*, fr. H. *saq*, a coarse cloth. (2) F. *sac*, a bag, fr. L. *saccus*, a sack. (3) F. *sec*, dry, fr. L. *siccus*, dry.]

SACKCLOTH (sak'kloth) *n.* cloth for sacks.

SACKFUL (sak'fool) *n.* as much as a sack will hold.

SACKING (sak'ing) *n.* cloth for sacks.

SACRAMENT (sak'ra-ment) *n.* a religious ordinance; the Lord's Supper. [L. *sacramentum*, an oath, fr. *sacrare*, to consecrate, fr. *sacer*, sacred.]

SACRAMENTAL (sak-ra-men'tal) *a.* pertaining to a sacrament.

SACRED (sā'kred) *a.* pertaining to God or religion; holy; inviolable. [M.E. *sacren*, pp. *sacred*, to render holy, fr. F., fr. L. *sacrare*, to consecrate, fr. *sacer*, holy.]

SACREDLY (sā'kred-li) *ad.* religiously.

SACREDNESS (sā'kred-nes) *n.* state or quality of being sacred.]

SACRIFIC (sa-krif'ik) *a.* used in sacrifice.

SACRIFICE (sak'ri-fis) *v.t.* to kill and offer to God in worship; give up with loss; devote; —*n.* an offering to God; any loss incurred. [F., fr. L. *sacrificium*, fr. *sacer*, holy, and *facere*, make.]

SACRIFICIAL (sak-ri-fish'al) *a.* relating to or performing sacrifice.

SACRILEGE (sak'ri-lej) *n.* violation of sacred things. [O.F., fr. L. *sacrilegium*, fr. *sacer*, sacred, and *legere*, to gather, to steal.]

SACRILEGIOUS (sak-ri-lē'jus) *a.* violating sacred things.

SACRIST (sā'krist) *n.* janitor; sexton.

SACRISTAN (sak'ris-tan) *n.* a sexton. [O.F. *sacristain*, fr. L. *sacer*.]

SACRISTY (sak'ris-ti) *n.* the vestry room.

SACROSANCT (sak'ru-sangkt) *a.* holy; inviolable. [L., fr. *sacer*, and (part.) *sanctus*, of *sancire*, to hallow.]

SAD (sad) *a.* sorrowful; serious; gloomy; sombre; calamitous. [O.E. *sæd*, sated, weary. Cf. Ger. *satt*.]

SADDEN (sad'n) *v.t.* or *i.* to make or become sad.

SADDLE (sad'l) *n.* a seat for the back of a horse;—*v.t.* to put a saddle on; burden. [O.E. *sadol*. Cf. Ger. *Sottel*.]

SADDLECLOTH (sad'l-kloth) *n.* cloth under the saddle.

SADDLER (sad'ler) *n.* a maker of saddles.

SADDLERY (sad'ler-i) *n.* trade of a saddler; materials or wares of a saddler.

Saddle.

SADDLETREE (sad'l-trē) *n.* the frame of a saddle.

SADDUCEAN (sad-ū-sē'an) *a.* pertaining to the Sadducees.

SADDUCEE (sad'ū-sē) *n.* a sect of the Jews which denied the resurrection. [H., fr. their reputed founder, *Zadok*, or fr. the *Zadokites*, a race of priests.]

SADLY (sad'li) *ad.* sorrowfully.

SADNESS (sad'nes) *n.* heaviness of heart.

SAFE (sāf) *a.* free from danger; secure;—*n.* a place to secure provisions, money, etc. [O.F. *sauf*, fr. L. *salvus*.]

SAFEGUARD (sāf'gärd) *n.* a thing that protects; a passport.

SAFELY (sāf'li) *ad.* securely.

SAFETY (sāf'ti) *n.* freedom from danger or loss.

SAFETY-LAMP (sāf'ti-lamp) *n.* a lamp covered with wire for use in mines.

SAFETY-VALVE (sāf'ti-valv) *n.* a valve by which a steam-boiler is preserved from bursting.

SAFFRON (saf'run) *n.* a yellow flower;—*a.* like saffron. [O.F. *safran*, fr. A., fr. *safra*, yellow.]

SAG (sag) *v.t.* or *i.* to bend; load; yield; lurch; stagger. [M.E. *saggen*. Cf. Ger. *sacken*, to sink.]

SAGA (sā'ga, sä'ga) *n.* a Scandinavian legend. [Icel., a tale. Cf. SAY.]

SAGACIOUS (sa-gā'shus) *a.* quick of scent; acute; judicious. [L. stem *sagac-*, of *sagax*, fr. *sagire*, to perceive quickly.]

SAGACIOUSLY (sa-gā'shus-li) *ad.* with quick discernment.

SAGACITY (sa-gas'i-ti) *n.* acuteness of scent; quick discernment; practical judgment.

SAGAMORE (sag'a-mōr) *n.* a North American Indian chief.

SAGE (sāj) (1) *a.* wise; discreet ;—*n.* a wise man; (2) a plant. [(1) F., fr. L. *sapius* (in *re-sapius*), wise, fr. *sapere*, to be wise. (2) O.F. *sauge*, fr. L. *salvia* (fr. its supposed power of healing), fr. *salvus*, safe.]

SAGELY (sāj'li) *ad.* wisely; prudently.

SAGITTAL (saj'i-tal) *a.* pertaining to an arrow. [L. *sagitta*, an arrow.]

SAGITTARIUS (saj-i-ta'ri-us) *n.* the archer; one of the twelve signs. [L. *sagitta*, an arrow.]

SAGO (sā'gō) *n.* granulated juice of a species of palm. [Malay.]

SAGOIN (sā'gŏŏ-in) *n.* a monkey of South America.

SAHIB (sā'ib) *n.* a title in India meaning master or sir. [Hind., fr. A. *sahib*, lord, master.]

SAID (sed) *pret.* and *pp.* of SAY.

SAIL (sāl) *n.* a ship's canvas; a ship;—*v.t.* or *i.* to move with sails on water; navigate; set sail; fly through. [O.E. *segel*. Cf. Ger. *Segel*.]

SAIL-LOFT (sāl'loft) *n.* a room where sails are made.

SAILOR (sā'ler) *n.* a seaman.

SAINFOIN (sān'foin) *n.* a leguminous plant used for fodder. [F. *sain*, wholesome, and *foin*, hay, fr. L. *sanum foenum*.]

SAINT (sānt) *n.* one eminent for piety; one of the blessed; one canonised;—*v.t.* to canonise. [O.F. *saint*, fr. L. *sanctus*.]

SAINTED (sān'ted) *a.* holy; sacred.

SAINTLY (sānt'li) *a.* resembling a saint.

SAINTSHIP (sānt'ship) *n.* character or qualities of a saint.

SAKE (sāk) *n.* cause; purpose; account; regard. [O.E. *sacu*, strife.]

SALAAM (sa-lām') *n.* a word of salutation in the East;—*v.t.* to salute; to greet. [A. =peace.]

SALACIOUS (sa-lā'shus) *a.* lustful; lewd. [L. *salax*, fr. *salire*, to leap.]

SALAD (sal'ad) *n.* food of raw herbs. [F. *salade*, fr. *salare* to salt, fr. L. *sal*, salt.]

SALAD-OIL (sal'ad-oil) *n.* olive oil.

SALAMANDER (sal-a-man'der) *n.* a small amphibious reptile. [F. *salamandre*, fr. L., fr. G. *salamandra*.]

SALAMANDRINE (sal-a-man'drin) *a.* like a salamander.

SALARIED (sal'a-rid) *a.* having a salary.

SALARY (sal'a-ri) *n.* a stated allowance for services; wages. [O.F. *salarie* = F. *salaire*, fr. L. *salarium*, salt money, fr. *sal*, salt.]

SALE (sāl) *n.* act of selling; auction; demand; price. [Scand.]

SALEABLE (sā'la-bl) *a.* fit for sale.

SALEABLENESS (sā'la-bl-nes) *n.* state of being saleable.

SALESMAN (sālz'man) *n.* one employed to sell goods.

SALIC (sal'ik) *a.* denoting a law which excludes females from the throne. [F. *salique*, belonging to the Salic tribe.] [ness.

SALIENCE (sā'li-ens) *n.* prominence; forward-

SALIENT (sā'li-ent) *a.* shooting forth; projecting; prominent. [L. (part.) stem *salient-*, of *salire*, to leap.]

SALIFIABLE (sal'i-fi-a-bl) *a.* capable of becoming a salt.

SALIFY (sal'i-fi) *v.t.* to form into a neutral salt. [L. *sal*, salt, and *facere*, to make.]

SALINE (sal-in, salin') *a.* salt; consisting of salt;—*n.* a salt spring. [F. *salin*, fr. L. *salinus*, fr. *sal*, salt.]

SALIVA (sa-li'va) *n.* the fluid secreted in the mouth; spittle. [F., fr. L. =a spittle.]

SALIVARY (sal'i-va-ri) *a.* secreting saliva, as the glands.

SALIVATE (sal'i-vāt) *v.t.* to excite an unusual discharge of saliva.

SALIVATION (sal-i-vā'shun) *n.* the act of secreting saliva; ptyalism.

SALLOW (sal'ō) (1) *a.* yellow and pale;—(2) *n.* a kind of willow. [(1) O.E. *salu*. (2) O.E. *sealh*.]

SALLOWNESS (sal'ō-nes) *n.* paleness tinged with yellow.

SALLY (sal'i) *n.* a sudden eruption of troops; outburst of fancy, wit, etc.;—*v.i.* to rush out suddenly. [F. *saillir*, to issue forth, fr. L. *salire*, leap.]

SALLY-PORT (sal'i-pōrt) *n.* a gate through which troops sally.

SALMAGUNDI (sal-ma-gun'di) *n* chopped meat and seasonings. [F. *salmigondis*, fr. It. *salame*, salt meat, fr. L. *sal*, salt, and (part.) *conditus*, of *condire*, to pickle.]

SALMON (sam'un) *n.* a large fish highly valued for food. [O.F. *saulmon*, fr. L. *salmo*, fr. *salire*, to leap.]

SALMON-TROUT (sam'un-trout) *n.* a trout resembling the salmon in colour; sea-trout.

SALOON (sa-lŏŏn') *n.* a spacious hall. [F. *salon*, fr. *salle*, fr. O. Ger. *Sal*, a dwelling.]

SALSIFY (sal'si-fi) *n.* a meadow plant with an edible root. [F., fr. It. *sassefrica*, goat's beard, fr. L. *saxum*, a rock, and *fricare*, to rub.]

SALT (sawlt) *n.* a substance used for seasoning;—*v.t.* to sprinkle with salt. [O.E. *sealt*. Cf. Ger. *Salz*; L. *sal*; G. *hals*.]

SALTATION (sal-tā'shun) *n.* act of leaping. [L. *saltare*, to dance, fr. *salire*, to leap.]

SALTATORY (sal'ta-tu-ri) *a.* for leaping or dancing.

SALTISH (sawlt'ish) *a.* somewhat salt.

SALTNESS (sawlt'nes) *n.* taste of salt.

SALTPETRE (sawlt-pē'ter) *n.* a mineral salt composed of nitric acid and potash. [O.F. *selpestre*, fr. Low L. *salpetra*, fr. L. *sal petrae*, salt of the rock.]

SALUBRIOUS (sa-lū'bri-us) *a.* healthful. [L. *salubris*, fr. *salus*, health.]

SALUBRITY (sa-lū'bri-ti) *n.* healthfulness.

SALUTARY (sal'ū-ta-ri) *a.* promoting health or safety. [L. *salutaris*, fr. *salus*, health.]

SALUTATION (sal-ū-tā'shun) *n.* act of saluting; greeting.

SALUTATORY (sa-lū'ta-tu-ri) *a.* containing or expressing welcome.

SALUTE (sa-lūt') *v.t.* to greet; kiss; honour; —*n.* act of saluting; a kiss; discharge of cannon. [L. *salutare*, to wish health to, fr. *salus*, health.]

SALVABLE (sal'va-bl) *a.* capable of being saved.

SALVAGE (sal'vij) *n.* reward for saving goods. [O.F. =a saying, fr. *salver*, fr. L. *scivare*, to save.]

SALVATION (sal-vā'shun) *n.* preservation from eternal misery; deliverance. [O.F., fr. L. *salvare*, pp. *salvatus* to save.]

SALVATION ARMY (sal-vā'shun-ar-mi) *n.* a quasi-military organisation for the revival of religion.

SALVE (salv, säv) *n.* a substance for covering sores; remedy. [O.E. *sealf*.]

SALVER (sal'ver) *n.* a piece of plate to present something on. [Sp. *salva*, fr. *salvar*, to taste the food of one to save him from poison, fr. L. *salvare*, to save.]

SALVO (sal'vō) *n.* an exception; military or naval salute with guns. [It. *salva* =a salute, fr. L. *salve*, hail!]

SALVOR (sal'ver) *n.* one who saves a ship or cargo at sea.

SAMBO (sam'bō) *n.* the offspring of a black person and a mulatto. [Sp. *zambo*, fr. L., fr. G. *skambos*, bow-legged.]

SAME (sām) *a.* identical; not different or other; mentioned before. [O.E.]

SAMENESS (sām'nes) *n.* entire likeness.

SAMIEL (sā'mi-el) *n.* a destructive wind in Arabia. [Turk.]

SAMPAN (sam'pan) *n.* a Chinese river-boat. [Malay, fr. Chin.]

SAMPLE (sam'pl) *n.* a specimen. [O.F. *sample*, fr. L. *exemplum*, example.]

SAMPLER (sam'plẹr) *n.* a pattern of work; one who makes up samples.

SANATORY (san'ạ-tu-ri) *a.* adapted to cure; healing. [L. *sanare*, to heal.]

SANCTIFICATION (sangk-ti-fi-kā'shun) *n.* act of sanctifying.

SANCTIFIER (sangk'ti-fi-ẹr) *n.* one who sanctifies; the Holy Spirit.

SANCTIFY (sangk'ti-fi) *v.t.* to make holy; secure from violation. [L. *sanctificare*, fr. *sanctus*, holy, and *facere*, make.]

SANCTIMONIOUS (sangk-ti-mō'ni-us) *a.* appearing holy; saintly; devout. [L. *sanctus*, holy.]

SANCTION (sangk'shun) *n.* that which confirms; ratification;—*v.t.* to ratify; give validity to; authorise. [L. (part.) *sanctus*, of *sancire*, to render sacred.]

SANCTITY (sangk'ti-ti) *n.* holiness; purity.

SANCTUARY (sangk'tū-ạ-ri) *n.* a sacred place; house of worship; place of refuge. [O.F. *sainctuarie*, a shrine, fr. L. *sanctus*, holy.]

SANCTUM (sangk'tum) *n.* a sacred place; private room. [L.]

SAND (sand) *n.* particles of stony matter;—*v.t.* to sprinkle with sand. [O.E.]

SANDAL (san'dal) *n.* a loose shoe. [F., fr. L., fr. G. *sandalon*.]

SANDALWOOD (san'dal-wood) *n.* wood of a low tree remarkable for its fragrance. [F. *sandaraque*, fr. L., fr. G. *sandarake*, fr. Skr. = the sandal-tree.]

SAND-GLASS (sand'glas) *n.* an instrument for measuring time by the running of sand.

Sandal.

SANDINESS (san'di-nes) *n.* a state of being sandy.

SANDSTONE (sand'ston) *n.* a stone composed of consolidated sand.

SANDWICH (sand'wich) *n.* pieces of bread and butter with a thin slice of ham or salted meat between them, said to have been a favourite dish of the Earl of *Sandwich*, who died 1792.

SANDY (san'di) *a.* full of sand.

SANE (sān) *a.* sound in mind; whole. [L. *sanus*.]

SANGAREE (sang'gạ-rē) *n.* a beverage of spiced wine and water. [Sp.]

SANGFROID (sang-frwaw') *n.* coolness; indifference. [F. *sang*, blood, and *froid*, cold.]

SANGUINARY (sang'gwi-nạ-ri) *a.* bloody; cruel.

SANGUINE (sang'gwin) *a.* full of blood; red; hopeful; confident. [F. *sanguin* fr. L. *sanguineus*, fr. *sanguis*, blood.]

SANGUINELY (sang'gwin-li) *ad.* with confidence.

SANGUINEOUS (sang-gwin'e-us) *a.* abounding with blood.

SANHEDRIM (san'he-drim) *n.* the supreme council of Jewish elders. [H.; G. *sun*, together, and *hedro*, a seat.]

SANICLE san'i-kl) *n.* a plant of several species used for healing. [F., fr. L. *sanare*, heal.]

SANIES (sā'ni-ez) *n.* a thin acrid matter from a wound. [L.]

SANITARY (san'i-tạ-ri) *a.* pertaining to, or designed to promote, health. [L. *sanitas*, health.]

SANITATION (san-i-tā'shun) *n.* sanitary science and its application.

SANITY (san'i-ti) *n.* soundness of mind or body.

SANK (sangk) *pret.* of SINK.

SANS-CULOTTISM (sanz-kū-lot'izm) *n.* extreme republicanism. [F., fr. *sans*, without, and *culotte*, breeches, fr. L. *sine*, and *culus*, the breech.]

SANSKRIT (san'skrit) *n.* the ancient language of Hindostan. [Skr. = perfected.]

SAP (sap) (1) *n.* vital juice of plants;—(2) *v.t.* or *i.* to undermine; subvert by digging. [(1) O.E. (2) O.F. *sappe*, fr. Late L. *sappa*, a pick, fr. G. *skaptein*, dig.]

SAPID (sap'id) *a.* well tasted; savoury. [F., fr. L. *sapidus*, fr. *sapere*, taste.]

SAPIDITY (sạ-pid'i-ti) *n.* taste; savour; savouriness. Also SAPIDNESS.

SAPIENCE (sā'pi-ens) *n.* wisdom.

SAPIENT (sā'pi-ent) *a.* wise; sagacious. [L. (part.) stem *sapient-*, of *sapere*, to be wise.]

SAPLING (sap'ling) *n.* a young tree.

SAPONACEOUS (sap-ṇ-nā'shus) *a.* having the qualities of soap. [L. stem, *sapon* = of *sapo*, soap.]

SAPONIFY (sạ-pon'i-fi) *v.t.* to convert into soap. [L. *sapo*, soap, and *facere*, to make.]

SAPPER (sap'ẹr) *n.* one who saps.

SAPPHIC (saf'ik) *a.* pertaining to Sappho, the poetess, or a kind of verse invented by her.

SAPPHIRE (saf'ir) *n.* a precious stone. [F., fr. L., fr. G. *sappheiros*, fr. H.]

SAPPINESS (sap'i-nes) *n.* juiciness; succulence.

SAPPY (sap'i) *a.* full of sap; juicy.

SARCASM (sär'kazm) *n.* a bitter sneer; satirical remark. [F., fr. L. *sarcasmus*, fr. G. *sarkazein*, to tear flesh like dogs, to sneer, fr. stem *sark-*, of *sarx*, flesh.]

SARCASTIC (sär-kas'tik) *a.* scornfully satirical or severe.

SARCASTICALLY (sär-kas'ti-kạl-i) *ad.* in a sarcastic manner.

SARCENET (särs'net) *n.* a thin silk. [O.F., fr. Late L. *sarcenatus*, fr. *Saracenus*.]

SARCOPHAGOUS (sär-kof'ạ-gus) *a.* flesh-eating.

SARCOPHAGUS (sär-kof'ạ-gus) *n.* a stone coffin. [L., fr. G. *sarkophagos*, fr. *sarks*, flesh, and *phagein*, eat.]

SARDINE (sär'den) (1) *n.* a small fish of the herring family;—(2) *n.* a precious stone. [(1) L. *sardinia*, fr. the island of *Sardinia*. (2) Fr. G. *sardios* (*lithos*), the Sardian (stone), fr. *Sardeis*, Sardis, in Asia Minor.]

SARDONIC (sär-don'ik) *a.* denoting a kind of forced, heartless, and bitter laughter or smile. [F. *sardonique*, fr. L., fr. G. *sardonios*, perh. fr. G. *sardonion*, a plant of *Sardinia*, which was said to screw up the face of the eater.]

SARDONYX (sär'don-iks) *n.* a precious stone of a reddish yellow colour. [G. *Sardonux*, Sardian onyx.]

SARSAPARILLA (sär-sạ-pạ-ril'ạ) *n.* a twining shrub used in medicine. [Sp.]

SASH (sash) (1) *n.* an ornamental silk band; —(2) *n.* a window-frame. [(1) Pers. (2) F. *chāsse*, fr. L. *capsa*, chest.]

SASSAFRAS (sas'ạ-fras) *n.* a kind of laurel, the wood of which is pungent and aromatic. [F., fr. L. *saxifraga*, fr. *saxum*, a stone, and *frangere*, to break.]

SAT (sat) *pret.* of SIT.

SATAN (sā'tan) *n.* the great adversary. [O.F. *Sathanas*, fr. Late L. *Satanas*, fr. H. = the enemy.]

SATANIC (sạ-tan'ik) *a.* having the qualities of Satan; very wicked.

SATCHEL (sach'el) *n.* a small bag used for books by schoolboys. Also SACHEL. [O.F. *sachel*, fr. L. *saccellus*, dim. of *saccus*, sack.]

SATE (sāt) *v.t.* to satisfy; glut; fill. [L. *satiare*, fr. *satis*, enough.]

SATEEN (sa-tēn') *n.* a glossy fabric of wool or cotton. [See SATIN.]

SATELLITE (sat'e-lit) *n.* a small planet revolving round a larger; an obsequious attendant. [F., fr. L. stem *satellit-*, of *satelles*, an attendant.]

SATIATE (sā'shi-āt) *v.t.* to fill or gratify to the utmost; glut;—*a.* filled to satiety. [L. (part.) *satiatus*, satisfied, fr. *satiare*.]

SATIETY (sa-tī'e-ti) *n.* fullness beyond desire or pleasure.

SATIN (sat'in) *n.* a glossy, close-woven silk. [F., fr. Late L. *setinus*, fr. *scla*, hair.]

SATINET (sat-i-net') *n.* a thin sort of satin; a woollen and cotton fabric.

SATINY (sat'i-ni) *a.* like or made of satin.

SATIRE (sat'ir) *n.* a discourse or poem exposing vice or folly; bitter invective or ridicule. [F., fr. L. *satira*, fr. *satura* (*lanx*, a dish), a full dish, a medley.]

SATIRICAL (sa-tir'i-kal) *a.* conveying satire; sarcastic.

SATIRICALLY (sa-tir'i-kal-i) *ad.* with satire.

SATIRISE (sat'i-riz) *v.t.* to expose by satire.

SATIRIST (sat'i-rist) *n.* one who writes satire.

SATISFACTION (sat-is-fak'shun) *n.* state of being satisfied; that which satisfies.

SATISFACTORILY (sat-is-fak'tu-ri-li) *ad.* so as to give content.

SATISFACTORY (sat-is-fak'tu-ri) *a.* giving content; making amends.

SATISFIABLE (sat'is-fi-a-bl) *a.* that may be satisfied. [satisfaction.

SATISFIER (sat'is-fi-er) *n.* that which makes

SATISFY (sat'is-fi) *v.t.* or *i.* to supply or please fully; discharge; convince; give content; atone. [F. *satisfaire*, fr. L. *satisfacere*, fr. *satis*, enough, and *facere*, make.]

SATRAP (sat'rap, sā'trap) *n.* the ruler of a province. [G. *satrapes*, fr. O. Pers. = the ruler of a region.] [saturated

SATURABLE (sat'ū-ra-bl) *a.* that can be

SATURATE (sat'ū-rāt) *v.t.* to fill to the full. [L. (part.) *saturatus*, soaked, of *saturare*, fr. *satur*, full.]

SATURATION (sat-ū-rā'shun) *n.* state of being filled.

SATURDAY (sat'ur-dā) *n.* the last day of the week. [O.E. *Sæter-dæg*, day of Saturn, L. *Saturnus*.]

SATURN (sat'urn) *n.* a remote planet. [L.]

SATURNALIA (sat-ur-nā'li-a) *n.pl.* festival of Saturn; unrestrained revelry. [L.]

SATURNALIAN (sat-ur-nā'li-an) *a.* dissolute.

SATURNINE (sat'ur-nin) *a.* grave; gloomy; dull.

SATYR (sat'er, sā'ter) *n.* a fabulous sylvan deity—half man, half goat. [L., fr. G. *saturos*.]

SAUCE (saws) *n.* something eaten with food to improve its relish; impudent language; —*v.t.* to apply sauce to; speak impudently to. [F., fr. L. *salsa*, neut. pl. of (part.) *salsus*, of *salire*, to salt, fr. *sal*, salt.]

SAUCEPAN (saws'pan) *n.* a stewing pan.

SAUCER (saw'ser) *n.* a vessel for a tea-cup.

SAUCILY (saw'si-li) *ad.* pertly.

SAUCY (saw'si) *a.* pert; impudent.

SAUNTER (sän'ter) *v.i.* to wander idly:— *n.* a stroll; place for sauntering. [M.E. *saunteren*, fr. O.F. *s'aventurer*, to risk oneself. See ADVENTURE. Some give F. *sainte terre*, Holy Land, from pilgrimages.]

SAUNTERER (sän'ter-er) *n.* one who wanders.

SAURIAN (saw'ri-an) *n.* a reptile covered with scales, as the lizard;—*a.* belonging to the saurians. [G. *sauros*, a lizard.]

SAUSAGE (saw'sij) *n.* a roll of minced meat stuffed into a skin. [F. *saucisse*, fr. Late L. *salcitia*, fr. (part.) *salsus*, salted.]

SAUTERNE (sō-tern') *n.* a French wine light in colour. [Fr. *Sauterne*, in the Gironde.]

SAVABLE (sā'va-bl) *a.* that can be saved.

SAVAGE (sav'ij) *a.* wild; uncivilised; cruel; —*n.* a wild person; brutal person; barbarian. [O.F. *salvage*, fr. L. *silvaticus*, pertaining to the woods, fr. *silva*, a wood.]

SAVAGELY (sav'ij-li) *ad.* barbarously.

SAVAGENESS (sav'ij-nes) *n.* state or quality of being savage.

SAVANT (sav'ong, sa-väng') *n.* a man of science or learning. [F.]

SAVE (sāv) *v.t.* to preserve; rescue; reserve; spare;—*v.i.* be economical;—*prep.* except. [F. *sauver*, fr. L. *salvare*, fr. *salvus*, safe.]

SAVELOY (sav'e-loi) *n.* a highly-seasoned sausage of pork. [F. *cervelat*, fr. It. *cervelata*, fr. *cervello*, brain, fr. L. *cerebellum*, dim. of *cerebrum*, the brain.]

SAVER (sā'ver) *n.* one who saves.

SAVING (sā'ving) *a.* frugal; incurring no loss; effecting salvation;—*n.* money saved; economy; *prep.* excepting.

SAVINGLY (sā'ving-li) *ad.* economically.

SAVIOUR (sāv'yur) *n.* one who preserves; Christ; the Redeemer. [L. *salvare*, save.]

SAVORY (sā'vur-i) *n.* an aromatic kitchen herb. [Fr. SAVOUR.]

SAVOUR (sā'vur) *n.* taste; odour; flavour; relish;—*v.i.* to have a taste or smell;—*v.t.* to taste; like. [F. *saveur*, fr. L. *sapor*, taste, fr. *sapere*, to taste.]

SAVOURINESS (sā'vur-i-nes) *n.* pleasing taste or smell.

SAVOURLESS (sā'vur-les) *a.* wanting taste.

SAVOURY (sā'vur-i) *a.* pleasing to the taste or smell.

SAVOY (sa-voi') *n.* a variety of cabbage for winter use. [*Savoy*, in France, since 1860.]

SAW (saw) (1) *n.* an instrument to cut wood; —*v.t.* or *i.* [*pret.* SAWED; *pp.* SAWED, SAWN] to divide with a saw;—(2) *n.* a proverb. [(1) O.E. *saga*. Cf. Ger. *Säge*. (2) O.E. *sagu*.]

SAWDUST (saw'dust) *n.* small fragments of wood made by the attrition of the saw.

SAW-PIT (saw'pit) *n.* a place for sawing timber.

SAWYER (saw'yer) *n.* one whose occupation is to saw wood, etc.

SAXON (sak'sn) *a.* pertaining to the Saxons; —*n.* the language of the Saxons. [O.E. *Seaxa*, *Seaxan*, fr. *seax*, a knife.]

SAY (sā) *v.t.* or *i.* [*pret.* and *pp.* SAID] to speak; utter; affirm; recite. [O.E. *secgan*. Cf. Ger. *sagen*.]

SAYING (sā'ing) *n.* something said; expression; maxim.

SCAB (skab) *n.* incrustation over a sore. [O.E. *scæb*, fr. Scand.]

SCABBARD (skab'ärd) *n.* sheath of a sword. [M.E. *scauberk*, perh. fr. O.F. *escaubere*, fr. Teut.] [scabs; paltry.

SCABBED (skab'ed, skabd) *a.* covered with

SCABBY (skab'i) *a.* full of scabs.

SCABIOUS (skā'bi-us) *a.* consisting of scabs.

SCABROUS (skā'brus, skab'rus) *a.* rough; rugged. [L. *scaber*.]

SCAFFOLD (skaf'uld) *n.* a staging for workmen; a stage for the execution of a criminal. [O.F. *escafaut* = F. *échafaud*, fr. L. *captare*, to try to seize, and *falco*, a scaffold. Doublet of CATAFALQUE.]

SCAFFOLDING (skaf'ul-ding) *n.* temporary frames or supports.

SCAGLIOLA (skal-yō'la) *n.* a species of stucco resembling marble. [It.]

SCALABLE (skā'la-bl) *a.* that may be scaled.

SCALADE (ska-lād') *n.* storm of a fortress with ladders.

SCALD (skawld) (1) *v.t.* to burn by a hot liquid;—*n.* a burn; scurf on the head;— (2) *n.* a Scandinavian poet. [(1) O.F. *escalder* = F. *échauder*, fr. Late L. *excaldare*, to bathe in warm water, fr. *ex*, from, and *calidus*, warm. (2) Scand.]

SCALE (skāl) (1) *n.* a thin plate covering a fish or reptile;—*v.t.* to deprive of scales; to peel;—*v.i.* to come off;—(2) *n.* a ladder; a series of steps or tones;—*v.t.* to mount on ladders; clamber up;—(3) *n.* the dish of a balance;—*v.t.* to weigh. [(1) O.E. *sceale*, the scale of a fish. Cf. Ger. *Schale*. (2) L. *scala*, a ladder, fr. *scandere*, to mount. (3) Scand.]

Fāte, fär, ado; mē, her; mine; nōte; tūne; moon.

SCALENE (skạ-lēn') *a.* having three sides and angles unequal. [L. *scalenus*, fr. G. *skalenos*, uneven.]

SCALINESS (skā'li-nes) *n.* quality of being scaly.

SCALL (skawl) *n.* scurf; leprosy. [Scand.]

SCALLOP, SCOLLOP (skal'up, skol'up) *n.* a genus of shell-fish; a curved indentation on the edge;—*v.t.* to cut into segments or scallops. [O.F. *escalope*, fr. Teut. Doublet of SCALP.]

Scallop.

SCALP (skalp) *n.* skin of the top of the head;—*v.t.* to take off the scalp. [Scand. Doublet of SCALLOP.]

SCALPEL (skal'pel) *n.* a surgeon's knife. [L. *scalpellum*.]

SCALPER (skal'per) *n.* a surgical instrument for scraping bones.

SCALY (skā'li) *a.* full of scales; rough.

SCAMMONY (skam'u-ni) *n.* a plant of the convolvulus family, used as a cathartic. [F., fr. L., fr. G. *skammonia*.]

SCAMP (skamp) (1) *n.* a knavish fellow;—(2) *v.t.* to do work perfunctorily. [(1) O.F. *escamper*, to flee, fr. It., fr. L. *ex*, out, and *campus*, field. (2) Icel.]

SCAMPER (skam'per) *v.i.* to run with speed or hurry. [Fr. SCAMP.]

SCAN (skan) *v.t.* to examine closely: count the poetic feet. [F. *scander*, fr. L. *scandere*, climb.]

SCANDAL (skan'dạl) *n.* offence; disgrace; defamatory speech. [F. *scandale*, fr. L., fr. G. *skandalon*, a stumbling-block.]

SCANDALISE (skan'dạ-līz) *v.t.* to offend; shock; disgrace.

SCANDALOUS (skan'dạ-lus) *a.* disgraceful; defamatory.

SCANDALOUSLY (skan'dạ-lus-li) *ad.* disgracefully; shamefully.

SCANDENT (skan'dent) *a.* climbing. [L. (part.) stem *scandent*-, of *scandere*, climb.]

SCANNING (skan'ing) *n.* act of resolving a verse into its component feet.

SCANSION (skan'shun) *n.* the act of scanning.

SCANSORIAL (skan-sō'ri-ạl) *a.* adapted to climbing.

SCANT (skant) *v.t.* to limit; straiten; restrain; —*a.* not full;—*ad.* not quite. [Scand.]

SCANTILY (skan'ti-li) *ad.* sparingly; narrowly.

SCANTINESS (skan'ti-nes) *n.* want of fullness or sufficiency.

SCANTLE (skan'tl) (1) *v.i.* to be deficient;—(2) *v.t.* to divide into thin pieces. [(1) Fr. SCANT. (2) O.F. *eschantillon*, a small cantle or fragment, fr. L. *ex*, out, and *cantel*, *chantel*, a cantel.]

SCANTLING (skant'ling) *n.* a small piece or quantity; narrow piece of timber.

SCANTY (skan'ti) *a.* narrow; small; bare; hardly sufficient.

SCAPE (skāp) *n.* a stem bearing the fructification without leaves. [G. *skapos*, shaft.]

SCAPEGOAT (skāp'gōt) *n.* one who suffers for the misdeeds of others. [Fr. ESCAPE.]

SCAPULA (skap'ū-lạ) *n.* the shoulder-bone. [L. *scapulœ*, the shoulder-blades.]

SCAPULAR (skap'ū-lạr) *a.* belonging to the shoulder or the scapula.

SCAR (skär) *n.* mark of a wound or sore; blemish;—*v.t.* to mark with a scar. [O.F. *escure*, fr. L., fr. G. *eschara*, a scar produced by burning.]

SCARCE (skärs) *a.* uncommon; rare. [O.F. *escars* = F. *échars*, niggardly, fr. Late L. *scarpsus*, fr. *excarpsus*, for L. (part.) *excerptus*, of *excerpere*, fr. *ex*, out of, and *carpere*, to pick.]

SCARCELY (skärs'll) *ad.* hardly; with difficulty.

SCARCITY (skär'si-ti) *n.* deficiency; rareness; dearth.

SCARE (skär) *v.t.* to terrify suddenly; drive away. [Scand.]

SCARECROW (skär'krō) *n.* a thing to frighten birds; any cause of fear.

SCARF (skärf) *n.* a loose covering of cloth; —*pl.* SCARFS;—*v.t.* to throw on loosely; join; piece. [O.E. *scearfe*, a piece.]

SCARFING (skär'fing) *n.* the joining of two beams into one. [Scand.]

SCARF-SKIN (skärf'skin) *n.* outer thin skin; cuticle.

SCARIFICATION (skar-i-fi-kā'shun) *n.* a slight incision of the skin.

SCARIFIER (skar'i-fī-er) *n.* one who or the instrument which scarifies.

SCARIFY (skar'i-fī) *v.t.* to scratch and cut the skin. [F. *scarifier*, fr. L. *scarificare*, fr. G. *skariphos*, an etching tool.]

SCARLATINA (skär-lạ-tē'nạ) *n.* scarlet fever. [It.]

SCARLATINOUS (skär-lạ-tē'nus) *a.* pertaining to scarlet fever.

SCARLET (skär'let) *n.* a deep red colour; —*a.* deeply red. [O.F. *escarlate* = F. *écarlate*, through Late L. *scarlatum*, fr. Pers. = scarlet cloth.]

SCARLET-BEAN (skär'let-bēn) *n.* a red bean. Also called SCARLET-RUNNER.

SCARLET-FEVER (skär'let-fē'ver) *n.* an infectious fever known by the red flush on the skin.

SCARP (skärp) *n.* the interior slope of a ditch. [F. *escarpe*. Cf. SCARF.]

SCATHE (skāth) *n.* damage; injury; waste; harm;—*v.t.* to do harm to; to damage; to waste. [O.E. *sceathu*. Cf. Ger. *Schade*, injury.]

SCATHFUL (skāth'fool) *a.* injurious; harmful.

SCATHING (skā'thing) *a.* withering; destroying.

SCATHLESS (skāth'les) *a.* without harm.

SCATTER (skat'er) *v.t.* to throw about loosely; strew; disperse;—*v.i.* to be dissipated. [O.E. *scateran*, a form of SHATTER.]

SCAUR (skawr) *n.* a precipitous bank or rock. [A Scot. form of SCAR.]

SCAVENGER (skav'en-jer) *n.* one employed to clean streets. [Orig. *scavager*, an inspector of goods for sale, and later of the cleansing of streets, fr. *scavage*, duty on goods for sale, fr. O.E. *sceawian*, to inspect.]

SCENE (sēn) *n.* a stage; place of action, occurrence, or exhibition; display of action or feeling; painted view; spectacle. [L. *scena*, fr. G. *skene*, a tent or stage.]

SCENERY (sē'ner-i) *n.* painted representation on the stage; aspect of a landscape.

SCENICAL (sen'i-kạl, sē'ni-kạl) *a.* dramatic; theatrical.

SCENOGRAPHIC (sē-nu-graf'ik) *a.* drawn in perspective.

SCENOGRAPHY (sc-nog'rạ-fi) *n.* representation in perspective. [G. *skene*, and *graphein*, write.]

SCENT (sent) *n.* odour; smell; chase pursued by the smell;—*v.t.* to smell; perfume; discern by the smell. [For *sent*; F. *sentir*, to feel, fr. L. *sentire*, to perceive.]

SCENTLESS (sent'les) *a.* having no smell.

SCEPTIC (skep'tik) *n.* one who doubts of all things, especially divine truth; an infidel. Also written SKEPTIC. [L. *scepticus*, fr. G. *skeptikos*, thoughtful.]

SCEPTICAL (skep'ti-kạl) *a.* doubting.

SCEPTICISM (skep'ti-sizm) *n.* universal doubt.

SCEPTRE (sep'ter) *n.* emblem of royalty. [F., fr. L., fr. G., *skeptron*, leaning staff, fr. *skeptein*, to prop.]

SCHEDULE (shed'ul) n. an inventory of property, debts, etc.; list. [O.F. = F. cedule, fr. L. schedula, dim. of scheda, a strip of papyrus.]

SCHEME (skēm) n. a plan; project; contrivance;—v.t. to plan; contrive. [L. schema, fr. G. schema, form, fr. schesein, to hold.]

SCHEMER (skē'mer) n. a projector; a contriver.

SCHISM (sizm) n. division or separation in a church. [L. schisma, fr. G. schizein, to split.]

SCHISMATIC (siz-mat'ik) n. one guilty of schism.

SCHISMATICAL (siz-mat'i-kal) a. pertaining to or partaking of schism.

SCHIST (shist) n. a rock of a slaty structure. [F. schiste, fr. G. schistos, easily cleft, fr. schizein, divide.]

SCHOLAR (skol'ar) n. a learner; man of letters.

SCHOLARLIKE (skol'ar-lik) a. like a scholar. Also SCHOLARLY.

SCHOLARSHIP (skol'ar-ship) n. learning; erudition; maintenance for a scholar.

SCHOLASTIC (sko-las'tik) a. pertaining to a school or to the schoolmen.

SCHOLASTICISM (sko-las'ti-sizm) n. the method or subtilities of the schools.

SCHOLIAST (skō'li-ast) n. a commentator.

SCHOLIUM (skō'li-um) n. an explanatory observation; marginal note. [G. scholion, interpretation.]

SCHOOL (skool) n. a place of discipline and instruction; the pupils; disciples; sect; system;—v.t. to instruct; admonish. [L. schola, fr. G. schole, leisure, a school.]

SCHOOL-BOARD (skool'bord) n. public body elected to see to the education of all children in a district.

SCHOOLHOUSE (skool'hous) n. a house for a school.

SCHOOLING (skool'ing) n. instruction.

SCHOOLMAN (skool'man) n. one versed in the divinity of the Middle Ages.

SCHOOLMASTER (skool'mas-ter) n. the master or teacher of a school.

SCHOOLMISTRESS (skool'mis-tres) n. a female teacher.

SCHOONER (skoo'ner) n. a vessel with two masts. [Orig. scooner, fr. Prov. E. scoon, to make a flat stone skip along the surface of water; O.E. scunian.]

SCIAGRAPHY (si-ag'ra-fi) n. the art of delineating shadows. [G., fr. skia, a shadow, and graphein, write.]

SCIATIC (si-at'ik) a. affecting the hip.

SCIATICA (si-at'i-ka) n. rheumatism in the hip. [Late L., fr. G. ischion, hip-joint.]

SCIENCE (si'ens) n. knowledge reduced to system under general facts or principles. [F., fr. L. scientia, fr. (part.) stem scient-, of scire, know.]

SCIENTIAL (si-en'shal) a. producing or according to science.

SCIENTIFIC (si-en-tif'ik) a. according to, or versed in, science. [L. scientia, and facere, make.]

SCIENTIST (si'en-tist) n. one versed in natural science.

SCILICET (si'li-set) ad. namely. [L.]

SCINTILLANT (sin'ti-lant) a. emitting sparks. [L. scintilla, a spark.]

SCINTILLATION (sin-ti-lā'shun) n. act of sparkling; a tremulous light.

SCIOLISM (si'u-lizm) n. superficial knowledge. [L. sciolus, dim. of scius, knowing, fr. L. scire, to know.]

SCIOLIST (si'u-list) n. one of superficial knowledge.

SCION (si'un) n. a shoot or twig; child or descendant of noble lineage. [O.F., fr. L. sectionem, a cutting, fr. secare, cut.]

SCIRRHOSITY (sir-os'i-ti, skir os'i-ti) n. induration of the glands.

SCIRRHOUS (sir'us, skir'us) a. indurated; knotty.

SCIRRHUS (sir'us, skir'us) n. a hard tumour in the flesh. [L., fr. G. skirros, a hard swelling.]

SCISSORS (siz'urz) n.pl. small shears. [M.E. sisoures, fr. O.F. cisoires, shears, fr. L. (part.) caesus, of caedere, to cut.]

SCOFF (skof) v.t. or i. to treat with scorn; mock;—n. mockery; derision. [Scand.]

SCOFFER (skof'er) n. one who scoffs.

SCOLD (skōld) v.t. or i. to chide rudely; rebuke; find fault;—n. a loud, clamorous woman. [D.]

SCOLDING (skōl'ding) n. act of chiding.

SCONCE (skons) n. a hanging candlestick; a bulwark; fort; headpiece; skull. [O.F. esconse, a hiding-place, also a dark lantern, fr. L. (part.) absconsus, of abscondere, to hide. Cf. ABSCOND.]

SCOOP (skoop) n. a large ladle or shovel;— v.t. to cut into a hollow; dig out; lade out. [Scand.]

SCOOP-NET (skoop'net) n. a net to sweep the bottom of a river.

SCOPE (skōp) n. sweep or range of the eye or mind; space; intention; drift. [It., fr. G. skopos, a mark, fr. skopein, to view.]

SCORBUTIC (skor-bū'tik) a. pertaining to, or diseased with, scurvy. [Late L. scorbutus, scurvy, fr. Teut.]

SCORCH (skorch) v.t. or i. to burn slightly; parch or shrivel; be burnt on the surface; be dried up. [O.F. escorcher, to flay, fr. L. ex, off, and stem cortic-, of cortex, bark.]

SCORE (skōr) n. a notch; twenty; a reckoning; account;—v.t. to notch; mark. [M.E., fr. Scand. Cf. SHEAR.]

SCORIA (skō'ri-a) n. dross or slag of metals in the furnace;—pl. SCORIÆ, volcanic ashes. [L., fr. G. skoria, dross, scum.]

SCORIFICATION (skō-ri-fi-kā'shun) n. act of reducing to dross.

SCORIFY (skō'ri-fi) v.t. to reduce to scoria. [G. skoria, dross, and L. facere, make.]

SCORIOUS (skō'ri-us) a. drossy.

SCORN (skorn) n. extreme contempt; object of contempt;—v.t. to hold in contempt; despise. [O.F. escorner, to mock at.]

SCORNER (skor'ner) n. one who scorns; a scoffer.

SCORNFUL (skorn'fool) a. disdainful; contemptuous.

SCORNFULLY (skorn'fool-i) ad. with disdain.

SCORPION (skor'pi-un) n. a reptile; the eighth sign of the zodiac. [F., fr. L., fr. G. skorpios.]

SCOT (skot) n. a portion of money assessed or paid; a tax; a fine. [O.F. escot, payment; fr. Icel. skot, a contribution. Cf. SHOOT.]

SCOT (skot) n. a native of Scotland. [O.E. Scottas, the Scots.]

SCOTCH (skoch) (1) a. pertaining to Scotland;—(2) to stop a wheel;—(3) v.t. cut slightly. [(1) Prov. E. (3) Scand.]

SCOTCHMAN (skoch'man) n. a native of Scotland. Also SCOTSMAN.

SCOT-FREE (skot'frē) a. excused from payment; unhurt.

SCOTTICISM (skot'i-sizm) n. an idiom of the Scots.

SCOTTISH (skot'ish) a. pertaining to Scotland.

SCOUNDREL (skoun'drel) n. a mean rascal. [Lowland Scots scunner, to disgust, fr. scunian, to shun, lit. one that shrinks, a loathsome fellow.]

SCOUNDRELISM (skoun'drel-izm) n. conduct of a scoundrel.

SCOUR (skour) v.t. to clean by rubbing; pass over quickly; range; purge violently. [O.F. escurer, fr. L. ex, and curare, to take great care of.]

SCOURER (skour'er) n. one who or that which scours.

SCOURGE (skurj) *n.* a whip; a lash;—*v.t.* to chastise. [O.F. *escorge*, fr. L. (part.) *excoriatus*, of *excoriare*, to flay off, fr. *corium*, leather.]

SCOURGER (skur'jer) *n.* one who scourges.

SCOUT (skout) (1) *n.* one sent to discover the movements of an enemy; a college servant;—*v.t.* to act as a scout;—(2) *v.t.* to sneer at; reject with disdain. [(1) O.F. *escoute*, a spy fr. L. *auscultare*, listen. fr. *auris* the ear. (2) Icel.]

SCOW (skow) *n.* a flat-bottomed boat. [D.]

SCOWL (skowl) *v.i.* to wrinkle the brows in displeasure;—*n.* a look of sullenness or anger. [Scand.]

SCRABBLE (skrab'l) *v.t.* or *i.* to scrape rudely; scribble. [Variant of *scrapple*, freq. of SCRAPE.]

SCRAG (skrag) *n.* something lean and thin. [Scand.]

SCRAGGINESS (skrag'i-nes) *n.* ruggedness of surface; leanness.

SCRAGGY (skrag'i) *a.* broken; lean and rough.

SCRAMBLE (skram'bl) *v.i.* to catch eagerly; climb;—*n.* act of scrambling or climbing. [Prov. E., allied to SCRABBLE.]

SCRAMBLER (skram'bler) *n.* one who scrambles.

SCRAMBLING (skram'bling) *n.* act of climbing;—*a.* straggling.

SCRANNEL (skran'el) *n.* slight; slender. [Prov. E. *scrannel*, lean.]

SCRAP (skrap) *n.* a little piece; fragment; crumb. [Scand.]

SCRAP-BOOK (skrap'book) *n.* blank book for preserving prints, extracts, etc.

SCRAPE (skrāp) *v.t.* to rub with something; remove by rubbing; collect together; save;—*v.i.* to make a harsh noise; play badly;—*n.* a bad situation; difficulty; a bow. [Scand.]

SCRAPER (skrā'per) *n.* an instrument for scraping and cleaning.

SCRAPING (skrā'ping) *n.* that which is rubbed off by scraping.

SCRATCH (skrach) *v.t.* or *i.* to tear the surface with the nails or claws;—*n.* a slight wound a sort of wig;—*pl.* ulcers on a horse's foot. [Scand.]

SCRATCHER (skrach'er) *n.* he or that which scratches.

SCRATCH-WIG (skrach'wig) *n.* a wig that covers only a part of the head.

SCRAWL (skrawl) *v.t.* or *i.* to write or mark awkwardly;—*n.* hasty or irregular writing. [Contr. of SCRABBLE.]

SCREAM (skrēm) *v.i.* to utter a shrill cry;—*n.* a shrill outcry. [Scand.]

SCREAMER (skrē'mer) *n.* an American wading bird.

SCREECH (skrēch) *v.i.* to shriek;—*n.* a harsh cry. [Scand. Cf. SHRIEK.]

SCREED (skrēd) *n.* a straight piece of wood by which the surface of plastering is levelled; a long piece. [O.E. *screade*, a shred.]

SCREEN (skrēn) *v.t.* to shelter; defend;—*n.* something that shelters; a partition. [O.F. *escren*=F. *écran*, fr. Teut.]

Screw.

SCREW (skrōō) *n.* a cylinder grooved spirally, and used as an engine of pressure;—*v.t.* to fasten with a screw; press; twist; oppress. [O.F. *escroue*.]

SCREW-DRIVER (skrōō'drī-ver) *n.* a tool for turning screw-nails.

SCREW-NAIL (skrōō'nāl) *n.* a small nail grooved like a screw.

SCRIBBLE (skrib'l) *v.t.* or *i.* to write without care; scrawl;—*n.* careless writing. [Freq. of SCRIBE, fr. L. *scribere*, write.]

SCRIBBLER (skrib'ler) *n.* a petty writer.

SCRIBE (skrib) *n.* a writer; notary; clerk; a doctor of law. [F., fr. L. *scriba*, fr. *scribere*, write.]

SCRIMMAGE (skrim'ij) *n.* a close, confused struggle. [Cf. SKIRMISH.]

SCRIMP (skrimp) *v.t.* to make too small or short; limit; stint;—*a.* short; scanty;—*n.* a miser. [O.E. *scrimpan*.]

SCRIP (skrip) (1) *n.* a bag;—(2) *n.* a certificate of stock. [(1) A.F. *escrepe*, fr. Scand. (2) Variant of SCRIPT, fr. L. (part.) *scriptus*, of *scribere*, to write.]

SCRIPT (skript) *n.* type in the form of written letters. [O.F. *escript*, fr. L. *scribere*.]

SCRIPTURAL (skrip'tū-ral) *a.* according to the Scriptures.

SCRIPTURE (skrip'tūr) *n.* the Old and New Testaments. [L. *scriptura*, fr. *scribere*, write.]

SCRIVENER (skriv'e-ner) *n.* one who draws contracts. [Orig. *scriven*, fr. O.F. *escrivain* =F. *écrivain*, fr. Late L. *scribanus*, fr. *scriba*, a scribe, fr. *scribere*.]

SCROFULA (skrof'ū-la) *n.* a disease affecting the glands, especially of the neck. [L. *scrofulæ*, fr. *scrofula*, dim. of *scrofa*, a sow.]

SCROFULOUS (skrof'ū-lus) *a.* diseased with scrofula.

SCROG (skrog) *n.* a thick, stunted shrub. [M.E. Cf. SCRAG.]

SCROGGY (skrog'l) *a.* thick and bushy.

SCROLL (skrōl) *n.* a roll of paper; a writing rolled up; a rough draft; architectural ornament. [Dim. of M.E. *scrowe*, fr. O.F. *escroue*.]

SCRUB (skrub) *n.* a worn brush; a mean drudge;—*v.t.* or *i.* to rub hard with something coarse. [O.E. *scrob*, a shrub.]

SCRUBBY (skrub'i) *a.* small; stunted; penurious.

SCRUPLE (skrōō'pl) *n.* a doubt; a weight of twenty grains;—*v.t.* or *i.* to doubt; hesitate. [F. *scrupule*, fr. L. *scrupulus*, a small stone, fr. *scrupus*, a sharp stone, anxiety.]

SCRUPULOSITY (skrōō-pū-los'i-ti) *n.* quality of being scrupulous.

SCRUPULOUS (skrōō'pū-lus) *a.* having doubts; cautious; conscientious.

SCRUPULOUSLY (skrōō'pū-lus-li) *ad.* with doubt or nicety.

SCRUTINEER (skrōō-ti-nēr') *n.* one who examines the votes at an election.

SCRUTINISE (skrōō'ti-nīz) *v.i.* to examine closely; investigate.

SCRUTINISER (skrōō'ti-nī-zer) *n.* one who searches closely.

SCRUTINOUS (skrōō'ti-nus) *a.* closely examining; captious.

SCRUTINY (skrōō'ti-ni) *n.* close inquiry; minute examination; examining the votes at an election. [O.F. *scrutine*, fr. L. *scrutinium*, fr. *scrutare*, to search even to the rags fr. *scruta*, trash.]

SCUD (skud) *v.i.* to run quickly; run before the wind in a gale;—*n.* act of running; loose vapoury clouds. [Scand.]

SCUFFLE (skuf'l) *n.* a confused quarrel;—*v.i.* to strive with close embraces. [Cf. SHUFFLE.]

SCUFFLER (skut'ler) *n.* one who scuffles.

SCULL (skul) *n.* a short oar; a boat;—*v.t.* to impel by oars, or by turning an oar at the stern. [Scand.]

SCULLER (skul'er) *n.* one who sculls; a boat rowed by two sculls.

SCULLERY (skul'er-i) *n.* a place for kitchen utensils. [O.F. *escuelle*, a dish fr. L. *scutella*, a salver; or, *sculler-y*, a variant of SVILLER. See SWILL.]

SCULLION (skul'yun) *n.* one that cleans kitchen utensils. [O.F. *escouillon*, a dishclout, fr. L. *scopa*, a broom.]

SCULPTILE (skulp'til) *a.* formed by sculpture.

SCULPTOR (skulp'tẹr) *n.* an artist in sculpture.

SCULPTURAL (skulp'tū-rạl) *a.* pertaining to sculpture.

SCULPTURE (skulp'tūr) *n.* the art of carving wood or stone into images; carved work; —*v.t.* to carve. [F., fr. L. *sculptura*, fr. (part.) *sculptus*, of *sculpere*, to carve.]

SCUM (skum) *n.* froth on the surface of liquor; —*v.t.* to take off the scum. [Scand.]

SCUMBLE (skum'bl) *v.t.* to spread or cover a painting with opaque colours to soften the effect. [Freq. of **SCUM**.]

SCUMMER (skum'ẹr). See **SKIMMER**.

SCUMMINGS (skum'ingz) *n.pl.* scum from boiling liquors.

SCUPPER (skup'ẹr) *n.* a hole to discharge water from the deck of a ship. [O.F. *escopir*, to spit out, fr. L. *expuere*, fr. *ex*, out, and *spuere*, to spit; or fr. D.]

SCURF (skurf) *n.* flaky matter formed on the skin; anything adhering to the surface. [O.E., fr. *sceorfan*, to scrape. Cf. Ger. *Schorf*.]

SCURFINESS (skur'fi-nes) *n.* state of being scurfy.

SCURFY (skur'fi) *a.* having scurf.

SCURRILITY (sku-ril'i-ti) *n.* vulgar, abusive language.

SCURRILOUS (skur'i-lus) *a.* grossly abusive; foul-mouthed. Also **SCURILE**. [L., *scurrilis*, fr. *scurra*, a buffoon.]

SCURRILOUSLY (skur'i-lus-li) *ad.* with low abuse.

SCURRY (skur'i) *v.i.* to hurry along; to scamper;—*n.* hurry; a flurry. [Fr. **SCOUR**.]

SCURVILY (skur'vi-li) *ad.* meanly.

SCURVY (skur'vi) *n.* a disease of the blood; —*a.* scurfy; low; mean. [Fr. **SCURF**.]

SCUTCHEON (skuch'un). See **ESCUTCHEON**.

SCUTTLE (skut'l) (1) *n.* a metal pail for coals;—(2) *a* hatchway; opening in the roof of a house;—*v.t.* or *i.* to cut large holes in a ship; sink by doing so in its bottom;—(3) *v.t.* or *i.* run away. [(1) O.E. *scutel*, fr. L. *scutella*, a dish, dim. of *scutra*, a dish. (2) O.F. *escoutille*, a hatchway, fr. D. (3) Scand. Cf. **SCUD**.]

SCYTHE (sīth) *n.* an instrument for mowing grass. [O.E. *sithe*.]

SEA (sē) *n.* a large body of salt water; ocean; high waves; surge; volume. [O.E. *sæ*.]

SEABOARD (sē'bōrd) *n.* the sea-shore;—*a.* adjoining the sea.

SEA-BORN (sē'born) *a.* born on the ocean.

SEA-BREACH (sē'brēch) *n.* an irruption of the sea.

SEA-BREEZE (sē'brēz) *n.* a current of air from the sea.

SEA-CALF (sē'käf) *n.* the seal.

SEA-CHART (sē'chärt) *n.* a chart of the sea-coast.

SEA-COAST (sē'kōst) *n.* the shore of the sea.

SEA-DOG (sē'dog) *n.* the dog-fish; seal; an old sailor.

SEAFARER (sē'fār-ẹr) *n.* a mariner; a seaman.

SEAFARING (sē'fār-ing) *a.* going to sea; employed in navigation.

SEA-FIGHT (sē'fīt) *n.* a naval engagement.

SEA-GAGE (sē'gāj) *n.* depth that a vessel sinks in water.

SEA-GIRT (sē'gẹrt) *a.* surrounded by the ocean.

SEA-GREEN (sē'grēn) *a.* having the colour of sea-water.

SEA-HORSE (sē'hors) *n.* the walrus; hippopotamus.

SEA-KALE (sē'kāl) *n.* a plant of the cabbage tribe.

SEAL (sēl) (1) *n.* a marine animal, fished for its oil and skin;—(2) *n.* a stamp with a device on it; wax impressed with a seal; —*v.t.* to fix a seal; fasten with a seal; ratify; confirm. [(1) O.E. *seolh*. (2) O.F. *seel*, fr. L. *sigillum*, a seal, dim. of *signum*, a mark.]

SEALER (sē'lẹr) *n.* one who seals.

SEALING (sē'ling) *n.* the business of fishing for seals.

SEALING-WAX (sē'ling-waks) *n.* a substance for sealing letters.

SEAM (sēm) *n.* the joining of two edges of cloth;—*v.t.* to join by sewing; make a seam in; scar. [O.E. *seam*, fr. *sewian*, to sew.]

SEAMAN (sē'man) *n.* a sailor.

SEAMANSHIP (sē'man-ship) *n.* skill in navigating.

SEAMLESS (sēm'les) *a.* having no seam.

SEA-MARK (sē'märk) *n.* a beacon; lighthouse.

SEAMSTER (sēm'stẹr) *n.* one who sews.

SEAMSTRESS (sēm'stres) *n.* a female whose occupation is sewing.

SEAMY (sē'mi) *a.* containing seams; showing them.

SEANCE (sā'ängs) *n.* session or sitting of a public body; a meeting of spiritualists. [F., fr. L. *sedere*, sit.]

SEA-PIE (sē'pī) *n.* a dish of paste and meat.

SEA-PIECE (sē'pēs) *n.* picture of a scene at sea.

SEAPORT (sē'pōrt) *n.* a harbour on the sea-coast.

SEAR (sēr) *v.t.* to burn the surface of anything; cauterise; make insensible;—*a.* dry; withered. [O.E. *sear*, dry.]

SEARCH (sẹrch) *v.t.* or *i.* to look or seek for; examine; investigate; put to the test;—*n.* a seeking; quest. [O.F. and F. *chercher*, fr. L. *circare*, go about, fr. *circus*, a circle.]

SEARCHABLE (sẹr'cha-bl) *a.* that may be searched.

SEARCHER (sẹr'chẹr) *n.* one who searches.

SEARCHING (sẹr'ching) *a.* trying; close.

SEAREDNESS (sēr'ed-nes) *n.* state of being hardened; insensibility.

SEA-ROOM (sē'rōōm) *n.* ample distance from land.

SEA-SHELL (sē'shel) *n.* a marine shell.

SEA-SHORE (sē'shōr) *n.* the coast of the sea; land adjacent to the sea.

SEASICK (sē'sik) *a.* affected with nausea at sea.

SEASIDE (sē'sīd) *n.* land near the sea.

SEASON (sē'zn) *n.* a division of the year; any time; period of time; fit or usual time;—*v.t.* or *i.* to prepare for use; accustom; give relish to; moderate; become fit or inured. [O.F. *seson* =F. *saison*, fr. L. (acc.) *sationem*, seed-time, fr. *serere*, sow.]

SEASONABLE (sē'zn-a-bl) *a.* in good time or season; opportune.

SEASONING (sē'zn-ing) *n.* that which seasons; act of drying.

SEAT (sēt) *n.* a chair; bench; place of sitting; mansion;—*v.t.* to place on a seat. [Icel.]

SEATING (sē'ting) *n.* material for seats.

SEAWARD (sē'ward) *a.* or *ad.* toward the sea.

SEAWEED (sē'wēd) *n.* a marine plant.

SEAWORTHINESS (sē'wur-THi-nes) *n.* fitness for a voyage.

SEAWORTHY (sē'wur-THi) *a.* able to encounter the violence of the sea.

SEBACEOUS (se-bā'shus) *a.* fat; like fat. [Late L. *sebaceus*, fr. L. *sebum*, tallow.]

SECANCY (sē'kạn-si) *n.* intersection.

Secant.

SECANT (sē'kạnt) *n.* a line that cuts another;—*a.* cutting. [L. (part. stem) *secant-*, of *secare*, to cut.]

SECEDE (se-sēd') *v.i.* to withdraw from fellowship or association. [L. *se*, aside, and *cedere*, go.]

SECEDER (se-sē'dẹr) *n.* one who secedes.

SECERN (se-sẹrn') *v.t.* to distinguish; secrete. [L. *se*, aside, and *cernere*, separate.]

SECERNENT (se-sẹr'nent) *a.* secreting;—*n.* a secreting vessel.

SECESSION (se-sesh'un) *n.* act of seceding.

SECLUDE (se-klŏŏd') *v.t.* to shut in retirement. [L. *secludere*, fr. *se*, aside, and *claudere*, shut.]

SECLUSION (se-klŏŏ'zhun) *n.* act of withdrawing; retirement. [L. (acc.) *seclusionem*, fr. (part.) *seclusus*.]

SECLUSIVE (se-klŏŏ'siv) *a.* that keeps in retirement.

SECOND (sek'und) *a.* following the first; original of two; next in position; inferior; —*n.* the next to the first; the sixtieth part of a minute; attendant in a duel;—*v.t.* to support; aid. [L. *secundus*, fr. *sequi*, follow.]

SECONDARY (sek'un-dạ-ri) *a.* subordinate.

SECONDER (sek'un-dẹr) *n.* supporter of a motion.

SECOND-HAND (sek'und-hand) *a.* not new.

SECONDLY (sek'und-li) *ad.* in the second place.

SECONDS (sek'undz) *n.pl.* a coarse kind of flour.

SECRECY (sē'kre-si) *n.* close privacy.

SECRET (sē'kret) *a.* concealed; unseen; reserved;—*n.* something unknown or hidden. [L. (part.) *secretus*, of *secernere*, put apart, fr. *se*, aside, and *cernere*, to separate.]

SECRETARY (sek're-tạ-ri) *n.* one who writes for others; the chief officer of a department. [O.F., fr. L. *secretum*, a secret.]

SECRETE (se-krēt') *v.t.* to put in a secret place; hide; conceal; separate and form, as sap, blood, etc.

SECRETION (se-krē'shun) *n.* act of secreting; matter or fluid secreted.

SECRETIVE (se-krē'tiv) *a.* pertaining to secretion; keeping secrets.

SECRETIVENESS (se-krē'tiv-nes) *n.* quality of being secretive; bump or organ of secrecy.

SECRETLY (sē'kret-li) *ad.* in a secret manner.

SECRETNESS (sē'kret-nes) *n.* state of being secret; keeping secret.

SECRETORY (se-krē'tu-ri) *a.* performing secretion.

SECT (sekt) *n.* men united in tenets. [F. *secte*, fr. L. *secta*, a school of philosophy, fr. (part.) *sectus*, of *secare*, to cut.]

SECTARIAN (sek-tā'ri-ạn) *a.* pertaining to a sect;—*n.* one of a sect.

SECTARIANISM (sek-tā'ri-ạn-izm) *n.* devotion to a sect.

SECTARY (sek'tạ-ri) *n.* a follower of a sect.

SECTION (sek'shun) *n.* a cutting off; part cut off; division; portion; intersection. [L., fr. *secare*, cut off.]

SECTIONAL (sek'shun-ạl) *a.* pertaining to a section.

SECTOR (sek'tẹr) *n.* a mathematical instrument. [Fr. L. *secare*, cut.]

SECULAR (sek'ū-lạr) *a.* worldly; not spiritual; —*n.* a layman. [L. *seculus*, fr. *seculum*, a generation.]

SECULARISE (sek'ū-lạr-iz) *v.t.* to convert to a secular use.

SECULARITY (sek-ū-lar'i-ti) *n.* a worldly disposition.

SECURE (se-kūr') *a.* free from fear or danger; safe;—*v.t.* to make safe; guarantee; fasten; get possession of. [L. *securus*, without care, fr. *se*, for *sine*, without, and *cura*, care.]

SECURELY (se-kūr'li) *ad.* so as to be safe.

SECURER (se-kū'rẹr) *n.* he or that which secures.

SECURITY (se-kū'ri-ti) *n.* freedom from danger; safety; pledge.

SEDAN (se-dan') *n.* a carriage for one, carried by two men. [Fr. *Sedan*, in France, where it was first made.]

SEDATE (se-dāt') *a.* composed; unruffled; calm and serious. [L. (part.) *sedatus*, of *sedare*, allay. Cf. *sedere*, to sit.]

SEDATELY (se-dāt'li) *ad.* with composure.

SEDATENESS (se-dāt'nes) *n.* calmness; serenity.

SEDATIVE (sed'ạ-tiv) *a.* allaying irritation; —*n.* a medicine that allays.

SEDENTARY (sed'en-tạ-ri) *a.* sitting much; requiring a sitting posture. [L. *sedentarius*, fr. *sedere*, to sit.]

SEDERUNT (se-dē'runt) *n.* a sitting or meeting of a court. [L. = ' they sat,' fr. *sedere*, to sit.]

SEDGE (sej) *n.* a coarse grass growing in swamps. [O.E. *secg*.]

SEDIMENT (sed'i-ment) *n.* that which settles at the bottom; lees. [L. *sedimentum*, fr. *sedere*, settle.]

SEDIMENTARY (sed-i-men'tạ-ri) *a.* pertaining to sediment.

SEDITION (se-dish'un) *n.* commotion against the state; insurrection. [L. (acc.) *seditionem*, fr. *se*, away, and (part.) *itus*, of *ire*, to go.]

SEDITIOUS (se-dish'us) *a.* engaged in sedition.

SEDUCE (se-dūs') *v.t.* to lead astray; corrupt. [L. *se*, aside, and *ducere*, lead.]

SEDUCER (se-dū'sẹr) *n.* one who seduces.

SEDUCIBLE (se-dū'si-bl) *a.* that may be seduced.

SEDUCTION (se-duk'shun) *n.* an enticing from virtue.

SEDUCTIVE (se-duk'tiv) *a.* enticing to evil.

SEDUCTIVELY (se-duk'tiv-li) *ad.* by seduction.

SEDULITY (se-dū'li-ti) *n.* great diligence; constant attention.

SEDULOUS (sed'ū-lus) *a.* very diligent; steady and persevering. [L. *sedulus*, fr. *sedere*, sit.]

SEDULOUSLY (sed'ū-lus-li) *ad.* with application; assiduously.

SEE (sē) (1) *n.* the seat of episcopal power; a diocese;—(2) *v.t.* [pret. SAW; pp. SEEN] to perceive by the eye; behold; discover; visit. [(1) F., fr. L. *sedes*, a seat. (2) O.E. *seon*. Cf. Ger. *sehen*.]

SEED (sēd) *n.* that which produces animals or plants; original; offspring; race;—*v.t.* or *i.* to sow; shed seed. [O.E. *sœd*, fr. *sawan*, sow.]

SEED-BUD (sēd'bud) *n.* germ of fruit.

SEED-CAKE (sēd'kāk) *n.* a sweet cake with aromatic seeds.

SEEDINESS (sē'di-nes) *n.* state of being seedy.

SEEDLING (sēd'ling) *n.* a plant springing from a seed.

SEEDSMAN (sēdz'man) *n.* one who deals in seeds.

SEED-TIME (sēd'tim) *n.* the time for sowing.

SEED-VESSEL (sēd'ves-el) *n.* the pericarp or case which contains the seed.

SEEDY (sē'di) *a.* full of seeds; run to seed; shabby; tipsy.

SEEING (sē'ing) *n.* vision;—*conj.* since.

SEEK (sēk) *v.t.* or *i.* [pret. and pp. SOUGHT] to look for; try to find or gain; solicit; endeavour. [O.E. *secan*, to follow. Cf. Ger. *suchen*.]

SEEM (sēm) *v.t.* to befit; become;—*v.i.* to appear; look like. [O.E. *seman*, to suit; or fr. Scand.]

SEEMING (sē'ming) *a.* appearing like; specious; —*n.* appearance; semblance.

SEEMINGLY (sē'ming-li) *ad.* in appearance.

SEEMLINESS (sēm'li-nes) *n.* comeliness.

SEEMLY (sēm'li) *a.* becoming; decent;—*ad.* in a suitable manner.

SEEN (sēn) *pp.* of SEE, perceived.

SEER (sēr) *n.* a prophet.

SEESAW (sē'saw) *n.* a reciprocating motion up and down or to and fro;—*v.i.* to move in this way. From the verb SAW.]

SEETHE (sēTH) *v.t.* to boil; decoct;—*v.i.* to be boiling. [O.E. *seothan*.]

SEETHER (sē'THẹr) *n.* a pot for boiling things.

SEGMENT (seg'ment) *n.* a part cut off; section; portion. [L. *segmentum*, fr. *secare*, cut.]

SEGREGATE (seg're-gāt) *v.t.* to separate; set apart. [L. (part.) *segregatus*, of *segregare*, fr. *se*, apart, and (stem) *greg-*, of *grex*, a flock.]

SEGREGATION (seg-re-gā'shun) *n.* separation from others.

SEIDLITZ (sed'litz) *n.* a saline water in Bohemia; a saline aperient powder. [*Seidlitz*, in Bohemia.]

SEIGNEURIAL (sē-nyòò'ri-al) *a.* manorial.

SEIGNIOR (sē'nyur) *n.* a lord. [F., fr. L. *senior*, elder, fr. *senex*, old.]

SEIGNIORAGE (sē'nyur-ij) *n.* a royal right.

SEIGNIORY (sē'nyur-i) *n.* a lordship; a manor.

SEINE (sēn, sān) *n.* a large fishing net. [F., fr. L. *sagena*, fr. G. *sagēne*, a fishing net.]

SEISMIC (sis'mik) *a.* belonging to earthquakes. [G. *seismos*, an earthquake.]

SEISMOLOGY (sīs-mol'ō-ji) *n.* science of earthquakes. [G. *seismos*, an earthquake, and *logos*, discourse.]

SEIZABLE (sē'za-bl) *a.* liable to seizure.

SEIZE (sēz) *v.t.* to take suddenly; grasp; apprehend. [O.F. *saisir*, fr. Teut.]

SEIZER (sē'zer) *n.* one who seizes.

SEIZIN (sē'zin) *n.* possession in deed or in law. [F. *saisine*.]

SEIZOR (sē'zer) *n.* one who takes possession.

SEIZURE (sē'zūr) *n.* act of seizing; the thing seized.

SELAH (sē'lä) *n.* in the Psalms, a pause or silence. [H.]

SELDOM (sel'dum) *ad.* rarely; not often. [O.E.]

SELECT (se-lekt') *v.t.* to choose from a number; pick out; cull;—*a.* taken from a number; well chosen. [L. (part.) *selectus*, of *seligere*, fr. *se*, aside, and *legere*, to choose.]

SELECTION (se-lek'shun) *n.* act of choosing; thing selected; a book of select pieces.

SELECTNESS (se-lekt'nes) *n.* the state of being select.

SELENOGRAPHY (sel-e-nog'ra-fi) *n.* a description of the surface of the moon. [G. *selene*, the moon, and *graphein*, describe.]

SELF (self) *pron.* or *a.* same;—*n.* one's own person; personal interest. [O.E.]

SELF-DENIAL (self-de-nī'al) *n.* the denial of personal gratification.

SELF-ESTEEM (self-es-tēm') *n.* good opinion of oneself. Also SELF-CONCEIT.

SELF-EVIDENT (self-ev'i-dent) *a.* needing no proof.

SELF-INTEREST (self-in'ter-est) *n.* selfishness.

SELFISH (sel'fish) *a.* regarding one's own interest solely.

SELFISHLY (sel'fish-li) *ad.* with undue self-love.

SELFISHNESS (sel'fish-nes) *n.* regard to one's own interest solely.

SELF-LOVE (self-luv') *n.* love of self.

SELF-SAME (self'sām) *a.* exactly the same; identical.

SELF-WILL (self-wil') *n.* one's own will; obstinacy.

SELL (sel) *v.t.* [*pret.* and *pp.* SOLD] to transfer property for money; betray for money;—*v.i.* to be sold; practise selling. [O.E. *sellan*, to hand over.]

SELLER (sel'er) *n.* one who sells.

SELVAGE (sel'vij) *n.* the edge of cloth. Also written SELVEDGE. [O.D.]

SELVES (selvz) *pl.* of SELF.

SEMBLANCE (sem'blans) *n.* likeness; appearance. [F. *sembler*, to resemble, fr. L. *similis*, like.]

SEMEIOLOGY (sē-mī-ol'ō-ji) *n.* doctrine of symptoms in disease. [G. *semeion*, a mark, *legein*, to say.]

SEMI-ANNUAL (sem-i-an'ū-al) *a.* half-yearly. [L. *semi*, half.]

SEMIBREVE (sem'i-brēv) *n.* a note of two minims. [L. *semi*, half.]

SEMICIRCLE (sem'i-ser'kl) *n.* half of a circle. [L. *semi*, half.]

SEMICOLON (sem'i-kō-lun) *n.* a point marked thus (;). [L. *semi*, half.]

Semicircle.

SEMI-DIAMETER (sem-i-dī-am'e-ter) *n.* half a diameter. [L. *semi*, half.]

SEMINAL (sem'i-nal) *a.* pertaining to seed; original; radical. [L. *semen*, stem *semin-*, of seed, fr. *serere*, sow.]

SEMINALITY (sem-i-nal'i-ti) *n.* power of producing or being produced.

SEMINARY (sem'i-na-ri) *n.* a place of education; college; academy.

SEMINATE (sem'i-nāt) *v.t.* to sow; propagate.

SEMINATION (sem-i-nā'shun) *n.* sowing; dispersion of seeds.

SEMIQUAVER (sem'i-kwā-ver) *n.* half a quaver. [L. *semi*, half.]

SEMITONE (sem'i-tōn) *n.* half a tone. [L. *semi*, half.]

SEMI-VOWEL (sem'i-vou-el) *n.* a consonant which makes an imperfect sound, as f, l, m, n, r, s. [L. *semi*, half.]

SEMOLINA (sem-u-lē'na) *n.* a preparation of the fine hard grains of wheat which do not pass through the sieve. [It. *semola*, fr. L. *simila*, fine wheat flour.]

SEMPITERNAL (sem-pi-ter'nal) *a.* everlasting. [L. *sempiternus*, fr. *semper*, always, and *eternus*, eternal.]

SEMPITERNITY (sem-pi-ter'ni-ti) *n.* duration without end.

SENARY (sen'a-ri) *a.* containing six. [L. *seni*, six each, fr. *sex*, six.]

SENATE (sen'at) *n.* a legislative body. [O.F. *senat*, fr. L. *senatus*, council of elders, fr. *senex*, *senis*, old, an old man.]

SENATOR (sen'a-ter) *n.* a member of a senate.

SENATORIAL (sen-a-tō'ri-al) *a.* pertaining to or becoming a senator.

SENATORSHIP (sen'a-tur-ship) *n.* the office of a senator.

SENATUS (se-nā'tus) *n.* the governing body in a university. [Cf. SENATE.]

SEND (send) *v.t.* or *i.* [*pret.* and *pp.* SENT] to cast or throw; cause to go or be conveyed; despatch; commission; diffuse; pitch forward. [O.E. *sendan*.]

SENESCENCE (se-nes'ens) *n.* a growing old. [L. (part. stein) *senescent-*, of *senescere*, to grow old, fr. *senex*, old.]

SENESCHAL (sen'e-shal) *n.* steward; head bailiff.

SENILE (sē'nil) *a.* belonging to old age. [L. *senilis*, fr. *senex*, old, an old man.]

SENILITY (se-nil'i-ti) *n.* old age.

SENIOR (sē'nyur) *n.* one older than another; —*a.* older in age or office. [L. comp. of *senex*, old.]

SENIORITY (sē-ni-or'i-ti) *n.* priority in age of office.

SENNA (sen'a) *n.* a leguminous plant and its leaves, which are cathartic. [It., fr. A.]

SENSATE (sen'sat) *a.* perceived by the senses. [L. *sensus*, feeling.]

SENSATION (sen-sā'shun) *n.* perception by the senses; excited feeling. [F., fr. L. (acc.) *sensationem*, fr. (part.) *sensus*, of *sentire*, to perceive.]

SENSE (sens) *n.* faculty by which external objects are perceived. [L. (part.) *sensus*, of *sentire*, to feel, to perceive.]

SENSELESS (sens'les) *a.* wanting sense or feeling; foolish.

SENSELESSLY (sens'les-li) *ad.* without sense; foolishly.

SENSIBILITY (sen-si-bil'i-ti) *n.* capability of sensation; acuteness of feeling; quick sympathy.

SENSIBLE (sen'si-bl) *a.* perceptible by the senses or mind; easily affected; cognisant; intelligent.

SENSIBLY (sen'si-bli) *ad.* perceptibly; with good sense.

SENSITIVE (sen'si-tiv) *a.* having acute sensibility; highly susceptible; shrinking from the touch.

SENSITIVELY (sen'si-tiv-li) *ad.* with nice sensibility.

SENSITIVENESS (sen'si-tiv-nes) *n.* the state or quality of being sensitive.

SENSITIVE-PLANT (sen'si-tiv-plant) *n.* a leguminous plant, the leaves of which shrink when touched.

SENSORIAL (sen-sō'ri-al) *a.* pertaining to the sensorium.

SENSORIUM (sen-sō'ri-um) *n.* the organ of sensation, supposed to be in the brain. [L. *sensus,* feeling.]

SENSUAL (sen'sū-al) *a.* pertaining or derived from the senses; carnal; voluptuous. [L. *sensus,* feeling.]

SENSUALISE (sen'sū-a-liz) *v.t.* to make sensual; debase by sensual pleasures.

SENSUALISM (sen'sū-al-izm) *n.* a state of subjection to sensual feelings or appetites.

SENSUALIST (sen'sū-al-ist) *n.* one devoted to sensuality.

SENSUALITY (sen-sū-al'i-ti) *n.* indulgence of sensual pleasures.

SENSUOUS (sen'sū-us) *n.* addressing the senses; connected with sensible objects.

SENT (sent) *pret.* and *pp.* of SEND.

SENTENCE (sen'tens) *n.* a judgment pronounced; a short saying; a period in writing;—*v.t.* to doom. [L. *sententia,* a way of thinking, fr. *sentire,* feel.]

SENTENTIAL (sen-ten'shal) *a.* comprising sentences.

SENTENTIOUS (sen-ten'shus) *a.* short and pithy.

SENTENTIOUSLY (sen-ten'shus-li) *ad.* in a sententious manner.

SENTENTIOUSNESS (sen-ten'shus-nes) *n.* quality of being sententious.

SENTIENCE (sen'shi-ens) *n.* faculty of perception or sensation. Also SENTIENCY.

SENTIENT (sen'shi-ent) *a.* having the faculty of perception. [L. (part. stem) *sentient-,* of *sentire,* feel.]

SENTIMENT (sen'ti-ment) *n.* a thought prompted by feeling; sensibility; opinion. [O.F. *sentement,* fr. L. *sentire,* to perceive.]

SENTIMENTAL (sen-ti-men'tal) *a.* abounding with sentiment.

SENTIMENTALIST (sen-ti-men'tal-ist) *n.* one who affects fine feelings.

SENTIMENTALITY (sen-ti-men-tal'i-ti) *n.* affectation of sensibility. Also SENTIMENTALISM.

SENTINEL (sen'ti-nel) *n.* a soldier on guard. [O.F. *sentinelle,* fr. L. *sentinella,* a watch, or fr. F. *sentinelle,* a dim. of *sentier,* a path.]

SENTRY (sen'tri) *n.* a soldier on guard; the duty of a sentinel. [O.F. *senteret,* a path, dim. of *sente,* fr. L. *semita,* a path.]

SEPARABLE (sep'a-ra-bl) *a.* that may be separated.

SEPARABILITY (sep-a-ra-bil'i-ti) *n.* quality of being separable.

SEPARATE (sep'a-rāt) *v.t.* or *i.* to disunite; withdraw;—*a.* divided; distinct. [L. (part.) *separatus,* of *separare,* to sever, fr. *se,* aside, and *parare,* to prepare.]

SEPARATELY (sep'a-rat-li) *ad.* singly; distinctly.

SEPARATION (sep-a-rā'shun) *n.* a disjunction; divorce.

SEPARATIST (sep'a-ra-tist) *n.* a dissenter.

SEPARATORY (sep'a-ra-tu-ri) *a.* serving to separate;—*n.* a chemical vessel for separating liquors.

SEPIA (sē'pi-a) *n.* the cuttle-fish; a dark or brown pigment;—*a.* denoting a drawing or sketch in water-colour with a dark background. [G. *sepia,* the cuttle-fish.]

SEPOY (sē'poi) *n.* a native of India in the military service of Europeans. [Hind. *sipahi,* horseman.]

SEPT (sept) *n.* a race; clan. [Perh. a variant of SECT.]

SEPTANGULAR (sep-tang'gū-lar) *a.* having seven angles. [L. *septem,* seven.]

SEPTEMBER (sep-tem'ber) *n.* the ninth month. [L.]

SEPTENARY (sep'te-na-ri, sep-ten'a-ri) *a.* consisting of seven. [L. *septenarius,* fr. *septem,* Septangular. seven.]

SEPTENNIAL (sep-ten'i-al) *a.* being every seventh year. [L. *septennis,* fr. *septem,* seven, and *annus,* year.]

SEPTIC (sep'tik) *a.* tending to promote putrefaction;—*n.* a substance promoting putrefaction. [G. *septikos,* putrefying.]

SEPTUAGENARIAN (sep-tū-a-je-nā'ri-an) *n.* one who is seventy years old. [L. *septuagenarius, septuaginta,* seventy.]

SEPTUAGESIMA (sep-tū-a-jes'i-ma) *n.* the third Sunday before Lent, (so called because it is seventy days before Easter.)

SEPTUAGINT (sep'tū-a-jint) *n.* the (LXX) Greek version of the Old Testament. [L. *septuaginta,* seventy.]

SEPULCHRAL (se-pul'kral) *a.* relating to burial; deep; hollow.

SEPULCHRE (sep'ul-ker) *n.* a grave; a tomb; —*v.t.* to bury. [O.F. *sepulcre,* fr. L. *sepulchrum,* fr. (part.) *sepultus,* of *sepelire,* bury.]

SEPULTURE (sep'ul-tūr) *n.* the act of burying a human being. [L., fr. *sepelire,* to bury.]

SEQUACIOUS (se-kwā'shus) *a.* following. [L. stem *sequae-,* of *sequor,* fr. *sequi,* follow.]

SEQUACITY (se-kwas'i-ti) *n.* tendency to follow.

SEQUEL (sē'kwel) *n.* a succeeding part. [F., fr. L. *sequela,* fr. *sequi,* follow.]

SEQUENCE (sē'kwens) *n.* order of succession; series.

SEQUENT (sē'kwent) *a.* following. [L. (part. stem) *sequent-,* of *sequi,* follow.]

SEQUESTER (se-kwes'ter) *v.t.* to separate; withdraw from; take possession of goods, property, etc., till claims are paid. [O.F. *sequestrer,* to sequester, fr. Late L. *sequestrare,* fr. *sequestor,* a depositary, fr. *sequi,* to follow.]

SEQUESTRATE se-kwes'trāt) *v.t.* to set apart.

SEQUESTRATION (sek-wes-trā'shun, se-kwes-trā'shun) *n.* a setting apart; seclusion.

SEQUESTRATOR (sek-wes-trā'ter, se-kwes-trā'ter) *n.* one who sequesters.

SERAGLIO (se-ral'yō) *n.* the palace of the Turkish sultan. [It. *serraglio,* fr. Late L. *serare,* to lock up, fr. L. *sera,* a door-bar. The word was confused with Per. *serai,* a palace.]

SERAPH (ser'af) *n.* an angel of the highest order. [H. *seraphim,* exalted ones.]

SERAPHIC (se-raf'ik) *a.* angelic; pure; sublime.

SERAPHIM (ser'a-fim) *n.pl.* of SERAPH.

SERE (sēr) *a.* dry; withered. [Cf. SEAR.]

SERENADE (ser-e-nād') *n.* music at night in the open air;—*v.t.* or *i.* to entertain with nocturnal music. [F., fr. It. *serenata,* fr. L. *serenus,* bright.]

SERENE (se-rēn') *a.* calm; unclouded; undisturbed; a title of honour. [L. *serenus,* clear.]

SERENELY (se-rēn'li) *ad.* calmly; quietly.

SERENITY (se-ren'i-ti) *n.* clearness; calmness.

SERF (serf) *n.* one in servitude; slave. [F., fr. L. *servus,* a slave.]

SERFDOM (serf'dum) *n.* state of a serf; slavery.

SERGE (serj) *n.* a thin woollen stuff. [F., fr. L. *sericus,* silken, belonging to the Seres, fr. G. *Seres,* Chinese.]

SERGEANCY (sár'jen-si) *n.* office of a sergeant.

SERGEANT, SERJEANT (sár'jent) *n.* a non-commissioned officer; a lawyer of the highest rank. [O.F *sergant* = F. *sergent*, fr. L. (part. stem) *servient-*, of *servire*, serve.]

SERIAL (sē'ri-al) *a.* pertaining to a series; —*n.* a tale, etc., issued in a series of numbers.

SERIALLY (sē'ri-al-i) *ad.* in a series.

SERIATE (sē'ri-at) *a.* arranged in a series. [L. *series*, a row.]

SERICEOUS (se-rish'us) *a.* silky. [L. *sericum*, silk, fr. G. *Seres*, Chinese.]

SERIES (sē'rēz, sē'ri-ēz) *n.* order; succession; course. [L. =a row, fr. *serere*, to join.]

SERIOUS (sē'ri-us) *a.* sober; grave. [F. *sérieux* fr. L. *serius*.]

SERIOUSLY (sē'ri-us-li) *ad.* gravely; solemnly; in earnest.

SERIOUSNESS (sē'ri-us-nes) *n.* gravity; earnest attention.

SERMON (ser'mun) *n.* a discourse on a text of Scripture. [L. (acc.) *sermonem*, of L. *sarmo*, a speaking, fr. *serere*, to join.]

SERMONISE (ser'mu-niz) *v.i.* to write or preach a sermon.

SERMONISER (ser'mu-ni-zer) *n.* one who writes sermons.

SEROSITY (se-ros'i-ti) *n.* the watery part of blood.

SEROUS (sē'rus) *a.* consisting of serum; thin; watery. [L. *serum*, whey.]

SERPENT (ser'pent) *n.* an animal that creeps; a firework; a bass wood musical instrument. [L. (part. stem) *serpent-*, of *serpere*, to creep, G. *herpein*.]

SERPENTINE (ser'pen-tin) *a.* winding, as a serpent;—*n.* a mineral.

SERRATE (ser'āt) *n.* indented like a saw. [L. *serratus*, fr. *serra*, a saw.]

SERRATURE (ser'a-tūr) *n.* a notching in the edge of anything.

SERRIED (ser'id) *a.* close; thick. [F. *serrer*, to press close, fr. L. *serare*, to bolt, fr. *serere*, to join.]

SERUM (sē'rum) *n.* thin part of the blood, or of milk. [L. whey, serum.]

SERVANT (ser'vant) *n.* one who labours for another.

SERVE (serv) *v.t.* to work for; obey; treat; deal out; be sufficient for; conduce to; worship;—*v.i.* to perform public or private duties; suit. [F. *servir*, fr. L. *servire*, serve.]

SERVER (ser'ver) *n.* one who serves; plate; salver.

SERVICE (ser'vis) *n.* duty of a servant; worship; military or naval duty; help; benefit; order or set of dishes. [L., fr. *servitium*, fr. *servire*, to serve.]

SERVICEABLE (ser'vi-sa-bl) *a.* that does service.

SERVILE (ser'vil) *a.* slavish; cringing.

SERVILITY (ser-vil'i-ti) *n.* mean submissiveness; obsequiousness.

SERVITOR (ser'vi-ter) *n.* a servant; an attendant. [L]

SERVITUDE (ser'vi-tūd) *n.* slavery; dependence.

SESAME (ses'a-me) *n.* an annual plant with oily seeds. [G. *sesame*, *sesamon*.]

SESSILE (ses'il) *a.* without a stalk. [L. *sessilis*, low, fr. (part.) *sessus*, of *sedere*, to sit.]

SESSION (sesh'un) *n.* a stated meeting of a public body; time or term of sitting. [L. (acc.) *sessionem*, fr. *sedere*, to sit.]

SESSIONAL (sesh'un-al) *a.* pertaining to sessions.

SET (set) *v.t.* or *i.* [*pret.* and *pp.* SET] to place; fix; determine; sharpen; spread; decline below the horizon; congeal; point;—*n.* a number of things suited to each other. [O.E. *settan.* Cf. Ger. *setzen.*]

SETACEOUS (se-tā'shus) *a.* bristly. [L. *seta*, a bristle.]

SET-OFF (set'of) *n.* an account set against another.

SETON (sē'tun) *n.* a thread to keep a wound open. [L. *seta*, a bristle.]

SETTEE (se-tē') *n.* a long seat with a back. [Perh. a variant of SETTLE.]

SETTER (set'er) *n.* a dog for hunting birds.

SETTLE (set'l) (1) *n.* a long bench with a. back;—(2) *v.t.* to establish; decide; compose; liquidate;—*v.i.* to sink down; become calm or clear; fix one's residence. [(1) O.E. *setl*, seat, fr. *sittan*, to sit. (2) O.E. *setlan*, fix.]

SETTLEMENT (set'l-ment) *n.* act of settling; place settled; a colony; jointure.

SETTLER (set'ler) *n.* one who settles; a colonist.

SETTLING (set'ling) *n.* act of adjusting, paying, subsiding, or hardening;—*pl.* sediment; lees.

SEVEN (sev'n) *a.* six and one. [O.E. *seofn.* Cf. Ger. *sieben.*]

SEVENFOLD (sev'n-fōld) *a.* seven times.

SEVENTEEN (sev'n-tēn) *a.* ten and seven. [O.E. *seofontiene.*]

SEVENTEENTH (sev'n-tēnth) *a.* the ordinal of seventeen.

SEVENTH (sev'nth) *a.* the ordinal of seven; —*n.* one part in seven; a musical interval.

SEVENTIETH (sev'n-ti-eth) *n.* the ordinal of seventy.

SEVENTY (sev'n-ti) *a.* seven times ten. [O.E. *seofontig.*]

SEVER (sev'er) *v.t.* to part violently; keep distinct;—*v.i.* to be rent asunder; be separate. [O.F. *sevrer*, fr. L. *separare*, separate.]

SEVERAL (sev'er-al) *a.* distinct; various; more than two; not many;—*n.* each; a separate place. [O.F., fr. L. *separare*.]

SEVERALITY (sev-er-al'i-ti) *n.* each by itself or taken singly; distinction.

SEVERALLY (sev'er-al-i) *ad.* separately.

SEVERALTY (sev'er-al-ti) *n.* a state of separation.

SEVERANCE (sev'er-ans) *n.* act of severing; separation.

SEVERE (se-vēr') *a.* grave; harsh; strict; difficult to endure; rigidly exact; searching. [F., fr. L. *severus*.]

SEVERELY (se-vēr'li) *ad.* with severity.

SEVERITY (se-ver'i-ti) *n.* harshness; rigour; austerity; strictness.

SEW (sō) *v.t.* to unite with needle and thread. [O.E. *siwian.*]

SEWAGE (sū'ij) *n.* refuse matter of a town carried off by sewers.

SEWER (sū'er) *n.* underground passage for carrying off water and filth from a town. [O.F. *seuviere*, *seviere*, a canal, fr. L. *ex*, out, and *aqua*, water.]

SEWER (sō'er) *n.* one who sews.

SEWERAGE (sū'er-ij) *n.* system of draining by sewers; the drainage carried off.

SEWING-MACHINE (sō'ing-ma-shēn) *n.* a machine for all kinds of needlework.

SEX (seks) *n.* the distinction of male and female; womankind. [L. *sexus*.]

SEXAGENARIAN (sek-sa-je-nā'ri-an) *n.* a person of sixty years of age. [L. *sexageni*, sixty each.]

SEXAGESIMA (sek-sa-jes'i-ma) *n.* the second Sunday before Lent; so called as being about the sixtieth day before Easter. [L. *sexagesimus*, sixtieth.]

SEXENNIAL (sek-sen'yal) *a.* lasting or happening once in six years. [L. *sex*, six, and *annus*, a year.]

SEXTANT (seks'tant) *n.* the sixth part of a circle; a nautical instrument for measuring the altitudes and angular distances of the sun, moon, etc. [L. *sex*, *six*.]

SEXTILE (seks'til) *n.* aspect of planets sixty degrees apart. [L. *sextus*, the sixth.]

SEXTON (seks'tun) *n.* an under officer of a church. [Contr. fr. **SACRISTAN.**]

SEXUAL (sek'sū-al) *a.* pertaining to sex.

SEXUALITY (sek-sū-a-l'i-ti) *n.* the state of being distinguished by sex.

SHABBILY (shab'i-li) *ad.* in a mean manner; raggedly.

SHABBY (shab'i) *a.* worn; ragged; mean; paltry. [Doublet of **SCABBY**; see **SCAB.**]

SHACKLE (shak'l) *v.t.* to fetter; chain; bind;—*n.pl.* fetters; handcuffs, etc. [O.E. *sceacul*, fetter.]

SHAD (shad) *n.* a fish of the herring family. [O.E. *sceadd.*]

SHADE (shād) *n.* interception of light; shelter; screen; degree of colour; a ghost; —*v.t.* to cover from light; obscure;—*n.pl.* place of the dead; deep obscurity. [O.E. *sceadu*, a shade.]

SHADINESS (shā'di-nes) *n.* state of being shady.

SHADOW (shad'ō) *n.* a figure formed by the interception of light; a representation; shade; shelter; faint appearance; anything unsubstantial;—*v.t.* to cloud; darken; represent faintly; follow, as a spy. [O.E. *sceadu*, a shade.]

SHADOWY (shad'ō-i) *a.* full of shade.

SHADY (shā'di) *a.* sheltered from light or heat; of doubtful honesty. [O.E. *sceadu*, shadow.]

SHAFT (shaft) *n.* an arrow; straight part of a column; passage into a mine; thills of a chaise; a long axis of machinery. [O.E. *sceaft.*]

SHAG (shag) *n.* rough hair-cloth; a kind of tobacco;—*a.* hairy; rough;—*v.t.* to make hairy or rough. [O.E. *sceacga*, a bush of hair.]

SHAGGINESS (shag'i-nes) *n.* state of being shaggy.

SHAGGY (shag'i) *a.* hairy; with rough, woolly hair.

SHAGREEN (sha-grēn') *n.* a kind of leather prepared from the skins of horses, sharks, etc.;—*a.* made of shagreen. [F. *chagrin*, fr. Turk. *saghrī*, the back of a horse.]

SHAH (shä) *n.* a Persian king. [Per.]

SHAKE (shāk) *v.t.* [*pret.* **SHOOK**; *pp.* **SHAKEN**] to agitate; make to tremble, waver, fear, etc.; trill;—*v.i.* to tremble; shiver;—*n.* vibratory motion. [O.E. *scacan.*]

SHAKER (shā'ker) *n.* one that shakes;—*pl.* a religious sect.

SHAKINESS (shā'ki-nes) *n.* instability; insecurity.

SHAKO (shak'ō) *n.* a kind of military cap. [Hung.]

SHAKY (shā'ki) *a.* feeble; unsteady.

SHALE (shāl) *n.* a husk; pod; a slaty rock found in the coal measures;—*v.t.* to peel; shell. [Ger. *Schale.*]

SHALL (shal) an auxiliary verb, used in forming the future tense, as *I shall go.* [O.E.]

Shako.

SHALLOP (shal'up) *n.* a large boat. [F. *chaloupe*; Ger. *Schaluppe.*]

SHALLOW (shal'ō) *a.* not deep; empty; superficial;—*n.* a place where the water is not deep. [Etym. doubtful.]

SHALLOWNESS (shal'ō-nes) *n.* want of depth.

SHALT (shalt) second person of **SHALL**.

SHAM (sham) *n.* false pretence;—*a.* false; counterfeit;—*v.t.* to pretend; deceive. [Fr. **SHAME.**]

SHAMBLE (sham'bl) *v.i.* to walk with awkward or unsteady gait; shuffle. [Etym. doubtful.]

SHAMBLES (sham'blz) *n.pl.* a place where butchers kill or sell meat. [O.E. *scamel*, a bench, fr. L. *scamellum*, for *scabellum*, dim. of *scamnum*, a bench.]

SHAMBLING (sham'bling) *n.* a shuffling gait.

SHAME (shām) *n.* sense or cause of disgrace; reproach;—*v.t.* to make ashamed. [O.E. *scamu*, modesty.]

SHAMEFACED (shām'fāst) *a.* bashful.

SHAMEFUL (shām'fool) *a.* disgraceful.

SHAMEFULLY (shām'fool-i) *ad.* disgracefully; ignominiously.

SHAMELESS (shām'les) *a.* destitute of shame.

SHAMELESSNESS (shām'les-nes) *n.* impudence.

SHAMMY (sham'i) *n.* leather made of the skin of the chamois.

SHAMPOO (sham-pōo') *v.t.* to rub and press the limbs after warm bathing; wash the hair with soap and water. [Hind.]

SHAMROCK (sham'rok) *n.* a trefoil clover plant; emblem of Ireland. [Ir. *seamrog.*]

SHANK (shangk) *n.* the bone of the leg; long part of a tool. [O.E. *scanca*, leg.]

SHANTY (shan'ti) *n.* a rude hut. [Ir.]

SHAPE (shāp) *v.t.* [*pret.* **SHAPED**; *pp.* **SHAPED** or **SHAPEN**] to form; mould; give figure to;—*n.* external form or figure; pattern. [O.E. *gesceap.*]

SHAPELESS (shāp'les) *a.* wanting regularity of form. [metrical.

SHAPELY (shāp'li) *a.* well formed; symmetrical.

SHARD (shärd) *n.* a fragment; a shell. [O.E. *sceard*, a fragment.]

SHARE (shär) *n.* a part; a plough-iron;—*v.t.* or *i.* to divide in parts; partake in; receive a portion. [O.E. *scearu*, (part.) fr. *sceran*, to tear.]

SHAREBROKER (shär'brō-ker) *n.* one who deals in stocks, shares, and other securities.

SHAREHOLDER (shär'hōl-der) *n.* one who holds a share in a joint property.

SHARER (shär'er) *n.* one who shares.

SHARK (shärk) *n.* a voracious fish;—*v.t.* to pick up hastily;—*v.i.* to swindle; cheat. [Perh. L. *carcharus*, fr. G. *karcharos*, jagged.]

SHARP (shärp) *a.* having a thin edge or fine point; keen; acute; eager; shrill;—*v.t.* to sharpen;—*v.i.* to grow sharp. [O.E. *scearp.* Cf. Ger. *scharf.*]

SHARP-CUT (shärp'kut) *a.* clearly outlined.

SHARPEN (shär'pn) *v.t.* or *i.* to make or grow sharp.

SHARPER (shär'per) *n.* a cheat.

SHARPLY (shärp'li) *ad.* keenly; severely.

SHARPNESS (shärp'nes) *n.* keenness of edge or point; acuteness.

SHARP-SET (shärp'set) *a.* very hungry.

SHARPSHOOTER (shärp'shōō-ter) *n.* a good marksman.

SHATTER (shat'er) *v.t.* to break in pieces; —*v.i.* to disorder. [Doublet of **SCATTER.**]

SHATTERS (shat'erz) *n.pl.* broken pieces; fragments. [easily broken.

SHATTERY (shat'er-i) *a.* of loose texture; easily broken.

SHAVE (shāv) *v.t.* or *i.* [*pret.* **SHAVED**; *pp.* **SHAVED**, **SHAVEN**] to cut or pare off; cut in thin slices; skim near; fleece. [O.E. *scafan.*]

SHAVER (shā'ver) *n.* one who shaves; a sharp dealer; a boy.

SHAVING (shā'ving) *n.* a thin slice.

SHAWL (shawl) *n.* a cloth to cover the neck and shoulders. [Per. *shal.*]

SHE (shē) *pron. fem.* standing for the name of female. [O.E. *seo*, fr. *heo*, an older fem.]

SHEAF (shēf) *n.* a bundle of stalks; any bundle;—*pl.* **SHEAVES**;—*v.t.* to bind in sheaves;—*v.i.* to make sheaves. [O.E. *sceaf*, fr. *scufan*, shove.]

SHEAR (shēr) *v.t.* [*pret.* **SHEARED**; *pp.* **SHEARED** or **SHORN**] to clip from the surface; reap;—*n.pl.* a cutting instrument with two blades. [O.E. *sceran*, shear.]

SHEARER (shēr'er) *n.* one that shears.
SHEATH (shēth) *n.* a case; a scabbard. [O.E. *sceth.* Cf. Ger. *Scheide.*]
SHEATHE (shēтн) *v.t.* to put in a case; cover.
SHEATHING (shē'тнing) *n.* the covering of a ship's bottom.
SHEATHY (shē'thi) *a.* forming a sheath.
SHEAVE (shēv) *n.* a wheel in a pulley. [Doublet of SHIVE.]
SHEBEEN (she-bēn') *n.* a house where intoxicating drinks are sold without a licence. [Ir.]
SHED (shed) (1) *n.* a slight building;—(2) *v.t.* [*pret.* and *pp.* SHED] to give forth; throw off; pour out. [(1) Doublet of SHADE. (2) O.E. *sccadan,* to separate. Cf. Ger. *scheiden.*]
SHEDDER (shed'er) *n.* one who sheds.
SHEEN (shēn) *n.* brightness; glitter. [O.E. *scene,* fair. Cf. Ger. *schon.*]
SHEENY (shē'ni) *a.* bright; glittering.
SHEEP (shēp) *n. sing.* and *pl.* a ruminant animal valued for its flesh and wool. [O.E. *seap.* Cf. Ger. *Schaf.*]
SHEEP-COTE (shēp'kōt) *n.* pen for sheep.
SHEEP-FOLD (shēp'fōld) *n.* fold for sheep.
SHEEPISH (shē'pish) *a.* like a sheep; timorous; modest.
SHEEPISHNESS (shē'pish-nes) *n.* bashfulness.
SHEEP'S-EYE (shēps'i) *n.* a sly, diffident, loving look.
SHEER (shēr) (1) *a.* pure; clear; mere; perpendicular;—(2) *v.i.* to deviate from a course;—*n.* the bend of a ship's deck. [(1) Icel. (2) O.E. *scir,* fr. Scand.]
SHEERS (shērz) *n.pl.* apparatus for raising heavy weights. [See SHEARS.]
SHEET (shēt) *n.* a broad expanse or piece of water, iron, cloth, paper, etc.; a rope to haul down the leeward corner of a sail. [O.E. *scyte,* a sheet. Cf. *sceotan,* to shoot.]
SHEET-ANCHOR (shēt'ang-ker) *n.* the largest anchor; last refuge.
SHEETING (shē'ting) *n.* cloth for sheets.
SHEET-IRON (shēt'i-urn) *n.* iron in plates or sheets.
SHEET-LEAD (shēt'led) *n.* lead in sheets.
SHEIK (shēk) *n.* an Arab chief. [A.]
SHEKEL (shek'el) *n.* a Jewish coin, worth about 2s. 6d. [H.]
SHEKINAH (shē-kī'na) *n.* the symbol of the Divine presence, which rested over the mercy-seat in the form of a cloud. [H. *shakhan,* to dwell.]
SHELF (shelf) *n.* a board supported to lay things on; a bank or rock under water;— *pl.* SHELVES. [O.E. *scilfe,* a plank.]
SHELFY (shel'fi) *a.* full of rocks and shoals.
SHELL (shel) *n.* a hard covering; outer part; framework;—*v.t.* or *i.* to remove the shell; cast the shell. [O.E. *scell.*]
SHELLAC (shel'ak, she-lak') *n.* resin-lac spread in thin plates. [SHELL-LAC.]
SHELL-FISH (shel'fish) *n.* fish covered with a shell.
SHELTER (shel'ter) *n.* a protection; refuge; —*v.t.* or *i.* to cover; shield; conceal; take shelter. [O.E. *scildtruma,* a guard.]
SHELTERLESS (shel'ter-les) *a.* without cover.
SHELVE (shelv) *v.t.* to furnish with shelves; put on a shelf; put aside; postpone;— *v.i.* to slope. [Fr. SHELF.]
SHELVING (shel'ving) *n.* fitting up shelves; materials for shelves.
SHELVY (shel'vi) *a.* abounding with sand-banks.
SHEPHERD (shep'erd) *n.* one that tends sheep. [O.E. *sceap-hyrde,* keeper of sheep.]
SHEPHERDESS (shep'er-des) *n.* a female that has the care of sheep.
SHERIFF (sher'if) *n.* an officer who administers the law in each county. [O.E. *scir,* a shire, and *gerefa,* a reeve.]

SHERRY (sher'i) *n.* a Spanish wine; so called from Xeres, in Spain.
SHIBBOLETH (shib'u-leth) *n.* the watch-word or test-word of a party. [H. =an ear of corn, or a stream.]
SHIELD (shēld) *n.* armour for defence; an escutcheon;—*v.t.* to protect. [O.E. *scild.* Cf. Ger. *Schild.*]
SHIFT (shift) *v.t.* or *i.* to change; remove; dress in fresh clothes; resort to:—*n.* a change; contrivance; resource; chemise. [O.E. *sciftan,* divide.]
SHIFTLESS (shift'les) *a.* lacking in expedients.
SHILLALAH (shi-lä'la) *n.* an oaken cudgel. [Fr. *Shillelagh,* a Wicklow barony, famous for oaks.]
SHILLING (shil'ing) *n.* a silver coin; sum of twelve pence. [O.E. *scilling.* Cf. Ger. *Schilling.*]
SHIMMER (shim'er) *v.i.* to gleam; glisten;— *n.* a glimmering. [O.E. *scimrian,* fr. *sciman,* to shine.]
SHIN (shin) *n.* fore part of the leg. [O.E. *scina.*]
SHINE (shin) *v.i.* [*pret.* and *pp.* SHINED or SHONE] to emit rays of light; be bright or conspicuous. [O.E. *scinan.*]
SHINGLE (shing'gl) (1) *n.* a thin board;— *v.t.* to cover with shingles;—(2) *n.* coarse pebbles. [(1) L. *scandula,* a wooden tile. (2) Orig. *single,* fr. Norw. *singel, singling,* shingle, fr. *singla,* freq. of *singa,* to ring.]
SHINGLES (shing'glz) *n.pl.* an eruptive disease. [L. *cingulum,* a girdle, fr. *cingere,* to gird.]
SHINING (shi'ning) *a.* bright in a high degree; radiant; conspicuous;—*n.* effusion of light; brightness.
SHIP (ship) *n.* a square-rigged vessel with three masts;— *v.t.* to put on board a vessel; hire for service in a ship; fix in its place;— *v.i.* to engage for service at sea. [O.E. *scip,* fr. *scippan,* to make, fr. *scea-pan,* to shape.]

Ship.

SHIPBOARD (ship'bōrd) *ad.* on board of a ship.
SHIP-BROKER (ship'brō-ker) *n.* an agent for the sale, cargoes, insurances, and outfit of ships.
SHIP-CHANDLER (ship'chand-ler) *n.* one who deals in canvas, cordage, and other furniture of ships.
SHIP-HOLDER (ship'hōl-der) *n.* one who holds a ship. Also SHIPOWNER.
SHIP-MASTER (ship'mas-ter) *n.* a master of a ship.
SHIPMENT (ship'ment) *n.* act of shipping.
SHIPPING (ship'ing) *n.* ships in general.
SHIPWRECK (ship'rek) *n.* the destruction of a ship by accident;—*v.t.* to ruin a ship by accident.
SHIPWRIGHT (ship'rit) *n.* a builder of ships.
SHIRE (shir) *n.* a county. [O.E. *scir,* fr. *sciran,* to cut off.]
SHIRK (sherk) *v.t.* or *i.* to avoid or get off from duty;—*n.* one who avoids duty. [Variant of SHARK.]
SHIRT (shert) *n.* a man's under-garment;— *v.t.* to cover with a shirt. [Scand.]
SHIVE (shiv) *n.* a slice; a fragment. [Scand. Icel. *skifa,* a slice; D. *schijf;* Ger. *Scheibe.*]
SHIVER (shiv'er) (1) *n.* a little piece;—*v.t.* or *i.* to break into small pieces;—(2) *v.t.* or *i.* shake. [(1) Fr. SHIVE. (2) Fr. QUIVER.]
SHIVERING (shiv'er-ing) *n.* a shaking with cold; dashing in pieces.

Fäte, fär, ado; mē, her; mīne; nōte; tūne; mōōn.

SHIVERY (shiv'er-i) *a.* easily broken.

SHOAL (shōl) (1) *n.* a crowd, as of fishes; (2) a sand-bank or bar;—*a.* shallow;—*v.i.* to become more shallow. [(1) O.E. *scolu*, company, fr. L. *schola*, school. (2) Scand.]

SHOALY (shōl'i) *a.* full of shoals.

SHOCK (shok) (1) *n.* a collision; a violent onset;—*v.t.* to strike with surprise, disgust, or terror;—(2) *n.* a group of sheaves of grain. [(1) Cf. D. *schok.* (2) Cf. D. *schocke.*]

SHOD (shod) *pret.* and *pp.* of SHOE.

SHODDY (shod'i) *n.* cloth made of old or refuse woollen goods;—*a.* of little value; inferior. [Cf. O.E. *sceadan*, to part.]

SHOE (shōō) *n.* a covering for the foot of man or beast;—*pl.* SHOES;—*v.t.* [*pret.* and *pp.* SHOD] to put on shoes. [O.E. *sceo.* Cf. Ger. *Schuh.*]

SHOEBLACK (shōō'blak) *n.* one that cleans shoes. [makes shoes.

SHOEMAKER (shōō'mā-ker) *n.* one who

SHONE (shon) *pret.* of SHINE.

SHOOK (shuk) (1) *pret.* and *pp.* of SHAKE; —(2) *n.* a bundle of staves. [(2) Fr. SHOCK. a group of sheaves.]

SHOOT (shōōt) *v.t.* or *i.* [*pret.* and *pp.* SHOT] to dart; jut; sprout; discharge, as a gun; —*n. t.* sprout or branch. [O.E. *sceotan.*]

SHOP (shop) *n.* a building for work or trade; —*v.i.* to visit shops for goods. [O.E. *sceoppa*, a treasury, a store-house.]

SHOPKEEPER (shop'kē-per) *n.* a merchant who sells in a shop.

SHOPLIFTER (shop'lif-ter) *n.* one who steals from a shop.

SHOPMAN (shop'man) *n.* one who serves in a shop.

SHOPPING (shop'ing) *n.* the act of visiting shops for the purchase of goods.

SHOP-WALKER (shop'wawk-er) *n.* attendant in a shop to direct and look after the customers.

SHORE (shōr) (1) *n.* coast;—(2) *n.* a prop; —*v.t.* to support by props. [(1) O.E. *score*, (2) Cf. O.E. *sceorian*, project.]

SHORELESS (shōr'les) *a.* having no shore.

SHORN (shorn) *pp.* of SHEAR.

SHORT (short) *a.* not long; brief; scanty; deficient; brittle. [O.E. *sceort.*]

SHORT-ALLOWANCE (short'a-lou-ans) *n.* allotment of provisions short of the regulated quantity.

SHORT-DATED (short'dā-ted) *a.* drawn and made payable at an early date.

SHORTEN (shor'tn) *v.t.* to make shorter.

SHORTENING (short'ning) *n.* act of contracting; something to make paste brittle.

SHORTHAND (short'hand) *n.* abbreviated writing.

SHORT-LIVED (short'livd) *a.* not living or lasting long.

SHORTLY (short'li) *ad.* quickly; briefly.

SHORTNESS (short'nes) *n.* brevity; conciseness; deficiency.

SHORT-RIB (short'rib) *n.* one of the lower ribs.

SHORTS (shorts) *n.pl.* coarse part of meal; small clothes.

SHORT-SIGHTED (short'sī-ted) *a.* unable to see far.

SHORT-WITTED (short'wit-ed) *a.* having little intellect or judgment.

SHOT (shot) (1) *pret.* and *pp.* of SHOOT:— *n.* act of shooting; a missile; ball; bullet; a marksman;—*v.t.* to load with ball;—(2) *n.* a reckoning. [(1) O.E. *sceotan*, shoot. (2) Icel. *skot.*]

SHOULD (shood) *imp.* of SHALL, denoting intention or duty.

SHOULDER (shōl'der) *n.* the joint that connects the arm with the body; upper joint of the foreleg of an animal cut for the market; a prominence;—*v.t.* to take on the shoulder; push rudely. [O.E. *sculdor.* Cf. Ger. *Schulter.*]

SHOULDER-BLADE (shōl'der-blād) *n.* the broad bone of the shoulder.

SHOUT (shout) *v.t.* or *i.* to utter loudly; cry aloud;—*n.* a loud cry. [Etym. unknown.]

SHOUTING (shou'ting) *n.* act of crying aloud.

SHOVE (shuv) *v.t.* or *i.* to push before one; drive along; push forward or off;—*n.* a push. [O.E. *scofian.*]

SHOVEL (shuv'l) *n.* a utensil for throwing earth, etc.;—*v.t.* to throw with a shovel. [O.E. *scofl*, fr. *scufan*, to shove. Cf. Ger. *Schaufel.*]

SHOW (shō) *v.t.* or *i.* [*pret.* SHOWED] *pp.* SHOWED, SHOWN] to exhibit; prove; direct; appear;—*n.* exhibition; sight. [O.E. *sceawian*, see. Cf. Ger. *schauen*, to behold.]

SHOWBREAD (shō'bred) *n.* bread presented in the Jewish sanctuary.

SHOWER (shou'er) *n.* a temporary fall of rain; a copious fall;—*v.t.* or *i.* to rain; bestow liberally. [O.E. *scur.* Cf. Ger. *Schauer.*]

SHOWERY (shou'er-i) *a.* subject to showers; rainy.

SHOWILY (shō'i-li) *ad.* in a showy manner.

SHOWY (shō'i) *a.* gaudy; fine.

SHRED (shred) *v.t.* [*pret.* and *pp.* SHRED] to cut into small pieces;—*n.* a small piece cut off; a fragment. [O.E. *screade.* Cf. Ger. *Schrot*; Scot. *screed.*]

SHREW (shrōō) *n.* an ill-tempered woman. [O.E. *screawa.*]

SHREWD (shrōōd) *a.* sagacious; sly.

SHREWDLY (shrōōd'li) *ad.* cunningly.

SHREWDNESS (shrōōd'nes) *n.* sly cunning; sagacity.

SHREWISH (shrōō'ish) *a.* like a shrew; illnatured; brawling.

SHRIEK (shrēk) *v.i.* to utter a shrill cry;— *n.* a shrill cry; a scream. [Variant of SCREECH.]

SHRIFT (shrift) *n.* confession made to a priest; absolution. [O.E. *scrift*, confession, fr. *scrifan*, to shrive.]

SHRIKE (shrik) *n.* a rapacious bird—butcher bird. [Scand. Cf. SHRIEK.]

SHRILL (shril) *a.* sharp; piercing, as sound. [M.E. Cf. Scot. *skirl.*]

SHRILLNESS (shril'nes) *n.* acuteness of sound.

SHRILLY (shril'li) *ad.* acutely.

SHRIMP (shrimp) *n.* a small shell-fish. [Cf. O.E. *scrimman*, dry up; Scot. *scrimpit*, pinched.]

SHRINE (shrin) *n.* a case or box, as for sacred relics; any sacred or hallowed place. [O.E. *scrin*, fr. L. *scrinium*, a desk, fr. *scribere*, to write.]

SHRINK (shringk) *v.t.* or *i.* [*pret.* and *pp.* SHRUNK] to contract; become or make less. [O.E. *scrincan.*]

SHRINKAGE (shring'kij) *n.* act or measure of shrinking.

SHRINKER (shring'ker) *n.* one who shrinks or avoids duty or danger.

SHRIVE (shriv) *v.t.* to hear or receive confession. [O.E. *scrifan*, to prescribe penance, fr. L. *scribere*, to write.]

SHRIVEL (shriv'l) *v.t.* or *i.* to contract into wrinkles; shrink. [Scand.]

SHROUD (shroud) *n.* a cover; a winding sheet;—*pl.* a range of ropes in a ship;— *v.t.* to shelter; dress for the grave. [O.E. *scrud*, a garment.]

SHROVETIDE (shov'tid) *n.* confession time; Tuesday before Lent. [O.E. *scrifan*, shrive.]

SHRUB (shrub) (1) *n.* a bush; a small woody plant;—(2) *n.* a liqueur of rum, lemon, etc. [(1) O.E. *scrob.* (2) Hind.]

SHRUBBERY (shrub'er-i) *n.* a collection or plantation of shrubs.

SHRUBBY (shrub'i) *a.* full of shrubs.

SHRUG (shrug) *v.t.* to contract, as the shoulders; —*n.* a drawing up of the shoulders. [Scand.]

SHUDDER (shud'ẹr) *n.* a tremor, as with horror;—*v.i.* to quake; tremble. [M.E. Cf. Ger. *schaudern.*]

SHUFFLE (shuf'l) *v.t.* to change the position of cards;—*v.i.* to prevaricate; evade;—*n.* a change in cards; a trick. [O.E. *scufan,* shove; a variant of **SCUFFLE.**]

SHUFFLER (shuf'lẹr) *n.* one who shuffles.

SHUFFLING (shuf'ling) *n.* evasion; irregular gait;—*a.* evasive.

SHUN (shun) *v.t.* to avoid; try to escape. [O.E. *scunian.*]

SHUNT (shunt) *n.* a siding off the main line of railway;—*v.t.* to drive or back into a railway siding. [M.E. *shunten,* to start aside, fr. O.E. *scyndan,* to hasten.]

SHUNTER (shun'tẹr) *n.* one who shunts.

SHUT (shut) *v.t.* or *i.* [*pret.* and *pp.* **SHUT**] to close. [O.E. *scyttan,* shut, fr. *sceotan,* to shoot.]

SHUTTER (shut'ẹr) *n.* that which closes.

SHUTTLE (shut'l) *n.* a weaver's instrument to shoot the threads. [O.E. *sceotan,* shoot.]

SHUTTLECOCK (shut'l-kok) *n.* an instrument used with a battledore.

SHY (shī) *a.* shunning society; reserved; coy; —*n.* start or swerving suddenly aside of a horse; a quick, jerking, or careless throw; —*v.i.* to start suddenly aside;—*v.t.* to fling; to toss. [O.E. *sceoh.* Cf. Ger. *scheu.*]

SHYLY (shī'li) *ad.* in a timid manner.

SHYNESS (shī'nes) *n.* reserve; coyness.

SIBILANT (sib'i-lạnt) *a.* hissing. [L. (part.) stem *sibilant-,* of *sibilare,* hiss.]

SIBILATION (sib-i-lā'shun) *n.* a hissing sound.

SICCATIVE (sik'ạ-tiv) *a.* drying. [L. *siccare,* fr. *siccus,* dry.]

SICCITY (sik'si-ti) *n.* dryness.

SICK (sik) *a.* afflicted with disease; inclined to vomit; disgusted; used by the sick. [O.E. *seoc,* fr. Ger. *siech.*]

SICKEN (sik'n) *v.t.* or *i.* to make or become sick.

SICKENING (sik'n-ing) *a.* disgusting; nauseating.

SICKISH (sik'ish) *a.* somewhat sick.

SICKISHNESS (sik'ish-nes) *n.* the quality of being rather sick.

SICKLE (sik'l) *n.* a reaping-hook. [O.E. *sicol,* fr. L. *secula,* a sickle, fr. L. *secare,* to cut.]

SICKLEMAN (sik'l-mạn) *n.* a reaper.

SICKLINESS (sik'li-nes) *n.* state of being sickly; unhealthiness.

SICK-LIST (sik'list) *n.* list of the names of the sick on board ship.

SICKLY (sik'li) *a.* unhealthy; faint.

SICKNESS (sik'nes) *n.* a morbid state of the body; disease.

SIDE (sīd) *n.* the broad part of a thing; party; interest;—*a.* lateral; indirect;— *v.i.* to lean to one part. [O.E. Cf. Ger. *Seite.*]

SIDE-CUT (sīd'cut) *n.* a road branching from the main one.

SIDEBOARD (sīd'bōrd) *n.* a side table to hold dinner utensils, etc.

SIDELONG (sīd'long) *a.* lateral; oblique.

SIDER (sī'dẹr) *n.* one who takes a side.

SIDEREAL (sī-dē're-ạl) *a.* pertaining to stars; sta . [L. stem *sider,* of *sidus,* a s ar.] rry

SIDEROGRAPHY (sī-dē-rog'rạ-fi) *n.* art or practice of steel engraving. [G. *siderites,* fr. *sideros,* iron, and *graphein,* engrave.]

SIDE-SADDLE (sīd'sad-l) *n.* a woman's saddle.

SIDEWISE (sīd'wīz) *ad.* on one side.

SIDING (sī'ding) *n.* lines of rails on which railway carriages are shunted.

SIDLE (sī'dl) *v.i.* to go side foremost.

SIDLING (sīd'ling) *ad.* with the side foremost.

SIEGE (sēj) *n.* a besetting a fortified place. [O.F. *sege* = F. *siège,* a seat, fr. Late L. *assedium* = L. *obsidium,* a siege, fr. *sedere,* to sit.]

SIESTA (si-es'tạ) *n.* a short sleep in the afternoon. [Sp., fr. L. *sexta (hora),* the sixth (hour) of the day; noon.]

SIEVE (siv) *n.* a small utensil for sifting. [O.E. *sife.* Cf. Ger. *Sieb.*]

SIFT (sift) *v.t.* to separate by a sieve; scrutinise. [O.E. *siftan.*]

SIFTER (sif'tẹr) *n.* he or that which sifts.

SIGH (sī) *v.i.* to emit breath audibly; lament; —*n.* a deep breathing. [O.E. *sican.*]

SIGHT (sīt) *n.* sense, act, or object of seeing. [O.E. *siht, gesiht,* fr. (part.) *ge-segen,* of *seon,* to see. Cf. Ger. *Sieht.*]

SIGHTLESS (sīt'les) *a.* wanting sight.

SIGHTLESSNESS (sīt'les-nes) *n.* the privation of sight.

SIGHTLINESS (sīt'li-nes) *n.* comeliness.

SIGHTLY (sīt'li) *a.* pleasing to the eye.

SIGN (sīn) *n.* something that represents or signifies; token; proof; wonder; constellation;—*v.t.* to subscribe one's name; mark. [F. *signe,* fr. L. *signum.*]

SIGNAL (sig'nạl) *n.* a sign to give notice;— *a.* eminent; remarkable. [F., fr. L. *signalis,* fr. *signum,* a sign.]

SIGNALISE (sig'nạl-īz) *v.t.* to make distinguished.

SIGNALLY (sig'nạl-i) *ad.* remarkably.

SIGNATURE (sig'nạ-tūr) *n.* a name or mark signed or impressed. [F., fr. Late L. *signatura,* fr. L. (part.) *signatus,* of *signare,* to sign.]

SIGNER (sī'nẹr) *n.* one who subscribes his name.

SIGNET (sig'net) *n.* a seal, or private seal. [F. dim. of *signe,* fr. L. *signum,* a mark.]

SIGNIFICANCE (sig-nif'i-kạns) *n.* importance; meaning; import.

SIGNIFICANT (sig-nif'i-kạnt) *a.* expressive of some fact or meaning.

SIGNIFICANTLY (sig-nif'i-kạnt-li) *ad.* with meaning.

SIGNIFICATION (sig-ni-fi-kā'shun) *n.* meaning by words or signs.

SIGNIFICATIVE (sig-nif'i-kā-tiv) *a.* having or expressing meaning.

SIGNIFY (sig'ni-fi) *v.t.* to make known; betoken; intimate; imply; mean. [F. *signifier,* to betoken, fr. L. *significare,* fr. *signum,* a sign, and *facere,* make.]

SIGNOR, SIGNIOR (sē'nyōr) *n.* an Italian word for Sir, Mr. [It.]

SIGN-POST (sīn'pōst) *n.* a post on which a sign hangs.

SILENCE (sī'lens) *n.* stillness; muteness; oblivion;—*v.t.* to still; stop;—*interj.* be silent.

SILENT (sī'lent) *a.* still; mute; quiet. [L. (part.) stem *silent-,* of *silens,* of *silere,* to be silent.]

SILENTLY (sī'lent-li) *ad.* without speech or noise.

SILEX (sī'leks) *n.* a flint and its metallic base. [L.]

SILHOUETTE (sil-ōō-et') *n.* an outline or profile filled in of a dark colour. [F., so called in derision, from Étienne de *Silhouette,* a French minister of finance, 1759.]

SILICIOUS (si-lish'us) *a.* pertaining to silex; flinty. [L. stem *silic-,* of *silex,* flint.]

SILIQUA (sil'i-kwạ) *n.* a pod with seeds fixed to both sutures. [L. *silicula,* dim. of *siliqua,* a pod or husk.]

SILK (silk) *n.* the fine, soft thread produced by the silk-worm, and cloth made of it; —*a.* consisting of silk. [O.E. *seolc,* fr. L. *sericum,* fr. G. (neut.) *serikon,* of *serikos,* pertaining to the Seres, fr. *Ser,* a native of China.]

SILKEN (sil'kn) *a.* made of silk; like silk; soft.

SILK-MERCER (silk'mẹr-sẹr) *n.* a dealer in silks.

SILK-WORM (silk'werm) *n.* a worm that produces silk.

SILKY (sil'ki) *a.* consisting of silk; soft.

SILL (sil) *n.* foundation timber of a house or window. [O.E. *syll*.]

Silk-worm.

SILLINESS (sil'i-nes) *n.* simple folly.

SILLY (sil'i) *a.* simple; weak; witless; foolish. [O.E. *scelig*, timely, fr. *sæl*, time. Cf. Ger. *selig*, happy.]

SILT (sil) *n.* salt mud or marsh. [Scand. = to drain.]

SILVA (sil'va) *n.* history of the forest trees of a country. [L.]

SILVAN (sil'van) *a.* pertaining to woods. [L., fr. *silva*, a wood or grove.]

SILVER (sil'ver) *n.* a metal of a white colour; —*a.* made of silver;—*v.t.* to cover with silver. [O.E. *seolfor*. Cf. Ger. *Silber*.]

SILVERLING (sil'ver-ling) *n.* a small silver coin.

SILVERSMITH (sil'ver-smith) *n.* one who works in silver.

SILVERY (sil'ver-i) *a.* resembling silver.

SIMARRE (si-mär) *n.* a lady's robe; a long scarf. [F. *simarre*, O.F. *chamarre*, fr. Sp. *chamarra*, a sheep-skin coat, prob. Basque.]

SIMIA (sim'i-a) *n.* the monkey ape. [L].

SIMILAR (sim'i-lar) *a.* like; resembling. [F., fr. L. *similis*, like.]

SIMILARITY (sim-i-lar'i-ti) *n.* resemblance; likeness.

SIMILARLY (sim'i-lar-li) *ad.* in a like manner.

SIMILE (sim'i-le) *n.* similitude. [L. (neut.) *similis*, like.]

SIMILITUDE (si-mil'i-tūd) *n.* likeness; resemblance; comparison.

SIMMER (sim'er) *v.i.* to boil gently. [A freq. of *sim*, the sound made in boiling.]

SIMNEL (sim'nel) *n.* a sweet cake. [O.F. *simenel*, fr. L. *simila*, fine flour.]

SIMONIACAL (sim-u-ni'a-kal) *a.* guilty or consisting of simony.

SIMONY (sim'u-ni) *n.* the crime of buying or selling of church preferment. [Fr. *Simon Magus*, who wished to purchase the power of conferring the Holy Spirit (Acts, viii.).]

SIMOOM (si-mööm') *n.* suffocating wind. [A. =to poison.]

SIMPER (sim'per) *v.i.* to smile in a silly manner; —*n.* an affected, foolish smile. [Scand.]

SIMPLE (sim'pl) *a.* single; plain; artless; unmingled; silly;—*n.* something not mixed; a medicinal herb. [F., fr. L. *simplex*, fr. *semel*, once, and *plicare*, fold.]

SIMPLENESS (sim'pl-nes) *n.* state or quality of being simple.

SIMPLER (sim'pler) *n.* one who collects simples; herbalist. Also **SIMPLIST**.

SIMPLETON (sim'pl-tun) *n.* a silly person.

SIMPLICITY (sim-plis'i-ti) *n.* singleness; plainness; artlessness.

SIMPLIFICATION (sim-pli-fi-kā'shun) *n.* act of making simple.

SIMPLIFY (sim'pli-fi) *v.t.* to make simple. [L. *simplex*, simple, and F. *fier* = L. *facere*, make.]

SIMPLY (sim'pli) *ad.* plainly; merely.

SIMULATE (sim'ū-lāt) *v.t.* to imitate; feign; counterfeit. [L. (part.) *simulatus*, of *simulare*, to make like, fr. *similis*, like.]

SIMULATION (sim-ū-lā'shun) *n.* act of feigning what is not true.

SIMULTANEOUS (sim-ul-tā'ne-us) *a.* being or happening at the same time. [Late L. *simultaneus*, fr. L. *simul*, together.]

SIMULTANEOUSLY (sim-ul-tā'ne-us-li) *ad.* at the same time.

SIN (sin) *n.* a violation of divine law, or rule of duty;—*v.i.* to depart knowingly from a rule of duty. [O.E. *synn*.]

SINAPISM (sin'a-pizm) *n.* a poultice of mustard-seed. [L., fr. G. *sinapi*, mustard.]

SINCE (sins) *prep.* after;—*ad.* from the time that;—*conj.* because; considering that. [M.E. *sithens*, fr. O.E. *siththam* = lit. 'after that,' fr. *sith*, late, and *tham*, dat. of *thæt*, that.]

SINCERE (sin-sēr') *a.* true; real; unfeigned. [F., fr. L. *sincerus*, perh. fr. *sine*, without and *cera*, wax.]

SINCERELY (sin-sēr'li) *ad.* truly; honestly.

SINCERITY (sin-ser'i-ti) *n.* freedom from disguise; honesty.

SINE (sin) *n.* a straight line from one end of an arch. [L. *sinus*, a curve.]

SINECURE (sī'ne-kūr) *n.* office with pay but without employment. [L. *sina*, without, and *cura*, care.] [sinecure.

SINECURIST (sī'ne-kūr-ist) *n.* one who has a

SINEW (sin'ū) *n.* a tendon; strength; muscle; —*v.i.* to unite as with a sinew. [O.E. *sinu*. Cf. Ger. *Sehne*.]

SINEWY (sin'ū-i) *a.* strong; muscular.

SINFUL (sin'fool) *a.* guilty of sin; unholy; wicked.

SINFULLY (sin'fool-i) *ad.* with sin.

SINFULNESS (sin'fool-nes) *n.* the state of being sinful.

SING (sing) *v.t.* or *i.* [*pret.* **SANG**, **SUNG**; *pp.* **SUNG**] to utter musical or melodious sounds; chant; celebrate. [O.E. *singan*. Cf. Ger. *singen*.]

SINGE (sinj) *v.t.* to burn the external part; scorch;—*n.* a slight burning of the surface. [O.E. *besengan*, lit. to make a singing or hissing noise, as in burning logs, fr. *singan*, to sing.]

SINGER (sing'er) *n.* one who sings.

SINGING (sing'ing) *n.* the act of uttering musical notes.

SINGLE (sing'gl) *a.* separate; individual; alone; unmarried; sincere;—*v.t.* to choose one from a number. [O.F., fr. L. *singulus*, one to each.]

SINGLE-ENTRY (sing'gl-en-tri) *n.* in bookkeeping, entry of transactions to one account only.

SINGLENESS (sing'gl-nes) *n.* simplicity; sincerity.

SINGLY (sing'gli) *ad.* individually; only; by oneself.

SING-SONG (sing'song) *n.* a drawling tone in singing.

SINGULAR (sing'gū-lar) *a.* particular; remarkable; rare; odd. [F., fr. L. *singularis*, fr. *singulus*, single.]

SINGULARIST (sing'gū-lar-ist) *n.* one who affects singularity.

SINGULARITY (sing-gū-lar'i-ti) *n.* peculiarity; oddity.

SINGULARLY (sing'gū-lar-li) *ad.* peculiarly; strangely; remarkably.

SINISTER (sin'is-ter) *a.* left; bad; unfair; unlucky. [L.]

SINISTRORSAL (sin-is-tror'sal) *a.* rising from the left to right, as a spiral line. [L. *sinistrorsus* = *sinistroversus*, fr. *sinister*, left, and (part.) *versus*, of *vertere*, to turn.]

SINISTROUS (sin'is-trus) *a.* on the left; perverse.

SINK (singk) *v.t.* [*pret.* **SUNK**, **SANK**; *pp.* **SUNK**] to immerse; depress; degrade; reduce; suppress; make by delving;—*v.i.* to fall down or to the bottom; fall gradually; enter into; decline;—*n.* a drain to carry off filthy water in a house. [O.E. *sincan*. Cf. Ger. *sinken*.]

SINKER (sing'ker) *n.* a weight as on a fish line to sink it.

SINKING-FUND (sing'king-fund) *n.* a fund to reduce a public debt.

SINLESS (sin'les) *a.* free from sin; innocent.
SINNER (sin'ẽr) *n.* a transgressor.
SIN-OFFERING (sin'of-ẽr-ing) *n.* a sacrifice for sin.
SINTER (sin'tẽr) *n.* dross of iron; a crystalline rock formed from mineral waters. [Ger.]
SINUATE (sin'ū-āt) *v.i.* to wind and turn. [L. (part.) *sinuatus*, of *sinuare*, bend, fr. *sinus*, a curve.]
SINUATION (sin-ū-ā'shun) *n.* a winding.
SINUOSITY (sin-ū-os'i-ti) *n.* the quality of winding in and out.
SINUOUS (sin'ū-us) *a.* winding in and out.
SINUS (sī'nus) *n.* a fold; opening; bay; recess; cavity. [L. =a bend, fold.]
SIP (sip) *n.* a taste, as of liquor;—*v.t.* or *i.* to draw into the mouth in small quantities. [M.E. *sippen.* Cf. O.E. *sypian*, to soak.]
SIPHON (sī'fun) *n.* a bent tube for drawing liquor from casks. [F., fr. G. *siphon*, a small pipe or reed.]
SIPPET (sip'et) *n.* a small sop.
SIR (sẽr) *n.* a title of address to a man; title of a baronet. [O.F. *sire*, fr. L. *senior*, an elder, comp. of *senex*, old. Cf. the form **SIRE, SENIOR, SEIGNIOR, SIGNOR**.]
SIRDAR (ser'dár, ser-dár') *n.* a native chief in Persia; in Egypt the commander-in-chief. [Hind.]
SIRE (sīr) *n.* father; male parent of a beast; term of address to a king;—*v.t.* to generate. [O.F., fr. L. *senior*, elder.]
SIREN (sī'ren) *n.* a mermaid noted for singing; —*a.* enticing; fascinating. [L., fr. G. *seiren*.]
SIRIUS (sir'i-us) *n.* a large bright star; the dog star. [G.]
SIRLOIN (sẽr'loin) *n.* the loin of beef. [O.F. *surlonge*, fr. *sur*, upon, and *longe*, loin.]
SIROCCO (si-rok'ō) *n.* a noxious south-east wind in Italy. [It., fr. A. = the east.]
SIRRAH (sir'a) *n.* sir—used in anger or in sport. [F., fr. L., an extension of **SIR**.]
SIRUP (sir'up) *n.* vegetable juice boiled with sugar. Also written **SYRUP**.
SISKIN (sis'kin) *n.* a small song-bird. [Low Ger.]
SISTER (sis'tẽr) *n.* a female born of the same parents as another. [O.E. *sweostor*. Cf. Ger. *Schwester*.]
SISTERHOOD (sis'tẽr-hood) *n.* a society of females.
SISTERLY (sis'tẽr-li) *a.* becoming a sister.
SIT (sit) *v.i.* [*pret.* and *pp.* SAT] to be placed; perch; rest; brood; meet officially;—*v.t.* to seat; keep the seat upon. [O.E. *sittan.* Cf. Ger. *sitzen*; L. *sedere*.]
SITE (sīt) *n.* a situation; local position. [F., fr. L. *situs*, a place, fr. (part.) *situs*, of *sinere*, to set down.
SITTING (sit'ing) *n.* act or time of resting; incubation; session.
SITUATED (sit'ū-ā-ted) *a.* being in any condition. [Late L. *situatus*, fr. L. *situs*, a site.]
SITUATION (sit-ū-ā'shun) *n.* relative position, location, or condition.
SITZ-BATH (sits'báth) *n.* a tub for bathing in a sitting posture. [Ger. *Sitz*, a seat, and **BATH**; Ger. *Sitzbad*.]
SIX (siks) *a.* five and one. [O.E. *siex.* Cf. Ger. *sechs*, L. *sex*, G. *hex*.]
SIXFOLD (siks'fōld) *a.* taken six times.
SIXPENCE (siks'pens) *n.* half a shilling.
SIXTEEN (siks'tēn) *a.* ten and six.
SIXTEENTH (siks'tēnth) *a.* the ordinal of sixteen.
SIXTH (siksth) *a.* the ordinal of six.
SIXTHLY (siksth'li) *ad.* in the sixth place.
SIXTIETH (siks'ti-eth) *a.* the ordinal of sixty.
SIXTY (siks'ti) *a.* six times ten.
SIZABLE (sī'za-bl) *a.* of a reasonable bulk. [See **SIZE** (1).]
SIZAR (sī'zar) *n.* a student at Cambridge of the rank below a pensioner. [F. *size*, an allowance of food.]

SIZE (sīz) (1) *n.* bulk; quantity;—*v.t.* to arrange according to size;—(2) *n.* a glutinous substance;—*v.t.* to cover with size. [(1) Contr. of **ASSIZE**. (2) It. *sisa*.]
SIZING (sī'zing) *n.* a kind of weak glue.
SIZY (sī'zi) *a.* glutinous; ropy.
SKATE (skāt) (1) *n.* a sliding shoe;—*v.i.* to slide with skates on the ice;—(2) *n.* a large flat fish. [(1) D. (2) Scand.]
SKATER (skā'tẽr) *n.* one who skates.
SKEDADDLE (ske-dad'l) *v.i.* to run away. [Etym. unknown.]
SKEIN (skān) *n.* a knot or number of knots of thread, silk, or yarn. [M.E. *escaigne*, fr. Celt.]
SKELETON (skel'e-tun) *n.* the bones of an animal retained in their natural position; framework; outline. [G. *skeleton*, a dried body, a mummy.]
SKETCH (skech) *n.* an outline; a rough draft;—*v.t.* or *i.* to draw the outline; make a rough draft; give the chief points of. [D., fr. It., fr. L. *schedius*, made offhand, fr. G. *schedios*, sudden.]
SKEW (skū) *a.* oblique; awry; —*ad.* obliquely. [Arch.] a slanting coping, as at the corner of a gable. [O.D. = to avoid.]
SKEWER (skū'ẽr) *n.* a pin to fasten meat;—*v.t.* to fasten with skewers. [*Shiver*, a splinter of wood.]
SKI (skē) *n.* a long flat piece of wood fastened to the foot for the purpose of travelling over snow. [Scand.]
SKID (skid) *n.* a short piece of timber; a slider; drag. [Scand. = a thin plank.]
SKIFF (skif) *n.* a small, light boat. [Doublet of **SHIP**. Cf. Ger. *Schiff*.]
SKILFUL (skil'fool) *a.* qualified with skill; experienced.
SKILFULLY (skil'fool-i) *ad.* with knowledge and dexterity.
SKILFULNESS (skil'fool-nes) *n.* dexterity.
SKILL (skil) *n.* familiar knowledge united to readiness of performance; dexterity;—*v.i.* to know or be knowing. [Scand.]
SKILLED (skild) *a.* having familiar knowledge.
SKILLET (skil'et) *n.* a small boiler. [L. *scutella*, a salver.]
SKIM (skim) *v.t.* or *i.* to take off scum; touch slightly. [Cog. with **SCUM**.]
SKIMMER (skim'ẽr) *n.* a utensil to take off scum. [off.
SKIMMINGS (skim'ings) *n.pl.* matter skimmed
SKIN (skin) *n.* covering of the flesh; hide; rind;—*v.t.* to deprive of the skin;—*v.i.* to form a skin over. [O.E. *scinn.* Cf. *schinden*, to flay.]
SKINFLINT (skin'flint) *n.* a niggard.
SKINNY (skin'i) *a.* consisting of skin only.
SKIP (skip) *v.t.* to pass over; omit;—*v.i.* to leap or spring lightly;—*n.* a leap; passing over. [Scand.]
SKIPPER (skip'ẽr) *n.* master of a ship. [D. *schipper*.]
SKIRMISH (skẽr'mish) *n.* a slight battle;— *v.i.* to fight slightly or in small parties. [O.F. *escaramouche*, fr. Teut.]
SKIRT (skẽrt) *n.* a border; the loose lower part of a woman's dress;—*v.t.* or *i.* to border; be on the border. [Scand. Variant of **SHIRT**.]
SKIT (skit) *n.* a jeer or jesting remark. [Scand.
SKITTISH (skit'ish) *a.* shy; timid.
SKITTISHLY (skit'ish-li) *ad.* shyly; timidly.
SKITTLES (skit'lz) *n.pl.* nine-pins. [Scand.]
SKIVER (skī'vẽr) *n.* split sheepskin. [Scand. Fr. rt. of **SHIVER**.]
SKULK (skulk) *v.i.* to lurk; hide. [Scand.]
SKULKER (skul'kẽr) *n.* one who skulks or avoids duty.

Skew.

Skew.

SKULL (skul) *n.* bone that encloses the brain. [Sw. dial. *skulle*.]

SKULL-CAP (skul'cap) *n.* a headpiece; a close-fitting cap.

SKUNK (skungk) *n.* a fetid carnivorous animal. [Amer. Indian.]

SKURRY (skur'i) *n.* haste; impetuosity. [See SCURRY.]

SKY (ski) *n.* the aerial region. [Scand. Cf. O.E. *scua*, G. *skia*, a shadow.]

SKYLARK (ski'lärk) *n.* a high-flying singing bird. [deck.

SKYLIGHT (ski'lit) *n.* a window in a roof or deck.

SKY-ROCKET (ski'rok-et) *n.* a species of fireworks. [royal.

SKY-SAIL (ski'säl) *n.* a small sail above the royal.

SKYWARD (ski'ward) *ad.* towards the sky.

SLAB (slab) *n.* a plane of stone; outside piece of sawed timber;—*v.t.* to cut slabs from. [Scand.]

SLABBER (slab'er) *v.i.* to slaver. [Cf. Ger. *schlabben*, lap.]

SLABBY (slab'i) *a.* glutinous; thick; dirty.

SLACK (slak) (1) *a.* loose; relaxed; remiss; —*v.t.* or *i.* to loosen; diminish speed; relax; repress. Also **SLACKEN**. *n.* small, broken coal. [(1) O.E. *sleac*. (2) Ger. *Schlacke*, dross.]

SLACKNESS (slak'nes) *n.* remissness.

SLAG (slag) *n.* dross of metal. [Scand. Cf. Ger. *Schlacke*, dross.]

SLAIN (slān) *pp.* of SLAY.

SLAKE (slāk) *v.t.* to quench, as thirst; mix with water, and reduce to powder as lime. [O.E. *sleacian*, grow slack.]

SLAM (slam) *v.t.* to shut with force;—*n.* a violent striking. [Scand. = to bang.]

SLANDER (slan'der) *v.t.* to injure by false reports; defame; calumniate;—*n.* false and malicious report; calumny. [O.F. *esclandre*, fr. L. *scandalum*, fr. G. *skandalon*. Variant of SCANDAL.]

SLANDERER (slan'der-er) *n.* a defamer.

SLANDEROUS (slan'der-us) *a.* defamatory.

SLANG (slang) *n.* low language. [Scand.]

SLANT (slant) *v.t.* or *i.* to turn or be turned obliquely; slope;—*a.* sloping;—*n.* a sloping direction; a gibe. [Scand.]

SLANTING (slan'ting) *a.* sloping; inclining.

SLANTWISE (slant'wiz) *ad.* obliquely.

SLAP (slap) *v.t.* to strike with open hand;— *n.* a blow with something flat. [Cf. Ger. *Schlappe*, a slap.]

SLAPDASH (slap'dash) *ad.* all at once; rashly.

SLASH (slash) *v.t.* or *i.* to make long cuts; strike at;—*n.* a long incision. [O.F. *esclachier eslecher*, to sever.]

SLAT (slat) *n.* a narrow strip of board. [O.F. *esclat*, a chip.]

SLATE (slāt) *n.* a flat piece of dark gray stone for covering buildings and writing on;— *v.t.* to cover with slate. [O.F. *esclat*, a splinter. Cf. Ger. *schleissen* to split.]

SLATER (slā'ter) *n.* one whose business is to slate buildings.

SLATTERN (slat'ern) *n.* a woman negligent of her dress and house. [Fr. freq. of Scand. *slat*, to strike.]

SLATTERNLY (slat'ern-li) *a.* like a slattern; slovenly.

SLATY (slā'ti) *a.* consisting of or like slate.

SLAUGHTER (slaw'ter) *n.* destruction of life; —*v.t.* to kill; slay; butcher. [Scand.: O.E. *sleaht*, fr. *slean*, to slay.]

SLAUGHTER-HOUSE (slaw'ter-hous) *n.* a house for butchering cattle.

SLAUGHTEROUS (slaw'ter-us) *a.* murderous.

SLAVE (slāv) *n.* a person held in bondage; a drudge. [O.F. *esclave*, fr. M. H. Ger. *Slave*.]

SLAVER (slā'ver) (1) *n.* a slave-ship; (2) (slav'-er)—*n.* spittle; drivelling;—*v.i.* to emit spittle;—*v.t.* to drivel. [(2) Icel. *slafra*, to slaver.]

SLAVERER (slav'er-er) *n.* a driveller.

SLAVERY (slā'ver-i) *n.* compulsory service; bondage. [beings.

SLAVE-TRADE (slāv'trād) *n.* traffic in human beings.

SLAVISH (slā'vish) *a.* servile; mean; laborious. [manner.

SLAVISHLY (slā'vish-li) *ad.* in a slavish manner.

SLAVISHNESS (slā'vish-nes) *n.* servility.

SLAY (slā) *v.t.* [*pret.* SLEW; *pp.* SLAIN] to put to death; kill. [O.E. *slean*, strike. Cf. Ger. *schlagen*.]

SLAYER (slā'er) *n.* one who kills.

SLEAVE (slēv) *n.* silk or thread untwisted;— *v.t.* to separate threads. [Etym. doubtful. Cf. Ger. *Schleife*, a loop.]

SLED, SLEDGE (sled, slej) *n.* a carriage on runners used over the snow;—*v.t.* to convey on a sled. [D.]

SLEDDING (sled'ing) *n.* the running of sleds; snow enough for sleds.

SLEDGE (slej) *n.* a.large hammer. [O.E. *slecg*, fr. *slean*, strike. Cf. Ger. *Schlägel*, a beater.]

SLEEK (slēk) *a.* smooth; glossy;—*v.t.* to make smooth and glossy. [Scand. Cf. Ger. *Schlick*, grease.]

SLEEKLY (slēk'li) *ad.* smoothly; softly.

SLEEKY (slē'ki) *a.* smooth and glossy.

SLEEP (slēp) *n.* repose; slumber;—*v.i.* [*pret.* and *pp.* SLEPT] to rest with the voluntary exercise of the powers of the mind suspended. [O.E. *slæpan*. Cf. Ger. *schlafen*.]

SLEEPER (slē'per) *n.* one who sleeps; a horizontal timber to support a weight, rails, etc.

SLEEPFUL (slēp'fool) *a.* inclined to sleep.

SLEEPINESS (slē'pi-nes) *n.* drowsiness.

SLEEPING SICKNESS (slē-ping-sik'nes) *n.* a peculiar disease common in many parts of the interior of Africa.

SLEEPLESS (slēp'les) *a.* having no sleep.

SLEEPLESSNESS (slēp'les-nes) *n.* want of sleep. [nambulism.

SLEEP-WALKING (slēp'waw-king) *n.* somnambulism.

SLEEPY (slē'pi) *a.* disposed to sleep; drowsy.

SLEET (slēt) *n.* rain and snow or hail falling together;—*v.i.* to snow or hail with rain. [Scand.] [sleet.

SLEETY (slē'ti) *a.* consisting of or bringing sleet.

SLEEVE (slēv) *n.* covering of the arm;—*v.t.* to put sleeves in. [O.E. *slíf*. Cf. Ger. *Schlauf*.]

SLEIGH (slā) *n.* a vehicle for travelling on snow. [See SLED.]

SLEIGHT (slīt) *n.* an artful trick; dexterity. [Scand.]

SLENDER (slen'der) *a.* thin and long. [O.D. *slinder*, thin.]

SLENDERNESS (slen'der-nes) *n.* smallness of diameter; slightness.

SLEPT (slept) *pret.* and *pp.* of SLEEP.

SLICE (slis) *n.* a thin piece cut off; a thin, broad knife;—*v.t.* to cut into thin pieces; divide. [O.F. *esclice*, fr. Teut. = to slit.]

SLIDDERY (slid'er-i) *a.* slippery.

SLIDE (slid) *v.t.* or *i.* [*pret.* SLID; *pp.* SLID, SLIDDEN] to move along the surface; slip; —*n.* a smooth, easy passage on something. [O.E. *slidan*.]

SLIGHT (slit) *a.* thin; weak; trifling;—*v.t.* to treat with neglect;—*n.* neglect. [O. Low Ger. Cf. Ger. *schlecht*, straight.]

SLIGHTLY (slit'li) *ad.* superficially.

SLILY (sli'li) *ad.* in a sly manner.

SLIM (slim) *a.* slender and long; weak. [O.D. = crafty. Cf. Ger. *schlimm*, bad.]

SLIME (slim) *n.* a glutinous substance; moist earth. [O.E. *slim*. Cf. Ger. *Schleim*.]

SLIMY (sli'mi) *a.* viscous; clammy.

SLING (sling) *n.* a weapon for throwing stones; a hanging bandage; a rope with hooks for hoisting;—*v.t.* [*pret.* and *pp.* SLUNG] to throw with a sling; hang or swing with a rope. [O.E. *slingan*, to turn in a circle. Cf. Ger. *schlinge*, to twine round.]

SLINK (slingk) *v.t.* or *i.* [*pret.* and *pp.* **SLUNK**] to sneak away. [O.E. *slincan*, to creep. Cf. Ger. *schleichen*.]

SLIP (slip) *v.t.* or *i.* to slide involuntarily; escape;—*n.* a sliding; a mistake; a twig; a narrow piece; a sloping bank for ship-building. [O.E. *slipan*. Cf. Ger. *schliefen*.]

SLIP-KNOT (slip'not) *n.* a knot that slips.

SLIPPER (slip'er) *n.* a loose shoe.

SLIPPERY (slip'er-i) *a.* smooth; unstable; uncertain; hard to keep or walk on.

SLIPSHOD (slip'shod) *a.* wearing shoes down at the heels.

SLIPSLOP (slip'slop) *a.* ill-made; feeble;— *n.* poor composition; bad liquor. [A duplication of **SLOP**.]

SLIT (slit) *n.* a long cut or rent;—*v.t.* [*pret.* **SLIT**; *pp.* **SLIT**, **SLITTED**] to divide length-wise. [O.E. *slitan*. Cf. Ger. *schleissen*.]

SLITTER (slit'er) *n.* one who, or that which, slits.

SLITTING-MILL (slit'ing-mil) *n.* a mill where iron bars are slit into nail rods, etc.

SLIVER (sli'ver, sliv'er) *v.t.* to divide into thin pieces;—*n.* a long slice cut off. [O.E. *slifan*, split.] [O.E. *sla*.]

SLOE (slō) *n.* the fruit of the blackthorn.

SLOOP (slōōp) *n.* a vessel having one mast only. [D.]

SLOP (slop) *v.t.* to make a puddle;—*n.* wetness by negligence; a mean liquor. [O.E. *sloppe*, puddle.]

SLOPE (slōp) *a.* inclin-ing; slanting;—*n.* a declivity;—*v.t.* or *i.* to form obliquely; incline. [O.E. *slupan*, to slip.]

SLOPING (slō'ping) *a.* oblique; inclined.

SLOPPY (slop'i) *a.* wet and dirty.

SLOPS (slops) (1) *n. pl.* dirty water; (2) ready-made clothes. [(1) See **SLOP**. (2) O.E. *slupan*, slip.]

Sloop.

SLOT (slot) (1) *n.* a broad, flat wooden bar; —(2) *n.* a hollow or depression. [(1) D. = a lock. (2) O.E. *slitan*, slit.]

SLOTH (slōth) *n.* sluggishness; a slow-moving animal. [O.E. *slæth*, fr. *slaw*, slow.]

SLOTHFUL (slōth'fool) *a.* idle; lazy; sluggish.

SLOUCH (slouch) *n.* a hanging down;—*v.t.* or *i.* to depress; stoop or bend down. [O.F. *esloucher*, fr. Scand.]

SLOUGH (slou) (1) *n.* a miry place;—(2) (sluf) *n.* the cast skin of a serpent, *v.t.* to cast off as a slough. [O.E. *sloh*, a hollow place. (2) Scand. Cf. Ger. *Slauch*, a skin.]

SLOUGHY (slou'i) *a.* miry; boggy.

SLOVEN (sluv'n) *n.* a man careless of dress and neatness. [O.D.]

SLOVENLINESS (sluv'n-li-nes) *n.* neglect of cleanliness; untidiness.

SLOVENLY (sluv'n-li) *a.* negligent of dress; untidy; disorderly.

SLOW (slō) *a.* not fast or quick; not prompt; tardy; dilatory. [O.E. *slaw*.]

SLOWLY (slō'li) *ad.* not quick; tardily.

SLOWNESS (slō'nes) *n.* state of being slow; want of readiness; dullness.

SLUBBER (slub'er) *v.t.* to do coarsely; daub. [D. *slobberen*.]

SLUDGE (sluj) *n.* mud; mire; melting ice or snow. [M.E. *sluche*. Doublet of **SLUSH**.]

SLUE (slōŏ) *v.t.* or *i.* to turn about its axis. [Scand.]

SLUG (slug) *n.* a drone; a kind of snail. [Scand.]

SLUGGARD (slug'ard) *n.* a person habitually lazy. [Dan. *slug*, drooping.]

SLUGGISH (slug'ish) *a.* habitually lazy; slothful; slow in motion.

SLUGGISHLY (slug'ish-li) *ad.* slothfully.

SLUGGISHNESS (slug'ish-nes) *n.* indolence; slowness.

SLUICE (slōōs) *n.* a stream of water issuing through a floodgate; a floodgate. [O.F. *escluse* = F. *écluse*, fr. Late L. *exclusa*, a flood-gate, fr. *excludere*, to shut out.]

SLUICY (slōō'si) *a.* falling, as from a sluice.

SLUM (slum) *n.* a low, dirty street or district. [See **ASYLUM**.]

SLUMBER (slum'ber) *v.i.* to sleep slightly; —*n.* light sleep. [M.E., with intrusive *b*, *slumeren*, fr. O.E. *sluma*. Cf. Ger. *schlummern*.] [bers.

SLUMBERER (slum'ber-er) *n.* one who slum-

SLUMBEROUS (slum'ber-us) *a.* inviting slumber; sleepy.

SLUMP (slump) (1) *v.i.* to sink through ice or snow into mud;—(2) *v.t.* to throw into a mass;—*a.* taken together; gross;—*n.* the gross amount. [(1) Imit. (2) Scand.]

SLUNG (slung) *pret.* and *pp.* of **SLING**.

SLUNK (slungk) *pret.* and *pp.* of **SLINK**.

SLUR (slur) *v.t.* to soil; sully; perform in a smooth, gliding manner;—*n.* a mark in music; disgrace. [O. D. = to trail (in mud).]

SLUSH (slush) *n.* watery mud or snow; refuse fat or grease for lubrication. [Doublet of **SLUDGE**.]

SLUT (slut) *n.* a woman who neglects dress and neatness. [M.E. *sluite*, fr. Scand. Cf. **SLOVEN**.]

SLUTTISH (slut'ish) *a.* negligent; dirty.

SLY (sli) *a.* artful; cunning; crafty. [M.E. *sligh*, fr. Scand. Cf. Ger. *schlau*.]

SLY-BOOTS (sli'bōōts) *n.* a sly person.

SLYLY (sli'li) *ad.* with art; slily.

SMACK (smak) (1) *v.i.* to kiss; crack as a whip;—*n.* a kiss;—(2) *n.* a coasting vessel; —(3) *n.* a flavour;—*v.i.* to have a taste. [(1) Sw. *smacka*, to smack. (2) D. (3) O.E. *smæc*, taste.]

SMALL (smawl) *a.* little in size, quantity, or degree; petty; weak; gentle; mean;—*n.* the slender part of a thing. [O.E. *smæl*. Cf. Ger. *schmal*.]

SMALL-ARMS (smawl'ärmz) *n.pl.* muskets, rifles, pistols.

SMALLISH (smaw'lish) *a.* somewhat small.

SMALLNESS (smawl'nes) *n.* state of being small.

SMALL-POX (smawl'poks) *n.* an eruptive disease. [E. **SMALL** and **POCK**.]

SMART (smärt) *a.* quick; active; brisk;— *v.t.* to have a keen pain. [O.E. *smeortan*, to feel pain. Cf. Ger. *schmerzen*.]

SMARTEN (smär'tn) *v.t.* to make smart.

SMARTLY (smärt'li) *ad.* briskly; wittily.

SMARTNESS (smärt'nes) *n.* the quality of being smart.

SMASH (smash) *v.t.* to dash to pieces. [E. **MASH**, to break up.]

SMATTER (smat'er) *v.i.* to talk superficially. [M.E. *smateren*, to make a noise.]

SMATTERER (smat'er-er) *n.* a person of superficial knowledge.

SMATTERING (smat'er-ing) *n.* slight know-ledge.

SMEAR (smēr) *v.t.* to daub; soil; pay over. [O.E. *smeru*, fat. Cf. Ger. *Schmeer*, grease.]

SMELL (smel) *v.t.* or *i.* [*pret.* and *pp.* **SMELLED** or **SMELT**] to perceive by the nose;—*n.* odour; scent. [M.E.]

SMELT (smelt) (1) *v.t.* to smelt ore;—(2) *n.* a small fish of the salmon family. [(1) Scand., Sw. *smälta*, to smelt. (2) O.E.]

SMELTER (smel'ter) *n.* one that smelts ore.

SMILE (smil) *v.i.* to look as when pleased;— *n.* a look of pleasure. [Scand.]

SMILING (smi'ling) *a.* appearing gay.

SMIRK (smerk) *v.i.* to smile affectedly;—*n.* an affected smile. [O.E. *smercian*, smile.]

SMITE (smīt) v.t. [pret. **SMOTE**; pp. **SMIT, SMITTEN**] to strike; kill; blast. [O.E. smītan. Cf. Ger. schmeissen.]

SMITH (smith) n. one who works in metals. [O.E. Cf. Ger. Schmied.]

SMITHERY (smith'ẹr-i) n. the work or workshop of a smith. Also **SMITHY**.

SMOCK (smok) n. a shift; a chemise. [O.E. smoc.]

SMOCK-FROCK (smok'frok) n. a coarse shirt or frock worn by farm labourers.

SMOKABLE (smō'kạ-bl) a. that may be smoked.

SMOKE (smōk) n. exhalation from burning substances;—v.i. to emit smoke;—v.t. to hang in smoke; use a pipe or cigar. [O.E. smocian, smoca. Cf. Ger. Smauch.]

SMOKELESS (smōk'les) a. having no smoke.

SMOKER (smō'kẹr) n. one who smokes.

SMOKY (smō'ki) a. emitting smoke; like smoke; obscure.

SMOOTH (smōōTH) a. even on the surface; glossy; easy; soft; mild; fawning;—v.t. to make smooth or easy; soften; palliate. [O.E. smethe.]

SMOOTHLY (smōōTH'li) ad. evenly; calmly.

SMOOTHNESS (smōōTH'nes) n. evenness; mildness; gentleness.

SMOTE (smōt) pret. of **SMITE**.

SMOTHER (smuTH'ẹr) v.t. to stifle or suffocate;—n. a smoke; thick dust. [O.E. smorian. Cf. Ger. schmoren, to stew.]

SMOULDER (smōl'dẹr) v.i. to burn slowly or without vent. [M.E. smolder, a stifling smoke. Cf. **SMOTHER**.]

SMOULDERING (smōl'dẹr-ing) a. burning and smoking without vent.

SMOULDRY (smōl'dri) a. burning and smoking without vent.

SMUDGE (smuj) v.t. to smear with dirt or smoke; blacken;—n. a dirty mark; stain. [Scand. Cf. Ger. Schmutz.]

SMUG (smug) a. neat; affectedly nice. [Scand. Cf. Ger. schmuck.]

SMUGGLE (smug'l) v.t. to import without paying duties; convey privately. [Teut. Cf. O.E. smugan, to creep; Ger. schmuggeln.]

SMUGGLER (smug'lẹr) n. one who smuggles.

SMUGGLING (smug'ling) n. unlawful exportation or importation of goods subject to duty.

SMUGNESS (smug'nes) n. neatness.

SMUT (smut) n. soot; foul matter;—v.t. or i. to mark with smut. [M.E. smotten, to foul, fr. Scand.]

SMUTCH (smuch) v t. to blacken with smoke.

SMUTTINESS (smut'i-nes) n. soil from smoke; obscenity.

SMUTTY (smut'i) a. soiled; obscene.

SNACK (snak) n. a share; repast. [M.E. snacchen. Doublet of **SNATCH**.]

SNAFFLE (snaf'l) n. a bridle with a bit without branches. [D. = nose. Cf. **SNAP**.]

SNAG (snag) n. a tooth standing out; a knot; a r ug branch. [Scand. = a tongue of land] h

SNAGGY (snag'i) a. full of knots or sharp points.

SNAIL (snāl) n. a slimy reptile. [O.E. snœgel, snegel, a snail. Cf. Ger. Schnecke.]

SNAKE (snāk) n. a kind of serpent. [O.E. snaca.]

SNAP (snap) v.t. to break short;—v.i. to bite at;—n. act of breaking suddenly. [D. Cf. Ger. schnappen.]

SNAPPISH (snap'ish) a. apt to snap; peevish.

SNARE (snār) n. any thing which entraps; a noose;—v.t. to ensnare. [O.E. snear, a string.]

SNARL (snārl) v.t. to entangle;—v.i. to growl, as a dog;—n. entanglement; a complicated difficulty. [D. Cf. Ger. schnarren.]

SNATCH (snach) v.t. to seize hastily; n. a hasty catch. [M.E. snacchen.]

SNEAK (snēk) v.i. to creep away privately; behave meanly. [O.E. snican, creep. Cf. **SNAKE**.]

SNEAKING (snē'king) a. mean.

SNEAKINGLY (snē'king-li) ad. slily; meanly.

SNEER (snēr) v.i. to show contempt by look, word, or tone; insinuate contempt;—n. a look or expression of disdain or contempt. [M.E. sneren. Cf. **SNARL**.]

SNEERER (snē'rẹr) n. one who sneers.

SNEERINGLY (snē'ring-li) ad. with a look of contempt or scorn.

SNEEZE (snēz) v.i. to eject air suddenly through the nose;—n. a single act of sneezing. [O.E. fneosan.]

SNEEZING (snē'zing) n. the act of ejecting air audibly through the nose.

SNIB (snib) v.t. to fasten; bolt;—n. catch of a door; latch. [Scot. Doublet of **SNUB**.]

SNICKER (snik'ẹr) v.i. to laugh with small catches of the breath. Also **SNIGGER**. [Imit.]

SNIFF (snif) v.i. or t. to draw air audibly up the nose; snuff; scent;—n. smell; scent; whiff. [Scand.]

SNIFT (snift) v.i. to snuff; smell. Also **SNIFTER**.

SNIGGLE (snig'l) v.t. to snare; catch;—v.i. to fish for eels. [Prov. E. snig, an eel.]

SNIP (snip) v.t. to cut off; nib;—n. a single cut; a clip or shred. [D. Cf. Ger. schnippen; conn. with **SNAP**.]

SNIPE (snīp) n. a small grallatorial bird; a blockhead. [Scand.]

SNIVEL (sniv'l) n. the running of the nose; —v.i. to run at the nose; cry. [O.E. snofel, mucus. Cf. **SNIFF**, **SNUFF**.]

SNOB (snob) n. one who affects gentility; a shoemaker. [Scand.]

SNOBBISH (snob'ish) a. like a snob; affected; pretentious.

SNOOZE (snōōz) v.t. to sleep; doze;—n. a short sleep; nap. [Conn. with **SNORE**.]

SNORE (snōr) v.i. to breathe with noise in sleep;—n. a breathing with noise. [O.E. snora, a snoring. Conn. with **SNARL**.]

SNORING (snō'ring) n. breathing noisily in sleep.

SNORT (snort) v.i. to force air through the nose with a noise. [O.E. snorten, to snore fr. Scand.]

SNOUT (snout) n. the long nose of a beast; end of a pipe; nozzle. [M.E. snoute.]

SNOW (snō) n. frozen vapour which falls in flakes;—v.i. to fall in flakes. [O.E. snaw; Ger. Schnee.]

SNOWBALL (snō'bawl) n. a ball of snow.

SNOWDRIFT (snō'drift) n. bank of snow.

SNOWDROP (snō'drop) n. a bulbous plant with white flower.

SNOWSHOE (snō'shōō) n. a frame to enable a person to walk on snow.

SNOWY (snō'i) a. full of snow; white.

SNUB (snub) v.t. to clip off; nip; check;— n. a rebuke; reprimand; knot in wood. [M.E. snibben, fr. Scand.]

SNUFF (snuf) (1) v.t. to nip off the top of a candle-wick;—(2) v.t. to sniff; to smell; to inhale;—v.i. to inhale air with noise; —n. pulverised tobacco snuffed up. [(1) M.E. snuffen, fr. Teut. Cf. Ger. schnaufen. (2) D.]

SNUFFERS (snuf'ẹrz) n.pl. an instrument to snuff candles.

SNUFFLE (snuf'l) v.i. to speak through the nose. [Fr. **SNUFF**.]

SNUFFLES (snuf'lz) n.pl. obstructions in the nose.

SNUFFY (snuf'i) a. soiled with snuff; musty.

SNUG (snug) a. lying close; private. [Scand.]

SNUGGLE (snug'l) v.i. to lie close.

SNUGLY (snug'li) ad. closely; safely.

SO (sō) ad. thus; in like manner or degree; on this account; at this time. [O.E. swa.]

SOAK (sōk) v.t. or i. to steep in a liquid; drench. [O.E. socian.]

SOAP (sōp) n. a compound of oil and alkali; —v.t. to rub with soap. [O.E. sape. Cf. Ger. Seife.]

SOAPY (sō'pi) a. like soap.

SOAR (sōr) v.i. to mount on the wing;—n. a towering flight. [F. essorer, to expose to air, to soar up, fr. L. ex, and aura, the air.]

SOB (sob) v.i. to sigh convulsively;—n. a convulsive cry. [Conn. with O.E. seofian, bewail.]

SOBER (sō'bẹr) a. serious; grave; temperate; not intoxicated;—v.t. to make sober or grave. [F. sobre, fr. L. sobrius, fr. se, apart, and ebrius, drunk.]

SOBERLY (sō'bẹr-li) ad. seriously.

SOBRIETY (sō-brī'e-ti) n. habitual temperance; gravity.

SOBRIQUET (sō-brē-kā') n. a nickname. [F., fr. O.F. soutzbriquet, a chuck under the chin, fr. L. sub, under, and briquet, breast.]

SOCAGE (sok'ij) n. a tenure of land under a certain service. [O.E. soc, a right of holding a court, fr. sacan, to contend.]

SOCIABILITY (sō-sha-bil'i-ti) n. disposition for society or conversation.

SOCIABLE (sō'sha-bl) a. conversable; familiar; friendly. [F., fr. L. sociabilis fr. sociare, to associate, fr. socius, a companion.]

SOCIABLY (sō'sha-bli) ad. conversably.

SOCIAL (sō'shal) a. pertaining to or fond of society; companionable. [L. socius, a companion.]

SOCIALISM (sō'shal-izm) n. the doctrine that a community of interests is the best form of society.

SOCIALIST (sō'shal-ist) n. advocate of Socialism.

SOCIALLY (sō'shal-i) ad. in a social manner.

SOCIETY (so-sī'e-ti) n. union of persons in one interest; an association; persons living in the same circle; social intercourse. [L. (acc.) societatem fr. socius a companion.]

SOCINIAN (sō-sin'i-an) n. one who denies the divinity and atonement of Christ. Fr. Socinus (16th century).]

SOCIOLOGY (sō-shi-ol'ō-ji) n. science of society and social institutions. [L. socius, a companion, and G. logia fr. legein, to speak.]

SOCK (sok) (1) n. a shoe for actors; a short stocking;—(2) n. a ploughshare. [(1) L. soccus, a light shoe. [2) O.F. soc, fr. Celt.]

SOCKET (sok'et) n. a hollow into which something is inserted; cavity of the eye, tooth, etc. [Dim. of SOCK.]

SOD (sod) n. earth with roots of grass; turf; sward;—v.t. to cover with turf. [Perh. as SODDEN, in wet weather.]

SODA (sō'da) n. fixed mineral alkali, the basis of common salt. [It., fr. L. solida, firm.]

SODALITY (so-dal'i-ti) n. fellowship. [L. (acc.) sodalitatem, fr. sodalis, a comrade.]

SODDEN (sod'n) pp. of SEETHE;—a. boiled; soaked and softened. [O.E. soden.]

SOFA (sō'fa) n. a long seat stuffed. [A.]

SOFFIT (sof'it) n. the under part of a lintel or ceiling. [F., fr. L. (part.) suffixus, of suffigere, to fasten beneath, fr. sub, under, and figere, to fix.]

SOFT (soft) a. easily yielding; smooth; mild; gentle in motion; easy. [O.E. soft.]

Soffit.

SOFTEN (sof'n) v.t. or i. to make or become soft.

SOFTISH (sof'tish) a. somewhat soft.

SOFTLY (soft'li) ad. tenderly; silently.

SOFTNESS (soft'nes) n. quality of being soft.

SOIL (soil) (1) v.t. or i. to daub; stain; make or become dirty;—n. spot; stain;—(2) n. upper stratum of the earth; mould; land; country. [(1) O.F. soillier, to wallow, fr. L. sus, pig. (2) O.F. soel, sueil, fr. Late L. solea, ground, fr. L. solea, sole; conn. with L. solum, ground.]

SOIREE (swä-rā') n. an evening party. [F., fr. soir, evening, fr. L. serus, late.]

SOJOURN (soj'urn, sō'jurn) v.i. to dwell for a time;—n. temporary abode. [O.F. sojourner, fr. L. sub, under, and diurnus, daily, fr. dies, a day.]

SOJOURNER (soj'ur-nẹr, sō'jur-nẹr) n. temporary resident, as a traveller.

SOL (sol) n. a note in music.

SOLACE (sol'as) v.t. to give comfort to; console; allay;—n. comfort in grief. [O.F. solas, fr. L. solatium, fr. (part.) solatus, of solari, to comfort in distress.]

SOLAR (sō'lar (a. pretaining to the sun. [L. solaris, pertaining to the sun, fr. sol, the sun.]

SOLD (sōld) pret. and pp. of SELL.

SOLDER (sod'er, sol'der) v.t. to unite with metallic cement;—n. metallic cement for lead. Also written SODER. [O.F. soudre, fr. L. solidus, firm.]

SOLDIER (sōl'jẹr) n. a man in military service; warrior. [O.F. =F. soldat, fr. L. solidus, a piece of money. the pay of a soldier.]

SOLDIERLY (sōl'jẹr-li) a. like a good soldier; warlike; brave.

SOLDIERSHIP (sōl'jẹr-ship) n. military character; martial skill.

SOLDIERY (sōl'jẹr-i) n. a body of soldiers.

SOLE (sōl) (1) n. bottom of the foot, or shoe; —v.t. to furnish with soles;—(2) a. single; alone;—(3) n. a marine flat fish, allied to the flounder. [(1) O.E. sole, fr. L. solea, fr. solum, the ground. (2) L. solus, alone. (3) L. solea.]

SOLECISE (sol'e-sīz) v.i. to commit solecism.

SOLECISM (sol'e-sizm) n. impropriety in language. [F. solécisme, fr. L. fr. G. soloikismos fr. soloikos, speaking incorrectly. Perh. fr. the corr. of the Attic dialect by the colonists of Soloi, in Cilicia.]

SOLECISTIC (sol-e-sis'tik) n. barbarous in phrase.

SOLELY (sōl'li) ad. singly; only.

SOLEMN (sol'em) a. religiously grave; marked with solemnity; serious; formal. [O.F. solempne =F. solennel fr. L. solemnis, solennis, fr. sollus. entire, and annus, a year.]

SOLEMNESS (sol'em-nes) n. solemnity.

SOLEMNITY (so-lem'ni-ti) n. a religious ceremony; seriousness.

SOLEMNISATION (sol-em-ni-zā'shun) n. celebration.

SOLEMNISE (sol'em-nīz) v.t. to celebrate; make serious.

SOLEMNISER (sol'em-ni-zẹr) n. one who performs a solemn rite.

SOLEMNLY (sol'em-li) ad. with religious reverence; gravely.

SOLENESS (sōl'nes) n. state of being alone.

SOL-FA (sol'fä) v.i. to sing the notes of the gamut. [It.]

SOLFEGGIO (sol-fej'ō) n. an exercise on the musical scale. [It., fr. solfa, the gamut.]

SOLICIT (so-lis'it) v.t. to ask with earnestness; try to obtain. [F. soliciter, fr. L. (part.) sollicitus, fr. sollus, whole, and (part.) citus, of ciere, to cite.]

SOLICITANT (so-lis'i-tant) n. one who solicits.

SOLICITATION (so-lis-i-tā'shun) n. entreaty.

SOLICITOR (so-lis'i-tẹr) n. one who solicits; a law agent; legal adviser.

SOLICITORSHIP (so-lis'i-tur-ship) n. office of a solicitor.

SOLICITOUS (so-lis'i-tus) a. anxious; careful.

SOLICITOUSLY (so-lis'i-tus-li) ad. with anxiety.

SOLICITRESS (so-lis'-i-tres) *n.* a female who solicits.

SOLICITUDE (so-lis'i-tūd) *n.* anxiety; carefulness.

SOLID (sol'id) *a.* firm; compact; sound;— *n.* a solid substance. [F., fr. L. *solidus*, firm.]

SOLIDARITY (sol-i-dar'i-ti) *n.* a complete union of interests. [F. *solide*, fr. L. *solidus*, solid.]

SOLIDIFY (so-lid'i-fī) *v.t.* to make solid. [L. *solidus*, and *facere*, make.]

SOLIDITY (so-lid'i-ti) *n.* state of being solid; compactness; firmness.

SOLIDLY (sol'id-li) *ad.* compactly.

SOLILOQUISE (so-lil'u-kwīz) *v.t.* to utter a soliloquy.

SOLILOQUY (so-lil'u-kwi) *n.* a talking alone. [L. *soliloquium*, fr. *solus*, alone, and *loqui*, to speak.]

SOLITAIRE (sol'i-tār) *n.* a recluse; an ornament for the neck; a game for one person. [F., fr. L. *solus*, alone.]

SOLITARILY (sol'i-ta-ri-li) *ad.* in solitude.

SOLITARINESS (sol'i-ta-ri-nes) *n.* forbearance of company; loneliness.

SOLITARY (sol'i-ta-ri) *a.* single; living alone; gloomy. [F. *solitaire*, fr. L. *solitarius*, fr. *solus*, alone.]

SOLITUDE (sol'i-tūd) *n.* state of being alone; a lonely life or place; desert.

SOLMISATION (sol-mi-zā'shun) *n.* reciting the *do*, *re*, *mi*, of the gamut; sol-faing. [F. *solmiser*, fr. the musical notes *sol*, *mi*.]

SOLO (sō'lō) *n.* a musical piece for a single voice or instrument. [It., fr. L. *solus*, alone.]

SOLSTICE (sol'stis) *n.* one of the two points where the sun ceases to recede from the equator; the time of this. [F., fr. L. *solstitium*, fr. *sol*, the sun, and *sistere*, cause to stand, fr. *stare*, to stand.]

SOLSTITIAL (sol-stish'al) *a.* belonging to a solstice.

SOLUBILITY (sol-ū-bil'i-ti) *n.* quality of being soluble.

SOLUBLE (sol'ū-bl) *a.* capable of being dissolved in a fluid. [L. *solubilis*, fr. *solvere*, to loosen.]

SOLUTION (so-lū'shun) *n.* the process of dissolving in a fluid; the mixture resulting from it; explanation. [L. (part.) *solutus*, loosened, of *solvere*, to loosen.]

SOLUTIVE (sol'ū-tiv) *a.* tending to dissolve.

SOLVABILITY (sol-va-bil'i-ti) *n.* solvency.

SOLVABLE (sol'va-bl) *a.* that may be solved.

SOLVE (solv) *v.i.* to explain; unfold; clear up. [L. *solvere*, loosen.]

SOLVENCY (sol'ven-si) *n.* ability to pay debts.

SOLVENT (sol'vent) *a.* dissolving; able to pay debts;—*n.* a fluid which dissolves any substance. [L. (part. stem) *solvent-*, of *solvere*, to loosen.]

SOLVER (sol'ver) *n.* one who solves or explains.

SOMATIC (sō-mat'ik) *a.* bodily; corporeal. [G. *soma*, the body.]

SOMATICS (sō-mat'iks) *n.* science of material bodies. Also **SOMATOLOGY**.

SOMBRE (som-ber) *a.* dark; gloomy; melancholy. [F. fr. L. *sub umbra*, under shade.]

SOMBROUS (som'brus) *a.* dark; gloomy.

SOME (sum) *a.* noting an indefinite number or quantity; more or less; a little; a portion. [O.E. *sum*.]

SOMEBODY (sum'bod-i) *n.* a person unknown or indeterminate.

SOMEHOW (sum'how) *ad.* one way or another.

SOMERSAULT, **SOMERSET** (sum'er-sawlt, sum'er-set) *n.* a leaping and turning heels over head; [M.F. *soubresault*, fr. L. *supra*, over, and *saltus*, a leap, fr. *salire*, to leap.]

SOMETHING (sum'thing) *n.* an indefinite thing or event; a portion;—*ad.* in some degree.

SOMETIME (sum'tim) *a.* having been formerly; —*ad.* at a time not fixed; once.

SOMETIMES (sum'timz) *ad.* at one time; at certain times; at intervals.

SOMEWHAT (sum'hwot) *n.* something more or less;—*ad.* in some degree or amount.

SOMEWHERE (sum'hwār) *ad.* in some place or another.

SOMNAMBULISM (som-nam'bū-lizm) *n.* a walking in sleep.

SOMNAMBULIST (som-nam'bū-list) *n.* one who walks in sleep. [L. *somnambulare*, fr. *somnus*, sleep, and *ambulare*, to walk.]

SOMNIFEROUS (som-nif'e-rus) *a.* tending to cause sleep. Also **SOMNIFIC**. [L. *somnus*, sleep, and *ferre*, bring.]

SOMNILOQUIST (som-nil'u-kwist) *n.* one who talks in sleep. [L. *somnus*, sleep, and *loqui*, speak.]

SOMNOLENCE (som'nu-lens) *n.* sleepiness.

SOMNOLENT (som'nu-lent) *a.* sleepy. [L. *somnolentia*, fr. *somnus*, sleep.]

SON (sun) *n.* a male descendant. [O.E. *sunu*. Cf. Ger. *Sohn*.]

SONATA (so-nä'ta) *n.* a musical composition for one or more instruments in three parts. [It., fr. L. *sonare*, sound.]

SONG (song) *n.* a poem; a hymn. [O.E. *sang*, fr. *singan*, to sing. Cf. Ger. *Gesang*.]

SONGSTER (song'ster) *n.* a singer.

SONGSTRESS (song'stres) *n.* a female singer.

SONNET (son'et) *n.* a poem in 14 lines working out one theme or thought. [F., fr. It. *sonetto*, fr. L. *sonus*, a sound.]

SONNETEER (son-e-tēr') *n.* a composer of sonnets.

SONOROUS (so-nō'rus) *a.* giving sound when struck. [L. *sonorus*, fr *sonor*, fr. *sonus*, a sound, fr. *sonare*, to sound.]

SONSHIP (sun'ship) *n.* the state of being a son.

SOON (sōōn) *ad.* in a little time; shortly after; immediately. [O.E. *sona*.]

SOOT (soot) *n.* a black powder formed by combustion;—*v.t.* to black with soot. [O.E. *sot*.]

SOOTH (sōōth) *n.* truth; reality;—*a.* true; pleasing. [O.E. *soth*, true.]

SOOTHE (sōōth) *v.t.* to quiet or please with soft words; assuage; soften. [O.E. *gesothian*, to confirm.]

SOOTHER (sōō'ther) *n.* one who soothes.

SOOTHSAY (sōōth'sā) *v.t.* to foretell; predict.

SOOTHSAYER (sōōth'sā-er) *n.* a predicter.

SOOTY (soot'i) *a.* containing or soiled by soot.

SOP (sop) *n.* anything dipped or soaked for food; anything given to satisfy;—*v.t.* to steep in liquor. [O.E., fr. *supan*, sip.]

SOPHISM (sof'izm) *n.* a fallacious argument; specious fallacy. [F. *sophisme*, fr. G. *sophisma*, fr. *sophizein*, to make wise, fr *sophos*, wise.]

SOPHIST (sof'ist) *n.* an insidious reasoner.

SOPHISTICAL (so-fis'ti-kal) *a.* pertaining to a sophist, or to sophistry.

SOPHISTICATE (so-fis'ti-kāt) *v.t.* to adulterate; corrupt.

SOPHISTICATION (so-fis-ti-kā'shun) *n.* act of adulterating; quibbling; a quibble.

SOPHISTRY (sof'is-tri) *n.* fallacious reasoning.

SOPORIFIC (sō-pu-rif'ik) *a.* causing sleep; somniferous. [F. *soporifique*, fr. L. *sopor*, a heavy sleep, and *facere*, make.]

SOPRANO (so-prä'nō) *n.* the highest kind of female voice; treble; one who sings the air or tune. [It., fr. L. *supra*, above.]

SORCERER (sor'ser-er) *n.* a magician; enchanter.

SORCERESS (sor'ser-es) *n.* an enchantress.

SORCEROUS (sor'ser-us) *a.* containing enchantments.

SORCERY (sor'ser-i) *n.* enchantment; witchcraft. [O.F. *sorcerie*, fr. Late L. *sortiarius*, one who tells fortunes by lots, fr. *sortire*, to cast lots, fr. stem *sort-*, of *sors*, a lot.]

SORDID (sor'did) *a.* filthy; mean; vile; avaricious. [F. *sordide*, fr. L. *sordidus*, fr. *sordere*, be dirty.]

SORDIDLY (sor'did-li) *ad.* meanly; basely; covetously. [ness.

SORDIDNESS (sor'did-nes) *n.* filthiness; mean-

SORE (sor) *n.* a painful or diseased place in the skin or flesh; grief;—*a.* tender; painful; grieved; vexed;—*ad.* greatly; painfully. [O.E. *sar*. Cf. Ger. *sehr* very.]

SORELY (sor'li) *ad.* with pain.

SORENESS (sor'nes) *n.* tenderness; painfulness.

SORORICIDE (so-ro'ri-sid) *n.* the murder or murderer of a sister. [L. *soror* a sister, and *caedere*, kill.]

SORREL (sor'el) (1) *a.* of a reddish-brown colour;—*n.* a reddish-brown colour;—(2) *n.* a plant allied to the dock. [(1) O.F. *sor* =F. *saure*, sorrel, fr. Low Ger. *soor* sear. (2) O.F. *sorel* (F. *surelle*), fr. *sur*, sour, fr. O. H. Ger. *sur* (Ger. *sauer*), sour.]

SORRILY (sor'i-li) *ad.* meanly; poorly.

SORROW (sor'o) *n.* pain produced by a sense of loss; regret; grief;—*v.i.* to mourn; grieve. [O.E. *sorg*. Cf. Ger. *Sorge*.]

SORROWFUL (sor'o-fool) *a.* causing or exhibiting sorrow; sad; dejected.

SORROWLESS (sor'o-les) *a.* free from sorrow.

SORRY (sor'i) *a.* grieved for something lost or past; poor; worthless. [O.E. *sarig*, fr. *sar*, pain.]

SORT (sort) *n.* a species; kind; manner;—*v.t.* or *i.* to arrange; put in classes; select; associate; suit. [O.F. *sorte*, fr. L. stem *sort-* of *sors*, a lot.]

SORTABLE (sor'ta-bl) *a.* that may be sorted.

SORTIE (sor'te) *n.* sally of troops from a besieged place. [F., fr. *sortir*, go out, fr. L. *surgere*, to rise up.]

SORTILEGE (sor'ti-lej) *n.* drawing lots; divination by drawing lots. [L. *sors sortis* a lot, and *legere*, gather.]

SOT (sot) *n.* a habitual drunkard. [O.E.]

SOTTISH (sot'ish) *a.* given to liquor; stupid; drunken.

SOTTISHNESS (sot'ish-nes) *n.* drunken stupidity.

SOU (soo) *n.* a French halfpenny; the 20th of a franc;—*pl.* **SOUS**. [F. *sou*, fr. It. *soldo*, fr. L. *solidus*, a coin.]

SOUCHONG (soo-shong') *n.* a kind of black tea. [F., fr. Chin.]

SOUGHT (sawt) *pret.* of **SEEK**.

SOUL (sol) *n.* the immortal spirit of man; life; intellect; essence; energy; a person. [O.E. *sawol*. Cf. Ger. *Seele*.]

SOULLESS (sol'les) *a.* without soul or spirit; mean.

SOUND (sound) (1) *n.* a noise;—*v.t.* to cause to make a noise;—*v.i.* to make a noise;—(2) *n.* a narrow sea;—(3) *n.* air-bladder of a fish;—(4) *v.t.* to measure the depth of;—*v.i.* to use the line and lead in finding the depth of water;—(5) *a.* safe; whole; healthy; correct; orthodox. [(1) O.F. *soner*, fr. L. *sonare*, fr. *sonus*, sound. (2) O.E. *sund*, a narrow arm of the sea, fr. *swimman*, to swim. Cf. Ger. *Sund*, a strait. (3) O.E. *sund* a swimming. (4) O.F. *sonder* to sound, fr. Late L. *subundare*, fr. *sub*, under and *unda*, a wave; F. *sonde*. (5) O.E. *sund*. Cf. Ger. *gesund*.]

SOUNDING (soun'ding) *n.* ascertaining the depth of water;—*pl.* a part of the sea in which the bottom can be reached.

SOUNDLESS (sound'les) *a.* that cannot be sounded.

SOUNDLY (sound'li) *ad.* justly; firmly; severely.

SOUNDNESS (sound'nes) *n.* entireness; health; solidity; validity.

SOUP (soop) *n.* a decoction of flesh, vegetables, etc. [F. *soupe*.]

SOUP-KITCHEN (soop'ki-chen) *n.* establishment to supply soup to the poor.

SOUR (sour) *a.* acid; tart; crabbed;—*v.t.* or *i.* to make or become acid or cross in temper. [O.E. *sur*.]

SOURCE (sors) *n.* a spring; fountain; origin; first cause. [O.F. *sorse* =F. *source*, fr. *sourdre*, fr. L. *surgere*, rise.]

SOURISH (sour'ish) *a.* somewhat sour.

SOURLY (sour'li) *ad.* with acidity.

SOURNESS (sour'nes) *n.* acidity; tartness; harshness.

SOUSE (sous) (1) *n.* pickle made of the ears and feet of swine; a plunge in water;—*v.t.* or *i.* to plunge in water; steep in pickle. [A variant of **SAUCE**.]

SOUTER (soo'ter) *n.* a shoemaker. [L. *suere*, sew.]

SOUTH (south) *n.* point toward the sun at noon;—*a.* in a southern direction;—*ad.* toward the south. [O.E. *suth*. Cf. Ger. *Süd*.]

SOUTH-EAST (south-est') *n.* a point between south and east.

SOUTHERLY (suTH'er-li) *a.* being at the south; coming from the south.

SOUTHERN (suTH'ern) *a.* belonging to the south.

SOUTHERN-WOOD (suTH'ern-wood) *n.* an aromatic plant.

SOUTHING (sou'THing) *a.* going towards the south;—*n.* course south.

SOUTHRON suTH'run) *n.* an inhabitant of the south.

SOUTHWARD (south'ward, suTH'ard) *ad.* towards the south.

SOUTH-WEST (south'-west) *n.* a point between south and west;—*a.* being at the south-west.

SOUTH-WESTER (south'-wester, sou-wes'ter) *n.* a wind from the south-west; a sailor's waterproof hat.

SOUVENIR (soo've-ner) *n.* a remembrancer. [F., a remembrance, fr. *souvenir*, to remember fr. L. *subvenire*, to come to mind, fr. *sub*, under, and *venire*, to come.]

SOVEREIGN (sov'rin, sov'e-rin) *a.* supreme in power;—*n.* a supreme ruler; a gold coin, value 20s. sterling. [O.F. *souverain*, fr. Late L. *superanus*, fr. *super*, *supra*, above.]

SOVEREIGNTY (sov'rin-ti, sov'e-rin-ti) *n.* supreme power.

SOW (sow) *n.* a female swine. [O.E. *sugu*, *su*.]

SOW (so) *v.t.* or *i.* [*pret.* **SOWED**; *pp.* **SOWED**, **SOWN**] to scatter as seed for growth; spread. [O.E. *sawan*. Cf. Ger. *säen*.]

SOWER (so'er) *n.* one who sows.

SOWN (son) *pp.* of **SOW**, scattered.

SPA (spa) *n.* a general name for springs of mineral water. [So called from *Spa*, south-west of Liege, Belgium.]

SPACE (spas) *n.* room; distance; interval;—*v.t* to arrange intervals between. [F. *espace*, fr. L. *spatium*, space.]

SPACIOUS (spa'shus) *a.* large in extent; ample; capacious.

SPADE (spad) *n.* an instrument for digging; a suit of cards. [O.E. *spædu*, *spada*. Cf. G. *spathe*, a broad blade of wood or metal.]

SPADEFUL (spad'fool) *n.* as much as a spade will hold.

SPAN (span) *n.* nine inches; the space from the end of the thumb to that of the little finger when both are extended; spread of an arch; space of time;—*v.t.* to measure by spans; arch over; embrace. [O.E. fr. *spannan*, to bind.]

SPANGLE (spang'gl) *n.* a small boss;—*v.t.* to set with spangles. [Dim. of *spang*, fr. O.E. *spange*, a metal clasp.]

SPANIEL (span'yel) *n.* a sporting dog;—*a.* fawning; obsequious. [M.E., fr. O.F. *espagneul* =F. *épagneul*, a Spanish dog, fr. Sp. *Espana*, Spain.]

SPANISH (span'ish) *a.* pertaining to Spain : — *n.* the language of Spain.

Spaniel.

SPANKER (spang'ker) *n.* the after sail of a ship or barque. [Cf. Dan. *spanke*, strut.]

SPANKING (spang'king) *a.* going free; dashing.

SPAR (spár) *n.* a long beam; nautical term for mast, yard, boom, and gaff;—*v.t.* to furnish with spars. [O.E., fr. *sparrian*, to fasten with a bar.]

SPARE (spâr) *v.t.* or *i.* to save; withhold; do without; part with; forbear; treat tenderly, be frugal;—*a.* frugal; superfluous; scanty; lean. [O.E. *sparian*, fr. *spœr*, spare.]

SPARENESS (spâr'nes) *a.* state of being spare.

SPARER (spâr'er) *n.* one who spares or saves.

SPARERIB (spâr'rib) *n.* rib of meat with little flesh on it.

SPARINGLY (spâr'ing-li) *ad.* in a sparing manner.

SPARK (spárk) (1) *n.* a particle of fire; (2) a gay man; lover. [(1) O.E. *spearca*. (2) Scand.]

SPARKISH (spár'kish) *a.* lively; gay.

SPARKLE (spár'kl) *n.* a little spark; lustre; —*v.i.* to emit sparks; glitter. [Freq. of SPARK (1).]

SPARKLER (spárk'ler) *n.* one who or that which sparkles.

SPARKLING (spárk'ling) *n.* glittering; brilliant; lively. [ling.

SPARKLINGLY (spárk'ling-li) *ad.* with twinkling.

SPARROW (spar'ō) *n.* a small familiar bird. [O.E. *spearwa*. Cf. Ger. *Sperling*.]

SPARRY (spár'i) *a.* resembling spar.

SPARSE (spárs) *a.* thin; scattered. [L. (part.) *sparsus*, fr. *spargere*, to scatter.]

SPARSELY (spárs'li) *ad.* thinly.

SPARTAN (spár'tan) *a.* pertaining to Sparta; brave; enduring.

SPASM (spazm) *n.* involuntary contraction of muscles; a sudden fit or effort. [F. *spasme*, the cramp, fr. L., fr. G. *spasmos*, fr. *spaein*, to draw.]

SPASMODIC (spaz'mod'ik) *a.* consisting in spasm; convulsive.

SPASTIC (spas'tik) *a.* pertaining to a spasm.

SPATTER (spat'er) *v.t.* to sprinkle on;—*v.i.* to sputter. [Freq. of *spat*, to splash.]

SPATULA (spat'ū-la) *n.* an apothecary's slice for plasters. [L., dim. of *spatha*, fr. G. *spathe*, a broad blade.]

SPAVIN (spav'in) *n.* a tumour on a horse's leg. [O.F. *esparvin* =F. *éparvin*, fr. Teut. = a sparrow.]

SPAVINED (spav'ind) *a.* affected with spavin.

SPAWN (spawn) *n.* the eggs of frogs and fishes;—*v.t.* or *i.* to deposit, as spawn. [O.F. *espandre*, fr. L. *expandere*, to spread out.]

SPAWNER (spaw'ner) *n.* the female fish.

SPEAK (spēk) *v.t.* or *i.* [*pret.* SPOKE, SPAKE; *pp.* SPOKE, SPOKEN] to say; talk; pronounce; utter words; converse. [O.E. *sprecan*. Cf. Ger. *sprechen*.]

SPEAKABLE (spē'ka-bl) *a.* that may be uttered; able to speak.

SPEAKER (spē'ker) *n.* one who speaks; the presiding officer in a deliberative assembly.

SPEAR (spēr) *n.* a pointed weapon; lance;— *v.t.* to stab with a spear. [O.E. *spere*. Cf. Ger. *Speer*; E. SPAR.]

SPEARMAN (spēr'man) *n.* one armed with a spear.

SPECIAL (spesh'al) *a.* particular; noting something more than ordinary. [Contr. fr. ESPECIAL.]

SPECIALITY (spesh-i-al'i-ti) *n.* peculiar case; special quality or object.

SPECIALLY (spesh'al-i) *a.* particularly.

SPECIALTY (spesh'al-ti) *n.* particularity ; a special contract under seal; that for which a person is distinguished.

SPECIE (spē'shi) *n.* coined money. [Abl. of L. *species*, kind.]

SPECIES (spē'shēz) *n.* sort; kind; class. [L., fr. *specere*, look, behold.]

SPECIFIC (spe-sif'ik) *a.* distinguishing one from another; comprehended under a kind; —*n.* a certain remedy.

SPECIFICALLY (spe-sif'i-kal-i) *ad.* definitely; particularly.

SPECIFICATION (spes-i-fi-kā'shun) *n.* act of specifying; thing specified.

SPECIFICNESS (spe-sif'ik-nes) *n.* quality of being specific.

SPECIFY (spes'i-fi) *v.t.* to mention particularly. [O.F., fr. Late L. *specificare*, fr. *species*, kind, and *facere*, to make.]

SPECIMEN (spes'i-men) *n.* a sample. [L. something shown, fr. *specere*, to see.]

SPECIOSITY (spē-shi-os'i-ti) *n.* fair outward show or appearance.

SPECIOUS (spē'shus) *a.* pleasing; appearing well at first sight; plausible. [F., fr. L. *speciosus*, fair to see, fr. *species*, look, fr. *specere*, to look.]

SPECIOUSLY (spē'shus-li) *ad.* with fair appearance.

SPECK (spek) *n.* a stain; a small spot;—*v.t.* to spot. [O.E. *specca*.]

SPECKLE (spek'l) *n.* a small speck;—*v.t.* to mark with spots.

SPECTACLE (spek'ta-kl) *n.* a show; sight; —*n.pl.* glasses to assist the sight. [L. *spectaculum*, fr. *spectare*, look at, fr. *specere*, to look.]

SPECTACULAR (spek-tak'ū-lar) *a.* pertaining to shows.

SPECTATOR (spek-tā'ter) *n.* a looker on; a beholder. [L.]

SPECTRAL (spek'tral) *a.* pertaining to a spectre.

SPECTRE (spek'ter) *n.* an apparition; ghost. [L. *spectrum*, image, fr. *specere*, to look.]

SPECTRUM (spek'trum) *n.* an image seen after the eyes are closed; exhibition of the colours of light separated by a prism. [L.]

SPECULAR (spek'ū-lar) *a.* like a mirror.

SPECULATE (spek'ū-lāt) *v.i.* to meditate; buy in expectation of a rise in price. [L. (part.) *speculatus*, fr. *speculari*, fr. *specula*, a look-out, fr. *specere*, to look.]

SPECULATION (spek-ū-lā'shun) *n.* mental view; act of speculating.

SPECULATIST (spek'ū-lā-tist) *n.* one who forms theories.

SPECULATIVE (spek'ū-lā-tiv) *a.* given to speculation; theoretical.

SPECULATOR (spek'ū-lā-ter) *n.* one who speculates.

SPECULUM (spek'ū-lum) *n.* a glass that reflects images; mirror. [L., fr. *specere*, look.]

SPEECH (spēch) *n.* language; discourse; oration. [O.E. *sprœc*, *spœc*. Cf. Ger. *Sprache*.]

SPEECHIFY (spē'chi-fi) *v.i.* to make a speech; harangue.

SPEECHLESS (spēch'les) *a.* not able to speak.

SPEED (spēd) *v.t.* or *i.* [*pret.* and *pp.* SPED] to hasten; despatch; aid; move quickly; succeed;—*n.* haste; despatch. [O.E. *sped*, haste, success.]

SPEEDILY (spē'di-li) *ad.* quickly; hastily.

SPEEDWELL (spēd'wel) *n.* a small herbaceous shrub.

SPEEDY (spē'di) *a.* quick; hasty.

SPELL (spel) (1) *n.* a charm;—(2) *v.t.* or *i.* [*pret.* and *pp.* SPELLED, SPELT] to name in order the letters of a word;—(3) *n.* a turn at work;—*v.t.* or *i.* take a turn at work. [(1) O.E. *spell spel* story magic charm. (2) M.E. *spellen* to spell, tell. (3) Fr. *spellian,* take one's place.]

SPELLER (spel'er) *n.* one that spells; a spelling-book.

SPELT (spelt) *n.* a kind of wheat; German wheat. [O.E.]

SPELTER (spel'ter) *n.* zinc. [D.]

SPENCER (spen'ser) (1) *n.* a kind of short coat worn by females;—(2) *n.* a fore and aft sail. [(1) Fr. Earl *Spencer,* d. 1845.]

SPEND (spend) *v.t.* [*pret.* and *pp.* SPENT] to consume; waste;—*v.i.* to make expense. [O.E. *spendan,* fr. L. *dispendere,* expend.]

SPENDTHRIFT (spend'thrift) *n.* a prodigal.

SPENT (spent) *a.* exhausted; spawned.

SPERM (sperm) *n.* animal seed; spawn of fishes; spermaceti. [F. fr. G. *sperma,* fr. *speirein,* to sow.]

SPERMACETI (sper-ma-se'ti) *n.* a fatty matter from the head of whales. [Literally whale-seed, fr. L. *sperma,* and G. *ketos,* any large sea-animal.]

SPERMATIC (sper-mat'ik) *a.* consisting of seed; seminal.

SPERM-OIL (sperm'oil) *n.* oil obtained from the spermaceti whale.

SPEW (spū) same as SPUE. [O.E. *spiwan.* Cf. Ger. *speien.*]

SPHENOIDAL (sfē-noi'dal) *a.* resembling a wedge. [G. *sphen,* a wedge, and *eidos,* likeness.]

SPHERAL (sfē'ral) *a.* like or inhabiting a sphere.

SPHERE (sfēr) *n.* a globe; orb; circuit; province;—*v.t.* to place in a sphere. [F. fr. L. *sphœra,* fr. G. *sphaira,* a ball.]

SPHERICAL (sfer'i-kal) *a.* having the form of a sphere; globular; round.

SPHERICALLY (sfer'i-kal-i) *ad.* in form of a sphere.

SPHERICITY (sfe-ris'i-ti) *n.* roundness.

SPHERICS (sfer'iks) *n.pl.* doctrine of the sphere; spherical geometry.

SPHEROID (sfē'roid) *n.* a body nearly spherical. [G. *eidos,* form.]

SPHEROIDAL (sfe-roi'dal) *a.* formed like a spheroid.

SPHERULE (sfer'ōōl) *n.* a little sphere.

SPHINX (sfingks) *n.* a monster with the body of a lion and the face of a woman. [L. fr. G. *sphinx,* literally the strangler fr. *sphingein,* to strangle.]

SPICE (spīs) *n.* an aromatic plant;—*v.t.* to season with spice. [O.F. *espice* =F. *épice,* fr. L. *species,* kind.]

Sphinx.

SPICERY (spī'ser-i) *n.* spices in general.

SPICULAR (spik'ū-lar) *a.* having a sharp point.

SPICULE (spik'ūl) *n.* a small granule or point. [L. dim. of *spica,* a spike.]

SPICY (spī'si) *a.* like spice; pungent; hot; showy; dashing.

SPIDER (spī'der) *n.* an insect that spins webs for catching prey. [O.E., fr. *spinnan,* spin. Cf. SPINDLE.]

SPIGOT (spig'ut) *n.* a peg to stop a cask. [Gael. Cf. L. *spica.*]

SPIKE (spīk) (1) *n.* an ear of corn;—*v.t.* to fasten with a spike;—(2) *n.* a long nail of iron or wood. [(1) L. *spica.* (2) Scand.]

SPIKELET (spik'let) *n.* a little spike.

SPIKENARD (spik'nard) *n.* a highly aromatic plant and its oil. [L. *spica nardi,* spike of nard. Cf. NARD.]

SPIKY (spī'ki) *a.* having a sharp point.

SPILE (spīl) *n.* a pin for a cask. [D.]

SPILL (spil) *v.t.* [*pret.* and *pp.* SPILLED, SPILT] to allow to run out or fall; shed;—*v.i.* to be lost by shedding. [O.E. *spillan,* fr. Teut. = to destroy.]

SPIN (spin) *v.t.* or *i.* [*pret.* and *pp.* SPUN] to draw out and twist into threads. [O.E. *spinnan.* Cf. Ger. *spinnen.*]

SPINAGE (spin'ij) *n.* a garden plant. Also SPINACH. [O.F. *espinache,* fr. Sp. *espinaca,* fr. A.]

SPINAL (spī'nal) *a.* belonging to the back-bone.

SPINDLE (spin'dl) *n.* a pin to form thread on;—*v.i.* to become thin or tall. [O.E. *spinl,* spinner. fr. *spinnan,* spin.]

SPINE (spīn) *n.* the backbone; a thorn. [O.F. *espine* =F. *épine,* fr. L. *spina,* a thorn.]

SPINET (spin'et) *n.* a musical instrument. [O.F. *espinette,* fr. It. *spinetta,* a spinet, a prickle, fr. L. *spina,* a thorn (so called because struck with a *spina,* or pointed quill).]

SPINIFEROUS (spi-nif'e-rus) *a.* bearing spines; thorny.

SPINNER (spin'er) *n.* one who spins; a spider.

SPINOSITY (spi-nos'i-ti) *n.* state of being spiny.

SPINOUS (spī'nus) *a.* full of spines; thorny. Also SPINOSE.

SPINSTER (spin'ster) *n.* a woman who spins; a maiden.

SPIRACLE (spī'ra-kl, spir'a-kl) *n.* a breathing-hole; any minute passage. [L. *spiraculum,* double dim. fr. *spirare,* to breathe.]

SPIRAL (spī'ral) *a.* winding like a screw. [L. *spira,* a coil.]

SPIRALLY (spī'ral-i) *ad.* in a spiral form.

SPIRE (spīr) (1) *n.* a winding line like a screw; curl;—(2) *n.* tapering body; steeple; stalk. [(1) F. fr. L. *spira,* fr. G. *speira,* a coil. (2) O.E. *spir,* a stalk.]

SPIREA (spī-rē'a) *n.* a genus of white flowering plants; meadow sweet.

SPIRIT (spir'it) *n.* breath; the soul; a ghost; mental force or disposition; liveliness; vigour; real meaning; alcohol;—*v.t.* to animate; excite. [L. *spiritus,* breath, fr. *spirare,* breathe.]

SPIRITED (spir'i-ted) *a.* full of life or fire; lively.

SPIRITLESS (spir'it-les) *a.* without spirit.

SPIRITOUS (spir'i-tus) *a.* refined; ardent.

SPIRIT-RAPPING (spir'it-rap-ping) *n.* pretended power of communicating with the spirits of deceased persons by raps or knocks.

SPIRITUAL (spir'i-tū-al) *a.* incorporeal; pertaining to the soul, the Holy Spirit, or sacred things; not lay or temporal.

SPIRITUALISE (spir'i-tū-al-īz) *v.t.* to give a spiritual meaning to; refine.

SPIRITUALISM (spir'i-tū-al-izm) *n.* doctrine that spirit exists independently of matter; belief that deceased persons can be communicated with by a spiritual *medium.*

SPIRITUALITY (spir-i-tū-al'i-ti) *n.* immateriality; spiritual nature or state of mind.

SPIRITUALLY (spir'i-tū-al-i) *ad.* in a spiritual manner.

SPIRITUOUS (spir'i-tū-us) *a.* consisting of spirit; ardent.

SPIRT. See SPURT.

SPIRY (spī'ri) *a.* of a spiral form; having spires.

SPISSATED (spis'a-ted) *a.* made dense or compact; thickened.

SPISSITUDE (spis'i-tūd) *n.* thickness of soft substances. [L. *spissus,* dense.]

SPIT (spit) (1) *n.* an iron prong; a point of land running into the sea;—*v.t.* to put on a spit;—(2) *n.* saliva; spittle;—*v.t.* or *i.* to eject spittle. [(1) O.E. *spitu.* Cf. Ger. *Spitze.* (2) O.E. *spittan.* Cf. Ger. *spützen.*]

SPITCHCOCK (spich'kok) *n.* an eel split and broiled;—*v.t.* to dress an eel thus. [SPIT-COCK.]

SPITE (spīt) *n.* rancorous ill will; grudge;—*v.t.* to treat maliciously; thwart; vex. [Contr. fr. **DESPITE.**]

SPITEFUL (spīt'fool) *a.* malicious; malignant.

SPITEFULLY (spīt'fool-i) *ad.* with malice.

SPITFIRE (spit'fīr) *n.* a violent, passionate person.

SPITTLE (spit'l) *n.* moisture of the mouth; saliva.

SPITTOON (spi-tōón') *n.* a vessel to spit in.

SPLASH (splash) *v.t.* or *i.* to spatter or dash with or in water or mud. [Variant of **FLASH.**]

SPLASHBOARD (splash'bōrd) *n.* a board over the wheels of a vehicle to prevent splashing. Also **SPLASHER.**

SPLASHY (splash'i) *a.* full of dirty water; wet and muddy.

SPLAY-FOOTED (splā'foot-ed) *a.* having the foot turned outward. [Contr. fr. **DISPLAY.**]

SPLEEN (splēn) *n.* the milt; ill humour; melancholy. [L., fr. G. *splen*, the milt or spleen.]

SPLEENY (splē'ni) *a.* angry; peevish.

SPLENDENT (splen'dent) *a.* shining; bright.

SPLENDID (splen'did) *a.* showy; magnificent. [L. *splendidus*, fr. *splendere*, to shine.]

SPLENDIDLY (splen'did-li) *ad.* with great show.

SPLENDOUR (splen'dur) *n.* great brightness; magnificence; brilliance. [L. *splendor*.]

SPLENETIC (sple-net'ik, splen'e-tik) *a.* full of spleen; sullen;—*n.* a peevish person.

SPLENIC (splē'nik, splen'ik) *n.* belonging to the spleen.

SPLICE (splīs) *v.t.* to unite, as two ends of a rope;—*n.* union of ropes by interweaving. [D. Cf. Ger. *splissen*.]

SPLINT (splint) *n.* a thin piece of wood used in setting a broken bone;—*v.t.* to tie with splints. [Scand.]

SPLINTER (splin'tẹr) *n.* a piece of wood or other substance broken off;—*v.t* or *i.* to split or rend into thin pieces.

SPLINTERY (splin'tẹr-i) *a.* like splinters.

SPLIT (split) *v.t.* or *i.* [pret. and *pp.* SPLIT] to divide lengthwise; rend; divide; burst; —*n.* rent; fissure; separation. [Scand. Cf. Ger. *spleissen*.]

SPLUTTER (splut'ẹr) *v.i.* to scatter saliva in speaking. or ink from the pen in writing;—*n.* bustle; stir. [Corr. fr. *sprutter* freq. of **SPROUT.**]

SPOIL (spoil) *v.t.* to take by force; plunder; corrupt; vitiate;—*v.i.* to practise robbery; decay;—*n.* plunder. [O.F. *espoille*, fr. L. *spolium*, booty.]

SPOILER (spoil'ẹr) *n.* one that spoils.

SPOKE (spōk) (1) *pret.* of **SPEAK**;—(2) *n.* the ray or bar of a wheel or ladder. [(2) O.E. *spaca*. Cf. Ger. *Speiche*.]

SPOKEN (spō'kn) *pp.* of **SPEAK.**

SPOKESHAVE (spōk'shāv) *n.* a kind of plane used by wheelwrights. [O.E. *spaca* spoke, and *scafan*, shave.]

SPOKESMAN (spōks'mạn) *n.* one who speaks for others.

SPOLIATION (spō-li-ā'shun) *n.* the act of plundering. [L. (part.) *spoliatus*, fr. *spoliare*, fr. *spolium*, spoil.]

SPONDAIC (spon-dā'ik) *a.* pertaining to a spondee.

SPONDEE (spon'dē) *n.* a poetic foot of two long syllables. [F., fr. L. *spondeus* (pes) fr. G. *spondeios* (pous), (a foot) of two syllables, much used in hymns sung at a *sponde*, or drink-offering, fr. *spendein*, to pour out.]

SPONGE (spunj) *n.* a porous marine substance; —*v.t.* to wipe out with a sponge; imbibe; live by mean arts. Also written **SPUNGE.** [O.F. *esponge*, fr. L., fr. G. *sponggia*.]

SPONGE-CAKE (spunj'kāk) *n.* a light sweet cake.

SPONGER (spun'jẹr) *n.* one who sponges.

SPONGINESS (spun'ji-nes) *n.* quality of being spongy.

SPONGY (spun'ji) *a.* porous; soft.

SPONSAL (spon'sạl) *a.* relating to marriage.

SPONSOR (spon'sẹr) *n.* one who becomes surety for another. [L. fr. (part.) *sponsus*, fr. *spondere*, to engage oneself.]

SPONTANEITY (spon-tạ-nē'i-ti) *n.* the quality of acting freely without constraint.

SPONTANEOUS (spon-tā"ne-us) *a.* voluntary; produced without external force. [L. *spontaneus*, fr. *sponte*. of free-will.]

SPONTANEOUSLY (spon-tā"ne-us-li) *ad.* of free-will; voluntarily.

SPOOL (spōól) *n.* a hollow cylinder used by weavers, etc. ;—*v.t.* to wind on spools. [D.]

SPOON (spōón) *n.* a small utensil for dipping up liquids. [O.E. *spon*, a cup.]

SPOONFUL (spōón'fool) *n.* as much as a spoon can hold.

SPOON-MEAT (spōón'mēt) *n.* food eaten with a spoon.

SPOONY (spōó'ni) *a.* being in love; soft; easily affected.

SPORRAN (spor'an) *n.* a pouch worn in front of the kilt. [Gael.]

SPORT (spōrt) *n.* play; mirth;—*v.i.* to play; make mirth. [Contr. fr. **DISPORT.**]

SPORTFUL (spōrt'fool) *a.* making sport.

SPORTIVE (spōr'tiv) *a.* merry; playful.

SPORTIVENESS (spōr'tiv-nes) *n.* playfulness.

SPORTSMAN (spōrts'mạn) *n.* one fond of or skilled in field sports.

SPORTSMANSHIP (spōrts'mạn-ship) *n.* practice or skill in field sports.

SPOT (spot) *n.* a stain; a blemish; a place; —*v.t.* to mark; tarnish; stain. [Perh. conn. with SPIT.]

SPOTLESS (spot'les) *a.* free from spots; pure.

SPOUSAL (spou'zạl) *a.* matrimonial;—*n.* marriage. [O.F. *espousailles*. fr. L. *sponsalia*.]

SPOUSE (spouz) *n.* a husband or wife. [O.F. *espouse* = F. *époux*, fem. *épouse*, fr. L. *sronsa*, a betrothed woman, fr. *spondere*, to promise.]

SPOUSELESS (spouz'les) *a.* having no husband or wife.

SPOUT (spout) *n.* a projecting mouth of a vessel; a pipe;—*v.t.* or *i.* to issue out of a narrow orifice; speak pompously. [Perh. fr. **SPROUT.** Cf. **SPURT.**]

SPOUTER (spou'tẹr) *n.* one who spouts speeches.

SPRAIN (sprān) *n.* excessive straining of the ligaments of the joints;—*v.t.* to overstrain the ligaments. [O.F. *espreindre* = F. *épreindre*, to press, fr. L. *exprimere*.]

SPRANG (sprang) *pret.* of **SPRING.**

SPRAT (sprat) *n.* a small fish of the herring family. [O.E. *sprott*. Cf. Ger. *Sprotte*.]

SPRAWL (sprawl) *v.i.* to lie with the limbs stretched out; spread ungracefully. [O.E. *spreawlian*, corr. fr. *spratile* or *sprottle*, to sprawl.]

SPRAY (sprā) *n.* (1) a small shoot; (2) any liquid blown or driven in small particles. (1) [Scand. (2) Low Ger. *Spret*, a drizzle.]

SPREAD (spred) *v.t.* or *i.* [pret. and *pp.* SPREAD] to extend; expand; diffuse;—*n.* extent; expansion. [O.E. *sprædan*. Cf. Ger. *spreiten*.]

SPREE (sprē) *n.* a merry frolic; drunken frolic. [Ir. = a spark.]

SPRIG (sprig) *n.* a small branch; twig;—*v.t.* to work with sprigs. [Cf. O.E. *sprœc*, a twig.]

SPRIGGY (sprig'i) *a.* full of sprigs or small branches.

SPRIGHT (sprīt) *n.* a spirit; a shade; an incorporeal agent; an apparition. [Variant of **SPRITE.**]

SPRIGHTFUL (sprīt'fool) *a.* gay; brisk; lively.

SPRIGHTLINESS (sprīt'li-nes) *n.* briskness; vivacity.

SPRIGHTLY (sprīt'li) *a.* brisk; lively; active; vigorous.

SPRING (spring) *v.i.* [*pret.* SPRANG, SPRUNG; *pp.* SPRUNG] to rise out of the ground; arise; start; bound;.—*v.t.* to fire, as a mine; crack, as a mast; open, as a leak:—*n.* the season of the year when plants begin to grow; a leap; a fountain. [O.E. *springan.* Cf. Ger. *sprengen.*]

SPRINGE (sprinj) *n.* a snare. [Fr. SPRING. Cf. Ger. *Sprenkel.*]

SPRINGHALT (spring'hawlt) *n.* a lameness in horses.

SPRINGINESS (spring'i-nes) *n.* elasticity.

SPRINGING (spring'ing) *n.* act of leaping.

SPRING-TIDE (spring'tīd) *n.* tide at the new and full moons.

SPRING-TIME (spring'tīm) *n.* the vernal season; spring.

SPRINGY (spring'i) *a.* containing springs; elastic.

SPRINKLE (spring'kl) *v.t.* or *i.* to scatter in drops. [O.E. *sprengan,* sprinkle. Cf. Ger. *sprenkeln.*]

SPRINKLING (spring'kling) *n.* act of scattering in small particles.

SPRITE (sprīt) *n.* a spirit; a ghost. [L. *spiritus,* spirit. Doublet of SPIRIT.]

SPROUT (sprout) *v.i.* to shoot; bud;—*n.* a shoot of a plant. [O.E. *aspreotan;* or fr. Low Ger. Cf. Ger. *spriessen.*]

SPRUCE (sproos) *a.* neat; trim. [O.F. *Pruce,* Prussia. Cf. Ger. *Preussen.*]

SPRUCELY (sproos'li) *ad.* with affected neatness.

SPRUCENESS (sproos'nes) *n.* neatness in dress.

SPRUNG (sprung) *pret.* and *pp.* of SPRING.

SPRY (sprī) *a.* nimble; active. [Scand.]

SPUD (spud) *n.* a narrow spade for rooting out weeds. [Scand.]

SPUE (spū) *v.t.* to vomit; eject from the stomach. Also written SPEW.

SPUME (spūm) *n.* froth; foam. [L. *spuma,* foam, fr. *spuere,* to spew.]

SPUMESCENCE (spū-mes'ens) *n.* frothiness.

SPUMOUS (spū'mus) *a.* consisting of froth or scum; foamy.

SPUNK (spungk) *n.* dry, rotten wood; resolute spirit. [Cf. Ir. *sponc,* tinder, fr. L., fr. G. *spongga,* a sponge.]

SPUNKY (spung'ki) *a.* spirited; active.

SPUN-YARN (spun'yärn) *n.* cord made of two or three rope yarns twisted.

SPUR (spur) *n.* an instrument with sharp points for horsemen;—*v.t.* to prick; incite; —*v.i.* to press forward. [O.E. *spora.* Cf. Ger. *Sporn.*]

SPURGALL (spur'gawl) *n.* a place excoriated by a spur.

SPURGE (spurj) *n.* a plant with an acrid, milky juice, used to remove corns. [O.F. *espurge* = F. *épurge,* fr. L. *expurgare,* purge, fr. *ex,* out of, and *purgare,* to clear.]

SPURIOUS (spū'ri-us) *a.* not genuine; false. [L. *spurius,* false.]

SPURIOUSLY (spū'ri-us-li) *ad.* falsely.

SPURIOUSNESS (spū'ri-us-nes) *n.* the state of being spurious.

SPURN (spurn) *v.t.* to reject with disdain. [O.E. *speornan;* conn. with SPUR.]

SPURRIER (spur'i-er) *n.* one who makes spurs.

SPURT (spurt) (1) *v.t.* to throw out a stream; —*v.i.* to issue forcibly or at intervals:—*n.* a sudden gush;—(2) *n.* short, impulsive effort. [(1) O.E. *spryttan,* to sprout. (2) Scand.]

SPUTTER (sput'er) *v.i.* to throw spittle; talk indistinctly. [Freq. fr. SPOUT, to throw out.]

SPUTTERER (sput'er-er) *n.* one who sputters.

SPY (spī) *v.t.* or *i.* to see at a distance; discover; detect; inspect secretly;—*n.* one who watches and conveys information secretly. [O.F. *espier,* fr L. *specere.*]

SPYGLASS (spī'glas) *n.* small telescope.

SQUAB (skwob) *a.* unfeathered; short and stout;—*n.* a young pigeon. [Scand.]

SQUABBISH (skwob'ish) *a.* thick; fat; heavy.

SQUABBLE (skwob'l) *v.i.* to wrangle;—*n.* a wrangle. [Sw. = a dispute.]

SQUABBLER (skwob'ler) *n.* a noisy, contentious person.

SQUAD (skwod) *n.* a company; a small party. [O.F. *esquadre,* fr. It. *squadra,* a squadron, fr. L. *exquadrare,* to make a square, fr. *ex,* and *quadrus,* four-cornered.]

SQUADRON (skwod'run) *n.* part of a fleet; a body of troops. [It. *squadrone,* fr. *squadra.*]

SQUALID (skwol'id) *a.* foul; filthy. [L. *squalidus,* fr. *squalere,* to be stiff. Cf. G. *skellein,* to dry.]

SQUALIDITY (skwo-lid'i-ti) *n.* foulness.

SQUALIDNESS (skwol'id-nes) *n.* foulness; filthiness.

SQUALL (skwawl) *n.* a sudden gust of wind; a loud scream;—*v.i.* to scream or cry out violently. [Scand. = to gush out.]

SQUALLER (skwaw'ler) *n.* one who screams or cries loudly.

SQUALLY (skwaw'li) *a.* subject to squalls.

SQUALOR (skwol'er, skwā'ler) *n.* filthiness.

SQUANDER (skwon'der) *v.t.* to spend lavishly. [Scand.; or, nasalised fr. Scot. *squatter,* to splash water about.]

SQUANDERER (skwon'der-er) *n.* a spendthrift.

SQUARE (skwār) *a.* having four equal sides and right angles;—*n.* a figure that is square, as a block of houses or a body of troops; a carpenter's tool; product of a number multiplied by itself; —*v.t.* to make square or equal; multiply a number by itself;—*v.t.* to suit. [O.F. *esquarre* = F. *équerre,* fr. L. *exquadrare,* to square, fr. *quadrus,* four-cornered, fr. *quatuor,* four.]

Square.

SQUASH (skwosh) *v.t.* to press into pulp; crush flat;—*n.* sudden fall of soft bodies; a kind of gourd. [O.F. *esquacher* = F. *écacher,* to crush, fr. L. *ex,* out, and *coactare,* force, fr. (part.) *coactus,* of *cogere,* to drive together.]

SQUAT (skwot) *v.i.* to sit upon the hams and heels;—*n.* the posture of sitting on the hams;—*a.* cowering; short and thick. [O.F. *esquatir,* to crush, fr. L. *ex,* out, and *coactare,* force, fr. (part.) *coactus,* of *cogere,* to drive together.]

SQUATTER (skwot'er) *n.* one who settles on new land without title.

SQUAW (skwaw) *n.* an Indian woman. [Amer. Ind.]

SQUEAK (skwēk) *v.t.* to utter a short, sharp, shrill sound;—*n.* a shrill sound. [Imit.]

SQUEAL (skwēl) *v.i.* to cry with a shrill sound;—*n.* a sharp, shrill, prolonged cry of a pig. [Scand.]

SQUEAMISH (skwē'mish) *a.* nice; fastidious. [Scand.]

SQUEAMISHLY (skwē'mish-li) *ad.* in a fastidious manner.

SQUEAMISHNESS (skwē'mish-nes) *n.* fastidiousness.

SQUEEZABLE (skwē'za-bl) *a.* that can be squeezed.

SQUEEZE (skwēz) *v.t.* or *i.* to press close;—*n.* close compression. [O.E. *cwysan,* crush.]

SQUIB (skwib) *n.* a firework; a lampoon;—*v.i.* to throw squibs. [Scand.]

SQUINT (skwint) *v.t.* or *i.* to look obliquely; —*n.* act or habit of squinting. [Scand.]

SQUIRE (skwīr) *n.* a gentleman next in rank to a knight; a country gentleman;—*v.t.* to attend as a squire. [Contr. fr. ESQUIRE.]

SQUIREEN (skwir-ēn') *n.* half squire, half farmer, in Ireland. [Dim. of SQUIRE.]

SQUIRM (skwĕrm) *v.t.* to twist and struggle; climb by embracing and scrambling. [Fr. *squir,* to jerk, fr. WHIRR.]

SQUIRREL (skwir'el) *n.* a small rodent animal with a bushy tail. [O.F. *escurel,* fr. Late L. *scurellus,* dim. of *sciurus,* fr. G. *skiouros,* squirrel, literally a shadow-tail, fr. *skia,* a shade, and *oura,* tail.]

SQUIRT (skwĕrt) *v.t.* or *i.* to eject fluid out of a narrow orifice; throw out;—*n.* a small syringe; a small, quick stream. [Low Ger. *swirtjen.*]

STAB (stab) *v.t.* or *i.* to pierce with a pointed weapon; kill; thrust; injure secretly;— *n.* a thrust; secret stroke or blow. [Gael. *stob,* a stake.]

STABILIMENT (sta-bil'i-ment) *n.* act of making firm; support.

STABILITY (sta-bil'i-ti) *n.* firmness.

STABLE (stā'bl) (1) *a.* fixed; durable;—(2) *n.* a house for beasts;—*v.t.* or *i.* to house, keep, or dwell in a stable. [(1) O.F. *estable,* fr. L. *stabilis,* fr. *stare,* to stand. (2) O.F. *estable,* fr. L. *stabulum,* a stall, fr. *stare,* stand.]

STABLING (stā'bling) *n.* stables in general.

STABLY (stā'hli) *ad.* fixedly; firmly.

STACK (stak) *n.* a pile of hay, grain, wood, etc.;—*v.t.* to pile in stacks. [Scand. =a heap.]

STADDLE (stad'l) *n.* a staff; a small tree. [O.E. *stathol,* a foundation. Cf. Ger. *Stadel.*]

STADIUM (stā'di-um) *n.* a furlong; forty rods; an oblong area or course.

STAFF (staf) *n.* a stick for support; five lines and spaces in music; a stanza; certain officers attached to an army; officials of a department;—*pl.* STAFFS or STAVES. [O.E. *staf* a staff. Cf. Ger. *Stab.*]

STAG (stag) *n.* male red deer. [Scand.]

STAGE (stāj) *n.* a raised floor; a theatre; any place of exhibition; distance between places in a road; degree of progress. [M.E. *estage,* a story, stage, stopping-place, fr. L. form *staticus,* fr. *stare,* to stand.]

STAGE-COACH (stāj'kōch) *n.* a public travelling carriage.

STAGER (stā'jĕr) *n.* one who has long acted on the stage of life.

STAGE-PLAYER (stāj'plā-ĕr) *n.* an actor of plays on the stage.

STAGEY (stā'ji) *a.* in the style of the stage; theatrical.

STAGGER (stag'ĕr) *v.i.* to reel in walking; begin to give way;—*v.t.* to make to hesitate; shock. [M.E. *stakeren,* fr. Scand. = to push.]

STAGNANCY (stag'nan-si) *n.* state of being without motion or flow.

STAGNANT (stag'nant) *a.* not flowing; impure; still.

STAGNATE (stag'nāt) *v.i.* to cease to flow; become motionless or dull. [L. (part.) *stagnatus,* fr. *stagnare,* to be still, fr. *stagnum,* a piece of standing water.]

STAGNATION (stag-nā'shun) *n.* cessation of flowing or action.

STAID (stād) *a.* steady; grave. [For *stay'd,* part. of STAY.]

STAIN (stān) *v.t.* to tinge; dye; discolour; disgrace;—*n.* a blot; spot; disgrace. [Contr. fr. DISTAIN, fr. O.F. *desteindre,* fr. *dis,* away, and *tingere,* to dye.]

STAINER (stā'nĕr) *n.* one who stains or dyes.

STAINLESS (stān'les) *a.* free from stains.

STAIR (stār) *n.* a step or series of steps for ascending or descending. [O.E. *stœger,* a stair, a step, fr. *stigan,* to ascend. Cf. Ger. *steigen,* to climb.]

STAIRCASE (stār'kās) *n.* the place for stairs.

STAKE (stāk) *n.* a sharpened stick of wood; a post; martyrdom; anything pledged in a wager;—*v.t.* to mark or defend with stakes; hazard; wager; pledge. [O.E. *staca.*]

STAKE-HOLDER (stāk'hōl-dĕr) *n.* one with whom the bets are deposited in a wager.

STALACTIC (sta-lak'tik) *a.* resembling an icicle; pertaining to stalactite.

STALACTITE (sta-lak'tīt, stal'ak-tīt) *n.* a mineral in form of an icicle. [G. *stalaktos,* trickling, fr. *stalazein,* to drip.]

STALE (stāl) (1) *a.* vapid and tasteless;—(2) *n.* a decoy;—(3) *n.* a long handle;—(4) *v.i.* to discharge urine. [(1) M.D. *stel,* old. (2) O.E. *stalu,* theft, fr. *stelan,* to steal. (3) O.E. *stela,* a stalk. (4) Ger. *stallen.*]

STALK (stawk) (1) *n.* the stem of a plant; —*v.t.* or *i.* to walk with long steps; strut; pursue deer or game. [(1) O.E. *stela.* (2) O.E. *stealcan,* to go warily.]

STALKER (staw'kĕr) *n.* one who stalks game; a kind of fishing net.

STALKY (staw'ki) *a.* resembling a stalk.

STALL (stawl) *n.* a stand for a beast; a bench; —*v.t.* to keep in a stall; induct. [O.E. *steall,* a station, a stall.]

STALLAGE (staw'lij) *n.* right of erecting stalls in a market; rent for the same.

STALL-FED (stawl'fed) *a.* fattened in a stable.

STALLION (stal'yun) *n.* a horse for stock. [O.F. *estalon* =F. *étalon,* fr. Late L. *equus ad stallum,* a horse at stall.]

STALWART (stal'wart) *a.* bold; strong;— *n.* a strong and sturdy person; a steadfast partisan. [O.E. *stœlwyrthe,* of use.]

STAMEN (stā'men) *n.* foundation; support; filament and anther of a flower;—*pl.* STAMENS, STAMINA. [L., a thread, also the warp, pl. *stamina,* fr. *stare,* to stand.]

STAMINA (stam'i-na) *n.* whatever constitutes the principal strength or support of anything; power of endurance.

STAMMER (stam'ĕr) *v.t.* or *i.* to halt or falter in speaking; stutter;—*n.* defective utterance. [O.E. *stamor.*]

STAMP (stamp) *v.t.* or *i.* to strike downward with the foot; impress; imprint; coin;— *n.* an instrument for making an impression; mark impressed; cast; form. [O.E. *stempan,* to stamp, tread. Cf. Ger. *stampfen.*]

STAMPEDE (stam'pēd) *n.* a sudden fright and running of cattle, horses, etc. [Sp. *estampido,* a crash.]

STAMPER (stam'pĕr) *n.* one who stamps; a tool for stamping.

STANCH (stänsh) *v.t.* or *i.* to stop from flowing; cease to flow. [O.F. *estancher* =F. *étancher,* fr. Late L. *stancare,* to stanch, fr. L. *stagnare,* be stagnant.]

STANCHION (stan'shun) *n.* an upright bar or beam used for a prop or support. [O.F. *estancon,* fr. *estancer,* to stop, fr. L. (part.) *stantia,* fr. *stare,* to stand.] [stopped.

STANCHLESS (stänsh'les) *a.* that cannot be

STAND (stand) *v.t.* or *i.* [*pret.* and *pp.* STOOD] to endure; sustain; abide by; be on the feet; cease to move; be firm; maintain a position;—*n.* a stop; station; musket and accoutrements. [O.E. *standan.* Cf. Ger. *stehen.*]

STANDARD (stan'dard) *n.* an established rule or measure; criterion; post; staff with a flag; ensign;—*a.* standing; legal; trusty. [O.F. *estendard,* an ensign, a standard measure, fr. Teut.]

STANDER (stan'dĕr) *n.* one who stands; a standard tree.

STANNARY (stan'a-ri) *n.* a tin-mine. [L. *stannum,* tin.]

STANNIC (stan'ik) *a.* of or pertaining to tin. Also STANNOUS.

STANZA (stan'zə) *n.* a staff or number of verses in poetry. [It., fr. L. (part.) *stantia,* fr. *stare,* to stand.]

STANZAIC 'stan-zā'ik) *a.* relating to stanzas.

STAPLE stā'pl) (1) *n.* loop of iron:—(2) *n.* mart for goods; the pile of textile fabrics; principal production;—*a.* chief; principal. [/1; O.E. *stapel,* a prop. '2) O.F. *estaple,* a general market, fr. Teut. =a heap, a storehouse.]

STAPLER (stā'plẹr) *n.* a dealer in staple commodities.

STAR (stär) *n.* a luminous body in the heavens: the mark (*); a badge of honour; a distinguished person;—*v.t.* to set or adorn with stars. [O.E. *steorra.* Cf. Ger. *Stern.*]

STARBOARD (stär'bŏrd) *n.* right side of a ship.

STARCH (stärch) *n.* a substance to stiffen cloth;—*a.* stiff; —*v.t.* to stiffen with starch. [O.E. *stearc,* strong. Cf. Ger. *stärke,* starch, fr. *stark,* strong.]

STARCHED (stärcht) *a.* stiffened with starch; stiff; formal.

STARCHEDNESS (stär'ched-nes) *n.* stiffness; formality of manner.

STARCHER (stär'chẹr) *n.* one who starches.

STARCHY (stär'chi) *a.* stiff; precise.

STARE (stär) *v.i.* to look with eyes wide open: —*n.* a fixed look. [O.E. *starian.*]

STARER (stär'ẹr) *n.* an eager gazer.

STAR-GAZER (stär'gāz-ẹr) *n.* one who observes the stars.

STARK (stärk) *a.* stiff; strong; mere; entire;—*ad.* wholly; entirely. [O.E. *stearc,* strong, stiff.]

STARLESS (stär'les) *a.* having no stars visible.

STARLIGHT (stär'līt) *n.* light from the stars; —*a.* lighted by stars.

STARLING (stär'ling) *n.* a bird of the sparrow family easily taught to whistle. [O.E. *stær,* a starling.]

STARRY (stär'i) *a.* adorned with stars.

START (stärt) *v.t.* or *i.* to rouse; set in motion ; begin ; move suddenly ; deviate ; wince ; broach;—*n.* a sudden motion; outset. [M.E. *sterten.* Cf. Ger. *sturzen.*]

STARTFUL (stärt' fool) *a.* apt to start; skittish.

Starling.

STARTLE (stär'tl) *v.t.* or *i.* to excite suddenly; surprise; shock; be alarmed. [Freq. of START.]

STARTLING (stärt'ling) *a.* suddenly surprising.

STARTUP (stärt'up) *n.* an upstart.

STARVE (stärv) *v.i.* to perish with hunger; —*v.t.* to kill with hunger or want. [O.E. *steorfan,* to die. Cf. *sterben,* to die.]

STARVELING (stärv'ling) *n.* he or that which is lean;—*a.* pining with want.

STARWORT (stär'wurt) *n.* a plant with radiated compound flowers.

STATE (stāt) *n.* condition; pomp; a community; civil power;—*v.t.* to express in words, in detail, or formally;—*a* public and ceremonial; royal. [O.F. *estat* = F., *état,* fr. L. *status,* fr. *stare,* stand.]

STATE-CRAFT (stāt'kraft) *n.* statesmanship; political dexterity.

STATED (stā'ted) *a.* fixed; established.

STATEDLY (stā'ted-li) *ad.* at fixed periods.

STATELINESS (stāt'li-nes) *n.* grandeur.

STATELY (stāt'li) *a.* lofty and grand; dignified;—*ad.* loftily.

STATEMENT (stāt'ment) *n.* account of facts, reasons, etc., verbally or in writing.

STATE-ROOM (stāt'rŏŏm) *n.* a reserved apartment in a vessel.

STATESMAN (stāts'man) *n.* one skilled in the art of government.

STATESMANSHIP (stāts'man-ship) *n.* qualifications, acts, or employments of statesmen.

STATICAL (stat'ik-al) *a.* pertaining to the science of bodies at rest. [G. *statike* (*episteme*), static science, fr. *statos,* placed standing, fr. *histemi,* I place.]

STATICS (stat'iks) *n.pl.* the science of bodies at rest. (G. *statike,* fr. *statikos,* at a standstill.]

STATION (stā'shun) *n.* situation; office; rank; a railway stopping-place;—*v.t.* to fix in a certain place. [F., fr. L. (acc.) *stationem,* fr. *stare,* to stand.]

STATIONAL (stā'shun-al) *a.* pertaining to a station.

STATIONARY (stā'shun-a-ri) *a.* fixed in a place; settled; not improving.

STATIONER (stā'shun-ẹr) *n.* one who sells paper pens, etc. [Fr. STATION: the first booksellers exhibiting their stock on stations or stalls.]

STATIONERY (stā'shun-ẹr-i) *n.* articles sold by a stationer, as paper, etc.

STATISTICAL (sta-tis'ti-kal) *a.* pertaining to statistics.

STATISTICIAN (stat-is-tish'an) *n.* one versed in statistics.

STATISTICS (sta-tis'tiks) *n.pl.* a collection of facts and figures respecting the civil condition of a people. [Fr. *statist,* fr. STATE.]

STATUARY (stat'ū-a-ri) *n.* art of carving images; a carver.

STATUE (stat'ū) *n.* an image carved in marble or bronze. ;F., fr. L. *statua,* fr. *statuere,* to cause to stand, fr. *stare,* to stand.]

STATUESQUE (stat-ū-esk') *a.* resembling a statue.

STATUETTE (stat-ū-et') *n.* a small statue.

STATURE (stat'ūr) *n.* the natural height of an animal. [L. *statura,* fr. *stare,* to stand.]

STATUS (stā'tus) *n.* standing; present condition; relative position. [L.]

STATUTABLE (stat'ū-ta-bl) *a.* made by, or conformable to, a statute.

STATUTE (stat'ūt) *n.* a law enacted by a legislature. [L. *statutum,* that which is set up, fr. *statuere,* to ordain, fr. *stare,* to stand.]

STATUTORY (stat'ū-tu-ri) *a.* established by statute.

STAUNCH (stänsh) *a.* firm; sound; true; steadfast. [See STANCH.]

STAVE (stāv) *n.* a thin piece of timber for casks; a staff; stanza;—*v.t.* [*pret.* and *pp.* STOVE or STAVED] to break or burst; push off; delay. [Variant of STAFF.]

STAY (stā) (1) *v.t.* or *i.* [*pret.* STAID or STAYED] to stop; delay; prevent; prop; abide; dwell; wait; trust;—*n.* stand; stop;— (2) *n.* a rope to support a mast. [(1) M.E. *estayer* to prop, fr. D.) =a prop. (2) O.E. *stæg.* Cf. Ger. *Stag.*]

STAYER (stā'ẹr) *n.* one who stays.

STAY-LACE (stā'lās) *n.* lace for stays.

STAYMAKER (stā'mā'kẹr) *n.* one who makes stays for females.

STAYS (stāz) *n.pl.* a bodice for females; any support.

STAY-SAIL (stā'sāl) *n.* a sail extended along a stay.

STEAD (sted) *n.* place; room; turn. [O.E. *stede,* a place. Cf. Ger. *Stadt.*]

STEADFAST (sted'fast) *a.* firm; constant. [O.E. *stedefæst,* firm in its place, fr. *stede,* and *fæst,* firm.]

STEADFASTLY (sted'fast-li) *ad.* firmly.

STEADFASTNESS (sted'fast-nes) *n.* firmness of mind or conduct.

STEADILY (sted'i-li) *ad.* with firmness.

STEADINESS (sted'i-nes) *n.* constancy.

STEADY (sted'i) *a.* firm; uniform;—*v.t.* to hold or keep firm; support.

STEAK (stāk) *n.* slice of beef, etc., broiled, or cut for broiling. [Scand. = broiled meat.]

STEAL (stēl) *v.t.* or *i.* [*pret.* STOLE; *pp.* STOLE, STOLEN] to take goods privately and unlawfully; pilfer; purloin. [O.E. *stelan.* Cf. Ger. *stehlen.*]

STEALER (stē'lēr) *n.* one who steals.

STEALTH (stelth) *n.* act of stealing; secret means.

STEAM (stēm) *n.* the vapour of water; —*v.i.* to rise in vapour; —*v.t.* to expose to steam. [O.E. *steam.* Cf. Ger. *Stum,* weather when snow or rain is drifted by the wind.]

STEAMBOAT (stēm'bōt) *n.* a vessel propelled by steam.

STEAM-ENGINE (stēm'en-jin) *n.* an engine worked by steam.

STEAMER (stē'mēr) *n.* a steamboat; a vessel in which articles are steamed.

STEAM-GAUGE (stēm'gāj) *n.* instrument to show the pressure of steam in the boiler.

STEED (stēd) *n.* a horse, *especially* a spirited horse for state or war. [O.E. *steda,* fr. *stud,* a stud.]

STEEL (stēl) *n.* iron with a small portion of carbon; a tool for sharpening knives upon; —*a.* made of steel; —*v.t.* to harden. [O.E. *style.* Cf. Ger. *Stahl.*]

STEEL-CLAD (stēl'klad) *a.* armed with steel.

STEELYARD (stēl'yard) *n.* a kind of balance for weighing. [The YARD in London where STEEL was sold to the German merchants.]

STEEP (stēp) (1) *a.* greatly inclined; —*n.* a precipitous place; —(2) *v.t.* to soak in a liquid; imbue. [(1) O.E. *steap,* high. (2) Scand. = pour out.]

STEEPLE (stē'pl) *n.* spire of a church. [O.E. *stypel,* fr. *steap,* steep.]

STEEPLECHASE (stē'pl-chās) *n.* a horse-race across the country.

STEEPNESS (stēp'nes) *n.* the state of being steep.

STEER (stēr) (1) *n.* a young ox; —(2) *v.t.* or *i.* to direct with the helm; pursue a course. [(1) O.E. *steor.* (2) O.E. *steoran, styran.* Cf. Ger. *steuern.*]

STEERAGE (stē'rij) *n.* room in the fore-part of a ship; act of steering; management.

STEERER (stē'rēr) *n.* one who steers; a pilot.

STEERSMAN (stērz'man) *n.* one who steers a ship.

STELLAR (stel'ar) *a.* relating to stars. [L. *stellaris,* fr. *stella,* a star.]

STELLATE (stel'āt) *a.* like stars.

STELLIFORM (stel'i-form) *a.* star-shaped. [L. *stella,* and *forma,* a form.]

STEM (stem) (1) *n.* the main body of a plant; stock of a family; —(2) *n.* prow of a ship; —(3) *v.t.* to oppose, as a current; stop. [(1) O.E. *stemn,* fr. *stefn.* (2) O.E. *stemn,* fr. *stefn,* prow of a ship. (3) Scand.]

STENCH (stensh) *n.* an offensive smell. [O.E. *stenc,* stink, fr. *stincan.*]

STENCIL (sten'sil) *n.* an open-work pattern over which colours are passed by a brush; —*v.t.* to paint or colour with stencils. [O.F. *estenceler,* fr. L. *scintilla,* spark.]

STENOGRAPHIC (sten-u-graf'ik) *a.* expressing in shorthand.

STENOGRAPHER (ste-nog'ra-fēr) *n.* one who writes in shorthand.

STENOGRAPHY (ste-nog'ra-fi) *n.* the art of writing in shorthand. [G. *stenos,* narrow, and *graphein,* write.]

STENTORIAN (sten-tō'ri-an) *a.* very loud; able to utter a loud sound. [G. *Stentor,* a herald spoken of by Homer, having a very loud voice.]

STEP (step) *v.i.* to move the feet; walk; —*v.t.* to set; fix the foot of a mast; —*n.* a pace; gait; degree. [O.E. *stepan,* go. Cf. Ger. *stapfe.*]

STEP-CHILD (step'child) *n.* a child by marriage only. [O.E. *steop,* orphaned.]

STEP-FATHER (step'fā-THēr) *n.* a father by marriage only.

STEP-MOTHER (step'muTH-ēr) *n.* a mother by marriage only.

STEPPE (step) *n.* a vast, uncultivated plain in Asia. [Russ. = heath.]

STEP-SON (step'sun) *n.* a son by marriage only.

STEREOSCOPE (stē're-u-skōp, ster'e-u-skōp) *n.* an optical instrument through which two objects appear as one. [G. *stereos,* and *skopein,* to view.]

STEREOTYPE (stē're-u-tīp, ster'e-u-tīp) *n.* fixed, immovable types; —*a.* done on fixed types; —*v.t.* to form or compose in fixed types. [G. *stereos,* firm, solid, and TYPE.]

STEREOTYPER (stē're-u-tī-pēr, ster'e-u-tī-pēr) *n.* one who makes stereotypes.

STERILE (ster'il) *a.* barren; unfruitful. [O.F., fr. L. *sterilis,* barren.]

STERILITY (ste-ril'i-ti) *n.* quality or state of being barren.

STERLING (stēr'ling) *n.* English money; —*a.* of the standard weight; genuine. [Etym. uncert. — perh. fr. *Esterlings,* men of the east, Hanse merchants of London.]

STERN (stern) (1) *n.* the hinder part of a ship; —(2) *a.* severe in look; harsh. [(1) Scand. (2) O.E. *styrne.*]

STERN-CHASER (stern'chā-sēr) *n.* a gun to fire from the stern.

STERNLY (stern'li) *ad.* harshly.

STERNMOST (stern'mōst) *a.* farthest astern.

STERNNESS (stern'nes) *n.* harshness.

STERNUTATION (ster-nū-tā'shun) *n.* the act of sneezing. [L. (acc.) *sternutationem,* fr. *sternutare,* sneeze, a freq. form of *sternuere,* sneeze.]

STERNUTATORY (ster-nū'ta-tu-ri) *n.* a substance which provokes sneezing.

STERTOROUS (ster'tu-rus) *a.* breathing heavily; snoring. [L. *stertere,* to snore.]

STETHOSCOPE (steth'u-skōp) *n.* an instrument used to distinguish sounds in the thorax. [G. *stethos,* the breast, and *skopein,* to see.]

STEVEDORE (stē've-dōr) *n.* one who contracts to load and unload vessels. [Corr. of Sp. *estivador,* a wool-packer, fr. L. *stipare,* to press together.]

STEW (stū) *v.t.* or *i.* to seethe; boil; —*n.* meat stewed; a hot-house. [O.F. *estuve,* a stove, fr. Teut. Cf. Ger. *Stube,* a heated room.]

STEWARD (stū'ard) *n.* a man who manages the affairs of another. [O.E. *stigweard,* fr. *stiga,* a stye, and *weard,* ward.]

STEWARDESS (stū'ar-des) *n.* a female waiter in a passenger ship.

STEWARDSHIP (stū'ard-ship) *n.* office of a steward.

STEW-PAN (stū'pan) *n.* pan in which things are stewed.

STHENIC (sthen'ik) *a.* attended with excessive action; inflammatory. [G. *sthenos,* strength.]

STIBIAL (stib'i-al) *a.* antimonial. [L. *stibium,* antimony.]

STICH (stik) *n.* a line or verse; a row or rank of trees. [G. *stichos,* a row, fr. *steichein,* to ascend.]

STICK (stik) (1) *n.* a piece of wood; —(2) *v.t.* or *i.* [*pret.* and *pp.* STUCK] to fix; adhere; hesitate; stop; stab; thrust in. [(1) O.E. *sticca.* (2) (Assumed) O.E. *stecan,* to stab.]

STICKINESS (stik'i-nes) *n.* quality of adhering.

STICKLE (stik'l) *v.i.* to contend obstinately. [See STICK.]

STICKLER (stik'lēr) *n.* an umpire; second; obstinate contender.

STICKY (stik'i) *a.* viscous; glutinous.

STIFF (stif) *a.* unbending; stubborn; formal; constrained. [O.E. *stif.*]

STIFFEN (stif'n) *v.t.* to make stiff; —*v.i.* to grow stiff.

STIFFLY (stif'li) *ad.* stubbornly; rigidly.

STIFFNESS (stif'nes) *n.* want of pliability; formality.

STIFLE (sti'fl) (1) *v.t.* to suppress; choke;— (2) *n.* knee-joint of a horse. [(1) Scand. (2) Fr. STIFF.]

STIGMA (stig'mạ) *n.* any mark of infamy: in *Botany* the top of the pistil. [G. *stigma,* mark of a pointed instrument, fr. *stizein,* to mark.]

STIGMATIC (stig-mat'ik) *a.* marked with a stigma.

STIGMATISE (stig'mạ-tiz) *v.t.* to mark with infamy.

STILETTO (sti-let'ō) *n.* a small dagger. (It. dim. of *stilo,* a dagger. fr. L. *stilus* a stake.]

STILL (stil) *v.t.* to silence; calm; quiet;— *a.* silent; motionless;—*ad.* to this time; nevertheless; notwithstanding. [O.E. *stille,* firm.]

STILL (stil) *v.t.* to distil:—*v.i.* to trickle down: —*n.* a boiler used in distillation. [L. *stillare,* to drop fr. *stilla,* a drop. contr. fr. E. DISTIL.]

STILL-BORN (stil'born) *a.* born lifeless.

STILLNESS (stil'nes) *n.* calm; quietness.

STILLY (stil'i) *a.* quiet; calm;—*ad.* silently; quietly.

STILT (stilt) *n.* a piece of wood with a rest for the foot, used in walking. [Scand. = a prop.]

STILTON (stil'tun) *n.* a rich kind of cheese. [Orig. made at *Stilton,* in Huntingdonshire.]

STIMULANT (stim'ū-lạnt) *a.* tending to excite action;—*n.* a stimulating medicine. [L. *stimulus,* for *stigmulus* a goad, fr. G. *stizein,* to prick.]

STIMULATE (stim'ū-lāt) *v.t.* to excite: instigate; stir

STIMULATION (stim-ū-lā'shun) *n.* the act of exciting.

STIMULATIVE (stim'ū-lā-tiv) *a.* tending to excite; stimulating.

STIMULUS (stim'ū-lụs) *n.* something that rouses either to mental action or to vital energy [L.]

STING (sting) *v.t.* [*pret.* and *pp.* STUNG] to pierce or pain acutely:—*n.* defensive weapon of a bee, wasp etc.: a thrust from it; anything pointed and painful. [O.E. *stingan,* sting.]

STINGILY (stin'ji-li) *ad.* with mean covetousness.

STINGINESS (stin'ji-nes) *n.* mean covetousness; avarice.

STINGLESS (sting'les) *a.* having no sting.

STINGY (stin'ji) *a.* meanly covetous: niggardly. [Fr. STING.]

STINK (stingk) *n.* an offensive smell;—*v.i.* to emit an offensive smell. [O.E. *stincan.*]

STINT (stint) *n.* a limit: restraint; task;— *v.t.* to limit; restrain. [O E. *styntan,* to stop.]

STIPEND (sti'pend) *n.* settled pay; wages; salary. [L. *stipendium,* fr. *stips* a gift, and *pendere,* to weigh or pay out.]

STIPENDIARY (sti-pen'di-a-ri) *a.* receiving a stipend.

STIPPLE (stip'l) *v.t.* or *i.* to engrave by means of dots instead of lines. [D. *stippelen,* to dot.]

STIPULATE (stip'ū-lāt) *v i.* to covenant. [L. *stipulari,* to bargain for.]

STIPULATION (stip-ū-lā'shun) *n.* an agreement: condition.

STIPULATOR (stip'ū-lā-tẹr) *n.* one who covenants or contracts.

STIR (stẹr) *v.t.* or *i.* to move: incite: rouse: be active: move about: to stir to action; —*n.* bustle: agitation: commotion. [O.E. *styrian.*]

STIRK (stẹrk) *n.* a young ox or heifer. [O.E. *styric,* fr. *steor,* a steer.]

STIRRUP (stir'up) *n.* an iron suspended by a strap for a horseman's foot. [O.E. *stiragp,* fr. *stigan,* mount, and *rap,* rope.]

STITCH (stich) *v.t.* to sew; join; —*v.i.* to practise sewing;—*n.* a single pass of a needle. [O.E. *stician,* to pierce.]

STIVER (sti'vẹr) *n.* a Dutch copper coin about three farthings. [D.]

STOAT (stōt) *n.* the ermine. [Scand.]

Stirrup.

STOCK (stok) *n.* body of a plant; progenitor of a family: a cravat; capital; store; cattle;—*pl.* frame in which the feet of criminals were confined; public funds;—*v.t.* to furnish or store. [O.E. *stocc.*]

STOCKADE (sto-kād') *n.* a line of stakes for a barrier;—*v.t.* to fortify with stakes. [Sp. *estaca;* F. *estocade,* fr. *estoc,* fr. Ger. *Stock,* a stick.]

STOCKBROKER (stok'brō-kẹr) *n.* one who deals in stocks.

STOCK-EXCHANGE (stok'eks-chānj) *n.* building where stocks are bought and sold; association of stockbrokers.

STOCKING (stok'ing) *n.* a covering for the foot and leg. [Fr. STOCK.]

STOCK-JOBBER (stok'job-ẹr) *n.* one who speculates in stocks.

STOCK-JOBBING (stok'job-ing) *n.* the dealing in the public stocks.

STOCK-STILL (stok'stil) *a.* motionless.

STOCKY (stok'i) *a.* thick and stout.

STOIC (stō'ik) *n.* one who affects indifference to pleasure or pain. [L. *Stoicus* fr. G. *stoikos* fr. *stoa,* a porch, esp. a porch in Athens where Zeno and his successors taught.]

STOICAL (stō'i-kạl) *a.* unfeeling; cold.

STOICISM (stō'i-sizm) *n.* insensibility to pleasure or pain.

STOLE (stōl) *n.* a long vestment. [L. *stola,* fr. G. *stole,* dress, fr. *stellein,* to array.]

STOLID (stol'id) *a.* stupid; foolish. [L. *stolidus.*]

STOLIDITY (sto-lid'i-ti) *n.* dullness of intellect; stupidity.

STOMACH (stum'ạk) *n.* the organ of digestion; appetite;—*v.t.* to brook or endure. [O.F. *estomac,* fr. L. *stomachus* fr. G. *stoma,* a mouth.]

STOMACHER (stum'ach-ẹr) *n.* ornament for the breast.

STOMACHIC (sto-mak'ik) *a.* strengthening the stomach; *n.* medicine for the stomach.

STOMACHLESS (stum'ạk-les) *a.* having no appetite.

STONE (stōn) *n.* a hard mass of earthy or mineral matter; a gem; concretion in the bladder: nut of a drupe; a weight of 14 pounds;—*a.* made of or like stone;—*v.t.* to pelt or kill with stones; free from stones. [O.E. *stan.* Cf. Ger. *Stein.*]

STONE-CHATTER (stōn'chat-ẹr) *n.* a lively singing bird, allied to the robin.

STONE-CUTTER (stōn'kut-ẹr) *n.* hewer of stones.

STONE-DRESSER (stōn'dres-ẹr) *n.* one who smoothes stones for building.

STONE-FRUIT (stōn'frōōt) *n.* fruit that contains a stone.

STONER (stōn'ẹr) *n.* one who kills with stones or walls with stones.

STONE-STILL (stōn'stil) *a.* motionless as a stone.

STONEWARE (stōn'wār) *n.* potter's ware.

STONINESS (stō'ni-nes) *n.* abundance of stones.

STONY (stō'ni) *a.* made of stones; full of stones: hard.

STOOD (stood) *pret.* of STAND.

STOOK (stook) *n.* a collection of sheaves set up. [Cf. Low Ger. *Stuke,* a bundle. Cf. STACK.]

STOOL (stool) *n.* a seat without a back. [O.E. *stol*. Cf. Ger. *stellen*, to place.]

STOOP (stoop) *v.i.* to bend forward; descend; yield;—*n.* act of stooping. [O.E. *stupian*.]

STOP (stop) *v.t.* to check ·motion; obstruct; hinder; intercept; close; regulate sounds; —*v.i.* to cease from motion; leave off;—*n.* cessation of motion; pause; a point in writing. [O.E. *stoppian*, stop up, fr. O.F. *estouper*. fr. L. *stupa*, tow, oakum.]

STOP-GAP (stop'gap) *n.* a temporary expedient.

STOPPAGE (stop'ij) *n.* act of stopping; state of being stopped.

STOPPER (stop'er) *n.* one who stops; that which closes the vent of a vessel; a short rope used in fastening;—*v.t.* to close or secure.

STOPPLE (stop'l) *n.* that which is used to close a bottle. [Dim. of STOP.]

STORAGE (stōr'ij) *n.* placing in store; rent for storing.

STORE (stōr) *n.* a large quantity; a warehouse;—*v.t.* to furnish; hoard; put in a warehouse. [O.F. *estor*, store, provisions, fr. L. *instaurare*, to provide.]

STOREHOUSE (stōr'hous) *n.* a magazine or repository.

STORIED (stō'rid) *a.* related in story; having stories.

STORK (stork) *n.* a large wading bird. [O.E. *storc*. Cf. Ger. *Storch*.]

STORM (storm) *n.* a violent wind; assault; commotion;—*v.t.* to attack by open force; —*v.i.* to blow with violence; rage. [O.E.]

STORMY (stor'mi) *a.* agitated with winds; violent.

STORY (stō'ri) (1) *n.* history; a tale;—*v.t.* to tell; relate;—(2) *n.* a stage, or floor, of a building. [(1) Contr. fr. HISTORY, fr. O.F. *estoire*, fr. L. *historia*. (2) O.F. *estorée*, a thing built, fr. L. *instaurare*, to build.]

STOUT (stout) *a.* large; strong; brave;—*n.* a kind of strong porter. [O.F. *estout*, stout, bold, for M.D. *stout*. Cf. Ger. *stolz*, bold.]

STOUTLY (stout'li) *ad.* strongly; lustily.

STOUTNESS (stout'nes) *n.* quality of strength; boldness.

STOVE (stōv) *n.* a place for a fire; an iron box for heating;—*pret.* of STAVE. [O.E. *stofa*. Cf. Ger. *Stube*.]

STOW (stō) *v.t.* to place or arrange compactly; pack. [O.E. *stow*, a place. Cf. Ger. *stauen*, to pack.]

STOWAGE (stō'ij) *n.* act of stowing.

STRABISMUS (stra-bis'mus) *n.* a habit of looking asquint. [G. *strabos*, squinting, fr. *strephein*, to twist.]

STRADDLE (strad'l) *v.t.* or *i.* to part the legs; walk with the legs apart. [Freq. of STRIDE.]

STRAGGLE (strag'l) *v.i.* to wander aside; ramble; be dispersed. [Freq. of M.E. *straken*, to wander.]

STRAGGLER (strag'ler) *n.* one who straggles.

STRAIGHT (strāt) *a.* not crooked; upward; direct;—*ad.* immediately. [O.E. *streht*, fr. *streccan*, stretch.]

STRAIGHTEN (strāt'n) *v.t.* to make straight.

STRAIGHTFORWARD (strāt'for-ward) *a.* going on in a straight course; downright; honest.

STRAIGHTLY (strāt'li) *ad.* in a direct line.

STRAIGHTNESS (strāt'nes) *n.* directness.

STRAIGHTWAY (strāt'wā) *ad.* immediately.

STRAIN (strān) *v.t.* to stretch; exert to the utmost; injure; constrain;—*n.* a sprain; force; song. [O.F. *estraindre*, fr. L. *stringere*, draw tight.]

STRAINER (strā'ner) *n.* an instrument for filtering.

STRAIT (strāt) *a.* narrow; close; strict;—*n.* a narrow pass; distress; difficulty. [O.F. *estreit*, narrow = F. *étroit*, fr. L. (part.) *strictus*, fr. *stringere*, to draw tight.]

STRAITEN (strāt'n) *v.t.* to make narrow or tight; distress.

STRAIT-JACKET (strāt'jak-et) *n.* dress used to restrain lunatics. Also STRAIT-WAIST-COAT. [ness.

STRAITNESS (strāt'nes) *n.* narrowness; strictness.

STRAKE (strāk) *n.* the iron band of a wheel. [Variant of STREAK.]

STRAND (strand) (1) *n.* shore or beach;— *v.t.* or *i.* to run aground; be driven ashore; —(2) *n.* one of the twists of a rope. [(1) O.E.; Ger. *Strand*. (2) D. *streen*, a hank of thread. Cf. Ger. *Strähne*.]

STRANGE (strānj) *a.* wonderful; foreign. [O.F. *estrange* = F. *étrange*, fr. L. *extraneus*, foreign, fr. *extra*, beyond.]

STRANGELY (strānj'li) *ad.* in a strange manner.

STRANGENESS (strānj'nes) *n.* oddness; singularity.

STRANGER (strān'jer) *n.* a foreigner; one unknown; a guest.

STRANGLE (strang'gl) *v.t.* or *i.* to choke; suppress; hinder from appearing. [O.F. *estrangler* = F. *étrangler*, fr. L. *strangulare*, fr. G. *stranggale*, a halter, fr. *stranggos*, twisted.]

STRANGLES (strang'glz) *n.pl.* swellings in a horse's throat.

STRANGULATION (strang-gū-lā'shun) *n.* the act of strangling; suffocation.

STRANGURY (strang'gū-ri) *n.* difficulty in discharging urine. [L. *stranguria*, fr. G. *stranggs*, a drop, and *ouron*, urine.]

STRAP (strap) *n.* a long strip of leather;— *v.t.* to beat or fasten with a strap. [O.E. *stropp*, fr. L. *struppos*. Cf. G. *strophos*, a twisted band.]

STRAPPING (strap'ing) *a.* tall, strong, and handsome.

STRASS (stras) *n.* a kind of flint glass. [Fr. Joseph *Strasser*, the inventor.]

STRATAGEM (strat'a-jem) *n.* artifice; trick. [F., fr. L., fr. G. *strategema*, the device of a general, fr. *strategos*, a general, fr. *stratos*, army, and *agein*, to lead.]

STRATEGIST (strat'e-jist) *n.* one skilled in military movements.

STRATEGY (strat'e-ji) *n.* science of, or skill in, great military movements.

STRATH (strath) *n.* a long, open valley. [Gael. = a valley, fr. L. *strata*, a street.]

STRATHSPEY (strath'spā) *n.* a lively Scotch tune or dance. [Fr. *Strathspey*, in Scotland.]

STRATIFICATION (strat-i-fi-kā'shun) *n.* arrangement into strata.

STRATIFIED (strat'i-fid) *a.* arranged in layers or beds.

STRATIFY (strat'i-fi) *v.t.* to form into layers. [F. *stratifier*, fr. L. *stratum*, and *facere*, to make.]

STRATUM (strā'tum) *n.* a layer, as of earth or rock; bed;—*pl.* STRATA. [L., fr. (part.) *stratus*, fr. *sternere*, to spread.]

STRAW (straw) *n.* a stalk of grain; mass of stalks;—*v.t.* to strew. [O.E. *streaw*. Cf. Ger. *Stroh*.]

STRAWBERRY (straw-ber'i) *n.* a plant and its fruit. [Fr. STRAW and BERRY.]

STRAW-COLOUR (straw'kul-ur) *n.* a beautiful yellowish colour.

STRAW-HAT (straw'hat) *n.* a hat of plaited straw.

STRAY (strā) *v.i.* to wander; rove;—*n.* a beast that wanders;—*a.* wandering. [O.F. *estraier*, to wander, fr. *estree*, a street, fr. L. *strata*, a road.]

STREAK (strēk) *n.* a line or long mark of different colour from the ground;—*v.t.* to mark with streaks; stripe. [O.E. *strica*, a line, fr. *strican*, to stroke. Cf. Ger. *Strich*; E. STRIKE.]

STREAKED (strēkt) *pp.* or *a.* striped.

STREAKY (strē'ki) *a.* marked with streaks; striped.

STREAM (strēm) *n.* a running water; a current; drift;—*v.t.* or *i.* to pour out or flow abundantly. [O.E. Cf. Ger. *Straum.*]

STREAMER (strē'mẹr) *n.* a flag; a beam of light.

STREAMLET (strēm'let) *n.* a small stream.

STREAMY (strē'mi) *a.* flowing with a current; floating in streaks.

STREET (strēt) *n.* a way or road in a city. [O.E. *strœt*, fr. L. *strata* (*via*), a paved (way). Cf. **STRATUM**; Ger. *Strasse.*]

STREET-DOOR (strēt'dōr) *n.* door opening on the street.

STRENGTH (strength) *n.* power to act; force; vigour. [O.E. *strengthu.* strength, fr. *strang*, strong.]

STRENGTHEN (streng'thn) *v.t.* or *i.* to make or grow strong.

STRENGTHENER (strength'nẹr) *n.* that which gives strength.

STRENGTHLESS (strength'les) *a.* destitute of strength.

STRENUOUS (stren'ū-us) *a.* eagerly pressing; active. [L. *strenuus*, vigorous.]

STRENUOUSLY (stren'ū-us-li) *ad.* with eager zeal.

STRENUOUSNESS (stren'ū-us-nes) *n.* eagerness; active zeal.

STRESS (stres) *n.* force; importance. [O.F. *estressier.* to pinch, and L. (part.) *strictus*, fr. *stringere*, to draw tight. Cf. **DISTRESS.**]

STRETCH (strech) *v.t.* or *i.* to draw out; expand; reach out; strain;—*n.* extension; effort; reach; utmost extent. [O.E. *streccan.* fr. *strœc* strong. Cf. Ger. *strack*, straight.]

STRETCHER (strech'ẹr) *n.* one that stretches; a piece of timber.

STREW (strōō, strō) *v.t.* to scatter. [O.E. *streowian.* Cf. Ger. *streuen*; L. *sternere.*]

STRIATED (strī'ā-ted) *a.* streaked. [L. *striare*, to furrow.]

STRIATION (strī-ā'shun) *n.* state of being finely channelled.

STRICKEN (strik'n) *pp.* struck. [Fr. **STRIKE.**]

STRICKLE (strik'l) *n.* an instrument for levelling corn in a measure. [Fr. **STRIKE.**]

STRICT (strikt) *a.* severe; close; rigid. [L. (part.) *strictus*, fr. *stringere*, to bind tight.]

STRICTLY (strikt'li) *ad.* rigorously.

STRICTNESS (strikt'nes) *n.* severity; rigour.

STRICTURE (strik'tūr) *n.* contraction; critical remark; censure.

STRIDE (strīd) *n.* a long step;—*v.i.* to walk with long steps. [O.E. *stridan.* Cf. Ger. *streiten*, to strive.]

STRIDENT (strī'dent) *a.* harsh; grating. [L. (part. stem) *strident-* fr. *stridere*, to make a creaking noise.]

STRIFE (strīf) *n.* contention; rivalship. [O.F. *estrif*, fr. Scand. ═strife.]

STRIKE (strīk) *v.t.* or *i.* [*pret.* **STRUCK**; *pp.* **STRUCK, STRICKEN**] to hit with force; dash; coin; let down; affect strongly; make, as a bargain; surrender; run aground; —*n.* ceasing from work and demanding higher wages. [O.E. *strican*, to go. Cf. Ger. *streichen*, to move.]

STRIKER (strī'kẹr) *n.* one who strikes.

STRIKING (strī'king) *a.* impressive; forcible; exact.

STRING (string) *n.* a slender line; a series; things filed;—*v.t.* [*pret.* and *pp.* **STRUNG**] to furnish with strings. [O.E. *strenge*, a cord, fr. *strang* strong. Cf. Ger. *strang*; E. **STRONG.**]

STRINGENCY (strin'jen-si) *n.* severe pressure.

STRINGENT (strin'jent) *a.* binding closely; pressing hard; urgent. [L. (part. stem) *stringent-.* fr. *stringere*, draw tight.]

STRING-HALT (string'hawlt) *n.* a twitching of a horse's legs.

STRINGLESS (string'les) *a.* having no strings.

STRINGY (string'i) *a.* ropy; fibrous.

STRIP (strip) *v.t.* to make naked; deprive; peel;—*n.* a long narrow piece. [O.E. *strypan*, to plunder. Cf. Ger. *streifen.*]

STRIPE (strīp) *n.* a line of a different colour; a lash;—*v.t.* to form with stripes. [D.]

STRIPLING (strip'ling) *n.* a youth. [Dim. of **STRIP.**]

STRIPPER (strip'ẹr) *n.* one who strips.

STRIVE (strīv) [*pret.* **STROVE**; *pp.* **STRIVEN**] to make effort; struggle; contend; aim. [O.F. *estriver*, fr. *estrif*, strive, fr. Scand.]

STRIVINGLY (strī'ving-li) *ad.* with laborious effort.

STROKE (strōk) (1) *n.* a blow; a dash; a touch; masterly effort; sound of a clock; sweep of an oar; a sudden attack of disease or affliction;—(2) *v.t.* to rub gently with the hand. [(1) O.E. *strican*, to strike. (2) O.E. *stracian*, a causal verb fr. *strican*, to strike.]

STROLL (strōl) *v.i.* to rove; ramble;—*n.* a ramble; excursion. [Etym. uncert.]

STROLLER (strō'lẹr) *n.* a rover; a vagrant.

STRONG (strong) *a.* having great power; healthy; solid; forcible; energetic; intoxicating; bright; intense. [O.E. *strang.* Cf. Ger. *streng.*]

STRONGHOLD (strong'hōld) *n.* a fortress.

STRONGLY (strong'li) *ad.* powerfully.

STROP (strop) *n.* a strip of leather for sharpening razors;—*v.t.* to sharpen. [O.E. *stropp*, a strap.] [structure.

STRUCTURAL (struk'tū-ral) *a.* pertaining to

STRUCTURE (struk'tūr) *n.* form; frame; an edifice. [L. *structura*, fr. (part.) *structus*, fr. *struere*, to join together.]

STRUGGLE (strug'l) *v.i.* to make great efforts with twistings of the body; contend; labour hard;—*n.* a violent effort; strife; agony. [M.E. *struystelen*, fr. Scand.]

STRUM (strum) *v.i.* to play badly on a stringed instrument. [Imit.; variant of **THRUM.**]

STRUMOUS (strōō'mus) *a.* having swellings in the glands. [L. *struma.*]

STRUMPET (strum'pet) *n.* a prostitute. [O.F. *strupe*, fr. L. *stuprum*, dishonour.]

STRUT (strut) *n.* an affected walk;—*v.i.* to walk affectedly. [Scand. Cf. Low Ger. *strutt*, rigid.]

STRYCHNINE (strik'nin) *n.* a vegetable poison. [G. *struchnos*, a kind of nightshade.]

STUB (stub) *n.* the stump of a tree. [O.E. *stybb.*]

STUBBLE (stub'l) *n.* stumps of rye, wheat, etc. [O.F. *estouble*, fr. L. *stipula*, dim. of *stipes*, a stalk.]

STUBBORN (stub'urn) *a.* inflexible in opinion; obstinate. [O.E. *stybb*, a stump.]

STUBBORNLY (stub'urn-li) *ad.* obstinately.

STUBBORNNESS (stub'urn-nes) *n.* obstinacy.

STUCCO (stuk'ō) *n.* a kind of fine plaster;—*v.t.* to plaster with stucco. [It.]

STUCK (stuk) *pret.* and *pp.* of **STICK.**

STUD (stud) (1) *n.* a small post; a button; a nail;—*v.t.* to set with studs;—(2) *n.* a set of horses. [(1) O.E. *studu*, a post. (2) O.E. *stod.* Cf. Ger. *Gestut.*]

STUDENT (stū'dent) *n.* one who studies. [L. (part. stem) *student-.* fr. *studere*, to study.]

STUDIED (stū'did) *a.* premeditated.

STUDIO (stū'di-ō) *n.* the workshop, especially of a sculptor;—*pl.* **STUDIOS.** [It. fr. L.]

STUDIOUS (stū'di-us) *a.* given to study; diligent; careful of.

STUDIOUSLY (stū'di-us-li) *ad.* with close application; carefully.

STUDY (stud'i) *n.* application to books; subjects of attention; a room for study; —*v.t.* or *i.* to apply the mind to. [O.F. *estudie* ═F. *étude*, fr. L. *studium*, zeal.]

STUFF (stuf) *n.* material; textile fabrics; cloth; worthless matter;—*v.t.* to fill full; fill with seasoning; fill the skin for preserving the form of an animal. [O.F. *estoffe* ═F. *étoffe*, fr. L. *stuppa*, tow.]

STUFFING (stuf'ing) *n.* that which is used for filling; seasoning.

STUFFY (stuf'i) *a.* close; ill-ventilated.

STULTIFY (stul'ti-fi) *v.t.* to make foolish. [L. *stultus*, foolish, and *facere*, to make.]

STUM (stum) *n.* wine revived by new fermentation. [D. *stom*.]

STUMBLE (stum'bl) *v.i.* to trip in walking; light upon by chance;—*n.* a trip; a blunder. [Doublet of STAMMER.]

STUMBLER (stum'bler) *n.* one who stumbles or blunders.

STUMBLING-BLOCK (stum'bling-blok) *n.* that which causes to err.

STUMP (stump) *n.* the part of a tree, limb. or other body left after the rest is cut off; one of the sticks of a wicket;—*v.t.* to knock down the wicket. [Scand.]

STUMPY (stum'pi) *a.* full of stumps; stubby.

STUN (stun) *v.t.* to make senseless by a blow; stupefy. [O.E. *stunian*, make a din, fr. *stun*, a din.]

STUNG (stung) *pret.* and *pp.* of STING.

STUNNER (stun'er) *n.* one who stuns; an extraordinary person or thing.

STUNT (stunt) *v.t.* to hinder from growth. [O.E. *stunt*, stupid.]

STUPE (stūp) *v.t.* to foment. [L. *stupa*, fr. G. *stuppe*, tow.]

STUPEFACTION (stū-pe-fak'shun) *n.* insensibility; torpor; stupidity.

STUPEFIER (stū'pe-fi-er) *n.* that which stupefies.

STUPEFY (stū'pe-fi) *v.t.* to deprive of sensibility. [L. *stupere*, be struck senseless, and *facere*, to make.]

STUPENDOUS (stū-pen'dus) *a.* astonishing in height or magnitude; wonderful. [L. *stupendus*, fr. *stupere*, be astonished at.]

STUPENDOUSLY (stū-pen'dus-li) *ad.* so as to excite astonishment.

STUPID (stū'pid) *a.* wanting sense; foolish; done without reason or judgment. [F. fr. L. *stupidus*, fr. *stupere*, be stupefied.]

STUPIDITY (stū-pid'i-ti) *n.* dullness of intellect; foolishness.

STUPIDLY (stū'pid-li) *ad.* foolishly; absurdly.

STUPOR (stū'per) *n.* suspension of sensibility; numbness. [L.]

STURDILY (stur'di-li) *ad.* stoutly; hardily.

STURDINESS (stur'di-nes) *n.* quality of being hardy.

STURDY (stur'di) *a.* stout; hardy; robust; forcible. [O.F. *estourdi*, stunned, rash.]

STURGEON (stur'jun) *n.* a large cartilaginous fish. [O.F. *esturgeon*, fr. Teut.]

STUTTER (stut'er) *v.i.* to stammer;—*n.* a hesitation in speech. [Cf. Ger. *stottern*.]

STUTTERER (stut'er-er) *n.* a stammerer.

STY (sti) (1) *n.* a pen for swine;— (2) *n.* a small ulcer on the edge of the eye-lid. Sometimes written STYE. [(1) O.E. *stigu.* Cf. Ger. *Steige.* (2) O.E. *stigend.* fr. *stiga*, to step up.]

STYGIAN (stij'i-an) *a.* infernal; dark; black. [L. *Stygius* fr. G. *Stux*, the Styx. *i.e.* the loathly fr. *stugein*, to hate.]

STYLAR (sti'lar) *a.* belonging to the style of a dial.

STYLE (stil) (1) *n.* manner of writing; title; graver;—*v.t.* to entitle; designate;—(2) *n.* pin of a dial; filament of a pistil. fr. L. *stilus*, a writing instrument. *stulos*, a pillar.]

Style. (1) F. (2) G.

STYLET (sti'let) *n.* a small poniard; a surgeon's instrument. [O.F.]

STYLISH (sti'lish) *a.* fashionable in form or manner; showy.

STYPTIC (stip'tik) *a.* that stops bleeding;—*n.* an astringent medicine. [F. fr. L. *stypticus* fr. G. *stuptikos*; fr. *stuphein*, contract.]

SUABLE (sū'a-bl) *a.* that may be sued at law.

SUASIBLE (swā'si-bl) *a.* that may be persuaded.

SUASION (swā'zhun) *n.* act of persuading. [F., fr. L. (acc.) *suasionem*, fr. *suadere*, to advise.]

SUASIVE (swā'siv) *a.* tending to persuade.

SUAVE (swāv, swov) *a.* agreeable; pleasant; bland. [F., fr. L. *suavis* sweet.]

SUBACID (sub-as'id) *a.* moderately acid.

SUBACTION (sub-ak'shun) *n.* act of reducing to any state.

SUBAGENCY (sub-ā'jen-si) *n.* a subordinate agency.

SUBALTERN (sub'al-tern su-bawl'tern) *a.* inferior; subordinate;—*n.* an inferior officer. [F., fr. L. *subalternus* fr. *sub*, under and *alternus*. one after another. fr. *alter*. the other.]

SUBALTERNATE (sub-al-ter'nat) *a.* succeeding by turns

SUBAQUEOUS (sub-ā'kwe-us) *a.* being under the surface of water. [L. *sub.* under. and *aqua*, water.]

SUBASTRAL (sub-as'tral) *a.* under the stars. [L. *sub*, under, and *astrum*, a star.]

SUBCOMMITTEE (sub-ku-mit'e) *n.* an under-committee.

SUBCONSCIOUS (sub-kon'shus) *a.* faintly conscious.

SUBCUTANEOUS (sub-kū-tā'ne-us) *a.* situated under the skin.

SUBDIVIDE (sub-di-vid') *v.t.* to divide a part into more parts.

SUBDIVISION (sub-di-vizh'un) *n.* a part of a division.

SUBDUABLE (sub-dū'a-bl) *a.* that may be subdued.

SUBDUE (sub-dū') *v.t.* to conquer; tame; soften. [O.F. *souduire*, fr. L. *sub* under, and *ducere*, lead.]

SUBDUER (sub-dū'er) *n.* he or that which subdues.

SUBEDITOR (sub-ed'i-ter) *n.* an under or assistant editor. [L. *sub*, under. and EDITOR.]

SUBITANEOUS (sub-i-tā'ne-us) *a.* sudden.

SUBJACENT (sub-jā'sent) *a.* lying under. [L. (part.stem) *subjacent-*, fr. *subjacere*, lie under.]

SUBJECT (sub'jekt) *a.* being under authority; liable;—*n.* one who lives under the power of another; object or matter handled; topic; theme. [L. (part.) *subjectus*, fr. *subjicere*, place or bring under.]

SUBJECT (sub-jekt') *v.t.* to bring under power; expose; cause to undergo.

SUBJECTION (sub-jek'shun) *n.* a being under control.

SUBJECTIVE (sub-jek'tiv) *a.* relating to the subject or to the point of view taken by the individual person.

SUBJECTIVITY (sub-jek-tiv'i-ti) *n.* that which relates to personal consciousness; individuality.

SUBJOIN (sub-join') *v.t.* to add at the end.

SUBJUGATE (sub'joo-gāt) *v.t.* to bring under power; conquer. [L. (part.) *subjugatus* fr. L. *subjugare*, fr. *sub*, under and *jugum*, a yoke.]

SUBJUGATION (sub-joo-gā'shun) *n.* act of subduing; subjection.

SUBJUNCTION (sub-jungk'shun) *n.* the act of subjoining.

SUBJUNCTIVE (sub-jungk'tiv) *a.* added; subjoined. [L. (part.) *subjunctus* fr. *subjungere*, to subjoin.]

SUBLET (sub-let') *v.t.* to lease, as lessee, to another person.

SUBLIMATE (sub'li-māt) *v.t.* to refine by heat; —*n.* product of sublimation. [L. (part.) *sublimatus*, fr. *sublimare*, to raise.]

SUBLIMATION (sub-li-mā'shun) *n.* the act of bringing solid substances to a state of vapour, which is then condensed.

SUBLIME (sub-lim') *a.* high; lofty; grand; noble;—*n.* the lofty or grand in thought or style;—*v.t.* or *i.* to exalt; sublimate. [L. *sublimis,* fr. *sublimare,* to raise.]

SUBLIMELY (sub-lim'li) *ad.* in a sublime or lofty manner.

SUBLIMITY (sub-lim'i-ti) *n.* loftiness of idea or language; nobleness of nature or character.

SUBLUNAR (sub-lŏŏ'nạr) *a.* being under the moon; earthly. [L. *sub,* under, and *luna,* moon.]

SUBMARINE (sub-mạ-rēn') *a.* under the water of the sea. [L. *sub,* under, and *mare,* the sea.]

SUBMERGE (sub-mẹrj') *v.t.* or *i.* to plunge under water; drown; sink. [L., fr. *sub,* under, and *mergere,* to plunge.]

SUBMERSION (sub-mẹr'shun) *n.* act of plunging under water.

SUBMISSION (sub-mish'un) *n.* act of yielding to authority; resignation.

SUBMISSIVE (sub-mis'iv) *a.* yielding to another; humble. [mission.

SUBMISSIVELY (sub-mis'iv-li) *ad.* with sub-

SUBMISSIVENESS (sub-mis'iv-nes) *n.* submissive disposition.

SUBMIT (sub-mit') *v.t.* or *i.* to yield to the power or opinion of another; refer; surrender; acquiesce. [L., fr. *sub,* under, and *mittere,* send.]

SUBNASCENT (sub-nas'ent) *a.* growing beneath something.

SUBORDINACY (sub-or'di-nạ-si) *n.* state of being subordinate.

SUBORDINATE (sub-or'di-nāt) *a.* inferior; subject;—*n.* an inferior;—*v.t.* to place in a lower order; subject. [L., fr. *sub,* under, and *ordinare,* to arrange, fr. *ordo, ordinis,* order.]

SUBORDINATION (sub-or-di-nā'shun) *n.* inferiority of position or rank.

SUBORN (sub-orn') *v.t.* to cause to take a false oath; procure privately; bribe. [F. *suborner,* fr. L. *subornare,* fr. *sub,* under, and *ornare,* to fit out.]

SUBORNATION (sub-or-nā'shun) *n.* act of suborning.

SUBORNER (sub-or'nẹr) *n.* one who suborns.

SUBPŒNA (sub-pē'nạ) *n.* a summons for witnesses;—*v.t.* to summon by subpœna. [L. *sub,* under, and *pœna,* punishment.]

SUBSCRIBE (sub-skrib') *v.t.* to sign one's name; attest; promise to give by writing one's name. [L., fr. *sub,* under, and *scribere,* write.]

SUBSCRIBER (sub-skri'bẹr) *n.* one who subscribes.

SUBSCRIPT (sub'skript) *a.* underwritten.

SUBSCRIPTION (sub-skrip'shun) *n.* the signing of a name; amount subscribed; attestation.

SUBSECTION (sub-sek'shun) *n.* division or part of a section.

SUBSEQUENCE (sub'se-kwens) *n.* the state of being subsequent.

SUBSEQUENT (sub'se-kwent) *a.* following in time or order; succeeding. [L. (part. stem) *subsequent-,* fr. *subsequi,* fr. *sub,* under, and *sequi,* to follow.]

SUBSEQUENTLY (sub'se-kwent-li) *ad.* later; afterwards.

SUBSERVE (sub-sẹrv') *v.t.* to serve subordinately or instrumentally; help forward. [L., fr. *sub,* under, and *servire,* to serve.]

SUBSERVIENCE (sub-sẹr'vi-ens) *n.* instrumental use.

SUBSERVIENT (sub-sẹr'vi-ent) *a.* helping to promote; acting as a tool.

SUBSERVIENTLY (sub-sẹr'vi-ent-li) *ad.* in a subservient manner.

SUBSIDE (sub-sid') *v.i.* to sink to the bottom; settle down; abate. [L., fr. *sub,* under, and *sedere,* sit down.]

SUBSIDENCE (sub'si-dens) *n.* act of sinking down.

SUBSIDIARY (sub-sid'i-ạ-ri) *a.* furnishing supplies; assisting. [L. *subsidium,* help.]

SUBSIDISE (sub'si-diz) *v.t.* to pay a subsidy to.

SUBSIDY (sub'si-di) *n.* aid in money. [L. *subsidium,* help.]

SUBSIST (sub-sist') *v.i.* to have existence;—*v.t.* to maintain. [L., fr. *sub,* under, and *sistere,* to stand.]

SUBSISTENCE (sub-sis'tens) *n.* real being; means of support.

SUBSISTENT (sub-sis'tent) *a.* having real being; inherent.

SUBSOIL (sub'soil) *n.* a bed of earth beneath the surface; soil. [L. *sub,* under, and SOIL.]

SUBSOLAR (sub-sō'lạr) *a.* being under the sun.

SUBSPECIES (sub-spē'shēz) *n.* division of a species.

SUBSTANCE (sub'stạns) *n.* a being; essential part; matter; property. [L. *substantia,* fr. *substare,* fr. *sub,* under, and *stare,* stand.]

SUBSTANTIAL (sub-stan'shạl) *a.* real; solid.

SUBSTANTIALITY (sub-stan-shi-al'i-ti) *n.* state of having real existence.

SUBSTANTIALLY (sub-stan'shạl-i) *ad.* in the main; essentially.

SUBSTANTIALS (sub-stan'shạlz) *n.pl.* essential parts.

SUBSTANTIATE (sub-stan'shi-āt) *v.t.* to prove or confirm.

SUBSTANTIATION (sub-stan-shi-ā'shun) *n.* act of making good by proper evidence.

SUBSTANTIVE (sub'stạn-tiv) *n.* a noun;— *a.* noting existence; real.

SUBSTITUTE (sub'sti-tūt) *n.* one put in place of another;—*v.t.* to put in the place of another; exchange. [L., fr. *sub,* under, and *statuere,* put.]

SUBSTITUTION (sub-sti-tū'shun) *n.* state of substituting or of being substituted.

SUBSTITUTIONAL (sub-sti-tū'shun-al) *a.* pertaining to substitution. Also **SUBSTITU-TIONARY.**

SUBSTRATUM (sub-strā'tum) *n.* a layer under something; basis.

SUBSTRUCTION (sub-struk'shun) *n.* an underbuilding. [L. (part.) *substructus,* fr. *substruere,* to build beneath.]

SUBSTRUCTURE (sub-struk'tūr) *n.* an underbuilding; foundation.

SUBTEND (sub-tend') *v.t.* to extend under; be opposite to. [L., fr. *sub,* under, and *tendere,* stretch.]

SUBTENSE (sub-tens') *n.* the chord of an arc.

SUBTERFLUENT (sub-tẹr'floo-ent) *a.* flowing beneath.

SUBTERFUGE (sub'tẹr-fūj) *n.* an artifice to escape; evasion. [L. *subterfugere,* flee secretly.]

SUBTERRANEAN (sub-te-rā'ne-ạn) *a.* being under the surface of the earth. [L. *sub,* under, and *terra,* earth.]

SUBTILE (sut'l, sub'til) *a.* fine; thin; acute; shrewd; crafty. [L. *subtilis,* fr. *sub,* under, and *tela,* a web.]

SUBTILISATION (sut-i-li-zā'shun, sub-ti-li-zā'shun) *n.* refinement.

SUBTILISE (sut'l-iz, sub'ti-liz) *v.t.* to make fine or thin; refine.

SUBTILITY (sut'l-ti, sub'til-ti) *n.* quality of being subtile.

SUBTLE (sut'l) *a.* acute; piercing; cunning; artful. [Contr. of SUBTILE.]

SUBTLETY (sut'l-ti) *n.* acuteness; shrewdness; cunning.

SUBTLY (sut'li) *ad.* artfully; nicely.

SUBTRACT (sub-trakt') *v.t.* to withdraw a part; deduct. [L., fr. *sub,* under, and (part.) *tractus,* fr. *trahere,* to draw.]

SUBTRACTION (sub-trak'shun) *n.* the taking a lesser sum from a greater; a withdrawing.

SUBTRACTIVE (sub-trak'tiv) *a.* tending to subtract.

SUBTRAHEND (sub'-tra-hend) *n.* number to be subtracted.

SUBURBAN (sub-ur'ban) *a.* being in the suburbs. [L. *suburbium*, fr. *sub.* under. and *urbs*, a city.]

SUBURBS (sub urbz) *n.pl.* confines of a city.

SUBVENTION (sub-ven'shun) *n.* act of coming in aid; government bounty, [L. *sub.* under. and *venire*, come.]

SUBVERSION (sub-ver'shun) *n.* total overthrow; ruin.

SUBVERSIVE (sub-ver'siv) *a.* tending to ruin.

SUBVERT (sub-vert') *v.t.* to overthrow; ruin. [L., fr. *sub* under and *vertere*, to turn.]

SUBVERTER (sub-ver'ter) *n.* one who overthrows.

SUCCEED (suk-sēd') *v.t.* or *i.* to follow in order; take the place of: obtain one's wish or object; prosper. [L. fr. *sub* under, and *cedere*, to go.]

SUCCESS (suk-ses') *n.* prosperous result of anything attempted.

SUCCESSFUL (suk-ses'fool) *a.* having accomplished what was desired or intended.

SUCCESSFULLY (suk-ses'fool-i) *ad.* prosperously.

SUCCESSION (suk-sesh'un) *n.* series of things; right of succeeding; lineage; race; rotation.

SUCCESSIONAL (suk-sesh'un-al) *a.* noting succession.

SUCCESSIVE (suk-ses'iv) *a.* following in order.

SUCCESSIVELY (suk-ses'iv-li) *ad.* in regular order.

SUCCESSLESS (suk-ses'les) *a.* having no success.

SUCCESSOR (suk-ses'er) *n.* one who succeeds another.

SUCCINCT (suk-singkt') *a.* compressed into a narrow compass; concise. [L. (part.) *succinctus*, fr. *succingere*, to gird below.]

SUCCINCTLY (suk-singkt'li) *ad.* briefly.

SUCCINCTNESS (suk-singkt'nes) *n.* conciseness; brevity.

SUCCORY (suk'u-ri) *n.* chicory; wild endive. [F. *chicorée* fr. L. *cichorium*.]

SUCCOUR (suk'ur) *v.t.* to relieve in distress; aid;—*n.* assistance in distress. [M.E. *socouren*, fr. O.F. *sucurre*, fr. L. *succurrere*, to run up to, fr. *sub*, near. and *currere*, run.]

SUCCOURER (suk'ur-er) *n.* a helper; deliverer.

SUCCOURLESS (suk'ur-les) *a.* destitute of help or relief.

SUCCULENCE (suk'ū-lens) *n.* juiciness.

SUCCULENT (suk'ū-lent) *a.* juicy. [L. *succulentus*, fr. *succus*, juice, fr. *sugere*, to suck.]

SUCCUMB (su-kum') *v.i.* to yield; sink under. [L., fr. *sub.* under, and *cumbere*, lie down.]

SUCH (such) *a.* of the like kind; the same that. [O.E. *swylc*.]

SUCK (suk) *v.t.* or *i.* to draw with the mouth; imbibe;—*n.* act of sucking; a small sip. [O.E. *sucan.* Cf. Ger. *saugen*.]

SUCKER (suk'er) *n.* one who or that which sucks; piston of a pump; a kind of pipe; shoot of a plant; fish of the carp family.

SUCKLE (suk'l) *v.t.* to nurse at the breast.

SUCKLING (suk'ling) *n.* a child at the breast.

SUCTION (suk'shun) *n.* act of drawing in. [M.F., fr. L. *sugere*, pp. *suctus*, to suck.]

SUCTORIAL (suk-tō'ri-al) *a.* adapted for sucking; adhering by suction.

SUDATION (sū-dā'shun) *n.* a sweating. [L., fr. *sudare*, to sweat.]

SUDDEN (sud'n) *a.* coming without previous notice; hasty; abrupt. [O.F. *soudain*, fr. L. *subitus*, that has come on suddenly.]

SUDDENLY (sud'n-li) *ad* unexpectedly.

SUDDENNESS (sud'n-nes) *n.* a coming unexpectedly.

SUDORIFIC (sū-du-rif'ik) *a.* causing sweat;—*n.* a medicine that causes sweat. [L. *sudor*, sweat. and *facere*, to make.]

SUDS (sudz) *n.sing.* water impregnated with soap, and worked up into froth. [O.E. *seothan*, to seethe.]

SUE (sū) *v.t.* to prosecute in law;—*v.i.* to make legal claim; plead; entreat. [O.F. *suir* = F. *suivre*, fr. L. *sequi*, to follow.]

SUET (sū'et) *n.* fat about the kidneys. [O.F *seu* = F. *suif*, fr. L. *sebum*, tallow.]

SUFFER (suf'er) *v.t.* or *i.* to undergo: endure allow; sustain loss. [O.F. *soffrir* fr. L. *sub*. under, and *ferre*, to bear.]

SUFFERABLE (suf'er-a-bl) *a.* that may be endured.

SUFFERANCE (suf'er-ans) *n.* permission endurance; patience.

SUFFERER (suf'er-er) *n.* one who undergoes suffering; one who permits.

SUFFERING (suf'er-ing) *n.* pain endured.

SUFFICE (su-fīs') *v.t.* to satisfy;—*v.i.* to be enough. [L. *sufficere* be sufficient, fr. *sub.* under, and *facere*, to make.]

SUFFICIENCY (su-fish'en-si) *n.* a full supply: ability; competence; conceit.

SUFFICIENT (su-fish'ent) *a.* adequate to wants; competent.

SUFFICIENTLY (su-fish'ent-li) *ad.* so as to satisfy.

SUFFIX (su-fiks') *v.t.* to add a letter or word; —(suf'iks) *n.* a letter or syllable added. [L. (part.) *suffixus*, fr. *suffigere*, to fix on, fr. *sub.* under, and *figere*, to fix.]

SUFFOCATE (suf'u-kāt) *v.t.* to choke by excluding air; stifle; smother. [L. (part.) *suffocatus*, fr. *suffocare*, fr. *sub* under, and *fauces*, the throat.]

SUFFOCATION (suf-u-kā'shun) *n.* the act of choking; strangling.

SUFFOCATIVE (suf'u-kā-tiv) *a.* tending to suffocate.

SUFFRAGAN (suf'ra-gan) *n.* an assistant bishop;—*a.* assisting. [L. *suffragari*, to support with one's vote.]

SUFFRAGE (suf'rij) *n.* a vote: united voice. [L. *suffragium*, a ballot. fr. *suffragari*, to vote for.]

SUFFRAGETTE (suf'ra-jette) *n.* a female agitator who demands the right of Parliamentary voting for women.

SUFFRAGIST (suf-ra-jist) *n.* one that has or exercises the right of suffrage; a voter.

SUFFUSE (su-fūz') *v.t.* to overspread, as with a fluid or colour. [L. (part.) *suffusus* fr. *suffundere*, to pour over. fr. *sub*, under and *fundere*, to pour.]

SUFFUSION (su-fū'zhun) *n.* act of suffusing.

SUGAR (shoog'ar) *n.* the juice of canes or other plants reduced to a concrete state;—*v.t.* to sweeten. [F. *sucre*, fr. Sp. fr. A. fr. Per. fr. Skr. =gravel, candied sugar.]

SUGAR-CANE (shoog'ar-kān) *n.* the cane whose juice produces sugar.

SUGAR-LOAF (shoog'ar-lōf) *n.* mass or cone of refined sugar.

SUGARY (shoog'a-ri) *a.* sweet.

SUGGEST (su-jest') *v.t.* to hint: intimate. [L. (part.) *suggestus*, fr. *suggerere*, fr. *sub*, under and *gerere*, to carry.]

Sugar-Cane

SUGGESTION (su-jes'tyun) *n.* hint: intimation.

SUGGESTIVE (su-jes'tiv) *a.* containing a hint.

SUGGESTIVENESS (su-jes'tiv-nes) *n.* quality of being suggestive.

SUICIDAL (sū-i-si-dal) *a.* of the nature of suicide.

SUICIDE (sū'i-sīd) *n.* self-murder; a self-murderer. [Coined fr. L. *sui*, of oneself and *cædere*, to kill.]

SUIT (sūt) *n.* a set; process; prosecution, one of the four sets of a pack of cards;—*v.t.* or *i.* to fit to or be fitted; become; agree. [F. *suite*, fr. L. *sequi*, to follow.]

SUITABLE (sū'ta-bl) a. fitting; becoming.
SUITABLENESS (sū'ta-bl-nes) n. fitness.
SUITABLY (sū'ta-bli) ad. fitly; properly.
SUITE (swēt) n. a train of attendants; a regular set or series. [F. Cf. SUIT.]
SUITER (sū'tur) n. one courting; one who sues; a petitioner.
SULKINESS (sul'ki-nes) n. silent or fitful sullenness.
SULKS (sulks) n.pl. a sulky mood or fit.
SULKY (sul'ki) a. silently sullen; sour. [O.E. solcen, dull, fr. solcan, to be slow.]
SULLEN (sul'en) a. gloomy; dark; malignant; morose. [O.F. solain, lonely, fr. L. solus, alone.]
SULLY (sul'i) v.t. or i. to soil; spot; tarnish. [O.E. sylian, to defile, fr. sol, mud.]
SULPHATE (sul'fat) n. a compound of sulphuric acid and a base. [See SULPHUR.]
SULPHUR (sul'fur) n. brimstone. [L.]
SULPHURATE (sul'fū-rāt) v.t. to combine with sulphur;—a. sulphury.
SULPHURET (sul'fū-ret) n. a combination of sulphur with an earth, metal, or alkali.
SULPHURIC (sul-fū'rik) a. pertaining to sulphur.
SULPHUROUS (sul'fū-rus) a. having the qualities of sulphur.
SULPHURY (sul'fur-i) a. partaking of sulphur; sulphurate.
SULTAN (sul'tan) n. Turkish emperor. [F., fr. A. sultan, victorious (also a prince).]
SULTANA (sul-tā'na) n. the Turkish empress; a kind of raisin.
SULTANIC (sul-tan'ik) a. belonging to the sultan.
SULTANSHIP (sul'tan-ship) n. state or office of the sultan.
SULTRINESS (sul'tri-nes) n. state of being sultry.
SULTRY (sul'tri) a. hot and close. [Corr. fr. SWELTRY.]
SUM (sum) n. the whole amount;—v.t. to collect into a total. [F., fr. L. summa, fr. summus, highest, superl. of supčrus, on high, fr. super, above.]
SUMLESS (sum'les) a. not to be counted.
SUMMARILY (sum'a-ri-li) ad. briefly.
SUMMARY (sum'a-ri) a. brief; short; concise;—n. an abridged account. [L. summa, the whole, fr. summus, highest.]
SUMMATION (su-mā'shun) n. the act of summing; aggregate. [See SUM.]
SUMMER (sum'er) n. the hot season. [O.E. sumer. Cf. Ger. Sommer.]
SUMMIT (sum'it) n. the highest point or degree.
SUMMON (sum'un) v.t. to call by authority; cite; call to action. [O.F. somoner, fr. L. summonere, fr. sub, under, secretly, and monere, warn.]
SUMMONER (sum'un-er) n. one who summons.
SUMMONS (sum'unz) n.sing. a citation.
SUMPTER (sump'ter) n. a pack-horse. [O.F. sommetier, a pack-horse driver, fr. Late L. sagmarius, fr. G. sagma, a pack-saddle, fr. sattein, to pack.]
SUMPTUARY (sump'tū-a-ri) a. regulating expenses. [L. sumptus, expense.]
SUMPTUOUS (sump'tū-us) a. characterised by expense and magnificence; costly. [L. sumptuosus, costly, fr. sumptus, expense.]
SUMPTUOUSLY (sump'tū-us-li) ad. in a magnificent manner.
SUMPTUOUSNESS (sump'tū-us-nes) n. magnificence; costliness.
SUN (sun) n. the luminary that enlightens and warms the earth and other planets; any beneficent centre;—v.t. to expose to the sun. [O.E. sunne.]
SUNBEAM (sun'bēm) n. a ray of the sun.
SUNBURNT (sun'burnt) a. scorched or browned by the sun's rays.
SUNDAY (sun'dā) n. the Christian Sabbath. [O.E. sunnan dæg. Cf. Ger. Sonntag.]

SUNDER (sun'der) v.t. to separate; divide. [O.E. syndrian, to separate, fr. sundor, apart.]
SUNDIAL (sun'dī-al) n. an instrument to show the time by the shadow of a style.
SUNDOWN (sun'doun) n. sunset.
SUNDRY (sun'dri) a. more than one or two; divers; several. [See SUNDER.]
SUNFISH (sun'fish) n. a large, flat, round sea-fish.
SUNFLOWER (sun'flou-er) n. a plant having a flower with a large disk and yellow rays.

Sundial.

SUNLIKE (sun'līk) a. resembling the sun.
SUNNY (sun'i) a. of or like the sun; bright; warm.
SUNRISE (sun'rīz) n. first appearance of the sun in the morning.
SUNSET (sun'set) n. disappearance of the sun at night.
SUNSHINE (sun'shīn) n. light of the sun;—a. bright with the sun's rays.
SUNSTROKE (sun'strōk) n. a nervous disease caused by exposure to the sun.
SUP (sup) v.t. or i. to take into the mouth, as liquid food; eat supper;—n. a small draught. [O.E. supan, to sip. Cf. Ger. saufen, to drink.]
SUPERABLE (sū'per-a-bl) a. that may be overcome. [L. superabilis, fr. super, over.]
SUPERABOUND (sū-per-a-bound') v.i. to be very abundant; be more than enough. [L. super.]
SUPERABUNDANCE (sū-per-a-bun'dans) n. more than is sufficient.
SUPERABUNDANT (sū-per-a-bun'dant) a. more than is sufficient.
SUPERADD (sū-per-ad') v.t. to add over and above. [L. super, over, and ADD.]
SUPERANNUATE (sū-per-an'ū-āt) v.t. to impair by old age. [L. super, above, and annus, a year.]
SUPERANNUATED (sū-per-an'ū-ā-ted) a. disqualified by old age.
SUPERB (sū-perb') a. proud; magnificent. [L. superbus, proud, fr. super, above.]
SUPERBLY (sū-perb'li) ad. grandly; splendidly.
SUPERCARGO (sū-per-kär'gō) n. one who has the care of a cargo. [L. super, over, and CARGO.]
SUPERCILIOUS (sū-per-sil'yus) a. haughty; dictatorial. [L. superciliosus, fr. supercilium, an eyebrow, fr. super, above, and cilium, eyelid.]
SUPERCILIOUSLY (sū-per-sil'yus-li) ad. haughtily.
SUPEREMINENCE (sū-per-em'i-nens) n. eminence above the common.
SUPEREMINENT (sū-per-em'i-nent) a. eminent in a high degree. [L. super, above, and EMINENT.]
SUPEREROGATION (sū-per-er-u-gā'shun) n. a doing more than duty. [L., fr. super, above, and erogare, to pay out.]
SUPEREROGATORY (sū-per-er'u-ga-tu-ri) a. exceeding the calls of duty.
SUPEREXCELLENCE (sū-per-ek'se-lens) n. superior excellence.
SUPEREXCELLENT (sū-per-ek'se-lent) a. very excellent. [L. super, over, and EXCELLENT.]
SUPERFICIAL (sū-per-fish'al) a. being on the surface; shallow. [L. superficialis, fr. super, above, and facies, the face.]
SUPERFICIALITY (sū-per-fish-i-al'i-ti) a n. state of being superficial; shallowness.
SUPERFICIALLY (sū-per-fish'al-i) ad. on the surface only.
SUPERFICIES (sū-per-fish'ēz) n. surface; exterior part of a thing. [L., fr. super, above, and facies, form, shape.]

SUPERFINE (sū-pẹr-fīn') *a.* very fine; over fine. [L. *super*, over, and FINE.]

SUPERFLUITY (sū-pẹr-flŏŏ'i-ti) *n.* abundance above necessity.

SUPERFLUOUS (sū-pẹr'floo-us) *a.* exceeding what is wanted; useless. [L. *superfluus*. fr. *superfluere*, to overflow, fr. *super*, above, and *fluere*, to flow.]

SUPERHUMAN (sū-pẹr-hū'man) *a.* beyond what is human. [L. *super*, beyond, and MAN.]

SUPERIMPOSE (sū-pẹr-im-pōz') *v.t.* to lay upon something else. [L. *super*, over, and IMPOSE.]

SUPERINCUMBENT (sū-pẹr-in-kum'bent) *a.* lying or resting on. [L. *super*, over, and INCUMBENT.]

SUPERINDUCE (sū-pẹr-in-dūs') *v.t.* to bring in as addition to something. [L. *super*, over, and INDUCE.]

SUPERINTEND (sū-pẹr-in-tend') *v.t.* to oversee. [L. *super*.]

SUPERINTENDENCE (sū-pẹr-in-ten'dens) *n.* act of overseeing.

SUPERINTENDENT (sū-pẹr-in-ten'dent) *n.* a manager; — *a.* directing.

SUPERIOR (sū-pē'ri-ur) *a.* higher; greater; — *n.* one higher or more excellent; a chief. [L. *superior*, comp. of *superus*, being above, fr. *super*, above.]

SUPERIORITY (sū-pē-ri-cr'i-ti) *n.* higher rank.

SUPERLATIVE (sū-pẹr'la-tiv) *a.* expressing the highest degree. [L. *superlativus*. fr. (part.) *superlatus*. fr *superferre*, fr. *super*, over, and *ferre*, to carry.]

SUPERLUNAR (sū-pẹr-lŏŏ'nar) *a.* being above the moon; not of this world. [L. *super*, above, and *luna*, the moon.]

SUPERMAN (sū'per-man) *n.* a higher order of man. [L. *super*, over.]

SUPERMUNDANE (sū-pẹr-mun'dān) *a.* being above the world.

SUPERNAL (sū-pẹr'nal) *a.* relating to things above; celestial. [L. *supernus*, fr. *super*, above.]

SUPERNATANT (sū-pẹr-nā'tant) *a.* swimming on the surface. [L. *supernatare*, swim above, fr. *super*, above, and *natare*, to swim.]

SUPERNATURAL (sū-pẹr-nat'ū-ral) *a.* being beyond the laws of nature. [L. *super*, beyond, and NATURAL.]

SUPERNATURALISM (sū-pẹr-nat'ū-ral-izm) *n.* doctrine of a divine or supernatural agency in the world.

SUPERNATURALLY (sū-pẹr-nat'ū-ral-i) *ad.* beyond the laws of nature.

SUPERNUMERARY (sū-pẹr-nū'me-ra-ri) *a.* exceeding the number necessary; — *n.* a person or thing beyond the stated number. [L. *supernumerarius*, fr. *super*, above, and *numerus*, a number.]

SUPERPOSITION (sū-pẹr-pō-zish'un) *n.* the order in which mineral strata are placed. [L. *super* above, and (part.) *positus*, of *ponere*, to place.]

SUPERSCRIBE (sū'pẹr-skrīb) *v.t.* to write on the surface, outside, or cover. [L. *super*, over, and *scribere*, write.]

SUPERSCRIPTION (sū-pẹr-skrip'shun) *n.* a writing over or on the outside.

SUPERSEDE (sū-pẹr-sēd') *v.t.* to take the place of; succeed; set aside. [L. *supersedere*, to sit above, fr. *super*, above, and *sedere*, to sit.]

SUPERSTITION (sū-pẹr-stish'un) *n.* rigour in religion; religious credulity; false faith; false fear. [L. (acc) *superstitionem*, fear of the gods, fr. *super*, above, and *sistere*, fr. *stare*, to stand.]

SUPERSTITIOUS (sū-pẹr-stish'us) *a.* addicted to superstition.

SUPERSTITIOUSLY (sū-pẹr-stish'us-li) *ad.* in a superstitious manner.

SUPERSTITIOUSNESS (sū-pẹr-stish'us-nes) *n.* quality of being superstitious.

SUPERSTRUCTURE (sū-pẹr-struk'tūr) *n.* that which is built on something. [L. fr. *super*, over, and *struere*, build.]

SUPERVENE (sū-pẹr-vēn') *v.i.* to come extraneously; occur. [L. *supervenire*. come over or upon, fr. *super*, above, and *venire*, to come.]

SUPERVENIENT (sū-pẹr-vē'nyent) *a.* added; additional.

SUPERVENTION (sū-pẹr-ven'shun) *n.* act of supervening.

SUPERVISAL (sū-pẹr-vi'zal) *n.* act of overseeing.

SUPERVISE (sū-pẹr-viz') *v.t.* to overlook; inspect. [L. *super*, over, and (part.) *visus*, fr. *videre*, see.]

SUPERVISION (sū-pẹr-vish'un) *n.* inspection; superintendence.

SUPERVISOR (sū-pẹr-vi'zẹr) *n.* an overseer.

SUPINE (sū'pin) *n.* a verbal noun. [L. *supinus*, bent, backward.]

SUPINE (sū'pin) *a.* lying on the back; indolent; careless.

SUPINELY (sū-pin'li) *ad.* indolently.

SUPINENESS (sū-pin'nes) *n.* indolence; heedlessness.

SUPPER (sup'ẹr) *n.* the evening meal. [O.F. *soper* = F. *souper*.]

SUPPERLESS (sup'ẹr-les) *a.* wanting supper.

SUPPLANT (su-plant') *v.t.* to displace by stratagem; take the place of. [F. *supplanter*. fr. L. *supplantare*, to trip up one's heels, fr. *sub*, under, and *planta*, the sole of the foot.]

SUPPLANTER (su-plăn'tẹr) *n.* one who supplants.

SUPPLE (sup'l) *a.* pliable; flexible; — *v.t.* or *i.* to make or become soft and pliant. [F. *souple*, fr. L. *supplex*, bending the knees, fr. *sub*, under, and *plicare*, to fold.]

SUPPLEMENT (sup'le-ment) *n.* an addition; — (sup-le-ment') *v.t.* to fill up; add to. [L. *supplementum*, fr. *supplere*, to fill up.]

SUPPLEMENTARY (sup-le-men'ta-ri) *a.* added to supply what is wanted. Also SUPPLEMENTAL.

SUPPLENESS (sup'l-nes) *n.* pliancy; flexibility.

SUPPLIANT (sup'li-ant) *a.* entreating; — *n.* an humble petitioner. [F., fr. L. (part. stem) *supplicant-*, fr. *supplicare*, to entreat.]

SUPPLICATE (sup'li-kāt) *v.t.* to entreat earnestly; address in prayer; — *v.i.* to petition; implore. [L. (part.) *supplicatus*, fr. *supplicare*, fr. *supplex*, kneeling down.]

SUPPLICATION (sup-li-kā'shun) *n.* humble petition; entreaty.

SUPPLICATORY (sup'li-kā-tu-ri) *a.* containing supplication.

SUPPLIER (su-pli'ẹr) *n.* one that supplies.

SUPPLIES (su-pliz') *n.pl.* things supplied.

SUPPLY (su-pli') *v.t.* to fill or furnish; — *n.* sufficiency for wants. [F., fr. L. *supplere*, fr. *sub*, under, and *plere*, fill.]

SUPPORT (su-pōrt') *n.* a prop; maintenance; — *v.t.* to prop; sustain; maintain. [L. *supportare*, fr. *sub*, under, and *portare*, carry.]

SUPPORTABLE (su-pōr'ta-bl) *a.* that may be supported.

SUPPORTER (su-pōr'tẹr) *n.* one who, or that which, supports; adherent; figure on each side of an escutcheon.

SUPPORTLESS (su-pōrt'les) *a.* having no support.

SUPPOSABLE (su-pō'za-bl) *a.* that may be supposed. [See SUPPOSE.]

SUPPOSAL (su-pō'zal) *n.* supposition.

SUPPOSE (su-pōz') *v.t.* to lay down or assume as true; imagine. [F. *supposer*, fr. L. (part.) *suppositus*, fr. *supponere*, fr. *sub*, under, and *ponere*, to place.]

SUPPOSITION (sup-u-zish'un) *n.* something supposed.

SUPPOSITIONAL (sup-u-zish'un-al) *a.* founded on supposition; hypothetical.

SUPPOSITITIOUS (su-poz-i-tish'us) *a.* not genuine; illegitimate.

SUPPRESS (su-pres') *v.t.* to crush; keep in; conceal; restrain from disclosure. [L. (part.) *suppressus*, fr. *supprimere*, fr. *sub*, under, and *premere*, to press.]

SUPPRESSIBLE (su-pres'i-bl) *a.* that may be suppressed or concealed.

SUPPRESSION (su-presh'un) *n.* act of suppressing.

SUPPRESSIVE (su-pres'iv) *a.* tending to suppress.

SUPPRESSOR (su-pres'er) *n.* one who suppresses.

SUPPURATE (sup'ū-rāt) *v.t.* or *i.* to generate pus. [L., fr. *sub*, under, and stem *pur-*, of *pus*, matter.]

SUPPURATION (sup-ū-rā'shun) *n.* a ripening into matter.

SUPPURATIVE (sup'ū-rā-tiv) *a.* promoting suppuration.

SUPRAMUNDANE (sū-pra-mun'dān) *a.* above the world. [L. *super*, above, and *mundus*, the world.] [ity.

SUPREMACY (sū-prem'a-si) *n.* highest authority.

SUPREME (sū-prēm') *a.* highest; chief;—*n.* the highest and greatest Being; God. [L. *supremus*, superl. of *superus*, fr. *super*, above.]

SUPREMELY (sū-prēm'li) *ad.* in the highest degree.

SURAL (sū'ral) *a.* pertaining to the calf of the leg. [L. *sura*, the calf of the leg.]

SURCEASE (sur-sēs') *v.t.* or *i.* to stop; leave off;—*n.* stop; cessation. [O.F. (part.) *sursis*, fr. *surseoir*, fr. L. *supersedere*, put off.]

SURCHARGE (sur-chárj') *v.t.* to overcharge; —*n.* excessive load. [F. *surcharger*.]

SURCINGLE (sur'sing-gl) *n.* a girth which passes over the saddle. [L., fr. *super*, over, and *cingulum*, a belt, fr. *cingere*, gird.]

SURCOAT (sur'kōt) *n.* a short coat worn over the other garments. [O.F. *surcote*, *surcot*, fr. *sur*, over, and *cote*, a garment.]

SURD (surd) *n.* a quantity whose root cannot be exactly expressed in numbers. [L. *surdus*, deaf.]

SURE (shóor) *a.* not liable to fail; certainly knowing; firm; confident; secure. [O.F. *seur* = F. *sûr*, fr. L. *securus*, safe, fr. *se*, apart, from, and *cura*, care.]

SURELY (shóor'li) *ad.* certainly; firmly.

SURENESS (shóor'nes) *n.* certainty.

SURETY (shóor'ti) *n.* certainty; security against loss; a hostage. [Doublet of SECURITY.]

SURETYSHIP (shóor'ti-ship) *n.* state of being surety for another.

SURF (surf) *n.* foam of the waves dashing upon the shore. [Fr. SOUGH, with r. intrusive. M.E. *swough*, fr. O.E. *swogan*, to make a rushing sound.]

SURFACE (sur'fis) *n.* the outside superficies. [F., fr. *sur*, fr. L. *super*, and FACE, fr. L. *facies*.]

SURFEIT (sur'fit) *n.* fullness by excess;—*v.t.* or *i.* to feed to excess; cloy. [O.F. *surfait*, fr. L. *super*, above, and *facere*, to make.]

SURFY (sur'fi) *a.* covered with surf.

SURGE (surj) *n.* a rising billow. [L. *surgere*, to rise.]

SURGEON (sur'jun) *n.* one who practises surgery. [F. *chirurgien*, fr. G. *cheirourgos*, fr. *cheir*, the hand, and *ergon*, work.]

SURGEONCY (sur'jun-si) *n.* the office of surgeon.

SURGERY (sur'jer-i) *n.* the art of healing external injuries of the body; a place for surgical operations, etc.

SURGICAL (sur'ji-kal) *a.* pertaining to surgery.

SURGY (sur'ji) *a.* rising in surges; full of surges.

SURLINESS (sur'li-nes) *n.* crabbedness.

SURLY (sur'li) *a.* cross and rude; crabbed; tempestuous. [O.E. *sur*, sour, or for *sir-ly*, = *sir-like*, arrogant.]

SURMISE (sur-miz') *v.t.* to imagine; suspect; —*n.* suspicion; conjecture. [O.F. *sur-mettre*, to accuse, fr. L. *super*, above, and *mittere*, send.]

SURMISER (sur-mi'zer) *n.* one who surmises.

SURMOUNT (sur-mount') *v.t.* to overcome. [F. *surmonter*, fr. *sur* (=L. *super*), and *monter*, to mount.]

SURMOUNTABLE (sur-moun'ta-bl) *a.* that may be overcome.

SURMOUNTER (sur-moun'ter) *n.* one who surmounts or overcomes.

SURNAME (sur'nām) *n.* a name added to the baptismal name;—*v.t.* to call by a family name. [Fr. F. *sur* (=L. *super*, over, and above, and E. NAME. Cf. F. *surnom*.]

SURPASS (sur-pas') *v.t.* to go beyond. [F. *surpasser*, to excel, fr. *sur*, beyond, and *passer*, to pass.] [ing others.

SURPASSING (sur-pas'ing) *ppr* or *a.* exceeding.

SURPLICE (sur'plis) *n.* a white garment for clergymen. [F. *surplis*, fr. L. *super*, over, and *pelliceus*, made of skins, fr. *pellis*, a skin.]

SURPLUS (sur'plus) *n.* excess beyond what is necessary; balance; residue. [F., fr. L. *super*, over, and *plus*, more.]

SURPLUSAGE (sur'plus-ij) *n.* surplus excess.

SURPRISAL (sur-pri'zal) *n.* act of surprising.

SURPRISE (sur-priz') *n.* taking unawares; wonder suddenly excited;—*v.t.* to come unexpectedly; excite wonder in. [O.F. *sorpris* =F. *surpris* (part.) of *sur-prendre*, fr. L. *super*, over, and *prehendere*, take.]

SURPRISING (sur-pri'zing) *a.* wonderful.

Surplice.

SURPRISINGLY (sur-pri'zing-li) *a.* in a surprising manner.

SURREBUTTER (sur-e-but'er) *n.* the plaintiff's reply to the defendant's rebutter. [See REBUT.]

SURRENDER (su-ren'der) *v.t.* or *i.* to deliver up; yield to another; resign;—*n.* the act of yielding to another. [O.F. *surrendre*, to give up, fr. L. *super*, over, and *reddere*, to restore.]

SURRENDERER (su-ren'der-er) *n.* one who makes a surrender.

SURREPTITIOUS (sur-ep-tish'us) *a.* done by stealth. [L., fr. (part.) *surreptus*, fr. *sur-ripere*, to take secretly, fr. *sub*, under, and *rapere*, to seize.]

SURREPTITIOUSLY (sur-ep-tish'us-li) *ad.* by stealth.

SURROGATE (sur'u-gāt) *n.* deputy of an ecclesiastical judge. [L. (part.) *surrogatus*, fr. *surrogare*, to substitute, fr. *sub*, under, and *rogare*, to ask.]

SURROUND (su-round') *v.t.* to encompass. [Fr. O.F. *suronder*, fr. L. *superundare*, to overflow.]

SURTOUT (sur-tòò') *n.* a close-fitting outer coat for men. [F. *sur* (L. *super*), over, and *tout* (L. *totus*,) all.]

SURVEILLANCE (sur-vāl'yans) *n.* watch; oversight. [F., fr. *surveiller*, watch over.]

SURVEY (sur-vā') *v.t.* to view attentively; measure. [O.F. *surveoir*, fr. L. *super*, over, and *videre*, see.]

SURVEY (sur'vā) *n.* a general view; plan or draft.

SURVEYOR (sur-vā'ur) *n.* one who measures land; an inspector of goods, highways, etc.

SURVEYORSHIP (sur-vā'ur-ship) *n.* office of a surveyor.

SURVIVAL (sur-vī'val) *n.* state of living beyond another.

SURVIVE (sur-vīv') *v.t.* to live after the death of another. [F. *survivre*, fr. L. *super*, over, and *vivere*, to live.]

SURVIVOR (sur-vī'ver) *n.* one who outlives another.

SURVIVORSHIP (sur-vī'vur-ship) *n.* state of being a survivor; right of a survivor.

SUSCEPTIBILITY (su-sep-ti-bil'i-ti) *n.* the quality of receiving impressions.

SUSCEPTIBLE (su-sep'ti-bl) *a.* capable of receiving; impressible; sensitive. [L. *susceptibilis*, fr. (part.) *susceptus*. fr. *suscipere*, to take up, fr. *sub*, and *capere*, to take.]

SUSCIPIENCY (su-sip'i-en-si) *n.* act or state or reception.

SUSPECT (sus-pekt') *v.t.* to mistrust; imagine without proof; think to be guilty. [F., fr. L. (part) *suspectus*, fr. *suspicere*, to look at secretly, fr. *sub*, under, and *specere*, to look.]

SUSPECTER (sus-pek'ter) *n.* one who suspects.

SUSPEND (sus-pend') *v.t.* or *i.* to attach to something; cause to cease for a time; delay; debar; stop payment; hang. [F. *suspendre*, fr. L. *sub*, under, and *pendere*, to hang.]

SUSPENDER (sus-pen'der) *n.* one that suspends;—*pl.* braces.

SUSPENSE (sus-pens') *n.* state of uncertainty.

SUSPENSION (sus-pen'shun) *n.* act of hanging up; temporary cessation.

SUSPENSORY (sus-pen'su-ri) *a.* that suspends.

SUSPICION (sus-pish'un) *n.* mistrust. [O.F. *suspeccion*, fr. L. *sub*, under, and *specere*, look at.]

SUSPICIOUS (sus-pish'us) *a.* apt to suspect.

SUSPICIOUSLY (sus-pish'us-li) *ad.* so as to excite suspicion.

SUSTAIN (sus-tān') *v.t.* to bear; endure; sanction; prolong. [L. *sustinere*, fr. *sub*, under, and *tenere*, hold.]

SUSTAINABLE (sus-tā'na-bl) *a.* that can be sustained.

SUSTAINER (sus-tā'ner) *n.* one who sustains.

SUSTAINMENT (sus-tān'ment) *n.* support.

SUSTENANCE (sus'te-nans) *n.* food that sustains; support.

SUSTENTATION (sus-ten-tā'shun) *n.* support; maintenance.

SUTLER (sut'ler) *n.* one who sells provisions and liquors in a camp. [D.]

SUTTEE (su-tē') *n.* a widow who is burnt on the funeral pile of her husband. [Skr. = a true wife.]

SUTTEEISM (su-tē'izm) *n.* self-immolation of widows in Hindustan.

SUTURAL (sū'tū-ral, sū-tū'ral) *a.* relating to a suture or seam.

SUTURE (sū'tūr) *n.* a seam; joint of the skull. [L. *sutura*, fr. (part.) *sutus*, fr. *suere*, to sew.]

SUZERAIN (sū'ze-rān) *n.* a feudal lord. [F. *suzerain*, paramount, a lord paramount.]

SWAB (swob) *n.* a mop for cleaning floors or decks;—*v.t.* to clean with a swab. [D.]

SWABBER (swob'er) *n.* one who uses the swab; a petty officer in a ship of war.

SWADDLE (swod'l) *v.t.* to swathe;—*n.* clothes wound round the body. [O.E. *swethel*, that which swathes, fr. *swathu*, a bandage.]

SWAG (swag) *v.i.* to sink by its weight; swing;—*n.* a bundle; stolen property. [Slang word.]

SWAGGER (swag'er) *v.i.* to boast; brag.

SWAGGERER (swag'er-er) *n.* one who brags.

SWAGGY (swag'i) *a.* hanging down.

SWAIN (swān) *n.* a rustic youth. [Scand. = boy, servant. Cf. O.E. *swan*, swineherd.]

SWALLOW (swol'ō) (1) *n.* a migratory bird; (2) the throat;—*v.t.* to take down the throat; engulf; absorb. [(1) O.E. *swealwe*. Cf. Ger. *Schwalbe*; O.E. *swelgan*.]

SWAM (swam) *pret.* of **SWIM.**

SWAMP (swomp) *n.* wet, soft, spongy ground;—*v.t.* to overset, as a boat in water. [Scand. = a sponge.]

SWAMPY (swom'pi) *a.* soft and spongy.

SWAN (swon) *n.* a large water-fowl. [O.E. Cf. Ger. *Schwan*.]

SWAP, SWOP (swop) *n.* a blow; exchange;—*v.t.* to strike with a long stroke; exchange or barter. [M.E. *swappen* to strike, to go swiftly.]

SWARD (swawrd) *n.* grassy surface of land; compact turf. [O.E. *sweard*, skin of bacon. Cf. Ger. *Schwarte*.]

SWARM (swawrm) *n.* a multitude;—*v.i.* to leave a hive in a body, as bees. [O.E. *swearm*.]

SWARTHY (swawr'thi) *a.* of a dark hue. [O.E. *sweart*. Cf. Ger. *schwartz*.]

SWASH (swosh) *v.i.* to dash noisily, as water;—*n.* splash of water; blustering noise. [Imit.]

SWASHBUCKLER (swosh-buk'ler) *n.* a bully.

SWATH (swawth) *n.* a line of grass, etc., cut down in mowing. Also **SWARTH.** [O.E. *swathu*, a track.]

SWATHE (swāth) *n.* a band or fillet;—*v.t.* to bind with cloth or bandages. [O.E. *beswethian*, bind. Cf. **SWADDLE.**]

SWAY (swā) *v.t.* or *i.* to wield; govern; move or wave; influence;—*n.* rule; command; power. [M.E. *sweien*. Cf. **SWAGGER.**]

SWEAR (swār) *v.i.* [*pret.* **SWORE;** *pp.* **SWORN**] to affirm with a solemn appeal to God for the truth of what is affirmed;—*v.t.* to put to an oath;—*n.* an oath. [O.E. *swerian.* Cf. Ger. *schwören*.]

SWEARER (swā'rer) *n.* one who swears.

SWEARING (swā'ring) *n.* act of swearing; profanity.

SWEAT (swet) *n.* moisture from the skin; labour;—*v.t.* or *i.* to emit moisture through the pores; toil; drudge. [O.E. *swat.* Cf. Ger. *Schweiss.*]

SWEATINESS (swet'i-nes) *n.* state of being moist with perspiration.

SWEATING-SYSTEM (swet'ing-sis-tem) *n.* employing persons at their own homes for low wages.

SWEATY (swet'i) *a.* moist with sweat.

SWEDE (swēd) *n.* a native of Sweden; a Swedish turnip.

SWEEP (swēp) *v.t.* [*pret.* and *pp.* **SWEPT**] to brush with a broom; carry along; carry off; strike with a long stroke; drag;—*v.i.* to pass swiftly or with pomp;—*n.* act of sweeping; compass; range; a large oar. [O.E. *swapan.* Cf. Ger. *schweifen.*]

SWEEPINGS (swē'pingz) *n.pl.* things collected in sweeping.

SWEEPSTAKES (swēp'stāks) *n.pl.* the whole money staked or won at a race.

SWEEPY (swē'pi) *a.* passing over with speed; wavy.

SWEET (swēt) *a.* pleasing to the taste or senses; fragrant; melodious; fresh; mild;—*n.* anything sweet; a term of endearment. [O.E. *swete.* Cf. Ger. *süss.*]

SWEETBREAD (swēt'bred) *n.* the pancreas of a calf or ox.

SWEETBRIER (swēt'brī-er) *n.* a thorny shrub of the rose kind which emits a very fragrant smell. [become sweet.

SWEETEN (swē'tn) *v.t.* or *i.* to make or

SWEETHEART (swēt'härt) *n.* a lover or mistress.

SWEETMEAT (swēt'mēt) *n.* fruit preserved.

SWEETNESS (swēt'nes) *n.* gratefulness to the taste, smell, or ear.

SWEET-WILLIAM (swēt-wil'yam) *n.* a garden flower of the pink species.

SWELL (swel) *v.t.* to dilate or extend;—*v.i.* to be inflated; heave; grow louder;—*n.* increase in size or sound; rise of ground; waves; a dandy. [O.E. *swellan.* Cf. Ger. *schwellen.*]

SWELLING (swel'ing) *n.* a tumour.

SWELTER (swel'tẹr) *v.t.* or *i.* to melt or be oppressed with heat. [O.E. *swelian*, to perish.]

SWELTRY (swel'tri) *a.* sultry.

SWERVE (swẹrv) *v.i.* to turn aside; deviate. [O.E. *sweorfan*, to rub, to move to and fro.]

SWIFT (swift) *a.* moving with celerity; rapid; speedy; fleet;—*n.* a small bird, like the swallow. [O.E. *swifan*, to move quickly.]

SWIFTLY (swift'li) *ad.* rapidly; with velocity.

SWIFTNESS (swift'nes) *n.* fleetness; speed; rapidity.

SWIG (swig) *v.t.* or *i.* to drink in large draughts; —*n.* a large draught. [O.E. *swelgan*, to swallow.]

SWILL (swil) *v.t.* to drink largely;—*n.* drink for swine. [O.E. *swilian*, to swill.]

SWIM (swim) (1) *v.t.* or *i.* [*pret.* **SWAM**; *pp.* **SWUM**] to move on a fluid; float;—*n.* act of swimming; air-bladder of a fish;—(2) *v.i.* to be dizzy or giddy. [(1) O.E. *swimman.* Cf. Ger. *schwimmen.* (2) O.E. *swima*, a swoon.]

SWIMMER (swim'ẹr) *n.* one who swims.

SWIMMING (swim'ing) *n.* act of floating on water; dizziness or giddiness.

SWINDLE (swin'dl) *v.t.* to defraud with deliberate artifice. [Ger. *schwindeln*, to be giddy, to cheat.]

SWINDLER (swin'dlẹr) *n.* a cheat.

SWINE (swin) *n.* *sing.* and *pl.* a hog. [O E. *swin.* Cf. Ger. *Schwein.*]

SWINEHERD (swin'hẹrd) *n.* a keeper of swine.

SWING (swing) *v.t.* or *i.* [*pret.* and *pp.* **SWUNG**] to move when suspended; whirl; cause to turn or be turned round; be hinged;—*n.* a waving motion; apparatus for swinging; free course. [O.E. *swingan*, to flutter. Cf. Ger. *schwingen.*]

SWINGE (swinj) *v.t.* to beat soundly. [O.E. *swengan*, to dash; causal of **SWING.**]

SWINGEL (swing'gl) *n.* that part of a flail that falls on the ground in threshing. [O.E. *swingell*, a whip, fr. *swingan*, to swing.]

SWINGER (swing'ẹr) *n.* one who swings.

SWINGLE (swing'gl) *v.t.* to clean flax by beating;—*n.* an instrument of wood like a knife for swingling flax. [O.E. *swingell*, fr. *swingan*, swing.]

SWINISH (swi'nish) *a.* like swine; gross.

SWISS (swis) *n.* a native of Switzerland; its language.

SWITCH (swich) *n.* a flexible twig; a movable rail;—*v.t.* to beat with a switch; transfer by a switch. [O.D. = a whip.]

SWITCHMAN (swich'man) *n.* one who tends a railway switch.

SWIVEL (swiv'l) *n.* a ring turning on a staple; a small gun that may be turned. [O.E. *swifan*, to move quickly.]

SWOLLEN (swōln) *pp.* of **SWELL.**

SWOON (swōōn) *v.i.* to faint;—*n.* a fainting fit. [O.E. *swogan*, to resound.]

SWOOP (swōōp) *v.t.* or *i.* to sweep down on; catch on the wing;—*n.* downward flight of a bird of prey. [O.E. *swapan*, rush. Cf. Ger. *schweifen*, to rove.]

SWORD (sōrd) *n.* a weapon for cutting or stabbing; death by the sword; war. [O.E. *sweord.* Cf. Ger. *Schwert.*]

SWORD-BELT (sōrd'belt) *n.* a belt to suspend a sword by.

SWORE (swōr) *pret.* of **SWEAR.**

SWORN (swōrn) *pp.* or *a.* of **SWEAR.**

SWOUND (swound) *v.i.* to swoon;—*n.* a swoon. [See **SWOON.**]

SWUM (swum) *pret.* and *pp.* of **SWIM.**

SWUNG (swung) *pret.* and *pp.* of **SWING.**

SYBARITE (sib'a-rīt) *n.* one addicted to luxury or pleasure. [L. *Sybaris*, a city in Italy, noted for effeminacy and luxury.]

SYCAMORE (sik'a-mōr) *n.* a species of fig-tree; maple-tree. Also **SYCOMORE.** [G. *sukomoros*, fr. *sukon*, a fig. and *moron*, black mulberry.]

SYCOPHANCY (sik'u-fan-si) *n.* mean flattery; servility.

SYCOPHANT (sik'u-fant) *n.* an obsequious flatterer; a parasite. [G. *sukophantes*, fr. *sukon*, fig. and *phainein*, show.]

SYCOPHANTIC (sik-u-fan'tik) *a.* servilely flattering.

SYCOPHANTISE (sik'u-fan-tiz) *v.i.* to play the sycophant.

SYLLABIC (sil-lab'ik) *a.* relating to syllables.

SYLLABICATION (si-lab-i-kā'shun) *n.* the formation of syllables.

SYLLABLE (sil'a-bl) *n.* a letter or combination of letters uttered by one articulation. [L. *syllaba*, fr. G. *sullabe*, that which is held together, fr. *sun*, with, and stem *lab-.* fr. *lambanein.* to take.]

SYLLABUS (sil'a-bus) *n.* an abstract; brief outline. [L., fr. G. *sun*, together, and *lambanein*, to take.]

SYLLOGISM (sil'u-jizm) *n.* an argument consisting of three propositions. [L. *syllogismus*, fr. G. *sullogismos.* a reckoning all together. a reasoning, fr. *sun*, together. and *logsesthai*, to reckon.]

SYLLOGISTIC (sil-u-jis'tik) *a.* consisting of a syllogism.

SYLVAN (sil'van) *n.* a fabled deity of the wood; a faun. [L. *silva*, a wood.]

SYMBOL (sim'bul) *n.* a type, emblem, or representation. [L. *symbolum*, fr. G. *sumbolon*, fr. *sun*, together, and *ballein*, to throw.]

SYMBOLICAL (sim-bol'i-kal) *a.* expressing by signs.

SYMBOLISE (sim'bu-liz) *v.t.* or *i.* to have resemblance; express or represent by symbol.

SYMBOLOGY (sim-bol'ō-ji) *n.* art of expressing by symbols. [tional.]

SYMMETRICAL (si-met'ri-kal) *a.* proportionate.

SYMMETRICALLY (si-met'ri-kal-i) *ad.* with due proportions.

SYMMETRISE (sim'e-trīz) *v.t.* to make proportionate.

SYMMETRY (sim'e-tri) *n.* adaptation of parts to each other or to the whole. [L. and G. *summetria*, fr. *sun*, with, and *metron*, measure.]

SYMPATHETIC (sim-pa-thet'ik) *a.* having a feeling in common with another.

SYMPATHISE (sim'pa-thīz) *v.i.* to feel with another; express sympathy.

SYMPATHY (sim'pa-thi) *n.* fellow feeling; compassion. [G. *sumpatheia*, fr. *sun*, with, and *pathos.* suffering.]

SYMPHONIC (sim-fon'ik) *a.* pertaining to a symphony.

SYMPHONIOUS (sim'fō'ni-us) *a.* agreeing in sound; harmonious.

SYMPHONIST (sim'fu-nist) *n.* a composer of symphonies.

SYMPHONY (sim'fu-ni) *n.* accordance of sounds; a musical composition for a full orchestra. [G. *sumphonia*, fr. *sun*, with, and *phone*, a sound.]

SYMPIESOMETER (sim-pi-e-zom'e-tẹr) *n.* an instrument for determining the pressure of the atmosphere. [G. *sun*, with, *piezein*, press, and *metron* measure.]

SYMPTOM (sim'tum) *n.* an indication of disease; sign. [F. *symptome*, fr. G. *sumptoma*, fr. *sumpiptein*, fall together.]

SYMPTOMATIC (sim-tu-mat'ik) *a.* indicating the existence of something else.

SYNÆRESIS (si-ner'e-sis, si-nē're-sis) *n.* contraction of a word by the omission of a letter. [G. *sunairesis*, a taking together.]

SYNAGOGUE (sin'a-gog) *n.* a Jewish assembly or place of worship. [G. *sunagoge*, an assembly, fr. *sun*, with, and *agein*, lead.]

SYNCHRONAL (sing'kru-nạl) *a.* happening at the same time; simultaneous. Also SYN-CHRONOUS. [time.

SYNCHRONISE (sing'kru-nīz) *v.i.* to agree in

SYNCHRONISM (sing'kru-nizm) *n.* concurrence of events in time; tabular arrangement of contemporary events. [G. *sunchronismos* fr. *sun*, together, and *chronos* time.]

SYNCOPATE (sing'ku-pāt) *v.t.* to contract, as a word; prolong a note in music. [Late L. (part.) *syncopatus* fr. *syncopare*, fr. G. *sun* together, and *koptein* cut.]

SYNCOPATION (sing-ku-pā'shun) *n.* contraction of a word; interruption of regular measure in music.

SYNCOPE (sing'ku-pē) *n.* elision of one or more letters of a word; a fainting fit. [G. *sun*, with, and *koptein* cut off.]

SYNCOPIST (sing'ku-pist) *n.* one who contracts words.

SYNCRETISM (sin'kre-tizm) *n.* an attempted union of different religious systems or principles. [G. fr. *sunkretizein*, to combine against.]

SYNDIC (sin'dik) *n.* a magistrate; an advocate. [L. fr. G. *sundikos*, an advocate, fr. *sun* with, and *dike*, justice.]

SYNDICAL (sin'dik-ạl) *a.* pertaining to syndicalism.

SYNDICALISM (sin-dik'ạl-ism) *n.* the policy of improving economic conditions by means of the general strike.

SYNDICALIST (sin'dik-ạl-ist) *n.* one who advocates syndicalism.

SYNDICATE (sin'di-kāt) *n.* office of a syndic; body of syndics; body of men united in some commercial transaction or speculation. [See SYNDIC.]

SYNOD (sin'ud) *n.* an ecclesiastical council; a conjunction of two or more stars. [L. *synodus* fr. G. *sunodos*, a meeting fr. *sun* together, and *hodos*, a way.]

SYNODIC (si-nod'ik) *a.* done by or pertaining to a synod; pertaining to a conjunction of planets or stars. Also SYNODICAL.

SYNODICALLY (si-nod'i-kạl-i) *ad.* by authority of a synod.

SYNONYM (sin'u-nim) *n.* a word which has the same meaning as another word. [G. fr. *sun*, with, and *onoma*, name.]

SYNONYMISE (si-non'i-mīz) *v.t.* to express the same meaning in different words.

SYNONYMOUS (si-non'i-mus) *a.* expressing the same idea or thing.

SYNONYMOUSLY (si-non'i-mus-li) *ad.* in the same sense.

SYNONYMY (si-non'i-mi) *n.* quality of expressing the same meaning in different words.

SYNOPSIS (si-nop'sis) *n.* a general view; conspectus; abstract;—*pl.* SYNOPSES. [G. fr. *sun*, with, together, and *opsis*, a view.]

SYNOPTICAL (si-nop'ti-kạl) *a.* affording a general view. [syntax.

SYNTACTIC (sin-tak'tik) *a.* pertaining to

SYNTAX (sin'taks) *n.* correct arrangement of words in sentences. [G., fr. *suntassein* put in order together fr. *sun*, together and *tassein*, *taxein*, to put in order.]

SYNTHESIS (sin'the-sis) *n.* composition, or the putting of two or more things together. [G., fr. *sun*, together and *thesis*, a placing fr. *tithemi*, I place.]

SYNTHETICAL (sin-thet'i-kạl) *a.* pertaining to synthesis or composition.

SYNTHETICALLY (sin-thet'i-kạl-i) *ad.* by synthesis; by composition.

SYRIAC (sir'i-ak) *a.* pertaining to Syria;—*n.* the language of Syria.

SYRIAN (sir'i-an) *a.* pertaining to Syria.

SYRINGA (sir-ing'ga) *n.* a genus of flowering plants—the lilac. [See SYRINGE.]

SYRINGE (sir'inj) *n.* a pipe for injecting liquids;—*v.t.* to inject or cleanse with a syringe. [L. stem *syring-* fr. *syrinx*, fr. G. *suringx*, a pipe, a reed.]

SYRUP (sir'up). See SIRUP.

SYSTEM (sis'tem) *n.* connection of parts or things; a whole connected scheme; regular order or method. [G. *sustema*, fr. *sun* together, and *histemi*, I place.]

SYSTEMATIC (sis-te-mat'ik) *a.* pertaining to system; methodical; duly connected.

SYSTEMISE (sis'te-mīz) *v.t.* to reduce to system or method. Also SYSTEMATISE.

SYSTOLE (sis'tu-lē) *n.* the shortening of a long syllable; contraction of the heart and arteries for expelling the blood and carrying on the circulation. [G. *sustole*, fr. *sun* together, and *stellein*, to place.]

SYSTOLIC (sis-tol'ik) *a.* relating to systole.

T

TAB (tab) *n.* a broad cap-string or border; a shoe-latchet. [Fr. TAPE.]

TABARD (tab'ard) *n.* a short gown; a herald's coat. [O.F.]

TABARET (tab'a-ret) *n.* a stout satin-striped silk used for hangings or coverings. [Fr. TABBY.]

TABBY (tab'i) *a.* brindled;—*n.* a coarse waved or watered silk; an artificial rock of lime, shells, gravel, etc.; a brindled cat. [F. *tabis*, fr. A. = a rich, watered silk.]

TABEFACTION (tab-e-fak'shun) *n.* a losing of flesh by disease.

TABEFY (tab'e-fī) *v.i.* to waste away by disease; lose flesh. [L. *tabes*, a wasting away and *facere*, make.]

TABERNACLE (tab'ẹr-na-kl) *n.* a tent; a temporary habitation; place of worship; —*v.i.* to reside for a time. [L. *tabernaculum*, dim. of *taberna*, a hut.]

TABID (tab'id) *a.* wasted by disease.

TABLE (tā'bl) *n.* an article of furniture with a flat surface; a board; a synopsis;—*v.t.* to lay on the table; form into a table. [L. *tabula*, a board.]

TABLEAU (tab'lō, tä-blō') *n.* a picture-like representation or still pantomime. [F., fr. L. *tabula*, a painting.]

TABLE-D'HOTE (tâb'l-dōt) *n.* a meal for several persons at the same hour, and for fixed prices. [F.]

TABLE-LAND (tā'bl-land) *n.* elevated flat land.

TABLET (tab'let) *n.* a little table; a flat surface.

TABLE-TURNING (tāb'l-tur-ning) *n.* movement of tables, ascribed by spiritualists to the agency of spirits.

TABOO (ta-bōō') *n.* a prohibition;—*v.t.* to forbid approach to; hold sacred. [Polynesian.]

TABOR, TABOUR (tā'bur) *n.* a small drum. [A. *tambur*.]

TABRET (tab'ret, tā'bret) *n.* a tabour. Also TABOURET.

TABULAR (tab'ū-lạr) *a.* having a flat surface; formed in laminæ or scales; arranged and classified in tables. [See TABLE.]

TACIT (tas'it) *a.* silent; implied. [L. (part.) *tacitus*, fr. *tacere*, to be silent.]

TACITLY (tas'it-li) *ad.* without words; by implication.

TACITURN (tas'i-turn) *a.* habitually silent; reserved. [L. *taciturnus*.]

TACITURNITY (tas-i-tur'ni-ti) *n.* habitual silence; reserve.

TACH (tak) *n.* a small nail; a rope; course of a ship; lease;—*v.t.* to fasten slightly;—*v.i.* to sail in tacks. [Scand.]

TACKET (tak'et) *n.* a small nail with a thick head.

TACKLE (tak'l) *n.* machines for raising weights; ropes and rigging of a ship;—*v.t.* to harness; seize. [Scand.]

TACKLING (tak'ling) *n.* rigging of ships; harness.

TACT (takt) *n.* nice perception in seeing what should be said or done; adroitness in speech or behaviour. [L. (part.) *tactus*, fr. *tangere*, to touch.]

TACTICAL (tak'ti-kәl) *a.* pertaining to tactics.

TACTICIAN (tak-tish'әn) *n.* one versed in tactics.

TACTICS (tak'tiks) *n.pl.* the science and art of manœuvring military and naval forces. [G. *taktikos*, fit for ordering or arranging.]

TACTILE (tak'til) *a.* susceptible of touch. [L. *tactilis*, fr. (part.) *tactus*, fr. *tangere*, to touch.]

TACTLESS (takt'les) *a.* wanting tact.

TACTUAL (tak'tū-әl) *a.* pertaining to touch.

TADPOLE (tad'pōl) *n.* a young toad or frog. [O.E. *tadie*, toad, and POLL, head.]

TAFFEREL (taf'e-rel) *n.* upper part of a ship's stern. Also **TAFFRAIL**. (D., fr. L. *tabula*, a table. Cf. Ger. *Tafel*.]

TAFFETA (taf'e-tә) *n.* a glossy silk stuff. [Per.]

TAG (tag) *n.* a metal at the end of a string; any slight appendage;—*v.t.* to fit with a point; fasten to; append. [Scand.]

TAIL (tāl) (1) *n.* the hinder part; end; (2) *n.* limitation. [(1) O.E. *tægl*, Ger. *Zagel*. (2) F. *taille*, a cutting. Cf. ENTAIL.]

TAILLESS (tāl'les) *a.* having no tail.

TAILOR (tā'lәr) *n.* one who makes men's clothes. [O.F. *tailleur*, fr. *tailler*, to cut.]

TAILORESS (tā'lur-es) *n.* a female tailor.

TAINT (tānt) *v.t.* or *i.* to infect; corrupt;—*n.* spot; blemish. [O.F.—F. (part.) *teint*, fr. *teindre*, to dye, fr. L. (part.) *tinctus*, fr. *tingere*, to dye.]

TAINTLESS (tānt'les) *a.* free from taint.

TAKE (tāk) *v.t.* [*pret.* TOOK; *pp.* TAKEN] to lay hold; capture; receive; choose; understand; assume; swallow;—*v.i.* to catch; please; have recourse to. [Scand.]

TAKING (tā'king) *a.* captivating.

TAKINGNESS (tā'king-nes) *n.* the quality of pleasing.

TALE (tāl) *n.* a story; number. [O.E. *talu*, fr. *tellan*, to tell.]

TALEBEARER (tāl'bār-әr) *n.* an officious informer.

TALENT (tal'ent) *n.* a weight; gift; faculty. [L. *talentum*, fr. G. *talanton*, a balance, a weight.]

TALENTED (tal'en-ted) *a.* possessing talents or abilities.

TALESMAN (tā'lēz-mәn, tālz'mәn) *n.* a juror taken from among the bystanders in court.

TALION (tal'i-un, tā'li-un) *n.* the law of retaliation—an eye for an eye, etc. [L. *talio*, like punishment, fr. *talis*, of such a kind.]

TALISMAN (tal'is-mәn) *n.* a magical charm engraved on metal or stone. [F., fr. A., fr. Late G. *telesma*, incantation, fr. *telein*, to consecrate.]

TALISMANIC (tal-is-man'ik) *a.* affording magical protection.

TALK (tawk) *n.* a familiar conversation; subject of discourse;—*v.i.* to converse familiarly; prate. [M.E. *talken*, fr. Scand.]

TALKATIVE (taw'kә-tiv) *a.* given to much talking; loquacious.

TALKER (taw'kәr) *n.* one who talks.

TALL (tawl) *a.* high in stature; lofty; long. [Etym. doubtful.]

TALLNESS (tawl'nes) *n.* height of stature.

TALLOW (tal'ō) *n.* hard fat of an animal;—*v.t.* to smear with tallow. [Teut.]

TALLOW-CHANDLER (tal'ō-chand-lәr) *n.* one who makes candles.

TALLY (tal'i) *n.* a notched stick for keeping accounts;—*v.t.* or *i.* to mark with notches; agree; correspond. [F. *taille*, a cutting, fr. L. *talea*, a cutting.]

TALLY-HO (tal'i-hō) *n.* the huntsman's cry to his hounds.

TALMUD (tal'mud) *n.* a book of Hebrew traditions and comments. [Chaldee = instruction.] [Talmud.]

TALMUDIST (tal'mu-dist) *n.* one versed in the Talmud.

TALON (tal'un) *n.* the claw of a bird of prey. [F., fr. L. *talus*, the heel.]

TALUS (tā'lus) *n.* slope of a rampart. [L.]

TAMABLE (tā'mә-bl) *a.* that may be tamed.

TAMARIND (tam'ә-rind) *n.* a tree and its fruit. [L. *tamarindus*, fr. A. = a ripe date, and *Hind*, India.]

TAMARISK (tam'ә-risk) *n.* a shrub with long white or pink flowers. [L. *tamariscus*.]

TAMBOUR (tam'bōor) *n.* a small drum; a kind of embroidery;—*v.t.* and *i.* to embroider on a cushion. [F. Cf. TABOR.]

TAMBOURINE (tam-boo-rēn') *n.* a kind of drum. [F. *tambourin*, fr. A.]

TAME (tām) *a.* mild; accustomed to man; spiritless;—*v.t.* to reclaim from wildness; subdue. [O.E. *tam*. Cf. Ger. *zahm*.]

TAMELESS (tām'les) *a.* wild; untamable.

TAMELY (tām'li) *ad.* with mean submission.

TAMENESS (tām'nes) *n.* gentleness.

TAMPER (tam'pәr) *v.t.* to meddle with; practise secretly. [Variant of TEMPER.]

TAMPION (tam'pi-un) *n.* the stopper of a cannon. [O.F. *tampon*, fr. D. *tap*, a bung.]

TAN (tan) *v.t.* to convert, as skin into leather; make brown;—*v.i.* to become tanned;—*n.* bark prepared for tanning. [Ger. *Tanne*, fir-tree.]

TANDEM (tan'dem) *a.* one after another;—*n.* a cycle on which two can ride, one in front of the other. [L. *tandem*, at length.]

TANG (tang) (1) *n.* a strong taste;—(2) *n.* a projection; the tongue of a buckle;—(2) *v.t.* to ring; to twang;—*v.i.* to ring;—*n.* sound; a twang. [(1) D. (2) Scand. (3) Imit.]

TANGENCY (tan'jen-si) *n.* touch. [See TANGENT.]

TANGENT (tan'jent) *n.* a right line touching a curve. [L. (part. stem) *tangent-*, fr. *tangere*, to touch.]

TANGIBILITY (tan-ji-bil'i-ti) *n.* quality of being tangible.

TANGIBLE (tan'ji-bl) *a.* perceptible by the touch.

TANGLE (tang'gl) *v.t.* or *i.* to unite confusedly; ensnare; entangle;—*n.* a knot of things; an edible sea-weed. [Scand. = sea-weed.]

Tangent.

TANGLY (tang'gli) *a.* covered with tangle.

TANK (tangk) *n.* a cistern; a reservoir. [Pg. *tanque*, fr. L. *stagnum*, a standing pool.]

TANKARD (tang'kard) *n.* a drinking-cup with a lid. [O.F. *tanquard*.]

TANNER (tan'әr) *n.* one who tans hides.

TANNERY (tan'әr-i) *n.* house for tanning.

TANNIN (tan'in) *n.* the astringent substance of bark. [Ger. *Tanne*, fir-tree.]

TANNING (tan'ing) *n.* the process of converting raw hides into leather by tannin.

TANTALISATION (tan-tә-li-zā'shun) *n.* act of tantalising.

TANTALISE (tan'tә-līz) *v.t.* to tease or torment with false hopes. [*Tantalus*, a Lydian king, condemned in Tartarus to perpetual thirst, with tempting fruits and water near him, which he never could reach.]

TANTALISING (tan'tә-lī-zing) *a.* tormenting.

TANTALISM (tan'tә-lizm) *n.* torment by vain hopes.

TANTAMOUNT (tan'ta-mount) *a.* equivalent; equal in value or meaning. [L. *tantus* so much, and **AMOUNT**.]

TANTIVY (tan-tiv'i) *ad.* swiftly; rapidly. [Perh. from the note of a hunting-horn.]

TANTRUM (tan'trum) *n.* a fit of ill-humour. [W.]

TAN-YARD (tan'yård) *n.* a yard where tanning is carried on.

TAP (tap) (1) *v.t.* to touch lightly;—*v.i.* to knock gently;—*n.* a gentle touch;—(2) *n.* a hole or pipe for drawing liquor; a plug or spile;—*v.t.* to broach. [(1) F. *taper,* to strike, fr. Low Ger. (2) O.E. *tœppa,* a tap.]

TAPE (tāp) *n.* a narrow fillet of woven work. [O.E. *tœppa,* a fillet.]

TAPER (tā'pẹr) *n.* a small wax candle;—*a.* long and slender;—*v.t.* or *i.* to make small; decrease gradually. [O.E. *taper.*]

TAPESTRY (tap'es-tri) *n.* cloth woven with figures. [F. *tapisserie,* fr. L. *tapete,* a carpet, fr. G. *tapes,* carpet.]

TAPE-WORM (tāp'wẹrm) *n.* a worm bred in the intestines.

TAPIOCA (tap-i-ō'ka) *n.* a farinaceous food prepared from *Cassava,* a Brazilian plant. [Braz.]

TAPIR (tā'pẹr) *n.* a thick-skinned quadruped with a short proboscis. [Braz.]

TAP-ROOM (tap'rŏŏm) *n.* a room where liquors are served. [See **TAP** (2).]

TAP-ROOT (tap'rŏŏt) *n.* the chief root. [See **TAP** (2).]

TAPSTER (tap'stẹr) *n.* one who draws liquors.

TAR (tår) *n.* a resinous substance obtained from pine-trees;—*v.t.* to smear with tar. [O.E. *teru.*]

TARDILY (tår'di-li) *ad.* with slow pace.

TARDINESS (tår'di-nes) *n.* slowness of motion: lateness.

TARDY (tår'di) *a.* noting a slow pace or motion; dilatory; late. [F. *tardif* fr. *tard,* fr. L. *tardus,* slow.]

TARE (tår) (1) *n.* a weed; vetch;—(2) *n.* allowance in weight for the cask or bag. [(1) Perh. fr. **TEAR**. (2) F. fr. Sp., fr. A. =what is rejected.]

TARGET (tår'get) *n.* a small shield; a mark to shoot at. [O.E. *targe,* fr. Scand.]

TARIFF (tar'if) *n.* a table of duties or customs. [F., fr. Sp., fr. A. = giving information, a tariff gving notice.]

TARN (tårn) *n.* a small mountain lake. [Scand.]

TARNISH (tår'nish) *v.t.* or *i.* to sully; lose brightness. [F. (part.) *ternissant* fr. *ternir*: O. H. Ger. =to darken.]

TARPAULIN (tår-paw'lin) *n.* canvas tarred. [Literally *tarred pauling,* or *pailing,* a covering. Cf. **PALL**.]

TARRY (tar'i) (1) *v.i.* to stay: continue; delay. (2) (tår'i) *a.* like tar. [(1) O.E. *teragn,* provoke. (2) See **TAR**.]

TART (tårt) (1) *a.* acid; sharp; severe;—(2) *n.* a kind of pie or pastry. [(1) O.E. *teart,* fr. *teran,* to split. (2) O.F. *tarte,* fr. L. (part.) *tortus,* fr. *torquere,* to twist.]

TARTAN (tår'tan) *n.* woollen stuffs checked with stripes of various colours. [F. *tiretaine,* linsey-woolsey.]

TARTAR (tår'tar) (1) *n.* an acid salt deposited from wine; concretion on the teeth;—(2) *n.* native of Tartary. [(1) F. *tartre,* fr. Late L. *tartarum,* fr. A. =dregs.]

TARTAREAN (tår-tå're-an) *a.* pertaining to Tartarus; hellish.

TARTAREOUS (tår-tå're-us) *a.* consisting of or like tartar.

TARTARIC (tår-tar'ik) *a.* pertaining to tartar.

TARTARISE (tår'ta-riz) *v.t.* to impregnate with tartar.

TARTARUS (tår'ta-rus) *n.* the infernal regions. [L., fr. G. *Tartaros.*]

TARTISH (tår'tish) *a.* somewhat tart.

TARTLY (tårt'li) *ad.* sharply; keenly.

TARTNESS (tårt'nes) *n.* sharpness; sourness: severity.

TARTUFFE (tår-tŏŏf') *n.* a hypocritical pretender in religion or morals. [Fr. the hero in a comedy by Molière.]

TAR-WATER (tår'waw-tẹr) *n.* a cold infusion of tar.

TASK (task) *n.* business or duty imposed: lesson; labour;—*v.t.* to impose a specific business. [O.F. *tasque* = F. *tâche,* fr. Late L. *taxa,* fr. *taxare,* to tax.]

TASK-MASTER (task'mas-tẹr) *n.* one who imposes tasks.

TASK-WORK (task'wurk) *n.* work set as a task; work done by the job.

TASSEL (tas'l) *n.* an ornamental bunch of silk. [O.F. fr. L. *taxillus* dim. of *talus* a die.]

TASTABLE (tås'ta-bl) *a.* that may be tasted.

TASTE (tåst) *v.t.* to perceive by the palate; partake of; experience;—*v.i.* to eat of: have the flavour of;—*n.* sense of tasting; a small portion; flavour; choice; intellectual relish or discernment. [O.F. *taster* = F. *tâter* fr. L. *taxare,* to touch repeatedly, fr. *tangere,* touch.]

TASTEFUL (tåst'fool) *a.* having a high relish: showing good taste.

TASTEFULLY (tåst'fool-i) *ad.* with good taste.

TASTELESS (tåst'les) *a.* having no taste; insipid.

TASTELESSNESS (tåst'les-nes) *n.* want of taste; insipidity.

TASTILY (tås'ti-li) *ad.* with good taste.

TASTY (tås'ti) *a.* having taste; according to good taste.

TATTER (tat'ẹr) *v.t.* to rend in pieces;—*n.* a torn piece; a rag. [Scand.]

TATTING (tat'ing) *n.* a kind of lace edging woven or knit from common thread. [Scand.]

TATTLE (tat'l) *v.i.* to tell tales:—*n.* idle, trifling talk. [M.E. *tatelen,* imit.]

TATTLER (tat'lẹr) *n.* an idle gossip.

TATTOO (ta-tŏŏ') (1) *n.* a beat of drums at night;—(2) *n.* figures stained on the skin;—*v.t.* to puncture the skin and stain the spots in figures. [(1) D., fr. *tap,* a tap, and *toe,* to (*i.e.* to close or shut the taps or drinking-houses at the beat of the drum). (2) Tahitian.]

TAUGHT (tawt) *pret.* and *pp.* of **TEACH**.

TAUNT (tånt, tawnt) *v.t.* to reproach with insulting words; revile; upbraid;—*n.* a gibe; scoff. [O.F. *tanter,* fr. L. *tentare,* try.]

TAURINE (taw'rin) *a.* relating to a bull.

TAURUS (taw'rus) *n.* the bull—one of the signs in the zodiac. [L., fr. G. *tauros.*]

TAUT (tawt) *a.* tight; fully stretched or extended. [Variant of **TIGHT**.]

TAUTOLOGICAL (taw-tō-loj'i-kal) *a.* repeating the same thing.

TAUTOLOGIST (taw-tol'ō-jist) *n.* one who uses tautology.

TAUTOLOGY (taw-tol'ō-ji) *n.* repetition of the same thing in different words. [G., fr. *tauto,* the same, and *logos,* speech.]

TAVERN (tav'ẹrn) *n.* a public-house; inn. [F. *taverne,* fr. L. *taberna,* a booth, fr. rt. of *tabula,* a board.]

TAVERN-KEEPER (tav'ẹrn-kēp-ẹr) *n.* one who keeps a tavern.

TAW (taw) (1) *v.t.* to dress white leather;—(2) *n.* a boy's marble. [(1) O.E. *lawian,* to prepare. (2) G., the letter т.]

TAWDRILY (taw'dri-li) *ad.* with excess of finery.

TAWDRINESS (taw'dri-nes) *n.* excess of finery.

TAWDRY (taw'dri) *a.* gaudy in dress; showy without taste. [Fr. St. *Awdrey,* and orig. implying bought at the fair of St *Awdrey* (17th Oct.), where laces and gay toys were sold.]

TAWER (taw'er) *n.* a dresser of white leather.
TAWNY (taw'ni) *a.* of a yellowish brown colour, like tan. [F. *tanné*, fr. Ger. *Tanne*, a fir-tree.]
TAWSE (tawz) *n.* a thick leather strap for chastising boys. [O.E. *tawian*, to scourge.]
TAX (taks) *n.* a rate assessed on a person for public use; any burdensome duty;—*v.t.* to lay a tax; accuse. [F. *taxe*, fr. L. *taxare*, value, fr. *tangere*, to touch.]
TAXABLE (tak'sa-bl) *a.* liable to be taxed.
TAXATION (tak-sā'shun) *n.* act of imposing taxes; impost.
TAXICAB (tak'si-kab) *n.* a motor-cab with a taximeter. Shortened form **TAXI**. [L. *taxare*, to value.]
TAXIDERMY (tak'si-der-mi) *n.* art of preserving skins of animals. [F., fr. G., fr. *taxis*, arrangement, and *derma*, a skin.]
TAXIMETER (tak-si'me-ter) *n.* a mechanical contrivance attached to certain cabs to record the distance travelled and the fare payable. [F. *taximètre*, fr. L. *taxare*, value, and G. *metron*, measure.]
TEA (tē) *n.* a plant or an infusion of it. [Chin.]
TEACH (tēch) *v.t.* [*pret.* and *pp.* **TAUGHT**] to instruct; inform; direct; counsel;—*v.i.* to practise teaching. [O.E. *tæcan*, show, teach. Cf. Ger. *zeigen*.]
TEACHABLE (tē'cha-bl) *a.* that may be taught.
TEACHABLENESS (tē'cha-bl-nes) *n.* aptness to learn.
TEACHER (tē'cher) *n.* an instructor.
TEA-CHEST (tē'chest) *n.* a box lined with lead, in which tea is imported.
TEA-CUP (tē'kup) *n.* a small cup in which tea is drunk.
TEAK (tēk) *n.* an East Indian tree or its valuable timber. [Malay.]
TEAL (tēl) *n.* a web-footed water-fowl. [M.E. *tele*.]
TEAM (tēm) *n.* horses or oxen harnessed together; a company. [O.E. *team*, offspring.]
TEAMSTER (tēm'ster) *n.* one who drives a team.
TEA-POT (tē'pot) *n.* a vessel in which tea is made.
TEAR (tēr) *n.* a water from the eyes. [O.E. *tær, tear*.]
TEAR (tār) *v.t.* or *i.* [*pret.* **TORE**; *pp.* **TORN**] to pull or burst asunder; lacerate. [O.E. *teran*. Cf. Ger. *zähren*.] [ing.
TEARFUL (tēr'fool) *a.* shedding tears; weeping.
TEARLESS (tēr'les) *a.* shedding no tears; unfeeling.
TEASE (tēz) *v.t.* to comb or card; raise a nap; vex. [O.E. *tæsan*, to pluck. Cf. Ger. *zeisen*.]
TEASEL (tē'zl) *n.* a burr used in dressing cloth. [O.E. *tæsel, tæsl*, the fuller's herb.]
TEA-SPOON (tē'spoon) *n.* a small spoon.
TEAT (tēt) *n.* the nipple. [O.E. *tit*.]
TECHNICAL (tek'ni-kal) *a.* pertaining to the arts or professions. [G. *teknikos*, fr. *techne*, an art.]
TECHNICALITY (tek-ni-kal'i-ti) *n.* quality of being technical.
TECHNICALLY (tek'ni-kal-i) *ad.* in a technical manner.
TECHNICS (tek'niks) *n.pl.* learning that respects the arts.
TECHNOLOGICAL (tek-nō-loj'i-kal) *a.* pertaining to technology.
TECHNOLOGY (tek-nol'ō-ji) *n.* a treatise on the arts. [G., fr. *techne*, an art, and *logos*, discourse.]
TECTONIC (tek-ton'ik) *a.* pertaining to building. [G. *tekton*, a carpenter.]
TE DEUM (tē-dē'um) *n.* a hymn of joy. [L.]
TEDIOUS (tē'dyus) *a.* tiresome from length or slowness; wearisome. [L. *tædiosus*, fr. *tædium*.]
TEDIOUSLY (tē'dyus-li) *ad.* wearisomely.

TEDIUM (tē'di-um) *n.* irksomeness.
TEEM (tēm) *v.i.* to be prolific;—*v.t.* to bring forth. [O.E., fr. *tyman, teman*.]
TEEMLESS (tēm'les) *a.* unfruitful.
TEENS (tēnz) *n.pl.* years between twelve and twenty.
TEETH (tēth) *n.pl.* of **TOOTH**.
TEETHE (tēth) *v.i.* to breed teeth.
TEETHING (tē'THing) *n.* first growth of teeth, or process by which they come through the gums.
TEETOTALISM (tē'tō-tal-izm) *n.* principle or practice of entire abstinence from intoxicating liquors. [*Tee* = *t*, and **TOTAL**; a stammering pronunciation of **TOTAL**, by Richard Turner, Preston, 1833.]
TEETOTUM (tē-tō-tum') *n.* toy like a top. [Formerly *T-totum*, from the *T* marked on it (L. *totum*, all).]
TEGULAR (teg'ū-lar) *a.* pertaining to tiles. [L. *tegula*, a tile, fr. *tegere*, to cover.]
TEGUMENT (teg'ū-ment) *n.* a covering. [L. *tegumentum*, fr. *tegere*, cover.]
TEGUMENTARY (teg-ū-men'ta-ri) *a.* relating to coverings.
TEINDS (tēndz) *n.pl.* tithes. [Scand. = a tithe.]
TELAUTOGRAPH (tel-au'tō-graf) *n.* a form of telegraph that transmits messages as set out by hand whether in writing or drawing. [G. *tele*, far, *auto*, self, and *graphein*, write.]
TELEGRAM (tel'e-gram) *n.* a telegraphic message or despatch. [G. *tele*, far, and *gramma*, that which is written, fr. *graphein*, to write.]
TELEGRAPH (tel'e-graf) *n.* a machine for communicating information by signals;—*v.t.* to convey by telegraph. [G. *tele*, far, and *graphein*, to write.]
TELEGRAPH-CABLE (tel'e-graf-kā'bl) *n.* a telegraphic line, consisting of one or more conducting wires, enclosed by an insulating and protecting material, to connect stations which are separated by a river, strait, or sea; ocean-cable.
TELEGRAPHIC (tel-e-graf'ik) *a.* pertaining to a telegraph.
TELEGRAPHIST (tel-eg'ra-fist, tel'e-graf-ist) *n.* one who works a telegraph.
TELEOLOGY (tel-e-ol'ō-ji) *n.* doctrine of the final cause of things. [G., fr. *telos*, the end, and *logos*, discourse.]
TELEPHONE (tel'e-fōn) *n.* an electrical apparatus for transmitting sound to a distance. [G. *tele*, afar, and *phone*, the voice.]
TELESCOPE (tel'e-skōp) *n.* an optical instrument for viewing distant objects. [G. *tele*, afar, and *skopein*, to view.]
TELESCOPIC (tel-e-skop'ik) *a.* pertaining to a telescope.
TELEWRITER (tel'e-rit-er) *n.* a telautograph.
TELL (tel) *v.t.* or *i.* [*pret.* and *pp.* **TOLD**] to relate; inform; count; give an account; take effect. [O.E. *tellan*. Cf. Ger. *zählen*.]
TELLER (tel'er) *n.* one who tells; a bank official who pays money on cheques.
TELL-TALE (tel'tāl) *n.* an officious informer;—*a.* telling tales.
TELLURIC (tel-ū'rik) *a.* pertaining to the earth. [L. stem *tellur-*, of *tellus*, the earth.]
TEMERITY (te-mer'i-ti) *n.* rash boldness. [F. *témérité*, fr. L. *temeritas*, fr. *temere*, by chance.]
TEMPER (tem'per) *n.* frame of mind; due mixture;—*v.t.* to mix in due proportion; modify; soften. [L. *temperare*, fr. *tempus*, time.]
TEMPERAMENT (tem'per-a-ment) *n.* constitution of the body or mind; disposition.
TEMPERANCE (tem'per-ans) *n.* moderate indulgence of the appetites.
TEMPERATE (tem'per-at) *a.* moderate; sober. [L. (part.) *temperatus*, fr. *temperare*.]
TEMPERATELY (tem'per-at-li) *ad.* with moderation.

TEMPERATURE (tem'per-a-tŭr) *n.* state with regard to heat or cold. [See TEMPERATE.]

TEMPEST (tem'pest) *n.* violent wind; a storm; commotion. [O.F. *tempeste*, fr. L. *tempestas*, a season, weather. fr. *tempus*, time.]

TEMPESTUOUS (tem-pes'tū-us) *a.* stormy; turbulent. [See TEMPEST.]

TEMPESTUOUSLY (tem-pes'tū-us-li) *ad.* with great violence.

TEMPLAR (tem'plar) *n.* one of a religious military order; a lawyer.

TEMPLE (tem'pl) (1) *n.* an edifice erected to some deity; a church;—(2) *n.* slope of the head. [(1) L. *templum.* (2) O.F., fr. L. *tempora,* the temples, pl. of *tempus,* time.]

TEMPLET (tem'plet) *n.* a piece of timber used in building. [L. *templatus,* vaulted, fr. *templum,* a small timber.]

TEMPORAL (tem'pu-ral) *a.* pertaining to the temple or to this life; not spiritual. [F., fr. L. *temporalis,* fr. stem *tempor-* fr. *tempus,* time.]

TEMPORALITY (tem-pu-ral'i-ti) *n.* a secular possession; revenue of a churchman.

TEMPORALLY (tem'pu-ral-i) *ad.* with respect to this life.

TEMPORARILY (tem'pu-ra-ri-li) *ad.* for a time only.

TEMPORARY (tem'pu-ra-ri) *a.* continuing for a time only; transient.

TEMPORISE (tem'pu-riz) *v.i.* to comply with the time or occasion; trim.

TEMPORISER (tem'pu-ri-zer) *n.* a time-server.

TEMPT (temt) *v.t.* to put to trial; test; try to persuade. [O.F. *tempter,* F. *tenter* fr. L. *tentare,* handle, test, fr. *tendere,* to stretch.]

TEMPTATION (tem-ta'shun) *n.* act of tempting; that which tempts.

TEMPTER (tem'ter) *n.* one who entices to evil; Satan.

TEMPTINGLY (tem'ting-li) *ad.* in a manner to attract or allure.

TEMPTRESS (tem'tres) *n.* a female tempter.

TEN (ten) *a.* twice five. [O E. *tien.* Cf. Ger. *zehn.*]

TENABILITY ten-a-bil'i-ti) *n.* state of being tenable. Also TENABLENESS.

TENABLE (ten'a-bl) *a.* that can be held. [F., fr. *tenir,* fr. L. *tenere,* to hold.]

TENACIOUS (te-nā'shus) *a.* holding fast; adhesive; stubborn. [L. stem *tenac-,* fr. *tenax,* fr. *tenere,* hold.]

TENACIOUSLY (te-nā'shus-li) *ad.* adhesively.

TENACITY (te-nas'i-ti) *n.* the quality of being tenacious.

TENANCY (ten'an-si) *n.* a holding or temporary possession.

TENANT (ten'ant) *n.* one who holds property of another;—*v.t.* to hold or possess as a tenant. [F. fr. L. (part. stem) *tenent-,* fr. *tenere,* to hold.]

TENANTABLE (ten'an-ta-bl) *a.* fit to be tenanted or occupied.

TENANTLESS (ten'ant-les) *a.* having no tenant.

TENANTRY (ten'an-tri) *n.* tenants in general.

TENCH (tensh) *n.* a fresh-water fish of the carp family. [O.F. *tenche,* fr. L. *tincta,* a tench.]

TEND (tend) (1) *v.t.* or *i.* to wait on or watch over;—(2) move in a certain direction; be inclined; contribute. [(1) Contr. fr. ATTEND. (2) F. *tendre,* fr. L. *tendere,* to stretch.]

TENDENCY (ten'den-si) *n.* drift; direction inclination.

TENDER (ten'der) (1) *n.* a small vessel that attends a larger; a carriage with fuel attached to a locomotive;—(2) *n.* an offer or proposal; thing offered;—*v.t.* to offer for acceptance;—(3) *a.* easily impressed or injured. [(1) See TEND (1). (2) L. *tendere.* (3) F. *tendre,* fr. L. *tener.*]

TENDERLY (ten'der-li) *ad.* gently; kindly.

TENDERNESS (ten'der-nes) *n.* softness; kindness.

TENDINOUS (ten'di-nus) *a.* full of tendons.

TENDON (ten'dun) *n.* a hard insensible cord by which a muscle is attached to a bone. [F., fr. L. *tendere,* to stretch.]

TENDRIL (ten'dril) *n.* clasper of a vine. [O.F. *tendrillons,* fr. L. *tener* delicate.]

TENEBROSITY (ten-e-bros'i-ti) *n.* darkness; gloom.

TENEBROUS (ten'e-brus) *a.* dark; gloomy obscure.

TENEMENT (ten'e-ment) *n.* a house; an apartment; anything that can be held by a tenant. [M.F. *tenement,* fr. L. *tenere,* to hold.]

TENET (ten'et) *n.* opinion; principle; doctrine. [L. *tenet,* he holds, fr. *tenere,* to hold.]

TENFOLD (ten'fōld) *a.* ten times more.

TENNIS (ten'is) *n.* a play with racket and ball. [Perh. fr. O.F. *tenies,* pl. of *tenie,* a fillet, fr. L. *tœnia.*]

TENON (ten'un) *n.* that part of timber which enters a mortise. [F., fr. *tenir,* fr. L. *tenere,* to hold.]

TENOR (ten'er) *n.* continued course; purport; part in music above the bass; one who sings tenor. [L., fr. *tenere,* to hold.]

TENSE (tens) (1) *a.* strained tight; rigid;—(2) *n.* inflection of a verb to express time. [(1) L. (part.) *tensus,* fr. *tendere,* to stretch. (2) O.F. *tens* = F. *temps,* fr. L. *tempus.* time.]

TENSENESS (tens'nes) *n.* state of being tense; rigidness; stiffness.

TENSION (ten'shun) *n.* act of stretching; stiffness.

TENSIVE (ten'siv) *a.* giving the sensation of tension or contraction.

TENSOR (ten'sor) *n.* a muscle that extends a part.

TENT (tent) (1) *n.* a pavilion or movable lodge; —*v.i.* to lodge in a tent;—(2) *n.* a roll of lint;—*v.t.* to probe; [(1) F. *tente.* fr. Late L. *tenta,* fr. L. *tendere,* stretch. (2) F. *tenter,* fr. *tentare,* to try, test. Cf. TEMPT.]

TENTACLE (ten'ta-kl) *n.* an organ of certain insects for feeling or motion. [F. *tentacule,* fr. Late L. *tentaculum,* fr. L. *tentare,* to feel, fr. *tendere,* to stretch.]

Tent.

TENTATIVE (ten'ta-tiv) *a.* trying; experimental. [F., fr. Late L., fr. L. *tentare,* to try.]

TENTER (ten'ter) *n.* a machine for stretching cloth;—*v.t.* to stretch on hooks. [F. *tenture,* fr. L. *tentura,* fr. *tendere,* to stretch.]

TENTH (tenth) *a.* the ordinal of ten;—*n.* one part in ten; a tithe.

TENTHLY (tenth'li) *ad.* in the tenth place.

TENUITY (ten-ū'i-ti) *n.* thinness; slenderness; rarity. [L. acc.) *tenuitatem,* fr. *tenuis,* thin.]

TENUOUS (ten'ū-us) *a.* thin; slender.

TENURE (ten'ūr) *n.* a holding of lands or tenements; manner or conditions of holding. [F., fr. Late L. *tenura,* fr. L. *tenere,* to hold.]

TEPEFACTION ('tep-e-fak'shun) *n.* act of warming.

TEPEFY (tep'e-fi) *v.t.* or *i.* to make or become moderately warm. [L. *tepere,* and *facere,* make.]

TEPID 'tep'id) *a.* moderately warm; lukewarm. [L. *tepidus* fr. *tepere,* to be warm.]

TEPIDNESS tep'id-nes) *n.* moderate warmth; lukewarmness. Also TEPIDITY.

TERAPHIM (ter'a-fim) *n.pl.* household images or idols. [H., images connected with magical rites.]

TERCENTENARY (ter-sen'te-na-ri) *n.* anniversary of 300 years. [L., fr. *ter,* three, and *centum,* a hundred.]

TEREBINTH (ter'e-blnth) *n.* a tree or shrub yielding turpentine. [L., fr. G. *terebinthos.*]

TERGIVERSATION (ter-ji-ver-sā'shun) *n.* a shifting or shuffling in conduct. [L. *tergiversari,* to turn one's back.]

TERM (term) *n.* a boundary; limited time; word; condition; time of session; rent-paying days;—*v.t.* to call; name. [F. *terme,* fr. L. *terminus,* a boundary.]

TERMAGANT (ter'ma-gant) *n.* a scolding woman;—*a.* boisterous; scolding; brawling. [M.E. *Termagant,* a supposed Saracen idol, appearing in old plays as a blustering character.]

TERMINABLE (ter'mi-na-bl) *a.* that may be bounded. [See **TERM.**]

TERMINAL (ter'mi-nal) *a.* ending; forming the end.

TERMINATE (ter'mi-nāt) *v.t.* to set the limit to a thing; put an end to; finish;—*v.i.* to end in space or time. [L. (part.) *terminatus,* fr. *terminare,*]

TERMINATION (ter-mi-nā'shun) *n.* a limit; end; result.

TERMINOLOGY (ter-mi-nol'ŏ-ji) *n.* explanation of terms. [L. *terminus,* term, and G. *logos,* discourse.]

TERMINUS (ter'mi-nus) *n.* a boundary; either end of a railway, etc.;—*pl.* **TERMINI.** [L.]

TERMLESS (term'les) *a.* unlimited.

TERN (tern) *a.* consisting of three. [L. *terni,* three each, fr. *tres,* three.]

TERNARY (ter'na-ri) *a.* proceeding by threes; —*n.* three. [See **TERN.**]

TERPSICHOREAN (terp-si-ku-rē'an) *a.* relating to dancing. [G. *terpsis,* delight, and *choros,* dancing.]

TERRACE (ter'as) *n.* a raised bank of earth; a flat roof. [F. *terrasse,* fr. It. *terrazza,* fr. L. *terra,* earth.]

TERRA-COTTA (ter'a-kot'a) *n.* a composition of clay and sand. [L. *terra,* and (part.) *cotta,* fr. *coquere,* to cook.]

TERRAPIN (ter'a-pin) *n.* a species of tortoise. [Amer. Ind.]

TERRAQUEOUS (te-rā'kwe-us) *a.* composed of land and water. [L., fr. *terra,* the earth, and *aqua,* water.]

TERRENE (te-rēn') *a.* pertaining to the earth. [L. *terrenus,* fr. *terra,* the earth.]

TERRESTRIAL (te-res'tri-al) *a.* belonging to or existing on the earth. [L. *terrestris,* fr. *terra,* the earth.]

TERRIBLE (ter'i-bl) *a.* that may excite terror; fearful; awful; shocking. [F., fr L. *terribilis,* causing terror, fr. *terrere,* to frighten.]

TERRIBLY (ter i-bli) *ad.* dreadfully; violently.

TERRIER (ter'i-er) *n.* a dog that pursues burrowing animals into their holes. [M.E. *terrere,* a 'burrow' dog, fr. L. *terra,* the earth.]

TERRIFIC (te-rif'ik) *a.* adapted to excite terror; dreadful.

TERRIFY (ter'i-fi) *v.t.* to frighten greatly. [L. *terrere,* and *facere,*]

TERRITORIAL (ter-i-tō'ri-al) *a.* pertaining to territory.

TERRITORY (ter'i-tu-ri) *n.* land or country belonging to a state or other body; domain. [F. *territoire,* fr. L. *territorium,* fr. *terra,* the earth.]

TERROR (ter'ur) *n.* great fear; dread; object of fear. [L., fr. *terrere,* to frighten.]

TERRORISM (ter'ur-izm) *n.* state of terror; government by terror.

TERSE (ters) *a.* neat; elegant; concise. [L. (part.) *tersus,* fr. *tergere,* to rub.]

TERSENESS (ters'nes) *n.* smoothness; neatness; conciseness.

TERTIAN (ter'shan) *a.* happening every third day. [L. *tertianus,* fr. *tertius,* the third, fr. *tres,* three.]

TERTIARY (ter'sha-ri) *a.* third; of the third formation. [See **TERTIAN.**]

TESSELLATE (tes'e-lāt) *v.t.* to form into chequered work. [L *tessella,* a little cube; dim. of *tessera,* a square piece.]

TESSELLATION (tes-e-lā'shun) *n.* the making of mosaic work.

TEST (test) *n.* a cupel to try metals; trial; standard; proof;—*v.t.* to put to the proof; examine critically. [O.F., fr. L. *testa,* an earthen pot.]

TESTACEOUS (tes-tā'shus) *a.* having a hard shell. [L. *testaceus,* fr. *testa,* a shell.]

TESTAMENT (tes'ta-ment) *n.* a will; one of the two divisions of the Scriptures. [L. *testamentum,* fr. *testari,* to be a witness.]

TESTAMENTARY (tes-ta-men'ta-ri) *a.* relating to a will.

TESTATE (tes'tāt) *a.* having made a will. [F. *tester,* fr. L. *testari,* to be a witness.]

TESTATOR (tes-tā'ter) *n.* one who leaves a will. [See **TESTATE.**]

TESTATRIX (tes-tā'triks) *n.* a female who leaves a will.

TESTER (tes'ter) (1) *n.* a flat canopy over a bed;—(2) *n.* one who tests. [(1) O.F. *testre,* fr. *teste*=F. *tête,* a head, fr. L. *testa,* a tile, the skull. (2) See **TEST.**]

TESTICLE (tes'ti-kl) *n.* an organ of animals. [L. *testiculus,* dim. of *testis,* a testicle.]

TESTIFY (tes'ti-fi) *v.t.* to give testimony. [L. *testificari,* fr. *testis,* a witness, and *facere,* make.]

TESTILY (tes'ti-li) *ad.* peevishly. [See **TESTY.**]

TESTIMONIAL (tes-ti-mō'ni-al) *n.* a certificate of character; something given as a mark of honour.

TESTIMONY (tes'ti-mu-ni) *n.* witness borne to a fact or truth; evidence; public declaration; the two tables of the law; divine revelation. [L. *testimonium,* fr. *testari,* to be a witness.]

TESTINESS (tes'ti-nes) *n.* peevishness. [See **TESTY.**]

TESTY (tes'ti) *a.* peevish; fretful. [O.F. *teste*=F. *tête,* the head.]

TETANUS (tet'a-nus) lock-jaw. [L., fr. G. *tetanos,* stretched, fr. *teinein,* to stretch.]

TETE-A-TETE (tāt-a-tāt') *n.* head to head; in private. [F.=head to head.]

TETHER (teth'er) *v.t.* to confine with a rope, as a beast;—*n.* rope or chain for tethering. [Orig. *tedder,* fr. M.E. *tedir.*]

TETRAGON (tet'ra-gun) *n.* a figure with four angles. [G., fr. *tetra,* four, and *gonia,* corner, angle.]

TETRAHEDRON (tet-ra-hē'drun) *n.* a figure of four equal triangles. [G., fr. *tetra,* four, and *hedra,* seat, base.]

TETRAMETER (te-tram'e-ter) *n.* a verse consisting of four measures or feet. [G., fr. *tetra,* four, and *metron,* a measure.]

TETRARCH (tet'rärk, tē'trärk) Tetrahedron. *n.* the governor of a fourth part of a province. [G., fr. *tetra,* four, and *arche,* ruler.]

TETRARCHATE (tet'rär-kat) *n.* office or jurisdiction of a tetrarch.

TETRASYLLABLE (tet-ra-sil'a-bl) *n.* a word of four syllables. [G. *tetrasullabos,* of four syllables.]

TETTER (tet'er) *n.* a cutaneous disease. [O.E. *teter.*]

TEUTONIC (tū-ton'ik) *a.* relating to the Teutons or ancient Germans. [L. *Teutones,* fr. Goth.]

TEW (tū) *v.t.* to work at; prepare for working; beat or dress;—*n.* materials for working. [O.E. *tawian.*]

TEXT (tekst) *n.* the original words of a book; words commented on; passage of Scripture. [L. *textus,* texture, structure, fr. (part.) *textum,* fr. *texere,* to weave.]

Fāte, fär, ado; mē, her; mine; nōte; tūne; mōŏn.

TEXT-BOOK (tekst'book) *n.* a book of general principles for students.

TEXTILE (teks'til) *a.* woven. [L. *textilis*, fr. *texere*, weave.]

TEXTUAL (teks'tū-al) *a.* contained in the text. [See **TEXT**.]

TEXTUALIST (teks'tū-al-ist) *n.* one versed in texts of Scripture; one who adheres closely to the text.

TEXTURE (teks'tūr) *n.* anything woven; web; manner of weaving or connecting one part with another. [L. *textura*, a web, fr. (part.) *textum*, fr. *texere*, pp. *textus*, weave.]

THALER (tä'lẹr) *n.* the German dollar, worth about 3s. [Ger.]

THAN (THan) *ad.* or *conj.* noting comparison. [M.E. *thanne*, *thonne*; O.E. *thonne*.]

THANE (thān) *n.* an old title of honour. [O.E. *thegn*, a soldier, a servant of the king, a nobleman.]

THANK (thangk) *v.t.* to express gratitude for a favour. [O.E. *thanc*, thought, content.]

THANKFUL (thangk'fool) *a.* full of gratitude.

THANKFULLY (thangk'fool-i) *ad.* with a grateful sense of favours.

THANKFULNESS (thangk'fool-nes) *n.* gratitude.

THANKLESS (thangk'les) *a.* unthankful; not obtaining thanks.

THANKLESSNESS (thangk'les-nes) *n.* want of gratitude.

THANK-OFFERING (thangk'of-ẹr-ing) *n.* a gift or acknowledgment of mercy received.

THANKS (thangks) *n.pl.* expression of gratitude.

THANKSGIVING (thangks'giv-ing) *n.* act of giving thanks; a day for expressing gratitude. [ing thanks.

THANKWORTHY (thangk'wur-THi) *a.* deserv-

THAT (THat) *a. pron.* designating a particular person or thing;—*conj.* noting cause or consequence. [O.E. *thæt*, neut. of **THE**. Cf. Ger. *dass*.]

THATCH (thach) *n.* straw for covering a roof; —*v.t.* to cover with straw. [O.E. *thæc*. Cf. Ger. *decken*, L. *tegere*.]

THATCHER (thach'ẹr) *n.* one who thatches houses.

THAW (thaw) *v.t.* or *i.* to melt, as ice or snow; —*n.* dissolution of frost. [O.E. *thawian*, to melt. Cf. Ger. *thauen*.]

THE (THe) *definite article*, denoting a particular person or thing. [O.E., common as an indeclinable relative. Cf. **THAT**, the neut of **THE**, or *se*.]

THEATRE (thē'a-tẹr) *n.* a play-house; a place of action or exhibition. [L. *theatrum*, fr. G. *theatron*, *theaomai*, I see.]

THEATRICAL (thē-at'ri-kal) *a.* pertaining to or suiting a theatre.

THEATRICALS (thē-at'ri-kalz) *n.pl.* dramatic performances.

THEE (THē) *pron.* objective case singular of **THOU**.

THEFT (theft) *n.* a felonious taking of property; thing stolen. [M.E. *thefte*, fr. O.E. *thiefth*, *theofth*, fr. *theof*. thief.]

THEINE (thē'in) *n.* the active principle in tea. [Mod. L. *thea*, tea.]

THEIR (THār) *pron. a.* belonging to them. Also **THEIRS**. [O.E. *thara*, of them, for older word, *hira*.]

THEISM (thē'izm) *n.* belief in a God. [G. *theos*, God.]

THEIST (thē'ist) *n.* one who believes in the being of a God.

THEISTICAL (thē-is'ti-kal) *a.* pertaining to theism.

THEM (THem) *pron.* objective case of **THEY**. [O.E. *tham*, for older form, *heom*.]

THEME (thēm) *n.* subject or topic. [F., fr. L. *thema*, fr. G. *thema*, fr. *tithenai*, to place.]

THEMSELVES (THem-selvz') *pron. pl.* **THEM** and **SELVES**.

THEN (THen) *ad.* at that time; in that case. [O.E. *thonne*. Doublet of **THAN**.]

THENCE (THens) *ad.* from that place or time; for that reason. [M.E. *thennes*, gen. of *thenne*, fr. O.E. *thanan*.]

THENCEFORTH (THens'fōrth) *ad.* from that time.

THENCEFORWARD (THens'for-wạrd) *ad.* from that time onward.

THEOCRACY (thē-ok'rạ-si) *n.* a government immediately directed by God. [G., fr. *theos*, a god, and *kratein*, rule.]

THEOCRATICAL (thē-u-krat'i-kal) *a.* pertaining to theocracy.

THEODOLITE (thē-od'u-līt) *n.* an instrument for measuring heights or distances. [Etym. uncert.]

THEOLOGIAN (thē-u-lō'ji-an) *n.* one versed in theology; a divine.

THEOLOGICAL (thē-u-loj'i-kal) *a.* pertaining to theology.

THEOLOGIST (thē-ol'u-jist) *n.* one versed in the science of divinity.

THEOLOGY (thē-ol'u-ji) *n.* the science of God and divine things. [G., fr. *theos*, a god, and *logos*, a discourse.]

THEOREM (the'u-rem) *n.* proposition to be proved by reasoning. [G. *theorema*, fr. *theorein*, to look at, fr. *theasthai*, see.]

THEORETICAL (thē-u-ret'i-kal) *a.* pertaining to theory; speculative.

THEORISE (thē'u-riz) *v.i.* to form theories; speculate.

THEORY (thē'u-ri) *n.* a supposition to account for or explain things; rules of art as opposed to practice. [G. *theoria*, fr. *theorein*, to look at.]

THEOSOPHY (thē-os'a-fi) *n.* direct philosophical knowledge of God. [G. *theosophia*, fr. *theos*, a god, and *sophia*, wisdom.]

THERAPEUTIC (ther-ạ-pū'tik) *a.* pertaining to the healing art. [G. *therapeutikos*, fr. *therapeuein*, take care of, heal.]

THERAPEUTICS (ther-ạ-pū'tiks) *n.* the part of medical science which treats of remedies and their action.

THERE (THār) *ad.* in that place. [O.E. *thær*.]

THEREABOUT (THār-ạ-bout') *ad.* near that place.

THEREAFTER (THār-af'tẹr) *ad.* after that.

THEREAT (THār-at') *ad.* at that place; on that account.

THEREBY (THār-bī') *ad.* by that; for that cause.

THEREFORE (THār'fur) *ad.* for that reason; consequently.

THEREIN (THār-in') *ad.* in that or this.

THEREOF (THār-ov') *ad.* of that or this.

THEREON (THār-on') *ad.* on that or this.

THERETO (THār-tŏŏ') *ad.* to this or that.

THEREUNDER (THār-un'dẹr) *ad.* under that.

THEREUNTO (THār-un-tŏŏ') *ad.* unto this or that.

THEREUPON (THār-u-pon') *ad.* upon that or this.

THEREWITH (THār-wiTH') *ad.* with that.

THEREWITHAL (THār-wiTH-awl') *ad.* along with that.

THERMAL (ther'mal) *a.* warm; tepid. [G. *thermai*, hot springs.]

THERMOMETER (ther-mom'e-tẹr) *n.* an instrument to measure heat. [G. *therme*, heat, and *metron*, measure.]

THERMOMETRICAL (ther-mu-met'ri-kal) *a.* pertaining to a thermometer.

THERMOTICS (ther-mot'iks) *n.pl.* science of heat. [G. *therme*, heat.]

THESAURUS (the-saw'rus) *n.* a treasury; a storehouse of literary information. [G.]

THESE (THēz) *pron. pl.* of **THIS**. [M.E. pl. of **THIS**.]

THESIS (thē'sis) *n.* a theme;—*pl.* **THESES**. [G., fr. *tithenai*, place set.]

Fāte, fär, ạdo; mē, hẹr; mīne; nōte; tūne; mŏŏn.

THESPIAN (thes'pi-an) a. a term applied to tragic acting. [G. *Thespis*, the founder of the Greek drama.]

THEURGY (thē'ur-ji) n. the art of doing supernatural things. [G. *theourgia*, fr. *theos*, a god, and *ergein*, to work.]

THEW (thū) n. sinew; strength;—pl. sinews. [O.E. *theaw*.]

THEY (THā) pron. pl. the persons or things. [Scand.]

THICK (thik) a. dense; close; crowded; frequent; foggy; dull; intimate:—ad. closely; in quick succession. [O.E. *thicce*.]

THICKEN (thik'n) v.t. or i. to make or become thick.

THICKET (thik'et) n. a wood with trees or shrubs closely set.

THICKLY (thik'li) ad. closely; densely.

THICK-SET (thik'set) a. closely planted; having a short, stout body;—n. a close hedge; a stout kind of cotton.

THIEF (thēf) n. one who steals. [O.E. *theof*. Cf. Ger. *Dieb*.]

THIEVE (thēv) v.i. to steal or practise theft.

THIEVERY (thē've-ri) n. the practice of stealing; theft.

THIEVISH (thē'vish) a. given to stealing.

THIGH (thī) n. part of the leg above the knee. [O.E. *theoh*.]

THILLS (thilz) n.pl. shafts of a wagon or other carriage. [O.E. *thille*, a board.]

THIMBLE (thim'bl) n. a metal cap for the finger in sewing. [O.E. *thymel*, a thumbstall, at first used on the thumb.]

THIN (thin) a. lean; slender; small; fine: —v.t. or i. to make thin; rarefy; become less dense or crowded. [O.E. *thynne*. Cf. Ger. *dünn*.]

THINE (THīn) a. belonging to thee. [O.E. *thin*, thy. Cf. Ger. *dein*.]

THING (thing) n. event or action; any substance; something. [O.E. Cf. Ger. *Ding*.]

THINK (thingk) v.t. or i. [pret. and pp. THOUGHT] to imagine; judge; purpose; consider. [O.E. *thencan*. Cf. Ger. *denken*.]

THINLY (thin'li) ad. in a scattered manner.

THIRD (therd) a. next to the second;—n. a third part; an interval of three tones in music. [O.E. *thridda*, fr. *threo*, three.]

THIRDLY (therd'li) ad. in the third place.

THIRDS (therdz) n.pl. the third part of an estate to which a widow is entitled by law.

THIRST (therst) n. a painful sensation from want of drink; eager desire for drink; longing for;—v.i. to feel thirst; desire vehemently. [O.E. *thyrst*. Cf. Ger. *Durst*.]

THIRSTINESS (thers'ti-nes) n. state of being thirsty.

THIRSTY (thers'ti) a. suffering from thirst; dry; parched; eagerly desiring.

THIRTEEN (ther'tēn) a. ten and three. [O.E. *threotyne*, fr. *threo*, three, and *tien*, ten.]

THIRTEENTH (ther'tēnth) a. the ordinal of thirteen.

THIRTIETH (ther'ti-eth) a. the ordinal of thirty.

THIRTY (ther'ti) a. thrice ten. [O.E. *thritig*.]

THIS (THis) a. or pron. denoting a specific person or project:—pl. THESE. [O.E. *thes*, masc. *theos* fem. *this* neut.]

THISTLE (this'l) n. a prickly plant; the emblem of Scotland. [O.E. *thistel*. Cf. Ger. *Distel*.]

THITHER (THiTH'er) ad. to that place; end or result. [O.E. *thider*.]

THITHERWARD (THiTH'er-ward) ad. toward that place.

THO (THō) contraction of THOUGH.

THOLE (thōl) n. a pin in the gunwale of a boat. Also written THOWL. [O.E. *thol*.]

THONG (thong) n. a strap of leather used for fastening. [O.E. *thwang*.]

THOR (thor, tor) n. the Scandinavian Jupiter or god of thunder. [Icel. *Thorr*.]

THORACIC (tho-ras'ik) a. pertaining to the breast. [See THORAX.]

THORAX (thō'raks) n. the cavity of the chest. [L., fr. G.]

THORN (thorn) n. a sharp woody spine; a prickly shrub; anything troublesome. [O.E. Cf. Ger. *Dorn*.]

THORNLESS (thorn'les) a. having no thorns.

THORNY (thor'ni) a. full of thorns.

THOROUGH (thur'u) a. passing through; complete; entire. [O.E. *thurh*; variant of THROUGH.]

THOROUGHBRED (thur'u-bred) n. bred from the best blood on both sides, as a horse.

THOROUGHFARE (thur'u-fār) n. a passage through; public street; right of passage.

THOROUGHLY (thur'u-li) ad. completely.

THORPE (thorp) n. a homestead; hamlet. [O.E. Cf. Ger. *Dorf*.]

THOSE (THōz) pron. pl. of THAT. [O.E. *thas*.]

THOU (THou) pron. denoting the person addressed. [O.E. *thu*.]

THOUGH (THō) conj. admitting; allowing. [O.E. *theah*, *theh*.]

THOUGHT (thawt) pret. and pp. of THINK; —n. that which the mind thinks; reasoning; deliberation; idea; opinion; care. [O.E. *thoht*, fr. *thencan*, to think.]

THOUGHTFUL (thawt'fool) a. given to thought; attentive; considerate.

THOUGHTFULLY (thawt'fool-i) ad. with contemplation.

THOUGHTFULNESS (thawt'fool-nes) n. deep meditation; consideration for others.

THOUGHTLESS (thawt'les) a. careless; inattentive; foolish.

THOUGHTLESSLY (thawt'les-li) ad. without thought; stupidly.

THOUGHTLESSNESS (thawt'les-nes) n. want of thought; heedlessness.

THOUSAND (thou'zand) a. or n. ten hundred. [O.E. *thusend*. Cf. Ger. *tausend*.]

THOUSANDFOLD (thou'zand-fōld) a. multiplied by a thousand.

THOUSANDTH (thou'zandth) a. ordinal of thousand.

THRALDOM (thrawl'dum) n. slavery; bondage; servitude.

THRALL (thrawl) v.t. to enslave;—n. a slave; slavery; bondage. [Scand. = a slave.]

THRASH (thrash) v.t. to beat out grain; beat soundly. [O.E. *therscan*. Cf. Ger. *dreschen*.]

THRASHER (thrash'er) n. one who thrashes grain; a large species of shark.

THRASHING-FLOOR (thrash'ing-flōr) n. a floor or area on which grain is beaten out.

THREAD (thred) n. a small twist of silk, cotton, etc.; a filament; spiral part of a screw; uniform tenor;—v.t. to put a thread in. [O.E. *thræd*, fr. *thræwan*, twist. Cf. Ger. *drehen*.]

THREADBARE (thred'bār) a. worn out; trite; hackneyed.

THREAT (thret) n. denunciation of punishment, loss, etc. [O.E. *threat*.]

THREATEN (thret'n) v.t. or i. to denounce evil against; menace; betoken evil; use threats. [O.E. *threotan*, to urge, to afflict.]

THREATENING (thret'ning) a. indicating danger; imminent.

THREE (thrē) a. two and one. [O.E. *threo*.]

THREEFOLD (thrē'fōld) a. three double.

THREEPENCE (thrē'pens, thrip'ens) n. three pennies.

THREESCORE (thrē'skōr) a. thrice twenty.

THRENODY (thren'u-di) n. a song of lamentation; funeral dirge. [G. *threnos*, a lament, and *ode*, a song.]

THRESH (thresh) v.t. to thrash.

THRESHOLD (thresh'ōld) n. the door sill; entrance; gate. [M.E. *threshwold*, fr. O.E. *threscwald*, fr. *therscan*, beat, and *wald*, wood.]

THREW (thrōō) pret. of THROW.

THRICE (thrīs) *ad.* three times.
THRID (thrid) *v t.* to slide through; thread. [Fr. THREAD.]
THRIFT (thrift) *n.* wise management; frugality; gain; a plant with rounded flowers. [Fr. THRIVE.] [successful economy.
THRIFTILY (thrif'ti-li) *ad.* with wise or **THRIFTLESS** (thrift'les) *a,* extravagant.
THRIFTY (thrif'ti) *a.* thriving by industry; frugal; careful; economical.
THRILL (thril) *v.t.* to pierce; affect strongly; —*v.i.* to feel a sharp shivering sensation; —*n.* a warbling; a shivering sensation. [O.E. *thyrlian.* to bore, fr. *thyrel.* a hole. Cf. Ger. *drillen.*]
THRIVE (thrīv) *v.i.* [*pret.* THRIVED; *pp.* THRIVED, THRIVEN] to prosper by industry; grow; flourish. [Scand. = to grasp.]
THRIVER (thrī'ver) *n.* one who thrives.
THRIVING (thrī'ving) *a.* flourishing; prosperous.
THROAT (thrōt) *n.* fore part of the neck. [O.E. *throte.* Cf. Ger. *Drossel.*]
THROB (throb) *v.i.* to beat forcibly; palpitate; —*n.* a strong pulsation. [M.E.]
THROE (thrō) *n.* extreme pain; anguish; pains of child-birth;—*v.i.* to agonise. [O.E. *threa,* suffering.]
THRONE (thrōn) *n.* a royal seat; sovereign power; a bishop's chair;—*pl.* spiritual powers;—*v.t.* to place on the throne. [O.F. fr. L. *thronus* fr. G. *thronos,* a seat.]
THRONG (throng) *n.* a crowd of people;—*v.t.* or *i.* to crowd together; fill; press or annoy with numbers. [O.E. *thrang* fr. *thringan.* to press.]
THROSTLE †thros'l) *n.* the mavis or songthrush; a machine for spinning. [O.E. Cf. Ger. *Drossel.*]
THROTTLE (throt'l) *n.* the windpipe;—*v.t.* or *i.* to choke by pressure; strangle. [Dim. of THROAT.]
THROUGH (thrōō) *prep.* from end to end; by means of;—*a.* from end to end. [O.E. *thurh.* Cf. Ger. *durch.*]
THROUGHLY (thrōō'li) *ad.* thoroughly.
THROUGHOUT (thrōō-out') *prep.* quite through; in every part.
THROVE (thrōv) *pret.* of THRIVE.
THROW (thrō) *v.t.* or *i.* [*pret.* THREW; *pp.* THROWN] to fling; cast; toss; turn; twist;—*n.* act of throwing; distance thrown; a cast; a fall. [O.E. *thrawan,* to twist. Cf. Ger. *drehen.*]
THROWSTER (thrō'ster) *n.* one who twists silk.
THRUM (thrum) (1) *n.* the ends of a weaver's threads;—*v.t.* to insert threads;—(2) *v.i.* to play coarsely. [(1) Scand. = the edge. Cf. Ger. *Trumm,* a fragment. (2) Scand.]
THRUSH (thrush) (1) *n.* a singing bird;—(2) *n.* ulcers in the mouth. [(1) O.E. *thrysce.* (2) O.E. *thyrre.* dry, and suffix *ise,* or *ish.*]
THRUST (thrust) *v.t.* [*pret.* and *pp.* THRUST] to push or drive with force;—*v.i.* to squeeze in; intrude; stab;— *n.* a pushing; stab. [Scand.]
THUD (thud) *n.* a blow or fall causing a dull, hollow sound. (O.E. *thyddan.*]

Thrust in fencing.

THUMB (thum) *n.* the short, thick finger;— *v.t.* or *i.* to handle awkwardly; play or soil with the thumb. [O.E. *thuma.*]
THUMP (thump) *v.t.* or *i.* to beat with something heavy; strike or fall with a heavy blow;—*n.* a heavy blow, fall, or sound. [Perh. imit.]
THUNDER (thun'der) *n.* the sound which follows lightning;—*v.t.* or *i.* to sound as thunder; give out with noise and terror. [O.E. *thunor.* fr. *thunian.* to rattle. Cf. Ger. *Donner.* L. *tonare.*]

THUNDERBOLT (thun'der-bōlt) *n.* a shaft of lightning. [thunder.
THUNDERCLAP (thun'der-klap) *n.* a burst of
THUNDERCLOUD (thun'der-kloud) *n* a cloud that threatens or discharges lightning and thunder.
THUNDEROUS (thun'der-us) *a.* producing or sounding like thunder. Also **THUNDERY.**
THUNDERSHOWER (thun'der-shou-er) *n.* a shower accompanied with thunder.
THUNDERSTRUCK (thun'der-struk) *a.* astonished with wonder.
THURIBLE (thū'ri-bl) *n.* a metal censer for burning incense. [L. *thuribulum.* fr. stem *thur-,* of *thus* incense.]
THURSDAY (thurz'dā) *n.* fifth day of the week. [O.E. *thunres* (gen. of *thunor* thunder). *dæg,* the day of Thor (so called because originally sacred to Thor. the god of thunder). Cf. Ger. *Donnerstag.*]
THUS (Thus) *ad.* so; in this manner. [O.E.]
THWACK (thwak) *v.t.* to beat; bang;—*n.* a heavy stroke. [O.E. *thaccian,* to stroke.]
THWART (thwawrt) *v.t.* to cross; oppose;— *a.* being across; crosswise;—*n.* bench on which the rowers sit. [Scand.]
THY (THĪ) *a.* belonging to thee. [Contr. of THINE.]
THYME (tīm) *n.* an aromatic herb. [L. *thymum,* fr. G. *thumos.* fr. *thuein,* to fill with sweet sme ls.]
THYMY (tī'mi) *a.* abounding with thyme; fragrant.
THYSELF (THĪ-self') *pron.* emphatical, thou or thee only.
TIARA (tī-ā'ra) *n.* an ornamental head-dress; mitre of the high priest; triple crown of the pope. [F. *tiare,* fr. L. fr G. *tiara,* a Persian head-dress, probably of Persian origin.]
TIBIAL (tib'i-al) *a.* pertaining to the large bone of the leg. [Fr. L. *tibia.*] [ing.]
TIC (tik) *n.* neuralgic pa'n. [F. *tic,* a twitch-
TICK (tik) (1) *n.* a large mite;—(2) *n.* case or cover of a bed;—(3) *n.* beat of a watch; small mark;—*v.i.* to beat; mark. [(1) Cf. Ger. *Zecke.* (2) G. *theke,* a case, fr. *tithemai.* I place. (3) Imit. Cf. Ger. *ticken.*]
TICKET (tik'et) *n.* a card entitling to some right or privilege;—*v t.* to distinguish by a ticket; put a ticket on; label. [Contr. fr. O.F. *etiquet,* a little bill or note, fr. Ger. *stecken,* to stick.]
TICKING (tik'ing) *n.* closely woven cloth for bed ticks. [See TICK (2).]
TICKLE (tik'l) *v.t.* to excite a thrilling sensation by the touch; please. [Freq. of TICK. to touch lightly.]
TICKLISH (tik'lish) *a.* easily tickled; unsteady; nice; critical.
TIDAL (tī'dal) *a.* relating to tides. [See TIDE.]
TIDE (tīd) *n* flowing of the sea. [O.E. *tid,* time. Cf. Ger. *Zeit.*]
TIDE-WAITER (tīd'wā-ter) *n* a man who watches the landing of goods.
TIDILY (tī'di-li) *ad.* with neatness.
TIDINESS (tī'di-nes) *n.* neatness and simplicity.
TIDINGS (tī'dingz) *n.pl.* news; intelligence.
TIDY (tī'di) *a* neat and simple; in good order;—*n.* an ornamental cover; a child's pinafore. [O.E. *tid* season.]
TIE (tī) *v.t.* to bind; fasten;—*n.* knot; obligation; bond; equa ity in numbers. [O.E. *tiegan,* fr. *tyge.* a rope.]
TIER (tēr) *n.* a row; a rank. [F. *tire,* fr. *tirer* draw.]
TIERCE (tērs) *n.* a cask of 42 gallons; a thrust; sequence of three cards. [O.F *tierz* fr. L. *tertia* (*pars*), a third (part) fr. *tres.* three.]
TIERCEL (tēr'sel) *n.* the male hawk; goshawk. [O.F. *tiercelet,* fr. *tiers* th third (so-called because the third in the nest is said to be a male.)
TIFF (tif) *n.* a draught of liquor; a slight quarrel. [Scand. = to sniff.]

TIFFANY 'tif'a-ni) *n.* a thin silk. 'Fr. *tiff* to deck.]

TIFFIN ,tif'in) *n.* in *India,* lunch. [For *tiffing,* sipping. fr. TIFF. a draught of liquor.]

TIG (tig) *n.* a child's game of chasing and touching. [*Tick* to touch.]

TIGER (ti'ger) *n.* a beast of prey: a young livery servant. [F. *tigre.* fr. L. *tigris.*]

TIGER-CAT (ti'ger-kat) *n.* a carnivorous animal smaller than the tiger.

TIGHT (tit) *a.* close: compact: taut: dear: slightly intoxicated· saving. [Scand. Cf. Ger. *dicht.*]

TIGHTEN (ti'tn) *v.t.* to make more tight.

TIGHTLY (tit'li) *ad.* closely: compactly.

TIGHTNESS (tit'nes) *n.* compactness: neatness: scarcity.

TIGRESS (ti'gres) *n.* a female tiger.

TIKE (tik) *n.* a clown: a dog. [Scand.]

TILE (til) *n.* a piece of baked clay for covering buildings:—*v.t.* to cover with tiles. [O.E. *tigele.* fr. L. *tegula* fr. *tegere.* to cover.]

TILER (ti'ler) *n.* one who covers buildings with tiles.

TILERY (ti'ler-i) *n.* place where tiles are made. Also **TILE-WORK.**

TILL (til) (1) *n.* a money-box: a drawer for holding cash:—(2) *prep.* or *ad.* until:—(3) *v.t.* to plough: cultivate. [(1) M.E. *tillen* to draw out. fr. O.E. *tyllan* in *fortyllan,* to draw aside. (2) Scand. ⁼to. (3) O.E. *tilian* to labour to till land. Cf. Ger. *zielen,* to arrange.]

TILLABLE (til'a-bl) *a.* that may be tilled. [See TILL (3).]

TILLAGE (til'ij) *n.* culture of land. [See TILL (3).]

TILLER (til'er) *n.* handle of a rudder: a husbandman.

TILT (tilt) *n.* a thrust: a military exercise: a large hammer: inclination forward:—*v.t.* or *i.* to raise one end of: incline: ride and thrust with a lance: forge with a tilt-hammer. [O.E. *tealt* unstable. Cf. Ger. *zelter.*]

TILTH (tilth) *n.* cultivation: cultivated land. [See TILL (3).]

TILT-HAMMER (tilt'ham-er) *n.* a heavy hammer in iron works. [See TILT.]

TIMBER (tim'ber) *n.* wood for building: trunk of a tree: beam: joist:—*v.t.* to furnish with timber. [O.E. *timber* material to build with. Cf. Ger. *Zimmer* an apartment.]

TIMBRE (tim'ber) *n.* quality of tone distinguishing voices or instruments. [O.F. a timbrel, fr. L *tympanum,* a drum.]

TIMBREL (tim'brel) *n.* a kind of drum. ⌈See TIMBRE.]

TIME (tim) *n.* absolute duration: a part of it: season: opportunity: allotted period: musical duration:—*v.t.* to adapt to the occasion: mark the time of. [O.E. *tima.*]

TIMEKEEPER (tim'ke-per) *n.* a clock or watch: one who keeps the time of workmen at work.

TIMELESS (tim'les) *a.* untimely: done at the wrong time. [in good time.

TIMELY (tim'li) *a.* in good time:—*ad.* early:

TIMEOUS (ti'mus) *a.* timely: early.

TIMEPIECE (tim'pes) *n.* a clock or watch.

TIME-SERVER (tim'ser-ver) *n.* one who complies with the times.

TIME-SERVING (tim'ser-ving) *a.* obsequiously complying with prevailing opinions.

TIMID (tim'id) *a.* wanting courage: fearful: timorous. [F. *timide.* fr. L. *timidus* fr. *timere,* to fear.]

TIMIDITY (ti-mid'i-ti) *n.* want of courage.

TIMIDLY (tim'id-li) *ad.* in a weak or timid manner.

TIMOCRACY (ti-mok'ra-si) *n.* government by men of property. [G. *timokratia* fr. *time* honour, and *kratein* to rule.]

TIMOROUS (tim'ur-us) *a.* fearful: timid. [L. *timor,* fr. *timere.*]

TIMOROUSLY (tim'ur-us-li) *ad.* with fear.

TIN (tin) *n.* a white metal much used:—*v.t.* to cover with tin. [O.E. Cf. Ger. *Zinn.*]

TINCTURE (tingk'tur) *n.* extract of a substance: tinge or shade of colour:—*v.t.·* to tinge: imbue. [L. *tinctura.* fr. (part.) *tinctus.* fr. *tingere.* to dye.]

TINDER (tin'der) *n.* anything used to kindle fire from a spark. [O.E. *tyndre.* Cf. Ger: *Zunder.*]

TINDER-BOX (tin'der-boks) *n.* a box for tinder.

TINE (tin) *n.* tooth of a harrow: spike of a fork. [O.E. *tind.* a point.]

TINFOIL (tin'foil) *n.* tin reduced to a thin leaf.

TINGE (tinj) *n.* a colour: dye: tincture:—*v.t.* to imbue: dye. [L. *tingere,* to dye.]

TINGLE (ting'gl) *v.i.* to feel a thrilling sensation of sound or pain. [M.E. *tinglen.*]

TINKER (ting'ker) *v.t.* to solder: mend: cobble: patch:—*n.* mender of old metal ware. [M.E. *tinkere.* Cf. Scot. *tinkler* a worker in tin.]

TINKLE (ting'kl) *v.i.* to make sharp sounds: —*v.t.* or *i.* to make or cause small sharp sounds: clink: jingle:—*n.* a single sharp sound. [Freq. of M.E. *tinken.*]

TINKLING (ting'kling) *n.* a small, quick, sharp sound.

TINMAN (tin'man) *n.* one who deals in tin.

TINMINE (tin'min) *n.* mine where tin is obtained. [cally sealed.

TINNED (tind) *a.* covered with tin and hermeti-

TINNER (tin'er) *n.* one who works in a tin mine. Also **TINSMITH.**

TINSEL (tin'sel) *n.* a shining dress stuff: ornamental lace: anything showy but of little value:—*a.* gaudy: superficial:—*v.t.* to deck with tinsel. [O.F. *estincelle.* a star-like ornament, fr. L. *scintilla,* a spark.]

TINT (tint) *n.* a slight colouring:—*v.t.* to colour: tinge. [Fr. L. *tingere,* pp. *tinctus,* dye.]

TINTINABULATION (tin-ti-nab-u-la'shun) *n.* ringing or tinkling of bells. [L. *tintinnabulum,* a little bell.]

TINY (ti'ni) *a.* very small. [Etym. doubtful.]

TIP (tip) (1) *n.* the end: the point:—*v.i.* to form a point: cover the end:—(2) *v.i.* lower one end. as a cart. [(1) M.E. (2) Scand.]

TIPPET (tip'et) *n.* a covering for the neck and shoulders. [L. *tapete* cloth.]

TIPPLE (tip'l) *v.t.* or *i.* to drink in small quantities: drink habitually or to excess. [Scand.]

TIPPLER (tip'ler) *n.* a drunkard.

TIPSY (tip'si) *a.* intoxicated: drunk. [Fr. TIPPLE.]

TIPTOE (tip'to) *n.* the end of the toes.

TIPTOP (tip'top) *n.* the highest degree:—*a.* most excellent.

TIRADE (ti-rad') *n.* a strain of censure or abuse. [F.. fr. It. *tirata,* fr. *tirare.* to draw.]

TIRE (tir) (1) *n.* a tier or row: a band of iron for a wheel: head-dress: apparel:—*v.t.* to adorn: dress:—(2) *v.t.* or *i.* to fatigue: weary: be exhausted. (1) Contr. fr. **ATTIRE.** (2) O.E. *teorian,* to be tired.

TIRED (tird) *a.* fatigued: weary.

TIRESOME (tir'sum) *a.* tedious: wearisome.

TISSUE (tish'u) *n.* cloth interwoven with gold or silver: organic substance:—*v.t.* to form tissue. [F. *tissu.* woven, fr. L. *texere.* to weave.]

TISSUE-PAPER (tish'u-pa-per) *n.* very thin gauze-like paper.

TIT (tit) *n.* a small horse: a tomtit. [Scand. ⁼a little bird.]

TITANIC (ti-tan'ik) *a.* gigantic. [Fr. *Titan,* in G. myth, one of the giants that warred against Jupiter.]

TITHABLE (ti-тна'bl) *a.* subject to tithes.

TITHE (titн) *n.* tenth of anything:—*v.t.* to levy a tenth. [O.E. *teotha,* the tenth, fr. *tien,* ten.]

TITILLATE (tit'i-lat) *v.t.* to tickle. [L. (part.) *titillatus,* fr. *titillare.*]

Fäte, fär, ado: me, her: mine: note: tune: möön.

TITILLATION (tit-i-lā'shun) *n.* act of tickling; any slight pleasure.

TITLE (tī'tl) *n.* an inscription; right; appellation of honour;—*v.t.* to name; entitle. [O.F. *i.*—F. *titre*, fr. L. *titulus*.]

TITLE-DEED (tī'tl-dēd) *n.* writing proving a man's right or title to real property.

TITMOUSE (tit'mous) *n.* a small bird. [M.E. *titmose*, fr. *tit*, small, and O.E. *mase*, a name for several small birds (not connected with MOUSE).]

TITTER (tit'ẽr) *v.i.* to laugh; giggle;—*n.* a restrained laugh. [M.E. *titeren*, to prattle, a repetition of *ti*. Cf. TITTLE-TATTLE.]

TITTLE (tit'l) *n.* a small particle; iota; jot. [O.E. *title*, fr. L. *titulus*.]

TITTLE-TATTLE (tit'l-tat'l) *n.* idle talk; an idle talker;—*v.i.* to prate; gossip.] Cf. TITTER.]

TITULAR (tit'ū-lẽr) *a* existing in name only. [L. *titulus*.]

TO (tōō) *prep.* toward, or moving toward. [O.E. Cf. Ger. *zu*.]

TOAD (tōd) *n.* a reptile. [O.E. *tadie, tadige*.]

TOAD-EATER (tōd'ē-tẽr)*n* a mean, obsequious sycophant. Also TOADY.

TOADSTOOL (tōd'stōōl) *n.* a fungus plant.

TOADYISM (tō'di-izm) *n.* sycophancy.

TOAST (tōst) *v.t.* or *i.* to dry and scorch at the fire; drink to the health of; name when so doing;—*n.* bread dried and scorched; a sentiment, etc., honoured by drinking. [O.F. *toster*, fr. L. (part.) *tostus*, fr. *torrere*, to roast.]

TOBACCO (tu-bak'ō) *n.* a narcotic plant. [Sp. *tabaco*, fr. Haytian, the tube or pipe in which the Indians or Caribs smoked the plant.] [tobacco.

TOBACCONIST (tu-bak'u-nist) *n.* a dealer in

TOCSIN (tok'sin) *n.* an alarm-bell. [O.F. *toquesin*, fr. *toquer*. to strike, and *sing* = F. *signe*. a sign, fr. L. *signum*.]

TODDLE (tod'l) *v.i.* to walk with short tottering steps. [Perh. a form of TOTTER.]

TODDLING (tod'ling) *a.* waddling, as children, in walking.

TODDY (tod'i) *n.* a mixture of spirit and water sweetened. [Hind., fr. Per. —a palm-tree.]

TOE (tō) *n.* one of the extremities of the foot. [O.E. *ta*. Cf. Ger. *Zehe*.]

TOFFY, TOFFEE (tof'i, tof'ē) *n.* a sweetmeat of sugar and butter. [Etym. uncert.]

TOGETHER (too-geᴛʜ'ẽr) *ad.* in company. [O.E.*togædere*, fr. *to*, to, and *geador*, together.]

TOGGERY (tog'ẽr-i) *n.* clothes; garments. [L. *toga*, a cloak.]

TOIL (toil) (1) *v.i.* to work hard;—*n.* hard labour;—(2) *n.* a net. [(1) O.F. *touiller*, to entangle, of uncert. etym. (2) F. *toiles*, nets, fr. *toile*, cloth, fr. L. *tela*, a web.]

TOILET (toi'let) *n.* a dressing-table; operation or mode of dressing. [F. *toilette*, dim. of *toile*, cloth. Cf. TOIL (2).]

TOILSOME (toil'sum) *a.* laborious; wearisome.

TOKAY (tō-kā') *n.* wine made at Tokay, in Hungary.

TOKEN (tō'kn) *n.* something intended to represent another thing; sign; symbol. [O.E. *tacen*, sign. Cf. Ger. *Zeichen*, a mark.]

TOLD (tōld) *pret.* and *pp.* of TELL.

TOLERABLE (tol'e-ra-bl) *a.* that may be endured.

TOLERABLY (tol'e-ra-bli) *ad.* moderately well.

TOLERANCE (tol'e-rans) *n.* act of enduring.

TOLERATE (tol'e-rāt) *v.t.* to allow by not hindering; suffer. [L. (part.) *toleratus*, fr. *tolerare*, to bear, fr. *tollere*, to lift up.]

TOLERATION (tol-e-rā'shun) *n.* act of tolerating; sufferance.

TOLL (tōl) (1) *n.* a tax for passing; a miller's portion of grain for grinding;—(2) *n.* sound of a bell;—*v.t.* or *i.* to ring a bell; sound, as a bell rung. [(1) O.E. *toll*, tax. Cf. Ger. *Zoll*. (2) M.E. *tollen*. Cf. O.E. *fortyllan*, allure.]

TOLL-BRIDGE (tōl'brij) *n.* a bridge where toll is paid for passing.

TOLL-GATE (tōl'gāt) *n.* a gate where toll is paid.

TOLL-GATHERER (tōl'gaᴛʜ-ẽr-ẽr) *n.* one who takes toll.

TOLL-HOUSE (tōl'hous) *n.* house where toll is taken.

TOMAHAWK (tom'a-hawk) *n.* an Indian hatchet;—*v.t.* to cut with a tomahawk. [Ind.]

TOMATO (tu-mā'tō, tu-mā'tō) *n.* a plant and its fleshy fruit, used raw or for sauces. [Mex.]

TOMB (tōōm) *n.* the grave; monument over a grave. [F. *tombe*, fr. L. *tumba*, fr. G. *tumbos*, a grave.]

TOMBOY (tom'boi) *n.* a romping girl. [Fr. *tom*, and BOY.]

TOMBSTONE (tōōm'stōn) *n.* a stone erected over a grave.

TOME (tōm) *n.* a volume of a large work; a ponderous book. [F., fr. L. *tomus*, fr. G. *tomos*, a piece cut off, fr. *temnein*, to cut.]

TOMFOOLERY (tom-fōō'lẽr-i) *n.* foolish trifling; knick-knacks; trinkets. [Fr. *tom*.]

TO-MORROW (tōō-mor'ō) *n.* day after the present.

TOMTIT (tom'tit) *n.* a small perching bird; titmouse. [*Tom*, a common name like Jack, and *tit*, as in TITMOUSE.]

TON (ton) *n.* the prevailing fashion. [F.]

TON (tun) *n.* weight of 2240 pounds avoirdupois. [O.E. *tunne*, a tun, tub. Cf. Ger. *Tonne*, cask.]

TONE (tōn) *n.* character of a sound or of the voice; harmony of colours; prevailing hue; state of mind or body; mood;—*v.t.* to utter with a whine; tune. [L. *tonus*, fr. G. *tonos*, a stretching, fr. *teino*, stretch.]

TONED (tōnd) *a.* having a tone.

TONELESS (tōn'les) *a.* without tone.

TONGS (tongz) *n.pl.* instrument to handle fire or heated metals. [O.E. *tange*. Cf. Ger. *Zange*.]

TONGUE (tung) *n.* the organ of taste and speech; language; utterance; fluency; any tapering point or projection;—*v.t.* to chide; scold. [O.E. *tunge*. Cf. Ger. *Zunge*, L. *lingua* (old form *dingua*.)]

TONGUE-TIED (tung'tid) *a.* having an impediment in speech.

TONIC (ton'ik) *a.* relating to sounds; giving tone or strength to the system;—*n.* a medicine that increases bodily strength. See TONE.

TONNAGE (tun'ij) *n.* amount of tons; duty by the ton.

TONQUIN BEAN (ton'kwin bēn) *n.* bean of a leguminous plant, used to scent snuff. [Guiana, *tonca*, the tree.]

TONSIL (ton'sil) *n.* a gland at the root of the tongue. [L. *tonsillae*, pl. a stake, dim. of *tonsa*, an oar.]

TONSILE (ton'sil) *a.* capable of clipping or being clipped. [L. *tonsilis*, fr. *tondere*, to clip.]

TONSORIAL (ton-sō'ri-al) *a.* pertaining to a barber or to shaving. [See TONSURE.]

Tonsure.

TONSURE (ton'shōōr) *n.* act of shaving off the hair. [L. *tonsura*, fr. (part.) *tonsus*, fr. *tondere*, to shave.]

TONTINE (ton-tēn') *n.* annuity or survivorship. [From its inventor, *Tonti*, an Italian, in the 17th century.]

TOO (tōō) *ad.* over; noting excess; also. [A form of *to*; lit. *added to*.]

TOOL (tōōl) *n.* an instrument; a hireling. [O.E. *tol*.]

TOOTH (tòòth) *n.* a bony substance in the jaw for chewing; a tine or prong;—*v.t.* to indent; furnish with teeth. [O.E. *toth*, pl. *teth*. Cf. L. stem *dent-*, of *dens*.]

TOOTHACHE (tòòth'āk) *n.* a pain in the teeth.

TOOTHLESS (tòòth'les) *a.* wanting teeth.

TOOTHPICK (tòòth'pik) *n.* an instrument to clean teeth.

TOOTHSOME (tòòth'sum) *a.* pleasing to the taste.

TOP (tòp) (1) *n.* the highest part;—*v.t.* or *i.* to cover on the top; tip; surpass; crop; rise above;—(2) *n.* a child's toy. (1) [O.E. *top*. Cf. Ger. *Zopf*. (2) M. H. Ger.]

TOPAZ (tō'paz) *n.* a mineral gem; the best are yellow in colour. [O.F. *topase*, fr. G. *topazion*.]

TOP-COAT (top'kōt) *n.* an overcoat.

TOP-DRESSING (top'dres-ing) *n.* manure laid on the surface of the land.

TOPE (tōp) *v.i.* to drink to excess. [Cf. F. *toper*, to agree.]

TOPER (tō'per) *n.* a tippler.

TOPIC (top'ik) *n.* subject of discourse. [G. *topika*, common-places, fr. *topos*, a place.]

TOPICAL (top'i-kal) *a.* pertaining to a place; local.

TOPMAST (top'mast) *n.* the mast next above the lower mast.

TOPMOST (top'mōst) *a.* uppermost; highest

TOPOGRAPHER (tō-pog'ra-fer) *n.* a writer o topography.

TOPOGRAPHICAL (top-ō-graf'i-kal) *a.* descriptive of a place.

TOPOGRAPHICALLY (top-ō-graf'i-kal-i) *ad.* by local description.

TOPOGRAPHY (to-pog'ra-fi) *n.* description of a particular place. [G., fr. *topos*, a place, and *graphein*, to describe.]

TOPPLE (top'l) *v.i.* to fall or pitch forward. [Freq. of TOP (1).]

TOPSAIL (top'sāl) *n.* sail extended on the topmast.

TORCH (torch) *n.* a light made of combustible matter. [F. *torche*, fr. L. (part.) *tortum*, fr. *torquere*, to twist.]

TORCH-LIGHT (torch'lit) *n.* a light of a torch or of torches.

TORMENT (tor'ment) *n.* misery; anguish; he who, or that which, causes pain. [L. *tormentum*, an engine for hurling missiles, fr. *torquere*, to turn.]

TORMENT (tor-mont') *v.t.* to torture; distress; vex.

TORMENTER (tor-men'ter) *n.* one who torments. Also written **TORMENTOR.**

TORN (tōrn) *pp.* of TEAR.

TORNADO (tor-nā'dō) *n.* a violent tropical wind. [Sp. *tornada*, fr. L. *tonare*, to thunder.]

TORPEDO (tor-pē'dō) *n.* the cramp-fish; a submarine apparatus for blowing up ships. [L., fr. *torpere*, to be stiff or torpid.]

TORPID (tor'pid) *a.* having lost the power of motion and feeling; dull; sluggish. [L. *torpidus*, fr. *torpere*, to be stiff.]

TORPIDITY (tor-pid'i-ti) *n.* numbness; insensibility; inactivity.

TORPOR (tor'per) *n.* numbness; sluggishness.

TORREFACTION (tor-e-fak'shun) *n.* the act of roasting.

TORREFY (tor'e-fi) *v.t.* to parch; roast; scorch. [L. *torrere*, to dry by heat, and *facere*, to make.]

TORRENT (tor'ent) *n.* a violent rushing stream. [L. (part. stem) *torrent-*, fr. *torrere*, to roast.]

TORRID (tor'id) *a.* burning; hot; parched or parching. [L. *torridus*, fr. *torrere*, to burn.]

TORSION (tor'shun) *n.* act of twisting. [F., fr. L. (acc.) *torsionem*, fr. *torquere*, to twist.]

TORSO (tor'sō) *n.* the trunk of a statue wanting head and limbs. [It. *torso*, stump, stalk.]

TORT (tort) *n.* wrong; injury done. [F., fr. L. (part.) *tortus*, fr. *torquere*, to twist.]

TORTIVE (tor'tiv) *a.* twisted; wreathed.

TORTOISE (tor'tis, tor'tus) *n.* an animal covered with a hard shell. [O.F. *tortis*, fr. Late L. *tortuca*, fr. *tortus*, twisted (from its twisted feet.)]

TORTUOUS (tor'tū-us) *a.* twisted; winding; crooked; deceitful. [L. *tortuosus*, fr. *tortus*, fr. *torquere*, to twist.]

Tortoise.

TORTURE (tor'tūr) *n.* extreme pain; anguish;—*v.t.* to put to the rack; inflict extreme pain; torment. [L. *tortura*, fr. (part.) *tortus*, fr. *torquere*, to twist.]

TORY (tō'ri) *n.* an extreme advocate of established institutions in state and church; conservative. [Fr. Ir. =a bog-trotter, and a pursuer (first used in the political sense about 1680).]

TORYISM (tō'ri-izm) *n.* the principles of Tories.

TOSS (tos) *v.t.* to throw up or with violence; agitate;—*v.i.* to roll and tumble;—*n.* act of tossing. [Scand.]

TOTAL (tō'tal) *a.* whole; complete;—*n.* the whole sum. [F., fr. L. *totus*, all.]

TOTALITY (tō-tal'i-ti) *n.* the whole sum, quantity, or amount.

TOTALLY (tō'tal-i) *ad.* wholly; completely; entirely.

TOTEM (tō'tem) *n.* a rude figure used as the family symbol among American Indians. [Amer. Ind.]

TOTTER (tot'er) *v.i.* to shake; be unsteady. [For *tolter*, fr. O.E. *tealt*, unstable.]

TOUCH (tuch) *v.t.* or *i.* to come or be in contact with; reach; handle or treat slightly; move; affect;—*n.* act or sense of touching; contact; hit; stroke; a little of. [F. *toucher*, to touch.]

TOUCHABLE (tuch'a-bl) *a.* that may be touched.

TOUCH-HOLE (tuch'hōl) *n.* vent of a firearm.

TOUCHINESS (tuch'i-nes) *n.* peevishness.

TOUCHING (tuch'ing) *a.* adapted to affect the feelings.

TOUCHSTONE (tuch'stōn) *n.* a criterion or test.

TOUCHWOOD (tuch'wood) *n.* decayed wood that easily takes fire.

TOUCHY (tuch'i) *a.* peevish; irritable.

TOUGH (tuf) *a.* not brittle; firm; stiff; tenacious; hard to chew. [O.E. *toh*. Cf. Ger. *zähe*.]

TOUGHEN (tuf'n) *v.t.* to make tough.

TOUGHISH (tuf'ish) *a.* somewhat tough.

TOUGHLY (tuf'li) *ad.* in a tough manner.

TOUGHNESS (tuf'nes *n.* firmness of cohesion; strength of texture.

TOUR (tòòr) *n.* a journey in a circuit; excursion; jaunt;—*v.i.* to make a journey. [F. fr. L. *tornus*, a wheel.]

TOURIST (tòòr'ist) *n.* one who makes a tour.

TOURNAMENT (tòòr'na-ment) *n.* martial sport on horseback. [O.F. *tornoiement*, fr. *tornoier*, to tilt, fr. *torner*, to turn, fr. L. *tornare*, to turn.]

TOURNIQUET (tòòr'ni-ket) *n.* a surgical instrument for stopping flow of blood in amputations. [F., that which turns about, fr. *tourner*, turn, fr. L. *tornare*.]

TOURNURE (tòòr-nūr') *n.* contour; shape; a bustle.

TOUSE (touz) *v.t.* or *i.* to pull or haul about; tear; rave. [Teut. Cf. Ger. *zausen*.]

TOUT (tout) *v.i.* to ply for or seek custom or customers;—*n.* a touter. [O.E. *totian*, to peep.]

TOUTER (tou'ter) *n.* one who hangs on to ply for customs or pick up racing information.

TOW (tō) *n.* coarse part of flax;—*v.t.* to draw by a rope. [O.E. *teon*, draw.]

TOWAGE (tō'ij) *n.* act of towing; price for towing.

TOWARD (tō'ard) *prep.* in the direction of; tending to;—*ad.* nearly; in a state of preparation;—*a.* ready to learn or do; apt. [O.E. *toweard*, future.]

TOWARDLY (tō'ard-li) *a.* ready to learn.

TOWARDNESS (tō'ard-nes) *n.* tractableness; readiness.

TOWEL (tou'el) *n.* a cloth for drying the skin after washing. [F. *touaille*, fr. O. H. Ger.]

TOWER (tou'er) *n.* a high edifice; a fortress; —*v.i.* to rise high; be lofty. [O.F. *tour* *tur*, fr. L. *turris*.]

TOWERING (tou'er-ing) *a.* very high; elevated; soaring.

TOW-LINE (tō'līn) *n.* a rope for towing.

TOWN (toun) *n.* a large collection of houses; the inhabitants. [O.E. *tun*, fence, farm, town.]

TOWNSHIP (toun'ship) *n.* territory of a town.

TOWNSMAN (tounz'man) *n.* one of the same town.

TOWN-TALK (toun'tawk) *n.* common discourse.

TOXICOLOGY (tok-si-kol'ō-ji) *n.* the science which treats of poisons. [G. *toxikon*, arrow-poison, and *logos*, a discourse.]

TOY (toy) *n.* a trifle; a plaything;—*v.t.* to dally; trifle. [D. = tools.]

TOYFUL (toi'fool) *a.* full of play.

TOYISH (toi'ish) *a.* given to dallying.

TOYSHOP (toi'shop) *n.* a shop where toys are sold.

TRACE (trās) *n.* a mark drawn; a footstep; vestige;—*v.t.* to delineate by marks; follow by the footprints. [O.F. *tracer* fr. L. (part.) *tractus*, fr. *trahere*, to draw.]

TRACEABLE (trā'sa-bl) *a.* that may be traced.

TRACES (trā'sez) *n.pl.* the straps by which a carriage is drawn by horses. [O.F. *trays*, fr. L. *trahere*, to draw.]

TRACERY (trā'ser-i) *n.* ornamental work. [See TRACE.]

TRACHEA (tra-kē'a, trā'ke-a) *n.* the windpipe. [L., fr. G. *tracheia*, rough.]

TRACK (trak) *n.* a footstep; path; course;—*v.t.* to follow by traces. [F. *trac*, fr. D. *trek* a drawing.]

TRACKLESS (trak'les) *a.* having no path.

TRACT (trakt) *n.* a space of indefinite extent; region; a short treatise. [L. (part.) *tractus*, fr. *trahere*, to draw.]

TRACTABILITY (trak-ta-bil'i-ti) *n.* the state or quality of being manageable. [See TRACTABLE.]

TRACTABLE (trak'ta-bl) *a.* easily managed; docile. [L *tractabilis*.]

TRACTABLY (trak'ta-bli) *ad.* with ready compliance.

TRACTILE (trak'til) *a.* that may be drawn out.

TRACTILITY (trak-til'i-ti) *n.* capacity of being drawn out at length.

TRACTION (trak'shun) *n.* act of drawing.

TRADE (trād) *n.* commerce; what one works at or deals in;—*v.t.* or *i.* to buy or sell; deal; traffic. [O.E. *tredan*, to step.]

TRADE-MARK (trād'märk) *n.* device used by manufacturers to identify their goods.

TRADE-PRICE (trād'prīs) *n.* price charged by wholesale dealers to retail traders.

TRADER (trā'der) *n.* one engaged in trade.

TRADESMAN (trādz'man) *n.* one who trades; a shopkeeper.

TRADE-UNION, TRADES-UNION (trādz'ūn-yun) *n.* a combination of workmen in a trade to maintain their rights.

TRADE-WIND (trād'wind) *n.* a periodical wind.

TRADITION (tra-dish'un) *n.* oral account transmitted from father to son. [L. (acc.) *traditionem*, fr. (part.) *traditus*, fr. *tradere*, to give up.]

TRADITIONAL (tra-dish'un-al) *a.* delivered by tradition.

TRADUCE (tra-dūs') *v.t.* to defame; slander; vilify. [L. *traducere*, fr. *trans*, across, and *ducere*, to lead.]

TRADUCER (tra-dū'ser) *n.* one who traduces; calumniator.

TRAFFIC (traf'ik) *n.* dealing for purposes of any kind; commerce; barter;—*v.t.* or *i.* to exchange; buy and sell; trade meanly. [F. *trafiquer* to traffic, fr. Late L. *vicare*, to exchange, fr. *vicis*, change.]

TRAFFICKED (traf'ikt) *pp.* of **TRAFFIC**.

TRAFFICKER (traf'i-ker) *n.* a trader.

TRAGEDIAN (tra-jē'di-an) *n.* an actor or writer of tragedies.

TRAGEDIENNE (tra-jē'di-en) *n.* a female tragic actress.

TRAGEDY (traj'e-di) *n.* a dramatic poem representing some action having a fatal issue; any sad or dreadful event. [L., fr. G. *tragodia*, a tragedy, literally a goat-song, because originally actors were dressed in goat-skins, fr. *tragos* a goat, and *odos*, a singer, fr. *aeidein*, to sing.]

TRAGICAL (traj'i-kal) *a.* relating to tragedy; fatal. Also **TRAGIC**. [event.

TRAGICALLY (traj'i-kal-i) *ad.* with a fatal

TRAIL (trāl) *v.t.* or *i.* to draw or be drawn along the ground;—*n.* a track; scent. [O.F. *trailler*, to tow a boat, fr. L. *trahere*, to draw.]

TRAIN (trān) *v.t.* to draw along; allure; break; exercise; educate; direct in growing;—*n.* tail of a gown; retinue; procession; line; series. [F. *trainer*, to draw through Late L., fr. L. *trahere*.]

TRAIN-BANDS (trān'bands) *n.pl.* militia.

TRAIN-OIL (trān'oil) *n.* oil from the fat of whales.

TRAIT (trā, trāt) *n.* stroke; line; touch; feature. [F. fr. L. (part.) *tractus*, fr. *trahere*, draw.]

TRAITOR (trā'ter) *n.* one who violates his allegiance or his trust. [O.F., fr. L. *traditor* fr. *tradere*, to deliver.]

TRAITOROUS (trā'tur-us) *a.* treacherous.

TRAITORESS (trā'tur-es) *n.* a female traitor.

TRAJECTION (tra-jek'shun) *n.* act of casting through.

TRAJECTORY (tra-jek'tu-ri) *n.* the orbit of a comet; a curve.

TRAM (tram) *n.* rail or track of a tram-road or tramway; shaft of a cart. [Scand. = a wooden doorstep.]

TRAMMEL (tram'el) *n.* a net; anything that confines or impedes; shackles; iron hook; —*v.t.* to confine; hamper; intercept. [O.F. *tramail*, a net, fr. L. *tres*, three, and *macula*, a mesh.]

TRAMONTANE (tra-mon'tān) *a.* being beyond the mountain. [F., fr. It., fr. L. *trans*, across, and stem *mont-* of *mons*, mountain.]

TRAMP (tramp) *v.t.* or *i.* to tread;—*n.* a foot journey; a vagrant. [M.E. Cf. Ger. *trampen*.]

TRAMPLE (tram'pl) *v.t.* to tread under foot. [Freq. of **TRAMP**.]

TRAM-ROAD (tram'rōd) *n.* a kind of railway for wagons. [cars.

TRAMWAY (tram'wā) *n.* a street railway for

TRANCE (trans) *n.* state of insensibility; ecstacy. [F. *transe*, fright, fr. L. *transire*, pass away.]

TRANQUIL (tran'kwil) *a.* quiet; calm; peaceful. [E., fr. L. *tranquillus*, at rest.]

TRANQUILLISE (trang'kwil-īz) *v.t.* to quiet; render calm; allay.

TRANQUILLITY (trang-kwil'i-ti) *n.* quietness; peaceable condition.

TRANQUILLY (trang'kwil-i) *ad.* peacefully; quietly.

TRANSACT (trans-akt') *v.t.* to do; perform; conduct;—*v.t.* to manage; do business. [L. (part.) *transactus*, fr. *transigere*, to complete, fr. *trans*, through, and *agere*, to do.]

TRANSACTION (trans-ak'shun) *n.* management; act; affair;—*pl.* reports of the proceedings of scientific associations.

TRANSACTOR (trans-ak'ter) *n.* one who transacts.

TRANSALPINE (trans-al'pin) *a.* being beyond the Alps in regard to Rome. [L., fr. *trans*, beyond, and *Alpinus*, of the Alps.]

TRANSATLANTIC (trans-at-lan'tik) *a.* being on the er side of the Atlantic. [L. *trans*, across.]oth

TRANSCEND (tran-send') *v.t.* or *i.* to rise above; surmount; surpass. [L., fr. *trans*, beyond, and *scandere*, climb.]

TRANSCENDENT (tran-sen'dent) *a.* surpassing; supreme.

TRANSCENDENTAL (tran-sen-den'tal) *a.* supereminent; beyond human knowledge or conception.

TRANSCENDENTALISM(tran-sen-den'tal-izm) *n.* a p i s ica system independent of inductiveo experience, and founded on *a priori* truths or principles.

TRANSCRIBE (tran-skrib') *v.t.* to write over again; copy. [L., fr. *trans*, across, and *scribere*, to write.]

TRANSCRIBER (tran-skri'ber) *n.* one who copies or transcribes. [original.

TRANSCRIPT (tran'skript) *n.* a copy from an

TRANSCRIPTION (tran-skrip'shun) *n.* the act of copying; copy.

TRANSEPT (tran'sept) *n.* the transverse part of a cruciform church. [L., fr. *trans*, across, and *septum*, an enclosure.]

TRANSFER (trans-fer') *v.t.* to remove from one place or person to another; convey. [L., fr. *trans*, across, and *ferre*, to bear.]

TRANSFER (trans'fer) *n.* removal; act of conveying to another; that which is conveyed.

TRANSFERABLE (trans-fer'a-bl) *a.* that may be conveyed. [transferring.

TRANSFERENCE (trans-fer'ens) *n.* act of

TRANSFIGURATION (trans-fig-ū-rā'shun) *n.* change of form or appearance.

TRANSFIGURE (trans-fig'ur) *v.t.* to change the external appearance of. [L. *transfigurare*, to change the figure, fr. *trans*, across, and *figura*, form.]

TRANSFIX (trans-fix') *v.t.* to pierce through. [L. *trans*, across, and (part.) *fixus*, fr. *figere*, to fasten.]

TRANSFLUENT (trans'flŏŏ-ent) *a.* flowing through. [L., fr. *trans*, across, and (part. stem) *fluent-*, fr. *fluere*, to flow.]

TRANSFORM (trans-form') *v.t.* to change the form; metamorphose. [L., fr. *trans*, over, and *formare*, to form.]

TRANSFORMATION (trans-for-mā'shun) *n.* change of form.

TRANSFUSE (trans-fūz') *v.t.* to pour into another. [L. *trans*, across, and (part.) *fusus*, of *fundere*, to pour out.]

TRANSFUSIBLE (trans-fū'zi-bl) *a.* that can be transfused.

TRANSFUSION (trans-fū'zhun) *n.* act of pouring from one into another.

TRANSGRESS (trans-gres') *v.t.* to pass beyond; break; violate;—*v.i.* to sin. [L. (part.) *transgressus*, fr. *transgredi*, to go across, fr. *trans*, across, and *gradi*, to pass.]

TRANSGRESSION (trans-gresh'un) *n.* violation of a law.

TRANSGRESSOR (trans-gres'er) *n.* one who breaks a law.

TRANSHIPMENT (tran-ship'ment) *n.* transferring from one ship to another.

TRANSIENT (tran'shent) *a.* passing; not lasting; fleeting; momentary. [L. (part. stem) *transient-*, fr. *trans*, beyond, and *ire*. go.]

TRANSIENTLY (tran'shent-li) *ad.* in passing; for a short time.

TRANSIENTNESS (tran'shent-nes) *n.* shortness of continuance.

TRANSIT (tran'sit) *n.* a passing as of goods through a country, or as a planet over the sun's disc. [L. *transitus*, a passing across, fr. *transire*, go over.]

TRANSITION (tran-sizh'un) *n.* a passage from one place, state, or subject to another; change.

TRANSITIONAL (tran-sizh'un-al) *a.* denoting transition.

TRANSITIVE (tran'si-tiv) *a.* expressing action passing from an agent to an object.

TRANSITORINESS (tran'si-tu-ri-nes) *n.* a passing with short continuance.

TRANSITORY (tran'si-tu-ri) *a.* continuing but a short time.

TRANSLATABLE (trans-lā'ta-bl) *a.* that may be translated.

TRANSLATE (trans-lāt') *v.t.* to remove; render into another language. [L. (part.) *translatus*, fr. *transferre*, to transfer.]

TRANSLATION (trans-lā'shun) *n.* a removal; that which is translated; a version.

TRANSLATOR (trans-lā'ter) *n.* one who translates.

TRANSLUCENT (trans-lŏŏ'sent) *a.* transmitting rays imperfectly. [L. (part. stem) *translucent-*, fr. *translucere*, shine through. Cf. LUCID.]

TRANSMARINE (trans-ma-rēn') *a.* lying beyond the sea. [L. *trans*, beyond, and *mare*, the sea.]

TRANSMIGRATE (trans'mi-grāt) *v.i.* to pass from one country or body to another. [L. *trans*, across, and *migrare*, to go.]

TRANSMIGRATION (trans-mi-grā'shun) *n.* a passing from one country or body to another.

TRANSMIGRATOR (trans'mi-grā-ter) *n.* one who transmigrates.

TRANSMIGRATORY (trans-mi'gra-tu-ri) *a.* passing from one place, state, or body to another.

TRANSMISSIBLE (trans-mis'i-bl) *a.* that may be transmitted. [L. *trans*, across, and (part.) *missus*, sent, fr. *mittere*.]

TRANSMISSION (trans-mish'un) *n.* act of sending from one place to another.

TRANSMISSIVE (trans-mis'iv) *a.* having power to transmit; derived.

TRANSMIT (trans-mit') *v.t.* to send from one to another. [L., fr. *trans*, across, and *mittere*, to send.]

TRANSMITTAL (trans-mit'al) *n.* transmission.

TRANSMUTABLE (trans-mū'ta-bl) *a.* that may be transmuted.

TRANSMUTATION (trans-mū-tā'shun) *n.* change into another substance.

TRANSMUTE (trans-mūt') *v.t.* to change into another substance or form. [L. *trans*, across, and *mutare*, to change.]

TRANSPARENCY (trans-pâr'en-si) *n.* the quality of being transparent; a picture on some material that can be seen through.

TRANSPARENT (trans-pâr'ent) *a.* that may be seen through distinctly; clear. [L., fr. *trans*, through, and *parere*, to appear.]

TRANSPIRABLE (tran-spir'a-bl) *a.* capable of being emitted through the pores.

TRANSPIRATION (tran-spi-rā'shun) *n.* act of passing through pores.

TRANSPIRATORY (tran-spir'a-tu-ri) *a.* pertaining to transpiration; serving to exhale.

TRANSPIRE (trans-pir') *v.t.* or *i.* to pass or exhale through the pores; emit; come to pass; become public. [L. *trans*, across, and *spirare*, to breathe.]

TRANSPLANT (trans-plànt') *v.t.* to remove and plant in another place. [F., fr. L. *trans*, and *plantare*, to plant. fr. *planta*, a plant.]

TRANSPLANTATION (trans-plàn-tā'shun) *n.* act of planting in another place.

TRANSPLANTER (trans-plàn'ter) *n.* one who transplants.

TRANSPLENDENCY (tran-splen'den-si) *n.* superior splendour.

TRANSPLENDENT (tran-splen'dent) *a.* resplendent in a high degree. [L. *trans*, through, and *splendere*, to shine.]

TRANSPORT (trans-pōrt) *n.* conveyance; carriage; a ship for carrying troops or stores; rapture; ecstacy;—(trans-pōrt') *v.t.* to carry from one place to another; carry into banishment; carry away with emotion or pleasure. [L., fr. *trans,* across, and *portare,* to carry.] [may be transported.

TRANSPORTABLE (trans-pōr'ta-bl) *a.* that

TRANSPORTATION (trans-pōr-tā'shun) *n.* act of conveying; banishment. [place.

TRANSPOSAL (trans-pō'zal) *n.* a changing of

TRANSPOSE (trans-pōz') *v.t.* to put in place of the other; change. [L. *trans,* across, and F. *poser,* to put, fr. L. *ponere,* to place.]

TRANSPOSITION (trans-pō-zish'un) *n.* change of places, words, or musical key.

TRANSPOSITIONAL (trans-pō-zish'un-al) *a.* pertaining to transposition.

TRANSUBSTANTIATE (tran-sub-stan'shi-āt) *v.t.* to change into another substance. [L. *trans,* across, and *substantia,* substance.]

TRANSUBSTANTIATION (tran-sub-stan-shi-ā'shun) *n.* a supposed change of the bread and wine in the eucharist into the body and blood of Christ.

TRANSUDE (tran-sūd') *v.t.* to pass through the pores. [L. *trans,* through, and *sudare,* to sweat.] [lying across.

TRANSVERSAL (trans-ver'sal) *a.* running or

TRANSVERSE (trans'vers) *n.* the longer axis of an ellipse;—(trans-vers') *a.* in a cross direction. [L., fr. *trans* across, and (part.) *versus,* fr. *vertere,* to turn.]

TRANSVERSELY (trans-vers'li) *ad.* in a cross direction.

TRAP (trap) (1) *n.* an instrument for snaring animals; ambush; stratagem;—*v.t.* or *i.* to catch in a trap; ensnare;—(2) *n.* an igneous rock;—(3) *v.t.* or *i.* adorn. [(1) O.E. *treppe.* (2) Scand. =a stair. (3) See TRAPPINGS.]

TRAPAN (tra-pan') *v.t.* to ensnare;—*n.* a snare. [O.F. *trappan* a snare, fr. O. H. Ger.]

TRAP-DOOR (trap'dōr) *n.* a door in a floor or roof which shuts like a trap.

TRAPEZE (tra-pēz') *n.* a swinging apparatus for acrobatic feats. See TRAPEZIUM.

TRAPEZIUM (tra-pē'zi-um) *n.* a plane figure contained under four right lines, of which no two are parallel. [G. *trapezion,* dim. of *trapeza,* a table, fr. *tetra* four and *pous podos,* a foot.]

TRAPPER (trap'er) *n.* one who sets traps to catch animals for their furs.

Trapezium.

TRAPPINGS (trap'ingz) *n.pl.* ornaments; external decorations. [F. *drap* fr. Late L. *drappus* cloth.]

TRASH (trash) *n.* any waste matter;—*v.t.* to lop or crop. [Scand.]

TRAVAIL (trav'āl) *v.i.* to toil; labour;—*n.* toil; labour; child-birth. [O.F., fr. Late L. *travaculum,* a shackle, fr. L. *trabs* a beam.]

TRAVEL (trav'el) *v.t.* or *i.* to walk; journey; pass from place to place; move or act;—*n.* journey; labour;—*pl.* account of a journey. [Variant of TRAVAIL.]

TRAVELLER (trav'el-er) *n.* one who travels.

TRAVERSABLE (trav'er-sa-bl) *a.* that may be traversed or denied.

TRAVERSE (trav'ers) *a.* lying across;—*v.t.* to cross; deny;—*n.* a denial. [L. *transversus* fr. *trans,* across, and (part.) *versus* fr. *vertere,* to turn.]

TRAVESTY (trav'es-ti) *n.* a burlesque translation; parody;—*v.t.* to turn into burlesque. [F. *travesti,* disguised, fr. L. *trans,* across, and *vestire,* to dress.]

TRAWL (trawl) *n.* a long bag-net for fishing in the deep sea;—*v.i.* to fish with this net. [O.F. *trauler,* to drag. Cf. TROLL.]

TRAWLER (traw'ler) *n.* one who, or vessel which, fishes with a trawl.

TRAY (trā) *n.* a salver for carrying dishes or serving tea, etc. [O.E. *trog,* a trough.]

TREACHEROUS (trech'er-us) *a.* faithless; perfidious.

TREACHERY (trech'er-i) *n.* violation of faith. [O.F. *tricherie,* fr. L. *tricae,* wiles.]

TREACLE (trē'kl) *n.* syrup from sugar; molasses. [O.F. *triacle,* fr. L. *theriacum,* fr. G. *theriaka* (*pharmaka*), antidotes against the bite of poisonous animals, fr. *therion,* a wild beast.]

TREAD (tred) *v.t.* or *i.* [*pret.* TROD; *pp.* TROD, TRODDEN] to set the foot; walk with measured step; copulate; crush; trample;—*n.* pressure with the foot; step. [O.E. *tredan.* Cf. Ger. *treten.*]

TREADLE (tred'l) *n.* the part of a loom which is moved by the foot. [See TREAD.]

TREASON (trē'zn) *n.* violation of allegiance; treachery; disloyalty. [O.F. *traison* =F. *trahison,* fr. *trahir,* fr. L. *tradere,* to betray.]

TREASONABLE (trē'zn-a-bl) *a.* partaking of treason.

TREASURE (trezh'ur) *n.* wealth accumulated; great abundance;—*v.t.* to lay up; hoard; value greatly. [O.F. *tresor* fr. L. *thesaurus,* fr. G. *thesauros.*]

TREASURER (trezh'ur-er) *n.* an officer who has charge of a treasury.

TREASURERSHIP (trezh'ur-er-ship) *n.* office of a treasurer.

TREASURE-TROVE (trezh'ur-trōv) *n.* money found in the earth of which the owner is unknown.

TREASURY (trezh'ur-i) *n.* a place where public money is kept; financial department of government.

TREAT (trēt) *v.t.* or *i.* to handle; negotiate; entertain; manage; use;—*n.* entertainment given. [O.F. *traiter,* fr. L. *tractare,* to handle, fr. (part.) *tractus,* fr. *trahere,* to draw.]

TREATISE (trē'tis) *n.* a written discourse; formal essay. [See TREAT.]

TREATMENT (trēt'ment) *n.* usage; management; behaviour; way of applying remedies.

TREATY (trē'ti) *n.* an agreement or compact between parties, usually states.

TREBLE (treb'l) *a.* threefold; playing or singing the treble;—*v.t.* or *i.* to make or become threefold;—*n.* highest part in music; the air. [O.F., fr. L. *triplus.*]

TREBLY (treb'li) *ad.* in a threefold number or quantity.

TREE (trē) *n.* the largest of the vegetable kind, consisting of a stem, roots, and branches. [O.E. *treow, treo.*]

TREFOIL (trē'foil, tref'oil) *n.* a three-leaved plant, as clover. [L. fr. *tres,* three, and *folium,* a leaf.]

TRELLIS (trel'is) *n.* a structure or lattice-work of iron. [F. *treillis,* fr. Low L. *trichila,* a bower.]

TREMBLE (trem'bl) *v.i.* to shake or quake; quiver. [F. *trembler,* fr. L. *tremulus,* fr. *tremere,* to shake.]

TREMBLER (trem'bler) *n.* one who trembles.

TREMBLING (trem'bling) *n.* act of shaking; quivering.

TREMENDOUS (tre-men'dus) *a.* awful; frightful; terrible. [L. *tremendus,* fr. *tremere,* to quake.]

TREMENDOUSLY (tre-men'dus-li) *ad.* in a manner to awaken terror.

TREMOR (trem'er, trē'mer) *n.* involuntary trembling. [L., fr. *tremere,* to tremble.]

TREMULOUS (trem'ū-lus) *a.* trembling; shaking. [trembling.

TREMULOUSNESS (trem'ū-lus-nes) *n.* act of

TRENCH (trensh) *v.t.* to cut or dig a ditch; fortify by digging;—*v.i.* to encroach;—*n.* a ditch; fosse. [O.F. *trencher* =F. *trancher,* to cut, fr. L. *truncare.*]

TRENCHANT (tren'shant) a. cutting; severe. [See TRENCH.]

TRENCHER (tren'sher) (1) n. one that digs a trench;—(2) n. a wooden plate. [(1) See TRENCH. (2) O.F. trenchoir, fr. trencher, cut.] [eater.

TRENCHERMAN (tren'sher-man) n. a great

TREPAN (tre-pan') n. a circular saw for perforating the skull;—v.t. to cut with a trepan. [F. fr. Late L. trepanum, fr. G. turpanon, fr. trupa, a hole.]

TREPIDATION (trep-i-dā'shun) n. confused alarm; trembling with fear. [L. trepidus, trembling.]

TRESPASS (tres'pas) v.i. to enter on another's property without right; intrude; injure; sin;—n. act of trespassing; injury; sin. [O.F. trespasser = F. trépasser, fr. L. trans, across, and passus, a step.]

TRESPASSER (tres'pas-er) n. one who trespasses; a sinner.

TRESS (tres) n. a lock of hair;—pl. ringlets. [F. tresse, fr. Low L. trica, fr. G. tricha, in three parts.]

TRESTLE (tres'l) n. a frame to support anything. [O.F. trestel = F. tréteau, perh. fr. L. transtrum, a transom.]

TRET (tret) n. an allowance for waste. [F. traite, a draught, fr. L. (part.) tractus, fr. trahere, to draw.]

TRIABLE (trī'a-bl) a. that may be tried. [See TRY.]

TRIAD (trī'ad) n. the union of three. [L. stem triad-, fr. trias, fr. G. trias, a triad, fr. treis, three.]

TRIAL (trī'al) n. attempt; examination by a test; judicial examination; suffering; temptation. [F. trier, cull, fr. L. terere, tritus, rub.]

TRIANGLE (trī-ang'gl, trī'ang-gl) n. a figure of three angles. [F., fr. L. triangulum, fr. tres, three, and angulus, an angle.]

TRIANGULAR (trī-ang'gū-lar) a. having three angles.

TRIBAL (trī'bal) a. belonging to a tribe.

TRIBE (trīb) n. a family; race; class. [L. tribus, orig. one of the three divisions of the Roman people, fr. tres, three.]

TRIBULATION (trib-ū-lā'shun) n. a great affliction; distress. [F., fr. L. (acc.) tribulationem, fr. (part.) tribulatus, fr. tribulare, to thrash, fr. tribulum, a sledge for rubbing out corn, fr. terere, to rub.]

TRIBUNAL (trī-bū'nal) n. a court of justice.

TRIBUNE (trib'ūn, trī'būn) n. a Roman magistrate; a platform. [L. tribunus, properly chief of a tribe, fr. tribus, tribe.]

TRIBUTARY (trib'ū-ta-ri) a. subject to tribute; contributing;—n. one subject to tribute. [L. tributarius.]

TRIBUTE (trib'ūt) n. a tax on a conquered country; personal contribution; acknowledgment paid. [L. tributum, tribute, fr. (part.) tributus, fr. tribuere, to grant, pay.]

TRICE (trīs) n. a short time; an instant. [Perh. fr. THRICE, or Fr. Sp. tris, a crack.]

TRICE (trīs) v.t. to haul and tie up.

TRICENTENARY (trī-sen'te-na-ri) a. comprising or happening in three hundred years;—n. a space or commemoration of three hundred years. [L. trecenti, three hundred.]

TRICEPS (trī'seps) n. a muscle with three heads. [L., fr. tres, three, and caput, head.]

TRICK (trik) (1) n. an artifice for the purpose of deception; clever contrivance to amuse, puzzle, or annoy; habit or manner;—v.t. to cheat; deceive;—(2) v.t. decorate; dress. [(1) Fr. O.F. tricher, cheat, fr. L. tricæ, wiles. (2) Celt.]

TRICKERY (trik'er-i) n. act or practice of playing tricks.

TRICKISH (trik'ish) a. somewhat tricky.

TRICKISHNESS (trik'ish-nes) n. state of being trickish.

TRICKLE (trik'l) v.i. to flow or drop gently. [M.E. triklen, for striklen, O.E. strican, to flow.]

TRICKSTER (trik'ster) n. one who plays tricks.

TRICKY (trik'i) a. given to tricks; artful; roguish. Also **TRICKSOME**.

TRICOLOURED (trī'kul-urd) a. of three colours. [F., fr. L. tres, three, and color, colour.]

TRICUSPID (trī-kus'pid) a. having three points. [L., fr. tres, three, and stem cuspid-, fr. cuspis, a point.]

TRIDENT (trī'dent) n. a sceptre with three prongs. [F., fr. L. (part. stem) trident-, fr. tres, three, and dens, a tooth.]

TRIDENTATE (trī-den'tāt) a. having three prongs.

TRIENNIAL (trī-en'i-al) a. being every third year. [L. triennium, fr. tres, three, and annus, a year.]

TRIENNIALLY (trī-en'i-al-i) ad. once in three years.

TRIER (trī'er) n. one who tries.

TRIFLE (trī'fl) n. a thing of little value or importance; a dish of sponge cakes and syllabub;—v.t. or i. to spend; waste; act or talk with levity. [O.F. trufle, dim. of truffe, a jest.]

TRIFLER (trī'fler) n. one who trifles.

TRIFLING (trī'fling) a. of little value or importance; trivial.

TRIFLINGLY (trī'fling-li) ad. without importance; with levity.

TRIFOLIATE (trī-fō'li-at) a. having three leaves. [L. tres, three, and folium, leaf.]

TRIFORM (trī'form) a. having a triple shape. [L., fr. tres, and forma, form.]

TRIFURCATE (trī-fur'kat) a. having three forks or prongs. [L., fr. tres, three, and furca, a fork.]

TRIG (trig) (1) v.t. to stop or fasten a wheel;—(2) a. trim; neat. [(1) D. (2) Scand.]

TRIGGER (trig'er) n. a catch of a wheel or gun. [D.]

TRIGLYPH (trī'glif, trig'lif) n. an ornament in Doric columns. [L. triglyphus, G. triglyphos, fr. treis, three, and glyphein, to carve.]

TRIGONAL (trig'u-nal) a. triangular.

TRIGONOMETRY (trig-u-nom'e-tri) n. the measuring of triangles. [G. trigonon, a triangle, and metron, a measure.]

TRIHEDRAL (trī-hē'dral) a. having three equal sides.

TRIHEDRON (trī-hē'drun) n. a figure having three equal sides. [G., fr. treis, three, and hedra, a base.]

TRILATERAL (trī-lat'e-ral) a. having three sides. [L. fr. tres, three, and stem later-, fr. latus, a side.]

Trihedron.

TRILITERAL (trī-lit'e-ral) a. consisting of three letters. [L. tres, three, and litera, letter.]

TRILL (tril) (1) n. a shaking of the voice;—v.t. or i. to quaver or shake;—(2) v.t. or i. flow in drops. [(1) It. trillo, shake. (2) Scand.]

TRILLION (tril'yun) n. a million of millions of millions. [Fr. trimillion.]

TRILOGY (tril'u-ji) n. a series of three dramas on one historical subject. [G., fr. treis, three, and logia, speech, fr. legein, to say.]

TRIM (trim) a. neat; in good order; nice;—v.t. or i. to put in order; clip; dress; arrange for sailing; fluctuate between parties;—n. dress; condition. [O.E. trum.]

TRIMLY (trim'li) ad. nicely; neatly.

TRIMMER (trim'er) n. one who trims; a political time-server.

TRIMMING (trim'ing) n. that which serves to trim;—pl. ornamental additions to a garment, dish, etc.

TRIMNESS (trim'nes) n. neatness.

Fāte, fär, ado; mē, her; mīne; nōte; tūne; mōŏn.

TRINAL (trī'nạl) a. threefold. [L. trini, three each.]
TRINITARIAN (trin-i-tā'ri-ạn) n. pertaining to the Trinity;—n. one who believes in the Trinity.
TRINITY (trin'i-ti) n. the union of three persons in one God. [L. (acc.) trinitatem, fr. trini, three each. fr. tres, three.]
TRINKET (tring'ket) n. a small ornament of little value. [Perh. fr. O.F. trenquer- a prob. form of trencher- to cut.]
TRINOMIAL (trī-nō'mi-ạl) a. consisting of three parts or terms. [L., fr. tres, three, and nomen, a name.]
TRIO (trē'ō, trī'ō) n. a piece of music for three performers. [It., fr. L. tres, tria, three.]
TRIP (trip) v.i. to step lightly; stumble;—v.t. to cause to trip;—n. a stumble; error; an excursion. [Teut.]
TRIPARTITE (trip'är-tīt, trī-pär'tit) a. divided into three parts. [L., fr. tres, three, and (part.) partitus, fr. partiri, to divide.]
TRIPARTITION (trī-pär-tish'un, trip-ạr-tish'un) n. a division by three, or into three parts.
TRIPE (trip) n. the intestines of ruminating animals, used as food. [Celt.]
TRIPEDAL (trip'e-dạl), trī-pē'dạl) a. having three e . [L., fr. tres, three, and pes, pedis, a foot.]et
TRIPETALOUS (trī-pet'ạ-lụs) a. having three petals or flower-leaves. [G., fr. treis, three, and petalon, a leaf.]
TRIPHTHONG (trif'thong, trip'thong) n. a union of three vowels in a syllable. [G., fr. treis, three, and phthongos, the voice, a sound.]
TRIPHTHONGAL trif-thong'gạl, trip-thong'gạl) a. pertaining to a triphthong.
TRIPLE (trip'l) a. treble; threefold;—v.t. to make threefold. [F., fr. L. triplus, threefold.]
TRIPLET (trip'let) n. three verses that rhyme; three of a kind.
TRIPLICATE (trip'li-kāt) a. threefold;—n. a third copy or thing. [L. (part.) triplicatus, fr. triplicare, to treble.]
TRIPLICATION (trip-li-kā'shun) n. act of making threefold. [threefold.
TRIPLICITY (tri-plis'i-ti) n. state of being
TRIPOD (trī'pod) n. anything standing on three feet. [G. treis, thrice, and stem pod-, of pous, a foot.]
TRISECT (trī-sekt') v.t. to cut into three equal parts. [L., fr. tres, three, and (part.) sectus, fr. secare, to cut.]
TRISECTION (tri-sek'shun) n. a division into three parts.
TRISYLLABIC (tri-si-lab'ik) a. consisting of three syllables.
TRISYLLABLE (trī-sil'ạ-bl) n. a word composed of three syllables. [G., fr. treis, thrice, and sullabe, a syllable.]
TRITE (trit) a. worn out; stale; hackneyed. [It. trito, fr. L. (part.) tritus, fr. terere, to rub.]
TRITELY (trit'li) ad. in a trite manner.
TRITENESS (trit'nes) n. a state of being trite.
TRITHEIST (trī'thē-ist) n. one who believes that the Trinity are three distinct Gods. [Pref. tri-, three, and THEIST.]
TRITON (trī'tun) n. a sea-demigod. [G. Triton.]
TRITURATE (trit'ū-rāt) v.t. to rub or grind to a fine powder. [L. (part.) trituratus, fr. triturare, fr. terere, to rub.]
TRITURATION (trit-ū-rā'shun) n. act of grinding to powder.
TRIUMPH (trī'umf) n. joy or pomp for victory or success;—v.t. to rejoice at success; obtain victory; exult over. [L. triumphus.]
TRIUMPHAL (trī-um'fạl) a. pertaining to or used in triumph.
TRIUMPHANT (trī-um'fạnt) a. celebrating victory; victorious. [triumph.
TRIUMPHANTLY (trī-um'fạnt-li) ad. with
TRIUMVIR (trī-um'vir) n. one of three men united in office. [L. gen. pl. of tres, three, and vir, a man.]

TRIUMVIRAL (trī-um'vi-rạl) a. pertaining to a triumvirate. [by three men.
TRIUMVIRATE (trī-um'vi-rạt) n. government
TRIUNE (trī'ūn) a. three in one. [L. tri-, three, and unus one.]
TRIVET (triv'et) n. a movable frame in a kitchen grate for hanging kettles on. [O.E. trevet, fr. L. stem triped- fr. tripes- three-footed.]
TRIVIAL (triv'i-ạl) a. trifling; light. [L. trivialis belonging to cross-roads, fr. tres, three, and via, way.]
TRIVIALITY (triv-i-al'i-ti) n. a trifling thing; trifling behaviour.
TROCAR (trō'kär) n. a surgical instrument to tap dropsical persons. [F. trois, three and carre, side, face.]
TROCHEE (trō'kē) n. a metrical foot, consisting of an accented and an unaccented syllable. [L. trochalus, fr. G. trochaios, running, fr. trechein, to run.]
TROD (trod) pret. and pp. of **TREAD.**
TRODDEN (trod'n) pp. of **TREAD.**
TROLL (trōl) v.t. to roll; sing loudly or freely; —v.i. to run about; fish by moving the bait quickly. [O.F. troller = F. trôler- to stroll. Cf. Ger. trollen, to roll.]
TROLLOP (trol'up) n. a slattern. [Fr. TROLL to roll.]
TROMBONE (trom'bōn) n. a brass wind instrument. [It., fr. tromba, a trumpet.]
TROMP (tromp) n. a blowing machine used in furnaces. [F.]
TROOP (trōóp) n. a number of people; company;—vl. soldiers collectively;—v.i. to gather in crowds; march in a company or in haste. [F. troupe; perh. fr. L. turba, a crowd.]
TROOPER (trōó'per) n. a horse-soldier.
TROPE (trōp) n. a figure of speech. [F. fr. L. tropus, fr. G. tropos, fr. trepein. to turn.]
TROPHIED (trō'fid) a. adorned with trophies.
TROPHY (trō'fi) n. a memorial of victory in battle. [F. trophée, fr. L. tropœum, fr. G. tropaion, monument of an enemy's defeat, fr. trepein, to turn.]
TROPIC (trop'ik) n. one of the two circles that bound the sun's declination north and south from the equator; one of two corresponding circles in the terrestrial globe;—vl. the regions lying between these. [L. tropicus. fr. G. tropikos. fr. trepein, to turn.]
TROPICAL (trop'i-kạl) a. incident to or between the tropics.
TROT (trot) v.i. to move in a trot;—n. a high pace of a horse. [O.F. troter fr. Late L. trotare, to go.]
TROTH (trōth) n. faith; fidelity. [Variant of TRUTH; O.E. treowth.]
TROUBLE (trub'l) v.t. to annoy; busy or engage overmuch;—n. that which annoys, disturbs, or affects. [O.F. tourbler = F. troubler fr. Late L. turbulare, fr. L. turbare to disturb, fr. turba, crowd.]
TROUBLER (trub'ler) n. one who troubles; disturber.
TROUBLESOME (trub'l-sum) a. giving trouble; annoying; wearisome; importunate.
TROUBLOUS (trub'lus) a. full of disorder; tumultuous.
TROUGH (trof) n. a long, hollow vessel; anything hollowed out. [O.E. trog troh.]
TROUNCE (trouns) v.t. to beat severely. [O.F. troncer to cut fr. trons a truncheon, fr. L. truncus a tree-trunk.]
TROUPE (trōóp) n. a company of players or performers. [F. Cf. TROOP.]
TROUSERS (trou'zers) n. loose pantaloons. Also written **TROWSERS.** [F. trousses, breeches, fr. O.F. trousser to pack. Cf. TRUSS.]
TROUSSEAU (trōó-sō') n. the lighter equipments of a bride. [F., dim. of trousse, a bundle.]

TROUT (trout) *n.* a fresh-water fish. [O.E. *truht*, fr. L. *tructa* fr. G. *troktes* a nibbler.]

TROVER (trō'vẹr) *n.* an action for goods found and refused to the owner. [O.F. *trover* = F. *trouver* to find, fr. Late L. *tropare* to compose.] [*treowian*, to trust.]

TROW (trō) *v.i.* to suppose or think. [O.E.

TROWEL (trou'el) *n.* a tool for laying bricks and stones in mortar. [O.F. *truele* fr. L. *trulla*, dim. of *trua*, a ladle.]

TROY-WEIGHT (troi'wāt) *n.* twelve ounces to the pound. [Fr. *Troyes* in France, where it was first adopted.]

TRUANT (trōō'ạnt) *a.* idle: wandering from duty;—*n.* one who absents himself from school or other duty. [F. *truand* a beggar, fr. Celt.]

TRUCE (trōōs) *n.* a temporary peace: brief quiet. [O.E. *treow* promise.]

TRUCK (truk) (1) *v.t.* or *i.* to barter;—*n* exchange of goods;—(2) *n.* a wheel; low cart; cap at the top of a mast. [(1) F. *troquer.* (2) L. *trochus* fr. G. *trochos* a wheel fr. *trechein* to run.]

TRUCKAGE (truk'ij) *n.* the practice of bartering. [See **TRUCK** (1).]

TRUCKLE (truk'l) *n.* a small wheel;—*v.i.* to yield obsequiously. [Dim. of **TRUCK** (2).]

TRUCKLE-BED (truk'l-bed) *n.* a bed that runs on wheels.

TRUCK-SYSTEM (truk'sis-tem) *n.* practice of paying wages in goods instead of cash. [See **TRUCK** (1).]

TRUCULENCE (truk'ū-lens) *n.* savage ferocity.

TRUCULENT (truk'ū-lent) *a.* fierce; cruel. [L. *truculentus* fr. *trux trucis* wild fierce.]

TRUDGE (truj) *v.i.* to travel on foot; travel with labour. [F. *trucher* to beg idly; or Scand.]

TRUE (trōō) *a.* agreeing with fact: real; actual; trusty; right; rightful. [O.E. *treove*, faithful. Cf. Ger. *treu*.]

TRUFFLE (truf'l) *n.* a kind of mushroom. [O.F., F. *truffe* fr. L. *tuber.*] [evident truth.

TRUISM (trōō'izm) *n.* an undoubted or self-

TRULY (trōō'li) *ad.* certainly; really.

TRUMP (trump) (1` *n.* a winning card;—*v.t.* or *i.* to take with a trump;—(2) *n.* a trumpet: —(3) *v.t.* to devise; forge. [(1) F. *triomphe* a card-game, a card in it, fr. L. *triumphus* triumph. (2) F. *trompe.* Cf. Ger. *Tromme.* E. **DRUM.** (3) F. *tromper* to deceive.]

TRUMPERY (trum'pẹr-i) *a.* empty talk; trifles.

TRUMPET (trum'pet) *n.* a wind instrument;— *v.t.* to proclaim by trumpet; sound the praises of. [F. *trompette.* dim. of *trompe.* a horn.]

TRUMPETER (trum'pe-tẹr) *n.* one who sounds a trumpet; a kind of pigeon.

TRUNCATE (trung'kāt) *v.t.* to cut off; lop; maim. [L. (part.) *truncatus* fr. *truncare* fr. *truncus*, a stump.]

TRUNCATED (trung'kā-ted) *a.* cut off short.

TRUNCATION (trung-kā'shun) *n.* the act of lopping.

TRUNCHEON (trun'shun) *n.* a short staff; a club;—*v.t.* to beat. [O.F. *tronçon* a thick stick, fr. *tronc.* a trunk. Cf. **TRUNK.**]

TRUNDLE (trun'dl) *v.i.* to roll on little wheels;—*n.* a little wheel; a low cart. [M.E. *trondeler.* to roll.]

TRUNK (trungk) (1) *n.* stem of a tree; body of an animal; a long tube: chest of clothes: —(2) *n.* the proboscis of an elephant. [(1) F. *tronc* fr. L. *truncus* maimed. (2) Orig. *trump* fr. F. *trompe.* a trumpet.]

Trunk-hose.

TRUNK-HOSE (trungk'hōz) *n.* full breeches extending from the waist to the middle of the thigh.

TRUNK-LINE (trungk'līn) *n.* main line of a railway.

TRUSS (trus) *n.* a bandage for ruptures; bundle of hay;—*v.t.* to pack or bind close. [O.F. *trosser* to pack up fr. (part.) *torṭus*, fr. *torquere*, to twist.]

TRUST (trust) *n.* confidence: reliance on; credit; charge; something entrusted;—*a.* held in trust;—*v.t.* to sell on credit; rely on: —*v.i.* to believe; expect. [Scand.]

TRUSTEE (trus-tē') *n.* one entrusted with anything. [trustee.

TRUSTEESHIP (trus-tē'ship) *n.* office of a

TRUSTER (trus'tẹr) *n.* one who trusts; one who executes a trust.

TRUSTILY (trus'ti-li) *ad.* faithfully; honestly.

TRUSTINESS (trus'ti-nes) *n.* fidelity; honesty.

TRUSTWORTHY (trust'wur-ṭhi) *a.* worthy of trust or confidence.

TRUSTY (trus'ti) *a.* worthy of trust.

TRUTH (trōōth) *n.* conformity to reality or fact; fidelity; a true statement or principle; veracity. [O.E. *treowthu*, fr. *treowe* true.]

TRUTHFUL (trōōth'fool) *a.* full of truth.

TRUTHLESS (trōōth'les) *a.* destitute of truth.

TRY (trī) *v.t.* to test; sift; examine judicially; experience; use as means;—*v.i.* to endeavour. [F. *trier.* fr. L. *terere*, to rub.]

TRYST (trist) *n.* an appointment to meet: place of meeting. [Variant of **TRUST.**]

TUB (tub) *n.* an open wooden vessel. [D.]

TUBE (tūb) *n.* a long. hollow pipe or cylinder. [F., fr. L. *tubus.*]

TUBER (tū'bẹr) *n.* a fleshy underground root, as the potato. [L. a hump- knob. Cf. *tumere*, to swell.]

TUBERCLE (tū'bẹr-kl) *n.* a small pimple. [L. *tuberculum*, dim. of *tuber.*]

TUBERCULOUS (tū-bẹr'kū-lus) *a.* full of pimples. Also **TUBERCULAR.**

TUBEROSE (tū'be-rōs) *n.* a plant with a tuberous root. [See **TUBER.**]

TUBEROUS (tū'be-rus) *a.* full of knobs or tubers.

TUBULAR (tū'bū-lạr) *a.* resembling or consisting of a pipe. Also **TUBULOUS.** [See **TUBE.**]

TUBULE (tū'būl) *n.* a small tube.

TUCK (tuk) (1) *n.* a long narrow sword;—(2) *n.* a fold in dress;—*v.t.* to thrust in or together; fold. [(1) O.F. *estoc*, a rapier (2) O.E. *tucian* to pull, fr. Low Ger. *tucken.* to pull, draw up.]

TUCKER (tuk'ẹr) *n.* a piece of dress for covering the breast.

TUESDAY (tūz'dā) *n.* third day of the week. [O.E. *Tiwesdœg* fr. *Tiw.* the god of war. and *dœg.* Cf. Ger. *Dienstag*; L. *dies Martis.*]

TUFT (tuft) *n.* a cluster of grass, etc.;—*v.t.* to separate into tufts; adorn with tufts. [F. *touffe*, fr. Teut.]

TUFTED (tuf'ted) *a.* growing in tufts. Also **TUFTY.**

TUG (tug) *v.t.* and *i.* to pull with effort;—*n.* a pulling with force. [Scand. = a rope.]

TUITION (tū-ish-un) *n.* guardianship; instruction; price of teaching. [F. fr. L. (acc.) *tuitionem*, fr. (part.) *tuitus.* fr. *tueri*, to watch.]

TULIP (tū'lip) *n.* a plant and flower. [M.F. *tulippe*, fr. It. *tulipano.* fr. Turk., fr. Per. = turban.]

TULLE (tōōl) *n.* a kind of lace or open network. [F., so called fr. *Tulle*, in France, where it was first made.]

TUMBLE (tum'bl) *v.i.* to fall down; roll about;—*v.t.* to throw headlong; turn over; throw about; *n.* a fall with rolling. [O.E. *tumpian*, to turn heels over heads.]

TUMBLER (tum'blẹr) *n.* one who tumbles; a large drinking-glass; a kind of pigeon.

TUMBRIL, TUMBREL (tum'bril, tum'brel) *n.* a ducking-stool; a cart with two wheels used by artillery forces. [O.F. *tomberel* = F. *tombereau*, fr. *tomber*, to fall over.]

TUMEFACTION (tū-me-fak'shun) *n.* a swelling; tumour.

TUMEFY (tū'me-fī) *v.t.* or *i.* to swell; rise in a tumour. [L., fr. *tumere*, to swell, and *facere*, to make.]

TUMID (tū'mid) *a.* swelled; distended; inflated; bombastic. [L. *tumidus*, fr. *tumere*, to swell.]

TUMOUR (tū'mur) *n.* a morbid swelling. Also written **TUMOR**. [L. *tumor*, fr. *tumere*, to swell.]

TUMP (tump) *v.t.* to heap earth round a plant; —*n.* a little hillock. [Celt.]

TUMULOUS (tū'mŭ-lus) *a.* full of heaps or hillocks. Also **TUMULOSE**.

TUMULT (tū'mult) *n.* wild commotion; uproar. [L. *tumultus*, fr. *tumere*, to swell.]

TUMULTUOUS (tū-mul'tū-us) *a.* conducted with tumult; disorderly; turbulent. Also **TUMULTUARY**.

TUN (tun) *n.* a large cask; a liquid measure equal to 252 gallons;—*v.t.* to put in a cask. [O.E. *tunne*.] [tune.

TUNABLE (tū'na-bl) *a.* that may be put in

TUNE (tūn) *n.* a series of musical notes; melody; air; harmonious arrangement; right disposition or humour;—*v.t.* to put in a state for harmonious sounds. [A.F. *tun*, fr. L. *tonus*, fr. G. *tonos*, a tone. Doublet of **TONE**.]

TUNER (tū'ner) *n.* one who tunes musical instruments.

TUNEFUL (tūn'fool) *a.* harmonious.

TUNIC (tū'nik) *n.* a kind of waistcoat; a membrane. [O.F. *tunique*, fr. L. *tunica*.]

TUNNEL (tun'el) *n.* a pipe for pouring liquor into vessels; a passage cut through a hill or under a river;—*v.t.* to make a passage through. [O.F. *tonnel* =*tonneau*, a pipe.]

TUNNY (tun'i) *n.* a very large fish of the mackerel family. [L. *thunnus*, fr. G. *thunein*, to dart along.]

TUP (tup) *n.* a ram. [Scand.]

TURBAN (tur'ban) *n.* a head-dress. [M.F. *turbant*, fr. Pg., fr. Per.]

TURBID (tur'bid) *a.* muddy; not clear. [L. *turbidus*, fr. *turba*, tumult.]

TURBIDNESS (tur'bid-nes) *n.* muddiness.

TURBOT (tur'but) *n.* a round, flat fish. [F., fr. L. *turbo*, a spinning-top.]

TURBULENCE (tur'bū-lens) *n.* tumult; confusion.

TURBULENT (tur'bū-lent) *a.* tumultuous; disorderly. [F., fr. L. *turbulentus*, fr. *turba*, disorder.]

TUREEN (tu-rēn') *n.* a large dish for serving soup at table. [F. *terrine*, fr. L. *terra*, earth.]

TURF (turf) *n.* a mass of earth filled with roots; sod; peat;—*v.t.* to cover with turf. [O.E. *turf*.]

TURFY (tur'fi) *a.* full of turf.

TURGENT (tur'jent) *a.* swelling; tumid. [L. (part. stem) *turgent-*, fr. *turgere*, to swell.]

TURGESCENCE (tur-jes'ens) *n.* state of being swelled.

TURGID (tur'jid) *a.* tumid; bombastic. [L. *turgidus*, swollen, fr. *turgere*, to swell.]

TURGIDITY (tur-jid'i-ti) *n.* a swelled state; tumidness; bombast.

TURKEY (tur'ki) *n.* a large fowl, a native of America;—*pl.* **TURKEYS**. [So called because it was believed to have come originally from Turkey.]

TURKISH-BATH (tur'kish-bath) *n.* a hot air sweating bath.

TURKOIS (tur-kois') *n.* a bluish gem. Also written **TURQUOISE**. [O.F.; first brought from Persia through *Turkey*.]

TURMERIC (tur'me-rik) *n.* an Indian plant used as a dye and as a chemical test. [Etym. doubtful.]

TURMOIL (tur-moil') *n.* great stir; trouble;— (tur-moil') *v.t.* or *i.* to harass; be disquieted. [Etym. doubtful.]

TURN (turn) *v.t.* or *i.* to move or go round; hinge; convert; shape; alter; divert;— *n.* act of moving round; a winding; change; brief walk; form; manner; good or bad act. [O.E. *tyrnan*, turn. Cf. Ger. *turnen*; F *tourner*; L. *tornus*, a lathe; G. *tornos*, a tool for drawing circles.]

TURNCOAT (turn'kōt) *n.* one who changes sides or principles.

TURNER (tur'ner) *n.* one who forms articles with a lathe; a kind of pigeon.

TURNERY (tur'ner-i) *n.* the art of forming by a lathe; things so formed.

TURNIP (tur'nip) *n.* an esculent root. [E. *turn*, something round, and O.E. *næp*, a turnip.]

TURNKEY (turn'kē) *n.* one who keeps the keys of a prison.

TURNPIKE (turn'pīk) *n.* a toll-gate; a road on which are turnpikes;—*v.t.* to form a turnpike.

TURNSOLE (turn'sōl) *n.* a very fragrant plant; heliotrope. [F., fr. *tourner*, to turn, and *sol*, the sun.]

TURNSTILE (turn'stīl) *n.* a revolving frame in a footpath.

TURPENTINE (tur'pen-tīn) *n.* a resinous juice from pine-trees. [O.F. *turpentine*, fr. L. *terebinthina* (*resina*), resin of the terebinth, fr. G. *terebinthos*, the terebinth-tree.]

TURPITUDE (tur'pi-tūd) *n.* baseness of principle or conduct. [L., fr. *turpis*, foul, base.]

TURRET (tur'et) *n.* a small tower. [M.F. *tourette* = F. *tourelle*, fr. L. *turris*, a tower.]

TURRETED (tur'e-ted) *a.* furnished with a turret; formed like a tower.

TURTLE (tur'tl) (1) *n.* a dove;—(2) *n.* a seatortoise. [(1) O.E., fr. L. *turtur*. Cf. Ger. *Turtel*; F. *tourterelle*. (2) Corruption of Pg. *tartaruga*, or Sp. *tortuga*. Cf. **TORTOISE**.]

TURTLE-DOVE (tur'tl-duv) *n.* a dove or pigeon.

TURTLE-SOUP (tur'tl-sōōp) *n.* soup made from the flesh of the turtle. [See **TURTLE** (2).]

TUSCAN (tus'kan) *a.* noting the oldest and simplest order of architecture; Doric. [Pert. to *Tuscany*, in Italy.]

TUSH (tush) *inter.* an expression of impatience or contempt.

TUSK (tusk) *n.* a long pointed tooth; a fish of the cod family. [O.E. *tusc*, *tux*.]

TUTELAGE (tū'te-lij) *n.* guardianship; protection; care. [L. *tutela*, fr. *tutari*, to guard, fr. *tueri*, to watch.]

TUTELARY (tū'te-la-ri) *a.* guarding; protecting.

TUTOR (tū'ter) *n.* one who instructs;—*v.t.* to instruct. [L., fr. *tueri*, to watch.]

TUTORAGE (tū'tur-ij) *n.* guardianship.

TUTORESS (tū'tur-es) *n.* a female instructor.

TUTORIAL (tū-tō'ri-al) *a.* belonging to, or exercised by, a tutor.

TWADDLE (twod'l) *v.i.* to prate;—*n.* silly talk. [For *twattle*, a variant of **TATTLE**.]

TWAIN (twān) *a.* two. [O.E. *twegen*.]

TWANG (twang) *v.t.* or *i.* to strike or sound with a quick, sharp noise;—*n.* a sharp, quick sound. [Same as **TANG**.]

TWEAK (twēk) *v.t.* to twitch;—*n.* a pinch. [O.E. *twiccian*, a variant of **TWITCH**.]

TWEED (twēd) *n.* a twilled woollen stuff;— *a.* made of tweed. [Fr. a mistaken reading of *tweel*, or **TWILL**.]

TWEEDLE (twē'dl) *v.t.* to handle lightly. [Etym. doubtful.]

TWEEZERS (twē'zers) *n.pl.* small nippers or pincers. [O.E. *tweeze*, *tweese*, a box for instruments; conn. with F. *étui*.]

TWELFTH (twelfth) *a.* the ordinal of twelve. [O.E. *twelfta*.]

TWELVE (twelv) *a.* two and ten. [O.E. *twelf*. Cf. Ger. *zwölf*.]

TWELVEMONTH (twelv'munth) *n.* a year.

TWENTIETH (twen'ti-eth) *a.* the ordinal of twenty.

TWENTY (twen'ti) *a.* twice ten. [O.E. *twentig*, fr. *twen*, *twegen*, two, and suffix *-tig* ten.]

TWICE (twis) *ad.* two times; doubly. [O.E. *twiges*, for *twiwa*.]

TWIG (twig) *n.* a small shoot or branch. [O.E. *twig*. Cf. Ger. *Zweig*.]

TWIGGY (twig'i) *a.* abounding in twigs.

TWILIGHT (twi'lit) *n.* light after sunset and before sunrise. [O.E. *twi*, double between, and LIGHT.]

TWILL (twil) *v.t.* to weave in diagonal ribs;— *n.* a ribbed textile fabric. [Low Ger. *twillen*, to double.]

TWIN (twin) *n.* one of two produced at a birth;—*a.* being one of two. [O.E. *getwinnas*, twins, fr. *twi*, two.]

TWINE (twin) *v.t.* or *i.* to twist; wrap closely round;—*n.* strong twisted thread; a twist. [O.E. *twin*, a double thread.]

TWINGE (twinj) *v.i.* to feel sharp pain;—*n.* a darting pain. [M.E. *twingen*, press. Cf. Ger. *zwingen*, to constrain.]

TWINKLE (twing'kl) *v.i.* to shine with a trembling, sparkling light;—*n.* a quick motion of the eye; instant. [O.E. *twinclian*.] [instant.

TWINKLING (twing'kling) *n.* a sparkling; an

TWIRL (twirl) *v.t.* to move or twirl round;— *n.* a quick turn. [O.E. *thweran*, to stir.]

TWIST (twist) *v.t.* to wind, as one thread round another; turn from the true form or meaning; insinuate;—*n.* a thread; cord; manner of twisting; a kind of tobacco. [O.E. =a rope, fr. *twi*, two.]

TWISTER (twis'ter) *n.* one who twists; instrument for twisting.

TWIT (twit) *v.t.* to reproach. [O.E. *ætwitan*, to reproach.]

TWITCH (twich) *v.t.* to pull suddenly; pluck; *v.i.* to be affected with a spasm;—*n.* a sudden pull; a twinge. [O.E. *twiccian*, to pluck. Cf. Ger. *zwicken*.]

TWITTER (twit'er) *v.i.* to make a noise, as swallows;—*n.* a small, tremulous noise. [Imit.] [*tu*, two.]

TWO (too) *a.* one and one. [O.E. *twegen*, *twa*.]

TWO-EDGED (too'ejd) *a.* having an edge on both sides.

TWOFOLD (too'fold) *a.* two of the kind.

TWO-FOOT (too'foot) *a.* measuring two feet.

TYMBAL (tim'bal) *n.* a kettledrum. [It. *timballo*.]

TYMPAN (tim'pan) *n.* a printer's frame on which the sheets are laid for printing. [G. *tumpanon*, a kettledrum.]

TYMPANUM (tim'pa-num) *n.* drum of the ear. [G. *tim'pa-num*) *n.* drum of the ear.

TYPE (tip) *n.* a mark; emblem; model; a printing letter. [F., fr. L. *typus*, fr. G. *tupos*, a blow, fr. *tuptein*, to strike.]

TYPHOID (ti'foid) *n.* a fever resembling typhus;. —*a.* resembling typhus fever. [G. *tuphoides* fr. *tuphos*, stupor, and *eidos*, likeness.]

TYPHOON (ti-foon') *n.* a tornado. [Pg. *tufão* fr. G. *tuphon*, a violent whirlwind, fr. *Typhon*, a giant struck with lightning by Jupiter.]

TYPHUS (ti'fus) *n.* a fatal kind of continuous fever, often epidemic. [G. *tuphos*, smoke, stupor, fr. *tuphein*, to smoke.]

TYPICAL (tip'i-kal) *a.* emblematical.

TYPICALLY (tip'i-kal-i) *ad.* in a figurative manner.

TYPIFY (tip'i-fi) *v.t.* to represent by an emblem. [G. *tupos*, and L. *facere*, to make.]

TYPOGRAPHER (ti-pog'ra-fer) *n.* a printer.

TYPOGRAPHICAL (ti-pu-graf'i-kal) *a.* pertaining to types or to printing.

TYPOGRAPHICALLY (ti-pu-graf'i-kal-i) *ad.* with types.

TYPOGRAPHY (ti-pog'ra-fi) *n.* the art of printing. [G. *tupos*, type, and *graphein*, to write.]

TYPOLOGY (ti-pol'o-ji) *n.* doctrine or treatise on Scripture types. [G. *tupos*, type, and *logos*, discourse.]

TYRANNICAL (ti-ran'i-kal) *a.* despotic; arbitrary; cruel. [G. *turannikos*, fr. *turannos*, master.]

TYRANNICALLY (ti-ran'i-kal-i) *ad.* in the manner of a tyrant.

TYRANNISE (tir'a-niz) *v.i.* to act as a tyrant. [See TYRANNY.] [despotic.

TYRANNOUS (tir'a-nus) *a.* cruel; arbitrary;

TYRANNY (tir'a-ni) *n.* arbitrary exercise of power; oppression; cruelty. [F. *tyrannie*, fr. Late L., fr. G. *turannia*.]

TYRANT (ti'rant) *n.* an arbitrary ruler; a cruel master; oppressor. [O.F. *tiran*] *tirant*, fr. L., fr. G. *turannos*, a sovereign.,

TYRIAN (tir'i-an) *a.* pertaining to Tyre; of a purple colour.

TYRO (ti'ro) *n.* a beginner; a novice. [L. *tiro*, a recruit.] [CZAR.

TZAR (tsar) *n.* Emperor of Russia. Also

TZARINA (tsä-re'na) *n.* Empress of Russia. Also CZARINA.

U

UBIQUITARY (ū-bik'wi-ta-ri) *a.* existing everywhere. Also UBIQUITOUS.

UBIQUITY (ū-bik'wi-ti) *n.* existence everywhere. [F. *ubiquité*, fr. L. *ubique*, everywhere, fr. *ubi*, where.]

UDDER (ud'er) *n.* the bags with the teats of a cow, etc. [O.E. *uder*. Cf. Ger. *Euter*; L. *uber*.]

UGLINESS (ug'li-nes) *n.* quality of being ugly.

UGLY (ug'li) *a.* offensive to the eye; hateful; ill-natured. [Scand.]

UKASE (ū-kās') *n.* an imperial order or decree in Russia. [Russ.]

ULCER (ul'ser) *n.* a sore that discharges pus. [F. *ulcère*, fr. L. stem *ulcer-*, of *ulcus*.]

ULCERATE (ul'ser-āt) *v.t.* or *i.* to affect with, or be formed into, an ulcer.

ULCERATION (ul-se-rā'shun) *n.* the act of ulcerating.

ULCEROUS (ul'ser-us) *a.* of the nature of an ulcer; having ulcers.

ULLAGE (ul'ij) *n.* what a cask wants of being full. [O.F. *ouillage*, fr. *ouillier*, to fill to the bung or eye, fr. L. *oculus*.]

ULNA (ul'na) *n.* the larger of the two bones of the fore-arm. [L. =elbow.]

ULT. (ult) contraction of ULTIMO, the last or preceding month. [L. *ultimo* (*mense*), in the last (month).]

ULTERIOR (ul-tē'ri-ur) *a.* lying beyond. [L. (comp.) *ulterior*, fr. *ulter*, beyond.]

ULTIMATE (ul'ti-māt) *a.* final; furthest. [Fr. L. (superl.) *ultimus*, fr. *ultra*, beyond.]

ULTIMATELY (ul'ti-māt'li) *ad.* finally; at last.

ULTIMATUM (ul-ti-mā'tum) *n.* final proposition or terms. [L.]

ULTRA (ul'tra) *a.* extreme;—*n.* one who advocates extreme measures. Also ULTRAIST. [L.]

ULTRAISM (ul'tra-izm) *n.* principles of men who advocate extreme views.

ULTRAMARINE (ul-tra-ma-rēn') *n.* a beautiful blue colour. [L. *ultra*, beyond, and MARINE.]

ULTRAMONTANE (ul-tra-mon'tān) *a.* beyond the mountains. [F. *ultramontain*, fr. L. *ultra*, and stem *mont-*, of *mons*, MOUNTAIN.]

ULTRAMONTANISM (ul-tra-mon'tā-nizm) *n.* extreme views of the pope's supremacy.

ULTRAMUNDANE (ul-tra-mun'dān) *a.* beyond the world. [L. *ultra*, beyond, and *mundus*, the world.]

ULTRONEOUS (ul-trō'ne-us) *a.* spontaneous; voluntary. [L. *ultroneus*, fr. *ultro*, of one's own accord.]

ULULATE (ul'ū-lāt) *v.i.* to howl. [L. (part.) *ululatus*, fr. *ulutare*, to howl; imit.]

UMBEL (um'bel) *n.* a collection of small flowers in a head. [L. *umbella*, a little shadow, fr. *umbra*. See UMBRAGE.]

UMBELLIFEROUS (um-be-lif'e-rus) *a.* bearing umbels.

UMBLES (um'blz) *n.* the entrails of a deer. [O.F. *nomble* = *lomble*, fr. *le*, the, and *omble*, fr. L. *umbilicus*, the navel.]

UMBRAGE (um'brij) *n.* a shade; resentment or offence. [O.F. *umbrage*, *ombrage*, fr. *ombre*, shadow, fr. L. (acc.) *umbram*.]

UMBRAGEOUS (um-brā'jus) *a.* shady.

UMBRELLA (um-brel'a) *n.* a portable screen from the sun or rain. [It. *ombrella*, dim. fr. L. *umbra*, a shade.]

UMPIRAGE (um'pir-ij) *n.* the decision of a dispute.

UMPIRE (um'pir) *n.* one to whose decision a dispute is referred. [O.F. *nomper*, *nompair*, without PEER, uneven, fr. *non*, not, and *pair*. See NONPAREIL.]

UN (un) a prefix; gives to words a negative sense, and is prefixed to adjectives adverbs, and participles, almost at pleasure. [E.]

UNABLE (un-ā'bl) *a.* not having power.

UNABRIDGED (un-a-brijd') *a.* not abridged or shortened.

UNACCENTED (un-ak-sen'ted) *a.* not accented.

UNACCEPTABLE (un-ak-sep'ta-bl) *a.* not acceptable.

UNACCOMMODATING (un-a-kom'u-dā-ting) *a.* not obliging.

UNACCOMPANIED (un-a-kum'pa-nid) *a.* unattended.

UNACCOUNTABLE (un-a-koun'ta-bl) *a.* not to be explained.

UNACCOUNTABLY (un-a-koun'ta-bli) *ad.* not to be explained. [unauthorised.

UNACCREDITED (un-a-kred'i-ted) *a.* unaccustomed.

UNACCUSTOMED (un-a-kus'tumd) *a.* not accustomed.

UNACQUAINTED (un-a-kwān'ted) *a.* not acquainted.

UNADORNED (un-a-dornd') *a.* not decorated.

UNADVISABLE (un-ad-vi'za-bl) *a.* not expedient.

UNADVISEDLY (un-ad-vi'zed-li) *ad.* inconsiderately; rashly.

UNAFFECTED (un-a-fek'ted) *a.* not affected.

UNAFFECTEDLY (un-a-fek'ted-li) *ad.* in sincerity; without disguise.

UNAIDED (un-ā'ded) *a.* not assisted.

UNALIENABLE (un-āl'yen-a-bl) *a.* that cannot be alienated.

UNALLIED (un-a-lid') *a.* having no alliance.

UNALLOYED (un-a-loid') *a.* not alloyed.

UNALTERABLE (un-awl'ter-a-bl) *a.* that cannot be altered; unchangeable.

UNALTERABLY (un-awl'ter-a-bli) *ad.* unchangeably.

UNAMBITIOUS (un-am-bish'us) *a.* not aspiring.

UNANIMITY (ū-na-nim'i-ti) *n.* agreement of a number of persons.

UNANIMOUS (ū-nan'i-mus) *a.* being of one mind. [L. *unanimus*, fr. *unus*, one, and *animus*, mind.]

UNANIMOUSLY (ū-nan'i-mus-li) *a.* with agreement of all.

UNANSWERABLE (un-àn'ser-a-bl) *a.* not to be refuted.

UNANSWERABLY (un-àn'ser-a-bli) *ad.* beyond refutation.

UNAPPEASED (un-a-pēzd') *n.* not pacified.

UNAPPRECIATED (un-a-prē'shi-ā-ted) *a.* not duly estimated.

UNAPPROACHABLE (un-a-prō'cha-bl) *a.* not to be approached.

UNAPT (un-apt') *a.* unfit; not ready.

UNARMED (un-ärmd') *a.* defenceless.

UNARRAIGNED (un-a-rānd') *a.* not brought to trial.

UNASCERTAINED (un-as-er-tānd') *a.* not certainly known.

UNASKED (un-askt') *a.* not asked; unsolicited.

UNASPIRING (un-as-pi'ring) *a.* not ambitious.

UNASSAILABLE (un-a-sā'la-bl) *a.* that cannot be assailed.

UNASSISTED (un-a-sis'ted) *a.* not aided.

UNASSUMING (un-a-sū'ming) *a.* not assuming; not forward.

UNATONED (un-a-tōnd') *a.* not expiated.

UNATTAINABLE (un-a-tā'na-bl) *a.* not to be obtained.

UNATTENDED (un-a-ten'ded) *a.* having no company.

UNAUTHENTIC (un-aw-then'tik) *a.* not genuine.

UNAUTHORISED (un-aw'thur-izd) *a.* not warranted. [able.

UNAVAILABLE (un-a-vā'la-bl) *a.* not available.

UNAVAILING (un-a-vā'ling) *a.* ineffectual; useless.

UNAVOIDABLE (un-a-voi'da-bl) *a.* that cannot be shunned.

UNAVOIDABLY (un-a-voi'da-bli) *ad.* inevitably.

UNAVOWED (un-a-voud') *a.* not acknowledged.

UNAWARE (un-a-wār') *a.* not aware; not knowing.

UNAWARES (un-a-wärz') *ad.* by surprise.

UNBALANCED (un-bal'anst) *a.* not balanced.

UNBAR (un-bär') *v.t.* to unfasten.

UNBEARABLE (un-bār'a-bl) *a.* not to be endured.

UNBECOMING (un-be-kum'ing) *a.* unsuitable.

UNBEFITTING (un-be-fit'ing) *a.* unsuitable.

UNBELIEF (un-be-lēf') *n.* infidelity.

UNBELIEVER (un-be-lē'ver) *n.* an infidel.

UNBELIEVING (un-be-lē'ving) *a.* not believing; infidel.

UNBEND (un-bend') *v.t.* to relax or slacken; cast loose.

UNBENDING (un-ben'ding) *a.* inflexible.

UNBENT (un-bent') *pp.* relaxed; unsubdued.

UNBIAS (un-bi'as) *v.t.* to free from bias.

UNBIASSED (un-bi'ast) *a.* free from partiality.

UNBIND (un-bind') *v.t.* to untie.

UNBIT (un-bit') *v.t.* to take bits from the mouth of.

UNBLEMISHED (un-blem'isht) *a.* free from blemish.

UNBLEST (un-blest') *a.* not blessed; unhappy.

UNBLUSHING (un-blush'ing) *a.* destitute of shame.

UNBOLT (un-bōlt') *v.t.* to remove a bolt from.

UNBORN (un-born') *a.* not born; future.

UNBOSOM (un-booz'um) *v.t.* to reveal.

UNBOUGHT (un-hawt') *a.* not purchased.

UNBOUND (un-bound') *a.* loose; not bound.

UNBOUNDED (un-boun'ded) *a.* having no limits.

UNBOUNDEDLY (un-boun'ded-li) *ad.* without bounds.

UNBRIDLE (un-bri'dl) *v.t.* to free from the bridle.

UNBROKEN (un-brō'kn) *a.* entire; whole.

UNBROTHERLY (un-bruTH'er-li) *a.* not becoming a brother.

UNBUCKLE (un-buk'l) *v.t.* to unfasten buckles.

UNBURDEN (un-hur'dn) *v.t.* to rid of a load; relieve. Also UNBURTHEN.

UNBURIED (un-ber'id) *a.* not interred.

UNBURNT (un-burnt') *a.* not scorched; not baked.

UNBUTTON (un-but'n) *v.t.* to loose buttons.

UNCANDID (un-kan'did) *a.* not candid.

UNCANONICAL (un-ka-non'i-kal) *a.* not according to the canons.

UNCEASING (un-sē'sing) *a.* not ceasing; continual.

UNCEASINGLY (un-sē'sing-li) *ad.* without intermission.

UNCEREMONIOUS (un-ser-e-mō'ni-us) *a.* not formal.

UNCERTAIN (un-ser'tin) *a.* not certain; doubtful.

UNCERTAINLY (un-ser'tin-li) *ad.* doubtfully.

UNCERTAINTY (un-ser'tin-ti) *n.* doubtfulness; want of certainty.

UNCHAIN (un-chān') *v.t.* to unbind.

UNCHALLENGED (un-chal-enjd') *a.* not objected to.

UNCHANGEABLE (un-chān'ja-bl) *a.* not subject to change; immutable.

UNCHANGEABLY (un-chān'ja-bli) *ad.* without change; immutably.

UNCHANGING (un-chān'jing) *a.* suffering no alteration.

UNCHARITABLE (un-char'i-ta-bl) *a.* wanting or contrary to charity.

UNCHARITABLENESS (un-char'i-ta-bl-nes) *n.* want of charity.

UNCHARITABLY (un-char'i-ta-bli) *ad.* with want of charity.

UNCHASTE (un-chāst') *a.* lewd; impure.

UNCHRISTIAN (un-kris'tyan) *a.* contrary to Christianity.

UNCHURCH (un-church') *v.t.* to expel from a church.

UNCIAL (un'shal) *n.* a large round letter used in ancient MSS. [L. *uncialis*, an inch long, fr. *uncia*, **INCH.**]

UNCIVIL (un-siv'il) *a.* unpolite; uncourteous in manners.

UNCIVILISED (un-siv'i-līzd) *a.* not civilised.

UNCIVILLY (un-siv'i-li) *ad.* rudely.

UNCLAD (un-klad') *a.* not clad.

UNCLE (ung'kl) *n.* a father's or mother's brother. [O.F. = F. *oncle*, fr. L. (acc.) *avunculum*, a mother's brother; dim. fr. *avus*, a grandfather.]

UNCLEAN (un-klēn') *a.* not clean; foul.

UNCLEANLY (un-klēn'li) *a.* foul; filthy; indecent.

UNCLEANNESS (un-klēn'nes) *n.* filthiness; incontinence.

UNCLOSE (un-klōz') *v.t.* to open.

UNCLOUDED (un-klou'ded) *a.* free from clouds.

UNCOCKED (un-kokt') *a.* not cocked; not turned up.

UNCOIL (un-koil') *v.t.* to unwind and open.

UNCOINED (un-koind') *a.* not coined.

UNCOMFORTABLE (un-kum'fur-ta-bl) *a.* affording no comfort.

UNCOMFORTABLY (un-kum'fur-ta-bli) *ad.* without comfort.

UNCOMMON (un-kom'un) *a.* rare; unusual.

UNCOMMONLY (un-kom'un-li) *ad.* unusually.

UNCOMPLAINING (un-kum-plā'ning) *a.* not murmuring.

UNCOMPROMISING (un-kom'pru-mī-zing) *a.* not agreeing to terms.

UNCONCERN (un-kun-sern') *n.* want of care or interest.

UNCONCERNED (un-kun-sernd') *a.* not anxious; indifferent.

UNCONCERNEDLY (un-kun-ser'ned-li) *ad.* without concern.

UNCONCERTED (un-kun-ser'ted) *a.* not planned together; independent.

UNCONDEMNED (un-kun-demd') *a.* not found guilty; not denounced.

UNCONDITIONAL (un-kun-dish'un-al) *a.* not limited by conditions.

UNCONDITIONALLY (un-kun-dish'un-al-i) *ad.* without conditions.

UNCONFORMITY (un-kun-for'mi-ti) *n.* incongruity. [genial.

UNCONGENIAL (un-kun-jē'nyal) *a.* not congenial.

UNCONNECTED (un-ku-nek'ted) *a.* not joined together; incoherent.

UNCONQUERABLE (un-kong'ker-a-bl) *a.* that cannot be subdued.

UNCONSCIONABLE (un-kon'shun-a-bl) *a.* unreasonable.

UNCONSCIONABLY (un-kon'shun-a-bli) *ad.* unreasonably.

UNCONSCIOUS (un-kon'shus) *a.* not knowing or perceiving.

UNCONSCIOUSLY (un-kon'shus-li) *ad.* without knowledge.

UNCONSCIOUSNESS (un-kon'shus-nes) *n.* want of perception.

UNCONSIDERED (un-kun-sid'erd) *a.* not thought of or attended to.

UNCONSTITUTIONAL (un-kon-sti-tū'shun-al) *a.* not constitutional.

UNCONSTITUTIONALITY (un-kon-sti-tū-shun-al'i-ti) *n.* opposition to the constitution.

UNCONSTITUTIONALLY (un-kon-sti-tū'shun-al-i) *ad.* in a manner not warranted by the constitution.

UNCONTESTED (un-kun-tes'ted) *a.* not contested.

UNCONTROLLABLE (un-kun-trō'la-bl) *a.* not to be controlled.

UNCONTROLLED (un-kun-trōld') *a.* not restrained.

UNCONTROVERTED (un-kon'tru-ver-ted) *a.* not called in question.

UNCONVERTED (un-kun-ver'ted) *a.* not regenerated.

UNCORK (un-kork') *v.t.* to draw the cork from.

UNCORRUPT (un-ku-rupt') *a.* not corrupt; pure.

UNCOUNTED (un-koun'ted) *a.* not numbered.

UNCOUPLE (un-kup'l) *v.i.* to loose; set loose.

UNCOUTH (un-kōōth') *a.* not rendered pleasing by familiarity; awkward. [O.E. *uncuth*, strange, fr. *un*, not, and (part.) *cuth*, known, fr. *cunnan*.]

UNCOUTHNESS (un-kōōth'nes) *n.* awkwardness.

UNCOVER (un-kuv'er) *v.t.* or *i.* to lay open; take off the hat.

UNCTION (ung'shun) *n.* act of anointing. [F., fr. L. *unctio*, fr. (part.) *unctus*, anointed, fr. *ungere*. See **UNGUENT.**]

UNCTUOUS (ung'tū-us) *a.* oily; fat; greasy.

UNCULTIVATED (un-kul'ti-vā-ted) *a.* not cultivated; rude; rough.

UNCURL (un-kurl') *v.t.* or *i.* to loose or fall from curls.

UNCURTAILED (un-kur-tāld') *a.* not shortened.

UNCUT (un-kut') *a.* not clipped; entire.

UNDATED (un-dā'ted) *a.* having no date.

UNDAUNTED (un-dawn'ted) *a.* fearless.

UNDAUNTEDLY (un-dawn'ted-li) *ad.* fearlessly.

UNDECEIVE (un-de-sēv') *v.t.* to free from deception.

UNDECIDED (un-de-sī'ded) *a.* not determined.

UNDEFILED (un-de-fīld') *a.* not polluted.

UNDEFINED (un-de-fīnd') *a.* not defined.

UNDENIABLE (un-de-nī'a-bl) *a.* that cannot be denied. [putably.

UNDENIABLY (un-de-nī'a-bli) *ad.* indisputably.

UNDER (un'der) *prep.* beneath; below; less than; during the time of; —*ad.* in a lower state or degree; —*a.* lower; subordinate. [O.E. Cf. Ger. *unter*.]

UNDERAGENT (un-der-ā'jent) *n.* a subordinate agent.

UNDERBID (un-der-bid') *v.t.* to bid or offer less.

UNDERBRUSH (un'der-brush) *n.* small trees and shrubs.

UNDERCHARGE (un-der-chárj') *v.t.* to charge insufficiently.

UNDERCURRENT (un'der-kur-ent) *n.* a current below.

UNDERESTIMATE (un-der-es'ti-māt) *v.t.* to rate beneath the real value.

UNDERFED (un-der-fed') *a.* insufficiently fed.

UNDERFOOT (un-der-foot') *ad.* beneath.

UNDERGO (un-der-gō') *v.t.* to bear; endure; pass through.

UNDERGRADUATE (un-der-grad'ū-āt) *n.* a student who has not taken his degree.

UNDERGROUND (un'der-ground) *a.* being below the surface of the ground.

UNDERGROWTH (un'der-grōth) *n.* shrubs which grow under trees.

UNDERHAND (un'der-hand) *a.* covert; secret; sly;—*ad.* by secret means.

UNDERHANDED (un-der-han'ded) *a.* clandestine.

UNDERIVED (un-de-rīvd') *a.* not borrowed.

UNDERLAY (un-der-lā') *v.t.* to lay under.

UNDERLET (un-der-let') *v.t.* to lease under another.

UNDERLIE (un-der-lī') *v.t.* to lie under.

UNDERLINE (un-der-līn') *v.t.* to mark with lines beneath the words.

UNDERLING (un'der-ling) *n.* an inferior.

UNDERMINE (un-der-mīn') *v.t.* to excavate beneath; injure clandestinely.

UNDERNEATH (un-der-nēth') *ad.* or *prep.* beneath. [**UNDER**, and *neath*, fr. O.E. *neothan.*]

UNDERPIN (un-der-pin') *v.t.* to lay the stones that support the sills of a building.

UNDERPINNING (un-der-pin'ing) *n.* the stones on which a building rests.

UNDERRATE (un-der-rāt') *v.t.* to rate below the value;—*n.* a price below the worth.

UNDERSCORE (un-der-skōr') *v.t.* to draw a line or mark under.

UNDERSELL (un-der-sel') *v.t.* to sell cheaper than another.

UNDERSET (un-der-set') *v.t.* to prop; support.

UNDERSET (un'der-set) *n.* a current of water beneath, contrary to the wind and the surface water moved by it.

UNDERSHOT (un'der-shot) *a.* moved by water passing under, as a wheel.

UNDERSIGN (un-der-sīn') *v.t.* to write one's name at the foot or end of; subscribe.

UNDERSIGNED (un-der-sīnd') *n.* the subscriber.

UNDERSOIL (un'der-soil) *n.* the soil beneath the surface.

UNDERSTAND (un-der-stand') *v.t.* or *i.* [*pret.* and *pp.* **UNDERSTOOD**] to comprehend; suppose to mean; be informed; learn. [O.E. *understandan*, to stand under, or in the midst of a thing.]

UNDERSTANDING (un-der-stan'ding) *n.* act or power of apprehending and comprehending; full knowledge; agreement between parties.

UNDERSTOOD (un-der-stood') *pret.* and *pp.* of **UNDERSTAND**.

UNDERSTRAPPER (un'der-strap-er) *n.* an inferior agent.

UNDERTAKE (un-der-tāk') *v.t.* or *i.* [*pret.* **UNDERTOOK**; *pp.* **UNDERTAKEN**] to take in hand; attempt; be bound to do.

UNDERTAKER (un-der-tā'ker) *n.* one who undertakes; one who manages funerals.

UNDERTAKING (un-der-tā'king) *n.* any work or project attempted or engaged in.

UNDERTENANT (un'der-ten-ant) *n.* the tenant of a tenant.

UNDERTOOK (un-der-took') *pret.* of **UNDERTAKE**.

UNDERVALUE (un-der-val'ū) *v.t.* to rate below the worth.

UNDERWOOD (un'der-wood) *n.* small trees.

UNDERWORK (un'der-wurk) (1) *n.* subordinate work;—(2) (un-der-wurk') *v.t.* to work for less.

UNDERWRITE (un-der-rīt') *v.t.* or *i.* subscribe one's name as insurer; practise the profession of insuring.

UNDERWRITER (un'der-rī-ter) *n.* an insurer.

UNDESERVED (un-de-zervd') *a.* not merited.

UNDESERVING (un-de-zer'ving) *a.* not deserving.

UNDESIGNED (un-de-sīnd') *a.* not intended.

UNDESIGNING (un-de-zī'ning) *a.* artless; sincere.

UNDESIRABLE (un-de-zīr'a-bl) *a.* not to be desired.

UNDETERMINED (un-de-ter'mind) *a.* not decided, settled, or defined.

UNDETERRED (un-de-terd') *a.* not restrained by fear or obstacles.

UNDEVIATING (un-de'vi-ā-ting) *a.* not deviating.

UNDIGNIFIED (un-dig'ni-fīd) *a.* not dignified.

UNDISGUISED (un-dis-gīzd') *a.* open; artless.

UNDISMAYED (un-dis-mād') *a.* not intimidated.

UNDISTURBED (un-dis-turbd') *a.* not disturbed.

UNDIVIDED (un-di-vī'ded) *a.* not divided.

UNDO (un-dōō') *v.t.* [*pret.* **UNDID**; *pp.* **UNDONE**] to reverse what has been done; unfasten; ruin.

UNDOER (un-dōō'er) *n.* one who brings to destruction.

UNDOING (un-dōō'ing) *n.* reversal; ruin.

UNDONE (un-dun') *pp.* reversed; ruined.

UNDOUBTED (un-dou'ted) *a.* not doubted.

UNDOUBTEDLY (un-dou'ted-li) *ad.* without a question; indisputably.

UNDRESS (un-dres') (1) *v.t.* to divest of clothes; strip;—(2) (un'dres) *n.* a loose dress.

UNDRESSED (un-drest') *a.* not attired; not cooked; not pruned or trimmed.

UNDUE (un-dū') *a.* not due; not right.

UNDULATE (un'dū-lāt) *v.t.* or *i.* to move backward and forward, as a wave. [L. (part.) *undulatus*, fr. *undulare*, fluctuate, fr. *unda*, a wave.]

UNDULATED (un'dū-lā-ted) *a.* waved; wavy.

UNDULATION (un-dū-lā'shun) *n.* a waving motion or vibration.

UNDULATORY (un'dū-lā-tu-ri) *a.* moving like waves; vibratory.

UNDULY (un-dū'li) *ad.* improperly; excessively.

UNDUTIFUL (un-dū'ti-fool) *a.* not dutiful.

UNDYING (un-dī'ing) *a.* not perishing; immortal.

UNEARNED (un-ernd') *a.* not gained or merited by labour.

UNEARTHLY (un-erth'li) *a.* not terrestrial; not human.

UNEASILY (un-ē'zi-li) *ad.* without ease or quiet.

UNEASINESS (un-ē'zi-nes) *n.* disquiet.

UNEASY (un-ē'zi) *a.* restless; disturbed.

UNEDUCATED (un-ed'ū-kā-ted) *a.* having no education.

UNEMBARRASSED (un-em-bar'ast) *a.* free from embarrassment.

UNEMBODIED (un-em-bod'id) *a.* incorporeal; immaterial.

UNEMPLOYED (un-em-ploid') *a.* not employed; idle.

UNENGAGED (un-en-gājd') *a.* not engaged.

UNENGLISH (un-ing'glish) *a.* not English.

UNENLIGHTENED (un-en-līt-nd) *a.* not enlightened.

UNEQUABLE (un-ē'kwa-bl) *a.* not uniform.

UNEQUAL (un-ē'kwal) *a.* not equal or even; inferior; unmatched; not uniform.

UNEQUALLED (un-ē'kwald) *a.* not equalled.

UNEQUALLY (un-ē'kwal-i) *ad.* in different degrees.

UNEQUIVOCAL (un-e-kwiv'u-kal) *a.* not doubtful or ambiguous.

UNEQUIVOCALLY (un-e-kwiv'u-kal-i) *ad.* without all doubt.

UNERRING (un-er'ing) *a.* committing no mistake; certain.

UNEVEN (un-ē'vn) *a.* not even; not level; irregular.

UNEVENNESS (un-ē'vn-nes) *n.* inequality of surface; want of uniformity.

UNEXCEPTIONABLE (un-ek-sep'shun-a-bl) *a.* not liable to objection.

UNEXCEPTIONABLY (un-ek-sep'shun-a-bli) *ad.* so as to be liable to no objection.

UNEXPECTED (un-eks-pek'ted) *a.* not expected; sudden.

UNEXPECTEDLY (un-eks-pek'ted-li) ad. suddenly.

UNEXPLORED (un-eks-plōrd') a. not explored.

UNEXPOSED (un-eks-pōzd') a. not exposed.

UNEXPRESSED (un-eks-prest') a. not mentioned.

UNFADED (un-fā'ded) a. not faded.

UNFADING (un-fā'ding) a. not liable to fade or wither.

UNFAILING (un-fā'ling) a. not failing; abiding.

UNFAIR (un-fâr') a. not fair; dishonest; disingenuous.

UNFAIRLY (un-fâr'li) ad. in an unfair or unjust manner.

UNFAIRNESS (un-fâr'nes) n. want of fairness, honesty, or impartiality.

UNFAITHFUL (un-fāth'fool) a. not faithful; perfidious; negligent.

UNFAITHFULNESS (un-fāth'fool-nes) n. quality of being unfaithful.

UNFALLEN (un-faw'ln) n. not fallen; upright.

UNFAMILIAR (un-fạ-mil'yạr) a. not common; unaccustomed.

UNFASHIONABLE (un-fash'un-ạ-bl) a. not according to the fashion.

UNFASHIONABLY (un-fash'un-ạ-bli) ad. so as not to be in the fashion.

UNFASTEN (un-fas'n) v.t. to loosen; unfix.

UNFATHOMABLE (un-faTH'um-ạ-bl) a. not to be fathomed.

UNFAVOURABLE (un-fā'vur-ạ-bl) a. not favourable.

UNFAVOURABLY (un-fā'vur-ạ-bli) ad. unpropitiously.

UNFEELING (un-fē'ling) a. void of feeling.

UNFEELINGLY (un-fē'ling-li) ad. with insensibility.

UNFEIGNED (un-fānd') a. real; sincere.

UNFEIGNEDLY (un-fā'ned-li) ad. without disguise.

UNFELT (un-felt') a. not felt or perceived.

UNFETTER (un-fet'ẹr) v.t. to unshackle; set free.

UNFILIAL (un-fil'yạl) a. not becoming a son or daughter.

UNFINISHED (un-fin'isht) a. not complete; imperfect.

UNFIT (un-fit') v.t. to disqualify;—a. not qualified; unsuitable. [tions.

UNFITNESS (un-fit'nes) n. want of qualifica-

UNFIX (un-fiks)' v.t. to loosen; unsettle.

UNFOLD (un-fōld') v.t. to expand; disclose; reveal.

UNFORBIDDEN (un-for-bid'n) a. not prohibited.

UNFORESEEN (un-fōr-sēn') a. not seen or expected beforehand.

UNFORETOLD (un-fōr-tōld') a. not predicted.

UNFORGIVING (un-for-giv'ing) a. not disposed to forgive.

UNFORMED (un-formd') a. not formed; not arranged.

UNFORTUNATE (un-for'tū-nāt) a. not successful.

UNFORTUNATELY (un-for'tū-nāt'li) ad. without success.

UNFOUNDED (un-foun'ded) a. having no foundation.

UNFREQUENTED (un-fre-kwen'ted) a. rarely visited.

UNFRIENDLY (un-frend'li) a. unfavourable.

UNFROCK (un-frok') v.t. to divest of priestly office or function.

UNFRUITFUL (un-frōōt'fool) a. not fruitful; barren.

UNFRUITFULNESS (un-frōōt'fool-nes) n. barrenness; unproductiveness.

UNFULFILLED (un-fool-fild') a. not fulfilled.

UNFURL (un-furl') v.t. to unfold; open or spread.

UNFURNISHED (un-fur'nisht) a. not supplied with.

UNGAINLY (un-gān'li) a. not expert; clumsy. [M.E. ungein, inconvenient, fr. E. **UN-**, and Scand.]

UNGENEROUS (un-jen'e-rus) a. illiberal; unkind; mean.

UNGENIAL (un-jē'nyạl) a. unfavourable to nature or to growth.

UNGENTLE (un-jen'tl) a. not gentle; wild.

UNGENTLEMANLY (un-jen'tl-mạn-li) a. unbecoming a gentleman.

UNGIRD (un-gẹrd') v.t. to loose from a band; unbind.

UNGODLINESS (un-god'li-nes) n. impiety.

UNGODLY (un-god'li) a. not fearing God; impious.

UNGOVERNABLE (un-guv'ẹr-nạ-bl) a. not to be restrained.

UNGOVERNABLY (un-guv'ẹr-nạ-bli) ad. so as not to be restrained.

UNGRACEFUL (un-grās'fool) a. wanting grace or dignity.

UNGRACIOUS (un-grā'shus) a. unpleasing.

UNGRACIOUSLY (un-grā'shus-li) ad. with disfavour; displeasingly.

UNGRAMMATICAL (un-grạ-mat'i-kạl) a. not according to grammar.

UNGRATEFUL (un-grāt'fool) a. unthankful.

UNGRATEFULLY (un-grāt'fool-i) ad. without gratitude.

UNGROUNDED (un-groun'ded) a. having no foundation; baseless.

UNGUARDED (un-gār'ded) a. not guarded; incautious. [tiously; carelessly.

UNGUARDEDLY (un-gār'ded-li) ad. incau-

UNGUENT (ung'gwent) n. an ointment. [L. unguentum, fr. unguere, anoint.]

UNGUENTOUS (un-gwent'us) a. like or partaking of ointment. [holy.

UNHALLOWED (un-hal'ōd) a. profane; un-

UNHAND (un-hand') v.t. to take the hands off; let go.

UNHAPPILY (un-hap'i-li) ad. unfortunately; miserably.

UNHAPPINESS (un-hap'i-nes) n. misfortune; infelicity.

UNHAPPY (un-hap'i) n. not happy; unfortunate.

UNHARMED (un-hârmd') a. unhurt; uninjured. [ness.

UNHARNESS (un-hâr'nes) v.t. to strip of har-

UNHEALTHFUL (un-helth'fool) a. insalubrious.

UNHEALTHINESS (un-hel'thi-nes) n. want of health; unsoundness.

UNHEALTHY (un-hel'thi) a. wanting health; sickly; insalubrious.

UNHEARD (un-hẹrd') a. not heard; unknown.

UNHEEDED (un-hē'ded) a. not regarded.

UNHEEDING (un-hē'ding) a. unmindful; inattentive.

UNHESITATING (un-hez'i-tā-ting) a. not hesitating.

UNHESITATINGLY (un-hez'i-tā-ting-li) ad. without hesitation.

UNHINGE (un-hinj') v.t. to take from the hinges; displace; unsettle. [etc.

UNHITCH (un-hich') v.t. to loose from a hook.

UNHOLINESS (un-hō'li-nes) n. want of holiness; impiety.

UNHOLY (un-hō'li) a. not holy; impious; profane.

UNHONOURED (un-on'urd) a. not treated with honour.

UNHOOP (un-hōōp') v.t. to divest of hoops.

UNHOPED (un-hōpt') a. not hoped for; unexpected.

UNHORSE (un-hors') v.t. to throw from the saddle.

UNHURTFUL (un-hurt'fool) a. not injurious.

UNICORN (ū'ni-korn) n. a fabulous animal with one horn. [F., fr. L. unicornis, one-horned, fr. unus, one, and cornu, horn.]

Unicorn.

UNIDEAL (un-i-dē'al) a. not ideal; real.
UNIFORM (ū'ni-form) n. the regimental dress of a soldier;—a. having the same form; undeviating; consistent with itself; agreeing with another. [L. uniformis, fr. unus, one, and FORM.]
UNIFORMITY (ū-ni-for'mi-ti) n. sameness; resemblance at all times.
UNIFORMLY (ū'ni-form-li) ad. in a uniform manner.
UNIMPASSIONED (un-im-pash'und) a. free from passion; calm; spiritless.
UNIMPEACHABLE (un-im-pē'cha-bl) a. not to be impeached.
UNIMPORTANT (un-im-pōr'tant) a. not important.
UNIMPROVING (un-im-prōō'ving) a. not tending to instruct.
UNINFLUENCED (un-in'floo-enst) a. not moved by motive or persuasion.
UNINFORMED (un-in-formd') a. not animated; not instructed.
UNINGENUOUS (un-in-jen'ū-us) a. not frank.
UNINHABITABLE (un-in-hab'i-ta-bl) a. not habitable.   [initiated.
UNINITIATED (un-i-nish'i-ā-ted) a. not in-
UNINJURED (un-in'jurd) a. unhurt.
UNINSTRUCTED (un-in-struk'ted) a. untaught; not having received instructions.
UNINSURED (un-in-shōōrd') a. not insured.
UNINTELLIGIBLE (un-in-tel'i-ji-bl) a. not to be understood.
UNINTELLIGIBLY (un-in-tel'i-ji-bli) ad. so as not to be understood.
UNINTENDED (un-in-ten'ded) a. not intended.
UNINTENTIONAL (un-in-ten'shun-al) a. not designed.
UNINTENTIONALLY (un-in-ten'shun-al-i) ad. without design.
UNINTERESTED (un-in'ter-es-ted) a. not having any interest in.
UNINTERESTING (un-in'ter-es-ting) a. not exciting interest.
UNINTERRUPTED (un-in-ter-rup'ted) a. not interrupted; not broken.
UNINVITED (un-in-vī'ted) a. not invited.
UNION (ūn'yun) n. act of uniting; concord; junction; combination. [F., fr. L. (acc.) unionem, oneness, fr. unus.]
UNIONIST (ūn'yun-ist) n. a lover of union.
UNIPAROUS (ū-nip'a-rus) a. producing one at a birth. [L. unus, one, and parere, bring forth.]
UNIQUE (ū-nēk') a. single in kind or excellence. [F., fr. L. unicus, single, fr. unus.]
UNISON (ū'ni-sun) n. agreement of sounds; concord. [F. unisson, fr. L. unus, one, and sonus, SOUND.]
UNISONOUS (ū-nis'u-nus) a. being in unison.
UNIT (ū'nit) n. one; the least whole number. [Short. fr. UNITY.]
UNITARIAN (ū-ni-tā'ri-an) n. one who denies the Trinity;—a. pertaining to Unitarians.
UNITARIANISM (ū-ni-tā'ri-an-izm) n. the doctrines of Unitarians.
UNITE (ū-nīt') v.t. to join together;—v.i. to become one; grow or act together. [L. (part.) unitus, made one, fr. unire, fr. unus.]
UNITEDLY (ū-nīt'ed-li) ad. with union or joint effort.
UNITY (ū'ni-ti) n. state of being one; agreement; harmony. [F., fr. L. unitatem, oneness, fr. uni-, for unus, one.]
UNIVALVE (ū'ni-valv) n. a shell having one valve only. [L. unus, one, and VALVE a two-leafed door, fr. valva, leaves of a folding door.]

Univalve.

UNIVALVULAR (ū-ni-val'vū-lar) a. having one valve only, as a shell.
UNIVERSAL (ū-ni-ver'sal) a. extending to all; whole; total.

UNIVERSALISM (ū-ni-ver'sal-izm) n. belief that all men will be saved.
UNIVERSALIST (ū-ni-ver'sal-ist) n. an adherent to Universalism.
UNIVERSALITY (ū-ni-ver-sal'i-ti) n. state of extending to the whole.
UNIVERSALLY (ū-ni-ver'sal-i) ad. throughout the whole.
UNIVERSE (ū'ni-vers) n. whole system of created things. [L. universus, turned into one, fr. uni-, for unus, one, and (part.) versus, fr. vertere, turn.]
UNIVERSITY (ū-ni-ver'si-ti) n. an institution where all the sciences and arts are studied. [F. université, fr. L. (acc.) universitatem.]
UNJOINTED (un-join'ted) a. having no joint.
UNJUDGED (un-jujd') a. not determined judicially.
UNJUST (un-just') a. contrary to justice or right.
UNJUSTIFIABLE (un-jus'ti-fī-a-bl) a. not to be justified or defended.
UNJUSTIFIABLY (un-jus'ti-fī-a-bli) ad. in a manner which can not be justified.
UNJUSTLY (un-just'li) ad. wrongfully.
UNKENNEL (un-ken'el) v.t. to loose or drive from a kennel; rouse from secrecy.
UNKIND (un-kīnd') a. not kind; not obliging.
UNKINDLY (un-kīnd'li) ad. with unkindness; unfavourably;—a. unfavourable.
UNKINDNESS (un-kīnd'nes) n. want of kindness or affection.
UNKNOWINGLY (un-nō'ing-li) ad. ignorantly.
UNKNOWN (un-nōn') a. not known.
UNLABOURED (un-lā'burd) a. not produced by labour; easy; free.
UNLACE (un-lās') v.t. to unfasten; loose the dress.
UNLADE (un-lād') v.t. to unload.
UNLADYLIKE (un-lā'di-līk) a. unbecoming a lady.   [latch.
UNLATCH (un-lach') v.t. to lift or loose a
UNLAWFUL (un-law'fool) a. not lawful; illegal.
UNLAWFULLY (un-law'fool-i) ad. in violation of law.
UNLAWFULNESS (un-law'fool-nes) n. illegality.
UNLEARN (un-lern') v.t. to forget what has been learned.
UNLEARNED (un-lernd') pp. forgotten.
UNLEARNED (un-lern'ed) a. ignorant; illiterate.
UNLEAVENED (un-lev'nd) a. not raised by leaven or yeast.
UNLESS (un-les') conj. except; if not. [Orig. on lesse (that), in less than.]
UNLETTERED (un-let'erd) a. unlearned.
UNLICENSED (un-lī'senst) a. not licensed.
UNLICKED (un-likt') a. rough; shapeless.
UNLIKE (un-līk') a. not like; dissimilar.
UNLIKELY (un-līk'li) a. not likely; improbable.   [blance.
UNLIKENESS (un-līk'nes) n. want of resem-
UNLIMBER (un-lim'ber) v.t. to remove the limbers from.
UNLIMITED (un-lim'i-ted) a. boundless; undefined; indefinite.
UNLINK (un-link') v.t. to disconnect.
UNLIQUIDATED (un-lik'wi-dā-ted) a. unsettled; unpaid.
UNLOAD (un-lōd') v.t. to disburden of a load.
UNLOCK (un-lok') v.t. to unfasten; open.
UNLOVELINESS (un-luv'li-nes) n. want of loveliness or amiableness.
UNLOVELY (un-luv'li) a. not amiable.
UNLUCKILY (un-luk'i-li) ad. unfortunately.
UNLUCKY (un-luk'i) a. unfortunate.
UNMAN (un-man') v.t. to deprive of strength; dishearten.
UNMANAGEABLE (un-man'ij-a-bl) a. not manageable or controllable.
UNMANLY (un-man'li) a. unsuitable to a man.
UNMANNERED (un-man'erd) a. uncivil; rude.

UNMANNERLY (un-man'ẽr-li) *a.* ill-bred; uncivil.

UNMARRIED (un-mar'id) *a.* not married.

UNMASK (un-màsk') *v.t.* to remove a disguise; expose.

UNMATCHED (un-macht') *a.* having no equal.

UNMEANING (un-mē'ning) *a.* having no meaning.

UNMEET (un-mēt') *a.* not fit or proper.

UNMENTIONABLE (un-men'shun-a-bl) *a.* not to be spoken of;—*pl.* trousers.

UNMERCHANTABLE (un-mẽr'chant-a-bl) *a.* not fit for the market.

UNMERCIFUL (un-mẽr'si-fool) *a.* having no mercy.

UNMERCIFULLY (un-mẽr'si-fool-i) *ad.* without mercy.

UNMERITED (un-mẽr'i-ted) *a.* not deserved.

UNMILITARY (un-mil'i-ta-ri) *a.* not according to military rules.

UNMINDFUL (un-mind'fool) *a.* forgetful; careless; inattentive.

UNMINGLED (un-ming'gld) *a.* not mixed.

UNMISTAKABLE (un-mis-tā'ka-bl) *a.* that cannot be mistaken.

UNMITIGATED (un-mit'i-gā-ted) *a.* not alleviated; not lessened. [age.

UNMOOR (un-mōor') *v.t.* to loose from anchor-

UNMOTHERLY (un-muTH'ẽr-li) *a.* not becoming a mother.

UNMUFFLE (un-muf'l) *v.t.* to take the covering off.

UNMURMURING (un-mur'mur-ing) *a.* not complaining.

UNMUSICAL (un-mū'zi-kal) *a.* not harmonious; harsh.

UNNATURAL (un-nat'ū-ral) *a.* contrary to nature.

UNNATURALLY (un-nat'ū-ral-i) *ad.* in opposition to nature.

UNNECESSARILY (un-nes'e-sar-i-li) *ad.* without necessity.

UNNECESSARY (un-nes'e-sa-ri) *a.* needless.

UNNEIGHBOURLY (un-nā'bur-li) *a.* not becoming a neighbour.

UNNERVE (un-nẽrv') *v.t.* to deprive of strength.

UNNOTICED (un-nō'tist) *a.* not observed.

UNNUMBERED (un-num'berd) *a.* not enumerated.

UNOBJECTIONABLE (un-ob-jek'shun-a-bl) *a.* not liable to objection.

UNOBSERVABLE (un-ob-zẽr'va-bl) *a.* not to be observed.

UNOBSERVING (un-ob-zẽr'ving) *a.* not noticing; inattentive. [ward.

UNOBTRUSIVE (un-ob-trōō'siv) *a.* not for-

UNOCCUPIED (un-ok'ū-pid) *a.* not possessed; being at leisure.

UNOFFENDING (un-u-fen'ding) *a.* not giving offence.

UNOFFERED (un-of'ẽrd) *a.* not presented for acceptance.

UNOFFICIAL (un-u-fish'al) *a.* not official.

UNOFFICIOUS (un-u-fish'us) *a.* not forward or intermeddling.

UNOPPOSED (un-u-pōzd') *a.* not opposed.

UNOSTENTATIOUS (un-os-ten-tā'shus) *a.* not making a showy display.

UNPACK (un-pak') *v.t.* to open.

UNPAID (un-pād') *a.* remaining due.

UNPALATABLE (un-pal'a-ta-bl) *a.* not relished; disagreeable.

UNPARALLELED (un-par'a-leld) *a.* having no equal.

UNPARDONABLE (un-pàr'dun-a-bl) *a.* not to be forgiven.

UNPARDONABLY (un-pàr'dun-a-bli) *ad.* beyond forgiveness.

UNPARLIAMENTARY (un-pàr-li-men'ta-ri) *a.* contrary to rules of debate.

UNPATRIOTIC (un-pā-tri-ot'ik) *a.* not patriotic.

UNPERCEIVABLE (un-pẽr-sē'va-bl) *a.* that cannot be perceived.

UNPHILOSOPHICAL (un-fil-u-sof'i-kal) *a.* not according to the principles of philosophy.

UNPIN (un-pin') *v.t.* to open what is pinned; unfasten.

UNPITIED (un-pit'id) *a.* not pitied.

UNPITYING (un-pit'i-ing) *a.* having or showing no compassion.

UNPLEASANT (un-plez'ant) *a.* not pleasant or pleasing. [agreeably.

UNPLEASANTLY (un-plez'ant-li) *ad.* dis-

UNPOETICAL (un-pō-et'i-kal) *a.* not according to poetry or its beauties.

UNPOLISHED (un-pol'isht) *a.* not polished; unrefined; rude.

UNPOLITE (un-pu-lit') *a.* wanting politeness; impolite.

UNPOLLUTED (un-pu-lū'ted) *a.* free from defilement.

UNPOPULAR (un-pop'ū-lar) *a.* not enjoying public favour; disliked by the people.

UNPRACTISED (un-prak'tist) *a.* not skilled by use or experience.

UNPRECEDENTED (un-pres'e-den-ted) *a.* having no precedent.

UNPREJUDICED (un-prej'oo-dist) *a.* free from bias.

UNPREMEDITATED (un-pre-med'i-tā-ted) *a.* not studied beforehand.

UNPREPARED (un-pre-pàrd') *a.* not prepared.

UNPREPOSSESSING (un-prē-pu-zes'ing) *a.* not having a winning appearance or manners.

UNPRETENDING (un-pre-ten'ding) *a.* not making pretensions.

UNPRINCIPLED (un-prin'si-pld) *a.* devoid of moral principle.

UNPRODUCTIVE (un-pru-duk'tiv) *a.* not fruitful; barren.

UNPROFESSIONAL (un-pru-fesh'un-al) *a.* not belonging to a profession.

UNPROFITABLE (un-prof'i-ta-bl) *a.* producing no profit or advantage.

UNPROFITABLY (un-prof'i-ta-bli) *ad.* without profit; uselessly.

UNPROGRESSIVE (un-pro-gres'iv) *a.* not advancing.

UNPROMISING (un-prom'i-sing) *a.* giving no promise.

UNPROMPTED (un-promp'ted) *a.* not instigated or suggested.

UNPROPITIOUS (un-pro-pish'us) *a.* not favourable. [tected.

UNPROTECTED (un-pro-tek'ted) *a.* not pro-

UNPROVED (un-prōōvd') *a.* not established by evidence or reasoning.

UNPROVOKED (un-pro-vōkt') *a.* not provoked.

UNPUBLISHED (un-pub'lisht) *a.* not published.

UNPUNISHED (un-pun'isht) *a.* not punished.

UNQUALIFIED (un-kwol'i-fid) *a.* not qualified; unfitted; unconditioned; absolute.

UNQUENCHABLE (un-kwen'sha-bl) *a.* not to be extinguished.

UNQUESTIONABLE (un-kwest'yun-a-bl) *a.* that is not to be doubted.

UNQUESTIONABLY (un-kwest'yun-a-bli) *ad.* beyond all doubt.

UNQUIET (un-kwi'et) *a.* uneasy; restless.

UNRAVEL (un-rav'l) *v.t.* to disentangle; solve.

UNREADY (un-red'i) *a.* not prepared.

UNREAL (un-rē'al) *a.* not real; unsubstantial.

UNREASONABLE (un-rē'zn-a-bl) *a.* irrational; excessive.

UNREASONABLENESS (un-rē'zn-a-bl-nes) *n.* quality of not being reasonable.

UNREASONABLY (un-rē'zn-a-bli) *ad.* immoderately; excessively.

UNRECORDED (un-rē-kor'ded) *a.* not narrated or registered.

UNREDEEMED (un-rē-dēmd') *a.* not redeemed; not ransomed; not paid.

UNREFINED (un-rē-find') *a.* not rectified or purified.

UNREGENERACY (un-re-jen'e-ra-si) *n.* state of being unrenewed.

UNREGENERATE (un-re-jen'e-rāt) *a.* not renewed in heart.

UNREGISTERED (un-rej'is-tẹrd) *a.* not entered in a register.

UNRELENTING (un-re-len'ting) *a.* feeling no pity.

UNRELIABLE (un-re-lī'ạ-bl) *a.* not to be depended upon.

UNREMITTING (un-re-mit'ing) *a.* continuing; persevering.

UNREPENTING (un-re-pen'ting) *a.* not sorrowful for sin.

UNREQUITED (un-re-kwī'ted) *a.* not recompensed.

UNRESERVE (un-re-zẹrv') *n.* perfect frankness.

UNRESERVED (un-re-zẹrvd') *a.* full; entire; open; frank.

UNRESERVEDLY (un-re-zẹr'ved-li) *ad.* without reservation.

UNRESISTING (un-re-zist'ing) *a.* not making resistance.

UNRESOLVED (un-re-zōlvd') *a.* not determined; not cleared up.

UNRESTRAINT (un-rẹ-strānt') *n.* freedom from restraint.

UNREWARDED (un-re-wawr'ded) *a.* not remunerated.

UNRIG (un-rig') *v.t.* to strip off tackle.

UNRIGHTEOUS (un-rīt'yus) *a.* not righteous; wicked; unjust.

UNRIGHTEOUSNESS (un-rīt'yus-nes) *n.* wickedness.

UNRIPE (un-rīp') *a.* not ripe; immature.

UNRIVALLED (un-rī'vạld) *a.* having no equal.

UNRIVET (un-riv'et) *v.t.* to loose from a rivet.

UNROBE (un-rōb') *v.t.* to disrobe.

UNROLL (un-rol') *v.t.* to open a roll.

UNROOF (un-rōōf') *v.t.* to strip off the roof.

UNRUFFLED (un-ruf'ld) *a.* calm; not agitated.

UNRULY (un-rōōl'i) *a.* ungovernable.

UNSADDLE (un-sad'l) *v.t.* to take the saddle from.

UNSAFE (un-sāf') *a.* not free from danger.

UNSAFELY (un-sāf'li) *ad.* not safely.

UNSAID (un-sed') *pret.* and *pp.* not said; recalled.

UNSALEABLE (un-sā'lạ-bl) *a.* that cannot be sold.

UNSANCTIFIED (un-sangk'ti-fīd) *a.* unholy.

UNSATISFACTORILY (un-sat-is-fak'tur-i-li) *ad.* so as not to satisfy.

UNSATISFACTORY (un-sat-is-fak'tu-ri) *a.* not affording satisfaction.

UNSATISFYING (un-sat'is-fī-ing) *a.* not giving satisfaction.

UNSAVOURY (un-sā'vur-i) *a.* having a bad taste; insipid.

UNSAY (un-sā') *v.t.* [*pret.* and *pp.* **UNSAID**] to recall; retract.

UNSCHOLARLY (un-skol'ạr-li) *a.* unlike or unbecoming a scholar.

UNSCREW (un-skrōō') *v.t.* to loose from screws.

UNSCRIPTURAL (un-skrip'tū-rạl) *a.* not agreeable to Scripture.

UNSCRUPULOUS (un-skrōō'pū-lus) *a.* having no scruples; unprincipled.

UNSEAL (un-sēl') *v.t.* to open what is sealed.

UNSEARCHABLE (un-sẹrch'ạ-bl) *a.* that cannot be explored; mysterious.

UNSEASONABLE (un-sē'zn-ạ-bl) *a.* untimely; unfit.

UNSEASONABLY (un-sē'zn-ạ-bli) *ad.* not in due season.

UNSEAT (un-sēt') *v.t.* to throw from a seat.

UNSEEMLY (un-sēm'li) *a.* unbecoming; improper;—*ad.* unbecomingly.

UNSEEN (un-sēn) *a.* not seen; invisible.

UNSELFISH (un-sel'fish) *a.* not selfish.

UNSERVICEABLE (un-sẹr'vi-sạ-bl) *a.* not fit for use.

UNSETTLE (un-set'l) *v.t.* to unfix; disturb.

UNSHACKLE (un-shak'l) *v.t.* to loose from shackles.

UNSHAKEN (un-shā'kn) *a.* not shaken; firm.

UNSHAPELY (un-shāp'li) *a.* not well shapen or formed. Also **UNSHAPEN**.

UNSHEATHE (un-shēтн') *v.t.* to draw from the sheath or scabbard.

UNSHELTERED (un-shel'tẹrd) *a.* not screened; not protected.

UNSHIP (un-ship') *v.t.* to take out of a ship.

UNSHOD (un-shod') *a.* not having shoes on.

UNSHRINKING (un-skringk'ing) *a.* not recoiling from danger, etc.

UNSIFTED (un-sif'ted) *a.* not sifted or examined.

UNSIGHTLINESS (un-sīt'li-nes) *n.* state of being unsightly.

UNSIGHTLY (un-sīt'li) *a.* unpleasing to the eye; ugly.

UNSKILFUL (un-skil'fool) *a.* wanting skill or dexterity.

UNSKILFULNESS (un-skil'fool-nes) *n.* want of skill.

UNSOCIABLE (un-sō'shạ-bl) *a.* not sociable.

UNSOCIABLY (un-sō'shạ-bli) *ad.* with reserve.

UNSOCIAL (un-sō'shạl) *a.* not agreeable in, or adapted to, society.

UNSOLD (un-sōld') *a.* not sold.

UNSOLICITED (un-so-lis'i-ted) *a.* not asked.

UNSOPHISTICATED (un-so-fis'ti-kā-ted) *a.* not adulterated; pure.

UNSORTED (un-sor'ted) *a.* not distributed into sorts.

UNSOUGHT (un-sawt') *a.* not searched for.

UNSOUND (un-sound') *a.* not sound; defective.

UNSOUNDNESS (un-sound'nes) *n.* defectiveness; infirmity.

UNSPARING (un-spār'ing) *a.* not sparing; liberal; not merciful.

UNSPEAKABLE (un-spē'kạ-bl) *a.* that cannot be uttered.

UNSPEAKABLY (un-spē'kạ-bli) *ad.* inexpressibly.

UNSPENT (un-spent') *a.* not spent.

UNSPOKEN (un-spō'kn) *a.* not uttered.

UNSPOTTED (un-spot'ed) *a.* not spotted; pure; immaculate.

UNSTABLE (un-stā'bl) *a.* not fixed or fast; unsteady.

UNSTAID (un-stād') *a.* not steady; mutable; fickle.

UNSTAINED (un-stānd') *a.* not stained or dyed; not dishonoured.

UNSTAMPED (un-stampt') *a.* not stamped or impressed.

UNSTEADY (un-sted'i) *a.* not steady; changeable; inconstant.

UNSTINTED (un-stint'ed) *a.* not limited.

UNSTOP (un-stop') *v.t.* to take a stopple from; open.

UNSTRING (un-string') *v.t.* to relax; loosen.

UNSTRUNG (un-strung') *a.* relaxed; loosened; untied.

UNSTUDIED (un-stud'id) *a.* not laboured; unpremeditated.

UNSUBSTANTIAL (un-sub-stan'shạl) *a.* not real; not solid.

UNSUCCESSFUL (un-suk-ses'fool) *a.* not meeting with success.

UNSUCCESSFULLY (un-suk-ses'fool-i) *ad.* without success.

UNSUITABLE (un-sū'tạ-bl) *a.* unfit; unbecoming.

UNSUITABLY (un-sū'tạ-bli) *ad.* in an unsuitable manner.

UNSUITED (un-sū'ted) *a.* not suited.

UNSULLIED (un-sul'id) *a.* not tarnished.

UNSUNG (un-sung') *a.* not recited in song.

UNSUPPORTED (un-su-pōr'ted) *a.* unsustained; not upheld.

UNSURPASSED (un-sur-past') *a.* not exceeded.

UNSUSCEPTIBLE (un-sus-sept'i-bl) *a.* not susceptible; unfeeling; insensible.

UNSUSPICIOUS (un-sus-pish'us) *a.* not having suspicion. Also **UNSUSPECTING**.

UNSUSPICIOUSLY (un-sus-pish'us-li) *ad.* without suspicion.

UNSUSTAINED (un-sus-tānd') *a.* not sustained or supported.

UNSWATHE (un-swāTH') *v.t.* to relieve from a bandage.

UNSWEPT (un-swept') *a.* not swept.

UNSYSTEMATIC (un-sis-te-mat'ik) *a.* wanting system.

UNTAINTED (un-tān'ted) *a.* not tainted.

UNTAMABLE (un-tā'ma-bl) *a.* that cannot be tamed or subdued.

UNTASTED (un-tās'ted) *a.* not tasted.

UNTAUGHT (un-tawt') *a.* not learned.

UNTAXED (un-takst') *a.* not charged with taxes; not accused.

UNTENABLE (un-ten'a-bl) *a.* not capable of defence or support.

UNTENANTED (un-ten'an-ted) *a.* unoccupied; having no tenant.

UNTHANKFUL (un-thangk'fool) *a.* not grateful.

UNTHANKFULLY (un-thangk'fool-i) *ad.* ungratefully.

UNTHANKFULNESS (un-thangk'fool-nes) *n.* ingratitude.

UNTHINKING (un-thing'king) *a.* thoughtless.

UNTHOUGHTFUL (un-thawt'fool) *a.* thoughtless.

UNTHRIFTY (un-thrif'ti) *a.* prodigal; not thriving.

UNTIDY (un-ti'di) *a.* not keeping or not kept in good order.

UNTIE (un-ti') *v.t.* to loose as a knot; unbind.

UNTIED (un-tid') *a* not tied; loose.

UNTIL (un-til') *prep.* or *con).* to the time, point, or degree that. [Goth. *und*, unto, and Scand. *till*.]

UNTIMELY (un-tim'li) *a.* unseasonable.

UNTIRING (un-tir'ing) *a.* indefatigable.

UNTO (un'tòò) *prep.* to. [Goth. *und*, up to, and E. to.]

UNTOLD (un-tōld') *a.* not told; not related.

UNTOUCHED (un-tucht') *a.* not handled; not attained; not affected.

UNTOWARD (un-tō'ard) *a.* froward; cross.

UNTRACTABLE (un-trak'ta-bl) *a* ungovernable; stubborn.

UNTRAINED (un-trānd') *a.* not disciplined; irregular.

UNTRAVELLED (un-trav'eld) *a.* not trodden by passengers; not travelled.

UNTRIED (un-trid') *a.* not tried or attempted.

UNTRODDEN (un-trod'n) *a.* not having been trodden or passed over.

UNTRUE (un-tròò') *a.* not true; false.

UNTRULY (un-tròò'li) *ad.* falsely; deceitfully.

UNTRUTH (un-tròòth') *n.* a falsehood.

UNTUNE (un-tūn') *v.t.* to put out of tune; disorder.

UNTWINE (un-twin') *v.t.* to untwist.

UNTWIST (un-twist') *v.t.* to separate twisted threads.

UNUSED (un-ūzd) *a.* not put to use; not accustomed.

UNUSUAL (un-ū'zhū-al) *a.* uncommon; rare; infrequent.

UNUTTERABLE (un-ut'ẽr-a-bl) *a.* that cannot be uttered.

UNVEIL (un-vāl') *v.t.* to throw off a veil.

UNVALUED (un-val'ūd) *a.* not prized or esteemed; neglected.

UNVARIED (un-vā'rid) *a.* not altered or diversified.

UNVARNISHED (un-vär'nisht) *a.* not varnished; plain.

UNVARYING (un-vā'ri-ing) *a.* not changing.

UNWARILY (un-wā'ri-li) *ad.* heedlessly.

UNWARINESS (un-wā'ri-nes) *n.* want of caution; heedlessness.

UNWARNED (un-wawrnd') *a.* not warned or cautioned.

UNWARPED (un-wawrpt') *a.* not warped or biased; impartial.

UNWARRANTABLE (un-wor'an-ta-bl) *a.* not justifiable.

UNWARRANTABLY (un-wor'an-ta-bli) *ad.* without authority.

UNWARRANTED (un-wor'an-ted) *a.* not authorised; not guaranteed.

UNWARY (un-wā'ri) *a.* not cautious.

UNWASHED (un-wosht') *a.* not washed; dirty.

UNWEARIED (un-wē'rid) *a.* not tired, or not tiring; indefatigable.

UNWEARIEDLY (un-wē'rid-li) *a.* without fatigue; indefatigably.

UNWEAVE (un-wēv') *v.t.* to undo what has been woven; unfold.

UNWELCOME (un-wel'kum) *a.* not welcome.

UNWELL (un-wel') *a.* not in good health.

UNWEPT (un-wept') *a.* not lamented.

UNWHOLESOME (un-hōl'sum) *a.* not healthy.

UNWHOLESOMENESS (un-bōl'sum-nes) *n.* unhealthiness.

UNWIELDINESS (un-wēl'di-nes) *a.* heaviness; bulkiness.

UNWIELDY (un-wēl'di) *a.* heavy; unmanageable.

UNWILLING (un-wil'ing) *a.* not willing; reluctant.

UNWILLINGLY (un-wil'ing-li) *ad.* with reluctance.

UNWILLINGNESS (un-wil'ing-nes) *n.* reluctance; disinclination.

UNWIND (un-wind') *v.t.* [*pret.* and *pp.* UNWOUND] to wind off; untwist.

UNWISE (un-wiz') *a.* not wise; injudicious.

UNWISELY (un-wiz'li) *ad.* imprudently.

UNWITTINGLY (un-wit'ing-li) *ad.* ignorantly.

UNWOMANLY (un-woom'an-li) *a.* unbecoming a woman.

UNWONTED (un-won'ted) *a.* unaccustomed; unusual.

UNWONTEDNESS (un-wōn'ted-nes) *n.* uncommonness; rarity.

UNWORN (un-wōrn') *a.* not worn; not impaired.

UNWORTHILY (un-wur'THi-li) *ad.* not according to dessert.

UNWORTHINESS (un-wur'THi-nes) *n.* want of worth.

UNWORTHY (un-wur'THi) *a.* undeserving.

UNWOUND (un-wound') *a.* wound off; untwisted.

UNWRITTEN (un-rit'n) *a.* not written; oral.

UNWROUGHT (un-rawt') *a.* not wrought or manufactured.

UNYIELDING (un-yēl'ding) *a.* stubborn; not pliant.

UNYOKE (un-yōk') *v.t.* to loose from a yoke.

UP (up) *ad.* aloft; out of bed; above the horizon; wholly; as far as. [O.E. *up*, *upp*. Cf. Ger. *auf*.]

UPAS (ū'pas) *n.* a large forest tree or its poisonous sap. [Malay.]

UPBRAID (up-brād') *v.t.* to charge with something wrong; reprove severely. [O.E. *up* upon, and *bregdan*, to BRAID, to seize.]

UPBRAIDER (up-brā'dẽr) *n.* one who reproaches.

UPHEAVAL (up-hē'val) *n.* a heaving up from beneath.

UPHEAVE (up-hēv') *v.t.* to heave or lift up from below.

UPHILL (up'hil) *a.* difficult; laborious.

UPHOLD (up-hōld') *v.t.* [*pret.* and *pp.* UPHELD] to hold up; support; maintain.

UPHOLDER (up-hōl'dẽr) *n.* one who upholds.

UPHOLSTERER (up-hōl'stẽr-ẽr) *n.* one who furnishes houses. [Fr. *upholdster*, for *upholder*, one that *holds up* for sale.]

UPHOLSTERY (up-hōl'stẽr-i) *n.* things furnished by upholsterers.

UPLAND (up'land) *n.* high land;—*a.* higher in situation.

UPLIFT (up-lift') *v t.* to raise aloft.
UPON (u-pon') *prep.* resting on; near to; in; besides; during; after. [O.E. *uppon*, fr. *upp*, UP.]
UPPER (up-ẹr) *a.* higher in place, rank, or office.
UPPERMOST (up'ẹr-mŏst) *a.* highest in place, rank, etc.
UPPISH (up'ish) *a.* assuming airs of superiority.
UPRAISE (up-rāz') *v.t.* to raise or exalt.
UPRIGHT (up'rit, up-rīt') *a.* erect; just.
UPRIGHTLY (up'-rit'li) *ad.* with honesty.
UPRIGHTNESS (up'-rit-nes) *n.* erectness; integrity; honesty.
UPRISING (up-ri'zing) *n.* act of rising; a steep ascent.
UPROAR (up'rŏr) *n.* great noise and disturbance. [D.]
UPROARIOUS (up-rŏr'i-us) *a.* making or attended by great noise; boisterous; disorderly.
UPROOT (up-root') *v.t.* to root up.
UPSHOT (up'shot) *n.* final issue; conclusion.
UPSTAIRS (up'stārz) *a.* in an upper-story;— *n.* an upper story;—(up-stārz') *ad.* towards, or in, an upper story.
UPSTART (up'stȧrt) *n.* one suddenly raised to wealth or power.
UPWARD (up'wȧrd) *a.* directed higher;— *ad.* toward a higher place; above; more than. Also **UPWARDS.**
URANIUM (ū-rā'ni-um) *n.* a rare iron-like metal. [See URANUS.]
URANOGRAPHY (ū-rȧ-nog'rȧ-fi) *n.* description of the heavens. [See URANUS, and G. *graphein*, write.]
URANUS (ū'rȧ-nus) *n.* one of the primary planets. [L., fr. G. *ouranos*, heaven.]
URBAN (ur'bȧn) *a.* of or belonging to a city. [L. *urbanus*, fr. *urbs*, city.]
URBANE (ur-bān') *a.* civil; courteous.
URBANITY (ur-ban'i-ti) *n.* politeness; civility.
URCHIN (ur'chin) *r.* a child; a hedgehog. [Through O.F., fr. L. *ericius*, hedgehog.]
URGE (urj) *v.t.* to press; impel; incite; importune. [L. *urgere*.]
URGENCY (ur'jen-si) *n.* pressing necessity; importunity.
URGENT (ur'jent) *a.* pressing; earnest. [L. (part. s'em) *urgent-*, urgent.]
URGENTLY (ur'jent-li) *ad.* with earnestness or importunity.
URINAL (ū'ri-nȧl) *n.* a convenience for discharging urine.
URINARY (ū'ri-nȧ-ri) *a.* relating to urine. Also **URINOUS.**
URINE (ū'rin) *n.* a fluid secreted by the kidneys. [F., fr. L. *urina*.]
URN (urn) *n.* a vessel or vase of various forms and for various uses. [F., fr. L. *urna*.]
URSIFORM (ur'si-form) *a.* bear-like in form.
URSINE (ur'sīn) *a.* pertaining to or resembling a bear. [Fr. L. *ursus*, a bear.]
URTICATION (ur-ti-kā'shun) *n.* stinging or whipping with nettles. [Fr. L. *urtica*, nettle.]
US (us) *pron.* objective case of WE. [O.E. (acc.) *us.* Cf. Ger. *uns.*]
USABLE (ū'zȧ-bl) *a.* that may be used.
USAGE (ū'zij) *n.* treatment; custom; practice.
USANCE (ū'zȧns) *n.* use; employment; interest of money.
USE (ūs) (1) *n.* act of employing; employment; utility; practice; custom; interest; (2) (ūz) *v.t.* to employ; handle; consume; habituate; treat;—*v.i.* be accustomed. [(1) F. *us*, fr. L. (acc.) *usum.* (2) F. *user*, fr. L., fr. (part.) *usus*, having used, fr. *ute.*]

USEFUL (ūs'fool) *a.* serviceable; profitable.
USEFULNESS (ūs'fool-nes) *n.* quality of being useful.
USELESS (ūs'les) *a.* having no use; answering no purpose.
USELESSLY (ūs'les-li) *ad.* without profit.
USELESSNESS (ūs'les-nes) *n.* unfitness for profitable use.
USHER (ush'ẹr) *n.* an introducer; an under teacher;—*v.t.* to introduce. [O.F. *ussier* = F. *huissier*, fr. L. (acc.) *ostiarium*, doorkeeper, fr. L. *ostium*, door.]
USQUEBAUGH (us'kwĕ-baw) *n.* a kind of whisky. [Ir., fr. *uisge*, water, and *beatha*, life.]
USUAL (ū'zhū-ȧl) *a.* customary; common. [L. *usualis*, fr. *usus*, USE.]
USUALLY (ū'zhū-ȧl-i) *ad.* customarily.
USUFRUCT (ū'zū-frukt) *n.* temporary use of land or property without power to alienate them. [L.]
USURER (ū'zhū-rẹr) *n.* one who practises usury.
USURIOUS (ū-zhū'ri-us) *a.* practising usury.
USURIOUSLY (ū-zhū'ri-us-li) *ad.* with usury.
USURP (ū-zurp') *v.t.* to seize and hold possession wrongfully. [F., fr. L. *usurpare*.]
USURPATION (ū-zur-pā'shun) *n.* illegal seizure or possession.
USURPER (ū-zur'pẹr) *n.* one who seizes power or property without right.
USURY (ū'zhū-ri) *n.* illegal interest for money. [F., fr. L. *usuria*, fr. *usus*, USE.]
UTENSIL (ū-ten'sil) *n.* an instrument; implement; tool; vessel. [F., fr. L. *utensilia*, fit for use, fr. *usus*, USE.]
UTERINE ū'tẹr-in) *a.* denoting one born of the same mother by a different father. [Fr. L. *uterus*, womb.]
UTILITARIAN (ū-til-i-tā'ri-ȧn) *a.* consisting in or pertaining to utility or utilitarianism;— *n.* one who practises utilitarianism.
UTILITARIANISM (ū-til-i-tā'ri-ȧn-izm) *n.* doctrine that the ground and the criterion of moral duty is utility, or the greatest happiness of the greatest number.
UTILISE (ū'til-iz) *v.t.* to make use of; turn to profitable use.
UTILITY (ū-til'i-ti) *n.* usefulness; production of good; profit. [F. *utilité*, fr. L. (acc.) *utilitatem*, utility, fr. *utilis*, fr. *uti*, to use.]
UTMOST (ut'mŏst) *a.* furthest; highest; greatest;—*n.* the most that can be. [O.E. *utemest*, double superlative of *ute*, OUT.]
UTOPIAN (ū-tō'pi-ȧn) *a.* fanciful; ideal. [Fr. *Utopia* = nowhere, fr. G. *ou*, not, and *topos*, place.]
UTRICLE (ū'tri-kl) *n.* a little bag. [L. dim. fr. *uter.*]
UTRICULAR (ū-trik'ū-lȧr) *a.* containing little bladders or bags.
UTTER (ut'ẹr) (1) *a.* farthest out; extreme; total; perfect;—(2) *v.t.* to speak; express; put in circulation. [(1) O.E. *uter*, outer, fr. *ut*, OUT. (2) O.E. *utian*, to put out, fr. *ut*, OUT.]
UTTERABLE (ut'ẹr-ȧ-bl) *a.* that may be expressed.
UTTERANCE (ut'ẹr-ȧns) *n.* manner of speaking; pronunciation; expression.
UTTERER (ut'ẹr-ẹr) *n.* one who pronounces or puts in circulation.
UTTERLY (ut'ẹr-li) *ad.* completely; totally.
UTTERMOST (ut'ẹr-mŏst) *a.* furthest; most remote;—*n.* greatest degree possible.
UVEOUS (ū'vē-us) *a.* like a grape. [L. *uva*, grape.]
UXORICIDE (uk-sor'i-sīd) *n.* murder or the murderer of a wife. [L. *uxor*, and *caedere.*]
UXORIOUS (uk-sō'ri-us) *a.* excessively or submissively fond of a wife. [L. *uxorius*, fr. stem *uxori-*, of *uxor*, wife.]

V

VACANCY (vā'kan-si) *n.* a void or gap between things; empty space; situation not filled up; leisure time; listlessness. [pied.

VACANT (vā'kant) *a.* empty; void; not occu-

VACATE (va-kāt') *v.t.* to make void; quit possession of. [L. (part.) *vacatus*, made empty, fr. *vacare*, to be empty.]

VACATION (va-kā'shun) *n.* intermission; break; recess; holidays; leisure.

VACCINATE (vak'si-nāt) *v.t.* to inoculate with cow-pox. [L *vaccinus*, belonging to cows, fr. *vacca*, a cow.]

VACCINATION (vak-si-nā'shun) *n.* inoculation with cow-pox.

VACCINE (vak'sin, vak'sīn) *a.* pertaining to or derived from cows or vaccination.

VACILLATE (vas'i-lāt) *v.i.* to waver; fluctuate. [L. (part.) *vacillatus*, fr. *vacillare*, to reel.]

VACILLATING (vas'i-lā-ting) *a.* inclined to fluctuate; inconstant.

VACILLATION (vas-i-lā'shun) *n.* a wavering of mind or purpose.

VACUITY (va-kū'i-ti) *n.* emptiness. [See **VACATE.**]

VACUOUS (vak'ū-us) *a.* empty; void.

VACUUM (vak'ū-um) *n.* empty space. [See **VACATE.**]

VADE-MECUM (vā'de-mē'kum) *n.* a handbook or manual for ready reference. [L. -go with me.]

VAGABOND (vag'a-bond) *n.* a vagrant; —*a.* wandering idly. [F., fr. L. *vagabundus*.]

VAGARY (va-gā'ri) *n.* a freak; a whim. [L. *vagari*, stroll about.]

VAGINAL (vaj'i-nal, va-gī'nal) *a.* pertaining to a sheath. [Fr. L. *ragina*.]

VAGRANCY (vā'gran-si) *n.* state or life of a vagrant.

VAGRANT (vā'grant) *a.* wandering; unsettled; —*n.* one who has no settled home; a sturdy beggar. [A.F. *wakerant*; O.F. *walerer*, to wander. 'Confused with L. *vagari*, but *not* derived from it.'—Skeat.]

VAGUE (vāg) *a.* unsettled; indefinite; uncertain; loose. [F. *vague*, wandering fr. L. *vagus*.]

VAIL. See **VEIL.** [O.F. *avaler*, to let fall down, fr. L. *ad vallem*, to the valley.]

VAIN (vān) *a.* unsatisfying; unreal; conceited; showy; fruitless; worthless. [F., fr. L. *vanus*, empty.]

VAINGLORIOUS (vān-glō'ri-us) *a.* excessively vain of one's own doings; boastful.

VAINGLORY (vān-glō'ri) *n.* empty pride.

VAINLY (vān'li) *ad.* in vain; proudly; ostentatiously.

VAIRY (vā'ri) *a.* charged with silver and azure colours. [F. *vair*, fr. L. *varius*.]

VALANCE (val'ans) *n.* drapery roun l the head of a bed. [Fr. *Valence* (L. *Valentia*), in France.]

VALE (vāl) *n.* a low ground; a valley. [F. *val*, fr. L. *vallis*, a valley.]

VALEDICTION (val-e-dik'shun) *n.* a bidding farewell. [L. (part.) *valedictus*, fr. *valedicere*, to say farewell, fr. *vale*, farewell.]

VALEDICTORY (val-e-dik'tu-ri) *a.* bidding farewell; —*n.* a farewell address.

VALENCIENNES (val-en-se-enz') *n.* a rich kind of French lace.

VALENTINE (val'en-tīn) *n.* a sweetheart chosen, or a letter sent, on Valentine's day.

VALET (val'et, val'ā) *n.* a man-servant; personal attendant. [F. *valet*, a groom. Doublet of **VARLET.**]

VALETUDINARIAN (val-e-tū-di-nā'ri-an) *a.* infirm in health; seeking health; —*n.* a man of a weak or sickly constitution. [L. *valetudin-*, stem of *valetudo*, health, fr. *valere*, to be strong.]

VALETUDINARY (val-e-tū'di-na-ri) *a.* sickly; infirm.

VALIANT (val'yant) *a.* intrepid in danger; performed with valour.

VALID (val'id) *a.* having sufficient force; sound; conclusive; legal. [L. *validus*, strong, fr. *valere*.]

VALIDITY (va-lid'i-ti) *n.* strength to prove or convince; soundness; justness.

VALIDLY (val'id-li) *ad.* justly; soundly; legally.

VALISE (va-lēs') *n.* a travelling-case. [F.]

VALLEY (val'i) *n.* a low place between hills; —*pl.* **VALLEYS.** [L. (acc.) *vallem*, fr. *vallis*, a vale.]

VALOROUS (val'ur-us) *a.* valiant; brave.

VALOUR (val'ur) *n.* courage; bravery; prowess; intrepidity. [O.F. *valor*, fr. L. (acc.) *valorem*, fr. *valor*, fr. *valere*, to be strong.]

VALUABLE (val'ū-a-bl) *a.* having value.

VALUATION (val-ū-ā'shun) *n.* act of fixing the value; appraisement; value set.

VALUE (val'ū) *n.* worth; price; rate; importance; —*v.t.* to estimate the worth; rate; appraise. [F. *valu*, part. of *valoir*, to be worth, fr. L. *valere*, be worth.]

VALUELESS (val'ū-les) *a.* having no value or worth.

VALUER (val'ū-er) *n.* an appraiser. Also **VALUATOR.**

VALVE (valv) *n.* a folding door; a lid opening only one way. [L. *valva*, a leaf of a folding door.]

VALVULAR (val'vū-lar) *a.* having valves.

VAMP (vamp) *n.* upper shoe-leather; —*v.t.* to mend. [F. *avant-pied*, fore-foot, fr. L. *ab*, *ante*, and *pes*, *pedis*, foot.]

VAMPIRE (vam'pir) *n.* a species of bat; a fabled demon. [Servian =a bloodsucker.]

VAN (van) (1) *n.* front of an army or a fleet; —(2) *n.* winnowing fan; —(3) *n.* a covered wagon for goods. [(1) Fr. O.F. *avant garde*, the vanguard of an army; F. *avant*, before, and O.F. *garde*, a guard. (2) F. *van*, fr. L. *vannus*, a fan. (3) Short for **CARAVAN.**]

VANDAL (van'dal) *n.* a barbarian; one hostile to arts and literature. [L., fr. Teut.]

VANDALIC (van-dal'ik) *a.* rude; barbarous.

VANDALISM (van'dal-izm) *n.* hostility to refinement of arts or letters.

VANDYKE (van-dīk') *n.* a small round neckerchief. [*Vandyke* (1599-1641), the painter.]

VANE (vān) *n.* a plate that shows the direction of the wind; the web of a feather. [O.E. *fana*, banner.]

VANGUARD (van'gârd) *n.* the troops in front; the first line. [See **VAN** (1).]

VANILLA (va-nil'a) *n.* a tropical plant used for seasoning ices, liqueurs, etc. [Sp., fr. L. *ragina*, sheath.]

VANISH (van'ish) *v.i.* to disappear; pass away. [L. *vanescere*, to become empty, fr. *vanus*, empty.]

VANITY (van'i-ti) *n.* empty pride; conceit; idle show; uncertainty; worthlessness.

VANQUISH (vang'kwish) *v.t.* to conquer. [Fr. A.F. *veincre*, to conquer, F. *vaincre*, fr. L. *vincere*.]

VANQUISHABLE (vang'kwish-a-bl) *a.* that may be conquered.

VANQUISHER (vang'kwish-er) *n.* one who conquers; a victor.

VANTAGE (van'tij) *n.* superiority; advantage. [Contr. of M.E. *avantage*, advantage.]

VANTAGE-GROUND (van'tij-ground) *n.* place or state which gives one an advantage over another. [stale.]

VAPID (vap'id) *a.* spiritless; flat. [L. *vapidus*,

VAPIDITY (va-pid'i-ti) *n.* the state of having lost life or spirit. Also **VAPIDNESS.**

VAPORATION (vap-u-rā'shun) *n.* act of converting into vapour.

VAPORISE (vā'pur-īz) *v.t.* to convert into vapour.

VAPOROUS (vā'pur-us) *a.* full of vapours; windy; unreal.

VAPOUR (vā'pur) *n.* a fluid rendered aeriform by heat;—*v.i.* to pass off in fumes: brag. [L. *vapor.*]

VAPOURABLE (vā'pur-a-bl) *a.* that may be converted into vapour.

VAPOUR-BATH (vā-pur-bath) *n.* a bath of vapour.

VAPOURER (vā'pur-ẹr) *n.* a boaster: braggart.

VAPOURS (vā'purz) *n.pl.* peevishness.

VAPOURY (vā'pur-i) *a.* full of vapours; splenetic.

VARIABLE (vā'ri-a-bl) *a.* changeable: unsteady. [L. *varius*, various.]

VARIABLENESS (vā'ri-a-bl-nes) *n.* aptness to change; inconstancy.

VARIABLY (vā'ri-a-bli) *ad.* changeably.

VARIANCE (vā'ri-ans) *n.* disagreement.

VARIATION (vā'ri-ā'shun) *n.* a change; deviation; difference; rate of change; musical embellishment.

VARICOSE (var'i-kōs) *a.* enlarged: dilated. [L. *varicosus.* fr. stem *varic-.* of *varix* dilated vein, fr. *varus,* crooked.]

VARIEGATE (vā'ri-e-gāt) *v.t.* to diversify. [L. *vario-.* fr. *varius.* of divers colours. and *-igare,* due to *agere,* to make.]

VARIEGATION (vā-ri-e-gā'shun) *n.* diversity of colours.

VARIETY (va-rī'e-ti) *n.* change; difference: a number of things, or one slightly differing.

VARIORUM (vā-ri-ō'rum) *a.* denoting an edition of the classics, with notes by various commentators. [L. *cum notis variorum.*]

VARIOUS (vā'ri-us) *a.* different; diverse: changeable; uncertain. [L. *varius* of divers colours.]

VARIOUSLY (vā'ri-us-li) *ad.* in different ways.

VARLET (vär'let) *n.* a footman; a low fellow. [O.F.] Doublet of **VALET.**

VARNISH (vär'nish) *n.* a viscid liquid laid on work to give it a gloss;—*v.t.* to lay varnish on; give a fair appearance to. [F. *vernis.* varnish.]

VARY (vā'ri) *v.t.* or *i.* to alter; diversify; differ: disagree. [F. *varier.* fr. L. *variare.* to vary, fr. *varius,* various.]

VASCULAR (vas'kū-lar) *a.* consisting of vessels. [L. *vasculum,* a small vessel, dim. of *vas* vessel.]

VASE (vās. vāz) *n.* an ornamental vessel of an antique pattern. [F. *vase,* a vessel, fr. L. *vasum.* allied to *vas,* a vessel.]

VASELINE (vas'e-lin) *n.* an ointment obtained from petroleum. [Ger. *Wasser* water. and G. *elaion,* oil.]

VASSAL (vas'al) *n.* a feudal tenant; bondsman; serf. [F., fr. Bret. *gwaz,* servant.]

VASSALAGE (vas'al-ij) *n.* dependence; subjection.

Vase.

VAST (vast) *a.* immense; great; numerous;—*n.* an empty space; boundless space. [F. *vaste.* fr. L. *vastus* great.]

VASTLY (vast'li) *ad.* exceedingly.

VASTNESS (vast'nes) *n.* immense extent; magnitude. amount, or importance.

VAT (vat) *n.* a large cistern for holding liquors; a measure. [O.E. *fœt,* a vessel, cask.]

VATICAN (vat'i-kan) *n.* the palace of the pope on the Vatican Hill in Rome; the papal power. [L. *Mons Vaticanus.* a hill in Rome.]

VATICINAL (va-tis'i-nal) *a.* containing prophecy.

VATICINATE (va-tis'i-nāt) *v.t.* or *i.* to prophesy; foretell. [L. (part.) *vaticinatus,* fr. *vaticinari,* to prophesy, fr. *vati-,* for *vates,* a prophet, and *-cin,* fr. *canere,* to sing, proclaim.]

VATICINATION (va-tis-i-nā'shun) *n.* prediction; prophecy.

VAUDEVILLE (vōd-vēl') *n.* a dramatic piece interspersed with light lively songs. [F., fr. *Val de Vire,* in Normandy.]

VAULT (vawlt) *n.* an arched roof; underground chamber with an arched roof; leap; bound ;—*v.t.* to arch ; roof with an arch ;— *v.i.* to curvet ; leap. [O.F. *volte,* a vault, fr. L. (part.) *volutus,* fr. *volvere,* to roll, turn round.]

VAULTED (vawl'ted) *a.* arched.

VAULTER (vawl'tẹr) *n.* a leaper or tumbler.

VAUNT (vawnt, vänt) *v.t.* or *i.* to boast of: make a vain display ;—*n.* vain boast. [F. *se vanter.* to boast: Late L. *vanitare,* to speak vanity. fr. L. *vanus.* vain.]

VAUNTINGLY (vawn'ting-li) *ad.* with boasting.

VEAL (vēl) *n.* flesh of a calf. [O.F. *veel* a calf, fr. L. (acc.) *vitellum,* dim. of *vitulus* a calf.]

VEDETTE (ve-det', vi-det') *n.* a sentinel on horseback. [M.F. *vedette,* a sentinel; It. *vedetta,* a horse-sentry, fr. L. *videre,* to see.]

VEER (vēr) *v.t.* or *i.* to turn; change direction. [F. *virer,* to turn.]

VEGETABLE (vej'e-ta-bl) *n.* a plant for the table;—*a.* of the nature of plants. [L. *vegetabilis.* full of life, fr. *vegetare* to quicken.]

VEGETAL (vej'e-tal) *a.* having power to cause growth.

VEGETARIAN (vej'e-tā'ri-an) *n.* one who holds that vegetables are the only proper food for man.

VEGETATE (vej'e-tāt) *v.i.* to grow as plants.

VEGETATION (vej-e-tā'shun) *n.* growth of plants.

VEGETATIVE (vej'e-tā-tiv) *a.* growing.

VEHEMENCE (vē'he-mens) *n.* violent activity or force.

VEHEMENT (vē'he-ment) *a.* acting with force: passionate; furious; earnest. [L. *vehement-,* stem of *vehemens.* passionate: lit. out of one's mind.']

VEHEMENTLY (vē'he-ment-li) *ad.* violently.

VEHICLE (vē'hi-kl) *n.* a carriage. [L. *vehiculum* fr. *vehere,* carry.]

VEIL (vāl) *n.* a cover to conceal the face: a curtain; a disguise;—*v.t.* to cover; hide. [O.F. *veile,* fr. L. *velum,* sail, covering. fr. *vehere,* carry.]

VEIN (vān) *n.* a vessel which returns the blood to the heart; current; seam; streak: train of thought; turn of mind. [F. *veine* fr. L. *vena,* a vein, fr. *vehere,* to carry.]

VEINY (vā'ni) *a.* full of veins; variegated.

VELLUM (vel'um) *n.* fine parchment. [O.F. *velin,* fr. L. *vitulinus,* fr. *vitulus.* a calf.]

VELOCITY (ve-los'i-ti) *n.* swiftness; celerity; speed. [M.F. *velocité,* swiftness, fr. L. (acc.) *relocitatem,* fr. *veloci-* stem of *velox,* swift.]

VELVET (vel'vet) *n.* a rich silk stuff with a nap;—*a.* like velvet; soft; smooth;—*v.t.* to paint velvet. [A.F. *veluet,* fr. Late L. *villutus,* shaggy, fr. L. *villus.* shaggy hair.]

VELVETEEN (vel-ve-tēn') *n.* cotton velvet.

VELVETY (vel've-ti) *a.* soft; like velvet.

VENAL (vē'nal) (1) *a.* mercenary;—(2) pertaining to veins. [(1) L. *venalis.* saleable, fr. *venus,* sale. (2) See **VEIN.**]

VENALITY (vē-nal'i-ti) *n.* mercenariness.

VEND (vend) *v.t.* to sell. [F. *vendre,* fr. L. *vendere,* to sell, fr. *venus-* sale, and *dare* to offer.]

VENDEE (ven-dē') *n.* one to whom a thing is sold.

VENDER (ven'dẹr) *n.* one who sells. Also **VENDOR.**

VENDIBLE (ven'di-bl) *a.* that may be sold.
VENDITION (ven-dish'un) *n.* the act of selling; sale.
VENDUE (ven-dū') *n.* public sale to the highest bidder.
VENEER (ve-nēr') *v.t.* to overlay or face with thin pieces of wood;—*n.* thin slices of finer wood for facing. [F. *fournir.* furnish.]
VENERABLE (ven'e-rạ-bl) *a.* worthy of veneration; aged.
VENERATE (ven'e-rāt) *v.t.* to regard with reverence. [L. *veneratus,* part. of *venerari,* to reverence.]
VENERATION (ven-e-rā'shun) *n.* the highest degree of reverence.
VENERATOR (ven'e-rā-tẹr) *n.* one who venerates.
VENEREAL (ve-nē're-ạl) *a.* relating to sexual intercourse. [L. *Venus, Veneris,* the goddess of love.]
VENERY (ven'e-ri) *n.* hunting; sexual intercourse. [M.F. *venerie,* hunting, fr. L. *venari,* hunt.]
VENESECTION (ven-e-sek'shun) *n.* act of opening a vein to let blood. [L. *vena,* vein, and **SECTION.**]
VENETIAN (ve-nē'shạn) *a.* belonging to or produced at Venice.
VENGEANCE (ven'jạns) *n.* infliction of pain in return for an injury; retribution. [F., fr. L. *vindicare,* avenge.]
VENGEFUL (venj'fool) *a.* vindictive; revengeful.
VENIAL (vē'ni-ạl) *a.* pardonable; excusable. [L. *venialis,* pardonable, fr. *venia,* forgiveness.]
VENISON (ven'i-zn, ven'zn) *n.* the flesh of deer. [M.F. *venaison,* fr. L. *venationem,* acc. of *venatio.* hunting.]
VENOM (ven'um) *n.* poison; malice. [L. *venenum.*] [ful; malicious.
VENOMOUS (ven'u-mus) *a.* poisonous; spite-
VENOUS (vē'nus) *a.* contained in veins.
VENT (vent) *n.* a passage for air, fluid, etc.; flue; escape;—*v.t.* to let out; utter; report. [M.F. *fente,* cleft, F. *fendre,* to cleave, fr. L. *findere,* to cleave.]
VENTAGE (ven'tij) *n.* a small hole.
VENTILATE (ven'ti-lāt) *v.t.* to fan; expose to air; submit to examination. [L. *ventilare,* to winnow, fr. *ventulus,* a light wind, fr. *ventus,* wind.]
VENTILATION (ven-ti-lā'shun) *n.* act of ventilating; state of being ventilated.
VENTILATOR (ven'ti-lā-tẹr) *n.* an instrument to introduce pure air.
VENTRAL (ven'trạl) *a.* belonging to the belly. [L. *ventralis,* fr. *venter,* belly.]
VENTRICLE (ven'tri-kl) *n.* a cavity in an animal body.
VENTRILOQUISM (ven-tril'u-kwizm) *n.* the art of speaking so that the voice seems to come from a distance. [L. *ventri-* stem of *venter,* the belly, and *loqui,* speak.]
VENTRILOQUIST (ven-tril'u-kwist) *n.* one who practises ventriloquism.
VENTURE (ven'tūr) *v.t.* or *i.* to have courage to do or undertake; run a risk; dare; hazard; risk;—*n.* a risking; hazard; stake. [F. *aventure,* a chance, fr. L. *ad,* and *venturus,* fut. part. of *venire,* come.]
VENTURER (ven'tūr-ẹr) *n.* one who ventures.
VENTURESOME (ven'tūr-sum) *a.* bold; daring. Also **VENTUROUS.**
VENUE (ven'ū) *n.* a neighbouring place; place where an action is laid. [M.F., fr. L. *venire,* come.]
VENUS (vē'nus) *n.* goddess of love; a planet. [L.]
VERACIOUS (ve-rā'shus) *a.* observant of truth. [L. *veraci-* stem of *verax,* true, and suffix, *-ous,* fr. *verus,* true.]
VERACITY (ve-ras'i-ti) *n.* agreement with fact; truth; habitual truthfulness.

VERANDA (ve-ran'dạ) *n.* an open portico. [Pg. *varanda,* fr. Sp. *vara,* a rod. fr. L. *vara,* a forked pole.]
VERB (verb) *n.* a word expressing being, doing, or suffering. [F. *verbe,* fr. L. *verbum,* a word.]
VERBAL (ver'bạl) *a.* uttered by the mouth; oral; literal;—*n.* a word derived from a verb. [pressed verbally.
VERBALISM (ver'bạl-izm) *n.* something ex-
VERBALLY (ver'bạl-i) *ad.* by word of mouth; orally.
VERBATIM (ver-bā'tim) *ad.* word for word.
VERBENA (ver-bē'nạ) *n.* a genus of plants with fragrant foliage and beautiful flowers. [L. *verbena,* leaves, twigs.]
VERBIAGE (ver'bi-ij) *n.* superabundance of words; wordiness. [L. *verbum,* a word.]
VERBOSE (ver-bōs') *a.* using more words than are necessary; wordy. [L. *verbum,* a word.]
VERBOSITY (ver-bos'i-ti) *n.* the use of too many words. [ness.
VERDANCY (ver'dan-si) *n.* greenness; raw-
VERDANT (ver'dạnt) *a.* green; fresh; flourishing; raw; ignorant. [O.F. *verd,* green, fr. L. *viridis.*]
VERDICT (ver'dikt) *n.* the decision of a jury in a case submitted to them. [M.E. *verdit,* fr. L. *vere dictum,* truly said.]
VERDIGRIS (ver'di-gris) *n.* rust of copper. [O.F.]
VERDURE (ver'dūr) *n.* greenness; freshness or vegetation.
VERGE (verj) (1) *n.* a rod; mace; shaft; edge; border; compass; range;—*v.i.* to tend downward; border upon. [(1) F. *verge,* fr. L. *virga,* a rod. (2) L. *vergere,* to tend towards.]
VERGER (ver'jer) *n.* a mace-bearer.
VERIFIABLE (ver'i-fi-ạ-bl) *a.* that may be verified.
VERIFICATION (ver-i-fi-kā'shun) *n.* act of verifying.
VERIFIER (ver'i-fī-ẹr) *n.* one who, or that which, proves a thing to be true.
VERIFY (ver'i-fi) *v.t.* to prove to be true; confirm. [M.E. *verifier,* fr. Late L. *verificare,* to make true, fr. L. *verus,* true, and *facere,* to make.]
VERILY (ver'i-li) *ad.* truly; certainly. [Fr. **VERY.**]
VERISIMILAR (ver-i-sim'i-lạr) *a.* probable; likely. [L. *verisimilis,* fr. *verus,* true, and *similis,* like.]
VERISIMILITUDE (ver-i-sim-il'i-tūd) *n.* resemblance to truth.
VERITABLE (ver'i-tạ-bl) *a.* agreeable to fact; true; actual. [L. *veritas,* truth.]
VERITY (ver'i-ti) *n.* truth; reality; a true fact or statement.
VERJUICE (ver'jŏŏs) *n.* a liquor expressed from green or unripe fruit. [F. *verjus;* lit. green juice, fr. L. *viridis,* green, and *jus,* juice.]
VERMICELLI (ver-mi-sel'i, ver-mi-chel'i) *n.* wheat paste made into long thin tubes. [It., fr. L. *vermis* worm.]
VERMICULAR (ver-mik'ū-lạr) *a.* like a worm. [L. *vermis,* worm.]
VERMICULATE (ver-mik'ū-lāt) *v.t.* to inlay in the form of worms.
VERMICULATION (ver-mik-ū-lā'shun) *n.* motion like a worm.
VERMICULE (ver'mi-kūl) *n.* a little worm or grub.
VERMIFUGE (ver'mi-fūj) *n.* a medicine to expel worms. [L. *vermis,* worm, and *fugare,* drive away.]
VERMILION (ver-mil'yun) *n.* cochineal; a bright red colour;—*v.t.* to tinge with red. [F., fr. L. *vermis,* worm.]
VERMIN (ver'min) *n.* all sorts of small noxious animals or insects. [F. *vermine,* fr. L. *vermis,* worm.]

VERMINATION (ver-mi-nä'shun) *n.* breeding of worms; griping of the bowels.

VERMINOUS (ver'mi-nus) *a.* full of, or caused by vermin.

VERMIVOROUS (ver-miv'u-rus) *a.* feeding on worms. [L. *vermis*, worm, and *vorare*, devour.]

VERNACULAR (ver-nak'ū-lar) *a.* native; belonging to one's own country. [L. *vernaculus*, native, fr. *verna*, a home-born slave.]

VERNAL (ver'nal) *a.* belonging to the spring or to youth. [L. *vernalis*, fr. *vernus*, belonging to spring, fr. *ver*, spring.]

VERSATILE (ver'sa-til) *a.* turning easily; easily applied; ready; unsteady; fickle. [L. *versatilis*, fr. *versare*, freq. of *vertere*, to turn.]

VERSATILITY (ver-sa-til'i-ti) *n.* quality of being versatile.

VERSE (vers) *n.* a line; a stanza; poetry; in the *Bible*, a short division of a chapter. [L. (part.) *versus*, fr. *vertere*, to turn.]

VERSED (verst) *a.* well skilled; practised. [F. *versé*, fr. L. *versari*, turn round.]

VERSIFICATION (vers-i-fi-kā'shun) *n.* the art of composing verses.

VERSIFIER (ver'si-fi-er) *n.* one who writes verses.

VERSIFY (ver'si-fi) *v.i.* to make verses;—*v.t.* to relate in verse; turn into verse. [L. *versificare*, to make verses, fr. *versus*, a verse, and *ficare*, fr. *facere*, to make.]

VERSION (ver'shun) *n.* translation; account; statement. [F., fr. L. (acc.) *versionem*, of *versio*, a translation, fr. (part.) *versus*, turned, fr. *vertere*, to turn.]

VERTEBRA (ver'te-bra) *n.* a joint of the spine:—*pl.* **VERTEBRÆ.** [L.]

VERTEBRAL (ver'te-bral) *a.* relating to the spine.

VERTEX (ver'teks) *n.* the crown or top of anything; the zenith. [L. *vertex*, top, pole of the sky, fr. *vertere*, to turn.]

VERTICAL (ver'ti-kal) *a.* being in the zenith; perpendicular.

VERTICALLY (ver'ti-kal-i) *ad.* in a vertical position.

VERTIGINOUS (ver-tij'i-nus) *a.* giddy; turning round.

VERTIGO (ver'ti-gō, ver-ti'gō) *n.* swimming of the head; dizziness. [L. *vertigo*, giddiness, fr. *vertere*, to turn.]

VERTU (ver'too) *n.* excellence and rarity in artistic productions. [See **VIRTU.**]

VERVE (verv) *n.* nervous energy; fire; lively spirit. [F.]

VERY (ver'i) *a.* true; real; actual;—*ad.* in a great degree. [O.F. *verai*, F. *vrai*, true, fr. L. *verus*, true.]

VESICATE (ves'i-kāt) *v.t.* to blister.

VESICATION (ves-i-kā'shun) *n.* act of raising blisters.

VESICLE (ves'i-kl) *n.* a little bladder or blister; small cavity or cell. [L. *vesicula*, dim. of *vesica*, bladder.]

VESICULOUS (ve-sik'ū-lus) *a.* consisting of vesicles. Also **VESICULAR.**

VESPER (ves'per) *n.* the evening star; evening; Venus;—*pl.* evening service;—*a.* pertaining to vesper or vespers. [Fr. L.; G. *hesperos.*]

VESSEL (ves'el) *n.* a hollow dish or utensil for holding things; a ship of any size; a canal or tube; an agent. [O.F. *vaissel*, a vessel, ship; late *vaisseau*, a vessel of any kind, fr. L. *vascellum*, a small vase, dim. of *vas*, a vase.]

VEST (vest) *n.* a waistcoat;—*v.t.* to clothe; put in possession;—*v.i.* to descend or pertain to. [L. *vestis*, a garment, clothing.]

VESTAL (ves'tal) *a.* pertaining to Vesta; pure; chaste;—*n.* a virgin consecrated to Vesta. [L. *Vesta.*]

VESTED (ves'ted) *a.* clothed; fixed; not contingent, as rights.

VESTIBULAR (ves-tib'ū-lar) *a.* pertaining to a vestibule.

VESTIBULE (ves'ti-būl) *n.* the porch or entrance of a house. [L. *vestibulum*, a forecourt, fr. *ve*, separated from, and *stabulum*, an abode.]

VESTIGE (ves'tij) *n.* a footstep; trace;—*pl.* small remains. [F. *vestige*, a foot-track, fr. L. *vestigium*, foot-track.]

VESTMENT (vest'ment) *n.* a garment.

VESTRY (ves'tri) *n.* a room in a church for vestments and parochial meetings; the managers of the secular affairs of a parish. [M.E. *vestrie*, short. fr. O.F. *vestiarie*, fr. L. *vestiarium*, a wardrobe, fr. *vestis*, garment.]

VESTURE (ves'tūr) *n.* a garment or articles worn; dress; clothing.

VESUVIAN (ve-sōō'vi-an) *a.* pertaining to Vesuvius;—*n.* a highly inflammable lucifer match.

VETCH (vech) *n.* a leguminous plant used for fodder. [O.F. *veche*, fr. L. *vicia.*]

VETERAN (vet'e-ran) *a.* long exercised; experienced;—*n.* one who has long served in war, art, or other occupation. [L. *veteranus*, experienced, fr. *vetus*, *veteris*, old.]

VETERINARIAN (vet-e-ri-nā'ri-an) *n.* one skilled in diseases of cattle.

VETERINARY (vet'e-ri-na-ri) *a.* pertaining to the art of healing the diseases of domestic animals. [L. *veterinarius*, of, or belonging to, beasts of burden, fr. *veterinus*, of beasts of burden.]

VETO (vē'tō) *n.* a prohibition; negative vote; —*v.t.* to withhold assent to; reject by vote. [L. *veto*, I forbid.]

VEX (veks) *v.t.* to tease; provoke; harass; irritate; trouble; distress. [F. *vexer*, fr. L. *vexare*, to harass.]

VEXATION (vek-sā'shun) *n.* act of vexing; state of being vexed; trouble; uneasiness.

VEXATIOUS (vek-sā'shus) *a.* harassing; distressing; troublesome.

VEXATIOUSLY (vek-sā'shus-li) *ad.* so as to give trouble or annoyance.

VIADUCT (vī'a-dukt) *n.* a structure by which a way is formed from one road to another. [L. *via ducta*, a road conducted across, fr. *via*, and (part.) *ducta* (fem.) of *ducere*, convey, carry.]

VIAL (vī'al) *n.* a small bottle. Also written **PHIAL.** [F., fr. L. *phiala*, fr. G. *phiale*, a shallow cup or bowl.]

Viaduct.

VIANDS (vī'andz) *n.pl.* dressed meat; victuals. [F. *viande*, meat, food, fr. L. *vivenda*, (neut. pl.) provisions, fr *vivere*, to live.]

VIATICUM (vī-at'i-kum) *n.* the communion given to a dying person. [L., fr. *via*, a way.]

VIBRATE (vī'brāt) *v.t.* or *i.* to move to and fro; oscillate; swing. [L. (part.) *vibratus*, fr. *vibrare*, to swing, shake.]

VIBRATION (vī-brā'shun) *n.* the act of vibrating.

VIBRATORY (vī'bra-tur-i) *a.* consisting of or causing vibrations.

VICAR (vik'ar) *n.* substitute; deputy. [F. *vicaire*, a deputy, fr. L. *vicarius*, a deputy.]

VICARAGE (vik'ur-ij) *n.* the benefice of a vicar.

VICARIOUS (vī-kā'ri-us) *a.* acting in place of another; performed or suffered in place of others.

VICARSHIP (vik'ar-ship) *n.* office or functions of a vicar.

VICE (vīs) (1) *n.* a blemish; fault;—(2) *n.* a small screw-press;—(3) a Latin prefix, denoting *in the place of.* [(1) F. *vice*, fr. L. *vitium*, blemish, fault. (2) O.F. *vis*, vice, a winding stair, fr. L. *vitis*, vine. (3) L. *vice*, in place of.]

VICE-ADMIRAL (vīs-ad'mi-rạl) *n.* an admiral of the second rank.

VICE-CONSUL (vīs-kon'sul) *n.* one acting for the consul.

VICEGERENT (vīs-jē'rent) *n.* an officer acting in place of another. [L. *vice*, in place of, and *gerent-* (pres. part. stem), fr. *gerere*, rule.]

VICEROY (vīs'roi) *n.* the representative of a king. [O.F.] [viceroy.

VICEROYALTY (vīs-roi'ạl-ti) *n.* the office of

VICINAGE (vis'i-nij) *n.* neighbourhood.

VICINAL (vis'i-nạl) *a.* near; bordering.

VICINITY (vi-sin'i-ti) *n.* neighbourhood; propinquity; adjoining country. [M.F. *vicinite*, fr. L. (acc.) *vicinitatem*, fr. *vicinus*, near, fr. *vicus*, village, street.]

VICIOUS (vish'us) *a.* immoral; wicked; corrupt; impure; unruly. [See VICE (1).]

VICIOUSLY (vish'us-li) *ad.* wickedly.

VICISSITUDE (vi-sis'i-tūd) *n.* alternation or change from one thing to another; ups and downs in human affairs. [L.]

VICTIM (vik'tim) *n.* a living being sacrificed; a sacrifice. [F. *victime*, fr. L. *victima*.]

VICTIMISE (vik'tim-īz) *v.t.* to make a victim of; cheat.

VICTOR (vik'tẹr) *n.* a conqueror. [L. *victor*, a conqueror, fr. *vic-*, base of *vincere*, to conquer.]

VICTORESS (vik'tu-res) *n.* a female who conquers. Also **VICTRESS.**

VICTORIA-CROSS (vik-tō'ri-ạ-kros) *n.* a bronze medal given for extraordinary bravery in the army or navy.

VICTORIOUS (vik-tō'ri-us) *a.* superior in contest; triumphant; successful.

VICTORIOUSLY (vik-tō'ri-us-li) *ad.* with conquest.

VICTORY (vik'tu-ri) *n.* success in contest; battle gained; triumph.

VICTUAL (vit'l) *v.t.* to supply with provisions. [M.E. *vitaille*, provisions, fr. Low L. (neut. pl.) *victualia*, fr. L. *victualis*, fr. *victu*, stem of *victus*, food.]

VICTUALLER (vit'l-ẹr) *n.* one who supplies provisions.

VICTUALS (vit'ls) *n.pl.* food prepared for the table; provisions.

VIDE (vī'dē) *n.* see—a word referring to something elsewhere. [L.]

VIDELICET (vi-del'i-set) *ad.* to wit; namely; viz. [L. *videre licet*, it is possible to see—hence, to wit.]

VIDIMUS (vid'i-mus) *n.* a statement, report, or summary of papers examined. [L. = we have seen, pret. of *videre*, to see.]

VIE (vī) *v.i.* to attempt to equal; strive for superiority. [M.E. *vien*, through F., fr. L. *invitare*, invite.

VIEW (vū) *v.t.* to see; behold; survey;—*n.* sight; survey; prospect; picture of a scene; opinion; intention. [Fem. of *veu* (part.) of O.F. *veoir*, F. *voir*, to see, fr. L. *videre*, to see.]

VIEWER (vū'ẹr) *n.* one who sees or examines.

VIEWLESS (vū'les) *a.* that cannot be seen.

VIGIL (vij'il) *n.* watch for religious exercises; evening before a fast or festival spent in devotion. [F. *vigile*, eve of a holy day, fr. L. *vigilia*, a watch, fr. *vigil*, watchful, fr. *vigere*, to be lively.]

VIGILANCE (vij'i-lạns) *n.* watchfulness.

VIGILANT (vij'i-lạnt) *a.* watchful; circumspect.

VIGNETTE (vin-yet', vi-net') *n.* an ornament on the title-page of a book. [F., dim. of *vigne*, a vine, fr. L. *vinea*, vine.]

VIGOROUS (vig'ur-us) *a.* strong in mind or body; forcible; energetic.

VIGOROUSLY (vig'ur-us-li) *ad.* with force.

VIGOUR (vig'ur) *n.* energy; force. [O.F. *vigor*, F. *vigueur*, fr. L. (acc.) *vigorem* of *vigor*, liveliness, fr. *vigere*, to be lively.]

VIKING (vīk'ing) *n.* a Scandinavian pirate chief. [Icel. *vikingr*, a warrior, rover, freebooter.]

VILE (vīl) *a.* contemptibly mean or low. [F. *vil*, fem. *vile*, base, fr. L. *vilis*, mean, base.]

VILELY (vīl'li) *ad.* basely; meanly.

VILENESS (vīl'nes) *n.* baseness.

VILIFICATION (vil-i-fi-kā'shun) *n.* act of defaming; abusive language.

VILIFIER (vil'i-fī-ẹr) *n.* one who defames.

VILIFY (vil'i-fī) *v.t.* to defame; traduce; debase. [L. *vilis*, vile, and *facere*, make.]

VILLA (vil'ạ) *n.* a country seat; a suburban mansion. [L., a farm-house.]

VILLAGE (vil'ij) *n.* a small collection of houses. [F. *village*, fr. L. *villaticus*, belonging to a farm-house, fr. *villa*.]

VILLAGER (vil'ij-ẹr) *n.* an inhabitant of a village.

VILLAIN (vil'ạn) *n.* a feudal serf; a vile, wicked person. [M.E., fr. A.F. *vilein*, fr. L. *villanus*, farm-servant, serf, fr. *villa*, farm.]

VILLAINOUS (vil'ạn-us) *a.* wicked; base.

VILLAINY (vil'ạn-i) *n.* extreme depravity; an atrocious crime.

VILLANAGE (vil'-ạn-ij) *n.* servitude.

VILLATIC (vi-lat'ik) *a.* pertaining to a village.

VINAIGRETTE (vin-ā-gret') *n.* a small box holding a sponge with aromatic vinegar. Also **VINEGARETTE.** [F. *vinaigre*, vinegar, fr. L. *vinum*, wine, and (acc.) *acrem* of *acris*, sharp.]

VINCIBLE (vin'si-bl) *a.* that may be overcome. [L., fr. *vincere*, to conquer.]

VINDICABLE (vin'di-kạ-bl) *a.* that may be vindicated.

VINDICATE (vin'di-kāt) *v.t.* to prove to be just or valid; defend; maintain; establish. [L. (part.) *vindicatus*, fr. *vindicare*, to claim.]

VINDICATION (vin-di-kā'shun) *n.* justification of a claim, act, or statement; defence; support.

VINDICATOR (vin'di-kā-tẹr) *n.* one who vindicates.

VINDICATORY (vin'di-kā-tu-ri) *a.* tending to vindicate; inflicting punishment.

VINDICTIVE (vin-dik'tiv) *a.* given to revenge. [Short. fr. F. *vindicatif* revenging, fr. L. (part.) *vindicatus*, fr. *vindicare*, avenge.]

VINDICTIVELY (vin-dik'tiv-li) *ad.* by way of revenge.

VINDICTIVENESS (vin-dik'tiv-nes) *n.* a revengeful temper.

VINE (vīn) *n.* a plant producing grapes; the slender, trailing stem of other plants. [F. *vigne*, fr. L. *vinea*, a vineyard, fr. *vinum*, wine.]

VINEGAR (vin'e-gạr) *n.* an acid liquor obtained from wine or beer. [O.F. *vin egre*, F. *vinaigre*, fr. L. *vinum*, wine, and *acer* sour.]

VINERY (vī'nẹr-i) *n.* a glass structure for rearing vines by artificial heat.

VINEYARD (vin'yạrd) *n.* a plantation of grape-vines.

VINOUS (vī'nus) *a.* having the qualities of wine.

VINTAGE (vin'tij) *n.* the harvest of vines; time of grape-gathering.

VINTAGER (vin'ti-jẹr) *n.* one who gathers the vintage.

VINTNER (vint'nẹr) *n.* a dealer in wines. [M.F. *vinetier* fr. Late L. *vinetarius* a wine-seller, fr. *vinetum*, a vineyard, fr. *vinum*, wine.]

VIOL (vī'nl) *n.* an old musical instrument superseded by the violin. [M.F. *viole*, fr. Low L. *vidula*, *vitula*.]

VIOLA (ve-ō'lạ, vē'u-lạ) *n.* a tenor violin.

VIOLABLE (vī'u-là-bl) *a.* that may be violated or broken.

VIOLATE (vī'u-lāt) *v.t.* to treat violently; abuse; transgress; profane; ravish. [L. (part.) *violatus*, fr. *violare.*]

VIOLATION (vī-u-lā'shun) *n.* act of violating.

VIOLATOR (vī'u-lā-tẹr) *n.* one who violates.

VIOLENCE (vī'u-lens) *n.* force; vehemence.

VIOLENT (vī'u-lent) *a.* acting with force; vehemence; outrageous; furious. [L. *violentus*, full of might.]

VIOLENTLY (vī'u-lent-li) *ad.* with force.

VIOLET (vī'u-let) *n.* a plant and its bluish sweet-scented flower;—*a.* bluish or light purple. [L. *viola.*]

VIOLIN (vī'u-lin, vī-u-lin') *n.* a stringed instrument of music; a fiddle. [It. *violino.*]

VIOLINIST (vī'u-lin-ist) *n.* a player on the violin.

VIOLONCELLO (vē-u-lon-chel'ō, vī-u-lon-sel'ō) *n.* a bass violin giving sounds an octave lower than the viola or tenor violin. [It. dim. of *violone*, a bass-viol.]

VIOLONE (vē-u-lō'nā) *n.* a bass violin giving sounds an octave lower than the violoncello; double bass.

VIPER (vī'pẹr) *n.* a kind of serpent. [F. *vipère*, fr. L. *vipera.*]

VIPEROUS (vī'pẹr-us) *a.* having the qualities of a viper.

VIRAGO (vi-rā'gō) *n.* a masculine woman; a termagant. [L.]

VIRGIN (vẹr'jin) *n.* a maid in her purity. [O.F. *virgine*, fr. L. (acc.) *virginem*, fr. *virgo*, a maid.]

VIRGINAL (vẹr'ji-nal) *a.* pertaining to a virgin; maidenly.

VIRGINITY (vẹr-jin'i-ti) *n.* maidenhood.

VIRGO (vẹr'gō) *n.* the virgin; a sign in the zodiac. [L.]

VIRIDITY (vi-rid'i-ti) *n.* greenness. [L. *viridis*, green.]

VIRILE (vir'il) *a.* belonging to males. [F. *viril*, manly, fr. L. *virilis*, fr. *vir*, a man.]

VIRILITY (vi-ril'i-ti) *n.* manhood.

VIRTU (vẹr'tōō) *n.* a love of the fine arts; taste for curiosities, articles of antique, or curious productions. [It., fr. L. *virtus.*]

VIRTUAL (vẹr'tū-al) *a.* in essence or effect, not in fact. [Low L. *virtualis*, fr. L. *virtus*, manly excellence.]

VIRTUALITY (vẹr-tū-al'i-ti) *n.* virtual character or power.

VIRTUALLY (vẹr'tū-al-i) *ad.* in substance.

VIRTUE (vẹr'tū) *n.* strength; moral goodness; efficacy. [F. *vertu*, fr. L. (acc.) *virtutem*, fr. *virtus*, manly excellence, fr. *vir*, a man.]

VIRTUELESS (vẹr'tū-les) *a.* destitute of virtue, power, or efficacy.

VIRTUOSO (vẹr-tū-ō'sō) *n.* one skilled in the fine arts. [It.]

VIRTUOUS (vẹr'tū-us) *n.* morally good; righteous; done from high motives; chaste.

VIRTUOUSLY (vẹr'tū-us-li) *ad.* in a virtuous manner.

VIRULENCE (vir'ū-lens) *n.* malignity.

VIRULENT (vir'ū-lent) *a.* malignant; poisonous; bitter. [L. *virulentus*, full of poison, fr. *virus*, poison.]

VIRUS (vī'rus) *n.* contagious or poisonous matter; the essence or spirit of anything hurtful. [L.]

VISAGE (viz'ij) *n.* the face; look. [F., fr. M.F. *vis*, visage, and suffix, *-age* (L. *-aticum*), fr. *visum*, acc. of *visus*, sight.]

VIS-A-VIS (vēz-a-vē') *ad.* opposite; face to face. [F., fr. L. *visus*, look.]

VISCERA (vis'e-rà) *n.pl.* the bowels. [L.]

VISCERAL (vis'e-ral) *a.* pertaining to the viscera.

VISCID (vis'id) *a.* glutinous; sticky. [L. *viscidus*, sticky, fr. *viscum*, bird-lime.]

VISCIDITY (vi-sid'i-ti) *n.* glutinousness.

VISCOSITY (vis-kos'i-ti) *n.* stickiness.

VISCOUNT (vī'kount) *n.* a title of nobility next below the earl. [A.F. *visconte*, F. *vicomte*, orig. the deputy of an earl, fr. L. *vice*, in place of, and (acc.) *comitem*, fr. *comes*, a count.]

VISCOUNTESS (vī'koun-tes) *n.* a viscount's wife.

VISCOUS (vis'kus) *a.* glutinous; adhesive.

VISIBILITY (viz-i-bil'i-ti) *n.* the state or quality of being visible.

VISIBLE (viz'i-bl) *a.* perceivable by the eye. [L. *visibilis*, that can be seen, fr. (part.) *visus*, fr. *videre*, to see.]

VISIBLY (viz'i-bli) *ad.* plainly; clearly.

VISION (vish'un) *n.* faculty of sight; anything seen; anything imaginary; divine revelation. [F., fr. L. (acc.) *visionem*, fr. *visio*, sight, fr. (part.) *visus*, fr. *videre*, to see.]

VISIONARY (vish'un-ar-i) *a.* imaginary; having no foundation;—*n.* one who forms impracticable schemes.

VISIT (viz'it) *v.t.* to go or come to see; call on; inspect;—*n.* act of going to see. [F. *visiter*, fr. L. *visitare*, to go to see, fr. *visere*, to behold, fr. *videre*, to see.]

VISITABLE (viz'i-tà-bl) *a.* in a state to receive visits. [another; visitor.

VISITANT (viz'i-tant) *n.* one who visits

VISITATION (viz-i-tā'shun) *n.* act of visiting; a judicial visit; retribution.

VISITOR (viz'i-tẹr) *n.* one who visits.

VISOR (viz'ọr) *n.* a mask; disguise. [M.E. *visere*, fr. M.F. *visiere*, fr. *vis*, the face, fr. L. *videre*, pp. *visus*, see.]

VISTA (vis'tà) *n.* a prospect or view through an avenue. [It., fr. L. *videre*, see.]

VISUAL (viz'ū-al, vizh'ū-al) *a.* belonging to the sight. [L. *visualis*, belonging to the sight, fr. *visu-*, stem of *visus*, sight, fr. *videre.*]

VITAL (vī'tal) *a.* pertaining to life; very important; essential. [F., fr. L. *vitalis*, belonging to life, fr. *vita*, life.]

VITALISATION (vī-tal-i-zā'shun) *n.* act or process of giving life to.

VITALISE (vī'tal-īz) *v.t.* to make alive; give life or spirit to.

VITALITY (vī-tal'i-ti) *n.* the principle of life; tenacity of life.

VITALLY (vī'tal-i) *ad.* in a manner affecting life; essentially.

VITALS (vī'talz) *n.pl.* parts essential to life.

VITIATE (vish'i-āt) *v.t.* to injure; impair; corrupt; deprave. [L., fr. *vitium*, fault.]

VITIATION (vish-i-ā'shun) *n.* depravation; corruption; invalidation.

VITREOUS (vit're-us) *a.* pertaining to; consisting of, or like glass. [L. *vitreus*, glassy, fr. *vitri-*, stem of *vitrum*, glass.]

VITRESCENCE (vi-tres'ens) *n.* state of being vitreous, or being convertible into glass.

VITRIFACTION (vit-ri-fak'shun) *n.* act of converting into glass.

VITRIFIABLE (vit'ri-fī-a-bl) *a.* that may be vitrified.

VITRIFY (vit'ri-fī) *v.t.* or *i.* to convert into or become glass. [L., fr. *vitrum*, glass, and *facere*, make.]

VITRIOL (vit'ri-ul) *n.* a sulphate of certain metals; sulphuric acid. [F., fr. L. *vitreolus*, glassy, fr. *vitrum*, glass.]

VITRIOLIC (vit-ri-ol'ik) *a.* pertaining to vitriol.

VITUPERATE (vī-tū'pe-rāt) *v.t.* to blame; be severe; abuse; scold. [L. (part.) *vituperatus*, fr. *vituperare*, to blame, fr. *vitium*, fault, and *parare*, prepare.]

VITUPERATION (vī-tū-pe-rā'shun) *n.* violent censure; abusive language.

VITUPERATIVE (vī-tū'pe-rā-tiv) *a.* containing censure.

VIVACIOUS (vi-vā'shus, vī-vā'shus) *a.* lively; active; animated. [L. (stem) *vivaci-*, of *vivax*, tenacious of life, fr. *vivere*, to live.]

VIVACIOUSLY (vi-vā'shus-li, vi-vă'shus-li) *ad.* with life or spirit.

VIVACITY (vi-vas'i-ti, vi-vas'i-ti) *n.* sprightliness; animation.

VIVANDIERE (vē-văng-di-ār') *n.* female sutler of a regiment. [F.]

VIVARIUM (vi-vā'ri-um) *n.* a building with ponds, cages, etc., for keeping living animals. [L.] [L.]

VIVA VOCE (vī'va vō'sē) by word of mouth.

VIVID (viv'id) *a.* lively; bright; striking. [L. *vividus*, lively fr. *vivere*, to live.]

VIVIDLY (viv'id-li) *ad.* with life and spirit; in glowing colours.

VIVIDNESS (viv'id-nes) *n.* life; liveliness.

VIVIFIC (vi-vif'ik) *a.* giving life.

VIVIFICATION (viv-i-fi-kā'shun) *n.* act of giving life.

VIVIFY (viv'i-fi) *v.t.* to impart life to; animate. [F. *vivifier*, to quicken, fr. L. *vivificare*, fr. *vivi-*, for *vivus*, living, and *ficare*, for *facere*, to make.]

VIVIPAROUS (vi-vip'a-rus) *a.* producing young alive. [L. *viviparus*, fr. *vivi-*, for *vivus*, living, and *parere*, to produce.]

VIVISECTION (viv-i-sek'shun) *n.* dissection of animals, while yet alive, for scientific purposes. [L. *vivus*, alive, and *sectio*, a cutting fr. *secare*, to cut.]

VIXEN (vik'sn) *n.* a she-fox; an ill-tempered woman. [O.E. *fyxen*, she-fox.]

VIZ (viz) *ad.* to wit; namely; same as *videlicet*. [L.]

VIZARD (viz'ard) *n.* a mask. [See VISOR.]

VIZIER (vi-zer') *n.* the Ottoman prime minister. [A.]

VOCABLE (vō'ka-bl) *n.* a word; name. [F., fr. L. *vocabulum*, an appellation, fr. *vocare*, call.]

VOCABULARY (vō-kab'ū-la-ri) *n.* a list of words arranged alphabetically and explained.

VOCABULIST (vō-kab'ū-list) *n.* compiler of a vocabulary.

VOCAL (vō'kal) *a.* uttered by the mouth. [F., fr. L. *vocalis*, fr. *voc-*, stem of *vox*, voice.]

VOCALISE (vō'kal-iz) *v.t.* to make vocal.

VOCALIST (vō'kal-ist) *n.* a vocal musician; public singer.

VOCALITY (vō-kal'i-ti) *n.* quality of being utterable by the voice.

VOCATION (vō-kā'shun) *n.* act of calling; occupation; trade. [F., fr. L. (acc.) *vocationem*, a calling, fr. (part.) *vocatus*, fr. *vocare*, to call.]

VOCATIVE (vok'a-tiv) *a.* calling;—*n.* the case in which a word is put when the person or thing is addressed. [L., fr. *vocare*, to call.]

VOCIFERATE (vō-sif'e-rāt) *v.i.* to cry out. [L. (part.) *vociferatus*, fr. *vociferari*, to lift up the voice, fr. *voci-*, stem of *vox*, voice, and *ferre*, to carry.]

VOCIFERATION (vō-sif-e-rā'shun) *n.* loud outcry; exclamation.

VOCIFEROUS (vō-sif'e-rus) *a.* clamorous.

VOE (vō) *n.* a creek or inlet of the sea. [Scand.]

VOGUE (vōg) *n.* fashion; mode; popular reception. [F.]

VOICE (vois) *n.* sound uttered by the mouth; a vote; mode of utterance; expression; mode of inflecting verbs; expressed opinion; vote;—*v.t.* to sound; report. [O.F. *vois*, F. *voix*, fr. L. (acc.) *vocem*, of *vox*, sound, voice.]

VOICELESS (vois'les) *a.* having no voice.

VOID (void) *a.* empty; unoccupied; null; unsubstantial;—*n.* an empty space;—*v.t.* to quit; eject; make of no effect;—*v.i.* to be evacuated. [O.F. *vuide*, *voide*, fr. L. *viduus*, deprived.] [or evacuated.]

VOIDABLE (voi'da-bl) *a.* that may be voided

VOIDANCE (voi'dans) *n.* ejection; vacancy.

VOIDER (voi'der) *n.* one that voids.

VOIDNESS (void'nes) *n.* emptiness.

VOLANT (vō'lant) *a.* flying; current; having the wings spread. [F. *volant* (part.) of *voler* to fly, fr. L. *volare*.]

VOLATILE (vol'a-til) *a.* evaporating quickly; flighty; lively. [F. *volatil*, flying, fr. L. *volatilis*, fr. *volatus*, flight, fr. *volare*, to fly.]

VOLATILISE (vol'a-til-iz) *v.t.* to cause to evaporate.

VOLATILITY (vol-a-til'i-ti) *n.* disposition to fly off in vapour; levity.

VOLCANIC (vol-kan'ik) *a.* produced by a volcano. [volcanic heat.

VOLCANISE (vol'ka-niz) *v.t.* to subject to

VOLCANO (vol-kā'nō) *n.* a mountain emitting fire and lava. [L. *Vulcanus*, god of fire.]

VOLE (vōl) (1) *n.* a deal at cards that draws all the tricks;—(2) *n.* a water-rat. [(1) F., fr. L. *volare*, to fly. (2) Fr. Norw. *voll*, field.]

VOLITION (vō-lish'un) *n.* the act of willing. [F., fr. Late L. *volitionem*, acc. of *volitio*, fr. L. *volo*, I wish.]

VOLLEY (vol'i) *n.* a discharge of small arms; —*pl.* **VOLLEYS**. [F. *volée*, a flight, fr. L. *volare*, to fly.]

VOLPLANE (vol'-plān) *n.* the descent of an aeroplane by gravity, at an angle. [L. *volare*, fly, and *planus*, level.]

VOLTAISM (vol'ta-izm) *n.* science of the chemical action of metals and liquids; galvanism. [It. *Volta*, the discoverer.]

VOLTIGEUR (vol-ti-zher') *n.* a light infantry soldier. [F.] [speech.

VOLUBILITY (vol-ū-bil'i-ti) *n.* fluency of

VOLUBLE (vol'ū-bl) *a.* fluent in words. [L. *volubilis*, easily turned about, fr. (part.) *volutus*, of *volvere*, roll.]

VOLUBLY (vol'ū-bli) *ad.* in a rolling or fluent manner.

VOLUME (vol'ūm) *n.* a roll; a book; dimensions; compass. [L. *volumen*, a roll or scroll, fr. *volutus*, *volvere*, to roll.]

VOLUMINOUS (vol-ū'mi-nus) *a.* consisting of many volumes; having written much; copious; diffuse. [own free-will.

VOLUNTARILY (vol'un-ta-ri-li) *ad.* of one's

VOLUNTARY (vol'un-tar-i) *a.* proceeding from choice; willing; free;—*n.* an air played at will. [L. *voluntarius*, willing, fr. *voluntas*, free will, choice.]

VOLUNTARYISM (vol'un-tar i-izm) *n.* principle of maintaining the church by the offerings of its people, apart from State aid or control.

VOLUNTEER (vol-un-tēr') *n.* one who serves by choice;—*v.t.* to engage voluntarily.

VOLUPTUARY (vō-lup'tū-a-ri) *n.* one given to luxury.

VOLUPTUOUS (vō-lup'tū-us) *a.* luxurious; sensual. [F. *voluptueux*, fr. L. *voluptuosus*, full of pleasure, fr. *voluptas*, pleasure, fr. *volo*, I wish.] [ously.

VOLUPTUOUSLY (vō-lup'tū-us-li) *ad.* luxuri-

VOLUTE (vō-lūt') *n.* a spiral scroll used in the Ionic capitals. [F., fr. L. *voluta*, fem. part. of *volvere*, to roll.]

VOMIT (vom'it) *v.t.* to eject from the stomach;—*n.* an emetic. [L. *vomitus*, a vomiting, fr. *vomere*, to vomit.]

VOMITORY (vom'i-tur-i) *a.* causing to vomit.

VORACIOUS (vo-rā'shus) *a.* greedy to eat; ravenous. [L. *voraci-*, stem of *vorax*, greedy to devour.]

Voluta.

VORACIOUSLY (vo-rā'shus-li) *ad.* greedily.

VORACITY (vo-ras'i-ti) *n.* greediness of appetite. Also **VORACIOUSNESS**.

VORTEX (vor'teks) *n.* a whirlpool;—*pl.* **VORTICES** or **VORTEXES**. [L.]

VORTICAL (vor'ti-kạl) *a.* having a whirling motion.

VOTARY (vō'tạ-ri) *n.* one devoted to any service or pursuit;—*a.* bound by a vow; consecrated; promised. [A word coined fr. L. *votum,* a vow, a wish.]

VOTE (vōt) *n.* expression of choice or opinion; suffrage; decision of a majority;—*v.t.* or *i.* to choose by vote; elect; determine; express one's choice. [L. *votum,* a vow, wish, fr. *votus,* part. of *vovere,* to vow.]

VOTER (vō'tẹr) *n.* one entitled to vote.

VOTIVE (vō'tiv) *a.* given by vow. [L. *votivus,* promised by vow.]

VOUCH (vouch) *v.t.* or *i.* to call to witness; declare; warrant; bear witness;—*n.* testimony. [M.E. *voucher,* fr. L. *vocare,* call.]

VOUCHER (vou'chẹr) *n.* one who vouches; a paper that confirms a receipt.

VOUCHSAFE (vouch-sāf') *v.t.* or *i.* to warrant safe; deign to grant; condescend; yield.

VOUCHSAFEMENT (vouch-sāf'ment) *n.* grant in condescension.

VOUSSOIR (vóō-swor') *n.* one of the stones of an arch. [F., through Low L., fr. L. *volutus,* fr. *volvere,* to roll.]

VOW (vou) *n.* a solemn promise to God; a formal promise of fidelity, affection, etc., —*v.t.* or *i.* to give or devote by solemn promise. [O.F. *vou, veu,* fr. L. *votum,* a vow.]

VOWEL (vou'el) *n.* a simple sound, as *a, e, o*; letter;—*a.* vocal. [O.F. *vouel,* F. *voyelle,* fr. L. *vocalis,* fr. *vox, vocis,* sound.]

VOYAGE (voi'lj) *n.* a journey by water;—*v.i.* to travel by sea. [O.F. *veiage,* fr. L. *viaticum,* provisions for a journey, fr. *via,* way.]

VOYAGER (voi'ij-ẹr) *n.* one passing by water.

VRAISEMBLANCE (vrā-sàng-blàngs') *n.* appearance of truth. [F.]

VULCAN (vul'kạn) *n.* the god of fire (Latin Mythology). [L.]

VULCANIC (vul-kan'ik) *a.* pertaining to Vulcan or to works in iron; volcanic; denoting the theory that all rocks are of igneous origin. Also **VULCANIAN.**

VULCANISE (vul'kạ-nīz) *v.t.* to harden india-rubber by treating it with heated sulphur.

VULCANITE (vul'kạ-nīt) *n.* india-rubber combined with sulphur.

VULGAR (vul'gạr) *a.* pertaining to common people; common; mean or low;—*n.* common people. [F. *vulgaire,* fr. L. *vulgaris,* belonging to the common people, fr. *vulgus,* the mob.]

VULGARISE (vul'gạr-īz) *v.t.* to make vulgar.

VULGARISM (vul'gạr-izm) *n.* a vulgar expression. [ness.

VULGARITY (vul-gar'i-ti) *n.* coarseness; rudeness.

VULGARLY (vul'gạr-li) *ad.* commonly coarsely. [Bible.

VULGATE (vul'gāt) *n.* Latin version of the Bible.

VULNERABLE (vul'ne-rạ-bl) *a.* that may be wounded. [L. *vulnerabilis,* liable to injury, fr. *vulner-,* stem of *vulnus,* a wound.]

VULNERARY (vul'ne-rạ-ri) *a.* useful in curing wounds.

VULPINE (vul'pin) *a.* pertaining to the fox. [L. *vulpinus,* fox-like, fr. *vulpes,* fox.]

VULTURE (vul'tūr) *n.* a large rapacious bird of prey. [L. *vultur,* a vulture, lit. a tearer, fr. *vulsi,* perf. of *vellere,* to pluck.]

VULTURINE (vul'tūr-in) *a.* of the nature of the vulture; rapacious.

W

WABBLE (wob'l) *v.i.* to move from side to side. [Low Ger. *wabbeln,* to wabble; cog. with Eng. *waver.*]

WAD (wod) *n.* a little mass or bundle; paper, tow, etc., to stop the charge of a gun;—*v.t.* to insert a wad. [Scand.]

WADDED (wod'ed) *a.* formed into a wad; quilted. [used in quilting.

WADDING (wod'ing) *n.* a wad; a soft stuff

WADDLE (wod'l) *v.i.* to walk like a duck. [Freq. of WADE.]

WADE (wād) *v.t.* or *i.* to walk through water; cross over; pass through. [O.E. *vadan.*]

WADER (wā'dẹr) *n.* one who wades; a long-legged bird that wades.

WAFER (wā'fẹr) *n.* a thin cake of bread; a thin leaf of paste;—*v.t.* to seal with a wafer. [O.F. *wafre,* fr. M.D. *waefel,* a wafer.]

WAFT (wàft) *v.t.* to bear through a fluid medium;—*v.i.* to float;—*n.* wave of the hand or of a flag; signal. [For *waff = wave,* to beckon.] [water.

WAFTAGE (wàf'tlj) *n.* carriage by air or

WAFTER (wàf'tẹr) *n.* he or that which wafts.

WAG (wag) (1) *n.* a merry droll fellow;—(2) *v.t.* or *i.* to shake or move to and fro. [(1) Jokingly for *waghalter,* one that deserves hanging. (2) Sw. *wagga.*]

WAGE (wāj) *v.t.* to lay a wager. [O.F. *wager,* to pledge, fr. Goth. *wadi,* a pledge.]

WAGER (wā'jẹr) *n.* something laid; a bet;—*v.t.* to offer a bet. [O.F. *wageure,* fr. Goth. *wadi,* a pledge.]

WAGES (wā'jes) *n.pl.* hire; reward of services.

WAGGERY (wag'ẹr-i) *n.* merriment; sport.

WAGGISH (wag'ish) *a.* merry; droll.

WAGGISHLY (wag'ish-li) *ad.* in sport.

WAGGLE (wag'l) *v.t.* or *i.* to wag; move from side to side; waddle. [Freq. of WAG.]

WAGON (wag'un) *n.* a vehicle on four wheels for carrying goods. [D. *wagen.*]

WAGONER (wag'un-ẹr) *n.* one who conducts a wagon.

WAGONETTE (wag-u-net') *n.* an open carriage with *vis-à-vis* seats; a drag.

WAGONING (wag'un-ing) *n.* business of transporting in a wagon. [species.

WAGTAIL (wag'tāl) *n.* a small bird of several

WAIF (wāf) *n.* goods found without an owner; a poor, homeless wretch. [Icel. *veif.*]

WAIL (wāl) *v.t.* or *i.* to weep audibly; lament; bemoan;—*n.* a cry of woe. [Icel. *væla, væla,* to wail.]

WAILING (wā'ling) *n.* loud weeping.

WAIN (wān) *n.* a wagon. [O.E. *wægn, wæn,* a wain, fr. *wegan,* carry.]

WAINSCOT (wān'skot) *n.* a wooden lining or boarding of the walls of rooms;—*v.t.* to line with boards. [D.]

WAIST (wāst) *n.* the part of the body below the ribs; middle of a ship. [O.E. *wearan,* grow.] [trousers, etc.

WAISTBAND (wāst'band) *n.* the band of

WAISTCOAT (wās'kōt) *n.* a garment worn under the coat.

WAISTER (wās'tẹr) *n.* a man whose station is in the waist of a ship.

WAIT (wāt) *v.t.* or *i.* to stay for; await; follow; remain;—*n.* staying for; ambush. [O.F. *waiter,* fr. *waite,* a watchman, fr. O. H. Ger. *Wahta,* a watchman.]

WAITER (wā'tẹr) *n.* an attending servant; a salver or tray.

WAITING-MAID (wāt'ing-mād) *n.* a female servant who attends a lady.

WAIVE (wāv) *v.t.* to relinquish. [A.F. *weiver,* to refuse, to abandon, fr. Icel. *veifa,* to flutter.]

WAKE (wāk) (1) *v.i.* to cease to sleep;—*v.t.* to rouse; put in action;—*n.* watch;—(2) *n.* track of a vessel in water. [(1) O.E. *wacan,* to arise, come to life. (2) Icel. *vök,* a hole (in the ice).]

WAKEFUL (wāk'fool) *a.* unable to sleep; vigilant.

WAKEFULNESS (wāk'fool-nes) *n.* inability to sleep; want of sleep.

WAKEN (wā'kn) *v.t.* or *i.* to rouse from sleep; stir up; be roused. [O.E. *wæcnan,* to be aroused, fr. *wacan,* to wake.]

WALE (wāl) *n.* a raised stripe or streak in cloth, or made by a rod or whip on the skin; —*pl.* strong planks along a ship's side;—*v.t.* to mark with wales. [O.E. *walu,* mark of stripes.]

WALK (wawk) *v.i.* to go by steps;—*n.* a gait; a path. [O.E. *wealcan,* to roll.]

WALKER (waw'ker) *n.* one who walks.

WALL (wawl) *n.* a work of brick or stone; side of a building; defence;—*v.t.* to enclose with a wall. [O.E. *weall,* fr. L. *vallum,* a rampart.]

WALLET (wol'et) *n.* a bag or knapsack. [M.E. *walet,* from *watel,* a bag.]

WALL-EYE (wawl'ī) *n.* a disease in the eye.

WALLFLOWER (wawl'flou-er) *n.* a plant having beautiful and fragrant yellow flowers.

WALLOP (wol'up) *v.i.* to boil; *v.t.* to beat soundly. [M.E. *waloper, galopen,* fr. O.F. *galoper,* to gallop, fr. Icel. *völlr,* a field.]

WALLOW (wol'ō) *v.i.* to roll on the earth; live in vice;—*n.* a rolling. [O.E. *wealwian,* to roll round.]

WALNUT (wawl'nut) *n.* a tree and its fruit. [O.E. *wealh,* foreign, and *hnutu,* nut.]

WALTZ (wawlts) *n.* a dance and a tune. [Ger. *Walzer,* fr. *walzen,* to roll.]

WALTZING (wawlt'zing) *n.* the act of dancing a waltz.

WAMPUM (wom'pum) *n.* shells or strings of shells used as money or for ornament by North American Indians. [Amer. Ind.]

WAN (won) *a.* having a pale and sickly hue. [O.E.]

WAND (wond) *n.* a small thin stick; a rod; staff. [Icel. *vöndr,* a switch.]

WANDER (won'der) *v.i.* to go astray; ramble; deviate; be delirious. [O.E. *wandrian,* wander.] [rambler.

WANDERER (won'der-er) *n.* a rover; a

WANDERING (won'der-ing) *n.* act of roving; deviation; rambling of the mind; raving.

WANE ((wān) *v.i.* to decrease;—*n.* decline; decrease. [O.E. *wanian,* fr. *wan,* wanting.]

WANNESS (won'nes) *n.* state of being pale and sickly.

WANT (wont) *n.* state of being without; need; scarcity; poverty;—*v.t.* or *i.* to need; wish for; fall short. [Icel. *vant.*]

WANTON (won'tun) *a.* moving loosely; frisky; unrestrained; licentious; *n.* a dissolute woman;—*v.i.* to frolic; play lasciviously. [O.E. *van-,* wanting, and *teon,* pp. *togen,* to draw.] [gayly.

WANTONLY (won'tun-li) *ad.* in a loose manner;

WANTONNESS (won'tun-nes) *n.* lasciviousness; recklessness.

WAR (wawr) *n.* contest carried on by force of arms; open hostility; enmity; the profession of arms; art of fighting;—*v.i.* to carry on war. [O. H. Ger. *Werra,* fr. *werran,* embroil.]

WARBLE (wawr'bl) *v.t.* or *i.* to sing in a quavering way; chirp; carol;—*n.* a quavering modulation; song. [O.F. *werbler,* fr. O. H. Ger. Cf. Ger. *wirbeln,* to warble.]

WARBLER (wawr'bler) *n.* a singing bird.

WAR-CRY (wawr'krī) *n.* alarm of war.

WARD (wawrd) *n.* a watch; custody; part of a lock; a person under a guardian;—*v.t.* or *i.* to guard; fend off. [O.E. *weardian,* protect, fr. *weard,* keeper.]

WARDEN (wawr'dn) *n.* a public officer; jailor; president of a college; manager of a church. [A.F. *wardein,* a guardian, O.F. *gardein,* fr. O.F. *warder, garder,* to guard, fr. O.E. *weardian,* to watch.]

WARDER (wawr'der) *n.* a keeper; a guard.

WARDROBE (wawrd'rōb) *n.* a place for clothes; wearing apparel. [O.F. *warderobe, garderobe.*]

WARD-ROOM (wawrd'rōōm) *n.* a room occupied by the lieutenants and surgeons of a warship.

WARDSHIP (wawrd'ship) *n.* guardianship.

WARE (wār) (1) *a.* wary; cautious;—*n.* a seaweed;—(2) *n.* article of merchandise. [(1) O.E. *wær,* cautious. (2) O.E. *waru,* wares.]

WAREHOUSE (wār'hous) *n.* a storehouse for goods; store;—*v.t.* to put in a store.

WARES (wārz) *n.pl.* goods; merchandise.

WARFARE (wawr'fār) *n.* military service; war; hostilities.

WARILY (wā'ri-li) *ad.* cautiously.

WARLIKE (wawr'lik) *a.* adapted to war; martial; military.

WARLOCK (wawr'lok) *n.* a male witch; a wizard. [O.E. *wær loga,* a truce-breaker, fr. *wær,* truth, and *leogan,* lie.]

WARM (wawrm) *a.* having moderate heat; zealous; keen; passionate; rich;—*v.t.* or *i.* to heat moderately; become animated. [O.E. *wearm.*]

WARMLY (wawrm'li) *ad.* with warmth.

WARMTH (wawrmth) *n.* moderate heat; ardour; enthusiasm.

WARN (wawrn) *v.t.* to caution against; admonish. [O.E. *wearnian,* to take heed, to warn.]

WARNER (wawr'ner) *n.* one who warns.

WARNING (wawr'ning) *n.* previous notice; a caution.

WARP (wawrp) *n.* thread that runs lengthwise in a loom; a rope used in towing;—*v.t.* or *i.* to turn or twist out of shape; pervert. [O.E. *weorpan,* throw, cast.]

WAR-PROOF (wawr'prōōf) *a.* able to resist attack;—*n.* tried valour.

WARRANT (wor'ant) *v.t.* to guarantee; assure; authorise; justify;—*n.* guarantee; security; writ. [O.F. *warantir,* to warrant, fr. O. H. Ger. *weren,* to certify.]

WARRANTABLE (wor'an-ta-bl) *a.* justifiable.

WARRANTEE (wor-an-tē') *n.* one to whom land, etc., is warranted.

WARRANTY (wor'an-ti) *n.* a deed of security; authority.

WARREN (wor'en) *n.* a place for rabbits, fowls, fish, etc. [O.F. *warenne,* fr. O. H. Ger. *warjan,* to protect.]

WARRENER (wor'en-er) *n.* keeper of a warren.

WARRIOR (wor'i-er) *n.* a soldier; a brave military man.

WART (wawrt) *n.* a hard excrescence on the skin. [O.E. *wearte,* a wart.]

WAR-WORN (wawr'wōrn) *a.* worn with war.

WARY (wā'ri) *a.* cautious; prudent. [See WARE.]

WAS (woz) past tense of the substantive verb *be.*

WASH (wosh) *v.t.* or *i.* to cleanse with or in water; wash away; cover with a thin coat of;—*n.* alluvial matter; a cosmetic; coating of metal or paint. [O.E. *wæscan.*]

WASH-BOARD (wosh'bōrd) *n.* a board next the floor; a board used in washing.

WASHER (wosh'er) *n.* one who or that which washes; a ring of metal or leather put under a nut or screw.

WASHERWOMAN (wosh'er-woom-an) *n.* a woman who washes clothes.

WASHY (wosh'i) *a.* watery; weak.

WASP (wosp) *n.* a genus of stinging insects. [O.E. *wæps.*] [like a wasp.

WASPISH (wos'pish) *a.* peevish; petulant;

WASPISHLY (wos'pish-li) *ad.* peevishly.

WASSAIL (wos'āl) *n.* a liquor made of wine or ale, sugar, nutmeg, and roasted apples; a drunken bout. [O.E. *weshal,* be in health.]

WASSAILER (wos'āl-er) *n.* a reveller; toper.

WAST (wost) past time, second person of the substantive verb, *be.*

WASTE (wăst) *v.t.* to devastate; destroy; spend; squander;—*a.* empty; desolate; unproductive; useless:—*n.* uncultivated land; useless expenditure; loss; refuse. -ᴜᴛ̤O.F. *wast*, fr. L. *vastus*, waste.]

WASTE-BOOK (wăst'book) *n.* a book in which rough entries of daily transactions are entered.   [destructive.

WASTEFUL (wăst'fool) *a.* lavish; extravagant:

WASTE-GATE (wăst'găt) *n.* a gate to discharge useless water.

WATCH (woch) *v.t.* or *i.* to keep in view; give heed to; guard; look out; keep guard;—*n.* act of looking out; guard; sentry; a pocket timepiece; place or time of watching. [O.E. *wacan*, to wake.]

WATCHER (woch'ẽr) *n.* one who watches.

WATCHFUL (woch'fool) *a.* careful to observe; guarding with caution; vigilant; attentive.

WATCH-GUARD (woch'gărd) *n.* chain or ribbon attached to a pocket watch.

WATCH-HOUSE (woch'hous) *n.* a house where watchmen are placed.

WATCHMAN (woch'mạn) *n.* a night-guard.

WATCHTOWER (woch'tow-ẽr) *n.* tower for a sentinel.

WATCHWORD (woch'wurd) *n.* a sentinel's night-word.

WATER (waw'tẽr) *n.* a transparent fluid; —*v.t.* or *i.* to irrigate; take in water. [O.E *wæter*.]

Watchtower.

WATER-CART (waw'tẽr-kărt) *n.* a cart filled with water for sprinkling the streets.

WATER-CEMENT (waw-tẽr-se-ment') *n.* a cement that hardens under water.

WATER-COLOUR (waw'tẽr-kul'ur) *n.* colour diluted and mixed with gum-water;—*a.* painted in water-colour.   [for water.

WATER-COURSE (waw'tẽr-kōrs) *n.* a channel

WATER-CURE (waw'tẽr-kūr) *n.* system of treating diseases with water; hydropathy.

WATERFALL (waw'tẽr-fawl) *n.* a cascade; a cataract.   [watery.

WATERISH (waw'tẽr-ish) *a.* like water;

WATERMAN (waw'tẽr-man) *n.* a boatman.

WATER-MELON (waw'tẽr-mel-un) *n.* a delicious fruit.

WATER-MILL (waw'tẽr-mil) *n.* a mill the machinery of which is driven by water.

WATER-POT (waw'tẽr-pot) *n.* a vessel to hold water.

WATER-POWER (waw'tẽr-pou-ẽr) *n.* mechanical power or action of water.

WATERPROOF (waw'tẽr-prŏŏf) *a.* not admitting water.

WATERSPOUT (waw'tẽr-spout) *n.* a whirling column of water at sea.   [to admit water

WATERTIGHT (waw'tẽr-tīt) *a.* so tight as not

WATERY (waw'tẽr-i) *a.* resembling or abounding in water; thin; insipid; vapid.

WATTLE (wot'l) *n.* a twig; a hurdle;—*v.t.* to plait twigs; bind with twigs. [O.E. *watel*. *watul*.]

WAVE (wāv) *n.* a moving swell of water:— *v.t.* or *i.* to play loosely; brandish; waft or beckon; give up; fluctuate. [O.E. *wafian*, to wave with the hand.]

WAVELESS (wāv'les) *a.* free from waves.

WAVELET (wāv'let) *n.* a little wave.

WAVE-OFFERING (wāv'of-ẽr-ing) *n.* an offering made by waving to the four cardinal points.

WAVER (wā'vẽr) *v.i.* to fluctuate; vacillate; be unsteady. [M.E. *waveren*, to wander about.]

WAVERER (wā'vẽr-ẽr) *n.* one who wavers.

WAV (wā'vi) *a.* playing to and fro; undulating.

WAX (waks) *n.* a tenacious substance formed by bees or in the ear; also one used to seal letters, and by shoemakers to rub their thread;—*v.i.* [*pret.* WAXED; *pp.* WAXED or WAXEN] to grow; increase; become;— *v.t.* to rub with wax. [M.E. fr. O.E. *weax*.]

WAXCLOTH (waks'kloth) *n.* cloth covered with ornamental figures in wax or oil; floorcloth.

WAXEN (wak'sn) *a.* made of wax.

WAX-END (waks'end) *n.* a thread pointed with a bristle and covered with shoemaker's wax.

WAXWORK (waks'wurk) *n.* figures formed of wax.   [not mealy.

WAXY (wak'si) *a.* soft like wax; adhesive;

WAY (wā) *n.* passage; road; direction; progress; means; manner; method; regular course. [O.E. *weg*.]

WAYBILL (wā'bil) *n.* a list of passengers and goods in a public conveyance.

WAYFARER (wā'făr-ẽr) *n.* a traveller. ʿWAY

WAYFARING (wā'făr-ing) *a.* travelling. and O.E. *faran*, to go.]

WAYLAID (wā'lād) *pret.* of **WAYLAY**.

WAYLAY (wā'lā, wā-lā') *v.t.* to beset by ambush.   [another on the way.

WAYLAYER (wā-lā'ẽr) *n.* one who watches

WAY-MARK (wā'mark) *n.* a mark to guide travellers.

WAYWARD (wā'wạrd) *a.* froward; perverse; wilful. [Fr. AWAY and WARD.]

WAYWARDLY (wā'ward-li) *ad.* perversely.

WAYWARDNESS (wā'ward-nes) *n.* state or quality of frowardness.

WE (wē) *pron. pl.* of **I**. [O.E.]

WEAK (wēk) *a.* feeble; soft; low; frail; unsteady; slight; inconclusive. [O.E. *wæcan*, to weaken, fr. *wac* weak.]

WEAKEN (wēk'n) *v.t.* to make weak; enfeeble.

WEAKLY (wēk'li) *ad.* in a feeble manner;— *a.* infirm.

WEAKNESS (wēk'nes) *n.* feebleness.

WEAL (wēl) *n.* happiness; prosperity. [M.E. *wele*, fr. O.E. *wela*, prosperity. Cf. O.E. *wel* well.]

WEALD (wēld) *n.* a wooded place or district; wold. [M.E. Cf. WILD.]

WEALTH (welth) *n.* affluence; riches; opulence. [M.E. *welthe*, fr. *wele* weal.]

WEALTHY (wel'thi) *a.* rich; opulent.

WEAN (wēn) *v.t.* to put from the breast; withdraw from any desire. [O.E. *wenian* accustom.]

WEANLING (wēn'ling) *n.* one newly weaned.

WEAPON (wep'un, wep'n) *n.* an instrument of offence or defence. [O.E. *wæpen*.]

WEAR (wār) *v.t.* or *i.* [*pret.* WORE; *pp.* WORN] to carry on the person; have the appearance of; consume by use, time, or friction; last under use; put a ship round; —*n.* act of wearing. [O.E. *werian*.]

WEARINESS (wēr'i-nes) *n.* state of being weary; fatigue.

WEARISOME (wēr'i-sum) *a.* tiresome.

WEARISOMENESS (wēr'i-sum-nes) *n.* tediousness; tiresomeness.

WEARY (wēr'i) *a.* tired; fatigued;—*v.t.* to tire; fatigue. [O.E. *werig* weary.]

WEASAND (wē'zạnd) *n.* the windpipe. [O.E. *wasend*, the gullet.]   [animal. [O.E.]

WEASEL (wē'zl) *n.* a small carnivorous

WEATHER (weᴛн'ẽr) *a.* state of the air as hot, dry, clear or the reverse;—*a.* windward; —*v.t.* to season; sail to the windward of; hold out against. [O.E. *weder*.]

WEATHER-BEATEN (weᴛн'ẽr-bē-tn) *a.* harassed or worn by the weather.

WEATHERBOUND (weᴛн'ẽr-bound) *a.* delayed by the weather.   [vane.

WEATHERCOCK (weᴛн'ẽr-kok) *n.* a turning

WEATHERGAGE (weᴛн'ẽr-gāj) *n.* that which shows the weather; windward position.

WEATHERGLASS (weᴛʜ'ẹr-glas) *n.* a barometer.

WEATHERWISE (weᴛʜ'ẹr-wiz) *a.* skilful in foretelling the weather.

WEAVE (wēv) *v.t.* [*pret.* WOVE; *pp.* WOVE, WOVEN] to unite threads so as to form cloth; intertwine; work into;—*v.i.* to practise weaving. [O.E. *wefan.*]

WEAVER (wē'vẹr) *n.* one who weaves.

WEB (web) *n.* anything woven; a film; a membrane uniting the toes of water-fowl; a roll of paper. [O.E. *webb.* a web.]

WEBBED (webd) *a.* having toes united by a membrane.

WEBBING (web'ing) *n.* a narrow fabric used variously. [feet.

WEB-FOOTED (web'foot-ed) *a.* having webbed

WED (wed) *v.t.* or *i.* to marry; unite closely. [O.E. *weddian* to pledge, engage, betroth, fr. *wedd*, a pledge.] [marriage.

WEDDING (wed'ing) *n.* nuptial ceremony;

WEDDING-FAVOUR (wed'ing-fā-vur) *n.* bunch of white ribbons pinned to the coat at a marriage.

WEDDING-RING (wed'ing-ring) *n.* ring put on the bride's finger during the marriage ceremony.

WEDGE (wedj) *n.* a piece of metal or of wood sloping to an edge for splitting;—*v.t.* to fasten, drive, or cleave with a wedge. [O.E. *wecg.*]

WEDLOCK (wed'lok) *n.* married state. [O.E. *wed*, pledge, and *lac*, a sport, a gift.]

WEDNESDAY (wenz'dā) *n.* the fourth day of the week. [O.E. *Wodnesdæg*, Woden's day.]

WEED (wēd) (1) *n.* a useless plant; anything useless;—*v.t.* to free from noxious plants; root out;—(2) *n.pl.* mourning garb, as of a widow. [(1) O.E. *weod.* (2) O.E. *wæde, wæd.*]

WEEDER (wē'dẹr) *n.* one who weeds.

WEEK (wēk) *n.* space of seven days. [O.E. *wice, wicu.*]

WEEKDAY (wēk'dā) *n.* any day except the Sabbath. [once a week.

WEEKLY (wēk'li) *a.* done every week;—*ad.*

WEEN (wēn) *v.i.* to think; fancy. [O.E. *wenan.* imagine.]

WEEP (wēp) *v.t.* or *i.* [*pret.* and *pp.* WEPT] to shed tears; bewail or bemoan. [O.E. *wepan*, to cry aloud.]

WEEPING (wē'ping) *n.* lamentation.

WEEVIL (wē'vl) *n.* an insect that injures grain. [O.E. *wifel.*]

WEFT (weft) *n.* the woof of cloth. [O.E. *weft* fr. *wefan*, weave.]

WEIGH (wā) *v.t.* to raise; find the heaviness of; equal in heaviness; take or give by weight; ponder;—*v.i.* to have weight; press heavily. [O.E. *wegan*, to bear.]

WEIGHER (wā'ẹr) *n.* one who weighs.

WEIGHT (wāt) *n.* heaviness; gravity; a metal standard for weighing; ponderous mass; pressure; importance.

WEIGHTLESS (wāt'les) *a.* light; unimportant.

WEIGHTY (wā'ti) *a.* heavy; important; grave; forcible.

WEIR (wēr) *n.* a dam to stop and raise the water of a stream; a fence of twigs set in a river to catch fish. Also **WEAR**. [O.E. *wer.*]

WEIRD (wērd) *n.* a spell or charm;—*a.* skilled in witchcraft; unearthly. [O.E. *wyrd* destiny.]

WELCOME (wel'kum) *n.* a kind reception;— *a.* received with gladness; grateful; pleasing; —*v.t.* to salute or entertain with kindness. [For WELL COME.]

WELCOMELY (wel'kum-li) *ad.* in a kind welcome manner.

WELD (weld) *v t.* to hammer into union, as heated metal;—*n.* a plant used as a yellow dye. [M.E. *well* fr. Sw. *välla.*]

WELDER (wel'dẹr) *n.* one who welds.

WELFARE (wel'fār *n.* health; happiness; prosperity. [O E. *wel*. well, and *faran* to fare go.]

WELKIN (wel'kin) *n.* the sky or region of clouds. [O.E. *wolcnu*, pl. of *wolcen*, cloud.]

WELL (wel) (1) *n.* a spring; an issue of water from the earth;—*v.i.* to issue forth; spring up;—(2) *a.* not sick; being in good state or favour;—*ad.* not amiss; rightly. [(1) O.E. *wella*, a spring. Cf. *weallan*, boil. (2) O.E. *wel*, well.] [perity.

WELLBEING (wel'bē-ing) *n.* welfare; pros-

WELL-BRED (wel'bred) *a.* having a polite education.

WELL-DONE (wel'dun) *inter.* rightly or nobly done.

WELL-MEANT (wel'ment) *a.* spoken or done in kindness.

WELLNIGH (wel'ni) *ad.* very nearly; almost.

WELLSPRING (wel'spring) *n.* source; fountain. [stances; well off.

WELL-TO-DO (wel'tòò-dòò) *a.* in easy circum-

WELT (welt) *n.* a border or edging;—*v.t.* to sew a welt on. [Cf. O.E. *wyltan*, to roll.]

WELTER (wel'tẹr) *v.i.* to roll about; wallow; tumble;—*n.* state of confusion; mess. [O.E. *wæltan*, roll.]

WEN (wen) *n.* a fleshy tumour. [O.E. *wenn.*]

WENCH (wensh) *n.* a young woman, usually of ill-fame;—*v.i.* to frequent the company of such. [M.E. *wenchel*, a child, fr. O.E. *wenclo*, children.]

WEND (wend) *v.t.* to direct; to betake; *v.i.* to go; to betake oneself. [O.E. *wendan*, go.]

WENT (went) used as the *prct.* of GO. [Orig. past tense of WEND.]

WEPT (wept) *prct.* of WEEP.

WERE (wẹr) used as the past tense, *pl.* of BE.

WERT (wẹrt) second person singular of the subjunctive past tense of BE.

WEST (west) *n.* the point where the sun sets; —*ad.* more westward;—*a.* situated toward the setting sun. [O.E.]

WESTERLY (wes'tẹr-li) *a.* toward or from the west.

WESTERN (wes'tẹrn) *a.* being in the west.

WESTWARD (west'wẹrd) *ad.* toward the west.

WET (wet) *a.* rainy; moist;—*n.* water; humidity;—*v.t.* [*pret.* and *pp.* WET] to moisten with a liquid. [O.E. *wæt.*]

WETHER (weᴛʜ'ẹr) *n.* a male sheep castrated. [O.E. *wither.*]

WETNESS (wet'nes) *n.* state of being wet

WHALE (hwāl) *n.* the largest of marine animals. [O.E. *hwæl.*]

WHALEBONE (hwāl'bōn) *n.* a firm elastic substance from the upper jaw of the whale.

WHALEMAN (hwāl'man) *n.* a person employed in the whale fishery.

WHALER (hwāl'ẹr) *n.* a ship or seaman employed in the whale fishery.

WHARF (hwawrf) *n.* a mole or quay for landing goods;—*pl.* WHARVES. [O.E. *wherf* bank to keep out water, fr. *hweorfan* to turn.] [wharf.

WHARFAGE (hwawr'fāj) *n.* fee for using a

WHARFINGER (hwawr'fin-jẹr) *n.* the keeper of a wharf.

WHAT (hwot) *pron. interrogative* of things, as **WHO** is of persons;—*pron. relative*, that which;—*inter.* how; how great, strange, etc. [O.E. *hwæt.*] [that.

WHATEVER (hwot-ev'ẹr) *pron.* being this or

WHATNOT (hwot'not) *n.* a piece of furniture with shelves for books ornaments, etc.

WHATSOEVER (hwot-sō-ev'ẹr) *pron.* whatever.

WHEAT (hwēt) *n.* a grassy plant and its seed which yields flour for bread. [O.E. *hwæte.*]

WHEAT-EAR (hwēt'ẹr) *n.* a small singing bird; fallow-finch. [WHITE and *arse.*]

WHEATEN (hwēt'n) *a.* made of wheat.

WHEEDLE (hwē'dl) *v.t.* or *i.* to entice by soft words; coax; flatter. [O.E. *wædlian*. to beg, fr. *wædl* poverty.]

WHEEDLER (hwē dlẹr) *n.* one who wheedles.

WHEEL (hwĕl) *n.* a circular frame of wood or metal turning on an axis;—*v.t.* to cause to move on wheels;—*v.i.* to turn. [O.E. *hweol.*] [with one wheel.

WHEELBARROW (hwĕl'bar-ō) *n.* a barrow

WHEELER (hwē'lẹr) *n.* one who turns or wheels; a shaft horse. [wheels.

WHEELWRIGHT (hwĕl'rīt) *n.* a maker of

WHEEZE (hwēz) *v.i.* to breathe hard. [O.E. *hwesan.*] [asthmatic.

WHEEZY (hwē'zi) *a.* affected with wheezing;

WHELK (hwelk) *n.* a pustule; a periwinkle; a kind of shell-fish. [O.E. *wiloc,* mollusc.]

WHELM (hwelm) *v.t.* to cover; immerse; overburden. [Scand.]

WHELP (hwelp) *n.* a puppy; a cub;—*v.i.* to bring forth young. [O.E. *hwelp.*]

WHEN (hwen) *ad.* at what time ; at the time that; while. [O.E. *hwænne.*]

WHENCE (hwens) *ad.* from what place ; from which place, source, etc.

WHENEVER (hwen-ev'ẹr) *ad.* at whatever time.

WHENSOEVER (hwen-sō-ev'ẹr) *ad.* at what time soever; whenever.

WHERE (hwăr) *ad.* at or in what place. [O.E. *hwær.*]

WHEREABOUT (hwăr'a-bout) *ad.* near what place; about which. Also **WHERE-ABOUTS.** [when in fact.

WHEREAS (hwăr-az') *ad.* considering; since;

WHEREAT (hwăr-at') *ad.* at which.

WHEREBY (hwăr-bī') *ad.* by which.

WHEREFORE (hwăr'fōr) *ad.* for which reason; for what reason.

WHEREIN (hwăr-in') *ad.* in which; in what.

WHEREOF (hwăr-ov') *ad.* of which; of what.

WHEREUPON (hwăr-u-pon') *ad.* upon or in consequence of which.

WHERESOEVER (hwăr-sō-ev'ẹr) *ad.* in what place soever.

WHERETO (hwăr-tōō') *ad.* to which; to what end. Also **WHEREUNTO.**

WHEREVER (hwăr-ev'ẹr) *ad.* at whatever place. [with what.

WHEREWITH (hwăr-with') *ad.* with which;

WHEREWITHAL (hwăr-wi-thawl') *ad.* wherewith. [Etym. unknown.]

WHERRY (hwer'i) *n.* a light, shallow boat.

WHET (hwet) *v.t.* to sharpen by friction; stimulate;—*n.* the act of sharpening; a stimulant. [O.E. *hwæt,* sharp, bold, brave.]

WHETHER (hweTH'ẹr) *pron.* which of the two. [O.E. *hwæther.*]

WHETSTONE (hwet'stōn) *n.* a stone for sharpening tools. [*hwæg.*]

WHEY (hwā) *n.* the thin part of milk. [O.E.

WHICH (hwich, *pron. interrogative,* who or what one of a number, sort, etc.;—*pron. relative,* that which. [O.E. *hwilc.*]

WHICHEVER (hwich-ev'ẹr) *pron.* whether one or other.

WHIFF (hwif) *n.* a puff of air;—*v.t.* or *t.* to emit whiffs; puff; smoke. [Imit.]

WHIFFLE (hwif'l) *v.t.* or *i.* to blow away; disperse; waver; prevaricate. [Fr. **WHIFF.**]

WHIFFLER (hwif'lẹr) *n.* a trifler.

WHIFFLETREE (hwif'l-trē) *n.* the bar to which traces are fastened. [Fr. **WHIFFLE,** to veer.]

WHIG (hwig) *n.* one of a political party;—*a.* pertaining to Whigs. [Contr. fr. *whiggamore.*]

WHIGGISH (hwig'ish) *a.* inclined to Whiggery.

WHIGGERY (hwig'ẹr-i) *n.* the principles of Whigs. Also **WHIGGISM.**

WHILE (hwil) *n.* time; space of time;—*ad.* during the time that; as long as;—*v.t.* to pass or spend idly. [O.E. *hwil,* a pause, a time.]

WHILST (hwilst) *ad.* while.

WHIM (hwim) *n.* a freak of fancy; caprice. [Icel. *hvima,* to have straying eyes.]

WHIMBREL (hwim'brel) *n.* a wading bird allied to the curlew. [Fr. **WHIMPER.**]

WHIMPER (hwim'pẹr) *v.i.* to cry with a whining voice. [Fr. **WHINE.**]

WHIMSICAL (hwim'zi-kạl) *a.* full of whims.

WHIMSICALLY (hwim'zi-kạl-i) *ad.* with freakishness.

WHIN (hwin) *n.* furze; gorse. [W. *chwyn* weeds, a single weed, furze.]

WHINCHAT (hwin'chat) *n.* a small singing bird allied to the stone-chat.

WHINE (hwin) *v.i.* to murmur in a plaintive tone;—*n.* a nasal tone of complaint. [O.E. *hwinan,* to whine.]

WHINNY (hwin'i) *v.i.* to neigh or cry like a horse. freq. of **WHINE.**

WHINSTONE (hwin'stōn) *n.* any hard, dark, unstratified rock. [Perh. corr. fr. *whenstone, quernstone,* stone suitable for querns.]

WHIP (hwip) *n.* a lash with a handle for punishing or driving; a driver; a small tackle for hoisting;—*v.t.* or *i.* to lash; sew lightly; snatch; move nimbly. [M.E. *whippen.* Cf. M.E. *wippen,* to jump up and down.]

WHIPHAND (hwip'hand) *n.* upper hand; advantage over.

WHIPPING (hwip'ing) *n.* act of striking.

WHIP-STOCK (hwip'stok) *n.* a whip-handle.

WHIR (hwẹr) *v.i.* to whirl round with noise; —*n.* noise made by rapid whirling. [Dan. *hvirre,* to twirl.]

WHIRL (hwẹrl) *v.t.* or *i.* to turn or revolve rapidly;—*n.* a rapid turning. [Icel. *hvirfla* to whirl.]

WHIRLIGIG (hwẹr'li-gig) *n.* a child's toy.

WHIRLPOOL (hwẹrl'pōōl) *n.* an eddy; a vortex of water.

WHIRLWIND (hwẹrl'wind) *n.* a stormy wind moving circularly.

WHISK (hwisk) *n.* a small besom;—*v.t.* to brush with a whisk; move rapidly. [Scand.]

WHISKER (hwis'-kẹr) *n.* long hair growing on the cheek. [grain, etc.

WHISKY (hwis'ki) *n.* spirit distilled from

WHISPER (hwis'pẹr) *v.t.* or *i.* to speak with a low voice;—*n.* a low, soft voice. [O.E. *hwisprian.*]

WHIST (hwist) *n.* a game at cards;—*a.* silent; mute. [Cf. HIST.]

WHISTLE (hwis'l) *n.* a sharp, shrill sound produced in various ways; a wind instrument; pipe or call;—*v.t.* or *i.* to make or utter a shrill sound; sound shrill; call. [O.E. *hwistlian.*]

WHISTLER (hwis'lẹr) *n.* one who whistles.

WHIT (hwit) *n.* smallest particle imaginable; point; jot. [O.E. *wiht.*]

WHITE (hwit) *a.* of the colour of snow; pale; pure;—*n.* a white colour; white part of the eye, an egg, or a target;—*v.t.* to make white. [O.E. *hwit.*] [delicate fish.

WHITEBAIT (hwit'bāt) *n.* a very small,

WHITE-BEAR (hwit'băr) *n.* the polar bear.

WHITE-FEATHER (hwit'feTH-ẹr) *n.* symptom of cowardice.

WHITEN (hwi'tn) *v.t.* to make white; bleach; —*v.i.* to become white. [white.

WHITENESS (hwit'nes) *n.* state of being

WHITESMITH (hwit'smith) *n.* a tinsmith.

WHITEWASH (hwit'wosh) *n.* a wash for the skin; lime and water;—*v.t.* to cover with whitewash; give a fair appearance to.

WHITEWASHER (hwit'wosh-ẹr) *n.* one who whitewashes.

WHITHER (hwiTH'ẹr) *ad.* to what place; to what point or degree. [O.E. *hwider.*]

WHITHERSOEVER (hwiTH-ẹr-sō-ev'ẹr) *ad.* to whatever place.

WHITING (hwi'ting) *n.* a sea-fish allied to the cod; clear ground chalk. [**WHITE.**]

WHITISH (hwi'tish) *a.* moderately white.

WHITLEATHER (hwit'leTH-ẹr) *n.* leather dressed with alum.

WHITLOW (hwit′lō) *n.* a tumour on the finger. [For *whick-flaw—i.e. quick,* the sensitive part under the finger-nail, and *flaw,* a crack.]

WHITTLE (hwit′l) *v.t.* or *i.* to pare or cut with a knife;—*n.* a small pocket-knife. [O.E. *thwitan,* to cut.]

WHIZ (hwiz) *n.* a humming and hissing sound; —*v.t.* to make such a sound. [Imit.]

WHO (hōō) *pron. interrogative,* which or what person;—*pron. relative,* the person which. [O.E. *hwa.*] [ever.

WHOEVER (hōō-ev′ẽr) *pron.* any person what-

WHOLE (hōl) *a.* all; entire; sound;—*n.* the entire thing. [O.E. *hal.*]

WHOLESALE (hōl′sāl) *n.* sale by the piece or large quantities;—*a.* trading in large quantities; general; charged to retailers, as price.

WHOLESOMENESS (hōl′sum-nes) *n.* salubrity; quality of contributing to health.

WHOLLY (hō′li) *ad.* totally; entirely.

WHOM (hōōm) *pron.* objective case of **WHO.**

WHOMSOEVER (hōōm′-sō-ev′ẽr) *pron.* objective case of **WHOSOEVER.**

WHOOP (hwōōp, hōōp) *n.* a loud eager cry; a hoot;—*v.t.* or *i.* to shout; hoot; insult with shouts. [F. *houper.*]

WHORE (hōr) *n.* a harlot;—*v.i.* to practise lewdness. [Scand.]

WHOREDOM (hōr′dum) *n.* lewdness; idolatry.

WHORL (hworl) *n.* arrangement of leaves in a circle round the stem. [O.E. *hweorfan,* to turn.]

WHOSE (hōōz) *pron.* possessive of **WHO.**

WHOSOEVER (hōō-sō-ev′ẽr) *a.* any person whatever.

WHY (hwī) *ad.* for what reason; wherefore. [O.E. *hwi.*]

WICK (wik) *n.* the cotton string of a candle or lamp. [M.E. *wicke,* fr. O.E. *weoce.*]

WICKED (wik′ed) *a.* evil; sinful; ungodly; malicious. [Literally rendered *evil,* fr. *wikke,* evil, weak; allied to **WEAK.**]

WICKEDLY (wik′ed-li) *ad.* in a wicked manner; viciously.

WICKEDNESS (wik′ed-nes) *n.* evil disposition or practice; crime; sin.

WICKER (wik′ẽr) *a.* made of twigs. [Cf. O.E. *wican,* to bend.]

WICKET (wik′et) *n.* a small gate; the frame of rods bowled at in cricket. [A.F. *wiket.*]

WIDE (wīd) *a.* having great extent each way; broad; extensive; distant;—*ad.* at a distance. [O.E. *wid.*]

WIDELY (wīd′li) *ad.* extensively.

WIDEN (wī′dn) *v.t.* or *i.* to make or grow wider. [side; width.

WIDENESS (wīd′nes) *n.* breadth from side to

WIDESPREAD (wīd′spred) *a.* extended far.

WIDGEON (wij′un) *n.* a waterfowl of the duck family. [O.F. *vigeon.*]

WIDOW (wid′ō) *n.* a woman bereaved of her husband;—*v.t.* to deprive of a husband. [O.E. *widwe, widuwe.*]

WIDOWER (wid′ō-ẽr) *n.* a man whose wife is dead. [widow.

WIDOWHOOD (wid′ō-hood) *n.* the state of a

WIDTH (width) *n.* extent from side to side.

WIELD (wēld) *v.t.* to employ; use; sway; handle. [O.E. *gewyldan,* to have power over.]

WIELDER (wēl′dẽr) *n.* one who wields.

WIELDY (wēl′di) *a.* manageable.

WIFE (wīf) *n.* the lawful consort of a man; —*pl.* **WIVES.** [O.E. *wif.*]

WIFEHOOD (wīf′hood) *n.* state or character of a wife.

WIG (wig) *n.* an artificial covering of hair. [Contr. fr. **PERIWIG.**]

WIGHT (wīt) *n.* a person; a being;—*a.* brave; powerful. [O.E. *wiht,* creature.]

WIGWAM (wig′wam) *n.* an Indian hut. [N. Amer. Ind. *wekouomut,* in his house.]

WILD (wīld) *a.* not tame; desert; savage; licentious; fanciful;—*n.* a forest; desert. [O.E *wilde.*]

WILDERNESS (wil′dẽr-nes) *n.* a wild region uncultivated and uninhabited. [O.E. *wilder,* a wild animal.]

WILDLY (wīld′li) *ad.* in a wild manner.

WILDNESS (wīld′nes) *n.* state of being wild.

WILE (wīl) *n.* a trick; sly artifice; stratagem; —*v.t.* to deceive. [O.E. *wil.*]

WILFUL (wil′fool) *a.* governed solely by one′s own will; done or suffered by design; stubborn.

WILFULLY (wil′fool-i) *ad.* with obstinacy.

WILFULNESS (wil′fool-nes) *n.* obstinacy of will; perverseness.

WILINESS (wī′li-nes) *n.* cunning; artfulness.

WILL (wil) *n.* the faculty of choosing; choice; inclination; command; testament;—*v.t.* or *i.* to determine; dispose by testament; decree; be willing;—*auxiliary verb, pret.* **WOULD.** [O.E. *willa,* will, fr. *willan,* to wish.]

WILLING (wil′ing) *a.* free to do; disposed; spontaneous; desirous.

WILLINGLY (wil′ing-li) *ad.* by free-will; cheerfully; gladly. [readiness.

WILLINGNESS (wil′ing-nes) *n.* free choice;

WILLOW (wil′ō) *n.* a tree with slender, pliant branches. [O.E. *welig.*]

WILY (wī′li) *a.* cunning; crafty; artful; sly.

WIMBLE (wim′bl) *n.* an instrument to bore holes. [M.E. *wimbil.* Cf. Dan. *vimmel,* a boring tool.]

WIN (win) *v.t.* [*pret.* and *pp.* **WON**] to gain; allure. [O.E. *winnan,* to struggle.]

WINCE (wins) *v.i.* to shrink or start back. [M. H. Ger.]

WINCH (winsh) *n.* an instrument to turn and strain forcibly. [O.E. *wince.*]

WIND (wind) (1) *n.* air in motion; breath; flatulence;—*v.t.* or *i.* (wind) to blow; winnow; sound; drive hard; recover breath. [O.E.]

WIND (wīnd) (2) *v.t.* [*pret.* and *pp.* **WOUND**] to turn; twist; meander; bend. [O.E. *windan.*]

WINDAGE (win′dij) *n.* the difference between the diameter of a gun and that of a ball. [See **WIND** (1).]

WIND-BOUND (wind′bound) *a.* detained by contrary winds.

WINDFALL (wind′fawl) *n.* fruit blown off; any unexpected benefit.

WIND-GALL (wind′gawl) *n.* a tumour on a horse′s fetlock. [air.

WIND-GUN (wind′gun) *n.* a gun discharged by

WINDINESS (win′di-nes) *n.* state of being windy.

WINDING-SHEET (wīnd′ing-shēt) *n.* a shroud for the dead.

WINDLASS (wind′las) *n.* a revolving cylinder used to raise weights. [Icel. *vindill,* a winder, and *ass,* a pole.]

WINDLESS (wind′les) *a.* calm; out of breath.

WINDMILL (wind′mil) *n.* a mill driven by wind.

WINDOW (win′dō) *n.* an opening for the admission of light; the frame in the opening. [Icel. *vindauga,* wind-eye.]

Windmill.

WINDOW-BLIND (win′dō-blīnd) *n.* a blind to obscure the light of a window.

WINDOW-CURTAIN (win′dō-kur-tin) *n.* a curtain hung inside and over a window.

WINDOW-GLASS (win'dō-glas) *n.* panes of glass for windows.

WINDOW-SASH (win'dō-sash) *n.* the frame in which glass is set. [breath.

WINDPIPE (wind'pīp) *n.* passage for the

WINDSAIL (wind'sāl) *n.* a canvas tube or funnel to convey air below a ship's deck.

WINDUP (wind'up) *n.* conclusion; concluding act.

WINDWARD (wind'ward) *a.* lying toward the wind;—*n.* the point from which the wind blows. [flatulent; empty.

WINDY (win'di) *a.* stormy; tempestuous;

WINE (win) *n.* fermented juice of grapes and of other fruits. [O.E. *win*, fr. L. *vinum*.]

WINE-BIBBER (win'bib-ẹr) *n.* a great drinker of wine. [wine.

WINE-CELLAR (win'sel-ạr) *n.* cellar for storing

WINE-COOLER (win'kŏŏ-lẹr) *n.* contrivance for cooling bottled wine for the table.

WINE-GLASS (win'glas) *n.* a small glass from which wine is drunk.

WINE-PRESS (win'pres) *n.* place in which grapes are pressed.

WING (wing) *n.* the limb of a bird; flight; side of a building, army. etc.; sidepiece; —*v.t.* to furnish with wings; wound in the wing. [Icel. *vœngr*.]

WINK (wingk) *v.i.* to shut and open the eyelids; connive;—*n.* a closing of the eyelids; a hint by the eye. [O.E. *wincian*.]

WINNER (win'ẹr) *n.* he that wins.

WINNING (win'ing) *a.* attracting; pleasing;— *n.* sum gained in games of competition.

WINNOW (win'ō) *v.t.* or *i.* to separate chaff from grain; sift. [O.E. *windwian*, fr. *wind*, wind.]

WINSOME (win'sum) *a.* cheerful and pleasing; attractive. [O.E. *wynsum*, fr. *wyn*, joy.]

WINTER (win'tẹr) *n.* the cold season;—*v.t.* or *i.* to pass the winter; feed during winter. [O.E. *winter*.] [cold; stormy.

WINTERLY (win'tẹr-li) *a.* suitable to winter;

WIPE (wīp) *v.t.* to clean by rubbing;—*n.* a rub; a stroke. [O.E. *wipian*.]

WIRE (wīr) *n.* a thread of metal;—*v.t.* or *i.* to bind with wire; telegraph. [O.E. *wir*.]

WIRE-DRAW (wīr'draw) *v.t.* to draw metal into wire; strain; spin out.

WIRE-DRAWER (wīr'draw-ẹr) *n.* one who forms wire by drawing. [gram.

WIRELESS (wīr'les) *a.* used as *n.* a Marconi-

WIRE-PULLER (wīr'pŏŏl-ẹr) *n.* one who pulls the wires; an intriguer.

WIRY (wī'ri) *a.* made of or resembling wire.

WISDOM (wiz'dum) *n.* knowledge properly used; prudence.

WISE (wīz) (1) *a.* having wisdom; judicious; prudent; grave;—(2) *n.* manner or way. [(1) O.E. *wis*. (2) O.E. *wise*, way fr. *wis*, wise.]

WISEACRE (wī'ză kẹr) *n.* a pretender to great wisdom. [Ger. *Weissager*, a soothsayer.]

WISELY (wīz'li) *ad.* judiciously.

WISH (wish) *v.t.* to desire or long for;—*v.i.* to have a desire;—*n.* desire expressed; thing desired. [O.E. *wyscan*, to wish.]

WISHER (wish'ẹr) *n.* one who wishes or expresses a wish. [desire.

WISHFUL (wish'fool) *a.* feeling or showing

WISHFULLY (wish'fool-i) *ad.* with desire.

WISP (wisp) *n.* a small bundle of straw or hay. [M.E. *wisp*, *wips*. Cf. **WIPE**.]

WISTFUL (wist'fool) *a.* thoughtful; expressing longing desire; eagerly attentive. [Variant of **WISHFUL**.] [desire.

WISTFULLY (wist'fool-i) *ad.* with longing

WIT (wit) *v.t.* to know;—*n.* understanding; sense; power of combining ideas in an unexpected or ludicrous manner; cleverness in repartee; a man of wit:—*pl.* presence of mind; sound judgment. [O.E. *witan*, to know.]

WITCH (wich) *v.t.* to charm;—*n.* a woman who practises sorcery. [O.E. *wicca*, wizard, *wicce*, witch.] [witches.

WITCHCRAFT (wich'krăft) *n.* the practices of

WITCHERY (wich'ẹr-i) *n.* enchantment; fascination.

WITH (with) *prep.* by, denoting cause, means, connection, contrast, succession, etc. [O.E.]

WITHDRAW (with-draw') *v.t.* or *i.* to take back; recall; retire. [back.

WITHDRAWAL (with-draw'al) *n.* a taking

WITHE (with, wīth) *n.* a willow twig. Also **WITH**. [O.E. *withig*, a willow.]

WITHER (wiTH'ẹr) *v.t.* or *i.* to dry up; waste; shrink; fade. [See **WEATHER**.]

WITHERS (wiTH'ẹrz) *n.pl.* the joint that unites the neck and shoulder of a horse. [O.E. *wither*, against.]

WITHHELD (with-held') *pret.* and *pp.* of **WITHHOLD**.

WITHHOLD (with-hōld') *v.t.* [*pret.* **WITHHELD**] to keep back.

WITHIN (wi-thin') *prep.* in the inner part;— *ad.* inwardly.

WITHOUT (wi-thout') *prep.* out; beyond;— *ad.* on the outside;—*conj.* unless; except.

WITHSTAND (with-stand') *v.t.* [*pret.* **WITHSTOOD**] to oppose; resist.

WITNESS (wit'nes) *n.* testimony; a person who sees and testifies;—*v.t.* to see; attest; subscribe as witness;—*v.i.* to bear testimony. [O.E., fr. *witan*, know.]

WITNESSER (wit'nes-ẹr) *n.* one who witnesses.

WITTED (wit'ed) *a.* endued with wit.

WITTICISM (wit'i-sizm) *n.* a phrase affectedly witty.

WITTILY (wit'i-li) *ad.* with wit.

WITTINGLY (wit'ing-li) *ad.* knowingly.

WITTY (wit'i) *a.* full of wit; smart; sarcastic; ingenious.

WIVES (wīvz) *n.pl.* of **WIFE**.

WIZARD (wiz'ạrd) *n.* one skilled in magical arts; a conjurer. [O.F. *guiscart*, fr. Icel. *vizkr*, clever, fr. *vita*, to know.]

WIZEN (wiz'n) *v.i.* to become dry and shrivelled;—*a.* dried up; weazen. [O.E. *wisnian*, to wither.]

WOE, WO (wō) *n.* a heavy calamity; sorrow; an exclamation of grief. [O.E. *wa*.]

WOEFUL (wō'fool) *a.* very sorrowful; full of distress; calamitous. [ably.

WOEFULLY (wō'fool-i) *ad.* wretchedly; miser-

WOLF (woolf) *n.* a rapacious animal allied to the dog; anything very destructive;—*pl.* **WOLVES**. [O.E. *wulf*.]

WOLFISH (wool'fish) *a.* like a wolf.

WOMAN (woom'ạn) *n.* the female of man; an adult female; a female servant. [O.E. *wifman*.]

WOMANHOOD (woom'ạn-hood) *n.* the state or qualities of a woman.

WOMANISH (woom'ạn-ish) *a.* feminine; effeminate.

WOMB (wŏŏm) *n.* a place where anything is produced; any deep cavity. [O.E. *wamb*.]

WOMEN (wim'en) *n.pl.* of **WOMAN**.

WONDER (won'dẹr) *n.* emotion of surprise; a strange thing; prodigy;—*v.i.* to be surprised. [O.E. *wundor*.]

WONDERFUL (wun'dẹr-fool) *a.* exciting surprise; astonishing.

WONDERFULLY (wun'dẹr-fool-i) *ad.* in a manner to excite surprise.

WONDERFULNESS (wun'dẹr-fool-nes) *n.* quality of being wonderful.

WONDERMENT (wun'dẹr-ment) *n.* surprise; astonishment.

WONDROUS (wun'drus) *a.* marvellous; strange. [manner-

WONDROUSLY (wun'drus-li) *ad.* in a surprising

WONT (wunt) *a.* accustomed;—*v.i.* to be accustomed;—*n.* custom; habit. [O.E. *wunian*, pp. *wunod*, dwell.]

WONTED (wun'ted) *a.* customary; usual.

WONTEDNESS (wun'ted-nes) *n.* state of being accustomed.

WOO (wōō) *v.t.* to solicit in marriage;—*v.i.* to make love. [O.E. *wogian.*]

WOOD (wood) *n.* a collection of trees; the solid part of trees; timber;—*v.t.* or *i.* to supply wood; take in wood. [O.E. *wudu.*]

WOODCOCK (wood'kok) *n.* a bird of the snipe species. [wood.

WOODCUT (wood'kut) *n.* an engraving on

WOODED (wood'ed) *a.* covered or supplied with wood.

WOODEN (wood'n) *a.* made of wood; hard.

WOOD-ENGRAVING (wood'en-grā'ving) *n.* art of engraving on wood; an engraving on wood. [wood.

WOODLAND (wood'land) *n.* land producing

WOODLESS (wood'les) *a.* destitute of wood.

WOOD-NYMPH (wood'nimf) *n.* a fabled goddess of the woods.

WOODY (wood'i) *a.* abounding with wood.

WOOER (wōō'er) *n.* one who solicits in marriage.

WOOF (wōōf) *n.* threads that cross the warp in weaving. [O.E. *owef,* woof.]

WOOL (wool) *n.* the fleece of sheep; any short, thick hair. [O.E. *wul.*]

WOOLLEN (wool'en) *a.* consisting of wool; made of wool;—*n.* cloth made of wool;— *pl.* woollen goods. [O.E. *wul.*]

WOOLLINESS (wool'i-nes) *n.* state of being woolly.

WOOLLY (wool'i) *a.* consisting of wool.

WOOL-PACK (wool'pak) *n.* a bag of wool.

WOOLSACK (wool'sak) *n.* a seat made of wool; the Lord Chancellor's seat.

WOOL-STAPLER (wool'stā-pler) *n.* one who deals in wool.

WORD (wurd) *n.* an oral or written discourse; sound which conveys an idea; message; promise; the Scriptures;—*v.t.* to express in words; phrase. [O.E. *word.*]

WORDINESS (wur'di-nes) *n.* verboseness.

WORDING (wur'ding) *n.* manner of expressing.

WORDY (wur'di) *a.* using many words; verbose.

WORE (wōr) *pret.* of WEAR.

WORK (wurk) *v.t.* or *i.* [*pret.* and *pp.* WORKED WROUGHT] to make or effect by labour; manage; influence; toil; carry on; operate; ferment; embroider;—*n.* labour for a purpose; manual labour; that on which one labours; the result of labour; product; performance; deed; a book; embroidery; manner of working; employment. [O.E. *weorc,* work.] [performs.

WORKER (wur'ker) *n.* one who works or

WORKHOUSE (wurk'hous) *n.* a house for employing the idle or the poor.

WORKING (wur'king) *n.* act of labouring; motion; operation; fermentation.

WORKMAN (wurk'man) *n.* man employed in manual labour; a skilful labourer; craftsman. [well-performed.

WORKMANLIKE (wurk'man-līk) *a.* skilful;

WORKMANSHIP (wurk'man-ship) *n.* work done; manner of making; skill.

WORKSHOP (wurk'shop) *n.* a shop where work is done.

WORLD (wurld) *n.* the earth; the universe; mankind; all which the earth contains. [O.E. *weorold.*]

WORLDLINESS (wurld'li-nes) *n.* predominant love of earthly things.

WORLDLING (wurld'ling) *n.* one devoted to worldly things.

WORLDLY (wurld'li) *a.* pertaining to this life; temporal; secular; carnal.

WORM (wurm) *n.* an insect that crawls; a reptile; anything spiral;—*v.t.* to work slowly and secretly;—*v.i.* to gain slowly and by imperceptible means. [O.E. *wyrm,* a wurm.] [worms.

WORM-EATEN (wurm'etn) *a.* gnawed by

WORMWOOD (wurm'wood) *n.* a plant with a bitter nauseous taste; a source of bitterness.

WORMY (wur'mi) *a.* abounding with worms.

WORN (wōrn) *pp.* of WEAR.

WORRIED (wur'id) *pp.* fatigued; harassed.

WORRY (wor'i) *v.t.* to tear with the teeth; harass; torment;—*n.* trouble; vexation. [O.E. *wyrgan,* strangle.]

WORSE (wurs) *a.* more bad; more sick;— *n.* the disadvantage;—*ad.* in a way more evil. [O.E. *wyrs, wyrsa.*]

WORSHIP (wur'ship) *n.* religious service; adoration; honour; respect; a title of honour;—*v.t.* or *i.* to adore; honour; perform religious service. [For *worthship.*]

WORSHIPFUL (wur'ship-fool) *a.* worthy of honour or respect.

WORSHIPFULLY (wur'ship-fool-i) *ad.* with worship or honour.

WORSHIPPER (wur'ship-er) *n.* one who worships.

WORST (wurst) *a.* bad, evil, or pernicious in the highest degree;—*n.* the most evil state; —*v.t.* to defeat; overthrow. [O.E. *wyrst, wyrsta.*]

WORSTED (woors'ted) *n.* a yarn from combed wool;—*a.* consisting of worsted; spun from wool. [Fr. *Worsted,* in Norfolk.]

WORT (wurt) *n.* a plant; a herb; new beer unfermented, or in the act of fermentation. [O.E. *wyrt,* a root.]

WORTH (wurth) *v.i.* betide, as woe *worth* the day;—*n.* value; price; importance; excellence;—*a.* equal in value to; deserving of. [O.E. *weorth.*] [well.

WORTHILY (wur'THi-li) *ad.* so as to deserve

WORTHINESS (wir'THi-nes) *n.* worth; desert; excellence.

WORTHLESS (wurth'les) *a.* having no worth, or value. [worth.

WORTHLESSNESS (wurth'les-nes) *n.* want of

WORTHY (wur'THi) *a.* deserving; excellent; —*n.* a man of eminent worth.

WOT (wot) *v.i.* to know; be aware of. [O.E. *wat,* present of *witan,* to know.]

WOULD (wood) *pret.* of WILL.

WOUND (wōōnd) *n.* a cut, stab, or bruise; hurt; injury;—*v.t.* to injure by violence; hurt; pain. [O.E. *wund.*]

WOUND (wound) *pret.* of WIND.

WOUNDING (wōōnd'ing) *n.* hurt; injury.

WOUNDY (wōōn'di) *a.* excessive; vastly great.

WOVE (wōv) *pret.* of WEAVE.

WRACK (rak) *n.* a sea-plant from which kelp is made; a flying cloud; rack. [O.E. *wræc,* exile, misery, fr. *wrecan,* to drive, to wreck.]

WRAITH (rāth) *n.* a spectre; apparition. [Scand.]

WRANGLE (rang'gl) *n.* an angry dispute;— *v.i.* to dispute noisily. [O.E. *wringan,* to wring, strain, press.]

WRANGLER (rang'gler) *n.* one who wrangles or disputes.

WRAP (rap) *v.t.* to roll or fold together; involve. [M.E. *wrappen, wlappen.*]

WRAPPER (rap'er) *n.* one who raps; a cover; a loose outer garment.

WRAPPING (rap'ing) *n.* a covering.

WRATH (rāth) *n.* violent anger; fury; rage; indignation. [O.E. *wrœththu.*]

WRATHFUL (rāth'fool) *a.* angry; enraged; expressing wrath.

WREAK (rēk) *v.t.* to inflict. [O.E. *wrecan.*]

WREATH (rēth) *n.* thing twisted; a garland; chaplet. [O.E. *wrœth,* a fillet.]

WREATHE (rēTH) *v.t.* or *i.* to twine or twist about; encircle; be intertwined.

WRECK (rek) *v.t.* or *i.* to damage or destroy; ruin; suffer loss or ruin;—*n.* destruction by sea; anything wrecked. [Same as WRACK.]

WRECKER (rek'er) *n.* one who plunders wrecks. [wrenna.]

WREN (ren) *n.* a small perching bird. [O.E.

WRENCH (rensh) *v.t.* to pull with a twist; strain; distort;—*n.* a twist; an instrument for turning bolts, etc. [O.E. *wrenc*, guile, fraud.]

WREST (rest) *v.t.* to take from by force; distort;—*n.* violent perversion. [O.E. *wræstan.*]

WRESTLE (res'l) *v.i.* to contend in grappling; struggle;—*n.* a contest between two to throw each other d_own. [O.E. *wræstlian*, fr. *wræstan*, to twist about.]

WRESTLER (res'ler) *n.* one skilled in wrestling.

WRESTLING (res'ling) *n.* the act of wrestling.

WRETCH (rech) *n.* a miserable person; a worthless fellow. [O.E. *wrecca*, an exile.]

WRETCHED (rech'ed) *a.* very miserable; worthless. [despicably.

WRETCHEDLY (rech'ed-li) *ad.* miserably;

WRIGGLE (rig'l) *v.t.* or *i.* to move to and fro with short motions. [D. *wriggelen.*]

WRIGHT (rit) *n.* an artificer or workman, usually in wood. [O.E. *wyrhta*, fr. *wyrht*, work.]

WRING (ring) *v.t.* [*pret.* and *pp.* **WRUNG**] to force by twisting and pressure; strain; extort; distress; distort;—*v.i.* to turn or twist. [O.E.]

WRINGER (ring'er) *n.* an extortioner; an apparatus for wringing water out of clothes after washing.

WRINKLE (ring'kl) *n.* a crease; furrow:—*v.t.* or *i.* to contract into furrows. [M.E. *wrinkel.*]

WRINKLY (ringk'li) *a.* full of wrinkles; liable to wrinkle.

WRIST (rist) *n.* the joint connecting the hand with the arm. [O.E.]

WRISTBAND (rist'band) *n.* the part of a sleeve that covers the wrist.

WRIT (rit) *n.* a writing; the Scriptures; a written document by which one is summoned or required to do something.

WRITE (rit) *v.t.* or *i.* [*pret.* **WROTE**; *pp.* **WRITTEN**] to form letters and words with pen or style; engrave; compose; record; communicate by letter; practise writing. [O.E.] [author.

WRITER (ri'ter) *n.* one who writes; clerk;

WRITHE (riŦH) *v.t.* or *i.* to twist; be distorted with pain. [O.E. *writhan.*]

WRITING (ri'ting) *n.* act of writing; that which is written; a book; a manuscript; —*pl.* official papers; deeds.

WRITTEN (rit'n) *a.* expressed in writing.

WRONG (rong) *n.* injustice; injury;—*a.* not right, true, or suitable; incorrect; evil:—*v.t.* to do injustice to; injure;—*ad.* not rightly; amiss. [O.E. *wrang.*]

WRONGDOER (rong'dŏŏ-er) *n.* one who commits any offence.

WRONGFUL (rong'fool) *a.* unjust; injurious.

WRONGFULLY (rong'fool-i) *ad.* unjustly; injuriously.

WRONGLY (rong'li) *ad.* unjustly; amiss.

WRONGOUS (rong'gus) *a.* illegal; unjust.

WROTE (rōt) *pret.* of **WRITE.**

WROTH (roth) *a.* very angry; enraged. [O.E. *wrath.*] [labour.

WROUGHT (rawt) *pret.* and *pp.* formed by

WRUNG (rung) *pret.* and *pp.* of **WRING.**

WRY (ri) *a.* twisted; distorted; wrested. [O.E. *wrigian*, twist.]

WYND (wind) *n.* a narrow lane. [O.E. *windan*, to turn round.]

X

XANTHIN (zan' thin) *n.* yellow dyeing matter in madder. [G. *xanthos*, yellow.]

XANTHOUS (zan'thus) *a.* yellow; denoting the fair races of mankind.

XANTIPPE (zan-tip'e) *n.* a female scold; shrew. [The wife of Socrates.]

XEBEC (ze'bek) *n.* a small three-masted vessel used in the Mediterranean. [Turk.]

XEROPHAGY (zē-rof'a-ji) *n.* the eating of dry meats; a kind of fast. [G. *xeros*, dry, *phagein*, to eat.]

XYLOGRAPHIC (zī-lō-graf'ik) *a.* belonging to wood-engraving.

XYLOGRAPHY (zī-log'ra-fi) *n.* the art of engraving in wood. [G. *xulon*, wood, and *graphein*, write.]

XYLOPHAGUS (zī-lof'a-gus) *a.* feeding on wood. [G. *xulon*, wood, and *phagein*, to eat.]

XYSTER (zis'ter) *n.* a surgeon's knife for scraping bones. [G. *xuster*, fr. *xuein*, to scrape.]

Y

YACHT (yot) *n.* a vessel for state, pleasure, or racing purposes;—*v.i.* to sail in a yacht. [D.]

YACHTSMAN (yots'man) *n.* one who keeps or sails a yacht; a sailor in a yacht. Also **YACHTER.**

YAHOO (yä'hŏŏ) *n.* a rude, boorish person. [Name given by Swift to a race of brutes.]

YAM (yam) *n.* a tropical root, somewhat like the potato. [Pg. *inhame*, a yam.]

YANKEE (yang'kē) *n.* a corrupt pronunciation of the French *Anglais*, *English*, by Indians; a New Englander; an American;—*a.* belonging to the United States.

YARD (yárd) (1) *n.* a measure of three feet; a long beam on a mast to which the square sails are tied;—(2) *n.* an enclosure. [(1) O.E. *gyrd*. (2) O.E. *geard*, enclosure.]

YARDSTICK (yárd'stik) *n.* a stick three feet in length.

YARN (yárn) *n.* spun wool, flax, or cotton; a story spun out. [O.E. *gearn.*]

YARROW (yar'ō) *n.* the plant milfoil. [O.E. *gearwe.*]

YATAGHAN (yat'a-gan) *n.* a long dagger. Also **ATAGHAN.** [Turk.]

YAW (yaw) *v.i.* to steer wild; fall from the course. [D.]

YAWL (yawl) *n.* a small ship's boat with four or six oars; a two-masted fishing boat. [D. *jol.*]

YAWN (yawn) *v.i.* to gape; open wide;—*n.* act of gaping. [O.E. *geonian.*]

YE (yē) *pron.* second person plural of **THOU.** [O.E. *ge.*]

YEA (yā) *ad.* yes; verily; certainly. [O.E. *gea.*]

YEAN (yēn) *v.t.* or *i.* to bring forth young. [O.E. *eanian.*]

YEANLING (yēn'ling) *n.* a young sheep.

YEAR (yēr) *n.* twelve months. [O.E. *gear.*]

YEARLING (yēr'ling) *n.* an animal a year old. [year;—*ad.* annually.

YEARLY (yēr'li) *a.* annual; coming every

YEARN (yern) (1) *v.i.* to feel earnest desire; to long;—(2) *v.i.* to grieve. [(1) O.E. *giernan*, fr. *georn*, desirous. (2) O.E. *eorn*, as in *eornful*, anxious.]

YEARNING (yẹr'ning) *n.* strong desire; tenderness;—*a.* longing.

YEAST (yēst) *n.* froth of liquors in fermentation; barm. [O.E. *gist.*]

YELL (yel) *v.i.* to utter a sharp outcry;—*n.* a hideous scream. [O.E. *gellan.*]

YELLOW (yel'ō) *a.* of gold colour;—*n.* a gold colour. [O.E. *geolu.*]

YELLOWISH (yel'ō-ish) *a.* moderately yellow.

YELP (yelp) *v.i.* to utter a quick, sharp cry; bark. [O.E. *gielpan.*]

YELPING (yel'ping) *n.* a barking shrilly.

YEOMAN (yō'mạn) *n.* a freeholder; farmer; —*pl.* **YEOMEN.** [M.E. *yoman vemen.* doubtless fr. an O.E. *gaman,* not found, but seen in Old Frisian *gaman,* villager, fr. *ga,* a village. Ger. *Gau,* district. *Man,* man.]

YEOMANRY (yō'mạn-ri) *n.* the collective body of yeomen.

YERK (yẹrk) *v.t.* or *i.* to strike suddenly; jerk; kick. [Fr. **JERK.**]

YES (yes) *ad.* yea; a word that affirms. [O.E. *gese,* fr. *gea,* yes indeed, and *swa,* so let it be.]

YESTERDAY (yes'tẹr-dā) *n.* the day last past; —*ad.* on the day last past. [O.E. *geostra,* and *dæg,* day.] [past.

YESTERNIGHT (yes'tẹr-nīt) *n.* the night last

YET (yet) *con.* nevertheless; however:—*ad.* besides; still; hitherto; after all. [O.E. *get.*]

YEW (ū) *n.* an evergreen tree. [O.E. *iw.*]

YIELD (yēld) *v.t.* to produce; afford; give up; concede;—*v.i.* to submit; comply with; give place to;—*n.* produce. [O.E. *gildan,* pay.]

YIELDER (yēl'dẹr) *n.* one who or that which yields.

YOKE (yōk) *n.* an instrument to connect oxen for work; bondage; a pair;—*v.t.* to connect; unite. [O.E. *geoc.*] [a companion.

YOKE-FELLOW (yōk'fel-ō) *n.* an associate

YOKEL (yō'kl) *n.* a country bumpkin.

YOLK (yōk) *n.* the yellow part of an egg. [O.E. *geolca, geolica,* fr. *geolu,* yellow.]

YON (yon) *a.* being at a distance, but within view;—*ad.* yonder. [O.E. *geon.*]

YONDER (yon'dẹr) *ad.* at a distance within view;—*a.* that or those there.

YORE (yōr) *ad.* of old time. [Fr. O.E. *geara,* of years; formerly gen. pl. of *gear.* year.]

YOU (ū) *pron.* second person singular or plural. [O.E. *eow.*]

YOUNG (yung) *a.* not long born;—*n.* the offspring of animals. [O.E. *geong.*]

YOUNGER (yung'gẹr) *a.* not so old as another.

YOUNGEST (yung'gest) *a.* having the least age.

YOUNGISH (yung'ish) *a.* rather young.

YOUNGSTER (yung'stẹr) *n.* a young lad; midshipman. Also **YOUNKER.**

YOUR (ūr) *pron. a.* belonging to you. [O.E. *eower.*] [only.

YOURSELF (ūr-self') *pron. emphatical,* you

YOUTH (yōōth) *n.* the early part of life; a young person; young persons collectively. [O.E. *geoguth,* fr. *geong,* young.]

YOUTHFOOL (yōōth'fool) *a.* young; fresh; vigorous.

YOUTHFULNESS (yōōth'fool-nes) *n.* the state of being youthful. [O.E. *geol.*]

YULE (ūl) *n.* the old name of Christmas.

Z

ZANY (zā'ni) *n.* a merry-andrew; buffoon. [It. *zanni,* a buffoon, fr. *Giovanni,* John.]

ZEAL (zēl) *n.* enthusiasm; passionate ardour. [G. *zelos* ardour.]

ZEALOT (zel'ut) *n.* one full of zeal.

ZEALOUS (zel'us) *a.* warmly engaged or ardent in anything.

ZEBRA (zē'brạ) *n.* an animal of the horse kind marked with stripes. [Afr.]

ZEBU (zē'bū) *n.* an East Indian bison. [F.]

ZEMINDAR (zem-in-dâr') *n.* a landowner in India under the government. [Per. *zamin,* land, and *dar,* holding.]

ZENANA (zē-nä'nạ) *n.* part of a house in India reserved for the women, fr. Per. *zanan,* pl. of *zan,* a woman.]

ZEND (zend) *n.* the primitive language of the Persians. [*Zend-avesta,* the sacred book of the Parsis.]

ZENITH (zen'ith) *n.* the point in the heavens vertical to the spectator. [F., fr. A. *samt,* a way.] [*zephuros.*]

ZEPHYR (zef'ẹr) *n.* a gentle west wind. [G.

ZERO (zē'rō) *n.* the cipher °; the point from which a thermometer is graduated. [It., fr. A. *sifr,* a cipher.]

ZEST (zest) *n.* orange peel cut thin; a relish; taste;—*v.t.* to give a flavour to. [G. *schistos* cleft, fr. G. *schizein,* to cleave.]

ZIGZAG (zig'zag) *a.* having frequent short turns:—*n.* something with short turns;—*v.t.* or *i.* to form or move in short turns. [F., fr. Ger. *zick-zack,* fr. *Zacke,* tooth.]

ZINC (zingk) *n.* a whitish metal. [Ger. *Zink,* zinc.]

ZINCODE (zing'kōd) *n.* the positive pole of a galvanic battery. [Ger. *Zink,* and G. *hodos,* way.]

ZINCOGRAPHY (zing-kog'rạ-fi) *n.* art of drawing on and painting from plates of zinc. [Ger. *Zink,* and G. *graphein,* to write.]

ZION (zī'un) *n.* a hill in Jerusalem; city or church of God. [H.]

ZODIAC (zō'di-ak) *n.* an imaginary circle in the heavens, containing the twelve signs and the sun's path. [F. *zodiaque,* fr. L. *zodiacus* fr. G. *zodiakos* the zodiacal circle. containing constellations represented by animals; fr. *zodion,* a small animal, dim. of *zoon,* animal.] [zodiac.

ZODIACAL (zō-di'ạ-kạl) *a.* pertaining to the

ZONE (zōn) *n.* a division of the earth: a girdle; circumference. [G. *zone.*]

ZONED (zōnd) *a.* wearing or having a zone.

ZONELESS (zōn'les) *a.* not having a zone.

ZOOGONY (zō-og'u-ni) *n.* science of the organic structure of animals.

ZOOGEOGRAPHER (zō-o-jē-og'rạ-fẹr) *n.* one who describes animals. [G. *zoon,* an animal, and *graphein,* to write.]

ZOOGEOGRAPHY (zō-o-jē-og'rạ-fi) *n.* the description of animals.

ZOOLITE (zō'u-līt) *n.* an animal substance petrified. [G. *lithos* stone.] [zoology.

ZOOLOGICAL (zō-o-loj'i-kạl) *a.* pertaining to

ZOOLOGIST (zō-ol'ō-jist) *n.* one versed in zoology.

ZOOLOGY (zō-ol'ō-ji) *n.* the natural history of animals. [G. *zoon* an animal, and *logos.* discourse.] [obtained from animal substances.

ZOONIC (zō-on'ik) *a.* pertaining to animals:

ZOONOMY (zō-on'u-mi) *n.* the laws of animal life. [G. *zoon,* an animal, and *nomos* law.]

ZOOPHYTE (zō'u-fīt) *n.* a body supposed to partake of the nature of an animal and of a plant. [G. *zoon.* an animal, and *phuton,* a plant.]

ZOUAVE (swäv, zōō-äv') *n.* name of an active and hardy body of soldiers in the French service. [F., fr. a tribe in Algeria.]

ZULU (zōō'lōō) *n.* a South African Kafir. [S. Afr.] [to zymology.

ZYMOLOGICAL (zī-mu-loj'i-kạl) *a.* pertaining

ZYMOLOGY (zī-mol'ō-ji) *n.* the doctrine of fermentation of liquors. [G. *zume,* ferment, and *logos,* a discourse.] [tion.

ZYMOTIC (zī-mot'ik) *a.* pertaining to fermenta-

ADDENDA.

AA (ä'-ạ) *n.* clinker lava.

AABEC (ä'-bek) *n.* an Australian bark used as a sudorific.

AAL (äl) *n.* an East Indian shrub of the madder family, or the red dye obtained from its root ; a tree of the terebinth family, in the Molucca Islands, with an aromatic bark, used in seasoning food.

ABACA (ab'-ạ-kạ) *n.* [Malay] Manilla-hemp.

ABACTINAL (ab-ak'-ti-nạl, -ak-tī'-nạl) *a.* [L. *ab* and G. *aktis, aktinos,* ray] pertaining to that part of a radiate opposite to the mouth ; aboral ; without rays.

ABATURE (ab'-ạ-tūr) *n.* [F.] the trail of a beast of chase.

ABORAL [ab-ō'-rạl) *a.* [*ab* and *oral*] pertaining to the part most remote from the mouth.

ACOUSTICON (ạ-kous'-ti-kon) *n.* [G.] an appliance to aid hearing.

AERIAL (ā-ē'-ri-ạl) *n.* and *a.* a collector or radiator used in wireless telegraphy. **AERIAL TORPEDO,** a powerful bomb discharged from aircraft.

AERO (G. *aēr*, air). **AEROBIOSCOPE** (ā-e-rō-bī'-ō-skōp) *n.* an apparatus for determining the number and the forms of micro-organisms in a given volume of air. **AERO-CAMERA,** a camera used in taking photographs of the ground from aircraft. **AERO-DENSIMETER** (ā-e-rō-deu-sim'-e-ter) *n.* a pressure gauge for gases. **AERODROME** (ār'-ō-drōm) *n.* [*cf. hippodrome*] a place for storing and overhauling flying machines. **AEROGRAM** (ār'-ō-gram) *n.* a message sent by wireless telegraphy. **AEROGUN** (ār'-ō-gun) *n.* an anti-aircraft gun. **AEROPHONE** (ā'-e-rō-fōn) *n.* an instrument for amplifying sound-waves. **AEROPLANE** (ār'-ō-plān) *n.* a flying machine using one or more planes as a support. **AEROSIDERITE** (ā-e-rō-sid'-e-rit) *n.* a meteorite composed chiefly of iron. **AEROSIDEROLITE** (see **SIDERO-LITE**). **AEROTROPIC** (ā-e-rō-trop'-ik) *a.* seeking air.

AERTON FAN (ār'-tun) *n.* a contrivance for clearing trenches of gas.

AETIAN (ā-ē'-shạn) *n.* [*Aetius*, of Antioch], one of the extreme Arians of the latter part of the fourth century.

AGRIMOTOR (ag-ri-mō'-tur) *n.* [L. *ager*, field, and *motor*] a motor vehicle or tractor used on the land.

AILERON (ā'-le-run) *n.* [F.] a part of the plane of an aeroplane that serves to balance and steer the machine.

AIR-BASE, *n.* a place used for housing, or directing the operations of air-craft. **AIR-CHAMBER,** *n.* an enclosed space containing air. **AIR-CRAFT,** *n.* the collective name for balloons, aeroplanes, etc. **AIR-DUCT,** *n.* a tube or passage conveying air. **AIR-LOOP,** *n.* a narrow window. **AIRMAN,** *n.* an aviator. **AIR-MECHANIC,** *n.* one employed on the repair of aircraft. **AIR-MONGER,** *n.* a visionary. **AIR-POCKET,** *n.* a more rarefied part of the atmosphere in which aircraft suddenly drop. **AIR-RAID,** *n.* an attack by aircraft. **AIR-SCOUT,** *n.* an airman acting as a scout. **AIR-SHIP,** *n.* a balloon or aeroplane, *esp.* if dirigible. **AIR-STONE,** *n.* a meteor.

ALBATROSS (al'-bạ-tros) *n.* a German aeroplane ; one of the bird-named aircraft used by the Germans.

ALBERIA (al-bē'-ri-ạ) *n.* [L. *albus*, white] a shield without armorial bearings or ornament.

ALEXIA (ạ-lek'-si-ạ) *n.* [G. *a.* without, and *legein*, to read] loss or impairment of the power to read.

ALPIGENE (al'-pi-jĕn) *a.* [root *gen*, produce] produced or growing in Alpine regions.

ALSATIAN (al-sā'-shạn) *n.* and *a.* a native of Alsace ; a resident in Alsatia ; of or pertaining to Alsace or Alsatia.

ALTAIC (al-tā'-ik) *a.* of or pertaining to the Altai Mts. ; Turanian. [Aquila.

ALTAIR (al-tār') *n.* [A.] the brightest star in

AMANDINE (am'-ạn-din) *n.* [F. *amande*, almond] the albuminous matter of sweet almonds ; anything, as cold cream, prepared from this.

AMATOL (am'-ạ-tol) *n.* an explosive consisting of ammonium nitrate and trinitrotoluene (T.N.T.) ; as in similar cases the name is made up of parts of the names of the ingredients used.

AMIDOL (am'-i-dol) *n.* a compound of phenol used in photography in developing bromide plates.

AMISSIBLE (ạ-mis'-i-bl) *a.* [L. *ab* and *mitto, missus,* send] liable to be lost.

AMMONAL (am'-ō-nạl) *n.* [*ammonia*] a high explosive containing aluminium, charcoal, ammonium nitrate.

ANGAREP (ang'-gạ-rep) *n.* [A.] a bedstead used in tropical Africa ; it consists of an ox-hide laced to a frame.

ANGARY (ang'-gạ-ri) *n.* [G.] forced service ; destruction by a belligerent of neutral property.

ANORTHOSCOPE (an-or'-thu-skōp) *n.* [G. *an, orthos,* straight, and *skopein,* to view] a toy by which distorted figures on one revolving disc appear as normal when viewed through slits in another.

ANTENNA, *n.* an aerial.

ANTHEMION (an-thē'-mi-un) *n.* [G.] the honeysuckle, palmette, or any conventional flower or leaf design in decorative art.

ANTHEROZOID (an-ther-ō-zō'-id) *n.* the male fertilising body in cryptogams.

ANTI-AIRCRAFT (an-ti-ār'-kraft) *a.* employed against aircraft. So, anti-submarine, etc.

ANTI-BURGHER (an-ti-bur'-ger) *n.* a member of that section of the Scottish Secession Church which separated from the "Burghers" in 1747 ; the "Anti-burghers" objected to the "Burgess oath," which seemed to them to recognise the Established Church.

ANZACS (án'-zaks) *n.pl.* the soldiers of the Australian and New Zealand Army Corps, the name being formed from the initials A.N.Z.A.C.

ARCATURE (ár'-kạ-tūr) *n.* [L. *arcus*, bow] a small arcade of little arches ; an arched balustrade [Arch.].

ARCHIES (ár'-chiz) *n.pl.* the anti-aircraft force ; also, the guns and shells. The name is said to have been given, owing to the fewness of the hits, from the song, "Archibald, certainly not."

AUSSIES (aw'-siz) *n.pl.* [*Australians*] Australian soldiers.

AVIATE (ā'-vi-āt) *v.i.* [L. *avis*, bird] to control or travel in an airship, flying machine, dirigible balloon, etc.

AVIATION (ā-vi-ā'-shun) *n.* the art of aviating.

AVIATOR (ā'-vi-ā-tur) *n.* one that aviates.

AVION (av-yong') *n.* [F. fr. L. *avis*, an aeroplane. [See **ADVICE**.

AVISO (ā-vē'-zō) *n.* [Sp.] an advice-boat.

B

BALAAM (bā'-lam) *n.* a disappointing prophet or ally; matter kept in stock to fill up gaps in a newspaper. **BALAAM-BOX**, the repository of such matter. The name is due to the prophet Balaam, who disappointed Balak (Numb. ch. 22, etc.)

BALLADE, Ballade Royal, Rhyme Royal, or Troilus Verse, consists, in its original form, of seven heroics, the first five rhyming at intervals, and the last two in succession.

BALLISTITE (bal'-is-tit) *n.* an improved form of gunpowder.

BANJO-FRAME, an apparatus for lowering and raising a ship's propeller.

BANK, *v.i.* to tilt sharply inwards in turning an aeroplane.

BARAD (ba-rad') *n.* [G. *barus*, heavy] the unit of pressure; a pressure of one dyne per square centimetre.

BAROGYROSCOPE (bar-ō-ji'-ro-skōp) *n.* [G. *baros*, weight, and *gyroscope*] a gyrostat used to exhibit the rotation of the earth.

BARRACOON (bar-a-kōōn') *n.* [Sp.] a barrack or enclosure for slaves or convicts.

BARRAGE, *n.* an offensive or defensive screen of artillery fire. [badger-dog.

BASSET (bas'-set) *n.* [F.] a short-legged

BENZOLISE (ben'-zol-iz) *v.t.* to mix with, or cause to unite with, benzene or any of its derivatives.

BENZYL (ben'-zil) *n.* the organic radical, C₆H₅CH₂.

BERTHA (ber'-tha) *n.* [*Bertha*, woman's name]; a German long-range gun; a deep collar worn on a low-necked bodice; in this sense also, **BERTHE** (berth).

BERTILLON SYSTEM (ber-til-lon') *n.* [French anthropologist, b. 1853]; a method of identifying criminals by means of various measurements.

BIBELOT (bib'-lō) *n.* [F.] a small object of art.

BIKE (bik) *n.* and *v.i.* shortened form of bicycle.

BIOGRAPH, **BIOSCOPE** (bi'-ō-graf, -skōp) *n.* [G. *bios*, life; *graphein*, write; *skopein*, view]. (See **KINEMATOGRAPH**).

BIOTICS (bi-ot'-iks) *n.* [G. *bios*, life] the functions or properties of living things; the science dealing with these.

BIPLANE (bi'-plān) *n.* an aeroplane with two planes, one above the other.

BISET (biz'-et) *n.* [F.] the rock-pigeon.

BISK (bisk) *n.* [F.] a rich soup made from meat or fish; a fine kind of ice-cream.

BLACK, *a.* **BLACK MARIA**, a van for conveying prisoners; a big enemy shell.

BLASTOMERE (blas'-to-mēr) *n.* [G. *blastos*, sprout, and *meros*, part] one of the segments into which the ovum divides.

BLASTULA (blas'-tū-la) *n.*; *pl.* blastulæ(-ē) the embryonic stage preceding the appearance of the blastodermic layers.

BLASTUS (blas'-tus) *n.* [G. *blastos*, a sprout] the plumule of grasses.

BLIGHTY (bli'-ti) *n.* [Hind.] Britain; a wound that leads to the soldier being sent home.

BLIMP (blimp) *n.* a small airship.

BLISTER, *n.* a protective outer hull below the water-line.

BLUNGE (blunj) *v.t.* [*cf. plunge*] to mix clay, etc., with water by means of a blunger, a kind of wooden shovel, or machinery.

BOCHE (bosh) *n.* [F. *caboche*. a head with reference to the size of the German head] a German.

BOEHMENISM (bā'-men-izm) *n.* [Jacob *Boehme*, German mystic, 1571-1634] a religious system resembling Quakerism.

BOLOISM (bō'-lō-izm) *n.* activity intended to weaken a country in time of danger; so called from Bolo Pasha, a Frenchman, executed in 1918 for German propaganda.

BOLOMETER (bo-lom'-e-ter) *n.* [G. *bolē*, a throw, and *metron*, measure] an instrument for measuring minute differences of radiant heat.

BOLSHEVIST, **BOLSHEVIK** (bol'-she-vist, bol-shev'-ik) *n.* [Russ. *bolshe*, comp. of *veliki*, great] an extreme revolutionary; a Maximalist; a believer in the right of the proletariat to supremacy.

BOMA (bō'-ma) *n.* [Afr.] a fenced enclosure.

BOMB, *v.t.* to attack with bombs. **BOMB-CRATER**, *n.* a large hole caused by the explosion of a bomb. **BOMBER**. *n.* a soldier that throws bombs; an aeroplane that drops bombs.

BOOLEY (bōō'-le) *n.* and *v.i.* [Celt. *buaile*, a fold] an upland settlement of villagers to which they removed with their families and cattle in summer; to remove to a booley.

BOREEN (bō-rēn') *n.* [Ir. *bōthar*, road] a narrow lane.

BORREEN-BRACK, **BARN-BRACK** (bor'-ēn-, bárn'-brak) *n.* [Ir.] "speckled cake," a cake with currants and raisins, eaten on Halloween.

BORZOI (bor'-zoi) *n.* [Russ.] the Russian wolf-hound.

BOSTON (bos'-tun) *n.* [*Boston*, Mass., U.S.] a game at cards somewhat like whist.

BOSWELLIAN (boz-wel'-i-an) *a.* in the manner of James Boswell, Dr. Johnson's biographer.

BOTULINE (bot'-ū-lin) *n.* [L. *botulus*, a sausage] a ptomaine poison found in unsound meat.

BOTULISM (bot'-ū-lizm) *n.* poisoning due to botuline.

BOUFFANT (bōō-fang') *a.* [F.] puffed out, as a skirt.

BOULANGISM (boo-lan'-jizm) *n.* [General *Boulanger*, French politician, 1837-1891] chauvinism mixed with personal ambition.

BOULTER (bōl'-ter) *n.* a long fishing-line with many hooks.

BOURASQUE (bōō-rask') *n.* [F.] a tempest.

BOURIGNIAN (bōōr-in'-yan) *a.* pertaining to Antoinette *Bourignon*, 1616-1680, who made religion a matter of inward illumination and emotion.

BOURSOCRAT (bōōr'-so-krat) *n.* a financial magnate.

BOUSTROPHEDON (bou-strof-ē'-don) *n.* and *adj.* [G.] turning like ploughing oxen from right to left and left to right alternately, like early Greek writing.

BOUTON (bōō'-ton) *n.* [F.] a button, a pimple.

BOUTONNIÈRE (bōō-ton-nyār') *n.* [F.] a button hole bouquet.

BOUTS-RIMÉS (bōō-rē-mā') *n.pl.* [F.] a game in which the players are required to complete verses of which the rhyming words are known.

BOYAU (bwa-yō') *n.*; *pl.* boyaux (bwa-yōz') [F.] a communication trench.

BRACKET, *v.i.* to determine the position of a target by means of ranging shots fired beyond and short of it.

Fāte, fär, ado; mē, her; mine; nōte; tūne; mōōn.

BRINOMETER (bri-nom'-e-ter) *n.* an Instrument for measuring the density of brine for curing.

BRIO (brē'-ō) *n.* [It.] liveliness, vivacity.

BRIOCHE (bri-osh') *n.* [F.] a sponge-cake.

BRIOLETTE (brē-o-let') *n.* [F.] a diamond, pear or drop shaped, cut with triangular or long facets.

BROCHÉ (bro-shā') *a.* [F.] woven with a raised design, brocaded, as fabrics; stitched as books.

BRUSQUERIE (brŏŏs'-ke-rē) *n.* [F.] brusqueness; a brusque expression or act.

BUCKEEN (buk-ēn') *n.* [Anglo-Ir.] a young man of the lower gentry who aped the wealthier.

BULGE, *n.* an outer protective hull, below the water-line.

BULIMIA (bū-li'-mi-á) *n.* [G.] morbid hunger; craze for reading.

BUMBO (bum'-bō) *n.* [It.] cold rum punch.

BUMMAREE (bum-á-rē') *n.* a middleman at Billingsgate.

BUZZ, *v.t.* to telephone in Morse;—*n.* a rumour. [Byron.

BYRONIC (bi-ron'-ik) *a.* in the manner of

C

CABOCHON (ka-bo-shong') *n.* [F.] a carbuncle-shaped gem cut but not faceted.

CABOTAGE (kab'-o-tij) *n.* [F.] coasting-trade.

CADET, *n.* a member of the Russian Constitutional Democratic party.

CÆSIUM (sē'-zi-um) *n.* [L. *cœsius,* bluish-gray] a silver-white alkali-metal.

CAHER (ká'-her) *n.* [Ir.] a circular stone fort.

CALAMANDER (kal-á-man'-der) *n.* [*Coromandel*] ebony wood used in cabinet-work.

CALAPITTE (kal'-á-pit) *n.* [Malay] a concretion found in the cocoa nut, worn by Malays as a charm.

CAMEMBERT (kam-áng-bār', kam'-em-bār) *n.* [F. village in Normandy] a small, rich, soft cheese.

CAMION (kam'-i-un) *n.* [F.] a heavy motor-vehicle used in military transport work.

CAMISARD (kam'-i-zárd) *n.* [F.] one of the Protestant insurgents of the Cevennes.

CAMMOCK (kam'-uk) *n.* [A.S.] a plant, the rest-harrow, etc.

CAMOUFLAGE (ká'-moo-flázh) *n.* [F.] disguise;—*v.t.* to disguise.

CAMOUFLET (ká'-moo-flā) *n.* [F. puff of smoke] a kind of mine.

CAMPAGNA (kam-pá'-nyá) *n.* [It.] a very level open plain, *esp.* that surrounding Rome.

CAMPIMETER (kam-pim'-e-ter) *n.* [L. *campus,* field, and G. *metron,* measure] a contrivance for determining the area of space-discrimination and colour-sense.

CAMSTON (kam'-stun) *n.* a kind of clay used to whiten objects, as doorsteps, etc.

CANAANITE (kā'-nan-īt) *n.* a descendant of Canaan; a native of Canaan. **CANANITE,** one of a body of Zealots hostile to Rome.

CANAPÉ (kan'-á-pā) *n.* [F.] a piece of fried bread with anchovies, etc.

CANCIONERO (kan-the-o-nē'-ro) *n* [Sp.] a collection of songs.

CANTHARUS (kan'-thá-rus) *n.* [L.] a large two-handled drinking-cup; a laver in the courtyard before ancient churches.

CANUCK (ka-nuk') *n.* a Canadian.

CAPORAL (kap'-u-rál) *n.* [F.] a French tobacco.

CAPOT (ka-pot') *n.* [F.] the winning of all the tricks at piquet and scoring forty;—*v.i.* to win all the tricks at piquet.

CARACT (kar'-akt) *n.* [G.] a character; sign; mark; a magical symbol or formula.

CARBORUNDUM-WHEEL, *n.* [*carbon,* and *corundum*] a machine used to grind, turn, and dress steel, etc.

CARREAU (ka-rō') *n.*; *pl.* carreaux (-rōz') [F.] a pane, small square, or diamond of glass; a quarrel, or arrow.

CARTOMANCY (kár'-tō-man-si) *n.* [Low **L.** *carta,* a card, and G. *manteia,* divination] divination by playing-cards.

CARTONNAGE (kár'-to-nij) *n.* [F. *carton*] pasteboard for book-covers, etc.; the casing of mummies.

CASHEL (kash'-el) *n.* [Ir.] a circular stone-fortification.

CASULA (kas'-ū-lá) *n.* [Low L.] a chasuble.

CAVATINA (ka-vá-tē'-ná) *n.* [It.] a short, simple song.

CAVETTO (ka-vet'-ō) *n.* [It.] a hollowed moulding; in decoration, the opposite of relief.

CAYUSE (ki-ūs') *n.* an Indian pony.

C.B.E., Commander of (the Order of) the British Empire. [celery.

CELERIAC (se-ler'-i-ak) *n.* turnip-rooted

CELTOMANIA (sel-to-mā'-ni-á) *n.* exaggeration of the importance of the Celtic race, language, and studies.

CEMBALIST (sem'-ba-list) *n.* a player on the cembalo; the pianist in an orchestra.

CEMBALO (sem'-ba-lō) *n.* [It.] a musical instrument with wire strings, as a dulcimer, harpsichord, piano.

CENACLE (sen'-a-kl) *n.* [F. fr. L.] a supper-room, *esp.* the scene of the Last Supper.

CENTILLION (sen-til'-yun) *n.* the hundredth power of a million.

CENTROID (sen'-troid) *n.* the centre of mass; the point of stress in speech-rhythm.

CENTRODE (sen'-trōd) *n.* the locus of the instantaneous centre of pure rotation.

CESSER (ses'-er) *n.* [F.] cessation of term, liability, etc. [Law.]

CHALUMEAU (shal-ū-mō') *n.* [F.] a musical instrument of the clarionet type; a shepherd's pipe.

CHASSE (shás) *n.* [F.] a small glass of spirits or liqueur taken after coffee.

CHASSÉ (shá'-sā) *n.* [F.] in dancing, a movement across, or to right and left; the gliding step used;—*v.i.* to make a chassé.

CHASSIS (shá'-sē) *n.* [F.] the base-frame of a gun-carriage, motor-car, etc.

CHATAUQUA (chaw-taw'-kwá) *n.* [American town] a meeting in connection with a system of reading circles and summer classes.

CHAUFFEUR (shō-fer') *n.* [F.] the driver of a motor-car.

CHELA (chā'-lá) *n.* [Hind.] a novice in esoteric Buddhism.

CHESSEL (ches'-el) *n.* [*cheese*] a mould used in cheese-making.

CIMBORIO (sim-bō'-ri-ō) *n.* [Sp.] a dome or lantern in a church.

CINCH (sinch) *n.* [Sp.] a saddle-girth;—*v.t.* to fasten a cinch round;—*v.i.* to tighten the cinch.

CINEMA (sin'-e-má) *n.* [G. *Kinema,* motion] a building used for kinematograph exhibitions; a picture house.

CINGLE (sing'-gl) *n.* [L. *cingulum*] a girth or belt.

CLOACA (klō-á'-ká) *n.*; *pl.* cloacæ (-á'-sē) [L.] a sewer; a privy; a sink of impurity; the excrementory cavity in birds, reptiles, e c.

CLOAM (klōm) *n.* [A.S.] earthenware; clay; —*a.* made of such.

CLOCHAN (klon'-an) *n.* [Ir.] a beehive-shaped hut.

CLOCHER (klō'-sher) *n.* [F.] a bell-tower; a belfry.

COALBOX, *n.* a kind of shell emitting, on bursting, a dark cloud of smoke.

Fāte, fár, ạdo; mē, her; mīne; nōte; tūne; mŏŏn.

COBURG (kō'-burg) *n.* [*Coburg*, Germany] a thin fabric of worsted and cotton or silk, twilled on one side.

CODE, *n.* a system of military or naval signals; a group of regulations; a private alphabet, or system of words representing others. (See **CIPHER**).

COHERER (ko-hē'-rẹr) *n.* a mechanical device that becomes an electrical conductor when acted on by wireless electric waves.

COLLINS (kol'-inz) *n.* [name of a character in *Pride and Prejudice*] a letter of thanks for hospitality.

COLOTOMY (ko-lot'-u-mi) *n.* [L. *colon* and G. *tomē*, a cutting] a surgical operation on the colon in order to form an artificial anus

COMPLUVIUM (kom-plŏŏ'-vi-um) *n.* [L.] a large square opening in the roof of a Roman house which admitted light and air, and through which rain-water reached the impluvium in the atrium below.

CONTEMPTIBLES, *n.pl.* a name adopted, usually in the form "Old Contemptibles," for the British Expeditionary Force of 1914; the Kaiser was reported to have referred to it as a "contemptible little army."

CONTINUATION-CLASS, SCHOOL, *n.* a class or school proposed for those that, having left school, have not yet reached eighteen years of age.

CONTORNO (kon-tor'-no) *n.* [It.] a contour or outline.

COPER (kō'-pẹr) *n.* a horse-dealer; [D. *kooper*] a floating grog-shop for North Sea fishers; also **COOPER**.

COPHOUSE (kop'-hous) *n.* a tool-house.

COPOS (kop'-os) *n.* [G.] a morbid lassitude.

COPPED (kopt) *n.* [A.S. *cop*, head] conical; peaked; pointed.

COQUELICOT (kok'-li-kŏ) *n.* [F.] orange red, the colour of the wild poppy.

COQUILLA (ko-kēl'-ya) *n.* [Sp.] the nut of a Brazil palm; its endosperm is used by button-makers and turners

COQUILLE (ko-kēl') *n.* [F.] the broad part of the guard of a sword-hilt.

CORROBOREE (ko-rob'-u-rē) *n.* a native Australian war-dance.

CORRODY (kor'-o-di) *n.* [Ir.] paid maintenance in a monastery.

COSTING (kos'-ting) *n.* the system of calculating the cost of production.

COUP (kŏŏ) *n.* [F.] a successful stroke or move. **COUP-DE-POING** (koo-dẹ-pwàng') *n.* a Palæolithic flint axe.

COUPON, *n.* this word was used during the war of 1914-18 for a ticket entitling the holder to a specified amount of some article of food.

COURBATURE (kŏŏr-bà-tŏŏr') *n.* [F.] myalgia.

COURY (kou'-ri) *n.* [Ind.] catechu produced by evaporating a decoction of the nuts of *Areca Catechu*.

CRUCIFIXION, *n.* a field punishment (No. 1) which includes tying the offender to the wheel of a gun-carriage.

CRUISKEN, CRUISKEEN (kroos'-ken, -kēn) *n.* [Ir.] a small cruse; a measure of whisky.

CRUIVE (krŏŏv) *n.* [Scot.] a pen for live stock; a pig-sty; a hovel; an apparatus for catching salmon.

CRULLER (krul'-ẹr) *n.* [D.] a cake cut out of dough, containing flour, sugar, butter, eggs, sour cream, and fried brown in boiling lard; often ring-shaped.

CRUMP (krump) *n.* [Imit.] the sound made by a high explosive missile.

CRYPTOPSYCHY (krip'-to-sī-ki) *n.* [G. *kruptos*, secret, and *psuchē*, the soul], subconscious mental phenomena.

CULVERTAGE (kul'-vẹr-tij) *n.* [O.F.] degradation of a vassal to the condition of a serf.

CUSHY (koosh'-i) *a.* [Hind. *khush*, pleasure] light; safe; said of jobs. One of the slang terms that became common during the war of 1914-18. A person holding such a post was called a Cuthbert, perhaps as living like St. Cuthbert, apart from the stress of the world.

CUTOSE (kū'-tos) *n.* [L. *cutis*, skin] the substance of the transparent film covering the aerial parts of plants.

CUT-OUT, *n.* an arrangement by which part of an electric circuit may be shut off.

CZECHO-SLOVAK (chek'-ō-slō'-vak) *a.* pertaining to the Slavonic racial group of Bohemia, Moravia, and N. Hungary;—*n.* a member of this group.

D

DALMATIAN (dal-mā'-shan) *a.* of or pertaining to Dalmatia;—*n.* a Dalmatian dog, the spotted coach-dog.

DALOYET (da-loi'-et) *n.* [Anglo-Ind.] an armed attendant; a peon.

DALT (dàlt) *n.* [Gael.] a foster-child.

DAMASSEÉ (dà-màs-sā') *a.* [F.] woven with a figured or flowered pattern;—*n.* Flemish linen so woven.

DANAKIL (dan'-a-kil) *n.* [A.] the tribes on the N.E. coast of Africa. [fine coal.

DANKS (dangks) *n.* black shale mixed with

DARDANIAN (dàr-dā'-ni-an) *a.* of or pertaining to Dardania, or ancient Troy;—*n.* a Trojan.

DAZZLE, *n.* a method of painting ships so as to give a false impression of their speed, direction, etc.

DÉCLASSÉ (de-klas'-sā) *a.* [F.] having lost caste or sunk socially.

DECODE (dē-kōd') *v.t.* to translate into ordinary language a code message.

DECURTATE (dē-kur'-tāt) *a.* [L] cut short; abridged.

DEFEATIST (de-fē'-tist) *n.* one accused of advocating measures tending to the defeat of his own country.

DEFLUENT (dē'-floo-ent) *n.* [L. *de* and *fluere*, to flow] the down-flowing part, as the lower end of a glacier;—*a.* down-flowing.

DELICATESSEN (del-i-ka-tes'-en) *n.pl.* [Ger.] table delicacies; confectionery; sweets.

DELUNDUNG (dē-lun'-dung) *n.* [E. Ind.] the weasel-cat of Java and Malacca.

DENGUE (deng'-gā) *n.* [Sp.] an acute tropical epidemic fever.

DENIGRATION (de-ni-grā'-shun) *n.* [L. *de* and *niger*, black] a blackening, *esp.* of a man's character.

DENTAGRA (den-tag'-ra) *n.* [L. *dens, dentis*, tooth, and G. *agra*, catching] a dentist's forceps; toothache.

DEODATE (dē'-ō-dāt) *n.* [L.] a gift from or to God.

DEPTH-CHARGE, -BOMB, *n.* a mine or bomb dropped into the sea for the purpose of destroying a submerged submarine.

DERBEND (der'-bend) *n.* [Turk.] a wayside Turkish guard-house on a mountain road.

DERBY SCHEME, *n.* a plan invented in 1915 by the Earl of Derby to secure volunteers for the army.

DOPE (dōp) *n.* [D.] any thick lubricant liquid; a kind of varnish; a drug;—*v.t.* to drug.

DORA (dō-ra) *n.* the Defence of the Realm Act, 1914, from the initials of the title.

DORMY (dor'-mi) *n.* as many holes ahead as there are holes to play. [Golf.]

DOSSAL (dos'-al) *n.* [L. *dorsum*, back] a hanging behind the altar or round the chancel.

DOSSER (dos'-er) *n.* [L. *dorsum,* back] a rich hanging of tapestry for the walls of a hall or the chancel of a church.

DOSSIER (dos'-yā, -i-er) *n.* [F.] a set of documents ; *esp.* the record of a person's antecedents.

DOUGHBOY (dō'-boi) *n.* an infantry man of the U.S. Army ; so called because of the globular buttons on his uniform.

DOUKHOBORS (dŏŏk'-ho-bors) *n.pl.* [Russ.] a religious sect somewhat akin in doctrine to the Quakers.

DRIFTER (drif'-ter) *n.* a fishing-boat using a drift-net, that is, a net kept erect by floats above and weights below.

DRISHEEN (drish'-ēn) *n.* [Ir.] a kind of black pudding.

DUD (dud) *n.* [Imit.] a shell that does not explode ; anything defective ; a useless person :—*a.* defective ; useless.

DUG-OUT, *n.* a shelter ; one recalled to active service.

DURALUMIN, DURALIUM (dū-ra-lū'-min, dū-rā'-li-um) *n.* [L. *durus,* hard, and *aluminium*] a strong, light alloy of aluminium.

DWALE (dwāl) *n.* [Icel. *drali,* sleep] the deadly nightshade ; an opiate. [Her.] sable.

DWANG (dwang) *n.* a large bar-wrench for tightening nuts.

DYAK (dī'-ak) *n.* one of the aboriginal race of Borneo.

DYARCHY (dī'-âr-ki) *n.* [G. *di-* and *archein,* to rule] government by two ; a division of powers between two authorities.

DYNACTINOMETER (din-ak-tin-om'-e-ter) *n.* [G. *dunamis,* force, *aktis, aktinos,* a ray, and *metron,* a measure] an instrument for measuring the actinic force of light.

DYOPHYSITE (dī-of'-i-zīt) *n.* [G. *duo,* two, and *phusis,* nature] a believer in the existence of two natures in Christ, a divine and a human.

DYOTHELISM (dī-oth'-e-lizm) *n.* [G. *duo,* two, and *thelō,* I wish] the doctrine that Christ had two wills, a divine and a human.

DYSPHAGIA (dis-fā'-ji-a) *n.* [G. *dus,* ill, and *phagein,* to eat] difficulty in swallowing.

DYSPHONIA (dis-fō'-ni-a) *n.* [G. *dus,* ill, and *phōnē,* a sound] difficulty in producing articulate sounds.

E

EMPENNAGE (ang-pe-nàzh') *n.* [F.] the arrangement of planes at the tail of a dirigible balloon for security and stability.

ENCÆNIA (en-sē'-ni-a) *n.* [G.] annual commemoration of founders at Oxford University.

ENCANTHIS (en-kan'-this) *n.* [G.] a small tumour in the inner angle of the eye.

ENJAMBMENT (en-jamb'-ment) *n.* [F.] in verse, the continuation of a sentence beyond the end of a line.

EOANTHROPUS (ē-o-an'-thru-pus) *n.* [G. *eōs,* dawn, and *anthrōpos,* man] a primeval type of man.

EPIGYNOUS (e-pij'-i-nus) *a.* [G. *epi* and *gunē,* woman] growing on the top of the ovary. [Bot.]

EPISPASTIC (ep-is-pas'-tik) *a.* [G.] blistering ; —*n.* a blister.

ESCALATOR (es'-ka-lā-tur) *n.* [L. *scala,* ladder] a moving stairway.

EUNOMIAN (ū-nō'-mi-an) *n.* a follower of Eunomius, a fourth century Arian.

EXCESS PROFIT DUTY, *n.* a tax on all profits above a certain level ; known briefly as E.P.D.

F

FANTOCCINI (fan-to-chē-nē) *n.pl.* [It.] mechanically-worked puppets ; a marionette show.

FARCEUR (fàr-ser') *n.* [F.] a joker or wag.

FARDAGE (fàr'-dij) *n.* [F.] loose wool, etc., used to pack cargo to prevent its shifting.

FAROUCHE (fa'-rōosh') *n.* [F.] sullen ; shy.

FIDDLEY (fid'-li) *n.* [*fiddle*] iron framework round opening of stokehold.

FIGARO (fig'-a-ro) *n.* a witty, tricky schemer in Beaumarchais' ' Barber of Seville ' ; a barber.

FILITE (fi'-lit) *n.* [L. *filum,* a thread] an Italian smokeless powder ; so called from its appearance ; *cf.* cordite.

FILM, *v.t.* to show or reproduce on a kinematographic-film.

FLAPPER, *n.* a young girl not yet out.

FLORILEGIUM (flôr-i-lē'-ji-um) *n.* [L. *flos, floris,* flower, and *legere,* gather] an anthology.

FLYING-BOAT, *n.* a combination of an aeroplane and a hydroplane.

FOKKER (fok'-er) *n.* a German aeroplane ; named from its inventor, a Dutchman.

FOOD-CARD, *n.* See COUPON.

FOURCHETTE (fŏŏr-shet') *n.* [F.] a small forked instrument used to support the tongue in cutting the frenum ; the forked piece between glove fingers.

FREE VERSE, *n.* rhythmic composition, without metre or rhyme, arranged in lines of different lengths as if it were verse.

FRENUM (frē'-num) *n.* [L. a bridle] a ligament restraining motion.

FREUDIAN (froi'-di-an) *a.* pertaining to the Austrian psychologist, Sigmund Freud, b. 1856, or his theories.

FRUCTUOUS (fruk'-tū-us) *a.* [L. *fructuosus*] full of, or producing, fruit.

FUBSY (fub'-zi) *a.* fat or squat.

FUSELAGE (fū'-ze-lij) *n.* [L. *fusus,* a spindle] the framework of the body of an aeroplane.

FUTURIST, *n.* one of a group of painters who regard their ideals and methods as those of the future.

G

GABY (gā'-bi) *n.* [Icel. *gapa,* to gape] a simpleton.

GADGET (gaj'-et) *n.* an appliance or contrivance for getting something done.

GALILEE (gal'-i-lē) *n.* a porch or chapel at the entrance of a church ; named perhaps as less sacred ; *cf.* Galilee of the Gentiles.

GALLOVIDIAN (gal-o-vid'-yan) *a.* belonging to Galloway :—*n.* a native of Galloway. Also **GALLWEGIAN, GALLOWEGIAN** (we-'ji-an).

GAMBA (gam'-ba) *n.* [It.] an organ stop with a violin or 'cello tone.

GAMETE (gam'-ēt) *n.* [G. *gamos,* marriage] a protoplasmic body that unites with another to form a zygote.

GARAGE (gar'-ij, ga-râzh') *n.* [F. *garer,* to shunt] building or shed for storing and repairing motor-cars, etc.

GAS, *v.t.* to overcome or kill by means of poison-gas. **GAS-HELMET, -MASK,** *n.* a contrivance to protect against poison-gas. **GAS-SHELL,** *n.* a shell for diffusing poison-gas.

GIGMILL (gig'-mil) *n.* a machine for raising nap on cloth ; a factory provided with such machines.

GLIDER, *n.* a fast flat-bottomed boat used to hunt submarines.

GOTHA (gō'-ta) n. [German town] a large German war-plane.

GOULARD (góo-lárd') n. [T. *Goulard*, French surgeon] a lotion of subacetate of lead in solution.

GOUSLY (gous'-li) n. an old form of harp used by the Slavonians. **GOUSLA**, n. a bard. **GOUSLO**, n. poetry recited by a gousla.

GOUSTY (gous'-ti) a. gusty; dreary.

GRAND FLEET, n. the main body of a fleet in time of war.

GRAPH (gràf) n. [G. *graphein*, to write] a diagram indicating any sort of relationship, chemical, algebraical, etc.; a gelatine copying apparatus;—v.t. to copy by means of such an apparatus.

GRAPPA (grä'-pə) n. [It.] a kind of brandy, made from the skins and stems of grapes.

GRATIN (grà-tang') n. [F.] a method of cooking so as to form a light crust; a dish so cooked.

GRATTOIR (gràt-wár') n. [F.] a flint implement; a scraper. [Archæol.]

GRYSBOK (gris'-bok) n. [D.] a small South African antelope.

GUACO (gwä'-kō) n. name of various tropical American plants used as antidotes to snakebites.

GUILD SOCIALISM, n. a proposal to restore the old guild organisation of industries on socialistic lines and to unite the different guilds in a national socialistic organisation. (See **GUILD** and **SOCIALISM**).

GUN-LAYER, n. an artilleryman whose duty it is to lay a gun on its target.

GUNNER'S-DAUGHTER, n. a gun to which sailors were lashed to be flogged. The victim was said to kiss or marry the gunner's daughter.

GYROSE (ji'-rōs) a. [*gyre*] folded and waved; twined round like a shepherd's crook; marked with wavy lines. [Bot.]

H

HAHNEMANNIAN (bà-ne-man'-i-ən) a. of or pertaining to C. F. S. Hahnemann (1755-1843), founder of homeopathy.

HANDLEY-PAGE (hand'-li-pàj) n. a kind of large aeroplane; named from the inventor.

HANGAR (hàng'-gər) n. [F.] a covered shed for carriages, etc.

HAY-BOX, n. a cooking-apparatus; named from the layer of hay used to retain heat.

HEMAL (hē'-məl) a. [G. *haima*, blood] of the blood; on the same side as the heart and the great blood vessels.

HEMATURIA (hē-mə-tū'-ri-ə) n. [G. *haima*, blood, and *ouron*, urine] the discharge of blood in the urine.

HERREROS (hẹ-rä'-rōz) n. pl. a negro race of what was German West Africa.

HIGH-BROW, a. intellectual;—n. an intellectual; a superior person.

HISTRION (his'-tri-on) n. [L.] a stage-player.

HOBO (hō'-bō) n. [Amer.] a shiftless wandering workman.

HOKEY-POKEY (hō'-ke-pō'-ke) n. hocus pocus;—[It.] a kind of ice-cream.

HONK (hongk) n. [Imit.] the sound of some kinds of motor-horns.

HUNGER-STRIKE. n. the voluntary starvation of prisoners to compel their release.

HUSH-BOAT, n. an armed vessel disguised as a peaceful one. Named from the secrecy with which they were first used.

HUSKY (hus'-ki) n. [Eskimo] an Indian sledge-dog; an energetic man.

HYDROPHONE (hī'-dro-fōn) n. [G. *phōnē*, a sound] an apparatus for detecting sound in, or the sound of, water.

HYDROPLANE (hī'-dro-plăn) n. a boat capable of rising partly above the surface of the water; a plane enabling a boat to do this.

HYDROVANE (hī'-dro-văn) n. [G. *hudōr*, water, and *vane*] the rudder of a submarine used in guiding the vessel up or down.

I

IDOL, n. idols of the tribe, cave, forum, theatre—fallacies due to limitations of the mind, personal causes, words, philosophical and logical prepossessions.

IDOLUM (i-dō'-lum) n.—pl. idola (-lə) [see **IDOL**] mental image; idea; fallacy.

IMPERIAL PREFERENCE, n. a system of differential duties so as to favour imports into the United Kingdom from other parts of the British Empire.

INTELLIGENTSIA (in-tel-i-jent'-si-ə) n. [It.] the intellectual classes.

INVAR (in'-vər) n. [*invar*(iable)] a steel containing 36% of nickel and having a very low coefficient of expansion; it is used in making such delicate contrivances as rangefinders.

IRON RATIONS n.pl. a soldier's emergency ration for one day.

J

JABOT (zhạ-bō') n. [F.] a frill of lace on a woman's bodice; formerly, a ruffle on a man's shirt-front.

JACK JOHNSON, n. a kind of large shell; named from a famous negro boxer.

JACTATION (jac-tā'-shun) n. [L.] act of throwing; extreme restlessness in disease; agitation of the body; boasting.

JADDIS (jad'-is) n. [E. Ind.] in Ceylon, a priest who officiates in the jacco, or devil's house.

JAEGER (yā'-gẹr) n. [Ger.] a huntsman; a sharpshooter.

JAMPAN (jam'-pan) n. [E. Ind.] a sedan-chair carried on bamboo poles by four bearers.

JAMRACH (jam'-rak) n. [name of dealer] a place where wild animals are kept for sale.

JARVEY (jàr'-vi) n. [*Jarvis*] a hackney-coach driver.

JAZZ (jaz) n. a roistering dance of negro origin;—v.i to dance the jazz.

JIG, n. in making duplicate parts, any tool or fixture used to guide cutting tools; a sieve or system of sieves used in separating ores.

JIM CROW, n. an old negro-minstrel song; a negro.

JIVA (jē'-vä) n. [Skr.] the individual soul, as distinct from the supreme soul.

JOY-RIDE, n. an illicit ride in a motor-car.

JOY-STICK. n. the starting-lever of an aeroplane.

JUDENHETZE (yóo'-den-het-ze) n. [Ger.] systematic persecution of Jews.

JUGO-SLAV (ū'-go-slav') n. one belonging to the southern Slav races.

K

KAGO (kag'-ō) n. [Jap.] a palanquin, *esp.* a chair of basketwork slung from a pole.

KAINITE (kī'-nit) n. [G. *kainos*, new] hydrous chloro-sulphate of magnesium and potassium; used as a fertiliser.

Fàte, fár, ạdo; mē, hẹr; mìne; nōte; tūne; mòon.

KANGAROO-CLOSURE, *n.* a means of expediting parliamentary business by confining discussion to selected amendments. See KANGAROO.

KAPELLMEISTER (kä-pel'-mïs'-tẹr) *n.* [Ger.] the director of an orchestra or choir.

KARAITE (kä'-rå-ït) *n.* [H.] one of a Jewish sect that interprets the Scriptures literally, rejecting Rabbinical tradition.

KATABOLISM (kạ-tab'-u-lizin) *n.* [G.] the breaking-down of protoplasm, as opposed to anabolism, the upbuilding process.

K.B.E. Knight Commander of (the Order of) the British Empire.

KINEMACOLOR (kin'-ẹ-mạ-kul-ẹr) *n.* the kinematographic production of pictures in natural colours

KULTURBUND (köól-toor-boond) *n.* [Ger.] an association formed in October, 1914, to impose on the rest of Europe German ideals of organisation in every department of life.

L

LACET (lạ-set') *n.* [*lace*] work of braid or tape shaped into a design with lace stitches.

LACHRYMATORY-SHELL, *n.* a tear-shell.

LAMPAS (lam'-pas) *n.* [F.] a material of silk and wool used in upholstery.

LAND-GIRL *n.* a girl employed on the land, *esp.* one that took up agricultural work during the war of 1914-1918.

LANT (lant) *n.* [A. S. *hland*, urine] stale urine ; used in scouring wool.

LEAD, *n.* a main conductor in electrical distribution.

LENINISM (lĕ'-nin-izm) *n.* [*Lenin*, leader of the Bolshevists] Bolshevism.

LENTITUDE (len'-ti-tūd) *n.* [L.] sluggishness.

LEPRECHAUN (lep'-re-kawn) *n.* [Ir.] a sprite ; a brownie.

LEWIS-GUN, *n.* [fr. name of inventor] a rapid-firing rifle, used as a machine-gun.

LEWISITE (lóó'-i-sı̆) *n.* [inventor's name] an explosive compound of a very deadly kind recently invented.

LIAISON OFFICER, *n.* an officer employed to keep touch between bodies of troops under different commands.

LINOTYPE (lin'-o-tïp) *n.* [*line-o'-type*] a machine for producing stereotyped lines of words, as a substitute for typesetting ; a line of type cast in one piece.

LIQUID-FIRE, *n.* burning petrol discharged against a foe.

LOOP. TO LOOP THE LOOP, *v.i.* to travel round a loop, as in an aeroplane, etc.

M

MAFFICK (maf'-ik) *v.i.* to exult riotously, as on the relief of Mafeking in 1900.

MAGNETO (mag-nĕ'-tŏ) *n.* a magneto-electric machine which ignites the explosive mixture in the cylinder of an internal-combustion engine.

MANCIPLE (man'-si-pl) *n.* [L. *manceps*, a purchaser] a purveyor, *esp.* of a college or of an inn of court.

MANCUNIAN (mang-kū'-ni-ạn) *n.* [L. *Macunium*, Manchester] a native of Manchester ; a pupil of the Manchester Grammar School.

MANUKA (mä'-noo-kạ, mạ-nóó'-kạ) *n.* a New Zealand shrub, its twigs are used to make brooms and its leaves by the bushmen as tea ; the tea-tree.

MARCONIGRAM (mär-kŏ'-ni-gram) *n.* a message sent by Marconi's system of wireless telegraphy.

MASSÉ (ma-sā') *n.* [F.] in billiards, a stroke made with the cue perpendicular or nearly so.

MAXIMALIST (mak'-sim-ạ-list) *n.* [*maximum*] a Bolshevist.

M.B.E., Member of (the Order of) the British Empire.

MECOMETER, MEKOMETER (me-kom'-ẹ-tẹr) *n.* [G.] *mẽkos*, length, and *metron*, measure] an instrument for measuring the length of a new-born child ; a range-finder.

MEMSAHIB (mem'-sä-ib) *n.* in India, a European married lady.

MENDELISM (men'-del-izm) *n.* [G. J. *Mendel* (1822-1884), Austrian priest] the theory of heredity based on Mendel's discovery that hybrids reproduce their parents' characteristics according to definite laws.

MENDELIAN (men-dĕ'-li-ạn) *n.* an exponent of Mendelism.

MENNONITE (men'-o-nit) *n.* [*Menno Simons* d. 1559] a sect of Protestants whose doctrines included some of those of the Baptists and the Friends.

MENSHEVIK (men-shev'-ik) *n.* [Russ.] a member of the moderate Russian revolutionary party.

MILLS-BOMB, *n.* a kind of hand-grenade; named from the inventor. [tion.

MINAUDERIE (mi-nŏ'-dẹr-i) *n.* [F.] affectation.

MINE-FIELD, *n.* an area in which mines have been laid. MINE-LAYER, *n.* a vessel employed in laying mines. MINE-SWEEPER, *n.* a vessel employed in picking up mines.

MINIÉ-RIFLE (min'-ĕ) *n.* [*Minie*, inventor] a rifle used to propel the ball invented by Minié.

MINOAN (mi-nŏ'-ạn) *a.* [*Minos*, King of Crete] relating to ancient Crete or its people.

MODIFICATION, *n.* a change in an organism due to the influence of the environment.

MOLLY MAGUIRE (mol'-i mạ-guir') *n.* a member of an Irish secret society (1843); its members were disguised as women, hence the name.

MOLOSSUS (mo-los'-us) *n.* [G.] a metrical foot of three long syllables.

MONEL METAL (mon'-el met'-ạl) *n.* a nickel-copper alloy.

MONOOUSIOUS (mon-o-óós'-i-us) *a.* [G. *monos*, single, and *ousia*, essence] having the same substance.

MONOPLANE (mon'-o-plän) *n.* an aeroplane with one supporting plane.

MORATORIUM (mor-ạ-tŏ'-ri-um) *n.* [L. *morari* to delay] an act authorising the suspension of payment by a bank or a debtor.

MORRIS TUBE, *n.* [Richard *Morris*, inventor] a small-bore barrel to be fixed on a rifle or gun for practice at close range.

MORTIER (mor-tyä') *n.* [F.] a cap of state.

MOTHER-SHIP, *n.* a warship that serves as a centre for submarines, etc.

MOTOR, *v.i.* to drive or ride in a motor-car ; —*v.t.* to convey in a motor-car.

MOTORIST (mŏ'-tur-ist) *n.* one that motors.

MOUCHARABY (móó-shar'-a-bi) *n.* [F.] a balcony enclosed with lattice-work ; an embattled balcony with parapet and machicolations.

MUSTARD GAS, *n.* one of the poison-gases; highly poisonous and irritant, with a faint garlic-like smell.

MYSTERY-SHIP, *n.* See HUSH-BOAT.

N

NEANDERTHALOID (nĕ-an'-dẹr-tal-oid) *a.* resembling the prehistoric skulls found in 1857 in a cave in the *Neanderthal*, a valley between Düsseldorf and Elberfeld.

NO-MAN'S-LAND, *n.* the ground between hostile trenches.

NON-PROVIDED, *a.* applied to schools not provided by a public authority.

NOSE-DIVE, *n.* a sudden plunge earthward by an aeroplane.

O

O.B.E., Officer of (the Order of) the British Empire.

OBSERVATION. This word is attached to such words as army, balloon, officer, post, to form compounds; it indicates the function of watching an enemy or noting what is happening within his lines.

OLID (ol'-id) *a.* [L.] rank-smelling; fetid.

OROGENY (o-roj'-e-ni) *n.* [G. *oros*, mountain, and *genesis*, beginning] the process of mountain formation.

ORTHOCENTRE (or'-tho-sen-ter) *n.* [G. *orthos*, right, and *centre*] the intersection of the perpendiculars from the vertices of a triangle to the opposite sides The triangle formed by joining the feet of the perpendiculars is called the pedal, or orthocentric, triangle.

OTTER-GEAR, *n.* an apparatus attached to the bow of a ship below the water-line to clear away fixed mines; on each side it carries a paravane.

P

PACHYMETER (pa-kim'-e-ter) *n.* [G. *pachus*, thick, and *metron*, measure] an instrument used to measure the thickness of glass, paper, etc.

PACIFIST PACIFICIST (pas'-i-fist, pa-sif'-i-sist) *n.* one opposed to war; an advocate of arbitration as a means of settling all international disputes.

PAIS (pā) *n.* [O.F.] the people from whom a jury is drawn.

PARAVANE (par'-a-vān) *n.* [G. *para* and *vane*] a contrivance for cutting the moorings of submerged mines.

PARSEVAL (par'-se-val) *n.* [inventor's name] a kind of airship.

PEKIN (pē-kin', -king') *n.* [fr. name of Chinese town] a kind of silk stuff; a civilian.

PEKINESE (pē-ki-nēz') *a.* of or pertaining to Pekin. **PEKINESE DOG,** *n.* a kind of Chinese dog.

PELOTA (pel-ō'-tà) *n.* [Sp.] a kind of tennis.

PENGUIN, *n.* one of the Women's Royal Air Force, who do not fly.

PERIPETY PERIPETEIA (per'-i-pet-i, per-i-pe-tī'-a) *n.* [G.] sudden change, *esp.* of fortune. [but more slowly.

PIAFFE (pi-af') *v.i.* [F.] to move as in trotting.

POILU (pwà-loo') *n.* [F., hairy] a French private soldier. [disable or kill.

POISON-GAS, *n.* a gas used in warfare to

PRIVAT DOCENT (prē-vat' dot-sent') *n.* [Ger.] a teacher in a university whose enrolment consists only of fees.

PROFITEER (prof-i-tēr') *v.i.* to make excessive profits at the expense of the public; —*n.* one that does this.

PROPORTIONAL REPRESENTATION, *n.* a method of securing a just representation in parliament of opinion in the country instead of a party majority; known as P.R. **PROPORTIONALIST,** *n.* one in favour of proportional representation.

PSYCHONEUROSIS (si-ko-nū-rō'-sis) *n.* [G. *psuchē*, soul, and *neuron*, nerve] mental derangement, without organic lesion, as in hypochondria.

PUCKA, PUKKA (puk'-a) *a.* [Hind.] of full weight; substantial; real; superior.

PUSSYFOOT (poos'-i-foot) *n.* an advocate of total prohibition.

Q

Q-BOAT, *n.* a mystery-ship.

QUONIAM (kwŏ'-ni-am) *n.* [L., since now] the part of the "Gloria in Excelsis" beginning "For Thou only art holy"; its musical setting.

R

RABI (rab'-i) *n.* [Hind.] the chief grain crop of India; it is reaped in the spring, hence the name.

RABOT (rab'-ut) *n.* [F., plane] a hard-wood block used in polishing marble.

RADIO (rā'-di-o) a combining element [L. *radius* and E. *radium*]. **RADIOACTIVE.** *a.* having the power of emitting invisible rays that penetrate opaque bodies and produce electrical effects. **RADIOMICROMETER** (-mi-krom'-e-ter), *n.* an instrument for measuring minute variations of heat. **RADIOPHONE** (rā'-di-o-fōn) *n.* [G. *phōnē*, voice] an instrument for the production of sound by means of radiant energy. **RADIO-SCOPY** (-os'-ko-pi) *n.* [G. *skopein*, to view] examination by means of Röntgen rays. **RADIOTELEGRAM,** *n.* a message sent by wireless telegram; often called Radio.

RAGLAN (rag'-lan) *n.* [Lord *Raglan*] a loose overcoat with large sleeves, or sleeveless and with a cape.

RALLI CAR, -CART (ral'-i) *n.* [personal name] a light two-wheeled trap for four.

RAMPLOR (ramp'-lur) *n.* [*ramp*] a gay rover.

RANCE (rans) *n.* a kind of red marble;— [F.] a rod, bar, or prop.

RANDEM (ran'-dem) *a.* [*random* and *tandem*] having three horses harnessed tandem.

RANGE-FINDER, *n.* an instrument for estimating the distance of a target.

RANKER (rang'-ker) *n.* an officer that has risen from the ranks.

REMISE, *n.* a coach-house; a carriage hired from a livery stable; in fencing, a thrust following up one that has missed before the opponent can recover;—*v.i.* to make a remise.

REMITTITUR (re-mit'-i-tur) *n.* [L., it is sent back] an order by a superior court sending back a case to an inferior court; the relinquishment by a successful litigant of part of his damages to save further proceedings.

REMONETISE (re-mun'-e-tiz) *v.t.* to restore as legal tender.

RENTIER (rän-tyā') *n.* [F.] one deriving income from invested capital.

REPERTORY THEATRE, *n.* one where a succession of plays is presented by the same company.

REPOUSSÉ (re-pŏŏ'-sā) *a.* [F.] hammered into relief from the reverse side;—*n.* metal work so produced. **REPOUSSAGE** (re-pŏŏ-sàzh', re-pŏŏs'-ij) *n.* the process of producing repoussé work or the work itself.

REPULPIT (rē-pŏŏl'-pit) *v.t.* to restore to the pulpit.

RESSALDAR (res-àl-dàr') *n.* [Hind.] a native captain in an Indian cavalry regiment.

RETENUE (re-te-noo') *n.* [F.] reserve; self-control.

REVANCHE (re-vàngsh') *n.* [F.] revenge.

RHINE (rīn) *n.* a large open ditch.

RHIZOGEN (rī'-zu-jen) *n.* [G. *rhiza*, root, and *gen*, producing] a plant parasitic on the roots of another.

RHIZOID (rī'-zoid) *a.* root-like ;—*n.* a hair-like filament of mosses, etc., serving for attachment.

RHOTACISM (rō'-ta-sizm) *n.* [G. *rhōtakizein*] the change of *s* into *r* ; excessive or peculiar pronunciation of *r*.

RHYOLITE (rī'-u-līt) *n.* [G. *rhuax*, a stream, and *lithos*, a stone] a kind of volcanic rock.

RHYPAROGRAPHY (rip-a-rog'-ra-fi) *n.* [G. *rhuparos*, dirty, and *graphein*, to write] genre and still-life painting, *esp.* of low subjects.

RHYSIMETER (rī-sim'-e-ter) *n.* [G. *rhusis*, a stream, and *metron*, measure] an instrument for measuring the velocity of fluids and the speed of ships.

RHYTON (rī'-tun) *n.* [G.] a drinking-horn, without a foot, generally ending in a beast's head.

RINFORZANDO (rin-fort-san'-dō) *a.* [It.] with special emphasis [Mus.] [ment.

RUN-ON VERSE, *n.* verse marked by enjamb-

S

SADISM (sā'-dizm) *n.* [F.] a form of sexual perversion marked by love of cruelty.

SAFFIAN (saf'-i-an) *n.* [Russ.] leather of a goatskin or sheepskin tanned with sumach and dyed in bright colours.

SAL (sāl) *n.* [Hind.] a large tree of India yielding valuable timber.

SALAMBA (sa-lam'-ba) *n.* a fishing contrivance used in the East.

SALANGANE (sal'-ang-gān) *n.* [F.] a Chinese swift whose nest is edible.

SALLENDERS (sal'-en-derz) *n.* dry eruption inside the hock of a horse's hind-leg. Also **SELLANDERS.**

SALLY-LUNN (sal'-i-lun) *n.* [name of a street vendor] a sweet, spongy tea-cake.

SALOPIAN (sa-lō'-pi-an) *a.* [*Salop*, Shropshire] pertaining to Shropshire ;—*n.* a native of Shropshire.

SALPINGITIS (sal-pin-jī'-tis) *n.* inflammation of a Eustachian or Fallopian tube.

SAM BROWN *n.* [inventor's name] a belt with a strap over the right shoulder.

SAMEL (sam'-el) *a.* [A.S. *sam*, half] imperfectly baked ; soft ; said of brick, etc.

SAMMY (sam'-i) *v.t.* to moisten hides with water ;—*n.* a machine for doing this.

SAMURAI (sām'-oo-rī) *n. sing.* and *pl.* [Jap.] under the old feudal system a member of the military class.

SANG (sāng) *n.* [Chin.] a Chinese wind instrument ;—[F.] blood [Her.] ; anthrax. **SANG-DE-BŒUF** (sāng-de-bŏof') *n.* [F.] a dark red found on antique Chinese pottery.

SANGAR, SANGA (sang'-gar, -ga) *n.* [Hind.] a stone breastwork.

SATSUMA (**WARE**) (sāt'-su-ma) *n.* [name of province] cream-coloured Japanese pottery.

SAUSAGE-BALLOON, *n.* a kind of observation balloon ; so called from its shape.

SAXE (saks) *n.* [*Saxony*] a kind of photographic paper.

SCOOTER (skŏo'-ter) *n.* [*scoot*, to move off fast] a small vehicle consisting of a plane surface on four wheels, on which one foot rests, guided by means of a handle.

SCREEVER (skrē'-ver) *n.* a begging-letter writer. [doing one's duty.

SCRIMSHANK (skrim'-shangk) *v.i.* to avoid

SCYPHUS (sī'-fus) *n.* [G.] a footless, bowl-shaped drinking-cup with two handles not carried above the rim ; [Bot.] a cup-shaped organ, as the crown of the corolla in the narcissus.

SEAPLANE (sē-plān) *n.* a form of aircraft employed in operations over water ; seaplanes may be carried on a flat-topped ship which serves as a depot and starting surface.

SELF-STARTER, *n.* an automatic contrivance for starting a motor-car ; a car so fitted.

SERINETTE (ser-i-net') *n.* [F.] an instrument for training song-birds.

SHADOW-DANCE, *n.* a dance in which the shadows of invisible dancers are thrown on a screen. **SHADOW-FIGURE,** *n.* a silhouette.

SHELL-SHOCK, *n.* a nervous disorder caused by the bursting of shells or bombs near the patient. [of hair.

SHOCKHEAD, *a.* having a thick, bushy head

SHOCK-TROOPS, *n.* those selected for some specially arduous and dangerous duty.

SHOEHORN (shŏo'-horn) *n.* a curved piece of horn or metal used in putting on a shoe.

SHOP-STEWARD, *n.* the trade-union representative of the workers in a factory, etc., in negotiating with the employers.

SILESIA (si-lē'-sha) *n.* [*orig.* made in *Silesia*] kinds of thin cloth used for blinds and dress-linings.

SINN FEIN (shin fān') *n.* [Ir., ourselves] an Irish revolutionary party. **SINN FEINER,** *n.* a member of this party.

SIPHONET (sī'-fun-et) *n.* one of two tubes through which aphides exude honeydew.

SIRVENTE (sir-vängt') *n.* [F.] a mediæval satirical song.

SMOKE-FLOAT, *n.* a floating contrivance for generating smoke, thrown overboard to produce a smoke-screen to conceal a ship.

SNIDER (snī'-der) *n.* [inventor's name] an early form of breechloading rifle.

SNIPE-HOLE, *n.* a shelter for a sniper.

SOPHIOLOGY (sof-i-ol'-u-ji) *n.* [G. *sophia*, wisdom, and *logos*, word] the natural history of science and philosophy.

SORDET, SORDINE (sor'-det, sor'-din, sor'-dēn) *n.* [L. *surdus*, deaf] a device to deaden the sound of a stringed instrument ; a damper. [of workers or soldiers.

SOVIET (sov'-yet) *n.* [Russ.] a council, *esp.*

SPARKING-PLUG, *n.* a contrivance for igniting the explosive mixture in the cylinder of a motor engine.

SPARTACIST (spär'-ta-sist) *n.* [*Spartacus*] a member of an extreme revolutionary party in Germany.

SPIRIT-PHOTOGRAPH, *n.* a photograph in which, it is pretended, are representations of inhabitants of the spirit-world.

SPOROGONIUM (spō-rō-gō'-ni-um) *n.* the so-called moss-fruit or capsule in which the spores are produced.

SPOROPHORE (spō'-ro-fōr) *n.* [G. *sporos*, a seed, and *phoros*, fruitful] the spore bearing part of a thallus ; the placenta in flowering plants ; a sporophyte, or the spore-bearing stage in the life-cycle of a plant.

SPOT-BARRED GAME, *n.* a game at billiards in which the spot-stroke may not be played more than twice in succession.

SPOT-LIGHT, *n.* the apparatus used to throw a strong light on a performer on the stage ; the light so thrown.

SQUARE-HEAD, *n.* a common name for a German in Latin countries.

STABAT MATER (stā'-bat mä'-ter) *n.* a Latin hymn on the agony of the virgin at the crucifixion ; its musical setting.

STABILISER (stā-bil-ī'-zer) *n.* a device for securing equilibrium.

STAITH (stāth) *n.* [A.S.] the extremity of a line of rails laid on a platform for discharging coals, etc., into a vessel ; a landing-stage, or stelling.

STALL *v.t.* to allow an aeroplane to lose momentum and fall.

STEREOBATE (ster'-e-o-bāt) *n.* [G. *stereos*, solid, and *batos*, fr. *bainein*, to go] the substructure of a building.

STEREO-ELECTRIC (ster'-e-o-e-lek'-trik) *a.* pertaining to electric currents produced by bringing together two solids of different temperatures.

STRADDLE (strad'-l) *v.t.* in naval gunnery, to bracket ; — *n.* a bracket.

STUNT (stunt) *n.* [*stent*] a special effort ; a prescribed task. [marine.

SUBMERGIBLE (sub-mer'-ji-bl) *n.* a sub-

SULPHONAL (sul'-fo-nąl) *n.* [*sulphur*] a hypnotic and anæsthetic drug ; akin to it is trional. [tax.

SUPER-TAX. *n.* a tax in addition to income-

SVELTE (svelt) *a.* [F.] lightly built ; supple (of the human figure) ; in art, free ; easy ; bold.

T

TAAL (tāl) *n.* [D.] Cape Dutch patois.

TANK (tangk) *n.* an armoured motor-vehicle used in trench warfare. **TANKER,** *n.* a steamer fitted with oil-tanks. [monoplane.

TAUBE (tou'-be) *n.* [Ger., a dove] a German

TAXIMETER (tak-sim'-e-ter) *n.* [F.] an automatic device fitted to a cab indicating distance travelled and fare due. **TAXI-CAB, TAXI,** *n.* a motor-cab fitted with a taximeter. **TAXI,** *v.i.* to drive in a taxi, or along the ground like a taxi (said of aeroplanes).

TEAR-SHELL (tĕr'-shel) *n.* a shell discharging an irritant gas that blinds by causing a profuse flow of tears.

TEREFA (te-rē'-fą) *a.* [H.] unclean, in reference to animals killed for food.

THRIP (thrip) *n.* [G.] a kind of insect.

TIERS ÉTAT (tyăr-ze-tà') *n.* [F.] the third estate of the realm ; the Commons.

TIM-WHISKY (tim-hwis'-ki) *n.* a kind of light one-horse chaise.

TINAMOU (tin'-ą-mòò) *n.* [F.] a South-American quail-like bird.

T.N.T., trinitrotoluene.

TRACTOR-PLANE, *n.* an aeroplane having the propeller in front. **TRACTOR-PLOUGH,** *n.* a plough drawn by a tractor.

TRAUMA (traw'-mą) *n.* [G.] an abnormal state of the body due to external injury.

TRENCH-WARFARE. *n.* warfare in which the opposing armies are entrenched, or dug-in ; opposed to open fighting.

TRIETERIC (tri-e-ter'-ik) *a.* [G.] triennial.

TRINITROTOLUENE (tri-ni-trō-tol'-ū-ēn) *n.* a high explosive derived from toluene.

TRIONYM (tri'-o-nim) *n.* [G.] a name of three terms. [three fixed planes.

TRIPLANE (tri'-plān) *n.* an aeroplane with

TROCO (trō'-ko) *n.* [Sp. *truco*, a kind of table] a game played on a lawn with wooden balls and a spoon-shaped cue ; lawn-billiards.

TROPHESY (trof'-e-si) *n.* [G. *trophē*, food] deranged nutrition from disorder of the motor nerve force pertaining to the nutritive function.

TROPHOTROPISM (trof'-ō-trō-pizm) *n.* [G. *trophē*, food, and *tropē*, a turning] the movements of the organs in a growing plant, as towards nutrient substances, due to the chemical nature of its surroundings.

TRYPANOSOME (trip'-ą-nu-sōm) *n.* [G. *trupanon*, borer, and *soma*, the body] one of an order of flagellate infusorians.

TUATH (tū'-ath) *n.* an ancient Irish territorial division.

U

U-BOAT, *n.* [Ger. *unterseeboot*] a German submarine.

V

VELITATION (vel-i-tā'-shun) *n.* [L.] a slight skirmish ; a controversy.

VERY LIGHT (vă'-ri) *n.* [inventor's name] a cartridge discharged from a large brass pistol to light up an area. [drug.

VERONAL (ver'-o-nąl) *n.* [*vernal*] a narcotic

VERS LIBRE (văr-lēbr) *n.* [F.] free verse, *q.v.*

VICKERS VIKING EAGLE *n.* a combination of aeroplane and seaplane ; an airship capable of resting on and rising from water.

VORTICIST (vor'-ti-sist) *n.* a futurist painter who finds objects a complex of vortices, while the cubist sees them as an aggregation of cubes.

W

WAAC (wak) *n.* a member of the Women's Army Auxiliary Corps, the name being formed from the initials. Similarly the members of the Women's Royal Naval Service were called Wrens.

(TO) WATER CAPITAL. To increase the number of shares, without increasing the assets, of a company.

WEISMANNISM (vis'-mą-nizm) *n.* [August *Weismann* (1834-1915), biologist] the theory that the germ has a continuous tendency to develop according to type and is not affected by the environment so that modifications are not transmissible by direct inheritance.

WHEEL, *n.* the return of a peculiar rhythm at the end of each stanza, *e.g.*, two short lines in rhyme. The bobwheel opens with a short line.

WHIPPET (hwip'-et) *n.* [*whip*, to move nimbly] a kind of racing dog, a cross between a greyhound and a spaniel ; a light, fast tank.

WILDEBEEST (wil'-de-bēst, wĕl'-de-bāst) *n.* [S. Afr. D.] the gnu.

WINDOW-DRESSING, *n.* the effective arrangement of goods in a window ; deceptive display.

WYKEHAMIST (wik'-am-ist) *n.* [Bishop *Wykeham*] a pupil, or former pupil, of Winchester College.

X

XENOPS (zē'-nops) *n.* [G. *xenos*, strange, and *ops*, face] a genus of South American tree-creepers, with short, turned-up bills.

Y

YERCUM (yer'-kum) *n.* [Tamil] the fibre of madar (or mudar), an East Indian shrub, whose root is used in medicine.

Z

ZANJE (zăn'-hā, than'-hē) *n.* [Sp. Amer.] an irrigating canal. **ZANJE-RO** *n.* the superintendent of a zanje who arranges for the distribution of the water.

ZANZE (zăn'-ze) *n.* [Afr.] a musical instrument of the xylophone type.

ZEPPELIN (zep'-e-lin) *n.* [Count Ferdinand *Zeppelin*, 1839-1918] a large dirigible airship.

ZIONIST (zi'-u-nist) *n.* an advocate of the colonisation of Palestine by modern Jews.

ZOOM (zòòm) *v.i.* [Imit.] to turn suddenly upwards at a sharp angle ; said of an aeroplane.

ZYGOTE (zi'-gōt) *n.* [G.] a body formed from the coalescence of two gametes ; a zygospore.

Fāte, fár, ądo ; mē, her ; mine ; nōte ; tūne ; mòòn.

PREFIXES AND AFFIXES.

PREFIXES.

a

a [A S.] on or in ; as abed, ashore, afield.
a [A.S. *ond*] over against ; as along.
a [A.S. *á*] used as an intensive prefix to verbs ; as arise, abide, affright.
a [A.S.] of or from ; as adown, anew.
a [A.S. *ge*] as aware.
a, at, old sign of *inf.* ; as ado.
a, an [G.] without, denoting privation ; as apathy, without feeling ; anarchy, without government.
a, ab, abs [L.] from or away ; as avert, abhor, abstain, abstract.
ad [L.] to, at ; with its different forms a, ac, af, ag, al, an, ap, ar, as, at ; as adhere, ascend, accept, affect, aggravate, allot, announce, appear, arrest, assent, attend.
all [A.S.] all ; as almighty, altogether.
amb, ambi, am [L.] on both sides, around ; as ambient, ambition, ambidexter, amputate.
amphi [G.] both, round about ; as amphibious amphitheatre.
an [F. *en*, L. *in*] as annoint. [analyse.
ana [G.] through, back, up ; as anatomy.
ante, anti, anci, ant, an [L.] before ; as antecedent, anticipate, ancient, antique, ancestor.
anti, ant [G.] opposite to, against ; as antipathy, antipodes, antagonist.
apo [G.] from ; as apostasy, apostate ; aph, in aphelion.
arch, archi, arche [G.] first, chief ; as in archangel, architect, archetype.
at [E] nearness ; as in atone. [authentic.
auto, auth [G.] self ; as autobiography,

B

be [A.S.] causative, as becloud ; privative, as behead ; intensive, as bespatter, bespeak, &c.
bis, bi, bin [L.] twice, double ; as biscuit, biennial, binocular.
by [A.S.] near, beside ; as bystander, bypath.

C

cata, cat, cath [G.] down, downwards, according to ; as cataract, catechism, catholic.
circum, circu [L.] round about ; as circumscribe, circumfluent, circumspect, circuit.
cis [L.] on this side ; as cisalpine.
con [L.] with its forms co, col, com, cor, coun, together with ; as connect, cohere, collect, compose, correct, council.
contra [L.] against ; as contradict, controvert
counter [F. *contre*] against ; as counteract.

D

de [L.] down, from, or off ; as deject, deter, defend.
demi [F.] half ; as demigod.
dia [G.] through ; as diameter, diaphanous.
di [G.] double ; as dilemma.
dis [L.] with its forms diff and di, off, asunder, away, out ; as dispel, disarm, dishonest, diffuse, divert.
dis [G.] two, twice ; as dissyllable.
dys [G.] ill, difficult ; as dysentery.

juxta

E

e, *see* ex.
e [A.S. *ge*] enough.
e [French phonetic addition] as in esquire.
ec [G.] out of ; as eccentric.
emb [A.S. *ymb-ryne*] a circuit ; as ember-days.
en, em, and im [F., L., and G.] in or on, also to make ; as encircle, encaustic, enfeeble, embark, immerge.
enter [F.] between, among ; as entertain.
ep, eph, epi [G.] upon ; as epoch, ephemeral, epitaph.
es [F.] out ; as escape.
eso [G.] in, into ; as esoteric.
eu, ev [G.] well ; as euphony, evangelist.
ex [L.] with its forms e, ef, &c., out from ; as exclaim, evade, effuse, effulgence.
ex [G.] from, out of ; as exodus.
exo [G.] without ; as exotic.
extra [L.] on the outside, beyond ; as extramural, extraordinary, extradition.

F

for [A S.] in place of ; as forasmuch.
for [A.S.] from, away, against ; as forswear, forbid. [forfeit.
for [F., L.] out of doors ; outside ; foreclose.
fore [A.S.] before ; as forerun, foretell.
forth [A.S.] forth ; as forthwith.
fro [Scand.] from ; as froward.

G

gain [Scand.] against ; as gainsay.

H

hemi [G.] half ; as hemisphere.
hetero [G.] other ; as heterodox.
holo [G.] entire ; as holograph.
homo [G.] same ; as homœopathy.
hyper [G.] over, above ; as hypercritical, hyperborean.
hypo, hyph, hyp [G.] under ; as hypocrite, hyphen, hypallage.

I

i [L.] not ; as ignoble.
i, y [A.S. *ge*] yclept, handywork.
in [L.] with its forms il, im, in, ir, in, into, upon ; as inter, illumine, impend, include, irrigate.
in [L.] with its forms il, im, ir, negative ; as infirm, illegal, immortal, irregular.
in, im [A.S.] in, on ; as inwrap, inward, imbed.
inter [L.] between ; as intercept, interpose, interval.
intra [L.] in the inside of, within ; as intramural.
intro [L.] into, within ; as introduce.
iss [F., from L. *ex*] out of ; as issue.

J

juxta [L.] close to, near ; as juxtaposition.

L

l, curtailment of *all* ; as lone.
l [Ar.] the ; as in lute.

M

male, mal, mau [L.] badly ; malefactor, maladroit, maugre.
meta, meth, met [G.] change ; as meta-morphose, method, meteor.
mid [A.S.] with ; as midwife.
mis [A.S. and Icel.] wrongly ; misdeed, mis-trust.
mis [F., L.] badly ; as mischief.
mono, mon [G.] single ; as monograph, monk.
multi, mult [L.] many ; as multiply.

N

n, as in newt, *i.e.*, as ewt, nickname (an ekename).
ne [L.] not ; as nefarious, neuter.
ne [G.] not ; as nepenthe.
nec [L.] not ; as neglect, negative.
non [L.] not ; as nonsense, nonage.

O

ob [L.] with its forms o, oc, of, op, os, against, in front, in or on ; as obloquy, omit, occur, offer, oppose, ostensible.
off [A.S.] off, from, away ; offal, offset.
on [A.S.] on ; onlooker.
or [A.S.] out ; ordeal.
out [A.S.] beyond ; as outdo, outrun.
over [A.S.] eminence or excess ; as overtop, overthrow.

P

palim, palin [G.] against ; as palimpsest, palindrome.
pan, panto [G.] all ; panacea, pantomime.
para, par, pa [G.] alongside, beyond, against ; as paradigm, parody, paisy.
pel, *see* per.
pene [L.] almost ; as peninsula.
per, par, pel, pil [L.] through, thoroughly ; as perfect, parson, pellucid, pilgrim.
peri [G.] round ; as perimeter, periphrasis, period.
pol, por, pour, pur [F.] other forms of L. *pro* ; as pollute, portend, pourtray, purvey.
post [L.] after, behind ; as postpone.
præ [L.] before ; as predict, precede, prevail.
preter [L.] beyond ; as preternatural.
pro [L.] forth, forward, for ; as proceed, proconsul, provoke, pronoun.
pros [G.] towards ; as proselyte.
proto, prot [G.] first ; as prototype, protoxide.

R

re, red, ren [L.] back ; as retract, redeem, render.

retro [L.] going backwards ; as retrograde, retrospect.

S

s, for se ; as in sober.
s, for dis ; as in spend.
s, for ex ; as in sample.
se, sed [L.] literally by itself, without, aside ; as seclude, sedition.
semi [L.] half ; semitone.
sine [L.] without ; as sinecure.
sub [L.] with its forms s, su, suc, suf, sug, sup, sus, so, under or after ; as subject, sombre, suspect, succeed, suffuse, suggest, suppose, sustain, sojourn.
subter [L.] under ; as subterfuge, subter-raneous.
super [L.] over, above, beyond; as super-structure, superfine, superadd.
supra [L.] over, above ; as superabundance, supernumerary, supramundane.
sur [F., L. *super*] as surmount, surprise.
syn [G.] with its forms sy, syl, sym, together, with ; as syntax, system, syllogism, sympathy.

T

t, at ; as in twit.
thorough [A.S.] through ; as thoroughfare.
to [A.S.] as in to-day, together.
to [A.S.] asunder ; as in the biblical to-brake.
trans, tran, tra, tres, tre [L.] beyond, over, through ; as transit, transcend, traduce, trespass, treason.

U

u [G.] not ; as Utopia.
ultra [L.] beyond ; as ultra-marine.
um [L.] same as non, not ; as umpire.
un [A.S.] not ; as unable, unseen ; before a verb, to do the opposite ; as unloose, untie, unfetter.
under [A.S.] under, below ; as underprop, undersell.
un, uni [L.] one ; as unanimous, unicorn.
up [A.S.] high, over ; as uplift, upset.

V

ve [L.] apart from ; vestibule.
vis, vice [F., L.] in place of ; viscount, viceroy.

W

wan [A.S.] wanting ; as wanton (wanting education).
with [A.S.] against, back ; as withstand, withdraw.

Y

y, *see under* i.

AFFIXES.

able [L. *abilis*] fit to be ; as portable.
ac [G. *akos*] pertaining to ; as elegiac.
aceous [L. *aceus*] having the qualities of ; as herbaceous.
acious [L. *ax, acis*] full of ; as audacious.
acity [L. *acitas*] power, abundance ; as capacity, loquacity.
acy [L.] act of doing, as conspiracy ; state, as celibacy.
ade [F.] relating to, pertaining to ; as decade.
age [L. *aticus*, F. *age*] act of doing, or thing done, locality ; as passage, parentage, postage, parsonage.

al [L. *alis*] belonging to ; as bridal, criminal, nuptial.
an, ain [L. *anus*] belonging or pertaining to, one who ; as guardian, human, librarian.
ana [L.] things belonging to, sayings ; as Johnsoniana.
ance, ancy [L. *antia*] state or being ; as ignorance, abundance, constancy, occu-pancy.
and, end [L. *andus, endus*] as viand, legend.
aneous [L. *aneus*] belonging to ; as extraneous.
ant [L. *ans, antis*] equivalent of E. *ing* ; as assistant, pleasant.

ar [L. *aris*] of or belonging to ; as globular, angular ; one who, as beggar.
ard [F.] one who ; as drunkard.
ary [L. *arius*] agent or doer, one who ; as secretary, missionary, lapidary ; —[L. *arium*] place where ; as seminary.
ass, ace [L. *aceus, acius*] cuirass, pinnace.
aster [L. *aster*] implying contempt ; as poetaster.
ate [L. *atus, ata, atum*] to make ; as regulate, deliberate ; one who, as delegate, potentate ; office, thing, as consulate, duplicate ; having full, as animate, adequate.
ative [L. *ativus*] having power ; as vegetative, creative.
atory [L. *atorius*] relating to, being ; as predatory, transitory.
ature [L. *atura*] state, form ; as creature.

B

ble, *see* able.
ble, ple [L. *plus*] fold ; as double, quadruple.
bund and **cund** [L. *bundus* and *cundus*] moribund, rubicund.

C

celli, cello [L. *culus* and *ellus*] diminutive ; as violoncello.
ch, augmentative ; as blotch.
cle, cule [L. *cuius*] particle, animalcule.
craft [A.S. *craft*] skill ; bookcraft, priestcraft.
cy [L. *tia*] being or state of being ; as clemency, delicacy, intimacy, infancy.

D

d, t, or **ed,** suffix of past tense ; did, felt, loved.
d, ed, denotes possession ; in nouns with passive meanings, as deed, seed ; in adjectives formed from nouns, as booted, feathered ; in past participles, as loved.
dom [A.S.] state, power ; as kingdom, earldom, dukedom, popedom, freedom.

E

ed [F.] having, action done ; as landed, finished.
ee [F., from L. *atus*] one who ; as lessee, trustee, referee, refugee.
eer [F. *ier*, L. *arius*] one who, agent or doer ; as muleteer, charioteer, mutineer, engineer.
el [L. *ellus,* or *illus*] diminutive ; as damsel.
el [A.S.] instrument ; as shovel.
en [A.S.] made of or belonging to ; as wooden, golden ; to make, as lengthen, strengthen.
en [A.S. *en*] diminutive ; as maiden.
en [A.S. *en*] vixen.
en [A.S. *n, ne, en*] *pp.* ; woven.
en [A.S. *an*] oxen, kine.
en [A.S.] to make ; darken.
ence, ency [L. *entia*] action, state or being ; as leniency, consistence, tendency, indolence, complacency.
ent [L. *ens*] being ; as president, opponent, different.
eous [L. *eus*] pertaining to, containing ; as aqueous.
er [A.S. *ere*] one who ; as maker, singer, writer.
er [A.S. *erian*] frequentative ; as flicker.
er more ; in comparative of adjectives, as greater.
erel [O.F.] little ; as pikerel, cockerel.
erie [L. *arium*] place where ; as menagerie.
erly [*ern, ly*] direction to or from ; southerly.
ern [L. *erna*] noun suffix ; cistern.
ern [A.S.] direction to or from, as eastern, western ; or belonging to, as modern
ery [F. *erie*] place, act, state ; as brewery, bribery, waggery.

es, or **s** [A.S. *as*] *pl.* suffix ; as foxes, boots.
escent [L. *escens*] growing, becoming ; as convalescent.
ese [L. *ensis*] belonging to ; as Japanese.
ess [F. *esse,* L. *issa*] *fem.* suffix of nouns ; as tigress, lioness.
est [A.S.] bringest, lovest.
est [A.S. *est*] *superl.* suffix in *adj.* ; as youngest.
et [F.] little ; as casket, tablet, floweret, rivulet.
etic [G. *etikos*] relating to ; as pathetic.
ette [F.] little ; as coquette.
ety [L. *etas*] state of ; as sobriety, anxiety.
ever [A.S.] every, any ; as whosoever, whoever.
ey [A.S. *ig*] consisting of ; as clayey.

F

fare, way ; as welfare.
fast [A.S. *faest*] firm, fast ; as steadfast.
fold [A.S. *feald*] *adj.* suffix ; as fourfold.
ful [A.S.] full of ; as joyful, useful, painful, delightful.
fy [F. *fier,* L. *facere*] to make ; as purify, fortify, diversify.

H

head, or **hood** [A.S. *had,* state] state or being ; as manhood, priesthood, neighbourhood.

I

i, *pl.* suffix of nouns, through Italian ; banditti.   [tian.
ian [L. *ianus*] *adj.* suffix ; as Arabian, Canaible [F., L. *ibilis*] able to be ; as flexible, accessible, possible.
ic, [L. and G.] belong to ; as gigantic, angelic, cubic.
ical, *adj.* suffix, belonging to ; as cubical, comical.
ice [L. *itium*] thing done ; as service, notice.
ice, ish [L. *ix, icis*] as pumice, radish.
icle [A.S. *gicel,* a piece of ice] as icicle.
ics [G. *ika*] in names of science ; as pneumaties, mathematics.
id [L. *idus*] belonging to ; as rabid, fervid.
ide [G. *eidos,* form] as bromide.
ie, y, diminutive ; as lassie.
ier [F. *ier*] one who ; as cavalier, hosier.
il, ile [L. *ilis*] able ; as civil, ductile.
ile [L. *ilis*] belonging to ; as juvenile, mercantile, gentile.
im, *pl.* suffix ; as cherubim.
ina, *fem.* suffix ; as Czarina.   [feline.
ine [L. *inus*] belonging to ; as divine, genuine.
ine [F. *ine,* L. *ina*] *fem.* suffix ; as heroine.
ing [A.S. *ende*] suffix of *ppr.* ; coming.
ing [A.S. *ung, ing*] noun suffix ; learning, dwelling.
ing [A.S. *ing*] son of ; as Manning, Harding ; also in names of animals, herring ; in coins, as farthing.
ion [L. *io*] being or state of being ; as creation.
ior [L.] more ; as superior, inferior.
ique [F., L. *iquus*] belonging to ; antique.
ish [A.S. *isc*] like ; as childish, girlish, foolish ; little, as brownish ;—[F. *iss,* L. *esc*] to make, as establish, finish.
ism, asm [G. *ismos, asmos*] act, being, or state of being ; as atheism, pleonasm.
ist, ast [G. *istes, astes*] one who ; as atheist, gymnast.   [ite, dynamite.
ite [G. *ites*] belonging to, one who ; as anchorite
ity [L. *itas*] being or state ; as ability, capability, inability.
ive [L. *ivus*] belonging to, having the power to ; as native, active, expansive, persuasive.
ix [L.] as executrix, testatrix.
ize [G. *izein*] to make ; as fertilize, realize, equalize, canonize, epitomize.

K

k, a verbal suffix ; as walk, talk.
kin [A.S.] little ; as lambkin, manikin.
kind [A.S.] race, sort ; as womankind, humankind, mankind.

L

l, le as verb suffix ; as kneel, drizzle.
lc, el [A.S.] denoting instrument, &c. ; as needle, navel.
lent [L. lentus] full of ; as benevolent, redolent, violent, virulent, corpulent.
less [A.S. leás] without ; as useless, worthless, valueless, tenantless.
let [el, le, and et] diminution, little ; as eaglet, streamlet. [like.
like [A.S. lic] like ; as warlike, saintlike, godling [A.S.] little, young ; as duckling, codling, darling ; something depreciatory, as hireling, groundling.
ling, long [A.S. lunga, linga] adv. suffix ; as sidelong, darkling.
lock [A.S. lác] noun suffix ; wedlock.
lock, lick [A.S. leác] a leek ; garlic, hemlock.
ly [A.S. lic] like ; as lordly, friendly, kingly manly.

M

meal [A.S. mǽlum] adv. suffix ; as piecemeal.
men [L. men] state, that which ; as regimen, acumen.
ment [F., L. mentum] act or state of ; as treatment, excitement, advancement, nourishment.
mony [F. monie, L. monium, monia] act or state of ; as parsimony, testimony, matrimony.
most [ma and est] greatest ; as uppermost, endmost, topmost.

N

n, in participles, denoting possession ; as broken, hewn.
nd [A.S.] ppr. suffix ; friend.
ness [A.S.] being or state of being ; as madness, blindness, kindness.

O

ock [A.S. uc] little ; as hillock.
oid, oidal [G. oeidés] colloid.
om [A.S. um] old dative ; as whilom.
on [L. onem] as felon.
on, one, oon [F. on, It. one] augmentative ; as balloon, flagon, trombone.
or [L.] one who ; as imitator, persecutor, author, factor.
ory [L. orius] belonging to or place where ; as olfactory, purgatory, prefatory, piscatory.
ose [L. osus] full of ; as verbose, jocose.
osity [L. ositas] abundance, state ; as verbosity, curiosity.
ot [F.] little ; as ballot, pivot ;—[G. otes] one who ; as patriot, zealot.
our [F. eur, L. or] state of being ; as honour, favour.
ous [L. us] full of ; as prosperous, lustrous, nervous, dubious, fibrous.
ow, w [A.S. u, we, uca] meadow, sparrow, straw.

R

r, er, verb suffix ; as chatter, titter.
re [A.S.] place ; as here, there.
red [A.S. rǽd] implying number ; as hundred.
red [A.S. rǽden, rule] state, those who ; as kindred.
ric [A.S. rice, dominion] dominion, region ; as bishopric.
right [A.S. riht] as upright, downright.
ry, ery [F. rie, erie] art, place ; as masonry, foundry ; also the result of action, as poetry ; action, as sorcery ; condition, as slavery ; forming collective n. as infantry.

S

s [A.S. es] marking the genitive case.
se [A.S. sian] to make ; as cleanse.
ship [A.S. scipe] state or quality ; as hardship, friendship.
sis [G.] action or state ; as thesis.
some [A.S.] full of ; as tiresome, quarrelsome, gladsome.
son, son ; as Johnson.
ster [A.S. estre] agent or doer ; as punster, gamester.
stress [A.S.] as songstress.
sy, se [G. sis] state ; as dropsy, eclipse.

T

t [L. tus] adj. and noun suffix ; as fact, exact.
t, for th, as height. [sixteen.
teen [A.S. týne] ten to be added ; as fifteen, ter, tre [G. tron] meter, centre.
ter, ther [A.S. der, ter] thither, after.
th, or t [A.S.] state or thing ; as birth, broth, light.
ther, ter, der [A.S. dor, ther, der] the agent, action ; as father, mother, slaughter, rudder.
tude [L. tudo] being or state of being ; as solitude, altitude, gratitude.
ty [A.S. tig] ten to be multiplied ; seventy.
ty [F. té, L. tas] being or state of being ; as captivity, poverty, rapidity.

U

ule, le [L. ulus] little ; as globule, circle.
und, ond [L. undus, F. ond] jocund, vagabond.
ure [L. ura, F. eur] act or state ; as verdure, mixture, capture, exposure.
urn [L. urnus] taciturn.
urnal [L. urnus] belonging to ; as diurnal.

W

ward [A.S.] in the direction of ; as hitherward, homeward, eastward.
ways [A.S.] way, manner ; as sideways, byeways, wrong-ways.
wise [A.S.] way, manner ; as likewise.

Y

y [A.S. e] place ; as smithy ;—[A.S. ig] as mighty ;—[A.S. i-an] as ferry.
y [F. ie, L. ia] abbey ;—[L. ivus] study ;—[L. ies] progeny ;—[L. ivus, F. if] massy ;—[G. ia] academy.
yer [A.S.] one who ; as lawyer.

Abbreviations Explained.

A.A.S. (*Americanæ Antiquarianæ Societatis Socius*) Fellow of the American Academy.
A.B. (*Artium Baccalaureus*), Bachelor of Arts.
A.B., able-bodied seaman.
A.C. (*Ante Christum*), before Christ.
A.D. (*Anno Domini*), in the year of our Lord.
Æt. (*Ætatis*), aged; of age.
A.M. (*Artium Magister*), Master of Arts. (*Ante Meridiem*), before noon. (*Anno Mundi*), in the year of the world.
An. (*Anno*), in the year.
A.R. (*Anno Regni*), in the year of the reign.
A.R.A., Associate of the Royal Academy.
A.R.S.A., Associate of the Royal Scottish Academy.
A.S., Anglo-Saxon.
A.U.C. (*Ab Urbe Condita*) in the year from the building of the city, *i.e.* Rome.

B.A., Bachelor of Arts.
Bart. or **Bt.**, Baronet.
B.C., before Christ.
B.C.L., Bachelor of Civil Law.
B.D., Bachelor of Divinity.
B.E., bill of exchange.
B.L., Bachelor of Law.
B.L., bill of lading.
B.M., Bachelor of Medicine.

C.A., Chartered Accountant.
C.B., Companion of the Bath.
C.E., Civil Engineer.
Cf. (*Confer*), compare.
C.J., Chief Justice.
C.M. (*Chirurgiæ Magister*), Master in Surgery.
C.M.G., Companion of the Order of St Michael and St George.
C.O.D., cash on delivery.
Com., commissioner; commodore; committee; commerce.
Con. (*Contra*), in opposition.
C.P., Common Pleas.
C.P.S. (*Custos Privati Sigilli*), Keeper of the Privy Seal.
Crim. Con., criminal conversation or adultery.
C.S. (*Custos Sigilli*), Keeper of the Seal; Court of Session.
C.S.I., Companion of the Star of India.

D.C.L., Doctor of Civil Law.
D.D. (*Divinitatis Doctor*), Doctor of Divinity.
Del. (*Delineavit*, he drew it), engraved on a copper-plate, with the name of the draughtsman.
D.G. (*Dei gratia*), by the grace of God.

D.P.H., Diploma in Public Health.
Dr., debtor; doctor.
D.Sc., Doctor of Science.
D.V. (*Deo volente*), God willing.

E.E., errors excepted.
E.G., (*Exempli gratia*), for example.
E. and O.E., errors and omissions excepted.
Et. al. (*Et alia*), and others.
Etc. (*Et cetera*), and so forth.
Ex. p. (*Ex parte*), a one-sided statement.

F. (**Fahr.**), Fahrenheit.
F.A.S., Fellow of the Antiquarian Society.
F.C., Free Church of Scotland.
F.D. (*Fidei Defensor*), Defender of the Faith.
F.H.S., Fellow of the Historical Society.
F.M., Field-marshal.
F.O.B., free on board.
F.P., fire-plug.
F.R.S., Fellow of the Royal Society.
F.S.A., Fellow of the Society of Arts.

G.A., General Assembly.
G.B., Great Britain.
G.C.B., Grand Cross of the Bath.
G.C.M.G., Grand Cross of St Michael and St George.
G.C.S.I., Grand Commander of the Star of India.
G.M., Grand Master.
G.P.O., General Post Office.
G.R. (*Georgius Rex*), George the King.
G.T., Good Templars.

H. or **Hr.**, hour.
H.B.M., His or Her Britannic Majesty.
H.C.M., His or Her Catholic Majesty.
Hil., Hilary.
H.M., His or Her Majesty.
Hon., Honourable.
H.R., House of Representatives.
H.R.H., His or Her Royal Highness.
H.S. (*Hic situs*), here lies.

Ib. or **Ibid.** (*Ibidem*), in the same place.
Id. (*Idem*), the same.
I.e. (*Id est*), that is.
I.H.S. (*Jesus Hominum Salvator*), Jesus the Saviour of Men.
Incog. (*Incognito*), unknown.
In loc. (*In loco*), in the place.
I.N.R.I. (*Jesus Nazarenus Rex Judæorum*), Jesus of Nazareth, King of the Jews.

I.O. of O.F., Independent Order of Odd Fellows.
I.O.U., I owe you.

J., Judge.
J.P., Justice of the Peace.

K., King.
K.A., Knight of St Andrew.
K.B., Knight of the Bath; King's Bench.
K.C., Knight of the Crescent; King's Counsel.
K.C.B., Knight Commander of the Bath.
K.C.H.G.O., Knight Commander of the Hanoverian Guelphic Order.
K.G., Knight of the Garter.
K.G.C., Knight of the Grand Cross.
K.G.C.B., Knight of the Grand Cross of the Bath.
K.G.F., Knight of the Golden Fleece.
K.M., Knight of Malta.
K.M.G., Knight of St Michael and St George.
K.P., Knight of St Patrick.
K.S.I., Knight of the Star of India.
Kt., Knight.
K.T., Knight of the Thistle.

L. (*Liber*), book.
L., (*Libra*), a pound in weight.
L., **l.**, or **£.**, a pound sterling.
L.C., Lord Chancellor.
L.C. or **l.c.** (*Loco citato*), in the place before cited.
L.C.J., Lord Chief Justice.
L.D.S., Licentiate in Dental Surgery.
LL.B. (*Legum Baccalaureus*), Bachelor of Laws.
LL.D., (*Legum Doctor*), Doctor of Laws.
L.S. (*Locus Sigilli*), Place of the Seal.
L.S.A., Licentiate of the Society of Apothecaries.
LXX., The Septuagint or Seventy.

M.A. (*Artium Magister*), Master of Arts; Military Academy.
M.B. (*Medicinæ Baccalaureus*), Bachelor of Medicine.
M.B. (*Musicæ Baccalaureus*), Bachelor of Music.
M.C., Member of Congress.
M.D. (*Medicinæ Doctor*), Doctor of Medicine.
M.E., Methodist Episcopal.
Mem. (*Memento*), remember; memorandum.
Mgr., Monsignor.
MM., messieurs; gentlemen.
M.N.S., Member of the Numismatic Society.
M.P., Member of Parliament.

M.P.S., Member of the Pharmaceutical Society.
M.R., Master of the Rolls.
M.R.A.S., Member of the Royal Academy of Science.
M.R.C.C., Member of the Royal College of Chemistry.
M.R.C.P., Member of the Royal College of Physicians.
M.R.C.S., Member of the Royal College of Surgeons.
M.R.C.V.S., Member of the Royal College of Veterinary Surgeons.
M.R.G.S., Member of the Royal Geographical Society.
M.S., manuscript.
M.S. (*Memoriæ sacrum*) sacred to the memory.
MSS., manuscripts.

N.B. (*Nota bene*), note well; take notice; North Britain.
Nem. Con., (*Nemine contradicente*), no one contradicting; unanimously.
Nem. Diss. (*Nemine dissentiente*), no one dissenting.
N.P., Notary Public.
N.S., New Style.

Ob. (*Obiit*), he died.
O.F., Odd Fellows.
O.H.M.S., On His or Her Majesty's Service.
O.S., Old Style.

P.C., Privy Councillor.
Ph.D., Doctor of Philosophy.
P.M. (*Post meridiem*), afternoon.
P.M., Postmaster.
P.M.G., Postmaster-General.
P.O., Post Office.
P.O.O., Post Office Order.
Pop., population.
PP. *or* **pp.,** printed pages.
P.P.C. (*Pour prendre congé*), to take leave.
Pro tem. (*Pro tempore*), for the time being.
Prox. (*Proximo*), next.

P.R.A., President of the Royal Academy.
P.R.S.A., President of the Royal Scottish Academy.
P.S. (*Post scriptum*), postscript.
P.T.O., please turn over.

Q.B., Queen's Bench.
Q.C., Queen's Counsel.
Q.D. (*Quasi dicat*), as if he should say.
Q.E.D. (*Quod erat demonstrandum*), which was to be demonstrated.
Q.E.F. (*Quod erat faciendum*), which was to be done.
Q.L. (*Quantum libet*), as much as you please.
Q.M.G., Quartermaster-general.
Q.P. (*Quantum placet*), as much as you please.
Q.S. (*Quantum sufficit*), a sufficient quantity; Quarter Sessions.
Q.V. (*Quod vide*), which see.
Q.V. (*Quantum vis*), as much as you will.

R. (*Rex*), King; (*Regina*), Queen.
R.A., Royal Academy or Academician; Royal Artillery.
R.A.M., Royal Academy of Music.
R.C., Roman Catholic.
R.C.M., Royal College of Music.
R.C.O., Royal College of Organists.
R.E., Royal Engineers.
R.M., Resident Magistrate.
R.N., Royal Navy.
Rom. Cath., Roman Catholic.
R.S.A., Royal Scottish Academy; Royal Society of Antiquaries.
Rt., Right.
Rt. Hon., Right Honourable.
Rt. Rev., Right Reverend.
Rt. Wpful., Right Worshipful.
R.V., Revised Version.

S.A., South Africa; South America; South Australia.
S.B.A., Society of British Artists.
Sc. *or* **Sculp.** (*Sculpsit*), engraved.
Scil. (*Scilicet*), to wit; namely.
S.P.G., Society for the Propagation of the Gospel.
S.P.Q.R. (*Senatus Populusque Romani*), Senate and People of Rome.
S.T.D. (*Sacræ Theologiæ Doctor*), Doctor of Divinity.
S.T.P. (*Sacræ Theologiæ Professor*), Professor of Theology.

T.O., turn over.
Tr., translation; transpose; treasurer.
Trin., Trinity.
T.T.L., to take leave.

U.K., United Kingdom.
Ult. (*Ultimo*), last, or the last month.
U.S., United States; (*Uti supra*), as above.
U.S.A., United States of America; United States Army.
U.S.M.A., United States Military Academy.
U.S.N., United States Navy.
U.S.S., United States Senate.

V. (*Vide*), see.
V.C., Victoria Cross.
V.D.M. (*Verbi Dei Minister*), Minister of the Word of God.
Viz. (*Videlicet*), namely; to wit.
V.P., Vice-president.
Vs. (*Versus*), against; in opposition.

W.S., Writer to the Signet.

&c (*Et cetera*), and so forth.

Foreign Words and Phrases,

ALPHABETICALLY ARRANGED, WITH ENGLISH TRANSLATIONS.

A

ab agendo (L.), from acting.
ab antiquo (L.), from ancient time.
ab extra (L.), from without.
ab initio (L.), from the beginning.
ab integro (L.), afresh; anew.
ab infra (L.), from within.
ab origine (L.), from the origin.
absque ulla conditione (L.), unconditionally.
a capite ad calcem (L.), from head to foot.
acerrima proximorum odia (L.), the quarrels of near relatives are the most bitter.
acta (L.), proceedings in court.
adagio (It.), slowly with grace.
ad arbitrium (L.), at pleasure.
ad astra per aspera (L.), to the stars through difficulties.
a dato (L.), from this time; from date.
ad captandum (L.), to attract or please.
ad captandum vulgus (L.), to catch the rabble.
ad eundem (L.), to the same point or degree.
ad finem (L.), to the end.
ad hominem (L.), to the interests or passions of the man.
ad infinitum (L.), to infinity.
ad interim (L.), in the meanwhile.
ad libitum (L.), at pleasure.
ad nauseam (L.), to the extent of disgusting.
ad referendum (L.), to be further considered.
Adressbuch (Ger.), a directory.
ad valorem (L.), according to the value.
ad vitam aut culpam (L.), during life or good behaviour.
æquam servare mentem (L.), to preserve an equal mind.
æquo animo (L.), with an equal mind; calmly.
affaire d'amour (F.), a love affair.
affaire d'honneur (F.), an affair of honour.
affirmatim (L.), in the affirmative.
a fortiori (L.), with stronger reason.
agenda (L.), things to be done; the business.
aide-de-camp (F.), an assistant to a general.
à l'abandon F.), at random.
à la bonne heure (F.), well-timed; at an early hour.
à l'abri (F.), under shelter.
à la française (F.), after the French mode.
à la mode (F.), according to the custom.
à l'anglaise (F.), after the English custom.
alere flammam (L.), to feed the flame.
à l'extrémité (F.), at the point of death; without resource.
al fresco (It.), in the open air.
alias (L.), otherwise.
alibi (L.), elsewhere.
à l'improviste (F.), unawares.
alla breve (It.), quickly.
alla zoppa (It.), in a halting or imperfect manner.
allegro (It.), cheerful; joyful.
allons (F.), come on; let us go.
alma mater (L.), a benign mother, generally applied to the University.
à louer (F.), for hire; to let.
à l'outrance (F.), to the utmost. (Wrongly written for *à outrances*).
al piu (It.), at most.

alter ego (L.), another self.
alter idem (L.), another of the same kind.
alto relievo (L.), in high relief.
amantium irae (L.), lovers' quarrels.
a maximis ad minima (L.), from the greatest to the least.
a mensa et thoro (L.), from bed and board.
amende honorable (F.), satisfactory apology.
amicus humani generis (L.), a friend of the human race.
à moitié de moitié (F.), by halves.
amor nummi crescit (L.), the love of money increases.
amoroso (It.), a lover; tenderly.
amor patriae (L.), love of country.
amour propre (F.), self-love; vanity.
Anglicè (L.), in English, or according to the English manner.
anguis in herba (L.), a snake in the grass.
animis opibusque parati, (L.), prepared with men and money.
animo et fide (L.), by courage and faith.
anno Domini (L), in the year of our Lord.
anno mundi (L.), in the year of the world.
anno urbis conditæ (L.), in the year the city (Rome) was built.
ante bellum (L.), before the war.
ante lucem (L.), before the light.
ante meridiem (L.), before noon.
anti (G.), against.
a posteriori (L.), from the effect to the cause.
a priori (L.), from the cause to the effect.
à propos (F.), to the point.
aqua tinta (It.), a mode of etching on copper.
aqua vitæ (L.), water of life, often applied to spirituous liquors.
arbiter elegantiarum (L.), an umpire in matters of taste.
arcades ambo (L.), both alike.
arcanum; *pl.* **arcana** (L.), a secret or secrets.
argumentum ad crumenam (L.), an argument to the purse; an appeal to interest.
argumentum ad invidiam (L.), an argument addressed to low passions or considerations.
argumentum ad judicium (L.), argument to the judgment.
argumentum ad populum (L.), an appeal to popular prejudice.
argumentum baculinum (L.), an appeal to force; club law.
ariston metron (G.), the middle course is the best; the golden mean.
arrectis auribus (L.), with attentive ears.
arrière pensée (F.), afterthought; a mental reservation.
ars longa, vita brevis (L.), art is long, but life is short.
artes honorabit (L.), he will honour the arts.
à tort et à travers (F.), at cross purposes.
at spes non fracta (L.), but hope is not broken.
auctor preciosa facit (L.), the author makes these things precious.
audaces fortuna juvat (L.), fortune favours the brave.
au désespoir (F.), in despair.
audi alteram partem (L.), hear the other side.
au fait (F.), well instructed; master of it.
au fond (F.), at the bottom.
auf wiedersehen ! (Ger.), till our next meeting.

au pis lealr (F.), at the worst.
aura popularis (L.), the gale of popular favour.
aurea mediocritas (L.), the golden mean.
aureola (L.), a nimbus.
au reste (F.), as for the rest.
au revoir (F.), adieu until we meet again.
auribus teneo lupum (L.), I hold a wolf by the ears; have caught a tartar.
auri sacra fames (L.), the accursed thirst for gold.
aussitôt dit aussitôt fait (F.), no sooner said than done.
aut amat aut odit mulier (L.), a woman either loves or hates.
aut Cæsar aut nullus (L.), Cæsar or no one.
aut disce aut discede (L.), either learn or depart.
aut vincere aut mori (L.), victory or death.
aux armes (F.), to arms.
auxilium ab alto (L.), help is from on high.
avant-courier (F.), a forerunner.
a verbis ad verbera (L.), from words to blows.
a vostra salute (It.), to your health.
à votre santé (F.) to your health.

B

bacio di bocca spesso cuor non tocca (It.), a kiss of the mouth often does not touch the heart
bagatelle (F.), a trifle.
bambino (It.) a figure or representation of the infant Christ.
banco regis (It.), on the king's bench.
bas-bleu (F.), a blue-stocking.
basis virtutum constantia (L.), steadiness or constancy is the foundation of all virtue.
batta (Hind.), an allowance or gratuity.
beatæ memoriæ (L.), of blessed memory.
beau idéal (F.), a perfect model of beauty.
beau monde (F.), the fashionable world.
beaux esprits (F.), gay spirits; men of wit.
bel esprit (F.), a brilliant mind.
bellum lethale (L.), a deadly war.
beneficium accipere, libertatem vendere (L.), to receive a favour is to sell your liberty.
bene placito (L.), at your pleasure.
benigno numine (L.), by the favour of Providence.
bis dat qui cito dat (L.), he who gives promptly gives twice as much.
bis vivit qui bene vivit (L.), he lives twice who lives well.
bizarre (F.), odd; fantastic.
bona fide (L.), in good faith; in reality.
bon-bon (F.), a sweetmeat; confectionery.
bon gré, mal gré (F.) willing or unwilling.
bonhomie (F.), good-natured simplicity.
boni pueri discunt (L.), good boys learn.
bonis nocet quisquis pepercerit malis (L.), he injures the good who spares the bad.
bon jour (F.), good-morning; good-day.
bonne bouche (F.), a delicate bit.
bon soir (F.), good-evening; good-night.
bon ton (F.), the height of fashion.
bonus (L.), a consideration for something received.
bon vivant (F.), a jovial companion.
bourgeois (F.), a citizen.
breveté (F.), patented.
brevi manu (L.), with a short hand; summarily.
Buchdruckerei (Ger.), printing-office.
brutum fulmen (L.), a loud but harmless menace.

C

caballero (Sp.), a gentleman.
cacoethes loquendi (L.), a rage for speaking.
cacoethes scribendi (L.), an itch for scribbling.
cetera desunt (L.), the remainder is wanting.
ceteris paribus (L.), other things being equal.
café (F.), coffee; coffee-house.
ça ira (F.), it will go.
calembour (F.), a kind of pun.

camarilla (Sp.), a secret council; clique.
camera (L.), the judge's private room in the court-house.
canaille (F.), the rabble.
candida pax (L.), white-robed peace.
cani capilli venient (L.), hoary hairs will come.
canis in præsepi (L.), a dog in the manger.
cantate Domino (L.), sing to the Lord.
cap-à-pie (F.), from head to foot; all over.
caput mortuum (L.), the worthless remains.
carbonari (It.), members of a secret society in Italy.
carpe diem (L.), enjoy the present day; seize the opportunity.
carte blanche (F.) a blank sheet of paper; full powers.
carte de visite (F.), a small photographic picture.
casus belli (L.), an occasion for war.
casus conscientiæ (L.), a case of conscience.
catena (L.), a chain.
causa sine qua non (L.), a condition which is indispensable.
caveat actor (L.), let the doer beware.
caveat emptor (L.), let the buyer beware.
cead mille failthea (Ir.), a hundred thousand welcomes.
cede Deo (L.) submit to Providence.
chacun à son goût (F.) every one to his taste.
Champs Elysées (F.), Elysian fields; a beautiful public park in Paris.
chapeau bas (F.), hats off.
chapeau de bras (F.), a military cocked hat.
châteaux en Espagne (F.), castles in the air; fanciful plans.
chef d'oeuvre (F.), a masterpiece.
chère amie (F.), a dear friend.
chiaroscuro (It.), in *painting*, the art of judiciously distributing light and shade.
chi tace confessa (It.), silence is confession.
chi va piano, va sano (It.), who goes softly, goes safely.
cicerone (It.), a guide who explains curiosities.
ci-devant (F.), former.
clarior e tenebris (L.), more bright from obscurity.
clarum et venerabile nomen (L.), an illustrious and venerable name.
clavis (L.), a key to something difficult.
Coena Domini (L.), the Lord's Supper.
cognoscente (It.), a connoisseur.
collectanea (L.), passages selected from authors.
comme il faut (F.), as it should be.
comment vous portez vous? (F.), how do you do?
commune bonum (L.), a common good.
communi consensu (L.), by common consent.
communibus annis (L.), on the annual average.
componere lites (L.), to settle disputes.
compos mentis (L.), of a sound mind.
con amore (It.), with love; earnestly.
concierge (F.), the keeper of a prison.
concordia res crescunt (L.), by harmonious action business is increased.
congé d'élire (F.), a leave to elect.
conscia mens recti (L.), a mind conscious of its integrity or honesty.   [law.
consensus facit legem (L.), consent makes the
consensus tollit errorem (L.), consent takes away an error.
consilio et animo (L.), by wisdom and courage.
constantia et virtute (L.), by constancy and virtue.
consuetudinis magna vis est (L.), great is the force of custom.
contrabandista (Sp.), smuggler.
contra bonos mores (L.), against good manners.
contretemps (F.), a mischance; disappointment.
conversazione (It.), conversation; a meeting for conversation.
corps diplomatique (F.), the diplomatic body.
corpus delicti (L.), the whole nature of the offence.

corpus juris canonici (L.), the body of the canon law.
corpus juris civilis (L.), the body of civil law.
corregidor (Sp.), a magistrate.
corrigenda (L.), things to be corrected.
cor unum, via una (L.), one heart, one way.
coup d'essai (F.), a first essay; attempt.
coup d'état (F.), a stroke of policy or of violence in state affairs.
coup de grâce (F.), a finishing stroke.
coup de main (F.), a sudden enterprise or effort.
coûte qui coûte (F.), cost what it may.
crassa negligentia (L.), gross carelessness.
credat Judæus Appella! (L.), Apella the Jew may believe it if he likes!
credenda (L.), things to be believed; articles of the Creed.
credit foncier (F.), loan on land security.
credit mobilier (F.), loan on personal security.
crescit eundo (L.), it increases as it goes.
crescit sub pondere virtus (L.), virtue grows under a weight or burden.
crimen falsi (L.), falsehood; perjury.
crimen læsæ majestatis (L.), high treason.
cruda, viridesque senectus (L.), a vigorous, green old age.
crux mihi anchora (L.), the cross is my anchor.
cui malo ? (L.), what evil will it do ?
cuisine (F.), kitchen; cookery.
cul de sac (F.), a blind alley.
cum grano salis (L.), with a grain of salt; with allowance for exaggeration.
cum multis aliis (L.), with many others.
cum privilegio (L.), with privilege.
currente calamo (L.), with a running or rapid pen.
custos morum (L.), the guardian of morality.

D

da capo (It.), from the beginning.
d'accord (F.), agreed; in tune.
da locum melioribus (L.), give place to your betters.
data (L.), things granted.
dat Deus incrementum (L.), God gives the increase.
debite justitiæ (L.), by debt of justice.
de bonne grâce (F.) with good grace; willingly.
debut (F.), first appearance in public.
deceptio visus (L.), an illusion of the sight.
de die in diem (L.) from day to day.
de facto (L.) from the fact.
dégagé (F.) easy.
dehors (F.), without.
Dei gratia (L.) by the grace of God.
de jure (L.), from the law; by right.
delirium tremens (L.), trembling madness; the drunkard's madness.
de lunatico inquirendo (L.), a commission to inquire as to a man's sanity.
de mal en pis (F.), from bad to worse.
de mortuis nil nisi bonum (L.) say nothing but good of the dead.
dénouement (F.) the unravelling of a plot.
de novo (L.), anew.
Deo favente (L.) with God's favour.
Deo gratias (L.), thanks to God.
Deo juvante (L.), with God's help.
de minimis non curat lex (L.) the law does not trouble itself about trifles.
Deo volente (L.), with God's will.
de profundis (L.), out of the depths.
dernier ressort (F.), a last resource.
desideratum (L.) a thing desired.
desunt cetera (L.) the remainder is wanting.
detour (F.) a circuitous march.
de trop (F.), too much, or too many.
detur pulchriori (L.), let it be given to the fairest.
Deus avertat (L.), God forbid.
Deus vobiscum (L.) God be with you.

devoir (F.) duty.
dictum de dicto (L.) report upon hearsay.
die wacht am Rhein (Ger.), the watch on the Rhine; the German national song.
dies faustus (L.) a lucky day.
dies iræ (L.), the day of wrath.
dies non (L.) in *Law*, a day on which judges do not sit.
Dieu défend le droit (F.), God defends the right.
Dieu et mon droit (F.), God and my right.
Dieu vous garde (F.), God bless you.
dignus vindice nodus (L.), a knot worthy to be untied or resolved.
dii penates (L.), household gods.
diis aliter visum (L.), to the gods it seemed otherwise.
dîtes moi s'il vous plaît (F.), tell me, if you please.
divide et impera (L.) divide and rule.
do ut des (L.), I give that you may give.
docendo discimus (L.), we learn by teaching.
dolce (It.), in *Music* soft and agreeable.
doloroso (It.), soft and pathetic.
Domine dirige nos (L.), O Lord, direct us.
Dominus providebit (L.), the Lord will provide.
Dominus vobiscum (L.), the Lord be with you.
double entendre (F.), a double meaning.
douceur (F.), sweetness; a bribe.
dramatis personæ (L.), characters represented in a drama.
droit des gens (F.), the law of nations.
duces tecum (L.), you shall bring with you; a subpœna.
ducit amor patriæ (L.), the love of country guides me.
dulce est desipere in loco (L.) it is pleasant to jest at the proper time.
dulce et decorum est pro patria mori (L.) it is sweet and glorious to die for one's country.
dum spiro spero (L.), while I breathe I hope.
dum vita est, spes est (L.), while there is life, there is hope.
durante bene placito (L.), during our pleasure.
durante vita (L.), during life.

E

eau de vie (F.) brandy.
ecce homo (L.) behold the man.
ecce signum (L.) behold the sign.
ecclesia non moritur (L.) the church does not die.
éclat (F.), splendour; pomp; glory.
e contra (L.), on the other hand.
e contrario (L.) on the contrary.
e converso (L.), conversely.
editio princeps (L.), the first edition.
ego et rex meus (L.), my king and I.
ego et tu sumus in tuto (L.), thou and I are in safety.
élite (F.) the best part.
emeritus (L.) one retired from official duties.
en ami (F.), as a friend.
en attendant (F.) in the meanwhile.
en avant! (F.), forward!
en foule (F.) in a crowd.
en masse (F.) in a body.
en passant (F.), in passing; by the way.
en plein jour (F.) in broad day.
en revanche (F.) in revenge.
en route (F.) on the way.
ense et aratro (L.) by sword and plough.
ens rationis (L.) a creature of reason.
entre deux feux (F.) between two fires.
entrée (F.), a made dish.
entremes (F.) small and dainty dishes set between the principal ones at table.
entre nous (F.) between ourselves.
eo nomine (L.) by that name.
e pluribus unum (L.) one composed of many.
erectus non elatus (L.) exalted not elated
e re nata (L.), for the occasion or exigency.

errare est humanum (L.), to err is human.
erratum (L.), an error;—*pl.* **errata**, errors.
esprit de corps (F.), general pride in one's school, regiment, political party, etc.
esse quam videri (L.), to be, rather than to seem. [all things.
est modus in rebus (L.)., there is a medium in
esto perpetua (L.), be thou perpetual.
et cetera (L.), and the rest; etc.
et cum spiritu tuo (L.), and with thy spirit.
et sic de ceteris (L.), and so of the rest.
et tu, Brute ! (L.), and thou, O Brutus !
eventus stultorum magister (L.), the result is the schoolmaster of fools.
e vestigio (L.), instantly. [caution.
ex abundanti cautela (L.), from excessive
ex abundantia (L.), out of the abundance.
exactement le même (F.), exactly the same.
ex animo (L.), heartily.
ex capite (L.), from the head; by memory.
ex cathedra (L.), from the chair; authoritatively.
excelsior (L.), higher.
exceptio probat regulam (L.), the exception proves the rule. [exceptions.
exceptis excipiendis (L.), with the necessary
excerpta (L.), extracts.
ex concesso (L.), from what has been conceded.
excudit (L.), he cut and fashioned.
ex curia (L.), out of court.
ex dono (L.), by the gift.
exempla sunt odiosa (L.), comparisons are hateful.
exempli gracia (L.), by way of example.
exeunt omnes (L.), all retire.
ex fumo dare lucem (L.), to give light out of smoke.
ex intervallo (L.), at some distance.
exit (L.), he goes out.
exitus ac a probat (L.), the result justifies the deed. t
ex luce lucellum (L.), a small gain out of light.
ex materna (L.), on the mother's side.
ex more (L.), according to custom.
ex necessitate rei (L.), from the necessity of the case.
ex nihilo nihil fit (L.), nothing comes of nothing.
ex officio (L.), by virtue of his office.
ex parte (L.), on one side only.
ex paterna (L.), on the father's side.
experimentum crucis (L.), a decisive experiment.
experto crede (L.), believe one who has tried or done the thing.
exposé (F.), an exposition; exposure.
expressis verbis (L.), in express terms.
ex professo (L.), professedly.
extempore (L.), without premeditation.
extra muros (L.), beyond the walls.
ex usu (L.), from or by use.
ex voto (L.), according to vow.

F

faber suæ fortunæ (L.), architect of his own fortune; a self-made man.
facile princeps (L.), the admitted chief.
facilis est descensus (L.), descent is easy.
facsimile (L.), a close imitation.
facta non verba (L.), deeds, not words.
fait accompli (F.), a thing already done.
fas aut nefas (L.), right or wrong.
fata obstant (L.), the fates oppose it.
faux pas (F.), a false step; a mistake.
fecit (L.), he made or drew it.
felo de se (L.), suicide.
festina lente (L.), hasten slowly; be quick, not rash.
fête (F.), a feast.
fête champêtre (F.), a rural feast.
feu de joie (F.), a firing of guns in token of joy; a bonfire.
fiat justitia, ruat cœlum (L.), let justice be done, though the heavens should fall.

fide, non armis (L.), by faith, not by arms.
fides et justitia (L.), fidelity and justice.
fides Punica (L.), Punic faith; treachery.
fidus Achates (L.), a faithful friend.
finem respice (L.), look to the end.
finis (L.), the end.
finis coronat opus (L.), the end crowns the work.
fiorituri (It.), flourishes in music.
flagrante delicto (L.), in the act of committing a crime.
flecti, non frangi (L.), to be bent, not to be broken.
fons malorum (L.), the source of misfortunes.
fortiter in re (L.), with firmness in acting.
fracas (F.), a slight quarrel.
fugit hora (L.), the hour flies.
functus officio (L.), out of office.
furor loquendi (L.), a rage for speaking.
furor poeticus (L.), poetical fire.
furor scribendi (L.), a rage for writing.

G

Gallicè (L.), in French.
garçon (F.), a boy; a waiter.
garde du corps (F.), a body-guard.
genus homo (L.), the human race.
genus irritabile vatum (L.), the irritable race of poets.
Germanicè (L.), in German.
gloria in excelsis Deo (L.), glory to God in the highest.
gratis (L.), for nothing.
gratis dictum (L.), mere assertion.
graviora manent (L.), greater trials await us.

H

habeas corpus (L.), in *Law*, a writ for delivering a person from imprisonment.
hac lege (L.), with this law or condition.
haud passibus æquis (L.), not with equal steps.
hauteur (F.), haughtiness.
haut goût (F.), high flavour.
hic jacet (L.), here lies.
hidalgo (Sp.), a man of noble birth.
hinc illæ lachrymæ (L.), hence these tears.
hoc age (L.), do this; attend to what you are doing.
hodie mihi, cras tibi (L.), to-day to me, to-morrow belongs to you.
homme d'esprit (F.), a man of talent or of wit.
homo sum, humani nihil a me alienum puto (L.), I am a man, and think nothing that relates to man indifferent to me.
honi soit qui mal y pense (F.), evil to him who evil thinks.
hors de combat (F.), out of condition to fight.
hortus siccus (L.), a collection of dried plants.
hôtel de ville (F.), a town hall.
hôtel Dieu (F.), the house of God; an hospital in Paris.
humanum est errare (L.), it is the lot of human nature to err.

I

ibidem, ibid. (L.), in the same place; *a note of reference.*
ich dien (Ger.), I serve.
id est (i.e.) (L.), that is.
il n'est sauce que d'appétit (F.), hunger is the best sauce.
imbroglio (It.), confusion; disorder.
imperium in imperio (L.), a government within a government.
imprimatur (L.), let it be printed.
imprimis (L.), in the first place; especially
impromptu (L.), without study.
in cœlo quies (L.), there is rest in heaven.

incognito (L.), unknown.
in commendam (L.), in trust or recommendation.
incredible dictu (L.), strange to say.
in curia (L.), in the court.
in dubiis (L.), in matters of doubt.
in equilibrio (L.), equally balanced.
in esse (L.), in being.
in extenso (L.), at full length.
in extremis (L.), at the point of death.
infinito (L.), perpetually.
in forma pauperis (L.), as a pauper.
in foro conscientiæ (L.), before the tribunal of conscience.
infra dignitatem (L.), below one's dignity.
in futuro (L.), in future; henceforth.
in initio (L.), at the beginning.
in limine (L.), at the threshold.
in loco (L.), in the place.
in loco parentis (L.), in the place of a parent.
in medias res (L.), into the midst of things.
in memoriam (L.), to the memory of.
in nubibus (L.), in the clouds.
in omnibus paratus (L.), prepared for all things.
in pace (L.), in peace.
in perpetuum (L.), for ever.
in posse (L.), in possible existence.
in præsenti (L.), at the present time.
in propria persona (L.), in person.
in puris naturalibus (L.), quite naked.
in re (L.), in the matter of.
in rerum natura (L.), in the nature of things.
in sæcula sæculorum (L.), for ever and ever.
in situ (L.), in its original situation.
instanter (L.), instantly.
in sta u quo (L.), in the former state or condition.
inter alia (L.), among other things.
inter nos (L.), between ourselves.
in toto (L.), in the whole; entirely.
intra muros (L.), within the walls.
in transitu (L.), on the passage.
in vacuo (L.), in empty space, or in a vacuum.
ipse dixit (L.), he said it himself; dogmatism.
ipsissima verba (L.), the very words.
ipso facto (L.), in or by the fact itself.
ipso jure (L.), by the law itself.

J

jacta est alea (L.), the die is cast.
januis clausis (L.), with closed doors.
je suis prêt (F.), I am ready.
jet d'eau (F.), a jet of water.
jeu d'esprit (F.) a witticism.
judicium Dei (L.), the judgment of God.
Jupiter tonans (L.), Jupiter the thunderer.
jure divino (L.), by divine law.
jure humano (L.) by human law.
juris peritus (L.), one versed in law.
jus civile (L.), civil law.
jus gentium (L.), law of nations.

K

Kaiser (Ger.), emperor.
kismet (A.) fate.
Kriegspiel (Ger.), a war game.
Kronprinz (Ger.), crown prince.
kudos (G.), glory; honour.
Kyrie eleïson (G.), Lord have mercy.

L

labore et honore (L.), by labour and honour.
l'allegro (It.), the merry man.
Landwehr (Ger.), the national militia.
lapsus calami (L.), a slip of the pen.
lapsus linguæ (L.), a slip of the tongue.
lares et penates (L.), household gods.
laus Deo (L.), praise to God.

lazzaroni (It.), street beggars.
le beau monde (F.), the fashionable world.
le savoir vivre (F.), acquaintance with life and manners.
le tout ensemble (F.), all together.
lex legum (L.), the law of laws.
lex loci (L.), the law or custom of the place.
lex non scripta (L.), the common law.
lex scripta (L.), statute law.
lex talionis (L.), the law of retaliation.
lex terræ (L.), the law of the land.
l'homme propose, et Dieu dispose (F.), man proposes, and God disposes.
liberum arbitrium (L.), free will or choice.
licentia vatum (L.), a poetical licence.
lis sub judice (L.), a case not yet decided.
lite pendente (L.), during the trial.
litera scripta manet (L.), the written letter remains.
literatim (L.), literally; letter for letter.
locum tenens (L.), a deputy or substitute.
locus sigilli (L.), the place of the seal.
locus standi (L.), a right to interfere.
lucidus ordo (L.), a clear arrangement.
Lustspiel (Ger.), a comedy.
lusus naturæ (L.), a sport or freak of nature.

M

ma chère (F.), my dear.
magna carta (L.) the Great Charter.
magna est veritas, et prevalebit (L.), truth is mighty, and will prevail.
magnas inter opes inops (L.), poor in the midst of great wealth.
magni nominis umbra (L.), the shadow of a great name.
magnum bonum (L.), a great good.
magnum opus (L.), a great work.
maintiens le droit (F.), maintain the right.
maison de ville (F.), the town-house.
maître d'hôtel (F.), a house-steward.
major domo (L.), master of the house; a steward.
mala fide (L.), treacherously.
mal à propos (F.), ill-timed.
malgré nous (F.), in spite of us.
mali exempli (L.), of a bad example.
malum in se (L.), a bad thing in itself.
malus pudor (L.), false shame.
mandamus (L.), we order; a judicial writ.
manu forti (L.), with a strong hand.
mater familias (L.), the mother of a family.
materia medica (L.), substances used in the healing art.
mauvais goût (F.), bad taste.
mauvaise honte (F.), false modesty.
maximum (L.), the greatest possible.
maximus in minimis (L.), very great in trifling things.
mea culpa (L.), by my fault.
mélange (F.), a mixture.
memento mori (L.), remember death.
memorabilia (L.), things to be remembered.
memoria in eterna (L.), in everlasting remembrance.
memoria technica (L.), an artificial aid to memory.
meo periculo (L.), at my own risk.
meum et tuum (L.), mine and thine.
mirabile dictu (L.), wonderful to be told.
mirabile visu (L.), wonderful to be seen.
modus in rebus (L.), a medium in all things.
modus operandi (L.), manner of operation.
modus vivendi (L.), mode or fashion of living.
mon ami (F.), my friend.
morceau (F.), a morsel.
more majorum (L.), after the manner of our ancestors.
more suo (L.), in his own way.
mors omnibus communis (L.), death is common to all.
mos pro lege (L.), custom for law.

motu proprio (L.), of his own accord.
multum in parvo (L.), much in little.
mutatis mutandis (L.), the necessary changes being made.
mutato nomine (L.), the name being changed.

N

Nachschrift (Ger.), postscript.
naiveté (F.), simplicity.
natale solum (L.), natal soil.
ne cede malis (L.), yield not to misfortune.
necessitas non habet legem (L.), necessity has no law.   [nor by bribe.
nec prece nec pretio (L.), neither by entreaty
ne exeat (L.), let him not depart.
nem. con. (nemine contradicente) (L.), without opposition.   [senting.
nem. dis. (nemine dissentiente) (L.), no one dis-
nemo me impune lacessit (L.), no one injures me with impunity.
nihil ad rem (L.), nothing to the point.
nihil debet (L.), he owes nothing; a plea, denying a debt.
nil admirari (L.), to wonder at nothing.
nil desperandum (L.), never despair.
nil dicit (L.), he makes no answer.
n'importe (F.) it matters not.
nisi prius (L.), unless before; a term applied to a court of law held by a single judge, with a jury.
noblesse oblige (F.), rank imposes obligations.
nolens volens (L.), whether he will or not.
noli me tangere (L.), don't touch me.
nolle prosequi (L.), to be unwilling to prosecute.
nominis umbra (L.), the shadow of a name.
nonchalance (F.), carelessness; indifference.
non compos mentis (L.), not of sound mind.
non constat (L.) it does not appear.
non est inventus (L.), he has not been found.
non libet (L.) it does not please me.
non liquet (L.), it is not clear.
non mi ricordo (It.), I do not remember.
non multa, sed multum (L.), not many things, but much.
non nobis, Domine (L.), not unto us, O Lord.
non nobis solum (L.), not merely for ourselves.
non obstante (L.), notwithstanding.
non omnis moriar (L.), I shall not wholly die.
non sequitur (L.), it does not follow; an unwarranted conclusion.
norma loquendi (L.), the rule of speaking.
nota bene (N.B.) (L.), mark well.
Notre Dame (F.), Our Lady; the name of a famous church in Paris.
n'oubliez pas (F.), don't forget.
nous verrons (F.) we shall see.
novus homo (L.), an upstart.
nunc aut nunquam (L.), now or never.
nunquam non paratus (L.), never unprepared.

O

obit (L.), he or she died.
obiter dictum (L.), a thing said incidentally.
observanda (L.), things to be observed.
obsta principiis (L.), resist the first beginnings.
omnes (L.) all.   [the good
omnia bona bonis (L.), all things are good to
omnia vincit amor (L.), love overcomes all things.   [things.
omnia vincit labor (L.), labour overcomes all
on dit (F.) they say; a flying rumour.
onus probandi (L.), the burden of proving.
operae pretium est (L.), it is worth while.
opus operatum (L.), the work done; work as a work.
ora et labora (L.), pray and work.
ora pro nobis (L.), pray for us.
ore rotundo (L.), with full voice.
O tempora ! O mores (L.), Oh, the times ! Oh, the manners.

P

pacta conventa (L.), the conditions agreed upon.
pactum illicitum (L.), an unlawful agreement.
padrone (It.), ruler; master.
pallida mors (L.), pale death.
papier maché (F.), a substance made of paper reduced to a pulp.
pares cum paribus (L.), equals with equals.
par excellence (F.), by way of eminence.
pari passu (L.), with equal pace; together.
pari ratione (L.), by similar reasoning.
par oneri (L.), equal to the burden.
pars minima sui (L.), the smallest part of the thing.
pars pro toto (L.), part for the whole.
particeps criminis (L.), an accomplice.
parvenu (F.), a new-comer; an upstart.
passe-partout (F.), a master-key.
passim (L.), everywhere.   [Prayer.
pater noster (L.), our Father; the Lord's
pater patriae (L.), father of his country.
patois (F.), a corrupt dialect.
pax in bello (L.), peace in war.
peccavi (L.), I have sinned.
penchant (F.), inclination; desire.
pendente lite (L.), pending the suit.
penseroso (It.) melancholy.
per aevum (L.), for ever.
per annum (L.), by the year.
per centum (L.). by the hundred.
per contra (L.), on the contrary.
per diem (L.), by the day.
pére de famille (F.), the father of a family.
per fas et nefas (L.), through right and wrong.
periculum in mora (L.), there is danger in delay.
per incuriam (L.), through negligence.
per interim (L.), in the meantime.
per mare per terras (L.), through sea and land.
per plures (L.), by the majority.
per saltum (L.), by a leap or jump.
per se (L.), by itself.
petitio principii (L.), a begging of the question.
petit-maître (F.), a fop.
pis aller (F.), the last shift.
pleno jure (L.), with full authority.
poco curante (It.), taking little trouble.
posse videor (L.), the appearance of being able
post restante (F.), to remain till called for.
post mortem (L.), after death.
post obitum (L.), after death.
postulata (L.), things required.
pour prendre congé (F.), to take leave.
praecognita (L.), things previously known.
praescriptum (L.), a thing prescribed.
prima donna (It.), the principal actress or singer.
prima facie (L.), on the first view.
primae viae (L.), the first passages.
primum mobile (L.), the first mover; the first impulse.
primus inter pares (L.), first among equals.
principia, non homines (L.) principles, not men
pro aris et focis (L.), for our altars and firesides
probatum est (L.), it is proved.
pro bono publico (L.), for the public good.
pro Deo et rege (L.), for God and the king.
procés verbal (F.), a written statement.
pro confesso (L.), as if conceded.
pro et con (L.) for and against.
profanum vulgus (L.), the vulgar throng.
pro forma (L.), for the sake of form.
pro hac vice (L.), for this turn or occasion.
pro loco et tempore (L.), for the place and time.
pronunciamiento (Sp.) a public declaration.
pro patria (L.), for our country.
pro rata (L.), in proportion.
pro re nata (L.), for a special emergency.
pro tanto (L.), for so much.
protégé (F.), one protected or patronised.
pro tempore (L.), for the time being.
proximo (L.), next month.

Q

qua (L.), in the character of.
quære (L.), query; inquiry.
quæritur (L.), the question arises.
quantum libet (L.), as much as you please.
quantum meruit (L.), as much as he deserved.
quantum sufficit (L.), a sufficient quantity.
quantum valeat (L.), for what it is worth.
quasi (L.), as if; in a manner.
quelque chose (F.), something ; a trifle.
quid nunc ? (L.), what now ?
qui docet discit (L.), he who teaches others learns himself.
quid rides ? (L.), why do you laugh?
quietus (L.), death; rest.
qui pense ? (F.), who thinks ?
qui vive ? (F.), who goes there ? on the qui vive, on the alert.
quoad hoc (L.), to this extent.
quo animo (L.), with what mind or intention.
quod avertat Deus ! (L.), which God avert !
quod erat faciendum (L.), which was to be done.
quod vide (L.), which see.
quo jure ? (L.), by what right ?
quo warranto ? (L.), by what authority ?

R

rara avis (L.), a rare bird; a prodigy.
recherché (F.), nice to an extreme; uncommon and desirable.
recte et suaviter (L.), justly and mildly.
rectus in curia (L.), upright in court; with clean hands.
reductio ad absurdum (L.), a reducing a position to an absurdity.
regina (L.), a queen.
regium donum (L.), a royal gift.
re infecta (L.), the business being unfinished.
rem acu tetigisti (L.), you have touched the matter with a needle, i.e. exactly.
renaissance (F.), revival, as of letters or art.
renovato nomine (L.), by a revived name.
requiescat in pace (L.) may he rest in peace.
rerum primordia (L.), the first elements of things.
res gestæ (L.), exploits.
res judicata (L.), a point already decided.
respice finem (L.), look to the end.
respublica (L.), the commonwealth.
résumé (F.), an abstract or summary.
resurgam (L.), I shall rise again.
rex (L.), a king.
rex non potest peccare (L.), the king can do no wrong.
rex nunquam moritur (L.), the king never dies.
rifacimento (It.), renewal; re-establishment.
rococo (It.), exaggerated ornament in architecture.

S

sal atticum (L.), attic salt; wit.
salus populi suprema est lex (L.), the welfare of the people is the supreme law.
salvo jure (L.), the right being safe.
salvo pudore (L.), without offence to modesty.
sanctum sanctorum (L.), holy of holies.
sang-froid (F.), indifference; apathy.
sans cérémonie (F.), without ceremony.
sans changer (F.), without changing.
sans-culottes (F.), ragged men; the lower class.
sans peur et sans reproche (F.), without fear and without reproach.
sans souci (F.), without care; free and easy.
sans tache (F.), stainless.
sartor resartus (L.), the tailor patched.
sauve qui peut (F.), save himself who can.
savant (F.), a learned man.
savoir faire (F.), ability; skill.

savoir vivre (F.), good breeding.
scienter (L.), knowingly; with skill.
scilicet (L.), that is to say; to wit.
secundum artem (L.), according to rule; scientifically.
secundum naturam (L.), according to the course of nature.
se defendendo (L.), in self-defence.
sederunt (L.), they have sat; a meeting.
semper idem (L.), always the same.
semper paratus (L.), always ready.
seriatim (L.), in order; one after another.
sic (L.), so; such.
sic est vita (L.), such is life.
sic itur ad astra (L.), such is the way to immortality.
sic passim (L.), so everywhere.
sic semper tyrannis (L.), ever so to tyrants.
sicut ante (L.), as before.
sic vos non vobis (L.), thus you do not labour for yourselves.
si je puis (F.), if I can.
sine cura (L.), without charge or care.
sine die (L.), without a day appointed.
sine dubio (L.), without doubt.
sine invidia (L.), without envy.
sine mora (L.), without delay.
sine odio (L.), without hatred.
sine prole (L.), without issue.
sine qua non (L.), an indispensable condition.
siste, viator (L.), stop, traveller !
sit tibi terra levis ! (L.), may the earth lie lightly upon thee !
sobriquet (F.), a nick-name.
soi-disant (F.), self-styled.
sotto voce (It.), in an under-tone.
soyez ferme (F.), be firm.
spero meliora (L.), I hope for better things.
spes mea Christus (L.), Christ is my hope.
spolia opima (L.), the richest booty.
sponte sua (L.), of one's own accord.
statim (L.), immediately.
stet (L.), let it stand.
stratum super stratum (L.), layer above layer.
stylo inverso (L.), with the back of the pen.
sua cuique voluptas (L.), every man has his own pleasures.
sub colore juris (L.), under pretext of law.
sub conditione (L.), under the condition.
sub judice (L.), under consideration.
sub pœna (L.), under a penalty.
sub rosa (L.), under the rose; privately.
sub silentio (L.), in silence.
suggestio falsi (L.), the suggestion of a falsehood.
sui generis (L.), of its own kind.
sui jure (L.), in one's own right.
summum bonum (L.), the chief good.
suo marte (L.), by his own strength.
suppressio veri (L.), suppression of the truth.
supra (L.), above.
suum cuique (L.), let each have his own.
suus cuique mos (L.), every one has his particular habit.

T

table d'hôte (F.), a common table for guests.
tabula rasa (L.), a smooth or blank tablet.
tædium vitæ (L.), weariness of life.
tant mieux (F.), so much the better.
tant pis (F.), so much the worse.
tapis (F.), the carpet.
Te Deum (L.), a hymn of thanksgiving.
te judice (L.), you being the judge.
tel maître, tel valet (F.), like master, like man.
telum imbelle sine ictu (L.), a feeble weapon thrown without effect.
tempus fugit (L.), time flies.
tenax propositi (L.), tenacious of his purpose.
terminus ad quem (L.), the end to be reached.
terminus a quo (L.), the starting-point.
terra firma (L.), solid earth; a safe footing.

terra incognita (L.), an unknown country.
toga virilis (L.), the gown of manhood.
totidem verbis (L.), in just so many words.
toties quoties (L.), as often as.
totis viribus (L.), with all his might.
toto cœlo (L.), by the whole heavens.
toujours prêt (F.), always ready.
tout-à-fait (F.), entirely; quite.
tout ensemble (F.), the whole taken together.
trait (F.), feature; arrow.
trans (L.), on the farther side.
transeat in exemplum (L.), may it pass into an example.
tria juncta in uno (L.), three joined in one.
trottoir (F.), side-walk.
tu quoque, Brute ! (L.), and thou, too, Brutus !
tutor et ultor (L.), protector and avenger.
tuum est (L.), it is your own.

U

uberrima fides (L.), implicit reliance.
ubi supra (L.), where above mentioned.
ultimatum (L.), the last or only condition.
ultimus (L.), the last.
ultra (L.), beyond.
una voce (L.), with one voice; unanimously.
un fait accompli (F.), an accomplished fact.
unique (F.), the only one of its kind.
uno animo (L.), with one mind or spirit.
usque ad aras (L.), to the very altars.
usque ad nauseam (L.), even to disgust.
usus loquendi (L.), usage in speaking.
utile dulci (L.), the useful with the pleasant.
ut infra (L.), as below.
ut prosim (L.), that I may do good.
ut quocunque paratus (L.), prepared for every event.
ut supra (L.) as above stated.

V

vade in pace (L.), go in peace.
vade mecum (L.), go with me; a constant companion.
væ victis (L.), woe to the vanquished.
valde deflendum (L.), greatly to be lamented.
valet de chambre (F.), an attendant; a footman.
vale (L.), farewell.
variæ lectiones (L.), various readings.
Vaterland (Ger.), native country; land of one's birth.
vaurien (F.), a worthless fellow.
veluti in speculum (L.), as in a mirror.
venire facias (L.), the writ for summoning a jury.
veni, vidi, vici (L.), I came, I saw, I conquered.
ventis secundis (L.) with prosperous winds.
vera pro gratiis (L.), truth before favours or benefits.
verbatim et literatim (L.), word for word and letter for letter.
veritas prævalebit (L.), truth will prevail.
versus (L.), against.
vestigia nulla retrorsum (L.), no steps backward; no going back.
vexata quæstio (L.), a disputed question.
via (L.), by the way of.
via media (L.), a middle course.
viaticum (L.), the Eucharist administered to the dying.
vice (L.), in the place of

vice versa (L.), the terms being exchanged.
vide et crede (L.), see and believe.
videlicet (viz.) (L.), to wit; namely.
videttes (F.), sentinels on horseback.
videtur (L.), it appears.
vide ut supra (L.), see what is stated above.
vi et armis (L.), by main force.
vi et arte (L.), by strength and skill.
vincit amor patriæ (L.), love of country prevails.
vinculum matrimonii (L.), the bond of marriage.
vires acquirit eundo (L.), she acquires strength in her progress, viz., fame.
vir sapit qui pauca loquitur (L.), he is wise who talks little.
virtu (It.), artistic merit.
virtuoso (It.), a man who has a taste for the fine arts:—pl. virtuosi.
virtus et veritas vincunt (L.), virtue and truth must prevail.
virtus in arduis (L.), courage in difficulties.
virtus incendit vires (L.), virtue fires the bodily strength.
virtute non viris (L.), from virtue not from men.
virtute officii (L.), by virtue of office.
vis a tergo (L.), a propelling force from behind.
vis-à-vis (F.), opposite; facing.
vis comica (L.), comic genius.
vis inertiæ (L.), the power of inertness.
vis major (L.) irresistible force.
vis medicatrix naturæ (L.), the healing power that lies in nature itself.
vis poetica (L.), poetic genius.
vis vitæ (L.), the vigour of life.
vita brevis, ars longa (L.), life is short, and art is long.
vivat regina ! (L.), long live the queen !
vivat respublica ! (L.), live the republic !
viva voce (L.), by the living voice; by oral testimony.
vive le roi ! (F.), long live the king !
vive, vale (L.), farewell, and be happy.
vivida vis animi (L.), the lively vigour of genius.
vocabula artis (L.), technical terms.
voilà tout (F.), that's all.
volo, non valeo (L.), I am willing but unable.
Vorwort (Ger.), preface.
vox et præterea nihil (L.), sound and nothing more.
vox faucibus hæsit (L.), the voice (or words) stuck in the throat.
vox populi, vox Dei (L.), the voice of the people is the voice of God.
vulgo (L.), commonly.
vulnus immedicabile (L.), an irreparable injury.
vultus est index animi (L.), the face is the index to the mind.

W

Wartezimmer (Ger.), waiting-room.
Was ist das? (Ger.), what is that?
Wasserkur (Ger.), water-cure.
Wasser-trinker (Ger.), a teetotaler.
Wochenblatt (Ger.), a weekly paper.
Wörterbuch (Ger.), a dictionary.

Z

Zauberflote (Ger.), the magic flute.
Zeitung (Ger.), a newspaper.
Zollverein (Ger.), a tariff union.
zonam perdidit (L.), he has lost his purse.

LONDON AND GLASGOW: COLLINS' CLEAR-TYPE PRESS.

Lightning Source UK Ltd.
Milton Keynes UK
UKOW06f2203180817
307520UK00022B/372/P